The Dictionary of Art

20

Mächtig

TO

Medal

GROVE

The Dictionary of Art

edited by JANE TURNER, in thirty-four volumes, 1996

Reprinted with minor corrections, 1998, 2002

This edition is distributed within the United Kingdom and Europe
by Macmillan Publishers Limited, London, and within the United States and Canada by
Grove's Dictionaries Inc., New York.

Text keyboarded by Wearset Limited, Sunderland, England
Database management by Pindar plc, York, England
Imagesetting by William Clowes Limited, Suffolk, England
Printed and bound by China Translation and Printing Services Ltd, Hong Kong

British Library Cataloguing in Publication Data

The dictionary of art
  1. Art - Dictionaries 2. Art - History -
    Dictionaries
  I. Turner, Jane
  703

ISBN 1-884446-00-0

Library of Congress Cataloging in Publication Data

The dictionary of art / editor, Jane Turner.
  p. cm.
  Includes bibliographical references and index.
  Contents: 1. A to Anckerman
  ISBN 1-884446-00-0 (alk. paper)
  1. Art—Encyclopedias.
  I. Turner, Jane, 1956–
N31.D5 1996   96–13628
703—dc20   CIP

Contents

List of Colour Illustrations

PLATE I. **Manuscript**

St Luke, miniature (189×147 mm) introducing the *Acts of the Apostles*, from a New Testament manuscript, Byzantine, mid-10th century (London, British Library, Add. MS. 28815, fol. 162*v*/Photo: British Library)

PLATE II. **Manuscript**

Illustration to Psalm 13, coloured line drawing from the Harley Psalter, 380×310 mm, from Christ Church, Canterbury, *c.* 1010–20 (London, British Library, MS. 603, fol. 7*v*/Photo: British Library)

PLATE III. **Manuscript**

Gasparo Padovano (attrib.): *Aristotle Seated*, frontispiece (367×257 mm) from Aristotle: *Historia animalium: De partibus animalium*, translated by Theodore of Gaza, written by Bartolomeo Sanvito, from Rome, *c.* 1473/4–80 (Rome, Vatican, Biblioteca Apostolica, MS. Vat. lat. 2094, fol. 8*r*/Photo: Vatican Museums)

PLATE IV. **Manuscript**

Boucicaut Master: *Pentecost*, miniature from the Boucicaut Hours, 274×190 mm, from Paris, after 1401 (Paris, Musée Jacquemart-André, MS. 2, fol. 112*v*/Photo: Institut de France, Musée Jacquemart-André)

PLATE V. **Manuscript**

1. Master of the Leaping Figures: *Calling of Jeremiah*, historiated initial (133×133 mm) from the Winchester Bible, 583×396 mm, from St Swithun's Cathedral Priory, Winchester, *c.* 1160 (Winchester Cathedral Library, vol. ii, fol. 148*r*/Photo: Dean and Chapter, Winchester Cathedral Office)

2. *Miracle of the Loaves and Fishes*, miniature (235×175 mm) from the Codex Escorial, Echternach school, 1043–6 (Madrid, Escorial, Biblioteca Monasterio S Lorenzo, Cod. Vit. 17, fol. 38/Photo: Ampliaciones y Reproducciones MAS, Barcelona)

PLATE VI. **Manuscript**

Bihzad (attrib.): *Caliph Ma'mun Visits a Turkish Bath*, miniature from Nizami: *Khamsa* ('Five poems'), 180×155 mm, from Herat, Afghanistan, 1494–5 (London, British Library, Or. MS. 6810, fol. 27*v*/Photo: British Library)

PLATE VII. **Marquetry**

Marquetry armoire attributed to André-Charles Boulle, wood, copper and shell with bronze trimmings, 1.49×2.71×0.61 m, from Paris, *c.* 1680–90 (Paris, Musée des Arts Décoratifs/Photo: Giraudon, Paris)

PLATE VIII. **Marquetry**

1. Marquetry piano, dyed and natural woods, engraved ivory, mother-of-pearl and abalone, l. 2.47 m, made by Erard and Co., London, with marquetry by George Henry Blake, *c.* 1840 (New York, Metropolitan Museum of Art/Photo: Metropolitan Museum of Art, Gift of Mrs Henry McSweeny, 1959; no. 59.76)

2. Marquetry cabinet, wood with bone pegs, 635×457 mm, from India, probably Goa, late 17th century (London, Victoria and Albert Museum/Photo: Board of Trustees of the Victoria and Albert Museum)

3. Marquetry writing-desk, wood, ivory and pigment with bronze trimmings, 202×440×283 mm, from southern Spain, Nasrid period, 14th century (Madrid, Museo Arqueológico Nacional/Photo: Museo Arqueológico Nacional)

General Abbreviations

The abbreviations employed throughout this dictionary, most of which are listed below, do not vary, except for capitalization, regardless of the context in which they are used, including bibliographical citations and for locations of works of art. The principle used to arrive at these abbreviations is that their full form should be easily deducible, and for this reason acronyms have generally been avoided (e.g. Los Angeles Co. Mus. A. instead of LACMA). The same abbreviation is adopted for cognate forms in foreign languages and in most cases for plural and adjectival forms (e.g. A.= Art, Arts, Arte, Arti etc). Not all related forms are listed below. Occasionally, if a name, for instance of an artists' group or exhibiting society, is repeated within the text of one article, it is cited in an abbreviated form after its first mention in full (e.g. The Pre-Raphaelite Brotherhood (PRB) was founded...); the same is true of archaeological periods and eras, which are abbreviated to initial letters in small capitals (e.g. In the Early Minoan (EM) period...). Such abbreviations do not appear in this list. For the reader's convenience, separate full lists of abbreviations for locations, periodical titles and standard reference books and series are included as Appendices A–C in vol. 33.

A.	Art, Arts	Anthropol.	Anthropology	Azerbaij.	Azerbaijani
A.C.	Arts Council	Antiqua.	Antiquarian, Antiquaries	B.	Bartsch [catalogue of Old Master prints]
Acad.	Academy	app.	appendix		
AD	Anno Domini	approx.	approximately	b	born
Add.	Additional, Addendum	AR	Arkansas (USA)	BA	Bachelor of Arts
addn	addition	ARA	Associate of the Royal Academy	Balt.	Baltic
Admin.	Administration			bapt	baptized
Adv.	Advances, Advanced	Arab.	Arabic	BArch	Bachelor of Architecture
Aesth.	Aesthetic(s)	Archaeol.	Archaeology	Bart	Baronet
Afr.	African	Archit.	Architecture, Architectural	Bask.	Basketry
Afrik.	Afrikaans, Afrikaner	Archv, Archvs	Archive(s)	BBC	British Broadcasting Corporation
A.G.	Art Gallery	Arg.	Argentine	BC	Before Christ
Agrar.	Agrarian	ARHA	Associate of the Royal Hibernian Academy	BC	British Columbia (Canada)
Agric.	Agriculture			BE	Buddhist era
Agron.	Agronomy	ARIBA	Associate of the Royal Institute of British Architects	Beds	Bedfordshire (GB)
Agy	Agency			Behav.	Behavioural
AH	Anno Hegirae	Armen.	Armenian	Belarus.	Belarusian
A. Inst.	Art Institute	ARSA	Associate of the Royal Scottish Academy	Belg.	Belgian
AK	Alaska (USA)			Berks	Berkshire (GB)
AL	Alabama (USA)	Asiat.	Asiatic	Berwicks	Berwickshire (GB; old)
Alb.	Albanian	Assist.	Assistance	BFA	Bachelor of Fine Arts
Alg.	Algerian	Assoc.	Association	Bibl.	Bible, Biblical
Alta	Alberta (Canada)	Astron.	Astronomy	Bibliog.	Bibliography, Bibliographical
Altern.	Alternative	AT&T	American Telephone & Telegraph Company	Biblioph.	Bibliophile
a.m.	ante meridiem [before noon]			Biog.	Biography, Biographical
Amat.	Amateur	attrib.	attribution, attributed to	Biol.	Biology, Biological
Amer.	American	Aug	August	bk, bks	book(s)
An.	Annals	Aust.	Austrian	Bkbinder	Bookbinder
Anatol.	Anatolian	Austral.	Australian	Bklore	Booklore
Anc.	Ancient	Auth.	Author(s)	Bkshop	Bookshop
Annu.	Annual	Auton.	Autonomous	BL	British Library
Anon.	Anonymous(ly)	Aux.	Auxiliary	Bld	Build
Ant.	Antique	Ave.	Avenue	Bldg	Building
Anthol.	Anthology	AZ	Arizona (USA)		

Bldr	Builder	Chin.	Chinese	Cur.	Curator, Curatorial, Curatorship
BLitt	Bachelor of Letters/Literature	Christ.	Christian, Christianity		
BM	British Museum	Chron.	Chronicle	Curr.	Current(s)
Boh.	Bohemian	Cie	Compagnie [French]	CVO	Commander of the [Royal] Victorian Order
Boliv.	Bolivian	Cinema.	Cinematography		
Botan.	Botany, Botanical	Circ.	Circle	Cyclad.	Cycladic
BP	Before present (1950)	Civ.	Civil, Civic	Cyp.	Cypriot
Braz.	Brazilian	Civiliz.	Civilization(s)	Czech.	Czechoslovak
BRD	Bundesrepublik Deutschland [Federal Republic of Germany (West Germany)]	Class.	Classic, Classical	$	dollars
		Clin.	Clinical	d	died
		CO	Colorado (USA)	d.	denarius, denarii [penny, pence]
Brecons	Breconshire (GB; old)	Co.	Company; County		
Brez.	Brezonek [lang. of Brittany]	Cod.	Codex, Codices	Dalmat.	Dalmatian
Brit.	British	Col., Cols	Collection(s); Column(s)	Dan.	Danish
Bros	Brothers	Coll.	College	DBE	Dame Commander of the Order of the British Empire
BSc	Bachelor of Science	collab.	in collaboration with, collaborated, collaborative		
Bucks	Buckinghamshire (GB)			DC	District of Columbia (USA)
Bulg.	Bulgarian	Collct.	Collecting	DDR	Deutsche Demokratische Republik [German Democratic Republic (East Germany)]
Bull.	Bulletin	Colloq.	Colloquies		
bur	buried	Colomb.	Colombian		
Burm.	Burmese	Colon.	Colonies, Colonial	DE	Delaware (USA)
Byz.	Byzantine	Colr	Collector	Dec	December
C	Celsius	Comm.	Commission; Community	Dec.	Decorative
C.	Century	Commerc.	Commercial	ded.	dedication, dedicated to
c.	circa [about]	Communic.	Communications	Democ.	Democracy, Democratic
CA	California	Comp.	Comparative; compiled by, compiler	Demog.	Demography, Demographic
Cab.	Cabinet			Denbs	Denbighshire (GB; old)
Caerns	Caernarvonshire (GB; old)	Concent.	Concentration	dep.	deposited at
C.A.G.	City Art Gallery	Concr.	Concrete	Dept	Department
Cal.	Calendar	Confed.	Confederation	Dept.	Departmental, Departments
Callig.	Calligraphy	Confer.	Conference	Derbys	Derbyshire (GB)
Cam.	Camera	Congol.	Congolese	Des.	Design
Cambs	Cambridgeshire (GB)	Congr.	Congress	destr.	destroyed
can	canonized	Conserv.	Conservation; Conservatory	Dev.	Development
Can.	Canadian	Constr.	Construction(al)	Devon	Devonshire (GB)
Cant.	Canton(s), Cantonal	cont.	continued	Dial.	Dialogue
Capt.	Captain	Contemp.	Contemporary	diam.	diameter
Cards	Cardiganshire (GB; old)	Contrib.	Contributions, Contributor(s)	Diff.	Diffusion
Carib.	Caribbean			Dig.	Digest
Carms	Carmarthenshire (GB; old)	Convalesc.	Convalescence	Dip. Eng.	Diploma in Engineering
Cartog.	Cartography	Convent.	Convention	Dir.	Direction, Directed
Cat.	Catalan	Coop.	Cooperation	Directrt	Directorate
cat.	catalogue	Coord.	Coordination	Disc.	Discussion
Cath.	Catholic	Copt.	Coptic	diss.	dissertation
CBE	Commander of the Order of the British Empire	Corp.	Corporation, Corpus	Distr.	District
		Corr.	Correspondence	Div.	Division
Celeb.	Celebration	Cors.	Corsican	DLitt	Doctor of Letters/Literature
Celt.	Celtic	Cost.	Costume	DM	Deutsche Mark
Cent.	Centre, Central	Cret.	Cretan	Doc.	Document(s)
Centen.	Centennial	Crim.	Criminal	Doss.	Dossier
Cer.	Ceramic	Crit.	Critical, Criticism	DPhil	Doctor of Philosophy
cf.	confer [compare]	Croat.	Croatian	Dr	Doctor
Chap., Chaps	Chapter(s)	CT	Connecticut (USA)	Drg, Drgs	Drawing(s)
		Cttee	Committee	DSc	Doctor of Science/Historical Sciences
Chem.	Chemistry	Cub.	Cuban		
Ches	Cheshire (GB)	Cult.	Cultural, Culture	Dut.	Dutch
Chil.	Chilean	Cumb.	Cumberland (GB; old)	Dwell.	Dwelling
				E.	East(ern)

EC	European (Economic) Community	figs	figures	Heb.	Hebrew
Eccles.	Ecclesiastical	Filip.	Filipina(s), Filipino(s)	Hell.	Hellenic
Econ.	Economic, Economies	Fin.	Finnish	Her.	Heritage
Ecuad.	Ecuadorean	FL	Florida (USA)	Herald.	Heraldry, Heraldic
ed.	editor, edited (by)	*fl*	*floruit* [he/she flourished]	Hereford & Worcs	Hereford & Worcester (GB)
edn	edition	Flem.	Flemish		
eds	editors	Flints	Flintshire (GB; old)	Herts	Hertfordshire (GB)
Educ.	Education	Flk	Folk	HI	Hawaii (USA)
e.g.	*exempli gratia* [for example]	Flklore	Folklore	Hib.	Hibernia
Egyp.	Egyptian	fol., fols	folio(s)	Hisp.	Hispanic
Elem.	Element(s), Elementary	Found.	Foundation	Hist.	History, Historical
Emp.	Empirical	Fr.	French	HMS	His/Her Majesty's Ship
Emul.	Emulation	frag.	fragment	Hon.	Honorary, Honourable
Enc.	Encyclopedia	Fri.	Friday	Horiz.	Horizon
Encour.	Encouragement	FRIBA	Fellow of the Royal Institute of British Architects	Hort.	Horticulture
Eng.	English			Hosp.	Hospital(s)
Engin.	Engineer, Engineering	FRS	Fellow of the Royal Society, London	HRH	His/Her Royal Highness
Engr., Engrs	Engraving(s)			Human.	Humanities, Humanism
		ft	foot, feet	Hung.	Hungarian
Envmt	Environment	Furn.	Furniture	Hunts	Huntingdonshire (GB; old)
Epig.	Epigraphy	Futur.	Futurist, Futurism	IA	Iowa
Episc.	Episcopal	g	gram(s)	ibid.	*ibidem* [in the same place]
Esp.	Especially	GA	Georgia (USA)	ICA	Institute of Contemporary Arts
Ess.	Essays	Gael.	Gaelic		
est.	established	Gal., Gals	Gallery, Galleries	Ice.	Icelandic
etc	*etcetera* [and so on]	Gaz.	Gazette	Iconog.	Iconography
Ethnog.	Ethnography	GB	Great Britain	Iconol.	Iconology
Ethnol.	Ethnology	Gdn, Gdns	Garden(s)	ID	Idaho (USA)
Etrus.	Etruscan	Gdnr(s)	Gardener(s)	i.e.	*id est* [that is]
Eur.	European	Gen.	General	IL	Illinois (USA)
Evangel.	Evangelical	Geneal.	Genealogy, Genealogist	Illum.	Illumination
Exam.	Examination	Gent.	Gentleman, Gentlemen	illus.	illustrated, illustration
Excav.	Excavation, Excavated	Geog.	Geography	Imp.	Imperial
Exch.	Exchange	Geol.	Geology	IN	Indiana (USA)
Excurs.	Excursion	Geom.	Geometry	in., ins	inch(es)
exh.	exhibition	Georg.	Georgian	Inc.	Incorporated
Exp.	Exposition	Geosci.	Geoscience	inc.	incomplete
Expermntl	Experimental	Ger.	German, Germanic	incl.	includes, including, inclusive
Explor.	Exploration	G.I.	Government/General Issue (USA)	Incorp.	Incorporation
Expn	Expansion			Ind.	Indian
Ext.	External	Glams	Glamorganshire (GB; old)	Indep.	Independent
Extn	Extension	Glos	Gloucestershire (GB)	Indig.	Indigenous
f, ff	following page, following pages	Govt	Government	Indol.	Indology
		Gr.	Greek	Indon.	Indonesian
F.A.	Fine Art(s)	Grad.	Graduate	Indust.	Industrial
Fac.	Faculty	Graph.	Graphic	Inf.	Information
facs.	facsimile	Green.	Greenlandic	Inq.	Inquiry
Fam.	Family	Gr.-Roman	Greco-Roman	Inscr.	Inscribed, Inscription
fasc.	fascicle	Gt	Great	Inst.	Institute(s)
fd	feastday (of a saint)	Gtr	Greater	Inst. A.	Institute of Art
Feb	February	Guat.	Guatemalan	Instr.	Instrument, Instrumental
Fed.	Federation, Federal	Gym.	Gymnasium	Int.	International
Fem.	Feminist	h.	height	Intell.	Intelligence
Fest.	Festival	ha	hectare	Inter.	Interior(s), Internal
fig.	figure (illustration)	Hait.	Haitian	Interdiscip.	Interdisciplinary
Fig.	Figurative	Hants	Hampshire (GB)	intro.	introduced by, introduction
		Hb.	Handbook	inv.	inventory

Inven.	Invention	m	metre(s)	Moldov.	Moldovan
Invest.	Investigation(s)	m.	married	MOMA	Museum of Modern Art
Iran.	Iranian	M.	Monsieur	Mon.	Monday
irreg.	irregular(ly)	MA	Master of Arts; Massachusetts (USA)	Mongol.	Mongolian
Islam.	Islamic			Mons	Monmouthshire (GB; old)
Isr.	Israeli	Mag.	Magazine	Montgoms	Montgomeryshire (GB; old)
It.	Italian	Maint.	Maintenance	Mor.	Moral
J.	Journal	Malay.	Malaysian	Morav.	Moravian
Jam.	Jamaican	Man.	Manitoba (Canada); Manual	Moroc.	Moroccan
Jan	January	Manuf.	Manufactures	Movt	Movement
Jap.	Japanese	Mar.	Marine, Maritime	MP	Member of Parliament
Jav.	Javanese	Mason.	Masonic	MPhil	Master of Philosophy
Jew.	Jewish	Mat.	Material(s)	MS	Mississippi (USA)
Jewel.	Jewellery	Math.	Mathematic	MS., MSS	manuscript(s)
Jord.	Jordanian	MBE	Member of the Order of the British Empire	MSc	Master of Science
jr	junior			MT	Montana (USA)
Juris.	Jurisdiction	MD	Doctor of Medicine; Maryland (USA)	Mt	Mount
KBE	Knight Commander of the Order of the British Empire	ME	Maine (USA)	Mthly	Monthly
		Mech.	Mechanical	Mun.	Municipal
KCVO	Knight Commander of the Royal Victorian Order	Med.	Medieval; Medium, Media	Mus.	Museum(s)
		Medic.	Medical, Medicine	Mus. A.	Museum of Art
kg	kilogram(s)	Medit.	Mediterranean	Mus. F.A.	Museum of Fine Art(s)
kHz	kilohertz	Mem.	Memorial(s); Memoir(s)	Music.	Musicology
km	kilometre(s)	Merions	Merionethshire (GB; old)	N.	North(ern); National
Knowl.	Knowledge	Meso-Amer.	Meso-American	n	refractive index of a medium
Kor.	Korean			n.	note
KS	Kansas (USA)	Mesop.	Mesopotamian	N.A.G.	National Art Gallery
KY	Kentucky (USA)	Met.	Metropolitan	Nat.	Natural, Nature
Kyrgyz.	Kyrgyzstani	Metal.	Metallurgy	Naut.	Nautical
£	libra, librae [pound, pounds sterling]	Mex.	Mexican	NB	New Brunswick (Canada)
		MFA	Master of Fine Arts	NC	North Carolina (USA)
l.	length	mg	milligram(s)	ND	North Dakota (USA)
LA	Louisiana (USA)	Mgmt	Management	n.d.	no date
Lab.	Laboratory	Mgr	Monsignor	NE	Nebraska; Northeast(ern)
Lancs	Lancashire (GB)	MI	Michigan	Neth.	Netherlandish
Lang.	Language(s)	Micrones.	Micronesian	Newslett.	Newsletter
Lat.	Latin	Mid. Amer.	Middle American	Nfld	Newfoundland (Canada)
Latv.	Latvian	Middx	Middlesex (GB; old)	N.G.	National Gallery
lb, lbs	pound(s) weight	Mid. E.	Middle Eastern	N.G.A.	National Gallery of Art
Leb.	Lebanese	Mid. Eng.	Middle English	NH	New Hampshire (USA)
Lect.	Lecture	Mid Glam.	Mid Glamorgan (GB)	Niger.	Nigerian
Legis.	Legislative	Mil.	Military	NJ	New Jersey (USA)
Leics	Leicestershire (GB)	Mill.	Millennium	NM	New Mexico (USA)
Lex.	Lexicon	Min.	Ministry; Minutes	nm	nanometre (10^{-9} metre)
Lg.	Large	Misc.	Miscellaneous	nn.	notes
Lib., Libs	Library, Libraries	Miss.	Mission(s)	no., nos	number(s)
Liber.	Liberian	Mlle	Mademoiselle	Nord.	Nordic
Libsp	Librarianship	mm	millimetre(s)	Norm.	Normal
Lincs	Lincolnshire (GB)	Mme	Madame	Northants	Northamptonshire (GB)
Lit.	Literature	MN	Minnesota	Northumb.	Northumberland (GB)
Lith.	Lithuanian	Mnmt, Mnmts	Monument(s)	Norw.	Norwegian
Liturg.	Liturgical			Notts	Nottinghamshire (GB)
LLB	Bachelor of Laws	Mnmtl	Monumental	Nov	November
LLD	Doctor of Laws	MO	Missouri (USA)	n.p.	no place (of publication)
Lt	Lieutenant	Mod.	Modern, Modernist	N.P.G.	National Portrait Gallery
Lt-Col.	Lieutenant-Colonel	Moldav.	Moldavian	nr	near
Ltd	Limited				

Nr E.	Near Eastern	Per.	Period	Ptg(s)	Painting(s)
NS	New Style; Nova Scotia (Canada)	Percep.	Perceptions	Pub.	Public
		Perf.	Performance, Performing, Performed	pubd	published
n. s.	new series			Publ.	Publicity
NSW	New South Wales (Australia)	Period.	Periodical(s)	pubn(s)	publication(s)
NT	National Trust	Pers.	Persian	PVA	polyvinyl acetate
Ntbk	Notebook	Persp.	Perspectives	PVC	polyvinyl chloride
Numi.	Numismatic(s)	Peru.	Peruvian	Q.	quarterly
NV	Nevada (USA)	PhD	Doctor of Philosophy	4to	quarto
NW	Northwest(ern)	Philol.	Philology	Qué.	Québec (Canada)
NWT	Northwest Territories (Canada)	Philos.	Philosophy	*R*	reprint
		Phoen.	Phoenician	*r*	*recto*
NY	New York (USA)	Phot.	Photograph, Photography, Photographic	RA	Royal Academician
NZ	New Zealand			Radnors	Radnorshire (GB; old)
OBE	Officer of the Order of the British Empire	Phys.	Physician(s), Physics, Physique, Physical	RAF	Royal Air Force
				Rec.	Record(s)
Obj.	Object(s), Objective	Physiog.	Physiognomy	red.	reduction, reduced for
Occas.	Occasional	Physiol.	Physiology	Ref.	Reference
Occident.	Occidental	Pict.	Picture(s), Pictorial	Refurb.	Refurbishment
Ocean.	Oceania	pl.	plate; plural	*reg*	*regit* [ruled]
Oct	October	Plan.	Planning	Reg.	Regional
8vo	octavo	Planet.	Planetarium	Relig.	Religion, Religious
OFM	Order of Friars Minor	Plast.	Plastic	remod.	remodelled
OH	Ohio (USA)	pls	plates	Ren.	Renaissance
OK	Oklahoma (USA)	p.m.	post meridiem [after noon]	Rep.	Report(s)
Olymp.	Olympic	Polit.	Political	repr.	reprint(ed); reproduced, reproduction
OM	Order of Merit	Poly.	Polytechnic		
Ont.	Ontario (Canada)	Polynes.	Polynesian	Represent.	Representation, Representative
op.	opus	Pop.	Popular	Res.	Research
opp.	opposite; opera [pl. of opus]	Port.	Portuguese	rest.	restored, restoration
OR	Oregon (USA)	Port.	Portfolio	Retro.	Retrospective
Org.	Organization	Posth.	Posthumous(ly)	rev.	revision, revised (by/for)
Orient.	Oriental	Pott.	Pottery	Rev.	Reverend; Review
Orthdx	Orthodox	POW	prisoner of war	RHA	Royal Hibernian Academician
OSB	Order of St Benedict	PRA	President of the Royal Academy	RI	Rhode Island (USA)
Ott.	Ottoman			RIBA	Royal Institute of British Architects
Oxon	Oxfordshire (GB)	Pract.	Practical		
oz.	ounce(s)	Prefect.	Prefecture, Prefectural	RJ	Rio de Janeiro State
p	pence	Preserv.	Preservation	Rlwy	Railway
p., pp.	page(s)	prev.	previous(ly)	RSA	Royal Scottish Academy
PA	Pennsylvania (USA)	priv.	private	RSFSR	Russian Soviet Federated Socialist Republic
p.a.	per annum	PRO	Public Record Office		
Pak.	Pakistani	Prob.	Problem(s)	Rt Hon.	Right Honourable
Palaeontol.	Palaeontology, Palaeontological	Proc.	Proceedings	Rur.	Rural
		Prod.	Production	Rus.	Russian
Palest.	Palestinian	Prog.	Progress	S	San, Santa, Santo, Sant', São [Saint]
Pap.	Paper(s)	Proj.	Project(s)		
para.	paragraph	Promot.	Promotion	S.	South(ern)
Parag.	Paraguayan	Prop.	Property, Properties	s.	solidus, solidi [shilling(s)]
Parl.	Parliament	Prov.	Province(s), Provincial	Sask.	Saskatchewan (Canada)
Paroch.	Parochial	Proven.	Provenance	Sat.	Saturday
Patriarch.	Patriarchate	Prt, Prts	Print(s)	SC	South Carolina (USA)
Patriot.	Patriotic	Prtg	Printing	Scand.	Scandinavian
Patrm.	Patrimony	pseud.	pseudonym	Sch.	School
Pav.	Pavilion	Psych.	Psychiatry, Psychiatric	Sci.	Science(s), Scientific
PEI	Prince Edward Island (Canada)	Psychol.	Psychology, Psychological	Scot.	Scottish
Pembs	Pembrokeshire (GB; old)	pt	part	Sculp.	Sculpture

SD	South Dakota (USA)	suppl., suppls	supplement(s), supplementary	Urb.	Urban
SE	Southeast(ern)	Surv.	Survey	Urug.	Uruguayan
Sect.	Section	SW	Southwest(ern)	US	United States
Sel.	Selected	Swed.	Swedish	USA	United States of America
Semin.	Seminar(s), Seminary	Swi.	Swiss	USSR	Union of Soviet Socialist Republics
Semiot.	Semiotic	Symp.	Symposium		
Semit.	Semitic	Syr.	Syrian	UT	Utah
Sept	September	Tap.	Tapestry	*v*	*verso*
Ser.	Series	Tas.	Tasmanian	VA	Virginia (USA)
Serb.	Serbian	Tech.	Technical, Technique	V&A	Victoria and Albert Museum
Serv.	Service(s)	Technol.	Technology	Var.	Various
Sess.	Session, Sessional	Territ.	Territory	Venez.	Venezuelan
Settmt(s)	Settlement(s)	Theat.	Theatre	Vern.	Vernacular
S. Glam.	South Glamorgan (GB)	Theol.	Theology, Theological	Vict.	Victorian
Siber.	Siberian	Theor.	Theory, Theoretical	Vid.	Video
Sig.	Signature	Thurs.	Thursday	Viet.	Vietnamese
Sil.	Silesian	Tib.	Tibetan	viz.	*videlicet* [namely]
Sin.	Singhala	TN	Tennessee (USA)	vol., vols	volume(s)
sing.	singular	Top.	Topography	vs.	versus
SJ	Societas Jesu [Society of Jesus]	Trad.	Tradition(s), Traditional	VT	Vermont (USA)
Skt	Sanskrit	trans.	translation, translated by; transactions	Vulg.	Vulgarisation
Slav.	Slavic, Slavonic			W.	West(ern)
Slov.	Slovene, Slovenian	Transafr.	Transafrican	w.	width
Soc.	Society	Transatlant.	Transatlantic	WA	Washington (USA)
Social.	Socialism, Socialist	Transcarpath.	Transcarpathian	Warwicks	Warwickshire (GB)
Sociol.	Sociology	transcr.	transcribed by/for	Wed.	Wednesday
Sov.	Soviet	Triq.	Triquarterly	W. Glam.	West Glamorgan (GB)
SP	São Paulo State	Tropic.	Tropical	WI	Wisconsin (USA)
Sp.	Spanish	Tues.	Tuesday	Wilts	Wiltshire (GB)
sq.	square	Turk.	Turkish	Wkly	Weekly
sr	senior	Turkmen.	Turkmenistani	W. Midlands	West Midlands (GB)
Sri L.	Sri Lankan	TV	Television		
SS	Saints, Santi, Santissima, Santissimo, Santissimi; Steam ship	TX	Texas (USA)	Worcs	Worcestershire (GB; old)
		U.	University	Wtrcol.	Watercolour
SSR	Soviet Socialist Republic	UK	United Kingdom of Great Britain and Northern Ireland	WV	West Virginia (USA)
St	Saint, Sankt, Sint, Szent			WY	Wyoming (USA)
Staffs	Staffordshire (GB)	Ukrain.	Ukrainian	Yb., Y.-b.	Yearbook, Year-book
Ste	Sainte	Un.	Union	Yem.	Yemeni
Stud.	Study, Studies	Underwtr	Underwater	Yorks	Yorkshire (GB; old)
Subalp.	Subalpine	UNESCO	United Nations Educational, Scientific and Cultural Organization	Yug.	Yugoslavian
Sum.	Sumerian			Zamb.	Zambian
Sun.	Sunday	Univl	Universal	Zimb.	Zimbabwean
Sup.	Superior	unpubd	unpublished		

A Note on the Use of the Dictionary

This note is intended as a short guide to the basic editorial conventions adopted in this dictionary. For a fuller explanation, please refer to the Introduction, vol. 1, pp. xiii–xx.

Abbreviations in general use in the dictionary are listed on pp. vii–xii; those used in bibliographies and for locations of works of art or exhibition venues are listed in the Appendices in vol. 33.

Alphabetization of headings, which are distinguished in bold typeface, is letter by letter up to the first comma (ignoring spaces, hyphens, accents and any parenthesized or bracketed matter); the same principle applies thereafter. Abbreviations of 'Saint' and its foreign equivalents are alphabetized as if spelt out, and headings with the prefix 'Mc' appear under 'Mac'.

Authors' signatures appear at the end of the article or sequence of articles that the authors have contributed; in multipartite articles, any section that is unsigned is by the author of the next signed section. Where the article was compiled by the editors or in the few cases where an author has wished to remain anonymous, this is indicated by a square box (□) instead of a signature.

Bibliographies are arranged chronologically (within section, where divided) by order of year of first publication and, within years, alphabetically by authors' names. Abbreviations have been used for some standard reference books; these are cited in full in Appendix C in vol. 33, as are abbreviations of periodical titles (Appendix B). Abbreviated references to alphabetically arranged dictionaries and encyclopedias appear at the beginning of the bibliography (or section).

Biographical dates when cited in parentheses in running text at the first mention of a personal name indicate that the individual does not have an entry in the dictionary. The presence of parenthesized regnal dates for rulers and popes, however, does not necessarily indicate the lack of a biography of that person. Where no dates are provided for an artist or patron, the reader may assume that there is a biography of that individual in the dictionary (or, more rarely, that the person is so obscure that dates are not readily available).

Cross-references are distinguished by the use of small capital letters, with a large capital to indicate the initial letter of the entry to which the reader is directed; for example, 'He commissioned LEONARDO DA VINCI . . .' means that the entry is alphabetized under 'L'.

M

[continued]

Mächtig, Hermann (*b* Breslau, Silesia [now Wrocław, Poland], 18 Aug 1835; *d* Berlin, 1 July 1909). German garden designer. He was one of the most important landscape gardeners in 19th-century Berlin and one of the last representatives of the school of garden design represented by PETER JOSEPH LENNÉ and his pupil Gustav Meyer. Mächtig trained in the school of gardening at the Wildpark in Potsdam (1854–6), himself becoming in 1865 an instructor there. In 1870 he became court gardener at Sanssouci, Potsdam, and in 1875, City Inspector of Gardens in Berlin, the right-hand man of Meyer, whom he succeeded as Director of Gardens in 1877. Mächtig's activity was confined to Berlin and its neighbourhood. Until 1888 he continued Meyer's plan for the park at Treptow; one of his early works, in 1879, was a design, possibly never carried out, for a children's playground in the old Sophia cemetery (Heinrich-Zille Park), with a flowerbed representing the ground-plan of a Baroque church. About 1880 he designed a monument to *Alexander von Humboldt* in the Humboldthain; a year later he laid out the central cemetery at Friedrichsfelde. Among his main tasks was the design of the areas of greenery in numerous Berlin squares such as the Pariserplatz (1880; destr.); the Dönhoffplatz (1886; altered); the Alexanderplatz (1889; altered); the Wilhelmplatz (*c.* 1890; not executed); and the Lützowplatz (*c.* 1900; altered). His best-known work is the Viktoriapark on the Kreuzberg (1888–94), where Karl Friedrich Schinkel's monument (1818–21) to the *Wars of Liberation* forms a special look-out point. Mächtig's earliest plans for this park, dating from 1880, included cascades that were later eliminated; one waterfall, constructed from irregularly sized boulders, which can be illuminated in colour, emphasizes a visual axis from the Grossbeerenstrasse to the *Kreuzberg* monument. This effect, which is further enhanced by Johann Heinrich Strack's base for the monument (1878), was not included in the original layout. Mächtig's plan was criticized as a sentimental dramatization of the romantic landscape garden. Among his later works were the Plänterwald in Treptow (finished in 1897) and his entry (1907) for the competition for the Schillerpark in Berlin-Wedding. On that occasion the decision went against Mächtig's ideas, favouring the more convincingly modern approach of Friedrich Bauer (1872–1937) and the 'reforming' school of landscape gardening that prevailed around 1900.

BIBLIOGRAPHY
F. Wendland: *Berlins Gärten und Parke* (Frankfurt am Main, Berlin and Vienna, 1979)
M.-L. von Plessen, ed.: *Berlin durch die Blume oder Kraut und Rüben: Gartenkunst in Berlin-Brandenburg* (Berlin, 1985), pp. 163–5
U. Kieling: *Berliner Baubeamte und Staatsarchitekten im 19. Jahrhundert* (Berlin, 1986), pp. 217–18
M. Nungesser: *Das Denkmal auf dem Kreuzberg von Karl Friedrich Schinkel* (Berlin, 1987), pp. 86–92
W. Ribbe und W. Schäche: *Baumeister, Architekten, Stadtplaner: Biographien zur baulichen Entwicklung Berlins* (Berlin, 1987), pp. 637–8
R. Stürmer: *Die historische Entwicklung des Viktoria-Parkes: Von den ersten Planungen Hermann Mächtigs 1879/80 bis zur Eintragung in das Baudenkmalbuch 1980* (Berlin, 1988)

MICHAEL BOLLÉ

Machuca, Pedro (*b* Toledo, *c.* 1490; *d* Granada, 4 Aug 1550). Spanish painter and architect. The form of his signature (*Petrus Machuca, Hispanus. Toletanus . . .*) on his earliest known work, the *Virgin of Succour* (1517; Madrid, Prado), suggests he was active at an early age in Italy. On the basis of the style of that work, a number of frescoes in the Vatican have been attributed to him, including *Isaiah Blessing Jacob*. Other works from the same period that have been attributed to him include a copy (Paris, Louvre) of the destroyed *Battle of Anghiari* by Leonardo da Vinci and two paintings of the *Virgin and Child* (Rome, Gal. Borghese, and Turin, Gal. Sabauda), some drawings and the original drawings for reproductive engravings by Marcantonio Raimondi and Agostino Veneziano.

The uncertain nature of these attributions have made it difficult to follow Machuca's early development as an artist. At first linked by critics with Michelangelo, Raphael and Fra Bartolommeo, he has also been considered an exponent of Italian Mannerism of the 1510s (Longhi, 1953) along with such painters as Perino del Vaga, Correggio and Domenico Beccafumi. It is more likely that he was connected from 1515 to 1516 with Raphael's workshop, where he would have learnt composition and depiction of the human form. Machuca's interest in strong nocturnal effects and his sometimes exaggerated use of gesture and pose also indicate the influence of Leonardo da Vinci. His eclecticism, which made him receptive to the art of Rosso Fiorentino, Andrea del Sarto and Sebastiano del Piombo, makes his work rather impersonal, and yet he has a surprising continuity of form.

The short account of Machuca's life written between 1554 and 1564 by Lázaro de Velasco suggests that the painter returned to Spain with his father, Jacopo Florentino, c. 1520. He is mentioned that year in a contract for the altarpiece of *Our Lady of Consolation* (destr.) in Jaén Cathedral, and the following year in a contract for the altarpiece of the *Holy Cross* in the Royal Chapel in Granada, where the panels of the *Agony in the Garden*, the *Taking of Christ* and the *Descent into Limbo* are probably his. He settled in Granada, marrying Isabel de Horozco, who bore him seven children, the third of whom, Luis Machuca (1525–71), became an architect. From 1526 Pedro was also active as an architect, but he continued to work on altarpieces in Toledo, including those of *St John the Evangelist* and *St Catharine* in the Chapel of Old Kings in the cathedral, commissioned for Diego López de Ayala (c. 1480–1549), and at the monasteries at Uclés and Granada, most of which disappeared during the Revolt of Granada (1568–70). Among other identified works are certain panels of the altarpieces of Nostra Señora de la Encarnación, Monachil, Granada, S María la Mayor in Ubeda and, perhaps painted by his son after his drawings, that of the chapel of S Pedro de Osma in Jaén Cathedral (all 1540s). Other generally accepted works, of which the dating is uncertain, include *Pentecost* (Ponce, Mus. A.), the *Descent from the Cross* (c. 1547; Madrid, Prado), the *Burial of Christ* in the Franciscan monastery of Coria, Cáceres, and a triptych of the *Virgin and Child*, *Adam and Eve* and *SS Sebastian and Roch* (Madrid, priv. col., see Buendía, fig. 20). These works show little general stylistic change from his early work in Italy, as is apparent in the *Descent from the Cross*, which for a long time was thought to have been painted in Italy. A comparison between the preparatory drawing (Paris, Louvre, Cab. Dessins, Inv. 6303) and the completed work suggests that Machuca's Spanish patrons called for certain changes, including the addition of references to Michelangelo and to Dürer's engravings, greater accentuation of gesture, more extreme foreshortening, more precise descriptive detail and greater narrative expression.

A similar eclecticism and consistency are apparent in Machuca's few architectural works, which began in 1526 with his involvement in the ephemeral decorations for the entry of the Emperor Charles V and the Empress Isabella of Portugal into Granada. For example, his designs for the wall fountain, the Pilar of Charles V and the Puerta de las Granadas for the Alhambra of Granada are reminiscent of his most important work, the Palace of Charles V, also in the Alhambra, the design (either by himself or based on a drawing submitted by Giulio Romano) and direction of which occupied him almost exclusively between 1527 and 1550. In 1526 Machuca combined the preliminary planning of the palace with the decoration and renovation of the new rooms (*quartos nuevos*) of the 14th-century Nasrid Palace, for which he designed a mantelpiece and three ceilings coffered in the Italian style (1528–33). The laying of the foundations of the new palace began in 1533, and when he died Machuca had completed the basic structure of the ground-plan, including the two finest and most stately façades, at the south and west, the east doorway (?1548), the crypt and body of the octagonal chapel (1538–50) and the foundations of the circular courtyard colonnade (1540; see fig.). His son Luis continued the courtyard, making only a few modifications (1556–

68), and built the arcade of Doric columns (1561). The construction of the exterior courtyards to the south and east with their various adjacent dwellings (servants' quarters, stables and ballroom), as seen in Machuca's plans (Madrid, Bib. Pal. Real, X-M-242, fasc. 2 of 1528, and plan no. 2 of 1529), was never realized.

The palace's ground-plan, based on a square perimeter with a circular patio contained within, demonstrates Machuca's knowledge of the formal experimentation that characterized the circle of Raphael and Antonio da Sangallo the younger in Rome during the 1510s. It is a curious symbiosis of forms, derived in its typology from the Italian urban palazzo and the *villa suburbana*. Machuca included in his treatment of the Classical orders theoretical references from Cesare Cesariano's edition of Vitruvius (Como, 1521), rather than sources he had seen himself in Italy, combined with decorative motifs more in the tradition of the Spanish than of the Italian Renaissance, such as the window finials and the sculptured reliefs commemorating the Emperor Charles V's victories at Tunis (1535) and Mühlberg (1547); yet he remained fundamentally true to the architectural trends of his last years in Italy. These recent Italian influences were always more important to Machuca than examples from Classical antiquity. For example, his projected ground-plans owed more to schemes by Raphael, Giuliano and Antonio da Sangallo than to antique Roman sources. Similarly, in his treatment of walls and the Classical orders, he followed Antonio da Sangallo and Raphael in his choice of staircase, oval

Pedro Machuca: circular courtyard colonnade (1540) of the Palace of Charles V, Alhambra, Granada, begun 1533

antechamber, ring-shaped vault with depressed barrel, Serliana, octagonal chapel and the rhythmic openings for recesses in the courtyard wall. Machuca retained the most orthodox Vitruvian precepts (optical corrections and tapered pilasters) of centralization and axial symmetry, thus bringing his work closer to these earlier sources than to Giulio Romano's contemporary but more Mannerist work. In Italian terms his integration of rustic masonry, and the orders in particular, and his formal planning of the scheme as a whole, were an innovation. In Spain, on the other hand, the classical treatment of the façades of the palace, the orthodox use of the orders, the details derived from Vitruvius, the dependence on a rigorous geometrical formula and the symmetry and proportions of the planning led to Machuca's palace being regarded as an 'imported' work and not as a Castilian building.

BIBLIOGRAPHY

M. Gómez-Moreno y González: 'Palacio de Carlos V', *Rev. España*, xviii (1885), pp. 191–225

M. Gómez-Moreno: 'Sobre el renacimiento en Castilla: En la Capilla Real de Granada', *Archv Esp. A. & Arqueol.*, iii (1925), pp. 1–40

——: *Las águilas del renacimiento español* (Madrid, 1941, 2/1983)

R. Longhi: 'Comprimari spagnoli della maniera italiana', *Paragone*, 43 (1953), pp. 3–15

A. Griseri: 'Perino, Machuca, Campaña', *Paragone*, viii/87 (1957), pp. 13–21

——: 'Nuove chede di manierismo iberico', *Paragone*, x/113 (1959), pp. 33–44

J. Hernández Perera: '"La Sagrada Familia" de Pedro Machuca en la catedral de Jaén', *Archv Esp. A.*, xxxiii (1960), pp. 79–81

A. Griseri: 'Berruguete e Machuca dopo il viaggio italiano', *Paragone*, xv/179 (1964), pp. 3–19

R. Longhi: 'Ancora sul Machuca', *Paragone*, xx/231 (1969), pp. 34–9

D. Angulo Iñiguez and A. E. Pérez Sánchez: *A Corpus of Spanish Drawings: I, 1400–1600* (London, 1975)

G. Previtali: *La pittura del cinquecento a Napoli e nel vicereame* (Turin, 1976)

N. Dacos: *Le logge di Raffaello: Maestro e bottega di fronte all'antico* (Rome, 1977)

R. Buendía: *El renacimiento*, iii of *Historia del arte hispánico* (Madrid, 1980)

N. Dacos: 'Pedro Machuca en Italie', *Scritti di storia dell'arte in onore di Federico Zeri* (Milan, 1984), i, pp. 332–61

E. E. Rosenthal: *The Palace of Charles V in Granada* (Princeton, 1985)

F. Marías: *El largo siglo XVI: Los usos artísticos del renacimiento español* (Madrid, 1989)

M. Tafuri: *Ricerca del rinascimento* (Turin, 1992)

FERNANDO MARÍAS

Machu Picchu. Pre-Columbian Inca citadel in Peru, 120 km north of Cuzco in the eastern Andes.

1. INTRODUCTION. Machu Picchu citadel was built on a saddle between the peaks of Machu Picchu and Huayna Picchu, 2743 m above sea-level in the Cordillera de Vilcabamba, probably late in the reign of Inca Pachacutec Yupanqui (*reg* 1438–71). Although there is no direct mention of the site by Spanish chroniclers, archival data suggest that it may have formed part of the Inca's private estate of Quentemarca. The site was rediscovered by the American explorer Hiram Bingham in 1911. Clearing, research and restoration was carried out by Yale University expeditions in 1911, 1912 and 1915, and the first plan of the site was drawn by Albert Blumstead. Fifty-two burial caves were excavated by George Eaton and Elwood Erdis. Further restoration and excavation at the site, and at several smaller locations in the immediate vicinity, has been conducted under the direction of the Instituto Nacional de Cultura since the 1950s.

1. Machu Picchu, general view

Machu Picchu site is an outstanding example of Inca architecture in its mature phase, displaying the canons of Inca construction and planning in an unusually homogeneous form. There the Inca architects achieved an equilibrium between uniformity and inventiveness in layout and demonstrated the use of classic Inca symmetry with a delicate new asymmetry, in harmony with an extraordinarily dramatic environment (see fig. 1; *see also* INCA, fig. 2). The forested slopes of the mountain-sides descend 610 m to the River Urubamba (Vilcanota), which circumvents the granite outcrop on three sides. The function of Machu Picchu citadel in its isolated location cannot be assessed in practical terms. The site offered natural security and privacy, and magnificent views for calendrical observations and sun worship, and was therefore probably an élitist centre with many shrines and facilities for carrying out ceremonial rituals.

2. ARCHITECTURE. The particular quality of Machu Picchu is its juxtaposition of the human scale of the architecture and the dramatic setting among precipitous mountains. The granite used in the construction was quarried *in situ* and worked into a variety of fitted masonry styles (*see* SOUTH AMERICA, PRE-COLUMBIAN, §III, 2(iii)). The finest examples are found in the fitted and graded, coursed rectangular style of the Torreón (see fig. 2a) and its associated walls, and in the softly sculptured, recessed joints of the polygonal and mixed styles in the Temple of the Three Windows (see fig. 2b). The monoliths and boulders are carved with planes, abstract forms and sometimes carved receptacles to receive offerings. Imprecisely fitted masonry and fieldstone construction were used for the less prestigious buildings, especially in some residential quarters, and sometimes for the gables of

2. Machu Picchu, plan, *c.* 1438–71: (a) Torreón Group; (b) Sacred Plaza with Temple of the Sun, Temple of the Three Windows and a priest's house; (c) Intihuatana hill; (d) Stairway of the Fountains; (e) burial caves; (f) Inca Palace; (g) residential groups; (h) residential groups; (i) Shrine Group; (j) Ingenuity Group and garden; (k) storehouses; (l) Little Huayna Picchu

structures. The latter were also sometimes constructed of adobe bricks.

In addition to the detailing of the architectural style and its use of regularly spaced trapezoidal doorways, niches and windows, both Machu Picchu and its outlying sites have a variety of intricate features: some of the steepest gables for carrying off rain; practical devices for fixing roofs and for shutting doorways; 'eye-bonders' (stones bored with holes) embedded in sloping gable walls; projecting stone pegs on external gable faces; barholds (small cylindrical stones placed vertically within a niche) and perforated stones at the edges of niches; and barhole perforations along the edge of a window.

The main ruins in the saddle are distributed around a long rectangular plaza and can be divided into the two sectors traditional in Inca urban planning—Hanan (upper) and Hurin (lower)—containing 143 main buildings and about 60 secondary structures. Only 80 of the main buildings appear to have been residential, with remarkably different group layouts and some highly specialized structures built in several contemporaneous masonry styles. Most buildings, however, are the more standard one-room structures arranged around open courts, in enclosures and/or along terraces. Back-to-back double structures occasionally divide two courtyards within a group, and some buildings have a second storey. Most of the remaining 63 buildings have an open front, and many have special features suggesting a ceremonial function—for example the Temple of the Sun (2b), the Temple of the Three Windows and the structures delimiting the space around the Intihuatana stone (2c; 'the tying post of the Sun', one of the most complete and beautiful examples known, carved with a sensitive and inventive arrangement of planes; *see* SHRINE (i), fig. 7). The mountain-side itself is landscaped by means of terraces, with drainage channels and stone stairways giving access to buildings and other terraces. The main stairway of the site, linking the two

sectors, is lined with 16 finely constructed and dramatically laid out fountain baths (2d).

The main groups in the Hanan sector include the Sacred Plaza (2b), with two open-fronted temples and a priest's house, and the Intihuatana hill (2c), connected to the Sacred Plaza by steps and bound front and back by terraces. These two groups, together with the area of rock and cave burials (2e) behind the Sacred Plaza, crown the Torreón Group (2a) and the Inca Palace below (2f). The Inca Palace comprises a controlled entrance to a group of two small, well-built rooms—one of which has an ante-chamber with a rock-carved drainage system—and a high, open structure. Beyond these are more domestic buildings (2g). On terraces behind the Torreón Group is a residential group of modest buildings arranged in pairs, having been converted from open structures to closed dwellings (2h). The Torreón Group comprises an irregular semicircular shaped tower enclosing a carved stone that may have been a sundial. This is built on a carved rock shrine with a variety of niches and features for displaying ritual objects. From the carved trapezoidal window of the Torreón, calendrical observations could be made to points in the surrounding mountains.

In the Hurin sector, the main Shrine Group (2i) contains structures with a variety of niches and irregularly shaped buildings. An open structure is built on a rock at an angle of 45°; the niches lining its walls have barholds carved in each side edge. Associated with this structure are a subterranean rock cavern and carved drainage holes, probably used for ritual purposes. The three or four residential groups in this sector are differentiated by the quality of the buildings and in their layout and access patterns. For example, one house in the Ingenuity Group (2j) has two boulders projecting through the floor that were carved into mortars. Two-storey storehouses (2k) overlook the terraces at the edge of the site.

To the north-west, the Hurin sector terminates in some boulders and two buildings beside Sacred Rock (Little Huayna Picchu; 2l). From here a steeply stepped road links Machu Picchu to the precipitous peak of Huayna Picchu. On that peak there are a few narrow terraces and structures, including the Temple of the Moon, an outstanding example of late Inca architecture situated on a descent from Huayna Picchu. It consists of two carved and masonry-built rock caverns, each surmounted by a building, linked by a stepped road and divided by an ornamental façade. The fine cutting and recessed detailing of some of the niches in the upper cavern, and the asymmetrical fluidity of the plan—in perfect relationship to the environment—is unsurpassed. At the south-eastern access to the main site, beyond and above a terrace system, a barrack-like building and several other structures overlook the saddle. Roads from Cuzco (south) and from the west converge on this spur, passing through a system of lookouts and checkpoints. Huiñay Huayna, Inti Pata, Phuyu Pata Marca and Sayac Marca are all sites on the road to the south.

BIBLIOGRAPHY

H. Bingham: *Machu Picchu: Citadel of the Incas* (New Haven, 1930/R 1973)

L. E. Valcárcel: *Machu Pijchu* (Buenos Aires, 1964)

V. Angles Vargas: *Machupijchu: Enigmatica ciudad inka* (Lima, 1972)

J. Hemming: *Machu Picchu* (New York, 1981)

——: *Monuments of the Incas* (Boston, 1982)

A. Kendall: *Aspects of Inca Architecture: Description, Function and Chronology*, 2 vols, Brit. Archaeol. Rep., Int. Ser., 242 (Oxford, 1985)

——: 'Inca Planning North of Cuzco, between Anta and Machu Picchu and along the Urubama Valley', *Recent Studies in Pre-Columbian Archaeology*, ed. N. Saunders and O. de Montmollin, Brit. Archaeol. Rep., Int. Ser., 421 (Oxford, 1988), pp. 457–88

J. H. Hyslop: *Inca Settlement Planning* (Austin, 1990)

ANN KENDALL

Machy, Pierre-Antoine de (*b* Paris, *bapt* 19 Sept 1723; *d* Paris, 10 Sept 1807). French painter and engraver. He was the son of a cabinetmaker and served his apprenticeship with Giovanni Niccolo Servandoni. He was approved (*agréé*) by the Académie Royale de Peinture, Paris, in 1755 and was received (*reçu*) three years later as a painter of architecture. He exhibited regularly at the Salon from 1757 to 1802. His views of the interiors of the Paris churches of Ste Geneviève and the Madeleine were painted from architectural plans and exhibited at the Salons of 1761 and 1763 respectively, earning Diderot's praise. At the Salon of 1763 de Machy also demonstrated his talent for painting contemporary events with a pair of pictures of the *Foire Saint-Germain* after the fire of 1762 (both Paris, Carnavalet) and a scene of the *Installation of Bouchardon's Statue of Louis XV* (untraced; engraved by Antoine François Hémery, *b* 1751), with the statue being placed on its pedestal in the Place Louis XV (now the Place de la Concorde). Later, however, de Machy suffered increasingly from comparison with other painters, especially those who, unlike himself, had studied in Italy. At the Salon of 1765 his *Inauguration of Ste Geneviève* and the *Building of the Halle au Blé* (both Paris, Carnavalet) were overshadowed by Servandoni's works, and in 1767 his pictures were totally eclipsed by the works of Hubert Robert, who had recently returned from Italy. At this exhibition Diderot found de Machy's pictures lacking in the quality of handling and Italian light effects that characterized Robert's painting.

De Machy continued to depict changes in the Parisian townscape in such works as the wash drawing of the *Demolition of the Hôtel Guénégaud in 1771* and the painting of the *Demolition of the Church of the Innocents in 1787* (both Paris, Carnavalet). The baptism of the Dauphin (Louis, son of Louis XVI) on 21 January 1782 occasioned two further pictures recording contemporary events, the *Arrival of the Queen at the Hôtel de Ville* for the baptism ceremony and the *Celebratory Firework Display at the Spanish Embassy*. He was made an adviser (*conseiller*) at the Académie Royale in 1775 and was appointed Professor of Perspective in 1786.

De Machy produced a number of decorative works. Dézallier d'Argenville's *Voyage pittoresque* (6/1778) records among others a background scheme in the church of St Roch, a set of paintings in the Palais-Royal and various *trompe l'oeil* effects in private garden locations. In the 1780s de Machy turned his talent for engraving to commercial use. At the Salon of 1781 he exhibited a set of views of Paris intended principally for engraving, colouring and sale by subscription. He continued to produce coloured prints after his own pictures and those of other artists, including an engraving (untraced) after a *Sleeping Child* by Murillo, inscribed and dated Madrid 1787.

After 1789 de Machy adapted his skills to revolutionary requirements, depicting the *Federation of the French* (14 July 1790), the *Festival of Unity* (10 Aug 1793), the *Festival of the Supreme Being* (8 June 1794) and *An Execution* (all Paris, Carnavalet). The less refined style of these later pictures and the profusion of badly drawn figures led Wilhelm to suggest that these works may have been painted by de Machy's son.

BIBLIOGRAPHY

A. J. Dézallier d'Argenville: *Voyage pittoresque des environs de Paris* (Paris, 1728, rev. 6/1778)

J. Cain: *Guide explicatif du Musée Carnavalet* (Paris, 1903)

D. Diderot: *Les Salons, 1759–1781*, ed. J. Seznec and J. Adhémar, 4 vols (Oxford, 1957–67)

J. Wilhelm: 'Une Peinture révolutionnaire de l'atelier d'Antoine de Machy', *Bull. Mus. Carnavalet*, i (1961), pp. 12–13

P. de la Vaissière: 'La Fédération des Français peinte par P.-A. de Machy: Essai d'iconographie de la fête de juillet 1790', *Bull. Mus. Carnavalet*, ii (1975), pp. 16–30

JOSHUA DRAPKIN

Machzor [Heb.: 'cycle']. Liturgical manuscript containing the prayers, liturgical hymns and Bible readings appropriate to each holy day of the Jewish yearly cycle. Such manuscripts first appeared in the 13th century in Jewish communities along the Rhine, becoming one of their most typical productions. These liturgical volumes were often large in format; the *machzor* was designed to be placed on the reading desk and read or chanted aloud by the *chazan* (cantor). The most splendid volumes, such as the Amsterdam Machzor (Amsterdam, Joods Hist. Mus.), were decorated and increasingly came to be illustrated.

The first elements of what became a definite iconographic programme appeared in the mid-13th-century Michael Machzor (Oxford, Bodleian Lib., Mich. MS. 617, 627). Only a few years later, the Laud Machzor (see fig.)

Illuminated page from the Laud Machzor, mid-13th century (Oxford, Bodleian Library, MS. Laud Or. 321, fol. 127v)

already exhibited the complete repertory, which was retained for approximately a century without noteworthy modifications. It included illustrations of Bible scenes related to texts read on particular holy days, for example the *Departure from Egypt* for Pesach (Passover); the *Divine Revelation on Mt Sinai* for Shavuot (Feast of Weeks); the *Sacrifice of Isaac* for Rosh ha-Shanah (New Year); and the *Hanging of the Sons of Haman* for Purim (Feast of Lots). Other illustrations were symbolic of biblical texts read on certain special Sabbaths: they included a weigher of shekels and a red heifer. A star and a crescent moon announced the beginning of a new month. Other representations evoked ritual actions and customs: the blowing of the *shofar* (ram's horn) for Rosh ha-Shanah; the *kapparah* (rite of expiation) for Yom Kippur (Day of Atonement); a tabernacle for Sukkot (Feast of Tabernacles).

Manuscripts particularly famous for their quality or their history include the Worms Machzor (Jerusalem, Jew. N. & U. Lib., Heb. MS. 4° 781), the Leipzig Machzor (Leipzig, Ubib., MS. V1102), the Dresden/Wrocław Machzor in two volumes (Dresden, Sächs. Landesbib., MS. Cod. A 46a, and U. Wrocław, Lib., MS. Or. I, 1) and the Tripartite Machzor (Budapest, Lib. Hung. Acad. Sci., MS. A. 384; London, BL, Add. MS. 22413; Oxford, Bodleian Lib., Mich. MS. 619). The last manuscript to use this programme fully (Darmstadt, Hess. Landes- & Hochschbib., Cod. Or. 13) dates from 1348, the year of the Black Death, for the unrest that followed this scourge largely put an

end to the production of *machzor* manuscripts. A *machzor* of more modest dimensions, with decorations only, was produced in the upper Rhine region (Jerusalem, Jew. N. & U. Lib., Hebrew MS. 80 5214). Exceptionally, some elements from the programme appeared in an Italian *machzor* of 1441 (Jerusalem, Schocken Lib., MS. 13873).

See also JEWISH ART, §V, 1; for further illustration *see* MICROGRAPHY.

BIBLIOGRAPHY
B. Narkiss and E. Katz: *Machsor Lipsiae* (Leipzig, 1964)
T. Metzger and M. Metzger: *Jewish Life in the Middle Ages: Illuminated Hebrew Manuscripts of the Thirteenth to the Sixteenth Centuries* (New York, 1982)
G. Sed-Rajna: *Le Mahzor enluminé* (Leiden, 1983)
M. Beit-Arié, ed.: *The Worms Mahzor* (Jerusalem, 1986) [facs. edn with commentaries]

GABRIELLE SED-RAJNA

Maciachini, Carlo (*b* Induno Olona, Varese, 2 April 1818; *d* Varese, 10 June 1899). Italian architect. He worked as a carpenter and then a cabinetmaker, continuing in these trades for many years, even after 1838, when he went to Milan to attend courses at the Accademia di Brera. By independent study he learnt the formal repertory of Western architecture, but he soon acquired his own personal style, which combined originality, balanced composition, attention to detail and imaginative interpretation, rather than passive imitation of earlier architectural forms. Maciachini's architectural work began when he won the competition for the Greek Orthodox church of S Spiridione in Trieste (1859–69), which he designed in a Byzantine style. He gained considerable fame with his entry for the competition (1863) for the Cimitero Monumentale, Milan. This Italian–Gothic project was his major work, and he supervised its execution until 1887. Many projects and building commissions followed, but he continued to enter competitions and maintained an interest, though only a marginal one, in applied industrial art. Through his particular interest in medieval motifs he was generally thought of as a follower of the neo-Gothic style. However, his attempt to reinterpret the architecture of the 13th, 14th and 15th centuries led to an inevitable eclecticism, though this was never exaggerated or coldly erudite. Medieval elements are found in his church of S Carlo (1890–97) in Biasca, Switzerland, and in his own house (1867; destr.) in Milan, where he experimented fully with the possibilities offered by a wide architectural frame of reference. In his work on existing buildings Maciachini showed a capacity for adaptation to the different styles suggested by the original structure, so as to produce a sense of formal unity. He created numerous façades; some of these were totally new, such as the front of S Maria del Carmine (1880), Milan, which he faced in a Lombard–Gothic style, and those of SS Flavio e Giorgio, Voghera, and Pavia Cathedral (1893–5), for which he had also designed the dome (1883–6). In his restorations, as at S Marco (1872–3), Milan, the distinction between newly designed elements and repaired old ones is often indefinable: Maciachini followed the common practice of analogical restoration, though in some cases he avoided the excesses of forced embellishments or inappropriate corrections.

BIBLIOGRAPHY
Catalogo della Biblioteca Maciachini, 1877 (Milan, 1877)
P. Mezzanotte: 'L'edilizia milanese dalla caduta del Regno Italico alla prima guerra mondiale', *Storia di Milano*, ed. G. Treccani degli Alfieri, xv (Milan, 1962), pp. 412–14
L. Franchini: 'Carlo Maciachini "intagliatore" a Varese', *Tracce*, iv (1983), pp. 319–28
——: 'Il cimitero monumentale di Milano nel dibattito sull'eclettismo nell'architettura funeraria', *A. Lombarda*, 68–9 (1984), pp. 79–95
——: 'Un architetto–restauratore lombardo del secondo ottocento: Carlo Maciachini', *A. Lombarda*, 83 (1987), pp. 97–120

LUCIO FRANCHINI

Macijauskas, Aleksandras (*b* Kaunas, 16 May 1938). Lithuanian photographer. He was abandoned as a child and trained as a toolmaker in a lathe factory. He graduated from the aviation training institution during his national service. In 1963 he became a member of the Kaunas photo-club and dedicated himself to photography. He began working as a photojournalist for the *Vakarines naujienos* newspaper in Kaunas in 1967. At that time he became involved with the theme of village markets. He achieved his first success in 1969, when he won an international photography competition in Czechoslovakia and was featured in the Czechoslovak *Revue fotografie*. This success changed his life: he was accepted as a member of the Union of Soviet Journalists and the Soviet state allocated him a flat. In 1973 he left his job in journalism and became the secretary of the recently founded Photographic Art Society of Lithuania in Vilnius. In 1979 he founded a new branch of the Society in Kaunas and its affiliated gallery of photography. In 1985 he founded the School of Photography for teenagers.

In his extensive series of photographs of Lithuanian *Village Markets* (begun 1972; see Mrázková and Remeš, nos 106–21) Macijauskas gathered much evidence of the social traditions of Lithuanian villagers, who since the Middle Ages have rallied after the harvest at big fairs to sell and buy things and to socialize. Macijauskas always used a wide-angle lens, which lessened the distance between photographer and subject and created images that appear heroic and poetic but at the same time ironic in their documentary immediacy; this pushes documentary evidence towards metaphor. In addition to his *Village Markets* he began in 1979 to photograph veterinary hospitals. Macijauskas's work was widely exhibited in Europe and admired for its documentary value and for its vitality. Together with his friend the photographer Antanas Sutkus (*b* 1938) Macijauskas prompted the creation of a school of Lithuanian photography.

BIBLIOGRAPHY
D. Mrázková and V. Remeš: *Another Russia: Through the Eyes of the New Soviet Photographers* (London, 1986)

DANIELA MRÁZKOVÁ

McIlworth, Thomas (*fl* New York, 1757–69/70). American painter. An itinerant New York artist, he is first noted as becoming a member of the St Andrews Society in New York in 1757. The following year, on 8 May, he advertised his skills as a portrait painter in the *New York Mercury*. Around 1761, following his marriage, McIlworth moved to nearby Westchester, where he remained briefly before settling for three years in upstate New York, in the Albany-Schenectady region. Apparently he returned to New York but soon afterwards departed for Montreal, where he is last recorded in October 1767.

Presumably born in America and self-taught, McIlworth was one of a number of migrant artists who painted in the prevailing provincial Rococo style. Several of his works were formerly attributed to Joseph Blackburn, who was active in America from 1754 to 1763. His portrait style is comparable with that of Copley's early works: distinctive traits in many of McIlworth's portraits include elongated faces, tightly drawn features and flushed skin tones. Among his best-known likenesses are those of the prominent Stuyvesant (e.g. 1760; New York, NY Hist. Soc.), Van Rensselaer (e.g. Albany, NY, Inst. Hist. & A.) and Livingston families of New York. A typical example is his portrait of *Philip Livingston* (New York, Brooklyn Hist. Soc.), a signatory of the Declaration of Independence.

BIBLIOGRAPHY
S. Sawitsky: 'Thomas McIlworth (Active 1758–*c.* 1769)', *NY Hist. Soc. Q.*, xxv (1951), pp. 117–39
S. K. Johnston: *American Paintings, 1750–1900, from the Collection of the Baltimore Museum of Art* (Baltimore, 1983), pp. 101–2

SONA K. JOHNSTON

McIntire, Samuel (*bapt* Salem, MA, 16 Jan 1757; *d* Salem, 6 Feb 1811). American architect, draughtsman and wood-carver. His father was a house carpenter, and with his two brothers he was brought up to the same trade. He went on to become a skilled draughtsman, thus qualifying himself to design buildings in whose construction he was to have no part. His work as a wood-carver included ships' figureheads, the decoration of interiors designed by himself and of furniture designed by others—he was not himself a furniture designer or maker—and a few pieces of sculpture (mostly symbolic eagles, portrait busts and reliefs). As an architect McIntire won many commissions and was second in importance only to Charles Bulfinch in New England during the early Federal period. As a result of the American War of Independence, Salem became a prosperous seaport, whose merchants were wealthy enough to commission large houses. McIntire was particularly fortunate, at the beginning of his career, in coming to the notice of one of the wealthiest Salem merchants, Elias Hasket Derby, who provided him with almost continuous employment until his death in 1799.

McIntire's architecture divides into two periods. In the first, starting in 1780 with his first house for Derby, he carried on the colonial Georgian tradition. His finest surviving building of this period is the Peirce–Nichols House (*c.* 1782), Salem, a three-storey clapboard building with giant Doric pilasters on the façade. The Doric orders and some interior details came from Batty Langley's *City and Country Builder's and Workman's Treasury of Designs* (1740). Among his other buildings of the period was the Salem Court House (1785; destr. 1839), his first civic building. In 1792 he submitted a design in a public competition for the United States Capitol (unexecuted). This design, which is indebted to James Gibbs's *Book of Architecture* (1728), marked the end of McIntire's early period. In 1793 McIntire made his first contributions to what has since been called the Federal style, with the Nathan Read House (destr. 1857), Salem, and the Lyman House, Waltham, MA. Two features characteristic of the

Federal style that appeared for the first time were the semi-circular porch with columns, in the Nathan Read House, and the oval room, in the Lyman House. In 1795 he received a commission for the Elias Hasket Derby Mansion (1795–9; destr. 1815) in Salem. This was Derby's grandest house, for which McIntire designed a façade with Ionic pilasters, balustrade and cupola. Inside, he combined an oval room, with a segmental portico over it, and an oval stair hall. He also supplied much of the carved ornament, which like his other later work derives from William and James Pain's *Practical House Carpenter* (London, 1790; Boston, 1796). McIntire's elegant South Church (1803–4), Salem, with its graceful steeple, burnt down in 1903. His surviving buildings in Salem include the John Gardner House (1804–5) and Hamilton Hall (1805–7), which housed the Salem assemblies. The John Gardner House is a perfectly proportioned brick mansion, with an imposing yet delicate Corinthian porch. It is undoubtedly McIntire's masterpiece. Inside, on mantelpieces and door surrounds, is some of his finest carved ornament, which typically combines chains of husks and classical frets with naturalistic foliage, vases of flowers, bowls of fruit and wheatsheaves. It shows the same skill and sensitivity as his furniture carving, the few authenticated examples of which have established him as one of the leading craftsmen of the period.

BIBLIOGRAPHY

Macmillan Enc. Architects

S. F. Kimball: *Mr Samuel McIntire, Carver: The Architect of Salem* (Portland, ME, 1940/*R* Gloucester, MA, 1966)

H. Comstock: 'McIntire in Antiques', *Antiques*, lxxi (1957), pp. 338–41 [summary of articles on McIntire as furniture carver]

B. W. Labaree, ed.: *Samuel McIntire: A Bicentennial Symposium, 1757–1957: Salem, 1957*

MARCUS WHIFFEN

McIntosh, W(illiam) Gordon (*b* Glasgow, 29 Nov 1904; *d* Pretoria, 27 July 1983). South African architect. He trained at the University of the Witwatersrand, Johannesburg (1923–7), in the Beaux-Arts tradition of Edwin Lutyens and Herbert Baker but was strongly influenced in his later development towards the newly emerging Modern Movement by his exposure to the work of van Heukelom and H. P. Berlage while on a student tour of Europe (1925–6). In 1929 McIntosh became South Africa's second architectural graduate. His early work included the A. G. Munro House (1932), Pretoria, one of the earliest and best examples of the International Style in this country and a landmark in South African architectural development. It demonstrates a simple, rational outward expression, the direct result of the internal regulation of the parts. In 1933, with Norman L. Hanson and Rex Martienssen, McIntosh co-edited and privately published the propagandist quarterly *Zerohour*, which aimed at focusing attention on the Modern Movement. It contained a manifesto and examples of the work of Le Corbusier, Walter Gropius and Mies van der Rohe, as well as examples of local avant-garde architecture including the Munro House. Other significant works by McIntosh in Pretoria include the H. Munro House (1935); W. G. McIntosh House (1936); and Henderson Mansions ('Whitecrook') (1940; destr. 1984), an austerely rationalist block of flats notable for the use of pilotis. McIntosh played a crucial role in the development of the International Style in South Africa, but its progress was halted by the outbreak of World War II. His later work, sometimes in association with others, included Caxton printing works (1947); the Poynton building (1950); and the notable Customs House and Assize building (1951), all in Pretoria, which show acknowledgement of climate, local influences and materials.

WRITINGS

with R. D. Martienssen and N. L. Hanson, eds: *Zerohour* (Johannesburg, 1933)

BIBLIOGRAPHY

N. L. Hanson and J. Fassler: 'House Brooklyn, Pretoria', *S. Afr. Archit. Rec.*, xxii/5 (1938), pp. 141–54

H. Casson: 'Modern Architecture in South Africa', *Archit. Rev.* [London], lxxxiii (1940), pp. 37–46

G. Herbert: *Martienssen and the International Style* (Cape Town, 1975)

CLYDE C. C. MEINTJES

McIntyre, (Robert) Peter (*b* Melbourne, 24 Aug 1927). Australian architect. He studied architecture at the University of Melbourne (1944–50 and 1955) and at the Royal Melbourne Technical College (1953). He rose to prominence when, with KEVIN BORLAND and John and Phyllis Murphy, he won the competition for the Olympic Swimming Pool, Melbourne (1952). In 1953 he formed a partnership of Borland, Murphy & McIntyre, which lasted three years. When the pool was completed in 1956 McIntyre joined his wife in the partnership of Peter & Dione McIntyre.

Unlike Borland, McIntyre retained his interest in structural expressionism and geometric forms, of which his house at 2 Hodgson Street, Kew, Melbourne (1953), is an example, its exposed frame raised on a central support against the flooding to which the site is susceptible. Beulah Hospital in north-west Victoria (also 1953) is less expressive but is a sensitive attempt to provide the shade and ventilation appropriate to the arid climate of the locality. After 1956 McIntyre designed two other swimming pools and experimented with frame and panel systems for housing. In 1961 his practice merged with that of his father, Robert H. McIntyre, to create McIntyre, McIntyre & Partners Ltd. As part of a consortium, 'Interplan', the firm was commissioned to prepare the Melbourne Strategy Plan in 1973–4, which determined much of the form of central Melbourne for a decade or more. In 1974 McIntyre designed Parliament Station for the Melbourne Underground Rail Loop Authority and converted the two-hectare Henry Jones Jam Factory building, South Yarra, Melbourne, into a shopping centre. Thereafter the practice undertook a number of planning commissions and housing and resort developments, of which Dinner Plain Alpine Village (1987–9) is the best-known. He was President of the Royal Australian Institute of Architects in 1973–4, became an Officer of the Order of Australia in 1982 and was appointed to a chair in architecture at Melbourne University in 1987.

WRITINGS

Cross-section (Melbourne, 1951–3)

with D. H. Wolbrink and G. J. Connor: *City of Melbourne Strategy Plan* (Melbourne, 1973)

'Struggle for Meaning', *Archit. Australia*, dxxix/5 (1990), pp. 30–33

BIBLIOGRAPHY
P. Goad: 'Optimism and Experiment', *Archit. Australia*, dxxix/5 (1990), pp. 34–53

MILES LEWIS

Maçip [Macip; Masip]. Spanish painters. (1) Vicente Maçip and his son (2) Juan de Juanes were probably the most significant artists in Valencia in the 16th century and beyond, at a time when the city was becoming a bridge for the entry of Renaissance ideals into Spain.

(1) Vicente Maçip (*b* ?Andilla, *c*. 1474–5; *d* Valencia, 1550). An appraisal of his art is based on the high altar in Segorbe Cathedral, comprising a series of panels with scenes from the *Life of the Virgin* (1528–30; *in situ*). These reveal the way in which the Valencian pictorial tradition of the previous century was gradually being discarded as elements of north Italian painting were introduced by Fernando Yáñez and Fernando de los Llanos. Maçip's use of solid architectural constructions to frame some of his paintings is also found in the work of Yáñez. The maturity evident in Maçip's Segorbe altarpiece is probably the result of a journey to Italy, which must have taken place before 1527, the year of the Sack of Rome, and the work is the clearest indication of the changes in Valencian art 20 years after Yáñez and Llanos. Three panels deriving from the Segorbe altarpiece are preserved in the church at Villatorca: two *Prophets* and the *Eucharistic Saviour*, of which the last is the most significant, as it anticipates what was to be achieved by Maçip's son, (2) Juan de Juanes, although here the feeling is more hieratic and less soft. The large panel of the *Baptism* (1535; Valencia Cathedral) has traditionally been attributed to Juanes, probably because for some years his fame eclipsed that of his father. In fact, it is a mature work by Maçip painted in collaboration with his son, the vigorous style of Maçip combining with the sweeter, softer approach of Juanes, who was then still deeply influenced by his father, although his hand is not difficult to determine. The circular paintings, the *Visitation* and the *Martyrdom of St Inés* (both *c*. 1535–45; Madrid, Prado), combine Maçip's austere classicism with elements taken from Raphael's frescoes in the Vatican Stanze. Outstanding in the first is the breadth of the scene portrayed, while the second is remarkable for the landscape, which has been given more attention than the actual event. In the same line of development are the *Fall of St Paul* (*c*. 1530–35; Valencia, Mus. Catedralicio-Dioc.) and the *Last Supper* (*c*. 1545; Valencia, Mus. B.A.).

BIBLIOGRAPHY
D. Angulo Iñíguez: *Pintura del renacimiento*, A. Hisp., xii (Madrid, 1954)

(2) Juan de Juanes [Joan de Joanes; Juan Maçip] (*b* Valencia, *c*. 1510; *d* Bocairente, Valencia prov., 21 Dec 1579). Son of (1) Vicente Maçip. His work is technically less precise than that of his father in the delineation of form; he preferred *sfumato* effects in modelling, very different from the sharper sculptural outlines of Maçip. In colour, Juanes preferred clear, luminous tones with which he achieved a characteristic Mannerist iridescence. His landscapes, too, differ from those of his father, becoming yet another decorative element. They often include classical ruins such as the pyramid of Caius Sextus or Egyptian obelisks, all of which are treated with the same delicacy and grace as his human forms.

Between 1530 and 1550 Juanes worked with his father, by whom he was strongly influenced, although his style was already distinctive and became increasingly so as he modelled himself more on Paolo da San Leocadia, Fernando Yáñez and Fernando de los Llanos. Father and son contracted jointly for some commissions, such as the St Eligius altarpiece (Valencia, S Martin) for the Silversmiths' Guild on 13 March 1536. Between 1547 and 1550 Juanes executed the retable at Fuente la Higuera, Valencia, in which the influence of the elder Maçip is still clear. There the compositions of the *Birth of the Virgin* and the *Pietà* follow closely those of his father in the high altar (1528–30) of Segorbe Cathedral, although his own style is expressed with a more marked delicacy and fluidity in the use of line and colour. In the panel paintings of the *Baptism* and *Christ among the Doctors* (both *c*. 1545–50; Palma de Mallorca Cathedral) the mature style of Juanes began to emerge, as is apparent in the expressions of the faces and in the landscape backgrounds.

Juanes's mature style is evident in his most important works, painted between 1550 and 1560. These include the two retables for side altars in the choir of S Nicolás, Valencia, belonging to the Woolcarders' Guild, which depict scenes from the lives of Christ and the Virgin, the miracles of St Michael and scenes from the Creation. All executed *c*. 1555, these show the influence of Leonardo, mediated through the work of Yáñez and Llanos. The three panels of the predella, the *Creation of Man, Mammals* and *Birds*, recall the treatment of the same subjects by Raphael in the Vatican Logge. A major work of this period is the *Virgin of the Mystic Marriage of the Venerable Agnesius* (*c*. 1560; Valencia, Mus. B.A.), which demonstrates Juanes's capacity for assimilation. It harmoniously combines certain elements from an earlier, almost miniaturist, style together with an acceptance of the Renaissance spirit introduced to Valencia by Yáñez and Llanos. Two subjects often depicted by Juanes, and of which he made several versions, were *Salvador mundi* (e.g. 1560–70; Valencia, Mus. B.A.) and *Ecce homo* (e.g. 1560–70; Madrid, Prado).

In the period between 1560 and 1570 Juanes moved towards the style of Raphael and current Roman academicism. The example of Raphael became the dominating influence; but there is no radical break, since Juanes remained true to his own convictions. The most characteristic works of this period are the panels of the great *St Stephen* altarpiece (Madrid, Prado; see fig.), painted for the parish church of St Esteban, Valencia. They were purchased from the church by Charles IV in 1801. These paintings show how Juanes had abandoned the hieratic qualities of medieval art, his work gaining a sense of movement and a more marked tendency to dramatize by means of facial expression. The changes in his painting around 1560 are the result of a visit to Italy, although the influences apparent in his work, and in particular that of Raphael, indicate that this was probably limited to Rome. The late works by Juanes, between 1570 and 1578, are most individual. They include *St Vicente Ferrer* (*c*. 1570; Villareal, Castellón, Parish Church, sacristy) and *St Tomás de Villanueva* (Keir, Scotland, Stirling-Maxwell col., see Albi Fita, pl. cxcv). These show that he had developed a style wholly different from that of his father.

Juan de Juanes: *Last Supper*, detail from the *St Stephen* altarpiece, oil on panel, 1.16×1.91 m, 1560–70 (Madrid, Museo del Prado)

Apart from painting religious subjects, Juanes also produced portraits and mythological works. Despite his considerable ability as a portrait painter, few examples have survived. His *Alfonso V of Aragon* (1557; Saragossa, Jordan de Urries priv. col., see Albi Fita, pl. cl) conveys a strong personality. Also extant is the series of 19 Valencian prelates commissioned for Valencia Cathedral (*c.* 1568; *in situ*). It is unlikely that the fine portrait of *Don Luis Castellá de Villanova* (Madrid, Prado) is by either Juanes or his father. In its treatment of a mythological theme, the *Judgement of Paris* (*c.* 1550; Udine, Gal. A. Ant. & Mod.), now attributed to Juanes, indicates the refined and cultured atmosphere then developing in humanist circles.

It is documented that towards the end of his life Juanes was at Bocairente working on an altarpiece, and there, in the presence of Cristóbal Llorens (*d*?1622), a notary, painter and his own pupil, he made his will on 20 December 1579, dying the following day. His remains were reburied in 1850 at the instigation of the Academia de S Carlos, in the crypt of the sepulchre of the Marquéses de Zanete in the chapel of Kings in the convent of S Domingo, Valencia, which became a pantheon for distinguished Valencians.

BIBLIOGRAPHY

D. Angulo Iñíguez: *Pintura del renacimiento*, A. Hisp., xii (Madrid, 1954)
J. Albi Fita: *Joan de Joanes y su círculo artístico* (Valencia, 1979)
Joan de Joanes (ob. 1579) (exh. cat., Madrid, Min. Cult.; Valencia; 1979–80)

ADELA ESPINÓS DíAZ

MacIver, Loren (*b* New York, 2 Feb 1909). American painter. She began painting at an early age and received her only year of formal training at the Art Students League, New York, when she was ten. She married the poet Lloyd

Frankenberg when she was 20, and her early work was inspired by their summers spent at Cape Cod, MA. From 1936 to 1940 she painted for the Federal Art Project of the Works Progress Administration (FAP/WPA). Mac-Iver's style was an evocative combination of abstract and realistic elements and showed little change after 1940. Her subject-matter was taken from the environment and includes both commonplace and unusual motifs: oil stains in a gutter, the arcs of windscreen wipers on a rainy night, a cracked window blind, her studio skylight and votive lights. Her stylistic approach is typified by *Hopscotch* (1940; New York, MOMA), in which a detailed rendering of a patch of blistered asphalt pavement next to the chalk marks of a child's game emerges from what appears to be an abstract pattern. Among her few depictions of people are portraits of poets as well as clowns and their paraphernalia. A trip to France, Italy, England, Ireland and Scotland in 1948 produced several landscapes and street scenes. Her interest in geology is exemplified in more exotic paintings, such as that of the eerie bauxite deposits in *Les Baux* (1952; Chicago, IL, A. Inst.). In 1947–8 she executed a series of murals for the ships of the Moore–McCormack and American Export lines.

BIBLIOGRAPHY

Contemporary Painters (exh. cat. by J. T. Soby, New York, MOMA, 1948)
Loren MacIver–Rice Pereira (exh. cat. by J. I. H. Baur, New York, Whitney, 1953)
Loren MacIver: Five Decades (exh. cat. by R. M. Frash, Newport Beach, CA, Harbor A. Mus., 1983)

JOHN I. H. BAUR

Mack, Heinz (*b* Lollar, nr Giessen, 8 March 1931). German painter and sculptor. He studied painting from

1950 to 1953 at the Staatliche Kunstakademie, Düsseldorf. In 1956 he passed his first degree in philosophy at Cologne university. Thereafter, consciously withdrawing from his early, informal painting, he developed his theory of 'dynamic structures', which he first introduced in 1958 in a manifesto-like essay 'Die Ruhe der Unruhe' in the first issue of the magazine *Zero*. He worked from a 'simple structure-zone' rather than a composition, to which from 1958 he gave practical expression in his vibration oil paintings and aluminium foil light reliefs. His collaboration with Otto Piene (from 1958) and with Günther Uecker (from 1961) led to the formation of the Zero group, which produced numerous projects of artificial light visions until 1966.

In 1959 Mack began his kinetic explorations including the *Rotors*; using structured aluminium foil and corrugated glass, he made the optical phenomenon of interference aesthetically visible in works such as *Silver Rotor* (1961–2; Brussels, Mus. A. Mod.). As stated in his essay of 1958, he wanted to extend the viewer's range of perception. As well as his relief and rotor works, from 1958 he produced steles, initially in aluminium, for example *Silver Stele* (aluminium stamped on to wood, 1966; Düsseldorf, Landeszentralbank). These anticipated Mack's concept of a 'light environment' as a means of structuring and extending both nature and the human environment. In 1963 he abandoned oil painting on canvas.

Mack's development reached a culmination in 1968, as he partly realized his *Sahara-Project*, planned from 1958 and first formulated in the third issue of *Zero*. In an unspoilt site on the edge of the Tunisian section of the Sahara Desert, he created an artificial garden out of sand-reliefs, artificial suns, walls of mirrors, light-reliefs, light-reflectors and other works for the shooting of the film *Tele-Mack*. In this work he realized his artistic concept of combining natural and technical elements. For the Olympic games in Munich in 1972 he created a cloud of light and water 36 m high (see Honisch, p. 423). An idea in 1974 for a *Peace Stele* 70 m high for the UN building in New York remained only a project, however. In the 1980s he began to explore sculpture in stone, chiselling dynamic, light-reflecting structures into stone steles.

WRITINGS

ed.: *Drei von hundert (tres de cien): Werkverzeichnis der Druckgraphik und Multiples* (Stuttgart, 1990)
ed.: *Skulptur im Raum der Natur* (Cologne, 1992)

BIBLIOGRAPHY

M. Staber: *Heinz Mack* (Cologne, 1968)
Mack: Objekte, Aktionen, Projekte (exh. cat., W. Berlin, Akad. Kst., 1972)
K. Weidemann: *Heinz Mack: Imaginationen, 1953–1973* (Berlin, 1973)
F. W. Heckmanns: *Heinz Mack: Handzeichnungen* (Cologne, 1974)
D. Honisch: *Mack: Skulpturen* (Düsseldorf and Vienna, 1986; Eng. trans., London, 1986)
Zero-Mack (exh. cat., ed. D. Stemmler; Mönchengladbach, Städt. Mus. Abteiberg, 1991)

STEPHAN VON WIESE

Mack, Ludwig Hirschfeld. *See* HIRSCHFELD-MACK, LUDWIG.

Mackay, David. *See under* MARTORELL, BOHIGAS, MACKAY.

Macke, August (Robert Ludwig) (*b* Meschede, Westphalia, 3 Jan 1887; *d* nr Perthes-les-Hurlus, Champagne, 26 Sept 1914). German painter. He began his artistic training in autumn 1904 at the Kunstakademie in Düsseldorf, but he was far more interested by the instruction at the Kunstgewerbeschule, run by Peter Behrens, where he attended evening courses given by the German printmaker Fritz Helmuth Ehmcke (1878–1965). Friendship with the playwrights of the Düsseldorfer Theater, Wilhelm Schmidtbonn and Herbert Eulenberg, awakened Macke's interest in the stage. With the German sculptor Claus Cito, he developed designs for stage sets, including those for a production of *Macbeth*, which led to an offer by the theatre to employ him, but Macke turned it down. In April 1905 Macke travelled with Walter Gerhardt, his future wife Elizabeth Gerhardt's brother, to northern Italy and Florence. His drawings of this period reveal freshness and a receptive sensibility. In July 1906 he travelled to the Netherlands and Belgium with Schmidtbonn, Eulenberg and Cito, continuing on with Schmidtbonn to London, where he visited the city's museums. In November 1906 he broke off his studies at the academy. After encountering French Impressionism on a trip to Paris in summer 1907, Macke began to paint in this manner; in autumn of that year he went to Berlin to join the studio of the German painter Lovis Corinth. However, work in the studio, and Corinth's way of suggesting corrections, did not suit Macke's temperament, nor did the city's oppressive atmosphere. He returned to Bonn in early 1908. His future wife's family provided him with the means for further travel, first to Italy and then together with his wife and her uncle Bernhard Koehler, who later became his patron, to Paris. Through Koehler he gained an insight into the art market in Paris and became acquainted with Ambroise Vollard. In 1908–9 Macke discharged himself from his one-year military service. Once again in Paris on his honeymoon in 1909, he met Louis Moilliet and, through him, Karl Hofer.

During this stay Macke seems to have been particularly impressed by Hofer and by the Fauves. He considered settling in Paris for a time, but decided in the end to accept Schmidtbonn's offer to go to the Tegernsee in Upper Bavaria. His extensive artistic output of this period reflects direct influences: in contrast to the brightly coloured, impressionistic manner of such paintings as *Washing in the Garden in Kandern* (1907, priv. col.) and *On the Rhine near Hersel* (1908; Bonn, Städt. Kstmus.) the pictorial composition is now more expansive, with clear forms built up out of large, contiguous planes. Hofer's influence is clear in *Dawn at Tegernsee* (1910; Munich, Lenbachhaus). The expressly simple composition is based on two clear contours on either side of a central axis: a hilly horizon above the surface of the lake and gentle waves on the sandy shore in the foreground. The light pastel colours were applied with a dry brush. Despite the reduction of compositional means, he successfully re-created an unmistakable and individual mood. *Portrait with Apples* (1909; Munich, Lenbachhaus), by comparison, betrays the influence of the Fauves.

In January 1910 Macke met FRANZ MARC for the first time during a visit to the latter's studio in Munich. It was the beginning of an intense artistic friendship, through which each, nevertheless, attained his individual artistic goals. In contrast to Marc, who restricted his themes to symbolic animal representations, Macke treated more traditional themes: portraits, still-lifes, interiors and landscapes, with and without figures. Meanwhile, however, his formal conceptions underwent increasing transformation. In winter 1910 Macke returned to Bonn. The view from his studio window there is captured in a number of works, for example in *St Mary's Church in the Snow* (1911; Hamburg, Ksthalle) and *Our Street in Grey* (1911; Munich, Lenbachhaus), in which the influence of the Fauves is still visible. Macke's meeting with Kandinsky and the other artists of the Neue Künstlervereinigung München (NKVM) took place in the same year. When Marc became a member of the NKVM in February 1911, artistic and theoretical convictions were at the centre of the discussions in their correspondence. Macke was invited to participate in the exhibition and to contribute to the *Der Blaue Reiter Almanach*, which Marc and Kandinsky were editing (*see* BLAUE REITER). Macke is represented in the latter by the essay 'Die Masken' and by reproductions of his painting *The Storm* (1911; Saarbrücken, Saarland-mus.; *see* GERMANY, fig. 24) and a drawing.

In the independent exhibition organized in December 1911 by Kandinsky and Marc at the Moderne Galerie Thannhauser, Munich, after differences between the members of the NKVM, Macke showed three works (as many as Kandinsky), and in the second exhibition, dedicated solely to graphic works, he was represented by 16 drawings, a contribution exceeded only by Klee, who showed 17 pieces. Although Macke's membership of the Blaue Reiter group constituted only one aspect of his career, and his critical distance from their declared intentions remained perceptible, his name is firmly associated with the group. In 1912 he took part in the *Sonderbund* exhibition in Cologne, exhibited in the Caro-Bube artists' union in Moscow and in the Cologne Secession, and he had his first one-man exhibition in the Moderne Galerie Thannhauser in Munich. In the work of this period it is clear that, after his brief pre-occupation with the symbolic–mystical, non-objective tendencies of the Blaue Reiter, Macke was reverting to representing impressions of the visible world, which corresponded more closely to his essential nature. A meeting with Robert Delaunay during a visit to Paris with Marc led to his appropriation of Cubist ideas, which became a dominant force in his work from then on, although he retained elements of objectivity. Examples of this are *Garden Restaurant* (1912; Berne, Kstmus.) and *Zoological Garden* (1912; Munich, Lenbachhaus). In 1912, too, the Futurists and their dynamic representation of time and movement became important for Macke's mode of representing animate nature. For the themes that he now preferred, such as strollers, dancers, tightrope walkers and acrobats, the process of crystallizing sequences of movement was crucially important, just as the motif of display windows with reflections of street life shows the influence of Delaunay. Among the best examples of these are *Couple in a Wood* (1912), *Evening* (1912; both priv. cols) and *Clothing Shop* (1913; Münster, Westfäl. Kstver.).

In 1913 Macke exhibited at the Galerie Arnold in Dresden and at Herwarth Walden's Sturm-Galerie in Berlin. The exhibitions of the Rhineland Expressionists in Bonn and the Erste Deutsche Herbstsalon in Berlin

August Macke: *Turkish Café*, oil on panel, 600×350 mm, 1914 (Munich, Städtische Galerie im Lenbachhaus)

received decisive impetus from his participation. In connection with these undertakings, Macke had moved with his family to Hilterfingen on Lake Thun in Switzerland. His paintings, now of such subjects as figure groups under trees, women in front of shop windows or strollers in the park, are among the finest of his mature works and show him as a representative of German EXPRESSIONISM. In pictures such as *A Promenade* (1913; Munich, Lenbachhaus) or *Sunlit Path* (1913: Münster, Stadtmus.) there is a paradisiacal calm in which man, individually or in groups, lingers in thoughtful contemplation, in complete harmony with nature. In February 1914 Macke accompanied Klee and Moilliet on the famous trip to Tunisia. The Tunisian watercolours are among the most important testimonies of classic modern art. The painting *Turkish Café* (1914; Munich, Lenbachhaus; see fig.) is one of the few compositions that were executed after his return, from drawings made on the trip. It was presented as a gift to Bernhard Koehler, who had made the trip possible. In August 1914 Macke was called up for military service; he was killed in the following month.

WRITINGS
'Die Masken', *Der Blaue Reiter Almanach*, ed. V. Kandinsky and F. Marc (Munich, 1912, rev. 1965)

W. Macke, ed.: *August Macke–Franz Marc: Briefwechsel* (Cologne, 1964)

W. Frese and E.-G. Güse, eds: *August Macke: Briefe an Elisabeth und die Freunde* (Munich, 1987)

BIBLIOGRAPHY

G. Vriesen: *August Macke* (Stuttgart, 1953/*R* 1957) [cat. rais. and bibliog.]

G. Busch and W. Holzhausen: *Die Tunisreise. Aquarelle und Zeichnungen von August Macke* (Cologne, 1958)

E. Erdman-Macke: *Erinnerung an August Macke* (Stuttgart, 1962)

August Macke, intro. by L. Lang (Leipzig, 1966)

August Macke: Aquarelle und Zeichnungen (exh. cat., Münster, Westfäl. Landesmus.; Bonn, Städt. Kstmus.; Krefeld, Kaiser Wilhelm Mus.; 1976–7)

August Macke und die Rheinische Expressionisten (exh. cat., Bonn, Städt. Kstmus.; Hannover, Kestner-Ges.; 1978–9)

August Macke: Retrospektive zum 100. Geburtstag (exh. cat., ed. E.-G. Güse; Münster, Westfäl. Landesmus.; Bonn, Städt. Kstmus.; Munich, Lenbachhaus; 1987) [extensive bibliog.]

A. von Friesen: *August Macke: Ein Maler-Leben* (Hamburg, 1989)

M. Moeller: *August Macke: Die Tunisreise* (Munich, 1989)

U. Heidrich: *August Macke: Zeichnungen* (Stuttgart, 1992)

August Macke: 'Gesang von der Schönheit der Dinge'. Aquarelle und Zeichnungen (exh. cat. by A. Firmenich and U. Heiderich, Emden, Ksthlle, 1992–3; Ulm, Ulm. Mus.; Bonn, Städt. Kstmus.; 1993)

B. Weyandt: *Farbe und Naturauffassung im Werk von August Macke* (Hildesheim, 1994)

ROSEL GOLLEK

McKean & Fairweather. Canadian architectural partnership formed in 1872 by John Thomas Chalmers McKean (*b* St Andrews, NB, 1840; *d* St John, NB, 22 Oct 1911) and George Earnest Fairweather (*b* St John, NB, 1850; *d* St John, NB, 16 Dec 1920). In 1870, following an apprenticeship with Vaux & Withers in New York, McKean opened a practice in St John, New Brunswick, which Fairweather joined. Their partnership flourished until 1880, when they lost to James Dumaresq in a competition for the New Brunswick Legislative Assembly building at Fredericton. This brief association produced many fine buildings and had a significant impact on the architecture of New Brunswick. Their projects included commercial buildings, churches and schools, and town halls in Fredericton (1875–6) and St John (1877–9), both New Brunswick. Their practice played an important role in the reconstruction of St John after it was devastated by fire in 1877. After 1880 McKean continued in private practice and was best known for his church of the Assumption, St John, completed just before his death. Fairweather also practised successfully and was highly respected for his construction expertise. He supervised construction on the Post Office building and the Bank of North America building, both in St John (n.d.), but is best remembered for his Episcopal Church (1890), Chatham, New Brunswick, and for Christ Church Cathedral (1907), Fredericton.

BIBLIOGRAPHY

R. G. Hill, ed.: *Biographical Dictionary of Architects in Canada, 1800–1950* (Toronto, 1986)

GRANT WANZEL, AARON BOURGOIN

Mackennal, Sir (Edgar) Bertram (*b* Melbourne, June 1863; *d* Devon, England, Oct 1931). Australian sculptor, active in Britain. He studied at the National Gallery of Victoria School in Melbourne from 1878 to 1882 and then on the suggestion of the English sculptor Marshall Wood (*d* 1882) he travelled to London, where he spent three months at the Royal Academy Schools in 1883. Finding the training there too academic Mackennal left and visited Paris and Rome, and in 1884 he set up a studio in Paris. He was helped financially by John Peter Russell, who also introduced him to Auguste Rodin. Mackennal found Rodin's work too revolutionary for his own tastes but did adopt aspects of Rodin's sensuous subject-matter. Also in Paris he met Alfred Gilbert, who advised him that his work would be better appreciated in England. In 1886 Mackennal became the head of the modelling and design department at the Coalport Potteries, Salop, England, and in 1887 he won the competition to design two relief panels for the façade of the Parliament House in Melbourne (*in situ*). His first real success came in 1893, when the plaster version of *Circe* (h. 2.8 m, incl. base, 1893; Melbourne, N.G. Victoria) was praised at the Paris Salon and at the Royal Academy in London the following year. It combined the various influences that he had been exposed to up to that time, including Rodin and Gilbert, his awareness of the former being revealed in the frieze of intertwined nudes on the base, a feature considered provocative by the hanging committee at the Royal Academy, who insisted on it being covered. Numerous commissions followed, including portrait busts of *Sarah Bernhardt* (*c.* 1893) and of *Dame Nellie Melba* (h. 1.98 m, incl. base, 1899; Melbourne, N.G. Victoria), which show his skilful assimilation of New Sculpture principles, and several public monuments, for example the Edward VII Memorial Arch in Calcutta (see CALCUTTA, fig. 2). During World War I he worked on his largest commission, *Apollo Driving the Horses of the Sun* (18.29×5.79 m; 1915), for the pediment of Australia House on The Strand in London; this was finally installed in 1924. In 1923 Mackennal became the first and only Australian sculptor to be elected an RA. In his later years his essentially conservative, classical style was seen as outdated and his reputation waned.

BIBLIOGRAPHY

N. Hutchinson: *Bertram Mackennal* (Melbourne, 1973)

G. Sturgeon: *The Development of Australian Sculpture, 1788–1975* (London, 1978), pp. 59–70

A. McCulloch: *Encyclopedia of Australian Art*, ii (Melbourne and London, 1984), pp. 741–2

GEOFFREY R. EDWARDS

Mackensen. Polish family of goldsmiths and metalworkers. Andrzej Mackensen I (*b* Delmenhorst, *c.* 1596; *d* Gdańsk, 1677–8) settled in Kraków before 1628 and moved to Gdańsk in 1643 where he lived until his death, working in the guild administration. He was the court goldsmith of the Polish kings Vladislav IV (*reg* 1632–48) and John Kasimir (*reg* 1648–68). Mackensen's impact on the artistic life of Gdańsk was considerable as he had many pupils. His important works include pieces (5 in Warsaw, N. Mus.) of a service originally consisting of 12 dishes, a gift from the city of Gdańsk to King John Kasimir, probably on the occasion of his marriage; the undersides are decorated with portraits of Polish kings. He executed elaborately ornamented secular and ecclesiastical works, both for Catholics, for example the monstrance at Pelplin (Dioc. Mus.), one of the first in Poland with radial aureola, and for Protestants, for example the pitchers for the Eucharist (St Petersburg, Hermitage). Together with JAN CHRYSTIAN BIERPFAFF he introduced shell-like motifs, influenced by the works of the Dutch van Vianen family, into Polish gold- and silverwork. Anne Mackensen, his daughter by his first wife, married the engraver Willem Hondius (ii); he also taught goldsmithing to his son Andrzej Mackensen II (*b* 1655; *d* Gdańsk, after 1701), who executed his masterpiece (destr.) for entry to the guild in the workshop of Piotr Rohde the younger (*c*. 1630–89) in 1685. Like his father he blended Mannerist traditions with Baroque stylization in his work, especially in repoussé figural scenes (e.g. chalice, 1689, at Mogilno, parish church). He also executed monumental works, for example the trophy composition chased from gilded sheet copper for the tomb at Węgrów of Jan Dobrogost Krasiński, who also commissioned the metal tomb plate with the figures of his two wives at Krasne parish church. Extant smaller works by Andrzej Mackensen II include ecclesiastical vessels (e.g. chalices at Pelplin and Piaseczno; monstrance at Starzyno, parish church).

BIBLIOGRAPHY

E. Czihak: *Die Edelschmiedekunst früherer Zeiten in Preussen*, ii (Leipzig, 1908), p. 67
J. Samek: 'Mackensen Andrzej I', *Polski słownik biograficzny* [Polish biographical dictionary], ed. E. Rostworowski, xviii (Kraków, 1959), pp. 82–4
J. Samek and M. Sławoszewska: 'Mackensen Andrzej II', *Polski słownik biograficzny*, ed. E. Rostworowski, xviii (Kraków, 1959), pp. 82–4
T. Rembowska: 'Andrzej Mackensen I: Złotnik gdański (XVII w.)' [Andrzej Mackensen I: the 17th-century goldsmith in Gdańsk], *Roc. Gdański*, xxiii (1964), p. 184
A. Fischinger: 'Uwagi nad twórczością Andrzeja Mackensena I: Złotnika krakowskiego i gdańskiego' [Remarks on Andrzej Mackensen I: goldsmith in Kraków and Gdańsk], *Sprawozdania Posiedzeń Kom. Naukowych Pol. Akad. Nauk Krakowie*, xiii (1970), p. 175

TADEUSZ CHRZANOWSKI

Mackensen, Fritz (*b* Greene, nr Einbeck, 8 April 1866; *d* Bremen, 1953). German painter. After attending the academies in Düsseldorf and Munich, in 1889 he moved to Worpswede, a village on the moors that he had visited regularly from 1884. The simple life of the peasants and bare landscape led Otto Modersohn (1865–1943), Hans am Ende and others to join him, forming the WORPSWEDE COLONY. He was thus part of the 19th-century movement that was rooted in the rejection of classical academic study, concern at the alienation of people from their environment by industrialization, the romantic move 'back to nature' and (in Mackensen's case) also in long-established nationalistic feelings. His quiet, clearly grasped representations of peasants engrossed in daily work reveal his ideal of a unity of humankind with nature, but they are still far removed from the poor conditions of reality. This may be the reason for Mackensen's rapid rise to popularity with the bourgeoisie. He achieved fame with his large painting *Religious Service on the Moor* (1886–95; Hannover, Hist. Mus. Hohen Ufer; for illustration *see* WORPSWEDE COLONY), in which a group of serious people in their Sunday clothes listens to a sermon in front of a row of peasant cottages.

Shortly after the artists' colony at Worpswede was established, Mackensen lost his place as leader among his artist colleagues because of his resistance to new developments, but he was the most successful among them in official artistic life. In 1908 he became a professor at the Kunsthochschule in Weimar and was made director in 1910, returning to Worpswede in 1918. In 1934 he led the building of the Nordische Kunsthochschule in Bremen.

After World War II he was unable to re-establish himself, and he died in poverty.

BIBLIOGRAPHY

U. Hamm: *Mackensen* (Munich, 1978)
For further bibliography *see* WORPSWEDE COLONY.

HANS GERHARD HANNESEN

Mackenzie. Scottish family of architects. Alexander Mackenzie (*d* 1827) was an architect–builder, active in Perth; his three sons became architects. His eldest son, William MacDonald Mackenzie (*b* 1797; *d* Perth, 15 Feb 1856), was City Architect for Perth and an accomplished Neoclassical designer whose work includes St Leonard's (1834), Perth. The second son, David Mackenzie, worked in Perth in 1830–42. The third son, Thomas Mackenzie (*b* Perth, Sept/Oct 1815; *d* Elgin, Grampian, 15 Oct 1854), the most important of this generation, practised in Aberdeen in 1835–9 in the offices of John Smith and of Archibald Simpson, and then in Elgin, in that of William Robertson, entering into partnership with Simpson's pupil James Matthews (1820–98) in 1844. Thomas Mackenzie worked mainly from Elgin and Matthews from Aberdeen. Thomas Mackenzie's preferred style was Italianate, as at Elgin Museum (1842), the Caledonian Bank (1852), Forres, Grampian, and the town hall (1853), Fraserburgh, Grampian. His largest buildings, however, were in other styles. He used Neo-classical for the Bank of Scotland (1847), Inverness, Neo-Tudor at Milne's Institution (1845), Fochabers, Grampian, and Jacobean Revival at Arndilly House (1850), Grampian. He befriended Robert William Billings (1813–74) on his tour that led to the latter's *The Baronial and Ecclesiastical Antiquities of Scotland* (4 vols, 1845–52) and used the Scottish Baronial style in the remodellings of Ballindalloch Castle (1847), Grampian, and Cawdor Castle (from 1851), Nairn, Highland, and at Dess House, Grampian, and Dall House, Tayside (both 1851).

Among the next generation, William MacDonald Mackenzie's son, David Mackenzie (1832–75), practised in Dundee. In 1870 Thomas Mackenzie's son, Alexander Marshall Mackenzie (*b* Elgin, 1 Jan 1848; *d* Culter, Grampian, 4 May 1933), reopened the Elgin office that had closed on his father's death, and in 1877 Matthews readmitted him to the Aberdeen office, where he had served his apprenticeship in 1863–8. His greatest work, among a prolific output of varying quality, was the enlargement of Marischal College, opened in 1906, and the associated Greyfriars Church, Aberdeen, a vast granite structure in the Perpendicular style. He was most influential as the exponent of a more liturgical arrangement in Presbyterian church design. The planning of his church (1883) at Craigiebuckler, Aberdeen, designed in an Early Pointed style, anticipated the aims of the Aberdeen (later Scottish) Ecclesiological Society, which was founded two years later. His work in restoring 15th- and 16th-century churches led to his interest in designing in a late Scottish Gothic style, as at Crathie (1895), Grampian, for Queen Victoria, and Cults West Church (1915), Grampian. The cathedral-like Lowson Memorial Church (1912–14), Forfar, Tayside, is an excellent example of the Society's ideals. He did much work in Aberdeen, for example New Buildings (1912) and Elphinstone Hall (1927) at King's

College, in a late Scottish Gothic style, and the Northern (now Commercial Union) Building (1883) and South Church (1892) in a Renaissance style.

In 1903 Alexander Marshall Mackenzie opened an office in London, with his eldest son Alexander George Robertson Mackenzie (*b* Aberdeen, 12 March 1879; *d* Bourtie, Grampian, 20 March 1963) in charge. Their first commission in London was the Waldorf Astoria Hotel (from 1903), Aldwych, followed by Australia House (1912–14), Aldwych, both of which show the younger Mackenzie's taste for Gallic historicism, which he had acquired from René Sergent, with whom he had worked in Paris. Despite amalgamation with the office of H. H. Wigglesworth (1866–1949) in 1927, the London office was difficult to maintain and in 1930 Alexander George Robertson Mackenzie returned to Aberdeen, where he designed the Northern Hotel (1938), Kittybrewster, Grampian, and Pittodrie Church (1939), Aberdeen, both in a bold 1930s modern style.

BIBLIOGRAPHY

W. Papworth, ed.: *A Dictionary of Architecture*, 11 vols (London, 1848–92) [article on Thomas Mackenzie]

The Aberdeen Press and Journal (5 May 1933; 11 Oct 1935; 21 March 1963)

Obituary, *The Builder*, cxiv (1933), p. 765

H. H. Wigglesworth: *An Appreciation of the Work of Alexander Marshall Mackenzie, LLD RSA FRIBA* (Edinburgh, 1933)

A. S. Gray: *Edwardian Architecture: A Biographical Dictionary* (London, 1985)

W. H. Watson: *A. Marshall Mackenzie: Architect in Aberdeen* (Aberdeen, 1985)

J. Gifford: 'Architects of the Highlands in the 19th Century: A Sketch', *Scot. Georg. Soc. Bull.*, no. 7 (1986), pp. 37–9

DAVID WALKER

Mackenzie, John. *See under* YOUNG & MACKENZIE.

McKenzie, Robert Tait (*b* Almonte, Ont., 26 May 1867; *d* Philadelphia, PA, 28 April 1938). Canadian sculptor and medallist. He was trained in medicine and taught physical education at McGill University, Montreal, and from 1904 at the University of Pennsylvania, Philadelphia. His lifelong interest in physical health and athletics informs his art, in which he was largely self-taught. His monumental works include the *Youthful Franklin* (bronze, 1911–14; Philadelphia, U. PA), a number of World War I memorials and the *Delano Memorial* (Washington, DC, Amer. Red Cross N.H.Q.), but it is as a modeller of statuettes representing sportsmen in action that he is best known. These naturalistic male nudes were much acclaimed in the early 20th century and resulted in many commissions for plaquettes and medals from sports and other organizations. The first of these was from the New York Public School Athletic League in 1906, and the last, in 1938, from the American Association of Anatomists. He exhibited his sculptures at the Royal Academy, and at the Fine Arts Society, London, occasionally, from 1907. His Olympic shield of 1932 (plaster; Philadelphia, U. PA, Jones Gal.) won that year's Olympic Art Award, and in 1936 he executed a plaster sketch of *Jesse Owens* (untraced). A large collection of his work is now in the J. William White Collection, University of Pennsylvania (Philadelphia, U. PA, Jones Gal.).

BIBLIOGRAPHY

DAB; Vollmer

L. Forrer: *Biographical Dictionary of Medallists* (London, 1902–30), viii, pp. 3–14

A. J. Kozar: *R. Tait McKenzie: The Sculptor of Athletes* (Knoxville, 1975)

J. McGill: *The Joy of Effort: A Biography of R. Tait McKenzie* (Bewdley, Ont., 1980)

Sculpture in Britain between the Wars (exh. cat., London, F.A. Soc., 1986), pp. 108–9

PHILIP ATTWOOD

McKim, Mead & White. American architectural partnership formed in September 1879 by Charles Follen McKim (*b* Isabella Furnace, PA, 24 Aug 1847; *d* St James, Long Island, NY, 14 Sept 1909), William Rutherford Mead (*b* Brattleboro, VT, 20 Aug 1846; *d* Paris, 30 June 1928) and Stanford White (*b* New York, 9 Nov 1853; *d* New York, 25 June 1906). This late 19th- and early 20th-century partnership produced over nine hundred executed designs for prestigious public and private commissions of all types, trained a generation of architects and, perhaps most importantly, created an evocative artistic climate that contemporary architects, artists and patrons believed to be an American Renaissance. Basing its work on a renewal of past forms it succeeded in establishing an architecture that evoked both the American past of the 17th and 18th centuries and the larger heritage of European classicism from antiquity through the Renaissance to the 18th century. Good craftsmanship was an ideal of the firm and its significant public and other important buildings were decorated by leading artists. Clients were wealthy, frequently from high society, and included prominent financiers and politicians. The firm designed large urban houses, country estates, commercial buildings, clubhouses and university campuses. Because its office was in New York, its work was largely in the north-east, though examples can be found in Virginia, the Midwest, Texas and California; the impact of the firm's work can be felt in nearly every town and city in America.

1. History of the firm. 2. Work. 3. Office organization. 4. Critical reception and posthumous reputation.

1. HISTORY OF THE FIRM. McKim, Mead and White worked as a partnership and sought to have their work thus identified, but contemporary accounts stressed their individual personalities. In these remembrances McKim appears as a calm and deliberate scholar with the office nickname of 'Bramante'; Mead as the quiet office manager known as 'Dummy'; and White as a mercurial redheaded playboy called 'Cellini'. These nicknames reflect their individual architectural preferences: McKim was the leading architectural theorist of the office, the style-setter, and his work tended to be grand and pompous; Mead did little actual design, concentrating on overseeing the working drawings and specifications; and White had a genius for designing ornament. All three partners had similar backgrounds; their families were members of the intellectual élite of the pre-Civil War years. McKim's father was an abolitionist and radical. Mead's father was a lawyer, and his family was connected to the radical religious sect of the Oneida community. Stanford White's father was a prominent music and literary critic. In contrast to their parents, McKim, Mead and White all turned to serving the new wealth, typified by the 'robber barons' who began

to emerge in the 1870s and would rule the new industrial America.

Charles McKim was the only member of the firm to be formally schooled as an architect. After a year studying engineering at Harvard University, he attended the Ecole des Beaux-Arts in Paris (1867–70) and returned to New York, where he entered the office of H. H. Richardson for two years. In 1872 he began to work independently, though he maintained a connection with Richardson's office, and became informally associated with William Mead until 1877 when a formal partnership was created. This partnership included William Bigelow, the brother of Annie Bigelow, whom McKim had married in 1874; when they divorced in 1879, Stanford White took William Bigelow's place in the firm. In 1885 McKim married Julia Appleton, a member of a wealthy Boston family; she died barely a year later. Extremely social, McKim devoted much of his later life to causes such as the World's Columbian Exposition (1893) in Chicago, IL, and the establishment of the American School of Architecture (later the American Academy) in Rome. In 1901–2 he became involved (with Daniel H. Burnham, Frederick Law Olmsted jr and Augustus Saint-Gaudens) in the McMillan Commission for the replanning of Washington, DC, the first large 'City Beautiful' project in America. In 1902–3 he served as president of the American Institute of Architects and helped to transform it from a gentlemen's club into an organization of political power.

William Mead attended Amherst College, MA, and was then apprenticed in the New York office of Russell Sturgis for two years (1867–70). Through his brother Larkin Mead (1835–1910), a sculptor, he studied informally at the Accademia di Belle Arti in Florence in 1871. His architectural work before joining McKim was undistinguished, and his role in the firm was that of office manager. The sculptor Augustus Saint-Gaudens, a close friend of all three partners, once did a cartoon labelled McKim and White, with kites flying in different directions and being held down by Mead. Mead married in 1884, and his personal life was uneventful.

Stanford White had a natural talent for drawing and studied briefly with painter and stained-glass artist John La Farge, but, perceiving the financial penury of an artist's life, he entered the office of H. H. Richardson in 1870. Richardson recognized White's illustrative and ornamental talents and gave him major responsibility for several houses including the William Watts Sherman House (1874–6), Newport, RI, designed in Richard Norman Shaw's Old English style. In 1878, feeling the lack of foreign training or experience, White left Richardson and travelled for over a year in Europe and England before returning and taking Bigelow's place in the New York office of McKim and Mead. Initially White was a junior member of the firm, specializing in interior decoration ornament and collaborating with artists such as Augustus Saint-Gaudens on pedestals. He also designed picture frames for many leading artists of the day (see FRAME, fig. 98). By the mid-1880s he became a full partner in the firm. He married Bessie Smith of Smithtown, Long Island, NY, in 1884. The high life of New York café society attracted him, and he designed not only buildings but also party and costume decorations. The lure of money and flesh led to a series of liaisons and White's fatal shooting (by Harry K. Thaw in 1906) because of his affair with Evelyn Nesbitt. The murder, ensuing trial and sensational publicity provided fodder for endless books, novels and films and ensured White a posthumous reputation that has little to do with architecture.

2. WORK.

(i) Early period. The work of McKim, Mead & White can be divided into three different periods that overlap chronologically but exhibit different characteristics. In the early period, from the mid-1870s to the mid-1880s, buildings have a lightness of form and are frequently asymmetrical in outline. Although McKim had attended the Ecole des Beaux-Arts, much of his and his partner's work of this time reflects the inspiration of the English Aesthetic movement. The buildings of the early period were eventually christened the SHINGLE STYLE; however, that term was unknown at the time, and they were referred to as either Queen Anne Revival or modernized Colonial Revival. It was the period of the great shingle-covered resorts and country houses clustered along the New Jersey shore, on Long Island and in Newport, RI. Much of the firm's reputation was made in Newport, where it was responsible for the design of the Casino (1879–81) and numerous cottages for wealthy New York clients.

The period is characterized by a picturesque attitude towards form, colour and space; buildings were designed from the inside out, with the plan determining outer form, as can be seen in the Isaac Bell House (1881–3; see fig. 1), Newport. However, both spatially and in massing, the work of McKim and his partners emphasizes the movement of the occupant through grand processional spaces, usually arranged about a central axis. The spaces are clearly arranged in a hierarchical manner, which makes the firm's work stand apart from that of contemporaries. McKim led in the investigation of American 17th-century colonial buildings, though his partners also had an interest in it. In the Queen Anne Revival, McKim perceived a wholeness of form and the germ of classicism that inspired his later work.

(ii) Consolidation period. McKim, Mead & White's second phase, the consolidation period, from the early 1880s through to the early 1890s, is marked by the increasing use of recognizable historical images and a greater visual weight to the buildings, e.g. the Romanesque Revival Ross Winans House (1882; for illustration *see* BALTIMORE). While buildings of the early period featured replicated colonial details, such as exaggerated goose-neck pediments, the entire building was now influenced by earlier architecture. Urban buildings dominated the firm's production at this time. The nascent classicism of the early phase became more obvious, as seen in the designs for the Henry G. Villard houses (1882–5), New York City, and the Commodore William Edgar House (1884–6), Newport.

The H. A. C. Taylor House (1883–5; destr. 1952), Newport, was derived from 18th-century New England Georgian houses, while the Edgar House resembled Southern plantation architecture. The buildings are heavier and more regular, and instead of the plan determining the

1. McKim, Mead & White: Isaac Bell House, Newport, Rhode Island, 1881–3; south-east view

outer form, as Beaux-Arts theory emphasized, the plan and form were conceived as a whole. During this period the partners investigated a number of older styles, such as Colonial Revival and Italian High Renaissance (e.g. the Villard houses), as well as François I (e.g. Mrs Mary Hopkins House, 1884–6, Great Barrington, MA) and Perpendicular Gothic (e.g. St Peter's, 1886–1905, Morristown, NJ).

(iii) High classical period. From the late 1880s into the 1910s the high classical period was based on a reinterpretation of classicism. Monumentality and associations with past civilizations, seen in the Boston Public Library (1887–95; fig. 2) or Pennsylvania Station (1902–11; destr. 1963–5), New York, reflect what McKim and his partners, and the artists with whom they collaborated, saw as an American Renaissance.

In the high classical period the drive towards preestablished order became more evident, along with the more literal quotation of historical reference especially in ornament. The full range of classical styles, from antiquity to the Italian, French and English Renaissances, along with American architecture of the 18th and 19th centuries were seen as the only suitable choices for the USA. McKim, Mead & White perceived America as a product of the classical Renaissance and the great awakening of the 15th and 16th centuries; America was the heir of the old world. Consequently American architecture and art should be a further development of this classical impulse; they should never strive for uniqueness, as did the work of Louis Sullivan or Frank Lloyd Wright. While the French Beaux-Arts heritage is of importance, McKim, Mead &

White's work is different; Harold Van Buren Magonigle (1867–1935), who had been trained at the Beaux-Arts and was also a McKim, Mead & White office member, wrote about the firm: 'The weak point of these men was their plan . . . McKim was the only one to enter the Ecole des Beaux-Arts, and plan never seems to have touched his consciousness' (Magonigle, p. 224). Magonigle criticized the lack of relationship between plan and elevation at the Boston Public Library, and, while the building does have a great sense of procession through different spaces, connections such as that between the stair hall and main reading room are awkwardly handled. The front elevation indicates a great two-storey palazzo and gives no indication of the tremendous third floor hall. The complexity of the interior spaces can only begin to be grasped on side elevations. Surviving correspondence and plans indicate that the outer impression of a building was always the major concern of the firm; functional considerations were suppressed or sometimes ignored for an evocative effect.

In the high classical period the picturesque effect and colour were toned down. Differences in colour abound, but lighter colours—pinks, whites, creams, tans, yellows—replaced the earlier, deeper and more earthy browns, greens, reds and greys. The Boston Public Library exemplifies this period and is a key building of late 19th-century America, its influence lasting well into the 1930s. For his design McKim was indebted to Henri Labrouste's Bibliothèque Sainte-Geneviève (1838–50), Paris, though he departed from the French prototype, significantly shortening the length and number of arches of the façade and making the library a free-standing palazzo, unlike its French

2. McKim, Mead & White: Boston Public Library, Boston, Massachusetts, 1887–95; Copley Square façade

prototype. The Boston Library, with its calm horizontal classicism, is across from Richardson's Trinity Church, with its dark colours and vertical organic picturesqueness. Details on the Library are drawn from Alberti's Tempio Malatestiano, Rimini, and Florentine palazzi, and instead of being a narrow rectangular block, as in Paris, McKim's building encloses a courtyard. The arcade of the courtyard is drawn from the Palazzo Cancelleria, Rome. Visualizing the structure as more than simply a building for housing books, McKim persuaded the Board of Trustees to commission leading artists to decorate it; among the many contributors were Pierre Puvis de Chavannes, Augustus Saint-Gaudens, Louis Saint-Gaudens (1854–1913), John Singer Sargent, Edwin Austin Abbey and Rafael Guastavino. Other buildings of this period follow the same general design development: they are classical and frequently replicate details, but as wholes they are new solutions and never imitations of other designs.

3. OFFICE ORGANIZATION. In actual methods of design the two main designing partners had different approaches. McKim was hesitant, as one office man, Henry Bacon, remembered: 'In [McKim's] sketch the idea was evident, but most indefinitely drawn; and in no stage of planning and designing did he make a definite line or contour' (Moore, p. 59). Designs controlled by McKim were constantly under revision, and in many cases substantial alterations were ordered after the building was well into construction. Later in his life he is remembered as 'designing out loud' or sitting at the draughtsman's table and calling out 'cyma recta; cyma reversa; fillet above', expecting these commands to be drawn out. In contrast, White was high-spirited, making instant decisions that frequently had to be corrected in construction, or, as Magonigle remembered, he would 'in five minutes make

a dozen sketches of some arrangement of detail or plan, slam his hand down on one of them—or perhaps two or three of them if they were close together—say "Do that", and tear off again' (Magonigle, p. 117).

McKim and White thought of themselves as artists working in architecture, and they tended to run the office as a French atelier, the partners acting as studio masters with draughtsmen assigned to them. During the first decade of the partnership intense collaboration existed, but thereafter each architect tended to handle his own projects and clients, though with design suggestions from the others. Mead ran the office, and—while he made a few design contributions, such as the plan for the Rhode Island State House (1891–1904), Providence, on which McKim was the partner-in-charge—his importance lay in trying to keep the office organized and supervising construction. Inevitably an office hierarchy did exist, and, while designers were clustered around McKim and White, there were also specialists in writing specifications, ink and linen working drawings, presentation drawings and model-making. As the scale of projects grew in the later 1880s, and a shift took place from the smaller resort cottage to large commercial buildings (e.g. the New York Life Insurance Co. buildings in Omaha, NB, and Kansas City, MO; 1887–90) and university campuses (e.g. Columbia University, 1892–1901 and 1903–30, New York; see fig. 3), the role of the partners in each project did diminish, and a particular office style dominated. The size of the office fluctuated; from a handful of men it grew to over a hundred at different periods, depending on the workload. All three of the partners made substantial sums of money, but the office also acted as a studio or training ground for many American architects who went on to important careers across the country. In addition to Bacon and Magonigle,

3. McKim, Mead & White: Low Library (1894–8), Columbia University, New York, 1892–1901 and 1903–30; from a photograph *c.* 1900

there were John Carrère, Thomas Hastings, Cass Gilbert, John Galen Howard (1864–1931), A. Page Brown (1859–96), Edward P. York (1865–1927), Philip Sawyer (1868–1949) and many others in New York and regional firms across America. After the death of White and McKim, several new partners were added, and Mead gradually withdrew from the business. The firm's name persisted until 1961; however, the last important work done in its classical style dated from the 1910s and 1920s (e.g. Minneapolis Institute of Arts, 1912–14, Minneapolis, MN; for illustration *see* MINNEAPOLIS).

4. CRITICAL RECEPTION AND POSTHUMOUS REPU-TATION. McKim, Mead & White's work was both widely accepted and understood by the public, in contrast to the general air of incomprehension that greeted the contemporary work of nascent Modernists such as Louis Sullivan or Charles Rennie Mackintosh. As spokesman, McKim made the firm's intentions clear, claiming that classicism was the only one universal language of architecture, and that Americans needed to go to Rome to establish 'standards within reach to stimulate our taste and inspire emulation' (Moore, p. 260). The American Renaissance mentality the firm created was two-sided: to emulate and to be nationalistic. As a belief, it played to American insecurity *vis-à-vis* Europe; America became the heir of all the great art, and indeed McKim, Mead & White inspired their clients to collect European Old Master paintings and other art objects on a grand scale. As McKim was a Bramante, his clients were Medicean princes—for example J. P. Morgan, who commissioned McKim to design his

library in New York (1902–6). But another side of the American Renaissance mentality was intensely nationalis-tic; it coincided with, and helped to celebrate, an American coming of age as a world power. The classical grandeur of the architecture clearly evoked an imperial stance to reflect the overseas colonial possessions that America gained in these years. President Teddy Roosevelt exemplified this new America, and for him McKim remodelled the interior of the White House, Washington, DC, in 1902–3. With McKim's help the plan of Washington, DC, was re-done by the McMillan Commission, and the earlier classical outline laid down by Pierre Charles L'Enfant in the 1790s (but subverted into a picturesque garden in the mid-19th century) was re-established and actually enhanced as a backdrop for great American dramas of ritual. These classical-Renaissance connections were fully understood at the time; one critical assessment of the firm's work in 1906 asked 'Cannot a very strong case be made in favor of a conscious, persistent attempt to adopt the architecture of the Renaissance to American uses?' (Desmond and Croly, p. 226). The answer was, of course, affirmative, with dissenters such as Louis Sullivan generally ignored.

The esteem in which McKim, Mead and White were held both in their lifetimes and afterwards is remarkable. McKim received two of the highest architectural honours: the gold medal of the Royal Institute of British Architects in 1903, and the gold medal of the American Institute of Architects in 1909. Well into the 1930s McKim, Mead & White, both personally and as a firm, were frequently ranked on a level with Bramante, Wren or Mansart. They were honoured abroad, and the first monograph on the firm came in 1924 from the English architect and educator Charles H. Reilly, who had used their drawings as teaching aids. While their reputations did suffer some diminishment in the 1930s and afterwards, with the onset of Modernism, the quality of their work was always respected. In the 1950s they were admired exclusively for their early shingle-covered buildings, while their classical work was disparaged. By the early 1970s their reputation began to be rehabilitated and the subsequent outpouring of scholarship by historians and literal quotation of their work by Postmodernist architects indicate a new level of appreciation.

UNPUBLISHED SOURCES

New York, Columbia U., Avery Archit. Mem. Lib. [drgs and major col. of White's pap.]
New York, Mus. City NY [firm's original glass pl. negatives of works in New York City and other bldgs]
New York, NY Hist. Soc. [major repository of firm's rec., drgs and ephemera]
Washington, DC, Lib. Congr. [McKim's personal and office corr.]

[Many individual buildings house collections covering that particular project (e.g. Boston Public Library, Newport Casino). Original materials relating to the firm's work before 1890 are scarce and seem to have been destroyed, at least in part.]

BIBLIOGRAPHY

G. W. Shelton: *Artistic Country-seats, Types of Recent American Villa and Cottage Architecture with Instances of Country Club-houses*, 2 vols (New York, 1886/R 1979)
R. Sturgis: *The Work of McKim, Mead & White*, Architectural Record Great American Architects (New York, 1895)
H. W. Desmond and H. Croly: 'The Work of Messrs. McKim, Mead & White', *Archit. Rec.*, xx (1906), pp. 153–246
A. H. Granger: *Charles Follen McKim: A Study of his Life and Work* (Boston, 1913)
A Monograph of the Works of McKim, Mead & White, 1879–1915, 4 vols (New York, 1915–20/R 1985); abridged student's edn, 2 vols (New York, 1925/R 1981) [illus. only, no text]
C. Reilly: *McKim, Mead & White* (London, 1924)
C. Moore: *The Life and Times of Charles Follen McKim* (New York, 1929/R 1970)
C. Baldwin: *Stanford White* (New York, 1931/R 1971)
H. V. B. Magonigle: 'A Half Century of Architecture', *Pencil Points*, xv (1934), pp. 115–18, 223–6
V. J. Scully jr: *The Shingle Style* (New Haven, 1955/R 1971)
L. Roth: *The Architecture of McKim, Mead & White, 1870–1920; A Building List* (New York and London, 1978)
R. G. Wilson, D. Pilgrim and R. Murray: *The American Renaissance, 1876–1917* (New York, 1979)
R. G. Wilson: 'The Early Work of Charles F. McKim: Country House Commissions', *Winterthur Port.*, xiv (1979), pp. 235–67
L. Roth: *McKim, Mead & White, Architects* (New York, 1983)
R. G. Wilson: *McKim, Mead & White, Architects* (New York, 1983)
P. R. Baker: *Stanny: The Gilded Life of Stanford White* (New York, 1989)
D. Garrard Lowe: *Stanford White's New York* (New York, 1992)

RICHARD GUY WILSON

Mackintosh, Charles Rennie (*b* Glasgow, 7 June 1868; *d* London, 10 Dec 1928). Scottish architect, designer and painter. In the pantheon of heroes of the Modern Movement, he has been elevated to a cult figure, such that the importance of his late 19th-century background and training in Glasgow are often overlooked. He studied during a period of great artistic activity in the city that produced the distinctive GLASGOW STYLE. As a follower of A. W. N. Pugin and John Ruskin, he believed in the superiority of Gothic over Classical architecture and by implication that moral integrity in architecture could be achieved only through revealed construction. Although Mackintosh's buildings refrain from overt classicism, they reflect its inherent discipline. His profound originality was evident by 1895, when he began the designs for the Glasgow School of Art. His decorative schemes, particularly the furniture, also formed an essential element in his buildings. During Mackintosh's lifetime his influence was chiefly felt in Austria, in the work of such painters as Gustav Klimt and such architects as Josef Hoffmann and Joseph Maria Olbrich. The revival of interest in his work was initiated by the publication of monographs by Pevsner (1950) and Howarth (1952). The Charles Rennie Mackintosh Society was formed in Glasgow in 1973; it publishes a biannual newsletter, has a reference library and organizes exhibitions. The Hunterian Art Gallery, University of Glasgow, which opened in 1981, holds the Mackintosh estate of drawings, watercolours and archival material as well as a collection of his furniture; the Glasgow School of Art and the Glasgow Art Gallery also have important collections.

1. Training and early work, to 1892. 2. Middle years, 1892–1913. 3. Final years, 1914 and after.

1. TRAINING AND EARLY WORK, TO 1892. On leaving school in 1884, Mackintosh became apprenticed to a Glasgow architect, John Hutchison (*c.* 1841–1908), concurrently attending evening classes at the Glasgow School of Art. He completed his apprenticeship in 1888, when he was taken on as a draughtsman in the architectural firm of Honeyman & Keppie, a well-established firm in Glasgow. Having won several prestigious prizes, culminating in the award of the Alexander Thomson Travelling Scholarship, he went to Italy in 1891 and spent some months travelling from Naples to Pavia. As a student he produced watercolour studies of Scottish architecture, ranging from a study of the ornate wall tombs in the graveyard of Elgin Cathedral (1889) to an atmospheric treatment of *Glasgow Cathedral at Sunset* (1890; both U. Glasgow, Hunterian A.G.). He used the architectural and topographical studies he made on tours and holidays as design sources. The watercolours he made in Italy are predominantly straightforward renderings of architectural elements, such as a transept doorway of Orvieto Cathedral or the brick tower of the Palazzo Pubblico in Siena capped by a stone belvedere; a panoramic vista of the *Lido at Venice* (1891; U. Glasgow, Hunterian A.G.) has the soft colouring and nebulous outlines associated with James McNeill Whistler.

2. MIDDLE YEARS, 1892–1913. On returning to Glasgow Mackintosh resumed work with Honeyman & Keppie, becoming a partner in 1904 and remaining with the practice until 1913. His views on Gothic architecture would have been reinforced by the founder of the firm, John Honeyman (1831–1914). Honeyman's interpretation of the Early English style in Landsdowne Church (1863), Glasgow, represents one of the city's most original Victorian churches; he was also responsible for the fabric of the medieval Glasgow Cathedral.

(i) Official architectural commissions. (ii) The Four. (iii) Interiors for the tea rooms. (iv) Domestic architectural commissions.

(i) Official architectural commissions. Mackintosh's earliest architectural work, the *Glasgow Herald* Building (1893–5), Mitchell Street, was produced in conjunction with the

firm's junior partner, John Keppie (1863–1945), a worthy but unimaginative architect who had trained in Paris at the Ecole des Beaux-Arts. Although the overall disposition of elements and details, such as the fenestration pattern and the flickering tongues of stone rising from the window surrounds, are familiar from Keppie's repertory, Mackintosh seems to have been allowed to introduce many of his own ideas. While possibly inspired by foliate, Gothic bosses, the vegetable carving on the rainwater-heads, corbels and keystones, particularly of the higher storeys, is a typical Mackintosh innovation. The two six-storey elevations are unified by a higher polygonal tower scaffolded at the angles by continuous pilaster strips. The top of the tower, which contains a water storage tank, is corbelled outwards like a bursting bud, so adding to the feeling of growth.

Few drawings survive for the *Glasgow Herald* Building or for the Queen Margaret Medical College (partly destr., substantially altered internally), Queen Margaret Drive, a pioneering college for women begun in 1895. Perspectives of both buildings were drawn by Mackintosh in his own distinctive style, revealing that for him the concept of a building extended to its immediate surroundings, including the planting. In the study for the Queen Margaret College tall damsels in loosely flowing robes loiter pensively on lawns spangled with aesthetically trimmed shrubs. Mackintosh's designs for the college also demonstrate his interest in vernacular architecture: the ashlar gabled walls inset with low windows and the L-plan, with the doorway in the re-entrant angle, are features of many Scottish tower-houses, although the cupola over the stair-tower is an importation from the east coast where the towers of the burgh tolbooths, as at Culross, Fife, are often of Dutch inspiration.

With the Martyrs' School (1895), Barony Street, the historical bias may be less obvious since Mackintosh was trying to attain a more Expressionist idiom. Like many Glasgow board schools, Martyrs' is constructed of red sandstone brought in by rail once the local sandstone quarries became exhausted. The plan conforms to the standard layout, which was governed by the requirement of separate entrances for boys and girls. A top-lit well lights a ground-floor drill hall over which galleries on all sides communicate with the classrooms, which were placed on the outer edges of the building to gain the maximum natural light. Over the hall and staircases exposed wooden rafters and ties are either pinned to the walls by brackets or rest on corbels. Although the construction is a standard exercise, the jointing anticipates Mackintosh's bolder carpentry in the museum roof of the Glasgow School of Art. Externally the clash of stereotyped and new forms may reflect compromises between Keppie and Mackintosh. The flowing Art Nouveau curves around doorways and windows occur on earlier works. Of greater interest are the groups of windows set on a continous bracketed sill, a concept that is neither unique nor new but is of interest when set against the individual verticality of a staircase pierced by a thermal window below oversailing rafter ends.

Similar unresolved compromises are found at Queen's Cross Church (1897), Maryhill Road, a job that would have gone to Honeyman & Keppie because of Honeyman's reputation in church circles. Although there is no mention in the surviving building records of Mackintosh's name, he alone could have devised the plethora of Art Nouveau details. Looser, more organic outlines have become heart-shaped tracery in the chancel window, while on the pulpit the intertwining of birds, foliage and circles refashion the traditions of Celtic art. The design of the corner tower was based on that of Merriot Church, Somerset, which Mackintosh had sketched. It was reproduced almost exactly with an entrance porch and a traceried window above on the main face and with an engaged stair-turret tucked into the corner. Most appealing to Mackintosh in the Somerset church tower was the marked entasis of its profile; the Queen's Cross tower has a similarly sturdy independence and is again the fulcrum for two different elevations. The more important south elevation has variations in height between one and two stages; while faithfully reflecting the internal placement of a gallery over a side aisle, this results in distressing changes in elevational scale. Throughout the design integrity is consistent with the structure since the buttresses carry exposed steel roof ties spanning the undivided interior; monotony is avoided by the broad chancel and use of galleries. The gallery fronts are dropped at intervals to allow the board ends to be fretted, a mannerism used more tellingly in the library of the Glasgow School of Art.

In 1895 a limited competition had been announced for the design of a building to house the Glasgow School of Art. Although the entries from nominated Glasgow firms were submitted anonymously, the authorship of Mackintosh's proposals could not have been mistaken. As the cost limit would not pay for the entire building, it had been decided to proceed with the construction in two phases. The first stage, begun in 1896, was the eastern half to just beyond the entrance; this was followed ten years later by the western portion. The Glasgow School of Art therefore demonstrates Mackintosh's organic planning whereby within a fixed frame elements are synthesized in response to changing design criteria. A good example is the introduction of the celebrated 'hen-run', a glazed corridor linking the eastern and western sections at second-floor level.

The school's site, a steep bluff falling from north to south, gives a huge increase in height between the entrance elevation on the north and the rear elevation to the south (see fig. 1). The difference is not just one of scale because each façade, being the revelation of inner functions, has an individual identity. On the north, with its banks of studios, the rhythmic sequence of metal-framed windows appears at a casual glance to be symmetrical, an illusion fostered by the equal lengths of railings flanking the entrance. Composed of small units indicating lesser volumes within, the elevation is marked out by an oriel window and seemingly off-centre doorway. This grouping of parts may be an updated detail from R. Norman Shaw's New Zealand Chambers (1872; destr.), London; the larger design components are an austere revision of Henry Wilson's Ladbroke Grove Library (1890), London, but without its plaintive historicism and emblematic sculpture.

Mackintosh's own use of history was evocative. On the east elevation of the School of Art the two vertical divisions recall one façade of the early 17th-century Maybole Castle, Strathclyde, a sketch of which by Mackintosh survives (U.

1. Charles Rennie Mackintosh: Glasgow School of Art, begun 1896; south-west view

Glasgow, Hunterian A.G.). Unfortunately the disparate fenestration of the east elevation of the School of Art fails to hold its own against the mass of walling. However, by the time the west elevation came to be built, the design had been unified by introducing lattice-framed bay windows. Used to light one floor they have a domestic scale imitating the prevailing fashion for bay windows in Glasgow's tenements and terraces; linked vertically, they correspond to Shaw's stacked grids (1867) at Leyswood, Groombridge, E. Sussex, and A. H. Mackmurdo's corner block at 25 Cadogan Gardens (1899), London. The novelty at the Glasgow School of Art is continuous glazing, which is freed from the library floor levels behind, an idea picked up perhaps from Alexander Thomson, who as early as 1871 had introduced a horizontal screen of glass, independent of the structure, on the top floor of his Egyptian Halls, Glasgow. In the twin stair towers of Scotland Street School (1904–6) Mackintosh left a void between the curved outer screen of glass and the staircase, two elements that were later united by Walter Gropius in the Fagus Factory (1911), Alfeld-an-der-Leine, Germany. At Scotland Street the separation permits an uninterrupted upward view through each tower to the traditional carpentry supporting the conical roof. The towers and the tall ranges of windows between them have their sources in the 16th-century Falkland Palace, Fife, which Mackintosh sketched (U. Glasgow, Hunterian A.G.).

The library (1907–9) of the Glasgow School of Art is one of Mackintosh's masterpieces. Whereas elsewhere in the school white interiors give spatial clarity and an exactness of definition, the wood-lined interior of the library is ambiguous despite its rigid geometry. On four sides a narrow gallery is supported by thin beams that project beyond the gallery front to engage the sides of eight free-standing posts. Set in two rows these posts define an inner zone, free of structural interruption, which houses a cluster of lamps with metal shades, like miniature black and silver skyscrapers, inset with pink and purple glass.

(ii) The Four. It was probably in 1893 that Francis H. Newbery (1855–1946), then director of the Glasgow School of Art, brought Mackintosh and Herbert MacNair, a colleague and friend in Honeyman & Keppie's office, into contact with the two MACDONALD sisters who were day students at the school. They were Frances, who married MacNair in 1899, and Margaret, who married Mackintosh in 1900. The group, which became known as the Four, displayed in their paintings and graphic designs a similarity of style and subject-matter. The significant characteristics are etiolated human figures (usually female) set against luminous but sombre backgrounds of blue or green; a pervasive symbolism hints at eroticism and pain, and there is often an overwhelming sense of desolation and despair. These ideals were also represented in the progressive art journal *The Studio*, whose first issue (with examples of C. F. A. Voysey's work and a cover by Aubrey Beardsley) was published in 1893. The Four exhibited at the Arts and Crafts Society in London in 1896, and their works were subsequently written up in *The Studio*; as a result they gained a following in Europe, being invited to furnish and decorate a room at the eighth exhibition of the Vienna Secession (1900) and at the Esposizione Internazionale d'Arte Decorativa in Turin (1902). These were the high-points of the Four's success. Thereafter it was Mackintosh alone who, by abandoning the self-indulgent introspection and mystical romanticism that typified the group's work, formulated a taut geometric and spatial discipline and became an artist of the first rank. As a result of Mackintosh's collaboration with MacNair and the Macdonald sisters, his potential as an artist of originality began to appear. Despite a dramatic change in content and form, however, he was still relying on the same colour range, using more intense acid blue and green tones. In his watercolour the *Harvest Moon* (1892; U. Glasgow, Hunterian A.G.) an androgynous angel stands before a full moon encircled by the angel's wings; in the foreground a tangle of twisted thorns are spotted with berries. Unlike the Macdonald sisters, Mackintosh avoided the obvious imitation of Beardsley's manner, showing a leaning towards abstract, philosophical ideas presented with ambiguous titles such as the *Tree of Personal Effort* (1895; Glasgow, Sch. A. Col.).

(iii) Interiors for the tea-rooms. The best-known Mackintosh interiors were those created for Miss Catherine Cranston's four tea-rooms in Glasgow: Buchanan Street (1896), Argyle Street (1897), Ingram Street (1900) and the Willow (1903), of which only the last-mentioned survives at 199 Sauchiehall Street. At this time tea-rooms in the city were

numerous and popular; when hung with paintings by the Glasgow Boys some of them became almost like art galleries. None could match the tea-rooms of Miss Cranston with their startling decorations and the provision of such amenities as billiard-rooms and ladies' rooms. The Buchanan Street tea-room was created behind an earlier neo-Flemish façade under the direction of the Glasgow designer George Walton (*see* WALTON, (2)). Mackintosh's contribution included mural decorations, the most striking of which was a frieze of stencilled women whose silhouettes, stiff and hieratic like Byzantine saints, were entwined with briars. As in his poster designs, Mackintosh used a flat technique, without shading or perspective, pale tones being highlighted by spots of primary colour. The roles of Walton and Mackintosh were reversed in 1897 in the Argyle Street tea-room, for which Mackintosh designed the furniture; in 1906 he added a basement, the Dutch Kitchen. The fireplace is framed by the swooping curves of a screen beyond which the wall is cross-hatched.

In furniture, as in other areas of design, it seems that there was an early affinity of approach and method between Mackintosh and MacNair; initially at least, the latter may have led the way, although in time Mackintosh's architectural discipline provided a more structural rationale. His early individual pieces of furniture made much use of dark or green-stained oak and often incorporated beaten metal figurative panels. With the commissions for the tea-rooms Mackintosh could extend his repertory and

experiment further by using the chairs to complement the interior decoration (*see* CHAIR, fig. 3) while defining a particular location. In the Dutch Kitchen, high-backed chairs were set in the inglenook; elsewhere the low Windsor chairs were a foil to the elaborate decorations on walls and piers.

In the Willow tea-room Mackintosh had total control of the project both inside and outside; his wife contributed some of the decorative motifs. On the ground floor he set up an unpainted frieze of plaster panels, their angular outlines leading the eye deeper into the stems and branches of the willow wood. Above, in the Room de Luxe, a leaded-glass frieze with pink and green insets was placed against white painted walls, and on the curved bay, leaf-shaped mirror glass shimmered like the stirring of willow leaves. Mackintosh had already developed in domestic commissions austere all-white ensembles of decoration with a few pieces of slender, white furniture, but such refinement of construction was not practical in a public place. In the Room de Luxe the chairs, of two sizes, are silver with purple upholstery; the tops of the higher chairs are pierced by a grid of squares, a favourite Mackintosh device.

(iv) Domestic architectural commissions. Mackintosh's earliest domestic commission of consequence was Windyhill, Kilmacolm, Strathclyde, built in 1899 for William Davidson (1861–1945). The house is aligned north to south

2. Charles Rennie Mackintosh: project for the Art Lover's House, colour lithograph, 394×529 mm, 1901 (Glasgow, University of Glasgow, Hunterian Art Gallery)

across a west-facing slope with an access road to the north, which dictated the position of the entrance. The plan of the house is very straightforward as the hallway leads into a broad corridor lying parallel to the three main rooms, each with a southern aspect. Mackintosh confined the service wing and staircase to separate units at the rear; although each reflects its internal function, the handling of the outlines and some awkward clashes in the juxtaposition of parts indicate that Mackintosh was using a vocabulary that he did not fully understand, having borrowed partly from others such as Voysey. While there are also stylistic incongruities on the south elevation, it is by contrast almost too plain. With its harled walls, deep openings, slate roof and chimney-stacks set on the end gables, it is like an overblown farmhouse.

Mackintosh further tested his ability as a house designer in his entry for the Art Lover's House, an international competition arranged by the *Zeitschrift für Innendekoration* (1900–01). Although the first prize went to another architect, M. H. Baillie Scott, the competition is chiefly remembered for Mackintosh's entry (see fig. 2), in which he eschewed the tricks of the English picturesque tradition, preferring the Scottish tradition of bold, unadorned massing and the external expression of staircases and chimneys, effects that do not rely on the reproduction of historical detail. The entry was a conceptual essay of the Modern Movement in which Mackintosh's idiosyncratic stamp was on everything, whether it was the knitting together of the

public rooms in a linear progression of functional importance, like an 18th-century apartment, or drawing a dark, sombre dining-room as was habitual in Glasgow. The house was built in Bellahouston Park, Glasgow, and completed externally in 1990–91.

Much of Mackintosh's career as an architect might have remained unfulfilled had he not been encouraged and sustained by a few determined and discriminating patrons such as the Glasgow publisher Walter Blackie (1860–1953). As a result of his friendship with Blackie's art director, Talwin Morris (1865–1911), Mackintosh was invited by Blackie in 1902 to design a family house, later known as the Hill House (now owned by NT Scotland). The chosen site, in upper Helensburgh, Strathclyde, is an exposed slope with a panoramic view of the Firth of Clyde. Before formulating a concept for the Hill House, Mackintosh invited Blackie to inspect Windyhill. Although the plan of the Hill House generated the form of the building, the relationships and scale of the main units as seen from the south have an uncanny resemblance to Crathes Castle, Grampian, a late 16th-century L-plan tower-house to which was added a plain two-storey wing to provide more commodious accommodation. There is much the same distribution of living and service requirements at the Hill House. The entrance is on the short, western side, thus ensuring maximum privacy for the occupants since the public rooms face south. Immediately beyond the entrance are a library and business-room with small, slit windows overlooking the approach to the house. From the outer hall a short flight of steps leads up to the main, dark-beamed hall (see fig. 3), providing circulation into the drawing-room and to the dining-room beyond. Thus the accepted principles of 19th-century country-house planning are followed, not only in the separation of zones according to function but also in the progression from public to semi-public to private areas. In the main hall, the principal staircase is partly enclosed by wooden uprights that repeat the vertical dimensions of the walls, which are interspersed with pale grey panels topped by coloured stencils. Characteristic oak furniture is pierced by squares; there are also squares on the pale grey carpet, emphasizing Mackintosh's comprehensive plan for the interior decoration..

3. FINAL YEARS, 1914 AND AFTER. In 1914, a year after leaving his architectural practice, Mackintosh and his wife moved to the village of Walberswick, Suffolk, where the Newberys had a holiday cottage. Mackintosh had an invitation from Austrian architects to travel to Vienna but was prevented from doing so by the outbreak of World War I. Instead he and his wife went to London, settling in Chelsea for the next eight years. Apart from designing textiles (see fig. 4), as well as some small decorative commissions for Miss Cranston and an aborted project for a group of studios, Mackintosh's only significant work during that period was the remodelling of 78 Derngate, Northampton, a brick terrace house. Mackintosh reshaped and extended the rear elevation using white concrete in the manner of the most advanced contemporary Austrian work; the interior can best be described as proto-Art Deco

3. Charles Rennie Mackintosh: Hill House, Helensburgh, Dunbartonshire, 1904; view of the main hall

with hard geometry and dazzling colours to relieve dark backgrounds. In 1923 Mackintosh and his wife went to Port Vendres, a French Mediterranean village on the Spanish border, where he devoted his time to painting watercolours.

In his architectural work Mackintosh had consistently displayed a fondness for stylized foliate patterns. His interest in nature had been revealed from 1901 onwards in a collection of botanical studies of individual flowers and shrubs usually sketched during holidays in England. What is remarkable is Mackintosh's ability combined with economy of effort, to delineate all stages in the plant's development while drawing attention to its structure. On retiring to Walberswick, Mackintosh resumed his flower studies, often choosing cultivated flowers as subjects, with a greater degree of finish, possibly with the intention of compiling a book.

At Port Vendres Mackintosh devoted his time to garnering a representative collection of watercolours for an intended exhibition in London. These still included flower studies, such as *Mimosa* and *Amelie-les-Bains* (both 1924; U. Glasgow, Hunterian A.G.), showing that his technique had not waned. The immediate vicinity of Port Vendres offered a diverse range of subjects, from the bustle of the quayside with its cranes and ships to the distant perspectives of mountain villages. In this varied landscape, baked by the summer heat, Mackintosh became so obsessed with the integrity and strength of structural form that village houses began to replicate rock formations, as in the *Village of La Lagonne* (*c.* 1924–7; Glasgow, A.G. & Mus.). In these late works, the relentless Mediterranean light suffuses the delicate watercolours, with their bright orange and blue splotches of roofs and water, reducing countryside and rocky slopes to flat, clearly defined planes without the distortion of shading. Buildings and landscape, having the same purity of form, are united in an overall pattern like a Mackintosh textile design.

On becoming ill in 1927, Mackintosh left France for treatment in London, where he died the next year.

See also CUTLERY, fig. 1.

BIBLIOGRAPHY

N. Pevsner: *Pioneers of Modern Design* (London, 1936, 3/1974)
——: *C. R. Mackintosh* (Milan, 1950); Eng. trans. in N. Pevsner: *Studies in Art, Architecture and Design*, ii (London, 1968), pp. 151–75
T. Howarth: *Charles Rennie Mackintosh and the Modern Movement* (London, 1952, 2/1977)
R. MacLeod: *Charles Rennie Mackintosh* (Feltham, 1968, rev. 1983)
Newslett.: Charles Rennie Mackintosh Soc. (1973–) [biannual newsletter]
R. Billcliffe: *Architectural Sketches and Flower Drawings by Charles Rennie Mackintosh* (London, 1977)
R. Billcliffe and P. Vergo: 'Charles Rennie Mackintosh and the Austrian Art Revival', *Burl. Mag.*, cxix (1977), pp. 739–46
J. Cooper, ed.: *Mackintosh Architecture* (New York and London, 1977, 2/1980)
R. Billcliffe: *Mackintosh Watercolours* (London, 1978)
——: *Charles Rennie Mackintosh: The Complete Furniture, Furniture Drawings and Interior Designs* (Guildford, 1979, rev. London, 3/1986)
W. Buchanan: 'Japanese Influences on the Glasgow Boys and Charles Rennie Mackintosh', *Japonisme in Art: An International Symposium: Tokyo, 1980*, pp. 290–301
R. Billcliffe: *Mackintosh Textile Designs* (London and New York, 1982)
A. R. Tintner: 'Furniture as Architecture: The Contribution of Charles Rennie Mackintosh', *J. Pre-Raphaelite Stud.*, iii (1982–3), no. 1, pp. 3–15; no. 2, pp. 1–8
Vienna 1900: Vienna, Scotland and the European Avant-garde (exh. cat. by P. Vergo, Edinburgh, N. Mus. Ant., 1983)

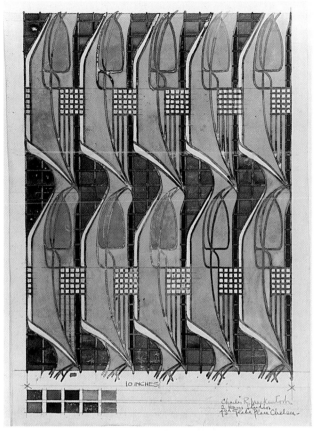

4. Charles Rennie Mackintosh: 'Tulip and Lattice' textile design, pencil, watercolour and gouache, 398×289 mm, *c.* 1915–23 (Glasgow, University of Glasgow, Hunterian Art Gallery)

Charles Rennie Mackintosh, 1868–1928 (exh. cat., ed. G. Laganà; Certaldo, Pal. Pretorio, 1988)
W. Buchanan, ed.: *Mackintosh's Masterwork: The Glasgow School of Art* (Glasgow, 1989)
P. Robertson, ed.: *Charles Rennie Mackintosh: The Architectural Papers* (Wendlebury, 1990)
J. Macaulay: *Glasgow School of Art* (London, 1993)
——: *Hill House* (London, 1994)
T. Neat: *Part Seen, Part Imagined: Meaning and Symbolism in the Work of Charles Rennie Mackintosh and Margaret Macdonald* (Edinburgh, 1994)
J. Steele: *Charles Rennie Mackintosh: Synthesis in Form* (London, 1994)

JAMES MACAULAY

Macklin, Thomas (*fl* 1787; *d* ?London, before 5 May 1800). English printseller and picture dealer. He began as a gilder of picture frames and later became a picture and print dealer. In 1787, inspired by the publicity surrounding the Shakespeare Gallery of John Boydell, he announced his own plan to commission 100 paintings illustrating the works of the English poets and to publish engravings after them. Artists such as Joshua Reynolds, Henry Fuseli and Angelica Kauffman contributed to the project, illustrating works primarily by 18th-century poets, such as Alexander Pope, James Thomson, William Collins and Thomas Gray. Unlike Boydell, Macklin acquired two paintings from Gainsborough, including his *Cottage Girl with Bowl of Milk* (1786; Cape Town, N.G.), which Macklin exhibited as *Lavinia*, a title inspired by Thomson's *Seasons* (1726–30). The first exhibition of Macklin's Poets' Gallery opened in Pall Mall, London, on 14 April 1788 with 19 paintings. The second, with 24 paintings, was held in his shop at 39 Fleet Street. Unfortunately fewer than 40 of the 100 paintings envisaged were completed, and only six numbers of *Macklin's British Poets*, with a total of 24 engravings by Francesco Bartolozzi, were published between 1788 and 1799.

In 1792 Macklin began publishing an illustrated Bible. Philippe Jacques de Loutherbourg provided most of the paintings for it, including *The Deluge* (1790s; London, V&A). Macklin also commissioned Benjamin West's *Christ Presenting a Little Child* (retouched 1801; London, Foundling Hosp.) and paid Reynolds 500 guineas for his *Holy Family* (c. 1788; London, Tate). *Macklin's Holy Bible* was completed in 1800, but the expenditure of over £30,000 on its production added to Macklin's increasing debts. In 1797 he was forced to sell the Bible paintings and those for the Poets' Gallery by lottery. After his death, those remaining with his firm were auctioned on 5–10 May 1800 and 27–30 May 1801.

WRITINGS
'Introduction', *Catalogue of the Third Exhibition of Pictures Painted for Mr Macklin by the Artists of Britain* (London, 1790)

BIBLIOGRAPHY
T. S. R. Boase: 'Macklin and Bowyer', *J. Warb. & Court. Inst.*, xxvi (1963), pp. 148–77
S. H. A. Bruntjen: *John Boydell, 1719–1804* (New York, 1985), pp. 118–21

SHEARER WEST

Mackmurdo, A(rthur) H(eygate) (*b* London, 12 Dec 1851; *d* Wickham Bishops, Essex, 15 March 1942). English architect and social reformer. He was an important figure in the Arts and Crafts Movement. He trained as an architect first with T. Chatfield Clarke (1825–95) and then with the Gothic Revivalist James Brooks (i). He was greatly influenced by John Ruskin (they travelled to Italy together in 1874), particularly on social and economic issues. Mackmurdo believed that his work should be socially as well as artistically significant. In design he valued tradition but sought a contemporary relevance, and he promoted the unity of the arts, with architecture as the central discipline. By 1884 he had moved away from the Gothic Revival style and adopted an eclectic use of Renaissance sources. Some of his designs have been described as proto-Art Nouveau and are thought to have influenced the emergence of this style in architecture and the applied arts in Britain and Europe in the 1890s and 1900s. His pattern designs for wallpaper and textiles incorporated swirling organic motifs (e.g. *Cromer Bird*, cretonne, c. 1884), while for three-dimensional and architectural work he often used a simplified version of classicism derived from English 18th-century sources. Brooklyn, a small, flat-roofed house (c. 1886; Private Road, Enfield, London), was designed in an austere and simple rationalized classical style in which the logic of constructional methods was emphasized in a way that heralds the work of architects such as C. F. A. Voysey.

About 1883 Mackmurdo formed the Century Guild of Artists with his former pupil Herbert Horne. During the

1880s Mackmurdo was responsible for the overall conception of the Guild's displays, for which he designed printed and woven textiles, wallpapers, furniture and metalwork. In 1890 Mackmurdo and Horne moved to 20 Fitzroy Street, London, where they formed an artistic community, jokingly known as the 'Fitzroy Settlement', which became a focus for advanced cultural gatherings. However, Horne's interests shifted, the Guild wound down and the partnership was dissolved in 1892. Mackmurdo continued to practise as an architect. In the 1890s he was using a less adventurous form of classicism. For a house at 25 Cadogan Gardens, Chelsea (c. 1899), he devised a composition in which the brickwork, divided into strips by vertically linked windows, is suggestive of a giant order of pilasters topped by an exaggerated cornice. The detailing is in the Queen Anne style.

After 1900 Mackmurdo retired from practice and moved to Essex to concentrate on his interests in social and economic reform. There he designed several buildings, including a house for his own use, Great Ruffins (c. 1902; Wickham Bishops). This has a tall central tower with flanking pavilions and is curiously Baroque in appearance. About 1925 Mackmurdo wrote an idiosyncratic 'History of the Arts and Crafts Movement' that remained unpublished. Many of his designs and examples of his work are in the collection of the William Morris Gallery, Walthamstow, London, which he helped to found.

UNPUBLISHED SOURCES
'History of the Arts and Crafts Movement', typescript, c. 1925, London, William Morris Gal.

WRITINGS
Wren's City Churches (Orpington, 1883)
'The Guild Flag's Unfurling', *C. Guild Hobby Horse*, i (1884), pp. 2–16

BIBLIOGRAPHY
N. Pevsner: 'Arthur H. Mackmurdo: A Pioneer Designer', *Archit. Rev.*, lxxxiii (1938), pp. 141–3; repr. in N. Pevsner: *Victorian and After*, ii of *Studies in Art, Architecture and Design* (London, 1968), pp. 133–9
E. Pond: 'Mackmurdo Gleanings', *Archit. Rev.*, cxxviii (1960), pp. 111–15
P. Stansky: *Redesigning the World: William Morris, the 1880s and the Arts and Crafts* (Princeton, 1985)

STUART EVANS

McKnight Kauffer, E(dward Leland). *See* KAUFFER, E. MCKNIGHT.

Maclagan, Sir **Eric (Robert Dalrymple)** (*b* London, 4 Dec 1879; *d* Spain, 14 Sept 1951). English museum curator. In 1905 he joined the Victoria and Albert Museum in London as an Assistant in the Department of Textiles; subsequently he moved to the Department of Architecture and Sculpture. His lifelong career at the Museum was interrupted during World War I, by a period of service (1916–19) in the Foreign Office and the Ministry of Information. In 1921 he became Keeper of the Department of Architecture and Sculpture. He concentrated on the study of Italian sculpture and he compiled, in collaboration with Margaret Longhurst, the Museum's *Catalogue of Italian Sculpture* (1932). Though superseded in 1964 by John Pope-Hennessy's *Catalogue of Italian Sculpture in the Victoria and Albert Museum*, Maclagan's work remains a monument of careful scholarship, which took full account of the advances made by Wilhelm von Bode in the study of sculpture.

As a museum curator he initiated some notable purchases, including a *Virgin and Child* by Desiderio da Settignano, another by Agostino di Duccio, and Gianlorenzo Bernini's bust of *Thomas Baker*. In 1924 he was appointed Director of the Victoria and Albert Museum. Although he concentrated on maintaining and expanding the Museum's reputation as a centre for scholarship, he did not neglect its more public role, encouraging inexpensive publications and the rearrangement of the labyrinthine galleries on a more logical basis. He was a gifted lecturer: in 1927–8 he was Charles Eliot Norton Professor at Harvard University, Cambridge, MA, his lectures appearing in 1935 as *Italian Sculpture of the Renaissance*. His interests were not confined to sculpture; his book on the Bayeux Tapestry, for example, enjoyed great success.

WRITINGS
Catalogue of Italian Plaquettes, London, V&A cat. (London, 1924)
with M. Longhurst: *Catalogue of Italian Sculpture*, London, V&A cat., 2 vols (London, 1932)
Italian Sculpture of the Renaissance (London, 1935)
The Bayeux Tapestry (London, 1943; rev. 3/1949)

BIBLIOGRAPHY
DNB

☐

MacLaren, James M(arjoribanks) (*b* Thornhill, Stirling, Central, 12 Jan 1853; *d* Hampstead, London, 20 Oct 1890). Scottish architect. He received his early training in Glasgow in the firm of J. J. Stevenson and Campbell Douglas (1828–1910); in the early 1870s he moved to London, where he worked with Richard Coad (1825–1900). He was particularly influenced by the contemporary work of Stevenson, E. W. Godwin and R. Norman Shaw. On 28 February 1883 MacLaren married Margaret M. MacColl, sister of the art critic D. S. MacColl, later Keeper of the Tate Gallery, London. MacLaren started his own practice in 1886. His first commission was for The Park, Ledbury, Hereford & Worcs, an old house to which he added a wing in the local vernacular style, with his first use of the angle turret that characterized many of his later designs. He retained his links with Scotland, working in particular for Donald Currie, chairman of the Union Castle steamship line, for whom he designed an L-shaped row of cottages, farmhouse and farm buildings (*c.* 1889–90) at the Glenlyon estate, Fortingall, Perthshire; these use white roughcast over stone as rendering, a refined version of a traditional Scottish feature, and the farmhouse has strong geometric lines. The small town hall (1889) at Aberfeldy, Tayside, has similar whitewashed rendering, sweeping gables and a rustic turret. MacLaren's stone observatory tower and wing (1887) for Stirling High School shows the influence of H. H. Richardson, with sculpture integrated into its rugged exterior. In London his most striking works are the houses at 22 Avonmore Road (1888; for the sculptor H. R. Pinker, 1849–1927), Kensington, and 10/12 Palace Court (1889–90; for Currie), Bayswater, which have unusual fenestration and bands of carved decoration. Among his last works was the Santa Catalina Hotel (1887–90; rebuilt except lodge), Las Palmas. MacLaren died young, but his influence through his membership of the Art Workers' Guild (from 1886) and his use and free interpretation of local styles and traditional local materials was considerable in the 1890s and 1900s among Arts and Crafts architects such as C. F. A. Voysey, E. S. Prior and Charles Rennie Mackintosh. His London practice was continued by the firm of Dunn & Watson.

BIBLIOGRAPHY
Obituary, *Builder*, lix (1890), p. 348; *Bldg News*, lix (1890), p. 672
H. S. Goodhart-Rendel: 'Rogue Architects of the Victorian Era', *RIBA J.*, n.s. 3, lvi (1949), p. 258
D. Walker: 'Charles Rennie Mackintosh', *Archit. Rev.* [London], cxliv (1968), p. 361
D. McAra: 'James MacLaren: An Architect for Connoisseurs', *Scot. A. Rev.*, xii/4 (1970), pp. 28–33
A. Service: 'James MacLaren and the Godwin Legacy', *Archit. Rev.* [London], cliv (1973), pp. 111–18
——: *Edwardian Architecture* (London, 1977)
A. Calder: 'James MacLaren', *Architects' J.*, cxci/3 (1990), pp. 34–53
James MacLaren, 1853–1890: Arts and Crafts Architect (exh. cat. by A. Calder, London, RIBA, Heinz Gal., 1990)

ALASTAIR SERVICE

McLaren, Sidney (*b* St Thomas, Jamaica, 1895; *d* St Thomas, 1979). Jamaican painter. A farmer for most of his life, he did not begin painting until he was nearly 70 years old. A series of successes in local exhibitions in his home town, Morant Bay, prompted him in 1970 to submit works to the Self-Taught Artist Exhibition, at the Institute of Jamaica in Kingston, where he won the first prize, and with it national fame and the affectionate nickname 'The Grandpa Moses of Jamaica'. With the exception of a few portraits, occasional religious paintings, a series of horses on the race-track, and dancers in the ballroom, the vast majority of his works are intricate depictions of the architecture and teeming streets of Kingston and other Jamaican towns. A keen sense of humour and love of anecdote, coupled with his cartoon-like drawing, bright colours and the wonderful (if accidental) spatial ambiguities of his 'self-taught' method, cause his works to exude a sense of joie de vivre that is unmatched in Jamaican art.

DAVID BOXER

McLean, Bruce (*b* Glasgow, 6 Nov 1944). Scottish performance artist and painter. He studied at Glasgow School of Art from 1961 to 1963, and from 1963 to 1966 at St Martin's School of Art, London, where he and others rebelled against what appeared to be the formalist academicism of his teachers, among whom were Anthony Caro and Phillip King. In 1965 he abandoned conventional studio production in favour of impermanent sculptures using materials such as water, along with performances of a generally satirical nature directed against the art world. In *Pose Work for Plinths I* (1971; London, Tate), a photographic documentation of one such performance, he used his own body to parody the poses of Henry Moore's celebrated reclining figures. When in 1972 he was offered an exhibition at the Tate Gallery, he opted, with obviously mocking intent, for a 'retrospective' lasting only one day.

In 1971 McLean established Nice Style, billed as 'The World's First Pose Band', while teaching at Maidstone College of Art. With them and in other collaborative performances (*Academic Board*, 1975; *Sorry! A Minimal Musical in Parts*, 1977; *The Masterwork: Award Winning Fishknife*, 1979), he continued to use humour to confront the pretensions of the art world and wider social issues such as the nature of bureaucracy and institutional politics.

From the mid-1970s, while continuing to mount occasional performances, McLean turned increasingly to painting, in a witty and subversive parody of current expressionist styles, and to ceramics.

BIBLIOGRAPHY
Bruce McLean Retrospective: 'King for a Day' (exh. cat., London, Tate, 1972)
Bruce McLean (exh. cat. by N. Dimitrijević, Basle, Ksthalle; London, Whitechapel A.G.; Eindhoven, Stedel. Van Abbemus.; 1981)
Bruce McLean: Berlin/London (exh. cat., ed. M. Francis; London, Whitechapel A.G., 1983)
Bruce McLean (exh. cat., Düsseldorf, Gal. Gmyzek, 1991)

MONICA BOHM-DUCHEN

Maclise, Daniel (*b* Cork, *bapt* 2 Feb 1806; *d* London, 25 April 1870). Irish painter, active in England. He grew up in Cork where his father had set up as a shoemaker after discharge from the British army. In 1822 Maclise went to the Cork Institute where he began to draw from the newly arrived collection of casts made after the antique sculpture in the Vatican, laying the foundation of the strong draughtsmanship that characterizes his mature work. Richard Sainthill, antiquary and connoisseur, encouraged Maclise and introduced him to local literary and artistic circles, which were influenced by the Romantic movement and interested in Irish antiquities and oral traditions. Maclise was a central figure in this early phase of the Irish revival, and maintained an interest in Irish subject-matter throughout his career; in 1833 he painted *Snap Apple* (Mrs Cantor priv. col.), and in 1841 contributed illustrations to Samuel Carter Hall's *Ireland: Its Scenery and Character*. When Sir Walter Scott visited Cork in 1825, Maclise made a sketch of him that was lithographed, and that inaugurated his public career. He set up a studio in Cork where he specialized in finely pencilled portrait drawings. During 1826 he travelled extensively in Co. Wicklow, Co. Tipperary and Co. Kerry, searching out picturesque views, although his landscape drawings were rather linear and old-fashioned, as in *Moar Abbey near Cashel* (1826; London, V&A).

To further his career, Maclise travelled to London in 1827 and entered the Royal Academy in 1828. He was successful as a student and left with the gold medal for history painting in 1831 for the *Choice of Hercules* (priv. col., see 1972 exh. cat., no. 63), a work indebted to the 18th-century British tradition of history painting. During the 1830s he developed a form of historical genre painting with a strongly literary flavour, influenced by the contemporary interest in 17th-century Dutch and Flemish genre painting; the composition and accessories in *Interview between Charles I and Cromwell* (1836; Dublin, N.G.) owe much to these models. Maclise's Romantic medievalism and Tory nostalgia for 'Young England' (which reflected his close friendship with Disraeli) can be seen in *Merry Christmas in the Baron's Hall* (1838; Dublin, N.G.). The theatre, and especially Shakespeare, was a lifelong interest of Maclise. All these concerns are evident in his highly dramatic paintings of the 1830s with their exaggerated characterization, such as the *Banquet Scene from 'Macbeth'* (1840; London, Guildhall A.G.).

Maclise was one of the Cork circle of journalists in *Fraser's Magazine*, contributing portrait caricatures to accompany William Maginn's racy comments. He also became a close friend of Dickens, Harrison Ainsworth, John Forster and the actor William Macready. These contacts resulted in some fine works, such as the 'Nickleby' portrait of Dickens (1839; London, N.P.G.), and book illustrations, notably those to Dickens's Christmas books including *The Chimes* (1844).

Maclise's mature style developed during the 1840s under the influence of continental art. In 1844 he visited Paris, where he was impressed by Paul Delaroche's hemicycle in the Ecole des Beaux-Arts. Through the propaganda of the *Art Journal* he was influenced by German book illustrators such as Moritz Retzsch and Rethel, a reflection of the rising interest in German civilization in England fostered by Prince Albert. Maclise absorbed their symmetrical compositions and symbolism, evidence of which is seen in the *Play Scene from 'Hamlet'* (1842; London, Tate), based on Retzsch's *Outlines to Shakespeare*, as well as in his illustrations to Thomas Moore's *Irish Melodies* (1845), Gottfried Bürger's *Leonora* (1847) and *The Norman Conquest* (1866). *Noah's Sacrifice* (1847; Leeds C.A.G.) is particularly close to the work of the Nazarenes.

The central event of Maclise's career was his commission to paint some of the mural decorations in the Houses of Parliament. He successfully entered the official competitions of 1844 and 1845, and was commissioned to paint two frescoes for the Chamber of the House of Lords, the *Spirit of Chivalry* and *Spirit of Justice*, which were in the hieratic medievalizing style favoured by Dyce, Eastlake and Prince Albert. Maclise became imbued with the high-minded ideals and style of contemporary German narrative art, which he related to themes that had personal meaning for him. In the succession of large paintings that he executed during the 1850s, for example *King Alfred in the Camp of the Danes* (1852; Newcastle upon Tyne, Laing A.G.) and the *Marriage of the Princess Aoife of Leinster with Richard de Clare, Earl of Pembroke (Strongbow)* (1854; Dublin, N.G.; see fig.), his nostalgic Celtic and Saxon Romanticism is attested to by the depiction of the enforced submission of these ancient societies to the invaders.

His large narrative subjects of the 1850s culminated in the cartoon of the *Meeting of Wellington and Blücher* for the Royal Gallery of the Palace of Westminster, which drew great acclaim when it was exhibited there in 1859. Maclise began painting the design in fresco on the gallery walls, but became disheartened by the awkward working conditions and the difficulty of unifying the complex detail of the cartoon in the medium. He was encouraged by Prince Albert to visit Germany in 1859 to study the stereochrome process, which he adopted on his return. He completed the *Meeting of Wellington and Blücher* in 1861 and its companion, the *Death of Nelson*, in 1865. Both of these gigantic paintings have all the factual historical detail so esteemed by Victorian critics and public. The works also show a largeness of scale and compositional arrangement deriving from continental art, while in personal terms they reflect Maclise's pessimism concerning the sufferings of war. The materials have deteriorated badly, but through the Art Union engravings of C. W. Sharpe (1874), the works became part of popular Victorian iconography. After Prince Albert's death in 1861, public interest in decorative schemes waned and Maclise's contract was terminated. In his last years, Maclise returned to

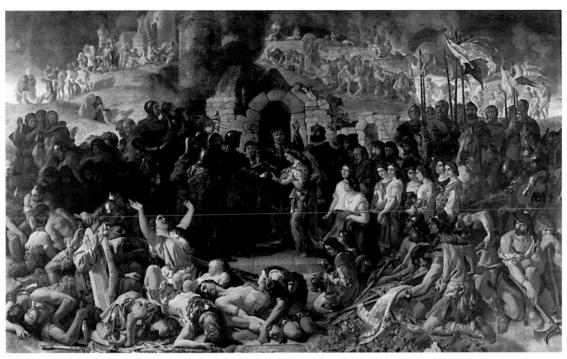

Daniel Maclise: *Marriage of the Princess Aoife of Leinster with Richard de Clare, Earl of Pembroke (Strongbow)*, oil on canvas, 3.09×5.05 m, 1854 (Dublin, National Gallery of Ireland)

literary subjects in paintings such as a *Winter Night's Tale* (*c.* 1867; Manchester, C.A.G.). He was elected RA in 1840 and was a regular Visitor in the schools. Maclise's personality is elusive; he was charming and genial although shy, but became withdrawn and depressed in later life.

BIBLIOGRAPHY

W. J. O'Driscoll: *A Memoir of Daniel Maclise, RA* (London, 1871)
R. Ormond: 'Daniel Maclise', *Burl. Mag.*, cx (1968), pp. 685–93
Daniel Maclise (exh. cat. by R. Ormond and J. Turpin, ACGB, 1972)
J. Turpin: 'German Influence on Daniel Maclise', *Apollo*, xcvii (1973), pp. 169–75
——: 'Daniel Maclise and his Place in Victorian Art', *Anglo-Irish Stud.*, 1 (1975), pp. 51–69
T. S. R. Boase: 'The Palace of History and Art: Painting', *The Houses of Parliament*, ed. M. H. Port (London, 1976), pp. 268–81
J. Turpin: 'Maclise as a Dickens Illustrator', *The Dickensian*, lxxvi (1980), pp. 66–77
——: 'Maclise as a Book Illustrator', *Irish A. Rev.*, ii/2 (1985), pp. 23–7

JOHN TURPIN

McLuhan, (Herbert) Marshall (*b* Edmonton, Alta, 21 July 1911; *d* Toronto, Ont., 31 Dec 1980). Canadian writer. McLuhan was a professor of literature, a James Joyce scholar and a witty analyst of modern systems of communication who became a guru figure and media personality during the 1960s. Some of the insights that he expressed in slogan-like phrases such as 'the medium is the massage [message]' and 'the global village' gained general currency.

As a student at the University of Manitoba, McLuhan studied engineering before moving on to literature. From 1934 to 1936 he continued his literary studies under F. R. Leavis and I. A. Richards at Trinity Hall, Cambridge. After teaching at various American universities, in 1946 McLuhan was appointed professor of literature at the University of Toronto. In 1963 he became Director of the Center for Culture and Technology there. Between 1953 and 1957 he and Edmund Carpenter edited the journal *Explorations*. McLuhan was a prolific writer and eventually became an oracle consulted by advertising firms and big business. He even made a guest appearance in one of Woody Allen's films.

The Mechanical Bride (1951), the first of McLuhan's three key texts, is an illustrated critique of magazine advertisements and posters, viewed as the 'folklore' of industrial man. *The Gutenberg Galaxy* (1962) is an examination of the invention of printing and its impact on social behaviour and on the relationship between the senses. It was followed two years later by *Understanding Media*, a detailed analysis of various kinds of communication viewed as extensions of the senses.

As a convert to Catholicism McLuhan began his media analysis with moralistic intent, but he soon concluded that this external vantage-point inhibited understanding. At the centre of his work is the idea that the content or message of mass media communications is much less important than their form or medium, though he did not consider these to be mutually exclusive.

Towards the end of the 1960s McLuhan collaborated with other writers and designers, such as Quentin Fiore and Harley Parker. The resulting series of books, *The Medium is the Massage* (1967) and *Through the Vanishing Point* (1968), was notable for the originality of its design and layout and was aimed at a mass audience.

Although McLuhan's name and ideas quickly faded from public consciousness, his impact was great as an explorer of the new post-war age of electronic technology. He was among the first to apply the methods of literary and artistic criticism to popular culture, to attempt a history of mass communication in terms of its impact on the human psyche and to examine the role of art and education in the age of mass media. Furthermore, he had an influence on the direction of art itself: his ideas were discussed at the ICA Independent Group meetings in the early 1950s when the British Pop art of Richard Hamilton and Eduardo Paolozzi was being formed.

Since McLuhan was not a systematic thinker and scorned consistency, his ideas aroused endless controversy. His mobile viewpoint militated against a profound understanding of the political and economic forces underpinning modern society. However, the weaknesses in his thought should be offset against his fecundity of imagination and his ability to popularize: like Andy Warhol, McLuhan mastered the media in order to reach a wider public beyond the academic world. Despite his non-judgemental stance a moral and political position was implied by his remark that 'education is civil defence against media fall-out'.

WRITINGS

The Mechanical Bride: Folklore of Industrial Man (New York, 1951)
The Gutenberg Galaxy (Toronto, 1962)
Understanding Media: The Extensions of Man (New York, 1964)
with Q. Fiore: *The Medium is the Massage: An Inventory of Effects* (New York, 1967)
with H. Parker: *Through the Vanishing Point: Space in Poetry and Painting* (New York, 1968)

BIBLIOGRAPHY

G. Stearn, ed.: *McLuhan Hot and Cool* (New York, 1967)
J. Miller: *McLuhan*, Modern Masters (London, 1971)

JOHN A. WALKER

Maclure, Samuel (*b* Sapperton, New Westminster, BC, 11 April 1860; *d* Victoria, BC, 8 Aug 1929). Canadian architect. He was the son of a British Army Royal Engineer and is reputed to have been the first white child born in the city of New Westminster. He was the foremost domestic architect in British Columbia during the period 1890–1920 and established a building style and form that gave Victoria and parts of Vancouver a distinctive Canadian west-coast flavour. Maclure was a self-taught architect, although he briefly studied painting at the Spring Garden Institute, Philadelphia, PA, in 1884–5. He opened his first practice in New Westminster in 1889 and moved to Victoria in 1892, where he had an office. In 1905 a practice was established in Vancouver in partnership with Cecil Croker Fox (1879–1916), who had trained in London with C. F. A. Voysey. The office closed with Fox's death at the Front in France in 1916. In 1920 the office reopened under Maclure's former apprentice, Ross A. Lort (1889–1968), who continued the practice after Maclure's death.

Noted mainly for his Tudor Revival house designs with their open plans and two-storey central halls, his buildings use native materials and local construction techniques. He pioneered a local variant of the Shingle style, worked in traditional board-and-batten, and after 1912 turned increasingly to a severe Edwardian classicism. The use of unbarked log-slab construction combined with fieldstone masonry was a feature of much of his work. Because of his meticulous supervision of construction and finely detailed plans and drawings, contractors added a surcharge to their estimates. His clientele, however, appreciated this attention to detail. He was noted for his ability to exploit the topography of the site: windows, porches and verandahs were aligned to capture the dramatic Pacific coast views. His commissions, for the social and political élite of the Province, were published in leading national and international journals such as *Canadian Architect and Builder, Canadian Homes and Gardens, Country Life, The Studio* and *Craftsman*.

During the course of Maclure's career, his offices were responsible for over 450 commissions including Government House (1900–3; destr. 1957), Victoria, BC, in collaboration with Francis Mawson Rattenbury, Hatley Park (1907), Colwood, a 'castle' and estate for industrialist and politican Robert Dunsmuir, managers' residences for the Bank of Montreal throughout British Columbia and numerous houses in the exclusive Shaughnessy Heights, a suburb of Vancouver financed by the Canadian Pacific Railway. Maclure was also well known for his garden and landscape designs that skilfully combined native flora and fauna with the plant materials and the natural design aesthetic of the English Arts and Crafts Movement. He was for many years consultant to the extensive public garden development of Mrs Butchart, near Victoria. Maclure's influence on British Columbia building design was so pervasive that into the 1940s government buildings and schools throughout the province emulated his early half-timbered commissions in Victoria's prestigious Rockland area.

BIBLIOGRAPHY

L. K. Eaton: *The Architecture of Samuel Maclure* (Victoria, BC, 1971)
M. Segger and D. Franklin: *Victoria: A Primer for Regional History in Architecture* (Watkins Glen, NY, 1979)
J. Bingham: *Samuel Maclure, Architect* (Ganges, BC, 1985)
M. Segger: *The Buildings of Samuel Maclure: In Search of Appropriate Form* (Victoria, BC, 1986)

MARTIN SEGGER

MacMonnies, Frederick William (*b* Brooklyn, NY, 28 Sept 1863; *d* New York, 22 March 1937). American sculptor and painter. During his apprenticeship in New York (1880–84) with Augustus Saint-Gaudens, who discovered and encouraged his talent, he rose from menial helper to assistant, studying in the evenings at Cooper Union and the National Academy of Design. Through Saint-Gaudens he met two architects who later became invaluable colleagues: Stanford White and Charles F. McKim, who lent him money in 1884 to go to Paris. He studied drawing at Colarossi's then went to Munich, attending drawing and portrait classes at the Academy (1884–5). In Paris he studied sculpture with Alexandre Falguière at the Ecole des Beaux-Arts, winning the Prix d'atelier in 1887 and 1888, worked in Antonin Mercié's studio, became Falguière's assistant and won honourable mention at the Salon of 1889 with a life-size *Diana* (plaster; untraced) modelled in Falguière's fluid manner.

Success brought MacMonnies American commissions and the independence to open his own studio. He created his first fanciful life-size fountain figures, *Pan of Rohallion* (1890; bronze original New York, Met.) and *Young Fawn with Heron* (1890; bronze original), for two country estates. These buoyant mythological creatures with vibrant surfaces in the Art Nouveau style introduced fountain sculpture as a new genre in America and inspired a whole generation of sculptors, many of whom were his students. MacMonnies had a lucrative bronze production of these and more serious works (including reductions in varying sizes), employing studio assistants and several French and American foundries. In 1891 he was the first American to be awarded a second-class medal at the Paris Salon. Of his two entries, the straightforward naturalism of the life-size bronze statue of *James S. T. Stranahan* (1891; Brooklyn, NY, Prospect Park) won popular approval. The other, *Nathan Hale* (New York, City Hall Park), an over-life-size bronze, although criticized for its lack of finish and for being 'too picturesque', achieved lasting success as a new expression of dramatic and uplifting sculpture. The plastic quality animating the Impressionist surface of this imaginary portrait heightens the emotion of the hero's last moment.

MacMonnies had great success at the World's Columbian Exposition of 1893 in Chicago with the 39-figure ensemble, Columbian Fountain, including the central group, *Barge of State* (destr.), a colossal temporary fountain made of staff (plaster and straw). This allegorical work of Beaux-Arts bravura became an icon of the American Renaissance. That same year the bronze life-size *Bacchante and Infant Faun* (New York, Met.), unveiled at the Boston Public Library (designed by McKim), scandalized Bostonians and had to be removed. When McKim presented it to the Metropolitan Museum of Art, New York, the realistic female nude attracted widespread attention. In the late 1890s MacMonnies returned to painting and subsequently alternated between the two media. Like James McNeill Whistler and the Impressionists, he admired the work of Diego Velázquez whose paintings he copied at the Prado in Madrid in 1904. MacMonnies taught painting with Whistler at the Académie Carmen and for almost two decades was a popular teacher of American artists in Paris and at his Giverny estate. His *Self-portrait* (*c.* 1904; New York, Met.) owes much to Velázquez, and his full-length portrait of *May Palmer* (1901–2; Bennington, VT, Mus.) displays a skill ranking with major contemporary portrait painters like his friend John Singer Sargent and Giovanni Boldini.

MacMonnies's most ambitious public monuments for America in the ten years following 1893 were for Prospect Park in Brooklyn, NY. The *Quadriga* and *Army* and *Navy* groups for the *Soldiers' and Sailors' Memorial Arch* (1898–1901; *in situ*) typify nationalistic outpourings in full-blown Beaux-Arts style. His uniquely eclectic French style merged neo-Baroque with Art Nouveau whiplash curves in the heroic bronze gatepost groups *Horse Tamers* (1900; *in situ*) for which MacMonnies was awarded a grand prize at the Exposition Universelle of 1900 in Paris. These near-mirror pairs of a mounted rider restraining another rearing horse were intended to represent man's mind pitted against brute force. He modelled them from live prancing horses at his Paris and Giverny studios. He used this technique for the bronze equestrian statues of *General Henry W. Slocum* (1896–1902) and *General George B. McClellan* (1903–7; Washington, DC, Connecticut Avenue), made for a Congressional commission initiated by Civil War veterans. The historical details of dress and regalia were carefully researched, a hallmark of his work.

MacMonnies's work never reflected modernist currents, despite his shift to direct carving in marble and the later influence of Auguste Rodin. On his return to New York at the end of 1915 he made another controversial work, *Civic Virtue* (1909–22), an over-life-size marble male nude with two sirens writhing at his feet. Public indignation forced its removal from City Hall Park, New York, to a plaza flanking Queens Borough Hall, New York. His last and most colossal monument was the 39.6 m high *Battle of the Marne* (or *Monument américain*) (1916–32; Meaux), the American nation's gift to France in return for the statue of *Liberty* (New York Harbor). The output of his years in New York included several dozen portrait busts in bronze, marble and oils. His first wife, Mary Fairchild MacMonnies Low (1858–1946), was a painter.

BIBLIOGRAPHY

D. M. Lockman: 'Interviews with Frederick MacMonnies, N. A.' (29 Jan and 16 Feb 1927), *DeWitt M. Lockman Collection of Interviews with American Artists* (New York, NY Hist. Soc.; microfilm, Washington, DC, Smithsonian Inst., Archv Amer. A.)
C. Taft: *The History of American Sculpture* (New York, 1930), pp. 332–55
W. Craven: *Sculpture in America* (New York, 1968, rev. 1984)
R. J. Clark: 'Frederick MacMonnies and the Princeton Battle Monument', *Rec. Mus. Princeton U.*, xliii/2 (1984) [comprehensive essays and bibliog., excellent pls]
American Figurative Sculpture in the Museum of Fine Arts, Boston (exh. cat., ed. K. Greenthal, P. M. Kozol and J. S. Ramirez; Boston, MA, Mus. F.A., 1986), pp. 293–8
The Beaux-Arts Medal in America (exh. cat. by B. A. Baxter, New York, Amer. Numi. Soc., 1988), pp. 7–9, 43, 45–6, 49, 56
Frederick William MacMonnies and Mary Fairchild MacMonnies: Two American Artists at Giverny (exh. cat. by E. A. Gordon and S. Fourny-Dargère, Vernon, Mus. Mun. Poulain, 1988) [comprehensive essays in Fr. and Eng. on painting and sculp.]

ETHELYN ADINA GORDON

MacNair, (James) Herbert (*b* Glasgow, 1868; *d* Innellan, Strathclyde, 1955). Scottish designer and teacher. Having trained as an architect alongside CHARLES RENNIE MACKINTOSH, he attended evening classes at the Glasgow School of Art between 1888 and 1894. After meeting the MACDONALD sisters (marrying Frances Macdonald in 1899) he began collaborating with them and Mackintosh (his future brother-in-law) on a number of designs which earned them the nickname 'the Spook School'. Much of his early work, including furniture, book illustrations and watercolours, was inspired by Celtic and medieval imagery. He later set up his own studio, but an extensive workshop fire destroyed many of his designs; however, a number of these were reproduced in *The Studio* magazine.

In 1898 MacNair accepted a teaching post, in design, at University College, Liverpool, and thus avoided the likelihood of any competition with Mackintosh. While in Liverpool he continued to receive a number of small, private commissions through friends and colleagues. His newly decorated home in Liverpool was featured in *The Studio* (summer 1901, pp. 116–19) alongside similar photographs of Mackintosh's flat in Glasgow. Striking similarities existed between the two interiors, with MacNair employing simple, white painted furniture against equally plain walls in a style reminiscent of mature Mackintosh. MacNair exhibited designs at the Vienna Secession of

1900 and the Esposizione Internazionale D'Arte Decorativa Moderna in Turin in 1902, thus gaining an enviable reputation in Europe. As a designer he lacked the genius of Mackintosh but in later years his enthusiasm as a teacher was particularly inspirational to younger artists.

BIBLIOGRAPHY

R. Billcliffe: 'J. H. MacNair in Glasgow and Liverpool', *Annu. Rep. & Bull., Walker A.G., Liverpool* (1970–71), pp. 48–74

PETER TROWLES

Macnee, Sir **Daniel** (*b* Fintry, Central, 1806; *d* Edinburgh, 17 Jan 1882). Scottish painter. He was educated in Glasgow where from the age of about 12 he studied drawing for approximately four years under the landscape painter John Knox (1778–1845) with Horatio McCulloch and William Leighton Leitch (1804–83). Macnee was first employed making anatomical drawings and then painting snuff boxes at Cumnock, Strathclyde. Aged about 19, he moved to Edinburgh to work for the engraver William Home Lizars, at the same time studying painting at the Trustees' Academy. He first exhibited chalk portraits in Edinburgh in 1826. He returned to Glasgow in 1830 and began to paint fancy heads and genre scenes, as well as portraits. Macnee was clever at catching a good likeness, and he soon gained popularity as a portrait painter. He rapidly built up a successful practice, contributing regularly to Glasgow and Edinburgh exhibitions, as well as to the Royal Academy in London, where his exhibited pictures were mainly portraits of Scottish worthies. Macnee's portrait of *Dr Wardlaw* (Glasgow, A.G. & Mus.), much admired by Théophile Gautier, was awarded a first-class gold medal at the 1855 Paris Exposition Universelle. His male portraits are extremely direct and strongly influenced by Raeburn, displaying free and rapid brushwork. His portraits of ladies were highly successful and included many of the local Scottish nobility. He also painted a few subject pictures such as *The Bracelet* (Edinburgh, N.G.).

After John Graham-Gilbert's death in 1866, Macnee was the leading portrait painter in the Glasgow region. He joined the Royal Scottish Academy in 1830 and on Sir George Harvey's death in 1876 was elected President, being knighted in 1877. He was highly popular and a famous raconteur.

DNB   BIBLIOGRAPHY

R. Brydall: *Art in Scotland: Its Origin and Progress* (Edinburgh, 1889), pp. 445–8

D. Irwin and F. Irwin: *Scottish Painters at Home and Abroad, 1700–1900* (London, 1975), pp. 310–11

CATHERINE WILLS

MacNicol, Bessie [Elizabeth] (*b* Glasgow, 15 July 1869; *d* Glasgow, 4 July 1904). Scottish painter. Associated with the younger members of the Glasgow Boys, she was the most important woman painter in Glasgow at the end of the 19th century. She studied at the Glasgow School of Art from 1887 until 1892. Francis H. Newbery (1853–1946), the headmaster, encouraged her to study in Paris at the Académie Colarossi. Her work was first noted at the 1895 Glasgow Institute Exhibition, and in 1896 she worked with E. A. Hornel and friends at the artists' colony at Kirkcudbright, Dumfries & Galloway. She painted *E. A. Hornel* (Broughton House, Dumfries & Galloway) in his studio, against a Japanese kakemono, and she was subsequently influenced by his oil painting technique and use of colour. Favourite subjects were young girls painted *en plein air* against trees in dappled sunlight, as in *A Girl of the 'Sixties'* (Glasgow, A.G. & Mus.). She painted other works, in watercolour as well as in oil, that show her interest in fashions of the past. In 1899 MacNicol married Dr Alexander Frew (1862–1908), a fellow artist who resumed his medical practice. Her large-scale nude study *Vanity* (priv. col., see Burkhauser, pp. 230–31) was exhibited at Munich in 1901. Her working life lasted only ten years, as she died in childbirth at the age of 34.

BIBLIOGRAPHY

P. Bate: 'In Memoriam: Bessie MacNicol', *Scot. A. & Lett.*, iii/3 (1904), pp. 197–208

A. Tanner: 'Bessie MacNicol', *'Glasgow Girls': Women in Art and Design, 1880–1920*, ed. J. Burkhauser (Edinburgh, 1990), pp. 192–9, 230–31

AILSA TANNER

Macomboa, Manuel Alves (*b* Lisbon, *c.* 1740; *d* Lisbon, 11 March 1815). Portuguese architect. He was a master carpenter in Lisbon during the rebuilding of the city after the earthquake of 1755. In 1773 he was summoned to Coimbra by King Joseph to work on projects at the University, where he became chief architect in 1782. He continued with the plans drawn up by William Elsden and played an important role in the replanning of the University following the education reforms of the Prime Minister, the Marquês de Pombal. Macomboa built the temporary Observatório Astronómico (1775–99), replacing that by Elsden (not completed), and he also carried out work during this period on houses rented by the University in the Rua do Norte.

Macomboa worked for the chapter of Coimbra Cathedral, making retables for the churches of S Julião in Figueira da Foz (1782) and at Assafarge, Coimbra (1791). He supervised building on churches under the patronage of Coimbra University, including the reconstruction (1780–90) of the church at Enxara do Bispo, Mafra. He acted as inspector of building works (1782–1805) at the convent of S Clara-a-Nova, Coimbra, and directed the building of its new aqueduct (1783–1800). In Viseu he supervised building work at the Misericórdia hospital (1799), where his Neo-classical style is apparent, as is his assimilation of Elsden's designs. During his long period of service to the University Macomboa was responsible for disseminating Neo-classicism through central Portugal.

BIBLIOGRAPHY

Viterbo: pp. 113, 447–57

V. Correia and N. Goncalves: *Inventário artístico de Portugal: Cidade de Coimbra* (Lisbon, 1947), pp. 107–8

L. Craveiro: *Manuel Alves Macomboa: Arquitecto da reforma pombalina da Universidade de Coimbra* (Coimbra, 1990)

LURDES CRAVEIRO

Maconde. *See* MAKONDE.

MacPherson, Margaret. *See* PRESTON, MARGARET.

Macpherson, Robert (*b* Forfarshire [now Tayside], 1811; *d* Rome, 17 Nov 1872). Scottish photographer and painter, active in Italy. He studied medicine at Edinburgh from 1831 to 1835 before deciding to become a painter. In 1840 he settled in Rome, where he belonged to the literary and artistic expatriate community. Among his acquaintances were the writers Robert and Elizabeth Browning and the art historian Anna Bronwell Jameson, whose niece, Gerardine Bate, he married in 1849. Macpherson made a living as a landscape painter and supplemented his income by buying and selling paintings. His most notable act of connoisseurship was the identification and acquisition of the *Entombment* of Michelangelo, now in the National Gallery, London.

After taking up photography in 1851, Macpherson became one of the most successful commercial photographers in Italy, calling himself an 'artist–photographer' and producing large albumen prints of views of Rome and architectural studies, for example *View of Rome from the French Academy, Monte Pincio*, taken probably before 1863. He used the wet collodion process at first and from *c*. 1857 the slower dry collodion process. He was also involved in evolving the process of photolithography (*see* LITHOGRAPHY, §I). His reputation was not confined to Italy. He contributed to exhibitions in London and Edinburgh, and in 1862 a large exhibition of his photographs was held at the Architectural Photography Association in London.

BIBLIOGRAPHY

M. Munsterberg: 'A Biographical Sketch of Robert Macpherson', *A. Bull.*, lxviii/1 (1986), pp. 142–53

JULIE LAWSON

Macrino d'Alba. *See* ALBA, MACRINO D'.

Macro, Cox (*b* Bury St Edmunds, Suffolk, 1683; *d* Norton, Suffolk, 2 Feb 1767). English patron, collector and physician. The son of a prosperous grocer and alderman, he studied divinity and medicine at Cambridge and Leiden. By the early 1730s he was chaplain and surgeon to George II but, rather than seek preferment at Court, he channelled his energies into collecting books, manuscripts and curiosities. He housed his collection at Little Haugh Hall, Norton, near Bury St Edmunds, where he had settled by 1719. After rebuilding the east façade of the house, Macro redesigned the interior staircase and commissioned the sculptor and painter Thomas Ross (*fl* 1730–46) to decorate it (paintings destr.). It was completed by Francis Hayman, who painted the stairwell's domed ceiling with *Fame Crowning Science* in 1743. From 1715 Macro patronized PETER TILLEMANS, who became a close friend. Tillemans provided over 20 paintings, including overdoors (*in situ*), an overmantel of *Little Haugh Hall* seen from beyond its gardens, and portraits of Macro's children, including *Master Edward and Miss Mary Macro* (*c*. 1733; Norwich, Castle Mus.). Following Tillemans's death at Little Haugh Hall in 1734, Macro commissioned a portrait bust of the artist from John Michael Rysbrack (1735; New Haven, CT, Yale Cent. Brit. A.), together with a self-portrait (untraced). An inventory, compiled in 1766, reveals that Macro also collected 17th-century Dutch paintings. Many of these were sold in 1819 although the residue, which includes a fine *Stag Hunt* by Abraham Hondius (see 1988 exh. cat., no. 72), is in the Castle Museum in Norwich.

UNPUBLISHED SOURCES

London, BL, Add. MS. 25473, fol. 29 [1766 inventory]

BIBLIOGRAPHY

N. Scarfe: 'Little Haugh Hall', *Country Life*, cxxiii (5 June 1958), pp. 1238–41

R. Raines: 'An Art Collector of Many Parts', *Country Life*, clix (24 June 1976), pp. 1692–4

Dutch and Flemish Painting in Norfolk (exh. cat. by A. W. Moore, Norwich, Castle Mus., 1988), pp. 43–5, nos 68, 71–3, 77–83

HUGH BELSEY

McTaggart, William (*b* Aros, Kintyre, Strathclyde [now Highland], 25 Oct 1835; *d* Broomiknowe, Lothian, 2 April 1910). Scottish painter. His love of the sea began in his childhood, spent on the west coast of Scotland. An aptitude for portrait painting led him to Edinburgh in 1852 where he became one of a brilliant generation of students under Robert Scott Lauder at the Trustees' Academy. In 1857 he visited the Art Treasures Exhibition in Manchester, seeing paintings by the Old Masters and by Constable and Turner, for both of whom he had a lifelong admiration.

McTaggart's early subjects were anecdotal and often included children. *Spring* (1864; Edinburgh, N.G.) shows two little girls lying beside a burn on a grassy bank of Pre-Raphaelite green. His Diploma painting *Dora* (1868–9; Edinburgh, Royal Scot. Acad.) illustrates Tennyson's poem, and the mother and child seated on the ground bear a resemblance to Millais's *Blind Girl* (1856; Birmingham, Mus. & A.G.) exhibited in Edinburgh in 1858. The harvest field behind the figures is freely painted, anticipating his later broad and sketchy manner, a lack of finish that was already offending the critics. Gradually sea and sky took over as the subjects of his paintings. Figures are absent or mere wraiths dissolved in the dazzling light reflecting off the water, no longer interrupting the atmospheric continuum. He refused a patron's request to introduce figures into *Summer Sundown: Tir-nan-og* (*c*. 1880; London, Tate), a painting in which his mature style is fully developed.

In the late 1880s he began to tackle the subject of emigration, perhaps because emigrant ships were a frequent sight off the west coast of Scotland. Of three versions, *The Emigrants: Rainbow Effect* (1891; Edinburgh, F.A. Soc.) is developed the furthest. Low, fast-moving rain clouds break over the sea and a rainbow throws its arc over the emigrants' ship. The transitory effect is brilliantly captured and clearly reflects the emotions of the passengers about to sail to a new life in faraway America. *Broken Weather, Port Seton* (1894; Kirkcaldy, Fife, Mus. & A.G.) is typical of McTaggart's maturity. He had worked outdoors for many years, but from the early 1880s even his largest canvases were painted in the open. He preferred virtually to complete a painting on the day it was begun, enabling him to capture transitory weather effects. The coarser canvas he adopted during this decade and his broader brush strokes were ideally suited to rough or choppy seas and scudding clouds.

McTaggart found watercolour a sympathetic medium. He used it until 1870 as an auxiliary to oils but came to value it as a medium in its own right, finding it ideal for capturing transient effects, such as in *In Father's Boat* (1873; Aberdeen, A.G.). He was Vice-President of the Scottish Watercolour Society founded in 1878 and he exhibited with it regularly.

McTaggart lived in Edinburgh, often spending the summer months at Machrahanish on the Atlantic coast of Kintyre or on the nearby Isle of Arran or at Carnoustie on the east coast, north of Dundee. In 1889 he moved to Broomiknowe, a village in Midlothian where he was to spend the last 20 years of his life. From this time he painted as many landscapes as seascapes. *Harvest, Broomiknowe* (Edinburgh, N.G.) is a typical example of the autumn subjects he favoured, perhaps because they were so different in tone and colour from the sea.

Although McTaggart's brushwork sometimes bears a superficial resemblance to that of the Impressionists, it is unlikely that they influenced him, as has been suggested. His intuitive approach took no account of theories of optics or physics and he often used nature merely as a tool for heightening the mood of his paintings, a practice totally alien to Impressionism.

BIBLIOGRAPHY
J. Caw: *William McTaggart: A Biography and an Appreciation* (Glasgow, 1917)
D. Irwin and F. Irwin: *Scottish Painters at Home and Abroad, 1700–1900* (London, 1975), pp. 365–71
Master Class (exh. cat., ed. L. Errington; Edinburgh, N.G., 1983)
William McTaggart, 1835–1910 (exh. cat. by L. Errington, Edinburgh, N.G., 1989)

FRANCINA IRWIN

Macuilxóchitl. *See* DAINZÚ.

Maculature. Print made by taking a second impression without re-inking the plate or block. The process is usually used to clean the plate, and the resulting image is weak and ghostly.

☐

MacWhirter, John (*b* Slateford, 27 March 1839; *d* London, 28 Jan 1911). Scottish painter. Abandoning an apprenticeship with the Edinburgh booksellers Oliver & Boyd, he entered the Trustees Academy in 1851 under Robert Scott Lauder and John Ballantyne (1815–97). He first exhibited at the Royal Scottish Academy at 14 and by 16 made the first of many continental tours. He later journeyed to Norway and Constantinople and across America.

Primarily a watercolourist, influenced by Turner, Millais and Horatio MacCulloch (1805–67), MacWhirter's paintings epitomized what Ruskin termed 'the contemplative order' of landscape. His early works are careful studies of botanical subjects and picturesque buildings, so meticulous that Ruskin bought 25 of them for teaching art at Oxford. Carefully annotated and catalogued alphabetically from 'animals' to 'windmills', the sketches were later worked up into landscape compositions. His foregrounds are almost Pre-Raphaelite in their sharp focus, containing trees, bright flowers, bracken, animals, water and buildings, more rarely marine subjects, and the distances are bathed in soft lights. He signed his work MacW or J MacW. Some landscape titles, such as *Night, Most Glorious Night, Thou Wert not Made for Slumber* (1874; Egham, U. London, Royal Holloway & Bedford New Coll.), suggest poetic stimuli, but others, such as *June in the Austrian Tyrol* (1892; London, Tate) or *Nature's Archway* (*c.* 1893; London, RA), were his stock-in-trade, and he preferred Italian and Scottish subjects.

MacWhirter first exhibited at the Royal Academy in 1865, and in 1867 he became an Associate of the Royal Scottish Academy. In 1869 he settled in London but would often return to Scotland to finish a painting. He was elected ARA in 1879; in 1880 he became Honorary Member of the Royal Scottish Academy and in 1893 RA. In later years, as a result of his financial success, he lived in an enormous Italian Renaissance revival mansion built for him by William Flockhart (1854–1913) at 1 Abbey Road, St John's Wood.

MacWhirter's work achieved wider circulation through coloured prints and etchings reproduced in the *Art Journal*. With his student contemporaries Pettie and Orchardson he illustrated the journal *Good Words* from 1860. In *Landscape Painting in Water-Colour* (1900) and the *MacWhirter Sketch Book* (1906), both with colour illustrations, he advised the student always to carry a notebook, to train the memory, to imitate nature and her moods closely, and to 'study Turner for light and atmosphere, Millais for everything'.

WRITINGS
Landscape Painting in Water-Colour (London, 1900)
The MacWhirter Sketch Book (London, 1906, rev. 1908)
Sketches from Nature (London, 1913)

BIBLIOGRAPHY
J. Dafforne: 'The Works of John MacWhirter', *A. J.* [London], xviii (1879), pp. 9–11
D. Irwin and F. Irwin: *Scottish Painters at Home and Abroad, 1700–1900* (London, 1975), pp. 359–60, 364–5

JANET COOKSEY

McWilliam, F(rederick) E(dward) (*b* Banbridge, Co. Down, 30 April 1909; *d* 13 May 1992). Irish sculptor. He studied painting at Belfast School of Art and at the Slade School of Fine Art in London (1928–31) before turning to sculpture in the early 1930s. His earliest wood carvings were influenced by archaic and primitive art, especially by African sculpture, and by Brancusi's pure reduction of figurative forms, as in *Figure* (1937; Brit. Govt A. Col.). After 1936 his work became increasingly Surrealist in spirit, and he was loosely associated with the British Surrealist group; *Eye, Nose and Cheek* (h. 889 mm, 1939; London, Tate) and other stone carvings of 1938–9 constitute an important contribution to Surrealist sculpture. In these works he developed Auguste Rodin's idea of the fragment with a disconcerting wit, distorting and displacing aspects of the human head in biomorphic configurations.

After spending most of World War II in service in India, McWilliam returned to London to teach at Chelsea School of Art and at the Slade, and he resumed working in a great variety of media, including terracotta, stone, wood and bronze. During the 1950s his work progressed from an attenuated, broken-surfaced figuration towards more hieratic symbolic forms, while retaining a characteristically fantastic or ironic aspect. His mechanomorphic bronze *Figures* of the early 1960s dynamically parody the reclining figures of his friend Henry Moore, while the *Bean* sculptures of 1965–6, with their swelling organic forms, at once celebrate and satirize sexuality. McWilliam's output is typified by a capricious and fanciful imagination, combined with a predisposition to work in series, exhaustively exploring a theme and then making a radical change in subject and style.

BIBLIOGRAPHY
R. Penrose: *McWilliam* (London, 1964)
F. E. McWilliam (exh. cat. by M. Gooding, London, Tate, 1989)
MEL GOODING

Mácza, János. *See* MATSA, IVAN.

Madagascar, Democratic Republic of [Repoklika De-mokratika n'i Madagaskar; formerly Malagasy Republic]. Island and country in the Indian Ocean, separated from the East African coast by the Mozambique Channel. The capital is Antananarivo (formerly Tananarive). Madagascar became fully independent in 1960.

1. Introduction. 2. Cultural history. 3. Art life and organization. 4. Funerary arts. 5. Body arts. 6. Domestic utensils. 7. Furniture. 8. Other arts.

1. INTRODUCTION. At *c.* 1600 km long and *c.* 560 km wide, Madagascar is one of the largest islands in the world. It has a diverse and original flora and fauna and sharply differing conditions of climate and environment. While the east of the island is dominated by tropical rainforest, the centre has high rolling grasslands with valley sides, many of which are terraced to assist in the irrigated rice cultivation that is distinctive of the region. The south and west of the island are mainly savannah and dry semi-desert, which support cattle-keeping peoples.

The island's population of *c.* 11,603,000 (UN estimate, 1989) comprises 18 officially recognized groups, some deriving from historical kingdoms or alliances and others designated partly for administrative convenience in the colonial period. Unsurprisingly, art styles and other cultural attributes do not correspond satisfactorily with the some-what arbitrary character of such ethnic boundaries. The largest of the Malagasy groups include the Merina (also known as Hova) and Betsileo, in the central part of the island; the Betsimisaraka, along its eastern coast; and the Sakalava, including the Vezo and Masikoro, in the west. Other peoples include the less populous Bara, Antandroy, Antanosy and the Mahafaly, all living in southern Mada-gascar. Regional distinctions in the arts may be attributable in some measure to the wide variation in the local raw materials. Inter-regional trade in both primary resources and artefacts, however, is well developed. This is particu-larly true for textiles, with silk, cotton and raffia being widely marketed, thus providing weavers with a range of fibres not otherwise produced in one locality. The Merina in particular have relied extensively on non-local materials to sustain their traditional textile industry. Ultimately, then, regional variations are not caused so much by local conditions imposing restrictions on artistic activity as by the differences in social institutions that provide the context for much visual art.

2. CULTURAL HISTORY. It is unclear when exactly Madagascar was first settled and stable communities first established. It is generally assumed that occupation must have begun *c.* AD 500 on the island's northern shores. By the 2nd millennium AD the island's coastline was widely settled and its interior penetrated. These first settlers are believed to have been both Austronesian and African. Many aspects of Madagascan culture have strong affinities with Asia, particularly South-east Asia, rather than with Africa. Archaeological and linguistic evidence indicates that the Malagasy people emerged from an intermingling of Asian and African peoples (Brown, 1978; Deschamps, 1960; Vérin, 1967, 1976). Malagasy is classed as an Austronesian language and contains remarkably few words of Bantu.

The building of the first stone mosque, by the 13th century, provides evidence of contact with the Arab–Swahili people, who were responsible for the development of town states along the East African coast and into the Comoro Archipelago (Vérin, 1986; Wright, 1984). Exten-sive trading networks resulted, with high-quality Chinese ceramics (both celadon glazed and blue-and-white porce-lain) and Near Eastern bowls being found in Madagascar, and stone bowls from the north of the island being traded to mainland Africa. Although the Islamic faith did not survive uninterrupted into modern times, Arab influences are evident in Madagascar in such arts as divination and geomancy. For example, in the south-east of the island an Arab script (*sorabe*, 'great writings') continued to be used into the 1980s at least by local scholars to record, in Malagasy, astrological, magical and historical details (Munthe, 1982).

European influences also played a significant part in Malagasy cultural life after the arrival of the Portuguese in 1500. Various countries sought, unsuccessfully, to estab-lish bases before it became a French colonial possession in 1896, and missionary activity, especially through the efforts of the London Missionary Society, was extensive. During the 19th century mission artisans taught a range of skills, including tanning, brickmaking, spinning, carpen-try, metalwork and painting, to local craftsmen. By the beginning of the 20th century paintings of Malagasy life were being produced by mission-trained artists, and these were often sold for the benefit of mission activities (for illustrations see 1986 exh. cat., pp. 25, 47, 71). Such schemes were developed under the system of Ateliers d'Art Appliqué, set up by the French to encourage local craft production in weaving, pottery, wood-carving and other skills. Madagascar returned to independent status in 1960. Following student protests and general anti-French feeling in the early 1970s, Madagascar's close relationship with its former colonial ruler changed completely, and the Democratic Republic of Madagascar was established in 1976.

Madagascar's mixed cultural ancestry is reflected in its traditional arts and technology. Architectural styles are strictly rectilinear, as in Asia, with no African round houses on the island. Equally, bellows used in iron working have a system of pipes and pistons not found in Africa. Weaving, however, shows a much broader range of influences. A version of the East African ground loom occurs in many parts of Madagascar, while the Zafimaniry use a backstrap loom of a type familiar from South and South-east Asia (see 1986 exh. cat., pp. 23–31; Mack, 1987).

As well as artefacts themselves, aspects of Malagasy design have been convincingly linked to South and South-east Asian and Near Eastern forms. Although this accords with the ultimate origins of many of the island's peoples, some eastern features were not introduced until the 19th century. At this time Jean Laborde, a Frenchman who had travelled in the area, brought to Madagascar such features as the carving of floral motifs on the massive stone doors, cornices and arches of Merina tombs.

In contrast, the wood sculpture found in Madagascar is often compared to that of East Africa. The tradition of chip-carved ornamentation, associated with Swahili art, is found also in Madagascar among the Zafimaniry, and Sakalava carvings of birds have been linked to the famous stelae surmounted by birds from the site of Great Zimbabwe. Another comparison is sometimes advanced between the commemorative *vigango* carvings of the Mijikenda in Kenya and such Malagasy objects as a particular Antandroy cenotaph (*see* §4 below) and the *aloalo* of the Mahafaly.

3. ART LIFE AND ORGANIZATION. Throughout Madagascar there is, traditionally, a rigid division of creative activities so that all weaving, basketry and pottery is done by women, whereas work in iron and wood-carving are male preserves. Although, in principle, all women are expected to weave, in practice some specialization occurs, with especially proficient weavers receiving local commissions and marketing their products more generally. Such towns as Arivonimamo for the Merina and Ambalavao for the Betsileo are centres for rural weavers in those localities (Augustins, 1971).

Among male crafts ironworking is the most strictly controlled. Under the Merina monarchy ironworking was the preserve of certain families. Elsewhere skills are passed on within kin groups, although there may be no ruling against others learning the relevant techniques. Specialization also occurs in wood-carving. Among the Zafimaniry certain villages specialize in blocking out such items as figures, stools, chairs and bowls. These are then taken to the studios at Ambositra to be finished by other carvers. Marquetry has also become a speciality in the area, although this is of a largely non-traditional kind, with a number of subjects having been suggested by local missionaries who have been seeking to diversify and commercialize traditional Zafimaniry skills (Coulaud, 1973; Vérin, 1964, 'Observations').

A non-traditional aspect of specialization has been the growth in the fame of individual artists. A number of sculptors, for example, have gained considerable reputations for the quality of their works, especially those produced in funerary contexts. The Antanosy carver Fesira was possibly the most talented of these, producing commemorative sculpture in the south-east of the island until his death in the 1940s (1986 exh. cat., pp. 90–92; *see also* §4 below). Among the Sakalava in the west, the best-known sculptors of the mid-20th century were Rasidany, Kabota and Tsivoloa (who carved among the Sakalava, although he was of Antanosy origin). All produced works in styles derived directly from tomb sculpture (1963 exh. cat.; Hardyman, 1968).

4. FUNERARY ARTS. Much of the wood sculpture and many of the textiles produced in Madagascar are occasioned by funerals; indeed the distribution of these two forms depends largely on regional differences in funerary practice. Broadly speaking, those peoples with a carved funerary image are not noted for producing funerary shrouds. Conversely, sculpture is not general in regions that extensively employ burial cloth. For the Malagasy, death is polluting, with pollution located in the fluids produced by the decomposition of the flesh. Funerary rites allow sufficient time for the corpse to become skeletal or at least symbolically 'dry' and thus free from pollution. By enabling the dead to join the clan ancestors in this appropriate condition, the living obtain vitality and well-being. In Madagascar there are three main ways of achieving the necessary phasing of the burial process. In some areas the body is first put in a temporary grave and then, after a year or more, exhumed and placed in the ancestral tomb, having by then substantially decomposed. Alternatively, the body may be allowed to decompose above the ground, with the polluting liquids being collected and disposed of separately from the corpse. Thirdly, the body may be permanently buried at death, and at some later date a monument or ancestor shrine will be erected. This will frequently be a carved pole with the skulls of sacrificed cattle attached, recalling the 'dryness' of the corpse in its resting place. Funerary cloth is important in the first of these methods, while sculpture is associated with the second and especially the third process.

(i) Sculpture. This takes two forms: sculpture erected away from the burial site as an ancestral shrine or cenotaph, and that placed directly on tombs. The latter is associated mainly with the Mahafaly, some groups of the neighbouring Antandroy and the Sakalava, especially in the area around Morondava. In addition, the Sihanaka and some Antaimoro clans in the south-east of the island place occasional figures at tombs (for illustrations see Decary, 1962). Although Malagasy has no word equivalent to 'sculpture', different forms have specific names. For example, among the Mahafaly, statues placed on tombs (*aloalo*; from *alo*, 'messenger') are stylistically and conceptually distinct from commemorative sculptures (*ajiba*), which are erected as cenotaphs when there is no body to bury.

Aloalo are pole sculptures with figurative images at the top and, often, at the bottom (see fig. 1). The length between is composed of circular motifs sometimes identified with the sun, hexagonal shapes and a design of paired crescents carved back to back. Although *aloalo* are usually placed only on the tombs of royal clans, some westerly groups of the Antandroy have bought the right to use them (Boulfroy, 1976; Schomerus-Gernböck, 1981). The figurative imagery of *aloalo* includes humped cattle, birds and, at the base, a single human figure. Cyclists, aeroplanes, policemen, colonial judges, hunters, drinkers and a funeral cortège have also been employed by 20th-century Mahafaly sculptors. Another change to traditional practice was that the sides of tombs, once exclusively in dressed stone, began to be cemented over and painted with a series of scenes, often recalling contemporary events. A similar evolution took place among the Antandroy, although here the painted image is abstract and geometric rather than figurative.

Among the Mahafaly, then, tomb imagery recalling the deceased by references to events of the times in which they lived was a late development. For its part, Sakalava sculpture has consistently reflected aspects of the funerary process rather than the deceased's individuality. Sakalava sculpture often portrays the regenerative passage of the deceased through a stage of pollution to rebirth as an ancestor, capable of bestowing blessings on the living. This is reflected in the subjects of tomb sculpture, which recall conception and birth. Subjects include naked figures sometimes portrayed in overtly sexual poses, with females carved proportionately larger than their male counterparts. Such sculpture is set up at the corners of the fenced-in, rectangular structure that forms the grave itself. Images used in conjunction with these human representations include birds, usually identified as herons, and double-headed pots (for illustrations see Oberle, pp. 130–40). In colonial times such traditional imagery was copied by local carvers who produced a variety of erotic images for sale. Sakalava carvers were also the source of a popular commercial image, known as *bibyolona*, a half-man half-beast figure said to derive from local mythology but carved for outsiders rather than for traditional use.

Cenotaphs (known by various names including *vatolahy*, 'male stone') are extensively distributed throughout Madagascar. Most serve to reunite the clan dead when this is not physically possible, either because someone has died far from home or the body has not been found. In some traditions individuals may be commemorated by a memorial placed separately from the tomb even though they are buried there in the normal manner. Cenotaphs commonly take the form of standing stones and cement obelisks, erected at roadsides or other public places. The obelisks often have motifs painted on their sides, showing cattle or other scenes recalling the life of the person commemorated. The standing stones are usually undecorated, although the Bara sometimes add a wood armature to the top of the stone, on which may be carved pictorial references to the property and position of the deceased.

Wood cenotaphs were also produced to commemorate kings or people of high rank. The most massive of these are of monumental height and made of exceptionally hard wood. These are called *teza*, a word suggesting hardness, and are made by the Betsileo. The sides are carved with various motifs, usually abstract but occasionally representing birds, oxen, horses or crocodiles. The significance of these images is unclear.

Figurative cenotaphs in wood are limited to the Mahafaly, Antandroy, Antanosy and Bara. Those of the Mahafaly (*ajiba*) are placed adjacent to the tomb rather than upon it (as are the funerary sculptures). Bara figurative memorials were displayed at such prominent places as markets or crossroads and, unlike the examples so far mentioned, portray the deceased as they were in life, with eyelids and beards added to the sculptures using the hair from cattle, and parasols or implements and weapons associated with the deceased added to identify and personalize the figure.

The style of Antandroy memorials varies greatly. While some resemble the naturalistic style seen among the neighbouring Antanosy (for illustration see 1986 exh. cat., p. 81), one figure is suggestive of Mijikenda funerary art from Kenya, having the same distinctive head, squared planklike body and incised decoration (for illustration see Urbain-Faublée, 1963, p. 56). In addition to this stylistic parallel, Mijikenda funerary practices are close to those of the Antanosy. Despite these resemblances, claims for cross-cultural influences are weakened by the atypicality

1. Mahafaly funerary posts (*aloalo*) on a tomb, south-west Madagascar; from a photograph by Hilary Bradt

of the Antandroy figure and the lack of any aesthetic similarities between the Mijikenda and Antanosy funeral figures.

Antanosy cenotaphs deserve separate consideration, being functionally different. The Antanosy bury their dead shortly after death in communal graves close to their villages. After the interment it is forbidden to visit the graves. Instead, cenotaphs, created later and placed at a separate and public place near by, act as memorials. Such cenotaphs commemorate those whose bodies are not incorporated in the ancestral grave in addition to recalling those who are. The resulting memorial sites can be extensive, and their construction has been interpreted as equivalent to the second phase of burial rites evident in other Malagasy traditions (1986 exh. cat.).

An accomplished carver of wooden funerary sculptures is Fesira (1986 exh. cat., pp. 90–93; Peyrot, 1973; Vérin, 1964, 'Observations'). His most renowned work is a memorial to a group of canoeists who drowned in an accident in the harbour at Tolanaro (formerly Fort Dauphin). The sculpture consists of a single upright block of wood with a series of scenes carved round its sides and, at its summit, a depiction of the canoeists themselves (see fig. 2). Other carved cenotaphs produced by Fesira include some single, naturalistic figures at a site to the west of Tolanaro. Fesira's speciality, however, was more complex works in which a single composition portrayed numerous

2. Antanosy funerary cenotaph by Fesira, wood, south-east Madagascar, *c.* 1930s; from a photograph by John Mack

scenes showing memorable events in the life of the deceased, or compositions showing the deceased sitting before his house while his family busy themselves with agricultural and domestic work. Another shows a man seated beside his motorcar, the first in the area (for illustration see 1986 exh. cat., p. 90). In these works, Fesira, who would have received his commission after the death of the individual, whom he may not have known, commemorated the subject not by representing their physical likeness, but by portraying events by which they were remembered.

(ii) Textiles. Burial shrouds, *lamba mena* ('red cloth'), are most extensively produced by the Merina and the Betsileo in the centre of the island who, together with the Bara, are the main practitioners of second burials. The shrouds need not incorporate the colour red. Instead the name refers to the fact that such textiles are colourful (Bloch, 1971, pp. 145–8) in contrast to the white shawls worn by the bereaved. Although cotton may be used by such peoples as the Betsileo, *lamba mena* are traditionally woven from silk. Indigenous varieties of silkworm produce thread both for a thick silk cloth that has the character of sacking and for a finer textile with a surface similar to that of silks from elsewhere. The shrouds are warp-striped, with bands of colour in varying widths. Although the range of colours used was traditionally quite small, commercial dyes have made possible a more extensive and vivid selection. Weftwise pattern is usually limited to geometric designs applied to the fringes of the cloth either as a floating weft pattern or picked out by the use of small beads traditionally made of metal (usually lead). In parts of the island that have no practice of second burial the body may nonetheless be enveloped in cloth or in matting of some kind: the Sakalava sometimes use raffia cloth, while the Zafimaniry employ the bast cloth that is their speciality.

In addition to using shrouds for second burial purposes, the Merina and, on occasion, the Betsileo, also periodically remove older remains from their communal tombs for a rewrapping ceremony known as *famadihana* (Bloch, 1971; Kottak, 1980, pp. 228–39). Although corpses are wrapped separately, they are not identified, and the *famadihana*, which involves removing bodies, carrying and, possibly, dancing with them, contributes to their physical disintegration and further jumbles up the bones. This accords with honouring not individuals but all the clan dead, and it explains why funerary sculpture, insofar as it commemorates and draws attention to specific people, is not a part of Merina or Betsileo culture.

5. BODY ARTS. The most varied of the traditional arts of Madagascar are arguably those associated with the body. Preferences in coiffure reflect region, sex and status, and each style has its appropriate local name. Among the Merina alone there were traditionally at least nine distinct fashions of female coiffure ranging from complex plaiting to the untressed style that has continued to be a sign of mourning for women. (Precise representations of hairstyle in Malagasy figurative sculpture provide an expression of identity when other features may be imprecise.) Cicatrization was once commonly applied to the face, shoulders and arms.

Personal ornamentation was also effected by the wearing of charms of which three basic types are known. Personal talismans (*ody*) may protect against physical danger from such causes as lightning or illness or may ensure wealth or well-being. Typically, charms comprise an active agent, for example earth taken from an ancestral tomb, carried in a container, frequently a cattle horn decorated with a beadwork sheath in colourful geometric patterns (for illustrations see Faublée, 1946, pp. 105–8). Small anthropomorphic containers in wood were also once used among the southern Merina (for illustrations see 1986 exh. cat., p. 53). These came apart at the waist, enabling the magical substances to be stored within. In place of the beaded sheath, such charm figures had a waistband of red cloth. Among the Sakalava and Bara carved representations of crocodiles have also been recorded as containers (for illustrations see 1986 exh. cat., p. 52; Faublée, 1946, p. 107).

The crocodile, one of Madagascar's few predatory animals, has a powerful iconographic significance, and its teeth are sometimes worn as a charm in their own right. During the 19th century this led to the development among the Merina ruling classes of gilt or silver charms that took the form of a heavily jewelled box of colourful beads or red, green and blue gems, with representations of crocodile teeth beneath attached to a decorated band (see fig. 3). These were worn across the chest or around the waist. The silver and bead examples are thought to be the older form (Edmonds, 1896, 'Mohara'; for illustrations see 1986 exh. cat., pls between pp. 48–9 and opp. p. 64).

Much personal jewellery combines decorative and talismanic qualities. This is particularly true of such silver

3. Merina jewelled gilt box and silk brocaded sash, l. 190 mm, from central Madagascar, *c.* 1820 (London, British Museum)

jewellery as chains, coins worn as medallions and necklaces, often with silver keys or small silver oxen attached (for illustrations see 1986 exh. cat., pp. 50–51). The latter are charms intended to bring wealth and are best known in central Madagascar. The silver came from melted-down coins that had been imported in insufficient quantities for them to be used as a viable currency. Through rarity, uncut coins acquired a special significance and continued to be used into the 1990s to seek ancestral blessings.

A second type of charm, *sampy*, was used by priests for the protection of a community (Berg, 1986). *Sampy* were often little more than bundles of wood, although one at least is described as having the appearance of a winged bird with a beaded body (Rainivelo, 1875). They were believed to have considerable powers and by the mid-19th century were ranked according to their attributed qualities. In 1869 all *sampy* were burned at the instigation of the Merina queen Ranavalona II who by then had converted to Christianity (Berg, 1986).

Certain charms (*mohara*) were reserved for use in warfare and were once common throughout the island. Those of the Bara were frequently representational, for example with warriors carrying small carved coffins to attract and trap the spirit of an enemy. The Bara also had larger, less portable images in the form of human heads on the tops of which were embedded magical substances. These substances could be transferred to the body of a warrior to protect him in warfare.

6. DOMESTIC UTENSILS. Containers are made for a variety of purposes, from honeypots to small boxes designed to keep fire-lighting equipment dry. The latter are made from wood by the Zafimaniry and, more often, in horn, by the Betsimisaraka. The most decorative larger containers are made by the Mahafaly and copied by the Antandroy and include figurative imagery on the body of the object and lids similar to that found on furniture panels (Faublée, 1946, p. 50; *see also* §7 below). Among the most elaborate of Malagasy domestic objects are spoons reserved for the eating of rice at ritual occasions. These, carved in wood or horn, have distinctive regional styles, some of which are figurative in conception. Vezo spoons have handles that schematically depict the human form. The Mahafaly carve strings of humped cattle along the length of the handle and, frequently, depict crocodiles curling round the bowl of the spoon.

Zafimaniry and Betsileo ironworkers make agricultural and domestic implements or spears, as well as lamps, which include in their construction elaborate decorative iron cattle 'horns' and skulls (for illustrations see Faublée, 1946, pp. 62, 64). Malagasy mats are used as flooring, for sleeping on, eating from, and as wall hangings. Their size and decoration vary with use. The most decorative, and the smallest, are those kept for laying out rice at a meal, and those displayed on walls inside dwellings. The latter often incorporate greetings or epithets of various kinds as part of the woven pattern (1986 exh. cat., p. 59).

7. FURNITURE. While the range of traditional Malagasy wooden furniture is limited, beds, found especially in central Madagascar, seem to have a long history and are probably not a European introduction. The bed of the Merina ruler Andrianampoinimerina in the royal enclosure at Ambohimanga dates to at least the late 18th century, a period before this part of the island was in regular contact with Europeans. Some older styles of bed had side panelling that included incised geometric decoration. By the early 19th century these panels began to incorporate more elaborate scenes in low relief showing such subjects as soldiers in European uniform comparable to those painted on the walls of the royal treasury at the same period (for illustrations see Loriman, pl. xi; Urbain-Faublée, 1963, pls between pp. 36–7). Similar panels were also produced by the Mahafaly, although the themes portrayed differ, including persons possessed by spirits, crocodiles or snakes devouring birds, and humped cattle. Such panels have various decorative purposes and may, among other uses, be attached to a shelf as an edging.

The Zafimaniry are, perhaps, the major furniture producers of modern times. Their best-known piece—a seat that fits together in two parts to give a form of wooden deckchair—is a style developed, under missionary direction, for commercial sale. A more traditional form is a round wooden stool with incised triangular patterns on the upper surface. These patterns are identical to the decorations found on Zafimaniry windows and doors, boxes, the backrests of looms and other domestic objects.

8. OTHER ARTS. Apart from funerary cloths, Malagasy textile manufacture includes cloth worn by the living (*lamba*). Cotton, raffia and bast are the usual fibres in which to clad the living. Equally, decoration is often limited to simple warp-striping. Ikat-dyed raffia cloth (*laimasaka*) was used by some Sakalava as an awning or mosquito net and, sometimes, as burial cloth. Such cloths (see fig. 4) incorporate figurative images and geometric patterning in a range of colours from browns and greens to the natural colour of the fibre. Until the 1960s these cloths were only made at the three centres of Kendreho, Ambatomainty and Besamampy (Heurtebize and Rakotoarisoa, 1974). Nevertheless, they are sometimes mistakenly treated as representative of Sakalava weaving as a whole.

An elaborate silk textile with detailed weft patterning running the length of the cloth was characteristic of Merina weaving until about the 1920s. Although the exact origins and functions of such cloth are not entirely clear, richly coloured cloth formed part of the dress of some Merina in the 19th century, and this may have included textiles with such extensive design. By the early 20th century such cloth was largely being acquired by Europeans. Many examples found their way into museum collections where they are usually identified as *lamba mena* because of their colourful design (*Notes on the Madagascar Collection*, 1906).

A final category of artistic output incorporates such objects with prestige implications as canes and staffs of office. Among the southern Betsimisaraka the major titleholder (*tangalamena*, 'red stick') carries a plain wood rod used, among other things, to address cattle at sacrificial

4. Sakalava, ikat-dyed raffia cloth (*laimasaka*), from western Madagascar (Chicago, IL, Field Museum of Natural History)

ceremonies. In northern Madagascar iron staffs were also used in ceremonies associated with spirit possession. Sculptured staffs are best known from the Sihanaka, where the characteristic form is a small paddle with an image such as that of humped cattle carved on the handle. One documented example is described as belonging to a magician (Faublée, 1946, p. 114).

BIBLIOGRAPHY

H. Loriman: *L'Art malgache* (Paris, n.d.)
P. Oberle: *Provinces malgaches* (Antananarivo, n.d.)
Rainivelo: 'The Burning of the Idol Ramahavaly', *Antananarivo Annu.*, i (1875), pp. 112–14
J. Sibree: 'Carving and Sculpture and Burial Memorials amongst the Betsileo', *Antananarivo Annu.*, i (1875), pp. 193–9

——: 'Decorative Carving on Wood, Especially on Burial Memorials', *J. Royal Anthropol. Inst. GB & Ireland*, xxi (1892), pp. 230–44

W. J. Edmonds: 'Bye-gone Ornamentation and Dress among the Hova Malagasy', *Antananarivo Annu.*, xxii (1896), pp. 469–77

——: 'The Mohara, or War Charm of Imerina', *Antananarivo Annu.*, xxii (1896), pp. 421–5

Notes on the Madagascar Collection, Philadelphia Museum (Philadelphia, 1906)

A. Grandidier: *Ethnographie de Madagascar*, 4 vols (Paris, 1908–28)

R. Boudry: 'L'Art décoratif malgache', *Rev. Madagascar*, xiii (1933), pp. 23–83

R. Linton: *The Tanala* (Chicago, 1933)

P. Heidman: 'Les Industries de tissage', *Rev. Madagascar*, xvii (1937), pp. 93–120

J. Faublée: *L'Ethnographie de Madagascar* (Paris, 1946)

R. Decary: *Moeurs et coutume des Malgaches* (Paris, 1950)

S. Bernard-Thierry: 'Les Perles magiques Madagascar', *J. Africanistes*, xxix (1959), pp. 33–90

H. Deschamps: *Histoire de Madagascar* (Paris, 1960)

A. Lavondes: *Art traditionnel malgache* (Tananarive, 1961)

R. Decary: *La Mort et les coutumes funéraires à Madagascar* (Paris, 1962)

M. Faublée and J. Faublée: 'Charmes magiques malgaches', *J. Africanistes*, xxiii (1963), pp. 139–49

M. Urbain-Faublée: *L'Art malgache* (Paris, 1963)

Art sakalava (exh. cat., Tananarive, U. Madagascar, 1963)

P. Vérin: 'Observations sur les monuments funéraires des Antanosy', *An. Malgaches*, iii (1964), pp. 47–51

——: 'Les Zafimaniry et leur art', *Rev. Madagascar*, xxvii (1964), p. 116

J. Vernier: 'Etude sur la fabrication des *lambamena*', *J. Africanistes*, xxiv (1964), p. 7–34

R. Decary: 'Les Anciennes Coiffures masculines à Madagascar', *J. Africanistes*, xxxv (1965), pp. 283–316

P. Vérin: 'Austronesian Contributions to the Culture of Madagascar', *East Africa and the Orient*, ed. N. Chittick and R. Rotberg (London, 1967), pp. 164–91

E. Vernier: 'Les Cannes cérémonielles à Madagascar', *Obj. & Mondes*, vii (1967), pp. 247–54

R. Decary: 'L'Art chez les Antandroy', *Civilis. Malgache*, ii (1968), pp. 253–67

J. T. Hardyman: 'Notes de sculpture sakalava', *Civilis. Malgache*, ii (1968), pp. 269–84

G. Augustins: 'Le Tissage dans la région d'Arivonimamo', *Taloha*, iv (1971), pp. 205–10

M. Bloch: *Placing the Dead* (London, 1971)

D. Coulaud: *Les Zafimaniry* (Tananarive, 1973)

Malgache, qui es-tu? (exh. cat., Neuchâtel, Mus. Ethnog., 1973)

G. Heurtebize and J.-A. Rakotoarisoa: 'Notes sur la confection des tissus de type *ikat* Madagascar', *Archipel*, viii (1974), pp. 67–81

N. Boulfroy: 'Vers l'art funéraire mahafaly', *Obj. & Mondes*, xvi (1976), pp. 95–116

N. J. Guernier: 'Wood Sculpting and Carving among the Betsileo', *Ethnographie*, lxxi (1976), pp. 5–22

P. Vérin: 'The African Element in Madagascar', *Azania*, xi (1976), pp. 135–51

M. Woulkoff: 'Notes sur les *aloalo* mahafaly', *Taloha*, vii (1976), pp. 113–18

M. Brown: *Madagascar Rediscovered* (London, 1978)

C. P. Kottak: *The Past in the Present* (Ann Arbor, 1980)

L. Schomerus-Gernböck: *Die Mahafaly* (Berlin, 1981)

L. Munthe: *La Tradition arabico-malgache* (Tananarive, 1982)

H. T. Wright: 'Early Seafarers of the Comoro Islands', *Azania*, xix (1984), pp. 13–59

G. M. Berg: 'Royal Authority and the Protector System', *Madagascar Society and History*, ed. C. P. Kottak and others (Durham, NC, 1986)

P. Vérin: *The History of Civilisation in North Madagascar* (Rotterdam, 1986)

Madagascar: Island of the Ancestors (exh. cat. by J. Mack, London, BM, 1986)

J. Mack: 'Weaving, Women and the Ancestors in Madagascar', *Indonesia Circ.*, xlii (1987), pp. 76–91

——: *Malagasy Textiles* (Princes Risborough, 1989)

JOHN MACK

Mada'in Salih. *See under* ARABIA, PRE-ISLAMIC, §§II, III, IV.

Madarász, Viktor (*b* Csetnek [now in Slovakia], 14 Dec 1830; *d* Budapest, 10 Jan 1917). Hungarian painter. He was an accomplished academic painter with a strong sense of national identity and a profound belief in his work. He was one of the first great masters of Hungarian history painting, but his tragic sense of history became dangerously exclusive in his work, which was strangely anachronistic by the second decade of the 20th century, when he was still trying to commemorate the tragic outcome of the fight for Hungarian independence in 1848–9. In his early work, however, his depictions of suffering and faith, his skill in evoking drama and his assurance of expression inspired respect.

Madarász came from a wealthy family that was deeply opposed to Habsburg rule, and he joined Kossuth's revolt as soon as it broke out in 1848. Although this military experience lasted barely a year, it had a permanent effect on his personal development. On returning home he resumed his study of law but also painted. His formal artistic training began in 1853 at the Akademie der Bildenden Künste in Vienna, and in 1855 he attended Ferdinand Georg Waldmüller's private school. Waldmüller's Biedermeier decorativeness had no effect on him, however, as is illustrated by his painting *The Fugitive's Dream* (1856; Budapest, N.G.). Already a Romantic by temperament, Madarász moved in 1856 to Paris, where he spent 14 years, taking part in Théophile Gautier's salons, becoming friendly with Victor Hugo and Baudelaire, and establishing his own style. He continued his studies at the Ecole des Beaux-Arts but left to become a pupil of Léon Cogniet, whose influence sealed his artistic development. Madarász's gentle, sentimental Romanticism, which overcame the strictures of academicism, was also modified by the instinctive Realism that he probably learnt from the example of Courbet.

In 1858 Madarász painted *Miklós Zrinyi, the Poet and Commander* (Budapest, N.G.), one of a series of works throughout his career in which he immortalized Hungary's rebel leaders, but characterized by a raw power absent from his later paintings. In the same year he painted *Felicián Zách* (Budapest, N.G.), which depicts the dramatic scene at Robert Károly's 14th-century court when Klara Zách, who has been seduced by one of the queen's relations, collapses and confesses to her father, who immediately determines to attack the royal family. Madarász was concerned to express emotional tension, enhanced by lighting effects. His best-known work is another Hungarian history painting, *László Hunyadi on the Bier* (see fig.). Hunyadi, a victim of Habsburg betrayal, was beheaded in 1457; in the picture his shrouded body lies on the bier while his mother and his lover can be seen embracing each other, broken with grief, as if mourning the death of a nation. Madarász's other large-scale works immortalizing tragic episodes of Hungarian history are less clearly focused. The Romantic atmosphere of such multi-figure works as *Blanka Teleki and Klára Leővey in Kufstein Prison* (1867; Budapest, N.G.) sits uneasily with his academic training, and many of his history paintings are marred by his ponderous, measured composition and doctrinaire depictions. Two of his works of 1868, however, are exceptional for their psychological drama: *Dobozi* and *Dozsa Nation* (both Budapest, N.G.) show idealized

Viktor Madarász: *László Hunyadi on the Bier*, oil on canvas, 2.43×3.12 m, 1859 (Budapest, Hungarian National Gallery)

heroes painted from below, giving the impression of figures expanding into the picture space filling the frame.

Madarász's work was acclaimed in Paris (he won the gold medal at the Salon in 1861), but in 1870 he returned to Hungary with his French wife. In 1871 his *Portrait of the Artist's Wife* (Budapest, N.G.) was his last harmonious and inspired work before the collapse of his career. Hungarian society had completely changed by the time he returned, but Madarász was incapable of adapting. In the 1870s he put two historical works into a competition but had no success. He continued nevertheless to experiment with complicated historical themes, treated in a more opulent and Baroque way (e.g. *Izabella Zápolya*, 1880; Budapest, N.G.), until 1880, when he gave up painting, prompted by his lack of success and consequent financial difficulties. He inherited his father's copper business in Budapest and became a merchant, but in 1902 the business failed, and Madarász attempted to revive his career as a painter. He painted landscapes (e.g. *Shepherd's Fire on the Plain*, 1905; priv. col., see Székely, p. 41) and portraits (e.g. *Washington Portrait*, 1912; priv. col., see Székely, p. 47), but with limited success. His emotions are muted in his late works, which still deal with the struggle for independence, but in a style that is more academic and

that eventually became naive and empty (e.g. *Insurrection*, 1913; Budapest, N. Mus.).

BIBLIOGRAPHY

Ö. Kacziány: 'Viktor Madarász', *Müvészet*, iii (1904), pp. 249–57
K. Lyka: 'Viktor Madarász', *Magyar mesterek* [Hungarian masters], (Budapest, n.d.), pp. 21–45
I. Csapláros: 'Théophil Gautier Madarász Viktor párizsi festményeiről' [Théophile Gautier on Viktor Madarász's Parisian work], *Magyar müvészet*, xii (1936), pp. 316–17
E. Petrovics: 'Madarász Viktor történeti jelentősége' [The historical significance of Viktor Madarász], *Élet és müvészet* [Life and Art] (Budapest, 1937), pp. 137–40
D. Radocsay: *Madarász Viktor, 1830–1917* (Budapest, 1941)
Z. Székely: *Madarász Viktor* (Budapest, 1954)

MÁRIA SZOBOR-BERNÁTH

Madden, Sir **Frederic** (*b* Portsmouth, 16 Feb 1801; *d* London, 8 March 1873). English antiquary, palaeographer and collector. The son of Captain William John Madden (*d* 1833) of the Royal Marines, he attended local schools in and around Portsmouth until 1818, finishing with a well-developed taste for independent study. Drawn to languages and a prodigious reader, he became an amateur antiquarian scholar with a special interest in the Middle Ages. He read Latin, Greek, French and Italian and mastered the dialectical forms of Norman-French and

Anglo-Saxon. He collected coins, seals and other curiosities; studied heraldry, genealogy and local history. Between 1824 and 1827 he worked for Henry Petrie, Keeper of Records in the Tower of London, transcribing manuscripts and documents. This work was the foundation of his expertise and lifelong devotion to palaeography. In 1826 he was employed by the British Museum as a part-time cataloguer and in 1828 joined its staff as Assistant Keeper in the Manuscript Department. He was appointed Keeper in 1837, a post he held until 1866. With Petrie's encouragement, Madden published his first major edition of medieval literature, *The Ancient English Romance of Havelok the Dane*, in 1828. The work set a standard in the field for its meticulous scholarship and effectively launched him as England's first professional and probably greatest palaeographer. He became a regular contributor to such journals as the *Gentleman's Magazine* and *Archaeologia* and continued to produce new editions of antiquarian subjects, including *William and the Werewolf* (1832), *Syr Gawayne* (1839) and *Gesta Romanorum* (1838). With Josiah Forshall (1795–1863), he edited the Wycliffite version of the English Bible (published 1850 in 4 vols), an undertaking that lasted 20 years. During his almost 30 years of service at the British Museum he amassed an exhaustive amount of fresh manuscript material and personally restored the extensive, fire-damaged Cotton Library collection. He was most popularly known for his dissertation presented in 1837 before the Society of Antiquaries on Shakespeare's name, which he argued should be spelt 'Shakspere'. His substantial diaries and papers were lodged with the Bodleian Library, Oxford, at his death, on the condition that they remain untouched until 1920.

BIBLIOGRAPHY

R. W. Ackerman and G. P. Ackerman: *Sir Frederic Madden* (New York and London, 1979)

T. D. Rogers, ed.: *Sir Frederic Madden at Cambridge* (Cambridge, 1980)

□

Maddock, Bea [Beatrice] **(Louise)** (*b* Hobart, Tasmania, 13 Sept 1934). Australian printmaker and painter. She studied at the Hobart Technical School (1952–6) and the Slade School, London (1959–61). Her woodcuts from the 1960s, influenced by Ernst Kirchner and Emile Nolde, show a lone figure tramping desolate streets. In her ironic self-portraits and in the symbol of Icarus (e.g. *Self-portrait with Icarus*, 1964; see *Bea Maddock*, p. 2), she developed the theme of loneliness and the isolation of the individual in a hostile or uncaring environment; this was a subject that had been treated by Melbourne artists in the 1950s, particularly Charles Blackman and Joy Hester.

In the 1970s Maddock produced large-scale photoetchings. She chose newspaper photographs of man-made disasters and anonymous crowd scenes to suggest a violent, chaotic world where the individual is reduced to a faceless blur on a black-and-white page. *No-where* (1974) and *Gauge* (1976) are grim, haunting prints in which advanced systems of information are seen as revealing only illusion and disorder. Maddock has also used words as images, giving them equal power as visual components and conjuring from them textual self-portraits. In *Going back* (1976) epigrammatic and lyrical notations from Maddock's diary are juxtaposed with a photograph of her home and

the drawn form of a favourite jacket. *Solitary* (1979; Canberra, N.G.), a painting that uses encaustic and collage, contains a dictionary definition of the word and thereby a 'definition' of Maddock herself. In the 1980s she produced books of hand-made paper with diary-like notations.

BIBLIOGRAPHY

J. Burke: 'Portrait of the Artist: Bea Maddock's Prints', *A. & Australia*, xvi/2 (1978), pp. 159–65

Bea Maddock, N.G. Victoria, Surv. 11 (Melbourne, 1980)

JANINE BURKE

Maderno, Carlo (*b* Capolago, nr Lugano, 1555–6; *d* Rome, 31 Jan 1629). Italian architect. One of the most important architects working in Rome at the beginning of the 17th century, he is credited by some with the revitalization of the dry, prosaic style that prevailed under Pope Sixtus V (*reg* 1585–90). His mature work, especially the vigorously articulated yet logical façade of S Susanna (1597–1603), is considered to be a harbinger of later stylistic development.

Maderno was so thoroughly enmeshed in the Roman practice of architecture that it is often difficult to isolate his personal contributions: throughout his career he collaborated with others, including Filippo Breccioli (*d* 1627), Bartolomeo Breccioli (*d* 1637) and Giovanni Vansanzio; he continued work begun by others, including FRANCESCO DA VOLTERRA, and initiated projects that were completed by others; he employed such standard Roman types as the two-storey church façade of Il Gesù and the plan and façade of the Palazzo Farnese; and he worked with a vocabulary of decorative elements derived from Michelangelo, Jacopo Vignola and other Roman architects. Yet he produced highly distinctive designs that set him apart from his contemporaries and made him a worthy model for his younger relative and (after 1619) assistant Francesco Borromini.

1. Early work and churches. 2. Secular architecture.

1. EARLY WORK AND CHURCHES. By at least 1576 Maderno had moved to Rome and was working there with his uncles Giovanni and Domenico Fontana, probably at first as a stuccoist. Domenico Fontana was the favoured architect of Cardinal Felice Peretti, who pursued an extensive programme of architectural and public works when he became Sixtus V. Maderno was closely involved with these projects, which included work on papal palaces, especially the Palazzo Quirinale, which Maderno later helped to complete (*see* ROME, §V, 26); the re-erection of the Vatican obelisk and the obelisks at S Maria Maggiore, S Giovanni in Laterano and the Piazza del Popolo (*see* FONTANA (iv), (2)); and aqueducts and other waterworks. It was in this context that he developed the formal and technical expertise that made him his uncle's successor as head of the family architectural concern in 1594 when Domenico Fontana finally left Rome for Naples.

Maderno's first important independent commission in Rome was the renovation (1597–1603) of S Susanna. The interior (previously rest. 1475–7) was revised, with an encrustation of stucco and painting on the walls and a coffered timber ceiling over the simple rectangular nave, and two pairs of curving staircases were built, descending to the oval crypt where an altar tabernacle evocative of

Michelangelesque forms in the façade (e.g. the triple-layered frame of the portal, the brackets composed of Ionic capitals above Doric triglyphs and the segmental pediments interrupted to make way for miniature triangular ones) are combined with Maderno's own distinctive detailing, notably the columns set into scooped-out channels in the wall and the spring-like volutes of the upper storey. The screen-like façade is both wider (in its lower storey) and taller than the simple, rectangular interior; indeed, the actual opening of the window that lights the upper part of the nave is barely visible behind the balustrade of the much grander window surround in the central bay of the upper storey.

Though employing Roman precedents, the façade of S Susanna did not form part of a sequence of church façade designs of this period; indeed, there is no such morphological sequence. Vignola's and della Porta's contrasting designs for Il Gesù are virtual contemporaries, and the variations worked on those two models in the following 30 years did not progress towards the hierarchical consistency and energy of Maderno's façade; nor did other architects follow Maderno's example. Maderno himself designed the body of the church of S Maria della Vittoria (1608–12), S Susanna's neighbour to the north, as a small, simplified version of Il Gesù; its façade, however, was not built until 1625–7 and then according to a design by Giovanni Battista Soria, who selected ornamental elements from S Susanna while eschewing its essential organization and energy.

Maderno was able to adapt his design to the much larger church of S Andrea della Valle; this had been begun in 1591 to a design by della Porta and Francesco Grimaldi, but only the first two bays of the nave were built before work stopped in 1600. Between 1608 and 1622 Maderno completed the body of the church, perhaps deepening the transept arms and the chancel, and constructed the drum and dome. The latter was based on that of St Peter's, the buttresses and ribs reduced from sixteen to eight and the proportions made taller. Maderno's design for the façade was engraved in 1624, but only its lower part, below the capitals of the first storey, was constructed (1626–7). Here he expanded the S Susanna design by using paired columns in the intermediate bays, but he obscured the clear layering of the bays by giving each ground-floor column its own pedestal and by shifting the paired columns of the upper storey into a single plane. He also eliminated the hierarchical progression toward the centre, instead filling all the bays with the same degree of ornament. The façade was completed in 1666 to a revised design by Carlo Rainaldi that was even farther removed from the model of S Susanna.

Maderno's most important project was the completion of St Peter's, where he had been appointed architect in 1603. After a century of discussion about the ultimate form of the church, it was finally decided that the centralized design, completed by the early 17th century, should be extended eastward with a nave, narthex and façade (*see* ROME, §V, 14(ii)(a) and fig. 37). Maderno tried to respect the centrality of Michelangelo's design in his extensions, but he eventually recognized that the church would become a longitudinal structure and that its façade would be an incident in a linear progression from the

1. Carlo Maderno: façade of S Susanna, Rome, 1597–1603

Early Christian examples was constructed. For the new façade Maderno used the common Roman type of two storeys joined by volutes, but he combined the compositional clarity of Vignola's unexecuted design for the façade of Il Gesù with the central concentration of Giacomo della Porta's built work (completed 1573), thus simultaneously rendering the old type with a new, lucid consistency and energy. At S Susanna (see fig. 1) the lower storey shows a systematic progression from the plain brick walls of the flanking monastery wings, their three bays marked by simple pilaster strips, to the outer bays of the travertine church façade proper, pilasters framing their low-relief ornaments; then to the intermediate bays, marked by half columns and with richly moulded niches containing figures of saints; and finally to the central bay, its single portal filling the entire space between the three-quarters columns. The hierarchy of the four clearly articulated layers, each progressively more ornate, in higher relief and projecting further forward, is pursued in the upper storey; there thick Composite pilasters replace the engaged Corinthian columns below, and tightly wound volutes on top of the outer bays of the lower storey press against the three upper bays. A triangular pediment surmounts the composition, its energetic verticality continued in candelabra-acroteria at the outer angles; and the balustrade that crowns the monastery wings mounts the pediment to its summit in an unorthodox manner.

obelisk in the Piazza through the nave to the great dome over the tomb of St Peter. He translated Michelangelo's continuous exterior wall of giant prismatic pilasters, entablature and attic into a symmetrical, hierarchically ordered façade of giant columns restraining the plastic substance of the wall beneath the entablature and attic. S Susanna provided the model for the progressive layering of the façade from pilaster-framed outer bays to the four central engaged columns, united beneath a triangular pediment (a residual image of the tetrastyle portico envisaged by Michelangelo), and also for such details as the columns set into channels in the wall and the moulded ornamental panels, niches and window-frames that fill the spaces between columns.

The decision to add bell-towers to the façade of St Peter's was taken by Pope Paul V in 1612, after construction of the façade was well under way. The tower bays, overlapping the pilasters at the ends of Maderno's façade, obscured the orderly composition of the façade, made it impossible to see Maderno's formal reference to Michelangelo's exterior forms and, because they were not completed but terminated at the height of the attic, produced the broad proportions with which so many observers have found fault. The façade was built between 1607 and 1625, and the nave was finally consecrated in 1626; the confessio was built to Maderno's design in 1615–16.

2. SECULAR ARCHITECTURE. In the same years in which his style as a church designer was emerging, Maderno demonstrated his expertise and originality in palace design. The Palazzo Mattei di Giove, Rome, built in three stages between 1598 and 1617, is set on a corner site and has two three-storey façades with regularly spaced windows and quoins at the angles, placing the building firmly within the prevailing Roman palace type; yet its fine brickwork (instead of the usual stucco) and carefully adjusted proportions set it apart from such predecessors as Domenico Fontana's Palazzo del Laterano and show it to be a worthy successor of Antonio da Sangallo (ii)'s Palazzo Farnese. The two portals, with superimposed frames and montages of capitals, triglyphs and eagles, are the secular companions of Maderno's details at S Susanna. The axis of the south portal (see fig. 2) extends through the small courtyard to terminate (originally) in a fountain niche in the centre of a three-bay bridge-loggia, beyond which is a small enclosed garden. The central arch was opened and the fountain removed in the late 17th or 18th century. The axis of the east portal is similarly stopped by the entrance to the main stair, with its splayed perspective jambs and vase-filled niche. Such closed axes appear repeatedly in Maderno's palaces and can be seen as a personal stylistic trait. The stair is complicated by turns to right and left, containing visitors within the space until they emerge in the upper loggia, where their vista is stopped by an antique figure in a shell-headed niche. On the *piano nobile*, the *sala* leads to ample linear suites of rooms, which, despite the site's irregularity, are regular rectangles, the differences between inside volumes and outer perimeter being taken up in walls of varying thickness. Maderno arranged these upper rooms with little regard for the pattern of walls on the ground floor, confident in his technical ability to place masonry walls over vaults. These planning traits also appear in his other buildings: the regular symmetry of the screen-like façades, as at S Susanna, gives no indication of the complex planning within.

Maderno's distinctive forms, perhaps developed in the context of his church designs, also appear in his contributions to the Villa Aldobrandini in Frascati. Most of the palace was built by Giacomo della Porta before 1602.

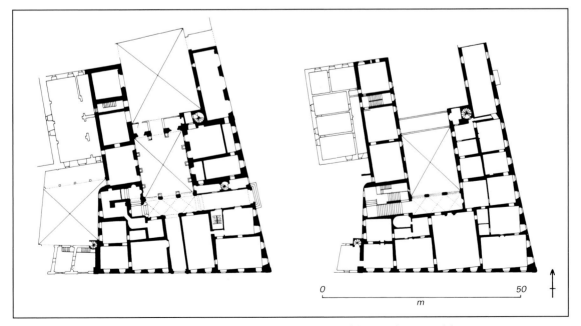

0   50
m

2. Carlo Maderno: plans of Palazzo Mattei di Giove, Rome, 1598–1617: (left) ground-floor; (right) *piano nobile*

Maderno and Giovanni Fontana then completed the outer and upper parts of the palace (1603–4) and built the water theatre that continues the axis of the site from the palace up the hillside (1603–21; *see* FRASCATI, fig. 1). The chimneys at the ends of the side terraces are buttressed by spring-like volutes that resemble those bracing the upper storey of S Susanna; and moulded, rectangular panels on the chimneys again recall those at S Susanna. In many of the other palaces for which documents attest Maderno's involvement, such as the Palazzo del Monte di Pietà (1623), the Barberini 'Casa Grande' ai Giubbonari (1622–4) and the Palazzo Ludovisi (1622–3; now Chigi-Odescalchi), his contributions can barely be isolated from those of earlier and later architects. At the Palazzo Borghese, Rome, however, his work (1611–14) was contained within the westernmost part of the wing stretching toward the Ripetta. Though altered later, it can be reconstructed in considerable detail that shows its stylistic consistency with Palazzo Mattei. Within the irregular perimeter of the small site, he arranged regularly shaped passages, stairs and rooms of contrasting volumes and functions; walls of varying thickness were used to accommodate these several shapes; and the lower floors were spanned with reinforcing tile arches that could support the walls of rooms above. The stair that rises through the middle of Maderno's addition is L-shaped at first but becomes U-shaped as it nears the *piano nobile* and continues thus to the attic, the upper landings being on the curve of the U. Instead of revealing these interior complexities, Maderno's addition to the south-west façade brings a regularity and order previously lacking on that side.

The three-dimensional imagination evident in Maderno's palaces, especially in their stairs, occurs elsewhere in his work. At the Borghese garden palace on the Quirinal (from 1611; now the Palazzo Pallavicini-Rospigliosi), the stairs that rise to the hanging garden change shape and direction several times, eventually vaulting over a fountain and pushing into the garden in concentric semicircular treads. At S Susanna two sets of bifurcated stairs curve downwards to the crypt, and at St Peter's the curving stairs of the confessio were occasioned by the complexities of relating the eccentrically located shrine of St Peter, considerably below the pavement of the new church, to the baldacchino and great domed crossing above.

The Palazzo Barberini, begun in December 1628, was the last and most complex of Maderno's palace designs, although it was largely executed by others. The basic idea for this palace (*see* ROME, §V, 24), with two separate wings in an H-plan, was conceived by its owner, Taddeo Barberini, nephew of Pope Urban VIII. Although many others contributed to the design, Maderno was in charge of design development. Here again can be seen his characteristic planning of eminently functional suites, closed axes (most notably in the deep, apsed entrance portico, the passage through which was cut only in the 1670s), the complex, three-dimensional arrangement of rooms on the several levels of the palace and the linking stairs. The great three-storey, seven-bay loggia of the west façade is surprising in the context of Maderno's oeuvre (or that of any other Roman architect in the 1620s), but the whole exterior is rendered in his distinctive style with such details as columns set within channels in the walls, splayed jambs (resembling those at the stair entrance in the Palazzo Mattei) in the third storey of the loggia, and the superimposed frames of the north portal.

Throughout his career, Maderno was involved with engineering projects. As well as his collaboration with Giovanni and Domenico Fontana, he worked on bridges and on the Fiumicino embankments at the mouth of the River Tiber (1608–12), and under Paul V he was appointed 'Architect of the Tibur'. He was consulted about the structural condition of older buildings, and his office made many routine surveys of buildings preliminary to their sale, estimates and evaluations, which were part of the daily practice of architecture in Rome. His grand designs for complex stairs and walls over voids may owe much to his intimate familiarity with ordinary Roman terraced housing, with its improvisatory arrangements of walls and, in particular, stairs.

Maderno's own estimation of his professional accomplishments is found on his tomb in S Giovanni dei Fiorentini, Rome, where it is related that he assisted Domenico Fontana in moving the Vatican obelisk from the side to the front of the church; he designed and built the nave and façade of St Peter's; and he moved an ancient column from the Basilica of Maxentius to a position in front of S Maria Maggiore (1613–14). The technical feats may be overlooked by modern critics, but they were highly respected in their time and indicative of the structural and constructional expertise that made possible some of Maderno's most interesting plans and designs.

BIBLIOGRAPHY

G. Baglione: *Vite* (1642); ed. V. Mariani (1935), pp. 307–9
N. Caflisch: *Carlo Maderno* (Munich, 1934)
K. Schwager: 'Kardinal Pietro Aldobrandinis Villa di Belvedere in Frascati', *Röm. Jb. Kstgesch.*, ix–x (1961–2), pp. 289–382
H. Hibbard: 'Scipione Borghese's Garden Palace on the Quirinal', *J. Soc. Archit. Historians*, xxiii (1964), pp. 163–92
H. Thelen: *Francesco Borromini: Die Handzeichnungen* (Graz, 1967)
G. Panofsky-Soergel: 'Zur Geschichte des Palazzo Mattei di Giove', *Röm. Jb. Kstgesch.*, xi (1967–8), pp. 109–88
H. Hibbard: *Carlo Maderno and Roman Architecture, 1580–1630*, Studies in Architecture, 10 (London and University Park, PA, 1971)
M. Bertoldi and others: 'Palazzo Mattei di Giove: Ricerca documentaria ed iconografica', *Boll. Cent. Stud. Stor. Archit.*, xxx (1983), pp. 63–73
——: 'Palazzo Mattei di Giove: Le fasi della costruzione e l'individuazione delle lavorazioni caratteristiche', *Ric. Stor. A.*, xx (1983), pp. 65–76
P. Waddy: *Seventeenth-century Roman Palaces: Use and the Art of the Plan* (New York, 1990)
C. Thoenes: 'Madernos St-Peter-Entwürfe', *An Architectural Progress in the Renaissance and Baroque: Sojourns in and out of Italy*, ed. H. A. Millom and S. Scott Munshower (University Park, PA, 1992), i, pp. 170–93

PATRICIA WADDY

Maderno, Stefano (*b* ?Rome, 1575; *d* Rome, 17 Sept 1636). Italian sculptor. He was one of the outstanding sculptors in Rome in the early 17th century, and his work, together with that of such sculptors as Pietro Bernini, Nicolas Cordier, Camillo Mariani and Francesco Mochi, is generally considered to mark a transition from the late Renaissance (or Mannerist) style to the early Baroque. He has long been considered a Lombard, but Donati (1945) questioned his northern origins on the basis of his death certificate, which gives Palestrina (30 km from Rome) as his place of birth. Pressouyre (1984) published the marriage contract drawn up between the sculptor and his second wife, Lucrezia Pennina, on 24 October 1611, which refers to both Maderno and his father as Roman, and drew attention to the artist's signature on his relief of *Rudolf II of Hungary Attacking the Turks* (1613–15) on the tomb of *Paul V* in S Maria Maggiore, Rome: STEPHANVS MA-DERNVS ROMANVS F.

Like many contemporary sculptors, Maderno began his career in Rome (before 1600) studying and restoring antique statues. The pronounced classicism of all his works is a product of this early training. He is best known for his marble statue of *St Cecilia* (1600) at the high altar of S Cecilia in Trastevere, Rome (see fig.). This work, which established Maderno's reputation, was commissioned by Cardinal Paolo Emilio Sfondrato, the titular cardinal of the church, who had undertaken extensive excavations of the building in the hope of finding the remains of St Cecilia. The discovery of her supposed entire and uncorrupt body on 20 October 1599 under the main altar was a momentous occasion in Rome, especially within the context of the Counter-Reformation. Sfondrato commissioned Maderno to reconstruct the altar and to carve, as its centrepiece, a statue of the recumbent saint.

Maderno depicted St Cecilia precisely the way Antonio Bosio described her at the moment of discovery: uncorrupt, lying on her side, clad in a dress, with her veiled head turned towards the ground (*Historia passionis SS Martyrum Caeciliae Virginis*, Rome, 1600). This gave rise to the assumption, fostered by Baglione and other writers, that the statue was based on direct study of the corpse. It is now generally recognized, however, that the statue is an ingenious invention of Maderno, indebted to ancient sculptures, such as the *Dead Persian* (Naples, Mus. Archeol. N.), and based on Bosio's description of St Cecilia's body as well as that found in the *Liber pontificalis*, which records Paschal I's reburial of the saint in AD 821.

The *St Cecilia* is a mature expression of Maderno's talent as a sculptor. The statue (1.31 m in length) is a work of classical simplicity and directness in presentation, which presages later developments in Baroque sculpture. It is designed to be seen from a single viewpoint and characterized by an emotive intensity, and a naturalism tempered by idealization that is also evident in contemporary works by Guido Reni in painting and Camillo Mariani in sculpture. The *St Cecilia* served as the model for a series of Roman Baroque statues of recumbent saints, including the *St Martina* (*c.* 1635; SS Luca e Martina) by Nicolò Menghini (*c.* 1610–55), Gianlorenzo Bernini's *Blessed Ludovica Albertoni* (1671–4; S Francesco a Ripa) and the *St Sebastian* (*c.* 1675; S Sebastiano fuori le Mura) by Giuseppe Giorgetti (*fl c.* 1668–80).

The *St Cecilia* was followed by a virtually uninterrupted series of commissions for monumental sculpture. In 1601 Maderno made a marble figure of *Prudence* for the tomb of *Cardinal Alessandrino* in S Maria sopra Minerva, Rome, a work of extreme classical severity, reminiscent of Andrea Sansovino. After his election to the Accademia di S Luca in 1607, he was engaged (1608–15) by Paul V to decorate the Pauline Chapel at S Maria Maggiore, Rome. For the exterior he carved, in collaboration with Francesco Caporale (il Sonzino; *fl* 1606–11), over-life-size travertine statues of *St Matthias* and *St Epaphras* (1608–9), figures of bold plasticity and movement. In 1610 he executed the model for the bronze relief of the *Miracle of the Snow* (depicting the legendary founding of the basilica) that surmounts the altar tabernacle in the chapel; it was cast in 1612 under the direction of Giulio Buratti (*d* 1652). From 1613 to 1615 Maderno carved the large marble relief of *Rudolf II of Hungary Attacking the Turks* for the tomb of *Paul V*. With its high horizon and stacked-up and overlapping figures, the relief conforms (as do the others on the tomb) to the conventions of the late 16th-century Lombard narrative relief style as established in S Maria Maggiore on the papal tombs (1585–90) in the chapel of Sixtus V. Yet in Maderno's work the figures have become larger, the movement and spatial complexity more acute, the carving deeper, and the play of light and shadow more dramatic, marking significant steps in the development of the Baroque relief.

Stefano Maderno: *St Cecilia*, marble, l. 1.30 m, 1600 (Rome, S Cecilia in Trastevere)

Among Maderno's other monumental sculptures for Roman churches are his reclining figures of *Peace* and *Justice* (1614), which crown the pediment of the high altar in S Maria della Pace. These allegorical statues demonstrate the sculptor's debt to both Classical antiquity and contemporary trends in painting, such as the work of Domenichino. According to Baglione, they so pleased their patron, Gaspare Rivaldi, that he bestowed on the sculptor a position in the customs office at the Port of Ripetta in Rome. Baglione's assertion, however, that Maderno's career as a sculptor came to a halt after receiving this position is unfounded. Documented works of 1624, 1628–9 and 1636 prove that he remained active as a sculptor for the rest of his life.

Perhaps Maderno's most important and characteristic works are his small terracotta models, bronzes and marbles derived, with varying degrees of freedom, from antique models and from works by Michelangelo and Giambologna. His signed and dated terracotta model of the *Farnese Hercules* (h. 525 mm, 1617; Oxford, Ashmolean) and the bronze variant (h. 560 mm) in Vienna, Hofburg-Schauräume, are, except for the overdeveloped musculature, faithful reproductions of the famous ancient statue. More inventive is his series of signed and dated terracottas representing the Labours of Hercules (Venice, Ca' d'Oro): *Hercules and the Nemean Lion* (h. 495 mm, 1621), *Hercules and Cacus* (h. 555 mm, 1621) and *Hercules and Antaeus* (h. 544 mm, 1622). These works, created *all'antica* but not dependent on specific ancient models, combine strong naturalism and studied classicism in dynamic compositions. Although the last of the series is known in two bronze replicas (Dresden, Skulpsamml.; Toledo, OH, Mus. A.), these terracottas, as well as others in St Petersburg (Hermitage), were certainly created as independent objects for collectors.

Maderno's work, like that of several of his contemporaries, marks a turning-point in the history of Italian sculpture. His most important and influential works—*St Cecilia*, the Pauline Chapel reliefs and his small terracottas and bronzes—bring together his lifelong interest in Classical antiquity and his concerns for naturalism and expression. As such, his sculpture presages that of Bernini.

BIBLIOGRAPHY

Thieme–Becker

G. Baglione: *Vite* (1642); ed. V. Mariani (1935), pp. 345–6

A. Venturi: *Storia*, xiii (1901–40), pp. 611–19

A. Muñoz: 'Stefano Maderno', *Atti & Mem. Reale Accad. S Luca; Annu.*, iii (1913–14), pp. 1–23

R. Wittkower: 'Ein Werk des Stefano Maderno in Dresden', *Z. Bild. Kst.*, lxii (1928), pp. 26–8

I. Robertson: 'Three Works Ascribed to Stefano Maderno', *Burl. Mag.*, lxix (1936), pp. 176–81

U. Donati: *Artisti ticinesi a Roma* (Bellinzona, 1942), pp. 412–32 [excellent plates]

A. Donati: *Stefano Maderno scultore, 1576–1636* (Bellinzona, 1945)

A. Nava Cellini: *Stefano Maderno* (Milan, 1966)

S. Pressouyre: *Nicolas Cordier: Recherches sur la sculpture à Rome autour de 1600*, 2 vols (Rome, 1984)

M. Smith O'Neil: 'Stefano Maderno's *Saint Cecilia*: A Seventeenth-century Roman Sculpture Remeasured', *Ant. B.A.*, 25–6 (1985), pp. 9–21

S. O. Androssov: 'Works by Stefano Maderno, Bernini and Rusconi from the Farsetti Collection in the Ca' d'Oro and the Hermitage', *Burl. Mag.*, cxxxiii (1991), pp. 292–7

STEVEN F. OSTROW

Madhhur, Tell. See under HAMRIN REGION.

Madhu. Indian miniature painters. Inscriptions of 1580–90 distinguish between Madhu Khurd ('the younger') and Madhu Kalan ('the elder'); in 1590–1605 reference is only to Madhu. The name Madhu, with no suffix, appears in the list of 17 prized artists compiled by Abu'l-Fazl in the 1590s for the *Āyīn-i Akbarī*, a contemporary account of court matters. Skill in portraiture was apparently a gift of both Madhu Kalan and Madhu Khurd; whether the Madhu referred to in the 1590s was one of these two is not yet clear.

In the *Tīmūrnāma* ('History of Timur'; *c.* 1584; Bankipur, Patna, Khuda Bakhsh, Lib.) Madhu Khurd was given three paintings to design in collaboration with other artists, while Madhu Kalan worked on one folio unassisted, was designer for one and worked as painter for Kesu Das on fol. 38*r*. The name Madhu appears as the ascription on fol. 60b in the *Khamsa* ('Five poems') of Nizami (*c.* 1585; Pontresina, Keir priv. col.) in collaboration with the designer Lal. Madhu Khurd, perhaps newly arrived in the workshop, was assigned more folios in the *Dārābnāma* ('Story of Darab'; *c.* 1583–6; London, BL, Or. MS. 4615). Madhu Khurd worked unassisted on five folios, while Madhu Kalan worked on one. It has been proposed that fol. 74a, assigned to Madhu Khurd, suggests in certain colour combinations and the swinging robes that this painter was of Ahmednagar (Deccani) origin (see 1982 exh. cat.). In the *Razmnāma* ('Book of wars'; 1586) and the *Rāmāyaṇa* (*c.* 1586; both Jaipur, Maharaja Sawai Man Singh II Mus., MS. AG. 1683–1850 and MS. AG. 1851–2026), Madhu Kalan was given sole responsibility for three folios and Madhu Khurd executed fols 114, 151 and 161 unassisted. Madhu Kalan was given paintings to colour, collaborating with the designers Daswanth (two fols), Jagan (two fols), Lal (two fols) and Makand (one fol.). Madhu Khurd was given less, collaborating with Basawan (two fols), Jagjivan (one fol.) and Lal (three fols). The inscription Madhu, without suffix, appears on fol. 121. In the *Rāmāyaṇa*, a Madhu Chela ('the disciple') is assigned one folio, Madhu Kalan seven and Madhu Khurd one. A study of the *Akbarnāma* ('History of Akbar'; *c.* 1590; London, V&A, MS. IS. 2–1896) reveals only one folio where Madhu Khurd was assigned the task of assisting with faces. The other miniatures have as inscriptions either Madhu Kalan or simply Madhu. In these paintings there is a consistent quality in the handling of those coloured by Madhu (14/117, 65/117) and those where solely the portraits were assigned to Madhu Kalan (20/117, 33/117, 49/117, 60/117, 91/117, 114/117). The quality of these portraits by Madhu Kalan is outstanding, and they are not comparable with the example by Madhu Khurd.

By the mid-1590s the suffix has disappeared. Madhu still seems to be used, particularly as a face painter. Work by Madhu also appears in the *Bāburnāma* ('History of Babar'; *c.* 1589; London, V&A and dispersed) and in the *Bahāristān* ('Spring garden') of Jami (dated 1595; Oxford, Bodleian Lib.; MS. Elliot 254); only a few artists worked on such de luxe manuscripts. Two folios of Madhu's work are also in the *Khamsa* of Nizami (1595; London, BL, Or. MS. 12208). It is interesting to note that Madhu was given greater responsibility for portraiture (16 fols) in the *Jami al-tavarikh* (dated 1596; Tehran, Gulistan Pal. Lib.) than any other painter. He worked as a designer on one painting but collaborated as a painter with the designers Basawan and Dharm Das. His work also appears in the *Khamsa* of Amir Khusrau Dihlavi (1597–8; Baltimore, MD, Walters A.G., MS. W.624), and his is one of the six names of artists involved in the 17 illustrations for the *Nafaḥāt al-uns* ('Fragrant breezes of friendship'; dated 1604–5; London, BL, Or. MS. 1362). Madhu was still working as a portrait artist in the *Akbarnāma* manuscript of *c.* 1596 (London, BL, Or. MS. 12988, and Dublin, Chester Beatty Lib., Ind. MS. 2), in which two folios have been attributed to him. He is also known to have worked for 'Abd al-Rahim Khan-i Khanan (*see* INDIAN SUBCONTINENT, §VI, 4(ii)(a)).

BIBLIOGRAPHY
The Imperial Image: Paintings for the Mughal Court (exh. cat. by M. C. Beach, Washington, DC, Freer, 1981)
The Art of the Book in India (exh. cat. by J. Losty, London, BL, 1982)
HEATHER ELGOOD

Madigan, Colin (Frederick) (*b* Glen Innes, NSW, 22 July 1921). Australian architect. He graduated from the Sydney Technical College in 1950, when functionalism was becoming canonical in Australian architecture and his concern, too, was with the creation of spaces that clearly communicated their making and their purpose. Madigan's early buildings, such as his own house in Sydney (1952), explored new ideas, including the skeletal construction that he abandoned in his first major work, the Dee Why Library (1967), Sydney, in which he coupled the heavy and romantic Brutalism of the Sydney area with a sophisticated use of steel. His firm's buildings for the High Court of Australia (1972–80, *see* AUSTRALIA, fig 6) and the Australian National Gallery (1973–82) stand adjacent to each other in the Parliamentary Triangle, Canberra. These are individualistic structures in which large glass surfaces play against dramatically placed concrete masses. High-quality finishes and careful, well-executed details are typical of the firm's work.

BIBLIOGRAPHY
Contemp. Architects
Archit. Australia (1982) [supernumerary issue]
J. Taylor: *Australian Architecture since 1960* (Sydney, 1986)
JENNIFER TAYLOR

Madinah, al-. *See* MEDINA.

Madinat al-Zahra' [Madīnat al-Zahrā'; Medinat al-Zahra; now Medina Azzahra]. Site in southern Spain, 6 km west of Córdoba, founded as a palace–city in 936 by the Umayyad caliph 'Abd al-Rahman III (*reg* 912–61). His son, the future al-Hakam II (*reg* 961–76), supervised the work of the architects Maslama ibn 'Abdallah and others. Sacked and destroyed by the Berbers in 1010, the site was repeatedly quarried for building materials. Excavations begun in 1911 have revealed the richness and variety of Umayyad secular architecture and its decoration (*see* ISLAMIC ART, §II, 5(iv)(a)) and confirm the glowing and unusually precise accounts of the city by chroniclers.

The site is a rectangle set east–west on the lower slopes of the Sierra Morena. Water was brought from mountain springs by a tunnelled and surface canal with stepped descents to the northern city wall. The site was enclosed in a rampart formed of two walls separated by a narrow corridor, except near the city gate (see fig. a) in the north where the wall was single. Arabic sources specify that the site was divided into three terraced zones. The Alcázar in the highest zone contained the caliph's private quarters (Arab. *dār al-mulk*; b) and those of his close associates. The middle zone housed the court and such workshops as the mint, moved from Córdoba in 947. The lowest zone contained gardens and, probably, the urban area, which remains unexcavated. Despite the relatively short period of occupation, several areas were modified and rebuilt, to judge from changes in orientation.

Partial excavation of the highest zone has revealed a series of reception halls and dwelling-rooms arranged around courts terraced across the slope. One of the earliest structures, the caliph's private quarters (b), stands on the highest terrace at the north-west of the excavated area. There may have ben a fortified area above it. A long room on the north has horseshoe arches at either end leading to alcoves, small chambers and courts. To its south lies a large central room with a tiled floor and alcoves and an external belvedere with three arches overlooking the terraces below. These quarters were later remodelled by al-Hakam II. To the east of and slightly below the caliph's quarters are courtyards (c, l) with dwelling-rooms.

A second terrace to the south and east contained the military headquarters (Arab. *dār al-jund*; d), dwellings of palace officials (e) and service areas. The *dār al-jund* (*c.* 958) has a transverse rectangular room with square chambers at either end that opens south on to a square court (f) surrounded by porticos. It opens north to a hall of five parallel perpendicular aisles separated by columns, piers and walls covered with plain stucco with moulding. Large horseshoe arches between the triple-arch arcades on either side of the central aisle modify this basilican scheme to create a somewhat cruciform plan. A zigzag ramp on the east connected the *dār al-jund* to a portico of 15 arches (g); the central arch originally supported a kiosk. A narrow road divided this terrace from the house of Ja'far (h), later chamberlain to al-Hakam II. It too has a transverse rectangular room and basilican area, but the central aisle opens on to a chamber with alcoves, courtyard and latrine. Another house (i) has two porticos and an eccentric pool in its garden. Between the houses stands a bath (j) built on the remains of a hall with parallel north–south aisles; the small ashlars used identify the bath as of the late 10th century. The north-west sector of the second terrace contains courts, storehouses, ovens and service quarters (k). A dwelling with a pillared court surrounded by rooms (l) has corner stairs that indicate it once had upper floors.

The third and lowest terrace contains the magnificent hall built by the caliph Abd al-Rahman III, now known as the Salón Rico (953–8; m). It is the focus of a large reception complex of structures and reflecting pools arranged in a cruciform garden parterre surrounded by towered walls. The remains of the building, which had been destroyed by fire, were discovered in 1944 and are being reconstructed with the fallen fragments of wall decoration placed on rebuilt walls and arches (*see* ISLAMIC ART, fig. 44). According to the contemporary historian Isa ibn Ahmad al-Razi, this structure, which he called the *majlis al-sharqī* ('eastern reception room'), was used for

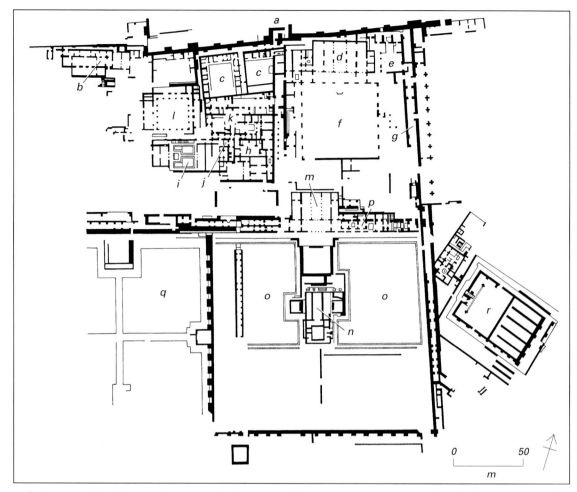

Madinat al-Zahra', plan of the highest zone, begun 936: (a) city gate; (b) Caliph's private quarters (*dār al-mulk*);(c) courtyards; (d) military headquarters (*dār al-jund*); (e) dwellings of the palace officials; (f) square court; (g) portico; (h) house of Ja'far; (i) house of the Patio of the Pool;(j) bath; (k) service quarters; (l) Court of the Pillars; (m) Salón Rico (*majlis al-sharqī*); (n) aisled hall; (o) pools; (p) annexe and baths; (q) cruciform garden; (r) mosque

the reception of kings, princes and ambassadors. The plan differs from the northern reception hall, for the three central aisles are integrated into a single space divided only by two horseshoe arcades. The outer aisles, however, which have vaulted alcoves at the north, have only single doors to the central chamber and the end chambers of the transverse rectangular main entrance room. In either outer wall a horseshoe arch, between square niches, rests on beautiful marble pilasters. The central hall was decorated with two pairs of niches, a marble dado, great stone tapestry panels with recessed borders carved with the tree of life, frames and horizontal panels with geometric designs. The arcades are richly ornamented with acanthus leaves. All this decoration was once highlighted with brilliant colouring. The magnificence and perfection of architectural space and decoration make the *majlis al-sharqī* the finest example of the court art of the Umayyad caliphate.

In the middle of the garden to the south stood an aisled hall supported by arcades (n) and surrounded on all sides

by pools (o) in which the *majlis al-sharqī* and this hall would have been reflected. An annexe to the east of this *majlis* contained baths and latrines (p); to the west were ramps and vaulted passages that led from the *majlis al-sharqī* and its parterres to a large cruciform garden (q) below the third terrace. From the east side of the terrace, the caliph descended to the mosque (r) by means of a bridge over a street and a passage in the thickness of the qibla wall of the mosque. The mosque, built on a platform to compensate for the slope of the land, had a square minaret with an internal octagonal staircase, porticoed courtyard and oratory with five arcaded aisles perpendicular to the qibla wall. The floor was tiled only in the *maqsūra* area in front of the mihrab.

The site of Madinat al-Zahra' has yielded notable finds in several media. A distinctive group of marble column capitals and bases have deeply carved and drilled acanthus decoration derived from Roman and Byzantine models, but geometricized and stylized. Often inscribed with the names of the ruler, supervisor of works and individual artisan, they can be dated precisely, allowing the evolution of Umayyad architectural ornament to be delineated. Several splendid ivory boxes were carved at the site, to judge from their inscriptions, in the second half of the 10th century (*see* CÓRDOBA (i), §2, and ISLAMIC ART, §VIII, 7). A bronze fountain-spout in the shape of a stag (Córdoba, Mus. Arqueol.; *see* ISLAMIC ART, fig. 141) found at the site represents the finest metalworking of the caliphal period.

Enc. Islam/2
                          BIBLIOGRAPHY
M. Gómez-Moreno: *El arte árabe español hasta los almohades, arte mozárabe* (1951), iii of *Ars Hispaniae* (Madrid, 1947–77)
B. Pavón Maldonado: *Memoria de la excavación de la mezquita de Medinat al-Zahra* (Madrid, 1966)
E. García Gómez: *Anales palatinos del califa de Córdoba al-Hakam II, por 'Isā ibn Ahmad al-Rāzī* (Madrid, 1967)
S. López-Cuervo: *Medina al-Zahra* (Madrid, 1983)
F. Hernández Giménez: *Madinat al-Zahrá'. Arquitectura y decoración. Nota preliminar: Purificación Marinetto Sánchez. Prólogo: Antonio Fernández-Puertas* (Granada, 1985)
                          ANTONIO FERNÁNDEZ-PUERTAS

Madonnero. Term of Venetian origin used generally to refer to any producer or purveyor of images of the Virgin. It was used specifically as early as the 15th century and as late as the 18th to designate a painter who specialized in devotional panels of a late Byzantine character. It is often used to signify painters of inferior talent, who executed either religious paintings derived from Byzantine prototypes in a weak, Italianizing style or subjects derived from Italian models in a pseudo-Byzantine manner. However, the artistic abilities of individual Madonneri varied widely, as did their artistic training. Whether Venetian, Cretan or Dalmatian in origin, they generally demonstrated little interest in experimentation, preferring a limited range of themes and stylistic continuity. Devotional images painted by Madonneri survive from the second half of the 15th century; production peaked in the latter half of the 16th century. After the fall of Constantinople (now Istanbul) in 1453, Greek artists moved to the Italian mainland or exported works of art there. Crete was an important centre of production, but others existed along the Dalmatian coast, in the Ionian islands, at Otranto and, of course, in Venice. As a result, some native Italian painters also adopted a Byzantine style and iconography when producing devotional panels for the popular market.

The Madonneri were mostly anonymous artists and craftsmen. Some may have been professional journeymen who learnt a late Byzantine manner from Greek artists, while others may have been connected to established workshops. Giovanni Bellini's workshop produced countless paintings of the Virgin. Although Bellini often evoked Byzantine archetypes in his half-length images, particularly after the mid-1470s, he is obviously not classed as a Madonnero, but lesser painters turned his inventions into formulae, sometimes applying a superficial Byzantine manner. The anonymous Madonnero found Bellini's studio to be a source of compositions for subjects such as the *Pietà with St John*, derived ultimately from Bellini's *Pietà* (Milan, Brera) and modelled after the *Pietà with St John* attributed to Bellini with workshop assistance (1490–1500; Berlin, Gemäldegal.). Thirteen copies have been identified, all unsigned and many executed in the Greek

manner, for example the *Pietà with St John* (Baltimore, MD, Walters A.G.), in which the hard edges, bronze colouring and stylized forms of the figures help to support the current attribution to a Madonnero of the Veneto–Byzantine school.

Several leading painters of the Cretan school popularized devotional images. A leading Madonnero was Andreas Ritzos (Andrea Rico or Rizzi) da Candia who belonged to a family of painters. The son of a painter, Andreas was active in Crete from 1451 to 1492, his son Nikolaos (1460–*c.* 1507) and his grandson Maneas (1528–71) continuing the tradition. Andreas was unusual in signing his paintings with inscriptions in both Greek and Latin. Furthermore, he was responsible for popularizing, if not inventing, the most common image of the Virgin used by Madonneri, the *Virgin of the Passion* (Florence, Uffizi, on dep. Fiesole, Mus. Bandini; see fig.). An epigram reveals the subject as the Virgin and Son confronted with foreknowledge of the Passion. The Child clutches his mother's hand and turns to the archangel Gabriel who holds the cross, crown of thorns and nails. In a curious detail, one sandal slips from the Infant's foot. The *Virgin of the Passion* may have been modelled after a Cretan icon of the *Virgin of Courage* (*Kardiotissa*), but Ritzos injected naturalism into the Christ Child's facial expression and pose. He signed the work, in Latin, on the lower edge.

Other examples of the *Virgin of the Passion* repeat the same formula, with slight variations in the decorative features (Parma, G.N.; St Petersburg, Hermitage; Princeton U., NJ, A. Mus.). Numerous copies survive from the hands of 16th- and 17th-century Madonneri, and the type spread through Italy. The gold background, two archangels

Andreas Ritzos da Candia: *Virgin of the Passion*, tempera on panel, 1.03×0.84 m, second half of the 15th century (Florence, Galleria degli Uffizi, on deposit Fiesole, Museo Bandini)

carrying symbols of the Passion and the arrangement of the figures suggest that the anonymous artist of the *Virgin and Child* (ex-Nelson–Atkins Mus. A., Kansas City, MO) employed the same prototype.

Nicola Zafuri was another Cretan painter who signed his works and supervised a workshop in Candia from the late 15th century to the early 16th. He evidently specialized in half-length images of the Virgin and Child holding a small globe. The iconography derives from the Byzantine images of 'she who points the way' (*hodegetria*), traditionally identified as the original image painted by St Luke. However, Italian artists of the early 14th century had invested the image with the powers of healing implied by the globe. Zafuri thus combined Western iconography and Byzantine style, as did other Madonneri who attempted to bridge the Eastern and Western traditions.

It is likely that Madonneri sold their works on the open market. Their pictures were modest in scale and design and were frequently displayed in a wall niche in the home. By the 16th century inventories of Venetian households often mention 'quadri de nostra Donna, Candioti' [from Crete] and the author Giovanni Battista Armenini lamented the practice of placing small panels of holy images 'alla greca' in so many private homes. It is likely that Madonneri also executed pictures for street tabernacles. Their work perpetuated the mystique of the Byzantine icon by adhering to a conservative, archaic style and by integrating Western motifs with Byzantine iconography.

BIBLIOGRAPHY
R. van Marle: *Italian Schools*, xviii (1923–38), pp. 544–51
S. Bettini: *La pittura di icone cretese–veneziana e i madonneri* (Padua, 1933)
F. Heinemann: *Giovanni Bellini e i belliniani*, 2 vols (Venice, 1959)
S. Ringbom: *Icon to Narrative: The Rise of the Dramatic Close-up in Fifteenth-century Devotional Painting* (Turku, 1965, rev. Doornspijk, 1984)
T. Gouma-Peterson: 'The Dating of Creto-Venetian Icons: A Reconsideration in the Light of New Evidence', *Allen Mem. A. Mus. Bull.*, xxx (1972), pp. 12–22
M. Cattapan: 'I pittori Pavia, Rizo, Zafuri da Candia e Papadopulo della Cavea', *Thesaurismata*, xiv (1977), pp. 225–34
M. Chatzidakis: 'La Peinture des "madonneri" ou "véneto-crétoise" et sa destination', *Venezia centro di mediazione tra Oriente e Occidente (secoli XV–XVI)*, ii (Florence, 1977), pp. 673–90
M. B. Fiorin: 'Mostra di icone al Museo Nazionale di Ravenna: Una proposta di lavoro', *A. Friuli, A. Trieste*, v–vi (1982), pp. 191–203
——: 'Nicola Zafuri, cretese del quattrocento, e una sua inedita "Madonna"', *A. Ven.*, xxxvii (1983), pp. 164–9
T. Gouma-Peterson: 'The Icon as Cultural Presence after 1453', *Icon*, ed. G. Vika (Washington, DC, 1988)

EUNICE D. HOWE

Madou, Jean-Baptiste (*b* Brussels, 3 Feb 1796; *d* Brussels, 3 April 1877). Belgian painter and lithographer. He was a pupil of Joseph François at the Académie in Brussels. Between 1814 and 1818 he was a clerk in the Ministry of Finance and until 1820 a topographical draughtsman in the Ministry of War. His work was then noticed by the publisher Jobard, who employed him as a lithographer of (largely unsigned) maps, book illustrations, vignettes and portraits. Around 1830 he began to publish in Brussels and Paris portraits and series of lithographs, for example the *Outskirts of Brussels* (1831), which first drew attention to his name. Madou's reputation was confirmed with the publication of *The Physiognomy of Society in Europe from 1400 to the Present Day* (1836), lithographs after his own watercolours. In the subsequent *Life of the Painters of the Flemish and Dutch School* (1842), Madou showed the taste for historical reconstruction that is also to be seen in the paintings he then began to produce, most of which were genre scenes set in the 18th century. These often show taverns, as in *The Spoilsport* (1854), or colourful, characterful crowds, as in *Village Politicians* (1871; both Brussels, Mus. A. Mod.). Madou brought a strong sense of humour to his evocation of the past in these pictures, while also showing his technical skill in the detail and finish of their treatment.

BIBLIOGRAPHY
A. Guislain: *Caprice romantique: Le Keepsake de M. Madou* (Brussels, 1947)
J. B. Madou (exh. cat., Brussels, Mus. Hôtel Charlier, 1964)
P. Roberts-Jones: 'Madou et Quetelet', *Bull. Classe B.-A.*, n.s. 5, lvi (1974), pp. 200–04
N. Walch: *J.-B. Madou, lithographe* (Brussels, 1977)
Cent Cinquante Ans de vie artistique (exh. cat., Brussels, Pal. Acad., 1980), pp. 59–60

RICHARD KERREMANS

Madox Brown, Ford. *See* BROWN, FORD MADOX.

Madras. City and manufacturing centre, capital of Tamil Nadu State, India. It has a fine, varied heritage of colonial architecture.

1. HISTORY AND URBAN DEVELOPMENT. There are ancient associations with early Christianity in the areas of Mylapore, Little Mount and St Thomas's Mount, where St Thomas the Apostle is said to have been martyred in AD 68. The Portuguese arrived in 1522, building the church of St Thomas (1547) and the cathedral of S Thomé south of the subsequent English settlement, and were expelled in 1672. The city was founded in 1639 by Francis Day, the agent from the nearby English factory or trading station, at Armagaum on territory ceded by the Raja of Chandragiri and was the first significant settlement of the British East India Company on the Indian subcontinent. In 1644 a small fort was built from which the city grew steadily, remaining the centre of English influence in the East until the emergence of Calcutta in the late 18th century.

Early European settlement was concentrated in Fort St George on the seashore, which came to be called Christian or White Town in contrast to Black Town (now George Town), which lay outside to the north. By 1659 White Town was enclosed and fortified, and by 1682 a masonry wall had replaced the mud ramparts around Black Town. Eight years later Madras had become a major city of over 300,000 people, laid out on a grid pattern and the earliest example of English urban planning in India. St Mary's Church (1678–80; damaged 1758, rest.), lying within the Fort area, was the centre of the original settlement. It was probably designed by William Dixon (*fl* 1675–82), master gunner of the Fort. It is a simple, robust building with a fluted spire, resembling an obelisk, which was added in 1795. It contains an important collection of funerary monuments by leading Neo-classical sculptors. Fort St George was reconstructed between 1755 and 1783 by a series of British military engineers, including Captain John Brohier and Colonel Patrick Ross, and became one of the most formidable forts in Asia. During the Wars of the Carnatic, Madras was the fulcrum of British power in the region. Taken by the French under Bertrand-François

Mahé de La Bourdonnais in 1746, it was restored to the British three years later and besieged again by Thomas-Arthur de Lally in 1758. A number of buildings of architectural and historic interest are concentrated within the Fort: notably Clive's House (*c*. 1750; altered) for Robert Clive, 1st Baron Clive of Plassey; Wellesley's House (*c*. 1770; now partly collapsed), once occupied by Arthur Wellesley, later 1st Duke of Wellington; the Arsenal (1772); the Accountant-General's Office (*c*. 1778–82); and the old Secretariat (1694; altered).

After 1760 greater security enabled expansion outside the Fort walls to the south, with garden houses built in spacious compounds. These classical colonial bungalows, known as Madras flat-tops, had colonnaded verandahs and were faced in chunam, a form of polished stucco made from burnt seashells. These were a distinctive form of local architecture. Other notable late 18th- and early 19th-century buildings outside the Fort include the old Madras Club (1832), off Mount Road, the Adyar Club (*c*. 1775) overlooking the River Adyar to the south, Brodie Castle (1776; now the College of Carnatic Music), also in Adyar, and Government House (*c*. 1817; now Raj Bhavan), Guindy. A Neo-classical style was also adopted for terraced public buildings, such as Bentinck's Building (*c*. 1800) in the inner city and the Customs Office (*c*. 1800) on First Line Beach, north of the Fort. The most opulent of the Neo-classical buildings is Old Government House, Mount Road, remodelled in 1800 by John Goldingham (*c*. 1765–1849) from an older Portuguese building for Edward, 2nd Lord Clive. Adjacent is the Banqueting Hall (1802; now Rajaji Hall), a monumental basilica with pediments once adorned with martial trophies celebrating British victories and marking a subtle change from mercantile to imperial attitudes in the early 19th century. This growth of imperial self-awareness was expressed in the two great churches of the period, St George's Cathedral (1816) and St Andrew's Kirk (1818–21), which, with its circular plan and dome modelled on St Martin-in-the-Fields, London, by James Gibbs, is the finest Neo-classical church in India. Both were the work of James Caldwell (1770–1863) and his assistant Thomas Fiott de Havilland (1775–1866), with porticos and spires influenced by those of St Martin-in-the-Fields. Indigenous buildings include the Big Mosque (1789) and the Thousand Lights Mosque (1800; altered), Mount Road.

In the later 19th century Madras became a centre of eclectic Indo-Saracenic architecture under the influence of ROBERT FELLOWES CHISHOLM, who arrived in Madras in 1865 and became Principal of the School of Industrial Art. Among an impressive series of Indo-Gothic and Indo-Saracenic buildings are the Presidency College (1865), Senate House (1874–9) and Chepauk Palace (1870; now the Board of Revenue Offices), all by Chisholm and situated along the Marina. The Law Courts (1888–92; see fig.) by J. W. Brassington (*fl* 1886–96), revised by Henry Irwin (1841–1922), are a spectacular work, with an eclectic profusion of Mughal domes, Buddhist stupas and canopied balconies and with the highest stage of the central tower forming a lighthouse. Irwin also designed the Victoria Memorial Hall and Technical Institute (1909; now Victoria Technical Institute Museum) based on the great principal gateway of Fatehpur Sikri; it forms part of a complex in

Madras, Law Courts, by J. W. Brassington and Henry Irwin, 1888–92

Pantheon Road that includes the Government Museum and National Art Gallery, which has a very fine collection of south Indian bronzes, miniatures and other artefacts. Among 20th-century additions, the University Examination Hall (1930) complements the skyline of the waterfront Marina with its distinctive helmet dome and red brick and stone detailing. The city contains the World Headquarters of the Theosophical Society, a group of buildings set in woodlands beside the River Adyar. There have been few post-war developments of any architectural significance.

BIBLIOGRAPHY
Mrs F. Penny: *Fort St George, Madras* (London, 1900)
D. Leighton: *Vicissitudes of Fort St George* (Madras, 1902)
H. D. Love: *Vestiges of Old Madras* (London, 1913)
M. Archer: 'Georgian Splendour in Southern India', *Country Life*, cxxxv (26 March 1964), pp. 728–31
S. Nilsson: *European Architecture in India, 1750–1850* (London, 1968)
M. Archer: 'Madras's Debt to a Father and Son', *Country Life*, cxlviii (17 Dec 1970), pp. 1191–3
P. Davies: *Splendours of the Raj: British Architecture in India, 1660–1947* (London, 1985)
S. Muthiah: *Madras Discovered* (Madras, 1987)

PHILIP DAVIES

2. ART LIFE AND ORGANIZATION. The local, largely Hindu, Dravidian culture that existed before 1638 revolved around religious needs and trading. The principal art forms were religious music and dance, most notably Carnatic music and *Bharatanatyam*, the oldest dance form. Crafts included the production of such religious and secular necessities as carved wooden spoons, clay pots, bronze

icons, frescoes, metalwork, decorative pottery, wooden architectural carvings, temple chariots and stone carvings.

In the late 18th century British settlers and traders started taking an interest in indigenous products and began to commission Western artefacts from Indian craftsmen. Around the mid-19th century Alexander Hunter, a surgeon living in Black Town, began to promote the deteriorating local crafts with his own money. Then, in 1850, the Government College of Arts and Crafts came into existence under the Director of Public Instruction. Renamed the School of Industrial Art, this institution was handed over to the Department of Industries and Commerce; in 1884 ERNEST BINFIELD HAVELL became its superintendent. The foundation of this college was responsible for encouraging such crafts as wood-carving, bronze-casting and painting, combining traditional skills and philosophy with Western ideas to produce a new visual arts tradition. Previously, Indian artists had carved and painted solely for the temples and royal patrons, but now British artists who visited India introduced them to the concept of painting for pleasure.

Two main branches of visual representation evolved in Madras. One was an extension of the Thanjavur school (paintings in gouache on wood covered in gessoed cloth then embellished with gold leaf) and was very Indian in character, with rich outlines and traditional naive styles; the other was influenced by Western techniques. In both cases, as the artists became important they began to express their own ideas, encouraged by their patrons. This marked the beginning of the contemporary art movement in south India. Naturally, other events and schools of art also influenced artists. Roy Chowdhary (1899–1975), the first Indian principal of the College of Art, was from Calcutta, and through him the Bengal School was influential. Since Chowdhary was a sculptor, several artists, such as Dhanapal (b 1919), Janakiram (b 1930), Kunvaraman (b 1937) and T. R. P. Mookiah (b 1937), followed his example. Other sculptors from Madras include Valsan Kolleri (b 1955), S. Nadagopal (b 1946), P. S. Nandan (b 1940) and Rajsekaran Nair (b 1957). K. C. S. PANIKER, another student of Chowdhary, was one of the first artists to use ideas abstracted from Tantric philosophy as a basis for his paintings. A dynamic person who encouraged the artistic movement and promoted abstract paintings, Paniker founded Cholamandal, an artists' settlement on the Coromandel coast, c. 32 km from Madras. In the early 1990s Cholamandal was the home of several artists, including the abstract painters Douglas (b 1951), Gopinath (b 1948) and Baghwan Chavan (b 1959). Akittam Narayan (b 1939), Viswanathan and Jaipal Paniker (b 1938) are all students of Paniker and members of the Progressive Painting Association of Madras who live elsewhere but whose roots can be traced back to Cholamandal. The first artists to paint within an Indian idiom were Srinivasulu, P. L. Narshima Murthy (b 1918) and Gokle; the following generation, who also used traditional iconography as a basis for their art, included Redappa Naidu (b 1932), Santhanaraj (b 1933), Ramanujam (b 1941–73) and Munnuswamy (b 1927). Many artists have been strongly influenced by the Carnatic musical school of Madras, a highly evolved and abstract vocal style, which, coupled with abstract philosophy, influenced and encouraged such artists as Gopinath, Douglas, Achutan Kudalur (b 1945) and P. Srinivasan (b 1951) to paint and sculpt abstract ideas. Other artists, such as R. B. Bhaskaran (b 1942), Nandagopal (b 1946), Janakiraman (b 1930), Muralidharan (b 1954), Santhanaraj and Premalata Hanumantha Seshadhari (b 1947), have been more influenced by folk forms.

In the late 20th century the government-funded Lalit Kala Akademi studios provide a workplace for several artists. The new spirit of industrial patrons, the entrepreneurial spirit of new art galleries, the increased activities of the music *sabha*s (gatherings) that attract people from around the world and the availability of affordable working space have encouraged new artists to use Madras as a base.

BIBLIOGRAPHY
Indian Art since the Early 40s: A Search for Identity, Artists' Handicraft Association of Cholamandal Artists' Village, Progressive Painters' Association (Madras, 1974)
S. Muthiah: *Madras Discovered* (Madras, 1987)

SHARAN APPARAO

Madrasa [Arab.: 'place of study'; also madrassah, medersa; Turk. *medrese*]. Islamic college of jurisprudence, often comprising an open or roofed court surrounded by large rooms for teaching and prayer and small rooms for accommodation.

1. History. 2. Architecture.

1. HISTORY. The functional origins of the madrasa lie in the MOSQUE, for, in addition to its primary role as a place of communal prayer, the mosque traditionally functioned as a centre of instruction and learning. There students would learn the Koran by heart and study the traditions of the Prophet (Arab. *hadith*), by which the proper Muslim life could be determined. When the science of jurisprudence began to develop, it was taught, like the ancillary literary arts, in the mosque. Although the mosque could provide housing for the occasional ascetic or wayfarer, it could not accommodate regular students and teachers; so as early as the 10th century independent lodging establishments were founded next to mosques. These mosque-hostels soon became essential for students and marked an intermediary stage in the evolution of the madrasa. The final stage, which took place in the early 11th century, was the development of the madrasa itself (literally, 'a place of study [of the law]'), an institution devoted exclusively to the teaching of jurisprudence and the housing of students, maintained by a pious endowment (*waqf*), often first administered by the founder and then later by his designated successors. The madrasa was often confounded with the ordinary mosque, because there was little functional differentiation between them: students and faculty might pray there, and sermons were preached in them. In principle, madrasas were distinguished from mosques by their residential units and the occasional presence of the tombs of their founders, which might be located in adjacent mausolea.

The Saljuq vizier Nizam al-Mulk (d 1092) is traditionally credited with being the first founder of madrasas, but this is hardly likely, since four famous examples already existed at Nishapur in north-east Iran in the first half of the 11th century. Nevertheless, his enthusiasm began a brilliant new period in the history of the institution; he founded madrasas throughout the Saljuq lands in Baghdad, Nishapur, Mosul, Herat and Merv, while his rivals and contemporaries followed suit elsewhere, as the madrasa was thought to be a primary weapon in the Sunni arsenal to counter the spread of Shi'ism. The Nizamiyya Madrasa that he founded in Baghdad remained the most notable in the city until the Abbasid caliph al-Mustansir (*reg* 1226–42) founded the Mustansiriyya Madrasa there in 1228 (for illustration *see* BAGHDAD); even so, the prestige of the Nizamiyya continued. The institution of the madrasa spread throughout Anatolia under the Saljuq dynasty of Rum (*reg* 1077–1307) and throughout northern Mesopotamia, Syria and Palestine under the Ayyubid dynasty (*reg* 1169–1260). The Ayyubid sultan Salah al-Din (*reg* 1169–93) had, after Nizam al-Mulk, the greatest reputation for building madrasas. The Ayyubid takeover of Egypt in 1171 from the Shi'ite Fatimid dynasty brought the madrasa there for the first time, although other institutions of learning, notably the 'house of knowledge' (*dār al-ḥikma*), had long been established there for the dissemination of Fatimid propaganda. Once introduced into Egypt, the madrasa flourished to an extraordinary degree under the patronage of the Ayyubids and their successors, the Mamluk sultans (*reg* 1250–1517), who saw it as a pious means of perpetuating their own names and

beliefs. By the mid-15th century there were 73 madrasas in Cairo, set up to instruct according to one or more of the four established schools of Islamic jurisprudence (*madhhab*)—Shafi'i, Maliki, Hanafi and Hanbali; the vast majority of madrasas, however, were established for the teaching of one rite only. The institution was introduced to North Africa under the Hafsid dynasty of Tunis (*reg* 1228–1574) and the Marinid dynasty of Morocco (*reg* 1196–1549), where it enjoyed great success; by contrast the Christian reconquest of Spain was too far advanced by the 13th century to allow madrasas to be founded anywhere outside of Granada, the Nasrid stronghold, where just one was built.

2. ARCHITECTURE. The architectural origins of the madrasa are thought to lie either in Transoxianan Buddhist monasteries or in the domestic architecture of the Iranian province of Khurasan, for such buildings had a central court surrounded by rooms for communal activities and individual accommodation. Excavations near BALKH in Afghanistan revealed remains of 7th- or 8th-century Buddhist monasteries with the four-iwan plan that became typical in later madrasas; no early house plans of the type are known, but later houses in Khurasan exhibit the four-iwan plan. Whatever gave rise to the form, the Saljuq

1. Domed chamber of the Karatay Madrasa, Konya, Turkey, 1251–2

enthusiasm for founding madrasas throughout their realm seems to have been accompanied by the adoption of a quasi-standard plan for all of them. Unfortunately, none of these early structures has survived, with the exception of a ruined madrasa at Khargird in eastern Iran (*see* ISLAMIC ART, §II, 5(i)(b)). Having at least one iwan and inscribed with the name of Nizam al-Mulk, this structure is thought to have been built as a centre of Sunni reaction against the Isma'ili Shi'ites who had effectively propagandized the region.

Over 50 madrasas survive from the period of Saljuq rule in Anatolia; they probably reflect lost architectural models from the Saljuq period in Iran (*see* ISLAMIC ART, figs 42 and 43). Located in cities, towns and villages, these madrasas show how far the institution had pervaded contemporary society. Although no single arrangement predominated, they were generally courtyard structures that provided places for teaching and prayer; each had a mausoleum, an elaborate façade (*see* MUQARNAS, fig. 1), often with one or more minarets, and usually no more than a dozen cells for students. The open court of some reflects the Iranian origins of the plan and its popularity elsewhere; in other cases a large domed chamber replaced the open court (see fig. 1), probably reflecting the contemporary Anatolian interest in domed mosques. Many of the buildings now considered madrasas may have been originally multipurpose institutions that also functioned as observatories, medical schools, hospitals or hospices.

In Syria the earliest surviving madrasa is that of Kumushtakin (Gümüshtekin) in Bosra, founded in 1136–7 (*see* BOSRA, §2). A small structure measuring less than 20×17 m, it has a central domed 'court' from which two lateral iwans and a prayer-hall open. Later examples in Damascus and Aleppo often have an open court but maintain the comparatively small scale, as they were inserted into a pre-existent urban environment. They announce their presence, therefore, with elaborate portals decorated with *muqarnas* hoods and domed mausolea of their founders jutting into the street. The free-standing

Firdaws Madrasa and congregational mosque (1235–7; *see* ISLAMIC ART, fig. 41) in ALEPPO is a notable exception, however, for it has several domed lateral chambers, an external iwan and two independent residential units with small courts, in addition to a large arcaded court with one iwan and a triple-domed prayer-hall.

In Egypt Salah al-Din ordered a madrasa built near the grave of the Imam al-Shafi'i in the Qarafa cemetery; it was completed in 1180, and it included a bath and other conveniences. The Spanish traveller Ibn Jubayr, who saw it three years later, was impressed by its size and splendour, but nothing of its original plan remains. Later rulers preferred to build within the city of Cairo itself; the confiscated Fatimid palaces that stood on either side of the main street provided the land for a series of funerary madrasas for the Ayyubid sultan Salih Najm al-Din Ayyub (1242) and his Mamluk successors. On increasingly narrow and oddly shaped plots, which reflected the rising value of the land, a half dozen splendid madrasas and allied institutions were built by al-Zahir Baybars I (Zahiriyya, 1262–3), Qala'un (1284–5), his son al-Nasir Muhammad (1295–1303) and their successors. Each of these buildings was oriented in two ways: their exteriors, marked by lavish portals, minarets and the mausolea of their founders, related directly to the street-plan, while their interiors—usually comprising paired iwans arranged around a court with subsidiary elements placed wherever space was available—were oriented towards the qibla.

These demands led necessarily to some rather bizarre plans. The largest (150×68 m) and most impressive of the Cairene madrasas is undoubtedly that of Hasan (1356–62), a largely free-standing building fronting on the maidan below the citadel (*see* CAIRO, §III, 9 and ISLAMIC ART, fig. 57). Uniquely, the complex combined madrasas for the four orthodox rites—each having its own court and residential units—with a congregational mosque and a tomb within an immense four-iwan scheme, the main iwan of which was built to surpass the arch of Ktesiphon. The exterior, dominated by the enormous dome under which the sultan's remains were to have been buried, was decorated with an impressive *muqarnas* portal and was to have had four slender minarets, but structural collapse reduced the number to two. The origins of the unusual plan have been sought variously in Saljuq Anatolia or Central Asia, but the most likely source is the slightly earlier mosque and tomb complex of the Mongol sultan Uljaytu at SULTANIYYA (*see* ISLAMIC ART, fig. 48) in northwest Iran. As land to build on became increasingly scarce in Cairo, the madrasas founded by the Circassian Mamluk sultans became smaller. They were wedged into irregular urban sites and often made up for their loss of horizontal space with vertical expansion on several floors. Only in the cemeteries were large plots still available, as can be seen in the madrasa–mausoleum complexes of Faraj b. Barquq (1410) and Qa'itbay (1472–4; *see* CAIRO, §III, 10 and ISLAMIC ART, fig. 58).

The Hafsids built the first madrasas in what is now Tunisia in the mid-13th century; 30 years later the Marinid sultans of Morocco followed suit. The funerary madrasa so common in the rest of the Islamic world, however, was almost unknown in the Maghrib, where the prevalence of

2. Bu 'Inaniya Madrasa, Fez, Morocco, 1350–55

Maliki law prohibited an individual from appointing himself the administrator of a pious endowment. Instead, most madrasas in North Africa were sponsored by the government, for only the ruler could afford the large sums involved, spent primarily to enhance his reign and realm. The almost total loss or transformation of the earliest Tunisian examples is compensated somewhat by the preservation in Morocco of a series of madrasas erected by the Marinids to combat both the heresy of their Almohad predecessors and the decentralizing effects of the Sufi movements that had brought the Marinids to power. Nestled into the dense and irregular urban fabric of Fez, Meknès, Sale and Tlemcen (now in Algeria), these madrasas generally present to the street only a magnificent stucco portal protected by an elaborate wooden awning. Within, a prayer-hall, teaching rooms, student cells and ablution facilities are arranged economically on several floors around an open central court. The interior decoration was formalized: typically, a geometric dado of mosaic faience is surmounted by an inscription band, geometric stucco panels and wooden consoles supporting the roof. The most elaborate example, the Bu 'Inaniya Madrasa of Fez, was erected by the sultan Abu 'Inan Faris between 1350 and 1355 (see fig. 2). Exceptionally, it contains a congregational mosque—indicated by a minaret—as well as a Koran school, water-clock and shops facing the street (*see* ISLAMIC ART, §II, 6(iv)(b)). The Marinid formula for madrasas was so successful that it continued virtually unchanged into the 16th century, when the Ben Yusuf Madrasa was built in Marrakesh.

Although the Saljuq madrasa in Anatolia was formally independent of the mosque, under the Ottomans madrasas became one of the typical dependencies of royal mosques (*see* ISLAMIC ART, §II, 7(i)). The Yıldırım Bayezit Mosque in Bursa (completed 1395) was accompanied by a madrasa and a tomb; within a century such grand complexes in Istanbul as that of Mehmed II and Süleyman (*see* ISTANBUL, §III, 9 and 10 respectively) incorporated several madrasas as well as a medical school, a hospital and other dependencies. These buildings, which were architecturally integrated through planning and design, formed essential parts of the overall architectural conception and graphically represented the nature of religious education in the Ottoman state (*see* KÜLLIYE).

In post-Mongol Iran the madrasa underwent little formal development, although remaining examples are some of the finest and most famous products of Iranian architecture. Typically, they continue to have open rectangular courts, usually with a central pool and two or more iwans flanked by residential cells. Some, such as the Muzaffarid madrasa at Isfahan (1366) and those flanking the Masjid-i Shah (17th century) in the same city, are subsumed within the larger architectural conception of the congregational mosque. Others, such as the madrasa of Ulughbeg (1417–20) at Samarkand, the Ghiyathiyya Madrasa (1444–5) at Khargird (*see* ISLAMIC ART, §II, 5(i)(b)) and the picturesque Madar-i Shah Madrasa (1706–14) at Isfahan, are independent structures.

For further illustrations *see* ISLAMIC ART, figs 59 and 61, and CENTRAL ASIA, fig. 13.

BIBLIOGRAPHY

Enc. Islam/2
C. Terrasse: *Médersas du Maroc* (Paris, 1927)
G. Marçais: *Architecture musulmane d'occident* (Paris, 1954)
K. A. C. Creswell: *The Muslim Architecture of Egypt*, ii (Oxford, 1959)
A. Kuran: *Anadolu medreseleri* [Anatolian madrasas] (Ankara, 1969)
M. Sözen: *Anadolu medreseleri: Selçuklular ve Beylikler devri* [Anatolian madrasas: Saljuq and Beylik period], 2 vols (Istanbul, 1970–72)
G. Makdisi: *The Rise of Colleges, Institutions of Learning in Islam and the West* (Edinburgh, 1981)
M. Meinecke: 'Rückschlüsse auf die Form der seldschukischen Madrasa in Irān', *Damas. Mitt.*, iii (1988), pp. 185–202
R. Hillenbrand: *Islamic Architecture: Form, Function and Meaning* (Edinburgh, 1994), pp. 173–252

JONATHAN M. BLOOM

Madrazo. Spanish family of artists, teachers, critics and museum directors. Its members included some of the most important artists in 19th-century Spain. (1) José de Madrazo y Agudo was a Neo-classical painter who had trained under David in Paris and also in Rome. He remained faithful to the tenets of Neo-classicism in subject-matter and style and became director of both the Real Academia de S Fernando and the Museo del Prado in Madrid. Two of his sons, (2) Federico de Madrazo y Küntz and Luis de Madrazo y Küntz (*b* Madrid, 27 Feb 1825; *d* Madrid, 9 Feb 1897), were also painters. Federico became the foremost portrait painter in Spain as well as holding all the significant posts in the art establishment. José's other sons were the art historian and critic (3) Pedro de Madrazo y Küntz, whose work includes studies of the Prado collection, and the architect Juan de Madrazo y Küntz (*b* Madrid, ?1829; *d* Madrid, 7 March 1880). The painters (4) Raimundo Madrazo Garreta and Ricardo Madrazo Garreta (*b* Madrid, 7 Feb 1852; *d* Madrid, 18 Aug 1917) were sons of Federico. Raimundo, who lived in Paris and New York, became a noted painter of society genre scenes and portraits.

BIBLIOGRAPHY

M. Ossorio y Bernard: *Galería biográfica de artistas españoles del siglo XIX* (Madrid, 1869, 2/1883–4/*R* 1975), pp. 397–406
B. de Pantorba: *Los Madrazo* (Barcelona, 1947)
J. de la Puente: 'Inovación y conservadurismo de los Madrazo', *Goya*, civ (1971), p. 98
M. Ealo de Sa: *José de Madrazo, primer pintor neoclásico de España* (Santander, 1981)
Gran enciclopedia de Madrid (Madrid, 1983) [articles on fam. members by M. Perez Posadas]
E. Arias Anglés: 'Influencias de John Flaxman y Gavin Hamilton en José de Madrazo y nueva lectura de *La muerte de Viriato*', *Archv Esp. A.*, lviii/232 (1985), pp. 351–62
Los Madrazo: Una familia de artistas (exh. cat., Madrid, Mus. Mun., 1985)

OSCAR E. VÁZQUEZ

(1) José de Madrazo y Agudo (*b* Santander, 22 April 1781; *d* Madrid, 8 May 1859). He studied in Madrid with the painters Cosme de Acuña and Gregorio Ferro, obtaining in 1803 a scholarship to study in Paris and Rome. He stayed in Paris for two and a half years, becoming one of the favourite pupils of Jacques-Louis David, who particularly admired his strictly Neo-classical *Christ in the House of Ananias* (*c*. 1805; Madrid, Prado). Madrazo moved *c*. 1806 to Rome, where he completed his training. His artistic personality was already formed, and he achieved great success with works such as the *Death of Viriatus, Leader of the Lusitanians* (Madrid, Prado) and the *Dispute between the Greeks and the Trojans over the Body of Patrocles*, designed for the gallery of the Palazzo del Quirinale in

Rome (*in situ*; preparatory drawing Madrid, Prado). He also painted portraits of several famous Italians, such as the sculptor *Antonio Canova* and the painter *Tommaso Camuccini*, and of the exiled Spanish monarchs *Charles IV* and *Maria Luisa*. These last works ensured him election as a member of the Spanish Academia de S Lucas.

On the Napoleonic invasion of Spain, Madrazo lost his scholarship and was briefly imprisoned in the Castel Sant'Angelo for refusing to recognize Joseph Bonaparte as king. With the restoration of Ferdinand VII to the Spanish throne, however, the scholarship was re-established and in 1814, when the 'old monarchs' Charles and Maria Luisa arrived in Rome, they made Madrazo painter to their Royal Chamber. In 1816 Ferdinand VII elected Madrazo painter to his own Royal Chamber and in 1818, when Madrazo returned to Spain, he obtained an important teaching position (Director del Colorido) at the Real Academia de S Fernando. In the same year he painted an equestrian portrait of *King Ferdinand VII* (Madrid, Mus. Romántico). After returning briefly to Rome until the death of the 'old monarchs' in 1819, Madrazo settled for good in Madrid. Because of his marriage, while in Rome, to Isabel Küntz, an Italian woman of noble Silesian origin and powerful social connections, Madrazo had been able to meet many of the most famous artists who passed through Rome, including the Germans Friedrich Overbeck, Peter von Cornelius and Johann Christian Reinhart. On his return to Spain, Madrazo attempted to bring the liberating influence of his wider European experience to bear on the teaching and organization of art in Spain.

At the Real Academia de S Fernando, where Madrazo became director in 1838, he introduced study from the live model and brought a considered programme of reform to bear on the old-fashioned teaching methods still in force there. His efforts as director of the Museo del Prado, from 1838 to 1851, were equally effective: he reorganized the collection, broadening it and laying the foundations for its future development. Madrazo also worked to encourage the progress of the arts in Spain through his post as painter to the court. Grasping the importance of the new technique of lithography, he went to Paris in 1825, with the King's agreement, to study this method of printmaking and, on his return to Madrid, founded the Real Establecimiento Litográfico. His own principal work in this medium was the important *Colección litográfica de cuadros del Rey de España, el Sr. D. Fernando VII*, published in Paris (1826–37). Madrazo also built up a valuable library and an important collection of older paintings.

Madrazo painted historical, religious and allegorical scenes and portraits, all regarded at that time as elevated genres, and generally adhered in style to the Neo-classicism imbibed under David. Among his history paintings are *Cincinnatus Called before the Supreme Power* and the *Grand Captain's Assault on Montefrío*. Notable among his religious works is the *Heart of Jesus with a Glory of Angels*, for the church of Las Salesas in Madrid (*in situ*). Of his allegorical paintings, *Dawn Conquering Night*, commissioned by Queen Maria Christina, and the *Triumph of Divine Love over Profane Love* are outstanding. Madrazo was also an exceptional portrait painter, showing restraint and elegance, and particular strength in drawing. His style

José de Madrazo y Agudo: *Self-portrait*, oil on panel, 730×560 mm, 1830–35 (Madrid, Museo del Prado)

is especially close to that of David in the portrait of *Don Manuel García de la Prada* (Madrid, Real Acad. S. Fernando). His portraits of women, such as that of *Queen Maria Christina*, are also excellent. Madrazo's style gradually evolved, however, from strict Neo-classicism, in the manner of David, towards a form of Romantic classicism. Among male portraits, that of the *Conde de Vilches* (1827; Madrid, Prado) and the *Self-portrait* (1830–35; Madrid, Prado; see fig.) show the artist's move towards Romanticism.

BIBLIOGRAPHY

B. de Pantorba: 'Don José de Madrazo', *A. Esp.*, xvi (1947)
—: *Los Madrazo* (Barcelona, 1947)
M. Ealo de Sa: *José de Madrazo, primer pintor neoclásico de España* (Santander, 1981)
E. Arias Anglés: 'Influencias de John Flaxman y Gavin Hamilton en José de Madrazo y nueva lectura de *La muerte de Viriato*', *Archv Esp. A.*, lviii/232 (1985), pp. 351–621
Los Madrazo: Una familia de artistas (exh. cat., Madrid, Mus. Mun., 1985), pp. 351–62

ENRIQUE ARIAS ANGLÉS

(2) Federico de Madrazo y Küntz (*b* Rome, 9 Feb 1815; *d* Madrid, 10 June 1894). Son of (1) José de Madrazo y Agudo. In 1818 the family returned from Rome to Madrid, where Federico studied painting under his father and the other leading Spanish Neo-classical painters Juan Antonio de Ribera and José Aparicio. Federico's *Continence of Scipio* (1831; Madrid, Real Acad. S Fernando Mus.) gained him the status of academician. It shows the French Neo-classical traditions instilled in him at the Madrid Academia by his professors, all pupils of Jacques-Louis David and Jean-Auguste-Dominique Ingres. Federico won immediate popularity in court circles with his sympathetic rendering of Ferdinand VII in the *King's Illness* (1832; Madrid, Patrm. N.), and that same year (1832) he was named Pintor Supernumerario de Cámara.

In 1833 Madrazo made his first trip to Paris to study the collections in the Louvre. He became acquainted with Ingres, who played a decisive role in the formation of his technique and style and whose portrait he painted (1833; New York, Hisp. Soc. America). He also became acquainted with and later painted the portrait of *Baron Isidore-Justín-Severin Taylor* (1837; Versailles, Château). Madrazo returned to Madrid in late 1833 to receive the medal of the Order of Isabel the Catholic and assume the post of Segundo Pintor de Cámara. His collaboration with the writer-critic Eugenio de Ochoa (1815–72) and their admiration for Parisian art journals such as *L'Artiste* led to the production of the key Spanish romantic journal, *El Artista* (1835–6). Contributors included artists and writers such as Valentín Carderera y Solano, Jenaro Pérez Villaamil and Federico's brother, the critic and lawyer (3) Pedro de Madrazo y Küntz. Federico contributed to this and other journals, such as *Semanario pintoresco español* and *El Panorama*, submitting lithographs as well as various articles on painting, restoration and essays in defence of the colourists Velázquez and Rubens.

Madrazo was in Paris again between 1837 and 1839, with hopes of finding patrons outside Madrid, where a virtual monopoly existed over court circle commissions (a monopoly later exercised by Madrazo himself). He was officially introduced into Parisian court circles through Baron Taylor and the writer Prosper Merimée (1803–70). His first major international success came with *Godofredo of Bouillon Proclaimed King of Jerusalem* (1837; Paris, Louvre), *Hugh Capet Proclaimed King* and *Charlemagne* (both 1838; Versailles, Château), commissioned by Louis-Philippe through Baron Taylor; they exemplify Madrazo's assimilation of French Romantic, medievalizing trends. In 1839 Federico travelled to Italy, visiting Milan, Florence, Perugia and Rome, where he met Ingres again and was introduced to one of the leaders of the German Nazarenes, Friedrich Overbeck. Madrazo's *Three Marys at the Sepulchre* (1842; Seville, Alcázar), with its devotional feeling, clarity of composition and colour, as well as emphasis on line and calm expressive quality (following the example of Ingres), can be linked with the ideas of the German Nazarenes whose aesthetic he helped to bring to Madrid.

In Madrid by 1842 Madrazo had again collaborated with Eugenio de Ochoa, on the art journal *En renacimiento* (1847), which promoted the notion of the 'regeneration' of a Spanish school of painting. Madrazo felt this regeneration would be accomplished through the expansion of the academic system. This was vigorously disputed by Federico's life-long rival, the history painter José Galofré, who believed an artistic revival could best be achieved through the deregulation, if not abolition, of the academic system, of which Madrazo was the leading representative. Madrazo and Galofré argued these issues through numerous articles and printed speeches made to the academies and legislative courts between 1850 and 1855.

Madrazo is best known for his highly polished, flattering portraits of the leading figures of Madrilene society around the mid-19th century. From the time of his return to Madrid in 1842 until his death, he executed over 600 portraits of the most prominent personalities of Isabelline society (including over 28 of Queen Isabella II herself). Other portraits were those of the leading bankers and industrialists (*José Güell*, 1858, Madrid, Bib. N.; *Marqués de Alcañices*, 1863, Madrid, priv. col.; *Nazario Carriquiri*, *c.* 1844, Madrid, priv. col.), as well as numerous artists and writers (*Carolina Coronado*, *c.* 1855, Madrid, Casón Buen Retiro; *Gertrudis Gómez de Avellaneda*, 1857, Madrid, Mus. Lázaro Galdiano; *Valentín Carderera y Solano*, 1833, Huesca, Mus. Huesca; *Mariano Fortuny y Madrazo*, 1867, Barcelona, Mus. A. Mod.; and *Eduardo Rosales Martínez*, 1867, Madrid, Casón Buen Retiro). Among his most dazzling works, however, are those of the aristocracy, such as the famous portrait of *Amalia de Llano y Dotres*, *Condesa de Vilches* (1853; Madrid, Casón Buen Retiro; see fig.), those of the *Duques de Medinaceli* (1854 and 1860; Madrid, priv. col.) and that of the *Duquesa de Fernán Núñez* (1854; Madrid, priv. col.). In all of these works the sitters are either standing or casually seated, and clothed in an array of fashions and regional costumes in richly coloured fabrics enhanced by highly reflective surfaces.

By 1867 Madrazo had become virtual dictator of the most important and influential art institutions and circles in Spain: Primer Pintor de Cámara (1857); Director of the Museo del Prado (1860); Professor of Colour and Painting at the Escuela Superior de Pintura, Escultura y Grabado,

Federico de Madrazo y Küntz: *Amalia de Llano y Dotres, Condesa de Vilches*, oil on canvas, 1.26×0.89 m, 1853 (Madrid, Casón de Buen Retiro)

Madrid (1863); and in 1866 the Director of the Real Academia de Bellas Artes de S Fernando. These posts, along with numerous commissions from prestigious personalities, made him the most sought-after and wealthiest of artists in 19th-century Spain. He received many awards, honorary academic memberships and various knighted orders from Milan and Rome, Belgium, France and Portugal.

BIBLIOGRAPHY

M. Ossorio y Bernard: *Galería biográfica de artistas españoles del siglo XIX* (Madrid, 1869 2/1883/*R* 1975), pp. 397–406

M. de Madrazo López: *Federico de Madrazo*, 2 vols (Madrid, 1921) [by Federico's grandson]

M. Herrero García: 'Un discurso de Madrazo sobre el arte religioso', *A. Esp.*, xiv (1942–3), pp. 13–14

M. de Madrazo López: *Historia del Museo del Prado, 1818–68* (Madrid, 1945) [incl. letters and docs]

B. de Pantorba: *Los Madrazo* (Barcelona, 1947)

C. González López: 'Federico de Madrazo y Küntz en el Paris romántico', *Estud. Pro A.*, iv (1975), pp. 28–36

——: 'El viaje de Federico de Madrazo a Alemania en 1853', *Rev. Ideas Estét.*, xxv/139 (1977), pp. 215–77

——: *Federico Madrazo y Küntz* (Barcelona, 1981)

M. E. Gómez-Moreno: *Pintura y escultura españolas del siglo xix*, xxxv of *Summa Artis* (Madrid, 1993), pp. 302–13

OSCAR E. VÁZQUEZ

(3) Pedro de Madrazo y Küntz (*b* Rome, 11 Oct 1816; *d* Madrid, 20 Aug 1898). Son of (1) José de Madrazo y Agudo. His activity covers a large part of the 19th century and had a considerable influence on the artistic world of Madrid. Having been exposed to painting from birth, he displayed an unusual erudition for his time in regard to both past and present art. After taking a law degree in Spain he moved to Paris, where he studied contemporary artistic trends and published several articles of criticism. He returned to Madrid in 1840 and, having earlier contributed to *El artista* (1835–6; *see* (2) above), he began writing for such publications as *El laberinto*, *El español* and *No me olvides*. Shortly thereafter, he was assigned the writing of the catalogue of the Museo del Prado in Madrid, the first edition of which appeared in 1843 and was followed by numerous other editions. Continuing his study of the Prado collection, in 1872 he published a volume on the Spanish and Italian schools in the *Catalogo descriptivo e histórico del Museo del Prado*. His work as a critic and archaeologist formed the basis of his contributions to the multi-volumed, multi-author works *Recuerdos y bellezas de España* (12 vols, Barcelona, 1839–65), *Monumentos arquitectónicos de España* (89 vols, Barcelona, 1884–92) and *España: Sus monumentos y su arte* (27 vols, Barcelona, 1884–92). Some of his best archaeological works date from the 1870s onwards when he published studies on silverwork, tapestries and enamel work. During those years he also contributed to numerous magazines, notably *La ilustración española y americana*. In 1884 in Barcelona he published the abundantly documented *Viaje artístico de tres siglos por las colecciones de cuadros de los reyes de España* and from 1895 to his death he was Director of the newly opened Museo de Arte Moderno in Madrid.

WRITINGS

Catalogo de los cuadros del Real Museo de Pintura y Escultura de S.M. (Madrid, 1843, 11/1893)

Catalogo descriptivo e histórico del Museo del Prado: Escuelas italianas y española (Madrid, 1872)

Viaje artístico de tres siglos por las colecciones de cuadros de los reyes de España (Barcelona, 1884)

Regular contributions to *El Artista* (1835–6), *El Español*, *El Laberinto*, *La ilustración española y americana* and *No me olvides*

BIBLIOGRAPHY

J. A. Gaya Nuño: *Historia de la crítica de arte en España* (Madrid, 1975)

M. DOLORES JIMÉNEZ-BLANCO

(4) Raimundo Madrazo Garreta (*b* Rome, 24 June 1841; *d* Versailles, 15 Sept 1920). Son of (2) Federico de Madrazo y Küntz. Because of his ability and training with his father, Federico, in the Real Academia de S Fernando in Madrid and with Léon Cogniet in Paris, he seemed destined to continue the family tradition of academic painting. However, due to the influence of the Belgian Alfred Stevens, of his brother-in-law, Mariano José Bernardo Fortuny y Marsal, and the Parisian environment, he exchanged dry historical painting (e.g. *Arrival in Spain of the Body of the Apostle St James*, 1858, and *Ataulfo*, 1860) for the preciousness of the *tableautin*, the small, intimate genre painting. He lived in Paris and New York and became so remote from Spanish artistic life that he and Fortuny y Marsal were the only Spanish artists not to participate in any national exhibition, and because of this the Spanish state never directly acquired their works. In 1882, with Giuseppe De Nittis, Stevens and the gallery owner Georges Petit, he co-founded the Exposition Internationale de Peinture, designed to promote foreign artists in Paris. Madrazo Garreta's most characteristic works are the female portrait and the witty and elegant genre painting, with soft, delicate tones and suggestive poses. The influence of the Rococo and of Japanese art is reflected in his painting, which expresses an exquisite aristocratic or bourgeois ideal, the illusion of a refined, sensual and superficial life. Consequently, his works are also described as representing the 'Parisian seraglio'. American collectors paid high prices for his paintings, for example Alexander Turney Stewart bought *Lady with a Parrot*; *Carnival Festival* (1878) was purchased by L. Wolfe; and *Girls at the Window* (1875) was bought by J. W. Vanderbilt, the last two now being in the Metropolitan Museum of Art, New York. His portraits were better received in Spain (e.g. the *Duquesa de Alba*, 1881; Madrid, Pal. Liria, Col. Casa Alba), although because of collectors such as Ramón de Errazu (*d* 1909), the Museo del Prado has a good number of his paintings (e.g. *After the Bath*).

JESÚS GUTIÉRREZ BURÓN

Madrazo, Mariano Fortuny y. *See* FORTUNY, (2).

Madrid. Capital and largest city of Spain, with a population in its metropolitan area of *c.* 3.8 million. It is the highest capital in Europe (*c.* 640 m) and is situated in central Spain, beside the Manzanares River and surrounded by a plateau.

I. History and urban development. II. Art life and organization. III. Centre of production. IV. Buildings.

I. History and urban development.

1. Before 1734. 2. 1734 and after.

1. BEFORE 1734. Although Madrid's earliest historians identified the Spanish capital with Ptolemy's 'Mantua Carpetana', the city actually owes its origins to the Muslim occupation of Spain (711–1492). Around 875 the Emir of Córdoba, Muhammad I, chose a strategic site, formed by

1. Madrid, Plaza de la Villa, with Casas Consistoriales, 1630–c. 1700

a rocky spur dominating the little river of Manzanares to the west and sloping sharply away to the south, in order to build a fortress from which he attempted to block the Christian advance towards the north of the Tagus valley. Following the usual layout of Muslim cities, each half of the town—the *alcazaba* to the north, dominated by the Alcázar, and the *medina* (the residential and market neighbourhood) to the south—had its own town wall; some remaining fragments of these can still be seen near the church of la Nuestra Señora de Almudena. After the reconquest of the city *c.* 1090, the city wall was extended towards the south-east to protect the new residential neighbourhoods there. It was still a defensive military structure, as was made clear in the *fuero* proclamation of 1202 (a franchise to enable people to settle there after the reconquest), until the Almohad incursions were stopped after the Battle of Las Navas de Tolosa (1212). From the end of the 13th century a Christian settlement divided into some ten parishes spread out towards the north and east as far as the Puerta del Sol, while at the same time various outlying suburbs grew up around the convents. The regular layout of such streets as the Calle de la Platería clearly

distinguished these new neighbourhoods from the original Muslim town with its winding lanes; indeed the *morería* (Moorish quarter) is still to be found there.

As early as the 14th and 15th centuries Madrid was receiving privileged treatment from the ruling Trastámara dynasty. They modified the Alcázar and made it one of their favourite residences, attracting a courtly circle of scholars and officials (*see also* §IV, 2 below). Similarly, Henry IV (*reg* 1451–77) initiated an attempt to develop commercial activity by creating a 'free market' on the Campo del Rey opposite the palace and by creating a number of market squares within the ramparts. He was responsible for the first regular layout of the Plaza S Salvador, where the church of that name was used for the meetings of the town council. The square later became the Plaza de la Villa, dominated by the Casas Consistoriales (City Hall) built between 1630 and the end of the century (see fig. 1). Henry also founded the royal monastery of S Jerónimo, which formed the eastern starting-point for the royal processions into the city, and hence also marked the beginning of the city's first main east–west axis. The greatest contribution of the Catholic monarchs Ferdinand

2. Madrid, Plaza Mayor, by Juan Gómez de Mora, 1617–19; rebuilt by Juan de Villanueva, from 1791

II and Isabella in the late 15th and early 16th centuries was the decision to cobble the streets and to create the opening formed by the long Calle de la Almundena in order to improve access to the Alcázar district.

From the reign of Charles V (*reg* 1517–56), who ordered the conversion of the Alcázar (*see also* HABSBURG, §I (5) and §IV, 2 below), Madrid underwent a spectacular population explosion. From 4060 inhabitants in 1530, the city grew by 1558 to 20,000, living in 3000 houses. The council's hesitation when faced with the king's demands for demolition in order to ease the circulation of traffic (e.g. of the Puerta de Guadalajara in 1538) was representative of the primacy that the municipality enjoyed over the monarchy in matters of urban development, but its agreement was representative of the way in which, from then on, bursts of rapid development coincided with periods when the sovereign was resident in Madrid. The city's central position, close to the site where the Escorial was being built (*see* ESCORIAL, §2), as well as the good condition of the palace, both contributed to the *capitalidad* of May 1561. This decision to establish the court in Madrid—which initially was by no means regarded as permanent—led to an urban explosion that did not stabilize until *c.* 1630; this at a time when other Spanish cities were already feeling the effect of the great crises of the 17th century, including a plague epidemic and loss of power in Europe. In 1598 Madrid had 60,000 inhabitants living in 8000 dwellings; in 1621 it had almost 150,000, and a new city wall had to be added in 1625 to replace that built in 1567.

Owing to the constraints of the *regalia deaposento* (a royal prerogative by which a proportion of the houses having more than one storey was requisitioned for the needs of the court), grandiose projects existed side by side with anarchic house-building until the end of the 16th century. An edict of 1565 was intended to provide *casas de aposento* (lodging houses) built on identical plans and exempt from royal privilege. As a result, and with a few exceptions, such as the palace of the Duques de Uceda (now the Consejo de Estado, built after 1613 to plans by Francisco de Mora) or that of the Duque de Pastrana (*c.* 1670), or a few Renaissance mansions such as the Casa del Campo or the Casa de las Siete Chimeneas (16th century; attributed to Juan de Herrera; largely reconstructed), the presence of the court in Madrid did not lead to the construction of a significant number of aristocratic residences until the 18th century. The most common type of mansion at this time was simply formed by a group of several adjoining houses grouped together by a single great gate. Nevertheless, Madrid was not slow to acquire all the administrative organizations corresponding to its status as capital city: a town planning council (Junta de Urbanismo; 1580s), a police board (1590) and a city architect (1592). The water supply was one of Madrid's urban planning successes, symbolized by idealistic plans to straighten the River Manzanares and the building of large numbers of public fountains from 1618 onwards. Other grandiose planning schemes, however, such as the building of monumental city gates or the construction of a cathedral near the palace, had to be abandoned because of economic difficulties. Under the direction of JUAN DE HERRERA, principal architect to Philip II, Madrid acquired the features that were to form the strongest points of its urban layout for over a century: the widening of the Calle Mayor, the construction (1580s) of the Puente de Segovia and the Calle de Segovia, and the design of the Plaza Mayor.

The Plaza Mayor was built in 1617–19 by Juan Gómez de Mora to plans by himself, his uncle Francisco de Mora (*see* MORA (i), (1) and (2)) and Herrera. Restored after the fires of 1631, 1672 and 1791, it played a vital role in Madrid's subsequent urban development, just as its equivalent did in almost every Spanish city. This was the centre for fairs, celebrations and trade, and the brick and stone Renaissance structure of the original Casa Panadería on the north side, replacing a bakery of 1590, set the tone for the 'post-Escorial' style of the whole; the square measures 121×85 m and its balconied houses stand over an arcaded passage running around the sides, lined with shops and bars. The present structure is the work of Juan de Villanueva (*see* VILLANUEVA, (2)), who rebuilt it after the fire of 1790 (see fig. 2). Madrid's other city squares, such as the Plaza de la Provincia opposite the Cárcel de Corte (1629; designed by Juan Gómez de Mora; now the Ministerio de Asuntos Exteriores), were born out of the natural meeting-points of the ancient roads leading into the city. Throughout the 17th century the city spread out along these same routes, particularly to the south-east towards the new Palacio del Buen Retiro (*see* §IV, 1 below) and the sanctuary of Atocha, or to the north around the Conde-Duque barracks (1717; by PEDRO DE RIBERA). Despite the creation of the Plaza Mayor and the regular

layout given to the Plaza del Palacio in 1675, however, the Madrid of the Habsburgs had neither the cathedral nor the great public or private buildings appropriate to its status as capital city, and it only acquired such status, in urban planning terms, at the end of the 18th century.

BIBLIOGRAPHY

A. Fernández de los Ríos: *Guía de Madrid* (Madrid, 1876/R 1976)
A. Gómez Iglesias: *Libros de acuerdos del Concejo madrileño, 1464–1600*, i (Madrid, 1932); ii (Madrid, 1970)
M. Molina Campuzano: *Planos de Madrid de los siglos XVII y XVIII* (Madrid, 1960)
Madrid hasta 1875: Testimonios de su historia (exh. cat., ed. M. Agulló y Cobo; Madrid, Mus. Mun., 1980)
V. Tovar Martín: *Arquitectura madrileña del siglo XVII* (Madrid, 1983)
A. Alvar Ezquerra: *Felipe II: La corte y Madrid en 1561* (Madrid, 1985)

VÉRONIQUE GERARD-POWELL

2. 1734 AND AFTER. In 1734 the royal palace was destroyed by fire. Philip V (*see* BOURBON, §II(1)), with whom palace-building was a habit, seized the opportunity to create a vast new edifice in his wife's Italian taste (*see* §IV, 2 below). The project generated more work in its turn: the recarving of the medieval street plan surrounding the palace site into the rational lines and right angles favoured by an enlightened age (see fig. 3). The triumph of reason in 18th-century Madrid is best represented, however, in the area east of El Buen Retiro, remodelled by VENTURA RODRÍGUEZ and Juan de Villanueva according to the civilized vision of Spain's enlightened despot, Charles III (*reg* 1759–88; *see* BOURBON, §II(4)), and incorporating rigidly intersecting avenues, classically inspired fountains, the triumphal arch of the Puerta de Alcalá (1764–78; for illustration *see* SABBATINI, FRANCESCO) and the Museo del Prado itself (1787), originally intended as

3. *View of Madrid, Calle de Atocha* by Antonio Joli, oil on canvas, 0.77×1.18 m, 1750 (Madrid, Palacio Liria, Colección Casa de Alba)

'a temple of useful knowledge' and in which the Academia de Ciencias was housed (*see* VILLANUEVA, (2), fig. 1).

Enlightened rule was unpopular in Madrid. Government campaigns for law and order and cleaner streets were resented as intrusive and provoked riots in 1766. The next king, Charles IV (*reg* 1789–1808; *see* BOURBON, §II(6)), continued policies of 'modernization' with less efficiency. The detested chief minister from 1792, MANUEL GODOY, appeared to defer excessively to revolutionary France. The riots of March 1808 were directed against the King and his minister in favour of the conservative heir, now proclaimed as Ferdinand VII. He ruled from March to May, but the main effect of the riots was to provide a pretext for the invasion of Spain and the reimposition of rational despotism under an intruded king, Joseph Bonaparte (*reg* 1808–13; *see* BONAPARTE, (3)). On 2 May 1808 the last popular riots against progressive reform were crushed by French soldiers. Goya's heroic and horrific canvases—the *Second of May 1808* and *Third of May 1808* (both 1808; Madrid, Prado; for illustration of the latter *see* GOYA, FRANCISCO DE, fig. 4), depicting respectively the rising in the streets and the execution of insurgents— helped to create a legend that these riots were the start of a national movement of resistance to French rule (*see also* GOYA, FRANCISCO DE, §3); the outcome represented the return of enlightened despotism with a vengeance.

Madrid bore the scars in its streets: houses of religion disappeared to make way for open squares; blocks were demolished to make the city easier to police. Some new squares were laid out, however, including those of Santa Catalina, Santa Ana, San Martín and San Ildesfonso, chiefly under the direction of the municipal architect Antonio López Aguado (1764–1840), following the old-fashioned but Francophile principles of Silvestre Pérez (1767–1825). At the beginning of the century Madrid had *c.* 175,000 people in 557 blocks of buildings; by 1831 the population had risen to 211,127, but the number of blocks had not yet recovered to the level preceding Bonaparte's reforms. When he was driven from power in 1813 by a combination of provincial resistance and English intervention, the ferocity of the reaction under the restored Ferdinand VII, who was to rule again until 1833, permanently changed the politics of Madrid. Henceforth popular sympathies were always aligned with progressive causes against the reactionary forces, who fought bitter rearguard actions through all the many political revolutions of 19th- and 20th-century Spain. In part, perhaps, the realignment was the result of long-term changes in society. The fast-growing population included a genuine working class, unbeholden to such traditional structures of authority as parishes and guilds. At the same time, their continued dependence on a local clientele gave workers a vested interest in the progressives' ideal of centralized government.

The advocates of progress clawed their way back into power in the early 1830s, with two major consequences for the topography of Madrid. The obliteration of the religious houses, which Joseph Bonaparte had begun, was completed by the policies of the secularist finance minister, Juan Álvarez Mendizábal (1790–1853), in 1835–6. The site of the decayed Palacio del Buen Retiro (*see* §IV, 1 below) became a municipal park—an urban reminder of a civilized

empire whose demise was officially acknowledged when the independence of Spain's former American colonies was recognized from 1836 onwards. Typical of the projects of this era was the creation of the majestic Plaza de Oriente out of a maze of old streets, begun by López Aguado and completed in the 1840s. In 1846 the town councillor Ramón Mesonero Romanez (1803–82), an enthusiast for straight streets, covered markets and shopping arcades, proposed radical remodelling that remained largely unrealized but influential for the rest of the century. Although there were new working-class districts further out, no part of Madrid better captures the expansive character of the second half of the 19th century than the costly grid of high-bourgeois streets known as the Salamanca district. The speculator who laid it out, on a vast and valuable site to the north-east of the Puerta de Alcalá, was JOSÉ SALAMANCA. The many stories told about him were sparks struck from his flashy way of life: his shady deals and rickety finances, which ended in his ruin, all seemed to sum up the effects of the 'gold fever' that was blamed for diverting capital from industrial investment into unproductive speculation; the considerable collection of paintings he had managed to acquire had to be sold in his own lifetime to help with his financial problems.

In 1854 a revolutionary mob burnt down Salamanca's own house. On the whole, however, the revolutionary interventions of the Madrid populace in the 19th century were on behalf of causes sponsored by the bourgeoisie. In 1854, for instance, the people endured four bloody days on the barricades in support of a coup by liberal generals. In 1868 they turned out to cheer a change of dynasty engineered by an alliance of professional men. Although there was a flurry of anarchist outrage in the 1860s, political change was made not in the streets but on the parade ground and in the cafés and clubs. The biggest project of the decade, the Biblioteca Nacional (*see* SPAIN, fig. 9), begun in 1866 by Francisco Jareño y Alarcón, was not completed until 1892 by Antonio Ruíz de Salces (1820–94). From 1875 until 1923 Spain experienced an unwontedly long period of constitutional stability. For much of it, urban planning in Madrid was able to make some show of keeping up with the increase of population. The city acquired its splendid markets, monuments of cast-iron engineering. The model for these was the Mercado de la Cebeda (1870–75), designed by Agustín Peró to be an irregular glass triangle erected on columns of English cast iron, enclosing over 6000 sq. m around a central fountain. The university city was laid out from 1927 on the old Moncloa estate to the west of Madrid, under the direction of Manuel López Otero (1885–1962). The Gran Vía, driven through the slums of the old town in 1910–36 under the direction of José López Sallaberri (*d* 1927), created the impressive view from the Plaza de Cibeles, which contributes so much to modern Madrid's European look (see fig. 4). Domestic electricity arrived, delayed by scandals, in 1915.

The working-class slums attracted few such conveniences. The refuse collection service in the 1920s reached only a third of the city, and the slum-dwellers were stricken by typhoid. Artisans easily outnumbered the genuine industrial proletariat until electrification and the economic opportunities of neutrality in World War I began to make

4. Madrid, view towards the Gran Vía from Plaza de Cibeles

Madrid's economy more productive. Industrial action, however, was replacing violence as Madrid's proverbial vice. Even the advent of the Second Republic in 1931 seemed only to release strikers' inhibitions rather than galvanize their loyalties, which were only aroused by the Civil War (1936–9). Madrid's citizens resisted the Nationalists with exemplary tenacity; paradoxically, however, the victory of the party of centralization favoured the prosperity and growth of the capital.

The rule of General Franco from 1939 to 1975 was disastrous for the environment. Subsidized heavy industry clouded the air with pollutants; trees were uprooted for traffic in the Paseo de La Castellana and the Calle Velázquez; banks replaced private villas on the best sites. Resources and demand nevertheless built up as wealth and population grew, and when democracy returned Madrid was ready for a cultural renaissance. From 1978 this was heavily subsidized from the cultural budget of the autonomous regional government established under the new constitution. In the 1980s programmes were launched to rehabilitate and restore old buildings and, in new inner-city housing projects, to evoke the distinctive classical style devised for 17th-century Madrid by Juan Gómez de Mora.

BIBLIOGRAPHY

F. Chueca Goitia: *Arte de España: Madrid y reales sitios* (Barcelona, 1958), pp. 39–108
P. N. Palacio: *Arquitectura y arquitectos madrileños del siglo XIX* (Madrid, 1973)
R. Carr: *Spain, 1808–1939* (Oxford, 1975)
E. Ruiz Palomeque: *Ordenación y transformaciones del casco antiguo madrileño durante los siglos XIX y XX* (Madrid, 1976)
M. Agulló y Cobo, ed.: *Madrid: Testimonios de su historia hasta 1875* (Madrid, 1980)
D. R. Ringrose: *Madrid and the Spanish Economy, 1560–1850* (Berkeley, 1983)
R. Gómez de la Serna: *Elucidario de Madrid* (Madrid, 1988)
H. Thomas: *Madrid: A Traveller's Companion* (London, 1988)

FELIPE FERNÁNDEZ-ARMESTO

II. Art life and organization.

1. Before 1700. 2. 1700 and after.

1. BEFORE 1700. During the medieval period the art life of Madrid was largely a reflection of events in the more dominant Toledo, but Philip II's decision in 1561 to establish his court in Madrid was decisive for its future. The population increased, and the nobility, high officials, the clergy, religious orders and nascent bourgeoisie gathered around the court and its institutions. The city began to attract numerous foreigners and in a short time had consolidated itself as Spain's political and cultural centre, although in religious matters it continued to be dependent on the archdiocese of Toledo. The formation of a distinctive 'school' of art in Madrid originated with Philip II's building of the Escorial and his improvements to other royal palaces, whose decoration would employ the services of the leading artists of the time (*see* ESCORIAL and §IV, 2 below). The dominance of artists from Toledo gave way at this point to those trained in Italy such as GASPAR BECERRA and JUAN FERNÁNDEZ DE NAVARRETE; the early deaths of both these painters, however, interrupted the King's plans, and Italian artists were brought in to the Escorial. By the late 16th century the monastery was a centre for the most recent developments in art and collecting; for his private quarters at the palace the King

collected works by such artists as Hieronymus Bosch and Titian, which to his mind equalled the official paintings for the monastery, such as those by Federico Zuccaro.

Outside the court, artistic life was more traditionally organized, with apprentices in workshops and studios under the instruction of a master. The medieval guilds and confraternities survived as auxiliary religious and technical institutions until the 18th century; painters' guilds were regulated by the *ordenanzas municipales* (1543). In 1603 an academy—modelled on those of Florence and Rome—was founded on the initiative of artists at the Escorial, ostensibly to protect the liberal status of painting and its scientific teaching, but in practice probably only to organize life drawing. The academy's short life was discussed in *Diálogos de la pintura* (Madrid, 1633) by Vicente Carducho, who, together with his contemporaries, was concerned less with the scientific nature of art than with the economic benefits that would accrue from an elevation in its status; similar arguments were put forward on behalf of the sculptors by Pedro Alonso de los Ríos in 1692. A second attempt to found a lasting academy was made by painters in 1620, who argued to Philip IV that such an establishment would prevent work being given to foreign artists.

Before the 17th century art in Madrid, as in the rest of Spain, was basically religious in character, but the king and the aristocracy imported secular Flemish and Italian works, and these were of great importance for the aesthetic training of Madrid artists of the Baroque period; the general diversification of genres that characterized painting in 17th-century Europe also occurred in Madrid, but with some variations. Mythological, landscape and genre paintings remained quite rare; still-life paintings (*bodegones*, flower paintings and *vanitas* paintings) followed the stylistic evolution of Baroque, and while they were in great demand for domestic decoration, they also provided opportunities for symbolism and complex allegories. The individual portrait was the last great European genre cultivated by painters in Madrid, who at first continued the representational forms of Mannerism (as in the works of ALONSO SÁNCHEZ COELLO) but then, through the influence of Titian and van Dyck, developed towards the forms of Velázquez and the painters of the second half of the 17th century. The technique of painting *al fresco* was dominated by Italians, from LUCA CAMBIASO to LUCA GIORDANO, while especially important in the development of Baroque illusionism were the 'Bolognese-style' artists Agostino Mitelli (*see* MITELLI, (1)) and ANGELO MICHELE COLONNA, who introduced *quadratura* to the city (1657–8).

The uniform character of the Madrid school was more evident in the work of lesser painters grouped around the masters. In the early 17th century the influence of the Escorial persisted in the work of Vicente Carducho (*see* CARDUCHO, (2)) and his followers and contemporaries, who progressively assimilated greater naturalism. While Velázquez was the artistic mentor at the court from his arrival there in 1622, the sphere of his influence was limited, and ANTONIO DE PEREDA and FRANCISCO COLLANTES were more popular. From 1650 major innovations were introduced by Francisco Rizi (*see* RIZI, (2)), Francisco de Herrera *el mozo* (*see* HERRERA, (2)) and JUAN CARREÑO DE MIRANDA, and the stylistic coherence of the school in the second half of the 17th century, with its blend of Italian and Flemish influences, was entirely derived from their work. Of importance during the reign of Charles II (1665–1700) was CLAUDIO COELLO, whose late work was dominated by a great serenity, but the culmination of Baroque in Madrid was represented by Luca Giordano in his paintings for the ceiling of the Casón de Felipe IV at the Buen Retiro, depicting the *Foundation of the Order of the Golden Fleece* (1697), and his frescoed frieze and vault of the imperial stairway in the Escorial (*see* ESCORIAL, fig. 4). At the end of the century another private academy was established in the studio of JOSÉ GARCÍA HIDALGO, where life drawing was practised (see fig.5).

The production of sculpture was of secondary importance to painting in Madrid's art life, and most notable works were imported, usually from Italy; indeed the possession of imported bronze and marble sculpture was a sign of social standing. Local sculptors generally produced religious works for private devotion. Although the most important sculptors' workshops were in Valladolid and Seville (*see also* SPAIN, §IV, 2), the capital began to exert some influence on retable design with the classicizing style used at the Escorial (e.g. the principal retable, in marble and jasper, designed by JUAN DE HERRERA and executed (1579–85) by Leone Leoni, Pompeo Leoni (*see*

5. José García Hidalgo: *Drawing Academy*, engraving, *c.* 1680–90; from *Principios para estudiar el nobilísimo y real arte de la pintura* (Madrid, Biblioteca Nacional)

LEONI), Jacopo da Trezzo I and Giovanni Battista Comane (*fl* 1579–81); *see also* ESCORIAL, §3). Other important Renaissance sculptures include the main retable (1545) by Francisco Giralte in the Capillo del Obispo, attached to the church of S Andrés, and the retable (1563; destr.) by Gaspar Becerra for the church of the Descalzas Reales. During the 17th century, however, sculpture in Madrid generally lacked stylistic coherence. The work of ANTONIO DE RIERA was influenced by Leone Leoni and Pompeo Leoni, while the sculptures of MANUEL PEREIRA display a struggle between equilibrium and emotiveness (e.g. *St Bruno*, before 1635; Burgos, Cartuja de Miraflores), midway between classicism and the dynamic Baroque of such contemporaries as JUAN SÁNCHEZ BARBA. Like many of his contemporaries, Sánchez Barba was aware of the theatricality of Bernini but preserved the broken drapery folds characteristic of Castilian workshops. At the end of the century retable sculptors began to relate their work more to architecture, and the classical style exemplified at the Escorial gave way to a tendency to intensify decorative, naturalistic and luminous effects; likewise, exuberant decoration came to be applied increasingly to buildings in what became known as the CHURRIGUERESQUE style.

BIBLIOGRAPHY
J. Gallego: *El pintor de artesano a artista* (Granada, 1976)
M. Agulló y Cobo, ed.: *Noticias sobre pintores madrileños de los siglos XVI y XVII*, intro. by A. E. Pérez Sánchez (Madrid, 1978)
F. Calvo Serraller: *Teoría de la pintura del Siglo de Oro* (Madrid, 1981)
J. J. Martín González: *Escultura barroca en España, 1600–1700* (Madrid, 1983)
M. B. Burke: *Private Collections of Italian Art in 17th-century Spain* (diss., New York U., 1984)
A. E. Pérez Sánchez: *Carreño, Rizi, Herrera y la pintura madrileña de su tiempo* (Madrid, 1985)
——: *Pintura barroca en España, 1600–1750* (Madrid, 1992)
                                ISMAEL GUTIÉRREZ PASTOR

2. 1700 AND AFTER. The accession to the throne of the Bourbon dynasty in 1700 ushered in for Madrid a new period of splendour in the arts, characterized to a great degree by the acceptance of French artistic styles and a tendency to eschew national trends. The presence on the throne of Philip V encouraged numerous foreign painters and sculptors to gather in the city in competition to enter his service. The monarch and his successors Ferdinand VI (*reg* 1746–59) and Charles III (1759–88) engaged many for the decoration of such palaces as the Palacio Real, rebuilt from 1738 (*see also* §IV, 2 below). Outside the royal palaces, the move from full Baroque towards the incorporation of Rococo features can be noted in such sculptural works as the *retablo mayor* (1720) in the church of the Orden de Calatrava, the last retable executed by José Benito de Churriguera (*see* CHURRIGUERA, (1)), and in the statues of the patron saints of Madrid (*St Isidore* and *St Mary*) on the Puente de Toledo, produced in 1723 by JUAN ALONSO VILLABRILLE Y RON. In painting, a national flavour was created by those Spanish painters who, aspiring to work at the court, abandoned their native cities to establish themselves in Madrid. Prominent among these was Antonio Palomino (*see* PALOMINO, (1) and SPAIN, fig. 16), born in Córdoba and perhaps more esteemed as a writer of treatises on art than as a painter, and JUAN BAUTISTA DE LA PEÑA, among whose most notable works was a portrait of *Ferdinand VI*. Foreign painters attracted

to the Spanish capital in search of royal commissions included ANDREA PROCACCINI and JEAN RANC, the latter of whom specialized in royal portraits (e.g. *Philip V of Spain*, *c.* 1723; Madrid, Prado), as well as Giambattista Tiepolo (*see* TIEPOLO, (1)) and ANTON RAPHAEL MENGS from Bohemia.

Of far-reaching importance for the art life of the city was the creation in 1752, under the patronage of Ferdinand VI, of the Real Academia de Bellas Artes de S Fernando, based closely on the French model (*see also* SPAIN, §XIV). The first directors of the Academia were men of Baroque training, but younger artists gradually came into the fold. Imbued with the culture of the Enlightenment, they turned for their inspiration to antiquity in search of beauty and equilibrium. Outstanding students at the Academia were accordingly awarded scholarships for study in Rome. Classical Roman models thus provided the source for many of the fountains erected in the Parque del Retiro and on the Paseo del Prado. Particularly worthy of note is that of Cybele (1780–86), designed by Francisco Gutiérrez (1727–82) and ROBERT MICHEL (i). The series of royal statues created by José Alvarez Cubero, such as that of *Queen Maria Isabel of Braganza* (*c.* 1816; Madrid, Prado; for illustration *see* ALVAREZ CUBERO, (1)), is an excellent example of the Neo-classical idiom.

The most extraordinary figure working in Madrid during this period was FRANCISCO DE GOYA, whose varied subjects included portraits of the royal family, of the upper nobility and intellectual figures of the day, and, particularly memorably, the tragic events of the War of Independence (or Peninsular War, 1808–13). Goya also produced cartoons, along with other leading court artists, for the Real Fábrica de Tapices y Alfombras de S Bárbara, which, together with the Real Fábrica de Cristales de la Granja de San Ildefonso and the Real Fábrica del Buen Retiro (producing porcelain; *see* §II, 2 below), supplied the royal family and other wealthy citizens with luxury furnishings and objects (*see also* SPAIN, §§XI, 4; VIII, 3; and VII, 4(ii)). In 1785 Charles III ordered the construction of a building to house large parts of the royal collections, and in 1818 the Real Museo de Pintura y Escultura was established in a building designed in 1787 by Juan de Villanueva as an Academia de Ciencias; in 1869 this became the Museo Nacional del Prado (*see* VILLANUEVA, (2), fig. 1).

In the middle of the 19th century, during the reign of Isabella II (1833–68), rigid academic discipline began to become more relaxed, and artists began to reveal a preference for treating subjects with more realism. Preeminent among such artists was JOSÉ PIQUER Y DUART, whose full-length marble statue of *Isabella II* (1855; see fig. 6) is in the Biblioteca Nacional. The other major figures of the 19th century, representing diverse pictorial trends, were the Neo-classical painters José de Madrazo y Agudo and his son Federico de Madrazo y Küntz (*see* MADRAZO, (1) and (2)), the *costumbrista* painter EUGENIO LUCAS VELÁZQUEZ, the Romantic EDUARDO CANO DE LA PEÑA and the history painter Eduardo Rosales Martínez (e.g. *Testament of Isabella the Catholic*, 1863; Madrid, Prado; for illustration *see* ROSALES MARTÍNEZ, EDUARDO). An important role in the artistic life of the capital was played by the Exposiciones Nacionales de Bellas Artes,

6. José Piquer y Duart: *Isabella II*, marble, 1855 (Madrid, Biblioteca Nacional)

The Salón had strong connections with the literary 'Generation of '27' and put forward opposition to the regional art of such figures as the Córdoban Julio Romero de Torres (1885–1930) and IGNACIO ZULOAGA, whose work was popular in the capital at the time. Cubism became a strong force in painting and sculpture, blending with more traditional approaches in the murals, portraits and landscapes of DANIEL VÁZQUEZ DÍAZ, whose work was to have considerable influence on later 20th-century Spanish painting; it also provided the inspiration for the early work of the sculptor ALBERTO, who, with BENJAMÍN PALENCIA and others, founded the Primera Escuela de Vallecas in 1925 to promote the study of landscape.

During the Second Republic (1931–6) tension heightened between supporters of traditional and avant-garde art; indeed, Madrid's less than whole-hearted commitment to artistic innovation was reflected in the fact that the Spanish pavilion at the Exposition Internationale des Arts Décoratifs et Industriels Modernes in Paris in 1937 featured avant-garde art produced largely outside the capital. In the post-war period JOSÉ SOLANA continued to advocate traditional images influenced by Goya and Spanish Baroque painters, but *Art informel* became firmly established in Madrid with the formation of the group El Paso (1957–60) by MANOLO MILLARES and ANTONIO SAURA; both painters were enthusiastic supporters of the abstract methods of action painting. In the 1960s a crisis of *Art informel* led in turn to Pop art and a revival of realism, the latter represented by the sculptures and paintings of ANTONIO LÓPEZ GARCÍA.

By the late 20th century Madrid was firmly established as a leading centre of the arts in Spain, its art life enhanced by a considerable number of museums, galleries and private foundations. Among the most notable are the Museo Arqueológico Nacional, the Museo de América, the Museo Nacional de Arte del Siglo XIX and, of course, the Museo del Prado, while the convents of the Descalzas Reales and the Salesas Reales contain valuable collections amassed as a result of royal donations and endowments. Private collections include that of the Palacio Liria, owned by the Duques de Alba, the Museo Cerralbo, now run by the Patrimonio Nacional, and the Museo Lázaro Galdiano, which houses an extremely varied collection from all over the world. There are also numerous foundations and galleries devoted largely to avant-garde art, including the Fundación Juan March, the Fundación Banco Exterior de España, the Galería Juana Mordó, the Galería Theo and the Centro Cultural de la Villa de Madrid. In the 1980s an attempt was made to give artistic experimentation official backing with the creation of the Museo de Arte Contemporáneo and the Centro de Arte Reina Sofía. Although historically not a major centre for dealing (*see also* SPAIN, §XII), Madrid now hosts the 'ARCO' Feria Internacional de Arte Contemporáneo, and several international auction houses now have offices there. Since 1992 most of the important THYSSEN-BORNEMISZA collection has been exhibited in the Palacio Villahermosa, opposite the Prado.

BIBLIOGRAPHY

J. Caveda: *Memorias para la historia de la Real Academia de San Fernando y de las bellas artes en España*, 2 vols (Madrid, 1867)
B. Pantorba: *Historia y crítica de las exposiciones nacionales de bellas artes celebradas en España* (Madrid, 1948; rev. 2/1980)

held from 1856 and sponsored by the State. Since the reign of Isabella II, the State had, however, generally lessened its patronage, being replaced by the new wealthy middle class; the Church, too, which had previously played such a central role, had become greatly weakened.

In the final decades of the 19th century new international influences reached Madrid, including Impressionism and other modernist movements such as Art Nouveau; the influence of these was particularly strong on graphic art. The appearance of avant-garde movements resulted in a gradual change in the very traditional tastes of the capital. The first signs of change came during the dictatorship (1923–30) of Primo de Rivera, when the Salón de Artistas Ibéricos was held in 1923 in the Parque del Retiro.

J. A. Gaya Nuño: *Arte del siglo XIX* (Madrid, 1966)

V. Bozal: *Historia del arte en España* (Madrid, 1978)

J. Brihuega: *Las vanguardias artísticas en España, 1909–1936* (Madrid, 1981)

G. Ureña: *La vanguardias artísticas en la posguerra española, 1940–1959* (Madrid, 1982)

P. Navascués Palacio: 'La época de la ilustración: La escultura y la pintura', *Historia de España Menéndez Pidal*, xxxi–xxxii (Madrid, 1987)

Y. Bottineau: *L'Art de cour dans l'Espagne des lumières, 1746–1808* (Paris, 1988)

Museos de Madrid: Guía de Madrid y región (Madrid, 1990)

ALBERTO VILLAR MOVELLÁN

III. Centre of production.

1. Metalwork. 2. Porcelain. 3. Hardstones.

1. METALWORK. The establishment of the court of Philip II in Madrid in 1561 prompted an extraordinary development in the production of ecclesiastical and secular metalwork and an abundance of craftsmen; during the mid-16th century there were 100 silversmiths in the city with an equal number of goldsmiths, among the most notable of whom were Francisco Alvarez (*d* 1576), creator of the biers and monstrance (1565–74) for the Ayuntamiento in Madrid, and his brother-in-law JUAN RODRÍGUEZ DE BABIA. From then onwards Madrid remained pre-eminent as a centre of Spanish metalwork, setting the stylistic and decorative trends for Hispanic silverwork and pioneering the organization of metalworkers' guilds. In 1575, for example, Madrid silverworkers established the Confraternity of St Eligius, which led to the development of similar guilds in other Spanish towns (*see* SPAIN, §IX, 1(ii)).

At the end of the 16th century a distinctive style emerged in Madrid. It was primarily architectural and marked by an austerity of form and the use of opaque enamels and engraved decorations (*see* SPAIN, §IX, 1(iii)). There were abundant commissions from ecclesiastical institutions, and from the king and the court. Production was very varied, of high quality and is considered the most original and distinctive phase of Hispanic metalwork. When the Bourbon king Philip V acceded to the throne in 1700, Spanish silverworkers started copying the late Baroque style (and later the Rococo style) of secular pieces imported from Paris for the Palacio Real and the production of the French craftsmen at the court. In ecclesiastical pieces the Spanish tradition continued. The arrival of King Charles III in Madrid in 1759 was followed by an influx at court of French and Italian metalworkers. The latter at times still employed the Rococo style but they also helped establish Neo-classicism, which appeared *c.* 1770 (as seen, for example, in Domingo de Urquiza's amphoras for oil in Burgos Cathedral) and became established in 1780 (*see* SPAIN, §IX, 1(v)). This stylistic development was further facilitated by the inauguration of the Real Escuela de Platería in Madrid in 1778, directed by ANTONIO MARTÍNEZ BARRIO. Production in Madrid continued to be abundant and of high quality until the Napoleonic invasion of 1808, when there was a certain decline, although the Neo-classical, Romantic and historical styles produced in the city influenced the rest of Spain throughout the 19th century. Industrial processes became widespread, and the Real Fábrica de Platería in Madrid promoted the adoption of new styles until it closed in 1869, having made several table services and dressing-table sets for the royal household (*see* SPAIN, §IX, 1(vi) and fig. 54). More silverwork pieces from Madrid have been preserved than from any other Spanish centre. They are usually marked either with the coat of arms topped by a tree (*madroño*) and a she-bear (the city coat of arms) or with a castle (the symbol of the court). From 1765 to 1934 the two hallmarks appeared together without distinction, accompanied by the year of manufacture. The hallmarkers who held public posts were nominated by the town council (those who stamped the object with the stamp of the town) and by the royal council (those who used the stamp of the court).

From the end of the 19th century to the Civil War (1936–9) traditional models were followed in the production of religious objects, especially in the workshops of Arte Granda. Few objects were designed in the *modernismo* (Art Nouveau) or Art Deco styles.

See also SPAIN, §IX, especially for bibliography.

JOSÉ MANUEL CRUZ VALDOVINOS

2. PORCELAIN. The two most important porcelain factories in Spain were located in Madrid. The Real Fábrica del Buen Retiro was named after the garden and palace on the outskirts of Madrid, where the factory was established in 1759 by Charles III, after he ascended to the Spanish throne. He was married to Maria Amalia of Saxony (1724–60), a member of the family of Saxon sovereigns who founded the porcelain factory at Meissen. Under her influence the porcelain factory of Capodimonte in Naples was created; when she moved to Spain she was accompanied by 53 artists from Capodimonte, with all the necessary material for the art to be continued in Madrid. In 1760 the Real Fábrica del Buen Retiro began to function with the Italian craftsmen and ten Spaniards under the direction of Gaetano Schepers. Giuseppe Gricci executed the Gabinete de la Porcelana (1760–65; *in situ*) at the Aranjuez Palace, near Madrid, which is totally covered with white porcelain plaques enhanced with coloured relief chinoiserie motifs, animals and plants. From 1770 to 1775 another Gabinete de la Porcelana, decorated in a similar style, was installed in the Palacio Real, Madrid (*see* CABINET (i)). Sculptures, dinner-services and imitation flower bouquets were also produced by the factory. Before 1789 soft-paste porcelain was manufactured, and the pieces executed in a Baroque style derived from that of Capodimonte. At the end of the 18th century, however, the Neo-classical style was introduced, and English Wedgwood Jasperwares were imitated. After the death of the King, a warehouse was opened for sales to the public. Until 1803 all the directors were Italian; between 1803 and 1808, however, the factory was directed by the Spaniard Bartolomé Sureda, who had visited France to study Sèvres porcelain. On his return hard-paste porcelain was introduced Buen Retiro, and the forms and decoration of Sèvres wares were copied. Despite these influences, and although some pieces are similar to those made at Sèvres, Buen Retiro porcelain is generally unmistakable. In the early 19th century Spanish fashion prevailed, but the factory was already in decline. The building, on a strategic site, was occupied by the French in 1808 and was completely destroyed on 10 August 1812.

In 1817 Maria Isabel of Braganza (1797–1818) persuaded her husband, Ferdinand VII, to create a new porcelain factory to replace the destroyed Real Fábrica del Buen Retiro. The workshops were constructed on the Moncloa site, then on the outskirts of Madrid, and after which the porcelain was named. All the surviving former workers from Buen Retiro were recruited, and the factory began to produce porcelain a few months after it was established. Its history, however, comprises a long series of intrigues and quarrels among artists, of technical failures and economic calamities, due to the use of antiquated equipment and techniques, and bad management. A crisis occurred in 1820 that ended with Sureda being named the new director. Moncloa porcelain is basically a fine ware, although it was soon replaced by cream-coloured earthenware in imitation of the English product. To offset the enormous production costs, the porcelain was sold to the public, who demanded more popular motifs. The typical design was a white background scattered with gold, stylized flowers and insets depicting popular characters or small vaguely Neo-classical pictorial landscapes. Sureda retired in 1829, leaving the factory, which had been destroyed by fire in 1825 and reconstructed in 1827, in an unfortunate state. The directors who succeeded him did not improve matters, and the factory was finally closed on 17 March 1850.

BIBLIOGRAPHY
L. de Mauri: *L'amatore di maioliche e porcellane* (Milan, 1951)
P. Navascués, C. Pérez and A. M. de Cossío: *Historia del arte hispánico*, v of *Neoclasicismo al modernismo* (Madrid, 1978)
N. Seseña Díez: 'Cerámica (siglos XIII–XVIII)', *Historia de las artes aplicadas e industriales en España*, ed. A. Bonet (Madrid, 1982)
W. Rincón García: *Las artes decorativas*, xxxv of *Historia de España* (Madrid, 1988)

CARLOS CID PRIEGO

3. HARDSTONES. The Laboratorio de Piedras y Mosaico, next to the Real Fábrica del Buen Retiro, in Buen Retiro park, was founded by Charles III in 1759 to specialize in the working of hardstones. As he had done at the Real Laboratorio delle Pietre Dure in Naples, he imported craftsmen from Florence; in October 1761 Domenico Stecchi (Domingo Stequi), active in the Opificio delle Pietre Dure in Florence, and Francesco Poggetti and his son Luigi Poggetti arrived in Madrid to practise their craft. In 1764 five artisans were employed under Stecchi and Francesco Poggetti, and by 1784 nineteen people were working under their direction. In 1786 Luigi Poggetti became the new director after Stecchi's death, while the administration—as distinct from its artistic supervision—was conducted until the end of the 18th century by two other Italians, the Bonicelli, who also superintended the Real Fábrica del Buen Retiro. Artists approved by the court were engaged to create designs that were then realized in pietre dure.

There are eight documented pietre dure mosaic tabletops (all Madrid, Prado) created by craftsmen at the Laboratorio, all finished before the death of Charles III in 1788. A ninth table (Lisbon, Pal. N. Ajuda), though not documented, undoubtedly belongs to the same series. The first of these to be made, decorated with a port scene surrounded by musical instruments, bears an inscription with the dates 1779–80 and the names of Domenico Stecchi, Francesco Poggetti and *Josh. Flipart Pintor de*

Cámara dei S. M. C. Although the name of Charles-Joseph Flipart (*fl* from 1753) appears only on this table, it seems likely that he designed the whole series. The two tables constructed last, with scenes of the games of *pelota* and shuttlecocks bordered by garlands, shells, flowers and fruits, show similarities with the figurative and ornamental designs of the painter Giuseppe Zocchi, whom Flipart may have known from the studio of the printmaker Joseph Wagner (1706–80) in Venice. Giovanni Battista Ferroni (*d* 1804), a bronze specialist, designed bronze mounts for the eight tables; these commissions are documented by a series of payments made to Ferroni from 1768 to 1796. In 1789 he is recorded as having designed and selected the stones for a cabinet to be made for Charles IV.

Other products of the Buen Retiro workshop include mosaic pictures, for example those of a *View of Bermeo*, based on a drawing by Luis Paret y Alcázar, and *Virgil's Tomb* (both Madrid, Prado) after Gaspar van Wittel. A sumptuous marble table centrepiece depicting a small temple (Malmaison, Mus. N. Château Bois-Préau), with polychrome stones and bronze ornaments chased by Ferroni, was begun in the 1790s. It was presented by Charles IV to Napoleon in 1808; in the same year the Laboratorio was destroyed in the Napoleonic Wars.

BIBLIOGRAPHY
M. Perez Villamil: *Artes e industrias del Buen Retiro* (Madrid, 1904)
J. M. Echalecu: 'Los talleres reales de ebanisteria, bronces y bordados', *Archv Esp. A.*, xxviii (1955), pp. 237–59
A. González-Palacios: *Mosaici e pietre dure*, ii (Milan, 1981), pp. 66–7
——: 'Il Laboratorio delle Pietre Dure del "Buen Retiro" a Madrid (1762–1808)', *Splendori di pietre dure: L'Arte di corte nella Firenze dei granduchi* (exh. cat., ed. A. M. Giusti; Florence, Pitti, 1988–9), pp. 260–67
A. M. Giusti: *Pietre Dure: Hardstones in Furniture and Decoration* (London, 1992)

ANNAMARIA GIUSTI

IV. Buildings.

1. BUEN RETIRO. Former royal palace in the east of Madrid, built from 1630 on the site of the Hieronymite monastery; the buildings are mostly no longer extant, and the extensive gardens are now a public park (the Parque del Retiro). Lying at the city's eastern gate, the monastery had played an important part in the life of the monarchy on such occasions as royal processions, funerals and religious festivals. JUAN BAUTISTA DE TOLEDO ordered the building of apartments there in 1561–3 for Philip II, backing on to the monastery church's northern chevet. In July 1630 the Conde-Duque de Olivares (*see* OLIVARES), First Minister under Philip IV (*reg* 1621–65), was named Alcalde del Cuarto de S Jerónimo and immediately ordered the building of an extension of the royal apartments towards the south. In July 1632 Olivares entrusted the further eastward extension of the apartments to the care of ALONSO DE CARBONEL, Aparejador Mayor (assistant architect-in-chief) of the royal building projects, under the direction of the Italian Giovanni Battista Crescenzi. Thanks to the generous financing of the project, and the plentiful supply of building land, the Plaza de Fiestas was laid out in 1633, enclosed by a three-storey building. In 1634 a further square was added to the north—larger still, but architecturally very simple—while to the east, towards the gardens, Carbonel built a rectangular ballroom in stone in 1637, known as the Casón de Felipe IV. This was

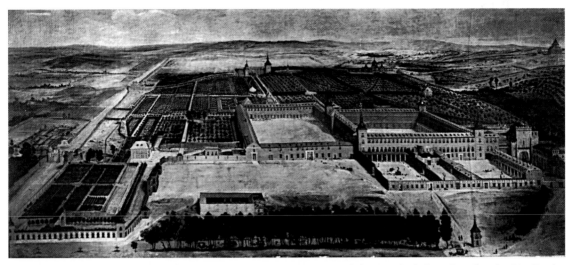

7. *View of the Palace of Buen Retiro*, by Jusepe Leonardo, 1.30×2.96 m, 1636–7 (Madrid, Palacio Real) formerly attributed to Juan Bautista Martínez del Mazo

followed by the Italianate theatre, the Coliseo de Comedias, built from 1638 by COSIMO LOTTI.

Apart from the latter two buildings, and despite a plan to construct the main building's façade from marble, the site generally reflected its hasty construction and its purely festive function: the design was simple, executed mainly in brick with stone door- and window-frames, with corner towers roofed in slate and balconies of wrought iron, the whole built around the square courtyard (see fig. 7). The interior decoration comprised paintings and sculptures from the royal collections, sometimes arranged by subject in different galleries and specifically commissioned for that purpose; these included battle scenes and equestrian portraits executed by DIEGO VELÁZQUEZ for the Salón de Reinos, a room that also housed works by such notable artists as ANTONIO DE PEREDA, Vicente Carducho (*see* CARDUCHO, (2)) and Francisco de Zurbarán (*see* ZUR-BARÁN, (1)). A fire in 1640 damaged a number of the paintings; some were replaced by Velázquez and others restored by ALONSO CANO. Some of the nine hermitages that were built (1633–40) throughout the park (five were by Carbonel) revealed greater architectural inventiveness than the main buildings and a greater concern for their interior decoration, as with the hermitage of S Antonio.

The perfunctory construction of the Buen Retiro and the court's irregular periods of residence led to the rapid deterioration of the buildings in general. This was partly remedied on occasion by restoration work: the Casón de Felipe IV was restored in 1692, and in 1697 Luca Giordano painted the *Foundation of the Order of the Golden Fleece* on its vaulted ceiling. Philip V (*reg* 1700–46) planned to renovate the palace and lay out the park along the lines of Versailles or Marly, but René Carlier's work (to plans by Robert de Cotte for a new palace and gardens; 1712–13; *see* COTTE, ROBERT DE, fig. 1) was abandoned; thus while the new Palacio Real was built (from 1738) on the ruins of the Alcázar, destroyed by fire in 1734, the sovereigns had to make do with a somewhat inferior residence. Alternative uses for the site were found in 1759, when

Charles III established the Fábrica del Buen Retiro there to manufacture porcelain, and also set up the Laboratorio de Piedras y Mosaico specializing in the working of hardstones (*see also* §III, 2 and 3 above). Occupation of the palace by Napoleonic troops in 1808, however, merely served to accelerate a general collapse into ruins that was in fact well under way. The west side of the palace was later built over, the rest of the complex becoming municipal property and the gardens being converted into the public Parque del Retiro, to which such buildings as the Velázquez Pavilion (1883; by Velázquez Bosco) were added. The remaining two buildings, the Salón de Reinos and the Casón de Felipe IV, became, respectively, the Museo del Ejército and an extension of the Museo del Prado.

BIBLIOGRAPHY
Y. Bottineau: 'Felipe V y el Buen Retiro', *Archv Esp. A.*, xxxi (1958), pp. 117–23; xxxii (1959), pp. 346–7
J. Brown and J. H. Elliott: *A Palace for a King: The Buen Retiro and the Court of Philip IV* (New Haven and London, 1980; Sp. trans., Madrid, 1981)
R. López Torrijos: *Lucas Jordán en el Casón del Buen Retiro* (Madrid, 1985)

2. PALACIO REAL. The first royal palace in Madrid was known as the Alcázar. It was initially a fortress built *c.* 875 by Muhammed I on a promontory that was soon incorporated into the north-west corner of the city walls. The Trastámara dynasty altered the structure *c.* 1390–1440, creating new towers around the military courtyard, a chapel and a room decorated with *Mudéjar*-style images. In 1536 Charles V, as part of his general initiative for improving a number of royal palaces, commissioned a major reworking of the palace: ALONSO DE COVARRUBIAS, aided and then replaced by Luis de Vega (see VEGA, DE, (1)), rearranged the palace around two patios in the Castilian proto-Renaissance style. The central double-square turning staircase (*doble claustral*) of 1536 was a notable contribution to the development of the imperial staircase and, to the south, the portal on the main façade (begun 1541)

8. Giovanni Battista Sacchetti: Palacio Real, Madrid, 1738–57

demonstrated an improved assimilation of Classical vocabulary. From 1559 the transformations ordered by Philip II concentrated on embellishing the interior decoration and improving the arrangement of the rooms. They reflected the King's eclectic taste: the Torre Dorada was influenced by Flemish designs, while the *pasillos* on the western wing, designed by JUAN BAUTISTA DE TOLEDO, were based on a Roman design. In the royal apartments the fresco and marble decorations (1562–84) by GASPAR BECERRA, Giovanni Battista Castello (*see* CASTELLO (i), (1)) and others were in a late Renaissance-Mannerist style.

The palace was briefly abandoned when the court moved to Valladolid (1601–5), but the extensions to the queen's apartment were subsequently continued under the direction of Francisco de Mora and resulted in the gradual building of a new main façade (1608–21), executed by Juan Gómez de Mora (*see* MORA, DE, (2)). The main body was in stone, enclosed between two brick corner towers, and made use of the Classical orders, with a portal at the centre; the whole was a picturesque version of the style associated with Juan de Herrera. The state rooms were in turn rearranged, and their decoration was developed around frescoes and the need to hang the paintings in the royal collection, which had expanded considerably with the addition of expressly commissioned works. Giovanni Battista Crescenzi and Diego Velázquez were responsible for the decoration, from 1630 to 1635 and from 1643 onwards respectively, and the influence of Italian art was uppermost (*see also* VELÁZQUEZ, DIEGO, §§3 and 5). Vicente Carducho and Angelo Nardi painted the vaults of the summer apartment, designed by Crescenzi in the north-west basement. Before his second trip to Italy (1649) Velázquez oversaw construction of the Octagonal Room

(1647–8) in the former central tower of the façade; with its lavish jasper and marble decoration it was intended to house Rubens's paintings and a number of sculptures. The central Salón de los Espejos (mirror room) was mainly built between 1656 and 1659. Arranged on two levels, it housed costly furniture and treasures from the picture gallery under a *quadratura* ceiling painted by Angelo Michele Colonna and Agostino Stanzani Mitelli; bronze eagles supported mirrors around the walls.

The key works carried out during Charles II's reign (1665–1700) included further frescoes, such as the decoration of the chapel (1692) by Luca Giordano. By enclosing the palace square between two rows of arcades, José del Olmo attempted in 1674 to turn it into a main courtyard. From 1711 the Bourbon king Philip V initiated plans to make the palace more comfortable and to adapt it to French taste, but the ambitious project (1715) of Robert de Cotte and René Carlier (*d* 1722) to create a French interior remained unexecuted. A fire on Christmas Eve 1734 destroyed nine centuries of history but enabled the new dynasty to build a palace to its own taste.

The new Palacio Real was built from 1738 to designs by GIOVANNI BATTISTA SACCHETTI, although FILIPPO JUVARRA had produced a more extravagant design (Madrid, Bib. N.), rejected by Philip V as too expensive. The new palace, built on a square ground-plan from Colmenar stone on a granite base, displays Italian and French Neoclassical influences (see fig. 8). In 1753 the decoration began under Corrado Giaquinto (*see* GIAQUINTO, CORRADO, §4); Anton Raphael Mengs and Giambattista Tiepolo took over in 1761–2 (*see* MENGS, (2), §3, and TIEPOLO, (1), §5). The palace's collection of paintings, sculptures and tapestries by leading Spanish, Italian, Flemish and French artists, which had suffered heavily in the fire of 1734, was increased by successive monarchs, notably Charles III (*reg* 1759–88; *see* BOURBON, §II(4) and SPAIN, §XII, 1). Among the works that survived the fire, however, were the gilt bronze lions (1561) by Giuliano Finelli in the red satin-lined Salón del Trono; the same room has a painted ceiling by Tiepolo, depicting the *Glory of Spain* (1762–4); ROBERT MICHEL (i) executed the stucco reliefs in the corners representing the *Four Seasons* (after 1749). Mengs decorated the ceiling of the Gran Comedor (formerly the Cuarto de la Reina) with the *Triumph of Aurora* (1762–4); and Francisco Bayeu (*see* BAYEU, (1)) also painted *al fresco* ceiling decorations. Also by Mengs is the unfinished altarpiece in the Capilla Real; the ceiling displays impressive paintings (1758–9) by Giaquinto who also painted the ceiling above the palace's main marble staircase (*see* GIAQUINTO, CORRADO, fig. 1); the staircase itself was designed by FRANCESCO SABBATINI in 1773–8. The palace also houses the Armería Real, the central feature of which is a collection made by the Holy Roman Emperor Charles V (*reg* 1517–56) of Flemish and German armour. In 1962 the Nuevos Museos were established in the north-west wing of the palace in order to exhibit properly the numerous paintings contained in the royal collection.

BIBLIOGRAPHY

F. J. Fabré: *Descripción de las alegorías pintadas en las bóvedas del Palacio Real de Madrid* (Madrid, 1829)

Y. Bottineau: 'L'Alcázar de Madrid et l'inventaire de 1686', *Bull. Hisp.*, lviii (1956), pp. 421–52; lx (1958), pp. 30–61, 145–79, 289–326, 450–83; lxxiv (1972), pp. 138–57

M. López Serrano, ed.: *El Palacio Real de Madrid* (Madrid, 1975)

F. J. de la Plaza Santiago: *Investigaciones sobre el Palacio Real nuevo de Madrid* (Valladolid, 1975)

V. Gerard: 'La fachada del Alcázar de Madrid, 1608–1630', *Cuad. Invest. Hist.* (1978), no. 2, pp. 237–51

——: 'Los sitios de devoción en el Alcázar de Madrid: Capilla y oratorios', *Archv. Esp. A.*, cxxiii (1983), pp. 275–84

——: *De castillo a palacio: El Alcázar de Madrid en el siglo XVI* (Madrid, 1984)

S. Orso: *Philip IV and the Decoration of the Alcázar of Madrid* (Princeton, 1986)

VÉRONIQUE GERARD-POWELL

Madurai. City in Tamil Nadu, India, and site of the Minakshi Sundareshvara temple, an important place of pilgrimage. It has been estimated that 15,000 people visit daily; 25,000 on Fridays, the day sacred to the goddess Minakshi (see Fuller).

1. HISTORY AND URBAN DEVELOPMENT. From an early period Madurai was associated with the PANDYA rulers as their capital. Greek geographers mention it as 'Modoura'. The earliest remains in the neighbourhood are rock-cut caves with short inscriptions (*c.* 2nd century BC). Accounts of the city are found in early Tamil literature, notably the poem *Maturaikkāñci*. The town was evidently laid out in a square following canonical prescription; the vestige of this scheme can be seen in the configuration of the central part of the city. Literary references make clear that a Shiva temple was a leading feature of Madurai. The god is praised in a number of 7th-century Tevaram 'Garland of God' hymns, in which the term *alavay* ('serpent-mouth') appears. This refers to a huge serpent girding the city protectively, its tail in its mouth. Central

to the cult is the divine marriage of Shiva as Chokkanatha (later Sundareshvara) to the goddess Minakshi, born in a sacrificial fire offered by the childless Pandya king and queen. Minakshi is, thus, a local princess, deified and absorbed into the 'great tradition' by becoming a consort of Shiva. She is also an invincible warrior goddess, Tatatakai. Before her marriage she fought off all other suitors, and annually, during the Navaratna festival, she is shut in her shrine for nine days as, clad in warlike red, she fights and destroys the Buffalo Demon. Minakshi is a powerful local divinity and protectress of Madurai in her own right.

The earliest temples of Shiva and Minakshi have not survived. In the early 14th century Malik Kafur, general of the KHALJI army, raided Madurai, and a local Sultanate was established. During this period the original Minakshi temple was apparently destroyed. There is still a Muslim population at Madurai and a number of important early Islamic monuments (see Shokoohy). The rising kingdom of VIJAYANAGARA gained control of Madurai in 1378. A governor (*nāyaka*) was appointed, which led to the establishment of a local NAYAKA lineage that lasted until the 18th century. The present Minakshi temple (*see* §2(i) below) dates from the centuries of Vijayanagara and Nayaka rule. Tirumalai Nayaka (*reg* 1623–59) renovated the Minakshi temple and built the Teppakkulam tank to the south-east of the city as well as a large palace (*see* §2(ii) below). Nayaka rule ended in 1739 when the Nawab of Arcot and Chanda Sahib took control of the city; Madurai became a possession of the East India Company in 1801. The Anglican church (*c.* 1875) was designed by Robert Fellowes Chisholm. The city continues to flourish, serving as the district administrative headquarters. Its population in 1990 was approximately 850,000.

Several places near Madurai are connected with local legends. Tirupparankunram, a massive rock some 6 km from the city, is sacred to Skanda (Murugan), the offspring of Shiva and Parvati. The site has a Nayaka-period temple and a number of 8th-century caves with relief sculptures; the Subrahmanya cave dates to 773. Alakarkoyil, some 20 km to the north, is sacred to Vishnu; he comes in procession to Madurai each year to give his sister in marriage to Sundareshvara. To the north-east is a large rock formation, clearly visible from Madurai. It resembles a slumbering elephant and is said to be an elephant conjured out of a sacrifice by Jainas with hostile intentions toward the temple; the elephant was stopped in its tracks by the god and has remained in the same spot to this day.

2. BUILDINGS.

(i) *Minakshi Sundareshvara Temple*. Located at the centre of Madurai is the vast temple enclosure (258×218 m). At its heart are two east-facing shrines, that on the proper right dedicated to the goddess Minakshi and the other to Shiva as Sundareshvara. Each shrine is set in its own walled area along with subsidiary shrines and pillared halls (*maṇḍapa*). The pillars of many of the halls are splendidly carved, as are the pillars adorning the verandah in front of the goddess shrine. A small shrine to the north-west of the Shiva temple is dedicated to the poets of the Tamil literary academy or Sangam and recalls the literary period

Madurai, Minakshi Sundareshvara Temple, *gopura* with upper part of the 'Golden Lily' tank, 17th century

of Tamil court poetry that acknowledged Madurai as its centre and arbiter of excellence. In front of the Minakshi enclosure is a courtyard with a large rectangular stepped pool known as the 'Golden Lily' tank. The largest of the *maṇḍapas* in the north-east corner of the complex houses a museum.

The temple's walls have a total of 11 *gopura* (entrance gateways), including one connecting the enclosures of the two main shrines. The four tallest *gopura* mark the north, south, east and west entrances from the surrounding streets. With their sweeping concave profiles and profusion of images, these gates are the most elaborate of their kind (see fig.). Like most of the Minakshi temple complex, they date to the Nayaka period. The sculpture and architectural ornaments of the gates were brightly repainted in the 20th century. The Pudu Mandapa, which extends eastward beyond the outer wall of the complex, was added by Tirumalai Nayaka in the second quarter of the 17th century. This long corridor-like hall is noteworthy for its carved piers and portrait statues of the Nayaka rulers (*see also* INDIAN SUBCONTINENT, §II, 8(ii)). At the eastern end of the Pudu Mandapa is the lowest storey of Tirumalai's massive but unfinished *gopura*.

(ii) Palace of Tirumalai Nayaka. This prominent building, erected by Tirumalai, is located in the south-east part of

the city, a short distance from the Minakshi temple. The palace complex occupied a large area (approximately 1.6 km sq.), but many structures were pulled down in the 18th century or incorporated into buildings in the surrounding streets. What remains is the enclosed court known as the Svarga Vilasam and a few adjoining structures. The audience chamber of the Svarga Vilasam is a vast hall (71.2 m×32.7 m) with arcades rising 12.2 m high. The architecture, a blend of Indo-Islamic and indigenous forms, recalls the royal buildings at HAMPI.

See also INDIAN SUBCONTINENT, §§III, 7(ii)(f), IV, 7(vi)(a) and V, 4(vii).

BIBLIOGRAPHY
K. Palaniappan: *The Great Temple of Madurai* (Madurai, 1963/R 1970)
K. A. Nilakanta Sastri: *A History of South India from Prehistoric Times to the Fall of Vijayanagara* (Madras, 1966)
A. V. Jeyechandrun, ed.: *The Madurai Temple Complex* (Madurai, 1974)
D. Devakunjari: *Madurai through the Ages* (Madras, [1979])
T. G. S. Balaram Iyer: *History and Description of the Sri Meenakshi Temple* (Madurai, 9/1982)
C. J. Fuller: *Servants of the Goddess: The Priests of a South Indian Temple* (Cambridge, 1984)
W. P. Harman: *The Sacred Marriage of a Hindu Goddess* (Bloomington, 1989)
M. Shokoohy: 'Architecture of the Sultanate of Ma'bar in Madura, and other Muslim Monuments in South India', *J. Royal Asiat. Soc. GB & Ireland*, n. s. 2, i (1991), pp. 31–92

J. MARR

Madurell i Marimón, Josep María [Madurell y Marimon, José María] (*b* Barcelona, 1893; *d* 1979). Spanish art historian. He studied science and architecture but abandoned these to dedicate himself to the history of art. In 1942 he was appointed archivist of the Archivo Histórico de Protocolos de Barcelona, where he conducted historical–literary research into both Catalonia and Aragon. His principal interest was the publication of documents on Catalan monuments and 15th- and 16th-century painting and silverwork. He undertook work on the history of printing, paper and the book trade in Barcelona and studied regional popular traditions. He had over 500 articles and studies published.

WRITINGS
'Los contratos de obras en los protocolos notariales y su aportación a la historia de la arquitectura', *Estud. Hist. & Doc. Archv Protocolos*, i (1948), pp. 105–99
'El pintor Lluís Borrassá', *An. & Bol. Mus. A. Barcelona*, vii (1949); viii (1950); x (1952) [whole issues]
El paper a les terres catalanes: Contribució à la seva història, 2 vols (Barcelona, 1972)
Claudi Bornat (Barcelona, 1973)

J. R. L. HIGHFIELD, ISABEL MORÁN SUÁREZ

Maeander. *See* MEANDER.

Maeda, Seison (*b* Gifu Prefect., 27 Jan 1885; *d* Kanagawa Prefect., 27 Oct 1977). Japanese painter. In 1901 he went to Tokyo, where he entered the painting school of Hanko Kajita (1870–1917). He formed a lasting friendship with fellow student Kokei Kobayashi. After 1914 Maeda was a central figure in the Inten, the exhibition of the Japan Art Institute. In 1922 he travelled to Europe as an overseas student of the Institute, and he was deeply impressed by Italian early Renaissance frescoes, which greatly influenced the development of his later style. He painted in the Japanese style (*Nihonga*; see JAPAN, §VI, 5(iii)) and worked in a variety of genres, including still-lifes and landscapes; he is best known, however, for such figure paintings as *Yoritomo in the Cave* (1929; Ogura Bunko Zaidan col.) and *Awaiting the Outset* (1955; priv. col.). In 1935 he became a member of the Imperial Art Academy, and in 1955 he was awarded the Order of Cultural Merit.

WRITINGS

Watakushi no rirekisho [Writings on my career] (Tokyo, 1969)

BIBLIOGRAPHY

Maeda Seison sakuhin shū [Collection of the works of Seison Maeda] (Tokyo, 1972)

YOSHIKAZU IWASAKI

Maegawa Kyoshū [Sekkokan] (*b* Osaka; *fl c.* 1777–1813). Japanese seal-carver. He learnt carving skills from his father, Maegawa Yūrin (1727–80), a seal-carver from the Osaka area, and also trained with the master of the Archaic school (Kotaiha), KŌ FUYŌ. Kyoshū engraved seals from a variety of materials and was especially adept at carving minute characters. In 1777 he gained fame by carving *c.* 150 characters from *Dokuraku'enki* by Shiba Onkō (1019–86) on a stone with a surface area of 300 sq. mm; he also engraved, on a stone surface of 31.0×26.5 mm, 360 characters from *Go Sekiheki no fu* ('Ode on the red cliff'; *c.* 1080) by the Chinese poet, painter and calligrapher Su Shi. He also came to appreciate the aesthetic quality of the Archaic character forms he had studied with Kō Fuyō and soon became a noted exponent of this style, publishing in 1778 the album *Keiko inshi* ('History of seal instruction'), designed in his own idiosyncratic way. Kyoshū favoured *usuyō* (thin-leaf) paper for the impression of seals and paid ingenious attention to colouring, mixing coral powder with his cinnabar ink.

He is regarded as the first Japanese professional seal-engraver, who established the making of seals as a trade with fixed rates for carving (*see also* JAPAN, §XVI, 20); it is said that he demanded a high price in advance for the seals he carved. Many literati of the late Edo period (1600–1868) owned his seals. He published many collections of seals, such as the *Sakukyō inpu* ('Sakukyō album', published *c.* 1800). He was reputedly buried, like his father, in the temple Daiunji in Kōzu. His son Juzan was also a seal-carver, and his pupils included Gō Hokusho (1798–1863). His carving style was continued by Hasegawa Ennen (1803–87), who edited the seal albums *Hakuaidōshū koinpu* ('Book of seals of the Hakuaidō [Hasegawa] collection'; 1860) and *Tōkōsai tenkoku inpu* ('Book of seals carved by Tōkōsai [Hasegawa]'; 1826–38).

BIBLIOGRAPHY

K. Nakai: *Nihon in jinden* [Accounts of Japanese seal-carvers] (Tokyo, 1915)

Y. Nakata, ed.: *Nihon no tenkoku* [Japanese seal-carving] (Tokyo, 1966)

N. Mizuta: *Nihon tenkoku shiron kō* [Study on the historical treatises of Japanese seal-carving] (Tokyo, 1985)

——: 'Horarezaru bohimei—Maegawa Kyoshū denkō' [Uncarved epitaph—a study of the biography of Kyoshū Maegawa, a famous seal-engraver in the Tokugawa era], *Kinran Tanki Daigaku Kenkyūjoshi*, 18 (1987), pp. 25–36

NORIHISA MIZUTA

Maeght. French dealers and publishers. Aimé Maeght (*b* nr St-Omer, 27 April 1906) first worked as a lithographic draughtsman and poster designer, joining the printing firm Robaudy in Cannes at the age of 20. In 1928 he married Marguerite Devaye (*b* Cannes, 25 April 1905; *d* 31 July 1977) with whom he opened a shop selling radios in 1932 while still working as a lithographer and advertising designer. In 1937 they opened the Galerie Arte in Cannes, where they exhibited the work of painters such as Georges Rouault, Jean Pougny, Roger Chastel, Henri Lebasque and Jean-Gabriel Domergue. With the encouragement of Pierre Bonnard, a friend of the Maeghts from 1941, and of Matisse and other artists and writers whom they met in the south of France, they decided to devote themselves to art publishing and dealing. In late 1945 they settled in Paris and opened the Galerie Maeght at 13, Rue de Téhéran with an outstanding exhibition of Matisse's work. They also embarked on an ambitious publishing programme, which included Kafka's *Description d'un combat* (illustrated by Jean-Michel Atlan, 1946), Tristan Tzara's *Parler seul* (illustrated by Miró, 1950), Pierre Reverdy's *L'Aventure méthodique* (illustrated by Braque, 1950) and from 1945 the series *Pierre à feu*, which collected together illustrated poems and prose works.

The Galerie Maeght mounted both thematic exhibitions such as *Black is a Colour* (1946) and *Surrealism in 1947* (organized by Breton and Duchamp) and a series of outstanding exhibitions devoted to artists such as Braque, Bram van Velde, Miró (from 1948), Léger (from 1949), Kandinsky, Alberto Giacometti, Chagall, Ubac and Calder. Aimé Maeght consistently refused to limit himself to any one movement, instead promoting the work of about 40 major painters. In later years he also exhibited the work of younger artists including Ellsworth Kelly (1953), Pablo Palazuelo (1955), Eduardo Chillida (1956), Jean-Paul Riopelle and Francis Bacon (1966), Paul Rebeyrolle and Antoni Tàpies (1967), Pol Bury (1969) and Valerio Adami (1970). Branches of the Galerie Maeght were later opened in Zurich (1970) and Barcelona (1974), and each maintained its own character.

From the time of his move to Paris, Aimé Maeght also became increasingly active as a publisher. The catalogue accompanying each of his exhibitions doubled as an issue of a magazine *Derrière le miroir* (253 issues), which was designed as a sumptuous large-format album illustrated with original lithographs and with reproductions and background material. In 1959 he established his own lithographic workshops, which were subsequently amalgamated with Imprimerie Arte (founded by the Maeghts' son Adrien), and began publishing monographs and catalogues raisonnés on major figures such as Braque and Miró. He also founded three highly esteemed if short-lived periodicals: *L'Éphémère* (20 issues, 1966–72), a quarterly literary journal run by Jacques Dupin, Gaëtan Picon, Yves Bonnefoy and Michel Leiris; *L'Art vivant* (57 issues, 1968–75), a provocative monthly magazine edited by Jean Clair, which covered the latest developments in contemporary art, film, music and dance; and *Argile* (24 issues, 1973–81), a poetry review, which, under the editorship of Claude Estéban, specialized in translation and previously unpublished works.

The most original achievement of the Maeghts, prompted by the death of their second son, Bernard, in 1953, was their decision to transform their home at Saint-Paul-de-Vence, near Nice, into a meeting-place for artists, the fondation Maeght. A centre designed by the Spanish

Catalan architect Josep Lluís Sert, a friend of Miró, was constructed in 1962–3 with the intention of bringing together many different functions; it includes well-lit exhibition halls opening on to gardens and patios, a sculpture park, artists' studios, a cinema, a concert hall and a reference library. The Maeghts financed the entire building and offered the best part of their private collection to the foundation, including major works by most of the painters they had exhibited, notably Bonnard, Léger, Miró and Giacometti. The self-financing institution holds concerts and major exhibitions every summer.

BIBLIOGRAPHY

Maeght éditeur (exh. cat., preface J.-L. Prat; Saint-Paul-de-Vence, Fond. Maeght, 1972)

La Fondation Marguerite et Aimé Maeght (exh. cat., intro. J. Meuris; Brussels, Mus. Ixelles, 1975)

L'Univers d'Aimé et Marguerite Maeght (exh. cat., intro. A. Chastel; Saint-Paul-de-Vence, Fond. Maeght, 1982)

ISABELLE MONOD-FONTAINE

Maejuk-hŏn. *See* YI YŎNG.

Maekawa [Mayekawa], Kunio (*b* Niigata, 14 May 1905; *d* Tokyo, 26 June 1986). Japanese architect. One of the masters of Japanese architecture in the period immediately after World War II, he was particularly known for his attempt to evolve an approach that synthesized Modernism and Japanese tradition. He studied architecture at the University of Tokyo, graduating in 1928. He then served a lengthy apprenticeship, first in the studio of Le Corbusier in Paris (1928–30) and then in the office of Antonin Raymond in Tokyo (1930–35). The extent to which Maekawa was influenced by Le Corbusier is apparent in his competition entry (1931; unexecuted) for the National Museum in Tokyo. Maekawa came to the fore with his designs for a series of prefabricated timber houses that were mass-produced between 1945 and 1950 in an effort to deal with the massive housing shortages that prevailed in Japan after the war. He came to maturity with his first major work in reinforced-concrete construction, the Nihon Sōgō Bank, built in downtown Tokyo in 1952. This success was followed by his monumental block of flats (1956) in the Harumi district of Tokyo. While influenced by Le Corbusier's Unité d'Habitation (1945–52), Marseille, Maekawa's mega-block departed from this model in many significant aspects, not least of which was the decision to abandon the typical cross-over maisonette section and to access the flats in two different ways: by single-loaded open corridors, and by stairs giving access to pairs of flats for two floors above each of the corridors. Maekawa's significant achievement in the Harumi flats was his successful integration of Western and Japanese domestic traditions, the living spaces of the flats being divided equally between dining areas with chairs and rooms furnished with *tatami* mats.

Maekawa's attempt to evolve a reinforced-concrete architecture that was specifically Japanese in feeling came to its early fruition with his City Hall (1958–60), Kyoto, and Metropolitan Festival Hall (1958–61; see fig.), Ueno Park, Tokyo, which was built opposite Le Corbusier's Museum of Western Art. The Japanese character of the Metropolitan Festival Hall was conveyed by three devices: a continuous monumental overhang running around the perimeter of the building, the thick, square, anti-seismic concrete columns, and the large, vertical masses clad in concrete, such as the fly-tower, auditorium and conference hall, by which the work is crowned. While Maekawa went on to simplify and discipline his own monumental concrete architectural language, most notably perhaps in his additions (1959–60) to Gakushūin University, Tokyo, a plastic language as compelling as the one evolved by his former assistant Kenzō Tange continued to elude him. He was, however, marginally more critical and reflective than Tange, as may be seen in his essay 'Thoughts on Civilization and Architecture' (1965), which emphasized the Japanese–Western disjunction evident in much of his work: 'We must go back to the beginnings of Western civilization and discover whether the power to bring about such an ethical revolution can really be found in the inventory of Western civilization itself. If not, then we

Kunio Maekawa: Metropolitan Festival Hall, Tokyo, 1958–61

must seek it, together with Toynbee, in the Orient or perhaps in Japan.' Maekawa's buildings of the 1970s and 1980s included several museums, among them the Museum für Ostasiatische Kunst (1977), Cologne. One of his finest later works, however, is the brick- and tile-faced 27-storey Kaijō Building (Tokyo Marine and Fire Insurance Company; 1974), Tokyo, in which the four-square trabeated system seems closer to the tectonic spirit of Louis Kahn than to Maekawa's former sculptural plasticity inspired by Le Corbusier.

See also JAPAN, §III, 5(ii).

WRITINGS
'Thoughts on Civilization and Architecture', *Bauen & Wohnen* [Zurich] (1965)
'My View of Architecture', *Architect: Journal of the Japanese Architects Association* (Autumn 1968)
'European Civilisation and Architecture', *Architect: Journal of the Japanese Architects Association* (Autumn 1969)

BIBLIOGRAPHY
U. Kultermann, ed.: *New Japanese Architecture* (New York, 1960)
'Kulturzentrum in Tokio', *Baukst & Werkform*, xv (March 1962), pp. 123–7
C. Oakham: 'Kunio Maekawa: Setting a Course for Japanese Architecture', *Prog. Archit.* (April 1965), pp. 168–79
A. Altherr: *Drei japanische Architekten: Mayekawa, Tange, Sakakura* (Teufen and Stuttgart, 1968)
'Tokyo Marine and Fire Insurance Company', *Japan Architect*, xlix/9 (1974), pp. 35–54
J. P. Noffsinger: *Kunio Mayekawa: Father of Modern Japanese Architecture* (Monticello, IL, 1979) [bibliog.]
D. B. Stewart: *The Making of a Modern Japanese Architecture, 1868 to the Present* (Tokyo and New York, 1987)

KENNETH FRAMPTON

Mael fsu (Mac Bratdan Ui Echan) (*fl* first half of the 12th century). Irish metalworker. He was probably trained by the metalworker Nechtain at Clonmacnois. Mael fsu's style, a mixture of revived INSULAR ART and imported Scandinavian styles, is similar to Nechtain's, a typical product of Clonmacnois, except that Mael fsu favoured the rounded Urnes manner of execution (*see* URNES, §1). Mael fsu was transferred to Roscommon, where he evidently founded a new workshop. This may be why his style is relatively individual; its strong Urnes cast prevents his work at Roscommon from being confused with products from Clonmacnois. Since Clonmacnois and Roscommon were the capitals of rival dynasties, this may have been an important consideration.

Two of Mael fsu's works survive. The Cross of Cong (Dublin, N. Mus.), dated by inscription to 1127–36, was made for Ruaidri Ua Conchobar, King of Connaught, to enshrine a fragment of the True Cross. The large, incomplete house-shaped shrine from Lemanaghan (Boher, Church, Co. Offaly) has no inscription, but its commission in 1166 was recorded in the *Annals of the Four Masters*. Another commission, recorded in 1170, does not name the artist and the object is lost, but it was made for Mael fsu's patrons and its description as 'an embroidering of gold' evokes his unique lacy openwork style.

It was rare for any craftsman to sign his work at this period, and rarer still for any commission to be recorded in the historical annals. That Mael fsu's existence was recorded in both ways suggests that he was highly esteemed. His surviving works show him to have been an exceptionally fine craftsman, but he was not an innovator: his style was the product of tradition and contemporary influence, and his surviving works, produced 30 years apart, are virtually identical in style. It was a style made obsolete by the new Anglo-Norman patrons who arrived after 1171. Their settling probably coincided with Mael fsu's death, and he had no successors.

BIBLIOGRAPHY
J. O'Donovan, ed.: *The Annals of the Kingdom of Ireland by the Four Masters: From the Earliest Period to the Year 1616* (Dublin, 1851)
W. Stokes, ed.: 'The Annals of Tigernach', *Rev. Celtique*, xvi (1895), pp. 374–419; xvii (1896), pp. 6–33, 116–263, 337–420; xviii (1897), pp. 5–59, 150–303, 374–91
Christian Art in Ancient Ireland, i, ed. A. Mahr (Dublin, 1932); ii, ed. J. Raftery (Dublin, 1941)
F. Henry: *Irish Art in the Romanesque Period* (London, 1967)
A. T. Lucas: *Treasures of Ireland: Irish Pagan and Early Christian Art* (Dublin, 1973)
Treasures of Ireland: Irish Art, 1500 BC–1500 AD (exh. cat., ed. P. Cone; New York, Met., 1977)
P. E. Michelli: *The Pre-Norman Crosiers of Ireland* (diss., Norwich, U. E. Anglia, 1987)
R. O'Floinn: 'Schools of Metalworking in Eleventh- and Twelfth-century Ireland', *Ireland and Insular Art*, ed. M. Ryan (Dublin, 1987)

PIPPIN MICHELLI

Maella, Mariano Salvador (*b* Valencia, 21 Aug 1739; *d* Madrid, 10 May 1819). Spanish painter and draughtsman. He was the son of a Valencian painter of the same name, and in 1751 he went to Madrid, where he studied drawing and modelling under the sculptor Felipe de Castro for two years. However, he felt painting to be his vocation and joined the students directed by Antonio González Velázquez at the Real Academia de S Fernando, where he completed his studies in 1757. In 1758, after an unsuccessful attempt to go to America, he went to Rome.

On returning to Spain in 1765, Maella was elected Académico de Mérito by the Real Academia, and he entered the circle of Anton Raphael Mengs, who, impressed by his fluency of brushwork, sense of colour and professionalism, protected and helped him. He shared with Francisco Bayeu a commission from Charles III in 1772 for frescoes depicting various saints and the *Immaculate Conception* in the dome of the chapel of the Palacio Real, and he was appointed Pintor de Cámara in 1774. Despite having a difficult relationship with Bayeu, he participated in a second joint commission from the King in 1775, for frescoes of the *Life of St Leocritia* in the cloister of Toledo Cathedral. Maella also worked for the Real Fábrica de Tapices, directing the work of younger artists and producing such cartoons as *Seascape* and *Fishermen* (both 1785; Madrid, Prado).

Maella was a prolific and diverse artist, producing portraits, landscapes, seascapes, battle scenes and historical and religious paintings. His portraits are in the style of Mengs, although the faces are warmer and softer. Court portraits, such as *Charles III Wearing the Robe of his Order* (1784; Madrid, Pal. Real), are among his most important works, although he was particularly adept at portraying children, as in the *Infanta Carlota Joaquina* (1785; Madrid, Pal. Moncloa). Surviving sketches and drawings indicate that he was also skilful at group portraits. Some of his drawings display elements of the Rococo style learnt in his youth and at times are reminiscent of the technique of Luca Giordano. In his religious paintings Maella often represented the traditional Spanish theme of the Immaculate Conception (e.g. 1787; Madrid, Mus. Mun.). Maella's paintings of saints show knowledge of works by Murillo, which he would have seen in the royal collections. The influence of Mengs is again noticeable in Maella's large-scale works, such as the frescoes depicting the *Apotheosis of Athena* (1789; El Pardo, Casita del Príncipe), but the tones are harsher.

Maella also produced excellent graphic work for the Real Academia de la Lengua's illustrated editions of the Roman historian Sallust (1777) and of Francisco Quevedo (1782). He also undertook the restoration of paintings in the royal collections and obtained commissions elsewhere in Spain, such as the fresco decorations on the dome of the chapel of the Venerable Palafox in Burgo de Osma Cathedral (*in situ*) and the canvases for the monastery of S Rosendo de Celanova, with themes associated with the Benedictine order (untraced).

Maella became Director of Painting at the Academia in 1794 and Director General there in 1795; in 1799 he became Primer Pintor del Rey. He collaborated with the French, however, during the Napoleonic invasion (1808), and he was decorated by the government of Joseph I. This led to his removal from court in 1814 on the return of Ferdinand VII, although he was still allowed an annuity 'by way of alms' in recognition of his artistic achievements and the role he had played in the reigns of the Bourbon kings Charles III and Charles IV. He was replaced in his official duties by Vincente López y Portaña.

BIBLIOGRAPHY

S. Alcolea: 'Mariano Salvador Maella, 1739–1819', *Register Kansas City Mus. A.*, iii/8–9 (1967), pp. 24–43

D. Mollinedo: 'Algunos dibujos de Mariano Salvador Maella', *Archv Esp. A.*, xlvi (1973), pp. 145–57

J. Camon, J. L. Morales and E. Valdivieso: 'Arte español del siglo XVIII', *Summa A.*, 27 (1984)

JUAN J. LUNA

Maelwael, Jan. *See* MALOUEL, JEAN.

Maes, Dirk. *See* MAAS, DIRK.

Maes, Nicolaes (*bapt* Dordrecht, Jan 1634; *bur* Amsterdam, 24 Dec 1693). Dutch painter. The son of the prosperous Dordrecht merchant Gerrit Maes and his wife Ida Herman Claesdr., Nicolaes Maes learnt to draw from a 'mediocre master' (Houbraken) in his native town before he studied painting with Rembrandt in Amsterdam. His training in Rembrandt's studio must have taken place between 1648/50 and 1653. By December 1653 Maes had settled in Dordrecht and made plans to marry, while a signed and dated picture of 1653 confirms that the 19-year-old artist had completed his training and embarked on an independent career. Maes continued to reside in Dordrecht until 1673.

1. Work. 2. Working methods and technique. 3. Patrons and followers.

1. WORK.

(i) Genre and history paintings. Maes's few pictures of biblical subjects and all his approximately 40 genre paintings date from *c.* 1653 to *c.* 1660. Though indebted to Rembrandt's example, the early religious works exhibit a precocious originality in the interpretation of the sacred text and iconographic tradition. For instance, in the *Expulsion of Hagar* (1653; New York, Met.) Hagar's inconsolable response to her dismissal and the characterization of Ishmael as a prematurely embittered outcast mark it as one of the most poignant renderings of a theme that was especially popular among Rembrandt's students. This and other biblical pictures are of cabinet size; *Christ Blessing the Children* (London, N.G.) is Maes's only religious work with lifesize figures.

For a brief period in the mid-1650s Maes ranked among the most innovative Dutch genre painters, owing to his talent for pictorial invention and for devising expressive poses, gestures and physiognomies. He adapted Rembrandt's brushwork and chiaroscuro to the scenes of domestic life that provided the favourite subject-matter for genre artists working in the third quarter of the century. The poetic deployment of light and shade and the adeptly designed figures invest his paintings of interior scenes with women absorbed in household tasks with an atmosphere of studious concentration. In pictures of spinners, lace-makers (e.g. *The Lacemaker*, 1655; Ottawa, N.G.) and mothers with children, dating from 1654 to 1658, household work assumes the dignity and probity claimed for it by contemporary authors of didactic literature on family life. Maes also executed a small group of works that show everyday events taking place on the doorstep of a private house. Some depict milkmaids ringing the doorbell or receiving payment for a pot of milk (e.g. London, Apsley House); others represent boys asking for alms from the residents. As in the interior scenes, Maes's pictorial gifts transformed these mundane transactions into events of solemn dignity. Another type of genre painting from the mid-1650s shows a single, nearly lifesize female figure in half or three-quarter length. An elderly woman says grace before a modest meal, prays amid *vanitas* symbols or dozes over a Bible (e.g. Brussels, Mus. A. Anc.), exemplifying, respectively, spiritual vigour and spiritual lassitude in old age.

Maes's most renowned genre paintings feature an interior with an eavesdropper who exposes the peccadilloes of another member of the household (e.g. London, Apsley House; see fig. 1). Dated or datable between 1655 and 1657, the six pictures of eavesdroppers and the closely related *Idle Servant* (1655; London, N.G.) and *Woman Picking the Pocket of a Sleeping Man* (Bangor, North Wales, Lady Janet Douglas-Pennant priv. col., see Sumowski, 1983, fig. 1344) employ gentle satire and an ingenious narrative structure to ridicule the vices of sloth, lust or anger. The eavesdropper or other principal figure smiles engagingly at the viewer and directs attention to a housewife scolding her husband, a kitchen maid asleep on the job or a servant entangled in the embrace of a lover. In these pictures and in the *Woman Plucking a Duck* of 1655 or 1656 (Philadelphia, PA, Mus. A.), Maes developed an innovative approach to the representation of interior space. He was among the first Dutch genre painters to depict the domestic interior not as a shallow, three-walled box but as a suite of rooms. His new disposition of domestic space resulted primarily from the narrative requirements of these paintings. While he demonstrably perused perspective handbooks, he resorted neither to a

1. Nicolaes Maes: *Lovers, with a Woman Listening*, oil on canvas, 578×631 mm, *c.* 1655 (London, Apsley House)

mathematically constructed space nor—with one exception—to *trompe l'oeil* illusionism. Maes pursued his experiments for only a brief period (1655–7), but his achievement exercised a decisive influence on the Delft painters Johannes Vermeer and Pieter de Hooch and thus had lasting consequences for the representation of interior space in 17th-century Dutch painting.

(ii) Portraits. While concentrating on his genre and history paintings, Maes embarked on a productive, 35-year career as a portrait painter. During the second half of the 1650s, when his output of subject pictures gradually diminished, his production of portraits steadily increased. Some 25 single, pendant and group portraits from the period 1655–60 have been preserved.

However, from *c.* 1660 until the end of his career, Maes worked exclusively as a portraitist. He settled in Amsterdam in 1673, making a bid to fill the vacancy left by the deaths of the portrait specialists Bartholomeus van der Helst and Abraham van den Tempel. Soon, wrote Houbraken, 'so much work came his way that it was deemed a

favour if one person was granted the opportunity to sit for his portrait before another, and so it remained for the rest of his life'. Hundreds of surviving portraits from the 1670s and 1680s corroborate Houbraken's report. Most are pendants in one of two favourite formats: a smaller rectangular canvas with a half-length figure within a painted oval; and a larger canvas with a three-quarter-length figure, usually shown leaning against a fountain, rock or column. In both types, the setting is often a garden or terrace before a sunset sky. There are several group portraits of children or families, depicting the sitters full length in landscape settings, but only one corporate group, the *Six Governors of the Amsterdam Surgeons' Guild* (1680–81; Amsterdam, Rijksmus.), is known.

2. Working methods and technique.

(i) Paintings. During his 40-year career, Maes's painting technique evolved continuously, but his exceptional skill with the brush never faltered. In the genre and history pictures of the prolific period 1653–5, his colour, chiaroscuro and brushwork owe a clear debt to Rembrandt's

work of the mid-1640s, particularly to the latter's *Holy Family in the Carpenter's Shop* (1645; St Petersburg, Hermitage). Maes restricted his palette to blacks, browns, whites and reds and employed techniques ranging from a meticulous 'fine painting' style in the description of wooden furniture or a wicker cradle to a grainy—occasionally even pastose—application of richly graduated tones in the execution of fabric and flesh. After the middle of the decade, he increasingly favoured a clearer light, smoother textures and more definite contours.

The early portraits developed differently. Apart from the evocative shadows that enrich a few of them, they scarcely recall the legacy of Rembrandt's teaching. Rather, Maes initially accommodated his style to the conservative Dordrecht tradition represented in the 1650s by Jacob Gerritsz. Cuyp, his son Aelbert Cuyp and the older Rembrandt pupil Samuel von Hoogstraten. Simple frontal poses, restrained conventional gestures, sober facial expressions, dark clothing rendered with tones of white, black and grey, and plain backgrounds or austere domestic settings characterize Maes's first essays in this field, dating from 1655–7 (e.g. the portrait of *Jacob de Witt*, 1657; Dordrecht, Dordrechts Mus.). In the portrait of the Dordrecht shipper *Job Cuijter and his Family* (1659; Raleigh, NC Mus. A.), which shows the family on a quay in Dordrecht harbour, Maes began to employ the lighter tonality, the pale red hues and the white highlights that also distinguish his latest subject picture, *Winter and Spring* (*c.* 1659–60; Oxford, Ashmolean).

Maes's mature style developed gradually during the 1660s in response to the Flemish mode of portraiture developed by van Dyck and introduced into the northern Netherlands in the previous decade by such artists as Govaert Flinck, Adriaen Hanneman and Jan Mijtens. From the early 1660s onwards, Maes regularly employed staging and accessories derived from Flemish portraiture. Although Houbraken reported that Maes once travelled to Antwerp, direct contact with Flemish painting contributed less to his development than his study of works by Mijtens, whose colouring and technique evidently inspired the glistening reds and blues and brilliant brushwork of his later paintings. Despite the general trend of his style, in some of his most sympathetic portraits of the 1660s Maes continued to utilize a plain background and a subdued palette (e.g. the *Portrait of a Widow*, 1667; Basle, Kstmus.).

The portraits of the 1670s and 1680s generally feature the same imaginary garden or architectural setting with a foreground composed of columns, fountains, terraces and billowing curtains, but they exhibit a novel repertory of graceful poses and refinements in technique and colouring. The pale, solidly modelled countenances preserve—according to Houbraken's reliable testimony—an accurate likeness of the sitter, but the brilliantly rendered hair and clothing increasingly dominate the image. Satiny fabrics in a broader and brighter range of reds, blues, oranges, golds and violets shimmer with dashing, scumbled highlights, while the elaborate curls of the period's long hairstyles are described with a breathtaking show of tonal painting in greys and browns (e.g. the *Portrait of a Young Man*; Munich, Alte Pin.; see fig. 2).

2. Nicolaes Maes: *Portrait of a Young Man*, oil on canvas, 1.15×0.91 m, *c.* 1675–80 (Munich, Alte Pinakothek)

(ii) Drawings. About 160 drawings by Maes have survived, making him one of the few outstanding Dutch genre painters of his generation whose practice as a draughtsman can be partially reconstructed. Many are working drawings, both compositional sketches and figure studies, for his genre and history paintings—only one rough design for a portrait survives (Besançon, Mus. B.-A & Archéol.), along with a few landscape drawings. For the compositional projects Maes used a variety of media: red chalk, pen and ink and combinations of chalk and wash or ink and wash. Most are cursory sketches, for example the study in pen and wash (Berlin, Kupferstichkab.) for *The Lacemaker* (1655; Ottawa, N.G.). The figure studies also exhibit a wide variety of media and techniques. They range from spare contours delineated with the pen or brush to exquisitely refined studies in red chalk (e.g. another study, Rotterdam, Boymans–van Beuningen, for *The Lacemaker*) to broadly pictorial drawings executed in a combination of chalk, ink, wash and bodycolour.

3. PATRONS AND FOLLOWERS. While early collectors of Maes's subject pictures remain unidentified, the known sitters in his portraits attest that in this field Maes enjoyed from the outset the patronage of Dordrecht's political and mercantile élite. Jacob de Witt, whom he portrayed in 1657, was a member of the city's Old Council and the father of Grand Pensionary Johan de Witt, the political leader of the United Provinces. A contract of 1658 records that Maes acquired a house from Job Cuijter in exchange for a cash payment and the portrait of Cuijter with his family. In 1659 or 1660 Maes painted a portrait of *Jacob Trip* (The Hague, Mauritshuis), the first of several pendant

portraits with Trip's wife Margaretha de Geer (both of whom were portrayed by Rembrandt about the same time). Among Holland's wealthiest families, the Trips and de Geers amassed fortunes from Swedish iron mines and the manufacture of armaments.

During his last years in Dordrecht and during his Amsterdam period, Maes continued to work for a varied clientele at the highest social levels, including the Utrecht University professor of theology Gijsbert Voet; the preacher Cornelis Trigland; Hieronymus van Beverningk, Treasurer-General of the United Provinces, diplomat and one time close confidant of Johan de Witt; the Amsterdam burgomaster Gerrit Hendriksz. Hooft; the Lieutenant-Admiral of Zeeland, Cornelis Evertsen; Laurent de Rasiere, a sea-captain in the service of the West India Company; and the Rotterdam burgomaster, silk-merchant and director of the East India Company Jan de Reus. A few of these portraits were reproduced in prints.

Maes's closest followers were the Dordrecht painters of portraits and genre scenes Reinier Covijn and Cornelis Bisschop (1630–74). Bisschop studied with Ferdinand Bol, but Covijn may have been Maes's pupil. Houbraken mentioned four minor artists as Maes's students: Jacob Moelaert (1649–c. 1727), Jan de Haen, Johannes Vollevens (1649–1728) and the poetess Margaretha van Godewijk (1627–77).

BIBLIOGRAPHY

A. Houbraken: *De groote schouburgh* (1718–21), ii, pp. 273–7

J. Veth: 'Aantekeningen omtrent eenige Dordrechtse schilders', *Oud-Holland*, viii (1890), pp. 125–42

C. Hofstede de Groot: *Holländischen Maler* (1907–28), vi (1915), pp. 479–622

A. Bredius: 'Bijdragen tot een biografie van Nicolaes Maes', *Oud-Holland*, xli (1923–4), pp. 207–14

W. Valentiner: *Nicolaes Maes* (Stuttgart, 1924)

W. Sumowski: *Gemälde der Rembrandt-Schüler*, iii (Landau in der Pfalz, 1983), pp. 1951–2174

——: *Drawings of the Rembrandt School*, viii (New York, 1984), pp. 3951–4489

W. Robinson: 'The Eavesdroppers and Related Paintings by Nicolaes Maes', *Holländische Genremalerei im 17. Jahrhundert, Symposium: Berlin 1984*, pubd in *Jb. Preuss. Kultbes.*, special issue iv (1987), pp. 283–313

——: 'Nicolaes Maes as a Draughtsman', *Master Drgs*, xxvii (1989), pp. 146–62

——: 'Nicolaes Maes: Some Observations on his Early Portraits', *Rembrandt and his Pupils: Papers Given at a Symposium in Nationalmuseum Stockholm, 2–3 October 1992* (Stockholm, 1993), pp. 98–118

WILLIAM W. ROBINSON

Maes Howe. Neolithic chambered tomb, dated to *c.* 2700 BC, on the Orkney mainland, Scotland, *c.* 14.5 km west of Kirkwall. Maes Howe is among the finest examples of Neolithic architecture in western Europe (*see also* PREHISTORIC EUROPE, §IV, 2). It is the type site for a local group of at least 11 passage graves, all characterized by a long passage leading to a large vaulted chamber with side-cells. Although these tombs are associated with carved megalithic decoration related to the art of Irish passage graves (*see* PREHISTORIC EUROPE, §IV, 3(i)), the Neolithic art at Maes Howe is confined to a series of engraved chevrons on the south-west buttress, comparable to decoration at the contemporary settlement of SKARA BRAE, also in Orkney.

The builders of Maes Howe handled the local flagstone with finesse to achieve a dry-stone structure of outstanding sophistication: together with its proximity to the stone

Maes Howe, interior of Neolithic chambered tomb, showing entrance, walling and buttresses, *c.* 2700 BC

circles of Brodgar and Stenness, the size and quality of the tomb suggest that it was intended to house the burial of a pre-eminent chieftain. The mound was first broken into in the 12th century AD, by Vikings who left runic inscriptions on the walls of the chamber. The tomb was cleared of debris and the runes first discovered by James Farrer in 1861, and subsequent excavations by V. Gordon Childe in 1954–5 and Colin Renfrew in 1973–4 elucidated the construction sequence of the mound and its surrounding earthworks.

A rocky knoll chosen as the site for the tomb was levelled shortly before 2700 BC to provide a flat platform on which to build. The inner structure of the tomb was built entirely in stone, and it consists of a vaulted chamber measuring 4.57 m square, with side-cells, entered through a passage 12 m long (see fig.). The chamber and cells were encased in a stone cairn with a carefully built outer face that created a stepped outline. The whole structure was then covered by a mound of earth and stones, now measuring 7.3 m high and 35 m in diameter at its base. Material for the mound was obtained from a wide, shallow ditch encircling it at a distance of *c.* 18 m; a low, stony bank was built along the outer lip of the ditch. The tomb's outer entrance could be closed by a large block of stone housed in a recess on the side of the passage. Roofed by flat lintels at a maximum height of 1.4 m, the passage is remarkable for the size of the stones used: for much of its length, the walls and roof consist of thin slabs measuring 5.6 m long × 0.17 m thick. In the chamber the walls initially rise vertically for 1.37 m, then for the next 1.2 m they converge slightly, simply by taking advantage of the oblique natural fracture of the sandstone flags. The corbelled roof survives to a height of 3.8 m and must originally have been finished with a lintel at about 4.5 m above the floor. Additional support for the weight of the roof was provided by a tall buttress bonded into each corner of the chamber, and where possible the walls were strengthened with slabs spanning the entire width of the chamber, often skilfully underpinned with slivers of stone. Each of the three walls not adjoining the passage has a raised entrance into a rectangular cell; three large blocks of stone found on the chamber floor appear to have been intended to close these. The only finds in the cells were a fragment of human skull and some animal bones.

Maes Howe is mentioned in *Orkneyinga Saga* (written *c.* AD 1200) as 'Orkhaugr', and it is clear, both from the saga and from the many runic inscriptions on the chamber walls, that the tomb was entered on more than one occasion in the 12th century AD. Several of the inscriptions refer to treasure, yet the original Neolithic burials are unlikely to have been accompanied by any object that a Viking would have regarded as treasure. Excavation of the bank encircling the tomb yielded evidence of refurbishment in the 9th century AD; it seems possible that this indicates re-use of the tomb for a Viking burial, the rich grave goods from which could have been robbed by later Norsemen and recorded in runes as treasure. Other carvings in the tomb include a dragon, a walrus and a serpent knot, all of Norse date.

BIBLIOGRAPHY

J. Farrer: *Notice of Runic Inscriptions Discovered during Recent Excavations in the Orkneys* (Edinburgh, 1862)
V. G. Childe: 'Maes Howe', *Proc. Soc. Antiqua. Scotland*, lxxxviii (1954–6), pp. 155–72
A. S. Henshall: *The Chambered Tombs of Scotland*, 2 vols (Edinburgh, 1963–72)
C. Renfrew: 'Investigations in Orkney', *Soc. Antiqua. London Res. Rep.*, xxxviii (London, 1979) [whole issue]

ANNA RITCHIE

Maesu. *See* CHO HŬI-RYONG.

Maewŏltang. *See* KIM SI-SŬP.

Maeyer, Marcel (de) (*b* St Niklaas, 23 July 1920). Belgian painter, art historian and teacher. He studied history and art history at the Rijksuniversiteit, Ghent (1938–42), subsequently becoming a curator until 1960 at the Koninklijk Museum voor Schone Kunsten in Antwerp, where he became the main specialist in the works of Ensor. From 1957 to 1986 he was a teacher and then a senior professor at the Rijksuniversiteit, Ghent. As a painter he was self-taught; his work was first exhibited in 1964 at the Galerie Ardetti in Paris and Galleria Ciranna, Milan, and until 1971 it was three-dimensional and dominated by the human figure. His series *Lives of the 12 Caesars* (after Suetonius) are assemblages of waste material (e.g. *The Fallen Emperor*, 1964; Brussels, Mus. A. Mod.). The *Death and Apotheosis of a Pope* series are polystyrene reliefs. He then experimented with terracotta. In 1967–8 he made 'picto-reliefs', such as *Paradise Lost*, which evokes a joyous profusion of plant life. His most striking official and public success came from 1971, when he became recognized as the most important Belgian hyperrealist painter. This phase ended *c.* 1978 with a series of monumental fragments of *Fairground Buildings*, in which he dealt directly with the problem of *trompe l'oeil* and the autonomy of abstract colouristic structures. In the 1980s he resumed a freer handling of materials associated with experiments in encaustic and in oils. These series include *Bouquet*, which chronicles the decay of flowers, as well as *Landscapes* and *Skies* (e.g. *Sky*, 1985; priv. col., see 1986 exh. cat., p. 71).

BIBLIOGRAPHY

P. Restany: 'Maeyer, l'intelligence de la technique', *Gal. A.*, xxii (Feb 1965), p. 4
Marcel Maeyer: Hyperrealism and Beyond (exh. cat. by L. Tegenbosch, Łódź, Mus. A., 1977) [Pol. and Eng.]
Marcel Maeyer (exh. cat. by C. Van Damme and H. Todts, Antwerp, Kon. Mus. S. Kst., 1986) [incl. cat. rai.]

HERWIG TODTS

Mafai, Mario (*b* Rome, 15 Feb 1902; *d* Rome, 31 March 1965). Italian painter. Mafai was the central figure of a group of artists called the SCUOLA ROMANA. His preference for lyrical, intimate subject-matter contrasted with the monumental neo-classicism of the Novecento Italiano. From 1922 until 1925 he attended the Accademia di Belle Arti in Rome. There he met his future wife, the artist Antonietta Raphael, who introduced him to the work of the Ecole de Paris. By 1927 the painter Scipione and the sculptor Marino Mazzacurati (1907–1969) gathered regularly in Mafai's studio, giving rise to an association known as the 'Scuola di Via Cavour'. During this period Mafai painted views of the River Tiber in a deliberately unschooled manner, self-portraits and still-lifes such as *Quartered Bullock* (1930; Milan, Brera), reminiscent of Chaïm Soutine. His series of still-lifes called *Dried Flowers* was begun after a year in Paris in 1930.

While Scipione went on to develop an increasingly expressionist style, Mafai responded to the formal research of Giorgio Morandi by stressing the tonal qualities in his paintings. This concentration on the subtle gradation of values endowed the commonplace objects of his still-lifes with a heightened, magical reality. After 1935 he developed veiled anti-Fascist themes in the *Demolition* series (*see* ROME, fig. 17), exhibited at the Galleria della Cometa in Rome in 1937. In *Demolition of the Suburbs* (1939; Rome, G.N.A. Mod.) the cross-sections of dilapidated houses allude to the razing of the city's working-class districts under the building programme instituted by Mussolini. In 1939 Mafai fled to Genoa fearing that his wife would be persecuted under the anti-semitic laws. Later that year he was conscripted into the military. He continued to paint still-lifes which by then often included mannequins, in a reworking of the ironic and hushed atmospheres characteristic of Pittura Metafisica. From 1940 to 1943 he painted *Fantasies*, a cycle of brutal scenes of Fascist horrors during the Resistance which was inspired by Goya's engraved series *Disasters of War*. Mafai returned to Rome in 1943 and continued working on his principal themes, also producing some abstract works during the 1950s.

BIBLIOGRAPHY

V. Martinelli: *Mario Mafai* (Rome, 1967)
Mafai: Mostra retrospettiva (exh. cat., Rome, Ente Premi Roma, 1969)
M. Fagiolo and V. Rivosecchi: *Mario Mafai* (Rome, 1986)

EMILY BRAUN

Maffei, Francesco (*b* Vicenza, 1605; *d* Padua, 2 July 1660). Italian painter. He probably trained with his father, Giacomo Maffei, before joining the workshop of the Maganza family in Vicenza. His early works, such as the *Ecce homo* (ex-Dianin priv. col., Padua, see Pallucchini, 1981, fig. 561), were influenced by the eclectic style, between Veronese and the Bassani, of Alessandro Maganza. The *St Nicholas and the Angel* (1626; Vicenza, S Nicola da Tolentino), with colours like those of Veronese, yet lighter, suggests Maffei's rapid development of an independent style that is both rugged and moving. His interest in narrative, already evident in scenes from the *Life of St Cajetan* (Vicenza, S Stefano), was developed in the later *Martyrdom of the Franciscan Minors at Nagasaki* (Schio, S Francesco), which is datable to about 1630. Here, the contrast between the pale, silvery tones of the background and the darker foreground figures is derived from Tintoretto, but the exaggerated Mannerist treatment of the main figures also recalls the art of such French engravers as Jacques Bellange and Pierre Brébiette. At the same time there is also an echo of the extreme stylizations of Giovanni Demio and, in the angels above, the marked influence of Veronese.

Towards 1638 Maffei was in Venice, where he became a collaborator of Santo Peranda (1566–1638) and finished Peranda's ceiling painting of *Paradise*, in the church of the Incurabili, and the altarpiece of the Pisani Chapel in S Nicola da Tolentino. In Venice, Maffei's art was enriched by contacts with the works of Johann Liss, Domenico Fetti and Bernardo Strozzi. He absorbed the late Mannerist elements of his provincial training into a freer and more Baroque style. His *Adoration of the Magi* (1640; Vicenza Cathedral), completed shortly after his return to Vicenza,

was inspired by Veronese's *Adoration of the Magi* (Vicenza, S Corona), but his handling is freer and more impetuous and the mood visionary. The picture is fully Baroque and is indebted to Rubens's treatments of this theme. The impact of 17th-century Lombard painting on Maffei's work, which critics have often stressed, is less easy to define. His *Translation of the Reliquaries of the Bishop-Saints Dominatore, Paolo and Anastasio* (Brescia, Old Cathedral) is spatially complex, with brilliantly free handling inspired by Tintoretto. The spectacular series of allegories in honour of the Podestà of Rovigo and of Vicenza (all 1644–56; Rovigo, Rotondo, and Vicenza, Mus. Civ. A. & Stor.) suggest the increasing complexity of Maffei's artistic sources. They unite the theatrical splendour of Veronese with a marked interest in portraiture and combine piety with passages of subtle Mannerist elegance. In the *Allegory in Honour of the Podestà Alvise Foscarini* (1648; Vicenza, Mus. Civ. A. & Stor.) the austere portrait of Foscarini is reminiscent of Velázquez, while the accompanying angel, derived from Liss, has an exuberance ultimately inspired by Rubens.

At the height of his success Maffei also painted mythological and biblical scenes with many figures. *Jephthah's Daughter* (Trent, Castello Buonconsiglio) and *Perseus and*

Francesco Maffei: *Perseus and Medusa*, oil on canvas, 1.3×1.6 m, 1650s (Venice, Galleria dell'Accademia)

Medusa (Venice, Accad.; see fig.), both datable to the 1650s, create powerful emotion and horror through boldly fragmented and dramatic close-up compositions and through the disturbing expressions and gestures of the figures, which may be stylistically indebted to the grotesque art of Pietro della Vecchia. Maffei here created a visionary world, which also unexpectedly returns to aspects of Mannerism, as in the *Sacrifice of Melchizedek* (Venice, Foscarini priv. col., see Pallucchini, 1981, fig. 591), which strikingly recalls Schiavone, although the form is predominantly Baroque.

The position of scenes from the *Life of the Virgin* (*c.* 1654) in the oratory of the Zitelle in Vicenza, high above the altar, allowed Maffei to experiment with daring perspectival effects. The cycle is distinguished by its unprecedentedly light tonality, indebted to Veronese, and by elegant figures reminiscent of Parmigianino. The cycle at the oratory of S Nicola da Tolentino in Vicenza (1655–7), with large canvases showing the *Miracles of St Nicholas*, is rich and more complex. The *Expulsion of the Rebel Angels* (1656; Venegona, Semin.), once in S Michele in Vicenza, constitutes a last homage to Tintoretto, yet the canvases of the final period of the artist in Padua, such as the *Adoration of the Magi* (Padua, S Tommaso Cantuariense), show at the end a return to the art of Veronese, modified by the grotesque from della Vecchia and with a richness that has a distinctly Baroque tone.

BIBLIOGRAPHY

N. Ivanoff: *Francesco Maffei* (Padua, 1942/R 1947)
F. Valcanover: 'Contributo alla conoscenza dell'ultimo Maffei', *A. Ven.*, iii (1949), pp. 114–18
Catalogo della mostra di Francesco Maffei (exh. cat., ed. N. Ivanoff; Vicenza, Basilica, 1956)
R. Pallucchini: 'Un fregio poco fortunato del Maffei', *A. Ven.*, xii (1958), pp. 134–40
R. Marini: 'La problematica maffeiana e un'opera inedita', *A. Ven.*, xv (1961), pp. 144–53
R. Pallucchini: *La pittura veneziana del seicento* (Milan, 1981), pp. 185–96

UGO RUGGERI

Maffei, Paolo Alessandro (*b* Volterra, 11 Feb 1653; *d* Rome, 1716). Italian antiquarian and writer. He belonged to one of the most illustrious Italian families, originally of Verona. After finishing his early studies, he was sent to Rome, where he lived with his uncle Ugo Maffei, the chargé-d'affaires for French business in the city. Thanks to the patronage of this powerful relative, he obtained a post in the Papal guard and meanwhile continued his studies of ancient authors. Taking advantage of his position, which gave him free access to the Roman museums and collections, he broadened his knowledge of the ancient monuments. He was over 50 years old when, in 1704, Domenico de Rossi published the work that perhaps remains his most important contribution, the *Raccolta di statue antiche e moderne*, an erudite commentary on 163 engravings, which also represented some modern works by Bernini and others. The illustrations were mainly done by French artists whom the author knew through his uncle. Three years later the same publisher produced a similar catalogue, the *Gemme antiche figurate*, with a commentary by Maffei.

WRITINGS

Raccolta di statue antiche e moderne (Rome, 1704)
Gemme antiche figurate (Rome, 1707)
as R. Romualdo: *Apologia del diario italico del P. Montfaucon* (Rome, 1710)

LUCA LEONCINI

Maffei, Raffaele [il Volaterrano] (*b* Rome, 1451; *d* Volterra, 1522). Italian official, writer and scholar. He followed the calling of his father Gherardo di Giovanni Maffei, a notary in the Camera Apostolica in Rome. In 1468 he entered the Curia as scriptor apostolicus, and in the following decade he lived with his brother Antonio Maffei in a house near S Eustachio, where a printing press was run for the benefit of Vatican secretaries with humanist interests. In 1479 Maffei entered the service of Cardinal Giovanni d'Aragona, son of Alfonso I, King of Naples, whom he accompanied to the court of Matthias Corvinus in Buda. Following his brief stay in Hungary, Maffei returned to Rome, taking part in archaeological excursions of the Accademia Pomponiana to ancient and Early Christian monuments. At his ancestral home in Volterra, Maffei hosted frequent meetings of humanists, many from Florence. He corresponded with Angelo Poliziano, Lorenzo the Magnificent and, following the fall of the Medici, Piero Soderini. His antiquarian pursuits, particularly as a translator of Aristotle, Procopius of Caesarea and Homer, culminated in his encyclopedia, the *Commentariorum urbanorum liber I–XXXVIII*, first published in 1506 and quickly disseminated throughout Europe. The work has three main divisions, the first part being *Geographia*, a descriptive atlas of the world modelled on Flavio Biondo's *Italia illustrata* (1453), on which Maffei published a commentary in 1527. *Anthropologia* includes a section on the popes and a short list of prominent artists and their work; this refers to Piero della Francesca's treatise *De Prospectiva pingendi*, as well as to paintings by such artists as Giotto, Mantegna, Leonardo, Perugino, Melozzo da Forlì and Ercole de' Roberti, whose works Maffei had seen in Hungary. He mistook Gentile Bellini for Giovanni Bellini in his reference to the decoration (destr. 1577) of the Sala del Maggior Consiglio in the Doge's Palace, Venice. Among sculptors, Maffei drew attention to Donatello and Antonio del Pollaiuolo, and he also mentioned three papal medallists: Andrea Guacialoti, whom he called Andreas Cremonensis, Cristoforo di Geremia of Mantua and Lysippus. Maffei claimed that Michelangelo would surpass all his contemporaries, as he had already with the *Pietà* (1498/1500) in the S Petronilla Chapel of St Peter's in Rome. Lastly Maffei noted the work of the Milanese sculptor Cristoforo Solari. The last section of Maffei's work, *Philologia*, follows book by book the Aristotelian corpus on natural and moral sciences. Disdaining the extravagance of papal Rome, Maffei retired in 1507 to Volterra, where he dedicated his remaining years to publications on such subjects as church reform, morality and Martin Luther, as well as writing poetry and an unpublished history of the pontificates of Julius II and Leo X. Maffei's tomb at S Lino in Volterra was executed by Silvio Cosini in 1522.

UNPUBLISHED SOURCES

Rome, Vatican, Bib. Apostolica, MS. Ottob. lat. 2377, fols 232–341 [*Raphaelis Volaterrani brevis sub Iulio Leoneque historia*]

WRITINGS

Commentariorum urbanorum liber I–XXXVIII: Item Oeconomicus Xenophontis ab eodem latio donatus (Rome, 1506)

BIBLIOGRAPHY

B. Falconcini: *Vita del nobil'uomo e buon servo di Dio, Raffaele Maffei detto il Volaterrano* (Rome, 1722)

P. Paschini: 'Una famiglia di curiali: I Maffei di Volterra', *Riv. Stor. Chiesa Italia*, vii (1953), pp. 337–76

PHILIP J. JACKS

Maffei, Scipione (*b* Verona, 1 June 1675; *d* Verona, 11 Feb 1755). Italian historian and writer. He was a member of the Veronese nobility and was educated at Jesuit colleges in Parma and Rome. He took part in the War of the Spanish Succession (1701–4) and afterwards became a member of the Accademia dell'Arcadia, a literary and philosophical society in Rome, absorbing its anti-Baroque attitudes and its demand for a new literature. He returned to Verona in 1705, where he continued to promote Arcadian ideas, founding the famous *Giornale de' letterati d'Italia* (1710) in Padua, which was followed between 1737 and 1740 by *Osservazioni letterarie*. The same themes appeared in his play *Merope* (1713), once considered the key work of 18th-century tragedy. In 1713 the late medieval codices of the Biblioteca Capitolare were discovered in Verona, followed two years later by the Roman tablets of the Accademia Filarmonica. These discoveries stimulated Maffei's passion for archaeology and palaeography. In these disciplines he collaborated with the most important scholars of the time, with whom he frequently corresponded. His activity in this area found expression both in his establishment of a lapidary museum, a collection of stone inscriptions in many languages together with pieces of antique sculpture, and in his masterpiece, the *Verona Illustrata* (1731–2), a work in eight volumes, which describes the city from the point of view of geography, history, archaeology and art using a documentary method based on original research. The book includes an essay on ancient theatres (published separately in 1728), and shows a precocious interest in Early Christian archaeology, the pictorial art of the Middle Ages and the particular qualities of the Veronese school of painting, the course of which is followed from its origins to the work of Paolo Caliari.

WRITINGS

Verona illustrata, 8 vols (Verona, 1731–2)

Museum Veronese (Verona, 1749)

BIBLIOGRAPHY

Studi maffeiani (Turin, 1909)

Miscellanea maffeiana (Verona, 1956)

A. Momigliano: *Il Contributo alla storia degli studi classici (Scipione Maffei)* (Rome, 1960)

G. Silvestri: *Scipione Maffei: Europeo del settecento* (Vicenza, 1968)

A. Bevilacqua: 'Scipione Maffei: Storico e critico d'arte', *Archv Ven.*, civ (1975), pp. 95–138

Atti del convegno: S Maffei e il museo maffeiano: Verona, 1983

F. Bernabei: 'La letteratura artistica', *Stor. Cult. Ven.*, v/1 (1985), pp. 485–508

FRANCO BERNABEI

Mafra. Town, 40 km from Lisbon, Portugal, entirely dwarfed by its palace-convent. In 1717 John V of Portugal, fulfilling a vow made in 1711, determined to rebuild a friary at Mafra for the Franciscans of Arrábida as thanks to God for the birth of a male heir. However, rather than housing about 13 members of the Order, as originally intended, the project dramatically expanded as the King appointed a vast team of workers. At its head was the German architect known in Portugal as JOÃO FREDERICO LUDOVICE, who had trained in Rome and had settled in Lisbon from 1701, and under him were the Milanese Carlos Baptista Garbo (*fl* 1698; *d* 1724), Custódio Vieira, Manuel da Maia and Ludovice's son António. The King also sought information about religious buildings in Rome from the Portuguese ambassador there and took advice from the Marquês de Fontes.

Between the laying of the foundation stone (17 Nov 1717) and the consecration ceremony in 1730 an army of masons, stone-cutters, carpenters etc from all over the kingdom gathered at Mafra; their numbers allegedly approached 45,000 as the project neared completion. A chronicler of the period recounts that a cloud of dust hung permanently over the site. The gigantic undertaking was made possible by the wealth of gold coming from Brazil at this time; this and the determination of the King explain the speed of execution. After the consecration, the lantern and some conventual areas were completed by contractors in 1735.

The plan of the palace-convent comprises two rectangles, with apartments on various floors. The rectangle containing the church and palace faces the town of Mafra and the sea, the more secluded rectangle being destined for the friars. In the centre of the main front (220 m long; for illustration *see* LUDOVICE, JOÃO FREDERICO) is the church, with two towers and a benedictional balcony like that at St Peter's in Rome, but intended for the King rather than the Pope; at either end is a square, domed pavilion. The whole façade, built mostly of local limestone, has an

Mafra, church of the palace-convent by João Frederico Ludovice, view of the dome above the crossing, 1730–35

urban air. The church, on a Latin cross-plan, is rather narrow and high (see fig.) and makes colourful use of marble. The adjacent sacristy, of yellow marble, combines rationality and sensitivity.

The interiors of the palace, such as the long scenographic gallery that runs parallel to the main façade, tend to be narrow, in the Portuguese tradition. The convent has housing for about 300 friars, in cells leading off long corridors on several floors. The most notable features are the magnificent library, the vestibule (lined with Italian statues of saints) and the staircase of honour, rather those of a palace than of a convent; the chapel of the Holy Land, a funerary chapel lined with black marble, the chapel of the Seven Altars, with its neo-Palladian loggia, and above all the Sala Elíptica, an unadorned chapter-room, the oval shape of which is a rarity in Portuguese Baroque architecture.

The chief influence at Mafra is the architecture of Baroque Rome, not only St Peter's but also Borromini and Rainaldi's S Agnese in Agone (1652–7). From Rome also came much of the statuary, including works by Carlo Monaldi, Giuseppe Baratta and others. However, unlike the Escorial in Madrid, to which it has been misleadingly compared, the distribution and articulation of spaces at Mafra make it clear that secular, courtly ideas predominated here, associated with the absolute power of John V. The vast complex, rhetorical and sublime, was the symbolic expression of his reign.

At a later stage the sculptor Alessandro Giusti worked at Mafra (1750–90), founding a school that trained several generations of Portuguese sculptors.

BIBLIOGRAPHY

R. Smith: 'João Frederico Ludovice, an Eighteenth-century Architect in Portugal', *A. Bull.*, xviii (1936)

A. de Carvalho: *A escultura em Mafra* (Mafra, 1956)

J. Fernandes Pereira: *Arquitectura barroca em Portugal* (Lisbon, 1986)

P. Varela Gomes: *O essencial sobre a arquitectura barroca em Portugal* (Lisbon, 1987)

JOSÉ FERNANDES PEREIRA

Magalhães, Mário Vieira de. *See* PORTO, SEVERIANO.

Magani, Mick (*b* Gatji Creek, Northern Territory, ?1920; *d* 1984). Australian Aboriginal painter. He was a member of the Mildjingi clan from the area of Gatji Creek in Central Arnhem Land in the Northern Territory. He had to leave the Methodist Mission station of Milingimbi after throwing a spear at one of the European staff; he subsequently spent some time in Fanny Bay Jail, Darwin. He later returned to Milingimbi and by the 1950s had become a prolific bark painter. Soon after the government settlement of Maningrida was established in 1957, Magani moved there and became one of the main ceremonial leaders of the community. He later moved back to his birthplace. His immense energy and humour was captured well in David Attenborough's account of him. His paintings are characterized by the black, red and white triangular-shaped Mildjingi cloud design but display great variety in their figurative content. A typical example is *Wongarr Spirits Return to Camp* (*c.* 1965; Canberra, N.G.). His work is well represented in the Ed Ruhe Collection, Lawrence, KS, and in the Australian National Gallery and the National Museum of Australia in Canberra.

BIBLIOGRAPHY

D. Attenborough: *Quest over Capricorn* (London, 1963), pp. 70–95

H. Groger-Wurm: *Eastern Arnhem Land*, i of *Australian Aboriginal Bark Paintings and their Mythological Interpretations* (Canberra, 1973), pp. 97–8, 106–7

HOWARD MORPHY

Maganza, Alessandro (*b* Vicenza, 1556; *d* after 1630). Italian painter and draughtsman. The son of Giambattista Maganza (*c.* 1509–86), he is the best-known member of a family of painters from Vicenza. According to Ridolfi, he was trained by his father and in the shop of Giovanni Antonio Fasolo, an associate and follower of Paolo Veronese. Lodi points out that Fasolo died in 1572 and that Alessandro spent the next four years in Venice. His work shows familiarity with the leading painters in Venice in this period: Jacopo Tintoretto, Veronese and Palma Giovane. In his first documented work, the *Virgin and Child with Four Evangelists* (1580) in the monastery of Monte Bérico, Vicenza, the figural types are close to Palma Giovane's; nothing extraneous is included in the symmetrical composition, and content is clearly stated. The severity is associated with a Counter-Reformation mentality, which Maganza maintained throughout his career. Its effect is partly mitigated by the juxtaposition of areas of deeply saturated colour, especially reds and blues. It is likely that he had studied Battista Zelotti's *Pentecost* (Vicenza, S Rocco) and his *Pentecost* and *Faith with the Four Evangelists* (Abbazia di Praglia, nr Padua, Benedictine monastery). The *Baptism of Christ* of 1591, also at Monte Bérico, clearly reveals the influence of Veronese's prototypes in both composition and the facial types of the angels. More thoroughly austere is the *Pietà* (*c.* 1600) in Vicenza Cathedral. The series of scenes of the *Passion* (1600–10) in the Cappella del Sacramento of the cathedral is closer to Tintoretto or Jacopo Bassano in its more active, robust style, as in the *Christ Being Nailed to the Cross*, in which Christ, a tumultuous crowd and the swooning Virgin are tightly packed and seen from a high viewpoint. The *Madonna of the Rosary* (*c.* 1610; Barbarano Vicentino, Parrocchiale) has a richly painted cornice, incorporating the *Stories of the Rosary*, which frames a straightforward representation of the *Virgin Enthroned with Saints*. Maganza frescoed the inner cupola of Palladio's Villa Rotonda, near Vicenza, with allegorical figures in colour, again recalling Veronese, and deities in monochrome; he also executed large ceiling canvases in tempera for the South and West rooms. His compositional pen sketches have occasionally been attributed to Veronese but are quite distinctive: rapid, skilful and competent, yet somewhat lacking in vitality. Examples include the *Vision of St Jerome* (Oxford, Christ Church) and the *Scene of Martyrdom* (Vienna, Albertina).

BIBLIOGRAPHY

C. Ridolfi: *Maraviglie* (1648); ed. D. von Hadeln (1914–24), ii, pp. 231–8

M. Boschini: *I Gioieli pittoreschi della città di Vicenza* (Venice, 1677), pp. 3–9, 30–34, 114–19

F. Lodi: 'Un tardo manierista vicentino: Alessandro Maganza', *A. Ven.*, xix (1965), pp. 108–17

C. Semenzato: *The Rotonda*, Corpus Palladianum, i (University Park, 1968), pp. 49–51, pls 33, 35, 36, 44–6, 49

E. Noè: 'Primo passo per Giambattista Maganza Senior', *A. Ven.*, xxx (1976), pp. 98–105

Palladio e la maniera (exh. cat. by V. Sgarbi, Vicenza, S Corona, 1980), pp. 106–20

DIANA GISOLFI

Magdeburg. German city and former archbishopric in Saxony-Anhalt, on the River Elbe. The town was established at an intersection for important trade routes on the west bank of the river, where it was fordable; a fortified trading settlement in the vicinity of the later cathedral close existed by AD 805. The old town grew up around three centres: the cathedral close, the Alter Markt with the Johanniskirche (destr. 1945), and a settlement around the Petrikirche (from 1380) and the Wallonerkirche. The cathedral close and the old town were legally and administratively separate. In 937 King Otto I founded the Benedictine monastery of St Mauritius, and, after Magdeburg had been made an archbishopric in 968 and the building became the cathedral, the monks moved into the newly founded monastery of Berge. The monumental imperial palace was situated north of the cathedral. The suburb of Sudenburg, the trading area under the protection of the castle, was first mentioned in 965. Under Archbishop Gero (reg 1012–23) the Ottonian fortifications of the town were extended, and the collegiate foundation of St Sebastian and the convent of Unsere Liebe Frau were founded. In the 11th century the old town was enlarged to include the parish of St Ulrich on the other side of the Breiter Weg. In 1213 the churches of St Jakob and St Katharine, which originally lay outside the old town wall, became parish churches. During the Romanesque period Magdeburg was a centre of brass production (see ROMANESQUE, §VI, 4(ii)). Under Archbishop Wichmann (reg 1152–92) the Alter Markt was enlarged; on it stood a statue of *Roland* and a stag monument (both destr. 1631) beside the statue of a horseman (copy *in situ*; original by Bamberg workshop that produced figures in the cathedral, Magdeburg, Kulthist. Mus.). Archbishop Albrecht II (reg 1205–32) began the rebuilding of the cathedral and extended the town wall; the new town is first mentioned in 1209. Magdeburg was destroyed by imperial troops under Johannes Tserklaes, Count of Tilly, in 1631, and only the cathedral and the convent of Unsere Liebe Frau were spared. The town was rebuilt in magnificent Baroque style under Burgomaster Otto von Guericke (1602–86), and from 1680 it was fortified to become the strongest fortress in Brandenburg-Prussia. The fortifications were razed in 1890. Four-fifths of the old town was destroyed in 1945, but it has been impressively rebuilt.

BIBLIOGRAPHY

E. von Niebelschütz: *Magdeburg* (Berlin, 1929)

H.-J. Mrusek: *Magdeburg* (Magdeburg, 1959)

E. Lehmann: *Der bezirk Magdeburg*, Dehio-Handbuch, ix (E. Berlin, 1974)

1. CATHEDRAL.

(i) Architecture. The cathedral is dedicated to SS Mauritius and Katharina. The Benedictine monastery founded in 937 by King Otto I as his burial place was converted to a cathedral from 955. In 968 Magdeburg became an archbishopric, and the cathedral was dedicated. An east crypt was consecrated by Archbishop Tagino (reg 1003–12) in 1008, and a further consecration took place in 1049 under Archbishop Hunfried (reg 1023–51). Parts of the Ottonian

church were excavated in 1901, 1920, 1926 and 1962. Of the porphyry, granite and marble columns brought by Otto I from Italy, twelve have been reused in the choir, nine are in the refectory ('sepultur'), eleven smaller ones are in the Lady chapel, and two are in the north transept gallery arcade. The Ottonian cathedral had an east choir with an apse flanked by towers, and a crypt with a horseshoe-shaped apse with five niches. The tombs of Otto I and his wife Edith (d 946) are supposed to have been situated in the two chambers in the lower storey of the north tower. The church had a continuous transept, an aisled nave and a sort of westwork with a crypt. In 1207 this building was gutted by fire.

In 1209 Archbishop Albrecht II laid the foundation stone for the new church, but a document of 1274 laments the incomplete state of the nave. In 1306–10 preparations were under way for building of the west front, although it was not completed until 1520, the last architect being Bastian Binder (*fl c.* 1515). In 1363 the splendid final consecration took place. Since 1567 the cathedral has been Protestant. The north tower was damaged during the siege of the city in 1631. The first general restoration was undertaken in 1826–34, and the cathedral was restored again after severe bomb damage in 1944–5, with services resumed in 1957.

The present cathedral is the first building in Germany constructed according to a French Gothic plan. It is a

1. Magdeburg Cathedral, exterior view of the choir from the east, begun *c.* 1209

cruciform, rib-vaulted basilica built of sandstone and is 111 m long internally. The transept has three square bays, the aisled nave has five; there is an ambulatory with radiating chapels, a choir gallery and a façade with two towers. The towers east of the transept were built only up to eaves level. In the first building campaign the four main piers of the two-bay choir and the ambulatory socle were constructed (see fig. 1); the interiors of the chapels are semicircular up to the level of the window sill, but their exteriors are polygonal from the foundations upwards. The decoration of the capitals is among the finest achievements of German Late Romanesque architectural sculpture. A second masons' workshop built the choir up to the string course below the gallery. The blind arcading of the exterior walls of the chapels, the bosses of the groin vaults and the round niches in the east wall of the transept are motifs from the Rhenish Transitional style. The main vessel of the choir, begun in 1220, was planned on the *Gebundenes System* (two aisle bays to each bay of the main vessel) using as a module the crossing square. The aisles are the same width as the choir ambulatory. From about 1230 a Cistercian workshop built the choir gallery, or *Bischofsgang*, which has elements from Burgundian Early Gothic. Characteristic features are the vaults with apexes of even height, but with (in part) stilted, round arches, descending to imposts at varying levels. The late Antique columns from the Ottonian cathedral are reused on the delicate compound piers of the ground storey. Above these are figures from an uncompleted portal set beside reliefs. The choir was finished after 1240 by a new master.

In the nave the galleries and *Gebundenes System* were discontinued; the side aisles are broader and the arcade arches wider, with two quadripartite rib vaults spanning each bay. The clerestory has two openings per bay, and the wall space between it and the arcade is blank. Between the two western towers is a narthex, the funerary chapel of Archbishop Ernst von Sachsen (*d* 1513), with a gallery over it. The west front is influenced by Strasbourg Cathedral. In front of the portal to the north transept is the Paradise Porch, with its jamb cycle of the *Wise and Foolish Virgins*. Although differences in the ornament and structure of the interior show changes of plan, the exterior of the nave is completely unified, characterized by low windows and ten gables. The distinctive choir forms a contrast. The total effect is of seriousness and majestic grandeur. The asymmetrically laid out cloister is on the south side of the church. Its east wing contains the two-aisled, ten-bay refectory, the Lady chapel and the Redekin Chapel founded in 1405. The two-storey south wing dates from the 12th century. The large four-bay sacristy of the 13th century in the west wing is also known as 'Cither' or St Maurice's Chapel.

BIBLIOGRAPHY
R. Hamann and F. Rosenfeld: *Der Magdeburger Dom* (Berlin, 1910)
W. Greischel: *Der Magdeburger Dom* (Berlin, 1929)
H. Giesau: *Der Dom zu Magdeburg* (Burg, 1936)
H.-J. Mrusek: *Drei deutsche Dome* (Dresden, 1963)
E. Schubert: *Der Magdeburger Dom* (Berlin, 1974; rev. Leipzig, 1984)

ERNST ULLMANN

(ii) Sculpture. Major works of figural sculpture survive from many phases of the cathedral's history. The earliest (now dispersed) are a group of ivories (*see* OTTONIAN ART, §VI). Stone reliefs depicting the *Beatitudes* and datable on stylistic grounds to *c.* the mid-12th century were probably part of the rood screen in the pre-1207 cathedral. Two brass tomb slabs of *Archbishop Friedrich von Wettin* (*d* 1152) and *Archbishop Wichmann* (*d* 1192), also from the old cathedral, demonstrate formal changes in the second half of the 12th century from a strictly geometrical treatment of the human figure to a looser, freer one (*see* ROMANESQUE, §VI, 4(ii)). Both slabs are from a foundry to which other works can be attributed, in particular the doors of Novgorod Cathedral, Russia (1152–4; *see* DOOR, §II, 1 and ROMANESQUE, §VI, 4(ii)).

The most important period for sculpture began with the rebuilding of the cathedral from 1209 and continued throughout the 13th century. Three distinct groups can be identified. The various fine capitals in the ambulatory have their antecedents in both 12th-century Lower Saxon architectural sculpture (e.g. Königslutter, SS Peter and Paul) and Rhenish and French art *c.* 1200 (*see also* GOTHIC, §III, 1(iii)(b)). Figures from a doorway, now in the high choir, are clearly later (*c.* 1220), and show the influence of sculptures at Notre-Dame, Paris (west doors), and Chartres Cathedral (south transept); they are the earliest indication in Germany of a familiarity with French High Gothic forms. Some 30 years later another workshop, probably from Bamberg and inspired by Reims, created sculptures of the *Wise and Foolish Virgins*, the *Church* and the *Synagogue*, *St Maurice* (in the choir), *St Catherine* (in the choir), the *Annunciation* (in the choir) and *Emperor Otto I* and his wife *Edith* enthroned (both in the nave). The vivid depiction of the emotions in the statues of the *Virgins* (see fig. 2) indicates a desire to involve the onlooker. The sculptures, which may originally have been placed against the rood screen, were subsequently (*c.* 1300) moved to the doorway of the north transept and, with those at Bremen and Strasbourg (*see* STRASBOURG, fig. 7), founded an iconographic tradition that persisted in Germany until the 16th century.

Later sculpture includes two late 13th-century standing figures of the *Virgin* (variations on a French theme). The tomb slab of *Archbishop Otto von Hessen* (*d* 1361) and the Elisabethaltar (*c.* 1360) have artistic links with sculptures in Brunswick or Erfurt and Halberstadt. The reliefs of the heavily restored choir-stalls (*c.* 1340–50) echo motifs from those (1308–11) of Cologne Cathedral. The tomb slab of *Archbishop Albrecht von Querfurt* (*d* 1403) is an isolated example of the Soft style. A *Man of Sorrows* with angels in the choir chapel and a *St Maurice* (1467) in the altar of the Ernstkapelle exhibit the love of detail characteristic of Late Gothic realism. From the end of the 15th century date a cenotaph for Empress Edith in very Late Gothic forms and the badly damaged *St Catherine* and *St Maurice* figures (*c.* 1515) from the north doorway; the period culminated in the tomb (1495, see Stafski, p. 65) of *Archbishop Ernst von Sachsen* (*d* 1513) by Peter Vischer the elder, which links Gothic construction with a new figural concept (*see* VISCHER, (2)). In the late 16th century and early 17th, memorial plaques of canons, the pulpit (1595–7) by Christof Kapup (*fl* before 1595) and works by Hans Klintzsch (*fl* 1590), Sebastian Ertle (*c.* 1570–*c.* 1612) and CHRISTOPH DEHNE were produced. The most important recent monument is Ernst Barlach's

2. Magdeburg Cathedral, portal of the north transept, the *Foolish Virgins*, h. *c.* 1.25 m each, *c.* 1260

memorial (1929) to those who died in World War I, which is a stirring condemnation of war.

BIBLIOGRAPHY

G. Deneke: *Magdeburger Bildhauer der Hochrenaissance und des Barock* (Halle, 1911)
H. Stafski: *Der jüngere Peter Vischer* (Nuremburg, 1962)
D. Schubert: *Von Halberstadt nach Meissen: Bildwerke des 13. Jahrhunderts in Thüringen, Sachsen und Anhalt* (Cologne, 1974), pp. 258–64, 285–305
E. Schubert: *Der Magdeburger Dom* (Berlin, 1974, rev. Leipzig, 1984)
M. Gosebruch: 'Die Magdeburger Seligpreisungen', *Z. Kstgesch.*, xxxviii (1975), pp. 97–126
K. Hardering: 'Kölner Motive am Magdeburger Chorgestühl', *Köln. Dombl.*, 1 (1985), pp. 53–62
Der Magdeburger Dom: Ottonische Gründung und staufischer Neubau: Leipzig, 1986
Gothic and Renaissance Art in Nuremberg, 1300–1550 (exh. cat., New York, Met., 1986), p. 382
K. Niehr: *Die mitteldeutsche Skulptur der ersten Hälfte des 13. Jahrhunderts* (Weinheim, 1992), pp. 108–25, 290–310

KLAUS NIEHR

Magenta, Giovanni Ambrogio. *See* MAZENTA, GIOVANNI AMBROGIO.

Maggi, Baldassare [Baltasar Maio da Vomio] (*b* Arogno, Ticino, before 1550; *d* Arogno, 29 March 1629). Italian architect, active in south Bohemia and Moravia. He reconstructed the castles of the Rožmberk dynasty at Česky Krumlov, where in 1580 he introduced an arcaded gallery into the great 13th-century tower, and Bechyně, to which he added a hall and new wings around a courtyard (1580–84). He was probably responsible for the Renaissance dwellings and a terrace (1581) added to the medieval fortress of Helfštejn in eastern Moravia. At Česky Krumlov he built the dormitory of the Jesuit College (1586–8) to a design by P. Alexander, and he built and decorated the villa of Kurzweil (now Kratochvíle; 1580–89; with Antonio Melana) for Vilém Rožmberk (*d* 1592) in a symmetrical ensemble with a chapel and a garden unusual at that time in central Europe, possibly influenced by the Neugebäude in Vienna.

For a related noble family, the Lords of Hradec, Maggi transformed the medieval castle of Frauenburg (now Hluboká) into a Renaissance mansion (re-Gothicized heavily in the 1840s). In the courtyard of the castle at

JINDŘICHŮV HRADEC he extended the line of Antonio Ericero's new block of the 1560s with a further addition in three storeys, joined to the main block by an arcaded wing attributed to Melana. Another arcaded wing was built by Antonio Cometta (*c.* 1555–1602) to Maggi's designs (1591). Cometta also built Maggi's rotunda (1591–3), with a tent-like roof, in the palace garden, one of the most interesting Renaissance architectural works in central Europe. At the Hradec castle in Telč, southern Moravia, Maggi built and decorated a new south wing, joined to the existing blocks with arcaded wings on two sides to form a five-sided courtyard. One of these sides opens on to an Italianate walled garden, similarly bordered with arcades, into which a Renaissance chapel penetrates, surmounted by a hall (1575–80). Maggi's works for the Bohemian and Moravian nobility were usually richly decorated with wall paintings and stuccowork or terracottas. They are of a north Italian Mannerist character; local influence is perceptible in articulated and graded contour of the upper parts of the rotunda, the chapel and hall at Telč, and the tower at Česky Krumlov.

BIBLIOGRAPHY

J. Krčálová: *Centrální stavby české renesance* [Centrally planned buildings of the renaissance in Bohemia] (Prague, 1974), pp. 18–26

——: 'Arts in the Renaissance and Mannerist Periods', *Renaissance Art in Bohemia* (London, New York, Sydney and Toronto, 1979), pp. 49–147

——: *Renesanční stavby Baldassara Maggiho v Čechách a na Moravě* [Renaissance buildings of Baldassare Maggi in Bohemia and Moravia] (Prague, 1986) [with archival sources and complete bibliog.]

J. KRČÁLOVÁ

Maggiolini, Giuseppe (*b* Parabiago, nr Milan, 13 Nov 1738; *d* Parabiago, 16 Nov 1814). Italian furniture-maker. He was the most renowned Italian furniture-maker of his time. He began his career as a carpenter in the monastery of S Ambrogio della Vittoria at Parabiago, near Milan, and from 1771 worked for Milanese and Genoese patrons. He was appointed cabinetmaker to Ferdinand (1754–1806), Archduke of Austria and Governor of Lombardy, and his wife, Maria Beatrice d'Este (1750–1829). Maggiolini's exceptional marquetry decoration was noticed in 1776 by the painter Giuseppe Levati (1729–1828) and by Marchese Pompea Litta, for whom he executed numerous pieces designed by Levati (drawings in Milan, Castello Sforzesco). Maggiolini also worked for Prince Eugène de Beauharnais, as well as for Stanislav II Poniatowski, King of Poland, and Queen Caroline of Naples (1782–1839). Designs for his inlay work were provided by such important artists as Andrea Appiani. Motifs include trophies of musical instruments, fruit, ribbons, volutes of acanthus leaves resembling cornucopias, bouquets of flowers and elements of Classical architecture (e.g. commode, 1790; Milan, Castello Sforzesco). These images were created from various stained and shaded woods, while the body of each piece of furniture was constructed in walnut. Maggiolini's son, Carlo Francesco Maggiolini, an able draughtsman and engraver, often worked with his father. After Giuseppe's death, Carlo Francesco continued the business with Cherubino Mezzanganica (*d* 1866) until 1834, when Mezzanganica inherited the workshop. All high-quality Italian marquetry furniture dating from the late 18th century is frequently indiscriminately attributed to Maggiolini's workshop. Those pieces that do not bear his signature can be identified by a mark depicting a furniture workshop and the inscription *con firma per esteso*. His works are in the collections of the Museo Civico and the Palazzo Reale, both in Milan.

BIBLIOGRAPHY

F. Meda: *Un centenario artistico* (Milan, 1914)

G. Marangoni: *Gli intarsi del Maggiolini* (Milan, 1918)

E. Sioli-Legnani: 'La mostra commemorativa di G. Maggiolini', *Riv. Milano* (Dec 1938)

G. Morazzoni: *Giuseppe Maggiolini* (Milan, 1953)

FERNANDA CAPOBIANCO

Maggiore, Giovanni Ambrogio (*b* ?Milan, *c.* 1550; *d* ?Rome, after 1 Feb 1598). Italian turner of ivory and wood. He or his brother, Dionigi Maggiore, with whom he worked for a while, succeeded in making a rotary lathe that was capable of producing not only the usual round turnings but also oblique forms. Little is known of the early stages of this invention; possibly the brothers based it on a project (now untraced) by Leonardo da Vinci. In 1573 a Milanese art dealer, Prospero Visconti, brought Maggiore to the attention of Crown Prince William, later William V, Duke of Bavaria (*reg* 1579–98), as an 'insignis faber' (noted craftsman) who knew how to turn oval frames. The Prince, who was interested in the discovery, brought Maggiore to Bavaria to work and to teach the new technique. In Munich, Maggiore passed on the technique to his pupils, and as early as 1576 Georg Wecker (*fl* 1575–1610), son of the court turner Hans Wecker (*d* 1577), took a new lathe and the new techniques to Saxony, leading to the development of the Dresden school of ivory turning. As a result of Prince William's unstable financial position, however, Maggiore received only temporary appointments, at the princely residence at Landshut and later in Munich. On New Year's Day 1575 Prince William presented his sister in Graz with one of the first examples of artistic turning; a small oval ivory box (Munich, Bayer. Nmus.) with portraits in tapestry of two of the Prince's children, it is dated 1576. In 1579 William was godfather to one of Maggiore's children. In 1582 William sent to the Medici in Florence a *Kontrafetkugel* (a turned series of nested ivory balls or other items, similar to 'Chinese balls') by Maggiore (Florence, Pitti), which was set up in the Tribuna of the Uffizi. In 1585 Philip II of Spain acquired a similar piece (untraced). A stacking box ascribed to Maggiore, painted by Joris Hoefnagel and dated 1586 (Vienna, Ksthist. Mus.), survives, as does a similar piece (Stockholm, Kun. Husgerådskam.), undated but certainly made before 1590, when the miniaturist left the court in Munich. Little is known of the later life of Maggiore. From Milan, he thanked William for a gift in 1593, and in 1595 Paolo Morigi praised him as a successful Milanese artist. In 1597 Grand Duke Ferdinand I de' Medici recommended Maggiore, 'il sordo delli ovati', to Rome, where he was still working on commissions for the Medici court in Florence by 1 February 1598.

BIBLIOGRAPHY

D. Diemer: 'Giovanni Ambrogio Maggiore und die Anfänge der Kunstdrechselei um 1570', *Jb. Zentinst. Kstgesch.*, i (1985), pp. 295–342

Prag um 1600: Kunst und Kultur am Hofe Rudolfs II (exh. cat., Essen, Villa Hügel, 1988; Vienna, Ksthist. Mus.; 1989), i, p. 529, no. 410

DOROTHEA DIEMER

Maggiotto [Fedeli]. Italian family of painters. (1) Domenico Maggiotto belonged to the group of 18th-century Venetian artists centred round Giovanni Battista Piazzetta, whose influential late Baroque style was based more on the effects of chiaroscuro than on colour. Domenico's son (2) Francesco Maggiotto was also a painter, although of lesser importance than his father.

(1) Domenico Maggiotto (*b* Venice, 1712; *d* Venice, 16 April 1794). He attended the school of Giovanni Battista Piazzetta in Venice from the age of ten, and until the latter's death (1754) he was active there as an assistant. His works between 1730 and 1750 are characterized by an adherence to the expressive formulae of Piazzetta and are concentrated exclusively on genre subjects, for example *Boy with a Flute* (*c*. 1745; Venice, Ca' Rezzonico). The plasticity of form and the strong preference for chiaroscuro effects are the most obvious characteristics of his works of this period, during which he collaborated on several large canvases painted by Piazzetta, including *Alexander before the Body of Darius* (*c*. 1745–7; Venice, Ca' Rezzonico). Following the death of Piazzetta, Maggiotto, clearly disorientated by the lack of firm guidance, developed a tendency towards impersonal eclecticism. At the suggestion of Giuseppe Angeli (1712–98), he completed, in lightened tones, the altarpiece of *St Nicholas and the Blessed Arcangelo Caneti* (1754) for S Salvatore, Venice, which had already been roughly sketched out by Piazzetta; he also produced two of the *Stations of the Cross* (1755) for S Maria del Giglio. A certain lack of experience with works on a large scale is also apparent, particularly in the rather cold and disunited quality of such works as the altarpiece of *St Bartholomew* (1758–9) in S Bartolomeo at Valnogaredo, near Padua.

From the time of Maggiotto's election to the Accademia di Belle Arti, Venice, in 1756, he developed a classicizing, narrative style; he produced numerous works of an anecdotal, moralistic and historical nature, for example *Volumnia and Coriolanus* (*c*. 1770; Padua, Mus. Civ.). However, he continued until the end of his career to produce genre scenes, for example *Man Looking at a Medal* (*c*. 1770; Milan, Treccani priv. col.) and *Restaurant Scene* (*c*. 1770; Rome, priv. col., see Martini, p. 553, no. 872), which also reveals the influence of Rembrandt's portraiture, perhaps resulting from Maggiotto's contacts with Giuseppe Nogari. Maggiotto was also important as a restorer of paintings.

BIBLIOGRAPHY
R. Pallucchini: 'Domenico Fedeli detto il Maggiotto', *Riv. Venezia*, 11 (1932), pp. 485–95
——: *La pittura veneziana del settecento* (Venice and Rome, 1960), pp. 160–61, 236
M. A. Bulgarelli: 'Profilo di Domenico Maggiotto', *A. Ven.*, xxvii (1973), pp. 220–35
E. Martini: *La pittura del settecento veneto* (Udine, 1982)
E. Merkel: 'Domenico Fedeli detto il Maggiotto', *Giambattista Piazzetta: Il suo tempo, la sua scuola* (exh. cat. by R. Pallucchini, Venice, Pal. Vendramin-Calergi, 1983), pp. 153–62
F. del Torre: 'Per un catalogo di Domenico Maggiotto', *Atti Ist. Ven. Sci., Lett. & A.*, cxlvi (1987–8), pp. 87–112
——: 'Nuovi documenti per Domenico Maggiotto', *A. Ven.*, xlii (1988), pp. 170–73

(2) Francesco Maggiotto (*b* Venice, 1738; *d* Venice, 13 Sept 1805). Son of (1) Domenico Maggiotto. He continued his father's innovations, while also being an eclectic follower of such major 18th-century Venetian painters as Giambattista Pittoni, Giambattista Tiepolo, Pietro Longhi (ii) and Francesco Zuccarelli. He studied with Michelangelo Morlaiter (1729–1806) and Pietro Novelli. His paintings include historical subjects, allegories (e.g. *Nature Presented to the Academy*, 1769; Venice, Gal. Venezia) and genre scenes that tend towards the didactic and moralistic, derived from the work of Longhi, which he knew through the engravings of Josef Wagner (1706–80). Within the circle of the Accademia in Venice, he was widely appreciated as a painter, and among his pupils were the most important Venetian artists of the early 19th century, including Lattanzio Querena (1768–1853), Carlo Bevilacqua (1775–1849), Natale Schiavoni (1777–1858) and Francesco Hayez.

BIBLIOGRAPHY
A. Tessier: 'Di Francesco Maggiotto pittore veneziano', *Archv Ven.* (1882), pp. 289–314
S. Sponza: 'Appunti su Francesco Maggiotto', *Not. Pal. Albani*, xiv/1 (1990), pp. 65–8
FILIPPO PEDROCCO

Mägi, Konrad (*b* nr Tartu, 1 Nov 1878; *d* Tartu, 15 Aug 1925). Estonian painter. Together with Kristjan Raud, Jan Koort and Nikolai Triik (1884–1940), Mägi was one of the first Estonian artists to break away from the official academic style of painting. In 1905 he entered the Baron Stieglitz Institute of Technical Drawing in St Petersburg but broke off his studies because of the revolutionary events of 1905. From 1907 he studied painting and sculpture in private academies in Paris. In 1908–10 he worked in Norway; his *Norwegian Landscape with Pine Trees* (*c*. 1910; Tallinn, A. Mus. Estonia) is typical of this period and was inspired by Germano-Dutch Impressionism. In 1912 he returned to Estonia, where he taught drawing, from 1914 in his own studio. At this time he was in a Fauvist phase and produced the first significant paintings of the Estonian landscape. *Vilsandi Motif* (*c*. 1913–14; Tallinn, A. Mus. Estonia), for example, is closer to an abstract representation of a locality than a precise portrayal of nature. In 1915–17 Mägi painted landscapes in the southern part of the country, while from around 1918 he used motifs from Võrtsjärv and Otepää, painted in darker colours than before, and to reflect the general mood of despondency he intensified the oppressiveness of the sky. He used the blue-black pigments of German Expressionism, as in the watercolour *Oberstdorf Landscape* (1922; Tallinn, A. Mus. Estonia), in which the contours of the individual mountains, valleys and woods create a distinctive flowing rhythm. Mägi also painted portraits, while his book illustrations were executed in a somewhat archaic Art Nouveau style. In 1922–3 he lived in Italy, where he added an understanding of colour, typical of Orphism, to previous Expressionist influences.

BIBLIOGRAPHY
Konrad Mägi (exh. cat. by T. Nurk, Tartu, Mus. A., 1969)
E. Pihlak: *Konrad Mägi* (Tallinn, 1979)
SERGEY KUZNETSOV

Magic lantern. Apparatus used to project an image, usually on to a screen, in use from at least the 17th century to the early 20th, the precursor of the modern slide projector. A transparent slide containing the image was placed between a source of illumination and a set of lenses to focus and direct the image. Although Athanasius Kircher is traditionally regarded as the first to outline the principles involved in the magic lantern in his book *Ars magna lucis et umbrae* (Rome, 1646, rev. Amsterdam, 1671), it is known to have been in use much earlier. Kircher's work is regarded as a development of the work of Giambattista della Porta (?1535–1615), who popularized the CAMERA OBSCURA and wrote *Magiae naturalis* (Naples, 1558). Although Kircher had apparent success in projecting images painted on strips of glass, improvements to the apparatus came about only following the investigations of such scientists as W. J.'s Gravesande (1688–1742). Early lanterns were crude, and the dependence on oil for illumination meant that most were fitted with a chimney in order to expel heat and fumes. Improvements in the magic lantern and the development of possibilities in the projection of optical effects were closely tied to the search for an illuminant that was stronger and more stable. When oil was finally superseded by limelight (lime ignited in oxy-hydrogen gas) and then by acetylene and the electric arc lamp, the magic lantern show was able to exploit sophisticated images involving effects of colour and movement; having been for a time the preserve of travelling showmen, the magic lantern was able to take its place among the major public optical spectacles of the 18th and 19th centuries.

Slides were hand-painted on glass until well into the 19th century. The ground pigments (occasionally watercolours) were diluted with varnish and blacked in with India ink. The spectacle itself usually demanded the use of strong colours, and sometimes an artist was employed simply to make the outlines of the image, leaving the rest to a colourist. Many 19th-century slides contain skilfully executed images—there was already a tradition of painting on glass (e.g. Thomas Gainsborough's slides for his 'show-box', 1780s; London, V&A)—while the cruder examples from the 18th and 19th centuries have a direct relation to images in contemporary popular prints. Few of the earlier slide painters' names are known, with the exception of the showman Etienne Gaspard Robertson (1763–1837), inventor of the *Fantasmagorie* spectacle (slides in Paris, Conserv. N. A. & Métiers), who also patented in 1799 a method of transferring an impression of a copperplate engraving on to glass. Despite the limitations of hand-painting, sophisticated optical effects were known, especially after the introduction of a method of imparting movement to figures in the early 18th century: this was generally achieved by pulling the slide across by hand, but the image could also be manipulated with the use of levers, and random movement could be created with the use of airstreams, for example. Panoramic slides and processional images (along with chase scenes) were especially popular. During the second half of the 19th century the painting, or at least colouring, of slides became a popular amateur pastime. The slide industry grew, and lantern shows became more popular and more ambitious. Vast spectacles involving sophisticated optical effects and simple narratives were produced, often before large audiences, as at the Royal Polytechnic Institution in London (slides now in London, Sci. Mus.; Oxford U., Mus. Hist. Sci.; and

elsewhere), where such images as the 'chromatrope' (a revolving kaleidoscopic slide) were used. One of the main developments of this period was the 'dissolving view', introduced *c.* 1837 by the projectionist Henry Langdon Childe (1782–1874); this created a simple but startling transformation scene not unlike the effect of the DIORAMA. This effect itself became so popular that 'dissolving views' became synonymous with 'lantern shows'.

Early magic-lantern spectacles had often consisted of supernatural images, sometimes projected on to smoke or a semi-transparent screen (e.g. Robertson's *Fantasmagorie*), which satisfied a public taste for the ghoulish and macabre. The magic lantern was also used for similar effects in the theatre. Gradually, however, as they became larger and involved more sophisticated optical effects, magic lantern shows were, by the 1860s at least, well on the way to becoming the most popular of all forms of public entertainment. In addition, around this time the photographic lantern slide (first developed *c.* 1858 by the Langenheim Brothers of Philadelphia) was introduced, although hand-painted slides were still being produced at the end of the 19th century. Photographic slides were still often coloured by hand, but along with the introduction of chromolithographic transfer, they ushered in a period of mass production. The possibility of photographic projection developed with the introduction of the gelatin dry-plate process, the achromatic lens and a powerful illuminant. The successful projection of detail became possible, and immediately the educational possibilities were exploited. The most popular subjects were works of art and topographical views. The teaching of art history, in particular, was transformed. The 'lantern lecture' became more of an instructional occasion. In Britain, for example, what had earlier been an optical spectacle became dominated by the Church and temperance societies for moral instruction. In this context a particularly successful photographic genre developed, the 'life-model series', in which a lengthy narrative illustrating some sternly moral tale or song was represented in a series of photographic scenes. In the USA a more secular context enabled one showman, Alexander Black (1859–1940), to produce narrative dramas lasting a whole evening, containing hundreds of slides. This meant that when the first film was produced in 1895 (the film projector itself being a modified magic lantern), there was already a public arena for cinema, which eventually usurped the magic lantern. It was not until after World War I, however, that the magic lantern ceased to be used for major public entertainments. By the late 20th century its modern equivalent, the slide projector, continued in use in instructional contexts and more private settings.

BIBLIOGRAPHY

T. C. Hepworth: *The Book of the Lantern* (London, 1889)
O. Cook: *Movement in Two Dimensions* (London, 1963)
C. W. Ceram: *Archaeology of the Cinema* (London, 1965)
J. Barnes: *Catalogue of the Collection: Barnes Museum of Cinematography, St Ives, Cornwall, England*, i–ii (St Ives, 1967–70)
J. Remise, P. Remise and R. Van de Walle: *Magie lumineuse: Du théâtre d'ombres à la lanterne magique* (Paris, 1979)
W. Hoffmann and A. Junker: *Laterna magica: Lichtbilder aus Menschenwelt und Gotterwelt* (Berlin, 1982)
H. B. Leighton: 'The Lantern Slide and Art History', *Hist. Phot.*, viii/1 (Jan–March 1984), pp. 107–18

J. Barnes: 'The Projected Image: A Short History of Magic Lantern Slides', *New Magic Lantern J.*, iii/3 (1985), pp. 2–7
L. Mannoni: *Le Grand Art de la lumière et de l'ombre: Archéologie du cinéma* (Paris, 1994)

KEVIN HALLIWELL

Magic Realism. Style of painting popular in Europe and the USA mainly from the 1920s to 1940s, with some followers in the 1950s. It occupies a position between Surrealism and Photorealism, whereby the subject is rendered with a photographic naturalism, but where the use of flat tones, ambiguous perspectives and strange juxtapositions suggest an imagined or dreamed reality. The term was introduced by art historian Frank Roh in his book *Nach-Expressionismus: Magischer Realismus* (1925) to describe a style deriving from Neue Sachlichkeit, but rooted in late 19th-century German Romantic fantasy. It had strong connections with the Italian Pittura Metafisica of which the work of Giorgio de Chirico was exemplary in its quest to express the mysterious. The work of Giuseppe Capogrossi and the Scuola Romana of the 1930s is also closely related to the visionary elements of Magic Realism. In Belgium its surreal strand was exemplified by René Magritte, with his 'fantasies of the commonplace', and in the USA by Peter Blume, as in *South of Scranton* (1930–31; New York, Met.). Later artists associated with Magic Realism include the American George Tooker (*b* 1920), whose best-known work *Subway* (1950; New York, Whitney) captures the alienation of strangers gathered in public, and the German Christian Schad, who also used the style in the 1950s. The later use of the term for types of non-Western, particularly Latin American fiction was not connected with the artistic application.

BIBLIOGRAPHY

F. Roh: *Nach-Expressionismus: Magischer Realismus* (Leipzig, 1925)
Neue Sachlichkeit and German Realism of the Twenties (exh. cat., intro. W. Schmied; London, Hayward Gal., 1978–9)
Realismo Magico: Pittura e scultura in Italia, 1919–1925 (exh. cat. by M. Fagiolo dell'Arco, Milan, Pal. Reale, 1989)

Magilp. *See* MEGILP.

Maginnis, Charles D(onagh) (*b* Londonderry, 7 Jan 1867; *d* Boston, MA, 15 Feb 1955). American architect and writer. He moved to the USA from Ireland at the age of 18. After an apprenticeship to Edmund M. Wheelwright in Boston, he established his own office, also in Boston, at about the turn of the century with Timothy Walsh (1868–1934). Among the Boston Gothicists headed by Ralph Adams Cram, Henry Vaughan (1846–1917) and Bertram Grosvenor Goodhue, Maginnis quickly established himself as a leader, best known for the magnificent Gothic Revival buildings of Boston College (begun 1909), for which the firm earned an American Institute of Architects Gold Medal. Like Cram, Maginnis's work was eclectic and included the Spanish-style Carmelite Convent (*c.* 1915), Santa Clara, CA, and the regal Classical Revival chapel of Trinity College (*c.* 1920), Washington, DC, as well as a number of churches in the Lombard style, for which he had a special affinity. The best of these is St Catherine's (1907), Spring Hill, Somerville, near Boston, MA. Important interior work by Maginnis in churches designed by others includes the high altar and baldacchino

of St Patrick's Cathedral, New York, and the entire chancel (1938) of H. H. Richardson's Trinity Church, Copley Square, Boston. Maginnis, who served as President of the American Institute of Architects, was given the institute's highest award, the Gold Medal, in 1948.

BIBLIOGRAPHY

S. Baxter: 'The Works of Maginnis and Walsh', *Archit. Rec.*, liii (1923), pp. 93–115
R. Walsh and A. Roberts, eds: *Maginnis, Charles Donagh: A Selection of his Essays and Addresses* (New Haven, 1956)

DOUGLASS SHAND-TUCCI

Magistris, Simone de (*b* Caldarola, Macerata, 1538; *d c.* 1611). Italian painter. He was the son of a painter, Giovanni Andrea de Magistris (*fl c.* 1510–60), and signed his first works, including the *Adoration of the Magi* (1566; Matelica, S Francesco), with his brother Giovanni Francesco de Magistris (*b* 1540). Simone's earliest independent painting, the *Nativity* (1570; Fabriano, Pin. Civ.), shows the influence of Pellegrino Tibaldi and the Zuccaro brothers. A brief stay at Loreto with Lorenzo Lotto left no trace on his style. Simone executed numerous paintings, mostly signed and dated, of variable quality and formulaic iconography, in small towns of the Marches and Umbria. The frescoes (1580–82) in the sanctuary of Macereto, near Visso, show a knowledge of the contemporary painters in Rome gained from a stay in the city (see Ponzi). His style did not evolve further, but in his better works there is a definite originality, as in the *Virgin and Child with SS Andrew and James* (1585; Osimo, Baptistery) and the *Death of St Martin* (1594; Caldarola, S Martino). His three canvases in S Maria, San Ginesio (Macerata), depicting the *Last Supper*, the *Road to Calvary* and the *Crucifixion* (all 1594), show an unrestrained expressiveness that suggests knowledge of northern European engravings.

BIBLIOGRAPHY

P. Zampetti: 'I pittori da Caldarola e Simone de Magistris', *Not. Pal. Albani*, ix/1–2 (1980), pp. 90–98
R. Petrangolini Benedetti Panici: 'Simone de Magistris', *Lorenzo Lotto nelle Marche: Il suo tempo, il suo influsso* (exh. cat., Ancona, Il Gesù, Francesco alle Scale and Loggia dei Mercanti, 1981), pp. 480–502
P. Zampetti: 'Simone de Magistris', *Andrea Lilli nella pittura delle Marche tra cinquecento e seicento* (exh. cat., Ancona, Pin. Com., 1985), pp. 175–85
E. G. Ponzi: 'Tra Roma e le Marche: Simone de Magistris, Antonio Tempesta e Domenico Malpiedi', *Prospettiva*, 57–60 (1989–90), pp. 99–107

ELISABETTA GIFFI PONZI

Magliabechiano [Gaddiano], Anonimo (*fl c.* 1537–57). Italian writer. The only known work by this anonymous writer is a manuscript (Florence, Bib. N. Cent., MS. Magl. XVII, 17), including biographies of major artists active in Florence from the late 13th century to the 16th, which was discovered in 1755 in the Magliabechiano collection of manuscripts and first published in 1892 (Frey). Its provenance can be traced back to descendants of the Gaddi family of artists, hence its alternative title. The provenance and the accuracy of the accounts of Gaddo, Taddeo and Agnolo Gaddi suggest that the family was known to the writer who was evidently a Florentine citizen, although probably not an artist. The manuscript begins with a list of artists of Classical antiquity and continues with biographies of artists in Florence from Cimabue to Michelangelo, but not in strict chronological order. There is also a brief section on Sienese artists. It ends with a list of artists' names, including Raphael and Sebastiano del Piombo, so arranged as to suggest that the work was to be continued. Bound with the main text is an account of buildings and works of art in Rome, written *c.* 1544–5, and of the Certosa del Galluzzo (also known as di Val d'Ema), near Florence, written in 1545 or after. Notes on works of art in Rome, Perugia and Assisi by another anonymous author are also included, and a copy of the introduction to Cristoforo Landino's commentary (Florence, 1481) on Dante's *Divine Comedy* that begins with an account of the artists of Classical antiquity derived from Pliny's *Natural History*.

The Anonimo manuscript is generally thought to have been written in 1542–8. The reference to Michelangelo's *Last Judgement* (Rome, Vatican, Sistine Chapel) indicates a date after 1541, and a *terminus ante quem* of 1557 is suggested by a note stating that the writer intended to include a life of Pontormo, who died in that year. A number of sources have been identified. For the section on ancient artists the writer consulted Pliny, either directly or via Landino, and the canon tables of Eusebius of Caesarea. The principal source for his account of Florentine artists, which is mentioned in the manuscript, is the Libro di Antonio Billi, a collection of notes probably dating from 1516–35, written or owned by Billi, a Florentine merchant (*see* BILLI, ANTONIO). The relationship between the two was noted by Milanesi. The Libro survives in two copies, both in the Biblioteca Nazionale Centrale, Florence: the Codex Petrei (MS. Magl. XIII, 89) and the Codex Strozziano (MS. Magl. XXV, 636). The Anonimo follows the latter most closely, although his account includes details and comments that do not appear in either copy of the Libro. This may indicate either that there was another, more complete, manuscript by the author of the Libro or that both used another source. Neither copy of the Libro begins with artists of the Antique: the Anonimo's account of Lorenzo Ghiberti's activities is taken virtually verbatim from Ghiberti's *Commentarii* (*c.* 1452–5) as is much of his information on Sienese artists. He consulted Angelo Poliziano's *Liber facetiarum* (1548) for his notes on Sandro Botticelli, and it is clear that he knew the *Cronica* of Giovanni Villani (*c.* 1275–1348). The Anonimo's text seems to be an elaboration of earlier sources (Kallab; Murray). The extent of his own contribution is difficult to assess, as his descriptions of works of art tend to follow established formulae. In some instances, he conflates or duplicates information obtained from different sources, indicating that he did not employ them critically. His biographies are factual accounts, without the narrative quality of Giorgio Vasari's *Vite* (1550, rev. 2/1568), but provide the fullest account of Italian art before Vasari.

WRITINGS
MS. (*c.* 1542–8; Florence, Bib. N. Cent., MS. Magl. XVII, 17); ed. C. Frey in *Il Codice magliabechiano cl. XVII 17, . . . scritto da Anonimo Fiorentino* (Berlin, 1892)
MS. (*c.* 1542–8; Florence, Bib. N. Cent., MS. Magl. XVII, 17); ed. A. Ficarra in *L'Anonimo Magliabechiano* (Naples, 1968)

BIBLIOGRAPHY
G. Milanesi: 'Documenti inediti riguardanti Leonardo da Vinci', *Archv Stor. It.*, 3rd ser., xvi (1872), pp. 219–30
C. von Fabriczy: 'Il libro di Antonio Billi e le sue copie nella Biblioteca Nazionale di Firenze', *Archv Stor. It.*, 5th ser., vii (1891), pp. 299–368
——: 'Il Codice dell'Anonimo Gaddiano (Cod. magliabechiano XVII, 17) nella Biblioteca Nazionale di Firenze', *Archv Stor. It.*, 5th ser., xii (1893), pp. 15–94, 275–334
W. Kallab: *Vasaristudien* (Vienna and Leipzig, 1908), pp. 178–207
P. Murray: *An Index of Attributions made in Tuscan Sources before Vasari* (Florence, 1959)
J. Schlosser-Magnino: *La letteratura artistica*, iii (Florence, 1964), pp. 190–92
Il libro di Antonio Billi (MS.; 1516–35); ed. F. Benedettucci (Rome, 1991)
HELEN GEDDES

Magnani, Giovanni Battista (*b* Parma, 21 Sept 1571; *d* Parma, 21 May 1653). Italian architect and designer. He may have been a pupil of Giovanni Battista Aleotti; he helped to complete Aleotti's design for the hexagonal church of S Maria del Quartiere (1604) in Parma. In 1605 or 1606 he produced a first design for the Altar of the Virgin in the right transept of Alessandro Balbi's church of the Madonna della Ghiara (1596) in Reggio Emilia. This was reconstructed in 1614, again to Magnani's design. He also designed the Altar of the City in the left transept of the church (1618). In 1608 he constructed the Altar of S Giuseppe in the church of S Maria della Steccata, Parma (modified in the 18th century). Magnani probably added the choir (1610) to S Maria del Quartiere and perhaps also built the adjoining convent. Other works in Parma include the Benedictine convent of S Paolo, where he designed the fountain cloister (1613–24) and perhaps the large stairway; and it is almost certain that he was responsible for the handsome campanile of S Giovanni Evangelista (1614). In 1622 Magnani was appointed City Architect of Parma. Later that year he reconstructed the church of S Alessandro in an interesting scenographic re-elaboration of Pellegrino Tibaldi's church of the SS Martiri (*c.* 1577), Turin. The side chapels are framed by Serlian windows that form a continuum with those of the presbytery. The ceilings are frescoed with *quadratura* paintings by Angelo Michele Colonna. In 1627–8 Magnani rebuilt the Palazzo Comunale (unfinished), which had collapsed in 1606. In 1628 he and Marcello Buttigli organized the temporary festive constructions for the formal entry of Margherita of Tuscany, the bride of Odoardo Farnese, 5th Duke of Parma.

BIBLIOGRAPHY
B. Adorni: *L'architettura farnesiana a Parma, 1545–1630* (Parma, 1974), pp. 62, 65, 71, 191–210
BRUNO ADORNI

Magnasco. Italian family of artists.

(1) Stefano Magnasco (*b* Genoa, *c.* 1635; *d* Genoa, *c.* 1670–73). Painter. He trained in Genoa in the workshop of Valerio Castello, whose influence can be seen in the *Mystic Marriage of St Catherine* (Genoa, priv. col., see Gavazza, 1987, fig. 179). Other painters he looked towards were Giovanni Benedetto Castiglione and Anthony van Dyck, as in the *Crucified Christ Comforted by an Angel* (Genoa, S Maria delle Vigne). The *Adoration of the Magi* (Genoa, priv. col., see Biavati Frabetti, fig. 7) shows a naturalism characteristic of early 17th-century Genoese painting.

Magnasco was in Rome *c.* 1655–60. The *Guardian Angel* (Genoa, S Teodoro), drawing on Pietro da Cortona's painting of the same subject (Rome, Pal. Corsini), and the *Triumph of David* (Novi Ligure, Coulant Peloso priv. col., see Gavazza, 1987, fig. 182), with its debt to Poussin, show him moving from Castello's manner to a more precise draughtsmanship, rounded forms and a clearly defined and limited palette.

The only paintings by Stefano Magnasco that can be securely dated, the *Miracle of St Uvo* (1663; Genoa, oratory of the SS Concezione) and the *Death of St Joseph* (1666; Genoa, Osp. Civ. S Martino), postdate his return to Genoa. Both evince an assimilation of Roman painting, with compositions reflecting the late devotional works of Cortona. However, other works from the period preceding his early death, such as *Moses Leading the Israelites out of Egypt* (priv. col., see Biavati Fabretti, fig. 23), return to a rich and luminous palette and an insistence on narrative realism and echo the work of Castiglione. Though Stefano Magnasco left many signed canvases, his eclecticism still offers problems in establishing his development.

BIBLIOGRAPHY

R. Soprani and C. G. Ratti: *Delle vite de' pittori, scultori ed architetti genovesi*, 2 vols (Genoa, 1768–9), i, pp. 349–50; ii, p. 156

E. Gavazza: 'Il momento della grande decorazione', *La pittura a Genova e in Liguria: Dal seicento al primo novecento*, ii (Genoa, 1971, rev. 1987), pp. 201–4, 257–60, n.6

G. Biavati Frabetti: 'Preliminari a Stefano Magnasco', *Paragone*, cccv/409 (1984), pp. 4–39

V. Belloni: *Scritti e cose d'arte genovese* (Genoa, 1988), pp. 166–74

FEDERICA LAMERA

(2) Alessandro Magnasco [Lissandrino] (*b* Genoa, 4 Feb 1667; *d* Genoa, 12 March 1749). Painter and draughtsman, son of (1) Stefano Magnasco. He did not study with his father, who died when he was a small child. He went to Milan, probably between 1681 and 1682, and entered the workshop of Filippo Abbiati (1640–1715). His *Christ Carrying the Cross* (Vitali, priv. col., see Franchini Guelfi, 1987, fig. 238) faithfully repeats the subject and composition of Abbiati's painting of the same subject (Pavia, Pin. Malaspina). Alessandro Magnasco's early works were influenced by the harsh and dramatic art of 17th-century Lombardy, with dramatic contrasts of light and dark and livid, earthy tones, far removed from the bright, glowing colours of contemporary Genoese painting. The depiction of extreme emotion in the *St Francis in Ecstasy* (Genoa, Gal. Pal. Bianco) was inspired by Francesco Cairo's *Dream of Elijah* (Milan, S Antonio Abate). However, Magnasco was already expressing himself in a very personal manner, with forms fragmented by swift brushstrokes and darting flashes of light. The *Quaker Meeting* (1695; ex-Viganò priv. col., see Franchini Guelfi, 1991, no. 18) is one of his first genre scenes. In this early period he specialized as a *figurista*, creating small human figures to be inserted in the landscapes and architectural settings of other painters. He also began collaborating with the landscape painter Antonio Francesco Peruzzini, with a specialist in perspective effects, Clemente Spera, and other specialist painters; it was not until between 1720 and 1725 that Magnasco himself began to create the landscapes and architectural ruins that provide the setting for his figures.

From about 1703 to 1709 Magnasco was in Florence, where he and Peruzzini worked for Grand Prince Ferdinand de' Medici and his highly cultured court. The *Journey of the Monks* (Turin, Gal. Sabauda), the *Old Woman and*

the Gypsies (Florence, Uffizi) and other paintings now in the Uffizi and Pitti in Florence were completed during this period. In the witty *Hunting Scene* (Hartford, CT, Wadsworth Atheneum) Magnasco portrayed himself and his friend the painter Sebastiano Ricci on a hunting expedition with Ferdinand de' Medici and his court. During these years Magnasco began to experiment with a wide range of subjects drawn from varied sources. He found inspiration in prints, such as those of the series on the *Quakers* after Egbert van Heemskerck, and painted three scenes inspired by Jacques Callot's *Misères de la guerre*: the *Inquisition* (Vienna, Ksthist. Mus.), the *Entry to the Hospital* (Bucharest, Mus. A.) and the *Sacking of a City* (Sibiu, Bruckenthal Mus.). He responded to the ironic low-life paintings by Dutch and Flemish artists, of which there were many in the Medici collections, and the lively court of Ferdinand encouraged an interest in burlesque art. Two popular literary genres, the Spanish picaresque novel and the literature of the *pitocchi* (sea beggars), which related the adventures of vagabonds, beggars, gypsies and footpads in tones ranging from the dramatic to the grotesquely comical, provided a further source of inspiration.

After returning to Milan, probably in 1709 (it is not known when he made the stay in Venice reported by his biographer, Carlo Giuseppe Ratti), Magnasco worked for the Lombard aristocracy, continuing to collaborate with Peruzzini and Spera but also experimenting with completely new subject-matter, as in the *Capuchin Friars' Refectory*, the *Capuchin Friars Studying* and the *Catechism in Church* (all Seitenstetten Abbey, Austria), painted between 1719 and 1725 for Conte Gerolamo Colloredo, the Austrian Governor of Milan. These works, and others completed during the succeeding period, such as the *Satire of the Nobleman in Poverty* (Detroit, MI, Inst. A.) and *The Synagogue* (Cleveland, OH, Mus. A.), suggest the artist's active participation in the intellectual debates of advanced aristocratic circles. His clients included such celebrated and progressive families as the Borromeo, the Archinto, the Arese, the Visconti and the Casnedi. In the first half of the 18th century in Milan, protests against corruption in the monastic orders, religious intolerance and social prejudice and ignorance began to be expressed in circles that were particularly sensitive to the new ideas of the Enlightenment emanating from France, Austria and the countries of northern Europe.

Magnasco returned to Genoa in 1735, remaining there until his death. His oeuvre shows contacts with the Genoese school in which his father had trained (Valerio Castello, Domenico Piola, Gregorio de' Ferrari), in its rhythmically disjointed brushwork and drapery and its flowing continuity of figures and gestures, as can be seen in *St Ambrose Expelling Theodosius from the Church* (Chicago, IL, A. Inst.) and the *Massacre of the Innocents* (The Hague, Mauritshuis). Yet in other ways his art contrasts sharply with the bright and glowing colours of Genoese decorative painting. In Magnasco's paintings the small figures are corroded by shadow, the colours are dull and leaden, almost monochromatic, and the swiftly executed brushstrokes are filled with tension. There is no serenity, and no easy visual pleasures are offered by his subjects, which express, particularly in the artist's final

Alessandro Magnasco: *Embarkation of the Galley Slaves in Genoa Harbour*, oil on canvas, 1.16×1.42 m, *c.* 1740 (Bordeaux, Musée des Beaux-Arts)

years, deeply felt moral judgements on the realities of the day, as in the *Arrival and Torture of the Prisoners* and the *Embarkation of the Galley Slaves in Genoa Harbour* (*c.* 1740; see fig.; both Bordeaux, Mus. B.-A.). The *Sacrilegious Theft* (Milan, Pal. Arcivescovile), an ex-voto completed in 1731 for S Maria at Siziano near Pavia depicting the Virgin putting to flight thieves who had broken into the church by night, seems to anticipate Goya in the terrifying presence of skeletons and the macabre nocturnal atmosphere, as do the four fearsome *Witches* (priv. col., see Franchini Guelfi, 1977, pls xli–xliv). In his final years Magnasco's rapid brushstrokes, as in the *Supper at Emmaus* (Genoa, Convent of S Francesco d'Albaro), suggest fleeting effects of light, dissolving solid forms, while in the *Entertainment in a d'Albaro Garden* (Genoa, Gal. Pal. Bianco) his total rejection of formal Rococo frivolity is expressed in the portrayal of the petty and futile life of an aristocratic family.

Magnasco left many drawings, and there is a large group in the Uffizi, Florence. *Woodcutters and Fishermen* and *Two Pilgrims and a Seated Woman* (both Florence, Uffizi) are characteristic of his fluid and expressive studies, in black and red chalk, for the figures that enliven his pictures. There are few compositional studies. He has evoked a variety of critical reactions. He was vastly successful during his own lifetime, as is shown by the large number of works by pupils and copyists that repeat the iconography and stylistic characteristics of his paintings. Forgotten during the 19th century, he was rediscovered in the early years of the 20th century by Benno Geiger, who compiled the catalogue of his works.

BIBLIOGRAPHY

R. Soprani and C. G. Ratti: *Delle vite de' pittori, scultori ed architetti genovesi*, ii (Genoa, 1769)
B. Geiger: *Alessandro Magnasco* (Berlin, 1914)
G. Delogu: *Pittori minori liguri, lombardi, piemontesi del seicento e del settecento* (Venice, 1931)
M. Pospisil: *Magnasco* (Florence, 1944)
B. Geiger: *Magnasco: I disegni* (Padua, 1945)
——: *Magnasco* (Bergamo, 1949)
A. Morassi: *Mostra del Magnasco* (Bergamo, 1949)
F. Franchini Guelfi: 'Alessandro Magnasco', *La pittura a Genova e in Liguria: Dal seicento al primo novecento*, ii (Genoa, 1971/R 1987)
——: *Alessandro Magnasco* (Genoa, 1977)
——: 'Magnasco inedito: Contributi allo studio delle fonti e aggiunte al catalogo', *Stud. Stor. A.*, v (1983–5), pp. 291–328
——: *Alessandro Magnasco* (Soncino, 1991)
——: 'Alessandro Magnasco', *Genova nell'età barocca* (Bologna, 1992), pp. 210–20
——: 'Alessandro Magnasco', *Kunst in der Republik Genua, 1528–1815* (Frankfurt am Main, 1992), pp. 201–13
——: 'Le 'macchiette' e i 'pensieri' di Alessandro Magnasco', *Disegni genovesi dal cinquecento al settecento* (Florence, 1992), pp. 235–63

FAUSTA FRANCHINI GUELFI

Magne. French family of architects. Auguste-Josephe Magne (*b* Etampes, 2 April 1816; *d* Paris, 15 July 1885) was the son of the architect Pierre Magne. He studied architecture at the Ecole des Beaux-Arts, Paris, where in 1838 he won second prize in the competition for the Prix de Rome. He spent much of his career in the architecture department of the city of Paris, where he built the church of St Bernard-de-la-Chapelle (1858–61), which has a Gothic Revival leadwork spire over the crossing, and several iron-framed market halls, usually in collaboration with his son Lucien Magne (*b* Paris, 7 Dec 1849; *d* Paris, 28 July 1916). Auguste-Josephe also built the theatre at Angers (1865–71), the mairie of Eaubonne (1869), near Paris, and the chapel and hospice (1872) at Albart (Cantal). Lucien began his career in the architecture department of the city of Paris as clerk of works (1873), inspector (1875) and architect (1885) to the Marché de la Chapelle. Other municipal works included the architectural elements of the monument (1889) to *Urbain Le Verrier* in front of the Observatoire, and the municipal wash-houses on the Seine to replace the 'bâteaux-lavoirs'. In 1874 he joined the Service des Edifices Diocésains, and he was appointed diocesan architect to Autun (1877) and Poitiers (1888). He also worked for the Commission des Monuments Historiques, being given responsibility for the départements of Maine-et-Loire and Seine-et-Oise (1878) and Bordeaux (1892). He was appointed Inspecteur-Général to the Commission in 1901 and architect of the church of Sacré-Coeur, Paris, in 1904. He also wrote on art history and taught at the Ecole des Beaux-Arts as professor of the history of architecture (from 1891) and at the Conservatoire National des Arts et Métiers at Poitiers (from 1899).

BIBLIOGRAPHY

Bellier de La Chavignerie–Auvray

L. Magne: *L'Oeuvre des peintres verriers français* (Paris, 1885)

——: *L'Architecture française du siècle* (Paris, 1889)

——: *L'Art appliqué aux métiers* (Paris, 1898)

J.-M. de Fêcamp: 'A.-J. Magne', *Congr. Archéol. France* (1934), p. 276

JEAN-MICHEL LENIAUD

Magnelli, Alberto (Giovanni Cesare) (*b* Florence, 1 July 1888; *d* Meudon, 20 April 1971). Italian painter. He was born into a wealthy family of textile traders and, on the death of his father in 1891, his education was supervised by his uncle Alessandro. From 1907 he taught himself to paint by visiting galleries and studying Quattrocento fresco cycles, especially those by Paolo Uccello and Piero della Francesca. From 1911, through the circle of Giovanni Papini and Ardengo Soffici, Magnelli came into contact with Futurism and the international avant-garde: he responded to Cubism through the reproductions in Guillaume Apollinaire's *Les Peintres cubistes: Méditations esthétiques* (Paris, 1913) but infused his large figures constructed from simplified curved planes with an individual use of bold colour (e.g. *Workers on the Cart*, 1914; Paris, Pompidou). In March 1914 he travelled with the poet Aldo Palazzeschi to join Soffici, Papini and Carlo Carrà in Paris, where he met Apollinaire, Henri Matisse, Pablo Picasso, Fernand Léger and others. Commissioned to expand his uncle's collection, Magnelli bought works by Picasso, Juan Gris, Carrà and three of the most controversial sculptures at the Salon des Indépendants:

Alexander Archipenko's *Medrano II* and *Carrousel Pierrot* (both 1913; New York, Guggenheim) and *The Boxers* (1913–14, New York, MOMA). The solidity and colour of his own work impressed Apollinaire, who encouraged Magnelli's move towards 'pure' painting.

Unable to return to Paris because of World War I, Magnelli used drawings made there as the basis for his first abstract paintings, characterized by angled planes of unmodulated colour (e.g. *Painting No. 0528*, 1915; Buffalo, Albright-Knox A.G. *See also* ITALY, fig. 40). These experiments were interrupted in 1916 by military training and ill health and, on returning to painting, he reintroduced the figure in a geometric form close to Synthetic Cubism. Their austerity gradually gave way to the celebratory nudes of the *Lyrical Explosion* series (1918). The widespread return to tradition after the war led Magnelli to execute figure studies and Tuscan landscapes in subdued tones. By 1925 this realism became tempered by brighter colour and by a reduction of modelling and perspective. Despite large one-man shows (Galleria Pesaro, Milan, 1929, and Galleria Bellenghi, Florence, 1930), Magnelli suffered a crisis of direction and temporarily abandoned painting. Although the extraction of marble at Carrara provided renewed inspiration, his coincidental move from the restrictive Fascist art world to Paris (October 1931) was equally important. The jagged, floating rock forms of the resulting *Stones* series, exhibited at the Galerie Pierre, Paris, in 1934 (e.g. *Stones No. 2*, 1932; Marseille, Mus. Cantini), paralleled Surrealism and the object paintings of Léger, with whom he re-established contact. They presaged his return to abstraction, a course encouraged by Enrico Prampolini. Together they participated in the Abstraction–Création group with Vasily Kandinsky, Piet Mondrian and Hans Arp, and Magnelli's clearly delineated abstract compositions were included in *Origines et développement de l'art international indépendant* (Paris, Jeu de Paume, 1937) and *L'arte concreta* (Milan, Gal. Il Milione, 1938).

With World War II Magnelli and his wife Susi Gerson formed a mutually supportive circle with Sonia Delaunay, Hans Arp and Sophie Taeuber-Arp at Grasse (Provence), where he made collages and paintings on gridded school slates (e.g. *Ardoise*, c. 1942; Basle, Kstmus.). His post-war reputation was established by one-man shows at the Galerie René Drouin, Paris (1947), and the Venice Biennale (1950), inspiring younger artists, such as Nicolas de Staël, Jean Dewasne and Piero Dorazio. In 1955 his uncle Alessandro's collection was dispersed, and Magnelli's earliest works came to public attention; critical disbelief over their early dates was refuted by surviving witnesses such as Palazzeschi. In 1959 he settled in Meudon, where he made many of his characteristic balanced late works (e.g. *Fiorenza*, 1962; Zurich, Ksthaus). He left works to Florence (Pitti) and Paris (Pompidou) on his death.

BIBLIOGRAPHY

Alberto Magnelli (exh. cat. by F. Russoli, M. Mendes and J. Lassaigne, Florence, Pal. Strozzi, 1963)

M. Mendes: *Alberto Magnelli* (Rome, 1964)

Magnelli, 1909–1918 (exh. cat. by J. Lassaigne and A. Lochard, Brussels, Pal. B.-A.; Paris, Mus. A. Mod. Ville Paris; 1973)

Magnelli nelle collezioni della Galleria d'Arte Moderna di Palazzo Pitti (exh. cat. by S. Pinto and A. Lochard, Florence, Pitti, 1973)

A. Maissonier: *Catalogue raisonné de l'oeuvre peint d'Alberto Magnelli* (Paris, 1975)

Alberto Magnelli: L'Oeuvre gravé (exh. cat. by A. Maissonier, Paris, Bib. N., 1980)

A. Maissonier: *Alberto Magnelli: Les Ardoises peintes* (St Gall, 1981)

Magnelli: Ardoises et collages (exh. cat. by D. Abadie and G. C. Argan, Paris, Pompidou; Grenoble, Mus. Grenoble; 1986–7)

Omaggio a Magnelli (exh. cat. by S. Salvi and M. Calvesi, Florence, Pal. Vecchio, 1988)

D. Abadie, ed.: *Magnelli* (Paris, 1989)

MATTHEW GALE

Magnesia on the Maeander [now Tekin]. Town in central Ionia (now western Turkey), which flourished in Hellenistic times. According to tradition, Magnesia was among the earliest Greek settlements in Anatolia and was found by the Aeolians from Thessaly. In the 7th century BC it was captured by the Lydian king Gyges (*reg* 680–652 BC) and destroyed by the Kimmerians *c.* 650 BC. After being rebuilt with help from Miletos, it fell to the Persians *c.* 530 BC, and in 460 BC they presented it to the exiled Athenian general Themistokles. The exact location of this early city is uncertain, but in 400–398 BC the Spartan general Thibron transferred the settlement to its present site beside Mt Thorax (Gümüş Daği), where the Archaic Sanctuary of Artemis Leukophryene stood. The reason for the transfer was to evade the silt carried down by the Maeander River. Although it retained its original name, the new settlement was not actually sited on the river but on its tributary, the Lethaeus (Gümüş Çay), on an important road between Ephesos, Priene and Tralleis.

The city remained under Persian control until liberated by Alexander the Great in 334 BC. Subsequently, under Seleucid rule and later under the Attalids of Pergamon, it developed into an important centre renowned for its grain production. It was among the few Asiatic cities to side with Rome against Mithridates of Pontos in 87 BC. Consequently, in Roman times Magnesia was a free city that claimed, according to a 3rd-century AD coin, to rank seventh in Asia. From Byzantine times until the 12th century AD it was an episcopal seat. The site was first explored in 1842–3 and systematically excavated in 1891–93.

The fortified city measured 1300×1100 m, with a grid of streets precisely orientated north–south and east–west. The principal surviving monument is the Temple of Artemis (late 3rd century BC–early 2nd). According to Vitruvius (*On Architecture*, III.ii.6) this pseudodipteral Ionic building was designed by HERMOGENES and built on the remains of an Archaic Temple of Artemis. It faced west, like the temples at Ephesos and Sardis, and had an opisthodomos. Its 8 by 15 columns and nine-stepped platform (67 by 41 m) made it the fourth largest temple in Asia Minor. The pronaos, with two internal columns and two *in antis*, was as big as the cella, which had six internal columns; the opisthodomos had two *in antis*. The temple's 200-m-long frieze depicting an *Amazonomachy* (Istanbul, Archaeol. Mus.; Paris, Louvre) appears to be the earliest figural frieze on the entablature of an Anatolian Ionic temple. The Attic column bases are also the earliest in Anatolia and were probably introduced by Hermogenes. In front of the temple stood a monumental altar of Pergamene type.

The replies of 70 cities invited to attend the festival of Artemis Leukophryene are recorded in inscriptions in Magnesia's agora, which covers some 26,000 sq. m, and in which stood a total of 420 columns as well as a propylon, a shrine of Athena and a fountain house. There was also a small Ionic prostyle Temple of Zeus Sosipolis (early 2nd century BC), also probably designed by Hermogenes. The temple faces west and has an opisthodomos; its frieze is uncarved. Its columns have eustyle spacing, again attributed to Hermogenes (Vitruvius: III.iii.6–8), with intercolumnar spaces of two and a quarter times the lower diameter. The agora, the Temple of Zeus and the theatre (4th century BC) are now covered by silt from the Gümüş Çay, so that only the remains of the Temple of Artemis, the Roman baths, odeion, gymnasium and stadium are visible.

BIBLIOGRAPHY

C. Humann: *Magnesia am Maeander* (Berlin, 1904)

A. von Gerkan: *Der Altar des Artemis-Tempels in Magnesia am Mäander* (Berlin, 1929)

A. Yaylali: *Der Fries des Artemisions von Magnesia am Mäander* (Tübingen, 1976)

A. Davesne: *La Frise du Temple d'Artémis à Magnesie du Méandre* (Paris, 1982)

O. Bingöl: 'Zu den neueren Forschungen in Magnesia', *Hermogenes und die hochhellenistische Architektur*, ed. W. Hoepfner and Schwandner (1990), pp. 63–8

——: 'Vitruvische Volute am Artemis-Tempel von Hermogenes in Magnesia am Mäander', *Istanbul. Mitt.*, xliii (1993), pp 399–415

ORHAN BİNGÖL

Magni, Cesare (*b* Milan, *c.* 1495; *d* Milan, 1534). Italian painter. He was the illegitimate son of Francesco Magni, a member of a prominent Milanese family. In 1511, while Fermo Tizoni's apprentice, he joined a protest against the officials of the Scuola di S Luca, Milan. In a will of 1524, Magni indicated that he wished to leave a drawing (untraced) of the Virgin in S Francesco (presumably a copy of all or part of Leonardo da Vinci's *Virgin of the Rocks*) to S Maria delle Grazie, Milan. In 1526 he painted a *St Apollonia* (untraced) for S Maria presso S Celso. An altarpiece of the *Virgin and Child with SS Peter and Jerome* (Milan, Bib. Ambrosiana) dates from 1530, while both the *Crucifixion* (Vigevano Cathedral) and the *Virgin and Child with SS Peter Martyr and Vincent Ferrer* (Codogno, S Biagio) are from 1531. Two years later he executed frescoes of *SS George and Martin* (Saronno, S Maria dei Miracoli) and a *Virgin and Child with SS Sebastian and Roch* (ex-Bodemus., Berlin) for the oratory of S Rocco at Codogno.

Magni is often considered one of the Milanese followers of Leonardo; he was, however, a generation younger than the Florentine's Lombard disciples. His surviving works, all from rather late in his short career, are strongly influenced by Bernardino Luini and his circle, by Cesare da Sesto and, indirectly, by Raphael.

BIBLIOGRAPHY

W. Suida: *Leonardo und sein Kreis* (Munich, 1929), pp. 226–7, 304–5

B. Berenson: *Central and North Italian Schools*, i (1968), pp. 86–7

M. T. Fiorio: 'Una scheda per Cesare Magni', *Paragone*, xxxiv (1983), pp. 94–9

J. Shell: *Painters in Milan, 1490–1530* (diss., New York U., 1986), pp. 774–95, *passim*

Disegni e dipinti leonardeschi delle collezioni milanesi (exh. cat., Milan, Pal. Reale, 1987–8)

P. C. Marani: *Leonardo e i leonardeschi a Brera* (Florence, 1987)

Pinacoteca di Brera: Scuole lombarda e piemontese, 1300–1535 (Milan, 1988), pp. 330–34 [entries by M. T. Fiorio and P. C. Marani]

J. Shell and G. Sironi: 'Copies of the *Cenacola* and the *Virgin of the Rocks* by Bramantino, Marco d'Oggiono, Bernardino de' Conti, and Cesare Magni', *Rac. Vinc.*, xxiii (1989), pp. 103–17

JANICE SHELL

Magni, Pietro (*b* Milan, 21 Oct 1817; *d* Milan, 20 Jan 1877). Italian sculptor. He studied briefly at the Accademia di Belle Arti di Brera in Milan and subsequently attended the studio of the Neo-classical sculptor Abbondio Sangiorgio (1798–1879). In his later artistic activity he was deeply influenced by the purity of the work of the Tuscan sculptor Lorenzo Bartolini, whose *Trust in God* (1834–6; Milan, Mus. Poldi Pezzoli; *see* BARTOLINI, LORENZO, fig. 2) he saw at the annual exhibition at the Brera in 1837. He made the traditional study trip to Rome, where, in 1849, during the unrest of the Risorgimento, he joined Giuseppe Garibaldi's ranks. Later returning to Rome, he achieved public prominence with his statue of *David Launching his Slingstone* (Milan, Gal. A. Mod.), which won the Premio Canonica at the Brera in 1850 and was exhibited there in 1851 and at the Exposition Universelle in Paris in 1855. At the Brera exhibition of 1853 he received great acclaim for his sober representation of *Socrates* (Milan, Gal. A. Mod.), but his most famous work is *Girl Reading* (Milan, Gal. A. Mod.), presented at the Brera in 1856 and copied on several occasions. This statue represents a moment of great formal equilibrium in Magni's career: it is a model of Romantic sculpture, demonstrating the 'study of reality, inspiration derived from everyday life, emphasis on content rather than form … carefully controlled by soft yet restrained modelling' (Piceni and Cinotti, p. 591). This balance was never again achieved by Magni, either in his large marble group of the *Nymph Aurisina* (1858; Trieste, Mus. Civ. Revoltella), which is characterized by an excessive display of exaggerated realism, or in his academic monument to *Leonardo da Vinci* (1859–72; Milan, Piazza della Scala). In 1860 Magni was appointed to one of the two chairs of sculpture that had been set up following the reorganization of the Accademia di Belle Arti di Brera. Between 1855 and 1867 he worked on the fabric of Milan Cathedral, creating statues of *St John of the Cross* (1860), *St Justin* (1863) and *St Eligius the Goldsmith* (1867) for its exterior.

BIBLIOGRAPHY

A. Caimi: *Delle arti del disegno e degli artisti nelle provincie di Lombardia dal 1777 al 1862* (Milan, 1862), pp. 185–7
G. Rovani: *Le tre arti considerate in alcuni illustri italiani contemporanei* (Milan, 1874), pp. 224–9
A. Caimi: 'Necrologio di Pietro Magni', *Atti della I. R. Accademia di belle arti in Milano* (Milan, 1877), p. 6
A. Ottino della Chiesa: 'Pietro Magni', *L'età neoclassica in Lombardia* (exh. cat., Como, Villa Olmo, 1959), p. 158
E. Piceni and M. Cinotti: 'La scultura a Milano dal 1815 al 1915', *Storia di Milano*, xv (Milan, 1962), p. 591
L. Caramel and C. Pirovani: *Galleria d'arte moderna: Opere dell'ottocento*, ii (Milan, 1975), pp. 342–3, nos 1356–9
E. Bariati: 'Pietro Magni', *Mostra dei maestri di Brera, 1776–1859* (exh. cat. by A. M. Brizio and others, Milan, Pal. Permanente, 1975), pp. 291–2

MARICA MAGNI

Magnum [Magnum Photos, Inc.]. International photographic agency, founded with offices in New York and Paris in April 1947 by the photographers Robert Capa, Henri Cartier-Bresson, Chim, George Rodger (*b* 1908) and William Vandivert (1912–*c*. 1992). In the period after World War II, when illustrated news magazines flourished, Magnum became the most famous of picture agencies. This was initally due to the reputation of its founder-members, who had photographed the Spanish Civil War (1936–9) and World War II (three of them as correspondents for *Life* magazine). Its celebrity was sustained by the success of its work, the quality of the photographers it continued to attract and by the deaths while on assignment of Capa (the driving force behind Magnum), Chim and Werner Bischof, the first new member to be admitted.

Magnum was founded as an independent cooperative agency whose members could for the first time retain copyright of their negatives. This ensures an increased income from resales and a high degree of control over how pictures are published, to prevent any distortion of their meaning. The members each hold an equal share in Magnum and make policy decisions collectively. Magnum finances photographers' projects and takes a percentage of their fees to cover administrative costs. This arrangement enables the photographers to travel and pursue their projects free from the usual constraints of agency work. Initially the company employed a number of freelance 'stringers' to supplement its income, but this practice declined as more members were admitted. Prospective members undergo a careful selection process. New offices opened in London in 1986 and in Tokyo in 1989. By the mid-1990s the membership had risen to forty and had included such photographers as Eve Arnold (*b* 1913), Bruce Davidson, Josef Koudelka, Marc Riboud (*b* 1923), Eugene Richards (*b* 1944) and Sebastião Salgado.

The freedom of Magnum's photographers to work on projects in which they were personally interested, in a supportive environment, contributed to a development in the expressive potential of photojournalism, particularly in its treatment of humanist themes. A corporate culture of social awareness, which had always been characteristic of documentary photography (*see* PHOTOGRAPHY, §II, 7 and 9), became the hallmark of Magnum. Initially this took the form of an idealism evident in the first group photoessays, such as 'People are People the World Over' (pubd. *Ladies Home J.*, 1947–8). By the 1960s, however, the series of uprisings, wars of independence and the protest movements in both East and West had redirected the course of what came to be termed 'concerned photography' by Cornell Capa (a former President of Magnum), and the work became more overtly critical. Thereafter, many of the photographers turned to more personal subjects, although in the 1980s Sebastião Salgado produced an impressive body of work in the developing nations, which furthered the agency's tradition of humanistic reportage.

From the 1960s changes occurred that influenced the agency's course in the following decades. Television superseded picture magazines, which had been the chief outlet for Magnum's work. As travel costs and office overheads rose sharply, the survival of the company came under threat, and increasingly the photographers had to take on commercial assignments in business and industry, advertising, exhibition-planning and film-making. Magnum remained a prestigious photographic agency, but its role was less pioneering than before.

PHOTOGRAPHIC PUBLICATIONS

Magnum's Global Photo Exhibition 1960 (exh. cat., Tokyo, Takashimaya Gal., 1960)

America in Crisis (New York, 1969)

After the War Was Over, intro. M. Blume (London, 1985)

A L'Est de Magnum (Paris, 1986)

In our Time, essay by F. Ritchin (London, 1989) [useful bibliog.]

BIBLIOGRAPHY

J. Morris: 'Magnum Photos: An International Cooperative', *US Camera 1954* (New York, 1953), pp. 110–60

'Magnum', *Creative Camera*, 57 (March 1969), pp. 94–115

H. Tardy: 'Magnum', *Reporter-Objectif*, 10 (Dec 1972), pp. 32–78

H. V. Fondiller: 'Magnum: Image and Reality', *35 mm Photography* (Winter 1976), pp. 58–103, 114–18

'Magnum', *Phototechniques*, v/10 (Nov 1977), pp. 27–66

NICK CHURCHILL

Magnus, Olaus. *See* MANSSON, OLAF.

Magosa. *See* FAMAGUSTA.

Magosaburō Ōhara. *See under* ŌHARA.

Magris, Alessandro. *See under* SUPERSTUDIO.

Magritte, René(-François-Ghislain) (*b* Lessines, Hainaut, 21 Nov 1898; *d* Schaerbeek, Brussels, 15 Aug 1967). Belgian painter, draughtsman, printmaker, sculptor, photographer and film maker. He was one of the major figures of SURREALISM and perhaps the greatest Belgian artist of the 20th century. His work, while lacking the drama of conventional stylistic development, continued to be admired during the later years of his life, in spite of changes in fashion, and can be said to have continued to grow in popularity and critical esteem after his death.

1. Life and work. 2. Working methods and technique.

1. LIFE AND WORK.

(i) Training and early work, 1916–25. (ii) First Surrealist works, 1926–30. (iii) The 1930s. (iv) World War II to the 1960s.

(i) Training and early work, 1916–25. Magritte studied from 1916 to 1918 at the Académie des Beaux-Arts in Brussels, producing his first paintings in an Impressionist manner. Under the supervision of the Belgian painter Gisbert Combaz (1869–1941), he produced his first posters, which were the first works he exhibited in 1919, such as *Pot-au-Feu Derbaix* (1918, Brussels, Mus. A. Mod.), a colour lithograph in a straightforward realist style. In 1919 he became interested in Futurism, which he had encountered in an exhibition catalogue, and painted a number of pictures such as *Youth* (1922; priv. col., see Waldberg, p. 65) in a related style. From the early 1920s he also came close to formal abstraction under the influence of Cubo-Futurism, in both prints and paintings such as *Women and Flowers* (1920; priv. col., see 1978–9 exh. cat., no. 2), but his doubts about abstract art led him to reintroduce more overt imagery into his work, especially after seeing a reproduction of Giorgio de Chirico's painting the *Song of Love* (1914) in 1922.

Impressed by the unconventional combination of objects in de Chirico's work, Magritte began to look for new subject-matter that would enable him to make reference again to the real world. The transition to a new style is visible in *Blue Cinema* (1925; Geneva, priv. col., see

Meuris, pl. 65). Although the composition is still dominated by flat geometric and stylized forms, they are more sharply outlined and more detailed than in earlier works. The border between interior and exterior cannot be precisely identified and an object shaped like a spinning top, clearly but meaninglessly present in the foreground of the painting, lends a sense of alienation to the scene. This transitional style was well suited to the advertising work that Magritte had taken on, and he used his experience of advertising in the combination of words and images in his paintings. Publicity work, including posters such as *Primevère* (Brussels, Mus. A. Mod.), covers for musical scores such as *Marche des snobs* (see Meuris, p. 188) and prospectus designs, remained part of Magritte's activity, particularly in the 1920s and 1930s.

(ii) First Surrealist works, 1926–30. Magritte played an important role in the foundation of the primarily literary Belgian Surrealist group in 1926. He was also active in the formation of the group's theories, which were developed independently from those of the French Surrealists, with whom he became better acquainted while living in Paris and participating in their activities from 1927 to 1930. While the French strove for a transcendent experience of reality through the expression of the unconscious, Magritte tried to reach the same goal by consciously disrupting conventions for representing reality. Wishing the identity of each image to be perfectly clear, without the distraction of a particular style, he perfected a deadpan form of representation to which he adhered except for two short periods during the 1940s. In order to express his views about mysterious and inexplicable levels of experience beyond surface appearances, he changed the conventional order of objects, altered form, created new objects and redefined the relationship of words to images.

From 1926 Magritte was able to devote himself exclusively to painting, having signed contracts with Paul-Gustave Van Hecke (1887–1967), co-founder of the Brussels galleries Sélection and Galerie Le Centaure. Van Hecke, who wrote the first significant article about Magritte's work, published in the periodical *Sélection* in March 1927, gave Magritte his first one-man show (consisting of 61 works) at Le Centaure a month later. The exhibition marked Magritte's emergence as a Surrealist, notably in the *Lost Jockey* (1926; priv. col., see Meuris, pl. 82), in which a figure on horseback is trying to escape from a mysterious place where interior and exterior are interwoven. The ground consists of linear forms in perspective suggesting the immeasurability of the monotonous landscape, with static forms suggestive of table legs taking the place of tree trunks. The individual elements in themselves are familiar from Magritte's previous work, since he had referred to the formal perfection of standardized factory products and had included such objects in his paintings from the early 1920s. The machine-turned spherical forms, used here to represent trees, appeared in other works as shadows or in place of mannequins in his advertising work of 1926–7 (see Roque, figs 235–71). Much later in life he returned to such motifs as stand-ins for nudes, for example in the *Age of Pleasure* (1948; priv. col.; see Waldberg, p. 131) and the *Difficult Crossing* (1964; Paris, Gal. Iolas; see Waldberg, p. 247).

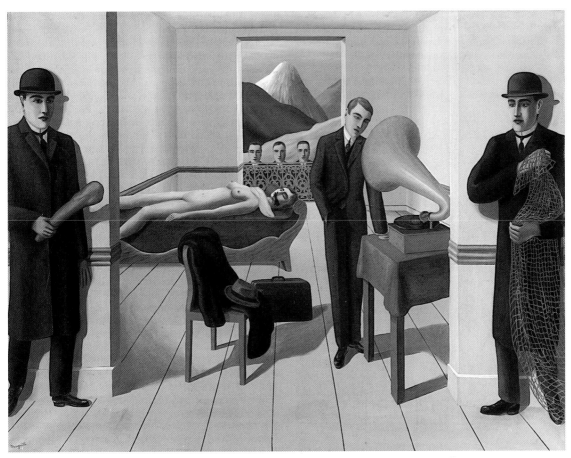

1. René Magritte: *Threatened Assassin*, oil on canvas, 1.52×1.95 m, 1927 (New York, Museum of Modern Art)

From the mid-1920s Magritte also created standardized human types, favouring especially the man in the bowler hat, who made the first of many appearances in the *Threatened Assassin* (1927; New York, MOMA; see fig. 1). The scene here, with its foreboding mood and narrative overtones, evokes the popular illustrated detective comic strips that interested Magritte. In this and other paintings of the second half of the 1920s, Magritte established the basis for both the style and the iconography of his later prolific production. Words and texts also began to play an important part in the paintings as a way of provoking an analysis of conventional assumptions, as in the *Treachery of Images* (1929; Los Angeles, CA, Co. Mus. A.; *see* TITLES, fig. 2), in which a precise image of a pipe is accompanied by an inscription, 'Ceci n'est pas une pipe', that draws our attention to the essential difference between an actual object and its representation in two dimensions.

(iii) The 1930s. In order to survive the Great Depression, in 1931 Magritte established Studio Dongo in Brussels with his brother Paul Magritte. In this small business they concerned themselves with aspects of publicity such as stands, displays, articles to be used in connection with advertising, posters, drawings, photo-montages and advertising texts. Although Magritte showed twice at the Palais des Beaux-Arts in Brussels in the 1930s (a one-man show of 59 works in 1933, followed by a group show with Man Ray and Yves Tanguy in 1937), he was temporarily left without a commercial outlet for his paintings on the closure of Le Centaure in 1930. The gallery's stock of *c.* 200 recent paintings by Magritte was purchased by his friend E. L. T. Mesens, who moved in 1938 to London, where he became director of the London Gallery. Through Mesens, Magritte gained greater recognition in Great Britain.

Although he admired de Chirico, who found poetry in the combination of normally unrelated objects, Magritte preferred to examine unexpected encounters between objects already in some way associated with each other. In the winter of 1932–3, for instance, he painted a birdcage containing an enormous egg, titling it *Elective Affinities* (priv. col.; see Waldberg, p. 228), after Goethe's novel *Die Wahlverwandtschaften* (1809). Often taking his titles from literature, films and musical scores on the completion of the picture, he invited friends, notably the writers Paul Nougé and Louis Scutenaire, to make suggestions. While the titles of his first Surrealistic paintings maintained a certain logic in relation to the imagery, from the 1930s words and images gradually acquired greater independence from each other, often retaining only an associative link. For example, he entitled a miniature reproduction in

2. René Magritte: *Red Model*, oil on canvas mounted on cardboard, 560×460 mm, 1935 (Paris, Pompidou, Musée National d'Art Moderne)

3. René Magritte: *Madame Récamier*, bronze, h. 1.2 m, 1967 (Paris, Pompidou, Musée National d'Art Moderne)

plaster of the *Venus de Milo*, a torso admired as the expression of feminine beauty in spite of the fact that it has no arms, the *Copper Handcuffs* (h. 370 mm, 1936; Paris, Charles Ratton priv. col.; see 1978–9 exh. cat., no. 200). Magritte continued to make frequent use of abstract forms, particularly in paintings that included texts, such as *Bel Canto* (1938; priv. col.; see Waldberg, p. 166), until the late 1930s. As a means of broadening the range of association, he sometimes represented an object undergoing metamorphosis into something else, as in the *Red Model* (1935; e.g. Stockholm, Mod. Mus.; Paris, Pompidou; see fig. 2), in which the pointed toes of a pair of boots become the toes themselves. Such strategies, drawing attention to the relationship between inanimate and living objects, were similar to those employed by other Surrealists (*see* METAMORPHISM). One constantly recurring motif is that of an enlarged leaf as a substitute for the foliage of a tree, as in the wall painting *Ignorant Faith* (1957; Charleroi, Pal. B.-A.). In other cases the metamorphosis was not simply of form but also of substance, with one material standing for another: the head of the *Copper Handcuffs*, for instance, is painted white to look like marble, but the body itself is a fleshy pink.

(iv) World War II to the 1960s. In reaction to the gloom of the war years, Magritte sought to exemplify the 'beautiful side' of life, from 1943 even making use of a parody of Impressionism with lighter colours, while maintaining the Surrealist character of the imagery. Although he was consciously mocking Impressionism in works such as *L'Eclair* (1944; Charleroi, Mus. Com. B.-A.), a bunch of grey flowers in loose, delicate brushstrokes, or the *Age of Pleasure* (1946; priv. col., see 1978–9 exh. cat., no. 135), with its travesty of Renoir's figure style, such works were strongly criticized in Surrealist circles. These were followed by a group of rapidly executed oil paintings and gouaches made in winter 1947–8 for his first one-man show in Paris, at the Galerie du Faubourg. For these whimsical works he employed a popular style related in some ways to Fauvism, in part as a way of attacking what he considered the superficiality of the French public. A typical example is the painting *Le Galet* (1948; Brussels, Mus. A. Mod.), in which a semi-nude woman is placed against a patterned background of broad strokes. During this time he also produced 77 drawings for a new illustrated edition of the Comte de Lautréamont's *Les Chants de Maldoror* (Brussels, 1948/*R* 1984).

Although even before World War II Magritte enjoyed considerable recognition by virtue of his participation in Surrealist group exhibitions, as well as through his one-man shows, he became internationally famous only after signing a contract in 1948 with Alexandre Iolas, the New York dealer who remained his agent until his death. He produced several privately commissioned portraits and from 1951 to 1961 also executed one ceiling painting and three wall paintings, for which he adapted motifs from his easel pictures. Having experimented from the 1920s with black-and-white still photography, borrowing subjects from his paintings in order to record unconventional staged situations, from 1956 he also made a number of brief and often comical Surrealist films, using friends as directors and actors. In 1967 he produced a series of wax sculptures based on his paintings; eight of these, including *Madame Récamier* (Paris, Pompidou; see fig. 3), after the painting by Jacques-Louis David, but with an L-shaped coffin in place of the high society figure, were cast in bronze after his death.

Magritte's critical and popular reputation alike continued to grow during and after the 1960s. He can be said to have exerted an influence on later generations of artists, particularly on Pop art and on conceptual art.

2. WORKING METHODS AND TECHNIQUE. Magritte made drawings of particular motifs as well as compositional studies for his paintings, discovering new ideas in the process of sketching. Most of his drawings were made for such purposes. He established the final composition on the canvas very precisely before building up the smooth surface of his paintings, which he wanted to be immaculate in their finish so that questions of technique would not distract the viewer's attention from the imagery. By availing himself, moreover, of an essentially naturalistic idiom, he avoided any suggestion of aesthetic preference. He made numerous gouaches and watercolours and from 1926 occasionally produced collages, sometimes in combination with different techniques; some of his paintings contain figures derived from papier collé.

Magritte was in the habit of repeating many of the same objects in new situations and also of exploiting the potential of a scene as a whole by executing variations on it. The *Secret Player* (1926; priv. col., see Waldberg, p. 199), which uses a setting nearly identical to that of the *Lost Jockey* of the same year, is an early example; further versions of the *Lost Jockey* itself, bearing the same title, were painted in the early 1940s. When his work began to gain greater recognition in the late 1940s, Magritte started to produce even more variations of particular pictures. For example, there are 16 versions in oil and *c.* 10 in gouache of the *Empire of Light* (e.g. the *Empire of Light II*, 1950; New York, MOMA), a nocturnal street scene set against a blue afternoon sky, with the first picture dating from 1949; elements from it also reappeared in one of the eight sections of his largest wall painting, the *Enchanted Realm* (4.3×71.2 m overall, 1953; Knokke-Heist, Casino Com.), a commissioned work executed under his supervision by Raymond Art and his assistants.

WRITINGS
Manifestes et autres écrits, preface M. Mariën (Brussels, 1972)
Quatre-vingt-deux lettres de René Magritte à Mirabelle Dors et Maurice Rapin (Paris, 1976)
La Destination: Lettres à Marcel Mariën (1937–1962) (Brussels, 1977)
A. Blavier, ed.: *Écrits complets* (Paris, 1979)

BIBLIOGRAPHY
P. Nougé: *René Magritte ou les images défendues* (Brussels, 1943)
L. Scutenaire: *René Magritte* (Brussels, 1964)
P. Waldberg: *René Magritte* (Brussels, 1965)
S. Gablik: *Magritte* (London, 1970)
R. Passeron: *René Magritte* (Paris, 1970; rev. 1972; Eng. trans., New York, 1980)
P. Robert-Jones: *Magritte, poète visible* (Brussels, 1972)
M. Foucault: *Ceci n'est pas une pipe* (Montpellier, 1973); Eng. trans. as *This is Not a Pipe* (Berkeley, CA, 1983)
U. M. Schneede: *René Magritte: Leben und Werk* (Cologne, 1973)
A. M. Hammacher: *René Magritte* (Paris, 1974; Eng. trans., New York, 1974; rev. London, 1986)
H. Torczyner: *René Magritte: Signes et images* (Paris, 1977); Eng. trans. as *Magritte: The True Art of Painting* (London and New York, 1979)
L. Scutenaire: *La Fidélité des images: René Magritte, le cinématographe et la photographie* (Brussels, 1978)
Rétrospective Magritte (exh. cat., essays L. Scutenaire, J. Clair and D. Sylvester; Brussels, Pal. B.-A.; Paris, Pompidou; 1978–9)
R. Calvocoressi: *Magritte* (Oxford, 1979, rev. 1984)
R. Schiebler: *Die Kunsttheorie René Magrittes* (Munich, 1981)
M. Paquet: *Magritte ou l'éclipse de l'être* (Paris, 1982)
——: *Photographies de Magritte* (Paris, 1982)
René Magritte und der Surrealismus in Belgien (exh. cat. by U. M. Schneede and others, Hamburg, Kstver., 1982)
G. Roque: *Ceci n'est pas un Magritte: Essai sur Magritte et la publicité* (Paris, 1983)
R. G. A. Kaulingfreks: *Meneer Iedereen: over het denken van René Magritte* (diss., Nijmegen, Kath. U., 1984)
René Magritte (exh. cat. by C. Goemans and E. L. T. Mesens, Lausanne, Fond. Hermitage, 1987)
J. Meuris: *Magritte* (Paris, 1988)
D. Sylvester: *Magritte* (London, 1992)
D. Sylvester, ed.: *René Magritte: Catalogue Raisonné*, 3 vols (London, 1992)
Magritte (exh. cat. by S. Whitfield, London, Hayward Gal., 1992)
René Magritte: La Période vache (exh. cat., Marseille, Mus. Cantini, 1992)

ANNEKE E. WIJNBEEK

Magro, Eduardo Adaro. *See* ADARO MAGRO, EDUARDO.

Magro, Guglielmo del. *See* GIRALDI, GUGLIELMO.

MA group. Hungarian group of artists and writers, active *c.* 1916 to 1926. It was associated with the journal *MA*, whose name was derived from the Hungarian for 'today', but it also refers to the movement Hungarian Activism (Hung.: Magyar Aktivizmus; *see* ACTIVISTS). Founded by the writer and artist LAJOS KASSÁK, *MA* first appeared in November 1916, and from then until it was banned on 14 July 1919 it was published in Budapest, at first edited solely by Kassák and by 1917 by Béla Uitz also. From 1 May 1920 until its demise in mid-1926 it was published in Vienna under Kassák's sole editorship. It was the most important forum for Hungarian Activism, and over the years its members included Sándor Bortnyik, Péter Dobrović (1890–1942), Lajos Gulácsy, János Kmetty, János Máttis Teutsch, László Moholy-Nagy, Jószef Nemes Lampérth, Béla Uitz among others. The first issue had a Cubist cover by the Czech artist Vincenc Beneš (see Kassák, p. 127) and an article by Kassák entitled 'A plakát es az uj festészet' ('The poster and the new painting', *MA*, i/1, pp. 2–4), which set the revolutionary tone of the group. The article suggested that painting should aspire to the same aggressive power as that achieved by posters: 'The new painter is a moral individual, full of faith and a desire for unity! And his pictures are weapons of war!.' Many members of the MA group did in fact produce posters during the short Communist regime under Béla Kun in 1919; Uitz, for example, designed *Red Soldiers, Forward!* (1919; Budapest, N.G.).

On 14 October 1917 the first exhibition organized by the MA group was held at 15 Visegrádi Street in Budapest with a one-man show of works by Máttis Teutsch. His paintings of this period were often near-abstract landscapes executed in bright colours and arabesque forms, as in *Bright Landscape* (1916; Pécs, Pannonius Mus.). From 1917 to 1918 another five exhibitions were organized by the group: the third in 1918 was a large group show with works by Bortnyik, Dobrović, Gulácsy, Kmetty, Máttis Teutsch, Nemes Lampérth, Uitz and others. One of the most radical artists at this time was Bortnyik, who produced works such as *Dynamic Composition* (1918; Budapest, N.G.), showing the influence of Futurism in its attempt to depict energy and dynamism. The seventh MA show, of graphic work, and the ninth of work by Bortnyik were held in 1919. Bortnyik's show included works such as *Red Locomotive* (1918; Budapest, N. Mus., Dept Mod. Hist.), which applied the techniques of Synthetic Cubism to a political subject. In 1919 *MA* came under attack from the paper *Ember* and also from Béla Kun, the latter claiming it to be a product of bourgeois decadence. Kassák published a letter of defence in *MA*, but by July 1919 the periodical had been banned, ostensibly due to a paper shortage.

The reappearance of *MA* in Vienna on 1 May 1920 under Kassák's editorship marked a new phase of Hungarian Activism. Kassák himself began to produce visual art and advocated a form of two-dimensional abstraction close to Constructivism and Suprematism. In 1921 he published the pamphlet 'Bildarchitektur' (repr. as 'Képarchitektúra', *MA* vii/4, 1922, pp. 52–4), which set out the new artistic credo. This bombastic essay linked the new art form, *Bildarchitektur*, with a new way of life, and it was seen stylistically by Kassák as an extension of Cubism, Expressionism and the *Merz* compositions of Kurt Schwitters: '*Bildarchitektur* is building on the flat surface ... For *Bildarchitektur* is art and art is creation and creation is everything.' Kassák began to produce works such as *Bildarchitektur* (1922; Budapest, N.G.), which use geometrical colour planes in a manner reminiscent of El Lissitsky's *Proun* projects. In the early 1920s Bortnyik also produced *Bildarchitektur* works, before turning to Surrealism with works such as the *Green Donkey* (1924; Budapest, N.G.). Moholy-Nagy's interest in Kassák's theories soon brought him into the international mainstream, and in 1923 he started to teach at the Bauhaus.

As well as Constructivism, the influence of Dada was also strong in this later phase of the MA group. Kassák for example produced collages and photomontages, such as *Hanged Man* (1920; Budapest, Lajos Kassák Mem. Mus.), that, like John Heartfield's photomontages, used aggressive social satire. Some of Moholy-Nagy's work, such as *H Relief* (1920; untraced, see J. Szabó: *A Magyar Aktivizmus története* [The history of Hungarian Activism], Budapest, 1971, pl. 132), resembled that of Schwitters. In 1922 Kassák and Moholy-Nagy's book *Buch neuer Künstler* (Vienna, 1922) was published, and it included illustrations of Constructivist, Futurist and Purist works together with some of cars and machines, reflecting the breadth of the MA group's interests at this time. Though maintaining contacts with many other European avant-garde circles, the MA group remained fairly isolated in Vienna, and in 1926 *MA* ceased publication. Lajos Kassák then returned to Hungary, where he founded the short-lived journal *Dokumentum*, while the other members pursued separate careers.

BIBLIOGRAPHY

L. Kassák: *MA* (Basle, 1968)

For further bibliography *see* ACTIVISTS and KASSÁK, LAJOS.

PHILIP COOPER

Magt, Leonhard (*fl* 1514; *d* Innsbruck, 1532). Austrian sculptor. It has been suggested that his early work may include some of the putti, usually ascribed to Sebastian Loscher (*fl* 1510–48), in the funerary chapel of the Fugger family in the Carmelite church of St Anna at Augsburg (endowed 1509 by Jakob Fugger II and his brothers), the earliest Renaissance monument in Germany. Magt's only documented activity is his contribution to the sculptural programme of the cenotaph of the *Holy Roman Emperor Maximilian I* in the Hofkirche at Innsbruck: the smaller than life-size statues of 23 Habsburg family saints including *St Maximilian, Bishop of Pannonia* and *St Reinhard*, which he worked up from designs provided by Jörg Kölderer (*fl* 1497–1540), the Emperor's court painter. In his drawings, Kölderer had differentiated the saints from one another almost entirely by means of differences in costume and attributes; Leonhard Magt was able to breathe life into them by giving each a highly individualized face and bearing, and voluminous drapery that is either stately or animated, as appropriate. Magt's wax models were cast in bronze by Stefan Godl. Originally 100 saints had been planned, but work on this part of the project was interrupted by the Emperor's untimely death in 1519.

BIBLIOGRAPHY

V. Oberhammer: *Die Bronzestandbilder des Maximiliangrabmales in der Hofkirche zu Innsbruck* (Innsbruck, 1935)

K. Oettinger: *Die Bildhauer Maximilians am Innsbrucker Kaisergrabmal* (Nuremberg, 1966), pp. 30, 65, 81–2

E. Egg: *Kunst in Tirol: Malerei und Kunsthandwerk*, 2 vols (Innsbruck, Vienna and Munich, 1970), pp. 334–9

JANE CAMPBELL HUTCHISON

Magubane, Peter (*b* Vrededorp, nr Johannesburg, 18 Jan 1932). South African photographer. Encouraged by the South African photographer Bob Gosani (1935–72) and the writer Can Themba (1923–67), he began his professional career with *Drum* magazine, first as a driver and messenger and then as a darkroom technician and photographer. He received further guidance from Jurgen Schädeberg (*b* 1931). In the 1950s he covered many important political events, including conferences of the African National Congress (ANC), treason trials and pass law demonstrations. In 1964–5 he worked in London and Boston, returning to South Africa in 1966 to work for the *Rand Daily Mail*. On several occasions he was subjected to police harassment and to periods of imprisonment, and in 1971 he was banned from practising photography for five years. When the order was lifted, he resumed work for the *Rand Daily Mail*. Coverage of the Soweto riots of 1976 earned him worldwide acclaim (e.g. 'The coffins of thirty of the Sharpeville dead were buried side by side', see *Magubane's South Africa*, p. 26) and led to a number of international photographic and journalistic awards, one of which was the American National Professional Photographers Association Humanistic Award in 1986, in recognition of one of several incidents in which he put his camera aside and intervened to prevent people being killed. He also took photographs for several United Nations agencies, including the High Commission for Refugees and UNICEF, being particularly committed to exposing the plight of children and documenting traditional societies. His photographs have appeared in *Life* magazine, the *New York Times*, *National Geographic* and *Time*.

PHOTOGRAPHIC PUBLICATIONS
Magubane's South Africa (New York, 1978)
Soweto Portrait of a City, text by D. Bristow and S. Motjuwadi (Cape Town, 1990)

LESLEY SPIRO COHEN

Mahābalipuram. *See* MAMALLAPURAM.

Mahan [Mahān]. Town in central Iran, 42 km south-east of Kirman. It is the site of a major shrine centre for the Sufi shaykh Nur al-Din Ni'matallah (*d* 1431), who moved there in 1406 and founded the Ni'matallahi order of dervishes. After his death a domed tomb chamber (1436) was erected by a follower, Ahmad I Vali (*reg* 1422–36), Bahmanid ruler of the Deccan and Bidar in India. The shrine was extensively enlarged by the Safavid ruler 'Abbas I (*reg* 1588–1629), and a forecourt with tall minarets at the gate was added under the Qajar dynasty (*reg* 1779–1924). The present complex, surrounded by beautiful gardens, comprises three open courts arranged on an axis. About 6 km to the west stands the ruined tomb of 'Abd al-Salam (*c.* 1450), said to have been one of Ni'matallah's teachers. A square chamber surmounted by a double dome, it preserves exterior decoration in glazed and unglazed brick.

BIBLIOGRAPHY
L. Golombek and D. Wilber: *The Timurid Architecture of Iran and Turan*, 2 vols (Princeton, 1988), pp. 394–5

Mahaut, Countess of Artois. *See* CAPET, (4).

Mahdaoui, Nja (*b* Tunis, 20 July 1937). Tunisian painter. He was educated at the Lycée Alaoui in Tunis and from 1959 to 1960 took courses in art history and painting at the Ecole Libre in Carthage. His work was noticed at this time by Ricardo Avérini, the director of the Centre Dante Alighieri in Tunis, and from 1965 to 1966 he attended the Accademia Santa Andrea in Rome, studying painting and the philosophy of art with Giotta Frunza, a student of Brancusi. He also learnt about Islamic and Far Eastern calligraphy with Father Di Meghio and participated in the creation of the first Association of Arab Artists in Italy. In 1967 he visited Yugoslavia, Bulgaria, Turkey and Russia, and from 1967 to 1968 studied at the Cité Internationale des Arts in Paris, where he attended courses at the Ecole du Louvre. In 1968 he was employed by the Société Tunisienne de Banque but the following year moved to Paris. He returned to live in Tunisia in 1977, and in the years 1978 and 1979 travelled to Saudi Arabia, Yemen, Syria and Algeria. In 1981 and 1984 he was commissioned for work in Saudi Arabia at Jeddah airport, the Islamic Bank and at the University of Riyadh. In his paintings during the 1960s he employed such motifs as masks, totem poles and calligraphy to create a lyrical abstract style. He produced his first paintings on parchment in 1972, became interested in weaving and carpet production in 1979, and began to paint on animal skins and on the human body in 1980. Calligraphy became the dominant theme in his work, with an emphasis on its visual qualities rather than its literal significance (*see* TUNISIA, fig. 1).

BIBLIOGRAPHY
E. J. Maunick: *Nja Mahdaoui* (Tunis, 1983)
Six peintres tunisiens contemporains (exh. cat., Paris, Mus. A. Mod. Ville Paris; Villeneuve d'Ascq, Mus. A. Mod. Nord; Paris, Mus. N. A. Afr. & Océan.; 1986–7), pp. 44–51

S. J. VERNOIT

Mahdia [al-Mahdiyya, Mahdiya, Mahdiyya]. Town on the east coast of Tunisia, 200 km south of Tunis. It was established in AD 912–13 by 'Ubayd Allah al-Mahdi (*reg* 909–34), founder of the Fatimid dynasty, on a previously uninhabited rocky peninsula. As his capital and refuge, the town was fortified with strong defences. Projecting about 1400 m into the sea, it was secured from attack by a thick sea wall, of which a section remains on the north, and a rampart and outer wall across the neck. Of the town's complex entrance, which included an iron gate decorated with bronze lions, only the much remodelled Skifa al-Kahla (*saqīfa al-kahla*, 'the dark vestibule') remains. Within the town, of which parts have been excavated, there was a palace for al-Mahdi, another for his son and successor al-Qa'im (*reg* 934–46), and underground storehouses, wells and cisterns. The mosque (916) was the first mosque built by the Fatimids. It is largely modelled on the Great Mosque of Kairouan, with nine naves perpendicular to the qibla wall, double colonnades along the axial aisle and a T-plan formed by a wide axial aisle and the aisle along the qibla wall, but the Fatimids replaced the massive minaret of the prototype with a monumental projecting portal (*see* ISLAMIC ART, fig. 34). The portal was flanked by bastions at the corners containing cisterns for rainwater. The original qibla wall was eroded by the sea, and the mosque was repeatedly restored, most recently in the 1960s, when it was reconstructed along its original lines.

In 948, having suppressed a revolt that had broken out five years earlier, al-Mansur (*reg* 946–53) moved the court to a new site on the outskirts of Kairouan, al-Mansuriyya, but Mahdia remained an entrepôt for Mediterranean trade. It again became the capital when the Zirid al-Mu'izz ibn Badis took refuge there from the Hilali bedouin in 1057. From this time onwards it was a capital under threat: it was repeatedly attacked by the Pisans, Genoese, Normans and Hammadids until the Norman Roger II seized it in 1148 and put an end to the Zirid dynasty. It remained a pawn in the struggles for control of the central Mediterranean, passing to the Almohads, Aragonese, Hafsids, Genoese, Turks and Spanish. The Burj al-Kabir (Borj el Kebir), a large square fortress, was erected in 1595 by Abu Abdallah Muhammad Pasha; it was remodelled in the 18th century to include projecting corner bastions with embrasures for cannon.

See also MAHDIA SHIPWRECK.

BIBLIOGRAPHY
Enc. Islam/2: 'Mahdiyya'
G. Marçais: *L'Architecture musulmane d'occident* (Paris, 1954)
A. Lézine: *Mahdiya: Recherches d'archéologie islamique* (Paris, 1965)
J. M. Bloom: 'The Origins of Fatimid Art', *Muqarnas*, iii (1985), pp. 30–38

Mahdia shipwreck. Source of a group of late 2nd-century BC Greek works of art. In 1907 an ancient shipwreck was located by sponge-divers in the waters off Mahdia on the east coast of Tunisia. The subsequent careful exploration of the ship and the lifting of its extensive cargo, carried out between 1908 and 1913, was the first operation of its kind in the Mediterranean. The principal cargo consisted of 60 marble columns, together with Ionic and Corinthian capitals, but also on board was a whole range of sculpture in both bronze and marble. The bronzes include an archaistic herm, a *Dancing Eros* (*see* GREECE, ANCIENT, fig. 150), three grotesque dancing dwarfs (with suspension rings attached), statuettes of *Eros with a Lyre*, satyrs, *Hermes* and actors, two lamp holders in the form of an Eros and a Hermaphrodite, and various assorted appliqués, vessels, candelabra (for illustration *see* CANDELABRUM (i)), lamps and couch attachments. The marbles, some badly corroded, include heads or busts of *Aphrodite*, *Artemis*, *Pan*, *Niobe* and a satyr and satyr-girl, as well as a statuette of *Artemis* and a partial torso of *Herakles*; in addition there were two marble kraters (large ornamental basins for garden furniture) with Dionysiac scenes, a candelabrum and four 4th-century BC Attic reliefs. With the exception of the last, which were being exported as 'antiques', the items were all new. The archaistic herm is signed by BOETHOS OF CHALKHEDON and was probably made *c.* 130–120 BC. There are good grounds for regarding the rest of the bronzes as coming from the same workshop, probably situated in Athens, and the marbles were certainly manufactured there in a NEO-ATTIC workshop about the same time. Pottery from the Mahdia wreck indicates that the vessel sank *c.* 100 BC: it was presumably on its way from Athens to Rome when it met disaster. The extent of the craze of the upper classes in Republican Rome for collecting Greek works of art is known from excavations of villas such as the Villa of the Papyri at Herculaneum (*see* HERCULANEUM, §III), as well as from literary sources such as Cicero's correspondence with Atticus, and the Mahdia shipwreck documents with especial clarity what must have been a booming industry and export trade for Greek sculptural workshops around the turn of the 2nd and 1st centuries BC. The finds are normally housed in Tunis (Mus. N. Bardo), but the bronzes were restored in the early 1990s in the Rheinisches Landesmuseum in Bonn, where they were the subject of a major temporary exhibition in 1993.

BIBLIOGRAPHY
W. Fuchs: *Der Schiffsfund von Mahdia* (Tübingen, 1963)

R. J. A. WILSON

Maher, George W(ashington) (*b* Mill Creek, WV, 25 Dec 1864; *d* Douglas, MI, 12 Sept 1926). American architect. He began his architectural training in 1878 in Chicago with the firm of Bauer & Hill and later joined the office of J. L. Silsbee (1845–1913), where he met George Elmslie and Frank Lloyd Wright. In 1888 he went into private practice with Charles Corwin; the partnership broke up in 1893 when Maher began a year of travel and study in Europe. On his return he established an independent practice in Chicago. His search for a modern, non-historic style led to the John Farson house in Oak Park, IL (1897). Its monumentality, formal symmetry, broad simple surfaces, rich materials and vaguely classical details are all hallmarks of Maher's personal style, to which he would return throughout his career. Except for the

period 1904–8, when he responded to the Austrian and English movements, in particular the work of J. M. Olbrich and C. F. A. Voysey, Maher's work shows little internal development.

BIBLIOGRAPHY
'Geo. W. Maher, a Democrat in Architecture', *W. Architect*, xx/3 (1914), pp. 25–9
J. W. Rudd: 'George W. Maher', *Prairie Sch. Rev.* i/1 (1964), pp. 5–10
H. A. Brooks: *The Prairie School* (Toronto, 1972)

PAUL KRUTY

Mahesh [Mahes; Maheśa] (*fl c.* 1560–1600). Indian miniature painter. An accomplished artist who contributed to at least a dozen manuscripts produced for the emperor Akbar (*reg* 1556–1605), he worked in a style that represents the mainstream of Mughal painting in the 1580s. His work is characterized by lively figures, bright colours and compositions in which surface design dominates and spatial recession is negligible. His name appears in a list of 17 painters in the *Āyīn-i Akbarī*, a contemporary account of Akbar's administration.

Paintings have been attributed to him (Beach) in such early manuscripts as the *Ṭūṭīnāma* ('Tales of a parrot'; *c.* 1570; Cleveland, OH, Mus. A., MS. 62.279, fol. 23*r*; alternatively dated *c.* 1560–65) and the *Ḥamzanāma* ('Tales of Hamza'; dated *c.* 1557–72 by the present author and alternatively *c.* 1562–77; e.g. Washington, DC, Freer, 60.15; and New York, Brooklyn Mus., 24.29). However, the earliest works with inscriptions actually naming Mahesh as the painter appear in the *Dārābnāma* ('History of Darab'; *c.* 1580; London, BL, Or. MS. 4615). He played a prominent role in the illustration of the imperial manuscripts of the two great Hindu epics translated into Persian for Akbar, the *Mahābhārata*, known as the *Razmnāma* ('Book of war') completed in 1586, and the *Rāmāyaṇa* ('Story of Rama'), apparently completed *c.* 1591–2 (both Jaipur, Maharaja Sawai Man Singh II Mus., MS. AG. 1683–1850 and MS. AG. 1851–2026). He was also assigned one painting in the small, fine *Dīvān* (collected poems) of Anvari (1588; Cambridge, MA, Sackler Mus., MS. 1960.117.15), which contains 15 miniatures by Akbar's finest artists.

Mahesh continued to rely on early Mughal figural and topographical conventions late in his career, even though the direction of Mughal painting was changing. His figures, endowed with pointed beards, blank eyes and little corporal modelling, tend to display emotion with furrowed brows or gaping mouths; his hills are rendered as pastel lobes with strong outlines and minimal internal articulation. Mahesh did not contribute to the de luxe manuscripts of Persian poetical works commissioned by Akbar in the 1590s; instead he was assigned to less prestigious projects such as the *Bābarnāma* ('History of Babar') manuscripts. However, the *Anvār-i Suhaylī* of 1596–7 contains a painting by him (Varanasi, Banaras Hindu U., Bharat Kala Bhavan, fol. 55). Two prolific Mughal painters, MISKIN and Asi, were Mahesh's sons and probably received their early training from him.

BIBLIOGRAPHY
Abu'l-Fazl: *Āyīn-i Akbarī* [Annals of Akbar] (*c.* 1596–1602); Eng. trans. in 3 vols: vol. i, trans. H. Blochmann, ed. S. L. Gloomer ([Calcutta], 1871/*R* Delhi, 1965); vols ii and iii, trans. H. S. Jarrett, ed. J. Sarkar (Calcutta, 1948–9/*R* New Delhi, 1972–3)

The Imperial Image: Paintings for the Mughal Court (exh. cat. by M. C. Beach, Washington, DC, Freer, 1981)

A. Schimmel and S. C. Welch: *Anvari's Divan: A Pocket Book for Akbar* (New York, 1983)

JOHN SEYLLER

Ma Hezhi [Ma Ho-chih] (*fl* Qiantang, Lin'an [now Hangzhou], Zhejiang Province, *c.* second half of 12th century). Chinese painter. A painter of classical themes at the Southern Song (1127–1279) court in Lin'an, modern Hangzhou, Zhejiang Province, Ma was known for his distinctive brushwork, marked by variations in hand pressure. However, the details of his life are obscure; sparse and contradictory information appears in different sources. A native of the Hangzhou area, Ma probably came from a humble family and did not interact with prominent men of letters, whose occasional poems and other writings might otherwise have mentioned his name.

Zhuang Su records that Ma studied for the national-level civil service examination to gain the title of *jinshi* and that he rose to become an executive in the Board of Works. A competing tradition, originating with a list of court painters compiled by the connoisseur Zhou Mi (1232–98), places Ma in the Imperial Academy rather than among educated officials working in the esteemed literati painting tradition (*see* CHINA, §V, 4). The question of whether Ma was primarily a scholar–painter or an Academy painter remains a live issue.

Despite the controversy over Ma's status, connoisseurs have generally agreed that his peculiarly vibrant brushwork characterizes him as a follower of the Tang (AD 618–907) virtuoso painter Wu Daozi, whose use of broken contour lines and variations in brush pressure suggested three-dimensional form and kinaesthetic energy. Since the Buddhist temples in which Wu created his wall paintings were mostly destroyed by Ma's time, it is likely that Ma learnt the style through the mediation of Wu's Northern Song (960–1127) followers. Particularly influential to Ma's artistic development was the 11th-century artist Li Gonglin, who tempered the extroverted Wu Daozi style with the introspection and elegance associated with such Six Dynasties (AD 222–589) painters as Gu Kaizhi and Lu Tanwei (*c.* 440–*c.* 500). Li's revival of archaic subjects and styles also provided important models for Ma and his contemporaries.

Connoisseurs traditionally characterized Ma's brushwork as *piaoyi* ('fluttering and untrammelled') and described his strokes with vivid metaphors, such as 'orchid leaf', 'willow leaf' or 'wasp waist'. His variations in brush pressure create a sense of life and movement in landscape forms as well as figures, and his technique of layering an area with multiple strokes of different tonalities and thickness enriches surface texture, as well as suggesting volume and depth. The flaring and ebbing of his brushlines create an impression of calligraphic brilliance while also

Ma Hezhi (attrib.): detail of an illustration to the 'Odes of Bin' from the *Shijing* ('Book of odes'), handscroll, ink and light colour on silk, 0.34×7.20 m, second half of the 12th century (New York, Metropolitan Museum of Art)

suggesting strong contrasts of light and shadow on three-dimensional forms. Ma's style was perhaps too individual to inspire later followers, indeed he had no major ones.

The subject for which Ma is best known is his illustration of the Mao version of the *Shijing* ('Book of odes'; see fig.) done for Emperor Gaozong (*reg* 1127–62), probably after his abdication. This consists of a group of handscrolls (New York, Met.; London, BM; Boston, Mus. F.A.; Kyoto, Fujii Yurinkan Mus.; Beijing, Pal. Mus.; Shenyang, Liaoning Prov. Mus.; and Shanghai Mus.) featuring pictures in ink and colours alternating with the texts of the 305 poems transcribed by Gaozong or his surrogates. The surviving illustrations are generally thought not to be the work of a single artist, although most seem to belong to the Southern Song period; it seems likely that Ma's designs were executed in multiple versions by other Court painters. There are many different compositions, including archaistic scenes with figures on blank ground, figures in full settings and innovative landscapes without figures.

Ma's surviving masterpiece is generally acknowledged to be his illustration, in ink and colour on silk, of Su Shi's *Chibi houfu* ('Second ode on the red cliff'; Beijing, Pal. Mus.). In contrast to other illustrators of the subject, who followed Su's text section by section, Ma attempted to capture the poetic flavour with a few suggestive images: the poet and his friends in a boat on a broad, moonlit river, a crane flying overhead and a prominent cliff. The flickering brushwork of the rocks and trees and the restless swirls of water masterfully evoke the poet's emotional state. The illustration is followed by Gaozong's transcription of the text in draft cursive (*zhangcaoshu*) calligraphy, with the seals of Gaozong's retirement palace. Ma's style is also exemplified by a pair of album leaves, *Old Tree by Water* and *Cranes Crying by a Clear Spring* (both Taipei, N. Pal. Mus.). In ink monochrome on paper, these display a rich variety of even more sensitive brushwork. Despite their current titles, they illustrate poems from the *Shijing* and may represent master drafts for the more formal *Shijing* scrolls. Although the tiny signatures on the two works may be later additions, the reliability of the paintings is attested by the seals of Ma's biographer Zhuang Su, who was an important collector and connoisseur.

BIBLIOGRAPHY

Franke: 'Ma Ho-chih'

Zhuang Su: *Hua ji buyi* [Painting continued: a supplement] (preface 1298/*R* Beijing, 1963), *juan* 1, p. 4

Xia Wenyan: *Tuhui baojian* [Precious mirror of painting] (preface 1365/*R* Taipei, 1974), *juan* 4, p. 95

Li E: *Nan Song yuanhua lu* [Record of Southern Song court painting], (preface 1721/*R* Taipei, 1974), *juan* 3

Zhuang Shen: 'Ma Hezhi yanjiu' [Research on Ma Hezhi], *Dalu Zazhi*, xi (1955), no. 3, pp. 11–15; no. 4, pp. 21–4

Xu Bangda: 'Chuan Song Gaozong Zhao Gou Xiaozong Zhao Shen shu Ma Hezhi hua *Mao shi* juan kaobian' [An examination and differentiation of the *Mao shi* scrolls transmitted as the calligraphy of Song emperors Gaozong and Xiaozong and painting of Ma Hezhi], *Gugong Bowuyuan Yuankan*, xxix (1985), no. 3, pp. 69–78

J. Murray: *Ma Hezhi and the Illustration of the Book of Odes* (Cambridge and New York, 1993)

JULIA K. MURRAY

Mahiṣūru. *See* MYSORE.

Mahlstick. Wooden rod, dowel or length of cane *c.* 1 m long, one end of which is covered by a small, ball-shaped pad of leather, cloth or cork. It is used by painters to steady the hand and keep it clear of the painting's surface. A mahlstick is held in the hand that is not actively painting. It is usually passed through the fingers and held rigid against the underside of the forearm, in a grip that also holds the palette and several spare brushes. The cushioned end is then supported against a convenient resting place, perhaps on the easel or on the edge of the stretcher or

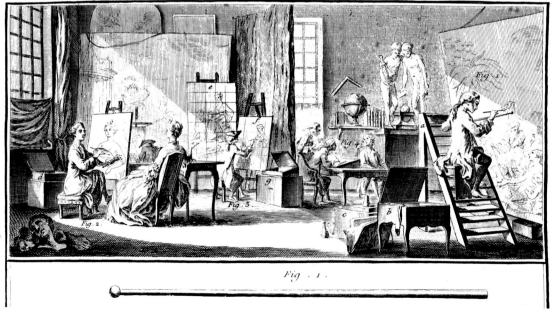

Mahlstick shown in use (top) and by itself (bottom); detail of an engraving from D. Diderot: *Encyclopédie, ou Dictionnaire raisonné des sciences, des arts et des métiers*, VIII (Paris, 1771), pl. 1

panel. Thus held, the mahlstick traverses the space in front of the painting, providing a rigid support for the hand holding the brush.

The mahlstick first appeared in the 16th century, coinciding roughly with the adoption of oil paint, and its use may have been further encouraged by the concurrent development of canvas supports. Neither wet oil paint nor flexible, insubstantial canvases allow the hand or arm to rest on the painting itself. In his *Arte de la pintura* (1649) Francisco Pacheco seemed to confirm this connection, when he remarked that most painters did not use mahlsticks for tempera (Zahira, pp. 146–7). Mahlsticks are shown in use on the title-page of a book of 1549 by Valentin Boltz (*Farbbuch oder Illuminierbuch*; Basle) and in a print of 1577 by Marcus Gheerhaerts the elder (the *Unlucky Painter*; Paris, Bib. N.). However, they are not shown consistently in painters' self-portraits or studio scenes until the 17th century. From then, they are almost always present. Mahlsticks appear in *St Luke Painting the Virgin and Child* (c. 1613; see OIL PAINTING, fig. 2), Velázquez's *Las Meninas* (1656; Madrid, Prado; see VÉLAZQUEZ, DIEGO, fig. 10), Rembrandt's *Self-portrait* (c. 1664; London, Kenwood House), Vermeer's *Allegory of Painting* (c. 1666–7; Vienna, Ksthist. Mus.; see MODEL, ARTIST'S, fig. 2) and Reynolds's *Self-portrait* (1753–4; London, N.P.G.). They are frequently shown or discussed in 18th-century sources (see fig.) and are the subject of some anecdotes in Antonio Palomino's treatise *El museo pictórico y escala óptica* (1715–24; Zahira, p. 50). A mahlstick in the form of Hogarth's 'Line of Beauty' appears in Paul Sandby's caricature of 1753, the *Author Run Mad* (example in London, BM). The use of the mahlstick has declined since the mid-19th century with the introduction of broader painting styles and the more robust use of oil paint.

BIBLIOGRAPHY
F. Schmid: *The Practice of Painting* (London, 1948)
V. Zahira, ed. and trans.: *Artists' Techniques in Golden Age Spain* (Cambridge, 1986)

JONATHAN STEPHENSON

Mahmud II. *See* OTTOMAN, §II (6).

Mahmud Muzahhib [Maḥmūd Muẓahhib] (*fl c.* 1500–60). Persian illustrator and illuminator. Mahmud Muzahhib ('the illuminator') was largely responsible for the transfer of styles from the Timurid ateliers at Herat to the Uzbek court at Bukhara following the Uzbek capture of Herat in 1507. His earliest works, such as the illustrations to a copy (ex-Paris, E. de Lorey priv. col.) of Jami's *Bahāristān* ('Abode of spring') are close to the style of BIHZAD, though lacking the originality of his model, and suggest that Mahmud was trained at Herat. His portrait of the Timurid bureaucrat 'Alishir Nava'i (Meshed, Imam Riza Shrine Mus.) is based on a prototype by Bihzad, except that the landscape in the original has been replaced by a plain gold ground. Of the many manuscripts made for 'Abd al-'Aziz, Khan of Bukhara from 1540 to 1549, Mahmud's illustrations to a copy (1542–9; Lisbon, Mus. Gulbenkian, N.177) of Sa'di's *Būstān* ('Orchard') define the highest levels of book illustration at Bukhara (*see* ISLAMIC ART, §III, 4(vi)(c)). They are the result of faultless technical control, but continually look back to the Timurid

past. Mahmud's style was mindlessly repeated by later artists to satisfy the needs of a rapidly expanding clientele.

BIBLIOGRAPHY
A. Sakisian: 'Maḥmūd Muḏhahīb—Miniaturiste, enlumineur et calligraphe Persan', *A. Islam.*, iv (1937), pp. 338–44
M. M. Ashraf-Aini: 'The School of Bukhara to *c.* 1550', *The Arts of the Book in Central Asia*, ed. B. Gray (Boulder, 1979), pp. 249–72

MILO CLEVELAND BEACH

Ma Ho-chih. *See* MA HEZHI.

Mahony, Marion. *See* GRIFFIN.

Maia, Antonio (*b* Carmópolis, 9 Oct 1928). Brazilian painter. He began painting while still living in his native state of Sergipe in north-eastern Brazil and was deeply affected by his native region. After moving to Rio de Janeiro in 1955 he briefly adopted an abstract style but in 1963 he returned to images of everyday life and popular religion in the north-east. He particularly favoured symbolically charged images of wooden ex-votos (arms, legs, hands, hearts and especially heads) depicted with a technical virtuosity that deliberately eschewed primitivism (*Walkers*, 1968; Curitiba, Mus. A. Contemp.). Visits to the United States in 1968 and to Europe (1969–72, staying longest in Barcelona) widened his contact with international art but did not draw him away from his own Brazilian subjects. In 1974 the Art Gallery of Ontario in Toronto acquired a series of paintings by him.

BIBLIOGRAPHY
C. Valladares: *Riscadores de Milagres* [Sketchers of miracles] (Rio de Janeiro, 1969)
W. Ayala: *A criação plástica em questão* [The plastic arts under debate] (Petrópolis, 1970)
O. de Araújo: 'Antonio Maia', *Visão da terra* (exh. cat., Rio de Janeiro, Mus. A. Mod., 1977), pp. 22–33
M. Machado da Silva: *Ex-votos e orantes no Brasil* [Ex-votos and orants in Brazil] (Rio de Janeiro, 1981)

ROBERTO PONTUAL

Maia, Manuel da (*b* Lisbon, *bapt* 5 Aug 1677; *d* Lisbon, 17 Sept 1768). Portuguese military engineer and urban planner. He was born into a humble family, and in 1698 he became assistant to Francisco Pimentel (1652–1706), an engineer who taught in the Ribeira das Naus (School of Fortification and Military Architecture) in Lisbon. He collaborated on the fortifications of Lisbon (1701), Estremoz (1703) and Abrantes (1705) and took part in the siege of Badajoz (1705). His competence in foreign languages led to his being appointed by the Junta dos Três Estados to produce translations of Antoine de Ville's *De la charge des gouverneurs des places* (Paris, 1639) and Johann Friedrich Pfeffinger the elder's *Nouvelle fortification* (Amsterdam, 1698); these were published in Lisbon in 1708 and 1713 respectively. Between 1713 and 1718 he constructed a plan of the city of Lisbon and *c.* 1719 a topographical model of the 'Buenos Aires' site (west Lisbon), where John V wanted to build a new royal palace and basilica.

From 1728 Maia was involved in plans for the Águas Livres aqueduct and was part of a team of engineers that directed the work after the resignation of Antonio Canevari. He was in sole charge of the project from November 1732 to September 1733 and wrote a work on the subject, *Considerações sobre o projecto da condução das Águas, chamadas Livres, ao Bairro Alto*, which he presented to the King on 6 November 1731. Though technically unoriginal, this study is interesting for the emphasis placed on purely functional rather than aesthetic considerations. His ideas, however, resulted in his being removed from the project at the end of 1733 (or the beginning of the following year, according to his account) because he opposed the King's wishes: John V wanted a monumental structure on the lines of the great Roman aqueducts of antiquity. In 1738, in a request for promotion, Maia claimed also to have carried out a survey of water resources and directed the project for the Mafra aqueduct (to supply the ambitious building ordered by John V), asserting that he had invented a new method of water transmission to avoid the expense of arches.

Besides being an engineer, Maia was archivist of the House of Braganza and contributed to the preparation of the catalogues of the royal library. He became a member of the Real Academia de História (10 December 1739), and soon afterwards John V conferred on him the patent of nobility, as Fidalgo da Casa Real (8 April 1740). In 1741 Maia compiled a report on the planning of a new parish in Lisbon (S Isabel), which was approved by royal decree on 13 April 1745. This laid down a series of recommendations relating to urban planning, which he had an opportunity to develop and implement in the following decade. In 1744, on the death of the Royal Architect, Custódio Vieira, Maia supervised the team responsible for the execution of the accepted plan of Nossa Senhora das Necessidades (Lisbon) by Vieita and was appointed to direct the implementation of these royal works.

Official recognition of Maia's professional status came slowly and in conjunction with three events: the deaths of John V in 1750 and of the Chief Engineer of the Kingdom Manuel de Azevedo Fortes (1660–1749) and the earthquake in Lisbon on 1 November 1755. That Maia only became Chief Engineer of the Kingdom on 24 January 1754 indicates a certain resistance to his nomination. In contrast to his predecessor, Maia was neither culturally nor ideologically in sympathy with the ideas of the Enlightenment, and on 8 July 1755 he denounced an 'enlightened mind' and Freemasonry. Following the earthquake, he was at once appointed to direct the work of reconstruction and was responsible for the choice of the teams of engineers connected with the Military Academy who prepared various plans. Six were drawn up in all, and these were submitted for the approval of King Joseph's powerful royal minister, Sebastião José de Carvalho e Melo (later Marquês de Pombal). In relation to this project, Maia wrote his important *Dissertações* (MS., 1755–6), in three parts with a supplement (MS., 1756) addressed to the president of the Casa de Suplicação, Pedro Henrique de Bragança Sousa Tavares Mascarenhas e Silva, 1st Duque de Lafões (1718–61). In the first part he set out five alternative proposals for the rebuilding of the city, considering the advantages and drawbacks of each. Although his preferred solution was that proposed in the fifth plan—to rebuild the city on another site to the west of the devastated area, leaving the reconstruction of the ruined centre to its fate, that is, to the free initiative of the proprietors—he was not averse to the fourth proposal. This involved rebuilding the destroyed area on a regular plan, radically

different from the old one in both organization and architectural design. The second part of his manuscript assumes the adoption of the fourth plan: Maia discussed the advantages of building the royal palace in another situation and suggested the urbanistic principles for the plan of the 'Baixa' (lower town). The third part includes four plans and five further schemes with various types of elevation and the cross-section of a street (divided into three parts) showing the respective infrastructures. As well as the supplement, he put forward two other plans for the Baixa, one of which, by Eugénio dos Santos, was approved and carried out.

Maia proved to be an excellent manager and urban planner, inspired more by practice than theoretical knowledge. However, the rebuilding of the city was innovative at an international level. He was not the author but only the adviser (or one of them) on the plan that was finally approved (*see also* POMBALINE STYLE). It is because of this that the new Lisbon could claim to embody a modern conception of the city, despite the fact that Maia had a typically 17th-century mentality. The *Dissertações* are fundamental for understanding the depth of consideration given to the problems of urbanization and the methodologies underlying the various solutions proposed. Nevertheless, it is unclear as to whether they were Maia's work alone or the result of prolonged discussion with other engineers under his orders, particularly Eugénio dos Santos. It has yet to be seen whether Maia's role in these projects was that of guardian angel or acting as a brace to restrict the creativity of the other architects and engineers involved.

BIBLIOGRAPHY

Viterbo

C. Aires: *História orgânica e política do exército português. Provas. História da engenharia militar portuguesa (subsídios), desde a fundação da monarquia até 1816*, v (Lisbon, 1902–32), pp. 128–33, 181–219 [incl. Maia's *Dissertações*]

——: *Manuel da Maia e os engenheiros militares portugueses no terramoto de 1755* (Lisbon, 1910)

E. dos Santos: 'Manuel da Maia e o aqueduto das Águas Livres', *Rev. Mun.*, xciv (1962), pp. 58–73 [includes Maia's *Considerações sobre o projecto da condução das Águas chamadas Livres ao Bairro Alto*]

J. A. França: *Une ville des lumières: La Lisbonne de Pombal* (Paris, 1965; Port. trans., rev. 5/1987)

J. E. C. H. Correia: 'Maia, Manuel da', *Dicionário da arte barroca em Portugal*, ed. J. F. Pereira (Lisbon, 1989)

W. R. F. da Silva: *Além da Baixa: Indícios de planeamento urbano na Lisboa setecentista*, 2 vols (MA thesis, Lisbon, U. Nova, 1990)

D. João V e o abastecimento da água a Lisboa, 2 vols (exh. cat., Lisbon, Pal. Galveias, 1990)

L. Ferrão: *A real obra de Nossa Senhora das Necessidades* (Lisbon, 1994)

LEONOR FERRÃO

Maiano [Majano], **da.** Italian family of artists. The brothers (1) Giuliano da Maiano, Giovanni da Maiano I (*b* Maiano, nr Florence, 1439; *d* Florence, 10 Aug 1478) and (2) Benedetto da Maiano ran one of the most versatile and productive workshops in Florence in the later 15th century. They were sons of the mason Leonardo d'Antonio da Maiano and were brought up in the quarry village of Maiano, outside Florence. Giuliano was the administrative head of the workshop, which produced secular and ecclesiastical furniture and executed sculpture in a wide variety of media, as well as designing and building numerous architectural projects. They worked throughout Tuscany and also in Naples. In a *catasto* (land registry declaration) of 1469 Giuliano gave his own age as 38 and those of Giovanni I and Benedetto as 31 and 28 respectively. Giovanni I is mentioned in payments (1473–7) for work at SS Annunziata, Florence, and is also named in the brothers' *catasti* of 1470 and 1480. Nothing is known of his specific contribution to the family's enterprises. (3) Giovanni da Maiano II was the son of (2) Benedetto da Maiano and was one of the first generation of Italian sculptors to introduce the Renaissance style to the English court at the time of Henry VIII.

BIBLIOGRAPHY

Thieme–Becker

L. Cèndali: *Giuliano e Benedetto da Maiano* (Sancasciano Val di Pesa, [1926])

(1) Giuliano da Maiano (*b* Maiano, nr Florence, 1432; *d* Naples, 17 Oct 1490). Architect, wood-carver and intarsia worker. As *capomaestro* of Florence Cathedral and Court Architect to Alfonso, Duke of Calabria (later Alfonso II, King of Naples), he was recognized in his lifetime as the outstanding architect of his generation. He made an important contribution to spreading the Renaissance style to southern Italy, and his ambition to enlarge the scale and scope of Italian architecture from the smaller scale employed in the early Renaissance, although not entirely successful, paved the way for the next generation's creation of the truly monumental architecture of the High Renaissance.

1. Life and work. 2. Working methods and technique.

1. LIFE AND WORK.

(i) Woodwork and intarsias. Although much of his posthumous fame rests on his work as an architect, Giuliano's earlier work in wood, which included intarsia work, earned him an equally high reputation. His first recorded commissions, for *all'antica* wooden panels and frames, were from the Florentine painters Neri di Bicci (payments from 28 Feb 1454/5–14 Nov 1472) and Cosimo Rosselli (payments, Aug 1456–March 1457 for a wooden frame (destr.) for the S Barbara altarpiece, originally in SS Annunziata, now Florence, Accad.). He also made a wooden bench (1455) for S Maria del Carmine in Florence and a wooden cross that was sold to Neri di Bicci on 24 April 1459. In addition, he accepted commissions for more ephemeral objects, including a float for the celebrations of the feast of St John the Baptist in Florence in 1461.

By 1461 Giuliano's workshop was well established, and he began to receive major commissions for entire ensembles of wooden church furnishings, including the choir benches, doors and sacristy cabinets for the Badia at Fiesole (payments 3 July 1461–2 Jan 1462/3) and the completion of panels and cabinets for the north sacristy of Florence Cathedral (commissions dated 20 July 1463 and 19 April 1465). The cathedral woodwork, the earliest complete surviving set of furnishings by Giuliano, shows him to have achieved full mastery of his craft. Five figures in two of the compositions showing the *Annunciation* and *St Zenobius between SS Eugenius and Crescenzo* were designed by Maso Finiguerra and coloured by Alesso Baldovinetti, so it is the design of the architectural settings and architectonic ornament that must be attributed to Giuliano. Indeed, the overall unity of the window wall points to a single designer. Giuliano provided arched frames for the iconic figure of *St Zenobius between SS Eugenius and Crescenzo* on the lower level and employed a deeply foreshortened perspective scheme for an elevated fictive loggia above. In the *Annunciation*, Maso's figures of the Virgin and Angel are not fully consonant with the daring illusionism Giuliano employed on the loggia in which the scene takes place. This only highlights Giuliano's exceptional inventiveness. The fictive architecture—the structural members, the framing panels and their ornament—are typical of the classically inspired architecture and architectural ornament of the generation following Brunelleschi; it also bears a strong resemblance to actual buildings designed or built by Giuliano in the next decade.

Giuliano received other commissions for woodwork, including wooden pulpits for S Maria Nuova, Florence (payment 5 April 1465), and for the collegiate church in San Gimignano (1469); the designs, but not the execution, of choir-stalls for Florence Cathedral (1471) and a similar commission for Pisa Cathedral (1477); and woodwork at SS Annunziata, Florence (1470s). He also provided cassoni, elaborate beds and other furniture for the Strozzi, Rucellai, Pazzi and other families in both Florence and Naples.

A letter of 3 April 1473 from Filippo Strozzi (i) and Lorenzo Strozzi in Florence to Filippo di Matteo Strozzi in Naples states that both Giuliano and his brother Benedetto were eager to take on three-dimensional work as opposed to woodwork. At about this time Benedetto started to work as a marble sculptor, and Giuliano took on major architectural commissions in Siena and Faenza. Giuliano's bottega, however, continued to receive commissions for woodwork throughout his lifetime. With Benedetto and a team of sculptors, he took on the commission for the new ceiling, doors and marble doorframes of the Sala dei Gigli in the Palazzo Vecchio, Florence (payments 28 Feb 1476–27 Nov 1481). On 8 January 1489–90 Giuliano was paid for the design of the coffered ceiling at S Eligio in Naples, and his name was included in an inscription on the choir-stalls in Perugia Cathedral, although these were executed largely by the del Tasso family, who must have been working to his designs.

(ii) Architecture. In 1461 Giuliano entered a competition for the design of an aedicula for the Madonna della Tavola in Orvieto Cathedral. Giuliano's other early work outside Florence included plans for enlarging the collegiate church in San Gimignano (payment 16 July 1466) and his subsequent erection of the chapel of S Fina in the same church (payment 16 May 1468), where he would seem to have been influenced by Bernardo Rossellino's and Antonio Rossellino's chapel of the Cardinal of Portugal in S Miniato al Monte, Florence.

In the 1460s Giuliano may also have begun work on the Palazzo Strozzino in Florence, which was left unfinished by Michelozzo in 1462. The irregular rustication and bold three-dimensionality of most of the ground storey shows the clear imprint of Michelozzo's style, but the shift to a much tauter surface and distinctly linear articulation in the last two courses of stonework are compatible with the sensibilities one might expect of an intarsia worker.

The upper storey is also planar, its minimal rustication delineated into neatly alternating narrow and wide courses that were inspired by the façade of Alberti's Palazzo Rucellai in Florence. The Strozzino rustication, however, is much more regular, the façade is not divided into bays, and the horizontal continuity of each storey is emphasized. The Palazzo Pazzi-Quaratesi, Florence, which is also usually attributed to Giuliano, has a similar articulation. Work there may have begun in 1462, when the major purchase of land on which to build was completed, and may have continued to the 1470s, for in 1478 Giuliano claimed that Jacopo de' Pazzi owed him money for some work in the Pazzi house in Florence, at a villa in Montughi and at Santa Croce, Florence. Some of the debt may have been for works in wood, but the design of the Pazzi courtyard shares numerous similarities with the cathedral intarsias (Haines, 1983), and the spare restraint of its façade links it to the Palazzo Spannocchi in Siena, built by Giuliano for Ambrogio Spannocchi, treasurer to Pope Pius II (payments 15 March 1473–1475).

In 1474 Giuliano was commissioned to rebuild Faenza Cathedral (1474–86; see fig.). He attempted to create a building more monumental in conception than earlier Renaissance architecture. He conceived of the nave of the basilica not as a Brunelleschian unity but as a series of ample square bays, each covered by a domical sail vault. Tall pilasters and slightly projecting architraves emphasize the division of space into bays so large that they require intermediate columnar supports. The articulation is severe, and the vaulting and alternating square piers and columns lend an almost neo-medieval aspect to the building. The decoration is minimal, the semi-dome of the apse is in the form of an outsized shell, and the nave capitals are singularly unexpressive. However, despite its large scale and careful articulation, the cathedral fails to live up to its monumental intention.

By the mid-1470s Giuliano was the leading architect of his generation, as his position as *capomaestro* (April 1477–2 May 1488) of Florence Cathedral would suggest. His plan for the placement of the doors on the façade of Brunelleschi's church of Santo Spirito, Florence, was chosen despite the fact that his design of three rather than four doors violated the master's original, much more daring, intentions. His long association with the fortification and perhaps the vaulting of the basilica in Loreto (1476–87) assured that his fame spread well beyond Florence. In 1482, for example, the city officials of Macerata sought his advice regarding the repair of the Palazzo Maggiore. He also attracted the attention of Cardinal Anton Giacomo Venieri of Recanati, who commissioned a palace in Recanati (begun 1477, left largely incomplete in 1479).

Giuliano accepted a wide variety of commissions, including the building of a castle at Montepoggiolo (1471), the expansion of one of the Strozzi palaces in Florence (1483) and the erection of a wooden tower at Pontormo (June 1485). He also seems to have provided designs for projects that he did not personally supervise, including those for S Maria del Sasso near Bibbiena (1486). Furthermore, he submitted designs for projects that were not carried out or not completed in his lifetime: the cloister of SS Flora e Lucilla in Arezzo (commissioned 27 April 1470, begun 1489), S Maria delle Carceri in Prato (20 April 1485, later reassigned to Giuliano da Sangallo) and a design (1490, unexecuted) for the façade of Florence Cathedral.

The last years of Giuliano's life were some of his most fruitful. From 1485 to 1490 he stayed largely in Naples in the service of Alfonso, Duke of Calabria, for whom he designed the elegant Porta Capuana (*see* NAPLES, fig. 2) in Naples, the adjacent Villa Duchesca (unfinished) and, most importantly, the villa at Poggio Reale (begun 1487; destr.), one of the most significant suburban residences of the Renaissance. The villa was a two-storey, rectangular structure with a large, brick-paved, interior courtyard located a few steps below ground-level. Four towers at the corners of the structure were joined to the core of the building by ground-floor porticos and arcaded loggias above, while a large fountain and flanking porticos extended along the axis of the structure into the extensive gardens. Thoroughly Classical in its inspiration, the design of Poggio Reale particularly appealed to architects of the 16th century. It influenced Baldassare Peruzzi's suburban Villa Farnesina in Rome, and Serlio published a plan and description of it in 1544. They must have admired its masterful use of geometry and the singularly successful manner in which it dissolved the usual boundaries between interior and exterior space. Whether the entire design can be credited to Giuliano, however, is not certain. The Duke employed and consulted numerous architects on the project, so the design may have resulted from group consultations. On the other hand, the plan seems surprisingly clear and coherent for a building designed by a committee. At the very least, Giuliano should be given credit for having guided the project to a most felicitous

Giuliano da Maiano: Faenza Cathedral, interior, rebuilt 1474–86

realization. The villa was already in use for a banquet in June 1489, so the speed of construction was also remarkable.

2. WORKING METHODS AND TECHNIQUE. Giuliano was the administrative head of a multifaceted workshop that produced secular and ecclesiastical furniture, sculpture in a wide variety of media and numerous buildings. Early in his career he seems to have engaged in many of these activities himself, but as his fame as an architect grew, he increasingly turned over certain operations to his brothers. Sometimes the brothers worked independently of each other, sometimes as partners; sometimes Giovanni I and Benedetto worked as Giuliano's subordinates, receiving payments on his behalf when he was outside Florence or ensuring that materials were sent to other sites, as, for example, on 24 May 1488, when Benedetto received a payment from the Gondi bank for 20,000 bricks destined for Naples. In addition, Giuliano provided designs for many types of work whose execution was subcontracted to other intarsia workers or builders, while his shop supplied several Florentine artists with panels and frames for their paintings.

Giuliano made great use of models and drawings (untraced), some of which are recorded in documents of the 1480s. In this manner he was able to engage in a large number of projects even when he could not be personally present for every phase of the construction. Through drawings designs could also be more easily explained to patrons, a number of whom took a sophisticated interest in architecture and exchanged drawings of their residences with one another. For instance, Giuliano carried drawings from Lorenzo the Magnificent to the Duke of Calabria.

BIBLIOGRAPHY

N. di Bicci: *Le Ricordanze, 10 Marzo 1453–24 Aprile 1475* (Florence, Bib. Uffizi, MS. 2); ed. B. Santi (Pisa, 1976)

G. Vasari: *Vite* (1550, rev. 2/1568); ed. G. Milanesi (1878–85), ii, pp. 467–75

L. Pecori: *Storia della terra di San Gimignano* (Florence, 1853)

G. Baroni: *La parrocchia di San Martino* (Florence, 1875)

G. Milanesi: *Nuovi documenti per la storia dell'arte toscana dal XII al XV secolo* (Rome, 1893), p. 155

C. von Fabriszy: 'Toscanische und oberitalienische Künstler in Diensten der Aragonesen zu Neapel', *Repert. Kstwissen.*, xx (1897), pp. 85–120 (87–9)

——: 'Giuliano da Maiano in Siena', *Jb. Preuss. Kstsamml.*, xxiv (1903), pp. 320–34

C. Grigioni: 'Il duomo di Faenza: Documenti inediti intorno alla sua costruzione e il documento decisivo sul nome del suo architetto', *Arte*, xxvi (1923), pp. 161–74

R. Mather: 'Documents Mostly New Relating to Florentine Painters and Sculptors of the Fifteenth Century', *A. Bull.*, xxx (1948), pp. 20–65 (37–40)

Mostra documentaria e iconografica di Palazzo Vecchio (exh. cat., Florence, Archv Stato, 1957), doc. 37, 38, 39, 40, 41

G. Marchini: *Giuliano da Maiano* (Florence, 1959)

G. Hersey: *Alfonso II and the Artistic Renewal of Naples, 1485–1495* (New Haven, 1969)

M. Salmi: 'Santa Maria delle Grazie ad Arezzo e il suo piazzale', *Commentari*, xx (1969), pp. 37–51

L. Borgo: 'Giuliano da Maiano's Santa Maria del Sasso', *Burl. Mag.*, cxiv (1972), pp. 448–52

B. Hellerforth: *Der Dom von Faenza: Ein Beitrag zur Problematik der Basilika-Architektur in der 2. Hälfte des Quattrocento* (diss., Bonn, Rhein. Friedrich-Wilhelms U., 1975)

D. Covi: 'A Documented Lettuccio for the Duke of Calabria by Giuliano da Maiano', *Essays Presented to Myron P. Gilmore*, ii (Florence, 1978), pp. 121–30

M. Haines: *The 'Sacrestia delle Messe' of the Florentine Cathedral* (Florence, 1983)

P. Nuttall: '"La Tavele Sinte Barberen": New Documents for Cosimo Rosselli and Giuliano da Maiano', *Burl. Mag.*, cxxvii (1985), pp. 367–72

(2) Benedetto da Maiano [Benedetto di Leonardo] (*b* Maiano, nr Florence, 1442; *d* Florence, 24 May 1497). Sculptor and wood-carver, brother of (1) Giuliano da Maiano. He was technically one of the most accomplished marble-carvers of the 15th century and the foremost sculptor in Florence of the generation following Bernardo Rossellino. Technical difficulties had been largely overcome by his predecessors, however, and he lacked the innovative qualities of Rossellino's generation. There are close parallels between Benedetto and his contemporary and sometime collaborator Domenico Ghirlandaio in their technical proficiency, powers of narrative expression, excellent portraiture and adherence to traditional techniques.

1. Life and work. 2. Working methods and technique.

1. LIFE AND WORK. Benedetto is first recorded as a woodworker. On 7 March 1467 he received payment for wooden panels that his older brother, Giuliano, had prepared for painters working in the chapel of the Cardinal of Portugal at S Miniato al Monte, Florence. His early training and first artistic activity appear to have been in the workshop of Giuliano. There he learnt the art both of intarsia and of wood-carving, which must have prepared him for his later career as stone-carver. The rich, decorative intarsia designs may also have contributed to the lavish quality of many of his mature works in marble.

Vasari told an apocryphal story that Benedetto abandoned working in wood when the inlaid panels of a pair of large chests (untraced) he had made for Matthias Corvinus, King of Hungary, fell apart after shipping; in fact he worked in this medium throughout his career, carving wooden angels that were painted and gilded by Neri di Bicci (23 March 1471–2), making a large intarsia chest for the personal papers of Filippo Strozzi (i) (8 May 1479), carving wooden frames for steel mirrors (one documented for the Strozzi family on 28 June 1482) and producing numerous crucifixes: one for Onofrio di Pietro of San Gimignano in 1474, another for the Strozzi Chapel in Lecceto (payment 22 June 1482), yet others listed in the inventory of his workshop after his death, and large crucifixes for the choir-screen of the charterhouse of Galluzzo (payment 12 August 1496) and Florence Cathedral (acquired from Giovanni II in 1509). He is also said to have completed Desiderio da Settignano's wooden statue of *St Mary Magdalene* (Florence, Santa Trinita), and the model he provided of the Palazzo Strozzi on 5 February 1491 must have been made of wood too.

Benedetto's first independent work in marble was the S Savino Monument (1468–71) in Faenza Cathedral. It is not in a fully mature style, but its six narrative reliefs, two free-standing statues and wide variety of architectural elements suggest something of the early influences on Benedetto. The organization of the monument derives from prototypes developed in the workshop of Bernardo Rossellino and Antonio Rossellino, as do the slight figures in the reliefs; however, the complex is more densely organized than anything produced by the Rossellini, and the conception of space within the narratives is unlike the restricted, even miniaturized settings used by them. Instead, Benedetto followed the example of Donatello and Ghiberti, cutting off figures and parts of his setting at both the top and sides of his scenes, as in *St Savino Heals a Blind Man*. In this monument Benedetto demonstrated his love of the richly ornamented surfaces and spatially complex but narratively clear reliefs that became characteristic of his mature work.

Benedetto's first important commission was the S Fina Monument in the collegiate church, San Gimignano (1472–7, inscribed 1475, last payment 13 Dec 1493), erected in the chapel of S Fina built by Giuliano da Maiano and frescoed by Domenico Ghirlandaio. The gilt marble monument takes up one wall of the chapel. Above an altar encrusted with rich decorative motifs stands a tabernacle with a relief of angels depicted in an architectural setting shown in raking perspective—possibly Benedetto was aware of the subtle effects achieved by Desiderio da Settignano. The scenes from the life of S Fina in the frieze above may owe their serene quality to the influence of Domenico Ghirlandaio. Above this is the saint's tomb, and still higher the Virgin and Child in high relief are displayed in a mandorla flanked by two flying angels. Illusionistic marble curtains are drawn back to reveal the monument. Originally two free-standing marble statues of kneeling angels flanked the monument (now by the high altar in the same church).

In 1473 Benedetto matriculated in the Arte dei Maestri di Pietra e Legname in Florence and then travelled to Rome, where he delivered an elaborate bed for the Duke of Calabria, before moving on to Naples, where he made preliminary studies for the marble tomb of *Matteo Strozzi* (*d* 1459; see Borsook, *Ant. Viva*, 1970). On 15 June 1475 Benedetto was paid for a marble bust of *Filippo Strozzi* (Paris, Louvre); its terracotta model (Berlin, Skulpgal.) possesses a good deal more life than the rather cool marble rendition. This is the only case in which both model and finished marble bust have survived from the 15th century.

Between 28 February 1476 and 27 November 1481 Giuliano and Benedetto were paid for work in the Palazzo Vecchio, Florence. Benedetto contributed the marble doorframes surmounted by statues between the Sala del Consiglio and the Sala dei Gigli. The elaborately decorative, classicizing doorframes are crowned with semicircular pediments flanked by candelabra and paired putti. Placed before the pediments on either side is a statue, the seated figure of *Justice* on one side and the young *St John the Baptist* on the other. The latter is inspired by Desiderio, but, like all of Benedetto's works, it is more straightforward in its conception and close in spirit to the work of Domenico Ghirlandaio.

In 1474 Benedetto signed and dated a meticulously detailed marble portrait bust of the wealthy Florentine merchant *Pietro Mellini* (Florence, Bargello). In 1478 he was again at work for Mellini, carving a marble tabernacle for holy oil at SS Fiora e Lucilla, Arezzo. A design for the portico of S Maria delle Grazie in the same town may also date from around this time. Mellini's last recorded commission, that for his own simple floor tomb and a magnificent marble pulpit (see fig.) over it in Santa Croce,

Benedetto da Maiano: marble pulpit, completed 1485 (Florence, Santa Croce)

Florence, is Benedetto's masterpiece. Completed by 19 May 1485, when Pietro Mellini made his final will and testament, the full-scale work was preceded by several models, three of which are preserved (London, V&A). A terracotta model for a relief of the *Dream of Innocent III* (Berlin, Bodemus) was also prepared, but the scene was abandoned in the final project. A model of the entire pulpit that was in the artist's studio at his death has not survived.

The pulpit is cleverly attached to one of the piers in the nave of the church, through which Benedetto excavated a staircase. The five relief scenes from the life of St Francis are powerfully clear and dramatic narratives illustrated with a kind of clear-eyed verism that is usually reserved for painting. The reliefs are separated by Corinthian colonettes, framed by finely carved classicizing mouldings, while below, closer to eye-level, the terminating corbel is overlaid with *tour de force* basketweave carving. The entire ensemble is of extremely high technical quality, one of the most remarkable works of relief sculpture of the later 15th century.

Similar in its complexity and virtuoso workmanship is the altar ciborium for S Domenico in Siena, which may also date from the 1480s. Earlier commissions include a ciborium for the collegiate church in San Gimignano and a holy water font for the Strozzi Chapel in Lecceto (payment 23 Jan 1482). In Loreto a lavabo and two glazed terracotta lunettes of Evangelists, which strongly resemble those in roundels at the base of the Siena ciborium, date from between 1480 and 1483.

Another major commission of the 1480s was the Annunciation Altar and marble furnishings for the Terranuova Chapel of the church of Monteoliveto Maggiore (now S Anna dei Lombardi), Naples. It was begun before 16 September 1489, when Joanna, Queen of Naples, requested duty-free passage of the carved marbles from Florence via Pisa to Naples; payments continued until 23 April 1491. The form of the altar, with a relief of the *Annunciation* flanked by niches containing statues of *St John the Baptist* and *St John the Evangelist*, is based on Antonio Rossellino's Piccolomini Altar in the same church. The detail and finishing are only slightly less meticulous than the Santa Croce pulpit, the saints are more substantial than Benedetto's earlier free-standing figures, and the central relief, with high-relief figures of the *Virgin and Angel* and a barrel-vaulted loggia leading to a garden, openly challenges painting's supremacy in the depiction of deep illusionistic space.

In the 1490s Benedetto's individual figures and the settings in which he placed them became increasingly large in scale and spare in detail. The sober dignity of a bust of *Giotto* for Florence Cathedral (*in situ*) and the relative restraint of the tomb monument of *Filippo Strozzi* (*d* 1491) in S Maria Novella (begun by 27 June 1491, payments continuing into 1497) marked a move away from the highly anecdotal and decorative quality of his earlier work towards more monumental forms and design. This is also evident in the broad figures in the unfinished *Coronation of Ferdinand of Aragon* (frags, Florence, Bargello), which he was working on in 1494 for the Porta Reale in Naples. In the S Bartolo Monument in S Agostino, San Gimignano (11 May 1492–23 July 1494), Benedetto increased the size of his figures, reduced the number of characters within his reliefs and provided architectural settings free of unnecessary detail. A *St Sebastian* and a *Virgin and Child* (both Florence, Misericordia), both left unfinished at his death, were also conceived along the same lines.

Benedetto's designs for the corner lanterns and torch holders of the Palazzo Strozzi, Florence (payment 12 March 1495), retained the decorative sense for which he was known in the 1480s, and the same may have been true of a design he submitted for a baptismal font in Pistoia (14 May 1497), but these were works intended as decorative fittings. Other surviving late works include a terracotta lunette of *St Lawrence* for the charterhouse of Galluzzo near Florence (payment 12 Aug 1496), which the della Robbia workshop glazed for Benedetto, and a bust of *Onofrio di Pietro* for the collegiate church in San Gimignano (commissioned 28 May 1493; San Gimignano, Mus. A. Sacra); both are notably more severe than his earlier, decorative works. His large wooden Crucifix in Florence Cathedral (acquired in 1509 from Giovanni II) is subtle in its rendering and, like a number of his late works, is characterized by a heightened idealization and grander dimensions that place it on the verge of the High Renaissance.

2. WORKING METHODS AND TECHNIQUE. Benedetto's sculptural ensembles show clearly that his workshop participated in their creation. In compositions that include symmetrical elements, one of the two complementary figures or architectural elements is regularly of superior

execution and can be credited to the master, while the second has been copied from its pair by an assistant. Full-scale models in terracotta, such as those that survive for the Santa Croce pulpit reliefs, must also have allowed Benedetto to maintain close control over his work while delegating a good deal of carving to assistants. Drawings would have been less useful in this regard, and although no drawings survive that can be firmly attributed to Benedetto, contemporary examples usually associated with Francesco di Simone Ferrucci suggest that they would have been useful for working out the complex interrelationships between the numerous component parts of Benedetto's monuments and altars, as well as suggesting to patrons the overall shape of a commissioned work. Other artists' drawings were also used by the sculptor, as in the case of Benedetto's bust of *Onofrio di Pietro*, which was not carved from life but from a drawing of the deceased.

Vasari claimed that he owned drawings by Benedetto and praised them highly. There is no indication that Benedetto did any carving outside Florence; his works for other cities were shipped in largely finished form and then installed under his supervision. His devotional works were often reproduced in stucco or terracotta: for example a marble relief of the *Virgin and Child* (Washington, DC, N.G.A.) served as a model for numerous terracottas and stuccos. Such artists as Neri di Bicci were engaged to paint these reliefs. Together with his brothers, Benedetto erected a tabernacle containing a terracotta *Virgin and Child* and a marble relief of the *Man of Sorrows* on their country property near Prato (relief dated 1480; now in Prato Cathedral).

BIBLIOGRAPHY

DBI: 'Benedetto di Leonardo, detto da Maiano'

G. Vasari: *Vite* (1550, rev. 2/1568); ed. G. Milanesi (1878–85), iii, pp. 333–46

P. Bacci: 'Documenti su Benedetto da Maiano e Andrea da Fiesole relative al "Fonte Battesimale" del Duomo di Pistoia', *Riv. A.*, ii (1904), pp. 271–84

A. Marquand: 'A Lunette by Benedetto da Maiano', *Burl. Mag.*, xl (1922), pp. 128–31

L. Dussler: *Benedetto da Maiano: Ein Florentiner Bildhauer des späten Quattrocento* (Munich, 1924)

M. Lisner: 'Zu Benedetto da Maiano und Michelangelo', *Z. Kstwiss.*, xii (1958), pp. 141–56

J. Pope-Hennessy: *Italian Renaissance Sculpture* (London, 1963, rev. 3/1981), pp. 289–92

E. Borsook: 'Documenti relativi alle cappelle di Lecceto e delle Selve di Filippo Strozzi', *Ant. Viva*, ix/3 (1970), pp. 3–20

——: 'Documents for Filippo Strozzi's Chapel in Santa Maria Novella and other Related Papers', *Burl. Mag.*, cxii (1970), pp. 737–45, 800–04

M. Lisner: *Holzkruzifixe in Florenz und in der Toskana von der Zeit um 1300 bis zum frühen Cinquecento* (Munich, 1970), pp. 76–82

D. Carl: 'Der Finaaltar von Benedetto da Maiano in der Collegiata zu S. Gimignano: Datierung, Rekonstruktion, Stil', *Münster*, xxvi (1973), pp. 285–7

A. Paolucci: 'I musici di Benedetto da Maiano e il monumento di Ferdinando d'Aragona', *Paragone*, xxvi/303 (1975), pp. 3–7

A. Tessari: 'Benedetto da Maiano tra il 1490 e il 1497', *Crit. A.*, 2nd ser., xxi/143 (1975), pp. 39–52; xxii/145 (1976), pp. 20–30

J. Russel Sale: *The Strozzi Chapel by Filippino Lippi in Santa Maria Novella* (diss., U. Pennsylvania, 1976), pp. 19, 524–6

D. Carl: 'Der Fina-Altar von Benedetto da Maiano in der Collegiata zu San Gimignano zu seiner Datierung und Rekonstruktion', *Mitt. Ksthist. Inst. Florenz*, xxii (1978), pp. 129–66

P. Morselli: *Corpus of Tuscan Pulpits, 1400–1550* (diss., U. Pittsburgh, 1979)

G. Radke: 'The Sources and Composition of Benedetto da Maiano's San Savino Monument in Faenza', *Stud. Hist. A.*, xviii (1985), pp. 7–27

Italian Renaissance Sculpture in the Time of Donatello (exh. cat., ed. A. Darr and G. Bonsanti; Detroit, MI, Inst. A., 1985), pp. 193–6

GARY M. RADKE

(3) Giovanni da Maiano II [John de la Mayn; Delamayne; Demayanns; Demyans; Dermyans; Mane] (*b* Florence, 1486–7; *d c.* 1542–3). Sculptor, son of (2) Benedetto da Maiano. It has erroneously been thought by some that he was the son of Giovanni da Maiano I. In 1507 he received a third of the inheritance his father had left him. On 4 August 1509 he rented, as a sculpture workshop, Benedetto da Maiano's (and subsequently Rustici's) old bottega on Via Castellacio in Florence. This was intended to continue for three years; however, on 8 January 1510 he withdrew without reason. He may at this point have accompanied Pietro Torrigiani northward. Alternatively, he may have been recruited by Torrigiani in 1519, together with the sculptor Benedetto da Rovezzano, when Torrigiani contracted with other Florentine sculptors, including Antonio Toto del Nunziata (Darr, 1980), to travel to England with him to assist on the altar of King Henry VII (frags, London, Westminster Abbey, Henry VII's Chapel) and the projected monumental tomb of King Henry VIII and his first wife, Catherine of Aragon, the latter commissioned to Torrigiani in January 1519 but never completed. Giovanni was certainly in England by 18 June 1521, when he wrote a letter to Cardinal Thomas Wolsey requesting payment for eight life-size painted and gilded terracotta roundels of Roman Caesars that he had made for the Cardinal for the exterior of Hampton Court near London (*in situ*; see Higgins). These are among the first evidence of Italian Renaissance style directly incorporated in English architecture. Additional busts of Caesars in roundels made of the same London yellow clay and red brick, and by the same hand, survive at The Vyne, Hants, in Hanworth and elsewhere. Presumably they originally formed a series (possibly of twelve Caesars) that decorated three of the Hampton Court gateways (made 1530–32). In the same letter Giovanni demanded payment from Wolsey for three Histories (i.e. Labours) of Hercules (untraced) that were probably also of painted and gilded terracotta. Also installed in a gateway of Hampton Court is a large terracotta relief bearing Wolsey's coat of arms, flanked by two standing putti, formerly bearing Wolsey's monogram and dated 1525, which may be by Giovanni or, more likely, initiated by Torrigiani and completed by Giovanni, possibly in conjunction with Benedetto da Rovezzano.

In 1527 Giovanni modelled and painted stucco and wood decorative furnishings for Henry VIII's Banqueting and Revels houses in Greenwich; he is mentioned working there with Ellys Carmyan and Vincent Volpe of Naples as a gilder for revels and is referred to as an Italian 'graver'—he may be the 'Maister Mane' paid for 'drawing the pictures' (see Auerbach). From 1528 he received an annual salary of £20 from Henry VIII, and in 1530 was paid for six painted, gilded and silvered 'Antique heads'. From 1530 to 1536 he collaborated with Benedetto da Rovezzano and other Italian and northern craftsmen on the revived project of a tomb for Henry VIII at Windsor, parts of the sculpture for which the King had taken over from Wolsey's aborted tomb project (1524–9). In 1536

Giovanni's and Benedetto's involvement on this important royal commission ended, and, despite later work by others, it was never completed. Between 1532 and 1536 Giovanni may have produced the screen of King's College Chapel, Cambridge (Auerbach), and he may have modelled the four terracotta tondi on the façade of the Holbein Gate at Whitehall Palace and various other busts and works in terracotta. He is not mentioned in England after 1536, and it is probable that he returned to Florence with Benedetto da Rovezzano, who was back by May 1543.

BIBLIOGRAPHY

DBI: 'Benedetto di Leonardo, detto da Maiano'; Thieme–Becker
A. Higgins: 'On the Work of Florentine Sculptors in England in the Early Part of the Sixteenth Century: With Special Reference to the Tombs of Cardinal Wolsey and King Henry VIII', *Archaeol. J.*, li (1894), pp. 129–220, 367–70
C. Beard: 'Torrigiano or da Maiano', *Connoisseur*, 84 (1929), pp. 77–86
E. Auerbach: *Tudor Artists* (London, 1954), pp. 17, 157, 176, 190
E. Luporini: *Benedetto da Rovezzano* (Milan, 1964), p. 169
A. Darr: *Pietro Torrigiano and his Sculpture for the Henry VII Chapel, Westminster Abbey* (diss., New York U., 1980)
S. Gunn and P. Lindley: *Cardinal Wolsey: Church, State and Art* (Cambridge, 1991), pp. 34, 47, 267, 280–82, 285
A. Darr: 'New Documents for Pietro Torrigiani and Other Early Cinquecento Florentine Sculptors Active in Italy and England', *Kunst der Cinquecento in der Toskana*, ed. M. Cämmerer (Munich, 1992), pp. 108–38

ALAN PHIPPS DARR

Mai-chi shan. *See* MT MAIJI.

Maiden Castle. Fortified hilltop site in Dorset, England. It has a long, if discontinuous, history of use as a settlement and ritual centre spanning over 4000 years from the beginning of the Neolithic period to late Roman times in the 4th century AD. However, the most important architecture at the site belongs to the period between 500 BC and AD 50, and the spectacular nature of these Iron Age remains has tended to obscure the significance of the earlier features. Maiden Castle was excavated between 1934 and 1937 by MORTIMER WHEELER; testing of his results took place in 1986 and 1987.

The eastern knoll of the hill was first occupied in the mid-4th millennium BC by a Neolithic settlement bounded by a system of ditches. After this settlement had gone out of use, a long mound known as a bank barrow was constructed: running for 546 m from the eastern knoll across the earlier ditches to the western knoll, it is the longest known example of its type. This monument was probably connected with ritual, as two child burials were found near the eastern end. During a gap in the occupation of the site a circular structure, probably a Bronze Age (*c.* 2300–*c.* 750 BC) round barrow, was erected on the western knoll. From *c.* 500 BC, during the Early Iron Age, the first hill-fort ramparts were constructed, enclosing the eastern knoll and largely following the line of the Neolithic ditches (for further discussion of Iron Age hill-forts *see* PREHISTORIC EUROPE, §VI, 2(i)). These timber-framed ramparts with their deep ditches were broken by entrances on the west and east; the latter was more elaborate, with two timber-lined entrance passages. This first hill-fort was then extended to enclose an area of 19 ha, encompassing the western knoll. Restructuring of the ramparts and elaboration of the gateways took place on at least two further occasions, the first when new ramparts were added (one on the north and two on the south), and again when all the ramparts were enlarged to the spectacular height of *c.* 20 m from the top of the bank to the bottom of the ditch. Although the full width of these defences was over 120 m, this distance was still within the range of a sling, and hoards of slingstones (up to 22,260 stones in one hoard alone) were found in piles near the entrances. The interior of the Iron Age fort was densely occupied by houses and stores, neatly arranged in streets. There is evidence of metalworking at the site, and many fine objects were recovered, including imported coral and elaborate horse trappings (Dorchester, Dorset Co. Mus.). Towards the end of the site's occupation 38 burials were made at the eastern entrance: some scholars believe these to have been victims of a Roman attack on Maiden Castle in AD 44 (one man's spine still had a Roman arrowhead in it, but it is not clear whether all the burials are war dead). A few years later the site was abandoned in favour of nearby Dorchester, but during the 4th century AD the hill became the site of a Romano-Celtic temple and an associated house.

BIBLIOGRAPHY

R. E. M. Wheeler: *Maiden Castle* (London, 1943)

SARA CHAMPION

Maidum [Arab. Maydūm]. Site of the first true pyramid in ancient Egypt. Maidum was first excavated by Flinders Petrie in 1891; it lies on the west bank of the Nile, 75 km south of Cairo. The pyramid was probably started by King Huni (*reg c.* 2600–*c.* 2575 BC) and completed by his successor, Sneferu (*reg c.* 2575–*c.* 2551 BC). It was originally conceived as a many-tiered structure, much like the earlier Step Pyramid of Djoser (*reg c.* 2630–*c.*2611 BC) at SAQ-QARA. The design was subsequently changed to that of a true pyramid when the steps were filled in and the sides were evenly cased with limestone. Although portions of these angled sides still remain around the base of the pyramid, all that can be seen on the site today are some of the original steps, making the whole appear as a tower set on a hill formed of the fallen stone debris covered in sand.

The 3rd and 4th Dynasty cemeteries clustered around the pyramid also hold an important position in the development of ancient Egyptian art, since these tombs added new themes to the repertory of scenes used by the artists. Beautiful examples of these come from the tomb of the vizier Nefermaat and his wife Itet, where unusual scenes from daily life were depicted, including the famous frieze of geese (Cairo, Egyp. Mus., JE34571; see fig.), elaborately painted over a coat of stucco, all that is left of a much larger scene of bird trapping. Another tomb, that of the army commander Rehotpe, yielded the seated limestone statues of the tomb owner and his wife Nofret (Cairo, Egyp. Mus., CG3, 4). Brightly painted, and with eyes inlaid in quartz and rock crystal, these remarkably preserved statues are masterful examples of early Old Kingdom sculpture.

BIBLIOGRAPHY

LÄ: 'Meidum'

I. E. S. Edwards: *The Pyramids of Egypt* (Harmondsworth, 1947; rev. 4/1991), pp. 71–8

R. J. LEPROHON

Maignan, Albert(-Pierre-René) (*b* Beaumont-sur-Sarthe, 14 Oct 1845; *d* Saint-Prix, 29 Sept 1908). French painter, illustrator and designer. In 1864 he left the Sarthe for Paris to study law. His studies did not prevent him from developing his gift for drawing and painting: he sketched views of Paris, copied works in the Louvre and entered the studio of Jules Noël in 1865. Having gained his law degree in 1866, Maignan was finally able to devote himself to painting. The following year his work was accepted by the Salon des Artistes Français, where he exhibited fairly regularly all his life. In 1869 he entered the studio of Evariste Luminais, keeping company with the group of artists brought together by Eugène Isabey.

Maignan developed ceaselessly, changing the sources of his inspiration and his technique and varying the range of his palette. His early landscapes were in the Barbizon style. Like Isabey he was interested in recording historic buildings and in perspective studies of streets. He was also fascinated by archaeological excavations and was an avid collector of classical and medieval antiquities. His early history paintings were influenced by Luminais; he constructed the events of the past with precision and an eye for the picturesque in such works as *Departure of the Norman Fleet* (1874; Nérac, Mus. Château Henri IV) and *Renaud of Burgundy Granting Letters of Enfranchisement to Belfort* (1879; untraced), his first official commission for a monumental decorative project. His first visit to Italy in 1875 encouraged him to lighten his palette; in Venice above all he discovered the importance of light in the perception of objects and the harmony it bestows on tones. He particularly admired the work of Carpaccio, Giambattista Tiepolo and Michelangelo, which influenced his monumental compositions. Italian settings featured in many of his history paintings. Maignan returned to Italy nine times in order to enrich his style and seek inspiration for his compositions. His paintings of the 1870s are distinguished by their generally sorrowful mood, as in such works as *Christ Calling the Suffering to Him* (1877; Paris, Petit Pal.), *Louis IX Consoling a Leper* (1878; Angers, Mus. B.-A.) and *Last Moments of Chlodobert* (1880; Melbourne, N.G. Victoria). For Maignan the lesson of history was essentially a moral one.

In the calm atmosphere of his home at Saint-Prix near Paris, and in the countryside where he walked at the end of each day, Maignan studied the mutability of nature and

Maidum, painted plaster frieze of geese from the tomb of Nefermaat, h. 270 mm, *c.* 2575 BC (Cairo, Egyptian Museum)

the vibration of light. As a result his painting became brighter, more luminous and serene, as in *Dante Meets Matilda* (1880; Amiens, Mus. Picardie). There was also a strongly Symbolist strain in much of his later work: the *Voices of the Tocsin* (1881) and the *Birth of the Pearl* (1892; both Amiens, Mus. Picardie). This strain is also evident in *Carpeaux* (1892; Paris, Mus. d'Orsay), which remains his most famous work. In it he accurately depicted the great sculptor's work, while also attempting to evoke its essentially dynamic quality. At the same time he meditated on the more general and ancient theme of artistic inspiration, all on a vast scale and with complex lighting effects.

In his many decorative schemes Maignan revealed his gifts for composition, the harmonious rendering of tones and the depiction of movement. He painted ceilings and panels: for example in the Salons des Lettres (completed 1893), Hôtel de Ville, Paris, Chambre de Commerce (1896), Saint-Etienne (1896), the Opéra Comique (1898), Paris, the Salle des Fêtes (1900), Exposition Universelle, Paris, and the Buffet in the Gare de Lyon (1900–05), Paris. He produced cartoons for the Gobelins and stained-glass designs. He also illustrated works by Victor Hugo and Alfred de Musset. Numerous prizes, honours and responsibilities punctuated his career, culminating in a medal of honour at the Salon of 1892 for *Carpeaux*, which was bought by the Musée du Luxembourg.

BIBLIOGRAPHY
H. Chantavoine: 'Albert Maignan', *Gaz. B.-A.*, n.s. 4, i (1909), pp. 36–48
D. Mallet: *Maignan et son oeuvre* (Mamers, 1913)
V. Alemany-Dessaint: *Albert Maignan: Artiste, peintre, décorateur* (diss., U. Paris, 1986)
Le Triomphe des mairies (exh. cat., Paris, Petit Pal., 1986), pp. 308–9

VÉRONIQUE ALEMANY-DESSAINT

Maiherpri, tomb of. Small, undecorated tomb (KV36) in the Valley of the Kings (Thebes) built for Maiherpri (*fl c.* 1400–*c.* 1390 BC), Egyptian warrior and courtier. Discovered substantially intact in 1899, it contained rich funerary equipment (Cairo, Egyp. Mus., CG 24001–100). Maiherpri was probably of Nubian origin; he was brought up in the royal nursery and later bore the title Fan-bearer, probably under Tuthmosis IV (*reg c.* 1400–*c.* 1390 BC) or Amenophis III (*reg c.* 1390–*c.* 1353 BC). His mummy lay in a wooden anthropoid coffin covered with gold leaf. This had been placed inside a rectangular outer case and a second anthropoid coffin, both decorated with designs in gold leaf on a black ground. Lying empty in the burial chamber was another anthropoid coffin of gilded wood; this was possibly intended to be the innermost case but was abandoned when it was found to be too large to fit inside the third coffin (see Reeves). A shrine-shaped chest, containing alabaster canopic jars, and many storage vessels of stone and pottery were also found. Exceptionally, in Maiherpri's Book of the Dead papyrus the owner's negroid traits were deliberately emphasized by the painter.

Among the vessels was a blue-glazed faience bowl of a type commonly found in 18th Dynasty tombs. The exterior has an open lotus design and inside, painted black, are *tilapia* fish, lotus flowers and gazelles, arranged asymmetrically. A core-formed jar of dark-blue glass, decorated with festoon designs in orange, green and white, is one of the earliest examples of its type. Also of particular interest

were a pair of leather quivers and two dog-collars, embossed with floral motifs and hunting scenes, and two gazelle-skin loincloths, discovered near Maiherpri's tomb by Howard Carter in 1902.

BIBLIOGRAPHY
G. Schweinfurth: 'Neue thebanische Gräberfunde', *Sphinx*, iii (1900), pp. 103–7
G. Daressy: *Fouilles de la Vallée des rois* (Cairo, 1902), pp. 1–61
C. F. Nims: *Thebes of the Pharaohs* (London, 1965), p. 146
J. Romer: *Valley of the Kings* (London, 1981), pp. 171–3, 185
C. N. Reeves: *Valley of the Kings: The Decline of a Royal Necropolis* (London, 1990), pp. 140–47

J. H. TAYLOR

Maiji shan. *See* MT MAIJI.

Maikop. *See* MAYKOP.

Mail art. *See* CORRESPONDENCE ART.

Maillart, Robert (*b* Berne, 6 Feb 1872; *d* Geneva, 6 April 1940). Swiss engineer and builder. He studied civil engineering (1890–94) at the Eidgenössische Technische Hochschule (ETH), Zurich, under Wilhelm Ritter (1847–1906), perhaps the greatest teacher of bridge design in the late 19th century. After graduating Maillart worked for Pümpin & Herzog (1894–6) and for the Tiefbauamt (1897–9), Zurich, where he designed his first major bridge, the Stauffacher, an unreinforced three-hinged concrete arch that followed Ritter's ideas. Maillart then moved (1899) to the design-construction firm of Frote & Westermann, Zurich, where he designed the first hollow box of concrete for the three-hinged arch over the River Inn (1901), Zuoz, for which Ritter acted as consultant.

Maillart founded his own design-construction firm in Zurich in 1902, specializing in reinforced concrete and becoming one of the first to develop its aesthetic potential. An early artistic masterpiece was the Rhine Bridge (1905; destr.), Tavanasa, in which the new hollow-box, three-hinged arch form was visually expressed, showing in profile the scientific diagram of internal forces. Its essential innovation, the integration of arch, walls and deck into a single structural element, was carried over into buildings by his development and tests (1908) of beamless floor slabs integrated with columns by broad 'mushroom' capitals, as seen in his warehouse (1910), Giesshübel, Zurich, and a filter building (1912) at Rorschach, in which he departed entirely from contemporary timber and metal framing structures. He also taught courses in reinforced concrete at the ETH in 1911–14. In 1914 he went with his family to Riga for the summer and was thence forced to St Petersburg by the onset of World War I. He built a series of large industrial buildings in Russia, but the Revolution closed his business and he barely escaped in 1918, returning to Geneva penniless and a widower.

In 1919 Maillart founded a new design office in Geneva, opening branches in Berne and Zurich (1924); by this time he had re-established himself and had begun designing new forms of startling originality. Among the first were bridge spans with light curved elements, as in his bridge over the Flienglibach (1923; removed), which was the first deck-stiffened arch bridge in concrete. He used the same idea for a shed roof (1924) at Chiasso, the form of which was derived from a hanging string analogy and stiffened by a pitched concrete roof. At Châtelard (1925) Maillart made the naturally stiff hollow-box aqueduct into one form by smoothly connecting it to slanting columns. The Valtschielbach Bridge (1925), Donath, was a technical masterpiece, its thin arch stiffened by a parapet that he lightened visually with an overhang. Maillart's most famous structure is the Salginatobel Bridge (1930), Schiers, a larger version of the bridge at Tavanasa; it is a pure structural form, and one in which all vestiges of masonry were removed. With the builder Florian Prader, Maillart won the design-construction contract by submitting the least costly design out of 19 entries, his structural forms being economical in the use of materials, yet providing immensely elegant solutions. His ideas developed rapidly, leading to the horizontally curved Landquart Bridge (1930; removed), Klosters; the skewed, double-arched Spital Bridge (1931), Berne; the counter-curved footbridge (1932) over the River Toss, near Winterthur; and his artistic masterpiece, the Schwandbach Bridge (1933; see fig.), Hinterfultigen, where he integrated a horizontally curved roadway with a vertically curved thin arch by trapezoidal cross walls.

In other developments Maillart gave his Thur Bridge (1933), Felsegg, a break at the crown that expressed the central hinge and allowed the quarter-span profile to be deeper. He also began to experiment with the cross walls, making them tilt-legged frames at Felsegg and X-shaped at Vessy (Arve Bridge, 1935); the abutment hinges at Felsegg and Vessy were expressed by moving them out into the span and designing buttresses to connect them to the foundations. Further experiments from 1932 involved the straight concrete beam, which, with its steel skeleton hidden, is often visually dead compared to the naturally expressive form of the arch; by 1935, with the Birs Bridge, Liesberg, Maillart had achieved an artistic solution by integrating the girder and columns through haunches, tapering the beam ends and spreading the columns bases to meet the foundations smoothly.

Maillart's pioneering shell structure for the Zementhalle at the Swiss National Exhibition (1939), Zurich, showed a maturity of form, the extreme thinness and full integration of which were possible largely because he visualized its performance as a combination of simple structures: the arch and the cantilever. His ideas and his elegant designs had a continuing influence on architects and engineers, as seen in the work of Félix Candela (*b* 1909), Heinz Isler (*b* 1926), Fazlur Khan (1930–82) and Christian Menn (*b* 1927). Maillart's ideas also helped writers and teachers rethink modern theories of art and engineering.

WRITINGS

'Leichte Eisenbeton-Brücken in der Schweiz', *Bauingenieur*, xii/10 (1931), pp. 165–71
'The Construction and Aesthetic of Bridges', *Concrete Way*, vi/6 (1935), pp. 303–9; trans. in *Génie Civ.*, cvi/xi (1935), p. 262
Numerous contributions to *Schweiz. Bauztg* (1901–38)

BIBLIOGRAPHY

S. Giedion: *Space, Time and Architecture: The Growth of a New Tradition* (Cambridge, MA, 1940, 5/1967), pp. 450–76
M. Bill: *Robert Maillart* (Zurich, 1949, 3/1969)
J. Abel, ed.: 'The Maillart Papers', *Second National Conference on Civil Engineering: History, Heritage and the Humanities: Princeton, 1972*
D. P. Billington: *Robert Maillart's Bridges: The Art of Engineering* (Princeton, 1979) [with list of writings and all known major bridges]

Robert Maillart: Schwandbach Bridge, Hinterfultigen, Switzerland, 1933

——: *Robert Maillart and the Art of Reinforced Concrete* (New York and London, 1990) [text in Eng. and Ger.]

DAVID P. BILLINGTON

Maillet, Jacques-Léonard (*b* Paris, 12 July 1823; *d* Paris, 14 Feb 1895). French sculptor. He studied at a local drawing school in the Faubourg Saint-Antoine, Paris, and then at the Ecole des Beaux-Arts, where he was a pupil of Jean-Jacques Feuchère and James Pradier. In 1847 he won the Prix de Rome. He then spent five years at the Académie de France in Rome, bringing back to Paris the group *Agrippina and Caligula* (marble, 1853; Saint-Germain-en-Laye, Château), his first Salon exhibit. Maillet specialized in decorative sculpture for public buildings and worked on the three great Parisian building projects of the second half of the 19th century, the Louvre, the Opéra and the Hôtel de Ville, as well as on numerous churches. In these works and such free-standing sculptures as the group *Agrippina Carrying the Ashes of Germanicus* (marble, 1861; Paris, Jard. Tuileries) he demonstrated his adherence to the Neo-classical style. He was also interested in technical developments, occasionally collaborating on mass-produced art objects, and invented a polychroming process.

BIBLIOGRAPHY

Lami

LAURE DE MARGERIE

Maillol, Aristide(-Joseph-Bonaventure) (*b* Banyuls-sur-Mer, 8 Oct 1861; *d* Perpignan, 24 Sept 1944). French sculptor, painter, designer and illustrator. He began his career as a painter and tapestry designer, but after *c.* 1900 devoted himself to three-dimensional work, becoming one of the most important sculptors of the 20th century. He concentrated almost exclusively on the nude female figure in the round, consciously wishing to strip form of all literary associations and architectural context. Although inspired by the Classical tradition of Greek and Roman sculpture, his figures have all the elemental sensuousness and dignity associated with the Mediterranean peasant.

Maillol first intended to become a painter and went to Paris in 1881, where he lived in extreme poverty. Three years later the Ecole des Beaux-Arts finally accepted him as a pupil, where he began studies under Alexandre Cabanel. He found the teaching there discouraging and his early painted work was more strongly influenced by Pierre Puvis de Chavannes, Paul Gauguin, and the Nabis group which he joined around 1894; the *Woman and the Wave* (*c.* 1898; Paris, Petit Pal.) is directly influenced by Gauguin's *Ondine* (1889; Cleveland, OH, Mus. A.). Maillol's profile portraits, such as *Profile of a Girl* (*c.* 1890; Perpignan, Mus. Rigaud), are reminiscent of Puvis, and in his decorative approach to composition, rejection of depth and use of bright, flat areas of colour Maillol reveals his affinities with the Nabis. These qualities are even more apparent in *The Washerwomen* (*c.* 1890; Switzerland, priv. col.), although the monumentality of the *Woman with a Parasol* (*c.* 1892; Paris, Mus. d'Orsay) shows the influence of Quattrocento fresco painting.

Sharing the same interest in the decorative arts as the Nabis and inspired by Gothic tapestries in the Musée de Cluny, Paris—which he considered to be on a par with the paintings of Paul Cézanne—Maillol set up a tapestry workshop at Banyuls on the Mediterranean coast in 1893. His tapestries have groups of flat, decorative figures disposed across a shallow space, and they are coloured with bright vegetable dyes obtained from plants which Maillol himself sought out. The workshop, with support from Princess Bibesco, who bought the elaborate *Music for a Bored Princess* (1897; Copenhagen, Kstindustmus.) and several other tapestries, continued until *c.* 1900 when eye disease forced Maillol to discontinue. His portrait was painted at this time by his friend the Hungarian painter József Rippl-Rónai (for illustration *see* RIPPL-RÓNAI, JÓZSEF). Having also taken up ceramics he then turned *The Wave* into a bas-relief (destr.; plaster-cast, Paris, Mus. d'Orsay). In his spare time Maillol sculpted. His flat figures carved from small blocks of wood show the influence of the sinuous lines of Art Nouveau, especially in such works as *The Dancer* (1895; Paris, Mus. d'Orsay) and *La Source* (*c.* 1896; France, priv. col.), which later developed into more geometric, elongated forms, for example *The Bather* (1899; Amsterdam, Stedel. Mus.). He also modelled small,

Aristide Maillol: *La Méditerranée*, marble, h. 1.10 m, 1927 (Paris, Musée d'Orsay)

bold nude figurines in terracotta, aiming at simplicity and density of construction. The dealer Ambroise Vollard made numerous bronze casts of them (e.g. *Leda*, which was much admired by Auguste Rodin, and *Women Wrestling*; both 1900). In 1902 Vollard gave Maillol his first exhibition, in which the tapestries and statuettes figured prominently.

In 1900 Maillol began work on his first major sculpture, a *Seated Woman* for which his wife posed, which was later named *La Méditerranée*. The first version (New York, MOMA), finished in 1902, was very close to his model. He noted, however, that it was not sufficient 'to have a model and to copy it. No doubt nature is the foundation of an artist's labours. . . . But art does not lie in the copying of nature' (Puig, 1965). Thus he resumed work and the definitive version (see fig.) was exhibited at the Salon d'Automne of 1905. He wanted the only meaning of this sculpture to reside in its formal beauty. With his acute sensitivity to form, he tightened the composition, which had been developed from a single viewpoint, into an almost perfect cube, simplifying the contours in the process. The sobriety and perfection of the form and gravity of *La Méditerranée* struck Octave Mirbeau and Maurice Denis as well as André Gide, who wrote (1905) of its 'silence'. All three saw Maillol as a classic artist in the mould of Cézanne.

These qualities also attracted two collectors: Count Harry Kessler (Graf Henry Kessler) ordered a marble version of *La Méditerranée* (Winterthur, Samml. Oskar Reinhart) as early as 1905 (the French state did not do so until 1923: Paris, Mus. d'Orsay) and bought several bronzes, among them the *Young Cyclist* (1907) and *Desire* (1905–7). In 1908 Kessler took Maillol to Greece and *c.* 1910 commissioned woodcut illustrations for a new edition of Vergil's *Eclogues*. The initial letters for the *Eclogues*, which was privately published in Weimar by Kessler in 1926–7, were cut by the English artist Eric Gill. Later books with woodcuts or lithographs by Maillol include *Daphnis and Chloe* (1937) by Longus and Paul Verlaine's *Chansons pour elle* (1939). The Russian collector Ivan Morosov, his other patron, bought the first bronze cast of *Pomona* (example Paris, Jardin Tuileries) and commissioned three other figures in gilded bronze: *Flora*, *Spring* and *Summer* (all Moscow, Pushkin Mus. F.A.). Although Maillol did not altogether abandon painting, he increasingly concentrated on sculpture. *Night* (1909) was followed by *Flora* and *Summer* (1911), *Ile de France* (1910–25), *Venus* (1918–28), *Nymphs of the Meadow* (1930–37), the *Memorial to Debussy* (marble, 1930–33; Saint-Germain-en-Laye) and *Harmony* (1944), all of which are composed and harmonious nude female figures that contrast sharply with his unusually dynamic *Action enchaînée* (1905–8) and *Mountain* (1937).

Maillol was commissioned to execute a number of monuments, the first of which was poorly received. As part of the memorial to the revolutionary *Louis-Auguste Blanqui* the *Action enchaînée* was erected at Puget-Théniers, Alpes-Maritimes, despite protests from municipal councillors that it was too extreme. In 1925 the town of Aix-en-Provence refused the memorial to *Cézanne* (stone; Paris, Mus. d'Orsay), which a committee of artists headed by Frantz Jourdain had commissioned in 1912. Maillol

also sculpted several war memorials. Three bas-reliefs were designed in the form of a triptych for the town of Banyuls (1933); of those memorials in the Pyrénées-Orientales, the *Douleur* (1922) in Céret is less original, echoing *La Méditerranée*, while the figures at Elne (1921) and Port-Vendres (1923) are recognizable as draped versions of *Pomona* and the memorial to *Cézanne*. The latter, reassembled after a sketch model of *c.* 1900, was also to serve as a point of departure for *Air* (1939; stone), part of the *Monument to Airmen* at Toulouse.

Maillol's work is widely distributed in the form of bronzes and lead casts. In 1964–5, 18 large bronzes were placed in the Jardins du Carrousel, Paris, thanks to the initiative of André Malraux and Dina Vierny, Maillol's last model.

BIBLIOGRAPHY
A. Gide: 'Promenade au Salon d'Automne', *Gaz. B.-A.*, n. s. 3, xxiii (1905), pp. 478–9
J. Cladel: *Maillol: Sa Vie, son oeuvre, ses idées* (Paris, 1937)
J. Rewald: *Maillol* (Paris, London and New York, 1939)
Hommage à Aristide Maillol (exh. cat., intro. J. Cassou; Paris, Mus. N. A. Mod., 1961)
R. Puig: 'La Vie misérable et glorieuse d'Aristide Maillol', *Tramontane*, 483–4 (1965), pp. 1–52
M. Guérin: *Catalogue raisonné de l'oeuvre gravé et lithographié de Aristide Maillol*, 2 vols (Geneva, 1965–7)
W. George: *Aristide Maillol et l'âme de la sculpture* (Neuchâtel, 1977)
Maillol (exh. cat., Perpignan, Mus. Rigaud, 1979)
W. Slatkin: *Maillol in the 1890s* (Ann Arbor, 1982)
G. Bresc-Bautier and A. Pingeot: *Sculptures du jardin du Louvre, du Carrousel et des Tuileries*, ii (Paris, 1986), pp. 286–305
La Sculpture française au XIXe siècle (exh. cat., ed. A. Pingeot; Paris, Grand Pal., 1986)
Maillol: 'La Méditerranée' (exh. cat., Paris, Mus. d'Orsay, 1986)
Maillol (exh. cat., St Tropez, Mus. Annonciade, 1994)

ANTOINETTE LE NORMAND-ROMAIN

Maillou [Desmoulins], **Jean-Baptiste** (*b* Quebec, 21 Sept 1668; *bur* Quebec, 18 Sept 1753). Canadian architect. He was apprenticed to, and occasionally collaborated with, Claude Baillif, as well as with other masons and contractors in New France, including his own brother Joseph Maillou (1663–1702). On the latter's death Maillou acquired 16 different architectural treatises of French origin, which had probably previously belonged to Baillif, and which influenced the style of his buildings. Maillou was involved in Quebec in building the church of St Nicolas and in rebuilding Notre-Dame des Victoires in 1723, in the second building campaign of Palais de l'Intendant in 1726 (with Gaspard-Joseph Chaussegros de Lery) and in the construction of the church of St Etienne in 1730. It is also generally believed that he participated in the early 18th century in the building of the majority of the stone parish churches that were then being set up in the colony, and his name is attached to the formalization of the prototype of the plan for such buildings. His activities also included stone cutting, masonry contracting, evaluation and land surveying, and he was assistant to the Chief Inspector of Highways. The French authorities gave him the title Architecte du Roi and *c.* 1700 put him in charge of the fortifications of Quebec.

BIBLIOGRAPHY
A. J. H. Richardson and others: *Quebec City: Architects, Artisans and Builders* (Ottawa, 1984)

RAYMONDE GAUTHIER

Nathan bar Simeon ha-Levi: *Codex Maimuni*, also known as the *Kaufmann Mishneh Torah*, by Maimonides, illuminated panel of the opening of Book V, 1296 (Budapest, Library of the Hungarian Academy of Sciences, MS. A77/II, fol. 48*r*)

Mailly, Simon de [Simon de Châlons] (*b* Châlons-sur-Marne; *d* ?Avignon, before 15 Oct 1563). French painter. He settled in Avignon, where documents and a number of works signed *Simon de Chalons* indicate his presence between 1535 and 1562. His technique and realist style suggest that he was trained in Flanders, and his work also has resemblances, albeit archaic and provincial, to the Italianate style of Frans Floris and his followers in Antwerp. De Mailly's borrowings from the work of Raphael, Albrecht Dürer and Michelangelo, presumably taken from engravings, are juxtaposed rather than combined in such works as the *Holy Kinship* (1543; Avignon, Mus. Calvet). Further examples of this mixture of Flemish and Italian influences are the *Incredulity of St Thomas* (1535; Paris, Louvre), the *Adoration of the Shepherds* (1548; Avignon, Mus. Calvet) and the *Road to Calvary* (1563; Avignon, Notre-Dame-des-Doms). De Mailly seems also to have painted copies or versions of works by other artists; examples of these are the pendants the *Virgin of Mercy* and *Ecce homo* after Andrea Solario (both 1543; Rome, Gal. Borghese). His archaic paintings demonstrate the provinciality of artistic life in the 16th century in a once flourishing centre far from Paris and Fontainebleau, the contemporary foci of artistic innovation in France.

BIBLIOGRAPHY
Thieme–Becker
P. de Chennevières-Pointel: *Essai sur l'histoire de la peinture française* (Paris, 1894)
G. Frizzoni: 'Rassegna d'insigni artisti italiani', *L'Arte*, ii (1899), p. 154–5
L. Cogliati-Arano: *Andrea Solario* (Milan, 1965)
Raphaël et l'art français (exh. cat., Paris, Grand Pal., 1983)
I. Compin, A. Roquebert, J. Foucart and E. Foucart-Walter: *Ecole française*, L–Z (1986), iv of *Catalogue sommaire illustré des peintures du Musée du Louvre et du Musée d'Orsay* (Paris, 1979–86)
La Peinture en Provence au XVIe siècle (exh. cat., ed. M. Laclotte; Marseille, Mus. B.-A., 1987), pp. 102–27, nos 20–31

PHILIPPE ROUILLARD

Maimonides manuscripts. Illuminated manuscript copies of the writings of the great Jewish philosopher Moses Maimonides (Moshe ben Maimon; 1138–1204). Of his many works, preserved in numerous manuscripts, the most widely disseminated was the *Mishneh Torah*, a codification of Jewish religious law. Several magnificent manuscripts, from different periods and locations, have survived. The oldest and most famous is the *Codex Maimuni*, also known as the *Kaufmann Mishneh Torah* (Budapest, Lib. Hung. Acad. Sci., MS. A77/I–IV; see fig.). It was copied in 1296 by Nathan bar Simeon ha-Levi, in north-eastern France. As well as frontispieces decorated in the Gothic style, the manuscript has in the margins biblical illustrations related to the text, and Maimonides's ideas about the Temple expressed in the form of diagrams. These were probably a part of the original manuscript, as they appear in most of the copies, particularly those made in France and the Germanic countries, and conform to those in a manuscript of Maimonides's commentary on the *Mishnah* (religious law), which may be in his own hand. In a copy of the *Mishneh Torah* (Jerusalem, Jew. N. & U. Lib., MS. 40 1193) made in northern Italy, possibly Perugia, the first 40 folios, decorated in the Bolognese style, have pictures that illustrate the text. In a particularly splendid manuscript (London, BL, Harley MS. 5698–9), copied in Lisbon in 1472 for the celebrated patron David ben Salomon ben David Gedaliah Ibn Yahyaa, only the frontispieces are decorated. An illustrated copy of Maimonides's great philosophical synthesis, the *Moreh Nebuchim* ('A Guide for the Perplexed'; Copenhagen, Kon. Bib., Codex hebr. XXXVII), was copied in 1348 in Barcelona by Levi Ben Isaac Hijo Caro and illustrated in the style of the Master of S Marco (*see* JEWISH ART, fig. 18). The three frontispieces depict the *Delivery of the Manuscript*, an *Astrology Lesson* and the *Vision of Ezekiel*. Maimonides's *Thirteen Principles of Faith* were included in a number of decorated compendia of ritual (e.g. Paris, Bib. N., Hebrew MS. 592).

BIBLIOGRAPHY
M. Meiss: 'Italian Style in Catalonia and a Fourteenth-century Catalan Workshop', *J. Walters A. G.*, iv (1941), p. 45
B. Narkiss: *Hebrew Illuminated Manuscripts* (Jerusalem, 1969), no. 47
G. Sed-Rajna: *Manuscrits hébreux de Lisbonne* (Paris, 1970), nos 1–4
R. Wishnitzer: 'Maimonides: Drawings of the Temple', *J. Jew. A.*, i (1974), pp. 6–27
G. Sed-Rajna: 'The Illustrations of the Kaufmann Mishneh Torah', *J. Jew. A.*, vi (1979), pp. 64–77
Codex Maimuni: Moses Maimonides' Code of Law (Budapest, 1984) [facs. edn; introductory articles by I. Twersky, A. Scheiber and G. Sed-Rajna]

GABRIELLE SED-RAJNA

Mainamati. *See* LALMAI-MAINAMATI.

Mainardi, Bastiano [Sebastiano] (*b* San Gimignano, 23 Sept 1466; *d* ?Florence, Sept 1513). Italian painter. Vasari mentioned that Mainardi was a pupil of Domenico Ghirlandaio and that he was still working in the studio at the time of his master's death. Vasari also claimed that Mainardi collaborated with Ghirlandaio on several works between 1475 and 1477, including the fresco decoration of the chapel of S Fina in the Collegiata, San Gimignano, and on the frescoes in the abbey of Passignano in Val di Pesa, near Florence. Given the dates of these works, it was thought that Mainardi was born between 1450 and 1460 and that he was, if not a contemporary of Ghirlandaio's, certainly one of his earliest collaborators, together with Ghirlandaio's brother Davide. The discovery that Mainardi was born in 1466 (Venturini) would suggest that the two painters' relationship was that of master and pupil, at least until the early 1480s. Certainly Mainardi could not have collaborated on the frescoes in the Collegiata.

Mainardi was the son of a wealthy apothecary in San Gimignano and was probably taken into Domenico Ghirlandaio's studio in the 1470s. From then on, he worked constantly with the Ghirlandaio family and continued to do so after Domenico's death in 1494, when his younger brothers, Davide and Benedetto Ghirlandaio, took over management of the studio. In June 1494 Mainardi married

Bastiano Mainardi: *Virgin and Child with St Justus and a Female Saint*, oil on panel, 1.61×1.55 m, 1507 (Indianapolis, IN, Museum of Art)

the brothers' half-sister, Alessandra (Venturini). Although it is difficult to define Mainardi's role in the Ghirlandaio studio, he presumably collaborated on the frescoes (1486–90) in the choir of S Maria Novella, Florence, since his portrait is included in the scene of *Joachim Driven from the Temple*. He was working for the studio in Pisa between the end of 1492 and the summer of 1494, and in 1493 he painted an *Assumption of the Virgin* (destr.) in the Palazzo dei Priori, Pisa.

Mainardi is first recorded working as an independent master on 20 July 1484, when he was paid for painting a screen (destr.) for the high altar in the Collegiata, San Gimignano. In 1487 he frescoed *St Gimignano Blessing Three Noblemen* in S Agostino, San Gimignano; the work (*in situ*) was commissioned by Fra Domenico Strambi, whose tomb beneath the fresco was completed the following year. For the same patron and in the same church, Mainardi frescoed *St Peter Martyr* (1488; destr. 17th century). Two frescoes representing *St Jerome* and the *Virgin and Child* in the chapel in the Bargello, Florence, date from 1490. The surviving early works are heavily influenced by Domenico Ghirlandaio. Vasari attributed the large fresco of the *Assumption of the Virgin with St Thomas* in the Baroncelli Chapel, Santa Croce, Florence, to Mainardi, adding that the cartoon was provided by Ghirlandaio. From these works it is difficult to define Mainardi's individual style, and numerous disparate products of Ghirlandaio's studio have been attributed to him. These include portraits (see Davies) and such drawings as the *Study of the Heads of Two Children* (Florence, Uffizi), which is connected to a series of tondi (e.g. Paris, Louvre) often attributed to Mainardi, but which should be regarded rather as products of Ghirlandaio's large bottega.

Mainardi's oeuvre has to be reconstructed around a single fresco cycle in the Cappella S Bartolo in S Agostino, San Gimignano. Originally the frescoes were signed and dated 1500 (Pecori). The Doctors of the Church are depicted in the quadripartite vault, and on the left wall *SS Gimignano, Lucy and Nicholas* are shown standing in a fictive loggia with pilasters and a frieze richly decorated with zoomorphic motifs and a landscape in the distance. A number of paintings in San Gimignano can be grouped around these frescoes and would seem to date from the turn of the 16th century. They include a large altarpiece of the *Virgin and Child with Six Saints*, which stylistically belongs to the late 15th century and would seem to have been painted with an assistant's help, two tondi of the *Virgin and Child* and a panel of the *Virgin and Child with SS Jerome and Bernard* dated 1502 (all San Gimignano, Mus. Civ.), all of which came from local monasteries. Other works of this date in San Gimignano include a tabernacle of the *Virgin and Child with Cherubim* in Via S Giovanni, and a series of lunettes of the Virgin and Child and busts of saints in the vestibule of the Ospedale di S Fina. Although he was still under the influence of Ghirlandaio, he seems also to have been influenced by such Florentine masters of the younger generation as Francesco Granacci, who was his fellow pupil in Ghirlandaio's studio. A fresco of a *Sacra Conversazione* in S Lorenzo in Cappiano, near Incisa, echoes some of Raffaellino del Garbo's stylistic traits. A *Pietà with SS John the Baptist and Paul* (Schwerin, Staatl. Mus.), usually attributed to Antonio da Viterbo

(*d* 1516), is stylistically very close to the frescoes in the Cappella S Bartolo, San Gimignano, and can be attributed to Mainardi. The panel was commissioned by Guglielmo Altoviti in 1500 for the chapel in the Palazzo Vicariato in Certaldo (Venturini).

The compositions of Mainardi's later works are repetitive, although in an attempt to bring his style up to date he simplified and softened the forms, perhaps influenced by Fra Bartolommeo and Mariotto Albertinelli, but above all under the influence of Ridolfo Ghirlandaio, in whose studio he almost certainly worked in the first years of the 16th century. Examples of this phase are the *Virgin and Child with SS Francis and Julian* (Palermo, Chiaramonte-Bordonaro priv. col., see van Marle, p. 221, fig. 150), painted in 1506 for Pietro Nori, a notary in San Gimignano employed by the Mainardi family (Venturini), and the *Virgin and Child with St Justus and a Female Saint* (see fig.). A banner of the *Holy Face* (San Gimignano, Mus. A. Sacra and church of the Compagnia della Misericordia) may also date from this period. Mainardi also undertook decorative work: he painted a plaster statue of the Virgin (untraced) for the rector of the Ospedale di S Fina, and in 1500 he gilded the marble tomb of S Bartolo, sculpted by Benedetto da Maiano, in the church of S Agostino, San Gimignano. In 1501 he frescoed a vault in the Collegiata in San Gimignano with blue sky and stars, and in 1504 and 1507 he decorated banners for the feast of S Fina.

BIBLIOGRAPHY

Thieme–Becker

G. Vasari: *Vite* (1550, rev. 2/1568); ed. G. Milanesi (1878–85), iii, pp. 263, 272, 275–7

L. Pecori: *Storia della terra di San Gimignano* (Florence, 1853), pp. 495–6, 522–3, 539–40, 545, 555

G. B. Cavalcaselle and J. A. Crowe: *Pittori fiorentini del secolo XV e del principio del seguente*, Stor. Pitt. It., vii (Florence, 1897)

R. van Marle: *Italian Schools* (1923–38), xiii, pp. 187–228

G. de Francovich: 'Sebastiano Mainardi', *Cron. A.*, iv (1927), pp. 169–93, 256–70

M. Davies: *The Earlier Italian Schools*, London, N.G. cat. (London, 1951, 2/1961/R 1986), pp. 220, 326

B. Berenson: *Florentine School* (1963), i, pp. 125–8

E. Fahy: *Some Followers of Domenico Ghirlandaio* (New York and London, 1976), pp. 190, 215–19

L. Venturini: *Bastiano Mainardi, pittore di San Gimignano, e altri problemi di pittura fiorentina tra la fine del quattrocento e l'inizio del cinquecento* (diss. U. Florence, 1988–9)

——: 'Tre tabernacoli di Sebastiano Mainardi', *Kermes*, xv (1992), pp. 41–8

——: *Maestri e botteghe: Pittura a Firenze alla fine del quattrocento* (exh. cat., Florence, Pal. Strozzi, 1992), pp. 151–2, 162, 214–16, *passim*

——: 'Il maestro del 1506: La tarda attività di Bastiano Mainardi', *Stud. Stor. A.*, v (in preparation)

LISA VENTURINI

Maindron, Etienne-Hippolyte (*b* Champtoceaux, Maine-et-Loire, 16 Dec 1801; *d* Paris, 21 March 1884). French sculptor. He studied at the Ecole des Arts et Métiers in Angers and from 1827 at the Ecole des Beaux Arts, Paris. He was a student and later an assistant of Pierre-Jean David d'Angers. He also collaborated with Henri-Joseph-François Triqueti on the bronze doors of La Madeleine (1834–41). A number of Maindron's own works represent confrontations between Christianity and paganism. He won great acclaim for his statue *Velléda* (plaster, exh. Salon 1839, Angers, Mus. B.-A.; marble, Paris, Louvre). The subject, from Châteaubriand's *Les Martyrs*, is a Druidic priestess, consumed by her passion for a Roman Christian, Eudore; she represents both the Gallic spirit and the death wish of the pagan world.

BIBLIOGRAPHY

Lami
Romantics to Rodin (exh. cat., ed. H. W. Janson and P. Fusco; Los Angeles, CA, Co. Mus. A., 1980)

PHILIP WARD-JACKSON

Maini, Giovanni Battista (*b* Cassano Magnano, Lombardy, 6 Feb 1690; *d* Rome, 29 July 1752). Italian sculptor. He went to Rome *c*. 1708 and joined the workshop of Camillo Rusconi with whom he worked for almost 20 years. His first important work, probably executed after a model by Rusconi, was a life-size marble monument to *Innocent X* (1729; Rome, S Agnese in Agone), which portrays the Pope kneeling behind his sarcophagus. For St Peter's Maini carved two over life-size marble statues of *St Francis of Paola* (1732; designed by Pietro Bianchi) and *St Philip Neri* (*c*. 1735), which formed part of the series showing the founders of the religious orders. He also carved a marble relief of the *Madonna of St Luke* (*c*. 1741–3) for the portico of S Maria Maggiore and one of *St John Preaching* (*c*. 1734) for the portico of S Giovanni in Laterano and designed the over life-size seated bronze statue of *Clement XII* (1734–5) for the Corsini Chapel in the same church. This replaced an earlier marble figure by Carlo Monaldi. For the same chapel he carved three over life-size marble figures for the monument to *Cardinal Neri Corsini* (1733–4). The classical pose and voluminous drapery of the Cardinal's figure resemble those of *Cardinal Girolamo Casanate* by Pierre Legros (ii) (Rome, Bib. Casanatense). The accompanying weeping putto, with its plump belly and swaying hip, is carved in the style of Bernini (e.g. Bernini's tomb of *Urban VIII*, Rome, St Peter's), and the posture of Maini's *Religion* owes much to Rusconi (e.g. the latter's statue of *Religion* on the monument to *Gregory XIII*; Rome, St Peter's). Maini was one of many sculptors who contributed life-size marble statues to the basilica at Mafra, Portugal, for which he carved figures of the archangels *Gabriel* and *Michael* (*c*. 1737). Another important commission was the *Oceanus* group for the Trevi Fountain, Rome, for which Maini executed drawings and models from 1734. His final full-scale stucco figures, later carved in marble by PIETRO BRACCI, were placed on the fountain between 1743 and 1759.

BIBLIOGRAPHY

J. Fleming and H. Honour: 'Giovanni Battista Maini', *Essays in the History of Art Presented to Rudolf Wittkower* (London, 1967), pp. 255–8
E. Kieven: 'Die Statue *Clemens XII* in Palazzo Corsini in Florenz: Ein Werk des Carlo Monaldi', *Mitt. Ksthist. Inst. Florenz*, xxix (1985), pp. 410–18
J. A. Pinto: *The Trevi Fountain* (New Haven, 1986) [contains a full disc. of the documentary background to the fountain]

FLAVIA ORMOND

Maino, Fray Juan Bautista (*b* Pastrana, Guadalajara, 1581; *d* Madrid, 1641). Spanish painter. He was born at the small court of the Prince of Eboli, Don Ruy Gómez de Silva. His father was Milanese and his mother of Portuguese origin. He went to Italy, probably before the end of the 16th century, and spent several years there. In Rome he was in contact with Annibale Carracci and Guido Reni and became familiar with the work of Caravaggio, which influenced him deeply. Given his father's Milanese origin, he probably also had contact with artists in Brescia, Cremona and Milan.

By 1611 Maino had returned to Spain and was working in Toledo Cathedral. In January 1612 he was commissioned to paint the retable and the frescoes on the lower part of the choir and the presbytery (*in situ*) of the Dominican convent of S Pedro Mártir, Toledo, and before the work was complete, he took religious orders there on 27 July 1614. The paintings for the retable reveal his mature and personal style. They are the *Adoration of the Shepherds*, the *Adoration of the Magi*, the *Resurrection* and the *Pentecost* (1611; all Madrid, Prado). The strong affinity with Caravaggio is seen in the *Adoration of the Shepherds*, in which the angels, depicted as ordinary street urchins, derive directly from the Lombard painter. Maino interpreted his study of the Roman art of Caravaggio in the manner of Orazio Gentileschi, showing a preference for light, intense colours, tight sculptural modelling and precise, incisive drawing that is revealed in the naturalistic details. In the predella paintings from the same altarpiece, *St John the Baptist in a Landscape* and *St John the Evangelist on Patmos* (both Madrid, Prado), Maino's debt to the Roman landscapes of Carracci, as well as the influence of Agostino Tassi and Adam Elsheimer, are seen in the scale and in the relationship between figures and landscape. This type of landscape painting, with its silver colouring, was new in Spain; it shows the method of Carlo Saraceni or of Gentileschi and can also be compared with the work of Netherlandish artists then in Rome. The fresco paintings at S Pedro Mártir are reminiscent of the early work of Guido Reni in terms of composition, use of colour, forms and figure types.

Some time before 1621 Maino went to Madrid, where he was appointed drawing-master to Prince Philip, who became Philip IV in 1621. He lived in the Dominican monastery Nuẹstra Señora de Atocha, which was under royal patronage. As artistic adviser to the King, Maino was able to influence the Court. In 1627 he was one of the panel of judges who gave first place to Diego Velázquez for his *Expulsion of the Moors* (untraced) in competition with Vicente Carducho, Eugenio Cajés and Angelo Nardi. In 1634–5 Maino painted the *Recovery of Bahía* (Madrid, Prado; see fig.), which was part of a series of victories by various artists for the Salón de Reinos, in the palace of the Buen Retiro, Madrid. This is perhaps his most important work, showing a taste for a limited range of colours and simplified volumes. In contrast to the more heroic and military tone of the other paintings in the series, especially those by Carducho, Félix Castelo and Cajés, Maino focused attention on the victims of war by placing them close to the foreground, thereby producing one of the most successful and original treatments of the theme.

Maino was one of the most interesting painters of his generation, working in a most advanced artistic language compared with his Spanish contemporaries. From his time in Italy and because of his particularly receptive sensibility, he created a personal style that revealed an early awareness of the art of Caravaggio while also reflecting aspects of classicism as developed by the Carracci family.

BIBLIOGRAPHY

E. Harris: 'Aportaciones para el estudio de Juan Bautista Maino', *Rev. Esp. A.*, xii (1934–5), pp. 333–9

Juan Bautista Maino: *Recovery of Bahía*, oil on canvas, 3.09 × 3.81 m, 1634–5 (Madrid, Museo del Prado)

D. Angulo Iñiguez and A. E. Pérez Sánchez: *Pintura madrileña del primer tercio del siglo XVI* (Madrid, 1969), pp. 299–325
F. Marías: 'Juan Bautista Maino y su familia', *Rev. Esp. A.*, xlix (1976), pp. 468–70
F. Cortijo Ayuso: 'El pintor Juan Bautista Maino y su familia', *Wad-al-Hayara*, vi (1978), pp. 285–92
G. Papi: 'Proporte per Juan Bautista Maino', *Studi di Storia dell'Arte*, iii (Todi, 1992), pp. 181–202
A. E. Pérez Sánchez: 'Juan Bautista Maino', *A. Crist.* (in preparation)

ALFONSO E. PÉREZ SÁNCHEZ

Mainssieux, Lucien (*b* Voiron, Isère, 4 Aug 1885; *d* 1958). French painter and illustrator. From 1887 to 1898 Mainssieux was confined to bed due to illness and it was then that his first interest in drawing developed. He was taught by Jules Flandrin, whose dogmatic, analytical approach to painting suppressed Mainssieux's spontaneity and enjoyment. From 1902 to 1910 he produced little work, concerning himself mainly with technical problems. In 1905 he moved to Paris, studying under Jean-Paul Laurens and meeting André Dunoyer de Segonzac, Jean-Louis Boussingault and Luc-Albert Moreau, whose artistic tastes he shared. Two years later he first exhibited some landscapes and portraits at the Salon des Indépendants, the former influenced by Andō Hiroshige as well as by Flandrin.

A trip to Italy in 1910 greatly affected Mainssieux's style; he was particularly impressed by the Classical architecture and sculpture. In 1913 a large decorative panel of Mount Palatino, near Rome, which he exhibited at the Salon d'Automne, attracted much critical acclaim. Thereafter he painted many Italian subjects, such as *Santa Francesca Romana* (1926; Paris, ex-Mus. Luxembourg). After World War I he went to Cagnes in Provence where he visited Auguste Renoir's studio, an experience that encouraged him to brighten his own colours. A travel scholarship in 1920 enabled him to visit Tunisia and after this he made many trips there and to Algeria. This resulted in many landscape and portrait works of Arab subjects, such as *Mosque at Mettouia* (1922; see Kunstler, pl. 10). The majority of Mainssieux's works were landscapes that show the influence of his favourite artist, Corot. He also illustrated various books such as Eugène Fromentin's *Un Eté dans le Sahara* and André Gide's *Amyntas*.

BIBLIOGRAPHY
Edouard-Joseph
C. Kunstler: *Lucien Mainssieux* (Paris, 1929)

□

Mainz. Capital city of Rhineland-Palatinate, Germany, on the left bank of the Rhine opposite the mouth of the Main.

It has a population of *c*. 187,000 (1984), and is the oldest settlement on the Rhine and the oldest archbishopric in Germany as well as being a university town. It was also a notable centre for tapestry-weaving from *c*. 1415 until the late 16th century.

For further discussion *see* GERMANY, §XI, 3(ii)–(iii).

1. History and urban development. 2. Buildings.

1. HISTORY AND URBAN DEVELOPMENT. The geographical position of Mainz in a fertile area at the intersection of ancient trade routes was an important factor in its development. The name derives from the Roman settlement of Mogontiacum, a military camp founded in 16 BC. Important Roman remains include the ruins of the aqueduct and the Column of Jupiter (AD 66; Mainz, Landesmus.). The camp and civilian settlement were declared a *civitas c*. 297 AD, and this became the capital of the province of Upper Germania that was formed *c*. 300. The town wall built at that time, with its medieval extension, formed the city boundary until the 19th century. After extensive destruction during the Migration period, the town recovered under Merovingian rule. St Boniface (*c*. 680–754) was appointed archbishop in 747. Archbishop Willigis (*reg* 975–1011) began the rebuilding of the cathedral complex.

In 1244, after a long struggle by the middle classes, Archbishop Siegfried II granted Mainz the privilege of self-government, and during the 13th century it became one of the richest and most powerful towns in Germany, known as 'Golden Mainz'. In 1254, with Worms and Speyer, it took over the leadership of the league of Rhenish towns. Its wealth and increasing power were reflected in numerous new buildings: *c*. 1300 more than 10 churches were under construction, and the cathedral was being enlarged. The Kaufhaus (destr.) was completed *c*. 1317 (*see* §2(ii) below). Buildings of the 13th and 14th centuries include the abbey of St Alban, the churches of St Quintin (*c*. 1300), St Christoph and St Emmeran (both 14th century; ruinous) and St Stephan (completed *c*. 1340; rebuilt), the Liebfrauenkirche (destr. early 19th century) and the churches of the Carmelites (*c*. 1350–1400), the Poor Clares, the Franciscans and the Dominicans. The invention *c*. 1446 by JOHANN GUTENBERG of printing with movable type had a decisive impact on intellectual life. A feud (1461–3) between archbishops Adolf II of Nassau and Dieter von Isenburg (*d* 1482) resulted in the sack of Mainz (1462) and the repeal of its privileges, but its status as the elector's residence from 1469 promoted court culture and increasing intellectual and cultural activity. The university was founded in 1477.

The important building works of the transition period between the Middle Ages and the Renaissance were the rebuilding of the Martinsburg (1478–82; destr. end 18th century; *see also* GERMANY, §V, 2(iii)) as the archbishop's residence and the raising of the west tower of the cathedral (1480). The central Marktbrunnen (1526) was the first Renaissance fountain north of the Alps. The arrival of the Jesuits in 1560 had a decisive influence on the appearance of the town. They occupied (1577–1773) the former Minorite monastery. During the Thirty Years War (1618–48) many art treasures were lost, although the grand-ducal palace was extended in 1627–78. A radical transformation of the town's appearance took place in the Baroque period. Noble families built town residences: Schönborner Hof (1668), Dalberger Hof (1715–18) and Osteiner Hof (1749). The earth ramparts begun *c*. 1655 were extended 1713–40 by MAXIMILIAN VON WELSCH. The prominent Neuer Brunnen was constructed in 1726. From the mid-18th century several costly churches were built: the Jesuitenkirche (1742–6; destr. 1805–11), the college and church of St Peter (1748–56), St Ignaz (1761–74) and the Augustinerkirche (1768–76).

The events of the French Revolution led to major losses of the town's historic fabric. In 1816 it became part of the Grand-Duchy of Hesse-Darmstadt; the university closed, and the town's importance declined. The city later became a centre for historical research, however, and an outward sign of this was the erection of the Gutenberg Monument (1873). The town's expansion (*see* KREYSSIG, EDUARD) led to the construction of the Neustadt (from 1872), the Kaiserstrasse (1875), the Rhine bridge (1880–85) and the Christuskirche (1897–1903). In the early 20th century the fortifications were demolished, resulting in industrial expansion in the north and suburban development in the south. During World War II 80% of the town was destroyed. Mainz has since regained its importance, however: the Johann Gutenberg University was refounded in 1946, the city became the capital of Rhineland-Palatinate in 1950, and the Rathaus was built in 1970–73.

BIBLIOGRAPHY

F. Arens: *Die Kunstdenkmäler der Stadt Mainz*, Die Kunstdenkmäler von Rheinland-Pfalz, iv (Munich and Berlin, 1961)

K. Schramm: *Mainz, Gegenwart und Geschichte: Ein Gang durch die 2000-jährige Stadt* (Mainz, 1963)

A. M. Reitzel: *Mainz: Kultur- und Wirtschaftschronik* (Munich, 1967)

K. Esser: *Mainz* (Munich and Berlin, 2/1969)

A. P. Brück and L. Falck, eds: *Geschichte der Stadt Mainz* (Düsseldorf, 1972–)

A. P. Falck and W. Jung: *Mainz* (Cologne, 1979)

VERENA BEAUCAMP

2. BUILDINGS.

(i) Cathedral. (ii) Kaufhaus.

(i) Cathedral. The cathedral of the archbishops of Mainz, who were high chancellors and electors of the Holy Roman Empire, is dedicated to SS Martin and Stephan and is one of the three 'imperial cathedrals' on the Rhine, the other two being Speyer and Worms. After Speyer, it is the earliest of the great German vaulted cathedrals, and it is an important example of Middle Rhenish Romanesque architecture.

(a) Architecture. As early as the 3rd and 4th centuries a Christian community existed at Mainz under a bishop; St Boniface elevated it to an archbishopric in the 8th century. The site of the Merovingian cathedral has not yet been clearly established. The cathedral constructed from *c*. 975 under Archbishop Willigis was an aisled basilica with a double chancel and a massive west transept, but it burnt down on the day of its consecration (30 August 1009). Archbishop Bardo (*reg* 1031–51) replaced it, and the new building with two chancels was consecrated in 1036, only to be burnt down in 1081. Remnants of the first structure preserved in the present cathedral include the lower storeys

of the circular staircase towers of the east façade and parts of the west end.

The present cathedral, in which the influence of Speyer is discernible, was built with the support of Emperor Henry IV. After his death in 1106 progress on the east chancel, nave and aisles was slow. Archbishop Adalbert I (*d* 1137) built the Gotthardkapelle (consecrated 1137) north of the west transept as the archbishop's family chapel. Its groin vaults are supported by piers on the ground floor and by columns on the upper floor, which is linked to it by an opening. The nave was completed by 1200, and subsequently the side aisles were replaced, and the west chancel and transept were rebuilt, the chancel square being enlarged to a trefoil formation with $\frac{3}{8}$ apses on three sides. The nave was given a new vault, and the sacristy was built between the west chancel and the transept. The cathedral was consecrated on 4 July 1239. Altar donations led to the construction of chapels to the north (1271–91) and south (1300–19). The east tower at the crossing was raised in 1361, the west towers much later (1480–90). The cloister was completed *c.* 1410, and the Nassau Chapel was founded in 1418 to commemorate two archbishops. The Memorie between the south aisle and the transept was originally a chapter house and later a memorial chapel for the canons. It is adjoined by the Gothic Nikolauskapelle. After a fire in 1767, the west end of the cathedral and the two west side towers were restored and the west tower rebuilt (completed 1774) by Franz Ignaz Michael von Neumann (1733–85). The restoration after the bombardment and fire of 1793 continued throughout the 19th century. The foundations were reinforced in the early 20th century. The cathedral was damaged during World War II (1942, 1944 and 1945) but has since been repaired.

The outward appearance of the cathedral is impressive. Both the east apse and the octagonal east crossing tower have dwarf galleries, while blind arches separate the windows of the apse. The chancel has massive corner piers and, in the gable, tall niches and a frieze of round-headed arches at the apex. The rich ornamentation of the two portals at the east ends of the aisles is reminiscent of Speyer and Lombardy. The outer nave walls are embellished with pilaster strips and friezes of round-headed arches. The articulation of the west end is especially lavish, with pier buttresses, friezes of round-headed arches and niches, deeply recessed windows, a dwarf gallery with paired windows, and rose windows in the west sides of the transept and in the chancel gables. On the inside the square east chancel is plain and is closed off at the sides from the adjoining structures, although from outside these resemble an east transept. The nave piers are in an alternating system in which piers incorporating demi-columns to support the arches of the vault (clearly demonstrating the influence of Speyer) alternate with simple rectangular ones. The piers continue up as flat pilasters framing the blind arches below the clerestory windows (see fig. 1). Each pair of windows is enclosed by a bay of the square groin vault. In the side aisles the capitals and bases show the influence of French Early Gothic. The west transept comprises three square bays. The shape of the crossing piers indicates that a rib vault was planned, but instead squinches link the structure to

1. Mainz Cathedral, interior of the nave looking east, consecrated 1239

an octagon over the crossing, which has three richly articulated storeys. In the west chancel, which has rib vaulting, the treatment of space as well as the rich articulation correspond to the German Late Romanesque style, but the construction shows the influence of French Gothic.

BIBLIOGRAPHY

R. Kautsch and E. Neeb: *Der Dom zu Mainz*, Die Kunstdenkmäler im Freistaat Hessen, ii/1 (Darmstadt, 1919)

G. Dehio and E. Gahl, eds: *Pfalz und Rheinhessen*, Hb. Dt. Kstdkml. (Munich and Berlin, 1951)

A. Schuchert: *Dom zu Mainz* (Mainz, 1963)

F. V. Arens: *Der Dom zu Mainz* (Darmstadt, 1981)

BETTINA GEORGI, ERNST ULLMANN

(b) Sculpture. The oldest sculptural decoration (probably *c.* 1100) in the cathedral is in the east apse. The ornamental and figurative forms, many just roughly hewn, are the work of Lombard masons. The blind arches and dwarf gallery on the exterior have cushion capitals with sculpted decorations. On the south-east doorway is an area that contains Corinthian capitals as well as being ornamented with haphazardly arranged battle scenes, probably symbolizing the fight between good and evil. There is similar sculptural work in the east apse and chancel.

The brass doors (*see* DOOR, §II, 1) cast by Master Berengar during the primacy of Willigis are in the Marktportal in the north aisle, built at the beginning of the 13th century as the main entrance to the cathedral. The brass doors were among the sources that inspired the tympanum above the portal, which depicts Christ enthroned in a mandorla borne by two angels and is executed in the Late Romanesque style. The Leichhofportal also dates from the first quarter of the 13th century. In the tympanum is a depiction of Christ between SS Boniface and Martin. In contrast to the frieze along the capital zone, which has Romanesque vegetal and figural sculpture, the tympanum exhibits hints of French Early Gothic influence.

The former west choir-screen (*c.* 1239; ded. 1243) by the Naumburg Master and his workshop was an outstanding example of Early Gothic sculpture (*see* GOTHIC, §III, 1(iii)(b)). Like the eastern choir-screen from the same workshop (remnants in Mainz, Bischöf. Dom- & Diözmus.), it was dismantled in 1682; only a few fragments (also Mainz, Bischöf. Dom- & Diözmus.) have been preserved. They include parts of a *Last Judgement* from the gable: the central section and two groups of the blessed and the damned. The famous *Bandaged Head* (see fig. 2), which shows traces of paintwork, was part of a spread-eagled figure from the screen vaulting and has been variously interpreted as representing the anointing of the king, 'cosmic man' or 'the new Adam'. A man rising from the dead, a grimacing devil's face and a number of architectural fragments have also been preserved. The *St Martin and the Beggar* or 'Bassenheim Rider' (*c.* 1240; Bassenheim, Kath. Pfarrkirche St Martin) was sculpted for Mainz Cathedral by the same workshop. The present appearance of the west chancel is dominated by the fine choir-stalls (completed 1767) by Franz Anton Hermann (*fl* 1733; *d* 1770).

The funerary monuments of the archbishops of Mainz, most of which stand upright against the nave piers, form an almost uninterrupted series from the 13th century to the 19th. The earliest are sarcophagus lids, the first and most important being that of *Archbishop Siegfried III von Eppstein* (*d* 1249), which shows the archbishop crowning two kings. The epitaph of *Archbishop Konrad II von Weinsberg* (*d* 1396), imported from Würzburg, was the first of a different type of monument, showing the deceased as a standing figure on an upright slab that was erected close to the place of burial. Three other important examples of this type by Hans Backoffen (*fl c.* 1505–19) are *Archbishop Berthold von Henneberg* (*d* 1504), *Archbishop Jakob von Liebenstein* (*d* 1508) and *Archbishop Uriel von Gemmingen* (*d* 1514). The most important 18th-century memorial is that of *Dean Ferdinand von der Leyen* (*d* 1714).

BIBLIOGRAPHY

R. Budde: *Deutsche romanische Skulptur, 1050–1250* (Munich, 1979), pp. 32, 91–2 [extensive bibliog.]

G. Kniffler: *Die Grabdenkmäler der Mainzer Erzbischöfe vom 13. bis zum frühen 16. Jahrhundert: Untersuchungen zur Geschichte, zur Plastik und zur Ornamentik*, Diss. Kstgesch., vii (Cologne and Vienna, 1979)

A. Legner: *Deutsche Kunst der Romanik* (Munich, 1982), pp. 50, 166

(ii) Kaufhaus. The former Kauf- und Tanzhaus (Exchange and Ballroom), completed *c.* 1317 and demolished in 1812–13, stood in the square called 'auf dem Brand', at the intersection of two routes outside the self-governing district, and was used principally for wholesale trade and as a customs house. It is possible to reconstruct it with considerable accuracy from a series of plans and views of the town dating mainly from the 17th and 18th centuries. It was a two-storey building on a trapeziform plan with an entrance on each side. Both storeys had three rows of five cross-vaulted bays, and the upper floor was reached by an

2. *Bandaged Head* from the former west choir screen of Mainz Cathedral, h. 250 mm, 1243 (Mainz, Bischöfliches Dom- und Diözesanmuseum)

external staircase. The outer walls were distinguished by different colours, and, with the exception of the main (south) façade, they were relatively simple in design, with a narrow string course separating the two storeys. Above the cornice, decorated with foliage, were crenellations surrounding open battlements, fortified by polygonal towers at the corners. The south façade had a rich figural cycle (usually dated *c.* 1317). Above the doorway was a free-standing sculpted figure of the *Virgin* (Mainz, Landesmus.), and in the gable above was a *Bishop Saint* (untraced), probably St Boniface. The crenellations held portrait panels of the seven electors and of *Ludwig the Bavarian* (reg 1314–47), with *St Martin on Horseback* in an extra gabled panel, larger than the crenellations, set in the middle axis of the panels (all Mainz, Landesmus.). The long-accepted attribution of another statue of the *Virgin* (Mainz, Landesmus.) to the cycle was convincingly refuted by Jung in favour of the *Virgin and Child* in the Catholic parish church of St Peter in Ketten, Gau-Bischofsheim.

BIBLIOGRAPHY

E. Schälicke-Maurer: 'Das alte Kaufhaus auf dem Brand in Mainz', *Mainz und der Mittelrhein in der europäischen Kunstgeschichte* (Mainz, 1966), pp. 315–54

G. Nagel: *Das mittelalterliche Kaufhaus und seine Stellung in der Stadt: Eine baugeschichtliche Untersuchung an südwestdeutschen Beispielen* (Berlin, 1971), pp. 73–95

W. Jung: 'Die Gottesmutter von Gau-Bischofsheim: Ein Steinbildwerk der Mainzer Dombauhütte aus der Zeit um 1320', *Kunst und Kultur am*

Mittelrhein: Festschrift für Fritz Arens zum 70. Geburtstag (Worms, 1982), pp. 66–73

ULRIKE LIEBL

Maiolica. Term used strictly to describe tin-glazed earthenware of Italian origin. The name may be derived from the imported lustrewares sent from Valencia via the Balearic island of Maiolica (now Mallorca) to Italy (*see* CERAMICS, colour pl. I, fig. 1 and ITALY, §VII, 1). (For an alternative derivation *see* MÁLAGA, §2.)

Mair, Johann Ulrich. *See* MAYR, JOHANN ULRICH.

Mair von Landshut (*fl c.* 1485–1510). German draughtsman, engraver and painter. The signature *Mair* appears on all but one of his twenty-two engravings and on one of three woodcuts. The rest of his posthumously acquired name derives from the Landshut coat of arms on the engraving *Hour of Death* (1499; Lehrs, no. 19), which presumably indicates that Mair was working there. Nine other engravings are dated the same year, the only date to appear on any of his engraved work. Former identification as Nicolaus Alexander Mair, a painter in Landshut documented in 1492, 1499 and 1514, has proved untenable. None of Mair's other dated works is earlier than 1495 or later than 1504, years in which he was also associated with Munich and Freising. Stylistic evidence suggesting he assisted Jan Polack *c.* 1490 in painting an altarpiece for St Peter in Munich tallies with an entry in the Munich tax records from 1490 that lists a 'Mair Maler von Freising'. In 1495 he executed a lunette panel with scenes from the *Life of Christ* for the sacristy of Freising Cathedral. He may also have worked temporarily in northern Italy, producing an *Ecce homo* (1502; Trent Castle) and two scenes of a martyrdom (Milan, Mus. Poldi Pezzoli).

The Freising lunette panel provides a good example of Mair's fantastic, stage-like architectural settings with multiple niches and platforms used to accommodate many-figured narrative scenes. The plain surfaces and building-block shapes of the architecture, albeit here decorated with much floral scrollwork, are not unusual in contemporary Bavarian painting, but this aspect of Mair's design also warrants comparison with the geometrically bold and simplified architectural forms of Konrad Witz from the 1430s and 1440s. Mair shared Witz's predisposition to reduce architectural forms and, in a larger sense, all physical appearances to a state of essential solids and voids.

Mair's reputation rests above all on his engravings and drawings. He customarily printed and drew on hand-tinted paper, then brushed on highlights in white or yellow. The coloured paper provided a ground tone for the modelling system and a foil to bring out the brilliance of the highlights. Unlike Dürer's use of a similar drawing technique to clarify the appearance of a solid body in space, Mair emphasized the decorative and atmospheric effects of the colour and highlights—perhaps inspiring Albrecht Altdorfer, whose drawings on toned paper, beginning in 1506, carry forth this graphic technique for related expressive ends. The visual effects that Mair achieved by printing on hand-coloured paper also anticipate by nearly a decade the chiaroscuro woodcuts of Lucas Cranach (i) and Hans Burgkmair I, who further developed a technique for making prints that resemble the appearance of drawings

on coloured paper. By the standards of such contemporaries as Martin Schongauer or the young Dürer, Mair's engravings have an undeniably naive and provincial character, but he remains notable for his technical inventiveness and distinct personality.

BIBLIOGRAPHY
Thieme–Becker
G. K. Nagler: *Monogrammisten* (1858–1920), i, pp. 428–30, no. 987
W. Hugelshofer: 'Zum Werk des Mair von Landshut', *Oberdeutsche Kunst der Spätgotik und Reformationszeit*, ed. E. Buchner and K. Feuchtmayr, Beiträge zur Geschichte der deutschen Kunst, i (Augsburg, 1924), pp. 111–19 [eight illus. of Mair's drgs]
F. Schubert: 'Mair von Landshut: Ein niederbayerischer Stecher und Maler des ausgehenden 15. Jahrhunderts', *Verhand. Hist. Ver. Niederbayern*, lxiii (1930), pp. 1–150
M. Lehrs: *Geschichte und kritischer Katalog des deutschen, niederländischen und französischen Kupferstichs im XV. Jahrhundert*, viii (Vienna, 1932), pp. 282–329
Albrecht Altdorfer und sein Kreis (exh. cat. by E. Buchner, Munich, Neue Staatsgal., 1938), pp. 125–33
M. Geisberg: *Geschichte der deutschen Graphik vor Dürer* (Berlin, 1939), pp. 206–7
A. Stange: *Deutsche Malerei der Gotik*, x (Munich, 1960), pp. 124–30
Fifteenth-century Engravings of Northern Europe (exh. cat. by A. Shestack, Washington, DC, N.G.A., 1967–8), no. 142
From a Mighty Fortress: Prints, Drawings and Books in the Age of Luther, 1483–1546 (exh. cat. by C. Andersson and C. Talbot, Detroit, MI, Inst. A., 1983), pp. 302–4
Albrecht Altdorfer: Zeichnungen, Deckfarbenmalerei, Druckgraphik (exh. cat. by H. Mielke, Berlin, Kupferstichkab., 1988), pp. 325–7 [three colour illus. of Mair's graphic work]

CHARLES TALBOT

Maison, Rudolf (*b* Regensburg, 29 July 1854; *d* Munich, 12 Feb 1904). German sculptor. He started to train as an architect at the Polytechnikum in Munich, but gave up after a short period to teach himself to sculpt. His work is typical of the Wilhelmine period; his 'anti-classicist' stance distanced him from the Munich school of sculpture founded by Ludwig von Schwanthaler, and most of his commissions came from Berlin and from Bremen. He completely followed the dictates of official art in his work for the Reichstag in Berlin, which included a life-size statue of *Otto the Great* (*c.* 1895–8; destr.); his monument to Emperor *Frederick III* was similarly conventional, while such works as his *Teuton Fleeing on Horseback* (bronze, *c.* 1890; Regensburg, Stadtmus.) or the small *Wotan* (bronze, *c.* 1890; Munich, Stadtmus.) conformed to the prevailing cult of Germanism.

However, Maison's recondite naturalism, in such works as the *Negro Attacked by a Panther* (early 1890s; untraced) and the monumental *Teichmann Fountain* (1899; Bremen), and his liking for polychrome sculpture were condemned by contemporary critics influenced by Adolf von Hildebrand's lean classicism. Maison said he was concerned only to express 'nobly perceived truth'. He also created a few neo-Baroque portrait busts in the style of Reinhold Begas, as well as some small pieces with a social message at the end of the 1880s, such as *Trapped* (c. 1889; untraced) and *Strike* (1889; untraced).

WRITINGS
Anleitung zur Bildhauerei (Leipzig, 1910)
BIBLIOGRAPHY
Thieme–Becker
F. von Ostini: 'Rudolf Maison', xvi of *Kunst für Alle* (Munich, 1900–01)
A. Heilmeyer: *Die Plastik des 19. Jahrhunderts in München* (Munich, 1931)
D. Schubert: 'Hinweis auf Rudolf Maison (1854–1904)', *Jb. Preuss. Kulthes.*, xiv (1977), pp. 281–91

G. Finckh: *Die Münchner Plastik der zwanziger Jahre unter Berücksichtigung der Entwicklung seit der Jahrhundertwende* (diss., Munich, Tech. U., 1987)

CLEMENTINE SCHACK VON WITTENAU

Maisoncelles, Jean de. *See* JEAN DE MAISONCELLES.

Maison de plaisance. Term of French origin used during the 18th century and the early 19th to describe rural and suburban houses planned as retreats by wealthy gentry and nobles. It is often considered synonymous with the German *Lusthaus* or *Lustgebaüde*, the Italian *vigna* and the English villa (*see* VILLA, §§III and IV). Its usage overlapped the meanings of the terms château, which properly implied a larger and more formal country house, and *pavillon de chasse*, a small but elegant hunting–lodge. Although not linked to a particular architectural style or plan configuration, it invoked associations of relatively intimate scale, attention to comfort in the layout and appointments of rooms, and coordination of architecture and landscape design. Maisons de plaisance reflected new patterns of sociability among the élite classes, characterized by a sensibility for intimacy, exquisite refinement and engagement with nature 'perfected' by art: themes portrayed early in the 18th century by Antoine Watteau's paintings of *fêtes galantes*. The concept of the maison de plaisance was disseminated in publications by such authors as Johann Bernhard Fischer von Erlach and especially Jacques-François Blondel and Charles-Etienne Briseux, who presented model houses suited for clients of various means and social rank, indications of the increasing diversity of architectural patronage. Noted examples of French maisons de plaisance, all near Paris, include the house built in 1714–17 (destr.) by Germain Boffrand for the Prince de Rohan at Saint-Ouen; the Petit Trianon (1762–8) for Louis XV at Versailles by Ange-Jacques Gabriel; and the pavilion (1770–71; remodelled) at Louveciennes commissioned by the Comtesse Du Barry from Claude-Nicolas Ledoux.

BIBLIOGRAPHY

J. B. Fischer von Erlach: *Entwurf einer historischen Architektur* (Vienna, 1721/*R* 1978)

J.-F. Blondel: *De la distribution des maisons de plaisance, et de la décoration des édifices en général*, 2 vols (Paris, 1737–8/*R* 1967)

C.-E. Briseux: *L'Art de bâtir des maisons de campagne, où l'on traite de leur distribution, de leur construction, et de leur décoration*, 2 vols (Paris, 1743, rev. 1761/*R* 1966)

W. Graf Kalnein and M. Levey: *Art and Architecture of the Eighteenth Century in France*, Pelican Hist. A. (Harmondsworth, 1972)

A. Blunt, ed.: *Baroque and Rococo: Architecture and Decoration* (New York, 1978)

RICHARD CLEARY

Maison du Roi [Fr.: 'King's household']. Part of the royal government in France from the 14th century, charged with the physical and spiritual care of the king and court. Its extensive administrative structure was staffed by venal office holders and large numbers of skilled professionals, clerks and menial employees. The Maison du Roi was the second of the four groups that made up the French court: (1) the Grands Officiers de la Couronne including the Chancellor (upon whom depended the councils, secretaries of state and the temporal government), the constable and marshals of France, the grand admiral, the grand master of the artillery and the highest dignitaries associated with the Maison du Roi; (2) the Maison Civile du Roi (which we refer to simply as the Maison du Roi); (3) the

Maison Militaire du Roi (the personal guard and troops of the king); and (4) the individual households of the queen, the Children of France (the legitimate children and grandchildren of the king or his predecessor) and the princes and princesses of the blood. The Maison du Roi was organized around high court officers and provided all the institutionalized services necessary for the king's daily needs, his religious life, his personal security, lodging, clothing, food and entertainments. The Maison du Roi included the three principal sources of state art patronage (*see* FRANCE, §XII) in the *ancien régime*: the Direction Générale des Bâtiments, Jardins, Arts, Académies et Manufactures du Roi (Directorate of Buildings, Gardens, Arts, Academies and Manufactures of the King), usually known as the Bâtiments du Roi; the Intendance de l'Argenterie, Menus Plaisirs et Affaires de la Chambre du Roi (Administration of the Silver, Miscellaneous Entertainments and Business of the Royal Chamber), usually known as the Menus Plaisirs du Roi; and the Intendance des Meubles de la Couronne (Intendency of the Movable Property of the Crown), usually known as the Garde Meuble de la Couronne. These three agencies were closely related, and the boundaries of their respective authority were frequently blurred.

I. Introduction. II. Bâtiments du Roi. III. Menus Plaisirs du Roi. IV. Garde Meuble de la Couronne.

I. Introduction.

The offices of the Maison du Roi had responsibility for the daily living arrangements of the king and his court from the smallest detail of his wardrobe to the construction of palaces and supervision of the king's properties. In the 17th and 18th centuries, several of the Grands Officiers de la Couronne had responsibility, at least traditional feudal and ceremonial responsibility, for many of the functions of the Maison du Roi. In practice, the appointed professional administrators often served two masters: one feudal and the other bureaucratic, the latter being the Secrétaire d'Etat charged with responsibility for the Maison du Roi. The five highest feudal offices of the crown were held by members of the oldest nobility in France. They were, in descending order of importance: (1) the Grand Aumônier de France (held in succession in the 18th century by four members of the Rohan family); (2) the Grand Maître de la Maison du Roi, always the head of the house of Condé, whose jurisdiction included the seven kitchen offices; (3) the Grand Chambellan, whose jurisdiction included all the sub-offices of the Chambre du Roi, including the secretaries of the Chambre who were the secretaries of state and thus directed the government, the four hereditary ducal Premiers Gentilhommes de la Chambre, the Intendance de l'Argenterie, Menus Plaisirs et Affaires de la Chambre du Roi, the Grand Maître de la Garde-Robe upon whom, in turn, depended the Garde Meuble de la Couronne; (4) the Grand Ecuyer de France, always from the household of the queen and a prince naturalized in France, and the Grand Veneur, responsible for the royal hunts and kennels; and (5) the Grand Prévôt, highest judge in the land. In a special and somewhat anomalous position was the Surintendant des Bâtiments du Roi. This post was not held by feudal right by a member of the old nobility but was held at different times by professional architects, royal favourites or holders of other government portfolios. The head of the Bâtiments swore his oath of loyalty directly into the hands of the king, a dignity otherwise reserved for the Grands Officiers de la Couronne. The Bâtiments was, however, one of the seven distinct divisions of the Maison du Roi and the only one not subordinate to one of the Grands Officiers de la Couronne. The Bâtiments nominally depended on the Secrétaire d'Etat charged with responsibility for the entire Maison du Roi. The Maison du Roi was feudal, venal and bound by a strict hierarchy in which the domestic arrangements of the court were inseparably linked with affairs of state. The number of sub-offices directing large departments comprising the Maison du Roi made appointments to its myriad posts a much sought-after means of rapid social mobility. Posts of high rank went to members of the old nobility; positions of middle rank might go either to members of the old nobility or to the recently ennobled; and lesser positions were filled by commoners of all ranks and wealth who sought social advancement and financial gain.

The origins of the Maison du Roi can be traced to the 13th century, when the Ostel le Roy is first mentioned. In the 14th century, in the reigns of Philip VI (*reg* 1328–50), Charles V and Charles VI, royal account-books show payments to a host of retainers including valets, cooks, falconers, pantrymen, washerwomen, armourers, clerks, chaplains, doctors, artists and workmen along with the higher offices of stewards, exchequer officers, tax-collectors, treasurers and masters of a royal mint. These itinerant kings took their household services with them because they could not afford to staff all the castles and town houses that they began to build for themselves. The 14th-century kings sent their *valet de chambre* and *valet de garde-robe* on in advance in charge of the servants who would prepare for their arrival. The next major change in the Maison du Roi came in the middle years of the reign of Francis I. After his return from captivity in Madrid, Francis moved the court from its previous itinerant existence in the Loire Valley to a more stable oscillation between his headquarters in Paris and the châteaux of Madrid, St Germain-en-Laye, La Muette de St Germain, Challuau, Fontainebleau and Villers-Cotterêts. This grander household included nobles living on royal pensions and gifts in addition to the commoners who served the person of the king. The extensive building programme pursued by Francis I was directly linked to the creation of a politically more centralized court served by and dependent on the Maison du Roi.

The Maison du Roi in its full extent and strictest organization was the creation of Louis XIV (*see* BOURBON, §I(8)) and his minister Jean-Baptiste Colbert (*see* COLBERT, (1)), who held several of its portfolios. Colbert centralized and coordinated the services previously provided by separate offices and servants in order to achieve the level of grandeur demanded by Louis XIV. However, he was unable to eradicate the inefficient system of venal offices that were sold for high sums in anticipation of a long-term sinecure and with work performed in large part by salaried clerks. In the course of the 18th century the real administrative work of the Maison du Roi was increasingly carried out by the ministerial bureaux, which laid the foundations for the bureaucratic administration of the 19th century and relegated the high officers of the royal household to ceremonial roles in the king's immediate entourage. The administrative reorganization of many departments in the 1770s removed a number of these redundant positions. The desperate condition of royal finances drastically affected royal patronage in the 18th century. The deficits inherited from Louis XIV's wars had not been overcome before succeeding unsuccessful wars plunged the crown into still deeper arrears. Accounting was eccentric, with the books for any given fiscal year staying open and unbalanced for years both before and after the year in question. Revenues anticipated in a particular year were spent in advance to pay for work accomplished in a previous year, while funds allocated for a specific year might not be received until many years later. Contractors and artists who took commissions from the crown risked being paid in promissory notes that might not be redeemable for several years, which created hardship for employees, contract workers, students on stipends and tradesmen for much of the 18th century.

The following descriptions of the organization and responsibilities of those branches of the Maison du Roi primarily responsible for art patronage are based on the formal scheme of the administrative hierarchy as described in official documents. In practice, personal rivalries, ambition and differences in competency, zeal or taste caused the boundaries of the authority of the offices both to vary and to change over time.

BIBLIOGRAPHY

A. Franklin: *Dictionnaire historique des arts, métiers et professions exercés dans Paris depuis le treizième siècle* (Paris and Leipzig, 1906)
J. Evans: *Art in Medieval France, 987–1498* (London, 1948)
A. Blunt: *Art and Architecture in France, 1500–1700*, Pelican Hist. A. (Harmondsworth, 1953, rev. 4/1980/*R* 1988)
M. Marion: *Dictionnaire des institutions de la France aux XVIIe et XVIIIe siècles* (Paris, 1972)
M. Antoine: *Le Gouvernement et l'administration sous Louis XV* (Paris, 1978)
R. E. Mousnier: *Les Institutions de la France sous la monarchie absolue, 1598–1789*, 2 vols (Paris, 1980; Eng. trans., Chicago, 1984)

II. Bâtiments du Roi.

1. Role of the Bâtiments. 2. History of the Bâtiments. 3. Organization from 1664.

1. ROLE OF THE BÂTIMENTS. As far as the arts are concerned, the Bâtiments was the most important branch of the Maison du Roi in terms of expenditure and the extent and expertise of its large staff. The post of Surintendant et Ordonnateur Général des Bâtiments was one of the seven independent offices of the Maison du Roi, and the holder was entitled to meet the king in formal decision-making sessions called the Travaux du Roi. He answered to the minister-secretary of state responsible for the Maison du Roi but had to address his budgets and requests for special funding to the Contrôleur Général des Finances. The post was at times a superintendency (1664–1708, 1715–36) and at times a directorate (1708–15, 1736–90). A *surintendant* had the *droit de signature*, the right to make expenditures from sources specifically assigned to his authority. A general directorate did not have its own

funds and had to submit an annual budget to the Contrôleur des Finances, who would allocate specific lines of income from the tax farm, from the sale of bonds or from the sale of wood in royal forests and parks as he saw fit, both for the regular maintenance expenses of royal properties, administrations and institutions (*entretiens fixes*) and for funds for repairs and new work (*dépenses estimatives*). With royal approval, major new projects or exceptional allocations required specific funding (*fonds libellés*). Thus a directorate was significantly less autonomous and less capable of achieving results than a *surintendance*.

The purview of the Bâtiments covered land, gardens, permanent structures of all kinds, allocation of space to occupants of those structures not governed by legal contracts and leases, and permanent decorations, sculpture and physical attachments to these properties and structures. As a general rule the Bâtiments was responsible for the actual structure and anything permanently attached to its interior—panelling, paintings, anything nailed or affixed to the walls, for example mantels, mirrors, tapestries—but not for such movable interior furnishings as draperies, carpets, furniture, fabrics, lighting fixtures or porcelain. In addition the head of the Bâtiments acted on behalf of the king as protector of the Royal Manufactories—the GOBELINS, Beauvais (*see* BEAUVAIS, §2), AUBUSSON, SAVONNERIE and, after 1780, the SÈVRES PORCELAIN FACTORY—and of the Académie Royale de Peinture et de Sculpture, the Académie Royale d'Architecture and their schools (*see* PARIS, §VI, 1 and 2) and the Académie de France in Rome. The Bâtiments was also charged with the protection of the royal collections of paintings, sculpture, drawings, prints and architectural designs (but not of jewels, books, curiosities or items of natural science). It maintained the royal nursery, which supplied plant stock for the gardens and parks, an inventory of marble in storage for sculpture, a studio of portrait copyists, a keeper of architectural plans, with a staff of draughtsmen to make working drawings, and keepers of pictures and of drawings.

2. HISTORY OF THE BÂTIMENTS. The history of French royal patronage of architecture is long and venerable. From the 13th century the Corporations du Bâtiment were overseen by a Charpentier Royal, who later came to be called the Maître des Oeuvres de Charpenterie du Roi. The earliest precursor of the Administration des Bâtiments du Roy dates to the 14th century and the reign of Charles V, when a Maître d'Oeuvre de Maçonnerie du Roi was appointed to oversee royal constructions. The first incumbent was Raymond du Temple, a mason from Paris trained in the guild system. His job was to produce initial designs for buildings and to coordinate the work of large groups of masons, carpenters, sculptors, painters and tapestry makers. In the 15th century, during the reign of Louis XI, an administrator with the title of Réformateur Général, Visiteur des Oeuvres, was placed in overall charge of royal works, which meant that the head architect was subordinate to a financial administrator. This post was first held by Gaspard Bureau (*d c.* 1469), a Parisian notary (notaries filled most of the financial administrative roles in the early history of the administration). Charles VIII was the first king to employ a royal architectural adviser, precursor of the Premier Architecte du Roi, when he appointed Fra

Giovanni Giocondo and the Neapolitan garden designer Pacello da Mercogliono. Under Charles VIII, the royal architectural adviser had no administrative duties but did have authority over the Maître d'Oeuvre de Maçonnerie du Roi, who was still charged with the actual execution of the works. Under Francis I three such posts existed simultaneously, nominally including administrative duties as architectural supervisor of design and construction. However, the appointment of Sebastiano Serlio in 1541 as 'peintre et architecteur ordinaire. . .de Fontainebleu' did not in fact carry with it the direction of any major project, and Serlio's activity in France was primarily as a writer and theorist.

For each royal property there might also be a separate appointment of *surintendant*. The architectural adviser and the master mason were subordinate to the superintendent or inspector general, who verified the fulfilment of contracts through site inspection using several *contrôleurs*, all of whom were notaries. Thus the administration was evolving into a financial department and a works department, both reporting to the *surintendant*. Francis I's first *surintendant*, named in 1528 to direct the work at Fontainebleau and Livry, was Florimond de Champeverne (*d* 1531), a notary from Paris who was Francis's trusted *valet de chambre*. After 1536, Francis I assigned the most important of the royal house superintendencies to the Minister of Finance. In 1536 Philibert Babou, Sieur de la Bourdaisière, a minister of finance and treasurer to Francis I, assumed the additional role of *surintendant* of many royal properties, though without a centralized administration. This explains how from 1546 to 1578 Pierre Lescot (*c.* 1510–78) could be given total charge for the conduct of work as *surintendant du Louvre* while another *surintendant* also appeared in the accounts of the Bâtiments du Roi. Partial centralization in the Bâtiments administration came when the responsibility of *surintendant* of all royal properties was combined in the person of the royal architect Philibert de L'Orme. In 1548 he held the posts of Inspector General of Buildings and Royal Architectural Adviser under Henry II. Dismissed by Francis II (*reg* 1559–60), in 1559 de L'Orme was replaced by Francesco Primaticcio, who filled the combined posts (with the exception of the Louvre) until his death. From 1570 to 1590 the responsibility for royal buildings was not always in the hands of a superintendent. Tristan de Rostaing directed the service as Commissaire Général des Bâtiments from 1570 with an architect as his adjunct, first (1571–8) Jean Bullant and then (1578–90) Baptiste Androuet Du Cerceau. In the late 16th century the superintendency of buildings was combined with the ministry of finance because of poor economic conditions and the small number of professional architects qualified to carry out administrative work. In 1592 the nomination of Pierre Biard (i) to serve as Surintendant des Bâtiments du Roi was rejected by the Cour des Comptes. The solution under Henry IV was to couple the management of the royal properties with financial rather than artistic expertise. While Louis Métezeau was named architect to the king, first the Marquis d'O (1535–94), and later Maximilien de Béthune, Duc de Sully (Conseiller des Finances from 1594, Surintendant des Finances from 1599 and Surintendant des Bâtiments from 1600 to 1610), held the combined posts of minister of finance and superintendent of buildings, but neither exercised serious control, permitting the effective leadership of the service to rest with the Intendant des Bâtiments Jean de Fourcy, Sieur de Corbinière (*intendant* from 1594, *surintendant* from 1610 to 1624).

During the reigns of Henry IV and Louis XIII increasing authority was vested in the *surintendant* and his administrative staff, with a commensurate diminution in the importance of the Premier Architecte du Roi. Under Henry IV the administration was also made responsible for direction of Royal Manufactories producing furnishings, decorative objects and hangings, and increased oversight, via the master mason, of professional standards of education and qualifications for craftsmen employed on royal projects. François Sublet de Noyers combined the Surintendance des Bâtiments with the responsibilities of Secrétaire d'Etat until his dismissal in 1643. He was succeeded by Le Camus, who served until 1656 when his chief clerk, Antoine de Ratabon, assumed the post. Jean-Baptiste Colbert went from the service of Cardinal Mazarin to the service of the young Louis XIV. Colbert, already Intendant des Finances, began preparing himself as early as 1662 to assume the Surintendance des Bâtiments in accordance with the pattern established under Henry IV. He purchased the post on 1 January 1664, when Ratabon resigned in pique at having been passed over as Vice-Protecteur of the Académie Royale de Peinture et de Sculpture in favour of Colbert, and held the two positions until his death in 1683, dramatically transforming the institutions of state art patronage. Under Colbert the title became Surintendant et Ordonnateur Général des Bâtiments, Arts, Tapisseries et Manufactures de France, and he used the relatively minor post to promote and control French arts and industries as part of his policy of mercantilism and enhancement of national prestige, adding the responsibilities of Contrôleur Général des Finances (1665) and the Ministry of the Navy (1669) to the office. The combined authority of his offices, in particular that of Contrôleur Général des Finances, allowed him to accomplish many of his goals: he founded the academies of Inscriptions et Belles-Lettres, of Music, of Architecture and the Académie de France in Rome (*see* PARIS, §VI, 1). His plan to create royal monuments had been formulated before he assumed the Surintendance des Bâtiments: to accomplish it he reorganized the staff of the Bâtiments and created an advisory council of literary men called the Conseil des Bâtiments, which gave advice on the projects for the Louvre.

The system of offices that had evolved since Francis I included separate salaried positions of Surintendant et Ordonnateur Général for each of the royal houses. When all the separate posts were bestowed on one person, as they were for Colbert and his successors, the combined remuneration amounted to a significant sum. However, the separate 'gages' were preserved, on the account-books, so there are multiple entries in the *Registres des Bâtiments* each year under 'gages des Officiers' paid to the same person in the various capacities in which he nominally served, while in fact all responsibility was vested in the one overriding post of Surintendant des Bâtiments. Under Colbert's system, the royally appointed Surintendant des Bâtiments controlled, through a network of *intendants* and other royal officials, all the royal houses, gardens and forests, the royal academies of architecture, of painting and of sculpture, the academy schools for artistic training and the royal manufactories of luxury goods (*see* FRANCE, §XV). The Bâtiments worked closely with the artistic services of the Chambre du Roi, the Menus Plaisirs and the Garde Meuble de la Couronne in caring for the royal collections, in choosing artists for important commissions and in managing the daily life and events of the court and of the organizations dependent on the crown. The Surintendant worked in concert with the services related to the management of royal properties and such public-works departments as the Service des Ponts et Chaussées, the Administration des Eaux et Forêts, the Ministry of the Navy (where artists supplied designs for the ornamental carvings on ships) and the governors of the provinces and corollary regional and municipal officials responsible for public works and royal monuments throughout the kingdom. Individual artists and entrepreneurs attached to the Bâtiments or the Menus Plaisirs could accept private work or commissions for other departments of the Maison du Roi. The Surintendant des Bâtiments dispensed his department's direct commissions, honours, positions and pensions to artists, architects and artisans. An artist or architect could have a career outside the orbit of the Bâtiments but could not rise to real prominence or gain any significant royal commission or favour without the good will of its head. The monarchy had taken over government of the arts, and in theory the State now had the means to carry out a coherent arts policy. In practice, this depended on the personality and gifts of the man who held the post and the attitude of the reigning monarch.

Colbert's policy of emphasizing a symbolic royal presence in the capital differed from Louis XIV's desire to create splendid châteaux to house the court and government outside Paris. Before Colbert's death, royal policy shifted from construction of the Cour Carrée of the Palais du Louvre in Paris to the vast works on the châteaux, gardens and aqueducts at Marly and Versailles. Louis XIV's surintendants des Bâtiments during the last 37 years of his reign were men driven by personal devotion to the king, and policies shifted to a more sycophantic effort to satisfy the taste and sense of self-importance of Louis XIV and to present the person of the king as quasi-divine and indissolubly linked with the concept of the State. From 1683 to 1708 the surintendants des Bâtiments were François-Michel Le Tellier, Marquis de LOUVOIS (1683–91), Edouard Colbert, Marquis de Villacerf (1691–9), and Jules Hardouin Mansart (1699–1708). The major accomplishment of this period was the creation of the château at Versailles (*see* VERSAILLES, §1) as an extension of the identity of Louis XIV as the embodiment of France's power and grandeur. The important projects of the later part of Louis XIV's reign are identified with Hardouin Mansart as Premier Architecte du Roi and, after 1699, as Surintendant des Bâtiments—the only architect after the 16th century to hold the post. He ran a large, well-organized architectural practice and brought his administrative skills to the direction of royal works, relying heavily on Robert de Cotte. Apart from Versailles and the Trianon, Hardouin Mansart is associated with the construction of the Hôtel des Invalides, the Place Vendôme, Paris, the château of Marly and other monuments and royal squares.

The office was demoted from Surintendant to Directeur et Ordonnateur Général des Bâtiments, Jardins, Arts, Académies et Manufactures du Roi in 1708 with the appointment of the Duc d'Antin, son of Madame de Montespan, and the only high-born courtier to hold the post. He brought no aptitude or special preparation to this delicate position, using the post to ingratiate himself with the aging Louis XIV, who in turn recognized d'Antin as a perfectly tame amateur. After the death of Louis XIV, the Bâtiments was again elevated to a *surintendance*, which it remained from 1716 to 1736. D'Antin's long tenure was noteworthy for the paucity of its accomplishments (apart from his commissions for new tapestry cartoons for the Gobelins, most notably from Antoine Coypel) and for the unfortunate tone of haughty remove he introduced into relations with artists.

While a *surintendance* was an effective administrative structure for concentrating fiscal and artistic oversight when particularly ambitious building campaigns were contemplated, combining the lesser post of director of works with that of controller of finances was an equally effective means of restricting expenditure in times of budgetary chaos, as was the case twice under Louis XV with Philibert Orry, Comte de Vignory, Contrôleur Général des Finances from 1730 and Directeur Général des Bâtiments from 1737 to 1745, and again briefly for the Abbé Terray in 1773. Orry attempted to stabilize the royal treasury in concert with the fiscal austerity of the government of Cardinal Fleury (1653–1743). He curtailed expenditures for the Bâtiments to counter-balance the fiscal crisis created by the War of the Austrian Succession (1741–8). He instituted the annual Salon exhibitions of the Académie Royale de Peinture et de Sculpture and reinstated the administrative discipline abandoned by the Duc d'Antin. As Louis XV matured, more work was commissioned for the King's personal use but very little for public works. Orry was dismissed from his posts in a controversy over contracts for the army commissaries in December 1745. He was replaced by Jean-Baptiste Machault d'Arnouville (1701–94) as Contrôleur Général des Finances and as Directeur Général des Bâtiments from 1745 to 1751 by Charles-François-Paul Lenormant de Tournehem, whose successor-designate, the Marquis de Marigny et de Menars, was appointed to succeed Tournehem in January 1746 and served from 1751 to 1773. Though Tournehem was Madame de Pompadour's uncle by marriage, and Marigny was her brother, her influence on the policies of the Bâtiments is exaggerated. All three shared the belief that popular esteem for Louis XV would be promoted by civic-minded projects, the most conspicuous of which were the creation of the Ecole Royale Militaire and the Ecole des Elèves Protégés (*see* PARIS, §VI, 1), the completion of the Place Louis XV (now Place de la Concorde), the opening of a proto-museum of the royal pictures displayed in the Palais du Luxembourg and the encouragement of luxury art manufactures as instruments of prestige and mercantilism. The reinvigoration of the royal academies, their schools and public exhibitions and the undertaking of major urban projects in Paris, particularly during Marigny's tenure, marked a dramatic reassertion of the role of royal patronage in the artistic life of the nation (*see* PARIS, §II, 4). These initiatives included the construction of the church of Ste Geneviève (Panthéon) by Jacques-Germain Soufflot, the effort to complete the Cour Carrée of the Louvre, the replanting of the Champs-Elysées and Claude-Joseph Vernet's commission for the series of paintings of the *Ports of France*. The projects most closely identified with Madame de Pompadour—the Ecole Militaire and her encouragement of the porcelain manufactory at Sèvres—were supported by private investment. The crisis in royal finances resulting from the debt created by the Seven Years War (1756–63) drastically reduced Marigny's commissioning plans.

Abbé JOSEPH-MARIE TERRAY, Contrôleur Général des Finances (1769–74), was named Directeur Général des Bâtiments from Marigny's resignation in August 1773 to August 1774, when the new king, Louis XVI (*reg* 1774–90), replaced him with his own appointees, the post of Contrôleur Général des Finances going to Anne-Robert-Jacques Turgot (1727–81) and Directeur Général des Bâtiments to Charles Claude de Flahaut de la Billarderie, Comte d'ANGIVILLER, the last tenant of the position under the *ancien régime*. D'Angivillier served from 1774 to 1790, when the Maison du Roi was suppressed, and he reorganized the administrative structure of the department and economized on salaries. He enjoyed a more stable and somewhat augmented budget, made significant acquisitions to enlarge the royal collections and commissioned both the *Great Men of France* sculptural series and narrative paintings to serve as cartoons for the Gobelins (among them J.-L. David's *Oath of the Horatii*; Paris, Louvre), as well as continuing the policy of urban improvements in Paris.

3. ORGANIZATION FROM 1664. The administration took on its fully evolved form, with all its branches reporting to and responsible to the Surintendant or Directeur, under Colbert. It was organized as an administrative hierarchy of individuals with a variety of assignments, which meant that several members could be involved with any given project. The essential element of Colbert's creation was a central administrative office, the Bureau de la Direction Générale des Bâtiments, housed in the Hôtel de la Surintendance des Bâtiments at Versailles. This executive secretariat was run by the Premier Commis du Bureau du Directeur Général des Bâtiments. This very important administrative post was held by men with legal training, usually notaries. The Premier Commis and his staff of eight clerks handled the voluminous correspondence, work orders, records and coordination of the administration. A second senior commissioner, the Commis des Bâtiments et Chef du Bureau de la Comptabilité, occupied himself with fiscal affairs as chief of the accounting staff. Also in the central office and reporting to the Surintendant or Directeur Général through the Premier Commis were the nine venal office-holders, each with their own offices and staffs. There were three treasurers, three *intendants et ordonnateurs généraux* and three *contrôleurs généraux des Bâtiments*. These appointments were one of the worst abuses in the system Colbert inherited and were not eliminated until the reorganization of the administration by d'Angiviller in 1776.

The major part of the administrative work was concerned with the management of and building projects for the royal palaces and châteaux. The *intendants* and *contrôleurs*—all professional architects—were charged with the planning, negotiations, coordination and assignment of work (the *intendants*) and the overseeing, inspection and assessment of work (the *contrôleurs*). Two internal panels in the executive secretariat—the Bureau d'Affaires et Discution des Bâtiments and the Bureau pour le Vérification et Enregistrement des Mémoires—each with its own Commis et Chef du Bureau and staff, prepared and assigned work and then evaluated reports from the several inspectors who were sent to the site to determine what the contractor should be paid. After the internal panels had evaluated and adjusted the invoices submitted by contractors, the Directeur Général would authorize the treasurers to make payment. Reporting to the *intendants généraux* and *contrôleurs généraux* were the *contrôleurs* of each of the organizational departments of the royal properties. These departments corresponded to palaces or groups of properties with the exception of the largest, the Département de Paris, which concerned itself with all the palaces and properties in the capital except those attached to other ministries and, after 1743, also included oversight of the Gobelins (*see* §IV below). The *contrôleurs* of the *départements* were also trained architects who directed repair work and new construction in the palaces and gardens assigned to them. Each *département* also had concierges, gardeners, warehouse men, fountain specialists, plumbers, locksmiths and labourers for routine maintenance under the direction of a non-professional *capitaine du château* and a venal governor of each château. Very large *départements*, such as Versailles, had a large number of employees; other smaller properties, or ones visited by the court less frequently, had far fewer. Plans for new construction or major repair were administered, in theory, by an *architecte ordinaire* in the executive secretariat who collaborated with the architect commissioned to do the work. This was, by precedent, the prerogative of the Premier Architecte du Roi; in practice, particularly under Marigny, many important royal commissions went to other architects. Many collateral services that supported the work of the Bâtiments were also linked through the executive secretariat, including the keeper of architectural plans, the marble depot, the nurseries, the team of surveyors, the surgeon and doctors employed by the service, the studio of copyist painters at Versailles, the warehouse, the keeper of the royal collection of paintings, the keeper of drawings, a historiographer and an iconographer (an engraver who recorded the royal works in images). There were three officers who communicated or worked directly with the Directeur Général without going through the Premier Commis—the Premier Architecte, the Premier Peintre and the Directeur of the Académie de France in Rome. The Directeur of the Académie de France reported on the financial and pedagogical aspects of his school and gave opinions on the potential of France's most promising painters, sculptors and architects. The other two officials not only worked intimately with the director but, depending on their personal relationships, met privately with the king, as was certainly the case for Charles Le Brun,

Hardouin Mansart and Anges-Jacques Gabriel. The holders of these positions served as advisers to the Directeur Général des Bâtiments, as directors of their respective royal academies and as principal executants of major royal commissions. The Premier Peintre would advise and oversee the keepers of the royal collections of painting and drawing, recommend acquisitions for the royal collections, evaluate the need for cleaning, care and framing of pictures and sculpture, advise on iconography and programme, suggest allocation of commissions and, at times, direct the Gobelins. The position of Premier Peintre became less important in the reign of Louis XV and was obviated for much of Marigny's tenure by the appointment of Charles-Nicolas Cochin (*see* COCHIN (ii), (2)), an engraver, as *chargé du détail des arts* in 1755. The Premier Architecte was more closely linked to the daily work of the Bâtiments; he, like the Premier Peintre, could continue to take private work and would, therefore, maintain his own studios and assistants. His private office, the most important and most active in France, was overseen by a carefully chosen Premier Dessinateur. Design work, whether for a royal or private commission, would be carried out in the private office of the Premier Architecte by his own draughtsmen. He would then coordinate construction working through his parallel subordinate in the Bâtiments administration, the *architecte ordinaire*, and with the appropriate *intendants* and *contrôleurs* on the site. Designs had to be approved by the Directeur Général, but when the Premier Architecte was working personally with the king, tension could arise as the Directeur was alienated from the process. Ultimately, the Directeur Général was responsible for representing the many interests of the institutions under his care to the king and his minister of finance, adjusting the priorities of his administration in concert with the needs and demands of the king, and selecting and sustaining the appropriate artists and assistants needed to accomplish his projects.

BIBLIOGRAPHY

C. de Pisan: *Le Livre des faits et bonnes moeurs de Charles V* (1405)

L. de Laborde: *Les Comptes des Bâtiments du roi (1528–1571)*, 2 vols (Paris, 1877–80)

H. de Luçay: *Des origines du pouvoir ministériel en France: Les Secrétaires d'état depuis leur institution jusqu'à la mort de Louis XV* (Paris, 1881), pp. 499–501

J. Guiffrey: *Comtes des Bâtiments du roi sous le règne de Louis XIV, 1644–1715*, 5 vols (Paris, 1881–1901)

F. Engerand: *Inventaire des tableaux commandés et achetés par la direction des Bâtiments du roi* (Paris, 1901)

M. Furcy-Raynaud: 'Directeurs généraux des Bâtiments du roi au XVIIIe siècle', *Studien aus Kunst und Geschichte Friedrich Schneider zum siebzigsten Geburtstag gewidmet von seinen Freunden und Verehrern* (Freiburg im Breisgau, 1906), pp. 533–9

P. Bonnefon: 'Charles Perrault commis de Colbert et l'administration des arts sous Louis XIV', *Gaz. B.-A.*, n. s. 2, xl (1908), no. 615, pp. 198–214; no. 616, pp. 340–52; no. 617, pp. 426–33

R. Guillemet: *Essai sur la surintendance des Bâtiments du roi dans le règne personnel de Louis XIV (1662–1715)* (Paris, 1908)

J. Locquin: *La Peinture d'histoire en France de 1747 à 1785* (Paris, 1912/R 1978)

R. Blomfield: *A History of French Architecture from the Death of Mazarin till the Death of Louis XV, 1661–1774*, 2 vols (London, 1921)

M. Furcy-Raynaud: *Inventaire des sculptures exécutées au XVIIIe siècle pour la direction des Bâtiments du roi* (Paris, 1927)

L. Hautecoeur: *Architecture classique* (1943–57), i–iv

J. Silvestre de Sacy: *Le Comte d'Angiviller: Dernier Directeur général des bâtiments du roi* (Paris, 1953)

Au Temps du Roi Soleil: Les Peintres de Louis XIV, 1660–1715 (exh. cat. by A. Schnapper, Lille, Mus. B.-A., 1968)

J. Coural: 'La Tapisserie', *Louis XV: Un Moment de perfection de l'art français* (exh. cat., Paris, Hôtel de la Monnaie, 1974), pp. 265–84

M. N. Rosenfeld: 'The Royal Building Administration in France from Charles V to Louis XIV', *The Architect: Chapters in the History of the Profession*, ed. S. Kostof (New York, 1977), pp. 161–79

C. Tadgell: *Gabriel* (London, 1978)

D. Gallet-Guerne and C. Baulez: *Versailles: Dessins d'architecture de la direction générale des Bâtiments du roi* (Paris, 1983)

B. Pons: *De Paris à Versailles, 1699–1736* (Strasbourg, [1985])

III. Menus Plaisirs du Roi.

The department of the Chambre du Roi served the person of the king directly. Its duties were the responsibility of the Grand Chambellan and were administered either by him personally or, in his absence and most often in practice, by his deputies the four Premiers Gentilhommes de la Chambre, who served yearly terms in rotation. The Premiers Gentilhommes were highly influential at court; they accompanied the king at all times and directed the Intendance de l'Argenterie, Menus-Plaisirs et Affaires de la Chambre du Roi, which touched the life of the king daily. Though referred to in short as Menus Plaisirs (for which there is no precise English translation), the full reference to Menus-Plaisirs et Affaires, implying 'various' or 'lesser' events of an ephemeral nature, gives a more accurate picture of this service, which was concerned with the pageantry of court life and the celebrations surrounding great events, including the highest ceremonies of State organized in part by the Menus Plaisirs and officiated by the Grand Maître des Cérémonies and performed by the *grands officiers* or members of the clergy. The Menus Plaisirs was administered by as many as three *intendants* who, although supposed to serve in rotation, for much of the 18th century performed specialized roles. The *intendants*, who had two secretariats, one in Paris and the other at Versailles, oversaw the Médecin du Roi, the Grand Maître de la Garde Robe, the two drama companies (the Comédie Française and the Comédie Italienne), a storehouse, the Musiciens du Roi and the artists who made designs for the events, wares and works of art, publications and performances overseen by the service. The principal artists included two sculptors, two painters, four draughtsmen and two *machinistes* (theatre-set builders). Other specialities were contracted out. This arrangement prevailed until 1780, when the service was reorganized under a single commissioner of the Maison du Roi.

The administration of the Menus Plaisirs had several quite distinct functions, which evolved and developed in response to the demands made on the service. It was responsible for the king's objects in precious metals and jewellery, the king's and the dauphin's wardrobes and linen, candles to illuminate the royal chambers, the king's doctor, music performed in the palace, the overseeing of the royal theatres in Paris and theatricals, balls and masquerades at court, purchases of gifts given by the king to authors, artists and churches, care of such temporary buildings as tents and wooden structures, and all aspects of ephemeral events (including triumphal entries, coronations, funerals and celebrations for marriages and births) from structures, music and costumes to fireworks and commemorative engravings.

The office of the Menus Plaisirs was created by Francis I and enlarged by Henry III. Royal entries and celebrations of treaties, births and weddings were undertaken collaboratively by the crown and the municipalities who were privileged to host them. The Menus Plaisirs was reorganized in 1660 by Nicolas Fouquet before his disgrace in 1661. The overseeing of the theatres in Paris was late to develop and at first more titular than real. Chappuzeau was director of the theatres from 1674 but was more a spokesman for the companies than a state authority. From 1760 the Comédie Française and the Comédie Italienne were governed by the four Premiers Gentilhommes de la Chambre and directed by the three *intendants* of the Menus Plaisirs, Fontpertuis, DENIS-PIERRE-JEAN PAPILLON DE LA FERTÉ and Delatouche. La Ferté, whose *Journal* is the primary published source for information about the workings of the Menus Plaisirs, was *intendant* and *contrôleur général* from 1756 until its reorganization in 1780 and then Commissaire until the Revolution. The various intendants before La Ferté merely executed the orders of the Premiers Gentilhommes who made the important decisions; La Ferté, as intendant-in-charge rather than in rotation, had much greater influence.

The artists of the Menus Plaisirs, who included Louis Le Vau and Le Brun, made significant contributions to the design of works of art and furniture, stage design, printmaking and architectural experimentation in temporary structures. Before 1756 the principal artist of the service, the Dessinateur de la Chambre et du Cabinet du Roi, played a central role, though it was never clearly defined. This important position was created in 1660 and held successively by Henry de Gissey (1660–73); Jean Berain I (1674–1711); Jean Berain II (1711–26); Juste-Aurèle Meissonnier (1726–50); René-Michel Slodtz (1750–64); and Michel-Ange Challe (1764–77). After 1777 the post was divided into three owing to the vastly increased activity of the department. Pierre-Adrien Pâris, an architect, held the post of Dessinateur du Cabinet; Louis-Jacques Durameau was named Peintre du Cabinet; and Jean-Michel Moreau was appointed Graveur du Cabinet. Other artistic functions might be assigned to the artists of the service who received contractual stipends paid either from the funds of the Menus Plaisirs or from the Cassette du Roi, the privy purse of the king. These artists were entrepreneurs and contractors for the service and intrigued for commissions and influence. The members of the Slodtz family, beginning as Sculpteurs des Menus Plaisirs, exercised an important influence on taste for more than 15 years before René-Michel Slodtz became Dessinateur. The artists of the Menus Plaisirs sometimes worked in collaboration with the Premier Architecte du Roi and the artists of the Bâtiments on projects that fell into the grey areas where the jurisdiction of the two services was vague, or where influence was applied to gain control of a project that ought logically to have come within the purview of the other: an example was the décor for the Théâtre des Petits Appartements, which should have been a Menus Plaisirs project but, owing to the influence of Madame de Pompadour, was managed by Marigny and the Bâtiments. By reverse token, the work on the Opéra in the château at Versailles was directed by Arnoult, the *machiniste* of the Menus Plaisirs, rather than by the architects of the

Bâtiments, owing partly to the need to complete the building for the wedding festivities of the Dauphin (later Louis XVI). The Menus Plaisirs only came to have a permanent headquarters in 1776, when La Ferté succeeded in having the Hôtel des Menus Plaisirs constructed in the Rue du Faubourg Poissonnière in Paris.

BIBLIOGRAPHY

A. Jullien: *L'Opéra sous l'ancien régime* (Paris, n.d.)

S. Chappuzeau: *Le Théâtre français* (Paris, 1674)

J. J. Guiffrey: 'Liste des peintres, sculpteurs, architectes, graveurs et autres artistes de la Maison du roi, de la reine ou des princes du sang aux XVIe, XVIIe, XVIIIe siècles', *Nouv. Archvs A. Fr.*, ii (1872), pp. 55–108

H. de Chennevières: *Les Menus-plaisirs du roi et leurs artistes* (Paris, 1882)

E. Boysse, ed.: *L'Administration des menus: Journal de Papillon de la Ferté, intendant et contrôleur de l'argenterie, menus-plaisirs et affaires de la Chambre du roi, 1756–1780* (Paris, 1887)

E. Pilon and F. Saisset: *Les Fêtes en Europe au XVIIIe siècle* (Saint-Germain, [1900])

J. C. Prodhomme and E. de Crauzat: *Les Menus-plaisirs du roi: L'Ecole royale du conservatoire de musique* (Paris, 1929)

G. Mourey: *Le Livre des fêtes françaises* (Paris, 1930)

F. Souchal: *Les Slodtz* (Paris, 1967)

A. C. Gruber: *Les Grandes Fêtes et leurs décors à l'époque de Louis XVI* (Geneva, 1972)

IV. Garde Meuble de la Couronne.

The stewardship of the movable property of the king was a responsibility of the minister of the Maison du Roi, who approved the activities of the Intendant et Contrôleur Général des Meubles de la Couronne. Before 1663, when Colbert created the Garde Meuble as an independent service, most of the objects it cared for were under the supervision of the Service de la Garde Robe de la Chambre du Roi, which had its expenses paid by the treasurer of the Argenterie and was a dependency of the Premiers Gentilhommes. In the 14th century, Jean Moynat, a *varlet de chambre et garde des chambres et tappis du Roy*, was a precursor of the *intendant*. The early history of the keepers of the king's collection is not well known. In the first decade of the 17th century Robert Marquelet is listed as Garde Meubles du Roy au Palais des Tuileries and Mathieu Jacquet de Grenoble as the Garde des Antiques du Roy from 1608 to 1610. Just before mid-century, Jean Mocquet is listed as Garde du Cabinet des Singularités du Roy en son Palais des Tuileries and Jehan Moyen as Commis par le Roy à la Garde et Magasin des Armes de sa Majesté in the abbey of St-Martin-des-Champs. Under Louis XIII there was already a position called Intendant des Meubles du Roy, held successively by Etienne de La Fond, Jacob de La Fond and Jean Dujon. During Mazarin's pre-eminence in the years before the personal reign of Louis XIV, the title of Contrôleur des Meubles de la Couronne was used successively for Roger Bonnars (1658), Paul Dujardin and Prosper Bauyn (1662), who was replaced in 1663 by Gédéon Berbier Du Metz (1626–1709), the first Intendant et Contrôleur Général des Meubles de la Couronne under the organization created by Colbert. Clearly subordinate to the *intendants* and *contrôleurs* was the post of Garde-Meubles de sa Majesté, held in 1616 by Jacques Valetz and, during the regency of Anne of Austria, by Charles Moymier. He was replaced in 1653 by Henry Guillain, who was supplanted for incompetence in 1665 by Louis Le Cosquino. Working with Du Metz, Le Cosquino created the first systematically organized numbered inventories of the royal furniture. His *Journal du Garde-meuble de la couronne et des maisons royales* and the *Inventaire général du mobilier de la couronne* are the sources for all studies of royal furniture.

From the Middle Ages the Garde Meuble had a special transportation service for moving hangings, tapestry, furniture and other necessities as the king travelled from palace to palace or ordered new furnishings for the succession of houses built by the crown. In the 18th century the wagons, with their distinctive cloth covers of blue sprinkled with gold fleurs-de-lis and embroidered with three crowns, were unmistakable as they moved to and from Paris and the royal châteaux. The Intendance des Meubles de la Couronne remained in existence up to the Revolution, with one reorganization in 1784.

The king's movable property overseen by this service as of 1663 comprised gold and silver jewellery and metalwork including silver gilt, filigree work, silver plate, serving pieces and table silver, gems, chapel silver, crystal, mirrors, tapestry—whether of gold and silver threads or wool and silk—rugs, pictures, busts and figures in marble and bronze, arms and armour, porcelain, chandeliers and crystal sconces, Venetian crystal, all sorts of furniture, brocades and gold or silver cloth, beds and bedding and canopies. It is not clear what pictures and sculpture would have been in the keeping of the Garde Meuble as opposed to that of the Bâtiments.

The Intendant et Contrôleur Général des Meubles de la Couronne executed orders given by or in the name of the king through an intermediary, usually the Secrétaire d'Etat à la Maison du Roi. His role was to take the orders of the royal family, have models made for approval and oversee final execution and installation; his service was responsible for moving and installing royal property and for its storage, maintenance and cleaning. The Mobilier de la Couronne was also charged with the protection of the crown jewels, sceptres, crowns and regalia. The first Intendant et Contrôleur des Meubles de la Couronne, Gédéon Berbier Du Metz, Comte de Rosnay, (in office 1663–1709), was succeeded briefly by his son, Jean Berbier Du Metz, 2nd Comte de Rosnay, who sold the post in 1712 or 1713. His successor was Moyse-Augustin de Fontanieu (in office 1712/13–57), who was succeeded in turn by his son Gaspard-Moyse-Augustin de Fontanieu, Marquis de Fiennes (1693–1767; in office 1757–67), who was succeeded by his own son Pierre-Elizabeth de Fontanieu (*d* 1784; in office 1767–83). The latter sold the post in 1783 to Marc-Antoine Thierry de Ville d'Avray (1732–92), whose son, Arnaud Thierry de Ville d'Avray, was summoned by Napoleon I in 1814 as Intendant Général du Garde-Meuble and reinstated some of the traditions of the service which continued into the 19th century.

In 1656 the Contrôleur des Meubles de la Couronne directed a staff including a Garde Général des Meubles, a garde-meuble at the Louvre, a garde-meuble in the Hôtel des Ambassadeurs Extraordinaires in the Rue de Tournon, Paris, and nine *garçons des meubles*. In the organization created by Colbert in 1663, the Intendant et Contrôleur Général had one Garde Général des Meubles, two inspectors and two staff, one for Paris and one for the châteaux. The staff for the châteaux was made up of keepers and workmen caring for the storerooms and immediate needs of each house. In Paris there was an extensive team that reached full elaboration after 1772, when the Garde Meuble moved to the building designed by Anges-Jacques Gabriel and constructed for its needs on the Place Louis XV (now Place de la Concorde), which housed the secretaries and commissioners, office boys, examiner (*vérificateur*), warehousemen and keepers, unskilled labourers, mechanics, armourers, seamstresses, upholsterers, polishers and porters. In 1785 there were forty-one employees in the Hôtel du Garde Meuble in Paris, fourteen at Versailles, three at Fontainebleau, three at Compiègne, six at Marly, three at Choisy, three at the Trianon, three at Rambouillet, and one each at Meudon, La Muette and Montreuil.

The Menus Plaisirs or the Bâtiments rather than the Garde Meuble was often responsible for furniture and silver commissions, particularly during the reign of Louis XIV when the major commissions were carried out on the budget of the Bâtiments. Commissions for furniture were put out to independent makers: Domenico Cucci and Pierre Gole were favoured during the period when Charles Le Brun was influential (1661–83); under Louvois, Jean Berain I, the Dessinateur de la Chambre du Roi in the service of the Menus Plaisirs, was a favourite furniture designer. After Louvois's death, André Charles Boulle was the designer preferred by the Marquis de Villacerf and Jules Hardouin Mansart. The Manufacture Royale des Meubles de la Couronne in the Gobelins' buildings in Paris, from which the more common name Manufacture des Gobelins derived, was the result of Colbert's plan, conceived in 1662, to bring the manufacture of furniture, carpets and tapestry under direct royal control. Under its first director, Charles Le Brun, a single *ébénisterie* workshop was created under Domenico Cucci, as well as several tapestry-weaving, bronze-casting and hardstone workshops (*see* GOBELINS, §1). In the 18th century the Garde Meuble had its own artists who provided designs for the *menuisiers* who executed the king's commissions. Eventually, only the tapestry workshops survived (they are still in production) and remained under the direction of the Bâtiments. Although the Garde Meuble was not necessarily responsible for making or buying furniture and furnishings, it was responsible for making an inventory of them and for their care and installation. Two categories of furniture were acquired, either by commission or purchase: cabinetwork (*ébénisterie*) and bronze furnishings were delivered complete from the maker; and seat furniture and beds were delivered bare and upholstered in the workshops of the Garde Meuble. The royal collection was constantly changing as objects were sold or given away as gifts and new suites of furniture were added.

While each royal house had its own furniture storerooms with a concierge in charge, the headquarters of the service—the Hôtel du Garde Meuble de la Couronne—was located from 1663 or 1664 to 1758 in the surviving parts of the Hôtel du Petit-Bourbon on the banks of the Seine and abutting the south-east corner of the Cour Carrée of the Louvre. The Petit-Bourbon was ordered to be demolished by Marigny in 1758 as part of the project to complete the Louvre and open a public space before the Colonnade. The Garde Meuble was moved in 1758 to

the Hôtel de Conti on the Quai de Conti almost immediately opposite, on the left bank of the Seine. For a brief time from 1768 to 1774, it was housed in the Hôtel des Ambassadeurs Extraordinaires or Hôtel d'Evreux (now Palais de l'Elysée). On the completion in 1772 of the new Hôtel du Garde Meuble at 2, Place Louis XV (now Place de la Concorde), the service moved to its custom-designed building, which housed workrooms, lodgings and public exhibition rooms in what was one of the more important proto-museums of the 18th century. In 1774 the service occupied the Hôtel du Garde Meuble de la Couronne (now the Ministère de la Marine) designed by Ange-Jacques Gabriel, which provided not only offices, lodgings, storerooms and workshops for all the specialized conservators but also vast, luxurious exhibition rooms in what was, in fact, a public museum of the decorative arts. When it opened to the public in 1778 there were rooms for arms and armour, the crown jewels and important furniture and, after 1785, galleries of bronzes and paintings. This vast treasure of royal patrimony was looted during the Revolution, and evidence of its contents and splendour can only be found in guidebooks to Paris published before 1789.

BIBLIOGRAPHY

L. Le Cosquino: *Journal du garde-meuble de la couronne et des maisons royales* (n.p., 1663)

J. J. Guiffrey: *Inventaire général des meubles de la couronne sous Louis XIV (1663–1715)*, 2 vols (Paris, 1885–6)

P. Verlet: *Le Mobilier royal français: Meubles de la couronne conservés en France avec une étude sur le garde-meuble de la couronne* (Paris, 1955/R 1990)

——: *French Royal Furniture* (London, 1963)

S. Schneelbalg-Perelman: 'Richesses du garde-meuble parisien de François Ier', *Gaz. B.-A.*, n. s. 5, lxvii (1971), pp. 255–304

C. Baulez: 'Identification de quelques meubles des collections de Versailles, Compiègne et Chantilly', *Bull. Soc. Hist. A. Fr.* (1977), pp. 161–70

'Melanges Verlet: Studi sulle arti decorative in Europa, III', *Antol. B. A.*, 31–32 (1987) [whole issue]

D. Alcouffe: 'Les Ventes de Louis XV', *De Versailles à Paris: Le Destin des collections royales*, ed. J. Charles (Paris, 1989), pp. 46–50

J. J. Gautier: 'Le Garde-meuble de la couronne sous Thierry de Ville d'Avray', *De Versailles à Paris: Le Destin des collections royales*, ed. J. Charles (Paris, 1989), pp. 51–9

B. Morel: 'Le Vol des joyaux de la couronne et leur destin sous la Révolution', *De Versailles à Paris: Le Destin des collections royales*, ed. J. Charles (Paris, 1989), pp. 70–78

J.-N. Ronfort: 'Le Mobilier royal à l'époque de Louis XIV et le garde-meuble de la couronne', *De Versailles à Paris: Le Destin des collections royales*, ed. J. Charles (Paris, 1989), pp. 15–39

ALDEN GORDON

Maisons, Marquis de. *See* LONGUEIL, RENÉ DE.

Maistora, Vladimir Dimitrov-. *See* DIMITROV-MAISTORA, VLADIMIR.

Maistre [Mestre], **(Le)Roy** [Roi] **(Leveson** [Leviston] **Laurent Joseph) de** (*b* Bowral, NSW, 27 March 1894; *d* London, 1 March 1968). Australian painter and designer. From 1913 to *c.* 1915 he studied art with Dattilo Rubbo (1870–1955) and music in Sydney. In 1919 he devised a colour–music theory that allied the colours of the spectrum to musical scales and, with fellow artist Roland Wakelin, held an exhibition of eleven paintings and five room designs based on this theory. The paintings, such as *Boat Sheds, Berry's Bay* (1919; priv. col., see Johnson, 1988, p. 33), are characterized by simplified forms, large areas of flat paint and heightened, non-representational colour. De Maistre was influenced by international art, but these works are a unique Australian hybrid of Post-Impressionism. Further experiments in 1919 led de Maistre to produce Australia's first abstract paintings: only one documented example is known—*Rhythmic Composition in Yellow Green Minor* (1919; Sydney, A.G. NSW). From 1923 to 1925 he was in Europe on a travelling scholarship. On his return to Sydney he held two solo exhibitions at the Macquarie Galleries (1926, 1928), worked on room and furniture designs and lectured on modern art. In 1930 he returned to London where he lived until his death.

De Maistre's work of the 1930s comprised mainly Surrealist paintings and renewed colour–music experiments, such as *Arrested Phrase from Beethoven's Ninth Symphony in Red Major* (1935; Canberra, N.G.). After 1940 he developed a decorative Cubist style. Following his conversion to Roman Catholicism in 1949 he concentrated on religious paintings (e.g. the *Stations of the Cross*, 1956; London, Westminster Cathedral), studio interiors (*Interior with Lamp*, 1953; London, Tate), flower paintings and portraits.

WRITINGS
'Modern Art and the Australian Outlook', *A. Australia*, n.s. 3, xiv (Dec 1925)
'Painting: Ingres to Cézanne', *New Britain* [London], i/8 (July 1933), p. 239

BIBLIOGRAPHY
J. Rothenstein: 'Roy de Maistre', *Modern English Painters*, ii: *Lewis to Moore* (London, 1956, rev. 2/1976), pp. 246–59, 329–30
Roy de Maistre: A Retrospective Exhibition of Paintings and Drawings, 1917–1960 (exh. cat., London, Whitechapel A.G., 1960)
H. Johnson: *Roy de Maistre: The Australian Years, 1894–1930* (Sydney, 1988) [detailed bibliog.]
——: *Roy de Maistre: The English Years 1930–1968* (Sydney, 1994) [detailed bibiliog.]

HEATHER JOHNSON

Maitani, Lorenzo (*b* Siena; *fl* 1290; *d* Orvieto, June 1330). Italian architect and ?sculptor. The first documentary reference to him occurs in a Sienese *catasto* (land registry declaration) of 1290. He was appointed *universalis caput magister* of Orvieto Cathedral in a contract drawn up on 16 September 1310, which required him to supervise the construction of the cathedral, as well as oversee the town's bridges and other civic structures. He spent the last two decades of his life at Orvieto, apart from a few periods of service elsewhere as an architectural consultant.

The contract of 1310 indicates that Maitani had initially been called to Orvieto from Siena when the newly built structure of the cathedral threatened to collapse. It is generally agreed that he was responsible for the series of remedial buttresses, four of which are still visible in the walls of the two side chapels off the transept. He worked on the roof, as is confirmed by a lost inscription on a decorated beam, bearing the architect's name and a date of 1327 (noted by Fumi, 1891). He is described in the contract as expert in buttressing, making roofs and 'walls figured with beauty'. This reference has led scholars to assume that he executed much of the sculpture on the lower part of the façade, although he is not explicitly described as a sculptor in any of the sources.

The design of the cathedral's west façade has been almost universally attributed to Maitani (*see* ORVIETO, fig. 3), and he is credited with having supervised its construction to the level of the gallery below the rose window. Two drawings (Orvieto, Mus. Opera Duomo), believed to be preliminary schemes for the façade, survive. The single-gable drawing is usually ascribed to an anonymous master presumed to have preceded Maitani at Orvieto by only a few years, while the three-gable drawing, which largely corresponds to the actual building, has been widely attributed to Maitani himself. The documentary basis for this is an inventory reference of 1356 mentioning a 'large parchment of the façade of the church of Santa Maria Maggiore drawn by Master Lorenzo Maitani'. Maitani apparently exercised strict control over the materials for the cathedral's construction and decoration in his capacity as *capomaestro*, judging from two entries in the cathedral treasury account books. The first is datable to 1321 and indicates that Maitani participated in the manufacture of gold glass for the mosaic inlay covering much of the façade. The second records that, in 1330, he was given bronze to cast the eagle of St John the Evangelist.

The extent of Maitani's involvement in the creation of the sculpture at the cathedral is disputed. The marble reliefs of *Genesis* and the *Last Judgement* on the first and fourth pilasters, the bronze and marble group in the main lunette of the façade, the bronze angels and the Evangelists' Symbols have been seen as stylistically related and have all been attributed to Maitani. The contract of 1310 did allow him to retain some assistants for the sculptural work on the façade, but it seems likely that these craftsmen had already begun the work under the supervision of an earlier master. The sole piece of documentary evidence explicitly linking Maitani with the sculpture is the document of 1330, noting the provision of the bronze for casting the eagle. The entry must, however, be interpreted with some caution: Maitani may simply have received the bronze in his role as *capomaestro*, in charge of the teams of sculptors working at Orvieto. If his activity as a sculptor is open to question, there is little doubt that Maitani was responsible for coordinating the design and decoration of the lower part of the west front.

Other works of sculpture attributed to Maitani, all of which may be seen at Orvieto, include two wooden crucifixes in the cathedral, a crucifix in S Francesco and the seated figure of *Christ* in the Museo Opera del Duomo. These attributions have been challenged with some justification by Weinberger (*EWA*), who suggested that they were executed by one of the masters whose work may be seen on the upper registers of the façade reliefs.

Maitani left Orvieto in 1317 and 1319–21 to advise the Perugians on the repair of their aqueducts. He was consulted about the work in progress on Siena Cathedral (1322), a castle at Montefalco (1323) and the repair of a castle at Castiglione del Lago (1325). During 1326 and 1327 he also repaired the town walls and gates in Orvieto, as well as the Palazzo del Comune.

For a full discussion of Maitani's work, *see* ORVIETO, §2 (ii).

UNPUBLISHED SOURCES
Orvieto, Archv Opera Duomo [Cathedral treasury account books]

BIBLIOGRAPHY
EWA
G. della Valle: *Storia del duomo di Orvieto* (Rome, 1791)
A. Rossi: 'Lorenzo ed Ambrogio Maitani al servizio del Comune di Perugia', *G. Erud. A.*, ii (1873), pp. 57–72

L. Fumi: 'La facciata del duomo di Orvieto: Lorenzo Maitani e i primi disegni', *Archv Stor. A.*, ii (1889), pp. 327–38
——: *Il duomo di Orvieto* (Rome, 1891)
A. Schmarsow: 'Das Fassadenproblem am Dom von Orvieto', *Repert. Kstwiss.*, xlvii (1926), pp. 119–44
W. R. Valentiner: 'Observations on Sienese and Pisan Trecento Sculpture', *A. Bull.*, ix (1927), pp. 177–220
G. de Francovich: 'Lorenzo Maitani scultore e i bassorilievi della facciata del duomo di Orvieto', *Boll. A.*, n. s., vii (1927–8), pp. 339–72
——: 'Un' Annunciazione in legno di Lorenzo Maitani', *La Diana*, iv (1929), pp. 171–80
E. Carli: *Le sculture del duomo di Orvieto* (Bergamo, 1947)
J. White: 'The Reliefs on the Façade of the Duomo at Orvieto', *J. Warb. & Court. Inst.*, xxii (1959), pp. 254–302
M. D. Taylor: *The Iconography of the Façade Decoration of the Cathedral at Orvieto* (diss., Princeton U., NJ, 1970)

CATHERINE HARDING

Maitec, Ovidiu (*b* Arad, 13 Dec 1925). Romanian sculptor. He studied sculpture at the Institute of Fine Arts 'N. Grigorescu' in Bucharest between 1945 and 1950. In 1950 he became a founder-member of the Union of Plastic Artists of Romania. From 1950 to 1956 he was a lecturer at the Institute of Fine Arts. In 1953 he made his début at the Official Salon in Bucharest, exhibiting sculptures inspired by Socialist Realism and by formal academicism. His masterly, naturalistic modelling is especially evident in public sculptures (e.g. *Miner*, plaster, 1957; Anina). In 1962, with *The Wall*, he began to explore different means of expression. Modelling was replaced by direct carving, bronze by wood and figuration by abstraction. The scale became more natural than monumental, as in *Angels* (walnut, 94×88×193 mm, 1971; London, Tate). Maitec used large pieces of hard wood, which he first attacked with saw and axe to achieve rough and gravitational volumes. Then he perforated the solid mass from different angles, creating a honeycomb structure penetrated by light. The immobility of the structure was broken through ingenious combinations, with hinges giving mobility to different parts and shutters (e.g. *The Tree*, 1422×558 mm, 1968; Bucharest, N. Mus. A.), inviting not only the eye but the hand of the viewer to participate in the continuous interplay. This synthesis between the craftsmanship of popular carving and modernism, between the legacy of Brancusi and Op art made Maitec one of the most original post-war Romanian artists. He also achieved recognition outside Romania, exhibiting at the Circle Gallery in London (1969); Kettle's Yard, Cambridge University (1973); Richard Demarco Gallery, Edinburgh (1974); and Bluecoat Gallery, Liverpool (1977). He also participated in the Venice Biennale (1968, 1972, 1980). His best-known monuments include those dedicated to Romanian Television, Bucharest (bronze, 1970), and to the national poet *Mihai Eminescu* (stone, 1975; Cluj-Napoca).

BIBLIOGRAPHY
Ovidiu Maitec (exh. cat. by J. Ede and B. Brezianu, U. Cambridge, Kettle's Yard, 1973)
Ovidiu Maitec: Expoziţie de sculptură (exh. cat., intro. M. Eliade; Bucharest, Gal. A. Dalles, 1985)

CĂLIN DAN

Maitland, Dick. See under CUBITT, JAMES.

Maitland, John, Duke of Lauderdale (*b* Lethington [now Lennoxlove], Lothian, 24 May 1616; *d* Tunbridge Wells, Kent, 20–26 August 1682). British statesman, patron and collector. A former Scottish Covenanter, Lauderdale went on to become a close supporter of Charles II. He was a member of the inner Cabal ministry and Secretary for Scotland, being appointed Lord High Commissioner in 1680. On his death he was described as 'the learnedest and most powerful minister of state of his age'; his London home, Ham House, near Richmond, Surrey, testifies to his reputation as a leading patron and collector.

Lauderdale's association with Ham House began in 1672 with his second marriage, to Elizabeth Murray, Countess of Dysart (*c.* 1626–98), who had inherited the house (built in 1610) from her father, William Murray, 1st Earl of Dysart (?1600–51). Between 1672 and 1674 the Lauderdales, using William Samwell (1628–76) as architect, greatly enlarged Ham House by adding a new suite of rooms along the south front; this takes in the space between the wings of the original building, to give a symmetrical structure with an unbroken Baroque frontage. The interior of the house was correspondingly rearranged and magnificently decorated. To John Evelyn, visiting the Lauderdales in 1678, Ham was 'indeed inferiour to few of the best Villas in Italy itselfe, the House furnished like a great Princes'. The most remarkable feature of Ham House is that its fabric has remained almost unaltered since Evelyn's time and that it retains all its 17th-century furnishings.

Lauderdale commissioned ceiling paintings in the Private and White Closets (*in situ*) from Antonio Verrio, whose studio was employed, together with a team of Anglo-Dutch artists and craftsmen, to refurbish and decorate the State Rooms. Much of this new decorative scheme consisted of paintings set within panelling, in the form of overdoors and overmantels. These included four marine paintings by Willem van de Velde II (*in situ*); paintings of birds, insects and landscapes, including *Plants, Insects and a Squirrel* by Abraham Begeyn and *Landscape with Cattle* by Dirck van den Bergen (both *in situ*); battle scenes and seaports by Thomas Wijck and Jan Wyck; bird paintings by Francis Barlow and strangely lit classical scenes by William Gouw Ferguson, such as *Classical Ruins* (*in situ*).

Peter Lely, who had earlier painted a portrait of the *Duchess of Lauderdale* (Ham House, Surrey, NT) and one of the *Duke of Lauderdale* (Edinburgh, N.P.G.), was commissioned to paint more recent portraits of the ducal couple, singly and together, such as the double portrait still hanging in the Round Gallery, Ham. The Duke also commissioned his portrait (pastel, 1674–5; Duchess's Bedchamber, Ham) from Edmund Ashfield; and another (Queen's Closet, Ham) from Cornelis Jonson van Ceulen I, who had earlier painted a double portrait of *Lauderdale with his Friend the Duke of Hamilton* (Inner Hall, Ham; copy at Lennoxlove, Lothian). These portraits, the decorative painting scheme and furniture such as the japanned chairs bought by Lauderdale in Amsterdam, made Ham strongly Dutch in character, in keeping with the taste prevailing in England in the 1670s and 1680s. The portraits in the Long Gallery, which included a portrait of the *Duchess of Lauderdale with a Black Servant* (*in situ*) by Peter Lely, were framed in a magnificent set of auricular ('Sunderland') frames (*see* FRAME, fig. 42).

A 1679 inventory also lists pictures—not all still at Ham—by Frans de Momper, Pieter van Roestraten, Philips Wouwerman, Hendrick van Steenwijk (ii) and Bartholomeus Breenbergh, as well as copies after Titian, including *Venus and the Organ Player* (original Paris, Louvre), Andrea del Sarto, Pier Francesco Mola and Jacopo Bassano. As their exact provenance is not stated, it is not certain whether they were bought by Lauderdale or by William Murray, his father-in-law, who lived at Ham House from the 1630s to 1654 and was a member of Charles I's Whitehall collecting group. Given the strong Dutch bias of the house, it seems likely that some of the Dutch pictures were bought by Lauderdale himself, while other works, such as the Italianate examples, were inherited from Murray.

Lauderdale undoubtedly benefited from his wife's connoisseurship, already apparent before their marriage; but he was well regarded in his own right as a bibliophile and collector of prints and drawings. Bishop Gilbert Burnet (1643–1715) described him as 'a curious Collector of Books and when in London would very often go to the Booksellers and pick up what curious Books he could meet with'. Lauderdale's library, consisting of rare and valuable works, including ones by William Caxton and Wynkyn de Worde, remained at Ham until 1930. His collection of prints and drawings, 'of Architecture, History and Roman Antiquities, by the most eminent European Masters' (a typical collection of this period) was sold in June 1689 in London.

DNB   BIBLIOGRAPHY
R. Law: *Memorials, or the Memorable Things that Fell Out within this Island of Britain from 1638 to 1684* (Edinburgh, 1818)
W. C. Mackensie: *The Life and Times of John Maitland, Duke of Lauderdale* (London, 1923)
J. Evelyn: *Diary*, ed. E. S. de Beer, 6 vols (Oxford, 1955)
M. Tomlin: *Ham House* (London, 1986)
                              DIANA DETHLOFF

Maitland [née McClymonds]**, Ruth (Esther)** (*b* Massillon, OH, 3 May 1885; *d* Los Angeles, CA, 16 Sept 1958). American collector. She received art works as gifts from her father at an early age and inherited his small collection of prints and mostly French mid-19th-century paintings, selling a portion of it primarily to acquire modern works by European and American artists, as well as a few Old Master prints. As a consequence of the growth of the collection an extensive remodelling of her and her husband's Georgian-style house in Bel Air, Los Angeles, was done by J. R. Davidson and George Howe in 1939–40.

Maitland's collection, which included *Italian Woman* (New York, Guggenheim) by Henri Matisse and works by Georges Braque, Paul Cézanne, Marc Chagall, Giorgio de Chirico, Salvador Dalí, Paul Klee, Joan Miró, Amedeo Modigliani, Pablo Picasso, Mary Cassatt, George Bellows and other artists, was amassed in a purely personal manner and not with a historical overview or with an emphasis on any particular school or movement. Moreover, she saw her acquisitions not so much as a collection but rather as a grouping of objects that she judged interesting. Her husband, apparently, did not actively participate in buying these works although exhibition catalogues sometimes list the collection under both of their names.

Maitland was actively involved in the artistic community in Los Angeles and was committed to the public display of art, including privately acquired works. Not only was her collection accessible to her large circle of friends and acquaintances, but she lent items to local and national exhibitions and donated *c*. 100 photographs by Edward Weston to the Los Angeles County Museum of Art in 1946. During her prolonged ill-health in the mid-1940s her collection was first placed into storage until her son and daughter, Walter McClymonds Maitland and Flora Maitland Dean, placed it on long-term loan at the Dickson Art Center of the University of California, Los Angeles, before it was dispersed between them.

UNPUBLISHED SOURCES
Santa Barbara, U. CA, A. Mus., Julius Ralph Davidson Papers
BIBLIOGRAPHY
Collection of Dr and Mrs Leslie M. Maitland (exh. cat., foreword A. Millier; Los Angeles, CA, Co. Mus. A., 1939)
An Exhibition: The Ruth McClymonds Maitland Collection (exh. cat., foreword V. Price; Los Angeles, UCLA, Dickson A. Cent., 1959)
W. H. Higgins: *Art Collecting in the Los Angeles Area, 1910–1960* (diss., Los Angeles, UCLA, 1963), pp. 221–35
                              NAOMI SAWELSON-GORSE

Maitland, William Fuller (*b* 10 March 1813; *d* Stansted, Essex, 15 Feb 1876). English collector. He was educated by private tutors until he went to Trinity College, Cambridge University, where he took a BA in 1835 and an MA in 1839. He had no formal artistic training but soon developed a strong interest in painting as well as an ability to detect worth in paintings and periods previously disregarded. He travelled widely in Italy and became familiar with the works of the early Italian masters, which he collected extensively. The paintings of Botticelli, Ambrogio de Predis, Franciabigio and others became an important part of his collection at a time when they were generally unappreciated by the rest of the art world. It seems likely that his passion for outdoor life was the prime motivation behind his extensive collecting of English landscape painting. After his death, the Royal Academy broke with tradition by voting to send its condolences to his widow, recognizing that Maitland had made a major contribution to the Old Masters exhibitions that they had held over many years. After his death nine of the most significant pictures in his collection were sold to the National Gallery in London; these include Botticelli's *Tondo: Adoration of the Kings* and Franciabigio's *Portrait of a Knight of St John* (1514).

DNB   BIBLIOGRAPHY
                              JULIAN SHEATHER

Maître François. *See* FRANÇOIS, MAÎTRE.

Maius, Jan. *See* VERMEYEN, JAN CORNELISZ.

Majano, da. *See* MAIANO, DA.

Majer, Jeremias. *See* MEYER, JEREMIAH.

Majiayao [Ma-chia-yao]. Neolithic site in Lintao County, Gansu Province, China. Excavated in 1921–3 by the Swedish archaeologist Johan Gunnar Andersson (1874–1960), it is the type site of the Majiayao phase (later part of the 4th millennium BC) of the Gansu or Western Yangshao culture (*see also* CHINA, §VII, 3(i)(b)).

Despite the discovery in 1975 of a knife made of bronze (an alloy of copper and 6–10% tin) dating from *c.* 3000 BC and some slag fragments (including copper, tin, lead and iron) that indicate bronze metallurgy at the Linjia site in Dongxiang County, Gansu Province, the Majiayao culture was definitely Neolithic. Agricultural tools such as hoes, axes, sickles, grinders and pestles are made of stone, and tools for hunting, fishing and domestic work, such as needles, awls, chisels, arrowheads and fish-hooks, are made of bone. There were also bone ornaments and pottery toys such as rattles. The limited bronze production was of little significance in the economy.

The lowest stratum of the excavations shows semi-subterranean houses of square or rectangular plan, with hearths and entrance stairs. Later houses were built at ground-level with sunken foundations. Walls were made of wattle and daub and reinforced with wooden posts. The roofs, which were probably thatched, were supported by wooden pillars and beams. Kilns were situated away from the dwellings, while burials were generally placed near the houses. In a large grave at Hetaozhuang, Minhe County, in Qinghai Province, many pieces of a wooden casket were found. At another site at Shangsunjia in Datong, Qinghai Province, a large painted pottery vessel was found broken into two halves, the upper half containing an adult male and the lower half an adult woman. The number of grave goods in the Majiayao tombs varied from a few to several dozen pieces of pottery, stone implements and bone artefacts, indicating the relative social status of the deceased.

Majiayao pottery has a fine red to buff body and a high lustre: it is either finished with black painted decorations or left plain, the surface polished smooth and ornamented with cloth or cord impressions. Shapes include bowls—with or without out-turned lips—jars with tall necks, small-mouthed jars, pointed bottles and bowls on stands. The motifs consist of animal and geometric patterns. Nearly all the painted pottery is decorated with black alone, but in a few pieces the black pattern is enhanced with red. Animal designs are mostly frogs and birds in more or less abstract form. Bird heads are shown in profile, and sometimes they are drawn into a curvilinear pattern, with the eye as a circle in a vortex surrounded by waves, giving the impression of endless movement (see fig.). The frog design is often combined with a net covering the body. Occasionally the legs and feet of the frog are used as a separate design on the sides of a bowl, with the legs interwoven like a vine and the feet represented as back-ward-curving branches. Geometric patterns include rows of parallel lines around the body, waves and oval or round spaces often filled with dots, stripes and/or curved lines. Net motifs are often combined with other geometric or animal designs. One low jar has a fake spout in the shape of a man's head, somewhat flattened, with a high brow, long nose and clearly defined eyes, nostrils and mouth formed as small openings (Xining, Qinghai Prov. Mus.). There is a scoop with a short handle in the shape of a human head, also fairly flat with a high brow and a long nose; the eyes and mouth are underlined with black circles (Stockholm, Östasiat. Mus.). The inside of one bowl is

Majiayao, polished jar with stylized bird's head in black paint on yellow-buff ground, h. 260 mm, late 4th millennium BC (Lanzhou, Gansu Provincial Museum)

decorated with a row of five dancing figures repeated three times holding each other by the hand and wearing what have been interpreted as penis sheaths (Xining, Qinghai Prov. Mus.). It is believed that this may be a scene from a shamanistic ritual.

BIBLIOGRAPHY

K. C. Chang: *The Archaeology of Ancient China* (New Haven, 1963, rev. New Haven and London, 4/1986), pp. 138–46
L. G. F. Huber: 'The Ma-chia-yao tradition', *Bull. Mus. Far E. Ant.*, 53 (1981), pp. 27–48
——: 'A Commentary on the Recent Finds of Neolithic Painted Pottery from Ta-ti-wan, Kansu', *Early China*, ix–x (1983–5), pp. 1–19
A. E. Dien, J. K. Riegel and N. T. Price, eds: *Prehistoric to Western Zhou* (1985), ii of *Chinese Archaeological Abstracts* (Los Angeles, 1978–85), pp. 266–70, 289–90

BENT L. PEDERSEN

Majolica. Term used to describe 19th-century decorative wares, covered in thick lead glazes and loosely based on Italian 16th-century maiolica. It was first introduced at the Minton Ceramic Factory in England.

Major, Máté (*b* Baja, 3 Aug 1904; *d* Budapest, 12 April 1986). Hungarian architect, architectural historian, theorist and teacher. He studied architecture at the Hungarian Palatine Joseph Technical University, Budapest, where an exhibition of modernist architecture in 1927 fired his interest. In 1933 he joined the Hungarian branch of CIAM and also joined the illegal Communist Party, remaining a member until his death. His semi-detached villa (1934),

Sasfiók Street, Budapest, like his other works, is built on the assimilation of Constructivist and Functionalist principles that became his hallmark. The severely geometrically arranged, flat-roofed building has a rendered white façade that contrasts with the precisely designed window apertures, the horizontal zone of windows and the similarly horizontal emphasis of the reinforced concrete construction. Major's writings argue for a Marxist interpretation of architectural history. In the 1950s, participating in a famous public debate, he opposed the Stalinist Socialist Realist style and, in the 1970s, he criticized efforts of the Peés group to create a national architectural style. He was a frequent contributor to architectural journals as well as being on the editorial board of the periodicals *Tér és forma* [Space and form] (1942–9); *Uj építészet* [New architecture] (1946–9); *Építés—Építészet* [Building—Architecture] (1949–51); and *Magyar Építőmüvészet* [Hungarian architecture] (1951–82). He was a professor of architectural history (1949–75) at the Technical University, Budapest, and a member (1960–63) of the executive committee of the Union Internationale des Architectes.

WRITINGS

Építészettörténet [The history of architecture] 3 vols (Budapest, 1954–60; Ger. trans., Berlin, 1976–84)

J. Bonta: 'Major Máté, 1904–1986', *Magyar Építőmüvészet*, lxxvii/3 (1986), p. 7

ÁKOS MORAVÁNSZKY, KATALIN
MORAVÁNSZKY-GYÖNGY

Major, Thomas (*b* 1714 or 1720; *d* London, 30 Dec 1799). English engraver. He trained in London under Gravelot, whom he accompanied to the Netherlands in 1745; he then travelled to Paris, to study under Jacques-Philippe Lebas at the Académie Royale de Peinture et de Sculpture and was befriended by an English-born engraver, André Laurent (1708–47). Major bought pictures in Paris that he took back to sell in London, where in 1749 he began to publish line-engravings, mostly of 17th-century paintings. In 1753 he became engraver to Frederick, Prince of Wales, and engraved several of the pictures in his collection. He issued collections of prints (title pages dated 1754 and 1768) and also engraved architectural plates, notably the *Ruins of Palmyra* (1753; H 939), the *Ruins of Balbec* (1757; H 936–8) and the *Ruins of Paestum* (1768; H 538–9); he published the latter himself and probably also wrote the text. He also imported prints and engraved some maps and contemporary pictures, such as the *Return from a Course on Lambourn Downs* (1756) after James Seymour. In 1756 Major was appointed Chief Engraver of Seals to the King; he was dismissed in 1760 but reinstated in 1768 after appealing on behalf of his eight children. He was overshadowed by the success of younger engravers, such as William Woollett; however, he broke ranks in 1770 by becoming the first Associate Engraver of the Royal Academy, a title offered as a sop to engravers since they were not permitted to be full Academicians. Major's only exhibit at the Royal Academy was the *Good Shepherd* (1776) after Murillo, possibly his last print. He retained his post as Chief Engraver of Seals and died quite rich.

UNPUBLISHED SOURCES

London, BM, Add. MS. 32,968m, fol. 272 [letter from Thomas Major to Charles Watson-Wentworth, 2nd Marquis of Rockingham]

BIBLIOGRAPHY

O'Donoghue; Thieme–Becker

T. Major: *Catalogue of Prints Engraved from the Finest Paintings* (London, 1754) [broadsheet, London, BM], repr. *Prt Q.*, i (1984), p. 19

R. Strange: *An Inquiry into the Rise of the Royal Academy* (London, 1775), pp. 112–28

C. Le Blanc: *Manuel de l'amateur d'estampes*, 4 vols (1854–89)

A. Graves: *The Royal Academy of Arts* (London, 1906), p. 168

F. Lugt: *Ventes* (1938–64)

H. A. Hammelmann: 'First Engraver at the Royal Academy', *Country Life*, cxlii (14 Sept 1967), pp. 616–18

E. Harris: *British Architectural Books and Writers, 1556–1785* (London, 1990), pp. 303–11 [H]

DAVID ALEXANDER

Majorana, Cristoforo (*b* Naples; *fl c.* 1480–94). Italian illuminator. Two manuscripts by this artist can be identified from surviving payment records in the Aragonese treasury: on 13 October 1480 he was paid for the illustration of 'Agostino super Salamis', a work that has now been identified as St Augustine's *Commentary on the Psalms* (London, BL, MSS Add. 14779–83), while a copy of Aesop's *Fables* (U. Valencia, Bib., MS. 758) has been linked to a payment made in 1481. Analysis of these documented volumes allows the partial reconstruction of the artist's career. Other work for the King of Naples, Ferdinand of Aragon, is recorded in numerous sources, but the manuscripts described in these commissions remain untraced. Majorana's hand has nevertheless been identified in a Breviary that once belonged to Ferdinand (*c.* 1480; Naples, Bib. N., MS. 1. B. 57). This was probably executed while Majorana was in the workshop of the Neapolitan illuminator Cola Rapicano, where he appears to have begun his career, as some pages reveal the hand of Nardo Rapicano, another member of the shop. Majorana also decorated several volumes for the libraries of both Cardinal Giovanni d'Aragona (1456–85) and Andrea Matteo Aquaviva d'Aragona, Duca d' Atri. His works for the latter include copies of Virgil's *Aeneid*, *Eclogues* and *Georgics*, now bound as one volume (1482–94; Leiden, Bib. Rijksuniv., MS. BPL 6B), and a copy of Ptolemy's *Cosmographia* (Paris, Bib. N., MS. lat. 10764). The Leiden copy of Virgil is an example of the numerous volumes Majorana decorated with frontispieces featuring classicizing architecture in a style that may have had its source in the manuscripts of the Venetian-Roman type that were circulated at the Aragonese court in Naples. It is also possible to detect in them influences from northern European, Florentine and Ferrarese manuscript illumination.

BIBLIOGRAPHY

T. De Marinis: *La biblioteca napoletana dei re d'Aragona*, 6 vols (Milan and Verona, 1947–69)

J. J. G. Alexander and A. C. de la Mare: *The Italian Manuscripts in the Library of Major J. R. Abbey* (Oxford, 1969)

A. Putaturo Murano: *Miniature napoletane del rinascimento* (Naples, 1973), pp. 34–8, 64–9

E. Cassee: 'La miniatura italiana in Olanda: Risultati di ricerche nella collezione della Biblioteca dell'Università di Leida', *La miniatura italiana tra gotico e rinascimento: Atti del II congresso di storia della miniatura italiana: Cortona, 1982*, i, pp. 155–74

A. C. de la Mare: 'The Florentine Scribes of Cardinal Giovanni of Aragon', *Il libro e il testo*, ed. C. Questa and R. Raffaelli (Urbino, 1984), pp. 245–93

J. P. Timmer: *Drie geïllumineerde Napolitaanse manuscripten uit de 15de eeuw, rich bevindende in de Universiteitsbibliotheek te Leiden* (diss., U. Leiden, 1984)

Dix siècles d'enluminure italienne (exh. cat., ed. F. Avril; Paris, Bib. N., 1984)

S. Gentile, ed.: *Vita e Favole di Esopo* (Naples, 1988) [on U. Valencia, Bib., MS. 758]

GENNARO TOSCANO

Majorca. *See under* BALEARIC ISLANDS.

Majorelle, Louis (*b* Toul, nr Nancy, 27 Sept 1859; *d* Nancy, 15 Jan 1926). French cabinetmaker. His father, Auguste Majorelle (*d* 1879), was a cabinetmaker and potter who specialized in reproduction 18th-century furniture and ceramics. Majorelle trained as a painter and studied under Jean-François Millet at the Ecole des Beaux-Arts in Paris (1877–9). Following his father's death in 1879 he abandoned painting and returned to Nancy to run the family business in partnership (until 1889) with his brother, Jules. They continued to produce furniture in Louis XV and Louis XVI revival styles but soon abandoned the production of ceramics.

Around 1894 Majorelle, under the influence of the Nancy glass- and cabinetmaker Emile Gallé, began to develop a more personal, Art Nouveau style and by 1897 he seems to have abandoned the revival styles altogether. The years between 1898 and 1908 were his most successful, and by 1910 he had retail stores in Nancy, as well as in Paris, Lyon and Lille. Along with furniture, a range of objects including lighting, metalwork and fabrics were produced in Majorelle's workshops. His reputation as the pre-eminent French cabinetmaker of the time was established at the Exposition Universelle of 1900 in Paris, where he exhibited an 'Orchid' bedroom suite, whose decoration, in the form of inlay and gilt-bronze mounts, is based on an orchid theme (e.g. desk; Paris, Mus. d'Orsay; chair; London, V&A; *see* FRANCE, fig. 61). Majorelle relied extensively on naturalistic ornament; however, his use of it was always more abstract than Gallé's. From 1901 Majorelle was a member of the Alliance Provinciale des Industries d'Art (later called the Ecole de Nancy). In 1904, at the Société Nationale des Beaux-Arts exhibition in Paris, Majorelle exhibited a dining-room *aux tomates*. His furniture in this period, in its sumptuousness, its use of lavish gilt-bronze mounts and its high-quality craftsmanship, rivals the best 18th-century French furniture. Between 1906 and 1908, probably due to the changing economic situation in France, Majorelle decided to mechanize his workshop. This, for the most part, marks the end of his more lavish production.

As a result of World War I, in 1914 Majorelle was forced to move to Paris where he worked as an interior decorator. In 1916 his factory in Nancy was destroyed by bombing, and in 1918 he returned to begin the task of rebuilding. By this time he had abandoned Art Nouveau, and his furniture of this period, much more restrained and rectilinear and less original than his earlier work, reflects the Art Deco style. Although a member of the jury, Majorelle exhibited a library *hors concours* at the Exposition Internationale des Arts Décoratifs et Industriels Modernes of 1925, in Paris. Alfred Lévy, who had worked as a designer for Majorelle for some years, took over the artistic direction of the firm on Majorelle's death.

BIBLIOGRAPHY

P. Juyo: *Louis Majorelle: Artiste, décorateur, maître ébéniste* (Nancy, 1927)

Art Nouveau in Belgium and France (exh. cat. by Y. Brunhammer and others, Houston, TX, Rice U. Inst. A., Rice Mus., 1976)

M.-C. Delacroix: 'Le Mobilier Majorelle', *L'Estampille* (Sept 1978), pp. 18–23

A. Duncan: *Art Nouveau Furniture* (New York, 1982)

DONNA CORBIN

Makart, Hans (*b* Salzburg, 28 May 1840; *d* Vienna, 3 Oct 1884). Austrian painter. He studied (1860–65) at the Akademie in Munich under the history painter Karl Theodor von Piloty whose influence is evident in Makart's *Death of Pappenheim* (1861; Vienna, Hist. Mus.). Makart visited London and Paris in 1862 and Rome in 1863. The *Papal Election* (1863–5; Munich, Neue Pin.) reveals Makart's skill in the bold use of colour to convey drama as well as his virtuoso draughtsmanship. Two decorative triptychs, *Modern Cupids* (1868; Vienna, Zentsparkasse), and the *Plague in Florence* (1868; Schweinfurt, Samml. Schäfer), brought Makart both fame and disapproval (mostly because they lacked a literary original) when exhibited in Munich in 1868. His plan for the second work (*c.* 1868; St Gall, Kstmus.; see fig.) shows a setting of sombre magnificence.

In 1869 the Emperor Francis Joseph summoned Makart to Vienna. It was hoped that he would contribute decorative schemes for some of the new Ringstrasse buildings then under construction. Makart's first years in Vienna were notable for several large-scale works that proved very influential on the further development of Viennese decorative painting. These included *Abundantia: The Gifts of the Earth, the Gifts of the Sea* (1870; Paris, Louvre), originally produced for the dining-room of the Palais Hoyos; the pictorial decoration for the study of the industrialist Nikolaus Dumba in his palace on the Ringstrasse (1871; Vienna, priv. col., see 1972 exh. cat.); and the large oil painting *Venice Pays Tribute to Caterina Cornaro* (1873; Vienna, Belvedere). During these years, Makart designed theatre curtains for various Viennese theatres, for example a *Midsummer Night's Dream* for the Stadttheater (1872; destr. 1874; pen and wash sketch, Vienna, Hist. Mus.) and *Bacchus and Ariadne* for the Komischer Oper (1873–4; destr. 1881; oil sketch, Vienna, Belvedere). Makart also swiftly established himself as a portrait painter of style and originality (e.g. *Dora Fournier-Gabillon*, 1880; Vienna, Hist. Mus.).

Makart spent the winter of 1875–6 with friends (including Lenbach) in Cairo, where he produced several pictures with an oriental setting (e.g. the *Hunt on the Nile*, 1875–6; Vienna, Belvedere, and *Cleopatra's Nile Journey*, 1875; Stuttgart, Staatsgal.; *see* AUSTRIA, fig. 16). In the autumn of 1876 Makart visited the Netherlands, after which he produced another monumental oil painting: *Charles V's Entry into Antwerp* (1877–8; Hamburg, Ksthalle), which he exhibited with great success at the Exposition Universelle in Paris in 1878. A year later, after taking up an appointment as professor of history painting at the Akademie der Bildenden Künste in Vienna, he produced the 'costumed' section of the great ceremonial procession that the city of Vienna organized to celebrate the silver wedding of Emperor Francis Joseph and Empress Elisabeth (large-scale sketches, Vienna, Hist. Mus.). This marked the peak

Hans Makart: *Plague in Florence*, sketch for room decoration, oil and photographs on canvas, 1.03×1.69 m, *c.* 1868 (St Gall, Kunstmuseum)

of Makart's popularity as an artist; after the procession his name was familiar to almost everyone in Vienna. Makart's last large-scale commission, in 1881, was for decoration for the main staircase of the new Kunsthistorisches Museum on the Ringstrasse. Lunette decorations were completed in 1883 (*in situ*), but the ceiling design only reached the stage of the sketch, the *Victory of Light over Darkness* (Vienna, Belvedere). The ceiling was finally completed by Mihály Munkácsy in 1890 (*in situ*).

During the last years of his life, overshadowed by worsening illness and increasing criticism of his output, Makart painted various architectural fantasies, for instance the *Design for a Palace of the Arts* (1883; Vienna, Belvedere), and some further monumental pictures, including the *Hunt of Diana* (1880; Sarasota, FL, Ringling Mus. A.) and a cycle incorporating subjects from the Nibelung legend, intended as a personal homage to Richard Wagner, whom Makart had always much admired (1883; Riga, Mus. Foreign A.; oil sketch *c.* 1880–83, Vienna, Belvedere). Makart had a decisive influence on shaping the character of a period of Viennese culture. For over a decade, his large, richly appointed studio was a focal point of Viennese society. He brought to Viennese art a new freedom of colour and range of subject-matter. With his enormous pictures, embodying highly personal interpretations of historical events, he was able to encourage the spectator to project himself into the pictures as if they were stage plays. The theatrical element was one of the most important in Makart's art, and also the aspect that had the strongest influence on younger artists. The division of public opinion into admiration and rejection remained with Makart, however, even in the days of his greatest renown. Soon after his death, his work met with hostility,

and the auction of his artistic estate, in spring 1885, yielded an extremely low figure.

BIBLIOGRAPHY

Thieme–Becker
Hans Makart (exh. cat., Vienna, Kstlerhaus, 1885)
Hans Makart (exh. cat., Salzburg, Landesgal., 1940)
E. Pirchen: *Hans Makart* (Vienna, 1954)
Makart und seine Zeit (exh. cat., Salzburg, Residenzgal., 1954)
B. Heinzl: 'Hans Makart', *Mitt. Österreich. Gal.*, xv/59 (1971), pp. 74–127
R. Mikula: *Studien zu Hans Makart* (diss., U. Vienna, 1971)
Hans Makart (exh. cat., Baden-Baden, Staatl. Ksthalle, 1972)
G. Frodl: *Hans Makart* (Salzburg, 1974) [cat. rais. with extensive bibliog.]
Hans Makart: Phantasien und Entwürfe (exh. cat., Vienna, Hermesvilla, 1975)
G. Frodl: 'Begegnung im Theater: Hans Makart und Gustav Klimt', *Mitt. Österreich. Gal.*, xxii/66–xxiii/67 (1978–9), pp. 9–36
Hans Makart: Zeichnungen und Entwürfe (exh. cat., Salzburg, Mus. Carolino Augusteum, 1984)
Das Zeitalter Kaiser Franz Josephs I, pt 1 (exh. cat., Schloss Grafenegg, nr Krems, 1985)
Hans Makart und der Historismus in Prag, Budapest und Wien (exh. cat., Vienna, Österreich. Gal., Schloss Halbturn, 1986)
Vienne 1880–1938: L'Apocalypse joyeuse (exh. cat., Paris, Pompidou, 1986)

GERBERT FRODL

Makhayev, Mikhail (Ivanovich) (*b* Smolenskoye, Vereysky district [now Moscow region], 1716-18; *d* St Petersburg, 25 Feb 1770). Russian draughtsman and engraver. He was the son of a priest, and from 1729 he studied at the St Petersburg Naval Academy. In August 1731 he was transferred to the instrument-making department of the Academy of Sciences, where he helped to make land-surveying instruments, including theodolites (a training that was of value when he later came to sketch views of St Petersburg); he also learnt how to carve moulds for dies under Georg Unfertsagt (1701–67); and he studied drawing under two members of the Academy staff, Ottmar Elliger II and Elias Grimmel (1703–58). In June 1743 Makhayev was made director of the cartographic and die-carving section of the Academy, and he was employed there for the rest of his life. Together with his pupils he helped to produce the *Atlas rossiyskoy imperii* ('Atlas of the Russian Empire'; 1740s); in addition, he provided inscriptions for diplomas for honorary members of the Academy, for porcelain snuff-boxes and for a large silver shrine at the tomb of *Aleksandr Nevsky* (early 1750s; St Petersburg, Hermitage).

Makhayev is chiefly known for his views of St Petersburg. His interest in perspective, which he originally took up 'for pleasure', led him to take a major part in creating several series of views of the city and its environs; these began with a commission from the Academy in the mid-1740s. The first series consisted of drawings for an engraved album containing a plan of St Petersburg and 12 views of its 'most famous avenues', published in 1753 to celebrate the capital's 50th anniversary. Makhayev made views of the city with the help of a camera obscura and other instruments; he then finished them in his workshop, adding details and staffage drawn from life. He was aided by his pupils Aleksey Grekov (1723/6–after 1770) and Ivan Lapin (1729/31–63). The finished drawings were approved by Giuseppe Valeriani (1708–62), who was in charge of the commission; they were then sent to be engraved by a large group of master craftsmen. Makhayev also took part in this work, marking the basic outlines on the grounded plate and carving the inscriptions for the various scenes. Most of Makhayev's original, delicate and skilful drawings for these prints were destroyed during the process of producing the engravings. Those drawings that have survived include the *Third Winter Palace Seen from Palace Square* (1750), the *Cour d'honneur of the Summer Palace on the Fontanka* (1749) and *Bol'shaya Nemetskaya Street Seen from the Main Apothecary's* (1751; all St Petersburg, Rus. Mus.). Together with Jean-Louis de Velli (1730–1804) Makhayev executed some drawings of the *Coronation of Catherine II* (1762–3; St Petersburg, Hermitage). In the 1750s and 1760s he produced a series of drawings of the surroundings of St Petersburg (Kamenny Ostrov, Tsarskoye Selo, Peterhof and Oranienbaum; surviving examples in St Petersburg, Rus. Mus., e.g. *View of the Menagerie at Tsarskoye Selo*, and in Moscow, Shchusev Res. & Sci. Mus. Rus. Archit.), as well as sets of small views of St Petersburg and Moscow, which are also known from engravings.

Makhayev's original drawings and the engravings from them are picturesque and full of animation and are typical of Russian graphic art in the Baroque style. The strictly organized construction is enriched by the use of aerial perspective, a generalization of architectural detail, the softening of line and the background contrast of light and shade, this last being a novelty in Russian drawing. The skilful introduction of small groups of people forming small genre scenes, and the many ships on the Neva, help to enliven the scene and also serve to indicate the scale of the buildings and avenues. Makhayev's views of St Petersburg continued the record of the city begun by Aleksey Zubov. They depict the city of the mid-18th century with its Baroque architecture, with a multitude of interesting details of everyday life, and provide valuable iconographic material.

During Makhayev's last years, he continued to work in the Academy, teaching in the field of die-carving, cartography and perspective. He also took part in planning and decorating the Tishinin family estate on the Volga. His last work consisted of a series of drawings of the *Kuskovo Estate* of Count Sheremetev near Moscow, which were engraved in Paris after the artist's death.

BIBLIOGRAPHY

G. Komelova: 'K istorii gravirovaniya vidov Peterburga i yego okrestnostey M. I. Makhayevym' [On the history of M. I. Makhayev's engravings of St Petersburg and its surroundings], *Trudy Gosudarstvennogo Ermitazha*, xi (1970), pp. 36–62

A. Alekseyeva: 'Dokumenty o tvorchestve Makhayeva' [Documents on the work of Makhayev], *Russkoye iskusstvo XVIII—pervoy poloviny XIX veka* [Russian art in the 18th and the first half of the 19th centuries] (Moscow, 1971), pp. 238–94

K. V. Malinovsky: *M. I. Makhayev, 1718–1770* (Leningrad, 1978)

G. KOMELOVA

Maki, Fumihiko (*b* Tokyo, 16 Sept 1928). Japanese architect, teacher, urban planner and writer. He studied with Kenzō Tange at the University of Tokyo (BArch, 1952), and then studied at the Cranbrook Academy of Art, Bloomfield Hills, MI (MArch, 1953), and at Harvard University, Cambridge, MA (MArch, 1954). From 1954 to 1956 he worked for Skidmore, Owings & Merrill in New York and Sert, Jackson & Associates in Cambridge, MA; he then taught at Washington University, St Louis (1956–62), and at Harvard (1962–5). In 1965 he returned to Tokyo and opened his own office. Maki's background enabled him to synthesize a comprehensive understanding of Western architecture with a Japanese sensitivity to scale and detail. He made his architectural debut as an urban planner and founder-member of the Metabolist group in 1960. While he remained a convinced modernist in his use of new technology, modular planning and standardized construction, he was also interested in a contextual approach to design. One of his principal ideas, developed with Masato Otaka, was 'group' or 'collective' form, which explored ways of grouping individual elements to make a larger whole. He applied these principles to his Hillside Terrace flats (1967–76) in Daikanyama, Tokyo, designed as a series of public, semi-public and semi-private spaces reinforcing the existing street pattern, and to the adjacent Royal Danish Embassy (1977–9). Maki's commissions were largely major public works such as museums, universities, libraries and exhibition centres. Examples include several buildings for the University of Tsukuba (1974–6); the National Museum of Modern Art (1983–6), Kyoto, which tempered quotations from early modern architecture with painstaking craftsmanship; and the Wacoal Art Centre (1985), Tokyo, whose 'spiral' façade is a geometrically ordered collage of different textures and elements, including modernist curved walls, a Japanese *shōji* window and classical 'temple' on top of the building. Maki taught at the University of Tokyo from 1965 and continued to teach in many universities outside Japan.

WRITINGS

Investigations in Collective Form (St Louis, 1964)

Movement Systems in the City (Cambridge, MA, 1965)

with N. Kawazoe: *What Is Urban Space?* (Tokyo, 1970)

BIBLIOGRAPHY

Japan Architect, 265 (1979) [whole issue]

New Public Architecture: Recent Projects by Fumihiko Maki and Arata Isozaki (exh. cat., New York, Japan Soc., 1985)

Space Des., cclvi (1986) [whole issue]

JACQUELINE E. KESTENBAUM

Mäkilä, Otto (*b* Turku, 9 Aug 1904; *d* Turku, 22 June 1955). Finnish painter. He studied at the Drawing School of the Turku Arts Association from 1920 to 1924. He initially concentrated on human subjects, using dense tones, and his paintings attracted attention at the Finnish art exhibition in Stockholm in 1929. His earliest stimulus came from his teacher Edwin Lydén (1879–1956)—also from Turku—who had become familiar with the work of Paul Klee and Kurt Schwitters in Munich. Mäkilä's style changed during his first trip to Paris in 1930–31. He began to concentrate on his individual vision in preference to painting from the model, creating fantastic, dream-like images with a refined use of colour. In 1939 Alvar Aalto helped him to obtain an invitation to the La Sarraz castle in Switzerland, whose owner, Hélène de Mandrot, was a generous patron. There he again came into contact with international art. Around this time he produced the significant works *Poésie* (1938), *They See what We Do not See* (1939, both Turku, A. Mus.) and *Summer Night* (1938; Helsinki, Athenaeum A. Mus.). He was caught up in the war on his return home from Switzerland via Paris, and he recorded his experiences in a number of works, including *Wanderings* (1940–41; Helsinki, Mika Waltari priv. col.), which, according to Mäkilä, depicts 'the aimless wandering of snatched souls—fallen soldiers—into the great unknown'.

After the war Mäkilä received another invitation to Switzerland, where he became inspired by abstract art. He continued, however, to produce works influenced by Surrealism, now more sombre and oppressive than in the 1930s (e.g. *Sirens*, 1947–8; Turku, A. Mus.). After 1948 Mäkilä's figures became more dehumanized, possibly in response to Picasso and Henry Moore, whose work he admired, and after a short while his work moved towards more abstract forms. Although he has been described as a leading Finnish Surrealist, Mäkilä was rather a mystic and visionary. From 1950 to 1955 he was a teacher and the Director at the Drawing School of the Turku Arts Association, and he was a major influence on the art life of Turku. As well as writing about art, he also produced a number of drawings and prints: sensitive, partly surrealistic line drawings or drypoint works, mainly figure groups or sketches for paintings.

WRITINGS

'Otto Mäkilän ajatuksia nonfiguratiivisestä taiteesta' [Otto Mäkilä's thoughts on non-figurative art], *Ateneumin Taidekokoelmat Museojulkaisu* (1957), no. 2, pp. 2–3

'Otto Mäkilän ajatuksia' [Otto Mäkilä's thoughts], *Taide* (1960), no. 3, pp. 136–8

BIBLIOGRAPHY

C.-J. af Forselles and L.-G. Nordström, eds: *Kymmenen taiteilijaa* [Ten artists] (Helsinki, 1962), pp. 51–8

L. Peltola: 'Uneksittu ja ajateltu maailma: Otto Mäkilä, mietelmiä' [A world of dreams and awareness: Otto Mäkilä, aphorisms], *Otto Mäkilä, 1904–1955* (exh. cat., Turku, A. Mus.; Tampere, A. Mus.; Helsinki, Athenaeum A. Mus.; 1986–7), Eng., pp. 56–75

U. Vihanta: *Unelmaton uni: Suomalaisen surrealismin filosofiskirjallinen ja psykologinen tausta: Otto Mäkilän surrealistinen taide* [Sleep without dreams: background to Finnish authors on surrealist philosophy and psychology, Otto Mäkilä's surrealist art] (Helsinki, 1992)

LEENA PELTOLA

Maki Ryōko (*b* Maki, Echigo, Niigata Prefect., 1777; *d* Edo [now Tokyo], 1843). Japanese calligrapher. During the mid-19th century he became one of the most celebrated calligraphers in Edo and was known as one of the Bakumatsu no Sanpitsu (Three Brushes of the late Edo period), along with NUKINA KAIOKU and ICHIKAWA BEIAN. He took his family name from the town of his birth and his artist's name from a nearby lake (*ko*), which was celebrated for its water chestnuts (*ryō*). Orphaned at a young age, Ryōko travelled to Edo to study with the famous scholar, poet and calligrapher KAMEDA BŌSAI. Because the form of eclectic Confucianism taught by Bōsai was frowned upon by the Tokugawa shogunate, Ryōko could not immediately aspire to a high governmental position, but he made rapid progress in his studies of philosophy, poetry and calligraphy. Unlike Bōsai, a masterly calligrapher with a highly idiosyncratic style in cursive script, Ryōko made thorough studies of all five principal scripts: seal (Jap. *tensho*; Chin. *zhuanshu*), clerical (Jap. *reisho*; Chin. *lishu*), regular (Jap. *kaisho*; Chin. *kaishu*), running (Jap. *gyōsho*; Chin. *xingshu*) and cursive (Jap. *sōsho*; Chin. *caoshu*). He learnt the styles of the great Chinese masters and developed a complete command of the brush.

Although Ryōko occasionally wrote out some of his own poetry, he more frequently chose classic texts from Chinese literature. In his younger days he demonstrated his study of styles of writing originating in the Song (AD 960–1279), Yuan (1279–1368) and Ming (1368–1644) periods and culminating in the work of DONG QICHANG. Later, however, Ryōko modelled his style more firmly on the tradition of the major Tang period (AD 618–907) masters. Ryōko's calligraphy displays strong horizontal and vertical strokes balanced by fluently curved strokes. Although his writing lacks great individuality, it is both forceful and elegant. Because several of Ryōko's works were reproduced in woodblock-book format, his calligraphy became a model for students and consequently exerted an influence on many artists of the later 19th century.

BIBLIOGRAPHY

C. Yamanouchi: *Kinsei jusha no sho* [Calligraphy of modern Confucianists] (Tokyo, 1980)

The World of Kameda Bōsai: The Calligraphy, Poetry, Painting and Artistic Circle of a Japanese Literatus (exh. cat. by S. Addiss, New Orleans, LA, Mus. A.; Seattle, WA, A. Mus.; Lawrence, U. KS, Spencer Mus. A.; Ann Arbor, U. MI, Mus. A.; 1984)

STEPHEN ADDISS

Makiya, Mohamed (Saleh) [Muhammad Salih] (*b* Baghdad, 1914). Iraqi architect and urban planner. He was educated at the Central Secondary School in Baghdad and then studied at Liverpool School of Architecture (BArch, 1941), Liverpool University (Diploma in Civic Design, 1942) and King's College, Cambridge (PhD, 1946). He returned to Baghdad in 1946 and established Makiya Associates, an architectural and planning consultancy practice. From 1947 to 1953 he worked for the Directorate General of Municipalities in Baghdad as an architect and urban planner. During the 1950s he designed houses and commercial buildings and became increasingly aware of the heritage of Iraqi architecture. In 1956 he was a visiting Fulbright scholar to the USA, and in 1959 he founded the first Department of Architecture in Iraq at the College of Engineering, Baghdad University, where he remained head of department until 1968. His small Khulafa Mosque (1960–63) in Baghdad, completed on a low budget, was his first important work. This mosque, built of concrete with brick decoration, was successfully integrated around the minaret of al-Ghazl (*c.* 1300). Urban conservation, regional architecture and continuity of an architectural heritage continued to preoccupy him, and he encouraged his students to record old buildings in Iraq by measuring them and drawing street elevations. In his own architecture he also became interested in the relationship between structural and non-structural elements. From 1963 to 1965 he was thrice visiting professor at the School of Architecture, University of Zaria, Nigeria, and in 1967 he became president of the Iraqi Architectural Association. From the late 1960s he devoted himself entirely to Makiya Associates. In 1967 a branch office was opened in Bahrain, which evolved into the head office, and in 1971 another office was established in Muscat, Oman. Here he worked on urban-planning proposals for the development of the city and the preservation of its old buildings. In 1974 a London office was established and further offices appeared in Kuwait, Doha, Abu Dhabi and Dubai. His work of the 1970s culminated in the Siddique Mosque (1978), Doha, and the Kuwait State Mosque (1976–84), Kuwait City, the largest building of his career. It accommodates 7000 people in a 5000 sq. m prayer hall, and has a large dome (diam. 26 m, h. 47 m), a minaret (h. 70 m) and a monumental entrance portico (h. 15 m). His reliance on concrete for this building, however, led to notable shortcomings. During the 1980s his work became increasingly monumental as he tried to reappropriate the heritage of Islamic architecture. He was encouraged in this direction by projects conceived by the Iraqi President Saddam Hussein, such as the competition for an enormous Baghdad State Mosque (1982) to accommodate 30,000 people. Makiya also produced the winning design in 1984 for the Ceremonial Parade Grounds in Tikrit, but neither project was realized.

WRITINGS

Influence of Climate on Architectural Development in the Mediterranean Region (diss., U. Cambridge, 1946)

BIBLIOGRAPHY

K. Makiya: *Post-Islamic Classicism: A Visual Essay on the Architecture of Mohamed Makiya* (London, 1990)

S. al-Khalil: *The Monument: Art, Vulgarity and Responsibility in Iraq* (London, 1991)
☐

Makka. *See* MECCA.

Makonde [Maconde]. Bantu-speaking people, numbering *c.* 350,000 by the 1990s, whose homeland is the densely thicketed Makonde Plateau south of the Ruvuma River valley in northern Mozambique. They are bounded to the west by the Makua and Yao and to the east by the Indian Ocean and by the Islamic Swahili and other coastal people. Another group of Bantu-speaking people whose homeland is north of the Rovuma River in Tanzania are also known

as Makonde. Except for a common language, these two peoples are no more closely related to each other than they are to the other Bantu-speaking peoples of the area. Tanzanian Makonde consider themselves a separate culture and refer to Mozambican Makonde as Maviha or Mawai. Before 1900 and colonization their cultural production was also distinctly different, as were their mask traditions. This entry focuses on the art of the Mozambican Makonde.

There are a number of important collections of Makonde art in Europe, particularly in Portugal (e.g. Lisbon, Mus. Ethnol. Ultramar), Germany (e.g. Stuttgart, Linden-Mus.; Leipzig, Mus. Vlkerknd.; Hamburg, Mus. Vlkerknd.; Berlin, Mus. Vlkerknd.; and Munich, Staatl. Mus. Vlkerknd.) and Great Britain (e.g. London, BM; Oxford, Pitt Rivers Mus.). The collections in Germany and Great Britain are mainly of Tanzanian Makonde art. There have been many exhibitions of Makonde art including a major show in Paris in the late 1980s (see 1989–90 exh. cat.).

1. HISTORY. Portuguese colonizers penetrated the Makonde Plateau in the 1910s. This led to a new form of patronage that was to transform Makonde art in the 20th century. Since they began carving for European patrons (Portuguese and German colonial administrators, missionaries and finally tourists and Western collectors), the Makonde have created a new livelihood for themselves and a controversial reputation in art circles. While art from both Makonde peoples is represented in early ethnographic collections, the art collected since the 1950s is almost exclusively the work of Mozambican artists who have migrated north to Tanzania for economic and political reasons. In 1970 there were at least 200 immigrant carvers in the region of Tanzania's capital, Dar es Salaam. For some time immigrant Makonde maintained a separate cultural identity, retaining such aesthetic practices as facial scarification, filing of teeth and the use of the women's lip-plug long after these practices had been abandoned by the Tanzanians. Among the second generation of immigrants these differences became less marked. Indeed, the Tanzanian government recognizes no distinction between the two Makonde peoples and has claimed the sculpture produced by Mozambican Makonde to be Tanzanian art. The marketing and export of wood-carvings, formerly in the hands of Asian and European traders, was nationalized in 1970. This policy has encouraged Tanzanian Makonde to enter the carving profession too, thus blurring further the distinctions between the two peoples.

2. PRE-COLONIAL ARTS. The major sculptural forms in the pre-contact period were female ancestor figures and masks. The ancestor figures are generally in a simple blocky style with a stiff frontality, and they are easily recognized by the distinctive lip-plug. The Mozambican Makonde *mapiko* helmet masks are often startlingly realistic. They have scarification patterns made from beeswax, filed teeth and human hair. Their production and use in boys' initiations continued into the 1990s. The face masks of the Tanzanian Makonde are usually in a simpler, blocky style, in which the lip-plug is emphasized. These masks, which also appeared among such neighbouring peoples as

the Makua, Yao and possibly Matambwe, performed as stilt masquerades (Wembah-Rashid).

3. COLONIAL AND POST-COLONIAL ARTS. Like other African cultures with mask and figure-carving traditions, the Mozambican Makonde initially responded to colonial patronage by modifying pre-existing sculptural forms to encompass new subject-matter. Genre figures based on the pre-colonial prototype of the ancestor figure were first produced in Mozambique. By the 1930s they were being made by immigrant Makonde carvers in southern Tanzania. Known in Kiswahili as *binadamu*, 'human beings', these figures saw the artists give full play to the introduction of caricature and narrative into what was previously a sacred form. Its most elaborate formulation has been the group sculpture in pole form, known in Tanzania as *ujamaa* ('family') (*see* AFRICA, fig. 25). Over time the *binadomu* carvings have lost their stiff frontality as the carvers have embraced an aesthetic of naturalism that continued to dominate *binadamu* carving into the 1990s at least.

The second and more controversial development has been that of the production of figures of bush spirits (*nnandenga* in the Makonde language, *shetani* in Kiswahili; see fig.). These were probably first produced in the 1950s as slightly distorted human forms (as bush spirits are said to be), but by 1970 they had developed into often highly abstract images with only vestiges of anthropomorphism. Due to the radical stylistic departure from the old style of carving, the genre has often been thought to have derived from modern European art forms. The evidence, however, points instead to a series of internal developments that have been encouraged, but not initiated, by external patronage. Because the Mozambican Makonde work in small kinship-based groups, the innovations of one artist are quickly picked up by others. This has resulted in a number of substyles of *shetani* figures traceable to individual carvers. A 'driftwood', or intentionally unfinished, style had a short life in the 1970s, but the better-known openwork, lattice-like style continued into the 1990s, as did the *ujamaa* family tree in the *binadamu* genre. Almost all *shetani* figures, as indeed almost all *binadamu* and *ujamaa* sculptures, are executed in African Blackwood (*Dalbergia melanoxylon*), often referred to as ebony.

A few sculptors have achieved international status as a result of their inclusion in major exhibitions. Works by John Fundi (1939–1991), for example, were exhibited in the *Magiciens de la Terre* exhibition (Paris, Pompidou, 1989). 'Makonde-style' paintings have also been produced. Works of this type by Georges Lilanga di Nyama (*b* 1934) were included in the *Out of Africa* exhibition (London, Saatchi Col.) in 1992. While the Makonde have invented several new forms for non-Makonde patrons, they have not extended this to their *mapiko* masks, which continue to be reserved for ritual use and to be carved from soft, light wood using the old style conventions.

BIBLIOGRAPHY

K. Weule: *Wissenschaftliche Ergebnisse meiner ethnographischen Forschungs-reise in den Südosten Deutsch-Ostafrikas*, Mitteilungen aus den Deutschen Schutzgebieten, Ergänzungsheft, 1 (Berlin, 1908); Eng. trans. by A. Werner as *Native Life in East Africa: The Results of an Ethnological Research Expedition* (London, 1909)
A. J. Dias: *Portuguese Contribution to Cultural Anthropology* (Johannesburg, 1961), chaps 2 and 3
J. Dias and M. Dias: *Vida social e rituel*, iii of *Os Macondes de Moçambique* (Lisbon, 1964–70)
W. Korabiewicz: *African Art in Polish Collections* (Warsaw, 1966)
J. A. Stout: *Modern Makonde Sculpture* (Nairobi, 1966)
H. Pollig, ed.: *Makonde: Eine ostafrikanische Dokumentation* (Stuttgart, 1971) [comprehensive bibliog.]
J. A. R. Wembah-Rashid: '*Isinyago* and *Midimu*: Masked Dancers of Tanzania and Mozambique', *Afr. A.*, iv/2 (1971), pp. 38–44
S. L. Kasfir: 'Patronage and Maconde Carvers', *Afr. A.*, xiii/3 (1980), pp. 67–70, 91–2
Art makondé: Tradition et modernité (exh. cat., Paris, Min. Affaires Etrangères, 1989–90)
Wooden Sculpture from East Africa from the Malde Collection (exh. cat., Oxford, MOMA; Plymouth, City Mus. & A.G.; Preston, Harris Mus. & A.G.; and elsewhere; 1989–90)
S. L. Kasfir: 'African Art and Authenticity: A Text with a Shadow', *Afr. A.*, xxv/2 (1992), pp. 40–53, 96–7

SIDNEY LITTLEFIELD KASFIR

Makoto Suzuki. *See* SUZUKI, MAKOTO.

Makovecz, Imre (*b* Budapest, 20 Nov 1935). Hungarian architect. In 1959 he graduated from the Technical University of Building and Transport Engineering, Budapest, and then worked for the state architectural offices BUVÁTI (1959–62) and SZÖVTERV (1962–71), both in Budapest. His early works, such as the Csákányosi Tavern (1968), Tatabánya, reflect the influence of Frank Lloyd

Makonde *shetani* figure sculpture by Dastani, wood, h. *c.* 600 mm, *c.* 1964 (Dar es Salaam, private collection)

Wright and Rudolf Steiner. After 1969, with others, he began studying human movement and its spatial contours, and he based his competition work 'Minimal Space' (1972; unexecuted) and the interior of the Funeral Hall (1974–7; with Gábor Mezei, b 1935), Farkasréti Cemetery, Budapest, on this research. While working in the state design architectural office VÁTI (1971–7) he designed the Cultural Centre (1974–7), Sárospatak, one of the most original post-war Hungarian buildings, whose U-shaped plan is inspired by the urban context. This partly two-storey, symmetrical building is dominated by the moulded, wave-shaped tiled roof. Above the main entrance the eye-shaped motifs of the balconies emphasize the centre of the façade. The roof interiors are wooden-beamed and supported by buttresses branching off columns, like branches of a tree. He was also concerned with Hungarian folk art and the legacy of Ödön Lechner and Károly Kós. The Leisure Centre (1977–9), Visegrád, is a simple, curved, wooden structure with a shingled roof and draws on his study of vernacular ornament. Rejecting the alienating and inhuman aspects of 20th-century architecture Makovecz created a unique, largely wood-based architecture derived from human and natural forms, even introducing branching tree trunks as supports for the structure of the Cultural Centre (1981), Zalaszentlászló, and Gubcsi Villa (1986), Budapest. He lectured at the Union of Hungarian Architects in Budapest (1971–3, 1982–4, 1986–8) and in 1984 he started an independent partnership, Makona, with Ágnes Kravár (b 1948) and Ervin Nagy (b 1950). Makoverz designed a number of village community centres, such churches as the Lutheran church (1986–90), Siófok and the Roman Catholic church (1988–90), Paks, and the Hungarian Pavilion (1990–92) for Expo' 92, Seville.

BIBLIOGRAPHY
Contemp. Architects
A. Komjáthy: *Makovecz Imre* (Budapest, 1977)
Makovecz Imre, intro. by J. Frank (Budapest, 1980)
Imre Makovecz, Hongaars architect [Imre Makovecz, Hungarian architect] (exh. cat., ed. T. Boersma; Rotterdam, Ned. Architectuurinst., 1989)
ÁKOS MORAVÁNSZKY, KATALIN MORAVÁNSZKY-GYÖNGY

Makovets. Association of Russian painters and graphic artists active in Moscow from 1921 to 1926. The name is that of the hill at Sergiyev Posad, on which the monastery of the Trinity and St Sergius, a centre of Russian Orthodoxy, is located, although until 1924 the group was known as the 'Art is Life' Union of Artists and Poets (Rus. Soyuz khudozhnikov i poetov 'Iskusstvo–zhizn'). Sergey Gerasimov, Lev F. Zhegin (1892–1969), Konstantin K. Zefirov (1879–1960), Vera Ye. Pestel' (1896–1952), Sergei M. Romanovich (1894–1968), Artur Fonvizin, Vasily Chekrygin, Nikolai M. Chernyshov (1885–1973), Aleksandr Shevchenko and others joined the association. They were greatly influenced by the aesthetics of Pavel Florensky, who was the spiritual leader of the group.

In 1922 two editions of a magazine, *Makovets*, were published, although the third issue was censored and exists only in manuscript. The members of Makovets criticized the avant-garde because, in their opinion, it was engaged solely in 'producing individual elements of form', which excluded the 'spiritual essence of the artist'; instead they proclaimed 'the end of analytical art' in favour of a new development and advocated uniting separate artistic elements 'in a powerful synthesis' (from 'Nash prolog' [Our prologue], *Makovets*, i). They believed that realism formed the basis of creative work, not narrow empirical realism but realism enriched with vivid religious experience. They based their ideas not on the medieval icon but rather on the art of the Renaissance, the Russian religious romanticism of the 19th century and the Symbolism of the early 20th. Most Makovets images contain an intimate, lyrical emotionality that borders on a mystical vision, as in Chekrygin's cosmic fantasies. The group's romantic idealism influenced a particular type of 'unofficial' realism distinguishable by its spiritual sincerity.

BIBLIOGRAPHY
Makovets, i–ii (1922)
B. Berman: 'Obshchestvo "Makovets"' [The Makovets association], *Tvorchestvo* (1980), no. 3, pp. 16–18
A. Kovalev: 'Makovets', *Iskusstvo* (1987), no. 12, pp. 32–41
Makovets, 1922–6: Sbornik materialov po istorii ob'yedineniya [Makovets, 1922–6: a collection of materials on the group's history], ed. Y. A. Ilyukhina and others (Moscow, 1994)
M. N. SOKOLOV

Makovsky. Russian family of artists. Yegor Makovsky (1800–86) was co-founder of the Moscow School of Painting, Sculpture and Architecture. His sons (1) Konstantin Makovsky, Nikolay Makovsky (1842–86) and (2) Vladimir Makovsky were all painters; Vladimir's daughter (4) Yelena Makovskaya-Luksh was a painter, sculptor and designer, while his son (3) Sergey Makovsky was an art critic.

(1) Konstantin (Yegorovich) Makovsky (*b* Moscow, 2 July 1839; *d* Petrograd [now St Petersburg], 30 Sept 1915). Painter. He produced historical and social scenes, as well as being a portrait painter of some renown, although his significance lies more in the role he played as a founder-member of the WANDERERS art society in late 19th-century Russia. He studied first at the Moscow School of Painting and Sculpture (1851–8), which had been co-founded by his father Yegor Ivanovich Makovsky (1800–86), under Mikhail Ivanovich Skotti (1814–61) and Sergey Konstantinovich Zaryanko, then from 1858 to 1863 at the Petersburg Academy of Arts. In 1862 he was awarded a Minor Gold Medal, but the following year, together with 13 other students, Makovsky rebelled against the theme set for the Grand Gold Medal competition and left the Academy with the title of Artist of the Second Degree. In 1863 he joined the Petersburg Artel of artists, the forerunner of the Wanderers and the most potent symbol of the break with classical tradition. The reversal of official policy that this engendered led to his being made an academician in 1867, in 1869 a professor and in 1898 a full member of the Academy. As a member of the Wanderers, Makovsky was most notable for his new subject-matter, namely the common people. However, he split with the society in 1883 and by 1891 had become a member of the newly formed and more Salon-orientated St Petersburg Society of Artists, of which he was subsequently to be president. Makovsky often veered towards sentimentalism, giving his works a cloying pathos, as in his portrait of the *Stasov Children* (early 1870s) and *Children Fleeing the Storm* (1872), or creating almost caricatured stylizations, as in the *Shrove-tide Fete on Admiralty Square, St Petersburg* (1869; all St Petersburg, Rus. Mus.).

BIBLIOGRAPHY
L. Tarasov: *K. Ye. Makovsky* (Moscow, 1948)
L. Pomytkina: *K. Makovsky: Vozzvanie Minina* [K. Makovsky: Minin's appeal] (Gor'ky (now Nizhniy Novgorod), 1978)

JEREMY HOWARD

(2) Vladimir (Yegorovich) Makovsky (*b* Moscow, 7 Feb 1846; *d* Petrograd [now St Petersburg], 21 Feb 1920). Painter, brother of (1) Konstantin Makovsky. He studied at the Moscow School of Painting, Sculpture and Architecture from 1861 to 1866 under Sergey Zaryanko and other artists. From 1872 Makovsky was a member of the WANDERERS (Peredvizhniki). In his early pictures, Makovsky usually portrayed contemporary manners and morals in a spirit of gentle irony, as in the *Lovers of Nightingales* (1872–3; Moscow, Tret'yakov Gal.). Such works reveal Makovsky's skill in defining precisely and carefully the role of each figure in the scene. In the mid-1870s Makovksy began to concentrate on the central theme of most of his subsequent work: the glaring social contrasts of Russian life. Through this theme he was able to give frank expression to his populist convictions and his sympathy for the world of the humble and downtrodden.

The most successful of Makovsky's mature paintings can be seen as dramatic but sophisticated 'urban novellas'. They deal with the sinister power of money, as in the *Bank Failure* (1881); with motherly love, as in *The Meeting* (1883; both Moscow, Tret'yakov Gal.), showing the meeting of a peasant woman and her son who has been sent off to study in the town; or with the ruin of a family and ensuing tragic estrangement, as in *On the Boulevard* (1886–7; Moscow, Tret'yakov Gal.), where the main characters are a tipsy factory hand playing the accordion and his despairing, downtrodden young wife. In a series of paintings from the end of the 1880s and the beginning of the 1890s Makovsky came close to the principles of *plein-air* painting as, for example, in the lyrical *Explanation* (1889–91; Moscow, Tret'yakov Gal.), which shows a dialogue between two lovers in an interior flooded with varying strengths of daylight through open doors and windows.

Makovsky made a considerable contribution to the developing iconography of the Russian revolutionary movement. Combining truth to appearances with psychological insight, he painted the exalted members of a group of liberal intelligentsia in the picture of the *Evening Party* (1875–97; Moscow, Tret'yakov Gal.), a canvas on the subject of the *Interrogation of the Female Revolutionary* (1904; Moscow, Cent. Mus. Revolution). Makovsky also painted portraits and illustrated books.

BIBLIOGRAPHY
G. A. Druzhenkova: *Vladimir Makovsky* (Moscow, 1962)
Ye. V. Zhuralova: *V. Ye. Makovsky* (Moscow, 1972)

M. N. SOKOLOV

(3) Sergey (Konstantinovich) Makovsky (*b* St Petersburg, 15 Aug 1877; *d* Paris, 13 May 1962). Art critic and historian, son of (2) Vladimir Makovsky. He was a leading figure in the poetic and artistic circles around the WORLD OF ART movement. He was a founder and editor of the journals *Staryye gody* (1907–17) and *Apollon* (1909–17). After the October Revolution of 1917, Makovsky emigrated to Czechoslovakia and there wrote *Siluety russkikh khudozhnikov* (Profiles of Russian artists, Prague, 1922) and *Narodnoye iskusstvo pod-karpatskoy Rusi* (Folk art of Sub-Carpathian Rus, Prague, 1925). He edited the literary-artistic section of the newspaper *Vozrozhdeniye* in 1926–32. In Paris after World War II he edited miscellanies of Russian émigré poetry and contributed to émigré newspapers and journals, being perhaps the foremost art critic of Russian emigration. He also published reminiscences, *Portrety sovremennikov* (Portraits of contemporaries, New York, 1955) and *Na Parnase 'Serebryanogo Veka'* (On the Parnassus of the 'Silver Age', Munich, 1962).

WRITINGS
Siluety russkikh khudozhnikov [Profiles of Russian artists] (Prague, 1922)
Narodnoye iskusstvo pod-karpatskoy Rusi [Folk art of Sub-Carpathian Rus] (Prague, 1925; Eng. trans., Prague, 1926)
Portrety sovremennikov [Portraits of contemporaries] (New York, 1955)
Na Parnase 'Serebryanogo Veka' [On the Parnassus of the 'Silver Age'] (Munich, 1962)

BIBLIOGRAPHY
Yu. Annenkov: Obituary, *Vozrozhdeniye*, cxxvi (June 1962), pp. 64–5
K. Pomerantsev: Obituary, *Mosty*, ix (1962), pp. 382–5

E. KASINEC, R. H. DAVIS JR

(4) Yelena (Konstantinovna) Makovskaya-Luksh [Luksch-Makowsky] (*b* St Petersburg, 13 Nov 1878; *d* Hamburg, 15 Sept 1967). Painter, sculptor, illustrator and designer, daughter of (2) Vladimir Makovsky. She studied in St Petersburg, first at the Tenisheva Drawing School (mid-1890s) and then briefly at the Academy of Arts, where she was taught painting by Il'ya Repin and sculpture by Vladimir Beklemishev (1861–1920). In 1898 she received a grant from the pacifist Jan Gotlib Bloch (1836–1902) for foreign study. She moved to Munich where she studied, simultaneously with Vasily Kandinsky, Alexey Jawlensky and Mstislav Dobuzhinsky, at Anton Ažbe's studio. She married the Austrian sculptor Richard Luksch (1872–1967) and the couple moved to Vienna, where Makovskaya-Luksh was the first female member of the Vienna Secession and a participant in the pioneering design cooperative Wiener Kunst im Hause.

As a permanent member of the WIENER WERKSTÄTTE from 1905, she made high-quality decorated fans, painted caskets, embossed silver and metal panels. Her other work included colour-glaze pottery reliefs on the theme of *Melpomene and her Choir* for the Vienna Bürgtheater (1905; now Hamburg, Mus. Kst & Gew.), as well as postcard designs and graphics for the periodicals *Ver Sacrum* and *Der lieber Augustin*. Around 1906 a Primitivist tendency emerged in her graphic art, first in her multi-figured illustrations to François Rabelais's *Gargantua* (1906–8; Hamburg, Ksthalle), then in her use of the Russian *lubok* print in her designs for a cycle of illustrated Russian proverbs (1908; Heusinger von Waldegg and Leppien, figs 74–95). Makovskaya-Luksh participated in numerous exhibitions, showing her painting, graphic art, sculpture and applied art designs in Vienna and St Petersburg between 1901 and 1912. She exhibited the symbolist painting *Adolescence* (now Vienna, Belvedere) at the 18th exhibition of the Vienna Secession in 1903. In 1907 she moved permanently to Hamburg where she taught at the Kunstgewerbeschule.

BIBLIOGRAPHY
J. Heusinger von Waldegg and H. Leppien: *Richard Luksch, Elena Luksch-Makowsky* (Hamburg, 1979)

JEREMY HOWARD

Makovský, Vincenc (*b* Nové Město, Moravia [now Czech Republic], 3 June 1900; *d* Brno, 28 Dec 1966). Czech sculptor. He studied at the Academy of Arts in Prague (1919–26), and he worked with Emile-Antoine Bourdelle in Paris from 1926 to 1930. In 1934 he co-founded the Surrealist group in Czechoslovakia. He taught at the Academy of Arts in Prague from 1952. His early work was influenced by Cubism, and especially by the work of Brancusi and Arp, as can be seen in *Sculpture on Fountain* (1930; Litomyšl, Reg. Mus.) and *Head* (1926–7; Prague, N.G., Zbraslav Castle), which counteracted the conventionality of Czech sculpture and concentrates on elementary shapes. The work *Torso* (1929; Hluboká nad Vltavou, Áléš Gal.) displays a wilfulness and animality that led, in the relief *Reclining Woman* (1929–30; Prague, N.G., Zbraslav Castle) with its brutal incorporation of metal hooks, to the disintegration of the figure. In 1933 Makovský produced *Relief* (Prague, N.G., Zbraslav Castle), an assemblage of cork, wax, paper, string and matches, which initiated a new period in Czech sculpture. Work from the Surrealist period of the early 1930s progressed towards a return to the Classical ideal, which reached a climax in the figural fountain for the square in Mělník (1935–8) and in the monument to *Comenius* (1957; Bethlehem, PA, Archv Morav. Church). After producing numerous effigies and statues, Makovský, following World War II, produced work on themes such as the *Victory of the Red Army over Fascism* (1955; Brno, Moravian Square). His strong sense of sculptural form and his synthetic ability ensured him an outstanding place in Central European art in the 20th century.

BIBLIOGRAPHY
J. B. Svrček: *Moderní výtvarné umění na Moravě* [Modern fine art in Moravia] (Brno, 1933), pp. 78–82
V. M. Nebeský: *L'Art moderne tchécoslovaque* (Paris, 1937), pp. 147–8
Vincenc Makovský (exh. cat., text M. Juříková; Prague, N.G., 1985)

JAROSLAV SEDLÁŘ

Makowski, Tadeusz (*b* Oświęcim [Auschwitz], 29 Jan 1882; *d* Paris, 1 Nov 1932). Polish painter, active in France. He studied at the Academy of Fine Arts in Kraków (1903–8) under Jan Stanisławski and Józef Mehoffer. From 1909 until his death he lived in Paris. Initially he painted landscapes, and he arrived at his own style via Post-Impressionism (1906–9) and Cubism (1912–14). Throughout his career his consistently flat, synthetic and rigorous composition, which was linear in his early works, began gradually to change into arrangements of simple, cubic bodies. Initially the rural landscape genre characteristic of the Kraków school was intensified and developed into poetic metaphors, timeless rural scenes composed with refined simplicity, at times resembling the work of Pieter Bruegel the elder (e.g. *Winter, c.* 1918; Warsaw, N. Mus.).

Makowski's most successful and best-known pictures (1925–32) are representations in which the main protagonists are doll-like children participating in concerts, masquerades and mysterious festivities, playing simple instruments and resembling their own toys. The laconic compositions assembled from cones, squares and circles are often grotesque portraits of child pierrots (e.g. *Village Concert*, 1922; Warsaw, N. Mus.). Their effect of transience is created with bright, transparent pastel tones that are darker in the interior scenes, and they often resemble puppet versions of Flemish genre painting (e.g. *Children at Table*, 1929; Paris, Mus. A. Mod. Ville Paris). The composition and mood alter when adults feature in the pictures. Makowski went on to produce portraits of character types (e.g. *The Shoemaker*, 1930; Warsaw, N. Mus.) and genre scenes.

WRITINGS
W. Jaworska, ed.: *Pamiętnik* [Diary] (Warsaw, 1961)

BIBLIOGRAPHY
W. Jaworska: *Tadeusz Makowski: Ein polnischer Maler in Paris* (Dresden, 1975)
——: *Tadeusz Makowski: Życie i twórczość* [Tadeusz Makowski: life and work] (Wrocław, 1976)

EWA MIKINA

Makowski, Zbigniew (*b* Warsaw, 31 Jan 1930). Polish painter, draughtsman and poet. He studied at the Academy of Fine Arts in Warsaw (1950–56) under the painter Kazimierz Tomorowicz (1893–1961). His first works, such as *An Interior with a Stool* (1956; Warsaw, N. Mus.), were paintings influenced by Polish Colourism, though he also made structural compositions of plaster casts with metal and wooden elements. He abandoned these experiments and in the 1960s began to explore the mysterious world of magic, astrology and the cabbala (e.g. *Vertical Garden*, 1961–2; Wrocław, N. Mus.). His calligraphic compositions, which he described as 'letters written to unknown addressees', make use of graphic signs, numerals, letters and geometrical figures. Meticulously executed in various techniques, such as ink on parchment or oil on panel, these compositions convey a whole range of symbolic meanings. They are bordered with long, written texts that introduce the artist's philosophical thoughts on existence and our cultural traditions, and evoke the world of pagan beliefs and Greek mythology, as in *Image* (1965; Wrocław, N. Mus.). He also painted Surrealist compositions with motifs of city landscapes, as in *Horizon of Consciousness* (1968; Warsaw, N. Mus.). With a similar multitude of graphic signs and the same care for detail, he created colourful images of an imaginary world. Inspired by literature, he included in some of his paintings appropriate quotations, for example from Homer.

BIBLIOGRAPHY
M. Hermansdorfer: 'Zbigniew Makowski', *Odra*, xii/5 (1972), pp. 83–5
Zbigniew Makowski (exh. cat., Wrocław, N. Mus., 1978)

ANNA BENTKOWSKA

Makron. *See* VASE PAINTERS, §II.

Maks, Cornelis Johannes [Kees] (*b* Amsterdam, 22 Aug 1876; *d* Amsterdam, 28 Oct 1967). Dutch painter and watercolourist. He lived in Amsterdam until 1901 and attended the Rijksakademie. He did not, however, complete his training, but Georg Hendrik Breitner taught him further. In 1901 Maks became a member of the artists' society Arti et Amicitiae, and he later joined the Nederlandsche Aquarellistenkring and the Nederlands Kunstenaarsgenootschap (Dutch Artists' Society). He lived and worked in Paris (1901–3), Spain (1903–4) and Rome (1904–5). In the latter city he regularly worked with Antonio Mancini. From 1907 he exhibited regularly at such painters' societies as the Onafhankelijken (Dut.: Independents) and St Lucas. He also took part in international exhibitions, including those of the Munich Secession (1910, 1911, 1912 and 1914) and the Salon d'Automne in Paris from 1910 to 1940; with his friend Kees van Dongen, he became particularly well known in France. He had a number of one-man shows, for example at Galerie Visconti (1924), at Durand-Ruel (1925, 1927, 1928 and 1930) and at Bernheim-Jeune in 1931. Various plans to settle in Paris did not, however, materialize.

Maks preferred to paint cheerful subjects such as circus scenes with clowns and dancers, for example *Clowns: The Three Fratellinis* (oil on canvas, *c.* 1920; Haarlem, Frans Halsmus.). In their broad brushstrokes and sometimes excessively strong colouring, many of his paintings, such as the *Furlane* (oil on canvas, *c.* 1913) and the *Painter and his Model* (oil on canvas, *c.* 1936; both Amsterdam, Stedel. Mus.), reflect the vital urge of the period and especially of the 'roaring twenties'.

Scheen

BIBLIOGRAPHY
H. Redeker and A. Venema: *C. J. Maks* (Amsterdam, 1976) [extensive bibliog.]

G. JANSEN

Maksimov, Vasily (Maksimovich) (*b* Lopino, nr Novaya Ladoga, St Petersburg region, 29 Jan 1844; *d* St Petersburg, 1 Dec 1911). Russian painter. The son of a peasant, he studied in the school for monastery novices and apprentice icon painters and entered the St Petersburg Academy of Arts in 1863. He had a passion for drawing and a strong sympathy with the growing tendency in Russian art towards realism and social criticism. He retained a deep relationship with the Russian countryside, and the life of the peasantry formed an important and constant theme in his work. In 1866, having completed the course of academic instruction, and following Ivan Kramskoy and the 'secession of the 14' in 1863, Maksimov refused to compete for the Grand Gold Medal and the right to a bursary for foreign travel, and he moved to a residence in the country, first in Tver' province, then from 1868 in the village of Chernavino in Novaya Ladoga district. Here Maksimov began enthusiastically producing pictures of the Russian peasantry, in whom he felt he found the living source of truth. In the painting *Grandmother's Tales* (1867; Moscow, Tret'yakov Gal.) the faces and poses of the peasants, fascinated by the old woman's stories, are filled with great human dignity. In 1872 Maksimov became a member of the WANDERERS. This was the period of his creative maturity and of his strong influence on Russian art. In 1875 he produced his most notable work, the *Arrival of the Sorcerer at the Peasant Wedding* (Moscow, Tret'yakov Gal.), a major work of Russian realism. It opened up new perspectives and surpassed his previous experiments. The psychological

Vasily Maksimov: *It's All in the Past*, oil on canvas, 720×935 mm, 1889 (Moscow, Tret'yakov Gallery)

intimacy of Maksimov's depictions found a powerful collective response, and it became characteristic of later works by the Wanderers. The poeticization of peasant life lost its earlier sweetness and ceased to be the object of a somewhat detached admiration, becoming instead an interweaving of fantasy and reality, beauty and squalor, the poetic and prosaic. For this picture and the picture the *Division of the Family* (1876; Moscow, Tret'yakov Gal.) Maksimov was awarded the title of Academician.

In the second half of the 1870s Maksimov's creative approach to the depiction of contemporary peasant life moved in an increasingly critical direction. Thus in the *Division of the Family* he showed, with candour and without embellishment, the cruel drama of the break-up of patriarchal family connections in Russia. The *Sick Husband* (1881; Moscow, Tret'yakov Gal.) shows the tragic fate of a poor peasant family losing its breadwinner. But even here the artist does not fail to notice purity of feelings, facial beauty and graceful movement in the peasant characters. In the 1880s, as before, Maksimov spent a large part of the time in the country, but he also travelled a great deal in the Volga regions, in Chernihiv and Kiev provinces and spent time in the Pskov area, where he drew landscapes on the Mikhaylovskoye and Trigorskoye estates, celebrating A. S. Pushkin's stays there. The most successful picture of this period is *It's All in the Past* (1889; Moscow, Tret'yakov Gal.; see fig.), an ironic description of the sad end of aristocratic estates, which outlive by centuries their once rich and distinguished owners, a picture that Maksimov repeated many times. In the 1890s there was a crisis in Maksimov's work; he had not understood the conflicts of the new era and was unable to find in the changing conditions and new artistic developments a role for his idealism. He stopped taking part in exhibitions and almost ceased to work, but the influence of his poetic approach to the life of the Russian peasantry re-emerged, although indirectly, in the work of several artists of the turn of the century who devoted themselves to this theme, in particular Andrey Ryabushkin.

WRITINGS
'Avtobiograficheskiye zapiski, s predisloviyem I. Ye. Repina' [Autobiographical sketches, with the assistance of I. Ye. Repin], *Golos minuvshego* (1913), nos 4–7

BIBLIOGRAPHY
A. Leonov: *Vasily Maksimovich Maksimov: Zhizn' i tvorchestvo* [Vasily Maksimovich Maksimov: life and work] (Moscow, 1951)
A. K. Lazuko: *Vasily Maksimov, 1844–1911* (Leningrad, 1982)

L. I. IOVLEVA

Malacca [Melaka]. Malaysian city and port. Strategically situated on the east coast of the Straits of Malacca, 147 km south-east of Kuala Lumpur and 245 km north of Singapore, Malacca was founded *c.* 1400 by a prince called Parameswara (*reg c.* 1400–24), who may have been a fugitive from Sumatra. The evidence of Chinese and Malay sources suggests that he was later converted to Islam and took the name of Iskandar Shah. During the 15th century Malacca became under its Muslim rulers the richest and most cosmopolitan entrepôt in South-east Asia and a major centre for the dissemination of Islam.

In 1511 Malacca was conquered by a small Portuguese force commanded by Afonso de Albuquerque. Making use of stones from the sultan's palace and the mosques that they had destroyed, the Portuguese constructed a fortress known as A Famosa, with walls 2.4 m thick, encircling the hill that later became St Paul's Hill. They held the city until 1641, when it was captured by the Dutch after a five months' siege. It remained a Dutch possession until 1795 when it was occupied by the British. In 1814 it was restored to Dutch rule, but under the terms of the Anglo-Dutch treaty of 1824 it was transferred permanently to Britain in exchange for Bengkulu (Bencoolen) in Sumatra. Under British rule, Malacca was one of the constituent crown colonies of the Straits Settlements, together with Penang and Singapore. In 1957 the Malay States and the Straits Settlements achieved independence in the Malayan Union, and in 1963 Malacca became one of the states of the Federation of Malaysia.

Nothing remains of the Malacca of the sultans before the Portuguese conquest, but the great wooden palace of Sultan Mansur Shah (*reg* 1458–77) has been imaginatively reconstructed from a detailed description in the Malay Annals (*Sejarah Melayu*), and it opened in 1984 as a museum with a display of Malay arts and a series of dioramas illustrating Malay court life in the 15th century. Of the various churches, palaces and public buildings built by the Portuguese within the walls of A Famosa, only the church of St Paul remains on the top of the hill of the same name. First built in 1512 and rebuilt by Duarte Coelho (*d* 1554) in 1521, probably on the site of an earlier Malay palace, and originally dedicated to Our Lady of the Assumption, the church was first used as a fort and an arsenal by the Dutch, then abandoned, and is now a roofless ruin. Against the walls are a number of finely carved granite tombstones of 16th-century Portuguese and 17th- and 18th-century Dutch settlers.

In 1807 the British completely destroyed all the Portuguese fortifications except for the south-eastern gate, known as the Santiago Gate, which had been reconstructed by the Dutch *c.* 1670 and adorned with a Dutch coat of arms and the cipher of the Dutch East India Company (VOC), and even this was only saved as a result of the direct intervention of Stamford Raffles. The most important buildings dating from the Dutch period are in the town square, often known as Red Square because of the distinctive red colour of the plaster covering the buildings surrounding it. On the east side of the square is the Stadthuys (1650), a three-storey brick building with external staircases giving access from the street to a verandah at first-floor level. It was formerly the town hall and the residence of the Dutch governor and is now a historical museum. On the north side is Christ Church (1753), a rather plain rectangular building built with bricks imported from the Netherlands; its triple-arched porch was added in the 19th century. It contains fine carved wooden pews, a brass lectern dated 1773 and other church furniture, and several 18th- and 19th-century Portuguese, Dutch and Armenian tombstones set into the floor. On the east side is the Post Office building, which has arcades and a Dutch gable.

The oldest Roman Catholic church in Malaysia still in use is St Peter's Church in the Bunga Raya district. It is used by the descendants of the Portuguese settlers who live in the Portuguese Settlement (founded 1930). Built in a curvilinear Baroque style with some Indian elements, characteristic of Portuguese architecture in Goa and Macau, it has a separate campanile containing a bell cast in Goa in 1608. The most important of the early mosques is the Terengkea Mosque on the western outskirts of the city, which was built in 1728, destroyed by the Dutch in 1756 during the Dutch–Bugis War and rebuilt in 1856 (*see* MALAYSIA, §II, 1(ii) and fig. 2). It has a three-tiered roof derived from Hindu–Javanese models and contains a notable wooden pulpit. The Kampung Keling Mosque (1748) in Jalan Tukang Emas also has a three-tiered roof and a hexagonal minaret. The pillars in the prayer-hall have Ionic capitals, and the walls are decorated with Portuguese glazed tiles. From the carved wooden ceiling hangs a fine Victorian chandelier. The mid-17th century Cheng Hoon Teng Temple is the oldest Chinese temple in Peninsular Malaysia. It has tiled roofs garishly and elaborately decorated with flowers and birds made of coloured glass and porcelain. The main hall is surrounded by four open courtyards. It is dedicated to Kwan Yin, the goddess of mercy, but it also contains Daoist, Buddhist and Confucian altars. The Sri Poyotha Vinayagar Moorthi Temple in Jalan Tukang Emas, Kampung Keling, is probably the oldest Hindu temple in Malaysia. It is built on land given by the Dutch authorities in 1781 to the Chittys, a community of Hindu south Indians settled in Malacca since the 15th century.

The community of people of Chinese descent known as Straits Chinese, Baba Nyonya or *peranakan* that emerged in Malacca in the 17th century and later in Penang and Singapore adopted an eclectic style of domestic architecture derived from the Chinese two-storey shop house (*see* MALAYSIA, §II, 2(ii)) and characterized by narrow façades and interiors stretching back through a series of rooms, frequently decorated with carved and gilded wood and lacquer and containing collections of Straits Chinese furniture, silver and ceramics. There are numerous houses in this style, the earliest dating from the 17th century, on both sides of Jalan Tun Tan Cheng Lock (formerly Heeren Street) at the centre of the Straits Chinese quarter. One of the most opulent of these houses, numbers 48 and 50, built in 1896, the residence of the wealthy Chan family, was made into a museum and opened to the public in 1985. It has Neo-classical columns, a fine teak-wood staircase, rattan window screens and archways carved with phoenix, dragon and floral motifs.

The most important buildings of the British period are the church of St Francis Xavier, a modified Gothic building with twin towers, built in 1849, and the former Malacca Club, now the Proclamation of Independence Memorial (Memorial Pengisytiharan Kemerdekaan) in Jalan Banda Hilir immediately to the east of the Santiago Gate, built *c*. 1912. The latter building is crowned with two onion domes copied from Islamic models. Near by is Bastion House built by the Dunlop Rubber Company in 1910 and now a bank. The bridge over the Malacca River was built in the late 19th century to replace a 17th-century structure, which in turn had replaced the original bridge a short way upstream.

BIBLIOGRAPHY
M. MacDonald: 'Malacca Buildings', *J. Malay. Branch Royal Asiat. Soc.*, xii/2 (1934), pp. 27–37
R. J. Wilkinson: 'The Malacca Sultanate', *J. Malay. Branch Royal Asiat. Soc.*, xiii/2 (1935), pp. 22–69
R. O. Winstedt: 'The Malay Founder of Medieval Malacca', *Bull. SOAS*, xii/3–4 (1948), pp. 726–9
C. C. Brown, trans.: 'Sejarah Melayu or "Malay Annals"', *J. Malay. Branch Royal Asiat. Soc.*, xxv/2–3 (1953) [whole issue]
Abdullah bin Abdul Kadir: *Hikayat Abdullah*; Eng. trans., ed. A. H. Hill (Kuala Lumpur and London, 1970)
C. M. Turnbull: *The Straits Settlements, 1826–1867* (London, 1972)
K. S. Sandhu and P. Wheatley, eds: *Melaka: The Transformation of a Malay Capital*, 2 vols (Kuala Lumpur, 1983)
B. Harrison: *Holding the Fort: Melaka under Two Flags, 1795–1845*, Monographs Malay. Branch Royal Asiat. Soc., Monograph 14 (Kuala Lumpur, 1985)

JOHN VILLIERS

Málaga [Arab. Mālaqa; anc. Malaca, Malaka]. Spanish port and provincial capital on the Mediterranean coast of Andalusia, with a population of *c.* 520,000. It was of particular artistic significance during the period of Islamic rule in the region, when it was an important centre of ceramic and textile production.

1. HISTORY AND URBAN DEVELOPMENT. Málaga was founded by Phoenician traders from Tyre in the 12th century BC and subsequently (6th–5th centuries BC) became subject to Carthage. Conquered by the Romans in 205 BC, it developed into one of the most active ports in the western Mediterranean. Strong ties with Byzantium did not prevent the city from falling to the Visigoths in 571. Remains from the antique period are few. They include parts of a Phoenician fortified wall at the Alcazaba and jewellery discovered in a tomb (Madrid, Mus. Arqueol. N.). Ruins of a temple, amphitheatre and aqueduct, as well as some significant examples of sculpture (Málaga, Mus. Arqueol. Prov.), remain from the Roman period. In 711 Málaga capitulated, without resistance, to the Moorish invasion and eventually grew to become one of the most important cultural and economic centres of Islamic Spain, especially after it became the port to Granada in the 13th century. The city never surpassed the splendour that it achieved during the subsequent Grenadine rule. The Alcazaba (partially destr. 1810–12; restorations under Jean Temboury, 1930s; see fig.) is the most important extant architectural work from Muslim Mālaqa. This fortress–palace was originally built on Phoenician and Roman ruins by 'Abdul-Rahman I, Umayyad (*reg* 756–88), but was later remodelled, especially the interior palace areas, by Yahya I, Hammudid (*reg* 1021–3, 1023–36). After the Zirid dynasty of Granada conquered Mālaqa, it was rebuilt by Badis (*reg* 1038–73). The subsequent Grenadine dynasty, the Nasrids, also made improvements to the Alcazaba. Early in the 14th century, Muhammad II (*reg* 1272–1302) extensively rebuilt the fortified and living areas. Subsequently Yusuf I (*reg* 1333–54) rebuilt the nearby fortress of Castillo de Gibralfaro (destr. 1810–12; in ruins), originally erected on Phoenician remains (*c.* 787) by 'Abdul-Rahman I. Yusuf I constructed a fortified wall to link the Gibralfaro with the Alcazaba, which was itself connected to the city ramparts (the latter also rebuilt by Yusuf I; destr. after 1916). Such an articulation of military architecture made of Mālaqa one of the best fortified coastal cities in the medieval western Mediterranean. Other important architectural examples of Muslim Mālaqa include the remains of the Atarazanas (destr. 1868), constructed by

Málaga, view from the west showing the Alcazaba and the Castillo de Gibralfaro

Yusuf I in the 14th century as a naval shipyard and arsenal. One of its portals, carrying a monumental white marble pointed horseshoe arch, has survived as the main entrance to the Alfonso XII market place, which was built on the site of the Atarazanas.

Captured in 1487 by the Catholic monarchs Ferdinand II of Aragón and Isabella of Castile, Málaga thereafter declined. Of the post-Islamic period in Málaga, the artistic endeavour of highest consequence is the cathedral (1528–1783; one tower unfinished), built on a Gothic plan but with classical details on the site of the city's main mosque by Diego de Siloe and Diego de Vergara (*d* 1582). José de Bada (1691–1756) continued work on the west nave and towers in 1722, introducing Baroque details in the looming four-storey façade, and Antonio de Ramos (*d* 1782) took over in 1755. Pedro de Mena arrived from Granada in 1658 to finish the carving of the cathedral's choir-stalls (*see* MENA, PEDRO DE). After completing the commission, he took permanent residence in the city, where he was active until his death (1688). The cathedral houses paintings and sculptures of important Renaissance and Baroque Spanish masters, such as Alonso Cano's masterpiece *Virgin of the Rosary* (1665–6). The city also has important works by FRANCISCO HURTADO IZQUIERDO (*camerín*, La Virgen de la Victoria, 1693–4) and Ventura Rodríguez (S Felipe de Neri, 1778–85).

Between the 17th and the 19th centuries the urban domestic architecture of the city and its hinterland was characterized by the use of the Málaga window. These ornately carved, enclosed wooden balconies developed from the *mashribiyya* of the Muslim period and became standard features of large houses. The wooden latticework enclosing these balconies was intended as a means of safeguarding the privacy of those within. This type of enclosed balcony was also widely built in other major urban centres of Andalusia and the Spanish New World (mainly in Peru, Ecuador and Colombia). In 1893 a very ambitious project to enlarge Málaga's port was initiated by the Crown. It called for the creation of a protected foreport and an inner harbour and the construction of vast warehouses and dockyards. When finally completed two decades later, it triggered an economic renaissance. In the late 20th century Málaga was the second most important port city (after Barcelona) of the Spanish Mediterranean. The city is also significant as the birthplace of Pablo Picasso, who received his early artistic training in the city.

2. CENTRE OF PRODUCTION. Under Islamic rule Mālaqa gained international fame for its ceramic production, which included dishes, lamps, architectural ornaments and well-heads. By the 10th century *cuerda seca* wares with various coloured glazes (white, green, purplebrown, yellow and reddish ochre) were being produced.

The date of the first production of lustreware in the city is disputed, but by the mid-13th century high-quality lustrewares were being made. Pieces made for the Nasrid nobility include the Fortuny Tablet (900×440 mm; Madrid, Inst. Valencia Don Juan), made for Yusuf III (*reg* 1408–17), and a series of vases made for the Alhambra palace in Granada. Ranging from 1.2 to 1.7 m tall, they are the largest lustre pots ever found and show the potters' mastery of this difficult technique (*see* SPAIN, fig. 43). Ceramics were exported to Europe and the Middle East from the 10th century, but the most important period for production was from the mid-13th century to the late 15th. The Mālaqa wares became known internationally by the 14th century as *opus de Melica*, giving rise to the European term maiolica (*see also* ISLAMIC ART, §V, 4(iv)). Textiles, especially different-coloured silks with gold fringes (Arab. *washy*), were also widely exported to Europe.

BIBLIOGRAPHY
F. Guillén Robles: *Málaga musulmana: Sucesos, antigüedades, ciencias, y letras malagueñas durante la edad media* (Málaga, 1880/R 1980)
S. Giménez Reyna: *Memoria arquelgica de la provincia de Málaga hasta 1946* (Madrid, 1947)
A. W. Frothingham: *Lustreware of Spain* (New York, 1951)
F. Percheles: *Las calles de Málaga* (Málaga, 1955)
L. Torres Balbás: *La alcaza y la catedral de Málaga* (Madrid, 1960)
Málaga: Museo Provincial de Bellas Artes (Málaga, 1961)
A. Caiger-Smith: *Lustre Pottery* (London, 1985), pp. 84–99
F. C. Lister and R. H. Lister: *Andalusian Ceramics in Spain and New Spain: A Cultural Register from the Third Century BC to 1700* (Tucson, AZ, 1987)

FRANÇOIS-AUGUSTE DE MONTÊQUIN

Malagasy Republic. *See* MADAGASCAR.

Malaguzzi-Valeri, Francesco, Conte (*b* Reggio di Emilia, 23 Oct 1867; *d* Reggio di Emilia, 23 Sept 1928). Italian art historian. Between 1890 and 1903 he did extensive research in the archives of Modena, Bologna and Milan, collecting materials for numerous books and articles on the art of these cities and also of Reggio di Emilia. His publications typically include archival documentation and rich photographic illustrations, which make them useful and authoritative today: for example *Giovanni Antonio Amadeo, scultore e architetto lombardo* (1904) remains the most important monograph on any native Lombard sculptor; its copious illustration presents a visual cross-section of the whole of Lombard Renaissance sculpture. *La corte di Ludovico il Moro* (1913–23) complements his monograph on Amadeo by portraying other aspects of the Lombard Renaissance: private life, major and minor painters, applied arts, literature and music. His primary expertise was in the Renaissance painting and sculpture of the regions that he studied, but his range was vast, including architecture, drawing, illumination and the decorative arts. He was co-director of *Rassegna d'arte* (1901–14) and founder and Director of *Cronache d'arte* (1924–8). In 1907 he was nominated an official at the Accademia di Belle Arti di Brera in Milan. He was Director of the Pinacoteca Nazionale in Bologna (1914–24) and was the major founder of a museum of decorative arts, the Museo d'Arte Industriale e Galleria Davia–Bargellini in Bologna (1924).

WRITINGS
Giovanni Antonio Amadeo, scultore e architetto lombardo (Bergamo, 1904)
La corte di Ludovico il Moro, 4 vols (Milan, 1913–23)

BIBLIOGRAPHY
A. M. Mucchi: 'Francesco Malaguzzi Valeri, 23 ottobre 1867–23 settembre 1928', *Cron. A.*, v (1928), pp. 327–46 [extensive bibliog.]

CHARLES R. MORSCHECK JR

Malakate. Greek family of sculptors. Jacob [Yacoumis] Malakate (*b* Tinos, ?1805; *d* Munich, 1903) and his brother Frangiskos Malakate (*b* Tinos, ?1815; *d* Athens, 1914) were both self-taught, and in 1835 they opened the first sculpture workshop in Athens, the Hermoglypheion, in response to the increasing need for sculptural work for buildings and monuments in the recently founded Greek capital. Their commissions, from both Greek and foreign architects active in Athens, were mainly for decorative architectural sculpture, but also for funerary columns, reliefs, crosses and busts as well as for the restoration of antiquities. Their style remained faithful to the popular classicizing spirit of mid-19th-century Athens. Most of their surviving works are at the First Cemetery in Athens (e.g. *Koumbaris* tombstone, 1859).

BIBLIOGRAPHY
S. Lydakes: *E ellenes glyptes* [The Greek sculptors] (Athens, 1981), pp. 30–43, 384–6
C. Christou and M. Koumvakali-Anastasiadi: *Modern Greek Sculpture, 1800–1940* (Athens, 1982), pp. 27–31, 167–8

EVITA ARAPOGLOU

Malangi, David (*b* Malanga, Northern Territory, 1927). Australian Aboriginal painter. A member of the Manharrngu clan of the Jinang language group from Central Arnhem Land, Northern Territory, he spent his early life at Milingimbi Methodist Mission, an island off the coast of Arnhem Land. In addition to painting he worked with cattle and made mud bricks for the missionary Edgar Wells. In 1960 he moved from Milingimbi to the mainland, where he established a settlement beside the lake at Yathalamarra. He achieved fame as an artist when in 1966 one of his early bark paintings was used as a design on the first Australian one-dollar note. The painting had been used without acknowledgement and without permission. Subsequently Malangi was paid Aus. £1000 and awarded a medal to commemorate the event. His early paintings (e.g. *Totems from the Artist's Country*, 1965; Melbourne, N.G. Victoria) impressed the collector Karel Kupka and are well represented in European collections (e.g. Basle, Mus. Vlkerknd., and London, BM). Malangi was artist-in-residence at Flinders University of South Australia, Bedford Park (1982) and the University of Sydney (1983), and in 1988 was invited to the opening of the *Dreamings* exhibition at the Asia Society Galleries in New York, which included paintings by him. Malangi's paintings have a high figurative content and many of them focus on themes from the life of Gumirringu, the great mythological hunter, as he journeyed through Manharrngu country (e.g. *Sacred Places at Milmindjarr*, 1982; Adelaide, S. Austral. Mus.).

BIBLIOGRAPHY
D. H. Bennett: 'Malangi: The Man who Was Forgotten before he Was Remembered', *Aboriginal Hist.*, iv/1 (1980), pp. 43–7
Dreamings: The Art of Aboriginal Australia (exh. cat., ed. P. Sutton; New York, Asia Soc. Gals; U. Chicago, IL, Smart Gal.; Melbourne, Mus. Victoria; Adelaide, S. Austral. Mus.; 1988–90), pp. 53, 68, 179

W. Caruana, ed.: *Windows on the Dreaming: Aboriginal Paintings at the Australian National Gallery* (Canberra, 1989), pp. 78–80

HOWARD MORPHY

Malani, Nalini (*b* Karachi [now in Pakistan], 19 Feb 1946). Indian painter and printmaker. She studied painting at the Sir Jamshetjee Jeejebhoy School of Art, Bombay, in 1964–9; she also worked in a studio at the Bhulabhai Memorial Institute, Bombay, between 1964 and 1967 with other painters, including performing artists. On a French Government scholarship she studied in Paris in 1970–72 (producing e.g. *Painting No. 16*, oil on canvas, 1.16×1.16 m, New Delhi, N.G. Mod. A.) and participated in international exhibitions and international festivals of arts in Tokyo, Cagnes-sur-Mer, Oxford and several cities in Germany. Her work can be categorized as the portrayal of Social Realism: interpreting the life of Indian middle-class families, their surroundings and activities with an illustrative configuration and expressionistic overtones imbued with naivety.

BIBLIOGRAPHY
J. Berger: *Art and Revolution* (New York, 1969)
G. Kapur: *Nalini Malani* (New Delhi, 1982)
Nalini Malani (exh. cat. by A. Sinha, Bombay, Pundole Gal., 1984)

ANIS FAROOQI

Mälardal school. Term applied to several workshops of wall painters, active between *c.* 1400 and the 1460s in the provinces around the lake of Mälaren, Sweden, and in Finland, showing many common stylistic features. Several of the workshops display, to varying degrees, traces of the *Schöne Stil*, the German and Bohemian version of International Gothic, characterized by soft drapery folds and elegant curved figures. Another characteristic feature is a sometimes rather graceful vine ornamentation surrounding the figures. Many of the paintings, however, are of a provincial character. Among the more important painters of this school are the Master of Fogdö (*see* MASTERS, ANONYMOUS, AND MONOGRAMMISTS, §I: MASTER OF FOGDÖ; JOHANNES ROSENROD), who signed the paintings in Tensta Church, near Uppsala, in 1437; the Master of Ärentuna (*fl c.* 1435–40); and the master of the paintings in Litslena Church, which have been dated to *c.* 1470 but which show stylistic features from the early half of the century. Since most painters of this school are anonymous, very little is known about their origin, although it is likely that some of the painters were Swedish. Stylistically, the Master of Ärentuna has much in common with Master Bertram in Hamburg and may have been German. His paintings are closely related to those in Vaksala and Färentuna, near Uppsala, and in the former Franciscan church in Arboga, Västmanland. The works in the sacristy in Kalanti, Finland, can also be compared with those in Vaksala, while those in Litslena Church, near Uppsala, show stylistic similarities with a number of wall paintings in the area of Uppsala and in Södermanland, for example in Strängnäs Cathedral (1462–3). The artists of the Mälardal school certainly had common roots in Swedish 14th-century wall painting; while their work did show various different stylistic features, these overlapped and make it difficult to isolate an 'Ärentuna school' or a 'Strängnäs

school'. The shared stylistic qualities are also, to a certain degree, more characteristic of the period than the region.

BIBLIOGRAPHY
L. Wennervirta: *Suomen keskiaikainen kirkkomaalaus* [Medieval church painting in Finland] (Porvoo and Helsinki, 1937), pp. 232–4 [summary in Ger.]
B. G. Söderberg: *Svenska kyrkomålningar från medeltiden* [Swedish church paintings from the Middle Ages] (Stockholm, 1951), pls 78–81, 88–90, 109–11, 121–2, 133–5, 140
H. Cornell and S. Wallin: *Stockholmer Malerschulen des 15. Jahrhunderts* (Stockholm, 1961), pls 1–28, 37–50
A. Nilsén: *Program och funktion i senmedeltida kalkmåleri: Kyrkmålningar i Mälarlandskapen och Finland 1400–1534* [Programme and function in late medieval wall painting: church painting in the Mälaren region and Finland 1400–1534] (Stockholm, 1986), pp. 9–10, 517, 544

ANNA NILSÉN

Malatesta. Italian family of rulers and patrons. (1) Sigismondo Pandolfo Malatesta, (2) Novello Malatesta and Galeotto Roberto Malatesta (*d* 1432) were the sons of Pandolfo III Malatesta (1370–1427), a condottiere and ruler of Bergamo, Brescia and Fano. When Pandolfo died, custody of his sons passed to his brother, Carlo Malatesta (1368–1429), ruler of Rimini and Cesena. Before Carlo died he secured the legitimization of his three nephews from Pope Martin V. The final division of Carlo's estate, as well as that of Pandolfo III, was made between Sigismondo and Novello in 1432 after Galeotto Roberto's death. To Sigismondo went Fano and Rimini, the latter unquestionably the most important possession, while Novello received the less important towns of Cesena and Cervia.

(1) Sigismondo Pandolfo Malatesta (*b* Rimini, 1417; *d* Rimini, 1468). At a very young age he distinguished himself as a condottiere in the service of the papacy, and from the 1430s he was involved in many of the important military engagements on the Italian peninsula. His fortunes began to wane, however, when in 1447 he deserted Alfonso I, King of Naples and Sicily (*reg* 1416–58). This desertion, his subsequent hostilities toward the Montefeltro and Sforza families, and his disregard in 1459 of peace terms proposed by Pope Pius II severely tarnished his reputation and heralded the eventual decline of his political and military fortunes. Although he continued to provide his services as a condottiere, fighting for Venice against the Turks (1464–5), his enemies had managed to reduce his base of power to Rimini alone by the time of his death.

In addition to his numerous political and military activities, Sigismondo made Rimini into an important, albeit small, centre of Renaissance art, science and learning. As there were few artists of note in 15th-century Rimini, he awarded his commissions to artists from other cities. Initially his patronage was influenced by the artistic direction taken by the Este court in Ferrara, with which he enjoyed a political alliance through his marriage in 1434 to Ginevra d'Este, daughter of Leonello d'Este, Lord of Ferrara; in the mid-1440s Pisanello, then employed by the Este, made medals of both Sigismondo and Novello. Sigismondo was one of the first Renaissance princes to grasp the possibilities of this art form as propaganda, and he commissioned no fewer than 15 medals from Pisanello. Sigismondo was also interested in the artistic developments in Florence. Filippo Brunelleschi is recorded in

Rimini in 1438, and his presence there may have been connected with the construction of the Castel Sigismondo (1437–46), which also served as Sigismondo's residence. In 1449 Sigismondo wrote to Giovanni de' Medici requesting the services of a good painter to decorate the chapels of the Malatesta and their dependants, ostensibly in the Gothic monastic church of S Francesco at Rimini, the burial site of his ancestors. Giovanni de' Medici seems to have recommended Fra Filippo Lippi, who painted for Sigismondo a *St Sigismund* and *St Jerome* (both untraced).

Sigismondo's greatest involvement with Florentine artists came with the reconstruction and decoration of S Francesco (*see* RIMINI, §1). His modest initial plans covered only new memorial chapels (1447–50) for himself and his mistress, Isotta degli Atti, whom he married *c.* 1454. The chapels were decorated by the Florentine sculptor Agostino di Duccio and the Tuscan painter Piero della Francesca, who created the fresco of *Sigismondo Malatesta Kneeling before St Sigismund*. Before he left Rimini, probably in 1457, Agostino was also responsible for most of the sculptural decoration inside S Francesco when Sigismondo decided to expand the project. His elegantly linear sculpture, which contemporaries considered antique in style and expression, was particularly well suited to the Renaissance environment established by Sigismondo in Rimini. Another Florentine, Maso di Bartolommeo, made an iron gate (destr.) for Sigismondo's memorial chapel. The contributions made by these artists and others to the interior of S Francesco were overshadowed when Sigismondo commissioned Leon Battista Alberti, the Florentine architect and theoretician, to renovate the exterior of the church (*c.* 1450). Alberti transformed the Gothic church into the neo-Roman Tempio Malatestiano, but his concept remains unfinished, and Matteo de' Pasti's foundation medal (1450; *see* RIMINI, fig. 3) is the only record of Alberti's original design. The medal indicates the intended construction of the upper storey of the façade, flanked by segmental half pediments and culminating in a single central bay, and a large rotunda surmounted by a hemispherical dome (*see* ALBERTI, LEON BATTISTA, fig. 1). The fidelity of the medal to Alberti's project is supported by Pasti's role as the architect responsible for the actual construction of the Tempio in Alberti's absence. In style and iconography the Tempio was classical and therefore pagan: Pius II described it as 'so full of pagan images that it seems like a temple for the worshippers of demons, and not for Christians'.

Sigismondo Pandolfo Malatesta has been represented traditionally as one of the most disreputable, though highly cultured, rulers and patrons of the Italian Renaissance: 'Unscrupulousness, impiety, military skill and high culture have been seldom so combined in one individual as in Sigismondo Malatesta' (Burckhardt). More recently, while not fully exonerating him, scholars have begun to question the testimony of his detractors. He was, however, unable to make Rimini a permanent home of the arts, and its cultural distinction lapsed with his death.

(2) Novello (Domenico) Malatesta (*b* 1418; *d* 1465). Brother of (1) Sigismondo Pandolfo Malatesta. Throughout his life he was overshadowed by his elder brother in political, military and cultural activities. A scholar and bibliophile, Novello commissioned and was responsible for the construction of the Biblioteca Malatestiana (1447–52) in the convent of S Francesco, Cesena, to the designs of the Umbrian architect Matteo Nuti. Particularly noteworthy is the scriptorium, with a barrel vault that spans the central of three aisles. The Biblioteca Malatestiana bears a striking resemblance to the library of S Marco, Florence, which Michelozzo di Bartolomeo built for Cosimo de' Medici in the 1430s.

BIBLIOGRAPHY
J. Burckhardt: *Die Kultur der Renaissance in Italien* (Basle, 1860; Eng. trans., London, 1873)
C. Ricci: *Il Tempio Malatestiano* (Rimini, 1925/*R* 1974)
C. Brandi: *Il Tempio Malatestiano* (Turin, 1956)
F. Arduini and others: *Sigismondo Pandolfo Malatesta e il suo tempo* (Vicenza, 1970)
P. J. Jones: *The Malatesta of Rimini and the Papal State: A Political History* (London and New York, 1974)
J. R. Hale, ed.: *A Concise Encyclopaedia of the Italian Renaissance* (London, 1981), pp. 196–7
ROGER J. CRUM

Malatya. *See* ARSLANTEPE.

Malaval, Robert (*b* Nice, 29 July 1937; *d* Paris, 9 Aug 1980). French painter and sculptor. From 1954 to 1960 he had various jobs unrelated to art, though he began painting in 1955. In 1958 he moved to the Alpes-Maritimes where he made a number of paintings of landscape details executed in sombre colours. He first exhibited in 1961 at a one-man show at the Galleria Alphonse Chave in Venice and in 1963 moved to Paris. From 1961 to 1965 he produced a series of works forming the cycle *White Food*, which he claimed was inspired by natural phenomena. It consisted of over 120 reliefs and sculptures and 130 drawings. The reliefs and sculptures were created largely from papier-mâché, then painted white, such as *Large White Food* (1962; Paris, Pompidou). The drawings, mainly produced in the latter part of the period, often depicted curious metamorphoses and intricate patterns, as in *Five Drawings that Follow Each Other* (1963; see exh. cat., pp. 17–21).

From 1965 to 1969 Malaval worked on the *Rose, White, Mauve* cycle, a series of paintings of female nudes executed in those colours, such as *Odile* (1966; see Lascaut, p. 47). In 1973 he produced the first works in which he incorporated glitter into the paint, such as *Bill Haley* (1974; see Lascaut, p. 56). In the last three years of his life he produced the cycle *Kamikaze, End of the World*, using large brushstrokes of thinly applied paint. Malaval committed suicide in 1980.

BIBLIOGRAPHY
Robert Malaval (exh. cat. by C. Malaval and M. Sanchez, Nice, Gal. A. Contemp., 1982)
G. Lascaut: *Robert Malaval* (Paris, 1984)
                                                                    □

Malawi, Republic of [Dziko La Malawi; formerly British Nyasaland]. Country in south-eastern Africa, bordered by Mozambique to the south and east, Zambia to the west and Tanzania to the north. The capital is Lilongwe. It became independent in 1964. One third of Malawi's total area of *c.* 118,500 sq. km is covered by Lake Malawi. The mountainous country has a sub-tropical climate, and its natural vegetation ranges from tropical savannah in the north to thornbush in the south. The population of 8,022,000 (UN estimate 1989) comprises the Tonga and Tumbuka in the north, the Maravi (including the Chewa) in the centre and south of the country, the Ngoni and Yao near the southern end of the lake, and other peoples. Most of the population follow traditional religions, and almost 90% practise subsistence farming. While Arabs and Portuguese have traded along the nearby Indian Ocean coast for centuries, non-Africans in fact had little impact on the region until the 1860s when the population was decimated by the East African slave trade. In 1891 the British Protectorate of Nyasaland was founded, followed by the establishment of missions and schools. Since 1900 there has been immigration from neighbouring Mozambique as well as from Europe and Asia. This entry covers the art produced in Malawi since colonial times. For art of the region in earlier periods, *see* AFRICA, §VII, 7.

Imported goods and ideas have almost eclipsed many traditional arts. These included the carving for indigenous use of ornamented furniture, household objects, human figures and smoking pipes. There has also been a decline in the production of finger rings, bracelets and anklets made of copper, brass, iron and ivory, and of beaded headdresses, necklaces and women's waist ornaments; the latter were made of colourful beads worked into patterns. Additionally the region was once renowned for the smelting and skilful working of iron implements and weapons, and for the manufacture of cotton cloth on broad horizontal looms. Some traditional art has continued undiminished into modern times. Fine masks and extraordinary basketry and fibre constructions are produced for the Gule Wankulu (Great Dance) performances of the ancient Maravi Nyau association. Face masks are made of a variety of materials and follow well-established conventions specific for each type. Kasiyamaliro and Chimkoko are enormous fibre sculptures animated with elegance and style by dancers inside them. Women still produce pottery vessels that are often incised with patterns, covered with graphite and burnished to a lustrous black. Handwoven mats and baskets can also be found throughout Malawi. Examples of the region's art and craft traditions can be seen at the Museum of Malawi, Blantyre.

Although the visual arts were not particularly encouraged by the government before independence, their development was assisted by the establishment of the University of Malawi, Zomba, in the late 1960s. In 1967 the first university-level art courses were offered at Soche Hill College, Blantyre, this art programme eventually becoming part of the Department of Fine and Performing Arts at Chancellor College, Zomba. From 1970 the accomplished sculptor Berlings Kaunda, with an art degree from Makerere College, Kampala, Uganda, was on the faculty. With a growing international reputation, Kaunda travelled to Japan in 1991 to oversee an exhibition of his work. He has also taught some of Malawi's finest artists and teachers, including Willie Nampeya (*b* 1947). Nampeya studied in London, earned an MFA in 1981 from the Pratt Institute, New York, and returned to Chancellor College to chair the fine-art section of the Department of Fine and Performing Arts in 1982. His work (in wood, stone, clay and concrete) is sometimes on a large scale, although he often produced smaller, more intimate pieces

Willie Nampeya: *Family*, polished granite, h. 356 mm, 1990 (Blantyre, Ministry of Education)

such as *Family* (see fig.). He received commissions from the architects Oldfield and Denn for wood, sculpture and clay reliefs (1985) for the Mount Soche Hotel in Blantyre and for a figurative work, *Mother and Child* (1990–92), several metres high in terrazzo-covered cement for an office complex in Lilongwe city centre by R. S. Mthawanji and Associates. Nampeya also exhibited works in oil, pastel and other media.

Like Nampeya, the artist Kay Chiromo (*b* 1951) served as head of the fine art section at the University of Malawi. He received an MFA from the Pratt Institute in 1986, and he illustrated books and produced a documentary video. His oil paintings are irregularly shaped canvases, their surfaces sometimes built up with fabric, sand or pebbles to produce a deep relief. His paintings have been exhibited at the 1982 United States Information exhibition in Lusaka, in a one-man exhibition in 1984 at the Africa Centre, London, at the Akwaa-Harrison Gallery, Toronto, and the Workshop Platform, Durban, in 1989.

In the early 1990s opportunities for contemporary artists included exhibitions organized by the Arts and Crafts Department of the Malawi Cultural Affairs Office, by the university art faculty and students and by other art organizations and individuals. Such artists as Alice Kaunda, Louis Dimowa, N. E. Kapitapita, Cuthy Mede and Tiona Mwera were exhibiting new work regularly. Various exhibitions without catalogues were held every few weeks at the French Cultural Centre, Blantyre. In addition, the textile firm of David Whitehead and Sons employed a group of artists, coordinated by Vina Simbale, who designed printed cotton cloth with colourful patterns based on indigenous themes, for both the home and export markets. A number of Malawi artists also worked in layout and as illustrators for newspapers, books and other materials produced by the Blantyre Print and Publishing Company and its affiliates. Brian Hara (*b* 1946), whose cartoon, 'Pewani', appeared in the *Malawi News*, produced a weekly illustrated feature article, 'Kwinyani', that commented satirically on current issues. Victor Kasinja (*b* 1957) drew the 'Joza' cartoon each week for the *Daily Times*. The Malawi Council for the Handicapped published cards, stationery and calendars with designs by disabled artists. A variety of paintings, batiks, craftwork, jewellery, masks and figures are made for export and for sale to tourists. Wooden bowls, platters, candle holders, cups and chairs, often with decorative borders, were produced by carvers' cooperatives in several parts of the country.

BIBLIOGRAPHY

L. Holy: *Masks and Figures from Eastern and Southern Africa* (London, 1967)
B. Blackmun and M. Schoffeleers: 'Masks of Malawi', *Afr. A.*, v/4 (1972), pp. 36–41, 69, 88
A. Nyambo: 'About my Art', *Baraza*, 3 (April 1986), pp. 69–73
L. B. Faulkner: 'Basketry Masks of the Chewa', *Afr. A.*, xxi/3 (1988), pp. 28–31, 86
Ndiwula (1988–) [Ann. newslett. of the museums of Malawi]
K. Chiromo: 'Malawian Craft', *African Crafts*, ed. L. Melgin (Helsinki, 1990), pp. 21–6

BARBARA WINSTON BLACKMUN

Malaysia. Country in South-east Asia, consisting of a federation of 13 states, 11 of which form West Malaysia in the Malay Peninsula at the southernmost tip of the South-east Asian mainland (see fig. 1), while the two states of Sarawak and Sabah, which surround Brunei in the north of the island of Borneo (formerly British North Borneo), comprise East Malaysia, situated some 650 km across the South China Sea.

For map of Brunei and East Malaysia *see* BRUNEI, fig. 1.

I. Introduction. II. Architecture. III. City planning. IV. Sculpture. V. Painting. VI. Metalwork. VII. Textiles. VIII. Theatre. IX. Other arts. X. Non-Malay arts. XI. Art education.

I. Introduction.

1. Geography, peoples and languages. 2. History. 3. Religion, iconography and subject-matter.

1. GEOGRAPHY, PEOPLES AND LANGUAGES. Both parts of Malaysia are dominated by high mountains and heavy tropical rain forest, with habitable lowland largely confined to the coastal zone, where small rivers have built up a fringe of deposits. In northern Borneo these tend to form mangrove swamps, which give way inland to low hills backed by east–west fold mountains, rising to the granite peak of Mt Kinabalu (4101 m)—Malaysia's highest mountain—in Sabah. Towards the end of the 20th century Malaysia became one of the richest countries of South-east Asia, as the world's leading producer of natural rubber, a major exporter of tin and pepper, and as a result of economic diversification through palm oil, pineapples, and oil production and tourism. Situated on the east coast of the Straits of Malacca, West Malaysia has long benefited from its position on this major trade route between the

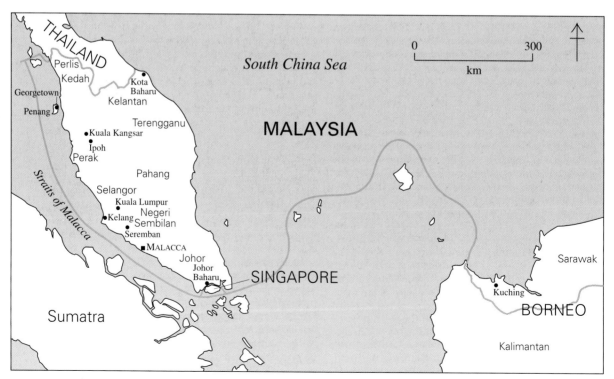

1. Map of West Malaysia; MALACCA has a separate entry in this dictionary

Indian Ocean and South-east Asia and, in consequence, has been influenced by many cultures.

Malaysia is characterized by an enormous ethnic and cultural diversity, with Malays of many different origins (47%), Chinese (34%; *see also* §II, 1(iii) below), Indians (9%) and Europeans, as well as a number of aboriginal peoples, such as the Ibans of Sarawak. The distribution, however, varies markedly between West and East Malaysia, Malays dominating the former, but the Chinese and Ibans more numerous in Sarawak. Malay is the official language of West Malaysia, with English in the East, although Chinese and Tamil are also important, and there is a wide range of lesser languages and dialects. Unfortunately, racial tensions are a problem, partly caused by the government's active promotion of Malay interests. Islam is the state religion.

BIBLIOGRAPHY
I. Carey: *Orang Asli: The Aboriginal Tribes of Peninsular Malaysia* (Kuala Lumpur, 1976)
Ooi Jin Bee: *Peninsular Malaysia* (London, 1976)

PHILIP STOTT

2. HISTORY. The extreme racial diversity of the peoples of South-east Asia is epitomized in Peninsular Malaysia, which was settled over a long period between *c.* 2500 and *c.* 1500 BC by peoples of Malay or Indonesian stock. They largely but not entirely superseded the aboriginal peoples in the area, who included the Semang and Senoi (Orang Asli), who speak Mon-Khmer languages and whose culture was originally characterized by the making of quadrangular stone adzes and unglazed cord-marked pottery. Among the earliest of these Malay migrants may have been the Jakuns (Orang Laut), who now live in the south of the Peninsula and are chiefly fishermen. During the 1st millennium BC the Bronze Age culture known as DONG SON after the type site in northern Vietnam spread throughout South-east Asia. Motifs found on Dong Son bronze artefacts occur in the traditional arts and crafts of many South-east Asian peoples, among them the Dayaks of Malaysia, and Dong Son bronze drums, bells and other objects have been found at several sites in the Peninsula including Selangor and Pahang and the lower courses of the Muar and Terengganu rivers, though it is not certain whether these were imported or manufactured locally. At about the same time trading contacts between South-east Asia and India and China were established along the maritime trade routes across the Indian Ocean and the South China Sea; the Straits of Malacca are strategically situated at the crossroads of these routes, so from an early date the Peninsula and Sumatra played an important part in the development of these links and in the dissemination of the religious and cultural influences associated with them, in particular those emanating from India.

The three earliest Indianized kingdoms of mainland South-east Asia were Funan, CHAMPA and Langkasuka, all of which date from the first two centuries AD and were located at key points along the sea route between India and China. Langkasuka, known to the Chinese as Langyaxiu, probably straddled the Peninsula from sea to sea and controlled the transpeninsular trade route. Its centre seems to have been in the Gulf of Thailand near modern Pattani, and it appears to have had close links with Kedah as well as with the port of Takola on the other side of the

Kra Isthmus, which has been tentatively identified with Takua Pa or with Trang, both now in Thailand. The presence of Buddhism in the area is attested by Buddhist inscriptions in Sanskrit dating from the 4th century and two Buddhist bronzes that may date from the 5th century found at Pengkalan Bujang on the lower reaches of the Bujang River in Kedah, and of Hinduism by Vaishnavite objects found at Kuala Selinsing in Perak. The Chinese annals describe the people of Langyaxiu as richly dressed and their cities as surrounded by brick walls and houses with double doors and pavilions. The state survived in some form or other until the 16th century.

In the 5th century AD the Sumatran kingdom of Srivijaya rose to pre-eminence. Srivijaya was a major commercial power, dominating the trade routes in the Straits of Malacca and the Sunda Straits and controlling much of Peninsular Malaysia, where its main centres were in Perak, Kedah and Perlis, and also an important centre of Mahayana Buddhism. Islam seems to have been introduced into the area as early as the late 7th century. Tombstones of that date in Perak and Terengganu inscribed with Koranic texts in Arabic may mark the burials of local inhabitants or Muslim immigrants.

The decline of Srivijaya from the 13th century was balanced by the rise of the East Javanese Hindu kingdom of Majapahit, which may have succeeded to suzerainty over Srivijaya's territories in Sumatra and the Peninsula as far north as Pattani. As early as 1275 the Javanese claimed Pahang as a dependency, and to this day there are Javanese words in the Malay dialect spoken in Kedah. In the late 14th century Majapahit claimed Tumasik (Singapore) as a dependency, but Tumasik later fell under the suzerainty of the Thai kingdom of Ayutthaya and it may have been the murder of the Thai governor of Tumasik that persuaded a Sumatran prince—whose title Parameswara means Prince Consort—and his Javanese wife to flee northwards and about 1400 to found MALACCA further up the Straits. Parameswara was converted to Islam *c.* 1414 and took the name Iskandar Shah. At first the new state of Malacca was under the suzerainty of the Thai kingdom of Ayutthaya, but until the arrival of the Portuguese its rulers maintained close ties with China. Malacca became a rich and cosmopolitan city, its prosperity based on its entrepôt trade in a wide variety of goods, especially Indonesian spices, and the leading maritime power in South-east Asia. It pursued an expansionist foreign policy, extending its control over Kedah, Pattani, the Riau and Lingga archipelagos and the riverine states of eastern Sumatra, and was an important centre for the diffusion of Islam in the Indonesian archipelago. In 1511 Malacca was conquered by the Portuguese and remained in their hands until 1641, when it was seized by the Dutch East India Company. During the 16th century, Minangkabaus from the highlands of central Sumatra crossed the Straits to settle in Negeri Sembilan north of Malacca and introduced their distinctive style of architecture into the area.

In 1786 the British gained their first foothold in Peninsular Malaysia by occupying the island of Penang. In 1819 Thomas Stamford Raffles founded SINGAPORE, and by the Anglo-Dutch treaty of 1824 Malacca was ceded to the British in exchange for Bengkulu (Bencoolen) in Sumatra. These three acquisitions formed the Straits

Settlements. During the 19th century the British gradually acquired control over the Malay sultanates of the Peninsula, in some cases by force, until 1919, when Terengganu finally accepted British rule.

In 1839 James Brooke arrived in Kuching in Sarawak from Singapore and, having successfully put down a rebellion by Illanun and Sea Dayak pirates for the sultan of Brunei, was persuaded to stay on as raja of Sarawak. Under his benign rule (*reg* 1841–68), and that of his nephew Charles (*reg* 1868–1917) and Charles's son Vyner (*reg* 1917–46), the so-called White Rajas, Sarawak enjoyed political stability and increasing prosperity based on the production of antimony, gold, pepper, oil, rubber, sago and birds' nests. Between 1882 and 1904 Sarawak added Baram, Trusan, Limbang and Lawas to its territories at the expense of Brunei. Sabah was originally shared between the sultans of Brunei and Sulu in the Philippines. In 1881, after a number of private individuals and companies had bought concessions to different parts of the territory and attempted unsuccessfully to exploit its resources of opium, timber and coal, it was finally acquired by the British North Borneo Company, which administered the territory under British government protection until 1946. Both Sarawak and Sabah have economies based chiefly on agriculture and forestry and a rich and varied culture.

During World War II both Peninsular Malaysia and Sabah and Sarawak were occupied by the Japanese. British rule was re-established in 1945, but the period of unrest that followed led in August 1957 to the independence of Malaya under its first prime minister, Tungku Abdul Rahman. In 1961 Tungku Abdul Rahman divulged his plan to bring about the unification of Malaya, Singapore, Sarawak, Brunei and Sabah in a Malaysian federation. This was a strictly political concept and was not intended to have any cultural or ethnic implications; the name Malaysia is not and never has been seen as synonymous with Malay. On 16 September 1963, in spite of hostility from Indonesia and the Philippines, the Federation of Malaysia came into being. Brunei refused to join and in 1965 the largely Chinese city of Singapore broke away to become an independent republic. The new nation developed rapidly to become one of the most stable and prosperous states in the region.

BIBLIOGRAPHY

R. J. Wilkinson: 'The Malacca Sultanate', *J. Malay. Branch Royal Asiat. Soc.*, xiii/2 (1935), pp. 22–69
R. O. Winstedt: 'A History of Malaya', *J. Malay. Branch Royal Asiat. Soc.*, xiii/1 (1935) [whole issue]; rev. as book (Singapore and New York, 1962)
——: *The Malays: A Cultural History* (Singapore, 1947/*R* 1981)
K. G. Tregonning: *Under Chartered Company Rule* (Singapore, 1958)
S. Runciman: *The White Rajahs: A History of Sarawak, 1841–1946* (Cambridge and New York, 1960)
C. D. Cowan: *Nineteenth Century Malaya: The Origins of British Political Control* (London and New York, 1961)
P. Wheatley: *The Golden Khersonese: Studies in the Historical Geography of the Malay Peninsula before AD 1500* (Kuala Lumpur, 1961/*R* 1966)
M. A. P. Meilink-Roelofsz: *Asian Trade and European Influence in the Indonesian Archipelago between 1500 and about 1630* (The Hague, 1962)
Wang Gungwu, ed.: *Malaysia: A Survey* (London and Dunmow, 1964)
B. W. Andaya and L. Y. Andaya: *A History of Malaysia* (London, 1982)
C. Leong: *Sabah: The First 100 Years* (Kuala Lumpur, 1982)
J. Ave and V. T. King: *Borneo: The People of the Weeping Forest* (Leiden, 1986)
J. Katharithamby-Wells and J. Villiers, eds: *The Southeast Asian Port and Polity: Rise and Demise* (Singapore, 1990)

3. RELIGION, ICONOGRAPHY AND SUBJECT-MATTER. The early migrants into Peninsular Malaysia were animists who worshipped ancestors and spirits and believed in the power of shamans and the sacredness of high places. Perhaps because these beliefs have much in common with Hindu Tantrism and Muslim mysticism, they have proved remarkably persistent in the face of later Hindu–Buddhist, Islamic and Western influences. Many of the non-Muslim peoples of East Malaysia are also still animists, notably the Bidayuhs (Land Dayaks) and the Melanaus of Sarawak, in spite of their proselytization by Christian missionaries in the 19th and 20th centuries and their increasing adoption of Western lifestyles. One of the tenets of Malay animism is that everything has a soul (Malay *semangat*) or a guardian spirit (*penunggu*). For example the special qualities of iron are thought to lie in its soul, so that when an iron *keris* (dagger) (see §VI, 2 below) is made special ceremonies must be performed to ensure that the virtue of the iron will remain in it and imbue it with magic powers. The *keris* smith is not merely a respected craftsman but has an almost priestly function, and his smithy becomes a sacred place. Likewise, a special knife (*tuai*) has to be used to harvest rice and handled in such a way as not to frighten the grains of rice and cause them to lose their *semangat*.

With the introduction of Indian religions into the Peninsula, Hindu incantations were adopted in these rituals. The court ceremonies of the Malay sultans still retain certain Hindu features, although, unlike Khmer and Thai rulers, the sultans do not have Brahmans at their courts. The title of the ruler of Perak, for example, can be proclaimed and his regalia handled only by a hereditary court functionary whose family is forbidden to eat beef and who claims descent from the vomit of Shiva's mount, the bull Nandi. Stories from the Hindu epics, the *Rāmāyaṇa* and *Mahābhārata*, provide much of the repertory of traditional Malay dance and drama, in particular of the shadow puppet play (*wayang kulit*), and the puppeteer makes offerings to Shiva before a performance (see §VIII, 2 below).

Islam has similarly accommodated many animist ideas, even though they are contrary to Islamic teaching, and the magic words of the ancient rituals are now taken from the Koran. Benevolent spirits are thought of as Muslims (*jin Islam*) and malevolent ones as infidels (*jin kafir*). Islamic influences on Malay dance and drama first appeared in the 15th century from India or from Java by way of Muslim Malacca, when, like the stories from the Hindu epics, Islamic stories such as the adventures of Amir Hamzah found their way into the *wayang* repertory.

Malaysia has far fewer Hindu and Buddhist monuments than most of its South-east Asian neighbours, and much of what little survives dates from the Srivijaya period (see §2 above and see also THAILAND, §II, 1(ii)). Srivijaya played a crucial part in the dissemination of Indian thought and art forms in Malaysia and western Indonesia, and Hindu and Buddhist art dating from the Srivijaya period in Malaysia shows strong affinities in form and iconography with Indian prototypes of the Gupta, post-Gupta, Pallava and Pala styles. Its main centres in the Peninsula were in Perak, Kedah and Perlis. One of the most important Hindu sites in Kedah is Candi Bukit Batu Pahat, near the

Merbok River, which is thought to date from the 9th or 10th century. It appears to be a classical representation of Mt Meru, the cosmic mountain, centre of the universe and abode of the gods. In the foundations six small stone caskets containing Shaivite ritual objects in gold and silver have been found; these include a seated female figure in gold leaf holding a trident and a lotus flower, a silver image of the bull Nandi and a small gold *linga* (all Kuala Lumpur, N. Mus.). Some Mahayana Buddhist bronze images have been found in Perak, including an eight-armed Avalokiteshvara (h. 855 mm) with a small image of Amitabha Buddha seated in a niche in the headdress, excavated in 1936 at Bidor and dating from between the 7th and the 10th centuries. In the Kurong Batang caves, near Kangar in Perlis, some finely modelled Mahayana Buddhist clay votive tablets of a type that occurs only in a small area between Perlis and the Kra Isthmus, and therefore presumably of local manufacture, have been found. They are 75×150 mm in diameter and date from between the 10th and the 12th centuries. On one side they depict a 12-armed Avalokiteshvara in a style related to that of the Pala dynasty, and on the other Buddhist texts.

Although the Islamic prohibition of the portrayal of human and animal forms has never been strictly observed in Malaysia, Islamic influence on Malaysian religious art is confined chiefly to the use of calligraphy and other aniconic motifs in the decorative arts, and to monuments such as mosques, shrines and cemeteries (*see* INDONESIA, §I, 3(iv)). Although Islam seems to have first reached the Peninsula as early as the 7th century, the earliest Malay inscription in Arabic script (Kuala Lumpur, N. Mus.), discovered at Kuala Berang some 50 km south-west of Kuala Terengganu, dates from 1303, and the earliest mosques in Malaysia only from the early 18th century. The numerous magnificent royal tombs and mausolea of all periods that exist throughout the Peninsula testify to the strength and persistence of Islamic concepts of monarchy in Malaysia. They range in date from the tomb of Alauddin Riayat Syah of Malacca (*reg* 1477–88) and his sister at Pagoh, about 29 km north-east of Muar, to the mausoleum of the royal family of Pahang near the mouth of the Pahang River, where Sultan Muktasim Billah Syah (*reg* 1917–30) is buried.

Christianity reached the Peninsula with the Portuguese conquest of Malacca in 1511 but has left little mark on Malaysian cultural life except among the Eurasian population of the Portuguese settlement in Malacca who are still Catholic in religion, speak a debased form of Portuguese known as Cristao and preserve some Portuguese customs.

BIBLIOGRAPHY
R. J. Wilkinson: 'Early Indian Influence in Malaysia', *J. Malay. Branch Royal Asiat. Soc.*, xiii/2 (1935), pp. 1–16
R. O. Winstedt: 'Indian Influence in the Malay World', *J. Royal Asiat. Soc. GB & Ireland* (1944), pp. 186–7
——: *The Malays: A Cultural History* (Singapore, 1947/R 1981)
Tempat-tempat bersejarah Malaysia/Malaysian Historical Sites, Persatuan Sejarah Malaysia (Kuala Lumpur, 1974, 2/1976) [bilingual text]
Syed Ahmad bin Jamal and Othman bin Mohd. Yatim: 'Srivijaya Art in Peninsular Malaysia', *The Art of Srivijaya*, ed. M. C. Subhadradis Diskul (Paris and Petaling Jaya, 1980), pp. 45–9
L. Chin: *Cultural Heritage of Sarawak* (Kuching, 1980)
JOHN VILLIERS

II. Architecture.

Few buildings constructed in Malaysia before the 19th century have survived in their original form, as they were made of wood. Indigenous architectural styles, which embraced important elements first of the Hindu–Buddhist and later of the Islamic traditions, also came to absorb Chinese and West European colonial influences.

1. Religious. 2. Secular and domestic.

1. RELIGIOUS.

(i) Hindu–Buddhist. At least 50 sites in the early Indianized state of Langkasuka, in the valley of the Bujang River, southern Kedah, have been traced. Langkasuka existed from the 2nd century AD, but flourished only from the late 5th century (*see* §I, 2 above). The sites consist mainly of the foundations of Hindu or Buddhist temples, constructed from laterite, bricks, river pebbles and granite blocks; their upper portions were probably of timber and other perishable materials which have long since disappeared. The most impressive of these remains is Candi Bukit Batu Pahat, the name of which indicates that it was made from hewn granite blocks. This temple, which may date to the 9th or 10th century, has both Mahayana Buddhist and Hindu features and was apparently erected in memory of a deceased ruler or official (*see* §I, 3 above). In East Malaysia, in the state of Sarawak, the recovery of ritual deposit boxes, similar to those retrieved from temple foundations in Kedah, indicates the existence of Tantric Buddhist structures there. But almost all the archaeological discoveries of Hindu and Buddhist monuments have been made on the west coast of Peninsular Malaysia, which is on the maritime trade route between India and the Indonesian archipelago.

Numerous late 7th-century inscriptions in Old Malay language found in Sumatra relate to the maritime kingdom of Srivijaya, which was renowned as a centre for the study of Mahayana Buddhism. Architectural remains, however, are scanty, though the brick bases of temples excavated on the west coast of Peninsular Malaysia and in southern Thailand may indicate that there were trading centres on these sites, their superstructures, again, having been of perishable materials.

BIBLIOGRAPHY
H. G. Quaritch Wales: 'Archaeological Researches on Ancient Indian Colonization in Malaya', *J. Malay. Branch Royal Asiat. Soc.*, xviii/1 (1940) [whole issue]
A. Lamb: *Chandi Bukit Batu Pahat* (Singapore, 1960)
——: 'Miscellaneous Papers on Early Hindu and Buddhist Settlement in Northern Malaya and Southern Thailand', *Fed. Mus. J.*, n. s., vi (1961) [whole issue]
O. W. Wolters: *Early Indonesian Commerce* (Ithaca, NY, 1967)
——: *The Fall of Srivijaya in Malay History* (London, 1970)
The Sensuous Immortals (exh. cat. by P. Pal, Los Angeles, CA, Co. Mus. A., 1977)
M. Jacq-Hergoualc'h: *La Civilisation des ports-entrepôts du Sud Kedah (Malaysia), Ve–XIVe siècle* (Paris, 1992) [Eng. summary]
KHOO JOO-EE

(ii) Islamic. Islam was first brought to South-east Asia by Middle Eastern and Indian Muslim traders. The earliest evidence of the presence of Islam in Peninsular Malaysia dates from the late 11th century, but documentation begins only during the reign of the first ruler of Malacca,

2. Terengkera Mosque, Malacca, Malaysia, 1728

Paramesvara (see §I, 2 above). Owing to its strategic location on the Straits of Malacca, the port state of Malacca became wealthy and powerful. Under its influence Islam spread as far north as Pattani in present-day Thailand and was reinforced by dynastic marriages of members of the Malaccan royal family throughout the Peninsula. No Malaysian mosque from this period has survived, but there is no doubt that the structure of the Great Mosque (Mesjid Agung) of Demak in north Java, built in 1477–9, which is the oldest mosque in Indonesia and is based on the traditional Javanese *pendopo*, or pillared pavilion, was a prototype for Malaysian mosques as it was for Indonesian.

The oldest mosques in Malaysia are the Peringgit Mosque (*c.* 1720), the Terengkera Mosque (1728; see fig. 2), the Kampung Hulu Malacca Mosque (*c.* 1728) and the Kampung Keling Mosque (1748), all in Malacca, and the Kampung Laut Mosque (*c.* 1730) in Kelantan. Although considerably smaller than the Demak Mosque (which has a base of almost 24 m sq. and a height of nearly 22 m), the Kampung Laut Mosque (nearly 16 m sq.; h. *c.* 11.5 m) and the Malacca mosques (similar in dimensions to the Kampung Laut structure) are clearly modelled on the Javanese building. All have triple-layered (*tangkup*) roofs with four central wooden pillars (*tiang seri*) supporting the topmost roof and two outer rows of columns (16 *tiang tegak* of 4.2 m and 24 *tiang serambi* of 2.14 m) supporting the other two roof layers. Originally the structures were entirely of timber, but during the 20th century some elements were replaced by brick or stone. The Javanese type predominates in traditional Malaysian mosques, though occasionally they incorporate features of indigenous palace architecture, as in the Langgar Mosque (1871), at Langgar, Kota Baharu, which resembles contemporary palaces built by Sultan Muhammad II of Kelantan.

A distinctive feature of Malaysian and Indonesian mosques is the subsidiary building (*serambi*) that is attached to one side. This is an open verandah used for meetings, classes and social gatherings. The old wooden mosques of Malaysia did not originally have minarets, and some still lack them. Added later, they are often in a radically different style, as, for example, the minarets in the style of a Chinese pagoda at the Terengkera and Kampung Keling mosques, the Mughal-influenced minaret of the Kampung Hulu Mosque and the European

tower at the Paloh Mosque (1912) in Ipoh, Perak. Although the mid-19th-century minaret at the Pulai Chondong Mosque in Kelantan is made of *cengal* wood (*Balanocarpus heimii*), minarets are usually of stone or plastered brick.

Although an early example was built in Penang in 1802 (the Kapitan Keling Mosque in Georgetown), the onion dome associated with Islam in the Middle East came into common use only *c.* 1900, coinciding with a return to fundamentalist attitudes among Malaysian Muslims. Since British colonial architects often drew on Indian models at that time, the domes of Malaysian mosques usually have the pointed, outward-bulging profile of Mughal buildings. Notable among these are the Ubudiah Mosque (1913) in Kuala Kangsar, Perak, where the minarets are crowned with umbrella-shaped *chatri*-like finials, the Jamek Mosque (1909) in Kuala Lumpur and the Perlis State Mosque (1972) in Kangar. The Zahir Mosque (1912) at Alor Star in Kedah clearly shows the influence of the mosque in Aceh, northern Sumatra, that its architects had studied.

Some mosques of the colonial period incorporate European styles. The Abu Bakar Mosque of Johor Baharu (1892) is in neo-Renaissance style, as is the Jamek Mosque (1925) of Muar, also in Johor state, while the Sultan Sulaiman Mosque (1932) in Kelang, Selangor, blends Islamic domes with Art Deco towers and turrets. Since independence in 1957, Malaysian architects have sometimes adopted contemporary styles, as in the National Mosque (1963–5) in Kuala Lumpur, a huge building with fan-pleated roof designed by Datuk Baharuddin bin Abu Kasim (*b* 1926), and in the Negeri Sembilan State Mosque in Seremban. The latter, designed in 1967 by Jurubena Bertiga and Ove Arup and Partners, has a soaring cantilevered concrete roof projecting from an octagonal core and epitomizes the trend away from the traditional mosque type in favour of either orthodox Middle Eastern or avant-garde international styles.

BIBLIOGRAPHY
Abdul Halim Nasir: *Mosques of Peninsular Malaysia* (Kuala Lumpur, 1984)
M. B. Hooker: *Islam in South-east Asia* (Leiden, 1988)
S. Vlatseas: *A History of Malaysian Architecture* (Singapore, 1990)

(iii) Straits Chinese. The Chinese population of Malaysia belongs to two main groups: immigrants who came from southern China from the 15th century, married Malay women and formed the first Baba or Straits Chinese communities, and those who came in the 19th century to work in the tin mines and on the rubber plantations and also intermarried with local Malays to form a later Baba community, centred mainly on the island of Penang. Temples are the most distinctive buildings of both these groups of Chinese immigrants. The construction principles, symbolism and decorative detail have changed very little over the centuries, so that the upcurving eaves, glazed tiles, ceramic roof decorations and predominantly red and gold coloration (for prosperity and happiness) of the Cheng Hoon Teng Temple (1645) in Malacca are very similar to the details of the 19th-century Tua Pek Kong Temple in Sarawak and the early 20th-century Chan See Shu Yuen Temple in Kuala Lumpur, to name only two.

BIBLIOGRAPHY
V. Purcell: *The Chinese in Southeast Asia* (London, 1965)

2. SECULAR AND DOMESTIC. Most of the peoples of Malaysia have an Austronesian culture heritage that they share with Indonesia, the Philippines and the Cham people in southern Vietnam. They also have connections with the contiguous civilizations of mainland South-east Asia. It is not surprising, therefore, that indigenous domestic architecture in Malaysia has traits in common with the architecture of these neighbours. Traditional Malay society was primarily rural, without large urban settlements until the rise of the Malacca sultanate in the 15th century. This may explain why monumentality is not characteristic of Malay architecture. Rather it embodies a harmony between local materials, cooperative communal labour and techniques, social traditions and the environment.

(i) Indigenous. (ii) Straits Chinese. (iii) Colonial and modern.

(i) Indigenous. More than 70% of Malaysia's population is still rural, living in small villages (*kampung*). Since the principal building material of all vernacular domestic architecture in Malaysia is timber and the tropical climate is destructive, there are no surviving domestic buildings from earlier than the 19th century. Palaces are similar in plan to ordinary dwelling houses but on a larger scale, built with a wider variety of materials, more subsidiary structures and more refined and elaborate carving. Typically, houses are raised on stilts and have palm thatch roofs, like those built in riverine and coastal Thailand, Laos and Cambodia as well as by the Minangkabau and Batak peoples of Sumatra and the Bugis of South Sulawesi. This elevation offers protection from floods (frequent in delta locations) and in earlier times gave security from marauding animals or human enemies; it has the incidental advantages of increasing air circulation by raising the structure above impeding ground planting and of providing a protected space beneath the house in which to keep animals and perform daytime tasks.

Various local hardwoods such as *cengal*, *petaling*, *meranti*, *merbau* and *damar laut* are used for the post-and-lintel frame with a central column (*tiang seri*) as structural and ritual centrepiece. The roof is usually in simple gable form (*bumbung panjang*), especially in the north-eastern states of Kedah, Perlis, Penang and Perak. There is typically a subsidiary, parallel lean-to roof over a verandah (*serambi*) flanking one or both sides of the main structure, and in larger houses and palaces there is also a small extension for the kitchen. Variants with gracefully curved gable beams, possibly influenced by Thai roof forms, are common in the western states of Kelantan and Terengganu; a fine example from the Royal Palace of Terengganu, the Istana Satu, has been dismantled and re-erected in the National Museum in Kuala Lumpur. Another gable variant occurs when the end beams project beyond the roof ridge and cross one another, as in the 1902–8 Royal Palace (Istana Lama) in Sri Menanti, Negeri Sembilan; this 'scissors' version is possibly derived from Bugis examples.

Double constructions comprising parallel gabled roofs are found in Malacca, where an open courtyard sometimes occurs between the two buildings. Hipped roofs (*bumbung lima*) also occur, as well as gambrel forms (*bumbung perak*), particularly in Perak, Pahang and Johor. These show Western influence but also resemble some Javanese models. In Negeri Sembilan the influence of Minangkabau culture from across the Straits of Malacca has resulted in roofs with ridge-poles curving up at the outer ends; in addition there is sometimes an upper roof with a similar profile. The 1612 *Sejarah Melayu* (Malay Chronicle) describes a palace in Minangkabau form built in the reign of Sultan Mansur Shah of Malacca (*reg* 1459–77). Another form (*bumbung limas*), pyramidal and probably deriving from Javanese models, is restricted to mosques and is often tiered.

Roof coverings are traditionally made from thatched palm leaf, a material much better suited to provide protection from the tropical sun than the metal roofs introduced in the 20th century. Ceramic tiles are found in Malacca houses, possibly reflecting the influence of Chinese settlers. Occasionally wooden shingles form the roof covering, as in the 1865 Minangkabau-style palace formerly at Ampang Tinggi, Negeri Sembilan, which is now a museum in Seremban.

Walls are made of prefabricated panels—either of timber, often carved with foliate or geometric forms, or of woven split bamboo—which are placed between the structural columns. Fastenings were traditionally all of wood, the metal nail being introduced only in colonial times. Ventilated gable ends, generous eaves that kept the sun from the walls and obviated closure during rainstorms, unglazed windows (sometimes filled with carved pierced screens) and internal spaces unobstructed by interior walls promote excellent air circulation and contribute to the successful adaptation of Malay architecture to the tropical climate. Access is by projecting stairs that sometimes lead to spacious entrance porches connecting with the verandah. Much of the social life takes place in these unenclosed areas, the inner room (*rumah ibu*) being used mostly for sleeping and praying.

Some of the people of Malaysia still live in their traditional longhouses, notably the Sakai peoples in the Peninsula and the Ibans (so-called Sea Dayaks) and Orang Ulu (Kayans, Kenyahs, Kelabits) in Sarawak. Longhouses are usually constructed near water, preferably at the confluence of a river and one of its tributaries, both for ease of communications and to ensure a water supply, and are grouped together to form a village community. Some longhouses are as much as 180 m long and 15 m wide and can accommodate 50 families or more, but the average size is sufficient only for 10 or 12 families. Since they are built entirely of wood, they decay quickly and have to be rebuilt every 10 or 15 years. As well as varying in size, the longhouses differ widely in their architecture, methods of construction and the arrangement of their interiors, but they usually have ridged roofs and are raised on wooden piles between 1 and 3 m high in order to increase the circulation of air, to provide space for livestock beneath and to give protection against vermin, flooding and enemy attack. The principal door is usually at the east end of the longhouse and is provided with a notched log or a ladder, which is pulled up at night. Parts of the building may be decorated with carvings. The carving on Kayan longhouses and funerary monuments (*see* §X, 1 below) is often of specially high quality. The interior is divided with partitions into apartments for each family, and a verandah running the whole length of the building and usually facing the river provides a communal living area. Rice, firewood, fishing nets, mats, tools and utensils are stored in a loft, and skulls from former headhunting expeditions are hung in the rafters.

BIBLIOGRAPHY
R. O. Winstedt: 'A History of Malaya', *J. Malay. Branch Royal Asiat. Soc.*, xiii /1 (1935), pp. 1–270; repr. as book (Singapore, 1936, rev. Kuala Lumpur, 1986)
Abdul Halim Nasir: *Panduan ke Tempat-Tempat Bersejarah: Guide to Historic Sites: Kelantan* (Kuala Lumpur, 1979)
Lim Jee Yuan: *The Malay House: Rediscovering Malaysia's Indigenous Shelter System* (Penang, 1987)
S. Vlatseas: *A History of Malaysian Architecture* (Singapore, 1990)

(ii) Straits Chinese. The most important contribution of the Chinese population to Malaysian domestic architecture is the shop house. These are typically two-storey, with commercial space at street level in front, and storage, living and sleeping quarters behind and above. They dominated the urban scene in Malaysian cities until high-rise developments after World War II began to obliterate them. In the first quarter of the 19th century, beginning during Sir Thomas Stamford Raffles's governorship of Bencoolen (Bengkulu) in Sumatra and his oversight of the new settlement in Singapore (founded 1819), the shop house was protected by decree from sun and rain by an arcaded roof over the pavement—the 'five-foot covered way'—that was a simple and effective adaptation of the design to climate. The shop house, which is deep and narrow and has interior courtyards for ventilation and light, is sometimes overtly Chinese in style, with gabled end walls, curved roof-tiles and pierced ceramic ventilation panels. Later examples often adopted Western details, with arched windows and elaborately carved pillars and pilasters. Their evenly spaced and harmoniously varied façades lend a pleasing scale to the streetscape. The post-World War II urge to demolish the shop house in the interests of increased density and stylistic modernization (and Westernization) was curbed by the last decade of the 20th century as urban planners came to appreciate the urban virtues of this pervasive South-east Asian building type.

BIBLIOGRAPHY
D. G. E. Hall: *A History of South-east Asia* (London, 1955, 3/1968/R 1976)
V. Purcell: *The Chinese in Southeast Asia* (London, 1965)
S. Vlatseas: *A History of Malaysian Architecture* (Singapore, 1990)

3. A. B. Hubbock: Railway administration building, Kuala Lumpur, Malaysia, 1900

(iii) Colonial and modern. The European colonial period in Malaysia began in 1511 when the Portuguese under Afonso de Albuquerque captured MALACCA in their attempt to gain a share of the profitable trade in spices from the Indonesian archipelago. Albuquerque built the fortress called A Famosa with stones taken from the sultan's palace and the mosques of the city. The oldest surviving colonial structure in Malaysia is the solid stone Santiago Gate, all that remains of A Famosa, which was rebuilt by the Dutch in the 17th century and almost entirely demolished by the British in 1807. The power of the Dutch East Indies Company (Vereenigde Oost-Indische Compagnie, or VOC) grew rapidly in the 17th century. Resenting the Portuguese control of the Straits, the Dutch attacked Malacca several times and finally, after a protracted siege, they captured the town in January 1641 and virtually destroyed it. The oldest intact colonial buildings in Malaysia, therefore, are those the Dutch built in Malacca, notably the Town Hall, built between 1641 and 1660. The simplicity, solid walls, flush end-gables and large windows reveal the Netherlandish inspiration of this three-storey structure.

During the 19th century the British gradually superseded the Dutch as the dominant colonial power in the area. Except for the imposing Neo-classical St George's Church in Penang (1818), however, little significant architecture remains from the early decades of British rule, as the administration of the Malay states remained largely in the hands of the indigenous rulers. In the mid-19th century, with the development of steam ships, the opening of the Suez Canal in 1869 and the industrialization of Britain, international trade expanded, as did the British presence in Malaya. A spate of building occurred at the end of the 19th century and early in the 20th. Some, neo-classical or neo-Renaissance, was to enhance British imperial status; some attempted to fuse Asian and European styles. Among impressive examples of the former are the colonnaded municipal building in Ipoh, the High Court in Kuching, the arcuated Civil Service buildings and cathedral of the Assumption in Penang, the pedimented and colonnaded Malay College in Kuala Kangsar, offices for the Chartered Bank throughout the region and the sultan of Johor's palace. Attempts to create a locally appropriate architecture produced several imposing if eclectic buildings, many designed by A. C. Norman or A. B. Hubbock, whose inspiration was Mughal India. In Kuala Lumpur, intricate Mughal arches embellish the High Court and the Secretariat building, while *chatri* confections crown the elaborately arcaded railway station and administration buildings (see fig. 3). This decorative blend of Indian Islamic with British imperial style sometimes provokes derision but has certainly created an architecturally unique fantasy.

Since independence in 1957 there has been a tendency to embrace international modern styles with high-rise office buildings and apartments. Typical examples include the vertically fenestrated Bangunan Datu Zainal Building, Kuala Lumpur (1978, Hijjas Kasturi Associates), the round glass tower of the Sabah Foundation Headquarters complex in Kota Kinabalu (1979, Wisma Akitek & James Ferrie International) and the glass-fronted Kompleks Nagaria (1986, Pakatan Reka) in Kuala Lumpur. Some buildings show efforts to adapt to the climate, such as the

Parliament House in Kuala Lumpur (1963, Jabatan Kerja Raya), which has an exterior concrete screen of pre-cast spandrels, and the Kuala Lumpur Dayabumi Complex (1984, BEP+MAA Akitek Sdn), which is screened by a metal grille with an Islamic design.

The growth of industrialization, Westernization, urbanism and population that followed independence caused rising prices for land, labour and materials and a public domestic housing problem. In many cases the attempt to solve it resulted in European solutions, either by the construction of high-rise apartment buildings (such as the 1958 Sulaiman Court, now demolished, and the 1985 Downtown Condominium, both in Kuala Lumpur) or by terrace houses where interior ventilation and protection from tropical rain and sun are inadequate.

Middle-class villas before World War II tended to incorporate in a grander version such indigenous vernacular features as construction on stilts, deep eaves and wide verandahs, just as planters' and officials' houses during the British colonial period in the 19th century were modelled on vernacular Malay architecture. Like low-cost housing, villa architecture after independence adopted international style, as in the house of the architect Kington Loo (1959) or Lai Lok Kun's The Hexagons (1971; both in Kuala Lumpur). During the 1980s there began a trend towards well-synthesized fusion of contemporary style with indigenous vernacular, as in the house of T. Y. Chiew (1980, CSL Associates, Selangor) and another for Ng Lu Pat (1984, Akitek MAA Sdn Bhd, Kuala Lumpur), or towards environmental consciousness as explored in the innovative Roof-Roof House (1984, T. R. Hamsah & Yeang Sdn Bhd, Selangor), where the concept of movable elements reacting to sun and breeze variables offers effective low-energy climate control.

After World War II some attempt was made to assert the distinctiveness of Malay culture by returning to indigenous architectural motifs. Most of the large buildings that resulted are hybrids with superficially applied features, such as the National Museum (1963, Ho Kwong Yew & Sons), which has an arbitrarily imposed traditional roof with 'scissors' eaves, and the Hilton Hotel (1973, BEP Akitek Sdn Bhd) in Kuala Lumpur, where a low entrance building with stylized indigenous roof sits incongruously in front of a tall tower. Deeper integration of local and international modern themes can be seen in the LUTH complex of 1986 (Hijjas Kasturi Associates Sdn, Kuala Lumpur), where the waisted round tower, with its five heavy vertical ribs suggesting the five pillars of Islam and its vertical fenestration ending in pointed arches, invokes Islamic form. In the 1980s and 90s the quest for a culturally and climatically appropriate architecture for Malaysia in the 21st century was articulated by several thoughtful Malaysian architects.

BIBLIOGRAPHY

M. MacDonald: 'Malacca Buildings', *J. Malay. Branch Royal Asiat. Soc.*, xii/2 (1934) [whole issue]
J. G. Butcher: *The British in Malaya, 1880–1941* (Kuala Lumpur, 1979)
J. Cooper, D. Dunster and D. Jones, eds: 'Vernacular, Pastiche, Modern?: The Search for a Malaysian Architecture', *ULA International Architect*, 6 (1984) [whole issue]
M. B. Ševcenko, ed.: *Design for High-intensity Development* (Cambridge, MA, 1986)
K. Yeang: *The Tropical Verandah City: Some Urban Design Ideas for Kuala Lumpur* (Selangor, 1986)
——: *Tropical Urban Regionalism: Building in a South-east Asian City* (Singapore, 1987)
Chan Chee Yoong, ed.: *Post-Merdeka Architecture: Malaysia, 1957–1987* (Kuala Lumpur, 1987)
S. Vlatseas: *A History of Malaysian Architecture* (Singapore, 1990)
D. Ng: *Penang: The City and Suburbs in the Early Twentieth Century* (Penang, n.d.)

HELEN IBBITSON JESSUP

III. City planning.

Most of the major urban settlements of Malaysia were built under the British administration between the late 19th century and independence in 1957. They are in marked contrast to the traditional coastal or riverine settlements and trading posts. During this period extensive building was fuelled by the income from trade and the exploitation of the Peninsula's commodities of tin and later rubber, a period that to a great extent fixed the urban patterns of the older parts of the major towns and cities along the west coast of Peninsular Malaysia, primarily Penang, Ipoh, Kelang, Kuala Lumpur, Seremban and Malacca down to Johor Baharu and Singapore. This resulted in the transformation of the traditional settlement pattern and the shifting of focus inland. The legacy of the British in these towns includes a random pattern of streets in the central business districts, the disposition of some of the key urban activities (such as the market square, and the cricket and parade ground with the country club and town hall facing it) and the ubiquitous development of low-rise shop houses (built mostly by the Chinese; *see* §II, 2(ii) above).

There was no evidence of formal urban planning until the 1920s and it was not until 1948 that the Municipal Ordinance gave powers for such planning. Previously, the sanitary boards in Penang and in Kuala Lumpur (set up in 1890) had simply managed their town's services under the jurisdiction of the British residents and governors. Another contribution to the rapid increase in urban settlements was the Emergency Resettlement Programme in the 1950s prompted by the anti-terrorist war of 1948–60. As the settlements expanded rapidly with the natural increase in population and migration into the cities, the common problems associated with rapid urban expansion, such as inadequate utilities and services, poor housing, squatters, traffic congestion and pollution, became increasingly difficult to resolve, and this led to measures to ensure more orderly growth. During the colonial era, certain aspects of urban planning had already been incorporated in various enactments, for example relating to utilities and public health. The most important were the Town Board Enactments or Council Ordinances. These various enactments were replaced in 1976 by the Local Government Act, which provided for a new system managed by local authorities. In the same year the British system of urban planning (i.e. the development plan system) was embodied in the Town and Country Planning Act. This instituted a uniform planning system to cover all the state in Peninsular Malaysia.

Kuala Lumpur, the capital city of Malaysia, was founded in 1859, 35 km inland from the Straits of Malacca, at the junction of the Kelang and Gombak rivers, a location originally known as Lumpur ('mud'), later becoming Kuala Lumpur ('muddy estuary'). It was created by Chinese immigrants engaged in tin-mining. When the British Resident was transferred to Kuala Lumpur in 1880, its shanty town image of predominantly timber buildings was changed to a more permanent settlement of brick buildings, the shop houses of old Kuala Lumpur (*see* §II, 2(iii) above). At the early stages, most of the urban development was concentrated on the eastern bank of the Kelang River, where the Chinese tin-miners and traders lived. The quarters of the British and other Europeans were on the west of the river. The city was gradually transformed into an administrative and commercial centre from the middle of the 20th century, which resulted in a rapid increase of the indigenous population (mainly Malays). The nucleus of the central area of Kuala Lumpur coincides with the Old Town constructed before 1884 and is defined by the areas reserved for the railway, the bus terminal and the central market. Around the mid-20th century, suburban residential and shopping areas began to be established around the fringes of Kuala Lumpur, notably Petaling Jaya, followed by satellite townships. The gradual decentralization of the urban centre, and amalgamation of resettlement villages (established during the anti-terrorist war between 1948 and 1960) with secondary centres linked to the central areas, have transformed Kuala Lumpur and its immediate environs into an extensive urbanized region.

Ipoh, the capital city of Perak state, was another important town in the Peninsula that developed and flourished in the 1880s through tin-mining. During this period Chinese immigrants and Europeans laid out the street patterns for the town, which owed its initial importance to its position as the highest navigable point on the Kinta River, and so became a natural staging-point and a market to the surrounding district. By *c.* 1900 brick buildings started to replace the wooden shacks of the mining town. Chinese shop houses proliferated (*see* §II, 2(ii) above), especially along the main streets traversing the town, many built with classical façades. The style combined stucco mouldings and pitched Chinese tiled roofs in bright colours, giving it its characteristic skyline. There is a fine ensemble of buildings formed by the cricket ground (Padang) and the various neo-classical colonial administrative buildings facing it, including the magnificent white Town Hall. By 1890 Ipoh had swollen to become the largest town in the Kinta Valley.

MALACCA, some 100 km south-east of Kuala Lumpur on the Straits of Malacca, contains the oldest European, Hindu, Chinese and Malay buildings in the country. Founded *c.* 1400, it developed under the Portuguese and later the British. Its architecture of shop houses and row houses is highly eclectic in style.

BIBLIOGRAPHY

L. Chin: *Cultural Heritage of Sarawak* (Kuching, 1980)
J. M. Gullick: *The Story of Kuala Lumpur (1857–1939)* (Singapore, 1983)
C. W. Harrison: *An Illustrated Guide to the Federated Malay States (1923)* (Kuala Lumpur, 1985)
R. O. Winstedt: *A History of Malaya* (Kuala Lumpur, 1986)
K. Yeang: *The Architecture of Malaysia* (Amsterdam, 1992)
S. R. Aiken: *Imperial Belvederes: The Hill Stations of Malaya* (Kuala Lumpur, 1993)

KEN YEANG

IV. Sculpture.

The surviving early sculpture of Malaysia, as elsewhere in South-east Asia, is entirely Hindu–Buddhist and derives ultimately from Indian models.

1. HINDU-BUDDHIST. Votive inscriptions in the Pallava script of southern India, found in the north-west of Peninsular Malaysia and on palaeographic evidence dated to the 4th and 5th centuries AD, are the earliest low-relief sculptures known in Malaysia. The earliest of these fragmentary stones has a beautifully carved stupa, and its inscription indicates that it was set up by a Buddhagupta, a master mariner. Of sculptures in the round, Hindu and Buddhist bronze images (7th–10th century), resembling their north Indian Gupta style prototypes but nonetheless distinct from them, have been discovered in the state of Perak south of Kedah (*see* §I, 3 above). The 9–11th-century Hindu–Buddhist sculptures in stone found in peninsular Thailand immediately to the north are monumental in character and closely resemble late Pallava and early Chola styles of southern India (*see* INDIAN SUBCONTINENT, §V, 6(vi) and 7(vi)).

BIBLIOGRAPHY

H. G. Quaritch Wales: 'Archaeological Researches on Ancient Indian Colonization in Malaya', *J. Malay. Branch Royal Asiat. Soc.*, xviii/1 (1940)
A. Lamb: 'Miscellaneous Paper on Early Hindu and Buddhist Settlements in Northern Malaya and Southern Thailand', *Fed. Mus. J.*, n. s. (1961)
S. J. O'Connor: 'Hindu Gods of Peninsular Siam', *Artibus Asiae*, suppl. xxviii (1972)
The Sensuous Immortals (exh. cat. by P. Pal, Los Angeles, CA, Co. Mus. A., 1977)

KHOO JOO-EE

2. ISLAMIC. About 90 km south-west of Kuala Lumpur is a group of menhirs on the site of the Keramat Sungai Udang (Saint of Prawn) River that are of a high order of aesthetic plasticity. The Sword Stone (2.52×0.66×0.32 m) has a stylized human form and the word 'Allah' carved in relief. The Rudder Stone (1.89×1.12×0.38 m) bears a landscape in low relief with mythical animals in curvilinear form echoing the elegant shape of the stone. Near by is a square-sectioned sandstone pillar that marks the grave of Shaykh Ahmad Mokhtar Ramli Ibni Marfu Talani (*d* 1467–8). Next to it, embedded in the ground, lies a flat, heart-shaped stone called the Shield Stone (1.17×1.35 m), in low relief with an eight-pointed star and a decorative motif of foliated 'clasps'. Together the stones form a symbolic link between the coming of Islam in the 15th century and the culture that preceded it.

The innumerable Batu Aceh tombstones (15th–19th century) found throughout Peninsular Malaysia have rich sculptural qualities. Rectangular or square, with Koran verses inscribed in panels, some have 'shoulders' with crocket-like wings extending on either side, round or eight-sided, topped with foliated finials.

Having an abundant supply of hardwood, the Malays excel in wood-carving, producing intricate works with sculptural qualities, such as wooden sail-guards for boats of east-coast peninsular Malaysia (based on the egret with foliated decoration), wooden coconut-graters in stylized animal form and the magnificent stylized dragon-head from the royal barge of Pahang state with its intricate foliation (*see also* §IX, 7 below).

In the 1970s Abdul Latiff Mohidin (*b* 1938) created reinforced-cement sculptures that reflect his early paintings (*see* §V, 2 below): the 'Langkawi' series of wall sculptures in painted wood. His *The Emerging Kubah* (1986) is a stainless steel sculpture. Syed Ahmad Jamal (*b* 1929), commissioned to execute a public sculpture based on Islamic principles, produced *Allah*, using *khat* (calligraphic) forms in stainless steel (1980); later he created *Lunar Peaks* (1986) and *Growth* (1987). Sculptors fundamentally committed to Islamic principles include Zakaria Awang, teacher in an art school. He too contrived a *khat* form, by means of lead weights suspended on transparent nylon strings to create a mystical effect. His sculpture *Tauhid* (1983) exudes a quality of calmness and spirituality (all works Kuala Lumpur, N.A.G.).

BIBLIOGRAPHY
Othman bin Mohd. Yatim: *Batu Aceh: Early Islamic Gravestones in Peninsular Malaysia* (Kuala Lumpur, 1988)
'Contemporary Islamic Art in Malaysia', *A. & I. World*, v (1988)
D. B. D. Pustaka: *Form and Soul: Syed Ahmad Jamal* (Kuala Lumpur, 1994)

SAYED AHMAD JAMAL

V. Painting.

No evidence survives of a painting tradition in Malaysia during the Hindu–Buddhist period, and before the arrival of Islam in the area virtually the only Malay paintings earlier than the 1930s are those found on manuscripts.

1. MANUSCRIPT. Manuscripts in the Malay language originate from present-day Indonesia, Malaysia, Singapore, Brunei and the southern parts of Thailand and the Philippines, and are generally written on paper in Jawi, a modified form of the Arabic script. The oldest Malay manuscripts extant date from the early 16th century, and the tradition of copying them lasted until the early 20th century. During this period Islamic manuscripts wholly or partially in Arabic were also produced in Peninsular Malaysia and Indonesia, and Arabic was the language of some diplomatic exchanges (*see* INDONESIA, §VII, 1(i)). Painting in Malay manuscripts is the exception rather than the rule, but at its best attains exquisite artistic heights. Most examples are either illuminated letters from rulers to other rulers or to high-ranking European officials—a fine early example is a letter to King James I of England from Sultan Perkasa Alam Johan of Aceh in Sumatra (1615; Oxford, Bodleian Lib., MS. Laud Or. Rolls. b. 1)—or illuminated frontispieces and colophons of literary and religious works, including the Koran.

Characteristic designs show a text block surrounded by rectangular borders, or a variety of single or multiple round, pointed and ogee arches (the last suggesting the

4. Colophon from the manuscript *Tāj al-Salāṭīn* ('Crown of Kings'), copied by Muḥammad bin 'Umar Syaikh Farid, each folio 250×180 mm, Penang, 1824 (London, British Library, Or. MS. 13295, fols 190*v*–191*r*)

influence of eastern Islamic manuscript painting from India), decorated with arabesques, geometric patterns and foliate and floral motifs. The main colours used are various shades of red and reddish brown, together with black, blue, green, ochre and yellow, often with the addition of gold, in both leaf and powder form. Chapter headings and key words and phrases may also be highlighted in red or gold, with coloured medallions and petal-like roundels as text markers. One of the most beautiful examples is a manuscript of the *Tāj al-Salāṭīn* ('The Crown of Kings'), copied in Penang in 1824 by Muḥammad bin 'Umar Syaikh Farid (London, BL, MS. Or. 13295; see fig. 4). In accordance with orthodox Islamic practice, figural painting in Malay manuscripts is rare and occurs only on a few late 19th-century examples, which betray contemporaneous popular Indian and European influences (e.g. the *Hikayat Hanuman* (Kuala Lumpur, U. Malaya Lib., MS. 30), which has many pencil-outline and watercolour illustrations). However, many magic and divination texts, which were often carried as charms, have crude anthropomorphic and zoomorphic illustrations in black and red ink, as can be seen, for example, in a charm book from Kelantan (*c.* 1906; U. London, SOAS, MS. 25030).

BIBLIOGRAPHY

M. C. Ricklefs and P. Voorhoeve: *Indonesian Manuscripts in Great Britain: A Catalogue of Manuscripts in Indonesian Languages in British Public Collections* (Oxford, 1977), pp. 103–71

A. T. Gallop: 'Malay Manuscript Art: The British Library Collection', *BLJ*, xvii/2 (Autumn 1991), pp. 167–89

A. T. Gallop with B. Arps: *Golden Letters: Writing Traditions of Indonesia/Surat Emas: Budaya Tulis di Indonesia* (London and Jakarta, 1991) [Bilingual text], pp. 33–72

A. T. Gallop: *The Legacy of the Malay Letter/Warisan Warkah Melayu* (London, 1994) [bilingual text]

ANNABEL TEH GALLOP

2. OTHER. Modern Malaysian painting dates from the 1930s but was first introduced by British colonial officers in the 18th and 19th centuries. The art of watercolour painting in the English tradition of Romantic treatment of the landscape influenced a whole generation of artists until after World War II. These Malaysian watercolours were generally idyllic landscapes of villages, rice-fields or palm-fringed beaches. A few personalities dominated the art scene of that time. Yong Mun Sen (1896–1962) produced simple landscapes in fluid washes of sun-filled scenes of coconut-palms and the simple life of country people, as well as some portraits, figural compositions and landscapes in oil. The watercolours of Abdullah Ariff (1904–62), by comparison, were technically more complex.

In the 1930s a number of immigrant artists introduced Western techniques and styles of painting derived from the art academies in southern China, among them Chuah Thean Teng (*b* 1914) who worked in Penang. Their academic training was evident in their handling of medium and their sense of plasticity of form, but they infused local elements into their work, such as lush tropical flora and scenes of urban and rural life. Teng developed batik as a medium for pictorial expression.

In the 1950s art groups and organizations were instrumental in the development of Malaysian art in response to the mounting impetus of the independence movement. The Arts Council, founded in 1952, organized art activities, while the Wednesday Art Group, established in 1952 and led by Peter Harris, an expatriate English art educator, introduced modern concepts of art to aspiring artists. In 1956 Mohd. Hoessein Enas from Indonesia established the Peninsular Artists' Movement, which was concerned with realistic figural presentation and identity. The National Art Gallery was established in 1958 and houses a national collection of works by Malaysian artists.

The artists of the 1950s and 1960s subscribed to the aesthetics of Abstract Expressionism. The gestural qualities of that expressive visual language appeal to the Malaysian temperament and sensitivity and have affinity with the calligraphic traditions of both the Malays and the Chinese. Among the leading artists of the period were: Abdul Latiff Mohidin (*b* 1938), whose haunting surrealistic forms drew inspiration from the region; Cheong Laitong (*b* 1932), who made use of calligraphic motifs; Dzulkifli Buyung (*b* 1948), who depicted scenes of childhood; Khoo Sui-Hoe (*b* 1939), notable for his dreamscapes; the symbolist painter Lee Joo For (*b* 1929); Nik Zainal Abidin (1933–93), who portrayed figures from the shadow puppet theatre; Patrick Ng Kah Onn (1932–91); Sayed Ahmad Jamal; and Yeoh Jin Leng (*b* 1929).

In the late 1960s Malaysian art changed as the second generation of post-war Malaysian artists became involved in international artistic developments. In contrast, in the 1970s artists became more involved with local materials and with their environment. Malaysian artists not only worked in the realm of Hard-edge, Minimalism, Pop (such as Joseph Tan (*b* 1941)), Op and other contemporary trends but also examined mystical and metaphysical values (such as Ismail Zain (1930–91) and Syed Thajudeen (*b* 1943)). Ibrahim Hussein (*b* 1936), Jolly Koh (*b* 1941), Redza Piyadasa and Choong Kam Kow (*b* 1934) also extended the boundaries of Malaysian painting, and Zulkifli Dahlan (1952–77) turned his skills to satires against social hypocrisy. Long Thien Shih (*b* 1946) and Raja Zahabuddin (*b* 1948) raised the art of printmaking to a high level of technical excellence while maintaining seriousness of content. During that decade, moreover, there was growing awareness of a common cultural heritage with other countries in South-east Asia.

This awareness continued to grow during the 1980s, alongside an increased sensitivity to Islamic values. Foremost among artists of this period were Ahmad Khalid Yusof (*b* 1934), Awang Damit (*b* 1956), Fauzan Omar (*b* 1951), Sharifah Fatimah Zubir (*b* 1948) and Suleiman Haji Esa (*b* 1941). The end of the 1980s was an active period, as Malaysian artists engaged increasingly with socio-political issues (e.g. Nirmala Shanmughalingham (*b* 1941), Lee Kian Seng (*b* 1948) and Ponirin Amin (*b* 1952)). There was also a revived interest in figural art and in ecology among the younger local-trained artists.

BIBLIOGRAPHY

D. D. Wharton: *Contemporary Artists of Malaysia* (Kuala Lumpur, 1971)

The Treatment of the Local Landscape in Modern Malaysian Art (exh. cat. by R. Piyadasa, Kuala Lumpur, N.A.G., 1981)

T. K. Sabapathy, R. Piyadasa and D. B. Dan Pustaka: *Modern Artists of Malaysia* (Kuala Lumpur, 1983)

Thirty Years of Malaysian Art (exh. cat. by S. A. Jamal, Kuala Lumpur, N.A.G., 1987)

T. Chee Khuan: *Penang Artists, 1920–1990* (Penang, 1990)

The Malaysianness of Malaysian Art: The Question of Identity (exh. cat. by Z. Ali, Kuala Lumpur, N.A.G., 1991)

K. Jit and others: *Vision and Idea: Relooking Modern Malaysian Art* (Kuala Lumpur, 1994)

SAYED AHMAD JAMAL

VI. Metalwork.

1. Introduction. 2. *Keris*. 3. Berel sets.

1. INTRODUCTION. There is an ancient tradition of intricate work in gold and silver in Malaysia, to which Malay, Indonesian, Chinese, Indian and Borneo peoples have all contributed, with a considerable cross-fertilization of ideas. Under the patronage of the Malay sultans, Malaysian craftsmen produced a wide range of gold and silver pieces for court use as regalia, plate, furnishings and personal ornament (*see* §IX, 4 below). Chased and repoussé gold and silver work is to be seen on *keris*, swords and spears (*see* §2 below). Boxes, trays, dishes and areca nut slicers for betel sets (*see* §3 below), boxes for cosmetics and tobacco, cuspidors, incense burners, bowls and water-jugs are all elegant in form. The more practical items are highly polished with restrained decoration; the rest have elaborate ornamentation. The decorated thrones and beds of Malay weddings gave opportunities for imaginative work in gold and silver leaf. The gilded silver plates (*bantal*) sewn on to the ends of pillows have become prized collectors' items. Best known and rarest of all the pieces are the *bunga mas*, trees made with gold flowers and silver leaves which were sent by Malay rulers as gifts or tribute to foreign potentates.

The favoured metal was pure gold, though it might be alloyed with other metals to produce a range of coloured golds. Much pre-20th-century silver was derived from melted-down coinage, so there is considerable variation in the composition of the metal, which frequently does not match the workmanship in quality. Techniques included chasing, repoussé and filigree. Filigree work of twisted wire and ribbon with spherical and faceted granules was sometimes mounted on a plain sheet of silver or gold. Focal points would be provided by the addition of precious and semi-precious stones in box or openwork settings. Depth was often added to such work by gilding the silver sheet or by chemically staining the underlying gold red or orange.

Malay designs follow Muslim conventions of geometric and vegetal patterns, concentrating on leaves (e.g. the breadfruit leaf), buds, tendrils, fruit and flowers (e.g. the eight-petalled lotus blossom), shapes that give serrated edges to a form or allow perforated patterns round edges. The interior may then be filled with intricate scrolling or geometric patterns. In Chinese and other designs animal and anthropomorphic figures are found, as well as cultur-ally specific symbols of good fortune. While ethnic attri-butions can generally be readily given to designs and motifs, it is often more difficult to do the same with workmanship.

Many of the best extant gold and silver pieces were made by craftsmen for the Peninsular courts of the 18th and 19th centuries, and for the wealthy Straits Chinese traders of the late 19th century and early 20th. Since then many of the classic forms have become obsolete, and a smaller modern industry has grown up, orientated to a fashion-conscious market, though there are still craftsmen who will make pieces in traditional styles to order in the more conservative states such as Kelantan. The Malohs, the traditional itinerant jobbing silversmiths for the Dayak peoples, find a declining market for their wares as people cease to wear traditional costume (*see also* §X, 1 below).

Brass was in common use everywhere for domestic ware until the increasing import of iron, steel and later aluminium and plastics drastically reduced its local mar-kets. Much of the brassware resembled the finer silver and gold pieces in form and decoration, though its greater weight and strength enabled more use to be made of perforated designs. Falling demand during the 20th century restricted craft production in brass to specialized local kitchenware, such as coconut presses, baking moulds and cooking pots. The state of Terengganu has a long tradition of brassworking. Here and there in other states craftsmen will still produce to commission, especially in Sabah and Sarawak, where brass is valued for jewellery and for household status objects such as betel boxes, gongs and kettles resembling Brunei ware. Terengganu smiths are famous for their *tembaga puteh* ('white brass') objects, using a secret 'brass' alloy which has a high proportion of nickel and zinc. Today they concentrate on high-value objects, such as betel sets, candlesticks, ritual washing equipment, incense burners and vases. These tend to be undecorated apart from scalloping of lips and edges and rely for their beauty on their elegant traditional shapes and high polish.

The work of the Selangor Pewter Company, founded in 1885, is well known internationally. It has concentrated on the best contemporary international design and, by using almost pure tin, has achieved a very fine satin polish on its wares. Elegant ewers, coffeepots, vases and tankards, plain or with simple incised pictures of, for example, palm trees, Malay houses and boats, are typical products suc-cessfully aimed at the high-quality souvenir market. Its range has expanded considerably to cater for the demands of pewter collectors, with such products as, for example, chess sets and miniature replicas of the *keris* displayed in the National Museum.

BIBLIOGRAPHY

H. L. Roth: *Oriental Silverware, Malay and Chinese: A Handbook for Connoisseurs, Students and Silversmiths* (London, 1910/*R* Kuala Lumpur, 1966, 1994, with intro. by S. Fraser-Lu)

J. H. Alman: 'Dusun Brasswork' *Sabah Soc. J.*, iii (1962), pp. 29–38

T. Harrisson and S. J. O'Connor: *Gold and Megalithic Activity in Prehistoric and Recent West Borneo* (Ithaca, NY, 1970)

M. Sheppard: *Taman Indera: A Royal Pleasure Ground: Malay Decorative Arts and Pastimes* (Kuala Lumpur, 1972)

V. T. King: 'Maloh Silversmiths', *Sarawak Gaz.*, ci (1975), pp. 114–15

Ho Wing Meng: *Straits Chinese Silver: A Collector's Guide* (Singapore, 1976, rev. 1984)

M. Sheppard: *Living Crafts of Malaysia* (Singapore, 1978)

L. Chin: *Cultural Heritage of Sarawak* (Kuching, 1980)

E. Moore: 'Peranakan Silver in Singapore', *A. Asia*, xii (1982), pp. 154–6

D. Ch'ng: 'Overseas Chinese Silversmiths', *A. Asia*, xiv (1984), pp. 100–06

A. A. Choo: *Silver*, National Museum: A Guide to the Collections (Sin-gapore, 1984)

B. Singh: *Malay Brassware*, National Museum: A Guide to the Collections (Singapore, 1985)

D. Ch'ng: 'Malay Silver', *A. Asia*, xvi (1986), pp. 102–9

V. T. King and Bantong Antaran: 'Some Items of Decorative Silverware in the Brunei Museum Ethnographic Collection', *Brunei Mus. J.*, vi/3 (1987), pp. 1–52

Mohd Kasim bin Haji Ali: *Gold Jewelry and Ornaments of Malaysia* (Kuala Lumpur, 1988)

V. T. King: 'Maloh, Malay and Chinese Silversmithing and Cultural Exchange in Borneo and Elsewhere', *Metalworking in Borneo: Essays*

on Iron and Silver-working in Sarawak, ed. J. W. Christie and V. T. King (Hull, 1988), pp. 29–56
S. Fraser-Lu: *Silverware of South-east Asia* (Singapore, 1989)
V. T. King: 'Brassware and Sarawak Cultures' and 'Silverware and Sarawak Cultures', *Sarawak Cultural Legacy*, ed. L. Chin and V. Mashman (Kuching, 1991), pp. 155–64, 165–75

2. KERIS. The *keris* is the traditional weapon of the Malay world and is credited with supernatural and magical powers. Since at least the 16th century the finest Malay craftsmanship in wood, ivory, precious metals and jewellery has been devoted to the making of *keris*. Ordinary *keris* were workmanlike weapons, while ceremonial *keris* became increasingly elaborate male adornments. During colonial times the wearing of *keris* by men was gradually restricted by law to use with ceremonial costume only, and their manufacture consequently went into steep decline. Since independence there has been a resurgence of interest and the *keris* has become an important symbol of Malaysian national identity. Today a few traditional craftsmen continue to make fine quality *keris* to order for ceremonial purposes. Some pre-17th century *keris* survive in museums, court regalias and royal collections, but most extant examples date from the 18th or 19th century.

Malay *keris* have four basic components: the blade (*mata*), including a lizard-shaped crosspiece (*ganja*) at the base; the cup (*pendongkok*) in which the hilt rests; the hilt (*hulu*); and the scabbard (*sarong*, composed of *sampir* or crosspiece and *batang* or main sheath). But there are variants such as the *keris majapahit*. In Malaysia many types survive as family heirlooms, the form of these depending on a family's origins. Blades are of steel and can be straight or wavy, the shape linked to the spiritual powers of the *keris* and the character of its owner. The base of the blade is drawn out into a hook projection (the 'elephant's trunk') and this area and the *ganja* are enhanced with spikes and notches. Blades are laminated and, by using acid to etch out differences between the iron and steel layers, patterns of dark and light lines (*pamor*) are produced creating a damascened effect. Blades are rarely polished but are sometimes inlaid in other metals with decorations such as *nāga*s (mythical serpents) and elephant heads or with Islamic inscriptions. While the blades are considered to be the most important part of the *keris*, much of its beauty lies in the superbly crafted sheaths and hilts. Fine and often rare hardwoods are carved and polished to bring out the beauty of the grain. Various ivories are also used, as well as chased and repoussé gold, silver and brass. The hilt cup is usually simply engraved cast brass, but it can be a brilliant piece of jewellery in filigree gold.

Severn types of *keris* are known to have been produced in Malaysia in quantity. Supposedly the most ancient of these is the *keris majapahit*, associated with the ancient Javanese empire of Majapahit and so with a pre-16th-century origin. Very convincing replicas are known to have been made in the 19th century and indeed are still being made in Terengganu. Variants of this form include the *keris picit*, which has a row of indentations in the blade that look as though they have been formed by the smith squeezing it while still red-hot between thumb and forefinger. The Pattani type, mainly found in Kelantan, is distinguished by its hilt, which has a head and a long extended nose or beak (the 'kingfisher' *keris*), and its sheath, which has a rounded crosspiece flared at both sides on top and a longish cylindrical sheath with a rounded end. Many *keris* of this type are entirely cased, hilt and sheath, with a brass, silver or gold sheet, decorated with leaf, tendril and floral motifs. The Peninsula type is the commonest in Malaysia, with a *pamor* blade of medium length, a *jawa demam* ('fever stricken', a figure bent at the shoulders with a bird-like head) hilt of half to three-quarter crank, and a sheath with a boat-shaped crosspiece, straight sides and a flat base, often achieved by the insertion of an additional piece. The Sumatran type is essentially derived from the Sumatran form through the Minangkabau people settled in Negeri Sembilan. It has a long thin blade, sometimes with *pamor*, sometimes blackened or polished, a straight or quarter-crank hilt with an elegantly carved 'horse's hoof' or 'flower' pommel, and a sheath with crescent moon crosspiece, rounded with an inserted round base, often in a V-shape. The finer examples have bands of decorated silver round the sheath. The Straits type has a strong, heavy blade of short to medium length with *pamor*, a fully cranked *jawa demam* hilt and a broad straight-sided sheath of elliptical cross-section, a flat base and a large squarish crosspiece. In the Peninsula these are particularly associated with Malacca, Johor and Singapore, but they were also common to the Riau-Lingga islands south of Singapore and the Malay-speaking states of the east Sumatran littoral, such as Palembang, where decorative patterns in enamel were applied to the sheath. The Bugis type was introduced into the Peninsula by the Bugis people of Sulawesi and is particularly associated with Selangor (for a description *see* INDONESIA, §VIII, 10). The Sulu or *sundang* type is an East Malaysian type associated with sea warfare and derives from Sabah and the southern Philippines. It is a long heavy sword or cutlass used for slashing rather than stabbing. The blade is often straight and polished, without *pamor*. An upright hilt with a beak pommel is firmly attached to it with one or two metal straps. The sheath is usually of wood, simply carved.

Whatever their style, the finest *keris* were made for the royal courts, which employed only the best craftsmen and reserved the use of gold for themselves. The courts determined the etiquette for their use and promulgated the legends of their deeds and the myths of their spiritual powers. Above all, they have preserved the finest examples in their regalias.

The Malays of the Peninsula also possess a wide variety of other well-crafted weapons. These include swords derived from Indian models, cutlass variants of the *parang*, a small hooked knife (*lawi ayam*), an Arabian-style knife (*beladau*), spears with *pamor* blades and carved wooden scabbards, set in elaborately decorated metal sockets, and firearms, particularly brass and bronze cannon on Portuguese and Brunei models. In all these the finest metalwork is to be seen on ceremonial spears, which still constitute an important part of royal regalias.

BIBLIOGRAPHY
W. Egerton: *An Illustrated Handbook of Indian Arms* (London, 1880)
G. C. Stone: *A Glossary of the Construction, Decoration and Use of Arms and Armor in All Countries and at All Times, Together with Some Closely Related Subjects* (Portland, ME, 1934, New York, rev. 1961)

G. B. Gardner: *Keris and Other Malay Weapons* (Singapore, 1936)

G. C. Woolley: 'The Malay Keris: Its Origin and Development', *J. Malay. Branch Royal Asiat. Soc.*, xx/2 (1947), pp. 60–103

A. H. Hill: 'The Keris and Other Malay Weapons', *J. Malay. Branch Royal Asiat. Soc.*, xxix/4 (1956) [whole issue]

Shahrum bin Yub: *Keris dan senjata₂ pendek* [Keris and short swords] (Kuala Lumpur, 1967)

M. Sheppard: *Taman Indera: A Royal Pleasure Ground: Malay Decorative Arts and Pastimes* (Kuala Lumpur, 1972)

——: *The Living Crafts of Malaysia* (Singapore, 1978)

Syed Ahmad Jamal: *Rupa dan Jiwa* [Form and spirit] (Kuala Lumpur, 1979)

E. Frey: *The Kris: Mystic Weapon of the Malay World* (Singapore and Oxford, 1986, rev. 1988)

LEWIS G. HILL

3. BETEL SETS. The ancient custom of betel-chewing may have originated in Malaysia, where it has been known for almost two millennia. In Malaysia, both sexes at all social levels chew betel, which plays an important symbolic role in betrothals and marriages. This ceremonial function necessitates elaborate containers made from the finest material available: metal. The choice of metal depends on its availability and the wealth and status of the owner. The earliest containers were made of gold, which was locally mined. Later, silver, an imported material, and such alloys as brass and bronze were used (*see* §1 above). A typical Malaysian metal betel set consists of a rectangular covered box, usually footed and decorated with a detailed abstract pattern, either geometric or arabesque. It contains four boxes for ingredients, such as slices of areca nut and lime paste. A removable tray is common. Round silver boxes are popular containers for individual ingredients. Most are portable and hang from a chain which can be secured to a belt. Many are in the shape of early European watchcases. The most common container for lime is a brass box shaped like a banana and decorated with an intricate floral scroll. For the betel leaves, a silver conical-shaped container with a finely detailed geometric design is popular. Betel-chewing in Malaysia was widespread until the 19th century, but since then many chewers have converted to tobacco.

BIBLIOGRAPHY

M. Sheppard: *Taman Indera: A Royal Pleasure Ground: Malay Decorative Arts and Pastimes* (Kuala Lumpur, 1972)

L. Chin: *Cultural Heritage of Sarawak* (Kuching, 1980)

DAWN F. ROONEY

VII. Textiles.

The production of traditional Malay textiles is largely confined to the north-eastern states of Kelantan and Terengganu, which, along with Pattani (now part of southern Thailand), have a cultural tradition dating back to the 1st century AD. Because of their relative isolation from the lanes of commerce during the last few centuries of European dominance, these states have retained more of their traditional Malay culture than the west-coast states, which have been subject to considerable Western and Chinese influence. There are still a number of tribal peoples in East Malaysia, the most notable being the Ibans of Sarawak, and the Rungus, Dusun and Bajau peoples of Sabah, who continue to weave traditional textiles (*see* §X, 1 below). The impact of changing lifestyles in the last half of the 20th century led to a drastic decline in weaving among these peoples.

1. KAIN SONGKET. The weaving of *kain songket*, a luxurious silk cloth patterned with gold supplementary wefts, which is considered to be the most traditional fabric of the Malay people for ceremonial wear, continues as a small cottage industry on the outskirts of Kota Baharu and Terengganu. In East Malaysia there are a few weavers in the Kuching and Mukah areas in Sarawak who produce an extremely fine *kain songket* in the Brunei tradition. On the east coast of Peninsular Malaysia the craft is organized at the village level by an entrepreneur, who receives orders for the cloth and supplies the weavers with dyed silk yarns, beaters and shuttles, which they use on their own looms. The entrepreneur may also make use of the services of a master weaver/designer, who visits the weavers at their homes and, for a small fee, assists them in setting up the loom for complex *songket* designs.

Kain songket is woven on a unique wooden-frame loom (*kek tenun*) consisting of a pair of transverse foot-treadles and a flat upright warp-beam fitted into slotted wooden guides suspended from a crossbeam at the top of the frame. The patterns for *kain songket* are set by carefully counting the warp threads in groups of three or five, lifting those required with a stick and looping them into groups with thick string to form bundles of *ikat butang*. At the time of weaving, the appropriate row of *ikat butang* threads is lifted and a shuttle of gold thread is inserted in the opening or 'shed' to form the weft and then anchored by two rows of plain thread in a plain weave.

Traditional *songket* patterns are either floral or geometric and are named after local flora, fauna and Malay cultural objects. They may be arranged in vertical, horizontal or diagonal rows, or in alternating motifs across the surface of the cloth. The cloth is traditionally divided into two distinct design areas: the *kepala* (head) and *badan* (body). The *kepala* consists of a decorative central panel embellished with two columns of triangular patterns called *pucuk rebung*. Floral motifs and small geometric designs fill the spaces between. The *badan* area usually has a plainer repetitive design and is separated from the *kepala* by floral border patterns. On some sarongs and shawls (*selendang*)

5. Malaysian headcloth or *kain destar* (detail), cotton ground with cotton and metallic threads, 1.06×1.02 m, from Sabah (Lewes, E. Sussex, private collection)

a smaller *kepala* area may appear at the warp ends of the cloth.

The Bajau (originally from the southern Philippines but later settled in the Kota Belud and Kudat areas in Sabah) use the *songket* supplementary weft technique to weave their distinctive, heavily starched headcloths (*kain destar*; see fig. 5) embellished with intricate geometric motifs in red, green, yellow and white on a black ground. Woven on a Filipino-style back-strap loom, the design shows strong affinities with headcloths of the Tausug of the Sulu Archipelago (*see* PHILIPPINES, §VII, 6). The headcloths are worn by men in almost every indigenous group in Sabah; each group has its own unique and imaginative methods of folding them.

2. OTHER WEAVING. The Bajau people also weave an all-purpose striped cotton material (*kain mogah*), embellished with small geometric motifs in a supplementary weft. The Rungus people of northern Sabah weave a distinctive indigo-coloured cotton cloth (*kain pudang*), patterned with wide warp bands decorated with geometric designs in white supplementary yarns. In Sarawak the Ibans in the Second and Third Divisions make use of two unique supplementary thread processes (*pilih* and *sungkit*) to produce traditional designs. In the *pilih* process bands of loose supplementary weft of alternating colours form a decorative background to the main weave, while in *sungkit* supplementary threads are inlaid into the weft with the aid of a needle.

Simply patterned stripes and plaids are popular for everyday cotton sarongs worn by men throughout Malaysia. These are usually woven on a loom called *kek Siam* (originally from Thailand), which has a self-releasing warp-beam, a metal beater, parallel foot-treadles and a box-shuttle device for faster weaving. The women of Kampung Peramu Pekan in Pahang have developed the weaving of vibrant plaids in silk into a flourishing cottage industry.

3. IKAT. The art of ikat (a resist-dye process in which yarns are tied in selected areas and then dyed so as to form a pattern when woven) is also practised in Malaysia. The greatest exponents of ikat are the Ibans, who make use of this difficult and very time-consuming technique to weave short ceremonial skirts for women (*bidang*), jackets (*kelambi*) and loincloths (*sirat*) for men and a blanket-sized textile (*pua kumbu*) of great ritual importance. Woven with a continuous warp on a back-strap loom, the palette for traditional Iban ikat is characterized by soft creamy-fawn shades enlivened by touches of chocolate brown and indigo against a brick-red ground. Iban textile designs are also remarkable for their spatial harmony, expressed in rows of vegetal, zoomorphic and anthropomorphic motifs cleverly linked by a series of hook and rhomb appendages into a skilfully integrated composition (*see also* §X, 1 below.)

North-eastern Malaya was at one time a notable centre for weft ikat. Until the early years of the 20th century, magnificent weft ikat cloth called *kain cindai* or *kain limar* was produced in Terengganu and Kota Baharu. It was made from the finest imported Chinese silk yarns delicately patterned with subtle arrowheads, zigzags, rhombs and small floral patterns against a rich ground of purple, deep brown and various vibrant reds. The patterning and cloth layout of *kain cindai* possibly owe their inspiration to imported Indian *patolu* double-ikat cloth and royal Cambodian textiles (*see* INDIAN SUBCONTINENT, §VI, 3(iii)(a); CAMBODIA, §V, 1). Beautiful two-tone *kain cindai* shawls with a red-coloured *kepala* area were highly prized by Malay women of rank and some continue to be worn on formal occasions by lovers of antique textiles.

4. BATIK. Weft ikat patterned silk cloth was superseded in Malaysia by a faster resist-patterning technique, that of batik (*see* INDONESIA, §V, 1), a method by which a wax compound is applied with a *canting*, a small copper vessel with a downward-pointing spout, to areas of previously woven cloth and acts as a resist during the dyeing process. In the 19th century, both in Java and Malaysia, batik patterns began to be stamped on to the cloth, rather than drawn. In this process a metal block (*cap*) of the desired design, made from soldered strips of copper or tin, is dipped into molten wax and stamped on to a plain piece of cloth.

Batik has been produced in Kelantan since 1910 and owes its origins to nearby Java. At the outset Malaysia turned to the commercialized outward-looking north-eastern coast of Java for inspiration rather than to the more conservative Central Java, the home of classical Indonesian batik, in which subdued shades of blue, brown and white are preferred. As a consequence, Malaysian batik is brightly coloured and shows considerable Western influence in its use of predominantly floral patterns. Since World War II, the craft has become very commercialized and the batik shirt and sarong have largely usurped *kain songket* as the preferred national dress. Numerous workshops are now producing batik designs on all weights of material, ranging from silk, satin, velvet and canvas to poplin, lawn, voile and cheesecloth. There is also a small but thriving *haute couture* industry, which produces unique hand-drawn and hand-painted batik fabrics for an exclusive clientele. To meet the demand from those of lesser means, many batik designs are now screenprinted rather than drawn or stamped.

5. GILDING AND GOLD EMBROIDERY. Batik or other cloth that is embellished with gold-leaf designs is known as *kain telepuk*. The area to be gilded is first smeared with gum arabic applied with a small hand-carved wooden design block. The same block is used to cut a pattern from gold foil which, when placed on the fabric, adheres to the glue. A sumptuous gold effect may also be achieved by embroidering couched gold thread designs on to a velvet-covered cardboard base. This embroidery technique (*tekat*) is used to decorate coverings and pillows for the bridal bed, prayer mats and ceremonial dish covers with delicate, interlacing floral patterns. In Kuching, the capital of Sarawak, a small group of women have revived the art of finely embroidering silk and muslin women's headcloths (*selayu*) with floral designs in flat gold thread.

BIBLIOGRAPHY
Kain serian songket [Silk *songket* cloths] (Kuala Lumpur, n.d.)
A. Haddon and L. E. Start: *Iban or Sea Dayak Fabrics and their patterns* (London, 1936)
A. H. Hill: 'Weaving Industry in Trengganu', *J. Malay. Branch Royal Asiat. Soc.*, xxii/3 (1949), pp. 75–84

J. M. Gullick: 'Survey of Malay Weavers and Silversmiths in Kelantan in 1951', *J. Malay. Branch Royal Asiat. Soc.*, xxv/1 (1952), pp. 134–48
J. Alman: 'Bajau Weaving', *Sarawak Mus. J.*, ix/15–16 (1960), pp. 603–18
Batek, Ikat and Pelangi and Other Traditional Textiles from Malaya (exh. cat. by B. A. V. Peacock, Hong Kong, Urban Council, 1977)
M. Shepherd: *Living Crafts of Malaysia* (Singapore, 1978)
——: *Taman Indera: A Royal Pleasure Ground: Malay Decorative Arts and Pastimes* (Kuala Lumpur, 1986)
S. Arney: *Malaysian Batik: Creating New Traditions* (Kuala Lumpur, 1987)
S. Fraser-Lu: *Handwoven Textiles of South-east Asia* (Singapore, 1988)
G. Mohd. Nawawi: *Malaysian Songket* (Kuala Lumpur, 1989)
G. I. Selvanayagam: *Songket: Malaysia's Woven Treasure* (Singapore, 1990)
SYLVIA FRASER-LU

VIII. Theatre.

The traditional drama of Peninsular Malaysia combines a wide variety of elements derived from different sources—indigenous Malay, Indian, Chinese, Arab, Javanese, Sumatran and Thai. These influences manifest themselves in the masks and costumes, the design of puppets, the dancing styles and techniques, the repertory, the language of performance and the music.

1. MASKS AND COSTUMES. Although masks have never played a central role in traditional Malay drama, two types may be distinguished: those of the *wayang Jawa* and those of the *mak yong, mek mulung* and *awang batil*.

A feature of ritual performances of the *wayang Jawa* (shadow theatre; see §2 below) is the *main topeng* (mask play), also known as *joget dalang* (dance of the puppet master). It was staged during the daytime, and preceded the ritual feast offered to propitiate the demon Betara Kala. The masks represent characters from the East Javanese tales of the adventures of Prince Panji, such as Ino, Jerudeh, Semar, Turas and Kalang, and reveal strong Javanese influence (see INDONESIA, §VI, 4(i)). The dance has apparently not been performed in Kelantan since the mid-20th century. An attempt was made to stage it in Pattani in 1971, but outside the context of a ritual *wayang* performance. Although the *main topeng* probably derives ultimately from the Javanese *wayang topeng*, it apparently consisted of a simple dance by the puppeteer (*dalang*) and two assistants, quite unlike the complex drama of the *wayang topeng* of Java.

The second type of mask is worn by the clowns of two genres of traditional drama found in Kedah: the *mak yong* and the *mek mulung*. (Masks are not employed in the Kelantan *mak yong*.) The predominant colours are red and black. In Perlis there is a third genre, the *awang batil*, in which the storyteller accompanies his chant by strumming with his fingers on a brass bowl (*batil*) and masks of the *mak yong* type are employed, one representing a captain (*hulubalang*), who summons people to the king's presence, and the other an astrologer (*nujum*). When either of these characters appears in the story, the teller dons the appropriate mask and describes the actions and acts the part of the character. The astrologer mask covers the whole face, the other leaves the mouth and chin exposed.

Of all the genres of traditional Malay drama, only the *mak yong* employs relatively elaborate costumes. In the *mek mulung*, where men play both male and female roles, the usual costume is a Malay tunic and short sarong worn over trousers, and a headcloth, for male characters, and

sarong and jacket (*kebaya*) for females. In the *mak yong*, where all roles except those of clowns are played by women, the principal female characters usually wear silk garments modelled to some extent on Kelantan and Pattani royal costume and consisting of a long-sleeved *kebaya* and sarong, embellished with waist-buckles, bracelets and anklets. The principal male characters wear a crown of stiff cloth, rising to a peak at the front, a tunic over which is draped a beaded collar, a knee-length sarong worn over trousers, and another sarong folded to form a waist-cloth. The two male clowns wore everyday peasant garb. Many illustrations of *mak yong* in modern publications are reconstructions of what is perceived to be traditional and 'original'.

Although the Thai *manora* is performed in northern Peninsular Malaysia, and the roles of females are often played by Malay males, it is more appropriately described in the context of Thai culture (see THAILAND, §IX, 2). The *bangsawan* or Malay opera, which developed in the latter part of the 19th century, employs a variety of costumes, the nature of which depends upon the setting of the play being performed. There is, however, a definite proclivity for a stylized form of 'Middle Eastern' dress: indeed, in Indonesia this play is usually called *stambul* (after Istanbul).

BIBLIOGRAPHY
J. Cuisinier: *Danses magiques de Kelantan* (Paris, 1936)
——: *Le Théâtre d'ombres à Kelantan* (Paris, 1957)
M. Sheppard: *Taman Indera: A Royal Pleasure Ground: Malay Decorative Arts and Pastimes* (Kuala Lumpur, 1972)
A. Sweeney: 'Professional Malay Storytelling: Some Questions of Style and Presentation', *J. Malay. Branch Royal Asiat. Soc.*, xlvi/2 (1973), pp. 1–53
Zaleha Abdul Hamid: *Permainan Mek Mulung* (Bangi, 1975)

2. WAYANG KULIT. Four genres of shadow theatre (*wayang kulit*) exist in Peninsular Malaysia. Two of these, the *wayang Siam* and the *wayang Jawa* (or *wayang Melayu*), are Malay forms, the references to Siam (Thailand) and Java indicating the local perception of the predominant influences in these types. The other two types are Thai and Javanese. The former, termed *wayang gedek* in Malay and found in the states adjacent to Thailand, is the Thai *nang talang* (see THAILAND, §IX, 1). The latter, performed in the Javanese-speaking areas of Johor and Selangor, is a version of the Javanese *wayang purwa* (see INDONESIA, §VI, 1(i)). The *wayang Siam* and *wayang Jawa* both exist in the states close to the Thai–Malaysian frontier: Kelantan, Terengganu, Kedah, Perlis, Perak and Pattani (Malay-speaking province of southern Thailand). The *wayang Jawa*, which has always depended upon the patronage of aristocrats, is now close to extinction. The *wayang Siam* has traditionally been much more popular, especially among the peasantry, and as recently as the 1970s it was one of the favourite entertainments in the rural areas of Kelantan and Pattani, the heart of Malay *wayang* country. Yet 20 years later it, too, had suffered a major decline in popularity.

Both Malay *wayang* are similar in technique, the main differences being in repertory, the iconography of the puppets, and the music. Both employ an operating box and place the screen slanting down towards the audience, as in Bali, which may represent a form of that earlier used

6. *Wayang Siam* shadow-puppets, episode from the *Rāmāyaṇa* depicting a battle between Hanuman and Ravana, from Kelantan, Malaysia

in Java. The Javanese origin of the Malay *wayang* is further suggested by the use of common technical terms.

The idea that the *wayang* is only a medium of artistic expression is a Western imposition, which may tend to obscure its traditional functions. The Malay *wayang* is a product of oral tradition and traditionally was at one and the same time a vehicle of general education, a way of communicating with the supernatural, a means of fulfilling aesthetic needs and a popular entertainment. Mass education and print literacy have gradually eroded most of these functions and brought about a redefinition of the elements of traditional Malay culture.

The basic core of the repertory of the *wayang Siam* (see fig. 6) is the 'Cerita Maharaja Wana', an oral tale roughly parallel to the Malay literary version of the Hindu epic, the *Rāmāyaṇa*. No two *dalang* produce identical versions, each preferring to alter and adapt the materials as he sees fit, and pupils rarely feel obliged to bind themselves to the repertory of their teachers. Nevertheless, all the versions possess a number of common features that distinguish them from the versions of other areas. Most of the motifs of these *wayang Siam* renderings occur in the Malay and/or Thai literary versions of the *Rāmāyaṇa*, and there is evidence that the *wayang Siam* version is the result of intermingling between these literary works or oral forms parallel to them. Much more frequently performed, however, are the offshoot tales (*cerita ranting*), which involve characters from the basic repertory and their descendants, but which have plots strongly influenced by the Javanese tales of the adventures of Prince Panji. Some of this influence may derive from the repertory of the *wayang Jawa*, which consists mainly of Malay versions of the Panji cycle. In addition, both *wayang Siam* and *wayang Jawa* occasionally performed 'Pandawa' tales, which derive from another major Hindu epic, the *Mahābhārata*.

The puppets of the *wayang Jawa* are largely modelled on the Panji figures of the Javanese *wayang gedog*, a variation of *wayang purwa*, the subject-matter of which is taken from the history of the last Hindu dynasties in Java, but the *wayang Siam* puppets possess a more distinctive style. Although at first glance the pinnacled crowns of royal male principals create the impression that the predominant influence is Thai, closer examination reveals an iconography that is typically Kelantanese. With the exception of clown figures, which have two movable arms, *wayang Siam* figures have only one arm articulated. Both males and females are depicted in profile, except for the shoulders and upper torso, which are *en face*. Feet are placed close together in a standing position, similar to that of Javanese puppets. The leaping pose of a few figures indicates Thai influence. Puppets may conveniently be classified according to nine character types, such as refined prince, ogre prince, sage, ape, coarse ogre officers (*patih*) and clowns. Although it is always possible to recognize the type to which a puppet belongs, it is often not possible to identify the individual, for, with the exception of about 30 chief characters (out of a set composed of over 200 puppets), the form of individuals is far from standardized. Nevertheless, although the *dalang* have introduced modern embellishments such as Malay national costume for some minor characters, even these puppets always fit the traditional stereotype. Predominant colours are red and green.

The *dalang*'s speech consists, on the one hand, of narrative and commentary spoken in his own voice, and, on the other, of the speech of his puppet characters; the character type determines the voice to be used. For clowns, however, the *dalang* has freedom to produce a variety of comic voices. The language is extemporized in performance and is a stylized form of the local dialect. The character type also determines the movements of the puppets. Various tunes are prescribed, first for the walking of each character type and second for other actions, such as battle, regardless of type. The music is played by an orchestra of nine to twelve musicians, with an oboe (*serunai*) accompanied by a variety of drums and gongs providing the melody.

Traditionally the *dalang* played an important role as a spirit medium in the ritual *berjamu* (feast) which was held to propitiate spirits, to release a person from a vow and to initiate a pupil. The *dalang*, in a state of trance, would feed the spirits, including those of his own puppets, who would possess him in turn. This ritual is a synthesis of Javanese *wayang* ritual and the rituals of local spirit mediums. It is now very rarely performed. (*See also* §1 above).

Most *dalang* live in rice-growing areas. *Wayang* performances were traditionally given to mark rites of passage, but in the 1960s they came to be organized mainly as commercial enterprises, with the sale of tickets. Even at the peak of the *wayang*'s popularity, few *dalang* lived entirely on their earnings from it, and most had a secondary occupation. Most *dalang* learn their art from a teacher, and their calling is not hereditary.

BIBLIOGRAPHY

A. Sweeney: *The Ramayana and the Malay Shadow-play* (Kuala Lumpur, 1972)

——: *Malay Shadow Puppets* (London, 1972)

——: *Authors and Audiences in Traditional Malay Literature* (Berkeley, 1980)
——: *A Full Hearing: Orality and Literacy in the Malay World* (Berkeley, 1987)
J. O. Miettinen: *Classical Dance and Theatre in South-east Asia* (Singapore, 1992)
P. Matsuky: *Malaysian Shadow Play and Music: Continuity of an Oral Tradition* (Kuala Lumpur, 1993)

AMIN SWEENEY

IX. Other arts.

1. Boats. 2. Ceramics. 3. Coins. 4. Dress. 5. Jewellery. 6. Kites. 7. Woodcarving.

1. BOATS. Boats and boatmaking have a long history in both Peninsular and East Malaysia. The early immigrants into Peninsular Malaysia were seafarers and used boats for transport, communication and commerce, from which contacts with other cultures resulted. As in many other South-east Asian cultures, boats were thought to be the vehicles that conveyed the dead to the afterlife. The bodies of the deceased were buried in boat-shaped coffins, and carvings and textiles were made depicting the soul of the ancestor sailing to the world of the dead. Ship of the dead motifs are still commonly used in textiles and wood- and stone-carvings in Malaysia and in the Indonesian archipelago.

Since the early immigrants into Peninsular Malaysia are believed to have gone on from there to settle in the islands of Indonesia, the Philippines and the Pacific, many Malaysian boatmaking traditions resemble those of Indonesia, Micronesia, Melanesia and Polynesia, and variants of the Malay for boat (*perahu*) occur in most Malayo-Polynesian languages. The most characteristic and universal of these crafts is the single outrigger canoe using a dugout or carvel-built hull. River boats usually have a dugout hull with a flat bottom, a sloping bow and stern held together with rattan and a canopy of cane and palm-leaf. The larger ones, called *kityup*, are used as houseboats. Rafts made of four parallel logs are occasionally used. The Iban people of Sarawak, East Malaysia, still make bark canoes similar to those found in the Solomon Islands. The Kenyah people, also of Sarawak, make very long bark canoes, often featuring a carved animal head at the stern. Most common in Malaysian waters are fishing boats, or *perahu payang*, used for drift-net fishing and local coastal trade. *Perahu payang* are built and carry large nets. Though there is no standard size, most are about nine metres overall. In the past the boats tended to carry a large press of sail, but today are usually run by diesel motors. Smaller canoes used for fishing have dugout hulls and a short mast. In Peninsular Malaysia, rulers and important dignitaries would travel sailing the inland waters in vast ceremonial boats called *perahu garai*, which were carvel-built with a dugout keel piece, a bamboo mast and canvas canopy. In the 19th century, the Brooke family, the white rajas of Sarawak, used a large pirate ship with two sails and two decks, 150 oarsmen and bronze cannons.

BIBLIOGRAPHY

R. Firth: *Malay Fishermen* (Hamden, CT, 1966)
J. Neyret: *Pirogues océaniennes* (Paris, 1976)
P. Bellwood: *Man's Conquest of the Pacific* (London, 1977)
Ethnographic Boat Models in the Royal Scottish Museum: A Catalogue of Traditional Watercraft from Africa, Asia, the Pacific and the Americas, Royal Scottish Museum (Edinburgh, 1984)

P.-Y. Manguin: 'Ship-shape Societies: Boat Symbolism in the Malay World', *Southeast Asia from the 9th to the 14th Centuries*, ed. D. B. Marr and A. C. Milner (Singapore, 1986)

NORA TAYLOR

2. CERAMICS. Neolithic wares dating from the 2nd millennium BC found in cave sites are among the earliest types of ceramics in Malaysia. Handmade jars, pots and bowls decorated with simple geometric designs are typical. This type of unglazed utilitarian earthenware was made until the 8th century AD, or perhaps later, when Chinese trade ceramics replaced it.

Peninsular Malaysia is a rich source of foreign ceramics because of its location on the east–west trade route between China and India. Types of Chinese trade wares found in quantity include celadons at Pengkalan Bujang in Kedah (10th century–mid-14th) and blue-and-white porcelains in the maritime state of Malacca (mid-15th century) and in the local kingdom of Johor (16th–17th century). Other ceramics include Thai and Vietnamese wares (14th–15th century) and Japanese ceramics (17th–19th century). Chinese-style glazed ceramics are still made in Malaysia by immigrant Chinese (from Guangdong and Fujian provinces) who arrived in the late 19th century and early 20th.

Unglazed earthenware for domestic use is made in rural parts of modern Malaysia. A gourd-shaped bottle used as a container for water is a well-known speciality of Sayong district, in Perak. A distinctive feature is its black burnished surface.

BIBLIOGRAPHY

L. Chin: *Cultural Heritage of Sarawak* (Kuching, 1980)

DAWN F. ROONEY

3. COINS. The earliest Islamic coinage in Peninsular Malaysia is a tin series struck by Malacca sultans between *c.* 1450 and 1511, for example those issued with calligraphic designs during the reign of Sultan Muzaffar Shah (*reg* 1445–59). The legends on Malacca tin were influenced by Indian coin design, notably from Gujarat (*see* INDIAN SUBCONTINENT, §VIII, 6). Following the conquest of Malacca by the Portuguese in 1511, a European-style coinage replaced the local series. During the 16th and 17th centuries, Johor played a major role in the development of Malay coinage, introducing an extensive series of octagonal gold *kupang* (0.60 gm) and *mas* (2.40 gm), including coins with Arabic calligraphic designs during the reign of Sultan Abdul Jalil Shah (*reg* 1623–77), as well as a large tin coinage that grew out of the Malacca experience. Johor's issues in turn influenced the coinage traditions of Kedah and Terengganu.

Another important area of gold-coin production, particularly during the 17th century, was Pattani–Kelantan. The most pervasive coin is a bull issue with *al-ādil* ('the Just') inscribed on the reverse which gradually took on the character of a *wayang* shadow-puppet figure. By the 19th century these gold issues had been replaced by a subsidiary tin coinage. A distinctive form of coinage, based on the old Malay tin ingot, is the *tampang* or 'tin hat' money of Pahang. The earliest dated coins were made in 1819; they continued as a major currency on the east coast until demonetized in 1889. In the north of Peninsular Malaysia, notably Singora, Patalung and Ligor (Nakhon Si Thammarat), areas under heavy Thai influence, bilingual and trilingual coinage was introduced in the second half of the 19th century. These cast-tin issues are inscribed in Chinese, Thai and Malay.

By the end of the 17th century, the gold issues of Johor, Pattani–Kelantan, Kedah, Terengganu and elsewhere were supplanted by Spanish silver as a medium of international trade. Indeed, Kedah issued a short-lived silver coinage in 1741 equal in weight to a Spanish *real*. As European silver gained in importance and popularity, only small, low-value tin coins were minted by local officials and merchants, most notably the Chinese. These issues continued to be made until the last decades of the 19th century, when they were replaced by British currency.

BIBLIOGRAPHY

F. Pridmore: 'The Native Coinage of the Malay Peninsula', *Spinks Numi. Circ.*, lxxvi/10 (1968)–lxxii/3 (1974)
W. Shaw and M. K. H. Ali: *Kedah Coins* (Kedah, 1970)
——: *Malacca Coins* (Kuala Lumpur, 1970)
——: *Tin 'Hat' and Animal Money* (Kuala Lumpur, 1970)
S. Singh: 'Tin and Gold Coins of the Malay States, 1400–1963', *Malaysia Numi. Soc. Newslett.*, vii/4 (1975)–ix/6 (1977)
R. S. Wicks: *A Survey of Native Southeast Asian Coinage Circa 450–1850: Documentation and Typology* (diss., Cornell U., NY, 1983)

ROBERT S. WICKS

4. DRESS. Traditional formal dress for Malay men, the *baju kurung*, consists of a long-sleeved silk or cotton tunic (*kurung*) with a 150 mm front opening secured by studs. Gusset inserts under the arms and side panels allow for ease of movement. This tunic, derived from Arab sources, is worn with matching loose-fitting, ankle-length trousers. Over this is worn a short sarong (*sampin*) which is secured at the waist with a wide cloth belt embellished with a large elliptical silver buckle (*pinding, see* §5 below). No *baju kurung* would be complete without the addition of a large distinctive headcloth (*kain destar* or *tengkolok*), which may be twisted and folded in a variety of ways according to the rank, occupation and location of the wearer. The regalia of the various heads of state may incorporate calligraphy as an integral feature of their design.

Traditional dress for Malay women consists of an ankle-length cotton or silk sarong folded into a pleat in the front. The sarong may be worn either with the knee-length, slightly flaring *kurung* (similar in tailoring to that of the men's except that the side panels are wider) or with the *kebaya* (a long-sleeved hip- or knee-length jacket with front panels and darts to ensure a smooth, contoured fit). The neckline may be edged with a small collar and lapels, while the front opening is usually fastened with a set of three ornamental pins (*kerongsang*). The *kebaya* is thought to have been inspired by the clothing worn by Portuguese women in 16th-century Malacca. Chinese women who have been in Malaysia for many generations (*nyonya*) also like to use a shorter *kebaya* of lace or a semi-sheer fabric with a batik sarong for everyday wear. Malay women may wear a long shawl (*selandang*) over the shoulders when they go out. Many also wrap a white or pastel-coloured cloth (*selayu*) over the head and shoulders when appearing in public.

See also §VII above.

BIBLIOGRAPHY

K. Sim: *Costumes of Malaya* (Singapore, 1963)

SYLVIA FRASER-LU

5. JEWELLERY. Traditional Malaysian gold and silver jewellery is often studded with precious and semi-precious stones. Techniques include repoussé, chasing, filigree, openwork, punching and granulation. Decoration takes the form of geometric and floral motifs derived from local flora and Chinese, Indian and Islamic sources. In East Malaysia, Chinese dominate the manufacture and marketing of gold and silver jewellery.

Women wear hair ornaments (*cucuk sanggul*), often flower-shaped, which may be burnt in charcoal to give the gold a reddish hue. Blouses are fastened with brooches or pins connected with chains (*kerongsang*) and flower-shaped earrings are worn, often set with precious stones. Men wear elaborate belt-buckles (*pinding*), usually consisting of a finely chased central medallion surrounded by vegetal decoration and a geometric border. Both sexes wear finger-rings, the men favouring large stones as settings. Women also adorn themselves with gold and silver necklaces, armlets and bangles. Special occasions, such as weddings, may be marked by the display of elaborate neck-chains, swathes of chain interspersed with decorated plaques. At weddings, moreover, the bridal couple will wear large quantities of heirloom jewellery. Tiaras and crowns are made for royalty. An unusual piece of jewellery once worn by young girls is the *caping*, a fig-shaped pubic plate of silver or brass, often intricately decorated with chasework. In Sabah and Sarawak, finger-rings, earrings, bracelets, armlets and anklets of heavy brass wire are still produced to commission.

Among aboriginal peoples of Peninsular Malaysia, headbands, necklaces and bracelets of fungus rhizomorphs are worn, partly for decoration and partly for magical protection. Leaf ornaments and everlasting flowers are also worn, as well as strips of barkcloth or pandanus (screw-pine) leaves, often fringed and painted in simple geometric patterns with charcoal and turmeric dyes. Women wear bamboo combs with scratched geometric and animal motifs. Necklaces of animal teeth, bone, Job's tears and European beads are also popular. Plaited rattan bracelets, armlets and leglets are used by both sexes, and porcupine quills may be worn in the nose by some groups.

BIBLIOGRAPHY

I. H. N. Evans: *The Negritos of Malaya* (Cambridge, 1937)
S. Fraser-Lu: *Silverware of Southeast Asia*, Images of Asia (Oxford, 1989)

SIAN E. JAY, with LEWIS G. HILL

6. KITES. Kite-flying in Malaysia was originally regarded as a means of communicating with sky spirits. Now it is a popular pastime, particularly in the states of Kelantan and Terengganu where kite-flying competitions are held. The most popular shape is the moon kite, though bird and animal shapes are also used. The kites usually measure *c.* 2.0×1.8 m, the frame being made from a light, flexible bamboo covered with up to three layers of paper, which together constitute the decoration. Kite makers may invent their own designs, but traditional Malay designs are also used. Leaf and flower patterns around the borders are frequently depicted, though a plain heart-shaped area is usually left in the centre of each wing.

BIBLIOGRAPHY

M. Sheppard: *Taman Indera: Malay Decorative Arts and Pastimes* (Kuala Lumpur, 1972)

——: *Mekarnya seni pertukangan Malaysia* [The flowering of crafts in Malaysia] (Kuala Lumpur, 1980)

SIAN E. JAY

7. WOOD-CARVING. In Malaysia's multicultural society, wood-carving traditions differ from one ethnic group to another. While the indigenous peoples both in the Peninsula and in Sarawak and Sabah (East Malaysia) carve human and animal figures, the Muslim Malays, owing to Islamic restrictions on representing anthropomorphic figures in art, employ their wood-carving skills to decorate the interior and exterior of their houses.

(i) Peninsular Malaysia. Traditional Malay houses are often embellished with wood-carving on posts, banisters, roof eaves, doorways, wall and window panels. Floral and geometric designs are prominent in these decorations, and the more elaborate they are, the higher the status of the owner of the house. The decorative fascia boards covering the roof and floor edges are called *awan larat* (floating clouds). Patterns of decoration also bear such names as *roda berpusing* (rotating wheel) and *bunga matahari* (sunflower). Ventilation is provided by fenestrations carved into window panels, which at the same time reduce glare. Wood-carvings on houses in Malacca are often painted, whereas in the rest of Malaysia they are usually left unpainted, so as to display the natural grain of the wood.

The most reputed Orang Asli wood-carvers are the forest-dwelling Mah Meri people of Pulau Carey *c.* 60 km west of Kuala Lumpur in the state of Selangor. The Mah Meri, who are a sub-group of the Senois, carve figurines out of the soft wood of trees that grow near the sea, using a *parang* (machete), a chisel and a mallet. They also carve ceremonial masks from *pulai* wood and images of their ancestors and of other spirits. They give to both masks and images the generic name of *moyang* (ancestor). *Moyang* images are used both as guardians to ward off evil spirits and sometimes in healing rituals. At least 200 types of *moyang* are known, each one with its own distinctive features. The Orang Asli also carve bamboo tube containers, blowpipes and wind instruments with finely incised designs.

The locally born Chinese population in Peninsular Malaysia, who are called *peranakan* or, more commonly, Baba Nyonya, and are concentrated chiefly in Malacca and Penang, and also in Singapore, make wood-carvings essentially as architectural decoration for buildings of all types. The most elaborate examples of this can be found in Malacca, where their ancestors came as traders and subsequently settled from the 15th to the 19th century. By combining designs and motifs from their native China with the use of local materials and techniques, the Straits Chinese created a unique and flamboyant style of ornamental wood-carving, generally in teak, ebony or rosewood, to adorn doors, panelling, window frames, staircases and pieces of furniture. The most frequently used motifs are dragon, phoenix and floral designs, and symbols of luck, fortune, longevity and happiness, while shop fronts are often carved with the names of their proprietors. One of Malacca's best-preserved Baba Nyonya houses is at 48 and 50 Jalan Tun Cheng Lok, built in 1896 by Chan Cheng Siew, a prosperous rubber planter. It was opened as a museum in 1985. Every surface in the interior is covered with carved rose-wood, gilded, lacquered or inlaid with mother-of-pearl. It has a teak staircase carved with longevity motifs and adorned with gold leaf. Much Straits Chinese furniture is made of ebony inlaid with mother-of-pearl. Sometimes the carved wood is covered with a coat of red lacquer and adorned with gold leaf. Red lacquer and gold doors and panels are made, as well as chests, beds and chairs.

BIBLIOGRAPHY

R. Werner: *Mah Meri of Malaysia: Art and Culture* (Kuala Lumpur, 1974)
F. Chia: *The Babas* (Singapore, 1980)
M. Sheppard: *Taman Indera: Malay Decorative Arts and Pastimes* (Kuala Lumpur, 1985)
W. Moore and I. R. Lloyd: *Malacca* (Singapore, 1986)
Lim Jee Yuan: *The Malay House* (Penang, 1987)

(ii) East Malaysia. In the East Malaysian states of Sabah and Sarawak in Borneo wood is commonly used to carve statuettes, especially for funeral rituals and magical ceremonies, to make masks and shields and to decorate houses. The tropical forests of the island provide a rich variety of wood types, and because wood comes from trees, which are believed to be the origin of all creation, it has a particularly important symbolic significance. Motifs include the tree of life, *nāga*s (mythical serpents), hornbills and various stylized vegetal and geometric motifs. To many of the ethnic groups in East Malaysia, birds and animals represent omens and auguries. For example, the Iban people of Sarawak believe the hornbill to be an ancestral messenger and therefore carve images of hornbills, which they adorn with jewels to appease the souls of the ancestors. The Kayan, Kenyah and Kelabit people believe that the *nāga* and the hornbill are the guardians of the higher world and accordingly carve these creatures on their shields as protective devices. Among the Ngajus, statuettes called *hampatong* are carved and kept in the home to bring good luck and ensure a good harvest. Sometimes miniature *hampatong* are placed in bamboo containers to provide protection. The Kenyah people place a wooden image of a guardian spirit called Bali Akang in the ground to protect the house or village from disease and danger. Among the Ibans ironwood is used for making blowpipes as well as small sticks called *tuntun*, which have a dark, smooth patina and are surmounted by a small human figure in a seated position with legs bent and chin resting on hands. *Tuntun* are used as charms or bait and as units of measure for hunting traps. Statuettes called *bilum* bearing the likeness of a sick person are carved out of the soft wood of the sago tree. Water is poured over them, collected in a cloth and applied to the part to be healed, after which they are discarded. No less elaborately carved than the *bilum* are tomb posts, or *keliring*, made to commemorate the death of a high-ranking person. These tomb posts are often carved with frightening motifs to protect the deceased from bad spirits. Bamboo is used for making wind instruments and tube containers, the surface often whittled into intricate patterns and the incisions dyed. Sword sheaths are also made of small wooden boards lashed together with creeper fibre or brass wire.

BIBLIOGRAPHY

L. Chin: *Cultural Heritage of Sarawak* (Kuching, 1980)
The Eloquent Dead: Ancestral Sculpture of Indonesia and Southeast Asia (exh. cat., ed. J. Feldman; Los Angeles, UCLA, Wight A.G., 1985)

J. P. Barbier and D. Newton, eds: *Islands and Ancestors: Indigenous Styles of Southeast Asia* (Munich, 1989)
H. Munan: *Sarawak Crafts* (Singapore, 1989)
B. Sellato: *Hornbill and Dragon: Arts and Culture of Borneo* (Jakarta and Kuala Lumpur, 1989)

X. Non-Malay arts.

1. EAST MALAYSIA. The Dayak peoples of East Malaysia are well-known for their artistic skills. The Kayan and Kenyah are accomplished in carving, beadwork, painting and forging ceremonial swords, the Ibans (Sea Dayaks) in weaving, the Penans in plaiting, the Bidayuhs (Land Dayaks) and Muruts in carving bamboo, the Kadazans (Dusuns) in decorative beadware and the Melanaus in wood-carving. Apart from its aesthetic dimensions, Dayak art is intimately related to religious ideas and practices concerning life, death and fertility. Everyday objects are frequently decorative, but there are also special, finely made pieces valued as heirlooms and exchanged as ritual gifts.

The Ibans are the only Malaysian Dayaks who weave decorative ceremonial cloths (*pua kumbu*), short skirts (*kain kebat*) and jackets (*kelambi*). Designs are incorporated by the warp ikat technique: the main motifs are given form by progressively dyeing areas of the background (commonly in reddish brown, indigo-blue, dark brown or black) to leave some warp in reserve. This produces a blurred, almost otherworldly effect. Motifs comprise naturalistic human and animal forms, including the crocodile and lizard, and non-representational lozenges, keys, spirals, dentates, zigzags and border stripes. (*See also* §VII, 3 above.)

The Penans manufacture pliable, closely woven rattan baskets (*ajat*) and mats (*uhu wai*) in diagonal weave, with complex designs picked out in black dye or by means of the natural colours of the rattan. These include stylized snakes of the underworld (nāga), upperworld hornbills (*kenyalang*), anthropomorphs (protective images) and key, spiral and other abstract forms. The Bidayuhs make a more austere, vertically and horizontally plaited carrying-basket (*tambok*), strengthened at corner and base with sticks. Its beauty comes from the simple, close weave contrasted with strategically placed, coloured vertical and horizontal bands. The Ibans plait rattan mats in which the designs are seen only when looked at obliquely so that the light falls on the raised parts of the weave. The variety of sun-hats made of overlapping pandanus and other palm leaves is bewildering, from the large, rounded, rather flat Kenyah hats covered with bead designs and pieces of coloured cloth (*sa'ong*) to the high, conical, coloured hats of the Bidayuh, Murut and Kadazan Dayaks.

Formerly, various Dayak groups made beautiful necklaces, bracelets and skull-caps from ancient beads of carnelian, agate, glass, amber, jade and bone, but small, monochrome glass beads have come to be commonly used for decoration on headbands, baskets (*see* BEADWORK, colour pl. I, fig. 2), boxes, baby-carriers, swordsheaths, skirts and jackets. Kayan and Kenyah beadwork is delicately executed. The most striking motifs serve as symbols of the aristocracy; they comprise for the Kenyahs the displayed human form (*kalong kelunan*), the human face or mask (*kalong ulu*), the dog-dragon (*asu/aso'*), the

tiger and the hornbill. The *aso'* is usually depicted with the body of a dog and a dragon-like snout, curled fangs and horns. The main motifs are linked and given uniformity by sprouting tendrils and spirals (*kelawit*). In contrast, Kadazan beadwork uses abstract key and rhomb patterns and conventionalized human forms.

The Kayans and Kenyahs also execute large-scale paintings on the longhouse dividing walls between apartments and charnel houses of aristocrats, using the same range of motifs as in their beadware. Some local painters, such as Jok Bato, have acquired a considerable reputation and have been commissioned by government departments and wealthy patrons to paint special pieces (see fig. 7). Other groups, such as the Kadazans and Ibans, produce painted Malay-like scrolls and coils on their funeral structures. Many Kayan, Kenyah and Iban designs, especially the *aso'*, hornbill and tendrils, are also used in tattooing. Iban men tattoo much of their body, Kayan and Kenyah females their arms and legs.

The Kayans and Kenyahs carve free-standing wooden human, *aso'* and hornbill figures, as well as incising them in wood. Frightening anthropomorphic protective figures

7. Jok Bato: 'Tree of Life' wall painting in the Kenyah–Kayan style, oil on white cotton cloth, 1.68×1.02 m, 1972 (Hull, private collection)

are placed at village entrances. Carved funerary monuments of aristocrats range from charnel houses (*salong*)—on one or more supports—to funeral posts (*kelirieng/liang*) decorated with incised demonic images. Demonic masks with protruding eyes and fangs are carved and worn during agricultural rituals. The Kayans and Kenyahs carve *aso'* and other designs in horn and bone for the hilts of ceremonial swords (*parang ilang*) and incorporate spirals, tendrils and inlaid brass circles on the blade of the sword. The coastal Melanaus carve sickness images (*bilum*) from sago pith; these are usually anthropomorphic, squatting or with legs crossed and with crosshatching on the body to produce a scaly effect. There is a variety of headdresses (crowns, braziers, turbans, horns); some *bilum* have wings, some have protruding tongues. The Ibans produce heavier, more blockish forms. Their wooden human and other figures are solid and have incised patterns (as with those in Bidayuh and Murut low-relief carving on bamboo) reminiscent of Malay arabesque designs. They also carve figures of hornbills, formerly used in head-hunting rituals, in softwood, with elaborate, exaggerated casque and tail and painted in green, yellow, red, white and black.

BIBLIOGRAPHY

H. Ling Roth: *The Natives of Sarawak and British North Borneo*, 2 vols (London, 1896)
E. B. Haddon: 'The Dog-motive in Borneo Art', *J. Royal Anthropol. Inst. GB & Ireland*, 35 (1905), pp. 113–25
O. Rutter: *The Pagans of North Borneo* (London, 1929)
A. C. Haddon and L. E. Start: *Iban or Sea Dayak Fabrics and their Patterns* (Cambridge, 1936)
W. Stöhr: *Das Totenritual der Dajak* (Cologne, 1959)
S. H. Sharples Gill: *Selected Aspects of Sarawak Art* (New York, 1968)
C. Zainie: *Handcraft in Sarawak* (Kuching, 1969)
H. L. Whittier: *Social Organization and Symbols of Social Differentiation: An Ethnographic Study of the Kenyah Dayak of East Kalimantan (Borneo)* (Michigan State University, 1973)
L. Chin: *Cultural Heritage of Sarawak* (Kuching, 1980)
N. J. Chadwick and P. P. Courtenay: *Punan Art and Artefacts* (Townsville, 1983)
M. Hitchcock: *Indonesian Textile Traditions* (Aylesbury, 1985)
V. T. King: 'Symbols of Social Differentiation: A Comparative Investigation of Signs, the Signified and Symbolic Meanings in Borneo', *Anthropos*, lxxx (1985), pp. 125–52
J. B. Avé and V. T. King: *People of the Weeping Forest: Tradition and Change in Borneo* (Leiden, 1986)
Chong Chin Seng: *Traditional Melanau Woodcarving (Bilum) in Dalat, Sarawak* (Kuching, 1987)

VICTOR T. KING

2. WEST MALAYSIA. The traditional decorative arts of the aboriginal peoples (Orang Asli) of Peninsular Malaysia employ geometric patterns. Generally these are incised on bamboo artefacts by males, or worked in basketry by females. Some painting of the designs on basketry and barkcloth has been recorded. Tattooing, body painting and patterned scarification, once practised by many groups, have largely disappeared.

Men use knives to produce elaborate patterns on blowguns, dart quivers, haircombs, hairpins, flutes, drinking vessels and charms. The Negritos, a group of Orang Asli who live in the interior highlands of the Peninsula, also decorate bamboo tubes used for arrow quivers and in birth and death rituals. They cut grooves through the outer skin of the bamboo and sometimes rub in charcoal and other dark substances to enhance the lines. The designs are incised in double rows with hatching between them and are mostly in bands round, across or down the object, with repeated oblique crosses, triangles, zigzags and bars. Less frequently, curved lines and representations of animals are incised.

Basketry is essentially a woman's art among the Orang Asli. Females prepare strips of plant fibre from pandanus, nipa, rattans and bamboos, and some of these are dyed before plaiting and weaving. Common products are finely worked baskets for carrying and storage. Mats (especially among the Proto-Malays), belts and small wallets for carrying betel ingredients are woven with elaborate coloured patterns. These patterns are geometric and, while resembling those of the incised work of the men, extend the range with waves and meanders.

Many patterns and designs were recorded and intensively studied at the end of the 19th century. There has been some controversy over their meanings since (see Skeat and Blagden; Evans, 1927). Most designs are stylized plants (e.g. flowers, rice grains, fruits). Others represent or take their names from animals (e.g. lizard, tortoise, python), and when applied to blowguns and dart and arrow quivers are associated with hunting magic. Some designs are purely decorative; some mark ownership; others are or were intended to protect the owner from misfortune and harmful spirits. Whatever the meaning of the patterns, it is doubtful whether the symbolism of many of the beautiful specimens preserved in early museum collections will ever be fully understood. With the increased absorption of the Orang Asli into Malay culture during the 20th century, and the development of a tourist market for aboriginal artefacts, understanding of the symbolism has declined and the emphasis has moved more to the decorative.

Two Senoi groups of Orang Asli are noted for their wood-carving today. The Mah Meri people (Besisi in early accounts) of Selangor produce grotesque masks and figures, and the Jah Heut (Jah Hut) of Pahang carve grotesque anthropomorphic figures. These modern hardwood sculptures began to be produced in the 1950s when the Department of Orang Asli Affairs encouraged some villagers to develop their carving skills commercially. After exhibitions in Kuala Lumpur the sculptures became something of a vogue for collectors. Most of the carvings are of spirits that bring misfortune, sickness and disease. They are inspired by simpler representations used in traditional curing rituals and ceremonials.

BIBLIOGRAPHY

W. W. Skeat and C. O. Blagden: *The Pagan Races of the Malay Peninsula*, 2 vols (London, 1906)
I. H. N. Evans: *Papers on the Ethnology and Archaeology of the Malay Peninsula* (Cambridge, 1927)
——: *The Negritos of Malaya* (Cambridge, 1937)
P. D. R. Williams-Hunt: *An Introduction to the Malayan Aborigines* (Kuala Lumpur, 1952)
Shahrum bin Yub: 'The Museums Department Collections Kuala Lumpur and Taiping of Mah Meri Sculpture', *Fed. Mus. J.*, n. s., ix (1964), pp. 52–67
R. Werner: *Mah Meri of Malaysia: Art and Culture* (Kuala Lumpur, 1974)
——: *Jah-hēt of Malaysia: Art and Culture* (Kuala Lumpur, 1975)
I. Carey: *Orang Asli: The Aboriginal Tribes of Peninsular Malaysia* (Kuala Lumpur, 1976)
M.-A. Couillard: *Tradition in Tension: Carving in a Jah Hut Community* (Penang, 1980)
Wazir-Jahan Begum Karim: *Ma' Betisek Concepts of Living Things* (London, 1981)

LEWIS G. HILL

XI. Art education.

Art education was developed only under British administration after 1945. When Malaysia gained its independence in 1957 art and crafts became a compulsory subject in primary schools and up to Form Three in secondary schools. To cope with the demand for specialist teachers, the Specialist Teachers' Training Institute at Cheras in Kuala Lumpur was established in 1960. There are at present 29 teacher-training institutions under the control of the Ministry of Education, and a general course in art education as an enrichment programme is provided.

In 1965, as part of the Government's social reconstruction programme, the Institute of Technology, MARA, was created to provide tertiary education exclusively for ethnic Malays or 'bumiputeras'. Set up some 25 km outside Kuala Lumpur in Shah Alam, its School of Art and Design provides three-year diploma courses in Painting, Sculpture, Printmaking, Textile and Fashion, Industrial Art, Fine Metal and Jewellery, Ceramics, Graphic Design, Photography and Music. All students are required to take a one-year pre-diploma course in Foundational Studies. A one year's art teacher's diploma course provides opportunities for diploma graduates to take up teaching as a career.

The Science University of Malaysia (Universiti Sains) in Penang was established in 1969. Here a full-time undergraduate programme of four years leading to the BA degree with Honours is offered by the School of Humanities. A minimum of five foundation courses are taken in the introductory year. Fine Arts and Critical Thinking are compulsory for Fine Arts major students. A minor specialization is also required for the degree course. Studio courses comprise Painting, Sculpture, Photography, Graphic Design and Printmaking. The Arts Centre conducts the bachelor's programme and also offers postgraduate master's and doctoral programmes. A one-year certificate creative course is offered to those without the minimum entry qualifications for the degree programme.

All teachers and staff of higher-education institutions in Malaysia are government employees, and the 29 state teacher-training institutions supply art teachers for primary schools. Art teachers for secondary schools are drafted from the the Institute of Technology, MARA, and the Science University of Malaysia.

Besides government institutions, there are a number of private art institutions, of which the Malaysian Institute of Art, established in 1967, is the largest. Three-year diploma courses in Fine Art, Printmaking, Graphic Design, Interior Design, Textile and Fashion Design, Industrial Design and Ceramics are offered. Other smaller institutions have developed in recent years to meet the increasing demand created by the commercial and advertising design industry in the country.

BIBLIOGRAPHY

E. W. Eisner and D. W. Ecker: *Readings in Art Education* (Lexington, MA, 1966)
V. Lowenfeld and W. Lambert Brittain: *Creative and Mental Growth* (New York, 1967)
S. Dodds, ed.: *Research Readings for Discipline-based Art Education: A Journey Beyond Creating* (Reston, VA, 1988)

YEOH JIN LENG

Malbin, Lydia Winston. *See* WINSTON.

Malbone, Edward Greene (*b* Newport, RI, Aug 1777; *d* Savannah, GA, 7 May 1807). American miniature painter. Like his boyhood friend Washington Allston, he was encouraged in his artistic pursuits by Samuel King, who lent him engravings to study. In autumn 1794 Malbone set himself up as a miniature painter in Providence, RI, where he worked for two years, achieving almost immediate success. His earliest miniatures, such as that supposedly of *Nicholas Brown* (1794; New York, NY Hist. Soc.), although somewhat primitive, demonstrate his precosity. The sitters' faces are modelled with a stippling technique and chiselled planes; their outlines are distinct and crisp. These first compositions all include a conventional portrait background, usually a red curtain pulled back to reveal a blue sky. Despite the laboured technique, they are lively, direct and sensitive. During the second half of the 1790s Malbone travelled the eastern USA in search of commissions. He renewed his friendship with Allston in Boston and later visited New York and Philadelphia. In 1801 he was in Charleston, where he befriended the miniature painter Charles Fraser, on whose work he had a strong influence. He developed a brilliant technique of delicate, barely perceptible crosshatching, using interwoven lines of pale colours to create graceful forms. His brushstroke became freer and more assured, and thin washes of light colour made the image softer and gave his work a luminous quality. In general he focused more closely on the subject.

In May 1801 Malbone and Allston sailed for London, where his portrait of Allston (Boston, MA, Mus. F.A.) particularly impressed Benjamin West. Unlike Allston, who preferred the work of earlier masters, Malbone was attracted to the paintings of Sir Thomas Lawrence. He also liked the miniatures of Samuel Shelley (1750–1808) and made a copy of the *Hours* (178 mm×152 mm; Providence, RI, Athenaeum), his largest miniature. Malbone remained in England for about six months. In his subsequent work his delicate brushstrokes became freer and slightly broader, with smoother transitions from one area of paint to another. His backgrounds, in which he now preferred a sky and clouds, were generally lighter. The overall size of the ivory support that Malbone used became larger, measuring up to 85×70 mm, and was generally an oval. Occasionally, towards the end of his career, he produced rectangular formats. He usually received £50 for each commission. About one fifth of his works are signed, more frequently his early ones, and in a variety of ways: *Malbone, EG Malbone*, EGM or EM, inconspicuously on the ivory. Sometimes he inscribed the backing card. His return to Charleston in December 1801 marked the beginning of his most prolific period. During the next five months his account-book shows that he averaged three miniatures a week. By 1805 he had contracted tuberculosis and by March 1806 had all but ceased painting.

BIBLIOGRAPHY

J. L. Brockway: 'Malbone: American Miniature Painter', *Amer. Mag. A.*, xx (1929), pp. 185–91
Catalogue of Miniatures and Other Works by Edward Greene Malbone, 1777–1807 (exh. cat., Washington, DC, N.G.A., 1929)
R. P. Tolman: *The Life and Works of Edward Greene Malbone, 1777–1807* (New York, 1958) [definitive study]
M. S. Sadik: 'Edward Greene Malbone (1777–1807)', *Colonial and Federal Portraits at Bowdoin College* (Brunswick, ME, 1966), pp. 123–30

DALE T. JOHNSON

Malbork [formerly Marienburg] **Castle.** Castle of the Teutonic Knights in northern Poland. The red-brick fortress of Malbork, the headquarters of the Order of Teutonic Knights from 1309 to 1457, is 48 km south-east of Gdańsk, on the right bank of the Nogat River. It is one of the most important architectural complexes in northern Europe.

The Teutonic Knights began building the castle *c.* 1274 on the western border of their territories, midway between Gdańsk and Elbląg, to complete the strategic network of castles along the Vistula River and the Baltic coast, from Toruń to Kaliningrad. The choice of Malbork reflects the importance that the Order attached to the acquisition of Pomerelia, the land lying on the west bank of the Lower Vistula, as the first step in an attempt to link up its eastern territories with those in the Holy Roman Empire.

The fortress, which was built in several stages, takes the form of three architectural groupings, each separated by a moat and protected by its own fortifications. The Upper Castle is the nucleus of the complex. To its north and set somewhat lower is the Middle Castle, consisting of three wings with the Grand Master's Palace projecting from it to the west (see fig.). The Lower Castle, incorporating a series of independent outbuildings, occupies a larger area to the north of the Middle Castle. The three castles are enclosed with the town in a common system of fortifications.

Building began with the Upper Castle, which has four wings round an inner courtyard with a surrounding curtain wall. The chapel and the chapter house on the first floor of the north wing were probably completed *c.* 1280, when the Knights and citizens of neighbouring Zantyr moved to Malbork. The east and west wings were added *c.* 1280–85, with the south wing closing the quadrangle *c.* 1285–1300. The courtyard was reached by a passageway leading from a wide portal set into a great niche. It has two storeys of arcades, thoroughly renewed in the 19th century, and a well. The ground-floor of the castle has large vaulted chambers and a kitchen in the west wing. The commander's lodgings were above the kitchen, and the brothers were accommodated in a large dormitory on the first floor of the east wing. Kilarski reconstructed the original form of the castle chapel as a nave of two bays without aisles, with quadripartite vaults, terminating at the east in a polygonal apse closed externally by a straight wall flush with the outer walls of the castle. Two sacristies were located in the slanting areas between the polygonal apse and the outer wall. The reconstruction of a sexpartite apse vault disproves earlier claims that the castle chapel inspired the development of tri-radial vaulting in the southern Baltic region. The chapel is rooted in a tradition of castle chapels, with particularly close parallels in Bohemia, such as Bezdez, Zvichov and Racibórz. In detail it follows Radzyń Castle chapel, begun before 1285.

The appearance of similar moulding profiles and overall measurements suggests that one workshop was involved in building all the major Teutonic castles: Brandenburg *c.* 1272 (65·4×52 m); Malbork *c.* 1274 (60.27×51.26 m); Lochstedt *c.* 1275 (53·7×47·7 m); and Radzyń *c.* 1285 (52·5×52 m). The origins of this workshop and the sources for the castle layout have long been controversial: earlier opinion favoured Italian, Thuringian or Danish origins, while suggesting the Teutonic Knights themselves did the building; it has also been suggested that Cistercian workshops were responsible, an argument supported by similarities in the austerity and massiveness of the brickwork as well as architectural detail between Malbork and the Cistercian abbeys at Chorin, Lehnin and Kołbacz.

The transfer of the Grand Master's headquarters from Venice to Malbork in 1309 initiated new projects. The chapter house was enlarged to incorporate the chapel gallery, and a residential west range, of which only the Great Refectory survives, was begun in the Middle Castle. The chapter house is divided into two aisles by three central supports and has star vaults composed of radiating triplets of ribs. At the west end of the chapel a narrow balcony modelled on the reliquary tribune of the Sainte-Chapelle, Paris, replaced an earlier gallery. The work must have been nearly complete in 1324 when the Grand Master took up residence. Clasen and Schmid have attributed

Malbork Castle, view from the north-west, showing (left) the Middle Castle and the Grand Master's Palace and (right) the Upper Castle, begun *c.* 1274

these projects to one man, the Master of the Lübeck Briefkapelle, while Frycz has suggested the involvement of the master responsible for Radzyń Castle and St James, Toruń. Although on plan the chapter house and the Great Refectory, based on Cistercian refectories such as those at Bebenhausen and Maulbronn, appear to be the work of one man, the different treatment of the vaults in three dimensions suggests two masters.

Under Grand Master Luther of Brunswick (1331–5), the chapel was extended eastwards beyond the walls and reconsecrated in 1344. A lower chapel was constructed beneath the extension as a mausoleum for the Grand Masters, dedicated to St Anne. This work is characterized by a profusion of sculptural decoration following the style of the original chapel portal sculpture of c. 1280. A Crucifixion group and a series of stucco apostles and female saints were inserted into the interior wall arcading of the upper chapel, while the tympana of the two St Anne's chapel porches were decorated by an elaborate programme based on the Life of the Virgin and the Finding of the True Cross. Around 1378 Venetian masters working in Prague were commissioned to decorate with mosaic the giant stucco Virgin (destr. 1945), on the outside of the east window of the upper chapel.

Major building activity ended at Malbork with the construction of the Grand Master's Palace from 1383 to 1399. The core of the palace was built on to the Great Refectory, with its entrance and chapel on the east side; the audience chambers were built into a block (36×21 m) projecting beyond the perimeter of the castle and dominating the view from the river. The exterior is marked by deep brick buttresses that run the full height of the building (27 m). These are bridged together at eaves level to form a defensive crenellated gallery. At second-floor level they are articulated by the introduction of granite columns that emphasize the location of the refectories and give more light to them. The two refectories are similar in plan, each with one central column of granite and vaults of radiating ribs. The Summer Refectory was glazed on three sides in two tiers of square traceried windows, while a series of wall paintings illustrating former Grand Masters decorated the Winter Refectory, executed by Master Peter in 1402. Clasen argued that the whole residence was inspired and modelled on the Palais des Papes at Avignon and built by Nicholas Fellenstein. Though an association with Avignon is generally accepted, a comparison with Fellenstein's other documented works, the fortifications to the Lower Castle (1418–20) and Bytów Castle (1398–1406), raises doubts over his involvement in the design.

After the war of 1454–66, the castle came into Polish hands and remained a royal residence until 1772, when it fell into disrepair. It was heavily restored by Schinkel (1817–42) and Steinbrecht (1882–1921). The Upper Castle was seriously damaged in World War II.

BIBLIOGRAPHY

K. Clasen: *Die mittelalterliche Kunst im Gebiete des Deutschordenstaates Preussens, die Burghauten* (Königsberg, 1927)

B. Schmid: *Die Marienburg* (Würzburg, 1955)

J. Frycz: 'Architektura zamków krzyżackich' [The architecture of the Teutonic Knights' castles], *Sztuka pobrzeżu Bałtyku* [Art of the Baltic coastlands] (1978), pp. 19–49

M. Kilarski: 'Pierwotna forma kaplicy zamkowej w Malborku' [The original form of Malbork Castle chapel], *Biul. Hist. Sztuki*, ii (1983), pp. 127–57

JACK LOHMAN

Malchair, J(ohn) B(aptist) (*b* Cologne, 1731; *d* Oxford, 12 Dec 1812). English painter and printmaker of German birth. The son of a watchmaker, he moved to England *c*. 1754 and taught music and drawing in London, Lewes and Bristol before settling in Oxford as a drawing-master and leader of the band at the city's Music Room. In 1763 he published 12 etchings of views near Oxford; further sets of etchings followed in 1771 and 1772. His only Royal Academy exhibit was a watercolour landscape, shown in 1773 when he was listed as an honorary exhibitor. There is no evidence that he sold his work. Nearly 500 drawings by Malchair are in the Ashmolean Museum, Oxford; these include unpretentious cottage subjects and panoramic views of the city (e.g. *Oxford in Flood Time, from Shotover Hill*, 1791) characterized by an atmospheric haziness achieved through blurred pencil lines and grey or pastel wash. Visits to north Wales in 1789, 1791 and 1795 encouraged him to use bolder grey washes, strong pencil lines and vertiginous mountain compositions as, for example, in *Moel y Ffridd* (1795; priv. col.; see Oppé, pl. iii, d).

As a teacher Malchair emphasized the importance of making studies direct from nature; his own low-key but spontaneous manner influenced the prominent amateur artists and collectors Heneage Finch, 4th Earl of Aylesford, Dr William Crotch (1775–1847) and Sir George Beaumont.

BIBLIOGRAPHY

H. Minn: 'Drawings by J. B. Malchair in Corpus Christi College', *Oxoniensia*, viii and ix (1943–4), pp. 159–68

P. Oppé: 'John Baptist Malchair of Oxford', *Burl. Mag.*, lxxxiii (1943), pp. 191–7

D. B. Brown: *Earlier British Drawings* (1982), iv of *The Ashmolean Museum Catalogue of the Collection of Drawings* (Oxford, 1988–), pp. 404–51

SUSAN MORRIS

Malcz [Malsch], Karol Filip (*b* Warsaw, 10 Aug 1797; *d* Czorków, 15 March 1867). Polish goldsmith. He was the son of an immigrant Saxon surgeon and a daughter of a Warsaw goldsmith, Anna Dorota Bandau (*c*. 1775–after 1842). He was initially apprenticed to the Warsaw goldsmith, Jan Maciej Schwartz (1772–1828), and later travelled throughout Europe on his apprenticeship journey. After his return to Poland he executed his masterpiece at his teacher's workshop and opened his own workshop in Warsaw in 1828. He obtained numerous awards and developed his workshop into a large enterprise, employing up to 50 people, including professional artists. The majority of products, however, were designed, and many made personally, by him (examples, Warsaw, Mus. Hist. City). Malcz's early wares exhibit Empire style features; his works include table services, candelabra and liturgical vessels. He later produced items in the revival styles, especially the Rococo Revival, and, towards the end of his life, his work became more eclectic. In 1864 he gave control of the factory to his partner August Teodor Werner (1836–1902).

BIBLIOGRAPHY
H. Lileyko: *Srebra warszawskie w zbiorach Muzeum Historycznego m. st. Warszawy* [Warsawian silver in the collection of the Warsaw Historical Museum] (Warsaw, 1879), pp. 63–4

TADEUSZ CHRZANOWSKI

Malczewski, Jacek (*b* Radom, 15 or 14 July 1854; *d* Kraków, 8 Oct 1929). Polish painter. He began his training in 1873 in Kraków's School of Fine Arts on the instigation of the historical painter Jan Matejko (1838–93). Malczewski was initially taught by Władysław Łuszczkiewicz (1828–1900) and Feliks Szynalewski (1825–92) and from 1875 worked exclusively under Matejko's supervision. In 1876–7 he studied under Ernest Lehmann (1814–82) at the Ecole des Beaux-Arts in Paris; here he began to abandon Matejko's historical subject-matter in order to tackle contemporary problems and give expression to his own experiences. He espoused the realism of, among others, Gustave Courbet and the Barbizon school. In 1877 he again studied under Matejko but broke away in 1879. In 1880 he travelled to Italy and in 1884 acted as draughtsman for an archaeological expedition to Asia Minor, visiting *en route* Vienna, Trieste, the Albanian coastline, Rhodes and Athens. His mature work dates from after a period spent in Munich in 1885–6.

Even in his earliest independent Parisian works, Malczewski treated patriotic–martyrologic subjects derived from the great Polish Romantic poet Juliusz Słowacki (1809–49), for example the tragic fate of the Polish insurgents deported to Siberia after the anti-Tsarist uprising of January 1863. The painting that won him renown was a huge composition entitled *Death of Ellenai* (2.12×3.70 m; completed 1883; Kraków, N. Mus.) inspired by J. Słowacki's epic *Anhelli*, which was first published in Paris in 1838. It initiated the long 'Siberian Cycle' of realistic works characterized by subdued, almost monochrome colour schemes (e.g. *Sunday at the Mine*, 1.18×1.80 m, 1882; *At the Halting-Place*, 305×385 mm, 1883; both Warsaw, N. Mus.). Realistic–naturalistic trends became more intense after Malczewski's journey to Munich in 1885–6, as in *Death at the Halting-Place* (530×1910 mm; 1891; Poznań, N. Mus.) and such portraits as that of *Fortunat Garlewski* (1.51×1.10 m; 1889; Poznań, N. Mus.). During the later 1880s, possibly under the influence of Witold Pruszkowski, Malczewski produced paintings on folk art fantasy themes, for example the *Water Nymphs* cycle (1887–8; Kraków, Jagiellonian U., Mus. F.A.) as well as his first allegorical compositions (*Three Arts of Painting*, 1886; untraced). In 1890 Malczewski travelled to Italy (where he returned once more in 1906) via Vienna, and in 1893 to Munich.

Malczewski's paintings of the early 1890s heralded a return to symbolism; they include *The Introduction: A Little Painter* (3.32×2.32 m; 1890; Kraków, N. Mus.) and *In the Whirl* (780×1500 mm; 1893; Poznań, N. Mus.). In 1894 he completed *Melancholy* (1.39×2.40 m; Poznań, N. Mus.) and in 1895–7 the *Vicious Circle* (1.74×2.40 m; Poznań, N. Mus.); these works convey the pessimism of the late 19th century that stemmed from the thwarted nationalism of the Polish people, interwoven with themes of destiny and the role of art. Around the turn of the century the new symbolic canon evident in Malczewski's painting was embodied in the works that were to win him a place as one of the foremost representatives of Polish modernism. This transformation took place under the influence of more extensive contact with the work of Arnold Böcklin, Fritz von Uhde, Hans Thoma and Franz von Stuck during his stay in Munich in 1893. It was also fuelled by Malczewski's idealistic–romantic imagination, manifested in an eclectic iconography, often drawn from Polish folk-tales, mythology and biblical subjects.

Several themes can be traced throughout Malczewski's career: patriotic–nationalistic motifs; 'existential' subjects, particularly the nature of death and artistic creation; and symbolic portraiture. Nationalistic themes are represented by such works as the triptych *Fatherland* (1903; Wrocław, N. Mus.) and the cycle the *Poisoned Well* (1905–6; Poznań, N. Mus.). Portraits include the *Polish Hamlet: Portrait of Aleksander Wielopolski* (1.00×1.48 m; 1903; Warsaw, N. Mus.), and among his symbolic compositions are a number with subjects drawn from Słowacki—for example later versions of the *Death of Ellenai* (1906–7; Poznań, N. Mus.; Warsaw, N. Mus.)—and many self-portraits. From 1898 his reflections on death became a distinct category of his work, in which he personified death as the Greek god Thanatos, represented as a young woman with a scythe (e.g. *Thanatos*, 450×575 mm; 1898–9; Warsaw, N. Mus.). The figure of Thanatos always appears as a liberator who brings consolation. Questions of destiny and artistic creation are treated in such works as *Artist's Inspiration* (800×630 mm; 1897; Kraków, Soc. Friends A.). Malczewski frequently personified these themes using the chimera–sphinx motif, made popular at the end of the 19th century, which might symbolize art (e.g. *Moment of Inspiration—The Harpy in Sleep* (725×920 mm; 1907; Poznań, priv. col.). From *c*. 1900 onwards the figure of the artist is personified by Malczewski himself (over 150 self-portraits exist). He identified himself variously with Christ (triptych, *Tribute Money*; 1908; Poznań, N. Mus.), with biblical characters (*Tobias and Parcae*; 0.56×1.25 m; 1912; Poznań, N. Mus.), and with saints (*St Francis*; 1.56×2.01 m; 1908; Warsaw, N. Mus.), and depicted himself in exotic costumes (*Self-portrait in a White Gown*, 930×780 mm; 1914; Kraków, N. Mus.). From the late 19th century onwards Malczewski's portraits of other sitters also assume a symbolic nature, as in his portrait of the critic and collector *Feliks Jasieński* (610×500 mm; 1905; Kraków, N. Mus.).

Malczewski's stylistic idiom was both traditional and innovative. It combined illusionistic verisimilitude and meticulous analytical line drawing with a simplified treatment of the main motif; traditional perspective with a suggestive, modernistic spatial sense; and delicate natural hues with deliberately harsh, aggressive dissonances. Malczewski's colouring of landscape elements is particularly subtle (e.g. *Landscape with Tobias*, 760×970 mm; 1904; Poznań, N. Mus.). Between 1896 and 1921 (with a break between 1914 and 1916, when he stayed in Vienna), Malczewski also taught, in particular from 1896 to 1900 and after 1910 at the School (later Academy) of Fine Arts in Kraków; he was Rector there in 1912–13 and 1913–14. During his final period Malczewski intensified the 'existential' aspects of his art in the autobiographical cycle *My Life* (begun 1914), as in *My Soul* (1×2 m; 1917; Warsaw, N.

Jacek Malczewski: *Polonia*, oil on canvas, 1025×730 mm, 1918 (Kielce, National Museum)

Mus.). Another of his major works is *Polonia* (see fig.), which encapsulates Malczewski's reflections on the Polish struggles for independence up to 1918.

Malczewski spent his last years on family estates in the Lesser Poland (Małopolska) region. From 1925 he ceased to paint due to failing eyesight. Throughout his career Malczewski exhibited widely both in Poland and abroad as a member of, among others, the 'Sztuka' ('Art') Society of Polish Artists and of the Vereinigung Bildender Künstler Österreichs Secession.

BIBLIOGRAPHY

SAP; Thieme–Becker

A. Heydel: *Jacek Malczewski: Człowiek i artysta* [*Jacek Malczewski: the man and the artist*] (Kraków, 1933)

Jacek Malczewski (exh. cat., ed. A. Ławniczakowa; Poznań, N. Mus., 1964)

J. Puciata-Pawłowska: *Jacek Malczewski* (Wrocław, 1968)

K. Wyka: *Thanatos i Polska czyli o Jacku Malczewskim* [Thanatos and Poland, that is, about Jacek Malczewski] (Kraków, 1971)

A. Jakimowicz: *Jacek Malczewski* (Warsaw, 1974)

A. Ławniczakowa: *Jacek Malczewski* (Warsaw, 1976) [good illus.]

Le Symbolisme en Europe (exh. cat., Rotterdam, Mus. Boymans-van Beuningen; Brussels, Musée Royaux B.-A.; Baden-Baden, Staatl. Ksthalle; Paris, Grand Pal.; 1976)

W. Juszczak: *Modernizm: Malarstwo polskie* [Modernism: Polish painting] (Warsaw, 1977)

A. Ławniczakowa: 'Das Gemälde "Melancholia" von Jacek Malczewski', *Polnische Malerei von 1830 bis 1914* (exh. cat., ed. J. C. Jensen; Kiel, Christian-Albrechts U., Ksthalle; Stuttgart, Württemberg. Kstver.; Wuppertal, Von der Heydt-Mus.; 1978–9), pp. 96–102

La Peinture polonaise du XVIe au début du XXe siècle (exh. cat., Paris, Grand Pal., 1979)

Malczewski (exh. cat. by A. Ławniczakowa; Stuttgart, Württemberg. Kstver.; Christian-Albrechts U., Ksthalle; Duisburg, Wilhelm-Lehmbruck-Mus.; 1980)

Symbolism in Polish Painting 1890–1914 (exh. cat., ed. A. Morawińska; Detroit, MI, Inst. A., 1984)

LIJA SKALSKA-MIECIK

Maldives, Republic of. Republic comprising an archipelago of an estimated 1196 coral islands and sandbanks with a total land area of *c.* 298 sq km in the centre of the Indian Ocean; the capital is Male. Only about 200 of the islands, all of which are low-lying, are permanently inhabited. The spoken and written language is Divehi, and the religion of the inhabitants is Sunni Muslim.

Little is known of the early history of the Maldives. They were probably settled in the 5th or 4th century BC by a Dravidian people from Kerala. These were followed by Sinhalese settlers from south India or Sri Lanka who brought Buddhism with them. The existence of Buddhism in the Maldives before the conversion to Islam in 1153 was demonstrated by H. C. P. Bell, the first Archaeological Commissioner of Ceylon (Sri Lanka), who visited the islands in 1879, 1920 and 1922 and published the most authoritative work on the country. The most impressive Buddhist remains are found on the larger islands in the south. On Gan, in Seenu, there was once a stupa and also a *bodhi* tree; however, the stupa was demolished by the British when they built an airstrip on the island during World War II. Buddhist artefacts have also been dug up at several sites. The conversion was initially marked by a period of iconoclasm, and in subsequent centuries deserted Buddhist sites were quarried for building materials. Other archaeological remains found in the Maldives include fragments of Chinese pottery, some of which were collected by John Carswell in Male in the early 1970s (see Carswell, 1975–7). In 1897 the Maldives became a British protectorate. They were ruled by a hereditary sultan until 1932, when a constitutional sultanate was formed. A republic was declared in 1953 under President Amin Didi, but he was overthrown within the year, and, after another referendum, the sultanate was restored. In 1965 the British protectorate ceased, and a third referendum in 1968 re-established a republican government under the presidency of Amir Ibrahim Nasir. Since the 1970s the influence of the outside world has become more intense in the Maldives, particularly as a result of tourism.

The widespread use of coral stone in the vernacular architecture of the Maldives appears to be a fairly recent phenomenon. When H. C. P. Bell arrived at Male in 1879, he found only one house of coral stone apart from the sultan's palace, but by the mid-20th century the larger part of Male was covered with buildings of coral stone and lime mortar, often plastered and whitewashed. Fine timber houses were, however, built before the 20th century; these often demonstrate exquisite skill in carpentry. Most houses have one or two storeys and originally had thatched roofs or roofs of Mangalore tiles imported from India; in the late 20th century corrugated iron sheets have become prominent. Cheaper houses are built of matting made of split bamboo or woven coconut fronds tied on timber frames; others are made of whitewashed canvas. A fear of malevolent spirits or jinns traditionally meant structures were built without windows; some old houses have a low barrier in front of the doorway to prevent evil spirits from entering.

There are many mosques and shrines throughout the Maldives, often with fine decoration. The congregational mosque at Male, known as the Hukuru Miskit, is the most important mosque in the archipelago. Initially constructed *c.* 1153, it was restored in 1338 and renewed and enlarged in 1656–7 by Sultan Ibrahim Iskandar (*reg* 1648–87), who also erected the minaret in 1674–5. Inside, it has turned columns painted in black and red lacquer, Koranic inscriptions on the cross beams, elaborate carvings on the wooden doorposts and screens and ornate carved coral tombstones. Male has numerous mosques and cemeteries, although many of the latter have been cleared to create space. Large areas of reef have also been reclaimed to prevent the city from overcrowding. In recent years modern building techniques have become more prominent, and hotels have been constructed.

According to François Pyrard de Laval, a Frenchman who lived in the Maldives from 1602 to 1607, certain crafts were confined to particular atolls. This is still partly true in the late 20th century, although increasingly artisans have moved to Male. Traditional crafts include lacemaking, which was done by women, and cloth-weaving, both of which have been unable to compete with imported, mass-produced goods. Stone-carving and metalworking, however, have been given a new lease of life by the tourist trade. Jewellers, formerly confined to Nilande Atoll, are now found throughout the archipelago. The lacquerwork industry, once a highly developed craft, especially in Baa Atoll, declined in the early 20th century, but it is still practised on Malosmadulu Atoll and at Male. Mat-weaving, another craft done chiefly by women, has been modified by the use of imported chemical dyes and the impact of tourism. It is centred in Suvadiva Atoll in the south, where rush is found in abundance. In 1952 the National Museum was founded in Male for the conservation and display of historical items.

BIBLIOGRAPHY

H. C. P. Bell: *The Maldive Islands: An Account of the Physical Features, Climate, History, Inhabitants, Production, and Trade* (Colombo, 1883)
A. Gray and H. C. P. Bell: *The Voyage of François Pyrard of Laval* (London, 1887)
H. C. P. Bell: *The Maldive Islands: Report on a Visit to Male, January 20 to February 21, 1920* (Colombo, 1921)
T. W. Hockly: *The Two Thousand Isles: A Short Account of the People, History and Customs of the Maldive Archipelago* (London, 1935)
H. C. P. Bell: *The Maldive Islands: Monograph on the History, Archaeology, and Epigraphy* (Colombo, 1940)
J. Carswell: 'China and Islam in the Maldive Islands', *Trans. Orient. Cer. Soc.*, xli (1975–7), pp. 119–98
——: 'Mosques and Tombs in the Maldive Islands', *A. & Archaeol. Res. Pap.*, ix (June 1976), pp. 26–30
A. Forbes and A. Ali: *Weaving in the Maldive Islands, Indian Ocean: The Fine Mat Industry of Suvadiva Atoll (Illustrated by Mats Held in the Collection of the Museum of Mankind)*, BM Occas. Pap., 9 (London, 1980)
C. Maloney: *People of the Maldive Islands* (Madras, 1980)
H. A. Maniku: *Malege Miskittah* (Male, 1980) [survey of mosques of Male in Divehi]
A. D. W. Forbes: 'The Mosque in the Maldive Islands: A Preliminary Historical Survey', *Archipel*, xxvi (1983), pp. 43–74
T. Heyerdahl: *The Maldive Mystery* (London, 1986)

S. J. VERNOIT

Maldonado, Tomás (*b* Buenos Aires, 24 April 1922). Argentine painter, graphic designer and theorist. He studied at the Academia Nacional de Bellas Artes in Buenos Aires from 1938. In 1944 he was a co-founder of the Argentine avant-garde review *Arturo*, which was concerned with both art and literature and led to the formation in 1945 of the ASOCIACIÓN ARTE CONCRETO INVENCIÓN, of which he was also one of the main instigators. In 1948 he travelled to Europe, where he came into contact with Max Bill and other Swiss Constructivists, whose example inspired him both as a painter and as a theorist on his return to Argentina. *Blue with Structure* and *A Form and Series* (both 1950, Buenos Aires, Mus. A. Mod.) are typical of a rigorous type of painting with which he became identified. He stressed the application of such ideas, moreover, not only to art but also to social and political concerns, seeking nothing less than the transformation of the physical environment in which we live. Such convictions gave coherence to all his activities from that time on, including his co-founding in 1951 of *Nueva Visión*, a review of visual culture, and his membership from 1952 of the ARTISTAS MODERNOS DE LA ARGENTINA.

In 1954 Maldonado left Argentina on Max Bill's invitation to teach at the Hochschule für Gestattung in Ulm, of which he became Rector from 1964 to 1966. Thereafter he lived and worked in Europe, apart from a spell of teaching at Princeton University's School of Architecture (1968–70). In 1971 he became professor of environmental planning at Bologna University, and in 1977 editor of the Italian magazine *Casabella*, through which he continued to promote his concept of culture as a totality, rejecting the notion of art, design and architecture as separate categories. He carried out research on education, semiology, the philosophy of language and applied experimental psychology.

WRITINGS
Avanguardia e razionalità (Turin, 1974)

BIBLIOGRAPHY
N. Perazzo: *El arte concreto en la Argentina* (Buenos Aires, 1983), pp. 143–7

NELLY PERAZZO

Mâle, Emile (*b* 1862; *d* Paris, 6 Oct 1954). French historian and writer. He was a pioneer in the study of medieval art. Following Adolphe-Napoléon Didron, who had shown the study of religious iconography to be a possible approach to the art of the Middle Ages, Mâle's achievement was to investigate and explain the sources that had inspired the iconography used by medieval artists; and ultimately, in a trilogy of works that remain standard texts, to put forward a unifying system, a 'summa' (as it has been called) covering all medieval art from the 12th to the 15th centuries.

Mâle was educated at the Ecole Normale Supérieure in Paris, and from 1886 he taught literature at the Lycée. In 1891 he published his first essay on the iconography of the Liberal Arts. This was followed by studies of the Romanesque capitals in the Musée des Augustins, Toulouse (1892), of the teaching of history of art (1894) and of the origins of French medieval sculpture (1895). In 1898 he began work on his doctoral thesis, which was published in 1902 as *L'Art religieux du XIIIe siècle en France* (translated as *The Gothic Image*), the work for which he is best known. In the introduction he referred to himself only as 'Professeur du Rhétorique au Lycée Lakanal', suggesting a certain caution on his part as to his own position and the possible reception of this work. He also expressed the modest wish that 'it may prove of service to historians of art'.

In *The Gothic Image* Mâle discussed much of the most common iconography and symbolism of the 13th century, drawing his examples from the decoration of the great French cathedrals. He was among the first to realize the Eastern origins of the symbolism he studied. Gothic art had been the subject of fashionable interest since the publication of Victor Hugo's *Notre Dame de Paris* (1831), but it was the accepted view to see it as somehow 'exalted' and separate from the 'debased' barbaric art of the centuries and styles preceding it. Although Mâle appears at this point to consider 13th-century art as a 'finished system', in 1908 he published *L'Art religieux de la fin du moyen âge en France*, in which he had come to see the iconography from the 13th to the 15th centuries in France as a coherent whole, exhibiting different styles only according to the artistic tastes of different ages. In 1922 he added a third volume, *L'Art religieux du XIIe siècle en France*, in which he traced the iconography of the Gothic and later periods back to its earliest appearance in Romanesque art, thereby creating for the first time a rational, overall study of this aspect of medieval art.

In 1908 Mâle was elected to the chair of medieval archaeology at the Sorbonne, becoming an honorary professor there in 1912; and in 1927 he was made honorary Director of the Ecole Française in Rome. He was a member of the Académie Française and many other learned societies throughout Europe; and he continued to revise and add notes to the many reprintings and translations of his works during the later years of his long life.

WRITINGS
L'Art religieux du XIIIe siècle en France (Paris, 1902); Eng. trans. as *The Gothic Image* (London, 1913)
L'Art religieux de la fin du moyen âge en France (Paris, 1908)
L'Art religieux du XIIe siècle en France (Paris, 1922); Eng. trans., with foreword by H. Bober (Princeton, 1978)
L'Art religieux après le Concile de Trent (Paris, 1932)
Religious Art from the Twelfth to the Eighteenth Century (London, 1949) [selections from the four works on relig. art]

BIBLIOGRAPHY
E. Lambert: 'Bibliographie de Emile Mâle', *Cah. Civilis. Méd.*, xi (1959)
Obituary: *Who Was Who*, v (London, 1961, rev. 3/1967)

JACQUELINE COLLISS HARVEY

Maler. German family of medallists and wax-modellers. Valentin Maler (*b* Jihlava, [Ger. Iglau], Bohemia, (now in Czech Republic), 1540; *d* Nuremberg, 1 Sept 1603) began his career in Joachimsthal as a coin engraver. In 1569 he settled in Nuremberg, where he worked until 1603, primarily as a portrait medallist, visiting many royal and episcopal courts in Prague, Munich, Dresden, Würzburg, Breslau (now Wrocław, Poland), Stuttgart and Bamberg. His medals were made both by striking and by casting from a model. The struck medals were often used as royal presentation pieces; several of them were struck at the Court of the Holy Roman Emperor Maximilian II, while some were struck later at the Court of his successor Emperor Rudolf II. Their subjects included *Maximilian*

II with an Eagle (several versions); *Emperor Rudolf II* (several versions, 1576 and 1589; Vienna, Ksthist. Mus.); and *Emperor Rudolf II and his Ancestors* (1590 and 1594). Several of the struck medals bore inscriptions. As a precaution against forgery, Maler obtained an Imperial privilege.

In casting medals from a model, Maler initially worked with wooden models, adding the lettering later: in this manner he made a portrait medal of *Ernst von Mengersdorf, Bishop of Bamberg* that was cast by the goldsmith Bernard Rehm. Subsequently Maler worked at the Court in Prague alongside Antonio Abondio, who was the first medallist to cast medals from wax models; from him Maler learnt the technique of working the wax models with a small chisel and of making several trial impressions with cheaper metals, before casting the final version in bronze or silver. Maler often painted his wax models with colourful decorations: almost all of these have been lost. In 1598 he failed to obtain the post of Master of the Nuremberg Mint and later died greatly in debt. His brother, Wenzel Maler, worked in Augsburg until *c.* 1605 and then moved to Nuremberg. The only medal known to be by him represents *Graf Wilhelm zu Zumden* and is signed with the monogram W.MO. Valentin Maler's son, Christian Maler (*b* Nuremberg, 11 July 1578; *d* after 1652), was a pupil of his father and took over his workshop after his death. Like his father, he travelled to many courts and was granted by successive Emperors the privilege of striking medals on his own premises. Most of his medals are struck and are of poor quality. They include *Frederick V, the Elector Palatine and his Wife, Elizabeth Stuart* (1615); the *Coronation of Frederick V and Elizabeth as King and Queen of Bohemia* (1619); and an equestrian portrait of the *Holy Roman Emperor Matthias as King of Hungary*. In 1630 he became die-cutter at the Mint in Vienna. Towards the end of his career he made a number of coins for Lübeck and a medal of *Frederick William of Brandenburg and Louise of Nassau-Orange*. Christian Maler also made portrait medals in coloured wax.

BIBLIOGRAPHY
Forrer
G. K. Nagler: *Monogrammisten* (1858–1920)
G. Habich: *Die deutschen Schaumünzen des 16. Jahrhunderts*, ii (Munich, 1934), nos 2621, 2853
R. A. Schutte: 'Medaillen, Münzen und Wachsbossierungen am Hofe Rudolfs II', *Prag um 1600: Kunst und Kultur am Hofe Rudolfs II* (exh. cat., Essen, Villa Hügel, 1988), pp. 575–96

M. J. T. M. STOMPÉ

Maler, Hans (i) (*b* Ulm, *c.* 1480; *d* ?Schwaz, Tyrol, *c.* 1526–9). German painter. He was first documented in Schwaz in 1517, and HM MZS, 'Hans Maler, Maler zu Schwaz', is inscribed on his portrait of *A Young Man* (1523; priv. col.; see 1906 exh. cat.), but his place of origin is noted on the reverse of his portrait of *Anton Fugger* (1524; ex-Děčín Castle, Czech Rep.) in the inscription 'HANS MALER VON ULM, MALER ZVO SCHWAZ'. He has been tentatively identified (Friedländer) as the painter (Ger. *Maler*) in Schwaz who in 1500 was reminded by the government in Innsbruck to deliver the portrait Emperor Maximilian I had commissioned of his late wife, *Mary of Burgundy*, and also with the painter Hans in Schwaz who in 1510 was paid for two portraits of *Mary of Burgundy*

MARIA REGINA
·1520·   Anno etatis·14·

Hans Maler: *Mary, Queen of Hungary*, oil on parchment on panel, 470×350 mm, 1520 (London, Society of Antiquaries of London)

(Vienna, Ksthist. Mus.; New York, Met.; see Egg). Judging by his oil paintings, he trained in Ulm with Bartholomäus Zeitblom or in his circle. His best works are portraits, with subjects generally appearing in bust-format, hands not shown, before a blue background that lightens towards the base. Only exceptionally do they establish eye-contact with the viewer: the diagonally placed pupils, which appear to tilt forwards, give the expression an uncertain quality. The bright flesh tint, with a hint of rose, and the jewellery and clothes were rendered with care and a fine sense of decorative values.

In 1517 Maler painted the portrait of *Sebastian Andorfer*, both bearded (New York, Met.) and shaven (priv. col., see 1983 exh. cat.). He painted several other portraits of men (e.g. Dresden, Gemäldegal. Alte Meister; Rome, Pal. Barberini; Vienna, Akad. Bild. Kst. and Gemäldegal. Akad. Bild. Kst.), and a few of burgher women. *Anna Klammer von Weydach, Frau Hermann* (Rotterdam, Mus. Boymans-van Beuningen) carries on its reverse side the finest of his painted coats of arms. Characteristic of his good-natured, decorative style is his double portrait of *Moritz Welzer von Eberstein and Maria Tänzl* (1524; Vienna, Akad. Bild. Kst.). Between 1519 and 1526 his main patrons were Archduke (subsequently Emperor) Ferdinand and members of the Augsburg merchant family of Fugger. In keeping with reality, the aristocratic subjects wore more extravagant jewellery and clothes and, to show off their rings, had their hands visible. Maler modelled his pictures on the court portraits Bernhard Strigel had painted in the

reign of Emperor Maximilian I, of which replicas were available. Archduke Ferdinand commissioned him to paint his wife *Anne of Hungary* (1503–47) in 1520 (Madrid, Mus. Thyssen-Bornemisza), in 1521 (Innsbruck, Tirol. Landesmus.) and in 1525 (Berlin, Gemäldegal.). He also painted the Archduke himself in 1521 (Dessau, Staatl. Gal.) and in 1525 (Vienna, Ksthist. Mus.; Florence, Uffizi) and Ferdinand's sister *Mary, Queen of Hungary* (1520; London, Soc. Antiqua.; see fig.; Schweinfurt, Samml. Schäfer). For the Fuggers he painted *Anton Fugger* (1525; Karlsruhe, Staatl. Ksthalle; Philadelphia, PA, Mus. A.), *Ulrich Fugger* (1525; New York, Met.) and *Jakob Fugger*, after a woodcut by Hans Burgkmair (ex-von Pannwitz priv. col., Haarlem; Mackowitz, fig. 31); all appear in replicas and copies.

Scholars have attributed to Maler a portrait of *A Young Lady* (1512; Düsseldorf, Kstmus.) and that of *Wolfgang Ronner* (1529; Munich, Alte Pin.), though the latter attribution is disputed (Lieb), as the picture shows a different hand. There was also controversy about Maler's original contributions to murals (1512–26) in the cloister of the Franciscan monastery in Schwaz, to the *Family Tree of Emperor Maximilian I* (c. 1510; Habsburgerstammbaum, Schloss Tratzberg, Tyrol), to some murals (c. 1512–16) in Schloss Tratzberg, Tyrol, and several altarpieces and individual religious pictures (cf. Mackowitz, Stange). A *Holy Family* (Sigmaringen, Fürst. Hohenzoll. Samml. & Hofbib.) carries the intertwined monogram MH, as does a drawn *Study of a Man's Head* (Karlsruhe, Staatl. Ksthalle). Maler used the study for an executioner in the *Martyrdom of St Bartholomew*, part of an apostle-altar of which two panels (Nuremberg, Ger. Nmus.; Schloss Tratzberg, Tyrol) show the martyrdom of apostles; the central picture shows the painting *Departure of the Apostles* (Schloss Tratzberg, Tyrol).

BIBLIOGRAPHY

M. J. Friedländer: 'Hans Maler zu Schwaz', *Repert. Kstwiss.*, xviii (1895), pp. 411–23; xx (1897), pp. 362–5

G. Glück: 'Hans Maler von Ulm, Maler zu Schwaz', *Jb. Ksthist. Samml. Wien*, xxv (1906), pp. 245–7

Early German Art (exh. cat., London, Burlington F.A. Club, 1906)

X. Weizinger: 'Die Malerfamilie der Strigel in der ehemals freien Reichsstadt Memmingen', *Festschrift des Münchener Altertumsvereins zur Erinnerung an das 50jährige Jubiläum* (Munich, 1914), pp. 145–6

N. Lieb: *Die Fugger und die Kunst im Zeitalter der Spätgotik und der frühen Renaissance* (Munich, 1952)

——: *Die Fugger und die Kunst im Zeitalter der hohen Renaissance* (Munich, 1958)

H. von Mackowitz: 'Der Maler Hans von Schwaz', *Schlern Schr.*, cxciii (1960)

E. Egg: 'Zur Maximilianeischen Kunst in Innsbruck', *Veröff. Tirol. Landesmus. Ferdinandeum*, xlvi (1966), pp. 31–3

A. Stange: 'Hans Maler: Neue Funde und Forschungen', *Jb. Staatl. Kstsamml. Baden-Württemberg*, iii (1966), pp. 83–106

K. Löcher: 'Studien zur oberdeutschen Bildnismalerei des 16. Jahrhunderts', *Jb. Staatl. Kstsamml. Baden-Württemberg*, iv (1967), pp. 31–5

The Northern Renaissance: 15th and 16th Century Netherlandish Painting (exh. cat., New York, Alexander Gal., 1983), nos 18, 19

KURT LÖCHER

Maler, Hans (ii). *See* KNIEPER, HANS.

Maler Müller. *See* MÜLLER, FRIEDRICH.

Mälesskircher [Mächselkircher; Maleskircher], **Gabriel** (*b c.* 1430; *d* Munich, 1495). German painter. His work, still distinctive despite considerable losses, forms an important branch of the little-researched Munich school of painting of the later 15th century. He probably trained in the Netherlands. In 1455 the 'jung maister Gabriel' was paid for miniatures in the Munich *Rechtsbuch* (Munich, Stadtarchv): research has shown this painter to be Mälesskircher. His most important commission, however, came from his brother-in-law Abbot Konrad Ayrinschmalz (*reg* 1461–92). This consisted of 13 apparently similar large retables and 2 smaller ones for the newly built nave (1471–6) of the church of the Benedictine monastery of St Quirin at Tegernsee. Archives give names of the patrons of the altars for whom Mälesskircher created the panels, and their years of execution. It can be inferred from the surviving fragments (e.g. Munich, Bayer. Nmus.; Schweinfurt, Samml. Schäfer) that the original works were winged altarpieces. The altarpieces were painted for the altars of the *Virgin* (1473); *St Quirinus* (1474); *St Benedict* (1475); *St Vitus and the Martyr Saints* (1476; see fig.); *Virgin Saints* (1476); *SS John and Paul* (1476); *All Souls* (1477); *Four Doctors of the Church* (1477); *St Sebastian* (1478); *St*

Martin (1478); *Four Evangelists* (1478); the *Three Kings* (1478); and the *Holy Spirit* (1478). The two small panels, which may not have been winged altarpieces, were for the *Poor Souls* altar and the *St Henry* altar.

Mälesskircher's work is distinguished by a delight in narrative and in the detailed depiction of everyday objects. On the basis of the paintings for the Lugano *Evangelists* altar, Stange went so far as to call him a genre painter. His figures and objects, which sometimes have a very fragile appearance, are firmly outlined. Mälesskircher also produced untraced works, mentioned in archives, for the monasteries in Raitenhaslach and Rottenbuch. Further paintings attributed to him, of uncertain origin, include *St Onophrius, St Oswald* and *?St Sigismund* (Freising, Diözmus.) and *SS Christopher and Onophrius* (Schweinfurt, Samml. Schäfer), while Stange suggested that a portrait of *A Master Builder* (?Jörg von Halsbach; Basle, Kstmus.) is Mälesskircher's. The painter held office in 1461 on the Munich town council as a representative of the four main guilds. He was a member of the outer council in 1469 and deputy mayor in 1485.

The Tegernsee Altar, painted *c.* 1445–50, was first separated from the work of Mälesskircher by Buchner (1938–9), who assigned it to an earlier MASTER OF THE TEGERNSEE ALTAR (*see* MASTERS, ANONYMOUS, AND MONOGRAMMISTS, §I), sometimes referred to as the 'Pseudo-Mälesskircher'.

Kindler

BIBLIOGRAPHY

E. Buchner: 'Der wirkliche Gabriel Mälesskircher', *Münchn. Jb. Bild. Kst*, n. s. 1, xiii (1938–9), pp. 36–45
A. Stange: *Deutsche Malerei der Gotik*, x (Munich and Berlin, 1960), pp. 75–80
S. Lampl: 'Die Klosterkirche Tegernsee', *Oberbayer. Archv*, c (1975), pp. 62–3
I. Lubbeke: 'Gabriel Mälesskircher: Heiligen Christophorus und Heiligen Onophrius', *Altdeutsche Bilder der Sammlung Georg Schäfer* (exh. cat., Schweinfurt, 1985), pp. 94–5

GISELA GOLDBERG

Gabriel Mälesskircher: *St Vitus Refuses to Go to the Banquet*, from the *St Vitus* altarpiece of St Quirin, Tegernsee, oil on panel, 779×448 mm, 1476 (Burghausen, Staatsgalerie)

Malevich, Kazimir (Severinovich) (*b* Kiev, 26 Feb 1878; *d* Leningrad [now St Petersburg], 15 May 1935). Russian painter, printmaker, decorative artist and writer of Ukranian birth. One of the pioneers of abstract art, Malevich was a central figure in a succession of avant-garde movements during the period of the Russian revolutions of 1905 and 1917 and immediately after. The style of severe geometric abstraction with which he is most closely associated, SUPREMATISM, was a leading force in the development of CONSTRUCTIVISM, the repercussions of which continued to be felt throughout the 20th century. His work was suppressed in Soviet Russia in the 1930s and remained little known during the following two decades. The reassessment of his reputation in the West from the mid-1950s was matched by the renewed influence of his work on the paintings of Ad Reinhardt and on developments such as Zero, Hard-edge painting and Minimalism.

1. Life and painted work. 2. Prints. 3. Writings.

1. LIFE AND PAINTED WORK.

(i) Before 1918. (ii) 1918–27. (iii) 1927–35.

(i) Before 1918. Malevich grew up in Ukraine. His father was of Polish origin and worked in the sugar factories in

Belopolye, but in 1896 the family moved to the Russian provincial town of Kursk, where both Kazimir and his father worked for the railway company. Malevich started painting at the age of 12 and for a brief period in 1895–6 he attended the Kiev School of Art. By 1904 he had saved enough money to study for a year in Moscow at the Stroganov School, and at the painter Ivan Rerberg's private school; he also studied at the Moscow School of Painting, Sculpture and Architecture, where painters such as Leonid Pasternak and Konstantin Korovin taught an Impressionist style of painting. In the autumn of 1905 Malevich was involved in the dramatic events of the 1905 Moscow uprising, although he avoided the subsequent repressions.

Malevich's earliest work was inspired by Impressionism. In some works painted in Kursk in 1904–5 (e.g. *Portrait of a Member of the Artist's Family*, 1904; Amsterdam, Stedel. Mus.) he applied a Divisionist technique, using white as the modifying element that pervaded the other colours of the spectrum. At the same time his drawings showed considerable influence from Symbolism and Art Nouveau, particularly in his graphic work intended for advertisements and illustrations.

In 1907 Malevich took part in the exhibition by the Association of Moscow Artists with artists such as Vasily Kandinsky, David Burlyuk, Aleksey Morgunov (1884–1935) and Mikhail Larionov, several of whom became his friends. In 1910 Larionov invited Malevich to join the newly formed exhibition group JACK OF DIAMONDS, which marked the turning-point in modern Russian painting; in 1912 he joined Larionov's breakaway group, DONKEY'S TAIL, renamed Target in 1913. The 1912 exhibition centred on Neo-primitive painting inspired by popular woodcuts (the *lubok*), signboard painting and folk art. Target was influenced by Cubist and Futurist art, and Larionov presented a new, almost non-objective concept named Rayism (Luchizm). After the demise of Target, Malevich quarrelled with Larionov and sided for some time with the St Petersburg avant-garde centred on the group Union of Youth (Soyuz Molodyozhi). He was now a leading member of the Russian Futurist group of artists, writers and poets.

In 1910 Malevich painted a series of large gouaches, including *Province* (Amsterdam, Stedel. Mus.) and *Village* (Basle, Kstmus.), which, despite the influence of both Cézanne and Fauvism, stand out as independent interpretations. These were characterized by heavy black contours and an intense colour scale and were divided into series of yellow, red and white. In his autobiography Malevich points to icon painting as a strong influence of his early years in Moscow. More influential were the private collections of works by Matisse and other contemporary French artists, which belonged to Sergey Shchukin and Ivan Morosov. Although Malevich continued to favour figure scenes of peasant and provincial life, dominated by a few figures occupying the foreground and most of the picture plane, he began to build the figures from conical and cylindrical forms in strong primary colours, as in *Peasant Woman with Buckets* and *The Woodcutter* (both 1912; Amsterdam, Stedel. Mus.; see fig. 1).

In his Cubo-Futurist paintings (1912–13) Malevich made less use of primary colours, concentrating on a multifaceted, Cubist-inspired style and colour range. His

1. Kazimir Malevich: *The Woodcutter*, oil on canvas, 940×715 mm, 1912 (Amsterdam, Stedelijk Museum)

work as designer for Kruchonykh and Matyushin's avant-garde opera *Pobeda nad solntsem* ('Victory over the sun', 1913) introduced him to three-dimensional constructions in the volumetric costumes, with words and pictorial elements on the backdrops alluding to the plot of the opera. One design showed a square divided diagonally, one half black, the other half white.

In 1914 Malevich exhibited only once in Russia, at the Jack of Diamonds exhibition, and at the Salon des Indépendants in Paris. He continued to use collage elements in his paintings, both as painted *trompe l'oeil* and as actual objects, combined with simple geometric shapes, often leaving large areas as blank colour fields (e.g. *Woman at Poster Column*, 1914; Amsterdam, Stedel. Mus.). Words or fragments of words provided a certain semantic value, as in an *Englishman in Moscow* (1914; Amsterdam, Stedel. Mus.). Malevich termed this combination of objects and words 'alogizm'. Early in 1915 he took part in the exhibition *Tramvay V* ('Tramway V'), and during the spring and summer he finally discarded all reference to figuration in favour of coloured plain geometric shapes on a white background (for illustration *see* SUPREMATISM). He saw his new Suprematist art as purely concerned with form, free from any analogical references, and he emphasized the purity of shapes, particularly of the square. The key painting of this series was *Black Square* (1915; Moscow, Tret'yakov Gal.), exhibited at the 1915 exhibition *Poslednyaya futuristicheskaya vystavka kartin: 0.10* ('The last futurist exhibition of paintings: 0.10') in Petrograd

2. Kazimir Malevich: *White Square on White*, oil on canvas, 794×794 mm, 1918 (New York, Museum of Modern Art)

(now St Petersburg), followed by *Black Circle* (untraced) and *Black Cross* (Paris, Pompidou).

Malevich often referred to the connection between this new Suprematist concept and his work from 1913, and on several later occasions he pre-dated his works from 1915 by two years. He explained Suprematism in his booklet *Ot kubizma i futurizma k suprematizmu* ('From Cubism and Futurism to Suprematism') issued for the *0.10* exhibition in 1915.

During the spring of 1916 Malevich worked with some of his friends on a journal entitled *Supremus* and produced a large number of Suprematist works (e.g. *Dynamic Suprematism*, 1916; London, Tate) until he was called up; his regiment was in Moscow at the time of the February Revolution in 1917. He planned to create a popular art school and joined the Left Front of the Arts, working to abolish the Academy of Arts and existing art institutions in Moscow. The Suprematist works of 1916 were formally more complex with a greater variety of colouring; this was followed by an extreme reduction of the colour range, leading to the series of *White on White* paintings (1917–18). The tilted *White Square on White* (1918; New York, MOMA; see fig. 2) was a counterpart to his initial Suprematist painting, *Black Square* (1915).

(ii) 1918–27. After the October Revolution of 1917 Malevich first sided with the Moscow anarchists, but when they were repressed he decided in April 1918 to work for NARKOMPROS, the People's Commissariat for Enlightenment, where he joined the Fine Arts department (IZO), the section that was to supervise museums, create exhibition centres and organize a state factory for the production of painters' materials. He then became a teacher at the Free Art Studios (Svomas) in Moscow. On the first anniversary of the Revolution, Malevich drafted designs for street decorations and painted the stage set for the performance of Mayakovsky's *Misteriya-Buffa*, directed by V. E. Meyerhold in Petrograd. At the Tenth State Exhibition: Non-objective Creation and Suprematism, held in Moscow (summer 1919), Malevich showed his series of *White on White* paintings, with Suprematist works by his followers, including ALEKSANDR RODCHENKO. That same summer Malevich was in Nemchinovka, near Moscow, completing the manuscript of a book entitled *O novykh sistemakh v iskusstve* ('On new systems in art').

Later in 1919 Malevich accepted an invitation to join the art school in Vitebsk (Viciebsk), directed by Marc Chagall. There, during Chagall's temporary absence, he soon established a movement of his own with student support, under the name UNOVIS (Affirmers of new art). After Chagall's enforced retirement in 1919/20 Malevich abandoned painting for several years, concentrating on teaching and writing, but continued to develop Suprematist ideas in his 'architectural' works, including cardboard models of Utopian towns, some of which were exhibited at a one-day exhibition in Vitebsk (1921). His interest in theoretical and philosophical topics increased. The rediscovered plaster models executed after his departure from Vitebsk, from 1923 to 1932 (Paris, Pompidou), consist of between 12 and 200 rectangular or cubic shapes, which Malevich described as movements of the square in space (e.g. falling) at different speeds. The maquettes, which he referred to as *arkhitektona*, are of two types: horizontal (*Alfa, Beta*) and vertical (*Gota, Gota 2a*). He considered the models as prerequisites for architectural projects and borrowed his term *arkhitektona* from Kant who used it in relation to the production of scientific knowledge, or 'the art of systematizing'.

The Unovis group, of which El Lissitzky was also a member, designed revolutionary posters (e.g. propaganda handbill *UNOVIS—We Want!*, c. 1920; see Schadowa, p. 298), textile patterns (e.g. 1919 watercolour design in St Petersburg, Rus. Mus.), signposts and street decorations (e.g. colour schemes for a speaker's platform, reproduced in *UNOVIS Almanac*, no. 1, 1920). Following an intervention from Narkompros, Malevich had to leave Vitebsk early in 1922, and he went to Petrograd with some of his pupils. An appeal to register Unovis as a public institution was declined, but the group was incorporated into the new Museum of Artistic Culture (Muzey Khudozhestvennoy Kul'tury), which housed a collection of modern Russian art, supposedly the first ever museum of modern art. In 1924 Malevich became the leader of Ginkhuk (formerly INKHUK), the Institute of Artistic Culture, which succeeded the museum.

Malevich continued to teach painting, but he also collaborated with his most advanced pupils on *arkhitektoniki*, which were shown at an exhibition in the Institute in 1926. The severe criticism that this exhibition received, along with increasing political pressure, led to the closure of the Institute in December 1926. Malevich had in vain applied for permission to take an exhibition about the Institute to Germany, where the work of the Bauhaus formed an interesting parallel, but he was allowed to show his own work in Warsaw and Berlin in 1927; many of the paintings and drawings and even some manuscripts were left behind on his hurried return to Leningrad at the beginning of June 1927 (now Amsterdam, Stedel. Mus.). After the closure of the Institute, Malevich and his group of advanced students were moved to the neighbouring State Institute of Art History (GIII), but even this position was now threatened.

(iii) 1927–35. Malevich had encouraged his pupils to work with design in various fields, including china. Within this area he confined himself to models for a cup and a teapot (1923; St Petersburg, Mus. China Factory; never in production). In 1929 his last retrospective exhibition in his lifetime was held in the Tret'yakov Gallery in Moscow. He was criticized as a painter, but his role in design was acknowledged. In 1929 he tried to exhibit in Germany with the left-wing Novembergruppe, but he was refused permission, and he was deprived of his post in the Institute, suffering great financial difficulties. Despite these setbacks he established links with the Futurist movement in Ukraine and wrote a series of articles for the journal *Nova generatsiya* (Kharkiv, 1928–30).

Malevich took up painting again in 1927, gradually returning to figuration, with portraits, landscapes and figure compositions. In his paintings he analysed his earlier figurative work of 1911–12 and developed frontal figure compositions, some of which, such as *Three Peasants* (after 1930; St Petersburg, Rus. Mus.), *Running Man* (1933–4) and *Man with Horse* (1933; both Paris, Pompidou), paid direct tribute to the oppressed peasant class; others, particularly drawings, referred to mystical and religious experience (for example, drawings for *Die gegenstandslose Welt*, Bauhausbücher, xi (Munich, 1927); now Basle, Kstmus.). A major state exhibition held in Moscow and Leningrad to mark the 15th anniversary of the Revolution was the last exhibition in which Malevich's works were featured; they were now shown under pejorative slogans. Malevich continued, however, to paint, draw and work on his writings, and in 1930 he taught a painting course to a group of amateur artists in the House of the Arts (Dom Iskusstva) in Leningrad.

In portraits of members of his family and friends (e.g. *Self-portrait*, 1933, St Petersburg, Rus. Mus.; *Female Portrait*, 1933, Moscow, Tret'yakov Gal.) and in many drawings from 1932 to 1933 Malevich tried to widen the artistic basis of the official Socialist Realist idiom by incorporating his experience from the Suprematist paintings and perhaps even patterns of icon painting. As a token of his intentions he continued to mark his works with the characteristic sign of the Suprematist black square. In 1934 he was found to be seriously ill with cancer. He planned his own funeral, and in the peasant tradition even designed his own coffin, decorated with a black square and circle (see Schadowa, p. 359). It was carried through the streets of Leningrad on a lorry, followed by many artists and friends, and after the cremation in Moscow the urn was placed in the fields near Nemchinovka.

For over 20 years Malevich's work was remembered only by a small group of artists and collectors in the Soviet Union and in Europe. Some works were on extended loan to the Museum of Modern Art in New York. In 1956–8 a large group of his paintings, originally shown in Berlin in 1927, were retraced and acquired by the Stedelijk Museum in Amsterdam. This led to renewed interest in his work, and Malevich has since been widely recognized as one of the major artists of the 20th century.

2. PRINTS. Malevich's earliest known print, the lithograph *Peasant Woman* (1913), was derived from a painting *Head of a Peasant Girl* (1912; Amsterdam, Stedel. Mus.) and mounted on the cover of the first edition of Aleksey Kruchonykh's *Porosyata* ['Piglets'] (St Petersburg, 1913). Malevich collaborated with Kruchonykh, from whom he learnt the technique of lithography, on illustrations to a series of small books and postcards in 1913. During World War I Malevich made propaganda posters in the style of popular woodcuts, illustrating short verses by, among others, Mayakovsky. His graphic work also included book covers (N. Punin: *Pervyy tsikl lektsiy* [First series of lectures], Petrograd, 1920; G. Petnikov: *Kniga izbrannykh stikhotvoreniy* [Book of selected poetical works], Khar'kov, 1930). Many of his prints were, however, executed by others after his drawings and paintings, as for example the book *Suprematizm: 34 risunkov* ('Suprematism: 34 drawings'; Vitebsk, 1920), which was supervised by El Lissitsky and printed by Unovis.

3. WRITINGS. Malevich's philosophical texts were, for a long time, virtually unknown. He published his first statement in 1913 and in 1915 wrote the booklet on Suprematism, *Ot kubizma i futurizma k suprematizmu*, which marks the beginning of his consistent activity as a writer; in 1919–20 he declared that he had abandoned painting in favour of writing. During his stay in Vitebsk he completed a large manuscript entitled *Suprematizm I–II*, dedicated to the philosopher and scholar Mikhail Gershenzon. The manuscript remained unpublished, but in 1922 he summarized some of his ideas in the book *Bog ne skinut* ('God is not cast down'). He continued to expand his ideas in new texts that focused on and were intended as modern parallels to Arthur Schopenhauer's *Die Welt als Wille und Vorstellung* (1818, 2/1844). Malevich called his work *Mir kak bespredmetnost'* ('The world as non-objectivity'); in it he described the experience of nature as a given fact, outside artistic or aesthetic laws, consciousness or thought. The object, according to Malevich, subjugates the will; the modern artist must therefore create new concepts of art as a form of cognition, taking as his point of departure Impressionism's occupation with light and colour. The modern artist must also aim at new relationships between technology, architecture and art. Malevich above all examined the non-objective form of thought and expression in relation to the structure of consciousness. A set of didactic charts (Amsterdam, Stedel. Mus.; New York, Met.) show Malevich's combination of formal, structural and psychological approaches to artistic analysis. They also demonstrate his notion of the 'additional element', a microstructure defining the stylistic development in works by Cézanne, the Cubists and in Suprematism. In the 1920s Malevich also wrote and published critical articles on architecture and film, and a large series of articles on the history of modern art from Cézanne to Suprematism, published in *Nova Generatsiya*.

UNPUBLISHED SOURCES
Amsterdam, Stedel. Mus. [texts and notebooks]

WRITINGS

Ot kubizma i futurizma k suprematizmu: Novyy zhivopisnyy realizm [From Cubism and Futurism to Suprematism: the new realism in painting] (Petrograd, 1915; rev. Moscow, 3/1916)

O novykh sistemakh v iskusstve [On new systems in art] (Vitebsk, 1919)

Bog ne skinut [God is not cast down] (Petrograd, 1922)

Mir kak bespredmetnost' [The world as non-objectivity] (MS.; 1922); first pubd in Ger. trans. as *Suprematismus: Die gegenstandslose Welt* (Cologne, 1962)

T. Andersen, ed.: *Essays on Art*, 4 vols (Copenhagen, 1968–78) [Eng. trans. of all major pubd and unpubd writings]

A. B. Nakov, ed.: *Malévitch: Ecrits* (Paris, 1975)

K istorii russkogo avangarda [Towards a history of the Russian avantgarde], ed. N. Khardziyev (Stockholm, 1976), pp. 85–127 [chap. from unfinished autobiog.]

BIBLIOGRAPHY

T. Andersen: *Malevich: Catalogue Raisonné of the Berlin Exhibition 1927, Including the Collection in the Stedelijk Museum, Amsterdam* (Amsterdam, 1970) [with bibliog. to 1968]

D. Karshan: *Malevich: The Graphic Work, 1913–1930—a Print Catalogue Raisonné* (Jerusalem, 1975)

Ye. F. Kovtun: 'K. S. Malevich: Pis'ma k M. V. Matyushinu' [K. S. Malevich: letters to M. V. Matyushin], *Yezhegodnik rukopis'nogo otdela Pushkinskogo doma na 1974* [Annual of the manuscript department of Pushkin house for 1974] (Moscow, 1976), pp. 177–94

A. B. Nakov: 'Malevich as Printmaker', *Prt Colr Newslett.* (March–April 1976), pp. 4–10

E. Martineau: *Malévitch et la philosophie* (Lausanne, 1977)

S. Compton: *The World Backwards: Russian Futurist Books, 1912–16* (London, 1978)

L. Schadowa: *Suche und Experimente: Aus der Geschichte der russischen und sowjetischen Kunst zwischen 1910 und 1930* (Dresden, 1978); Eng. trans. as L. A. Zhadova: *Malevich: Suprematism and Revolution in Russian Art, 1910–1930* (London, 1982)

Kasimir Malewitsch zum 100. Geburtstag (exh. cat., ed. A. Gmurzynska; Cologne, Gal. Gmurzynska, 1978) [Ger. and Eng. text, with otherwise unpubd docs; several drgs reproduced are not authentic]

Malévitch (exh. cat. by J.-H. Martin, Paris, Pompidou, 1978) [selective bibliog. 1968–77]

Malévitch 1878–1978: Actes du colloque international, tenu au Centre Pompidou, Musée national d'art moderne, Paris, les 4 et 5 mai 1978

J.-H. Martin and P. Pedersen: *Malévitch: Oeuvres de Casimir Séverinovitch Malévitch, 1878–1935, avec en appendice les oeuvres de Nicolai Souétine, 1897–1954*, Paris, Pompidou cat. (Paris, 1980) [incl. the architectonic models rediscovered and restored 1978–80]

Kazimir Malewitsch (1878–1935): Werke aus sowjetischen Sammlungen (exh. cat., ed. E. Kowtun; Düsseldorf, Städt. Ksthalle, 1980)

E. F. Kovtun: 'Kazimir Malevich', *A. J.* [New York], xli/3 (1981), pp. 234–41

G. Demosfenova, ed.: *Malevich, Artist and Theoretician* (London, 1990)

J.-C. Marcadé: *Malévitch* (Paris, 1990)

Kazimir Malevich, 1878–1935 (exh. cat., Washington, DC, N.G.A.; Los Angeles, Armand Hammer Mus. A.; New York, Met.; 1990–01)

G. Steinmüller: *Die suprematistischen Bilder von Kasimir Malewitsch* (Cologne, 1991)

D. Sarabyanov and others: *Kazimir Malevich* (Moscow, 1993)

For further bibliography see USPENSKY, PYOTR.

TROELS ANDERSEN

Malfray, Charles (*b* Orléans, 19 July 1887; *d* Dijon, 28 May 1940). French sculptor. He came from a long line of masons and was trained at the Ecole des Beaux-Arts in Orléans. In 1904 he was sent to Paris, entering the Ecole des Beaux-Arts in 1907. He fought in World War I and was seriously gassed. After the war he soon resumed his sculptural work, and in 1920 he was awarded second place in the Prix de Rome and also won the Blumenthal prize.

In 1921 Malfray was commissioned to produce a war memorial for Pithiviers, which he entitled *Fright* (see exh. cat., pl. 2). This caused much controversy among those accustomed to more academic works. Similar problems arose over his commission in 1922 for the war memorial at Orléans, *To Glory*. Only after a fierce struggle could he persuade the authorities not to have the work destroyed. This large bronze sculpture, 14 m high, embodied all of his feelings for the misery of war and was hence perceived as inappropriate as a memorial. After a long period of financial hardship he was offered the chair of sculpture at the Académie Ranson in Paris in 1930 on the recommendation of Aristide Maillol. At last established as a sculptor, he then received various public commissions in the 1930s, such as *Spring* for the Palais de Chaillot in Paris (1937) and the *Spring of Taurion* (1938) for a public garden in Limoges. He died while at work on an immense triptych *The Dance.*

BIBLIOGRAPHY

Charles Malfray, 1887–1940: Sculpture and Drawings (exh. cat., London, Marlborough F. A., 1951)

R. Maillard, ed.: *Dictionnaire univers de l'art et des artistes* (Paris, 1967)

□

Malhoa, José (*b* Caldas da Rainha, 28 April 1855; *d* Figueiró dos Vinhos, 26 Oct 1933). Portuguese painter. He studied at the Academia de Belas-Artes in Lisbon, where he acquired a lifelong taste for landscape painting from Tomás José da Anunciação and learnt the technique of portraiture from Miguel Ângelo Lupi. He became known as a landscape and animal painter when his canvas the *Invaded Cornfield* (Lisbon, priv. col.; see 1983 exh. cat.), showing calves eating crops, was shown at the Madrid Exhibition of 1881. He failed to win a state scholarship to study abroad, and was accordingly one of the few Naturalist artists of his generation to embark on a career rooted in the Portuguese tradition. He belonged to the Grupo do Leão (1881–9) and was thus in contact with António Silva Porto, who had studied in Paris and had assimilated the values of *plein-air* painting and Barbizon Naturalism. The influence of Silva Porto is evident in Malhoa's *Paul from the Other Side* (Caldas da Rainha, Mus. Malhoa), painted in 1885 to decorate the walls of the Cervejaria do Leão de Ouro, Lisbon, headquarters of the first generation of Naturalist painters (including Silva Porto, António Ramalho, João Vaz, Columbano Bordal Pinheiro) and the source of their group name. Malhoa introduced figures into his landscapes, increasingly making them *costumbrista* (realistic genre) scenes, and came to specialize in regional and popular subjects. From the *Viaticum at the End* of 1884 (priv. col.; see 1983 exh. cat.) to *The Betrothed* of 1933 (Caldas da Rainha, Mus. Malhoa), he exhaustively treated the events of Portuguese rural life at the end of the 19th century: festivals, processions, harvests, work in the fields. His favourite scenery was that of Estremadura, especially the country around Figueiró dos Vinhos, a peaceful provincial town where he had a summer villa from about 1895. His work's originality lay not in its monotonous subject-matter but in the spontaneity with which he conveyed the rural life and the sincerity with which he portrayed his models. Two works deserve special mention: *Clara* (1903; Caldas da Rainha, Mus. Malhoa) and *Cócegas* (1904; Rio de Janeiro, Mus. N. B.A.). Both of these paintings, one of a country girl washing clothes by a river, the other of a couple resting in the hay, demonstrate the plastic qualities of his painting, his vigorous brushstrokes and intense colours.

In the field of *costumbrismo*, Malhoa left two outstanding canvases, which, although of interiors, are still characteristic of his work: *The Drunkards* (1907; Caldas da Rainha, Mus. Malhoa) and *O Fado* (1910; Lisbon, Mus. Cidade; see fig.). The first is a rural scene, with half a dozen peasants sitting round a table after drinking the new wine, the other a low-life study of a prostitute listening to a *fado* singer. Apart from their solid technique these paintings have a realism and intimacy rare in Portuguese painting. This applies to *O Fado* in particular, where these qualities are conveyed by the light and the objects reflected in a mirror. In the late 1910s and the 1920s Malhoa painted middle-class subjects set in the cosmopolitan life of the capital city (e.g. *Autumn*, 1918; Lisbon, Mus. N. A. Contemp.). In these the juxtaposition of tones approaches the Impressionist manner.

Malhoa also painted portraits: one of his best-known is that of *Laura Sauvinet* (1888, Caldas da Rainha, Mus. Malhoa), in which he employs a conventional romantic treatment, evident likewise in that of *Prince Luis Filipe*, whom he painted in 1892 (Vila Viçosa, Ducal Pal.) and in 1908 (Caldas da Rainha, Mus. Malhoa). However, the portraits of his wife (1912) and of *Agostinho Fernandes* (1926; both Caldas da Rainha, Mus. Malhoa) and of *Dr Anastâcio Gonçalves* (Lisbon, Casa Mus. Gonçalves) have greater psychological depth as well as an elegance appropriate to their bourgeois, cosmopolitan subjects.

Malhoa was, in addition, active as a decorative and history painter. In 1888 he won a competition to decorate the Câmara Municipal in Lisbon with a painting of the *Departure of Vasco da Gama* (1889), and he painted other historical subjects for the Ajuda Palace (1890), the Constituent Assembly (1891) and the Military Museum (1907–8; all *in situ*). Outstanding is the epic series of *Discoveries* for the Military Museum (*in situ*), which is distinguished by Malhoa's realistic treatment of the historical figures. History yields to fable in the *Lovers' Isle* (*c.* 1907), a scene from this series, inspired by Canto IX and *Os Lusíadas* (Lisbon, 1572) by Luiz de Camoês, a pretext for a nude model in a landscape background, a subject rarely explored in Naturalist painting. Other, more conventional, history paintings are the ambitious *Ultimo interrogatório do Marquês de Pombal* (1892; Lisbon, Mus. N. A. Contemp., on dep. Caldas da Rainha, Mus. Malhoa) and the portrait of *Queen Leonor* (1926; Caldas da Rainha, Mus. Malhoa). These are somewhat theatrical and lack the colourful vitality and realism of his genre paintings, evidence that Malhoa was most at ease depicting the spectacle of daily life.

José Malhoa: *O Fado*, oil on canvas, 1.50×1.83 m, 1910 (Lisbon, Museu da Cidade)

Malhoa received many distinctions in Portugal and abroad, including medals at the Exposition Universelle in Paris (1900) and at the international exhibitions of Berlin (1896), Madrid (1901), Rio de Janeiro (1908), Barcelona (1910), Buenos Aires (1910) and San Francisco (1915). He was represented in the Paris Salons between 1897 and 1912, and awarded the Légion d'honneur in 1905. The Museu José Malhoa was founded at Caldas da Rainha in 1934.

BIBLIOGRAPHY

J. D. Ramalho Ortigão: *Arte portuguesa*, 3 vols (Lisbon, 1943–7), ii
A. Montes: *Malhoa* (Caldas da Rainha, 1950)
J.-A. França: *A arte em Portugal no século XIX*, 3 vols (Lisbon, 1966), ii, pp. 277–90
Cinquentenário da morte de José Malhoa (exh. cat., Lisbon, Inst. Port. Patrm. Cult., 1983)
Soleil et ombres: L'Art portugais du XIXe siècle (exh. cat., ed. J. -A. França and L. Verdelho da Costa; Paris, Petit Pal., 1987), pp. 209–19

LUCILIA VERDELHO DA COSTA

Mali, Republic of [République du Mali; formerly French Sudan]. Country in north-west Africa. It is bordered by Algeria to the north, Niger to the east, Mauritania and Senegal to the west, and Burkina Faso, Côte d'Ivoire and Guinea to the south. The capital is Bamako.

1. GEOGRAPHY AND CULTURAL HISTORY. Half of Mali's *c.* 1,280,000 sq. km is desert, supporting nomadic herding. In the southern part of the country, a mixture of savannah and forest, arable and livestock farming are practised, especially along the fertile banks of the Niger, which flows through Mali for 1600 km. The area that is now Mali was once occupied by the medieval empires of Ghana (?4th–11th centuries), Mali (13th–16th centuries) and Songhay (*c.* 1460–1591), all of which flourished on revenues from taxes levied on the trans-Saharan gold trade. Between 1880 and 1898 the area was conquered by the French, becoming part of French West Africa. In 1920 the distinct territory of French Sudan (Soudan Français) was formed, and by 1947 the country's present borders were established. From 1958 to 1960 the region was part of the federation of ex-French African states, becoming fully independent in 1960. Mali's present population of 7,960,000 (UN estimate, 1989) is ethnically and linguistically very diverse. This has meant a long history of co-existence between Muslim and non-Muslim peoples, and, in general, Malian culture combines elements of both. French is the language of government. This entry covers art in Mali since colonial times; unlike other countries in western Africa, however, Mali produced little specifically colonial art other than architecture (*see* §2 below). Contemporary 20th-century Malian artists have found their greatest inspiration in native traditions; indeed the poverty of the country seems to have encouraged the production and exploration of folk art forms.

For the arts of the area in earlier times *see* AFRICA, §VII, 3 and MIDDLE NIGER CULTURES. *See also* BAMANA, DOGON, FULANI, MOSSI, SENUFO, TIMBUKTU and TUAREG.

2. ARCHITECTURE. Malian architecture is based largely on the continuation of traditional forms and techniques. The cities of Djenné, founded in the 11th century AD (added to the UNESCO catalogue of historical monuments in 1989), and Timbuktu, founded *c.* 1100, represent the centres of ancient West Sudanese mud architecture, which is characterized by two-storey, rectangular houses with flat roofs. Built of sun-baked mud-bricks, and plastered with mud, these houses feature decorative conical projections on the tops of walls, with visual emphasis placed on entrances. The traditional architecture of Djenné was taken up by the French and transformed into a 'Neo-Sudanese' style, which was first used in a fort (destr.) built in Ségou by Léon Underberg (*d* 1891), the first commander of the city after conquest, in 1891–2 on the ruins of the palace of Ahmadou Tall (*reg* 1861–90), king of the Tukulor empire of Ségou. Later examples of the style can be seen in the colonial government offices of Bamako and Ségou, and in the Red Market, Bamako. The Friday Mosque (1906–7), Djenné, by Ismaila Traoré, may not be as attractive or elegant as many of the small village mosques of the 19th century, but it remains the largest mud building in Sub-Saharan Africa. Its eastern façade, adorned with three tower-like minarets with rectangular cross-sections, served as the model for several new mosques. An innovation of the mosque at Djenné was the staircase inside one of its minarets leading up to the flat roof.

Mixtures of mud and cement have been used in post-colonial architecture, which frequently draws on the Neo-Sudanese style. For example, the Medical Assistance Clinic in Mopti (1974; awarded the Aga Khan Award for Architecture in 1980), by the French architect André Ravéreau, uses earth and concrete and follows the layout of a traditional village, with one- and two-storey units. In southern Mali round houses with conical grass roofs continued to be built in the 20th century, but Dogon architecture has been increasingly influenced by the Islamic architecture of Djenné.

3. TEXTILES. Among other traditions still practised in the 20th century is the manufacture of textiles, which has a long history dating from at least the 11th century. Particularly characteristic is the weaving of narrow strips (up to 210 mm wide), which are sewn together with deliberate irregularities introduced into the motif. Embroidery, practised in such commercial centres as Djenné and Timbuktu, also continues to play an important role in Malian fashion, both in the flowing robes of the national dress (the *boubou*), with its colourful imported silks, and in more modern styles. Woollen blankets are produced by the stock-breeding Fulani and are traded as far as Ghana. The resist-dyeing of cloths with indigo is another Malian speciality. Dyeing is traditionally done by Soninke women of noble birth, and the centres of production continue to be Nioro du Sahel and Kayes. Also typical, in this case of the Bamana and Maninka, is the resist-dyeing of handspun, handwoven, unstretched, narrow-band cotton cloths painted with mud in a series of production stages. Called *bogolanfini* (see fig. 1), these cloths are traditionally worn by young women after circumcision, during the wedding ceremony and after childbirth. Increasingly secularized since independence, the mud-painted cloths have undergone an imaginative reinterpretation, especially since 1978, when a collective of six artists called the Groupe Bogolan Kasobane was formed in Bamako to revitalize the technique. The artists worked together using motifs drawn from traditional African sculpture, ancient Egyptian art

S. Sinaba (*b c.* 1950), a self-taught artist, produced many such paintings in Bamako, particularly during the 1980s. Two late 20th-century Malian artists who gained recognition for their work are Ismael Diabate (*b* ?1945) and Abdoulaye Konate (*b* 1953). The former, educated at the Institut National des Arts, Bamako, had international exhibitions in Tunis, Moscow, Beijing, Paris, Stockholm and elsewhere, but in Mali exhibitions of his work (16 of which took place in the 1970s and 1980s) have been held in such venues as the Catholic Mission, Ségou, because of the lack of galleries. Perhaps partly because of this scarcity of exhibition space, Diabate earns his living as a teacher. Konate, also educated at the Institut National des Arts (although he finished his education in Havana), was employed as a painter in the early 1990s by the Musée National du Mali, Bamako. In 1994 he had his first international exhibition at the Institut du Monde Arabe, Paris.

5. SCULPTURE. Modern Malian sculpture has drawn on such existing traditional forms as terracotta figures, small bronze statues, wooden sculptures and masks. Some older types of mask (e.g. the elephant) have become unpopular, while new characters have been introduced, such as the Learned Muslim, the Annoying Tourist, with camera, and the White Anthropologist, with pen and notebook (for illustrations see 1991 exh. cat.). The best-known mask forms derive from the puppet shows that are held after harvesting in the Ségou region for the entertainment of the rural community. Performed by youth groups, these parodies employ gaudily painted masks and figures made of several parts. Theatre performances (*koteba*) with a similar content are also held in the outer residential areas of Bamako.

6. ART LIFE AND ORGANIZATION. Into the 1990s the most outstanding works of such Malian folk arts as textiles, woven mats, ceramics and painted calabashes continued to be given as wedding presents. Women have played a central role in their manufacture, commissioning objects, formulating specific requests and exercising quality control. The once-important role of secret societies and age-sets as commissioners of masks and figures has diminished under the influence of Islam. Some formal art education is provided by the Institut National des Arts, Bamako, set up by the French administration in 1932 as the Maison des Artisans and given its new name in 1966. Even in the early 1990s, however, leading artists were still chiefly self-taught or came from tradition-oriented social backgrounds. A biennial arts festival, held in Bamako, is intended to encourage artistic appreciation and participation and to lessen the differences between the capital and the remote hinterland. Also meant to foster artistic production is the Association Nationale des Artistes du Mali, which was established in the 1980s in recognition of the difficulties faced by Malian fine artists. The Musée National du Mali, Bamako, was founded in 1982, and a regional branch museum was opened in Gao in the early 1980s. The main centres for trade in contemporary Malian fine art, however, continue to be Paris and New York.

1. Mud-painted cotton cloth (*bogolanfini*), 1.43×0.65 m, Bamana, Beledougou region, Mali (Basle, Museum für Völkerkunde)

and comics. Clothes made from this type of cloth became the popular dress of young intellectuals. In his fashion houses in Paris and Bamako, international Malian couturier Chris Seydou (*d* 1994) used *bogolanfini* materials in his designs.

4. PAINTING. Painting was used traditionally to embellish masks, a practice that has continued with such 20th-century introductions as new colours and enamel paints. Naive painting, however, spontaneous in expression but of varying standards, has been used for advertising in hairdressers, tailors, butchers and bars (see fig. 2).

2. Painted wall advertisement for a butcher's shop, Bamako, Mali; from a photograph by Bernard Gardi, 1985

BIBLIOGRAPHY

P. Brasseur: *Bibliographie générale du Mali*, Institut Français d'Afrique Noire, Catalogues et Documents, xvi and xvi-l, 2 vols (Dakar, 1964–76)

R. Boser-Sarivaxévanis: 'Aperçus sur la teinture à l'indigo en Afrique occidentale', *Verhand. Natforsch. Ges. Basel*, lxxx–lxxxi (1969), pp. 151–208

L. Prussin: *The Architecture of Djenné: African Synthesis and Transformation* (diss., New Haven, Yale U., 1973)

J.-B. Cuypers: 'De architectuur in Mali/L'Architecture du Mali', *Africa–Tervuren*, xxvii/2 (1981), pp. 33–45

S. C. Brett-Smith: 'Symbolic Blood: Cloths for Excised Women', *Res*, 3 (Spring 1982), pp. 15–31

J.-P. Vuilleumier: 'Museum Programming and Development', *Museum: Rev. Trimest.*, xxxii/2 (1983), pp. 94–7

B. Gardi: *Ein Markt wie Mopti: Handwerkerkasten und traditionelle Techniken in Mali*, Basl. Beitr. Ethnog., xxv (Basle, 1985)

J.-L. Bourgeois: 'The History of the Great Mosques of Djenné', *Afr. A.*, xx/3 (1987), pp. 54–63, 90–92

Mali: Land im Sahel (exh. cat. by B. Gardi, Basle, Mus. Vlkerknd., 1988)

S. Domian: *Architecture soudanaise: Vitalité d'une tradition urbaine et monumentale—Mali, Côte d'Ivoire, Burkina Faso, Ghana* (Paris, 1989) [well illustrated]

F. B. Keita and L. Albaret: *Bogolan et arts graphiques du Mali* (Paris, 1990)

P. Maas and G. Mommersteeg: *Djenné: L'Architecture africaine en argile* (Amsterdam, 1991)

S. Sibide: 'L'Exposition au Musée National du Mali', *Arte in Africa/Art in Africa*, ii, ed. E. Bassani and G. Speranza (Florence, 1991), pp. 172–96

Africa Explores (exh. cat., ed. S. Vogel; New York, Cent. Afr. A., 1991)

VIDEO RECORDING

Togu na and Cheko: Change and Continuity in the Art of Mali (Washington, DC, Nat. Mus. Afr. A., 1989) [½" videotape]

BERNARD GARDI

Ma Lin. *See* MA, (2).

Malinalco. Site of a 16th-century rock-cut Aztec temple, *c.* 60 km south-east of Mexico City. The temple at Malinalco is an example of a widespread type of ritual building described in 16th-century ethno-historical texts and associated with the cult of the earth. Its monolithic inner chamber is the only excavated example to have survived intact. The temple forms part of a ritual and administrative centre built at the hilltop Matlazinca town of Malinalco after it had been incorporated into the Aztec empire. The

buildings were begun in 1501, under the Aztec ruler Ahuizotl (*reg* 1486–1502), as extensions of the symbolic architectural system developed in Tenochtitlán; they are compactly arranged along an artificial terrace partly carved from the steeply sloping mountainside. The façade comprises two sections. Sculptured guardian figures flank the foot of a flight of 13 steps ascending the lower platform. Similar figures flank the front of the upper temple chamber; another figure forms part of the centre of the 3rd to 6th steps, in which the most important sculpture is a large relief carving of a serpent-like mask framing the chamber doorway. The carved mask functions as a hieroglyph for *oztotl* (Náhuatl: 'cave'), signalling that the door was an entrance to the earth's interior. In front of, east of and to the north-east of this main temple are several less well preserved structures, including three small pyramidal platforms (two circular and one rectangular); a second circular chamber cut into the cliff, with a shallow rectangular antechamber; and a larger rectangular chamber with two portals.

In the main temple the interior space of the circular temple chamber is articulated by a curving stone bench abutting the rear wall. Stone representations of two eagle pelts and a central feline hide are carved symmetrically on the bench. A third stone eagle pelt is carved in the centre of the floor, and immediately behind it is a small circular opening cut into the bedrock, giving symbolic access to the subterranean fastness of the mountain. The connection between these emblematic animals and the chamber as a place of communion with the earth lies at the heart of the meaning and function of the Malinalco temple. The earth was regarded in essentially female terms by the Pre-Columbian peoples of Central Highland Mexico. In creation myths many groups, including the Aztecs, traced their beginnings to emergence from the earth. The earth's procreative properties were represented in the myriad forms of deities associated with fertility and the agricultural cycle. In this ancient chthonic schema, the earth was perceived as physical habitat and provider, a hallowed progenitor and mythic household of ancestral household spirits. The use of caves as places for rites of passage, such as coronation ceremonies, was also widespread. At Malinalco the temple was an architectural cave, where traditional communications were maintained with the animistic forces residing in the earth's interior.

The imagery of eagles and felids affirmed the religious connection betweeen the earth and imperial government. Feline and eagle seats were emblems of military authority as well as seats of rulership. At Tenochtitlán (see MEXICO CITY, §I) emperors sat on thrones covered with eagle and ocelot hides and adorned with eagle plumes. At Malinalco the sculpted feline figure hide at the centre of the rock-cut bench served as the principal seat of imperial authority, while the carved eagle pelts on either side were the seats of other military officers of the Aztec administration. Dancing figures of anthropomorphic jaguars and eagles, surrounded by various symbolic references to warfare, are carved in low relief on two wooden drums or *huéhuetls* from Malinalco (Mexico City, Mus. N. Antropol.; Tenango, Mus. Arqueol. Estado México). In front of, east of and to the north-east of this main temple are several less well preserved structures, including three small pyramidal-platforms (two circular and one rectangular); a second circular chamber cut into the cliff, with a shallow, rectangular antechamber; and a larger rectangular chamber with two portals.

The hole in the floor of the temple chamber was essential to the connection between the earth and the royal administrators, since it was required that rulers—in order to take office—perform a rite of passage in which drops of their own blood were offered to the earth as a sacrificial confirmation. Such sacrifices are depicted on the Tizoc and Ahuizotl Stone from Tenochtitlán (Mexico City, Mus. N. Antropol.). After the blood offering, the ruler would emerge from the temple–cave, symbolically 'reborn' in his new social role. Architecturally the Malinalco temple functioned on two levels as a place for communication with chthonic powers, where Aztec overlords performed the rites to certify their government in this conquered province, and as a three-dimensional ideogram, an earth–temple where cosmological and royal symbols told of the legitimacy of the Aztec rulers and of the corresponding incorporation of conquered territory into the larger social-sacred cosmos of Tenochtitlán's empire.

BIBLIOGRAPHY
J. G. Payon: *La Zona arqueológica de Tecaxic-Calixtlahuaca y los Matlazincas* (Mexico City, 1936)
——: *Los Monumentos arqueológicos de Malinalco* (Mexico City, 1947)
R. Mendoza: 'World View and the Monolithic Temples of Malinalco, Mexico: Iconography and Analogy in Pre-Columbian Architecture', *Actes du XLIIème congrès international des americanistes: Paris, 1976*, pp. 63–80
R. F. Townsend: 'Malinalco and the Lords of Tenochtitlán', *The Art and Iconography of Late Post-Classic Central Mexico: Dumbarton Oaks, 1977*, pp. 111–40
——: *State and Cosmos in the Art of Tenochtitlán* (Washington, DC, 1979)
——: 'Coronation at Tenochtitlán', *The Aztec Templo Mayor*, ed. E. Boone (Washington, DC, 1987), pp. 371–407

RICHARD F. TOWNSEND

Malines. *See* MECHELEN.

Malinovsky, Aleksandr. *See* BOGDANOV, ALEKSANDR.

Mall, shopping. *See under* SHOPPING CENTRE.

Mallarmé, Stéphane (*b* Paris, 18 March 1842; *d* Valvins, 9 Sept 1898). French poet. Like his predecessor among French poets, Charles Baudelaire, and his successor, Paul Valéry, he loved all forms of art, especially painting and music. More than either, he had an acute sense of his time and immediate sympathy and empathy with virtually all the major, and many of the minor, avant-garde artists of the Third Republic. He was closely involved in Impressionism from its origins. He had an exceptional gift for friendship and brought warm appreciation and intelligent encouragement to great and small, inducing his friend Henri Roujon, Directeur des Beaux-Arts, to purchase for the State James Abbott McNeill Whistler's *Arrangement in Grey and Black: Portrait of the Artist's Mother* (1871), Auguste Renoir's *Young Girls at the Piano* (1892; both Paris, Mus. d'Orsay) and works by struggling artists. His relations with the visual arts are attested in four main ways: he inspired numerous portraits and illustrations of his work; he drew suggestions for his own poetry from paintings or drawings; he published art criticism; and above all, he left an extensive correspondence.

The best portraits of Mallarmé are Edouard Manet's oil painting (1876; Paris, Mus. d'Orsay); the etching by Paul Gauguin with a raven behind the poet's head (Jan 1891); and especially Whistler's superb lithograph (Nov 1892), which was used as the frontispiece to *Vers et prose* (1893). Mallarmé died before Whistler could complete an etching and a portrait in oils. Renoir's portrait (1892; Versailles, Château) did not please Mallarmé: he felt it made him look like 'a prosperous financier'. A woodcut by Félix Vallotton (1896) and a lithograph by Edvard Munch (1897) were more successful; the latter was derived from one of several remarkable photographs of Mallarmé by Nadar. The most significant illustrations of Mallarmé's works are those by Manet: the six lithographs for Mallarmé's translation of Edgar Allan Poe's *The Raven* (1875) and the four woodcuts, hand-tinted by the artist, for *L'Après-midi d'un faune* (1876): one is directly derived from a sketch by Katsushika Hokusai. Mallarmé planned to have his collected prose writings (*Pages*, 1891; originally entitled *Le Tiroir de laque*) illustrated by Degas, Mary Cassatt, Berthe Morisot, John-Lewis Brown and Renoir, who alone fulfilled his promise: his etching of a nude illustrating the prose poem 'Le Phénomène Futur' formed the frontispiece. Ambroise Vollard planned editions of Mallarmé's *Hérodiade* illustrated by Edouard Vuillard and of his experimental poem 'Un coup de dés' illustrated by Odilon Redon: nothing came of the first; Redon, however, executed four lithographs (one of which was lost), but the poem appeared posthumously without the illustrations. Later Raoul Dufy illustrated his *Madrigaux* (1920) and Henri Matisse his *Poésies* (1932).

Visual sources are much less important in Mallarmé's poetry than in that of Théophile Gautier or Baudelaire, but they need further examination. It is unlikely, as has been suggested, that Gustave Moreau's *The Apparition* (1876; Paris, Louvre) inspired Mallarmé's 'Le Cantique de Saint Jean'. François Boucher's *Pan and Syrinx* (1759; London, N.G.) may well be reflected in a central passage of *L'Après-midi d'un faune*. Mallarmé collaborated with Jean-François Raffaëlli in *Les Types de Paris* (1889): two sonnets and six quatrains illustrate drawings by Raffaëlli, mostly from tiny preliminary sketches, while some of Raffaëlli's final versions probably reflect Mallarmé's poems. The lively, charming drawings and the witty little poems are in perfect harmony. The episode is fully documented in Mallarmé's correspondence, which also throws much light on his relations with artists (including the sculptors Cyprian Godebski (1835–1909), Albert Bartholomé and, above all, Rodin) and sometimes comments on their work, notably that of Claude Monet and of Odilon Redon.

Mallarmé's published art criticism includes brief notes in the gossip columns of the London *Athenaeum*, mainly praising Manet but also disparaging Ernest Meissonier; an important article in the Edinburgh *Art Monthly Review* on 'The Impressionists and Edouard Manet' (1876); 'Le Jury de peinture pour 1874 et M. Manet' (1874), a vigorous defence of the painter; and the splendid preface to the catalogue of the Berthe Morisot retrospective exhibition of 1896, which he organized with Monet, Renoir, Edgar Degas and especially his ward Julie Manet, Berthe Morisot's daughter, whose diary confirms Mallarmé's place as an outstanding witness of one of the greatest periods of French painting.

WRITINGS

H. Mondor and G. Jean-Aubry, eds: *Oeuvres complètes* (Paris, 1945, rev. 1951/*R* 1971)
'Compléments et suppléments', i, *Fr. Stud.*, xl/1 (1956), pp. 13–25; ii, *Fr. Stud.*, xli/2 (1987), pp. 155–80; iii, *Fr. Stud.*, xliv/2 (1990), pp. 170–95; iv, *Fr. Stud.*, xlv/2 (1991), pp. 166–94; v, *Fr. Stud.*, xlvii/2 (1993), pp. 172–201; vi, *Fr. Stud.*, xlviii/1 (1994), pp. 17–49 [addns to *Correspondance*]
H. Mondor, ed.: *Correspondance*, with J.-P. Richard (vol. i); with L. J. Austin (vols ii–xi), 11 vols (Paris, 1959–85)
H. Mondor and L. J. Austin, eds: *Les 'Gossips' de Mallarmé: 'Athenaeum' 1875–1876* (Paris, 1962)

BIBLIOGRAPHY

H. Mondor: *Vie de Mallarmé*, ii (Paris, 1941–2)
L. J. Austin: 'Mallarmé and the Visual Arts', *French 19th-century Painting and Literature*, ed. U. Finke (Manchester, 1972), pp. 232–57
——: 'Mallarmé: Critique d'art', *The Artist and the Writer in France: Essays in Honour of Jean Seznec* (Oxford, 1974), pp. 153–60
E. Souffrin-Le Breton: 'The Young Mallarmé and the Boucher Revival', *Baudelaire, Mallarmé, Valéry: New Essays in Honour of Lloyd Austin* (Cambridge, 1982), pp. 283–313
P. Florence: *Mallarmé, Monet and Redon: Visual and Aural Signs and the Generation of Meaning*, Cambridge Studies in French (Cambridge, 1986)
L. J. Austin: *Poetic Principles and Practice* (Cambridge, 1987)
——: *Essais sur Mallarmé* (Manchester, 1994)

LLOYD JAMES AUSTIN

Málles Venosta [Ger. Mals im Vinschgau], **S Benedetto**. Benedictine church in the Italian Tyrol, *c.* 50 km west of Merano. It is most notable for its 9th-century frescoes, which are among the few examples of monumental painting to survive from the Carolingian period (*see* CAROLINGIAN ART, §IV, 1). Built *c.* AD 816, the church contains a simple rectangular space, its east wall punctuated by three narrow niches for altars. The central niche contains a fresco of *Christ* standing between two angels. The slightly smaller lateral niches contain representations of *St Gregory the Great* (left) and *St Stephen* (right). Immediately to the left of the central niche is a standing male figure, in secular costume, holding a sword; in a corresponding position to the right is a priest with a square halo, holding a model of the chapel (*see* CAROLINGIAN ART, fig. 4). These two paintings, of higher quality than

the other frescoes, probably represent donors. The paintings were originally surrounded with decorative stuccowork, fragments of which are preserved (Bolzano, Mus. Civ.). On the north wall, the frescoes in the lower register are almost entirely lost. The upper register has scenes from the early *Life of St Paul*, including the *Stoning of St Stephen* and the *Conversion of St Paul*, and representations of four tonsured clerics, one of whom is Gregory the Great. These frescoes have often been compared to those at nearby Müstair, but, although both cycles are assigned to the 9th century, there are no close stylistic similarities between them.

BIBLIOGRAPHY

U. Theil and E. Theil: *St Benedikt in Mals* (Bolzano, 1973)
N. Rasmo: *Karolingische Kunst in Südtirol* (Bolzano, 1981), pp. 19–32, 41–5; pls 16–43, 61–8, IX–XX, XXX–XXXII
E. Rüber: *St Benedict in Mals* (Frankfurt am Main, 1991)

DON DENNY

Mallet, Jean-Baptiste (*b* Grasse, 1759; *d* Paris, 16 Aug 1835). French painter. A pupil of Simon Julien in Toulon, he was then taught by Pierre-Paul Prud'hon in Paris. He exhibited at every Salon between 1793 and 1827, obtaining a second class medal in 1812 and a first class medal in 1817. He executed very few portraits (*Chénier*, Carcassonne, Mus. B.-A., is an exception), preferring to paint nymphs bathing and graceful classical nudes such as the *Graces Playing with Cupid* (Arras, Abbaye St Vaast, Mus. B.-A.). He established his reputation with gouache genre scenes of fashionable and often libertine subjects, always elegant and refined, in the style of Louis-Philibert Debucourt and Louis-Léopold Boilly, and remarkable for the delicacy and brilliance of their brushwork: for example *At the Laundry Maid's* and the *Painful Letter* (both Paris, Mus. Cognacq-Jay). They reveal a knowledge of 17th-century Dutch painting in the treatment of details (transparent crystal, reflections on silk or satin) as well as the choice of themes: *Military Gallant* (Paris, Mus. Cognacq-Jay). Mallet's meticulously precise paintings are one of the best records of fashionable French furnishings and interiors at the end of the 18th century and the beginning of the 19th. They were very popular and widely disseminated in prints.

During the Restoration Mallet adopted the TROUBADOUR STYLE, producing very small paintings with a porcelain-like quality, elegant details and an extremely refined treatment of contrasting light effects, for example *Education of Henry IV* (exh. Salon 1817; Pau, Mus. N. Château) and *Genevieve of Brabant Baptizing her Son in Prison* (exh. Salon 1824; Cherbourg, Mus. Henry). Mallet achieved a synthesis of his early amorous works, the Dutch style and Troubadour painting in the *Gothic Bathroom* (exh. Salon 1810; Dieppe, Château-Mus.), in which he combined a Gothic window, a rich lustre reminiscent of Gerrit Dou and a female nude, smoothly glazed in the manner of Adriaen van der Werff. He painted fewer outdoor scenes, such as *St John the Baptist as a Child Washing* (1820; Paris, Louvre), a family scene that is similar, in its intimist feeling and delicacy of lighting, to the style of Hortense Haudebourt-Lescot.

BIBLIOGRAPHY

J. Renouvier: *Histoire de l'art pendant le Révolution* (Paris, 1863), pp. 188–90

P. Marmottan: *L'Ecole française de peinture (1789–1830)* (Paris, 1886), pp. 263–6

De David à Delacroix: La Peinture française de 1774 à 1830 (exh. cat., Paris, Grand Pal., 1974), pp. 532–5

MARIE-CLAUDE CHAUDONNERET

Mallet-Stevens, Robert (*b* Paris, 24 March 1886; *d* Paris, 8 Feb 1945). French architect, designer and writer. His father, Maurice Mallet, was an important paintings dealer and appraiser, and one of the first to promote the work of Impressionist painters. While studying at the Ecole Spéciale d'Architecture in Paris (1903–6), Robert Mallet-Stevens frequently visited his family in Brussels, where he observed the construction of the Palais Stoclet (1905–11), designed by Josef Hoffmann for Mallet-Stevens's uncle, Baron Stoclet. Hoffmann's influence can be seen in Mallet-Stevens's earliest designs for villas such as the Ecorcheville house (1914; 2nd version, Paris, Mus. A. Déc.). The graphic style of the villa design, the smooth white façades and rigorous geometry of the masses were derived from the Palais Stoclet. Mallet-Stevens's series of drawings for city buildings (1917) were similar in style and were published as *Une Cité moderne* (1922). His villa at Hyères (1923–6; *see* FRANCE, fig. 14) for Charles, Vicomte de Noailles, revealed a style that had been influenced by contact with the De Stijl group. Simple prisms project laterally, in a series of terraces, from a central staircase that acts as the vertical counter-weight to the composition. Jacques Lipchitz, Henri Laurens, Jozseph Czaky and Constantin Brancusi were chosen by Mallet-Stevens to provide the bas-reliefs and other sculptures for the villa. In 1928 the villa was used as the film set for *Les Mystères du château du dé* by Man Ray.

From 1924 to 1930 Mallet-Stevens executed numerous important commissions. His garage for Alfa-Romeo in Paris (1925; destr.), with its concrete and metal façade, was much imitated in Paris. For the Exposition Internationale des Arts Décoratifs et Industriels Modernes (1925) in Paris, Mallet-Stevens's Pavillon de Tourisme, including an unusual tower composed of reinforced concrete, was one of the few examples of modern architecture to be exhibited. Between 1926 and 1927 Mallet-Stevens constructed the Rue Mallet-Stevens, Paris (modified 1951), comprising five detached houses built of rough concrete. The effect of the sculptural design relied on the dramatic play of light and shadow on boldly juxtaposed cubes and cylinders.

In 1929 Mallet-Stevens was a founder-member of the UNION DES ARTISTES MODERNES, an avant-garde group of architects, artists and designers. He also began to abandon his severe machine aesthetic. His last villa, the Cavroix (1931–2), Croix, was inspired by W. M. Dudok's Hilversum Raadhuis (1927–31, Netherlands) and the architecture of Frank Lloyd Wright. The villa was faced in brick, and its bold geometrical forms were more monumental than his earlier designs. Although Mallet-Stevens frequently called on colleagues to design the interiors of his villas, he also designed furniture. His most important pieces were the tubular-steel and wood furnishings for his own villa in the Rue Mallet-Stevens and for the Villa Cavroix.

Mallet-Stevens's last major constructions were five pavilions for the Exposition Internationale des Arts et Techniques dans la Vie Moderne in Paris (1937). His Pavillon de l'Electricité was noteworthy for an enormous screen incorporated into the façade, on to which films could be projected for outdoor viewing. He was particularly interested in film as a medium for promoting public acceptance of modern architecture. Between 1919 and 1929 Mallet-Stevens designed at least ten film sets. The most remarkable of his designs were the Cubist-inspired sets for *L'Inhumaine* (1923) and *Le Vertige* (1926), both directed by Marcel L'Herbier. In 1929 he published an important study on film set design, 'Le Décor moderne au cinema', and continued to write on architecture and design for French journals until his death.

WRITINGS
Une Cité moderne, preface F. Jourdain (Paris, 1922)
'Le Décor moderne au cinema', *A. Cinéma*, vi (1929), pp. 1–23

BIBLIOGRAPHY
L. Moussinac: *Mallet-Stevens* (Paris, 1931)
D. Deshoulières and H. Janeau: *Robert Mallet-Stevens: Architect* (Paris, 1980)
Rob. Mallet-Stevens: Architecture, mobilier, décoration (exh. cat., ed. P. Sers; Paris, Mairie XVIe, 1986)

SUZANNE TISE

Mallia [Malia]. Minoan palace and town on Crete, which flourished *c.* 1900–*c.* 1425 BC. The palace stands on a small, fertile plain on the north coast of Crete, about 36 km east of Herakleion. It is relatively well preserved, and restoration has been kept to a minimum. While it is less elaborate than the Minoan palaces of Knossos and Phaistos it is nonetheless impressive. Excavations in the vicinity have revealed extensive remains of the town, while cemeteries have been found between the palace and the sea. The site was first excavated by JOSEPH HAZZIDAKIS in 1915 and 1919. The French School of Archaeology in Athens took over in 1922, and by 1926 had effectively revealed the whole palace, although their programme of excavation and research continued into the late 20th century. Important finds, including those cited below, are housed in the Archaeological Museum, Herakleion.

Evidence for Early Minoan (*c.* 3500/3000–*c.* 2050 BC) occupation at Mallia takes the form of traces of buildings beneath the palace and simple burials in the cemetery area, where natural fissures in the rock were used. The First Palace was constructed *c.* 1900 BC, but little survives, so that the visible remains (see fig.) belong mainly to the

Mallia, aerial view from the south of the palace and town, *c.* 1900–*c.* 1425 BC

Second Palace, built in Middle Minoan (MM) IIIA (*c.* 1675–*c.* 1635 BC) after a major destruction. It may have followed the plan of the First Palace quite closely. The Second Palace survived until the end of Late Minoan (LM) IB (*c.* 1425 BC), when it was burnt in the wave of destructions that overwhelmed most Cretan sites.

Like the palaces of Knossos and Phaistos, the Second Palace at Mallia was constructed around an open-air central court orientated roughly north–south. It was built largely of local grey limestone and reddish sandstone, with extensive use of mud-brick. Architectural refinements common at Knossos and Phaistos, such as the use of thin gypsum slabs to cover walls and floors, are absent, giving it a more provincial air. Nonetheless, it had the staterooms, storage areas, domestic and cult rooms typical of all the Minoan palaces, and traces of painted plaster show that some walls and floors were decorated, although no substantial wall paintings survive.

The most carefully designed and constructed, and therefore probably the most important, group of rooms lies directly to the west of the central court. A spacious pillared hall may have had state or ceremonial functions. North of this the grand staircase led to an upper storey, which no longer survives, while further north is the so-called loggia, a room opening on to the central court, from which it is reached by four steps. The loggia is in a position analogous to that of the throne room at Knossos, and both may have had important religious functions. Finds in the room adjoining the loggia to the north-west included an elaborately carved schist axe in the form of a leopard and a bronze ceremonial sword with a rock-crystal pommel, perhaps offerings or religious paraphernalia of the Proto-Palatial (*c.* 1900–*c.* 1650 BC) or early Neo-Palatial (MM IIIA) periods.

The palace's vast stores were kept in rows of long, narrow magazines along its west and east sides and in eight circular granaries at its south-west corner. An elegant suite of apartments at the north-west has been identified as the principal residential quarters. They feature characteristic Minoan light wells to illuminate inner areas, as well as pier-and-door partitions that allowed rooms to be closed off in winter and open in summer. Two further ceremonial swords, one with the relief figure of an acrobat decorating its pommel, were found in this area (LM IA, *c.* 1600–*c.* 1480 BC).

On the north side of the central court is a large room with six square pillars, which perhaps served as a kitchen, beneath a pillared banqueting hall at first-floor level. Paved courtyards flanked the palace to the west and east, and the main approach was apparently the broad paved way leading to the central court from the south, although other entrances existed on all sides.

Impressive town houses of the Second Palace period have been found to the east, south and west of the palace, but the remains of the First Palace period town are more unusual. A series of semi-basement rooms and a large open courtyard directly to the north-west of the palace perhaps constituted a council chamber and assembly place. Extensive and elaborate mud-brick structures further to the west were probably connected in some way with the First Palace, since they contained elaborate reception rooms, large cult rooms and offices with a Linear A archive, and were adjoined by a seal-maker's workshop. Finally, to the north, in the area of the Minoan cemeteries, stands the stone-built Chrysolakkos ('pit of gold') complex, a curious structure perhaps used for funerary rituals and as an ossuary. From here came the famous gold pendant showing two bees or wasps around a granulated gold disc possibly representing a honeycomb (MM II, *c.* 1800–*c.* 1650 BC; *see* MINOAN, fig. 24).

BIBLIOGRAPHY
J. W. Graham: *The Palaces of Crete* (Princeton, 1962)
G. Cadogan: *Palaces of Minoan Crete* (London, 1980)
H. van Effenterre: *Le Palais de Mallia et la cité minoenne*, 2 vols (Rome, 1980)
O. Pelon and others: 'Mallia', *The Aerial Atlas of Ancient Crete*, ed. J. W. Myers, E. E. Myers and G. Cadogan (Berkeley, 1992), pp. 173–83

J. LESLEY FITTON

Mallo, Cristino (*b* Túy, Pontevedra, 23 Aug 1905). Spanish sculptor. He settled in Madrid in 1923, studying there at the Escuela de Bellas Artes de San Fernando until 1927, and on graduating he began to frequent artistic and literary gatherings. He was awarded the Premio Nacional de Escultura in 1933, a controversial choice for someone so young. While teaching sculpture in Salamanca from 1935 to 1936 he befriended the painter José Solana. He returned to his work as a sculptor in 1940, after the Spanish Civil War, employing a lyrical realism that reflected his preference in subject-matter for typical popular figures of the day, such as *The Concierge*, *The Flathunter* and *The Female Assistant*. In 1947, at the Galería Estilo in Madrid, Mallo held the first of his rare one-man exhibitions; he achieved considerable success at the Venice Biennale in 1952, and in 1954 he was awarded the Primera Medalla de Escultura at the Exposición Nacional de Bellas Artes, but he subsequently exhibited rarely. His monumental, classicizing works, such as *Nude* (h. 1.7 m, bronze, 1954; Madrid, Mus. A. Contemp.), nevertheless continued to receive recognition: in 1973 he was made a member of the Academia de Bellas Artes de San Fernando and in 1983 he was awarded the Medalla de Oro in the fine arts.

BIBLIOGRAPHY
Cristino Mallo (exh. cat., ed. F. C. Goitia and A. M. Novillo; Madrid, Mus. A. Contemp., 1985)

M. DOLORES JIMÉNEZ-BLANCO

Mallo, Maruja (*b* Vivero, nr Lugo, 6 Jan 1902; *d* Madrid, 6 Feb 1995). Spanish painter. She studied painting at the Escuela de Bellas Artes, Madrid (1926). After a journey to the Canary Islands in 1927, her work was presented to the public by José Ortega y Gasset and his *Revista de Occidente*. Her first exhibition firmly established her among the avant-garde. Through a grant from the Junta para Ampliación de Estudios she travelled to Paris in 1932, where she came into contact with the Surrealists. She exhibited at the Galerie Pierre in 1933 and met André Breton and Picasso. On her return to Spain she worked at the Escuela de Cerámica designing plates. In 1937 she settled in Argentina, giving lectures there and in Montevideo, Chile and Bolivia. She exhibited in various Latin-American countries and in New York. She renewed contact with Spain in 1948 but did not return there permanently until 1965. She was awarded the gold medal for fine arts from the Ministry of Culture in 1982 and from the city of Madrid in 1990.

Mallo's work can be divided into different stages. The first began in 1928 with *Fairs* and *Prints*; the former show strong colouring, and the latter rigorous geometry. They communicate the painter's love of popular fiestas, but are not without some satire. The early *Prints* were followed by *cinemáticas* and *románticas*, which reconciled several aspects of the painter's creative spirit. She soon turned her attention towards a darker, more painful world. This was her period of depicting detritus, skeletons and refuse, for example the series *Sewers and Belfries*, perhaps considered the height of her Surrealist work and the reason for Breton's admiration (*Scarecrow*, 1932; Breton priv. col., see Gómez de la Serna, pl. xvi). On her return to Spain in the 1930s, with Benjamin Palencia and others she became an important member of the Escuela de Vallecas, in which the artists spent time in discussion, organizing outings into the countryside and observing nature. During this period she executed her purest and most geometric paintings: *Rural Constructions* (1934; priv. col., see Gómez de la Serna, pl. xx); *Country Buildings* (1934; priv. col., see Gómez de la Serna, pl. xxi); her scenery for the opera *Clavileño*, based on an episode in *Don Quijote*; and her ceramic designs. Land, ears of corn and rural life, allied with her love for geometric form, came together in *Surprise of Wheat* (1936; priv. col., see Gómez de la Serna, pl. xxxiii). This began her *pintura del trabajo*, an affectionate approach to social consciousness through the female form: harvesting in *Song of the Ears of Corn* (1939; Madrid, Mus. A. Contemp.) and fishing in *The Sea's Message* (1937; priv. col., see Gómez de la Serna, pl. xxxviii). The same theme continued in *Supremacy of the Races*, a series of flatly painted portraits of women with huge features emphasizing different racial characteristics.

Mallo's meeting with Chilean poet Pablo Neruda and her visit to Easter Island inform her *naturalezas vivas* (the opposite of *naturalezas muertas*, or still-lifes), with shells, roses, starfish, algae and jellyfish painted in a Surreal, geometric world. These paintings mark the beginning of her last creative phase, a journey towards the heavens, and her world began to be peopled by strange beings, as in the series *Dwellings in the Void*, for example *Airagu* (1979; Madrid, Mus. A. Contemp.).

WRITINGS
Lo popular en la plástica española a través de mi obra (Buenos Aires, 1937)
'El Surrealismo a través de mi obra', *El Surrealismo* (Madrid, 1983)

BIBLIOGRAPHY
R. Gómez de la Serna: *Maruja Mallo* (Buenos Aires, 1942) [incl. essay by Mallo: 'Proceso histórico de la forma en las artes plásticas']
J. Cassou: *Maruja Mallo: Arquitecturas* (Madrid, 1949)
C. de la Gandara: *Maruja Mallo* (Madrid, 1978)
Maruja Mallo (exh. cat., ed. F. Rivas and J. Pérez de Ayala; Madrid, 1992)
Maruja Mallo (exh. cat., Santiago de Compostela, Cent. Galego A. Contemp., 1993)
JUAN PÉREZ DE AYALA

Mallorca. *See under* BALEARIC ISLANDS.

Mallowan, Sir Max (Edgar Lucien) (*b* London, 6 May 1904; *d* Oxford, 19 Aug 1978). English archaeologist. He was Professor of Western Asiatic Archaeology at the Institute of Archaeology, University of London, from 1947 until 1962, when he was made a fellow of All Souls College, Oxford. He was elected a Fellow of the British Academy in 1955. His first wife, whom he married in 1930, was the novelist Agatha Christie (1890–1976).

Mallowan was known primarily for his archaeological research into ancient Mesopotamia. He assisted Sir Leonard Woolley in the excavations at Ur (1925–31) and then worked with R. Campbell Thompson at Nineveh (1931–2), where he dug a sounding down to bedrock that greatly elucidated the different phases of Mesopotamian prehistory. At Arpachiyah, near Nineveh (1933), he helped to establish the chronology of Halaf pottery, which dates from the late 6th to 5th millennia BC; much of this pottery is beautifully painted with dots, geometric shapes and stylized motifs, often arranged in chequerwork patterns or friezes. Next he worked at two sites in the Khabur basin in North Syria, Chagar Bazar (1935–7) and Tell Brak (1937–8). At the latter he found many figurines of the late 4th millennium BC known as 'eye idols' and a large administrative building of *c.* 2300 BC, probably founded by the Akkadian king Naram-Sin. The crowning achievement of Mallowan's career was his work at Nimrud (1949–63), during which he recovered a large number of important works of art, particularly ivories, dating from the Late Assyrian period (9th–7th centuries BC). Among these were two panels, overlaid with gold and encrusted with lapis lazuli and cornelians, showing lionesses attacking Nubians (Baghdad, Iraq Mus.; London, BM).

WRITINGS
Nimrud and its Remains, 2 vols (London, 1966)
Mallowan's Memoirs (London, 1977)

BIBLIOGRAPHY
J. E. Curtis, ed.: *Fifty Years of Mesopotamian Discovery* (London, 1982)
JOHN CURTIS

Malmesbury Abbey. Former Benedictine abbey in Wiltshire, England, founded in the 7th century, dedicated to SS Peter and Paul. Of the church built from *c.* 1115 only the nave (*c.* 1160) survives. This has pointed main arcades on columnar piers, rib-vaulted aisles, an elaborate round-headed gallery, and a clerestory with wall passage, the windows of which were rebuilt in the 14th century, when the Romanesque wood roof was replaced by the present lierne vault. Little remains of the west doorway. The south porch preserves one of the richest programmes in English Romanesque sculpture.

The south doorway has three continuous orders with symmetrical foliage and a tympanum with *Christ in Majesty* in a mandorla held by two angels. The porch has two side tympana, each with six *Apostles* in high relief with a flying angel above inspired by Anglo-Saxon iconography. The entrance arch has eight continuous orders, the third, fifth and seventh with Old and New Testament scenes and *Virtues* overcoming *Vices* set in medallions; the remainder are carved with geometric foliage. The idea for the sculptured porch may derive from south-western French work, for example as at Moissac (*see* MOISSAC, ST PIERRE), and certain details find parallels at Aulnay-de-Saintonge (*see* AULNAY, ST PIERRE). The iconography of the scenes, however, is primarily Anglo-Saxon, and the immediate stylistic sources are probably Bishop Roger of Salisbury's work at Old Sarum Cathedral and Sherborne Castle, and derivatives at Lullington, Somerset, and the panel of the *Elect in Heaven* on the west front of Lincoln Cathedral.

BIBLIOGRAPHY

H. Brakspear: 'Malmesbury Abbey', *Archaeologia*, lxiv (1913), pp. 399–436

G. Zarnecki: *Later English Romanesque Sculpture, 1140–1210* (London, 1953), pp. 40–43

K. J. Galbraith: 'The Iconography of the Biblical Scenes at Malmesbury Abbey', *J. Brit. Archaeol. Assoc.*, n.s. 2, xxviii (1965), pp. 39–56

MALCOLM THURLBY

Malmö. City and seaport in Skåne, Sweden, situated on the Öresund. It is first documented in 1275, when, with Skåne, it belonged to Denmark, in whose possession it remained (with two short breaks in the 14th century) until 1658. The wealth of Malmö was derived from its strong connection with the Hanseatic League, and, as the centre of the Oresund herring industry, in the 17th century the city was as important as Copenhagen. St Peter's Church was begun *c.* 1300 (*see* §1 below), and 16th-century buildings include the town hall (1546; restored several times) and Malmöhus Castle, which was founded in 1434 and rebuilt from 1537 to 1542 by Christian III of Denmark, Norway and Sweden (*reg* 1534–59). The castle was badly burnt in 1870 and later restored. Since 1937 it has been the Malmöhus Museum.

1. ST PETER'S. The new town church, begun *c.* 1300, was built on the model of the brick Gothic churches of the north German Hansa towns (so-called *Backsteingotik*). It consists of a three-aisled, vaulted basilica with an ambulatory and five slightly projecting chapels. St Peter's, rather unusually for this type of brick church, has a transept; although this barely projects in plan, its exterior is strongly marked by tall windows and rich blind arcading. The church's buttressing system is entirely preserved.

The west tower collapsed in 1420 and again in 1442. The present tall west tower was begun just after, and the high copper spire was added in the 1890s. The original tower stood over the westernmost bay of the nave, and the great piers that supported its eastern side survive inside the church. In the roof space can be seen remains of the tower walls. The west wall of the tower is thought to have projected some distance from the west wall of the church. The tower seems to have collapsed northwards, destroying both the main vault and that of the north aisle, but the star vault of the south aisle seems to have survived undamaged. This is the earliest star vault in the region.

The chapels were built during the 15th century. The Merchants' Chapel, north of the west tower, has two bays; it contained the altar of the Holy Redeemer and the Virgin and has a richly decorated exterior with blind arcading and niches with figured reliefs in chalk. The interior has sculpted vault consoles and partly preserved wall paintings (early 16th century), which are characterized by exuberant creepers swarming with figured scenes and grotesques. Among the subjects is a sequence showing the *Dance of Death*, including scenes with Death dancing with a king, a bishop and a pope. The interior of the church contains a large amount of good-quality 17th-century furnishings, including numerous epitaphs.

BIBLIOGRAPHY

A. U. Isberg: *Malmö stads 600-års-jubileum, 1319–1919* (Malmö, 1919)

T. Wåhlin: *Malmö S:t Petri kyrka* (Malmö, 1919)

S. Rosborn: 'Krämarnas kapell i S:t Petri kyrka' [The Merchants' Chapel in St Peter's Church], *Elbogen*, viii/4 (1978), pp. 21–48

MARIAN ULLÉN

Malmström, Johan August (*b* Vastra Ny, Östergötland, 14 Sept 1829; *d* Stockholm, 18 Oct 1901). Swedish painter. He studied first at the Kungliga Akademi för de Fria Konsterna in Stockholm (1849–56) and then briefly in Düsseldorf. From 1857 to 1863 he worked in Paris under Thomas Couture, and while there he copied the works of Titian in the Louvre. During this period he also visited Rome, and after leaving Paris in 1863 he travelled back via Italy, Munich and Berlin, reaching Sweden in early 1864. While in Paris he painted *Ingeborg Receiving the News of the Death of Hjalmar* (1859; Stockholm, Nmus.), a subject derived from Norse mythology and executed in a Romantic style. The *Battle of Bravalla* (*c.* 1861; Stockholm, Nordiska Mus.) is painted in the same manner. In 1867 he became a professor at the Akademi in Stockholm, a post he held until 1894, and was its director from 1887 to 1893. In 1868 he began a series of illustrations for *Frithjof's Saga*, confirming his love for epic subjects, and he also produced illustrations for the *Saga of Ragnar Lodbrok* (1880). His interest in Scandinavian culture led to a series of works derived from the Russian-Swedish war over Finland of 1808–9, including a number of grey-toned paintings illustrating Johan Ludvig Runeberg's the *Grave of Perrho*, which he presented to the Kungliga Tekniska Högskola in Stockholm. Malmström also painted much gentler subjects, as in the dreamy *Dance of the Elves* (1866; Stockholm, Nmus.) and a number of pictures of children, such as the *Last Pair Out* (Stockholm, Nmus.). During the 1890s he painted several watercolours of the Swedish landscape, such as *Landscape* (Stockholm, Nmus.).

See also SWEDEN, §VII, 1 and fig. 23.

BIBLIOGRAPHY

R. Muther: *The History of Modern Painting* (London, 1896), iii, p. 350

H. Wieselgran: *Johan August Malmström* (Stockholm, 1904)

C. Laurin and others: *Scandinavian Art* (New York, 1922)

Málnai, Béla (*b* Budapest, 14 Dec 1878; *d* Budapest, 31 Aug 1941). Hungarian architect and editor. He received his diploma in 1901 from the Hungarian Palatine Joseph Technical University, Budapest. After a study trip to western Europe, he worked first with Ödön Lechner, then with Béla Lajta. From 1908 to 1911 he edited the architectural journal *A Ház*, in which, inspired primarily by the Garden city movement and the efforts of M. H. Baillie Scott, he advocated the building of detached family houses on estates. From 1907 to 1914 he worked in partnership with Gyula Haász (1877–1945) in Budapest. Their first commission was a group of four-storey residential blocks built (1909–10) around an enclosed court on Hungária Boulevard, Budapest, as part of a municipal housing plan. Most of the partnership's later works were middle-class residential blocks, in a severe, unornamented style with a few classicizing features, such as pedimented gables, colonnades and friezes, influenced by the Biedermeyer revival *c.* 1910. The partnership's most notable building, combining office and residential uses, is the former headquarters of the Hungarian–Czech Industrial Bank

(1912; now National Bank of Hungary), Nádor Street, Budapest. Situated on a corner site, its two lower levels were occupied by the bank, and the upper four by flats. The medium-sized windows that pierce the stone façade of the upper stories contrast with the much bigger windows below, while both are set off by the metal and glass corner balconies. In the 1920s Málnai's work followed the prevalent official trend of neo-historicism, for example in his villa (1927), Szarvas Gábor Road, Budapest, while in the 1930s he made much use of Functionalism, as in the residential block (1935), Pozsonyi Road, Budapest.

BIBLIOGRAPHY
P. Relle: *Béla Málnai* (Geneva, 1931)
Z. Mendöl: *Málnai Béla* (Budapest, 1974)
ÁKOS MORAVÁNSZKY, KATALIN MORAVÁNSZKY-GYÖNGY

Malnaia, Guccio di. *See* GUCCIO DI MANNAIA.

Malosso, il. *See* TROTTI, GIOVANNI BATTISTA.

Malouel [Maelwael; Malwael; Maulouel; Meluel], **Jean** [Jan; Jehan] (*b* ?Nijmegen *c.* 1365; *d* Dijon, 12 March 1415). ?North Netherlandish painter, active in Burgundy. He was the son of the heraldic artist Willem Maelwael and uncle of the Limbourg brothers. First recorded as a painter in 1382, he is then documented on 20 September 1396 for a commission to provide designs for textiles with decorative armorial bearings for Queen Isabeau of Bavaria, wife of Charles VI, for which he received payment on 27 March 1397. By 5 August 1397 he was in Dijon, where he succeeded Jean de Beaumetz as court painter and Valet de Chambre to Philip the Bold, Duke of Burgundy. Malouel was highly paid, and his annual pension was considerably more than that of Beaumetz or of the sculptor Claus Sluter. One of the first works Malouel produced for the Duke was a painting of the *Apostles with St Anthony* (untraced), paid for on 11 November 1398, which the Duke is known to have kept in his private oratory. On 18 March 1398 wooden supports were purchased for Malouel to paint five large altarpieces for the Charterhouse of Champmol, outside Dijon. The subject-matter of the paintings is not specified in the document, although the dimensions of the panels are given. The *Martyrdom of St Denis* (Paris, Louvre; for illustration *see* BELLECHOSE, HENRI) has been identified as one of these five panels, on the basis of its possible provenance and its dimensions, which correspond approximately to those given in the document. In May 1416, however, Henri Bellechose received pigments to 'perfect' a painting of the Life of St Denis, and this document, in conjunction with the earlier one, has been interpreted to suggest that Bellechose completed a work left unfinished by Malouel. A rereading of the 1398 document and the absence of any discernible evidence of collaboration on the *St Denis* panel has led to its attribution to Henri Bellechose alone (Reynaud, 1961).

A *Pietà* tondo (Paris, Louvre; see fig.) is dated *c.* 1400–04, and bears on the reverse the painted Burgundian coat of arms in the form adopted by Philip the Bold, whose date of death provides a *terminus ante quem*. This, and its provenance from the Burgundian Collection, suggests that the *Pietà* was produced for Philip the Bold and painted by

Jean Malouel (attrib.): *Pietà*, panel, tondo, diam. 645 mm, *c.* 1400–04 (Paris, Musée du Louvre)

his court painter, Malouel. Its style has been compared both to Parisian manuscript illumination and to the work of such Sienese painters as Lippo Memmi and Simone Martini. In 1401 Malouel was at the ducal residence at Conflans (outside Paris), where he installed some paintings for Margaret of Flanders, Duchess of Burgundy (1350–1405), and he was in Paris and Arras for a few weeks in 1402. During 1401–3 Malouel, assisted by Herman of Cologne, painted and gilded the life-size statues on Claus Sluter's Well of Moses (1395–1404; Dijon, Charterhouse of Champmol; *see* FRANCE, fig. 33; *see also* RENAISSANCE, fig. 3) for Philip the Bold.

After the Duke's death, Malouel was employed by his successor, John the Fearless, for whom he decorated armour, painted the ducal arms and devices and executed other works in the Charterhouse, including the decoration of the monastery parlour. In 1406 he made a number of harnesses for the Duke and his officers on the occasion of a joust held at Compiègne for the marriage of the Duc de Touraine. He also painted, in 1410, the tomb effigies of *Philip the Bold* and *Margaret of Flanders* (Dijon, Mus. B.-A.), executed by Claus Sluter, Jean de Marville and Claus de Werve. One of Malouel's last documented works, *c.* 1412–13, was a portrait of *John the Fearless* (untraced) made as a gift for John I, King of Portugal. This portrait may be similar in appearance to a number of later portraits of the Duke (e.g. Chantilly, Mus. Condé; Versailles, Château). Meiss and Eisler have attributed the *Virgin and Child with Angels* (tempera on gold cloth; Berlin, Gemäldegal.) to the later part of Malouel's career, *c.* 1405–12. In late 1413 Malouel travelled back to Nijmegen, which he may also have visited in 1405. After Malouel's death, Henri Bellechose succeeded him as court painter.

BIBLIOGRAPHY
A. Kleinclausz: 'Les Peintres des Ducs de Bourgogne, II', *Rev. A. Anc. & Mod.*, xx (1906), pp. 161–76

F. Gorissen: 'Jan Maelwael und die Brüder Limbourg: Eine Nimweger Künstlerfamilie um die Wende des 14. Jahrhunderts', *Gelre*, liv (1954), pp. 153–221
——: 'Jan Maelwael, die Brüder Limbourg und der Herold Gelre: Nachträge und Berichtungen', *Gelre*, lvi (1957), pp. 166–78
C. Sterling: 'Portrait Painting at the Court of Burgundy in the Early 15th Century', *Crit. A.*, vi (1959), pp. 289–312
M. Meiss and C. Eisler: 'A New French Primitive', *Burl. Mag.*, cii (1960), pp. 232–40
N. Reynaud: 'A propos du Martyre de St Denis', *Rev. Louvre*, xi (1961), pp. 175–6

Malqata. *See* THEBES (i), §XII.

Malraux, (Georges-)André (*b* Paris, 3 Nov 1901; *d* Créteil, 23 Nov 1976). French writer and government minister. He became well known as a writer of novels of heroism and adventure, especially *Les Conquérants* (Paris, 1928) and *La Condition humaine* (Paris, 1933), and as a leader of the Resistance. He had an interest in art, however, and at the age of 19 he became art director for the publisher Simon Kra's Editions du Sagittaire, and at 20 took charge of Kahnweiler's Editions de luxe, for which Malraux himself wrote *Lunes en papier* (Paris, 1921), a fictional work illustrated by Fernand Léger. In 1926–7 he founded two successive but short-lived publishing companies of his own, A la Sphère and Aux Aldes, to produce illustrated limited editions, and from 1928 to 1936 he was in charge of the art book department of Gallimard.

Prior to World War II Malraux began work on his first major art book, *La Psychologie de l'art*, whose first volume, *Le Musée imaginaire*, was published by Albert Skira in 1947, shortly after a brief text entitled *Dessins de Goya au Musée du Prado*. In both works, Malraux the man of action and Malraux the contemplator of art fused in his vision of the artist as a catalyst for change, through whom the past could be absorbed and transformed. The originality of *La Psychologie de l'art* lay in Malraux's use of the concept of the creative artist to refute the then fashionable idea of Western civilization's inevitable decline; for Malraux, culture represented man's triumph over the past and his own fate. To support his argument, he provided examples from a vast range of civilizations and historical periods and introduced the idea of 'the imaginary museum'. Museums had radically altered our way of seeing, affording hitherto unthinkable possibilities of comparison and divorcing works from their original functional context, thereby intellectualizing art; a crucifix, for instance, had come to be seen as sculpture. While museums were inevitably incomplete in their coverage, they could be supplemented by art books. Here the role of photography had been crucial: extensive comparisons of artefacts across time and space had only become possible with the advent of appropriate technology, particularly colour photography, and the history of art was conditioned by the evidence provided by photography. Such comparisons shifted the emphasis from individual works to the relationships between them; although the physical attributes of works of art as objects were often lost in reproduction, the characteristics of style could thus be made more apparent. A large part of the impact of *La Psychologie de l'art* was attributable to its striking appearance, the effect of the 376 reproductions and their judicious arrangement. Malraux himself drew a parallel between the art book and film, both suggesting as much by the framing and succession of shots as by each individual image. Many of Malraux's ideas were indebted to those of contemporaries such as Elie Faure (1873–1937) and Henri Focillon, but their impact resulted from the force of their verbal and visual presentation. Malraux adopted a similar approach in the three volumes of *Le Musée imaginaire de la sculpture mondiale*, but in this work the 700 black-and-white photographs dominated the brief introductory text.

In 1960 Malraux became the founder and director of Gallimard's series of books on the art of the world known as L'Univers des formes and continued to display his global cultural knowledge and his ability to detect affinities between works of art from varied times and places. At the end of 1945 he became Minister of Information under General De Gaulle for a period of two months, and in 1959 De Gaulle's first Minister of State for Cultural Affairs, a post he held more or less continuously for the next ten years. Among his most notable achievements in that decade were the cleaning and preservation of historic buildings in Paris, sending the *Mona Lisa* to the USA for exhibition and commissioning Marc Chagall to paint the ceiling of the Paris Opéra. In the belief that all Frenchmen should have access to the best of their cultural heritage as well as to contemporary artistic practice, Malraux instituted the Maisons de la Culture, which aimed to attract new classes of people to the arts, especially outside Paris. The first of these, at Bourges, was opened in 1964, and further centres were later set up in provincial towns such as Amiens, Grenoble and Reims. As a statesman, Malraux was as tireless and eloquent an advocate of the power and significance of artistic creation as he was as a writer.

WRITINGS
Esquisse d'une psychologie du cinéma (Paris, 1946); Eng. trans. in *Reflections on Art*, ed. S. Langer (Baltimore, 1958), pp. 317–27
Dessins de Goya au Musée du Prado (Geneva, 1947)
La Psychologie de l'art, i: *Le Musée imaginaire* (Geneva, 1947; Eng. trans. as *Museum without Walls*, New York, 1949), ii: *La Création artistique* (Geneva, 1948; Eng. trans. as *The Creative Act*, London, 1949/*R* New York, 1950), iii: *La Monnaie de l'absolu* (Geneva, 1950; Eng. trans. as *The Twilight of the Absolute*, New York, 1951); rev. as *Les Voix de silence*, 4 vols (Paris, 1951; Eng. trans., New York, 1953)
Saturne: Essai sur Goya (Paris, 1950; Eng. trans., London, 1957)
Le Musée imaginaire de la sculpture mondiale, 3 vols (Paris, 1952–4)
La Métamorphose des dieux, i: *Le Surnaturel* (Paris, 1957; Eng. trans. as *The Metamorphosis of the Gods*, New York, 1960), ii: *L'Irréel* (Paris, 1974), iii: *L'Intemporel* (Paris, 1976)
Antimémoires (Paris, 1967; Eng. trans., New York, 1968) [autobiography]
La Tête d'obsidienne (Paris, 1974; Eng. trans. as *Picasso's Mask*, New York, 1976)

BIBLIOGRAPHY
G. Picon: *Malraux par lui-même* (Paris, 1953)
C. D. Blend: 'Early Expressions of Malraux's Art Theory', *Romanic Rev.*, liii (1962), pp. 199–213
W. Righter: *The Rhetorical Hero: An Essay on the Aesthetics of André Malraux* (London, 1964)
P. Sabourin: *La Réflexion sur l'art d'André Malraux* (Paris, 1972)
J. Lacouture: *André Malraux: Une Vie dans le siècle* (Paris, 1973; Eng. trans., London, 1975)
André Malraux (exh. cat., Saint-Paul-de-Vence, Fond. Maeght, 1973)
M. de Courcel, ed.: *Malraux: Life and Work* (London, 1976)
W. Langlois, ed.: 'Malraux et l'art', *Rev. Lett. Mod.* (1978) [whole issue]
M. Cazenave, ed.: *André Malraux* (Paris, 1982) [43 of a series of monographs]

VALERIE HOLMAN

Mal'ta. Upper Palaeolithic site at a village on the River Belaya, 85 km west of Irkutsk in eastern Siberia. It was excavated in 1928 by Mikhail M. Gerasimov (1907–70), who continued to work there until 1959. An extended line of dwellings along the river was uncovered. They are circular in plan and include semi-dugouts with walls strengthened by stone slabs and large bones, with central hearths and conical roofs of poles covered with skins. Many artefacts were discovered (e.g. Moscow, Hist. Mus.; St Petersburg, Peter the Great Mus. Anthropol. & Ethnog.), including about 30 anthropomorphic statuettes, together with maquettes, figurines of water-fowl and a rhinoceros, mostly made of mammoth tusk, and a bone plate with engraved images of a mammoth. The female figures have sloping shoulders, flat, pendulous breasts incised with sharp lines, and stomachs separated from their legs by similar incised lines. Typical are statuettes of women with sculpted faces and bodies that are not hypertrophic (unlike European examples), as well as some with extended, spindly trunks, occasionally marked by transverse incisions intended to represent fur garments with hoods. Holes bored in some statuettes and sculptures of flying swans suggest that they were used as pendants. Also a pendant is a flat piece of mammoth tusk with circles and spirals picked out in points on one side and an engraved image of a snake on the other. Stylistically similar artefacts have been found at Buret' in the Irkutsk region.

BIBLIOGRAPHY

M. M. Gerasimov: *Mal'ta: Paleoliticheskaya stoyanka* [Mal'ta: a Palaeolithic site] (Irkutsk, 1931)
——: 'Paleoliticheskaya stoyanka Mal'ta (raskopki, 1956–1957 gg.)' [The Palaeolithic site of Mal'ta (excavations, 1956–1957)], *Sov. Etnog.*, iii (1958), pp. 28–52
A. A. Formosov: 'Neopublikovannyye proizvedeniya iskusstva paleoliticheskoy stoyanki Mal'ta' [Unpublished works on the art of the Palaeolithic site of Mal'ta], *Sov. Arkheol.*, iv (1976), pp. 180–84

V. YA. PETRUKHIN

Malta, Republic of. Island country located 93 km south of Sicily in the Mediterranean Sea between Italy and North Africa. The three inhabited islands—Malta, Gozo and Comino—comprise an area of 316 sq. km.

I. Introduction. II. Prehistoric and Classical. III. Middle Ages and after.

I. Introduction.

The five Maltese islands were settled in the 5th millennium BC and are rich in prehistoric remains (*see* §II below). Malta was colonized by the Phoenicians in the 7th century BC and was later ruled by the Carthaginians until it became part of the Roman Empire in 218 BC. Many architectural and sculptural remains testify to the peace and prosperity of the Roman period. After AD 395 the islands came under Byzantine rule, which lasted until the Arab conquest of 870. From 1090, as part of the kingdom of Sicily, Malta was ruled by the Normans, the Angevins and the Aragonese. In 1530 Charles I, King of Spain (*reg* 1516–56), granted the islands to the Knights of St John Hospitaller, under whose rule Malta flourished, attracting artists and architects from mainland Italy (*see* §III, 1 below). Napoleon expelled the knights in 1798, and in 1814 Malta elected to become part of the British Empire. It was granted full independence in 1964.

BIBLIOGRAPHY

B. Blouet: *A Short History of Malta* (Gerards Cross, 1967)

II. Prehistoric and Classical.

Malta has a heritage of prehistoric art out of all proportion to its size, the roots of which are still unexplained. The islands' remoteness prevented them from being overwhelmed by foreign influences, and the powerful local religion, with its unique megalithic temples, provides a context for this art; moreover, the availability of a soft, fine-grained local limestone may have encouraged the production of the islands' characteristic sculpture. None of these alone, however, is sufficient explanation for the unique art that flourished there in prehistoric times. Unless otherwise noted, all the prehistoric finds mentioned may be found in the National Museum of Archaeology, Valletta.

The earliest known Neolithic (c. 5000–c. 4000 BC) settlers introduced a competent and attractive, but not particularly artistic, style of pottery from Stentinello in Sicily by c. 5000 BC, characterized by impressed designs filled with a white paste. This first cycle of cultural development produced only a few stylized and markedly steatopygous female figurines in terracotta. The faces are reduced to backward-sloping triangles with eyes, nose and mouth summarily represented, similar to marble Cycladic figurines, though a millennium earlier in date.

Around 4000 BC new immigrants from Sicily initiated a second and more striking cycle of development, called the Copper Age (c. 4000–c. 2500 BC). Pottery developed increasingly elegant forms, and painted decoration was abandoned, though the incised designs were regularly given a red ochre incrustation. These designs became more and more curvilinear and inventive in the Ggantija phase (c. 3500–c. 3000 BC), with no two vessels bearing identical patterns. In the succeeding Tarxien phase (c. 3000–c. 2500 BC), the more lightly scratched designs became stereotyped in simple volutes or diagonal latticing. Other decorative techniques were introduced, however, such as applied pellets, rosette fluting and inlaying with a band of clay fired to a different colour.

There are a surprising number of sculpted pieces from this phase, modelled in terracotta or carved in stone; interpretation is always difficult, but the larger ones must surely portray divinities. A statue just inside the main entrance of the temple at Tarxien shows an obese human figure wearing a skirt; though its upper half has been destroyed, it must originally have stood some 3 m high. There are smaller portrayals of the same supposed deity from Tarxien and Ta' Silg and a notable series from Hagar Qim. Some are standing, some seated on a kind of throne or on the ground with feet tucked in. Heads were often made separately and set in sockets in the neck; two such unattached heads (Victoria, Gozo, Mus. Archaeol.) were found in the Ggantija temple on Gozo. Although the corpulence of these statues is strongly emphasized, the sex of the figure is, puzzlingly, not shown. The commonly used label, 'fat ladies', may well be correct, but it is not obviously so. The smaller figurines, on the other hand, show no such inhibitions. The so-called 'Venus' of Hagar Qim (see fig. 1) is a very delicately modelled standing female figure, 129 mm high though now lacking head and

1. 'Venus' of Hagar Qim, stone, h. 129 mm, from Hagar Qim, Malta, *c.* 3000–*c.* 2500 BC (Valletta, National Museum of Archaeology)

feet. The 'Sleeping Lady' of Hal Saflieni is equally clearly female, lying on a four-legged bed 122 mm long, with a hand under her head and a cloth draped over her hips. There are even smaller pieces, down to a seated but headless figure only 30 mm high, and miniature animal amulets of stone and shell. Unlike the highly skilled workmanship exhibited in the larger pieces, a few of the smaller human figures can only be described as grotesque: one of these is pierced with sharp flint blades, which looks suspiciously like a case of witchcraft. These exceptions serve to illustrate an artistic achievement of the highest order in the majority of sculpted works.

Excavations at the Xaghra Circle, Gozo, from 1987 to 1993 have added to this range of corpulent sexless figures. They include two seated side by side on a bed, another much fragmented standing figure, all three skirted, in stone and originally painted, and fifteen ceramic sitting figures. All are of the highest quality. A set of nine stone heads, eight human and one pig, on plank- or rod-like bodies, some well finished but others barely roughed out, are much more puzzling. Equally unexpected were eight animal phalanges, as small as 14 mm in length, their articular ends carved into minute human heads.

The prehistoric Maltese also sculpted rectangular blocks of stone up to 3 m long with beautifully executed relief designs, mostly based on spirals with fishtail ends. The main series comes from the Tarxien temples (originals in Valletta, N. Mus. Archaeol.; copies on site). The spirals may form a single or double running row or appear in opposed pairs, and the finest are on two thin slabs erected as screens, each about 1.4×1.1 m. Four spirals of up to four turns appear in relief on each, emphasized by a regularly pitted background, probably originally painted in red, all within a raised frame. Spirals, pitting and frame can all be matched, separately or together, by artefacts on other temple sites. Two blocks from Tarxien exhibit a variation of the repertory, with rows of sheep and other animals in relief, and two wall slabs show a bull on one, a bull and sow on the other, though some doubt the

identification. Other sites have yielded depictions of a fish and a snake.

All of this material was discovered in the remarkable stone temples for which Malta is famous. These were erected *c.* 3500–*c.* 2500 BC, making them the oldest free-standing stone architecture known. They were a purely indigenous development, neither influenced by nor influencing areas outside the islands. A typological sequence for the temples, from simple to more complex, has been established, generally corroborated by the development of associated successive styles of pottery.

In its final form, the Maltese temple consisted of a forecourt overlooked by a concave vertical façade of large stone slabs, a truly megalithic architecture with blocks weighing up to an estimated 19 tonnes. The first course was set on edge as orthostats, with face exposed, higher courses lying in the more usual horizontal position. In the rear wall, these orthostats alternate with others set radially, an effective way of ensuring greater stability. The entrance doorway and inner passages were of trilithon construction, with orthostatic jambs supporting horizontal lintel slabs. From a central court, lobate chambers, usually, if not very precisely, referred to as apses, open to right and left. Ahead, a third apse resulted in a trefoil plan; in later temples, a second passageway here led to a second pair of apses and a central niche. It has been suggested that the plan is based on the outline of the 'fat lady' statues, the apses representing hips, shoulders and head, though this seems at best speculative. Apse walls were either orthostatic or cyclopean (of irregular large blocks) and were originally plastered. The interior was completely roofed, usually, it is assumed, with timber rafters, brushwood and clay. In at least one case, the smaller chambers of the Central Temple at Tarxien, the upper courses of well-squared blocks have an inward slope that implies the use of a corbelled roof. The sophistication of the architecture is emphasized by the presence of several contemporary representations of these buildings in stone or terracotta, including plans, elevations and three-dimensional models. The most remarkable depicts a façade, finely carved in white limestone (fragmentary; original w. *c.* 400 mm), found beside the central altar of the Southern Temple. It is difficult to explain any of these other than as architect's 'drawings', appearing here at a date before *c.* 2500 BC.

The frequent occurrence of relief decoration on well-shaped, free-standing blocks found in these structures strongly suggests their use as altars; the presence of these and the monumental form of the architecture support the interpretation of these buildings as temples. Human skeletal remains are not normally found, though animal bones are common, presumably the remains of sacrifices. Graphic support for this interpretation came in 1915, when Themistocles Zammit discovered within a niche cut into an altar slab at Tarxien a flint knife-blade (l. 110 mm), together with sheep and cow bones. In the pottery too, stereotypical offering bowls predominate heavily over more obviously domestic forms.

The Hypogeum of Hal Saflieni (*c.* 3000 BC) at Pawla differs from the other temples in that it was not erected above ground but hewn out of the solid rock, its deepest levels more than 10 m beneath the surface. Its central chambers are carved to imitate the trilithon doorways and corbel-vaulted roofs of the free-standing temples, and the walls bear ochre-painted spiral patterns that survive no-where else. Its main purpose was clearly for burial. A rough estimate at the time of excavation (1905–11) by Zammit counted the remains of over 6000 individuals, though since these burials span at least seven centuries, they need imply a settlement at any one time of no more than some 300 people. A second newly discovered hypogeum of natural caves is currently under study within the Xaghra Circle on Gozo. Tarxien also yielded human remains, but here the burials were cremations in jars of a later style. One with a date of 3880±150 BP (BM-141) provides a useful *terminus ante quem*, since this cemetery overlies the already ruined temple.

The artistic and cultural development of the temple builders appears to have been cut short *c.* 2500 BC, to be replaced by that of new immigrants who used the first bronze to be found on the islands. How this happened is a matter of intense scholarly debate. The technical skills of the newcomers, while competent relative to the stand-ards of the time, fell far short of the achievements of the temple builders. Simple stone huts, the most basic flat axes and daggers of bronze, and pottery mostly very plain and functional, though occasionally attractively decorated, suggest a far lower artistic level. A few terracotta figurines from Tarxien offer the only glimpse of higher things. Most consist of a disc with typical geometric incised decoration, which has been turned into a stylized female body by the addition of a simple knob as head, two bosses to represent breasts, and a pair of marginally more naturalistic legs, bent as if seated. Rather finer are two figurines with more recognizable features and bold headdresses but no decoration.

Indigenous culture was brought to a close by the Phoenician occupation of the islands in the 7th century BC. Metal objects from this period are particularly rich, consisting of gold beads, silver bracelets with gold foil, and gold rings and amulets; silver jewellery was more common in the 6th and 5th centuries BC. The common Phoenician motifs of griffins, palmette and ringed solar disc occur on one 7th-century gold bracelet, while a gold amulet depicts the Egyptian gods Horus and Anubis. Also from the 7th century BC is a bronze torch-holder with leaf-shaped supports. A bronze figurine representing Ho-rus, with a falcon's head, solar disc and rearing hooded cobra, dates to the 6th century BC; inside the hollow body was discovered a papyrus fragment bearing a Phoenician inscription.

Under succeeding domination by Carthage, Greece (culturally but not politically) and Rome, Malta became a backwater for over a thousand years, until the coming of the Knights of St John in 1530. From the Roman period survive some life-size or larger marble statues of draped female figures (?2nd century AD; Rabat, Malta, Roman Villa and Mus. Ant.), whether empresses, goddesses or both is not clear. They are sadly mutilated and the heads are missing, but the quality of their workmanship is patently high. Also in Rabat are two troughs of local limestone set with exceptionally fine mosaics (1st century BC–1st century AD), probably Pergamene, one depicting a satyr being tormented by a maenad, the other a child with flowers and fruits. These would have been set as expensive centre-pieces in otherwise unexceptional mosaic floors.

BIBLIOGRAPHY

T. Zammit, T. E. Peet and R. N. Bradley: *The Small Objects and the Human Skulls Found in the Hal Saflieni Prehistoric Hypogeum* (Malta, 1912)

T. Zammit and C. Singer: 'Neolithic Representations of the Human Form from the Islands of Malta and Gozo', *J. Royal Anthropol. Inst. GB & Ireland*, liv (1924), pp. 67–100

T. Zammit: *Prehistoric Malta: The Tarxien Temples* (Oxford, 1930)

J. D. Evans: *Malta* (London, 1959)

D. Trump: 'A Prehistoric Art Cycle in Malta', *Brit. J. Aesth.*, iii/3 (1963), p. 237

J. D. Evans: *The Prehistoric Antiquities of the Maltese Islands* (London, 1971)

M. Ridley: *The Megalithic Art of the Maltese Islands* (Christchurch, 1971)

D. Trump: *Malta: An Archaeological Guide* (London, 1972)

H. Lewis: *Ancient Malta: A Study of its Antiquities* (Gerrard's Cross, 1977)

T. Gouder: 'Phoenician Malta and Some Amulets from Phoenician Malta', *Heritage: Enc. Malt. Cult. & Civilis.*, i (1979–80), pp. 173–85, 311–35

C. Malone and others: 'The Death Cults of Prehistoric Malta', *Sci. American*, cclxix (1993), pp. 110–17

DAVID TRUMP

III. Middle Ages and after.

1. Architecture. 2. Painting. 3. Sculpture. 4. Furniture. 5. Ceramics and glass. 6. Metalwork. 7. Textiles. 8. Patronage and museums.

1. ARCHITECTURE. An abundance of fine limestone and the absence of timber have meant that from earliest times the Maltese have had to fashion an architecture based on masonry construction, often providing a field for rich carving (*see* §II above). The traditional Maltese house has thick walls pierced by small openings, with floors and flat roofs constructed of stone slabs supported on stone cross-arches. Rectangular buildings, clustered and piled together, give a homogeneous character to the islands. The reorganization of church parishes in 1436 prompted the building of small, single-cell churches with shallow-pitched stone roofs and small bellcotes, the en-trance approached from a small, low-walled atrium that acted as an ecclesiastical sanctuary beyond the jurisdiction of the civil courts.

The arrival of the Knights of St John (*see* KNIGHTS HOSPITALLER) in 1530 gradually transformed the scale and opulence of civil and military architecture. Abandon-ing the old capital, Città Vecchia (now Mdina), in the middle of the island, they made their headquarters at Birgu (now Vittoriosa) on a creek off the Grand Harbour (see fig. 2), building their houses and offices with plain stone façades, their windows and doors decorated with bulbous mouldings characteristic of Renaissance Malta. Italian engineers planned an 'ideal' Renaissance capital city on a peninsula between the two main harbours, protected by bastions and high stone curtain walls. Construction was delayed by the Turkish siege of 1565, but after this was raised and financial aid began to flow in, Francesco Laparelli (1521–70) was commissioned to prepare a grid-iron plan for the fortified city. His Maltese assistant, Gerolamo Cassar (1520–86), who had trained in Rome, continued the work after Laparelli left; he built most of the auberges, or hostels, for the different languages of the Order, as well as the Palace of the Grand Masters and the magnificent barrel-vaulted St John's Co-Cathedral, all in the new city called Valletta and designed in an austere Mannerist style.

2. Malta, Valletta, view looking east over the Grand Harbour towards Fort St Angelo

A late form of Renaissance architecture is found in the delicately carved work of Tommaso Dingli (1591–1666), particularly at Attard and the old parish church at Birkirkara, but it was Roman Baroque that was to plant the most impressive stamp upon Malta. Lorenzo Gafa (1630–1710) rebuilt the cathedral at Mdina and several parish churches, the best of which is at Zejtun and reveals his ability to mould powerful domes, façades and internal spaces. Military engineers, including the Italians Pietro Paolo Floriani (1585–1638) and Antonio Maurizio Valperga, built vast Baroque sweeps of bastioned fortified lines at Floriana and Cottonera, with richly carved gateways encrusted with armorial bearings and symbols of war. Many palaces and churches in Valletta display a late flowering of Baroque. Soon each town was crowned by a large domed church, often with twin western towers. Largely rebuilt after the earthquake of 1693 (although some fine Siculo-Norman palaces had survived), the old fortified hilltop capital of Mdina is preserved as a homogeneous Baroque city. Towards the end of the Knights' rule there emerged a more classical style, in which Giuseppe Bonici (1707–99) designed the Customs House and the Italian Stefano Ittar (d 1790) the library, both in Valletta. Both buildings are clearly articulated with symmetrical plans and precise detailing characteristic of Neo-classicism.

In 1798 the British aided a Maltese uprising against French occupation and in turn occupied the islands, building many impressive detached forts, in particular S Leonardo (1872), south-east of the Grand Harbour, and forts Bingemma, Mosta and Madliena (1878) on the Victoria Lines near Mosta. They enlarged the dockyards, where William Scamp (1801–72) built an imposing bakery, and they completed St Paul's Anglican cathedral in Valletta; the Opera House (1860–66; destr.) by Edward M. Barry was in its ostentation quite out of scale in Valletta, a city unknown to the designer.

Since the 1960s attempts have been made to design a modern Maltese architecture with national characteristics, the best work being done by the Maltese architect Richard England (b 1937). His buildings, like the church at Manikata, suggest sculpted forms that relate to the indigenous architecture of the islands.

BIBLIOGRAPHY

G. Bosio: Istoria della sacra religione militare di S. Giovanni Gerosolimitano, 3 vols (Rome, 1594–1602)
G. F. Abela: Della descrizione di Malta, v (Malta, 1647)
J. B. Ward-Perkins: 'Mediaeval and Early Renaissance Architecture in Malta', Antiqua. J., xxii (1942)
H. Braun: An Introduction to Maltese Architecture (Valletta, 1944)
H. Luke: Malta: An Account and an Appreciation (London, 1949)
H. P. Scicluna: The Church of St. John in Valletta (Rome, 1955)
Q. Hughes: The Building of Malta: 1530–1795 (London, 1956, rev. 1967/R Malta, 1986)

——: *Fortress: Architecture and Military History in Malta* (London, 1969)

——: 'Malta: Past, Present and Future', *Archit. Rev.* [London], cxlvi (July 1969), pp. 1–82 [special issue]

——: '"Give me Time and I Will Give you Life": Francesco Laparelli and the Building of Valletta, Malta, 1565–1569', *Town Planning Rev.*, xlix (Jan 1978), pp. 61–74

C. Knevitt: *Connections: The Architecture of Richard England, 1964–84* (London, 1984)

L. Mahoney: *A History of Maltese Architecture* (Malta, 1988)

Q. Hughes: *Malta: A Guide to the Fortifications* (Valletta, 1993)

QUENTIN HUGHES

2. PAINTING. The history of painting in Malta since the late Middle Ages is a reflection of its position as a Latin Christian, central Mediterranean island. The earliest surviving works are icons of Siculo-Byzantinesque inspiration painted on the walls of built or rock-cut churches. The political connection with the Aragonese court (1282–1530) produced one important masterpiece, a polyptych of *St Paul* (Mdina, Cathedral Mus.) that is stylistically attributable to the circle of Lluís Borrassà and was presumably painted in Cataluña. The Renaissance arrived on the islands with the Sicilian followers of Antonello da Messina, whose sister was married to the Maltese Giovanni de Saliba (*fl* 1469–1510). Giovanni's painter sons, Pietro (*fl* 1497–1530) and Antonio (*c.* 1466–*c.* 1535), were active in Malta together with their cousin Salvo d'Antonio, the son of Antonello's brother Giordano.

The Knights of St John, who settled on the island in 1530, brought with them artistic treasures, including the early 12th-century icon of the *Virgin of Damascus* (Valletta, Greek Orthodox Church), which has origins similar to the *Madonna of Vladimir* (Moscow, Tret'yakov Gal.) but may be an earlier work, and a triptych of the *Deposition* (Mdina, Cathedral Mus.) from the circle of Jan van Scorel. Important works, such as a *Crucifix* attributed to Polidoro da Caravaggio (Valletta, St John's Co-Cathedral), were meanwhile commissioned, and after the founding of Valletta in 1566 noteworthy artists were invited to the island. First to come was Matteo Perez d'Aleccio (1547–1616), who painted frescoes for the Palace of the Grand Masters and altarpieces for several churches, including the Conventual Church. He was succeeded by the Florentine Filippo di Benedetto Paladini, whose prestige influenced the formation of a vernacular Late Mannerist school.

Caravaggio lived in Malta from July 1607 to September 1608 and painted the *Beheading of St John the Baptist* and the *Penitent St Jerome* (Valletta, St John's Co-Cathedral), besides other canvases that have either left the island or are untraceable. His artistic heir was a painter of mediocre ability called Cassarino about whom nothing is known. Two more gifted Caravaggisti who worked for Maltese patrons were the Sicilians Pietro Novelli and Mario Minniti. Other works came from more distant artistic centres. A painting of the *Immaculate Conception* (Gozo, Qala Sanctuary) shows affinities with the style of Federico Barocci, to whom it has traditionally been ascribed. More certainly attributed is the canvas of *Christ Embracing the Cross* by Guido Reni (Valletta, N. Mus.), which was acquired for the Palace of the Grand Masters.

Mattia Preti moved to the island in 1661, bringing with him his personal brand of Baroque formed of a synthesis of Neapolitan Caravaggism and Venetian opulence (*see* PRETI, MATTIA, §4). His paintings on the vault of St John's

Co-Cathedral in Valletta are his masterpieces and arguably the most successful ceiling decoration of the 17th century south of Rome. Preti ran a busy bottega and was exceedingly prolific, and his impact on the subsequent development of Maltese painting was tremendous. Among his disciples the most noteworthy was Giuseppe d'Arena, who in spite of his limited ability occasionally produced good works.

The indigenous Late Mannerist tradition produced a significant artist in Stefano Erardi (*see* ERARDI), who widened his artistic vocabulary to include elements of Neapolitan Baroque. In the work of Alessio Erardi one notices the crystallization of a Maltese Baroque school, which produced two noteworthy artists in GIAN NICOLA BUHAGIAR and FRANCESCO ZAHRA. Contacts with Naples became closer. Francesco du Mura painted an *Allegory of Malta* for the Palace of the Grand Masters (Valletta, Mus. F. A.), while Sebastiano Conca produced devotional works, including an altarpiece of the *Holy Family* (Cospicua, St Joseph).

The more intellectual approach of the Roman school made itself felt through the Maltese works of Agostino Masucci and Benedetto Luti, and its impact was intensified by ANTOINE DE FAVRAY, who settled on the island. Links were forged with the Accademia di S Luca in Rome during the last two decades of the Knights' rule and in the early British period. The Maltese artists who were trained there, such as SALVATORE BUSUTTIL and PIETRO PAOLO CARUANA, moved in the circle of Tommaso Minardi, whose sweetly pious works of Raphaelesque inspiration enjoyed great appeal. The HYZLER brothers, Giuseppe and Vincenzo, became active among Friedrich Overbeck's Nazarenes. Their academic art received official encouragement but was never really popular.

The Romantic Movement made a belated appearance in the works of GIUSEPPE CALÌ, whose technically superb paintings were often unashamedly melodramatic. His rival Lazzaro Pisani carried the Neo-classical tradition into the 1930s. The founding in 1921 of a Government School of Art at Valletta fostered a new interest in the visual arts; in the immediate post-World War II period it matured into a revival that brought Maltese painting in line with contemporary European currents. The artistic orientation was at first provided by the Regia Accademia of Rome, where such talented young artists as ANTON INGLOTT, GIORGIO PRECA and WILLIE APAP were sent to complete their studies. These painters were an inspiration to the young rebel artists who in 1952 formed the Modern Art Circle, from whose ranks the leading artists of contemporary Malta emerged.

BIBLIOGRAPHY

M. Buhagiar: *The Iconography of the Maltese Islands, 1450–1900: Painting* (Malta, 1988)

——: 'The Artistic Legacy of the Order in Malta', *The Order's Early Legacy in Malta*, ed. J. Azzopardi (Malta, 1989)

——: 'Paintings in Gozo: A Brief Analytical History', *Gozo: The Roots of an Island*, ed. C. Cini (Malta, 1990)

A. Espinoza-Rodriguez: *Paintings at the National Museum of Fine Arts in Malta* (Malta, 1990)

3. SCULPTURE. The history of sculpture in Malta follows the same pattern as that of painting. A limestone relief of two standing saints (Victoria, Gozo, Flklore Mus.)

seems to come from a Siculo-Byzantinesque milieu, but the dumpy proportions and non-idealized schematization suggest an awareness of Romanesque. This is further confirmed by two 16th-century limestone medallions of *St Peter* and *St Paul* (Rabat, Malta, Wignacourt Mus.), which are obviously based on Romanesque prototypes.

In the late 15th century contacts were established with the Palermo workshop of Domenico Gagini, who produced a baptismal font for Mdina Cathedral. Domenico's son Antonello also worked for patrons in Malta, where his works include a white marble *Virgin and Child* (1504; Rabat, Gesù); towards the end of his life his workshop produced the sarcophagus of Grand Master L'Isle Adam (Valletta, St John's Co-Cathedral).

In 1530 the Knights of St John brought to Malta two significant works: a stained-wood statue of *St John the Baptist* in an archaic Early Gothic idiom (Dingli, parish church) and an early 16th-century polychrome relief of *St Anne* (Valletta, Fort St Elmo), remarkable for its closely knit composition and tender humanity. A life-size gessoed and painted wooden Crucifix (Rabat, collegiate church) is presumably an Italian late Renaissance work and may also have close associations with the Knights.

After the founding of Valletta in 1566, the most important works centred round St John's Co-Cathedral, the inside walls of which are decorated with high-relief carvings designed by Mattia Preti (*see* PRETI, MATTIA, §4) and executed in stone by Sicilian and Maltese craftsmen. The crowning glory of the church is the white marble group of the *Baptism* by Giuseppe Mazzuoli, which is set off by a Berniniesque gilt-bronze *Gloria* by Giovanni Giardini da Forlì. Mazzuoli was also responsible for the memorial to *Grand Master Perellos*, which has a classical grandeur and restraint compared to the Baroque exuberance of the Florentine Massimiliano Soldani, who is represented by two signed marble and bronze memorials and who gave Malta its finest public monument, the bronze statue of *Grand Master Vilhena* at Floriana. Other monuments in the Co-Cathedral have been ascribed to Giovanni Battista Foggini and Ciro Ferri, while Alessandro Algardi is associated with a bronze relief of *Christ* on the tympanum of the west façade and with a life-size wooden Crucifix inside the church. In 1680 Algardi also produced a gilt-bronze medallion with a relief of the *Beheading of St Paul* for the grotto of the saint at Rabat; this grotto contained other important works, including a stained wood statue of *St Luke* (Valletta, N. Mus.; see fig. 3) in the Roman Baroque tradition by Pietro Papaleo. The influence of such works was instrumental in fostering a Maltese Baroque tradition of devotional and processional statues and church decoration and ornamentation, often at grass-roots level.

The only Maltese sculptor to attain international repute was Melchiorre Gafa (1635–67); he settled in Rome, where he attracted the favourable attention of Gianlorenzo Bernini and was regarded as the most gifted young sculptor of the second generation of the Roman High Baroque. The vernacular tradition produced a gifted artist in MARIANO GERADA, who was allegedly trained in Spain and worked exclusively for churches, specializing in painted wood processional statues. Vincenzo Dimech showed a

3. Pietro Papaleo: *St Luke*, stained wood, h. 1.60 m, from the grotto of St Paul, Rabat, Malta (Valletta, National Museum of Malta, Auberge de Provence)

familiarity with Neo-classicism and received official commissions for work in Malta and the Ionian Islands.

The British introduced the Neo-classical commemorative monument in cemeteries and public gardens. Most surviving examples are of unknown authorship, but the white marble bust in the memorial to *Admiral Sir Henry Hotham* (Valletta, Upper Barracca Gdns) has recently been associated with Bertel Thorvaldsen. Worthy of note is the memorial to *Louis Charles d'Orléans* (Valletta, St John's Co-Cathedral) consisting of a wall-plaque by Jean-Baptiste Augustin and Felix Fortin and a sarcophagus with a recumbent figure of the Count by James Pradier. In the later part of the 19th century works were commissioned in Italy from Pietro Tenerani and Giuseppe Valenti; the latter enjoyed popularity for his Diamond Jubilee monument of *Queen Victoria* in Valletta.

The first half of the 20th century was dominated by Antonio Sciortino (1879–1947), who was for a time Director of the British Academy in Rome. His greatest work is probably the *Eucharistic Congress Memorial* at Floriana but *Les Gavroches* (Valletta, Upper Barracca Gdns) is also of artistic interest. The example of Sciortino brought about an awakening in Maltese sculpture that produced two artists of note in GEORG BORG and Vincent Apap (*b* 1909).

BIBLIOGRAPHY

E. Sammut: 'Melchior Gafa: Maltese Sculptor of the Baroque', *Scientia* [Malta], xxiii (1957), pp. 117–39

J. A. Cauchi: 'St John's: Works of Art Reconsidered', *The Church of St John in Valletta, 1578–1978* (exh. cat., ed. J. Azzopardi; Valletta, St John's Mus., 1978), pp. 9–15

M. Buhagiar: 'The Early Artistic Legacy of the Order of Malta: Sculpture', *The Order's Early Legacy in Malta*, ed. J. Azzopardi (Malta, 1989)

——: 'The St Peter and St Paul Medallions', *St Paul's Grotto, Church and Museum at Rabat, Malta*, ed. J. Azzopardi (Malta, 1990)

E. F. Montanaro: 'Popular Statuary', *Maltese Baroque*, ed. G. Mangion (Malta, 1990)

——: 'The Sculptures at the Grotto of St Paul', *St Paul's Grotto, Church and Museum at Rabat, Malta*, ed. J. Azzopardi (Malta, 1990), pp. 41–5

4. FURNITURE. The poverty of Maltese architecture in the late Middle Ages gave little scope for interior decoration. Moorish-style houses had stone benches, called *dukkien*, which served as seats and on which mattresses were spread at night. The few property inventories that survive from the 15th and 16th centuries make no mention of chairs and usually list only one European-style bed, whereas references to tables and to chestnut and red deal coffers are common. High-quality furniture was found only in important churches. The Cathedral at Mdina had choir-stalls with inlaid wood panels of saints and Bible scenes, manufactured at Catania, Sicily, by Pariso and Pietro Antonio Calacura between 1482 and 1487, and a painted and carved gilt-wood exposition-throne, which is possibly 15th century and perhaps of Sicilian make. However, the art of wood-carving was known to the island and is mentioned in a document (1496) of an artisan named Antonio Carastu.

After 1530 the presence on the island of the Order of the Knights of St John brought a demand for fine furniture that was first satisfied by foreign, mostly Italian, cabinet-makers, who were gradually supplanted by Maltese craftsmen. A local school specializing in veneer and richly inlaid work was well established by the middle of the 17th century. The style was eclectic, showing the influence of heterogeneous continental models. Chests-of-drawers veneered in carob- and olive-wood and decorated with inlaid animal, bird and plant motifs in orange-wood were common; many carried ebonized mouldings, and almost all had bun feet. The Conventual Church in Valletta contains church furniture of excellent craftsmanship dating from between the late 16th and 17th centuries, including gilt walnut choir-stalls, and a richly carved and gilt-wood lectern with four high-relief scenes from the *Life of St John the Baptist*.

The French influence became increasingly pronounced in the 18th century when cabriole legs and serpentine fronts became fashionable. Painted and gilt red deal furniture was also in demand: a remarkable example is the *bombé* two-drawer chest (1732–6; Valletta, N. Mus.; see fig. 4) decorated with eight-pointed crosses and shields with the arms of Grand Master Antonio Manoel de Vilhena (1722–36). This decorative tradition is reflected in the trestle beds with ornate headboards carrying medallions with religious symbols or holy effigies. In the 18th century the Maltese wall-clock developed, consisting of a painted dial with large Roman numerals, and decorated with landscape scenes or ornate motifs; finer examples had doors fitted with blown glass.

4. Two-drawer *bombé* chest, red deal and gilt, 1732–6 (Valletta, National Museum of Malta, Auberge de Provence)

In the 17th and 18th centuries centres of production were set up in Senglea and Vittoriosa, where skilled artisans, or *ebanisti*, satisfied the requirements of the island's numerous churches, establishing a vernacular Baroque tradition that survived until the first decades of the 20th century. In the 19th century inlays of classical squares and urn and star motifs were used, but the shapes remained basically Baroque. The British introduced mahogany, and under their influence drum- and sofa-tables and larger centre tables became fashionable, as did frame sofas, armchairs and chairs, which were generally decorated with lion motifs or grotesque animal heads and scrolls. Two other new items of furniture were the bureau-bookcase, often double-domed and veneered in olive-wood with orange-wood inlays, and the longcase clock. The last of the great craftsmen was EMMANUELE BUHAGIAR, who specialized in wood-inlaying and was a gifted designer.

BIBLIOGRAPHY

J. Galea-Naudi and D. Micallet: *Antique Maltese Furniture* (Valletta, 1989)

5. CERAMICS AND GLASS. After 1530 the activities of the Knights Hospitaller in caring for the sick are reflected in the many extant ceramic drug jars. Most are tin-glazed earthenware decorated with blue, yellow, green, and orange leaves, tendrils, flowers and fruit in imitation of Venetian ware, but the place of manufacture was probably Sicily. Some have medallions with saints or mythological figures and the coats of arms of Grand Masters. One particularly fine example is an owl-shaped jar (Valletta, N. Mus.), which was apparently ordered by Grand Master Manoel Pinto de Fonseca (1741–73). During the 18th and 19th centuries ceramics were not produced, and it was only after World War II that serious interest in the art was revived.

All glassware was imported into Malta until the 1960s, when glass-blowing was introduced as a tourist-orientated industry. Between 1530 and 1798 most ornamental glass came from Murano, Venice, but Silesian and Bohemian glass was also in demand. Individual items were sometimes made to order and engraved with armorial shields and commemorative inscriptions. Important works include a Silesian glass decanter (Valletta, N. Mus.), decorated with the coat of arms of Grand Master Antonio Manoel de Vilhena (1722–36) set against a trophy of arms, and a polygonal bottle (Valletta, N. Mus.)—probably Bohemian—which belonged to the Bailiff of Brandenburg, Fra Franz Anton von Schonau von Schwenstatt (*d* 1743).

MARIO BUHAGIAR

6. METALWORK.

(i) Gold and silver. As few Maltese gold and silver objects dated before the 16th century survive, the history of gold and silver in Malta commences with the advent of the Order of St John in 1530. In Malta the Knights Hospitaller applied the laws and regulations, based on the *Code d'Amboise* or *Pragmaticae Rhodiae F. Emerici Damboyse*, by which they had governed in Rhodes from 1309 to 1522. One of their first decrees ordered the establishment of consuls for silversmiths and goldsmiths. They enjoyed precedence over all other consuls and had the right to vote in the Consiglio Popolare, the representative council of Malta.

The *Code d'Amboise* empowered the consuls to exercise strict vigilance over the conduct of craftsmen, to ascertain that fake gems were not passed as genuine, that rings were not made hollow and filled with lead, that the gold and silver were of the required fineness and that silver was given an assay mark. Unauthorized melting of precious metals was prohibited, buying and selling strictly controlled, and prices officially assessed. The *Code d'Amboise* was amended and updated by several Grand Masters in later years. In 1640 Jean Paul Lascaris de Castellar (Grand Master, 1636–57) ordered that gold articles manufactured in Malta were to be of not less than 21 carats, and those of silver not less than 10 ounces of fine silver to the pound (1 Maltese pound of silver equals 12 ounces). The standard of gold was raised to 22 carats and that of silver to $10\frac{1}{2}$ ounces. From the same year craftsmen were required to have their own special mark, to be stamped on each work within 12 hours of completion. In 1778 the price of 22 carat gold was fixed at 33 scudi per ounce.

Like craftsmen elsewhere, goldsmiths were grouped in religious guilds or confraternities. In Malta they chose St Helen as their patron saint. Their chapel in the church of St Paul Shipwrecked, Valletta, contains a sanctuary lamp (1745) decorated with scenes from the life of St Helen and an inscription recording Giovanni Bessiere (1741–5), the consul for silversmiths, as its donor. Membership was obligatory, and every goldsmith applying for a licence had to pay a fee, which contributed to the upkeep of the chapel. St Helen's day, 18 August, was observed as a holiday by all goldsmiths. The confraternity of goldsmiths was dissolved in 1903.

In Valletta, Malta, the Order of St John had the Sacra Infermeria, one of the finest hospitals in Europe, in which the Knights and Maltese of all classes, as well as galley crews and slaves, were given the best medical care available. Silver plate was used to serve food to the Knights and the Maltese patients, while galley crews and slaves were supplied with pewter vessels. Hospital silver was mostly of plain workmanship, without flourishes or ornament. An account of the Infirmary silver plate of 1725, entitled *Notizia della Sacra Infermeria e della carica delli Commisarij delle povere inferme* (Rome, 1725), lists a total of no less than 1140 pieces weighing 1235 pounds. The Comun Tesoro (Treasury) of the Order, with the Langues of France and Aragon (two of the eight chapters of the Order), were responsible for the supply and maintenance of the silver. Each piece bore the mark of an Aragonese knight, Fra Giovanni Villargut, who in 1443, when the Order was still in Rhodes, made an endowment of 4000 Catalan soldi for the supply of silver to the Infirmary. When the Order's property was seized during the French Revolution, the Order was forced to convert most of the hospital plate into coin.

On two different occasions in the history of the Order, Malta suffered great losses in its gold and silver plate. In 1760 following a threat of a punitive expedition from the Turks, the Council ordered the meltdown of all silver that was not in use at the Infirmary, the Conventual Church (St John's Co-Cathedral) or the Palace of the Grand Masters, in order to provide funds for the defence of the island. In 1798 French forces under Napoleon forced the Knights Hospitaller to withdraw from Malta and ordered the seizure of all gold, silver and precious stones in the Conventual Church, the auberges of the Order and the Palace of the Grand Masters. The gold was converted into ingots, while silverware was sold locally for currency. The remaining silver was coined to provide for the French soldiers' upkeep.

Besides hospital plate, Maltese artisans also manufactured plate for the galleys of the Order. The use of silver on its ships had been sanctioned in 1624, on condition that the fineness should be $10\frac{1}{2}$ deniers, and that the cutlery on the *Capitana* or flagship should not exceed 60 pieces or 40 on the galleys. Unfortunately, no galley pieces have survived.

Gold and silver filigree work, still manufactured in Malta to a high standard, is thought to have been introduced in the 17th century from Sicily, then under Spanish rule, and is thus of Spanish taste. One of the earliest pieces of Maltese filigree work is a silver reliquary (*c.* 1726) donated by Antonio Manoel de Vilhena (1722–36), which is still in use at St John's Co-Cathedral in Valletta. One of the finest filigree bracelets is of 17 carat gold (1830; ex-De Piro priv. col., Lija, Malta) made by the Maltese goldsmith Michele Metropoli (*fl* 1830s). It is 37.5 mm wide, is in six hinged parts and has an elaborate design of scrolls, volutes and cable motifs.

All parish churches in Malta possess substantial quantities of gold and silver in the form of altar-fronts, chalices, statuettes, sanctuary lamps, candlesticks, ewers, cruets, ciboria, tabernacles etc. Most articles were donated by either the ruling class, the nobility or parishioners. Grand Master Gregorio Carafa (Grand Master, 1680–90), for example, donated a silver candlestick to the nunnery of St Ursola, Valletta, in the 1680s. The finest examples of Maltese church silver in existence are the silver gates (see fig. 5) in the chapel of the Blessed Sacrament in St John's Co-Cathedral. The gates were made in Malta in 1752 probably by Francesco Assenza (*fl* 1725–52).

5. Silver gates, attributed to Francesco Assenza, wings 2.4×2.0 m, centre gates w. 1.7 m, chapel of the Blessed Sacrament, St John's Co-Cathedral, Valletta, 1752

The earliest known piece of Maltese domestic silver is a gilt flask (*c.* 1636–57) bearing the crest of Grand Master Jean Paul Lascaris de Castellar (London, V&A). It has an oval base, a bulbous body, a narrow neck with a screw-cap in the form of a double-headed eagle and brass chains. Trays, salvers and basins were popular among wealthy Maltese families. Trays are generally round and elaborately embossed with designs of foliage, scallop shells, cornucopia and acanthus leaves, and they usually bear the reigning Grand Master's coat of arms and the family crest. Glove-trays or *guantieri*, of Italian inspiration, were very common in Malta from the 16th century. Unlike salvers, *guantieri* are mostly oval and usually very richly embossed or chased (e.g. in London, Mus. Order St John).

Another notable type of Maltese silverware is the écuelle, generally embossed with motifs from nature, such as foliage, flowers, fruit and birds. The handles are extremely elaborate, and the Maltese Cross often surmounts the dome-shaped cover. Three fine specimens of 18th-century Maltese écuelles form part of the Lady Julia Inglefield bequest to the Museum of the Order of St John, London. The lucerna, or Maltese oil-lamp, was also popular during the 18th century.

The earliest known Maltese silver coffeepot (untraced) was made *c.* 1710 and had a plain bulbous body on a low moulded foot, a domed lid and a silver handle set opposite the spout. A fluted pear-shaped body, with a domed lid surmounted by an acorn and a wooden handle, was common in the 18th century, but following discoveries during the excavations of Herculaneum and Pompeii, the low moulded base was replaced by caprine legs. Spouts underwent a number of changes in the 19th century, terminating in representations of bird and animal heads. Sugar bowls followed the general pattern and decoration of the coffeepots. Silver teapots were introduced in Malta after the advent of British rule in 1814 and usually had a round moulded foot, a wooden handle in line with the spout and a wooden knob surmounting the domed lid. Maltese milk-jugs were unknown prior to the 19th century because orange-blossom water instead of milk was added to coffee.

Another interesting piece of goldsmiths' work was the Sword of Honour (untraced) made by Saverio Satariano (*fl* 1789–1807), presented in 1807 to Sir Alexander Ball, the first British Civil Commissioner in Malta. In 1944 Field-Marshal John Vereker, 6th Viscount Gort, Governor of Malta, was presented with an equally fine gold sword (Penshurst Place, Kent) in recognition of his leadership in the defence of the island during World War II.

BIBLIOGRAPHY
A. Critien: *Holy Infirmary Sketches* (Malta, 1946)
V. F. Denaro: *The Goldsmiths of Malta and their Marks* (Florence, 1972)
J. Findlater and P. Willis: *Silver at St John's Gate: Maltese and Other in the Collection of the Museum of the Order of St John* (London, 1990)
J. Farrugia: *Antique Maltese Domestic Silver* (Valletta, 1992)

(ii) Base metals. Malta does not possess any mineral resources; all locally made metal objects, whether of gold, silver or base metal, are produced from imported ingots. A small mine was, however, mentioned by G. F. Abela and G. A. Ciantar in *Malta illustrata* (1772). They described a cast-iron statue dedicated to the metallurgist and metalworker *Glauco Chio*, who flourished towards the end of the seventh century BC and is considered to be the inventor of the method for the fusion of metals (*Enc. It.*). This statue was made by smelting local ore for 34 hours in furnaces operated by bellows. This mine was permanently closed in 1460, but its location has never been identified.

The Knights Hospitaller, on their arrival in Malta in 1530 from Rhodes, adopted the same regulations for workers in base metals as for goldsmiths and silversmiths (*see* §1 above). They appointed a consul for blacksmiths who controlled the opening of new workshops and the granting of licences. Blacksmiths, founders and farriers,

6. Wrought-iron Spanish window, 2.50×1.35 m, from the Auberge de Castille, Valletta, 1741

officially recognized by 1538, obtained further recognition by later Grand Masters. Workers in base metal were grouped in a special guild and had a chapel dedicated to St Eligius in the church of St Paul Shipwrecked, Valletta.

The Knights Hospitaller had a large arsenal and a well-equipped foundry in which church-bells and such military equipment as shields, halberds, mortars and iron and bronze cannons were cast. The Order's principal church, St John's Co-Cathedral in Valletta, has a set of eight fine bells, dating from 1636 to 1749, some of which were cast in the Order's foundry. Some of the founders studied metallurgy in Turin; among the best known are the TRIGANCE family, Vincenzo Menville (*fl* 1715–38) and Louis Bouchut. In 1734 Bouchut (*fl* 1734) was commissioned to cast a bronze statue of Grand Master Antonio Manoel de Vilhena (1722–1736), probably designed by Feliciano de Savasse, a masterpiece of sculpture that graces a square in Floriana.

Wrought-iron has been a speciality of Maltese artisans since the 16th century. At first they worked on arms and armour, but, after the initiation of an extensive programme of building by the Order of St John, began producing door-knockers, window and door grilles, stair and balcony railings, gates and the Spanish windows (see fig. 6) that decorate many buildings in Valletta and Mdina. There is an area in Valletta still known as the Smithies' Bastion, due to the large number of blacksmiths who had workshops in that street.

Enc. It.

BIBLIOGRAPHY
T. Zammit: *Valletta: An Historical Sketch* (Malta, 1908/*R* 1928)
A. Mifsud: 'I nostri consoli e le arti ed i mestieri', *Archv Melitense*, iii/2 (1934), pp. 36–82
M. Galea: *Malta: More Historical Sketches* (Malta, 1971)

MICHAEL ELLUL

7. TEXTILES.

(i) Woven. The production of cotton developed during the Middle Ages and became increasingly important under the Knights Hospitaller, especially in the 18th century, when fustian caps, quilts and coverlets were exported to France, Portugal and Spain. Sailcloth was also woven, and woollen yarn was used to weave heavy covers, rugs and such items as large haversacks. In spite of economic depression during and after the Napoleonic wars, the cotton industry continued to flourish. Up to World War I coarse cotton and finer-quality fabrics in imitation of foreign goods were manufactured locally in a variety of weaves on traditional handlooms. Since the early 1960s modern technology has been introduced, and with the influx of tourists weavers have expanded their production to include skirts, handbags, belts, ties, wall tapestries and rugs. These are also sold abroad in Britain, Italy, the USA, Canada and Germany. Many of the knitted and crochet designs on bedspreads, clothing and home furnishings are traditional, and there is a steady demand for sheep's wool rugs and blankets.

(ii) Lace. Malta is renowned for its production of bobbin lace, which was probably made there as early as the 16th century. It developed into a thriving industry mainly serving the domestic market, but in the late 18th century and early 19th it suffered from the general collapse of the lace trade. In 1833 Lady Hamilton-Chichester (formerly

Honoria Blake), who had been living in Malta for more than a decade, brought lacemakers from Genoa, and the industry was revived. Bobbin lace spread to the neighbouring island of Gozo, encouraged by two priests, Canon Salvatore Bondì (1790–1859) and Father Joseph Diacono (1847–1924). It developed a character of its own, loosely based on 19th-century Genoese lace but formed largely of wheat-ear motifs, linked by twisted threads and with a limited use of clothwork tapes. The lace was made of cream or black silk, and the eight-pointed Maltese Cross (the emblem of the Knights Hospitaller) was a prominent feature in the geometric patterns. Maltese lace was sent to the international exhibitions in London (1851 and 1880), and its commercial potential led British missionaries in China and India to copy it and to introduce local patterns. Lacemaking continued to thrive in the late 20th century as a cottage industry in Gozo, stimulated by tourist demand for a wide variety of lace-edged products, as well as all-lace runners, tablecloths, shawls and mantillas.

BIBLIOGRAPHY

G. F. Abela: *Della descrittione di Malta* (Malta, 1647), pp. 102, 132
T. McGill: *Handbook, or Guide for Strangers Visiting Malta* (Malta, 1839), pp. 23–4
A. Ferres: 'Dr D. Salvatore Bondì', *L'Arte*, xciii (1866), pp. 3–4
E. Mincoff and M. S. Marriage: *Pillow Lace* (London, 1907), p. 21
B. Blouet: *The Story of Malta* (London, 1967), pp. 32, 130–34
T. L. Huetson: *Lace and Bobbins: A History and Collector's Guide* (Cranbury, New Jersey, 1973), p. 31
P. Mizzi: 'Dun Gużepp Diacono', *Heritage*, xliii (1982)
S. M. Levey: *Lace: A History* (Leeds, 1983), pp. 95, 104
C. Azzopardi: *Gozo Lace: An Introduction to Lace-making in the Maltese Islands* (Gozo, 1991) [72 prickings in folder at back]

J. CASSAR-PULLICINO

8. PATRONAGE AND MUSEUMS. The single most consistent patron of the arts in Malta since at least the late Middle Ages has been the Church. Indeed, before the arrival of the Knights of St John in 1530, the Church appears to have been the sole *raison d'être* for art production. With the arrival of the Knights of St John and especially after 1571, by which time Valletta had been built, art in Malta received a tremendous boost. The new city was studded with the finest of palaces, churches, auberges and residences, which the Knights proceeded to decorate with works of art worthy of their glorious chivalric past and noble ancestry. Local aristocratic families, emulating the trends set by the Knights, began patronizing foreign and important local artists to decorate their residences.

It was only towards the middle of the 17th century that patrons outside the Church and the Order emerged. Although of no outstanding artistic merit, an important early collection of some 150 portraits of distinguished Maltese was put together by the physician Fra Giuseppe Zammit (1646–1740) and donated to the Jesuit College in Valletta, where it still remains. The commissioning of portraits and the collecting of works of art became very fashionable in the 18th century, from which time date certain important private collections, notably that of Marquis Carlo Antonio Barbaro (1721–93) at Marnisi, an estate near Zejtun, and the Valletta collection of Count Saverio Marchese (1757–1833). The bequest of a good part of the latter to the cathedral subsequently formed the nucleus of the Cathedral Museum, opened in 1969 at the former Mdina Seminary (built 1733).

The other principal church museums in the Maltese Islands are the St John's Museum in Valletta, the St Paul's Collegiate Church Museum at Rabat, both on Malta, and the Cathedral Museum at Victoria on Gozo. The main state museums include the National Museum of Archaeology, the Museum of Fine Arts, both in Valletta, the Museum of Archaeology at Victoria, Gozo, together with a number of smaller repositories annexed to important excavation sites. Notable among these is the Roman Villa and Museum of Antiquities at Rabat.

The genesis of the Museums Department can be traced to 1903, when a committee was set up to establish a museum in Valletta to be built around an existing collection of antiquities, mainly bequeathed by Fra Giovanni Francesco Abela (1582–1655) to the Jesuit College in 1637, and until 1903 kept at the so-called Gabinetto delle Antichità at the public library; the museum opened in 1905 at Palazzo Xara, Valletta. In 1922 the Museums Department was founded with Professor (later, Sir) Themistocles Zammit (1864–1935) as its first Director (1922–35), aided by three assistant curators, one of whom was Vincenzo Bonello (1891–1969), who from 1922 to 1937 was responsible for the Fine Arts Section. More spacious premises were sought at the Auberge d'Italie in 1925, and following World War II the collection was moved to the centrally sited Auberge de Provence, where the ground floor was occupied, as it still is, by the Archaeological Section, and the *piano nobile* by the Fine Arts Section. In 1974 the exquisite Baroque De Sousa Palace in Valletta became the new Museum of Fine Arts.

BIBLIOGRAPHY

G. Wettinger: 'Artistic Patronage in Malta: 1418–1538', *Hal Millieri: A Maltese Casale, its Churches and Paintings*, ed. A. T. Luttrell (Malta, 1976), pp. 108–19
J. Azzopardi: 'Count Saverio Marchese (1757–1833): His Picture Gallery and his Bequest to the Cathedral Museum', *Proceedings of History Week 1982*, ed. M. Buhagiar (Malta, 1983), pp. 28–43
A. Bonanno: 'Giovanni Francesco Abela's Legacy to the Jesuit College', *Proceedings of History Week 1983*, ed. M. Buhagiar (Malta, 1984), pp. 27–37
J. Azzopardi: *The Museum of St Paul's Collegiate Church, Wignacourt College, Rabat, Malta* (Malta, 1987)
A. Espinoza Rodriguez: 'The Painting of the Cathedral Dome at Mdina: A Case Study on Ecclesiastical Patronage in Malta in the 19th and Early 20th Centuries', *Proceedings of History Week 1986*, ed. J. F. Grima (Malta, 1991), pp. 39–68
S. Fiorini: 'Artists, Artisans and Craftsmen at the Mdina Cathedral in the Early Sixteenth Century', *Melita Hist.*, x/4 (1992), pp. 321–52
J. Gash: 'Painting and Sculpture in Early Modern Malta', *Hospitaller Malta: 1530–1798*, ed. V. Mallia-Milanes (Malta, 1993), pp. 509–603
S. Fiorini: 'The Earliest Surviving Accounts Books of the Cathedral Procurators: 1461–1499', *Proceedings of History Week 1992*, ed. S. Fiorini (Malta, 1994)

STANLEY FIORINI

Maltai. Village in northern Iraq, near Dohuk *c.* 70 km north of Mosul, notable as the site of four Neo-Assyrian rock reliefs. On the cliffs south of the village, about 200 m above the Rubar-e Dohuk River valley, four reliefs (each *c.* 6×2 m) are carved on the limestone rock face. The panels all depict the same nine figures arranged in a single line: two images of the Assyrian king, and seven gods all facing left, wearing horned crowns and standing or sitting on the backs of mythical creatures (*see* MESOPOTAMIA, fig. 7). As identified by Julian Reade (in *RLA*), the figures (from left to right) are as follows: first, the Assyrian king faces right in a pose of worship; second, the state god, Assur, stands on the dragon of the Babylonian god Marduk and a horned lion; third, Ninlil/Mulissu, consort of Assur, sits on a throne on the back of a lion; fourth, the moon god Sin stands on a lion-dragon. The identity of the fifth god is uncertain: Reade suggests the sky god Anu or, less probably, Enlil, standing on the dragon of Marduk. Sixth, the sun god Shamash stands on a horse; seventh, the weather god Adad, holding lightning bolts in his hands, stands on a lion-dragon, accompanied on one panel by a bull; and eighth, some form of the goddess Ishtar stands on a lion. At the right is the Assyrian king again, this time facing left. None of the panels is inscribed, so their date has been a matter for discussion. On the basis of a somewhat similar rock relief at BAVIAN, the Maltai sculptures are generally attributed to Sennacherib (*reg* 704–681 BC). The god Assur's association with the dragon of Marduk points to a date after Sennacherib's destruction of Babylon in 689 BC, when Assur usurped Marduk's role as king of the gods. The purpose of the reliefs is also uncertain. Nearly identical reliefs, also ascribed to Sennacherib, were reported by Reade north of Mosul at Faida, near modern al-Kosh. Those reliefs, like the one at Bavian, mark a Sennacherib canal, and it has been suggested by Reade that the Maltai reliefs might be associated with a water project involving the River Rubar-e Dohuk, although no such canal system has been identified.

BIBLIOGRAPHY

F. Thureau-Dangin: 'Les Sculptures rupestres de Maltai', *Rev. Assyriol.*, xxi (1924), pp. 185–97
W. Bachmann: *Felsreliefs in Assyrien*, Wiss. Veröff. Dt. Orient-Ges. (Leipzig, 1927)
R. M. Boehmer: 'Die neuassyrischen Felsreliefs von Maltai (Nord-Irak)', *Jb. Dt. Archäol. Inst.*, xc (1975), pp. 42–84 [good illustrations]
J. Börker-Klähn: *Altvorderasiatische Bildstelen und vergleichbare Felsreliefs*, 2 vols, Baghdader Forschungen (Mainz, 1982)
RLA [article by J E. Reade, 1987–90]

JOHN M. RUSSELL

Maltese [Fieravino], **Francesco** (*fl* Rome, *c.* 1610–60). Italian painter. He was a painter of still-lifes like his contemporary Benedetto Fioravanti, with whose works Maltese's have been confused. In 17th-century documents and inventories, however, a distinction between their paintings is made. The name of Maltese first appears in a Barberini inventory (1631–6), which lists 'six paintings in oil on paper, of varied flowers', and then in numerous inventories ending with that (1659) of the collection of Archduke Leopold William of Austria, in which his works are distinguished from those of Fioravanti. Maltese's style is puzzlingly close to that of Evaristo Baschenis and Bartolomeo Bettera, yet it seems more probable that it had its roots in a Roman tradition of still-life. Often including carpets, his still-lifes are painted with thick strokes in a forcefully realistic manner, like the later work of Michelangelo Pace del Campidoglio, the Pseudo Caroselli, Meiffren Conte and Giuseppe Recco. Engravings made by Jacobus Coelemans (*b* 1654) in 1703 and 1704 of two paintings entitled *Still-life with Musical Instruments* (both untraced) and inscribed *Le Maltois pinxit* record the works that may be most securely attributed to Maltese.

They are monumental compositions, showing tables loaded with many objects. The paint surface of other still-lifes attributable to Maltese, such as the *Still-life with Jewelcase Bearing the Barberini Crest* (priv. col.), is lively.

BIBLIOGRAPHY

C. de Bie: *Het gulden cabinet* (1661)
A. Félibien: (1666–8; rev. (1725)
M. Aronberg Lavin: *Seventeenth-century Barberini Documents and Inventories of Art* (New York, 1975)
L. Salerno: *La natura morta italiana, 1560–1805* (Rome, 1984), pp. 182–7
La natura morta in Italia (exh. cat., ed. E. A. Safarik and F. Bottari; Milan, 1989), ii, pp. 768–9

UGO RUGGERI

Malton, Thomas, the younger (*b* London, 1748; *d* London, 7 March 1804). English painter and draughtsman. The son of Thomas Malton the elder (1726–1801), a cabinet-maker, perspective lecturer and architectural draughtsman, from whom he received early instruction, Thomas the younger attended the Royal Academy Schools, London, from 1773. He received a Premium from the Society of Arts in 1774 (followed by a Royal Academy Schools gold medal for a theatre design in 1782). In 1777 he made architectural drawings in Bath (e.g. *Royal Crescent, Bath*; Bath, Victoria A.G.); he also painted scenery for Covent Garden Theatre, London, during this period and exhibited architectural drawings at the Royal Academy between 1773 and 1803. From 1783 he practised as a drawing-master, specializing in perspective. Among his pupils was J. M. W. Turner, who later, in 1811, in his lectures as Professor of Perspective at the Royal Academy praised Malton's skill. In 1791 Malton issued proposals for publishing by subscription *A Picturesque Tour through the Cities of London and Westminster*, a collection of etchings with coloured aquatint based on his own drawings, which he published the following year. His vision of London is that of a bright, clean city with grandiose architecture and a stratified, but harmonious, population. *King's Mews, Charing Cross* (*c.* 1792; London, BM), an etched outline with watercolour, is an example of his precise style; he chose a low viewpoint to enhance the drama of the building and put in shadows throughout with crisp grey wash, before adding delicate local colours. This sense of architectural grandeur and use of precise perspective influenced the early watercolours of Turner and Thomas Girtin. Malton's aquatint *View from Scotland Yard*, with its counterpoint of silhouetted mooring posts, City of London skyline and cloud-flecked sky, continues the tradition established by Canaletto of Thames views that are both topographically accurate and concerned to convey atmosphere.

Malton was a leading producer of London topographical views and attracted many imitators at a time when the wars with France increased patriotic pride in the capital. In his views he sought to combine architectural accuracy with a sense of the city's social make-up. His success depended on topicality, and he modified views, updated fashions in dress and included the latest alterations to buildings before publishing them. In his last years he worked on a series of *Picturesque Views in the City of Oxford* (1802). His brother James Malton (?1766–1803) was also an authority on perspective and a fine architectural draughtsman; his several publications include *A Picturesque and Descriptive View of the City of Dublin* (1792–7) and *A Collection of Designs for Rural Retreats or Villas* (1802).

PRINTS

A Picturesque Tour through the Cities of London and Westminster, 2 vols (London, 1792)
Picturesque Views in the City of Oxford (1802)

BIBLIOGRAPHY

M. Hardie: *The Eighteenth Century* (1966), i of *Water-colour Painting in Britain* (London, 1966–8), pp. 177–8
A. Wilton: *British Watercolours, 1750 to 1850* (Oxford, 1977), p. 191
British Landscape Watercolours, 1600–1860 (exh. cat. by L. Stainton, London, BM, 1985), p. 34

SUSAN MORRIS

Maluku [Moluccas]. *See under* INDONESIA.

Malvasia, Carlo Cesare, Conte (*b* 18 ?Sept/Dec 1616; *d* 9 March 1693). Italian writer, painter, collector, antiquarian and lawyer. He won a reputation when still young for his poems, which were influenced by Cesare Rinaldi and by Claudio Achillini, a follower of Giambattista Marino. Like many aristocrats, he also studied painting under Giacinto Campana (*b* 1600) and Giacomo Cavedone. A prominent member of the literary academy 'dei Gelati' in Bologna, he went to Rome in 1639, soon after graduating in Law. There he joined the two major literary academies 'degli Umoristi' and 'dei Fantastici'. He also met Cardinal Giovan Francesco Ginetti and Cardinal Bernardino Spada; the latter probably introduced him to Alessandro Algardi. He returned to Bologna in 1646, where from 1647 he was senior lecturer in Law at the university. In 1652 he published his first work on art, *Lettera a Monsignor Albergati. . .*, a perceptive description of the *Supper in the House of the Pharisee* (1652; Bologna, Certosa) by Giovanni Andrea Sirani (1610–70). In 1653 he obtained a degree in theology and nine years later he was appointed a canon in Bologna Cathedral. Besides frequent visits to Rome, in 1664 Malvasia went to Padua and Venice, where he met Marco Boschini and Nicolas Régnier; in 1666 he visited the Marches and Florence, where he became acquainted with Cardinal Leopoldo de' Medici, whom he later advised on paintings and drawings for his collection. In Rome in 1665 he met Pierre Cureau de la Chambre, an admirer of Bernini, who secured him the favour of King Louis XIV and the attention of the Académie Royale de Peinture et de Sculpture.

In 1678 Malvasia published his *Felsina pittrice*, a history of painting in Bologna presented through biographies of Bolognese artists, which he had conceived in the 1650s or early 1660s and researched exhaustively. It remains the foundation of the history of art in Bologna. Written in the tradition of Giorgio Vasari's *Vite. . .* (1550) but without Vasari's belief in the supremacy of Florentine and Tuscan painting, it promotes a new and passionate appreciation of Bolognese art, championing the originality and diversity of Bolognese painters on the basis of painstakingly collected data and documents. The text is divided into four sections, dealing respectively with the primitives, the innovative art of Francesco Francia, the art of the Carracci and, finally, biographies of Malvasia's contemporaries, among them Guido Reni, Domenichino, Francesco Albani and Guercino. Malvasia's prose style, in contrast to the pure Tuscan of Vasari, reflects the idiomatic language of his native Bologna, blending fantasy and anecdote with elaborate Baroque conceits and metaphors. In 1686 this work was followed by his *Le pitture di Bologna*, a small yet rich guide for the educated viewer, which proved immensely popular and was reprinted seven times between 1704 and 1792. In 1694 he celebrated the Carracci school in his *Il Claustro di S Michele in Bosco di Bologna*, of particular value as it was illustrated by engravings of the already damaged frescoes.

Malvasia's opinions and methodology were opposed by Roman and Florentine art theorists and sparked a long debate. Filippo Baldinucci's *Apologia*, in the first volume of his *Notizie di professori del disegno. . .*, is a woefully inadequate reply to Malvasia's attack on Florentine supremacy, for Baldinucci simplified the argument, presenting it as a product of obsessive local patriotism, similar to that which had inspired the Venetian Marco Boschini, and failing to grasp the importance of Malvasia's new historiographical method. Malvasia's methodology also contrasted sharply with that of Giovanni Pietro Bellori, who, in his *Vite*, used historical material to support his classicist position, whereas Malvasia's *Felsina Pittrice* is more empirical and allows a greater freedom of aesthetic viewpoints. In 1703 Vincenzo Vittoria (1650–1712), encouraged by Carlo Maratti, published his *Osservazioni sopra il libro della Felsina Pittrice per difesa di Raffaello*, a Roman reply to Malvasia's position.

In the 18th century Malvasia's Baroque prose style was deeply unfashionable; in the 19th his Bolognese language was condemned and his validity as a source questioned. At the beginning of the 20th century he fell increasingly into disrepute, partly because of his assumed (but never proven) forgeries, and partly because of his attacks on specific issues, such as the role he played in applying the idea of eclecticism to the Carracci. It was not until the 1980s that Malvasia's original message began to be revalued, and his historical and cultural value reassessed.

WRITINGS

The only conspicuous collection of Malvasia's manuscripts known so far is in the Biblioteca Comunale dell'Archiginnasio, Bologna. For details see A. Sorbelli: *Inventari dei manoscritti delle biblioteche d'Italia* (Florence, 1933), liii.
Lettera a Monsignor Albergati. . . in ragguaglio d'una pittura fatta ultimamente dal Signor Giovan Andrea Sirani (Bologna, 1652)
Felsina pittrice: Vite de' pittori bolognesi, 2 vols (Bologna, 1678); ed. G. Zanotti, 2 vols (Bologna, 1841)
[Lettera] *Agl'Illustrissimi Signori Confaloniere e Senatori dell'Assonteria di Militia e Magistrati per gli pittori. . .* (Bologna, 1685)
Le pitture di Bologna che nella pretesa e rimostrata in hora da altri maggiori antichità ed impareggiabile eccellenza nella pittura, con manifesta evidenza di fatto rendono il Passaggero disingannato ed instrutto (Bologna, 1686)
Il Claustro di S Michele in Bosco di Bologna dipinto dal famoso Ludovico Carracci e da altri maestri usciti dalla sua Scuola (Bologna, 1694)

BIBLIOGRAPHY

D. Mahon: *Studies in Seicento Art and Theory* (London, 1947)
——: 'Eclecticism and the Carracci: Further Reflections on the Validity of a Label', *J. Warb. & Court. Inst.*, xvi (1953), pp. 303–41
A. Arfelli: 'Il viaggio del Malvasia a Milano e notizie su Ercole Procaccini il giovane', *A. Ant. & Mod.* (1961), pp. 470–76
L. Grassi: *Teorici e storia della critica d'arte – Parte seconda: L'età moderna: Il seicento* (Rome, 1973)
G. Perini: 'Il lessico del Malvasia nella sua *Felsina pittrice*', *Stud. & Prob. Crit. Test.*, xxiii (1981), pp. 107–29
F. Bologna: *La coscienza storica dell'arte d'Italia* (Turin, 1982), pp. 127, 131–3, 135–8, 143

L. Marzocchi, ed.: *Scritti originali del Conte Carlo Cesare Malvasia spettanti alla sua 'Felsina pittrice'* (Bologna, 1983); review by G. Perini in *Stud. & Prob. Crit. Test.*, xxix (1984), pp. 211–20

G. Perini: 'L'epistolario del Malvasia – Primi frammenti: le lettere all' Aprosio', *Stud. Seicent.*, xxv (1984), pp. 183–230

C. Dempsey: 'Malvasia and the Problem of the Early Raphael and Bologna', *Stud. Hist. A.*, xvii (1986), pp. 57–70

G. Perini: 'Central Issues and Peripheral Debates in Seventeenth-century Art Literature', World Art: Themes of Unity in Adversity. *Acts of the XXVI International Congress of the History of Art: Washington, DC, 1986*, i/1, pp. 139–43

GIOVANNA PERINI

Malyan, Tall'i [anc. Anshan]. Iranian site and capital of the ancient Elamite state, on the plateau north-west of Shiraz, which was occupied at least from the early 3rd millennium BC to the end of the 2nd millennium, and again during the Sasanian period (AD 224–651). Five seasons of excavations were conducted by William Sumner in the 1970s, and the finds are preserved in the Archaeological Museum in Tehran. In the early 3rd millennium BC the material culture of Malyan was equivalent to the Proto-Elamite phase of Susa (*see* ELAMITE). Multicoloured wall paintings with crenellations and sigmoidal curves also known in glyptic art have been found in a large public structure. Between *c.* 2800 and *c.* 2000 BC there was limited occupation at Malyan. Seals and seal impressions from the early 2nd millennium BC are comparable to those at Susa, with presentation scenes and animals depicted in a similar style; there is also buff pottery painted in black with geometric patterns and birds. During the subsequent period (*c.* 1600–*c.* 1250 BC) the painted decoration on the pottery is simpler. A large public structure of the Middle Elamite period (*c.* 1250–*c.* 1000 BC), with piers around a courtyard, contained evidence of craft activities. Inscribed tablets were found describing the movement of precious metals, foodstuffs and animal products. Seal impressions show humans riding equids, and an unusual series of impressions has cuneiform wedges made by an object decorated with granulated gold beads. A Sasanian kiln and a burial containing coins and a dagger are the evidence for the final stage of occupation.

BIBLIOGRAPHY
W. M. Sumner: 'Excavations at Tall-i Malyan, 1971–1972', *Iran*, xii (1974), pp. 155–80

——: 'Analysis of Material from Tall-i Malyan, 1975', *Proceedings of the IVth Annual Symposium on Archaeological Research in Iran: Tehran, 1975*, pp. 85–109

E. Carter and M. W. Stolper: 'Middle Elamite Malyan', *Expedition*, xviii (1976), pp. 33–42

W. M. Sumner: 'Excavations at Tall-i Malyan (Anshan) 1974', *Iran*, xiv (1976), pp. 103–15

J. W. Nickerson: 'Malyan Wall-paintings', *Expedition*, xix (1977), pp. 2–6

J. R. Alden: 'Excavations at Malyan, Part 1: A Sasanian Kiln', *Iran*, xvi (1978), pp. 79–86

J. M. Balcer: 'Excavations at Tal-i Malyan, Part 2: Parthian and Sasanian Coins and Burials (1976)', *Iran*, xvi (1978), pp. 86–92

I. M. Nicholas: 'Investigating an Ancient Suburb: Excavations at the TUV Mound', *Expedition*, xxiii (1981), pp. 39–47

E. Carter and M. W. Stolper: *Elam: Surveys of Political History and Archaeology* (Berkeley, 1984)

W. M. Sumner: 'The Proto-Elamite City Wall at Tall-i Malyan', *Iran*, xxiii (1985), pp. 153–61

HOLLY PITTMAN

Malyavin, Filipp (Andreyevich) [Maliavine, Philippe] (*b* Kazanka, Samara region [now Orenburg region], 10 Oct 1869; *d* Nice, July, 1940). Russian painter and draughtsman. He studied icon painting at the St Panteleimon monastery, Agios-Oros, Greece, from 1885 to 1891. He then enrolled at the Academy of Arts in St Petersburg, where he stayed until 1899, taking lessons from Il'ya Repin, one of his principal influences, before embarking on his career as a painter. At the 1900 Exposition Universelle in Paris he was awarded a gold medal for his picture *Laughter* (Venice, Ca' Pesaro), a celebration of peasant women. Malyavin enjoyed a certain success for his many vivid, colourful portrayals of peasant women, further examples being *Peasant Woman in Yellow* (1903; Nizhniy Novgorod, A. Mus.) and *Whirlwind* (1906; Moscow, Tret'yakov Gal.). He was also noted for his fine portraits of contemporaries, such as *Grabar* (1895) and *Somov* (1895; both St Petersburg, Rus. Mus.).

The tempestuous decorative colour of Malyavin's canvases and the harsh, impulsive rhythms of his drawings make his work a transitional link between the Russian Art Nouveau and Expressionism. But he did not go over to the avant-garde, after the October Revolution moving closer to the artists of AKhRR [The Association of Artists of Revolutionary Russia], taking part in their first exhibition in 1922. Although he produced a number of political portraits just after the Revolution, including sketches of Lenin (1920; Moscow, Cent. Lenin Mus.; London, BM), Lunacharsky and Trotsky (both priv. coll., London), Malyavin emigrated to France in 1922 where he continued to paint mainly those recurring themes that had first brought him success, for example *Russian Peasants* (1925; Riga, Latv. Mus. A.).

BIBLIOGRAPHY
V. Pica: *Philippe Maliavine* (Milan, 1929)

N. Alexandrova: *Filipp Malyavin* (Moscow, 1966)

O. Zhivova: *Filipp Andreyevich Maliavin* (Moscow, 1967)

Malyutin, Sergey Vasil'yevich (*b* Moscow, 22 Sept 1859; *d* Moscow, 6 Dec 1937). Russian painter and designer. He attended the Moscow School of Painting, Sculpture and Architecture in 1881–90, studying under Vladimir Makovsky, Vasily Polenov and Illarion Pryanishnikov, and joined the Wanderers (Peredvizhniki) in 1891. At first Malyutin supported the traditions of narrative Realism, as is clear from paintings such as *Peasant Girl* (1890; Moscow, Tret'yakov Gal.), although he quickly developed other interests in the popular arts and crafts, in history painting and in *plein-air* painting.

Like other Russian artists of his time such as Ivan Bilibin, Nicholas Roerich, the Vasnetsov brothers and Mikhail Vrubel', Malyutin turned for inspiration to Russian folklore, ancient history and the domestic arts, as in his panoramic *Battle of Kulikovo* for the Historical Museum in Moscow (1898) and in his invention in 1889 of the *matryoshka* (Russian stacking doll), which, misleadingly, has now been accepted as an integral part of traditional Russian folk art. In the 1890s he worked at the ABRAMTSEVO colony, producing stage and book designs, for example the edition of *Ruslan and Lyudmila* (Moscow, 1899), contributing to the revival of old arts and crafts and adapting the decorative elements of Russian tiles, embroidery and wood-carving to the concepts of Art Nouveau. By the early 1900s Malyutin was regarded as a leader in the creation of a new school of design that stressed intense ornament, bright colours and exaggerated, serpentine forms, as in his buildings and furniture for Princess Mariya Tenisheva's estate at Talashkino near Smolensk. His decorative imagination was recognized by the World of Art artists in St Petersburg, who invited him to their exhibitions and reproduced his works in their journal, *Mir Iskusstva*. In 1903 Malyutin moved back to Moscow and applied his decorative talent to one of the most prominent examples of Moscow Art Nouveau architecture with his mosaic panels for the Pertsov apartment house (1905–7) at Soymonovsky Proyezd on the Moskva River embankment.

Malyutin joined the Union of Russian Artists in 1903, an affiliation that marked his new orientation towards portraiture and landscape painting in the style of Arkhipovor Grabar'. His self-portraits and portraits of the early 1900s, often in pastel, were psychologically incisive if somewhat conservative in style, for example the portraits of *Valery Bryusov* (1913; Moscow, Lit. Mus.) and *Viktor Vasnetsov* (1915; Nizhny Novgorod, A. Mus.). Malyutin's renewed interest in the analytical portrait facilitated his acceptance of the new Realism after the October Revolution, as in his portrait of the writer *Dmitry Furmanov* (1922; Moscow, Tret'yakov Gal.), and in 1922 he became a founder-member of the Association of Artists of Revolutionary Russia. As a bridge between the traditions of 19th-century Realism and the Socialist Realism of the 20th century, Malyutin exerted a considerable influence on the younger generation of Russian traditionalist painters, such as Alexandr Gerasimov and Arkady Plastov.

BIBLIOGRAPHY

G. Golynets: *Sergey Vasil'yevich Malyutin* (Leningrad, 1974)

S. V. Abramova: *Zhizn' khudozhnika S. Malyutina* [The Life of the Artist S. Malyutin] (Moscow, 1978)

G. Golynets: *S. Malyutin: Izbrannye proizvedeniyya* [S. Malyutin: selected works] (Moscow, 1987)

JOHN E. BOWLT

Mamallapuram [Māmallapuram, Skt Mahāmallapuram; Mahābalipuram, Kāḍalmalai]. Temple site 50 km south of Madras, India; once a ceremonial centre and port of the PALLAVA dynasty, and now a popular resort.

1. SITE NAME AND CHRONOLOGY. The name Mamallapuram links the site to Narasimhavarman I (*reg* AD 630–*c.* 668), from whose title, Mahamalla ('the Great Wrestler'), its name derives. The still-prevalent alternative, Mahabalipuram, emerged later when mythic recollection of Vishnu's humbling of the demon king Bali proved stronger than local memory of the historical Pallavas. From at least Marco Polo's time until Pallava inscriptions were deciphered in the mid-19th century, mariners knew the site by the name Seven Pagodas, prompting in turn legends of temples lost to the sea beyond the now solitary Shore Temple. In Vaishnava hymns of the Pallava period the site is known as Kadalmalai ('Mount by the sea') from the boulder-strewn hill that lies parallel to the shore, half a kilometre inland.

Although the dating of the site is debated, the majority of art historical remains can be assigned to the mid-7th century reign of Narasimhavarman Mahamalla, eponym of the site. While some scholars have credited these monuments to the patronage of Mahamalla's father, Mahendravarman I (*reg c.* AD 570–630; Ramachandran, Hirsh), or to Mahamalla's great-grandson, Rajasimha (*reg* AD 690–728; Nagaswamy, Ramaswami), the attribution to Narasimha Mahamalla himself is corroborated by ample literary, epigraphic, stylistic and iconographic evidence. First the *Avantisundarikathā*, Dandin's Sanskrit romance, testifies to the currency of the name Mahamallapuram in the late

1. Mamallapuram, Pandava Rathas, view from the north-west, *c.* AD 650–*c.* 675

7th century, i.e. before the reign of Rajasimha (who also appropriated the title Mahamalla as one among hundreds). Second, the list of imperial titles engraved on the Dharmaraja Ratha (*see* §3 below) includes the proper name Narasimha (twice) and the epithet Mahamalla (Hultzsch, Srinivasan). In palaeographic terms these epigraphs are earlier than comparable inscriptions on Rajasimha's Kailasanatha Temple in KANCHIPURAM and elsewhere. Third, the Dharmaraja Ratha and its companion shrines (see fig. 1), several contemporary caves and narrative low reliefs exemplify a 'classical' phase in the stylistic development of Pallava sculpture, one that is distinguishable from the Mahendra-period style that preceded it and the 'embellished style' of Rajasimha that followed. Finally, the site's finest sculptural achievement, a unique cliffside low relief alternatively known as Arjuna's Penance of the Descent of the Ganges, is best understood as a mythic eulogy of Narasimhavarman I Mahamalla, its probable patron. (For illustration and a more detailed discussion *see* INDIAN SUBCONTINENT, §IV, 7(vi)(a).)

2. CAVE TEMPLES AND RELIEFS. Two cave temples that seem, on stylistic grounds, to predate the more numerous mid-7th century monuments were excavated at opposite ends of the kilometre-long hill that defines the axial centre of Mamallapuram. The cave situated in the north-west (facing towards the Pallavas capital of Kanchipuram, 65 km away) is popularly known as the Kotikal Mandapam ('Fort-rock chamber'). That a fort once existed is indicated by an extensive series of rock-cut notches and grooves for securing walls that once rimmed the entire hill, defending no-longer extant palace structures at the summit. Recent excavations in rubble mounds near a monolithic lion throne have disclosed a vault (6 m sq.) cut 3 m deep into the bedrock and lined with brick partitions. The Kotikal Mandapam consists of a modest sanctum (1 m sq.) and a rough-hewn porch (6×2 m) fronted by two square-sectioned pillars *in antis*. Characteristic of

2. Mamallapuram, Mahishasuramardini Mandapam, north panel, depicting Durga slaying the buffalo demon, and lion pillar of the interior porch of the central sanctum, 7th century AD

many early cave temples in the south-east, the middle third of both pillars is chamfered to give the appearance of an octagonal spacing block between two cubes. From the sanctum wall projects a rudimentary structural elevation simulating basement string courses, plank pilasters and a roll cornice with empty dormer-like arches. A pair of female guardian figures carved in low relief flank the entrance, indicative by gender of a sanctuary intended for the victory goddess, Durga.

At the south-east end of the hill and oriented towards the winter sunrise, the Dharmaraja Mandapam is a more elaborate exemplar of this archaic Pallava cave type insofar as its architectural simulations are much more crisply cut and multiplied to include two pillared fore-chambers (the *mukha-* and *ardha-mandapas*) and three sanctuaries. The deities to whom they were originally dedicated cannot be determined. The *dvārapāla* (Skt 'doorkeepers') that once guarded the central sanctum and might have indicated its dedication were subsequently chiselled away. They were probably plastered over with Shaiva guardians when an anachronistic inscription was engraved on the cave's south wall. Attributable to Parameshvaravarman I (*reg* 669–90), it is verbatim copy of the dedication of the Ganesha Ratha (*see* §4 below).

Seven cave temples were either finished or brought nearly to completion at various points around the central hill during Mahamalla's reign. Listed clockwise from the east (in *pradaksina* or circumambulatory order), they are the Panchapandava, Ramanuja, Mahishasuramardini, Adi Varaha, Koneri, Trimurti and Varaha Mandapams. All of these are comparable in scale and basic configuration to the earlier Shiva Gangadhara cave at Tiruchi, dating from the time of Mahendravarman (*reg c.* 570–630; *see* INDIAN SUBCONTINENT, fig. 207). The Mamallapuram caves, however, reflect an infinitely richer vision. In place of the austere cube-and-octagonal pillars, their façades are framed by sculptured columns of great complexity, distinguished as a group by shafts embodying seated lions (see fig. 2). (Exceptions are the Koneri Mandapam, with its slender, archaicizing shafts of the Mahendra type, and the Trimurti cave, which has no porch at all.) Bracketed between floral mouldings and crowned with fluted cushion capitals, these lion shafts constitute heraldic allusions to the patron, Narasimha, whose name recalls the myth of Vishnu as 'man-lion', who emerged from a pillar. Increased attention was devoted to figural sculpture in the Mamallapuram caves. As a rule, all interior walls are framed with copiously detailed base mouldings and ornamented cornices, which together serve to showcase life-sized narrative reliefs depicting major Brahmanical myths, set like *tableaux vivants* on a shallow stage. These works are unsurpassed anywhere in India for their apparent naturalism, intrinsic beauty and convincing sense of movement. For example, in the panel from which the Mahishasuramardini Mandapam takes its name (see fig. 2), the goddess Durga, 'slayer of the buffalo demon', surges forward in a company of spirit dwarves (*bhūta-ganas*), while the satanic prince hesitates and falls back. Usually her triumph is visualized in iconic certitude, Durga standing over an already beheaded foe; but here superiority of character, or spirit, is captured before its proof in a physical act. The viewer is drawn into the suspenseful moment before the climax and allowed to savour the odds before a heightened appreciation of the victory registers.

The increased emphasis on sculpture during the mid-7th century is most evident in the unique panoramic low relief covering two large boulders on the eastern side of the hill. This celebrated work, variously identified as the 'Penance of Arjuna' or 'Descent of the River Ganga' and praised for its complex composition, close observation of nature, dynamism and balance, is one of the most compelling creations of India's sculptors (*see* INDIAN SUBCONTINENT, fig. 208).

3. PANDAVA RATHAS. Situated nearly one km south of the main hill, the five monolithic temples known as the Pandava Rathas (see fig. 1 above) are ascribed to Narasimha Mahamalla. They appear to have no precedent in earlier Indian art, constituting as they do free-standing sculptural replicas of several temple types whose antecedents, structures of brick and timber, have not survived.

The simplest is the Draupadi Ratha, which takes the form of a hut with thatched roof. The external niches house female guardians and images of Durga. Two nearby boulders have been carved in the form of a lion and bull. The Bhima Ratha is a rectangular structure with pillared verandah on one of the long sides; the parapet is edged with miniature shrines and the barrel-vaulted superstructure fitted with projecting dormers. The Nakula and Sahadeva Ratha takes an apsidal form and has a small projecting porch. Directly adjacent is a boulder carved in the shape of an elephant. The Dharmaraja Ratha, the most elaborate temple of the group, has a multi-tiered superstructure with each level edged by aediculae. The summit is crowned by an octagonal domed cupola. Porches on each side have pillars with lion-bases, as in the other temples. The walls contain a variety of images framed by pilasters (see Srinivasan); most depict manifestations of Shiva, including the half-female Ardhanarishvara and Harihara, the half-Vishnu composite (above which the patron's name, 'Shri Narasimha', is inscribed). The Arjuna Ratha is a smaller version of the Dharmaraja.

In stylistic terms they share with the Mahamalla-period caves a wonderful equilibrium between contrasting elements: architectural components never overwhelm figural work; horizontal and vertical articulations of form effectively counterbalance one another (whereas verticality predominates in subsequent periods); daring empty spaces in both architectural and figural contexts maximize the effectiveness of judiciously applied ornamentation; likewise, purely decorative effects are never elaborated at the expense of iconographic significance.

4. SHORE TEMPLE AND OTHER MONUMENTS. Departure from this 'classical' Pallava style, and the emergence of an 'embellished' aesthetic (*alaṃkṛta*), is first apparent on the Ganesha Ratha, a monolithic temple with a rectangular plan and barrel-vaulted superstructure, located north of the Pandava Rathas. Its dedicatory inscription can be securely attributed to Mahamalla's grandson, Parameshvaravarman I. The stylistic shift is completed during the reign of Rajasimha Narasimha II. It is typified by the Shore Temple, located east of the main hill beside the sea, which constitutes one of the earliest structural

monuments of the Pallavas (*see* INDIAN SUBCONTINENT, fig. 64). The complex consists of ruined forecourts and an irregular cluster of three sanctums. The main sanctum and the smaller one adjacent to it were dedicated to Shiva as Rajasimheshvara and Kshatriyasimheshvara (see Rangacharya). The intervening space between these two temples is occupied by a rectangular cella containing a recumbent figure of Vishnu. The largest sanctum is surrounded by a weather-worn wall, creating a circumambulatory passage. A hallmark of Rajasimha-period temples is the rampant lion pilaster (*see* INDIAN SUBCONTINENT, fig. 65).

Similar pilasters appear on the Olakkanneshvara Temple, situated on the highest point of the site near the lighthouse, and on the Yali Mandapam, or Tiger Cave, near the beach, 3 km north at Shalwvankuppam. The Atiranacandeshvara Cave, also at Shaluvankuppam and Mukunda Nayanar structural temple, at the northern outskirts of Mamallapuram, may also be assigned to Rajasimha, by the inscriptions of the former and the Somaskanda iconography of both. This iconography, showing Shiva enthroned with his wife Uma and son Skanda, was a popular metaphor for the royal family among the later Pallavas.

BIBLIOGRAPHY

Dandin: *Avantisundarī of Ācārya Daṇḍin* (*c.* 7th century), Trivandrum Sanskrit Series, no. 172 (Trivandrum, 1954)
E. Hultzsch: 'The Pallava Inscriptions of the Seven Pagodas', *Epig. Ind.*, x (1909–10), pp. 1–14
G. Jouveau-Dubreuil: 'Les Antiquités de l'époque Pallava', *Rev. Hist. Inde Fr.*, i (1916), pp. 1–78; Eng. trans. as *Pallava Antiquities*, 2 vols (i, London, 1916; ii, Pondicherry, 1918)
H. Longhurst: *Pallava Architecture*, Mem. Archaeol. Surv. India, nos 17, 33, 40 (Simla, 1924; Calcutta, 1928, 1930)
V. Rangacharya: 'Two Inscriptions of the Pallava King Rajasimha-Narasimhavarman II', *Epig. Ind.*, xix (1927–8), pp. 105–15
R. Nagaswamy: 'New Light on Mamallapuram', *Trans. Archaeol. Soc. S. India*, (1960–62), pp. 1–50 [Silver Jubilee vol.]
K. R. Srinivasan: *Cave-temples of the Pallavas*, Architectural Survey of Temples, i (New Delhi, 1964)
W. Willetts: *An Illustrated Annotated Bibliography of Mahabalipuram, on the Coromandel Coast of India, 1582–1962* (Kuala Lumpur, 1966)
T. N. Ramachandran: 'Mamallapuram', *Marg*, xxiii (1970), pp. 23–118
S. Sivaramamurti: *Mahābalipuram* (3rd ed. New Delhi, 1972)
M. Lockwood, G. Siromoney and P. Dayanandan: *Mahabalipuram Studies* (Madras, 1974)
J. Dumarçay and F. L'Hernault: *Temples Pallava construits* (Paris, 1975)
N. S. Ramaswami: *Mamallapuram* (Madras, 1975)
K. R. Srinivasan: *The Dharmarāja Ratha and its Sculptures: Mahābalipuram* (New Delhi, 1975)
N. S. Ramaswami: *Mamallapuram: An Annotated Bibliography* (Madras, 1980)
M. Lockwood: *Māmallapuram and the Pallavas* (Madras, 1982)
M. Meister, ed.: *South India: Lower Drāviḍadēśa, 200 B.C.–A.D. 1324*, (1983), i/1 of *Enc. Ind. Temple Archit.*
S. Muthiah, ed.: *Mahabalipuram* (Madras, 1985)
M. Hirsh: 'Sources for the Figural Sculpture of Mamallapuram' (diss., New York U., 1986)
——: 'Mahendravarman I Pallava: Artist and Patron of Māmallapuram', *Artibus Asiae*, xlviii (1987), pp. 109–30
M. Rabe: 'The Monolithic Temples of the Pallava Dynasty: A Chronology' (diss., Minneapolis, U. MN, 1987)

MICHAEL D. RABE

Mamluk [Arab. *mamlūk*: 'slave']. Name applied to two distinct sequences of Islamic rulers in northern India and the Levant from the 13th century. Many but not all of the rulers were manumitted slaves of Turkish origin, hence the common names of the lines.

I. Mu'izzi Mamluks of Delhi. II. Mamluks of Egypt and Syria.

I. *Mu'izzi Mamluks of Delhi.*

This quasi-dynastic line of Turks conquered and ruled northern India from 1206 to 1290. The line of sultans is known as the Mu'izzi Mamluks of Delhi because Qutb al-Din Aybak (*reg* 1206–10) was originally a slave of the GHURID king Mu'izz al-Din Muhammad; two later sultans, Shams al-Din Iltutmish and Ghiyath al-Din Balban, were also manumitted slaves. As a trusted lieutenant, Qutb al-Din extended Ghurid power over the Gangetic doab. In Delhi he initiated the construction of the Quwwat al-Islam Mosque (*see* DELHI, §III, 1) and in AJMER the Arhai Din ka Jhompra Mosque. These are the earliest and most important monuments of the Sultanate period. Iltutmish (*reg* 1211–36) consolidated Mamluk rule from the Indus to eastern India, building extensively at Delhi, Badaon and elsewhere. The most impressive buildings in Delhi are the extensions to the Quwwat al-Islam Mosque and his own tomb, situated near by. After the death of Iltutmish, a conflict ensued between his heirs and the nobles. Five rulers acceded to the throne within a decade. Finally, in the absence of a direct heir, Ghiyath al-Din Balban (*reg* 1266–87) came to power. Although he restored order to the Sultanate, few building projects appear to have been undertaken. The most notable is Balban's tomb, now in ruins. Balban was succeeded by his grandson Mu'izz al-Din Kaiqubad (*reg* 1287–90). He shifted the capital to Kilokari, close to the present headworks of the Okhla Canal. The site is marked by a few ruins. Balban's line was abruptly ended in 1290 when the KHALJI dynasty seized power.

See also INDIAN SUBCONTINENT, §III, 6(ii)(b).

BIBLIOGRAPHY
Enc. Islam/2: 'Dilhi Sultanate'
Minhaj al-Din 'Uthman al-Juzjani: *Tabaqāt-i Nāṣirī* [An account of Nasir (al-Din Mahmud)] (*c.* 1259–60); Eng. trans. by H. G. Raverty, 2 vols (London, 1881/*R* New Delhi, 1970)
Ziya al-Din Barani: *Tārīkh-i Fīrūz Shāhī* [History of Firuz Shah] (MS. 1357; Calcutta, 1860–62; Aligarh, 1957) [extracts trans. in Eng. in H. Elliot and J. Dowson: *History of India as Told by its Own Historians (The Muhammedan Period)*, iii (London, 1866–77/*R* Allahabad, 1964), pp. 93–268 and *J. Asiat. Soc. Bengal* (1869), pp. 181–220; (1870), pp. 1–51, 185–216; (1871), pp. 217–47]
R. C. Majumdar, ed.: *The Delhi Sultanate*, vi of *The History and Culture of the Indian People* (Bombay, 1960/*R* 1967)

R. NATH

II. *Mamluks of Egypt and Syria.*

This name was given to the sequence of sultans and patrons who ruled in the Levant from 1250 to 1517, of whom the majority were of slave (Arab. *mamlūk*) origin. Coups d'état, civil wars and assassinations played a greater role than hereditary succession in determining who occupied the throne, although 15 of the descendants of (2) Qala'un eventually succeeded him. In the first half of the period (to 1382), Qipchaq Turks tended to predominate, and the line is often known as Bahri after their barracks on the Nile (*al-baḥr*), while in the second half of the period most of the sultans and leading figures were Circassians recruited in the northern Caucasus, and the line is often known as the Burji after their barracks in the Cairo Citadel (*al-burj*). In both periods, however, mamluks of Mongol, Georgian, Slav, Greek, German, Hungarian and even Chinese origin were known. Once acquired as slaves, the majority of them went into the royal barracks in Cairo where they were trained in the arts of warfare, instructed in the rudiments of Islam and taught to speak and write Arabic. They were then manumitted and given positions of responsibility in the army or royal household.

1. Introduction. 2. Individual patrons.

1. INTRODUCTION. Mamluks monopolized the highest administrative offices, closely supervising the Arabs and Copts who worked in the chancery and financial bureaux. Freeborn subjects found it hard to rise to positions of power, and even the freeborn sons of mamluks usually found it impossible to emulate the careers of their fathers. Nevertheless, those who pursued careers in commerce, religion and scholarship or who achieved subaltern ranks in the army played an important role as cultural mediators between the Turkish culture of their fathers and the Arab culture of the non-mamluks. Moreover, the mamluks' desire to ensure the future of their wives and descendants by means of religious endowments protected from state taxation or confiscation (*waqf; see* ISLAM, §III) may explain the large number of mosque and tomb complexes that the military élite endowed. Most mamluks, however, practised Islam with all the zeal of the newly converted.

In the late 13th century the Mamluks defeated both the remaining Crusader states in Syria and Palestine and the Mongol ILKHANID dynasty of Iran and Iraq, who repeatedly invaded Syria but failed to gain any permanent foothold there. To strengthen their legitimacy against their non-Muslim enemies, the Mamluks set up a 'shadow caliphate' in Cairo and maintained a loose suzerainty over the Holy Cities in Arabia. Cairo became the cultural centre of the Arab Islamic world, attracting refugees from the east and the west, where the Christian reconquest in Spain had gained new momentum. During the third reign of (3) al-Nasir Muhammad (1310–41) there was a lull in internal factional strife and foreign aggression, and it was one of the great ages for Mamluk patronage of the arts. Few of his descendants, however, effectively controlled either the empire they inherited or those who pretended to serve them, yet by the end of the Bahri period the Mamluk sultans reigned over an area that included large areas of southern and eastern Turkey as well as eastern Libya.

From the 1360s the supply of Turkish slaves dried up, and mamluks of Circassian origin began to predominate in the élite. Nevertheless, they took Turkish names, and Turkish continued to be the lingua franca of the élite. During the early Circassian period civil war and factional strife reached new levels, and in 1400 the Mamluk army fell apart before it could give battle to Timur (*see* TIMURID, §II(1)), who went on to sack Aleppo and Damascus virtually unopposed. Under (9) Barsbay (*reg* 1422–38) Mamluk fortunes partially revived. Throughout the 15th century the Mamluks held their own against foreign threats, despite increasing pressures along the northern and eastern frontiers, and by the end of the century an international court culture flourished among the Mamluks, the Ottoman dynasty in western Anatolia, and the Qaraqoyunlu and Aqqoyunlu dynasties in eastern Anatolia. Under (10)

Qa'itbay (*reg* 1468–96) programmes of fiscal, legal and military reform were pursued and a renaissance of the arts encouraged. The penultimate ruler (11) Qansuh al-Ghawri (*reg* 1501–16) presided over the Indian summer of Mamluk literary and artistic culture, as Portuguese fleets appeared in the Indian Ocean and the Red Sea to threaten the Eastern spice trade that had supported the Mamluk regime for 250 years. Simultaneously the Mamluks drifted into conflict with the Ottomans over suzerainty in eastern Anatolia, and in 1516–17 the Ottomans conquered Syria and Egypt.

The arts in the Mamluk lands were remarkably conservative in form and subject during the two and a half centuries of Mamluk rule, although elsewhere in the Islamic world the arts changed significantly. The typical building (*see* ISLAMIC ART, §II, 6(iii)(a)) combined one or more religious and charitable institutions, such as a mosque, madrasa, *khānaqāh*, elementary school, hospital and drinking-water dispensary, with the tomb of the founder in irregular stone buildings wedged into the dense urban fabric of Mamluk cities. Elaborate portals, slender multi-storey minarets and intricately carved stone domes over the tomb punctuated the exterior of these structures and served to draw attention to their presence. Elegant Arabic inscriptions in a variety of scripts accompanied by repeated vegetal and geometric motifs are constant features of Mamluk art and architectural decoration, although some early Mamluk inlaid metalwork (*see* ISLAMIC ART, §IV, 3(iii)(a)) and enamelled glass (*see* ISLAMIC ART, §VIII, 5(ii) and figs. 234–5) are decorated with figural motifs and even narrative scenes. The technical and decorative achievements of Egyptian potters in earlier centuries were not continued during the Mamluk period, although a wealth of imported Far Eastern goods introduced new ceramic shapes, decorative schemes (e.g. blue-and-white) and motifs (e.g. lotus and peony scrolls; *see* ISLAMIC ART, §V, 4(ii)). Although the art of the illustrated book (*see* ISLAMIC ART, §III, 4(v)(a)) was not as important as it was in contemporary Iran, magnificent mammoth copies of the Koran were produced for reading and display in Mamluk religious foundations (*see* ISLAMIC ART, §III, 3(i)). Fine silk textiles were produced throughout the period (*see* ISLAMIC ART, §VI, 2(ii)(b)), and knotted carpets with distinctive octagonal patterns are known from the 15th and 16th centuries (*see* ISLAMIC ART, §VI, 4(iii)(b)).

The most characteristic feature of Mamluk art is the emblem (often incorrectly known as a blazon) that identified an object (or even a building) as belonging to the household of an amir who held a specific office. Although the earliest emblems were strictly pictorial, such as the cup, penbox or polo stick, signifying the offices of cupbearer, secretary and polo-master, by the mid-14th century rulers incorporated their official titles into epigraphic blazons, while other mamluks developed complex composite emblems.

BIBLIOGRAPHY

Enc. Islam/2: 'Rank' [emblem]
The Mosques of Egypt, Ministry of Waqfs, 2 vols (Cairo, 1949)
D. S. Rice: 'Studies in Islamic Metalwork, IV', *Bull. SOAS*, xv (1953), pp. 489–503
K. A. C. Creswell: *The Muslim Architecture of Egypt*, ii (Oxford, 1959)
I. M. Lapidus: *Muslim Cities in the Later Middle Ages* (Cambridge, MA, 1967)
U. Haarman: *Quellenstudien zür frühen Mamlukenzeit* (Freiburg, 1970)
J. Rogers: 'Seljuk Influence on the Monuments of Cairo', *Kst Orients*, vii (1970), pp. 40–68
M. Meinecke: 'Zur mamlukischen Heraldik', *Mitt. Dt. Archäol. Inst.: Abt. Kairo*, ii (1972), pp. 213–65
J.-C. Garcin: *Un Centre musulman de la Haute-égypte médiévale: Qus* (Cairo, 1976)
C. Kessler: *The Carved Masonry Domes of Mediaeval Cairo* (London, 1976)
D. Ayalon: *Studies on the Mamluks of Egypt, 1250–1517* (London, 1977)
D. Haldane: *Mamluk Painting* (Warminster, 1978)
D. Ayalon: *The Mamluk Military Society* (London, 1979)
C. Petry: *The Civilian Elite of Cairo in the Later Middle Ages* (Princeton, 1981)
Renaissance of Islam: Art of the Mamluks (exh. cat. by E. Atıl, Washington, DC, N. Mus. Nat. Hist.; Minneapolis, MN, Inst. A.; New York, Met. and elsewhere; 1981)
E. Ashtor: *Levantine Trade in the Later Middle Ages* (Princeton, 1983)
Muqarnas, ii (1984) [whole issue devoted to papers selected from a symposium on the arts of the Mamluks]
D. Behrens-Abouseif: *The Minarets of Cairo* (Cairo, 1985)
P. M. Holt: *The Age of the Crusades: The Near East from the Eleventh Century to 1517* (London, 1986)
R. Irwin: *The Middle East in the Middle Ages: The Early Mamluk Sultanate, 1250–1382* (London, 1986)
D. James: *Qur'āns of the Mamlūks* (New York, 1988)
E. Whelan: 'Representations of the *Khāṣṣakīyah* and the Origins of Mamluk Emblems', *Content and Context of Visual Arts in the Islamic World*, ed. P. P. Soucek (New York, 1988), pp. 219–53
M. Meinecke: *Die mamlukische Architektur in Ägypten und Syrien* (Glückstadt, 1993)

ROBERT IRWIN

2. INDIVIDUAL PATRONS.

(1) Baybars I [al-Zāhir Rukn al-Dīn Baybars al-Bunduqdārī] (*b* ?1233; *reg* 1260–77; *d* Damascus, 1277). A Qipchaq Turk bought for the service of the antepenultimate AYYUBID sultan of Egypt, al-Malik al-Salih Najm al-Din, Baybars reduced the remaining Ayyubid possessions in Syria and drove the Crusaders from most of the Levant. He refortified nearly every important citadel in the region and endowed many public and pious foundations in Cairo, Damascus and Jerusalem. The Zahiriyya Madrasa in Cairo (1262–3; destr. 19th century), on a site of the eastern Fatimid palace, was built adjacent to and on the model of the madrasa and mausoleum of Baybars's master, al-Salih. The Syrian style portal, with striped masonry and a MUQARNAS vault, set the style for the period. Baybars's congregational mosque (1266–9; *see* CAIRO, §III, 7) was erected as part of the Sultan's campaign to break the Shafi'i monopoly on religious affairs. In Damascus he restored the Umayyad Mosque (1269) and built the famous Qasr al-Ablaq ('Striped Palace'; destr.). Baybars was buried in Damascus in the Dar al-'Aqiqi, a palatial residence immediately across from the Madrasa al-'Adiliya built by the ZANGID Nur al-Din (*reg* 1146–74); the residence was then transformed into the Zahiriyya Madrasa. The most notable parts of the building are its grand portal, an iwan preceding a small prayer-hall, and the mausoleum. The architect, Ibrahim b. Ghana'im, signed his name in the *muqarnas* vault of the portal, which resembles that of the lost Zahiriyya Madrasa in Cairo, and the same architect is known to have designed Baybars's in suburban Damascus. Bold inscriptions follow the yellow-and black-striped masonry across the portal, beneath an accomplished *muqarnas* vault. The lower part of the interior of the mausoleum is richly decorated with marble panelling and mosaic in marble and glass, recalling the techniques and style of decoration associated with the

Umayyad caliphs (*reg* AD 661–750; *see* UMAYYAD, §1). These were revived in the mid-13th century and further developed by a group of artisans assembled by Baybars to restore the Dome of the Rock (before 1272) and the Aqsa Mosque in Jerusalem; their use in Baybars's mausoleum linked it with those pious works.

Enc. Islam/2

BIBLIOGRAPHY
K. A. C. Creswell: *The Muslim Architecture of Egypt*, ii (Oxford, 1959), pp. 142–77
M. Meinecke: 'Das Mausoleum des Qala'un in Kairo: Untersuchungen zur Genese der mamlukischen Architekturdekoration', *Mitt. Dt. Archäol. Inst.: Abt. Kairo*, xxvii (1971), pp. 47–80
A.-A. al-Khowaiter: *Baybars the First* (London, 1978)
J. M. Bloom: 'The Mosque of Baybars al-Bunduqdārī in Cairo, *An. Islam.*, xviii (1982), pp. 45–78

(2) Qala'un [al-Manṣūr Sayf al-Dīn Qalā'ūn al-Alfi; Kalawun] (*b c.* 1220; *reg* 1280–90; *d* 11 Nov 1290). Like (1) Baybars I, Qala'un was a Qipchaq Turk bought for the service of the Ayyubid sultan al-Malik al-Salih. An ally of Baybars, Qala'un was active in the turbulent politics of the first decades of Mamluk rule, extending Baybars's campaign against the Crusaders and fighting the Nubians and the kings of Little Armenia. Qala'un also continued his predecessor's campaign of fortification, but is best known for his religious and charitable complex (1284–5; *see* CAIRO, §III, 8; *see also* ISLAMIC ART, fig. 56). Built in an unusually short time on the site of the western Fatimid palace, from which spolia were taken, Qala'un's complex comprises a madrasa, mausoleum and minaret, as well as a hospital, elementary school and fountain (largely destr.). The hospital was built to fulfil a vow Qala'un had made when he received treatment at the hospital established by the Zangid Nur al-Din (*reg* 1146–74) in Damascus. The octagonal plan of the mausoleum and its marble decoration were probably inspired by the Dome of the Rock in Jerusalem in an attempt to underscore Qala'un's claim to be heir to the glory of the Umayyad caliphs (*reg* AD 661–750; *see* UMAYYAD, §1).

BIBLIOGRAPHY
Enc. Islam/2: 'Kalāwūn'
K. A. C. Creswell: *The Muslim Architecture of Egypt*, ii (Oxford, 1959), pp. 190–212

Basin made for the Mamluk sultan al-Nasir Muhammad, brass inlaid with gold and silver, diam. 536 mm, from Egypt or Syria, *c.* 1330 (London, British Museum)

M. Meinecke: 'Das Mausoleum des Qala'un in Kairo: Untersuchungen zur Genese der mamlukischen Architekturdekoration', *Mitt. Dt. Archäol. Inst.: Abt. Kairo*, xxvii (1971), pp. 47–80

(3) Al-Nasir Muhammad [al-Nāṣir Nāṣir al-Dīn Muḥammad ibn Qalā'ūn] (*b* Cairo, 1285; *reg* 1293–4, 1299–1309 and 1310–41; *d* Cairo, 1341). Son of (2) Qala'un. His mother was the daughter of a Mongol immigrant. The child Muhammad was placed on the throne by a junta of amirs professing loyalty to the house of his father, but the Amir Kitbugha ((*reg* 1294–6) sent the youth into exile a year later. In 1299 he was brought back, only to withdraw in 1309, but he returned definitively in 1310 to rule for three decades of unparalleled peace and prosperity. Egyptian merchants took luxury goods to Saray Berke on the Volga, capital of the Golden Horde, the Mamluks' traditional ally against the ILKHANID dynasty of Iran, and brought back wood, fur and slaves. Tentative cultural and commercial contacts had already been established with the Ilkhanids, but the conclusion of a peace treaty in 1322 expanded them considerably, and Iranian craftsmen may have come to Cairo to work on architectural projects. In 1325 al-Nasir sent an expedition to assist the RASULID rulers of the Yemen, an important market for Egyptian inlaid metalwork and enamelled glass. He maintained a large harem and had many children; most of his eleven daughters married prominent amirs, and he was followed on the throne by eight of his sons, two of his grandsons and two of his great-grandsons.

An earthquake in 1303 and a great fire in 1321 encouraged new building in Cairo (*see* CAIRO, §I, 2), which was already burgeoning as a result of the canal al-Nasir had dug, allowing Cairo to spread to the west and engulf its former suburbs. Al-Nasir's passion for architecture amounted to a mania, and his patronage mixed a concern for civic improvement with aesthetic delight. Royal building in Cairo included a complex (1295–1304), which he took over from Kitbugha, next to that of Qala'un; it comprised a madrasa and his tomb. The Striped Palace (Qaṣr al-Ablaq) was al-Nasir's major undertaking in the Cairo citadel (*see* CAIRO, §III, 5), although only the adjoining mosque (1318; enlarged 1335) survives. Amirs such as Sayf al-Din Tankiz al-Husami (*d* 1340), Baktimur al-Silahdar (*d* 1300), Qawsun (*d* 1342) and Bashtak (*d* 1341) accumulated vast fortunes and emulated royal patronage on a smaller though still princely scale. Ibn Battuta (1304–*c.* 1370), the Moroccan traveller who visited Egypt during al-Nasir's reign, praised the Sultan's construction of a great Sufi convent outside Cairo and commented that his favoured amirs vied with one another in the founding of mosques and religious institutions. While governor of Damascus (1312–40), Tankiz erected or repaired 40 buildings in Syria; in Jerusalem he constructed in al-Nasir's name the long portico on the western side of the Haram enclosure and the Bab al-Qattanin (Gate of the Cotton Sellers), and the Dome of the Rock and the dome of the Aqsa Mosque were repaired.

Al-Nasir Muhammad was a prominent patron of the arts, partly because of his long reign. Bearing his name or attributed to him are about 30 inlaid brasses (see fig.), a dozen enamelled glass mosque lamps and a few single-volume copies of the Koran (e.g. Cairo, N. Lib., 4). The inlaid brasses include two boxes (Cairo, Al-Azhar Mosque, and Berlin, Mus. Islam. Kst) for 30-volume manuscripts of the Koran. During al-Nasir's long reign the figural compositions associated with inlaid metalwork in the Mosul style were increasingly supplanted by bold and majestic inscriptions bearing the patron's names and titles in *thuluth* script, and this new epigraphic style characterized most later Mamluk metalwork (*see* ISLAMIC ART, §IV, 3(iii)). This epigraphic style is also seen on enamelled glass mosque lamps bearing the names and titles of al-Nasir or other contemporary patrons (*see* ISLAMIC ART, §VIII, 5(ii)). Magnificent manuscripts of the Koran show the impact of contemporary Ilkhanid work, and a splendid 30-volume copy commissioned by the Ilkhanid ruler Uljaytu (Cairo, N. Lib., MS. 72) may have been one of the gifts Uljaytu's son exchanged with al-Nasir after the peace treaty was signed.

BIBLIOGRAPHY

Ibn Faḍl Allah al-'Umarī (d 1349): *Masālik al-abṣār fī mamālik al-amṣār* [Ways of seeing regarding provinces that have cities in them], i, ed. A. F. Sayyid (Cairo, 1985)
Aḥmad ibn 'Alī al-Maqrīzī (1364–1442): *al-Mawā'iẓ wa'l-i'tibār bi-dhikr al-khiṭaṭ wa'l-āthār* [Exhortations and consideration for the mention of districts and monuments], 2 vols (Cairo, 1853)
K. A. C. Creswell: *The Muslim Architecture of Egypt*, ii (Oxford, 1959), chap. 25
L. Golvin: 'Quelques Notes sur le Sūq al-Qaṭṭanīn et ses annexes à Jerusalem', *Bull. Etud. Orient.*, xx (1967), pp. 101–17
J. M. Rogers: 'Evidence for Mamluk-Mongol Relations, 1260–1360', *Colloque internationale sur l'histoire du Caire: Caire, 1969*, pp. 385–404
V. Meinecke-Berg: 'Quellen zur Topographie und Baugeschichte in Kairo unter Sultan an-Nāṣir b. Qalā'un', *Z. Dt. Mrgländ. Ges.*, suppl. 3 (xix, Deutscher Orientalistentag, 1975), pp. 538–50
J. W. Allan: *Islamic Metalwork: The Nuhad es-Said Collection* (London, 1982), nos 14–15
ROBERT IRWIN

(4) Baybars II [Rukn al-Dīn Baybars al-Jāshankīr] (*reg* 1309; *d* Cairo, 16 April 1310). Mamluk of (2) Qala'un. He was co-regent with the amir Salar (*d* 1310) for Qala'un's son (3) al-Nasir Muhammad during his second reign (1299–1309). Baybars then seized power for himself, but his reign lasted only until al-Nasir Muhammad could organize an army in Syria, return to Cairo and have Baybars strangled. Baybars's funerary complex in the eastern quarter of Cairo comprised a large Sufi convent (Arab. *khānaqāh*; 1306–10), begun while he was still regent, accompanied by a hospice (*ribāṭ*; destr.), housing 400 and 200 Sufis respectively. Some building materials, including decoration, were taken from a Fatimid palace on the site. Endowment documents describe the building and the operation of its institution in detail. Baybars also commissioned an unusually large seven-volume manuscript of the Koran (1304–6; London, BL, Add. MS. 22406–12) for the *khānaqāh*. Totalling well over 1000 folios, the manuscript was mentioned in the endowment deed and reportedly cost 1600 dinars. It was made by a team of artists comprising the calligrapher Ibn al-Wahid, the two master illuminators Sandal and Muhammad ibn Mubadir and their assistant Aydughdi ibn 'Abdallah al-Badri.

BIBLIOGRAPHY

Enc. Islam/2
K. A. C. Creswell: *The Muslim Architecture of Egypt*, ii (Oxford, 1959), pp. 249–54
D. James: 'Some Observations on the Calligraphers and Illuminators of the Koran of Rukn al-Din Baybars al-Jashnagir', *Muqarnas*, ii (1984), pp. 147–57

L. Fernandes: 'The Foundation of Baybars al-Jashankir: Its *Waqf*, History, and Architecture', *Muqarnas*, iv (1987), pp. 21–42
D. James: *Qur'āns of the Mamlūks*, no. 1 (New York, 1988)

(5) Hasan [Nāṣir al-Dīn Ḥasan] (*b* ?1336; *reg* 1347–51, 1354–61; *d* Cairo, 9 March 1362). Son of (3) al-Nasir Muhammad. The young Hasan was proclaimed sultan under the control of a regent. After a brief attempt at independence, he was deposed in favour of one of his brothers, then returned to power—again under the control of a series of senior amirs. He was again deposed and, only in his mid-twenties, murdered by a cabal of amirs. In addition to these internecine struggles, Hasan's reign was marked by wars against the kings of Little Armenia and in the Hijaz, and the appearance of the Black Death in Syria and Egypt. Hasan is best remembered for his mammoth funerary complex (1356–62; *see* CAIRO, §III, 9 and ISLAMIC ART, fig. 57) and its fine fittings, including dozens of enamelled glass lamps (*see* ISLAMIC ART, §VIII, 5(ii)) and a set of superb bronze-plated doors later expropriated by al-Mu'ayyad Shaykh for his complex (*see* DOOR, fig. 7). Many of the immense manuscripts of the Koran usually associated with the patronage of (6) Sha'ban II may have been intended for this building.

BIBLIOGRAPHY

Enc. Islam/2

(6) Sha'ban II [al-Ashraf Nāṣir al-Dīn Sha'bān II] (*b c.* 1353; *reg* 1363–77; *d* Cairo, March 1377). Son of (5) Hasan. During his reign, despite domestic strife, commerce grew with Venice, and Cilicia was conquered. Although Sha'ban was never independent of his regents, by the end of his reign he was deemed an effective and pious ruler but was murdered while trying to make the pilgrimage to Mecca. The structure in Cairo known as the madrasa of Umm al-Sultan Sha'ban (1369) was ordered, according to historical sources, by Sha'ban's mother Khwand Baraka, or, according to the inscriptions, by the Sultan himself for her. It comprises a portal, four-iwan madrasa and two mausolea with ribbed domes. Oversized for the narrow street on which it stands, the building has a striped façade that shows the increasing dryness and low relief characteristic of later Mamluk architecture. Sha'ban also built a complex (destr.) near the citadel with a *khānaqāh*, madrasa and mosque. His name also appears on a small number of enamelled glass and inlaid brass objects. Several huge and stunningly elaborate illuminated manuscripts of the Koran were completed during his reign and represent the best of Mamluk illumination. They feature double-page frontispieces and finispieces, elaborate chapter headings and marginal ornament lavishly executed in gold, along with lapis lazuli, red and other colours, and often employ geometric designs, based particularly on multi-pointed stars and the radial extensions of their sides.

BIBLIOGRAPHY

J. W. Allan: 'Sha'ban, Barquq and the Decline of the Mamluk Metalworking Industry', *Muqarnas*, ii (1984), pp. 85–94
C. Kessler: 'Mecca-oriented Urban Architecture in Mamluk Cairo: The Madrasa-mausoleum of Sultan Sha'ban II', *In Quest of an Islamic Humanism*, ed. A. H. Green (Cairo, 1984), pp. 98–108

(7) Barquq [al-Ẓāhir Sayf al-Dīn Barqūq ibn Anas] (*b* ?1336; *reg* 1382–9, 1390–99, *d* Cairo, 20 June 1399). Barquq was purchased in the Crimea and brought to Cairo during the reigns of the last descendants of (2) Qala'un and members of the Bahri line. He served the most powerful amirs and was involved in their intrigues, becoming the regent of yet another child sultan before seizing power for himself and becoming the first sultan of the Circassian or Burji line of Mamluks. Unseated and imprisoned briefly in Transjordan, he returned to Cairo within the year. Barquq was a powerful soldier and a contemporary and foe of Timur, but he did little else for Egypt except to build a large madrasa (1398) on the central artery of Cairo near the madrasas of al-Salih Najm al-Din Ayyub, Baybars I, Qala'un and al-Nasir Muhammad. The complex of Barquq comprises a mausoleum, minaret and four-iwan madrasa with residential and service rooms packed around the main elements. The interior of the mausoleum is richly panelled in marble, and the qibla wall of the prayer-hall also bears marble panelling, but otherwise the building is poor in marble, brass and fine wood, which were growing scarce in financially troubled 14th-century Egypt.

BIBLIOGRAPHY

Enc. Islam/2: 'Barḳūḳ'
M. Rogers: 'The Stones of Barqūq, *Apollo*, ciii (April 1976), pp. 307–13
S. L. Mostafa: *Madrasa, Hanqāh und Mausoleum des Barqūq in Kairo* (Glückstadt, 1982)
J. W. Allan: 'Sha'ban, Barquq and the Decline of the Mamluk Metalworking Industry', *Muqarnas*, ii (1984), pp. 85–94

(8) Faraj [al-Nāṣir Nāṣir al-Dīn Faraj] (*b* Cairo, 1389; *reg* 1399–1405, 1405–12; *d* Damascus, 28 May 1412). Son of (7) Barquq. His mother, Shirin, was Greek. He succeeded on Barquq's death and within five months emerged from the tutelage of the mamluk amirs. He was deposed briefly in 1405 and ultimately forced from the sultanate and executed by amirs he could not control. During his reign the finances of the Mamluk empire declined still further, amid the turmoil caused by the incessant conflict among the leading amirs. Faraj built a mosque and fountain (*sabīl*, 1408) in Cairo and a massive funerary *khānaqāh* (1400–11) in the eastern cemetery. An arcade connected the modest tomb of Barquq's father, Sharaf al-Din Anas, to the complex. The *khānaqāh* unusually has arcades around the courtyard and a hypostyle prayer-hall, which is flanked by two domed mausolea, one for himself, his father and his male relatives and the other for his female relatives. The mausolea feature openwork wooden screens, marble panelling, painted decoration and fine cenotaphs.

BIBLIOGRAPHY

Enc. Islam/2: 'Faradj'
S. L. Mostafa: *Kloster und Mausoleum des Farağ b. Barqūq* (Glückstadt, 1968)
——: *Moschee des Farağ ibn Barqūq in Kairo* (Glückstadt, 1972)

(9) Barsbay [al-Ashraf Sayf al-Dīn Barsbay] (*reg* 1422–38; *d* Cairo, 7 June 1438). Mamluk of (7) Barquq. He seized the sultanate and proclaimed a series of xenophobic, discriminatory and oppressive policies. Achieving victory in a campaign against Cyprus, he attained only stalemate in a war with the Aqqoyunlu in upper Mesopotamia. Barsbay escaped the most common fate of Mamluk sultans, deposition and execution, by dying of the plague. The economic decline of Egypt at this time may be judged by the remark of the Mamluk antiquarian al-Maqrizi (*d* 1442) that while brasswork inlaid with silver had been popular, in his day only a few metalworkers still produced such vessels, and others bought up inlaid vessels to remove

their precious inlays. Maqrizi's observations are borne out by the quantity and quality of most surviving pieces, and many tinned copper vessels were produced as the brass-working industry declined. Barsbay nevertheless commissioned several magnificent manuscripts of the Koran (Cairo, N. Lib.), which were endowed to his madrasa (1424), one of three extant buildings he founded. The complex, in the centre of Fatimid Cairo, comprised a public fountain, primary school minaret, mausoleum and four-iwan madrasa. An original ceiling that has survived in the iwan opposite the qibla iwan is a colourful and richly gilded composition of gored domelets and intersecting six-lobed rosettes filled with strapwork and arabesque. Barsbay's mausoleum, mosque and *khānaqāh* in the eastern cemetery (1432) was an immense structure, conventional in design and ornament, but only part of it is preserved. He also ordered a congregational mosque (1437) in the town of al-Khanka north of Cairo.

BIBLIOGRAPHY

Enc. Islam/2
Aḥmad ibn 'Alī al-Maqrīzī (1364–1442): *al-Mawā'iz wa'l-i'tibār bi-dhikr al-khiṭaṭ wa'l-āthār* [Exhortations and consideration for the mention of districts and monuments], 2 vols (Cairo, 1853)
A. Darrag: *L'Egypte sous le règne de Barsbay* (Damascus, 1961)
L. E. Fernandes: 'Three Sufi Foundations in a Fifteenth-century *Wakfiya*', *An. Islam.*, xvii (1981), pp. 141–56

□

(10) Qa'itbay [al-Ashraf Sayf al-Dīn Qā'itbāy al-Ẓāhirī] (*b c.* 1413; *reg* 1468–96; *d* Cairo, 1496). Purchased in 1435 by (9) Barsbay, he rose steadily in the Mamluk hierarchy until Timurbugha (*reg* Dec 1467–Feb 1468) appointed him commander-in-chief. After Timurbugha's deposition, Qa'itbay was acclaimed sultan and reigned until he abdicated in favour of his son the day before his death. Qa'itbay was highly cultured and personally austere: he wrote poetry and mystic litanies in Arabic, Arabic-Turkish and Turkish. His architectural patronage, for which surviving endowment deeds are an important but not always reliable source, extended throughout the realm and supported religious aims. The most important of his extant works in Cairo include the madrasa and mausoleum in the northern cemetery (1472–4; *see* CAIRO, §III, 10 and ISLAMIC ART, fig. 58), another madrasa at Qal'at al-Kabsh (1475–6) and a third on Roda Island (1481–90), a water-dispensary and Koran-school (1479) and two caravanserais (1477 and 1480), as well as a new gate and minaret for the Azhar Mosque and minbars for the *khānaqāh* of Faraj and the mosque of Mu'ayyad Shaykh. In Jerusalem Qa'itbay sponsored the Ashrafiyya Madrasa (1482) and an exquisite fountain (1482; see fig.) inside the Haram enclosure. Mamluks of German origin are said to have built Qa'itbay's fort in Alexandria (1477–99). In the 1470s and 1480s he had parts of the Prophet's mosque in Medina restored, and over the following years he founded madrasas in Mecca and Medina and a string of hostels along the pilgrimage route. European pilgrims report that he was unusually tolerant of Christian rebuilding in Jerusalem and Bethlehem. The cultivated grand amirs were also important literary and architectural patrons. The palace of Yashbak min Mahdi (*d* 1482) in the Matariyya district of Cairo made a great impression on visiting Europeans, and the architectural foundations he constructed were admired by contemporaries.

Deeply incised and elaborately carved tracery patterns are commonly found on the façades and domes of Qa'itbay's buildings, and his wooden minbars (e.g. London, V&A) have unusually elaborate inlay. Many of the designs are also found in the fine illuminated manuscripts commissioned by the Sultan. A distinct revival of inlaid metalwork occurred during his reign, although the engraving was not as elaborate as the work of earlier centuries (*see* ISLAMIC ART, §IV, 3(iii)(b)). Knotted carpets may also have been produced during his reign, for the composite heraldic emblem peculiar to the Sultan and two of his mamluks appears on some carpets (*see* ISLAMIC ART, §VI, 4(iii)(b)).

BIBLIOGRAPHY

Enc. Islam/2: 'Ḳā'it Bāy'

Ibn Iyās (1448–*c.* 1524): *Badā'i' al-zuhūr fī-waqā'i' al-duhūr* [The wonders of blossoms concerning events of the times], iii, ed. P. Kahle and M. Mustafa (Istanbul, 1936); Fr. trans. by G. Wiet as *Histoire des Mamlouks circassiens* (Cairo, 1945)

L. A. Mayer: *The Buildings of Qaytbay as Described in his Endowment Deed* (London, 1938)

A. S. Melikian-Chirvani: 'Cuivres inédits de l'époque de Qa'itbay', *Kst Orients*, vi (1969), pp. 99–133

O. Grabar: 'The Inscriptions of the Madrasah–mausoleum of Qaytbay', *Near Eastern Numismatics, Iconography, Epigraphy and History: Studies in Honor of George C. Miles*, ed. D. Kouymjian (Beirut, 1974), pp. 465–8

S. Tamari: 'Al-Ashrafiyya: An Imperial Madrasa in Jerusalem', *Atti & Mem. Accad. N. Lincei, Atti Cl. Sci. Morali*, xix (1976), pp. 537–68

C. Kessler and M. Burgoyne: 'The Fountain of Sultan Qaytbay in the Sacred Precinct of Jerusalem', *Archaeology in the Levant: Essays for Kathleen Kenyon*, ed. R. Moore and P. Parr (Warminster, 1977), pp. 251–68

D. Behrens-Abouseif: 'The North-eastern Extension of Cairo under the Mamluks', *An. Islam.*, xvii (1981), pp. 157–90

C. Petry: 'A Paradox of Patronage during the Later Mamluk Period', *Muslim World*, lxxiii (1983), pp. 182–207

A. W. Newhall: *The Patronage of the Mamluk Sultan Qa'it Bay, 872–901/1468–1496* (diss., Cambridge, MA, Harvard U., 1987)

A. G. Walls: *Geometry and Architecture in Islamic Jerusalem: A Study of the Ashrafiyya* (London, 1990)

C. F. Petry: *Twilight of Majesty: The Reigns of the Mamlūk Sultans al-Ashraf Qāytbāy and Qānṣūh al-Ghawrī in Egypt* (Seattle and London, 1993)

ROBERT IRWIN

(11) Qansuh [Kansawh] **al-Ghawri** [al-Ashraf Qānṣūh al-Ghawrī] (*b c.* 1440; *reg* 1501–16; *d* Marj Dabiq, 24 Aug 1516). Circassian mamluk of (10) Qa'itbay. He served in many positions of authority around the Mamluk empire before being elevated to the sultanate at the age of 60. His death in battle with the Ottomans north of Aleppo spelt the end of the Mamluk empire. Despite the precarious finances and deteriorating military situation, Qansuh followed Qa'itbay's lead in building in Cairo (*see* ISLAMIC ART, §II, 6(iii)(a)). His works include several mosques, an aqueduct, a gate to a covered market, a large commercial building (Arab. *wakāla*) and his most imposing work, a pair of buildings that includes his madrasa, his mausoleum, a public fountain, a primary school, a *khānaqāh* and a palace (1503–4). The exterior design and decoration of these paired buildings is a somewhat less successful version of that of the Qa'itbay complex, although their siting and arrangement are well calculated for maximum impact on the passer-by. The Sultan, a bibliophile who could read Persian, had many copies of the *Shāhnāma* ('Book of kings') in his library. He commissioned a Turkish translation of the text from the poet Sharif Amidi, and a copy (Cairo, 1511; Istanbul, Topkapı Pal. Lib., H. 1519) was

Fountain inside the Haram enclosure, Jerusalem, 1482; sponsored by Qa'itbay

illustrated with 62 paintings modelled on those in his Persian copies (e.g. Istanbul, Topkapı Pal. Lib., H. 1506) with added Egyptian details of architecture, furniture and costume. He also commissioned an anthology of Turkish poetry including some of his own verses (Berlin, Staatsbib., MS Or. Oct. 3744), and the frontispiece was probably painted by one of the artists who worked on the *Shāhnāma* (*see* ISLAMIC ART, §III, 4(v)(a)).

BIBLIOGRAPHY

Enc. Islam/2: 'Ḳānṣawh al-Ghawrī'

E. Atıl: 'Mamluk Painting in the Later Fifteenth Century', *Muqarnas*, ii (1984), pp. 159–71

C. F. Petry: *Twilight of Majesty: The Reigns of the Mamlūk Sultans al-Ashraf Qāytbāy and Qānṣūh al-Ghawrī in Egypt* (Seattle and London, 1993)

☐

Mammisi [Copt.: 'place of birth']. Type of small temple that first appeared in Egypt in the 30th Dynasty (380–343 BC) and became a common feature of Egyptian temple complexes in the Greco-Roman period (332 BC–AD 395). The name was invented by the French Egyptologist Jean-François Champollion (1790–1832) to describe the buildings devoted to the birth rites of the mother-goddess (usually Isis or Hathor). The birth house was invariably an annexe within the enclosure wall of a large temple such as those at Edfu, Dendara, Philae and Armant. The concept of such a building developed out of the birth scenes of Queen Hatshepsut (*reg c.* 1479–*c.* 1458 BC) at the Deir el-Bahri temple and the birth chamber of Amenophis III (*reg c.* 1390–*c.* 1353 BC) at the Luxor temple (*see* THEBES (i), §§III and IV). The rites of the goddess, as she gave birth to her son Horus or Ihy, followed on from the rites performed in the chambers associated with the god Osiris.

The plan of the *mammisi* developed from the peripteral temple of the New Kingdom (*see* EGYPT, ANCIENT, §VIII, 2(i)), and the small temple at El-Kab (dedicated by Tuthmosis III to the vulture-goddess Nekhbet) may have been a prototype for it. The basic plan is rectangular, with an ambulatory (often columned) surrounding the sanctuary. Two *mammisi*s were constructed at DENDARA, one dating to the reign of Nectanebo I (*reg* 380–362 BC) and the other to the reigns of Trajan (*reg* AD 98–117) and Hadrian (*reg* AD 117–38). The *mammisi* of Nectanebo I consists of a court, paved with various stones including basalt and alabaster, surrounded by a low wall and entered through a palmiform screen. An open hall leads to a sanctuary, in which the decoration shows Amun, instead of Horus, as father of Ihy, son of Hathor. The scenes, similar to those in other *mammisi*s, include Amun announcing the birth of Ihy, the god Khnum modelling the child on a potter's wheel, Khnum and Thoth leading Hathor to the birthplace, Amun recognizing the child, Thoth promising long life and many jubilees, the child being nourished and enthroned before the Ennead (a group of nine divinities) of Karnak, and Anubis rolling the full moon along to assure the child's future. The figures in the decoration of the earliest Dendara *mammisi* were covered in a thin sheet of gold leaf held in place by gum.

The Roman *mammisi* at Dendara has a columned screen wall surrounding the main structure in order to obscure the view of processions within. The temple includes guardian sphinxes, a hall of offering, a sanctuary, stairs to the roof and crypts. A type of column peculiar to the *mammisi* is one with a composite capital surmounted by a block with the figure of Bes, god of births, on all four sides, found at Edfu and Dendara. At the Philae *mammisi* the column incorporates the figure of Hathor instead.

LÄ

BIBLIOGRAPHY
M. de Rochemonteix and E. Chassinat: *Le Temple d'Edfou* (Paris, 1892; Cairo, 1918–)
G. Benedite: *Le Temple de Philae*, 2 fascs (Paris, 1893–95)
F. Daumas: *Les Mammisis de Dendara* (Cairo, 1959)
H. Junker and E. Winter: *Das Geburtshaus des Tempels der Isis in Philä* (Vienna, 1965)

ANN BOMANN

Mamontov, Savva (Ivanovich) (*b* Yalutorovsk, Tyumen' Province, 15 Oct 1841; *d* Moscow, 6 April 1918). Russian industrialist and patron. He was educated at the Mining Institute in St Petersburg and the Law Faculty of Moscow University. He made his fortune in the building of the railways. During the 1870s he spent a few years in Italy studying painting and art history and taking singing lessons. In Rome and Paris Mamontov met and became friends with the painters Vasily Polenov and Il'ya Repin, the sculptor Mark Antokol'sky and the art historian Adrian Prakhov (1846–1916). This group formed the foundation of the circle at the estate of ABRAMTSEVO, which Mamontov purchased in 1870.

Mamontov invited numerous artists to Abramtsevo, and they were inspired by the creative atmosphere and the picturesque surroundings. Some of them lived and worked there for a large part of the summer, and among the works painted there were Valentin Serov's *Girl with Peaches*

(1887), Mikhail Nesterov's *Vision of the Boy Bartholomew* (1889–90) and Viktor Vasnetsov's series of fairytale paintings (*Alyonushchka, Bogatyrs* etc; for illustration *see* VASNETSOV, VIKTOR). Mamontov's opinions were highly valued among the artists, as was his ability to inspire. According to Viktor Vasnetsov, 'there was in him a sort of electric current that ignited other people's energies. God gave him a special talent for stimulating the creativity of others' (Pakhomov, p. 112).

The first museum of Russian folk art was opened in Abramtsevo in May 1885. All the members of the Abramtsevo circle took part in collecting items for the museum, a particularly large contribution being made by Mamontov's wife Yelizaveta Mamontova and the artist Yelena Polenova. The desire for a collective creative effort on the part of the members of the circle led to the building of the Abramtsevo Church (1881–2), which was designed by Viktor Vasnetsov and makes deliberate use of medieval Russian architecture. Vasnetsov, Repin, Antokol'sky, Polenov and Nikolay Nevrev all contributed to the decoration of the church and the painting of the iconostasis, in which the images of the saints resemble ancient Russian epic heroes or hermits.

Mamontov also organized theatrical performances at Abramtsevo, in which the performers included not only artists but also such leading figures of the theatre as Konstantin Stanislavsky. Out of this developed Mamontov's idea of creating the first privately owned Moscow opera, to which he devoted several hundred thousand roubles as well as his organizational abilities. The opera was opened in 1885. In contrast to the established opera companies, Mamontov regarded his opera as a synthesis of the arts, and accordingly he attracted not only such prominent musicians as the singer Fyodor Shalyapin [Chaliapin] and the composers Sergey Rachmaninov and Mikhail Ippolitov-Ivanov, but also equally outstanding artists such as Serov, Konstantin Korovin, Aleksandr Golovin, Isaak Levitan and Mikhail Vrubel'. This project originated the concept of the 'theatre artist' in Russia. Mamontov's opera was noted for its innovative style and its use of Russian national motifs.

WRITINGS
Vospominaniya o russkikh khudozhnikakh [Memoirs of Russian artists] (Moscow, 1950)

BIBLIOGRAPHY
N. Pakhomov: *Abramtsevo* (Moscow, 1958)
D. Z. Kogan: *Mamontovskiy kruzhok* [The Mamontov circle] (Moscow, 1970)
M. Kopshitser: *Savva Mamontov* (Moscow, 1972)
For further bibliography *see* ABRAMTSEVO.

OXANA CLEMINSON

Mamoru Yamada. *See* YAMADA, MAMORU.

Mampukuji. *See* MANPUKUJI.

Mamurra. *See under* VITRUVIUS.

Man, Felix H(ans) [Baumann, Hans Felix Siegismund] (*b* Freiburg im Breisgau, 30 Nov 1893; *d* London, 30 Jan 1985). British photographer, writer and collector of German birth. He began to study fine art and art history in Munich and Berlin in 1912, but had to interrupt his studies in 1914 on the outbreak of World War I. While serving as an officer at the front he began to take photographs. He resumed his studies in 1918 and in 1926 moved to Berlin, where he worked as an illustrator. Soon he gave up drawing and concentrated on photography, adopting his professional name in 1929. Between 1929 and 1934 he worked for the *Münchner Illustrierte Presse* and the *Berliner Illustrierte Zeitung*, for which he travelled all over Europe and North Africa and spent eight months in Canada.

Man was a leading photojournalist who contributed particularly to what later became known as 'candid camera' photography. His use of the light available instead of a flash made him unobtrusive, allowing him to catch his subjects unawares. Forced out of Germany by the Nazis, Man emigrated in 1934 to London, where he co-founded the *Weekly Illustrated* and worked for the *Daily Mirror* and later for the *Picture Post*. He also contributed to *Life Magazine* and to the *Sunday Times*. In 1958 he moved to Switzerland, later settling in Rome. In his later life he devoted most of his time to collecting and writing about lithographs, on which he became a leading authority.

WRITINGS
150 Years of Artists' Lithographs, introduction J. Laver (London, 1953)
Artists' Lithographs: A World History from Senefelder to the Present Day (London and New York, 1970)

BIBLIOGRAPHY
Felix H. Man: Photographs and Picture Stories, 1915–1975 (exh. cat., Stockholm, Fot. Mus., 1975)
Felix H. Man: 60 Years of Photography (exh. cat., foreword C. M. Kauffmann, London, V&A, 1983)

ASTRID SCHMETTERLING

Manaku (*b* Guler, *c.* 1700; *d c.* 1760). Indian painter, elder son of the painter PANDIT SEU and brother of NAINSUKH. Manaku figures in the controversial colophon of a famous *Gīta Govinda* series of 1730. Although no place name is given in the colophon, it is more than likely that Manaku continued to work near his father in the small but lively principality of Guler. In 1736 he appears to have gone on a pilgrimage to Hardwar, where he made an entry in the priest's register in his own hand, using the Takri hill-script. Two portraits of Manaku have survived (Chandigarh, Govt Mus. & A.G.; New Delhi, N. Mus.). The earlier shows him as a mature man of about 40, wirily built, with an erect stance and a thin, remarkably sensitive face. The appearance is noble and notably self-assured. On his forehead Manaku wears the prominent caste-mark of a devout person, a double crescent line with a dot below it. The second portrait shows Manaku decidedly heavier and older, aged somewhere between 55 and 60. In this portrait he again appears simply but elegantly dressed; a prominent jewelled bracelet on his right wrist is perhaps a token of royal favour brought in carefully by the painter. Nothing more is known of Manaku's movements, and there are no dated works bearing his name after 1730. His name appears on two other paintings: one, *Krishna Playing Blind Man's Buff with his Friends* (*c.* 1750–55; New York, Kronos Col.), is ascribed to him; the other (*c.* 1760s; London, V&A), by an unknown artist, mentions that he rewarded the painter with a gold ring set with a precious stone.

The development of Manaku's work paralleled that of his father in many ways: an initial adherence to the basic vocabulary of the family style; then a very carefully considered response to the stimulus of naturalism while staying within the framework of the family style; and finally an accentuated spurt towards that naturalism, opening up new possibilities for the next generation. Manaku did not, however, start from the point where his father left off but went through all his own stages of growth and development. His earlier work, the *Siege of Lanka* series of *c.* 1725 (examples in Boston, MA, Mus. F.A.; Bombay, Prince of Wales Mus.) and *Gīta Govinda* of 1730 (examples in Chandigarh, Govt Mus. & A.G.; Karachi, N. Mus. Pakistan; Lahore Mus.), already shows him as a master turning out paintings that are at once majestic and innovative. He seems to have been a thinking painter, delighting in taking on fresh, untouched subjects and conceiving a series of works in densely packed sequences, and was practically the inventor of the youthful, lively Krishna so often seen as a divine lover in Pahari paintings. He also visualized a grand series on the *Bhāgavata purāṇa* theme (examples in Chandigarh, Govt Mus. & A.G.; Lahore Mus.; Udaipur, Rajasthan Orient. Res. Inst.), treating early sections that were never before, and have seldom since, been depicted. The series was left unfinished, later episodes existing only in the form of drawings. Manaku's sense of colour was impeccable, his line always firm and fluent. Where the narrative allows no change of locale, he shifted the elements—water, trees and rocks—in the composition with consummate ease. Capable from a very young age of rendering studied individual figures, he did not use these gifts indiscriminately, adhering to iconic forms in the treatment of myths. In the minor characters, however, he brought his powers of observation into play, turning out sensitive character studies of men of different ranks and callings, combining gravity with liveliness. There is in Manaku's work great energy, but also a certain restraint; deep emotion, but no sentimentality. He had two sons, Fattu and Khushala, who were also painters.

See also INDIAN SUBCONTINENT, §V, 4(iv).

BIBLIOGRAPHY
M. S. Randhawa: *Basohli Painting* (New Delhi, 1959)
M. C. Beach: 'A Bhagavata Purana from the Punjab Hills and Related Paintings', *Bull. Mus. F.A., Boston*, lxiii (1965)
W. G. Archer: *Indian Paintings from the Punjab Hills*, i (London, 1973)
F. S. Aijazuddin: *Pahari Paintings and Sikh Portraits in the Lahore Museum* (London, 1977)
B. N. Goswamy: *Essence of Indian Art* (San Francisco, 1986)
Pahari Masters: Court Painters of Northern India (exh. cat. by B. N. Goswamy and E. Fischer, Zurich, Mus. Rietberg, 1992), pp. 239–66

B. N. GOSWAMY

Manalt, Antonio Viladomat y. *See* VILADOMAT Y MANALT, ANTONIO.

Manara, Baldassare (*fl* 1526; *d* Faenza, 1546–7). Italian potter. He was a member of an important family of maiolica potters in Faenza; his father Giuliano Manara and his uncle Sebastiano worked in Faenza, as several documents prove. Baldassare was one of the most eminent artists working in Faenza during the first half of the 16th century. A series of documents refer to his workshop in the S Clemente district of the city, and he left many works, signed with the monogram BM or his signature in full, dated between 1528 and 1542. Manara was an exponent of the *istoriato* (narrative) genre, in which despite being inspired by many of Raphael's subjects taken from prints, he also derived some elements of form and colour from *istoriato* maiolica made in Urbino (as in a shallow bowl decorated with the *Triumph of Time*, 1530–35; Oxford, Ashmolean). Historians often regard Manara as the single greatest influence on maiolica production in Faenza during the second *istoriato* period.

BIBLIOGRAPHY

C. Grigioni: 'Documenti relativi alla famiglia Manara', *Faenza*, xx (1932), pp. 152–80
G. Liverani: 'Sul disco di B. Manara con l'effigie di Battistone Castellini', *Faenza*, xxviii (1940), pp. 78–82

CARMEN RAVANELLI GUIDOTTI

Mañara Vicentelo de Leca, Miguel (*bapt* Seville, 3 March 1627; *d* Seville, 9 May 1679). Spanish patron, painter and writer. He was the most remarkable of the patrons of the Baroque period in Seville. He came from a wealthy family, and his father owned an unremarkable collection of paintings. Mañara was a painter of some ability; his works were in several Sevillian collections. He led a dissolute existence until a series of family deaths prompted him to repent and adopt a devout and ascetic way of life. In 1662 he joined the Hermandad de la Santa Caridad, a Sevillian confraternity dedicated to providing Christian burial for criminals condemned to death. The following year he was elected head of the brotherhood, retaining the post until his death. Under Mañara's leadership the brotherhood became a dominant spiritual and social force in caring for the sick and poor of Seville. He oversaw all aspects of the society's activities, from writing the new rule to raising funds for new buildings. He paid close attention to the completion and decoration of the church in the Hospital de la Caridad (*see* SEVILLE, §IV, 4). The church of the Hospital de la Caridad was finished in 1670, and Mañara commissioned Bartolomé Esteban Murillo to decorate the nave with six paintings: *Moses Sweetening the Waters of Mara* and the *Miracle of the Loaves and Fishes* (both *in situ*), the *Prodigal Son* (Washington, DC, N.G.A.), *Christ Healing the Sick at the Pool of Bethesda* (London, N.G.), the *Liberation of St Peter* (St Petersburg, Hermitage) and *Abraham and the Three Angels* (Ottawa, N.G.). Bernardo Simón de Pineda won the competition for the principal retable in 1670 (completed by 1674), which established a new type in Seville. The central sculpture on the retable of the *Entombment* (*in situ*) was by Pedro Roldán, and the polychroming and gilding were by Juan de Valdés Leal. In 1672 Valdés Leal painted his two masterpieces for the church, *In Ictu oculi* (*see* VALDÉS LEAL, (1), fig. 2) and *Finis gloriae mundi* (known as the 'Hieroglyphs of Death'), located under the raised choir at the entrance, and Murillo added the altarpieces *St John of God Assisting a Sick Man* and *St Elizabeth of Hungary Tending the Sick* (both *in situ*). In 1674 a church inventory set out the decorative programme. The six nave paintings by Murillo, together with the *Entombment* on the principal retable, represent the six biblical acts of mercy, the sacred prototypes for the activities of the brotherhood. The two paintings by Valdés Leal illustrate the worthlessness of worldly ambitions and the inevitable conquest of Man's vanity by Death, as well as indicating the necessity to lead a life of charity in order to achieve salvation. These extraordinary images illustrate the ideas of Mañara as presented in his *Discurso de la verdad* (1671). Mañara possessed unusual aesthetic sensitivity in selecting the artist temperamentally suited to a particular subject. Murillo, Valdés Leal and Simón de Pineda were members of the brotherhood. They understood Mañara's philosophy and translated it brilliantly into their individual media.

BIBLIOGRAPHY

J. de Cardenas: *Breve relación de la muerte, vida y virtudes del venerable caballero D. Miguel de Mañara Vicentelo de Leca* (Seville, 1679)
F. de Borja Palomo: *Noticia histórica de la Santa Casa de la Caridad de Sevilla y de los principales objetos artísticos que en ella se conservan* (Seville, 1862)
F. Collantes de Terán y Delorme: *Memorias históricas de loas establecimientos de Caridad de Sevilla y descripción artística de los mismos* (Seville, 1884)
J. Gestoso y Pérez: *Sevilla monumental y artística*, iii (Seville, 1892)
C. López Martínez: 'La Hermandad de la Santa Caridad y el venerable Mañara', *Archv Hispal.*, ii (1943), pp. 25–48
J. M. Granejo: *D. Miguel Mañara* (Seville, 1963)
J. Brown: 'Hieroglyphs of Death and Salvation: The Decorations of the Church of the Hermanadad de la Caridad, Seville', *A. Bull.*, lxxxv (1970), pp. 265–77
E. Valdivieso and J. M. Serrera: *El Hospital de la Caridad de Sevilla* (Seville, 1980)

DUNCAN KINKEAD

Manastir. *See* BITOLJ.

Manaure, Mateo (*b* Uracoa, Monagas, 18 Oct 1926). Venezuelan painter and graphic designer. He studied painting at the Escuela de Artes Plásticas in Caracas (1942–6). At the age of 21 he won the highest award for national painters and went to France. He was a member of the Venezuelan group in Paris, Los Disidentes, who opposed traditional Venezuelan landscape painting. At this time he produced works of an abstract–lyrical tendency, which he varied so that they approached geometric abstraction. In 1952 he returned to Caracas, where, between 1953 and 1955, he executed a series of murals for the university campus. In 1957, with the sculptor Carlos González Bogen (*b* 1920), he founded in Caracas the Cuatro Muros gallery, with the purpose of propagating abstract art in Venezuela. Manaure was also one of the pioneers of graphic design in Venezuela. In 1958–67 he returned to easel painting, with works whose lyrical figuration and subjective landscapes border on the oneiric. Subsequently his art began to show the influence of Constructivism (e.g. *Polychromed Columns*, 1976; Caracas, Mus. A. Contemp.). This continued to rival his earlier lyricism as the dominant element in his work.

BIBLIOGRAPHY

Diccionario de las artes visuales en Venezuela, i (Caracas, 1973), p. 143
C. Barceló: *De la abstracción a la figuración: El cambio de tendencia en cuatro pintores venezolanos* (diss., Caracas, U. Central de Venezuela, 1988)

CRUZ BARCELÓ CEDEÑO

Mancadan, Jacobus Sibrandi (*b* Minnertsga, Friesland, *c.* 1602; *d* Tjerkgaast, Friesland, 4 Oct 1680). Dutch painter and government official. He married in 1634 and served as burgomaster of Franeker from 1637 to 1639 and of Leeuwarden in 1645. His primary occupation, however, was painting, and in 1648 he paid for the purchase of a house in Leeuwarden with some of his own pictures. He was buried in Leeuwarden.

Mancadan, who possibly started his career as a painter in middle age, had a highly individual style. He painted

Jacobus Sibrandi Mancadan: *Peat-cutting at Wildervank near Groningen*, oil on canvas, 1.31×1.82 m, *c.* 1650 (Groningen, Groninger Museum)

two types of landscapes: Italianate and native Dutch. Among the first group are a number of Arcadian subjects, including a scene from P. C. Hooft's play, *Granida and Daifilo* (Groningen, Groninger Mus.). Other scenes of shepherds with their flocks near ruins may also have been intended as illustrations to pastoral literature. He was apparently inspired by the early landscapes of Salvator Rosa, although there is no evidence that he ever travelled to Italy. The second group of landscapes depicts the local Frisian countryside: these include a *Landscape with Farms in Friesland* (Leeuwarden, Fries Mus.); a woodland view; and a seascape that may have been painted on the Zuyder Zee coast of Friesland. Mancadan's large painting of *Peat-cutting at Wildervank near Groningen* (Groningen, Groninger Mus.; see fig.), a subject rarely depicted by his contemporaries, occupies a special place within his oeuvre, since he owned a part share in a peat-bog in south-eastern Friesland. His compositions are typified by a scheme of diagonals, with a massive group of mountains or a ruin on one side, flanked by a distant view, with a few figures or animals acting as a foil. The mountainous landscapes, with or without ruins, usually include goats and sheep or cows. His figures can always be recognized by their strangely crooked posture. His subdued palette of browns and greens for the landscapes and ruins is enlivened only by the occasional use of red in the shepherds' clothing. Only a few of the paintings are fully signed; others are monogrammed, but most are unsigned.

The inventory of Mancadan's estate (part of the van Harinxma thoe Slooten family archive; Leeuwarden, Rijksarchf Friesland) includes over 100 paintings and more than 300 drawings. Many of these, depicting landscapes with animals, were probably by him. The only named artists in the inventory are his Frisian contemporaries Margaretha de Heer (*fl* 1650) and Guilliaum de Heer (*d* 1681). He also possessed a considerable collection of books on historical and theological subjects, including Classical texts as well as later Latin and Italian books and contemporary sources on the new Dutch Republic.

BIBLIOGRAPHY

A. Heppner: 'J. S. Mancadan: Neue Funde, sein Leben und sein Werk betreffend', *Oud-Holland*, li (1934), pp. 210–17

C. Boschma: 'Nieuwe gegevens omtrent J. S. Mancadan', *Oud-Holland*, lxxxi (1966), pp. 84–106

C. BOSCHMA

Mancheng [Man-Ch'eng]. Site of two royal Western Han (220 BC–AD 9) tombs in south-western Mancheng County, Hebei Province, China. The tombs were discovered in 1968 at the end of passages cut 53 m into the solid rock hillside. From inscriptions on some of the bronze burial goods the tombs have been attributed to Liu Sheng, Prince Jing of Zhongshan (*d* 113 BC), a son of Emperor Jingdi (*reg* 157–141 BC), and to his wife, Dou Wan.

The tombs are a good early example of the horizontal pit grave that gradually replaced the older vertical pit grave (*see* CHINA, §II, 6(ii)). Both tombs are laid out on a palatial

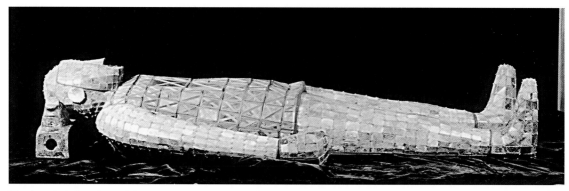

Mancheng, jade funeral suit of the princess Dou Wan, l. 1.71 m, Western Han period, 220 BC–AD 9 (Baoding, Hebei Provincial Museum)

scale: Liu Sheng's measures *c.* 52×37 m in area. They face east and have huge central banqueting and audience halls, stabling for horses and storerooms. The wings and central chambers, wooden with tiled roofs, imitate contemporary architecture. The burial chambers are lined with stone slabs, and the coffins are of lacquered wood with jade inlay on a marble bed. Tomb 1 contained sixteen horses and six chariots, the axles and shafts of which were decorated with gold and silver, some inlaid with precious stones, and Tomb 2 contained thirteen horses and four chariots.

The approximately 3000 objects from the two tombs are varied and rich, among the most impressive found in any Han burial. They include cooking utensils, earthenware dishes, weights, bronzes, lacquerware, stone and pottery figures, silks, gold and silver, weaponry, jades, ceramics and armour (*see* CHINA, §XIII, 1). Two small leopards, decorated in parcel gilt and inlaid with hardstones, gold and silver, acted as weights to hold down the funeral pall of one tomb occupant; four leopards were found in total. A bronze lamp (h. 480 mm; Baoding, Hebei Prov. Mus.), a masterpiece of bronze sculptural art, depicts a maidservant holding a lamp in her left hand, with her right hand and arm acting as the lampshade and smoke flue. The inscription 'Changxin Palace' indicates it was made for royalty; it was probably inherited by Dou Wan. Another notable bronze item is a *boshan* incense burner (h. *c.* 250 mm; Baoding, Hebei Prov. Mus.), with a lid shaped like a mountain peak (representing the Daoist Immortals' home) and pierced with holes for the smoke to escape. It is inlaid with gold and beautifully decorated with miniature animals and birds in a landscape setting. (For further discussion of bronzes from the Mancheng tombs *see* CHINA, §VI, 3(v)(b) and fig. 166.)

The jade burial suits from these two tombs illustrate the contemporary belief that jade prevents the body from decomposing and thus enables the deceased to enjoy an afterlife. The use of burial suits was restricted to the upper classes. According to sumptuary regulations, emperors' suits were sewn with gold thread, those of princes with silver and those of concubines and sisters of empresses with bronze thread; the reconstructed suits of Liu Sheng and Dou Wan were sewn with gold, indicating the general lack of observance of such laws. Liu Sheng's suit was 1.88 m long and comprised 2498 pieces, while Dou Wan's

was 1.71 m long, containing 2160 pieces (see fig.). They were constructed by means of sewing through small holes in the corners of each piece. It has been estimated that it probably took ten years' labour to produce such made-to-measure suits.

BIBLIOGRAPHY
J. J. M. de Groot: *The Religious System of China*, i (Leiden, 1892/*R* Taiwan, 1964), pp. 269–74, 277–9
'Mancheng Han mu fajue jiyao' [Brief record of the excavation of the Han tombs at Mancheng], *Kaogu* [Archaeology] (1972), no. 1, pp. 8–18, 28
'Mancheng Han mu "Jinlü yuyi" de qingli he fuyuan' [Conservation and restoration of the jade costumes sewn with gold thread from the Han tombs at Mancheng], *Kaogu* [Archaeology] (1972), no. 2, pp. 39–47
J. Fontein and Tung Wu: *Unearthing China's Past* (Boston, 1973)
Mancheng Han mu fajue baogao [Excavation report of the Han tombs at Mancheng], 2 vols (Beijing, 1980)
Wang Zhongshu: *Han Civilization* (New Haven and London, 1982)
J. Rawson, ed.: *The British Museum Book of Chinese Art* (London, 1992), p. 333

CAROL MICHAELSON

Manchester. English metropolitan city, occupying the south-east angle of the North West region. It is significant historically as a dramatic illustration of early urban industrialization (*c.* 1780–1840) and as a prime Victorian city. It was then the hub of the world trade in cotton textiles and enjoyed political influence as the promoter of the economic ideal of Free Trade. Its wealth and independence produced ambitious patronage which is expressed in many of its institutions and excellent 19th-century architecture. The modern city is a centre for finance, commerce and higher education. It is relatively small (population 407,000) but its conurbation, Greater Manchester (population *c.* 2.5 million), is the third largest in Britain, and 11 million people live within 80 km of the city's centre.

1. History and urban development. 2. Art life and organization.

1. HISTORY AND URBAN DEVELOPMENT. Manchester stands centrally in a deep western embayment of the Pennines, where rivers and historic routes intersect. The principal river, the Irwell, a tributary of the Mersey, provides access to the sea. Manchester's name has a pre-Roman derivation, but the city's earliest physical remains are Roman. The *castrum* of Mamucium, in the area known as Castlefield, was abandoned *c.* 500 AD, and the modern city grew from its successor located 1.6 km upstream to the north where, on the east bank, the medieval town grew and flourished through the production and marketing of

textiles. Across the river the neighbouring town of Salford developed. Manchester extended slowly to the south and east until more vigorous expansion began early in the 18th century.

The surviving buildings of pre-industrial Manchester are notable but few. The modern cathedral (from 1847) was formerly the medieval parish church. It was made collegiate and rebuilt from 1421, and its great size (l. *c.* 65 m) testifies to the town's wealth at that time. Heavily restored in the 19th and 20th centuries, it is most distinguished for an exceptionally fine range of oak choir-stalls (*c.* 1505–10). Adjacent is the priests' college, which was splendidly converted from 1653 to house a hospital and a library to commemorate Humphrey Chetham (1580–1653), their benefactor. Chetham's library, created free and public in 1653, was unsurpassed among town libraries until the 1850s and remains invaluable to scholars. Outside the old town, the handsome, galleried church of St Ann (1709–12) and a few houses and terraces are all that survive of the early 18th-century town that appears in attractive contemporary prospects such as Samuel Buck's of 1728.

The early industrialization and subsequent commercial advance of Manchester were facilitated by improvements in transport, and its history is associated with the development of both canals and railways. From 1761 it received coal and cheaper food, and from 1776 cotton, by the innovative Bridgewater Canal. A new terminus, which opened in 1764 at Castlefield, became an entrepôt and an industrial district. As textile manufacture was mechanized, factory production evolved, and from the 1780s the textile mill became ubiquitous: more than 50 had opened in Manchester by 1802. Industry straddled two new canals at Ancoats, to the north-east of the town (*see* URBAN PLANNING, fig. 8). The largest mills, for example Murray's (built from 1798), are vast seven- and eight-storey blocks that were capable of working continuously. Engineering works and the crowded dwellings of the new working classes completed the industrial scene. All the world came to view the new phenomenon. Some were horrified, while others believed it heralded a miraculous new age: to Thomas Carlyle in 1839 smoky Manchester was 'sublime as a Niagara, or more so'. The industrial sites are still impressive.

There was more to Manchester than industrialism. Science, medicine and pioneering social investigation were also promoted, and several buildings of advanced Neo-classical design were executed, such as the Portico Library (1802–6), Mosley Street, and the Exchange (1806–9; destr. *c.* 1868), both by Thomas Harrison; and Charles Barry's Royal Manchester Institution (1824–35, since 1882 the City Art Gallery). Parliamentary representation was obtained in 1832, and much-needed reforms followed the town's incorporation in 1838. Sweeping changes also occurred as commerce progressively expanded. Land values rose, and banks and blocks of four- and five-storey commercial warehouses replaced houses and factories. By 1853, when city status was granted, Manchester's Victorian character had emerged.

Architecturally, the ever-adaptable palazzo mode, introduced locally by Barry's highly sophisticated Athenaeum (1836–9), Princess Street, found peculiarly Mancunian expression. Leading resident practitioners adopted it with great ingenuity for all purposes, and especially for commercial warehouses, of which there is a handsome range (1850–60) by Edward Walters (1808–72) in Charlotte Street. Other notable palazzi are Heywood's Bank (1848), St Ann Street, by John Edgar Gregan (1813–55), and the Free Trade Hall (1853–6, by Walters; destr. World War II; rebuilt 1950–51), Peter Street, which eponymously commemorates the success in 1846 of the campaign, largely conducted from Manchester, for the repeal of the Corn Laws.

Civic needs and ambitions soon required buildings for new or enlarged functions. The Assize Courts (1859–64; destr. *c.* 1956) by ALFRED WATERHOUSE was influential typologically and as an early essay in Ruskinian Gothic, which quickly supplanted the palazzo mode. It was also realized that civic schemes could be used to make urban improvements, and the creation of Albert Square (1863–67) exemplified this. It provided a setting for a monumental ciborium (1862–67) designed by THOMAS WORTHINGTON for the memorial statue (1862–5) of Albert, Prince Consort, by Matthew Noble. The adjacent site was chosen for the building of a new town hall. For this the council organized a two-stage competition which *The Builder* described as 'for the age and country, an immense innovative stride'. Waterhouse won the commission and developed his scheme from 1867 to 1877 to produce a masterwork of the century (see fig. 1; for plan *see* TOWN HALL, fig. 4). The decoration of the Great Hall includes 12 wall paintings on Manchester's history (1878–87; *see* BROWN, FORD MADOX, §3). Simultaneously (1868–72) another civic work was in hand, Worthington's Police and

1. Manchester Town Hall by Alfred Waterhouse, 1867–77; view from the first-floor lobby

Magistrates' Courts in Minshull Street. This and other buildings, for example Owens College (1869–1903, by Waterhouse; from 1880 the Victoria University of Manchester), further illustrate the flowering of Ruskinian Gothic that is Manchester's second distinctive architectural form.

Despite a rise in population to more than 390,000 by 1851, Manchester and Salford remained remarkably compact, and most of the urban area fell within a radius of 1.3 km. Thereafter the absorption of neighbouring townships and the provision of public transport produced growth. In the new suburbs numerous churches were built, including works of great quality by either leading national or distinguished local architects, for example G. F. Bodley's influential church of St Augustine (1870–74; for illustration *see* BODLEY, G. F.), Pendlebury, and Edgar Wood's proto-Expressionist First Church of Christ, Scientist (1903–07), in Victoria Park. The churches are matched by notable houses, especially Edgar Wood's own house (1914–16) at 224 Hale Road, Hale, Cheshire, outstanding for its sculptural modelling, flat-roofed construction and dynamically patterned decoration.

Architectural eclecticism undermined stylistic consistency in the decades about 1900. An exception is the John Rylands Library (1890–99), Deansgate, designed by Basil Champneys. It is an elaborate Mancunian finale to the Gothic Revival but is significant nationally. In contrast to its delicate intricacy, warehouse building entered its final stage with a brassy series of large, steel-framed structures (1906–12) built in the Whitworth Street area solely for the packing and dispatch of goods. The cotton industry reached its peak in 1913, but few warehouses were built after World War I and the commercial office gradually became Manchester's staple building.

Manchester benefited from the completion in 1894 of the Manchester Ship Canal (l. 57.94 km), which opened the region directly to seaborne trade and ended its long dependence on Liverpool. The new port, located in Salford, at times ranked third in national importance. It stimulated massive modern industrial expansion, which broadened the regional economy and sustained it as the cotton trade dwindled almost to extinction by *c.* 1955.

Manchester's urban life was characterized between the wars by vigorous municipal action. In the city E. Vincent Harris extended the civic centre with two large new buildings, the Central Library (1925–34) and the Town Hall Extension (1925–37). Skilfully disposed, they relate effectively to Waterhouse's Town Hall and, in the other direction, to St Peter's Square and the Cenotaph (1924, by Sir Edwin Lutyens). Another ambitious scheme to relieve overcrowded housing became practicable in 1926, and a plan was commissioned in 1927 from R. Barry Parker (1867–1947) for a satellite garden city to house 80,000 people at Wythenshawe, extending the city's southern boundary. Construction started in 1931, but it was halted by World War II.

The city suffered spectacular but limited wartime damage. After 1945 an immense regional transformation occurred as traditional industries disappeared, Salford docks closed and Manchester's population declined by one third. The city remained buoyant, however, although

lacking its former status and municipal power. Its postwar architectural progress had been regrettably pedestrian. Wythenshawe, its most outstanding 20th-century venture, caught by slump, war and post-war expediency, emerged as more suburb than city, but its early stages are admired by historians of town planning. With notable exceptions that include the imaginative reuse of some historic buildings, contemporary standards have generally prevailed. The best of the city's new offices are two towers on Miller Street that are part of a development for the Co-operative Insurance Society and the Co-operative Wholesale Society (C.W.S.; 1953–63) by Gordon Tait (of Sir John Burnet, Tait and Partners) in association with G. S. Hay (Chief Architect to the C.W.S.); and the National Westminster Bank, formerly the District Bank (1966–9), King Street, by Casson, Conder and Partners. Despite losses and blemishes the centre retains an appreciable identity and a legible history that is diversely, and on occasions magnificently, enriched architecturally.

BIBLIOGRAPHY

S. Austin and others: *Lancashire Illustrated* (London, 1831)
T. Carlyle: *Chartism* (London, 1839); repr. in *Works*, xxix, pp. 181–2
Builder, xxv (1867), p. 223
C. H. Reilly: *Some Manchester Streets and their Buildings* (London, 1924)
C. Stewart: *The Architecture of Manchester: An Index of the Principal Buildings and their Architects, 1800–1900* (Manchester, 1956)
——: *The Stones of Manchester* (London, 1956)
W. H. Chaloner: 'Manchester in the Latter Half of the Eighteenth Century', *Bull. John Rylands Lib.*, xlii (1959), pp. 40–60
N. J. Frangopulo: *Rich Inheritance* (Manchester, 1962)
A. Briggs: *Victorian Cities* (London, 1963)
O. Ashmore: *The Industrial Archaeology of Lancashire* (Newton Abbot, 1969)
N. Pevsner: *Buildings of England: South Lancashire* (Harmondsworth, 1969)
D. Sharp: *Manchester* (London, 1969)
P. Atkins: *Guide across Manchester* (Manchester, 1976/R 2/1987)
J. H. G. Archer, ed.: *Art and Architecture in Victorian Manchester* (Manchester, 1985)

JOHN H. G. ARCHER

2. ART LIFE AND ORGANIZATION. Manchester was never an important art centre, and although some of the wealth created there in the 19th century was spent on art, the city had a philistine reputation. The Bridgewater and Peel collections of Old Masters were bought in the early 19th century with money made in Manchester, but neither collection was formed or kept in the city. In Queen Victoria's reign the Manchester art market was strong, and Thomas Agnew, chief of the local art dealers, promoted the taste for contemporary pictures among industrialists and merchants such as the Ashtons of Hyde—the brothers Samuel Ashton (*d* 1861) and Thomas Ashton (1818–98)—Henry McConnel (1801–71) and Sam Mendel (1810/11–84).

The greatest contribution of Manchester to the fine arts was the Art-Treasures Exhibition of 1857 (often referred to as the Manchester Art-Treasures Gallery), the most important art exhibition of the century in Britain (see fig. 2 and EXHIBITION, fig. 4), which took place in a specially designed temporary building at Old Trafford. Its success was based on the riches of British private collections, mostly unconnected with Manchester. That it was held there showed the determination of Manchester's leading citizens, such as Sir Thomas Fairbairn, to bring culture to

2. Manchester, Art-Treasures Exhibition, modern masters section, 1857; from a photograph by P. H. Delamotte (Manchester, Central Reference Library)

the seat of industry, but the exhibition was a private rather than a civic enterprise, and it led to no permanent institution in the city. The greatest act of civic patronage was the commissioning of the Manchester Town Hall murals (1878–93) from Ford Madox Brown, an unexpected but successful choice.

The first annual exhibition of modern art was held in 1827 by the Royal Manchester Institution, founded in 1824 by private subscription. It also formed a small permanent collection. In 1882 Manchester Corporation took over the collection and the building, which became the Manchester City Art Gallery, and acquisitions began in earnest with the purchase of modern British paintings, in particular by the Pre-Raphaelites and their followers (e.g. Ford Madox Brown's *Work*, 1852–65; John Everett Millais's *Autumn Leaves*, 1856; D. G. Rossetti's *Astarte Syriaca*, 1875–7). The collections later broadened in scope to include costume, decorative arts and some European paintings. The Whitworth Institute was established in 1889 out of funds endowed by the Manchester armaments manufacturer Sir Joseph Whitworth (1803–87). Now called the Whitworth Art Gallery, with fine collections of modern art and watercolours, prints and textiles, it has been part of the University of Manchester since 1958. The Royal Peel Park Museum, renamed the Salford Museum

and Art Gallery, was founded in 1849, the first municipal gallery to be set up after the Museums Act of 1845. Its chief distinction is the large L. S. Lowry collection. The Manchester Art Museum, founded by T. C. Horsfall (1844–1932) to bring art to the working-class district of Ancoats, opened in 1886 (it became part of the City Art Gallery in 1918 and closed in 1939). The Cornerhouse, a centre for contemporary art exhibitions, was opened in 1985.

There were only private art academies in Manchester until 1838, when the Government School of Design opened its first provincial branch there. A historical exhibition of local artists held at Peel Park in 1857 led in 1859 to the formation of the Manchester Academy of Fine Arts, an exhibiting society that still continues. The Manchester School of Art, now part of Manchester Metropolitan University (formerly Polytechnic), opened in 1878. Among painters born in or associated with the city are a number of minor talents, including William Marshall Craig (*c*. 1765–1828), Frank Stone, William Bradley (1801–57), Henry Liverseege, Robert Crozier (1815–91), Frederic Shields and Randolph Caldecott. In the 1870s and 1880s the Manchester school of painters, chief among whom were James Hey Davies (1844–1930), Richard Gay Somerset (1848–1928) and Anderson Hague (1850–1916), exhibited Barbizon-like landscapes, mainly of the Lake District and North Wales. The first artist of note to record the appearance of the city was the Frenchman Adolphe Valette (1876–1942), who came to Manchester as an art student and stayed on to teach life drawing to, among others, L. S. Lowry, the city's only native artist to make a major and original contribution to British painting. Unlike many Mancunian artists, Lowry never left the area, and he made its industrial environment, buildings and working people his central concern.

BIBLIOGRAPHY

C. P. Darcy: *The Encouragement of the Fine Arts in Lancashire, 1760–1860* (Manchester, 1976)
Presents from the Past (exh. cat., Bolton, Mus.; Oldham, Lib. & A.G.; Stockport, Mun. Mus.; 1978)
A Century of Collecting, 1882–1982: A Guide to the Manchester City Art Galleries (Manchester, 1983)
J. H. G. Archer, ed.: *Art and Architecture in Victorian Manchester* (Manchester, 1985) [extensive bibliog.]
M. Harrison: 'Art and Philanthropy: T. C. Horsfall and the Manchester Art Museum', *City, Class and Culture*, ed. A. J. Kidd and K. W. Roberts (Manchester, 1985), pp. 120–47

JULIAN TREUHERZ

Manchester, 4th Earl and 1st Duke of. *See* MONTAGU, (2).

Mancini. Italian family of patrons. They are documented in Rome from the Middle Ages and frequently held civic office. Their patronage became important in the 17th century. Paolo Mancini (*b* Rome; *d* Rome, ?Dec 1635) founded (1602) the Accademia degli Umoristi, a leading literary circle in Rome. His two sons Lorenzo Mancini (*b* Rome 1602; *d* Rome, 14 Oct 1650) and Francesco Maria Mancini (*b* Rome, 20 Oct 1606; *d* Marino, 28 June 1672) gained prominence through Lorenzo's marriage in 1634 to a sister of JULES MAZARIN. The Mancini family's activities thereafter became largely dependent on Mazarin's patronage. Lorenzo was named Maestro di Strade in 1644, and after his death his family moved to the French court. There his five daughters, known as the 'Mazarinettes', married into French and Italian aristocratic families. Francesco became a cardinal in 1660 and remained in Rome. Lorenzo's only surviving son, Filippo Giuliano Mancini Mazarin, Duc de Nevers (*b* Rome, 26 May 1641; *d* Paris, 8 May 1707), was Mazarin's Roman heir, and he commissioned Carlo Rainaldi to provide designs for renovations and additions to the Palazzo Mancini, Rome, which took place *c*. 1687–9. Rainaldi had previously been commissioned by Cardinal Mazarin to provide a project for the palace (1660; unexecuted); he also renovated the Mancini chapel in S Maria d'Aracoeli, Rome, probably in the 1670s. The line ended with Filippo's grandson, Louis-Jules Barbon Mancini-Mazarin, Duc de Nivernais (*b* Paris, 16 Dec 1716; *d* Paris, 25 Feb 1798). As French Ambassador to the Holy See (1749–52), Nivernais sponsored festivals in the Piazza Farnese.

BIBLIOGRAPHY

G. Dethan: *Mazarin et ses amis* (Paris, 1968); Eng. trans. as *The Young Mazarin* (London, 1977)
A. Schiavo: *Palazzo Mancini* (Palermo, 1969)

SUSAN KLAIBER

Mancini, Antonio (*b* Albano Laziale, 14 Nov 1852; *d* Rome, 28 Dec 1930). Italian painter. He entered the Istituto di Belle Arti, Naples, at the age of 12; while still an adolescent he produced accomplished works such as *Head of a Young Girl* (1867; Naples, Capodimonte). On his graduation in 1873, Mancini, together with Francesco Paolo Michetti and Vincenzo Gemito, was at the forefront of VERISMO in Neapolitan art. Sharing a studio with Gemito, he painted the street boys, musicians and dancers of Naples, creating an anti-academic, popular art. His patron, Albert, Count Cahen of Antwerp (1846–1903), encouraged him to visit Paris in 1875, where he met Manet and Degas. After a second visit in 1877, he lightened his previously sombre palette and his style moved away from sensual modelling to become more decorative.

Through the 1880s and 1890s Mancini's work became increasingly flamboyant in the use of both colour and impasto. His output was dominated by society portraits, although he often returned to the genre subjects of his youth and also painted many self-portraits. The grandiose *Marchese Capranica del Grillo* (1889; London, N.G.) is a striking example of his mature work. In his late paintings Mancini was preoccupied with surface texture, using thick impasto and adding materials such as coloured glass and foil to enhance the luminous colours of his canvases. Though considered by John Singer Sargent to be the best contemporary Italian painter, Mancini only became a member of the Accademia Nazionale di S Luca in 1929.

BIBLIOGRAPHY

Bolaffi; Comanducci
C. Maltese: *Realismo e verismo nella pittura italiana dell'ottocento* (Milan, 1967)
F. Bellanzi: *Antonio Mancini* (Milan, 1978)

□

Mancini, Domenico (*fl* Venice, 1511). Italian painter. The only evidence for his existence is an inscription in a painting of the *Virgin and Child with an Angel* (Lendinara Cathedral), which reads *opus • dominicj mancinj/ venetj • p • / • 1511*. The painting was first recorded in 1652 (1984 exh. cat.), in S Francesco, Lendinara. In 1795 Brandolese reported that it was part of a triptych, the side panels of which (untraced) each contained pairs of apostles. The Lendinara picture is derived from the central section of Giovanni Bellini's altarpiece (*Virgin and Child Enthroned with Saints*) in S Zaccaria, Venice, dated 1505. The poses of the Virgin and Child are almost identical in the two pictures, but the musician angel is different from Bellini's in pose and holds a lute rather than a *lira da braccio*. Closer parallels to this figure appear in various pictures by Francesco Bissolo, but these may all be later.

The importance of the Lendinara altarpiece lies less in its dependence on Bellini than in its links with works associated with the circle of Giorgione. The arrangement of folds of the left sleeve of the Virgin and of the lower right section of her robe is identical to that in the corresponding sections of the *Madonna and Child with SS Anthony and Roch* (Madrid, Prado), usually attributed to Giorgione or early Titian. Scholars have suggested that Mancini copied the figure of the Virgin from the S Zaccaria altarpiece and these drapery sections from the Prado picture. No convincing explanation of why he should have done so has been offered, however, and it could be argued that Mancini himself painted the Prado *Madonna*. The impact of Giorgione's innovations is most evident in the angel, which is painted with saturated colours, very soft modelling and loose brushwork, especially in the curls. Physiognomically the head is close to that of the wife in *Christ and the Woman Taken in Adultery* (Glasgow, A. G. & Mus.), another picture generally given to Titian or Giorgione. Zampetti (1955 exh. cat.) tentatively assigned the Glasgow painting to Mancini, a view which has much to recommend it. Trevisani (1984 exh. cat.), noting that there are pentiments in the head of the angel, argued that it was repainted by Dosso Dossi in or after 1516. This seems implausible, even though the stylistic parallels with Dosso's work are undeniable, but Dosso may well have been influenced by Mancini.

Other pictures have been assigned to Mancini on the basis of their supposed similarity to the Lendinara panel; the most convincing attribution is a *Virgin and Child with Two Saints* (ex-Gamba priv. col., Florence; see Berenson, pl. 692). Probably because of the lack of documentary evidence of his activity, however, most scholars have been reluctant to suppose that Mancini was more than a minor and unproductive follower of Bellini. Since very few documents survive from this period concerning Venetian painters even of the stature of Giorgione and Titian, the possibility that he was much more important than is now generally supposed cannot be excluded.

BIBLIOGRAPHY

P. Brandolese: *Del genio de' Lendinaresi per la pittura e di alcune pregevoli pitture di Lendinara* (Padua, 1795), pp. 7–9
J. Wilde: 'Die Probleme um Domenico Mancini', *J. Ksthist. Samml. Wien*, vii (1933), pp. 97–135
Giorgione e i Giorgioneschi (exh. cat., ed. P. Zampetti; Venice, Doge's Pal., 1955), pp. 110–13
B. Berenson: *Venetian School* (1957)
The Genius of Venice, 1500–1600 (exh. cat., ed. J. Martineau and C. Hope; London, RA, 1983), pp. 168–70 [entries by F. L. Richardson]
Restauri nel Polesine (exh. cat., ed. A. della Valle; Rovigo, Accad. Concordi, 1984), pp. 133–66 [full discussion and technical report on the Lendinara panel by F. Trevisani]

CHARLES HOPE

Mancini, Francesco (*b* S Angelo in Vado, 24 April 1679; *d* Rome, 1758). Italian painter. He was trained in Bologna in the school of Carlo Cignani, and his art is rooted in the classicist tradition of Bologna and Emilia Romagna. His achievements can be measured not only by his official appointments (French Academician, 1732; associate and regent of the Congregazione dei Virtuosi al Pantheon, 1743, 1745; principal of the Accademia di S Luca, 1750–51) but also by the numerous commissions, almost exclusively ecclesiastical, that he obtained both in Rome and in the provinces. These made a significant contribution to the development of the form and iconography of the altarpiece.

Mancini's early period is not well documented: the only canvases that remain from it are the *Chariot of the Sun* (Forlì, Pal. Albicini), which is clearly influenced by Correggio, two more solemn and measured canvases, *Union of the Greek and Latin Churches* and *Gregory and Gratian, Compilers of the Sacred Canons*, and the fresco of the *Triumph of Eternal Wisdom* (1714; Ravenna, Bib. Com. Classeuse).

The later works of Mancini are better documented. In 1719 he won the commission for the frescoes in Foligno Cathedral: the apse fresco of *St Felician Commending the City of Foligno to Religion* (1722–3) and the fresco in the presbytery of *St Felician in Glory* (1723–4). Here, he renewed Maratti's compromise between classical and Baroque traditions and replaced the airy and spirited compositions of the 17th century with more static and carefully composed groups of figures. By 1725 Mancini had moved to Rome, and in that year was elected a member of the Accademia di S Luca. His moderately theatrical style became marked by a search for sobriety and clarity harmonized, in its most felicitous moments, with brilliant execution and refined colour.

Other works that can be securely dated are the fresco of the *Assumption of the Virgin* (1730) in the dome of S Filippo, Perugia, again influenced by Maratti; the canvas of *SS Anna and Joachim with the Virgin* (1732; Perugia, Gal. N. Umbria), which is closely modelled on 16th-century traditions; the fresco showing the *Assumption of the Virgin* and the four canvases illustrating scenes from the *Life of the Virgin* (all 1737; Macerata, Madonna della Misericordia), carried out with a rare freshness of touch; the altarpiece with *St Filippo Neri in Glory* (1738) in S Filippo, Macerata (also the location of an impressive and dramatic undated *Crucifixion*); the *Blessed Gambacorti Establishing his Order* (1740; Pisa Cathedral), a work of sober and devout naturalism; and *Christ in Glory with Saints* (1750; Fabriano, SS Biagio e Romualdo).

The works of uncertain dating are numerous and include: *Christ Appearing to SS Clement and Augustine* (Urbino, Pal. Ducale), which retains a pyramidal composition; the *Domine quo vadis?* (Città di Castello, Pin. Com.), which reflects the direct influence of Annibale Carracci; and the notable group remaining in S Angelo in Vado, the artist's home town, including the *Vision of St Filippo Benizi*, *St Pellegrino Laziosi Healed by the Crucifix* and the *Virgin with the Seven Founding Saints* in the church of S Maria dei Servi.

Of Mancini's most famous work, *St Peter Healing the Cripple*, there remains only a mosaic copy (Rome, St Peter's, chapel of the Colonna), which reveals a grandiose compositional rhythm in keeping with the classicism of Pompeo Batoni. Altarpieces by Mancini in several Roman churches (S Gregorio al Celio, S Maria Maggiore, S Maria della Scala) are rather uninspired; they are merely reworkings of similar compositions limited by the demands of an obligatory and repetitive iconography. He showed greater originality when he painted on a smaller scale, as in the *Rest on the Flight into Egypt* (Rome, Pin. Vaticana), a tender and intimate interpretation of the theme, enriched by a refined technique and colour. In his few secular works, such as *Flora* (Rome, Accad. N. S Luca), the fable of *Cupid and Psyche*, frescoed on the vault of the coffee-house at the Palazzo Colonna, Rome, and *Cupid and Pan* (Rome, Pin. Vaticana), there blossoms a pleasant Arcadian spirit that recaptures the grace and lightness of the Rococo.

BIBLIOGRAPHY

Thieme–Becker [with bibliog. before 1929]
E. Filippini: *Gli affreschi del Mancini nel duomo di Foligno* (Pesaro, 1917)
N. Ridarelli: 'Un pittore del settecento, Francesco Mancini', *Rass. March.* (1923), p. 322
O. Montenovesi: 'Francesco Mancini e la sua opera pittorica', *Riv. Stor. Benedettina* (1925), pp. 35–44

E. Berti Toesca: 'Francesco Mancini a palazzo Colonna', *L'Arte*, xiv (1943), pp. 7–13

Il settecento a Roma (exh. cat., ed. De Luca; Rome, Pal. Espos., 1959), p. 145

G. Sestieri: 'Profilo di Francesco Mancini', *Stor. A.*, xxix (1977), pp 67–79

A. C. Toni: 'La pittura del '700 nel maceratese', *Stud. Maceratesi*, xii (1978), pp. 122–45

S. Rudolph: *La pittura del '700 a Roma* (Milan, 1983), pls 416–24

A. Fucili Bartolucci: 'Pittura devozionale e patetismo metastasiano: Mancini, Lazzarini, Ceccarini e Lapis', *Arte e cultura nelle province di Pesaro e Urbino* (Venice, 1986), pp. 454–7

G. Sestieri: *La pittura del settecento* (Turin, 1988), pp. 46, 49

M. Rosaria Valazzi: 'La pittura del settecento nelle Marche', *La pittura in Italia: Il settecento* (Milan, 1989), i, pp. 378–9

EMILIA CALBI

Mancini, Giulio (*b* Siena, 21 Feb 1558; *d* Rome, 22 Aug 1630). Italian physician, art historian and connoisseur. His medical career culminated with his appointment in 1623 as personal physician to Urban VIII. His interest in the arts, notably painting and dance, cannot be securely dated before 1617 when he started writing his most famous work, *Alcune considerazioni appartenenti alla pittura come di diletto di un gentilhuomo nobile*, and its twin *Alcune considerationi intorno a quello che hanno scritto alcuni autori in materia della pittura* (completed in 1621 but with later emendations). The first is divided into ten sections: the first two (20 folios) are introductory and theoretical; the following four (94 folios) are historical, organized by periods and schools; and the last four (46 folios) discuss topics that would interest collectors, including observations on how to distinguish quality, or an original work from a copy, or the age of a painting, as well as how to buy, frame, install and conserve them. The second work is divided into three sections: first a critique of Giovanni Paolo Lomazzo, including his etymology of *pingere*, his praise for the serpentine figure, and his emphasis on movement in painting which, according to Mancini, is necessarily static (18 folios); there then comes a critique of Giorgio Vasari, concentrating on factual errors but also discussing errors of judgement and taste, notably his Tuscan bias (68 folios); finally there are brief descriptions of the lives of painters who had started working or had established a reputation only after Vasari's *Vite* of 1568 (86 folios).

Although both works remained in manuscript until 1956, their influence was considerable during the 17th and 18th centuries. One manuscript was owned by Cassiano dal Pozzo, and this or other versions were cited or plagiarized by Fabio Chigi (later Alexander VII), Secondo Lancellotto (1583–1643), Giovanni Baglione, Giovanni Pietro Bellori, Conte Carlo Malvasia, Filippo Baldinucci, Giovanni Gaetano Bottari and Guglielmo Della Valle. Mancini is now consulted most often as a source for factual information concerning attribution and provenance, although his reliability in these matters cannot be assumed. Among those who provided him with information, and possibly even interpretation, were Ottaviano Macherino, Domenico Passignano and Teofilo Gallaccini, who dedicated his *Trattato sopra gli errori degli architetti* (written 1625) to Mancini.

Mancini is also valued as a rare commentator on early 17th-century taste in Roman painting. His classicizing taste was not as rigorous as that of Giovanni Battista Agucchi nor as generous as that of Vincenzo Giustiniani. On the one hand he rejected the serpentine line as an ideal form, insisted that the principal figure should be placed in the centre of the composition, and identified beauty with decorum, but he virtually ignored Agucchi's central thesis of an ideal beauty. He thought that Caravaggio and the Carracci had invented distinct, if not opposing styles, but found that both should be valued as modern correctives to a general decline of painting in the late 16th century. He said that although Caravaggio might have erred somewhat with his 'unnatural' lighting and, paradoxically, his dependence on nature and her models, he nevertheless merited his important position as head of one of four modern 'schools'. (The other three consisted of the Carracci, Cavaliere d'Arpino and a miscellaneous group of late Mannerists.) Caravaggio's followers, including Ribera and Bartolomeo Manfredi, also commanded Mancini's respect.

Mancini anticipated the developments that would be labelled 'connoisseur' in late 17th-century France and England: 'My intention is not to propose precepts pertinent to painting or its production such as those treated by Dürer, Gaurico, Leonardo, Vasari, Lomazzo and Zuccaro, since this is not my profession; rather I propose to consider the various means by which a dilettante (*un huomo di diletto*) of similar learning as myself can easily pass judgement on paintings, collect them and display them.' He wrote that before a collector can decide whether or not the price of any painting is a just one, he must determine when and where it was done and, if possible, who did it. Mancini was particularly concerned with the problem of detecting copies and forgeries. Questions of technique (types of colours and varnishes) were considered by him, but only to the extent that they helped the collector to arrive at an attribution.

Mancini's comprehensive system of historical periods was probably motivated by the collector's need to classify, but may also be the result of his Aristotelian education at the University of Padua. He was probably drawn to Vasari's biological model of progress and decline ('Art, like man, is born, grows, ages and dies') because its organic basis appealed to him as a physician. His cycle that featured the Trecento as childhood, the Quattrocento as youth, *c.* 1500–50 as maturity and after 1550 as senility gave him second thoughts because it placed Caravaggio and the Carracci among the senile. He therefore relabelled the 'age of senility' the 'succeeding age', so leaving its final decline unspecified. The notion of the Carracci as a new Renaissance was not developed until later. Mancini found that in addition to historical influences on an artist's style, nations also have aesthetic inclinations, and he explained this by means of physiology. However, unlike Vasari, he had little interest in the artist's character and its stylistic reflections.

Mancini also made significant contributions to the study of Roman and Sienese medieval painting. Whereas it had been studied earlier by antiquarians and historians interested in medieval customs and artefacts, Mancini, who believed that art was less useful than pleasurable, became interested in medieval painting for its aesthetic qualities. He examined medieval painting as a connoisseur and with a care and attentiveness that previous writers had reserved only for painting from the 14th century onwards.

Two shorter and less discursive works by Mancini should be noted. The *Viaggio per Roma per vedere le pitture* (*c.* 1620–24) was written for the gentleman connoisseur, not for the pilgrim, and so may be claimed as the first guidebook to Rome that departs from the medieval *Mirabilia* type. The *Breve ragguaglio delle cose di Siena* (written in the mid-1620s) includes notices of Sienese painters, sculptors and architects as well as their work.

WRITINGS

Viaggio per Roma per vedere le pitture (*c.* 1620–24), ed. L. Schudt, Röm. Forsch. Bib. Hertziana, iv (Leipzig, 1923)

Considerazioni sulla pittura (*c.* 1621), ed. A. Marucchi, 2 vols (Rome, 1956–7) [with extensive notes and excellent intro. by L. Salerno]

BIBLIOGRAPHY

D. Mahon: *Studies in Seicento Art and Theory* (London, 1947), pp. 32–8, 279–331

L. Salerno: 'Sul Trattato di Giulio Mancini', *Commentari*, ii/1 (1951), pp. 26–39

——: 'Giulio Mancini e le cose di Siena', *Scritti di storia dell'arte in onore di Lionello Venturi*, ii (Rome, 1956), pp. 9–17

G. Previtali: *La fortuna dei primitivi dal Vasari ai neoclassici* (Turin, 1964), pp. 46–50

M. Capucci: 'Dalla biografia alla storia: Note sulla formazione della storiografia artistica Seicento', *Stud. Seicent.*, ix (1968), pp. 92–5

J. Hess: 'Note manciane', *Münch. Jb. Bild. Kst*, xix (1968), pp. 103–20

C. M. Strinati: 'Studio sulla teorica d'arte primoseicentesca tra manierismo e barocco', *Stor. A.*, xiii (1972), pp. 67–8, 76–7

L. Grassi: *Teorici e storia della critica d'arte: L'età moderna; il Seicento* (Rome, 1973), pp. 32–5, 97–8

PHILIP SOHM

Mancoba, Ernest (Methuen) [Ngungunyana] (*b* Turffontein, Johannesburg, 29 Aug 1904). French sculptor, painter and draughtsman of South African birth. He attended an Anglican teachers' training college, Grace Dieu, near Pietersburg (1920–29), both as student and as teacher. He enrolled at the University of Fort Hare where he studied English, history and psychology, intending a career in journalism, and graduated from the University of South Africa (BA 1937). Although he won acclaim in 1929 for a religious carving, *Bantu Madonna* (Johannesburg, A. G.), he gave up carving in 1950 and thereafter devoted himself to painting and drawing. Mancoba gained from his mother Florence (*née* Mangqangwana) a lasting reverence for their Fingo histories, the African philosophy of the brotherhood of man, and for poetry, in particular that expressing the 'unsayable' of experience. During the mid-1930s his friend the sculptor Lippy Lipschitz (1903–80) introduced him to the sculptor Elza Dziomba (1902–70) and brought to his attention Paul Guillaume's and Thomas Munro's book *Primitive Negro Sculpture* (1926). Guillaume's analysis of African sculpture particularly affected Mancoba's approach and kindled an enduring respect for older African art. Mancoba's imagery, technique and style changed systematically in accordance with the notion of the 'unsayable' and his interest shifted from descriptive to interpretative carving. Mancoba left for Paris in 1938 and enrolled at the Ecole des Arts Décoratifs. (He became a naturalized French citizen in 1961.) With the Danish sculptor SONJA FERLOV MANCOBA (they married in 1942) he explored automatism, emphasizing autonomy of line and colour wash (drawings in Silkeborg, Kstmus.). He was interned during World War II, after which he lived in Denmark, encountering like-minded artists in the groups Høst (Harvest) in 1948–9 and in

COBRA in 1950. At the centre of Mancoba's expression is a configuration that conjures up associations with the Kanaga masks of the DOGON of Mali (e.g. *Drawing*, 1960; Copenhagen, Stat. Mus. Kst) and the reliquary figures of the KOTA (ii) of Gabon (e.g. *Painting*, 1971; Århus, Kstmus., and *Painting*, 1973; Silkeborg, Kstmus.). He evoked these ancestral images by means of, and within a field of, seemingly impulsive brushstrokes. Later (*c.* 1990) he developed a personal calligraphy of script-like characters in his ink and pastel drawings (Copenhagen, Gallerie Mikæl Andersen) that simultaneously masks and reveals the presence of three or more ancestral images, holding in suspension memories and the unknown.

BIBLIOGRAPHY

W. Stokvis: *Cobra* (Amsterdam, 1974)

Ernest Mancoba (exh. cat. by T. Andersen, Silkeborg, Kstmus., 1977)

L. Bouquin: *Fonds national d'art contemporain*, Paris, Louvre cat. (Paris, 1989)

E. Rankin: *Images of Wood* (Johannesburg, 1989)

E. Miles: *Lifeline out of Africa: The Art of Ernest Mancoba* (Capetown, 1994)

ELZA MILES

Mancoba, Sonja Ferlov. *See* FERLOV MANCOBA, SONJA.

Mandalay [Ratanapunja]. City in Upper Burma on the Irrawaddy River. The last capital of the Burmese kings, it was founded in 1857 by King Mindon (*reg* 1853–78). Its square citadel (2 km on each side) was defended by a rampart with 12 fortified gates, each surmounted by a tiered wooden pavilion (Burm. *pyatthat*), and five bridges spanning a moat over 68 m wide. At its centre stood the wooden royal palace (*see* BURMA, §II, 1(iii)(d)), which was destroyed by fire during World War II. Straight roads, the most important one on the eastern side, divided the space between the rampart and the palace enclosure into large squares where the senior officials had their residences.

The streets outside this fortified citadel also followed a regular grid plan. They were punctuated by several landmarks, the first being Mandalay Hill, where there were numerous great religious foundations, among them the Ku-tho-daw where 729 stone slabs were engraved in 1857 with sacred Buddhist texts, each one protected by a small stone pavilion. European architecture has left its mark on Mandalay, through Italian and other exiled architects or engineers working for King Mindon and his successors, even on major monuments such as the Atu-mashi Monastery, a composite structure of stone with a timber frame, the Kin-wun-min-gyi Monastery, a wooden version of a Renaissance palace, and the Yaw-min-gyi Monastery, built of stone. The Shwe-nan-daw Monastery, built in 1880 from parts of the royal palace, retains well-conserved wooden carving (*see* BURMA, figs 10 and 27). The Mahamuni Temple, a large complex, has been heavily restored in recent times.

BIBLIOGRAPHY

Taw Sein Ko: 'The Mandalay Palace', *Archaeol. Surv. India Annu. Rep.* (1902–3), pp. 95–103

V. C. Scott O'Connor: *Mandalay and Other Cities of the Past in Burma* (London, 1907/*R* Bangkok, 1987)

C. Duroiselle: 'Taitkaw and Sangyaung Monasteries, Mandalay', *Archaeol. Surv. India Annu. Rep.* (1912–13), pp. 87–119

——: *Guide to the Mandalay Palace* (Rangoon, 1925/*R* 1963) [reprint illus.]

Maung Maung Tin and T. O. Morris: 'Mindon Miu's Development Plan for the Mandalay Area', *J. Burma Res. Soc.*, xlix/1 (1966), pp. 29–34

U Myo Myint Sein and others: 'Kon-baung hkit hnaung phon-gyi kyaung-mya' [Monasteries of the later Konbaung period], *Tekkathou pyinnya padetha sa Sheì Myan-ma ein-myà zaung*, v/4 (1970), pp. 269–92

U Aung Thaw: *Historical Sites in Burma* (Rangoon, 1972/*R* 1978)

U Kan Hla [S. Ozhegov]: 'Traditional Town Planning in Burma', *J. Soc. Archit. Hist.*, xxxvii/2 (1978), pp. 92–104

PIERRE PICHARD

Mandasor [anc. Daśapura]. Site of ancient city and modern town in the Avanti region on the upper fringe of the Malwa plateau in Madhya Pradesh, India. The ancient city that once stood here, apparently well known in the GUPTA period (4th century AD–late 5th), is mentioned in the poems of Kalidasa. Inscriptions record building activity in that period, but no temples survive. However, a mid-5th century stele (h. 3m) depicting Shiva with his riotous attendants (Skt *gaṇa*) has been found at Mandasor. It may be regarded as the Avanti parallel to the Mathura images of *c.* AD 435, although a greater plasticity and softer rendering of volume is evident in this regional style. The face of the Mandasor Shiva has been cut away and fitted with a replacement of *c.* 11th century, a common practice to make worn or damaged religious images suitable for worship.

A square pillar with Vaishnava and Shaiva scenes probably dates from the 7th century and a number of stray architectural fragments from the 9th to 11th centuries. The present fort, built on a vast mound and dating to the late Sultanate period (*c.* 15th century), contains only a few 20th-century government buildings. Antiquities from nearby sites brought to Mandasor Fort include a gateway jamb (h. 5.6 m) from the village of Khilichipur. It carries reliefs of a river goddess and a guardian figure at the base, with amorous couples (*mithuna*) in panels above, a configuration similar to a temple door. Though often placed in the 6th century, the jamb probably dates to *c.* AD 475, as the modelling is similar to the Sarnath Buddhas of that date, though lacking their linear precision and crisp chiselling. A Kubera image was also found at Khilichipur (see Schastok).

The town of Mandasor, located slightly to the south of the fort, has gates that are fine specimens of provincial Mughal architecture. The old portions of the town contain many stately homes of the 19th and early 20th centuries.

See also INDIAN SUBCONTINENT, §IV, 6(iv)(b).

BIBLIOGRAPHY

J. Williams: 'The Sculpture of Mandasor', *Archv Asian A.*, xxvi (1972–3), pp. 50–66

J. C. Harle: *Gupta Sculpture* (Oxford, 1974)

K. Mankodi: 'A Carved Pillar from Mandasor', *J. Ind. Soc. Orient. A.*, xi (1980), pp. 34–42

S. Schastok: 'The Sixth Century Kubera Image from Mandasor', *Chhavi*, ii (Varanasi, 1981), pp. 105–8

J. Williams: *The Art of Gupta India: Empire and Province* (Princeton, 1982)

The Sculpture of India, 3000 BC–1300 AD (exh. cat. by P. Chandra, Washington, DC, N.G.A., 1985)

R. Salomon: 'New Inscriptional Evidence for the History of the Aulikaras of Mandasor', *Indo-Iran. J.*, xxxii (1989), pp. 1–36

MICHAEL D. WILLIS

Mande. Broad group of peoples who inhabit parts of a number of West African countries from Sudan to Guinea-Bissau. Variants of the Mande language are spoken by such peoples as the MENDE of Sierra Leone and Liberia, and the GURO of the Côte d'Ivoire. Many Mande traditions are influenced by Islam.

□

Mander, van. Dutch family of artists of Flemish origin. The most famous member of the family, (1) Karel van Mander I, although a noted painter and draughtsman, is known primarily as the author of the *Schilder-boeck* ('Book of painters'), which follows the example of Vasari's *Vite* (van Mander is sometimes referred to as the 'Dutch Vasari') and includes biographies of Italian and northern European artists as well as containing practical advice. His son Karel van Mander II (*b* Courtrai, *c.* 1579; *d* Delft, 13 June 1623) was a tapestry designer who worked for Christian IV of Denmark, and his grandson (2) Karel van Mander III also worked at the Danish court, as a portrait painter and decorative artist.

(1) Karel van Mander I (*b* Meulebeke, nr Courtrai, West Flanders, 1548; *d* Amsterdam, 11 Sept 1606). Poet, writer, painter and draughtsman.

1. Life. 2. Writings. 3. Artistic work.

1. LIFE. Before 1568 van Mander was apprenticed to Lucas de Heere, a painter and poet in Ghent, and afterwards to Pieter Vlerick (1539–81) in Courtrai and Doornik. Between *c.* 1570 and 1573 he lived in his native Meulebeke, where he applied himself to writing plays and poetry. In 1573 he went to Italy, where he first paid a brief visit to Florence; in Terni he was commissioned to paint a fresco for a count of the *St Bartholomew's Night Massacre*, in which the death of Gaspard de Coligny in 1572 was represented. Three sections of the fresco, restored and partly overpainted, are still extant in the Palazzo Spada Terni. In Rome he met Bartholomeus Spranger and became a close friend of Gaspard Heuvick (1550–after 1590) from Oudenaarde, who was working in Bari and elsewhere. In 1577, or shortly afterwards, van Mander was working in Basle; he then moved on to Krems. Spranger encouraged him to go to Vienna, where he worked with Hans Mont on the triumphal arch on the Bauermarkt, erected for the occasion of Rudolph II's arrival in July 1577. After this, van Mander returned to Meulebeke, passing through Nuremberg on the journey. Because of the religious turmoil and uprising against the Spanish, van Mander and his family, who were Mennonites, kept wandering from place to place; he stayed in Courtrai and Bruges and finally fled from the southern Netherlands to Haarlem, where he arrived penniless but remained for 20 years.

In 1584 van Mander became a member of Haarlem's Guild of St Luke. He is said to have set up a sort of academy in Haarlem at this time with Hendrick Goltzius and Cornelis Cornelisz. van Haarlem, but hardly anything is known about this project. In 1586 he worked on a gateway for the entry of Robert Dudley, Earl of Leicester, into the city; after a difficult beginning, he established his reputation with this project. In 1603 he retreated to Zevenbergen, a house between Haarlem and Alkmaar, where he wrote the greater part of his *Schilder-boeck*. In June 1604 he moved to Amsterdam, where he died a poor man with outstanding debts. Jacques de Gheyn II made a drawing of him on his deathbed (Frankfurt am Main, Städel. Kstinst. & Städt. Gal.). No fewer than 300 mourners accompanied his coffin to the Oude Kerk, where he is buried.

2. WRITINGS.

(i) Poet and man of letters. (ii) The *Schilder-boeck*.

(i) Poet and man of letters. Van Mander initially followed the style of the *rederijkers* (rhetoricians) but soon changed his manner under the influence of Renaissance literature. In Haarlem he was an important member of the Flemish chamber of rhetoricians called De Witte Angieren (The White Carnations), founded in 1592, for which he designed a blazon. Van Mander had a good command of Latin and Greek as well as French and Italian. Among the works he translated were Virgil's *Bucolics and Georgics* (1597), Ovid (1604) and the *Iliad* (1611); his own writings include *De harpe* ('The harp'; 1599), the *Kerck der deught* ('Church of virtue'; *c.* 1600) and the *Olijfbergh* ('Mount of Olives'; 1609). He also devised numerous inscriptions for prints, to which he always added his own motto, *Eén is nodigh* ('One thing is necessary'). Van Mander was a broad-minded spirit for his time; he took a stand against Calvinism as well as Roman Catholicism. With Jan Baptiste van der Noot (*c.* 1540–*c.* 1595) and Jan van Hout (1542–1609), he is one of the best poets of the early Dutch Renaissance, whose work influenced Bredero (1585–1618) and others.

(ii) The 'Schilder-boeck'. The first edition was published in Haarlem in 1604; the second edition, which includes an anonymous biography of van Mander, appeared in 1618

1. Karel van Mander I: *Schilder-boeck*, title-page to the second edition (Amsterdam, 1618)

(see fig. 1). The *Schilder-boeck*, regarded as an art-historical source of great importance, consists of six sections.

(a) 'Het leerdicht' ('The didactic poem'). This is a treatise (in verse) on the theory of painting rather than a technical guide based on practice. Also known as the *Grondt der edel vry schilderconst* ('Foundations of the noble free art of painting'), it comprises 14 chapters: an introduction in which the poet addressed himself to young artists, followed by chapters on drawing, the rules of proportion, pose, composition, invention, disposition (temperament), the handling of light, landscape, animals, drapery, the combination of colours, painting, colour and the meanings of colour. Van Mander based his *Leerdicht* on the medieval tradition of didactic poetry and on the French *poésie scientifique*. He used a great many literary sources, Classical as well as later, the most important of which were Alberti, Vasari and Walter Rivius. Van Mander's approach can be described as scientific, historical, philosophical and astrological. In order to illustrate the various aspects of painting, he often referred to famous works of art or celebrated artists, who excelled in one way or another. For example, he used the Farnese *Flora* (Naples, Capodimonte) to illustrate drapery, Titian as the champion of brilliant flesh tone and Pieter Bruegel the elder as the master of landscape painting. In between, the poet offered various allegorical interpretations and explanations for the meaning of numerous symbols. He was the first art theorist to devote a whole chapter exclusively to landscape. In essence, the *Leerdicht* was an attempt to establish the superiority of the 'free and noble art of painting' over the crafts and trades; a similar argument ran through contemporary Italian art theory. Van Mander complained bitterly about the fact that as a painter he was forced to be a member of the same guild as tinkers, tinsmiths and rag-and-bone men, something he regarded as humiliating.

(b) 'Het leven van de antieke schilders' ('The lives of the ancient painters'). This section of the *Schilder-boeck*, dated 1603, is largely based on part XXXV of Pliny the elder's *Natural History*. Pliny's encyclopedia existed in a number of edited versions with explanatory notes, a number of which were known to van Mander, though he seems to have drawn primarily on the French translation by Antoine du Pinet (1562). After the introduction, in which van Mander commented on the origins of painting and sculpture—citing Homer and the reckoning of years by Olympiads—he gave biographical descriptions of Greek and Roman painters, beginning with Gyges, the first painter in Egypt. He also provided accounts of the earliest examples of Etruscan sculpture in Chiusi, Viterbo and Arezzo. The longest description is devoted to Apelles. Apart from discussing the work of ancient artists, van Mander included numerous anecdotes about the deceptive nature of realistic or naturalistic painting: Zeuxis deceived birds with real-looking painted grapes, while Parhasius deceived Zeuxis with a *trompe l'oeil* painted cloth apparently covering a painting. In the 16th century and early 17th Pliny's book was mainly influential as an iconographical source; one good example is his description of Apelles' *Hercules aversus*, the hero seen from behind, which gave rise to a number of such images, including Hendrick Goltzius's famous

engraving of the Farnese *Hercules* seen from behind (B. 143).

(c) 'Leven van moderne beroemde Italiaanse schilders' ('Lives of famous contemporary Italian painters'). This section is a translated and adapted version of Vasari's *Vite*. Van Mander made a critical selection from the original text, cut down the longer passages and left out most of the portrait painters, whom he thought less important; he also discarded all decorative artists. His translation is reliable and demonstrates his good command of Italian. In the final chapters van Mander added a number of artists who had not been included by Vasari (who died in 1574). These final chapters form van Mander's most original contribution to the discussion of contemporary Italian artists; they introduce Jacopo Bassano, Federigo Zuccaro, Federigo Barocci, Palma Giovane and Cavaliere d'Arpino. The section is rounded off with two general chapters, one about Italian artists 'now working in Rome', the other about Italian painters 'working in Rome in my time, between 1573 and 1577'. Van Mander collected the material for these two chapters himself; he assembled information from Dutch artists active in Italy after 1577, such as Goltzius and Jacob Matham. Van Mander is notable for being the first literary source for Caravaggio, whose innovative naturalism he strongly opposed; he made no attempt to conceal this bias, for he believed that artists should be selective and copy only what seemed most beautiful in nature. This idealism in the representation of reality was a legacy of the Italian Renaissance, the prime exponent of which was Raphael.

(d) 'Levens van de beroemde Nederlandse en Hoogduitse schilders' ('The lives of famous Netherlandish and High German painters'). This is the most original and important part of the *Schilder-boeck*. It laid the foundations of the history of Dutch and German painting before 1604. Among the author's sources were the writings of Domenicus Lampsonius, Lucas de Heere, Marcus van Vaernewijck and Pieter Coecke van Aelst, as well as letters, manuscripts, anecdotes he had heard and his own experience and memories. The first biography deals with Hubert and Jan van Ecyk. Jan is compared to Masaccio and deemed the pioneer and innovator of early Netherlandish painting due to his legendary invention of oil paint. The next two chapters are about the south Netherlandish artists Hugo van der Goes and Rogier van der Weyden. In the discussion of 15th-century artists, the emphasis is placed primarily on Haarlem as the cradle of north Netherlandish painting, with Albert van Ouwater, 'Dirck van Haarlem' (i.e. Dieric Bouts) and Geertgen tot Sint Jans as the key figures. Haarlem seems to have been to van Mander, who, after all, worked there for 20 years, what Florence was to Vasari. The discussion of 16th-century painters is longer and more informative. There are important chapters on Dürer, Holbein and Pieter Bruegel the elder. The work of the 'prodigy' Lucas van Leyden he thought to equal Dürer's achievements. Van Mander was concerned with the glory of Dutch art, for, as he proudly declared, he did not travel abroad to learn about art, 'although Vasari wrote otherwise'. There are further important chapters largely devoted to the lives and works of contemporary artists such as Goltzius and Cornelis van Haarlem. The elaborate description of Spranger, who became a friend of van Mander's in Rome and Vienna, is also full of vital information. This section, moreover, provides numerous facts about collectors and about paintings destroyed by iconoclasts or subsequently lost. The section ends with a discussion of some younger Dutch painters active shortly after 1600, such as Paulus Moreelse, who by 1604 had already achieved fame as a portrait painter. The index includes the names of almost 200 Netherlandish painters active before 1604, arranged alphabetically by their Christian names.

(e) 'Uitleg en verklaring van de symboliek van de Metamorphosen van Ovidius' ('Interpretation and explanation of the symbolism in Ovid's "Metamorphoses"'). The importance of this part lies in its useful iconological information. In the artist's biography incorporated in the second edition of the *Schilder-boeck*, van Mander is reported to have taught his colleagues in Haarlem 'the Italian method, something which can be seen from the *Metamorphoses* designed by Goltzius'. Goltzius worked on these illustrations in close collaboration with van Mander; they began in 1587–8 but never got beyond the fourth book. There are 52 anonymous engravings, but only 6 of the original drawings have survived (Reznicek, nos 99–104; and the drawing of *Apollo and Daphne*, Amiens, Mus. B.-A.). The explanations in this section of the *Schilder-boeck* make it possible to interpret the symbolic and moral significance of a number of van Mander's own drawings, for example that of *Ixion* (Paris, Louvre), which deals with punishment, ingratitude and false wisdom.

(f) 'Hoe de figuren worden uitgebeeld, hun betekenis en wat zij voorstellen' ('How to render figures, what they mean and what they represent'). In this part of the book van Mander provided his readers with iconographical–iconological guidelines in the manner of Cesare Ripa and others. Mythological gods and animals are dealt with first, then the various parts of the body, then trees and plants. Finally, van Mander discussed the abstract notions underlying these images. For instance, *c.* 1600 a tortoise alluded not only to slowness but also to the idea that women should stay indoors; a pair of bent knees indicated subjection; and a reed meant lack of resolution.

3. ARTISTIC WORK. Van Mander's own work as an artist reflects his theoretical writings, and although there are only a few paintings by him, a considerable number of his drawings have been preserved, as well as at least 150 engravings after his designs. These show that he was interested primarily in 'instructive history'—that is religious (see fig. 2), mythological and moral–allegorical subjects— and in peasant scenes. That he believed that artists should not blindly follow nature explains why he himself never aimed at achieving realistic effects in his work. Most important to him was the poetic approach of 'historia'; his dictum was Horace's 'UT PICTURA POESIS'. His drawings and paintings thus include neither portraits (with the exception of a signed *Portrait of a Man*, Vienna, Ksthist. Mus.) nor domestic scenes of the kind drawn by Goltzius and Jacques de Gheyn II, nor, for that matter, pure

2. Karel van Mander I: *Christ with the Twelve Apostles*, pen and brown ink, grey wash, 172×307 mm, *c.* 1588–1600 (Brussels, Bibliothèque Royale Albert 1er)

landscapes, animal or still-life pictures. He regarded portrait painting as an inferior, profit-seeking affair, citing Michiel van Mierevelt as an example. Landscapes could be amusing, 'droll' in his view, for instance the farm landscapes near Utrecht by Abraham Bloemaert. As an artist, and as a theorist, van Mander was one of the last serious followers of the Italian Renaissance in the Netherlands. When, *c.* 1600, a new generation of artists began to move in the direction of 'realism', van Mander no longer took part in artistic developments.

(i) Drawings. There are *c.* 70 surviving drawings by van Mander, 46 of which were catalogued by Elisabeth Valentiner in 1930. Only one drawing can be attributed to him with certainty from the period before 1583, the year he came to Haarlem: the *Flight into Egypt* (Dresden, Kupferstichkab.), which corresponds to an engraving of the same subject by Cherubino Alberti (B. 15). The early style points to the influence of Jan Speeckaert and Spranger. Later, van Mander seems to have been especially influenced by Cavaliere d'Arpino, as can be seen in the red chalk drawing of *Neptune* (Berlin, Kupferstichkab.; not accepted by Valentiner). After Goltzius's return from Italy in 1591, van Mander gradually reduced the amount of exaggerated movement in his figures, and his compositions generally became more balanced, with a greater sense of depth. Among his finest drawings are those of *Apollo and Daphne* and *Pan and Syrinx* (both Florence, Uffizi), which are in the manner of Spranger, and that of *Diana and Actaeon* (Bremen, Ksthalle; see fig. 3), which shows a splendid use of colour and seems related in concept to van Mander's lost tapestry designs. Besides religious and mythological subjects, he also represented peasant scenes in imitation of Pieter Bruegel. His brilliant

watercolour sketches in the Italian manner were based on woodcuts after Parmigianino.

Most of van Mander's designs for engravings, which were executed by Jacques de Gheyn II, Jacob Matham, Zacharias Dolendo and others, have been lost, but the prints show him to have been an imaginative inventor. The captions underneath the prints often help elucidate the symbolical meaning of the image, which usually has some underlying Christian moral; they were written either by van Mander himself or by Latin schoolmasters in Haarlem, such as Franco Estius (*b c.* 1544) and Theodore Schrevelius.

Van Mander's drawings include no academic studies of nudes, which is curious, given his alleged involvement with an academy in Haarlem where artists could draw models and make use of other facilities. His drawing of a *Male Nude* (Amsterdam, estate of J. Q. van Regteren Altena, see Valentiner, no. XI), seen from behind in an elegant pose, seems to have sprung from the artist's imagination rather than anything he might have seen in reality. And although there are a number of academic drawings of Classical statues by Goltzius, no such works by van Mander survive. Possibly they were lost *en bloc.*

(ii) Paintings. There are approximately 30 surviving paintings by van Mander, on copper, panel and canvas; they were catalogued by Leesberg in 1994. The earliest painting—the altarpiece of *St Catherine*—was made for the clothmakers' guild in the St Maartenskerk in Courtrai (1582; *in situ*). It was painted shortly before the artist moved from Flanders to Haarlem. Stylistically, it is close to the work of the so-called Flemish Romanists, such as Michiel Coxie, who were influenced by 16th-century Italian art (*see* ROMANISM). The overall impression is rather stiff

3. Karel van Mander I: *Diana and Actaeon*, pen and brown ink, brown wash, heightened with white, on pink prepared paper, 315×419 mm, *c.* 1588 (Bremen, Kunsthalle)

and old-fashioned, as if the artist had learnt practically nothing in Italy. Van Mander seems to have deliberately adapted his style to what was then the fashionable taste in Flanders.

Most of van Mander's paintings, however, were carried out in the northern Netherlands after 1583. Yet his colours continue to betray his Flemish background; they are similar to those of the Bruegel family: usually brown in the foreground, green in the centre and pale blue in the background. The figures are clothed in gentle tones, with sufficient contrasts of yellow, red and blue. The compositions are schematic and follow the rules set out in the *Schilder-boeck*: clusters of trees on the edges, a distant view in the middle (often showing a river winding through a landscape) and the narrative taking place in the foreground. Typical examples are the *Continence of Scipio* (Amsterdam, Rijksmus.) and *Mankind before the Flood* (Frankfurt am Main, Städel. Kstinst. & Städt. Gal.; see fig. 4). On the *verso* of the former, van Mander painted an appropriate allegorical scene, something he did in a few other cases as well. His landscapes reveal the influence of Gillis van Coninxloo, with whom he collaborated on several occasions; van Mander, for example, painted the figures in van Coninxloo's *Judgement of Midas* (Dresden, Gemäldegal. Alte Meister).

WRITINGS

Het schilder-boeck, waer in voor eerst de leerlustighe iueght den grondt der edel vry schilderconst in verscheyden deelen wort voorghedraghen: Daer nae in dry deelen t'leuen der vermaerde doorluchtighe schilders des ouden, en niewen tyds [The book of painters, in which firstly the foundation of the noble free art of painting is set out in several parts for the eager student: then in three parts the lives of the celebrated illustrious painters of old and new times] (Haarlem, [1603]–1604; rev. Amsterdam, 1618/*R* Utrecht, 1969)

BIBLIOGRAPHY

GENERAL

H. E. Greve: *De bronnen van Carel van Mander* [The sources of Carel van Mander] (The Hague, 1903)

R. Jacobsen: *Carel van Mander (1548–1606): Dichter en prozaschrijver* (Rotterdam, 1906)

H. Miedema: *Karel van Mander: Het bio-bibliografisch materiaal* (Amsterdam, 1972)

THE 'SCHILDER-BOECK'
Het leerdicht

O. Hirschmann: 'Beitrag zu einer Kommentar von Karel van Manders *Grondt der edel vry schilderconst*', *Oud-Holland*, xxxiii (1915)

R. Hoecker: *Das Lehrgedicht des Karel van Manders*, Quellen & Stud. Holland. Kstgesch., viii (The Hague, 1915)

H. Miedema: 'Karel van Mander's *Grondt der edel vry schilder-const*', *J. Hist. Ideas*, xxxiv (1973), pp. 653–68

——: *Karel van Mander: 'Der grondt der edel vry schilder-const'*, 2 vols (Utrecht, 1973); review by E. K. J. Reznicek in *Oud-Holland*, lxxxix (1975), pp. 102–28; and by L. de Pauw-de Veen in *Simiolus*, ix (1977), pp. 183–6

Leven van de antieke schilders

H. Miedema: *Karel van Mander: 'Het leven der oude antijcke doorluchtighe schilders'* (Amsterdam, 1977)

4. Karel van Mander I: *Mankind before the Flood*, oil on copper, 310×255 mm, 1600 (Frankfurt am Main, Städelsches Kunstinstitut und Städtische Galerie)

Leven van de Italiaanse schilders

H. Noe: *Karel van Mander in Italie* (The Hague, 1954)
Leven der moderne beroemde Italiaansche schilders; ed. H. Miedema (Alphen aan den Rijn, 1984)

Leven van de Nederlandse en Hoogduitse schilders

Levens van de beroemde Nederlandse en Hoogduitse schilders; ed. and Fr. trans. by H. Hymans, 2 vols (Paris, 1884–5); ed. and Ger. trans. by H. Floerke, 2 vols (Munich and Leipzig, 1906); ed. and Eng. trans. by C. van de Wall (New York, 1936) [unreliable]
A. F. Mirande and G. S. Overdiep: *'Het schilder-boeck' van Karel van Mander* (Amsterdam and Antwerp, 1950)
W. Waterschoot: *Ter liefde der const* [For the love of art] (Leiden, 1983)

ARTISTIC WORKS

Thieme–Becker; Wurzbach
E. Valentiner: *Karel van Mander als Maler* (Strasbourg, 1930)
W. Bernt: *Die niederländischen Maler des 17. Jahrhunderts*, 4 vols (Munich, 1948–62); Eng. trans., 3 vols (London and New York, 1970), ii, pp. 73–7
——: *'Die niederländischen Zeichner des 17. Jahrhunderts*, 2 vols (Munich, 1957–8), ii, no. 386
E. K. J. Reznicek: *Die Zeichnungen von Hendrick Goltzius*, 2 vols (Utrecht, 1961)
——: 'Een en ander over van Mander', *Oud-Holland*, cvii (1993), pp. 75–83
M. Leesberg: 'Karel van Mander as a Painter', *Simiolus*, xii (1993/4), pp. 5–57

E. K. J. REZNICEK

(2) Karel van Mander III (*b* Delft, 1610; *d* Copenhagen, *bur* 6 April 1670). Painter, grandson of (1) Karel van Mander I. After his father's death in 1623, the 13-year-old Karel III and his mother Cornelia Rooswijck moved to Denmark. From 1623 to 1629 Karel III trained with Pieter Isaacsz., and from 1631 he worked as a portrait painter to the royal family. In 1635 he received financial support from Christian IV to travel to the Netherlands and Flanders (where he visited the workshops of Rembrandt and Rubens) and then to France, Italy and Spain.

On his return to Denmark in 1638, Karel III became court painter, working in an eclectic style primarily influenced by Rembrandt and Rubens. Although his compositions tend to be traditional, he managed to break away from the rigidity of Danish portrait painting by his use of vivid colour and free handling of the brush. In both the equestrian portrait of *Christian IV* (1642) and the full-length portrait of the King (1643–4; both Hillerød, Frederiksborg Slot), the influence of Frans Hals, Rubens and van Dyck is evident. After Christian IV's death, van Mander III worked for his successor, Frederick III, and between 1650 and 1660 his portraits with innovative blue backgrounds made him very popular. The portrait of *Prince Jørgen* (1660; Hillerød, Frederiksborg Slot) is painted in the fashionable 'heroic style' of the time whereby the subject is depicted in Classical or mythological costume.

Van Mander III also worked as a decorative painter, and his *Abraham Blessing Melchizedek* for the chapel of Frederiksborg Castle (1642; *in situ*), since cut down, was inspired by Rembrandt. For the Amalienborg in Copenhagen, van Mander III produced five ceiling paintings with concert and drinking scenes, presumably symbolizing the *Five Senses*, the compositions of which were borrowed from ceiling paintings by Orazio Gentileschi and Agostino Tassi in the Palazzo Pallavicini-Rospigliosi in Rome.

BIBLIOGRAPHY

O. Andrup: 'Noter verdrørende Karel van Manders biografi' [Notes concerning Karel van Mander's biogrqaphy], *Kstmus. Årsskr.*, xx–xxi (1933–4), pp. 141–82
——: 'Noter om Karel van Mander' [Notes on Karel van Mander], *Kstmus. Årsskr.*, xxvi (1939), pp. 100–113
H. Gerson: *Ausbreitung und Nachwirkung der holländischen Malerei des 17. Jahrhunderts* (Haarlem, 1942), pp. 463–5
P. Eller: 'Karel van Mander', *Billedkunst og Skulptur: Rigetmaend lader sig male, 1500–1700* [Painting and sculpture: statesmen have themselves painted, 1500–1700], ii of *Dansk kunsthistorie* [Danish art history] (Copenhagen, 1973), pp. 165–91

M. J. T. M. STOMPÉ

Mandijn [Mandyn], **Jan** (*b* Haarlem, *c.* 1500; *d* Antwerp, 1559). South Netherlandish painter of north Netherlandish origin. He was trained in Haarlem but moved to Antwerp before 1530. Pieter Aertsen was living with Mandijn *c.* 1535, when Aertsen moved from Amsterdam to Antwerp. In 1537 Mandijn painted a copper memorial plaque for the Bishop of Dunkeld in Scotland, and he collaborated on the decoration of triumphal arches for Philip II's entrance into Antwerp in 1549. He took on pupils in Antwerp until 1559, the best known of whom are Hans van der Elburcht (*fl* 1536–53), Gillis Mostaert and Bartholomäus Spranger. The connection with Mandijn may explain the common stylistic features of the work of Aertsen and van der Elburcht.

On the basis of Mandijn's only surviving signed work, the *Temptation of St Anthony* (Haarlem, Frans Halsmus.), he is called a follower of Hieronymus Bosch. The painting is certainly inspired by Bosch's work, but Mandijn painted in a freer, looser manner, and the colours and fantastic creatures are less harmonious, to the extent that the whole has a less powerful expression. These features characterize a whole series of Antwerp 'devil pictures' that have been attributed to him, such as the *Temptation of St Christopher* (Munich, Alte Pin.). The distinction between the style of these works and that of Pieter Huys is not, however, always clear. There is also doubt about the authenticity of the signature on the *Temptation of St Anthony*, since archival evidence indicates that Mandijn could not write. It has also been suggested that Mandijn can be identified with the anonymous Master of SS Paul and Barnabas, the painter of *SS Paul and Barnabas at Lystra* (Budapest, Mus. F.A.), whose style falls between that of Pieter Coecke van Aelst, Jan van Amstel and Jan Sanders van Hemessen.

BIBLIOGRAPHY
L. Van Puyvelde: *La Peinture flamande au siècle de Bosch et Brueghel* (Paris, 1962), pp. 69–72
G. Unverfehrt: *Hieronymus Bosch: Die Rezeption seiner Kunst im frühen 16. Jahrhundert* (Berlin, 1980)
J. Bruyn: 'De Meester van Paulus en Barnabus (Jan Mandijn) en een vroeg werk van Pieter Aertsen', *Rubens and his World: Aangeboden aan R. A. d'Hulst* (Antwerp, 1985), pp. 17–29

ELS VERMANDERE

Mändl [Mandl], **(Michael) Bernhard** (*b* Prague, *c.* 1660; *d* Salzburg, 23 April 1711). Austrian sculptor of Bohemian origin. He is first recorded after his arrival in Salzburg *c.* 1690, where his first signed work was the marble *Horse Tamer* group (1695; Salzburg, Sigmundsplatz), probably executed to a design by Johann Bernhard Fischer von Erlach. In it Mändl is referring back to the antique groups on the Piazza Quirinale in Rome. The group's balanced composition was greatly admired, and it was the inspiration for the *Horse Tamer* group installed in the 1720s in front of Schloss Belvedere in Vienna. Mändl's marble statues of *St Peter* and *St Paul* (1697) flanking the doorway of Salzburg Cathedral, whose positioning echoes the contemporary placing of wooden figures over altars, are typical of his work, with their soft, rounded modelling. *St Paul*'s downcast eyes are fixed on the viewer, while the opposite movement of his body draws the eye up the façade of the cathedral to the gable figures, which had been installed *c.* 1650. Johann Bernhard Fischer often employed Mändl for decorative sculpture on his Salzburg buildings, including the Hofstall (1694), Dreifaltigkeitskirche (1699–1702), Ursulinenkirche (1702) and Kollegienkirche (1707).

BIBLIOGRAPHY
L. Pretzell: *Salzburger Barockplastik* (Berlin, 1935), pp. 52–9

JOHANNES RAHMHARTER

Mandorla [It.: 'almond']. Almond-shaped light enclosing the whole of a sacred figure.   □

Mandu [Mandoo]. Fortified town *c.* 98 km south of Indore in Madhya Pradesh, central India. The town flourished under the PARAMARA dynasty at the end of the 10th century but fell into Muslim hands in 1303 at the time of 'Ala' al-Din Khalji (*reg* 1296–1316) and was later chosen as the capital of the sultanate of Malwa by Hushang Shah Ghuri (*reg* 1405–35), who renamed it Shadiabad (City of Joy). Little remains from the pre-Islamic period apart from the foundations of the fort, founded in the 6th century, which were incorporated into the walls of the new town. Begun by Dilavar Khan Ghuri (*reg c.* 1401–5) and completed by Mahmud Shah Khalji I (*reg* 1436–69), this lies south of the citadel and is surrounded by fortified walls *c.* 41 km long running around the upper contours of

the hills. A large part of the land within the walls was never occupied by buildings and was left as gardens, farmland and forest dotted with pavilions and tombs. The architecture of Mandu is rooted in the style of the TUGHLUQ sultanate of Delhi but displays many local features, such as marble and stucco inlaid with coloured stone and extensive use of tiles.

The citadel is entered through a complex fortified gateway with three portals, the arches of which are constructed of red and grey stone and decorated with spearhead fringes in the Delhi style of the 13th and 14th centuries. Inside, the palace buildings include two audience halls—the ruinous Gada Shah Dukkan ('Gada Shah's Shop') and the smaller but well-preserved Hindola Mahal ('Swing Palace'). These are similar in plan, each consisting of a vaulted audience hall with a two-storey structure at one end, the throne-room being on the upper level overlooking the hall. The entrance façade of the Gada Shah Dukkan has retained some of its elaborate marble inlay. In the centre of the citadel are two large tanks: the Kapur Talao on the east and the much larger Munja Talao on the west. Among the residential palaces constructed around these is the impressive late 15th-century Jahaz Mahal ('Ship Palace'; *see* INDIAN SUBCONTINENT, fig. 94); set between the two reservoirs, this is a large, multi-storey building with a skyline of domed pavilions and a complex hydraulic system that provided water for fountains and pools constructed on its upper levels. Near the palaces is the mosque of Dilavar Khan Ghuri, which has a flat-roofed colonnaded court. It was built in 1405 with spoil from older temples and was later connected to the palace complex and used as the royal mosque. It is slightly larger than the mosque of Malik Mughith (1431–2) in Mandu town, which again was built with temple spoil; the design of the latter incorporates a domed entrance pavilion and another three domes over the prayer-hall. The finely carved columns of the two mosques are the only remains of the Hindu temples that once stood in Mandu.

In the centre of the old town, the Jami' Masjid commenced by Hushang Shah and completed by Mahmud Khalji in 1454 is built on a grand scale around a central courtyard standing on a massive platform, with three large domes over the prayer-hall and a domed entrance chamber. The style of this chamber, with its three openings at each side and four smaller domes at the corners of the roof, is repeated in the tomb of Hushang Shah (*c.* 1440), which is set in a courtyard to the west of the mosque (see fig.). To the east of the mosque and facing its entrance stand the ruins of the tomb of Mahmud Khalji, which was originally a square, domed chamber; its remaining piers also display traces of marble inlay. The tomb stands on the arched platform of an earlier building, known as the Ashrafi Mahal, which was probably a theological college or madrasa. One of the corner towers of the Ashrafi Mahal was in the form of a huge minaret, over 50 m tall and faced with green marble, which was built by Mahmud Khalji as a sign of his victory over Rana Kumbha of Mewar (*reg c.* 1433–68). The minaret, now fallen, was standing during the Mughal period and is described in the memoirs of the emperor Jahangir. The form of the two royal tombs seems to have been the inspiration for numerous lesser tombs built in the fields within the walls.

In 1526 Mandu fell into the hands of the Gujarat sultan Bahadur Shah (*reg* 1526), who put an end to the Malwa sultanate, and the region remained under Gujarat until 1534, when the Mughal emperor Humayun (*reg* 1530–40, 1555–6) took over the fort and for a short time made it his residence. In the subsequent struggle between Humayun and Sher Shah Sur (*see* SUR (ii)), Mandu changed hands several times between local commanders and was finally taken by Daulat Khan, who ruled as Sultan Baz Bahadur from 1555 to 1566, when he was deposed by Akbar (*reg* 1556–1605). At the southern end of the walled area is a large enclosure that seems to have been intended as the site of Baz Bahadur's citadel; inside is the Baz Bahadur Palace, founded by Nasir al-Din in 1508 and subsequently adapted by Baz Bahadur. Its buildings are set around two courtyards near a tank known as the Riwa Kund. Another building, the Rupmati Pavilion, set on a vantage-point overlooking the southern valley, is said to have been the residence of Baz Bahadur's beloved, Rupmati, but from the content of an inscription it appears that the building is earlier and may have been restored or extended by Baz Bahadur. The Mughal emperors seem to have been impressed by the architecture of Mandu. Akbar visited the town four times, and Jahangir admired its buildings in his memoirs, noting the seven-storey victory minaret and the then newly constructed Nilkantha Palace, still preserved, which overlooks the wooded valley west of the town. The influence of Mandu architecture was particularly strong on Shah Jahan (*reg* 1628–58), who was the governor of the region for a long period and repaired many of the older palace buildings as well as constructing some of his own. These include a palace to the west of the Munja Talao and probably another north of the Kapur Talao; the latter, now known as the Gada Shah House, has interior wall paintings. The later buildings of Shah Jahan in Delhi and Agra, which are renowned for their marble inlay and the display of water, may owe much of their inspiration to the architecture of Mandu.

See also INDIAN SUBCONTINENT, §III, 6(ii)(e).

BIBLIOGRAPHY
C. Harris: *The Ruins of Mandoo* (London, 1860)
J. M. Campbell: 'Mandu', *J. Bombay Branch Royal Asiat. Soc.*, xix (1902), pp. 154–201
E. Barnes: 'Dhar and Mandu', *J. Bombay Branch Royal Asiat. Soc.*, xxi (1904), pp. 339–91
G. Yazdani: *Mandu, the City of Joy* (Oxford, 1929)
R. Ettinghausen and others: 'In Praise of Mandu', *Marg*, xiii/3 (1959)
D. R. Patil: *Mandu* (New Delhi, 1971/*R* 1982)

MEHRDAD SHOKOOHY

Mandylion of Edessa. Term for a miraculous image (untraced) of Christ, believed to date from the 1st century AD. It is one of a number of holy images 'not made by human hands' whose origins are obscured in legends of the early Christian East. In the late 6th century the image was first mentioned as a miraculous icon. The fully developed 8th-century version of the legend relates how King Abgar V (*reg* 4 BC–AD 50) of Edessa (now Urfa in Turkey) commanded a portrait to be made of Christ but received instead a cloth miraculously imprinted with Christ's features (*see* EARLY CHRISTIAN AND BYZANTINE ART, fig. 67). The image became known as the Holy Mandylion (Arab. *mandil*: 'small cloth'). The fame and

Mandu, tomb of Hushang Shah, *c.* 1440

importance of the Edessan image grew as the need increased to counter arguments against the cult of images. During the Iconoclastic Controversy (726–843) the Mandylion (though still in Arab-occupied Edessa) was cited frequently by Iconophiles as proof of Christ's endorsement of image making. In 944 it was brought from Edessa to Constantinople and honoured as a prime relic of the Orthodox Church and remained there until the Crusader conquest of Constantinople in 1204, when it was sold to the French and taken to the Sainte-Chapelle in Paris. It was almost certainly lost during the French Revolution (1789–99), although attempts have been made (without success) to identify the Mandylion with the Holy Shroud in Turin Cathedral.

There is little evidence that copies of the Mandylion were made before its transfer to Constantinople: the image entered Christian iconography during the 11th and 12th centuries, first in manuscript picture cycles that were elaborated to accompany narratives of the Edessan legend and then as part of a fixed scheme of images in church decoration. Although these representations adhere to early descriptions of the Mandylion (the so-called Eastern type of Christ, long-haired and bearded), stylistically they differ considerably, according to local and period influences.

BIBLIOGRAPHY
E. von Dobschütz: *Christusbilder: Untersuchungen zur christlichen Legende*, i (Leipzig, 1899)
A. Grabar: *La Sainte Face de Laon: Le Mandylion dans l'art orthodoxe* (Prague, 1931)
K. Weitzmann: 'The Mandylion and Constantine Porphyrogennetos', *Cah. Archéol.*, xi (1960), pp. 163–84
A. Cameron: *The Sceptic and the Shroud* (London, 1980)

SARAH MORGAN

Mane, John. *See* MAIANO, DA, (3).

Mané-Katz [Katz, Mané] (*b* Kremenchug, Ukraine, 5 June 1894; *d* Tel Aviv, 9 Sept 1962). French painter and sculptor of Ukrainian birth. He came from an orthodox Jewish family; his father was sexton of a synagogue, and he was originally intended to become a rabbi. After studying at the School of Fine Arts in Kiev, he visited Paris for the first time in 1913 and enrolled in Fernand Cormon's class at the Ecole des Beaux-Arts, where his fellow students included Chaïm Soutine. He was influenced by Rembrandt, by the Fauves (especially Derain) and, briefly, by Cubism.

Mané-Katz returned to Ukraine after the outbreak of World War I. There he was appointed professor at the academy in Khar'kov (now Kharkiv) in 1917, after the Revolution. He left again for Paris in 1921, this time with the intention of taking as his principal theme life in the ghettos of Eastern Europe, the rabbis and Talmudic students, the fiddlers and drummers, comedians and beggars, for example in the *Eternal People (Am Israel Hai)* (1938; Haifa, Mané-Katz Mus.); he also painted a number of landscapes and flower studies. His style became expressionist and baroque, with loose brushwork and rhythmical forms. He obtained French citizenship in 1927 but after the fall of France took refuge from 1940 to 1945 in New York, where he also began to make a few sculptures, such as the *Double-bass Player* (bronze, h. 610 mm, 1943; see Aries, i, p. 194). After the war his paintings became much bolder in their colours and patterning. He made a number of visits to Israel and left the works in his possession to the town of Haifa, where they formed the basis of a museum devoted to his work.

BIBLIOGRAPHY
J.-M. Aimot: *Mané-Katz: L'Art et la vie* (Paris, 1933)
M. Ragon: *Mané-Katz* (Paris, 1960)
R. S. Aries: *Mané-Katz, 1894–1962: The Complete Works*, 2 vols (London, 1970 and 1972)

RONALD ALLEY

Mánes. Bohemian family of artists. The most notable members were the landscape painter and lithographer (1) Antonín Mánes and his son (2) Josef Mánes, who was an illustrator, designer and draughtsman as well as an influential painter. Antonín's brother Václav Mánes (1793–1858) was head of the Prague Academy of Fine Arts for a short while, and Antonín's children Antonína, Amálie (1817–83) and Quido (1828–80) were also painters.

(1) Antonín Mánes (*b* Prague, 3 Nov 1784; *d* Prague, 23 July 1843). Painter and lithographer. He studied at the Prague Academy of Fine Arts and in the landscape school of Karel Postl, which he took over on his tutor's death. He elevated landscape painting into a recognized sphere of artistic endeavour in Prague, which led to the landscape school being fully incorporated into the Academy, where Mánes was a professor from 1836 to 1843. In the early 1830s he published for his students a lithographic album of the study of tree types (*Baumschlagstudien*). He completed several of Postl's last paintings, introducing new life into them through work on detail. He enriched landscape painting by including realistic domestic motifs and features from the Bohemian countryside. In his first mature work, *Landscape with Royal Summer Residence* (1816; Prague, N.G.), he introduced motifs from Prague architecture.

Mánes never visited Italy, as did his brother Václav Mánes and František Tkadlík, but this led him to pay more attention to his native landscape, which, by the 1820s, he portrayed with great delicacy. He combined a Romantic approach to nature with concepts from Dutch landscape painting. For example *Landscape with Ruin (Abbey at Kelso)* (1827; Prague, N.G.) is probably influenced by Thomas Gray's *Elegy Written in a Country Churchyard* (1751) as well as by the versions of *Jewish Cemetery* by Jacob van Ruisdael (second half of 17th century; Detroit, MI, Inst. A., and Dresden, Gemäldegal. Alte Meister). Patriotic historicism in landscape painting had concentrated on castles and fortifications in Bohemia; Mánes transferred this subject-matter from media such as watercolours to oil painting. From the 1830s his oil paintings concentrated less on composed landscape and pageantry and more on domestic motifs, sometimes depicting stormy moods of nature (e.g. *Kokořín Castle*, 1839; Prague, N.G.).

In Mánes's later works even his large paintings were characterized by increasing emphasis on the accuracy of the depiction of the motifs, as in *Křivoklát Castle* (1842; Prague, N.G.). At the same time he widened the spectrum of his *plein-air* studies, which he had been painting in oils since the 1820s. His paintings of the early 1840s, in which he captured the atmosphere of the countryside (e.g. *St John under the Cliffs* (1840); Prague, N.G.), had much in common with the work of his son Josef.

BIBLIOGRAPHY
E. Reitharová: *Antonín Mánes* (Prague, 1967)
M. Nováková: 'A. Mánes', *Die tschechische Malerei des XIX. Jahrhunderts* (exh. cat. by J. Kotalík, Vienna, Belvedere, 1984), pp. 41–2

(2) Josef Mánes (*b* Prague, 12 April 1820; *d* Prague, 9 Dec 1871). Painter, illustrator, designer and draughtsman, son of (1) Antonín Mánes. He began his studies in 1835 at the Prague Academy of Fine Arts under his uncle Václav Mánes and under both František Tkadlík and Christian Ruben (1805–75). From 1844 to 1846 he studied in Munich, where he gained a thorough knowledge of Munich painting. He also travelled in central Europe and spent time in Vienna. The work of Moritz von Schwind was of particular interest to him, as was to a lesser extent that of Bonaventura Genelli and Ludwig Richter. From the early 1840s, apart from portraits and studies depicting various moods of mountainous landscapes, or motifs such as *The Wanderer* (Ostrava, A.G.), his paintings largely reflect Romantic sources. In 1846 he exhibited *Meeting of Petrarch and Laura in Avignon* (Prague, N.G.) in Munich and Prague.

Mánes's initial ambition was to paint academically esteemed monumental and historical subjects, but increasing conflicts with Ruben, the director of the Academy, and the development of Bohemian nationalism after the defeat of the 1848 revolution deprived him of the prospect of an academic career, as it had his older contemporary, Josef Hellich. Mánes belonged to the prominent opposition group, the Association of Fine Artists (1848–56), and to the nationally orientated group of writers, musicians and designers, the ARTISTIC FORUM (Umělecká Beseda). In 1849 he was a portrait painter at the regional anti-imperial congress at Kroměříž in Moravia; later he joined in many Bohemian and Slovak activities and was one of the first Bohemian artists to apply himself to folklore. On several journeys to Poland, Silesia, and around Moravia and Slovakia he undertook studies for an unpublished album of Slavonic national costumes, which he originally wanted to publish with his brother Quido, whose portrait he painted in 'Mazurian' dress at the artists' ball of 1847 (Prague, N.G.). He also illustrated folk-songs: in 1845 he contributed to a collection with illustrations by students from the Prague Academy (published by Haas brothers, Prague). From 1856 he illustrated songs on his own.

Mánes made a study of country people, mainly at Haná in Moravia where he often stayed with his friends and patrons, the family of Count Sylva-Taroucca. Paintings for his hosts included *Life at a Nobleman's Residence*, a cycle of watercolours (Prague Castle) and variations on that cycle (Prague, N.G.). At Haná he began a series of small paintings in the 1850s that contain something of the sensuality of colour and light and the intimacy of the Rococo Revival (e.g. *Outing III*; Prague, N.G.; or *In Summer (Red Parasols)*; untraced). He was in touch with Carl Spitzweg, but genre painting did not represent the core of his work as it did with Spitzweg and Quido Mánes. He produced many small humorous drawings and watercolours, often on writing paper or in diaries, for example *Caricatures of Schools of Painting* (c. 1860; Prague, N.G.) and other cartoons in *St Luke's Book*, a portfolio of humorous drawings and texts by different authors (mostly 1850s; Prague, N.G.). As well as drawings with humorous or ironic contents, he created fairy-tale scenes combining his own sensual studies of nature with allegorical and fantastic compositions, as in the pencil drawings *Gardener and Flowers* and *Dusk* (both early 1850s; Prague, N.G.) or in *Cave of Venus* (1867–9; Prague, N.G.). The Association of Fine Artists used his designs for their lithographs *Honeymoon at Haná* (1850) and *Home* (1856; both Prague, N.G.).

Throughout the 1850s, in addition to his work as a painter, especially of portraits, Mánes was occupied with illustrations and designs, many of which were not realized. He created designs for industrial and applied art, including bookbindings, for example *Perly české* ('Czech pearls'), a collection of poems and prose (1855; copy in Vienna, Österreich. Nbib.). He produced illustrations, mainly for the Prague publishers Bellmann & Kober, including the cover for *Slovenské pověsti* ('Slovak tales') by Božena Němcová (1857). The pinnacle was meant to be an illustrated edition of *Rukopis královédvorský* (Králův Dvůr manuscript), a romantic forgery of early medieval chronicles of Bohemian history. Only the first two parts were realized, in which figural scenes and decorative ornament appear above the text (Prague, 1860). In *Home*, in the *Musica* cycle (after 1855; Prague, N.G.) and in the Králův Dvůr illustrations Mánes characterized the Bohemian people by means of figurative types, and also by combining the lyrical expression of the figures and scenes with a certain monumentality. In many of his works he used native Bohemian ornament, usually Romanesque, often with vernacular elements, and he enlivened them with Gothic decorative schemes.

From the late 1850s Mánes designed many large-scale works, some prestigious, including painted banners as well as the design of figural medallions (1863) for the doors of the church of SS Cyril and Methodius in the Prague suburb of Karlín. The Old Town Hall clock in Prague (1865; original in Prague, Mus. City) consists of 12 calendar medallions symbolizing the union of the people and the soil within the rhythm of time, as in medieval examples; it is a synthesis of Mánes's artistic characteristics. His legacy, especially his 'national' figurative type and his lyricism,

was taken up by the following generation of Bohemian painters and sculptors. This generation began work in the 1870s and was associated with the decoration of the National Theatre in Prague (e.g. Mikoláš Aleš, Felix Jenewein, František Ženíšek and Josef Myslbek). The generation of the 1890s, including Alphonse Mucha, also claimed him as their predecessor.

See also JEWISH ART, fig. 7.

BIBLIOGRAPHY

K. B. Mádl: *Josef Mánes* (Prague, 1905)
A. Matějček and others: *Dílo Josefa Mánesa* [The work of Josef Mánes], 4 vols (Prague, 1920–40)
J. Loriš: *Mánesovy podobizny* [Mánes's portraits] (Prague, 1954)
J. Neumann: *Modern Czech Painting and the Classical Tradition* (Prague, 1958)
O. Macková: *Josef Mánes* (Prague, 1970)
E. Reitharová: 'Josef Mánes—Rané dílo: Katalog díla z let 1830–48' [Josef Mánes—early work: catalogue of work from the years 1830–48], *Umění*, xix (1972), pp. 29–73
Josef Mánes, 1820–1871 (exh. cat. by J. Kotalík, Prague, N.G., 1972)
H. Volaková: *Josef Mánes, malíř vzorků a ornamentu* [Josef Mánes, painter of patterns and ornaments] (Prague, 1981)
M. Nováková: 'J. Mánes', *Die tschechische Malerei des XIX. Jahrhunderts* (exh. cat. by J. Kotalík, Vienna, Belvedere, 1984), pp. 42–5
Krajina v díle Josefa Mánesa [Landscape in the work of Josef Mánes] (exh. cat. by G. Kesnerová, Prague, N.G., 1991)

ROMAN PRAHL

Manes, Pablo Curatella. *See* CURATELLA MANES, PABLO.

Manessier, Alfred (*b* Saint-Ouen, nr Amiens, 5 Dec 1911). French painter and decorative artist. His earliest training was at the Ecole des Beaux-Arts at Amiens. In 1929 he moved to Paris, where he registered to study architecture at the Ecole des Beaux-Arts, although he did not complete the course. He made copies of Old Master paintings at the Louvre and frequented the Académies Libres. At the Académie Ranson in 1935 he met Roger Bissière, who was teaching there, and became friendly with a small group of his students: Jean Le Moal (*b* 1909), Jean Bertholle (*b* 1909) and the sculptor Etienne-Martin. He exhibited for the first time with them in 1938 at the Galerie Breteau in Paris. In 1943 he went on a Trappist retreat and became a believer, an event that was to leave its mark on all his work. He executed several commissions for stained-glass windows for churches in France and abroad, in 1948–50 at the church at Bréseux, Doubs; in 1953 at the church of St-Pierre, Trinquetaille, Arles; in 1957 at the Chapel of Sainte-Thérèse de l'Infant Jésus et de la Sainte Face, Hem, Nord (for which he also designed a Benediction cape and five chasubles in 1957 and 1958–9), and in All Saints church, Basle (1952).

Manessier is rare among 20th-century painters in his concentration on religious themes. After 1945 he adopted an abstract style, developing signs based on the cross and the crown of thorns as Christian symbols, as in *Crown of Thorns* (1951; Essen, Mus. Flkwang). The range of colours in his paintings, severe and opalescent at first, gradually became darker and more dramatic, for example *Requiem for November 1956* (1956/7; Stuttgart, Staatsgal.). Manessier's aesthetic position was allied to a typically French tendency of the 1950s in which the abstract and the figurative were considered interchangeable. Although he was awarded a major prize for painting at the Venice Biennale in 1962, his reputation subsequently went into eclipse for about twenty years, in part because of his decision to exhibit only on rare occasions and to live in seclusion near Chartres.

BIBLIOGRAPHY

J. Cayrol: *Manessier* (Paris, 1955, rev. 1966)
M. Brion: *L'Art abstrait* (Paris, 1956)
M.-G. Bernard: *Catalogue of the Galerie de France* (Paris, 1970)
J. Hodin: *Manessier* (Bath, 1972)

DORA VALLIER

Mánes Union of Artists [Czech Spolek výtvarných umělců Mánes]. Czech association of painters, sculptors, architects, critics and art historians, active from 1887 to 1949. It was founded in 1887 by students at the Prague Academy of Fine Arts whose aim was to develop the Bohemian artistic traditions embodied in the work of Josef Mánes (*see* MÁNES, (2)) and of artists of the older generation such as Mikoláš Aleš, whom they elected as their first president. In the mid-1890s, when the union comprised almost the entire younger generation of artists, it specifically associated itself with the Secessionist movement in central Europe. In the autumn of 1896 it started publishing the first Czech art journal, *Volné směry*, and from 1898 onwards it organized exhibitions that expressed the new artistic values, both as regards the choice of works and the methods of presentation. Among the leading personalities were the sculptor Stanislav Sucharda, the painter Jan Preisler and the architect Jan Kotěra. The union collaborated with the Hagenbund of Vienna, and established many contacts with Paris and other artistic centres. Members systematically brought modern European art to the notice of the Bohemian public, organized the Rodin retrospective exhibition of 1902, for which the society built a *fin-de-siècle* exhibition pavilion to Kotěra's design, and also mounted numerous other exhibitions. In 1911 the younger generation, led by Emil Filla, left the union and founded the GROUP OF PLASTIC ARTISTS. When the latter fell into decline during World War I, the majority of those who had left returned to the Mánes Union, occupying a decisive position in it during the inter-war period. In 1930 the union opened a functionalist exhibition building, designed by Otakar Novotný. In the 1930s it supported contemporary artistic trends and provided a venue for avant-garde architects and Surrealist artists. In 1936, when the photographic section was founded, the union brought together the avant-garde of the 1920s and 1930s at the International Exhibition of Photography. The last influx of strength into the union was linked with the generation that matured in the late 1930s, including Josef Istler, Václav Tikal, Zdeněk Sklenář and Karel Černý. Soon after the Communist putsch in Czechoslovakia in 1948 the union went into decline.

SVU

BIBLIOGRAPHY

Mánes (exh. cat. by J. Kotalík, Prague, Mánes Exh. Hall, 1987)
L. Bydžovská: *Spolek výtvarných umělců Mánes v letech, 1887–1907* [Mánes Union of Artists, 1887–1907] (diss.)

LENKA BYDŽOVSKÁ

Manet, Edouard (*b* Paris, 23 Jan 1832; *d* Paris, 30 April 1883). French painter and printmaker. Once classified as an Impressionist, he has subsequently been regarded as a Realist who influenced and was influenced by the Impressionist painters of the 1870s, though he never exhibited with them nor adopted fully their ideas and procedures. His painting is notable for its brilliant *alla prima* painterly technique; in both paintings and prints he introduced a new era of modern, urban subject-matter. In his relatively short career he evolved from an early style marked by dramatic light-dark contrasts and based on Spanish 17th-century painting to high-keyed, freely brushed compositions whose content bordered at times on Symbolism.

1. Life and work. 2. Technique. 3. Character and personality. 4. Critical reception and posthumous reputation.

1. LIFE AND WORK.

(i) 1832–59. (ii) 1859–65. (iii) 1865–70. (iv) 1870–79. (v) 1879–83.

(i) 1832–59. Manet was the eldest of three sons of Auguste Manet, a distinguished civil servant in the Ministry of Justice, and Eugénie Désirée Fournier, daughter of a diplomatic envoy to the Swedish court. Although he showed talent for drawing and caricature at an early age, his career as an artist began only after his secondary education at the Collège Rollin and two attempts to enter the Naval College, in which he failed even after a training voyage to Rio de Janeiro (1848–9). Encouraged as a schoolboy in his love of art by his maternal uncle Edouard Fournier and by his school-friend Antonin Proust, later to become Minister of Fine Arts, he enrolled, with Proust, in the atelier of Thomas Couture in September 1850. Among his earliest extant works are copies made in the Louvre after Venetian and Florentine Renaissance Masters and Dutch genre painters. His eclecticism reflected the example of Couture, who also taught the traditional techniques and colour formulae that Manet was later to abandon. During his six years of training with Couture, Manet did not enter the Prix de Rome, preferring to visit museums in Belgium, Holland, Germany, Austria and Italy. In February 1856 he established his own studio, and in 1857 he went again to Florence.

(ii) 1859–65. By 1860 Manet had moved his studio twice and had set up home with Suzanne Leenhoff, his family's piano teacher, who became his wife in 1863. Manet's earliest independent works such as his portrait of *Mme Brunet* (?1860; New York, priv. col., see Rouart and Wildenstein, no. 31) are dark in tone and are indebted to earlier artists, notably Velázquez, Rubens and Italian Renaissance Masters. His first Salon entry—the *Absinthe Drinker* (1859; Copenhagen, Ny Carlsberg Glyp.)—was refused in 1859, in spite of favourable comment from Delacroix. The *Spanish Singer* (1860; New York, Met.) and his portrait of *M. and Mme Manet* (1860; Paris, Mus. d'Orsay) were accepted in 1861 (the Salon was then biennial), winning an honourable mention and one favourable review. In the same year he also showed work at a private gallery and at the Imperial Academy in St Petersburg. Manet's hopes for early success, inspired by these auspicious beginnings, were soon disappointed.

Manet's art showed marked change and maturation during 1862. The enormous canvas the *Old Musician* (Washington, DC, N.G.A.) still referred to Spanish and other Old Master painting but introduced the subject of marginal city life, while the smaller *Music in the Tuileries Gardens* (1862; London, N.G.; *see* FÊTE CHAMPÊTRE, fig. 3) was his first straightforward image of a contemporary urban scene. In such works as *Music in the Tuileries Gardens* and the *Street Singer* (*c*. 1862; Boston, MA, Mus. F.A.) he identified himself with the dandy in pursuit of the 'heroism of modern life', reflecting his close association with Charles Baudelaire. A number of pictures were shown in an exhibition at the Galerie Martinet in early 1863, when the first clear signs of unfavourable critical reception emerged.

The three paintings Manet submitted to the Salon of 1863 were refused along with so many other works that the Emperor instituted a 'Salon des refusés', at which the *Déjeuner sur l'herbe* (Paris, Mus. d'Orsay; see fig. 1) was the centre of a critical storm, in part for its challenging subject-matter and in part for its innovative colour and brushwork. Controversy greeted his accepted Salon entries for many years thereafter, reaching its height in the scandal provoked by his *Olympia* (Paris, Mus. d'Orsay; *see* REALISM, fig. 2), painted in 1863 but first shown in 1865. In *Déjeuner sur l'herbe* and *Olympia* an element of ironic mockery colours the homage paid to Italian Renaissance art. In poses derived from works by Raphael and Titian, Manet presented on the one hand a foursome of profligate youths picnicking and bathing in compromising circumstances while mimicking idealized river gods of antiquity,

and on the other, a heroic but brazen nude figure of a reclining modern courtesan in the pose and setting of Titian's *Venus of Urbino* (1538; Florence, Uffizi). In these, as in several works of 1862 and later, Manet depicted a favoured model, Victorine Meurend. Scholarship has shown these famous compositions to assimilate to Old Master designs the spirit of the popular libertine lithographic and photographic imagery that had become part of the visual culture of mid-19th-century France. By inserting a vulgar modernity into the complex web of references in these paintings, Manet put himself in a theoretical position similar to that of Gustave Courbet, whose work had shocked the French public and critics in the 1850s; but Manet's urban emphasis and a cool, unmodulated paint surface were foreign to Courbet's art.

Acting on his lifelong conviction that the Salon was the place to compete, Manet continued to submit works with varying success: *Episode at a Bull-fight* (?1864–5; fragment, Washington, DC, N.G.A.) and *Dead Christ and Angels* (1864; Washington, DC, N.G.A.) were accepted in 1864, *Jesus Mocked by Soldiers* (1865; Chicago, IL, A. Inst.) in 1865 with *Olympia*. He enjoyed a certain notoriety and was considered the leader of a 'school' that included Edgar Degas and the younger Impressionists whom he saw regularly at the Café Guerbois. In the summer of 1865,

1. Edouard Manet: *Déjeuner sur l'herbe*, oil on canvas, 2.08×2.65m, 1863 (Paris, Musée d'Orsay)

following the critical fiasco of *Olympia*, he travelled to Spain where he first saw major works by Goya and Velázquez. Although he had previously painted many pictures with Spanish themes, he was newly inspired by the formal and colouristic features of Spanish painting to produce such paintings as *Matador Saluting* (1866–7; New York, Met.).

Manet played an important part in the revival of original etchings. His career as a printmaker, though it presents problems of chronology, seems to have begun in 1860, with one lithographic caricature and a number of etchings. He showed etchings in 1862 at the print publisher and dealer Cadart's and became a founder-member of the Société des Aquafortistes under whose auspices he issued a portfolio of etchings the same year. This portfolio was reissued with some changes and additions in 1874. Etching was his favoured medium until the late 1860s, after which lithography became more important.

(iii) 1865–70. Emile Zola, writing in *L'Evénement* on the Salon of 1866, launched a spirited defence of Manet, whose *The Fifer* (1866; Paris, Mus. d'Orsay) and the *Tragic Actor* (1865; Washington, DC, N.G.A.) had been rejected by that year's Salon jury. In 1867 he published a fuller biographical and critical study. This support gained Zola the friendship of Manet who painted his portrait in 1868 (Paris, Mus. d'Orsay). The portrait shows the impact on Manet's art of Japanese woodblock prints, newly available in Paris since the opening of Japan to the West in 1853. A tendency toward flattened space and unmodulated areas of colour, already present in such earlier works as *Mlle Victorine in the Costume of an Espada* (1862; New York, Met.), was reinforced, and Japanese artefacts began to appear as accessories. Zola's criticism pointed out these features in Manet's art and argued that he was primarily interested in the act of painting and of representing visual experience rather than in the subject-matter depicted. This approach, intended to defuse hostile reactions to the somewhat shocking subject-matter of *Déjeuner sur l'herbe* and *Olympia*, had the added effect of aligning Manet's art with the prevailing avant-garde theory of Art for Art's Sake.

Not having been invited to participate in the Exposition Universelle of 1867, Manet set up a private exhibition of 50 of his works next to the exposition grounds in a specially constructed pavilion that was ignored by the public and press alike. Manet had, however, published a catalogue with a short, unsigned preface (repr. in Moreau-Nélaton, 1926, i, pp. 86–7), one of the few statements about his art that can be attributed to his own ideas (it has been presumed that he received help from his literary friends). In it the importance of exhibiting is stressed, and his work is characterized as 'sincere', one of the watchwords of the Realist movement.

In 1867 Manet undertook to paint a vast canvas representing the execution of the Emperor Maximilian, an event that had taken place in Mexico on 19 June of that year. Five versions of this composition exist: a full-scale oil study (Boston, MA, Mus. F.A.), a group of fragments from a dismembered canvas (London, N.G.), a lithograph (see 1977 exh. cat., no. 54), a small definitive sketch (Copenhagen, Ny Carlsberg Glyp.) and the definitive

canvas (Mannheim, Ksthalle). Drawing inspiration from Goya's *Third of May 1808* (1814; Madrid, Prado) and contemporary pictorial reportage, Manet created a Realist image devoid of any romantic commentary such as that found in Goya. The charge of lack of interest in his subject is difficult to sustain in this case in view of the time and energy he devoted to it. More persuasive is the proposal that understatement for greater effect (litotes) was his aim (1983 exh. cat., p. 18). Early in 1868 Manet was advised by the administration that his painting of the execution would not be accepted at the next Salon and that authorization to publish the lithograph of it would not be granted. Although Manet defended himself on artistic grounds through notices by journalist friends, it is clear that the subject was calculated to embarrass the imperial regime, an intention that accords with his lifelong Republican sympathies.

In the summer of 1868 Manet met the painter BERTHE MORISOT who was briefly his pupil; she married his brother, Eugène, in 1874, and also modelled for several pictures, including *Resting, Portrait of Berthe Morisot* (1870; Providence, RI, Sch. Des., Mus. A.). The most celebrated of these works, *The Balcony* (1868–9; Paris, Mus. d'Orsay), was accepted at the Salon of 1869, together with *Luncheon in the Studio* (1868; Munich, Neue Pin.). These two pictures were Manet's masterpieces of the late 1860s and display many of his abiding qualities. The most prominent tones were flatly applied and unusual: silky black for Léon Leenhoff's jacket in the *Luncheon* and piercing green for the railings in *The Balcony*. He employed the traditional compositional formulae of earlier art but with minimal spatial recession, creating awkward disjunctions of scale, particularly in the *Luncheon*. Nor do his figures relate in any conventional formal or psychological sense. A mood of enigmatic isolation pervades both the bohemian interior of the *Luncheon* and the more elegant exterior of *The Balcony*.

In 1869 another painter, EVA GONZALÈS, became Manet's student and posed for a portrait (London, N.G.) shown in the Salon of 1870. Although his direct effect on Morisot and Gonzalès was considerable, his influence was far broader, and his position as head of a school was acknowledged by the Café Guerbois group and by contemporary critics.

In 1868 and 1869 Manet and his family had holidays at Boulogne-sur-Mer, where he made a number of marine paintings, ferry departures and beach scenes (e.g. *Folkestone Boat, Boulogne*, 1869; Philadelphia, PA, Mus. A.). His early attraction to the sea is perhaps reflected in his summer sojourns at various maritime resorts between 1868 and 1873, interrupted only by the Franco-Prussian war and civil strife of 1870–71.

(iv) 1870–79. In early 1870 Manet fought a duel with the journalist-critic Louis-Edmond Duranty, whose friend he nevertheless remained, and made common cause with other artists in an attempt to effect changes in the selection of Salon jurors. With the approach of the Prussian Army in September 1870 he sent his family to a resort in the Pyrenees, and joined the National Guard. After the end of the siege of Paris in February 1871, he rejoined his family and remained in the provinces until the days

immediately following the 'bloody week' of 21–28 May. A federation of artists under the short-lived Paris Commune had elected him a delegate in his absence, but this organization soon evaporated. Manet's attitude towards the Commune is not documented, but scholarship on the lithographs he made following its bloody events (*Civil War* and *The Barricade*; see 1977 exh. cat., no. 72) suggests that although he did not side actively with the Commune, he did oppose its suppressors (*Art Journal*, 1985, pp. 36–42).

The war of 1870 divided Manet's career into two distinct halves. A number of profound changes in his life and art marked the beginning of the second decade of his professional career. In 1872 he moved his studio to the Rue de Saint-Pétersbourg near the Place de l'Europe, and he and his circle abandoned the Café Guerbois for the Café de la Nouvelle Athènes in the Place Pigalle, then in a newly constructed area of Paris. He travelled in the Netherlands in 1872, renewing his acquaintance with the works of Dutch Masters, especially those of Frans Hals, an experience that is reflected in *Le Bon Bock* (Tyson priv. col., on loan to Philadelphia, PA, Mus. A.); this painting was shown in the Salon of 1873 to unexpected critical acclaim from formerly hostile quarters and equally unexpected adverse criticism from his friends. In 1872 he sold 24 pictures to the dealer Durand-Ruel. He also acquired a new circle of friends who came to his studio, which had become the focus of his social as well as his professional life. At the centre of this circle were Nina de Callias, a somewhat unconventional woman of wealth, generosity and talent, and Stéphane Mallarmé, who replaced Baudelaire, who had died in 1867, in the painter's affections. Among those who frequented their salons were artists, poets, writers, composers and journalists, including Marcellin Desboutin, Verlaine, Leconte de Lisle, Villiers de l'Isle-Adam, Jean Richepin, Henri Rochefort, François Coppée and Anatole France.

In his paintings of the early 1870s, Manet began to adopt a higher-keyed coloration and henceforth dispensed with dark backgrounds, as, for example, in *The Railroad* (Washington, DC, N.G.A.) of 1872–3. Equally new was an extreme freedom and sketchiness of brushwork, as in the portrait of Nina de Callias called *Woman with Fans* (Paris, Mus. d'Orsay) of 1873–4. These new features of Manet's art can be traced to his association with the younger generation of Impressionist painters, who exhibited together for the first time in 1874. (Manet was invited to exhibit but declined.) He spent the summer of 1874 at his family property at Gennevilliers, near Argenteuil, where Claude Monet was at work, and where he also saw Gustave Caillebotte and Auguste Renoir. There he painted *Argenteuil* (Tournai, Mus. B.-A.) and *Boating* (New York, Met.), the major works cited as evidence of Impressionist influence on his art, largely because of their subject-matter (boating on the Seine) but also for their high colour values and intensities and their broken brushwork. Manet travelled to Venice in 1875, where he painted in brilliant, quasi-Impressionist style such works as *Grand Canal at Venice* (1875; Shelburne, VT, Mus.).

In the 1870s the Salon juries continued to be ambivalent about accepting Manet's pictures. In 1874 *Argenteuil* was accepted; in 1875 *The Linen* (Merion Station, PA, Barnes Found.) and *The Artist* (1875; São Paulo, Mus. A. Assis Châteaubriand) were refused. The jury of 1877 accepted one picture (*Faure as Hamlet*; Essen, Mus. Folkwang) and refused another (*Nana*; Hamburg, Ksthalle; *see* FRANCE, fig. 26). In 1878 he avoided competing for admission to the Exposition Universelle by exhibiting work publicly in his own studio.

Manet's friendships with writers and poets led him to collaborative ventures in printmaking. In 1869 he had made a lithographic poster, *Cats' Rendezvous*, for Champfleury's book *Les Chats*, and in the early 1870s he made several etchings as illustrations; these collaborations with writers provided the basis for the 20th-century LIVRE D'ARTISTE. In 1874 a volume of poems by Charles Cros with etched illustrations by Manet appeared. In 1875 he created his masterpiece of this genre, the illustrations for Mallarmé's translation of *The Raven* by Edgar Allan Poe. Many of the prints considered among Manet's most important were not published during his lifetime, and several were never published at all, extant only in a few artist's proofs.

(v) 1879–83. Manet was installed in his last atelier at 77 Rue d'Amsterdam in April 1879. By this time the illness that was to take his life had begun to manifest itself, and he spent annual extended curative sojourns in the country near Paris. During these periods he amused himself by painting small still-lifes and flower-pieces (see fig. 2) and writing letters decorated with charming watercolours (1983 exh. cat., nos 191–205). In 1881 he received a second-class medal and was thereafter excused from jury

2. Edouard Manet: *White Lilac in a Glass*, oil on canvas, 540×410 mm, 1880 (Berlin, Nationalgalerie)

submission. At the end of that year, with his friend Antonin Proust installed as Minister of Fine Arts, Manet was made Chevalier de la Légion d'honneur, a recognition some thought he should have refused.

Contemporary Paris was the subject of his last major painting and his swan-song at the Salon of 1882, a *Bar at the Folies-Bergère* (U. London, Courtauld Inst. Gals.; see fig. 3). The figure of the cashier at one of the bars in the largest and most sumptuous place of entertainment in the city presides like a goddess over her domain, depicted in strokes of shattering light and colour. Her centred, frontal figure and her moon-like face with its dreamy expression (seen as sad or weary by some) make of her an urban icon flanked by a still-life of bottles, fruit and flowers. She stands in front of a mirror that reflects the auditorium balcony with its seated spectators, as well as the back of the cashier herself and the patron who faces her on the other side of the counter. The scene is an amalgam of disparate areas in the Folies-Bergère, mediated by the equivocal mirror represented as though parallel to the picture plane and the counter but reflecting the woman and the customer as though at an angle. The liberties Manet took with perspective have been much discussed; it can be concluded that Symbolism won out over Realism; the reflection is necessary to the theme. In popular imagery from 1830 to 1880 *la dame du comptoir* always appears with the still-life of her counter in front of her and her reflection, often displaced, in the mirror behind her. Manet underlined this tradition by exaggerating the reflection's displacement.

By September 1882 Manet's condition had deteriorated enough to prompt him to write his will. On 20 April 1883 his left leg was amputated, and on 30 April he died, probably of tertiary syphilis complicated by gangrene. He was buried on 3 May at the Passy cemetery, his coffin borne by pallbearers including Proust, Zola and Monet.

Manet's influence on his successors was paradoxically both negligible and enormous. He had few significant imitators, yet he has been universally regarded as the Father of Modernism. With Courbet he was among the first to take serious risks with the public whose favour he sought, the first to make *alla prima* painting the standard technique for oil painting and one of the first to take liberties with Renaissance perspective and to offer 'pure painting' as a source of aesthetic pleasure. He was a pioneer, again with Courbet, in the rejection of humanistic and historical subject-matter, and shared with Degas the establishment of modern urban life as acceptable material for high art. Manet's art, like the contemporary and analogous Realist and Naturalist movements in French literature, occupies a central place within the larger framework of a new modernist culture that was to affect the evolution of these arts in France well into the 20th century.

2. Technique.

(i) Painting. Manet was the last great French painter to receive a long and academic training. His technical development, therefore, has particular significance for the evolution of 19th-century art. Once he had graduated from Couture's atelier, he disowned his master's technique as he had disdained while a student the posturing models

and the universal insistence on the importance of the nude. He retained for life, however, the use of studio aids and gadgets such as plumb lines and black mirrors and continued throughout his career to outline figures and objects with paint in a kind of brushed drawing derived from Couture's sketching method. His major break with earlier technique was to abandon the practice of covering the canvas with a dark, usually brown, tone upon which the composition was then built up with heavier layers of pigment and translucent glazes. In Manet's mature early style, most passages present a firm, opaque paint layer, and there is little glazing; each colour was selected and applied, from the start, for its final effect (*alla prima* painting). If, after a day's work, he was not satisfied with any completed passage, he scraped it down to the canvas and began again the next day with fresh colours. (Pentiments seen in radiographs represent changes made, sometimes years later, after the original version had dried.)

Manet's adoption of the *alla prima* technique served both practical and expressive purposes and had far-reaching effects on the art of his younger colleagues. The procedure was useful for completing a passage, or a whole painting, in a day. Manet insisted on having his subject before him while painting, a practice adopted and considerably extended by the Impressionists. Their capturing of moments of light and weather in the permanent medium of oil, often executed out of doors, depended absolutely on *alla prima* technique, as time could not be allotted to the drying of intermediate paint layers. Although there have been revivals of complex Old Master techniques, the methods of Manet and the Impressionists have gradually become the standard practice in oil painting in the 20th century.

Among the idiosyncratic features of Manet's style was his simplification of form by letting one stroke or area of paint of a single colour (a *tache*) stand for a more complex reality. This Tachism, though on a larger scale, stood behind the Impressionists' re-creation of the visible world in small dabs of paint. Another, related feature was his fairly consistent omission of intermediate values between extremes of light and dark, producing dramatic contrasts that are most vivid in his early work. This simplification of the rendering of curved surfaces contributed to the 'flatness' of many three-dimensional forms in his work, for instance the nude in *Déjeuner sur l'herbe* and the figure of *Olympia*. In both, shadow is reduced to a band-like outline. These forms are not, however, composed simply of flat, unified colour. Under raking light one can see that his brush followed the roundness of the form. Broader shadows were brushed in where needed but minimized in the painting's final state, and in the nude of the *Déjeuner* there are slight variations in colour throughout of a sort that Titian or Rubens would have achieved by letting the ground show through. For Manet, each of these passages represented the choice of a colour, mixed and brushed on, making his task more difficult since it was carried out without the traditional formulae of layering. The challenge of rendering a particular optical reality excited Manet and gave to his art a peculiar freshness and novelty disturbing to many in his time. The same method was applied to portraiture, and despite Manet's neutral approach to psychological expression as an indicator of 'character', his

3. Edouard Manet: *Bar at the Folies-Bergère*, oil on canvas, 0.96×1.30m, 1882 (London, University of London, Courtauld Institute Galleries)

portraiture is faithful in a photographic sense to the features of his sitters, whether or not a portrait was intended (and was probably influenced by photography).

Manet was as ready to simplify in composition as in the rendering of surfaces. Several works painted in the 1860s were subsequently reduced by simply cutting up the canvas (e.g. *Surprised Nymph*, 1861; Buenos Aires, Mus. N. B.A.). The *Dead Toreador* (?1864–5; Washington, DC, N.G.A.) as shown in 1864 was part of a much larger composition. Although this work may have been cut down in response to adverse criticism of its perspective, other examples suggest a more positive attempt at simplification. X-radiography has provided insight into Manet's working methods in general and especially in the *Execution of Maximilian*, which was repeatedly revised to achieve a starker, simpler statement (1986 exh. cat., pp. 48–64).

(ii) Drawing. Manet was primarily a painter and did not produce an enormous body of drawings, even though many have surely been lost. The extant drawings are, however, impressive in their own right and are consistent with the paintings in character. A large number of early drawings in pencil or chalk after figures in Old Master paintings reveal a bold, almost aggressive use of outline, drastically simplifying the means of representation in the original, yet maintaining its style and expression. Certain later drawings, heightened with watercolour, that seem to

be compositional studies for well-known paintings were probably made after completion of the painting, perhaps with reproductive etching in view. Among a varied sequence of figure studies leading to the great nudes of 1863 is a pencil-and-ink wash drawing of a seated bather (London, priv. col.) that brilliantly displays Manet's early mastery of wash drawing. Many portrait sketches were made in this rapid, summary technique which was later turned to account in illustrative prints. Between 1879 and 1882 he produced a series of pastel portraits of women that fully exploits the fragile delicacy of the medium, for example *Irma Brunner* (*c.* 1880; Paris, Louvre). Manet's line, whether executed in pencil, pen or wash, is firm, laconic and precise in its representational function, bold and clear in its expression.

(iii) Printmaking. Manet had a thoughtful and sometimes adventurous approach to printmaking. He produced few prints of any kind after 1875. His etchings were chiefly reproductive of his paintings (e.g. *Dead Christ and Angels*, *c.* 1866–7; see 1977 exh. cat., no. 51), whereas many of the lithographs were on topical and independent, often popular, subjects. His earliest etchings were influenced by the conservative style of Alphonse Legros, who taught him the technique. He achieved mastery of the medium between 1860 and 1862, the year in which the portfolio was published by Cadart. Manet incorporated aquatint and

4. Edouard Manet: *The Races*, lithograph, 390×512mm, 1865–72 (Cambridge, MA, Fogg Art Museum)

other etched tones, and drypoint, into his copperplate repertory, and he relied heavily on the advice and help of colleagues in the biting and printing of his plates. He pursued tonal effects, through both hatched line and aquatint, particularly in the rendering of paintings, a practice at variance with the 'pure etching' ideals of the Société des Aquafortistes. He was much influenced by the etchings of Goya, especially in his use of aquatint (*Au Prado*, *Fleur exotique*). Since many of his later etchings were made for publication in books, they are much smaller than the imposing early portfolio etchings. He used photographs to reduce and reverse paintings for reproduction in prints, for example *Jeanne—Spring* (1882; see 1977 exh. cat., no. 107).

Manet was slower to take up lithography. He seems to have composed *The Balloon* (1862; see 1977 exh. cat., no. 28) directly on to a stone offered him by Cadart. The result was never published, deviating so markedly from the stylistic norms of commercial lithography in its very freely sketched manner that the printer refused to make more than trial proofs. While several crayon lithographs were executed in a more conservative style, *The Races* (1865–72; Cambridge, MA, Fogg; see fig. 4) stands out as Manet's most exuberant and striking work in this medium. Exploiting the broad characteristics of the lithographic crayon throughout, his free, energetic line became in one area a scribble that some have interpreted as a precocious modernism, others an expression of frustration over a failed composition. The stone was probably not printed in his lifetime and impressions are extremely rare. He made sheet music cover illustrations for the music and lyrics of friends in the manner of commercial lithographers and treated the tragic events of 1871 in a broad manner related to that of *The Races* in, for example, *The Barricade* (1871; see 1977 exh. cat., no. 72). The seven-colour lithograph *Polichinelle* (see 1977 exh. cat., no. 90) of 1874 was probably heavily dependent on the help of printers in making the colour separations and therefore comparatively timid in technique.

In 1874–6 Manet turned from the familiar commercial crayon medium to a transfer process for a group of prints culminating in his illustrations for *The Raven* (pubd 1875). In this technique, derived from transfer lithography, he was able to exploit his mastery of wash drawing in rapid, evocative sketches on transfer paper subsequently transferred to zinc plates which were etched and printed probably in the relief process of gillotage (1985 exh. cat., p. 115). It is characteristic of Manet's boldness and his openness to new ideas that he should have approached this project using a technique probably untried for such a purpose.

Spontaneity, directness and simplicity were Manet's aim. He bent every technique to these expressive purposes and in doing so created an art that is unique and consistent in producing an effect of immediacy and freshness.

3. CHARACTER AND PERSONALITY. Manet was a well brought up and financially independent member of the old bourgeoisie. Though educated according to the conventions of his class, he retained little interest in reading and wrote almost nothing but letters His mode of life was discreetly bohemian: he lived with Suzanne Leenhoff for

years before their marriage but did not disclose the arrangement even to his most intimate friends. He cut the public figure of a dandy. It is reported by Proust that, although he affected the drawling speech and slouching gait of a Parisian urchin, he never succeeded in looking anything but aristocratic. Blond, blue-eyed and of sunny disposition, he was a witty conversationalist and had charismatic allure for men and women alike. An impressionable youth at the time of the Revolution of 1848, he retained Republican sympathies throughout his life, associating with political liberals and radicals but apparently engaging in no political activities other than occasionally creating works of art that could be seen as offensive to the regime of Napoleon III and the conservative early Third Republic. His association with other men of talent included not only Degas and the Impressionist circle, as well as Henri Fantin-Latour (who had painted his portrait in 1867; for illustration *see* FANTIN-LATOUR, (2)), but a number of major literary figures, including Baudelaire, Théodore de Banville, Zola and Mallarmé. He was a gregarious man who adored society and maintained a salon in his own studio that included radical friends and demimondaines.

Manet's personality had a darker side, reflected in his frequent discouragement over his failure to win success and acclaim at the Salon, in his duel with Duranty and in a serious nervous depression in 1871. Occasional pictures express this side of his psyche, such as *The Suicide* of 1881 (ex-Hatvany Col., Budapest), painted at a time when a friend lay gravely ill and Manet himself was already in the grip of his final illness. However, by far the majority of his pictures and the accounts of his friends reveal a temperament basically happy and at ease with the world, even in his last years when physical disability made standing at his easel difficult. It was during this period that he painted the *Bar at the Folies-Bergère* (see fig. 3 above), a work epitomizing the pleasure he took in the life around him, in the image of woman and in the sheer act of looking.

4. CRITICAL RECEPTION AND POSTHUMOUS REPUTATION. Manet was one of many avant-garde 19th-century painters who endured vilification and sarcasm for the novelty of their work. He nevertheless found a few sympathetic critics. The most articulate of these was Zola, who championed Manet's early work and, despite later quarrelling with him, wrote the introduction to Manet's memorial exhibition catalogue in 1884. Mallarmé wrote a profound appreciation of Manet in 1876 that acknowledged his historic connection with Impressionist painting and his engagement with the contemporary world. In contrast with the rich and poetic art of past ages, he praised Manet for his sincerity and simplicity.

By the time of his death, Manet had gained a grudging reputation as an important and influential innovator but had found few understanding defenders. His reputation has risen steeply, and the body of historical and critical writing on his career is extensive. Several of his close friends produced monographic witness accounts of his life: Edmond Bazire, his first biographer; Antonin Proust, his friend since school days; and Théodore Duret, the critic, who compiled the first oeuvre catalogue. Manet benefited from the rise in the reputation of Impressionism, but it was only in the 20th century that independent studies of his life and work were produced. German scholars were the first to treat Manet's art in its historical context (H. von Tschudi, 1902; J. Meier-Graefe, 1912); Etienne Moreau-Nélaton provided the first detailed documentation of his career (1926).

By the 1920s, with formalist criticism dominant, Manet's art was appreciated primarily as 'pure painting'. This critical view continued well into the post-World War II era but was challenged at the time of the centenary exhibition in Paris of 1932. Left-wing intellectuals saw Manet's apparent lack of interest in subject-matter not as a virtue but as a sign of the bourgeois formalism rejected by Marxist aesthetics. A variation on this view was revived in the 1980s by T. J. Clark.

In 1954 a book by the Swedish artist-critic Nils Gösta Sandblad gave Manet studies a new direction. Concentrating on subject-matter and social context as much as on form, Sandblad anticipated the trend in the 1960s and 1970s, seen especially in American art history and criticism, towards the iconographic study of modern art. Writings by Reff, Fried, Hanson, Farwell and others in America, and Hofmann in Germany, have added to Manet's reputation for formal artistry an equal reputation for social engagement and profound awareness of tradition. Research in the 1980s based on X-radiography has sought to establish Manet's working procedures with greater precision. The literature on Manet has from the beginning been marked by wide differences of interpretation that may in part be traced to the protean and enigmatic quality of his creative genius.

WRITINGS

Tableaux de M. Edouard Manet (exh. cat., Paris, 1867)

BIBLIOGRAPHY

CATALOGUES RAISONNÉS

E. Moreau-Nélaton: *Manet: Graveur et lithographe* (Paris, 1906)
L. Rosenthal: *Manet: Aquafortiste et lithographe* (Paris, 1925)
A. Tabarant: *Manet: Histoire catalographique* (Paris, 1931)
P. Jamot, G. Wildenstein and M. L. Bataille: *Manet*, 2 vols (Paris, 1932)
M. Guérin: *L'Oeuvre gravé de Manet* (Paris, 1944/R Amsterdam and New York, 1969)
S. Orienti: *L'opera pittorica di Edouard Manet* (Milan, 1967; Fr. trans., intro. D. Rouart, Paris, 1967; Eng. trans., intro. P. Pool, New York, 1967)
A. de Leiris: *The Drawings of Edouard Manet* (Berkeley, 1969)
J. C. Harris: *Edouard Manet: Graphic Works, a Definitive Catalogue Raisonné* (New York, 1970)
D. Rouart and D. Wildenstein: *Edouard Manet: Catalogue Raisonné*, 2 vols (Geneva, 1975)
J. Wilson: *Edouard Manet: L'Oeuvre gravé, chef-d'oeuvre du Département des estampes de la Bibliothèque Nationale, Paris* (Ingelheim-am-Rhein, 1977)

MONOGRAPHS

E. Zola: *Ed. Manet: Etude biographique et critique* (Paris, 1867)
E. Bazire: *Manet* (Paris, 1884)
T. Duret: *Histoire d'Edouard Manet et de son oeuvre* (Paris, 1902, 3/1919 with suppl., 4/1926)
H. von Tschudi: *Edouard Manet* (Berlin, 1902)
J. Laran and G. Le Bas: *Manet* (Paris, [1910])
J. Meier-Graefe: *Edouard Manet* (Munich, 1912)
A. Proust: *Edouard Manet: Souvenirs* (Paris, 1913)
E. Waldmann: *Edouard Manet: Sein Leben und sein Kunst* (Berlin, 1923)
J. E. Blanche: *Manet* (Paris, 1924; Eng. trans., London, 1925)
E. Moreau-Nélaton: *Manet raconté par lui-même*, 2 vols (Paris, 1926)
R. Rey: *Manet* (Paris, 1938; Eng. trans., New York, 1938)
G. Jedlicka: *Edouard Manet* (Zurich, 1941)

P. Courthion and P. Cailler: *Manet raconté par lui-même et par ses amis*, 2 vols (Geneva, 1945, 2/Lausanne, 1953; Eng. trans., New York, 1960)
M. Florisoone: *Manet* (Monaco, 1947)
A. Tabarant: *Manet et ses oeuvres* (Paris, 1947)
G. H. Hamilton: *Manet and his Critics* (New Haven, 1954/R New York, 1969)
N. G. Sandblad: *Manet: Three Studies in Artistic Conception* (Lund, 1954)
G. Bataille: *Manet* (Lausanne, 1955; Eng. trans., New York, 1983)
J. Richardson: *Edouard Manet: Paintings and Drawings* (London, 1958/R 1982)
H. Perruchot: *La Vie de Manet* (Paris, 1959; Eng. trans., New York, 1962)
P. Courthion: *Edouard Manet* (Paris, 1961; Eng. trans., New York, 1962)
G. Hopp: *Edouard Manet: Farbe und Bildgestalt* (Berlin, 1968)
W. Hofmann: *Nana: Mythos und Wirklichkeit* (Cologne, 1973)
G. Mauner: *Manet, peintre-philosophe: A Study of the Painter's Themes* (University Park, PA, 1975)
T. Reff: *Manet: Olympia* (New York, 1976)
A. C. Hanson: *Manet and the Modern Tradition* (New Haven, 1977)
J. Wilson: *Dessins, aquarelles, eaux-fortes, lithographies, correspondance* (Paris, 1978)
B. Farwell: *Manet and the Nude* (New York, 1981)
N. Ross: *Manet's 'Bar at the Folies-Bergère' and the Myths of Popular Illustration* (Ann Arbor, 1982)
T. J. Clark: *The Painting of Modern Life: Paris in the Art of Manet and his Followers* (New York, 1985)
W. Hofmann: *Edouard Manet: Das Frühstück im Atelier* (Frankfurt am Main, 1985)
K. Adler: *Manet* (Oxford, 1986)
H. Rand: *Manet's Contemplation at the Gare Saint-Lazare* (Berkeley, 1987)

EXHIBITION CATALOGUES

Exposition des oeuvres de Edouard Manet (exh. cat., preface E. Zola; Paris, Ecole N. Sup. B.-A., 1884)
Manet and the Post-Impressionists (exh. cat., London, Grafton Gals, 1910)
Manet (exh. cat., preface P. Valéry; Paris, Mus. Orangerie, 1932)
Edouard Manet, 1832–1883 (exh. cat. by A. C. Hanson, Philadelphia, PA, Mus. A., 1966)
Manet and Spain: Prints and Drawings (exh. cat. by J. Isaacson, Ann Arbor, U. MI, Mus. A., 1969)
Edouard Manet: Das graphische Werk (exh. cat. by J. Wilson, Ingelheim, Int. Tage, 1977)
Manet: Dessins, aquarelles, eaux-fortes, lithographies, correspondance (exh. cat. by J. Wilson, Paris, Gal. Huguette Berès, 1978)
Edouard Manet and the Execution of Maximilian (exh. cat., Providence, RI, Brown U., Bell Gal., 1981)
Manet and Modern Paris (exh. cat. by T. Reff, Washington, DC, N.G.A., 1982)
Edouard Manet, 1832–1883 (exh. cat. by F. Cachin, C. Moffett and J. Wilson Bareau, Paris, Grand Pal.; New York, Met.; 1983)
The Prints of Edouard Manet (exh. cat. by J. M. Fisher, Washington, DC, Int. Exh. Found., 1985)
The Hidden Face of Manet (exh. cat. by J. Wilson Bareau, U. London, Courtauld Inst. Gals, 1986) [pubd as suppl., *Burl. Mag.*, cxxviii (1986)]
Manet (exh. cat. by M. Wivel, Copenhagen, Ordrupgaardsaml., 1989)
Manet: The Execution of Maximilian: Painting, Politics and Censorship (exh. cat. by J. Wilson-Bareau, London, N.G., 1992)
Manet: The Execution of Maximilian (exh. cat., ed. J. Wilson-Bareau; London, N.G., 1992)

SPECIALIST STUDIES

S. Mallarmé: 'The Impressionists and Edouard Manet', *A. Mthly*, i (1876), pp. 117–21; Fr. trans., *Gaz. B.-A.*, n. s. 6, lxxxvi (1975), pp. 147–56
Amour A. (May 1932) [issue ded. Manet; essays by P. Jamot, R. Huyghe and G. Bazin]
M. Fried: 'Manet's Sources: Aspects of his Art, 1859–1865', *Artforum* (March 1969) [whole issue]
J. Clay: 'Fards, onguents, pollens', *Bonjour Monsieur Manet* (exh. cat., Paris, Pompidou, 1983), pp. 6–24
D. Druick and P. Zegers: 'Manet's "Balloon": French Diversions, the Fête de l'Empereur 1862', *Prt Colr Newslett.* (May–June 1983), pp. 37–46
A. J. [New York], xlv (Spring 1985) [issue ded. Manet]

BEATRICE FARWELL

Manetti, Antonio (di Tuccio) [di Marabottino] (*b* Florence, 6 July 1423; *d* Florence, 26 May 1497). Italian writer.

He came from a long-established Florentine family of merchants and was himself joint owner of a silk warehouse. He was a friend of the neo-Platonist philosopher MARSILIO FICINO, whose cultural interests included architecture. In his youth Manetti was also acquainted with FILIPPO BRUNELLESCHI, and he later acquired a reputation as an expert in architecture and related disciplines, in which connection he held some administrative and consultative posts in Florence: in 1466 he was Councillor (*operaio*) at the Ospedale degli Innocenti and in 1491 a member of the jury, with the title of *architectus*, in the competition for the façade of Florence Cathedral. No architectural works can be attributed to him with certainty, however, as architects and woodworkers of the same name were active in Florence at that time. His interest in architecture was expressed in two manuscripts that are now generally recognized to be his work, *Vita di Filippo Brunelleschi* and *Huomini singhularii in Firenze dal MCCCC. innanzi*. The latter contains concise biographies of two theologians, four humanists and eight artists from Florence, among whom the dominant figure is Brunelleschi. These biographies are preceded by a translation from Latin of the second part of Filippo Villani's *De origine civitatis Florentiae et de eiusdem famosis civibus*.

The *Vita* was conceived as an appendix to the *Novella del Grasso*, a lengthy version of the famous mocking anecdote thought to have been invented by Brunelleschi himself. The text is written in the Florentine vernacular and possibly dates from the early 1480s. It breaks off at the description of the beginning of the work on Santo Spirito, owing to either an interruption in the writing or a mutilation of the original manuscript. Four copies survive, one of which is autograph (Florence, Bib. N. Cent., MS. II, ii, 325, fols 295r–312v). The *Vita* was the first really comprehensive biography of a single artist to appear in the early Renaissance, and it was used by Giorgio Vasari. It was also one of the major documents that described the relationship established in the 15th century between Brunelleschi and the vernacular culture of Florence. In his manuscript Manetti sought to define, in opposition to some contemporary ideas, the development and physical appearance of the master's works, reaffirming Brunelleschi's fundamental role in introducing the new 'antique' style of architecture. The information is most reliable when it rests on the author's personal testimony or on the literal quotation of public documents (a technique that Manetti was the first to employ in artistic biography).

WRITINGS

Vita di Filippo Brunelleschi (MS., ?1480s; Florence, Bib. N. Cent.; Eng. trans., ed. H. Saalman (University Park, PA, 1970); ed. D. de Robertis, intro. G. Tanturli (Milan, 1976)
Huomini singhularii in Firenze dal MCCCC. innanzi (MS., 1494–7; Florence, Bib. N. Cent. Conventi Soppressi, G.2. 1501, fols 141r-142r); ed. G. Milanesi in *Operette istoriche, edite ed inedite, di Antonio Manetti* (Florence, 1887), pp. 159–68

BIBLIOGRAPHY

G. Benivieni: 'Dialogo di Antonio Manetti cittadino fiorentino circa al sito, forme et misure dello 'Inferno' di Dante Alighieri', *Dante Alighieri: Commedia di Dante'* (Florence, 1506); ed. N. Zingarelli (Città di Castello, 1897)
P. Murray: 'Art Historians and Art Critics, iv: "XIV uomini singhularii in Firenze"', *Burl. Mag.*, xcix (1957), pp. 330–36
G. Tanturli: 'Le biografie d'artisti prima del Vasari', *Il Vasari storiografo e artista: Atti del congresso internazionale nel IV centenario della morte: Arezzo and Florence, 1974*, pp. 275–98

A. Rochon: 'Une Date importante dans l'histoire de la "Beffa: La nouvelle du Grasso Legnaiuolo"', *Formes et significations de la 'Beffa' dans la littérature italienne de la Renaissance*, ed. M. Marietti and others (Paris, 1975), pp. 211–338
G. Tanturli: 'Per l'interpretazione storica della "Vita del Brunelleschi"', *Paragone*, xxvi/301 (1975), pp. 5–25
Filippo Brunelleschi: La sua opera e il suo tempo: Atti del convegno internazionale di studi: Florence 1977, pp. 459–69, 923–32
D. Zervas: 'The Parte Guelfa Palace, Brunelleschi and Antonio Manetti', *Burl. Mag.*, cxxvi (1984), pp. 494–9
R. Pacciani: 'La fondazione della nuova basilica di San Lorenzo a Firenze: i committenti, l'opera, Antonio di Tuccio Manetti', *Prospettiva* (1994), pp. 75–6

RICCARDO PACCIANI

Manetti, Antonio di Ciaccheri (*b* Florence, *c.* 1402; *d* Florence, 8 Nov 1460). Italian carpenter and architect. He was the son of a Florentine merchant and writer, Manetto Ciandi. As early as October 1432 he was paid for wooden models relating to the construction of the dome of Florence Cathedral, a task probably passed to him by Filippo Brunelleschi. Before 1436 he was working on the model for the upper section of the dome and on detailed parts, such as screws and the high scaffolding, for the special crane intended to hoist building material up to the dome. In 1434 he produced two models (destr.) for the high altar of the cathedral, based on a design by Brunelleschi, as well as seven models (destr.) for the side altars. He was also involved, in 1438, with the installation of the organs in their galleries and produced two models for the cathedral lantern competition held in 1436. One of these was from a design by Brunelleschi; the other was Manetti's own, although according to Antonio di Tuccio Manetti this was almost identical with Brunelleschi's design. However, Manetti did make an independent contribution to part of the marquetry cupboards for one of the cathedral sacristies, the Sagrestia delle Messe (1436–42), which were begun by Agnolo de' Cori.

From 1447 Manetti received payments for a model that may have represented Michelozzo da Bartolomeo's restructuring of the church of SS Annunziata, Florence. He also produced models for the small Chiostro dei Voti in front of the church, and for the outer door leading on to the Piazza della SS Annunziata (1453). Several courtyards and cloisters dating from the same period (1446–55) have been attributed to Manetti, including the Canonica at S Lorenzo, the Spinelli Cloister of Santa Croce, both in Florence, as well as at Badia a Settimo, Impruneta and Montepulciano. These are articulated with slender Ionic columns of *pietra serena* and have no cornices or horizontal emphasis. In later cloisters the columns are more slender and support Corinthian or Composite capitals. In 1452, after the dismissal of Michelozzo, Manetti was put in charge of the Office of Works of Florence Cathedral. He was involved mainly with continuing work on the lantern, for which he had already invented (1444) a revolving crane to hoist the large sections of marble. Manetti also constructed a model for the exterior gallery of the dome and wooden decorations (destr.) such as lamps, tabernacles, processional floats for chapels, as well as stalls for the new choir. Manetti was ordered by the Florentine government to present Francesco Sforza, Duke of Milan, in March 1459/60 with a design for a fortified stronghold at Pisa, but this was considered impractical and 'too splendid'.

In 1455 Manetti was involved with the Villa Medici at Fiesole and at the nearby convent of S Gerolamo, once attributed to Michelozzo. In 1457 he took over the construction of the church of S Lorenzo, particularly the dome and the nave chapels. Both elements were later criticized by Brunelleschi's biographer and by Vasari because they were considered to differ from the original plan. The dome was criticized because it lacked a light source, while the chapels were considered too small and not well proportioned to the rest of the architecture. In 1459 Manetti was put in charge of Brunelleschi's church of Santo Spirito where he is traditionally attributed with covering the convex curves of the original exterior with a straight wall. In the same year at SS Annunziata, he worked on the completion of the large cloister and strengthened the foundations of the choir tribune. In 1460, together with Michelozzo and Giovanni da Gaiole, Manetti was called upon by the Ufficiali della Torre to judge a project for an artificial lake at Mantignano, which would contain the waters of the Arno. In 1460 he supplied a model for the Cardinal of Portugal Chapel in the church of S Miniato, Florence. However, the chapel as executed probably follows the designs of the circle of Antonio Rossellino.

BIBLIOGRAPHY

DBI; Thieme–Becker

A. di Tuccio Manetti: *Vita di Filippo di Ser Brunellesco* (*c.* 1487); ed. H. Saalman (Pennsylvania and London, 1970), pp. 110–15, 149–53

G. Gaye: *Carteggio inedito d'artisti dei secoli XIV, XV, XVI*, i (Florence, 1839), pp. 169–71

C. Guasti: *La cupola di Santa Maria del Fiore, illustrata con i documenti di archivio dell'opera secolare* (Florence, 1857)

C. Von Fabriczy: 'Brunelleschiana', *Jb. Kön.-Preuss. Kstsamml.*, xxvii (1907), pp. 53–5

G. Poggi: 'Il Duomo di Firenze', *It. Forsch. Kstgesch.*, ii (1909), pp. 208, 214, 234, 239, 240, 270

H. Saalman: 'Tommaso Spinelli, Michelozzo, Manetti and Rosselino', *J. Soc. Archit. Historians*, xxv (1966), pp. 151–64 (155,158)

I. Hyman: 'Toward Rescuing the Lost Reputation of Antonio di Manetto Ciaccheri', *Essays Presented to Myron P. Gilmore*, ii (Florence, 1978), pp. 261–80

F. Borsi, G. Morolli and F. Quinterio: *Brunelleschiani* (Rome, 1979), pp. 34–45, 106–13, 260–76

H. Saalman: *Filippo Brunelleschi: The Cupola of Santa Maria del Fiore* (London, 1980)

FRANCESCO QUINTERIO

Manetti, Rutilio (*b* Siena, *bapt* 1 Jan 1571; *d* Siena, 22 July 1639). Italian painter. He was a student of the Late Mannerist artists Francesco Vanni and Ventura Salimbeni. His earliest paintings, and especially his frescoes illustrating the *Story of St Catherine and Pope Gregory* (1597; Siena, Pal. Pub.) and his altarpiece of the *Baptism* (1599–1600; Siena, S Giovannino in Pantaneto), are strongly influenced by their works and also those of Federico Barocci. Although his style changed considerably during his career, Manetti never fully abandoned the fleshy, oval facial types with delicate, sweet features and the cluttered compositions that typify Sienese Mannerism. From 1600 to 1610 his paintings, for example the fresco cycle of the *Story of St Roch* (1605 to 1610; Siena, S Rocco alla Lupa), drew on

Rutilio Manetti: *Musicians and Card Players*, oil on canvas, 1.21×1.80 m, *c.* 1626 (Siena, Monti dei Paschi, on loan to Siena, Collezioni Chigi-Saracini)

the clear narrative style, naturalistic light effects and particularized figure types of Florentine painters such as Bernardino Poccetti and Domenico Passignano.

By the early 1620s Manetti had turned to Roman and Bolognese sources. Although the painter is not documented in Rome, it is generally assumed that he was there some time between 1616 and 1621. From Guercino, Caravaggio and the Caravaggisti (especially Artemisia Gentileschi and Orazio Gentileschi, Cecco del Caravaggio and Bartolomeo Manfredi) his paintings gained a sense of naturalism, solidity of form and drama, both in terms of lighting and evocative gesture. In this style he executed a number of important commissions for altars (e.g. *St Alexander Liberated by an Angel*, 1625; Vinci, S Ansano in Greti) and easel paintings (e.g. *Samson and Delilah*, c. 1625–7; Mexico City, Inst. N.B.A.). After 1625 he also produced a number of Caravaggesque gaming and concert scenes in the manner of Gerrit van Honthorst and Valentin de Boulogne (e.g. *Musicians and Card Players*, c. 1626; see fig.); in these half-length figures are grouped densely around a table that is lit by a single bright candle. In the *Assumption of the Virgin* (1632; Forlì, S Mercuriale), Manetti called on the Bolognese work of Guido Reni and particularly Giovanni Lanfranco. He learnt not only from their dramatic compositions but also from their clear light, which crisply defines the forms and highlights drapery shapes. His last paintings were largely executed by his son Domenico Manetti (*b* 1609), a less gifted painter, and other workshop assistants, and they are not generally well thought of.

BIBLIOGRAPHY
C. Brandi: *Rutilio Manetti, 1571–1639* (Siena, 1931)
C. del Bravo: 'Su Rutilio Manetti', *Pantheon*, xxiv (1966), pp. 43–51
A. Bagnoli: 'Aggiornamento di Rutilio Manetti', *Prospettiva*, xiii (1978), pp. 23–42
——: *Rutilio Manetti: 1571–1639* (Florence, 1978)

Manfredi, Bartolomeo (*b* Ostiano, nr Mantua, *bapt* 25 Aug 1582; *d* 12 Dec 1622). Italian painter. In the 17th century he was known throughout Italy and beyond as Caravaggio's closest follower and his works were highly prized and widely collected. More than simply aping Caravaggio's style, Manfredi reinterpreted his subjects and rendered new ones, drawing upon Caravaggio's naturalism and dramatic use of chiaroscuro. His paintings were often praised by his contemporaries as equal to Caravaggio's and he was subsequently emulated and imitated by other Roman Caravaggisti during the 1610s and 1620s. Yet by the 18th century his works were forgotten or confused with those of Caravaggio himself, and he is today among the most enigmatic Italian Baroque painters.

He learnt the principles of painting in Milan, Cremona and Brescia, and moved to Rome probably c. 1605, perhaps earlier (Mancini). There he studied with Cristoforo Roncalli (Baglione) and may have been Caravaggio's assistant, although this seems unlikely since Caravaggio strongly objected to imitators, and Manfredi's biographers would probably have related such important information. He is first documented in Rome in 1610, and his name appears frequently in parish records until 1622, often with those of his servants and assistants. He apparently never inscribed his paintings; no work displays his signature or a date, and no evidence such as contracts or letters related

to extant paintings by Manfredi, or records of payments to him, is known. Efforts to identify his pictures are further complicated by the broader problem of discerning individual hands among the Caravaggisti. It is therefore difficult, if not impossible, to construct a strict chronology for his paintings, although his general development is distinguished by a progression away from Caravaggio's artistic ideals towards a more personal artistic conception.

The early period, from which few originals survive, is the most problematic. It is the least documented phase, and there are numerous copies and variants of lost compositions. Yet a small, varied group of works reveal, in their sharply defined forms and choice of subjects (allegories, mythologies and genre scenes), his close and direct dependence on Caravaggio's youthful paintings. The *Chastisement of Cupid* (Chicago, IL, A. Inst.; see fig. 1), which was probably painted c. 1607, is thought to be Manfredi's earliest extant painting. Its bright, saturated colours and sharply defined forms are characteristic of late Roman Mannerism. The dramatic composition, violent action and strong chiaroscuro, however, betray Manfredi's knowledge and mastery of Caravaggio's tenebrism (seen for example in the latter's *Martyrdom of St Matthew*; Rome, S Luigi dei Francesi). A physiognomic type that appears in the *Chastisement* remained virtually unchanged throughout Manfredi's career: figures with oval faces, broad noses, flaring nostrils and full lips, heavy, puffy eyes, and pronounced brows and chins. These features generically reveal Manfredi's interest in Caravaggio's early secular paintings,

1. Bartolomeo Manfredi: *Chastisement of Cupid*, oil on canvas, 1.75×1.30 m, c. 1607 (Chicago, IL, Art Institute of Chicago)

such as his *Concert of Youths* (New York, Met.). Manfredi's lost *Allegory of the Four Seasons* (ex-Scialiapin Col., Paris; see 1987 exh. cat., p. 62), known through an excellent copy (Dayton, OH, A. Inst.), also dates from his early career, as does the *Bacchus and Drinker* (Rome, Pal. Barberini). In all of these the figures are shown in rather shallow, confined interiors, an element found in all of Manfredi's works. The space is defined by raking light and a dark background wall.

In Manfredi's mature period the variety of compositional schemes yielded to much more regular, formulaic and frieze-like compositions with half-length figures, and he adopted themes foreign to Caravaggio's oeuvre, such as tavern scenes. The brilliantly contrasting colours and clear light of his youthful works were replaced by a limited palette of warm colours and by moist, atmospheric effects. The start of this period is marked by his *Assembly of Drinkers* (*c.* 1610; priv. col., on dep. Los Angeles, CA, Co. Mus. A.), based on Caravaggio's *Calling of St Matthew* (Rome, S Luigi dei Francesi) in which a group of half-length figures is shown seated at a table in a shallow space defined by chiaroscuro. The palette is sombre, although the horizontal composition is animated by the staccato organization of expressive hands and tilted heads. His depictions of carefree gatherings of merrymakers greatly inspired other Caravaggisti. Foreign painters in particular recognized Manfredi's skill at capturing human nature through direct observation and at portraying everyday events with uncommon sensitivity—what Sandrart called the '*Manfrediana methodus*'. Many of his subjects were strictly secular. Unlike Caravaggio, his work is more decorative than didactic. The symmetrical, isocephalic composition of the *Concert* and *Card Players* (*c.* 1612; Florence, Uffizi; both destr. 1993) is typical of the painter's fully developed method of spatial organization. The brushwork is generally freer, the colours darker and the paint more liquid than in earlier works.

Although Manfredi is known primarily for his depictions of secular subjects, he also executed numerous private religious paintings. These he often cast in the guise of genre scenes. He painted several versions of *Christ Crowned with Thorns* (one example, Springfield, MA, Mus. F.A.). The *Christ Driving the Money-changers from the Temple* (*c.* 1613; Libourne, Mus. B.-A. & Archéol.; see fig. 2), which contains an architectural setting and a dramatic group of fleeing figures indebted to Caravaggio's *Martyrdom of St Matthew*, served as a source for Valentin de Boullogne, Cecco del Caravaggio and Theodoor Rombouts, among others.

Manfredi was highly successful, according to Mancini, and some of the most important collectors in Rome and Tuscany owned his works, among them Vincenzo Giustiniani and Ferdinando I de' Medici. Mancini also relates that the Accademia dei Pittori in Florence requested Manfredi's portrait. Although his biographers state that he executed a small number of public works, none is recorded in Roman guide books. By 1615 his fame had spread beyond central Italy. In that year, Giulio Cesare Gigli's

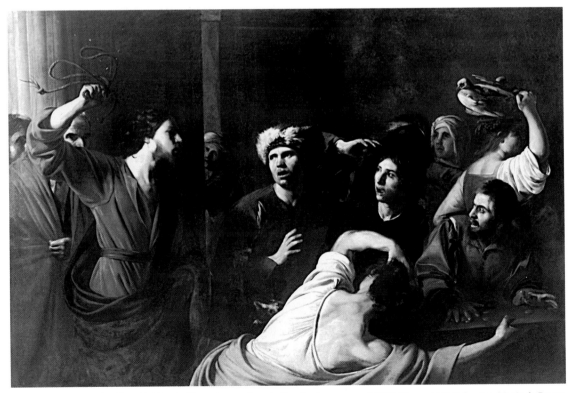

2. Bartolomeo Manfredi: *Christ Driving the Money-changers from the Temple*, oil on canvas, 1.68×2.44 m, *c.* 1613 (Libourne, Musée de Beaux-Arts et d'Archéologie)

poem *La pittura trionfante* (published in Venice) briefly mentions Manfredi.

His last phase reveals an expressive, freer use of paint and more rapid brushstroke that was inspired by his awareness of Caravaggio's late, more broadly executed paintings. Compositionally and technically the *Tribute Money* (*c.* 1618; Florence, Uffizi) is indebted to the *Toothpuller* (Florence, Depositi Gal.), now thought by many scholars to be a late work by Caravaggio himself rather than by one of his followers. Manfredi may have seen this painting on an unrecorded trip to Florence. In the *Christ Appearing to the Virgin after the Resurrection* (*c.* 1621; Florence, Gregori priv. col.; see 1987 exh. cat., p. 85), probably the artist's last known picture, his freer style is most evident. Passages of heavy impasto and thinly brushed areas of paint enliven its surface. The highlights are dull and the flesh unnatural and waxy; the quickly painted, 'disjointed' figures of Christ and the Virgin are also remarkable for being full-length and life-size.

Although Baglione lists Manfredi's name among notables who died during the papacy of Paul V (1605–21), a notice of Manfredi's death is dated 12 December 1622. Joachim von Sandrart was the first writer to recognize that Manfredi himself initiated an independent and flourishing form of Caravaggism. In his *Teutsche Academie*, he used the term 'Manfredi Manier' to describe the paintings of the Flemish artist Gerard Seghers. He also wrote that Nicolas Régnier worked in the 'methodum' of Manfredi, and that Valentin was a follower of Caravaggio and Manfredi. No works can be certainly assigned to Manfredi's known assistants. Though no documentary evidence connects them, the earliest extant works of Régnier and Nicolas Tournier come so close to Manfredi's style that it is likely that they studied with him.

BIBLIOGRAPHY

G. Baglione: *Vite* (1642); ed. V. Mariani (1935), p. 159

G. P. Bellori: *Vite* (1672); ed. E. Borea (1976), p. 234

J. von Sandrart: *Teutsche Academie* (1675–9); ed. A. R. Peltzer (1925), p. 170

R. Longhi: 'Ultimi studi sul Caravaggio e la sua cerchia', *Proporzioni*, i (1943), pp. 5–63

G. Mancini: *Considerazioni sulla pittura* [written between 1614 and 1630]; ed. A. Marucchi, commentary, L. Salerno, 2 vols (Rome, 1956–7), i, p. 251; ii, p. 151

B. Nicolson: 'Bartolomeo Manfredi', *Studies in Renaissance and Baroque Art Presented to Anthony Blunt on his 60th Birthday* (London, 1967)

Caravaggio and his Followers (exh. cat., ed. R. E. Spear; Cleveland, OH, Mus. A., 1971)

A. Brejon de Lavergnée: 'New Paintings by Bartolomeo Manfredi', *Burl. Mag.*, cxxi (1979), pp. 305–10

B. Nicolson: *Caravaggism in Europe*, 3 vols (Oxford, 1979, rev. L. Vertova, Turin, 1990)

J. P. Cuzin: 'Manfredi's *Fortune Teller* and Some Problems of the *Manfrediana methodus*', *Bull. Detroit Inst. A.*, lviii (1980), pp. 14–25

K. Garas: 'Unbekannte italienische Gemälde in Gotha: Probleme um Bigot und Manfredi', *Acta Hist. A. Acad. Sci. Hung.*, xxvi (1980), pp. 265–83

A. Moir: 'An Examination of Bartolomeo Manfredi's *Cupid Chastised*', *Mus. Stud.*, xi (1985), pp. 157–67

G. Merlo: 'Precisazioni sull'anno di nascita di Bartolomeo Manfredi', *Paragone*, xxxvii (1986), pp. 42–6

R. Morselli: 'Bartolomeo Manfredi and Pomarancio: Some New Documents', *Burl. Mag.*, cxxix (1987), pp. 666–8

Dopo Caravaggio, Bartolomeo Manfredi e la Manfrediana methodus (exh. cat., ed. M. C. Poma; Cremona, Mus. Civ. Ala Ponzone, 1987) [excellent pls]

E. Parlato: 'Manfredi's Last Year in Rome', *Burl. Mag.*, cxxxiv (1992), p. 442

JOHN J. CHVOSTAL

Manfredino (d'Alberto) da Pistoia (*fl* 1280–93). Italian painter. In 1280 he was paid for (lost) frescoes in the chapel of S Procolo, Pistoia Cathedral. His next known activity was in 1292, when he signed a fresco cycle in S Michele de Fassolo, Genoa, as *Magister Manfredinus Pistoriensis*. Only detached fragments survive (Genoa, Mus. S Agostino), but they reveal that Manfredino was one of the more eloquent artists of the late 13th century. The dynamic pose and physical solidity of the *St Michael* shows a keen and intelligent response to the art of Cimabue, whose example can be seen in the modelling and facial construction of the figures in the other major surviving fragment, the *Anointing at Bethany*. Here Manfredino adds to the traditional Byzantine iconography a sympathetic and psychologically alert sense of the dramatic undertones and a remarkably ambitious and detailed backdrop of a city scene. The last record of his activity is in a Genoese document of 1293.

BIBLIOGRAPHY

I. M. Botto, ed.: *Museo di S Agostino* (Genoa, n.d.), pp. 85–6

F. Alizeri: *Notizie dei professori di disegno in Liguria*, i (Genoa, 1873)

R. Van Marle: *Italian Schools*, i (1923), pp. 296–8

C. B. Dufour and others: *La pittura a Genova e in Liguria dagli inizi al cinquecento* (Genoa, 1970), pp. 27–36

JOHN RICHARDS

Mangbetu. Central Sudanic-speaking people living on the northern edge of the rain-forest in north-eastern Zaïre. The largest groups bordering the Mangbetu are the Zande to the north and west, the Barambo and Bua to the west, the Bodu and Mayogo to the south and the Mamvu to the east. The art typically classified as Mangbetu comprises works in wood, ivory, copper, iron, clay and other natural materials. Such prestige objects as harps, knives, trumpets, boxes and pots include a portrayal of the most distinctive Mangbetu feature, an elongated cranium formed by binding the heads of infants until the skull hardens into the desired shape (*see* AFRICA, fig. 88). Other prestigious art forms, such as the king's musical instruments, hats and weapons, are of superior craftsmanship, and they are decorated with geometric designs. Everyday objects, including well-made furniture, pots, tools and clothing, are also decorated with geometric patterns.

The major museum collections (e.g. Tervuren, Kon. Mus. Mid.-Afrika; New York, Amer. Mus. Nat. Hist.) are the results of American and Belgian scientific expeditions to the Mangbetu region between 1907 and 1915. German acquisitions from the same period are distributed among many German, and other European, ethnographic museum collections. A major exhibition of the art of the Mangbetu and neighbouring peoples was held at the American Museum of Natural History, New York, in 1990 (see 1990 exh. cat. for an authoritative and well-illustrated account).

1. PRE-COLONIAL ARTS. In the 19th century the Mangbetu-Mabiti clan conquered many of the peoples between the Uele and Nepoko rivers and united them into several small kingdoms. When the German botanist Georg Schweinfurth visited the northern Mangbetu in 1870 he marvelled at the high level of their culture. Nangazizi, the

Mangbetu king, Mbunza, dancing before his wives in the assembly hall in Nangazizi, Central Africa; engraving after the drawing by Georg Schweinfurth in *Im Herzen von Afrika* (Leipzig, 1873)

village of King Mbunza, had several thousand inhabitants, and in the court complex was an assembly hall that could accommodate hundreds of people and that ranks among the largest buildings in pre-colonial Sub-Saharan Africa (see fig.). Men and women of the Mangbetu nobility took great care in personal dress and adornment, and meticulous craftsmanship was evident in the geometric designs on metalwork, pottery, basketry, architecture and woodwork.

While Schweinfurth's descriptions and his drawings are generally reliable, he did not accurately perceive the nature of King Mbunza's rule, a factor that has led to problems in our understanding of pre-colonial Mangbetu art. Schweinfurth's assumption that the Mangbetu controlled a large, powerful and highly centralized kingdom has been generally accepted, and it has been deduced from this that all the art from the area was of Mangbetu origin. Mangbetu political achievement was significant in the region, but the kingdoms did not exist long enough, nor were they powerful enough, to have been responsible for all the regional styles. Styles assumed by scholars to be Mangbetu are often part of a wider regional-style area, formed over many centuries of regional interaction. Distinctions between Mangbetu and non-Mangbetu are also unclear, because each group conquered by the Mangbetu brought its separate styles to the kingdoms. Since early European collectors rarely knew exactly where or why an object was created or the ethnic origin of its creator, many separate pre-colonial artistic traditions have been grouped together as Mangbetu.

These problems of identification may be illustrated with reference to anthropomorphic objects. Even though

Schweinfurth and many later observers noted that the Mangbetu had no tradition of anthropomorphic carving, many anthropomorphic objects do exist (*see* AFRICA, fig. 138). Unfortunately, the supposedly distinctive feature of Mangbetu cranial elongation gives few clues to the origins of such art, because this feature was widely copied by non-Mangbetu subjects and neighbours, both as an actual bodily practice and in art. There is some evidence to suggest that those neighbours and subjects who had anthropomorphic art traditions may have been the first to carve these elongated heads. Presumably, these art styles were taken up by the Mangbetu courts in the late 19th century.

2. COLONIAL ARTS. A new period in Mangbetu art accompanied the beginning of the colonial era (1891). Because the Mangbetu efforts at political centralization seemed to indicate social 'evolution', European colonial officers, missionaries and travellers celebrated and even elevated the importance of the Mangbetu kingdoms. Evidence of advancement was seen in the realism of Mangbetu anthropomorphic works and in what was perceived as an aesthetic sensibility superior to that of other African peoples. This resulted in extensive European patronage of anthropomorphic objects and in official encouragement of such Mangbetu showpieces as the painted village of Chief Ekibondo, where both the outside and inside walls of buildings were covered with geometric patterns in white, black and ochre. Moreover, missionaries, administrators and other foreigners began to tutor artists of the region in styles pleasing to Europeans.

There were at least two other significant changes during the colonial period. First, wider travel helped homogenize regional styles while also bringing in ideas from other peoples outside the region. Second, the Mangbetu responded to European tastes. Mangbetu rulers, especially those close to larger European posts in the north, welcomed visitors, impressed them with decorated villages, entertained them with dances and gave them objects made by Mangbetu artists. By the early 1900s artists throughout the region were creating pieces with anthropomorphic forms for sale to Europeans. Such new forms of Mangbetu art as cephalomorphic pots also appeared (*see* AFRICA, fig. 77). These seem to have been made almost exclusively for Europeans. Mangbetu artists also began to produce in ivory such European items as shoehorns, salt-cellars, napkin-rings and forks.

BIBLIOGRAPHY
G. A. Schweinfurth: *Im Herzen von Afrika* (Leipzig, 1873); Eng. trans. as *The Heart of Africa: Three Years' Travels and Adventures in the Unexplored Regions of Central Africa from 1868 to 1871*, 2 vols (London, 1873/R New York, 1874) [numerous later editions and reprints]
——: *Artes Africanae: Abbildungen und Beschreibungen von Erzeugnissen des Kunstfleisses Centralafrikanischer Völker/Illustrations and Descriptions of Productions of the Industrial Arts of Central African Tribes* (Leipzig and London, 1875) [Ger. & Eng. text]
W. Junker: *Reisen in Afrika, 1875–1886*, 3 vols (Vienna, 1889–91; Eng. trans. by A. H. Keane, London, 1890–92)
G. Casati: *Dieci anni in Equatoria* (Milan, 1891); Eng. trans., 2 vols (London, 1891)
A. Hutereau: 'Notes sur la vie familiale et juridique de quelques populations du Congo Belge', *An. Mus. Congo Belge, Anthropol. & Ethnog.*, ser. 4, i/1 (1909) [whole issue]
E. Schildkrout, J. Hellman and C. A. Keim, 'Mangbetu Pottery: Tradition and Innovation in Northeast Zaire', *Afr. A.*, xxii/2 (1989), pp. 38–47
African Reflections: Art from Northeastern Zaire (exh. cat. by E. Schildkrout and C. Keim, New York, Amer. Mus. Nat. Hist., 1990)
Mangbetu: Art du cour africain de collections privées belges (exh. cat. by H. Burssens with A. Guisson, Brussels, Gal. Kredietbank, 1992)
CURTIS A. KEIM

Mange, Ernest (Robert de Carvalho) (*b* São Paulo, 28 Dec 1922). Brazilian engineer, architect and urban planner. He graduated in civil engineering from the Polytechnic School of the University of São Paulo in 1945, and in 1947–48 he worked with Le Corbusier in Paris. In 1955 he became an associate of Ariaki Kato (*b* 1931) in PLANEMAK (Planejamento de Edifícios e Cidades Ltda), a partnership that specialized in a variety of design and engineering projects such as hydroelectric, mining and railway installations, the underground railway in São Paulo, industrial and administrative buildings. The construction of large-scale hydroelectric installations in sparsely populated areas of the interior involved the creation of new towns such as those planned by Mange along the Paraná river: Jupiá (1961–70) with 15,000 inhabitants, Ilha Solteira (1966–74) with 45,000 inhabitants, Itaipú (1976–8) and Porto Primavera (1978) with 24,000 inhabitants; the Tocantins river: Tucuruví (1975–9); and the Jamari river: Samuel (1981–3). Some of these townships were temporary camps, but the permanent work was very extensive and demonstrated the importance of thoughtful planning in the transfer of thousands of workers and their families from one region to another with the minimum of disruption. Other projects undertaken by Mange, all solidly planned and appropriately detailed, included various technical schools for the Serviço Nacional de Aprendizagem

Industrial (1952–6), the elegantly sited Banco América do Sul (1965), Avenida Brigadeiro Luis Antonio, São Paulo, the Municipal Building (1970) at Cubatão, with its excellent system of ventilation and protection from the sun, and the Ciba Geigy Laboratories (1974–6), with 40,000 sq. m of floor space. Later projects involved mine construction and the industrial processing of rare minerals in Amazonia. Mange received a PhD and became a Professor at the University of São Paulo in 1963.

BIBLIOGRAPHY
'Escola de Engenharia de São Carlos', *Habitat*, vi/33 (1956), pp. 44–9
'Usina Limoeiro, Rio Pardo, Esi de Sao Paulo Realização da Companhia Hidroeléctrica do Rio Pardo', *Habitat*, vi/35 (1956), pp. 56–60
'Planejamenio em Urubupunga, E. R. Carvalho Mange, Engenheiro, Ariaki Kato, Arquiteto', *Acrópole*, 289 (1962), pp. 1–11
PAULO J. V. BRUNA

Mangi. *See* CHŎNGJO.

Mangiarotti, Angelo (*b* Milan, 26 Feb 1921). Italian architect and designer. After graduating from the Polytechnic of Milan (1948), he worked independently in Milan and in Chicago, where he became visiting professor at the Institute of Design, Illinois Institute of Technology (1953–4). There he met Walter Gropius, Ludwig Mies van der Rohe and Konrad Wachsmann and studied their works carefully. Mies van der Rohe's emphasis on structure as the basis of form is reflected in his work, as is his interest in traditional Japanese architecture. Mangiarotti was particularly interested in construction techniques, and he developed increasingly sophisticated structural systems comprising prefabricated column or pilaster and beam components. The first example to be realized was the Church of Mater Misericordiae (1957), Baranzate, Milan, a graceful prefabricated concrete structure of rectilinear form with double cross-braced roof beams running the length of the nave. The quality and interest of the industrial buildings of the 1960s and 1970s lies in the clarity of the relationships between structural elements and the enclosing envelopes, which are often treated like transparent skins. The elegant Elmag Factory (1966) at Monza is perhaps the best-known of this period. The importance that Mangiarotti placed on the structural joint as generator of form is evident in both his architectural and product design. Examples include the prestressed structural systems for industrial application of 1976, or those designed for railway stations in and around Milan and the 'Eros' series of tables (1975), in which the leg joints are formed in the marble tops. Less well-known but also refined in the use of materials and techniques are the villa (1957) at San Martino di Castrozza, Trento (1957), and the flats at Via Gavirate (1957) and Via Quadronno (1960) in Milan, and at Monza (1977), or, more typical of Mangiarotti's structural virtuosity, the single-storey prefabricated houses (1962) at Marcianese, Casserta.

WRITINGS
with I. Kawahara, eds: *Angelo Mangiarotti, 1955–1964* (Tokyo, 1964)

BIBLIOGRAPHY
I. Kawahara and others: 'Mangiarotti's Sumptuous World', *Space Des.*, cxxix (1975), pp. 5–99
E. D. Bona: *Angelo Mangiarotti: Il processo del costruire* (Milan, 1980)
ANDREA NULLI

Mangin, Joseph François (*fl* 1794–1818). French architect, active in the USA. He had already been trained in France when he arrived in the USA in 1794, where he joined his brother, Charles Mangin, in New York. For several years he served as an engineering adviser for the city fortifications, and in 1796 he became a city surveyor. With his brother he designed the Park Theater (1795–9) and independently the New York State Prison (1797). Mangin collaborated in 1802 with JOHN McCOMB in the winning submission for the New York City Hall, which is his only surviving building in the USA. It is probable that the French Neo-classical character of the winning design was largely Mangin's, although the construction (1803–12) was supervised by McComb, who introduced more English-derived details in the interior. After New York City Hall, Mangin independently designed an early building for St Patrick's Cathedral (1809–15) and the Wall Street Presbyterian Church (1810), both in New York.

BIBLIOGRAPHY

DAB; *Macmillan Enc. Architects*
'Joseph François Mangin': *National Cyclopedia of American Biography* (New York, 1936), xxv, pp. 289–90
T. F. Hamlin: *Greek Revival Architecture in America* (New York and Oxford, 1944)
D. Stillman: 'Artistry and Skill in the Architecture of John McComb, jr' (diss., Newark, U. DE, 1956)
——: 'New York City Hall: Competition and Execution', *J. Soc. Archit. Historians*, xxiii (1964), pp. 129–42

LELAND M. ROTH

Mangione, Salvatore. *See* SALVO.

Manglard, Adrien (*b* Lyon, 10 March 1695; *d* Rome, 1 Aug 1760). French painter, draughtsman and engraver, active in Italy. The son of a modest painter and godson of Adriaen van der Cabel, he learnt figure painting with Frère Imbert in Lyon. He travelled to Rome in 1715, where he spent much of his time making studies of ships (Paris, Mus. A. Déc.) and even of Turks and camels (Paris, Ecole N. Sup. B.-A.). He also trained in the studio of Bernardino Fergioni (1674–1738) and learnt from those artists in the circle of the sculptor Pierre Legros (ii), who was to purchase two seascapes by Manglard before 1719. His skill as a marine painter was such that his career advanced rapidly: prestigious clients included Victor Amadeus II, Duke of Savoy and King of Piedmont, who bought two matching pieces from him in 1726 (Turin, Gal. Sabauda), and Philip, Duke of Parma (*d* 1765), who acquired a pair in 1759 (Colorno, Pal. Ducale), and the Rospigliosi family in Rome, for whom he produced a number of pictures (Rome, Mus. N. Romano).

In 1734 Manglard was approved (*agréé*) by the Académie Royale de Peinture et de Sculpture in Paris and received (*reçu*) as a full member two years later. In 1735 he was accepted into the Accademia di S Luca in Rome, to which he presented *The Calling of the Apostles* (Rome, Accad. N. S Luca), the figures for which were inspired by Bolognese models, and in 1741 he joined the Virtuosi al Pantheon. Painting on canvas, often in a large format, Manglard concentrated on seascapes throughout his career, for example *Shipwreck in a Storm* (Guéret, Mus. Guéret), but he also painted landscapes and *vedute*, for example *View of the Palazzo Rospigliosi* (Rome, Pal. Braschi). He also revealed himself to be an interior decorator of great talent

with the Sala delle Marine (1748) in the Palazzo Chigi, Rome. He engraved 44 plates after his own paintings of landscapes, marines and antique buildings in 1753–4 (Rome, Ist. N. Graf.), and the sale made after his death revealed the true extent of his passion for collecting. An album of his figure and other studies is in Paris (Ecole N. Sup. B.-A.). Manglard discovered his own style by accommodating Northern realism within the classical idealism of Claude Lorrain; this he passed on to Claude-Joseph Vernet, who may have trained in his studio and who rapidly surpassed him.

BIBLIOGRAPHY

O. Michel: 'Adrien Manglard, peintre et collectionneur (1695–1760)', *Mél. Ecole Fr. Rome: Moyen Age, Temps Mod.*, xciii (1981), pp. 823–926
S. Maddalo: *Adrien Manglard (1695–1760)* (Rome, 1982)

OLIVIER MICHEL

Mangold. American painters.

(1) Robert (Peter) Mangold (*b* North Tonawanda, NY, 12 Oct 1937). He first trained at the Cleveland Institute of Art from 1956 to 1959, and then at Yale University, New Haven, CT (BFA, 1961; MFA, 1963). In 1961 he married Sylvia Plimack, and they moved to New York. Robert Mangold's early work consisted largely of monochromatic free-standing constructions displayed against the wall, such as *Grey Window Wall* (oil on plywood, 2.44×2.29 m, 1964; destr., see 1982 exh. cat., no. 1); their architectonic forms and grey tonal scale led to their association with Minimalism. The almost sculptural quality of this work was soon abandoned in favour of shaped and multipartite canvases such as *Cool Grey Area with Curved Diagonals* (1966; New York, Guggenheim). Mangold's consistent use of flat colour and geometry in such works as *Red X within X* (1980; San Francisco, CA, MOMA) was modified by a consistent manipulation of the painting's edge and by an illusionism that distinguished his work from the sober immediacy of Minimalism. The book *Six Arcs* (New York, 1978) was designed and illustrated by Mangold himself.

BIBLIOGRAPHY

L. Lippard: 'Silent Art: Robert Mangold', *Changing Essays in Art Criticism* (New York, 1971), pp. 130–40
Robert Mangold (exh. cat. by D. Waldman, New York, Guggenheim, 1971)
Robert Mangold (exh. cat. by N. Spector, La Jolla, CA, Mus. Contemp. A., 1974)
Robert Mangold: Four Large Works (exh. cat., Basle, Kstmus., 1977)
Robert Mangold: Schilderijen/paintings, 1964–1982 (exh. cat., Amsterdam, Stedel. Mus., 1982)
Robert Mangold: Painting, 1971–84 (exh. cat., Akron, OH, A. Mus., 1984)
J. Gruen: 'Robert Mangold: "A Maker of Images—Nothing More and Nothing Less"', *ARTnews*, lxxxvi/6 (1987), pp. 132–8

(2) Sylvia Plimack Mangold [née Plimack] (*b* New York, 18 Sept 1938). Wife of (1) Robert Mangold. She attended Cooper Union College, New York, from 1956 to 1959 before going to Yale University, New Haven, CT (BFA, 1961). After returning to New York in 1961 she made carefully rendered paintings of abstract grid patterns and other precise designs. Her penchant for realism soon evolved into a style of painting: an indefinite field often provided the ground for a softly illusionistic landscape, which was depicted using a variety of *trompe l'oeil* devices. By painting the masking tape or ruler that fixes her image to its surroundings, as in *Taped and Defined in Fall* (oil on canvas, 1979; Indianapolis, IN, Mus. A.), she challenged the objectives of realist painting. In addition to her paintings, she also produced pastels, and she published an illustrated book *Inches and Field* (New York, 1978).

BIBLIOGRAPHY
Sylvia Plimack Mangold (exh. cat. by A. Miller-Keller, Hartford, CT, Wadsworth Atheneum, 1980)
Sylvia Plimack Mangold: Paintings, 1965–1982 (exh. cat., Madison, WI, A. Cent., 1982)

DERRICK R. CARTWRIGHT

Mangone, Giovanni (*b* Caravaggio; *d* Rome, before 27 June 1543). Italian architect and sculptor. He was a pupil of the sculptor Andrea di Piero Ferrucci. From *c.* 1527 to 1532 he was supervisor of the Fonte di S Pietro, Rome. He was conservator of the gilded ceilings of the basilica of S Maria Maggiore until 1541, and from *c.* 1542 he was also the architect to the Camera Apostolica (Vatican Works Office), a post he held until his death. For Angelo Massimo, Mangone constructed the Palazzo di Pirro (initiated *c.* 1533). In this, his first architectural work, he appears as a faithful follower of the severe style of Antonio da Sangallo (ii) with whom he worked on the decorations (1534) for the coronation of Pope Paul III and the fortifications (1537–43) of Rome. In 1535 he worked on the palazzo in Rome of Giacomo Simonetta, Cardinal of Perugia, and in 1536 he planned alterations to the convent of the Serviti attached to the church of S Marcello al Corso. In the same year, he executed the monument to Cardinal Eckervoirt in the church of S Maria dell'Anima, Rome, in a style influenced by Andrea Sansovino. This work and the monument (1538) to Cardinal Magalotti in the church of S Cecilia in Trastevere, Rome, represent the sculptural production attributed to Mangone. In his last years he carried out valuations and, at an unspecified time, worked on the church of S Luigi dei Francesi (before ?1531), laying out the architectural arrangement (later altered) of the internal decoration. In *c.* 1543 he worked on the fortification of the Sermoneta in Lazio. Other buildings attributed to him, all in Rome, include the Palazzo Alicorni in Borgo (destr. 1931; later rebuilt) and the Palazzetto dei Vellis in Piazza S Maria di Trastevere. Mangone's architecture is characterized by his great attention to proportion and balance, revealing his training as a sculptor in the precise design of the mouldings.

BIBLIOGRAPHY
Thieme–Becker
C. Tolomei: *Delle lettere libri sette* (Venice, 1547), p. 105
G. Vasari: *Vite* (1550, rev. 2/1568); ed. G. Milanesi (1878–85), iv, p. 480
G. Milanesi: 'Stima di un lavoro di Giovanni Mangone', *G. Erud. A.*, iv (1875), pp. 152–3
A. Bertolotti: *Artisti lombardi a Roma nei secoli XV, XVI e XVII*, i (Milan, 1881), pp. 43–7
G. Caetani: *Domus Caietana*, ii (San Casciano in Val di Pesa), p. 65
A. Venturi: *Storia*, x (1935), pp. 273–6
G. Giovannoni: 'Giovanni Mangone, architetto', *Palladio*, iii (1939), pp. 97–112
P. Portoghesi: *Roma del rinascimento* (Venice, 1970), pp. 237, 498
C. L. Frommel: *Der römische Palastbau der Hochrenaissance*, i (Tübingen, 1973), p. 54
M. Tafuri: 'Antonio da Sangallo il giovane e Jacopo Sansovino: Un conflitto professionale nella Roma medicea', *Antonio da Sangallo il giovane: La vita e l'opera*, ed. G. Spagnesi (Rome, 1986), pp. 90–91
S. Benedetti and G. Zander: *L'arte in Roma nel secolo XVI*, i of *L'architettura* (Bologna, 1990)
M. Tafuri: *Ricerca del rinascimento: Principi, città, architetti* (Turin, 1992), p. 209

ADRIANO GHISETTI GIAVARINA

Mangones, Albert (*b* Port-au-Prince, 26 March 1917). Haitian architect and sculptor. He studied from 1939 to 1942 at the College of Architecture, Cornell University, Ithaca, NY, where he was awarded the Sand Goldwin Medal. His early works, such as the Théâtre de Verdure (1949), the Cité Militaire (1956–7), a social urban development for the military, and the Régie du Tabac (1958), an industrial complex, all in Port-au-Prince, are characterized by simple geometrical lines and large openings in order to integrate the structure with the environment. The materials used include cement blocks, bricks and cobblestones. He was influenced by Le Corbusier, Frank Lloyd Wright and the latter's pupil Henry Klumb (*b* 1905). He also built many villas, notably the Sheila Burns Villa (1956), Diquini, and his own residence (1966), Martissant, as well as the Villa Créole Hotel, Pétion Ville, and the Habitation Leclerc Hotel (1974), Port-au-Prince. Mangones's statue of *St Domingue Marron* (bronze, 1968) and his design for its site in the Place du Marron Inconnu, Port-au-Prince, established his international reputation. The statue, representing a kneeling slave blowing the conch of freedom, illustrated a postage stamp commemorating the United Nations Universal Declaration of Human Rights (1989). After 1978 he undertook the preservation of the historic site combining the Citadelle La Ferrière, the Palace of Sans-Souci and the site of Ramiers in the north of Haiti. In 1979 he was appointed Director of the Institut de Sauvegarde du Patrimonie National (ISPAN), Haiti.

BIBLIOGRAPHY
B. Raymond: 'Haitian Hideaway: Architect Albert Mangones', *Interiors*, cxxxiii/8 (1974), pp. 98–105
E. I. Christensen: *The Art of Haiti* (New York, 1975), pp. 50, 69–70

BENJIE THÉARD

Manguin, Henri(-Charles) (*b* Paris, 23 March 1874; *d* St Tropez, 25 Sept 1949). French painter. He studied under Gustave Moreau at the Ecole des Beaux-Arts in Paris from late 1894, befriending his fellow students Albert Marquet, Henri Matisse, Jean Puy and Georges Rouault, who were among those later to be labelled the Fauves (*see* FAUVISM) when they exhibited together at the Salon d'Automne in 1905. Manguin's *Nude in the Studio* (1903; Canada, priv. col., see L. Manguin and C. Manguin, p. 67), in its rejection of local colour, conspicuously broken brushstroke and subversion of traditional perspective, is an early example of his Fauvist style, which was considerably less revolutionary than that of Matisse or Maurice de Vlaminck. The picture is, however, given a personal twist by Manguin's unusual framing devices and ambiguous space, for example in his use of a theoretically impossible reflection in a mirror to produce a picture within a picture. The disjunction that was noted at the time by Guillaume Apollinaire between Manguin's use of heightened, unnaturalistic colour and straightforward, almost academic drawing style is evident in a *Self-portrait* (1905; France, L. Manguin priv. col., see L. Manguin and C. Manguin, p. 11), in which broadly brushed areas and patches of colour break down traditional illusionism by drawing attention to the canvas surface.

Manguin had exhibited for the first time at the Salon des Indépandants in 1902, before becoming secretary of the Salon d'Automne, to which he would contribute

Henri Manguin: *Gulf of St Tropez*, oil on canvas, 630×730 mm, 1918 (Paris, Pompidou, Musée National d'Art Moderne)

regularly until his death. He continued to meet other avant-garde artists, including Paul Signac in 1905 and Henri-Edmond Cross in 1906, and on enrolling at the Académie Ranson in 1908 he renewed his friendship with Marquet. Nevertheless his association with the most radical form of Fauvism, as represented by *Fourteenth of July at St Tropez, the Harbour—Left Side* (1905; Mme G. Holstein priv. col., see L. Manguin and C. Manguin, p. 17), was to prove short-lived.

It was through Signac that Manguin came to know St Tropez in 1905, and he continued to make regular visits there, painting many views of the town and its environs, for example *Lane in St Tropez* (1905; St Petersburg, Hermitage). Meanwhile he travelled extensively, to Naples, Lausanne and Antwerp, and to areas of France such as Normandy, Brittany and Provence, all of which had associations with previous painters such as Boudin, Gauguin and van Gogh.

Unlike his contemporaries, who seemed intent on a critical examination of their medium, Manguin concentrated on joyous and stylish effects of colour and composition, working mainly on small canvases, which were easy to transport and sell, and on charming and intimate, rather than aggressive or daring, subjects, including landscapes such as the *Gulf of St Tropez* (1918; Paris, Pompidou; see fig.), still-lifes such as *Green Tray* (1912; Zurich, Ksthaus) and nudes, for which his wife Jeanne often posed, such as *Bather at Cavalière, Jeanne* (1906; Moscow, Pushkin Mus. F.A.).

Rest (1919; Geneva, Petit Pal.) retains Manguin's extremely vivid range of colours with shrill green shadows, but the picture is traditionally composed, using the carpet and divan on either side of the seated model as a means of defining spatial depth and to provide a framework for the decorative exuberance of arabesques and patterns reminiscent of Matisse. Manguin can indeed be credited with popularizing earlier pictorial devices originally judged too extreme. In *Sea Bream and Condiments* (1928; Lausanne, priv. col., see Cabanne, p. 145) the tilting of the table towards the picture plane and the treatment of the folded tablecloth in the foreground clearly allude to Cézanne, while the relationships of the different colour surfaces again recall Matisse. It was this very restraint that made his work appealing to many private collectors, particularly Sergey Shchukin, while excluding it from most of the great international museums.

BIBLIOGRAPHY
Gustave Moreau et ses élèves (exh. cat., ed. J. Cassou; Marseille, Mus. Cantini & Gal. Faïence, 1962)
P. Cabanne and others: *Henri Manguin* (Neuchâtel, 1964)
Henri Manguin, 1874–1949: Erste deutsche Retrospektive (exh. cat. by J. Goldman, W. Berlin, Neuer Berlin. Kstver., 1970)
Manguin in America: Henri Manguin, 1874–1949 (exh. cat. by W. E. Steadman and D. Sutton, Tucson, U. AZ Mus. A.; New York, Cult. Cent.; Los Angeles, UCLA, Wight A.G.; Athens, U. GA Mus. A.; 1974)
Henri Manguin, 1874–1949 (exh. cat. by J.-P. Manguin and A. Mousseigne, St Tropez, Chapelle de la Miséricorde, 1976)
L. Manguin and C. Manguin, eds: *Henri Manguin: Cat. raisonné de l'oeuvre peinte* (Neuchâtel, 1980) [cat. by M.-C. Sainsaulieu]
Manguin parmi les Fauves (exh. cat. by P. Gassier, L. Manguin and M. Hahnloser, Martigny, Fond. Pierre Gianadda, 1983)

VANINA COSTA

Mangup. Medieval fortress on an isolated plateau in the Crimea, 20 km from BAKHCHISARAY. In the centre of the plateau are the ruins of a large 6th-century AD basilica, thought to have been dedicated to SS Constantine and Helen. The building (31.5×28 m) comprises a nave and two aisles with two galleries and two apses. The central apse is trihedral and has a triple-stepped synthronon, and the southern apse is semicircular. The walls were frescoed, and remnants of a mosaic floor have been found in the nave and narthex. A fragmentary inscription including the name of Justinian I was discovered in the western part of the building. Other finds include capitals of Prokonnesian marble.

The site, known in the 7th and 8th centuries AD as Doros, was fortified in the second half of the 6th century by Byzantines from Cherson with their Goth and Alan confederates. Walls with square towers protected the slopes and the three ravines that bisect the northern part of the plateau. The defended area covered 90 ha, making it the largest fortress in the Crimea until the 13th century. At the end of the 8th century the fortress was captured by the Khazars, and the late 10th century stratigraphic levels of the site are marked by fires and demolitions. In the first half of the 14th century a town developed on the plateau. It was the capital of the principality of Theodoro, the rulers of which were probably members of the aristocratic Trebizond house of Gavras and vassals of the Tatar Khan. In the 1360s the Byzantine walls were restored, and a citadel was built on the Teshkli-burun promontory. In the 1380s a second line of defences was erected to protect the built-up area. The citadel is cut off from the plateau by a defensive wall with a projecting three-storey donjon, which has an entrance gate decorated with carved ornament in the north-east wall. In the middle of the promontory stands an octagonal church, a unique Crimean example of this type. Ranged along the edge of the precipice and cut into the rock are casemates overlooking the main road, which wound round the foot of the promontory and passed into the town by way of the main gates in the Kapu-dere ravine. In 1425 a palace complex was built in the middle of the plateau 150 m south-west of the basilica. A small church (14th–15th century) was excavated in 1912 in the north-east of the site, and the lower part of a relief depicting St George was discovered. In 1475, after a six-month siege, the town was taken by the Ottomans, who used heavy siege artillery against its walls. The fortress remained a regional centre until the beginning of the 18th century, and it was abandoned at the end of the century.

BIBLIOGRAPHY
N. V. Malitsky: 'Zametki po epigrafike Mangupa' [Remarks on the epigraphy of Mangup], *Izvestiya Inst. Istor. Mat. Kul't.*, lxxi (1933)
A. A. Vasiliev: *The Goths in the Crimea* (Cambridge, MA, 1936)
Mat. Issledovaniya Arkheol. SSSR, xxxiv (1953)
A. G. Gertsen: 'Krepostnoi ansambl' Mangupa' [Fortification ensemble of Mangup], *Materialy po arkhaeologii, istorii i ethnographii Tavrii* [Materials on the archaeology, history and ethnography of the Tavria] (Simferopol, 1990)
——: 'Archaeological Excavation of Karaite Settlements in the Crimea' *Proceedings of the 11th World Congress of Jewish Studies. Division B. The History of the Jewish People. v.1. Second Temple Period to Modern Times* (Jerusalem, 1994)

A. G. GERTSEN

Manière criblée [Fr.: 'sieved manner']. Term used for an early tonal DOTTED PRINT, with punched and stamped decoration, made with METALCUT during the second half of the 15th century in Germany and France.

□

Manière de lavis. *See* WASH MANNER and *under* AQUATINT.

Manila. Capital of the Philippines, on the shores of Manila Bay, west central Luzon, at the mouth of the Pasig River. The city of Manila (population 1.6 million) is the centre of Metro Manila (population over 8 million), which includes Quezon City, Pasay Makati and other suburbs. After Spanish occupation of the Philippines, the walled town of Intramuros was founded (1571) on the site of a Muslim settlement. Long before Spanish colonization, merchants of the locality traded with southern China. Excavations at grave sites in Santa Ana, further upstream on the Pasig, have yielded Chinese trade pottery, proof of extensive trade relations, and locally manufactured ornaments that indicate a degree of technological sophistication.

From 1571 to 1815 Manila was the entrepôt of the Spanish galleon trade. Trade goods and raw material from the Philippines and elsewhere in East Asia were amassed in Manila and sent annually to Acapulco in Mexico (*see* PHILIPPINES, §I, 2). Ivory carvings, *piña* (a gossamer cloth made from pineapple fibre), canvas, shawls and furniture were among the trade goods manufactured in the Philippines. Silk was imported in large quantities from China. In exchange came food, clothing, furniture, books, crystals and other artefacts from Europe, as well as silver from Mexico. The missionary orders introduced European architectural styles, modified by their building experience in Mexico, and encouraged religious painting by organizing workshops in their monasteries. The church and monastery of S Agustín in Intramuros is an excellent example of the fruit of this missionary patronage (*see* PHILIPPINES, §II, 1(ii)(b)). Churches such as S Agustín, S Ana, S Pedro Makati and S Sebastián, built during the Spanish colonial period, house artefacts and furniture fashioned in the Hispanic tradition but with oriental elements.

With the increase of foreign trade during the mid-19th century, an educated merchant class, composed of Mestizos and Europeans, became the new art patrons. Some of their houses—a blend of native, Chinese and European artistic traditions—are still standing in the business districts

Manila, Cultural Center of the Philippines, by Leandro Locsin, founded 1966, opened 1969; eastern elevation

of Binondo and Quiapo. Local portrait painters and miniaturists including Damian Domingo (*c.* 1790–?1841), Justiniano Asuncion (1816–96), Juan Arceo (*c.* 1795–*c.* 1865) and Antonio Malantic (*c.* 1820–*c.* 1885) were busy painting portraits for this class. Art became professionalized with the establishment of the Obras Públicas (1867) to supervise building works, and the Academia de Pintura y Dibujo (1850). (*See also* PHILIPPINES, §V, 1.)

In 1908 the University of the Philippines was established, with a School of Fine Arts under Rafael Enriquez (1850–1927). His successor Fabian de la Rosa (1869–1937) popularized landscape and genre painting, but it was Fernando C. Amorsolo (1892–1972), a product of this school, who set the model for Philippine art with his genre works. Reacting against the conservatism of Amorsolo and the classicist sculptor Guillermo Tolentino (1890–1976), in the 1930s Victorio Edades (1895–1985) engaged in a lively debate that opened the door to modern art in all its forms.

Early in the 20th century the city's layout and appearance were transformed by the Plan for Manila (1905) of DANIEL H. BURNHAM and the architecture of William E. Parsons (1872–1939). The two Americans introduced wide streets, open areas and civic buildings (*see* PHILIPPINES, §§II, 1(iii) and III). During the period of American rule (1898–1946), Neo-classicism became the standard for civic architecture, while Art Deco and Art Nouveau became popular for theatres, business establishments and private houses. The Metropolitan Theater of Manila (1931), designed by Juan Arellano (1881–1960), is the best known Art Deco work.

Two of the country's oldest art schools are located in Manila: the College (former School) of Fine Arts of the University of the Philippines and the College of Architecture and Fine Arts of the University of Santo Tomás, which trained most of the artists active since the 1960s. Since World War II new styles of art and architecture have appeared ranging from those inspired by ethnic designs and traditions to Post-modernism (*see* PHILIPPINES, §V, 3). The Art Association of the Philippines, founded in 1947 by Purita Kalaw-Ledesma, is the country's biggest and oldest artists' association; its initial membership came from the alumni of the University of the Philippines School of Fine Arts.

The National Museum of the Philippines (founded 1901) houses a representative collection of Filipino paintings, including works by two 19th-century masters, Juan Luna y Novicio (1857–99) and Felix Resurreccion Hidalgo (1853–1913). The Metropolitan Museum of Manila (1976) has a permanent collection of Western art and is the venue for exhibitions on loan from foreign museums and for exhibits of contemporary Filipino artists. The Cultural Center of the Philippines (1966; see fig.), apart from its permanent collection of theatre-related arts, has galleries for exhibits of contemporary art. In addition to these public institutions, the privately owned Ateneo Art Gallery (1960), Ayala Museum (1967) and Lopez Museum (1969) have collections of Filipino art. Galleries are numerous, although some only have brief existences. The first to open after World War II, the Philippine Art Gallery (1951) founded by Lyd Arguilla, no longer exists. The Luz Gallery, established in 1960, is the oldest and most prestigious in the country.

BIBLIOGRAPHY

P. Ortiz Armengol: *Intramuros de Manila de 1571 hasta su destrucción en 1945* (Madrid, 1958)
D. Castaneda: *Art in the Philippines* (Quezon City, 1964)
M. Duldulao: *Contemporary Philippine Art: From the Fifties to the Seventies* (Manila, 1972)
P. Kalaw-Ledesma: *The Struggle for Philippine Art* (Manila, 1974)
N. Zafra: *The Colonization of the Philippines and the Beginnings of the Spanish City of Manila* (Manila, 1974)
R. R. Reed: *Colonial Manila: The Context of Hispanic Urbanism and Process of Morphogenesis* (Berkeley, Los Angeles and London, 1978)
P. Kalaw-Ledesma: *Edades: National Artist* (Manila, 1979)
G. Casal and others: *The People and Art of the Philippines* (Los Angeles, 1981)
V. de la Torre: *Landmarks of Manila* (Manila, 1981)
M. Duldulao: *A Century of Realism in Philippine Art* (Manila, 1982)
F. de Leon, Jr, ed.: *Philippine Art and Literature* (New York, 1982)
W. Klassen: *Architecture in the Philippines* (Cebu City, 1986)
C. Reyes, ed.: *Conversations on Philippine Art* (Manila, 1989)

R. M. Zaragoza: *Old Manila* (Singapore, 1990)
J. T. Gatbouton and others, eds: *Art Philippines* (Manila, 1992)

R. JAVELLANA

Manini, Luigi (*b* Crema, 8 March 1848; *d* Brescia, 1936). Italian architect and stage designer, active in Portugal. He studied at the Accademia di Brera (now Accademia di Belle Arti), Milan, under Carlo Ferrario (1833–1907), stage designer at La Scala, Milan. Manini was appointed stage designer of the Teatro S Carlos, Lisbon, in 1879, at a time when the theatre received the most important European operatic productions. In this position he succeeded his compatriot Giuseppe Cinatti and, like his predecessor, in addition to his work in the theatre he designed houses for middle-class clients with a taste for his late Romantic façades, influenced by scenery design. He carried over into his architectural designs his passion for painting and for *trompe l'oeil* landscapes, and his principal achievements were decorative: the interior decoration of the Teatro do Funchal, Madeira; the ceiling of the Teatro S João, Oporto; and the winter garden (1893) of the Teatro Dona Amélia, Lisbon. His contributions to the layout of the terrace of the Palácio da Cidadela, Cascais, and the Portuguese Pavilion at the Exposition Universelle, Paris (1900), were similar. In his best-known buildings Manini evolved a highly wrought version of the Late Gothic Manueline style, saturating façades with superimposed ornament as if he was a goldsmith. For royal patrons he designed a country house (1887–1907; now the Palace Hotel) in this style, set in the Buçaco forest. At Sintra, a town full of Manueline associations, he designed his most elaborate and celebrated homage to that era in the house (begun 1904) for the wealthy António Augusto de Carvalho Monteiro. At the beginning of a century that saw the triumph of Functionalist architecture, Manini was formally and aesthetically an architect who belonged to the past. He returned to Italy in 1913.

BIBLIOGRAPHY
'Palácio de António Augusto de Carvalho Monteiro', *Arquit. Port.*, (Aug–Sept 1917)
J.-A. França: *A arte em Portugal no século XIX*, ii (Lisbon, 1966), pp. 168–170, 189–90

RAQUEL HENRIQUES DA SILVA

Maniple. *See under* VESTMENTS, ECCLESIASTICAL, §1(ii).

Manizer, Matvey (Genrikhovich) (*b* St Petersburg, 17 March 1891; *d* Moscow, 20 Dec 1966). Russian sculptor. He studied at the Academy of Arts in St Petersburg (1911–16) under the Russian sculptor Vladimir A. Beklemishev (1861–1920) and G. R. Zaleman (1859–1919). Between 1918 and 1920, while participating in the 'Monumental Propaganda Plan', he produced the cement relief *The Worker* (1920–21; Moscow, Petrovsky Arcade). Essentially a social realist, in his style he sought to soften his cold, academic manner with elements of genre and literary narrative and with slight Art Nouveau tendencies of naturalism. In the early 1920s he worked on portrait figures of Lenin, and he produced many monuments of him, which were erected in various towns in the USSR. The most notable is that at Lenin's birthplace of Ulyanov (now Simbirsk), on the high bank of the Volga (bronze and granite, 1940). The scrupulous style of his modelling

became more generalized here, accentuated by the dynamic turn of the figure in space. He sculpted a series of monuments to the poet *Taras Shevchenko* that were erected in the Ukraine, the most famous being the monument in Kharkiv (granite and bronze, 1935), executed with Iosif Langbard, in which the heroes of Shevchenko's works are represented alongside the figure of the poet himself in a spiral-like composition; among them stands out the figure of the farmworker Katerina with her child, which Manizer recreated as an independent work in plaster (1935; Moscow, Tret'yakov Gal.). He also created a figure of the young heroine of World War II *Zoya Kosmodem'yanskaya* (bronze, 1942; Moscow, Tret'yakov Gal.). The free-standing statue depicts the partisan setting out on a military operation and became the basis for the monument erected in her home town of Tambov in 1947. Manizer was also responsible for the sculptures installed at Moscow Metro underground stations, such as those at Revolution Square (1938) and Izmaylovskaya (1944). The bronze statues at Revolution Square station are particularly interesting as they fully embody the aesthetic of social realism.

WRITINGS
Skul'ptor o svoyey rabote [The sculptor on his work], 2 vols (Leningrad and Moscow, 1940–52)
P. M. Sysoyev, ed.: *Manizer Matvey Genrikhovich* (Moscow, 1970)

BIBLIOGRAPHY
V. V. Yermonskaya: *M. G. Manizer* (Moscow, 1961)
P. M. Sysoyev: *Leniniana skul'ptora M. G. Marizera* [The Leniniana of the sculptor M. G. Manizer] (Moscow, 1984)

R. YA. ABOLINA

Manjuwi. *See* GURRUWIWI, MANDJUWI.

Mankes, Jan (*b* Meppel, 15 Aug 1889; *d* Eerbeek, 23 April 1920). Dutch painter, draughtsman and printmaker. Between 1904 and 1908 he studied at the stained-glass studio of J. L. Schouten in Delft; he also took evening classes at the Koninklijke Academie van Beeldende Kunsten in The Hague. He was taught by Hermanus Veldhuis (1878–1952). At the suggestion of Antoon Derkzen van Angeren, he decided to become an independent artist. In 1909 he moved with his parents to De Knijpe near Heerenveen. From 1909 until 1915 he had business contacts with the art dealer J. C. Schüller (1871–1915) in The Hague who, until his death, bought everything that he produced. From 1910 he made penetrating self-portraits (e.g. *Self-portrait with Owl*, 1911; Arnhem, Gemeentemus.), as well as a great number of small-scale precisely observed scenes of animals from his immediate environment. The landscapes breathe a dreamy atmosphere. Mankes started etching in 1912. In the same year Schüller organized a successful exhibition of Mankes's work at the Larense Kunsthandel, Amsterdam. In this period Mankes saw exhibitions of the work of van Gogh and Katsushika Hokusai, whose influences are evident in his work. He also began to make woodcuts in 1913. In 1916 Mankes and his wife moved to Eerbeek, but tuberculosis made working increasingly difficult and led to his death. A large collection of his work is housed in the Gemeentemuseum in Arnhem.

BIBLIOGRAPHY
A. Plasschaert, J. Havelaar and A. Mankes-Zernicke: *Jan Mankes* (Wassenaar, 1927)
Jan Mankes, 1889–1920 (exh. cat., Leeuwarden, Fries Mus., 1979)

Jan Mankes: Schilderijen, tekeningen en grafiek [Jan Mankes: painting, drawings and graphics] (exh. cat., Heerenveen, Hist. Mus.; Arnhem, Gemeentemus.; Dordrecht, Dordrechts Mus.; 1989)

JOHN STEEN

Manley, Edna (*b* Bournemouth, 1 March 1900; *d* Kingston, Jamaica, 10 Feb 1987). Jamaican sculptor. The daughter of an English cleric and his Jamaican wife, she studied sculpture in London at the Regent Street Polytechnic, the Royal Academy Schools and St Martin's School of Art. In 1921 she married her Jamaican cousin Norman Manley and in 1922 she travelled with him to Jamaica. Her work in Jamaica in the 1920s and early 1930s strongly reflected the current Vorticist and Neo-classical trends in British sculpture. The influence of Frank Dobson and Jacob Epstein is particularly marked. Her subject-matter, however, revealed a strong identification with Jamaica and its people. Throughout this period her work was exhibited in England, where she was associated with the London Group, to which she was admitted in 1930. Her work in the late 1930s became increasingly political, reflecting the social upheavals of the time and her husband's involvement with the establishment of a viable political framework for his country. Indeed, with their powerful insistent rhythms, and the essential leitmotifs of the head straining upwards towards a vision, or downwards in suppressed anger, works like *Negro Aroused* (1935; *see* JAMAICA, fig. 5), *The Prophet* (1936; Kingston, Inst. Jamaica N.G.), *Pocomania* (1936; Kingston, priv. col.) and *Tomorrow* (1939, Wales, priv. col.) have become virtual icons of that period of Jamaican history; a period when black Jamaicans were indeed aroused, demanding a new and just social order.

In the 1940s Manley retreated into a private, Blakean world and produced a series of carvings marked by their extreme subjectivity and almost painterly approach to form and surface. *Horse of the Morning* (1943; Kingston, Inst. Jamaica N.G.) and *Land* (1945; Kingston, Jamaica, U. W. Indies) are key works of the period. The 1950s and 1960s was a period during which teaching duties, political activity and her role as wife of the Premier of Jamaica (1955–62) clearly affected her work. It was notable for major commissions like the *Crucifix* (1950) for All Saints Church, Kingston, *He Cometh Forth* (1962), an allegory celebrating Jamaican independence, for the Sheraton Hotel, Kingston, and the monument to the national hero *Paul Bogle* (1965) for Morant Bay, Jamaica. After her husband's death in 1969, Manley created a last series of wood carvings, attempting to deal with his death and her own grief. *The Angel* (1970; Kingston, parish church), *Mountain Women* (1970; Philadelphia, PA, priv. col.) and *Journey* (1973; Kingston, Inst. Jamaica N.G.) are key examples. Her subsequent works, modelled and cast in various materials, reflect a variety of concerns. Chief among these is *The Ancestor* (1978), a symbolic self-portrait in which the artist has become the ancestral spirit that nourishes successive generations. In 1985 she stopped sculpting altogether and turned to painting.

WRITINGS
R. Manley, ed.: *Edna Manley, The Diaries* (Kingston, 1990)

BIBLIOGRAPHY
W. Brown: *Edna Manley: The Private Years, 1900–1938* (London, 1975)
D. Boxer: *Edna Manley: Sculptor* (Kingston, 1990)

DAVID BOXER

Mann, Alexander (*b* Glasgow, 22 Jan 1853; *d* London, 26 Jan 1908). Scottish painter. The second son of James Mann, merchant and collector, he took drawing lessons from the age of ten with Robert Greenlees (1820–94) and then attended evening classes at the Glasgow School of Art, where Greenlees was headmaster. In 1877 he went to Paris and enrolled at the Académie Julian, and then studied under Mihály Munkácsy and from 1881 to 1885 under Carolus-Duran. Influenced by the Hague school and by Jules Bastien-Lepage, his picture *A Bead Stringer, Venice* gained an honourable mention at the Salon in 1885. After a public controversy over this painting when it was exhibited at the Royal Glasgow Institute, Mann settled in England, at West Hagbourne, Berks, and later in the neighbouring village of Blewbury, where he painted a series of views of the Downs and portraits of country people. He also had a studio in Chelsea, London. In 1886 he was invited to become the first Scottish member of the New English Art Club and was joined by several of his friends, notably John Lavery, Thomas Millie Dow (1848–1919) of the Glasgow Boys and Norman Garstin. Mann travelled extensively in Britain, paying several visits to the coast in Angus and Fife, and to Walberswick, Suffolk. His travels also covered Europe and the Americas, and from 1890 to 1892 he lived with his family in Tangiers. He kept in touch with Paris all his life. He recorded his visits and ideas for studio compositions in sketchbooks, using photography as well to assist his memory of a subject. His liveliest and most colourful works are the oil sketches executed on small mahogany panels. The larger paintings tend to be more subdued in colouring, sometimes containing an element of mystery. He frequently used his own children as models and gave away many of his paintings to family and friends. In 1995 Mann's work was exhibited in London at the Barbican and in Dublin at the Hugh Lane Municipal Gallery of Modern Art.

BIBLIOGRAPHY
J. Caw: *Scottish Painting Past and Present, 1620–1908* (Edinburgh, 1908)
N. Garstin: Obituary, *The Studio*, xlvi (1908), p. 300
Alexander Mann, 1853–1908 (exh. cat., foreword C. Newall; London, F.A. Soc., 1983)
S. Moore: 'Poetic Eclecticism: Alexander Mann at the Fine Art Society', *Country Life*, clxiii (21 April 1983), p. 1007
R. Billcliffe: *The Glasgow Boys* (London, 1985)
Alexander Mann: Sketches and Correspondence with his Wife and Family (exh. cat., intro. M. Hopkinson; London, F.A. Soc., 1985)
New English Art Club Centenary Exhibition (exh. cat. by A. Robins, London, Christie's, 1986)

HELEN PICKTHORN

Mann, George R. *See under* ECKEL & MANN.

Mann, Sir Horace [Horatio] (*b* London, Aug 1706; *d* Florence, 16 Nov 1786). English diplomat, collector and patron. He is best known for his correspondence with Horace Walpole. In 1738 Mann was appointed assistant to the English Resident at the Tuscan court in Florence, a post obtained through the influence of Sir Robert Walpole, his distant kinsman; he remained in Florence for the rest of his life, becoming a baronet in 1755, a Knight of the

Bath in 1768 and Envoy and Plenipotentiary in 1782. His duties entailed entertaining British visitors making the Grand Tour, as well as spying on the exiled Stuart court in Rome; he excelled at the former but was less successful in the world of espionage. Horace Walpole visited him in 1739; the ensuing correspondence, which lasted 47 years and numbered over 1800 letters, and which Walpole intended for publication, records the gossip and politics of England in Walpole's brilliant epistolary style, and the daily activities of Florentine aristocrats and English visitors in Mann's more pedestrian manner. Mann probably eked out his salary by commissions to purchase art and antiquities for wealthy tourists. He gave Walpole works attributed to Donatello and Cellini, and antiquities for the gardens of Strawberry Hill, such as a small bronze bust of *Caligula*, discovered at Herculaneum. He also helped and patronized resident and visiting British artists; among them were Robert Adam (i), Johan Zoffany, who included Mann in a prominent position in his group portrait, the *Tribuna of the Uffizi* (1772–5; Windsor Castle, Berks, Royal Col.), and Thomas Patch, who portrayed Mann in a caricature group (1760s; Exeter, Royal Albert Mem. Mus.) and dedicated to him the *Life of the Celebrated Painter Masaccio* (1770), his important record of Masaccio's frescoes in S Maria del Carmine, Florence.

BIBLIOGRAPHY

W. S. Lewis, ed.: *The Yale Edition of Horace Walpole's Correspondence*, xvii–xxvii (London and New Haven, 1955–71)

I. G. Sieveking: *The Memoir of Sir Horace Mann* (London, 1912)

J. Fleming: *Robert Adam and his Circle* (London, 1962)

O. Millar: *Zoffany and his Tribuna* (London, 1966)

H. M. M. Acton: *Three Extraordinary Ambassadors* (London, 1983)

DAVID RODGERS

Mannaia, Guccio di. *See* GUCCIO DI MANNAIA.

Mannerism [It. *maniera*]. Name given to the stylistic phase in the art of Europe between the High Renaissance (*see* RENAISSANCE, §4) and the BAROQUE, covering the period from *c*. 1510–20 to 1600. It is also sometimes referred to as late Renaissance, and the move away from High Renaissance classicism is already evident in the late works of Leonardo da Vinci and Raphael, and in the art of Michelangelo from the middle of his creative career. Although 16th-century artists took the formal vocabulary of the High Renaissance as their point of departure, they used it in ways that were diametrically opposed to the harmonious ideal it originally served. There are thus good grounds for considering Mannerism as a valid and autonomous stylistic phase, a status first claimed for it by art historians of the early 20th century. The term is also applied to a style of painting and drawing practised by artists working in Antwerp slightly earlier, from *c*. 1500 to *c*. 1530 (*see* ANTWERP MANNERISM).

1. History of the term. 2. Historical context. 3. Formal language. 4. Iconography and theory. 5. Spread and development.

1. HISTORY OF THE TERM. The multitude of opposing tendencies in 16th-century art makes it difficult to categorize by a single term, a difficulty increased by the importance Mannerism placed on conflict and diversity. The word 'maniera' was first applied to the visual arts in 1550 by Giorgio Vasari. He used the words 'maniera greca'

to describe the Byzantine style of medieval artists, which yielded to the naturalism of the early Renaissance, and he wrote of the '*maniera*' of Michelangelo, which deeply influenced later 16th-century art. This gave rise to the modern concept of Mannerism as a description for the style of the 16th century. Although in 18th- and 19th-century art theory Mannerism was regarded as marking a decline from the High Renaissance, in the early 20th century critics recognized its affinities with contemporary artistic movements, and Mannerist art was highly esteemed. At the same time its importance in leading to the Baroque was appreciated, as were those aspects that opposed the classical stability of the High Renaissance.

2. HISTORICAL CONTEXT. Mannerist art can be understood only in the context of profound social, religious and scientific turmoil. The Reformation officially started when Martin Luther nailed up his theses in 1517; the Counter-Reformation opposition started from the time of the Council of Trent in 1545. The Protestant doctrine of justification by faith challenged fundamental Catholic dogmas, and the Church of Rome could no longer exert its spiritual authority effortlessly, even in areas where the Counter-Reformation prevailed. The Sack of Rome in 1527 was interpreted as a retribution for moral decline and the glorification of luxury and sensuality. North of the Alps the structure of society was destabilized by the Peasants' Wars of 1524–5 in Germany. The discovery of the New World in the late 15th century and the early 16th must have had an equally momentous impact on the Christian West's concept of itself. The Old World could no longer see itself as the centre of the earth, but was revealed as a relatively small area within an immeasurable and largely still unexplored whole with incalculable potential. On top of this came Copernicus's recognition of the heliocentric planetary system (*c*. 1512). A completely new view of the world came into being. The varied forms of Mannerist art evolved against this background. The art of the 16th century as a whole reflects deep doubts over the classical principles, normative proportions and lucid space of the High Renaissance. Mannerism may be described as the most wilful and perverse of stylistic periods.

3. FORMAL LANGUAGE.

(i) Movement. (ii) Spiritual intensity. (iii) Space. (iv) The fusion of the arts. (v) Anti-classicism and subjective expression.

(i) Movement. For the first time in Western art the painting and sculpture of the 16th century made the optical suggestion of movement a central creative concern. In painting this mainly affected subjects that suggest the passage of time, such as the Assumption of the Virgin or scenes from the Life of Christ, such as the Deposition and the Entombment. Examples include the *Lamentation* by Pontormo (1525–8; Florence, S Felicità; *see* PONTORMO, fig. 2), Tintoretto's *Bacchus and Ariadne* (*c*. 1575; Venice, Pal. Ducale) and, north of the Alps, Pieter Bruegel the elder's *Parable of the Blind* (1568; Naples, Capodimonte; *see* BRUEGEL, (1), fig. 6). In sculpture this interest in movement inspired the creation of single figures or groups of figures that can be viewed from all sides, rather than from a single point; just as the figure seems to be in perpetual movement, so the spectator is encouraged to

keep moving around it. Giorgio Vasari coined the expression '*figura serpentinata*' (serpentine line) to describe this concept. The style was developed by Benvenuto Cellini in his *Perseus with the Head of Medusa* (1545–54; Florence, Loggia dei Lanzi; *see* CELLINI, BENVENUTO, fig. 6) and subsequently by Giambologna in such works as *Mercury* (1580; Florence, Bargello) and the *Rape of a Sabine* (1582; Florence, Loggia dei Lanzi; *see* GIAMBOLOGNA, fig. 2).

(ii) Spiritual intensity. Endeavours to depict the spiritual were equally characteristic of Mannerism, especially in the field of painting. Medieval artists set weightless figures against a spaceless gold ground to suggest the realm of the Divine; in the Renaissance an interest in naturalistic description and anatomy subordinated the depiction of the transcendental. In Renaissance art the 'miracle is a process like any other earthly event' (Frey). For example, in Raphael's *Disputa* the heavenly and earthly spheres are bound together by being represented with equal reality. Mannerism, however, developed new means of distinguishing between the earthly and the divine, and in Mannerist art 'the world beyond intrudes into the world below' (Frey). The High Renaissance had paved the way for this process: Raphael, for instance, suggested the miraculous in the *Liberation of St Peter* (1514; Rome, Vatican, Stanza di Eliodoro) through the representation of light.

A new painterly concept was the necessary basis for representing the spiritual. In 15th-century painting line dominated over colour. Line fixes an object on a flat surface, making it appear tangible and real. Leonardo da Vinci countered this with a new emphasis on colour, as in the *Virgin with Child and St Anne* (*c.* 1508; Paris, Louvre). In his art line gave way to the subtle modulation of tone, and this concept deeply influenced 16th-century painting, especially in Venice and Emilia. Forms become less tangible and clearly defined, and while line primarily appeals to the intellect, colour speaks first and foremost to the emotions. Thus the conditions were set for the viewer to be overwhelmed by the miracle made visible in the picture.

This new potential was most fully realized in pictures of apparitions and visions. Titian's *Virgin and Child with SS Francis and Aloysius and the Donor Alvise Gozzi* (1520; Ancona, Pin. Com.), in which the Virgin miraculously appears to saints and to the donor, Alvise Gozzi, was of fundamental importance to the development of this theme. Many of Parmigianino's paintings, such as the *Vision of St Jerome* (commissioned 1526; London, N.G.) and the *Virgin and Child with SS Mary Magdalene, John the Baptist and the Prophet Zachariah* (*c.* 1530; Florence, Uffizi), were influenced by this work by Titian. Even the events described in the New Testament as taking place in this world were transposed into the divine realm, as in Titian's late version of the *Annunciation* (before 1566; Venice, S Salvatore) and Tintoretto's *Last Supper* (1592–4; Venice, S Giorgio Maggiore). Both the interest in movement and the representation of saintly visions and ecstasies were features developed by Baroque artists.

(iii) Space. Closely linked with giving visible expression to the spiritual was the endeavour to represent the infinite. In both architecture and painting the Renaissance had

created space that was clearly defined on all sides. The viewer was provided with a definite frame and a fixed viewpoint. In the 16th century this situation was reversed. This development took place in stages. Initially the construction of pictorial space began to dominate over the animation of the surface. Here again the roots of the change can be found in the High Renaissance. Raphael's *School of Athens* (completed 1512; Rome, Vatican, Stanza della Segnatura; *see* ITALY, fig. 32) and the *Expulsion of Heliodorus* (1512–14; Vatican, Stanza di Eliodoro), in compositions based on the same principles, demonstrate the development from the primacy of surface to the primacy of space. In the second stage the space represented in pictures is seemingly extended into infinity: as in Francesco Salviati's fresco *Bathsheba Going to David* (1552–4; Rome, Palazzo Sacchetti), Tintoretto's *Rediscovery of the Body of St Mark* (before 1566; Milan, Brera) or Giambologna's relief of the *Rape of a Sabine* (1582; Florence, Loggia dei Lanzi; *see* GIAMBOLOGNA, fig. 2). In the final stage, the side boundaries, too, are made transparent or even removed, as for example in Tintoretto's painting of the *Transportation of the Body of St Mark* (1562; Venice, Accad.) or Parmigianino's *Madonna of the Long Neck* (1534–40; Florence, Uffizi; *see* PARMIGIANINO, fig. 3). This last painting also epitomizes a further defiance of High Renaissance lucidity: the architectural features and figures are no longer rationally united. Data relating to proportion and perspective space are at variance with one another, as is also the case in Pontormo's earlier panels illustrating the *Story of Joseph* (1515–18; London, N.G.).

North of the Alps the impression of infinite space was conveyed by means different from those used in Italian painting, as northern artists were less skilled in the refinements of mathematical perspective. The world landscape (*Weltlandschaft*), seen from a bird's-eye viewpoint, was created in such works as Albrecht Altdorfer's *Battle of Alexander* (1529; Munich, Alte Pin.; *see* GERMANY, fig. 18) and Joachim Patinir's *Charon Crossing the Styx* (*c.* 1510–20; Madrid, Prado; *see* PATINIR, JOACHIM, fig. 2; *see also* PERSPECTIVE, colour pl. VIII, fig. 2).

Developments in architecture were closely bound up with those in painting. The ideal of the centralized plan was abandoned in favour of the elongated axis. The administrative building of the grand duchy of Tuscany, the Uffizi (*see* VASARI, (1), fig. 6), started in 1560 and designed by Vasari, was laid out according to this principle. The concept of a long gallery building, which was to be a constant component of grand houses and castles until the 19th century, became a favourite element in secular architecture. For example, Rosso Fiorentino created the Galerie François I at Fontainebleau in 1533–40 (5 m wide and 58 m long). In the 1580s Duke Vespasiano Gonzaga had the Palazzo del Giardino built at his residence in Sabbioneta, probably to designs by Vincenzo Scamozzi, on a narrow, seemingly unending axis. The blurring of fixed side limits that can be observed in painting, however, also had parallels in architecture. Michelangelo in particular in his designs (1516) for the façade of S Lorenzo in Florence (not implemented), the New Sacristy (1519–33) at S Lorenzo and the vestibule of the Biblioteca Laurenziana (both from 1524; *see* MICHELANGELO, §I, 4) treated the wall in a way that defies the normative proportions and clarity of the High Renaissance. Not only is the wall more sculpturally modelled than ever before, but there is no clear surface to act as a point of reference for the projecting and receding architectural elements; where the wall and thus the spatial boundary lies is debatable. In addition, Michelangelo no longer made a precise distinction between the façade and the inner wall; in the vestibule of the Biblioteca Laurenziana and in the New Sacristy the observer is confronted with four inward-turning façades.

Another characteristic of Mannerist art with regard to treatment of space is the lifting of boundaries—or blurring of them—in a variety of ways. This applies especially to the boundary between the artistic space (in the work of art) and the real space. A distinction can be made between the passive and active removal of this aesthetic boundary: when it is lifted passively the artistic space appears to be a continuation of the real space, while when it is lifted actively elements or figures from the artistic space appear to step out into real space. Important preliminary stages of this process are again discernible *c.* 1500 (e.g. the altar wall of the Strozzi Chapel painted by Filippino Lippi at S Maria Novella, Florence). In 1516–17 Baldassare Peruzzi painted the Sala delle Prospettive in the Villa della Farnesina in Rome, in which a painted architectural colonnade opens out over a view of Rome. In the Sala dei Cento Giorni (1546; Rome, Pal. Cancelleria) Vasari successfully achieved a disorientating play with the spatial boundaries,

while with the Sala dei Cavalli (1525–35; Mantua, Palazzo del Te) GIULIO ROMANO blurred the division between artistic and real space, and between architecture, painting and sculpture. With the frescoes (1561–2) in the Villa Barbaro at Maser, Paolo Veronese went farthest along this path (*see* VERONESE, PAOLO, §I, 3; for illustration *see* ILLUSIONISM, colour pl. IV). An important example of these trends north of the Alps is the painting in 1578–80 of the Narrentreppe and the Wartstube at Burg Trausnitz, outside Landshut, by Alessandro Scalzi.

(iv) The fusion of the arts. In all the examples given so far it is clear that conditions specific to the individual art forms were removed. The possibility of replacing one art form with another—for example, sculpture and architecture with painting, or architecture with sculpture—is most powerfully rooted in the work of Michelangelo (the nude figures that appear to be painted sculptures in the ceiling of the Sistine Chapel in the Vatican, 1508–12). This trend developed fully in the next generation. When CORREGGIO decorated the Camera de S Paolo at the monastery of S Paolo in Parma (*c.* 1518–19) not only did he make it impossible to see where the ceiling ended, but he also used painting to suggest the presence of sculpture and architectural elements. Veronese opened the boundaries between architecture, sculpture and painting farther than anyone else in his decorations at the Villa Barbaro at Maser.

Boundaries were overstepped in other respects too—here verging on the bizarre: for example, when buildings

1. Giambologna: allegory of the *Apennines*, brick and volcanic lava, h. 11 m, 1570–80, Pratolino, near Florence

were created in the form of figural sculptures (*c.* 1580) in the garden at the Villa Orsini in Bomarzo (*see* BOMARZO, SACRO BOSCO), or when sculpture sprang directly out of nature, as in the allegorical figure of the *Apennines* (1570–80; see fig. 1) by Giambologna in the park at Pratolino, above Florence.

(v) Anti-classicism and subjective expression. 16th-century art rejected the classical principles of the High Renaissance. However, this alone does not make it Mannerist, as this further requires, among others, a predilection for the depiction of the abnormal and an emphasis on the subjective. Indeed, since the reassessment of Mannerism at the beginning of the 20th century, these latter aspects of 16th-century art have been much over-emphasized. In this context, the distortion of the human figure, often with the object of making it more expressive (a trend that is therefore allied with Expressionism), is of primary importance. Thus Rosso Fiorentino had no doubt studied Michelangelo, but he gave to his heroic figures seemingly arbitrary proportions and forms, summarizing and generalizing detail, as in *Moses Defending Jethro's Daughters* (1523; Florence, Uffizi; see fig. 2) and the *Deposition* (1521; Volterra, Pin. Com.; *see* ROSSO FIORENTINO, fig. 1). In Florentine painting in particular figures were often elongated, while the heads remained relatively small, as in

2. Rosso Fiorentino: *Moses Defending Jethro's Daughters*, oil on canvas, 1.60×1.17 m, 1523 (Florence, Galleria degli Uffizi)

Pontormo's portrait of *Alessandro de' Medici* (*c.* 1525; Lucca, Mus. & Pin.), his *Visitation* (*c.* 1530; Carmignano, S Michele) and his frescoes (1523–5) in the Certosa del Galluzzo, near Florence. In northern and central Italy the same phenomena occurred, as in Parmigianino's *Madonna of the Long Neck* or Tintoretto's *Christ before Pilate* (1566–7; Venice, Scu. Grande di S Rocco). The work of El Greco is especially influenced by this anti-classical approach to the figure. The Milanese painter Giuseppe Arcimboldi came close to the style of Surrealism when he assembled human heads exclusively from realistically reproduced plant details (e.g. *Winter*, 1563; Vienna, Ksthist. Mus.) or placed figures in dreamlike contexts.

In general terms between 1400 and 1600 three stages of development in the representation of the human figure in art can be identified. In the early Renaissance the ideal was to show man as he appears naturally. There followed, in the High Renaissance, a desire to create ideally beautiful figures and to overcome the blemishes of nature. The ideal of Mannerism was to go beyond the natural reality and to distort figures in the interests of subjective expression.

In architecture classical forms are used in a fanciful and complex way that defies the rules of Classical architecture. Typical examples of this are the Palazzo del Te in Mantua, built *c.* 1525–35 by Giulio Romano (*see* GIULIO ROMANO, fig. 3), the courtyard face of which is structured *all'antica*, but with the masonry irregularly divided and with every third triglyph on the frieze threatening to slip out of place; the courtyard façade of the Palazzo Pitti in Florence, which adopts the Classical orders—Doric, Ionic and Corinthian—but where the actual load-bearing members, the columns, are given virtually no visual impact; or Palladio's Villa Rotonda (started in 1553; *see* PALLADIO, ANDREA, fig. 5), which externally embodies the idea of the centrally planned building to perfection, while the central space within is so poorly lit that the visitor has the impression of being drawn outwards by the horizontal shafts of light coming from the four entrances. Thus the centripetal principle of the centrally planned building is reversed into its centrifugal opposite.

4. ICONOGRAPHY AND THEORY. Mannerism is also distinguished by its intellectually complex iconography. Agnolo Bronzino's painting of the *Allegory of Venus* (*c.* 1544–5; London, N.G.; *see* BRONZINO, AGNOLO, fig. 2) is as typical in this respect as Benvenuto Cellini's salt cellar (Vienna, Ksthist. Mus.; *see* CELLINI, BENVENUTO, fig. 4) with its heavy burden of mythological references, both works made for Francis I. Cellini himself said that he was well aware that he did not approach his work like many ignorant artists who, although they could produce things that were quite pleasing, were incapable of imbuing them with any meaning. Pieter Bruegel the elder drew much of his iconography from proverbs and folklore, attaining a similar intellectual sophistication.

The art theory of the Mannerist period was concerned with aesthetic problems rather than with the empirical problems of perspective, proportion and anatomy that had absorbed 15th-century writers. Venetian and Florentine theorists debated the primacy of *colore* and *disegno*; PARAGONE, a debate over whether painting or sculpture was the superior art form, raged; and in the late 16th century the question of the relationship between the creative idea (the 'concetto') and the model in nature was discussed by such theorists as Giovanni Paolo Lomazzo.

5. SPREAD AND DEVELOPMENT. In the 1520s Mannerism was established as a style in Rome by the late work of Raphael and that of his followers, Giulio Romano and Perino del Vaga, and in Florence by the work of Pontormo and Rosso Fiorentino. After the Sack of Rome (1527), the style spread to other Italian centres (Giulio Romano worked in Mantua, Sanmicheli in Verona and Parmigianino in Parma) and Florentine art of the mid-16th century may be described as mature Mannerism, the principal exponents of which were Bronzino, Vasari, Salviati and Giambologna. The FONTAINEBLEAU SCHOOL was influential in the spread of Mannerism throughout Europe. The Italians Rosso, Cellini and Primaticcio were associated with it, and Rosso and Primaticcio, in the Galerie François I (1533–40), created a rich and intricate decorative style. The style was developed by Jean Goujon and Germain Pilon and, in the reign of Henry II, by such French artists as Jacques Androuet Du Cerceau the elder, who were influenced by developments in the Netherlands. In the Netherlands many artists who had visited Italy, among them Frans Floris and Marten de Vos, created a Mannerist style, and pattern-books such as those of Cornelis Floris, combining the Italian grotesque with scrolling and strapwork, had a decisive effect in the second half of the 16th century, especially on architectural decoration north of the Alps. A highly sophisticated Mannerism flourished at the Wittelsbach court of Albert V in Munich and the Habsburg court of Rudolf II in Prague.

In northern European art Mannerism continued well into the 17th century, but in Italy the Baroque style was established by c. 1600. The Mannerist interests in movement and expression were more prophetic of future developments than the static images of the High Renaissance. In many ways early Baroque art united these elements with High Renaissance clarity and naturalism.

BIBLIOGRAPHY

EWA [with full bibliog. and list of sources]
G. Vasari: *Vite* (1550, rev. 2/1568); ed. G. Milanesi (1878–85)
G. P. Lomazzo: *Trattato dell'arte della pittura, scultura e architettura* (Milan, 1584)
——: *Idea del tempio della pittura* (Milan, 1590)
J. van Schlosser: *Die Kunstliteratur* (Vienna, 1924) [contains most sources]
H. Hofmann: *Hochrenaissance, Manierismus, Frühbarock: Die italienische Kunst des 16. Jahrhunderts* (Zurich and Leipzig, 1939)
R. Zürcher: *Stilprobleme der italienischen Baukunst des Cinquecento* (Basle, 1948)
De triomf van het Manierism (exh. cat., ed. M. van Luttervelt; Amsterdam, Rijksmus., 1955)
W. Friedländer; *Mannerism and Anti-Mannerism in Italian Painting* (New York, 1957)
E. Battisti: *Rinascimento e barocco* (Turin, 1960)
G. Briganti: *La maniera italiana* (Rome, 1961)
F. Württenberger: *Der Manierismus* (Vienna, 1962)
F. Baumgart: *Renaissance und Kunst des Manierismus* (Cologne, 1963)
J. Pope-Hennessy: *Italian High Renaissance and Baroque Sculpture*, 3 vols (London, 1963)
L. van Puyvelde: *Die Welt von Bosch und Breughel: Flämische Malerei im 16. Jahrhundert* (Munich, 1963)
D. Frey: *Manierismus als europäische Stilerscheinung: Studien zur Kunst des 16. und 17. Jahrhunderts* (Stuttgart, 1964)
A. Hauser: *Der Ursprung der modernen Kunst und Literatur: Die Entwicklung des Manierismus seit der Krise der Renaissance* (Munich, 1964); Eng. trans. as *Mannerism*, 2 vols (London, 1965)
J. Shearman: *Mannerism* (Harmondsworth, 1967)
G. Kauffmann: *Die Kunst des 16. Jahrhunderts* (Berlin, 1972)
H. Kozakiewiczowie and S. Kozakiewiczowie: *The Renaissance in Poland* (Warsaw, 1976)
M. Wundram: *Renaissance und Manierismus* (Stuttgart and Zurich, 1985)

MANFRED WUNDRAM

Mannerist Workshop. *See* VASE PAINTERS, §II.

Mannheim. German university town and river port in Baden-Württemberg, lying at the confluence of the rivers Rhine and Neckar. It flourished particularly in the 18th century as the court of the Electors Palatine of the house of Wittelsbach and preserves many features from that period, despite severe damage in World War II. The small fishing village of 'Manninheim' is first documented in the Lorsch Codex of AD 766. In the 13th century Eichelsheim Castle (destr. 1622), the most important Rhine customs post in the Palatinate, was founded close by. The modern town of Mannheim, however, was founded on 27 March 1606, shortly before the outbreak of the Thirty Years War (1618–48), under Elector Palatine Frederick IV (*reg* 1583–1610), based on a citadel (Friedrichsburg) intended as a bastion of Calvinism against the Catholic powers. The Dutch engineer Barthel Janson was in charge of work on the fortifications from 1606 to 1610. The design may have been based on the ideal plan published by Pietro Cataneo in *I quattro primi libri dell'architettura* (Venice, 1554) and on theoretical discussion in Daniel Speckle's *Architectura von Vestungen* (Strasbourg, 1584). The town and the citadel were separate but interlinked: the former was contained within a regular, bastioned decagon, into which half the heptagonal citadel was inserted, the length of one side of the decagon being exactly equal to the radius of the citadel. The town, already with a grid plan, was protected by eight bastions.

During the Thirty Years War (1618–48) the fortress was taken four times: by imperial troops in 1622 and 1635, by the Swedes in 1632 and by the French in 1644. In 1649 Elector Charles Ludwig (*reg* 1649–80) returned to his principality, and rebuilding of the devastated town began on the old ground-plan in 1652. To attract new residents the privileges granted in 1607 were extended to include the freedom to trade, and between 1652 and 1679 the population, swollen by Walloon and Huguenot immigrants, grew to almost 10,000. Mannheim was reduced to rubble by the French on 5 March 1689, but by 1698 Elector John William had engaged Baron Menno van Coehorn (and after his death the engineers de Robiano and Nottum) to redesign the fortifications.

After 1720, when Elector Charles Philip (*reg* 1716–42) moved his court to Mannheim, there was an upsurge of prosperity with accompanying building activity, under both Charles Philip and his son-in-law Charles Theodore (*see* WITTELSBACH, II(4)). On the site of the ruined citadel was built an enormous palace (see fig.), modelled on Versailles in France. The project, directed successively by Jean Clemens de Froimont (*fl* 1717–26), Guillaume Hauberat, Alessandro Galli-Bibiena and NICOLAS DE PIGAGE,

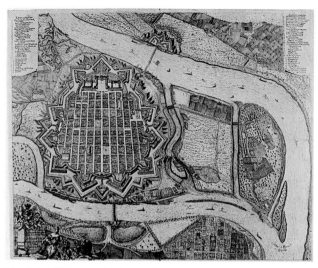

Mannheim, 1758; engraving by Joseph Anton Baertels (Mannheim, Städtische Kunsthalle Mannheim)

cost more than 1 million gulden, and it was finally completed only in 1760. The Schloss has a U-shaped ground-plan with wings and a *cour d'honneur*; on the side facing the town two further wings were added, each round an inner courtyard. The *corps de logis* was finished in 1731, and in 1737 work started on the opera house; PAUL EGELL, the Asam brothers and members of the Kobell (i) family carried out interior decorations in the Schloss. The building was almost completely burnt out in World War II; restoration has centred on the *corps de logis* and the grand staircase. Most of the rest of the site is occupied by the University.

Fortified gates gave access to the municipal area between the Rhine and the Neckar; and the grid plan of the city streets, which gives Mannheim its character, still survives. Apart from the Schloss and nearby palaces of the nobility, such as the Palais Bretzenheim (1782–8; rest.) by Peter Anton von Verschaffelt, the Baroque skyline was dominated by churches and public buildings: the Rathaus with the Marktkirche (1705–10; rest.) by Johann Jakob Rischer (1662–1755) on the market square; the Kaufhaus (1736); the Jesuit church (1738–60; rest.), modelled by Galli-Bibiena and Franz Wilhelm Rabaliatti (1716–82) on Il Gesù in Rome. Beside the church stands Rabaliatti's five-storey Observatory (1772–4); and from the same decade dates von Verschaffelt's massive Arsenal (1777).

The later buildings, and the Schloss itself, were completed under Charles Theodore, who also made Mannheim a major centre of culture and learning. He founded the Academia Theodoro Palatina in 1763, a Deutsche Gesellschaft in 1775 and a drawing academy with an antiquities collection. In 1782 the Nationaltheater produced the first performance of Friedrich Schiller's *Die Rauber*, and under the Elector's patronage the court orchestra became a major force in European music.

Mannheim's great period ended after 1777, when the Bavarian branch of the Wittelsbach family died out and Charles Theodore inherited the Duchy of Bavaria, moving the court to Munich in 1778. The town was bombarded

by the French in 1795 (Galli-Bibiena's opera house in the palace was destroyed), and in 1799–1801 Austrian forces razed the fortifications; their line is now marked by a ring road. With the advent of industrialization in the second half of the 19th century the town expanded, with a new phase of achitectural vitality that in the first decade of the 20th century seemed to illustrate through church buildings the debate between historicism and *Jugendstil*. Other notable examples of the period, all in the area round the Friedrichsplatz, include the water tower (1886; by Gustav Halmhuber), the Congress Centre (1903; by Bruno Schmitz) and Hermann Billing's City Art Museum (1905–7).

Grove

BIBLIOGRAPHY

F. Walter: *Geschichte Mannheims von den ersten Anfang bis zum Übergang an Baden (1802)* (Frankfurt am Main, 1977)
H. Huth, ed.: *Die Kunstdenkmäler des Stadtkreises Mannheim*, 2 vols (Munich, 1982)

KAI BUDDE

Manning, Eleanor (*b* Boston, MA, 1884; *d* 1973). American architect. She received her architectural training at the Massachusetts Institute of Technology (MIT), Cambridge, MA, graduating in 1905. In 1913 she and Lois Howe (1864–1964), who also had graduated in architecture at MIT (1890), became partners and operated one of the most successful women's architectural firms of the period. Mary Almy (1883–1967) later joined the partnership. The firm specialized in low-income housing. In 1924 they designed a series of houses in Mariemont, OH, a model industrial suburb of Cincinatti that had been designed by American planner John Nolen (1869–1937). Manning concentrated on low-income housing, designing Old Harbor Village (built 1937), the first public housing in Boston, while Howe focused on single-family suburban houses. Although the partnership dissolved due to the Depression, Manning continued to practise and teach, working with her husband, Johnson O'Connor, for his Human Engineering Laboratory and the Johnson O'Connor Research Foundation, and participating as one of the 17 architects on Old Harbor Village.

BIBLIOGRAPHY

J. Paine: 'Pioneer Women Architects', *Women in American Architecture: A Historic and Contemporary Perspective*, ed. S. Torre (New York, 1977)
D. Cole: *The Lady Architects: Lois Lilley House, Eleanor Manning and Mary Almy; 1893–1937* (New York, 1990)

LELAND M. ROTH

Mannlich, Johann Christian von (*b* Strasbourg, 2 Oct 1741; *d* Munich, 3 Jan 1822). German painter, lithographer and administrator. He received his first training from his father, Konrad Mannlich (1701–58), court painter to Christian IV, Duke of Zweibrücken. In 1758 he was sent to the drawing academy at Mannheim by Christian IV, and in 1762–3 accompanied him to Paris, where he met François Boucher, Carle Vanloo and also Christoph Gluck and Diderot. His work from this period reveals the influence of French Rococo, for example in *The Surprise* (a scene from 'Blaise the Shoemaker', an opera by F.-A. Danican Philidor; Regensburg, Staatsgal.). He studied in Paris under Boucher in 1765–6, at the Académie de France in Rome under Charles-Joseph Natoire in 1767–70 and also visited Naples; on his return journey to

Germany he met Anton Raphael Mengs in Florence. During 1770–71 he made a great many copies of paintings, including one after Raphael's *Madonna della sedia* and another after Correggio's *Madonna of St Jerome* (both Munich, Bayer. Staatsgemäldesammlungen, depot). His portrait of *Duke Christian IV* (Munich, Bayer. Staatsgemäldesammlungen, depot) dates from the same period, during which Mannlich's painting moved towards Neoclassicism and to some extent towards 17th-century Dutch painting. He undertook many commissions for hunting paintings after the tradition of Daniel Hien (1725–73), such as *Two Canadian Foxes* (1781; Speyer, Hist. Mus. Pfalz). In 1772 he was appointed court painter to the dukes of Zweibrücken, and inspector of the ducal picture collections in 1773; during the same period he returned to Paris with Christian IV where he met Greuze, Jean-Honoré Fragonard and Joseph Vernet.

After Christian IV's death in 1775, Mannlich was appointed Baudirektor in Zweibrücken, which involved him in supervising the building of Schloss Karlsberg; he also produced numerous architectural designs, some of which were executed, such as the Gesellschaftstheater at Zweibrücken (destr.; see Weber, 1987, pp. 244–5). In 1788 he became director in charge of all fine arts; thus in 1793 he evacuated all the paintings and the graphic collection to Mannheim, and when Maximilian IV Joseph, Elector of Bavaria, came to power in 1799 he transferred both collections to Munich. He became court painter to Maximilian and general director of all Bavarian galleries and art institutes. A central administrative authority was created under his direction; he drew up catalogues and new inventories, arranged for the paintings in the royal galleries in Munich and Schleissheim to be re-hung, and founded subsidiary galleries. He had considerable influence on the young generation of painters, such as Max Joseph Wagenbauer, Georg Wilhelm Issel and Simon Warnberger, although he himself now had little time to paint: his late work was close to that of the Nazarenes. He was ennobled in 1808.

Mannlich also worked as a lithographer, directing the production of *Les Oeuvres lithographiques par Strixner, Piloti et Compagnie* (1810–16) and *Königlich Baierischer Gemäldesaal zu München und Schleissheim* (1817–21), to which he also contributed his own plates. He was a prolific writer and produced books and works of poetry illustrated with his own lithographs, such as *Aesculap's Hahn und Amor's vergiftete Fackel* (Munich, 1812).

WRITINGS
Mémoires de M. Mannlich (MS., Munich, Staatsbib.); ed. E. Stollreither (Berlin, 1910)

BIBLIOGRAPHY
B. Speth: 'Aus dem Leben des Königlich Bayerischen Central Gallerie-Direktors Johann Christian von Mannlich', *Schorns Kstbl.*, 43 (1822), p. 169; 44, p. 174

E. Sichel: *Der Hofkünstler Johann Christian von Mannlich* (Forchheim, 1932)

B. Roland: *Die Malergruppe von Pfalz-Zweibrücken* (Baden-Baden and Strasbourg, 1959)

W. Becker: *Paris und die deutsche Malerei 1750 bis 1840* (Munich, 1971)

Johann Christian von Mannlich (exh. cat. by W. Weber, Kaiserslautern and Zweibrücken, 1972)

B. Roland: 'Johann Christian von Mannlich und die Förderung junger Künstler', *Stimme Pfalz*, xxv (1974)

B. Hardtwig: *Nach-Barock und Klassizismus* (1978), *Gemäldekataloge der Bayerischen Staatsgemäldesammlungen Neue Pinakothek* (Munich, 1978)

W. Weber: *Schloss Karlsberg* (Homburg-Saarpfalz, 1987)

RÜDIGER AN DER HEIDEN

Manno. Italian family of painters. Antonio Manno (*b* Palermo, 1739; *d* Palermo, 1831) worked as a decorative painter in Palermo and western Sicily. He was trained in the school of Vito d'Anna (*d* 1769), a successful painter who worked in the manner of Corrado Giaquinto, and Antonio's early work, the *Virgin Passing the Flag to Ruggero, Conqueror of the Saracens* (Palermo, Mus. Dioc.), was thought by contemporaries to have been painted by d'Anna. In 1759 Manno helped to complete d'Anna's decoration of the Villa Filippina in Palermo. His manner then moved away from Giaquinto towards a more classical manner, derived from Maratti through d'Anna and Batoni. Of the many fresco decorations he executed in the noble properties of Palermo, only those in the Palazzo Calderone Fatta (1771) survive. By 1780 the great number of Antonio's commissions obliged him to enlist the help of his brother, Vincenzo Manno (*b* Palermo, *c.* 1760; *d* Palermo, *c.* 1821): the frescoes in the church at Santo Stefano Quisquina (1780), in Mdina Cathedral, Malta (1790–94), and in S Lorenzo in Trapani (1800) are examples of their collaboration. On 19 September 1788 Antonio was elected to the Accademia di S Luca. His last work was the fresco decoration of Nicosia Cathedral (1810). Francesco Manno (*b* Palermo, 20 Dec 1754; *d* Rome, 18 June 1831), another brother, was also trained in Palermo under Vito d'Anna and then moved to Rome in 1786, where he frequented the studio of Francisco Preciado de la Vega. Francesco was introduced, through Cardinal Maffei, to Pompeo Batoni and was acquainted with Felice Giani. In 1786 he won the Balestra prize at the Accademia di S Luca, Rome, with the painting of *Clelia Crossing the Tiber* (Rome, Accad N. S Luca). A popular religious painter, he produced a number of paintings for the canonization of saints (many untraced). Between 1791 and 1793 he executed several ornamental overdoor panels for the Palazzo Altieri, Rome. On 13 July 1794 he became a member of the Accademia dei Virtuosi del Pantheon. A favourite of Pope Pius VI, Francesco was appointed Painter of the Sacred Apostolic Buildings (1800). In 1808 he worked in S Lorenzo in Lucina on paintings celebrating the canonization of St Francesco Caracciolo and on decorations in the Alaleoni Ruspoli Chapel. Beginning in 1812 he worked in the Palazzo del Quirinale, first for Napoleon, and then at the request of Pope Pius VII. Only the ceiling fresco in the Sala degli Ambasciatori (1822–3), showing the *Judgement of Solomon*, with two flanking allegorical tondi, survives. In 1818 he frescoed in situ the vault of SS Vincenzo ed Anastasio. Throughout his career he sent paintings back to Sicilian churches, and in 1830 he returned to Sicily and frescoed (*in situ*) some of the rooms in the Palazzo Arcivescovile, Monreale.

BIBLIOGRAPHY
S. Rudolph, ed.: *La pittura del '700 a Roma* (Milan, 1983), p. 784

C. Siracusano: *La pittura del '700 in Sicilia* (Rome, 1986), pp. 345–58, 399–405

——: 'La pittura del '700 in Sicilia', *La pittura in Italia: Il settecento*, ed. G. Briganti, ii (Milan, 1989, rev. 1990), pp. 516–30, 780

DONATELLA GERMANÒ SIRACUSA

Mannozzi, Giovanni. *See* Giovanni da San Giovanni.

Manohar [Manohara] (*fl c.* 1580–1620). Indian miniature painter, son of Basawan. Known mainly for exquisite court scenes and detailed historical paintings produced for the Mughal emperors Akbar (*reg* 1556–1605) and Jahangir (*reg* 1605–27), Manohar excelled in recording the trappings of power: the architecture, costume, carpets and luxury objects so important to Mughal rulers. He developed a precise miniaturistic technique that complemented the accuracy of his observations, using colour to great effect in paintings that are notable for their brilliant patterns and subtle rhythms.

Though Manohar studied and worked with his father, he was selective in the aspects of style he adopted in his own work. The earliest illustration with an inscription naming Manohar is a scene showing himself at work in a manuscript of the *Gulistān* ('Rose garden') of Sa'di (1581; London, Royal Asiat. Soc., Pers. MS. 258) commissioned by the Emperor Akbar. Much of the work was probably substantially retouched by Basawan, which is hardly surprising, since the young Manohar seems no older than 13 in the painting.

There are no contemporary historical references to Manohar, but many works inscribed with the artist's name survive, and these provide a framework for further attributions. Illustrations with inscriptions naming him as artist are included in several manuscripts of the 1580s and early 1590s, including a *Khamsa* ('Five poems') of Nizami (*c.* 1585; Richmond, Surrey, Keir priv. col., fol. 195b), a *Bābarnāma* ('History of Babar'; *c.* 1590; London, BL, Or. MS. 3714, fol. 283b) and an *Akbarnāma* ('History of Akbar'; *c.* 1590 or before; London, V&A, IS. 2-1896). However, Manohar emerges as a fully mature artist only in manuscripts of the middle and late 1590s that are associated with the imperial capital at Lahore, where he may have worked. These include manuscripts of the *Khamsa* of Nizami (1595; London, BL, Or. MS. 12208, fols 13*v*, 17*r* and 132*r*) and a *Khamsa* of Amir Khusrau Dilhavi (1597–8; dispersed; folio inscribed to Manohar: New York, Met., 13.288.33). His illustrations for a second *Akbarnāma* (*c.* 1596–7; London, BL, Or. MS. 12988, fols 34a and 138a; Dublin, Chester Beatty Lib., MS. 3, fols 32b, 57a, 212a and 212b; and dispersed) are among the finest Mughal historical scenes. The individuality of the portraiture and the ability to unite spatial depth with effective surface design are particularly notable. Manohar was one of the first Mughal artists to create realistic representations of actual buildings and architectural complexes.

Manohar studied and adapted many of the European prints that were readily available at the court of the emperors Akbar and Jahangir. On occasion, Basawan and Manohar both worked from the same source. Manohar tended to use a harder line, to create more solid contours, and to include more brilliant, clear colours. In the late 16th century, he made a series of portraits of Sultan Murad (1570–99), Jahangir's younger brother (examples in Jaipur, Maharajah Sawai Man Singh II Mus.; New Delhi, N. Mus.; Washington, DC, Freer). While he may have worked especially for that prince (they must have been almost exactly the same age), it is more likely that he moved freely within the imperial circle, painting various family members.

Manohar: *Akbar Receiving Mirza' Aziz Koka*, opaque watercolour and gold on paper, 181×121 mm, *c.* 1602–4 (Cincinnati, OH, Cincinnati Art Museum)

Akbar Receiving Mirza' Aziz Koka (*c.* 1602–4; Cincinnati, OH, A. Mus.; see fig.), inscribed 'the work of Manohar Das', is one of the finest known portraits of the elderly emperor, and superb depictions of Jahangir have also survived, including *Jahangir Drinking Wine under a Canopy* (*c.* 1605; London, BM). Several pages of the imperial *Jahāngīrnāma* ('History of Jahangir'; dispersed), the official illustrated memoirs of the Emperor, were apparently assigned to Manohar. *Jahangir in Darbar* (*c.* 1620; Boston, MA, Mus. F.A.), with dozens of individual portraits of courtiers and a rich display of Mughal textiles and jewellery, bears the inscription 'work of the humble house-born' and has been attributed either to Manohar working alone or to Manohar and Abu al-Hasan (both the sons of court painters) working together.

A portrait of Manohar at about the age of 40 by the painter Daulat is found in the album the *Muraqqa'-i gulshan* (Tehran, Gulistan Pal. Lib., MSS. 1663–4, fol. 44), part of a border decoration depicting several Jahangir-period artists. Manohar seems to have ended his career *c.* 1620 with no perceptible decline of his powers.

See also Indian subcontinent, §V, 4(i)(c).

BIBLIOGRAPHY
G. Lowry: 'Manohar', *The Grand Mogul: Imperial Painting in India, 1600–1660* (exh. cat. by M. C. Beach, Williamstown, MA. Clark A. Inst.; Baltimore, MD, Walters A.G.; Boston, MA, Mus. F.A.; New York, Asia Soc. Gals; 1978–9)
M. C. Beach: *Imperial Image: Paintings for the Mughal Court* (Washington, DC, 1981)

MILO CLEVELAND BEACH

Manolo [Hugué, Manuel Martínez] (*b* Barcelona, 30 April 1872; *d* Caldes de Montbui, Barcelona, 1 Nov 1945). Spanish sculptor, painter and draughtsman. The difficult circumstances of his childhood and youth were not at all propitious for an artistic training, but he made the most of Barcelona before leaving in 1900 for Paris, where he remained until 1910. Essentially self-taught, he associated with artists based at the Bateau-Lavoir and with writers such as the Greek-born French poet Jean Moréas. Eventually he decided it would be better for his work if he lived somewhere more peaceful and closer to Spain, so with the financial security of a contract with Daniel-Henry Kahnweiler in 1910 he settled in Céret, a small town in the Pyrenees, remaining there until 1915 and living there again from 1919 to 1927 after a period in Barcelona and Arenys de Munt.

Manolo assimilated a wide range of sources including Egyptian and Classical art, Gothic sculpture and Cubism, but the main point of departure for his marriage of idealistic Naturalism and Expressionism was in the art of Rodin. In many respects he is comparable with Aristide Maillol in his feeling for the grandiose and for simplicity, but he had a greater interest in capturing movement and in exploiting a gallery of popular types with great vitality and intensity. Consistently devoted to the human figure, even in his earliest works he demonstrated his ability to handle a variety of specific types and different materials, as in *Woman Harvesting* (bronze, h. 440 mm, 1913; New York, MOMA), *Toreador* (stone, 400×300 mm, 1914; Barcelona, Mus. A. Mod.) and *Woman's Head* (terracotta, h. 280 mm, 1919; Copenhagen, Stat. Mus. Kst). By close observation he was able to identify in his models elements through which he could express his ideas. Working slowly and using sketches or maquettes when moving towards cast bronzes, he succeeded in externalizing these ideas in reliefs or in the round. His preferred materials were plaster or clay, their pliability helping him to overcome the physical weakness of his hands.

Manolo eventually settled in Caldes de Montbui, in the province of Barcelona, attracted by the medicinal springs and by the simplicity of the surroundings. He remained in touch with the artistic activity of Barcelona and Paris and continued to base his sculptures, such as *The Bacchante* (bronze, h. 500 mm, 1934; Barcelona, Mus. A. Mod.) and *Seated Woman* (bronze, h. 900 mm, 1930–31; Barcelona, Ajuntament), on simple and well-defined geometrical shapes such as the cube or sphere, triangle or parallelogram. This formal emphasis elevated what might otherwise have seemed trivial or picturesque beyond an anecdotal level. He was attracted by the graceful figures of dancers and bullfighters and by scenes of popular interest, and he also attained a high level in his treatment of the nude, and his portrait busts, in particular, are distinguished by their psychological insights. He achieved a marked plastic intensity and a strong expressiveness without affectation, and although he is known principally as a sculptor with a large and varied output, he was also a versatile and accomplished painter and draughtsman. In works such as *Self-portrait* (watercolour and pastel, 1927) and the painting *Working in the Countryside* (1942; both Caldes de Montbui, Mus. Manolo) he used colour to convey form, modelling, light and subtle atmosphere. He also designed jewellery characterized by an elegant symbolism and monumentality.

WRITINGS
M. Hugué: *Poesías* (Barcelona, 1972) [inc. essays by D. H. Kahnweiler, M. Blanch and J. Corredor Matheos]

BIBLIOGRAPHY
J. Pla: *Vida de Manolo contada per ell mateix* (Sabadell, 1928; Sp. trans., Madrid, 1930); rev. as *Vida de Manolo* (Barcelona, 1947)
P. Pía: *Manolo* (Paris, 1930)
V. Crastre: *Manuel Hugué dit Manolo* (Marseille, 1933)
R. Benet: *El escultor Manolo Hugué* (Barcelona, 1942)
Manolo: Plastik und Zeichnungen (exh. cat. by D. H. Kahnweiler, Dortmund, Mus. Ostwall, 1963)
Tramontane, no. 3 (1967) [issue ded. to Manolo]
M. Blanch: *Manolo: Escultura, pintura, dibujo* (Barcelona, 1972)
Manolo Hugué: Escultures, pintures, dibuixos (exh. cat. by M. Blanch, Barcelona, Dau al Set, 1975)
Manolo Hugué (exh. cat. by M. Donale and M. Blanch, Barcelona, Mus. A. Mod., 1990)
On Classic Ground: Picasso, Léger, de Chirico and the New Classicism, 1910–1930 (exh. cat. by E. Cowling and J. Mundy, London, Tate, 1990), pp. 158–64

MONTSERRAT BLANCH

Manpukuji [Mampukuji; Ōbakuzan]. Temple site in Uji, Kyoto Prefecture, Japan. It is the headquarters of the Ōbaku sect of Zen Buddhism and is important as a centre for the diffusion in Japan of Chinese arts of the Ming period (1368–1644). Many of its original buildings still stand.

1. HISTORY. In the mid-17th century, amid the upheaval following the fall of the Ming dynasty in China, monks of the Linji (Jap. Rinzai) sect of Zen (Chin. Chan) Buddhism from southern China (*see* BUDDHISM, §III, 10) began emigrating to Japan, settling in NAGASAKI, Kyushu, where a large Chinese community had gathered. In Japan they found the Rinzai sect well established, though with different religious orientations. In order to distinguish themselves from the Japanese sect, the Chinese monks called their sect Ōbaku (Chin. Huangbo), after Mt Huangbo in Fujian province, the site of their home temple, Wanfu si.

Yiran (Jap. Itsunen; 1601–68), abbot of Nagasaki's Chinese temple Kōfukuji, invited the abbot of Wanfu si at Mt Huangbo, Yinyuan Longqi (Jap. INGEN RYŪKI), to come to Japan. Ingen arrived in Nagasaki in 1654, 12 years after Itsunen, accompanied by twenty monks and ten artisans and helpers. With the assistance of the influential Japanese Rinzai monk Ryūkei Shōsen (1602–70) from Myoshinji in Kyoto, Ingen met the Tokugawa shogun Ietsuna (1641–80) in Edo (now Tokyo) in 1658. The following year he was granted permission to construct a temple headquarters for the Ōbaku monks in Uji. Work began in 1661 with the west abbot's quarters (*hōjō*). The temple was officially opened in 1663, but construction continued until 1693, when the Sōmon (side gate) was completed. The site was named Ōbakuzan and the temple Manpukuji (the Japanese pronunciation of Wanfu si).

2. ARCHITECTURE AND LAYOUT. Manpukuji was consciously designed in emulation of Chinese Ming-period temples of the late 16th century and the early 17th. The main buildings were constructed of teak imported from Thailand. Chinese influences are apparent in architectural details such as patterns on the railings in the shape of *manji* (swastikas or signs of divine quality or good fortune; Skt *śrīvatsa* and *svastika*), curved and carved stone column bases, round windows, arched stucco gateways, tiled interior floors on which individual round straw cushions are placed, dolphin-shaped roof ornaments and sharply upturned roof eaves. Other Chinese-style features include wooden tablets carved with the gates' or buildings' names set above or flanking doorways; covered porticos, with ribbed, slightly arched ceilings, which connect the buildings; and pathways with large inset square stones laid point to point. The arrangement of the buildings and certain architectural features, such as the covered porticos and two-storey Sanmon (Triple or Mountain Gate; 1678), are reminiscent of the earliest Japanese Zen temples of the late Kamakura period (1185–1333), which also adhered more closely to orthodox Chinese styles.

The main buildings of the temple complex are asymmetrically placed on a long central axis leading from west to east. The Sōmon is the first to be encountered on entering the complex, slightly north of the main axis. To its right is the Hōjōchi (Setting-free Pond) surrounded by a rare early garden (1664), which lies directly in front of

Manpukuji, Daiyū Hōden (Main Buddha Hall), entrance and portico, 1668

the Sanmon. Beyond that is the Tennōden (Hall of Heavenly Kings; 1668), followed by the Daiyū Hōden (Main Buddha Hall; 1668), noted for its carvings of peaches in inset panels on the main doorway (see fig.), and the lecture or dharma hall (*hattō*; 1662). Other important buildings are the kitchen (*saidō*; 1668), south of the Daiyū Hōden, the founder's hall (*kaisandō*; 1675) and the east abbot's quarters (*higashi hōjō*), with its adjoining south garden (1663), south of the *hattō*. Many of these buildings are designated Important Cultural Properties.

3. ARTISTIC AND CULTURAL INFLUENCE. Until 1739 the temple's abbots were exclusively Chinese émigrés, whose influence on artistic, daily and religious practices at Manpukuji was, and remains, profound. The first Japanese abbot was Ryōtō Gentō (1663–1746). Much art is associated with Ōbaku Zen in general and with Manpukuji in particular, the latter housed largely in the Bunkaden (Culture Hall; 1972). Among the examples of Chinese Ming-style sculpture produced for Manpukuji, the first was made by Fan Daosheng (Jap. Han Dōsei; 1635–70), who worked at Manpukuji from 1663 to 1665. His most important works at the temple are a set of the *Eighteen Rakan* in the Daiyū Hōden and a figure of *Hotei* (Chin. Putai; one of the seven gods of good fortune) in the Tennōden, both of which date from 1663.

Since the Ōbaku monks were learned scholars, well versed in the classical Chinese literati tradition, many Chinese literati paintings and works of calligraphy, books of poetry, philosophy, religion and history were deposited at Manpukuji. This collection, as well as the spiritual guidance of the monks themselves, attracted the attention of Japanese intellectuals, who eagerly flocked to Manpukuji in order to learn more of Chinese arts and culture, at a time (Edo period, 1600–1868) when travel to China was restricted by law. Important paintings brought to Manpukuji from China include albums of *Patriarchs* (1654) and *Eighteen Kannon* (Skt Avalokiteshvara; the *bodhisattva* of mercy) by Chen Xian (*fl* 1634–54) and the *Bodhisattva Muryōju Meditating* by Ding Yunpeng (*c.* 1575–1638). Works by émigré Chinese monks include scrolls of the *Eighteen Rakan* (Skt *arhat*; enlightened persons) and a triptych of Shaka (Skt Shakyamuni; the historical Buddha) and his two attendant *bodhisattva*s, Fugen (Skt Samantabhadra) and Monju (Skt Manjushri) by Itsunen, all inscribed by Ingen Ryūki, and two *Taima maṇḍala*s and a portrait of the priest *Mokuan* by Dokutan (Chin. Duchan; 1628–1706).

Major paintings by Japanese Ōbaku artists include a set of *Eighteen Rakan* by Chin Jōtoku (1648–1703) and a portrait of *Ingen* by Kita Genki (*fl* 1664–98). Monks at Manpukuji also contributed to the development of Japanese literati painting (*Nanga* or *Bunjinga*; see JAPAN, §VI, 4(vi)(d)), of *Zenga* ('Zen pictures') during the Edo period (see JAPAN, §VI, 4(vii)) and of calligraphy (see JAPAN, §VII, 2(vi)). The bold, thick style of Ōbaku calligraphy is best represented by the works of three Manpukuji monks, Ingen, Mokuan Shōtō (1611–84) and SOKUHI NYOITSU, who are collectively known as the Ōbaku Sanpitsu (Three Brushes of Ōbaku). Artists of other schools were also associated with Manpukuji: Kanō Tan'yū (see KANŌ, (11)) painted a *Shaka* triptych in emulation of Itsunen's and similarly inscribed by Ingen; the literati painter Ike Taiga (*see* IKE, (1)) decorated *fusuma* (sliding paper doors) with the finger-painting (*shitōga*) *Five Hundred Rakan* (*c.* 1764; Kyoto, N. Mus.; Imperial Cultural Property), which is considered one of his masterpieces; and ITŌ JAKUCHŪ created a brush portrait of the Ōbaku priest *Hoan Joei* (1797).

An Ōbaku monk named Kō Yūgai or Baisaō (Old Tea Seller; 1675–1763) is credited with spreading the custom of drinking *sencha* (infused tea) to the general population by selling it in Kyoto and is usually considered to be the father of *senchadō* (the *sencha* ceremony) in Japan. Manpukuji houses a memorial hall to Baisaō, the Baisadō (Hall of Selling Tea), and the headquarters of the Zen Nihon Senchadō Renmei (All-Japan Sencha Ceremony League), which includes the Yuseiken (House of Voices) Tea House (all 1928), containing several rooms and a garden with Chinese-style details.

BIBLIOGRAPHY

A. C. Soper: *The Evolution of Buddhist Architecture in Japan* (Princeton, 1942/*R* New York, 1978)
Y. Hayashi, ed.: *Ōbaku bunka* [Ōbaku culture] (Uji, 1972)
M. Fuji and Z. Abe: *Manpukuji* (1977), ix of *Koji junrei, Kyoto* [Pilgrimage to the temples of Kyoto] (Kyoto, 1976–8)
Ōbaku: Zen Painting and Calligraphy (exh. cat. by S. Addiss, Lawrence, U. KS, Spencer Mus. A.; New Orleans, LA, Mus. A.; 1978)
Y. Hayashi, ed.: *Ōbaku bijutsu* [Ōbaku art] (Uji, 1982)
——: *Mokuan* (Uji, 1983)
——: *Ōbakusan Manpukuji rekidai gazō shū* [Collection of portraits of successive generations of Ōbaku Manpukuji abbots] (Uji, 1983)
J. Stanley-Baker: 'The Ōbaku Connection: One Source of Potential Chinese Influence on Early Tokugawa Painting', *Sino-Japanese Cultural Interchange: Aspects of Archaeology and Art History*, ed. Yue-him Tam, i (Hong Kong, 1986), pp. 99–154
M. Ōtsuki, S. Katō and Y. Hayashi, eds: *Ōbaku bunka jinmei jiten* [Biographical dictionary of Ōbaku culture] (Kyoto, 1988)
S. Hayashi, ed.: *Ōbaku sanpitsu* [The three brushes of Ōbaku] (Uji, 1989)
Ingen zenshi to Ōbakusō no kaiga ten [Priest Ingen and Ōbaku sect painting] (exh. cat., Kobe, City Mus., 1991)
P. J. Graham: 'A Heterodox Painting of Shussan Shaka in Late Tokugawa Japan', *Artibus Asiae*, li/3–4 (1991), pp. 275–92; lii/1–2 (1992), pp. 131–45
Tokubetsuten, Ingen zenshi seikatsuyonhyakunen kiuen: Ōbaku zen to geijutsu [Special exhibition, commemorating the 400th anniversary of the birth of Priest Ingen: Ōbaku zen and art] (exh. cat., Gifu, 1992)
Ōbaku no bijutsu [Ōbaku art] (exh. cat., Kyoto, N. Mus., 1993)

PATRICIA J. GRAHAM

Man Ray [Radnitzky, Emmanuel] (*b* Philadelphia, PA, 25 Aug 1890; *d* Paris, 18 Nov 1976). American photographer and painter. He was brought up in New York, and he adopted the pseudonym Man Ray as early as 1909. He was one of the leading spirits of DADA and SURREALISM and the only American artist to play a prominent role in the launching of those two influential movements. Throughout the 1910s he was involved with avant-garde activities that prefigured the Dada movement. After attending drawing classes supervised by Robert Henri and George Bellows at the Francisco Ferrer Social Center, or Modern School, he lived for a time in the art colony of Ridgefield, NJ, where he designed, illustrated and produced several small press pamphlets, such as the *Ridgefield Gazook*, published in 1915, and *A Book of Diverse Writings*.

Man Ray was a frequent visitor to Alfred Stieglitz's influential gallery, 291 (*see* <TWO NINE ONE>), where he was introduced not only to a dizzying array of European contemporary art, from Auguste Rodin's drawings to collages by Braque and Picasso, but also to photographs by Stieglitz and others. Like many American artists, he was also greatly influenced by the avant-garde art exhibited at the ARMORY SHOW. He pursued his interest in the flatness of modern abstraction in a series of paintings and collages that culminated in his masterpiece from this period, the *Ropedancer Accompanies herself with her Shadows* (1916; New York, MOMA). Inspired by a performance of a circus tight-rope walker, he composed the painting by arranging large pieces of coloured paper on the canvas. Once painted, the flat, brilliantly hued 'shadows' created a powerful overall design.

Demonstrating a flair for diplomacy, which later served him well among the Surrealists, Man Ray was one of the few artists to be admitted to both of New York's avant-garde circles. He attended Walter Arensberg's Salon and, at Marcel Duchamp's invitation, also became a founder-member, with patron Katherine Dreier, of the SOCIÉTÉ ANONYME, one of the first organizations to promote and collect avant-garde art. In 1921 Man Ray collaborated with Duchamp on *New York Dada*, one of the first official chronicles of the movement.

By 1921 Man Ray was eager to experience his European influences first-hand. A timely sale of paintings to the industrialist Ferdinand Howald provided him with the funds for a trip to Paris. Unlike many American artists who spent only a short time in Paris, Man Ray made it his home for 20 years, while remaining firm about his identity as an American. There he was an influential member of the international Dada and Surrealist circles of artists and writers, which included Tristan Tzara, Jean Cocteau, Max Ernst, Dali, Paul Eluard, Picasso and André Breton. Free to experiment, he produced works in a variety of styles and in many different media; in 1922 he began to exploit his personal variant of the photogram, which he called the 'rayograph', a method of producing images directly from objects on photo-sensitive paper. His rayographs were usually made with recognizable objects combined in an apparently casual and arbitrary way. A group of such images was published in 1922 with the title *Les Champs délicieux* (see fig.), with an introduction by Tristan Tzara. Tzara and other colleagues from this late Dada milieu, which prefigured the Surrealist movement, appreciated the transformation of ordinary objects into mysterious images. Man Ray himself equated his technique with painting, stating in letters that he was 'painting with light'. Although he continued to paint and make objects such as *Emak Bakia* (cello fingerboard and scroll with grey hair; 1926, untraced; replica 1962, New York, MOMA) throughout his career, it was as a photographer that he made his greatest impact on 20th-century art.

The more commercial aspects of Man Ray's photography provided him with a steady income. Famous as a portrait photographer, in the 1920s and 1930s he was also one of the foremost fashion photographers for magazines such as *Harper's Bazaar*, *Vu* and *Vogue*. Begininning in the late 1920s he experimented with the Sabattier, or solarization process (*see* PHOTOGRAPHY, §I), a technique that won him critical esteem, especially from the Surrealists. Many of the central figures of Surrealism—Breton, Magritte, Dali—followed his example in using photography in addition to other media. Other photographers, such as

Man Ray: Untitled 'rayograph', gelatin-silver print, 227×175 mm; from *Les Champs délicieux* (Paris, 1922), pl. I (New York, Museum of Modern Art)

Maurice Tabard and Raoul Ubac, were directly inspired by Man Ray's techniques, while photographers such as André Kertész and Brassai were indirectly influenced by his innovative approach to the medium.

Man Ray also made substantial contributions to avant-garde film. In his earliest incursion into film, *Le Retour à la raison*, made in 1923 for the Dada soirée du Coeur à Barbe, Man Ray created the first 'cine-rayographs', sequences of cameraless photographic images. Later films, *Emak Bakia* (1926), *L'Etoile de mer* (1928) and *Les Mystères du Château de Dé* (1929), have become classics of the Surrealist genre, along with films by Luis Buñuel, Dali and Hans Richter.

Man Ray left Paris at the onset of World War II and spent the war years in Los Angeles, where he concentrated on painting and making objects. There and on his return in 1951 to Paris, where he lived for the rest of his life, he continued to pursue the many strands of his art that had already marked him as one of the century's most innovative artists.

WRITINGS
Man Ray: *Self-portrait* (Boston, 1962)
Man Ray: *Objects of my Affection*, preface J.-H. Martin (Paris, 1983)
PHOTOGRAPHIC PUBLICATIONS
Les Champs délicieux: Album de photographies (Paris, 1922)
BIBLIOGRAPHY
A. Jouffroy: *Man Ray* (Paris, 1972)
R. Penrose: *Man Ray* (London, 1975)
A. Schwarz: *Man Ray: The Rigour of the Imagination* (New York, 1977)
J.-H. Martin: *Man Ray Photographs* (New York, 1983)
M. A. Foresta and others: *Perpetual Motif: The Art of Man Ray* (New York, 1988)
Man Ray, 1890–1976 (exh. cat., Antwerp, Ranny Van de Velde Gal.; London, Serpentine Gal., 1994–5)

MERRY A. FORESTA

Mansart. French family of architects. Absalon Mansart (*d* 1610) was a carpenter whose son (1) François Mansart became one of the most important architects of the mid-17th century in France, perfecting a subtle and distinctively French classicism. After François's death, his great-nephew (2) Jules Hardouin Mansart, who became the most important architect at the court of Louis XIV, added the name of Mansart to his own, as did his cousin Pierre Delisle, thereby ensuring that it was carried through to a dynasty of architects in the next generation and, at the same time, enhancing their own reputations. Jules Hardouin's brother Michel Hardouin (1647–87) was a draughtsman and contractor and worked with Jules on some of his projects; he was appointed Contrôleur des Bâtiments at Versailles in 1684. Jules Hardouin's grandsons Jean Hardouin Mansart de Jouy (?1700–54) and (3) Jacques Hardouin Mansart de Sagonne also became architects, the latter producing some of the most Baroque developments of French classicism.

(1) François Mansart (*bapt* Paris, 23 Jan 1598; *d* Paris, 23 Sept 1666). He was one of the most skilful architects of his generation, redefining French architecture by applying classical forms to building types for which they were not originally intended with such ingenuity and sophistication that in his hands the French château and town house (hôtel) effectively became classical building types in their own right. Pierre Lescot and Salomon de Brosse had already made significant progress in this regard, although Lescot's pioneering work in the 1540s was apparently not generally appreciated, while de Brosse was less meticulous, frequently obscuring his designs with rustication in the manner of Jacopo Vignola. Mansart was strongly influenced by these two French architects, but he also absorbed something of the structural and geometrical ingenuity of Philibert de L'Orme, derived from traditional French masonry techniques, as well as adapting the systematic brick-and-stone style of the civil works associated with Henry IV, King of France (*reg* 1589–1610). By combining these elements and exploring, insofar as was possible, the forms of antiquity, Mansart produced designs that were truly classical without being dry or mechanical.

1. Training and early works, to *c.* 1635. 2. Hôtel de La Vrillière, Blois, Maisons and Val-de-Grâce, *c.* 1635–45. 3. Late works, after 1645.

1. TRAINING AND EARLY WORKS, TO *c.* 1635. Mansart was trained successively by his father, by his brother-in-law, the sculptor Germain Gaultier (1571–1624), who was active in Rennes, and by an uncle, Marcel Le Roy (*d* 1647), who was a mason and building contractor. As far as is known, however, he received no formal education and never travelled outside France. In 1621 Mansart was sent to Toulouse to work on the construction of the Pont Neuf over the Garonne, which was undertaken by Marcel Le Roy and his associates; Mansart may have played a part in the design of the bridge itself and of the triumphal arch

(destr.) that was constructed at one end. Certainly he seems to have been influenced by the highly articulated classical façades of town houses in the city. His first recorded architectural commission was to design the façade of the church of the Feuillants (1623) in the Rue St Honoré, Paris. This is based closely on the upper storeys of de Brosse's façade (1616) for the Gothic church of St Gervais, Paris, but it incorporates rusticated pyramids and other iconographical references not present in the model.

During the 1620s and early 1630s Mansart carried out a number of relatively small-scale commissions, modifying three existing châteaux (Berny, Coulommiers and Plessis-Belleville), building one new one (Balleroy in Normandy), remodelling an existing town house (the Hôtel de l'Aubespine, Paris) and designing two altars (St Martin-des-Champs and Notre-Dame, Paris) and a small church (Ste Marie-de-la-Visitation in the Rue St Antoine, Paris; see

LE FAMEVX FRONTISPICE DV TEMPLE DE S.ᵗᵉ MARIE
Situé à Paris Rue Saint Antoine   Au dessing de F. Mansart

1. François Mansart: elevation of Ste Marie-de-la-Visitation, Rue St Antoine, Paris, 1632–33; engraving by Pierretz

fig. 1). Only the château of Balleroy and Ste Marie-de-la-Visitation survive, both of which reveal Mansart's remarkable facility in handling building masses, even at this early stage in his career. The stylistic vocabulary of Balleroy (*c.* 1626), near Bayeux, is similar to that of the Place des Vosges (1605), Paris, which was laid out for Henry IV, although the château is built of rough brownish-yellow local stone, not brick, with lighter dressed stone trim at the windows and quoins. The compositional effect depends on the relationship of the main block to the two single-storey pavilions standing at right angles to it on a terrace. The main block is divided into three parts, each of three bays; the central unit has three storeys, and the others have two. Each unit has a slight accent on its central bay and, in the Henry IV manner, a separate, high, hipped roof, the middle one distinguished by a flat top surmounted by a belvedere lantern. The interplay of these finely proportioned parts and the spaces between them is particularly harmonious, while the successive rises in level emphasize the tall central unit, giving it a remarkably dominating effect over the main entrance of the château. (For an illustration *see* STAIRCASE, fig. 3.)

The church of the Visitation (1632–4) features a circular domed nave set in the centre of a quadrangular space. Access is through a vestibule, the side walls of which are angled in towards the axis of the nave, which is encircled by three curved chapels. The oval dome above the central chapel is pierced to admit light from a tall lantern. The decoration mixes High Renaissance and Mannerist forms. Here, as in every project, Mansart demonstrated his ability to rethink the standard building layouts accepted at the time and to propose new, if not radically different, solutions. He also discarded much of the mannered and over-worked traditional decoration of the period in favour of a purer and more classical style.

2. HÔTEL DE LA VRILLIÈRE, BLOIS, MAISONS AND VAL-DE-GRÂCE, *c.* 1635–45. In 1635 Mansart received two commissions, both of which gave him an opportunity to exercise his powers of inventiveness and imagination on a grand scale. For Louis Phélypeaux de La Vrillière, the Secretary of State, he designed one of the largest town houses in Paris, and for Louis XIII's brother, Gaston d'Orléans, he prepared a scheme for a magnificent palace of vast proportions at BLOIS that would probably have been regarded as the greatest creation of French classical architecture had it been completed. In his project for Blois (1635–9) Mansart introduced planning that was almost as bold as the contemporary work of Francesco Borromini in Italy. He produced the appearance of symmetry within an unsymmetrical layout, so that the scheme has none of the monotonous regularity sometimes associated with classical architecture. The unfinished Orléans wing (see fig. 2), which was the only part of the château to be built at this time, gives an impression of the grandeur and subtlety of the whole project. The well-proportioned and clearly articulated, pilastered wall surfaces, with trophies and garlands discreetly placed under the pediments, are typical of Mansart's work of this period, as are the carefully modulated frontispieces, which recede with height. The *corps de logis* has short wings projecting at each end of both façades. The manner in which these had to be

accommodated on the existing site means that the central axes of the two main elevations are not aligned. Each façade appears symmetrical, however, and their axial discrepancy is disguised internally by the position of the staircase. Similar ingenuity ensures that the significant differences of level between the town and courtyard elevations do not prevent the same classical order appearing at the same level on both façades.

Inside the Orléans wing, the grand staircase (not finally completed until the 20th century) rises to the first floor in three flights round the sides of a square well. Access to the remaining storeys is by other stairs, but the grand stairwell itself rises the full height of the building. At the top of the first floor the well is partially roofed by a coved stone ceiling, open in the centre to allow an oblique view of the gallery above, giving access to the top-floor rooms. The vertical view, on the other hand, rises ultimately to a dome, supported on pendentives and lit from second-floor windows that cannot be seen from below: a Baroque use of dramatic lighting in the context of a classical simplicity of colour and materials.

The Hôtel de La Vrillière (*see* LA VRILLIÈRE, LOUIS PHÉLYPEAUX DE) was typical of a number of town houses built in Paris in the 1630s, with a gallery wing *en retour* beside the garden and the stair set in a pavilion to one side of the main court wing, thus enabling a complete suite of rooms to be laid out in this wing. The main layout, however, follows the usual plan of three wings around a court, closed by a screen wall. The same problem occurs as at Blois, in that the elevation on the garden side is not coaxial with that of the much shorter court side, but the plan is manipulated with great ingenuity to conceal this discrepancy. It is difficult to assess the respective roles of Mansart and his contemporary and rival, Louis Le Vau, in developing this type of layout, as both of them adopted it simultaneously, Le Vau in 1634–7 at the Hôtel de Bautru (*see* LE VAU, (1), §1). In 1642 Mansart extended the old Hôtel St Paul for Léon Bouthillier, Comte de Chavigny, taking great care to match his new design with the wall treatment and layout of the original house. At the Hôtel de Chevry-Tubeuf (1644; now part of the Bibliothèque Nationale), which he extended for Cardinal Jules Mazarin, he introduced a new suite at one end of the main court wing with more elaborate galleries running back beside the garden. He reputedly offended the Cardinal while engaged on this work, however, and was replaced by the architect Pierre Le Muet.

In 1642 Mansart was commissioned to design the Château de Maisons (now Château de Maisons-Laffitte), Yvelines, near Paris, for René de Longueil, who proved to be his most satisfactory patron, for his wealth increased as the work proceeded. Mansart was for once able to pursue his search for perfection, and every part of the scheme, from the subterranean vaults and unusually deep foundations to the finest decorative detail, was designed and executed with the utmost care and precision (*see* LONGUEIL, RENÉ DE). A splendid site was chosen on the banks of the Seine near the forest of Saint-Germain, and an elaborate series of forecourts, entrance gates and avenues was laid out, with the main avenue leading astutely

2. François Mansart: courtyard façade of the Orléans wing, château of Blois, 1635–9.

3. François Mansart: courtyard façade of the Château de Maisons (now Maisons-Laffitte), Yvelines, 1642–51

towards the château of Saint-Germain, where the king frequently stayed. The plan of Maisons comprises a single two-storey block with a finely modulated central frontispiece. Two short wings, each the same height as the main block, project at the ends and continue forwards in single-storey units. The façade of the château (see fig. 3) represents an improved version of that developed at Blois, with simplified window-frames and more varied relationships of coupled columns and pilasters. Both the court and garden frontispieces are highly complex three-dimensional compositions, diminishing in weight with each successive storey so that the layout of columns and pilasters differs at each level. On one side of the outer forecourt stood one of the largest stables in France, containing a riding-school and an elaborately decorated watering-place, preceded by a frontispiece that rivalled that of the château itself.

Much of Mansart's interior decoration at Maisons survives intact. The vestibule, ungilded and built of stone and uncoloured stucco, is articulated with Roman Doric columns and pilasters. Allegorical reliefs adorn lunettes over the doors and other openings, while eagles perch on the cornices. The grand staircase rises round the sides of a square, domed well, as at Balleroy and Blois. The walls of the stairwell are adorned with panels surmounted by putti executed by Philippe Buyster after models by Jacques Sarrazin. The balustrade consists of a series of interlocking stone arcs, surmounted by leaf capitals, which support the broad stone baluster. (For further discussion *see* CHÂTEAU.)

In 1645 Mansart was appointed by the queen, Anne of Austria, to add a church and palace to the convent of the Val-de-Grâce (*see* PARIS, §V, 5 and fig. 37), which she frequently visited on retreat. For this project Mansart devised a highly imaginative scheme (see fig. 4) based on the Escorial in Spain, where Anne had spent her youth. His design for the church was original in many respects, with bell-towers flanking the nave and a projecting single-storey entrance portico, more reminiscent of his château frontispieces than of a conventional church front. The portico was possibly influenced by that on the north side of Jacques Le Mercier's church of the Sorbonne (1635–48). The plan of the church of the Val-de-Grâce is characterized by a dominant central domed space at the crossing, surrounded by three equal apses for the choir and transepts, a layout reminiscent of that adopted by Andrea Palladio for Il Redentore (1576–80), Venice, where there is a similar play on circular forms. The whole of the domed space is located in a square block that projects slightly beyond the walls of the nave. After work on the scheme had proceeded for a year, Mansart was dismissed, possibly because of the excessive cost of the scheme, due in part to the unsuitable character of the site and perhaps because of Mansart's inability to commit himself to a final plan. Nevertheless, although the palace was never built, the church itself was begun under his direction, and he was responsible for the walls of the nave, with their giant Corinthian pilasters, up to the entablature, and for the lower storey of the façade.

3. LATE WORKS, AFTER 1645. After the setback at the Val-de-Grâce and during the ensuing civil wars of the

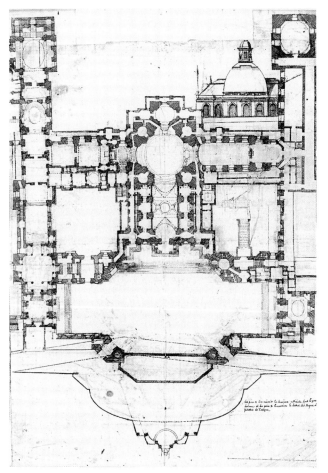

4. François Mansart: plan of the church, convent and palace of the Val-de-Grâce, Paris, partially executed, *c.* 1645 (Paris, Bibliothèque Nationale, Cabinet des Estampes)

Fronde (1648–53), Mansart designed and modified a series of private houses in Paris for the bourgeoisie and minor nobility. In these, particularly at the Hôtel de Jars (1648–50; destr.) and the Hôtel de Guénégaud-des-Brosses (?1653), his style became even more plastic with simpler decorative elements, while at the Hôtel de Guénégaud-Nevers (1648–52; destr.), the Hôtel de la Bazinière (1653–8; destr.) and the Hôtel de Condé (1645–51 and 1664–5; destr.) he showed great ingenuity in exploiting restricted sites and adapting existing layouts. In these later town houses Mansart developed a series of stairs that became progressively more animated and curvilinear in form, culminating in those at the Hôtel d'Aumont (1665; stair destr.) in the Rue de Jouy, Paris, which tapered and curved so that they returned on themselves within the width of the stair cage.

Contrary to the claims of the *Mansarade* (1651), a pamphlet attacking the architect, Mansart always seems to have respected the work of his predecessors when modifying existing buildings. This is particularly true in the case of his work (1660–61) on the Hôtel de Carnavalet, where he was at great pains to preserve and enhance the street doorway designed by Pierre Lescot a century before, and which was located in the new two-storey block built by Mansart to replace the screen wall that ran between the side wings. The wings themselves were raised by one storey, and the first-floor rooms they now accommodated were thus carried round all four sides of the courtyard. A sculpture by Jean Goujon was retained over the entrance door, where added emphasis was given to the rusticated surround with the use of vermiculation. The plain rustication of the side pavilion façades forms the base for the first-floor composition, where widely spaced coupled pilasters support a broken-based pediment in a way that recalls the château of Maisons.

Mansart was never again given the opportunity to design a complete château, but he was commissioned to modify a number of existing châteaux and carried out pioneering work in the layout of terraces, gardens and water features. There is evidence that his garden designs at Maisons, Fresnes, Limours, Petit-Bourg and Gèsvres established a standard for the latter part of the 17th century and greatly influenced André Le Nôtre, who also studied under him as part of his training (*see* GARDEN, §VIII, 4(ii)). Little remains of these schemes or of Mansart's late work generally, but a surviving pavilion at the château of Gèsvres suggests that Mansart's work of this period took on something of the *terribilità* associated with the late style of Michelangelo.

In 1657 Mansart submitted a proposal for the completion of the church of the Minimes, Paris, consisting of a high pyramidal composition with a dome and flanking bell-towers, similar to Borromini's church of S Agnese (1653–5) in the Piazza Navona, Rome, and modelled on centralized Italian designs of the High Renaissance. This famous *portail* was never completed, and the section that was built has been destroyed.

With the appointment in 1661 of Jean-Baptiste Colbert as a Conseiller du Roi, Mansart briefly returned to favour at the court of Louis XIV and received two important royal commissions: for the construction of a funerary chapel for the Bourbon family at Saint-Denis and for the completion and extension of the Louvre. Neither of these projects was executed, however, partly because of the changing tastes and requirements of the court and partly because of Mansart's difficult temperament. His designs for the Bourbon chapel proposed a vast centralized domed composition at the east end of Saint-Denis Abbey, which already possessed the domed, if incomplete, Valois chapel. Several smaller domed chapels to house the tombs were to be grouped round the central space, which was to have been surmounted by a complex cut-off dome lit internally by concealed windows. The similarity to Italian High Renaissance schemes became even more apparent than before, while it was also the logical conclusion to a series of experiments with centralized spaces in Mansart's ecclesiastical designs, which can be traced back to his church of the Visitation. As with his scheme for the Louvre, Mansart here found himself preparing schemes in rivalry with Gianlorenzo Bernini, who had been summoned to France by Colbert in 1665.

Mansart's work on the Louvre (*see* PARIS, §V, 6(ii)) was probably the most extraordinary and frustrating episode in his whole career. Louis Le Vau, who had already prepared schemes for completing the Cour Carrée with the addition of an east wing, was rejected by Colbert, and in 1664 Mansart was asked to submit a design. Inspired by the importance of the commission, he produced not one but an extensive series of designs, in which almost every conceivable form of building round an open courtyard was developed, as well as some in which the court was abandoned altogether. These were not sketchy or empirical schemes, but real alternatives based on a close understanding of the requirements of the King and courtiers and ingeniously related to the existing buildings on the site. Mansart was asked to select one or two specific designs to present to the King for his approval, but he refused to do so, claiming that, for such an important work, he did not want to limit himself to one scheme, preferring to retain the freedom to improve and alter the designs so that a perfect building might result. He was dismissed, but he continued to work on variant schemes for the Louvre, while a number of other architects submitted their proposals, many of them based on his own. Mansart was not entirely ignored, however, for even after his death the King retained the right to consult his designs. These, together with other drawings by Mansart, were guarded by his closest relatives, including his great-nephews Jules Hardouin Mansart and Jacques Gabriel IV, who drew on his work for many of their own schemes. Many of the drawings were later destroyed in a fire at the workshop of the cabinetmaker André-Charles Boulle, but a number that were inherited by Robert de Cotte eventually passed to the Bibliothèque Nationale, Paris.

Mansart's name is associated with the mansard roof (*see* ROOF, §2), although he did not invent this type, which had already been used by Pierre Lescot at the Louvre in 1551 and is derived from Italian sources. It is no accident, however, that this roof carries Mansart's name (albeit a corruption), for he exploited it consistently and ingeniously throughout his work and developed a three-pitched variety that does not appear to have been used by other architects.

Outside France, particularly in England and Sweden, the influence of Mansart's architecture was considerable. Christopher Wren, who met Mansart in Paris in 1666, owed a great deal to him, as did Nicodemus Tessin (i), the Swedish court architect, while in Austria his influence is manifest in the work of Johann Bernhard Fischer von Erlach. After a decline in popularity, his reputation was reinstated in France towards the end of the 17th century and in the 18th, and his designs were again widely imitated and admired, notably by Jacques-François Blondel.

BIBLIOGRAPHY

A. F. Blunt: *François Mansart and the Origins of French Classical Architecture* (London, 1941)
L. Hautecoeur: *Architecture classique* (1943–57)
A. F. Blunt: *Art and Architecture in France, 1500–1700*, Pelican Hist. A. (Harmondsworth, 1953, rev. 1957)
M.-A. Fleury: 'Les Dispositions testamentaires etc. de François Mansart', *Bull. Soc. Hist. A. Fr.* (1956), pp. 228–53
A. J. Braham: 'Mansart Studies I: The Val-de-Grâce', *Burl. Mag.*, cv (1963), pp. 351–63
J.-P. Babelon: 'L'Hôtel de Guénégaud-des-Brosses', *Paris & Ile-de-France: Mém.*, v (1964), pp. 161–76
W. P. J. Smith: 'Mansart Studies II: The Val-de-Grâce', *Burl. Mag.*, cvi (1964), pp. 106–15
——: 'Mansart Studies III: The Church of the Visitation in the Rue Saint-Antoine', *Burl. Mag.*, cvi (1964), pp. 202–15
A. J. Braham and W. P. J. Smith: 'François Mansart's Work at the Hôtel de Chavigny', *Gaz. B.-A.*, lxv (1965), pp. 317–30
——: 'Mansart Studies V: The Church of the Minimes', *Burl. Mag.*, cvii (1965), pp. 123–32
E. J. Ciprut: 'Oeuvres inconnues de François Mansart', *Gaz. B.-A.*, lxv (1965), pp. 39–50
J. Dupont and R. Vassas: 'Le Domaine de Maisons à Maisons-Laffitte', *Mnmts Hist. France*, iii (1967), pp. 14–39
W. P. J. Smith: 'L'Hôtel de La Bazinière', *L'Urbanisme de Paris et l'Europe, 1600–1680* (Paris, 1969), pp. 71–84
——: 'Redécouverte de François Mansart', *Archeologia*, xli (1971), pp. 52–67
A. J. Braham and W. P. J. Smith: *François Mansart* (London, 1973)
J.-P. Babelon: 'François Mansart: Dieu de l'architecture?', *Bull. Mnmtl*, cxxxiii (1975), pp. 311–20
C. Mignot: 'Travaux récents sur l'architecture française du Maniérisme au Classicisme', *Rev. A.*, xxxii (1976), pp. 78–85

PETER SMITH

(2) Jules Hardouin Mansart (*b* Paris, 16 April 1646; *d* Marly, 8 May 1708). Great-nephew of (1) François Mansart. He was the leading court architect under Louis XIV. Much of his career was spent completing the château of Versailles, but he also built numerous houses for the nobility, public squares and churches—most notably his masterpiece, the Dôme des Invalides, which incorporated elements of the Baroque and represented a distinct development of French classicism.

1. Life and work. 2. Critical reception and posthumous reputation.

1. LIFE AND WORK.

(i) Training and early works, to 1675. (ii) Dôme des Invalides, Versailles, Marly and other work, begun 1676–81. (iii) Late works, 1681 and after.

(i) Training and early works, to 1675. He was the son of the painter Raphaël Hardouin (*d* 1660) and Marie Hardouin (née Gaultier), the niece of François Mansart. His father was a mediocre painter but worked with François Mansart on the Hôtel de Condé and Hôtel de Carnavalet; when he died, his widow and two sons were taken in by Mansart, and Jules Hardouin began his career with his great-uncle, working on Mansart's later projects. There is little doubt that he subsequently benefited from Mansart's reputation after he added the name to his own following Mansart's death: he became known in his own lifetime as 'Monsieur Mansart', and as a result there is still confusion about the attribution of some buildings.

Hardouin Mansart began his independent career carrying out his own designs immediately after Mansart's death. In 1667 he built a large house in Paris on land he owned in the Rue des Tournelles; this he later enlarged (from 1687) to become his own residence, the Hôtel de Sagonne, named after the Bourbon estate he acquired in 1693. In 1669–72 he built a small town house for Henri de Guénégaud adjacent to the large house on the Quai de Seine built for the same patron by François Mansart. It later became known as the Petit Hôtel de Conti (now part of the mint), and it reveals his skill in making the best use of a restricted site, recalling in its sober style François Mansart's Hôtel Guénégaud-des-Brosses. In 1670–71 Hardouin Mansart built three identical villas (all destr.) at Versailles for the Comte de Soissons, the Duc de Créqui and the Maréchal de Bellefond. Each had a long, rectangular plan in two storeys, with a low, austere façade composed of a single storey accented with channelled stonework and crowned by a roof with dormer windows.

In 1672, however, he abandoned this enterprise and concentrated on providing designs for the Hôtel de Bouillon (destr.) at Versailles. This was similar in plan but with a particularly elegant arrangement of its variously shaped rooms. The façade was more classical due to the presence of an attic over the ground floor, a continuous balustrade above the cornice and a frontispiece of paired giant columns framing the entrance arch. In 1673 he visited Languedoc, apparently sent there by Jean-Baptiste Colbert, chief minister to Louis XIV, to inspect work on the Canal des Deux-Mers. On the way he produced a design for the Hôtel de Ville (1673–5) at Arles, which was inspired by Louis Le Vau's recent work at Versailles. Hardouin Mansart may also have been responsible for the great flat, pierced vault that spans its entrance hall—a masterpiece in the tradition of French stonework.

In the mid-1670s Hardouin Mansart began to work for the King, perhaps on the recommendation of André Le Nôtre. In 1675 he designed the King's Pavillon du Val, a small building at the end of the terrace at Saint-Germain-en-Laye, which represents the perfect culmination of his early work. The layout is ingenious, with one wing next to the central salon containing four rooms of varying shapes fitted into a square plan and all heated by a common stove; the building's elegant, arcaded single storey was crowned originally by a mansard roof (replaced in the 19th century by an additional storey). At the same time he was working on the enlargement of a château at Clagny (destr. 1769), begun by Antoine Le Pautre for Mme de Montespan but by then considered too modest. There he added two low projecting wings (a design that prefigures the solution he later adopted at Versailles; see §(ii) below); he also replaced the attic with an upper floor of rectangular bays and enriched the front wings with superimposed columns or pilasters and triangular pediments. In addition, he arranged one wing as a gallery between two drawing-rooms, an idea that again was taken up in his work at Versailles.

(ii) Dôme des Invalides, Versailles, Marly and other work, begun 1676–81. The success of the Pavillon du Val and Clagny earned Hardouin Mansart the favour of the King and marked the beginning of his brilliant official career. In 1675 Louis XIV nominated him to the Académie Royale d'Architecture, and in 1676 he was commissioned to build the church of the Hôtel des Invalides (see PARIS, §V, 7 and fig. 41), after Libéral Bruand, who designed the rest of the complex, failed to produce a satisfactory scheme. For this almost monastic establishment for disabled soldiers, Hardouin Mansart created a bipartite building: the first part, a nine-bay nave for the pensioners, has a barrel vault and side aisles with tribunes opening through flattened arches, following 17th-century French models. The second part, beyond, is the 'great church', the Dôme, in the form of a Greek cross inscribed in a square and vaulted by a dome on a drum—a plan that Hardouin Mansart borrowed from his great-uncle's designs for the 'rotunda' Bourbon chapel at Saint-Denis Abbey. These two parts were linked by an oval sanctuary housing a canopy (copied from the church of Val-de-Grâce, Paris) over a double-sided altar, which allowed celebration of the mass to face either residents or visitors. The pensioners' nave was completed rapidly (1676–9), while the Dôme progressed more slowly; the major part of the work was finished only in 1691, the decoration carried out from 1699 and the whole building consecrated in 1706.

The Dôme des Invalides is a masterpiece of French classical architecture. Its centralized plan is a perfect example of the type, the central area opening not only into the arms of a Greek cross but also diagonally into corner chapels through openings in the piers supporting the dome. Free-standing columns in front of the piers give an air of magnificence to the central space, which is lit from different levels: through the transept windows, the windows in the drum and, via an aperture in the dome, through attic windows (invisible from within) that illuminate a second, painted dome above.

The exterior of the church (see fig.1) was conceived to give maximum emphasis to the dome, which dominates all the other buildings of the Invalides as well as the church itself. This was achieved by the insertion of an attic storey over the drum and by the graceful silhouette of the outer dome, with its extremely tall lantern and crowning obelisk, together reaching more than 100 m above the ground. Consequently the square, flat-roofed body of the building supporting it appears somewhat low and squat beneath

1. Jules Hardouin Mansart: Dôme des Invalides, Paris, begun 1676

this mass, recalling the horizontality of Hardouin Mansart's domestic architecture. In order to integrate the body of the church with its drum, dome and lantern, he was obliged to enrich it with a powerful frontispiece of columns and pediment that draw the eye up through the attached columns of the drum towards the dome.

The whole building is given an upward movement by the accentuation of the central axis at all levels: a central niche was inserted on the upper level of the frontispiece, and, contrary to the classical tradition, a solid support instead of a void was placed on the central axis at each level of drum, dome and lantern. This concern with vertical movement in contrast to the solidity of the base, together with sculptural effects created by the accumulation of columns and the projection of the drum buttresses, as well as the rich colouristic qualities of the ostentatious display of gilded trophies cascading between the ribs of the dome, may all be interpreted as Baroque. In Hardouin Mansart's case, this is explained not by contact with Italian art—of which he had no direct knowledge—but through the continuing influence of the fashions of his youth and of François Mansart's design for the Bourbon chapel at Saint-Denis.

From the time of his adoption by the King, Hardouin Mansart became the most fashionable of architects. In 1675 he was commissioned to enlarge the hôtel of the Duc de Chaulnes, situated behind the Place Royale (now Place des Vosges), Paris, and at Versailles he built a symmetrical companion to the Pavillon de Bellefond; the latter two buildings were each given an additional storey in 1682 and used to house the King's kennels. They were

characteristic of his style: long, low, two-storey buildings crowned by a balustrade concealing the roof. For the Président de Nicolay he built a château at Prèsles (1676; destr.). He remodelled the Vieux Château at Meudon for the Marquis de Louvois from 1678, redecorating it again for the Grand Dauphin in 1705, when a new château or guest wing was added (all destr. 1803). In 1679 he produced designs for the Hôtel de Noailles, Saint-Germain-en-Laye; only the ends survive, but engravings by Pierre-Jean Mariette show that it was a very simple building with a horizontal emphasis but with a triple-arcaded entrance embellished with a columned frontispiece similar to the Hôtel de Bouillon at Versailles. From 1680 he rebuilt the Château de Dampierre for the Duc de Chevreuse, adding two floors of simple rectangular bays and columned porticos to the central section. Designs for a house at Versailles for the Maréchal de Lorge (destr.) date from 1681.

Meanwhile, in 1676 Hardouin Mansart had begun work at the château of Versailles with designs for lodges in the Bosquet de la Renommée; each of these two square pavilions (destr.) had bevelled interior angles, pediments on all four sides and were crowned by domes. Soon afterwards, in 1678, he was commissioned to design new additions for the château itself (see VERSAILLES, §1). His Galerie des Glaces (Hall of Mirrors) replaced Louis Le Vau's recessed first-floor terrace in the centre of the garden front, requiring Hardouin Mansart also to redesign the entire garden façade to incorporate the projecting wings of Le Vau's scheme, which became the Salon de la Guerre and the Salon de la Paix. For this scheme he used

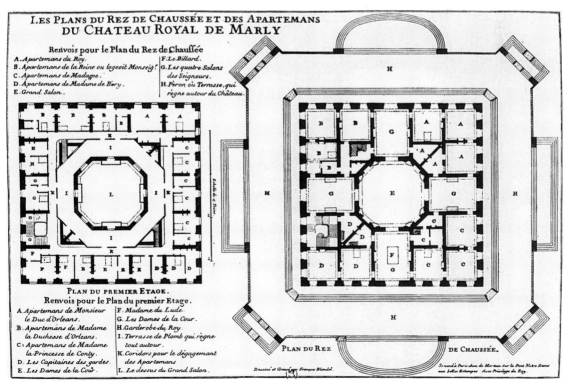

2. Jules Hardouin Mansart: plan of the Pavillon du Roi, château of Marly, 1679

round-headed windows on the first floor and a central hexastyle frontispiece based on Le Vau's lateral façades. Long north and south wings were then added in the same style but with a different rhythm in the projections. These additions have been criticized for destroying the scale and effect of Le Vau's building, but they provided Louis XIV with the grand ceremonial court setting that he sought, enhanced by the richness of the interior decoration by CHARLES LE BRUN.

Hardouin Mansart designed several other structures at Versailles. Those of the late 1670s and early 1680s include two blocks of stables opposite the entrance front; these buildings, the Grande Ecurie and Petite Ecurie, have deeply concave façades, which helped to balance the spread of the château's north and south wings imposed by the inverted trapezoidal plan of the site. The new orangery in the garden, which replaced Le Vau's, was planned in 1681 but was not begun until three years later. It has a rusticated, single-storey façade with particularly imposing arcades; the interior galleries, however, have plain barrel vaults without even an impost moulding, creating a monumental effect worthy of the Antique. His other principal works at Versailles, the Grand Trianon and the chapel, were built later (see §(iii) below).

In 1679 Hardouin Mansart also provided designs for buildings and gardens at MARLY (destr.), intended as a retreat for the King. For this he developed an innovative overall plan consisting of a square, two-storey pavilion for the King, raised on a low terrace at the head of twelve separate smaller pavilions for the courtiers, aligned in two rows on either side of a slightly sunken parterre. The Pavillon du Roi was a centrally planned Palladian type but further refined in the skilful arrangement of rooms in its

3. Jules Hardouin Mansart: façade of the Royal Chancellery (now Ministry of Justice), Place Vendôme, Paris, 1699

corners (see fig. 2). The horizontal emphasis of the façade, crowned by a balustrade interrupted only by a central pediment, would be entirely consistent with his earlier works were it not for the addition of painted decoration consisting of giant pilasters and *trompe l'oeil* reliefs created by Le Brun.

(iii) Late works, 1681 and after. In 1681, in recognition of his services, Hardouin Mansart was appointed Premier Architecte du Roi, a post that gave him both responsibility for the royal works and authority over the other architects and draughtsmen in the royal office of works. During the next few years he started to work on all outstanding projects in the office and soon had to engage assistants in order to meet the workload. In addition to François d'Orbay, Le Vau's assistant, who continued to work at Versailles until his death in 1697, Hardouin Mansart's chief assistants were Augustin-Charles d'Aviler (from 1684 to 1691); Pierre Lassurance, employed in 1684 and to whom the diarist Louis de Rouvroy, Duke of Saint-Simon, attributed a major role in Mansart's production (see LASSURANCE, (1), and §2 below); and Germain Boffrand (from 1686 to 1700). The most important, however, was Robert de Cotte, who had been associated with him since 1676, became his brother-in-law in 1682 and quickly became his principal collaborator.

In addition to continuing works, Hardouin Mansart was also involved in numerous fresh projects. The church of Notre-Dame at Versailles, built on a traditional plan with a façade of two superimposed orders and flanking towers, dates from 1684. The following year he designed the Capuchin convent in Paris (destr. 1806) and the façade for the Palais des Etats, Dijon, with a pediment carried on Doric columns, together with the Place Royale in front of it; this was a simple screen of rusticated arches laid out on a semicircular plan.

Hardouin Mansart later designed a regularly planned palace at Dijon (1688), to be created by the unification of the Palais des Etats and the Logis du Roi. In 1685 he designed the large residential college at Saint-Cyr on a square plan (for illustration see AUGUSTINIAN CANONS), and in 1687 the church of Notre-Dame at Chantilly and the partial reconstruction of the old château there (destr. 1799); the skilful arrangement of the latter made it possible to correct the irregular layout of the original building.

Other works by Hardouin Mansart in the 1680s included his urban plans for Paris and the Grand Trianon at Versailles. For the buildings of the circular Place des Victoires (1685; altered, see FRANCE, fig. 9), Paris, he used the traditional Italian façade design of a giant pilaster order over a rusticated, arcaded ground floor. A similar design was used in the first version (1685) of his plan for the Place Vendôme (formerly Place Louis-le-Grand), which proposed an arcaded square with buildings housing the royal library and academies. Due to financial difficulties this was not executed, and only in 1699 was a revised version built by Hardouin Mansart. The final form of the Place Vendôme (see PARIS, fig. 4) incorporates bevelled interior corners to the rectangular plan, which has only two openings, one at each end, forming a principal axis. The elements of the earlier façade design remained unchanged, with elegant, restrained, slightly projecting classical Corinthian temple fronts placed at the centres of the long sides and in the bevelled corners; round-headed dormer windows have curved frames that hint at the Baroque (see fig. 3). Hardouin Mansart's skill in designing grand settings was here clearly expressed in urban form. The Grand Trianon (*see* VERSAILLES, §3, and fig. 3) was built in 1687 as the 'Trianon de Marbre', a group of simple one-storey arcaded blocks replacing Le Vau's earlier buildings of the 'Trianon de Porcelaine'; the central block was left as an open colonnade between court and garden, the King's own idea, and a new wing, the 'Trianon-sous-Bois', was added. The design prefigured the work of Ange-Jacques Gabriel in its austere refinement of style.

The outbreak of the War of the Grand Alliance (1688–97) paralysed the activities of the royal office of works, and during this period Hardouin Mansart worked only for private patrons. For Barbezieux he built the small Château de L'Etang (1695; destr.); this was in the sober style of his early houses but was distinguished by a concave façade, in the corners of which he placed a spiral stairway on one side and an oval room on the other. The château of Boufflers (destr.) was unremarkable except for the flattened arches above its windows. The Hôtel de Lorge (1697; destr. 1778), Paris, consisted of a central block opening at ground-floor level on to both courtyard and garden; the upper storey was lit by fully arched windows that anticipated the fashions of the 18th century.

In 1699 Hardouin Mansart was appointed Surintendant des Bâtiments du Roi, and thereafter he had the power to approve payment for the projects he had himself designed in his role as Premier Architecte. Meanwhile, the return of peace allowed work to continue on existing projects and even the start of some new ones, and he was obliged to increase the workforce in his department by taking on the draughtsman Pierre Le Pautre (i) and setting up a drawing office at each of his residences in Paris, Versailles and Marly.

In addition, Robert de Cotte was appointed head of the Paris office as Architecte Ordinaire and given the post of Contrôleur des Bâtiments for the Paris region. It was at about this time that Hardouin Mansart, who was made Comte de Sagonne in 1693, became the powerful figure described by Saint-Simon—one whose organizational structure was interpreted as being proof of his own artistic inadequacy (*see* §2 below). While it is true that the interior design of his projects underwent a marked change at this time under the influence of such assistants as de Cotte and Le Pautre (e.g. in the King's new apartments at Versailles), the architectural designs nevertheless remained within the style of his earlier work.

The two-storey royal chapel at Versailles, begun in 1699 to plans prepared in 1689, has a Classical order of tall Corinthian columns at the upper level where the King's gallery, entered from his suite in the château, was placed; these columns support an entablature from which the vault springs, and they lend an air of nobility and lightness to the chapel (see fig. 4). The Château Neuf at Meudon, built for the dauphin in 1706–9, was Hardouin Mansart's last major work (*see* BOURBON, §I(9)). Only the ground

4. Jules Hardouin Mansart: royal chapel, Versailles, begun 1699

floor survives, but it continued Mansart's usual type of austere, astylar façade; it did, however, represent a step forward in interior planning, since there was a transverse corridor at all levels, running the length of the building between the two suites of rooms. His project of 1706 for modifications to the Primatiale at Nancy was also a development on a grandiose scale of the basic principles employed at Notre-Dame, Versailles, and the Dôme des Invalides.

2. CRITICAL RECEPTION AND POSTHUMOUS REPUTATION. Hardouin Mansart's brilliantly successful career attracted the malevolent envy of his contemporaries. His working methods and the role of his assistants were misunderstood, causing him to be regarded as an imposter who had been clever in attracting the King's favour and in exploiting the talent of his own employees. Saint-Simon reinforced this judgement of his authoritarian manner, and it is a view that continued to influence historians. In 1921 it was confirmed by Blomfield, and later scholarship concentrated above all on the re-evaluation—to the detriment of Hardouin Mansart—of the work of the assistants he supposedly exploited: Lassurance and Le Pautre (see Kimball) or François d'Orbay (see Laprade). This view must be qualified by two concrete observations: Hardouin

Mansart had already conceived his most important work (Clagny, the château of Versailles, Marly and the Dôme des Invalides) before he became Premier Architecte and thus before he had the services of these assistants; moreover, despite the diversity of his successive assistants, his work possesses an undeniable stylistic unity.

The characteristic features of a 'Hardouin Mansart style' can be readily identified. Layouts are generally open (e.g. Clagny, Versailles, Trianon), the only exception being the public squares that, in accordance with French tradition, are tightly closed. Interior plans either strive for geometric harmony, based where possible on symmetry (e.g. Dôme des Invalides, Marly, stables at Versailles), or demonstrate particular skill in combining rooms of various shapes (e.g. Le Val, Chantilly, L'Etang). Façades are characterized by a horizontal emphasis (e.g. Clagny, Versailles, Trianon), achieved by the absence of vertical accents—except in the form of domes—and by the use of columned frontispieces to embellish the entrances. These follow the French Renaissance tradition in acting as screens of applied decoration in front of the building rather than being an integral part of the structure. Also typical is Hardouin Mansart's austerity regarding architectural ornament, which is often reduced to simple rustication channels. Fenestration is frequently arched at the window-head, not only on the ground floor (e.g. orangery at Versailles, Trianon, public squares) but also on upper floors (Versailles, Hôtel de Lorge, attic of the Dôme).

By contrast, the interior decoration of his buildings evolved considerably during his career; he was clearly not personally responsible for this development but relied on the talent of younger collaborators, for example Robert de Cotte and Pierre Le Pautre. At the time of Hardouin Mansart's death in 1708, interior decoration was dominated by the so-called Régence style, which anticipated Rococo. However, the architecture itself, which remained under his control, developed in the direction of elegance and convenience of planning and towards a sober and unified style—features that remained the basis of French academic architecture until the death of Ange-Jacques Gabriel (1782). That Hardouin Mansart deliberately strove for this style is without doubt, for when Nicodemus Tessin (ii), architect to Karl XII, King of Sweden, complimented him (not without a certain irony) in 1699 on having eliminated the element of triviality from French buildings, it was taken by Hardouin Mansart as true praise and, apparently moved, he claimed this simplicity was more difficult to master than other styles.

It can therefore be said that Hardouin Mansart is responsible for the contradiction existing between exteriors and interiors that typifies French architecture and design in the first half of the 18th century. It is, however, essential to recognize his decisive role in the development of the classical tradition from the work of François Mansart to that of Ange-Jacques Gabriel, as well as his creation of some of the most original masterpieces of French architecture.

BIBLIOGRAPHY

G. Pérau: *Description historique de l'Hôtel royal des Invalides* (Paris, 1756/R 1974)
R. Blomfield: *History of French Architecture, 1661–1774* (London, 1921)
F. Kimball: *The Creation of the Rococo* (Philadelphia, 1943)
A. Marie: *Marly* (Paris, 1947)
L. Hautecoeur: *Architecture classique*, ii (1948), pp. 527–688
A. Blunt: *Art and Architecture in France, 1500 to 1700*, Pelican Hist. A. (London, 1953, rev. 4/1982)
E. J. Ciprut, ed.: 'L'Auteur de l'église des Capucines', *Bull. Soc. Hist. A. Fr.* (1956), pp. 259–63
P. Bourget and G. Cattaui: *Jules Hardouin-Mansart* (Paris, 1960)
A. Laprade: *François d'Orbay: Architecte de Louis XIV* (Paris, 1960)
M. Petzet: 'Quelques Projets inédits pour la chapelle de Versailles', *A. France*, i (1961), pp. 315–19
B. Jestaz: 'Jules Hardouin-Mansart: L'Oeuvre personnelle, les méthodes de travail et les collaborateurs', *Position Thèses Ecole Chartes* (1962), pp. 67–72
——: 'J. Hardouin-Mansart et l'église des Invalides', *Gaz. B.-A.*, ii (1965), pp. 59–74
P. Reuterswaerd: *The Two Churches of the Hôtel des Invalides* (Stockholm, 1965)
J. Garms: 'Les Projets de Mansart et de Boffrand pour le palais ducal de Nancy', *Bull. Mnmtl*, cxxv (1967), pp. 231–46
J. Levron: *L'Eglise Notre-Dame de Versailles* (Lyon, 1968)
J. Boyer: 'Jules Hardouin-Mansart et l'hôtel de ville d'Arles', *Gaz. B.-A.*, ii (1969), pp. 1–32
B. Jestaz: 'Le Trianon de marbre ou Louis XIV architecte', *Gaz. B.-A.*, ii (1969), pp. 259–86
P. Simonin: 'La Cathédrale de Nancy: J. Hardouin-Mansart et la genèse d'une grande église classique', *Pays Lorrain*, li (1970), pp. 107–38
B. Jestaz: L'Hôtel de Lorge et sa place dans l'oeuvre de J. Hardouin-Mansart', *Bull. Mnmtl*, cxxix (1971), pp. 161–81
A. Marie and J. Marie: *Mansart à Versailles*, 2 vols (Paris, 1972)
D. Meyer: 'A propos du péristyle du Grand Trianon', *Rev. A.*, xv (1972), pp. 79–80
G. Weber: 'Der Garten von Marly', *Wien. Jb. Kstgesch.*, xxviii (1975), pp. 55–105
——: *Brunnen und Wasserkünste in Frankreich im Zeitalter von Louis XIV* (Worms, 1985)
B. Jestaz: 'Documents sur l'oeuvre de J. Hardouin-Mansart à Chantilly', *Bull. Mnmtl*, cxlix (1991), pp. 7–75

BERTRAND JESTAZ

(3) Jacques Hardouin Mansart de Sagonne (*b* Trévolles, Bourbonnais, 1703; *d* 1758). Grandson of (2) Jules Hardouin Mansart. He became a member of the Académie Royale d'Architecture in 1735 and was appointed Architecte du Roi in 1742. His style is characterized by undulating façades and elaborate, ornamental interiors, which reflect the influence of his frequent collaborator, Nicolas Pineau. His best-known work is the church of St Louis (1743–54) at Versailles. The central part of the façade, with its ten Doric and six Ionic columns, resembles St Roch (1736), Paris, by Robert de Cotte, although the tighter setting of the orders at St Louis accentuates the verticality of the design, while the angles of the corner towers are inflected outwards in a Baroque gesture. Mansart de Sagonne was assisted in this project by Pineau, who designed the interior and may have made suggestions for the exterior as well. They worked together again on the design of the Maison des Dames de St Chaumond (1754; destr.), Paris, which included an undulating façade reminiscent of work by Guarino Guarini, and ornamental masks, such as that of *Wisdom* over the door. The Hôtel Claustrier (1752), Paris, again displays Rococo exuberance in the use of a serpentine balcony, but by this time the style was losing favour with patrons and was being criticized for its lack of clarity and order. Mansart de Sagonne is credited with numerous other designs, including several schemes for the Place Louis XV (now Place de la Concorde), Paris, which were not executed. His style represents the most baroque departure from French classicism to be built at a time when a move towards Neo-classicism was imminent.

BIBLIOGRAPHY
C. Gallet: *St Louis de Versailles* (Paris, n.d.)
L. Deshairs: *XVIIIe siècle, époque de Louis XV: Nicolas et Dominique Pineau: 208 dessins* (Paris, 1910)
S. Granet: 'Les Origines de la Place de la Concorde à Paris', *Gaz. B.-A.*, liii (1959), pp. 153–66
M. Gallet: *Paris Domestic Architecture of the Eighteenth Century* (London, 1972)
W. G. Kalnein and M. Levey: *Art and Architecture of the Eighteenth Century in France*, Pelican Hist. A. (Harmondsworth, 1972)

KATHLEEN RUSSO

Mansdale, van. *See* KELDERMANS.

Mansel Talbot, Thomas. *See* TALBOT, THOMAS MANSEL.

Mansfeld, Al(fred) (*b* St Petersburg, 2 March 1912). Israeli architect, theorist and teacher, of Russian birth. He studied (1931–3) at the Technische Hochschule, Berlin, and then (1933–5) at the Ecole Spéciale d'Architecture, Paris, under Auguste Perret. He moved to Palestine in 1935 and set up in private practice in Haifa in 1938. Between 1951 and 1959, in partnership with Munio Weinraub, he designed his first important buildings, including the Institute for Hebrew Studies (1956) at the Hebrew University of Jerusalem; the Mansfeld Residence (1957), Mount Carmel, Haifa; and the Hydrotechnical Institute (1957), Technion, Haifa. With Dov Karmi and Arieh Sharon, he was among the initial wave of foreign-born Israeli architects who introduced European Modernist design concepts to Israel. He moved gradually from formalism to a contextual, open-ended architecture that allowed for flexibility and growth in keeping with the vision of a new country. Mansfeld's best-known work is the Israel Museum (1960–65, with Dora Gat), Jerusalem, which he called his 'new Acropolis'. A cluster of interconnected buildings set on a terraced hilltop, it is integrated with a spacious sculpture garden designed by Isamu Noguchi. The scheme includes separate pavilions, including the Shrine of the Book (*see* JERUSALEM, fig. 4), each with an umbrella-canopy roof springing from a central pylon and freeing the walls from their load-bearing role. The site was planned to accommodate more buildings as the museum collections grew, fulfilling the architect's philosophy of controlled expansion. He was a senior lecturer (1949–70) and professor (from 1970) in architecture at Technion, Haifa, and between 1968 and 1970 he was President of the Israeli Institute of Architects.

WRITINGS
Designing with Open-ended, Cumulative Systems (Haifa, 1975)

BIBLIOGRAPHY
W. Sandberg: 'The Israel Museum in Jerusalem', *Mus.: Rev. Trimest.*, xix (1966), pp. 15–22
A. Harlap: *New Israeli Architecture* (East Brunswick, NJ, and London, 1982)

Manship, Paul (Howard) (*b* St Paul, MN, 25 Dec 1885; *d* New York, 1 Feb 1966). American sculptor. He grew up in St Paul, MN, where he attended evening classes at the St Paul Institute of Art from 1892 to 1903. In 1905 he went to New York and studied at the Art Students League, before becoming an assistant to the sculptor Solon Borglum (1868–1922). The following year Manship moved to Philadelphia to study at the Pennsylvania Academy of Fine Arts. In 1909 he won the Prix de Rome and attended the American Academy in Rome (1909–12). During this period he not only received rigorous technical training but also toured Italy, Greece and Egypt, where he became the first of many modern American sculptors who were attracted to the abstract qualities of Etruscan, ancient Greek and Egyptian art.

Manship returned to the USA in 1912 and, once established in New York, developed a style of simplified contours and bold asymmetrical design, favouring bronze as a medium. His work was highly praised, and he received many commissions for public monuments, architectural sculpture, small bronze figures and medals. One of his best-known works, the fountain sculpture *Prometheus* (bronze, h. 5.5 m, 1933–8), serves as the focal point of Rockefeller Plaza, New York. Like many of his sculptures, it depicts a sleek, streamlined figure moving through space, and the void is treated with as much importance as the solid.

WRITINGS
Paul Manship (New York, 1947)

BIBLIOGRAPHY
E. Murtha: *Paul Manship* (New York, 1957)
Paul Howard Manship, an Intimate View: Sculpture and Drawings from the Permanent Collection of the Minnesota Museum of Art (exh. cat. by F. Leach, St Paul, MN Mus. A., 1972)
Paul Manship: Changing Taste in America (exh. cat, St. Paul, MN Mus. A., 1985)
S. Rather: *The Origins of Archaism and the Early Sculpture of Paul Manship* (diss., Newark, U. DE, 1986)
R. Silberman: 'Thoroughly Modern Manship', *A. America*, lxxiv/1 (1986), pp. 111–15
Paul Manship (exh. cat. by H. Rand, Washington, DC, N. Mus. Amer. A., 1989)

JANET MARSTINE

Mansson, Olaf [Magnus, Olaus] (*b* Linköping, Oct 1490; *d* Rome, 1 Aug 1557). Swedish writer and cartographer. He was titular archbishop of Uppsala. He travelled through much of Scandinavia on a mission to combat Lutheranism, collecting as he went information concerning the local topography, folklore and customs. In 1523 he fled the Swedish Reformation and lived thereafter in exile, first in Danzig (now Gdańsk) and then in Rome. He continued to travel, however, and collected notes in the North Sea and Baltic regions. His *Carta marina* (1539) was the culmination of his accumulated research: a large-scale map of Scandinavia printed from wood-blocks, with more than 100 miniature engravings illustrating the costumes, commerce, warfare, skills in craftsmanship and superstitious beliefs of its peoples as well as the fauna of the different parts. The work has provided a detailed record of Scandinavian life in the early 16th century. The engravings, which were probably prepared from sketches made by Mansson, are remarkably skilful. Although the artist has not been identified, the style suggests that he was Italian. The map had a marked influence on a number of major map cycles and on the work of map-makers of subsequent generations, such as Gerardus Mercator (1512–94). The companion volume to the *Carta marina*, the *Historia de gentibus septentrionalibus* (1555), provides descriptions of the topography, ethnography, natural history and political conditions of the countries depicted on the *Carta* and is illustrated with copies of the engravings from the *Carta*, although these were executed by a far inferior artist.

WRITINGS

Carta marina et descriptio septentrionalium terrarum ac mirabilium rerum in eis contentarum diligentissime elaborata (Venice, 1539)

Historia de gentibus septentrionalibus earumque diversis statibus, conditionibus, moribus, itidem superstitionibus, disciplinis, exercitiis, regimine, victu, bellis, structuris, instrumentis, ac mineris metallicis, et rebus mirabilibus (Rome, 1555); Eng. trans. as *A Compendious History of the Goths, Swedes and Vandals and Other Northern Nations* (London, 1658)

BIBLIOGRAPHY

E. Lynam: *The 'Carta marina' of Olaus Magnus, Venice 1539 and Rome 1572* (Jenkintown, 1949)

E. R. Knauer: *Die 'Carta marina' des Olaus Magnus von 1539: Ein kartographisches Meisterwerk und seine Wirkung* (Göttingen, 1981)

K. Johannesson: *Gotisk Renässans* (Stockholm, 1982)

Mansueti, Giovanni (di Niccolò) (*fl* Venice, 1485–1526/7). Italian painter. The large number of signed pictures, several of which are dated, provides a clear idea of his style and forms a firm basis for further attributions. His earliest known work is the *Symbolic Representation of the Crucifixion* (London, N.G.), signed and dated 1492, by which time he was clearly already a mature master. The *Miracle of the True Cross at the Campo di S Lio* (1494; Venice, Accad.) is one of two works he made for the *Miracles of the True Cross* cycle for the Scuola Grande di S Giovanni Evangelista, Venice. The signature declares the artist to be a pupil of Gentile Bellini, whose influence is evident in the pictorial composition, with its decoratively repetitive treatment of shapes and colours. As in Bellini's paintings for the same cycle, Mansueti provides a topographically accurate record of an actual location in Venice; and with an even greater tendency than Gentile towards pedantic literalness, he packed his scene with stiff ceremonious figures in contemporary costume, and with a wealth of anecdotal detail.

Mansueti also executed a number of altarpieces and smaller devotional works, but his most characteristic and successful productions were narrative canvases of this type, painted for the meeting-rooms of the Venetian confraternities. Apart from the pair for the Scuola di S Giovanni Evangelista, the most important include the *Arrest of St Mark* for the chapel of the silk-weavers in the church of the Crociferi (1499; Vaduz, Samml. Liechtenstein), and three paintings for the *Life of St Mark* cycle for the Scuola Grande di S Marco, Venice (two in Venice, Accad.; one in Milan, Brera), datable on circumstantial evidence to *c.* 1518–26. All four of these works, which portray scenes from St Mark's apostolic activity in Alexandria, include a profusion of pseudo-Islamic elements, reflecting the 'oriental mode' then fashionable in Venice. Most of his narrative paintings include portraits of confraternity officers, and it may be that Mansueti painted more independent portraits than is generally realized. It is difficult, if not impossible, to discern any development in his art: the Scuola Grande di S Marco paintings, although contemporary with Titian's *Pesaro* altarpiece (1526; Venice, S Maria Gloriosa dei Frari), are distinguishable from works of the 1490s only to the extent that they appear more tired and repetitive. Many of these late paintings include motifs taken directly from Giovanni Bellini (for whom he seems occasionally to have worked as an assistant), Cima or Vittore Carpaccio. Documents indicate that he remained in Venice throughout his life, dying there between September 1526 and March 1527 (Ludwig).

BIBLIOGRAPHY

A. M. Zanetti: *Della pittura veneziana* (Venice, 1771), pp. 42–4

G. Ludwig: 'Archivalische Beiträge zur Geschichte der venezianischen Malerei', *Jb. Kön.-Preuss. Kstsamml.*, xxvi (1905), pp. 61–9 [doc.]

S. Moschini Marconi: *Gallerie dell'Accademia di Venezia: Opere d'arte dei secoli XIV e XV* (Rome, 1955), pp. 134–9

S. Miller: 'Giovanni Mansueti: A Little Master of the Venetian Quattrocento', *Rev. Roum. Hist. A.*, xv (1978), pp. 77–115 [full bibliog.]

H. W. van Os and others, eds: *The Early Venetian Paintings in Holland* (Maarsen, 1978), pp. 106–9 [entry by B. Groen]

T. Pignatti, ed.: *Le scuole di Venezia* (Milan, 1981)

J. Raby: *Venice, Dürer and the Oriental Mode* (London, 1982)

P. Humfrey: 'The Bellinesque Life of St Mark Cycle for the Scuola Grande di San Marco in Venice in its Original Arrangement', *Z. Kstgesch.*, xlviii (1985), pp. 225–42

P. F. Brown: *Venetian Narrative Painting in the Age of Carpaccio* (New Haven and London, 1988)

PETER HUMFREY

Mansur [Ustad Mansur] (*fl c.* 1590–1630). Indian miniature painter. He was the leading painter of animal and bird studies at the courts of the Mughal emperors Akbar (*reg* 1556–1605) and Jahangir (*reg* 1605–27). He is mentioned more frequently than any other artist in Jahangir's memoirs, the *Tūzuk-i Jahāngīrī*, a clear indication of the esteem in which he was held. By 1618/AH 1027, the Emperor had granted him the title Nādir al-'Asr ('wonder of the age').

The earliest known illustrations by Mansur, datable to *c.* 1590, are animal studies. However, as a young trainee artist in the Mughal workshops his contribution to these works was limited to colouring in and completing the designs by older, master painters. The *Bāburnāma* ('History of Babur') manuscript of 1589 (London, V&A, and dispersed) and the *Akbarnāma* ('History of Akbar') manuscript of *c.* 1590 (London, V&A, MS.IS. 2–1896) include fully reliable attributions to this period. The 1589 *Bāburnāma* also contains the earliest-known studies of individual animals by Mansur working alone. On these illustrations his name is frequently preceded by the honorific Ustad ('master'). The format of these compositions includes some landscape elements, and the forms are often set against areas of uncoloured paper. By 1589 this was clearly a well-established compositional custom, used by several artists in this *Bāburnāma*. Its roots can be found in earlier Persian works and in academic paintings of the Ming dynasty (1368–1644) imported into India; the works of Lü Ji, for example, are compositional prototypes for those studies at which Mansur excelled. The frequent references to the 'picture galleries of China' in 16th-century Mughal historical texts implies an awareness of the Chinese traditions indicated by these animal studies. Not an initiator himself, Mansur carefully refined the compositional and technical innovations of other artists. Two additional *Bāburnāma* sets of *c.* 1595 (London, BL, Or. MS. 3714) and 1598 (New Delhi, N.Mus.) include animal studies by Mansur working alone.

While these manuscripts illustrate the meticulous accuracy and acute observation of Mansur's bird and animal paintings, a later *Akbarnāma* (*c.* 1596; London, BL, Or. MS. 12988, and Dublin, Chester Beatty Lib., Ind. MS. 2) reveals clearly that his weakness was the human figure. He shows an inability to master the physiognomic accuracy

BIBLIOGRAPHY
A. K. Das: 'Ustad Manṣūr', *Lalit Kala*, xvii (1974), pp. 32–9
——: 'Some More Manṣūr Drawings', *Lalit Kala*, xviii (1977), pp. 26–30
——: *Mughal Painting during Jahangir's Time* (Calcutta, 1978)
The Grand Mogul: Imperial Painting in India, 1600–1660 (exh. cat. by M. C. Beach, Williamstown, MA, Clark A. Inst.; Baltimore, MD, Walters A.G.; Boston, MA, Mus. F.A.; New York, Asia Soc. Gals; 1978–9), pp. 137–43

MILO CLEVELAND BEACH

Mansur: *Turkey Cock*, miniature from an album leaf, tempera, 235×165 mm, *c.* 1612 (London, Victoria and Albert Museum)

or depth of characterization developed by other Mughal artists. The decorative patterns in architecture and textiles, however, are handled with superior craftsmanship and parallel the brilliance of his illuminations in a manuscript of the *Khamsa* ('Five poems') of Amir Khusrau Dihlavi dated 1597–8 (Baltimore, MD, Walters A.G., MS. W. 624). It is now fully evident that Mughal court painters were assigned those subjects at which they were most skilled; thus, Mansur was able to develop his special talent for natural history subjects. That these include plants is proved by Jahangir's statement in the *Tūzuk-i Jahāngīrī* that Mansur painted more than one hundred of the flowers of Kashmir. *Western Asiatic Tulip* (Aligarh, Muslim U., Maulana Azad Lib.) remains the most reliably authentic of these floral studies.

The *Tūzuk-i Jahāngīrī* also reports that Mansur was frequently asked to paint birds (see fig.), animals and flowers that specifically interested the Emperor. These were then usually bound into albums. Following accepted practice, such works were often copied by other artists and provided with inscriptions stating that they were the work of Ustad Mansur. The identification of the artist's authentic work is therefore an especially controversial subject. Most reliable are paintings made for such specific manuscripts as the *Bāburnāma* sets noted above. These provide a solid basis for further attributions.

See also INDIAN SUBCONTINENT, §V, 4(i)(c) and fig. 264.

Mansurov, Pavel (Andreyevich) [Mansouroff, Paul] (*b* St Petersburg, 26 March 1896; *d* Nice, 2 Feb 1983). Russian painter and theorist. He studied at various institutions between 1909 and 1917, including the School of the Society for the Encouragement of Arts in St Petersburg (1911–15), but his real interest in painting began after his encounters with the artists of the avant-garde, especially Kazimir Malevich and Vladimir Tatlin (in whose studio he worked in 1917–19). In 1919 Mansurov joined Mikhail Matyushin's experimental Studio of Spatial Realism at Svomas (the Free Art Studios) in Petrograd (now St Petersburg), took part in the First State Free Exhibition of Works of Art and contributed to the establishment of the Museum of Artistic Culture in Petrograd.

In 1923 Mansurov helped to organize special research departments within the Museum, which in 1924 were consolidated into Ginkhuk (*see* INKHUK). Like his colleagues Pavel Filonov and Matyushin, Mansurov was drawn to the connections between art and natural form, and he used his position as head of the Experimental Department at Ginkhuk to pursue this line of inquiry. While there (until 1925), Mansurov had access to laboratories, studios and display cases, used the collection of the Museum as a reference guide and had several talented assistants. His basic theoretical aim was to demonstrate that the true work of art was like an efficient mechanical structure, which, in turn, was like a bird, a dog or a tree. The charts that Mansurov used at the Museum of Artistic Culture and Ginkhuk (see 1963 exh. cat., pp. 151–7) demonstrate his attempts to draw visual parallels between art and nature: for example, next to his own abstract studies of *Painterly Formulae* and *Painterly Tensions* (many Milan, Lorenzelli A.) are to be found a stuffed bird, a hunk of wood and a collage with a butterfly attached to a piece of wood. The Ginkhuk tabulations also emphasize Mansurov's basic principle concerning the economic system of colour and form in nature, showing diagrams and photographs of rock formations, feathers, fossils, spiders' webs etc.: structures that bring to mind the concurrent work of Naum Gabo, Gustav Klucis, Aleksandr Rodchenko and Tatlin.

Mansurov left the USSR in 1928, settling in Paris the following year, where he continued to work on his geometric abstractions. With the encouragement of Sonia Delaunay he also turned to textile design, but studio painting remained his primary concern, and he continued the same kind of experimental abstract studies throughout his life (e.g. *Painting*, 1965; Paris, Pompidou).

BIBLIOGRAPHY
Mansurov/Mansouroff (exh. cat., Milan, Gal. Lorenzelli, 1963)
T. Omuka: 'A Short Note on Paul Mansouroff', *Sov. Un./Un. Sov.*, iii/2 (1976), pp. 188–96

Mansouroff: Opere 1918–1980 (exh. cat., Rome, Carpine, 1985)
Mansurov (exh. cat., Milan, Lorenzelli A., 1987)

JOHN E. BOWLT

Mantai. Port, occupied from the 2nd millennium BC to *c.* AD 1000, near modern Mannar in north-west Sri Lanka. Mantai was the port for the inland capital at ANURADHA-PURA and an important link in the maritime network between the Mediterranean, the Indian Ocean and East Asia; during its final phase, it was one of Asia's most important trading emporia. Its growth must have been dependent on the surplus capital generated by the agricultural development of the northern dry zone, with its sophisticated irrigation system of canals and tanks (reservoirs). The primary reason for Mantai's development as an emporium was its location at the end of a narrow channel transversing the chain of reefs, known as Adam's Bridge, that prevent the passage of large-scale shipping. Ships from the Near East and East Asia were able to meet at Mantai and exchange goods via the channel. Evidence of the Sasanian and Islamic presence was found in excavations in 1980–84. Quantities of early Islamic pottery and glass, ceramics of the Chinese Tang period (AD 618–907) and imports from the south Asian mainland testify to the variety of material objects traded. The climatic conditions of the monsoon belt are such that no trace remained of the vast amount of perishable goods such as textiles and spices that must also have been traded.

Mantai has been identified as the Persian colony referred to by Cosmas Indicopleustes in the 6th century AD that controlled the export of Chinese silk to the West. A baked clay bulla found at the site, bearing three seal impressions—of a quadruped, a Nestorian cross and an old Persian inscription—is of the Sasanian period (3rd–7th centuries AD). The Islamic glass includes a lustre-painted sherd (*c.* 9th–10th centuries AD) and the pottery lustre-decorated ware, Samarra-type splashed ware and imitation Chinese white ware of the same period (*see also* ISLAMIC ART, §V, 2(ii)). The Chinese pottery includes white wares, *sancai* (Chin.: 'three-colour' wares), and painted stoneware and fragments of relief-impressed ewers from the kilns at Changsha, Hunan Province. South Asian pottery includes a red polished ware sherd from a sprinkler, stamped with a monkey and a crocodile and three Brahmi characters; this is the earliest depiction of a well-known Indian fable, later translated from Sanskrit to Persian as one of the *Kalīla and Dimna* stories.

Mantai was also a major manufacturing site, particularly for bangles of chank shell and for polished quartz and glass beads. The quartz beads were drilled using a double diamond bit, and are the earliest evidence for the use of industrial diamonds. The glass beads, of the Indo-Pacific type, were widely exported as far afield as Korea and east Africa. After the Chola invasion, the site was sporadically occupied. A number of sherds of the fine Chinese white ware with a faint blue-green transparent glaze known as *quingbai* ('bluish white') of the 12th century were found on the surface. Dressed stones from Mantai were used for the construction of the Portuguese fort across the Straits of Mannar in the 17th century. A modern Hindu temple at the centre of the site is based on a much older structure.

See also CHINA, §VII, 4(iv).

BIBLIOGRAPHY
J. Carswell: 'China and Islam in the Maldive Islands', *Trans. Orient. Cer. Soc.*, xli (1977), pp. 121–98
——: 'China and Islam: A Survey of the Coast of India and Ceylon', *Trans. Orient. Cer. Soc.*, xlii (1977–8), pp. 24–68
——: 'China and the West: Recent Archaeological Research in South Asia', *Asian Affairs*, xx/1 (Feb 1989), pp. 37–44.
——: 'The Port of Mantai, Sri Lanka', *Rome and India: The Ancient Sea Trade* (Milwaukee, WI, 1991), pp. 197–203

JOHN CARSWELL

Mantegazza. Italian family of sculptors. The brothers Cristoforo Mantegazza (*d c.* 1481) and Antonio Mantegazza (*d* 1495) were, with Giovanni Antonio Amadeo, major sculptors in Milan during the later 15th century. Their dates of birth are unknown, and no documented or signed work exists by either. The earliest documentation of their activities records Cristoforo at the Certosa di Pavia (*see* PAVIA, §2(i)) in 1464 working with other sculptors to furnish stones carved as arches, vaults and columns for the walls of the nave (Dell'Acqua, 1948). Also in 1464 he worked in the Certosa's two cloisters, making capitals for the large cloister. In 1465 he designed wooden models for the terracotta capitals in the large cloister, working with the sculptor Rinaldo de' Stauris (*fl* 1461–90; Dell'Acqua, 1948). On 26 August 1467 Cristoforo was given six pieces of marble for works to be made for the Castello Sforzesco, Milan (Dell'Acqua, 1948).

Both brothers were active at the Certosa di Pavia by 1472; its prior repaid their work with a house in Milan at the beginning of the next year. In 1473 they were consulted by Galeazzo Maria Sforza, Duke of Milan, concerning a bronze equestrian sculpture of his father, Francesco I Sforza, a commission eventually given to Leonardo da Vinci. The documentation here refers to them as goldsmiths (*orevexi*). Also in 1473 the brothers, on a recommendation from Galeazzo Maria, were charged on 7 October to execute the façade of the church of the Certosa. On 20 August 1474 the Mantegazza brothers ceded half the work on the façade to Amadeo. In 1476 the Mantegazza presented unspecified works to the Certosa, and in 1478 they, together with Amadeo, presented architectural furniture and sculpture. In 1477 and again in 1480 the Duke reminded the prior to treat the Mantegazza well and not to delay in paying them. Cristoforo Mantegazza had died by February 1482, when his brothers Antonio and Giorgio and his daughter Costanza were paid for his works for the façade. Antonio appears to have kept his studio until 1489, when he gave it up to Alberto Maffiolo da Carrara (*fl* 1488–99). In the succeeding years he remained in contact with the monks, if only as a contractor. In 1495 Antonio was replaced as ducal sculptor by Cristoforo Solari and is presumed to have died.

Attempts to distinguish the individual hands of the brothers have been inconclusive, although scholars have provided some plausible solutions. A particular style of angular, flattened figures and drapery has been associated with both their names. Recalling flattened crumpled paper, the 'cartaceous' style characterizes much Milanese sculpture of the later 15th century. It appears that this style should now be associated only with Antonio; Cristoforo is responsible for some softer and more curving sculptures

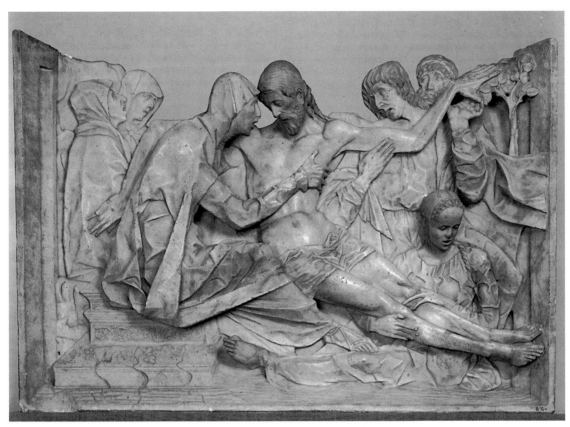

Antonio Mantegazza: *Lamentation*, marble relief, 1470s (London, Victoria and Albert Museum)

at the Certosa, including some of the *Old Testament* reliefs on the church façade (Morscheck, 1978).

A document of 12 October 1478 identifies two medallions of the *Doctors of the Church*, sculpted under the Certosa's *tiburio*, as by the Mantegazza brothers and two by Amadeo. The document also refers to a marble *Pietà* in a double chapel and an Angera stone *Madonna* keystone of the same chapel and identifies them as by the Mantegazza (Morscheck, 1984, p. 29). Morscheck (1978, pp. 225–9) identified a keystone in a double chapel in the Certosa as the *Madonna* keystone mentioned in the 1478 document and determined that its Late Gothic style must be associated with Cristoforo rather than Antonio Mantegazza. On the basis of this keystone, he then associated Cristoforo with the *St Jerome*, one of the four Doctors of the Church carved in the *tiburio*, and a number of similar corbels and capitals in the large cloister (Morscheck, 1984, p. 29; Bernstein, 1972, pp. 79f). He also associated Cristoforo with the triangular relief of *God the Father* (now above the refectory door) from the *Old Testament* cycle for the façade of the Certosa (*in situ*; also examples in Pavia, Mus. Certosa; Milan, Castello Sforzesco). These reliefs were probably placed there no earlier than 1515 (Morscheck) and may not have been intended for their present site.

To Antonio Mantegazza have been attributed many works in the cartaceous style, including the *Lamentation* in the Capitolo dei Fratelli of the Certosa (*see* PAVIA, fig. 2); another *Lamentation* (London, V&A; see fig.), which may be the *Pietà* described in 1478 in the double chapel in the Certosa; Old Testament *Creation* and *Expulsion* scenes for the façade of the Certosa; and some of the *New Testament* scenes on the right side of the façade of the Certosa. Also attributed to Antonio are the Foulc *Madonna* (Philadelphia, PA, Mus. A.) and *Faith*, *Hope* and *Charity* (all Paris, Louvre).

BIBLIOGRAPHY

G. L. Calvi: *Notizie sulle vite e sulle opere dei principali architetti, scultori e pittori che fiorirono in Milano durante il governo dei Visconti e degli Sforza*, ii (Milan, 1865)

C. Magenta: *I Visconti e gli Sforza nel Castello di Pavia*, 2 vols (Milan, 1893)

——: *La Certosa di Pavia* (Milan, 1897)

G. A. Dell'Acqua: 'Problemi di scultura lombarda: Mantegazza e Amadeo', *Proporzione*, ii (1948), pp. 89–108

E. Arslan: 'Sui Mantegazza', *Boll. A.*, xxxv (1950), pp. 27–34

J. Pope-Hennessy: *Italian Renaissance Sculpture* (London, 1958, rev. New York, 1985), pp. 325–6, 364

G. A. Dell'Acqua: *Arte lombarda dai Visconti agli Sforza* (Milan, 1959), p. 91

A. M. Romanini: 'L'incontro tra Cristoforo Mantegazza e il Rizzo nel settimo decennio del quattrocento', *A. Lombarda*, ix (1964), pp. 91–102

J. G. Bernstein: 'The Architectural Sculpture of the Cloisters of the Certosa di Pavia' (diss., New York U., Inst. F.A., 1972)

C. R. Morscheck: *Relief Sculpture for the Façade of the Certosa di Pavia, 1473–1499* (New York and London, 1978), pp. 225–35

M. G. Albertini Ottolonghi: 'Per i Mantegazza: Note sui capitelli pensili dei chiostri della Certosa di Pavia', *La scultura decorativa del primo rinascimento; Atti del I. convegno internazionale di studi: Pavia, 1980*, pp. 113–28

C. R. Morscheck: 'Keystones by Amadeo and Cristoforo Mantegazza in the Church of the Certosa di Pavia', *A. Lombarda*, lxviii–lxix (1984), pp. 27–37

ANDREA S. NORRIS

Mantegna, Andrea (*b* Isola di Carturo, nr Padua, 1430–31; *d* Mantua 13 Sept 1506). Italian painter and print-maker. He occupies a pre-eminent position among Italian artists of the 15th century. The profound enthusiasm for the civilization of ancient Rome that infuses his entire oeuvre was unprecedented in a painter. In addition to its antiquarian content, his art is characterized by brilliant compositional solutions, the bold and innovative use of perspective and foreshortening and a precise and deliberate manner of execution, an aspect that was commented upon during his lifetime. He was held in great esteem by his contemporaries for his learning and skill and, significantly, he is the only artist of the period to have left a small corpus of self-portraits: two in the Ovetari Chapel; his presumed self-portrait in the *Presentation in the Temple* (Berlin, Gemäldegal.); one in the Camera Picta (Mantua, Pal. Ducale) and the funerary bust in his burial chapel in S Andrea, Mantua, designed and probably executed by himself. His printmaking activity is technically advanced and of great importance, although certain aspects of the execution remain to be clarified. Due to the survival of both the Paduan and Mantuan archives Mantegna is one of the best-documented artists of the 15th century.

I. Life and work. II. Working methods and technique.

I. Life and work.

Mantegna's date of birth is gleaned from an inscription (recorded by Scardeone, 1560) on an altarpiece (ex-S Sofia, Padua; untraced) stating that the work was painted in 1448 when the artist was 17. He is presumed to have been born at Isola di Carturo, where the birth of his brother Tommaso is recorded. His father Biagio was a carpenter. By 1442 he had been taken on as a pupil by Francesco Squarcione who legally adopted him. In 1448, following disagreements, Mantegna made himself independent of Squarcione. By this time he probably already knew Jacopo Bellini, whose daughter Nicolosia he was to marry in 1452 or 1453. Mantegna claimed (in 1456) that he had painted many works while in Squarcione's workshop but none of these is known. From the late 1440s Mantegna was associated with a circle of scholars and professionals in Padua, and they helped form his interest in the civilization of Classical antiquity. Among them were the Venetian notary Ulisse degli Aleotti (1412–68) and the epigrapher and doctor of medicine Giovanni Marcanova (*d* 1467). Mantegna must also have studied the works that Tuscan artists had produced in the Veneto, notably the frescoes of Filippo Lippi (*c*. 1443; untraced) for the chapel of the Podestà in the basilica of S Antonio (the Santo), Padua; Ucello's series of *Famous Men* (*c*. 1445; Padua, Casa Vitaliani; untraced); Andrea Castagno's frescoes (1442; Venice, S Zaccaria, chapel of S Tarasio) and the attributed mosaic of the *Death of the Virgin* (early 1440s; Venice, S Marco, Mascoli Chapel) and, most important, the work of Donatello, who was in Padua from 1443 to 1453. Donatello's sculptures for the basilica of the Santo

and the equestrian monument of *Gattamelata* (1447–53; Padua, Piazza del Santo; *see* DONATELLO, fig. 4) introduced to the region the modern Florentine manner together with a whole new repertory of forms. In 1448 Mantegna formed a partnership with Niccolò Pizzolò, a talented painter and modeller who had worked as an assistant to Donatello.

1. Paintings and drawings. 2. Engravings.

1. PAINTINGS AND DRAWINGS.

(i) Padua, to 1460. (ii) Mantua, 1460–88. (iii) Rome, 1488–1490. (iv) Mantua, *c*. 1490–1506.

(i) Padua, to 1460.

(a) Youthful easel pictures. (b) Ovetari Chapel decoration. (c) Altarpieces. (d) Other frescoes and easel pictures.

(a) Youthful easel pictures. Mantegna's development was extraordinarily precocious and his earliest securely attributable easel picture, the *St Mark* (Frankfurt am Main, Städel. Kstinst.), dating from the late 1440s, displays many characteristics that became distinctive features of his style. The saint is seen through a round-headed marble window, a pictorial device that permitted the artist to control the relationship between the painted space and the viewer's space. The swag of fruit and foliage, much used by members of Squarcione's workshop, is a variation of an antique motif, and the embroidered edge of the Saint's tunic, embellished with pearls, is executed with studied realism. The fictive cartellino is signed in a latinate form but it was only after his move to Mantua that Mantegna signed in a consistent and accurate Latin form. The *St Jerome* (São Paolo, Mus. A.) is a more problematic attribution, having more in common stylistically with Bolognese or Ferrarese painting, but if it is a work of Mantegna it must date from about the same time as the *St Mark*. Mantegna was in Ferrara, briefly, in 1449; he was commissioned to paint a double-sided portrait of the *Marchese Lionello d'Este and Folco da Villafora* (untraced), a remarkably prestigious commission for such a young artist.

(b) Ovetari Chapel decoration. In May 1448 Mantegna and Pizzolò were commissioned to paint one half of the funerary chapel of Antonio Ovetari in the church of the Eremitani, Padua. The other half was to be executed by the more established Muranese partnership of Antonio Vivarini and Giovanni d'Alemagna. The chapel was bombed in 1944 and all that survives are Mantegna's two *St Christopher* scenes and the *Assumption of the Virgin*, which had been transferred to canvas in the early 1880s because of their poor state of conservation. Fragments of other frescoes remain but are unmounted and not on display. The comments that follow, therefore, are based mainly on photographic evidence. (For colour plates of the destroyed scenes, see G. Fiocco: *Paintings by Mantegna.*) According to the 1448 contract, Mantegna and Pizzolò were assigned the decoration of the left wall (scenes of *St James*), the chapel tribune and the execution of a terracotta altarpiece. Following a dispute between the two, however, their partnership was dissolved in September 1448 and, according to the arbitration, Mantegna was to execute all the *St James* scenes, excepting that of the saint's martyrdom, three of the five tribune vault figures— *St Paul*, *St Peter* and *St Christopher*—and the left side of

the tribune arch. His tribune figures (1449–50) are characterized by a weightiness and solidity that recalls the similar figures by Castagno (1442) in the tribune of the chapel of S Tarasio at S Zaccaria. Of the six *St James* scenes, which are based on the Gospel narratives and on the account in *The Golden Legend*, the first, at upper left, is the *Calling of SS James and John* (1450). Set in a landscape with an impressive ensemble of rocks towering above the figure group, it gives an early indication of the artist's fascination with geological formations and all types of stone. The adjacent *Preaching of St James* (1450) shows a more developed narrative sense and is Mantegna's earliest attempt at an *all'antica* setting, although the pulpit from which St James preaches could hardly be described as rigorously classical. The two scenes in the middle register (both 1450–51), the *Baptism of Hermogenes* and the *Trial of St James*, are linked by a unified perspective system and by the putto-bearing swags with the arms of Antonio Ovetari quartering those of his widow, Imperatrice Capodilista, which illusionistically hang across and in front of both pictorial fields. The *Trial of St James* displays a significant advance on the *Preaching* scene above it in terms of its Classical setting and the *all'antica* detail. The triumphal arch in the background is generally modelled on the now-destroyed Arch of the Gavi (Verona) and the inscription on it is taken from an antique slab formerly at Monte Buso, outside Padua. The throne of Herod Agrippa

is a classicizing invention, the zoomorphic supports of which probably depend on those that appear on Donatello's sculpture of the *Virgin and Child Enthroned* in Il Santo. The musculated cuirass with cingulum worn by the soldier on the left, sometimes identified as a self-portrait, shows an accurate understanding of Roman armour. At this date no more convincing rendition of a Classical scene had been realized. The compositional dynamic in the *St James* frescoes owes a debt to Donatello's reliefs for the Santo altar, both in the figure groupings and in the relationship of figures to architecture.

In 1450 Giovanni d'Alemagna died and Vivarini abandoned the Ovetari project soon after. Bono da Ferrara and Ansuino da Forlì were enlisted to execute the *St Christopher* scenes on the right-hand wall, on which no start had been made, and they probably worked under the direction of Pizzolò. During a caesura in the chapel's execution, between 1452 and 1453, Mantegna took on at least two other commissions, the lunette fresco depicting *SS Anthony and Bernardino* for Il Santo and the *St Luke* altarpiece (1453–4; Milan, Brera), both discussed below. In 1453 Pizzolò was killed and Mantegna acquired sole responsibility for the completion of the Ovetari Chapel decoration. This included the tribune fresco of the *Assumption of the Virgin* (c. 1456), the two remaining *St James* scenes and the two remaining *St Christopher* scenes (1453–7). In the bold and ambitious *St James Led to Martyrdom*

1. Andrea Mantegna: *Martyrdom of St Christopher* (1453–7; detail), fresco on the right-hand wall of the Ovetari Chapel, church of the Eremitani, Padua

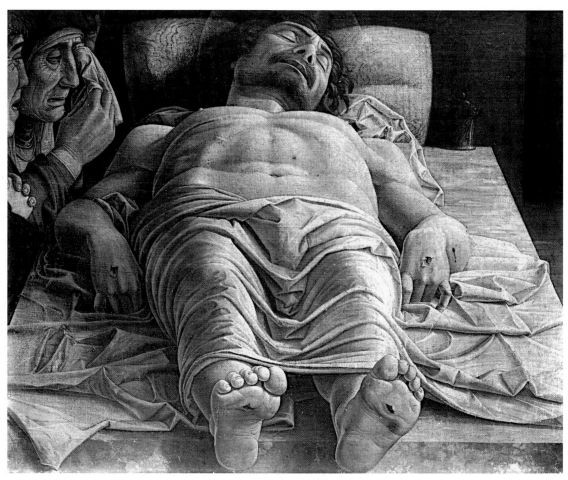

2. Andrea Mantegna: *Dead Christ*, tempera on canvas, 680×810 mm, *c.* 1500 (Milan, Pinacoteca di Brera)

(probably 1453–4) Mantegna adopted a very low viewpoint and established the vanishing-point of the perspective beneath the base-line of the composition. This had the effect of making the architectural setting more dominant and impressive. The figural composition was worked out in a pen-and-ink drawing (London, BM) in which, interestingly, the viewpoint is much higher and the pivotal figure of the soldier with a shield is absent. The neighbouring scene of the *Martyrdom of St James* had been allocated to Pizzolò and must therefore have been painted by Mantegna between 1453 and February 1457, when all the parts left unfinished by the former were said to have been completed.

The chronology of the scenes of the *Martyrdom of St Christopher* (see fig. 1) and the *Removal of the Body of St Christopher* on the right-hand wall is more difficult to determine. They are not named in the documents that relate to a dispute of 1457 concerning Mantegna's works in the chapel, and this has led some scholars to conclude that they should be dated later (Davies, Romanini, Paccagnini, Lightbown). The documents do not explicitly exclude a dating of between 1453 and 1457 and stylistically the frescoes fit neatly into this period. The *St Christopher*

scenes share a unified perspectival and architectural stage-like setting and are separated visually and notionally by an illusionistically painted Ionic column. King Dagnus's palace is decorated with Classical ornament and carved portrait-bust diptychs and inset with coloured marble medallions reminiscent of Leon Battista Alberti's design for the Tempio Malatestiano at Rimini. Mantegna's figures are in contemporary dress to conform with the scenes above. The saint's body in the right-hand scene is shown in extreme foreshortening, a foretaste of the virtuoso effects later achieved by Mantegna in his decoration of the Camera Picta and in his *Dead Christ* (Milan, Brera; see fig. 2). Vasari, in his description of these frescoes, which derived from a dependable source, identified several portraits.

The *Assumption* (1456–7) was probably the last fresco to be painted by Mantegna. Originally the area behind the altar was to be frescoed with a Christ blessing (possibly an Ascension scene), but Antonio Ovetari's executors decided in 1454 to change the iconography to the Assumption of the Virgin. Mantegna turned to advantage the limitations imposed by the compressed space available, boldly bringing two of the apostles on to the viewer's side of the painted architectural setting and emphasizing the sense of receding space with a low viewpoint.

Scardeone and Vasari recorded that Mantegna's *St James* frescoes in the Ovetari Chapel were criticized by Squarcione as being dull in colouring and that as a result the artist responded by brightening his palette for the *St Christopher* scenes. From the photographic evidence these do appear less sombre, and it has been argued that this softer mode of expression was due to Mantegna's contact with the Bellini (Cavalcaselle). More serious was Squarcione's claim that Mantegna's figures were characterized by the hardness of antique marble figures and had nothing of the softness of natural and living things, an appraisal that has become a touchstone of negative criticism of the artist ever since (Berenson, Longhi).

(c) Altarpieces. Mantegna painted the high altarpiece of S Sofia, Padua, in 1447–8, for the Paduan master-baker Bartolommeo di Gregorio (*d* 1447). It showed the Virgin and was elaborately and proudly signed *Andreas Mantegna Pat. an. septem & decem natus, sua manu pinxit, M.CCC.XLVIII* (Scardeone). Payments totalling nearly 46 ducats, a very substantial sum, are recorded. The painting was probably removed from the church in the late 16th century and was subsequently lost.

The *St Luke* altarpiece (1453–4; Milan, Brera) executed for the reformed Benedictines of S Giustina, Padua, retains the traditional polyptych format with gilded backgrounds and varying figure-scale common in Veneto altarpieces of the 1430s and 1440s. Indeed, it is likely that Mantegna was instructed to take as his model the polyptych that Vivarini and d'Alemagna painted for the Benedictine abbey of Praglia, outside Padua (1448; Milan, Brera). The two paintings share many features, including the full-length standing saints in the lower register and the central image on a larger scale crowned by a *Pietà*; this is flanked in the upper register by three-quarter-length saints. Mantegna, however, updated the formula by employing a unified perspective scheme for the marble platform on which all the saints of the lower register, including the larger figure of the titular saint, are placed and achieved an overall sense of chromatic harmony through the gently rhythmical alternation of pink and black draperies. He developed the perspectival logic of the lunette scene of *SS Anthony and Bernardino* (see below) and showed the figures of the upper register (with the exception of the *Pietà* group) in slight *di sotto in sù* perspective. St Luke is shown in full frontal view, seated at a scribe's desk working with the miniaturist's red and black ink: the figures are drawn with subtlety and precision of line. Commissioned by the abbot Mauro dei Folperti on 10 August 1453 and completed in November 1454, the altarpiece originally had a carved and gilded frame, which must surely have made the anomalies of figure scale less apparent. The artist's signature appears illusionistically carved on the marble column supporting St Luke's writing desk ('OPVS/ANDREAE/MANTEGNA').

3. Andrea Mantegna: *Crucifixion*, tempera on panel, 670×930 mm, 1456–9 (Paris, Musée du Louvre)

It may have been the *St Luke* altarpiece commission that brought Mantegna to the attention of Gregorio Correr, nephew of Cardinal Antonio Correr who had sponsored the reform of the Benedictines of S Giustina. Gregorio was the abbot of the Benedictine monastery of S Zeno in Verona and commissioned Mantegna to paint the high altarpiece. The format of the S Zeno Altarpiece (1456–9; *in situ*), a unified scene showing the *Virgin and Child with Saints* and extending over three large panels, also has precedents in the work of Vivarini and d'Alemagna (for example, the triptych for the Scuola della Carità, 1446; Venice, Accad.), but it has frequently been proposed that Donatello's altar in Il Santo, as it was set up in 1450, had a direct bearing on Mantegna's figure groups and their enclosed architectural setting, as well as on the design of the altarpiece's elaborate (surviving) classical frame. In an open pavilion supported by marble piers decorated with carved medallions of Classical subject-matter, the Virgin sits enthroned, with the Christ Child, attended by musician angels. In the left panel stand SS Peter, Paul, John the Evangelist and Zeno, Bishop and patron saint of Verona. A compositonal drawing at Chatsworth, Derbys (inv. no. L.718), shows this group with some slight differences of pose and viewpoint. In the right panel are SS Benedict, Lawrence, Gregory Nazianzen and John the Baptist. Remarkably, seven out of eight saints hold books in their hands, a fact that undoubtedly reflects the scholarly concerns of the patron, Gregorio Correr, a devout Christian humanist, and the monks of S Zeno. The altarpiece was commissioned from Mantegna in 1456, executed over the next three years in Padua and delivered to Verona in the second half of 1459. The date 1433, which appears on the lower edge of the carpet beneath the Virgin, corresponds to the year in which Correr received the monastery of S Zeno *in commendam*. The altarpiece is impressive for the sheer conceptual logic of its design, and for the complete integration of the figures, sculpture, architecture, multifarious decorative details and carved frame into a unified whole. Mantegna even appears to have arranged for a window to be opened in the choir of the church so that the lighting of the picture, which is from upper right, might correspond to the source of real light and thus appear even more convincing. The three predella scenes show the *Agony in the Garden* (Tours, Mus. B.-A.), the *Crucifixion* (Paris, Louvre; see fig. 3) and the *Resurrection* (Tours, Mus. B.-A.). In the *Crucifixion* the scene is set on a raised rocky plateau with the walled city of Jerusalem in the background. The archaeological detail of costume and armour is impressive, if not completely accurate. Mantegna seems to have been the first artist to realize that the Romans did not have stirrups.

(d) Other frescoes and easel pictures. Mantegna's lunette fresco depicting *SS Anthony and Bernardino* supporting a wreath with the monogram of Christ (1452; Padua, Mus. Antoniano) was painted above the main door of Il Santo. It is noteworthy for the illusionism achieved with the adoption of the low viewpoint. The *St Euphemia* (1454; Naples, Capodimonte) shows a development of some of the characteristics of the Frankfurt *St Mark*, and it, too, is painted on canvas. The saint appears full-length and life-size, exerting a forceful physical presence in the marble

arch. The cartellino inscribed with the artist's name and the date in Roman majuscules testifies both to Mantegna's increasing skill in illusionistic rendering of materials and to his study of Classical epigraphy. The painting was probably executed as an altarpiece although there is no record of its early provenance.

With the *Presentation in the Temple* (*c.* 1455; Berlin, Gemäldegal.; see fig. 4) Mantegna established a new and influential pictorial format, the narrative half-length scene. Conceived as a pictorial equivalent to relief sculpture in its horizontal composition and in the absence of background detail, Mantegna played up the illusionism of the picture by setting the figures behind a marble window and arranging for the cushion beneath the Christ Child to protrude into the viewer's space. The inclusion of what is generally accepted as a self-portrait head on the extreme right and the identification of the woman on the left as Nicolosia Bellini may mean that the painting is a votive picture painted to commemorate the safe delivery of a child, perhaps Francesco Mantegna, the artist's first son. The style of the picture would anyway accord well with a date close to that of the *St Euphemia*.

The dating of the *Adoration of the Shepherds* (New York, Met.), a work of which the authorship has been unjustly questioned, is not easy to determine, although there is general agreement that it falls in the decade of the 1450s. The early provenance of the picture, combined with what is purported to be an Este emblem in the picture (the wattle fence), has prompted the suggestion (1992 exh. cat.) that it was painted for Borso d'Este, Duke of Ferrara, in the early 1450s. The painting, originally on panel but transferred to canvas in 1924, is characterized by the miniature-like quality of the execution, particularly apparent in the minute gold brushstrokes employed for the highlights of the Virgin's robe and for the heads of the cherubs that surround her, and the brilliant palette. The slightly uneasy amalgamation into a single composition of what are essentially self-sufficient figural groups would support an early dating for the picture. The shepherds are sometimes said to depend on Netherlandish figure types.

Somewhat similar in character, although a more ambitious and more fully successful composition, is the *Agony in the Garden* (London, N.G.), an image of great narrative tension and clarity. Christ kneels in a *profil perdu* view before a natural rock formation resembling an altar, his form set against a distant view of Jerusalem, conceived as an oriental Classical city with buildings inspired by famous Roman monuments. The Apostles, statue-like, sleep, oblivious to the approach of Judas and the soldiers, while Christ, in a curious deviation from traditional iconography, is visited by putti bearing the instruments of the Passion. It has been proposed (1992 exh. cat.) that since the *Agony in the Garden* probably shares the same early provenance of the *Adoration of the Shepherds* it too may have been a commission from Borso d'Este. Compared with the Tours version of this subject, the London picture would appear to reflect a more sophisticated appreciation of the narrative content of the Gospel episode and its affective potential, which would suggest a later date, at the end of the 1450s, although Tietze-Conrat and Camesasca date it as early as 1450. In March 1459 Mantegna was engaged on a small work for Jacopo Marcello, a work that is sometimes

4. Andrea Mantegna: *Presentation in the Temple*, oil on canvas, 670×860 mm, *c.* 1455 (Berlin, Dahlem, Gemäldegalerie)

identified with the *St Sebastian* (Vienna, Ksthist. Mus.). Of very refined execution, redolent with Classical learning, from the representation of the ruined architecture to the Greek inscription, the picture illustrates the maturity of Mantegna's classicism just before his removal to Mantua. Other pictures that can be assigned to the 1450s with some degree of plausibility are the *Infant Redeemer* (Washington, N.G.A.), the Butler *Madonna and Child* (New York, Met.) and another, extraordinarily tender, representation of the *Virgin and Child* (Berlin, Gemäldegal.), which shares some of the characteristics of Donatello's reliefs of the subject.

By the end of the 1450s Mantegna had accepted the invitation from Ludovico II Gonzaga, 2nd Marchese of Mantua, to become his court painter. The invitation was made in 1456 and Mantegna gave a positive response by the end of the year, because in January 1457 Ludovico wrote and thanked him for agreeing to enter his service. The artist, however, was unable to go immediately because of his commitment to complete the S Zeno Altarpiece. There is evidence, too, that he may have had some misgivings about taking up a court post. About March 1458 Ludovico sent his architect Luca Fancelli to Padua to settle the terms on which Andrea would move to Mantua and in January 1459 he granted him the privilege

of bearing the Gonzaga device of a sun in splendour with the motto *par un désir*, which Ludovico had used since 1448. It was probably on a visit to Mantua at this time that Mantegna painted the portrait of *Cardinal Ludovico Trevisan*, also known as *Cardinal Mezzarota* (Berlin, Gemäldegal.), who was in the town for the ecumenical council of 1459–60. In this work Mantegna emulated the pose and *gravitas* of Roman portrait busts. He eventually moved permanently to Mantua in 1460.

(ii) Mantua, 1460–88. Mantegna's terms of employment in Mantua were generous. In return, as court painter he was expected to work exclusively for the Gonzaga, overseeing the decoration of their palaces, making portraits, designing tapestries, heraldic devices, vases and whatever else his patrons required.

(a) Castello di S Giorgio and portraits. The artist's first important task in Mantua was the decoration of the new chapel in the Castello di S Giorgio, the late 14th-century fortified residence overlooking the River Mincio. The chapel no longer survives, and the painted elements were dismantled in the 16th century. Although the documentation is incomplete, it is possible to reconstruct the appearance of the chapel partially. It was square in plan

and had a small dome resting on four arches; there was a niche rising above the altar. In type it probably resembled the approximately contemporary chapel of the Perdono in the Palazzo Ducale at Urbino. Its decoration engaged Mantegna into the mid-1460s.

Three paintings in the Uffizi are associated with the scheme—the *Adoration of the Magi*, the *Circumcision* and the *Ascension*—together with a fourth in the Prado, Madrid, the *Death of the Virgin*, the upper part of which is the fragment in the Pinacoteca Nazionale at Ferrara showing *Christ with the Virgin's Soul*. These four panels, and there were probably others, would have been set in gilded wooden panelling. Iconographically, the quartet of surviving pictures suggests a combined Marian and Christological cycle. The *Adoration of the Magi*, which is slightly concave in form and lit from the front, would have been set above the altar, probably opposite a small window. Its hard-edged drawing, brilliant chromatic range and use of gold places it in close stylistic proximity to the *Crucifixion* in the Louvre. The *Circumcision* scene combines three episodes from the Gospels: the Circumcision of Christ, his Presentation in the Temple and the Purification of the Virgin. These scenes are linked typologically to the Old Testament scenes presented in feigned relief in the lunettes. Such a purposeful, many-layered presentation of the story suggests some special significance in a contextual sense, although it is difficult to determine precisely what this might have been. The Temple setting is of extraordinary richness and illustrates an unprecedented confidence in handling architectural elements and devising variegated marble types. The *Death of the Virgin* conforms to the account in *The Golden Legend* and is compositionally close to the Venetian mosaic scene attributed to Castagno mentioned above. It includes Mantegna's only topographical view, showing with a limpid focus the Ponte di S Giorgio, linking the Castello with the Borgo di S Giorgio.

Documents indicate that as court painter Mantegna frequently had to make portraits, both drawn and painted, on canvas and on panel. Among the few that have survived is the small panel portrait of *Francesco Gonzaga* (Naples, Capodimonte), Ludovico's second son, dressed in the robes of a protonotary apostolic and thus dating from before his appointment to the cardinalate in December 1461. Portraiture was one aspect of his work in which Mantegna did not always satisfy his patrons, and even Ludovico admitted in 1475 that although Mantegna was a great artist his portraits were perhaps lacking in grace (Signorini, 1985). In 1466 Mantegna was sent to Florence by Ludovico. It was probably during this visit that he painted the striking *Portrait of a Man* (Florence, Pitti) usually identified as Carlo, the illegitimate son of Cosimo de' Medici.

(b) Camera Picta. Ludovico's principal commission from Mantegna was an historiated portrait gallery for the Palazzo Ducale, Mantua; this mural decoration took the artist nearly ten years to complete. The so-called Camera Picta (1465–74), also known as the Camera degli Sposi, shows the Marchese and his consort, Barbara of Brandenburg, together with their children, friends, courtiers and animals engaged in professional and leisurely pursuits, illustrating the present successes and alluding to the future

ambitions of the Gonzaga dynasty. The gallery represents the culmination of a series of secular decorative schemes for palace interiors in northern Italy in the 14th and 15th centuries, and the illusionism of the painted vault (*see* ILLUSIONISM, fig. 1) establishes its status as the progenitor of Correggio's ceilings and those of the Baroque. The Camera Picta is a room with a square plan (8.1× 8.1m). An inscription, simulating graffiti, on the embrasure of the north window, *1465.d.16.iunii*, indicates the date of the official commencement of the decoration.

Mantegna devised an integrated scheme according to which the room is conceived as a pavilion, open on the sides and topped by an elaborate architectural framework perforated by a Classical oculus. As custom and practical considerations dictated, the ceiling must have been painted first. Inset within the classical intersecting ribs are roundels with simulated marble busts of the first eight Caesars. The roundels are surrounded by wreaths supported by putti strongly reminiscent of those painted by Castagno on the soffit of the arch of the chapel of S Tarasio in S Zaccaria, Venice. The oculus represents a tour de force of *di sotto in sù* illusionism. Winged putti, drastically foreshortened, play among the openings in the balustrade while women courtiers and domestics look into the room with a mixture of curiosity and amusement.

Over the fireplace on the north wall is the so-called *Court Scene*. Ludovico is shown surrounded by members of his family and to the right stand retainers wearing the Gonzaga colours. The Marchese is shown in conversation with his secretary, Marsilio Andreasi, while his dog Rubino rests comfortably under his chair. This image of the reigning marchese is that of an active paternalist governor, head of a secure dynasty. The figures stand before and behind the painted piers, which are crowned by real stone corbels from which the ceiling vaults spring. Mantegna subtly combined fictive elements with real ones, adapting viewpoints so that the spectator is constantly under pressure to believe the illusion and enter into the fiction of the represented scenes. Although it has been claimed that the *Court Scene* illustrates a specific historical moment (Signorini), it is more likely that it should be understood as an idealized group portrait of the ruler and his family. In 1470 the ambassadors of the Duke of Milan were taken to see the room and they witnessed that this wall was already completed.

On the west wall, adjacent to the *Court Scene* (which is painted largely in secco, hence its poorer state of preservation), is the *Meeting Scene*, representing an open-air encounter between Ludovico and his second son, Cardinal Francesco. Again it is unlikely that a specific moment is intended since among the other figures in the scene are the Holy Roman Emperor Frederick III, who never visited Mantua, and Christian I, King of Denmark and brother-in-law of Barbara of Brandenburg, who was in Mantua in 1474. A Classical city, exquisitely executed, dominates the landscape background behind the figures. In the lunettes are Gonzaga devices and above them are painted simulated reliefs set against painted gold mosaic backgrounds showing scenes from the stories of Arion, Hercules and Orpheus, which symbolically allude to Gonzaga virtues. Above the doorway in the west wall are putti bearing an inscribed stone slab in which Mantegna dedicated 'this slight work' (*OPVS HOC TENVE*) to Ludovico and Barbara. It is dated 1474. Despite the proclaimed modesty, Mantegna was doubtless counting on the viewer's awareness that *'tenue'* could also mean 'subtle' or 'fine' and a few centimetres away amidst the foliage decoration of the pilaster on the right he introduced his self-portrait.

(c) *Relationship with the Gonzaga.* Mantegna was employed by three generations of Gonzaga and held in great esteem and affection by all of them. Ludovico was a model of patience in dealing with the artist's difficult character and slow work rate. He made him gifts of land, notably a plot just outside the city centre near Alberti's S Sebastiano, where Mantegna set about constructing a grandiose dwelling that still survives; the foundation stone is dated 18 October 1476. Square in plan with a circular courtyard, the house is of considerable architectural interest and reflects Mantegna's desire to emulate a Classical town house. The Gonzaga valued his antiquarian knowledge; there is a letter of 1472 from Cardinal Francesco to Ludovico asking that Mantegna be sent to the baths of Porretta so that Francesco, who was taking the waters, could discuss with him his collection of antique bronzes. The artist had his own collection of antiquities, which Lorenzo de' Medici came to see in 1483, and in 1506 he sold a valuable bust of the *Empress Faustina* (probably the exemplar in the Palazzo Ducale, Mantua) to Isabella d'Este. It was almost certainly Federico I Gonzaga, Ludovico's successor, who commissioned the *St Sebastian* (Paris, Louvre). The picture, painted in the early 1480s, was probably intended as an altarpiece for the Sainte-Chapelle at Aigueperse in the Auvergne (where it hung until the French Revolution), where Chiara Gonzaga, Federico's daughter, went to live after her marriage in 1481. The idealized figure of the saint is set against a temple fragment painted with a masterly sense of the texture of both carved and broken rock. Mantegna juxtaposed the saint's real foot with a foot fragment of a statue, playing on the *paragone* theme in a demonstration of the versatility of painting. The landscape background is close to that in the *Meeting Scene* in the Camera Picta, confirming the works' chronological proximity. Francesco Gonzaga, Federico's successor, was also appreciative of Mantegna's abilities, making him a grant of land in 1492 in recognition of his painted works for the family.

(iii) *Rome, 1488–c. 1490.* Mantegna was summoned to Rome in 1488 by Pope Innocent VIII to paint the Belvedere Chapel in the Vatican. Unfortunately, the chapel was destroyed in 1780, but a fairly full description of its fresco decoration survives. Above the altar was the *Baptism*, which Vasari described in some detail, while on the entrance wall was a *Virgin and Child with Saints*, life-size, with the Pope being commended to the Virgin's protection by St Peter. The *Beheading of the Baptist* was represented on the wall facing the entrance wall, and there were also small-scale narrative scenes of the *Annunciation*, *Nativity* and the *Adoration of the Magi*, and eight full-length figures representing Virtues. Mantegna included an inscription in which he declared himself a Palatine Count and Knight of the Golden Spur, the former title probably given to him by the Pope and the latter by Federico I

Gonzaga. According to the humanist and poet Battista Fiera, the chapel excited the Romans 'for its marvellous minuteness of workmanship'. It was in Rome, according to Vasari, that Mantegna painted the *Madonna of the Quarries* (Florence, Uffizi), a tiny picture of great delicacy of execution in which the Virgin and Child are set against a vast landscape dominated by a fantastic basaltic rock formation at the base of which are quarrymen engaged in carving. The picture was seen by Vasari in the collection of Francesco de' Medici.

Mantegna's sojourn in Rome appears to have had little effect on his art. The only evidence that he made drawings after the antiquities in Rome is an ink-and-chalk drawing, of disputed attribution (Vienna, Albertina; see 1992 exh. cat., no. 145), the *recto* of which shows a section of a Trajanic relief on the Arch of Constantine and the *verso* a detail of a Greco-Roman relief. There is no significant alteration in the style or content of the *Triumphs of Caesar*, which Mantegna had begun before going to Rome and continued painting after his return.

(iv) *Mantua, c. 1490–1506.*

(a) *Triumphs of Caesar.* (b) *Studiolo* of Isabella d'Este. (c) Altarpieces. (d) Easel pictures and other works.

(a) *Triumphs of Caesar.* The series (London, Hampton Court, Royal Col.), the clearest and most potent testimony of Mantegna and his Gonzaga patrons' devotion to the cult of antiquity, is composed of nine large canvases (each 2.66×2.78 m) and has as its principal theme the Gallic triumph of Julius Caesar, an exemplary role model for the Gonzaga. In his depiction of the standard bearers (Canvas I), trophy and bullion bearers (Canvases II and III), sacrificial oxen and elephants (Canvases IV and V), captives (Canvas VII) and musicians (Canvas VIII), Mantegna followed the descriptions of Roman triumphs given in the ancient sources, principally Plutarch, Appian and Suetonius. It seems likely that he made use of the compendium of triumphal literature entitled *Roma triumphans*, published (*c.* 1472) by Flavio Biondo in Mantua, which transcribes or paraphrases the ancient accounts. Mantegna supplemented this information with his own knowledge of antique visual sources for the costumes, arms, siege-engines and buildings. Elsewhere he used his imagination to create motifs that have no textual source. The *Triumphs* should not be understood as an accurate archaeological reconstruction of an antique ovation, but rather as a passionate re-creation of a Roman triumph, which seeks to make the world of antiquity come alive.

The identity of the patron, the precise chronology of the *Triumphs*, their original location, and even whether the series is complete or not (Martindale and Lightbown argue that it is not), are issues that remain unresolved. The canvases are first mentioned in a letter of August 1486, and it has been argued that Mantegna may have completed the last surviving canvas as late as 1505 (Hope). Since the imagery of the *Triumphs* makes no specific allusion to any of the marchesi, or indeed to the Gonzaga family, and because the date of the earliest reference to the pictures does not *per se* exclude any of Mantegna's three Gonzaga patrons, the case for patronage has been made on the basis of trying to match the character of the enterprise to the character and patronage activities of a particular marchese. On balance, the arguments in favour of Francesco seem strongest. The intended location of the series is not known, and the use of some of the canvases as theatrical decoration in the 1490s and early 1500s suggests that they may not have had a permanent site from the beginning. The series was acquired from the Gonzaga by Charles I in 1629 and has been in England ever since. The fame of the work was immediate and was propagated by engravings after Mantegna's original drawn designs and subsequently by reproductive woodcuts and painted copies.

(b) Studiolo of Isabella d'Este. Isabella d'Este, consort of Francesco Gonzaga, commissioned from Mantegna two allegories for her first *studiolo*, in the Castello di S Giorgio. Mantegna's first painting for her was the so-called *Parnassus* (Paris, Louvre), begun in 1495–6 and completed in 1497. The combination of the familiar mythological subject-matter of the illicit union of Mars and Venus, the parents of Cupid, with the less familiar dance of the Muses on Mt Helicon and the winged horse Pegasus giving birth to the fount of Hippocrene alludes to the harmony of love and the arts, although the precise meaning of the allegory remains elusive (which may have been intentional). The picture is executed with a fineness of touch and sureness of outline that set the standard of execution for the other painters who contributed pictures to the scheme, Perugino and Lorenzo Costa, whose works did not please Isabella as much as those by Mantegna. A detailed programme drawn up by the Mantuan humanist and Hebrew scholar Paride da Ceresara for Perugino's picture survives and similarly complex literary programmes may have been provided for Mantegna's pictures. Highly sophisticated in their intellectual content, refined in execution and compositionally elaborate, the pictures for Isabella's *studiolo* reflect perfectly the cultivated and elitist courtly milieu for which they were created.

Mantegna's second picture, *Pallas Expelling the Vices from the Garden of Virtue* (1499–1502; Paris, Louvre; *see* ALLEGORY, fig. 4), is unequivocal in its moralizing intention. The goddess erupts into the Garden of Virtue which has been overtaken by ugly and deformed personifications of the Vices, most of them identified by inscriptions, while in the sky the rightful residents of the Garden, Temperance, Fortitude and Justice, wait to return. Paride da Ceresara's participation in devising the programme of this allegory is suggested by the presence of the Hebrew inscription on the anthropomorphic tree on the left of the composition. Despite the pictorially unpromising theme Mantegna's unfailing draughtsmanship, his extraordinary attention to minute detail and the brilliance of wit apparent in the grotesque personifications make the picture wholly compelling.

(c) Altarpieces. To celebrate Francesco Gonzaga's victory against the French at Fornovo in 1495, an altarpiece was commissioned from Mantegna to decorate a newly constructed chapel in Mantua dedicated to the Madonna of Victory (1495–6; Paris, Louvre; *see* fig. 5). The altarpiece was originally to have the iconographic form of a Madonna della Misericordia protecting Francesco, his

5. Andrea Mantegna: *Madonna of Victory*, ?tempera on canvas, 2.80×1.64 m, 1495–6 (Paris, Musée du Louvre)

brothers and his wife, but in the event only Francesco was shown, in full armour, with the warrior saints Michael and George, the patron saints of Mantua, Andrew and Longinus, and SS Elizabeth and John the Baptist. The Virgin is seated with the Child on a raised throne beneath a fruit-laden canopy, extending her hand in protection over the Marchese. Camesasca has accurately characterized the *Madonna of Victory* as a 'colossal miniature'. The heavy theatricality and monumental character of the composition anticipates the altarpieces of the 16th century.

These aspects of the picture were further developed by Mantegna in the so-called *Trivulzio Madonna* (1496–7; Milan, Castello Sforzesco), painted for the Olivetan monks of S Maria in Organo in Verona. Here Mantegna employed the low viewpoint of the *Triumph* scenes, with the foreground figures of St John the Baptist and St Jerome, gracefully elongated, standing on the base-line of the composition on a surface that slopes away from the picture plane. By contrast, the Virgin in her mandorla of cherubs, whose heads dissolve into cloud (an effect that anticipates Correggio and Raphael), is shown frontally. The altarpiece is dated 15 August 1497, the feast of the Assumption, and although not strictly an Assumption scene, allusion to that iconography is implied. The sobriety of this picture, which contrasts sharply with the courtly richness of the *Madonna of Victory*, is entirely appropriate to its monastic context.

The altarpiece showing the *Virgin and Child with Mary Magdalene and St John the Baptist* (London, N.G.) is completely undocumented. The refined classicism of the composition, the elongated figures and the sharply defined folds and *cangiantismo* of the robes suggest a date in the 1490s close to the two large altarpieces.

(d) Easel pictures and other works. Mantegna's late devotional works are characterized by a great depth of feeling and by profoundly meditated pictorial solutions. The half-length narrative type devised in the 1450s is further developed in the *Adoration of the Magi* of the 1490s (Malibu, CA, Getty Mus.) and the contemporary *Ecce homo* (Paris, Mus. Jacquemart-André), both executed in distemper on a cloth support. The *Dead Christ* (Milan, Brera), with the bold foreshortening of the Christ figure and the broken flesh of the stigmata, make this a deeply moving image whose sense of tragedy is heightened by the expressions of the devastated mourners and by the sombre colouring. A painting of this subject, perhaps this very work, was in Mantegna's house at his death, a fact that, taken in conjunction with the style of the picture, the subdued tonalities in particular, and the extreme emotionalism, suggests a date of *c.* 1500. Other late devotional works include the *Descent into Limbo* (Princeton, NJ, Johnson priv. col.), which in its preternatural rendition of the earth and rocks in the foreground is very similar to the *Madonna of the Quarries* and to the *Man of Sorrows with Two Angels* (Copenhagen, Stat. Mus. Kst.). In the latter picture Mantegna imitated the light effects of Bellini in the sky and clouds. The image projects a rarefied sense of dramatic tragedy through the combined effect of the realistically rendered details of the porphyry tomb and the winding sheet and the stylized expressions of grief imprinted on the heads. The same combination of realism and stylization is apparent in the haunting late *St Sebastian* (Venice, Ca' d'Oro), which was also in Mantegna's studio at his death. Abstracted from any narrative context, the elegant elongated figure is about to step out of a marble frame, like that of the *St Euphemia* or the *St George* (probably 1470s; Venice, Accad.), giving rise to a most graceful contrapposto pose. In the lower right-hand corner a snuffed-out candle bears a cartellino with a Latin inscription which states: 'Nothing stands firm except the divine; all else is smoke', a dictum perhaps composed by Mantegna himself and perhaps indicative of the increasing sense of frustration and disillusionment that appears to have marked his final years. Among the Virgin and Child pictures that should be dated late are the one in the Poldi Pezzoli Museum, Milan (probably 1490s), and the Altman *Madonna and Child* (*c.* 1495–1505; New York, Met.).

Mantegna's grisailles were painted to simulate marble or bronze reliefs. They were intended to be appreciated as virtuoso representations, on the model of the *trompe l'oeil* works described by Pliny, but they were also demonstrations of the conceits of art imitating art and painting

outdoing sculpture. Their appearance in Mantegna's oeuvre in the 1490s corresponds with the contemporary development of a classicizing relief style in Veneto sculpture. The grisailles are small in scale and show Old Testament or Classical subjects. The distemper on canvas technique, with its dry matt look, was particularly appropriate for the realistic representation of shallow relief sculpture. A fine example of this new category of painting is the *Judith with the Head of Holofernes* (late 1490s; Dublin, N.G.), in which the grey canvas preparation is made to act as the mid-tone between the white highlights and the dark shadows. The figural monochromatic scene is set against a coloured slab of marble, the patterning of which is designed to resemble, but not to imitate, a particular kind of stone, and perhaps here too Mantegna was exercising his powers of invention. Another example is the *Samson and Delilah* (late 1490s; London, N. G.; see fig. 6), which interprets the subject in a strong moralizing key as an admonition against excessive drinking and combines this with a warning concerning the wiles of evil women. Mantegna's most ambitious monochrome painting is the *Introduction of the Cult of Cybele to Rome* (1505–6; London, N. G.), executed for Francesco Cornaro in Venice. It illustrates an episode from the story of the Roman Cornelia family in imitation of a Classical frieze set against two different types of coloured marble. The scene is presented *di sotto in sù*, and it is clear that the painting was intended to hang high, probably in a small study. Mantegna by this late stage in his career had acquired an extraordinary confidence for dealing with recondite Classical subject-matter in an entirely convincing way.

6. Andrea Mantegna: *Samson and Delilah*, distemper on canvas, 470×370 mm, late 1490s (London, National Gallery)

Mantegna also painted '*bronzi finti*', or fictive bronzes, in which he created the metallic effect by painting the highlights in shell gold over the distemper technique employed for the fictive stone reliefs. A superlative example of this is the *?Sibyl and Prophet* (*c.* 1495; Cincinnati, OH, A. Mus.), which achieves an effect ultimately more pictorial than sculptural. The *Tuccia* and the *Sophonisba* (both *c.* 1500; London, N. G.) are also fictive bronzes but painted in tempera and gold on panel. They may have been intended to decorate furniture.

Mantegna executed some highly finished drawings towards the end of his career; these appear to constitute some of the earliest examples of what have been called 'presentation drawings', drawings made as finished works of art and often intended as gifts. Among them are the *Judith with the Head of Holofernes* (Florence, Uffizi), signed and dated 1491, and the coloured drawing of *Mars, Diana and (?)Iris* (1490s; London BM). The *Allegory of the Fall of Ignorant Humanity* ('*Virtus combusta*', 1490–1506; London, BM), which is associated in style and subject-matter with the *studiolo* pictures, is probably in the same category. It formed the template for the design of the upper half of the print attributed to Giovanni Antonio da Brescia. The lower half, inscribed *Virtus deserta*, must depend on a lost Mantegna drawing.

Mantegna's burial chapel, dedicated to St John the Baptist, is in S Andrea, Mantua; it has frescoed decoration that was probably executed by his son Francesco. Canvas paintings include a *Baptism*, perhaps designed by Andrea but whose execution is not worthy of him, and a frieze-like altarpiece depicting the *Families of Christ and John the Baptist*. The latter is at least in part by Mantegna. The bronze bust of Mantegna set in a roundel against a porphyry background was probably made by the artist. It is modelled on the Roman *imago clipeata* portraits. The artist is portrayed crowned with a wreath, identifying himself as the 'painter-laureate', or the new Apelles, a title often applied to him by his contemporaries.

2. ENGRAVINGS. Mantegna's prints are the finest examples of copperplate-engraving in 15th century Italy, compositionally elaborate and technically advanced. He was a pioneer in the medium and was probably responsible for the technical innovation of combining drypoint and burin to broaden the tonal range. With the exception of Antonio Pollaiuolo's print of *Battling Nudes* (*c.* 1470), the large dimensions of Mantegna's engravings are unprecedented. Initially he appears to have been interested in the expressive and artistic potential of the medium and only subsequently in its potential for disseminating his '*invenzioni*' and for financial return, at which point he enlisted the services of professional engravers, such as Giovanni Antonio da Brescia and possibly the young Giulio Campagnola.

Although there is disagreement as to whether Mantegna cut his own plates, there is good reason to believe that he did cut some of them, notably the seven prints attributed to the artist by Kristeller; the *Virgin and Child* (B. 8), the two parts of the *Battle of the Sea Gods* (B. 17 and 18), the *Risen Christ with SS Andrew and Longinus* (B. 6), the two *Bacchanals* (B. 19 and 20) and the *Entombment* (B. 3). These are works of extremely high quality and represent what must be the culmination of a process of increasing familiarity with the technical problems of the medium. Recently the case has been made for adding four more engravings to the canon of autograph prints. These are more experimental in character (three of them unfinished) and sometimes clumsy in execution, testifying to the artist's first uncertain steps in the medium. They are the co-called *Flagellation with a Pavement* (B. 1), the *Descent into Limbo* (B. 5; these two were engraved on either side of the same plate), the *Deposition* and the *Entombment with Four Birds* (B. 2A; these two also engraved on either side of the same plate and accepted as Mantegna's by Bartsch; for all the above see 1992 exh. cat.). It is difficult to establish a chronology for Mantegna's prints, but it seems certain that none predates the artist's move to Mantua. From a letter of 1475 written by an engraver called Simone Ardizzone da Reggio to the Marchese Ludovico, it appears that at this date Mantegna was considering employing a professional engraver, and so it has been argued that most of his prints date from before that time (Landau). The *Entombment*, which exists in two states, is probably Mantegna's first experiment in using the drypoint technique. The first state shows that the design had been executed wholly in drypoint and the resulting print has poor contrast of tone and is illegible in parts. The much improved second state shows that the plate was recut with a burin, and the clarity and range of tone is far superior (see 1992 exh. cat., cat. nos 38 and 39).

The most ambitious print is the *Battle of the Sea Gods*, which is composed of two sheets and is more than 800 mm long. The Classical subject-matter has been interpreted as an allegory of Envy, since the emaciated hag who presides over the battling Tritons and Icthyocentaurs bears a tablet inscribed with the word INVID (Jacobsen), although the subject may have a specific literary source. Mantegna's intention in designing this composition must have been to create an authentic-looking Classical scene that imitated the appearance and effect of a Roman frieze. The *Bacchanal with a Wine Vat* and the *Bacchanal with Silenus* were conceived in a similar spirit but lack the moralizing content.

Mantegna's prints were recognized as important works from an early date. Dürer made drawn copies of the right half of the *Battle of the Sea Gods* and the *Bacchanal with Silenus* (both 1494; Vienna, Albertina). Engraved copies of some of the prints were made in Mantegna's own lifetime, sometimes in reverse and presumably most of them under his supervision. There are several prints by other engravers after Mantegna's drawings, and these probably date from quite late in his career.

II. Working methods and technique.

Mantegna's painting technique presents some very interesting characteristics. Among them are the frequent use of a canvas support, unusual in 15th-century Italy, the frequent use of distemper (pigment bound in animal size) and his propensity for using gold (usually in the form of shell gold, gold powder bound in size) right up to his death, by which time its use had largely gone out of fashion.

Panel paintings by Mantegna, on the other hand, generally conform to traditions current in Italy in the period. Most of the panels of the *St Luke* altarpiece, for example, are made from the commonly used white poplar, although some are black poplar. On the white gesso layer that was customarily laid on panel supports, Mantegna made quite careful underdrawings, probably with a brush and sometimes with the aid of a cartoon, as can be seen in infra-red reflectograms of some of the figures in his painting of the *Ascension* (Florence, Uffizi). In his tempera paintings on panel Mantegna sometimes made use of oil-glazes, for example in the garland of the *St Mark* (Frankfurt am Main, Städel. Kstinst. and Städt. Gal.) and probably for the copper resinate greens of the foliage in the *Agony in the Garden* (London, N.G.), some of which have turned brown. Mantegna seems to have varnished all his tempera paintings on panel to give them a glossy, reflective finish, and the letter he wrote to Ludovico Gonzaga in 1464 saying that he 'could not yet varnish the panels because the frames are not gilded' suggests that varnishing was the very last thing he did.

One of the advantages of using canvas was that it was cheaper and could be easily transported, as Montegna himself acknowledged in a letter to Marchese Ludovico (1477). The pictures for Isabella d'Este's *studiolo* are executed in tempera (pigment bound in an egg medium), except for the areas of blue paint, which are in oil on canvas, and were varnished with high-quality varnish, purchased in Venice. This had the effect of saturating the colours and gave the surface a precious vitreous quality. Mantegna's propensity for using distemper on canvas was governed by the optical and aesthetic effects that could be achieved using this technique, which gives results very similar to fresco. The low refractive index of the medium means that the pigments are closer in appearance to their dry state than when they are bound in other media. Once settled in Mantua, Mantegna had few opportunities to paint in fresco, a technique in which he excelled, and this may partly account for his frequent use of distemper on canvas. The *Triumphs*, which have the character and are of the scale of wall paintings, appear to be painted in distemper, although their state of preservation is so poor and the pictures have been so mistreated over the centuries that it is hard to be certain. Usually executed on a very fine linen support, the pictures in distemper are executed over a layer of size, sometimes coloured. Occasionally, as in the *Introduction of the Cult of Cybele to Rome* (London, N.G.), the paint is applied over a fine layer of gesso. It is generally accepted that pictures in this technique were never intended to be varnished, although most of them subsequently have been, causing a saturation of colour that the artist never intended and an overall darkening of tone due to the varnish impregnating the paint layer and the support. One picture that has escaped this fate is the *Ecce homo* (Paris, Mus. Jacquemart-André), which also happens to be glued to its original panel backing. As a result, it has preserved its fresh matt appearance and constitutes a touchstone for Mantegna's paintings in this technique. Most of the late grisailles (e.g. *Samson and Delilah*, London, N.G.; *Judith with the Head of Holofernes*, Dublin, N.G.) are in the distemper technique, which was particularly suited to imitating the dry appearance of carved stone.

Mantegna worked with great precision, leaving very little to chance. He worked methodically and, by all accounts, very slowly. Few pictures reveal significant pentiments, and in general his underdrawing was so carefully executed that when he came to paint he rarely had to make departures from the drawn lines. A drawing for the engraving of the *Risen Christ with SS Andrew and Longinus* in Munich (Staatl. Graph. Samml.; illus. in 1992 exh. cat., no. 44) shows how fastidious he was in preparing the design that was to be engraved on the copperplate. The drawing is highly finished in all its details and includes an important correction to the head of Christ. At a certain point the artist must have decided the inclination of the head was not quite right and so he cut it out of the sheet and pasted it back on at the correct angle. This is not to say that his drawings lack spontaneity; on the contrary, the preparatory pen studies (U. London, Court. Inst. Gals) for the engraving of the *Flagellation with a Pavement* are vibrant sketches that show a brilliantly inventive mind thinking out loud.

BIBLIOGRAPHY

EARLY SOURCES

G. Vasari: *Vite* (1550, rev. 2/1568); ed. G. Milanesi (1878–85), iii
B. Scardeone: *Historiae de urbis patavinae antiquitate et claries civibus patavini* (Padua, 1560)

MONOGRAPHS AND EXHIBITION CATALOGUES

H. Thode: *Mantegna* (Bielefeld and Leipzig, 1897)
P. Kristeller: *Andrea Mantegna* (London, 1901); 2nd edn, with fuller documentary appendix (Berlin and Leipzig, 1902)
C. Yriarte: *Mantegna* (Paris, 1901)
E. Tietze-Conrat: *Mantegna: Paintings, Drawings, Engravings* (London, 1955)
G. Fiocco: *L'arte di Andrea Mantegna* (Venice, 1959)
Andrea Mantegna (exh. cat., ed. G. Paccagnini; Mantua, Pal. Ducale, 1961)
R. Cipriani: *Tutta la pittura del Mantegna* (Milan, 1962)
E. Camesasca: *Mantegna* (Milan, 1964)
M. Bellonci and N. Garavaglia: *L'opera completa del Mantegna* (Milan, 1967)
G. Fiocco: *Paintings by Mantegna* (London, 1978) [includes colour plates of the Ovetari frescoes]
R. Lightbown: *Mantegna* (Oxford, 1986)
Andrea Mantegna (exh. cat., ed. J. Martineau; London, R.A., 1992); review by M. Hirst, *Burl. Mag.*, cxxxiv (1992), pp. 318–21

MANTEGNA IN PADUA

V. Lazzarini and A. Moschetti: *Documenti relativi alla pittura padovana del secolo XV* (Venice, 1908/R Bologna, 1974)
P. Kristeller: 'Francesco Squarcione e le sue relazioni con Andrea Mantegna, *Rass. A.*, ix (1909), no. 10, pp. iv–v; no. 11, pp. iv–v
E. Rigoni: 'Nuovi documenti sul Mantegna' (1927–8), reprinted in *L'arte rinascimentale in Padova. Studi e documenti* (Padua, 1970)
H. Tietze: 'Mantegna and his Companions in Squarcione's Workshop', *A. America* (1942), pp. 54–60
V. Moschini: *Gli affreschi del Mantegna agli Eremitani di Padova* (Padua, 1944)
G. Fiocco: *La Cappella Ovetari* (Milan, 1953; Eng. trans., Oxford, 1979) [See also G. Fiocco exh. cat.]
C. Paccagnini: 'La cronologia della Cappella Ovetari', *Atti del congresso sull'arte e la cultura a Mantova: Mantova, 1961*
L. Puppi: 'Osservazioni sui riflessi dell'arte di Donatello tra Padova e Ferrara', *Atti dell'VIII convegno (Inst. N. Stud. Rinascimento): Donatello e il suo tempo': Firenze 1966*, pp. 307–29
A. M. Romanini: 'L'itinerario pittorico del Mantegna nel primo rinascimento padano-veneto', *Arte in Europa: Scritti in onore di E. Arslan* (1966), pp. 437–64
L. Puppi: *Il trittico di Andrea Mantegna per la Basilica di San Zeno Maggiore in Verona* (Verona, 1972)
——: 'Nuovi documenti (e una postilla) per gli anni padovani del Mantegna', *Ant. Viva*, xiv (1975), pp. 3–11
M. Dunkelman: 'Donatello's Influence on Mantegna's Early Narrative Scenes', *A. Bull.*, lxii (1980), pp. 226–35

S. Bandera Bistoletti : *Il polittico di San Luca di Andrea Mantegna (1453-1454) in occasione del suo restauro* (Florence, 1989)

MANTEGNA IN MANTUA

F. Arcangeli: 'Un nodo problematico nei rapporti fra L. B. Alberti e il Mantegna', *Convegno di studi sul Sant'Andrea di Mantova e L. B. Alberti: Mantova, 1974*, pp. 189–203

C. Elam: 'Mantegna in Mantua', *Splendours of the Gonzaga* (exh. cat., ed. D. Chambers and J. Martineau; London, V&A, 1981), pp. 15–25

L. Ventura: 'La religione privata: Ludovico II, Andrea Mantegna e la Cappella del Castello di San Giorgio', *Quad. Pal. Te*, vii (1987), pp. 23–34

The 'Camera degli Sposi'

C. Paccagnini: 'Appunti sulla tecnica della Camera Picta di Andrea Mantegna', *Studi in onore di Mario Salmi* (Rome, 1961), pp. 395–403

C. M. Brown: 'New Documents on Mantegna's Camera degli Sposi', *Burl. Mag.*, cxiv (1972), pp. 861–3

R. Signorini: 'Lettura storica degli affreschi della Camera degli Sposi di A. Mantegna', *J. Warb. & Court. Inst.*, xxxviii (1975), pp. 109–35

——: 'L'autoritratto del Mantegna nella Camera degli Sposi', *Mitt. Ksthist. Inst. Florenz*, xx (1976), pp. 205–12

C. Lloyd: 'An Antique Source for the Narrative Frescoes in the Camera degli Sposi', *Gaz. B.-A.*, xci (1978), pp. 119–22

A. Tissoni Benvenuti: 'Un nuovo documento sulla Camera degli Sposi del Mantegna', *Italia Med. & Uman.*, xxiv (1982), pp. 357–60

R. Signorini: *Opus Hoc Tenue: La Camera dipinta di Andrea Mantegna* (Mantua, 1985)

D. Arasse and C. Cieri Via: 'A proposito della Camera degli Sposi: Una discussione di metodo', *Quad. Pal. Te*, vi (1987), pp. 19–22

M. Cordaro: 'Aspetti del modo di esecuzione della Camera Picta di Andrea Mantegna', *Quad. Pal. Te*, vi (1987), pp. 9–18

The 'Triumphs of Caesar'

E. K. Waterhouse, C. H. Collins-Baker and J. Macintyre: 'Mantegna's Cartoons at Hampton Court', *Burl. Mag.*, lxiv (1934), pp. 103–7

A. Luzio and R. Paribeni: *Il 'Trionfo di Cesare' di Andrea Mantegna* (Rome, 1940)

M. Vickers: 'The Intended Setting of Mantegna's *Triumphs of Caesar*, *Battle of the Sea Gods* and *Bacchanals*', *Burl. Mag.*, cxx (1978), pp. 365–70

A. Martindale: *The 'Triumphs of Caesar', by Andrea Mantegna in the Collection of H.M. The Queen at Hampton Court* (London, 1979)

C. Hope: 'The Chronology of Mantegna's *Triumphs*', *Renaissance Studies in Honour of Craig Hugh Smyth*, ed. A. Morrogh and others (Florence, 1985), ii, pp. 297–316

C. Hope: 'The *Triumphs of Caesar*', *Andrea Mantegna* (exh. cat., ed. J. Martineau; London, RA, 1992), pp. 350–92

The 'Studiolo' of Isabella d'Este

E. Tietze-Conrat: 'Mantegna's *Parnassus*: A Discussion of a Recent Interpretation', *Art. Bull.*, xxxvi (1949), pp. 126–30

E. H. Gombrich: 'An Interpretation of Mantegna's *Parnassus*', *J. Warb. & Court. Inst.*, xxvi (1963), pp. 196–8

A. Martindale: 'The Patronage of Isabella d'Este at Mantua', *Apollo*, lxxix (1964), pp. 183–91

E. Verheyen: *The Paintings in the Studio of Isabella d'Este at Mantua* (New York, 1971)

V. Tátrai: 'Osservazioni circa due allegorie del Mantegna', *Acta Hist. A. Acad. Sci. Hung.*, xviii (1972), pp. 233–50

P. W. Lehmann: 'The Sources and Meaning of Mantegna's *Parnassus*', *Samothracian Reflections: Aspects of the Revival of the Antique*, ed. P. Lehmann and C. Lehmann (Princeton, 1973), pp. 59–178

Lo Studiolo d'Isabella d'Este (exh. cat., ed. S. Béguin; Paris, Louvre, 1975)

R. Jones: 'What Venus Did with Mars: Battista Fiera and Mantegna's *Parnassus*', *J. Warb. & Court. Inst.*, xliv (1981), pp. 193–8

Late works and miscellaneous

A. Luzio : 'La *Madonna della Vittoria* del Mantegna', *Emporium*, x (1899), pp. 359

F. Hartt: 'Mantegna's *Madonna of the Rocks*', *Gaz. B.-A.*, xl (1952), pp. 329–42

M. Levi d'Ancona: 'Il Mantegna e la simbologia: Il *S Sebastiano* del Louvre e quello della Ca' d'Oro', *Commentari*, xxiii (1972), pp. 44–52

A. Portioli: 'La chiesa e la *Madonna della Vittoria* di Andrea Mantegna in Mantova', *Atti & Mem. Accad. N. Virgil. Mantova* (1984)

R. Jones: 'Mantegna and Materials', *I Tatti Studies: Essays in the Renaissance*, ii (Florence, 1987)

MANTEGNA AND ANTIQUITY

I. Blum: *Mantegna und die Antike* (Strasbourg, 1936)

A. M. Tamassia: 'Visioni di antichità nell'opera di Mantegna', *Atti Pont. Accad. Romana Archeol.*, xxviii (1956), pp. 213–49

F. Saxl: 'Jacopo Bellini and Mantegna as Antiquarians', *Lectures*, i (London, 1957), pp. 150–60

P. D. Knabenshue: 'Ancient and Medieval Elements in Mantegna's *Trial of St James*', *A. Bull.*, xli (1959), pp. 59–73

M. Meiss: 'Towards a More Comprehensive Renaissance Palaeography', *A. Bull.*, xlii (1960), pp. 97–112

V. Fasolo: 'L'inspirazione romana negli sfondi architettonici di Mantegna', *Palladio*, xiii (1963), pp. 79–84

E. Battisti: 'Il Mantegna e la letteratura classica', *Arte, pensiero e cultura a Mantova nel primo rinascimento in rapporto con la Toscana e con il Veneto: Atti del convegno internazionale di studi sul rinascimento: Firenze, 1965*, pp. 103

C. M. Brown: 'A Sketchbook after the Antique Known to Andrea Mantegna', *Mitt. Ksthist. Inst. Florenz*, xvii (1973), pp. 153–9

M. Vickers: 'The Palazzo Santacroce Sketchbook: A New Source for Andrea Mantegna's *Triumphs of Caesar*, *Bacchanals* and *Battle of the Sea Gods*', *Burl. Mag.*, cxviii (1976), pp. 824–34

M. Billanovich: 'Intorno all'IUBILATIO di Felice Feliciano', *Italia Med. & Uman.*, xxxii (1989), pp. 351–8

DRAWINGS AND ENGRAVINGS

E. Tietze-Conrat: 'Was Mantegna an Engraver?', *Gaz. B.-A.*, xxiv (1943), pp. 375–81

A. E. Popham and P. Pouncey: *Italian Drawings in the Department of Prints and Drawings in the British Museum: The Fourteenth and Fifteenth Centuries*, 2 vols (London, 1950)

Prints by Mantegna and his School (exh. cat. by D. Alston, C. Burman and D. Landau, Oxford, Christ Church, 1979)

D. Landau: 'Mantegna as Printmaker', and S. Boorsch: 'Mantegna and his Printmakers', *Andrea Mantegna* (exh. cat., ed. J. Martineau; London, RA, 1992), pp. 44–54, 56–66

TECHNIQUE AND MATERIALS

Lo Studiolo d'Isabella d'Este (exh. cat., ed. S. Béguin; Paris, Louvre, 1975)

M. Hours and others: 'L'Analyse des peintures du Studiolo d'Isabella d'Este au Laboratoire de recherche des Musées de France', *An. Lab. Rech. Mus. France* (1975), pp. 21

S. Bandera Bistoletti: *Il polittico di San Luca di Andrea Mantegna (1453-1454) in occasione del suo restauro* (Florence, 1989)

K. Christiansen: 'Some Observations on Mantegna's Painting Technique', and A. Rothe: 'Mantegna's Paintings in Distemper', *Andrea Mantegna* (exh. cat., ed. J. Martineau; London, RA, 1992), pp. 68–78, 80–88

J. Dunkerton: 'Mantegna's Painting Techniques', *Lectures on Mantegna*, ed. F. Ames-Lewis (in preparation)

GABRIELE FINALDI

Mantelpiece. *See* CHIMNEY-PIECE.

Manteño. Pre-Columbian culture that flourished on the Pacific coast of Ecuador *c.* AD 800–*c.* 1500. Manteño artisans were skilled in metalworking, especially copper, in textile-weaving and in ceramics, but it was the late elaboration of free-standing stone sculpture that introduced a novel dimension to their artistic production.

Despite its limited repertory, Manteño sculpture stands as one of the rare pre-Inca stoneworking traditions in the northern Andes. Best known are the seats (see fig.) and stelae sculpted from monolithic blocks of stone of variable quality and thickness, according to the locally available raw materials. Several hundred examples, in varying states of repair, have been recovered from the abandoned ruins of major Manteño ceremonial and political centres such as Cerro Jaboncillo, Cerro de Hojas and AGUA BLANCA, all in the south of Manabí Province. Both the type of stone used and the details of stylistic treatment differ from site to site, suggesting the existence of local schools of artisans. Almost invariably either a feline or a crouching male prisoner is depicted under the U-shaped arms of the seats. Although zoomorphic shamans' stools of wood are widespread among the lowland tropical forest cultures of the New World, the Manteño seats also served to denote hierarchical ranking analogous to that of the Incas. The Spanish chronicler Guaman Poma de Ayala described how the type and size of seat awarded to an official in the political hierarchy was carefully graded according to his status. The stone stelae are engraved with images featuring the 'heraldic woman' motif and a reptilian 'earth monster', both of which were evidently integral elements of a seasonal fertility cult. Other forms found in the corpus of Manteño stone sculpture include free-standing human and zoomorphic figures in a rigidly constrained style reminiscent of Aztec monumental stone sculpture (*see* MESOAMERICA, PRE-COLUMBIAN, §IV, 4(ii)(b)), and tiered columns incorporated into houses and public buildings as post supports.

BIBLIOGRAPHY

M. H. Saville: *Antiquities of Manabí*, 2 vols (New York, 1907–10)
E. Estrada: *Prehistoria de Manabí*, Museo Victor Emilio Estrada, iv (Guayaquil, 1957)
——: *Arqueología del Manabí Central*, Museo Victor Emilio Estrada, vii (Guayaquil, 1962)
B. J. Meggers: *Ecuador* (London, 1965)
M.-I. Silva: *Pescadores y agricultores de la costa central del Ecuador: Un modelo socio-economico de asentamientos precolombinos* (MA thesis, Urbana, U. IL, 1984)
A. M. Mester: *The Pearl Divers of Los Frailes: Archaeological and Ethno-historical Explorations of Sumptuary Good Trade and Cosmology in the North and Central Andes* (diss., Urbana, U. IL, 1990; microfilm, Ann Arbor, 1990)
C. McEwan: 'Sillas de poder', *5000 años de ocupación—Parque Nacional Machalilla*, ed. P. Norton (Quito, 1992)

COLIN MCEWAN, with MARIA-ISABEL SILVA

Mantes, Notre-Dame. Former collegiate church in Yvelines, France. Both Louis VII (*reg* 1137–80) and Philip II Augustus (*reg* 1180–1223) were titular abbots. No documentation for the building survives but stylistic evidence dates it to *c.* 1170–*c.* 1220. Details of both design and ornament recall Notre-Dame, Paris. The apsidal chapels and the chapel of Navarre on the south of the choir are additions of the 14th century. The gallery was spanned by decidedly curious transverse barrel vaults, which were replaced throughout most of the nave in the 14th century. In 1794 the pavement and portal jambs were destroyed. In 1851–4 Alphonse Durand (1813–82) replaced the north tower with a replica of its southern counterpart and linked the two with a gallery.

Two 12th-century sculpted portals survive on the west front. The earlier portal (*c.* 1170) on the left depicts the *Three Marys at the Tomb* on the lintel with the enthroned, resurrected Christ on the tympanum. The arrangement and figure style of the standing prophets in the archivolt is very close to the north transept Porte des Valois at Saint-Denis Abbey. The central doorway is slightly later. Its programme, the *Death and Assumption of the Virgin* on the lintel, the *Coronation of the Virgin* on the tympanum and the *Tree of Jesse* on the archivolt, is often presumed to derive from the west portal of Senlis Cathedral, but the expanded Marian cycle suggests that this was not its sole source and no sculptor worked on both portals. Stylistically the central portal derives from the left portal and hence possibly from the Valois portal of Saint-Denis, if one accepts an early date for the latter, while both ultimately

Manteño stone seat, supported by crouching male figure, from Cerro de Hojas, *c.* AD 800–*c.* 1500 (Brussels, Musées Royaux d'Art et d'Histoire)

derive from Mosan metalwork and manuscript illuminations. Four jamb heads discovered in 1857 are in the church. The right portal was added in 1300 and is very closely related to the south transept Calende portal at Rouen Cathedral.

BIBLIOGRAPHY

J. Bony: 'La Collégiale de Mantes', *Congr. Archéol. France*, civ (1946), pp. 163–220
W. Sauerländer: *Gotische Skulptur in Frankreich, 1140–1270* (Munich, 1970; Eng. trans., London, 1972)
D. C. Brouillette: *The Early Gothic Sculpture of Senlis Cathedral* (diss., U. California, Berkeley, 1981), pp. 445–501

Mantilla, Francisco de Burgos. *See* BURGOS MANTILLA, FRANCISCO DE.

Mantovano. *See* SCULTORI.

Mantovano, Marcello. *See* VENUSTI, MARCELLO.

Mantovano, Rinaldo. *See* RINALDO MANTOVANO.

Mantua [It. Mantova]. North Italian city in the Lombard plain, situated on the River Mincio *c.* 16 km north of its confluence with the River Po. Here the Mincio widens into a series of swampy lakes that once surrounded the city but now bound it on the west, north and east. Occupied successively by Etruscans, Gauls and Romans, although never a settlement of any significance, Mantua first claimed fame as the birthplace in 70 BC of the poet Virgil, whose head sometimes appeared on coins (earliest example 1256) and, set within a quarter of St George's cross, is borne on the city's coat of arms.

The city developed only from the 9th century AD. Its proximity to the River Po, the main link between the central Lombard cities and Ferrara and Venice, enabled it to exert some fiscal control over river traffic. It also straddled the land routes from Padua to Cremona and Parma, but Mantua was always relatively isolated, the only town in a flat region, some of which was forest or marsh and much of which subject to flooding. The economy was based on agriculture, although in the 13th century a cloth industry developed, its masters soon dominating the merchants' guild. Later on, silk textiles were manufactured, but on a modest scale, and Mantua remained dependent on its larger neighbours, above all on Venice. The city's heyday came between the 14th century and the early 17th, under the rule of the GONZAGA family. Major patrons of all the arts, the Gonzagas expanded and transformed the city, employing such architects as Leon Battista Alberti, Giulio Romano and Antonio Maria Viani. To their court they attracted painters, among them Andrea Mantegna and Peter Paul Rubens, musicians (Claudio Monteverdi) and goldsmiths and metalworkers (Antico). What were probably the earliest tapestry workshops in Italy grew up under Gonzaga patronage (*see* §3 below). In the early 17th century a large part of the family's collections was sold to Charles I of England, and after the sack of the city by imperial troops during the War of Succession many of the more portable items from the Gonzaga inventory left Mantua, to be dispersed in collections across Europe, although much of the family's legacy is still to be seen in the city.

1. History and urban development. 2. Art life and organization. 3. Centre of tapestry production.

1. HISTORY AND URBAN DEVELOPMENT.

(i) Before 1328. (ii) 1328–1707. (iii) After 1707.

(i) Before 1328. Mantua began to emerge as an urban community under its own bishops in the 9th century and under the counts of Canossa in the 11th. The original cathedral of S Pietro, the abbey of S Andrea (founded 1037) and the Romanesque rotunda of S Lorenzo (1082) date from this time; the relic of the Blood of Christ, Mantua's outstanding sacred treasure, was deposited in S Andrea in 1048, its annual display becoming the city's principal religious festival. St Anselm (*d* 1086), Bishop of Lucca and adviser to Countess Matilda of Canossa, was buried in the cathedral, but his cult did not survive beyond the 15th century.

In 1115 the city threw off the Canossa overlordship and became an independent commune, usually loyal to the Holy Roman emperors. By about 1200 communal Mantua was growing rapidly. Alberto Pitento achieved some control over the waters of the Mincio by building in 1190 the Ponte dei Mulini (destr. 1944), a causeway bridge bearing 12 mills, which linked the city to its suburb of Porto on the northern shore. The city, with the cathedral at its centre, had spread westwards beyond its original walls as far as S Andrea and S Lorenzo. Evidence of the early public buildings of the commune is fragmentary, but the 'Arengario' survives, a high brick vault bearing a loggia.

The building sequence of the Palazzo del Podestà (Broletto) and the Palazzo della Ragione is difficult to clarify—both are now dated from the 13th century; but the Palazzo della Ragione, overlooking the principal market-place (Piazza dell'Erbe), is probably partly on the site of an earlier building and was undergoing improvements as late as *c.* 1460 to designs by Leon Battista Alberti. By the beginning of the 13th century the city, divided into four districts, had expanded westwards to a new line of walls beside the Rio, a canal linking the middle and lower lakes; beside this boundary, which emphasized Mantua's character as a defensible island, were built the conventual churches of the principal mendicant orders, S Francesco (badly damaged 1944–5; rest. 1952) and S Domenico (destr. except tower 1926). By the 1240s, however, a third wall was being built still further west.

In 1273 the Bonacolsi family seized power. From the years of their rule date the earliest parts of what became the Palazzo Ducale—the Domus Magna and the Palazzo del Capitano. However, in 1328 the Gonzaga family took control of the city in a *coup d'état*, an event commemorated in the *Expulsion of the Bonacolsi from Mantua* (Mantua, Pal. Ducale; see fig. 1) painted in 1494 by Domenico Morone, which also illustrates the vast open space (Piazza Sordello) created by the demolitions in this area by *c.* 1400.

(ii) 1328–1707. The Gonzagas, proprietors of large estates in the southern part of the Mantuan dominion, increased their wealth through contracts of military service with such major Italian powers as Venice, Milan, Florence and the Papacy, by marriage with influential dynasties, and by the acquisition of imperial titles (Marchese 1433; Duke 1530). Both lay and ecclesiastical government came under their control, the bishopric being held by members of the family from 1466 over most of the following two centuries. Mantua's urban society and economy were not wholly parasitic upon the court; there was some resurgence in the cloth industry by the middle of the 15th century, and the merchants' guild flourished although it had no political power. The Gonzaga regime offered some degree of stability and the rule of law; it was little troubled by opposition.

The city's urban expansion continued despite physical disadvantages: Pope Pius II noted it was built on a swamp (*Commentaries*, Book II), dusty in summer, muddy in winter; those who suffered from its fever-bearing mosquitoes included Giulio Romano's assistants and Benvenuto Cellini. The first panoramic view of Mantua is a wall painting from the early 15th century, uncovered in 1981 in a warehouse that may originally have been the office of the *massaro* (economic administrator). It shows a water-girt city of brick houses, towers and churches huddled within its walls, linked to the mainland on the north and east by the Ponte dei Mulini and the Ponte di S Giorgio (destr. 1920), the surrounding landscape studded with castles. The schematic depiction gives no idea of the street layout or identifiable rendering of individual buildings. Under Francesco I Gonzaga (*reg* 1382–1407), Bartolino da Novara built the Castello S Giorgio by the lake east of the city, which was itself reorganized into 20 districts (*rioni*) and its statutes revised. The façade of the cathedral was added by Pierpaolo and Jacobello DALLE MASEGNE

1. Domenico Morone: *Expulsion of the Bonacolsi from Mantua*, oil on canvas, 1.65×3.15 m, 1494 (Mantua, Palazzo Ducale)

from 1395 to 1403; although now destroyed, it appears in Morone's *Expulsion of the Bonacolsi from Mantua* (see fig. 1).

Under Gian-Francesco Gonzaga (*reg* 1407–44), subsequently the 1st Marchese, the school of Vittorino da Feltre made Mantua a centre of humanistic education and values, and in these years some of the most familiar features of the city centre were established. In the absence of local stone, brick was the principal building material, as for the high bell-tower of S Andrea (1416); terracotta was sometimes used for such details as capitals and doorframes, seen in the house of the Milanese merchant, Giovanni Boniforte da Concorezzo, built in 1455. Over the portico above his shop (facing S Andrea) are curiously fretted terracotta window-cases and carved stone friezes showing woolsacks and items of merchandise, including combs, bowls, gloves, stirrups and saddlebags.

It was, however, Marchese Ludovico Gonzaga (*reg* 1444–78) whose initiatives reflected Renaissance architectural theory emanating from Florence. Although he already had a Florentine architect in LUCA FANCELLI, in 1459–60 he was consulting Leon Battista Alberti over a programme of urban renewal. Mantua's streets were paved, and the votive church of S Sebastiano was begun to an innovative Greek-cross design by Alberti; and in 1472 work began on the rebuilding of S Andrea to a revised design by the same architect (*see* ALBERTI, LEON BATTISTA, §III, 2(iii) and figs 4–8). The latter, a huge new building that dominates the city centre, remains the major monument to Ludovico's architectural patronage. Its portico inspired by Roman triumphal arches and the vast scale of its interior, with coffered vaulting and side chapels instead of aisles, exerted a strong influence upon church design in Rome, Milan, Venice and elsewhere.

Other civic projects sponsored by Ludovico were the rebuilt Palazzo della Ragione, the adjacent tower with its elaborate astrological clock (1473; rest. 1989) by Bartolomeo Manfredi, a new market-hall (Casa del Mercato; destr.), and a civic hospital (now offices of the Polizia Stradale, Piazza Virgiliana) designed by Luca Fancelli, begun in 1450 and in operation by 1472. At this time, too, the streets leading to the market-place beside S Andrea assumed their present character, with prominent merchants' houses surmounting porticoed shop-fronts. Some of the original marble columns with a variety of devices on their capitals and certain of the original buildings survive, although only faint traces remain to suggest the effect produced by painted stucco walls. The porticoed 15th-century exterior to the meeting-house of the merchants' guild has a capital bearing their device of an eagle above a woolsack.

Marchese Federico I (*reg* 1478–84) added the Domus Nova to the Ducal Palace complex, and further urban development occurred under Marchese Federico II (*reg* 1519–40), subsequently the 1st Duke. GIULIO RO-MANO, who came to Mantua in 1524, combined the roles of court painter and building overseer. A palace built for Marchese Francesco II (*reg* 1484–1519) near S Sebastiano was superseded after *c.* 1525 by Giulio's project on the site of the Gonzaga stables, the eccentric Palazzo del Te (*see* GIULIO ROMANO, fig. 3 and GROTTO, fig. 1); he also designed for Federico's bride the Palazzina Palaeologa (destr.). As supervisor of the city's streets and housing, Giulio is credited with the layout of straight streets and patrician palazzi with gardens that still continued westwards, and he may have been responsible for the porticoed bridge over the Rio at the fish market, and in 1536 for a new meat market building. He also redesigned the interior of the cathedral (1545–6), remodelling the nave along the lines of an Early Christian basilica in Rome.

The reign of Duke Guglielmo Gonzaga (1550–87) probably marked Mantua's zenith of prosperity and efficient government, the population reaching 35,000 in the

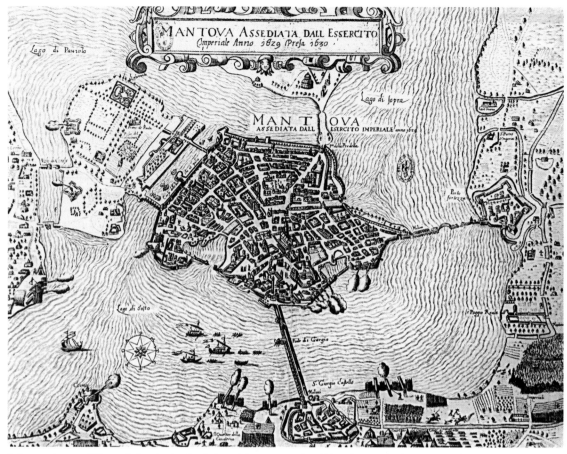

2. Panoramic map of Mantua during the siege by the imperial army, engraving, 370×475 mm, 1629–30 (Mantua, Biblioteca Comunale)

1560s. Thereafter the city declined, the direct Gonzaga line ending at the death of Duke Vincenzo II in 1627, leading to the War of Succession (1628–31), the sack of the city by imperial troops (see fig. 2), plague in 1630 and the accession of a French-sponsored cadet line of the Gonzaga dynasty, which itself died out in 1707. Printed panoramic views of Mantua in these years, in particular those by Gabriele Bertazzolo, published in 1596 and 1628, provide striking images of fortified strength, orderly layout and ample population. In the early 17th century, development westwards was still proceeding. Among notable buildings designed by ANTONIO MARIA VIANI were the churches of S Orsola and S Maurizio (begun 1608–9) and the imposing palace (now the Palazzo di Giustizia) with its façade of gigantic herms, completed 1604 for the Vescovato branch of the Gonzaga family.

The Palazzo Ducale, a court city within a city, extending over a vast area and incorporating many loosely connected buildings from the Palazzo del Capitano to the Castel S Giorgio, was further enhanced by the construction (1561–72) of the palatine church of S Barbara, designed by GIOVANNI BATTISTA BERTANI, which became famous for its choral functions and special liturgy. Other extensions to the complex were carried out by Viani for Duke Vincenzo I (reg 1587–1612). The quasi-sacral and sanctimonious character that Gonzaga rule had acquired was

sustained under Duke Ferdinando (reg 1613–25), who added to the palace a miniature version of the Scala Santa (formerly misidentified as the Apartments of the Dwarfs), intending it to become an additional focus of pilgrimage for the cult of the Holy Blood.

(iii) After 1707. In 1707 Mantua, always in theory a fief of the Holy Roman Empire, became virtually a provincial and military base of the imperial government in Vienna. There was still some notable building even after the decline of the Gonzagas. Churches such as S Barnaba and residences such as the Palazzi Canossa, Cavriani, Sordi, Bianchi (later the Bishop's Palace) and d'Arco indicate that this was not a time of stringency for local landowners or the clergy, despite economic reforms that greatly reduced their privileges. From 1733 to 1765 work was resumed on S Andrea, which was completed with a high drum and cupola designed by Filippo Juvarra. A new façade, designed by Niccolò Baschieri (fl 1760s), a military engineer from Rome, was imposed on the cathedral. The palace of the Academy of Letters and Sciences (Accademia Virgiliana), founded in 1768, had its façade completed in 1773 by Giuseppe Piermarini and the adjacent Teatro Scientifico by Antonio Galli-Bibiena was built in 1767 (destr.). The Palace of Studies of the Jesuits, completed only in 1763, was expropriated ten years later after the expulsion of the Order, which had controlled higher education in Mantua since 1624; part of the building became the civic library, opened in 1780. The architectural expression of this Mantuan revival was carried forward by the Veronese Paolo Pozzo (1741–1803), Professor of the Academy and city architect. An enthusiast for Neo-classical improvements, he imposed some modifications upon the design of the Palazzo del Te, but his plan for a new façade for the Ducal Palace was rejected.

The 18th century ended with the city's worst involvement in war: sieges by Napoleon's troops (1796–7), recapture by the Austrians (1799) and reassignment to France by the Treaty of Lunéville (1801). After the end of French occupation in 1814 a more repressive imperial government followed, which tightened its grip after 1848. Subsequently a centre of Risorgimento patriotism, Mantua joined the New Kingdom of Italy in 1866.

Over this period the suppression of religious communities, combined with the impact of war, brought much ruination to the city; religious houses were converted to secular use: the Jesuit church of Santa Trinità, despoiled of Rubens's paintings, underwent further damage by fire, before being constructed as a military store in 1852–3. Despite the prevailing dinginess, however, the upper classes had resumed the building of palatial residences after 1815, and the Teatro Sociale was opened in 1822.

Since the 19th century there has been much further destruction of significant buildings. The Palazzina Palaeologa was destroyed in 1898; from 1905 the remains of the city walls and gateways were demolished; the city was damaged in World War II. Restoration of historic churches (e.g. S Sebastiano, 1925; S Francesco, 1952) has not always been sensitive; and by the early 1950s the central part of the Rio had been covered by a new commercial and business quarter. The older core of the city has, however, been relatively well conserved, with few additions, the most notable of which is Aldo Andreani's Camera di Commercio of 1913, which, with its Moorish, late Art Nouveau features, is the most original building in Mantua since the Palazzo del Te.

2. ART LIFE AND ORGANIZATION. Virgil, who publicized Mantua's legendary foundation and supposedly historical beginnings as an Etruscan city (*Aeneid* X.196–206), not only brought fame to the city; his works provided painters there (including Rubens) with subject-matter. Monuments commemorating him extend from two 13th-century sculptures of the seated writer (see fig. 3, and Mantua, Pal. Ducale) to the 20th-century memorial by Luca Beltrami, which was inaugurated in 1930. Others, or projects for them, do not survive, among them the statue destroyed by Carlo Malatesta in 1397 and the project for which there is a drawing by Andrea Mantegna (Paris, Louvre).

Most artists and other professional experts during Mantua's heyday were brought in from elsewhere, as they may have been earlier: the first signed work of art in Mantua, a 13th-century *Virgin and Saints* on a wall of the Palazzo della Ragione, is by one 'Grixopolus', probably from Parma. It is remarkable that unlike Padua, Bologna or Ferrara, for example, Mantua seems to have been without its own characteristic workshop traditions of

3. Statue of seated Virgil, façade of the Palazzo del Podestà, Piazza Broletto, Mantua, 13th century

painting. Very little survives at all before 1400, the principal works (in S Francesco and in the Palazzo Ducale) being attributed to Stefano da Verona; no names emerge of Mantuan masters. Yet in 1380 Gian Galeazzo Visconti, later 1st Duke of Milan, sent to Mantua for good painters (*bonos depictores*), so there may have been native talent. Even in better recorded times, painters of Mantuan origin were few and undistinguished, for example Rinaldo Mantovano, an assistant of Giulio Romano, or the latter's disciples, such as IPPOLITO ANDREASI and Lorenzo Costa (ii), who was born and died in Mantua, although his parents were not from there. A similar dearth of native sculptors is rather less surprising, in view of the lack of stone quarries in the region to stimulate a working tradition; apart from the two figures of Virgil already mentioned, and the tomb effigy of *Margherita Malatesta* (*c.* 1400; formerly in S Francesco, now Pal. Ducale), there are very few surviving examples of sculpture by any hand from late medieval Mantua.

Goldsmiths, whose guild statutes date from 1310, did flourish in Mantua, and they achieved some distinction in the Renaissance. Cristoforo di Geremia, who worked for Marchese Ludovico Gonzaga in the 1460s, appears to have specialized in the design of objects, including medals, based on the Antique. One of his pupils was probably Bartolommeo Melioli (1448–1514), who had a shop near S Lorenzo and was a supervisor of the Mantuan mint *c.* 1492; another remarkable medallist, also an official of the mint, was Gian Marco Cavalli; a third was Sperandio, who also worked for Marchese Francesco II. The Mantuan mint, which lasted from the 10th century until 1785, had already begun producing gold and silver coins of high quality and denomination in the 1430s. It was then that Gian-Francesco, the first Gonzaga marquis, was granted the imperial privilege of having his head represented on coins; these finer coins, imitations of those produced by the Venetian mint, may, like medals, have been principally commemorative. The most distinguished of 15th-century Mantuan goldsmiths was probably Piero Jacopo Alari Bonacolsi, known as 'Antico', a pioneer in the art of small neo-antique bronze-castings.

The related arts of printing and engraving were also practised early in Mantua. Four of the earliest incunabula (1472–4) were printed by Pietro Adamo de' Micheli (*c.* 1441–81), the son of a Mantuan lawyer; he learnt the technique from the Butzbach brothers who had come from near Mainz. Early printed books and book illustrations in Mantua were few and mostly of inferior quality, whereas engravings were pioneered there at an early date. Zoan Andrea was in practice with his friend Simone Ardizone da Reggio, and Simone complained in September 1475 that not only their stock but their persons had been attacked, for which he blamed Mantegna. It may have been that some of Mantegna's drawings were pirated; Mantegna himself was practising engraving in Mantua by the 1490s, and the tradition was continued with great distinction by others such as Giorgio Ghisi.

Art in Mantua was very much the business of the court, and most major works were by distinguished non-Mantuans either invited to work there or given specific commissions by members of the Gonzaga family or their foreign consorts, such as Isabella d'Este (*see* ESTE (i), (6)), a notable collector, who resided in Mantua from 1490 to 1539. Some arts, such as tapestry-weaving, which probably found its first Italian home at Mantua, may have been entirely dependent on court patronage (*see* §3 below). There were important non-Mantuans who remained in Mantua for long periods and whose local influence went far beyond the court apartments they decorated. One was ANDREA MANTEGNA, who arrived as court painter in 1460 and stayed almost without interruption until his death in 1506; he designed not only his own house in the city but also his funerary chapel in the church of S Andrea. The other was Giulio Romano, who arrived as court painter in 1524. Giulio (as well as also leaving his own house behind) inspired many of the city's painters and

architects, most notably the Mantuan Giovanni Battista Bertani, who designed the first court theatre (1549, destr. 1591) and painted scenery for its productions. The house Bertani designed for himself also survives. Mantua is exceptional in containing three houses that leading Renaissance artists designed and (at least briefly) themselves inhabited.

Duke Vincenzo I brought Rubens to Mantua in 1600; his most significant work there is the *Adoration of the Trinity* (1604–5; Mantua, Pal. Ducale), painted for the Jesuit church, Santa Trinità. Rubens was never given an official position, but his compatriot Frans Pourbus (ii) was court painter from 1600 to 1609 and produced a series of formal state portraits (many dispersed, some Mantua, Pal. Ducale) of Vincenzo and his family.

Paradoxically, it was not until after the Gonzaga period that a native painter of exceptional skill appeared in Giuseppe Bazzani, who became director of the new Accademia di Belle Arti. From its foundation in 1752 this academy promoted the use of the ducal palace as a museum, where its collections of antique sculpture were exhibited. (Subsequently the museum has incorporated many different collections and retains only a fraction of the Gonzaga inheritance.) The moving spirit behind the academy as a school of design, which existed until 1796, was Giovanni Cadioli (1710–67), who was also a pioneer in the study of the history of art in Mantua and in 1763 published a description of its artistic monuments.

BIBLIOGRAPHY

GENERAL

G. Cadioli: *Descrizione delle pitture, sculture ed architetture che si osservano nella città di Mantova e nei suoi contorni* (Mantua, 1763)

L. C. Volta and G. Arrivabene: *Compendio cronologico critico della storia di Mantova dalla sua fondazione sino ai nostri tempi*, 5 vols (Mantua, 1807–33)

C. D'Arco: *Delle arti e degli artifici di Mantova*, 3 vols (Mantua, 1857–9/*R* 1975)

W. Braghirolli: *Lettere inedite di artisti del secolo XV cavate dall'archivio Gonzaga per nozze Cavriani-Sordi* (Mantua, 1878)

P. Torelli and A. Luzio: *L'archivio Gonzaga di Mantova*, i (Ostiglia, 1920), ii (Verona, 1922) [introductory essays and bibliog. as well as lists of the archives]

D. E. Rhodes: 'A Bibliography of Mantua', *La bibliofilia*, lvii–lviii (1955–6, 1964) [for early printed books]

G. Coniglio and L. Mazzoldi, eds: *Mantova: La storia*, 3 vols (Mantua, 1958–63)

E. Faccioli, ed.: *Mantova: Le lettere*, 3 vols (Mantua, 1959–63)

G. Paccagnini and others, eds: *Mantova: Le arti*, 3 vols (Mantua, 1960–65)

[Each of the series has an additional volume of illustrations and extensive bibliog.]

Mantova e i Gonzaga nella civiltà del rinascimento: Atti del convegno organizzato dall'Accademia Nazionale dei Lincei e dall'Accademia Virgiliana: Mantova, 1974

M. Vaini: *Mantova nel Risorgimento: Itinerario bibliografico* (Mantua, 1976)

C. Pecorari: 'La pianta di Mantova disegnata e incisa dal Bertazzolo nel 1596', *Civiltà Mant.*, xi (1977), pp. 325–48

A. Franchini and others, eds: *La scienza a corte* (Rome, 1979)

U. Bazzotti and A. Belluzzi: *Architettura e pittura all'Accademia di Mantova, 1752–1802* (Florence, 1980)

Splendours of the Gonzaga (exh. cat., ed. D. Chambers and J. Martineau; London, V&A, 1981) [full bibliog.]

P. Carpeggiani and I. Pigliari: *Mantova: Materiali per la storia urbana dalle origini all'ottocento* (Mantua, 1983)

Mantova nel settecento (exh. cat., ed. A. Belluzzi; Mantua, Pal. Ragione, 1983)

M. A. Grignani and others, eds: *Mantova 1430: Pareri a Gian Francesco Gonzaga per il governo*, Fonti per la storia di Mantova e del suo territorio (Mantua, 1990)

R. Signorini, ed.: *Andrea da Schivenoglia, 'Cronaca di Mantova'*, Fonti per la storia di Mantova e del suo territorio (in preparation)

SPECIALIST STUDIES

A. Magnaguti: *Studi intorno alla zecca di Mantova 1433–1627*, 2 vols (Milan, 1913–15)

P. Carpi: 'Giulio Romano ai servizi di Federico Gonzaga', *Atti & Mem. Accad. N. Virgil. Mantova*, xi–xiii (1918–1920), pp. 35–150

A. Magnaguti: *Le medaglie mantovane* (Mantua, 1921)

E. Rosenthal: 'The House of Andrea Mantegna in Mantua', *Gaz. B.-A.*, xv (1962), pp. 327–48

G. Paccagnini: *Il Palazzo Ducale di Mantova* (Turin, 1969)

K. W. Forster: 'The Palazzo del Te', *J. Soc. Archit. Hist.*, xxx (1971), pp. 267–93

Il Sant'Andrea di Mantova e Leon Battista Alberti: Atti del convegno di studi organizzato dalla città di Mantova con la collaborazione dell'Accademia Virgiliana nel quinto centenario della basilica di Sant'Andrea e della morte dell'Alberti, 1472–1972: Mantova, 1972

K. W. Forster and R. J. Tuttle: 'The Casa Pippi: Giulio Romano's House in Mantua', *Architectura* [Munich], iii (1973), pp. 104–7

C. Perina: 'Bertanus invenit: Considerazioni intorno su alcuni aspetti della cultura figurativa del cinquecento a Mantova', *Ant. Viva*, xiii/4 (1974), pp. 18–23

E. J. Johnson: *S Andrea: The Building History* (University Park, PA, and London, 1975) [some transcripts faulty]

R. Signorini: 'Marmi della casa di mercante', *Civiltà Mant.*, x (1976), pp. 53–68

D. S. Chambers: 'Sant'Andrea at Mantua and Gonzaga Patronage', *J. Warb. & Court. Inst.*, xl (1977), pp. 99–127

C. Vasic Vatovec: *Luca Fancelli architetto: Epistolario gonzaghesco* (Florence, 1979)

E. Marani: *La masseria di Mantova e i suoi affreschi* (Mantua, 1983)

D. Ferrari: *Mantova nelle stampe* (Brescia, 1985)

R. Signorini: *Opus hoc tenue: La camera dipinta di Andrea Mantegna* (Mantua, 1985) [lavish illustrations, documentation and bibliog.]

R. Margonari: 'Figure eminenti dell'arte mantovana dal 1900 al 1950', *Civiltà Mant.*, n.s., 12 (1986), pp. 69–82

R. Signorini: *L'ostensorio sognato: Breve guida alla conoscenza del ripristinato orologio pubblico di Mantova* (Mantua, 1989)

D. S. CHAMBERS

3. CENTRE OF TAPESTRY PRODUCTION. The earliest published record of a northern European tapestry-weaver in Italy is of Nicolò di Francia, who in early 1420 was in Mantua weaving a tapestry for Gianfrancesco Gonzaga, 1st Marchese of Mantua, from a cartoon by Giovanni Corradi; Nicolò seems to have stayed in Mantua for only a year. In 1421–2 Maria di Bologna is recorded as having the qualification of master of hangings, although it is not clear whether she was weaving or repairing tapestries. Zanino di Francia is first recorded in 1422 and worked for the Gonzaga until 1442, weaving several bench-backs.

After working for the Este in Ferrara, the peripatetic Brussels master Rinaldo Boteram (pseud. di Gualtieri; *fl* 1438–81) moved to Mantua in 1449, in one of the earliest of numerous exchanges of tapestries and tapestry-weavers between the Gonzaga and Este families. Cartoons were provided by the painter Giacomo Bellanti di Terra d'Otranto. In 1457 Boteram, with a recommendation from Ludovico II Gonzaga, went to Modena and then Venice. Until at least 1480, however, Boteram continued to import northern European tapestries for the Gonzaga. In 1465 Maffeo de Mafeis (*fl* 1462–8) began a set of fine, large tapestries, with silk and gold-thread highlights, from cartoons by Andrea Mantegna (see Kristeller, p. 524), who is also said to have designed the tapestry of the *Annunciation* (Chicago, IL, A. Inst.). In 1466 the master Zohanne de Franza (pseud. Giovanni or Zanino di Francia; *fl c.* 1466–91; *d* ?1507) was recommended to Marchesa

Barbara from Ferrara by Bengarda Gonzaga. Other weavers, Simone (1469) and Lorenzo and Ruggiero (from 1471) who were listed as *tappezzieri*, may have woven either tapestries or rugs. From 1475 to 1478 the upholsterer Francesco degli Acerbi worked for the Gonzaga, and in 1493 Master Bartolomeo had a tapestry workshop in Mantua.

Documents from the 16th century seem to indicate that the Gonzaga attempted to have always at least one tapestry master in their employ. Various weavers are documented as working in Mantua until 1511. Information is then scarce until 1538, when a tapestry-weaver called Giuseppe is mentioned. In 1539 Federico II Gonzaga invited NICOLAS KARCHER to come from Ferrara to establish a court workshop. Karcher brought ten other weavers with him, probably including his father, Aluisio Karcher (1455–1540). Until this time 16th-century production of tapestries appears to have been limited, and weavers may have worked mainly on smaller pieces and repairs. An antependium of the *Annunciation* (*c.* 1509; Chicago, IL, A. Inst.) with the arms of Francesco II Gonzaga is from a cartoon strongly influenced by Mantegna.

Following the lead of his cousin Ercole II d'Este, Federico II Gonzaga doubtless planned a major tapestry-decorating campaign with Karcher's workshop, which under Cardinal Ercole Gonzaga continued the 15-piece *Playing Putti* (five complete tapestries and two fragments, Lisbon, Mus. Gulbenkian; one complete piece and one fragment in other collections) from cartoons by Giulio Romano. After an eight-year sojourn in Florence, Karcher returned to Mantua (1554), and his workshop's major project, probably from cartoons by several different painters, was the six *Stories of Moses* and the accompanying *spalliera* of *Putti with Garlands* (four in Milan, Mus. Duomo; three destr.), which were later given to San Carlo Borromeo (1538–84). No tapestry-weavers are documented in Mantua after Karcher's death in 1562. Despite having weavers in Mantua, the Gonzaga never abandoned the tradition of importing tapestries from north of the Alps, some of which were woven from their own cartoons.

BIBLIOGRAPHY

A. Bertolotti: 'Le arti minori alla corte di Mantova nei secoli xv, xvi e xvii: Ricerche storiche negli archivi mantovani', *Archv Stor. Lombardo*, v (1888), pp. 259–318, 980–1075

P. Kristeller: *Andrea Mantegna* (Berlin and Leipzig, 1902)

M. Viale Ferrero: *Arazzi italiani* (Milan, 1961)

D. Heinz: *Europäische Wandteppiche* (Brunswick, 1963), pp. 260–64

M. Viale Ferrero: *Arazzi italiani del cinquecento* (Milan, 1963), pp. 18–22, 50–55

C. H. Brown and G. Delmarcel: 'Les Jeux d'enfants: Tapisseries italiennes et flamandes pour les Gonzague', *RACAR*, xv/2 (1988), pp. 109–21

N. Forti Grazzini: 'Arazzi', *Giulio Romano* (exh. cat., Mantua, Pal. Ducale and Mus. Civ. Pal. Te, 1989), pp. 466–79

C. Adelson: 'On Benedetto Pagni da Pescia and Two Florentine Tapestries: The Allegorical "Portière" with the Medici-Toledo Arms', *Kunst des Cinquecento in der Toskana*, ed. M. Kämmerer (Munich, 1992), pp. 185–96

C. H. Brown and G. Delmarcel: *The Tapestries of the Gonzaga* (in preparation)

CANDACE J. ADELSON

Mantz, Werner (*b* Cologne, 28 April 1902; *d* Eijsden, Netherlands, 12 May 1983). German photographer. He took his first photographs of Cologne and its surroundings at the age of 14. He studied photography from 1920 to

1921 at the Bayrische Lehr- und Versuchsanstalt in Munich. After working as a portraitist and advertising photographer he was discovered in 1926 by the Cologne architect Wilhelm Riphahn (1889–1963), whose Cologne housing estates he photographed sympathetically for the next five years. He did similar work for many other architects, including Klemens Klotz, Erich Mendelsohn, Bruno Paul and others. His photographs of Wilhelm Riphahn's Kalkerfeld estate and *Kölnische Zeitung* building in Cologne were particularly well known, as were those of Erich Mendelsohn's Rudolf Mosse Pavilion at the Pressa exhibition, Cologne, 1928. With the stagnation of Neue Sachlichkeit architecture at the beginning of the 1930s, Werner Mantz moved to the Netherlands, where, after a number of government contracts photographing buildings, bridges and so on for the Rijkswaterstad, he opened a portrait studio.

PHOTOGRAPHIC PUBLICATIONS

Portfolio Werner Mantz, Gal. Schürmann & Kicken (Aachen, 1977)

BIBLIOGRAPHY

Werner Mantz: Fotografien 1926–1938 (exh. cat. by K. Honneff, Bonn, Rhein. Landesmus., 1978)

Werner Mantz: Architekturphotographie in Köln 1926–1932 (exh. cat. by R. Misselbeck, Cologne, Mus. Ludwig, 1982)

REINHOLD MISSELBECK

Manual, manuscript. Technical handbook on manuscript painting. Most such manuals are short sections within manuscripts containing miscellaneous texts, rather than independent books. Among the many manuals on painting techniques, few are solely devoted to manuscript painting (*see* TREATISE, §II). The famous treatises of THEOPHILUS and CENNINO CENNINI contain only brief references to manuscripts in the sections on pigments, ink and the application of gold. Some texts on pigments seem to be primarily concerned with their use for painting in books: Heraclius' DE COLORIBUS ET ARTIBUS ROMANORUM; the 12th-century *De coloribus et mixtionibus*, which was added to the 8th- or 9th-century MAPPAE CLAVICULA; the treatise (*c.* 1300) of Peter of St Omer; and several 15th-century technical treatises. In some of these works it is evident that the author was a practising craftsman, whereas others are collections of pigment recipes, without detailed practical instructions.

Three late medieval and two 16th-century treatises are devoted entirely to manuscript illumination and contain detailed practical accounts of the techniques involved (*see also* MANUSCRIPT, §III, 3): how to prepare pigments and mix them with a medium, how to lay gold on a gesso or bole ground or with a mordant, how to mix different pigments, how to model in light and shade using the appropriate colours on a ground colour, and how to make glues and size. There is little or no discussion about underdrawing. The most important of these texts is a late 14th-century Italian treatise known as DE ARTE ILLUMINANDI (Naples, Bib. N., MS. XII.E.27). It contains 32 short sections of which about half are concerned with the use of pigments. The constituents of each pigment—mineral, plant or artificial—are listed with some comment

Manuscript manual, opening from the Göttingen Model Book illustrating the stages of painting acanthus leaf decoration, each folio 155×105 mm, 15th century (Göttingen, Niedersächsische Staats- und Universitätsbibliothek, MS. Uffenb. 51, fols 3v–4r)

on their use for various purposes. Before the pigments are discussed the media in which they are mixed are described: glair and solutions of gum arabic, gum tragacanth or honey. Later in the treatise there are sections on the methods of their preparation. The mixing of pigments is described, and their application for modelling flesh. There are also recipes for glue and size. The methods of applying gold leaf and 'artificial' gold are the subject of several sections. The treatise also covers the preparation and application of gesso and Armenian bole. Similar in content is a 15th-century Portuguese treatise in Hebrew (Parma, Bib. Palatina, De Rossi MS. 945), written by Abraham ben Judah ibn Hayyim, and probably an expansion of a 13th-century original. It has 46 sections, of which over 30 refer to pigments and the application of gold for manuscript illumination.

The 15th-century Göttingen Model Book (Göttingen, Niedersächs. Staats- & Ubib., MS. Uffenb. 51) is of a different character. It is in three sections, beginning with a detailed account of painting, in various colours, the large modelled acanthus leaves used in contemporary German manuscript illumination; each stage in the application of colour is accompanied by an illustration (see fig.). There follows an unillustrated text describing first the bole ground required for gilded areas, and then the pigments and how to grind them and mix them in various media. The last section instructs on the painting of chequered circles of various combinations of colours and gold and is accompanied by illustrations showing each stage of the painting. The short work ends with a description of the method of manufacturing artificial gold. The two 16th-century printed treatises, the *Illuminierbuch* (Basle, 1549) by Valentin Boltz (*d* 1560) and the anonymous English *Arte of Limming* (London, 1573), were written after the great age of manuscript illumination, when it was used only for relatively small-scale production. The treatises are similar in content to *De arte illuminandi*, but rather fuller in some sections.

BIBLIOGRAPHY

M. P. Merrifield: *Original Treatises Dating from the XIIth to the XVIIIth Centuries on the Arts of Painting*, 2 vols (London, 1849/*R* New York, 1968)
J. O. Halliwell: *Early English Miscellanies in Prose and Verse* (London, 1855), pp. 72–91 [a 15th-century Eng. treatise]
C. J. Benziger: '*Illuminierbuch*: Valentin Boltz von Ruffach, 1549', *Sammlung maltechnischer Schriften*, ed. E. Berger (Munich, 1913); as *Illuminierbuch* (Munich, 1988)
D. S. Blondheim: 'An Old Portuguese Work on Manuscript Illumination', *Jew. Q. Rev.*, xix (1928–9), pp. 97–135
D. V. Thompson: '*De arte illuminandi': The Technique of Manuscript Illumination* (New Haven, 1933)
——: 'The Liber Magistri Petri de Sancto Audomaro *De coloribus faciendis*', *Technical Studies in the Fine Arts*, iv (1935), pp. 28–33
F. Avril: *La Technique de l'enluminure d'après les textes médiévaux: Essai de bibliographie* (Paris, 1967) [typescript]
L. van Acker, ed.: *Petri de Sancto Audomaro, 'Librum de coloribus' faciendis*, Corpus Christianorum, Continuatio Medievalis, xxv (Turnhout, 1972), pp. 145–98
H. Lehmann-Haupt: *The Göttingen Model Book: A Fifteenth Century Illuminator's Manual* (Columbia, MO, 1972, rev. 1978)
C. S. Smith and J. G. Hawthorne: '*Mappae Clavicula*: A Little Key to the World of Medieval Techniques', *Trans. Amer. Philos. Soc.*, n. s., lxiv/4 (1974) [whole issue]
F. Brunello, ed.: '*De arte illuminandi*' *e altri trattati sulla tecnica della miniatura medievale* (Vicenza, 1975)

The Arte of Limming: A Reproduction of the 1573 Edition Newly Imprinted, intro. M. Gullick (London, 1979) [facs.]

NIGEL J. MORGAN

Manuel. *See* DEUTSCH.

Manuel I, King of Portugal. *See* AVIZ, (6).

Manuel do Cenáculo, Frei. *See* VILAS BOAS, MANUEL CENÁCULO.

Manueline style. Architectural style, identified by Francisco Adolfo de Varnhagen (1816–78; *see* PORTUGAL, §XVII) and named after Manuel I, King of Portugal (*see* AVIZ (6)), that drew much of its symbolism and ornament from the voyages made by Portuguese navigators in the 15th century. These led to the exploration of Africa and the discovery of the ocean routes to the Far East and inspired tremendous cultural vitality. It is a specifically national style, the origins of which also lay in Portugal's decisive rejection of Spanish influence after an attempt by John I, King of Castile and León (*reg* 1379–90), to take the throne of Portugal was defeated by John I, King of Portugal (*reg* 1385–1433), at the Battle of Aljubarrota (1385). The first intimations of the new style may perhaps be detected in the west façade and Founder's Chapel of the monastery of Batalha, mostly built *c.* 1386–1438 by John I as an offering of thanks for his victory.

The great advances in shipbuilding, navigation and marine technology presided over by John's son, Henry the Navigator (1394–1460), made possible the discoveries of the late 15th century and the riches that resulted from the Portuguese monopoly over trade with the East and Brazil, given papal blessing by the Treaty of Tordesillas (1494). The Manueline style was the architectural celebration of this astonishing success. Its forms are those of the Late Gothic: the vaults, pointed arches, relatively narrow windows and general proportions are not far from the contemporary Hispano-Flemish style in Castile. What is extraordinary and characteristic is the rich and complex ornament, often carved in great depth, with liberal use of foliate and nautical imagery. The leading figure was DIOGO BOITAC, who designed the church (*c.* 1494–8) of the Franciscan monastery, the Convento de Igrejia do Jesus in Setúbal, with its twisted piers in the nave. He is also documented at the monastery of Batalha, where the tracery in the arcade screens of the Claustro Real has fantastic ornament, perhaps partly derived from Islamic filigree-work, incorporating the cross of the Order of Christ, armillary spheres and bizarre foliage patterns. There is further exuberant Manueline decoration in the Unfinished Chapels (for illustration *see* BATALHA), notably in the portal designed by MATEUS FERNANDES I, which has cusped and lobed forms reminiscent of Indian architecture.

A new Hieronymite monastery, directly funded by revenues from trade with India, was built from 1501 at Belém, near Lisbon, on the site of a chapel where voyagers had traditionally prayed before embarking. Boitac was largely responsible for the church, which has aisles of the same height as the nave in the manner of a hall church (*see* BELÉM (i)). The very tall, slender columns have rich, plastic ornament in which Renaissance motifs are already visible. Diogo de Arruda's design for the west front (*c.* 1510–14) of TOMAR ABBEY is one of the most extraordinary achievements of the Manueline. There are huge, round angle buttresses, flanking a rectangular window, with a smaller circular window over, and a balustrade above (for illustration *see* ARRUDA, (1)). These elements are decorated with fantastic elaboration, with ropes, branches, seaweed and coral forms woven into an unprecedented kind of ornament. Two great string courses of knotted ropes divide the façade, and around the buttresses are gigantic garters, alluding to the English alliance and to Manuel's investiture with the Order of the Garter by Henry VII, King of England. Francisco de Arruda designed the Tower of Belém (1514–21), close to the Hieronymite monastery. This was intended as both a fort and a ceremonial gateway to Lisbon, with the machicolation and battlements of contemporary fortifications, dressed with the rich sculptural ornament of the style (for illustration *see* BELÉM (i)).

Several other buildings received Manueline additions or alterations, such as Alcobaça Abbey, where the vestibule and doorway to the sacristy have rich foliate ornament. The University chapel at Coimbra, a relatively simple structure, has windows and a portal (after 1517) in the style, with characteristic cusped, lobed and interlacing ornament. The style was short-lived, however, for Manuel I died in 1521, and his successor, John III, showed more interest in the Renaissance style. Even if the Manueline represented the end of a stylistic era, rather than a beginning, it may be seen as the origin of Portugal's independent national tradition in the visual arts and as a remarkable instance of architecture directly related at a symbolic level to contemporary events.

BIBLIOGRAPHY
W. C. Watson: *Portuguese Architecture* (London, 1908)
R. dos Santos: *Arquitectura em Portugal* (Lisbon, 1929)
E. Delmar: 'The Window at Thomar: A Monument to Vasco da Gama, the Portuguese Argonaut', *A.Q.* [Detroit], x (1947), pp. 203–12
R. C. Smith: *The Art of Portugal, 1500–1800* (London, 1968)

STEPHEN BRINDLE

Manufacture Royale des Meubles de la Couronne. *See* GOBELINS.

Manuscript [Lat.: 'written by hand']. In its broadest sense, a handwritten BOOK, ROLL, tablet or other form of portable means for storing information. Many different materials have been used for the production of manuscripts, the choice of which depends largely on geographical availability, the stage of technological development and prevailing traditional values. These factors have in turn frequently played an important part in deciding the shape and appearance of the manuscript itself, as well as influencing the SCRIPT. The introduction to this article discusses the various forms that manuscripts have taken in different cultures and periods; the rest of the article focuses, however, on the Western tradition. Manuscripts in other civilizations are discussed in detail under the appropriate country or civilization heading and especially in the following articles: CHINA, §XIII, 3; INDIAN SUB-CONTINENT, §V, 1(v)(b); and ISLAMIC ART, §III. For additional references to manuscripts throughout the world *see also* the Index.

I. Introduction. II. Production and trade. III. Illumination.

I. Introduction.

Clay tablets (see fig. 1) were used extensively as a writing material between *c.* 3000 BC and the 7th century BC in Mesopotamia (*see* MESOPOTAMIA, §I, 2(i)(c)) and other regions of the ancient Near East (*see* ANCIENT NEAR EAST, §I, 3); the script impressed on them, with a reed stylus while the clay was still wet, was one of the earliest systematic forms of writing. Inscribed tablets manufactured from water-cleaned clay were sun-dried or baked in a kiln (according to the importance of the text they were meant to store). Their individual size varied, the most popular formats being the cylinder and the oblong brick with convex sides. As a result of their role in the social and economic life of the ancient city states, clay tablets were stored in special libraries attached to temples and palaces, where they were foliated, indexed (according to the first sentence) and arranged on shelves in the appropriate order.

In ancient China bamboo strips strung together to form rolls were widely used, first for administrative records but later also for literary, philosophical and other compositions (*see* CHINA, §XIII, 3). It has been suggested that the shape of the bamboo cane determined the vertical direction of Chinese script. Wood slips, often with notches on one or both ends for binding them together, may have been imitations of earlier bamboo models, a change made necessary when Chinese administration moved to areas

1. Two scribes registering the spoils from a city, one writing with a stylus on a clay tablet, the other with a pen on a leather or papyrus roll, detail from a gypsum relief, '*Palace without Rival*', Nineveh, second half of the 7th century BC (London, British Museum)

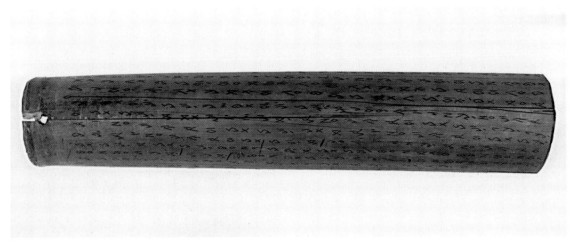

2. Bamboo manuscript, l. 425 mm, from Sumatra, 19th century (London, British Library, Or. 5309)

where the bamboo cane was rarer. Bamboo manuscripts, their texts incised with a sharp knife, are also found in Indonesia (see fig. 2). Wood, freely available in most parts of the world, has always been a popular writing material. Extant wooden writing boards from ancient Egypt date from as far back as the Middle Kingdom (*c.* 2008–*c.* 1630 BC; *see* EGYPT, ANCIENT, fig. 79); wooden tablets in various shapes and sizes, either covered with plaster, mud, brick dust or wax, lacquered and polished or more usually left in their natural state, were used in Mesopotamia, China and the Mediterranean countries of Classical antiquity (*see* BOOK, fig. 2). Greek and Roman writing tablets, consisting of rectangular boards with a slightly hollowed-out surface filled with wax and laced together not unlike a modern loose-leaf binding, were one of the most popular forms of manuscript and were referred to in Latin as a 'codex'.

A material that needs only a moderate amount of processing to make it suitable for writing is tree bark (Lat. *liber*). In India the earliest extant birch-bark folios, cut, polished and oiled, are fragments of Buddhist works written at the beginning of the Christian era (*see* INDIAN SUBCONTINENT, §VI, 1(v)(b)), but there is some evidence that birch-bark manuscripts existed at the time of Alexander the Great's invasion (326–325 BC). The long, narrow shape of some early examples has provoked speculation about possible connections with Greek papyrus rolls; however, most extant Indian birch-bark manuscripts clearly copy the shape of the palm leaf (see below), and in Kashmir from the 15th century, even that of the codex. In Sumatra long sheets of coarse bark, folded like a concertina, served until the modern era as notebooks for Batak medicine men. Bark was also used in this form by the Mayas and Aztecs of Pre-Columbian America (*see* MESOAMERICA, PRE-COLUMBIAN, §VII, 2).

The palm leaf, which has a long tradition of use for manuscripts, had a lasting and decisive influence not only on the shape of the manuscript but also on the development of a large number of scripts in India and South-east Asia (*see* INDIAN SUBCONTINENT, §VI, 1(v)(b) and fig. 234). Unlike wood and bamboo, palm leaves require a simple manufacturing process of boiling and drying to render them suitable for writing. A pile of leaves (inscribed on both sides), usually between 30 and 50 mm wide and 300–420 mm long, and secured between two wooden covers (see fig. 3), was, until the beginning of the 20th century, the most common form of the handwritten book in South and South-east Asia (*see* BURMA, §V, 2(i) and THAILAND, §VI, 1(ii)). After the introduction of paper to India by the Muslims in the early 13th century, certain types of manuscripts retained the characteristic oblong shape of palm-leaf manuscripts and even the blank space in the text, originally left by the scribe to provide room for the cord; this became a focal point for decoration.

Skin made into leather (by curing, processing and manipulation; for an explanation of these techniques *see* LEATHER, §2(i)) is impervious to water and is thus durable as a writing material. The earliest extant examples of ancient Egyptian leather manuscripts date from *c.* 2500 BC; leather was also an established writing material in Western and Central Asia. It has also always played an important part in Jewish ritual; for example, the Torah scroll kept in the synagogue is always made of skin. Since only one side is normally suitable for writing, leather promoted the roll format.

Silk, cotton and linen, originally used for clothing, became, during certain periods and in certain circumstances, established forms of writing material. Perhaps best known are the linen wrappings of Egyptian mummies inscribed with passages from the Book of the Dead (*see* EGYPT, ANCIENT, §XII, 2(v)). In India pieces of cotton, cut to size and treated with a paste made of rice or wheat flour, were, until the 20th century, used for the writing of texts and, in Karnataka (formerly the State of Mysore), for accounts. In Burma cotton cloth was sometimes cut into palm-leaf shaped pieces, which were stiffened with black lacquer, a slow and painstaking process during which letters were inlaid with mother-of-pearl. Manuscripts manufactured from cloth were not restricted to the East: Livy (59 BC–AD 17) described the *libri lintei*, the linen books used in Rome during his lifetime. Silk, the most expensive textile, was first produced in China, where references to it

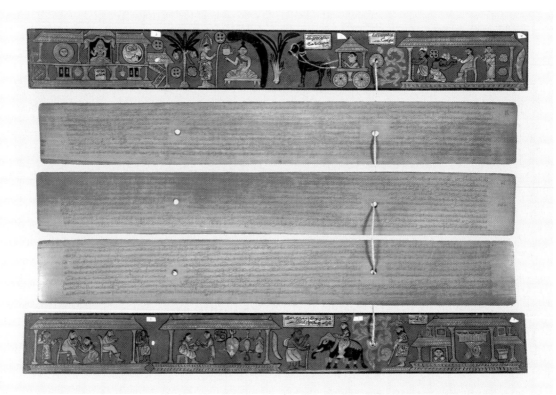

3. Palm-leaf manuscript with painted wooden covers, 50×410 mm, from Kandy, Sri Lanka, 18th century (London, British Library, Or. 6660.71)

as a writing material in the 5th and 4th centuries BC imply frequent use (*see* CHINA, §XIII, 3). Silk, however, was at all times a costly commodity, and eventually a recycling process, by which old silk rags could be pulped and the resulting mixture spread thinly on to a frame, led to the production of silk 'paper'.

One of the most durable forms of writing material is metal. This quality made it well suited for documents of a legal nature: bronze tablets inscribed with the Roman laws were supposedly kept in the Capitol; in South and Southeast Asia it was customary, until the 19th century, to record grants of land on (often palm-leaf shaped) copperplate charters, which served the recipients as title deeds (see fig. 4). The earliest extant, inscribed copper plate comes from the Indus valley (*c.* 2800 BC), although its exact purpose is uncertain. Lead, both pliable and durable, could be beaten into thin sheets and if necessary rolled up for storage; Pliny and Pausanius made reference to this custom. Gold and silver were used, especially in the East, to stress the value of a religious text, to gain special merit by commissioning such an expensive work, to express proper respect for the position of the person to whom a

4. Charter written on copper in Sanskrit and Tamil, 80×275 mm, from southern India, AD 769–80 (London, British Library, Ind. Ch. 4)

letter was addressed or simply to draw attention to one's own wealth and status. Two beaten-gold sheets, for example, inscribed with a famous Pali verse, were found inside a brick (probably the foundation stone) of a Burmese Buddhist structure dating from the 5th or 6th century AD. In Sri Lanka, according to tradition, the entire Theravada Buddhist canon was written on golden plates in 88 BC, and as late as the 18th and 19th centuries South-east Asian princes sometimes wrote their letters on thin sheets of pure gold.

The plant *Papyrus cyperus*, after which papyrus is named, was extensively cultivated in the ancient Nile Delta. As a writing material it was prominent for over three millennia, first in Egypt, and later also in Greece and Rome (*see* PAPYRUS). Although other materials were used simultaneously, none was as serviceable or as pleasing, and none could be produced as readily in equally large quantities. Once the papyrus had been prepared, several sheets were glued together to form a roll, which was inscribed on one side only. At the beginning of the Christian era papyrus became increasingly scarcer and, in consequence, more expensive. Traditional Egyptian society and economy, which had fostered its use and production, had disintegrated, and from *c.* AD 400 the parchment manuscript in codex form took precedence over the papyrus roll. After the 10th century the use of papyrus as a writing material rapidly declined, and by the 14th century it was more or less extinct.

Although the invention of parchment had traditionally been associated with the city of Pergamon in the 2nd century BC, its earlier use elsewhere has been established (*see* PARCHMENT, §2). The transformation of leather into parchment involves a fairly complex manufacturing process (*see* PARCHMENT, §1). Early fragments have survived from the 2nd century BC, but it was not before AD 200 that parchment started to rival papyrus in the Roman world, and two more centuries passed before it was used for the highest quality books. At about the same time the codex began to replace the roll format, since there was no longer any need to write on one side only. In Europe, parchment was the most common material for manuscripts until the end of the Middle Ages when it was eventually supplanted by paper.

The invention of paper, which lends itself with equal ease to the roll and the codex form of the manuscript, is traditionally attributed to Cai Lun, a minister at the court of the Eastern Han emperor Hedi, in AD 105 (*see* CHINA, §XIII, 18). Among the factors that stimulated the process was the ever growing cost of silk, the knowledge of how to produce silk 'paper' and the cumbersome nature of bamboo books. The basic ingredient of paper is macerated vegetable fibre; the manufacturing process is skilful and, like that of papyrus, a triumph of traditional technology (*see* PAPER, §I). Paper reached Europe a millennium after its invention by a tortuous and uncertain route. By the 12th century the Muslims had introduced it via the Middle East and North Africa to Spain and Sicily. When the Muslims lost Spain in 1492, the art of paper-making passed into the hands of less skilled Christian craftsmen. Its quality almost immediately declined, but during the following century paper became firmly established in western Europe. Although paper lacks the 'life' of parchment, it is

better suited for taking an impression from type or an engraved plate. In the 15th century its cheapness and availability played an important part in facilitating the explosion of PRINTING, which ultimately heralded the decline of the handwritten book or manuscript.

BIBLIOGRAPHY

F. A. Ebert: *Zur Handschriftenkunde* (Leipzig, 1820)
F. Madan: *Books in Manuscript* (London, 1920)
D. Diringer: *The Hand-produced Book* (London, 1953)
——: *The Illuminated Book: Its History and Production* (Cambridge, 1958, rev. London, 1967)
T. S. Pattie and E. G. Turner: *The Written Word on Papyrus* (London, 1974)
A. Gaur: *Indian Charters on Copper Plates* (London, 1975)
——: *Writing Materials of the East* (London, 1975)
J. I. Whalley: *Writing Implements and Accessories* (New York, 1975, 2/1980)
——: *The Pen's Excellence: Calligraphy of Western Europe and America* (New York, 1980)

ALBERTINE GAUR

II. Production and trade.

Manuscripts have been produced in the Latin West from around the 5th century AD. Although the introduction of printing in the mid-15th century signalled a decline, the handwritten book has continued to be produced, if more rarely, into the modern era. This article is concerned with the production and trade of manuscripts in Europe during the medieval, Renaissance and modern periods; for manuscripts in other traditions see under the relevant cultural and geographical articles.

1. Medieval. 2. Renaissance. 3. Modern.

1. MEDIEVAL. During the medieval period broad changes in the production and trade of manuscripts took place by which there was a gradual transition from monastic 'scriptorium'-based production to a more secularized and urban-centred context.

(i) Early medieval. (ii) Romanesque. (iii) Gothic.

(i) Early medieval. In the Late Antique period the efforts of such influential writers as Jerome (*c.* 342–420) and Cassiodorus in the promulgation of good clear texts and the copying of both secular and theological material formed the basis of the early medieval library. Jerome was among the first to encourage the copying of books as a monastic duty, while Cassiodorus set about creating communities where texts would be copied and preserved. In his *Institutiones* (6th century) he outlined the technical practices for copying and binding books, and these served as the basis for this activity for his communities at Vivarium in Calabria and were, in general, followed by other communities throughout the Middle Ages. Rome continued to be a centre for the acquisition of books until at least the time of Benedict Biscop and Bede (*c.* 673–735; see below), but this was exceptional during the early medieval period when, until the 12th century, the training of scribes, illuminators and bookbinders was closely linked to the monastic community. The famous colophon added by the priest Aldred in the Lindisfarne Gospels (late 7th century; London, BL, Cotton MS. Nero D. IV), explaining which members of the community wrote and bound the Gospels, is evidence of this.

During the pre-Carolingian period a number of major European centres were established for the production of books. Their existence was mainly the result of the missionary activity of Irish monks, notably St Columba (*c.* 540–615) who founded communities at Luxeuil (*c.* 590) and Babbio (610) among others. The most lavishly illustrated manuscripts at this time were the great Gospel books that were produced in Ireland and Northumbria in some quantities (*see* INSULAR ART, §3). Major centres of Benedictine monasticism were also established almost simultaneously. After the foundation of Montecassino *c.* 529, the influence of St Benedict (*c.* 480–*c.* 547) spread from Rome and reached England in 597 when St Augustine (*d c.* 605) was sent by Pope Gregory I to convert the south of England (*see* BENEDICTINE ORDER, §1). This missionary activity resulted in the transportation of such books as the St Augustine Gospels (late 6th century; Cambridge, Corpus Christi Coll., MS. 286), probably a Roman product brought with the Saint's mission or soon after. Benedict Biscop founded the twin monasteries of Monkwearmouth–Jarrow between 664 and 685, after the victory of the Roman party at the Synod of Whitby in 664. It was after this that Abbot Coelfrith's Bible, the Codex Amiatinus (before 716; Florence, Bib. Medicea-Laurenziana, MS. Amiatinus 1), a copy of Cassiodorus' Codex Grandior (a huge one-volume Bible or pandect executed at Vivarium), was made for presentation to the pope at Monkwearmouth–Jarrow.

St Willibrord (658–739) and St Boniface (*c.* 675–754/5) continued missionary activity on the Continent, founding monasteries at ECHTERNACH (698/9) and at Fulda (744). The Willibrord or Echternach Gospels (*c.* 700; Paris, Bib. N., MS. lat. 9389) is probably one of the books that the saint brought to the Abbey. Testimony to the learning and ability of Northumbrian churchmen of this period is Alcuin of York (735–804), who, together with such others as Paul the Deacon, was called on to reform Merovingian practices in the copying of books. During his abbacy (796–804) and those of his successors at St Martin, Tours, a number of single-volume Bibles were produced (*see* TOURS, §2(i) and fig. 2). A scriptorium also appears to have developed around Charlemagne's court at Aachen; this Court School was later also patronized by Lothair I (*reg* 840–55) and Charles the Bald (*see* CAROLINGIAN ART, §IV, 3). Another school, also originating at the court, produced work in a more classicizing style, perhaps suggesting the influence of Byzantine artists. The greatest product of this school, the Coronation Gospels of Charlemagne (8th century; Vienna, Schatzkam.; *see* CAROLINGIAN ART, fig. 7 and GERMANY, fig. 14), apparently found in the tomb of Charlemagne by Otto III, contains the enigmatic name 'Demetrius' and has miniatures painted on purple-dyed leaves, typically found in Byzantine manuscripts.

Apart from Tours the foundations associated with the emperor's close associates and relatives at Reims and Metz were prominent in the production of manuscripts in the Carolingian period. It is from these centres that the Gospels of Archbishop Ebbo of Reims (before 835; Epernay, Bib. Mun., MS. 1; for illustration *see* AUTHOR PORTRAIT) and the Sacramentary of Archbishop Drogo of Metz (mid-9th century; Paris, Bib. N., MS. lat. 9428; *see* MISSAL, fig. 1) belong. The location of the so-called Court School of Charles the Bald remains enigmatic, but it is likely that it represents a group of special commissions

that should not be considered the product of a scriptorium in the normal sense. Among the most impressive products of Charles the Bald's reign is the Bible of San Paolo (*c.* 870; Rome, S Paolo fuori le Mura; *see* CAROLINGIAN ART, fig. 8), probably made in Reims. Manuscripts were produced at a number of other centres including Salzburg, St Gall, Fleury and Lorsch.

During the Ottonian period there was a shift away from these centres (*see* OTTONIAN ART, §IV, 2). Traditionally Reichenau has been singled out as the main centre from which most manuscripts emanated, but Trier (*see* TRIER, §2(ii)) and Lorsch were also important centres of production. It seems probable that such manuscripts as the Codex Egberti (Trier, Stadtbib., MS. 24) were made at Trier, although in this case monks from Reichenau were also involved. The Liuthar group of manuscripts, named after a Gospel book (Aachen, Domschatzkam.), which includes a miniature of the monk Liuthar presenting the Gospels to Otto III (for its attribution to Reichenau, *see* OTTONIAN ART, §IV, 2(ii)(a)), is less easily located; it seems that artists, even if monks, could travel freely even at this early date. Other major centres developed during the 11th century at Echternach (see colour pl. V, fig. 2), Cologne, Regensburg and Salzburg, all of which had their own accomplished scriptoria.

In England the revival of scriptoria can be traced back to the reign of Alfred the Great; this revival peaked during the last decades of the 10th century, particularly in the south of England at Winchester and Canterbury (see colour pl. II and ANGLO-SAXON ART, §IV, 2). The so-called Winchester school (*see* WINCHESTER, §II), the work of which is exemplified by the great Benedictional of St Aethelwold (*c.* 980; London, BL, Add. MS. 49598; *see* ANGLO-SAXON ART, fig. 9), appears to have trained artists who eventually travelled to many parts of England and France. The scriptorium at Canterbury (*see* CANTERBURY, §II) appears to have been slightly less influential, but scribe–artists such as Eadui, a monk of Christ Church, who almost certainly wrote and illuminated such manuscripts as a Gospels (Hannover, Kestner-Mus. MS. WM XXIa 36) and contributed to the Harley Psalter (*c.* 1000; London, BL, Harley MS. 603; see colour pl. II and ANGLO-SAXON ART, fig. 10), must have been quite well known during their lifetime.

In Spain centres developed under semi-royal patronage at Oviedo under Alphonso III and at León under Ordoño II (*reg* 910–25) in the 10th century. Evidence of work carried out under the Muslims at Córdoba has survived only in small quantities. Apart from the early Bibles from León (e.g. 960; León, Mus.-Bib. Real Colegiata S Isidoro Cod. 2), remarkable products of Spanish manuscripts were the sumptuously illustrated copies of the Commentary of Beatus of Liébana (*d* 798) on the Apocalypse (e.g. Madrid, Escorial, Bib. Monasterio S Lorenzo, Cod. II. 5), a type of book unknown in the rest of Europe.

(ii) Romanesque. During the late 11th century and the early 12th there was an increase in the production of large Bibles for monastic institutions throughout Europe; nearly every large scriptorium associated with a monastery appears to have been producing Bibles at this time (*see* BIBLE, §I, 1). An important area for this production was

the valley between the Rhine and Meuse rivers. The monasteries of Stavelot, Floreffe and Averboden all possessed such manuscripts. In England, far from putting a stop to the production of manuscripts, the conquest by the Normans gave it new impetus, with libraries restocking on a more systematic basis.

In southern Italy a unique type of liturgical manuscript, the Exultet roll, was produced, notably in the Benevento and around Montecassino (e.g. Bari Cathedral Archivio, Cod. 1; for illustration *see* EXULTET ROLLS), the miniatures of which are heavily influenced by Byzantine work. During the 11th century Montecassino was a major centre, producing manuscripts that often emphasized its own role in the Church, such as saints' lives (e.g. the *Lives of SS Benedict, Maurus and Scholastica*, late 11th century; Rome, Vatican, Bib. Apostolica, MS. Vat. lat. 1202; *see* MONTE-CASSINO, §2(i) and fig. 2). From *c.* 1100 manuscripts of some importance were once more produced in Rome, in the scriptorium of S Cecilia (e.g. the Gospel lectionary; Florence, Bib. Medicea–Laurenziana, MS. Plut. 17.27; *see* ROMANESQUE, fig. 57). Florence and other Tuscan centres produced large Bibles during the 12th century.

During the 12th century there was a major shift away from centres of production associated almost exclusively with monastic or (on occasion) court patronage to a more secularized basis for production (*see* ROMANESQUE, §IV, 2(ii)). The Winchester Bible (Winchester Cathedral Lib.; for illustration see colour pl. V, fig. 1 and WINCHESTER BIBLE) is a good example of this transition. It was produced over a long period (*c.* 1160–90) by artists of diverse origins. Some of these artists, for example, are also associated with the decoration of the wall paintings in Winchester Cathedral, while some of the work is particularly close to the paintings from the chapter house (partly destr. 1936) of the monastery at Sigena in Spain. It seems quite clear that the Bible was not illuminated by the 'Winchester scriptorium'. The same principle applies to the work associated with St Albans (*see* ST ALBANS, §2) or Bury St Edmunds (*see* BURY ST EDMUNDS, §2). It is unlikely that either the Alexis Master of the St Alban's Psalter (Hidesheim, St Godehardkirche) or Master Hugo of the BURY ST ED-MUNDS BIBLE (*c.* 1135; Cambridge, Corpus Christi Coll., MS. 2) was trained in the scriptoria of either of these monasteries (*see* ROMANESQUE, figs 63 and 64). Although the writing of books by monks continued, the best illuminators were not necessarily trained in the monastic scriptorium that provided their patronage.

(iii) Gothic. The establishment of non-monastic schools led to the incorporation, from the 12th century on, of the great medieval universities of Bologna, Padua, Paris, Oxford, Cambridge, Prague and Heidelberg, which provided the major impetus for book production outside a monastic context (*see* BOLOGNA, §II, 1, and GOTHIC, §IV, 2(i)). Theological texts such as the main gloss on the Bible, the *Glossa ordinaria*, the *Historia scholastica* of Peter Commestor (*d* 1179) and later the work of St Thomas Aquinas and the *Postillia litteralis* of Nicholas of Lyra, were all required university reading. They were also expanded during the 12th to 14th centuries as teaching methods developed: the *Historia scholastica*, for example, was supplemented by Peter Lombard's *Sentences*, which

became a leading text book. The republication of the *Corpus juris civilis* at Bologna led to similar developments in canon law with various collections of commentaries earning canonical status: Gratian's *Decretals* eventually gained almost mythical authority (*see* DECRETAL). A gloss similar to the theological glosses was also supplied for the *Corpus juris civilis*.

The requirements of university students affected the production of books in several ways. A new form of Bible, small and in one volume for greater portability, was developed and copied in large numbers, initially in Paris, and then in other university towns. The need for students to own or borrow books also led to the development of a more efficient means of production referred to as the '*pecia*' system, whereby gatherings or sections (*peciae*:

5. Medieval manuscript of a legal textbook, Bologna, late 13th century (Oxford, Bodleian Library, MS. Holkham misc. 47, fol. 254*r*); *pecia* note in inner margin above miniature

'pieces') of books were rented out to students who could read or copy them in instalments. Notes in these books often indicate the cost of a *pecia*, particularly in scholarly books from Oxford, Paris and Bologna (see fig. 5). The system allowed several scribes to copy from a single text simultaneously.

At the same time the structure of prayer, established under the monastic system, became more accessible for private devotion by the laity through such liturgical books as the Breviary and Psalter. The latter became one of the most frequently illustrated texts during the late 12th century and the early 13th. The text of the Little Office of the Virgin, which had originated in the Breviary, was often appended to the Psalter, and by the mid-13th century, as the BOOK OF HOURS, it became an independent book, acquiring other devotional material throughout the Middle Ages. As a shorter version of the cycle of daily prayers found in the Breviary, the Book of Hours became the most popular devotional book for the laity (see colour pl. IV). Other secular reading material became available in much larger quantities throughout Europe as texts began to be translated and written in the vernacular. The bestiary, which had originated in the 12th century in monastic libraries, became a popular picture book; herbals on the other hand are less well preserved during this period. The growth of interest in Joachimist writings appears to have influenced the development in England and later the rest of Europe of extensively illustrated Apocalypse manuscripts, often with the 12th-century commentary of Berengaudus, and some written in Anglo-Norman, for example the Douce Apocalypse made for Prince Edward, later Edward I, and Eleanor of Castile (*c.* 1270; Oxford, Bodleian Lib., MS. Douce; *see* APOCALYPSE, fig. 2 and GOTHIC, fig. 73). Manuscripts of Saints' lives were also popular in the 13th century, but it was the growth of interest in Romances (*see* ROMANCE, MANUSCRIPT, §1), Histories and 'Mirrors for Princes' (books of instruction on kingly behaviour; *see* CHRONICLES AND HISTORIES, MANUSCRIPT), reflecting the values of courtly life, that marks a change of outlook in the later medieval period. Edward III, for example, owned or borrowed several books of this kind such as the Walter of Milemete Treatise (Oxford, Christ Church Lib., MS. 92) and Bruno Latini's *Li Livre dou trésor* (Paris, Bib. N., MS. fr. 571). French translations of the Bible and later English and German versions herald important developments in the history of Western culture. The *Bible historiale*, a compilation of biblical history and legend, translated into French, survives in a number of French 14th-century copies.

The scribes and artists who illuminated these books appear to have worked in particular districts in the major cities of Europe (*see* GOTHIC, §IV, 3): in Paris the tax registers suggest an enclave of illuminators, scribes and stationers on the left bank; in London a similar area around Fleet Street was established; at Oxford the area around Catte Street was used by illuminators. The process of making a book for a secular owner became more standardized during the 13th century. A patron might go to a bookseller (*libraire*), who would be asked to commission a book from the illuminators and scribes working in the vicinity. The surviving documentary evidence suggests that court artists who also painted on a larger scale often

practised manuscript illumination, but this rarely occurred the other way around. Family workshops are suggested by the documents with husband, wife and sons and daughters taking part in the production of a manuscript, and some women seem to have carried on work after being widowed.

Some illuminators appear to have been more peripatetic than others. There is evidence that some artists and scribes migrated from England to Paris, while others from Paris appear to have worked in Bologna. After the sack of Constantinople in 1204, artists from the Byzantine Empire were attracted to Bologna. The analysis of painting styles in manuscripts is clouded by such considerations, since the neat divisions by scriptoria, which have been suggested by scholars for the earlier period, cannot be applied so easily to the period after 1200; indeed it is doubtful whether a view that does not allow for artists and scribes moving freely from the earliest period is a valid one. During the 14th century and later, artists working in Paris in particular appear to have been drawn to this centre from the Netherlands, making it impossible to identify a clearcut 'ethnic' style with a particular city or country. The removal of the papal court to Avignon (1309) resulted in the establishment of a centre there that attracted artists from Italy and northern Europe, who worked on books side by side with local illuminators.

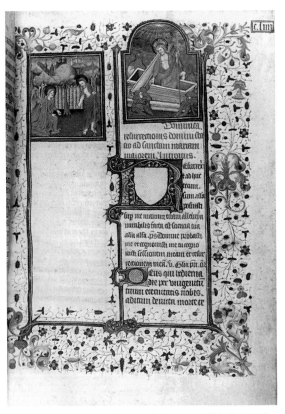

6. Medieval manuscript of a Missal, Rouen, *c.* 1430–50 (London, Sotheby's, 26 Nov 1985, lot 120, fol. 9*r*); a blank space has been left for the insertion of a coat of arms

Towards the end of the 14th century a much more systematized production began to break down the 'bespoke trade'. Evidence survives of books being produced ready-made with spaces left for armorials (see fig. 6) and special prayers to be inserted for the individual who eventually bought the book. There are indications that peripatetic artists worked for monastic institutions on their way from one commission to another, and artists who worked for particular bibliophiles also appear to have had peripatetic lives, for example the Limbourg brothers. The systemized production of Books of Hours in such centres as Bruges in the 15th century heralds the advent of printing long before the first printed books were produced.

BIBLIOGRAPHY

P. A. Delalain: *Etude sur le libraire parisien du XIIIe au XVe siècle d'après les documents publiés dans le cartulaire de l'Université de Paris* (Paris, 1891)

P. Blanchon-Lasserve: *Ecriture et enluminure des manuscrits du IXe au XIIe siècle: Histoire et technique* (Solesmes, 1926)

J. Destrez: *La Pecia dans les manuscrits universitaires du XIIIe et du XIVe siècle* (Paris, 1935)

J. W. Thompson: *The Medieval Library* (New York, 1957)

G. Pollard: 'The University and the Book Trade in Medieval Oxford', *Misc. Med.*, iii (1964), pp. 336–44

D. Diringer: *The Illuminated Book: Its History and Production* (London, 1967)

F. Baron: 'Enlumineurs, peintres et sculpteurs parisiens du 14ème et 15ème siècles d'après les Archives de l'Hôpital Saint-Jacques', *Bull. Archéol. Cté Trav. Hist. & Sci.*, n.s., 4 (1969), pp. 37–121; (1970–71), pp. 77–115

J. J. G. Alexander: *Norman Illumination at Mont St Michel, 966–1100* (Oxford, 1970)

C. R. Dodwell: *Painting in Europe, 800–1200*, Pelican Hist. A. (Harmondsworth, 1971); rev. as *The Pictorial Art of the West, 800–1200* (1993)

F. Dressler, ed.: *Scriptorium Opus: Schreiber-Mönche am Werk. Festschrift Prof. Dr. Otto Meyer zum 65. Geburtstag* (Wiesbaden, 1971)

W. Koehler: 'Buchmalerei des frühen Mittelalters', *Fragmente und Entwürfe aus dem Nachlass*, ed. E. Kitzinger and F. Mütherich (Munich, 1972)

O. Pächt and D. Thoss: *Die illuminierten Handschriften und Inkunabeln der Österreichischen Nationalbibliothek I: Französische Schule*, 2 vols (Vienna, 1974)

C.-M. Kauffmann: *Romanesque Manuscripts, 1066–1190* (1975), iii of *A Survey of Manuscripts Illuminated in the British Isles*, ed. J. J. G. Alexander (London, 1975–)

J. Folda: *Crusader Manuscript Illumination at Saint Jean d'Acre, 1275–1291* (Princeton, 1976)

E. Temple: *Anglo-Saxon Manuscripts, 900–1066* (1976), ii of *A Survey of Manuscripts Illuminated in the British Isles*, ed. J. J. G. Alexander (London, 1975–)

R. Branner: *Manuscript Painting in Paris during the Reign of St Louis* (Berkeley, 1977)

K. Weitzmann: *Late Antique and Early Christian Book Illumination* (London, 1977)

J. Williams: *Early Spanish Illumination* (London, 1977)

J. J. G. Alexander: *Insular Manuscripts from the 6th to the 9th Century* (1978), i of *A Survey of Manuscripts Illuminated in the British Isles*, ed. J. J. G. Alexander (London, 1975–)

F. Avril: *Manuscript Painting at the Court of France: The Fourteenth Century (1310–1380)* (London, 1978)

B. Bischoff: *Paläographie des römischen Altertums und des abendländischen Mittelalters* (Berlin, 1979); Eng. trans. by D. Ó'Crónín and D. Ganz as *Latin Palaeography* (Cambridge, 1990)

A. von Euw and J. M. Plotzek: *Die Handschriften der Sammlung Ludwig* (Cologne, 1979–85)

F. Avril and Y. Załuska: *Manuscrits enluminés d'origine italienne, VIe–XIIe siècles* (Paris, 1980)

N. J. Morgan: *Early Gothic Manuscripts, 1190–1285*, 2 vols (1982–8), iv of *A Survey of Manuscripts Illuminated in the British Isles*, ed. J. J. G. Alexander (London, 1975–)

——: 'Aspects of Colour in English and French Manuscript Painting of the Late 13th Century', *Europäische Kunst um 1300*, ed. G. Schmidt and E. Liskar (Vienna, 1983), pp. 111–16

F. Avril, M-T. Gousset and C. Rabel: *Manuscrits enluminés d'origine italienne, XIIIe siècle* (Paris, 1984)

L. E. Boyle: *Medieval Latin Palaeography* (Toronto, 1984)

Ornamenta Ecclesiae, 3 vols (exh. cat., ed. A. Legner; Cologne, Josef-Haubrich-Ksthalle, 1985)

R. S. Wieck: *The Book of Hours in Medieval Art and Life* (London, 1988)

J. J. G. Alexander: *Medieval Illuminators and their Methods of Work* (New Haven and London, 1992)

M. A. Michael: 'English Illuminators c. 1190–1450: A Survey from Documentary Sources', *Eng. MS. Stud., 1100–1700*, iv (1993), pp. 62–113

M. A. MICHAEL

2. RENAISSANCE. Traditional means of making handwritten and decorated manuscripts were maintained during the Renaissance. Urban production for a largely lay audience predominated in 15th-century Europe where manuscript output peaked in the years just after 1450. Booksellers and artisans struggled to meet the enthusiastic demand created by a socially diverse and increasingly literate urban clientele as well as the court aristocracy. The style of manuscript decoration described as 'Renaissance' developed early in Italy, where copies of humanist texts took on the forms and content of Classical antiquity (see colour pl. III). The French and Netherlandish luxury markets were known for their illustrated romances, moralized Classical texts, and historical chronicles. Bibles and vernacular devotional tracts continued to be made in a diminishing number of monastic houses in the north Netherlands and Germany. Throughout Europe the most popular personal religious book was the Book of Hours, typically produced in an urban, secular context (*see* BOOK OF HOURS, §3).

There was no tidy division of labour in manuscript production, but, as in previous centuries, independent artisans worked in sequence from the preparation of parchment to writing, decoration and illumination and, finally, binding. Documents for 15th-century Florence, Rouen and Paris show that the artisans involved in manuscript production generally occupied neighbouring ateliers; this arrangement must have made placing orders and serial production an expedient process. The planning and sometimes the financing of the entire expensive process was often undertaken by the bookseller (*librarius*), who was often the scribe and not infrequently also author or translator and even the binder. In such a thriving centre as Florence, VESPASIANO DA BISTICCI, supported by the book-collecting Medici family and responding to humanist scholarship, is by far the best-known bookseller. Enterprising Italian manuscript booksellers also provided the marketing substructure for the production of printed books (*see* BOOK ILLUSTRATION, §I, 2). Scribes and booksellers in the Netherlands, especially in the neighbouring cities of Ghent and Bruges, undertook large-scale projects of illuminated manuscripts for the dukes of Burgundy, and there was also a lively export market. Two bookseller–scribes, Jean Wanquelin of Mons (*d* 1453) and Nicolaas Spierinck of Ghent (*d* 1499), exemplify the complexities of such endeavours. Paris, as a capital city responsive to a university, a king and a growing merchant class, had for centuries supported a thriving book trade. Elsewhere in France, production was not always as centralized.

The sheer quantity of late 15th-century manuscript Books of Hours from such centres as Paris, Rouen and

7. *Author Writing and Presenting his Book to King Francis I,* 252×174 mm; frontispiece miniature from Guillaume Budé: *Institution d'un prince, c.*1518–19 (Paris, Bibliothèque de l'Arsenal, MS. 5103, fol. 1*v*)

Bruges reveals a degree of 'industrial' production and a wide-ranging export business. The traditional use by illuminators of patterns and models allowed replication and speed, as well as uniformity. Leaves of text were sent to outside illuminators, who might also supply single-leaf miniatures for a bookseller's stock. Illuminators might also be involved in decorating printed books (e.g. *see* VENICE, §III, 1). Changing patterns of collaboration and book format in the 16th century suggest that manuscript artisans became itinerant, moving around when important, but increasingly rare, projects presented themselves.

Manuscripts were ordered and paid for in numerous and sometimes indirect ways, especially in the case of ducal and royal commissions. Court officials knowledgeable about books could serve as intermediaries with booksellers, or even deal directly with the independent artisans. The stages of work in large, elaborate commissions were often directly supervised and paid through the intermediary of an author who was neither bookseller nor scribe, as in the case of Jean Thenaud for the French king Francis I in 1536. Following on from the activity of Jean Fouquet and in response to French court patronage, the area around Tours remained a magnet for luxury illuminated manuscript production well into the 16th century,

notably in the work of Jean Bourdichon. In Italy aristocratic patrons such as the Este rulers in Ferrara, the Gonzaga in Mantua, the Sforza in Milan, the Aragonese kings of Naples and the popes in Rome attracted book artists and painters.

Trade in manuscripts prospered with the increasing ease of communication in Europe, through which bankers, diplomats, high-ranking clerics and nobles travelled and exchanged gifts. Manuscripts continued to be moved great distances as the result of inheritance; whole libraries were seized as war booty. Individually commissioned, decorated manuscripts of popular stories, prayerbooks and presentation volumes of new texts, for example the tract for the education of Francis I presented by the humanist Guillaume Budé (1468–1540; see fig. 7), continued to be sought after well into the 16th century. Such manuscripts retained their powers of political persuasion and aesthetic seduction far beyond their ostensible textual contents or market value.

The expansion of printing throughout Europe in the 1470s rechannelled the demand for books, and the new technology satisfied new expectations. While handwritten copies of intellectually utilitarian texts all but disappeared from everywhere except court circles, luxury decorated manuscripts survived for almost a century, coexisting with the parallel development of printing production.

BIBLIOGRAPHY

J. Pichon and G. Vicaire: *Documents pour servir à l'histoire des libraires de Paris, 1486–1600* (Paris, 1895), pp. 225–38
C. Bühler: *The Fifteenth-century Book: The Scribes, the Printers, the Decorators* (Philadelphia, 1960)
A. De Schryver: 'Nicolas Spierinck, calligraphe et enlumineur des Ordonnances des états de l'hôtel de Charles le Téméraire', *Scriptorium*, xxiii (1969), pp. 434–58
H. Lehmann-Haupt, ed.: *The Göttingen Model Book* (Columbia, 1972)
J. Farquhar: *Creation and Imitation: The Work of a Fifteenth-century Manuscript Illuminator* (Fort Lauderdale, 1976), pp. 41–3, 61–74
B. Gagnebin: 'L'Enluminure de Charlemagne à François I', *Genava*, n. s., xxiv (1976), pp. 5–200
J. Farquhar and S. Hindman: *Pen to Press: Illuminated Manuscripts and Printed Books in the First Century of Printing* (Baltimore, 1977)
L. Armstrong: *Renaissance Miniature Painters and Classical Imagery: The Master of the Putti and his Venetian Workshop* (London, 1981), pp. 1–6
P. Saenger: 'Silent Reading: Its Impact on Late Medieval Script and Society', *Viator*, xiii (1982), pp. 367–414
N. Davis: 'Beyond the Market: Books as Gifts in Sixteenth-century France', *Trans. Royal Hist. Soc.*, xxxiii (1983), pp. 69–88
E. König: 'The Influence of the Invention of Printing on the Development of German Illumination', *Manuscripts in the Fifty Years after the Invention of Printing*, ed. J. Trapp (London, 1983), pp. 85–94
H.-J. Martin: 'La Révolution de l'imprimé', *Le Livre conquérant* (1983), i of *Histoire de l'édition française*, ed. H.-J. Martin and R. Chartier (Paris, 1983–), pp. 145–61
A. Van Buren: 'Jean Wauquelin de Mons et la production du livre aux Pays-Bas', *Publn Cent. Eur. Etud. Burgondomédianes*, xxiii (1983), pp. 53–74
C. Bozzolo, D. Coq and E. Ornato: 'La Production du livre en quelques pays d'Europe occidentale aux XIV et XV siècles', *Scr. & Civiltà*, viii (1984), pp. 129–60
R. Watson: *The Playfair Hours: A Late Fifteenth Century Illuminated Manuscript from Rouen* (London, 1984), pp. 31–4
A. de la Mare: 'New Research on Humanistic Scribes in Florence', *Miniatura fiorentina del rinascimento, 1440–1525: Un primo censimento*, ed. A. Garzelli, i (Florence, 1985), pp. 395–600
A. Guidotti: 'Indagini su botteghe di cartolai e miniatori a Firenze nel xv secolo', *La miniatura italiana tra gotico e rinascimento. Atti del II congresso di storia della miniatura italiana: Cortona, 1982*, ii (Florence, 1985), pp. 473–507
D. Muzerelle: *Vocabulaire codicologique: Répertoire méthodique des termes français relatifs aux manuscrits* (Paris, 1985), figs 17–63, 283–325

C. de Hamel: *A History of Illuminated Manuscripts* (Boston, 1986), p. 183

M. Rouse and R. Rouse: *Cartolai, Illuminators, and Printers in Fifteenth-century Italy: The Evidence of the Ripoli Press* (Los Angeles, 1988), pp. 17–19, 49–68

J. Lemaire: *Introduction à la codicologie* (Louvain-la-Neuve, 1989), pp. 203–5

F. Avril and N. Reynaud: *Les Manuscrits à peintures en France, 1440–1520* (Paris, 1993)

MYRA D. ORTH

3. MODERN. The notion of the modern manuscript is contradictory, since the values that underlie it are fundamentally different from those applicable to manuscripts made before the advent of printing: the unique nature of a manuscript is incompatible with the multiple production of the printed book. Once printing had satisfied the needs of readers, the production of handwritten, decorated and even illustrated books would appear to be contrary to progress. Yet the links between the page and its decoration, the word and the image, have long commanded the attention of artists, and the handmade book retains its place as a work of art. In the modern period the term 'manuscript' is rarely used in its strict sense to denote a handwritten book.

From the start printed books co-existed with manuscripts (*see* §2 above). Indeed initially they were often designed to imitate them. Until the mid-16th century the tradition of the illuminated manuscript persisted, changed only in that sections of the book might now be printed (*see* BOOK ILLUSTRATION, §I): the main text, the decorative borders, or even a woodblock printed illustration illuminated by hand using gold and colours. In the following centuries the art of manuscript illumination based on medieval techniques fell into disuse. Fine book design concentrated on the production of printed texts, with decoration based chiefly on the elaborate TITLE-PAGE. Although artists might design the illustration for a book, few artists were concerned with the making of the book as a whole. An exception was WILLIAM BLAKE who, as both writer and artist, designed, wrote and illustrated a number of texts, both his own (*Songs of Innocence*, 1789) and others' (e.g. the *Poems of Mr Gray*, 1797, to a commission by John Flaxman). The latter, an amalgam of words and pictures on the page, using pale washes of watercolour to integrate the imagery with the text, draws little from the medieval tradition. Furthermore, it was designed with a printed version to follow, as was so often the case.

The 19th-century revival of interest in the illuminated manuscripts was fuelled by both an interest in medievalism (by such figures as George Gilbert Scott I, A. W. N. Pugin and John Ruskin among others) and the mid-century religious revival epitomized by the Oxford movement, by which there was a return to ritual and the Roman tradition. Long-hidden medieval manuscripts were rediscovered and appreciated primarily as works of art, redolent of medieval values of craftsmanship. In the 1880s and 1890s the market for medieval manuscripts flourished, while a parallel market for single illuminated leaves was an indication that the interest centred on design rather than the original purpose of the book. Books were written about medieval methods of illuminating, the history of illumination and the grammar of ornament as a guide to both the modern designer and the amateur illuminator.

8. Manuscript written and decorated by William Morris: *A Book of Verse*, 279×203 mm, 1870 (London, Victoria and Albert Museum, MS. L. 131–1953, p. 11)

William Morris consulted and copied manuscripts in the British Museum, London, and the Bodleian Library, Oxford, developing his ideas about ornament and book design; he also built up his own very fine collection of medieval manuscripts from *c.* 1880 until his death. During the 1870s he wrote and illuminated a number of manuscripts, including his own *A Book of Verse* (see fig. 8) and a number of copies of Edward Fitzgerald's *Rubaiyat of Omar Khayyam*, richly decorated in gold and colours and using the complex foliate patterning that was later to appear in designs for other media. His biggest manuscript project was to be the writing and illumination of Virgil's *Aeneid*, which was conceived and developed in 1874–5 with Edward Burne-Jones, but was abandoned. In this and other calligraphic works Morris developed his aesthetic ideals of book design, expressed in his published lecture on *The Ideal Book*.

It is in the fine press books of the latter part of the 19th century and the 20th (e.g. Kelmscott, Doves, Ashendene, Vollard and Kahnweiler and still continued in the work of such presses as Kaldeway Press) that the traditional elements of design—the quality of the material and the relationship between text, decoration and illustration—continue to be emphasized (*see* BOOK ILLUSTRATION, §V). The artists' books (*see* LIVRE D'ARTISTE) of the 20th century show no more concern than Morris with the means of creation, although the concept of creation remained all-important. In the work of such artists as Pablo Picasso (in his publications for Ambroise Vollard), of Filippo Tommaso Marinetti in stating the Futurist's vision, of the formulators of Dada such as Max Ernst and André Breton, or the 'book-works' of contemporary artists, books are no longer illustrated texts, but exploit the juxtaposition of images and words as a means of expression, using a variety of media. The overriding concern of such modern works is for originality of artistic expression.

BIBLIOGRAPHY

H. N. Humphreys: *Illuminated Books of the Middle Ages (Printed in Colours by Owen Jones)* (London, 1844–99)
O. Jones: *Grammar of Ornament* (London, 1856)
D. Diringer: *The Hand-produced Book* (London and New York, 1953)
E. M. Garvey, ed.: *The Artist and the Book, 1860–1960, in Western Europe and the United States* (Boston, 1961)
P. Needham, ed.: *William Morris and the Art of the Book* (New York, 1976)
W. Morris: *The Ideal Book: Essays and Lectures on the Arts of the Book*, ed. W. S. Peterson (Berkeley, 1982)
C. Hogben: *From Manet to Hockney: Modern Artists' Illustrated Books* (London, 1985)
J. Lyons, ed.: *Artists' Books: A Critical Anthology and Sourcebook* (Rochester, NY, 1985)

CLAIRE DONOVAN

III. Illumination.

Strictly, the embellishment of a manuscript using burnished gold, the term is more usually and widely applied to denote all types of manuscript decoration or illustration, whether or not this involves the use of gold.

1. Introduction. 2. Survey. 3. Materials and techniques. 4. Conservation.

1. INTRODUCTION. Handwritten texts have been ornamented and illustrated from the earliest times and in diverse parts of the world. In the East, in Arabia, Persia, Turkey, India, China, Japan and South-east Asia, there was a long tradition, paralleling that in the West, but more enduring, lasting even into the 19th century in some regions. In Central America the few surviving Maya and Aztec illustrated texts of the 14th to 16th centuries are evidence of their interest and skill in this form of painting. This article focuses on the Western tradition; for the discussion of decorated and illustrated manuscripts in other traditions see under the relevant geographical or cultural heading.

The tradition in the West is represented by a rich heritage, beginning with the books and papyri of the ancient and Classical Mediterranean (*see* EGYPT, ANCIENT, §X, 4; PAPYRUS; and ROLL) and continuing unbroken from the 6th to the 15th centuries in Christian medieval Europe up to the final flowering during the Renaissance (*see* §2 below), at the same time extending into such areas as the Byzantine (*see* EARLY CHRISTIAN AND BYZANTINE ART, §V) and Jewish (*see* JEWISH ART, §V, 2) worlds. The regions most active in the production of illuminated manuscripts were Austria, England, France, Germany, Italy, the southern Netherlands, Spain and the Byzantine centres in Greece, Asia Minor, Armenia and Georgia. Less consistently active, but important during certain periods, were Syria, Coptic Egypt and Ethiopia, Ireland, the northern Netherlands, the regions around the River Meuse,

Scandinavia and the Slav lands of Bohemia, Bulgaria, Croatia, Russia and Serbia. For further discussion see under the relevant geographical heading.

The earliest Western examples of illustrated texts are fragmentary Egyptian papyri of the 20th century BC (e.g. *see* BOOK, fig. 5) and the Books of the Dead, which have small drawn or painted vignettes set within the columns of text (*see* EGYPT, ANCIENT, figs 75 and 76). Greek papyrus fragments with a similar format of illustration, from the 2nd century BC, have been excavated in Egypt. Survivals from the Roman period are scarce, and those from before the 5th century AD consist almost entirely of papyrus fragments from Egypt. It is not until the 4th century AD that the numbers of surviving manuscript books on parchment gradually increase. From the 8th century on in Europe and the Byzantine world, large quantities of illuminated books are extant, reaching a peak in the first half of the 15th century. The great European tradition of manuscript illumination slowly came to an end in the first half of the 16th century as the printed book supplanted the handwritten one (*see* PRINTING). The only successful, if short-lived, modern revival was that of the ARTS AND CRAFTS MOVEMENT in the 19th century (*see also* §II, 3 above). For discussion and illustration of the stylistic development of illuminated manuscripts *see* EARLY CHRISTIAN AND BYZANTINE ART, §V, 2; INSULAR ART, §3; CAROLINGIAN ART, §IV, 3; ANGLO-SAXON ART, §IV, 2; OTTONIAN ART, §IV, 2; ROMANESQUE, §IV, 2; and GOTHIC, §IV.

For certain periods and regions our knowledge of painting is derived almost entirely from illuminated manuscripts. Thousands of medieval examples survive, many having hundreds of pages with decoration and illustration. These far exceed the number of surviving examples of painting on walls, panels, canvas and in stained glass. Thus manuscripts provide vital and abundant material for the study of stylistic developments in painting and for the study of religious and secular iconography. Preserved in the closed pages of books, protected from the effects of wear and damage over the centuries, most manuscript painting has a freshness of colour that is hardly diminished.

BIBLIOGRAPHY

Dict. Middle Ages: 'Manuscript Illumination'; *EWA*: 'Miniatures and Illumination'; *LM*: 'Buchmalerei'; *RDK*: 'Buchmalerei'
J. A. Herbert: *Illuminated Manuscripts* (London, 1911/*R* Bath, 1972)
A. Boeckler: *Abendländische Miniaturen bis zum Ausgang der romanischen Zeit* (Leipzig, 1930)
K. Weitzmann: *Ancient Book Illumination* (Cambridge, MA, 1959)
D. Formaggio and C. Basso: *La miniatura* (Novara, 1960)
S. Mitchell: *Medieval Manuscript Painting* (London, 1965)
D. Diringer: *The Illuminated Book* (London, 1967)
P. d'Ancona and E. Aeschlimann: *The Art of Illumination* (London, 1969)
B. Narkiss: *Hebrew Illuminated Manuscripts* (New York, 1969)
K. Weitzmann: *Illustrations in Roll and Codex* (Princeton, 1970)
L. Donati: *Bibliografia della miniatura* (Florence, 1972)
H. D. L. Vervliet, ed.: *The Book through Five Thousand Years* (London, 1972)
D. M. Robb: *The Art of the Illuminated Manuscript* (London, 1973)
F. Unterkircher: *Die Buchmalerei: Entwicklung, Technik, Eigenart* (Vienna, 1974)
O. Mazal: *Buchkunst der Gotik* (Vienna, 1975)
H. Zotter: *Bibliographie faksimilierte Handschriften* (Graz, 1976)
J. Gutmann: *Hebrew Manuscript Painting* (New York, 1978)
O. Mazal: *Buchkunst der Romanik* (Vienna, 1978)
J. Backhouse: *The Illuminated Manuscript* (Oxford, 1979)

D. Diringer: *The Book before Printing: Ancient, Medieval and Oriental* (New York, 1982)

R. G. Calkins: *Illuminated Books of the Middle Ages* (London and New York, 1983)

C. de Hamel: *A History of Illuminated Manuscripts* (Oxford, 1986, rev. 1994)

O. Pächt: *Book Illumination in the Middle Ages* (Oxford, 1986/R 1994)

2. SURVEY. The illumination of a manuscript serves a variety of purposes. It may be purely decorative or else illustrative (and often both), rendering the appearance of a text more attractive or communicating in visual form its narrative or ideas. It may also function to emphasize important sections or divisions of a text. The history of the forms of manuscript illumination is thus inevitably linked to the history of the texts that were required to be illustrated, and the needs and tastes of the readers of those texts. For some books it was necessary to mark the beginnings of significant texts. For others, pictorial illustration was required to assist the text description: for example diagrams in scientific works or illustrations of plants, animals and birds in works on natural history. In some cases lavish decorative borders and frontispieces, purple-dyed parchment with writing in gold, and rich displays of heraldic devices were used to signify the wealth of the owner. For books used in the liturgy, such as Gospel books or Missals, richness of decoration and illustration signified an offering worthy of God; many of these would be used only a few times a year on the greatest feast days

of the Church. The study of the ways in which books were decorated must be placed, therefore, within the context of their patronage and use.

(i) Forms of illumination. (ii) Types of illustrated text.

(i) Forms of illumination. Various formats were used for the decoration and illustration of a text, using one or a combination of several elements: miniatures, decorated or historiated initials, line-endings and borders (see fig. 9). These were integrated with the text into a total system of ornamentation. In different periods and regions more or less emphasis was placed on these elements of the decoration; their position in relation to the text block also changed as styles developed. A scribe might either impose certain constraints on the format of the decoration or collaborate closely with the artist to coordinate its design with that of the text. In such cases a choice would be made between single, double or triple columns of text. If the illustrations were to be inserted within the text, the scribe would leave appropriate spaces, or, in the case of historiated or decorative initials, he would indent the text. If heavy, decorative borders were intended as a frame for the text, the size of the text block was reduced accordingly.

(a) Miniatures. Miniatures occur in a variety of formats (*see* MINIATURE, §I): they may be full-page or smaller, or divided into such units as squares or medallions. Miniatures, framed or unframed, may stand independently

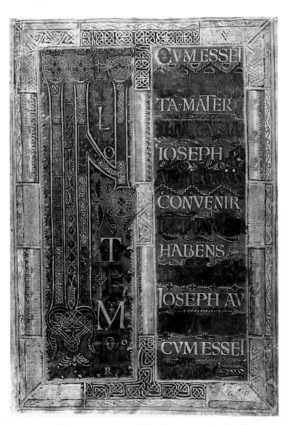

9. Opening from the Godescalc Evangeliary, showing a miniature of the *Fountain of Life* and a decorated initial from a reading for Christmas Eve and borders, *c.* 781–3 (Paris, Bibliothèque Nationale, MS. nouv. acq. lat. 1203, fols 3*v*–4*r*)

without text, or be set at the head of or within the text block, or even outside the text, in the margins. They might act as single illustrations, for instance donor or AUTHOR PORTRAITS, or be part of a series of illustrations, forming a narrative cycle. In their relation to the text, miniatures of later periods tended to become less integrated with the text and more like independent paintings; this development was often emphasized by *trompe l'oeil* effects.

(b) Initials. Emphasis of the first letter or section of a text through size, colour or decoration occurred in books of the Late Antique period and may have begun even earlier (for further discussion *see* INITIAL, MANUSCRIPT). In 4th- and 5th-century manuscripts these initials were taller than the rest of the text. In 6th-century Italian, French, Spanish and early Byzantine manuscripts the first enlarged letter was often placed in the margin of the text block, extending above and below the line. The stems of these early decorative initials were often filled with ornamental patterns. Probably beginning in Ireland, also in the 6th century, the letters after the initial of the first word were progressively diminished in size until they reached that of the normal script. A further development was to diminish the size of the letters over several words, or line by line, at the beginning of the text (for illustration *see* LINDISFARNE GOSPELS). This method of treating the initial had a lasting influence on European illumination, particularly in Carolingian manuscripts.

In Insular manuscripts decorative initials were usually filled and surrounded by patterns of abstract and animal ornament (*see* INITIAL, MANUSCRIPT, fig. 1). Interlace patterns continued to be used in Carolingian (*see* CAROLINGIAN ART, fig. 9) and Ottonian illumination, replacing the geometric and vegetal patterns, occasionally combined with fish and birds, used in 6th- and 7th-century Italian and Merovingian manuscripts; in a few cases, from the 7th century on, heads or figures were placed within the initials. In Continental manuscripts, and occasionally in Insular manuscripts, animals, fish, birds and human figures were used to form the stems of the initials, a practice continued in early Carolingian examples and endlessly exploited in later centuries. In Romanesque works the initial was often formed of human figures, dragons, lions and other animals and birds, and filled with ornamental foliage that was inhabited by creatures usually engaged in combat (*see* INITIAL, MANUSCRIPT, fig. 2 and ROMANESQUE, fig. 61).

Historiated initials, containing narrative subjects, were first extensively developed in Carolingian art (for illustration *see* GOSPEL BOOK) but continued to be used alongside decorative initials in the Romanesque period (*see* INITIAL, MANUSCRIPT, fig. 3), becoming the main form for Gothic initials. In these, the repertory of fantastic dragons, hybrids and combat scenes continued to be used in the stems of historiated initials and in the surrounding borders; ornamental foliage served to decorate lesser initials. The early medieval tradition of interlace ornament and entwined foliage stems was revived in 15th-century Italian humanist manuscripts.

(c) Borders. The text block, miniatures and initials were sometimes provided with borders or frames, although in some manuscripts the plain parchment border might form a frame to the text block, or the text itself might frame the illustrations (for further discussion *see* BORDER, MANUSCRIPT). Plain or ornamented frames were traditionally used in Classical art, often incorporating architectural structures (e.g. columns, capitals, bases, entablatures and pediments). Such framing devices were adopted in Late Antique manuscripts, although the only text to be framed was that on the title-page. Title-pages and incipit pages continued to include ornamental and architectural frames in 7th-century Merovingian manuscripts, a tradition that developed into the framed text pages found in a few 8th-century books (*see* TITLE-PAGE, fig. 1). The architectural frame of late antiquity continued to be influential, often forming the upper part of frames in Carolingian, Anglo-Saxon, Ottonian and Romanesque manuscript painting. The development of this type is most clearly seen in the Evangelist portraits of Gospel books produced between *c.* 700 and *c.* 1200. Ornamental frames were used for the decorative carpet pages of Insular manuscripts. These became rich and heavy in Carolingian manuscripts of the Court school in the late 8th century, appearing not only on the incipit pages but sometimes on every text page. Such elaborate frames, often surrounding a single full-page initial, are also characteristic of Anglo-Saxon (*see* ANGLO-SAXON ART, fig. 9) and Ottonian illumination of the 10th and 11th centuries, and in certain parts of Europe continued to be used for this purpose into the 12th century.

The development of frames in Byzantine manuscripts shows less variation. The plain bar frame, occasionally containing foliate ornament and sometimes ornamented at the corners, was the favoured system in most Byzantine books, although architectural arcades were used for framing canon tables in Gospel books (*see* §(ii)(a) below). Characteristic of Byzantine manuscripts are the large ornamental headpieces placed above the beginning of a text or in the Canon Tables of Gospel books, and containing foliage and birds (for further discussion *see* EARLY CHRISTIAN AND BYZANTINE ART, §V, 2(ii)(f) and figs 60 and 62).

In the Gothic period, from the mid-13th century, the main interest in framing was to provide elaborate borders for the text rather than for the illustrations. During the 13th century, beginning in England, France and Italy (particularly Bologna), the stems of the initials were extended into the border by means of various decorative devices (*see* BORDER, MANUSCRIPT, fig. 1): pen flourishes in coloured inks and foliate and dragon forms. These extensions, forming bars, might link up several initials on a page, eventually forming a continuous border around part of the page. At the same time free-standing figural scenes, animals, birds and fantastic forms were placed at the foot of the text in the border (*see* BAS-DE-PAGE); by the end of the 13th century border bars became the stage for these *bas-de-page* scenes. Simultaneously, borders were extended to frame all four sides of the text at the major divisions of the book, and were composed of figures, fantastic hybrids, animals, birds and ornamental foliage on a bar base (*see* GOTHIC, fig. 74). This type of border was fully developed during the first half of the 14th century (*see* BORDER, MANUSCRIPT, fig. 2).

PLATE I

Manuscript

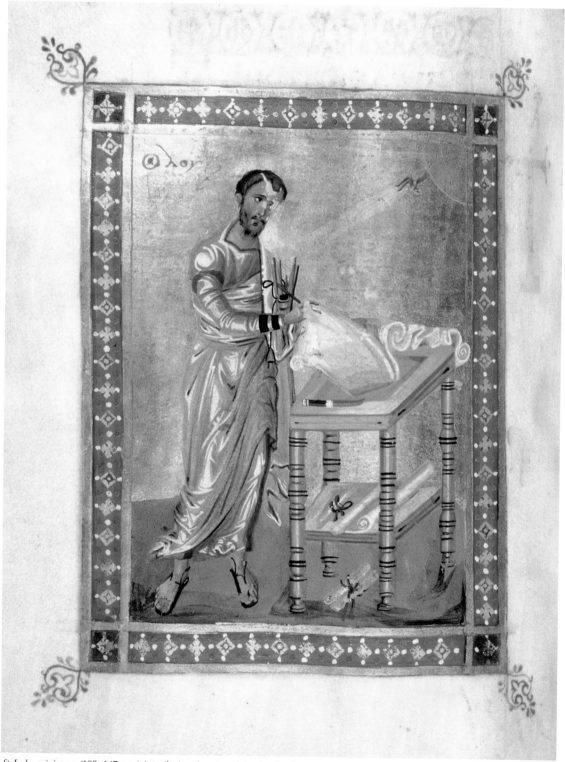

St Luke, miniature (189×147 mm) introducing the *Acts of the Apostles*, from a New Testament manuscript, Byzantine, mid-10th century (London, British Library, Add. MS. 28815, fol. 162)

Illustration to Psalm 13, coloured line drawing from the Harley Psalter, 380×310 mm, from Christ Church, Canterbury, *c.* 1010–20 (London, British Library, MS. 603, fol. 7*v*)

PLATE III

Manuscript

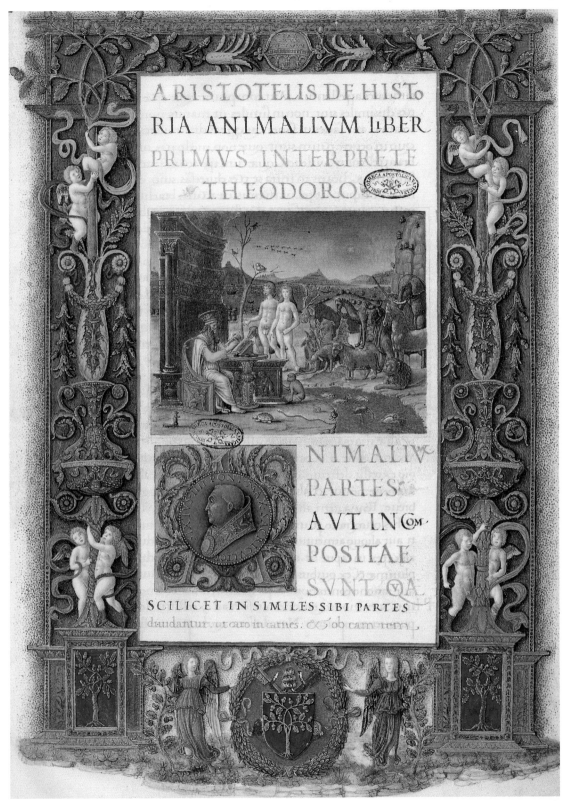

Gasparo Padovano (attrib.): *Aristotle Seated*, frontispiece (367×257 mm) from Aristotle: *Historia animalium: De partibus animalium*, translated by Teodoro Gaza, written by Bartolomeo Sanvito, from Rome, *c.* 1473/4–80 (Rome, Vatican, Biblioteca Apostolica, MS. Vat. lat. 2094, fol. 8*r*)

Boucicaut Master: *Pentecost*, miniature from the Boucicaut Hours, 274×190 mm, from Paris, after 1401 (Paris, Musée Jacquemart-André, MS. 2, fol. 112*v*)

PLATE V

Manuscript

1. Master of the Leaping Figures: *Calling of Jeremiah*, historiated initial (133×133 mm) from the Winchester Bible, 583×396 mm, from St Swithun's Cathedral Priory, Winchester, *c.* 1160 (Winchester Cathedral Library, vol. ii, fol. 148*r*)

2. *Miracle of the Loaves and Fishes*, miniature (235×175 mm) from the Codex Escorial, Echternach school, 1043–6 (Madrid, Escorial, Biblioteca Monasterio S Lorenzo, Cod. Vit. 17, fol. 38)

Bihzad (attrib.): *Caliph Ma'mun Visits a Turkish Bath*, miniature from Nizami: *Khamsa* ('Five poems'), 180×155 mm, from Herat, Afghanistan, 1494–5 (London, British Library, Or. MS. 6810, fol. 27*v*)

PLATE VII   Marquetry

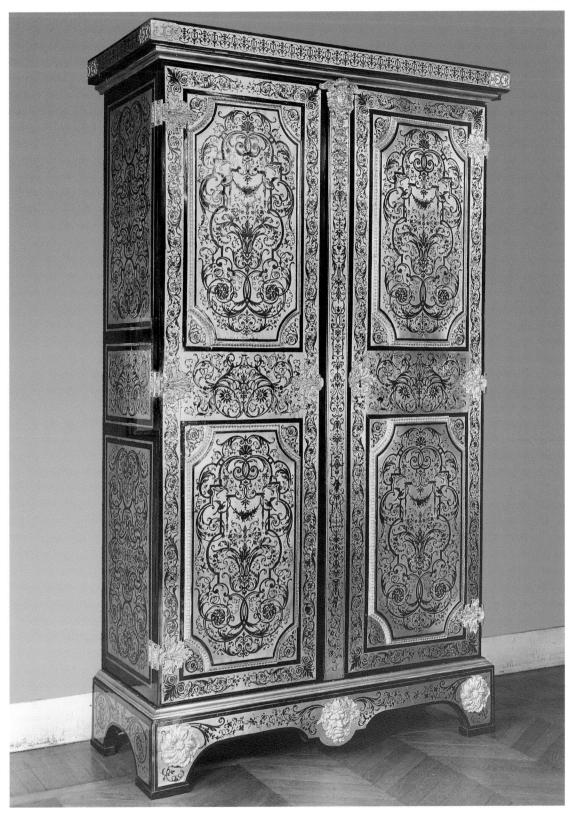

Marquetry armoire attributed to André-Charles Boulle, wood, copper and shell with bronze trimmings, 1.49×2.71×0.61 m, from Paris, *c.* 1680–90 (Paris, Musée des Arts Décoratifs)

1. Marquetry piano, dyed and natural woods, engraved ivory, mother-of-pearl and abalone, l. 2.47 m, made by Erard and Co., London, with marquetry by George Henry Blake, *c.* 1840 (New York, Metropolitan Museum of Art)

2. Marquetry cabinet, wood with bone pegs, 635×457 mm, from India, probably Goa, late 17th century (London, Victoria and Albert Museum)

3. Marquetry writing-desk, wood, ivory and pigment with bronze trimmings, 202×440×283 mm, from southern Spain, Nasrid period, 14th century (Madrid, Museo Arqueológico Nacional)

In the second half of the 14th century borders developed into distinct regional types. In France ornamental foliage was used for wide, lace-like borders, which continued into the 15th century, framing miniatures, as well as the text. In England the grotesque type of border also gave way to foliage forms, but with heavier leaves and sprays than in France. By the end of the 14th century the acanthus foliage used by Italian illuminators was taken up in France and England and continued to be used extensively during the 15th century, thereby introducing more colour and heavier forms into borders. In Italy figure, bird and animal elements continued to be used in border decoration in the second half of the 14th century and the early 15th, particularly in Lombardy. In France, England and the southern Netherlands variations on the types evolved by *c.* 1400 characterize 15th-century borders. In the third quarter of the 15th century Netherlandish illuminators introduced a *trompe l'oeil* type of border, also adopted in England and France, in which flowers, insects and domestic utensils were painted on to a broad border, giving the illusion that real objects had been placed on the page (*see* BOOK OF HOURS, fig. 1; and BORDER, MANUSCRIPT, fig. 3). In Italy *c.* 1450 borders in early humanistic manuscripts were composed of solidly framed panels with white interlace and intertwining foliage ornament or acanthus, derived from antique sources. These became richer during the 15th century, with bright colours and a range of

10. Psalms 147–50 and canticle (*Confitebor tibi*); from a Psalter illustrated with historiated initials and line-endings, from ?Paris, *c.* 1280 (Cambridge, University Library, MS. Ee. iv. 24, fol. 35*v*)

Classical motifs such as cameo heads, putti, grotesques *all'antica* and various foliage forms (see colour pl. III).

(d) Line-endings. Another form of decoration was the line-ending, used to fill lines not completely filled by the text. In some Insular manuscripts decorative ornament or animals were occasionally placed in these spaces. In the 12th century scribes increasingly filled them with simple, decorative, penwork flourishes. By *c.* 1200 illuminators started to paint ornament, animal and bird forms at the end of all those lines not filled with text, which helped to balance the text area with the painted illumination of the initial. During the 13th century line-endings became more elaborate (see fig. 10), and in the 14th century, with the development of grotesques, they became integrated with the similar repertory of the border motifs (*see* GOTHIC, fig. 80).

BIBLIOGRAPHY
A. Schardt: *Das Initial* (Berlin, 1938)
E. A. Van Moé: *Illuminated Initials in Medieval Manuscripts* (London, 1950)
J. Gutbrod: *Die Initiale in Handschriften des achten bis dreizehnten Jahrhunderts* (Stuttgart, 1965)
L. M. C. Randall: *Images in the Margins of Gothic Manuscripts* (Berkeley, 1966)
D. Debes: 'Das Figurenalphabet', *Beitr. Gesch. Bwsn*, iii (1968), pp. 7–134
C. Nordenfalk: *Die spätantiken Zierbuchstaben* (Stockholm, 1970)
J. J. G. Alexander: *The Decorated Letter* (London, 1978)
For further bibliography see §1 above.

(ii) Types of illustrated text. The history of manuscript illumination is part of the history of manuscript production and its patronage (*see* §II above). Illuminated books were considered luxury books compared with those without decoration. The degree of luxury varied considerably, and by the late medieval period certain texts, above all Books of Hours, were produced in exceedingly rich editions by artists of great talent, as well as in simpler versions by mediocre painters.

See also ROMANESQUE, §IV, 2(iii); and GOTHIC, §IV, 2(i).

(a) Liturgical and devotional. The Christian Church required illuminated books both for the liturgy (of the Mass and of the Divine Office) and for private devotion. The liturgical book that was most extensively and richly decorated in the early medieval period was the GOSPEL BOOK, which was used in the ceremony of the Mass; produced in luxury editions in both the Latin West and the Byzantine East, it is perhaps the most impressive of all medieval books. Its illustration centred on full-page portraits of the Four Evangelists as authors, preceding each of their Gospels (*see* AUTHOR PORTRAIT; and EARLY CHRISTIAN AND BYZANTINE ART, fig. 57). From the 7th century, beginning in Insular manuscripts, a large decorative initial introducing the text of the Gospel was painted on the facing page (*see* LINDISFARNE GOSPELS). The same format for the Evangelist portrait occurs in Byzantine art, but with a much smaller initial and usually a headpiece (*see* EARLY CHRISTIAN AND BYZANTINE ART, §V, 2(ii)(b) and fig. 60). An area for ornamental illumination was the concordance of Gospel text passages, compiled by Eusebios of Caesarea, and known as the CANON TABLE: arches, pediments and tympana supported on columns with capitals were used to frame these tables. In the Anglo-Saxon, Carolingian and Ottonian periods these luxury

11. *Ascension*; miniature from the Breviary of Jean sans Peur, from Paris, *c.* 1415 (London, British Library, Harley MS. 2897, fol. 188*v*)

Gospel books continued to be produced (*see* CAROLIN-GIAN ART, fig. 7; and OTTONIAN ART, figs 4 and 6), sometimes in even more elaborate versions, with full-page miniatures of narrative scenes from the life of Christ. By the Romanesque period luxury Gospel books became rarer, and from the 13th century on their production ceased almost entirely. In the Gothic period, although a few illuminated Evangeliaries (Gospel Lectionaries) were produced, Missals, containing the Gospel passages read at Mass, were used instead (see below).

Other early medieval liturgical books with rich decoration include the Sacramentary (*see* ANGLO-SAXON ART, fig. 11; and MISSAL, fig. 1), the Benedictional (*see* ANGLO-SAXON ART, fig. 9) and the Pontifical (for further discussion and illustration *see* SERVICE BOOK). From the 13th century the most splendidly embellished liturgical books were the MISSAL and the BREVIARY (see fig. 11), and their companion books containing the music for the Mass and the Divine Office, the Gradual and the Antiphonal (*see* CHOIR-BOOK and fig. 2). Luxury Pontificals continued to be produced, above all in 14th- and 15th-century France. Sometimes forming part of the Pontifical, but often a

separate book, the ritual of the coronation of kings and queens survives in several de luxe copies from late medieval England and France.

The Bible, either complete or in volumes with the text of one or more of the biblical books, was illustrated perhaps as early as the 3rd century AD. The narrative illustration of the Old Testament was often extensive, with numerous pictures. For example, the Byzantine Octateuchs (11th–13th centuries), containing the first eight books of the Old Testament, were illustrated with several hundred framed, narrative miniatures scattered throughout the text; Byzantine manuscripts of the book of Job are equally fully illustrated (*see* EARLY CHRISTIAN AND BYZANTINE ART, §V, 2(ii)(c)). Whether or not the New Testament was provided with such profuse illustration has been debated. By the 10th century, in Byzantine and Ottonian manuscripts (see colour pl. I), New Testament illustrative cycles were extensive, and it has been argued (although not unanimously agreed) that these may have been based on 4th- or 5th-century prototypes. Similarly, it is unclear whether the illustration of Carolingian and Byzantine Psalters of the 8th to 10th centuries was derived from Early Christian cycles. Although the illustration of every psalm was rare (*see* UTRECHT PSALTER), decorated or historiated initials usually marked the major liturgical divisions of the text (for further discussion and illustration *see* PSALTER). Byzantine Psalters were illustrated either with full-page miniatures of the Life of King David (for illustration *see* PARIS PSALTER), or with literal illustrations in the margins (for illustration *see* CHLUDOV PSALTER). Psalters were subsequently produced in enormous numbers, and from the 12th century, when they were used for private devotion, they became even more profusely decorated (e.g. *see* ROMANESQUE, fig. 70; and QUEEN MARY PSALTER). During the 13th century Books of Hours began to take over this role, becoming the most important and abundantly illustrated of lay devotional books in the later medieval period (for further discussion and illustration *see* BOOK OF HOURS, §2).

Complete Bibles of large format were produced in the Carolingian period; these combined full-page, framed frontispieces (*see* CAROLINGIAN ART, fig. 8) with figural scenes to some of the biblical books. In Spain in the 10th and 11th centuries such Bibles were also produced, but usually with coloured drawings for the frontispieces and less luxurious ornamentation than in the Carolingian examples. In the 12th century throughout Europe, but particularly in Austria, England, France, Germany, Italy and the Mosan region, the Bible replaced the Gospel book as the large-scale de luxe illuminated text. Most Bibles of this kind were made for the Benedictines, Cistercians and for the Augustinian and Premonstratensian canons. They were very large in format with figural frontispieces (e.g. *see* ROMANESQUE, figs 59, 64 and 65) or large historiated initials at the beginning of the books (for illustration *see* WINCHESTER BIBLE). In the 13th century Bibles became smaller, and their illustration was mostly restricted to small-scale historiated initials (for further discussion and illustration *see* BIBLE, §II, 1). From the 13th century picture Bibles became more popular, while from the 14th century in France illustrated versions of the vernacular

French paraphrase of the Bible, the *Bible historiale*, were developed (*see* BIBLE, §I, 3(iii)).

Another biblical book with a tradition of illustration from the Carolingian period was the Apocalypse. Essentially a picture book, it was usually provided with an accompanying theological commentary, which may have been didactic in purpose. Two commentaries, the late 8th-century Spanish one of Beatus of Liébana (*d c.* 798), and that (*c.* 1100) of Berengaudus, were the most popular. The illustrations to these are usually framed, occasionally full-page, but most often set within the text or at the head of the page (*see* APOCALYPSE, §1 and figs 1 and 2). Other devotional texts popular with the laity, and often with a didactic purpose, were books of religious instruction on Christian doctrine and morality. These seldom contained pictures, although the *Somme le roi*, written for Philip III of France (*reg* 1270–85) by his Dominican confessor, is a notable exception. Many costly examples survive from the late 13th century onwards, from England and France. Guillaume de Deguilleville's *Pèlerinage de la vie humaine*, an allegorical pilgrimage, was also popular in illustrated copies. Similarly, the French translation of St Augustine's *City of God* was also provided with elaborate figural decoration in the 14th and 15th centuries.

Related to literary texts (*see* §(d) below) in their form of illustration are SAINTS' LIVES. From the 10th century on they were provided with cycles of narrative illustration either with pictures set into the text or as full-page miniatures (*see* ROMANESQUE, fig. 60). From the early 14th century, above all in France, many illustrated copies were produced of the compilation of saints' lives, the *Golden Legend*, by JACOPO DE VORAGINE. Collections of the miracles of the Virgin, for example that of Gautier de Coincy, have also survived in many illuminated copies. In Byzantine art an equivalent frequently illustrated collection of saints' lives is the Menologion of Symeon Metaphrastes (*see* EARLY CHRISTIAN AND BYZANTINE ART, §V, 2(v)(e)).

(b) Scholarly. Theological works, above all the biblical commentaries of the early Church Fathers, Ambrose, Augustine, Gregory and Jerome, were often ornamented. From the Carolingian period these texts were supplemented by the works of, among others, Alcuin and Rabanus Maurus, and subsequently by such 11th- and 12th-century theologians as Bernard of Clairvaux, Hugh of St Victor, Peter Comestor and Peter Lombard. These works did not lend themselves readily to narrative illustration, and were usually decorated with author portraits and ornamented initials (see fig. 12). The study of the works of Aristotle became more widespread in the 13th century and essential as part of the university syllabus. Collections of his works and commentaries on them by St Thomas Aquinas and others were produced in large numbers, usually illustrated with historiated initials containing scenes of teaching or philosophers debating, combined with decorative borders extending from their stems.

Expensive copies of law books, both canon and civil, were produced largely in the university towns of Bologna and Paris during the later medieval period. Gratian's *Decretum* and various subsequent collections of decretals were more frequently illustrated than books of civil law (for further discussion and illustration *see* DECRETAL; and

12. *Gregory the Great*; historiated initial from Gregory the Great: *Homilies on Ezekiel*, from St Albans, 1168–83 (Stonyhurst, Lancs, Stonyhurst College, MS. 7, fol. 3v)

BOLOGNA, §II, 1 and fig. 3). Among civil law books, the *Digest* of Emperor Justinian I and various national collections of laws were occasionally decorated with miniatures. Sermons were rarely illustrated except in Byzantine manuscripts. Numerous copies with extensive picture cycles survive of the *Homilies* of Gregory Nazianzus; as his sermons have many allusions to the Bible and occasionally also to Classical literature, they provided varied scope for illustration. Another collection of homilies, that of James of Kokkinobaphos, is found in luxury illuminated copies (*see* EARLY CHRISTIAN AND BYZANTINE ART, §V, 2(ii)(d) and fig. 63).

(c) 'Scientific'. Scientific or pseudo-scientific texts had a long tradition of illustration beginning in antiquity. The BESTIARY, HERBAL and various MEDICAL ILLUSTRATED BOOKS were all illustrated either with unframed coloured pictures, framed miniatures or historiated initials (see fig. 13). Books on astronomy, especially Cicero's commentary on Aratus, were illustrated with images of the constellations, also derived from Late Antique cycles, as is shown by the surviving Carolingian copies; up to the 12th century the human and animal personifications of the constellations follow these antique prototypes. Illustrated books on astrology are frequent in the 14th and 15th centuries throughout Europe: for example, among others, the *Liber introductorius* of Michael Scotus and the *Sphaera* translated from the Arabic of Abu Ma'Shar (Albumasar; for further discussion and illustrations *see* ASTROLOGICAL AND ASTRONOMICAL MANUSCRIPTS).

(d) Literary and historical. Among Classical literature, although the works of Homer, Virgil and TERENCE had

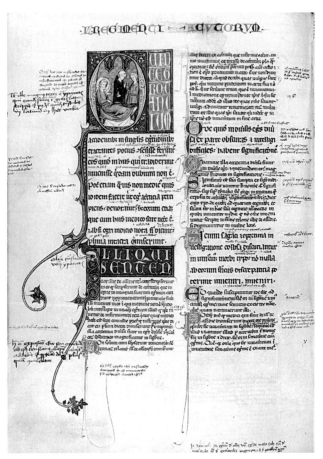

13. *Doctors Discussing a Patient*, miniature from Hippocrates: *Liber regimenti auctorum*, from Paris, second half of the 15th century (Vienna, Österreichische Nationalbibliothek, Cod. 2315, fol. 100*v*)

been illustrated in late antiquity, only Terence's plays were copied and illustrated in the early medieval and Romanesque periods (*see* ROMANESQUE, fig. 62). Arthurian literature became popular in the 12th century, but it was only in the 13th century, with the increase in secular patronage, that narrative cycles began to appear as historiated initials or small miniatures, set within the text in such works as Wolfram von Eschenbach's *Parzifal* and *Willehalm*, the *Lancelot del lac* and the *Queste de Saint Graal*. In the 14th and 15th centuries, in French, Netherlandish, German and Italian manuscripts, illustrated versions of Arthurian and other chivalric romances were popular, with either framed miniatures or historiated initials. This period is characterized by the widespread translation of literary works into the vernacular. Romance literature, derived from Classical antiquity, above all the life of Alexander and compilations of the stories of the Trojan war, was translated into French, English and German and given extensive narrative illustrations: for example Benoît de Sainte-Maure's *Roman de Troie*, John Lydgate's *Troy Book* and Raoul Lefèvre's *Recueil des histoires de Troie*, which was made for Burgundian patrons in the second half of the 15th century (for further discussion and illustration *see* ROMANCE, MANUSCRIPT).

Also translated from Latin into French and extensively illustrated were, among others, the works of Caesar, Livy, Quintus Curtius Rufus, Sallust, Valerius Maximus and Xenophon. Ovid was read in the *Ovide moralisé*, a moralized version of the *Metamorphoses*, often illustrated.

Of the works of contemporary writers, the *Decameron* of Boccaccio, the *Divine Comedy* of DANTE ALIGHIERI, the *Roman de la rose* of Guillaume de Lorris and Jean de Meung, and the *Epistre d'Othéa* of CHRISTINE DE PIZAN were the most popular texts for illustration. The Italian and Latin works of Boccaccio were not elaborately illustrated in Italy but were frequently produced as luxury copies with many pictures in French versions, particularly in the *Des Cas des nobles hommes et femmes*. Collections of the poetry of the German minnesingers and of the French poet Guillaume de Machaut also exist in richly illuminated copies.

Other, less obviously literary works include books on hunting and travel. The *Cynegetica* of Pseudo-Oppian is illustrated in a few Byzantine manuscripts, which may suggest that it had been illustrated in late antiquity. In the West there is no tradition derived from antiquity and only in the Gothic period in Italy and France are treatises on hunting provided with accompanying series of pictures. The book on falconry (*c.* 1250) by the emperor Frederick II, *De arte venandi cum avibus*, survives in several copies and has painted illustrations set in the margin. The most popular works on hunting, the *Livre de chasse* of Gaston Phébus and the *Livre du roy Modus et de la reyne Ratio* of Henri de Ferrières (see fig. 14), both in French, were not illustrated until *c.* 1400. They were provided with framed miniatures, set in the text, depicting the various types of animals and birds hunted and the care of hunting dogs and falcons. Numerous 15th-century copies by French and Netherlandish illuminators exist of these books. Travel books were illustrated in England from the 11th century, for example the compilation the *Marvels of the East*. In the 14th and 15th centuries the travels of Marco Polo and of Sir John Mandeville, describing journeys to the East, exist in a few luxury copies with many pictures (for further discussion and illustration *see* TRAVEL MANUSCRIPTS).

Historical works such as the Alexandrian World Chronicle first had pictures set in or beside their text in antiquity. Throughout the early medieval period chronicles were relatively simply illustrated with coloured drawings. During the Gothic period such illustrated chronicles as the *Grandes Chroniques de France*, Jean Froissart's *Chronicles* and Rudolf von Ems's *Weltchronik* became more popular, and luxury copies with many framed miniatures or historiated initials were produced in France, the Netherlands and Germany. Compilations of the history of antiquity such as the *Histoire ancienne jusqu'à César*, the *Faits des Romains* and *Roméléon* were also popular in illustrated versions, as was the French translation of the *Jewish Antiquities* of Flavius Josephus (for further discussion and illustrations *see* CHRONICLES AND HISTORIES, MANUSCRIPT).

BIBLIOGRAPHY

Exhibition catalogues and catalogues of libraries, in which the majority of the manuscripts described are illuminated, are listed alphabetically by country.

ARMENIA

L. A. Dournovo: *Miniatures arméniennes* (Erevan, 1969)

au ꝓꝛꝭ ꝉꝓꝮꝭ Ꝉꝭ ꝛꝯꝯꝟ ꝛꝯꝼꝉ ꝃꝯꝯꝓ   ꝈꝭꝛꝯꝮꝯ ꝺꝯꝼꝯꝛꝯꝟꝯꝙ ꝼꝯꝛꝯ ꝃꝯꝯꝓꝯꝥ ꝯ ꝛꝯ

14. *Hunting Scene*; miniature from Henri de Ferrières: *Livre du roy Modus et de la reyne Ratio*, from the Netherlands, 15th century (Brussels, Bibliothèque Royale Albert 1er, MSS 10218–9)

AUSTRALIA

M. M. Manion and V. F. Vines: *Medieval and Renaissance Illuminated Manuscripts in Australian Collections* (London, 1984)

AUSTRIA

F. Wickhoff: *Beschreibendes Verzeichnis der illuminierten Handschriften in Österreich*, 7 vols (Leipzig, 1905–15)

Vienna

R. Beer: 'Les Principaux Manuscrits à peintures de la Bibliothèque impériale de Vienne', *Bull. Soc. Fr. Repr. MSS Peint.*, ii (1912), pp. 5–53; iii (1913), pp. 5–55

H. J. Hermann: *Die illuminierten Handschriften und Inkunabeln der Nationalbibliothek in Wien*, 15 vols (Leipzig, 1923–36)

E. Trenkler, K. Holter and K. Oettinger: 'Les Principaux Manuscrits à peintures de la Bibliothèque nationale de Vienne', *Bull. Soc. Fr. Repr. MSS Peint.*, xx–xxi (1937–8) [whole issues]

F. Unterkircher: *European Illuminated Manuscripts in the Austrian National Library* (London, 1967)

O. Pächt and D. Thoss: *Französische Schule: Die illuminierten Handschriften und Inkunabeln der Österreichischen Nationalbibliothek*, 2 vols (Vienna, 1974–7)

O. Pächt and U. Jenni: *Holländische Schule: Die illuminierten Handschriften und Inkunabeln der Österreichischen Nationalbibliothek* (Vienna, 1975)

H. Buschhausen, H. Buschhausen and E. Zimmermann: *Die illuminierten armenischen Handschriften der Mechitaristen-Congregation in Wien* (Vienna, 1976)

Französische Gotik und Renaissance in Meisterwerke der Buchmalerei (exh. cat., ed. D. Thoss; Vienna, Österreich. Nbib., 1978)

O. Pächt, U. Jenni and D. Thoss: *Flämische Schule: Die illuminierten Handschriften und Inkunabeln der Österreichischen Nationalbibliothek*, 2 vols (Vienna, 1983–90)

Flämische Buchmalerei: Handschriftenschätze aus dem Burgunderreich (exh. cat., ed. D. Thoss; Vienna, Österreich. Nbib., 1987)

BELGIUM

Treasures of Belgian Libraries (exh. cat., Edinburgh, N. Lib., 1963)

Bruges

Tentoonstelling van miniaturen en boekbanden [Exhibition of miniatures and bookbindings] (exh. cat., Bruges, Stadhuis, 1927)

Vlaamse kunst op perkament, handschriften en miniaturen te Brugge van de 12de tot de 16de eeuw [Flemish art on parchment, manuscripts and miniatures in Bruges from the 12th to the 16th century] (exh. cat., Bruges, Gruuthusemus., 1981)

Brussels

E. Bacha: *Les Très Belles Miniatures de la Bibliothèque royale de Belgique* (Brussels, 1913)

C. Gaspar and F. Lyna: *Les Principaux Manuscrits à peintures de la Bibliothèque royale de Belgique*, i and ii (Paris, 1937–45/R Brussels, 1984–7); iii, ed. C. Panteng (Brussels, 1989)

L. Gilissen and H. Liebaers: *La Librairie de Bourgogne* (Brussels, 1970)

BRITISH ISLES

Trésors des bibliothèques de l'Ecosse (exh. cat., Brussels, Bib. Royale Albert 1er, 1963)

Cambridge

M. R. James: *A Descriptive Catalogue of the Manuscripts of the Fitzwilliam Museum* (Cambridge, 1895)

——: *A Descriptive Catalogue of the McClean Collection of Manuscripts in the Fitzwilliam Museum* (Cambridge, 1912)

Illuminated Manuscripts in the Fitzwilliam Museum (exh. cat., ed. F. Wormald and P. Giles; Cambridge, Fitzwilliam, 1966)

F. Wormald and P. M. Giles: *A Descriptive Catalogue of the Additional Illuminated Manuscripts in the Fitzwilliam Museum* (Cambridge, 1982)

Glasgow

N. Thorp: *The Glory of the Page: Medieval and Renaissance Illuminated Manuscripts from Glasgow University Library* (London, 1987)

Holkham

L. Dorez: *Les Manuscrits à peintures de la bibliothèque de Lord Leicester à Holkham Hall, Norfolk* (Paris, 1908)

W. O. Hassall: *The Holkham Library* (London, 1970)

London

W. de Gray Birch: *Early Drawings and Illuminations with a Dictionary of Subjects in the British Museum* (London, 1879)

G. F. Warner: *Illuminated Manuscripts in the British Museum*, 4 vols (London, 1899–1903)

Series of Reproductions from Illuminated Manuscripts, London, BM cat., 5 vols (London, 1907–65)

J. A. Herbert, ed.: *Schools of Illumination*, London, BM cat., 6 vols (London, 1914–30)

E. G. Millar: 'Les Principaux Manuscrits à peintures des bibliothèques de Londres', *Bull. Soc. Fr. Repr. MSS Peint.*, iv (1914–20), pp. 83–149

Catalogue of Miniatures, Leaves and Cuttings from Illuminated Manuscripts, London, V&A cat. (London, 1923)

E. G. Millar: 'Les Principaux Manuscrits à peintures du Lambeth Palace à Londres', *Bull. Soc. Fr. Repr. MSS Peint.*, viii (1924), pp. 1–66; ix (1925), pp. 5–19

D. H. Turner: *Early Gothic Illuminated Manuscripts in the British Museum* (London, 1965)

——: *Romanesque Illuminated Manuscripts in the British Museum* (London, 1966)

Illuminated Manuscripts Exhibited in the Grenville Library, London, BM cat. (London, 1967)

J. J. G. Alexander: *Catalogue of Illuminated Manuscript Cuttings in the Wallace Collection* (London, 1980)

T. Kren: *Renaissance Painting in Manuscripts: Treasures from the British Library* (London, 1983)

Manchester

M. R. James: *A Descriptive Catalogue of Latin Manuscripts in the John Rylands Library at Manchester* (Manchester, 1921)

Oxford

O. Pächt and J. J. G. Alexander: *Illuminated Manuscripts in the Bodleian Library*, 3 vols (Oxford, 1965–73)

A. G. Hassall and W. O. Hassall: *Treasures from the Bodleian Library* (London, 1976)

I. Hutter: *Corpus der byzantinischen Miniaturenhandschriften*, *Oxford*, 4 vols (Stuttgart, 1977–93)

M. B. Parkes: *The Medieval Manuscripts of Keble College, Oxford* (London, 1979)

J. J. G. Alexander and E. Temple: *Illuminated Manuscripts in Oxford College Libraries* (Oxford, 1985)

CZECH REPUBLIC

M. Bohatec: *Illuminated Manuscripts* (Prague, 1970) [on Czech cols]

EGYPT

Sinai

K. Weitzmann and G. Galavaris: *The Monastery of Saint Catherine at Mount Sinai: The Illuminated Greek Manuscripts*, i (Princeton, 1990)

FRANCE

V. Leroquais: *Les Sacramentaires et les missels manuscrits des bibliothèques de France* (Paris, 1924)

P. Lauer: *Les Enluminures romanes des manuscrits de la Bibliothèque nationale* (Paris, 1927)

V. Leroquais: *Les Livres d'heures manuscrits de la Bibliothèque nationale* (Paris, 1927; suppl. Mâcon, 1943)

P. Neveux and E. Dacier: *Les Richesses des bibliothèques provinciales de France*, 3 vols (Paris, 1932)

V. Leroquais: *Les Bréviaires manuscrits des bibliothèques publiques de France* (Paris, 1934)

——: *Les Pontificaux manuscrits des bibliothèques publiques de France* (Paris, 1937)

——: *Les Psautiers manuscrits des bibliothèques de France* (Paris, 1940–41)

Les Manuscrits à peintures du VIIe au XIIe siècle (exh. cat., ed. J. Porcher; Paris, Bib. N., 1954)

Les Manuscrits à peintures du XIIIe au XVIe siècle (exh. cat., ed. J. Porcher; Paris, Bib. N., 1955)

Autun

Trésors manuscrits de la Bibliothèque d'Autun (exh. cat., Autun, Bib. Mun., 1980)

Le Livre au siècle des Rolin (exh. cat., Autun, Bib. Mun., 1985)

Chantilly

J. Meurgey: *Les Principaux Manuscrits à peintures du Musée Condé à Chantilly* (Paris, 1930)

Chartres

Y. Delaporte: *Les Manuscrits enluminés de la Bibliothèque de Chartres* (Chartres, 1929)

Dijon

C. Oursel: 'Les Manuscrits à miniatures de la Bibliothèque de Dijon', *Bull. Soc. Repr. MSS Peint.*, vii (1923), pp. 5–33

Y. Załuska: *Manuscrits enluminés de Dijon* (Paris, 1991)

Lyon

F. Cotton: 'Les Manuscrits à peintures de la Bibliothèque de Lyon', *Gaz. B-A.*, lxv (1965), pp. 265–320

Paris

La Collection Wildenstein, Musée Marmottan (Paris, n.d.)

A. Boinet: 'Les Manuscrits à peintures de la Bibliothèque Sainte Geneviève', *Bull. Soc. Fr. Repr. MSS Peint.*, v (1921)

C. Couderc: *Les Enluminures des manuscrits du moyen âge de la Bibliothèque nationale* (Paris, 1927)

H. Martin and P. Lauer: *Les Principaux Manuscrits à peintures de la Bibliothèque de l'Arsenal à Paris* (Paris, 1929)

H. Omont: *Miniatures des plus anciens manuscrits grecs de la Bibliothèque nationale* (Paris, 1929)

G. de la Batut: 'Les Principaux Manuscrits à peintures conservés à la Bibliothèque Mazarine à Paris'. *Bull. Soc. Fr. Repr. MSS Peint.*, xvi (1933), pp. 5–62

Les Plus Beaux Manuscrits français à peintures du moyen âge de la Bibliothèque nationale (exh. cat., Paris, Bib. N., 1937)

J. Porcher: *Manuscrits à peintures offerts à la Bibliothèque nationale par le comte Guy de Boisrouvray* (Paris, 1961)

F. Avril and Y. Załuska: *Manuscrits enluminés d'origine italienne: VIe–XIIe siècles*, Paris, Bib. N. cat. (Paris, 1980)

Trésors de la Bibliothèque de l'Arsenal (exh. cat., Paris, Bib. N., 1980)

F. Avril and others: *Manuscrits enluminés de la péninsule ibérique*, Paris, Bib. N. cat. (Paris, 1983)

F. Avril and M.-T. Gousset: *Manuscrits enluminés d'origine italienne: XIIIe siècle*, Paris, Bib. N. cat. (Paris, 1984)

Dix siècles d'enluminure italienne (exh. cat., ed. F. Avril; Paris, Bib. N., 1984)

F. Avril and P. D. Stirnemann: *Manuscrits enluminés d'origine insulaire, VIIe–XXe siècle*, Paris, Bib. N. cat. (Paris, 1987)

Reims

Les Plus Beaux Manuscrits de la Bibliothèque de Reims (exh. cat., Reims, Bib. Mun., 1967)

Troyes

L. Morel-Payen: *Les Plus Beaux Manuscrits et les plus belles reliures de la Bibliothèque de Troyes* (Troyes, 1935)

Les Richesses de la Bibliothèque de Troyes (exh. cat., Troyes, Bib. Mun., 1951)

GEORGIA

S. Amiranshvili: *Gruzinskaya miniatyura* (Moscow, 1966)

GERMANY

R. Bruck: *Die Malerei in den Handschriften des Königreichs Sachsen* (Dresden, 1906)

L. Olschki: *Manuscrits français à peintures des bibliothèques d'Allemagne* (Geneva, 1932)

E. Rothe: *Medieval Book Illumination in Europe* (London, 1966) [on the libraries of the former E. Germany]

H. Frühmorgen-Voss and N. H. Ott: *Katalog der deutschsprachigen illustrierten Handschriften des Mittelalters* (Munich, 1986–)

Bamberg

H. Fischer: *Mittelalterliche Miniaturen aus der Staatsbibliothek in Bamberg*, 2 vols (Bamberg, 1926–9)

Berlin

P. Wescher: *Beschreibendes Verzeichnis der Miniaturhandschriften der Kupferstichkabinett der Staatlichen Museen in Berlin* (Leipzig, 1931)

Zimelien: Abendländische Handschriften des Mittelalters aus den Sammlungen der Stiftung Preussischer Kulturbesitz (exh. cat., W. Berlin, Staatsbib. Preuss. Kultbes., 1976)

Das christliche Gebetbuch im Mittelalter (exh. cat., W. Berlin, Staatsbib. Preuss. Kultbes., 1980)

H.-E. Teitge and E.-M. Stelzer: *Kostbarkeiten der Deutschen Staatsbibliothek (Berlin DDR)* (Leipzig, 1986)

Glanz alter Buchkunst: Mittelalterliche Handschriften der Staatsbibliothek preussischer Kulturbesitz Berlin (exh. cat., W. Berlin, Staatsbib. Preuss. Kultbes., 1988)

Darmstadt

E. Zimmermann and K.-H. Staub: *Buchmalerei in Darmstadt: Illuminierte Handschriften der Hessischen Landes- und Hochschulbibliothek Darmstadt* (Munich, 1979)

Düsseldorf

G. Gattermann: *Kostbarkeiten aus der Universitätsbibliothek Düsseldorf* (Wiesbaden, 1989)

Erlangen

E. Lutze: *Die Bilderhandschriften der Universitätsbibliothek Erlangen* (Erlangen, 1936)

Frankfurt am Main

G. Swarzenski and R. Schilling: *Die illuminierten Handschriften und Einzelminiaturen des Mittelalters und der Renaissance in Frankfurter Besitz* (Frankfurt, 1929)

Fulda

H. Köllner: *Die illuminierten Handschriften der Hessischen Landesbibliothek Fulda* (Stuttgart, 1976)

Heidelberg

A. Oechelhäuser: *Die Miniaturen der Universitätsbibliothek zu Heidelberg* (Heidelberg, 1887–95)

W. Werner: *Cimelia Heidelbergensia: Illuminierte Handschriften der Universitätsbibliothek Heidelberg* (Wiesbaden, 1975)

Hildesheim

M. Stähli and H. Härtel: *Die Handschriften im Domschatz zu Hildesheim* (Wiesbaden, 1984)

Karlsruhe

Initial und Miniatur: Buchmalerei aus neun Jahrhunderten in Handschriften der Badischen Landesbibliothek (exh. cat., ed. E. J. Beer; Karlsruhe, Bad. Landesbib., 1965)

Kassel

H. Broszinski: *Kasseler Handschriftenschätze* (Kassel, 1985)

Konstanz

W. Irtenkauf: *Bibliophile Kostbarkeiten: Handschriften aus der Konstanzer Dombibliotheken* (Konstanz, 1987)

Leipzig

D. Debes: *Leipziger Zimelien: Bücherschätze der Universitätsbibliothek* (Wiesbaden, 1989)

Munich

G. Leidinger: *Miniaturen aus Handschriften der Kgl. Hof- und Staatsbibliothek in München*, 6 vols (Munich, 1913–21)

——: *Meisterwerke der Buchmalerei aus Handschriften der Bayerischen Staatsbibliothek* (Munich, 1920)

Bayerns Kirchen im Mittelalter: Handschriften und Urkunden aus bayerischen Staatsbesitz (exh. cat., Munich, Bayer. Staatsbib., Munich, 1960)

Treasures of the Bavarian State Library (exh. cat., Munich, Bayer. Staatsbib., Munich, 1970)

E. Klemm: *Die romanische Handschriften der Bayerischen Staatsbibliothek: Die Bistümer Regensburg, Passau und Salzburg* (Munich, 1979)

U. Bauer-Eberhardt: *Die italienischen Miniaturen des 13.–16. Jahrhunderts*, Munich, Staatl. Graph. Samml. cat. (Munich, 1984)

Münster

J. Lammers: *Buchmalerei aus Handschriften vom 12. bis zum 16. Jahrhundert* (Münster, 1982)

Stuttgart

W. Irtenkauf: *Stuttgart Zimelien* (Stuttgart, 1985)

S. von Borries Schulten and A. Butz: *Katalog der illuminierten Handschriften der Württembergischen Landesbibliothek, Stuttgart: Die romanischen Handschriften*, 2 vols (Stuttgart, 1987)

Würzburg

Kostbare Handschriften (exh. cat., Würzburg, Ubib., 1982)

GREECE

Athens

A. Marava-Chatzinicolaou and C. Toufexi-Paschou: *Catalogue of Illuminated Byzantine Manuscripts of the National Library of Greece*, 2 vols (Athens, 1978–85)

Mt Athos

S. M. Pelekanidis and others: *The Treasures of Mount Athos*, 3 vols (Athens, 1974–9)

HUNGARY

I. Berkovits: *Illuminated Manuscripts in Hungary* (Shannon, 1969)

ITALY

Mostra storica nazionale della miniatura (exh. cat., Rome, Pal. Venezia, 1954)

A. Daneu Lattanzi: *I manoscritti ed incunaboli miniati della Sicilia* (Palermo, 1965–84)

Assisi

M. Assirelli, M. Bernabo and G. Bigalli Lulli: *I libri miniati di età romanica e gotica* (Assisi, 1988)

Cava dei Tirreni

M. Rotili: *La miniatura nella Badia di Cava*, 2 vols (Cava dei Tirreni, 1976–8)

Florence

G. Biagi: *Riproduzione di manoscritti miniati di codici della Biblioteca Medicea Laurenziana* (Florence, 1914)

R. Chiarelli: *I codici miniati del Museo di S Marco a Firenze* (Florence, 1968)

A. Morandini: *Biblioteca Medicea Laurenziana* (Florence, 1986)

C. Di Benedetto: *Biblioteca nazionale centrale* (Florence, 1989)

M. C. Castelli and A. Gardin: *I codici miniati della Fondazione Horne* (Florence, 1990)

Friuli

G. C. Menis and G. Bergamini: *La miniatura in Friuli* (Udine, 1972)

Genoa

D. Puncuh: *I manoscritti dalla Raccolta Durazzo* (Genoa, 1979)

Lodi

A. Novasconi: *Le miniature di Lodi* (Lodi, 1976)

Milan

F. Carta: *Codici corali e libri a stampa miniati della Biblioteca nazionale di Milano* (Rome, 1891–5)

M. Salmi and C. Santoro: *I codici miniati della Biblioteca Trivulziana* (Milan, 1958)

R. Cipriani: *Codici miniati dell'Ambrosiana* (Venice, 1968)

M. L. Gengaro and G. V. Guglielmetti: *Inventario dei codici decorati e miniati della Biblioteca Ambrosiana, sec. VII–XIII* (Florence, 1968)

C. Marcora: *I libri d'ore della Biblioteca Ambrosiana* (Milan, 1973)

Modena

M. Salmi and D. Fava: *I manoscritti miniati della Biblioteca Estense di Modena* (Florence, 1950)

P. Di Pietro Lombardi: *Biblioteca Estense, Modena* (Florence, 1987)

Padua

A. Barzon: *Codici miniati della Biblioteca Capitolare della città di Padova* (Padua, 1950)

G. Abate and G. Luisetto: *Codici e manoscritti della Biblioteca Antoniana col catalogo delle miniature* (Vicenza, 1975)

Parma

A. Ciavarella: *Codici miniati della Biblioteca Palatina di Parma* (Milan, 1964)

Perugia

A. Caleca: *Miniatura in Umbria: La Biblioteca Capitolare di Perugia* (Florence, 1969)

Piacenza

A. G. Quintavalle: *Miniature a Piacenza* (Venice, 1963)

Rimini

G. M. Canova, P. Meldini and S. Nicolini: *I codici miniati della Gambalunghiana di Rimini* (Rimini, 1988)

Rome

S. Beissel: *Vatikanische Miniaturen* (Freiburg im Breisgau, 1893)

A. Muñoz: *I codici greci miniati delle minori biblioteche di Roma* (Florence, 1905)

H. Tietze: *Die illuminierten Handschriften der Rossiana* (Leipzig, 1911)

Il libro della Bibbia (exh. cat., Rome, Vatican, Bib. Apostolica, 1972)

Quarto centenario della Biblioteca Apostolica Vaticana, 1475–1975 (exh. cat., Rome, Vatican, Bib. Apostolica, 1975)

Libri manoscritti e stampati del Belgio nella Biblioteca Vaticana (exh. cat., Rome, Vatican, Bib. Apostolica, 1979)

C. Gnoni Mavarelli: *I libri d'ore francesi e fiamminghini della Biblioteca Riccardiana* (Rome, 1986)

Biblioteca Palatina (exh. cat., Heidelberg, Heiliggeistkirche, 1986)

G. Morello: *Die schönsten Stundenbücher aus der Biblioteca Vaticana* (Rome, 1988)

A. M. Stickler and L. E. Boyle: *The Vatican Library: Its History and Treasures* (New York, 1989)

Biblioteca Apostolica Vaticana: Liturgie und Andacht im Mittelalter (exh. cat., Cologne, Erzbischöf. Diöz.-Mus., 1992)

Siena

B. Klange Addabbo: *Codici miniati della Biblioteca comunale degli Intronati di Siena: Sec. XI–XII* (Siena, 1987)

Trento

M. Bernasconi, L. Dal Poz and M. G. Ciardi Dupré dal Poggetto: *Codici miniati della Biblioteca comunale di Trento* (Florence, 1985)

Turin

C. Segre Montel: *I manoscritti latini dal VII alla metà del XII secolo* (1980), i of *I manoscritti miniati della Biblioteca nazionale di Torino* (Turin, 1980–89)

N. U. Gulmini: *I manoscritti greci* (1989), ii of *I manoscritti miniati della Biblioteca nazionale di Torino* (Turin, 1980–89)

Venice

S. der Nersessian: *Manuscrits arméniens illustrés des XIIe–XIVe siècles de la Bibliothèque des Pères Mékhitaristes de Venise* (Paris, 1936–7)

I. Furlan: *Codici greci illustrati della Biblioteca Marciana*, 4 vols (Milan, 1973–81)

Verona

A. Piazzi and G. Zivelonghi: *La tradizione veronese nelle miniature dei codici capitolari*, Verona, Bib. Capitolare cat. (Verona, 1984)

LUXEMBOURG

B. Weicherding-Goergen: *Les Manuscrits à peintures de la Bibliothèque nationale de Luxembourg* (Luxembourg, 1968)

J. Christophory: *150 Manuscrits précieux du IXe au XVIe siècles conservés à la Bibliothèque nationale de Luxembourg* (Luxembourg, 1989)

NETHERLANDS

A. W. Byvanck: 'Les Principaux Manuscrits à peintures conservés dans les collections publiques du royaume des Pays-Bas', *Bull. Soc. Fr. Repr. MSS Peint.*, xv (1931)

The Hague

A. W. Byvanck: 'Les Principaux Manuscrits à peintures de la Bibliothèque royale du Pays-Bas et du Musée Meermanno-Westreenianum à la Haye', *Bull. Soc. Fr. Repr. MSS Peint.*, viii (1924)

Verluchten handschriften uit eigen bezit, 1300–1550 (exh. cat., The Hague, Rijksmus. Meermanno-Westreenianum, 1979)

Schatten van de Koninklijke Bibliotheek (exh. cat., The Hague, Rijksmus. Meermanno-Westreenianum, 1980)

Liturgische handschriften uit der Koninklijke Bibliotheek (exh. cat., The Hague, Rijksmus. Meermanno-Westreenianum, 1983)

J. T. Brandhorst and K. H. Broekhuysen-Kruijer: *De verluchte handschriften en incunabeln van de Koninklijke Bibliotheek* (The Hague, 1985)

Utrecht

K. van der Horst: *Illuminated and Decorated Medieval Manuscripts in the University Library Utrecht* (Utrecht, 1989)

NEW ZEALAND

M. M. Manion, V. F. Vines and C. de Hamel: *Medieval and Renaissance Manuscripts in New Zealand Collections* (London, 1989)

POLAND

Z. Ameisenowa: 'Les Principaux Manuscrits à peintures de la Bibliothèque Jagellonienne de Cracovie', *Bull. Soc. Fr. Repr. MSS Peint.*, xvii (1933), pp. 5–119

M. Jarosławiecka-Gasiorowska: 'Les Principaux Manuscrits à peintures du Musée des Princes Czartoryski à Cracovie', *Bull. Soc. Fr. Repr. MSS Peint.*, xviii (1935), pp. 5–203

S. Sawicka: 'Les Principaux Manuscrits à peintures de la Bibliothèque nationale de Varsovie, du Château royal et des bibliothèques des Zamoyski à Varsovie, du Séminaire de Płock et du Chapitre de Gniezno', *Bull. Soc. Fr. Repr. MSS Peint.*, xix (1936)

PORTUGAL

R. Dos Santos: 'Les Principaux Manuscrits à peintures conservés au Portugal', *Bull. Soc. Fr. Repr. MSS Peint.*, xiv (1930), pp. 1–32

RUSSIA

A. de Laborde: *Manuscrits à peintures de l'ancienne Bibliothèque impériale de St. Pétersbourg* (Paris, 1937–8)

V. D. Likhachova: *Byzantine Miniature: Masterpieces of Byzantine Miniature of IXth–XVth Centuries in Soviet Collections* (Moscow, 1977)

I. P. Mokretsova and V. L. Romanova: *Les Manuscrits enluminés français du XIIIe siècle dans les collections soviétiques, 1200–1300*, 2 vols (Moscow, 1983–4)

SCANDINAVIA

M. Mackeprang: *Greek and Latin Illuminated Manuscripts, X–XIII Centuries in Danish Collections* (Copenhagen, 1921)

H. Hermansson: *Icelandic Illuminated Manuscripts in the Middle Ages* (Copenhagen, 1935)

Gyllene böcker [Golden books] (exh. cat., ed. C. Nordenfalk; Stockholm, Nmus., 1952)

C. Nordenfalk: *Bokmålningar från medeltid och renässans i Nationalmusei samlingar* [Manuscript painting from the Middle Ages and Renaissance in the collections of the National Museum] (Stockholm, 1979)

Medeltida bokillustrationer [Medieval book illustrations] (exh. cat., Uppsala, Ubib., 1980)

SOUTH AFRICA

P. E. Westra: *Medieval and Renaissance Manuscripts in the Grey Collection: A Preliminary Catalogue* (Cape Town, 1984)

SPAIN

J. Dominguez Bordona: *Manoscritos con pinturas* (Madrid, 1933)

Miniatures espagnoles et flamandes dans les collections d'Espagne (exh. cat., Brussels, Bib. Royale Albert 1er, 1964)

A. Domínguez Rodríguez: *Libros de horas del siglo XV en la Biblioteca nacional* (Madrid, 1979)

SWITZERLAND
Basle

K. Escher: *Die Miniaturen in Basler Bibliotheken* (Basle, 1917)

Berne

O. Homburger: *Die illustrierten Handschriften der Burgerbibliothek, Bern* (Berne, 1962)

Geneva

H. Aubert: 'Les Principaux Manuscrits à peintures de la Bibliothèque publique et universitaire de Genève', *Bull. Soc. Fr. Repr. MSS Peint.*, ii (1912), pp. 55–107

L'Enluminure de Charlemagne à François I: Manuscrits de la Bibliothèque publique et universitaire de Genève (exh. cat., Geneva, Mus. Rath, 1976)

Lucerne

J. Schmid: *Schöne Miniaturen aus Handschriften der Kantonsbibliothek* (Lucerne, 1941)

Sion

J. Leisibach: *Livres sédunois du moyen âge. Enluminures et miniatures: Trésors de la Bibliothèque du chapitre de Sion* (Sion, 1985)

UNITED STATES OF AMERICA

Illuminated Books of the Middle Ages and the Renaissance (exh. cat., ed. D. Miner; Baltimore, MD, Walters A.G., 1949)

Illuminated Greek Manuscripts from American Collections (exh. cat., ed. G. Vikan; Princeton U., NJ, A. Mus., 1973)

The Last Flowering: French Painting in Manuscripts, 1420–1530, from American Collections (exh. cat., ed. J. Plummer; New York, Pierpont Morgan Lib., 1982)

Baltimore

S. Der Nersessian: *Armenian Manuscripts in the Walters Art Gallery* (Baltimore, 1973)

L. M. C. Randall: *Medieval and Renaissance Manuscripts in the Walters Art Gallery*, 2 vols (Baltimore, 1989–92)

Boston

J. Oliver: *Manuscripts Sacred and Secular from the Collections of the Endowment of Biblical Research and Boston University* (Boston, 1985)

Cambridge

Illuminated and Calligraphic Manuscripts (exh. cat., ed. W. H. Bond; Cambridge, MA, Harvard U., Houghton Lib., 1955)

Late Medieval and Renaissance Illuminated Manuscripts, 1350–1525, in the Houghton Library (exh. cat., ed. R. S. Wieck; Cambridge, MA, Harvard U., Houghton Lib., 1983)

Chicago

P. Saenger: *A Catalogue of the pre-1500 Western Manuscript Books at the Newberry Library* (Chicago, 1989)

Ithaca

R. G. Calkins: 'Mediaeval and Renaissance Illuminated Manuscripts in the Cornell University Library', *Cornell Lib. J.*, xiii (1972), pp. 1–95

Malibu

A. von Euw and J. M. Plotzek: *Die Handschriften der Sammlung Ludwig*, 4 vols (Cologne, 1979–85)

New Haven

W. Cahn and J. Marrow: 'Medieval and Renaissance Manuscripts at Yale: A Selection', *Yale U. Lib. Gaz.*, lii (1978), pp. 173–284
B. Shailor: *The Medieval Book* (New Haven, 1988)

New York

M. R. James: *Catalogue of Manuscripts and Early Printed Books from the Libraries of William Morris, Richard Bennett, Bertram, Fourth Earl of Ashburnham and Other Sources now Forming a Portion of the Library of J. Pierpont Morgan* (London, 1906–7)
Treasures from the Pierpont Morgan Library (exh. cat., New York, Pierpont Morgan Lib., 1957)
M. Harrsen: *Central European Manuscripts in the Pierpont Morgan Library* (New York, 1958)
J. Plummer: *Manuscripts from the William S. Glazier Collection* (New York, 1959)
Medieval and Renaissance Manuscripts in the Pierpont Morgan Library (exh. cat., New York, Pierpont Morgan Lib., 1974)

Princeton

A. Bennett and J. Preston: *Illuminated Manuscripts in Princeton* (Princeton, 1990)

San Marino

C. W. Dutschke: *Guide to the Medieval and Renaissance Manuscripts in the Huntington Library* (San Marino, 1989)

Washington, DC

S. Der Nersessian: *Armenian Manuscripts in the Freer Gallery of Art* (Washington, DC, 1963)
Medieval and Renaissance Miniatures from the National Gallery of Art (exh. cat., ed. G. Vikan; Washington, DC, N.G.A., 1975)
S. Schutzner: *Medieval and Renaissance Manuscript Books in the Library of Congress*, i (Washington, DC, 1989)

3. MATERIALS AND TECHNIQUES. Knowledge of the materials and techniques involved in manuscript painting is derived first from medieval technical treatises (*see* CENNINI, CENNINO; MANUALS, MANUSCRIPT; and THEOPHILUS), second from TECHNICAL EXAMINATION, which has been undertaken on only a very small number of manuscripts, and third, not always with certainty, from direct observation.

The materials used in the production of Western manuscripts may be divided into the support (*see* §I above), ink, pigments and the media in which they are mixed, and finally the gold and its ground. The most usual supports for Western medieval manuscripts are PARCHMENT and PAPER. Sheets of these were folded and cut according to the size of the double page required. A number of folded sheets, usually eight or ten, constitute a 'gathering', and several gatherings make up a book. Before the book was assembled, however, the double sheets were ruled with horizontal lines for the text and vertical lines for the columns and borders of the text block, often referred to as the 'ruling pattern'. Ruling was done either in drypoint, with the blunt end of a STYLUS, resulting in an indentation in the parchment, or leadpoint (plummet) or silverpoint, resulting in pale grey lines, or in ink. Once one sheet had been ruled out, this pattern could be transferred to a number of sheets laid beneath it by means of guiding marks pricked through the sheets with a sharp instrument. These 'prickmarks' are visible on many medieval manuscripts at the very edge of the sheet, although frequently they have been cropped during binding (for illustration *see* CODICOLOGY).

Carbon-based and metal tannate inks were the most usual media for writing in Western manuscripts (*see* INK, §§I, 1(ii) and II, 2(i)). Red, green, purple and blue pigments were also used for writing, as well as for the decorative penwork flourishes of line-endings and border ornament; in English manuscripts, especially during the Anglo-Saxon period, such pigments were also used for drawing figures in outline (*see* ANGLO-SAXON ART, §IV, 2 and fig. 10). The substances used for pigments vary considerably, but, unless scientific analysis has been carried out, it is almost impossible to identify them with certainty. Most of the pigments used for manuscript painting occur naturally, either as minerals or as organic compounds derived from plants, but some artificial pigments were also manufactured (for a detailed discussion *see* PIGMENT, §I). As many of the substances exist only in certain parts of Europe or Asia, a trade in pigments developed, with apothecaries often supplying artists. Some pigments such as lapis lazuli, which is found only in Afghanistan (see colour pl. VI), were understandably costly. The binding medium with which pigments were most commonly mixed was glair, made from the white of an egg, beaten for a long time, and then allowed to settle until it became clear again; this liquid was then mixed with a little water. The instructions for making glair in medieval technical treatises are very precise, even specifying the type and age of the eggs to be used. For some pigments the treatises suggest the addition of egg yolk to glair, while an alternative was a solution of GUM in water.

The survival of several unfinished manuscripts makes it possible to discern the stages involved in their decoration and illustration. In addition, some manuscripts contain small marginal notes, instructing the artist on what to depict or the colours to use, while others have faint trial sketches in silverpoint or leadpoint; such marginal notes or sketches would usually be erased in the final stages.

Once the text had been copied, with appropriate spaces left by the scribe for the illustrations, the first stage in the process of decoration could begin: this was to draw out the design of the frame, ornament and figures in silverpoint or leadpoint. Often the illuminator would then work up these sketches in ink lines. If gold leaf was to be used, this was applied and burnished before the paint was laid on (see fig. 15). On rare occasions silver leaf was also used, but its tendency to tarnish quickly made it unsuitable (*see* §4 below). If the gold was to be burnished, it was laid over a smoothed GROUND of raised gesso, sometimes mixed with Armenian bole (a red clay; *see also* GILDING, §I, 1(i)). Once applied, the gold leaf was burnished with a polisher, for which a large animal's tooth is often recommended in the treatises. Gold leaf could alternatively be applied on an adhesive (mordant) rather than on gesso, but in this case it could not be burnished. In many manuscripts punched geometrical or foliage patterns would be made

15. *Angel Carrying John to New Jerusalem*; illustration from the Douce Apocalypse showing underdrawing, ink outline, wash and gold leaf, from London, *c.* 1270 (Oxford, Bodleian Library, MS. Douce 180, p. 92)

on the burnished gold. Occasionally similar patterns would be painted on to the polished gold in powdered (shell) gold. Such powdered gold, mixed in a gum solution and applied with a brush, could also be used for details and highlights in the painting.

The next stage was the painting, when the pigments were applied with an animal-hair brush (usually squirrel) and possibly also in many cases with a quill pen. In most manuscripts there is only a two-stage application of colour, although three-stage coloration does occur. Some of the unfinished manuscripts show the first stage, the application of a flat ground colour, sometimes slightly varied in tone according to the placing of highlights or shadows. The next stage was the use of a darker shade to paint in the shadow areas. Highlights in early medieval and Roman-esque manuscripts are applied with streaks of white or sometimes gold paint, often in patterned forms. From the second half of the 13th century on, after applying the shadow colour, the illuminator would apply highlights in a lighter tone than the ground colour so as to create fully modelled effects. Streaks of white continued to be used to

enhance the highlights, and these, combined with dots in white paint, are frequently found for foliage ornament. In the 14th and 15th centuries more sophisticated modelling was achieved by a variety of techniques, including stippling. Hatched, painted lines in gold on a flat colour ground are frequently used in 15th-century manuscripts to create modelled forms. As a final stage, it was necessary to re-emphasize some of the figure and drapery outlines as well as more detailed areas in black or brown ink, using a quill or fine brush.

Some manuscripts were not illustrated with full-colour painting and gold illumination, but had outline or tinted drawings. In the latter, ink or coloured drawings were given substance and body by the application of light colour washes to indicate shadow areas and the tints of garment and flesh areas. In some cases the colour was applied as a light overall wash with little interest in modelling. These drawing techniques, although used all over Europe, were particularly popular in English manuscripts from the 10th to the 14th centuries. In France and the Netherlands during the 14th and 15th centuries monochrome tinted drawings developed into grisaille painting, in which tones of grey, black or brown were highlighted with white. Grisaille painting was sometimes combined with areas of full colour (*see* GRISAILLE, §1(iii)).

See also GOTHIC, §IV, 3(ii) and (iii).

BIBLIOGRAPHY

RDK: 'Farbe, Farbmittel'

M. P. Merrifield: *Original Treatises . . . on the Arts of Painting*, 2 vols (London, 1849/*R* New York, 1968)

C. J. Benziger: *Valentin Boltz von Ruffach, Illuminierbuch (1549)* (Munich, 1913/*R* Munich, 1988)

D. V. Thompson: 'Liber de coloribus illuminatorum sive pictorum', *Speculum*, i (1926), pp. 280–307, 448–50

D. S. Blondheim: 'An Old Portuguese Work on Manuscript Illumination', *Jew. Q. Rev.*, xix (1928–9), pp. 97–135

D. V. Thompson: 'The *De Clarea* of the so-called Anonymous Bernensis', *Techn. Stud. Field F.A.*, i (1932), pp. 9–19, 70–81

——: 'The Art of Limning', *Techn. Stud. Field F.A.*, ii (1933), pp. 35–7

——: 'The *ricepte daffare piu colori* of Ambrogio de Ser Pietro da Siena', *Archeion*, xv (1933), pp. 339–47

D. V. Thompson and G. H. Hamilton, eds: *An Anonymous Fourteenth-century Treatise, 'De arte illuminandi': The Technique of Manuscript Illumination* (New Haven, 1933)

D. V. Thompson: 'Medieval Color Making', *Isis*, xxii (1935), pp. 456–68

——: 'Medieval Parchment Making', *The Library*, xvi (1935), pp. 113–17

——: 'The Liber Magistri Petri de Sancto Audomaro *De coloribus faciendis*', *Techn. Stud. Field F.A.*, iv (1935), pp. 28–33

——: 'More Medieval Color Making', *Isis*, xxiv (1935–6), pp. 382–96

——: *The Materials and Techniques of Medieval Painting* (London, 1936/*R* New York, 1956)

H. Roosen-Runge: 'Die Buchmalerei-Rezepte des Theophilus', *Münchn. Jb. Bild. Kst*, iii–iv (1952–3), pp. 159–72

S. Waetzoldt: 'Systematisches Verzeichnis der Farbnamen', *Münchn. Jb. Bild. Kst*, iii–iv (1952–3), pp. 150–58

H. Roosen-Runge and A. E. A. Werner: 'The Pictorial Techniques of the Lindisfarne Gospels', *Evangeliorum Quattuor Codex Lindisfarniensis*, ed. T. D. Kendrick, T. J. Brown and R. L. S. Bruce-Mitford, ii (Lausanne, 1960), pp. 263–77

S. M. Alexander: 'Medieval Recipes Describing the Use of Metals in Manuscripts', *Marsyas*, xii (1964–5), pp. 34–51

——: 'Base and Noble Metals in Illumination', *Nat. Hist.*, lxxiv/10 (1965), pp. 31–9

F. Avril: *La Technique de l'enluminure d'après les textes médiévaux: Essai de bibliographie* (Paris, 1967)

H. Roosen-Runge: *Farbgebung und Technik der frühmittelalterlichen Buchmalerei* (Munich, 1967)

C. R. Dodwell: 'Techniques of Manuscript Painting in Anglo-Saxon Manuscripts', *Sett. Studio Cent. It. Stud. Alto Med.*, xviii (1970), pp. 643–62

L. van Acker, ed.: *Petri de Sancto Audomaro: Librum de coloribus faciendis*, Corpus Christianorum continuatio mediaevalis, xxv (Turnhout, 1972), pp. 145–98

J. L. Ross: 'A Note on the Use of Mosaic Gold', *Stud. Conserv.*, 18 (1973), pp. 174–6

F. Brunello, ed.: '*De arte illuminandi' e altri trattati sulla tecnica della miniatura medievale* (Vicenza, 1975)

M. Frinta: 'On the Punched Decoration in Medieval Panel Painting and Manuscript Illumination', *Conservation and Pictorial Art*, ed. N. Brommelle and P. Smith (London, 1976), pp. 54–60

U. Schiessl: *Musivgold*, *Maltechnik*, 87 (1981), pp. 219–30

H. Kühn and others: *Farbmittel: Buchmalerei, Tafel- und Leinwandmalerei* (Stuttgart, 1984)

V. Trost: *Skriptorium: Die Buchherstellung im Mittelalter* (Heidelberg, 1986)

J. J. G. Alexander: *Medieval Illuminators and their Methods of Work* (New Haven and London, 1992)

C. de Hamel: *Scribes and Illuminators*, Medieval Craftsmen (London, 1992)

NIGEL J. MORGAN

4. CONSERVATION. Since most manuscript painting remains within a closed book, it is protected from light and atmospheric pollution and buffered by the bulk of pages from rapid changes in humidity; it thus often retains all its original crispness and brilliance. Once the book is opened, progressive and irreversible deterioration starts to take place because of the effects of light (photochemical changes), which fade organic pigments and blacken vermilion. Other pigments are discoloured by atmospheric gases: traces of hydrogen sulphide can convert lead white and red lead to black lead sulphides; oxygen will tarnish silver, turning the shiny metallic foil to a dull grey or black. Of these only blackened lead white can be treated, by oxidizing it to white lead sulphate. The copper-based pigments, malachite, azurite and verdigris, can also become destructive. They undergo a chemical reaction with the cellulose, causing the paint to turn brown and embrittling the parchment, a process probably exacerbated by damp and dirt. It has also been suggested that the application of a solution of magnesium or calcium salts will inhibit the decomposition process.

The parchment is prone to fungal, rodent and insect damage. This may be treated by fumigation and secure, dry storage. Parchment is very sensitive to fluctuations in humidity, shrinking and buckling in dry air. A desiccated and distorted sheet can be made to relax by treatment in a humidifying tank, and much of its flatness is then recovered by placing it in tension and letting it dry slowly. Caution must be exercised, however, when painting is involved, as this treatment can lead to loss of adhesion between paint and page. A relative humidity of 55–60% at temperatures between 15.5°C and 21°C is considered the optimum for most organic materials. In the absence of air-conditioning, manuscripts can be buffered from the effect of rapid moisture change by wrapping them in textiles and storing them in rooms that contain such hygroscopic materials as carpets and curtains, rather than on bare shelves in cold storage vaults.

Tears and holes in parchment are fairly simply repaired using parchment insets and size made from parchment clippings. Crumbling, flaking and blistering paint is much harder to conserve because the unvarnished pigments are so sensitive: their brightness, opacity, texture, even their colour being affected by changes to the medium. Intervention should be avoided wherever possible, but when absolutely necessary, adhesive is carefully injected along the crack lines to secure flaking paint and a diluted form applied by spray or soft brush to consolidate crumbling areas. The adhesives are usually the same as the paint medium (egg white, gum or parchment size), but where persistent flaking occurs, as on the smoothly polished pages of Byzantine manuscripts, traditional materials are simply not strong enough to correct the trouble. Certain acrylic polymers and adhesives based on cellulose have come close to meeting the strict requirements of manuscript conservators. Since manuscript painting is always unvarnished, the removal of later paint is virtually impossible. For this reason the practice of touching in losses and damages is no longer considered acceptable.

BIBLIOGRAPHY

H. Plenderleith and A. Warner: *The Conservation of Antiquities and Works of Art* (Oxford, 1956/*R* 1974)

I. Bikova and others: 'Conservation Methods for Miniature Paintings on Parchment: Treatment of the Paint Layer', *Conservation and Restoration of Pictorial Art*, ed. N. Brommelle and P. Smith (London, 1976)

I. Mokretsova: 'Treatment of a Greek 13th Century Manuscript', *Reprints of the International Council of Museums Meeting* (Ottowa, 1981)

CATHERINE HASSALL

Manutius, Aldus (*b* Bassiano, ?1450; *d* Venice, 6 Feb 1515). Italian printer, publisher, teacher and translator. He studied in Rome and Ferrara and spent some time in Mirandola with Giovanni Pico (1463–94). In 1483 he was tutor to the Pio family. He formed a project to publish Greek texts and in 1489–90 moved to Venice, where soon afterwards he published the *Musarum panegyris* (1491). His Greek publications formed the core of his activities: he issued *c.* 30 first editions of literary and philosophical Greek texts including a five-volume Aristotle (1495–8). The first book printed with his own newly cut Greek type was the *Erotemata* (1495) by Constantine Lascaris (1434–?1501). Three further Aldine Greek types were developed, the last in 1502. Manutius established a pre-eminent position in Venetian publishing and in 1495 entered into a formal partnership with Andrea Torresani, his future father-in-law, and Pierfrancesco Barbarigo. His total output has been estimated at 120,000 or more copies. One of his most significant innovations was the production of small-format editions of Classical texts, starting with those of Virgil in 1501, produced in comparatively large print runs of 1000, the earliest precursor of the modern paperback. Typographically his major achievement was the type cut by Francesco Bologna, il Griffo, for Pietro Bembo's *De Aetna* (February 1495), a truly modern type still used in modified form. His activities as a teacher, scholar and translator were of equal importance to his printing work: his academy included among its associates Erasmus, Pietro Bembo, Andrea Navagero (1483–1529) and Fra Giovanni Giocondo of Verona.

See also TYPOGRAPHY.

BIBLIOGRAPHY
M. Lowry: *The World of Aldus Manutius: Business and Scholarship in Renaissance Venice* (Oxford, 1979)
N. Barker: *Aldus Manutius and the Development of Greek Script and Type in the Fifteenth Century* (Sandy Hook, 1985)
H. G. Fletcher: *New Aldine Studies. Documentary Essays on the Life and Work of Aldus Manutius* (San Francisco, 1988)

LAURA SUFFIELD

Manwaring, Robert (*fl* London, 1760–*c.* 1770). English furniture designer and cabinetmaker. He was recorded as working in the Haymarket, London, from 1760 until 1766, but no furniture documented or labelled from his workshop has been identified. In 1760 he contributed 50 designs to *Houshold Furniture in Genteel Taste*, sponsored by a Society of Upholsterers and Cabinetmakers, and in the same year he published the *Carpenter's Compleat Guide to the Whole System of Gothic Railing*, which consisted of 14 plates. There followed the *Cabinet and Chair-maker's Real Friend and Companion* in 1765, with designs for 100 chairs in Gothic, chinoiserie, Rococo and Rustic styles. A second edition, virtually unaltered, appeared in 1775. In 1766 he brought out the *Chair-maker's Guide*, containing 'upwards of Two Hundered New and Genteel Designs . . . for Gothic, Chinese, Ribbon and other chairs'; it includes two plates from William Ince and John Mayhew's *Universal System of Household Furniture* and at least six from Matthias Darly's *New-Book of Chinese, Gothic & Modern Chairs*.

In his preface to the *Cabinet and Chair-maker's Real Friend and Companion* Manwaring wrote, 'I have made it my particular Study to invent such Designs as may be easily executed by the Hands of a tolerable skilful Workman', and there have survived a number of chairs, particularly in the Rustic style intended for 'Summer Houses' that follow his designs. The perspective of his designs is faulty, and indeed Thomas Sheraton considered his designs 'worthless'. Two 'dressing chairs' (pl. 16 in the *Cabinet and Chair-maker's Real Friend and Companion*) seem to anticipate the 1820s Rococo Revival style.

WRITINGS
The Carpenter's Compleat Guide to the Whole System of Gothic Railing (London, 1760)
The Cabinet and Chair-maker's Real Friend and Companion (London, 1765, 2/1775)
The Chair-maker's Guide (London, 1766)

BIBLIOGRAPHY
G. Beard and C. Gilbert, eds: *Dictionary of English Furniture Makers, 1660–1840* (Leeds, 1986)

JAMES YORKE

Mányoki, Adám (*b* Szokolya, Hungary, 1673; *d* Dresden, 6 Aug 1757). Hungarian painter. The son of a Calvinist clergyman of noble birth, he was adopted at the age of 12 by a military judge and brought up in Celle, in northern Germany. He trained under the Hamburg artist Andreas Scheits (*c.* 1655–1737) and studied works by Nicolas de Largillierre in the castle of Salzdahlum. In 1703, he moved to Berlin and worked as a portrait painter at the Prussian court. No early oil paintings are known for certain, although scholars date an expressive, youthful *Self-portrait* (Budapest, N.G.) to this time. In 1707, the Princess Charlotte Amalia Rákóczi persuaded Mányoki to return to Hungary, whereupon he entered the service of Ferenc II Rákóczy (1676–1735), Prince of Transylvania. In 1709, the Prince sent him to the Netherlands to continue his studies and in particular to learn the art of engraving. After the defeat of the Hungarian struggle for independence from Austria, led by the Prince, Mányoki followed Rákóczy into exile in Danzig (now Gdańsk, Poland), where he painted the Prince's portrait (Budapest, N.G.), a half-length figure of particular dignity and solemnity and perhaps his most important work. After the Prince left Danzig, Mányoki worked in Warsaw; in 1713 he painted several portraits of Poles: of King *Augustus II*, of his ministers and courtiers, of *Count Heinrich Fleming* (all Warsaw, N. Mus.), and of the royal mistresses, including *Countess Aurora Königsmarck*, *Anna Cosel* and *Anna Orzelska* (Warsaw, Łazienki Pal.).

In 1714 Mányoki moved to Dresden and in 1717 took up an appointment as painter to the Saxon court. Portraits commissioned by Augustus II and the court, in Berlin, Dessau and elsewhere, reveal the influence of the French portrait painters Hyacinthe Rigaud and Nicolas de Largillierre. In 1723 Mányoki received permission to return to Hungary, where he hoped to reclaim family possessions. *En route*, in Vienna, he produced portraits of the imperial family: the *Archduchesses Maria Theresa and Maria Anna* (Schleissheim, Neues Schloss). With the exception of journeys to Vienna and Bohemia, Mányoki stayed in Hungary for about seven years. During this time he painted portraits of *János Podmaniczky* and of his family (Budapest, N.G. and Hung. N. Acad. Sci.) and of *Pál Ráday* and of his family (Budapest, Ráday Lib. Mus. Relig. A.). These differed sharply from his Dresden court portraits both in approach and in execution. For the milieu of his mainly Protestant Hungarian patrons Mányoki produced less elaborate, more austere pictures, which suited the rural Hungarian nobility's traditional ancestral galleries.

In 1731 Mányoki was again in Germany, working in Berlin, Leipzig and Dresden. In 1737 he returned to the post of court painter in Dresden, although he received less favour at the court of Augustus III (1696–1763), who gave preference to the French court painter, Louis de Silvestre. Mányoki's works from this time include portraits of *Augustus III* and *Count Georg Wilhelm Werthern* (Budapest, N.G.). During the 1730s and 1740s Mányoki produced numerous portraits of patricians, scholars and artists in Leipzig and Dresden; these include *Johann Melchior Dinglinger* (Dresden, Grünes Gewölbe) and *Johann Alexander Thiele* (Dresden, Gemäldegal. Neue Meister), paintings that reiterate the sumptuous presentation and intricate structure of Baroque court portraits but attempt to depict character in a more direct and emphatic manner. Many of these late works are only known from engravings, by Martin Bernigeroth (1713–67) and Johann Gottfried Bodenehr (1696–1743) among others. Some, including the once highly praised portrait of *Christian Ludwig von Hagedorn*, have disappeared without trace; several have survived but were long attributed to other artists. Although contemporary records confirm that Mányoki also experimented with genre-like portraits, it seems that he was unable to meet the new demands associated with the rise of Rococo. He died neglected and in poverty. Several letters and contemporary documents offer insight into Mányoki's personality and artistic outlook. The most important source of facts about Mányoki's life and work is provided by Christian Ludwig von Hagedorn, who came to know Mányoki in Dresden and regarded him very highly.

BIBLIOGRAPHY

Thieme–Becker
C. L. von Hagedorn: *Lettre à un amateur de la peinture* (Dresden, 1755)
T. Baden: *Briefe über die Kunst von und an Ch. L. v. Hagedorn* (Leipzig, 1797)
B. Lázár: *Mányoki Ádám: Élete és művészete* [Adám Mányoki: life and work] (Budapest, 1933)
K. Garas: *Magyarországi festészet a XVIII. században* [Hungarian painting in the 18th century] (Budapest, 1955)
Mányoki Ádám: Emlékkiállítás [Adám Mányoki: memorial exhibition] (exh. cat., Budapest, Mus. F.A., 1957)

KLÁRA GARAS

Manzi-Joyant. French firm of dealers. Michele Manzi (*b* Naples, 29 Sept 1849; *d* Paris, 1915) was an Italian printmaker. He studied at the military academies of Naples and Turin and became a professor of topography at the Scuola di Guerra in Turin. In 1872 he moved to Paris, where he became friendly with a group of other expatriate Italians that included Federico Zandomeneghi, Giovanni Boldini and Giuseppe De Nittis. In 1881 he took charge of the heliogravure workshop of Adolphe Goupil and Vincent van Gogh (1820–88), the painter's uncle; there he perfected the technique of chromotypogravure. Among his works was a celebrated album of facsimiles of drawings (1896–8) by his friend Edgar Degas. Maurice Joyant (*b* Mulhouse, 16 Aug 1864; *d* Paris, 1930) was the nephew of the painter Jules-Romain Joyant (1805–54) and a lifelong friend of Henri de Toulouse-Lautrec, whom he met at the Lycée Fontanes in 1872–3. Joyant replaced Théo van Gogh (1854–91) as a director of BOUSSOD, VALADON & Cie and in 1891 played an important role in persuading the French State to purchase James McNeill Whistler's *Arrangement in Grey and Black No. 1: Portrait of the Artist's Mother* (1871; Paris, Mus. d'Orsay). In 1893 Boussod, Valadon & Cie organized the first retrospective of Toulouse-Lautrec's work and five years later held an exhibition of his work at Goupil's gallery in London.

In 1898 Manzi and Joyant joined Jean Boussod to form the firm Jean Boussod, Manzi, Joyant & Cie, which was principally engaged in publishing prints. On Boussod's death in 1907 Manzi and Joyant opened their own gallery at 15 Rue de la Ville-l'Evêque, Paris, and became increasingly active as dealers in modern pictures and objects of vertu. They also held important auctions, such as those of the collections of Henri Rouart (1912) and Roger Marx (1919). Manzi was himself a collector of French and East Asian porcelain (collection sold in 1919) and was responsible, for example, for forming Comte Isaac de Camondo's magnificent collection of Japanese prints (Paris, Mus. Guimet). The Galerie Manzi-Joyant organized the posthumous retrospective of Toulouse-Lautrec in 1914; and Joyant was instrumental in persuading the Comtesse Adèle de Toulouse-Lautrec to give her collection of her son's work to the Musée Toulouse-Lautrec at Albi. On Manzi's death, however, increasing financial difficulties forced Joyant to sell Manzi's estate in 1919 (Paris, Gal. Manzi, Joyant & Cie, 13–14 March) to pay the gallery's creditors. Joyant's biography of Toulouse-Lautrec, published in 1926–7, remains the most vivid account of that artist's life and work.

WRITINGS
M. Joyant: *Henri de Toulouse-Lautrec, 1864–1901*, 2 vols (Paris, 1926–7)

BIBLIOGRAPHY
A. Alexandre: 'La Collection Manzi', *Collection Manzi: Tableaux, pastels, aquarelles, dessins* (sale cat., Paris, Gal. Manzi, Joyant & Cie, 13–14 March 1919), pp. i–xii
M. Barbin and C. Bouret: *Inventaire du fonds français après 1800*, Paris, Bib. N., Dept Est. cat., xv (Paris, 1985), pp. 154–7
S. Monneret: *L'Impressionnisme et son époque: Dictionnaire international*, i (Paris, 1987), pp. 394–5, 492–3

Manzini, Andrea di Giusto. See ANDREA DI GIUSTO.

Manzo (y Jaramillo), José (María) (*b* Puebla, 1789; *d* Puebla, 1860). Mexican architect, sculptor, painter, lithographer and teacher. He was the leading figure in Puebla in the fields of architecture, sculpture, painting and drawing during the early 19th century. He was Director of the Academia de Dibujo in Puebla from its foundation in 1814, and the first recipient of a scholarship from the academy, which allowed him to go to Paris (1824–7), where he studied architecture, drawing and lithography. He also visited museums, factories and prisons, intending to introduce French developments and systems into Puebla. On his return to Mexico he devoted himself to intense public activity, architectural reform, painting, lithography and teaching, and experiments in industrialized production. Among his most important sculptural works is the completion (1819) of the *ciprés* (altarpiece with baldacchino) for Puebla Cathedral, which had been left unfinished on the death of Manuel Tolsá. It combines a high altar, a sepulchral monument and a sanctuary of the Virgin, and it is one of the most spectacular examples of Mexican Neo-classicism. From 1829 Manzo y Jaramillo worked on restructuring the interior of the cathedral with the aim of achieving a Neo-classical stylistic unity. Besides a number of oils and drawings, he left a book of notes and watercolours that he made during his European travels.

BIBLIOGRAPHY
I. Katzman: *Arquitectura del siglo XIX en México* (Mexico City, 1973)
A. Alcocer: *La arquitectura de la ciudad de Guanajuato en el siglo XIX* (Mexico, 1988)

MÓNICA MARTÍ COTARELO

Manzoni, Piero (*b* Soncino, Cremona, 13 July 1933; *d* Milan, 6 Feb 1963). Italian painter and conceptual artist. He was self-taught as an artist. Shortly after he began painting he started to question the traditional aims and methods of the artist, expressing the nature of his searching in both writings and the objects that he produced. With Ettore Sordini (*b* 1934), Camillo Corvi-Morra and Giuseppe Zecca he co-edited the manifesto *Per la scoperta di una zona di immagini* (Milan, 1956). A manifesto with the same title written by Manzoni alone appeared almost immediately afterwards (1956–7). In his text he stressed the relationship between artistic expression and the collective unconscious, arguing that through extreme self-awareness the artist is able to tap mythological sources and to realize authentic and universal values; the canvas should remain an area of freedom in which the artist may go in search of primal images.

Around 1957 Manzoni began the *Achromes* series. Some were executed in raw gesso that had been scratched and scored, and others, for example *Achrome* (1959; Paris, Pompidou), consisted of cut or pleated canvas and kaolin. Although Manzoni had discovered the work of Yves Klein in early 1957 and apparently had been profoundly impressed, his own *Achromes* signify something different from Klein's monochromatic works: the desire to create a space devoid of any image of colour, mark or material.

In early 1958 Manzoni began to call into question the nature of the art object in works that prefigured CONCEPTUAL ART. In April he packaged his first precisely measured *Line* in a cardboard tube, a theme that he continued to evolve, for example *Line 1000 m Long* (1961; New York, MOMA; see fig.). Also in spring 1958 he began signing his name on living people and issuing them with certificates of authenticity (see 1971 exh. cat., pl. 99). He did not, however, exhibit his living sculptures until 1961. In 1958 he also began producing do-it-yourself pneumatic sculptures, each of which consisted of a balloon and a tripod packed in a wooden case. The purchaser was free to inflate the balloon himself; however, should he wish Manzoni to do the job, he would have to pay for the artist's breath.

Towards the end of 1959, with Vincenzo Agnetti (1926–81) and Enrico Castellani, Manzoni published *Azimut*, a magazine that set itself in opposition to the established organ of the Milanese avant-garde, *Il Gesto*. Soon afterwards, Manzoni and Castellani opened Galleria Azimut, which featured the work of Manzoni at its inauguration and on several other occasions during the short span of its existence, including an event in summer 1960 for which the public was invited to 'collaborate directly' in the

Piero Manzoni: *Line 1000 m Long*, chrome-plated metal drum containing roll of paper with ink line drawn along its 1000-m length, 514×390 mm, 1961 (New York, Museum of Modern Art)

consumption of the artist's work; during the 70 minutes that the exhibition lasted, Manzoni made hard-boiled eggs, signed them with his thumb print and distributed them to gallery visitors.

During the last years of his life Manzoni continued producing *Achromes* using a vast range of new materials: wads of cotton, canvas or cotton chemically treated so that changes in temperature would alter the colour, dinner rolls sealed in plastic and covered with kaolin, waste paper, stones and other materials (*see* ITALY, fig. 46). During this period he realized his most monumental work, *Socle of the World* (1961), an iron block that was installed in the sculpture park at the Angligården, Herning, Denmark, and supposedly served as the 'base of the world'.

BIBLIOGRAPHY
Piero Manzoni (exh. cat., Milan, Gal. Schwartz, 1964)
V. Agnetti and others: *Piero Manzoni* (Milan, 1967)
Piero Manzoni (exh. cat., ed. G. Celant; Rome, G.N.A. Mod., 1971)
Sarenco, ed.: *Piero Manzoni: Opere & giorni* (Villanuova sul Clisi, 1973)
J. Van der Marck: 'Piero Manzoni: An Exemplary Life', *A. America*, lxi (May 1973), pp. 74–81
Piero Manzoni: Paintings, Reliefs and Objects (exh. cat., London, Tate, 1974)

LAURAL WEINTRAUB

Manzù [Manzoni], **Giacomo** (*b* Bergamo, 22 Dec 1908; *d* Rome, 17 Jan 1991). Italian sculptor, draughtsman, painter, printmaker and stage designer. A mainly self-taught artist, working outside the avant-garde, Manzù developed a sculptural language unusual in that, while devoted primarily to the naturalistic, pre-modernist traditions of the free-standing human figure and the bas-relief, its strong design and imaginative qualities enabled it to avoid academicism. Manzù came from a poor family and at 13 started work as a gilder and stuccoist soon learning the skill of carving and the properties of wood, stone and plaster. Although ignorant of contemporary art and interested in painting only as a curiosity, he looked avidly at Greek art and the works of Michelangelo in reproduction and at 15 was captivated by the natural tactile qualities of Aristide Maillol's sculpture, which he also discovered in a book. While doing his military service in Verona in 1927, he was strongly affected by the reliefs on the doorway of S Zeno Maggiore and the equestrian statue of *Can Grande della Scala.*

Manzù travelled to Paris in 1928 in order to see Maillol's work, but his financial resources enabled him to stay only a few days. He then settled in Milan, broadening his political and cultural awareness through contact with painters, poets and journalists. In 1929 he was commissioned to decorate a chapel of the Università Cattolica del Sacro Cuore with saints and decorative works (*in situ*) and was thus enabled to devote himself full-time to sculpture. From 1929 to 1934 Manzù created polychrome stuccoes, painted terracottas, marble works in the round and bas-reliefs that recalled Etruscan, early Christian and medieval art, for example *Circus Scene* (wrought copper, 1932; New Jersey, L. A. Kolker priv. col., see Rewald, pl. 1), His more immediate influences were, however, the sculpture of Medardo Rosso and Ernesto de' Fiori (1884–1945). Until the late 1930s Manzù's two main themes were everyday life and scenes from the Bible, for example *Annunciation* (polychrome stucco, 1931; Milan, M. Grosso priv. col., see Rewald, pl. 4), the latter indicating less a religious conviction than a familiarity with the subject, absorbed during his strictly Catholic upbringing. His severe self-criticism led him to destroy many of his early works in 1933 and 1934 on his return to Bergamo.

In 1934 Manzù visited Rome, where he was able at last to study Classical marble sculpture at first hand and where the sight of the Pope flanked by two cardinals in St Peter's struck him as a singularly timeless image, almost like a sculptural group. The experience led him to produce his first sculpture of a *Cardinal* (bronze, 1938; Rome, G.N.A. Mod.), which was a recurring subject (e.g. *Cardinal*, bronze, 1947–8; London, Tate; see fig.). Back in Milan he continued to investigate different materials, executing his first bronze sculptures in 1934, and natural forms, especially the human body, for example in the crouching figure of David (1939–40, bronze; Ardea, nr Rome, Rac. Amici Manzù), in which movement is conveyed by the tension and expressive force of the overall shapes and anatomical details.

In the late 1930s Manzù introduced several new subjects to which he returned consistently for many years, using various media, until he felt he had exhausted both their pictorial and emotive possibilities. These included the life-size nude *Francesca Blanc* (e.g. bronze, *c.* 1941–50; Ardea, Rac. Amici Manzù); *Girl on a Chair* (e.g. bronze and lead, 1948; Turin, Gal. Civ. A. Mod.) and from 1941 scenes of the Crucifixion and Deposition, for example *Christ with a General* (bronze bas-relief, *c.* 1947; Ardea, Rac. Amici Manzù), Christian themes to which he at first introduced

Giacomo Manzù: *Cardinal*, bronze, h. 505 mm, 1947–8 (London, Tate Gallery)

elements reflecting contemporary violence, as part of a fierce critique of the Fascist dictatorship, without recourse to melodrama or overt polemicism. He also produced numerous variations on the theme of artist and model, treated with great naturalness and intimacy, particularly in paintings, drawings and prints, for example in the etchings *Painter and Model I–III* (1970).

Manzù's ideological development from anti-Fascism to Marxism during World War II did not prevent his returning to religious themes. In 1947 he entered the competition for the doors of St Peter's in Rome, for which the set subject was the Triumph of the Saints and Martyrs. After meeting Pope John XXIII (1881–1963), Manzù obtained permission to produce the *Door of Death* (bronze, 1964–7; *in situ*; see DOOR, fig. 6), which he felt to be a more suitable subject and which represents the threshold to another world rather than simply a backdrop or a screen. The overall pictorial effect and the palpable sense of space are here created by the folds of the drapery defining the bulk of the figures. Another monumental bronze door (1965–8; *in situ*; see DOOR, fig. 6) followed for the Grote Kerk in Rotterdam, this time on the theme of *War and Peace*, in which the image of mother and child becomes a symbol of a longed-for world. Manzù's delight in the innocence of youth, evident in earlier works such as *Playing Child* (bronze, 1943–52; Bristol, Mus. & A.G.), remained a favourite subject, notably in the series of sculptures of his children, which have an admirable spontaneity, for example *Giulia and Mileto on a Cart* (bronze, 1968; Ardea, Rac. Amici Manzù).

Apart from his more important activities as a sculptor, Manzù also made paintings and drawings characterized by a stripped-down naturalism, sometimes in preparation for a sculpture, such as *Reclining Woman* (pen and ink on paper, 1937; London, Tate), one of a series of studies for *Susanna* (bronze, 1942–52; London, Tate). His other activities included book illustrations, jewellery and stage design, for example for Stravinsky's *Oedipus rex* (Rome, Teatro dell'Opera, 1964) and Wagner's *Tristan und Isolde* (Venice, Teatro la Fenice, 1971). He also taught from 1941 to 1954 at the Accademia di Belle Arti in the Brera, Milan, and from 1954 to 1966 at Oskar Kokoschka's Internationale Sommerakademie für Bildende Kunst in Salzburg. In 1964 he settled in Ardea, near Rome, where the Raccolta Amici di Manzù, a branch of the Galleria Nazionale d'Arte Moderna, holds a large selection of his work.

BIBLIOGRAPHY

B. Joppolo: *Giacomo Manzù* (Milan, 1946)
A. Pacchioni: *Giacomo Manzù* (Milan, 1948)
E. Hüttinger: *Giacomo Manzù* (Amriswil, 1956)
C. L. Ragghianti: *Giacomo Manzù* (Milan, 1957)
C. Brandi: *Studi per la porta di San Pietro di Giacomo Manzù* (Milan, 1964)
A. Ciranna: *Manzù: Catalogo dell'opera grafica, 1929–1968* (Milan, 1968)
C. B. Pepper: *Un artista e il Papa* (Milan, 1968)
M. De Micheli: *Giacomo Manzù* (Milan, 1971)
J. Rewald: *Giacomo Manzù* (Milan, 1973) [definitive monograph, excellent illus.]
B. Heynold-von Graefe: *L'improvviso di Manzù* (Turin, 1974)
Giacomo Manzù (exh. cat. by A. Rohrmorer and E. Lack, Salzburg, Mus. Carolino Augusteum, 1974)
Giacomo Manzù (exh. cat. by R. Rewald, Rome, Ist. It.-Lat. Amer., 1975)
E. De Filippo: *Manzù: Album inedito* (Rome, 1977)
Il muro dell'Odissea (exh. cat. by C. Brandi and G. C. Argan, Rome, Studio A. A2, 1977)
Giacomo Manzù: Esposizione per le celebrazioni del suo settantesimo anno (exh. cat. by C. Brandi and R. Siviero, Florence, Accademia, 1979)
Manzù: 100 Works, 1938–1980 (exh. cat. by U. Parricchi, Hamilton, A.G., 1980)
'Hommage à Manzù', *XXe Siècle*, lviii (1984) [anthol. of crit. texts]
Giacomo Manzù (exh. cat. by M. Bogiancino, G. C. Argan and C. Brandi, Florence, Villa Poggio Imperiale, 1986)
Manzù (exh. cat., ed. L. Velani; Edinburgh, N.G. Mod. A.; Liverpool, Walker A.G.; Oxford, MOMA; 1987)
J. Shabel Manzù and others: *Manzù pittore* (Bergamo, 1988)
Manzù (exh. cat. by P. Portoghesi, F. Minervino and R. Bossaglia, Milan, Pal. Reale and Mus. Duomo, 1988–9)
C. Brandi and others: *Manzù, le porte* (Milan, 1989)
Manzù e il sacro (exh. cat. by L. F. Capovilla, G. Pellegrini and M. Calvesi, Bergamo, Pal. Ragione, 1991; Venice, Correr, 1991–2)

PIERO PACINI

Manzuoli, Tommaso. *See* SAN FRIANO, MASO DA.

Maori. Polynesian-speaking people inhabiting the area now known as New Zealand (Aotearoa) from the earliest times. They are descended from Eastern Polynesian canoe-builders and fisher people who migrated from the archipelagos that include the Society Islands and the Marquesas. Known as Hawaiki, this departure point may have been not one but many islands. Maori society consists of *c.* 13 tribal groups or nations (*iwi*), made up of clans or sub-tribes (*hapu*); each tribal group claims stewardship of and traditional residence within a particular territory. In the late 20th century Maori descendants numbered *c.* 404,000,

some 12% of the total population of New Zealand, and the majority lived in the northern part of North Island (Te Ika a Maui).

1. Before *c.* 1900. 2. After *c.* 1900.

1. BEFORE *c.* 1900.

(i) History. (ii) Architecture and carving. (iii) Canoe-building. (iv) Fibre art. (v) Tattoo.

(i) History. The earliest Maori sites excavated reveal settled occupation from the 11th and 12th centuries, so the actual arrival of Eastern Polynesian canoe voyagers probably occurred up to five or six generations before, from *c.* AD 900. Cooler climatic conditions resulted in the failure of most of the tropical food sources and garment fibre plants that they brought with them, though *taro* (*Colocasia antiquorum*) grew in the warmer northern regions, and the *kumara* (*Ipomea batatas*) flourished. Art was produced by all members of the tribe, although certain media and forms (e.g. architectural ornamentation, tattoo, dog-skin and feather weaving and weaponry design) were undertaken by learned specialists (*tohunga*). Central to the production of art was the concept of *tapu*: controlling access to resources and information and guarding the traditions, thus ensuring the arts' survival. *Tapu* also sustained a relationship to the realm of the deceased, the source of most arcane knowledge and inspired direction.

Maori art changed over the 1000 years following the initial settlement. This history is recorded in a chronology formulated by S. M. Mead, which describes the changes in style using a metaphor of growth, in both English and Maori (see Mead, ed., 1984, pp. 73–5). During the initial Seeding phase (Nga Kakano; *c.* AD 900–*c.* 1200), the 'seeds' sown by the original settlers included tattoo, canoe construction, adzes and fish-hooks, the rectangular house, bark-cloth manufacture, netting and plaiting techniques and the *patu*, a small cleaver. Local materials were used, but the objects' forms and compositions reflected examples found in the Polynesian islands of origin. Maori oral literature also tells of return voyages to the Central Pacific.

In the Growth phase (Te Tupunga; *c.* 1200–*c.* 1500) offshoots grew from the original forms. Isolation within a new physical and climatic environment required new rituals. The potential of nephrite (*pounamu*) and argillite (*pakohe*) was realized. An important object from this period is the Lake Ngaroto sculpture known as Uenuku (Te Awamutu, Dist. Mus.; see Mead, ed., 1984, p. 183). The clean, straight lines of this wood-carving culminate in a curvilinear shape that anticipates later trends, while also resembling the crested-headdress motif of Hawaiian art. Another fine work is a carved wooden lintel (*pare*) or ridge-carving found at Lake Tangonge, near Kaitaia (see fig. 1). This has an ABA composition, with B a central figure, or head facing outward, flanked by smaller heads or profiled avian–human (*manaia*) figures, an arrangement that prevails in the next style period. Both the Kaitaia carving and the Uenuku sculpture were ornamented with V-shaped notches, a motif characteristic of Te Tupunga that continued into the next period. It also occurred on stone, bone and ivory objects, and on such smaller items as whaletooth ornaments, filed argillite pendants and chevroned amulets. Motifs and designs inspired by the

1. Maori lintel (*pare*) or ridge-carving, wood, w. 2.26 m, from Lake Tangonge, near Kaitaia, *c.* 1200–*c.* 1500 (Auckland, Institute and Museum)

natural world were also used extensively; fish and bird forms were popular, shaping the surfaces of amulets, fish-hooks and lures.

More extensive fibre and plaitwork probably developed in this period too, as local resources were adapted. Basic mat-making, netting and basketry remained the same, but in textile manufacture, with the demise of *aute* (*Broussonetia papyrifera*), the bark cloth (*tapa*) resource plant, a new technology evolved, rooted in *harakeke* (*Phormium tenax*), or New Zealand flax. Long, durable fibres were processed through single- and double-pair twining techniques to produce serviceable garments for all seasons. Due to the perishable nature of fibre, there is little archaeological evidence to show when this development took place.

The Flowering phase (Te Puawaitanga; *c.* 1500–*c.* 1800) is often referred to also as the Classic phase of Maori art. Notching and chevrons, although retained for the first few decades, were eclipsed by the emergence of a curvilinear style, as artists broke away from the conventions of a rectilinear patterning based on the straight lines and matrices of plaiting and basketry. This stylistic evolution may be traced in such smaller items as hair combs. The simple rectangular style worn in the Growth phase was replaced by a rounded, intricately patterned form. Te Puawaitanga was a period of dramatic expansion, during which ornamentation blossomed. Canoes were spectacular, houses and storehouses elaborately constructed and embellished, and personal dress and adornment became consciously glamorous. Spiralling lines were inscribed on wood, bone, stone, ivory and tattooed on the human body. Maori art had developed its own distinctive character.

There followed Contact and Transition (Te Huringa; from *c.* 1800). During the 19th century Christianity undermined and destabilized tribal belief systems, and the Maori's economic and spiritual base—the land—was rapidly alienated. Some tribal representatives and the white-settler Government signed the Treaty of Waitangi in 1840 to protect the interests of both parties, but it became clear that settler expansion was a greater priority to the Government. During the hostilities that followed, in particular the Maori Wars (1860–72), over three million acres of Maori land were confiscated. Such foreign diseases as chicken pox and measles worsened their predicament, and by the turn of the century the Maori population had plunged to 42,000, compared to an estimate of 200,000 at the time of first contact. Yet Maori art, and art production, demonstrated an extraordinary resilience and vigour. The use of metal transformed the arts of carving, tattoo, canoe and house construction. The dynamic balance of plain and embellished surfaces was lost beneath a profusion of ornamentation. Paint became a popular medium in house ornamentation; and wool and candlewick were eagerly appropriated by garment weavers, for their colour range and immediate utility.

(ii) Architecture and carving. The early settlers brought with them the rectilinear floor-plan of Eastern Polynesia. One of the oldest sites excavated is the 12th-century Moikau house, with floor dimensions of 6×3.5 m, situated in the south-east region of the North Island. Suiting the cooler climate, this form endured through the ensuing centuries, with some modification in size and decoration. By the late 18th century chiefly dwellings were elaborately carved, and measured 6–10 m long and 3.5–5.5 m wide. Houses and utensils were profusely decorated, a favourite figure being the volute. With the introduction of metal, the technology of housebuilding and design became more sophisticated.

One outstanding early example of a Maori house survives. This is Te Hau Ki Turanga, whose designer, architect and principal carver, Raharuhi Rukupo (*c.* 1790-1873), is still acclaimed. Construction began in 1842 and was completed a few years later. Rectangular, with a shallow front verandah, this house has two central poles supporting a central beam, from which rafters extend, culminating above upright wall panels. The front and rear walls are also panelled by vertical carvings, and the ceiling is lined with *kakaho* (*Arundo conspicua*). The exterior is ornamented with carved and painted gable boards (*maihi*) supported by elaborate uprights on either side (*amo*), and the front central pillar is crowned with a decorative mask (*koruru*). The threshold (*paepae*) across the verandah is also ornamented. Deeper relief and complex surface carving indicate the use of metal tools. Such houses were, and continue to be, the centres of diverse activity: death rituals, weddings, meetings, inaugurations and other ceremonies. Te Hau Ki Turanga was purchased by the Government from the people of the Ngati Kaipoho tribe in 1868 and is on permanent display in the Museum of New Zealand, Te Papa Tongawera, Wellington (see Mead, ed., 1984, pl. 13).

Both men and women participated in the construction of Te Hau Ki Turanga and other such houses. The carved panels (*poupou*; see fig. 2) are linked by insulating lattices (*tukutuku*), which are vertical and horizontal slats of narrow wood laced together in geometric patterns of flax, *pingao* (*Demoschoenus spiralis*) or *kiekie* (*Freycinetia banskii*). Based on rectilinear and chevron forms, named after parts of the natural world, *tukutuku* was made by women, working in pairs one on either side of the panel. The rafter painting (*kowhaiwhai*) was also women's work in many tribal regions. (For an illustration of an ancestral ridgepole support post *see* PACIFIC ISLANDS, fig. 12.)

Storehouses (*pataka*), set above ground on one or four sturdy, carved supports, were also elaborately ornamented, with carved panels flanking the exterior, but not the interior, walls. Like the chiefly houses, they exhibited and often literally contained the material wealth of the tribe. Whereas the dwelling house's iconography comprised abstracted ancestral figures and historical narrative, the *pataka*'s art comprised schematic whales, birds and other edible creatures, symbolizing abundant food supply.

Portable and more functional items were also carved: weaponry and jewellery, food bowls and garden implements, mortuary caskets and fishing gear. The different woods included: *totara* (*Podocarpus totara*) and *kauri* (*Agathis australis*) for general works; *matai* (*Podocarpus spicatus*) for musical instruments; and *manuka* (*Leptospermum scoparium*) and *pohutukawa* (*Metrosideros excelsa*) for weaponry. Whale ivory and teeth were popular for jewellery and some weaponry, and whale, dog and human bone was used for musical instruments, fishing gear and personal adornment. Nephrite was greatly prized for weaponry and jewellery, for example *patu* (*see* PACIFIC ISLANDS, fig. 14), as well as the more functional artists' tools, adzes and chisels; argillite was worked too. Basalt and greywacke were also made into weapons and adzes, sinkers and small deity figures. Where it occurred, pumice was used to make mortuary caskets, figurines and small containers. Prevalent surface motifs included the spiral, the *manaia* (human–avian profile) and incised parallel lines. Although many scholars insist that carving was an exclusively male occupation, this is countered by the evidence of a strong oral tradition that records the activities of female artists.

(iii) Canoe-building. The first settlers brought an extensive canoe-building heritage to the islands of New Zealand, derived from their experience of crossing the Pacific Ocean. That heritage was further expanded, peaking with the magnificent carved vessels, *waka taua*, that greeted the early European travellers (*see* PACIFIC ISLANDS, fig. 8). The huge forest trees, sheltered waterways and plentiful fibre resources contributed to their development. *Waka taua* consisted of several sections of worked timber, usually *kauri* or *totara*, bound together with cordage of *harakeke*. Three pieces comprised the hull, the mid-section being the longest and widest, locking in at either end to bow and stern. Subsequently, remarkable lengths were achieved, but the average size was *c.* 20–30 m. The average crew-size was *c.* 50, but in the larger craft, with men sitting four or five abreast amidships, a crew of up to 140 has been recorded. Depth was acquired by gunwales fastened to the upper edge of the hull, running from fore to aft on either side, usually *c.* 200–250 mm wide and carved in a frieze-like pattern of rhythmic, moving figures. Tufts of seabird feathers were fixed to the cordage.

An elaborate bow-piece (*tauihu*) was set on the bow, a humanoid figure in an aggressive posture, with out-thrust tongue, and arms extended backwards. The *tuere*-prow type, trapezoid in shape, was less common, with eel-like figures framing intricate spirals. On either side of the

2. Maori house side-panel (*poupou*), wood, 1.12 m, from Whangara (possibly from the house owned by Hinematioro, a leading member of the Te Aitanga-a-Hauiti *hapu* of the Ngati Porou tribe), 18th century; recovered 1885 (Auckland, Institute and Museum)

bowpiece, on extended frames of *kareao* supplejack (*Rhipogonum scandens*), was fixed a circle of seabird feathers (*karuatua*), an ornamental navigational aid made by women. Positioned on the canoe stern was the stern-piece (*taurapa*), an upright panel, often carved, set against a leaning figure to oversee the crew. *Taurapa* could be up to 2.5 m long and 0.4 m across, and were enhanced by *puhi ariki*, a cape or streamers of dyed flax fibre (*muka*), entwined with seabird feathers.

Sails were rigged on long-distance voyages around the coast and between islands. *Harakeke* was used, and the sole extant example, dating from the early 19th century (London, BM), measures 4.4 m high, being 0.3 m wide at the apex and 2 m across at the top. *Raupo* or bullrush fibre (*Typha augustifolia*) was preferred, for its lightness, and some vessels were rigged with as many as three separate sheets. They were plaited in the chequerwork (*takitahi*) weaving technique.

(iv) Fibre art. Basic household equipment, such as floor-mats, containers, sleeping-mats and blinds, were manufactured by the plaiting technique of winding dextral and sinistral blades of fibre along a fixed commencement edge. This technique was brought from Eastern Polynesia and was adapted to the local resources, primarily *harakeke* and to a lesser degree *kiekie* and *pingao*. While most items were crafted for everyday use, they were variously patterned, and coloured with vegetable dyes and matter: *tanekaha* (*Phyllocladus trichomanoides*) for reddish tan, *raurekau* (*Coprosma australis*) for gold, and *paru*, a dense swamp mud that produced black. These were also used in garment manufacture. Sleeping-mats (*takapau wharanui*) and baskets (*kete*) were often fine works, particularly in aristocratic homes, with a finely plaited finish and bright geometric patterns.

Harakeke was the principal fibre source for garment-making, processed and manipulated in a variety of ways. *Toi* (*Cordilyne indivisa*) was used in rain-capes. Incidental, disposable garments like belts, girdles and chaplets were made from *paopao* (*Scirpus lacustris*) and *karetu* (*Heirochloe redolens*), perishable and quickly replaced. Other materials included dog-skin and dog-hair, selected feathers and, in a few recorded instances, human hair (used in the *taniko* borders of fine cloaks).

Oral literature records elaborate ceremonial costumes, and woven fragments of both ceremonial and everyday clothing have emerged from excavations and burial sites. Because of the paucity of material, textile-weaving techniques are not evident until the Flowering phase.

Fibre was drawn out from the flax plant by scraping with a mussel shell, after removal of the inner and outer edges and the butt of the blade. The hard green chaff would come away, leaving the silky fibre (*muka*). Maori weaving is always worked from left to right, horizontally, with suspended, vertical fibres (*whenu*) being twined together by horizontal fibres (*aho*) manipulated by the weaver. Three principal techniques were employed: single-pair twining (*whatu aho patahi*), double-pair twining (*whatu aho rua*) and *taniko*, which developed from the *whatu aho patahi*. *Taniko* involves the use of coloured threads to produce geometric patterns in red, black and white, and it

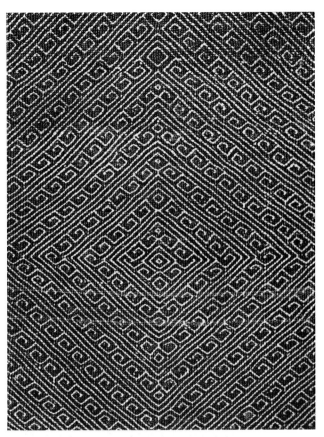

3. Detail of *taniko* border of Maori cloak (*kaitaka*), fibre, before 1770s (Stockholm, Etnografiska Museum)

was used to ornament hems and borders of chiefly garments (see fig. 3).

Everyday wear was simple, consisting of penis cords attached to a belt (*tu ure*) for men, and waistcloths or disposable grass aprons (*maro*) for women. In cold or inclement weather both men and women wore coarsely woven cloaks. For special occasions and to display social position and affluence, dress could be very elaborate. Cloaks of dogskin or dog-fur were the ultimate prestige garments (see fig. 4). Backed by a dense fabric of closely woven flax fibre, dogskin cloaks were formed of contrasting black–brown or black and white panels, emphasizing the height and vertical lines of the wearer; *taniko* was another visual device. Dogskin garments (*ihupuni* or *topuni*) had enormous symbolic value, because the pet dog (*kuri*) was greatly prized as a chief's accoutrement, and its demise resulted in the decline of this style. Dogskin cloaks were also presented as protective war garments, and tribal histories record their role in political negotiation and economic exchange.

Textiles draped toga-like around the body (*kaitaka*) were also popular, with borders of *taniko* ornamenting a shaped and gored cloak of finely processed fibre. Wool and candlewick, but especially coloured wool, were eagerly appropriated by weavers, although liable to moth infestation. Many of the finest examples of *kaitaka* and *paepaeroa*

4. Maori dogskin cloak (*kaha-kuri*), New Zealand flax and strips of haired dogskin, 1.24×1.41 m, early 19th century (Wellington, Museum of New Zealand, Te Papa Tongarewa)

(a cloak with vertical *aho* or weft lines), dating from the early 19th century, include accents of coloured wool and, occasionally, cotton thread. Although not common at the time of European contact, the feather cloak was to become a significant symbol of Maori nationhood and personal status, replacing the *ihupuni* and *kaitaka*. It is based on the thrummed cloak (*korowai*), which consists of fibre thrums or tassels (*hukahuka*) attached to the fabric foundation (*kaupapa*). *Korowai* were reportedly worn by women as an overgarment above the *mai* (a basic wraparound cloth), which was of highly processed fibre, bleached and soft, worn next to the skin. Rain-capes, though more functional than decorative, were also manufactured, with much coarser *whenu* and *aho*, and lighter processing of the fibre.

Maori textile art has often been regarded as primarily the domain of women, although tribal history and contemporary practice reveal a continuing contribution of men. Related to this is the comparative cultural value of the carver's art to the weaver's; as recently as the early 19th century a war canoe was exchanged for a *kaitaka*, demonstrating that a finely made textile had equal value to a *wakataua*.

(v) Tattoo. Tattoo (*moko*) was the mark of aristocracy, adulthood and achievement. As the tattooing process shed blood and brought risk of infection, it was tightly ritualized and regulated by *tapu*, a series of stringent prohibitions concerning food consumption and human contact. It varied between genders and social classes, and was executed by a highly skilled *tohunga*, who often travelled from one community to the next, working on commission. For this reason, although particular families may have claimed certain designs as part of their clan heritage, often a *tohunga*'s artistry would be shared across tribal boundaries. Both men and women practised the art.

Unlike the puncture technique of other Polynesian tattoo, *moko* actually gouged, the chisel incising the skin

to create a scarred channel of tissue into which pigment was applied. Chisels (*uhi*) were of nephrite, albatross and human bone, sharpened to a cutting edge. This edge was either smooth or serrated with comb-like teeth; the average blade was about 5 mm wide and lashed to a hafted handle. Different patterns required different blades: parallel curving lines had teeth set apart, and deep grooves demanded a straight edge. The *uhi* was dipped in pigment, set against the skin and, rhythmically, lightly tapped by the operator, to the accompaniment of a chanted monotone. An assistant, usually an apprentice, stretched and manipulated the skin to facilitate penetration. Pigment consisted of soot mixed into a fine oil base; the soot came from burning the powdered resin of the *kauri* or the *kahikatea* (*Podocarpus excelsum*) trees, or the *awheto hotete* (*Cordiceps robertsii*), a parasitic fungus. The tint varied from dense blue-black to a blackish green. Pigment containers reflected the art and the wealth of the artist. Often disposable, in light pumice or wood, some were ornately carved. The special feeding devices, used by the person being tattooed (*korere*, or funnels), were no less elaborate.

Design varied according to gender. Men were tattooed on the face (for illustration *see* TATTOO), generally first on one side, then on the other; the process was completed over a lifetime. Spirals and curvilinear patterns enhanced the wearer's own features. The hips, buttocks, groin and thighs (almost to the knee) were also patterned, often reflecting the *waituhi* motifs of rafter, gourd and calabash painting. Women's tattoo was generally less complex, though oral history and some ethnographic records tell of chiefly female warriors with fully patterned faces and/or thighs. The principal focus was the chin area, including the upper lip and nostrils, balanced by a diamond-shaped design between the eyebrows. Elegant lines on the sides of the neck, from the ear to the shoulder, were also worn, and across the abdomen and into the groin area. Spirals and abstract forms decorated the shoulders, and more vertical motifs flattered the thighs and the calves. Genital tattoo, though extremely rare, occurred in both sexes.

The tradition of severing and embalming the tattooed heads of enemies created a macabre but intense interest among non-Maori in the late 18th century and early 19th, before the traffick was outlawed. Many, perhaps hundreds, became trade items, particularly in exchange for firearms; to meet the demand, prisoners of war and low-born slaves were slain and then tattooed. Those of vanquished chiefs, however, are often fine examples of the artistry of *moko*. *Moko* was deplored by missionaries and discouraged by settlers; Robley records that the last male *moko* was probably carried out during the nationalist revival at the time of the 1860s land wars. By then, iron, copper and metal chisels had come into use, most commonly for the women's chin tattoo (*kauae moko*).

BIBLIOGRAPHY

The writings and drawings of the early European visitors to New Zealand are important sources for the history of Maori art. The works listed below will guide the reader to both the published accounts and archive holdings.

A. Hamilton: *The Art Workmanship of the Maori Race in New Zealand*, 5 pts (Wellington, 1896–1900); repr. as 1 vol. (Wellington, 1901), also as *Maori Art* (London, 1972)

H. G. Robley: *Moko: Or Maori Tattooing* (London, 1896)

H. L. Roth: *The Maori Mantle* (Halifax, 1923)

E. Best: *The Maori*, Mem. Polynes. Soc., v, 2 vols (Wellington, 1924)

——: 'The Maori Canoe', *NZ Dominion Mus. Bull.*, 7 (Wellington, 1925/*R* 1976)

P. Buck [Te Rangi Hiroa]: *The Coming of the Maori* (Wellington, 1949)

S. M. Mead: *Traditional Maori Clothing: A Study of Technological and Functional Change* (Wellington, 1969)

N. Prickett, ed.: *The First Thousand Years: Regional Perspectives in New Zealand Archaeology* (Palmerston North, NZ, 1982)

S. M. Mead, ed.: *Te Maori: Maori Art from New Zealand Collections* (Auckland and New York, 1984) [pubd in conjunction with exh., New York, Met.]

S. M. Mead: *Te Toi Whakairo: The Art of Maori Woodcarving* (Auckland, 1986)

M. Prendergast and B. Brake: *Te Aho Tapu/The Sacred Thread: Traditional Maori Weaving* (Auckland, 1987)

N. Te Awekotuku: *Mane Wahine Maori: Selected Writings in Maori Women's Art, Culture and Politics* (Auckland, 1991)

R. Neich: *Painted Histories: Early Maori Figurative Painting* (Auckland, 1993)

NGAHUIA TE AWEKOTUKU

2. AFTER *c.* 1900. In the early decades of the 20th century the New Zealand Government sought to revive Maori arts, and in 1927 a School of Maori Arts and Crafts (now the New Zealand Maori Arts and Crafts Institute) was established in Rotorua. The School tended to encourage the following of fixed rules about colour, form, media, gender roles and even narrative, rules that came to be challenged by Maori artists after World War II. Meeting-houses, the focal point for Maori art forms—carving, weaving, painting—had by the late 19th century already radically integrated European materials, tools and structural and aesthetic approaches to architecture, decoration and figurative depiction. This Maori readiness to adapt in the face of change gained in importance when the large-scale movement of Maori people from rural tribal bases to urban centres and their cultural interaction with Pakeha (white settlers) increased markedly after World War II. In 1936 only 9.3% of the total Maori population were based in the cities, but by 1966 this figure had risen to 54.5%. Many Maori artists became schoolteachers, for example SANDY ADSETT, employed as arts-and-crafts advisers. Other artists, such as SELWYN MURU, have also worked as teachers.

The study of Western art by artists from strong rural Maori communities helped create exciting cross-cultural possibilities. Maori art in the late 1950s and 1960s was characterized by assimilations of Western aesthetic and Maori culture, experimentation with new materials and technology, and greater exposure to the New Zealand public through gallery exhibitions. For FRED GRAHAM, the British sculptors Barbara Hepworth and Henry Moore provided important models for sculptural work, suggesting new ways of working with materials, particularly wood, from 1962. Their concentration on the formal qualities of materials, the organic, curvilinear treatment of surfaces and their balance of flat and rounded forms were inspirational. Contact with white New Zealand sculptors influenced Graham to try moving Maori art away from such materials as wood and from the intricate surface decoration traditional in Maori carving. When working on public sculptures Graham used other media, such as copper and stainless steel. ARNOLD MANAAKI WILSON, the first Maori to graduate with honours from a school of fine arts (University of Auckland, 1955), exploited Brancusi's dictum that 'What is real is not the external form but the essence of things'. Already interested in the embodiment of man (*tangata*), Wilson sensed in Brancusi's work similar references to the power of human form evident in traditional Maori posts, such as markers of land (*pou whenua*).

Western influence is even stronger in the work of Maori who have had first-hand experience of European art during their formative years. RALPH HOTERE and MATT PINE attended the Central School of Art and Design, London, studying graphic art and design. Pine's experience with formalist and minimalist forms of sculpture in England in the 1960s led him to focus on the architectural structure and detail of cultural forms such as the carved meeting-house (*whare whakairo*). Hotere's work bears affinity with the aesthetic of such American abstract painters as Frank Stella.

The sculpture *Te Maaoorii* by Selwyn Muru exemplifies his life-long interest in the work of Picasso, especially his assemblage methods (see fig. 5). The sculpture is a response to the 1984 exhibition *Te Maori* (New York, Met.; see Mead, ed., 1984), its lengthened vowels encouraging correct pronunciation. *Te Maaoorii* is a complex synthesis of tradition and innovation. The main material used is *kauri* timber from local demolition sites, *kauri* being one of the major woods used in traditional Maori carving. The S-bend copper pipe on top of the figure's head suggests a top knot, the classical form of hairstyle in the late 18th century. Cast-iron engine parts and a metal rod allude to sexual organs. Overall there is here a robust sense of humour about the body and bodily functions that is typical of traditional Maori carving.

From 1959 until his death in 1972, PINE TAIAPA, the Tikitiki master carver (*tohunga whakairo*), made himself available to many young Maori artists wishing to deepen their knowledge and experience of Maori art. The Department of Education employed him to instruct Maori arts-and-crafts advisers in carving, weaving and history. Maori legends were a recurring theme in Maori art in the early 1960s. The Maori creation belief—the separation of Ranginui (sky-father) and Papatuanuku (earth-mother)—is often evident in the work of both PARATENE MOKO PUORONGO MATCHITT and CLIFF WHITING. Whiting's 15 years of research into Maori community art forms culminated in the large customboard mural *Te wehenga o Rangi Raua ko Papa* ('The separation of Rangi and Papa'; 1965–76; Wellington, NZ, N. Lib.). The mural used materials, forms and techniques essential to Maori art, and in integrating all three major meeting-house art forms Whiting offered an economic and culturally viable alternative to the traditional meeting-house aesthetic. The most spectacular extension of Whiting's mural is *Te whaneke-tanga o Tainui* ('The history of Tainui'; 1974–5), designed by Matchitt for the Kimiora dining-hall, Turangawaewae Marae, Ngaruawahia. This articulates the history of the Tainui confederation of tribes, adopting many of Whiting's innovations but on a larger scale.

Since the late 1970s a growing number of Maori women artists have contributed to the development of Maori art. Traditional Maori art forms undertaken by women, particularly weaving, have continued to be practised by such

5. Selwyn Muru: *Te Maaoorii*, mixed media, h. 3.0 m, 1986 (Auckland, private collection)

meeting-house has not been reflected in exhibited art. It has been male Maori artists who have dominated public gallery exposure and key developments in community art since the mid-1960s. Emerging Maori women artists have sought to redress this imbalance. Painters such as EMILY KARAKA, ROBYN KAHUKIWA and KURA TE WARU REWIRI and the fibre artist AROMEA TAHIWI have all been involved in developing Maori art forms from a female perspective. The use of figurative carving in Karaka's, Rewiri's and Kahukiwa's painting has been a further challenge to an art form traditionally considered a male domain. Aromea Tahiwi is one of a number of weavers who have contributed to developments in Maori art. In her fibre work *Ka hao te rangatahi* ('The new net goes fishing'; 1990; Melbourne, Mr and Mrs Beade priv. col.) she made inventive use of traditional weaving techniques, materials and motifs.

Maori versatility is further shown by the development from the rain-cape of the *piupiu*, a thrummed skirt possessing a remarkable acoustic quality. Women's chin tattoo (*Kauae moko*; *see* §1 above) declined in popularity in the mid-20th century, but by the late 1940s chisels (*uhi*) had been replaced by iron needles, and chins were tattooed by the puncture technique.

BIBLIOGRAPHY

J. Mcpham: *The Story of Te Hono Ki Rarotonga Carved Meetinghouse and the Hine Matikotai Dining Hall, Pakirikiri Marae, Tokomaru Bay* (Gisborne, n.d.)
Contemporary Maori Art (exh. cat. by F. Davis, Hamilton, NZ, Waikato Mus. A. Hist., 1977)
W. Renwick: *Art in Schools: The New Zealand Experience* (Wellington, 1978)
P. Cape: *New Zealand Painting since 1960: A Study in Themes and Developments* (Auckland, 1979)
S. Mead and B. Kernot, eds: *Art and Artists of Oceania* (Palmerston North and Mill Valley, CA, 1983)
K. Mataira: *Maori Artists of the South Pacific* (Raglan, 1984)
S. Mead, ed.: *Te Maori: Maori Art from New Zealand Collections* (Auckland and New York, 1984) [pubd in conjunction with exh., New York, Met.]
E. Eastmond and M. Penfold: *Women and the Arts in New Zealand: Forty Works, 1936–86* (Auckland and Harmondsworth, 1986)
D. Nicholas: *Seven Maori Artists* (Wellington, 1986)
Aspects of Recent New Zealand Art: Sculpture (exh. cat. by A. Johnston, Auckland, C.A.G., 1986)
M. Pendergrast and B. Brake: *Te Aho Tapu: The Sacred Thread: Traditional Maori Weaving* (Auckland, 1987)
R. Panoho: *Developments in Maori Art: Paratene Matchitt* (diss., U. Auckland, 1988)
A. Taylor: *Maori Folk Art* (Auckland, 1988)
R. Neich: *Painted Histories: Early Maori Figurative Painting* (Auckland, 1993)

RANGIHIROA PANOHO

Mao Tse-tung. *See* MAO ZEDONG.

Mao Zedong [Mao Tse-tung] (*b* Shaoshan, Hunan Province, 26 Dec 1893; *d* Beijing, 9 Sept 1976). Leader of the People's Republic of China from 1949 to 1976. His importance in art history derives from his writings on art and his status as an icon. In his *Talks at the Yan'an Forum on Literature and Art*, delivered in May 1942, Mao established the Chinese Communist Party's attitude to art, which contrasted strongly with traditional Chinese concepts of art but had much in common with contemporary ideas in the Soviet Union. Mao believed art to be inherently class-based and sought to harness it to serve political struggle. He extolled the so-called 'mass style', which, it

outstanding exponents as RANGIMARIE HETET and her daughter DIGGERESS (RANGITUATAHI) TE KANAWA. However, the gender balance that Whiting believes is fundamental to the unity and harmony of art forms in the was proclaimed, was a fusion of the thoughts and feelings of the artist with those of the peasants and workers. This form of SOCIALIST REALISM, which incorporated aspects of Chinese folk art, came to characterize Chinese art until after Mao's death. In art, as in other aspects of life under Mao, deviation from the party line was not tolerated and was met with severe punishment (*see also* CHINA, §XV, 2(ii)).

As leader of China, Mao became the focus of a cult of personality, and his image became an object of near-religious veneration. This phenomenon had its parallels not only in the 20th century, when other dictators such as Lenin were similarly exalted, but also in the godlike status that had traditionally been accorded to China's emperors. Every office or classroom had a photograph or painting of Mao, every town a statue: his image was to be found even on key-rings. He was represented in a variety of guises—the great philosopher, the man of the people advising the peasants, the national hero swimming across the Yangzi River—all of them calculated to emphasize various qualities of his leadership. This movement reached its tumultuous peak during the Cultural Revolution (1966–76), but even after his death Mao's image was used in a talismanic fashion. It was also appropriated by political groups as an emblem of legitimacy; for example, during the pro-democracy demonstrations in Tiananmen Square, Beijing, in 1989 it was used by the students as a symbol of resistance to Deng Xiaoping and Li Peng, the government leaders at the time. In the 1990s such Chinese artists as Yi Youhan (*b* 1943), Li Shan (*b* 1944) and Wang Ziwei (*b* 1963) adapted the idiom of Pop art to show Mao in a way that recalled, both in style and in the conscious lack of idealism, the portraits of Mao by Andy Warhol (e.g. *Mao*, 4.44×3.47 m, 1973; Chicago, IL, A. Inst.). The contrast with the sincere devotion that earlier artists had striven to convey and inspire with their depictions of Mao was intentional and obvious.

WRITINGS
'Talks at the Yenan Forum on Literature and Art', *The Period of the War of Resistance against Japan (II)* (1965), iii of *Selected Works of Mao Zedong* (Beijing, 1961–77), pp. 69–98

BIBLIOGRAPHY
New Art from China: Post-1989 (exh. cat., Hong Kong, A. Fest.; Taipei, Hanart Gal.; Oxford, MOMA; London, Marlborough F.A.; 1993–4)

Map. Image of the earth, seas or stars projected on a flat surface. Its contents represent the distribution of a variety of phenomena in space: continents and oceans, mountains and flatlands, rivers and lakes, countries and their subdivisions, cities and towns. Through much of history the central part of a map represented the known and faded outward into the unknown. This phenomenon of decreasing knowledge and accuracy was doubtless responsible for the cartographer's tendency to fill unknown spaces with imaginary creatures, monsters of sea and land, ships on the seas, rulers and cities on land. Jonathan Swift summed up this characteristic of maps in his *On Poetry* (177–80):

So Geographers in Afric-Maps
With Savage-Pictures fill their Gaps;
And o'er unhabitable Downs
Place Elephants for want of Towns.

The earliest decorative–artistic elements on maps are anthropomorphic representations of the principal winds. On a 10th-century world map, in a manuscript of Isidore of Seville's *Etymologia* (Rome, Vatican, Bib. Apostolica, MS. Reg. Lat. 1260, fol. 39), the four principal winds are represented in the four corners of the map, each riding what appears to be a leather sack. This particular image can be plausibly traced back to the cave of winds of Aeolus in the *Odyssey*. Winds continued to be part of the artistic vocabulary of cartographers until well into the 16th century. Artistic details on maps may be defined as serving one or more of these purposes: to embellish an otherwise purely utilitarian, linear image of the earth; to provide representations of man and his works as well as creatures of man's imagination; and last, but not least, as Swift defined it, to fill in the blank spaces.

1. The origins of cartography. 2. Western world maps. 3. Sea charts. 4. Printed maps and atlases. 5. Wall maps. 6. Tapestry maps. 7. Later developments.

1. THE ORIGINS OF CARTOGRAPHY. The earliest known attempts to present the topography of a given area in a two-dimensional form are found on clay tablets from Mesopotamia. An example of *c.* 1500 BC (Jena, Friedrich-Schiller-U., Hilprecht Samml.) bears a map of Nippur, on which are marked the city's principal buildings, gates and rivers, all of which are identified in Sumerian and Akkadian. A Babylonian world map from Sippar (7th–6th century BC; London, BM), more ambitious in scope, portrays the world in a series of concentric circles centred on Babylon; its concept of a circular world surrounded by water was to recur in Europe until the 16th century AD. Elsewhere in the ancient world the Egyptians developed surveying techniques, and a number of architectural plans have survived (e.g. London, U. Coll., Petrie Mus. Egyp. Archaeol.), but the only known map in the modern sense is the so-called Turin Mine Plan (Turin, Mus. Egizio; *see* EGYPT, ANCIENT, §XVI, 11).

Chinese cartography was technically much further advanced than that in the Ancient Near East. The earliest extant Chinese maps were engraved on stone in the 12th century AD, but cartography flourished from at least *c.* 1137 BC, when there is an account of a map depicting the whole of China. About 450 BC an official topographical description was issued with maps, and further surveys were made in the second half of the 3rd century BC. The maps were painted on bamboo, silk or, from the late 2nd century BC, paper (*see* TOPOGRAPHY, fig. 1). The works of Pei Xiu (AD 224–71) were to become the basis of later Chinese cartography, although this was modified when the introduction of Buddhism from India brought with it the concept of a disc surrounded by water. Sea maps and charts were also produced, covering coastlines as far as the Persian Gulf. The earliest extant examples of maps in Japan, preserved in the Shōsōin repository in Nara, are ink drawings on linen or rice-paper of reclaimed land, dating from the Heian period (AD 710–94). It is said that the first map of the whole of Japan was done by the priest Gyōgi (also known as Gyōgi Bosatsu or Bodhisattva Gyōgi; AD 668–749). In the 17th century, with the importation of European maps and improved printing techniques, cartography flourished in Japan and resulted in high-quality examples, such as the *Dai Nihon enkai jissoku zenzu* ('The complete surveyed coastal map of Great Japan', 1821; Tokyo, N. Mus.).

In the Americas primitive cartography is well represented by the easily portable birch bark maps used by the indigenous people of North America. The Eskimos of Greenland developed both two- and three-dimensional maps. The latter were sometimes modelled in sand in relief, with villages and islands marked by wood and stones. Lengths of wood with features carved into the edges were also used for elaborate schematic maps of the coastline. In Central America much of the evidence for cartography among the Aztecs and Maya has been destroyed (*see* MESOAMERICA, PRE-COLUMBIAN, §VI), but there is enough to indicate its use both in cartographic histories and in representations of the area under a town's control.

2. WESTERN WORLD MAPS. Although Herodotus of Halikarnassos mentioned the production of world maps in Greece in the second half of the 5th century BC, the number of surviving Greek and Roman maps or map fragments is very small. The most important illustrate the manuscripts of the manuals of Roman land surveyors, the *agrimensores* or *gromatici*, although the only elements that may be considered as remotely artistic are the symbols used to represent settlements. The *Tabula Peutingeriana* (Vienna, Österreich. Nbib., Cod. 324), a 13th-century copy of a road map of the Roman empire, which was compiled possibly as early as the 2nd century AD, bears, in addition to town and city symbols, a handful of more elaborate

images. As the major roads, such as the Via Appia, are shown as emanating from Rome, the city is represented by a goddess presiding over the centre of the empire's road system. The port of Rome, Ostia, is shown as it was in the 2nd century AD.

The largest number of surviving medieval maps are the *mappae mundi*, world maps conforming to one of several late Classical and medieval concepts of the world. The best-known of these are the tripartite maps (see fig. 1) that represent the earth as a flat disc, divided into three continents (Europe, Asia and Africa); these are usually defined as 'T-in-O' maps. The 'O' stands for the ocean surrounding the earth disc; the vertical stroke of the 'T' represents the Mediterranean, dividing Europe and Africa; the left side of the horizontal stroke of the 'T' is the River Don, dividing Europe and Asia, while the right side is the River Nile, dividing Africa and Asia. Half of the earth disc is occupied by Asia, with the other half equally divided between Europe and Africa. The 'T-in-O' maps are theocentric and anthropocentric and may be viewed as symbolic, with the threefold division standing for the Trinity and the three continents for the inheritance of Noah's three sons. There are very few artistic and decorative elements in the early *mappae mundi*; it is only after 1200 that an increasing number of pictorial representations are added to the linear, two-dimensional map, except for the simplistic image of mountains and mountain systems.

The largest and most heavily decorated of medieval world maps was the Ebstorf *mappa mundi* (Ebstorf Abbey, destr. 1943), known through excellent full-scale facsimiles. Its Christian symbolism is unmistakable: the head of Christ is at the top of the map (orientated to the east), his hands are shown in the north and south and his feet in the west. Jerusalem is at the centre of the map, as was usual in the medieval Christian view of the world, corresponding to the biblical statement placing it there. Those parts that portray the known world of the time are illustrated by places and real people who are part of the cartographer's world. Further out, mythological–historical elements take over, drawn from medieval or Classical texts: thus the Amazons are shown in the east, earthly Paradise is illustrated by Adam, Eve and the serpent, while Africa, occupying the southern margins of the world map, is peopled by monsters of every variety as described by late Classical writers, for example in Solinus' work on the marvels of the world (*Collectanea rerum memorabilium, c.* AD 200).

It seems possible to draw a parallel between the functions of these *mappae mundi* of the later Middle Ages and certain features of the great cathedrals. The sole surviving large medieval world map (13th century; Hereford Cathedral; see fig. 2) probably served as a means of showing pilgrims and visitors the *fabrica mundi* in considerable detail, just as stained-glass windows, sculptures and bas-reliefs provided images of the lives of saints, kings, queens and biblical personages.

3. SEA CHARTS. The medieval *mappa mundi* was a product of the scholarly world. Although it may be traced back to Roman antecedents, its two-dimensional aspect represents a marked step back when compared with the insistence of Greco-Roman writers on a spherical earth. It

1. 'T-in-O' map, painted parchment, 13th century (London, British Museum, MS. 28681, fol. 9*r*)

is probable that a new kind of map, the navigation chart, based on practical observation rather than scholarly speculation, was developed from the early 11th century. Its beginnings are unknown, but its use by mariners is well documented from the mid-13th century, and the first datable examples were probably drawn at the end of that century.

The nautical or sea chart, often referred to as a 'portolan chart' (from It. *portolano*, Gr. *periplos*: a set of written sailing directions that can be traced back to the first centuries of the Christian era), was a tool of the sea trade. Its purpose was to enable the navigator to set his course from one port to the next, using simple navigational aids. The sea chart was utilitarian, practical and devoid of extraneous elements, showing coastlines, coastal cities and an intricate network of rhumb-lines indicating the wind directions as represented by the compass: 4, 8, 16 or 32 lines radiating from several points on the chart. As maritime trade expanded rapidly, at first within the Mediterranean and later including the marginal seas of Europe, the 'portolan chart' enabled the navigator to reach his destination. Few charts designed for shipboard use have survived. However, in the late 14th century chartmakers began to add artistic features, and examples made to ornament the walls of counting houses or for use in libraries display both the artistic and cartographic talents of the maker. An early 15th-century contract drawn up between the factor of a Florentine merchant and a Barcelona chartmaker, the representative of one of the leading schools of sea chart design in the earlier stages of the art, clearly defined the decorative elements to be included in the chart. There were to be 165 people and animals, 25 ships, 140 trees and 340 banners standing for cities and castles. The chart thus united the skills of the chartmaker with those of a miniaturist.

At first the sea chart was restricted to the Mediterranean and the Black Sea. Gradually it came to include the Atlantic and the Mediterranean shores of the Iberian peninsula and north-west Africa. From the 16th century the waters of northern Europe were included, and eventually all the world's seas were covered. As the area encompassed by the charts extended, so did the decorative and artistic content. In the earliest surviving sea charts colour was limited to the network of rhumb-lines, corresponding to the winds as shown in the compass rose, with different colours being used for the four principal winds and for the subordinate ones that make up the complete network of 32 winds. At first coastal settlements were marked only by name, but later the more important were identified by the use of banners with the coat of arms of the controlling power. Major ports, most frequently Venice and Genoa, were shown in bird's-eye views; ships were drawn on the open seas, with their rigging illustrating current techniques of ship and sail design. The inland areas of remote, exotic places, especially north Africa, include representations of kings sitting in their tents, which are open to the viewer. A handful of charts, or maps based on their design, include information about inland areas, both textual and pictorial, which represented the state of contemporary knowledge. The best-known and most important among these was the Catalan Atlas (Paris, Bib. N., MS. Esp. 30), drawn by a Catalan cartographer and presented to Charles V of

2. *Mappa mundi*, painted parchment, 13th century (Hereford Cathedral)

France in 1375. Some of its illustrative material refers to information contained in the writings of Marco Polo (*c.* 1254–1324).

The first major centres of sea chart design were Italy and Catalonia, whose cartographers dominated the trade in the 14th and 15th centuries. Later, Portuguese, French, Flemish, Dutch and English practitioners also produced charts. By the late 16th century sailing charts had become outstanding examples of the miniaturist cartographer's art, employing colour and a wealth of illustrative material. Flags and coats of arms remained among the dominant elements of the artistic vocabulary, and to these were added the imagery of native peoples in distant lands, as well as their flora and fauna. Without exception, all manuscript sea charts from the 13th century to the early 18th were drawn on parchment.

4. PRINTED MAPS AND ATLASES. The first printed map was published in 1472; it was a rather plain version of a 'T-in-O' type medieval world map. For the next hundred years or so, printed maps, whether of the world or its component parts, remained plain, linear works without ornamental features. A few of them are decorated with the portraits of important cartographers. Those illustrated in the first half of the 16th century were generally based on maps by Claudius Ptolemy (*fl* 2nd century AD), the cartographer and astronomer whose *Geographia* revolutionized geography and cartography in the 15th and 16th centuries, and the Florentine explorer and navigator Amerigo Vespucci (1454–1512). Ptolemy's *Geographia*, later manuscript versions of which were accompanied by maps,

set forth the basic principles of cartography, including the directions for projecting the spherical surface of the earth on flat paper.

One of the first printed maps to employ artistic concepts and fit the framework within an artistic design was a world map made by Georg Braun (1542–1622), a well-known illustrator. This was printed in Cologne in 1574. The design fits within the body of a double-headed eagle, symbol of the Holy Roman Empire. Within the wings of the eagle there are nearly 100 coats of arms, the body of the eagle is the world map, and on the margins are the planets and the signs of the zodiac. During the last third of the 16th century mapmakers began using various ornamental forms on woodcut and engraved maps. These included vignettes to represent important cities and towns, portraits of rulers and images of the officials and military in their employ. Animals such as elephants, representative of the fauna of exotic places, decorated maps of remote parts of the world. The tools of important trades, such as navigation, became an accepted adjunct of the map itself. A good example of this latter type is the title-page of *Spieghel der zeevaerdt* (Leiden, 1583–5) by Lucas Waghenaer (1533/4–1606), a Dutchman and the most popular maker and publisher of printed, rather than manuscript, sea charts of the late 16th century and the 17th. The London edition, entitled the *Mariners Mirrour* (1588), shows mariners, a ship and some of the important tools of the navigator: magnetic compass, lead-line, quadrant, Jacob's staff, astrolabe and dividers.

During the 16th century another element appeared on printed maps, the CARTOUCHE, which was to become an integral part of map design and provide engravers with unlimited opportunities to display their artistic skills. A cartouche may be defined as an embellishment, often in the form of a scroll, that encloses a title, legend or name. William Folkingham (*fl* 1610), an English surveyor, referred to it as a 'compartiment, blankes or Figures bordered with Anticke Boscage or Grotesco-Worke'. In its early form the cartouche simply displayed the title of the map. Its abstract ornament was borrowed from the general vocabulary of woodcutters and engravers. The frame of the early cartouche could be defined by strapwork, with few non-generalized features, displaying the heads of deities, putti or, occasionally, heads of animals. These designs were borrowed from Italian, Flemish and Dutch pattern books published for the use of engravers, goldsmiths, printers and cartographers.

During the last third of the 16th century the northern and southern Netherlands became the centre of European map-printing. At first the trade and craft was centred on Antwerp, which was ruled by Spain, the leading colonial power of the time, but early in the 17th century, with the rise of Dutch sea power and the emergence of the Netherlands as one of the leaders of world trade, the centre moved to Amsterdam. Cartographers of the 16th century were generally conservative in their use of artistic features, restricting them to a few embellishments of the map. Artistic design was best displayed on the title-page of an ATLAS, a new and increasingly important form of map publishing. The first atlases were *ad hoc* volumes, sets of maps bound together to respond to the demands of the cartographer's clientele.

A typical example from the 17th-century Dutch 'Golden Age' is a world atlas, first published in 1606 by Jodocus I Hondius (i). Many maps in this had been incorporated originally in the atlas of Gerardus Mercator (1512–94), first published in 1595. Mercator was a Flemish engraver and instrument-maker who settled in Duisburg and became one of the greatest cartographers of all time. The title-page of the first volume of his atlas may be considered an intimation of the later development of map- and atlas-making, incorporating both allegory and abstract designs. The leading map publishing houses of 17th-century Amsterdam were those of the Blaeu and Jansson families, who produced luxurious atlases destined for the libraries of royal and merchant princes.

A map entitled *Leo Belgicus*, published in 1610 by Pieter van den Keere (1571–1646), is a fine early example of Dutch artistic skill in cartography: the lion's body incorporates the territory of the Low Countries, the title cartouche is 'held' by two fishermen, symbolic of the sea's importance to the region, engravings on the top of the map illustrate costumes and occupations, with farm scenes at the bottom, and along both sides are views of cities with their coats of arms. The cartouche containing the scale of the map is ornamented with *vanitas* symbols, an hour-glass and a skull.

Atlas maps of the 17th century display a number of artistic additions, including the cartouche, which frame the title, dedication, symbols used and scale of the map. Scenes characteristic of the region often portray farm activities and farmers, costumes worn and the coats of arms of the map's dedicatee. Maps of Oxfordshire and Cambridgeshire provide good examples of these additions; John Speed, a leading British cartographer, was the first to include the coats of arms of the colleges comprising the universities of Oxford and Cambridge, with a group of two or more dons in academic dress portrayed in one of the corners.

World maps of the 17th century display an extensive repertory of decorative elements, both symbolic and realistic. These might include the four elements, the ages of mankind, symbolic figures of the twelve months of the year and of the four seasons, portraits of important cartographers, costumes of various countries and social classes, exotic peoples, the seven wonders of the ancient world and the seven planets. Maps covering the great rivers of the world, such as the Danube, Rhine and Dnepr, might carry an allegorical portrait of the river and appropriately smaller figures symbolizing its tributaries. The map entitled *Belgii Novi, Angliae Novae* (Amsterdam, 1651), by Jan Janssonius (1588–1664), bears images of the native fauna of the New World, including bear, deer, otter, weasel and beaver. On some maps natural wonders, such as the Niagara Falls, or scenes of trade in distant lands, were used as decorative elements. Maps mainly displaying parts of the oceans can bear either symbolic scenes (Neptune, mermen, mermaids and tritons) or realistic ones (men working at sea, fishermen and whalers).

The cartouche evolved, during the last quarter of the 17th century and the 18th, into a minor art form of its own. The most developed examples appear on maps published by two German map publishing houses, Homann and Seutter. To the decorative elements of the earlier

3. Map of Harz Mountains with scenes of mining, engraving, image area 485×560 mm, published by Homann, Nuremberg, c. 1740

cartouche were added portraits of rulers, warlords and religious figures (e.g. priests of Israel, popes, Knights of Malta); scenes of mining (see fig. 3), trading and industry; costumes of city and country folk; weapons and battle scenes; city plans and bird's-eye views. Most maps contain the coats of arms of the dedicatee or of the principal protagonists of battles shown. On some 18th-century maps artistic and geographic features appear to vie for prominence.

5. WALL MAPS. Maps had an important place as wall hangings in the decorative scheme of mid-17th-century Dutch homes, and they often appear in the background of paintings by Johannes Vermeer (e.g. *Woman Reading a Letter*, c. 1662–5; Amsterdam, Rijksmus.; *Officer and Laughing Girl*, c. 1658–61; New York, Frick; *see* SCIENCE AND ART, fig. 4). He carefully copied them from the finest contemporary products, which are well provided with fashionable ornamental features.

Another category of artistic cartography consists of maps actually painted on walls, generally in fresco, as part of a scheme of interior decoration. Early examples at Rome include the world map, *Orbis pictus*, on the wall of the Porticus Vipsania (destr.), which was built after the death of Marcus Vipsanius Agrippa (c. 64–12 BC); another example is the map commissioned by Pope Zacharias

(*reg* 741–52) for the loggia of the Lateran Palace. Their existence is well documented, but no trace of either has survived. A world map was painted on a wall of the Sala dello Scudo ('Hall of the Coat of Arms') in the Doge's Palace in Venice in 1342; it was overpainted several times, most recently in 1750, leaving the features of the first map unknown. One of the apartments of the Palazzo Venezia in Rome is still called the Sala del Mappamondo ('Hall of the World Map'), though the map itself, mentioned in 1534, has long since been painted over.

The oldest surviving example of these ornamental wall maps is a set of maps of the world according to the Ptolemaic canon, painted by Ignazio Danti on the doors of storage cabinets in the Guardaroba at the Palazzo Vecchio in Florence. They were commissioned by Cosimo I de' Medici, begun by Danti in 1562 and completed by Stefano Buonsignori, an Olivetan monk, in 1575. The set consists of 27 maps of parts of the world, copied from contemporary editions of Ptolemy's *Geographia*; a large contemporary globe stands in the middle of the room.

Another set of maps was frescoed on the walls of the west wing of the Farnese family's country residence (*see* CAPRAROLA, VILLA FARNESE, §1), forming part of the overall scheme of decorations of the ceremonial floor, the *piano nobile*. The frescoes of the Sala del Mappamondo (see fig. 4) were completed in 1574 by two painters

4. Wall maps frescoed in panels of the Sala del Mappamondo, Villa Farnese, Caprarola, near Rome, 1574

working from the best maps then available. They include a world map (7.5×4.5 m), and maps of the four continents, Italy and the Holy Land. The ceiling shows the celestial hemispheres, while lunettes over doors and windows contain portraits of great explorers. The hall was untouched until restoration in the 1960s and is an outstanding example of the Renaissance manner of representing earth and heavens in one harmonious whole.

Pope Pius IV (reg 1559–66) and his immediate successors had two very large hemispheres and maps of the continents painted on the walls of the Terza Loggia of the Vatican Palace. The Galleria delle Carte Geografiche in the Vatican was decorated by Danti from 1580 to a commission by Pope Gregory XIII. There are 32 large maps in the gallery and 8 small ones representing all of Italy and the papal territory of Avignon: on one side of the gallery are those parts of the country facing west, towards the Tyrrhenian Sea, and on the other side those facing east, to the Adriatic. Several town plans and views of seaports include a remarkable bird's-eye view of the city of Rome. To complete the decorative scheme, paintings representing major miracles are set in the coffered ceiling next to the map of the region where the miracle took place.

6. TAPESTRY MAPS. Maps woven into tapestries are a small but unusual category of decorative maps. Sultan Mehmed II (reg 1444–81), the conqueror of Constantinople, is reputed to have commissioned a Byzantine scholar to design a map based on the Ptolemaic world map, which he had woven in tapestry in the imperial workshop. A set of ten tapestry maps, representing the defeat of the Spanish Armada, was commissioned by the Lord High Admiral, Charles Howard of Effingham (1536–1624), from the Dutch painter Hendrik Vroom and woven by Frans Spiering (c. 1550–1630) from 1592 to 1595 (ex-Pal. Westminster, London; destr. by fire in 1834). They are known from engravings by John Pine (1690–1756) published in 1753. The Sheldon family of Weston, Warwicks, produced elegant maps of several English counties in the early 17th century, including one of Middlesex (London, V&A), based on the map of c. 1575 of Christopher Saxton (c. 1542–1606).

7. LATER DEVELOPMENTS. During the mid-18th century a series of geographical surveys (*see* SURVEYOR) were instituted through which, by rigorous field measurements, cartography became a more scientific undertaking, culminating in the Carte Géométrique de la France, which was authorized in 1748 and published in 182 sheets. Cartouches were employed throughout the 18th century and into the early 19th, but then cartography was increasingly the domain of accurate, painstaking surveys, and maps, which once bore images and illustrations, became instruments of scientific, political, economic and military importance. In the 20th century the functional aspects of map design, which had co-existed with the decorative elements from the beginning, became the dominant concern. In an attempt to improve the effectiveness of the map as a means of communication, developments in the understanding of the psychological bases of perception (colour, shape, size, texture etc) were explored and employed in late 20th-century map design.

See also TOPOGRAPHY, §1.

BIBLIOGRAPHY
L. Bagrow: *Geschichte der Kartographie* (Berlin, 1951); Eng. trans., ed. R. A. Skelton (Cambridge, MA, 1964)
R. A. Skelton: *Decorative Printed Maps of the 15th to 18th Centuries* (London and New York, 1952/R 1965)
The World Encompassed (exh. cat., ed. L. A. Brown; Baltimore, MD, Walters A.G., 1952)
H. Harms: *Künstler des Kartenbildes* (Oldenburg, 1962)
D. Grosjean and R. Kinauer: *Kartenkunst und Kartentechnik vom Altertum bis zum Barock* (Berne and Stuttgart, 1970)
Karte als Kunstwerk: Dekorative Landkarten aus Mittelalter und Neuzeit (exh. cat. by T. Seifert, Munich, Bayer. Staatsbib., 1979)
D. Woodward, ed.: *Art and Cartography: Six Historical Essays* (Chicago, 1987)
GEORGE KISH

Ma-Pe-Wi. *See* HERRERA, VELINO.

Mappae clavicula [Lat.: 'Little key of painting']. Medieval compendium of recipes. It possibly originated in northern France or Germany. Like the COMPOSITIONES VARIAE, it can be related to knowledge of ancient Egyptian origin and early Greek alchemist texts. Some of its recipes are literal translations of texts in the Leiden papyrus (3rd century AD; Leiden, Rijksmus. Oudhd., MS. X). The *Mappae clavicula* has descriptions of the nature and preparation of various minerals, herbs, woods, stones and chemicals. It contains recipes for making glues, solder and pigments and many recipes of a metallurgical nature. It also has instructions for dyeing both textiles and skins for parchment in purple, for writing in gold and silver and for making gold leaf.

The most complete copy of the *Mappae clavicula* is in a 12th-century manuscript (Corning, NY, Mus. Glass, Phillipps MS. 3715), which was published in transcript in 1847. An earlier copy is dated to the 10th century (Sélestat, Bib. Human., MS. 17), while the earliest fragments of the *Mappae clavicula* are in a late 8th- or early 9th-century bifolium in Klosterneuburg (Bib. Augustin. Chorherrenstiftes). A copy is known to have existed at Reichenau Abbey in 821, and recipes from the *Mappae clavicula* are now extant in some 80 manuscripts dating from the 9th to the 17th centuries. The first 11 chapters of Phillipps

MS. 3715—describing pigments, their mixtures and concordances of colours—are a separately compiled group of recipes from the 12th century, prefixed to the *Mappae clavicula* text. The *Mappae clavicula* contains all but 26 of the recipes of the *Compositiones variae* and seems to derive from it, either directly or via a closely related tradition.

BIBLIOGRAPHY
T. Phillipps: 'Letter from Sir Thomas Phillipps, Bart, F.R.S., F.S.A., Addressed to Albert Way, Esq., Director, Communicating a Transcript of a MS. Treatise on the Preparation of Pigments, and on Various Processes of the Decorative Arts Practised during the Middle Ages, Written in the Twelfth Century, and Entitled Mappae clavicula', *Archaeologia*, xxxii (1847), pp. 183–244
H. Roosen-Runge: *Farbgebung und Technik frühmittelalterlicher Buchmalerei: Studien zu den Traktaten 'Mappae clavicula' und 'Heraclius'*, 2 vols (Munich, 1967)
C. S. Smith and J. G. Hawthorne: '*Mappae clavicula*: A Little Key to the World of Medieval Techniques', *Trans. Amer. Philos. Soc.*, lxiv (1974) [whole issue]
A. WALLERT

Mapplethorpe, Robert (*b* New York, 4 Nov 1946; *d* Boston, 9 March 1989). American photographer, sculptor and collagist. In the early 1970s, after studying at the Pratt Institute of Art in Brooklyn (1963–70), he produced a number of assemblages and collages from magazine photographs often altered by spray painting. In one such work, *Julius of California* (1971; Charles Cowles priv. col., see Marshall, p. 21), he drew a circle around the male figure's genitals as a subversion of the usual practice of censorship. He soon began to take his own black-and-white photographs with a Polaroid camera, incorporating them into collages (e.g. *Self-portrait*, 1971; Charles Cowles priv. col., see Marshall, p. 17) or arranging them in sequences, as in *Patti Smith (Don't Touch here)* (1973; artist's col., see Marshall, p. 27), a portrait of the poet and singer who was one of his favourite models. Within a year of showing his Polaroids in his first one-man show (New York, Light Gal., 1973) he began to use a large format press camera, followed soon afterwards by a Hasselblad. As his interest in photography increased, so he looked more closely for guidance to such earlier photographers as Nadar, Julia Margaret Cameron and F. Holland Day. His photographs of the later 1970s include a number of homo-erotic, sado-masochistic images, such as *Helmut* (1978; see Marshall, p. 70). Here, as in other works, the presentation of a carefully posed figure against a plain paper or cloth backdrop creates a strong formal structure in counterpoint to the shock value and intensity of the subject-matter. This formal emphasis is even more apparent in the flower and still-life works, such as *Pan Head and Flower* (1976; Holly Solomon priv. col., see Marshall, p. 46).

In the 1980s Mapplethorpe's photographs became more elegantly formal and correspondingly less sexually charged. He took numerous shots of muscular, often black, men such as *Andre* (1984; Washington, DC, N. Mus. Amer. A.) and also produced an entire series in the 1980s devoted to the female body-builder Lisa Lyon. Making use of various processes, including not only gelatin silver prints but also platinum prints on paper or linen and photogravures, he used strong lighting and sharp focus to achieve rich tonal contrasts. During the 1980s he continued to produce still-lifes and flower studies as well as a number of portraits of friends, celebrities and artists, such as that of the photographer *Cindy Sherman* (1983; see 1988 exh. cat., p. 62). Although he worked primarily in black and white, in the late 1980s he produced a series of still-life dye transfer prints, such as *Poppy* (1988; see Marshall, p. 191). He recorded his deteriorating health from AIDS in a group of harrowing self-portraits emphasizing his ravaged features.

An exhibition of Mapplethorpe's photographs in Cincinnati in 1990 involved Dennis Barrie, Director of the Contemporary Arts Center, in an obscenity charge, of which he was later cleared.

PHOTOGRAPHIC PUBLICATIONS
Certain People: A Book of Portraits, essay by S. Sontag (Pasadena, 1985)

BIBLIOGRAPHY
Robert Mapplethorpe, 1970–1983 (exh. cat. by S. Morgan and A. Hollinghurst, London, ICA, 1983)
R. Marshall: *Robert Mapplethorpe* (New York, 1988) [with additional essays by R. Howard and I. Sischy]
Mapplethorpe: Portraits (exh. cat. by P. Conrad, London, N.P.G., 1988)
LEE FONTANELLA

Maqhubela, Louis Khela (*b* Durban, Natal, 1939). South African painter, active in the UK. He began his training as an artist in 1957 at the Polly Street Art Centre under Cecil Skotnes and Sydney Kumalo. The stylistic choices presented to him involved two broad streams: the realistic depiction of everyday life in 'township scenes' or by contrast a more symbolic and abstract form of expression, as explored at that time by artists in contact with modernism. Maqhubela was one of many black urban artists who came to prominence during the surge of artistic activity in the 1960s. He exhibited in commercial galleries in Johannesburg, which became meeting places for artists of any colour, contributing to a dialogue that attempted to bypass the restrictions of apartheid. Maqhubela was particularly interested in the abstract work of the South African painter Douglas Portway (*b* 1922), which was of significant and lasting influence. By winning the Artists of Fame and Promise award he was able to travel to Ibiza in Spain in 1973, in search of Portway. However, Portway had already left for St Ives in Cornwall, England, and so Maqhubela travelled there and spent a short period working with him. Maqhubela spent many difficult years attempting to establish himself in the UK and dealing with the hardships of life in exile. In 1984 Maqhubela was given a grant to study at Goldsmiths College, University of London, and from 1985 to 1987 at the Slade School of Art where he obtained a diploma in Fine Art, with printmaking his major subject. He continued to exhibit in both South Africa and London and had a studio in Stockwell, London.

BIBLIOGRAPHY
The Neglected Tradition: Towards a New History of South African Art (1930–1988) (exh. cat. by S. Sack, Johannesburg, A.G., 1988–9), pp. 17–18, 60, 111–12
STEVEN SACK

Maqṣūra. Enclosed area in a mosque reserved for the use of the sovereign. In the earliest years of Islam, the MIHRAB seems to have maintained its pre-Islamic meaning as the place of a ruler and fulfilled the functions in the mosque that would later be associated with the *maqṣūra*. After the *maqṣūra* was introduced into the general plan of the mosque, the mihrab assumed its present form of a concave niche. According to Islamic traditions, the third caliph 'Uthman (*reg* AD 644–56) introduced the *maqṣūra* at the mosque of Medina to protect himself from assassination. Initially a wall of mud-brick pierced with openings to allow the congregation to see the caliph when he led prayer, it was later replaced by a permanent structure in stone. Under the Umayyad dynasty (*reg* 661–750) provincial governors followed the caliph's lead, building themselves *maqṣūra*s in the principal mosques of Basra, Kufa, Damascus and Fustat (Old Cairo). In the second half of the 8th century the early Abbasid caliphs ordered *maqṣūra*s removed from mosques because they considered them an impious Umayyad innovation, but this edict seems to have had little or no effect, and the numbers of *maqṣūra*s increased.

The earliest extant *maqṣūra* is the one completed in AD 965 for the congregational mosque of Córdoba (*see* ISLAMIC ART, fig. 45). It was and remains the most elaborate *maqṣūra* in the western Islamic lands, comprising an ensemble some 20 m wide of three domed triple bays in front of and on either side of the mihrab. A door on one side of the mihrab led to a closet; that on the other allowed communication to the caliphal palace via a passageway within the wall of the mosque. Although the metal railing dividing the *maqṣūra* from the rest of the mosque is modern, the remarkable screen of intricately carved intersecting cusped arches above it clearly defines this special area and separates it from the rest of the mosque. Each of its three bays is marked by an extraordinary ribbed dome, the central one revetted with mosaics like those covering the surrounds of the mihrab and the flanking doors of the qibla wall. The lower walls are decorated by a dado of carved marble panels.

The *maqṣūra* erected by the Zirid ruler al-Mu'izz ibn Badis (*reg* 1016–62) for the Great Mosque of Kairouan in Tunisia (see fig.) is quite different but no less impressive. In this case an area to the right of the minbar is enclosed by an elaborate wooden screen well over a man's height. The turned wooden grilles of the *maqṣūra* itself are framed with splendid vegetal and epigraphic ornament, testifying to the continuous vitality of joinery and carving techniques in 11th-century North Africa. The first Almohad congregational mosque of Marrakesh (begun 1147) was equipped with a wooden *maqṣūra* said to be able to hold more than 1000 men. When the ruler entered the mosque, a counterbalance mechanism raised the *maqṣūra* from the floor; when he left, the *maqṣūra* automatically sank back into the ground. Excavation at the site produced foundations consistent with the medieval descriptions, although no other parts of this extraordinary construction remain.

The term *maqṣūra* additionally came to refer to other rooms or special spaces in the mosque. Ibn Jubayr, who travelled to Damascus in 1184, stated that the mosque there had three *maqṣūra*s: one built by the first Umayyad caliph Mu'awiya (*reg* AD 661–80), which Damascenes claimed to be the first ever built; the New Maqṣūra, which was apparently erected when the caliph al-Walid rebuilt the mosque early in the 8th century; and a third used by members of the Hanafi rite for study and prayer. The Fatimid caliph al-Hafiz (*reg* 1130–49) erected a *maqṣūra* in the Azhar Mosque in Cairo. It consists of a domed bay,

Maqṣūra, Great Mosque, Kairouan, Tunisia, 11th century

elaborately decorated in carved stucco, located on the court façade in front of the aisle leading to the mihrab. Its original purpose is unknown, but nothing suggests that it was reserved particularly for the use of the ruler. It is formally similar to the axial domed bays between the courtyard and the prayer-hall found at the congregational mosques of Kairouan and Tunis, but the function of these domed structures has not yet been determined. In Morocco, the word *maqṣūra* refers to the room to the left and behind the mihrab from which the imam emerges to lead prayer; the ruler's enclosure is called the *afrāgh*.

No early *maqṣūra per se* survives from Iran. The six bays surrounding the mihrab of the 10th-century mosque at Na'in, ornamented with richly carved stucco, are the most sumptuously decorated parts of the mosque. Although no screen divides this area from the rest of the mosque, the heightened decoration suggests that the area can reasonably be termed a *maqṣūra*. An inscription dated 1115 from the congregational mosque at Qazvin refers to the area in front of the mihrab covered by the huge single dome as a *maqṣūra* and indicates that the political and religious associations of the form were still alive in Iran under the Saljuq dynasty. Indeed, the identification of the Qazvin dome as a *maqṣūra* suggests that the dome in front of the mihrab at Isfahan's Friday mosque, added in 1086–7 by the Saljuq vizier Nizam al-Mulk, was also a *maqṣūra*. This huge interior (diam. 15 m) dome was the first of its type erected in Iran and seems to have been directly inspired by that of the congregational mosque at Damascus. Soon Iranian urban and village mosques alike began to be built with a dome in front of the mihrab; the political significance must have become nil as the dome became a cliché in mosque design.

In Turkey, the *maqṣūra* seems never to have existed, although most Ottoman royal mosques had a *loge* (*hünkâr mahfili*) reserved for the sultan's use. The earliest certain example is at the Yeşil Cami at Bursa (1412–19), where a splendid tiled and gilt *loge* on the axis of the mihrab is approached by twin staircases flanking the entrance vestibule and overlooking the prayer-hall. After the conquest of Constantinople (now Istanbul) in the mid-15th century, the imperial *loge* became an elevated screened platform in a corner, normally the south-east, of the mosque. Although this type is presumed for the mosque of Mehmed II (1463) in Istanbul, the earliest extant examples are found in the mosques of Beyazid II (*reg* 1481–1512) in Edirne and Istanbul where the *loge*s are supported on handsome marble columns. Later examples were augmented by external loggias and retiring rooms, and special entrances and ramps allowed the sultan to arrive in the mosque without passing through the congregation. The Arab historian Ibn Khaldun (*d* 1382) believed that the *maqsūra* was an Islamic invention, but the Ottoman variants seem to combine a vague knowledge of the Islamic type with more proximate experience of the imperial boxes of Byzantine religious architecture.

BIBLIOGRAPHY
K. A. C. Creswell: *Early Muslim Architecture*, 2 vols (Oxford, 1932–40, 2nd edn of vol. 1, 1969)
G. Goodwin: *A History of Ottoman Architecture* (Baltimore, 1971)
S. S. Blair: *The Monumental Inscriptions of Early Islamic Iran and Transoxiana* (Leiden, 1992)
JONATHAN M. BLOOM

Maquette [Fr.: 'scale model']. Small wax or clay model used as a preliminary sketch, usually for a piece of sculpture or for presentation to a client for approval.

RUPERT FEATHERSTONE

Mar, 6th and 11th Earl of. *See* ERSKINE, JOHN.

Marabitti, (Francesco) Ignazio (*b* Palermo, 6 Jan 1719; *d* Palermo, 9 Jan 1797). Italian sculptor. His father, Pietro Marabitti, was a wood-carver and mosaic restorer active in Palermo during the first quarter of the 18th century, and his elder brother Lorenzo was a sculptor who worked to Procopio Serpotta's designs. Ignazio probably trained first under Giacomo Serpotta's brother-in-law, Gioacchino Vitagliano (1669–1739), assisting him with the sculptural elements that decorate the entrance wall of the church of Il Gesù in Palermo (before 1739; Palermo, Casa Professa dei Gesuiti), including the small statue of the *Christ Child* above the door. Between *c.* 1740 and 1745 Marabitti studied in Rome under Filippo della Valle. His return to Palermo in 1746 coincided with the decline of the Serpotta studio, and Marabitti was able to establish, with the help of a large studio, his position as Sicily's foremost sculptor in marble. His style is lively and rhetorical but not innovative, resembling that of Tommaso Righi (1727–1802), another of della Valle's pupils. However, his grandiose and festive funerary monuments decorated with putti, allegorical figures and swags of drapery, such as those to *Eustache de Laviefiulle* (1754) and *Carlo Filippo Cottone, Prince of Castelnuovo* (1764; both Palermo, Church of the Cappuccini), represent a break with Sicilian tradition.

Marabitti's works include monumental statues of the *Virgin with SS Lucy and Marziano* (1753) and *SS Peter and Paul* (1757) for the exterior of Syracuse Cathedral, large-scale pictorial reliefs such as his masterpiece, the *Glory of St Benedict* (1776; Monreale Cathedral), and the allegorical statue of the *Genius of Palermo* (1778; Palermo, Villa Giulia).

BIBLIOGRAPHY
G. Bozzo: *Le lodi dei più illustri siciliani trapassati ne' primi 45 anni del secolo XIX* (Palermo, 1851)
R. Giudice: *F. I. Marabitti* (Palermo, 1935)
D. Malignaggi: 'Ignazio Marabitti', *Stor. A.*, xvii–xix (1973)
T. Fittipaldi: 'Sculture inedite di Ignazio Marabitti', *Napoli Nob.*, xv/3–4 (1976), pp. 65–105
A. Nava Cellini: *La scultura del settecento* (Turin, 1982), pp. 85–8
DONALD GARSTANG

Maragall (i Gorina), Joan [Juan] (*b* Barcelona, 10 Oct 1860; *d* Barcelona, 20 Dec 1911). Spanish Catalan writer. He has been called perhaps the greatest poet working in Spain in the 19th century. He was born into a well-to-do family and studied law, a profession that he abandoned to devote himself to literature. An extremely erudite man, he wrote lyrical prose and poetry in Catalan and Spanish, and translated the works of Goethe, Novalis and Maurice Maeterlinck. He also introduced the writings of Ibsen, Nietzsche, Henry George, Ruskin, Ralph Waldo Emerson and others into Spain. He wrote articles of a socio-political nature on aesthetics and Catalan patriotism for the *Diario de Barcelona*. In his writings there are echoes of late Romanticism and influences of Symbolism and *fin-de-siècle* Decadence, although he was predominantly a writer of modernism during the Catalan *Renaixença* (Renaissance), at which time he collaborated on the magazine *L'Avenç* (Forward). He was an important enricher of the Catalan language, which he raised to a new cultural level, but his overriding love of Catalonia did not prevent him from being loyal to Spain. In contrast with the positivism of his time, his writings contain a profound spirituality, and he saw the world and its beauty as an authentic paradise, a work of divinity.

WRITINGS
Cant espiritual [Spiritual song]
La vaca cega
Oda infinita (Barcelona, 1886)
Poesías (1895)
Visions i cants [Visions and songs] (1900)
Elogios (1906–9)
Regular contributions to *L'Avenç* [Forward] (1886–90) and *Diario de Barcelona* (1890)

BIBLIOGRAPHY
M. S. Oliver: *Maragall publicista* (Barcelona, 1911)
P. Javier de Arenys: *Maragall y su obra* (Barcelona, 1914)
M. de Riquer and J. M. Valverde: 'Joan Maragall', *Historia de la literatura universal*, viii (Barcelona, 1986), pp. 363–6, 396
CARLOS CID PRIEGO

Maragha [Marāgha; Maraghe; Maragheh]. Town in East Azerbaijan province, north-west Iran. A settlement has existed at Maragha since pre-Islamic times, but the city flourished from the 12th century to the 14th when it was the seat of several local dynasties, such as the Ahmadilis and the Ildeñizids, and became a capital of the Ilkhanid empire. The most remarkable buildings are a group of five tomb towers that document the development of glazed-tile decoration in Iranian architecture. They vary in plan, but they are all two-storey constructions with stone crypts supporting brick superstructures and conical or pyramidal roofs. The earliest is the square tomb known as the Gunbad-i Surkh ('Red tomb'; 1147–8; 8.44 m on a side), built for the amir 'Abd al-'Aziz. It shows a restrained use of glazed decoration in light blue that complements the reddish brick. The anonymous cylindrical tomb tower (1167) shows a more extensive use of light-blue tile, and the nearby decagonal Gunbad-i Kabud ('Blue tomb'; 1196–7; diam. 9.0 m) is almost enveloped in a glazed web. Tile mosaic in three colours (light and dark blue and white) appears on the two tomb towers from the 14th century, the 8.33 m square Gunbad-i Ghaffariya built for Shams al-Din Qarasunqur (*d* 1328), a Mamluk amir who was governor of Azerbaijan for the Ilkhanids, and the cylindrical Joi Burj ('Blue tower'; *c.* 1330; diam. 11.83 m).

When Maragha became the capital of the Ilkhanids in Iran in 1258, the ruler Hulagu ordered the construction of an observatory for the noted astronomer Nasir al-Din Tusi. This observatory was the first of its kind: it cost 20,000 dinars, its instruments cost another 30,000 and it had ample endowments. Excavations on a hill north of the present town have revealed an outer wall enclosing several buildings for scientific and educational use. The central tower (diam. 45 m) had a long corridor with a stone mount for a giant metal quadrant set along the meridian. Scientific instruments, including a mural quadrant, an armillary astrolabe, solsticial and equinoctial armillaries, and a device having two quadrants for simultaneous measurement of the horizon coordinates of two stars, were prepared there under the direction of a Damascene, Mu'ayyad al-Din al-'Urdi. A brass celestial globe signed by Muhammad ibn Mu'ayyad al-'Urdi (1278; Dresden, Math.-Phys. Salon) is inlaid with silver dots marking the position of stars and engraved with the outlines of the conventional figures of the constellations. Illustrated manuscripts were also prepared under court patronage at Maragha. 'Abd al-Hadi ibn Muhammad ibn Mahmud ibn Ibrahim of Maragha translated the Arabic text of Ibn Bakhtishu's *Manāfi' al-ḥayawān* ('Usefulness of animals') into Persian at the behest of Sultan Ghazan, and an illustrated copy, one of the earliest Persian manuscripts to survive, was produced at Maragha in 1297 or 1299 (New York, Pierpont Morgan Lib., M. 500; *see* ISLAMIC ART, §III, 4(v)(b)). The 94 illustrations vary in style; some are conservative while others show the impact of new Chinese models.

BIBLIOGRAPHY
H. J. Seemann: 'Die Instrumente der Sternwarte zu Maragha nach den Mitteilungen von al-'Urdi', *Sber. Phys. Mediz. Soz. Erlangen*, lx (1928), pp. 15–126
A. Godard: 'Les Monuments de Marāgha', *Soc. Etud. Iran. & A. Persan*, ix (1934)
——: 'Notes complémentaires sur les tombeaux de Maragha', *Athar-é Iran*, i (1936), pp. 125–60
D. Wilber: *The Architecture of Islamic Iran: The Il Khānid Period* (Princeton, 1955)
P. Vardjavand: 'Rapport préliminaire sur les fouilles de l'observatoire de Maraqé', *Monde Iran. & Islam*, iii (1975), pp. 119–24
——: 'La Découverte archéologique du complexe scientifique de l'observatoire de Maraqé', *Akten des VII. internationalen Kongresses für iranische Kunst und Archäologie: Munich 1976*, pp. 527–36
A. Daneshvari: 'Complementary Notes on the Tomb Towers of Medieval Iran. I: Gunbad-i Kabud at Maraghe 593/1197', *Art et société dans le monde iranien*, ed. C. Adle (Paris, 1982), pp. 287–95

Maragliano, Antonio Maria (*b* Genoa, 18 Sept 1664; *d* Genoa, 7 March 1739). Italian sculptor and wood-carver. In 1680 he entered the workshop of his uncle, the sculptor Giovanni Battista Agnesi, as an apprentice, but he also attended the workshop of the furniture-maker Pietro Andrea Torre (*d* 1668). By 1688 he already had his own workshop in partnership with Giovanni Battista Pedevilla. The success of his work soon enabled him to open an independent workshop, where he was assisted by pupils, among them his own son, Giovanni Battista Maragliano (*d* after 1762). His early works include *St Michael and Lucifer* (1694; Celle Ligure, oratory of S Michele) and *St Sebastian* (1700; Rapallo, oratory of the Bianchi), both processional *casse*: groups of polychrome wooden statues made to be carried in procession by the religious confraternities on feast days. The larger part of Maragliano's production consists of such monumental groups, in which the scenes from a saint's life (ecstasy, martyrdom etc) are represented in a theatrical manner, expressing devotional wonder and intense emotional involvement. The lively colouring of the sculptures was done by specialist polychrome painters, at times under the supervision of Maragliano himself. Among the most famous of these *casse* are *SS Anthony Abbot and Paul the Hermit* (Mele, Genoa, oratory of S Antonio Abate) and *St Francis Receiving the Stigmata* (1708–9; Genoa, SS Concezione). He also produced small statues for crèches, sculpted altar groups such as the grandiose *Deposition* (Genoa, Church of the Visitation) and made processional Crucifixes for confraternities (e.g. Genoa, oratory of S Antonio Abate alla Marina). In all these works Maragliano's virtuoso skills are evident in the delicacy of the modelling and the rendering of movement. The painters Domenico Piola, Paolo Girolamo Piola and Gregorio de' Ferrari often provided him with designs and ideas. His later works (e.g. *Annunciation*, 1725; Savona, oratory of the Cristo Risorto) reveal the new expressive freedom of the Rococo style. Only two works by his son Giovanni Battista are documented: a processional Crucifix (1714; Bogliasco, oratory of S Chiara) and the *cassa* of the *Annunciation* (1762; Noli, S Pietro), both refined sculptures in polychrome wood showing his father's influence. Giovanni Battista was killed in Lisbon by some of his pupils.

BIBLIOGRAPHY
C. G. Ratti: *Vite de' pittori, scultori ed architetti genovesi*, 2 vols (Genoa, 1768–9/R 1965), ii, pp. 165–73
G. Colmuto: *L'arte del legno in Liguria: A. M. Maragliano (1664–1739)* (Genoa, 1963)
F. Franchini Guelfi: *Le casacce: Arte e tradizione* (Genoa, 1973)
La Liguria delle casacce (exh. cat. by F. Franchini Guelfi, Genoa, Pal. Reale, 1982)
M. Tassinari: 'La cassa dell'Annunziata di Noli', *Riv. Ingauna & Intemelia*, xxxviii/1–2 (1983), pp. 62–4
F. Franchini Guelfi: 'Le casse processionali: Immagine devozionale e sacra rappresentazione', 'La scultura lignea', *La scultura a Genova e in Liguria dal seicento al primo novecento*, i (Genoa, 1987), pp. 265–70, 286–7 [with bibliog.]

FAUSTA FRANCHINI GUELFI

Marajó. Island between the mouth of the River Amazon and the Rio do Pará, Brazil. It covers an area of approximately 48,000 sq. km and is almost completely flat, apart from a few low hillocks; its south-western half is covered in forest, while the rest is open country, with some forested tracts in the littoral areas and along the rivers. In the rainy season poor drainage turns the fields into an immense lake. Over a long period Marajó's archaeological wealth attracted explorers, whose expeditions resulted in several collections now in various museums. The earliest systematic investigation was by Betty Meggers and Clifford Evans in 1948–9 and resulted in the first complete survey of the prehistoric occupation of the island. Excavations carried out for the Museu Paranese Emilio Goeldi, Belém, in the 1960s under the direction of N. Figueiredo and M. Simões complemented and enlarged upon these findings. Archaeological evidence suggests that the island was the site of successive occupations represented by a sequence of five phases beginning *c.* 1100 BC and continuing into the 19th century AD; the best known is the Marajoará phase (*c.* AD 400–*c.* 1300).

Marajoará woman's pubic cover (*tanga*), terracotta with painted decoration, 150×120 mm, *c.* AD 400–*c.* 1300 (Pará, private collection)

These phases were based on pottery sequences, which in the past were used both to elaborate a general picture of Marajó culture and to support the argument that these peoples originated outside the Amazon Basin. Later studies, however, suggest that the horizons and traditions with which these pottery phases may be associated are more likely to have had an Amazonian origin. Since the 1980s excavations with new theoretical bases and methodology have concentrated on sites belonging to the Marajoará phase, and these should produce important contributions to the question of the origin of the inhabitants of Marajó.

The earliest occupation, known as the Ananatuba phase, is dated *c.* 1100–*c.* 200 BC. It extended throughout an area that included the central north coast and the southern edge of Lake Arari, as far as the Camarà River. The people lived in *palafitas* (huts built on piles), generally constructed along the banks of small rivers. The density of pottery fragments found at Ananatuba sites is high, and the occupation levels are deep, suggesting prolonged residence. Most of the pottery is simple, a small proportion being decorated with incisions or bands of red paint. Tubular pottery smoking pipes also occur.

The Mangueiras phase, dated *c.* 1000 BC–*c.* AD 100, extended over a slightly larger area of the same region and co-existed with the Ananatuba over a long period. The dwellings of the Mangueiras were also huts on piles, arranged in circles close to navigable rivers. Their pottery is more fragile and has a higher proportion of decoration. Besides fragments of containers, pipes, ear-plugs, lip-plugs and, occasionally, figurines occur.

The first evidence for the Formiga phase belongs to a period close to the disappearance of the Mangueiras, *c.* AD 100. This phase lasted only a short time, until *c.* AD 400. Its dwellings were generally in open country, on *tesos* (small hillocks that remained above flood level) along the rivers. The pottery, which includes few decorated fragments, seems less sophisticated than that of preceding phases.

The earliest date for the Marajoará phase is *c.* AD 400. This distinctive culture occupied an area of about 25,000 sq. km in the centre of the eastern part of the island, around Lake Arari. Traces of the Marajoará are found on numerous artificial terraces measuring 3–7 m in height and 1–100 ha in area. Some of the terraces were built especially for burials, others for residential and ceremonial purposes. The houses were of adobe resting directly on the ground. Primary burial, secondary burial with urns and cremation were all practised. The material culture was elaborate and diverse and varied with the passage of time; the pottery is outstanding for its patterns and the degree of its finish. The modelling is still rather coarse, but the decoration includes complex combinations of incision, scraping, excision and polychrome painting using vermilion, yellow, white, black and brown (see fig.). Geometric designs reveal sophisticated stylizations of anthropomorphic and zoomorphic motifs, which underwent changes with the passage of time. Features such as the creation of the large terraces, the degree of elaboration of the pottery and the differential treatment of the dead, together with the extensive territory and the size and number of sites, suggest that Marajoará society was highly stratified, with a political élite and division of labour among specialists.

The exuberant culture of the Marajoarás was followed after *c.* AD 1200 by the Aruã phase, characterized by very simple pottery, almost all utilitarian and lacking the patterns and skill evident in earlier phases. Glass beads of European provenance are often found in association with the pottery. The Aruã practised secondary burial in large urns that were not interred but arranged in groups on the surface of the ground. Their dwellings, in villages of *palafitas* on small natural elevations that remained above flood level in the rainy season, were sited along navigable streams in the forest near the coast. European colonizers found the Aruã living on the islands of Mexiana and Caviana as well as along the shores of Marajó.

BIBLIOGRAPHY

B. J. Meggers and C. Evans: 'Archeological Investigations at the Mouth of the Amazon', *Bureau Amer. Ethnol. Bull.*, cxlvii (1957) [whole issue]

N. Figueiredo and M. F. Simões: 'Contribuição à arqueologia da fase Marajoará', *Rev. Mus. Paulista*, xiv (1963), pp. 455–65

M. F. Simões: 'Resultados preliminares de uma prospecção arqueológica na região dos riós Gaiapi e Camará (Ilha de Marajó)', *Antropologia*, ii (1965), pp. 207–24

——: 'The Castanheira Site: New Evidence on the Antiquity and History of the Ananatuba Phase (Marajó Island, Brazil)', *Amer. Ant.*, xxxiv (1969), pp. 402–10

A. C. Roosevelt: *Archaeological Research on Marajó Island, Brasil* (New York, 1986)

FERNANDA DE ARAUJO COSTA

Mařák, Julius (Eduard) (*b* Litomyšl, 21 March 1832; *d* Prague, 8 Oct 1899). Czech painter, draughtsman and printmaker. He studied at the Prague Academy of Fine Arts under Max Haushofer between 1852 and 1858, and subsequently privately at Munich under Leopold Rottmann (1812–81) and Eduard Schleich. From 1858 to 1887 he lived mainly in Vienna, where his work increasingly epitomized late-Romantic taste. The principal Czech landscape painter of his generation, he specialized in forest scenes, often choosing low viewpoints and confined compositions which show the forest at its most untouched and impenetrable. In addition to paintings he was also known for engravings and large charcoal drawings (e.g. *Oak*; Prague, N.G.; part of the series *Austrian Forest Scenes*, 1878). Mařák also produced decorative works, including views of Czech and Austrian towns, originally in Franz Josef Bahnhof, Vienna (studies; Plzeň, A.G. W. Bohemia), and depictions of places important in Czech mythology and history at the National Theatre and National Museum in Prague (e.g. *Říp*, sketch 1882–3; Prague, N.G.). In 1887 he became rector at the Prague Academy, where he was an influential teacher and encouraged the practice of *plein-air* painting.

BIBLIOGRAPHY

J. Loriš: *Julius Mařák* (Prague, 1955)
J. Neumann: *Modern Czech Painting and the Classical Tradition* (Prague, 1958), pp. 41–5
Julius Mařák (exh. cat. by J. Boučková, Pardubice, E. Boh. Gal., 1981) [bibliog., résumé in Ger.]
M. Nováková: 'Julius Mařák', *Tschechische Kunst, 1878–1914* (exh. cat., ed. J. Kotalík; Darmstadt, Ausstellhallen Matildenhöhe, 1984), ii, pp. 200–02

ROMAN PRAHL

Marascalchi [Marescalchi; Mariscalchi], **Pietro de'** [lo Spada] (*b* Feltre, *c.* 1520; *d* Feltre, 1589). Italian painter. His first known work, a crowded *Virgin and Saints* (1545–7; Feltre, S Martino), is a curious mixture of traditional elements derived from the Feltre painter Lorenzo Luzzo, with Emilian Mannerist influence, probably from Parma. The impact on Marascalchi of the work of the Venetian Jacopo Bassano was also of critical importance. Marascalchi's celebrated altarpiece, the *Adoration of the Shepherds* ('*Madonna della Misericordia*', *c.* 1560; Feltre Cathedral), also shows the influence of Giovanni Demio. An exercise in pictorial dynamism, it is notable for its rich colours and for the cluster of supplicants spiralling around the Virgin, who is portrayed in equally energetic torsion. The free and vibrant predella scenes from the *Life of the Virgin* are characteristic of the small-scale painting that Marascalchi favoured. The small altarpiece of the *Virgin and Child Enthroned with SS Victor, Michael and Angel Musician* (San Giustina Bellunese, S Michele) dates from the same time.

This successful and creative period ended by 1564, when Marascalchi signed and dated the *Virgin and Child with Saints* (Malibu, CA, Getty Mus.). The hieratic *St John the Baptist* (Feltre Cathedral) is of a similar date. Marascalchi's many later altarpieces are conventionally structured, archaic in their composition and often show a repetition of physical types. An exception is the small *Feast of Herod* (1575; Dresden, Gemäldegal. Alte Meister), Marascalchi's last dated work, which with its almost Rococo informality, once led to the suggestion that he was a precursor of El Greco.

BIBLIOGRAPHY

R. Pallucchini: 'Petro de Mariscalchi: Un manierista di provincia', *Da Tiziano a El Greco* (exh. cat., Venice, Doge's Pal., 1981), pp. 208–15
V. Sgarbi: 'Pietro de Mariscalchi', *The Genius of Venice* (exh. cat., ed. C. Hope and J. Martineau; London, RA, 1983), pp. 183–5
S. Claut: '"Regesto" Marascalchi', *Archv Stor. Belluno, Feltre & Cadore*, ccxlvi (1984), pp 21-7
——: 'Novità, divagazioni e note su Pietro Marascalchi', *A. Ven.*, xxxviii (1984), pp. 46–56

SERGIO CLAUT

Marathon. Narrow coastal plain hemmed in by mountains in south-east central Greece, which was densely occupied during the entire Bronze Age, especially in the west near the mountain passes connecting it to the rest of Attica. The region contains the remains of three known Early Helladic (EH) fortified settlements situated within 3 to 5 km of each other: Kato Souli to the east, Agriliki to the west and Plassi, the only one even partially excavated, on the coast between them. At Plassi a thick wall with a gate flanked by a tower enclosed a large Middle Helladic (MH) building covering cist graves of the same period and housing a pottery kiln at one end. About 2.5 km inshore, at Tsepi, lies an extensive EH cemetery of regularly aligned family cist graves, marked off by rows of stones and poorly furnished with imported Cycladic artefacts. Further west, near the entrance to the Vrana Valley, are four low MH tumuli (*c.* 8–17 m in diameter). They consist of an earth fill held in place by a low circular wall and overlaid with stones, and cover one-, two- or three-chambered cists lined and roofed with stone slabs and containing contracted burials dating from the late 17th to the 13th century BC. One such cist held the skeleton of a mutilated horse. The two largest and earliest tumuli include an inner stone ring surrounding the main burial. Finally a tholos tomb near by (*c.* 1400 BC) has two burial shafts, which contained a gold cup and some pottery. Two sacrificed horses were also buried in the dromos. This pattern of occupation persisted into historical times engendering many local cults and legends. Later remains in the area include the tombs of the Athenians and Plataians killed at the battle of Marathon (490 BC) and the estate of Herodes Atticus (2nd century AD).

BIBLIOGRAPHY

S. Marinatos: 'Anaskaphai Marathonos' [Excavations at Marathon], *Praktika Athen. Archaiol. Etaireias* (1970), pp. 5–28
——: 'Marathon', *Athens An. Archaeol.*, iii (1970), pp. 63–8
——: 'Further News from Marathon', *Athens An. Archaeol.*, iii (1970), pp. 153–66
——: 'Further Discoveries at Marathon', *Athens An. Archaeol.*, iii (1970), pp. 349–66

□

Maratti [Maratta], **Carlo** (*b* Camerano, 18 May 1625; *d* Rome, 15 Dec 1713). Italian painter, draughtsman and printmaker. He was the last major Italian artist of the classical tradition that had originated with Raphael, and his pre-eminence among the artists of his time marks the triumph of classicism. Nonetheless his art unites the virtues of *disegno* and *colore*, and he created a grandiose and decorative style that satisfied the demands of the Church. At the same time his late works had a grace and refinement that anticipated the development of the Rococo and Neoclassicism.

1. Training and early life. 2. Work.

1. TRAINING AND EARLY LIFE. Carlo Maratti was the son of the Dalmatian Tommaso Maratti and Faustina Masini, and his half-brother Bernabeo Francioni was also a painter. His first biographer, Bellori, described how as a boy Maratti made copies of the coloured engravings of saints that were sold in Camerano, and how Bernabeo showed some of these copies to Andrea Camassei, who advised that Maratti should be brought to Rome. He

moved to Rome in 1636, supported by Corintio Benicampi, a friend of his father and secretary to the Pope's nephew, Taddeo Barberini. This was in the year of the celebrated debate held at the Accademia di S Luca between the supporters of *disegno*, led by Andrea Sacchi, and those of *colore*, who followed Pietro da Cortona: it would have interested Maratti, who later united the virtues of both parties. Bernabeo introduced him to Sacchi, whose workshop he entered in 1637 and with whom he stayed until the latter's death in 1661. He followed the usual practice of Roman studios, making copies after the Antique and after the celebrated works of the Renaissance and early 17th century. He also attended the theoretical discussions that took place at Sacchi's studio, where the most eminent Roman artists gathered and drew from life. A large group of drawings (Windsor Castle, Berks, Royal Lib.; Madrid, Real Acad. S Fernando, Mus.) support Bellori's statement that Maratti copied the frescoes by Raphael in the Vatican Stanze; others reveal his study of the works of Annibale Carracci, Domenichino and Guido Reni. The sources state that in this first stage of his training he was forbidden to use colour; the emphasis was on drawing. His earliest drawings, in red chalk on green or blue paper, demonstrate the decisive influence of Sacchi and laid the foundations for his absolute mastery of draughtsmanship.

2. WORK.

(i) Subject compositions. (ii) Portraits. (iii) Designs for sculpture and architecture.

(i) Subject compositions.

(a) Early years, to 1661. (b) Mature years, 1662–*c.* 1680. (c) Final years, *c.* 1680–1713.

(a) Early years, to 1661. Maratti's earliest works are untraced: Bellori cited two half-figures of *St Peter* and *St Paul*, a *David Victorious* and an *Assumption of the Virgin*, painted for Benicampi, and, presumably through the mediation of Benicampi, a *Birth of the Virgin* for a convent in Nocera Umbra. The earliest surviving work is the *Glory of Saints* (1645; Monterotondo Cathedral), commissioned by Taddeo Barberini before his departure for France in 1645. It was probably around 1646 to 1648 that Maratti undertook a journey to Camerano and Ancona in the Marches (Bellori), during which he was able to see works by Titian and by local artists. In 1648 in Rome he collaborated on *Constantine Ordering the Destruction of Pagan Idols*, one of the frescoes for S Giovanni in Fonte, the baptistery of S Giovanni in Laterano. It was based on drawings and cartoons by Sacchi, who directed the decoration. Maratti's first independent public work in Rome, in which he first moved away from Sacchi's dominance, is the *Adoration of the Shepherds* (1650; Rome, S Giuseppe dei Falegnami). The female figure, with its large eyes and oval face framed by strands of dark hair, was characteristic of the painter's early phase. It would seem, however, that this work was preceded by a considerable output; Bellori relates that his brother Bernabeo kept his first earnings, which Maratti then reclaimed *c.* 1650. On the basis of drawings in the Academia de S Fernando in Madrid and a drawing in the Künsthalle, Düsseldorf, a group of works have been assigned to the period immediately before and contemporaneous with the altarpiece of S Giuseppe dei Falegnami. These drawings include studies both for this

altarpiece and for other works: the figures in Gaspard Dughet's *Landscape with Dido and Aeneas* (London, N.G.), the *Virgin with Saints* in the parish church of Camerano, the *Preaching of St John the Baptist* (Pau, Mus. B.-A.) and the *Sacrifice of Noah* (untraced; known through an engraving and an oval version, perhaps painted by Sacchi, in Chatsworth, Derbys). Maratti's collaboration with Dughet suggests his rising popularity with a circle of distinguished private collectors.

The *Adoration of the Shepherds* marked his début in the public domain and the start of an uninterrupted flow of official commissions. The 1650s were decisive for his development. The influence of Sacchi remained, both in the classical rhythms of his compositions and in his Venetian painterliness; but he also explored other sources. The colour and chiaroscuro, best displayed in *St Rosalía among the Plague Sufferers* (before 1660; Florence, Gal. Corsini priv. col.), suggest the work of Giovanni Lanfranco, while the delicacy of the figures is indebted to Guido Reni. Pietro da Cortona became an invigorating influence, especially after 1656, when both artists worked for Pope Alexander VII on the decoration of the gallery of the Palazzo del Quirinale. In spite of remaining connected to the workshop of Sacchi, Maratti acted independently, and the works from these years display characteristics that make them original and individual. His style, less revolutionary than that of his young contemporaries, such as Pier Francesco Mola or Giovanni Battista Gaulli, perfectly fulfilled the requirements of the high dignitaries of the Roman Church for an official art that continued the classical tradition and was both grandiloquent and decorative.

The most important of Maratti's works from the early 1650s is the *Peace of Augustus* (Lille, Mus. B.-A.), commissioned by Louis Phélypeaux de La Vrillière, for the upper gallery of the Hôtel de la Vrillière, Paris. In this picture Maratti was in competition with the most distinguished artists working in Rome: Guido Reni, Guercino, Nicolas Poussin, Alessandro Turchi and Pietro da Cortona, all of whom had contributed heroic subjects from ancient history to La Vrillière's gallery. The picture suggests Maratti's deep knowledge of the Classical world; both the dress and decorative detail reveal his knowledge of Roman sculpture, and the frieze-like composition and some of the figures appear to have been inspired by the reliefs of Augustus' Ara Pacis (*see* ROME, fig. 22). Between 1651 and 1656 Maratti decorated the Cappella Alaleona in S Isidoro, Rome; for this he painted three altarpieces—the *Marriage of the Virgin*, the *Death of St Joseph* and the *Flight into Egypt*—as well as the frescoed lunettes, of *St Joseph's Dream* and the *Adoration of the Shepherds*, and the fresco in the cupola of *St Joseph in Glory*. Here he moved towards a more Baroque composition, with figures in movement, and strong contrasts of light and shadow. From the same period are the frescoed figures of *Prudence* and *Innocence* and the altarpiece of the *Adoration of the Magi* (all Rome, S Marco), commissioned by Niccolò Sagredo (1606–76), the Venetian ambassador in Rome. The altarpiece suggests the influence of Guido Reni and, in the figure of the Virgin, of François Du Quesnoy's *St Susanna* (Rome, S Maria di Loreto). In the *St Augustine* in S Maria dei Sette

Dolori, Rome, the artist used glowing, Venetian-inspired colour.

Pope Alexander VII commissioned many works from Maratti, notable among which is the *Visitation* (1656) for the church of S Maria della Pace, Rome (*in situ*). This is an accomplished composition, with many figures in movement, ideal beauty and elegant gesture; the ample clothing envelops the figures in a mass of folds set off by the light and demonstrates the influence of Gianlorenzo Bernini. Maratti also contributed a fresco, the *Adoration of the Shepherds*, to the decoration of the Palazzo del Quirinale, which was directed by Pietro da Cortona; here, for the first time, he used the light colours that were to characterize his later work. The commissions of the later 1650s, such as the *Submission of Victor IV to Innocent II* (Rome, Santa Croce in Gerusalemme) and *Summer* (Ariccia, Pal. Chigi), with fruit and flowers painted by Mario dei Fiori, demonstrate his brilliant synthesis of the light and movement of the Roman Baroque with the ideal beauty of antique art.

(b) Mature years, 1662–c. 1680. In the 20 years following the death of Sacchi Maratti won international renown; his patrons were from pre-eminent families and included Lorenzo Colonna and members of the Barberini, Chigi, Spada, Rospigliosi, Cybo, Pallavicini and Altieri. He directed one of the leading workshops in Rome, in terms of both the numbers and quality of those who worked there, making sketches and preparatory drawings for works that were executed by his most outstanding pupils. In the early 1660s he worked on the decoration of the Cappella de' Sylva in the Roman church of S Isidoro, a project directed by Bernini; Maratti contributed the oval canvas of the *Immaculate Conception* over the main altar. This picture shows the Virgin with the Christ Child in her arms, helping her to kill the serpent of heresy; it became widely known through copies and engravings, and its iconography was immensely influential. In the same period Maratti continued a series of *Apostles* for the Palazzo Barberini (*in situ*), which had been commissioned from Sacchi by Cardinal Antonio Barberini. The project, completed with the *St Matthew* in the late 1690s, constitutes a direct precedent to the sculpted *Apostles* (Rome, S Giovanni in Laterano) that he designed later.

Maratti's activity in cities outside Rome began in the same decade; he painted two altarpieces, the *Visitation* and the *Flight into Egypt*, for the Chigi Chapel in Siena Cathedral, where he again collaborated with Bernini. The *Immaculate Virgin with Saints* for the Sienese church of S Agostino dates from *c.* 1665. It was probably around this time that he executed a group of about 14 delicate etchings, either signed or attributed to him, in which representations of scenes from the *Life of Mary* predominate (Bartsch, pp. 24–37); the composition of the etched *Visitation* is close to that of the painting in Siena Cathedral.

In 1664 Maratti became principal of the Accademia di S Luca, where, in the same year, Bellori delivered his lecture on 'L'Idea del pittore, dello scultore e dell'architetto', published as a prologue to his *Vite* in 1672; this formulated the classicist theory of art, the practice of which is so perfectly represented by Maratti. As principal, Maratti was concerned to raise the status of the artist in society. For the training of the young artists

he recommended the study of Classical sculpture and, above all, life drawing; the artist should select from nature that which was beautiful and reject the ugly. He was also influential in the Académie de France in Rome through his friendship with its director, Charles Errard.

In 1672 Maratti travelled to Loreto to restore works by Annibale Carracci, Federico Barocci and Lorenzo Lotto (Bellori), and in that year executed the *Virgin with Saints* for the altar in the Altieri Chapel of the Roman church of S Maria sopra Minerva (*in situ*). In both style and iconography this work is seminal to Maratti's conception of the altarpiece; it is a balanced and harmonious composition, in which classical and monumental forms are enhanced by the clear light and rich, pure colours. Despite their idealization, each of the figures remains individual. In this and contemporary works, for example the *Miracle of St Filippo Benizzi* (Rome, Pal. Altieri), the effects of light, the white flesh, full forms and complicated, harmonious patterns of dark hair of the female figures, suggest a response to the large altarpieces of Guercino. After Raphael, Maratti was perhaps the most supremely gifted in inventiveness as a painter of the Virgin and Child (e.g. Vienna, Ksthist. Mus., and Florence, Bib. N. Cent.). It was this important aspect of his art that won him the sobriquet Carluccio delle Madonne. He did not, however, paint an exaggerated number of such works as his detractors claimed when they asserted that he was only capable of painting small devotional scenes.

In 1674 Maratti received a new commission from Pope Clement X: the great fresco, the *Triumph of Clemency*, for the audience room in the Palazzo Altieri, Rome. The programme was devised by Bellori and the fresco constitutes a manifesto of classicism, in opposition to the contemporary Baroque style of Gaulli. The composition is clearly contained within the frame and uses only those figures necessary to illustrate the allegorical theme, the title of which plays on the name of the Pope. Even the dancing cupids, bearing symbols, are limited to those relevant to the theme. Each figure, carefully studied, has individual significance and yet is integrated into an overall harmony. The light colours set off the clarity of the composition. The room remained unfinished due to the death of the Pope; preparatory drawings reveal that it was intended to include lunettes and pendentives with religious allegories on the theme of the four corners of the world, and scenes relating to the history of Rome.

In 1676 Maratti painted the ostentatious *Death of St Joseph* for the chapel of Empress Eleanor of Austria (1655–1720) and the equally grandiose *Death of St Francis Xavier* (Rome, Il Gesù) as well as the *Martyrdom of SS Blaise and Sebastian* (Genoa, S Biagio) for the Roman church of S Carlo ai Catinari. *SS Carlo and Ignatius Adoring the Virgin* (*c.* 1675; Rome, S Maria in Vallicella), commissioned by the Marchese Orazio Spada, introduces the more refined elegance that was to characterize his later style. His work of the 1670s culminated in the series of the *Four Seasons* (untraced), commissioned by Cardinal Portacarrero for the king of Spain, Charles II, and known through engravings and the preparatory drawings, and in work on the *Apollo and Daphne* (1681; Brussels, Mus. A. Anc.; see fig. 1), executed for Louis XIV. This was one of the most celebrated works of the time, to which Bellori

1. Carlo Maratti: *Apollo and Daphne*, oil on canvas, 2.21×2.34 m, 1681 (Brussels, Musée d'Art Ancien)

dedicated a eulogistic pamphlet, and which earned the painter the title of Royal Painter to the French Court. To Bellori the work illustrated the Classical doctrine of UT PICTURA POESIS, which claimed equal value for painting as for poetry. He also wrote that Maratti sought, in the figure of Daphne (inspired by the *Venus de' Medici*; Florence, Uffizi), to express the *affetti*, while in the Apollo (based on the *Apollo Belvedere*; Rome, Vatican, Mus. Pio-Clementino) he sought to express the idea of beauty.

(c) Final years, c. *1680–1713.* After the death of Bernini, Maratti became the most important artist of the time and the head of the most influential studio since that of Annibale Carracci; with Bellori he promoted and encouraged the arts. However, fewer works have been preserved from this period. Illness may have caused his output to diminish, and many works remain untraced. His position in the artistic and social life of Rome had increased considerably, and his activities were not centred exclusively on painting. Pope Innocent XI appointed him keeper of Raphael's Vatican Stanze. Italian and foreign collectors consulted him as a connoisseur of ancient art. For such patrons as Cardinal Paolo Savelli, Prince Livio Odescalchi, Ferrante Caponi or the Marchese Nicolò Maria Pallavicini, Maratti executed mythological works, such as the *Rape of Europa* (Dublin, N.G.) and *Venus, Ceres and Bacchus*, known through drawings, as well as private devotional works. Among his admirers were British Grand Tourists and other British collectors.

In the mid-1680s Maratti decorated his country house at Genzano with frescoes of mythological subjects; his social standing is suggested by his owning both this house and a Roman palazzo and a rich art collection. The latter belonged in part to his second wife Francesca Gommi, the mother of his daughter Faustina (*b* 1680), whose features, known through his portrait of her (*c.* 1698; Rome,

Pal. Corsini), served as the model for many female figures in his late work. In the 1680s Maratti finished the important commission for the Cappella della Presentazione in St Peter's, for which he executed the cartoons for the lunettes and the pendentive mosaics. Among them is the famous *Judith with the Head of Holofernes*. The *Virgin Immaculate with SS Gregory, John Chrysostom, John the Evangelist and Augustine* (*c.* 1686; Rome, S Maria del Popolo, Cybo Chapel; see fig. 2) is a measured and, to a certain degree, cold composition, but it presents its subject forcefully and is a clear precedent of 18th-century Neo-classicism. The *Death of the Virgin* (*c.* 1686; Rome, Villa Albani) was painted for Cardinal Alderano Cybo (1613–1700) and is distinguished by its accomplished treatment of the drapery; the commission for *St Carlo Borromeo Received into Glory with SS Ambrose and Sebastian below* (1680–85; Rome, S Carlo al Corso) was apparently accepted to discredit accusations that he was unable to paint large-scale pictures.

2. Carlo Maratti: *Virgin Immaculate with SS Gregory, John Chrysostom, John the Evangelist and Augustine*, oil on canvas, *c.* 1686 (Rome, S Maria del Popolo)

At the turn of the century political and economic factors caused official and aristocratic patronage to decline. Maratti became active as a restorer. Before 1695, Francesco di Parma had commissioned him to restore the Raphael frescoes in the Villa Farnesina and those by Annibale Carracci in the Palazzo Farnese. In 1702 Maratti was appointed Director of the Antiquities of Rome, and Pope Clement XI proposed that he undertake the restoration of the frescoes by Raphael in the Vatican Stanze. In 1700 he was again elected principal of the Accademia di S Luca, a responsibility that was renewed in perpetuity in 1706, an unprecedented honour. In this late period his important works include the *Baptism* (1699; Rome, S Maria degli Angeli), the large canvases (1692–1702) painted for the Baptismal Chapel in St Peter's (*in situ*), as well as the cartoons for the pendentives for the Cappella del Coro there. Distinguished by its ravishing colour is the *Virgin of the Rosary with Saints* (1695) for the oratory of S Cita, Palermo (*in situ*). The *Apparition of the Virgin to St Andrea Corsini* for the chapel of the Palazzo Corsini in Florence (*in situ*), the *Virgin with Saints* (1700–09) for the church of S Filippo Neri in Turin (*in situ*), commissioned by Emanuel-Philibert of Savoy, and the *Baptism* (1710) for the Certosa di S Martino in Naples are Maratti's last works. In this final period of his life, he prepared drawings and sketches and continued to lead the workshop, but the works were executed by assistants, among them Giuseppe Bartolomeo Chiari, Andrea Procaccini and Agostino Masucci. He continued to produce mythological and pastoral works (e.g. the *Judgement of Paris*, 1708; St Petersburg, Hermitage), which reflect the spirit of the literary movement of the Accademia degli Arcadi and its search for grace and feminine beauty.

When Maratti was 81 years old, his sight deteriorated and his hand shook, making painting very difficult. Nevertheless, he continued to direct his workshop, and some contemporary documents suggest that he continued to paint after this date. A document of 1710 regarding the great canvas of *St Peter Baptizing the Centurion Cornelius* (1711; Urbino, S Francesco) for the Baptismal Chapel in St Peter's, entrusted to his disciple Andrea Procaccini, reveals that the painting was not to be exhibited in the chapel before being retouched first by Maratti. On his death, at the age of 88, Maratti received exceptional honours: his coffin was carried by members of the Accademia di S Luca and his funeral and burial in S Maria degli Angeli were attended by all the members of the Accademia and of the Compagnia dei Virtuosi del Pantheon.

(ii) Portraits. Maratti was a distinguished portrait painter, whose blend of realism and an idealizing elegance ensured his immediate success. Such portraits as *Andrea Sacchi* (*c.* 1655; Madrid, Prado) are characterized by simplicity of composition and intense concentration, but he gradually developed a more decorative Baroque style, indebted to Anthony van Dyck or Philippe de Champaigne, as in the portrait of *Cardinal Antonio Barberini* (*c.* 1660; Rome, Pal. Barberini). The splendour of the draperies in such works and the rich and brilliant colour are combined with allegorical or mythological elements or themes derived from ancient history, as in the portrait of *Robert Spencer*

(c. 1661) and the portrait of *Wentworth Dillon* (c. 1665; both Althorp House, Northants). His portraits have something in common with contemporary French portraiture, on which he may have had some influence. His *Pope Clement IX* (1669; Rome, Pin. Vaticana; see fig. 3) unites realism and psychological depth with rich draperies and an evocation of wisdom and dignity; it echoes Renaissance portraits by Titian and Raphael, as well as Velázquez's *Pope Innocent X* (1650–51; Rome, Gal. Doria-Pamphili; *see* VELÁZQUEZ, DIEGO, fig. 6).

In the 1670s Maratti executed a notable series of portraits, such as those of the British Grand Tourists in Rome: *Thomas Isham* (c. 1677; Lamport Hall, Northants) and *Charles Fox* (c. 1679; Earl of Ilchester priv. col.); others remain untraced, such as those of *Charles Errard* and *Michelangelo de la Chaussé*, known through drawings and engravings, or that of *Giovanni Pietro Bellori* (Rome, priv. col.). These are all more idealizing works and incorporate references to the sitter's occupation (Bellori, for example, is seated in front of books written by himself); the more ample draperies add to the decorative aspect of these pictures. His *Self-portrait* (after 1695; Brussels, Mus. A. Anc.) is an outstanding act of self-glorification, showing the artist, rejuvenated, idealized and ennobled, against a landscape background; a female figure personifying Painting is shown inscribing his name on Minerva's shield. In *Cleopatra Dissolving the Pearl* (c. 1692; Rome, Mus. Pal. Venezia) the artist painted his daughter Faustina as Cleopatra; and in the grandiose *Marchese Nicolò Maria Pallavicini with the Artist* (1706; Stourhead, Wilts, NT; see fig. 4), one of the most ostentatious portraits of the Roman Baroque, Maratti appears seated

4. Carlo Maratti: *Marchese Nicolò Maria Pallavicini with the Artist*, oil on canvas, 3.00×2.13 m, 1706 (Stourhead, Wilts, NT)

3. Carlo Maratti: *Pope Clement IX*, oil on canvas, 1.45×1.16 m, 1669 (Rome, Pinacoteca Vaticana)

on the right accompanied by the Graces and painting the heroically clad Marchese, whom Glory crowns with laurel and to whom Genius (based on the *Apollo Belvedere*, Rome, Vatican, Mus. Pio-Clementino) indicates the Temple of Virtue in the background.

(iii) Designs for sculpture and architecture. On the death of Pope Innocent XI in 1689, his nephew Livio Odescalchi commissioned Maratti to design the Pope's tomb (1701; Rome, St Peter's); it was executed by the French sculptor Pierre-Etienne Monnot. Maratti's activity as a director or designer of sculptural decorations was concentrated in the period 1689 to 1713, although it was by no means a new activity—years before he had presented drawings for the monument to Raphael in the Pantheon. In the Academia de S Fernando in Madrid there are various studies by him for an entrance to a chapel, an organ loft and a series of funerary and fountain monuments. He also collaborated with Monnot on the tomb of *John Cecil, 5th Earl of Exeter* (erected 1704) for the church of St Martin in Stamford, Lincs (*in situ*), and c. 1695 he made preparatory drawings for his own funerary monument (completed in 1704; Rome, S Maria degli Angeli), which was executed by the sculptor Francesco Moratti (d 1719). He was also involved in a series of sculptures of *Apostles* for S Giovanni in Laterano, Rome (*in situ*), commissioned in 1701; numerous preparatory drawings of *St John, St Matthew* and *St Peter* survive for these works, which were executed by

Monnot and Camillo Rusconi, among others, and finished after Maratti's death. Maratti's sculptural style is closer to that of Bernini than to the more rigorous classical style of younger sculptors. Nevertheless, the elegant and rhetorical attitudes of the Apostles are derived from the grandiose figures in Maratti's altarpieces.

BIBLIOGRAPHY

G. P. Bellori: *Vita di Guido Reni, Andrea Sacchi e Carlo Maratti* (MS., 1695); ed. M. Piacentini (Rome, 1942) [follows MS. of 1695, Rouen, Bib. Mun.]
N. Pio: *Vite* (1724); ed. C. Enggass and R. Enggass (Vatican City, 1977)
L. Pascoli: *Vite* (Rome, 1730–36)
G. P. Bellori and others: *Vita di Carlo Maratta pittore* (Rome, 1732)
P. Picca: 'Carlo Maratta', *Rass. March.*, iv (1909), pp. 53–7
C. Lorenzetti: 'Carlo Maratti, la sua giovinezza a Roma', *L'Arte*, xvii (1914), pp. 135–52
O. Kutschera-Woborski: 'Ein kunsttheoretisches Thesenblatt Carlo Marattas und seine ästhetischen Anschauen "Graphische Künste"', *Mitt. Ges. Vervielfält. Kst* (1919), suppl., pp. 9–29
C. Lorenzetti: 'A proposito di due opere giovanili di Carlo Maratti non ricordate dal Bellori', *Rass. March.*, iii (1924–5), pp. 331–7
R. Wittkower: 'Die vier Apostelstatuen in Mettelschiff von S Giovanni in Laterano in Rom', *Z. Bild. Kst*, lx (1926–7), pp. 2–20
M. Loret: 'Carlo Maratti e gli scultori delle statue degli Apostoli in S Giovanni in Laterano', *Archv Italia & Rass. Int. Archv.*, 2nd ser., xi (1935), pp. 140–44
E. Raffaele: *Notizie nella famiglia del pittore Carlo Maratti* (Monza, 1943)
A. Mezzetti: 'Contributi a Carlo Maratti', *Riv. Ist. N. Archeol. & Stor. A.*, iv (1955), pp. 253–354
——: 'Carlo Maratti, altri contributi', *A. Ant. & Mod.* (1961), pp. 377–87
H. Dowley: 'Carlo Maratti, Carlo Fontana and the Baptismal Chapel in St Peter's', *A. Bull.*, xlvii (1965), pp. 57–81
H. Ost: 'Ein Rühmesblatt für Raphaël bei Maratti und Mengs', *Z. Kstgesch.*, xxviii (1965), pp. 281–98
W. Witzthum: 'V. M. Nieto Alcaide, Carlo Maratti, quarenta y tres dibujos de tema religioso', *Master Drgs*, iii (1965), pp. 174–5
E. Schaar and A. Sutherland Harris: *Die Handzeichnungen von Andrea Sacchi und Carlo Maratta* (Düsseldorf, 1967)
F. R. di Federico: 'Documentation for the Paintings and Mosaics of the Baptismal Chapel in St Peter's', *A. Bull.*, l (1968), pp. 194–8
E. Schaar: 'Carlo Marattas *Tod des Heiligen Franz Xaver* in Gesù', *Kunsthistorischen Studien Hans Kauffmann, 70 Geburtstag* (Berlin, 1968), pp. 247–64
M. Mena: 'Some Drawings by Carlo Maratta and Niccolò Berrettoni for the Altieri Palace in Rome', *Master Drgs*, xiii (1975)
——: 'Dibujos de Carlo Maratta en colecciones madrileñas', *Mitt. Ksthist. Inst. Florenz*, i (1975)
J. Westin and R. Westin: *Carlo Maratti and his Contemporaries: Figurative Drawings from the Roman Baroque* (Pennsylvania, 1975)
P. Bellini: *Italian Masters of the Seventeenth Century (1983)*, 47 [XXI/ii] of *The Illustrated Bartsch*, ed. W. Strauss (New York, 1978–), pp. 21–55
D. L. Bershad: 'The Newly Discovered Testament and Inventories of Carlo Maratti and his Wife Francesca', *Antol. B. A.*, xxvi (1985), pp. 65–85
M. Mena: 'Carlo Maratti e Raffaello', *Raffaello e l'Europa: Atti del IV Corso Internazionale di Alta Cultura*, Accad. N. Lincei (Rome, 1990)

MANUELA B. MENA MARQUÉS

Marbling. *See under* PAPER, DECORATIVE.

Marburg, Elisabethkirche. Early Gothic church in Hessen, Germany, and the centre of the cult of St Elisabeth of Hungary (1207–31; *can* 1235). Established during the 12th century, Marburg was promoted as the cult centre by the Teutonic Order, and Emperor Friedrich II emphasized its importance to imperial politics in the east by crowning the saint's head reliquary with a gold crown from his own treasury.

1. ARCHITECTURE. In 1228 the widowed Landgräfin Elisabeth of Thuringia founded a hospital to the north of the modest castle of the Landgraves of Thuringia, where she was buried in 1231. The day after her burial miracles started to occur at her grave. The foundations excavated in the 19th century under and to the east of the north transept of the present building indicate that there was an elongated single-cell church with an apse and presumably a west tower. In 1234 the hospital was taken over by the Teutonic Order, of which Elisabeth's brother-in-law, Landgraf Konrad (*d* 1240), became Grand Master in 1239. The present church was founded in 1235 and the saint's body translated in 1249/50. It was used as the church of the Teutonic Order, as the burial church of St Elisabeth and as the burial place of the Landgraves of Thuringia.

The church has a trefoil-plan choir, a three-aisled hall nave and twin towers on the west façade. Each polygonal apse has a single straight bay, and the nave has six bays leading to the west block. The general consecration took place on 1 May 1283, but the towers were still being constructed in 1314. The building was restored between 1854 and 1861 and in 1930–31. The exterior and interior are severely articulated and sparingly decorated; freely handled foliate ornament is found only on the doors and the capitals. The walls are pierced by two rows of traceried two-light windows, identical in size with an oculus, similar to those at Reims Cathedral (those on the axis of each apse are cusped). The large west window below a richly ornamented stepped gable was made after 1290 and influenced by the cathedrals of Strasbourg and Freiburg im Breisgau. The quadripartite rib vaults rest on slender supports; unlike the Liebfrauenkirche at Trier, to which the Elisabethkirche may be related, there are no shaft rings to break the vertical lines.

Contrary to earlier belief, the hall nave is part of the original design (see fig.). The *piliers cantonnés* are topped by imposts with wreaths of foliage, corresponding to the pre-mid-13th-century western piers at Reims Cathedral.

Marburg, Elisabethkirche, interior looking east, founded 1235

Up to the third bay from the east the wreaths of foliage use Rémois leaf forms, but after that the leaves are closely related to foliage at Amiens Cathedral. The original unified concept for the interior, with white pointing on a pinky-red background, ochre-coloured ribs, and arches picked out in white, was whitewashed in the 19th century. The furnishings are unusually complete and stylistically unified: the stained glass (from *c.* 1240 to the first half of the 14th century; *see* GOTHIC, §VIII, 5), the wall altars and wall painting (consecrated in 1294 and 1298) and a variety of sculpture (*see* §2 below).

Along with the Liebfrauenkirche (1233–43, 1273–83) in Trier and the choir of the Cistercian church of Marienstatt (1243–1324) at Streithausen in the Westerwald, the Elisabethkirche is one of the earliest buildings east of the River Rhine to show the strong influence of the cathedrals of Reims and Soissons. It is still uncertain, however, if the trefoil choir was inspired by the Early Gothic examples at the cathedrals of Noyon, Soissons and Cambrai and at Chaalis Abbey rather than Romanesque choirs of similar plan in the Rhineland. Equally undecided is the influence of the polygonal transepts of the Liebfrauenkirche at Trier, whether the Elisabethkirche's function as a burial church demanded a central plan, or whether it was influenced by the Teutonic Knights' church (1222–3) at Tartlau (now Prejmer, Romania). Nor can the conjecture that the building was intended largely for prestige purposes be proved for certain, and in some respects it cannot be justified. The hall reflects contemporary developments in Westphalia: Herford Minster (*c.* 1228–50), Paderborn Cathedral (after 1235) and Haina Abbey church (*c.* 1240–50).

BIBLIOGRAPHY

K.-W. Kästner: *Die Elisabethkirche zu Marburg und ihre künstlerische Nachfolge*, i (Marburg, 1924)

W. Meyer-Barkhausen: *Die Elisabethkirche in Marburg* (Marburg, 1925)

H. Bauer: *St. Elisabeth und die Elisabethkirche zu Marburg* (Marburg, 1964)

J. Michler: 'Die Langhaushalle der Marburger Elisabethkirche', *Z. Kstgesch.*, xxxii (1969), pp. 104–32

A. Tuczek: 'Das Masswesen der Elisabethkirche in Marburg und der Liebfrauenkirche in Trier', *Hess. Jb. Landesgesch.*, xxi (1971), pp. 1–99

J. Michler: 'Die Elisabethkirche zu Marburg als Schöpfungsbau der deutschen Gotik', *Hess. Heimat*, xxvii (1977), pp. 95–104

700 Jahre Elisabethkirche in Marburg, 1283–1983: Die Elisabethkirche: Architektur in der Geschichte (exh. cat., ed. H.-J. Kunst; Marburg, Schloss, 1983)

J. Michler: *Die Elisabethkirche zu Marburg in ihrer ursprünglichen Farbigkeit*, Quellen und Studien zur Geschichte des deutschen Ordens, xix (Marburg, 1984)

N. Nussbaum: *Deutsche Kirchenbaukunst der Gotik* (Cologne, 1985), pp. 57–62

GÜNTHER BINDING

2. SCULPTURE. The sculpture in the Elisabethkirche, dating mainly from the High Middle Ages, forms a compact set of ecclesiastical furnishings that is unique in Germany, as the sculpture from portals, brackets, tombs and altars, both relief and free-standing, survives unaltered. At the Elisabethkirche it was not only the latest models that were followed, but those that could be best adapted to the church's requirements. On the west portal (*c.* 1280) the *Vierge dorée* (*c.* 1260) of Amiens Cathedral was used as a model and modified to the tympanum position to act as a focal point in the context of the Teutonic Order's Marian leanings. St Elisabeth's mausoleum (*c.* 1280) has a stone canopy with burial relief (*c.* 1350) added to the front

of the sarcophagus; a gold shrine to St Elisabeth (before 1249–50) stands in the sacristy. For the high altar (consecrated 1290) with its stone altarpiece, a style inspired by sculpture on the outer west portal at Freiburg im Breisgau Cathedral was deemed appropriate, both in size and expression, for the backdrop of saints who accompany the displays of relics. The tombs of the early Landgraves (*c.* 1320) contain references to the latest Parisian styles, as in the tomb by Pépin de Huy (*fl* 1312-23) of *Robert d'Artois* (*d* 1317). On the choir-screens (*c.* 1320–30) hosts of saints with coldly uniform drapery watch over the knights of the Teutonic Order. They reveal the stylistic influence of Cologne and Lorraine. The church also contains memorial plaques from the 13th to the 16th centuries and five wooden, winged altarpieces (early 16th century) by Ludwig Juppe.

BIBLIOGRAPHY

R. Hamann: *Die Plastik*, ii of *Die Elisabethkirche zu Marburg und ihre künstlerische Nachfolge*, ed. R. Hamann and K. Wilhelm-Kästner (Marburg, 1929)

U. Geese: 'Die hl. Elisabeth im Kräftefeld zweier konkurrierender Mächte: Zur Ausstattungsphase der Elisabethkirche zwischen 1280 und 1290', *700 Jahre Elisabethkirche in Marburg, 1283–1983* (exh. cat., Marburg, Schloss, 1983), i, pp. 55–67

A. Köstler: *Ausstattung der Marburger Elisabeth Kirche: Die Ästhetisierung des Kultraums im Mittelalter* (Berlin, 1995)

ANDREAS KÖSTLER

Marc, Franz (Moriz Wilhelm) (*b* Munich, 8 Feb 1880; *d* nr Verdun, 4 March 1916). German painter. He decided to become a painter in autumn 1900, after initially intending to study philosophy and theology. He began his training at the Akademie der Bildenden Künste in Munich under Gabriel von Hackl (1843–1926) and Wilhelm von Dietz (1839–1907) and worked in the style of Munich landscape painting. His early *Portrait of the Artist's Mother* (1902; Munich, Lenbachhaus) reveals in its form and construction that he already possessed an astonishing mastery of traditional artistic means. From summer 1902 onwards, increasingly self-taught, he worked at Kochel in Upper Bavaria, often on the alpine slopes of the Staffelalm. In May 1903, thanks to his excellent command of French (his Huguenot mother came from Alsace), he accompanied a friend on a study trip to Paris. On his return to Munich he gave up his studies at the Akademie. In his studio in the Kaulbachstrasse he devoted himself primarily to illustrations of poems by Richard Dehmel, Carmen Sylva, Hans Bethge and others, which were published posthumously by Anette von Eckhardt in 1917 in Munich under the title *Stella Peregrina*.

In spring 1906 Marc accompanied his brother Paul Marc to Greece. His few works from this year are limited to realistic animal and landscape studies. In spring 1907, during another brief trip to Paris, he was deeply impressed by the work of van Gogh and Gauguin as well as by Egyptian and medieval sculpture. For financial reasons, he gave lessons in anatomical drawing. He spent summer 1908 with his future wife, Maria Franck, making nature studies at Lenggries in Bavaria. The painting *Larch Sapling* (1908; Cologne, Mus. Ludwig) shows for the first time the influence of van Gogh. In Lenggries he developed further his preoccupation with animals, their habits and their characteristic ways of moving: they appeared to him to be of a purer, less corrupt nature than man. He studied horses at pasture for weeks at a time, and cows and deer in the wild, and he sculpted in clay in addition to his graphic and painted efforts. The naturalistic character still dominates the works of this period, even when the surface treatment of the paintings increasingly reveals the stylistic influence of van Gogh. Even the works of the following year spent in Sindelsdorf in Upper Bavaria, such as *Oak Sapling* (1909; Munich, Lenbachhaus) or *Crouching in the Reeds* (1909; Münster, Westfäl. Landesmus.), continue to reveal the influence of this artist and culminated in a picture painted at the end of the year, *Cats on a Red Cloth* (1909–10; Munich, priv. col.), in which extremely intense colour is used for the first time.

In January 1910 Marc was visited by the young painter Auguste Macke and his uncle Bernhard Koehler, who later became patron of them both. A close friendship developed between the two painters. Marc was able to exhibit his work for the first time in February in Brakl's modern art gallery in the Goethestrasse in Munich. He visited Koehler in Berlin and in July 1910 was given by him a monthly stipend in exchange for an option on his future paintings. Marc then moved to Sindelsdorf in Upper Bavaria, giving up his studio in Munich. In September 1910, fascinated by the second exhibition of the NEUE KÜNSTLERVEREINIGUNG MÜNCHEN (NKVM), he met the painters in this group: Kandinsky, Alexei Jawlenski, Gabriele Münter, Marianne Werefkin and others. *Nude with Cat* (1910; Munich, Lenbachhaus) shows a new monumentality in its pictorial construction and an intensity of colour reminiscent of the Fauves. Although Marc at first continued producing paintings with a naturalistic palette, such as *Grazing Horses I* (1910; Munich, Lenbachhaus), his style was changing significantly, for example in *Grazing Horses IV (The Red Horses)* (1911; formerly Hagen, Folkwang-Museum), a painting that was later impounded as decadent and auctioned in 1939 at the Galerie Fischer, Lucerne.

In February 1911 Marc became a member of NKVM. In May he held his second exhibition at the Galerie Thannhauser in Munich's Theatinerstrasse. Marc's artistic intentions coincided with Kandinsky's, with whom he had become friends, both feeling themselves called upon to contribute through their painting to a spiritual renewal of Western culture. They found inspiration in the religious folk art of Upper Bavaria and employed the formal simplicity of its means, particularly that of painting behind glass, in their own endeavours. Working entirely within the tradition of Western religious art, both sought to convey a spiritual message. Marc used animals as symbolic figures and called upon the viewer's powers of association to disclose his works' meaning. The problems this posed led to disagreements within NKVM and ultimately to the resignations of Kandinsky and Marc, the two most important members, who then put on their own exhibition in December 1911, with the famous title *Der Blaue Reiter*; Marc was represented by four pictures. Both painters are listed as editors in the almanac *Der Blaue Reiter*, which came out in May 1912, and which is recognized as one of the most important artistic manifestos of the 20th century (*see* BLAUE REITER). In it, contemporary artists articulated in a series of essays the underlying motivations for modern art, and reproductions of their works appeared in the context of illustrations of Western religious art and non-European art. Marc was represented by the essays 'Geistige Güter', 'Die Wilden Deutschlands' and 'Zwei Bilder'; a reproduction of his painting *The Steer* (1911; New York, Guggenheim); and two woodcuts. The continual artistic interchanges while the almanac and the exhibition were in preparation helped to focus and intensify the form and colour of Marc's work, and increased its expressive power. He sought to reduce the natural multiplicity of detailed forms to an almost geometrical simplicity, as is seen in *Yellow Cow* (1911; New York, Guggenheim), *Small Blue Horses* (1911) and *Small Yellow Horses* (1911; both Stuttgart, Staatsgal.).

In autumn 1912 Marc and Macke visited Robert Delaunay in Paris. This meeting and the confrontation with the intellectual foundations of French Cubism proved to be of immense importance for both. The principle of the transitory condition of all living things and their interpenetration, the simultaneity and inseparability of spirit and matter, is reflected in pictures such as *In the Rain* (1912), *Deer in the Convent Garden* (1912; both Munich, Lenbachhaus), and one of Marc's major works, *The Tiger* (1912; see fig.). In this work the figure of the dangerous, cunning animal appears crouching and yet ready to spring in the midst of formal structures whose crystalline construction corresponds to that of the physical presence of the animal. No dualism of any sort between animate and inanimate nature is shown. The indivisibility of all being was the essential spiritual message.

In the summer of 1913 in Sindelsdorf, Marc's large, major compositions were painted: the *Impoverished Land of Tyrol* (1913; New York, Guggenheim), *Tower of the Blue Horses* (1913; ex-Berlin, Neue N.G., lost since 1945), *Fate of Animals* (1913; Basle, Kstmus.), as well as *Mandrill* (1913) and *Picture with Cattle* (1913; both Munich,

Franz Marc: *The Tiger*, oil on canvas, 1.11×1.11 m, 1912 (Munich, Städtische Galerie im Lenbachhaus)

Staatsgal. Mod. Kst). In all of them the subject stands almost entirely fractured into prismatic structures of various colours. Simultaneously, he produced the first designs for a planned illustrated Bible (to include illustrations by Kandinsky and others), himself undertaking the Book of Genesis.

In autumn 1913 Marc took part in the organization of the first Deutscher Herbstsalon, initiated by Herwarth Walden in Berlin. In early 1914 he moved from Sindelsdorf to a house in Ried, near Benediktbeuern and, at the prompting of Hugo Ball, occupied himself briefly with ideas for a staging of Shakespeare's *The Tempest* that nevertheless failed to come to fruition. In the few months before the outbreak of World War I, the last large, almost completely non-objective compositions were made, such as *Birds* (1914; Munich, Lenbachhaus), *Playing Forms* (1914; Essen, Mus. Flkwang) or *Fighting Forms* (1914; Munich, Staatsgal. Mod. Kst), all of them reflecting a search for metaphysical regularities. On the outbreak of war Marc registered as a volunteer. His letters from the front and his sketchbook, the only pictorial expression of this period, were published under the title *Franz Marc, Briefe, Aufzeichnungen, und Aphorismen* by Paul Cassirer in 1920. Marc was killed near Verdun.

WRITINGS

with V. Kandinsky: *Der Blaue Reiter* (Munich, 1912/R 1965/R 1976)
Franz Marc: Briefe, Aufzeichnungen, und Aphorismen (Berlin, 1920)
August Macke–Franz Marc: Briefwechsel (Cologne, 1964)
K. Lankheit, ed.: *Franz Marc: Schriften* (Cologne, 1978)
——: *Wassily Kandinsky und Franz Marc: Briefwechsel* (Cologne, 1983)

BIBLIOGRAPHY

A. Schardt: *Franz Marc* (Berlin, 1936)
Franz Marc: Das graphische Werk (exh. cat. by H. C. von Tavel, Berne, Kstmus., 1967)
K. Lankheit: *Franz Marc: Katalog der Werke* (Cologne, 1970)
——: *Franz Marc: Sein Leben und seine Kunst* (Cologne, 1976)
F. S. Levine: *The Apocalyptic Vision: The Art of Franz Marc as German Expressionism* (New York, 1979)
Franz Marc, 1880–1916 (exh. cat., ed. M. Rosenthal; Berkeley, U. CA, A. Mus., 1979)
Franz Marc, 1880–1916 (exh. cat., ed. R. Gollek; Munich, Lenbachhaus, 1980)
R. März: *Franz Marc* (Berlin, 1984)
P. K. Schuster: *Postkarten an den Prinzen Jussef von Franz Marc* (Munich, 1988)
M. Rosenthal: *Franz Marc* (Munich, 1989)
Franz Marc: Zeichnungen und Aquarelle (exh. cat. by M. M. Moeller, Berlin, Brücke-Mus.; Essen, Mus. Flkwang; Tübingen, Ksthalle; 1989–90)
S. Partsch: *Franz Marc: 1880–1916* (Cologne, 1990)
H. Düchting: *Franz Marc* (Cologne, 1991)
Franz Marc: Kräfte der Natur–Werke, 1912–1915 (exh. cat. by E. Franz, Munich, Staatsgal. Mod. Kst; Münster, Westfäl. Landesmus.; 1993–4)

ROSEL GOLLEK

Marcahuamachuco. Site of Pre-Columbian culture, flourishing *c.* AD 400–*c.* 1000, in the northern Peruvian highlands near the modern town of Huamachuco, Sánchez Carrión Province. The site ranges across the top of a hilly plateau 3.8 km long and approximately 500 m wide. The plateau itself is elevated 3400–3600 m above sea-level and is enclosed on three sides by steep cliffs and gorges up to 1000 m deep. The site is important for its architecture and architectural stone-carving.

Max Uhle visited the site in 1900 and made the first scientifically recorded collections; in 1941 Theodore D. McCown made an extensive study of the ruins, collecting more artefacts. Both their collections are housed in the Robert H. Lowie Museum of Anthropology at the University of California, Berkeley. John P. Thatcher conducted surveys in the late 1960s and early 1970s, and a Canadian project directed by John and Theresa Topic, with the collaboration of H. Stanly Loten and Marie-Ann Geurts, began a study of the site in 1981.

Hills define sectors of the site: Cerro Viejo in the northeast, Cerro de los Corrales and Cerro de las Monjas in the centre and Cerro del Castillo in the south-east. The earliest occupation of the site appears to have occurred at Cerro Viejo slightly before AD 400. Soon after this date, however, buildings were erected across the entire plateau, and construction of monumental buildings continued until *c.* AD 1000.

Early buildings at Cerro Viejo were single-storey structures with flat earthen roofs supported by roof beams resting on stone corbels set into the walls. Parapets pierced by drains carried rain-water off the roofs. Most later buildings are multi-storey; buildings with two storeys are common, but a few have three storeys, and the Castillo (see below) is four or five storeys high in places. The upper floors of multi-storey buildings are usually supported by stone corbels, but sometimes the joists are set directly into the walls. Roofs of later buildings often rest directly on top of the walls, but they are sometimes supported by corbels set slightly below the wall tops.

Walls were built in a distinctive masonry style, in which large blocks of stone, often 1 m or more in length, were laid on carefully prepared beds of small stones. Although mud mortar was used, the strength of the walls results from the tight fit of the stones. This style of masonry can be traced back to the Pre-Ceramic period at LA GALGADA. The corners of the buildings are especially distinctive, being constructed in a pleasing technique known as long-and-short work in which long blocks are alternately set vertically and horizontally.

The focal-point of the site is the Castillo, a massive construction that comprises multi-storey curvilinear and rectangular buildings, with an artificial mound crowning the highest point of the site. Many of the other buildings are also located to accentuate the natural topography of the site, giving the impression that the architecture has grown out of the bedrock. Perhaps because of this tendency to emphasize the natural features, large areas—especially hollows and gradual slopes—were never built upon.

There are three major classes of buildings: curvilinear galleries, circular galleries and niched halls. Curvilinear galleries are typically located along the edges of cliffs and serve to define the site perimeters at Cerro Viejo and Cerro del Castillo. They are often two storeys high, 2–3 m wide, and sometimes more than 200 m long. This length is subdivided into a series of rooms served by multiple entrances. There are at least nine circular galleries (varying in plan from almost circular to oval to irregularly curved), all located on the Cerro de los Corrales and on the Cerro de las Monjas. These are similar in most respects to the curvilinear galleries but completely enclose a central patio in which other, rectangular, buildings are located. The best preserved circular gallery is about 60 m in diameter and had from one to three storeys; originally it probably had four entrances on the ground-floor and access from all three levels to the central patio.

Niched halls are voluminous roofed spaces, rectilinear in plan and typically two to three times the width of the galleries. Sometimes they are multi-storey, and in these cases the hall is usually located on the second storey. They have from one to four entrances in the front wall and, if multi-storey, usually a number of entrances in the rear wall of the ground-floor. They are characterized by a row of niches, measuring *c*. 750 mm square, on the interior of the back wall and sometimes the interior and exterior of the front wall. In one of the best preserved examples, the hall measures *c*. 10×60 m and is set on the second floor. It has rectangular niches on the interior back wall and decorative stepped niches on the exterior front wall. A window and four entrances are set in the front wall; the entrances are reached from the roof of a single-storey annexe in front of the building. Ground-floor doorways connect with the annexe and with open areas at the rear of the building.

The contemporaneous HUARI culture adopted some of these architectural forms, though not the distinctive masonry style. Huari administrative centres display the niched hall and the multi-storey gallery, adapted to a rectangular form. Since one such administrative centre was near the Inca capital of Cuzco, it is possible that the Incas also borrowed some architectural forms derived from Marcahuamachuco.

The stepped design that occurs as a decorative niche in some of the halls also occurs carved in high relief on rectangular stone slabs, which may have been made to be set into walls. There are also stones sculptured in the round in the form of human heads. Often quite lifelike, they have stone pegs or tenons in the back, which can be inserted into walls. The stone sculpture is related to the RECUAY style, especially that found at Pashash.

BIBLIOGRAPHY

T. D. McCown: *Pre-Incaic Huamachuco: Survey and Excavations in the Region of Huamachuco and Cajabamba*, U. CA Pubns Amer. Archaeol. & Ethnol., xxxix (Berkeley, 1945)

J. R. Topic: 'A Sequence of Monumental Architecture from Huamachuco', *Perspectives on Andean Prehistory and Protohistory*, ed. D. Sandweiss (Ithaca, 1986), pp. 63–84

——: 'Hurari and Humachuco', *Huari Administrative Structure: Prehistoric Monumental Architecture and State Government* (Washington, DC, 1991)

JOHN R. TOPIC

Marçais, Georges (*b* 1876; *d* 1962). French historian. He was trained as a painter and an engraver. A visit to his brother, William, who was director of a school in Algeria, led Georges to the study of Arabic, a thesis on the Berbers in North Africa and a life devoted to Islamic art in North Africa. He was professor at the University of Algiers (1919–44). Marçais was a prolific writer on subjects ranging from history to ethnography and technology, but the main thrust of his work was architecture, and *L'Architecture musulmane d'occident* remains the standard work on the subject. Beyond the clarity of expression that characterizes most of his work, his importance lies in the presence of two ideologically significant, although not fully expressed, themes. One is the nurturing of a western Islamic (Spanish and North African) artistic and cultural regionalism with a Roman substratum, which he set up in opposition to a supposed pan-Islamic cultural unity centred on the Middle East. As a consequence, Marçais helped to develop local as well as national museums as a focus for local pride in art. The second is the organization of the history of Islamic art by dynasties, so that stylistic variations are more clearly uncovered than through the study of constant diachronic cultural forms. This conception lessens the power and significance of any one monument, but lets readers and visitors feel that what they see is deeply wedded to the land that surrounds it and to the people and events that made it. In addition to books and surveys of architecture, Marçais wrote a number of articles dealing with the central questions of Islamic art such as urbanism, the representation of living beings and the arabesque. With acuity and precision, he drew attention to what is essential in a work of art and what features are peculiar to Islamic art.

WRITINGS

with W. Marçais: *Les Monuments arabes de Tlemcen* (Paris, 1903)

Coupoles et plafonds de la Grande Mosquée de Kairouan (Paris, 1925)

Manuel d'art musulman: L'Architecture: Tunisie, Algérie, Maroc, Espagne, Sicile, 2 vols (Paris, 1926–7)

Les Faïences à reflets métalliques de la Grande Mosquée de Kairouan (Paris, 1928)

Le Costume musulman d'Alger (Paris, 1930)

Tunis et Kairouan (Paris, 1937)

'Les Broderies turques d'Alger', *A. Islam.*, iv (1937), pp. 145–53

'Remarques sur l'esthétique musulmane', *An. Inst. Etud. Orient.*, iv (1938), pp. 55–71

'Les Figures d'hommes dans bois sculptés d'époque fatimite conservés au Musée Arabe du Caire', *Mélanges Maspero*, iii (1940), pp. 241–57

'La Conception des villes dans l'Islâm', *Rev. d'Alger*, ii (1945), pp. 517–33

La Berbérie musulmane et l'orient au moyen âge (Paris, 1946)

L'Art de l'Islam (Paris, 1947)

'Nouvelles remarques sur l'esthétique musulmane', *An. Inst. Etud. Orient.*, vi (1947), pp. 31–52

with L. Poinssot: *Objets kairouanais, IXe au XIIIe siècle: Reliures, verreries, cuivres et bronzes, bijoux*, 2 vols (Tunis, 1948–52)

'Salle, antisalle: Recherches sur l'évolution d'un thème de l'architecture domestique en pays d'Islâm', *An. Inst. Etud. Orient.*, x (1952), pp. 274–301

L'Architecture musulmane d'occident: Tunisie, Algérie, Maroc, Espagne et Sicile (Paris, 1954)

with L. Golvin: *La Grande Mosquée de Sfax* (Tunis, 1960)

L'Art musulman (Paris, 1962)

OLEG GRABAR

Marçal [Marzal] de Sas, Andrés (*fl c.* 1393–1410). ?German painter, active in Spain. He came to the Valencia region from Germany: a Valencian document of 1396 specifically refers to him as *pintor almany*. The epithet 'Sas' may possibly refer to Saxony. He has been called 'the leading exponent of his art in Valencia for over a decade' (Kauffmann). Altogether 17 documents relating to him have been identified, some of which refer to commissions carried out with such painters as Pere Nicolau and Gonçal Peris. The only documented work that can be identified, however, is a panel of the *Incredulity of St Thomas* (see fig.) in the chapter house of Valencia Cathedral; this is almost certainly a fragment of the retable of *St Thomas the Apostle* for the cathedral, which is referred to in a receipt signed by Marçal de Sas on 20 March 1400. There are otherwise real difficulties in distinguishing Marçal's work from that of his collaborators, notably Pere Nicolau with whom he was in partnership. Marçal de Sas is last mentioned in April 1410 in 'grave poverty and illness', when the city council of Valencia granted him free lodging in recognition of his work.

Andrés Marçal de Sas: *Incredulity of St Thomas*, tempera on panel, *c.* 1400 (Valencia Cathedral)

Marçal de Sas's style as seen in the *Incredulity of St Thomas* has been characterized by Post as being harsh and Germanic, although there does not seem to be any contemporary German work with which it can be compared and which shows this harshness. A possible parallel exists, however, with Bohemian painting, for example the Třeboň retable of *c.* 1380 (Prague, N.G.). At all events the circle influenced by Marçal de Sas shows recognizable traits, such as angular types with elongated noses, distinct from contemporary work in Catalonia. By comparison with the *Incredulity of St Thomas*, Post made a tentative attribution to Marçal de Sas or his circle of a long list of retables and panels, notably the large altarpiece of *St George* (tempera on panel, 6.6×5.5 m; London, V&A), which Kauffmann has shown almost certainly came from the chapel of the meeting-house of the municipal militia of Valencia known as the Centenar de la Ploma, whose insignia it bears. The retable comprises two large superimposed central panels, depicting *St George and the Dragon* and the *Defeat of the Moors by the Christian Army under James I of Aragon (1237)*, surmounted by the *Virgin and Child* and *Christ with Angels*. The lateral panels bear 16 scenes of the *Life and Martyrdom of St George* and Evangelists surrounded by angels, with Apostles and prophets on the pilasters and outer frame; the damaged predella shows 10 scenes of the *Passion*. The work is distinguished by its naturalism, sharply individualized and expressive faces and the strong contrasts drawn between the good and bad characters, the latter being caricatured. The combination of realistic features (e.g. the torture scenes), accuracy of observation (e.g. the armour in the battle scenes), courtly elegance and a liking for surface decoration has suggested the influence of early 15th-century Franco-Flemish painting (e.g. the work of the Boucicaut Master). The predominant use of gold for the backgrounds, however, is unlike the more developed landscapes and interiors seen in contemporary Italian and French painting. For these reasons, Kauffmann has suggested that the retable dates from *c.* 1410–20, arguing that Marçal de Sas probably continued to be active after 1410.

BIBLIOGRAPHY

J. Sanchis y Sivera: *La catedral de Valencia* (Valencia, 1909)
——: *Pintores medievales de Valencia* (Barcelona, 1914)
C. R. Post: *A History of Spanish Painting*, iii and iv/2 (Cambridge, MA, 1930–33)
L. Cervero y Gomis: *Pintores valentinos, su cronología y documentación* (Valencia, 1964)
M. Kauffmann: 'The Altarpiece of St George from Valencia', *V&A Mus. Yb.*, ii (1970), pp. 65–100

J. R. L. HIGHFIELD

Marca-Relli, Conrad (*b* Boston, 5 June 1913). American painter. He studied briefly at the Cooper Union Institute in New York in 1930, and from 1935 to 1938 he participated in the WPA/FAP, for which he painted both easel pictures and murals. His work was strongly influenced at this time by that of Giorgio de Chirico. By the early 1950s he was producing essentially abstract works, some of them very large, which consist of a layering of biomorphic canvas shapes painted in bright or sombre colours and collaged to the support; in their lingering allusions to figurative and landscape forms, and in the particular quality of their interlocking shapes, they bear comparison with works produced by de Kooning in the late 1940s. Like de Kooning, he was rare among the painters associated with Abstract Expressionism in retaining such a strong attachment to subject-matter, as revealed even in his use of titles such as *The Battle* (1956; New York, Met.).

Marca-Relli continued in the 1960s to explore the potential of collage but became more concerned with cut-out and broken forms, incorporating not only the textured surfaces of canvas but also more unyielding materials such as plastics, metals and rivets (see 1970 exh. cat.). After treating colours at maximum intensity, with an abundant and forceful disposition of forms, he gradually evolved a more subdued idiom, in which colours and shapes are rigidly controlled and masterfully enhanced by their formalized presentation against the background. A typical example of this period is *Dissenters* (1956; New York, Whitney).

BIBLIOGRAPHY

P. Tyler: *Marca-Relli* (Paris, 1960)
H. H. Arnason: *Conrad Marca-Relli* (New York, 1963)
Marca-Relli (exh. cat. by W. C. Agee, New York, Whitney, 1967)
Conrad Marca-Relli (exh. cat., New York, Marlborough-Gerson Gal., 1970)
G. Miracle and H. Rosenberg: *Marca-Relli* (Barcelona, 1976)

ALBERTO CERNUSCHI

Marcel-Lenoir [Oury, Jules] (*b* Montauban, Tarn-et-Garonne, 12 May 1872; *d* Montricoux, Tarn-et-Garonne, 7 Sept 1931). French painter, printmaker and poet. He was the son of a jeweller and at an early age learnt how to produce lithographs and etchings. He quickly established a reputation as a creator of illuminated Symbolist works such as the gouache *The Monster* (1897; Paris, Flamand-Charbonnier priv. col.; see 1972 exh. cat., p. 64). This was executed in an Art Nouveau style and depicted the common Symbolist theme of woman as the destructive temptress of man. Four works, including this, were shown at the sixth SALON DE LA ROSE+CROIX at the Galerie Georges Petit in Paris (1897), and he had similar works published in periodicals such as *L'Estampe moderne*, *L'Aube* and *Le Courrier français*.

Marcel-Lenoir's first paintings were produced with a palette knife or by using paint straight from the tube, as in *A Review in the Cours Foucault in Montauban* (1907; Toulouse, Mus. Augustins). He produced other townscapes also, such as *View of Montauban: The Place de la Préfecture* (1911; Toulouse, Mus. Augustins), but was most interested in religious subjects. He held strong mystical religious beliefs which were mixed with an idealist Symbolist aesthetic, leading to such works as the *Second Crucifixion* (1910; Montauban, Mus. Ingres). Most notably, however, he produced a number of large religious frescoes such as *Crowning of the Virgin*, executed from 1921 to 1922 for the Institut Catholique at Toulouse. This huge work, 7 m high×17 m long, is considered his masterpiece. He also produced decorations for the church at Ribeauvillé, Haut-Rhin. His book of poems *Raison ou déraison du peintre Marcel-Lenoir* (1908) was published by the Abbaye de Créteil artists.

WRITINGS
Raison ou déraison du peintre Marcel-Lenoir (Paris, 1908)

BIBLIOGRAPHY
E. Boissier: *L'Enlumineur Marcel-Lenoir, l'homme et l'oeuvre* (Paris, *c.* 1900)
S. Fumet: *Marcel-Lenoir: L'Homme et l'oeuvre* (Paris, 1926)
French Symbolist Painters: Moreau, Puvis de Chavannes, Redon and their Followers (exh. cat. by G. Lacambre and others, London, Hayward Gal., 1972), pp. 64–5

Marcellini, Carlo Andrea (*b* Florence, *c.* 1644; *d* Florence, 22 June 1713). Italian sculptor, stuccoist and architect. After training in Florence as a goldsmith, he studied with the painter Felice Ficherelli. In 1671 he went to Rome, having been chosen for the Tuscan Accademia Granducale. He studied sculpture under Ercole Ferrata and Ciro Ferri, showing a predilection for modelling rather than the marble carving expected by his patron, Cosimo III de' Medici, Grand Duke of Tuscany. In 1672 he won first prize at the Accademia di S Luca for a terracotta relief of *Decaulion and Pirra*. He modelled the angels (1673–4) for the ciborium at the Chiesa Nuova (S Maria in Vallicella), which was designed by Ferri and cast by Stefano Benamati, and a terracotta relief of the *Fall of the Giants* (1674), pendant to a Niobid relief by Giovanni Battista Foggini (both Florence, Mus. Opificio Pietre Dure). When recalled to Florence in 1676, he was working on a more than life-size marble bust of *Galileo Galilei* (Florence, Mus. Stor. Sci.), a blocky image, ruggedly carved even in its finished portions.

In Florence, Marcellini worked repeatedly as an assistant under other artists, especially Foggini. From the latter's designs he produced his principal marble work, the relief of *God the Father with Angels* (1683) in the Corsini Chapel, S Maria del Carmine, and his only marble statue, the *St Dominic* (1692) in the Feroni Chapel, SS Annunziata. The lively marble relief of putti (1680s) in the main chapel at S Maria Maddalena de' Pazzi are attributed to him (designs by Ferri); they resemble his most successful creations, which are primarily stucco angels in large decorative schemes, for example those of 1702 in the sacristy of SS Michele e Gaetano. His works in stucco enrich such Florentine buildings as the Palazzo Ginori (1697–1700), S Frediano (1700) and SS Annunziata (nave) as well as several buildings elsewhere in Tuscany, including the chapel of S Giovanni Gualberto at Vallombrosa (1695–7) and S Lucia alla Castellina in Sesto Fiorentino (1704).

Marcellini's architectural projects included renovation of S Giovanni di Dio (from 1702), Florence, where he was later buried. He also produced festival designs. In 1699 and 1703 he executed marble busts of *Cosimo III* now in Florentine churches, the former at S Maria Nuova and the latter at S Jacopo sopr'Arno. A letter of 1687 (Lankheit, Doc. 318) mentions him among the best sculptors in the city, after Massimiliano Soldani and Foggini, but his erratic behaviour ultimately cost him his court patronage. A poet and satirist, he vented his anger in satirical verse (Lankheit, Doc. 22).

BIBLIOGRAPHY
Thieme–Becker
K. Lankheit: *Florentinische Barockplastik: Die Kunst am Hofe der letzten Medici, 1670–1743* (Munich, 1962)
La civiltà del cotto: Arte della terracotta nell'area fiorentina dal XV al XX secolo (exh. cat., ed. A. Paolucci and G. Conti; Impruneta, Sala Loggiata Silvani, 1980), pp. 132–3
E. L. Goldberg: *Patterns in Late Medici Art Patronage* (Princeton, 1983), pp. 140, 145, 156, 158, 160, 226
E. Chini: *La chiesa e il convento dei Santi Michele e Gaetano a Firenze* (Florence, 1984), esp. pp. 161, n. 170; 185–6, 231–2
M. Visona: *Carlo Marcellini, accademico 'spiantato' nella cultura fiorentina tardo-barocca* (Ospedaletto, 1990)

ALISON LUCHS

Marcello [Adèle d'Affry; Duchessa da Castiglione Colonna] (*b* Fribourg, 6 July 1836; *d* Castellammare, Italy, 14 July 1879). Swiss sculptor and painter. While studying sculpture in Rome under Heinrich Max Imhof, she married in 1856 Carlo, Duca da Castiglione Colonna, who died of typhoid the same year. Her meeting with Auguste Clesinger and Jean-Baptiste Carpeaux in Rome in 1861 reaffirmed her artistic vocation. She had already fallen under the spell of Michelangelo, feeling the significance of the name she shared with his paragon, Vittoria Colonna. In Paris she figured prominently at the court of Napoleon III in the 1860s and presented at the Exposition Universelle of 1867 a group of eight works, some of which had been shown in the preceding years at the Paris Salon and the Royal Academy in London. The works shown included a full-length statue of *Hecate* (marble, 1866; Montpellier, Esplanade de Celleneuve), an imperial commission. The bulk of her exhibit, however, consisted of historical and poetic busts, some of them pastiches of Renaissance and Rococo styles, such as *Bianca Capello* (marble version, 1872; Fontainebleau, Château), or *Marie-Antoinette at Versailles* (plaster, 1866; marble version, after 1879; Fribourg, Mus. A. & Hist.). A number of portraits of contemporaries, busts and statuettes form part of her bequest to her native town. Her most successful full-length figure, the bronze *Pythian Sibyl* (1867–70), placed in the Paris Opéra in 1875, represents its subject writhing in the throes of inspiration. She also executed drawings, pastels and paintings, including some fancy pieces in an 18th-century style (e.g. *Woman with a Pitcher*, 1873; Fribourg, Mus. A. & Hist.).

BIBLIOGRAPHY
H. Bessis: *Marcello sculpteur* (Fribourg, 1980)
La Sculpture française au XIXe siècle (exh. cat., ed. A. Pingeot; Paris, Grand Pal., 1986)

PHILIP WARD-JACKSON

March (i). Spanish family of painters.

(1) Esteban March (*b* Valencia, *c.* 1610; *d* Valencia, *c.* 1668). He was one of the outstanding pupils of Pedro Orrente. March's energetic narrative style is best appreciated in his battle scenes, which were favoured by his middle-class patrons, although he also painted religious works. His apprenticeship with Orrente is apparent in an early work, *Crossing of the Red Sea* (signed, *c.* 1640; Madrid, Prado). The types and attitudes of the figures recall the paintings of Orrente, but the lively brushwork is characteristic of March. According to Palomino, Esteban March was an unpredictable man, and his highly-strung temperament is often expressed in his battle scenes, for example the *Triumph of David*, *Surrender of a Fortress* and *Joshua Halting the Sun* (all Valencia, Mus. B.A.). The compositions of his work are often derived from Flemish and Italian engravings of the work of such artists as Antonio Tempesta. The brushwork in his paintings is lively and sketch-like, and this characteristic is intensified in his numerous drawings of battle scenes (Madrid, Prado; Florence, Uffizi; Madrid, Real Acad. S Fernando, Mus.; Valencia, Mus. B.A.). March also practised portraiture, of which two drawings, a *Self-portrait* and *Portrait of the Artist's Son, Miguel* (*c.* 1650; both Madrid, Prado) are extant.

BIBLIOGRAPHY
A. A. Palomino de Castro y Velasco: *Museo pictórico* (1715–24), pp. 888–90
M. S. Soria: 'Esteban March: Baroque Battle and Portrait Painter', *A. Bull.*, xxvii/2 (1945), pp. 109–23
M. A. de Orellana: *Biografía pictórica valentina* (Madrid, 1930, Valencia, 2/1967), pp. 185–201
F. B. Domenech, ed.: *Los Ribalta y la pintura valenciana de su tiempo* (Madrid, 1987), pp. 289–93
D. Angulo Iñiguez and A. E. Pérez Sánchez: *Valencia, 1600–1700* (1988), iv of *A Corpus of Spanish Drawings* (London, 1975–), pp. 34–8

FERNANDO BENITO DOMENECH

(2) Miguel March (*b* Valencia, *c.* 1638; *d* Valencia, *c.* 1670). Son of (1) Esteban March. He was trained by his father, and sources mention work in all genres, including battle scenes, his father's speciality. Miguel, however, died young, and there are few paintings known by him. His signed *St Roch and an Angel Assisting Plague Victims* (Valencia, Mus. B.A.) is dynamically composed along a diagonal that bisects the picture. The chiaroscuro of the large, naturalistic figures is more emphatic than that of March's contemporary Jeronimo Jacinto Espinosa and shows the influence of Jusepe de Ribera and Neapolitan painting. Four genre-like *Allegories* (Valencia, Mus. B.A.)

combine the themes of the Seasons, the Senses and Time, with moralizing overtones. March also painted still-lifes: a pair of game pieces, signed and dated 1661 (Valencia, Marques de Montortal priv. col.), are set in extensive landscapes, with small figures of hunters. Such 'open-air' still-lifes, also painted by the Valencian Tomás Hiepes, were known in the 17th century as *bodegones de país*. A volume of figure and drapery studies in black lead has been recently discovered and attributed to March.

BIBLIOGRAPHY
M. A. de Orellana: *Biografía pictórica valentina* (Madrid, 1930, Valencia, 2/1976), pp. 207–10
Pintura española de bodegones y floreros de 1600 a Goya (exh. cat. by A. E. Pérez Sánchez, Madrid, Prado, 1983), pp. 104, 138–9, 211; nos 117–20
D. Angulo Iñiguez and A. E. Pérez Sánchez: *Valencia, 1600–1700* (1988), iv of *A Corpus of Spanish Drawings* (London, 1975–), p. 10, nos 145–6, 149–258

PETER CHERRY

March (ii). German family of architects.

(1) Otto March (*b* Berlin, 1 Oct 1845; *d* Berlin, 1 April 1913). As a student at the Bauakademie and the Preussische Akademie der Künste in Berlin, March was taught by Richard Lucae, Johann Heinrich Strack and Martin Gropius. He then worked (1872–4) for Heinrich von Ferstel in Vienna. He entered the Prussian civil service in 1874 but left in 1880 to set up in practice as a private architect. He had a large clientele among German industrialists, for whom he designed substantial and elegant country houses and villas. His early style was German Renaissance Revival, for example the Villa Holtz (1881–2) in Charlottenburg, Berlin, but later he looked for inspiration to England and the domestic designs of R. Norman Shaw, W. E. Nesfield and T. E. Collcutt. Having visited England repeatedly from 1888, he revealed particularly marked English influences in his Queen Anne Revival design for the Villa Vörster (1893–4), Cologne. As an architect, however, March was versatile. His department store, the Neue Friedrichsstrassestore (1895), Berlin, used three-storey bays of glass and iron. His innovative design for the municipal theatre in Worms (1889–90; destr. 1922) attracted much interest. In it he attempted to revive the principles of Shakespearean theatre by building part of the stage out into the auditorium. He also pioneered race-course and stadium design. His Deutsches Stadion (1912; remodelled 1935), Berlin, for the intended Olympic Games of 1916 (cancelled due to World War I) set new standards for modern sports complexes. He published widely on the theory of architecture, particularly on Protestant church building. An early supporter of the urban-planning movement, he initiated the urban-planning competition of 1909 called 'Die Grosse Berlin' and organized the first international urban-planning exhibition (1910) in Berlin.

WRITINGS
Berlin und seine Bauten (Berlin, 1896)
BIBLIOGRAPHY
Macmillan Enc. Architects; *NDB*; Thieme–Becker; Wasmuth
W. March, ed.: *Otto March: Reden und Aufsätze* (Tübingen, 1972)
S. Muthesius: *Das englische Vorbild*, Studien zur Kunst des 19. Jahrhunderts, xxvi (Munich, 1974)
B. Edle von Germersheim: *Unternehmervillen der Kaiserzeit, 1871–1918* (Munich, 1988)

(2) Werner March (*b* Berlin, 17 Jan 1894; *d* Berlin, 11 Jan 1976). Son of (1) Otto March. He studied architecture at the Technische Hochschule in Dresden and received his diploma with distinction at the Technische Hochschule in Charlottenburg, Berlin (1919). In 1920 he became a pupil in German Bestelmeyer's master-class at the Akademie der Künste in Berlin and in 1922 passed the examination to become a government architect in Berlin. His first major work was the Deutsches Sportforum (1926–8), Berlin, which he subsequently enlarged to form a part of the complex that he planned for the Olympics in Berlin (1936). This consisted of a series of sports buildings and tracks planned around the Olympiastadion (1934–6), his best-known building. The elliptical stadium is designed in a severe classical style with an external colonnade of square piers without bases or capitals. This was the style generally prescribed by Adolf Hitler for major public buildings, and the stadium is one of the most impressive monuments of the Third Reich; it was, however, a style that the Nazis appropriated rather than created, as the earlier Sportforum building demonstrates.

In 1946 March moved to Minden in Westfalen, where he was involved in many rebuilding projects, particularly churches and administration buildings, for example the Landeszentralbank (1949), Münster, and the land-utilization plan for Wetzlar (1952). He was Professor of Urban Development at the Technische Universität of Berlin between 1954 and 1959. Between 1961 and 1964 he was Chairman of the regional group for Berlin at the Deutsche Akademie für Städtebau und Landesplanung. He was also the Chairman of the German regional group for Berlin at the Bund Deutscher Architekten between 1930 and 1962.

Vollmer

BIBLIOGRAPHY

W. Hegemann: *Werner March* (Berlin, Leipzig and Vienna, 1930)
B. Miller Lane: *Architecture and Politics in Germany, 1918–45* (Cambridge, MA, 1968)

BRIGITTE JACOB, WOLFGANG SCHÄCHE

Marchand, André (*b* Aix-en-Provence, 10 Feb 1907). French painter, illustrator, stage designer and tapestry designer. He started painting at the age of 13 in spite of his family's categorical opposition to art as a profession, and six years later he moved to Paris to pursue his vocation. He was self-taught. He began exhibiting at the Salon d'Automne in Paris in 1932 and at the Salon des Indépendants from 1933, when he was producing stark realist paintings of figures in desolate landscapes, such as *The Strangers* (1935–6; Paris, Pompidou).

Marchand was prone to striking changes in his style and technique, ranging from Ingres-style drawings between 1933 and 1937 to a developing interest in the 1940s in more textured surfaces and a more stylized form of representation, as in *Landscape with Olive Trees* (1943; see 1963 exh. cat., no. 18), in which the angular branches of the trees create an almost abstract pattern. In the early 1950s, in such works as *The Window (Arles)* (1952; see 1963 exh. cat., no. 41), which features a pair of identically dressed women framed by a decorative architectural setting, he turned again to a more serene play of flat shapes, this time using clearly outlined, unmodelled forms. He came close to calligraphic abstraction in such paintings as the *Light of the Bird* (1955; Paris, Pompidou), which consists of linear bird-like forms over large areas of washes of colour. He travelled widely and remained sensitive to the atmosphere and colour of particular places, which he sought to transpose into his work, as in *Light and Bird* (1955; Paris, Pompidou). In *Night on the Beach* (1959; see 1963 exh. cat., no. 74) the silhouettes of elongated female figures are woven into a striated patterned surface representing their outdoor setting.

Although Marchand was considered part of the FORCES NOUVELLES and was a close friend of Francis Gruber, his work was distinguished by its joyful and celebratory moods. Only in occasional works, such as *The Room* (1955; Paris, Pompidou), in which a faceless seated figure is shown isolated in a bare and confined interior space, did he hint at the existential outlook of other painters working in France immediately after World War II. In the 1960s he came close to abstraction in more thickly and spontaneously painted works such as *Mistral in the Mediterranean* (1962–3; see 1963 exh. cat., no. 104), while maintaining a clear link with landscape subject-matter.

Marchand also executed designs for tapestries in the mid-1940s, illustrated books such as an edition of André Gide's *Les Nourritures terrestres* and created stage sets, for example for productions at the Opéra-Comique in Paris of the ballet *Suite provençale* by Darius Milhaud and of the opera *Mireille* by Charles Gounod.

BIBLIOGRAPHY

André Marchand (exh. cat. by J. Kober, Paris, Gal. Maeght, 1946)
J. Lassaigne: *André Marchand* (Paris, 1946)
André Marchand (exh. cat., intro P. Vorms; The Hague, Gemeentemus., 1951)
André Marchand (exh. cat. by J. Bonnet, Geneva, Gal. Motte, 1953)
G. P. Brabant: *André Marchand* (Paris, 1954)
Cent tableaux par André Marchand (exh. cat., intro. J. Lassaigne; Paris, Gal. Charpentier, 1956)
André Marchand: Exposition rétrospective, 1933–1963 (exh. cat., preface B. Dorival; Arles, Mus. Réattu, 1963)

Marchand, Jean (Hippolyte) (*b* Paris, 21 Nov 1882; *d* Paris, 1941). French painter, printmaker and illustrator. He studied part-time at the Ecole des Beaux-Arts in Paris from 1902 to 1906 under Léon Bonnat and Luc Olivier Merson and briefly in 1909 at the Académie Vitti under Henri Martin. He experimented with Cubism and to a lesser extent with Futurism and participated in the Salon de la Section d'Or in 1912 (*see* SECTION D'OR (ii)), but his subsequent work showed a greater affinity with that of Cézanne and with the revival of classicism sometimes referred to as the 'retour à l'ordre'. He remained faithful in his later paintings to an essentially naturalistic style, which he applied to both landscapes, such as *Landscape at Vence* (1927; London, Tate), and studies of the human figure, for example *Maternity* (1921; London, Tate), which combine a serene mood with a monumentality of form.

Marchand lived for two years in Syria and the Middle East in the late 1920s and painted two of his most remarkable decorative murals there, at the Palais de la Résidence in Beirut in 1928 and at the Syrian pavilion at the Colonial Exhibition at Vincennes in 1931. He also illustrated a number of books with lithographs and woodcuts, including *Chemin de croix* (1918) by Paul Claudel and Paul Valéry's *Le Serpent* and *Le Cimetière marin* (both 1927).

BIBLIOGRAPHY
P. Chabaneix: *Jean Marchand* (Paris, 1935)
Jean Marchand, 1882–1941: Retrospective Exhibition. Paintings from the Estate of the Late Mme. Marchand (exh. cat., London, Crane Kalman Gal., 1967)

ALBERTO CERNUSCHI

Marchand, J(ean) [John] **Omer** (*b* Montreal, 28 Dec 1873; *d* Montreal, 11 June 1936). Canadian architect. His serious architectural studies began in 1893 when he was sent to the Ecole des Beaux-Arts in Paris. He remained in France for ten years, earning a French government diploma and various awards of merit for architecture. In 1900 the French Ministry of Works commissioned him to design and manage the Canadian Pavilion at the Exposition Universelle in Paris. Upon his return to Montreal (1903), Marchand joined in partnership with architect Stevens Haskell (*d* 1913), and he is known to have practised for a period in Winnipeg, Manitoba (*c.* 1905–8). He is remembered principally for his work on the reconstruction of Ottawa's Parliament building, which was devastated by fire in 1916. The restoration work carried out by Marchand and architect John Pearson (1867–1940) between 1919 and 1927, incorporated a new, Gothic Revival Peace Tower with clock face and carillon bells. It rose beside the older building replete with pointed roof, stone-dressed quoins, and window openings and gargoyles. In 1927 Marchand served for one year as consultant architect to the City of Montreal and was a member of the Board of Trustees of the National Gallery of Canada, Ottawa. He was also responsible for the design of a number of important ecclesiastical buildings (e.g. St Boniface Basilica (1908), Winnipeg; partly destr. by fire, 1968), hospitals and schools in Manitoba and Quebec. Following World War I he built the Juvenile Court and the Water Works pumping station, both in Montreal. He remained active throughout his life, and just prior to his death he had been invited by the French Ministry of Industry and Commerce to assist in the plans for the Exposition Internationale des Arts et Techniques dans la Vie Moderne in Paris (1937).

BIBLIOGRAPHY
Obituary, *RIBA J.* (5 Sept 1936), pp. 1050–51
T. Ritchie: *Canada Builds, 1867–1967* (Toronto, 1967)

Marchand–amateur [Fr.: 'dealer–collector']. Term used to describe a dealer in works of art who actively forms a collection of his own, independently of his business interests. The most notable example was the 18th-century *marchand–amateur* P.-J. Mariette (*see* MARIETTE, (4)).

COLIN J. HARRISON

Marchands-merciers. Parisian guild of merchants selling luxury goods. The name has no direct translation, as it derives from the incorporation of the mercers (textile merchants) and jewel merchants. It was the third of the six guilds of merchants in Paris, and was subdivided into twenty classes by the types of goods available for sale. The 13th class was allowed to sell a wide variety of works of art, which included not only paintings and prints but also all manner of items including furniture, light fittings, bronzes, marble and clocks. Although the merchants were, in theory, regulated by the guild system as to the types of goods they were permitted to sell, in practice several classes frequently overlapped. A large number of *marchands-merciers* were established in the Rue Saint-Honoré, and advertisements in the form of trade cards or shop signs—for example, *L'Enseigne de Gersaint* by Antoine Watteau (1721; Berlin, Schloss Charlottenburg; *see* DRESS, fig. 43)—often listed or illustrated the marvellous array of goods available.

The *marchands-merciers* relied on a number of sources for their stock. They sold goods supplied by specialized craftsmen in Paris and other major European centres of production, work that was either fully complete or needed embellishment with such additional materials as gilt-bronze mounts or inlays of lacquer, hardstones or porcelain. English-made goods were extremely popular from the mid-18th century, East-Asian lacquer and porcelain were imported via merchants in the Netherlands and items from the Near- and Middle East via Venice. Goods were purchased from factories throughout Europe (for example the Sèvres Porcelain Factory, which offered a 12% discount, later reduced to 9%), acquired from other *marchands-merciers* or from private individuals; some *marchands-merciers* sold 'second-hand' goods, thus acting as the equivalent of modern-day antique dealers. The day-book of LAZARE DUVAUX gives some idea of the range and quality of the goods available, although most *marchands-merciers* tended to specialize to some degree in the stock available. As well as trading in goods, the *marchands-merciers* introduced new forms and fashions on to the market. They were directly responsible for the creation of novel forms and luxury items that were made up of a combination of different materials. *Etuis* (small cases for holding small articles), jewellery or snuff-boxes (e.g. gold, tortoise-shell and gem snuff-box, 1725–6; Paris, Louvre), would be made by goldsmiths to the *marchands-merciers'* specification and then sold in the latter's establishments. The *marchands-merciers* were also instrumental in further developing the practice of fitting porcelain with gilt-bronze mounts. East-Asian porcelain was especially prized for its monochrome or crackled glazes and was fitted with gilt-bronze mounts reflecting the prevailing French style (e.g. pair of Chinese porcelain ewers, *c.* 1745–9; London, Wallace). The Vincennes Porcelain Factory produced porcelain flowers that the *marchands-merciers* set on gilt-bronze stems and also commissioned them to mount other items. It may have been the *marchands-merciers* who steered Sèvres towards producing vases in imitation of East-Asian porcelain. It is probable that the *marchand-mercier* Antoine Dulac (*fl* 1759–before 1765) was responsible for the design (*c.* 1763–4) of the *goût grec* mounts seen on surviving examples of Sèvres pot-pourri vases (e.g. at Waddesdon Manor, Bucks, NT). European and East-Asian porcelains were transformed by the addition of mounts into clocks, candelabra, pot-pourri vases and *garnitures de cheminée*. Panels of Japanese lacquer taken from screens and cabinets were given new settings in contemporary French furniture by such leading cabinetmakers as Martin Carlin, or set in such smaller items as boxes, trays or inkstands. Under the direction of such *marchands-merciers* as Simon-Philippe Poirier (?1720–85) and DOMINIQUE DAGUERRE (his partner after 1772), Sèvres porcelain plaques were fitted to secrétaires, *guéridons* and work tables (e.g. *bonheur-du-jour* by Carlin, 1766; Paris, Mus. Nissim de Camondo).

Marchands-merciers supplied goods to the Garde Meuble de la Couronne, the Menus Plaisirs du Roi, members of the royal family and court and an international clientèle. Many customers held open accounts at the *marchands-merciers*, who also undertook to clean, repair or restore goods, or arrange for them to be packed and shipped abroad. The *marchands-merciers* both held and attended sales, acting either on their own behalf or for clients, prepared catalogues for clients and valued goods and property.

BIBLIOGRAPHY

L. Courajod, ed.: *Livre journal de Lazare Duvaux, marchand-bijoutier ordinaire du roy, 1748–1758*, 2 vols (Paris, 1873)
P. Verlet: 'Le Commerce des objets d'art et les marchands merciers à Paris au XVIIIe siècle', *An., Econ., Soc., Civilis.*, xiii (1958), pp. 10–29
G. Wildenstein: 'Simon-Philippe Poirier, fournisseur de Madame du Barry', *Gaz. B.-A.*, lx (1962), pp. 365–77
C. Sargentson: *The Merchants of Luxury Goods in Eighteenth Century Paris* (MA thesis, London, Royal Coll. A., 1988)
J. Whitehead: 'The Marchands-Merciers and Sèvres', *International Ceramics Fair and Seminar* (London, 1993), pp. 36–43

BET McLEOD

Marchant, Nathaniel (*b* Sussex, 1739; *d* London, 24 March 1816). English gem-engraver and medallist. He first came to notice as the main prizewinner of the London Society of Arts' premiums for intaglio-engraving between 1762 and 1766. He was a pupil of Edward Burch and briefly studied drawing at the St Martin's Lane Academy (1766), but, inspired by the 3rd Duke of Richmond's gallery of casts, he soon pursued an original line, concentrating on engraving in intaglio copies of ancient sculptures (see fig.). He exhibited (1765–74) with the Society of Artists, of which he became a fellow and briefly a director; in the last two years he sent his submissions from Rome, where he had gone to study the monuments of antiquity in the original. There he created remarkable gems after ancient reliefs and statues, many of them only recently excavated or in private, princely collections. At first he worked for patrons at home, principally for George Spencer, 4th Duke of Marlborough; for the Rev. Francis Henry Egerton, later 8th Earl of Bridgwater, he engraved *Priam at the Feet of Achilles* (sard, 1784; Belton House, Lincs, NT). In time he became recognized as the only rival to Giovanni Pichler, then considered the foremost engraver in Rome. For Roman princes, as well as English and foreign visitors on the Grand Tour, he engraved not only ancient subjects (e.g. *Marcus Aurelius*, sard, ?1783; London, BM) but also skilful portraits, modelled from life (e.g. *Sir Charles Bingham, Earl of Lucan* and his wife, *Lady Lucan*, both sard, *c.* 1780; ex-Spencer priv. col., see Seidmann). For Louisa, Countess of Albany, he cut a portrait of *Dante* (exh. RA 1783; paste copy, Montpellier, Bib. Ville) as a present for Count Alfieri, and for Sir Richard Worsley he engraved a *Pericles*, a *Niobe* and the *Death of General Wolfe*, a bold excursion into modern history (exh. RA 1783; Brocklesby Park). His portrait of *Pope Pius VI* (cornelian; untraced) was in the Vatican Cabinet until 1798. These works of his maturity, some as large as 30 mm, exhibit bold, uncluttered lines and planes in heads and busts and bring out fully the beauty of Marchant's preferred sardonyx or sard (e.g. *Achilles*, sard,

Nathaniel Marchant: intaglio head of 'Isis', after a marble bust, traditionally known as 'Clytie', in the Charles Townley collection, cornelian, h. 26 mm; one of six intaglios by various artists set in a gold necklace together with a cameo, l. 200 mm, made in Italy, *c.* 1805 (London, British Museum)

1772–88; London, BM); while figure groups, such as the *General Wolfe* and *Bacchus and a Bacchante* (sard, 1772–83; London, BM, *see* GEM-ENGRAVING, fig. 16; unsigned version, St Petersburg, Hermitage), are distinguished by the delicate modelling of his often attenuated figures and a brilliantly handled recession of planes.

After Marchant's return to London in 1788, he prepared a selection from his gems in plaster impressions; his *Catalogue* (1792) was widely subscribed to. Having exhibited at the Royal Academy since 1781, he was elected ARA in 1791 and hoped for early election as a full Academician; but, despite his high standing as the foremost English gem-engraver of his day, he did not achieve this goal until 1809. Sociability and connoisseurship procured him a wide circle of acquaintances among artists as well as *cognoscenti*; he was an intimate of Charles Townley and the Rev. Clayton Mordaunt Cracherode, who bequeathed six gems by Marchant to the British Museum, including the widely copied *Grief of Achilles* (cornelian, 1772–8; destr.). Marchant's popularity in aristocratic Whig circles is reflected in the commissions he received for portraits of the statesmen *Earl Spencer* (exh. RA 1791), *William Wyndham* (1794; both cornelian, London, BM), *William Pitt* (paste, before 1811; London, V&A) and *Charles James Fox* (exh. RA 1797; untraced). In 1797 Marchant was appointed to the Royal Mint, where he modelled a fine head of George III (used for the gold guinea and half-guinea, 1813), and in 1800 to the Stamp Office, which provided him with an official apartment in Somerset House, London, where he died after a lengthy illness. An inscribed monument by John Flaxman marks his tomb in the church at Stoke Poges, Bucks.

WRITINGS

A Catalogue of 100 Impressions from Gems, Engraved by Nathaniel Marchant (London, 1792)

BIBLIOGRAPHY

S. Boardman and D. Scarisbrick: *The Ralph Harari Collection of Finger Rings* (London, 1977)

G. Seidmann: 'Nathaniel Marchant, Gem-engraver', *Walpole Soc.*, liii (1987), pp. 1–105 [fully illustrated cat. rais.]

GERTRUD SEIDMANN

Marchesi, Giuseppe (*b* Bologna, 1699; *d* Bologna, 1771). Italian painter. After initially studying with Aureliano Milani, he entered the studio of MARCANTONIO FRANCESCHINI, whose refined classical style had a decisive influence on his development. His first independent work was the huge *Rape of Helen* (1723; Bologna, Pal. Mentasti). During the 1730s he proved himself to be a capable practitioner of large-scale fresco painting with his ambitious decoration of the vaults and cupola of S Maria di Galliera, the Oratorian church in Bologna. Franceschini's influence is particularly evident in Marchesi's interpretation of Ovidian pastoral myths, where his suave, languorous figures, his comely maidens and scantily clad nymphs represent the transformation of Franceschini's elegiac classicism into an elegant late Baroque idiom with clear analogies to Rococo. Marchesi was among the more prominent painters in Bologna in the mid-18th century and an active member of Bologna's Accademia Clementina, which Franceschini had founded. His works must have had a particular appeal to English patrons, as many of them have been discovered in English country-house collections, for example a series of paintings of the *Four Seasons* (Bologna, Pin. N.) that was sold at Agnews, London, 22 May 1966.

BIBLIOGRAPHY

G. Cavazzoni Zanotti: *Storia dell'Accademia Clementina di Bologna*, 2 vols (Bologna, 1739), ii, p. 167

M. Oretti: *Notizie de' professori del disegno, cioè pittori, scultori ed architetti bolognesi e de' forestieri di sua scuola* (MS. B.123–35, Bologna, Bib. Com. Archinnasio, *c.* 1760), fol. 134

L. Lanzi: *Storia pittorica dell'Italia* (Bassano, 1809), v, p. 180

R. Roli: 'Per la pittura del settecento a Bologna: Giuseppe Marchesi', *Paragone*, 261 (1971), pp. 15–30

——: *Pittura bolognese, 1650–1800* (Bologna, 1977), pp. 103–4, 274–5

L'Arte del seicento emiliana, la pittura Accademia Clementina (exh. cat., Bologna, Pal Podestà, Pal. Dire Enzo, 1979), pp. 45, 79–81

DWIGHT C. MILLER

Marchesi, Pompeo (*b* Saltrio, nr Como, 7 Aug 1783; *d* Milan, 6 Feb 1858). Italian sculptor. He studied at the Accademia di Belle Arti in Milan under the aegis of the Neo-classicist Giuseppe Franchi (1731–1806). In 1804 he won a government scholarship to continue his education in Rome, where he remained for five years, studying under Antonio Canova. During this period he sent at least two examples of his work to the Pinacoteca di Brera, Milan, including the plaster low relief of *Socrates Urging Alcibiades to Leave a Brothel* (1807; Milan, Gal. A. Mod.). Returning to Milan, in 1811 he won first prize for sculpture in a government-sponsored competition, with a terracotta group, completed in Rome, of the *Belvedere Torso Restored and Assembled with the Apollo* (1811; Milan, Gal. A. Mod.). By 1810 he had already begun his lifelong collaboration with the cathedral works of Milan Cathedral, for which he created numerous statues of saints, including the prophets *Ezekiel* and *Amos* (1810–11) for the cathedral's façade. In 1813 he was summoned by the architect Luigi Cagnola to take part in the sculptural decoration of the Arco della Pace, Milan, for which he created various marble reliefs, including the *Foundation of the Kingdom of Lombardy and Venice* (1829–30) and the *Occupation of Lyon* (*c.* 1813–26); he used models created by Camillo Pacetti before 1814

Pompeo Marchesi: monument to *Francis I of Austria*, 1841 (Freiheitsplatz, Graz)

for the two *Victories* on the front facing the countryside and sculpted the colossal statues of the rivers *Adige* and *Tagliamento* for the crown of the arch.

In 1826 Marchesi was summoned to the Accademia in Milan to serve temporarily as professor of sculpture, a post that he held from 1838 to 1852. He was extremely active throughout this period: a favourite of the Austrian government, he obtained many public and private commissions, which allowed him to open a studio attended by numerous pupils and assistants and also visited by sovereigns, artists and intellectuals. The most obvious sign of the favour he enjoyed was the gift from the city of Milan of a new studio, opened in 1835 by the Austrian viceroy, Archduke Ranieri, following the destruction of his old one in a fire the previous year. An extremely prolific artist, his most memorable works include the monument dedicated to *Emanuel-Philibert of Savoy* (1835) for the Cappella Reale in Turin Cathedral and the monuments to the Habsburg emperor *Francis I of Austria* in the Freiheitsplatz in Graz (1841; see fig.) and in the Burgplatz of the Hofburg, Vienna (completed 1846). He also produced a series of funerary stelae and portrait busts, the most outstanding being his marble busts of *Antonio Canova* and *Andrea Appiani* (both 1835; Milan, Gal. A. Mod.). It was precisely because of the vastness of his output, rather than its quality, that Marchesi had such a strong influence on the development of early 19th-century Milanese sculpture. He was 'partly spoiled … by the … conflicting trends of the two styles of teaching in Milan and Rome, which he was never able to synthesize in a vital way' (1959 exh. cat., p. 46), and, overburdened with work, he produced essentially academic and affected sculpture.

BIBLIOGRAPHY
Enc. It.; Thieme–Becker
A. Caimi: *Delle arti del disegno e degli artisti nelle provincie di Lombardia, dal 1777 al 1862* (Milan, 1862), pp. 164–8
L'età neoclassica in Lombardia (exh. cat. by A. Ottino della Chiesa, Como, Villa Olmo, 1959), pp. 45–6, 164
L. Caramel and C. Pirovano: *Galleria d'arte moderna: Opere dell'ottocento*, ii (Milan, 1975), pp. 352–5, nos 1704–95
A. Finocchi: 'Pompeo Marchesi', *Mostra dei maestri di Brera, 1776–1859* (exh. cat. by A. M. Brizio and others, Milan, Pal. Permanente, 1975), pp. 165–9
M. di Giovanni: 'Pompeo Marchesi', *Scultura romantica e floreale nel duomo di Milano* (exh. cat. by R. Bossaglia, M. di Giovanni and V. Caprara, Milan, Mus. Duomo, 1977–8), pp. 10–11
A. Sassi: *Pompeo Marchesi scultore* (Saltrio, 1983)

MARICA MAGNI

Marchesini, Alessandro (*b* Verona, 30 April 1663; *d* Verona, 27 Jan 1738). Italian painter and agent. He is traditionally believed to have trained with Biagio Falcieri (1628–1703). At the age of 17 he moved to Bologna, where he entered the workshop of Carlo Cignani. His first commission after his return to Verona was for the fresco decoration of the vault of S Domenico (1687), with scenes glorifying the saint, set in a *quadratura* framework by Carlo Tedesco. The style is heavily Baroque. In 1690–91 Marchesini painted a *Jonah* for S Niccolò, Verona; this remains within a Veronese tradition, whereas his *Assumption of the Virgin* for S Biagio (1692; Breonio, SS Marziale e Giovanni) and his *Purification of the Virgin* (1699; Verona, Pal. Scaligero, Notai Chapel) contain references to the Bolognese art of the Carracci.

In 1700 Marchesini moved to Venice, where he painted two works (untraced) for S Silvestro. He remained in Venice until 1737 and specialized in making small-scale copies of works by the Old Masters to decorate private houses, thereby imitating a wide variety of styles. His most memorable independent works are the two paintings of *Christ Blessing the Little Children* (1708; Bologna, priv. col., see Pallucchini, fig. 1171), which attain the light elegance of the Emilian late Baroque. His later *Triumph of Apollo* (after 1720; Pommersfelden, Schloss Weissenstein) reveals, in its radiant colours and the airiness of its composition, his development of an international Rococo style. Marchesini was also active as an agent and adviser, notably to STEFANO CONTI, who in 1725 acquired four paintings by Canaletto on Marchesini's recommendation.

BIBLIOGRAPHY
La pittura a Verona tra seicento e settecento (exh. cat., ed. L. Magagnato; Verona, Gran Guardia, 1978), pp. 153–8
R. Pallucchini: *La pittura veneziana del seicento*, i (Milan, 1981), p. 356
F. d'Arcais: 'La decorazione della chiesa di S Domenico a Verona', *A. Ven.*, xxxvi (1982), pp. 167–76

FILIPPO PEDROCCO

Marchi, Giuseppe (i) (*b* Oro, Italy; *fl* Sweden, 1694–1705). Italian stuccoist, active in Sweden. Among his works are the ceilings of the Spökslott (1697–1702) in Drottninggatan, Stockholm, and in the city palace (1704) of the Stenbock family. His work is more delicate, soft and 'floating' than that executed by members of the school of Carlo Carove; and although he used the same types of ornament, he made more of the shell motif. Thus his style was more modern than that of contemporary stuccoists in Sweden, save those working in the Royal Palace, Stockholm, by the end of the 17th century from the directions of Nicodemus Tessin (ii), and was in accordance with contemporary Italian-made work in Germany. Marchi also produced three decorative borders (1705) between the walls and vault in the House of the Nobility in Stockholm, in the main hall of Drottningholm Castle near Stockholm and the great hall of the Salsta mansion (both 1701–2) in Uppland.

BIBLIOGRAPHY
Thieme–Becker
Spökslottet: Kunst- och kulturhistoriska studier [The ghost mansion: studies in the history of art and culture] (Stockholm, 1927)
S. Karling: 'Les Stuccateurs italiens en Suède', *Riv. Archeol. Prov. & Ant. Dioc. Como*, ii (1964), pp. 291–301 [special issue: *Arte e artisti dei laghi lombardi*]
G. Beard: *Stucco and Decorative Plasterwork in Europe* (London, 1983), p. 69

TORBJÖRN FULTON

Marchi, Giuseppe (Filippo Liberati) (ii) (*b* Rome, *c.* 1721–2, or, less likely, *c.* 1735; *d* London, 2 April 1808). Italian painter and engraver, active in England. He was chief studio assistant to Joshua Reynolds, who brought him to England in 1752 and painted his portrait (*c.* 1753; London, RA). He attended the St Martin's Lane Academy, London, and exhibited portraits in oil as well as mezzotints at the Society of Artists (1766–75), but he never exhibited at the Royal Academy. He became a director of the Society of Artists in 1775.

Marchi worked for Reynolds between 1752 and 1792, except for a brief period (1768–9) when he tried to establish himself as an independent painter, first in London and then at Swansea. Very few pictures by him can be identified: *Thomas Jones* (Cardiff, N. Mus.) and *Major John Jones* (1768; sold London, Sotheby's, 24 Nov 1965, lot 85;

see Waterhouse, p. 231) are portraits closely dependent on Reynolds both in style and in the way the sitter is presented, while that of *Jane Deere* (priv. col., see 1948 exh. cat., no. 63) is less derivative. Marchi returned to work with Reynolds and seems to have received a salary of £100 a year. He was not mentioned in Reynolds's will, but—as reported in the *General Evening Post*—Mary Palmer, Reynolds's niece, arranged that he continue to receive his salary. In addition to such routine studio jobs as setting his master's palette and painting drapery in portraits, Marchi had charge of Reynolds's 'Sitter Books' (appointment diaries) and was one of his most trusted copyists. He was probably responsible for many of the replicas of popular pictures that issued from Reynolds's studio. Marchi's close familiarity with Reynolds's technique made him, especially after his master's death, an invaluable restorer and repairer of Reynolds's pictures, as noted in the long obituary he received in the *Gentleman's Magazine*.

BIBLIOGRAPHY

Obituary, *Gent. Mag.*, lxxviii (1808), p. 372

W. T. Whitley: *Artists and their Friends in England, 1700–1799*, 2 vols (London, 1928/*R* London and New York, 1968)

Portraits from Welsh Houses (exh. cat., Cardiff, N. Mus., 1948)

E. K. Waterhouse: *Dictionary of British 18th-century Painters* (Woodbridge, 1981)

DAVID MANNINGS

Marchionni, Carlo (*b* Rome, 10 Feb 1702; *d* Rome, 28 July 1786). Italian architect, sculptor, draughtsman and designer. He owed his career to the patronage of cardinals Alessandro Albani (*see* ALBANI, (2)) and Annibale Albani. Like the Marchionni family, the Albani family came from the Marches. Marchionni first trained as a sculptor, then studied architecture at the Accademia di S Luca in Rome under Filippo Barigioni, winning the first prize in 1728, his final year. Marchionni's prizewinning drawings demonstrated his exceptional talent as a draughtsman, always far greater than his inspiration as an architect. Cardinal Alessandro Albani engaged him to build his villa in Anzio as early as 1728 and in 1734 commissioned Marchionni to design the façade of the collegiate church at Nettuno. Both are conventional works carrying the imprint of the Accademia, revealing a clear commitment to the past in their use of 17th-century architectural motifs. Marchionni worked as a sculptor between 1730 and 1748. His most interesting sculptural work is the tomb of *Benedict XIII* (completed 1739) in S Maria sopra Minerva, Rome, commissioned by Cardinal Alessandro Albani. As well as the overall design, Marchionni also executed the relief depicting the 1725 Lateran Council on the sarcophagus. His work as a sculptor revealed his dependence on traditional, late Baroque Roman style, drawing inspiration from Camillo Rusconi. Other projects included statuary (1741) for the façade of S Maria Maggiore; a statue of *Benedict XIV* (1743) for Santa Croce in Gerusalemme; a statue of *St Ignatius* (1748) for S Apollinare; and busts of founders (*c.* 1745) for the Collegio di Propaganda Fide, all in Rome. He created reliefs depicting scenes from the *Life of the Virgin* (1747) for the chapel of St John the Baptist in S Roch in Lisbon, and he also executed reliefs for the chapel of the Madonna del Voto (1748) in Siena Cathedral and the tomb (1747) of *Cardinal Giacomo Milli* in the church of S Crisogono, Rome.

Marchionni's rise to become one of the foremost architects in Rome began only after 1750, helped by the departure of Ferdinando Fuga and Luigi Vanvitelli for Naples. Thanks to the two Albani cardinals, Marchionni succeeded Vanvitelli as architect to the papal *camera* in 1752 and took over from Filippo Barigioni in 1754 as Architetto Revisore at St Peter's, becoming head (1773) after Vanvitelli's death. Because Vanvitelli lived in Naples, Marchionni was effectively responsible for all work done at St Peter's after 1754, including decorations for special festivals. As architect to the *camera*, he also successfully carried out an ambitious engineering project, further extending the harbour at Ancona.

Marchionni's versatility is best expressed in his drawings, some 600 of which have been preserved (large numbers in New York, Cooper-Hewitt Mus.; Rome, Villa Torlonia; and U. Würzburg, Wagner-Mus.). These drawings demonstrate his rich and prolific output as a designer of reliefs, tombs, ceiling paintings, villas, churches and particularly settings and decorations for festivals; he also produced landscape sketches, caricatures and visiting cards. In his architectural designs, motifs from both the 16th and 17th centuries are mixed in a collage-like way and woven together into complex forms and images. The way fragmentary individual motifs are combined together produces a picturesque composition that plays with the allusive nature of the details. He thus interlocked pedimental forms, a reversion to Michelangelo and Gian Giacomo della Porta, and combined them with tendrils, masks and trophies in the manner of Borromini and Pietro da Cortona. Marchionni's greatest talent as a designer lay in the field of festive decorations. His designs included those for the canonization of St Catherine dei Ricci in S Maria sopra Minerva in Rome (1746) and such festive façades as that of the Palazzo della Valle in Rome (1747) celebrating the elevation of Carlo Vittorio delle Lanze as cardinal. Marchionni also designed the decorations for the funeral services of King Augustus III of Poland (1764) and King Charles Emanuel III of Sardinia (1773) in S Salvatore in Lauro, Rome. These ephemeral designs, some asymmetric in composition and lively in outline, sparkle with imagination and are an expression of purest Rococo.

Marchionni's reputation as an architect is based on two buildings in Rome: the Villa Albani for Cardinal Alessandro Albani and the sacristy of St Peter's. The Villa Albani (*see* ROME, §V, 27; *see also* ITALY, fig. 108) was located outside the Porta Salaria, and the Cardinal intended it to house his famous collection of antiquities. The main building, the Palazzina (see fig.), was constructed in 1755, and the interior decoration was completed *c.* 1762. The Villa Albani must have developed as a kind of collaboration between the client, his adviser and the architect, although their respective contributions have not been precisely identified and Marchionni had a free hand in the design of the exteriors. He was also able to exploit his subtle decorative talents to the full in the splendid interior furnishings, inserting antique reliefs in doorframes, chimneypieces and wall decorations in an impressive and innovative way and lining the sculptural niches with mirror-glass. The sacristy of St Peter's, Rome, was started in 1776 under Pope Pius VI and attracted strong criticism even from Marchionni's contemporaries. It was the Pope's wish

Carlo Marchionni: façade of the Palazzina (1755), Villa Albani (now Villa Torlonia), Rome

that Marchionni should base his ideas on designs (from 1715 to 1732) by Filippo Juvarra. The huge dimensions of St Peter's made it difficult to give suitable proportions to an adjacent building. Marchionni resolved the problem with a centrally planned octagonal building with a dome, flanked by two lower wings to accommodate the canons at the rear. Set slightly away from the basilica, the building answered functional requirements and was skilfully structured. The sacristy epitomizes past Roman building tradition very much in the style of the Accademia, but, by the time it was completed (1785), it was stylistically antiquated.

In contrast to his decorative designs, Marchionni's buildings display a certain uniformity of style. Façades are rather flat and serve as a foil for the decorative elements that articulate the buildings. Marchionni's work as a whole, which also included S Domenico (1763) in Ancona and the Maddalena (1765) in Messina, reveals an ability to use the Roman architectural tradition of the 16th and 17th centuries to good effect, but it lacks innovation. A stylistic division between real and ephemeral architecture is typical of the period but is rarely as pronounced as in Marchionni's work. Apart from Filippo Juvarra, Marchionni was the most inventive architectural draughtsman in 18th-century Rome. His designs are pictorial compositions with immense aesthetic appeal that almost lose their relationship to their real objective, making each drawing a work of art

in its own right. Marchionni became an 'Accademico di merito' of the Accademia in Rome in 1740 and its Principe in 1775. His career is a perfect illustration of the system of patronage based on local connections and the continued protection of his patrons. His work demonstrates both the high standard of the Roman Accademia and the lack of interest showed by an established Roman artist in the emerging Neo-classicism. Marchionni's son Filippo Marchionni (1732–1805) continued work on the harbour at Ancona under Pope Pius VI, building the lighthouse and the Porta Pia (1785).

UNPUBLISHED SOURCES

Rome, Archv Cent. Stato [drgs and doc.]
Rome, Accad. N. S. Luca, Archv Stor.

BIBLIOGRAPHY

Macmillan Enc. Architects
R. Berliner: 'Zeichnungen von Carlo und Filippo Marchionni', *Münch. Jb. Bild. Kst*, ix–x (1958–9), pp. 267–396
J. Gaus: *Carlo Marchionni: Ein Beitrag zur römischen Architektur des Settecento* (Cologne, 1967)
M. L. Polichetti: 'Il Vanvitelli e i Marchionni: Carlo e Filippo nelle opere architettoniche di Ancona', *Atti & Mem. Reale Deput. Stor. Patria Marche*, viii (1975), pp. 177–94
A. Gambardella: *Architettura e committenza nello Stato Pontificio tra barocco e rococò* (Naples, 1979)
W. F. Cousins: 'Concorso Clementino of 1728', *Architectural Fantasy and Reality: Drawings from the Accademia Nazionale di San Luca in Rome, Concorsi Clementini, 1700–1750*, ed. H. Hager and S. S. Munshower (University Park, PA, 1981), pp. 96–9

H. Hager: 'Gian Lorenzo Bernini e la ripresa dell'alto barocco nell'architettura del settecento romano', *Atti del convegno Bernini e il barocco europeo: Roma, 1981*, ii, pp. 469–96

S. Röttgen: 'Die Villa Albani und ihre Bauten', *Forschungen zur Villa Albani: Antike Kunst und die Epoche der Aufklärung*, ed. H. Beck and P. Bol (Berlin, 1982), pp. 59–184

L. Arcangeli: 'Una "Deliziosa" per gli Albani ed altri progetti di Carlo Marchionni nella Biblioteca Civica di Iesi', *Stud. Settecento Romano*, i–ii (1985–6), pp. 129–46

E. Debenedetti, ed.: 'Carlo Marchionni: Architettura, decorazione e scenografia contemporanea', *Stud. Settecento Romano*, iv (1988) [whole issue on Marchionni and contemporary artists]

Jörg Garms: 'Due parrocchiali nelle Marche ed altre chiese di Carlo Marchionni: Architettura, città, territorio. Realizzazioni e teorie tra illuminismo e romanticismo', *Stud. Settecento Romano*, viii (1992), pp. 131–147

ELISABETH KIEVEN

Marchiori, Giovanni (*b* Caviola d'Agordo, nr Belluno, 30 March 1696; *d* Treviso, 2 Jan 1778). Italian sculptor. He may have trained with Andrea Brustolon, but his style was more influenced by the elegant classicism of such Venetian sculptors as Giuseppe Torretti and Antonio Corradini. His first recorded work is a wooden sacristy cupboard (*c.* 1715) for the parish church at Caviola, and before 1738 he had carved the six marble *Sibyls* and the seven marble *Apostles* for S Maria degli Scalzi, Venice. The signed marble statues of *St Alexis* and *St Juliana* for the Servite church in Venice (now in Fratta Polesine, Parish Church) were completed in 1738, and there followed low reliefs in wood, showing scenes from the *Life of St Roch* (1741) for the Scuola di S Rocco, Venice, which were distinguished by their varied compositions and elaborate settings, enriched by surprisingly naturalistic architecture and landscape. In 1743 Marchiori completed works for S Rocco, Venice, a marble relief of the *Glory of St Roch* over the entrance (now replaced by a bronze copy) and the marble figures of *David with the Head of Goliath* and *St Cecilia*. These, his most celebrated works, look forward, in their extreme refinement and formal beauty, to Neo-classicism, although their lively outlines and picturesque qualities remain Rococo. Marchiori's output was vast, and his most significant works in Venice include the marble relief of the *Pool of Bethesda* (1753; Venice, S Simeon Piccolo) and the marble *St Peter* (1753; Venice, S Maria della Pietà). Between 1765 and 1767 he spent some time in Treviso, where he made two powerful marble statues of *Hope* and *Faith* (Treviso, S Maria Maddalena), characterized by the rhythmic and sensual beauty of broad folds of drapery. His marble figures of *Cybele* and *Saturn* are in the garden of the Schloss Nymphenburg, Munich. His work may have had a formative influence on Antonio Canova.

BIBLIOGRAPHY

G. Mariacher: 'Sculture ignote di Giovanni Marchiori', *Arte in Europa: Scritti di storia dell'arte in onore di Edoardo Arslan*, 2 vols (Milan, 1966), ii, pp. 831–7

C. Semenzato: 'Giovanni Marchiori', *La scultura veneta del seicento e del settecento* (Venice, 1966), pp. 59–61, 133–4

P. Rossi: 'L'attività di Giovanni Marchiori per la Scuola di S Rocco', *A. Ven.*, xxxvi (1982), pp. 262–7

CAMILLO SEMENZATO

Marchis, Alessio de (*b* Naples, 1684; *d* Perugia, 1752). Italian painter and draughtsman. Pio's biography (1724) reports that at the age of 17 he moved from Naples, his native city, to Rome, where he studied for 18 months with Philip Peter Roos and then completed his training by studying the work of Gaspard Dughet and painting subjects from life. He painted landscapes, portraying the most picturesque aspects of nature quickly and almost impressionistically, to obtain a highly decorative effect. In Rome he received commissions from such noble families as the Teodoli, Albani and Ruspoli. In 1715 he frescoed the two main rooms of the ground-floor apartment of the Palazzo Ruspoli (Rome, Via del Corso) with landscapes and views (destr.). On this project he collaborated with such distinguished painters as Antonio Amorosi and Andrea Locatelli to create a decorative complex that included seascapes, *bambocciate* (low-life subjects), history paintings and mythological themes.

After being imprisoned for a period (Pio) for having set fire to a hayloft with the intention of painting a fire from life (Lanzi), de Marchis was patronized by the Albani, the family of the then pope, Clement XI. This allowed him to work at Urbino, where, in the Palazzo Albani, he painted a ceiling and panels beneath windows with landscapes and seascapes. Other notable works from this time include the thickly impastoed imaginary landscapes painted on the upper doors and on the lower part of an *armadio* (Urbino, oratory of S Giuseppe). In 1739 he was given the task of frescoing the 'woodland and countryside' scenes in the chapel of the Collegio Gregoriano, Urbino. Other paintings by him were preserved in the picture galleries of Urbino's noble families together with works by his son Eugenio (*b* 1714). Recently a sizeable group of landscape paintings in the chapterhouse of S Lorenzo Cathedral, Perugia, has been attributed to de Marchis.

De Marchis's early period in Rome allowed him to study 17th-century landscape painting through the works of the northern painters who were present in the capital and with whose works his own paintings and drawings are often confused. However, the inspiration behind de Marchis's compositions can be traced back to the influence of another Neapolitan, Salvator Rosa. The contrasts of light and the rapid brushwork, full of nonchalantly applied colour effects, lend his landscapes a romantic atmosphere, far removed from the arcadian style then fashionable in Rome. One of his finest and best-known paintings is the *Landscape with Herd* (Rome, Pal. Barberini, on dep. Tivoli, Villa d'Este), which shows a peasant and his herd outlined by the light and placed in a luxuriant, dewy setting. A group of 40 drawings (Rome, Gab. N. Stampe) by de Marchis, many of them signed, has survived, providing a greater knowledge of him as a draughtsman than as a painter. His favourite medium in these landscape drawings was red chalk with reddish-brown watercolour wash, applied in a free and spontaneous manner. His motifs are at times taken from life and sometimes echo those of other artists.

BIBLIOGRAPHY

Thieme–Becker

N. Pio: *Vite* (1724); ed. C. Enggass and R. Enggass (1977), pp. 142–3

B. Orsini: *Guida al forestiere per l'augusta città di Perugia* (Perugia, 1784); ed. B. Toscano (Treviso, 1973), pp. 97, 104, 177, 181, 268, 329, 342

L. Lanzi: *Storia pittorica della Italia*, ii (Bassano, 1809), p. 169

S. Siepi: *Descrizione topologica-istorica della città di Perugia* (Perugia, 1822), pp. 147, 177, 344, 446, 644, 660, 662, 678, 739, 837, 895

M. Chiarini: 'Alessio de Marchis as a Draughtsman', *Master Drgs*, v/3 (1967), pp. 289–91

——: *I disegni italiani di paesaggio dal 1600 al 1750* (Treviso, 1970), pp. 70–71

Painting in Italy in the Eighteenth Century (exh. cat., ed. A. M. Clark; Chicago, IL, A. Inst.; Minneapolis, MN, Inst. A.; Toledo, OH, Mus. A.; 1970–71), p. 230

A. Busiri Vici: *Trittico paesistico romano del '700: Paolo Anesi, Paolo Monaldi, Alessio de Marchis* (Rome, 1975)

G. Michel and O. Michel: 'La Décoration du Palais Ruspoli en 1715 et la redécouverte de "Monsu Francesco Borgognone"', *Mél. Ecole Fr. Rome: Moyen Age, Temps Mod.*, i (1977), pp. 265–340

M. Chiarini: 'Il paesaggio a Roma fra sei e settecento', *Ant. B. A.*, iii/9–12 (1979), pp. 144–54

SOPHIE ANNE GAY

Marcillat, Guillaume de.

See GUILLAUME DE MARCILLAT.

Marciniec, Marcin

(*b* Kraków *c.* 1460; *d* Kraków, *c.* 1518). Polish goldsmith. He was born to a Kraków family of goldsmiths and was head of the goldsmiths' guild for several terms from 1486. He worked for Elizabeth Habsburg (1438–1505), consort of King Kasimir IV (*reg* 1447–92), and for her sons, King John Albrecht (*reg* 1492–1501), King Sigismund I (*reg* 1506–48) and Cardinal Frederick Jagiellon (1468–1503). Marciniec ran a large workshop, with more than 20 pupils, and made both ecclesiastical and secular silverware and jewellery. Many of his works have been destroyed, and others are only attributed to him. The octagonal box reliquary for the head of St Stanislas (Kraków, Wawel Cathedral), commissioned from Marciniec in 1504 by the royal family and Bishop Jan Konarski (1447–1525), is covered with Late Gothic tracery, plant motifs and cameos. On its sides are eight scenes from the life of the patron saint of Poland, modelled after engravings in pattern books and exhibiting the influence of the work of Veit Stoss I. Other works by Marciniec, for example the Late Gothic chalice from Wieliczka Parish Church covered with thistle motifs, the sceptre presented by Cardinal Jagiellon to the Jagiellonian University in Kraków and the cross given by the Cardinal to Gniezno Cathedral, are attributions. Adopting Flamboyant style motifs from pattern books, Marciniec's works are characterized by restrained decoration, a sense of proportion and—especially in casts—a high technical level. His brother Stanisław Marciniec (1464–1521) and his nephew Andrzej Marciniec (*fl* 1522–37) also worked as goldsmiths, the latter attaining the position of the royal goldsmith; no works by them have been identified, however.

BIBLIOGRAPHY
H. Kopydłowski: 'Marcin Marciniec złotnik krakowski' [Marcin Marciniec the Krakovian goldsmith], *Biul. Hist. Sztuki*, xvi (1954), pp. 235–44

J. Samek: 'Marciniec Marcin', *Polski słownik biograficzny* [Polish biographical dictionary], xviii (Kraków, 1959), pp. 586–7

TADEUSZ CHRZANOWSKI

Marck, Erard

[Eberhard; Evrard; Evard] **de la** (*b* Sedan, 31 May 1472; *d* 1538). South Netherlandish ecclesiastic and patron. He studied at the University of Cologne and then at the Papal Curia. Between 1500 and 1505 he was a regular visitor at the court of Louis XII of France (1462–1515) and at the Vatican, where he enjoyed the favour of Pope Julius II. In 1505 he was elected prince-bishop of Liège, a position he held up to his death. He amassed a considerable fortune and was an important patron of the arts, instrumental in introducing Renaissance art to the Netherlands at an early date. He built (*c.* 1526) an episcopal palace in Liège that reflects his familiarity with the French Renaissance châteaux and through them of Italian Renaissance styles of building. The interiors were painted by Lambert Lombard, who was official painter to Marck from 1532. According to a custom of the period, Erard endowed a number of churches and monasteries within the principality with stained glass depicting his portrait and coat of arms. His ecclesiastical patronage was focused on Liège Cathedral, which he presented in 1512 with numerous precious liturgical objects including the famous reliquary bust of *St Lambert*. In 1527 he commissioned a monumental tomb for himself, to be placed in the choir of the cathedral; this was one of the first Netherlandish funerary monuments in the Renaissance style. Marck also had an important collection of tapestries. The discovery of his inventories has revealed the extent of this collection, comprising nearly 250 tapestries, including a large number made for the Habsburg court, which Marck acquired as a result of his political alliance with the Habsburgs.

BIBLIOGRAPHY
P. Harsin: *Le Règne d'Erard de la Marck, 1505–1538: Etudes critiques sur la principauté de Liège, 1477–1795*, ii (Liège, 1955)

J. K. Steppe and G. Delmarcel: 'Les Tapisseries du Cardinal Erard de la Marck, prince-évêque de Liège', *Rev. A.* [Paris], xxv (1974), pp. 35–54

S. Collon-Gevaert: *Erard de la Marck et le palais des princes-évêques à Liège* (Liège, 1975)

G. Delmarcel: 'La Vie de la Vierge, deux nouvelles tapisseries du Cardinal Erard de la Marck', *Archivum artis Lovaniense: Bijdragen tot de geschiedenis van de Kunst der Nederlanden opgedragen aan prof. em. Dr. J. K. Steppe* (Leuven, 1981), pp. 225–37

□

Marcks, Gerhard

(*b* Berlin, 18 Feb 1889; *d* Burgbrohl, nr Cologne, 13 Nov 1981). German sculptor, draughtsman and printmaker. He first sculpted animals while studying under Richard Scheibe. After World War I his interest in classicism gave way to the influence of Expressionism and of the *Sturm* artists, as part of a search for a new spirituality. This new style of work can be seen in *Woman Suckling* (gold-plated limewood relief, 1919; Bremen, Marcks-Haus). Walter Gropius, who founded the Bauhaus in Weimar in 1919, asked Marcks to establish a ceramics workshop for the school in the nearby village of Dornburg. With his students he set out to create a Bauhaus ceramics ethic of simplicity and honesty of design as determined by the materials used and the function of the object. In stylistic terms he combined geometry with a local pottery tradition. He was also inspired by Lyonel Feininger to make woodcuts of rural genre themes.

In 1925 Marcks left the Bauhaus in protest at Moholy-Nagy's principle of 'Art and technology—a new unity', which became an organizing policy of the Bauhaus. After a short stay in Paris, he returned to Halle and to the Kunstgewerbeschule Burg Giebichenstein and renewed his interest in the figure, in elastic volume and drawing. While on a fellowship in Greece the affinity he felt with archaic sculpture led him to a form of abstraction based on the human body but subject to its own laws. This development resulted in monumental figures such as *Kneeling Woman* (stone, 1928; Bremen, Marcks-Haus). Considered to be a degenerate artist, he was dismissed from his teaching post by the Nazis because of his support of Jewish colleagues, his non-conformist, non-ideologically committed sculpture, and his friendship with other artists regarded as degenerate, including Ernst Barlach and Käthe Kollwitz (*see* ENTARTETE KUNST).

To escape from German government supervision, Marcks went to Italy in 1935, where he lived and worked in the Villa Romana in Florence and the Villa Massimo in Rome. In the late 1940s and 1950s he was very influential on younger artists but his own work of this period showed vacillation and a melancholy mood, for example in *Ver Sacrum* (bronze, 1943) and *Tantalus* (bronze, 1944; both Bremen, Marcks-Haus; see fig.). After World War II he was appointed professor of sculpture at the Landeskunstschule, Hamburg. In spite of primitive working conditions, *c.* 1950 he created monuments to those who died in the war. Occasionally he called upon earlier ideas, drawings and mythological themes, for example in *Prometheus in Chains* (bronze, 1948; version in Baltimore, MD, Mus. A.). He also completed Ernst Barlach's frieze for the Katharinenkirche, Lübeck, as well as carrying out important commissions for the cities of Cologne, Hamburg, Mannheim and others.

By the early 1950s Marcks was considered a master of a new morality in German sculpture. During the 1950s and 1960s Marcks was working outside the mainstreams of art. He travelled to Spain, Africa, the USA and Mexico, and to Greece, which he considered his spiritual home. In 1951 he settled in Cologne and in the last years of his life produced pastels. In 1971 the Gerhard Marcks Museum was founded in Bremen, where his sculpture the *Musicians of Bremen* was erected in the Marktplatz in 1951. The

Gerhard Marcks: *Tantalus*, bronze, 490×325 mm, 1944 (Bremen, Gerhard Marcks-Haus)

museum houses a collection of *c.* 350 sculptures as well as all his prints (900) and 12,000 sketches and preparatory model drawings.

PUBLISHED WRITINGS

'Wie kam ich zur Tiergestaltung', *Bild. Kst*, 1/30 (1955), p. 30
Hans Purrman—Gerhard Marcks, eine Künstlerfreundschaft: Briefwechsel (Bremen, 1986)

BIBLIOGRAPHY

G. Busch and M. Rudloff: *Gerhard Marcks: Das plastische Werk, Werkzeichnis* (Berlin, 1977)
J. J. Keller: *Gerhard Marcks und Griechenland* (Starnberg, 1979)
G. Busch: *Buch der Holzschnitte* (Düsseldorf, 1984)
Gerhard Marcks: Skulpturen, Ölkreiden, Aquarelle, Zeichnungen (exh. cat., W. Berlin, Gal. Nierendorf, 1986)
Gerhard Marcks, 1889–1981: Retrospective (exh. cat., ed. M. Rudloff; Cologne, Mus. Ludwig; W. Berlin, N.G.; Bremen, Marcks-Haus; 1989)
K. Lammek: *Gerhard Marcks: Das druckgraphische Werk* (Stuttgart, 1990)
M. Rudloff: *Gerhard Marcks und die Antike* (Bremen and Heidelberg, 1993)

MARTINA RUDLOFF

Marco da Ravenna. *See* DENTE, MARCO.

Marco di Costanzo. *See* COSTANZO, MARCO (DI).

Marconi. Polish family of artists of Italian origin. The Italian architect Francesco Marconi had two sons, Leandro Marconi (1763–1837), an architect, painter and stage designer who was active in Rome and taught at the Accademia delle Belle Arti in Bologna, and Giovanni Battista Marconi, an architect and painter who worked in Mantua. Leandro's son Ferrante Marconi (1798–1868), a sculptor, went to work in Poland at the request of his older brother (1) Henryk Marconi; Ferrante's son Leonard Marconi (1836–99) was born in Warsaw and worked in Poland as an architect and sculptor. Of (1) Henryk's eight children, Karol Marconi (1826–64) was a painter working in Poland and Italy, while (2) Leandro Jan Ludwik Marconi and (3) Władysław Marconi were both architects.

(1) Henryk [Enrico] **Marconi** (*b* Rome, 7 Jan 1792; *d* Warsaw, 21 Feb 1863). Architect. He began his training under his father Leandro Marconi and studied at both the University and the Accademia delle Belle Arti in Bologna (1806–10). From 1811 he taught drawing at the college at Lugo di Faenza and was also active as an architect in both Faenza and Bologna. In 1822 Ludwik Pac, a general in the Polish army, brought him to Poland to finish the construction of a Gothic Revival palace at Dowspuda, near Suwałki (destr.; only the portico survives). During his first 15 years in Poland, Marconi was constrained to tailor his own rather catholic tastes to the dominant preference, especially in government circles, for a monumental Neo-classicism, although he did try, with some success, to promote both neo-Renaissance and Gothic Revival designs where patrons were interested. His treatise *O porządkach architektonicznych* ('On the architectural orders'; 1828) reflects his attempt to accommodate his views to those of the Warsaw architectural community.

Examples of Marconi's earlier work in Poland are the rebuilding of Ludwik Pac's palace (1822–8; destr. 1944; rebuilt 1947–51) at Miodowa Street, Warsaw, a Doric temple (1834) for the Natolin residence of Aleksander Potocki and his wife Anna and a pump-room (1835) for the spa at Busko, near Kielce. During this period he also lectured at the Road and Bridge Engineering School of

Warsaw University (1824) and held several official posts: from 1826 he was Construction Councillor and from 1827 a member of the General Building Council of the State Commission for Internal Affairs and Police.

After a trip to England in 1836, a change in his stance on architecture is reflected in the second edition of his treatise. The views expressed here clearly reflect those of the circle of the Ecole Polytechnique in Paris, whose members held that the styles of all epochs were equal and could be used in combination. The 12 issues of Marconi's *Zbiór projektów architektonicznych* ('Selection of architectural designs'; 1838–42) increased their readers' familiarity with the wide range of possibilities available. Marconi's success by this time ensured that he received a large number of commissions during the following years, both from wealthy private patrons and from the Church. Private commissions included a Gothic Revival tomb (1836) for *Stanisław Kostka Potocki and his Wife Aleksandra* in Wilanów and two neo-Renaissance palaces in Novy Świat, Warsaw, that of Andrzej Zamoyski (1846; destr. 1939–44; rebuilt 1948–50) and the Branicki palace (1853–6; destr. 1944; rebuilt 1946–9). Among the churches he designed were those of St Charles Borromaeus (1841–3) in Chłodna Street, Warsaw, and All Saints (1859–63) in Grzybowski Square in Warsaw, both built in the neo-Renaissance style.

Marconi's most significant contribution to Warsaw architecture during this phase, however, lay in his public buildings. His work here not only reflected the evolving demands of the typical 19th-century metropolis for new types of architecture (the railway station or the office block) but also took advantage of the increased scope for size and strength of construction offered both by advances in building techniques and by the invention of new building materials, such as cast iron. Important large-scale projects undertaken by Marconi in Warsaw included the St Lazarus Hospital (*c.* 1840; destr. 1939–44) in Książęca Street, the station (1844–5; destr. 1925–30) of the Warsaw–Vienna railway, the water tank (1852) in the Saxon Gardens and other structures connected with the new water supply systems Marconi designed at this time, the Europejski Hotel (1855; destr. 1944; rebuilt 1949–51) in Krakowskie Przedmieście and the office building (1856; destr. 1944; rebuilt 1950 and 1962–71) of the Land Credit Society in Kredytowa Street. While Marconi certainly moved with the times, some of the fundamental concepts underlying his architectural thought may be traced to his study of later 18th-century practice and theory. His own work reflected, for example, a strict distinction in the design of public urban buildings and those intended for garden or rural settings. He generally retained symmetry, axiality and regularity of scale and decoration in his own town buildings while allowing those designed for the outskirts (the Novy Świat palaces) an asymmetrical plan, variety of scale within the parts and variety of texture on the wall surfaces. As well as leaving a vast body of Warsaw architecture as a model for his followers, Marconi was also active as a teacher, in 1851 taking on the post of Professor of Architecture at the School of Fine Arts in Warsaw. Among his more successful pupils were Jan Heurich the Elder (1834–87), Adolf Schimmelpfenning (1834–94) and Franciszek Tournelle (1818–80).

WRITINGS

O porządkach architektonicznych [On the architectural orders] (Warsaw, 1828, rev. 2/1837)

Zbiór projektów architektonicznych [Selection of architectural designs], 12 issues (Warsaw, 1838–42)

(2) Leandro Jan (Ludwik) Marconi (*b* Warsaw, 23 April 1834; *d* Montreux, 8 Oct 1919). Architect, son of (1) Henryk Marconi. He first practised under the supervision of his father, with whom he collaborated, for example on the construction of St Anne's church in Wilanów, which he finished (before 1870) after his father's death. His work represented the more mature, selective phase of historicism: he only rarely combined elements from different styles within one work, borrowing mostly from a repertory of French and Italian Renaissance forms as well as from Polish Neo-classical architecture. His wealth allowed him to pick and choose among potential patrons, but he recognized the attractions of working only for the richest clients as these could be persuaded to ensure the use of superior materials and a more perfect finish in implementing a design. From this point of view he was an exception among architects in Warsaw in the last quarter of the 19th century.

Marconi worked mainly in and around Warsaw, and town residences and country villas dominated his output. Among his commissions were the rebuilding (1868) of the 'Artichoke' Villa in Ujazdowskie Avenue on the outskirts of Warsaw for his father, a house (1874; destr.) for Stanisław Zamoyski in Warecka Street in Warsaw and a palace (before 1880) for the Tyszkiewicz family at Waka, near Vilnius (Lithuania), which he based on the Neo-classical design of the late 18th-century Łazienki Palace in Warsaw. Marconi did, however, take on both church and public commissions in Warsaw and elsewhere. He designed the Commercial Bank (1873; destr. 1944; rebuilt after 1950) in Traugutta Street, the synagogue (1875; destr. 1943) in Tłomackie Street and the church (1875) at Czyżew, near Ostrów Mazowiecki.

(3) Władysław Marconi (*b* Warsaw, 29 Feb 1848; *d* Warsaw, 4 June 1915). Architect, son of (1) Henryk Marconi and brother of (2) Leandro Jan Marconi. He graduated from the Academy of Arts in St Petersburg in 1874 and subsequently worked both in Warsaw and in other areas of Poland. His historicist style borrowed mostly from classical and Baroque elements, and his appreciation for the building methods and techniques of the past was increased through his active role in the Society for the Protection of Historical Monuments, of which he was a founder-member (in 1906). Among Władysław's Warsaw designs were the offices (1898–1901; destr. 1944) of the Russia Insurance Company in Marszałkowska Street, the Bristol Hotel (1900–02) and many houses, such as that designed for the collector and painter Antoni Strzałecki (1844–1935) in Ujazdowskie Avenue (1904–7). Marconi also undertook valuable conservation work, for example at the Wilanów Palace (1893–1906) and in the town houses in the Old Town Market Square (complete project 1910–20). Outside Warsaw Marconi was likewise engaged in a variety of projects: he designed the Karski Palace (*c.* 1900) at Włostów, near Sandomierz, and the church at Otwock (1892), near Warsaw. He also worked on the large restoration project (1902) in the castle at Pieskowa Skała, near

Kraków. Between 1894 and 1900 Marconi and his brother Jan Marconi (1845–1921) published the *Album Marconich* ('Marconi album'), a series of volumes of Polish monuments illustrated with Władysław's own photographs. Marconi was also active and influential as a publisher of two professional architectural journals *Przegląd Techniczny* ('Technical Review'; from 1897) and *Architekt* (from 1900/01).

BIBLIOGRAPHY

S. Łoza: *Henryk Marconi i jego rodzina* [Henryk Marconi and his family], Mistrzowie Architektury Polskiej [Masters of Polish architecture] (Warsaw, 1954)

A. Rottermund: *Katalog rysunków architektonicznych ze zbiorów Muzeum Narodowego w Warszawie* [Catalogue of architectural designs in the collections of the National Museum in Warsaw], Biblioteka Muzealnictwa i Ochrony Zabytków, ser. A, vi (Warsaw, 1970)

M. Rudowska: 'Warszawskie Konkursy Architektoniczne w latach 1864–1898' [Warsaw architectural competitions in the years 1864–1898], *Stud. & Mat. Teor. & Hist. Archit. & Urb.*, x (1972), pp. 27–38

P. Marconi, A. Cipriani and E. Valeriani: *I disegni di architettura storica della Accademia di San Luca*, i (Rome, 1974), p. 45

T. S. Jaroszewski and A. Rottermund: *Katalog rysunków architektonicznych Henryka i Leandra Marconich w Archiwum Głównym Akt Dawnych w Warszawie* [Catalogue of architectural designs by Henryk and Leandro Marconi in the Main Archives of Old Documents in Warsaw], Biblioteka Muzealnictwa i Ochrony Zabytków, ser. A, xi (Warsaw, 1977)

T. S. Jaroszewski: *O siedzibach neogotyckich w Polsce* [On Gothic Revival residences in Poland] (Warsaw, 1981)

T. S. Jaroszewski and A. Rottermund: 'La famiglia dei Marconi in Polonia', *Zeszyty Naukowe U. Jagiellon.*, dcxxviii/71 (1982), pp. 129–42

ANDRZEJ ROTTERMUND

Marconi, Rocco (*fl* Venice, 1504–29). Italian painter. He is mentioned (Ridolfi, Boschini, Zanetti) as being a native of Treviso, but signed himself *venetus* in the contractual document for an altarpiece for Treviso. He may have been born in Venice to parents originating from Bergamo (Ludwig). He is documented for the first time as a witness in 1504, and then several times until 1529, including in 1517 as an auditor of the Guild of Painters, a sign that by this time he was already established. He spent over 25 years in the workshop of Giovanni Bellini, and during this period, either in the 1490s or perhaps the late 1480s, he produced three paintings of the *Virgin and Child* (Strasbourg, Mus. B.-A.; ex-Czernin priv. col., Vienna), all signed *Rochus de Marchonib*. These are exact copies of Bellini's *Virgin and Child* (*c.* 1485–90; Atlanta, GA, High Mus. A.), on which it is sometimes thought that Marconi collaborated. On the basis of these signed works others have been attributed, most of which are now reattributed to the Venetian Master of the Incredulity of St Thomas. Thus there are only three or four certain works from the years Marconi spent with Bellini. On Bellini's death (1516) Marconi moved to the workshop of Palma Vecchio and adjusted his style accordingly, although his figures retained some of the rigid quality that was characteristic of Bellini's art. He specialized mainly in paintings of *Christ and the Adulteress* and *Christ with Martha and Mary*, although many that have been attributed to him are undoubtedly not by his hand. From this second phase of his career there is also the signed altarpiece of *Christ Blessing, with Two Saints* (Venice, S Giovanni e Paolo). It is painted in his characteristic mixture of styles derived from Bellini and Palma Vecchio, which cannot be said of two other works that have been attributed to him: the *Christ with SS Peter and John the Baptist* (Venice, Accad.) and the altarpiece in the Alte Pinakothek in Munich. It seems to the present writer that these are unlikely to have been painted by Marconi.

BIBLIOGRAPHY

C. Ridolfi: *Meraviglie* (1648); ed. D. von Hadeln (1914–24), p. 237

M. Boschini: *Le ricche miniere della pittura veneziana* (Venice, 1664), pp. 25, 412, 467, 521, 566

A. M. Zanetti: *Della pittura veneziana* (Venice, 1771), pp. 208–10

G. Ludwig: 'Archivalische Beiträge zur Geschichte der venezianischen Kunst', *Jb. Kön.-Preuss. Kstsamml.* (1905), suppl., pp. 136–42

F. Gibbons: 'Giovanni Bellini and Rocco Marconi', *A. Bull.*, xliv (1962), pp. 127–34

P. L. de Vecchi: 'Rocco Marconi', *I pittori bergamaschi dal XIII al XIX secolo: Il cinquecento*, i (Bergamo, 1975), pp. 345–59

M. Lucco: 'Marconi, Rocco', *La pittura in Italia: Il cinquecento*, ed. G. Briganti, 2 vols (Milan, 1987, rev. 1988), ii, p. 763 [with bibliog.]

MAURO LUCCO

Marco Romano (*fl* 1317/18). Italian sculptor. He is known from a single surviving sculpture, the effigy of *St Simon* in S Simeone Grande, Venice. The tomb, commissioned to preserve the relics of the Saint, no longer survives. An inscribed tablet accompanying the effigy records the names of the clerics who commissioned the monument, the sculptor's name MARCUS ROMANUS and the date 4 February 1317 (NS 1318). The style of the statue in its confident treatment of the supine figure and the summary but convincing delineation of drapery folds points to a sculptor of considerable skill and experience who was outside the mainstream of early 14th-century Venetian sculpture. The expressive head with its prominent cheekbones, furrowed brow and heavy features and the realistic detail of the teeth just showing between strong lips, suggest knowledge of the work of Giovanni Pisano and, in particular, his series of prophets and sibyls for Siena Cathedral. Remarkably progressive in comparison to contemporary Venetian sculpture, *St Simon* was to provide the starting-point for subsequent tomb effigies in the Veneto: that of the *Blessed Oderico da Pordenone* (1331) by Filippo de Santi for S Maria del Carmine, Udine, is the most significant.

Other works plausibly attributed to Marco Romano include a group of capitals on the Doge's Palace, Venice; the over life-size sculptures of the *Virgin and Child*, *St Omobono* and *St Imerio* on the façade of Cremona Cathedral; and, in Tuscany, the monument to *Porrina* in the Collegiata, Casole d'Elsa, and, less convincingly, the figure of *Christ* in wood from a crucifix in S Agostino, Colle Val d'Elsa. Whether Marco Romano actually came from Rome or not is unknown, certainly no work by him in that city has been identified. It has sometimes been assumed that the Marco Veneto who signed two capitals in the cloister of S Matteo, Genoa, in 1308 and 1310 was the same person. The style of these works, however, precludes this possibility.

BIBLIOGRAPHY

W. Wolters: *La scultura veneziana gotica (1300–1460)*, 2 vols (Venice, 1976), pp. 22, 24, 28

G. Previtali: 'Alcune opere "fuori contesto": Il caso di Marco Romano', *Boll. A.*, xxii (1983), pp. 43–68

Scultura dipinta: Maestri di legname e pittori a Siena, 1250–1450 (exh. cat., Siena, Pin. N., 1987), pp. 30–35

BRENDAN CASSIDY

Marcoussis, Louis [Markus, Louis Casimir Ladislas] (*b* Warsaw, 10 Nov 1878; *d* Cusset, nr Vichy, 22 Oct 1941). French painter and printmaker of Polish birth. The second son in a cultivated family of Jewish origin that had converted to Catholicism, he began studying law in Warsaw but left to enrol in the Academy of Fine Arts in Kraków. When he refused to follow decorative arts and design, potentially useful in the family's carpet manufacturing business, his father cut off his allowance, reinstating it only after he won honours in drawing and decided to continue his studies in Paris. In 1903 he enrolled under Jules Lefebvre at the Académie Julian in Paris, where he became friendly with Roger de La Fresnaye and the French painter Robert Lotiron (1886–1966). A casual student, he spent most of his time visiting the Louvre, salon exhibitions, galleries and cafés until 1905, when the subvention from home ended. The first work he exhibited in Paris was an Impressionist landscape at the Salon d'Automne in 1905. Now obliged to support himself, he took advantage of his facility as a draughtsman and submitted illustrations to Parisian magazines of humour and fashion: *Vie parisienne*, *Le Journal* and *Assiette au beurre*. He continued to paint and by 1907 had moved into the orbit of Fauvism. A chance encounter with Guillaume Apollinaire and Georges Braque at the Cirque Médrano in 1910, by which time he was living in bourgeois comfort with Marcelle Humbert as a highly successful illustrator, changed the course of Marcoussis's life. Presented to Picasso, Marcoussis was startled by Cubism; Picasso in turn was taken with Marcelle, whom he renamed Eva and swept off to Avignon, Ceret and Sorgues. Freed of the pressures of maintaining a middle-class apartment, Marcoussis began to associate with Apollinaire and other younger poets and to experiment with the new painting. At the urging of Apollinaire he changed his surname to that of a small village in the district of Essonne. Although he exhibited in the Section d'Or (*see* SECTION D'OR (ii)) exhibition of 1912, the year in which he etched Apollinaire's portrait (Philadelphia, PA, Mus. A.), his own brand of Cubism was closer to that of the Montmartre artists Picasso and Braque than to that of the PUTEAUX GROUP. Like the former he favoured still-life and subjects that made reference to music, but his approach to form remained readable, his Cubist treatment more moderate. He gave up illustration only in 1913, the year in which he married the Polish painter Alicia Halicka; among his last caricatures is one lampooning Cubism. A typical example of his pre-war work is *The Cellist* (1914; Washington, DC, N.G.A.).

Marcoussis's development was interrupted by World War I. He served in the French army with distinction, rose to be a decorated Lieutenant and on the basis of his service was able to attain French nationality. On a return trip to Poland in 1919 he was charmed by a folk-art form that consisted of painting on the rear side of glass. He adapted this technique to the Cubist vocabulary, creating a pleasing decorative art that was also his solution to the making of paintings that also declared themselves as objects. Until late 1928 Marcoussis, never a productive artist, finished about three such paintings per month, almost all of them still-lifes dominated by fish. Typically he exploited correspondences between forms, for example rhyming the shape of a fish with that of a cloud and relating both to a patch of wood-grain. For the first six years the mood of these still-lifes was wistful and humorous. Many were sent to Pierre Emile Legrain to be framed in a fashion that emphasized their object quality; Marcoussis also designed other objects for Legrain to execute, including inlaid furniture. Around 1926, in such works as the *Knifed Dove* (1927; priv. col., see Lafranchis, p. 256), the mood of Marcoussis's paintings began to change, with dead birds, knives, partly open doors and ominous shadows dominating. At this time he again took up serious printmaking, illustrating a volume of poems by Tristan Tzara (*Indicateur des chemins de coeur*, Paris, 1928), then a series of plates to accompany an edition of Gérard de Nerval's *Aurelia* (Paris, 1930) and, most important, a set of ten etchings, *Planches de salut* (Paris, 1931), conceived as homages to his favourite authors, which were published by his dealer Jeanne Bucher. They were followed in 1933 by a suite of etchings entitled *Eaux-fortes théâtrales pour Monsieur G.*, based on Marcel Jonhandeau's *Monsieur Godeau intime* (Paris, 1926), and in 1933–4 by 40 plates illustrating Apollinaire's *Alcools* (see Lafranchis, pp. 329–35).

From the mid-1920s Marcoussis's association with so many poets linked to Surrealism had an effect on his style, which by 1927 had already loosened in pictorial organization in a series of landscapes painted at Kérity in Brittany. He returned to the human figure in *Three Poets* (oil on canvas, 1.63×1.31 m, 1929; Paris, Pompidou), a fanciful triple portrait of Max Jacob, Apollinaire and André Salmon. Marcoussis rarely made prints after his paintings, but he sometimes followed the reverse procedure, concentrating the calm and silence he sought by an adroit manipulation of light effects in the black-and-white medium. In order to supplement his income during the 1930s he taught printmaking at the Académie Moderne in the Montparnasse district of Paris, and he began to work as a decorator and art collecting adviser to the cosmetics manufacturer Helena Rubinstein; for her fashionably modern home, designed by Louis Süe, he executed his largest oil painting, *Anabase* (3.4×2.5 m, 1936; priv. col., see Lafranchis, p. 277). In his last paintings, in which he made reference to prehistoric art, realistic elements such as a horse or a frog yield a Surrealist shock by their integration into compositions that are overwhelmingly geometric and abstract. His last prints, *Les Devins* (see Lafranchis, nos G 195–210), a set of ten made in 1940–41, which combine portrait heads and the tools of both divination and art-making, reflect the doubly depressing effects of the German invasion (which forced him to move with his wife to unoccupied France, near Vichy) and the lung cancer that claimed his life.

BIBLIOGRAPHY
A. Halicka: *Hier* (Paris, 1946)
J. Lafranchis: *Marcoussis: Sa vie, son oeuvre* (Paris, 1961) [incl. cat. rais. of his work in all media]
Marcoussis (exh. cat., ed. J. Cassou; Paris, Mus. N. A. Mod., 1964)
Marcoussis: L'Ami des poètes (exh. cat., ed. J. Cassou; Paris, Bib. N., 1972)
Souvenir de Marcoussis (exh. cat., Paris, Pompidou, 1978)
D. Robbins: 'Louis Marcoussis', *The Société Anonyme and the Dreier Bequest at Yale University: A Catalogue Raisonné*, ed. R. L. Herbert, E. S. Apter and E. K. Kenney (New Haven, CT, 1984), pp. 435–8

DANIEL ROBBINS

Marcovaldo, Coppo di. *See* COPPO DI MARCOVALDO.

Marcu, Duiliu (*b* Calafat, 23 March 1885; *d* Bucharest, 9 March 1966). Romanian architect, urban planner, teacher and theorist. He graduated in 1906 from the Academy of Architecture, Bucharest, and in 1912 from the Ecole des Beaux-Arts, Paris. His early buildings were influenced by the 'neo-Romanian' style of ION MINCU, which tended towards Byzantine Revival decoration. Marcu's buildings in this style include the Polytechnic (1923), theatre and students hostel (1924), all in Timișoara, as well as the Romanian Pavilion at the Exposició Internacional (1929), Barcelona. He then developed a practical architecture that primarily addressed public needs and was characterized by a severe mood imparted by strongly balanced horizontals and verticals, rectangular plans and volumes and 20th-century techniques and materials, such as reinforced concrete, steel and glass. The luxurious façades are finished with marble and travertine. Examples in Bucharest include the Autonomous Monopolies Building (1934–41; now the Ministry of Industry) at Calea Victoriei 152, the Romanian Railways Building, Palatul CFR (1936–47; with Ștefan Călugăreanu (1904–75) and P. E. Miclescu (*b* 1901); now the Ministry of Transport and Telecommunications) and the Magistrates' Credit Building (1937–8), Magheru Boulevard 22–4, the façade of which closely resembles those by Horia Creangă. Marcu also executed major urban planning projects at Unirea Square (1926), Oradea, the city centre (1935–6), Buzău, and the civic centre (1943–5), Brașov, and wrote studies in this field. Between 1929 and 1957 he taught at the Ion Mincu Academy of Architecture, Bucharest. He was also a member of the Romanian Academy from 1943 and president (1952–66) of the Romanian Architects Union.

WRITINGS
Problema sistematizării orașelor în România [The problem of town planning in Romania] (Bucharest, 1963)

BIBLIOGRAPHY
G. Ionescu: *Arhitectura în România de-alungul veacurilor* [Architecture in Romania over the centuries] (Bucharest, 1982), pp. 583, 596, 598, 601

CODRUȚA CRUCEANU

Marcuard, Robert Samuel (*b* 25 Dec 1756; *d* London, ?before 1788). English engraver. He entered the Royal Academy Schools in London as an engraver on 31 May 1777. He was a pupil of the stipple engraver Francesco Bartolozzi, whose portrait by Joshua Reynolds he engraved in 1784; he probably remained in Bartolozzi's employ. Nearly all his signed stipple prints were of allegorical or fancy pictures, notably after William Hamilton and Angelica Kauffman. Marcuard probably died very young, as the latest of his prints is dated 1786, and in 1788 a sale of the drawings of Robert Marcuard of North End, Hammersmith (Bartolozzi's address) was advertised.

UNPUBLISHED SOURCES
London, V&A, *Press Cuttings Relating to the Arts*, ii, p. 384 [newspaper advertisement for a sale of Marcuard's drgs]

BIBLIOGRAPHY
DNB; Thieme–Becker
A. W. Tuer: *Bartolozzi and his Works* (London, 1882/rev. 1885)
A. De Vesme and A. Calabi: *Francesco Bartolozzi* (Milan, 1928)

DAVID ALEXANDER

Marcus, Jacob Ernst (*b* St Eustatius, 19 March 1774; *d* Amsterdam, 2 Oct 1826). Dutch draughtsman and printmaker. In 1783 he moved to Amsterdam where he trained as an engraver and draughtsman with Steven Goblé (1749–99) and Reinier Vinkeles. While at the municipal drawing academy he was awarded the third, second and first prize in 1793, 1797 and 1798 respectively. In 1801 he founded the drawing society, Kunst zij ons doel ('Let art be our aim') with Harmanus Fock (1766–1822), Harmanus Vinkeles (1745–after 1817) and others. Marcus became especially famous for a series of 105 prints published as *Studiebeelden en fragmenten* ('Studies and fragments') (begun in 1807), which was intended as an aid to draughtsmen and engravers. Marcus's etchings are characterized by a delicate handling of the medium, which often resembles copper engraving. They were based on his own drawings as well as those of Willem Hendrik Caspari (1770–1829), Wybrand Hendriks, Wouter Johannes van Troostwijk and others and give a light-hearted, natural and poignant impression of the Dutch way of life at the beginning of the 19th century. In 1815 Marcus was awarded a silver medal for his printed oeuvre by the Nederlandsche Huishoudelijke Maatschappij (Dutch Domestic Society) in Haarlem. In 1816 his series went out of print for lack of interest but was later reissued. From 1820 he was one of the directors of the Koninklijke Akademie van Beeldende Kunsten in Amsterdam, where he taught engraving.

BIBLIOGRAPHY
J. Knoef: *Tussen rococo en romantiek* [Between Rococo and Romanticism] (The Hague, 1943), pp. 155–68
Jacob Ernst Marcus graveur en takenaar. St Eustatius 1774–1826, Amsterdam (exh. cat., Willemstad, Curaçaos Mus.; Aruba, Cult. Cent.; Amsterdam, Rijksmus.; 1972)
P. Knolle: 'Modeltekenaars in zakformaat: Een aan J. E. Marcus (1774–1826) toegeschreven tekening', *Ned. Ksthist. Jb.*, 38 (1987), pp. 172–84

FRANS GRIJZENHOUT

Marcus Aurelius. *See* AURELIUS, MARCUS.

Marczibányi. Hungarian family of collectors. Various members of the family, who resided in the county of Trencsén (now Trenčín, Slovakia), were interested in Hungarian and European cultural history. István Marczibányi (1752–1810) acted in 1802 as an important patron of the Hungarian National Museum in Budapest: according to the museum's first catalogue in 1825, he gave the institution a large part of his collection. His brother, Imre Marczibányi (*b* after 1753; *d* 1824), was particularly interested in Italian bronzes. According to the family tradition, the 48 pieces of his collection came from the Hungarian sculptor István Ferenczy, who, as Canova's pupil, spent several years in Rome. This claim is supported by the close relationship between Imre's collection and that of Ferenczy, now in the Museum of Fine Arts in Budapest. Imre's collection came into the possession of Antal Marczibányi (1793–1872). After his death it reached different branches of the family and, apart from a few pieces, disappeared into the art market. Most of the bronzes were Italian works from the Cinquecento (e.g. by Andrea Riccio, Alessandro Vittoria, Giambologna and Francesco Segala). Other notable examples included a *St Christopher* (1407; Boston, MA, Mus. F.A.) by a Florentine master; a superb south German *Venus and Cupid* (Toronto, A.G. Ont.);

and a *God and Goddess* (Budapest, Mus. F.A.) by the school of Segala.

BIBLIOGRAPHY
G. Entz: 'I bronzetti della collezione Marczibányi', *Acta Hist. A. Acad. Sci. Hung.* (1955), pp. 215–34

GÉZA ENTZ

Marczyński, Adam (*b* Kraków, 24 June 1908; *d* Kraków, 13 Jan 1985). Polish painter, sculptor and draughtsman. Between 1930 and 1936 he studied at the Academy of Fine Arts, Kraków. During the 1930s he had contacts with the Kraków group. The simplified form of his early compositions, most of which were destroyed in World War II, was at that time a popular interpretation of Expressionism and Cubism, while the treatment of the subject and subtle range of colour link these works to the Polish school of colourism. Between 1945 and 1955 he produced drawings and monotypes of transparent composition and delicate line. His fascination with motifs from everyday life and nature (without conflicting with the doctrines of Socialist Realism, which he managed to bypass) produced intimate and lyrical works, ranging from realism to modernist compositions resembling at times the drawings of Paul Klee or Yves Tanguy (e.g. *Herbarium*, *c*. 1955).

From the outset of the *Hard Facts* (Pol. *Konkrety*) series (1959) Marczyński completely changed his style, creating assemblages from rusty sheet metal, fibreboard, tar, cinders and veneer. In 1961 he superimposed on these works trusses made from thin fibreboard battens, which introduced a certain order to the composition. The *Variable Systems* series (1963) contains reliefs with a distinctive vertical batten, with movable plates affixed to the surface. In 1967 Marczyński produced his *Variable Reflexes*, and the hitherto complex material and compositional structures made way for box-reliefs. The batten truss was replaced by a geometric construction of flat hexagons completely filling the rectangle of the relief. The boxes, with their internal walls painted in garish, electric colours enclosed with silver revolving plates mounted vertically or horizontally, produced a kaleidoscopic effect of colour on the surface of the relief. The *Interventions* event (1970) involved the arrangement of individual boxes in a forest on tree trunks and ushered in the extensive *Decompositions* series, in which the compositionally coherent relief breaks down into a spatial, sculptural system of boxes arranged about a central form, giving a sense of order to the composition as a whole. In the 1980s Marczyński started working on small white cardboard reliefs (unrealized) reminiscent of Elementarism.

BIBLIOGRAPHY
B. Kowalska: *Twórcy-postawy: Artyści mojej galerii* [Creators–attitudes: artists from my gallery] (Kraków, 1981)
J. Pollakówna: *Malarstwo polskie między wojnami 1918–1939* [Polish painting between the wars, 1918–39] (Warsaw, 1982)
Adam Marczyński, 1908–1985 (exh. cat., ed. J. Chrobak; Kraków, Office A. Exh., 1985)

EWA MIKINA

Mardakan. Village and region in Azerbaijan. Its defensive castles were a part of a system of fortifications in the northern Apsheron Peninsula that included fortresses in BAKU and the settlements of Ramana and Nardaran. The earliest surviving fortress, built by ʿAbd al-Majid ibn Masʿud in 1232, is a cylindrical donjon (h. 12 m) crowned by a row of merlons and machicolations and surrounded by a wall strengthened by semi-cylindrical buttresses. In the 14th century a rectangular fortress (h. 22 m) with corner columns and merlons was built in a keep (28×25 m) protected by three-quarter towers. In later times the fortresses in Mardakan served as refuges for local feudal overlords, for the last fortress (1720–21; destr.) was built by the ruler of Baku, Mirza Muhammad Khan. These fortresses, like other buildings in Mardakan, were constructed of large blocks of locally quarried yellowish limestone. Other noteworthy monuments include the mosque of Shah Tuba (1482), a rectangular building with a large central dome, several domed mausolea (15th–17th century) for local holy men and two 19th-century baths, Qazym Hammam and Khanbaba Hammam. During the oil boom of the 1860s Mardakan, with its moderate sea climate, became a summer resort for the gentry of Baku. The main street was extended, and villas were built between it and the sea to the north. The Asadullayev Villa (1897–1901), for example, is set in a freely landscaped park. From the gate in the style of a Roman triumphal arch, the main avenue leads to a two-storey pavilion facing the sea. Near by is the three-storey villa, its façade overlooking an avenue leading to a round pool (diam. 35 m). The ground-floor has an open colonnade supporting a glazed veranda on the main floor.

BIBLIOGRAPHY
Y. A. Pakhomov: 'Staryye oboronnyye sooruzheniya Absherona' [Ancient defensive buildings in Apsheron], *Trudy Inst. Istor. A. Bakikhanova*, i (1947)
Arkhitektura Azerbaydzhana: Epokha Nizami [The architecture of Azerbaijan: the epoch of Nizami] (Baku, 1947) [col. of articles]
M. Useynov, L. Bretanitsky and A. Salamzade: *Istoriya arkhitektury Azerbaydzhana* [The history of the architecture of Azerbaijan] (Moscow, 1963)
S. S. Fatullayev: *Gradostroitel'stvo Baku, XIX–nachala XX vekov* [Town planning in Baku in the 19th century and early 20th] (Leningrad, 1978)

E. R. SALMANOV

Mardall, Cyril. See *under* YORKE, ROSENBERG & MARDALL.

Mardan [Hoti-Mardan]. Town on the Kalpani River, in the centre of the Peshawar Valley, *c.* 50 km north-east of Peshawar, Pakistan. The town originally developed from two separate villages: Hoti, the headquarters of an important local khan; and Mardan, the site of a British cantonment (1852–1947) that was the military base of Queen Victoria's Own Corps of Guides and the administrative centre of the district. The town retains its military associations as the headquarters of the Punjab Regiment.

In the early 20th century a mound (61×30×9 m) of uncertain date still survived beside the High School, albeit covered with graves and deeply cut for soil on all sides. Although it was never excavated, potsherds suggest that it had been a settlement site. There is no record of any Buddhist remains within the vicinity. Numerous Gandharan sculptures are said to be 'from Mardan', but this is a secondary attribution resulting from the fact that, in the 19th century, excavated finds from Gandharan sites in the region were all initially stored at Mardan awaiting orders for their ultimate destination, during which time records of site provenance were often lost. In 1904, for example, the Assistant Commissioner at Mardan handed over 227 'remnants of earlier collections' to the Archaeological Survey of India. An important collection of Gandharan sculptures was also made over the years by officers of the Guides Corps. These pieces were used to decorate a fireplace, sundial and the regimental mess but have since been transferred to the Peshawar Museum.

BIBLIOGRAPHY

M. A. Stein: *Report of Archaeological Work in the North-west Frontier Province and Baluchistan*, pt 1, section iii (Peshawar, 1905), p. 8

'List of Ancient Monuments in the Frontier Circle', *Archaeol. Surv. India, Annu. Rep. Frontier Circ.* (1915–16), app. v, p. 35

J. Marshall: *The Buddhist Art of Gandhāra* (Cambridge, 1960) [illustrates sculptures from the Guides' Col.]

E. Errington: *The Western Discovery of the Art of Gandhāra and the Finds of Jamālgarhī* (diss., U. London, SOAS, 1987), pp. 154–5, 210–14, 367–70, figs 7.4–7, 53, 211

——: 'Towards Clearer Attributions of Site Provenance for Some 19th-century Collections of Gandhāra Sculpture', *South Asian Archaeology 1987*, ed. M. Taddei, ii (Rome, 1990), pp. 765–7

E. ERRINGTON

Mardel, Carlos [Mardell, ?Károly] (*b* ?Hungary, *c.* 1695; *d* ?Lisbon, 1763). Architect of Hungarian origin, active in Portugal. He lived in England and France and fought as a military officer in the imperial wars in Central Europe before going to Portugal in 1733. There his part in the development of secular architecture during the reigns of kings John V and Joseph I was very important. Mardel's style was formed essentially by central European late Baroque and Rococo and the formal secular architecture of French Classicism. As an engineer his experience was invaluable in the immense project for the reconstruction of Lisbon from 1755. His work also shows an ability to incorporate local Portuguese characteristics, and he aimed to combine the official courtly Joanine style with the vernacular Portuguese tradition of the *estilo Chão* or Plain Style favoured by other military engineers active in Lisbon. Mardel brought to Pombaline architecture his own elegance, lightness and imagination, qualities that stand beside the radical simplicity seen in the work of Eugénio dos Santos.

Mardel came to Portugal to work as an engineer on the monumental Águas Livres aqueduct (1729–48) that John V gave to the city of Lisbon. He took charge of the project when the water supply reached Lisbon, and he designed the great enclosed reservoir, the Casa das Águas Livres or Mãe de Água (1750–54), the starting-point at Amoreiras for the channels feeding the city's fountains. Mardel also designed the Arco das Amoreiras or triumphal arch (1746–8) that commemorates the completion of the aqueduct. Inserted in the structure of the aqueduct, it is a splendid celebration of royal power employed for the benefit of the people. The impressive arch is framed with Tuscan pilasters supporting a triangular pediment crowned with one of the aqueduct 'ventilators' in the form of a little classical aedicule, a feature that Mardel favoured. The design of the Mãe de Água, where the water flows in a cascade into an enormous basin, is equally distinctive; a large rectangular space is covered with cross vaults at the same height throughout, and it is one of the finest pieces of functional contemporary architecture.

Connected with this project are the designs for fountains made by Mardel (drawings; all Lisbon, Mus. Cidade). Those that were actually built include the carefully sited Chafariz do Rato (1753), which is composed in two stages, at street level for animals and with lateral steps leading to an upper basin for human use, all set in a finely moulded frame and surmounted by a pediment with pinnacles on each side. The more monumental Chafariz da Esperança (1756–8) is also constructed in two sections on different levels, a type that Mardel seems to have invented, but the effects on the back panel are more scenographic and the decoration more elaborate, with flat pilasters and Rococo ornament.

Mardel's designs for fountains (all *c.* 1752) in various parts of Lisbon that were never built include that of S Catarina, similar in composition to the Esperança but more monumental; that of S Pedro de Alcântara, in the form of an octagonal high tower crowned by a bulbous Rococo dome; and the alternative designs for the fountain-monument to John V, which show elements of French and Austrian influences.

In 1747 Mardel was appointed architect to the royal palaces, the Monastery of Batalha and the region of the Alentejo in succession to Custódio José Vieira. In 1749 he became Architect to the Military Orders and of the Lisbon fortifications, becoming an Engineer Colonel in 1751. After the earthquake in 1755, he was principal assistant to Eugénio dos Santos in drawing up the alternative plans for the reconstruction of Lisbon, and at the death of dos Santos in 1760 Mardel was put in charge of completing the whole project; this involved making changes where needed in the existing plans. His overall part is more in terms of the architectural forms than of the scheme of urban planning, but he was responsible for the unrealized programme for the western area of the city (Lisbon, Mus.

Carlos Mardel (attrib.): north façade of the palace of the Marquês de Pombal, Oeiras, 1737–40

Cidade). His main contribution was the detailed plan (Lisbon, Mus. Cidade) for the Rossio of Dom Pedro IV (*c.* 1756). He designed the homogeneous elevations that were intended to unify the whole square and which included on equal terms the hospital, the Dominican convent and the Paço dos Estãos. Mardel followed the general lines imposed by EUGÉNIO DOS SANTOS for the whole district of the Baixa. He also introduced a specific rhythm to the design, achieved through his effective articulation of each of the sections that were divided by pilasters and that have alternating bay and flat windows. Throughout he used double hipped roofs, a design from central Europe and a feature he introduced to Portugal. The Rossio scheme was altered by Reinaldo Manuel dos Santos after 1763; this is apparent at the ends of the square, but the essential elements of Mardel's programme were constructed, and the discreet elegance of its design was an important contribution to the Lisbon recreated under the 1st Marquês de Pombal, Sebastião José de Carvalho e Melo.

The Palácio Aranha, designed by Mardel (1734–43 and 1756), was built in the Junqueira as a country house by the River Tagus for Lázaro Leitão Aranha, a new type of patron and a canon and principal of the Patriarchate from 1718 until his death in 1767. The extended façade of one storey, with the chapel at one end, is in the tradition of the Portuguese country house, but the design also offers innovative solutions. The composition is in five sections; the main entrance is not central but set in one of the towers flanking the house, which frame the central section with their high double hipped roofs.

In the design for the palace for the Marquês de Pombal at Oeiras (see fig.), now the property of the Fundação Calouste Gulbenkian, which has been attributed to Mardel on the basis of style, he used a French scheme of the early 17th century in the composition of the principal north façade consisting of a central block with a triangular pediment preceded by an enclosed courtyard. The façade has turrets surmounted by double hipped roofs at the corners, one of which contains the chapel.

Mardel designed the church of St John of Nepomuk, Lisbon (destr.). He was involved in restoration work at S Clara-a-Nova, Coimbra (design by João Turriano), where he built the portal (1761), and where the design of the large cloister (*c.* 1750–55) has been attributed to him. There his own distinctive style is combined with architectural forms represented in Coimbra by the small cloister of the Colégio da Sapiência. In 1752 he made the plans for the Colégio de S Paulo, Coimbra, which was ultimately built after 1755 to the design of Mateus Vicente de Oliveira. Mardel was also commissioned to remodel the Noviciado da Cotovia in the Colégio dos Nobres, Lisbon, which was in turn remodelled later as the 19th-century polytechnic school, in Neo-classical style.

BIBLIOGRAPHY
F. Têles de Menezes e Vasconcelos: *Carlos Mardel: Elementos para a história da arquitectura portuguesa do século XVIII* (diss., U. Lisbon, 1955)
H. Wohl: 'Carlos Mardel and his Lisbon Architecture', *Apollo*, xcvii (1973), pp. 350–59
J.-A. França: *Lisboa pombalina e o iluminismo* (Lisbon, 1977)
J. E. Horta Correia: *Vila Real de Santo António: Urbanismo e poder na política pombalina* (diss., U. Lisbon, 1984)

JOSÉ EDUARDO HORTA CORREIA

Marden, Brice (*b* Bronxville, NY, 15 Oct 1938). American painter and printmaker. He studied at Boston University School of Fine and Applied Arts, receiving his BFA in 1961, and from 1961 to 1963 at Yale University School of Art and Architecture in New Haven, CT. Settling in New York in 1963, in the following year he produced his first single-panel monochromatic paintings, such as *Decorative Painting* (1964; priv. col., see 1975 exh. cat., pl. 1), through which he contributed to the emerging aesthetic of MINIMALISM. In such works he reacted against the dominance of gestural techniques in second generation Abstract Expressionism by emphasizing the subtlety of surface and colour within the spatial and structural limits of the rectangle. Bringing together the painterly quality of Abstract Expressionism with the intellectual rigours of Minimalism, Marden achieved a balance between emotional intensity and formal simplicity.

In his early paintings Marden left a bare narrow margin at the bottom edge of the thickly worked surface of oil mixed with wax to allow the observer to be witness to the process. In later works such as *Winter Painting* (3 panels, 1.83×3.05 m overall, 1973–5; Amsterdam, Stedel. Mus.) he developed subtle colour combinations by joining together panels of a single colour in either vertical or horizontal formats. From 1975, when he began making annual visits to Greece, he took inspiration from the light and colour of its landscape and also made reference to mythology in his choice of titles, as in *Thira* (16 panels, 2.44×4.57 m overall, 1979–80; Paris, Pompidou). After preparing designs for stained-glass windows for Basle Cathedral in 1977, a commission that occupied him until 1985, he became interested in expressing in his paintings the conditions of colour and light in architecture. He also began to allude to traditional themes, for example in *Humilatio* (1978; Cologne, Mus. Ludwig), one of a series of five paintings, each on four panels, expressing different spiritual or emotional states—disquiet, reflection, inquiry, submission and merit—through colour and form.

After producing a series of 25 etchings, *Etchings to Rexroth* (1985–7), in which he made reference to Chinese ideograms, he introduced a network of meandering lines into his paintings. These works (see 1988 exh. cat.), for which monochrome panels now acted as background colour fields, provided a dramatic departure from his previous style, but they continued to stress the importance of touch, surface, colour and tone.

WRITINGS
'Three Deliberate Grays for Jasper Johns', *A. Now*, iii/1 (1971)
BIBLIOGRAPHY
L. R. Lippard: 'The Silent Art', *A. America*, lv/1 (1967), pp. 58–63
Brice Marden's Drawings, 1963–1973 (exh. cat. by D. Ashton, Houston, 1974)
Brice Marden (exh. cat. by L. Shearer, New York, Guggenheim, 1975)
R. White: 'Interview', *View* [Oakland], iii/2 (1980) [interview with artist]
Brice Marden (exh. cat. by R. Smith and S. Bann, London, Whitechapel A.G.; Amsterdam, Stedel. Mus.; 1981)
Brice Marden: Recent Paintings & Drawings (exh. cat., essay J. Yau, London, Anthony d'Offay Gal., 1988)

PAULINE I. A. BULLARD

Mardersteig, Hans [Giovanni] (*b* Weimar, 8 Jan 1892; *d* Verona, 27 Dec 1977). German typographer and printer, active in Italy. In 1917 he was curator of the modern section of the major German 19th- and 20th-century art exhibition in Zurich and was employed by the publishing house of Kurt Wolff (1887–1963), where he edited the modern art and literary review *Genius*, before taking over book production. Wolff moved to Munich (1919), and Mardersteig set up his own press (1922), using type from the remains of Giambattista Bodoni's printing works, a hand press and specially commissioned paper. Early works from his Officina Bodoni, at Montagnola di Lugano, were simply produced and without illustrations; from 1936 illustrated books were printed. Mardersteig had a deep knowledge of and passion for early types and printing and reprinted early treatises on letter forms. The Officina specialized in the reconstruction of rare alphabets from books and from 1926 used those of John Baskerville, Pietro Bembo, Adobe Garamond and Nicolas Jenson, as well as types specially cut for the press, notably Zeno, Griffo and Dante. In 1927 the Officina moved to Verona, having won the commission to produce a state edition of the complete works of Gabriele D'Annunzio; all 49 volumes were completed by 1936. In 1935 Mardersteig acted as consultant to the Collins Cleartype Press in Glasgow and developed a new type for them called Fontana. After World War II Mardersteig set up a mech-anized press, the Stamperia Valdonga, which set a high standard for Italian book-printing and produced high-quality projects, such as Ricciardi's Italian classics series. The Officina continued to flourish, producing *c.* 100 more books. In 1962 Mardersteig was awarded the gold medal for Benemeriti della Cultura.

WRITINGS

H. Schmoller, ed.: *Die Officina Bodoni. Das Werk einer Handpress, 1923–1977* (Verona, 1979; Eng. trans., Verona, 1980)

BIBLIOGRAPHY

Giovanni Mardersteig, stampatore, editore, umanista (exh. cat., Verona, Castelvecchio, 1989)

H. Schmoller: *Two Titans* (New York, 1990)

LAURA SUFFIELD

Mardi Gras. *See under* CARNIVAL.

Mardikh, Tell. *See* EBLA.

Mare, John (*b* New York, 1739; *d* Edenton, NC, after June 1802–before April 1803). American painter. Little is known of his artistic training, although his portraits have the same terse and stiff qualities associated with the painter Thomas McIlworth. After 1759 Mare is recorded in Albany, NY. His earliest surviving portrait is that of *Henry Livingston* (priv. col.), signed and dated 1760. In 1766 he was commissioned by the Common Council of New York to execute a portrait of *George III* (destr.). His two most engaging portraits are those of *Jeremiah Platt* (New York, Met.) and *John Keteltas* (New York, NY Hist. Soc.), both painted in 1767. His best work can be distinguished by his devotion to details: the lovingly rendered Chippendale chair in *Jeremiah Platt* or the *trompe l'oeil* house-fly poised on John Keteltas's wristband. Fewer than a dozen portraits by Mare survive. Lack of success may have contributed to his departure for Albany once again in 1772. He painted his last surviving portrait, *Dr Benjamin Youngs Prime* (New York, NY Hist. Soc.), in New York in 1782 and within four years had moved to Edenton, NC, where he abandoned painting for business.

BIBLIOGRAPHY

H. B. Smith: 'John Mare (1739–c. 1795), New York Portrait Painter, with Note on the Two William Williams', *NY Hist. Soc. Q.*, xxxv (1951), pp. 355–99

H. B. Smith and E. V. Morris: 'John Mare: A Composite Portrait', *NC Hist. Rev.*, xliv (1967), pp. 18–52

H. B. Smith: 'A Portrait by John Mare Identified: "Uncle Jeremiah"', *Antiques*, ciii (1973), pp. 1185–7

RICHARD H. SAUNDERS

Marées, Hans (Reinhard) von (*b* Elberfeld, 24 Dec 1837; *d* Rome, 5 July 1887). German painter, draughtsman and sculptor. Marées was a leading representative of the later 19th-century return to Renaissance models, especially the use of figure painting in large-scale decorative schemes.

1. TRAINING, EARLY WORK AND TRAVELS, TO 1870. He studied in Berlin (1853–5), first at the Akademie and then in the studio of the equestrian painter Carl Steffeck. The historical and military scenes of Adolph Menzel were also an important influence. Apart from a few portraits and a number of small landscapes, Marées concentrated mainly on equestrian and military pictures in the Berlin tradition. He continued to paint pictures of this kind even after moving, in 1857, to Munich, where he remained until 1864: for example *Ulans on the March* (1859; Munich, Neue Pin.). In the early 1860s a marked Dutch influence, particularly that of Rembrandt, became apparent in Ma-rées's work, and it is possible that he visited the Nether-lands during this period. The self-portraits, such as that of 1862 (Munich, Neue Pin.), are notable for strong chiaro-scuro effects and an unmistakable psychological intensity. Marées also revealed a penchant for self-dramatization, which he shared with the young Rembrandt. In the *Double Portrait of Marées and Lenbach* (1863; Munich, Neue Pin.) he recorded the close but troubled relationship between the two artists. In the summer of 1863 Marées was commissioned to design several decorative panels with mythological scenes for the St Petersburg house of the banker and collector Baron A. Stieglitz. While working on these, Marées also produced a separate painting, *Diana Resting* (1863; Munich, Neue Pin.). The direction Marées's work was now to take is seen in his use of rich colour glowing in the dark of the forest clearing of this scene, which is suggestive of the influence of Venetian painting, especially the work of Titian. Such features are also found in the otherwise more Dutch-influenced painting the *Watering Place* (1864; Munich, Schack-Gal.).

In 1864 Adolph Friedrich Graf von Schack commis-sioned both Lenbach and Marées to go to Italy, primarily to make copies of Old Master paintings for him. Over the next two years Marées painted four copies from paintings by Palma Vecchio, Titian, Velázquez and Raphael (copies now all Munich, Schack-Gal.). These, however, were not so much painstaking reproductions of the originals as evidence of an independent exploration of the subjects. This approach encouraged even greater receptivity to the composition, colouring and subject-matter of Old Master paintings, qualities reflected in Marées's original compo-sitions. *Roman Landscape I* (1868; Munich, Neue Pin.) is reminiscent of scenes of figures in imaginary idyllic settings by Giorgione and Titian. In 1868 Schack, disappointed with Marées's copies, withdrew his financial support, but from 1869 Marées was able to rely on Konrad Fiedler, whom he had met in Italy three years earlier. With Fiedler, Marées travelled in 1869 to Spain, France and the Netherlands. This reinforced the influence of Old Master painting (especially the work of Rubens), but it also brought Marées's attention again to French painting, especially that of Delacroix. The latter's influence is to be found in the work Marées did on his return to Germany: for example in the glowing red cloak and dramatic shadows in the landscape background of *St Martin and the Beggar* (1870; Winterthur, Stift. Oskar Reinhart).

2. BERLIN AND ITALY, 1870 AND AFTER. In 1870 Marées rented a studio in Berlin to share with the sculptor Adolf von Hildebrand, whom he had met in Italy in 1867 and who now became Marées's pupil. The influence of Old Master paintings on Marées's work persisted, as seen in the *Portrait of My Brother, Georg von Marées* (1871; Munich, Neue Pin.), whose appearance recalls that of Venetian nobles. In 1873, Marées was commissioned by the zoologist Anton Dohrn to decorate the newly established Stazione Zoologica in Naples. Marées collaborated in the project with Hildebrand, who designed and painted the *trompe l'oeil* architectural decoration, while Marées contributed five large scenes, showing the life of the fishermen in the Bay of Naples (the *Fishermen Set Off*, the *Fishing Boat*), groups of male and female figures in the orange groves of Sorrento, and the artist friends seated beneath a trellis (*Pergola*) (all 1873; *in situ*). Marées also produced a number of oil paintings as studies for these frescoes, such as *Oarsmen* (1873; Berlin, Neue N.G.). While incorporating elements seen in Marées's earlier work, such as portraiture and the use of idyllic settings, the Naples frescoes as a whole point to the work Marées was to produce during the later years of his career, above all in the orange grove scene with male figures of distinct ages, and the depiction of a nude male shown reaching up to pick the ripe fruit from the tree. Such scenes were intended by Marées to serve as exemplary images of human life conducted in a world of perfect economic, social and emotional relations, and a deeply earnest tone is detectable in them all. After completing the frescoes, Marées spent two years with Hildebrand in Florence, where he painted five rather sombre self-portraits. He also pursued the idyllic theme of some of the Naples frescoes in works such as *Three Youths under Orange Trees* (1875–80; Munich, Neue Pin.; see fig.). The physical beauty of the figures and the almost programmatic distribution of poses invite a largely formal perception of the scene.

An interest in the figure in largely formal terms may also reflect Marées's role as teacher to a series of sculptors, starting in 1876 with A. J. W. Volkmann and continuing with Peter Bruckmann (*fl* 1850–91) and Louis Tuaillon. In the early 1880s Marées tried his own hand at sculptural work; in 1882 he produced a clay model of a figure of *Nestor* (destr.), which he planned to execute in marble. For his pupils he frequently sketched sculptural projects, for example the design for Volkmann's *Amazon Watering her Horse* (1886; priv. col., see 1987 exh. cat., pl. 111). Sculptural interests are also seen in the provision of

Hans von Marées: *Three Youths under Orange Trees*, oil on panel, 1.87×1.45 m, 1875–80 (Munich, Neue Pinakothek)

elaborate *trompe l'oeil* bases and frames for several of Marées's large-scale late works, substantially preserved only in the case of the second version of the triptych *The Hesperides* (1884–7; Munich, Neue Pin.; usually assumed to be close in design to the first version of 1879, destr.). With this work and the three other triptychs of his last years, Marées appears to have been striving for a form of *Gesamtkunstwerk*: a complete pictorial, decorative and architectural entity distinct from the individual work of painting or sculpture as traditionally produced by the artist and consumed by his public. While both the pale, life-size nude male and female figures of the three scenes and the deep red of the background of the base are in themselves solemnly imposing elements, Marées's overall conception also allows for elements of gentle humour, such as the dog shown lying under the central *trompe l'oeil* wall fountain, which appears to look up as if just woken by the spectator. Out of the *Hesperides* compositions, Marées subsequently developed two very different versions of the *Golden Age* (1879–80 and 1880–83; both Munich, Neue Pin.). In the first, attention is focused on the figure of a young boy, who is marked out by his enquiring air. The second version presents a more complex interaction of adult figures, with the central male figure in the background a self-portrait of the artist, removed beyond the majority of his fellow men and women with their unthinking pursuits of needs and pleasures. The experiments in technique Marées often made while working on such large-scale paintings led to extensive reworking, and the condition of many deteriorated rapidly.

During his last years Marées returned to Christian themes with two versions of a triptych: the *Three Knights* (1881, left and middle panels destr., right panel, Berlin, Neue N.G., 1885–7, all three canvases, Munich, Neue Pin.). Once again, an elaborate *trompe l'oeil* setting was initially planned, as shown in a chalk and pencil sketch from 1885 (Berlin, Alte N.G.). While the three sections are of equal shape and size, they show enormous range in both colour and composition: at the left *St Martin and the Beggar* in a bleak winter landscape is a scene of sombre tones and subdued mood; at the centre *St Hubert Kneeling before the Stag* is shown in a picturesque wooded setting, against a softly gleaming sky; at the right the boldly coloured figure of *St George Slaying the Dragon* is both violent and grandiose.

In 1883, Marées painted his last *Self-portrait* (Munich, Neue Pin.) of a total of 15. In the final picture there is a sense of apprehension but also a feeling of dignity prompted by the artist's pride in his calling. The total of 800 drawings left by Marées constitutes a large part of his oeuvre, but Marées himself saw these largely as no more than preparations for finished work.

WRITINGS
A.-S. Domm, ed.: *Briefe* (Munich, 1987)

BIBLIOGRAPHY
K. Fiedler: *Bilder und Zeichnungen von Hans von Marées* (Munich, 1889)
H. Wölfflin: 'Hans von Marées', *Z. Bild. Kst*, iii (1892), pp. 73–9
J. Meier-Graefe: *Hans von Marées: Sein Leben und Werk*, 3 vols (Munich and Leipzig, 1909–10)
A. Neumeyer: 'Hans von Marées and the Classical Doctrine in the Nineteenth Century', *A. Bull.*, xx (1938), pp. 291–311
B. Degenhart: *Marées Zeichnungen* (Berlin, 1953)
——: *Hans von Marées: Die Fresken in Neapel* (Munich, 1958)
L. D. Ettlinger: 'Hans von Marées and the Academic Tradition', *Yale U. A. Bull.*, xxxiii/3 (1972), pp. 67–84
G. Schiff: 'Hans von Marées and his Place in Modern Painting', *Yale U. A. Bull.*, xxxiii/3 (1972), pp. 85–102
U. Gerlach-Laxner: *Hans von Marées: Katalog seiner Gemälde* (Munich, 1980)
Hans von Marées: Zeichnungen (exh. cat., Wuppertal, Von der Heydt-Mus., 1987)
Hans von Marées (exh. cat., ed. C. Lenz; Munich, Neue Pin. and Schack-Gal., 1987–8) [with critical essays and complete bibliography]
Hans von Marées und die Moderne in Deutschland (exh. cat., Bielefeld, Städt. Ksthalle; Winterthur, Kstmus.; 1987–8)

CHRISTIAN LENZ

Marell [Marrel; Marrellus; Marzell; Morrel; Morsel], **Jakob** (*b* Frankenthal, 1613/14; *d* Frankfurt am Main, *bur* 11 Nov 1681). German painter, active also in the northern Netherlands. He was the grandson of a French goldsmith, Claude Marrel, who had settled in Frankfurt am Main in the 16th century, and the only notable pupil of the Frankfurt still-life artist Georg Flegel. Jakob's earliest known paintings date from 1634. One is from Utrecht, where Marell stayed until 1651, not only painting but also dealing in art and flower-bulbs. In 1651 he settled permanently in Frankfurt, where he married the widow of Matthäus Merian I and continued dealing in art. In 1661 his *Artliches und Kunstreiches Reissbuchlein für die ankommende Jugend zu lehren Insonderheit für Mahler, Goldschmied und Bithauern* was published. Remaining in contact with the Netherlands, he returned to Utrecht occasionally from 1664.

Marell's strength lay in naturalistic portrayal of flowers and animals in still-lifes. His flower arrangements were usually seasonally accurate: for instance the *Cartouche with Flower Decoration and Imaginary Architecture* (*c.* 1650; Darmstadt, Hess. Landesmus.) has only spring flowers. The cartouche contains a view of the Roman Capitol with plants from southern Europe: the device of a garland with an empty centre was possibly derived from Daniel Seghers. The central axis of the flower arrangements is generally emphasized by a lily or tulip, with the irregular lush bunches set against smooth vases. Marell was clearly influenced by Ambrosius Bosschaert (i), Roelandt Savery and Jan de Heem I.

BIBLIOGRAPHY
G. Bott: 'Stilleben des 17. Jahrhunderts: Jakob Marell', *Kst Hessen & Mittelrhein* (1966), pp. 85–117
P. Mitchell: *European Flower Painters* (Schiedam, 1981), pp. 166–7

A. GERHARDT

Marescalco, il. *See* BUONCONSIGLIO, GIOVANNI.

Marey, Etienne-Jules (*b* Beaune, 5 March 1830; *d* Paris, 16 May 1904). French photographer. His photographic research was primarily a tool for his work on human and animal movement. A doctor and physiologist, Marey invented, in 1888, a method of producing a series of successive images of a moving body on the same negative in order to be able to study its exact position in space at determined moments, which he called 'chronophotographie'. He took out numerous patents and made many inventions in the field of photography, all of them concerned with his interest in capturing instants of movement. In 1882 he invented the electric photographic gun using 35 mm film, the film itself being 20 m long; this photographic gun was capable of producing 12 images per second on a turning plate, at 1/720 of a second. He began to use transparent film rather than sensitized paper in 1890 and patented a camera using roll film, working also on a film projector in 1893. He also did research into stereoscopic images. Marey's chronophotographic studies of moving subjects were made against a black background for added precision and clarity. These studies cover human locomotion—walking, running and jumping (e.g. *Successive Phases of Movement of a Running Man*, 1882; see Berger and Levrault, cat. no. 95); the movement of animals—dogs, horses, cats, lizards, etc.; and the flight of birds—pelicans, herons, ducks etc. He also photographed the trajectories of objects—stones, sticks and balls—as well as liquid movement and the functioning of the heart. He had exhibitions in Paris in 1889, 1892 and 1894, and in Florence in 1887.

PHOTOGRAPHIC PUBLICATIONS
Le Vol des oiseaux (Paris, 1890)
Le Mouvement (Paris, 1894)

BIBLIOGRAPHY
R. Lecuyer: *Histoire de la photographie* (Paris, 1945), pp. 176–80
E.-J. Marey, 1830–1904: La Photographie du mouvement (exh. cat., Paris, Pompidou, 1977)
Regards sur la photographie en France au XIXe siècle, Berger–Levrault (Paris, 1980)

PATRICIA STRATHERN

Márffy, Ödön (*b* Budapest, 30 Nov 1878; *d* Budapest, 3 Dec 1959). Hungarian painter. He studied in Paris at the Académie Julian and the Ecole des Beaux-Arts between

1902 and 1904. In 1906 he exhibited at the Salon d'Automne. He was influenced by Fauvism and especially by Matisse. In 1907 he returned to Hungary, where he became a member of THE EIGHT (iii) and exhibited with them from 1909 until they disbanded in 1912. During this period his paintings emphasize the structural components of the composition. In certain pictures, for example the *Old Customs at Vác* (*c.* 1910; Budapest, N.G.), thick contours delimit balanced forms; in others (e.g. *Constructivist Self-portrait*, *c.* 1914; Budapest, N.G.), the same contours become lines of force dividing the composition into turbulent surfaces. The early paintings *Forest Path* and *Green Room* (both 1910; Budapest, N.G.) show the influence of both Cézanne and van Gogh, respectively. From 1919 Márffy responded to Post-Impressionism and the Ecole de Paris, developing his own style only in the 1930s, when he abandoned painting from direct observation. He used sensuous opal colours that blur the content, but he retained a strict compositional formula, as in *Zdenka Lying*, *Woman with a Lacy Shawl* and *Rowers* (all 1930s; Budapest, N.G.). Márffy became one of the leading figures in the artistic life of Hungary between the World Wars. From 1927 to 1938 he acted as president of the New Society of Fine Artists (KÚT). He exhibited often, in New York and Washington in 1928 and finally at the Ernst Museum, Budapest, in 1958.

BIBLIOGRAPHY
A. Kárpáti: 'Márffy Ödön művészete' [The art of Ödön Márffy], *Literatura*, iv (1929), pp. 356–60
L. Zolnay: *Márffy Ödön* (Budapest, 1966)
K. Passuth: *Márffy Ödön* (Budapest, 1978)

MÁRIA SZOBOR-BERNÁTH

Margall, Francisco Pi i. *See* PI I MARGALL, FRANCISCO.

Margaret, Queen of Spain. *See* HABSBURG, §II(6).

Margaret of Austria. *See* HABSBURG, §II(6).

Margaret of Austria, Duchess of Savoy. *See* HABSBURG, §I(4).

Margaret of Burgundy. *See under* BURGUNDY, (5).

Margaret of Parma. *See* HABSBURG, §II(4).

Margarito d'Arezzo [Margaritone] (*fl c.* 1250–90). Italian painter. The only documentary record of Margarito dates from 1262, when he was living in Arezzo. The nature and distribution of his surviving works suggest a thriving practice and a steady demand for his skills throughout Tuscany. Margarito's fame outside Italy rests partly on Vasari's account, partly on his easy identifiability among a host of anonymous contemporaries (most of his paintings are signed) and partly on the role imposed on him by 19th-century critics as an epitome of that barbarism into which Italian painting was deemed to have fallen by the late 13th century. Margarito seems to stand rather outside the main line of painting in Tuscany and has at times been dismissed as reactionary or provincial. Establishing a chronology for his work in the absence of any surviving dates is problematic.

The earliest of Margarito's signed panels may be the *Virgin and Child* in S Maria, Montelungo (Arezzo), on which a (possibly unreliable) date of 1250 was recorded in the 18th century. This is stylistically close to two other panels, an upright *Virgin and Child Enthroned with Four Saints* (Washington, DC, N.G.A.; see fig.) and a dossal with the *Virgin and Child, Angels, Saints and Scenes from the Lives of SS John the Evangelist, Benedict, Catherine and Margaret*, from S Margherita, Arezzo (London, N.G.). The exceptional degree to which the Virgin's head extends beyond the main rectangle of the Washington panel distinctly recalls the design of the Bigallo Master's panels; Margarito may have trained in Florence, possibly in the circle of the Bigallo Master. The painting style, however, is clearly different, and formative contact with the art of the Middle East has also been suggested (Longhi). The Washington panel illustrates most of the fundamental

Margarito d'Arezzo: *Virgin and Child Enthroned with Four Saints*, tempera on panel, 970×495 mm, *c.* 1265–75 (Washington, DC, National Gallery of Art)

characteristics of Margarito's art. The keynote, far more than with his immediate predecessors or successors, is symmetry. The Virgin's knees are level with each other, and, although the lateral position of her left foot makes some concession to the already established tradition of displacing and raising one of the legs, there is no corresponding sense of the structure of the lower body beneath the drapery. The alignment of her right foot down the clearly marked central axis of the panel, with the hem of her skirt falling into symmetrical folds on either side, reinforces the essentially flat design, as does the non-spatial presentation of the throne. The central section of the London dossal, where the Virgin is seated on the Throne of Solomon and enclosed within a mandorla of exquisite delicacy, emphasizes the predominantly two-dimensional and decorative nature of Margarito's style. Even if Margarito had begun his career as early as 1250, the type of Byzantine crown worn by the Virgin on the Washington and London panels is old-fashioned.

Most of Margarito's extant work consists of full-length images of *St Francis*. At least eight survive. They are of great importance in the development of a more humane and eloquent iconography for the Saint. Three, of virtually identical design (Siena, Pin. N.; Zurich, Ksthaus; Ganghereto, S Francesco), recall the small figure (probably of St Benedict) flanking the Washington *Virgin and Child* and may be dated to the same period (*c*. 1265–75). Heads and hands are very large, and the displaced left foot still gives no real sense of the implied stance. These images, however, are more approachable than earlier versions by Berlinghieri and others, and the Saint's eye-contact with the spectator is much more a matter of establishing a dialogue than of imposing authority. In two more examples in Rome (Pin. Vaticana; S Francesco a Ripa) Margarito adopted more elongated proportions, with smaller heads. Modelling is more pronounced and drapery patterns more complex. In the Vatican panel the Saint's head tilts quizzically to one side, and in the S Francesco version his weight is now decisively and visibly on one leg, and the corresponding sway of the other much more marked. Yet another version (Arezzo, Gal. & Mus. Med. & Mod.) has the boss of the knee pushing forcefully through the drapery.

If this sequence of Margarito's work is correct it shows a response to naturalistic developments that his early work had seemed to bypass. The work of his major contemporaries may have affected him. The figure of Christ on a dossal of the *Virgin and Child with New Testament Scenes* (*c*. 1285; Monte S Savino, S Maria delle Vertighe) is reminiscent of the equivalent in Coppo di Marcovaldo's *Virgin* (*c*. 1270; Orvieto, S Maria dei Servi), and the fuller and more continuous modelling of the Virgin's face, still marked with intense blobs of red on the cheeks, may reflect the same kind of influence, although the essential amiability, the symmetrical design and the decorative play of line remain unaffected by the drama of Coppo's style.

BIBLIOGRAPHY

G. Vasari: *Vite* (1550, rev. 2/1568); ed. G. Milanesi (1878–85), i, p. 593 [as Margaritone]
L. Dami: 'Opere ignote di Margarito di Arezzo e lo sviluppo del suo stile', *Dedalo* (1925), pp. 537–49
E. Sandberg Vavalà: *La croce dipinta italiana e l'iconografia della passione* (Verona, 1929/*R* Rome, 1980), pp. 641–6
R. Longhi: 'Giudizio sul duecento' [1939], *Proporzioni*, ii (1948), pp. 5–54; also in *Opere complete di Roberto Longhi*, vii (Florence, 1974), pp. 1–18
A. del Vita: 'La Madonna delle Vertighe di Margarito d'Arezzo', *Arti: Rass. Bimest. A. Ant. & Mod.*, v (1942–3), p. 199
E. B. Garrison: *Italian Romanesque Panel Painting: An Illustrated Index* (Florence, 1949), pp. 22–3; nos 51, 54–8, 60, 226, 237, 358, 365
F. R. Shapley: *Paintings from the Samuel H. Kress Collection*, i (London, 1967), p. 3
B. Berenson: *Central and North Italian Schools*, i (1968), pp. 244–5
A. M. Maetzke: 'Nuove ricerche su Margarito d'Arezzo', *Boll. A.*, lvii (1973), pp. 95–112
E. Castelnuovo, ed.: *La pittura in Italia: Il duecento e il trecento* (Milan, 1986), pp. 634–6

JOHN RICHARDS

Marhia. *See* DEORI KALAN.

Mari [now Tell Hariri]. Capital of an important kingdom of the 3rd millennium BC and the early 2nd, situated in Syria on the River Euphrates. A sequence of palaces culminated in that of King Zimri-Lim in the first half of the 18th century BC, which incorporated earlier structures and was decorated with wall paintings. An archive found in this palace has helped to establish a close chronology and has illuminated this whole period of history. Sculpture was excavated in all levels but was particularly rich in the mid-3rd-millennium BC temples. Mosaic panels have also survived.

Mari was established 120 km south of the confluence of the Euphrates with the River Khabur and 15 km north of the present-day frontier dividing Syria and Iraq. The Euphrates is the main link between Mesopotamia and Anatolia and crosses the north Syrian route to the Levant and eastern Mediterranean. This meant that Mari was well placed to control trade. The city's ruins cover an area 1400 m square, on the middle terrace of the river valley *c*. 2.5 km west of the river's current course. The city was protected in this way from normal annual floods, and a circular *levée* was constructed against exceptional flooding. A canal from the Euphrates provided both a water supply and access to the river trade that guaranteed the city's wealth.

1. DISCOVERY AND EXCAVATION. Tell Hariri is some way off the route along the edge of the western plateau and did not attract the attention of early 20th-century travellers until the accidental discovery by some bedouin of a statue drew archaeologists to the site. An expedition led by A. Parrot identified the site as Mari, following the discovery in the Temple of Ishtar of a statue inscribed with the name of Lamgi-Mari, King of Mari. Parrot worked at the site for 20 seasons between 1933 and 1972. Since 1979 the excavations have been directed by Margueron. Material from Mari is in the Musée du Louvre, Paris, the Damascus National Museum, the Aleppo National Museum and the Dayr al-Zawr Museum, Syria.

2. HISTORY. The main tell's present asymmetry is explained by its partial erosion. The city was originally circular and at the time of its foundation would have had an intramural diameter of almost 2 km. It must have been founded at the beginning of the Early Dynastic period, in the early 3rd millennium BC, when the whole region was being developed with large-scale irrigation and navigable canals.

The city had a relatively short life, for it was destroyed *c.* 1760 BC and in 1758 BC by Hammurabi, King of Babylon, upsetting the balance of power on which Mari's existence depended. Nothing is known of the first centuries of the city's existence, beyond its general layout and its large initial size. Major changes were made during the Early Dynastic III period, including the installation of drainage networks and the extension of the palace. It seems that Mari continued to prosper into the Akkadian period. Some of the official monuments were then destroyed, which should perhaps be interpreted as evidence of unrest. After this began a long period when Mari was ruled by the Shakkanakku (governors); the construction of numerous buildings indicates the city's importance. There is little information about Mari at the beginning of the 2nd millennium BC, and its final half-century (1810–1760 BC) is the period about which most is known, not only concerning the city, but on the Near East as a whole, owing to the exceptional find of cuneiform texts in the Old Babylonian palace. During this period the city was dominated in turn by Yahdun-Lim, Shamshi-Adad I of Assur and Zimri-Lim.

3. PLANNING AND ARCHITECTURE. Excavation has made it possible to deduce something of the city's organization, though it is more difficult to form an idea of its evolution. A permanent feature was its concentric plan, with roads radiating from the city centre. Roads also ran down into the southern half of the city, with transverse streets intersecting at an angle and dividing up the different quarters. The great royal palace, the Temple aux Lions, and its high terrace, the Massif Rouge, and the palace of the Shakkanakku lie in the city centre. None of the residential districts has been studied, apart from the 'pre-Sargonic' (Early Dynastic) district, to the east of the

Temple of Ishtar, which was apparently a commercial neighbourhood.

Mari's architecture has some original features that are only rarely mixed with those of Mesopotamia or Syria. In the Early Dynastic period buildings were often arranged round a central space. This was particularly true of domestic architecture but is sometimes also seen in sacred architecture as in the temples of Ishtar, Ishtarat and Ninni-Zaza. There was also a type of sanctuary with a more compact design (as in the Temple of Ninhursag and the Massif Rouge), which may be related to the tower-shaped sanctuaries of Syria known from terracotta models (*see* MASKANA). The 'pre-Sargonic' palace dates from this period. It is so far unique, not only because of its excellent state of preservation but also because of its design and the length of time it was in use. Indeed, there are four levels, several of which have at least 2 m of deposit. Its Sacred Enclosure retained the same basic plan throughout the sanctuary's history, and the extent of its outbuildings (most of which have not been excavated) is without parallel. Another unique building belongs to the Akkadian period, marked by the beginning of rule by the Shakkanakku; a large hall some 16 m square is divided into three aisles by great pillars of unbaked brick. This hall may have been the throne-room of a palace. The period of the Shakkanakku is the best known architecturally because many of its buildings continued in use until the destruction of the city. The design of the Temple aux Lions is closely related to that of the elongated temples common in Syria since the beginning of the Bronze Age. Sanctuaries are often associated with a high terrace, a combination again found in Syrian temples. Little is known of domestic architecture, but the palace of the Shakkanakku and the great Palace of the Rulers—also called the Palace of Zimri-Lim (see fig. 1)—a large part of which dates from this period, are clear examples of the official architecture of

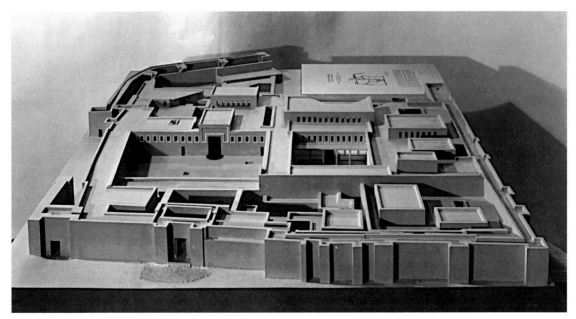

1. Mari, Palace of the Rulers (Palace of Zimri-Lim), 2nd millennium BC; reconstruction

Mesopotamia. Beneath apparent anarchy this architecture is strictly ordered, with well-controlled internal organization and a division into specialized units. The official complex in the Palace of Zimri-Lim must have been splendid, with its Palm Court decorated with large wall paintings and its monumental throne-room.

4. SCULPTURE, PAINTING AND OTHER ARTS. Although Mari is rich in architecture, it is even richer in other art forms. When excavated, the temples and palaces contained a large quantity of remarkable objects, despite pillage and abandonment. Mari seems to have been an exceptional centre, always enjoying a connection with Syria or Mesopotamia and yet developing an originality that has not always been appreciated.

2. Mari, 'goddess with the flowing vase', white stone, h. 1.4 m, from the Temple aux Lions, 18th century BC (Aleppo, National Museum of Aleppo)

Statuary at Mari is outstanding, although here again Mesopotamian influence is clear. Details of costume and headdress are always carefully rendered. The Early Dynastic III period is by far the best represented. Some pieces are stereotyped, for instance the squat statue of *King Lamgi-Mari* (Aleppo, N. Mus.), which nevertheless has an unusual power of expression. In another sculpture (Paris, Louvre) *Ebih-Il* is shown seated; his enigmatic smile, the quality of carving and the contrasting materials (a light-coloured stone with lapis lazuli and bitumen eyes) make this a masterpiece. The cross-legged gypsum statue of the musician *Ur-Nanshe* (Damascus, Mus. N.) is a highly original piece. Only statues of the governors *Ishtup-Ilum* (Aleppo, N. Mus.) and *Idi-Ilum* (Paris, Louvre) have survived from the period around 2000 BC, though that of *Puzur-Ishtar* (Istanbul, Archaeol. Mus. and Berlin, Pergamonmus.), found in Babylon, belongs to the same group; all three figures stand with hands clasped, but the first is stiff and heavy. The 'goddess with the flowing vase' (18th century BC; Aleppo, N. Mus.; see fig. 2), found in the official part of the great royal palace, is a unique piece, produced when the mastery of the sculptors in Mari was at its height. The figurines of two naked goddesses, one in bronze and one in ivory, are smaller but just as remarkable (Damascus, Mus. N.); they were found in the 'Treasure of Ur', a collection of Early Dynastic objects of various provenances, including a votive bead inscribed with the name of Mes-ane-pada of Ur.

In Mari mosaic panels of shell and coloured stones set in bitumen were particularly highly prized. Unfortunately, no complete composition has survived, and only scattered fragments and disconnected remains have been found in the temples. Their quality, however, suggests that in this field, too, Mari equalled or surpassed its Mesopotamian neighbours. One particularly significant scene is that of the sacrifice of a ram, two examples of which (Damascus, Mus. N.) have been found in the temples of Shamash and of Dagan; the power of Mari's engravers is clearly shown.

The particular way in which the palace was destroyed preserved the remains of large wall paintings in the rubble of the Palm Court (Court 106) and of Court 132. Two offering scenes (*see* SYRIA-PALESTINE, fig. 10), although incomplete, show the scope of the compositions and the principles on which they are based. The well-preserved southern wall of Court 106 still bore an exceptional composition (1.75×2.50 m) of Zimri-Lin being invested as king by the goddess Ishtar. The composition and motifs reveal the painters' creative power and the diversity of their inspiration.

BIBLIOGRAPHY

Syria, xvi–lii (1935–75) [preliminary excav. reps]
A. Parrot: *Le Temple d'Ishtar*, Mission Archéologique de Mari (Paris, 1956)
——: *Le Palais*, 3 vols, Mission Archéologique de Mari (Paris, 1958–9)
——: *Le Temple d'Ishtarat et de Ninni-Zaza*, Mission Archéologique de Mari (Paris, 1967)
——: *Le 'Trésor' d'Ur*, Mission Archéologique de Mari (Paris, 1968)
——: *Mari, capitale fabuleuse* (Paris, 1974)
MARI (1982–)
J. Margueron, B. Pierre-Muller and M. Renisio: 'Les Appartements royaux du premier étage dans le palais de Zimri-Lim', *MARI*, vi (1990), pp. 433–51
B. Pierre-Muller: 'Une Grande Peinture des appartements royaux du palais de Mari (salles 219–220)', *MARI*, vi (1990), pp. 463–558

J.-C. MARGUERON

Maria. *See* AVIZ, (12).

Maria I, Queen of Portugal. *See* BRAGANZA, (9).

Maria II, Queen of Portugal. *See* BRAGANZA, (12).

Maria, Francesco di (*b* Naples, ?1623; *d* Naples, 1690). Italian painter. He was the most fervent supporter of the classical tradition working in Naples in the second half of the 17th century. He was taught by his father, but later became a follower of Domenichino and, during several visits to Rome, came into contact with the circle of classical artists led by Andrea Sacchi and Nicolas Poussin. His interest in the Antique and in the Old Masters was encouraged by Salvator Rosa. Yet di Maria also responded to the more painterly art of Lanfranco, Luca Giordano and Mattia Preti, and his art unites the colour of Giordano with an emphasis on *disegno* and on intellectual complexity. His early works include a *St Anne* (1640–53; Naples, church of the Girolamini) and *The Drummer* (Cefalù, Mus. Mandralisca). A series of altarpieces included the *Calvary* and the *Ecstasy of St Teresa of Avila* (both 1660; Naples, S Giuseppe a Pontecorvo) and the monumental *St Gregory Thaumaturgus* (*c.* 1660) for S Gregorio Armeno, where di Maria also frescoed a chapel with scenes from the *Life of St Gregory Thaumaturgus* (1660–70). These works suggest the influence of Charles Mellin (in Naples 1643–7), Simon Vouet and Lanfranco. Di Maria enjoyed a high reputation as a portrait painter; one of the few surviving portraits is of *Cardinal Ascanio Filomarino* (Florence, Gal. Corsini). English patrons, among them John Cecil, 5th Earl of Exeter, also received portraits, biblical scenes and mythological pictures (untraced). Among di Maria's last works were frescoes (1684; untraced) in S Luigi di Palazzo, Naples. He was an influential teacher whose pupils included Paolo de Matteis, Andrea Malinconico (1624–98) and Giacomo Farelli.

BIBLIOGRAPHY
C. Fiorillo: 'Francesco di Maria', *Napoli Nob.*, xxii/5–6 (1983), pp. 183–209; xxiii/1–2 (1984), pp. 25–54
Civiltà del seicento a Napoli, 2 vols (exh. cat., ed. S. Cassani; Naples, Capodimonte, 1984–5)
DONATELLO GERMANÒ SIRACUSA

Maria Giovanna Battista, Duchess of Savoy. *See* SAVOY, §II, (9).

Marialva, 1st Marquês de [Meneses, Antonio Luis de; Cantanhede, 3rd Conde de] (*b* 1597; *d* 1695). Portuguese patron. He became a national hero for his part in the defence of Portugal against Spanish invasion after Portugal declared its independence of Spain and John IV was proclaimed king in 1640. He was created Marquês de Marialva by Alfonso VI in 1661 and was among those who concluded the peace treaty with Spain in 1668. He was heir to possessions in the neighbourhood of Coimbra, where in the 16th century members of his family had commissioned important works from João de Ruão. These included the rebuilding of the church of Our Lady of the Assumption, Atalaia, near Tomar, the limestone retable of the *Virgin of Mercy* (*c.* 1530–35) in the funerary chapel of Dom Jorge de Meneses at Varziela, near Cantanhede, and the chapel of the Sacrament (1545) in the parish church

at Cantanhede. The Casa Solar at Cantanhede, which belonged to the family, is now the town hall. The principal act of patronage by the Marquês was the foundation (1680) of the monastery of S Pedro de Alcantara (partially destr. 1755) in Lisbon, commemorating the victories against the Spanish at Linhas de Elvas (1659) and Montes Claros (1665), in both of which he was involved. Serving as the mausoleum of the Marquês and of several of the leading families in the 17th and 18th centuries, the building comprises the funerary chapels of the Lencastre family, designed by João Antunes. The Marialva palace in Lisbon was destroyed in the earthquake of 1755. A portrait of the *Marquês de Marialva* (priv. col.), in his later years and painted by an unknown artist, was afterwards engraved.

BIBLIOGRAPHY
V. M. Godinho: 'Restauração', *Dicionário da história de Portugal*, ed. J. Serrão (Lisbon, n.d.)
F. Lacerda: *Panegyrico ao . . . D. António Luis de Meneses, Marquês de Marialva* (Lisbon, 1674)
T. Santa Marta: *Elogio histórico da ilustríssima casa de Cantanhede-Marialva* (Lisbon, 1751)
V. Correia: *Distrito de Coimbra* (1952), iv of *Inventário artistico de Portugal* (Lisbon, 1943–)
Monumentos e edifícios notáveis do distrito de Lisboa, 6 vols (Lisbon, 1962–75)
LUISA ARRUDA

Mariana Islands. Group of sixteen islands, of which six are inhabited, in the western Pacific Ocean, *c.* 2250 km south of Japan. The islands comprise the US territory of Guam and the self-governing Commonwealth of the Northern Mariana Islands, which has close ties with the USA. The islands are usually classified as Micronesian. The indigenous islanders, the Chamorros, were conquered by Spanish settlers in the 17th century, and the population subsequently declined drastically. During the 18th and 19th centuries the islands' culture developed as an amalgam of Chamorro and Spanish elements, the latter coming mainly from Spain, but also from Mexico and the Philippines. In view of this early European domination, pre-Spanish Chamorro art in perishable materials has long disappeared. Since the earliest European accounts of the Marianas do not mention distinctive secular or religious material culture or art forms, it seems probable that Chamorro artistic expression was primarily channelled into functional design in the production of canoes, tools, pottery and other utilitarian objects. It seems that tattoo was not practised.

There are, however, numerous early archaeological sites on all the main islands. These consist of double rows of *latte* (stone columns) usually in sets of eight or ten, each with a shaft and a cup-shaped capstone, that served as house-posts for the erection of wooden structures. At some of the larger sites the columns are set end-to-end in rows to form a linear 'village', with the largest and most impressive *latte* at the centre. For unknown reasons, the ancient Chamorros at some point decided to increase the size of these structures; the largest standing *latte* recorded is the 'House of Taga', which bears the name of a legendary giant (see fig.). It has 12 columns and formed the central structure of a large beach village. The house was not a temple (it was surrounded by domestic debris) but was more likely a men's house or the residence of a chief. Even larger shafts and capstones have been found left

Mariana Islands, *latte* known as the 'House of Taga', h. of each column 5.5 m, on the island of Tinian, probably 14th century or later

unfinished in a quarry at As Nieves on Rota. Neither the 'House of Taga' nor the As Nieves site have been accurately dated, but they are probably no earlier than the 14th century. The Spanish conquest ended the *latte*-building period of Marianas culture. All archaeological work and collections related to the Mariana Islands are centred at the Bernice P. Bishop Museum, Honolulu, Hawaii.

BIBLIOGRAPHY

EWA: 'Micronesian Cultures'

G. Anson: *A Voyage round the World in the Years 1740–44* (London, 1748)

L. M. Thompson: *Archaeology of the Mariana Islands*, Bishop Mus. Bull., c (Honolulu, 1932)

——: 'The Function of *Latte* in the Marianas', *J. Polynes. Soc.*, xlix/195 (1940), pp. 447–65

A. Spoehr: 'Marianas Prehistory: Archaeological Survey and Excavations on Saipan, Tinian, and Rota', *Fieldiana Anthropol.*, xlviii (1957)

P. R. Henrickson: 'Two Forms of Primitive Art in Micronesia', *Micronesica*, iv (1968), pp. 39–48

F. R. Reiman: *An Archaeological Survey and Preliminary Excavations on the Island of Guam, Mariana Islands, 1965–1966* (Guam, 1977)

B. M. Cooper: 'A Small Collection of Artifacts from the Marianas Islands', *Ann. Rep. Mus. Anthropol.*, U. MO, vii (1979–80), pp. 43–58

L. Hanson and F. A. Hanson: *The Art of Oceania: A Bibliography*, Ref. Pubns A. Hist. (Boston, MA, 1984)

W. N. Morgan: *Prehistoric Architecture in Micronesia* (Austin, TX, 1988/R London, 1989)

ALEXANDER SPOEHR

Mariani, Camillo (*b* Vicenza, ?1567; *d* Rome, July 1611). Italian sculptor, painter and architect. He received his early training as a sculptor in Vicenza, in the workshop of Lorenzo and Agostino Rubini (*fl* late 16th century). Deeply influenced by the style and method of Alessandro Vittoria, Lorenzo Rubini's brother-in-law, Mariani enjoyed an active career in his native city and beyond from *c.* 1584 until his departure for Rome in 1597. Around 1584 he helped to carry out the stucco figural decoration of Andrea Palladio's Teatro Olimpico, Vicenza, and his most important independent early commission (*c.* 1596) consisted of six elegant life-size stucco statues, representing members of the Cornaro family, for the main salon of Palladio's Villa Cornaro, Piombino Dese. These works, stylistically

close to Vittoria's sculpture, are characterized by a largeness of form, an emotive intensity and expressive movement.

In Rome after 1597 Mariani played a key role, together with Nicolas Cordier, Stefano Maderno and others, in the large architectural and decorative enterprises of Clement VIII and Paul V. Among other works for Clement VIII Mariani modelled the colossal allegorical stucco figures of *Justice* and *Fortitude* (1599–1600) above the nave arch of the Clementina Chapel in St Peter's, and he carved the marble statues of *St Peter*, *St Paul* and *Religion* (1604) for the Aldobrandini Chapel in S Maria sopra Minerva. Paul V employed him as a member of the team of sculptors that carried out the sculptural decoration of the Pauline Chapel in S Maria Maggiore; he contributed models (1609–10) for the bronze angels surrounding the icon of the Virgin on the altar-tabernacle, the marble statue of *St John the Evangelist* to the left of the altar, and the large marble relief of the *Siege of Strigonia* on the tomb of *Clement VIII* (both begun 1610).

The masterpieces of Mariani's Roman period are his eight monumental stucco figures of saints (1599–1600) in niches in the church of S Bernardo alle Terme. These figures reveal the sculptor's debt to the style of Vittoria and, more significantly, demonstrate his importance to the development of the early Baroque. The statues have robust three-dimensional volume and weight and are endowed with a profound sense of life and energy. Chiaroscuro effects are achieved through subtle and bold modelling of surfaces, and each of the saints is characterized psychologically and spiritually by means of pose, expression and gesture. Through their dynamic stances and directed glances, these figures engage the spectator and activate the space of the church.

In addition to his work in stucco and marble, Mariani also produced medals and small-scale bronzes, among the latter *St Crescentino and the Dragon* (h. 830 mm, 1596; Urbino, Pal. Mun.). One painting, a *Flight into Egypt* (Florence, Roberto Longhi priv. col.), has been identified by Middeldorf as by Mariani, and Fiocco (1940–41 and 1968) has argued convincingly that the sculptor, a close friend of Vincenzo Scamozzi, designed the façade of S Pietro, Vicenza, and the main salon of the Villa Cornaro, Piombino Dese. Mariani raised the art of stucco sculpture to an unprecedented position in Rome, and his dynamic, pictorial and highly expressive style was of fundamental importance to his pupil, Francesco Mochi, and to the second generation of sculptors in the papal capital.

BIBLIOGRAPHY

G. Baglione: *Vite* (1642); ed. V. Mariani (1935), pp. 113–14

A. Venturi: *Storia*, x/3 (1937), pp. 349–77

G. Fiocco: 'Camillo Mariani', *Arti: Rass. Bimest. A. Ant. & Mod.*, iii (1940–41), pp. 74–86

A. Riccoboni: *Roma nell'arte: La scultura nell'evo moderno dal quattrocento ad oggi*, i (Rome, 1942), pp. 130–34

V. Martinelli: 'Le prime sculture di Camillo Mariani a Roma', *Venezia e l'Europa. Atti del XVIII congresso internazionale di storia dell'arte: Venezia, 1955*, pp. 306–11

M. C. Dorati: 'Gli scultori della Cappella Paolina in Santa Maria Maggiore', *Commentari*, xviii (1967), pp. 231–60

G. Fiocco: 'Camillo Mariani e Palladio', *Boll. Cent. Int. Stud. Archit. Andrea Palladio*, x (1968), pp. 164–9

S. Pressouyre: 'Actes relatifs aux sculptures de la chapelle Aldobrandini à Sainte Marie-de-la-Minerve à Rome', *Bull. Soc. N. Antiqua. France* (1971), pp. 195–206

U. Middeldorf: 'Camillo Mariani, scultore-pittore', *Burl. Mag.*, xcviii (1976), pp. 500–03

R. C. Burns: *Camillo Mariani: Catalyst of the Sculpture of the Roman Baroque* (diss., Baltimore, MD, Johns Hopkins U., 1979)

STEVEN F. OSTROW

Mariano [Rodríguez, Mariano] (*b* Havana, 1912; *d* Havana, 26 May 1990). Cuban painter. He studied briefly in 1936 in Mexico under Manuel Rodríguez Lozano and took part in the 'Modern Cuban painters' exhibition at the Museum of Modern Art, New York, in 1944. He made his name in the 1940s with bold paintings of fighting cocks (e.g. *Cock-fight*, 1942; see *MOMA Bull.*, 1944, p. 11) but these were followed by three decades of less vital work. From 1960 he specialized in landscapes and flora, for example *From the Mountains to the Plain* (1963; Havana, Mus. N. B.A.).

BIBLIOGRAPHY

A. H. Barr, jr: 'Modern Cuban Painters', *MOMA Bull.*, xi/5 (1944), pp. 2–14

Pintores y guerrillas: El deber de todo revolucionario es hacer la Revolución (exh. cat., Havana, Casa Américas, 1967)

RICARDO PAU-LLOSA

Mariano del Buono di Jacopo (*b* Florence, 1433; *d* Florence, ?19 Nov 1504). Italian illuminator. His output appears to be divided into two main phases: the early phase is characterized by an exuberant style; the later (after 1478), for which he is best known, is less vivacious, due to the constant intervention of mediocre collaborators. In 1464 Mariano illuminated Livy's *History of Rome* (Florence, Bib. Riccardiana, MS. 484), formerly attributed to the Master of the White Scrolls because of an incorrect interpretation of the motif of white scrolls, which were seen as a stylistic peculiarity rather than as characteristic of a certain type of book. A feature of Mariano's early work is the use of innovative design, even within traditional graphic schemes. He preferred portraits to narrative scenes and his portraiture reflects a more complex range of influences, including such artists as Piero della Francesca and Antonio del Pollaiuolo, and such Classical motifs as the bust. Pairs of putti, three-dimensional candelabra and a vast assortment of animals can often be seen in the backgrounds.

Among the codices featuring white scrolls is a manuscript of Plutarch's work (1469; Modena, Bib. Estense, MS. lat. 429); the initials frequently contain representations of themes that are typical of cassone panels: the journey, the couple, the drama of love. In the depiction of *Theseus and the Minotaur* in the initial of the proem by the translator Antonio da Todi, Mariano shows the suffering minotaur with a bleeding face that is more like that of a dead Christ than the traditional image of sinful brutality; this anticipates Sandro Botticelli's *Pallas and the Centaur* (1480–85; Florence, Uffizi). Another early work is St Augustine's *City of God* (London, BL, Add. MS. 15246). Among the themes used by Mariano during the 1460s is a symbolic *Woman in Profile* with a little dog jumping into her lap, found in a miscellany (Milan, Castello Sforzesca, MS. 817, fol. 1). In a *Fior di virtù* (Florence, Bib. Riccardiana, MS. 1774) a variety of animals are similarly correlated with moral classifications.

The manuscript (finished 1477; Florence, Bargello, MS. 68) illuminated for the hospital of S Maria Nuova in Florence reveals the stylistic change in Mariano's work. It also contains work by Gherardo di Giovanni del Foro, Felice di Michele (*d* 1518), Antonio di Domenico and Girolamo da Cremona. The manuscript, presumably executed over a long period, contains examples of Mariano's early and later work, the latter suggesting his acquaintance with Girolamo da Cremona in the new conception of the figure and the transformation of the borders. Similarly, in the copy of Virgil's *Aeneid* (Florence, Bib. Medicea-Laurenziana, MS. Plut. 39.6) illuminated for Francesco Sassetti, Mariano shows his familiarity with the antique. The Classical subjects—the *Abduction of Helen*, the *Judgement of Paris*, the *Departure of Aeneas*, the *Wooden Horse*—are inserted into 15th-century urban scenes. Classical references also appear in the three-volume *History of Rome* by Livy (Munich, Bayer. Staatsbib., Clm. 15731–3) made for Johannes Vitéz, of which Mariano illuminated the frontispieces. This small book is a celebratory cycle in which the Labours of Hercules and Stories of Ancient Rome are evoked in terms that later became common in 16th-century iconography. The influence of the art of Girolamo da Cremona emerges in a vernacular version of the *History of Rome* (U. Valencia, Bib., MS. 757). Portraits of famous people are found in this manuscript and are common in the *Scriptores historiae Augustae* and the *Storie di Roma* by Eutropius and Paul the Deacon (Melbourne U., MS. 219) executed for Lorenzo the Magnificent in 1479. The motif of the famous man in a pattern of white scrolls appears again in the *History of Rome* (New York, Pub. Lib., Spencer MS. 27) executed later for Matthias Corvinus.

In 1484 Mariano illuminated Nesi's *De moribus* (Florence, Bib. Medicea-Laurenziana, MS. Plut. 77.24), dedicated to Piero, son of Lorenzo the Magnificent. The medallions in the frontispiece are related to work by Pollaiuolo, Botticelli and others. The Book of Hours (*c.* 1488; Waddesdon Manor, Bucks, NT, MS. 16), decorated for the wedding of Maddalena de' Medici and Francesco Cybo, has substantial contributions from Mariano's bottega. The importance of his bottega is witnessed by the presence of collaborators throughout his work.

BIBLIOGRAPHY

M. Levi d'Ancona: *Miniatura e miniatori a Firenze dal XIV secolo al XVI secolo* (Florence, 1962), pp. 175–81

A. Garzelli: 'Micropittura su temi virgiliani prima e dopo Apollonio di Giovanni: Apollonio, Giovanni Varnucci, Mariano del Buono e altri', *Scritti di storia dell'arte in onore di Federico Zeri*, i (Milan, 1984), pp. 147–62

——: *Miniatura fiorentina del Rinascimento, 1440–1525*, i (Florence, 1985), pp. 189–215

PATRIZIA FERRETTI

Maria-Theresa, Queen of Hungary and Bohemia. *See* HABSBURG, §I(21).

Ma'rib. *See under* ARABIA, PRE-ISLAMIC, §§I–III.

Marie, Princesse d'Orléans. *See* ORLÉANS, (9).

Marie-Antoinette, Queen of France. *See* BOURBON, §I(12).

Marie de' Medici, Queen of France. *See* BOURBON, §I(6).

Mariën, Marcel (*b* Antwerp, 29 April 1920; *d* Brussels, 19 Sept 1993). Belgian writer, painter, collagist, draughtsman and sculptor. He left school at the age of 14 and in 1937 met Magritte, and the Belgian writers Louis Scutenaire (1905–87) and Paul Nougé (1895–1967), through whom he soon became drawn into the Surrealist movement. Though largely involved with writing poetry and essays, like many Surrealists he also produced collages, such as *La Traversée du rêve* (1938–45; Paris, Gal. Isy Brachot). Also in 1937 he participated in his first Surrealist exhibition, *Surrealist Objects and Poems*, organized by E. L. T. Mesens at the London Gallery in London. From 1940 to 1941 he was held prisoner in Germany. On his return to Belgium he founded the publishing house L'Aiguille Aimantée, which issued Paul Eluard's *Moralité du sommeil* in 1941. In 1943 he published the first monograph on Magritte and two years later took part in the important exhibition of Belgian Surrealism at the Galerie La Boëtie in Brussels. In 1946 he edited the special issue of the American periodical *View* devoted to Belgian Surrealism.

Like Magritte and others, Mariën rebelled against André Breton's doctrinaire approach to Surrealism and in 1947 launched an open attack on him. He favoured instead the greater independence and vigour of its Belgian manifestation. From then on he rarely used the word 'Surrealism' of his own work, feeling it too closely linked to Breton. From 1954 to 1960 he edited the review *Les Lèvres nues* and in 1959 directed the film *L'Imitation du cinéma*, banned in France. From 1967 he regularly exhibited collages, paintings, drawings and sculptures. In the true spirit of Surrealism, these shock the viewer by their juxtaposition of unexpected elements.

WRITINGS

Magritte (Brussels, 1943)
L'Activité surréaliste en Belgique (Brussels, 1979)
Le Radeau de la mémoire (Brussels, 1983) [autobiog. work]

BIBLIOGRAPHY

Contemp. Artists (1977)
Le Mouvement surréaliste à Bruxelles et en Wallonie (exh. cat., Paris, Cent. Cult. Wallonie Bruxelles, 1988)

□

Marienburg Castle. *See* MALBORK CASTLE.

Marieschi, Michele [Michiel] **Giovanni** (*b* Venice, 1 Dec 1710; *d* Venice, 18 Jan 1743). Italian painter and engraver. His first biographers, Orlandi and Guarienti (1753), stated that Marieschi worked in Germany early in his career and then returned to Venice, where he established himself as a painter of 'beautiful views of the Grand Canal, and of churches and palaces'. Yet there is no other evidence for this journey and Marieschi's early training remains problematic. It seems likely that he began his career as a stage designer: his first recorded activity, in 1731, was the preparation, on behalf of the impresario Francesco Tasso (*fl* 1725–*c*. 1740), of the setting for the Venetian celebration of Carnival Thursday in the Piazzetta. He then, influenced by Marco Ricci and Luca Carlevaris, began to paint capriccios and *vedute*. His early capriccios, such as the pair *Capriccio with Classical Ruins and Bridge*

Michele Giovanni Marieschi: *Town on a River with Shipping*, oil on canvas, 607×918 mm, *c*. 1735 (London, National Gallery)

and *Capriccio with Roman Arch and Encampment* (mid-1730s; Naples, Mus. Civ. Gaetano Filangieri), are indebted to Ricci, although they lack his solemnity and magnificence. Marieschi's blend of medieval and Classical ruins in a serene Venetian landscape is more picturesque and romantic. Marieschi began to paint *vedute* having been encouraged by Canaletto's great success with the genre; examples such as the *S Maria della Salute* (1733–5; Paris, Louvre), the *Piazzetta dei Leoni* and the *Grand Canal at Ca' Pesaro* (1734–5; both Munich, Alte Pin.) are distinguished from Canaletto's work by their exaggerated perspective, more atmospheric colour and the spirited handling of the small figures. Two capriccios, the *Town on a River with Rapids* (London, N.G.) and the *Town on a River with Shipping* (London, N.G.; see fig.), both charmingly picturesque scenes with watermills and crumbling towers, date from the mid-1730s. Marieschi began to etch in the 1730s, and his theatrical setting, *A Palace Courtyard* (mid-1730s; Succi, 1987, cat. no. 1), is the only direct evidence of his work as a stage designer.

In 1735 Marieschi went to Fano, where his continuing interest in stage design is suggested by two drawings (untraced) that were engraved by Giuseppe Camerata II (1718–1803) and Francesco Tasso for inclusion in *Solenni esequie di Maria Clementina Sobieski, Regina dell'Inghilterra, celebrate nella chiesa di S Paterniano a Fano* (e.g. Venice, Correr), published by Gaetano Fanelli in 1736. In 1736 Marieschi's most important patron, Johann Matthias, Graf von der Schulenburg, commissioned a 'quadro della Corte di Palazzo', identifiable with the *View of the Courtyard of the Palazzo Ducale* (1736; sold London, Christie's, 2 July 1976; see Succi, 1989, figs 87 and 88), and a 'veduta di Rialto', identifiable with the *View of the Rialto with the Entry of the Patriarch* (1737; Claydon House, Bucks, NT). These two works, characterized by their deep space and theatrical splendour, are Marieschi's first documented paintings. In 1738 Schulenburg commissioned six small architectural views (untraced) and in 1741 two *vedute* (untraced). In the same years Marieschi started to paint an important series of six *vedute*, which in the 18th century hung in the palace of Sanssouci, Potsdam, and of which two pairs (1735–6; 1737–9) are now in the Schloss Charlottenburg, Berlin; a further pair, the *Grand Canal at San Samuele* and the *Grand Canal at Cannaregio* (1742–3), are in the Gemäldegalerie of the Bodemuseum, Berlin. The latter pair, with larger figures and a darting, sparkling touch close to that of Giovanni Antonio Guardi, is characteristic of Marieschi's final phase. In 1741 he published a set of etchings comprising a *Self-portrait* and 21 views of Venice, entitled *Magnificentiores selectioresque urbis Venetiarum prospectus* (Succi, 1987, nos 2–23). His late capriccios include the *Capriccio with Elegant Figures* and the *Capriccio with Equestrian Monument* (both 1741–2; Stuttgart, Staatsgal.). According to tradition, his death was caused by overwork. Francesco Albotto (1721–57) was Marieschi's most able pupil.

BIBLIOGRAPHY
Mariette; Thieme–Becker
P. A. Orlandi and P. Guarienti: *Abecedario pittorico* (Venice, 1753), p. 380
G. Fogolari: 'Michele Marieschi, pittore prospettico veneziano', *Boll. A.: Min. Pub. Instruzione*, vii (1909), pp. 241–51
A. Morassi: *Michele Marieschi* (Bergamo, 1966)
D. Succi: *Michiel Marieschi* (Turin, 1987) [cat. rais. of prts]
R. Toledano: *Michiel Marieschi: L'opera completa* (Milan, 1988)
Capricci veneziani del settecento (exh. cat., ed. D. Succi; Gorizia, Mus. Prov. Stor. & A., 1988), pp. 166–205
Marieschi tra Canaletto e Guardi (exh. cat., ed. D. Succi; Gorizia, Mus. Prov. Stor. & A., 1989) [with bibliog.]
D. Succi: *Michiel Marieschi* (in preparation) [cat. rais. of ptgs]

DARIO SUCCI

Mariette. French family of engravers, print publishers and dealers, collectors and a writer. (1) Pierre Mariette (i) and his son (2) Pierre Mariette (ii) were wealthy and influential print publishers in 17th-century Paris. Pierre (ii)'s son (3) Jean Mariette published *L'Architecture française*, an important collection of engravings of modern French buildings, and formed a fine collection of prints and drawings. His son (4) Pierre-Jean Mariette continued the family business. He also expanded the collection of drawings to make it one of the most celebrated ever assembled by a private individual. In addition he researched the voluminous notes on art and artists that were posthumously published as the *Abécédario*, the best-known of his writings on the history of art.

UNPUBLISHED SOURCE
Paris, Archvs N., Minutier central, MS. fonds cix, reg. 203, 14 Dec 1657 [*Vente Pierre I Mariette à son fils Pierre II*]

BIBLIOGRAPHY
F. Lugt: *Marques* (1921), no. 1787
J. R. Thomé: 'Le Commerce des estampes au XVIIe siècle: Les Mariette (1)', *Courrier Graph.*, vi/23 (1939), pp. 29–30
R.-A. Weigert: 'Le Commerce de la gravure au XVIIe siècle en France: Les Deux Premiers Mariette et François Langlois, dit Ciartres', *Gaz. B.-A.*, n. s. 6, xli (1953), pp. 167–94

(1) Pierre Mariette (i) (*b* Paris, 1596; *d* Paris, 18 Dec 1657). Engraver, print dealer and publisher. By 1633, the date of his marriage to Geneviève Lenoir, daughter of a bookseller, he was living in the Rue Saint-Jacques at the sign of the elephant. As well as engravings he sold maps, illuminated manuscripts, religious prints, 'coquilles d'or' and German silver. In 1634, the year he probably travelled to Italy, he was noted also as a picture dealer. His acquisition in 1637 of Jean Messager's print shop and in 1644 of that of Melchior Tavernier, the publisher of Abraham Bosse and others, significantly increased the stature of Mariette's business, which henceforth was known by Messager's sign, 'L'Espérance'. Pierre Mariette (i) was one of the principal publishers of the prints of Stefano della Bella. In addition to engravings after works by Jacques Blanchard, Claude Vignon, Titian and others, the five presses owned by Pierre (i) published original engravings by Daniel Rabel, François Collignon, Israël Silvestre and Michel Lasne. He was also closely associated with a number of painters, including Charles Le Brun. In 1651 he married as his second wife Catherine de Bray (*d* 1658), sister of a publisher.

UNPUBLISHED SOURCE
Paris, Archvs N., Minutier central, MS. fonds cix, reg. 225, 16 Jan 1658 [*L'Inventaire après décès de Pierre I Mariette*]

BIBLIOGRAPHY
R.-A. Weigert: 'Stefano della Bella et trois de ses éditeurs parisiens', *Bull. Mus. B.-A. Alger* (1950), pp. 167–88

(2) Pierre Mariette (ii) (*b* Paris, 1634; *d* Paris, Aug 1716). Print dealer and publisher, son of (1) Pierre Mariette (i). His mother was Geneviève Lenoir. In 1655 he married Madeleine de Collemont, widow of François Langlois, called Ciartres, one of the most prominent print-sellers on the Rue Saint-Jacques. Mariette thereby acquired Langlois's fabulous stock of plates and engravings, to which he added that of his father's business, which he purchased from the ailing dealer in 1657 for 30,000 livres. Madeleine and Pierre (ii)'s principal shop maintained Langlois's name, the 'Librairie des Colonnes d'Hercule', while the other continued as 'L'Espérance'. After Madeleine's death in 1661, an inventory of the comprehensive collection of prints, which Pierre (ii) had enriched with his own acquisitions, was valued at 70,000 livres. Pierre (ii) frequently wrote his name and date of acquisition on the reverse of the prints that passed through his hands. Among works by 17th-century artists he published prints after Nicolas Poussin, portraits by Robert Nanteuil and ornamental works, particularly those of Jean Le Pautre. In 1664 Pierre (ii) married Marie Piget, the daughter of a book dealer.

UNPUBLISHED SOURCE

Paris, Archvs N., Minutier central, MS. fonds cix, liasse 204, 23 March 1658 [*Vente François Foucault, Pierre II Mariette et Madeleine de Colemont*]

BIBLIOGRAPHY

R. Froté: 'De François Langlois à Pierre II Mariette (étude d'inventaires inédits ou le commerce de l'estampe à Paris de Callot à Watteau)', *Gaz. B.-A.*, n. s. 6, cii (1983), pp. 111–20

(3) Jean Mariette (*bapt* Saint-Benoît, July 1660; *d* Paris, 20 Sept 1742). Engraver, print dealer and publisher, and collector, son of (2) Pierre Mariette (ii). His mother was Madeleine de Collemont, and he studied painting under his brother-in-law Jean-Baptiste Corneille. He gave up painting in favour of engraving and the family business. After his father's death in 1716, he took over the 'Librairie des Colonnes d'Hercule', the business at the sign of 'L'Espérance' being inherited by his elder brother Pierre-Joseph Mariette (1656–1729). He produced nearly 900 prints after artists such as Domenichino, Poussin, Le Brun and Corneille, as well as prints after his own designs. He specialized in the design of vignettes, frontispieces, portraits and other decorations for books. In 1727 he began to publish *L'Architecture française*, a five-volume collection of plans, elevations and cross-sections of modern French buildings, which is one of the most important sources for the study of French classical architecture. Jean Mariette was considered by his contemporaries as the greatest connoisseur of prints of his time. He had connections with many important collectors, one of his best clients being Prince Eugene of Savoy. He continued to enlarge both the stock inherited from his father and the Mariette private collection, the best of which he had inherited. This included over 300 prints by Rembrandt, as well as sheets by or after Rubens, Dürer, Callot and many others. He had a particular predilection for the prints of Marcantonio Raimondi, Callot and Hollar, but also added to the collection graphic works by contemporary artists, many of whom were his associates and friends. His numerous documents on art and artists provided the basis for the studies of his son (4) Pierre-Jean Mariette.

WRITINGS

L'Architecture française, 5 vols (Paris, 1727–38/*R* 1927–9) [the reprint in 3 vols with an introduction by L. Hautecoeur]

BIBLIOGRAPHY

Mariette (iii, pp. 264–5)

F. Lugt: *Marques* (1921), no. 1488

J. R. Thomé: 'Le Commerce des estampes au XVIIe siècle: Les Mariette (2)', *Courrier Graph.*, iv/25 (1939), pp. 27–32

A. Mauban: *L'Architecture française de Jean Mariette* (Paris, 1945)

(4) Pierre-Jean Mariette (*b* Paris, 7 May 1694; *d* Paris, 10 Sept 1774). Print dealer, publisher, collector and writer, son of (3) Jean Mariette. He received a classical education at the Collège des Jésuites in Paris and spent the years 1717–18 in Vienna, supervising the cataloguing of the collection of prints owned by Prince Eugene of Savoy, for whom he later acted as an agent. During the following two years he travelled throughout Italy, making copious notes on works of art. Around 1720 he returned to Paris, where he joined the circle of the noted collector Pierre Crozat (*see* CROZAT, (1)). Among those whom he met was the antiquary and connoisseur the Comte de Caylus, who became a close friend. In 1724 Pierre-Jean married Angélique-Catherine Doyen, the daughter of a notary. He assisted his father at the 'Librairie des Colonnes d'Hercule', and by 1732 was apparently running the family print and publishing businesses. In 1735, with Charles-Antoine Coypel and the Abbé Jourdain, he was reorganizing the prints in the Bibliothèque Royale.

Pierre-Jean Mariette was respected not only for his expertise in drawings and prints but also for his knowledge of the history of art. His father's vast collection of notes on artists and original and reproductive prints provided the foundation for his own careful observations, to which he added information from his many correspondents throughout Europe, who included the Abbé Barthélemy, Anton-Maria Zanetti (i) and Francesco Maria Gabburri. His notes, which comprise ten manuscript volumes (Paris, Bib. N., Cab. Est.) of commentary on *Abecedario pittorico* (1704, rev. 1719) by PELLEGRINO ANTONIO ORLANDI, were intended to serve two major projects, which remained unfinished at his death: a history of engraving and a dictionary of artists. These notes also formed the basis for his unpublished commentary on Vasari's *Vite* (Paris, Louvre, Cab. Dessins) and were used by Caylus for his manuscript *Vies d'artistes du XVIIIe siècle*. Selections from them were published over the period 1851–62 by Chennevières and Montaiglon. Other important works by Mariette include *Lettre sur Leonardo da Vinci*, published in 1730 as the preface to an album of etchings by Caylus after caricatures attributed to Leonardo and owned by Jean Mariette; and a translation of Horace Walpole's *Anecdotes of Painting in England*. His *Traité des pierres gravées* (1750) on the subject of engraved gems was praised for being clear, comprehensive and accurate. Mariette also published important books on architecture, including an augmented edition of Augustin-Charles d'Aviler's *Cours d'architecture* (1738). His special interest was provenance, and his 1741 sale catalogue of the Crozat collection was the first to use provenances to verify attributions and the first to place the individual works within their time, defining their specific characteristics and comparing them to other works of art.

In 1750 Mariette decided to concentrate on his activities as a historian and connoisseur. He sold the stock of his shop to five associates and purchased a house at Croissy-sur-Seine as well as the office of Contrôleur Général de la Grande Chancellerie. Two years later he sold his publishing business. In October 1761 Mariette was made a Chevalier des Ordres du Roi.

As a collector, Mariette lacked the great wealth of his predecessors Everard Jabach or Crozat, many of whose drawings entered his collection, but distinguished himself by the consistently high quality of his drawings, which he selected after a critical study of their attributions, based partially on provenance. He preferred, if the choice had to be made, exceptional works by secondary artists to secondary works by famous artists; but he nevertheless owned important drawings by Raphael and Michelangelo, including the latter's drawing of his own hand (Paris, Louvre). At the time of his death Pierre-Jean Mariette owned over 3400 mounted drawings (some of which he hung under glass on the wall) and approximately 6000 drawings in portfolios. He especially admired Italian art but also had 1000 French drawings including fine works by Claude Lorrain and Nicolas Poussin, as well as his own contemporaries (see fig.), 16 drawings by Dürer, including the *Small Owl* (Vienna, Albertina), and works by Rubens, Anthony van Dyck and Velázquez. He disliked, however, the work of the popular Dutch minor masters.

Mariette inherited important drawings by Stefano della Bella, Jacques Callot and early 18th-century French artists associated with the 'Librairie des Colonnes d'Hercule'. Other works were purchased from, exchanged with, or given by collectors and his many artist friends, including Rosalba Carriera, François Boucher, Charles-Joseph Natoire, Hubert Robert, and the van Loo family. Important drawings came from the 1732 sale of the *ébéniste* ANDRÉ-CHARLES BOULLE and especially from the 1741 Crozat sale, from which Mariette purchased 132 of the 149 studies by Annibale Carracci for the ceiling of the Palazzo Farnese, Rome. The provenance of many of his drawings included Giorgio Vasari, Peter Lely, Queen Christina of Sweden and other famous collectors. Mariette's drawings are identifiable by his mark, a capital M within a circle, and his characteristic mounts: thick blue paper trimmed with black lines surrounding a pattern of gold and grey and ornamented with a cartouche bearing the name of the artist and sometimes information regarding the provenance.

In addition to the drawings, Mariette also owned an important collection of engravings, many of them inherited from other family members. There were approximately 1300 prints by Callot and over 400 by Rembrandt, a copy of van Dyck's *Iconography*, and engravings after portraits. He had a valuable library of art books and a few paintings, among which were Watteau's *Shepherds* (Berlin, Schloss Charlottenburg) and Poussin's *Bacchanal* (London, N.G.). His numerous sculptures included 20 terracotta models by his friend Edme Bouchardon, by whom he also owned drawings.

Mariette's will stipulated that his collections be sold and the proceeds shared by his wife and four children. Louis XVI was offered the collection, but his offer of 300,000 livres was refused by the family, and the collections were sold at auction in Paris in 1775–6. Among the buyers were the Crown (1000 drawings now Paris, Louvre, Cab. Dessins), Louis-François, Prince de Conti, Paul Randon de Boisset, and other notable collectors, French and foreign.

WRITINGS

Abécédario de P.-J. Mariette et autres notes inédites de cet amateur sur l'art et les artistes (MS., Paris, Bib. N., Cab. Est.); ed. P. de Chennevières and A. de Montaiglon, 6 vols (Paris, 1851–62/*R* 1966)

Lettre sur Leonardo da Vinci (Paris, 1730)

Description sommaire des dessins des grands maistres d'Italie, des Pays-Bas et de France, du cabinet de feu M. Crozat. Avec des réflections sur la manière des dessins des principaux peintres par P.-J. Mariette (Paris, 1741) [Crozat collection sale cat.]

Description sommaire des pierres gravées du cabinet de feu M. Crozat (Paris, 1741) [Crozat collection sale cat.]

Lettre de M. M . . . à un ami de province au sujet de la nouvelle fontaine de la rue de Grenelle, au Fauxbourg Saint-Germain des Prez (Paris, 1746) [in praise of Bouchardon's new Paris fountain]

Traité des pierres gravées, 2 vols (Paris, 1750/*R* Florence, 1987)

Catalogue des tableaux et sculptures du cabinet de feu M. le Président de Tugny et de M. Crozat (Paris, 1751)

Description sommaire des statues du cabinet de feu M. Crozat (Paris, 1751) [Crozat collection sale cat.]

Description des travaux qui ont précédé, accompagné et suivi la fonte en bronze de la statue équestre de Louis XV par Bouchardon (Paris, 1768)

BIBLIOGRAPHY

F. Basan: *Catalogue raisonné des différents objets de curiosités dans les sciences et les arts qui composaient le cabinet de feu M. Mariette, Contrôleur Général de la Grande Chancellerie de France, Honoraire Amateur de l'Académie Royale de Peinture et de celle de Florence* (Paris, 1775) [served as catalogue for the sales of 1–27 Feb, 13 May 1775 and days following, and 15 Nov 1775–30 Jan 1776]

'Le Catalogue de la vente Mariette par F. Basan', *Mercure de France* (1775), p. 136

A.-J. Dumesnil: *Histoire des plus célèbres amateurs français et de leurs relations avec les artistes*, i (Paris, 1858/*R* Geneva, 1973)

A.-C.-P. Caylus: *Correspondance inédite avec le Père Paciaudi, théatin (1757–1765), suivi de celles de l'abbé Barthélemy et de P. Mariette avec le même*, 2 vols (Paris, 1877)

Pierre-Jean Mariette by Jean-Baptiste Massé, black and red chalk, 188×146 mm, 1735 (Oxford, Ashmolean Museum)

Lady Dilke: *French Engravers and Draughtsmen of the XVIIIth Century* (London, 1902)

F. Lugt: *Marques* (Amsterdam, 1921), no. 1852 [full account of drawings collection and sales]

Mariette et son temps: Le Cabinet d'un grand amateur (exh. cat., Paris, Louvre, Cab. Dessins, 1967) [with full bibliography]

B. Scott: 'Pierre-Jean Mariette, Scholar and Connoisseur', *Apollo*, xcvii (1973), pp. 54–9

H. Marx: 'Pierre Jean Mariette und Dresden', *Dresdn. Kstbl.*, xxiii/3 (1979), pp. 77–87

F. Viatte: 'A propos de Vasari historien et collectionneur: Un Dessin de Giovanni Angelo Canini pour *Le Vite* de Vasari', *Rev. Louvre*, xxix/4 (1979), pp. 277–9 [discusses Mariette's annotated copy of Vasari's *Vite*]

D. Le Marois: 'Les Montages de dessins au XVIIe siècle: L'Exemple de Mariette', *Bull. Soc. Hist. A. Fr.* (1982), pp. 87–96

AMY L. WALSH

Mariette, (François-)Auguste(-Ferdinand) [Mariette Pasha] (*b* Boulogne, 11 Feb 1821; *d* Cairo, 19 Jan 1881). French Egyptologist. His interest in Egypt may date from 1837, when a hieroglyphic inscription in the Musée Municipal in Boulogne aroused his curiosity and he began to learn to read hieroglyphics, using the grammar and dictionary compiled by Jean-François Champollion (1790–1832), who in 1822 had deciphered the Rosetta Stone. Mariette's first Egyptological task was to order some papers left him by a cousin, Nestor Lhôte (1804–42), a former pupil of Champollion. In 1849 he was offered a junior post at the Musée du Louvre, Paris. He taught himself Coptic and wrote a *Bibliographie copte* (1849) of texts in the Louvre.

In 1850 Mariette was sent by the Ministry of Public Instruction to acquire ancient manuscripts from Coptic monasteries in Egypt; when admission to the monasteries was delayed, he diverted his resources to excavations at SAQQARA. From November 1850 to November 1851 he uncovered the avenue of sphinxes leading to the Serapeum, the burial place of the sacred Apis bulls of Memphis (*see* EGYPT, ANCIENT, fig. 31). The tombs yielded rich finds, and in August 1851 the French government extended Mariette's funding for a further two years' work at the Serapeum. In the meantime, he encountered difficulties over the right to continue excavations and the ownership of the objects found. Early in 1852 the Ottoman viceroy, Abbas Pasha, and the French government came to a compromise whereby the Louvre gained possession of *c.* 7000 objects already discovered, and further French excavations were permitted, provided that their finds remained in Egypt. In November 1854 Mariette returned to Paris where he reported on his work to the Académie des Inscriptions et Belles-Lettres, and in 1855 he was appointed Assistant Curator at the Louvre. After travelling to Berlin and Turin to see other Egyptian antiquities, Mariette returned to Cairo in 1857. In 1858 Said Pasha, the new viceroy, appointed him Director of the Service des Antiquités and agreed to his establishment of an Egyptian museum. From this time onwards Mariette lived permanently in Egypt. The Service was created to protect monuments and prevent the illegal removal of antiquities from Egypt, and it was responsible for large-scale excavations, in particular at Saqqara, Abydos, Tanis, Dendara and in Nubia. As Director, Mariette was given the Ottoman rank of a Bey of the first order and sent as the Egyptian representative to the Great Exhibition in London in 1862. Mariette's Egyptian Museum at Bulaq near Cairo was opened by Said Pasha's successor, Ismail Pasha, in 1863. It was severely damaged by flooding of the Nile in 1868 and replaced by a new museum in Cairo in 1889 under the directorship of Mariette's successor, Gaston Maspero (1846–1910). Mariette is known in the history of music for providing the plot for *Aida* (1871) by Giuseppe Verdi (1813–1901).

WRITINGS

Bibliographie copte (1849)

'Renseignements sur les soixante-quatre Apis trouvés dans les souterrains du Serapeum', *Bull. Archéol.*, iv (1855); as book (Paris, 1856)

Choix de monuments et de dessins découverts pendant le déblaiement du Serapeum de Memphis (Paris, 1856)

Abydos: Description des fouilles exécutes sur l'emplacement de cette ville (Paris, 1869)

Aperçu de l'histoire d'Egypte (Paris, 1874)

Notice sur la vie et les travaux de François-Auguste-Ferdinand Mariette-Pacha (Paris, 1883)

G. Maspero, ed.: *Les Mastabas de l'Ancien Empire* (Paris, 1889)

ANNE PUETZ

Marigliano [Mariliano; Marliano; Merigliano; Miriliano], **Giovanni** [Giovanni da Napoli; Giovanni da Nola] (*b* Nola, *c.* 1488; *d* Naples, 1558). Italian wood-carver and sculptor. He trained in Naples as a wood-carver under Pietro Belverte (*d* 1513), executing polychromed wooden reliefs (1507; Naples, S Lorenzo; destr.) and crib figures (1507; Naples, S Domenico Maggiore). In 1508 he and Belverte assisted Tommaso Malvito (*fl* 1484–1508) on a frame for an image of *St Anne* and on doors at the Ospizio dell'Annunziata, Naples. Marigliano continued to work almost exclusively in Naples. His first independent commissions were the frame for the *Virgin and Child* (1511; Naples, S Pietro ad Aram) by Antonio da Rimpacta (*fl* 1509–11) and the altar frame for Bartolommeo de Lino's *Virgin and Saints* (1513; Castelluccio, S Francesco). Around 1524 he carved crib figures for S Maria del Parto, Naples, and collaborated on the marble tomb of the Viceroy of Sicily *Don Ramón de Cardona* (*d* 1522; Catalonia, Bellpuig, S Nicolás), a monument that reflects Andrea Sansovino's tomb designs and the decorative style imported by the Spanish sculptor Bartolomé Ordoñez. The lyrical tomb of *Antonia Guadino* (*c.* 1530; Naples, S Chiara) depicts the figure as a sleeping antique Cleopatra. In 1532 he completed the altar of the *Madonna del soccorso*, commissioned by the Liguoro family (Naples, S Anna dei Lombardi), a pendant to another altar by Girolamo da Santacroce (*c.* 1502–*c.* 1537) for the del Pezzo family in the same church. Both follow earlier Tuscan models, and the juxtaposition highlights Marigliano's awkward figure designs and his dependence on other sculptors' formulae. His altar of the *Madonna della neve* (1536; Naples, S Domenico Maggiore) represents a more classical solution, as did his monument to *Guido Fieramosca* (*c.* 1535–6; church of Montecassino Abbey; destr.). These precede the bizarre designs for the three tombs of the brothers Sigismondo, Ascanio and Jacopo Sanseverino (1539–46; Naples, SS Severino e Sossio), who were poisoned (1516) by their uncle. Here Marigliano's training in wood-carving is revealed in the armour-clad figures, like wooden lay-figures perched on their severely architectonic ledges. The grandiose tomb of the Viceroy of Naples (*reg* 1532–53) and his consort, *Don Pedro of Toledo and Maria Ossorio Pimental* (*c.* 1540–46; Naples, S Giacomo degli Spagnoli), combines Lombard influences with Giovanni Angelo Montorsoli's classical style, derived from Michelangelo, detectable also in such later marble figures as the *St Peter* in the Cappella Caracciolo (1547; Naples, S Giovanni Carbonara). Marigliano's last surviving sculpture, the *Deposition* (*c.* 1549; Naples, S Maria delle Grazie a Caponápoli), is a highly emotive scene.

BIBLIOGRAPHY
Thieme–Becker
A. Venturi: *Storia* (1901–40), X, i, pp. 715–44
A. Borzelli: *Giovanni Miriliano o Giovanni da Nola scultore* (Naples, 1921)
M. Collareta: 'Un busto napoletano a Washington', *Paragone*, xxxviii/443 (1987), pp. 53–5
ANTONIA BOSTRÖM

Marigny, Marquis de. *See* POISSON, (2).

Marika. Australian Aboriginal family of painters and printmakers. (1) Mawalan Marika was the father of the painter (2) Wandjuk Marika. His three daughters, Bayngul Marika (*b* 1927), Dhuwarrwarr Marika (*b* 1949) and (3) Banduk Marika, were also artists.

BIBLIOGRAPHY
W. Caruana, ed.: *Windows on the Dreaming: Aboriginal Paintings at the Australian National Gallery* (Canberra, 1989), pp. 110–13, 114–17

(1) Mawalan Marika (*b* ?1908; *d* 1967). He was a member of the Riratjingu clan of the Yolngu-speaking peoples of north-east Arnhem Land, N. Territory. Born before intensive European colonization, he moved into the newly established mission station of Yirrkala in 1935. Bark paintings by Marika were among the first commissioned by the missionary Wilbur Chaseling in the 1930s, and examples from this period are in the state museums in Sydney, Melbourne and Brisbane. He assisted the anthropologists Charles Mountford, Ron Berndt and Catherine Berndt, and much of the rich literature on Arnhem Land song-poetry has its origins in his work with them (e.g. *Turtle and Oystercatcher*, 1952; Adelaide, S. Austral. Mus.). In 1959 he produced a series of paintings commissioned by Stuart Scougall and Tony Tuckson for the Art Gallery of New South Wales in Sydney, including his renowned painting of the Djankawu sisters giving birth, *Scenes from the Djanggawal Myth* (*c.* 1959). These paintings were characterized by the grandeur of their conception and their representation of myths in episodic form. With Narritjin Maymurru and Munggurrawuy Yunapingu he developed a narrative mode that was characteristic of much Yirrkala art of the 1960s to the 1980s. In 1962 he played a leading role in producing painted panels on Yolngu religious themes, which were installed in Yirrkala Church, contributing to the regional syncretism. He played a role in increasing the economic and cultural opportunities open to Yolngu women by encouraging his daughters as well as his sons to paint. Previously women had not been allowed to produce sacred paintings.

BIBLIOGRAPHY
R. M. Berndt, ed.: *Australian Aboriginal Art* (Sydney, 1964), pp. 81–2
VIDEO RECORDINGS
I. Dunlop: *In Memory of Mawalan* (Sydney, 1981)

(2) Wandjuk Marika (*b* 1927; *d* 1987). Son of (1) Mawalan Marika. He was taught to paint at an early age by his father, and he worked with him subsequently both as an interpreter and on some of his paintings. His own paintings include *Djang'kawu Story* (1960; Melbourne, N.G. Victoria). Through his role as an interpreter for anthropologists, missionaries and politicians, he became a cultural ambassador for north-east Arnhem Land people. In 1973 he was one of the founder-members of the Aboriginal Arts Board, and in 1979 he became its Chairman. His official duties left him little time for painting, although towards the end of his life he produced a series on the Djankawu mythology (e.g. the *Birth of the Djang'kawu Children of Yelangbara*, 1982; Canberra, N.G.). In style and content his paintings are similar to his father's later works, although some of the figurative representations are more elaborate. He claimed to have introduced an olive colour into Yolngu art, produced by mixing manganese and yellow ochre; the same colour was, however, also used occasionally by Maymurru.

BIBLIOGRAPHY
A. P. Elkin, R. M. Berndt and C. H. Berndt: *Art in Arnhem Land* (Melbourne, 1950), pp. 44, 70, 90–91, 95, 97, 102
J. Isaacs: Obituary, *A. Mthly* [Australia], iii (1987)

(3) Banduk Marika (*b* Yirrkala, 1954). Daughter of (1) Mawalan Marika. She learnt to paint in the traditional medium of ochres on bark but subsequently gained a reputation as a printmaker, initially producing linocuts before moving on to other lithographic processes. Her prints are based on themes of Yolngu mythology (e.g. *Muka Milnymirri Three Snakes*, linocut, 1987; see Isaacs, 1989, p. 20). She lived in Sydney from 1980 to 1988; during this time she was artist in residence at Canberra School of Art (1984) and at Flinders University of South Australia, Bedford Park (1986). Her first solo exhibition was at the Old Meadows Gallery, Blacktown, Sydney. In 1987 the Australian Museum, Sydney, held an exhibition focusing on her work and that of her sisters Bayngul Marika and Dhuwarrwarr Marika. In 1988 she returned to Yirrkala, where for a time she managed the Yirrkala community art and craft business. She was one of the artists who was commissioned to produce a print for the *The Bicentennial Portfolio* exhibition in 1988 (Canberra, N.G.), and in 1990 she was appointed a member of the Council of the Australian National Gallery, Canberra.

BIBLIOGRAPHY
R. Butler: 'From Dreamtime to Machine Time', *Imprint*, xxi/3–4 (1986), pp. 7–14
J. Isaacs: 'The Marika Sisters at the Australian Museum', *A. Mthly* [Australia], iii (1987)
——: *Aboriginality, Contemporary Aboriginal Paintings and Prints* (Brisbane, 1989), pp. 20–23
HOWARD MORPHY

Marilhat, Prosper(-Georges-Antoine) (*b* Vertaizon, Puy-de-Dôme, 26 March 1811; *d* Paris, 13 Sept 1847). French painter. He painted his first landscapes and family portraits at Thiers and in the Auvergne before moving to Paris in 1829. After working as the pupil of Camille Roqueplan he was engaged by Baron Karl von Hügel for an expedition to the Near East (1831–3), from which he brought back numerous studies. He visited Greece, Syria, Lebanon and Palestine, stayed in Egypt from October 1831 to May 1833 and returned by way of Rhodes and Corfu. Cairo, the villages of the Delta and Upper Egypt proved to be sources of inspiration for later works. At Alexandria he painted theatre sets and numerous court

Prosper Marilhat: *Syrian Arabs on a Journey*, oil on canvas, 280×500 mm, 1844 (Chantilly, Musée Condé, Château de Chantilly)

portraits (more than 80, according to Gérard de Nerval: 'Les Artistes français à l'étranger, par L. Dussieux', *L'Artiste*, x (15 March 1853), p. 60). Despite further trips to Italy (1835), the Midi, the Pyrenees (1836) and Normandy (1843), the Near East and the Auvergne remained his major themes. *Ezbekiyah Square* (1834; untraced, engraving in Paris, Bib. N.), the *Recollection of the Countryside near Rosetta* (1835; untraced, engraving in Paris, Bib. N.) and the illustration of the *Countryside near Luxor* published (Paris, 1835) by the engraver Léon de Joannis (*fl* 1808–50) brought him to the attention of the public. Although *Twilight* (1836; untraced, engraving in Paris, Bib. N.) was refused by the Salon in 1836, his pastel drawing of the *Villa Pamphili* (Paris, priv. col.) was engraved by Eugène Ciceri (Paris, Bib. N.).

During the late 1830s Marilhat concentrated on historical and poetical landscapes, influenced by Neo-classicism, by Théodore Caruelle d'Aligny particularly, and by his friend Corot. D'Aligny's influence is apparent, for example, in the *Pastoral Scene* (1837; Le Mans, Mus. Tessé). The press criticized the coldness and artifice of his compositions but praised his *Tomb of Sheik Abou-Mandour* (1837; untraced) and his *Delta* (1839; untraced). His collaboration in the production of 86 drawings for the *Journey from Syria* (1837) and the *Journey from Asia Minor* (1838), published by the archaeologist Léon de Laborde, confirmed his reputation as an Orientalist. From 1840 Marilhat returned to his Egyptian and Auvergnat subjects, though he now darkened his palette. His work also became more naturalistic as he began to depict subjects traditionally associated with the Barbizon painters, including the Forest of Fontainebleau and Chevreuse. The seven royal commissions executed between 1843 and 1845 are evidence of his fame at this time. The *Return from Château*

d'Eu (1844; Versailles, Château) was commissioned after Queen Victoria's visit to Louis-Philippe in 1843 and executed with Eugène Lami. Marilhat's success culminated in the exhibition of eight major works at the Salon of 1844, including *Recollections of the Banks of the Nile* (untraced), *Egyptian Town at Twilight* (1844; untraced, engraving in Paris, Bib. N.) and *Memories of the Area around Thiers* (1844; untraced, engraving in Clermont-Ferrand, Bib. Mun.). His commissioned individual and family portraits, particularly his graphite pencil drawings, are distinguished by a fine linear style reminiscent of Ingres that suggests the character and social status of the sitter, for example in *Mme Madieu* (1838; Paris, priv. col.). Marilhat lapsed into insanity and died aged 36. He left many unfinished paintings; when the contents of his studio were sold (13–15 Dec 1847) 281 works were listed.

Marilhat's stylistic development falls into five phases. His early picturesque landscapes (1828–31) give way to more balanced compositions (1831–5), notable for their vigorous colours and warm light. Between 1835 and 1839 Marilhat worked in an academic style. His mature works (1839–45), with their full forms and technical perfection, pleased his admirers despite their over-reliance on the effects of shadow. His last works (1846–7) show a marked decline in their conception and execution. Marilhat's Orientalist works present a vision of Egypt that is at once authentic and idealized. He depicted both the everyday life of the region and the grandeur of its ruins and mosques. He produced individual studies of typical characters—hookah smokers, Nubian warriors and fellah musicians—and integrated carefully grouped objects and figures into daguerreotype-like landscapes to produce a tranquil, meditative effect. Works such as *Syrian Arabs on a Journey*

(1844; Chantilly, Mus. Condé; see fig.) suggest the immutable characteristics of the Near East. His French landscapes similarly combine naturalistic themes (forest edges, cattle pens, storm effects and rocks damp with water) with a treatment that is akin to the clarity and harmony of Poussin's work. The paintings suggest the influence of Claude Lorrain's golden skies and diffuse light, while their poetic atmosphere arises partly from references to Classical mythology and partly from Marilhat's vision of a world in which exuberant palm leaves, sleepy waters and twilight effects invite the viewer to fall into reverie. His colour, bright at first, was later softened into half-tones, though he remained a scrupulously precise draughtsman and his works have a documentary value. His watercolours rival those of John Frederick Lewis in their refinement.

Marilhat was, together with Delacroix and Alexandre-Gabriel Decamps, an important and influential figure in the development of French Orientalist painting. His numerous imitators included the painters Théodore Frère (1814–88) and Narcisse Berchère (1819–91), while Eugène Fromentin, captivated by his elegant style, modelled his works on Marilhat from 1843 to 1861. Reproductions of Marilhat's work by 46 engravers, and copies of his work by William Leighton Leitch (1804–83), William Forrest (1805–89) and Henry Warren (1794–1879), increased his reputation until 1886. Thereafter, though valued by Monet and Degas, his work suffered a period of obscurity until 1960, when it was rehabilitated. There is a large collection of prints after his paintings in the British Museum, London.

WRITINGS
'Marilhat paysagiste: Fragments de ses lettres inédites', *Mag. Pittoresque*, xxiv (1856), pp. 347–50, 370–71, 403–4

BIBLIOGRAPHY
T. Gautier: 'Prosper Marilhat', *Rev. Deux Mondes*, xxiii (1848), pp. 56–75
G. A. Delafoulhouze: 'Notice sur Prosper Marilhat, peintre de paysage', *Mém. Acad. Sci., B.-Lett. & A. Clermont-Ferrand*, iv (1862), pp. 27–49
H. Gomot: *Marilhat et son oeuvre* (Clermont-Ferrand, 1884)
M. Delotz: *Prosper Marilhat (1811–47): Visite chez son neveu* (Thiers, 1913)
R. Bonniot: 'Le Peintre auvergnat Prosper Marilhat (1811–47): Etude iconographique', *Auvergne Litt.*, cxci (1966), pp. 3–28
D. Menu: 'L'Orient de Prosper Marilhat d'après quelques inédits', *Inf. Hist. A.*, xviii (1973), pp. 62–9
——: 'Un Paysagiste français du XIXe siècle: Prosper Marilhat et l'Auvergne', *Auvergne Lit.*, ccxviii–ix (1973), pp. 159–76
——: 'Portraits et figures d'Orient à propos de dessins de Prosper Marilhat au Musée des Beaux-Arts de Lyon', *Bull. Mus. & Mnmts Lyon.*, v/2 (1973), pp. 21–33
——: 'Prosper Marilhat à l'époque romantique', *Médec. Fr.*, ccxliii (1973), pp. 25–40
——: 'L'Orient gravé d'après P. Marilhat', *Marseille*, xcvii (1974), pp. 47–56
——: *Prosper Marilhat (1811–47)*, 2 vols (diss., U. Dijon, 1979)

DANIÈLE MENU

Marillier, Clément-Pierre (*b* Dijon, 28 June 1740; *d* Boissise, nr Melun, 11 Aug 1808). French draughtsman. Having first studied painting in Dijon, in 1760 he became Noël Hallé's pupil in Paris, but, needing to earn a living, by 1762 he had changed to a career as an illustrator. Like Charles Eisen, whose associate he became, he devoted himself mainly to illustrating the amorous poetry of such writers as François-Thomas de Baculard d'Arnaud (*Anecdotes et nouvelles*, 1767–75, later published as a collection in *Epreuves du sentiment*, Paris, 1775) and Claude-Joseph

Dorat (notably the *Oeuvres complètes*, Amsterdam, 1772–3). He was at home with courtly and slightly erotic subjects, treated with wit and delicacy, but was less successful with the serious subjects he wanted to treat in the 1780s, including 150 drawings for the two-volume *L'Abrégé de l'histoire universelle en figures* (Paris, 1785–90) and the 300 drawings (some of which Marillier commissioned from Nicolas-André Monsiau) for the *Holy Bible* in 12 octavo volumes (Paris, 1789–1804). A contract that he signed with the publisher Defer de Maisonneuve shows that Marillier was to be paid 4000 livres for these 300 drawings. Such an output allowed him to live in some comfort at Boissise, where during the period of the French Revolution (1789–95) he found a role in organizing the national festivals in Melun.

BIBLIOGRAPHY
R. Portalis: *Les Dessinateurs d'illustrations au XVIIIème siècle*, i (Paris, 1877), pp. 364–86
T. Lhuillier: 'Le Dessinateur Marillier: Etude biographique suivie d'un catalogue chronologique de son oeuvre', *Réun. Soc. B.-A. Départs*, x (1886), pp. 368–404
G. N. Ray: *The Art of the French Illustrated Book, 1700 to 1914* (New York, 1986), p. 86 [examples of Marillier's original drgs]

CHRISTIAN MICHEL

Marimon, José María Madurell y. *See* MADURELL I MARIMÓN, JOSEP MARÍA.

Marin, John (*b* Rutherford, NJ, 23 Dec 1870; *d* Cape Split, ME, 1 Oct 1953). American painter and printmaker. He attended Stevens Institute in Hoboken, NJ, and worked briefly as an architect before studying at the Pennsylvania Academy of the Fine Arts in Philadelphia from 1899 to 1901 under Thomas Pollock Anshutz and Hugh Breckenridge (1870–1937). His education was supplemented by five years of travel in Europe where he was exposed to avant-garde trends. While abroad he made etchings of notable and picturesque sites, for example *Campanile, S Pietro, Venice* (1907; see Zigrosser, no. 57), which were the first works he sold.

Marin returned permanently to the USA in 1911, settling in New York and devoting the rest of his long career to painting views of the city and country. His art initially reflected the impact of Impressionism and Post-Impressionism. During the next decade he first moved towards a modernist artistic statement, seen in his views of New York and nearby Weehawkin, New Jersey. The *Weehawkin* series (watercolour, 1910; New York, Met.) reveals a Fauvist handling and choice of colour, and an abstract sense of design, while the New York images demonstrate the artist's willingness to fragment and distort a scene for expressive purposes. Marin was one of the first artists to convey the 20th-century city in modern pictorial terms: in works such as *Brooklyn Bridge* (watercolour, c. 1912; New York, Met.) the urban landscape seems to erupt; buildings and streets break apart, heaving under the pressure of the frenetic pace and congestion of city life.

During the 1920s Marin's handling became even more expressive and abbreviated, at times calligraphic, seen for example in *Lower Manhattan (Composing Derived from Top of Woolworth)* (watercolour, 1922; New York, MOMA); objects were further simplified into fractured coloured planes; directional lines suggesting movement were added and borders painted and fragmented. His city images underwent a major transformation in the 1930s, as the figures increased in scale and became more important elements in the scenes, demonstrated in *Untitled (Figures in Downtown New York City)* (drawing, 1932; artist's estate, see 1971 exh. cat., p. 58). His style did not change substantially thereafter, although it became increasingly expressionistic.

The natural landscape was equally important to Marin. Both in his art and in his writings he revealed a unique sensitivity to and love of nature. He travelled frequently, visiting New Jersey, upstate New York, New England, New Mexico and Canada, to capture the nuances of varied moods in response to nature. Stylistically his landscapes parallel the evolution of the city views. They culminate in what have become perhaps his best-known works, the images of the sea along the Maine coast that he created during the 1930s, for example *Composition, Cape Split, Maine, No. 3* (oil on canvas, 1933; Santa Barbara, CA, Mus. A.); these convey a primeval power.

Although he could be lyrical, Marin brought a rare vigour and intensity to the medium of watercolour. He approached it as both a painting and a graphic medium. He used oils sporadically from the early 1900s, the *Weehawkin* series including his most extensive early work in the medium. He did not, however, begin to devote a significant amount of his attention to oil painting until the 1930s.

Marin was one of the few early American modernists who received substantial attention and critical praise throughout most of his career. Upon his return from abroad, he became a member of the avant-garde circle centred around Alfred Stieglitz, and his work was shown on a regular basis at Stieglitz's galleries from 1909. As a result of his first retrospective, held in 1920 at the Daniel Gallery, New York, the collector Ferdinand Howald (1856–1934) became Marin's first important patron. Marin was also one of the first American artists to be accorded a retrospective exhibition by MOMA (1936), New York.

PUBLISHED WRITINGS
H. J. Seligman, ed.: *Letters of John Marin* (New York, 1931)
D. Norman, ed.: *The Selected Writings of John Marin* (New York, 1949)
C. Gray, ed.: *John Marin by John Marin* (New York, 1977)

BIBLIOGRAPHY
John Marin (exh. cat., essays by H. McBride, M. Hartley and E. M. Benson, New York, MOMA, 1936/*R* 1966)
M. Helm: *John Marin* (Boston, 1948)
John Marin in New Mexico: 1929 & 1930 (exh. cat. by V. D. Coke, Albuquerque, U. NM, A. Mus., 1968)
C. Zigrosser: *The Complete Etchings of John Marin: Catalogue Raisonné* (Philadelphia, 1969)
S. Reich: *John Marin: A Stylistic Analysis and Catalogue Raisonné*, 2 vols (Tucson, 1970)
John Marin: 1870–1953 (exh. cat. by L. Curry, Los Angeles, CA, Co. Mus. A., 1971)

ILENE SUSAN FORT

Marin, Joseph-Charles (*b* Paris, 1759; *d* Paris, 18 Sept 1834). French sculptor. He emulated the graceful Rococo style of his master, Clodion, and enjoyed a successful career, working largely for private patrons and exhibiting at the Paris Salon from 1791 to 1833. Most of his works are terracotta busts, statuettes and groups made in imitation of Clodion's erotic Rococo female figures, but with an added touch of realism and a more marked interest in varieties of texture. Among them are a *Bust of a Girl* (Paris, Mus. Jacquemart-André), the statuettes *Ganymede* and *Hebe* (Bayonne, Mus. Bonnat) and the *Young Girl with a Dove* (1791; Paris, Louvre). More severe is his group *Canadian Indians at their Infant's Grave* (1794; ex-Pierre Decourcelle priv. col., Paris). In 1801 he won the Prix de Rome for sculpture with the classicizing plaster bas-relief of *Caius Gracchus Leaving his Wife Licinia to Rejoin his Partisans* (Paris, Ecole N. Sup. B.-A.). This work and the bold and free terracotta sketch of *Roman Charity* (*c*. 1805; Besançon, Mus. B.-A. & Archéol.) show that Marin was able to produce original works in different styles. In 1805 he was made a professor at the Académie de France in Rome; in the same year he finished the marble tomb of *Pauline de Montmorin, Comtesse de Beaumont* (Rome, S Luigi dei Francesi), commissioned by François-René, Vicomte de Chateaubriand. Marin's most famous work is the marble *Bather* (1808; Paris, Louvre) in the Neo-classical style. His reputation was in decline before 1820, and he lived in some poverty towards the end of his life.

BIBLIOGRAPHY
P. Bonnefon: 'Quelques Lettres inédites du sculpteur J.-C. Marin', *Chron. A. & Curiosité* (1901), 35, pp. 283–5; 36, pp. 290–92; 39, pp. 315–17; 41, pp. 331–2; (1902), 1, pp. 2–5; 2, p. 13; 3, pp. 1–20; 4, pp. 28–9; (1906), 6, p. 45; 7, p. 53; 10, pp. 77–8
Collection Pierre Decourcelle: Tableaux anciens, aquarelles, pastels, dessins, sculptures de l'Ecole Française (Paris, 1911), pp. 133–4
S. Rubenstein: 'French Eighteenth-century Sculpture in the Collection of Mortimer Schiff', *A. America*, xii (1924), pp. 67–75
P. Pradel: '*La Baigneuse* de Marin', *Mus. France*, xiii (1948), pp. 112–14
M. Quinquenet: *Un Elève de Clodion: Joseph-Charles Marin* (Paris, 1948)
France in the Eighteenth Century (exh. cat. ed. D. Sutton; London, RA, 1968), nos 810–12
R. Rosenblum: 'Caritas Romana after 1760: Some Romantic Lactations', *ARTnews Annu.*, xxxviii (1972), pp. 43–63
The Age of Neo-classicism (exh. cat., Council of Europe 14th exh.; London, 1972), no. 404
Skulptur aus dem Louvre: 89 Werke des französischen Klassizismus, 1770–1830 (exh. cat., ed. J.-R. Gaborit; Duisburg, Lehmbruck-Mus.; Karlsruhe, Städt Gal. Prinz-Max-Pal.; Gotha, Schloss Friedenstein; 1989–90), pp. 128–9, 292, 318

MICHAEL PRESTON WORLEY

Marinali. Italian family of sculptors. Francesco Marinali (*b* 17 Oct 1609; *d* after 1655) was a sculptor in Angarano, who moved to Bassano after the birth of his sons (1) Orazio Marinali, Francesco Marinali the younger (1647–after 1717) and (2) Angelo Marinali. The family subsequently established (*c*. 1668) a workshop in Vicenza and were active throughout the Veneto in the late 17th century and early 18th. Other sculptors employed in the Marinali workshop included Angelo De Putti (*fl* 1699–1725) and Giacomo Cassetti (1682–1757). The workshop was directed by Orazio, and while Francesco the younger was only an executor and not the creator of original works, Angelo played an important role. Like Orazio he had a distinctive style and carried out independent commissions.

(1) Orazio Marinali (*b* Angarano, 24 Feb 1643; *d* Vicenza, 7 April 1720). The most celebrated member of the family, he trained in Venice with Josse de Corte, the leading sculptor in the city at that time, whose dramatic power and feeling for chiaroscural effects Orazio adopted. De Corte's influence is to be found most clearly in Orazio's early works, such as the marble statues of the *Virgin and Child with SS Dominic and Catherine* (1679), made for the altar of the Rosary in S Nicolò, Treviso, and the *Virgin and Child with Saints, Angels and Putti*, made for the cathedral in Bassano del Grappa. Orazio became a prolific sculptor of religious works, and he was active in towns throughout the Veneto. Most of his works are initialled 'O.M.'. Although he collaborated with his brother Angelo on numerous occasions, Orazio remained the dominant partner. In 1681, for example, the city of Bassano del Grappa commissioned from both Marinali brothers the statue of *St Bassano*, the city's patron saint, for the main square (*in situ*). One of Orazio's own particularly successful projects was his decoration for the church of S Maria di Monte Berico, Vicenza, executed between 1690 and 1703. Here he provided numerous imposing statues of saints and reliefs in *pietra tenera* (a soft limestone from near Taranto) for the exterior and stucco figures of four prophets and marble Holy Water stoups for the interior. In 1704 he completed the high altar of S Giuliano, Vicenza, with marble figures of the *Risen Christ with Saints*. Nearly all the sculptures there are signed by him. He later (1715–17) executed the marble figures of the *Guardian Angel* and the *Angel Gabriel* for the altar of SS Sacramento in S Giovanni Battista, Bassano.

Orazio, whose sculptures are solid and massive but nevertheless display vivacity and naturalism, also carried out a number of secular commissions, including the decoration of palaces, gardens and parks. He made many garden statues, including the pastoral fancy-dress masqueraders for the Villa Lampertico at Montegaldella near Vicenza (mostly executed by workshop assistants). Other sets of figures include those he made for the Parco Revedin-Bolasco at Castelfranco, the Villa Trissino near Vicenza and the particularly fine *Seasons* in the Giardino Barnabo, Venice. The Marinali workshop was known also for the production of male and female marble busts, the former often characterized by almost grotesque exaggeration. Examples are at the Villa Pisani at Stra, two male busts are at Linz (Stadtmus.). Two self-portraits in stone by Orazio are extant (Bassano del Grappa, Mus. Civ.; Vicenza, Mus. Civ. A. & Stor.); numerous terracotta *bozzetti* also survive (same museums) and confirm his sculptural sensitivity. This sensitivity is also apparent in a notable album of his drawings (Bassano), which contains numerous imaginative examples of his favourite themes.

(2) Angelo Marinali (*b* Angarano, 24 May 1654; *d* Vicenza, 1702). Brother of (1) Orazio Marinali. He played an important part in the Marinali family's Vicenza workshop but also undertook independent work. Notable examples are the marble allegorical figures and a ciborium with saints in S Luca, Verona, and the marble and stucco figures of saints and allegories for S Nicolò, Verona, the churches of S Antonio Abate and S Nicolò on the Lido, Venice, and the churches of S Corona, S Giuliano and S Maria dei Servi in Vicenza. The figures of *St Augustine* and *St Ambrose* (S Nicolò al Lido) are particularly imposing. Angelo's style is distinguished from that of his brother Orazio by a less dramatic chiaroscuro and by a greater softness of light, which introduces a sweeter and more

elegiac note, although the formal character of his figures is close to his brother's work.

BIBLIOGRAPHY
P. M. Tua: *Alcune opere poco note di Orazio Marinali* (Bassano, 1927), p. 10
C. Tua: 'Orazio Marinali e i suoi fratelli', *Riv. A.*, n. s. 2, xvii (1935), pp. 281–322
G. Fasolo: 'I Marinali', *Odeo Olimpico* (1942), pp. 45–75; (1943), 207–29
A. M. Semenzato: 'Per un catologo degli scultori Orazio e Angelo Marinali', *Crit. A.* (1956), pp. 589–91
F. Barbieri: 'Terrecotte, marini e disegni dei Marinali presso il museo civico di Vicenza', *Studi in onore di F. M. Mistrorigo* (Vicenza, 1958), pp. 111–97
P. Toniato: 'La scuola dei Marinali', *A. Veneta* (1964)
L. Puppi: 'Nuovi documenti sui Marinali', *Atti Ist. Veneto Sci., Lett. & A.*, cxxv (1966–7), pp. 195–215

CAMILLO SEMENZATO

Marinatos, Spyridon (Nikolaos) (*b* Kephallenia, 1901; *d* Thera, 1 Oct 1974). Greek archaeologist and historian. After graduating at Athens in Classical Philology and Archaeology (1919), Marinatos began his career with the Archaeological Service in Crete. Rapid promotion (Ephor, 1921) culminated in the Directorship of Herakleion Archaeological Museum (1929), after two years of study in Germany. For the next decade he excavated many Minoan sites, including Nirou Chani, Amnisos, Tylissos and Arkalochori. His energy and elegant, often bold, interpretations brought him the rewards first of the Directorship of the Service (1937) and then of a chair at Athens (1939). The last he held until 1968, though being twice recalled to the Service (1955–8; 1967–74). On the mainland he concentrated on Mycenaean matters, conducting excavations at Mycenae, around Pylos (1952 onwards) and at Marathon (1969–71), and producing many articles on aspects of Mycenaean culture, often set within a wider Aegean and Mediterranean perspective. Yet he also found time to work on Crete (Vathypetro, 1949–51), and after 1967 in particular at Akrotiri on Thera, where his discovery of a Late Bronze Age settlement preserved under volcanic debris was not only his crowning achievement, but a vindication of much of a theory, proposed in 1939, concerning Thera and the decline of Neo-Palatial Crete. His death resulted from an accident there while excavating. Bronze Age archaeology was not his only sphere of interest: excavations at the Geometric sanctuary of Dreros (1936), and at Thermopylae (1939) and Helike (1960–66), as well as publications on Hellenistic sculpture (1923), Byzantine icons (1921) and sundry philological matters all bear witness to his wide-ranging intellect and contributed to his international reputation.

WRITINGS
'The Volcanic Destruction of Minoan Crete', *Antiquity*, xiii/52 (Dec 1939), pp. 425–39
Excavations at Thera: Preliminary Reports, 7 vols (Athens, 1968–76)
Kreta, Thera und das mykenische Hellas (Munich, 1973)
BIBLIOGRAPHY
S. Iakovides: Obituary, *Gnomon*, xlvii (1975), pp. 635–8

D. EVELY

Marine painting. Term used to describe a variety of painted subjects ranging from the sketchiest of beach scenes to the carefully detailed ships' portraits commissioned by naval officers and ship-owners. There is no clear division between marine painting and landscape painting, and many of the most vivid portrayals of the sea have been painted by artists with little or no first-hand experience of ships. In the 17th and 18th centuries marine paintings were variously described as 'sea-pieces', 'seascapes', 'marines' and 'ship-paintings'. The most popular subjects were sea battles, harbours, shipwrecks and estuary scenes. During the 19th century other subjects were added to the repertory including pictures of the seaside, fishing boats, yachts and vistas of the open sea.

1. EARLY HISTORY. Marine art can be traced back to the wall paintings of royal barges in Egyptian tombs dated 1360 BC. The voyages of Odysseus were illustrated on Greek vases of the 5th century BC. Glimpses of ships and ports appear in medieval manuscripts and in the frescoes and altarpieces of the early Renaissance in Italy. The story of Jonah and the Whale and the legend of St Nicholas of Myra, patron saint of sailors, provided opportunities to paint shipwrecks and storms. Among the finest of these early examples of marine painting is Vittore Carpaccio's *Legend of St Ursula* (1495; Venice, Accad.; *see* CARPACCIO, (1), fig. 4). Maps and charts are another early source. The voyages of the great explorers in the 16th century resulted in the production of beautifully drawn maps, which are frequently decorated with pictures of ships and sea monsters. Closely linked with these maps are aerial views of towns, the most notable examples being those of Venice and Antwerp with numerous vessels moored along the waterfront.

The aerial view resulted in two pictures that occupy a key place in the development of marine painting: the so-called *Portuguese Carracks* (1520; London, N. Mar. Mus.), which was painted by a north European artist, probably Cornelis Anthonisz.; and Pieter Bruegel the elder's *View of Naples* (Rome, Gal. Doria-Pamphili). These two pictures, together with the famous *Storm at Sea* (Vienna, Ksthist. Mus.), long associated with Bruegel but now generally attributed to Josse de Momper II, were forerunners of the great age of marine painting that was centred on the Netherlands in the 17th century.

2. SUBSEQUENT DEVELOPMENT.

(i) *The Netherlands.* The first of a long line of Dutch marine artists was Hendrick Cornelis Vroom. Much influenced in his early years by Paul Bril, he began with landscapes and townscapes but moved on to sea battles, storms and harbour scenes. He was followed by Adam Willaerts, who specialized in colourful embarkation scenes. Jan Porcellis introduced a very different mood with his sombre seascapes and his low-key renderings of fishing boats in humble settings. He led the way for a generation of talented artists including Jan van Goyen, Aelbert Cuyp and Simon de Vlieger. Van Goyen's silvery palette and cloudy skies are a distinctive feature of his river scenes. Cuyp's contribution was the acute observation of sunlight and reflections, the *Passage Boat* (London, Buckingham Pal. Royal Col.) being a spectacular example. De Vlieger painted cool, grey pictures of windswept beaches and rocky coasts. He was a friend of Willem van de Velde the elder and the teacher of Willem van de Velde the younger.

The van de Veldes were an impressive team, the elder making on-the-spot drawings of warships and naval actions, while his son used the information for his masterful paintings. The younger van de Velde painted storms and calms, as in *Dutch Vessels Inshore, and Men Bathing* (or *Calm: A Wijdschip and a Kaag in an Inlet close to a Sea Wall*, 1661; London, N.G.; see fig.), with equal ability, and his work was admired and copied by generations of marine artists. The only two artists of his day who could challenge his supremacy were Jan van de Cappelle and Ludolf Bakhuizen. The former was a gifted amateur artist who painted estuary scenes shimmering with sails and watery reflections beneath billowing clouds. Bakhuizen was as skilful as van de Velde in the drawing of ships and produced seascapes of great power with dramatic use of light and shade. Other accomplished marine artists from this golden age were Abraham Storck, who specialized in harbour scenes, Hendrick Dubbels, Abraham van Beyeren and Reinier Nooms (also called Zeeman).

(ii) *Britain.* The van de Veldes emigrated to England in 1672 and established a flourishing school of marine painting in London. Isaac Sailmaker and Peter Monamy were among their many followers. Samuel Scott depicted sea battles in the manner of the van de Veldes but also painted a number of finely observed views of the Thames, which show the beginnings of an English style. This was taken a stage further in the mid-18th century by Charles Brooking, an artist who received scant recognition in a short life dominated by illness. His sparkling seascapes are notable for their exquisitely drawn ships and subtle portrayal of wind and weather. Brooking was followed by two generations of professional marine artists who recorded the sea battles and shipyards of the later 18th century. They were mostly ex-shipwrights or former seamen and included John Cleveley, Dominic Serres, Nicholas Pocock, Francis Holman (*fl* 1760–90) and Thomas Luny.

Many of the landscape artists associated with the Romantic movement in England turned to the sea as a source of inspiration. Philippe-Jacques de Loutherbourg, who settled in London in 1771, produced a number of shipwreck pictures in the style of Joseph Vernet; he also painted sea battles, the most impressive being his huge canvas of the *Battle of the Glorious First of June* (1794; London, N. Mar. Mus.). J. M. W. Turner devoted much of his long and successful life to the portrayal of the sea in all its moods. *The Shipwreck* (1805; London, Tate) is an awesome vision of the destructive power of a storm. Turner's similar mastery of the sunlit calm is demonstrated in one of the most beautiful of all marine paintings, *Dordrecht: The Dort Packet-boat from Rotterdam Becalmed* (1818; New Haven, CT, Yale Cent. Brit. A.).

An artist who emerged from Turner's shadow and became the leading marine painter of his day was Clarkson Stanfield. A former seaman and a theatrical scene-painter, he was particularly adept at painting the surface of the sea and the weather-beaten timbers of jetties. The pre-eminent figure after Stanfield's death was E. W. Cooke, who painted meticulously rendered pictures of Dutch fishing boats and English coastal scenes. Two artists who specialized in panoramic vistas of the open sea were John Brett and Henry Moore (1831–95), while W. L. Wyllie painted

Marine painting by Willem van de Velde II: *Calm: A Wijdschip and a Kaag in an Inlet close to a Sea Wall* (or *Dutch Vessels close Inshore at Low Tide*), oil on canvas, 632×722 mm, 1661 (London, National Gallery)

everything from battle-cruisers and ocean liners to tug-boats and yachts.

It is sometimes assumed that marine painting in England suffered a sharp decline in the 20th century, but this is not the case. In Cornwall the artists of the Newlyn school, led by Stanhope Forbes, produced some brilliantly observed studies of the local fishing boats and harbours. The two world wars provided a huge variety of subjects for official war artists, some of whom—Charles Pears (1873–1958), Norman Wilkinson, Edward Wadsworth, Montague Dawson (1895–1973) and Richard Eurich (*b* 1903)—later turned their talents to the more peaceful subject-matter of yachts and coastal views.

(iii) USA. By the end of the 19th century American artists had produced a number of seascapes remarkable for their originality and freshness of vision. A forerunner was the British artist Robert Salmon, who settled in Boston in 1829, but the first American painter to specialize in marine subjects was Fitz Hugh Lane. His pictures of sailing craft in sheltered bays have an extraordinary stillness and clarity

of light. *Owl's Head, Penobscot Bay* (1862; Boston, MA, Mus. F.A.) is typical, showing a schooner becalmed beneath a pearly sky. The landscapes and seascapes of Martin Johnson Heade also have a static quality, but that of the calm before the storm. His *Thunderstorm over Narragansett Bay* (1868; Fort Worth, TX, Amon Carter Mus.) is an astonishing work in which fishermen and sailing boats are starkly illuminated against a black sea and threatening thunder clouds. Usually linked with the work of Lane and Heade is Frederick Edwin Church: he made his name with *Niagara* (1857; Washington, DC, Corcoran Gal. A.), a minutely observed study of the vast, curving expanse of water viewed from the very edge of the falls. Church also painted stormy coast scenes and ships among the icebergs of the Arctic.

The most gifted and versatile of the American landscape and seascape painters was Winslow Homer. Equally adept in watercolours and oils, he painted a variety of subjects in a dashing style. *Breezing up* (1876; Washington, DC, N.G.) captures the excitement of sailing a small boat on a sparkling, summer day. His later works are more sombre. The *Fog Warning* (1885; Boston, MA, Mus. F.A.) is one of many paintings showing the local fishermen battling with the elements off Cape Cod. In dramatic contrast to Homer's seascapes are the river scenes of Thomas Eakins. Fascinated by photography and perspective, Eakins constructed his pictures with elaborate care: his masterpiece, *Max Schmitt in a Single Scull* (1871; New York, Met.), is a painting of astonishing brilliance and technical skill.

(iv) France. In France many of the greatest seascapes were painted by landscape painters. The first of these was Claude Lorrain, with his imaginary harbours bathed in sunlight. Claude-Joseph Vernet, a specialist, earned a reputation as the most accomplished marine painter of the mid-18th century. He perfected a successful formula for dramatic shipwrecks and picturesque seaports. In 1753 he received a royal commission to paint all the ports of France, and, of the 15 pictures he completed, 13 hang in the Musée de la Marine and 2 in the Musée du Louvre, Paris. Théodore Gericault and Gustave Courbet, though not marine specialists, cannot be ignored here. The *Raft of the Medusa* (1819; Paris, Louvre; *see* GERICAULT, THÉODORE, fig. 3) is one of the most powerful of all images of the sea. Courbet was inspired by his first sight of the Mediterranean to paint the *Artist on the Seashore at Palavas* (1854; Montpellier, Mus. Fabre) and later painted *Stormy Sea*, or '*The Wave*' (1869; Paris, Louvre) in which heavy seas break on a desolate beach. Less dramatic but full of poetry are the marines of Charles-François Daubigny. *Etretat* (Glasgow, Burrell Col.) is a deceptively simple picture of a bay with distant sails beneath a summer sky. Daubigny made several visits to England between 1866 and 1870 and painted some atmospheric views of the Thames.

One of the few French artists to concentrate exclusively on marine subjects was Eugène Boudin. Son of a ship's captain, Boudin painted harbour scenes alive with light and movement, while his breezy depictions of fashionable crowds on the beaches of Deauville and Trouville brought him considerable success. Marine subjects frequently appear in the work of some of the French Impressionists. Manet and Seurat painted harbours, Alfred Sisley was fond of river scenes (*see* IMPRESSIONISM, colour pl. VII), but it was Monet who made the most significant contribution. *Impression: Sunrise* (1874; ex-Mus. Marmottan, Paris; *see* IMPRESSIONISM, fig. 1), the picture that gave its name to the whole movement, was an oil-sketch of the harbour at Le Havre. Monet also painted numerous beach scenes at Fécamp and Etretat, river scenes with boats at Argenteuil and a dazzling series of paintings of the Thames showing Waterloo Bridge and the Houses of Parliament in different lights.

BIBLIOGRAPHY

J. Wilmerding: *A History of American Marine Painting* (Boston, MA, 1968)
D. Cordingly: *Marine Painting in England: 1700–1900* (London, 1974)
W. Gaunt: *Marine Painting: An Historical Survey* (London, 1975)
E. H. H. Archibald: *Dictionary of Sea Painters* (Woodbridge, 1981)
M. Russell: *Visions of the Sea* (Leiden, 1983)

DAVID CORDINGLY

Marinetti, (Emilio) [Angelo; Carlo] **Filippo Tommaso** (*b* Alexandria, 22 Dec 1876; *d* Bellagio, 2 Dec 1944). Italian writer and theorist. He was educated by Jesuit monks in Alexandria until 1893, when he moved to Paris. Having obtained a Baccalauréat, he studied law at the Università degli Studi di Genova, from which he graduated in 1899. In 1898 he published poetry for the first time, in particular the free verse *Les Vieux Marins*: this was awarded a prize by Gustave Kahn and the Symbolist poet, Catulle Mendès, and was recited by Sarah Bernhardt at the 'Samedis populaires' held at her theatre in Paris. In late 1898 Marinetti settled in Milan where he was to found and run the international review *Poesia* (1905–9), in which Symbolist poets and forerunners of free verse collaborated. However, he maintained close links with French culture. In Paris he published the epic poem *La Conquête des étoiles* in 1902 and his first satirical tragedy *Le Roi bombance* in 1905; the latter, still influenced by Symbolism and Alfred Jarry, was not performed until 1909, at the Théâtre de l'Oeuvre in Paris. In 1907 he visited the Abbaye de Créteil, whose circle heavily influenced Marinetti's Futurist ideas.

In 1909 Marinetti published his 'Manifeste de fondation du Futurisme', which aroused immediate international repercussions (*see* FUTURISM). This manifesto proclaimed a new kind of poetry, exalting the love of danger, aggression, speed and war ('the war's only hygiene') and the excitement of great crowds, revolutions, industry and technology. Marinetti urged the destruction of museums, libraries and academies. His ideas were extended to figurative art in the *Manifesto dei pittori futuristi* (1910), signed by Giacomo Balla, Umberto Boccioni, Carlo Carrà, Luigi Russolo and Gino Severini. In 1910 the manifestos were declaimed in riotous soirées throughout Italy. Marinetti also publicized Futurism abroad, where it had an important influence, for example on CUBO-FUTURISM in Russia. Marinetti visited St Petersburg and Moscow in 1910 and 1913, and London in 1911, when he gave a lecture on Futurism at the Lyceum Club. On that occasion he challenged to a duel an Irish journalist who had denigrated the Italian army. During 1911 Marinetti fervently supported the Italian campaign in Libya, in which he served as a war correspondent for *L'Intransigeant*. He also reported in 1912 on the war in the Balkans. In the same year Marinetti presented Futurist exhibitions in Paris, Berlin, Brussels and also in the Sackville Gallery in London, where the catalogue contained English translations of key Futurist manifestos. Marinetti had an important influence in Britain on CHRISTOPHER NEVINSON and on the development of VORTICISM, even though Ezra Pound was to describe the Italian as a 'corpse' in the Vorticist manifesto published in *Blast* in 1914.

In May 1912 Marinetti published the 'Manifesto tecnico della letteratura Futurista', which was to revolutionize poetic techniques and contemporary prose. Marinetti declared the abolition of syntax, punctuation, adjectives and adverbs and instead proposed placing nouns at random and using verbs in the infinitive: 'after free verse, behold words at last in freedom.' The typography of the printed 'words in freedom' (*parole in libertà*) developed so that on the page the poems had expressive pictorial qualities (e.g. *A Tumultuous Assembly, Numerical Sensibility*; see fig.). These works were highly influential on the

Filippo Tommaso Marinetti: *A Tumultuous Assembly, Numerical Sensibility*, collage, after 1918 (private collection)

figurative use of words in Futurist paintings by such artists as CARLO CARRÀ. In Paris from 1912 to 1914 Marinetti frequently visited Guillaume Apollinaire, Blaise Cendrars, Max Jacob, Pierre Reverdy and the artist–poet Pierre Albert-Birot, all of whom were greatly influenced by the 'free words' of the Futurists. In Italy, after initial conflicts, Marinetti formed an alliance with Ardengo Soffici and Giovanni Papini, from 1913 using their review *Lacerba* to publish his ideas. His Futurist theories developed to cover areas other than literature and the visual arts: for example in 1914 he organized a series of conferences in London launching the manifesto *Abbasso il tango e Parsifal* condemning two dance styles that he considered decadent and degenerate. As well as dance, Marinetti's ideas concerned music, drama, film and such applied arts as industrial and graphic design, ceramics, textiles, bookbinding and metalwork. He also himself experimented with the plastic arts, for example in the *Self-portrait (Dynamic Combination of Objects)* (priv. col., see Belloli, 1982, p. 86), made of polychrome woods, matchboxes, various brushes and a grey silk handkerchief, hung from the centre of the main ceiling of the Doré Gallery in London in 1914.

At this time Marinetti strenuously supported Italian intervention in World War I. In Milan in September 1914 the Futurists, led by Marinetti, fought each other as a pro-war demonstration, and on a similar occasion in 1915

Marinetti was arrested together with the future Fascist leader Benito Mussolini. Marinetti encouraged the Futurists to depict warlike subjects in their paintings (e.g. Severini's *Cannon in Action*, 1915; Frankfurt am Main, Städel. Kstinst.). In July 1915 Marinetti volunteered for the Lombard cyclists battalion, in which he was wounded and decorated for bravery. On his return he again became involved with politics, founding the Futurist Political Party in February 1918. This was anti-clerical, anti-monarchist, nationalist and proposed left-wing policies. Mussolini used its support in his rise to power in 1922, even though policy differences quickly appeared. Marinetti continued to support FASCISM, even though the regime favoured a classical figurative style of art, which most of the first generation of Futurist artists adopted. Marinetti, however, persisted in promoting Futurist ideas and art.

In 1920 Marinetti constructed his first *Free-word Tactile Tables* (e.g. 'Paris–Soudan': *Tavola tattile in libertà*, 1920; Rome, Luce Marinetti priv. col.), which anticipated the 'poem-objects' of Dada and Surrealism, and in 1921 he published the 'Manifeste du tactilisme'. In 1925 he moved to Rome where he continued to direct the Futurist movement, which had its headquarters in his house. In 1929 he was first made a member of the Reale Accademia d'Italia and then asked to direct the Secretariat of the Accademia's Classe Arti e Lettere. In the late 1920s and

1930s Marinetti supported the phase of Futurist painting known as AEROPITTURA. He himself practised and theorized about 'aeropoesia', poetry concerned with the sensation and speed of flight. In 1933 he produced *Futurist Words in Freedom/Tactile, Thermic, Olefactory*, printed in coloured lithographs on metallic panels as pages of the *Libro di latta aggressivo e contundente* (1933), the world's first experimental object–book of poetry, produced by the Lito-latta Nosenzo of Savona in a limited edition of 250 for bibliophiles and edited by the Futurist poet Tullio d'Albisola.

Marinetti's aggressive nationalism reappeared in October 1935, when he went as a volunteer to the Italian war of conquest in Ethiopia (1935–6). His fascination with technology and warfare continued to inspire his poetry. In 1939 he created the 'poesia dei tecnicismi', which brought into poetic language terms specific to science, technology and contemporary arts and also utilized neologisms of the worlds of labour, finance and modern economics. In 1942 he celebrated with 'poesia armata' the military campaigns of the Axis powers in World War II. On 20 July 1942 he enrolled as a volunteer at the Russian Front, fighting in the battles of the Don, but was repatriated through illness after four months. In September 1944 in Venice, convalescing after an operation brought about by war fatigue, he gave to the Futurist painter and writer Giovanni Acquaviva (1900–72) his last Futurist manifesto *La Patriarte* (International Institute of Studies in Futurism, Milan, unpubd), in which he proposed an art of renewed expressive synthesis. In October 1944 he moved to Bellagio di Como where he was appointed keeper of the archives of the disbanded Accademia d'Italia and died soon after.

WRITINGS

Les Vieux Marins (Paris, 1898)
La Conquête des étoiles (Paris, 1902)
Le Roi bombance (Paris, 1905)
'Manifeste de fondation du Futurisme', *Le Figaro* (20 Feb 1909), p. 1
Mafarka le futuriste (Paris, 1910)
Le Futurisme (Paris, 1911)
La Bataille de Tripoli (Milan, 1912)
Zang-Tum-Tumb (Milan, 1914)
Guerra sola igiene del mondo (Milan, 1915)
Les Mots en liberté futuristes (Milan, 1919)
Futurismo e fascismo (Milan, 1924)
Libro di latta aggressivo e contundente (Savona, 1933)
L'aeropoema del golfo della Spezia (Milan, 1935)
Il poema africano della Divisione 28 Ottobre (Milan, 1937)
Il poema non umano dei tecnicismi (Milan, 1939)

BIBLIOGRAPHY

T. Pànteo: *Il poeta Marinetti* (Milan, 1908)
I. Domino: *F. T. Marinetti* (Palermo, 1911)
B. H. Samuel: *Essay on F. T. Marinetti* (London, 1914)
E. Settimelli: *Marinetti: L'uomo e l'artista* (Milan, 1921)
C. Pavolini: *Marinetti* (Rome, 1924)
R. J. Salas: *Marinetti* (Rio de Janeiro, 1926)
V. Schilirò: *Marinetti e il futurismo* (Bronte, 1929)
B. Corra: *Marinetti poeta* (Rome, 1938)
V. Dattilo: *Il pensiero di Marinetti* (Naples, 1938)
A. Viviani: *Il poeta Marinetti* (Turin, 1940)
G. Lipparini: *Marinetti* (Rome, 1941)
C. Belloli: *Marinetti: Presente!* (Milan, 1943)
F. Bellonzi: *La poesia di Marinetti* (Urbino, 1943)
W. Vaccari: *Vita e tumulti di Marinetti* (Milan, 1959)
L. De Maria, ed.: *Teoria e invenzione Futurista* (Verona, 1968) [sel. writings, incl. examples cited in the text]
G. Lista: *Marinetti* (Paris, 1976)
C. Belloli: *Iconografia di F. T. Marinetti, fondatore del Futurismo* (Milan, 1982)
J. P. Andreoli: *Marinetti et le premier manifeste du Futurisme* (Ottawa, 1986)
For further bibliography *see* FUTURISM.

CARLO BELLOLI

Marini, Marino (*b* Pistoia, 27 Feb 1901; *d* Viareggio, 6 Aug 1980). Italian sculptor, painter, draughtsman and printmaker. He studied at the Accademia di Belle Arti in Florence, joining in 1917 the classes in engraving and painting given by Galileo Chini and in 1922 those in sculpture under Domenico Trentacoste. He drew small subjects from life, such as flowers, birds and insects, and he also modelled and painted. After military service in 1924, he settled in Florence, where he opened his first studio. He worked intensively, experimenting with different materials, from terracotta to wood and plaster combined with paint, which he also sometimes used with bronze in order to accentuate forms and express movement. Marini made his début as a sculptor in 1928, when he exhibited at *La mostra del Novecento toscano* at the Galleria Milano in Milan. His sculptures of this period were free of any ornament or descriptive detail: they referred to history and occasionally to the fascinating symbolism of Roman and Etruscan statuary, or the Etruscan-inspired sculpture of Arturo Martini or the traditions of the Tuscan Quattrocento. Marini's work developed a mysterious mythical quality, for example in *People* (1929; Milan, Gal. A. Mod.), a small, coloured terracotta statue.

During the 1920s Marini travelled frequently to Paris, where he met Picasso, Laurens, Braque, Lipchitz and Maillol. In 1929, however, he settled in Lombardy at the invitation of Arturo Martini as his successor in the teaching of sculpture at the Scuola d'Arte della Villa Reale in Monza. He exhibited at the *Seconda mostra del Novecento italiano* in Milan in 1929 and subsequently in the group's exhibitions in Nice (1929), Basle (1930), and Helsinki and Stockholm (1931). In 1932 he had his first one-man exhibition at the Galleria Milano. In the 1930s he again travelled extensively in Europe, visiting Holland, England, Belgium, Austria, Germany and above all Paris, where he was able to renew contact with avant-garde artists such as Tanguy, De Chirico, Campigli and Kandinsky. He was a guest at all the major Italian exhibitions of the 1930s, including the Venice Biennales, the Milan Triennales and the Rome Quadriennales: in 1935 he received his first official recognition, winning the first prize for sculpture in the second Rome Quadriennale. His work in the 1930s was characterized by the continuing use of antique references and a formal quality of static equilibrium. For example, the heroic cycle of *Horsemen* begun in 1936 was marked by a search for balance between the juxtaposed masses of compact blocks of stone: the works were firmly established in the sculptural tradition of the Italian Novecento, for example the four bronze casts of the *Gentleman on Horseback* of 1937 (h. 1.56 m, version, Ottawa, N.G.).

In 1940 Marini resigned from his teaching post in Monza and became Professor of Sculpture at the Accademia di Belle Arti di Brera in Milan. During World War II he was in Locarno, where he befriended Giacometti, Fritz Wotruba and Hermann Haller. During this time he sculpted sensual, enigmatic female nudes, sometimes lacking head or arms in order to stress their resemblance to fragments of antique sculpture. These included the *Pomona* series and *Adolescent Girl* (1943; see fig.). In 1946 he

Marino Marini: *Adolescent Girl*, bronze, h. 1.13 m, 1943 (Florence, Museo Marino Marini)

returned to Milan. From his home–studio near the Accademia in the late 1940s he arrived at the culmination of the monumental expression of the previous decade. In his return to sculpture, painting and engraving he produced variations on the theme of *Horsemen*, *Warriors* and *Jugglers*, which expressed ever more urgently Marini's anguish over the uncertainties of the time. They symbolized the destruction of the myth of the heroic victor. In contrast with the noble figures of the 1930s, the *Horsemen* reappeared in 1946 as disorientated, tragic characters (e.g. *Horseman*, bronze, 1.64×1.55×0.67 m, 1947; London, Tate). A sense of tension is conveyed by the contrast between the horizontal lines of the vast back, long lowered neck and flattened head of the horse, and the vertical horseman, erect with fear. The harshness of the image is increased by the simplification of the forms, the rider without ears and with round, sunken eyes. Moreover, the overall balance between the juxtaposed masses enhances the expressionistic tragedy of the whole. As well as using bronze, Marini appreciated that the simplicity of stone and particularly clay and wood was well suited to this drastic simplification of form. He also developed the same theme in painting (e.g. *Horsemen*, mixed media, 1946; Antwerp, Openluchtmus. Beeldhouwkst Middelheim).

Marini visited the USA in 1950 for an exhibition at the gallery of the dealer Curt Valentin in New York. There Marini befriended such artists as Lipchitz, Alexander Calder, Arp, Lyonel Feininger and Max Beckmann. The success of his exhibition far exceeded even the most optimistic predictions and introduced him to the American art market. Other accolades followed, such as the sculpture prize at the Venice Biennale of 1952 and the Feltrinelli international prize for sculpture at the Accademia dei Lincei, Rome, in 1954. Marini's American experiences also contributed to a new artistic liberty: expressionistic vitality and a tragic sense found form in such abstract works as *Miracle* (1959–60; Turin, Gal. Civ. A. Mod.) and *Horseman* (1958–9), an open-air war memorial in The Hague.

In the 1960s Marini had further important exhibitions, including a one-man show at the Kunsthaus, Zürich (1962), and a retrospective in the Palazzo Venezia in Rome (1966). He also produced a long series of busts of contemporaries (e.g. *Henry Moore*, bronze, 1962; London, N.P.G.). However, distorted abstract works recalling animal or human forms predominated in both his sculpture and painting, which took on greater importance with intensified colour. The large abstract stone sculptures of the 1970s (e.g. *Ideal Composition*, l. 2.26 m) are characterized by extremely rough surfaces and, on occasion, energetic paintwork (e.g. *Idea of the Miracle*, h. 2.43 m, both 1971; Florence, Mus. Marino Marini). There are museums devoted to Marini's work in Milan, Pistoia and Florence.

BIBLIOGRAPHY

E. Trier: *The Sculpture of Marino Marini* (London, 1961)
P. Waldberg and G. di San Lazzaro: *Marino Marini: L'opera completa* (Milan, Paris and New York, 1970, rev. 1974)
C. Pirovano: *Marino Marini scultore* (Milan, 1972)
XXe siècle [Paris] (1974) [supernumerary issue ded. Marini]
G. Ruggeri: *Io sono un etrusco, Marino Marini* (Bologna, 1978)
Marino Marini: L'Oeuvre gravé complet, 1914–1977 (exh. cat., Paris, Mus. A. Mod. Ville Paris, 1978)
Centro di documentazione dell'opera di Marino Marini del comune di Pistoia (Pistoia, 1979)
K. Azuma: *Marino Marini* (Milan, 1980)

Marino Marini: Sculture, pitture, disegni dal 1914 al 1977 (exh. cat., ed. M. De Micheli; Venice, Pal. Grassi, 1983)

L. Papi: *Marino Marini pittore* (Ivrea, 1987) [in Eng. and It.]

C. Pirovano, ed.: *Marino Marini*, Florence, Mus. Marino Marini cat. (Florence, 1988)

Marino Marini (exh. cat. by C. Pirovano, E. Steingräber and M. De Micheli, Milan, Pal. Reale and Mus. Marino Marini, 1989–90)

Marino Marini: Catalogo ragionato dell'opera grafica (incisioni e litografie), 1919–1980 (Livorno, 1990)

M. Marini: *Vita con Marino* (Milan, 1992)

SILVIA LUCCHESI

Marinid [Merinid]. Islamic dynasty that ruled in northwest Africa from 1196 to 1465. The Marinids, a tribe of nomadic Zanata Berbers, took MARRAKESH from the last ALMOHAD ruler in 1269 and extended their power in the 14th century. Abu'l-Hasan 'Ali (*reg* 1331–48) conquered all of North Africa, thus reconstituting the great Almohad empire, but was unable to sustain rule in Tunisia and was forced to withdraw in 1341. His son Abu 'Inan Faris (*reg* 1348–59) renewed the successful campaign against the HAFSID realm of Tunis, but was obliged to withdraw hurriedly. The dynasty then began a decline that ended in its extinction in 1465, although a collateral branch, the Wattasids, continued to rule in Fez until 1549.

Marinid rule was marked by an unprecedented flourishing of literature, due to the patronage of the first generation of sovereigns. Their architectural legacy (*see* ISLAMIC ART, §II, 6(iv)(b)) was considerable, beginning with Abu Yusuf Ya'qub (*reg* 1258–86) who founded New Fez (Arab. *fās al-jadīd*; *see* FEZ) where he built his palace, a mosque and a MADRASA, the second of its kind in Morocco. The mosque at Taza and the great mosque of al-Mansura near TLEMCEN with its lavishly decorated minaret are attributed to Abu Ya'qub Yusuf (*reg* 1286–1308). Numerous houses and palaces were built under the Marinid princes, who also completed the various urban fortifications begun by Abu Yusuf Ya'qub (*see* MILITARY ARCHITECTURE AND FORTIFICATION, §IV, 3). Abu'l-Hasan 'Ali was the most prolific builder of the dynasty, and his works include the necropolis at Chella (*see* RABAT), numerous madrasas and mosques. Abu 'Inan Faris constructed madrasas at Fez and MEKNÈS, both of which are known eponymously. Marinid architectural decoration is characterized by an abundance of sculpted stucco and wood and tile on façades and courtyards, a style partly inspired by Nasrid architecture of Granada, but also preserving purely Moroccan characteristics.

Many Marinid foundations were embellished with fine objects. Bronze chandeliers, such as the ones made for mosques in Taza and Fez, continue Almohad traditions (*see* ISLAMIC ART, §IV, 3(iv)). Wooden minbars, such as the one in the mosque at Taza, also continue the proportions and techniques of strapwork decoration established in earlier centuries, but are decorated with ebony and ivory inlays (*see* ISLAMIC ART, §VII, 2(i)). Fine silk textiles were undoubtedly produced under the Marinids, but only two banners (Toledo, Mus. Catedralicio), both made at Fez and captured at the battle of the Rio Salado in 1340, are known to have been woven in North Africa (*see* ISLAMIC ART, §VI, 2(ii)(a)). A rare example of a Marinid manuscript is a copy of the Koran (Paris, Bib. N., MS. arab. 423) commissioned by Abu 'Inan Faris.

BIBLIOGRAPHY

Enc. Islam/2

R. Le Tourneau: *Fez in the Age of the Marinids* (Norman, OK, 1961)

J. Revault, L. Golvin and A. Amahan: *Palais et demeures de Fès* (Paris, 1985)

LUCIEN GOLVIN

Marino, Giambattista [Giovan Battista; Gian Battista] (*b* Naples, 18 Oct 1569; *d* Naples, 25 March 1625). Italian poet, patron and art theorist. He was the most famous Italian poet of the late 16th century and early 17th and was also perhaps the most celebrated and pensioned literary courtier of his age. He abandoned his initial study of law in Naples and by his early twenties was established among the Neapolitan *literati*, securing employment as a secretary to the nobility. His facility in obtaining the sponsorship of nobility and royalty led to his presence in the most illustrious courts and households of his time. In 1600 he went to Rome, and after 1602 he became attached to the court of Cardinal Pietro Aldobrandini, with whom he moved to Ravenna after 1605. By 1609 his benefactor was the Duke of Savoy, Carlo Emmanuele I, in Turin.

Marino's position in the history of art theory is due to *La Pittura* (Turin, 1614), the first of his *Dicerie sacre*. It includes a discussion of the art of *disegno*, which was a preferred theme of Renaissance art theorists; in Marino's case probably inspired by Federico Zuccaro's distinctions between *disegno esterno*, drawing and its technical requirements, and *disegno interno*, the conceptual act. When discussing the latter, Marino laid emphasis on *fantasia* as the primary component of individual creativity and thereby gave theoretical justification to the new inventive spirit of the Baroque. In 1615 he left Italy for Paris at the invitation of Queen Marie de' Medici, and he remained in France for eight years. In Paris he became friendly with Poussin and commissioned from him a series of drawings illustrating Ovid's *Metamorphoses* (Windsor Castle, Royal Lib.; Budapest, Mus. F.A.); he also encouraged him to go to Italy.

As a poet Marino was immensely industrious and prolific. His works were characterized by a great fertility of invention and historical erudition. They were worldly, lascivious and frequently impious. Critics later applied his name derisively to the 'Marinisti' poets of early 17th-century Italy whose literary Mannerism (*il marinismo*) derived from Marino's studied use of metaphors and conspicuous conceits. His personal interest in the arts and his activities as a patron and collector are intimately linked in his verse anthology, *La Galleria* (Venice, 1620), a compilation of over 600 poems, which Marino claimed were inspired by and each to be illustrated by an engraving of a drawing or painting by a well-known artist. The anthology was subdivided into: Fables, Caprices, Histories, Sculpture, Portraits, Reliefs, Models and Medals. Marino's letters record his solicitations for works of art for *La Galleria*, although many requests remained unfulfilled. In some cases the poem, or at least its subject, was supplied to the artist before the work of art was made: in others Marino composed poems about existing works, some of which he may have hoped to secure for his own collection. *La Galleria*, when published, contained few of the engravings originally planned, but those that did materialize suggest that Marino preferred not the Italian Mannerists with whom his poetry has been stylistically linked (Ackerman; Viola), but the works of his contemporaries, many of whom he knew (e.g. Bernardo Castello, Bartolomeo Schidone, Giovanni Battista Trotti, Sinibaldo Scorza), and masters of the High Renaissance (e.g. Raphael, Titian). His poetry achieved enormous popular success, especially the epic poem *Adone* (1622). He returned to Rome in 1623, and was exultantly welcomed there, and then moved to Naples, where he died. His friendship with Poussin, whose career in Rome flourished after Marino introduced him to Marcello Sacchetti, was honoured by the painter after Marino's death in a painting known either as *Apollo and the Muses on Parnassus* or the *Apotheosis of the Poet* (*c.* 1632; Madrid, Prado), which depicts the poet's allegorical entry on to Mount Parnassus.

WRITINGS
Dicerie sacre del Cavalier Marino (Turin, 1614)
La Galleria (Venice, 1620); ed. M. Pieri, 2 vols (Padua, 1979) [incl. a disc. of the artists and works of art associated with Marino's poems]
Adone (Paris, 1622)

BIBLIOGRAPHY
A. Borzelli: *Storia della vita e delle opere di Giovan Battista Marino* (Naples, 1898/*R* 1927) [incl. the publishing history of Marino's works]
G. G. Ferrero: *Marino e i Marinisti* (Milan, 1954)
J. Costello: 'Poussin's Drawings for Marino and the New Classicism', *J. Warb. & Court. Inst.*, xviii (1955), pp. 296–317
G. Ackerman: 'Gian Battista Marino's Contribution to Seicento Art Theory', *A. Bull.*, xliii (1961), pp. 326–36
G. E. Viola: *Il verso di Narciso, tra tesi sulla poetica di Giovan Battista Marino* (Rome, 1978) [discusses Marino's taste and collct.]

Marino di Siressea. *See under* REYMERSWAELE, MARINUS VAN.

Marinot, Maurice (*b* Troyes, 20 March 1882; *d* Troyes, 8 Feb 1960). French glassmaker and painter. Although he trained as a painter and exhibited with the Fauves at the Salon d'Automne in 1905, he developed an enthusiasm for glass after visiting a glass factory at Bar-sur-Seine in 1911. At first he designed glass wares and enamelled plain glass with graceful figures and floral designs combined with such decorative motifs as rosettes and palmettes. He considered himself an opponent of the Art Nouveau style and was closely associated with the international trend towards an austere, decorative style. The architect André Mare (1887–1932) invited him to take part in the Maison Cubiste organized by the Puteaux group, which was presented at the Salon d'Automne of 1912, in which such artists as Jacques Villon, Raymond Duchamp-Villon, Roger de La Fresnaye and Marie Laurencin participated. His work was noticed by the art dealer André Hébrard who regularly exhibited Marinot's glass at his gallery in the Rue Royale, Paris. From 1920 Marinot began to create blown glass, a technique in which he became supremely successful. In 20 years he produced over 2000 pieces (e.g. bottle and stopper, *c.* 1925; London, V&A). The variety of his work is extraordinary: his first pieces were transparent, while later coloured vases were created by sandwiching a layer of opaque, coloured glass between sheets of clear, colourless glass. Some items were decorated further with cut, engraved and acid-etched geometric designs (*see* FRANCE, fig. 72), while others contained trapped air bubbles or swirls of colour. Each object was therefore unique,

and, although most were functional (jugs, vases and bowls), they were often abstract in form. Marinot's work was highly acclaimed at the Exposition Internationale des Arts Décoratifs et Industriels Modernes of 1925 in Paris. In 1937 the Bar-sur-Seine Glassworks was destroyed by fire, and due to ill-health Marinot was forced to abandon his work in glass and thereafter devoted himself to painting and drawing.

BIBLIOGRAPHY
G. Janneau: *Le Verre et l'art de Marinot* (Paris, 1925)
J. Bloch-Demant: *Le Verre en France d'Emile Gallé à nos jours* (Paris, 1983)
Maurice Marinot, peintre et verrier (exh. cat., ed. M. Hoog and C. Giraudon; Paris, Mus. Orangerie, 1990)
MICHEL HOOG

Marinus. *See* GOES, MARINUS ROBYN VAN DER.

Marinus de Seeu. *See under* REYMERSWAELE, MARINUS VAN.

Marinus van Reymerswaele. *See* REYMERSWAELE, MARINUS VAN.

Mario dei Fiori [Nuzzi, Mario] (*b* Rome, 19 March 1603; *d* Rome, 14 Nov 1673). Italian painter. He was the first and most famous Roman painter to specialize in flowerpieces and one of only four still-life artists included by Leone Pascoli in his collection of artists' biographies. The early sources and old inventories attribute many flower paintings in distinguished Roman collections to the Caravaggesque painter Tommaso Salini, and since the 18th century Mario's name has been linked with his, and it has been assumed that he trained with Salini. This apprenticeship is difficult to document, yet a comparison of Mario's pictures with inventory descriptions of works by Salini confirms that Mario was influenced by his art. To the minute observation of various kinds of flowers, Mario added a refined sense of design and an interest in effects of light, still linked to Caravaggio in the use of a dark background. He also responded to the art of the Neapolitan flower painter Paolo Porpora, who was in Rome from the early 1650s, in the service, as was Mario, of Cardinal Flavio Chigi.

Signed or documented works, which might suggest Mario dei Fiori's artistic development, are rare. His earliest dated work appears to be a *Garland with the Dream of Jacob* (1650), one of a series of four *Garlands* (all Madrid, Escorial) that have scenes drawn from the Old Testament in their centres. Of the many recorded in the early inventories of Roman collections, the only identifiable works associated with Mario are five canvases (all 1659; Ariccia, Pal. Chigi) painted for Cardinal Flavio Chigi. One is a portrait of *Mario dei Fiori* by Giovanni Maria Morandi (1622–1717). The other four form the series of the *Four Seasons*, each one of which has flowers painted by Mario together with figures by other artists: *Spring* has figures by Filippo Lauri, *Summer* by Carlo Maratti, *Autumn* by Giacinto Brandi and *Winter* by Bernardino Mei. Mario also collaborated with Maratti in the decoration of two painted mirrors (1660) for the great gallery of the Palazzo Colonna, Rome (*in situ*), which reveal the influence of Porpora's vivid colour and rigorous sense of reality. The individual flowers are studied with such attention that, using colour and the contrast of light and shade, the artist succeeds in rendering their textures while his composition is naturalistic rather than purely decorative. Giovanni Stanchi (1608–after 1673) contributed two painted mirrors to the series, yet the rich and refined compositions of Mario contrast with the dry and flat decorations of Stanchi. Five canvases (all Madrid, Prado), overdoors all of the same size, have been attributed to Mario since the 18th century. Laura Bernasconi is the only pupil of his mentioned in the sources. The intense naturalism of Mario's work was not continued by other artists in Italy, and such painters as Giovanni Stanchi, Niccolò Stanchi (1626/36–c. 1690) and Pietro Paolo Cennini (1661–1739) merely produced trivial, decorative works until the middle of the 18th century. However, the pictures Mario sent to Spain had a deep effect on flower painters there, particularly on Juan de Arellano.

BIBLIOGRAPHY

L. Pascoli: *Vite*, ii (Rome, 1736)

G. Bartocci: 'Della patria del pittore Mario Nuzzi de' Fiori', *Atti & Mem. Deput. Stor. Patria Marche*, viii (1961), pp. 197–8

V. Golzio: 'Mario de' Fiori e la natura morta', *L'Urbe*, xviii (1965), pp. 1–9

A. E. Pérez Sánchez: *Pintura italiana del siglo XVII en España* (Madrid, 1965)

L. Salerno: *La natura morta italiana, 1560–1805* (Rome, 1984)

L. Laureati: 'Mario de' Fiori', *La natura morta in Italia*, ii (Milan, 1989)

L. Salerno: *Nuovi studi sulle nature morte italiane* (Rome, 1989)

LAURA LAUREATI

Mariotto di Nardo (*fl* Florence, 1394–1424). Italian painter. He was the son of the sculptor Nardo di Cione (*fl c.* 1480; namesake of the painter) and was probably trained by his father (Boskovits, 1975). Mariotto's interest in sculpture and his almost obsessive rendering of plastic form in painting remain constant factors in his style, which is easily identifiable and markedly different from that of his contemporaries.

Numerous surviving documents relating to Mariotto di Nardo indicate that he was much sought after as a painter for both public and private commissions in Florence. From 1394 to 1404 he may have been working as the principal artist for the Cathedral for which he executed a large number of paintings, most of which have not survived. Three panels from an altarpiece survive, bust-length figures of *Christ, St Ambrose* and *St Augustine* (1402–4; Florence Cathedral).

Around 1400 Mariotto was employed on the fresco decoration of two of the most important churches in Florence: S Maria Maggiore and Orsanmichele (fragments of both cycles *in situ*). For the officials of Orsanmichele he also executed frescoes in their residence, including a *Virgin and Child Enthroned with Saints* (*in situ*). At this stage of his career he was also commissioned to paint illuminated manuscripts, which brought him in contact with the manuscript workshop at S Maria degli Angeli, Florence. This contact had a considerable influence on his style. Examples of his work in this medium include two fragments of *St Lawrence* (Cambridge, Fitzwilliam) and *St Mary Magdalene* (Berlin, Kupferstichkab.).

In 1400 Mariotto may have accompanied Lorenzo Ghiberti to Pesaro, possibly at the request of Pandolfo Malatesta, the ruler of the city. Ghiberti mentioned the journey in his *Commentarii* but failed to give the name of his companion. However, the hypothesis that it was Mariotto (Salmi) is substantiated by the existence in Pesaro of a triptych of the *Virgin and Child with SS Michael and Francis* (Pesaro, Mus. Civ.), dated 1400, by Mariotto.

A large number of securely attributed works by Mariotto survive. These include an altarpiece of the *Virgin and Child with Saints* for the church of S Donnino at Villamagna, Bagno a Ripoli (*in situ*); a triptych of the *Assumption of the Virgin* with *St Jerome* and *St John the Evangelist* (1398; Fiesole, Fontelucente Church); a polyptych of the *Virgin and Child with Saints* and a predella with scenes from the *Life of the Virgin* (Florence, Accademia) from the convent of S Gaggio, Florence; the *Coronation of the Virgin* (Florence, Certosa del Galluzzo, Pin.); the *Trinity* (Impruneta, S Maria); and an altarpiece of the *Virgin and Child Enthroned with Saints* for S Leolino at Panzano in Chianti (*in situ*).

As Mariotto's career progressed, so his paintings became increasingly repetitive and acquired traditional traits. Given that his paintings are often of little more than artisan quality, his success in his own day has perplexed critics, but it was evidently based on his works of the late 14th century, which introduced to Florence elements of Late Gothic taste, such as oblique perspective, nervous tension of the figures and deserted, rocky landscapes.

BIBLIOGRAPHY

Colnaghi

L. Ghiberti: *I commentarii* (MS., Florence, Bib. N. Cent. II.1.33, *c.* 1447–8); ed. J. von Schlosser (Berlin, 1912), p. 45

G. Vasari: *Vite* (1550, rev. 2/1568); ed. G. Milanesi (1878–85), i, p. 610

O. Sirèn: 'Alcuni pittori che subirono l'influenza di Lorenzo Monaco', *Arte*, vii (1904), pp. 337–55

O. H. Giglioli: 'Mariotto di Nardo e la sua tavola d'altare per la Pieve di Villamagna presso Firenze', *Illustratore fiorentino*, n. s., iii (1906), pp. 67–70

O. Sirèn: 'Gli affreschi nel Paradiso degli Alberti: Lorenzo di Niccolò e Mariotto di Nardo', *Arte*, xi (1908), pp. 179–86

H. Horne: 'A Commentary upon Vasari's Life of Jacopo del Casentino', *Riv. A.*, vi (1909), pp. 165–84

G. Poggi: *Il duomo di Firenze* (Berlin, 1909)

R. Piattoli: 'Un mercante del trecento e gli artisti del suo tempo', *Riv. A.*, xi (1929), pp. 396–437, 537–79

R. Offner and K. Steinweg: *Corpus* (New York, 1930), section III, ii, iii

——: 'The Mostra del Tesoro di Firenze Sacra', *Burl. Mag.*, lxiii (1933), pp. 166–78

M. Salmi: 'Lorenzo Ghiberti e Mariotto di Nardo', *Riv. A.*, xxx (1955), pp. 147–52

B. Berenson: *Florentine School*, i (1968), pp. 129–34

M. Boskovits: 'Sull'attività giovanile di Mariotto di Nardo', *Ant. Viva*, vii/5 (1968), pp. 3–13

——: 'Mariotto di Nardo e la formazione del linguaggio tardo-gotico a Firenze', *Ant. Viva*, vii/6 (1968), pp. 21–31

U. Procacci: 'L'affresco dell'Oratorio del Bigallo e il suo maestro', *Mitt. Ksthist. Inst. Florenz*, xviii (1973), pp. 135–52

M. Boskovits: *Pittura fiorentina alla vigilia del rinascimento* (Florence, 1975), pp. 139–41, 388–402

R. Fremantle: *Florentine Gothic Painters* (London, 1975), pp. 451–9

CECILIA FROSININI

Mari Republic. *See under* RUSSIA, §XII, 3.

Maris. Dutch family of painters. The family consisted of three brothers: the eldest was (1) Jacob Maris, who started as a figure painter but later turned to painting town- and landscapes. He was one of the leading painters of the HAGUE SCHOOL, along with Jozef Israëls and Anton Mauve. His brother (2) Matthijs Maris painted fantastic castles and scenes with figures. The youngest brother was

(3) Willem Maris, known primarily for his paintings of cattle at pasture and ducks by the waterside. In the 1860s all three shared a studio in The Hague.

BIBLIOGRAPHY

Scheen

P. Zilcken: *Les Maris: Jacob—Matthijs—Willem* (Amsterdam, 1896)

M. Rooses, ed.: *Het schildersboek: Nederlandsche schilders der negentiende eeuw, in monographieën door tijdgenooten* [The book about painters: Dutch painters of the 19th century, in monographs by contemporaries], 3 vols (Amsterdam, 1898–1900), ii, pp. 2–16, 99–113; iii, pp. 2–21

D. Croal Thomson: 'The Brothers Maris (James—Matthew—William)', *The Studio* (1907) [special number]

Maris tentoonstelling (exh. cat., The Hague, Gemeentemus.; Amsterdam, Stedel. Mus.; 1935)

A. M. Hammacher: 'Kroniek: De drie Marissen in het Haagsche Museum', *Elsevier's Geïllus. Mdschr.*, xlvi/91 (1936), pp. 131–4

M. H. W. E. Maris: *De geschiedenis van een schildersgeslacht* [The history of a family of painters] (Amsterdam, 1943)

J. de Gruyter: *De Haagse school*, ii (Rotterdam, 1969), pp. 16–28, 31–60

The Hague School: Dutch Masters of the 19th Century (exh. cat., ed. R. de Leeuw, J. Sillevis and C. Dumas; London, RA; The Hague, Gemeentemus.; Paris, Grand Pal.; 1983)

De Haagse school: De collectie van het Haags Gemeentemuseum (exh. cat., The Hague, Gemeentemus., 1988)

J. de Raad and T. van Zadelhoff: *Maris, een Kunstenaarsfamilie* (Zwolle, 1991)

(1) Jacob(us Hendricus) Maris

(*b* The Hague, 25 Aug 1837; *d* Karlsbad, 7 Aug 1899). By the age of 12 he was apprenticed to Johannes Stroebel (1821–1905), and from 1850 he attended classes at the Academie in The Hague. In 1854 he accompanied his teacher, Huib van Hove (1814–64), to Antwerp, where he attended evening classes at the Academie for two years and made contact with Louis Meijer, the marine painter. In 1855 he was joined in Antwerp by his brother (2) Matthijs Maris, with whom he shared a workshop and house. For a short period their friend and fellow student Laurens Alma-Tadema came to live with them. They lived on Matthijs's grant and made small paintings, based on 17th-century Dutch genre pictures, for the American market.

In 1857 Jacob returned to The Hague, where he was joined by Matthijs the following year. In 1859 and 1860 William I's daughter, Marianne of Orange Nassau, Princess of Prussia (1810–83), commissioned them to make copies (untraced) of a number of portraits of the Orange-Nassau family; this provided the two brothers with an opportunity to work in Oosterbeek, the Dutch equivalent to the French Barbizon, and in Wolfheze, and, in 1861, to travel to Germany, France and Switzerland. By the time they finally returned to the Netherlands, the money had run out. Jacob subsequently helped to complete paintings by Meijer. In 1865 he went to Paris again; there he collaborated with Adolphe Artz and others, and worked in the studio of Ernest Hébert, under whose influence he began to paint a series of 'Italiennes' (e.g. *Girl Knitting on a Balcony, Montmartre*, 1869; The Hague, Gemeentemus.). Around 1865 Jacob visited Barbizon and Fontainebleau in France. The influence of this trip can be seen in the *View of Montigny-sur-Loing* of 1870 (Rotterdam, Mus. Boymans–van Beuningen), which is indebted not only to Barbizon painters such as Camille Corot but also to Dutch 17th-century masters, in particular Vermeer. This painting is, moreover, one of Jacob's earliest river city views and foreshadows his long 'grey period'.

In 1867 Jacob married Catharina Horn. In 1869 Matthijs came to live with them in Paris. Jacob returned to The Hague in 1871, after which he painted figures only rarely. There exist, however, a few watercolours with figures,

Jacob Maris: *Five Windmills*, oil on canvas, 0.82×1.29 m, 1878 (Utrecht, Centraal Museum)

mostly members of his own family; one such is *The Duet* (*c.* 1878; The Hague, Gemeentemus.), showing his two young daughters. The character of his work changed: he applied himself more and more to painting landscapes and townscapes in a rather vigorous style, and his oil paintings and watercolours became more daring. His landscapes were mostly based on the view from his studio, while the townscapes were often fantasies based on existing buildings. The *Truncated Windmill* (1872; Amsterdam, Rijksmus.) marks the beginning of Jacob's 'grey period', typified by the *Five Windmills* (1878; Utrecht, Cent. Mus.; see fig.). The most extreme example from this period is the *Allotments near The Hague* (The Hague, Gemeentemus.). Although Jacob was, with Jozef Israëls and Anton Mauve, one of the leading figures of the Hague school, and his influence on other artists was considerable, his only pupils apart from his younger brother (3) Willem Maris were Willem de Zwart and Bernard Blommers. Jacob's influence can be seen, for example, in the interest in the effects of light that Mauve began to display in his work. Like Jan Hendrik Weissenbruch, Jacob often produced several paintings of the same theme; there are at least 12 different versions of the *Canal near Rijswijk* (version, 1885; New York, Frick), oil paintings and watercolours as well as one etching. The same applies to the Grote Kerk in Dordrecht, which the artist painted over and over from various viewpoints (e.g. *Dordrecht—the Grote Kerk*; Montreal, Mus. F.A.). Jacob was in fact responsible for the rediscovery of Dordrecht's historic architecture, which had been ignored for many years.

BIBLIOGRAPHY

C. Vosmaer: *Jacob Hendrik Maris* (The Hague, 1883)
P. Zilcken: *Le Peintre Jacob Maris* (The Hague, 1889)
——: 'Jacob Maris', *Gaz. B.-A.*, n. s. 3, xxiii (1900), pp. 147–55
J. Kalff jr: *Jacob Maris* (Haarlem, 1902)
T. de Bock: *Jacob Maris* (Amsterdam, 1903) [with Eng. text]
Selected Works by James Maris, Anton Mauve, H. Fantin Latour (exh. cat., London, Fr. Gal., 1910)
J. Veth: 'Jacob Maris', *Kst & Kstler*, ix/1 (1911), pp. 15–25
K. Erasmus: 'Jacob Maris', *Kst Alle: Mal., Plast., Graph., Archit.*, xxvii/11 (1912), pp. 261–8

(2) Matthijs [Matthias] **Maris** (*b* The Hague, 17 Aug 1839; *d* London, 22 Aug 1917). Brother of (1) Jacob Maris. In 1851 he was apprenticed for one year to Isaac Elink Sterk (1808–71); from 1852 to 1855 he attended classes at the Academie in The Hague, and in 1854 he joined the studio of Louis Meijer, where his brother Jacob was also working. It was due to Meijer that in 1855 he was granted a monthly allowance by Queen Sophie to continue his training in Antwerp, where he moved in with Jacob. Through his studies at the Academie, Matthijs met the German painter Georg Laves, who introduced him to the work of the 19th-century German Romantic painters, in particular Ludwig Richter.

In 1858 Matthijs returned to The Hague, where he again moved in with his brother, who had returned earlier. They received financial support from Princess Marianne; this enabled them not only to stay in Oosterbeek and Wolfheze, but also to undertake a journey to Germany, France and Switzerland in 1861. This trip had a tremendous influence on Matthijs's development: in particular, the castle and cathedral at Lausanne, with its surrounding wooden cottages, appealed strongly to his imagination. The skyline of Lausanne is a motif that recurs frequently in Matthijs's work. At this time his choice of subject-matter began to crystallize: his preferred themes were townscapes with only a faint resemblance to reality, portraits and figure paintings. One watercolour inspired by the journey (and by the work of Richter) is the *Christening Procession at Lausanne* (The Hague, Gemeentemus.), a work that in 1863, after the personal mediation of Willem Roelofs, earned him honorary membership of the Société Belge des Aquarellistes in Brussels. After this, however, his success dwindled; in the following years he was attacked by the press, and his work met with fierce criticism, which depressed him severely. In 1869, on his family's advice, he decided to join Jacob once again, in Paris. Both brothers witnessed the Franco-Prussian War (1870–71), and Matthijs experienced the revolt of the Communards (1871) at first hand. Jacob returned to The Hague before the revolt, but Matthijs remained in his beloved Montmartre. During this period he painted his finest works; for example *Souvenir d'Amsterdam* (1871; Amsterdam, Rijksmus.), which was praised highly by van Gogh, and *Butterflies* (1874; Glasgow, Burrell Col.), a theme that recurs frequently in his work. Gradually people became interested in his work again, and, with the arrival of his younger sister in Paris, he managed to recover from the deep depression he had suffered since 1871.

Through the assistance of the art dealer Goupil, Matthijs came in contact with Daniel Cottier (1838–91), a Scottish art dealer active in London. In 1877 Matthijs decided to move to London, where he stayed permanently, living with Cottier until 1887. Although the dealer took him on journeys to Norway, Brittany and Paris, Matthijs felt rather disappointed in him, and their relationship deteriorated over the years. He moved house again but painted little in the following 19 years, plagued by poverty, loneliness and suspicion. He withdrew into a world of fantasy; in this period he painted virtually monochrome grey dream landscapes with dark veiled figures, such as the *Enchanted Castle* (Oss, Gemeente Mus. Jan Cunencent.). In his last years he ceased painting, and he was supported financially by the art dealer Elbert J. van Wisselingh (*d* 1912).

BIBLIOGRAPHY

C. J. Holmes: 'The Landscapes of Matthew Maris', *Burl. Mag.*, x (1906–7), pp. 348–54
P. Zilcken: 'Matthijs Maris', *A. & Artistes*, xii (1911), pp. 266–71
E. Luther Cary: 'A Comment on Matthew Maris', *A. America*, ii (1914), pp. 134–47
D. Croal Thomson: 'Matthew Maris', *The Studio*, lxxii (1917), pp. 46–51
P. Buschmann: 'Matthew Maris', *Burl. Mag.*, xxxii (1918), pp. 4–9
D. Croal Thomson: *Matthew Maris: An Illustrated Souvenir* (London, 1918)
E. D. Fridlander: *Matthew Maris* (London, 1921)
H. E. van Gelder: 'Matthijs Maris: Documenten', *Oud-Holland*, xliv (1927), pp. 35–43, 103–11
——: *Matthijs Maris* (Amsterdam, 1939)
Matthijs Maris: 1839—17 augustus—1939 (exh. cat., The Hague, Gemeentemus., 1939)
Matthijs Maris (exh. cat., The Hague, Gemeentemus., 1974)
J. F. Heijbroek: 'Matthijs Maris en het *Souvenir d'Amsterdam*', *Amstelodamum*, lxii (1975), pp. 14–18
——: 'Matthijs Maris in Parijs: 1869–1877', *Oud-Holland*, lxxxix (1975), pp. 266–89
H. E. M. Braakhuis and J. van der Vliet: 'Patterns in the Life and the Work of Matthijs Maris', *Simiolus*, x (1978–9), pp. 142–81
T. B. Brumbaugh: 'A Matthijs Maris Correspondence', *Oud-Holland*, xcv (1981), pp. 88–96

J. F. Heijbroek: 'Tekeningen van Matthijs Maris uit het bezit van Ernest Fridlander', *Bull. Rijksmus.*, xxxiii (1985), pp. 110–23 [Eng. summary, pp. 139, 144]

(3) Willem [Wenzel] **Maris** (*b* The Hague, 18 Feb 1844; *d* The Hague, 10 Oct 1910). Brother of (1) Jacob Maris. He received his training as a painter from his brothers, (1) Jacob Maris and (2) Matthijs Maris. Although he briefly attended evening classes at the Academie in The Hague and was advised by the animal painter Pieter Stortenbeker (1828–98), he was basically self-taught; he was the only 'self-made' man in the circle of Hague school artists. In 1862 he visited Oosterbeek where he met Anton Mauve, with whom he established a long friendship. In the same year he first entered a painting, *Cows on the Heath* (untraced), in the *Tentoonstellung van Levende Meesters* [Exhibition of Living Masters] in Rotterdam. The themes of cows at pasture and ducks by the side of a ditch, which characterized the Dutch polder landscape in summer, became his hallmark. In the following year he exhibited *Cows by a Pool* (The Hague, Gemeentemus.; see fig.) in The Hague; it received discouraging reviews, as did the picture entered by his brother Matthijs. Painted in 1863, this work already employs Willem's main motif and shows his attention to the handling of light (with effects of haze and backlighting).

In 1863 Willem moved into a house in The Hague, where he shared a studio with his two brothers, who had already established themselves there. In 1865 he travelled along the Rhine with his friend Bernard Blommers; they shared a studio in The Hague from 1868 and frequently went to the Mauritshuis together to copy paintings. The only extant painting from this journey is *Herdboys with Donkeys* (1865; The Hague, Gemeentemus.), attributable to this time not from the theme (donkeys were occasionally used as a motif by Hague school painters) but from the wide river landscape. In 1867 Willem briefly went to Paris, where Jacob was then living, but he soon left. During this short period, however, he may well have seen works by the painters of the Barbizon school. In 1871 he travelled to Norway. With the exception of three foreign journeys, Willem spent his entire life in and around The Hague and led a much more settled life than his brothers.

It is difficult to determine the chronology within Willem's oeuvre, in the first instance because the choice of motifs is so limited and secondly because he stopped dating his painting after the 1860s. However, his early work is characterized by subdued greyish-white and green tones, coinciding with the 'grey period' of the Hague school, while after 1880 his brushstrokes became broader and the subdued tones were replaced by much warmer colours. He was a master of depicting ducks, both in watercolour and oil. Constant Artz (1870–1951), also famous for his paintings of ducks, borrowed the motif from Willem and is thus known as his imitator, while the German artist Franz Grässel (1861–1948) also followed his example. In 1876 Willem founded the Hollandsche Teeken-Maatschappij (Dutch Drawing Society) with Anton Mauve and Hendrik Willem Mesdag. George Hendrik Breitner was his pupil for a short period. Willem Maris met with little success early in his career but later obtained recognition, even on an international level. One of his sons, Simon Willem Maris (1873–1935), became a painter.

BIBLIOGRAPHY

H. de Boer: *Willem Maris* (The Hague, 1905)

C. H. Tiepen, ed.: *Willem Maris' herinneringen* [Willem Maris's memoirs] (The Hague, 1910)

M. D. Henkel: 'Willem Maris', *Kunstchronik*, n.s., xxii (1911), pp. 74–5

Selected Pictures by Johannes Bosboom and William Maris (exh. cat., London, Fr. Gal., 1911)

Willem Maris: *Cows by a Pool*, oil on canvas, 360×620 mm, 1863 (The Hague, Gemeentemuseum)

W. Sickert: 'An Early Landscape by William Maris', *Burl. Mag.*, xxvii (1915), p. 175

FRANSJE KUYVENHOVEN
bibliography by GEERT JAN KOOT

Mariscal. Mexican family of architects. Nicolás Mariscal (*b* Mexico City, 1875; *d* Mexico City, 13 April 1964) and his brother Federico Mariscal (*b* Querétaro, 1881; *d* Mexico City, 19 Aug 1969) both received a Neo-classical architectural education at the Academia Nacional de Bellas Artes in Mexico City, graduating in 1899 and 1903 respectively. Despite this traditional background they showed themselves predisposed to change, especially with respect to a national architecture. Both later became professors at the Escuela Nacional de Arquitectura, Mexico City, of which Federico was also director between 1935 and 1938. Nicolás Mariscal is particularly notable for his militancy on behalf of his profession in Mexico, which he defended against the privileges of the engineers. This activity culminated in 1919 with the creation of the Sociedad de Arquitectos Mexicanos. From 1899 to 1911 he published the prestigious magazine *El Arte y la Ciencia*. In this and in his *Teoría de la arquitectura* (1903) he was able to express innovative ideas. His works include the monument (1923) to *Cristo Rey* (Christ the King), a pilgrimage chapel topped with a statue designed by Fidias Elizondo (1881–1979), on Cerro del Cubilete, Guanajuato, and some houses in the capital.

Federico Mariscal designed a number of important buildings in Mexico City. Examples include the Inspección de Policía building (1906), in a neo-Gothic style; two identical banks (1909; with Nicolás Mariscal); the Esperanza Iris Theatre (1917), with its neo-Baroque tendencies; and the Tostado Ateliers (1923) of neo-colonial inspiration. Between 1930 and 1934 he completed the Palacio de Bellas Artes (begun 1904 by Adamo Boari; see MEXICO, fig. 5), with an Art Deco interior of Maya inspiration. This capacity for innovation can be seen further when, in 1950, working in partnership with his sons Enrique Mariscal (1918–72) and Alonso Mariscal (1914–58), he built the Registro Público de la Propriedad, Mexico City, in a strictly Modernist style. Federico Mariscal was a strong proponent of Mexico's national architecture. On the one hand, he issued various publications to draw attention to the architectural heritage of the country, both pre-Hispanic and colonial (*La patria y la arquitectura nacional*, 1915, and *Estudio arquitectónico de las ruinas Mayas*, 1928). On the other hand, he was militantly involved in the Ateneo de la Juventud, proposing the creation of a neo-colonial architecture as an adequate expression of national architecture at the time, a proposal that had the support of many of his colleagues.

BIBLIOGRAPHY
A. & Cienc. (1899–1911)
I. Katzman: *La arquitectura del siglo XIX en México* (Mexico City, 1973)
L. Noelle and D. Schavelzon: 'Un monumento efímero de Federico Mariscal', *An. Inst. Invest. Estét.*, 55 (1986), pp. 161–9

LOUISE NOELLE

Marismas del Guadalquivir, Marqués de Las. *See* LAS MARISMAS DEL GUADALQUIVIR, Marqués de.

Marisol (Escobar) (*b* Paris, 22 May 1930). French–Venezuelan sculptor. After studying painting at the Ecole des Beaux-Arts, Paris (1949) and then at the Art Students League (1950) and the Hans Hofmann School (1951–4) in New York, she developed an interest in Mexican, Pre-Columbian and American folk art and turned her attention to sculpture. In her early work she fashioned small, animated figurines out of bronze, terracotta and wood, often placing these pieces in compartmentalized, glass-fronted boxes, for example *Printer's Box* (1958; Mr and Mrs Edwin A. Bergman priv. col., see 1966 exh. cat., no. 4). In 1961 she began to incorporate drawing, painting, and *objets trouvés* into complex, life-size figure arrangements. Cast fragments of her own body and images of her face frequently appear in her works from this decade, many of which address the position of women in modern society. *Women and Dog* (1964; New York, Whitney) depicts a group of fashionable middle-class housewives parading in public wearing blank, mask-like expressions; other works depict farm women and socialites in similarly constrained poses.

Marisol's images of contemporary culture, at once deadpan and satirical in tone, were produced in the context of Pop art; the personal, enigmatic, often primitive elements of her work, however, set it apart from the mainstream of the movement. In the early 1970s she carved small, exotic fishes out of mahogany, with her own face on their polished, colourful bodies, and produced a series of prints and drawings with erotic, often violent overtones, such as *Double Flower* (coloured pencils and crayon, 1973; see 1975 exh. cat., no. 1). In the 1980s she returned to large-scale figural assemblages, creating a series of portrait 'homages' to well-known contemporary artists and personalities.

BIBLIOGRAPHY
Marisol (exh. cat., Chicago, IL, A. Club, 1966)
Marisol (exh. cat., ed. L. Shulman; Worcester, MA, A. Mus., 1971)
Marisol: Prints, 1961–73 (exh. cat., ed. J. Loring; New York, Cult. Cent., 1973)
C. Nemser: 'Marisol', *Art Talk: Conversations with 12 Women Artists* (New York, 1975), pp. 179–200
New Drawings and Wall Sculptures by Marisol (exh. cat., New York, Sidney Janis Gal., 1975)

NANCY RING

Maritain, Jacques (*b* Paris, 18 Nov 1882; *d* Toulouse, 28 April 1973). French philosopher and writer. He was a Catholic philosopher and for many years taught at the Institut Catholique, Paris. After serving as French ambassador to the Vatican (1945–8), he continued his university teaching career at Princeton, NJ, and elsewhere in North America.

In *Art et scolastique* (1920) Maritain formulated a theory of art and beauty based on Aristotle and St Thomas Aquinas. Art (in the sense of craft) is a form of practical as opposed to speculative intelligence, the fine arts being distinguished from the useful arts in that they create a work of beauty that reflects the divine beauty. His most important book in Aesthetics, *Creative Intuition in Art and Poetry* (1953), an expanded version of the 1952 A. W. Mellon Lectures in the Fine Arts, develops the theme of the earlier book. Maritain suggested that works of art result from the poet's 'intuition' or the painter's 'vision', which is a kind of non-conceptual knowledge

(knowledge through 'connaturality') consisting in 'affective union' between the artist's subjectivity and the outer world. This knowledge is expressed through the work itself and is said to be conveyed by a 'spiritualized emotion' that gives form to the work. Maritain attacked formalism and the doctrine of Art for Art's Sake and in *The Responsibility of the Artist* (1960) developed an ethics of art. He was a friend of the artist Georges Rouault and wrote critical essays on Rouault, Chagall and Severini, among others.

WRITINGS

Art et scolastique (Paris, 1920); Eng. trans. by J. W. Evans as *Art and Scholasticism* (New York, 1962)

Frontières de la poésie et autres essais (Paris, 1935); Eng. trans. of last three chapters as *Art and Poetry* (New York, 1943)

Creative Intuition in Art and Poetry, Bollingen Series, XXXV/i (New York, 1953)

The Responsibility of the Artist (New York, 1960)

BIBLIOGRAPHY

J. Dunaway: *Jacques Maritain* (Boston, 1978), chap. 8

JENEFER ROBINSON

Marius, G(erharda) H(ermina) (*b* Hengelo [Overijssel], 7 June 1854; *d* The Hague, 8 Nov 1919). Dutch art historian and painter. After studying under the painter J. Striening (1827–1903) in Deventer and under August Allebé at the Amsterdam Kunstacademie, she settled in The Hague. Initially she concentrated on the human figure, but gradually her talent for still-life became evident in watercolours that were visionary and lyrical rather than being actual depictions of concrete form. In 1893 Marius began writing criticism for the periodical *De Nederlandse spectator*, publishing frequently thereafter under the pseudonym 'G'.

After 1904 she abandoned painting and devoted herself primarily to writing, producing reflective and aesthetically well-balanced articles and essays that appeared in Dutch periodicals, including *De gids, De nieuwe gids, De kroniek, Elsevier's geïllustrierd maandschrift, Onze kunst* and *Woord en beeld*. Her magnum opus, *De Hollandsche schilderkunst in de negentiende eeuw*, was the first inclusive overview of Dutch art in the 19th century and remained the standard work for long afterwards. However, critics objected to what they considered her disproportionate emphasis on the Hague School, which was imputed to her admiration for various artists whom she knew personally, such as Anna Abrahams (*b* 1849) and Suze Robertson.

WRITINGS

De Hollandsche schilderkunst in de negentiende eeuw [Dutch painting in the 19th century] (The Hague, 1903/rev. 2, ed. W. Martin, 1920) [containing biography, pp. viii–xii]; Ger. trans. (1906); Eng. trans. by A. Texeira de Matthos (London, 1908/rev. Woodbridge, 1973)

with P. A. M. Boele van Hensbroek: *Het museum Mesdag en zijne stichters* [The Mesdag Museum and its founders] (Amsterdam, 1909)

BIBLIOGRAPHY

J. Veth: 'De Hollandsche schilderkunst in de negentiende eeuw' [Dutch painting in the 19th century], *XXe Eeuw* (1907), pp. 352–68 [review]

G. van Wezel: 'Waarde Mejuffrouw Marius, brieven van J. Toorp' [Dear Ms Marius, letters from J. Toorp], *Jong Holland*, ii (1986), pp. 2–28

WILLEM FREDERIK RAPPARD

Marius Pictor. *See* DE MARIA, MARIO.

Mark, William (*b* Scarsdale, Victoria, 12 June 1868; *d* Melbourne, 7 Oct 1956). Australian enamellist, jeweller and silversmith. He trained in Melbourne under J. R. Rowland and in the late 1890s travelled to England, where he worked for a time in the London workshop of Nelson Dawson (1859–1942). By the end of 1900 he had joined C. R. Ashbee's Guild of Handicraft, and he subsequently moved with the Guild to Chipping Campden, Glos. Though an accomplished silversmith and jeweller, Mark's skill lay in enamelwork. He and F. C. Varley were largely responsible for the fine painted enamels produced by the Guild. He worked independently in Chipping Campden after the Guild failed in 1907 and eventually returned to Australia in 1920. He established a studio at his home in Melbourne, where he stayed until his death. The greater part of his production comprised ecclesiastical commissions, notably the silver and enamel processional cross (designed by Louis Williams; *c.* 1931) of St Paul's Cathedral, Melbourne, and the plate and fittings (*c.* 1924) of the Warrior's Chapel, Christ Church Cathedral, Newcastle, NSW.

BIBLIOGRAPHY

A. Crawford: *C. R. Ashbee: Architect, Designer and Romantic Socialist* (New Haven and London, 1985)

Treasures from Australian Churches (exh. cat. by J. O'Callaghan, Melbourne, N.G. Victoria, 1985)

JUDITH O'CALLAGHAN

Markelius, Sven (Gottfrid) (*b* Stockholm, 25 Oct 1889; *d* Stockholm, 27 Feb 1972). Swedish architect. He was educated at the Royal Institute of Technology and the Academy of Arts in Stockholm in 1910–15 and then travelled on the Continent, returning to practise in the office of Erik Lallerstedt. He developed an early interest in housing and planning and was one of the founder members of CIAM in 1928. He was an author of *Acceptera*, the manifesto of Swedish Functionalism (Stockholm, 1931). From 1938 he directed the development department of the National Board of Building.

Markelius adapted his first major project, Helsingborg Concert Hall, in line with current taste from the classical competition entries of 1925–8 into the purely Functionalist design that was eventually executed in 1930–32: the auditorium is a simple steel-framed box, with a low wing containing the lobby and curved cloakrooms, all faced with smooth white stucco. The windows are metal-framed. For this building he also designed stacking chairs in plywood, as well as some steel-tube furniture. The Students' Union building at the Royal Institute of Technology in Stockholm (with Uno Åhrén; 1928–30) is likewise an important work of early Swedish Functionalism; he planned a series of villas on the same lines. More significant, however, are his contributions to standardized housing; his pioneering collective building, a service block of flats at John Ericsongatan 6 in Stockholm (1934–6) was carefully planned to combine flats of economic layout with a restaurant, day nursery and other services.

The Stockholm Builders Association premises (1935) is a rational office block, where the roof storey has a free layout with undulating wall and ceiling panelling. Markelius developed this vocabulary on a large scale during the 1940s and 1950s, for example at the Civic Halls in Linköping (1948–54) and Stockholm (1956–60); the latter is a vast complex including a large auditorium and a theatre. He also designed the Social and Economic Council meeting room for the United Nations Headquarters in New York (1953). As City Planning Director in Stockholm from to 1944 to 1954 he directed the planning of new outer suburbs on the subway such as Vällingby (1950–56), the preparation of the master plan of 1952 and redevelopment plans for the city centre, including the Hötorg redevelopment scheme, where he designed one of the five tower blocks.

BIBLIOGRAPHY
G. E. Kidder Smith: *The New Architecture of Europe* (London, 1961)
S. Ray: *Il contributo svedese all'architettura contemporanea e l'opera di Sven Markelius* (Rome, 1969)
P. G. Råberg: *Funktionalistiskt genombrott* [The emergence of Functionalism] (Stockholm, 1970)
Nordisk klassicism/Nordic Classicism, 1910–1930 (exh. cat., ed. S. Paavilainen; Helsinki, Mus. Fin. Archit., 1982)
H. O. Andersson and F. Bedoire: *Swedish Architecture* (Stockholm, 1986)

Market, covered. Enclosed or partially enclosed building for the exchange of goods. The presence of a covered market is one of the earliest indications of a settlement's status as a city. There may, for example, have been a market at Çatal Hüyük (7th–6th millennia BC). In ancient Greece stoas were sometimes used for commercial activities (*see* STOA), and more elaborate examples might have incorporated rows of shops, as at the North Agora (4th century BC) of Miletos. As early as the 4th century BC Aristotle advocated the creation of separate agoras for public affairs and commerce. The Stoa of Attalos (2nd century BC) at Athens is a two-aisled stoa with twenty small square shops on each floor (*see* ATHENS, §II, 2(i)(a)). In Rome the commercial functions of the Forum Romanum were moved to adjacent sites, and the first macellum was built in the 3rd century BC. Permanent market buildings, which varied greatly in layout, became the norm throughout the empire, for they regularized the commercial activities in a single structure. Files of shops or stalls were often arranged to frame open rectangular courts, within which some examples, such as those at Leptis Magna (9–8 BC; for illustration *see* MACELLUM) and PUTEOLI (late 1st century AD), contain a round building. Perhaps the most impressive Roman market was the multi-level Markets of Trajan (*c.* AD 100–112; *see* ROME, ANCIENT, §II, 2(i)(e) and fig. 30), which was terraced into the slope of the Quirinal Hill.

The Islamic world inherited the tradition of covered markets and courts surrounded by shops on several storeys. These buildings were called by various names (*see* CARAVANSERAI) and were used as warehouses, workshops, sections of the main market, accommodation or for a combination of these functions. The ground floor might accommodate shops or animals. Such buildings were usually the product of state sponsorship to encourage trade and were sometimes devoted to particular items, such as cloth, oil or soap. Some were intended for the use of foreign merchants, for example for the French at Tunis after 1574 and for the Venetians at Cairo and Aleppo.

One of the oldest surviving covered markets is the Khan al-Mirjan (1359) at Baghdad, with a central space roofed with transverse barrel vaults. Most extant commercial buildings in the Islamic world, however, were built after 1500. There are four notable examples of the courtyard type at Aleppo, while the Wakala of Qa'itbay (1480) and the Wakala of Qansuh al-Ghawri (1505), both in Cairo, combine commercial and residential functions. Such markets were often integrated into networks of covered streets known as souk (Arab. *sūq*) and bazaar (Pers./Turk. *bāzār*; *see also* ISFAHAN, §3(v)), which may have developed by walling in and roofing Classical colonnades, for example at Aleppo (see Sauvaget). In Cairo, Aleppo and other major cities this linear arrangement was transformed into a grid of intersecting market streets, which linked commercial structures with courts (*see* ISTANBUL, §III, 14).

Expanding commercial activity in Europe in the Middle Ages led to the development of new building types. At Como, for example, the ground floor of the town hall, the Broletto (completed 1215; rebuilt 15th century), is divided into two aisles by a central row of four piers. This space was considered an extension of the adjacent market-place, and privileged goods, such as iron, wine, herbs and salt, were sold from the arcades of the porch. Similar structures were built for several centuries and formed the basis of the English market hall (e.g. 16th century; Horndon on the Hill, Essex) and the First Town House (1657–8; destr.) at Boston, MA (*see* BOSTON, §I, 1). The growing power of merchants in northern Europe was marked by a sequence of increasingly magnificent market halls, such as the Lakenhalle (1200–1304) in Ypres, which incorporated the town hall, law courts, prison and a chapel (*see* TOWN HALL, §2).

In the 19th century metallic canopies were developed for commercial architecture. François-Joseph Bélanger replaced the wooden dome of the Halle au Blé, a circular granary in Paris, with the first full cast-iron and glass dome (1808–13). This technique was quickly adopted to span commercial arcades in Europe and North America: impressive early examples include the Providence Arcade (1828–9, by Russell Warren and James C. Bucklin) in Providence, RI, and the Passage Pommeraye (1843), Nantes. Similar techniques have been adopted in the creation of later commercial developments, such as the DEPARTMENT STORE and the SHOPPING CENTRE.

BIBLIOGRAPHY
Enc. Islam/2: 'Funduḳ'; 'Ḳayṣariyya'; 'Khān'
J. Sauvaget: *Alep: Essai sur le développement d'une grande ville syrienne, des origines au milieu du XIXe siècle* (Paris, 1941)
W. MacDonald: *The Architecture of the Roman Empire* (New Haven and London, 1965–86), i, pp. 75–93; ii, pp. 116–17
N. Pevsner: *A History of Building Types* (Princeton, 1976), pp. 235–56
E. Sims: 'Trade and Travel: Markets and Caravanserai', *Architecture of the Islamic World: Its History and Social Meaning*, ed. G. Michell (London and New York, 1978), pp. 80–111
S. Kostoff: *A History of Architecture: Settings and Rituals* (New York and Oxford, 1985)   ☐

Märklin, Konrad. *See* MERKLIN, KONRAD.

Markó. Hungarian family of artists. (1) Károly Markó (i) moved in 1832 from Hungary to Italy, where he spent most of the rest of his career. The rest of his family followed in 1838, and his three sons were all active in Italy, although (2) Károly Markó (ii) eventually settled in Moscow, (3) András Markó worked primarily in Vienna and (4) Ferenc Markó settled in Hungary.

(1) Károly Markó (i) (*b* Lőcse [now Levoča, Slovakia], 25 Sept 1791; *d* Villa Appeggi, nr Florence, 19 Nov 1860). Painter, teacher and illustrator, active in Italy. He studied in Kolozsvár (now Cluj, Romania) and Pest and in 1822 at the Akademie der Bildenden Künste in Vienna. His early paintings are of Hungarian landscapes (e.g. the *Danube Bank at Óbuda*, 1821). In 1830 he painted his best-known early work, the *Castle Hill at Visegrád* (Budapest, N.G.), which amalgamated natural elements and patriotic sentiments through its reference to the heroic past. In 1832 he moved to Rome, and in 1833 he illustrated *Perlen der heiligen Vorzeit* (Ofen, 1821; Hung. trans. by F. Kazinczy as *A Szent Hajdan Gyöngyei*, Budapest, 1830), the poems of János Pyrker, the Bishop of Eger. His main interest, however, was in painting landscape studies (e.g. *Roman Campagna*, 1838; Budapest, N.G.) and depicting the lives of the Italian peasants (e.g. *Grape Harvest*, 1835–6; priv. col.). In 1838 he lived in San Giuliano and in 1843 in Florence, where he became a teacher at the Accademia di Belle Arti. He moved to Villa Appeggi, near Florence, in 1847. His animated depictions of the natural world were influenced by the landscapes of Poussin and Claude, but the natural elements in his works always formed part of an ideal landscape. In the lit middle ground between the dark foreground and the blue sky in the distant background he placed biblical figures (e.g. *Abraham Receiving the Angel*, 1849) and mythological characters (e.g. the *Death of Eurydice*, 1847; Budapest, N.G.) or native peasants (e.g. *Landscape of Appeggi*, 1848; Budapest, N.G.). In 1845, however, he had participated in the architectural competition for the Hungarian parliament, and in his later career he became closely involved with Hungarian art life. During a visit to Pest in 1853 he was warmly received, and his impressions of Hungary appear in *Hungarian Plain Landscape with Well* (Budapest, N.G.). In the same year he became preoccupied with Hungarian historical themes, painting several versions of *Béla IV's Escape* (Budapest, Szilárd Vilmos priv. col.). He sent many pictures back to Hungary to be shown in the exhibitions of the Artists Association of Pest, and he included numerous Hungarian artists among his pupils. A large part of his artistic estate was bought by the Hungarian National Museum in Budapest.

BIBLIOGRAPHY

T. Szana: *Markó Károly és a tájfestészet* [Károly Markó and landscape painting] (Budapest, 1898)

G. Keleti: *Idősb Markó Károly* [Károly Markó the elder] (Budapest, 1899)

O. G. Pogány: *Idősb Markó Károly* (Budapest, 1954)

E. Bodnár: *Idősb Markó Károly* (Budapest, 1980/*R* 1982)

Idősb Markó Károly (exh. cat., ed. E. Bajkay, O. Hessky and E. Bodnar; Budapest, N.G., 1991) [incl. detailed bibliog.]

(2) Károly Markó (ii) (*b* Budapest, 22 Jan 1822; *d* Moscow, 1891). Painter, son of (1) Károly Markó (i). He studied in the landscape painting department of the Akademie der Bildenden Künste in Vienna (1836) and from 1838 under his father in Italy. In 1843 he visited Rome and Florence, and in 1845 he took part in the exhibitions of the Società Promotrice di Belle Arti in Florence. From 1851 to 1854 he lived in Vienna, showing his paintings in the exhibitions of the Österreichische Kunstverein (e.g. *Carrara Landscape*, 1852). His work was also exhibited in Milan, Genoa and Livorno, and he sent some paintings to be shown in the Budapest Artists Circle

and in the Hungarian National Fine Arts Association exhibitions. He became an honorary member of the academies in Florence, Genoa, Perugia and Urbino. His landscapes were painted in his father's style (e.g. *Sunset*, 1861; Budapest, N.G.), although they were freer, stronger, less detached and used colder colours. In some of them he used forest motifs (e.g. *Wooded Landscape*, 1861). He painted a number of scenes of Rome and Carrara as well as *Dante's Meeting with Virgil* (1865). In 1885, at the invitation of a Russian princess to whose daughter he had given drawing lessons in Florence, he settled in Moscow. After his death 34 of his paintings and sketches, including *Landscape in the Rain* and *Hill Road with Houses*, were returned to Hungary; some of these were bought by the Hungarian National Museum and Hungarian National Gallery in Budapest.

See also SCUOLA DI STAGGIA.

BIBLIOGRAPHY

Thieme–Becker

J. Kopp: *Markó Károly ismeretlen levelei* [Károly Markó's unknown letters] (Budapest, 1942), p. 223

E. Bodnár: 'Magyar festők Itáliában' [Hungarian painters in Italy], *Művészet*, x (1967), p. 3

(3) András Markó (*b* Vienna, 29 Sept 1824; *d* Villa Tivoli, Tuscany, 12 July 1895). Painter and draughtsman, son of (1) Károly Markó (i). He studied first in Florence and then in 1851 at the Akademie der Bildenden Künste in Vienna under Carl Rahl. In the early 1850s he exhibited with the Artists Association of Pest and the Hungarian National Fine Arts Association; in 1852 and 1854 his Italian landscapes were shown, and in 1854 he also exhibited his *Hungarian Landscape* (Budapest, N.G.) in Milan. He worked primarily in Vienna, painting Romantic genre pictures and landscapes. Like his father, he was attracted to the beauty of the Italian landscape, which he populated with shepherds and goatherds. Some of his best works are his charcoal drawings, which are also peopled with peasants, for example *Italian Landscape with Bridge* and *The Cows*. He was a successful animal painter, as in *Oxen Herders on the Bridge* (1876; Budapest, N.G.) and also painted biblical scenes, such as *Ruth and Boaz* (1882). His work the *Marble Mountains of Carrara* was shown in 1882 at the Contemporary Arts Museum, Budapest, and was bought by the royal private collection. He was one of the founder-members of the Hungarian Fine Arts Association in 1894.

See also SCUOLA DI STAGGIA.

BIBLIOGRAPHY

Thieme–Becker

D. Pataky: *A magyar rajzművészet* [Hungarian drawing] (Budapest, 1960), p. 17

Művészet Magyarországon, 1830–1870 [Art in Hungary, 1830–1870], ii (Budapest, 1981), pp. 275, 450

K. Lyka: *Nemzeti Romantica: Magyar Művésiet, 1850–1867* [National Romanticism: Hungarian art, 1850–1867] (Budapest, 1982), p. 81

(4) Ferenc Markó (*b* Kismarton, 1832; *d* Budapest, 3 Aug 1874). Painter and draughtsman, son of (1) Károly Markó (i). He studied first with his father then for two years at the Accademia di Belle Arti, Florence, where he concentrated on life drawing and figure painting. He took part in the struggle for Italian independence and was imprisoned (before 1853) for his political drawings. Subsequently he painted landscapes of the Appennines and of

Rome and Carrara. In 1853 he moved permanently back to Hungary. Although he was interested in the Hungarian countryside and particularly the Hungarian Plain, whose hamlets he depicted in romantic drawings and whose farm life he painted in *Shepherd on a Donkey* (1854), he moved away from his father's style and subject-matter. He began instead to give a new emphasis to the agricultural labourers and the life of the simple man, rather than to the idealized landscape. In 1859 he painted *Visegrád* (Budapest, N.G.), a contrast to the historical scenes and heroic depictions favoured by many 19th-century Hungarian painters. The development of his painterly style, which was characterized by a lively everyday atmosphere, was influenced by the Viennese Biedermeier genre painting and by the Munich school. He took part in the exhibitions of the Pest Artists Association and the Österreichische Kunstverein. At the age of 40 he went mad, dying not long after. His most successful paintings, such as *Young Woman in the Stream* (1855) and *Corn Harvester* (1863), are in the Hungarian National Gallery in Budapest.

Thieme–Becker

BIBLIOGRAPHY

Művészet Magyarországon, 1830–1870 [Art in Hungary, 1830–1870], ii (Budapest, 1981), pp. 357–8, 447–8

K. Sinkó: 'Az Alföld és az alföldi pásztorok felfedezése a Külföldi és a hazai képzőművészetben' [The Hungarian Plain and Hungarian shepherds in foreign and Hungarian art], *Ethnographia*, i–iv (1989), pp. 121–54

JÚLIA PAPP

Markov, Vladimir (Ivanovich) [Matvejs, Voldemārs Hans] (*b* Riga, 13 Oct 1877; *d* St Petersburg, 16 May 1914). Latvian artist and theorist, active in Russia. He trained at the Riga art school of Benjamin Blum (1861–1949) before moving to St Petersburg and entering the Academy of Arts in 1906. As the principal spokesman for the St Petersburg art society, the UNION OF YOUTH (1910–14), he published articles defending the group's artistic experiments, organized its early exhibitions and travelled to western Europe to establish links with the German and French avant-garde. In 1910 his programme for the re-examination of the formal principles of art was manifested in two Union of Youth exhibitions in St Petersburg and Riga and in his article on the 'Russian Secession'. He explored the move from Symbolist-Impressionism to Neo-primitivism and the overlap between them, and indicated the continuing emphasis on spiritual content in Russian art combined with the call for a new social and cultural awareness. His article on the principles of the new art (1912) and his book on artistry (1914) recommend an intuitive, subjective approach to art invoked through empathy and altered states of consciousness. Such a position provided a theoretical basis for the new developments in the art of Kazimir Malevich, Pavel Filonov, Ol'ga Rozanova and Mikhail Larionov (Cubo-Futurism, analytical art and Rayism), as well as the *zaum* ('transrational') aesthetic promoted by ALEKSEY KRUCHONYKH. Markov's last essays—which included analyses of Chinese poetry, Easter island sculpture and African art—were grounded in his attempt to redefine the principles of beauty and to re-establish the essential relationship, lost in the alienated world of the Russian art establishment, between modern artists and the world they perceived and experienced; here he concentrated more on plastic and literary principles, analysing creative form from the viewpoint of material conditions and the artist's psyche.

WRITINGS

'Russkiy Setsession (po povodu vystavki "Soyuza molodyzhi" v Rige)' [The Russian Secession (concerning the Union of Youth exhibition in Riga)], *Rizhskaya mysl'* [Riga thought], 908 (11 Aug 1910), p. 3; 909 (12 Aug 1910), p. 3

'Printsipy novogo iskusstva' [The principles of the new art], *Soyuz molodyozhi*, 1 (1912), pp. 5–14; 2 (1912), pp. 5–18

Iskusstvo ostrova Paskhi [The art of Easter Island] (St Petersburg, 1914)

Printsipy tvorchestva v plasticheskikh iskusstvakh: Faktura [Creative principles in the plastic arts: artistry] (St Petersburg, 1914)

Svirel' Kitaya [The Chinese flute] (St Petersburg, 1914)

Iskusstvo negrov [Negro art] (Petrograd, 1919)

BIBLIOGRAPHY

J. Bowlt: *Russian Art of the Avant Garde* (London, 1988)

J. Howard: *The Union of Youth* (Manchester and New York, 1992)

Marks. Symbols put on a work of art to denote such things as the identity of the craftsman or the owner, the source or destination of the object, or its quality.

1. Architecture. 2. Ceramics. 3. Furniture. 4. Metalwork. 5. Collectors'.

1. ARCHITECTURE. The use of masons' marks incised on building stones has received much scholarly attention, but the nature of the evidence makes it difficult to produce a coherent account of their origin and use in the medieval masons' craft. Two kinds of mark were made: position marks and banker marks. The former, usually simple in character, were inscribed by the mason hewers and used to identify a stone for its particular place in the building. In some buildings these position marks have survived on the exterior surfaces of the stone, but many more were probably inscribed on surfaces that are no longer visible. Inscribing position marks was by no means a universal practice, and it is not clear how the masons kept track of unmarked stones. Identifying marks may have been painted on, as they are in present-day European building lodges, where the finished carved stones are indexed with stencilled numbers and letters.

The banker mark identified the mason who carved the stone at his banker in the building lodge. The origins and intended use of banker marks are not entirely understood. Not every stone was identified by the mark of the mason who carved it. In England banker marks may have been developed for two reasons (Coulton): first, for quality control in a large building project where a number of less-skilled masons were employed; second, from the 13th century, when taskwork began to be used alongside, or sometimes instead of, the direct labour system, banker marks identified stones carved by task so that the masons could be paid appropriately (*see* MASON (i), §II, 2). In Germany from the second half of the 12th century, banker marks were used on simpler squared stones (Friederich), which indicated that they, too, helped to record the production of ashlars by men less skilled than the free-masons, who carved mouldings and figurework. By contrast, the carvers of these complex stones could be more easily identified, and few mouldings or figures have banker marks.

The banker mark eventually came to identify the mason himself when he permanently assumed its use as a kind of signature. Illiterate craftsmen could use the marks as legal signatures: as late as the mid-16th century more than half the carpenters in the Carpenters' Company of London inscribed their marks as signatures in the company's record books. A mark then became identified with a particular family of masons, with the father's mark slightly modified and adopted by his son or sons and perhaps grandsons or other relatives. Several of the famous 15th-century families of German master masons, for example the PARLER, BÖBLINGER, ENSINGER and RORICZER families, left examples of these closely related sets of marks. Those of important masters were sometimes carved on to a heraldic shield and set into a prominent place in the building, such as the keystone of a vault, or even on a portrait of the master mason himself. Examples of the latter are the busts of Mathias of Arras and Peter Parler in Prague Cathedral (see PARLER, (3), fig. 2), and of ANTON PILGRAM in the Stephansdom, Vienna.

By the time these 'master marks' had come into use, the masons' mark had clearly become an honorific signature. Its acquisition was a matter of considerable importance to the masons and served as one more way of certifying that a mason had learnt his trade. While the masons' mark was not mentioned in the Regensburg Ordinance of 1459, a book of regulations concerning the activities of masons (see MASON (i), §III, 2), it received prominent notice in the Ordinance compiled in 1462 by a regional meeting of northern German masons at Torgau, 50 km north-east of Leipzig. If a journeyman came to a project and requested that a mark be assigned to him, and if the master and journeymen of the project certified that he knew the art and craft of masonry, then he would be given his own mark. No master was allowed to assign a mark to his apprentice before he had completed his apprenticeship; on the other hand, the master was forbidden to delay the assignment of a mark beyond 14 days after completion of the apprenticeship. The master was also to pay for bread, meat and wine for a meal with ten journeymen to celebrate the assignment of the mark to the apprentice. If more than ten were invited, the apprentice had to share the cost of the meal.

BIBLIOGRAPHY

F. Rziha: 'Studien über Steinmetz-Zeichen', *Mitt. Ksr.-Kön. Zent.-Comm. Erforsch. & Erhaltung Kst- & Hist. Dkml.*, n. s., vii (1881), pp. 26–49, 105–17; ix (1883), pp. 25–45
K. Friederich: *Die Steinbearbeitung in ihrer Entwicklung vom 11. bis zum 18. Jahrhundert* (Augsburg, 1932)
R. H. C. Davis: 'Masons' Marks in Oxfordshire and the Cotswolds', *Rep. Oxon Archaeol. Soc.*, lxxxiv (1938), pp. 69–83
G. G. Coulton: *Art and the Reformation* (Cambridge, 1953)
R. H. C. Davis: 'A Catalogue of Masons' Marks as an Aid to Architectural History', *J. Brit. Archaeol. Assoc.*, 3rd ser., xvii (1954), pp. 43–76
H. Sauer: 'Die Steinmetzzeichen des Aachener Domes', *Z. Aachen. Geschver.*, lxxiv-lxxv (1962–3), pp. 467–76

LON R. SHELBY

2. CERAMICS. For centuries potters throughout the world have adopted the practice of marking their wares. From the 6th century BC Greek vases exist that are sometimes signed by both the potter and the painter (see VASE PAINTERS, §I), while from the 1st century BC to the 7th century AD *terra sigillata*, or Samian ware, which frequently bore the names or seals of the makers (see ROME, ANCIENT, §X, 8(i)), was made at various centres throughout the Roman Empire. Kiln marks are found on Japanese ceramics from the 3rd century AD (see JAPAN, §VIII, 1(vi)).

Rare pieces of Chinese porcelain survive from the early 14th century, bearing marks incised into the clay; but the practice of writing the reign title of the incumbent emperor in underglaze blue was not widely used until the reign of the Xuande emperor (1426–35). Other marks were used, but these were usually marks of good omen or commendation. It is dangerous to rely entirely on the marks found on Chinese wares as a means of dating, as it was quite acceptable, especially during the reign of the Kangxi emperor (1662–1722), to show reverence for previous periods by applying an earlier mark, often of the Chenghua emperor (1465–87) (see CHINA, figs 232 and 233).

During the Middle Ages in Europe there was little production of fine pottery, and the practice of marking wares appears to have lapsed. In the Middle East, however, Mesopotamian potters sometimes applied dedicatory inscriptions or a rather vague signature. No regular marking was used by the potters in Spain who from the 15th century produced lustrewares. In the 16th century Italian maiolica was occasionally signed with the potter's name and the date and city of his birth. It was probably the Italian potters' familiarity with Far and Near Eastern ceramics that inspired the mark of the dome of Florence Cathedral, which is sketched on some of the extremely rare examples of 16th-century Medici porcelain (see FLORENCE, §III, 1). During the 17th century more regular marks were used on Italian maiolica, for example the shield of Savona or the lighthouse of Genoa. Such marks do not identify the potter, which is also true of the numerous devices on 17th- and 18th-century Delftware; there were often the names of the breweries that had formerly occupied the premises where the potteries were situated.

The first true factory mark is that of the crossed swords, which was adopted from the arms of Saxony and used by the Meissen Porcelain Factory from c. 1722. Other continental European factories in the mid-18th century followed this fashion and marked their wares with devices taken from the state coat of arms or the patron's initials. The Swedish factories of Rörstrand and Marieberg marked many of their wares with the date of manufacture and the painter's mark, in addition to the recognized factory mark. In Berlin the Royal State Factory adopted the mark of a sceptre in underglaze blue from 1763, and a further enamel mark was added at the time of decoration. While the majority of these marks are in underglaze blue, a few factories, such as the Nymphenburg Porcelain Factory, impressed their mark into the clay prior to firing.

The crossed swords of Meissen became so universally recognized that many factories introduced marks that were similar enough to confuse the purchaser, and the English porcelain factories of Bow, Worcester, Derby, Lowestoft and Coalport at times blatantly copied this mark. The most imitated French mark is that of the royal cipher of interlaced Ls, which was introduced at the factory of Vincennes c. 1750 and continued after the move to Sèvres in 1756. From 1753 this cipher usually enclosed a date letter and showed the initials or device of the painter and, occasionally, the gilder. This method of marking was used until 1793, after which further written or printed datable marks were invariably applied.

From the mid-18th century many European potters impressed the name of the factory or that of the owner into the unfired clay, using letters resembling printers' type, as in the WEDGWOOD mark, but from *c.* 1800 printed marks, or backstamps, usually in underglaze blue, were generally used by the major factories, especially if the decoration had been applied by transfer printing. Many of these marks included the name or the initials of the potter, the location of the factory and the name of the pattern. The inclusion of the name of the country of origin usually indicates a date after 1891, to comply with the American McKinley Tariff Act, while the addition of the words MADE IN followed by the country of origin is more likely to indicate a date in the 1920s. Similarly the addition of LIMITED in any form was rarely added prior to *c.* 1880. It should be remembered that marks incised into the clay or applied in underglaze blue prior to glazing must have been applied at the time of manufacture, whereas enamel or gilt marks applied over the glaze after firing could have been added at a later date in order to deceive.

BIBLIOGRAPHY

J. P. Cushion and W. B. Honey: *Handbook of Pottery and Porcelain Marks* (London and New York, 1956, rev. London, 4/1990)

J. P. Cushion: *Pocket Book of English Ceramics Marks and those of Wales, Scotland and Ireland* (London, 1959); 4th edn as *British Ceramic Marks* (London, 1994)

S. E. Vingedal: *Porslinsmärken* (Stockholm, 1959)

L. Danckert: *Manuel de la porcelaine européenne* (Fribourg, 1973)

J. P. O'Neill, ed.: *Sèvres Porcelain: Makers and Marks of the 18th Century* (New York, 1986)

JOHN CUSHION

3. FURNITURE. On medieval and later European and North American furniture, marks indicating the origin or date of a piece may be found on the wood, on other materials used in its construction or on metal mounts. As in other types of decorative art, marks were increasingly applied from 1800, when the Industrial Revolution and improved means of transport allowed markets and trade to expand. Marks on wood were carved or incised; stamped with dies; branded with a hot iron; written in pencil, pen or paint; stencilled; incorporated into the motifs in the veneer; or applied using paper labels or transfers (decals).

Types of carved marks include dates, initials and heraldic devices, which may be those of the original owner; plain pieces occasionally bear marks that were carved later in an attempt to render them more valuable. Incised marks often appear inside the piece or on the back. After 1700 crude Roman numerals, including IIII for IV, were customarily scratched inside the frames of seats on sets of chairs. These functioned as inventory numbers, and similar marks on the removable frames of upholstery (e.g. seats) ensured that they were returned to their correct location. Other incised marks served to guide the craftsman assembling the piece.

Marks made by impressing a cold metal die in the wood began to be used in the late 17th century. The best-known are *estampilles* incorporating the name, or occasionally the initials, of *maîtres ébénistes* and *menuisiers* in Paris; these first appeared *c.* 1725 and were required by the Corporation des Menuisiers-Ebénistes for every item produced in the craftsman's workshop between 1751 and 1791. Struck on the carcass, under the top or under the seat, the one or more *estampilles* indicate the shop that made, finished, retailed or even repaired the piece. Sometimes employed in other French centres, they were revived after the French Revolution and continued as late as the 1930s (for interpretation of these marks see Verlet and Ledoux-Lebard).

Stamped marks found on furniture in the British tradition include the initials of makers of cane chairs in the late 17th century, of individual journeymen, shops and, in some instances, the owner, the most significant of the last type being the crowned royal cipher found on the furnishings of palaces and government buildings. In the USA some furniture of *c.* 1800 was branded with the name of the owner or merchant. Occasionally a craftsman signed the marquetry or decoration, as in the case of the furniture produced in the workshops of Emile Gallé in Nancy, France, which often incorporates his signature. Signatures and monograms are a distinctive feature of objects of the Arts and Crafts Movement and of Art Nouveau. Pen or pencil marks, often found in drawers or under tops, may identify the maker or a tradesman; in many cases, however, they relate to a former owner. Painted, pen, pencil, chalk or stencilled marks including a number may coincide with an inventory. Those relating to furniture that belonged to Louis XIV (reprinted in Guiffrey) have helped to identify a number of important pieces.

Although paper labels and trade cards appeared *c.* 1700, they only became a common form of marking after 1800. As with much printed material, a date can be deduced from the style of lettering and graphic design, and the business name and address verified against city directories and tax lists. The name on a label may be the maker, retailer or even a business that stored or repaired the piece. (English examples are illustrated in Heal; a comprehensive listing is in Beard and Gilbert.) After 1900 paper labels were occasionally forged.

By the late 19th century, standard trademarks began to be common, mainly in the form of paper labels, transfers or impressed stamps. These are frequently located on drawers or back boards. Some quality furniture bears a small metal or ivory coloured tablet giving the name and address of the maker or retailer. Impressed or written numbers on furniture manufactured after 1800 may represent the model, an order number or some other business code. Sometimes these are traceable. Registration, patent and copyright marks, or numbers generally, indicate an origin in the 19th century or later. Non-Western furniture was rarely marked until after 1891, when British and American customs regulations required all imported goods to be marked with the name of the country of origin. Locks, hinges, castors and ornamental mounts sometimes bear marks. Superior British locks manufactured between 1800 and 1890 may bear the stamp PATENT alongside the crowned initials of the reigning sovereign.

BIBLIOGRAPHY

J. Guiffrey: *Inventaire général du mobilier de la couronne sous Louis XIV*, 2 vols (Paris, 1885–6)

A. Heal: *The London Furniture Makers from the Restoration to the Victorian Era, 1660–1840* (London, 1953/R 1972)

P. Verlet: *Les Meubles français du XVIIIe siècle*, 2 vols (Paris, 1956)

D. Ledoux-Lebard: *Les Ebénistes parisiens du XIXe siècle, 1795–1870: Leurs oeuvres et leurs marques* (Paris, 1965, rev. and enlarged, Paris, 1984)

G. Beard and C. Gilbert: *The Dictionary of English Furniture Makers, 1660–1840* (London, 1986)

A. Pradère: *French Furniture Makers: The Art of the Ebéniste from Louis XIV to the Revolution* (London and Malibu, 1989)

C. PETER KAELLGREN

4. METALWORK. Symbols or letters have commonly been applied to a piece of metalwork to identify where it was assayed and thus to warrant or guarantee its fineness. Such marks are often called hallmarks, after the Goldsmiths' Hall in London. There are also a variety of other marks, however, that signify a range of information; these are also occasionally referred to as hallmarks. Most marks are punched to appear in relief. Assaying and hallmarking regulations vary throughout the world, but few countries have centralized systems of control, or vest these in entirely independent agencies, as in Britain. Only makers' marks and alloy quality marks have been used, albeit unsystematically, in the USA. This article is concerned primarily with an overview of the history of marks on metalwork. Further information on marking in specific centres of production is given within the relevant articles on cities (where subdivided, under the heading 'Centre of production') and on countries and civilizations (under 'Metalwork').

(i) Precious metals. (ii) Base metals.

(i) Precious metals. The need to protect the public from silver, copper, bronze or lead that had been gilded and from work with a lower content of precious metal than claimed resulted in the introduction of systems of control marks. In ancient Rome they were used to certify the weight of pieces and, from the 4th century AD, the manufacturer. A system of applying control stamps to gold and silver objects was used under imperial authority in Byzantium during the 6th and 7th centuries AD. These stamps essentially pertained to the traffic of precious metal objects and taxation, but they also identify the reigns of the emperors and the individual workshops. The assaying or testing of the metal content of gold and silver has medieval origins. Assay grooves are formed when a sample of metal is removed to be assayed. Marks were used in the Middle Ages in western Europe, principally France, England and the Netherlands, to control the minimum fineness of gold and silver. Throughout Europe guilds of goldsmiths assayed and marked gold and silver objects as well as regulating membership (see fig. 1). Sometimes guilds also marked goldsmiths' weights to show that they had been standardized.

In France the guilds of certain towns were active in hallmarking before 1300. In 1238 Henry III of England laid down that all silverware should be of the 'sterling standard', or 92.5% pure silver, the remaining proportion normally being copper added to harden the metal. In England the Worshipful Company of Goldsmiths began to assay or test precious metals at their Hall in London in 1300, taking their example from France and perhaps immigrant goldsmiths from the 'east' (i.e. northern Europe), who could well have introduced and regulated their 'easterling' standard before this date. The first hallmark used in England was a crowned or uncrowned leopard's

1. Marks and names of goldsmiths in Ghent, bronze sheet, 260×141 mm, 1454–81 (Ghent, Oudheidkundig Museum van de Bijloke)

head, which indicated the Goldsmiths' Company's satisfaction that the object touched was either gold or silver of the required minimum standard; that is, either sterling silver or gold 'of the touch of Paris' (19.2 carats in 1300; 18 carats from 1478; and 22 carats from 1576). The leopard's head is now the London Assay Office hallmark, but until the 18th century it was frequently used in major provincial assaying towns (e.g. York and Exeter) in addition to their own town marks.

In 1355 the use of makers' marks and date marks was introduced in Montpellier, France. In England makers' marks (see fig. 2(i)a) were used from 1363; at this time they usually consisted of symbols rather than initials. Makers' marks were used to avoid confusion concerning the origin of a piece at the hall; all goldsmiths had to mark

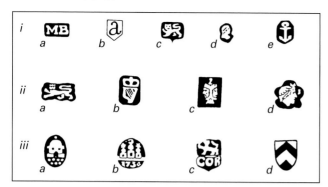

2. Silver marks: (i) marks from a piece by Matthew Boulton, 1798: (a) maker's mark; (b) date letter; (c) lion passant guardant; (d) sovereign's head duty mark for George III; (e) Birmingham assay office; (ii) European fineness marks: (a) London, *c.* 1600; (b) Ireland, from 1637; (c) Spanish Netherlands, 18th century; (d) Austria, 1866–72; (iii) Town marks: (a) Bergen, 18th and 19th centuries; (b) Copenhagen, from 1608; (c) Córdoba, 15th and 16th centuries; (d) Neuchâtel, 1820–66

their own wares in advance of assaying with punches approved by the guild and recorded at the hall (see fig. 1). Punches are still ordered through the relevant assay office. In Spain town marks were required from 1401 (see fig. 2(iii)c). They also became obligatory in Germany.

Also in Montpellier a cycle of date letters, based on the letters of the alphabet running in cycles of 20 to 26 characters, was developed in 1427 to indicate the year of assaying of a piece. Date letters also acted as a safeguard on the honesty of the assay master and his employees in their term of office, which could thus be identified. A similar system was adopted in Paris in 1461 and in England in 1478 (2(i)b). Not until the mid-19th century was there a serious attempt by the antiquary Charles Octavius Swinnerton Morgan (1803–88) to identify each date letter. The typeface is changed after every cycle, both in design and case, and cycles can easily be confused. Many edicts concerning marking in the South Netherlands survive from the 14th and 15th centuries. Brussels gained its first hallmark, the lion of Brabant, at the beginning of the 14th century. Laws governing Scottish marking were introduced in 1457. By contrast, in Augsburg and Nuremberg, two of the main German centres of gold and silver production, marks were not used consistently until the 16th century. Marking procedures in Rome were codified at this point. In Russia the earliest marks date from the mid-17th century, and marking did not become mandatory until 1700.

Perhaps the best-known of all English standard hallmarks is the lion passant guardant (2(i)c), which was taken from the arms of England. It was used from 1544 until 1821–2, when it was superseded by the lion passant standard hallmark. The maker's mark, date letter and subsequently the lion passant were also applied to gold until 1844. In 1697, as a result of the passing of the Wrought Plate Act, the new, higher Britannia standard was set for silver of 95.8% fineness. The Act was designed to frustrate the melting down of sterling silver specie or coin and to enforce the smelting of bullion silver from fresh supplies. New marks were required, and the lion passant was changed to a seated figure of Britannia, which

was used together with the lion's head erased hallmark. All goldsmiths' makers' marks were re-engraved to show the first two letters of each surname instead of their initials, as before. In 1720 the sterling standard was restored. The Britannia standard, with appropriate mark or marks, remains optional. The use of the same marks for gold and sterling silver in England caused some confusion, although during the period of Britannia Standard silver the old marks continued to be used for gold, apart from the maker's mark, the new form of which was adopted, as on the ewer and basin (1701; Chatsworth, Derbys) by Pierre Platel.

After periods of excise duty evasion, in 1784 the government reimposed its tax in England and Scotland and added a compulsory duty mark, which consisted of the reigning sovereign's head (2(i)d). The Hibernia duty mark was introduced by the Dublin Assay Office in Ireland in 1730. Similarly, in France marks were used to indicate that tax had been paid on a piece. The British duty particularly influenced the output of the new flourishing manufacturing and assaying cities of Birmingham and Sheffield, which had received their new assay offices and town marks, of an anchor (2(i)e) and a crown respectively, in 1773. After the duty was abolished in 1890, sovereigns' heads continued to be used optionally as hallmarks on such special occasions as the coronation in 1953, or the Silver Jubilees in 1935 and 1977. Likewise, Ireland has also used commemorative marks, for example the one used in 1987 to celebrate the 350th anniversary of the first Irish hallmark, the harp crowned (2(ii)b).

French marks were suspended during the Revolution. Napoleon abolished the guilds and changed the laws regulating marking. In 1811 a French system of marks was adopted in Italy. Three years later a national system of marking replaced the systems used by individual cities in the Netherlands. Chinese silver made for export in the late 18th century and the 19th often included pseudo-English marks (*see* CHINA, §X, 2).

On the introduction of 18 carat gold in England in 1798 the numerals 18 in a separate punch, and a crown, were used to signify gold for the first time. From 1816 an additional sun in splendour mark was applied to 22 carat gold, perhaps intended for mounted items only, and then in 1844 the numeral 22 was authorized, along with the crown, or gold mark, introduced in 1798. From 1842 imported gold- and silverwork was subject to testing and, from 1867, to the application of the foreign origin mark, which consisted of the letter F in an elliptical escutcheon, together with appropriate hallmarks. The latter practice was discontinued from 1904.

Sheffield was forbidden to mark gold until 1904, when a rose town mark was enforced. The British Hallmarking Act of 1973, enforced from 1 January 1975, successfully standardized procedures for hallmarking both gold and silver in all four remaining United Kingdom assay offices: London and Birmingham retained their marks. Sheffield adopted the rose mark for both silver and gold, although confusion still arises concerning silver-gilt items assayed there; and the Edinburgh Assay Office's standard hallmark was changed from a thistle to a lion rampant. A common date letter system using the same typeface and a sequence of 25 letters was also agreed upon; it changed at the quarter-century and was subject to further international centralization. Platinum was also included in the legislation for assaying for the first time; it was allocated a distinct orb in a pentagon mark. Various conventions arranged through the European Free Trade Association and the European Community have attempted to standardize internationally recognized finenesses and assay marking procedures since 1975. Convention marks must include a sponsor's mark (the mark of the maker or firm that commissioned the smith), the convention control mark (a set of balance scales), a fineness mark and an assay office mark.

BIBLIOGRAPHY

M. Rosenberg: *Die Goldschmiede-Merkzeichen* (Frankfurt am Main, 1890, rev. in 4 vols, 3/1922–8)
C. J. Jackson: *English Goldsmiths and their Marks* (London, 1921, *R*/1948)
E. Beuque: *Dictionnaire de poinçons officiels français et étrangers: De leur création (XIVe siècle) à nos jours*, 2 vols (Paris, 1925–8)
S. G. Ensko: *American Silversmiths and their Marks* (New York, 1948, 3/1980/*R* 1983)
E. C. Dodd: *Byzantine Silver Stamps* (Washington, DC, 1961)
W. R. T. Wilkinson: *A History of Hallmarks* (London, 1971, rev. 1975)
F. Bradbury: *Book of Hallmarks* (Northend, 1975)
Les Poinçons de garantie internationaux pour l'argent (Paris, 1975); Eng. trans. as *International Hallmarks on Silver Collected by Tardy* (Paris, 1985)
J. Divis: *Silver Marks of the World* (London, 1976)
Touching Gold and Silver (exh. cat., London, Goldsmiths' Co., 1978)
C. Blair, ed.: *The History of Silver* (London, 1987)
J. Cherry: *Goldsmiths*, Medieval Craftsmen (London, 1992)
P. Pazzi: *I punzai dell'argenteria veneta*, 2 vols (Treviso, 1992)

(ii) Base metals. Since base metals are more plentiful and of lower value than precious metals, legislation concerning their marking tends to be found in the protective clauses of precious metal statutes. In Britain, for example, Sheffield plate manufacturers were permitted to apply their maker's marks only from 1774, and by the end of the 19th century strict rules were enforced to prevent the electroplating industry from confusing the public with such ambiguous marks as crowns and anchors, which could be mistaken for sterling silver town marks.

Touches, or marks, are found on pewter, particularly that from northern Europe from the 15th and 16th centuries. In Paris pewterers had to mark all hammered work from 1382, which may have given rise to the hammer mark. Many guilds required origin or standard marks. There were also city, town, quality, standard, ownership, maker's and capacity confirmation marks. In England, following the example of the Goldsmiths' Company, the Worshipful Company of Pewterers (which received its first charter in 1474) required each member to apply a mark in case any wares should not reach the required quality and standard. Unfortunately, the table or touch plate that recorded the makers' marks was destroyed in the Great Fire of London in 1666, but a new one (London, Pewterers' Co.) that commenced in 1667 records 1071 makers from the period 1640 to *c*. 1840. Cotterell records the marks of 6000 pewterers to that date in England, and over 11,000 German pewter marks are known. So-called hallmarks were also applied from *c*. 1630 to *c*. 1725 to reinforce the deceptive resemblance to silver that new and polished pewter can have. This practice was never approved of by the Pewterers' Company and was the subject of frequent complaints made by the wardens of the Goldsmiths' Company; the practice was also pursued in

continental Europe and the American colonies. Marking of pewter was strictly controlled in Sweden in the 17th century. At the end of the 17th century a mark that consisted of a crowned X was introduced; it originally denoted the quality of metal composition in England and Germany. In time this mark became meaningless. Likewise, a crowned rose, an angel and a LONDON mark became common in England but were widely imitated in the rest of Europe. Many good pieces remained unmarked in spite of regulations, and with the Arts and Crafts Movement the value of a maker's mark or emblem was newly recognized. German Kayzerzinn and Orivit pewterware, for example, competed with the 'Tudric' line marketed by Liberty's of London *c*. 1900, and their wares were marked accordingly. Much pewter was silver-plated, and many items followed silver designs closely.

Ormolu (gilt bronze) is not normally marked unless taxed, as it was in France for a short period during the reign of Louis XV, when a crowned C was applied. During the Empire period such manufacturers as Pierre-Philippe Thomire stamped their identity as a matter of advertisement and prestige. Some manufacturers had their names cast into objects, especially those made of iron. In the area of copper- and brassware, marks were used mainly by such manufacturers and designers as W. A. S. Benson during the Arts and Crafts period.

BIBLIOGRAPHY

H. H. Cotterell: *Old Pewter: Its Makers and Marks* (London, 1969)
J. L. Scott: *Pewter Wares from Sheffield* (Baltimore, 1980)
V. Brett: *Phaidon Guide to Pewter* (Oxford, 1981), pp. 230–41
P. Hermann: *Die Merkzeichen der Nürnberger Rotschmiede* (Munich, 1981)
J. M. Burks: *Birmingham Brass Candlesticks* (Charlottesville, 1986)

JOHN K. D. COOPER

5. COLLECTORS'. A small, identifying mark is sometimes affixed to a drawing or print, or the mounts thereof, to indicate ownership and/or authenticity. Collectors, agents, heirs, executors and curators employ collectors' marks to affirm legitimate ownership, authorized sale or inclusion within a designated corpus, such as the contents of a museum, library or the studio of a deceased artist. For permanence, collectors' marks are usually handwritten, ink-stamped or blind-stamped on the *recto* or *verso* of an object or on the mount. The most popular forms include shields and armorial crests, paraphs (marks or flourishes under signatures) and inscriptions, flowers, stars, animals or other objects, or names, initials and monograms (see figs 3 and 4). Occasionally a distinctive ornamental border or the decoration of a mount may serve as a sort of collectors' mark, since such embellishments can often be identified with specific collections.

The practice of affixing identifying marks was developed in the early 17th century as an outgrowth of the practice of designing mounts of uniform size and type of ornament, a custom that originated in the 16th century with Giorgio Vasari (*see* VASARI, (1)), the first systematic and historically minded collector of drawings. While such mounts facilitated storage and reduced the risk of damage through handling, the collector's mark originated from a need to account for and record large quantities of works on paper. It appeared initially in the early 17th century, when large collections were routinely sold *en bloc*.

3. Collectors' marks of Jonathan Richardson sr and Sir Joshua Reynolds on Annibale Carracci's *Man Wearing a Hat* (New York, Pierpont Morgan Library)

national collections. As signs of a common past ownership, collectors' marks make possible the association of individual works with celebrated collections, from Vasari, Nicholas Lanier, Peter Lely, the Dukes of Devonshire, Pierre-Jean Mariette, Joshua Reynolds, Thomas Lawrence and the de Goncourt brothers through to Franz W. Koenigs (1881–1941). They testify to the bonds of artistic appreciation across the centuries. The mark of a collection of distinction will always add value, both aesthetic and commercial, to the work on which it is placed.

The need for an authoritative manual reproducing and describing all known collectors' marks was already recognized in the 18th century, but it was not until 1921, when FRITS LUGT published *Les Marques de collections de dessins et d'estampes*, that such an ambition was realized. In 1956 Lugt published a supplement, and since that date the project has been continued under the auspices of the Institut Néerlandais, Paris, the foundation to which he bequeathed his own collection and his documentary archives. Lugt's reference joins detailed biographical information and sales information to the register of marks it reproduces and thus serves as a vast compendium of reliable, factual information.

BIBLIOGRAPHY

F. Lugt: *Marques* (1921)
——: *Marques*, suppl. (1956)

BEVERLEY SCHREIBER JACOBY

A drawing or print bearing one or more collectors' marks discloses the permanent, symbolic record of its own provenance or history of ownership. Collectors' marks form part of the history of taste. They serve to document the contents of collections long dispersed as well as helping to trace the sources and sequence of acquisitions of large

4. Collectors' marks of Sir Joshua Reynolds and Sir Peter Lely on Paolo Farinati's *Figure of a Woman* (New York, Pierpont Morgan Library)

Marks, Henry Stacy (*b* London, 13 Sept 1829; *d* London, 9 Jan 1898). English painter. He studied with J. M. Leigh (1808–60) from 1847 and in January 1851 enrolled at the Royal Academy Schools. In 1852 Marks and P. H. Calderon spent five months studying in Paris under François-Edouard Picot and at the Ecole des Beaux-Arts. The next year he made his début at the Royal Academy Summer Exhibition, where he exhibited annually until 1897. He was elected ARA in 1871 and RA in 1878. Marks was a key member of the ST JOHN'S WOOD CLIQUE and a notorious practical joker.

Marks's early work was literary (especially Shakespearean), genre and often lightly humorous, as in *Toothache in the Middle Ages* (exh. London, RA 1856; untraced, see *Pen and Pencil Sketches*, i, opp. p. 56). During the 1850s he produced designs for the firm of Clayton & Bell, and in 1859 he painted the chancel arch of All Souls, Halifax. In the 1860s he painted furniture for William Burges and was the pseudonymous reviewer 'Drypoint' of the *Spectator*. In the 1870s Marks began to concentrate on painting animals, especially birds, which dominated the rest of his career. Among the best known of these is the series of 12 panels painted for the Duke of Westminster (1877–80; Eaton Hall, Ches) and a painting of a group of parrots, *A Select Committee* (1891; Liverpool, Walker A.G.). Marks was also a prolific watercolour painter.

WRITINGS

Pen and Pencil Sketches, 2 vols (London, 1894)

BIBLIOGRAPHY

B. Hillier: 'The St John's Wood Clique', *Apollo*, lxxix (1964), pp. 490–95
Great Victorian Painters (exh. cat. by R. Treble, ACGB, 1978), pp. 56–7
'*And When Did You Last See Your Father?*' (exh. cat. by E. Morris and F. Milner, Liverpool, Walker A.G., 1992), pp. 1–28, 32, 61–5

PHILIP MCEVANSONEYA

Márkus, Géza (*b* Budapest, 6 April 1872; *d* Budapest, 8 Dec 1912). Hungarian architect and designer. He worked from the age of 17 as a drawing assistant, first with the master builder József Gutwillig and then with Vilmos Freund (1846–1920) in Budapest. His decorative talent led him to become assistant to Alajos Hauszmann, one of the leading Hungarian exponents of late Eclecticism, whom he assisted in designing the Court of Justice (1891–6; now Museum of Ethnography), Budapest. After 1896 Márkus worked independently and was also active as a critic. The most significant and characteristic of his few surviving buildings is the 'Ornate House' (1902), Kecskemét, a former casino and residential block, which now houses the Kecskemét Gallery. It is two storeys high, and its façades bear striking moulded forms reminiscent of the folk pottery of the district. The decoration of fiery coloured enamels from the ZSOLNAY CERAMICS FACTORY follows a pattern of embroidery motifs. The roof, chimney tops and dormer windows are virtually non-figurative ceramic sculptures. The ornamented façade of the Erdey Sanatorium (1904), Bakács Square, Budapest, although similarly conceived, is not quite as organically assembled. Between 1904 and 1908 Márkus took part in the reconstruction of a number of theatres and entertainment halls in Budapest, such as the rebuilding of the Orfeum as the Royal Theatre, the internal refurbishment of the Jardin de Paris music hall and of the Endre Nagy cabaret (with Frigyes Spiegel; all destr.; see Gerle, Kovács and Makovecz, pp. 134–6). His last work, the People's Opera House (1911–12; now rebuilt as the Erkel Theatre), on which he was assisted by KOMOR & JAKAB, contained Hungary's first auditorium in reinforced concrete. Márkus also designed memorials, sepulchres (e.g. tomb of Sándor Erkel, 1904, and tomb of János Jankó, 1905; both Budapest, Kerepesi Cemetery; both with Ede Kallós, sculptor) and innovative stage sets, but he is best known as one of the first and perhaps most original followers of the *fin-de-siècle* movement, associated with Ödön Lechner, to develop a Hungarian national style.

BIBLIOGRAPHY

J. Gerle: 'Márkus Géza: A káprázatok építésze' [Géza Márkus: the architect of illusions], *Magyar Építőművészet*, lxxv/5 (1984), pp. 54–5

J. Gerle, A. Kovacs and I. Makovecz: *A századfordulő Magyar építészete* [Hungarian architecture at the turn of the century] (Budapest, 1990)

ÁKOS MORAVÁNSZKY,
KATALIN MORAVÁNSZKY-GYŐNGY

Marlborough, 1st Duke of. *See* CHURCHILL, JOHN.

Marle, (Valentin) Raymond [Raimond] **(Silvain) van** (*b* The Hague, 28 June 1887; *d* Perugia, 17 Nov 1936). Dutch art historian, active in France and Italy. He studied in Paris at the Ecole des Chartes and the Ecole Pratique des Hautes Etudes, taking his degree at the Sorbonne in 1910, finally becoming a doctor of the Faculty of Letters at the University of Paris. From 1918 onwards van Marle lived in Perugia. He is best known for his monumental 19-volume series entitled *The Development of the Italian Schools of Painting*, which developed out of his earlier writings on art. Van Marle combined connoisseurship with an idiosyncratic and broad methodology, which he described as a 'history on broad lines, estimating psychological developments, judging works of art on broad aesthetic lines, caring more about the intelligence of attributions

than their rightness'. Also of considerable value to students and art historians are his publications on iconography. History, theology, astrology and mysticism were all subjects that fascinated van Marle and influenced his writing.

WRITINGS

Le Comté de Hollande sous Philippe le Bon (1428–1467) (The Hague, 1908)

Hoorn au moyen âge: Son histoire et ses institutions jusqu'au début du seizième siècle (The Hague, 1910)

An Outline of Manichaeism (1912–13)

De mystike leer van Meister Eckhart (Haarlem, 1916)

Recherches sur l'iconographie de Giotto et de Duccio (Strasbourg, 1920)

Simone Martini et les peintres de son école (Strasbourg, 1920)

La Peinture romaine au moyen âge: Son développement du sixième jusqu'à la fin du treizième siècle (Strasbourg, 1921)

The Development of the Italian Schools of Painting, 19 vols (The Hague, 1923–38)

Iconographie de l'art profane au moyen-âge et à la renaissance, et la décoration des demeures, 2 vols (The Hague, 1931–4)

BIBLIOGRAPHY

A. M. Hind: Obituary, *Burl. Mag.*, lxx (1937), pp. 46–7

Marliani, Giovanni Bartolomeo (*b* Robbio, territory of Lomellina, 1488; *d* Rome, 1566). Italian antiquarian. Marliani left his native Milan to study at the University of Padua, where he came in contact with Giovanni Morone, later Cardinal. In Rome he became a friar at S Agostino and member of a religious confraternity (Compagnia di S Apollonia). He published works on Roman law, history, topography and numismatics, among which the most significant was his archaeological guidebook, *Topographia antiquae Romae* (Rome, 1534; *see also* ROME, §III, 1(i)). A revised text with woodcut illustrations and dedicated to Francis I of France, *Urbis Romae topographia*, followed in 1544. For various reconstructions of ancient monuments in plan, elevation and section, Marliani relied on the *Libro terzo dell'architettura* of SEBASTIANO SERLIO, published in Venice in 1540. The *Urbis Romae topographia* was republished with Fulvio Orsini's commentary by J. G. Graevius in *Thesaurus antiquitatum Romanarum* (Leiden, 1694–9). Another copy (Modena, Bib. Estense) is bound with other treatises by Marliani, including *De Foro Romano contra novam et stultam opinionem cujusdam Strepsiadis* ('On the Forum Romanum, against the new and foolish theory of a certain Strepsides'). Marliani was the first to publish the inscriptions of the consular Fasti in the same year of their discovery in the Forum Romanum and transfer to the Capitoline. The *Consulum dictatorum censorumque Romanorum . . .* (Rome, 1549) was reprinted in Venice in 1555 and expanded for Antonio Blado's lavishly engraved publication of 1560, the *Annales consulum dictatorum censorumque Romanorum a condita urbe usque ad Ti. Caesarem.*

BIBLIOGRAPHY

A. Bertolotti: 'Bartolomeo Marliano: Archeologo nel secolo XVI', *Atti & Mem. RR. Deput. Stor. Patria Prov. Emilia*, n. s., iv/2 (1880), pp. 107–38

P. Jacks: *The Antiquarian and the Myth of Antiquity. The Origins of Rome in Renaissance Thought* (Cambridge, 1993), pp. 206–27

PHILIP J. JACKS

Marlik [Pers. Mārlīk]. Site in the Gilan Province of northwest Iran, in which is located the royal cemetery of an Indo-Iranian kingdom of the late 2nd millennium BC and the early 1st. It is one of five apparently related sites in the valley of the Gawhar Rud and was excavated in 1961–2 by Ezat Negahban. Finds are in the Archaeological Museum, Tehran.

The people of Marlik, who left no written records except for two cylinder seals with fragmentary inscriptions, seem to have belonged to a group of Indo-Iranians, possibly the Marda or Amarda, who entered Iran and settled along the northern slopes of the Elburz mountains and the southern shores of the Caspian Sea during the second half of the 2nd millennium BC. They established a strong kingdom in this area and used the crest of a natural hill for their royal cemetery for at least two or three centuries between the 14th and 10th centuries BC.

Excavation revealed 53 roughly constructed stone tombs, all from the same period, which varied in size from 7×5 m to 1.5 m square. They contained rich objects of gold, silver, bronze, pottery and glass (see ANCIENT NEAR EAST, fig. 24). The burial arrangements at Marlik can be illustrated by the contents of a large oval-shaped tomb, apparently belonging to a warrior king, which contained a skeleton lying on its side on a long stone slab. Beneath him were several large daggers and spearheads, while behind lay a broken gold bowl with repoussé designs of gods and goddesses. Scattered over the skeleton were fragments of cloth and numerous embossed gold buttons that had apparently decorated the burial clothes, along with gold, red cornelian and shell beads, gold pendants, a gold chain and hair holder, bronze buttons and silver loops. Under and around the burial slab were fragments of a bronze quiver and decorated leather quiver cover, bronze cymbals, belts, tools and equipment and pottery human figurines and vessels. Elsewhere in the tomb were pottery and bronze cooking vessels containing animal and bird bones, a bronze ladle and skewer, many bronze figurines of wild game, a bronze model of oxen, yoke and plough and three pottery animal figurines. A small adjacent tomb contained a set of horse teeth, a bronze horse bit and bronze loops. Other less organized but equally rich tombs seem, from their contents, to have belonged to women and children.

The most striking objects from Marlik are the many thin-walled, finely chased ritual vessels of gold. Winged bulls, griffins, phoenixes, unicorns, eagles, wild boar, mountain goats and gods and goddesses decorate these vessels, often with part of the design, such as the animal heads, hammered out from the body of the vessel in high relief (see fig.). A smaller number of silver vessels and some fragmentary bronze vessels exhibit the same type of relief designs.

Also of apparent ritual significance are the many figurines, both human and animal. The metal figurines include a small hollow gold torso of a king with separate crown and earrings, and two female figures of solid bronze. The hollow red pottery male and female figurines are particularly striking. These have flat triangular faces with open mouths, attenuated arms, massive buttocks and lower limbs and carefully detailed and exaggerated sexual organs. The many hollow pottery animal figurines include the humped bull, stag, ram, mule, horse, bear, leopard and dog. These figurines, up to 375 mm high and 350 mm long, are made in red or grey pottery and are simple and

Marlik, ritual vessel, gold, h. 190 mm, 12th–11th centuries BC (Tehran, Archaeological Museum)

beautifully stylized. Almost half are humped bulls with the hump greatly exaggerated, and a hump may also be added to other species of animal. On most of these figurines the muzzle is extended into a spout, the ears are pierced (some still carry simple gold or bronze earrings), and the body is streamlined with tapering conical legs. The surface is usually highly polished and burnished, sometimes pattern burnished or decorated with incised patterns. (For an illustration of a zebu-shaped vessel from Marlik see AMLASH REGION.)

The animal figurines of cast bronze are much smaller but equally varied, including humped bull or ox, stag, mountain goat, ram, horse, leopard, wild boar and dog. Some are quite natural in form and attitude, while others are more stylized, with extreme exaggeration of a characteristic feature such as hump or horns.

The abundant jewellery from Marlik is mostly of gold, with lesser amounts of silver, bronze and other materials. Gold necklaces have quadruple spiral, pomegranate, animal head and other beads, and gold beads can be combined with such materials as red cornelian, faience and agate. Gold pendants are found in the form of a pomegranate and pomegranate cluster, double eagle head, granulated cage and other granulated designs, and there are a very large number of embossed disc pendants. Among the gold bracelets are several decorated with animal heads. Other gold jewellery includes earrings, rings, forehead bands and hair holders, embossed gold disc buttons up to 165 mm in diameter, gold leaves, pins and an elaborate belt buckle set with red cornelian and lapis lazuli. The tomb also contained a variety of domestic tools and utensils and large numbers of weapons and other military equipment.

The objects from Marlik exemplify an artistic style that combined elements from the existing cultures of the Iranian plateau, Elam and neighbouring areas with local traditional patterns. The influence of this style can be seen in the art of the later Medes, Achaemenids, Assyrians, Urartians, Cimmerians and Scythians.

BIBLIOGRAPHY
E. O. Negahban: *Marlik: A Preliminary Report on Marlik Excavation* (Tehran, 1964, R 1977)
——: 'Notes on Some Objects from Marlik', *J. Nr E. Stud.*, xxiv (1965), pp. 309–27
——: 'Seals of Marlik', *Akten des VII. Internationalen Kongresses für iranische Kunst und Archäologie: München, 1976*, pp. 108–37
——: 'Pottery and Bronze Human Figurines of Marlik', *Archäol. Mitt. Iran* (1980)
——: 'Maceheads from Marlik', *Amer. J. Archaeol.*, lxxxv (1981), pp. 367–78
——: *Metal Vessels from Marlik*, Prähistorische Bronzefunde, ii/3 (Munich, 1983)
——: *Weapons from Marlik* (in preparation)

EZAT O. NEGAHBAN

Marlow, William (*b* London, 1740; *d* Twickenham, nr London, Jan 1813). English painter. From *c.* 1756 to 1761 he was a pupil of Samuel Scott, the topographical and marine painter; he also studied at the St Martin's Lane Academy, London. Throughout his career Marlow made oils and watercolours of London views, for example *Near Westminster Bridge, Evening* (London, Guildhall A.G.), which shows his balanced, classical sense of composition, sensitivity to lighting effects and smooth handling of oil paint. Between 1765 and 1766 Marlow travelled in France and Italy, making numerous drawings of ruins, which provided the subjects for many paintings finished on his return to London. *An Oxcart in the Grotto of Posillipo* (*c.* 1770; New Haven, CT, Yale Cent. Brit. A.) exemplifies his bold, blue-toned watercolour style, with washes applied in loose blotches to emphasize the picturesque roughness of masonry and terrain. The handling has much in common with Canaletto, whom Marlow copied; a letter of 1771 from Horace Walpole to Sir Horace Mann (see 1956 exh. cat., p. 3) records that two views of Verona by Marlow were mistakenly sold as Canalettos. Marlow specialized in souvenirs of the Grand Tour, portraits of country houses, seascapes and river scenes. He visited many parts of Britain and Ireland in search of subjects, such as *Powys Castle, Montgomeryshire* (U. Manchester, Whitworth A.G.). He exhibited at the Incorporated Society of Artists from 1767, was made a Fellow in 1771 and Vice-President in 1778. He exhibited at the Royal Academy, London, from 1788 to 1807 but never sought membership.

Marlow was commercially successful; he rented a country house at Twickenham from 1775 and moved there permanently ten years later. By the late 1780s he was in semi-retirement, preferring to make telescopes and other scientific instruments. However, a financial downturn may have prompted his production of six etched *Views in Italy* (1795; set of proof impressions in London, BM). He is also thought to have designed the seals for the original 13 United States of America. His achievement as a topographical painter lies in his technical versatility, which allowed him to encompass both the tranquil compositions and cool lighting of British scenes and the picturesque roughness and more intense light of Italian views.

BIBLIOGRAPHY
William Marlow (exh. cat., ed. J. L. Howgego; London, Guildhall A.G., 1956)
M. Hardie: *Water-colour Painting in Britain*, i (London, 1966), pp. 170–71
M. J. H. Liversidge: 'Six Etchings by William Marlow', *Burl. Mag.*, cxxii (1980), pp. 549–53
British Watercolors: Drawings of the Eighteenth and Nineteenth Centuries from the Yale Center for British Art (exh. cat., ed. S. Wilcox; New Haven, CT, Yale Cent. Brit. A., 1985)

SUSAN MORRIS

Marly, château of. French royal château 27 km west of Paris in the Yvelines département. It was built in 1679–83 for Louis XIV as an annexe to Versailles by Jules Hardouin Mansart, Charles Le Brun and André Le Nôtre (see fig.). The buildings were sold at the French Revolution (1789–95) and demolished in the 19th century, but the site still shows the main outlines of the gardens.

Louis XIV bought the land at Marly in 1677, the year before the final enlargement of Versailles, which had originally served him as a maison de plaisance for privileged house parties. He needed a new base for such activities and chose to build at Marly where the site takes the form of a vast re-entrant, of which the principal contour line follows the shape of a capital U opening towards the valley of the Seine to the north. The high, wooded hills gave a pleasing sense of privacy and with it intimacy and exclusiveness. At the focal point of the re-entrant was built the Pavillon du Roi, a two-storey house with a square ground-plan and with four identical façades (*see* MANSART, JULES HARDOUIN, fig. 2). In the earliest designs these façades are blank except for the quoins. This was because the rich architectural detail of fluted Corinthian columns and bas-reliefs was achieved by mural painting, mostly by Jacques Rousseau. The effect was highly colourful. The pilasters imitated the red marble of Languedoc and the podium *verde antico*; the bas-reliefs were picked out in gold against

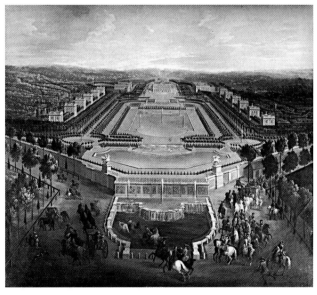

Château of Marly, begun 1679; from a painting by Pierre-Denis Martin (*c.* 1663–1742), oil on canvas, 1.37×1.55 m, 1722 (Versailles, Musée National du Château de Versailles et de Trianon)

a royal blue. On the same contour line that forms the two arms of the U to the north were built twelve small pavilions, six on each side, for the King's guests. The designs for these by Hardouin Mansart varied between façades proportioned to the Doric or Ionic order and ornately Baroque compositions with caryatids and panels in low relief. They faced inwards, over a series of terraced walks, to the Grande Pièce d'Eau, which occupied the centre of the re-entrant. To east and west, and set closer in, were the chapel and Salle des Gardes enclosing an entrance court to the east of the Pavillon du Roi and a building always known as the 'Perspective' to the west. It took its name from the great architectural *trompe l'oeil* painted by Rousseau. The effect was like that of an open peristyle, similar to the one at the Trianon de Marbre at Versailles. Between its stately rows of columns appeared two long, colonnaded wings framing a distant prospect of classical landscape. The octagonal Salon was the centre of the Pavillon du Roi and the centre of life at Marly. On four sides glazed doors each gave access to a vestibule. On the other facets were four fireplaces surmounted by tall, round-arched mirrors. The Salon occupied the full height of the building; a Corinthian order marked the ground floor and upheld an elaborate entablature. At first-floor level the pilasters were replaced by caryatids.

In 1694 Hardouin Mansart took over responsibility for the gardens from Le Nôtre. The gardens were divided into four main areas: that immediately surrounding the château; the central axis to the north with three large *pièces d'eau*; the Bosquets de Louveciennes to the east; and the Bosquets de Marly to the west. The principle of the bosquet, with its high, flat walls of hornbeam, forming an open-air extension to the apartments, is well illustrated here in the names—the Vestibule de la Table, the Cabinet de la Belle Vue and the Salon du Couchant. The gardens were well supplied with water by the gigantic pump known as the Machine de Marly (completed 1684), which forced the water of the Seine up to a reservoir above the gardens. The garden sculpture at Marly was of a more bucolic and light-hearted character than that at Versailles. It included a number of individual marble statues making up dynamic but dispersed groups, among them *Hippomenes* by Guillaume Coustou (i) and *Atalanta* by Pierre Le Pautre (ii) (both Paris, Louvre). The most famous statues at Marly were Antoine Coyzevox's equestrian groups of *Mercury* and *Fame* (Paris, Louvre) replaced in 1745 with Coustou's *Roaring Horses*.

BIBLIOGRAPHY
J. Marie and A. Marie: *Marly* (Paris, 1947)
I. Dunlop: *Versailles* (London, 1956, rev. 1970)
A. Marie: 'Marly. Son jeu de construction reconstitué pièce par pièce', *Conn. A.*, 246 (1972), pp. 58–65
J. Feray: 'Épaves de Marly', *Bull. Soc. Hist. A. Fr.* (1979), pp. 111–13
I. Dunlop: *Royal Palaces of France* (London, 1985)
IAN DUNLOP

Marmey, Jacques (*b* Marseille, 27 March 1906; *d* 1988). French architect, active in Morocco and Tunisia. He grew up in Morocco and then trained at the Ecole des Beaux-Arts in Paris (1928–33), working in the studio of Emmanuel Pontrémoli. From an early stage he was interested in regional styles, and he claimed to have learnt most about architecture from studying the convents on Mt Athos,

Greece, which he visited in 1930. He returned to Morocco in 1933, and over the next decade he designed many religious and academic buildings, notably the Saffarin *madrasa* (*c*. 1935), Fez, an Islamic college, and the university (1935) at Qarawiyyin, Fez; in this work he was deeply influenced by the style and construction methods of traditional Islamic architecture of the region. His synthesis of European modernism and North African tradition is particularly evident in his Tunisian work. He was invited by Bernard Zehrfuss to join the team working on the reconstruction of Tunisia in 1943. As Chief Architect in the Studies and Works Division, he was responsible for several important projects, including a reception centre for the war-wounded (1944) in Tunis, an administration building (*c*. 1945) at Bizerte Zarzouna and the Lycée (1949–55) at Carthage. In these, as in his private houses like the Ces House (1945; with Paul Herbe and Michel Patout), Hammamet, and the Patout House (1950), Sidi Bou Said, he found a freedom to depart from the typological constraints of his Moroccan work by adapting traditional forms to modern buildings. After a brief period in the Lebanon, he returned to Tunisia in 1960. Besides much else, he built the Reqqada Palace (1965; now the Musée d'Art Islamique), near Kairouan, for the Tunisian president Habib Bourgiba.

BIBLIOGRAPHY
M. Breitman: 'Jacques Marmey', *AAP Envmt Des.*, 1 (1985), pp. 6–65
——: 'Entre rationalisme et tradition', *Archit. Aujourd'hui*, 259 (1988), p. 28
NAOMI STUNGO

Marmion, Simon [Louthe Master; Master of the St Bertin Altar] (*b* Amiens, *c*. 1425; *d* Valenciennes, 25 Dec 1489). French illuminator and painter. He was trained in Amiens and established a productive workshop in Valenciennes, but at the end of his career appears to have had connections with manuscript painting in the southern Netherlands. Although no signed or documented works survive, many illuminated manuscripts and some panel paintings have been convincingly attributed to him and his workshop. On the basis of these he has been recognized as an important figure in the development of both French and Netherlandish painting.

1. DOCUMENTATION AND ATTRIBUTIONS. Documentary references to the Marmion family of painters from Amiens were first assembled by Hénault. Simon's father, Jean Marmion, is mentioned for the first time in 1426. In 1449 Simon is first documented, assisting his father, and by 1450 he was already working in Amiens independently. He was called to Lille in 1454 to take part in the preparations for the 'banquet du faisan' given by Philip the Good, Duke of Burgundy. In 1458 he is mentioned as the owner of an estate in Valenciennes, suggesting that he had lived there for some time before. Records from Valenciennes concerning the artist's finances occur regularly until his death. In 1465 he married Jeanne de Quaroble in Valenciennes. Further documents indicate commissions outside Valenciennes: in 1464–5 he painted a statue of the *Virgin* for Cambrai Cathedral; in 1467 Philip the Good commissioned a Breviary from him (for which Charles the Bold made the final payments in 1470); in 1468 he joined the painters' guild of Tournai; in

1484 he painted a *Virgin* as an epitaph for Pierre Dewez, Canon of Cambrai Cathedral.

Despite the relatively large number of documents naming Marmion, no surviving work by him is fully authenticated (but see below), and his oeuvre, therefore, is based on attributions. These centre on two stylistically close works from the late 1450s, commissioned by Guillaume Fillastre, Abbot of St Bertin, Saint-Omer: the first, an altarpiece of chased and gilded silver (destr. 18th century) with painted wings (Berlin, Gemäldegal.; London, N.G.), was ordered for his abbey (*see* §2 below); the second, a copy of the *Grandes Chroniques de France* (St Petersburg, Rus. N. Lib., MS. Erm. fr. 88), completed before 1460, was painted for Guillaume for presentation to Philip the Good. In neither case is the artist documented. Nevertheless, their attribution to Simon Marmion, and that of a large group of stylistically related works, seems likely in the light of the coincidence of their chronology (based on stylistic considerations) with the documented biographical details known for Marmion, and of their exceptional quality, which matches the artist's reputation among contemporaries. In a poem written after his death by Jean le Maire, Marmion was praised as the 'prince de l'enluminure', who also painted panels, altarpieces and chapels. Scholars have emphasized that the specific aesthetic qualities that contemporaries praised in Marmion correspond exactly to the works attributed to him (e.g. Sterling).

Although the attribution to Marmion of the St Bertin Altar has been challenged by some (Warren Hoffman, 1973; Hindman; Dogaer), the artist's oeuvre has generally been accepted (*see also* §2(ii) below) and is supported by further evidence: Pächt's publication (1979) of the study of a hoopoe (Vienna, Österreich. Nbib., Cod. min. 42, fol 55r), inscribed 'Simon Mormion myt der handt' ('by the hand of Simon Mormion'), has shown that the drawing is comparable with birds depicted in the borders of manuscripts attributed to Marmion's circle on other grounds; Hindman (in Kren 1992) has identified two detached leaves (New York, Met.) with the documented Breviary of Charles the Bold, the first time a surviving work has been related to the documentary evidence.

2. LIFE AND WORK.

(i) To *c.* 1474. (ii) *c.* 1474 and after.

(i) To c. *1474.* Marmion appears to have trained with a group of illuminators centred around the Master of Mansel and the Master of Guillebert de Mets. Marmion's earliest works are probably miniatures in manuscripts begun by these Masters: for example, around 1455 he completed (fols 351r–474v) the illumination of a copy of Jean Mansel's *Fleur des histoires* (Brussels, Bib. Royale Albert 1er, MSS 9231–2), begun by the eponymous master; similarly, he worked on a *Livre des propriétés des choses* (London, BL, Cotton MS. Aug. A. VI), begun by the Master of Guillebert de Mets. Marmion's miniatures in the Thérouanne Pontifical (Haarlem, Teylers Mus., MS. 77), painted *c.* 1455–6 for David of Burgundy (1425–96), are indeed close to the style of the Master of Mansel. Apart from his work on the St Petersburg *Chroniques*, which was certainly complete before 1460, and probably around 1457, other work of

1. Simon Marmion (attrib.): *St Bertin Founding the Monastery*, detail from left wing (h. 560 mm) of the St Bertin Altar, 1455–9 (Berlin, Gemäldegalerie)

this period includes the miniatures in a Pontifical for Sens Cathedral (Brussels, Bib. Royale Albert 1er, MS. 9215), which already look forward to his work of the 1460s.

The most important of the panels attributed to Marmion are the painted wings of the St Bertin Altar. Those in Berlin have a pronounced horizontal format and are painted on both sides. They are supplemented by the small vertical-format panels in London, which originally formed part of the extension of the altarpiece. When closed, the wings show a central *Annunciation*, flanked by *Prophets*, and the *Evangelists*, all painted in grisaille to create the illusion of sandstone figures standing in niches. This effect is accentuated by the inscriptions below the figures, which are painted as if they were chiselled in stone. The inner sides show, from the left, the *Patron* in full regalia at a prie-dieu and nine scenes from the *Life of St Bertin*, set in landscapes (see fig. 1) or in monastic buildings. A *Crucifixion* panel (Philadelphia, PA, Mus. A.) is of central importance, showing close parallels with Marmion's depictions of the *Crucifixion* in the Sens Pontifical (fol. 129r; see fig. 2) and in the prayer-book of Philip the Good (1462–5; Paris, Bib. N., MS. nouv. acq. fr. 16428, fol. 84r). Stylistically, the *Miracle of the True Cross* panel (Paris, Louvre) can be connected with the Philadelphia *Crucifixion*. A small panel with the Mass of St Gregory (1460–65; Toronto, A.G. Ont.), published by Sterling, shows striking correspondences with the picture of the same subject in the much later Huth Book of Hours (1475–80; London, BL, Add. MS. 38126, fol. 125v).

(ii) c. *1474 and after.* The only firmly dated manuscript attributed to Marmion is a copy of Guy de Turno's *Vision*

2. Simon Marmion (attrib.): *Crucifixion*; miniature from the Sens Pontifical,
c. 1455 (Brussels, Bibliothèque Royale Albert 1er, MS. 9215, fol. 129*r*)

de l'âme and *Visions de Tondal* (Malibu, CA, Getty Mus.,
MSS 30–31), copied in 1474 by David Aubert in Ghent
for Margaret of York (1446–1503). Marmion's 20 miniatures, depicting Tondal's apparent death and journey
through hell and paradise, are among the most remarkable
creations of 15th-century illumination. The artist transformed the story into pictorial narrative in a masterly way,
apparently without earlier models to follow. The borders
of the manuscript are filled with single clusters of a slim,
elegantly curved acanthus in gold-brown and blue, among
which nature studies are arranged (oak leaves with acorns
in shell-gold are especially frequent). This distinctive
border decoration allows the identification of other works
with similar borders: a Book of Hours (San Marino, CA,
Huntington Lib. & A.G., MS. 1173) for the Berlaymont
family; a copy of the *Instruction d'un jeune prince* (Cambridge, Fitzwilliam, Founder's Bequest, MS. 165); and a
Livre des sept âges du monde (Brussels, Bib. Royale Albert
1er, MS. 9510, fols 12*r*, 34*v*). After the end of Burgundian
rule in 1477, Marmion (like the illuminators of Ghent and
Bruges) seems to have concentrated on producing Books
of Hours, for which there was commercial demand.

De Schryver observed that Marmion's late miniatures
show a more highly developed conception of space than
his earlier works, and that they are framed by *trompe l'oeil*
borders typical of the GHENT-BRUGES SCHOOL. He thus
attempted to separate these late works from Marmion's
oeuvre and to attribute them to the Louthe Master, named
after a Book of Hours (Leuven, U. Catholique, Archvs,
MS. A. 2), which bears the coat of arms of the English
Louthe family. The relatively early appearance of *trompe*

l'oeil borders in Marmion's work may, however, be explained by his frequent contact with Netherlandish painters
during the late stages of his career: he collaborated several
times with the Master of the Dresden Prayerbook, for
example in the Huth Hours; with Lieven van Lathem (e.g.
Vienna, Österreich. Nbib., Cod. 1857, fol. 35*v*; Paris, Bib.
N., MS. nouv. acq. fr. 16428); and with the Master of
Mary of Burgundy (e.g. Cambridge, MA, Harvard U.,
Houghton Lib., MSS typ. 443–443.1).

Nevertheless, the details of the circumstances in which
these late works were produced remain unexplained: in a
few cases miniatures by Marmion have obviously been
inserted into manuscripts (e.g. Naples, Bib. N., MS. I.
B. 51; Munich, Bayer. Staatsbib., Clm. 28345); in a Missal
(Turin, Bib. Reale, MS. Varia 186) for Claudio Villa,
possibly produced in Brussels, a canonical miniature
(fol. 142*v*) by Marmion was incorporated. This may have
been done after Marmion's death. Moreover, too little
attention has been paid to Marmion's influence on manuscript illumination in Ghent and Bruges. In several later
Books of Hours, for example, familiarity with the Huth
Hours is clear (e.g. early 16th-century; London, Soane
Mus., MS. 4*r*). Finally, another Book of Hours illuminated
by Marmion (New York, Pierpont Morgan Lib., M. 6),
occupies a special position as the manuscript was written
in Burgundy. The supposition of a Louthe Master contributes nothing to the elucidation of these matters.

3. STYLE. The greatest colourist of his time, Marmion
displays in his work a highly individual palette composed
entirely of light (almost pastel) colours, among which
delicate shades of grey and violet are especially prominent.
His daring depiction of the sky in a *Crucifixion* (London,
V&A, MS. Salting 1221, fol. 18*v*), in shell gold and pale
violet, with yellow clouds, is unique among contemporary
illumination. The same is true of a Paradise landscape
(Malibu, CA, Getty Mus., MS. 30, fol. 33*v*), where the
celestial quality is conveyed through the highlighting of
the colours including the green of the meadows and the
blue shading. Marmion produced perhaps the earliest fully
developed pure landscape picture, showing a river with
ships in the *Livre des propriétés des choses* (London, BL,
Cotton. MS. Aug. A. VI, fol. 245*r*). Deep blue skies, which
become considerably lighter towards the horizon, are
characteristic of his landscapes, their particular effect due
to the use of hatching to mark the gradation, rather than
variations of tone. The soft-textured trees, mostly bright
green, are also distinctive. Buildings are brought to the
front edge of the picture, for example on the inner sides
of the St Bertin Altar where they contain and plausibly
unify scenes from the *Life of St Bertin*.

The artist's rather doll-like figures, mostly with thin,
fragile-looking arms, are stereotyped, as are the serious
faces of the women and the male heads (among which the
figure of an elderly man with a long fleecy beard is
recurrent). The predilection for van Eyckian fantastic,
oriental-style headdresses is retained throughout Marmion's work. His use of orange to outline fingers and
shade faces is striking. For garments, as well as vivid green,
he used light greys, bright blues, salmon red and brown.
He excelled in depicting shimmering effects and thin,
translucent cloth, for example in veils. The fall of the folds

is worked with finely placed shell gold. Despite his talent as a colourist, he also painted miniatures in highly developed grisaille technique, as in three Books of Hours (Tournai, Bib. Ville, MS. 122; Madrid, Bib. N., MS. Res. 149; Turin, Mus. Civ., MS. 558). His panel paintings also reflect his work as an illuminator, in their brilliant colouring and the concentration on tiny details. In the figure types and their relation to the space around them the influence of Dirk Bouts can be seen.

BIBLIOGRAPHY

C. Dehaisnes: *Recherches sur le retable de Saint Bertin et sur Simon Marmion* (Lille and Valenciennes, 1892)

S. Reinach: 'Un Manuscrit de Philippe le Bon à la bibliothèque de Saint-Pétersbourg', *Gaz. B.-A.*, n. s. 2, xxix (1903), pp. 265–78

——: 'Un Manuscrit de la bibliothèque de Philippe le Bon à Saint-Pétersbourg', *Mnmts Piot*, xi (1904)

M. Hénault: 'Les (Jéhan, Simon, Mille et Colinet) Marmion, peintres amiénois du XVe siècle', *Rev. Archéol.*, n. s. 3, ix (1907), pp. 119–40, 282–304, 410–24; x (1908), pp. 108–24

F. Unterkircher and A. De Schryver: *Gebetbuch Karls des Kühnen vel potius Stundenbuch der Maria von Burgund* (Graz, 1969) [facs. and commentary]

E. Warren Hoffman: 'Simon Marmion Reconsidered', *Scriptorium*, xxiii (1969), pp. 243–71

——: 'Simon Marmion or "The Master of the Altarpiece of Saint-Bertin": A Problem in Attribution', *Scriptorium*, xxvii (1973), pp. 263–90

S. Hindman: 'The Case of Simon Marmion: Attributions and Documents', *Z. Kstgesch.*, xl (1977), pp. 185–204

E. Warren Hoffman: 'A Reconstruction and Reinterpretation of Guillaume Fillastre's Altarpiece of St-Bertin', *A. Bull.*, lx (1978), pp. 634–49

O. Pächt: 'La Terre de Flandres', *Pantheon*, xxxvi (1978), pp. 3–16

——: '"Simon Marmion myt der handt"', *Rev. A.*, 46 (1979), pp. 7–15

C. Sterling: 'Un Nouveau Tableau de Simon Marmion', *Racar*, vii (1981), pp. 3–18

Renaissance Painting in Manuscripts: Treasures from the British Library (exh. cat., ed. T. Kren; Malibu, CA, Getty Mus.; New York, Pierpont Morgan Lib.; London, BL; 1983–4), pp. 31–9

G. Dogaer: *Flemish Miniature Painting in the 15th and 16th Centuries* (Amsterdam, 1987), pp. 51–5, 140–43

T. Kren, ed.: *Margaret of York, Simon Marmion and the 'Visions of Tondal'* (Malibu, 1992) [articles by B. Brinkmann, G. Clark and S. Hindman]

Les Manuscrits à peintures en France, 1440–1520 (exh. cat. by F. Avril and N. Reynaud, Paris, Bib. N., 1993–4)

BODO BRINKMANN

Marmitta, Francesco (*b c.* 1460; *fl ?*1505). Italian illuminator, painter and gem-engraver. According to Vasari, Marmitta lived in Parma and, after training as a painter, became an engraver of gemstones, 'closely imitating the ancients'. Although no signed work is known, he is mentioned in verses prefacing a manuscript of Petrarch's *Canzoniere* and *Trionfi* (Kassel, Landesbib., MS. Poet.4°.6) as the illuminator of the accompanying miniatures. This poem, written by Jacobus Lilius, the patron and scribe of the manuscript, praises Marmitta by comparing him with two of the greatest artists of antiquity, Apelles and Lysippos. Marmitta's familiarity with ancient art is particularly evident in the cameos with Classical figures inset in the frames of the miniatures. These are modelled as if in three-dimensions and, with other illusionistic devices featuring Classical motifs, suggest his knowledge of illumination of the 1470s and 1480s from the Veneto. An equally important influence is the work of the Ferrarese painter Ercole de' Roberti. Marmitta's highly personal figure style, characterized by slender, slightly elongated forms, well modelled but full of nervous energy, clearly derives from Roberti's work of the 1480s such as the *Israelites Gathering Manna* (London, N.G.).

Marmitta's distinctive style has been recognized in other manuscripts, including a Book of Hours from the Durazzo collection (Genoa, Bib. Berio) and a Missal commissioned by Cardinal Domenico della Rovere (Turin, Mus. Civ. A. Ant.). The Missal, Marmitta's only clearly datable work, was made as a gift for Turin Cathedral between 1498 and 1501. It appears to be later than the Petrarch. The surer draughtsmanship and less intense compositions may reflect the influence of the calm, idealized style of Lorenzo Costa (ii) in his Bolognese period (1483–1506). The development towards a quieter figure style is taken a stage further in the Durazzo Hours, where the miniatures are free from fussy detail and tranquil settings are effectively used for subjects often treated with genuine pathos. The scribe of this manuscript, Pierantonio Sallando, worked in Bologna after 1483, which confirms the Bolognese connection in Marmitta's work.

An apparent preparatory drawing for the miniature of the *Entombment* in the Durazzo Hours (London, BM) and two drawings of the *Virgin and Child* of the same period (London, BM) are in a style that strongly suggests knowledge of Raphael's work in Florence of *c.* 1505. Indeed, the *Entombment* drawing was formerly attributed to Raphael. Marmitta's late style, further characterized by an interest in effects of light and shade, may also be seen in a large altarpiece of the *Virgin and Child with SS Benedict and Quentin* (Paris, Louvre). A passage in Francesco Maria Grapaldi's *De partibus aedium* (1506 edn) confirms that

Francesco Marmitta: *Flagellation*, oil on panel, 358×250 mm, ? before 1498 (Edinburgh, National Gallery of Scotland)

Marmitta worked as a painter of altarpieces. One other panel painting, a small *Flagellation* (Edinburgh, N.G.; see fig.), has been attributed to Marmitta. Comparison with the Petrarch suggests that this is an early work. Marmitta's work as a gem-engraver is now known only through the cameos illuminated in his manuscripts. Vasari recorded that he taught the art to his son Ludovico Marmitta (*fl* 1534), who practised it successfully in Rome.

BIBLIOGRAPHY

G. Vasari: *Vite* (1550, rev. 2/1568); ed. G. Milanesi (1878–85), v, p. 383

R. Longhi: *Officina ferrarese* (Rome, 1934, rev. Florence, 2/1956), pp. 93–4

P. Toesca: 'Di un pittore e miniatore emiliano: Francesco Marmitta', *L'Arte*, xvii (1948), pp. 33–9

A. E. Popham and P. Pouncey: *Italian Drawings in the Department of Prints and Drawings in the British Museum: The Fourteenth and Fifteenth Centuries* (London, 1950), pp. 106–7

P. Pouncey: 'Drawings by Francesco Marmitta', *Proporzioni*, iii (1950), pp. 111–13

L. A. Pettorelli: 'La miniatura a Parma nel rinascimento', *Parma A.*, ii (1952), pp. 107–17

M. Levi D'Ancona: 'Un libro d'ore di Francesco Marmitta da Parma e Martino da Modena al Museo Correr', *Boll. Mus. Civ. Ven.*, xii (1967), pp. 9–28

J. J. G. Alexander: *Italian Renaissance Illuminations* (London, 1977), pp. 26, 34, 118–19

G. Mariani Canova: *Miniature dell'Italia settentrionale nella Fondazione Giorgio Cini* (Vicenza, 1978), pp. 34–5

D. A. Brown: 'Maineri and Marmitta as Devotional Artists', *Prospettiva* [Florence], 52–3 (1988–9), pp. 99–308

THOMAS TOLLEY

Marmolejo, Pedro de Villegas. *See* VILLEGAS MARMOLEJO, PEDRO DE.

Marmorstein, Martin. *See* MUNKACSI, MARTIN.

Marmottan, Paul (*b* Paris, 27 Aug 1856; *d* Paris, 1932). French writer and collector. Destined by his father for a career in law, he completed his studies in Paris in 1880 and in 1882 became councillor at the Prefecture in Evreux, a post he resigned on the death of his father in 1883. From his father Jules Marmottan (1829–83), he inherited a large fortune and his collection of Northern paintings, sculptures and tapestries from the Middle Ages and Renaissance. He then devoted himself to historical studies and collecting art. He was most interested in the period of the First Empire and travelled all over Europe to see Napoleonic sites, visiting Waterloo five times. His book *L'Ecole française de peinture 1789–1830* (1886) surveyed the work of numerous painters of the period and revealed his dislike for 18th-century art. In the introduction, he criticized the way art appreciation was led by fashion rather than understanding. He had a special interest in the history of Italy under the Empire which led to books such as *Les Arts en Toscane sous Napoléon. La Princesse Elisa* (1901). Among his favourite artists were minor figures working in Italy, such as Louis Gauffier and François-Xavier Fabre. This interest in forgotten painters of the past was confirmed by his 1913 monograph on Louis-Léopold Boilly.

As a collector Marmottan specialized mainly, though not exclusively, in art of the First Empire, acquiring paintings, furniture and other *objets d'art* from this period. He intended his collection to form a public museum; after he had filled his mansion at Auteuil in Paris, he had a special pavilion built at Boulogne-Billancourt near by. On his death his property and its contents were bequeathed to the Académie des Beaux-Arts and formed the basis of the Musée Marmottan in Paris.

WRITINGS

L'Ecole française de peinture 1789–1830 (Paris, 1886)

Les Arts en Toscane sous Napoléon. La Princesse Elisa (Paris, 1901)

Le Peintre Louis-Léopold Boilly (1761–1845) (Paris, 1913)

BIBLIOGRAPHY

D. Sutton: 'L'Europe sous les Aigles', *Apollo* (June 1976), pp. 458–63

Art in Early XIX Century France (exh. cat. by G. Bernier, London, Wildenstein's, 1981) [intro. about Marmottan]

☐

Marochetti, Carlo [Charles], Baron (*b* Turin, 14 Jan 1805; *d* Passy, Paris, 29 Dec 1867). Italian sculptor. His father, Vincenzo Marochetti, was a prominent advocate and functionary. The family moved to Paris shortly after Carlo's birth. Marochetti trained with François-Joseph Bosio and, after failing to win the Prix de Rome, travelled to Italy in 1822 at his own expense. On his return he showed *Young Girl with a Dog* (Turin, Castello d'Agliè) at the Salon of 1827. His exhibit at the Salon of 1831, *Rebel Angel* (plaster; untraced), established his allegiance to the Romantic cause. Marochetti succeeded in projecting this Romanticism in public monuments: in his marble relief of the *Battle of Jemmapes* (1833–4) on the Arc de Triomphe and, in a more original form, in the group of the *Assumption of the Magdalene* (marble, 1834–44) for the church of the Madeleine, Paris, the latter an apotheosis deriving from the Baroque, but strongly symmetrical and denuded of scenic apparatus. Marochetti's monumental Romanticism received wider exposure in a gift he made to his native city, the equestrian statue of *Duke Emanuel-Philibert of Savoy* (bronze, 1833–7; Turin, Piazza San Carlo). This is characterized by a degree of historical drama unprecedented at that time in public statuary. In recognition of this gift, Marochetti was made a Baron of the Kingdom of Sardinia. The success of this statue resulted also in the commission for a bronze equestrian statue of *Ferdinand, Duc d'Orléans* (1844) for the courtyard of the Louvre (now Château d'Eu, Seine-Maritime); here Marochetti went to the opposite extreme of literal modernity. Resentment against Marochetti, viewed by many as a courtly foreign interloper, came to a head over the preparations for the tomb of Napoleon in the Invalides, when it was thought he had attempted to bypass competition. An equestrian statue of Napoleon, eventually commissioned in 1842 for the Esplanade des Invalides, was never permanently erected. Simultaneously, and with a conspicuous disregard for patriotism, Marochetti was working on his equestrian statue of the *Duke of Wellington* for Glasgow (bronze, 1841–4).

After the revolution of 1848, Marochetti settled in England. The plaster model of his equestrian *Richard Coeur de Lion*, exhibited at the entrance to the Crystal Palace in 1851 (bronze; London, Pal. Westminster), brought him acclaim, though purists objected to its picturesque style. In England Marochetti produced many public portrait statues. A group of these, executed in the early 1860s and celebrating men of practical achievement—*Isambard Kingdom Brunel* (bronze, 1859–61, erected 1877; London, Victoria Embankment), *Robert Stephenson* (bronze, 1861, erected 1871; London, Euston Station), *Jonas Webb* (bronze, after 1862; Cambridge, Corn Exchange)—is remarkable for mundane realism. In funerary monuments and memorials, where Marochetti continued to deploy his large-limbed angels, his romantic lyricism was unabated, as in the marble-and-bronze tomb of *Queen Victoria and Prince Albert* (1864–8; Frogmore House, Berks, Royal Col.; see TOMB, §VI and fig. 19), or in the *Mourning Seraph* (1862–3) erected over the well in the Kanpur Memorial Churchyard, India. There was considerable opposition to a number of Marochetti's monumental projects in England, but he enjoyed the favour of the court and, although at this time no sculptor to the Queen was officially appointed, he occupied the position in all but name. In 1866 he was elected RA.

While resident in England, Marochetti worked on some major commissions for both France and Italy, sending to Turin a second, and highly elaborate, equestrian monument, this one of *King Charles-Albert* (bronze, 1861). He ardently advocated sculptural polychromy. His experiments in this line included a statuette of Queen Victoria as *Queen of Peace and Commerce* (untraced, see *Gaz. B.-A.*, xvi (1864), p. 566), and such extant busts as *Princess Gouramma of Coorg* (tinted marble, 1856; Osborne House, Isle of Wight, Royal Col.).

BIBLIOGRAPHY
DNB; Lami
M. Calderini: *C. Marochetti* (Turin, 1927)
G. Hubert: *Les Sculpteurs italiens en France, sous la Révolution, l'Empire et la Restauration (1790–1830)* (Paris, 1964)
B. Read: *Victorian Sculpture* (London, 1982)

PHILIP WARD-JACKSON

Marold, Luděk (*b* Prague, 7 Aug 1865; *d* Prague, 1 Dec 1898). Czech painter and illustrator. He studied (1881–2) at the Academy in Prague and then (1882–7) at the Akademie in Munich under Ludwig von Löfftz (1845–1910) and the Greek painter Nikolaos Gysis. In Munich he was a member of the Verein Tschechischer Künstler, and he also embarked on a career as an illustrator, contributing drawings and sketches in various media to the German periodical *Fliegende Blätter* and the Czech magazine *Zlatá Praha* among others (original drawings in Prague, N.G., Convent of St Agnes). On his return to Prague he studied (1887–9) at the Academy under Maximilián Pirner and simultaneously at the School of Decorative Art. He first exhibited his work publicly in 1888, showing to great acclaim a carefully observed but attractively stylized treatment of an urban genre subject, the *Egg Market in Prague* (1888; Prague, N.G., Convent of St Agnes).

In 1889 Marold won a grant to enable him to study decorative art in Paris, where he remained until 1897. He soon gained a reputation for the scenes of the fashionable world of aristocrats, artists and adventurers that he contributed to such leading French magazines as *Le Monde illustré* and *L'Illustration*. He also illustrated books and designed posters (original drawings in Prague, N.G., Convent of St Agnes; books and posters in Prague, Mus. Dec. A.). In 1892 he won a gold medal at the Munich Weltaustellung for his work as an illustrator.

Marold's oil paintings from the 1890s usually treat the same themes as those of his sketches and his published illustrations, as in the small compositions an *Exciting Read* (1892) and a *Kiss under the Parasol* (*c.* 1895; both Prague, N.G., Convent of St Agnes). The decorative use of line and surface is invariably balanced by a strong sense of depth and structure and by an evident concern for clarity of exposition. Larger ambitions were evident in Marold's last work, a panorama of the 15th-century *Battle of Lipany*, prepared in collaboration with other artists for the *Výstava architektury a inženýrství* ('Exhibition of engineering and architecture') in Prague in 1898 (now Prague, Park Cult. & Rest., Pav.).

BIBLIOGRAPHY
P. Wittlich: *Česká secese* [The Czech Secession] (Prague, 1982)
Die tschechische Malerei des XIX. Jahrhunderts aus der Nationalgalerie Prag (exh. cat., ed. J. Kotalík; Vienna, Belvedere, 1984)
Tschechische Kunst 1878–1914 (exh. cat., Darmstadt, Ausstellhallen Mathildenhöhe, 1984)
T. Vlček: *Praha 1900* (Prague, 1986)
J. Brabcová: *Luděk Marold* (Prague, 1988)

ELIZABETH CLEGG

Marolles, Michel de, Abbé de Villeloin (*b* Château de Marolles, Génillé, Indre-et-Loire, 1600; *d* Paris, 6 March 1681). French collector, genealogist, translator and writer. He was the son of the eminent soldier Claude de Marolles. In 1609 he was granted the abbey of Beaugerais and in 1626 that of Villeloin. In 1628 he entered the household of Charles I de Gonzague, Duc de Nevers, who appointed him tutor to his grandson. He found a friend and protectress in Louise-Marie de Gonzague, daughter of the Duc de Nevers and future queen of Poland. From about 1644 he dedicated himself to study; he translated many Latin texts and began to search for prints. He acquired all or part of the collections of Delorme (possibly Charles de l'Orme, *d* 1655), Claude Maugis, Jacques Kerver (*d* 1583) and probably Denis Pétau (1583–1652), of G. N. La Reynie (1625–1709) and Desneux de La Noue. In 1655 he owned 80,000 prints; ten years later he owned 123,000. He published a catalogue of them in 1666 with a preface on the usefulness of engraving. In 1667 Jean-Baptiste Colbert acquired this collection for Louis XIV's library for 28,000 livres, followed by two gratuities of 12,000 livres, one in 1668 and the other in 1669. The prints were classified sometimes by artist and sometimes by subject. More than 6000 Old Masters were represented, including Raphael, Marcantonio Raimondi, Lucas van Leyden, Rembrandt, Peter Paul Rubens, the Wierix family, Robert Nanteuil and Claude Mellan; there was also an exceptional set of 500 Italian chiaroscuro woodcuts. These collections, bound in 520 leather-covered volumes stamped with the royal arms, were the origin of the Cabinet des Estampes of the Bibliothèque Nationale in Paris.

Having sold one collection, Marolles began another. He bought the second part of the Delorme collection and that of Père Henry de Harlay. In 1672, when he published the catalogue of this collection, accompanied by a list of artists' monograms (one of the first known), it comprised 111,424 items, including 10,576 drawings, among them portraits by Nicolas Lagneau, Daniel Dumonstier and François Quesnel. His acquaintance with the artists Abraham Bosse, François Chauveau, Gregoire Huret, Michel Lasne, Claude Mellan, Gilles Rousselet and Claude Vignon facilitated his acquisitions. This collection, which he was unable to sell to the king, was dispersed after his death. In 1674 he published a history of art in quatrains, *Le livre de peintres et des graveurs*. It was merely a resumé of a voluminous history of painting that he intended to publish but of which no trace can be found. In 1677 there also appeared his *Paris, ou description de cette ville*, for which his friends supplied him with much material.

Marolles is sometimes identified with the Démocède of Jean de La Bruyère's *Caractères*. Mellan in 1648, Nicolas Poilly in 1656 and Nanteuil in 1657 engraved his portrait. At the age of 55 he compiled his *Mémoires* (Paris, 1655).

WRITINGS
Mémoires, 3 vols (Paris, 1656/*R* Amsterdam, 1755)
Catalogue des livres d'estampes et de figures en taille douce (Paris, 1666)
Catalogue des livres d'estampes et figures en taille douce (Paris, 1672)
Le Livre de peintres et des graveurs (Paris, 1677/*R* 1855, 1872)
Paris, ou description de cette ville (Paris, 1677/*R* 1879)

BIBLIOGRAPHY
G. Duplessis: 'M. de Marolles, abbé de Villeloin, amateur d'estampes', *Gaz. B.-A.*, n. s. 1, i (1869), pp. 523–32
L. Bosseboeuf: *Michel de Marolles, abbé de Villeloin: Sa vie et son oeuvre* (Tours, 1902)
L. R. Metcalfe: 'Prince of Print-collectors: Michel de Marolles, abbé de Villeloin (1600–1681)', *Prt Colr Q.*, xi (1912), pp. 317–40
F. Lugt: *Marques* (1921), i, no. 1855
J. Adhémar: 'L'Abbé de Marolles', *Bull. Club Fr. Médaille*, xxviii (1972), pp. 20–25

VÉRONIQUE MEYER

Maron, Anton von (*b* Vienna, 1733; *d* Rome, 1808). Austrian painter. He studied at the Vienna Akademie and, in 1755, he went to Rome, where he was based for the rest of his life. From 1756 to 1761 he was first the pupil then the assistant of Anton Raphael Mengs. In 1765 he married Mengs's sister, the miniature painter Theresia Concordia Mengs. After collaborating on Mengs's fresco paintings in Rome (at S Eusebio and the Villa Albani; both *in situ*), Maron, working independently in Rome, spent some time on altar pictures (S Maria dell'Anima) and on various decorative projects. Mengs's influence is evident in Maron's ceiling pictures of the casino of the Villa Borghese (1784; *in situ*), where five paintings tell the *Story of Aeneas and Dido* in the style of *quadri riportati*, using clear construction, sharply defined drawing and a historical concept based on antiquity. Although he received many commissions for this type of work, Maron's true gifts lay in the field of portraiture. Along with Pompeo Batoni, Maron was the most celebrated portrait painter in 18th-century Rome, and he received an enormous number of commissions from princes, diplomats and church dignitaries and from English aristocrats visiting Rome as part of their Grand Tour. Maron painted such sitters in the same style as did Batoni, usually full-length and life-size, in elegantly fashionable dress, against backgrounds of Classical sculptures and views of Rome. Portraits such as those of *Francis, Prince of Anhalt Dessau* (Wörlitz, Staatl. Schlösser & Gtn), *Sir Robert Clive* (1776; Rome, priv. col., see Röttgen, fig. 227), *Sir Archibald Menzies* (Cambridge, MA, Busch-Reisinger Mus.) or *Cardinal Franz Hrzan* (Rohrau, Schloss) are distinguished not only by their elegant presentation and harmonious delicacy of colouring but also by strong characterization: the sitter's activity and interests are conveyed with insight.

Some of Maron's portraits, especially those of his relations or friends (e.g. *Johann Joachim Winckelmann*, 1768; Weimar, Schlossmus.) or his *Self-portrait* (Florence, Uffizi), may be regarded as among the best examples of portrait painting in the late 18th century. Maron's ability to portray such sitters honestly, yet in an advantageous light, ensured favours and commissions from the Austrian imperial family. In 1771 he was summoned to Vienna by the Empress Maria-Theresa to paint the portraits of the imperial family and to help with the planned reorganization of the Akademie. Maron fulfilled the first of these assignments in Vienna, making studies and sketches (Vienna, Ksthist. Mus.) for portraits of *Empress Maria-Theresa* in widow's weeds, a portrait of *Emperor Joseph* and a posthumous portrait of *Emperor Francis I* (1772–3), but he completed the final paintings (1773; Vienna, Ksthist. Mus.) after returning to Rome. Maron was ennobled by the Empress in recognition of his services and entrusted with directing the studies of Austrian scholarship holders in Rome.

Maron was highly regarded in Rome, becoming a member of the Accademia di S Luca in 1766, then a professor and the Secretary there. He was one of the leading personalities in the German artistic circle centred on Winckelmann and Mengs and, with them, resolutely propagated the ideas and artistic concepts of Neo-classicism, in particular the need for a break with the illusionistic ceiling painting of the Baroque period. Maron's ceiling paintings, both in the casino at the Villa Borghese and in the Palazzo Altieri, were presented to the viewer as if they were easel paintings (foreshortening, vertical perspective and architectural framing were avoided), and subjects were taken from Classical mythology and ancient history. It seems that most of Maron's work in the later 18th century was on such subjects, for example *Leda* (St Petersburg, Hermitage), or the *Return of Orestes* (1786; untraced), for an English patron; but only a few such pictures by him have been preserved. Maron's position in Rome became increasingly difficult, however, towards the end of the century: the Revolution and the difficulties caused by wars against Napoleon drastically reduced the possibilities of commissions. Maron tried his luck in Genoa in 1791–2, painting a further series of important portraits there. He spent the last ten years of his life in Rome, forgotten and neglected. His works, especially portraits, were sometimes confused with works by Mengs or Batoni, so that Maron was for a long time not fully appreciated.

BIBLIOGRAPHY
F. Noack: *Das Deutschtum in Rom* (Berlin, 1927)
S. Röttgen: '"Antonius de Maron faciebat Romae": Intorno all'opera di Anton von Maron a Roma', *Artisti austriaci a Roma* (Rome, 1972), pp. 1–17

KLARA GARAS

Marone, Roberto. See RAFFAELLO DA BRESCIA.

Marot. French family of artists of Netherlandish origin. (1) Jean Marot I, son of Girard Marot, a cabinetmaker, worked as engraver and architect; little remains of his architectural projects, but his engravings of architectural designs, highly regarded in his lifetime, have become one of the most important sources for an understanding of French architecture before the great building campaigns of Louis XIV. One of his brothers, Jean-Baptiste Marot (*b* 1632), appears to have been a painter. One of Jean Marot's own sons, (2) Daniel Marot I, was a successful engraver in Paris, until anti-Protestant legislation obliged him to emigrate to the Netherlands, where he became principal designer to William of Orange; Jean Marot's other son, Jean Marot II, probably worked with his father as an engraver and, later, as an architect of the Bâtiments du Roi in Nantes and Paris between 1686 and 1702. Daniel Marot's son, (3) Daniel Marot II, worked as a decorative painter on a number of his father's projects.

(1) Jean Marot I (*b* Paris, 1619; *d* Paris, 15 Dec 1679). Engraver and architect. He is celebrated for his engravings of architectural views. As a young man, he worked for Israël Silvestre, supplying his publications with architectural engravings, while Silvestre himself engraved the landscapes and Jean Le Pautre was responsible for some of the figures. Marot also produced a book with 44 plates after Vitruvius, Vincenzo Scamozzi, Palladio and Philibert de L'Orme. The first of his major works, the *Recueil des plans, profils, et élévations de plusieurs palais, chasteaux, églises, sépultures, grotes et hostels bâtis dans Paris*, known as the *Petit Marot*, is undated, but internal evidence suggests it was produced between 1654 and 1660. The 116 plates include views of the then most important buildings in Paris, such as the Palais du Luxembourg and the Hôtel de Liancourt by Salomon de Brosse; the Hôtel Carnavalet by Pierre Lescot and François Mansart; the Hôtel de Jars by Mansart; and the Hôtel de Bretonvilliers by Louis Le Vau. Other engravings depict various châteaux, such as the château of Maisons-Lafitte by Mansart and the château of Coulommiers-en-Brie by Brosse (see fig.). Also included are designs, thought to be Marot's own, for the façade of a church, the gate of a city and a tomb.

About 1670 Marot published *L'Architecture françoise*, known as the *Grand Marot*, with 120 plates. Like its predecessor, it shows ground-plans, façades and cross-sections of the most important buildings in Paris and its environs. It includes 10 plates of triumphal arches designed by Marot himself; these may reflect his official position as Architecte du Roi, the title by which he was described at his death. As in Mansart's designs, the arches, severe and geometric in outline, are decorated with classical ornaments, such as swags and volutes. It is not known whether these designs were ever carried out. Marot also published several suites of designs for vases, ironwork, chimney-pieces and ceilings, describing them as based on the Antique; but the vases, for example, for which there are some 50 designs, are clearly based on the work of 16th-century artists, such as Jacques Androuet Du Cerceau the elder; they are carried out in the bold, exuberant style popular in the middle of the century.

Marot's work as architect is more difficult to define; he may have worked primarily as a designer of interiors. On the plan for a grotto for a hôtel particulier in the Rue St Antoine, Paris, Antoine Le Pautre is described as the architect, and Marot as the designer. Marot was to be paid 4000 livres for this work, to be carried out in the spring of 1669. In the same year he is recorded in the Comptes des Bâtiments du Roi for decorative ornaments in the balconies of the apartments of the Duchesse de la Vrilliere and Marquise de Montespan at Saint Germain. Marot's published designs for the Hôtel de Pussart, the Hôtel de Montemart and the Hôtel de Monceaux show him working in the style of Mansart and Le Vau, adding no significant ideas of his own.

In 1727 Pierre-Jean Mariette republished the *Grand Marot* with 227 plates; the additional designs include views of the Palais du Louvre and the Tuileries in Paris and the château of Blois, as well as the church of the Sorbonne and Val-de-Grâce in Paris. Plates from the *Grand Marot* were also used in publications by Jacques-François Blondel, confirming the importance of these designs for 18th-century architects.

PRINTS

Recueil des plans, profils, et élévations de plusieurs palais, chasteaux, églises, sépultures, grotes et hostels bâtis dans Paris (Paris, *c.* 1660–70/*R* Farnborough, 1969) [facsimile edition]

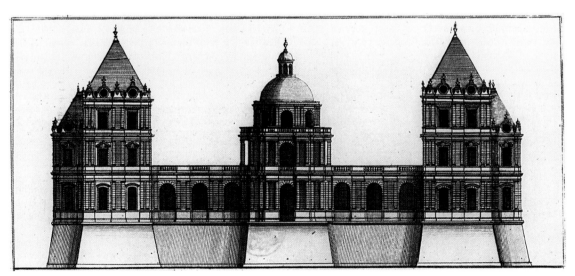

Jean Marot I: *Château de Coulommiers-en-Brie* (by Salomon de Brosse), engraving; from his *Recueil des plans, profils, et élévations de plusieurs palais, chasteaux, églises, sépultures, grotes et hostels bâtis dans Paris* [the *Petit Marot*] (Paris, *c.* 1660–70)

L'Architecture françoise (Paris, *c.* 1670); rev. as vol. iv of P.-J. Mariette: *L'Architecture française* (Paris, 1727/*R* 1970)

Recueil de diverses pièces modernes d'architecture et nouvelles inventions de portes, cheminées, ornemans et autres (Paris, 1755)

BIBLIOGRAPHY

Thieme–Becker

A. Mauban: *Jean Marot: Architecte et graveur parisien* (Paris, 1944)

ADRIANA TURPIN

(2) Daniel Marot I (*b* Paris, 1661; *d* The Hague, 4 June 1752). Architect, designer and engraver, active in the Netherlands, son of (1) Jean Marot I. He probably trained with his father, whom he assisted with the publication of the *Grand Marot*, a monumental series of engravings of contemporary French architecture. Some of the 196 prints in this series, such as the view of the front of the royal abbey of Val-de-Grâce in Paris, were signed by Daniel Marot. From 1677 he worked independently as an engraver, making engravings for such artists as Jean Le Pautre and Jean Bérain I, and his collaboration with them, particularly with Bérain, had a lasting influence on his work. Bérain, who in 1674 was appointed Dessinateur du Cabinet et de la Chambre du Roi, was responsible in this capacity for the decorations at all court celebrations and ceremonies; Marot made prints from some of his designs, such as those for Lully's opera *Le Triomphe de l'amour* (1681) and for the funeral in 1683 of Queen Marie-Thérèse, wife of Louis XIV. It is probable that at a later stage in his career Marot himself worked as royal designer.

However, in October 1685 Louis XIV revoked the Edict of Nantes, which in 1598 had guaranteed freedom of worship to France's Protestant subjects. In 1686 Marot, like thousands of other Huguenots, fled to the Netherlands. There he was soon noticed by the Stadholder William III of Orange Nassau and his courtiers as someone who was familiar with the latest developments in French art and the style of the French court. In the Netherlands the notion of using a designer to secure a unified domestic interior had not yet taken root. Dutch architects only occasionally involved themselves with features of the interior; in most cases they provided bare buildings, for which they had designed at most the door frames and chimney-pieces. It was up to the patron to order wall hangings, furniture and silver from the appropriate craftsmen; consequently the interior thus created was a combination of the unrelated ideas of a number of artists. William III appointed Marot the court's principal designer, responsible for unifying the style of both interiors and gardens. He was also put in charge of the decoration of celebrations and state banquets.

Marot's first work in his new capacity was probably a print depicting a ball held in 1686 at the Huis ten Bosch, near The Hague, by Mary Stuart, wife of William III, to celebrate his birthday. In the same year Marot designed the staircase decorations for the newly completed palace at Zeist (started in 1677) of Willem Adriaan, Count of Nassau-Odijk. Marot probably also designed the decorations for the Willemszaal in the same building. Some years later he worked on a staircase similarly decorated with illusionistic painting for Het Loo, Apeldoorn, built as a hunting-lodge (1685–6) for William III by Johan van Swieten (*d* 1695) and Jacob Roman. In 1688 William III and Mary became King and Queen of England. Het Loo, being now too small for the enlarged royal household, was

extended and renovated (from 1690) to become the royal summer residence, a process in which Marot was closely involved (*see* HET LOO). He designed the dining-room in 1692, and, as well as executing the designs for the decoration of the principal staircase, he redesigned the upper hall and the royal apartments (see fig.) in the main building. He probably also had a hand in a renovated design for the garden (*see* GARDEN, fig. 53).

Between 1694 and 1697 Marot was at William and Mary's court in England, but his work there, such as that for the interiors and gardens of Hampton Court, London, has not been securely identified. On his return to the Netherlands, he worked between 1697 and 1700 for Arnold Joost van Keppel, 1st Earl of Albermarle (1669–1718), designing interiors (destr.) and gardens for the de Voorst house near Zutphen, built *c.* 1695 by Roman. In 1698 Marot designed the Trêveszaal, the meeting-room in the Binnenhof, The Hague, of the States General of the Dutch Republic. He was thus able to carry out his ideas for palatial settings for court life on the French model.

After William III's death in 1702, commissions from the court declined, and so Marot was obliged to take on work for townspeople. He lived in The Hague until 1704, when he moved to Amsterdam to work for a new circle of patrons, the Amsterdam regent class; he obtained commissions for interior decorations at a time when the large 17th-century canalside houses were being refurbished in the new taste, with wall panelling, rich stuccowork on the ceilings and spacious staircases crowned with Baroque skylights. He appears to have produced no new large-scale buildings in Amsterdam, and to have made few contributions to Amsterdam citizens' country houses. While in Amsterdam he also worked for John William Friso, Stadholder of Friesland (*reg* 1696–1711), at Oranienstein Castle, where new state apartments and a staircase were laid out in 1707–9 after Marot's designs.

At the same period Marot resumed his former career as an engraver. He supplemented many of his earlier designs (*see* DISPLAY OF ART, fig. 10) with new ideas; the engravings, published from 1703 in suites of about six sheets, display the extent of his creativity (*see* UPHOLSTERY, fig. 1). The designs encompass the whole of fashionable court life, ranging from such individual items as clocks, chairs, beds and ornaments to complete interior designs for houses and palaces, decorative arches for festive processions, stage sets and gardens with coordinated features such as vases, sculptures and fountains. Marot was also able to provide appropriate posthumous settings, as shown by his designs for funerary monuments. His prints, which from 1712 were also published as collected sets, were apparently a great success, and probably the most important factor in the renewal of interest in The Hague in Marot's art.

Marot drew his new patrons from the cultivated upper class in The Hague, the holders of important posts in the Dutch government, who wanted town houses in the French taste, like those that they had seen in Paris and that Marot had reproduced in his prints. The many important commissions they granted Marot persuaded him to settle in The Hague. His most important works there after 1702 included the house at Noordeinde that he rebuilt in 1707 for François Fagel (1659–1746), Secretary

Daniel Marot I: bedroom of Queen Mary II (*c.* 1692); at the Rijksmuseum Paleis, Het Loo, Apeldoorn, 1662–95; restored

of the States General. As well as a series of new rooms with stucco ceilings, Marot designed for it a garden pavilion, connected to the house by a long gallery. In 1715 Cornelis van Schuylenburch (1683–1763) commissioned Marot to convert two old houses in the row on the Hofvijver opposite the Binnenhof into one large town mansion. Marot designed the new grand façade in natural stone, seven bays wide; the entrance and the balcony and windows above were surrounded with elegant scrolls and flower tendrils, while the façade was crowned with a balustrade above the cornice, with a Baroque crest on the central axis. This was one of the earliest examples in the Netherlands of the application to an exterior of typical Louis XIV-style of ornament, derived from interior design. Johan Hendrik van Wassenaer-Obdam (*d* 1745), a Dutch nobleman and member of the Council of State, commissioned Marot *c.* 1717 to design for him a mansion on the corner of the Kneuterdijk. The design cut across the corner, so as to accommodate in the middle an impressive entrance, surmounted by a dome. In 1734–6 the wealthy Adriana Margareta Huguetan (*d* 1752) had a palatial residence (now the Royal Library) built on the Lange Voorhout; the façade was probably the work of Jan Pieter van Baurscheit (ii), while Marot was responsible for designing

the interior. He was also closely involved (1734–9) with extensions to the Huis ten Bosch for William Charles Henry Friso of Orange Nassau (later the Stadholder William IV). To the compact block built by Pieter Post in 1645–7 he added two extended wings, for which he designed elegant rooms. The entrance was given a splendid entrance hall and made part of a striking frontage.

The patrons that Marot worked for in The Hague were on the whole a younger generation than those who employed him in William III's day. In working for them he did not need to adapt his style radically to conform to new developments in France, where the lighter Régence style and, from *c.* 1730, the elegant and asymmetrical Rococo were in turn replacing the more grandiose Louis XIV style. The shapes and concepts of French 17th-century interior design remained for him the model on which he continued to produce variations throughout his career, symmetry and monumentality in particular being more important to him than grace or elegance. It was his younger collaborators, such as Baurscheit, who introduced the new designs to the Netherlands.

Marot did not involve himself fully in every one of his projects. On occasions his contribution was limited to providing a few drawings, while the artists, masons, stuccoists and sculptors also made important contributions to the design. Although the part he played is not always absolutely clear, his contribution to the total scheme remains highly significant; without him, the inclination to imitate French art would have produced a much more sterile result. It was he who possessed the necessary imagination to carry out a design through to the smallest detail, and to adapt successfully French aristocratic taste to a Dutch scale.

BIBLIOGRAPHY
P. Jessen: *Das Ornamentwerk des Daniel Marot* (Berlin, 1892)
M. Ozinga: *Daniel Marot: De Schepper van den Hollandschen Lodewijk XIV–stijl* [Creator of the Dutch Louis-XIV style] (Amsterdam, 1938)
P. Thornton: *Seventeenth-century Interior Decoration in England, France and Holland* (New Haven and London, 1978, R 4/1990)
H. W. M. van der Wyck: *De Nederlandse buitenplaats* [The Dutch country house] (Alphen aan den Rijn, 1983)
J. Rosenberg, S. Slive and E. H. ter Kuile: *Dutch Art and Architecture, 1600–1800*, Pelican Hist. A. (Harmondsworth, 1984), pp. 411–13
K. A. Ottenheym, W. Terlouw and R. van Zoest, eds: *Daniel Marot: Vormgever van een deftig bestaan* [Designer of a stately way of life] (Zutphen, 1988)
P. Spies and S. van Raaij: *In het gevolg van Willem III & Mary: Huizen en tuinen uit hun tijd* [In the train of William and Mary: the houses and gardens of their time] (Amsterdam, 1988)
R. van Zoest and X. van Eck: *Huis Schuylenburch* (The Hague, 1988)
K. A. OTTENHEYM

(3) Daniel Marot II (*b* London, 16 June 1695; *d* The Hague, 14 May 1769). Painter and draughtsman, son of (2) Daniel Marot I. He worked with his father until the latter's death. His first dated drawings are of 1716. It is possible that he was involved, as a decorative painter, in the important commissions for town houses that his father undertook in The Hague; documents of 1735 mention payments to the painter Marot for a small painting in the anteroom of the king's apartments at the palace of Huis ten Bosch. On a drawing (1742) showing Count Bentheim's and Count van der Duyn's encampment in the Haagse Bosch, Marot refers to himself as a painter. After his father's death, he is said to have continued to paint decorations for grottoes and garden pavilions.

Marot's surviving drawings show that he specialized in town views and landscape painting; there are several views of houses and gardens in The Hague, as well as imaginary landscape scenes. One undated drawing (London, BM), which shows figures dancing and merrymaking in a garden setting, gives a good indication of his light and decorative style. In 1764 he entered the Lepers' Hospital in The Hague and died there five years later.

BIBLIOGRAPHY
Thieme–Becker
ADRIANA TURPIN

Maróti, Géza (Rintel) (*b* Barsvörösvár (now Červený-Hrádok, nr Zlaté Moravce, Slovakia), 1 March 1875; *d* Budapest, 6 May 1941). Hungarian architect and sculptor. He studied in Budapest and then at the Akademie der Bildenden Künste, Vienna, where he became interested in architecture through producing ornamental sculpture. About the turn of the century he was commissioned by various architects to design the ornament for Secessionist buildings, and between 1905 and 1913 he taught ornamental modelling to architectural students at the Hungarian Palatine Joseph Technical University, Budapest. His decorative architectural schemes ranged from the use of severe, academic historicist motifs, through a free-flowing floral and figural style, to the vernacular-inspired style of the Secession, which he used in his exhibition pavilions, where he also employed elements of Finnish National Romanticism as well as Hungarian folk art. One example is his Hungarian Pavilion (1906), with József Fischer (*b* 1873), for the Esposizione Internationale del Sempione, Milan. Between 1908 and 1921 he delivered designs for decorative work on Adamo Boari Dandini's Opera House (inaugurated 1934; now Palacio de Bellas Artes), Mexico City, which is distinguished by its huge concentric glass roof composition, with figurative and geometric designs and subtle colour effects. The cupola is decorated on the exterior with monumental female figures. In 1927 at the invitation of his friend Eliel Saarinen, who was working on the designs for the Cranbrook Academy of Art, Bloomfield Hills, MI, Maróti went to the USA to design its sculptural embellishments, but by 1929 he had left Cranbrook to work in Albert Kahn's office in Detroit. He designed classicizing forms for elegant Art Deco façades, façade sculptures and interiors, for example for the Fisher Building Passage (1927), Detroit.

BIBLIOGRAPHY
J. Gerle: 'Maróti Géza építészet és szobrászat határán' [Géza Maróti: on the border of architecture and sculpture], *Magyar Építőművészet*, 6 (1983), pp. 50–51
ÁKOS MORAVÁNSZKY,
KATALIN MORAVÁNSZKY-GYÖNGY

Maroto, Fray Diego (*b* 1620; *d* Lima, *c.* 1701). Peruvian architect. He was a friar of the Dominican order in Lima and one of the most active architects in Peru during the second half of the 17th century. His earliest known work was a new plan (1643) for the cathedral at Trujillo, on the north coast. However, all his known works from 1659 were in Lima: that year he signed a contract to repair the water system in the main cloister of the convent of Nuestra Señora de la Concepción, and in 1663 the Sagrario was begun to his designs on the Plaza de Armas. Following the earthquake of 1678, Maroto took charge of the reconstruction of the transept of S Domingo and designed a new dome using *quincha*, a light construction of plastered reeds on a timber frame, an anti-seismic system first used in Peru in 1657 by Constantino de Vasconcelos. Maroto also rebuilt (1678–81) the second-storey arcades of the main cloister of the Dominican monastery in Lima to a design inspired by Vasconcelos's main cloister at S Francisco (1669–74), where oval lunettes alternate with arcaded openings. Between 1685 and 1687 he was Master of the Works in Lima and *alarife*, Surveyor and Inspector of Public Works. After the earthquake of 1687, with the *alarifes* Pedro Fernández de Valdez and Manuel de Escobar, he surveyed the damage to the cathedral and other major buildings, and his detailed report survives.

WRITINGS
Declaración de Fr. Diego Maroto, Maestro de Reales Fábricas (1687, Lima, Archv Gen. N.); transcribed in 'El terremoto del año 1687', ed. D. Angulo in *Rev. Archv N. Peru*, xii/2 (1939), pp. 131–7

BIBLIOGRAPHY
E. Harth-Terré: *Artífices en el virreinato del Perú* (Lima, 1945), pp. 202, 210, 220
J. Bernales Ballesteros: 'Apuntes para la historia de El Sagrario de la catedral de Lima', *Mercurio Peru.*, 455 (1965), pp. 159–73
HUMBERTO RODRÍGUEZ-CAMILLONI

Marouflage. Technique of fastening a canvas painting on to a solid support, such as a wall or a wooden or synthetic board. White lead in oil is the traditional adhesive for fastening painted canvas to internal walls as decoration. Reversible synthetic adhesives are used for marouflaging damaged or delicate canvases on to rigid supports as an alternative to lining.

RUPERT FEATHERSTONE

Marquand, Henry G(urdon) (*b* New York, 11 April 1819; *d* New York, 26 Feb 1902). American businessman, philanthropist and collector. Born into a family of silversmiths, he first worked in real estate in New York and then moved into banking and investment. In 1874, together with his brother Frederick and other investors, he purchased the St Louis, Iron Mountain & Southern Railroad; from 1875 to 1881 he served as its vice-president and in 1881 as president, and he continued to serve as director of this railroad and its later parent organization, the Missouri Pacific, until his death.

Marquand was a member of the original group of 50 prominent New Yorkers who met in 1869 to plan the organization of the Metropolitan Museum of Art and to raise an endowment. After he had retired in 1881, he was able to devote his energies to civic activities, primarily to the successful development of the Metropolitan. From 1882 to 1889 he served as its treasurer, and from 1889 until his death as president. In 1886 he gave the Metropolitan $10,000 for the purchase of a collection of sculptural casts and $30,000 for the endowment of a museum art school. He continued his benefactions by enabling the Museum to purchase for $15,000 from Jules Charvet the Charvet Collection of antique glass and by obtaining for the institution reproductions of medieval carvings, Renaissance ironworks, metal reproductions of gold and silver objects in the Imperial Russian Museum, and English and Old Master paintings; these gifts elicited the comment from Russell Sturgis that Marquand 'bought like an Italian Prince of the Renaissance' (Kirby, preface).

The 50 paintings given by Marquand between 1888 and his death contributed to establishing the Metropolitan as one of the most important museums in the world. The collection includes four works by Rembrandt, two by Anthony van Dyck, three by Peter Paul Rubens, two by Jan van Eyck, four by Frans Hals and Johannes Vermeer's *Young Woman with a Water Jug*, as well as paintings by Diego Velázquez, Gabriel Metsu, Gerard ter Borch (ii), Francisco de Zurbarán, Thomas Gainsborough and William Hogarth, among others. Tompkins suggested that Marquand's 'eye for quality may even have influenced the future trend of collecting in America' (p. 74). These works, which represent Marquand's interest in helping the Metropolitan create a historically representative collection, were never hung in Marquand's home, having gone directly from Europe to the museum. Marquand's private collection emphasized contemporary works, including a large number of French Salon paintings, which may have been intended for the museum but were later sold at auction. His richly furnished and artistically decorated home received great public attention, for it boasted a Grecian drawing-room, a Moorish smoking-room and a Japanese morning-room.

UNPUBLISHED SOURCES
Washington, DC, Smithsonian Inst., Archvs Amer. A. [clippings in the Florence N. Levy col.]

BIBLIOGRAPHY
DAB
Twelfth Annual Report of the Trustees of the Association of the Metropolitan Museum (New York, 1882), pp. 215–16
Pictures by Old Masters: The Henry G. Marquand Collection of Old Masters and Pictures of the English School in Gallery No. 6, New York, Met. cat. (New York, 1896)
T. E. Kirby, ed.: *Illustrated Catalogue of the Art and Literary Property Collected by the Late Henry G. Marquand* (New York, 1903)
The Marquand Residence (New York, [?1905])
L. Lerman: *The Museum: One Hundred Years and the Metropolitan Museum of Art* (New York, 1969)
C. Tompkins: *Merchants and Masterpieces: The Story of the Metropolitan Museum of Art* (New York, 1970)
E. McFadden: *The Glitter and the Gold* (New York, 1971)
LILLIAN B. MILLER

Marque, Albert (*b* Nanterre, Hauts-de-Seine, 14 July 1872; *d* 1947). French sculptor. Although he attended evening drawing classes and worked in a stone-cutter's workshop, he was largely self-taught and turned down an offer to work in the studio of Hubert Ponscarme. Marque exhibited at the Salon de la Société Nationale in Paris from 1899 to 1904, at the Salon des Indépendants from 1902 and later at the Salon d'Automne and elsewhere. His conservative style was inspired by that of Jean-Baptiste Carpeaux, Jules Dalou and Jean-Baptiste Pigalle, and, though also influenced by classical and Renaissance models, his sculpture has a charm characteristic of the 18th century. He invariably worked in bronze or terracotta producing small-scale female heads and figures. At the Salon des Indépendants in 1902 he exhibited a sculpture of a girl's head, which attracted the attention of Maurice Denis. He also made portrait busts (e.g. *Honoré Daumier*; Paris, Bib. A. & Archéol.). In addition to such autonomous works, he designed decorative sculpture for furniture, architecture and domestic objects, as in the *Naiad* (see Vaillat, p. 275) designed for a pedestal bowl. He also created numerous low reliefs such as *Maternity* (see Vaillat, p. 276). Examples of his work were included in the important exhibition *Les Maîtres de l'art indépendant*, held in Paris in 1937. At the Salon d'Automne Marque exhibited the Florentine-style *Bust of a Small Girl* (terracotta, *c.* 1905; Paris, Pompidou), in the same room as paintings by Matisse, Derain, Othon Friesz, Maurice de Vlaminck and others. This prompted the famous comment from the critic Louis Vauxcelles: 'Un Donatello au milieu des fauves', which christened Fauvism.

BIBLIOGRAPHY
L. Vaillat: 'L'Art décoratif: Albert Marque', *A. & Artistes*, xv (April–Sept 1912), pp. 274–8
A. Salmon: *La Jeune Sculpture française* (Paris, 1919), p. 65
ALBERTO CERNUSCHI

Marques, Agostinho (*fl* Braga, 1692–1717; *d* Braga, 1720). Portuguese cabinetmaker and metalworker. The most outstanding characteristic of his documented works—all commissioned by religious institutions—is his use of *pau preto* (Brazilian rose-wood), either solid or thickly veneered on to chestnut, worked *em espinhado* (in a herring-bone pattern) decorated with parallel grooves, mouldings and, more rarely, with *almofadados* (pillow panelling). In the contracts signed by Marques with the chapter of Braga Cathedral and various convents and Misericórdia churches in northern Portugal he is referred to as the *enxamblador da Cónega* (joiner) responsible for executing both the woodwork and decorative metalwork of the furniture commissioned. The application of pierced and gilded brass plaques in the form of borders, rosettes in relief, enormous escutcheons and impressive handles is a constant feature of his work. He played an important role in northern Portuguese furniture-making for the uniformity of his production. He specialized in balustrades, for example those for the pulpit of the Misericórdia church in Vila do Conde (1692), for the chapels in the church of the Jesuit college in Braga (1700) and for the church of Nossa Senhora do Pópulo, Braga (1701). From 1697 to 1717 he also made a wide variety of sacristy furnishings, which included chests-of-drawers, wardrobes and tables for the Benedictine monastery in Rendufe, the Misericórdia church and the church of Nossa Senhora do Pópulo, both in Braga, the Misericórdia church at Ponte da Barca, the Cistercian monastery of S Maria at Bouro and the church of S Miguel at Refoios de Lima. His other works include sacristy doors and lampstands with spiral or baluster turning. His son, Joseph Marques Reis, who also specialized in ecclesiastical furniture, continued his father's work during and after the latter's lifetime at the same address in Rua da Cónega in Braga.

BIBLIOGRAPHY
R. Smith: 'Os arcazes e armários da sacristia da sé do Porto', *Bol. Cult. Camâra Mun. Porto*, xxxii/3–4 (1969), pp. 809–32
——: *Agostinho Marques, enxamblador da Cónega: Elementos para o estudo do mobiliário em Portugal* (Oporto, 1974)

MARIA HELENA MENDES PINTO

Marques (Lucas), Diogo (*fl* 1594–1640). Portuguese architect. He was an important figure in the development of the 'Plain style', a term used by Kubler to define the rather austere interpretation of Renaissance architecture found in Portugal. In 1594 Marques was appointed to one of the three royal apprenticeships to study architecture in Lisbon, created by Philip I (Philip II of Spain) in 1584, under Filippo Terzi. His major works were as architect to the Benedictine Order as part of their programme of building renovation, a post to which he was appointed in 1600; by that year he was also a Royal Architect. In 1604 he designed the Benedictine monastic church of S Bento, Oporto, in a style that is characteristic of Portuguese Mannerist architecture. S Bento has a wide façade arranged on four levels and a large thermal lunette constrained by volutes. The interior follows the pattern established by Terzi at S Vicente de Fora (1582–1605), Lisbon, of a broad undivided nave, coffered barrel vault and *sotocoro* narthex (choir over the narthex porch). The nave at S Bento was finished in 1640, although work continued until 1707. In 1602 Marques took over and completed the church of S Bento (1598–1634; destr. 1932), Coimbra, by Baltasar Alvares; in 1616 he replaced Pero Fernandes de Torres as Master of Works at the Convent of the Military Order of Christ at Tomar.

BIBLIOGRAPHY
F. Sousa Viterbo: *Dicionário histórico e documental dos architectos, engenheiros e construtores portugueses ou a serviço de Portugal*, ii (Lisbon, 1904)
R. dos Santos: *Oito séculos de arte portuguesa*, ii (Lisbon, 1966)
G. Kubler: *Portuguese Plain Architecture: Between Spices and Diamonds, 1521–1706* (Middletown, 1972)

Marqués, Francisco Domingo y. *See* DOMINGO Y MARQUÉS, FRANCISCO.

Marquesas Islands. Polynesian archipelago located *c.* 1500 km north-east of Tahiti in the South Pacific. It consists of two groups of mountainous islands, of which Hivaoa, Tahuata and Fatuhiva in the south-east and Nukuhiva, Uapou and Uahuka in the north-west are inhabited. The islands form part of French Polynesia. Almost every aspect of Marquesan daily and ceremonial life reflected the inhabitants' aesthetic sense. Marquesan technical expertise has produced some of the best-known and most celebrated art works of the Pacific region. There are some stylistic differences between objects produced in the various islands, especially between the two major groups, but on the whole Marquesan art shows a remarkable homogeneity. Early works were collected by Capt. James Cook (1728–79) during his second voyage (1772–5), from which much material survives (see 1979 exh. cat.). Between the 18th century and the mid-19th neither the objects nor the decorative motifs used by the Marquesans underwent any fundamental changes, although the introduction of metal tools encouraged the development of sculpture. After 1850, however, these art traditions either came to an end or were altered substantially.

Marquesan artists specialized in particular art works or techniques, such as carving statues, clubs and fan handles; building houses and canoes (*see* PACIFIC ISLANDS, §II, 3); making ornaments; and tattoo. They are known to have used such tools as adzes, chisels, awl heads and polishing instruments, sometimes made from shells but more often from volcanic rock. With these tools they carved wood and stone sculptures and also worked shells, mother-of-pearl, tortoiseshell, sperm-whale ivory, bone and pigs' teeth. Iridescent headdresses and gorgets were made from bundles of coloured feathers obtained from cocks, tropic-birds and green pigeons, bunches of white beards and red or black seeds, tied and fixed on coir-fibre bands or plaits (e.g. Oxford, Pitt Rivers Mus.; Dublin, Trinity Coll.). Warriors and dancers also wore belts, bracelets and anklets made of human hair. Fine wickerwork decorated with human or animal forms was used to cover the hilts of large clubs and chiefs' staffs.

Marquesan architecture was characterized by rectangular, often very high, platforms built from large, unworked blocks of stone. These served as foundations for houses, dance areas and places for ritual. The roofing was joined by ornamental bindings made of coloured coconut fibre. Geometrical designs were carved on the main pillars, and the façades of sacred houses were often decorated with anthropomorphic poles.

The most complex and highly developed art form was tattoo (*see also* PACIFIC ISLANDS, §II, 2(i)). So much time and attention was given to it that it was not unusual for old men to have their entire bodies covered with black motifs. Bands of simple geometric designs, in the form of rectangles, triangles, squares, diamonds and herringbone patterns, were often combined. Their repetition created new patterns, which, in turn, were framed by light areas to produce other decorative schemes. Single motifs or their combinations, such as a 'little man' reduced to a few lines, or two eyes represented by concentric circles, are also found on petroglyphs. The repertory of designs used by tattoo artists were engraved on bamboo-canes. They were also reproduced on the outer surfaces of a wide variety of utilitarian and ceremonial objects, including eating bowls, cups made from coconuts, lids made from gourds, club heads, drum bases, tortoiseshell ornaments and models of canoes.

The carving on such prestigious objects as fan handles combines flat engraving and low and high relief (e.g. Salem, MA, Peabody Mus.). On handles small figural representations are devoid of design elements, since they would be difficult to make out. Instead small designs are spread out flat in bands above and below the human figures, as if the two types of configurations (representations of human figures and graphic signs) were complementary. From the elegantly worked miniatures on ivory ear ornaments to the massive monumental statues, all the human representations conform to an established model. Viewed face on, they usually exhibit a perfect lateral symmetry in relation to the vertical axis, and the three sections of the head, body and legs are evenly and rhythmically divided. The cylindrical head is characterized by eyes set on the sides, an elongated mouth and double spiral ears. The arms are folded on to the stomach at an angle of *c.* 120°. The back is flat with unpronounced buttocks and the legs are slightly bent. Attractive heads in the round were carved on the ends of boxes with lids and around the edges of large dishes. Human figures were also used to decorate canoes and the steps of ceremonial stilts (see fig.). Large, imposing wooden or stone statues dominated sacred or forbidden places, dedicated to the dead and to religious ceremonies, and small single or double sculptures were used for propitiatory rites during the main fishing season.

BIBLIOGRAPHY
W. C. Handy: *Tattooing in the Marquesas*, Bishop Mus. Bull., i (Honolulu, 1922/*R* 1971)
E. S. C. Handy: *The Native Culture in the Marquesas*, Bishop Mus. Bull., ix (Honolulu, 1923/*R* 1971)
R. Linton: *The Material Culture of the Marquesas Islands*, Mem. Bishop Mus., viii/5 (Honolulu, 1923)
——: *Archaeology of the Marquesas Islands*, Bishop Mus. Bull., xxiii (Honolulu, 1925)
K. von den Steinen: *Die Marquesaner und ihre Kunst: Primitive Südseeornamentik*, 3 vols (Berlin, 1925–8/*R* New York, 1969)
W. C. Handy: *L'Art des Iles Marquises* (Paris, 1938)
J. Guiart: *Océanie*, A. Mankind (Paris, 1963); Eng. trans. by A. Christie as *The Arts of the South Pacific* (New York, 1963)
T. Barrow: *Art and Life in Polynesia* (London, 1972), pp. 92–101
'*Artificial Curiosities': Being an Exposition of Native Manufactures Collected on the Three Pacific Voyages of Captain James Cook, R.N.*, Bishop Mus. Special Pubn, lxv (exh. cat. by A. Kaeppler, Honolulu, Bishop Mus., 1978), pp. 87–8, 122–32
The Art of the Pacific Islands (exh. cat. by P. Gathercole, A. L. Kaeppler and D. Newton, Washington, DC, N.G.A., 1979), pp. 87–8, 123–32
P. Ottino and M. N. de Bergh: 'Les Isles Marquises', *A la recherche des anciens Polynésiens* (1986), iv of *Encyclopédie de la Polynésie* (Papeete, Tahiti, 1985–7), pp. 105–20
A. Lavondès: 'Le Corps, le vêtement et la parure', *La Vie quotidienne dans la Polynésie d'autrefois* (1986), v of *Encyclopédie de la Polynésie* (Papeete, Tahiti, 1985–7), pp. 83–4
——: 'Les Arts', *La Vie quotidienne dans la Polynésie d'autrefois* (1986), v of *Encyclopédie de la Polynésie* (Papeete, Tahiti, 1985–7), pp. 89–110
P. Ottino and M.-N. de Bergh: *Hiva Oa: Images d'une mémoire océanienne* (Papeete, Tahiti, 1991)

ANNE LAVONDÈS

Marques de Oliveira, João (*b* Oporto, 23 Aug 1853; *d* Oporto, 9 Oct 1927). Portuguese painter and draughtsman. In 1864 he entered the Academia de Belas-Artes, where he studied drawing under João António Correia and was a pupil of António José da Costa (*b* 1840). He completed the course in history painting in 1873, when he went to Paris with a state scholarship and on 17 March 1874 was admitted into the Ecole des Beaux-Arts to study with Alexandre Cabanel. He was an outstanding draughtsman and was awarded medals for figure drawing in 1875 and 1876. He painted a *Self-portrait* (1876; Caldas da Rainha, Mus. Malhoa) which shows his qualities as a figure painter in an academic style. His training in Cabanel's studio is reflected in *Prodigal Son* (1877) and *Cephalus and Procris* (1879; both, Oporto, Mus. N. Soares dos Reis), paintings which he exhibited in 1880 at the Salon of the Sociedade Promotora de Belas-Artes, Lisbon, where his affiliations with French academic painting were recognized by the critics. The influence of Cabanel is also seen in *Daphnis and Chloe* (1879; Oporto, Mus. N. Soares dos Reis) in the treatment of the female nude and the luminous flesh tones.

Though Marques de Oliveira exhibited two portraits in the Paris Salon in 1876 and 1878, he was also interested in landscape painting and, with António da Silva Porto,

Marquesas Islands, ceremonial stilts, wood and sennit, h. 1.93 m, steps h. 0.33 m (Paris, Musée de l'Homme)

introduced the practice of painting out of doors to Portugal. As a naturalistic painter following Barbizon lines he moved away from academic conventions, and his landscapes sometimes show pre-Impressionist tendencies reminiscent of Boudin. His rendering of the Portuguese countryside had no parallel in Portugal, except in the work of António Carneiro at the beginning of the 20th century.

Marques de Oliveira travelled in Belgium, the Netherlands and England, and in 1877–8 he concluded his studies with a visit to Italy. On his return to Portugal in 1879 he settled in Oporto where in 1881 he became Professor of Drawing in the Academia de Belas-Artes, and in 1895 he succeeded J. A. Correia in the chair of History Painting. With António Soares dos Reis he co-founded the Centro Artístico Portuense (Oporto Artistic Centre) in 1881. He exhibited his landscapes in the Salons of the Sociedad Promotora de Belas-Artes, Lisbon, in 1880 and 1884 with scenes such as *Beach at Póvoa do Varzim* (1884; Lisbon, Mus. N. A. Contemp.), a view of a transparently luminous beach, bathed in a rosy light, that dissolves in impressions of colour. These land- and seascapes convey an understanding of light and of atmospheric values that is rare in contemporary Portuguese painting. His later landscapes acquired a new precision in their structure and use of colour: his visions came to life, and the little figures or silhouettes which dotted his beaches, as in *Póvoa do Varzim: Impression* (undated; Caldas da Rainha, Mus. Malhoa) were replaced by holiday scenes or genre pictures, such as *Waiting for the Boats* (1892; Lisbon, Mus. N. A. Contemp.), in which the drawing is more defined, standing out against a clearer light. He became Director of the Escola de Belas-Artes, Oporto, where he was an outstanding teacher and where he trained a new generation of artists.

BIBLIOGRAPHY

J. Costa: *O pintor Marques de Oliveira* (Oporto, 1929)
Diogo de Macedo: *Marques de Oliveira, Artur Loureiro: Dois naturalistas* (Lisbon, 1953)
J.-A. França: *A arte em Portugal no século XIX*, ii (Lisbon, 1966), pp. 34–7

LUCÍLIA VERDELHO DA COSTA

Marques dos Santos, Joaquim (*fl* Aveiro, 1782). Portuguese sculptor. His activity, and that of his son Manuel Marques de Figueiredo, is associated with the popular taste in the second half of the 18th century for large religious groups of figures in the form of nativity cribs executed in glazed and painted terracotta for churches and convents. This vogue can be compared with the popularity of such cribs in Naples, and the involvement of leading contemporary sculptors ensured that a high artistic level was often attained in these elaborate compositions that appealed to late-Baroque taste. Most of these groups have been dismantled, but the elegance of Marques dos Santos's figures is seen in the crib (Aveiro, Mus. Reg.) modelled in partnership with Bartolomeu Gaspar for the convent of Sá, Aveiro. Another of Marques dos Santos's most attractive works is a terracotta relief, representing the Virgin surrounded by angels appearing as advocates of the souls of penitents in purgatory, a small-scale treatment of the popular cult of the *alminhas*, or souls in purgatory, signed and dated July 1782 (Aveiro, Mus. Reg.).

BIBLIOGRAPHY

F. de Pamplona: *Dicionário de pintores e escultores*, v (Lisbon, 1959), p. 145
R. C. Smith: *The Art of Portugal, 1500–1800* (London, 1968), p. 168

ANTÓNIO FILIPE PIMENTEL

Marquet, Albert (*b* Bordeaux, 26 March 1875; *d* Paris, 14 June 1947). French painter and draughtsman. In 1890 he was taken by his family to live in Paris so that he could study drawing at the Ecole Nationale Supérieure des Arts Décoratifs. There he met Henri Matisse, with whom he formed a lasting friendship and with whom he studied from 1894 to 1898 at the Ecole des Beaux-Arts under Gustave Moreau. In the Louvre, Marquet made copies after Poussin, Velázquez, Claude Lorrain and particularly Chardin, of whose *House of Cards* he produced copies in 1894 and 1904 (Montmédy, Mus. Bastien-Lepage, holds what is considered the later of the two).

Tentative early works by Marquet such as *Portrait of the Artist's Mother* (1894; San Francisco, priv. col., see 1988 exh. cat., no. 1), suggesting the influence of Fantin-Latour, were soon succeeded by landscape paintings such as *Parisian Suburb* (1897; Besançon, Mus. B.-A. & Archéol.), in which he began to simplify the subject into broad areas of colour. *Nude*, sometimes known as *Fauve Nude* (1898; Bordeaux, Mus. B.-A.), painted in Matisse's company shortly before they left Moreau's studio, was one of the earliest works in which he used separate brushstrokes of vivid colour, prefiguring the style that was later to be called FAUVISM.

Marquet found it difficult at first to sell his works, but in 1900 he was hired with Matisse to paint the Art Nouveau ornaments of the Grand Palais for the Exposition Universelle. In 1901 he participated in the Salon des Indépendants and produced his first painting of the *Apse of Notre-Dame de Paris* (Besançon, Mus. B.-A. & Archéol.), announcing his habit of using the banks of the Seine as subject-matter. To this he soon added a preference for broader and more colourful brushwork.

Marquet exhibited at Berthe Weill and the Galerie Druet, Paris, from 1902, and from 1903 at the Salon d'Automne. At the Salon of 1904 he made his first sale to the state, the *Trees at Billancourt* (*c.* 1898; Bordeaux, Mus. B.-A.), and in the Salon of 1905, which marked the emergence of Fauvism, his own relation to the movement began to be defined. Although his technique and use of colour were less violent than those of such artists as Vlaminck or Derain, in 1906 he produced some of his best and most characteristic Fauve paintings, for example *14th of July at Le Havre* (Bagnols-sur-Cèze, Mus. Bagnols-sur-Cèze), *Posters at Trouville* (Mr & Mrs J. H. Whitney priv. col., see 1975 exh. cat., p. 39) and the *Beach at Fécamp* (Paris, Mus. d'Orsay). It was during this period also that, under the influence of Japanese brush paintings, he devised a remarkably animated and spontaneous form of India ink drawing, for example in *Dancing Couple* (1904), one of the group of figure drawings now in the Musée des Beaux-Arts, Bordeaux.

Subsequently, Marquet worked in more tonally quiet colours, but with the yellows, greens and greys expressing the nuances of light on water, his favourite subject, as in *Pont Saint-Michel and the Quai des Grands-Augustins* (1910–11; Paris, Pompidou; see fig.). In Paris he almost always

Albert Marquet: *Pont Saint-Michel and the Quai des Grands-Augustins*, oil on canvas, 650×810 mm, 1910–11 (Paris, Pompidou, Musée National d'Art Moderne)

lived on the quais of the Seine, from which he was able to paint the river. He also travelled constantly, visiting all the coasts of France and spending time in England, the Netherlands, Sweden, Germany, Italy, Spain, Egypt and the USSR. These trips are recorded in a number of paintings in which he responded to the light and atmospheric conditions characteristic of each place, as in the *Port of Hamburg* (1909; Hamburg, Ksthalle). After his first stay in Algiers in 1920, where he met Marcelle Martinet, whom he married in 1923, he spent several successive winters in North Africa; one of his most decorative and luminous pictures, the *Window at La Goulette* (1926; Bordeaux, Mus. B.-A.), was painted in Tunisia during one such visit.

Marquet was timid and discreet as a person, perhaps because of his near-sightedness and a limp, and he shied away from any official honours. Nevertheless his late paintings, such as the *Pont Neuf at Night* (1935–9; Paris, Pompidou) and *View of Algiers* (1939; Bordeaux, Mus. B.-A.), continued to testify to the acuteness of his observation and freshness of vision.

BIBLIOGRAPHY

G. Besson: *Marquet* (Paris, 1929)
A. Rouveyre and G. Besson: *Marquet: Dessins* (Lanzac, 1943)
M. Marquet: *Marquet* (Paris, 1951)
F. Daulte and M. Marquet: *Marquet* (Lausanne, 1953)
F. Jourdain: *Marquet* (Paris, 1959)
Albert Marquet (exh. cat. by J. Cassou and M. Sembat, Bordeaux, Gal. B.-A.; Paris, Mus. Orangerie; 1975)
Albert Marquet (exh. cat. by M. Marquet, F. Daulte and M. Paret, Lausanne, Fond. Hermitage, 1988)

JEAN SELZ

Marquetry. Pattern or design assembled from small, shaped pieces of veneer. With marquetry the entire surface, including the background, is veneered, whereas with inlay, with which marquetry is historically associated, the pattern pieces are laid into a solid ground (*see* WOOD (i), §III, 5). The term 'intarsia' derives from 15th-century Italian inlay and is commonly used in continental Europe to describe both techniques.

1. Materials and techniques. 2. History.

1. MATERIALS AND TECHNIQUES. The design is drawn on strong paper and transferred by needle-pricking the outlines to create a copy marked with tiny holes. (The master patterns are often kept, so designs may be repeated over a long period.) Powder, usually a carbon or vegetable

black, is then used to dust or pounce the design through these holes on to further pieces of paper, which will be used as guides when cutting the veneer.

The veneers, contrasted by colour and grain, are then prepared. The technique basic to marquetry involves cutting bundles of veneer, interleaved with paper and sandwiched together in layers. These bundles, known as parcels, are protected front and back by waste veneers, one of which carries a piece of paper with the design. In the 17th and 18th centuries the veneers were heavy: it is common to find examples up to 4 mm thick in work of that date (compared to the modern 0.5 mm), so most parcels contained only three veneers. In early marquetry the sawing was often crude, but methods were improved in the early 17th century with the development of the fretsaw frame, originally made from a bow of wood, which held a fine blade suitable for cutting intricate designs. Initially the saw was used vertically (*see* WOOD, fig. 9), but later a horizontal position was found to admit more light. The 'French horse' or 'cutter's donkey', which holds the saw in guides and so guarantees a 90° saw-cut, was invented *c.* 1780. It enables a skilled craftsman to follow complex patterns with ease, aided by a foot strap or pedal, which controls the vice and leaves his hands free to work the parcel of veneers around the saw as it moves.

The sawing is done from the centre outwards, and each piece of veneer is then lightly stuck on paper, vellum or linen. This assembly is then pinned on to the carcass, which has been previously been covered with a layer of glue, and a large, hot wooden panel is clamped on top of it. The underside of this panel, or caul, is slightly convex, which ensures that no glue is trapped under the veneer when the clamps are tightened. The heat of the panel resoftens the glue, and when it has set again, the caul is removed, the paper peeled off and the marquetry panel polished. In the finest work the ground veneer is laid on the furniture carcass first, and the pattern shapes inlaid into the ground veneer, using the technique most inlayers continue to call intarsia.

Marquetry is generally used to describe curvilinear designs, whereas the term parquetry is applied to the creation of veneered geometric patterns, including rhomboid, herringbone, chessboard and *trompe l'oeil* chequered effects. For the last, each element forms a diamond or parallelogram, its widest angle 120°; parcels of three are sawn in a mitre box, then assembled with the grains directed to form visual 'cubes'. Designs can be framed by decorative cross-banding composed of narrow strips or lines (strings) of box, holly, ebony, metal or ivory, or by check or herringbone patterns; the designs are varied and wide.

The woods used in marquetry include such native European timbers as plane, sycamore, walnut, mulberry, laburnum, hawthorn, holly, box, lime, cedar, olive, fruit-woods, thuya, bog yew and bog oak, as well as a variety of exotic, imported woods. Ebony was among the first tropical woods to be employed, beginning in the early 16th century, but by the 17th and 18th centuries satin-wood, purple-wood (amaranth), king-wood, rose-wood, amboyna, tulip-wood and padauk also became available. The dark brown of bog yew and the black of bog oak are the result of chemical changes occurring naturally during the trees' decades of immersion in peat bogs. Both were frequently used in place of ebony, set off against such pale woods as holly and sycamore. Light-coloured woods were often dyed, possibly by soaking or fuming. Decorative 'leaves' cut from ivory or bone were sometimes stained green, and to brighten the effect of ivory inlay whiting was mixed with clear fish glue. Scorching the wood in shallow trays of heated sand achieved remarkable effects of animation, light and shade. From *c.* 1760 the wood pieces were sometimes engraved for finer detail; later, the scored lines were inked to emulate penwork. Another practice was to induce colour changes in the wood of living trees; the application of ferrous oxide to the roots of sycamore trees, for example, produced a silvery-grey wood known as hare-wood.

Marqueries of ebony, brass and tortoiseshell are known as boullework. Prior to roller presses, the brass or pewter sheets were cast and beaten by hand to the thickness required, and the design was sometimes engraved in the metal before sawing. The tortoiseshell was, in fact, the shell of marine turtles, generally Hawksbill and Green turtle: the Hawksbills' thin 'blond' shell with random mottle was considered superior. The shells were flattened and thinned by being boiled in salt-water and placed under pressure, though some thick shells were reduced by laborious hand-scraping. The colour was achieved not by dyeing the shell, but by adding coloured pigments to the animal glue adhesive, which then showed through the semi-translucent shell. The favoured hues were vermilion, umber, yellow or white. These were sometimes mixed with gold and silver powders, though on important furniture the finest gold leaf was often used. A similar practice was applied to horn, which was also translucent. Another method of elaboration was to inlay into brass or pewter grounds fine miniature paintings executed in oil or tempera on good rag-paper. Their surfaces were protected by horn, which allowed the picture to show through and so served the role that hardened plastic sheet plays today. Mother-of-pearl is a hard, brittle substance that cracks easily; nonetheless it sometimes appeared in boullework. The pieces of shell were obtained from the abalone and other molluscs and came in a range of shades. They were cut with the finest piercing or jewellers' saws and were polished and engraved.

Until the 20th century hot and cold animal glues, made from bone, skin and hide, provided the adhesives for marquetry work; there were also fish glues. These organic adhesives are neither water nor heat proof, but they form a flexible bond that allows the wood to move in response to changes in temperature and humidity. Modern adhesives include polyvinyl acetate and a variety of synthetic resins. However, many craftsmen still use animal glues because of their easy reversibility, which enables them to rectify any mistakes.

2. HISTORY. Geometric marquetry veneers were used in the ancient world, for example in Egypt where craftsmen decorated low tables and coffers with coloured woods in herringbone and basketweave designs (e.g. the funerary furnishings from the tomb of Tutankhamun, 14th century BC; Cairo, Egyp. Mus.; *see* WOOD, colour pl. III, fig. 1).

The practice fell into disuse prior to the Middle Ages but re-emerged in Germany and the Low Countries in the early 17th century. From there it spread to France and England, where it reached the peak of sophistication in the 18th century. The resurgence of marquetry decoration was stimulated by improved sawing techniques, particularly in Germany where the first water-driven veneer mills were established by the late 1600s. As Europe became increasingly prosperous, there was a demand for more luxurious furniture. A wide range of tropical woods was imported, and with marquetry the craftsman could utilize small pieces of these to advantage and could incorporate other such valuable materials as ivory and tortoiseshell.

The origins of marquetry lay in Italian intarsia work, which had been used since the 14th century to decorate furniture and architectural woodwork (e.g. the studio of Federigo da Montefeltro, 1476; Urbino, Pal. Ducale; *see* STUDIOLO, fig. 1). Inlay satisfied the Italian love of surface decoration and was thought to be more durable than painted wood. The designs included plant arabesques, geometric mosaic (known as *certosina*) and ingenious architectural perspectives. Many of the pictorial compositions were closely linked to advanced ideas in early Renaissance painting, and such artists as Piero della Francesca and Lorenzo Lotto were known to have supplied craftsmen with designs (e.g. the choir-screen and stalls designed by Lorenzo Lotto, 1524–30; Bergamo, S Maria Maggiore). Admired throughout Europe, Italian inlay was copied and eventually surpassed by south German craftsmen during the 16th century. Augsburg was particularly known for this type of work, of which the most outstanding example is the *Wrangelschrank* (1566; Münster, Westfäl. Landesmus.), with its illusionist pictorial panels.

In England 'markatre' furniture is mentioned in Tudor inventories, and a few rare pieces survive from this period. The best known is the so-called 'Aeglantyne' table (Hardwick Hall, Derbys, NT), made in 1567 for Elizabeth Talbot, Countess of Shrewsbury. The top has an elaborate marquetry design of flowers, musical instruments, playing cards and strapwork surrounding the Talbot–Cavendish coat of arms.

Given the German and Elizabethan examples, it is evident that inlay and marquetry were both practised quite early in northern Europe. In the 17th century, however, marquetry became the dominant form in the hands of Dutch and Flemish cabinetmakers. The extensive trading links of the Low Countries gave them access to an array of tropical woods, and they soon mastered the new techniques of veneering and marquetry. They introduced oyster-work, small, ringed patterns made up of veneer pieces cross-cut from branches of walnut, laburnum and olive trees, and created vivid floral designs, frequently derived from Dutch flower paintings, on cabinets, chests and table-tops (*see* WOOD, colour pl. IV, fig. 2). The finest Dutch floral marquetry was executed between 1660 and 1700 and characterized by designs of bouquets or large blossoms overflowing vases or urns (e.g. the cabinet attributed to Jan van Mekeren, *c.* 1700; Amsterdam, Rijksmus.; see fig. 1).

Intarsia work, Italian in influence, had been practised in France throughout the 16th century, and Flemish-style

1. Marquetry cabinet attributed to Jan van Mekeren, oak, veneered with other woods including king-wood, ebony, rose-wood, olive-wood and sycamore, 2.05×1.73×0.61 m, made in the Netherlands, *c.* 1700 (Amsterdam, Rijksmuseum)

marquetry soon became fashionable in the 17th century. There was close interchange between France and the Low Countries. Jean Macé (*c.* 1602–72), for example, who is said to have introduced the craft to the French, trained in Middelburg, Zeeland, *c.* 1620, and on his return to France became a specialist in the laying of patterned floors. His *parquet marqueté* commissioned by Anne of Austria for the Palais-Royal was the wonder of Paris, and thereafter the term 'parquetry' was associated with floors and furniture embellished with geometric patterning. A Dutch master craftsman, Pierre Gole, who worked at the Gobelins from *c.* 1653, was probably responsible for introducing the art of floral marquetry and pewter inlay. A specifically French contribution, however, was boullework, the complex marquetry of brass, pewter and tortoiseshell perfected by André Charles Boulle (e.g. the commode for Louis XIV's bedroom at the Grand Trianon, 1708–9; Versailles, Château; for illustration *see* FRANCE, fig. 54). In boullework the veneers were often used in a reciprocal fashion, either within the same piece of furniture or on two complementary pieces: a tortoiseshell ground inlaid with brass formed the 'first part', a brass ground inlaid with shell the 'counter part'. The technique was particularly suited to designs in the style of Jean Berain I, with whom Boulle had collaborated, and was practised widely in France, Germany and England.

Marquetry was introduced to England by Dutch and French Huguenot craftsmen, who settled there in large numbers in the late 17th century. One of these, Gerrit Jensen, worked for the royal household from *c.* 1680 to 1715 and became the first London cabinetmaker of note. He specialized in metal inlay, similar to boullework, as well as in arabesque and scrolling 'seaweed' marquetry (e.g. the writing-table attributed to Jensen, *c.* 1690; Windsor Castle, Berks, Royal Col.). Arabesque and 'seaweed' marquetry was especially popular in England, as were Dutch- and Flemish-style floral designs (e.g. the Anglo-Dutch side chair, *c.* 1720; London, V&A, W. 40–1953) and geometrically patterned figured veneers (e.g. one of a pair of cabinets veneered in 'oyster' lignum vitae, *c.* 1660–69; Windsor Castle, Berks, Royal Col.; see fig. 2). Similar figured veneers appeared in American colonial furniture, for example in a William and Mary style desk (New York, Met., 10.125.75) made in Massachusetts between 1700 and 1730.

The celebrated *ébénistes* at work in France during the 18th century produced some of the finest marquetry in the history of the craft. During that period furniture was still largely ranged against the walls of rooms, so surface interest was of paramount importance. The craftsmen mastered the technique of applying marquetry veneers to curved surfaces, and this practice was further developed with the spread of Rococo styles; gilt-bronze mounts protected the thin edges of veneers as furniture forms became more serpentine. The woods included king-wood,

satin-wood, purple-wood, rose-wood and amboyna: by the 1770s a total of over 50 exotic varieties and some 40 native ones were recorded.

At the beginning of the 18th century symmetrically patterned veneers of matched, figured burl or with striped grain were the chief form of marquetry (e.g. the commode attributed to Charles Cressent, 1730–35; London, Wallace; for illustration *see* RÉGENCE STYLE); these were set off by cross-banding, achieved by running narrow strips of cross-cut veneer at right angles to the grain of the background veneer. Later three-dimensional geometric patterns came into favour, as well as pictorial scenes with architectural views, hunts, trophies, floral and still-life arrangements. Many *ébénistes*, for example Jean-François Oeben (*see* FRANCE, fig. 55) and Jean-Henri Riesener, combined geometric and pictorial marquetry in one piece of furniture (e.g. chest-of-drawers by Riesener, 1776; Waddesdon Manor, Bucks, NT; see fig. 3). The designs of the panels, which were intended to emulate painting, were sometimes taken directly from engravings; craftsmen dyed, etched, stained and scorched the wood pieces to enhance the detail and create an illusion of depth. The construction of these scenes was highly specialized work, and busy, or less skilled, craftsmen could buy prefabricated panels from other tradesmen. Towards the end of the century there was a move away from such elaborate marquetry. David Roentgen, in particular, whose marquetry work was Neo-classical yet delicately naturalistic, preferred from *c.* 1780 to use figured veneers and geometric forms.

After 1760 classical ornament was increasingly adopted for marquetry furniture in France, Britain, the Netherlands, Germany, Italy and Scandinavia; eventually it reached Spain, Portugal (e.g. Neo-classical commode, *c.* 1785; Lisbon, Mus. N. A. Ant.) and the USA (e.g. gentleman's secretaire, *c.* 1810–20; New York, Met., 67.203). In Italy the best-known practitioner was Giuseppe Maggiolini of Milan. His rectilinear furniture featured marquetry veneers with antique ornaments, quivers of arrows, birds, ribbons and trophies (e.g. commode, 1790; Milan, Castello Sforzesco). Georg Haupt was a German-trained Swede whose work for the Swedish crown displayed the popular royal insignia of a vase-shaped sheaf of corn (e.g. commode, 1779; London, V&A, 1108–1882). In England marquetry was revived in the 1760s by John Cobb, Pierre Langlois and, later, John Linnell (i) and Thomas Chippendale (ii). Sophisticated marquetry furniture in light-coloured woods was executed according to designs by Robert Adam (i) (e.g. the commode attributed to William Ince and John Mayhew, 1773–4; London, Osterley Park House, NT).

In the early 19th century the French Empire style was influential throughout Europe, reaching as far as Russia. Such Napoleonic motifs as trophies, armour, laurel wreaths and eagles were evident in marquetry 'still-lifes' in all lands subject to Napoleon's campaigns. In England marquetry patterns in early Regency furniture were mostly confined to central fan motifs and border designs of bellflowers. There was, however, a revival of boullework, led by George Bullock, which employed a system of repetitive inlay as used by Charles Percier. In this, the ground of stained veneer and the metal ornament, usually of pewter or brass, were stamped together and cut out in

2. Marquetry cabinet, one of a pair, veneered with lignum vitae and mounted in embossed silver, 1.5×1.9×0.5 m, *c.* 1660–69 (Windsor Castle, Berks, Royal Collection)

3. Marquetry chest-of-drawers by Jean-Henri Riesener, oak veneered with purple-wood, 1.72×0.90×0.64 m, made in France, 1776 (Waddesdon Manor, Bucks, NT)

a single mechanical process (e.g. mixed metal-and-tortoise-shell marquetry writing-table, *c.* 1815; London, Wallace). Throughout the 19th century there was a fashion in England for Tunbridge ware, a type of fine, wood mosaic decoration that had been used for small articles since the late 17th century and was made principally in the area of Tunbridge Wells, Kent.

Elsewhere, there were spasmodic revivals of marquetry, for example in the USA, where Peter Glass (1824–95), an English-born, European-trained inlayer, created unique, high-quality marquetry designs (e.g. the sewing-table attributed to Peter Glass, 1865–75; New York, Met., 1978.284). In France the tradition persisted in luxury furniture right through to the Art Nouveau period, when floral marquetry was revitalized by Emile Gallé and Louis Majorelle. Art Deco designers continued to use marquetry in floral bouquets (e.g. armoire by Jacques-Emile Ruhlmann; *c.* 1922; Paris, Mus. A. Déc; *see* ART DECO, fig. 2) and in geometric designs composed of figured or cross-cut woods.

See also colour pls VII and VIII.

BIBLIOGRAPHY
J. A. Roubo: *L'Art du menuisier ébéniste*, III/iii of *L'Art du menuisier* (Paris, 1774/*R* 1977)
P. Macquoid and R. Edwards: *The Dictionary of English Furniture*, 3 vols (London, 1924–7, rev. 1954/*R* Woodbridge, Suffolk, 1983)
P. Verlet: *Le Mobilier royal français*, 2 vols (Paris, 1945–55; Eng. trans., London, 1963)
H. Hayward, ed.: *World Furniture* (London, 1965)
W. A. Lincoln: *The Art and Practice of Marquetry* (London, 1971)
G. de Bellaigue: *Furniture, Clocks and Gilt Bronzes*, i of *The James A. de Rothschild Collection at Waddesdon Manor* (London and Fribourg, 1974)
P. Ramond: *La Marqueterie* (Dourdan, 1978)
A. Duncan: *Art Deco Furniture: The French Designers* (London, 1984)
F. Collard: *Regency Furniture* (Woodbridge, Suffolk, 1985)
M. A. V. Gill: *Tunbridge Ware* (Aylesbury, Bucks, 1985)
H. Flade: *Intarsia: Europäische Einlegekunst aus sechs Jahrhunderten* (Munich and Dresden, 1986)
D. Hawkins: *The Techniques of Wood Surface Decoration* (London, 1986)

Marrakesh [Arab. Marrākush; Fr. Marrakech]. Moroccan city in the province of the same name. Until *c.* 1890 the town was known as Morocco or Morocco City. Situated in the arid Haouz plain north of the High Atlas Mountains, it is the southernmost of the four imperial cities of Morocco. Its walls of red clay and its low houses give the city a more African aspect than Fez, Meknès or Rabat. The urban development of the city was determined by its location amid palm and olive groves, planted when the city was founded. The city comprises two distinct parts: the medina in the east, itself subdivided into the old town centre in the north and the royal quarter in the south; and the modern city in the west. One of the most important administrative, economic and touristic centres in Morocco, it is known for its ancient ramparts, mosques, tombs and picturesque souks.

Marrakesh was founded *c.* 1062 by the Almoravid ruler Yusuf ibn Tashufin (*reg* 1061–1106) as a military encampment for the expansion of his Saharan Berber dynasty north towards the Atlantic plains. The town became important first as a regional commercial centre, then as an administrative centre and finally as the capital city of an empire. The city received its water supply via subterranean channels (Arab. *khaṭṭāra*, Pers. *qanāt*) that originate in the Atlas Mountains. Part of the first rammed-earth wall (*c.* 1120) surrounding the city still stands, and most of the gates date from the Almoravid period, although they have been modified so many times that their original appearance has changed beyond recognition. The radial concentric plan of the medina also dates from this time. The site of the Almoravid palace, Qasr al-Hajar, has been identified, but the only surviving building is the Qubbat Barudiyyin (or Ba'diyyin; 7.3×5.4 m), once the centrepiece of the ablution complex for the Almoravid congregational mosque. It is an elegant pavilion that documents the impact of such Andalusian decorative motifs as ribbed domes and intersecting horseshoe arches on local architectural styles.

The Almohads (*reg* 1130–1269) took the city in 1147 and turned it into a political, intellectual and artistic centre. Their kasba, a royal city in the south of the medina, was later used by the Sa'dian dynasty (*reg* 1511–1659), and the only remains from the Almohad period are the mosque of the kasba, which has a plan similar to that of the Hasan Mosque at RABAT, and a monumental stone gate, Bab Agnaw, which is beautifully decorated with interlaced designs and inscriptions. The most prestigious monument in the medina of Marrakesh is the Kutubiyya ('Booksellers') Mosque (1147–58), which has an elegant stone minaret (h. 67.5 m) decorated at the top with multicoloured ceramic tiles. The mosque, with its T-shaped plan, lambrequin arches and stucco decoration, is a masterpiece of Almohad architecture (*see* ISLAMIC ART, §II, 5(iv)). Gardens with reservoirs situated west and south of the city also date from this period.

In 1269 Marrakesh was taken by the Marinids (*reg* 1196–1465), who neglected it in favour of Fez. Some mosques, such as those of Sidi Muhammad ibn Salih (1331) and Harat al-Sura, as well as the rather insignificant ruins of the madrasa of Abu'l-Hasan (*reg* 1331–48), date from this period, but Marrakesh was not one of the Marinids' creative centres. Under the Sa'dian dynasty the city once more became a capital and was enriched by the addition of many sumptuous buildings. The magnificent Ben Yusuf Madrasa (1564–5), once thought to be a restoration of a Marinid foundation, is one of the finest examples of Sa'dian religious architecture. Mosques in the medina include the mosque of Bab Dukkala (1557) and the mosque of al-Muwassin (Mwasin; 1562–72) with its fountain, bath and madrasa. Other important Sa'dian foundations are the Shrub wa Shuf ('Drink and gaze') Fountain and the funeral complexes of Sidi Bel 'Abbas (1605 and later) and Sidi Ben Sulayman (Sliman) al-Jazuli (*c.* 1554; rest. 18th century). On the site of the Almohad kasba, the Sa'dian sovereigns erected a royal town with palaces, gardens, a customs house, prisons, an assembly area (Arab. *mashwar*) and a dynastic necropolis, which remains one of the most elegant monuments in all Morocco (*see* ISLAMIC

ART, fig. 75). The ruined al-Badi' Palace, intended for official receptions, is an inordinately enlarged version of the Court of the Lions at the Alhambra in Granada (*see* GRANADA, §III, 1 and PALACE, §III).

Marrakesh did not remain the capital under the 'Alawi dynasty (*reg* 1631–), but Muhammad III ibn 'Abdallah (*reg* 1757–90) actively restored the ancient religious monuments and erected a palace complex in the south of the city. A district was developed forming a triangular projection north of Bab Taghzut, thereby incorporating the mosque of Sidi Bel 'Abbas. Al-Hasan (*reg* 1873–95) was proclaimed sovereign there before being recognized at Fez; his son and successor 'Abd al-'Aziz (*reg* 1895–1907) frequently stayed there. Many mosques were built, such as those of Sidi Ishaq, Darb al-Badi', Darb al-Shtuka, Dar al-Makhzan and 'Ali al-Sharif. Other notable buildings include the mausoleum of Sidi 'Abd al-'Aziz and the madrasa of Ibn Salih. High-ranking officials maintained magnificent palaces, such as the Dar Si Sa'id (late 19th century; transformed into a museum of Moroccan art) and the Dar al-Glawi (early 20th century). The al-Ma'muniyya Palace, built in an 18th-century palm grove, has been transformed into the Mamounia Hotel; the Bahia Palace (late 19th century) was designed by al-Hajj Muhammad ibn Mekhi al-Mifioui. These 'Alawi buildings tend to be somewhat monotonous, but they do not deserve the disdain with which they have been treated by archaeologists. The French took the city in 1912, and a modern town was added. A private museum of Islamic art has been created by Yves St Laurent and Pierre Bergé in the home of LOUIS MAJORELLE. The city continues to be a luxury winter resort for Europeans, and notable residences have been built in a neo-traditional style (*see* MOROCCO).

BIBLIOGRAPHY
Enc. Islam/2: 'Marrākush'
J.-P. Gabriel-Rousseau: *Le Mausolée des princes saadiens à Marrakech*, 2 vols (Paris, 1925)
J. Meunié and H. Terrasse: *Recherches archéologiques à Marrakech* (Paris, 1952)
——: *Nouvelles Recherches archéologiques à Marrakech* (Paris, 1957)
G. Deverdun: *Marrakech, des origines à 1912*, 2 vols (Rabat, 1959–66)
MARIANNE BARRUCAND

Marralwanga, Peter (Djakku) (*b* Kalerrkiwerr, N. Territory, 1916; *d* 1987). Australian Aboriginal painter. His language group was Kunwinjku, and he belonged to the clan Kardbam. Through his experience of ceremonial performance and through his intimate knowledge of local landscape, Marralwanga gained considerable social stature. He lived primarily by hunting and gathering and participating in traditional ceremonies. In the 1940s he visited the mission town of Oenpelli, which later became a major centre for the production of arts and crafts, and he lived in the Maningrida government settlement briefly during the 1960s. In the 1970s he eventually settled at a camp called Marrkolidban, where he lived with Yirawala, who taught him how to transpose the designs he had learnt as ceremonial body paintings into paintings suitable for sale. Marralwanga continued painting for the Aboriginal art cooperative at Maningrida until his death. The subjects of his paintings were the important creator beings of the local region, often shown in animal form. While the shape of the figures suggested an animal manifestation, Marral-wanga, like Yirawala before him, used the internal deco-ration of the figure to suggest its creative potential. In a work such as *Ngalyod the Rainbow Serpent* (1982; Robert Holmes à Court priv. col., see 1988 exh. cat., p. 31) he used inventive patterns of multicoloured cross-hatching called rarrk to suggest a link between the figure and ceremonial themes. Works such as *Ngalyod the Rainbow Serpent, Son of Yinarna* (*c.* 1977; Canberra, N.G.) reveal his mastery in achieving a harmonious relationship be-tween the shape of the figure and the bright patterns of infill used to suggest the symbolic potential of the subject.

BIBLIOGRAPHY
L. Taylor: 'Ngalyod, Creator of the Country', *Creating Australia: 200 Years of Art, 1788–1988* (exh. cat., ed. D. Thomas; Sydney, Int. Cult. Corp. Australia, 1988), p. 31
——: 'Western Arnhem Land, Figures of Power', *Windows on the Dreaming*, ed. W. Caruana (Sydney, 1989), p. 37
LUKE TAYLOR

Marriott, Alvin (*b* St Andrew, Jamaica, 29 Dec 1902; *d* 20 Sept 1992). Jamaican sculptor. He was initially self-taught, but later attended the Camberwell School of Arts and Crafts, London. He worked as a furniture carver in the 1930s for the Jamaican Art Deco furniture designer Burnett Webster (*b* 1909). His own work of this period was influenced by Art Deco and by Edna Manley. Grad-ually it became more academic, and he became Jamaica's most popular monumental sculptor. Among his best-known works are monuments in Kingston to Jamaica's national heroes, including Norman Manley (1971) and Alexander Bustamante (1972), as well as to the reggae singer Bob Marley (1985). He worked in various materials, including bronze, but was at his best as a wood-carver. His outstanding achievement is the carved ceiling deco-ration and lectern of the university chapel, University of the West Indies, Mona, Jamaica.

BIBLIOGRAPHY
Jamaican Art 1922–1982 (exh. cat. by D. Boxer, Washington, DC, Smithsonian Inst.; Kingston, Inst. Jamaica, N.G.; 1983)
VEERLE POUPEYE

Marsal, Mariano Fortuny y. *See* FORTUNY, (1).

Marseille [Marseilles; anc. Gr. Massalia; Massilia]. Second largest city in France and capital of the Bouches-du-Rhône *département*. It is situated near the mouth of the River Rhône on the Golfe du Lion on the north coast of the Mediterranean Sea. Its history and urban development, from its foundation by the Phocaeans in the 6th century BC (*see* §1 below), are largely dependent on its topography. Situated at the end of a sheltered cove and surrounded by hills, the city relies heavily on its port, which provides its livelihood. Its present triangular area, surrounded by ancient ramparts, is the same as that of the Roman city and was also the basis of the first medieval and modern urban plan, though originally only 50 ha in size. Continual development has eradicated most of the early city, leaving little evidence of its history and few remains of buildings. One of the few extant early buildings is St Victor, founded

1. Marseille, ancient Roman storage jars (*dolia*), h. over 2 m (Marseille, Musée des Docks Romains)

in the 5th century and rebuilt in its present form in the 13th century (*see* §4 below).

1. History, urban development and art life. 2. Centre of ceramics production 3. St Victor.

1. HISTORY, URBAN DEVELOPMENT AND ART LIFE.

(i) Massalia. It is the oldest city in France, founded *c.* 600 BC by Greek settlers from Phocaia in Asia Minor. The area was undoubtedly found congenial because of the hot, Mediterranean landscape and climate of Provence, similar to that of areas already colonized; because of the easy defensibility of the site, on a promontory with a narrow-necked natural harbour; and because it was a convenient port for the river traffic of the Rhône and trade with the interior of Gaul. Massalia soon became one of the most powerful and prosperous Greek cities of the west; indeed, its own colonies stretched from Nice to Ampurias in Catalonia. The city assumed a significant role in the distribution of Greek products and Greek culture in south and central Gaul, and in the early days it rivalled Carthage for the Spanish metal trade. A treasury building for the Massaliots was constructed at Delphi before the end of the 6th century BC. Its citizens chose the wrong side in the conflict between Caesar and Pompey, but Caesar spared the city when he took it in 49 BC, and it seems to have retained something of its independent status.

Unfortunately most of the ancient city has been obliterated by modern development. Destruction of parts of the city during World War II revealed the remains of a Greek theatre with circular *orchestra* just north of the old harbour; an interesting detail is the ridge or lip on the tiered stone seats to protect the backs of the spectators from the feet of those sitting behind (a feature also found in some theatres in Sicily and the eastern Mediterranean). The Musée des Docks Romains occupies part of an ancient warehouse adjacent to the Roman quayside, stretching along most of the harbourside; it preserves a large number of huge storage jars (*dolia*; see fig. 1).

The discoveries made during the Bourse excavations are preserved in the Jardin des Vestiges (Marseille, Mus. Hist.) and include an inland extension of the harbour; a stretch of the city walls and a gateway, both built of large, carefully cut blocks of stone; part of an ancient road with grooves cut into the paving slabs to prevent horses slipping; a section of a Hellenistic (323–31 BC) aqueduct; a well-preserved merchant ship; and a very large freshwater basin or cistern with overshot water-wheel, which was evidently used for supplying ships with drinking water.

In 1994 two Greek vessels (probably 6th–5th century BC) and three Roman ships (1st–2nd century AD) were discovered next to the city hall, along with remains of docks, warehouses and a 6th-century BC Greek shipyard containing many unfinished boats.

BIBLIOGRAPHY
M. Clerc: *Massalia: Histoire de Marseille dans l'antiquité, des origines à la fin de l'empire romain de l'ouest*, 2 vols (Marseille, 1927–9)
F. Villard: *La Céramique grecque de Marseille* (Paris, 1960)
M. Escalon de Fonton, ed.: *Naissance d'une ville: Marseille* (Aix-en-Provence, 1979)
M. Euzennat: 'Ancient Marseille in the Light of Recent Excavations', *Amer. J. Archaeol.*, lxxxiv (1981), pp. 133–40
A. L. F. Rivet: *Gallia Narbonensis* (London, 1988)
A. King: *Roman Gaul and Germany* (London, 1990)
J. Bromwich: *The Roman Remains of Southern France* (London, 1993)
P. G. Bahn: 'Ancient Ships in Marseille', *Archaeology*, xlvii/3 (1994), p. 15

JEFFREY HILTON

(ii) Modern city. Although Marseille was an important Mediterranean port from the 13th century to the 16th, its urban development did not essentially begin until the 17th century, when Louis XIV decided to enlarge the city in 1660. Wishing to break the independent spirit of the townspeople, he had the main gate and part of the ramparts demolished and instructed Louis Nicolas, Chevalier de Clerville (1610–77), and later Sébastien Leprestre de Vauban, to build two strong fortresses at the entrance to the port: Fort St Nicolas to the south and Fort St Jean to the north. Fort St Jean, surrounded by a strong limestone wall, is composed of several buildings, the oldest of which is the 13th-century church built by the Knights Hospitaller. A later square tower (1447; enlarged 1664) was built by René I. Fort St Nicolas, flanked by four bastions, has a more classical layout. Neither citadel was intended for defensive purposes but rather to act as a sentinel. The King's plans for fortification allowed him to enter the city as conqueror and to subdue it. He wanted to make it France's chief port on the Mediterranean, and in 1666 he ordered it to be enlarged, declaring it a free port in 1669.

In the late 17th century and throughout the 18th there was extensive urban planning. Such public buildings as the Hôtel de Ville (rebuilt 1666–70) and the arsenal, both by Gaspard Puget (1615–*c.* 1683), the Hôtel-Dieu (reconstructed on Mansart's plans in the 18th century, with east staircase (1785) by Jean Esprit Brun, and rebuilt under the Second Empire on Félix Blanchet's plans) and the opera house (by Charles Joachim Bénard, 1787; destr. by fire 1919, rebuilt 1921–4 by Gaston Castel, Raymond and Ebrard) were either enlarged or newly built and decorated, and the Church endowed the city with new church buildings, convents, seminaries and hospices. Hôtels and country houses were built or enlarged as the fortunes of their owners would permit. Few buildings remain from this period, most having been destroyed in the French Revolution (1789–95) or demolished or refurbished as part of 19th-century building schemes. The most renowned artist who worked in the city in the 17th century was PIERRE PUGET (see fig. 2). He was commissioned to produce designs (Marseille, Mus. B.-A.) for a Place Royale, although it was never built. He did, however, draw up the plans for the Hospice de la Charité, begun in 1671. The building has an austerity of design on both its exterior and interior and surrounds an elliptical chapel on three sides; in the 1990s it was converted into a cultural centre. St Cannat, a 16th-century church, in late Provençal Gothic style, has a later façade (1739) with sculptures by Antoine Duparc (*b c.* 1680; *d* 1755). The Carthusian church, with a colonnaded façade in classical style, was built in the late 17th century. Two important artists working in the city in the 18th century were Michel Serre (1653–1733), who painted principally for churches but who also executed a *View of the Cours during the Plague of 1720* and *View of the Hôtel de Ville during the Plague of 1720* (both 1721; Marseille, Mus. B.-A.) and FRANÇOISE DUPARC, who came from a well-known family of artists and who painted and exhibited portraits and genre scenes in England and Russia as well as France. In the 18th century Marseille also became an important centre for the production of faience (*see* §3 below).

By the mid-18th century the areas to the east and south of Marseille beyond the original ramparts were becoming urbanized, but to a more symmetrical and well-defined plan than that of the central core. However, much of the population still wished to live in the area around the harbour: houses and churches developed on its north side, while buildings devoted to the arts were constructed on its south side. Although the plague of 1720 had decimated the population and had virtually ruined Marseille's maritime commerce, there was a gradual recovery during which the city widened its circle of trading nations to include Russia and the American colonies of Great Britain. By the time of the French Revolution in 1789 Marseille was flourishing and prosperous, having also developed a solid trading base with the eastern Mediterranean: soap factories and fez and card manufactories were established in the city. However, during the Reign of Terror Marseille became a city 'without name', being known as 'Sans nom', and lost 60% of its conventual heritage. The politician Count Mirabeau introduced the libertarian ideals of the Revolution to its citizens, and the Marseille Federalists marched to Paris singing the anthem of the Rhine army, which was heard for the first time at the Club des Fédérés in Marseille and was to become the *Marseillaise*, the national anthem of France. The city's mercantile livelihood suffered during the reign of Napoleon I. A continental blockade on trade was imposed by the English and lasted four years. It was not until the restoration of the Bourbons in 1814 that the city again began to prosper. France's conquest of Algeria in 1830 played a determining role, as the port was used as a base of operations in the Mediterranean. The physical appearance of Marseille thus began to improve: public works linked as much to industrial as to urban needs were undertaken. Such major thoroughfares as Rue Impériale, Rue Colbert, Avenue du Prado and the Corniche were laid out, and the Canal de la Durance was built. Soap factories, flour mills, sugar and sulphur refineries and metal- and tile-works were founded. With the opening of the Suez Canal (1869), the city extended its trade with the Far East and became, more than ever, the 'Port of the Orient'.

During the Second Empire (1852–70) Marseille became an international commercial centre. The influx of Italians and Spanish into the city encouraged the establishment of banking organizations and brought about massive construction. Such buildings as the Préfecture (1867), begun by François Auguste Martin (1828–77), with decoration realized by François-Joseph Nolan (1804–83), the stock exchange (1852; now the chamber of commerce and the Musée de la Marine et de l'Economie de Marseille) by Pascal Coste, the cathedral (1852–93) by Léon Vaudoyer (*see* VAUDOYER, (2) and fig. 2), which combines Roman, Byzantine, medieval and Renaissance forms, and Notre-Dame-de-la-Garde (1853–74) and the Palais Longchamp (1862–9; now the Musée des Beaux-Arts), both by JACQUES-HENRY ESPÉRANDIEU, helped re-establish Marseille as an important city. From that time it grew considerably, especially to the north and the east. Dwellings were built

2. *Pierre Puget*, engraving by Charles Dupuis after the painting by François Puget, *c.* 1715–25 (Marseille, Musée de l'Histoire de Marseille)

without any coherent plan in the suburbs and along rural routes. A new port was constructed, and inner harbours were developed to the north at La Joliette. Marseille now became the principal producer of such traditional products as soap and sugar. It imported raw materials, processed them and sold them to the French colonies. A powerful middle class of industrialists, ship-owners and businessmen arose. In the 19th century several important artists had associations with the city, among them Cézanne, PAUL GUIGOU, Jean-Antoine Constantin, Augustin Aubert (1781–1857), Emile Loubon (1809–63), François Barry (1813–1905) and Marius Engalière (1824–57). Honoré Daumier was born in Marseille, as was ADOLPHE MONTICELLI, who established his career there. Views of the port and the Canebière, Marseille's main promenade, were rendered by a number of artists, among them Lucien Marcélin Gautier (*b* 1850; see fig. 3).

From 1914 Marseille's history was linked to the history of France at war, and the city was no longer able to maintain its autonomous character. However, it was a refuge for people in transit, especially in World War II. In 1942–3 it was occupied by the Germans, and at this time much of the Old Town near the port was blown up under Hitler's orders; the harbour front was later reconstructed by Fernand Pouillon. After the war, several mass-housing developments were built on the outskirts, including the Unité d'Habitation (1948–54; for illustration *see* BRUTALISM) by LE CORBUSIER. Various artists painted scenes of the lively commerce of the port, among them Paul Signac.

3. Lucien Marcélin Gautier: *La Canebière*, lithograph, 1883 (Marseille, Musée de l'Histoire de Marseille)

BIBLIOGRAPHY
E. Parrocel: *L'Art dans le Midi* (Marseille, 1881)
A. Alauzen: *La Peinture en Provence du XIVe siècle à nos jours* (Marseille, 1962)
E. Baratier, ed.: *Histoire de Marseille* (Toulouse, 1973)
C. Carrière: *Négociants marseillais au XVIIe siècle* (Marseille, 1973)
C. Carrière, M. Courdurié and F. Rebuffat: *Marseille, ville morte, la peste de 1720* (Marseille, 1978)
La Peinture en Provence au XVIIe siècle (exh. cat. by H. Wytenhove, Marseille, Mus. B.-A., 1978)
C. Carrière: *Le Port mondial au XVIIIe siècle* (Marseille, 1979)
R. Duchêne, ed.: 'Marseilles au XVIIe siècle', *Rev. Marseille*, 122 (1980) [special issue]
P. Urbain: *Architectures historiques à Marseille* (Aix-en-Provence, 1987)
E. Témine: *Histoire des migrations à Marseille*, 4 vols (Aix-en-Provence, 1989–92)

MYRIAME MOREL-DELEDALLE

2. CENTRE OF CERAMICS PRODUCTION. The first faience factory in the region of Marseille was established *c.* 1677 in Saint-Jean-du-Désert by Joseph Clérissy (?1644–85), a potter from Moustiers. The Clérissy family directed the factory from 1679 to 1733. The earliest wares were Baroque in form and the decoration almost always in monochrome blue, usually with manganese outlines. Designs were after Simon Vouet or Nicolas Poussin, as seen in the circular plate painted with the *Adoration of the Magi*, after Poussin, inscribed on the front 'Fait à Marseille chez F. Viry 1681' (Paris, Louvre). Picturesque scenes and chinoiseries were also employed, for example on the baluster vase painted with scenes from the story of Orpheus and Eurydice (Marseille, Mus. A. & Trad. Pop. Terroir Marseill.), as was the decoration after Jean Berain I. Imported wares from Savona or Genoa in Italy also influenced decoration during the late 17th century. In 1710 Joseph Fauchier (*d* 1751), a potter from Saint-Jean-du-Désert, set up a factory in Marseille, which continued to be directed by the Fauchier family until 1789. Fauchier introduced figures (e.g. statue of the *Virgin and Child*,

c. 1735; ex-Tessier priv. col.) and specialized in wares decorated with naturalistc flowers. Other notable factories were those of Joseph Leroy (1750–58) and Joseph Gaspard Robert (*c.* 1750–93), which during the 1750s both employed a looser form of the style used on Rouen wares known as the *style rayonnant*. Pierrette Candelot (1709–94), the widow of Claude Perrin (1696–1748), took over the running of the Perrin faience factory after her husband's death. Henceforth it was known as Veuve Perrin, and the wares were marked with the initials VP. The factory was renowned for its decoration of polychrome, naturalistic floral sprays and insects. The Rococo forms were often painted with a pink or green edge (e.g. circular plate; Marseille, Mus. Cantini). A turquoise enamel was developed between 1763 and 1765, while chinoiseries after Jean-Baptiste Pillement and exotic flowers were employed, as was similar decoration in monochrome green and red. Masonic symbols and alphabets, often on a yellow ground (e.g. oval platter; Sèvres, Mus. N. Cér.) were produced from the 1760s. Of particular regional interest were the wares decorated with naturalistic marine trophies and fish (e.g. terrine and dish; Marseille, Mus. Grobet-Labadié), quayside scenes after Claude-Joseph Vernet and views of the port of Marseille. The numerous other factories in the town produced wares with similar decoration. In 1765 Honoré Savy (1725–90), who had been associated with the Veuve Perrin and Leroy factories, and who had become a member in 1765 of the Académie Royale de Peinture et de Sculpture de Marseille, applied for a privilege to experiment with porcelain. In the *Guide marseillais* of 1793 he is described as a porcelain and faience manufacturer, as were Bonnefoy, Veuve Perrin and Robert. Porcelain produced by these factories is decorated in a similar style to the faience.

BIBLIOGRAPHY
H. J. Reynaud: *Faïence de Marseille: XVIIe et XVIIIe siècles* (Geneva and Marseille, 1951)
M. Desnuelle: *Faïence à Marseille au XVIIe siècle: Saint-Jean-du-Désert* (Avignon, 1984)
Faïence de Marseille: Saint-Jean-du-Désert (exh. cat., Marseille, Mus. Grobet-Labadié, 1985–6)
H. Amourie: *La Faïence de Marseille au XVIIIe siècle: La Manufacture de la veuve Perrin* (Marseille, 1990)

BET McLEOD

3. ST VICTOR. The abbey was founded by the monk John Cassian (*c.* AD 360–*c.* 432) in the 5th century AD on the site of a 3rd-century necropolis overlooking the port of Massalia. In the early 10th century it was settled by Benedictine monks, and during the 11th and 12th centuries it was a wealthy and powerful abbey. Although it remained significant in an urban context, contributing to the defence of the port, it suffered a loss of prestige after the mid-12th century.

The development of the site began in the 5th century, when a small basilica was built with adjoining atrium and several additional buildings. This Early Christian church was situated next to a rock tomb, the legendary burial place of St Victor. Under the abbots Wilfred (*reg* 1005–20) and Isarn (*reg* 1020–47), the early constructions were enlarged towards the north, thereafter serving as a crypt area for a new upper church consecrated in 1040. Only parts of this church are preserved: the extant north porch with its classical capitals and the wall in the north aisle of the present church. The tombstone of abbot Isarn, the style of which is unique in the area of Marseille, was made soon after his death in 1047 and was originally located in the crypt.

The present church was built in a second major campaign in the first half of the 13th century by the sacrist Hugh de Glazinis (*d* 1250). The construction necessitated further modifications of the crypt area. The new upper church consists of a nave with four bays and two side aisles. The precise arrangement of the east end is unknown, as transept and choir were reconstructed in the mid-14th century. It was at this time that the abbey received its fortified character with crenellated outer walls. Nothing has survived of the monastic buildings that originally surrounded the church.

BIBLIOGRAPHY
F. Benoît: *L'Abbaye de Saint-Victor et l'église de la Major à Marseille*, Petites Monographies Grands Edifices France (Paris, 1936)
G. Drocourt-Dubreuil: 'Saint-Victor de Marseille: Art funéraire et prière des morts aux temps paléochrétiens (IV–V siècles)', *Doc. Hist., Archéol. & Archit.*, ii (1989)

ALEXANDRA KENNEDY

Marseus van Schrieck, Otto. *See* SCHRIECK, OTTO MARSEUS VAN.

MARS Group [Modern Architectural Research Group]. Organization of British architects, designers, engineers and journalists that was started in 1933 and dissolved in 1957. The MARS Group formed the British section of the CIAM and was established by Wells Coates with the architects E. Maxwell Fry and David Pleydell-Bouverie and the critics Philip Morton Shand, Hubert de Cronin Hastings and John Gloag. Its initial membership, mostly young architects with little experience of building, included the partners of Connell Ward and Lucas, and Tecton; the writers John Betjeman and James Richards; and Ove Arup. With *c.* 24 members by 1934, it grew to a peak of 120 by 1938, but the group was most significant in policy-making within the CIAM during the 1950s.

MARS worked as a pressure group within the struggle to improve public housing and amenities. Its first public statement appeared as an architectural and social investigation of Bethnal Green, London (1934), which demonstrated the severe deprivation in that area. Despite the success of this exposition, Berthold Lubetkin and Francis Skinner of Tecton became exasperated at the lack of positive action and left the group in 1935 to form the Architects and Technicians Organisation (a key group of mixed professions campaigning for better housing rights and, subsequently, in defiance of official policy on air raid precautions).

After 1935 the MARS Group's main strategy was to promote widespread acceptance of modern architecture, culminating in the exhibition *New Architecture* (1938) in London, a stylish presentation conceived by Godfrey Samuel, with separate sections by individual members under a general layout designed by László Moholy-Nagy (prior to his departure for the USA) and completed by Misha Black (1910–77). Although well attended—it was opened by Le Corbusier—it was criticized for not confronting the wider social implications of modern architecture. In 1942 the Group published a Plan of London, an ambitious redevelopment proposal for the capital. This was largely the work of the MARS Town Planning Committee under refugee members Arthur Korn and Arthur Ling (*b* 1913) with E. Maxwell Fry and Eileen Brown and William Tatton-Brown (*b* 1910). Referred to as a master plan, it envisaged a linear layout based on a rationalized traffic network, with London broken down into neighbourhood units, each of a fixed size. Its publication provoked much dissent from within the group and therefore cannot be seen as a collective statement. Younger architects who became members in the post-war years were critical of past policy and opposed to the CIAM Athens Charter evolved in 1933. This came to a head at CIAM IX held at Aix-en-Provence in 1953, when English and Dutch protesters, including Peter Smithson and Alison Smithson, William Howell, Jacob Bakema and Aldo Van Eyck, formed the breakaway Team Ten after the Congress. Both CIAM and MARS Group were dissolved in 1957.

WRITINGS
New Architecture (exh. cat., London, 1938)
MARS Report (London, 1944–5) [only three issues appeared: nos 1 and 2 are on urban plan. and no. 3 is a record of proc. at the RIBA confer. in London in 1945, held to discuss mod. archit.]
Turn Again (exh. cat., London, 1955) [a presentation to improve new bldg in the City of London]

BIBLIOGRAPHY
D. Lasdun: 'MARS Group, 1953–57', *Architect's Y-b.*, viii (1957), pp. 57–61
E. M. Fry: 'The MARS Plan of London', *Perspecta*, xiii (1971), pp. 162–73
L. Campbell: 'The MARS Group, 1933–1939', *Trans. RIBA*, viii (1986), pp. 72–86
M. Reading: *A History of the MARS Group, 1933–45* (diss., U. Bristol, 1986)

MALCOLM READING

Marsh, Sir **Edward (Howard)** (*b* London, 18 Nov 1872; *d* London, 13 Jan 1953). English civil servant, collector and patron. Educated at Westminster School, London, and Trinity College, Cambridge, he entered the Colonial Office and spent his career in the civil service, retiring in 1937 when he was awarded the KCVO. In London Marsh met young artists and painters, whom he assisted financially. He edited a series of anthologies of modern poetry entitled *Georgian Poetry* and translated works by La Fontaine and Horace.

'Eddie' Marsh, as he was generally known, began collecting under the direction of the painter Neville Lytton. He initially bought Old Master works and then concentrated on British painting, purchasing, for example, Richard Wilson's *Cader Idris* (*c.* 1765–7; London, Tate). He borrowed £2400 from his father to purchase Sir Herbert Percy Horne's magnificent collection of 200 early English watercolours; but the rest of his collection was formed mainly with a little family money and his salary. On average he spent only £200–300 a year on pictures. After buying Duncan Grant's *Parrot Tulips* (Southampton, C.A.G.) in 1911, Marsh became a committed collector of such contemporary painters as Stanley Spencer, Walter Sickert, John and Paul Nash, David Bomberg and Mark Gertler. Marsh was a trustee of the Tate Gallery, London, and was on the committee of the Contemporary Art Society, through which he left most of his pictures to galleries in Britain and the Commonwealth.

WRITINGS
A Number of People (London, 1939)

BIBLIOGRAPHY
DNB
C. Hassall: *Edward Marsh: Patron of the Arts* (London, 1959)
An Honest Patron: A Tribute to Sir Edward Marsh (exh. cat., ed. B. Putt and L. Johnson; Liverpool, Bluecoat Gal., 1976)

DAVID BUCKMAN

Marsh, Reginald (*b* Paris, 14 March 1898; *d* Dorset, VT, 30 July 1954). American painter, printmaker and illustrator. He returned from France to the USA with his American parents, Fred Dana Marsh (1872–1961) and Alice (née Randall) Marsh, who were also artists, in 1900. In 1920 he graduated from Yale University, New Haven, CT, where he had been art editor and cartoonist for the *Yale Record*. He moved to New York and became staff artist for *Vanity Fair* and the New York *Daily News*. By 1923 he had begun painting scenes of street life in New York in oil and watercolour. His first one-man show was held at the Whitney Studio Club in 1924. In 1925 he joined the *New Yorker*, to which he contributed regularly until 1931.

In 1925 Marsh travelled with his first wife, sculptor Betty Burroughs, to Europe where he studied and copied the works of the Old Master painters such as Peter Paul Rubens, Rembrandt and Michelangelo, whom he particularly admired for their ability to organize large figure groups. In 1927–8 he studied at the Art Students League in New York under Kenneth Hayes Miller, who encouraged him to paint the earthy vitality and social landscape of life in New York, subjects typical of AMERICAN SCENE PAINTING. Marsh painted and made prints of scenes such as *Dance Marathon* (engraving, 1932; Storrs, U. CT, Benton Mus. A.), Times Square, the 'El' or elevated railway, and the Bowery, often taking preparatory photographs, for example those of *Lifeguards* (New York, Mus. City NY) at Coney Island, for the painting of the same title (tempera on panel, 1933; Athens, U. GA Mus. A.).

In 1929 Marsh was shown by Thomas Hart Benton how to use egg tempera, the medium in which most of his street scenes of the 1930s are painted. In the 1940s he experimented with the 'Maroger medium', an oil emulsion formula promoted by Jacques Maroger of the Musée du Louvre, Paris, who believed it to have been used by some Old Master painters. In the last two decades of his life Marsh continued to depict the same themes, for example *The Bowery—Strokey's Bar* (tempera on panel, 1953; New York, Whitney).

WRITINGS
'Let's Get Back to Painting', *Mag. A.*, 37 (1944), pp. 292–6

BIBLIOGRAPHY
N. Sasowsky: *Reginald Marsh: Etchings, Engravings, Lithographs* (New York, 1956)
L. Goodrich: *Reginald Marsh* (New York, 1972)
N. Sasowsky: *The Prints of Reginald Marsh* (New York, 1976)
M. Cohen: *Reginald Marsh's New York: Paintings, Drawings, Prints and Photographs* (New York, 1983)
R. Walker and V. F. Brooks: 'The Rembrandt of Coney Island', *ARTnews*, lxxxii/7 (1983), pp. 28–31

M. SUE KENDALL

Marshal, Alexander (*b* ?1610–20; *d* London, 7 Dec 1682). English painter, merchant and plantsman. During the 17th century, as a result of world exploration, many new botanical species were brought to Europe, arousing considerable interest in natural history. Among the many collectors, gardeners and artists inspired by the new flowers and plants was Marshal, who was described in 1650 by Samuel Hartlib as a merchant by profession and a great florist (i.e. grower). According to Hartlib, Marshal had by this date produced a book of botanical drawings for the eminent gardener and collector John Tradescant the elder (presumably the book, now lost, recorded in John Tradescant the younger's *Musaeum Tradescantianum* of 1656). Although Marshal seems to have been a talented amateur of independent means who painted for his own amusement, he had a high contemporary reputation, and he was singled out as a painter of flowers and fruit in Sir William Sanderson's *Graphice* (1658). Among his surviving works are miniature copies after van Dyck and a modified copy of John Hoskins (i)'s miniature portrait of *Katherine Bruce, Countess of Dysart* (1649; Ham House, Surrey, NT), which substitutes for Hoskins's background the only known view of the original north front of Ham House. At least two still-lifes in oil on panel are known, including *Flowers in a Delft Jar* (New Haven, CT, Yale Cent. Brit. A.), which probably dates from his later years.

Marshal is best known for his *Florilegium* (Windsor Castle, Berks, Royal Col.), a volume of exquisitely detailed watercolour and gouache studies of exotic plants, which he painted during the last two decades of his life. He was particularly interested in pigments, and in a letter read to the Royal Society in 1667 he explained that in his search for colours that 'will be as fresh a hundred years hence, as when you saw them last' he had made many experiments with pigments extracted from 'flowers, or berries, or gums, or roots', and that he used these in both water and oil media.

UNPUBLISHED SOURCES
Lord Delamere priv. col. [S. Hartlib: *Ephemerides*, unpubd MS.]

BIBLIOGRAPHY
E. Croft Murray: *Catalogue of Drawings in the British Museum*, i (London, 1960), pp. 440–46
J. A. Mears: 'An Analysis of Information Preserved in a Recently Identified Collection of Insect Drawings by Alexander Marshal', *History in the Service of Systematics* (London, 1981), pp. 87–94
P. Leith-Ross: 'A Little-known Botanical Artist: Alexander Marshal', *Apollo*, cxix (1984), pp. 104–7
J. Roberts and J. Fisher: *Mr Marshal's Flower Album from the Royal Library at Windsor Castle* (London, 1985)

PRUDENCE LEITH-ROSS

Marshall. English family of sculptors and master masons.

(1) Edward Marshall (*b* 1597/8; *d* London, 10 Dec 1675). He was apprenticed to the mason John Clarke (*c.* 1585–1624), had his own workshop by 1628–9, held office in the Masons' Company of London and was appointed Master Mason to the Crown at the Restoration of the monarchy in 1660, retiring in 1673. He signed the memorial brass with finely detailed effigies of *Sir Edward and Lady Filmer* (*c.* 1629; East Sutton, Kent, SS Peter and Paul) and carved a number of other church monuments, notably that to *Henry Curwen* (1638; Amersham, Bucks, St Mary), shown standing in awkward contrapposto between the doors of his tomb, which is held open by angels.

During the 1650s Marshall undertook building work for private clients. He executed the designs of his friend John Webb (i) at the Vyne, Hants, where he built the portico in 1654, and at Gunnersbury House (1658; destr. 1800), Middx. At Aynho Park, Northants, he appears to have acted as architect and executant for the building campaign which began during the 1660s.

(2) Joshua Marshall (*bapt* London, 24 June 1628; *d* London, 6 April 1678). Son of (1) Edward Marshall. He succeeded his father in the royal service and also had a large mason-contracting business. During the 1670s he was much involved with the reconstruction of the public buildings of the City of London, being responsible, under Christopher Wren, for six churches and, in part, for St Paul's. As a sculptor of church monuments, he showed little talent, his designs depending heavily on his father's work.

Colvin; Gunnis
M. Whinney: *Sculpture in Britain, 1530–1830*, Pelican Hist. A. (Harmondsworth, 1964), pp. 31–3, 63–4
H. M. Colvin, ed.: *1660–1782* (1973), v of *The History of the King's Works* (London, 1963–82)

ADAM WHITE

Marshall, Ben(jamin) (*b* Seagrave, Leics, 8 Nov 1768; *d* London, 24 July 1835). English painter. The son of Charles and Elizabeth Marshall, he spent his childhood at Seagrave. During the 1780s he is believed to have taken drawing instruction from John Boultbee (1753–1812), although as late as 1791 his profession was recorded (on his brother-in-law's will) as schoolmaster. In this year he was introduced by William Pochin, MP, of Barkby Hall, Leics, to the portrait painter Lemuel Francis Abbott with whom he subsequently embarked on an apprenticeship. This seems not to have lasted, for he completed a painting of a horse for George, Prince of Wales (later George IV), in 1792 (the first of several such commissions in the 1790s); this belies the traditional story that he turned to sporting art after seeing Sawrey Gilpin's *Death of the Fox* on exhibition at the Royal Academy in London in 1793.

Between 1795 and 1810 Marshall occupied a studio at 23 Beaumont Street, St Marylebone, London (later the address of H. B. Chalon). From here he built up a strong sporting art practice, taking on John Ferneley and Abraham Cooper (1786–1868) as pupils and concentrating on hunting and racing. He also executed occasional non-sporting portraits; his best-known is the full-length *Daniel Lambert* (1806; Leicester, Mus. & A.G.), a likeness of the celebrated fat man who was among Marshall's close friends. His friendship with the printmaker John Scott (1774–1828) led to many of his sporting pictures being engraved for the *Sporting Magazine*, a journal to which he probably made additional contributions as a racing correspondent (he is thought to have been the writer behind the pseudonyms 'Observator' and 'Breeder of Cocktails').

An informed understanding of racing was considered by most patrons to be a requisite quality in any 19th-century sporting artist, and Marshall certainly enjoyed the full confidence of his employers and the associated rewards. In 1812 he moved to a studio in Newmarket, Suffolk, to capitalize on this further. He sustained injuries in a severe coaching accident in 1819, and this may have restricted his output for some years afterwards, even though no consequent loss of quality is apparent in his later work (as is often maintained). He returned to London in 1825. Although he was admired by sporting enthusiasts for his skilful delineation of horseflesh and his ability to evoke the atmosphere of sporting events, his naturalistic human portraiture, for example *Sir Charles Bunbury with Cox, his Trainer, and a Stable Lad* (?1801; London, Tate), and his earthy, unidealized landscapes (which occasionally include a foreground signature 'scraped' illusionistically on to muddy turf) have earned him recognition in broader and more critical circles.

One of Marshall's sons, Lambert Marshall (1809–70), supposedly named after Daniel Lambert, also practised as a painter; 26 of his pictures were engraved for the *Sporting Magazine*, but few survive. In *Sultan at the Marquess of Exeter's Stud, Burghley House* (1826; New Haven, CT, Yale Cent. Brit. A.) there is evidence of a substantial contribution from his father—as, it was alleged, was usually the case with his work. Lambert Marshall appears to have given up painting after his father's death; on his own death certificate his profession is listed as weaver.

BIBLIOGRAPHY
W. S. Sparrow: *George Stubbs and Ben Marshall* (London, 1929)
A. Noakes: *Ben Marshall, 1768–1835* (London, 1978)

STEPHEN DEUCHAR

Marshall, Sir John (*b* Chester, 19 March 1876; *d* Guildford, 17 Aug 1958). English archaeologist, active in India. Educated at Dulwich College and King's College, Cambridge, Marshall was introduced to archaeology at the British School at Athens and took part in excavations in Crete. In 1902 he succeeded JAMES BURGESS as Director-General of the Archaeological Survey of India, in which position he promoted both the conservation of existing structures and new site surveys and excavations.

In 1913 Marshall launched the first and largest project of his career: the exploration of TAXILA in ancient Gandhara (now in Pakistan), where he continued extensive excavations until 1934. Marshall initially set out to unearth what he imagined to be a lost 'Greek city' and 'the enduring legacy of Hellenistic culture'. As it gradually became apparent that numerous cities, destroyed and rebuilt by successive invaders, had existed around the site, Marshall concentrated his efforts on the full excavation of the Parthian city at Sirkap and on the partial excavation of the early 3rd-century BC Maurya city buried in the Bhir Mound. He endeavoured to preserve all the structural remains he uncovered in order to enable later archaeologists to form their own judgements regarding the sites.

Marshall's second major excavation project was in the Indus Valley. Following the pioneering discovery of MOHENJO-DARO by Rakhaldas Banerjee (1886–1930), Marshall's excavations between 1922 and 1927 confirmed the existence of the Indus civilization, which ranked in importance with ancient Mesopotamia and Egypt. Marshall also devoted time to conservation, preparing a comprehensive Antiquities Law, along the lines of those developed by the British in western Asia and Greece, and writing the *Conservation Manual* (1923), a guide for archaeological officers and others entrusted with the care of ancient monuments in India.

Between 1912 and 1919 Marshall undertook restoration work and fresh excavations at the early Buddhist monuments of SANCHI in central India. Conservation projects followed at the BAGH caves and at Lahore fort, where the tile mosaics were a main concern. Marshall also took a special interest in the restoration of Mughal gardens around tombs and palaces.

As an archaeologist, Marshall's contribution lay mainly in meticulous observation and the organization and classification of data, and less in analysis and explanation. He was appointed C.I.E. in 1910, knighted in 1914, and elected F.B.A. in 1936.

WRITINGS

A Guide to Sanchi (Calcutta, 1918)
A Guide to Taxila (Calcutta, 1918)
Tile Mosaics of the Lahore Fort (Calcutta, 1920)
Conservation Manual (Calcutta, 1923)
with others: *The Bagh Caves in the Gwalior State* (London, 1927)
Mohenjodaro and the Indus Civilisation, 3 vols (London, 1931)
with A. Foucher: *The Monuments of Sanchi*, 3 vols (London, 1940)
Taxila, 3 vols (Cambridge, 1951)
The Buddhist Art of Gandhara (Cambridge, 1960)

BIBLIOGRAPHY

DNB, Suppl., 1951–1960 (Oxford, 1971)
F. R. Allchin and D. K. Chakrabarti, eds: *A Source-book of Indian Archaeology* (New Delhi, 1979)
D. K. Chakrabarti: *A History of Indian Archaeology from the Beginning to 1947* (New Delhi, 1988)

TAPATI GUHA THAKURTA

Marshall, William (*fl c.* 1617–50). English engraver. His extant works as a line-engraver comprise over one hundred portraits and perhaps twice as many book illustrations, title-pages and occasional broadsheets. His earliest dated engravings are the amusing title-pages to Richard Brathwait's *Solemne Joviall Disputation Briefly Shadowing the Law of Drinking* and the *Smoaking Age with the Life and Death of Tobacco* (both 1617), which may have been plagiarized from Netherlandish prints. Much of Marshall's work was made after portraits in oils by contemporary artists, although he hardly flattered their work. This can be seen by comparing van Dyck's portrait of *William Laud, Archbishop of Canterbury* (1635; Cambridge, Fitzwilliam) with Marshall's engraving after it for the second edition of the lawyer Nicholas Fuller's *Argument of N.F. in the Case of F. Lad and R. Maunsell, his Clients* (1641), a defence of personal rights against ecclesiastical power first published in 1607, or Edward Bower's *Sir Thomas Fairfax on Horseback*, which Marshall engraved for Joshua Sprigg's *Anglia Rediviva* (1647). On occasion, however, Marshall engraved from his own drawings, and these, although slight, do show a certain wit and naive charm.

Marshall's best-known works are the 40 relatively refined engravings made for Francis Quarles's *Emblemes* (1635), half the total number of illustrations used in the book. Quarles, along with George Withers whose *Emblemes* was published the same year, introduced the EMBLEM BOOK, long popular on the Continent, into England; this may explain why Marshall cribbed as heavily as he did from two Jesuit examples, Herman Hugo's *Pia desideria* (1624) and the *Typus mundi* (1627), both of which were published in Antwerp. During the civil wars of the 1640s Marshall was employed by the Royalists to produce propaganda for their cause. His *Eikon Basilike: The Pourtraicture of his Sacred Majestie in his Solitudes and Sufferings* (1648), issued after Charles I's execution in January 1649, helped propagate the memory of a Martyr King; engraved in no less than eight versions, *Eikon Basilike* was perhaps the best-known English print of the 17th century. (Examples of Marshall's work are in London, BM.)

BIBLIOGRAPHY

A. M. Hind: *The Reign of Charles I*, ed. M. Corbett and M. Norton (1964), iii of *Engraving in England in the Sixteenth and Seventeenth Centuries* (Cambridge, 1952–64), pp. 102–92
R. T. Godfrey: *Printmaking in Britain: A General History from its Beginnings to the Present Day* (Oxford, 1979), p. 17

CHRISTOPHER FOLEY

Marshall, William Calder (*b* Edinburgh, 18 March 1813; *d* London, 16 June 1894). Scottish sculptor. He studied at the University of Edinburgh and began his artistic training at the Trustees' Academy in 1830. In 1834 he moved to London, where he attended the Royal Academy Schools and worked for Sir Francis Chantrey and Edward Hodges Baily. He lived in Rome from 1836 to 1838; there he studied antique sculpture and admired Neo-classical works. He became a companion of the sculptors John Gibson, Lawrence Macdonald and R. J. Wyatt and began to model Classical subjects, such as *Hebe Rejected* (marble, 1837; Edinburgh, N.G.).

Marshall's first major success came in 1846: as a result of the Westminster Hall competition, he was chosen to execute the marble statues of *Edward Hyde, 1st Earl of Clarendon* (1852), and *John, Lord Somers* (1855), both for the House of Lords. In the competition of 1857 for the Duke of Wellington monument at St Paul's Cathedral, he won first prize, although the commission was obtained by Alfred Stevens. Marshall produced some notable commemorative statues, among them *Sir Robert Peel* (marble, 1853; Manchester, Piccadilly Gdns) and *Dr Edward Jenner* (bronze, 1858; London, Kensington Gdns). He also designed the pediment sculpture for Bolton Town Hall (*c.* 1870) and the stone group representing *Agriculture* (*c.* 1865) for the Albert Memorial in Hyde Park, London.

Marshall's ideal sculpture takes its subjects from Shakespeare, Milton, English history and the Bible, as well as from Classical authors. Informed by Neo-classical principles of composition and modelling, his works, such as the *First Whisper of Love* (marble, 1846; Dublin, Royal Dublin Soc.), are characteristically Victorian in their narrative interest and sentimental appeal. Many of his designs were engraved in the *Art Journal*; others were commissioned by the Art Unions and pottery manufacturers for reproduction in statuary porcelain. Marshall was made RA in 1852 and Chevalier of the Légion d'honneur in 1871.

UNPUBLISHED SOURCES
London, RA [Marshall's papers]

BIBLIOGRAPHY
DNB; Gunnis
Obituary, *A. J.* [London] (1894), p. 286
Obituary, *The Times* (19 June 1894)
R. L. Woodward: *19th Century Scottish Sculpture* (PhD diss., U. Edinburgh, 1977)
B. Read: *Victorian Sculpture* (New Haven, 1982)

MARTIN GREENWOOD

Marshall Islands, Republic of. Two chains of atolls in the central Pacific Ocean (4–14°N., 160–173°E.), consisting of Ratak ('sunrise') to the east and Ralik ('sunset') to the west. The total land area of the 30 atolls, comprising more than 1150 individual islets and 5 single coral islands, is only 181 sq. km, and the estimated population (1993) is 53,000. The capital is Majuro. The Marshall Islands were formerly administered by Germany, Japan and finally the USA as a Trust Territory under the United Nations. In 1979 they became the self-governing Republic of the Marshall Islands, and in 1986 a Compact of Free Association was established with the USA. Although the small specks of land are very isolated and separated by extreme distances, the Marshall Islanders have a homogeneous culture and language with only slight differences between the two chains. Historically, communication between islands was frequent, whether for warfare, trade or visiting relatives and friends. Since all the islands are coral atolls the materials available for artistic production are limited. Traditionally, aesthetic expression was concentrated on such utilitarian items as outrigger canoes, clothing, tools and on designs woven in both mats and the thatch of houses. In the late 20th century handicrafts predominated, and many traditional objects were no longer used, although older people still possessed the necessary knowledge and skill to produce them. Collections of artefacts are held by the Field Museum of Natural History in Chicago and Bishop Museum in Honolulu.

One of the most outstanding achievements of the Marshall Islanders is the outrigger canoe. Traditionally, three types were developed: the *walap*, a sailing canoe large enough to carry up to 100 people and supplies for voyages lasting several months; the *tipnol*, carrying up to 20 people and very fast and efficient, being used for sailing between atolls; and the *korkor*, a small canoe for fishing and sailing within a lagoon. The *walap* was no longer made regularly by the 1990s, although a few older men had the knowledge and skill to produce them. In 1992 a 15.24-m Enewetak *walap* was built and completed a 240-km ocean voyage in the Cook Islands at the fourth Pacific Festival of Arts inRarotonga. In 1994 an 18.25-m *walap* was planned to be built on Ujae atoll. The *tipnol* and especially the *korkor*, however, were still made and used on the outer islands. The traditional design and construction were followed, although some elements, such as the ropes and sails, may differ from earlier workmanship. There are several hull shapes and types of these canoes, which vary according to their intended use. The unique and effective design of the outrigger platform with its booms leading to the outrigger is noted for its strength and flexibility under severe ocean conditions. These canoes were sleek in design and always finely carved from *ma* (breadfruit tree; *Artocarpus incisus*), *lukwej* (*Calophyllum inophyllum*) or mahogany or other hardwood driftwood. They attest both the seafaring knowledge and the artistic skill of the Marshall Islanders. Navigational knowledge was recorded in stick charts that represented diagrammatically the movements of the sea around the islands. These have become popular handicraft items.

Most adult women continue to make woven or plaited products for home use or to sell as handicrafts. All such items are made from pandanus leaf (*maan*) or the transparent outer skin of a new coconut leaf (*kimej*). The *maan* or *kimej* is woven around the rough and fibrous skin of the coconut midrib (*malwe*), which is pliable and ideal for shaping baskets and other types of frames. All mats are made from *maan*, although they sometimes incorporate other types of fibres to make different superimposed designs.

The traditional dress of Marshallese women was a soft and very finely plaited mat (*nieded*) made from strips of pandanus leaf (*c.* 3–4 mm wide) woven into elaborate designs. Usually a complicated border pattern of other materials was added. The women wore the skirt-like *nieded* by wrapping one around the front and another around the back, secured with a belt resembling a cummerbund. The skill, technique, design and aesthetic appeal of the *nieded* has continued to be exemplified into the late 20th century in such woven or plaited handicraft items as bowls, trays, wall hangings, baskets, purses and mats.

Another traditional art form was tattoo. Both men and women had intricate designs tattooed on their arms, chests and backs (*see* PACIFIC ISLANDS, §II, 2(iii)). A traditional type of flower headband or *wutwut* has continued to be made, and the various methods of braiding and combining different types of flowers make it a popular and fragrant gift.

BIBLIOGRAPHY
EWA: 'Micronesian Cultures'
A. Krämer and H. Nevermann: *Ralik-Ratak (Marshall-Inseln)* (1938), II/B/xi of *Ergebnisse der Südsee-Expedition, 1908–1910*, ed. G. Thilenius (Hamburg, 1913–36)
W. Davenport: 'Marshall Islands Cartography', *Expedition*, vi/4 (1964), pp. 10–13; also in *Micrones. Reporter*, xii/8 (1964), pp. 5–8
E. H. Bryan, ed.: *Life in the Marshall Islands* (Honolulu, 1972)
L. Hanson and F. A. Hanson: *The Art of Oceania: A Bibliography*, Ref. Pubns A. Hist. (Boston, MA, 1984)
The Art of Micronesia (exh. cat. by J. Feldman and R. Rubinstein, Honolulu, HI A.G., 1986)
J. Milford: *Decorative Marshallese Baskets* (Los Angeles, CA, 1991)

CAROL CURTIS

Marstrand, Wilhelm (Nicolai) (*b* Copenhagen, 24 Dec 1810; *d* Copenhagen, 25 March 1873). Danish painter and illustrator. He was a student of C. W. Eckersberg at the Kunstakademi in Copenhagen (1825–33). His art reflects his constant observation of the world around him, in particular middle-class society, and the narrative element dominated his pictures of crowds in the city streets. Throughout his life he sought inspiration from literature and the theatre. In his early genre painting *Moving Day Scene* (1831; Nivå, Nivaagaards Malsaml.) it was the popular novelty of vaudeville that interested him. The *October Festival* (1839; Copenhagen, Thorvaldsens Mus.) reveals how Marstrand's five-year stay (1836–41) in Italy opened his eyes to the classical ideal of beauty. It was, however, an ideal that found little response in contemporary Denmark, and he turned towards a more anecdotal and humorous approach. In *Scene of Country Life* (1843; Copenhagen, Kon. Dan. Kstakad.), painted as a set subject for the Kunstakademi, Marstrand took as his theme a scene from *Erasmus Montanus*, a play by the 18th-century Danish poet and playwright Ludvig Holberg. Thereafter Holberg's comedies provided an inexhaustible source that satisfied Marstrand's need to pursue his investigations of human character. Family life similarly interested him throughout his career, as in his *Scene of Daily Life* (1857; Copenhagen, Stat. Mus. Kst). Such group portraits as *The Waagepetersen Family* (1836; Copenhagen, Stat. Mus. Kst) show an equal concern to depict the quiet details of Danish domestic life. Marstrand continued to travel abroad in search of inspiration. His stay in Venice in 1853–4 was particularly important; his studies there of the great Venetian painters improved his understanding of the handling of colour, as seen clearly in the many historical and religious paintings of his last years. Of particular interest is his mural decoration of Christian IV's chapel in Roskilde Cathedral (1864–6) with scenes from the life of the Danish monarch. Marstrand's paintings have a certain facetiousness which often obscures a much deeper philosophical content. For this reason, it is his drawings that arouse more admiration. In these drawings, many of which are housed in Copenhagen (Stat. Mus. Kst and Hirschsprungske Saml.), Marstrand captures the spirit of his time with sharp satire.

BIBLIOGRAPHY

K. Madsen: *Wilhelm Marstrand* (Copenhagen, 1905)

V. Andersen: *Holberg billedbog* [Holberg picture-book] (Copenhagen, 1922)

Danish Painting: The Golden Age (exh. cat. by K. Monrad, London, N.G., 1984), pp. 172–7

G. Valentiner: *Scenebilleder: Wilhelm Marstrand* [Stage pictures: Wilhelm Marstrand] (Copenhagen, 1992)

Wilhelm Marstrand (exh. cat., ed. G. Valentiner; Nivå, Nivaagaards Malsaml., 1992)

ELISABETH CEDERSTRØM, GITTE VALENTINER

Marsy [de Marsy; Marcy; Marsi; Mercy; Mersy]. French family of sculptors. Jaspard Marsy (1600–74) had two sons celebrated for their work together, Gaspar(d) Marsy (*b* Cambrai, 1624; *d* Paris, 10 Dec 1681) and Balthazar(d) Marsy (*b* Cambrai, *bapt* 6 Jan 1628; *d* Paris, 16 May 1674); two other sons who seem to have been minor collaborators with them; and a daughter, Jeanne, who married the sculptor Pierre Legros (i). Jaspard himself, of whose origins and training virtually nothing is known, was the dominant figure in the artistic life of Cambrai during the second quarter of the 17th century. He possessed great versatility and was in continual demand for his skills as a figure-sculptor, carver of epitaphs and rood screens, restorer, architect, and commercial dealer of materials. From the 1650s he worked in Paris.

Gaspar and Balthazar received their early training in sculpture from their father but in 1648 moved to Paris in search of greater opportunities. They stayed for a year in the house of a wood-carver (whose name is not known), then devoted some time to private study. Between 1651 and 1656 they perfected their skills in the workshops of Jacques Sarazin, François Anguier, Gérard van Opstal and Philippe de Buyster. They were known at first as specialists in the art of stucco relief, and they took part in 1655–60 in the decoration of the interiors of the Hôtel de la Vrillière, the Château du Bouchet (destr.) and a number of mansions in the Marais district, including the Hôtel Salé (now the Musée Picasso). In 1658, working under the direction of Charles Errard (ii), they modelled a major part of the stucco decorations in the two northern rooms of the summer apartments of the Queen Mother, Anne of Austria, in the Louvre. They invested the money thus earned in land, apartment houses, works of art and the stock market. The scope of their commercial activity was sufficiently wide to preclude the need for them to travel to Italy, the usual goal of young French sculptors at the time.

Gaspar and Balthazar reached their artistic maturity just as Charles Le Brun, Louis XIV's new Premier Peintre, was assembling his team of decorators. Their first royal commission, on which they worked in 1663–4 with François Girardon and Thomas Regnaudin, was for the ceiling decorations, in stucco, of the Galerie d'Apollon in the Louvre. Over the next ten years the Marsy workshop, under Le Brun's direction, was responsible for a series of important works for the gardens of Versailles, including the Siren and Dragon Fountains (lead, both 1666–7; destr.); the marble group of the *Horses of Apollo* (1667–72), originally right niche of the *Grotte de Thétys*, now part of Hubert Robert's *Bains d'Apollon*); the Fountain of Latona (1667–70; central group in marble, metamorphosed figures in lead); and the lead Fountain of Bacchus (1672–5; now lacking its four accessory groups, three of which function as independent fountains in the Trianon gardens). From 1670 to 74 the brothers played leading roles in two other large programmes of sculpture at Versailles: the decoration of the main garden façade, to which they contributed eight statues, a series of trophies, at least ten keystone masks and twenty-four reliefs of children at play (the latter destr. during construction of the Galerie des Glaces); and the stucco ornamentation of the ceilings of the King's great apartments. Of their final joint work, the tomb of *John II Kasimir*, former King of Poland (*c.* 1674–5; Paris, St Germain-des-Prés), only the marble effigy is extant; the stone captives and stucco angels disappeared at the time of the Revolution (1789–95).

Throughout their partnership the Marsy brothers lived and worked in extraordinary harmony. Almost invariably they received joint commissions calling for ensembles of two or more figures, either on common or separate pedestals. For these commissions, it seems, they divided the labour into equal shares; each figure was executed from beginning to end by the same brother. Their contemporaries were struck by the similarity of their individual styles, and it is extremely hazardous to attempt to identify each brother's work.

Every extant sculpture by the Marsy brothers was made to the design of another artist (usually Le Brun, but occasionally, during their early Parisian career, Charles Errard or Louis Le Vau), who provided them with drawings and verbal instructions. The sculptors responded with their own drawings and models, which were discussed and finally approved by their superiors before work began on the final piece. They were permitted to introduce new formal language while respecting the iconography of the original drawings. The Marsy brothers were at their best in interpreting dramatic subject-matter, and Le Brun, conscious of the strengths of each of his sculptors, selected them for many of the most physically and emotionally charged works at Versailles. For important companion pieces he often pitted the older Marsy against Girardon, who exhibited a more restrained classical spirit. Both brothers, but especially Gaspar, had a deep respect for the historical masters, and a number of expressions, gestures, and compositional devices in Marsy works can be traced to Antique sculptures and to Italian Renaissance and Baroque paintings.

Gaspar was a member of the Académie Royale de Peinture et de Sculpture for 24 years, rising through the ranks to the office of *adjoint-recteur*. He delivered two theoretical lectures to the students, one of which contains some interesting personal reminiscences as well as an analysis of ancient Greek sculpture. Balthazar did not enter the Académie Royale until the year before his death.

After his brother's death, Gaspar produced the Fountain of Enceladus (lead, 1675–6), the Fountain of Fame (lead, 1676–80) and the marble statues of *Morning* and *Noon* (1674–80) for the gardens of Versailles; the marble figures of *Religion* ('*Liberality*') and *Valour* at the lower angles of the tomb of *Henri de la Tour d'Auverge, Maréchal de Turenne* (1676–80), formerly in Saint-Denis, now at Les Invalides, Paris; and one of the stone reliefs on the Porte Saint-Martin (1677) in Paris. Between 1679 and his death in 1681, Gaspar collaborated with Anselme Flamen. Unlike the earlier Marsy partnership, the two artists seem to have worked together on several large compositions, such as *Mars* (1679) and the *Victory of France over the Empire* (1680–81/2), both in the forecourts of the château of Versailles. It is known that Flamen, working from Marsy's models, completed the tomb of the Duc Anne de Noailles (1680/81–3, destr.) for the church of St Paul in Paris and the *Abduction of Orithyia by Boreas* (1677, 1684–7), a marble group for the gardens of Versailles (now Paris, Louvre).

BIBLIOGRAPHY

Lami; Souchal

Guillet de Saint-Georges: 'Gaspard et Balthazar Marsy', *Mémoires inédits. . .des membres de l'Académie Royale*, ed. L. Dussieux and others, 2 vols (Paris, 1854)

A. Parent: 'Un Tailleur d'images cambrésien: Jaspard Marsy', *Rev. N.*, vii (1921), pp. 249–57

F. Machelart: *Naissance et développement de l'art baroque en Cambrésis* (diss., U. Lille, 1977)

F. Souchal: 'De Cambrai à Versailles: Les Frères Marsy', *Rev. N.*, lxii (1980), pp. 383–413

T. Hedin: 'Exemple d'une collaboration d'artistes: The Partnership of Gaspard Marsy and Anselme Flamen (1679–1681)', *Gaz. B.-A.*, xcviii (1981), pp. 103–14

T. Hedin: *The Sculpture of Gaspard and Balthazard Marsy* (Columbia, 1983)

THOMAS F. HEDIN

Marsyas Painter. *See* VASE PAINTERS, §II.

Martanda. Temple site on a high plateau overlooking the Kashmir Valley, Jammu and Kashmir, India. The Surya Temple, built by the Karkota king Lalitaditya (*reg c.* AD 724–*c.* 760) is the earliest surviving Hindu temple in Kashmir. The main shrine, measuring some 19×11 m, stands on a high plinth in a rectangular colonnaded court (80.5×52 m) surrounded by 84 small shrines. This layout, together with the use of tall ribbed pillars and pilasters in the entrance porch and the repeated motif of a trefoil arch within a triangular pediment, gives a strong feeling of Bactrian Hellenistic influence. Indeed, the earlier Buddhist monasteries of the region were directly influenced by the architecture of Gandhara and Bactria, and the style remained current in both Buddhist and Hindu buildings in Kashmir until the 13th century AD (*see* INDIAN SUBCONTINENT, §III, 5(i)). The entire temple is built of large blocks of dressed grey limestone held together by mortar and dowels. The large entrance portico, where the once profuse decorations have nearly disappeared owing to the friability of the stone, is on the west. There is a small tank in front of the main shrine, and traces of foundations in the four corners of the court suggest that the temple originally formed a quincunx. The main shrine consists of a portico (Skt *ardhamaṇḍapa*), an entrance hall (*antarāla*) and a sanctum (*garbhagrha*). The roof is lost; however, the monumental triple doorway before the sanctum—consisting of a trilobate arch inside a tall triangular pediment standing on engaged pilasters—still exists. The design of this doorway is repeated in miniature on pilasters to either side and as large niches on two small shrines flanking the portico. Both the portico and the entrance hall are richly ornamented with carved images: the river goddesses Ganga and Yamuna are shown on both sides of the entrance hall, and standing, three-headed images of Vishnu wearing a three-pointed crown and a garland also appear (for a discussion of Vishnu and of Surya as the solar form of the deity, *see* INDIAN SUBCONTINENT, §II, 1). The insides of the trefoil arches of the portico and entrance hall are also decorated. The cells around the court are formed by columns and pilasters supporting tall pediments over trefoil arches; larger shrines are built into the centre of the northern and southern sides. The fluted columns stand on built-up bases and are crowned by small cushion motifs and capitals; their Hellenistic appearance is enhanced as the beams they support are ornamented with a dentil design.

BIBLIOGRAPHY

P. Brown: *Indian Architecture, Buddhist and Hindu Periods* (?Bombay [1941], rev. Bombay, 1956)

R. C. Kak: *Ancient Monuments of Kashmir* (New Delhi, 1971)

S. L. Huntington: *The Art of Ancient India: Buddhist, Hindu, Jain* (New York and Tokyo, 1985)

J. MARR

Martellange, Etienne [Ange, Etienne Martel] (*b* Lyon, 1568/9; *d* Paris, 3 Oct 1641). French architect, painter and draughtsman. He was the grandson of a painter of stained glass and son of a painter from Lyon, and he began his own career as a painter. Martellange trained in Italy from 1586 to 1587 with François Stella (1563–1605), and in 1590 he entered the Jesuit Order at Avignon, with the title of Pictor, taking his vows as a coadjutor brother at Chambéry in 1603; he was not, however, ordained a priest.

Martellange worked throughout France, producing architectural plans and some competent watercolour views of Jesuit establishments where work was in progress (e.g. *see* AVIGNON, fig. 1). Drawings and estimates were sent to the Jesuit Order in Rome and served as a basis for decisions by the leaders of the Order on the building projects in hand. From the study of his drawings (Paris, Bib. N.) it is possible to reconstruct a list of more than 20 Jesuit houses and colleges on which Martellange worked. His active career began in 1605–6 at Moulins (college) and Le Puy (church and college) and included the colleges at Carpentras (1607), Blois, Bourges and Chambéry, as well as work at Dijon (1611), Besançon, Dôle and Lyon (1609–19), where he also designed the church of the Trinity (1617–22). Martellange's college plans usually consisted of two or three rectangular courtyards with the church along one side of the court. The churches generally followed Italian Jesuit prototypes in having a nave with shallow recesses between the abutments of the transverse arches and galleries above. Ornament was minimal, his overriding concerns being economy and utility.

In 1625 Martellange's design for the Jesuit church of St Louis, Rue St Antoine, Paris, received endorsement from the authorities in Rome, and the foundation stone was laid in 1627. However, two years later he was replaced by François Derand in the continuing construction of the church and its façade, although Martellange's supporters thought Derand's design would weaken the church. Meanwhile, Martellange had begun work in 1628 on the chapel at Clermont College, Rue St Jacques, Paris, and from 1630 he designed and built the Jesuit noviciate (destr.) in the Rue Pot-de-Fer, which was completed in 1642. The church, and in particular the restrained classicism of its façade (copied from Giacomo della Porta's S Maria dei Monti in Rome), exerted considerable influence on French religious architecture in the 17th and 18th centuries and helped establish Martellange as one of the most important Jesuit architects in France.

BIBLIOGRAPHY
E. Charvet: *Etienne Martellange* (Lyon, 1874)
H. Bouchot: 'Notice sur la vie et les travaux d'Etienne Martellange', *Bib. Ecole Chartes*, xlvii (1886), pp. 17–52, 208–25
R. Blomfield: *A History of French Architecture*, 2 vols (London, 1911)
L. Hautecoeur: *Architecture classique* (1943–57), i, pp. 250–52; ii, pp. 940–49
P. Moisy: 'Martellange, Derand et le conflit du baroque', *Bull. Mnmtl*, cx (1952), p. 237
——: *Les Eglises des Jésuites de l'ancienne assistance de France* (Rome, 1958)
J. Vallery-Radot: *Le Recueil des plans d'édifices de la Compagnie de Jésus conservé à la Bibliothèque Nationale de Paris* (Rome, 1960)
——: 'Le Séjour de Martellange à Rome en 1586 et 1587', *Rev. Louvre* (1962), pp. 205–16
Saint-Paul-Saint-Louis: Les Jésuites à Paris (exh. cat., Paris, Carnavalet, 1985)

JEAN-PIERRE BABELON

Martelli. Italian family of patrons and collectors. Members of the family held important political positions in Florence, especially during the 15th century. One of their most important acts of patronage, recorded by Vasari, was the commissioning by Roberto Martelli (1408–64) of several sculptures from Donatello, including the famous statue of *St John the Baptist as a Youth* (*c*. 1455; Florence, Bargello). Although the accuracy of Vasari's information has been questioned, some recently discovered unpublished documents have enabled a partial confirmation of the attribution (see Civai, 1988–9, pp. 40–59; 1989). During the 16th century the family gave important commissions to Lorenzo di Credi, Giorgio Vasari I, Andrea Sansovino and Giovanni Francesco Rustici in connection with the decoration of family chapels in the basilica of S Lorenzo and the churches of S Frediano in Florence and S Agostino in Rome. In the 17th century the Martelli constructed their sumptuous chapel (1634–42) in the baroque church of SS Michele and Gaetano in Florence and created the nucleus of their picture gallery. During the 18th century the gallery was enriched with frequent acquisitions and became one of the outstanding private collections in Florence, one noted for the quality of its works and for the modernity of its taste (e.g. Domenico Beccafumi's *Cult of Vesta*; Florence, Pal. Martelli). The family has been extinct, in the main line, since 1986. Most of the painting collection is owned by the Seminario Arcivescovile di Firenze and is held at the Palazzo Martelli in Florence.

BIBLIOGRAPHY
G. Vasari: *Vite* (1550; rev. 2/1568); ed. G. Milanesi, ii, vi, vii (1878, 1881, 1881)
A. Civai: 'Donatello e Roberto Martelli: Nuove acquisizioni documentarie' *Donatello-Studien. Atti del convegno, Kunsthistorischen Institut in Florenz: Firenze 1986*, pp. 253–62
——: *Dipinti e sculture in casa Martelli: Storia di una collezione patrizia fiorentina dal quattrocento all'ottocento* (Florence, 1990)
——: 'La quadreria Martelli: L'allestimento tardosettecentesco alla luce di un catalogo figurato', *Stud. Stor. A.*, i/1 (1990), pp. 285–99

ALESSANDRA CIVAI

Martelli, Diego (*b* Florence, 28 Oct 1839; *d* Florence, 20 Nov 1896). Italian critic and patron. Born into an intellectual and liberal family, he studied natural sciences at the University of Pisa, intermittently, from 1856 to 1861. In 1855 his drawing teacher Annibale Gatti (1827–1909) introduced him to the Caffè Michelangiolo, where the politically and artistically radical members of the Florentine art world congregated. There he met and befriended the MACCHIAIOLI, becoming their dedicated supporter, patron, theorist and unflagging defender.

From 1861 he gathered his artist friends at his estate in Castiglioncello, on the coast near Livorno, where the group would often spend the summer sketching and painting. Regular visitors were Giuseppe Abbati (1836–68), Telemaco Signorini, Odoardo Borrani (1834–1905), Raffaello Sernesi (1838–66), Vincenzo Cabianca (1827–1902), Giovanni Fattori, Federico Zandomeneghi, Giovanni Boldini and the art dealer Luigi Pisani (1824–95). Martelli's friendship and patronage were particularly valuable to Abbati and Fattori, personally and professionally, throughout their lives.

In 1867 Martelli founded, directed and financed the *Gazzettino delle arti del disegno*, a short-lived weekly art journal, and in 1873 he co-founded *Il giornale artistico*, which ran for a similarly brief period. The *Gazzettino* was the vehicle for his championship of progressive art against academic conventionalism. It earned him an international reputation, for in 1869 he was commissioned to organize the biographies of contemporary Italian artists for the *Allgemeines Künstler-Lexikon* (Leipzig, 1872–85, 3 vols, letters A and B), for which he wrote five essays. As a critic he contributed to numerous journals and also lectured. His approach to art history was inspired by the theories of Pierre-Joseph Proudhon and Hyppolite Taine that art is a function of biological inheritance, environmental conditions and social evolution. Like them, he saw a correlation between greatness in art and its closeness to reality, with the artist playing the crucial role of intermediary. His interests encompassed European art movements and especially French painting, on which he wrote extensively. He took four trips to Paris. On his last one (1878–9), as correspondent to the Exposition Universelle of 1878 for several Italian journals, he met the protagonists and writers of the Impressionist movement and established links with Degas, Camille Pissarro and Manet. His assessment in various articles of the modernity that distinguished Degas and Manet from the other Impressionists demonstrates his perceptiveness as a critic. His lecture, 'Gli Impressionisti', delivered at the Circolo Filologico in Livorno after his return in 1879, holds a distinguished place in 19th-century Italian art criticism for its lucid exposition of the Impressionist scientific attitude and technique.

Martelli continued his championship of the Macchiaioli even when his financial situation became desperate, and in the 1880s he endeavoured to have paintings by Silvestro Lega and Sernesi included in the newly established Galleria Nazionale d'Arte Moderna in Rome. The biographical essays he wrote on Abbati, Adriano Cecioni, Giovanni Costa, Signorini and Lega constitute the first critical recognition of the works of the Macchiaioli. He ably captured the complexities of the artists' efforts and technical problems. His last major lecture, 'Romanticismo e Realismo nelle arti rappresentative' (1895), delivered as part of a series of lectures for the inauguration of the first Venice Biennale, distils his ideas on art and its history and reveals his knowledge and appreciation of contemporary Italian and French art, up to and including the Neo-Impressionists. His collection of just over a hundred paintings, etchings, drawings and sculptures, which he bequeathed to the city of Florence (Pitti), constitutes, together with the collection of Cristiano Banti (1824–1904), the largest public collection of Macchiaioli works in the world. His collected manuscripts, in four volumes (DXIII and DXIV), together with his correspondence, are held at the Biblioteca Marucelliana, Florence.

WRITINGS
Gazzettino delle arti del disegno (Florence, 1867/*R* 1968)
A. Boschetto, ed.: *Scritti d'arte di Diego Martelli* (Florence, 1952)
A. Marabottini and V. Quercioli, eds: *Diego Martelli: Corrispondenza inedita* (Rome, 1978)

BIBLIOGRAPHY
B. M. Bacci: *Diego Martelli, l'amico dei 'Macchiaioli'* (Florence, 1952)
P. Dini: *Diego Martelli* (Florence, 1978)
E. G. Calingaert: *Diego Martelli, a Man of the Twentieth Century in the 1800s: Art Criticism and Patronage in Florence, 1861–1896* (MA thesis, Washington, DC, American U., 1985)
N. Broude: *The Macchiaioli: Italian Painters of the Nineteenth Century* (New Haven and London, 1987)
EFREM GISELA CALINGAERT

Martens, Conrad (*b* London, 1801; *d* Sydney, 21 Aug 1878). Australian painter, lithographer and librarian of English birth. Son of a London merchant, he studied *c*. 1816 under Copley Fielding. His training was as a watercolourist and his most important works are watercolours, although he also produced paintings in oils. His early work displays the taste then current for the Picturesque. Francis Danby, David Cox and Turner were artists he admired. Martens left for India in 1832 or 1833 but at Montevideo joined Charles Darwin's expedition, replacing Augustus Earle as topographical draughtsman aboard the *Beagle*. The work strengthened his observation of detail and skill as a draughtsman. He left the expedition in October 1834 and, travelling via Tahiti and New Zealand, arrived in Sydney in April 1835. There he worked as a professional artist, in the 1840s and 1850s producing lithographic views of the Sydney area to augment his income. In 1863 he was appointed Parliamentary Librarian, which secured his finances. The skills he had acquired aboard the *Beagle* helped to gain him commissions to depict the estates around Sydney. However, his admiration for Turner, and with this the desire to elevate landscape as a subject, prompted him to subordinate line to mood in a Romantic treatment of the landscape. His thoughts were clearly stated in a lecture on landscape painting given in 1856 at the Australian Library, Sydney (see Smith, 1975). His ability in the handling of light and colour is evident in his watercolours of Sydney Harbour and the Blue Mountains. Martens did much to advance the English watercolour tradition in Australia, and he is regarded as one of the most important colonial watercolourists. His work is represented in all the Australian state galleries and in the Dixson Gallery of the State Library of New South Wales, Sydney.

BIBLIOGRAPHY
L. Lindsay: *Conrad Martens: The Man and his Art* (Sydney, 1920, rev. 2/1968)
B. Smith: *Place, Taste and Tradition: A Study of Australian Art since 1788* (Sydney, 1945, rev. Melbourne, 1979)
——: *European Vision and the South Pacific* (Oxford, 1960)
B. Smith, ed.: *Documents on Art and Taste in Australia: The Colonial Period, 1770–1914* (Melbourne, 1975), pp. 97–111
M. Holloway: 'Australian Landscape Painting', *Apollo*, cxviii (1983), pp. 245–51
ROSEMARY T. SMITH

Martens, Friedrich von (*b* Venice, 1809; *d* Paris, 1875). French printmaker and photographer. Of German origin, he lived most of his life in Paris and exhibited prints of city scenes and seascapes at the Salon from 1834 to 1848. Among his views of cities were those of Coblenz, Cologne, Frankfurt, Lausanne, Le Havre, Mainz, Orléans, Paris, Rouen, Stuttgart, Trieste and Venice. In 1845 he invented the first panoramic camera, called the Megaskop-Kamera or Panorama-Kamera, which used curved daguerreotype plates and had a visual angle of 150°. The lens was rotated to scan the desired scene; a curved plate was essential to minimize aberration, but made development of the plates difficult. Nevertheless he managed to produce a number of high quality panoramas, such as *Panoramic View of Paris from the Louvre* (1847; Rochester, NY, Int. Mus. Phot.). He gave a detailed account of his invention to the Académie des Sciences in Paris in June 1845. In 1851 he exhibited at the Great Exhibition in London a number of albumen prints of architectural views, for which he was awarded the Council Medal. In the early 1850s he took a number of panoramic views of the Alps using talbotypes instead of daguerreotypes. One of these taken of Mont Blanc, in 14 parts, was exhibited at the Exposition Universelle in Paris in 1855.

BIBLIOGRAPHY

J. M. Eder: *History of Photography* (New York, 1945), pp. 255–6, 329

A. Gernsheim and H. Gernsheim: *The History of Photography* (London, 1969), pp. 119, 196

□

Martial Potémont, Adolphe(-Théodore-Jules) (*b* Paris, 10 Feb 1828; *d* Paris, 14 Oct 1883). French printmaker and painter. He studied under Léon Cogniet and Félix Brissot de Warville (1818–92). His earliest known work is a series of 300 etchings of Paris, *Ancien Paris* (Paris, 1862–6). He then produced several series of prints depicting various contemporary aspects of the city, such as *Paris sous la Commune, Paris incendié, Les Femmes de Paris pendant le siège* and *Paris pendant le siège* (all Paris, 1871). His best works, however, are the delightful *Notes et lettres manuscrites* (Paris, 1867) and *L'Exposition universelle* (Paris, 1878), which describe the 1867 and 1878 exhibitions and are illustrated with his own lively drawings. In 1873 his book on etching, *Nouveau traité de la gravure à l'eau-forte pour les peintres et les dessinateurs*, was published in Paris. Among his few surviving paintings is the *Vue générale de la Ville de Paris* (Paris, Carnavalet).

BIBLIOGRAPHY

J. G. Grand-Carteret: *Les Moeurs et la caricature en France* (Paris, 1888)

F. L. Leipnik: *History of French Etching* (London, 1924)

ETRENNE LYMBERY

Martí Alsina, Ramón (*b* Barcelona, 10 Aug 1826; *d* Barcelona, 22 Dec 1894). Spanish Catalan painter. He enrolled when he was 14 in the Escuela de la Lonja, Barcelona, where he remained for 5 years. In 1848 he went to Paris, where the paintings of Eugène Delacroix and especially of Gustave Courbet influenced his work. Martí Alsina's *Sìesta*, with its realism that recalls Courbet, has often been called one of the most beautiful paintings of 19th-century Spain. Also significant are his paintings of the female nude, depicted without any romantic idealization and showing the effect of the passage of time on his models. His most important work, however, was as a landscape painter, and he has been seen as the creator of realistic Catalan landscapes. His studies from life of the countryside, woods and seascapes convey an optimistic view of nature. He also excelled in urban scenes, such as *View of Boulevard Clichy* (Barcelona, Col. Mata), which clearly anticipates the Impressionist movement.

BIBLIOGRAPHY

J. A. Gaya Nuño: *Arte del siglo XIX*, A. Hisp., xix (Madrid, 1966)

A. M. Arias de Cossio: *Pintura del neoclasicismo al modernismo* (Madrid, 1979)

JUAN NICOLAU

Martienssen, Rex (Distin) (*b* Queenstown, Cape Province, 26 Feb 1905; *d* Pretoria, 23 Aug 1942). South African architect and writer. He was appointed lecturer at the University of the Witwatersrand and an editor of the *South African Architectural Record* in 1932, both under G. E. Pearse's tolerant tutelage. For the next decade he dominated the School of Architecture and the journal, using them as levers to bring about an architectural revolution, which swept South Africa into the mainstream of the Modern Movement. He was the principal motivator of the small revolutionary cadre, and, with Gordon McIntosh and Norman Hanson, stood at the heart of that band of enthusiasts that Le Corbusier dubbed the 'Transvaal Group'. Martienssen's writing, a heady mixture of erudition and passionate advocacy, articulated the philosophy and provided the informational data base; his teaching enlightened and inflamed the younger generation. His friendship with Le Corbusier gave status and legitimization to the geographically and culturally isolated group.

Martienssen was a talented designer, but not a compulsive architect. His few buildings should be considered as teaching exemplars, which demonstrate an architectural point, rather than as the productive continuum of architectural practice. His short-lived association with John Fassler and Bernard Cooke (1934–5) produced some unexecuted projects and a few outstanding buildings, such as House Stern and Peterhouse, which were the enduring monuments of the period. Internationally recognized as a member of CIAM's executive, he also achieved acclaim as a Classical scholar with his *The Idea of Space in Greek Architecture* (pubd posthumously) and other writings. His own house in Johannesburg (1939–40), his last work, while Corbusian in its interior, revealed a search for classical serenity in its ordered façade.

WRITINGS

with W. G. McIntosh and N. L. Hanson, eds: *Zerohour* (Johannesburg, 1933)

'Constructivism and Architecture: A New Chapter in the History of Formal Building', *S. Afr. Archit. Rec.*, vii (1941), pp. 241–72

The Idea of Space in Greek Architecture: With Special Reference to the Doric Temple and its Setting (Johannesburg, 1956)

BIBLIOGRAPHY

N. L. Hanson and others: 'Rex Distin Martienssen: In Memoriam', *S. Afr. Archit. Rec.*, ii (1942) [special issue]

G. Herbert: *Martienssen and the International Style: The Modern Movement in South African Architecture* (Cape Town, 1975)

R. Lewcock: 'The Legacy of Martienssen', *Archit. Assoc. Q.*, ix/2–3 (1977)

GILBERT HERBERT

Martin (i). Swedish family of artists.

(1) Elias Martin (*b* Stockholm, *bapt* 8 March 1739; *d* Stockholm, 25 Jan 1818). Painter and engraver. After training in his father's joinery shop and with the painter Friedrich Schultz (1709–69), he was engaged to design ornamentation for ships of the coastal fleet at Sveaborg (Finland). There he also taught drawing to the son of Field Marshal Count Augustin Ehrensvärd (1710–72) while himself learning printmaking techniques from the Field Marshal. During this period Martin produced accurate studies of Finland's coastal scenery and the Sveaborg fortress (e.g. Stockholm, Nmus.), as well as purely imaginary landscapes based on engravings. In 1766 he went to

Paris and with Alexander Roslin's help was able to study under Joseph Vernet at the Académie Royale de Peinture et de Sculpture. A direct result of his studies was a *View of Paris from the Quay Beneath the Pont Neuf* (1766–7; Stockholm, Nmus.).

In 1768 Martin settled in London, and in 1769 he entered the Royal Academy of Arts as a student; by 1771 he was an Associate of the Academy. The influence of landscapes by Richard Wilson and Paul Sandby unleashed his potential as a colourist: *c.* 1772–3 he abandoned his method of first making an outline wash drawing and then colouring it; instead he intensified the brilliance and space-creating potential of colour by juxtaposing tints. His composition echoed that of Canaletto, with an often unbroken horizon and broad expanse of sky. In particular Martin recorded views of many country houses (e.g. *Pope's Villa at Twickenham*, 1773; Stockholm, Nmus.), and he made a major contribution to English landscape painting. He also executed caricatures (e.g. Stockholm, Nmus.), though eschewing Hogarth's satirical and moralizing attitude, and his everyday episodes are portrayed with great sympathy. His figure drawing was often made expressive by his calligraphic manner and distorted proportions (e.g. *The Two Murderers in Macbeth*, 1770s; Stockholm, Nmus.). Presumably Horace Walpole had this in mind when he accused Martin of poor draughtsmanship and also when he voiced doubts about his edition of engravings (1779), which were to serve as educational aids.

On his return to Stockholm in 1780 Martin was already a celebrity in his native Sweden. In 1781 he became a member of the Swedish Royal Academy of Fine Arts, and in 1785 he was appointed professor there. In 1788–91 he was again in Britain. Though his *View of Stockholm from Mosebacke* (*c.* 1795; Stockholm, Stadshuset) is one of his major works, he was a stranger to the pure townscape. He was fascinated more by the meeting of town and country-side that he found around Stockholm; ironworks were another common motif (e.g. *Ironworks at Österby or Söderfors*, pencil, grey wash and watercolour, after 1780; Stockholm, Nmus.). In the 1790s his Romantic landscapes became increasingly pantheistic, with a sublime treatment of light and darkness. Martin was the doyen of 18th-century Swedish landscape painters.

(2) Johan Fredric Martin (*b* Stockholm, *bapt* 8 June 1755; *d* Stockholm, 28 Sept 1816). Engraver and etcher, brother of (1) Elias Martin. In 1770 he joined his elder brother in London, where he learnt various printmaking techniques from Francesco Bartolozzi and assisted his brother. Back in Sweden (1780) Johan Fredric Martin worked more independently, producing, for example, a set of engraved portraits, the *Swedish Gallery* (1782–3; see Frölich, 1939). He did, however, continue to etch copies of his brother's landscape views in outline, which were then being hand-coloured. Aquatint versions of these prints were later published under the title *Swedish Views* (1805–12; see Berenfelt, 1965, p. 199, fig. 142).

BIBLIOGRAPHY
R. Hoppe: *Målaren Elias Martin* [The painter Elias Martin] (Stockholm, 1933)
H. Frölich: *Bröderna Elias och Johan Fredric Martins gravyrer* [The engravings of the brothers Elias and Johan Fredric Martin] (diss., U. Stockholm, 1939)
G. Berenfelt: *Svensk landskapskonst* (Stockholm, 1965)
U. Cederlöf: *Svenska teckningar 1700-talet* [Swedish drawings of the 18th century] (Stockholm, 1982) [with Eng. summary]
MAGNUS OLAUSSON

Martin (ii). English family of potters. The first Martin-ware, a hard, salt-glazed stoneware, was produced in 1873 at the Fulham Pottery, London. From 1877 to 1914 it was made at Southall, London. The four brothers—Robert Wallace Martin (*b* London, 4 May 1843; *d* London, 10 July 1923), Charles Douglas Martin (*b* London, Sept 1846; *d* London, June 1910), Walter Fraser Martin (*b* London, Oct 1857; *d* London, 8 March 1912) and Edwin Bruce Martin (*b* London, 25 Dec 1860; *d* London, 2 April 1915)—worked as a team, from the initial throwing to the eventual selling of the products from their shop at 16 Brownlow Street, High Holborn, London, which opened in 1878 but closed after a fire in 1903. Wallace modelled and threw the wares, Walter, the technician, was the glaze and clay specialist, Edwin was the decorator, and Charles managed both the business and the shop.

Prior to 1880 the wares were of simple and conventional form, such as vases, but the Martin tradition and name were built upon the production of grotesque and bizarre animal forms, for example the 'Martin birds' (examples in London, V&A), and jugs in the form of grotesque heads (examples in London, V&A). After 1900 the forms and decoration were simplified, influenced both by Japonisme (*see* ENGLAND, fig. 65) and Art Nouveau. The Martin brothers were among the forefront of studio potters in the late 19th century. Pitshanger Manor, London, has a renowned collection of Martinware.

BIBLIOGRAPHY
G. Godden: *British Pottery* (London, 1974)
M. Haslam: *Martin Brothers: Potters* (London, 1978)
JOHN MAWER

Martin (iii). English painters and sculptors. In 1930 (1) Kenneth Martin married Mary Balmford ((2) Mary Martin), with whom he formed an artistic partnership. Although they took different directions in the development of their artistic practices, they both worked consistently within the disciplines and conventions of Constructivism. With a small number of other British artists, such as Victor Pasmore and Anthony Hill, the Martins succeeded in developing a type of abstraction that was as radically different from the pre-war work of Ben Nicholson and the other artists associated with the manifesto *Circle* of 1937 as it was from contemporary lyrical abstraction, or Tachism, which flourished in France.

BIBLIOGRAPHY
Mary Martin, Kenneth Martin (exh. cat., ACGB, 1970)

(1) Kenneth Martin (*b* Sheffield, 13 April 1905; *d* London, 18 Nov 1984). He studied at the Sheffield School of Art (1921–3, 1927–9) and the Royal College of Art, London (1929–32). His early work was figurative, but he came to regard his emergence as an artist as dating from a series of carefully designed, abstract paintings of 1948–9, such as *Composition* (1949; London, Tate). He was later unwilling to show any of the earlier work, even in a retrospective context. His principal achievement, however, was in the field of constructions. From 1951 to 1967 he dedicated himself to renewing the tradition that had begun with the mobiles of Aleksandr Rodchenko and Alexander Calder. His own constructions, sometimes static and sometimes relying on natural or mechanical movement, were more exact and methodical than these earlier examples. Most often they made use of prefabricated metal components, arranged in spiralling structures, for example *Screw Mobile* (1956; Lisbon, Fund. Gulbenkian). The rigour and regularity of the construction was, however, offset by the unpredictable effects of light and ambiance. Many of these works were on a miniature scale, but during this period Martin also completed a number of successful public commissions, such as the *Fountain in Stainless Steel* (1961) for Brixton College of Further Education and the *Construction in Aluminium* (1967) for the Engineering Laboratory, Cambridge.

After his wife's death, Martin turned almost exclusively to painting. His first works in the *Chance and Order* series date from 1969; the series was to engage his attention for the next 15 years. He relied on the operation of chance, usually through throwing a die, to give him certain number sequences, which he then carefully plotted through structures of line on squared graph-paper. These initial drawings, which gave the number sequence as well as the resultant composition, were the basis of the larger paintings. This way of working is remarkable in that it enables others to retrace the stages through which the painting developed: Martin recognized this aspect by calling some of his last works *History Paintings*, that is, works that told their own history. At the same time the spectator's attention is concentrated on the brilliant pictorial qualities of the finished object. Martin did not believe in flat, 'hard-edge' painting but used the brush to enliven his surfaces and relieve them of any mechanical connotations. In this he was at variance with the tradition of Constructivist art associated with the Bauhaus, recalling instead the thickly worked surfaces of Malevich and, beyond them, Impressionist methods of evoking the presence of light.

Martin was a leading figure in the renewal of the Constructivist tradition in sculpture and painting. His influence as a teacher (1946–68) at Goldsmiths' College, London, and mentor for the succeeding generation of British Constructivist artists was considerable, and the clarity and cogency of his writings carried his distinctive ideas to a wider public, in Britain, Europe and the USA. His contribution to British art in the post-war period was recognized in the award of the OBE (1971), in his honorary doctorate of the Royal College of Art (conferred 1976) and in his receipt of the Midsummer Prize of the City of London (also 1976).

WRITINGS
'Construction from Within', *Structure*, vi/1 (1964), pp. 3–4; repr. in *The Tradition of Constructivism*, ed. S. Bann (New York, 1974/*R* 1990)
'Movement and Expression', *DATA: Directions in Art, Theory and Aesthetics*, ed. A. Hill (London, 1968), pp. 68–75
Chance and Order (London, 1979) [sixth William Townsend Memorial Lecture]

BIBLIOGRAPHY
Chance and Order: Drawings by Kenneth Martin (exh. cat., London, Waddington Gals, 1973)
Kenneth Martin, 2 vols (exh. cat., London, Tate, 1975) [incl. large selection of Martin's writings and essays by other artists and critics]
Kenneth Martin (exh. cat., New Haven, CT, Yale Cent. Brit. A., 1979)
Kenneth Martin: The Late Paintings (exh. cat., ACGB, 1985)

(2) Mary Martin [née Balmford] (*b* Folkestone, 16 Jan 1907; *d* London, 9 Oct 1969). Wife of (1) Kenneth Martin. She studied at Goldsmiths' School of Art (1925–9) and went on to the Royal College of Art (1929–32), where she met and in 1930 married Kenneth Martin. Like her husband, she set little store by her early work; she dated her career as an artist from 1950, when she painted her first abstract pictures.

The influence of the American painter and relief-maker Charles Biederman was important to Mary Martin at this stage. From 1951 she worked almost exclusively with constructed reliefs. However, she saw her own work as a process of 'building' rather than 'abstracting', as Biederman did. By 1955 she had learnt to use a variety of industrial materials, including perspex, formica and stainless steel. Her sureness of touch in combining these different materials was as apparent in *Perspex Group on Orange (E)* (1967; Exeter, Royal Albert Mem. Mus.) as in her last works in stainless steel, formica and wood, of which one characteristic example, *Cross* (1968; Liverpool, Walker A.G.), was joint winner of the first prize in the John Moores Liverpool Exhibition, held a month after her death. The logic of her structures likewise followed quite simple progressions and permutational patterns. Her work was most often small in scale and intimate in its effect. However, she demonstrated how successfully she was able to work on an environmental scale in a number of imaginative commissions, such as the *Wall Construction* (1969) for the University of Stirling.

WRITINGS
'Reflections', *DATA: Directions in Art, Theory and Aesthetics*, ed. A. Hill (London, 1968), pp. 95–100

BIBLIOGRAPHY
Mary Martin (exh. cat., London, Tate, 1984)

STEPHEN BANN

Martin V, Pope. *See* COLONNA, (1).

Martin, Agnes (Bernice) (*b* Maklin, Sask., 22 March 1912). American painter of Canadian birth. She grew up in Vancouver and moved to the USA in 1932, taking American citizenship in 1940. She began making art in the early 1940s, while living in New York, where she studied at Columbia University (1941–2, 1951–2) and intermittently in New Mexico, where she studied briefly at the University of New Mexico at Albuquerque (1946–7), also teaching painting there from 1947 to 1948. She returned to New York in 1957, living in Coenties Slip, two blocks of artists' lofts near South Ferry, where she met other painters such as Ellsworth Kelly, Jack Youngerman (*b* 1926), Robert Indiana and James Rosenquist while basically living a reclusive life.

Martin held her first one-woman exhibition at the Betty Parsons Gallery in New York in 1958. She constructed her paintings on a rational grid system, superimposing a network of pencilled lines and later coloured bands on fine-grained canvas stained with washes of colour in such a way as to reconcile these apparently antithetical elements. Often the impression is conveyed that the colour is floating off the canvas, with the delicately drawn pencil marks hovering within the edges of the canvas but not quite touching them, as in *White Flower* (1960; New York,

Guggenheim) or *Morning* (1965; London, Tate). These paintings were influential on the development of MINIMALISM in the USA, especially on the wall drawings executed in coloured pencils by Sol LeWitt, although Martin regarded her use of grids as a development from the 'all-over' compositional methods of Abstract Expressionism. She persistently rejected the suggestion that her paintings were conceived in response to the landscape of New Mexico, where she settled again in 1967 and where she chose to work most of her life.

From 1967 Martin concentrated on writing, but when she returned to painting in 1974 she continued refining the idiom that she had established in the early 1960s, favouring geometric structures of uniform bands of evanescent colour in works such as *Untitled Number 3* (1974; New York, Pace Gal.; see 1977 exh. cat., p. 16). Her convictions about the emotive content of her work, underlying its apparent reticence and austerity of form, were cogently expressed in a lecture, 'We Are in the Midst of Reality Responding with Joy', delivered at Yale University, New Haven, CT, in 1976 (printed in full in 1977 exh. cat., pp. 17–39).

WRITINGS

D. Schwarz, ed.: *Writings/Schriften* (Winterthur, 1992)

BIBLIOGRAPHY

Agnes Martin (exh. cat., foreword S. Delehanty; essay L. Alloway; Philadelphia, U. PA, Inst. Contemp. A., 1973) [with texts by artist]

L. Alloway: 'Agnes Martin,' *Artforum*, xii/4 (1973), pp. 32–7

Agnes Martin: Paintings and Drawings 1957–1975 (exh. cat., essay D. Ashton; ACGB, 1977) [with essay by artist]

Agnes Martin (exh. cat. by B. Haskell, A. C. Chave and R. Krauss, New York, Whitney, 1992) [with selected writings by artist]

KLAUS OTTMANN

Martin, David (*b* Anstruther, Fife, 1737; *d* Edinburgh, 1798). Scottish painter and engraver. He was a pupil of Allan Ramsay from *c.* 1752; in 1755 he joined Ramsay in Rome, where he remained for over a year, studying under the patronage of Robert Alexander, an Edinburgh banker. On Ramsay's return to Britain, Martin worked for him in London until 1775, painting most of the drapery work during the early and middle 1760s. By 1766, when he engraved Ramsay's portrait of *Jean Jacques Rousseau* (Edinburgh, N.G.), he was earning over £300 a year as assistant and copyist. He began his independent practice while still engaged in Ramsay's studio: his finest early portrait is that of *Benjamin Franklin* (1767; Washington, DC, White House Col.); it is informal and intimate, and it was described by Horace Walpole as 'a great likeness'. Although Martin's preferred format was three-quarter length, in the late 1770s he attempted full-lengths of *Henry, 2nd Earl Bathurst* (Oxford, Balliol Coll.), and *William, 1st Earl of Mansfield* (Scone Pal., Tayside).

After Ramsay's death in 1784 Martin settled in Edinburgh, where he established himself as the leading Scottish portrait painter, until Henry Raeburn superseded him in the late 1790s. In 1791 Martin was chosen, in preference to Raeburn, to paint *Sir James Pringle of Stitchell* (Edinburgh, Archers' Hall), the President of the Royal Company of Archers; but the younger artist was already a serious rival, and there is evidence in some of Martin's later works, such as *Provost Murdoch of Glasgow* (*c.* 1790; Glasgow, A.G. & Mus.) of stylistic borrowing from Raeburn,

particularly in the freer, bolder handling. Martin's early style depends heavily on Ramsay, and his grander compositions derive from Joshua Reynolds.

BIBLIOGRAPHY

H. Walpole: *Anecdotes of Painting in England* (1762–71); ed. R. N. Wornum (1849)

A. Smart: *The Life and Art of Allan Ramsay* (London, 1952)

D. Irwin and F. Irwin: *Scottish Painters at Home and Abroad, 1700–1900* (London, 1975)

D. Macmillan: *Scottish Art, 1460–1990* (London, 1990)

DAVID RODGERS

Martin, Edgar. *See under* SCHMIDT, GARDEN & MARTIN.

Martin, Etienne. *See* ETIENNE-MARTIN.

Martin, Fredrik (Robert) (*b* Stockholm, 8 May 1868; *d* Cairo, 13 April 1933). Swedish diplomat, scholar, collector and dealer. In 1884 he became assistant at the ethnographical museum in Stockholm, and by 1890 he was assistant at the archaeological museum. He combined his interests in ethnography and archaeology on a visit to Siberia (1891–2), publishing his findings in *L'Age du bronze au Musée de Minoussinsk*. He then turned to Islamic art, travelling widely and collecting in Russia, the Caucasus, Central Asia, Egypt and Turkey. He began to acquire Islamic book paintings at Bukhara in 1894 and in the following year sold 387 oriental manuscripts to the University Library at Uppsala. In the winter of 1896 he excavated at Fustat (Old Cairo), returning with several thousand ceramic fragments. In 1897 he exhibited his collection at Stockholm. About this time he formed the opinion that manuscripts had been the chief disseminators of ornamental motifs in the Islamic world. From 1903, when he was attached to the Swedish Embassy in Istanbul as dragoman, he acquired a number of precious manuscripts and albums, and he also probably formed in these years a collection of etchings of views of Istanbul, portraits of sultans and political pictures that went to Lund University. He published *A History of Oriental Carpets before 1800*, an important study that brought attention to examples in Swedish collections, and was the first to use depictions of carpets in Islamic paintings for dating purposes. He was involved with the Munich exhibition of Islamic art in 1910 and contributed to the catalogue. His interest in the arts of the book culminated in *The Miniature Painting and Painters of Persia, India and Turkey*, which emphasized the achievement of Persian painting in the 15th century. His collection was exhibited at the Victoria and Albert Museum, London in 1924.

WRITINGS

L'Age du bronze au Musée de Minoussinsk (Stockholm, 1893)

A History of Oriental Carpets before 1800 (Vienna, 1906–8)

The Miniature Painting and Painters of Persia, India and Turkey (London, 1912)

Lustre on Glass and Pottery in Egypt from the Period of Hadrian to Saladin (Faenza, 1929)

SBL

BIBLIOGRAPHY

T. J. Arne: 'Fredrik Martin', *Fornvännen*, iii (1935), pp. 129–36 [with bibliog. of Martin's writings]

S. J. VERNOIT

Martin, Henri(-Jean-Guillaume) (*b* Toulouse, 5 Aug 1860; *d* La Bastide-du-Vert, Lot, Nov 1943). French painter. After winning the Grand Prix at the Ecole des

Beaux-Arts in Toulouse, he moved to Paris (1879) to study at the Ecole des Beaux-Arts there under Jean-Paul Laurens, who encouraged his interest in Veronese and other Venetian painters. The literary inspiration of his early work was reflected in such paintings as *Paolo de Malatesta and Francesca da Rimini in Hell* (1883; Carcassonne, Mus. B.-A.) based on Dante, for which he won a medal at the Salon of 1883. During his subsequent study in Rome, however, on a fellowship awarded to him at the Salon, he was attracted both by the brilliant Italian light and by the paintings of Giotto and his contemporaries.

On his return to Paris (1889), Martin experimented with pointillism, which he sometimes applied to allegorical subjects, for example *Festival of the Federation* (1899; Toulouse, Mus. Augustins). In the 1890s his work showed links with Symbolism and the themes of dreams and reverie. A Baudelairean pessimism fills such paintings as *To Each his Chimera* (1891; Bordeaux, Mus. B.-A.), *Man between Vice and Virtue* (1892) and *Towards the Abyss* (1892; both Toulouse, Mus. Augustins); for his idealized images of women as nymphs or muses, for example *Muse* (*c.* 1898; Paris, Mus. A. Déc.), the ethereal figures were literally dematerialized by the use of a pointillist technique. He exhibited eight paintings in the first Salon de la Rose+Croix (1892), the acclaimed showcase for mystical art.

Parallel with his production of small oil paintings, Martin worked on large-scale decorative commissions including a series of decorative panels for the Salle des Illustrés in the Capitole of Toulouse, followed by murals for the new Hôtel de Ville in Paris (1895–6). In the latter, particularly in his treatment of Apollo and the muses in the Salle d'Introduction, he combined official portraits with allegorical figures in a dreamy landscape that incorporated pointillist brushwork and techniques of academic drawing. These idyllic themes culminated in *Serenity* (1898; Paris, Mus. d'Orsay), a large easel painting. After 1900 Martin employed allegory in his murals only within the context of a celebration of nature, as in *Mowers* (1903; Toulouse, Capitole), in which the sun-drenched fields and the brilliant vegetation of the Midi were praised for their representation of the timelessness of ordinary labour and humanity's harmonious co-existence with nature. The triptych format alludes to the interrelationship between the cycle of the seasons and the passage of man's life, a popular theme at the end of the 19th century.

Martin was much in demand as a muralist in the early 1900s, and he was cited by some as heir to Puvis de Chavannes. His work includes panels in the Mairie of the 10e arrondissement, Paris; the Hôtel Terminus, Lyon; La Caisse d'Epargne, Marseille (1904); and the Sorbonne (1908), the Palais Royal (1914) and the Conseil d'Etat (1922) in Paris.

BIBLIOGRAPHY
L. Bénédite: 'La Lyre et les muses par Henri Martin', *A. & Déc.*, i (1900), pp. 1–10
A. Ségard: *Peintres d'aujourd'hui: Les Décorateurs*, ii (Paris, 1914), pp. 3–58
J.-R. de Brousse: 'Henri Martin', *A. Méridional*, 41 (1939), pp. 4-5
French Symbolist Painters, (exh. cat. by P. Jullian, A. Bowness and G. Lacambre, London, Hayward Gal., 1972), pp. 71–3
Autour de Lévy-Dhurmer (exh. cat., Paris, Grand Pal., 1973), pp. 66–8
R. Pincus-Witten: *Occult Symbolism in France* (New York, 1976), pp. 131–2
T. Greenspan: *'Les Nostalgiques' Re-examined: The Idyllic Landscape in France, 1890–1905* (diss., New York, City U., 1981), pp. 288–301

TAUBE G. GREENSPAN

Martin, Homer Dodge (*b* Albany, NY, 28 Oct 1836; *d* St Paul, MN, 12 Feb 1897). American painter. He was largely self-taught, although he studied briefly with James MacDougal Hart and was encouraged by Erastus Dow Palmer. He specialized in scenes of Lake George, Lake Ontario and the Adirondacks in New York State. These are depictions of the wilderness, exclusive of figures, in the realistic manner of the Hudson River school, for example *Upper Ausable Lake* (1868; Washington, DC, N. Mus. Amer. A.). There are preliminary pencil sketches for several early oil paintings.

After 1876, when Martin first visited England and became casually acquainted with Whistler, his painting style became looser and more preoccupied with colour. It was at this time that he started working in watercolour. In the early 1880s he spent four years in France, settling in the Normandy coast near Trouville. Martin returned to America in 1886, where he painted French, Adirondack and Newport landscapes from memory as his eyesight was failing. In 1893 his work was exhibited at the Chicago Columbian Exposition. His best landscapes are the *Harp of the Winds* (1895; New York, Met.) and *Adirondack Scenery* (1895; New York, priv. col., see Mandel, 1973, *Archv Amer. A. J.*, fig. 3).

BIBLIOGRAPHY
E. G. D. Martin: *Homer Martin: A Reminiscence* (New York, 1904)
F. J. Mather jr: *Homer Martin: Poet in Landscape* (New York, 1912)
D. H. Carroll: *Fifty-eight Paintings by Homer D. Martin* (New York, 1913)
P. C. F. Mandel: *Homer Dodge Martin: American Landscape Painter, 1836–1897* (diss., New York U., 1973)
——: 'The Stories behind Three Important Late Homer D. Martin Paintings', *Archv Amer. A. J.*, xiii/3 (1973), pp. 2–8

PATRICIA C. F. MANDEL

Martin, Jean (*d* 1553). French writer, translator and diplomat. He was secretary, first to Massimiliano Sforza, Duke of Milan, and then in 1530 to Robert, Cardinal de Lenoncourt. He was renowned as a popularizer in France of Italian Renaissance architecture. To disseminate this new style he translated, into French, the Italian and Latin treatises of Serlio (Books I and II, 1545), Vitruvius (1547) and Alberti (1553) and such works as Colonna's *Hypnerotomachia Poliphili* (1546). Martin rendered into French the Latin funerary oration for Francis I and collaborated with JEAN GOUJON and Jean Cousin (i) on organizing the decorations for the triumphal entry of Henry II into Paris (1549). It is not certain whether he ever visited Italy. He is known to have frequented humanist circles, where his friends included Serlio, who supervised the translations of his works. As a writer Martin was admired by his contemporaries, among them Joachim Du Bellay, and by Ronsard, who wrote a Pindaric ode in his honour and also an epitaph, which appeared posthumously in Martin's edition of Alberti's work on architecture.

Martin's translations were lauded in his own time, as witness Jean Bullant in the preface to Alberti: 'Translated by Jean Martin, Parisian, to whom is due great praise for the studies of architecture, for having clarified and put in our language so excellent a book and many others from which one can derive great pleasure'. Posterity has been less kind, especially concerning the Vitruvius translation (in which the portrait on the title-page in the edition illustrated by Jean Goujon may be of *Jean Martin*). In his *Holomètre* (1555), the mathematician Abel Foullon challenged Martin's authorship of the translation, and successive translators, such as Jean Guardet and Dominique Bertin (1559) and Claude Perrault (1673), criticized Martin's errors, his lack of literary style and his insufficient understanding of architectural terminology. The ultimate blow was delivered by François Blondel (1673), who thought the translation of Vitruvius less intelligible than the original text. Although acknowledged to be lacking in literary or scientific value, Martin's translations were nevertheless important in educating the artisan/worker class, providing both theories and practical information on building methods.

BIBLIOGRAPHY
P. Marcel: *Jean Martin* (Paris, 1898, rev. 1927)

NAOMI MILLER

Martin, Jean-Baptiste [Martin des Batailles] (*b* Paris, 1659; *d* Paris, 1735). French painter. According to Pierre-Jean Mariette, he trained in the studio of Laurent de La Hyre (1606–56). There the Marquis de Vauban noticed his skill in making accurate drawings of plans and elevations of fortified sites and introduced him to the battle painter ADAM FRANS VAN DER MEULEN, who from 1664 was employed by Louis XIV, mainly to paint scenes commemorating Louis's military triumphs, many of which were used as tapestry designs. He quickly became van der Meulen's closest and chief collaborator. Indeed, the closeness of collaboration between the master and his pupils created a homogeneous style, in which the hand of the individual is difficult to determine. On van der Meulen's death (1690), Martin and Sauveur Lecomte (?1659–95) were ordered to complete the series of twelve paintings showing the *King's Conquests*, seven of which were still unfinished. On Lecomte's premature death in 1695, he was replaced by another of van der Meulen's pupils, Pierre-Denis Martin (Martin *le jeune*; *c.*?1663–1742), who is generally assumed, without evidence, to have been Jean-Baptiste Martin's nephew. By 1699 the two Martins had completed the series, and the paintings were installed at the château of Marly (destr.). Martin had meanwhile acted as official artist on Louis XIV's campaigns in the Dauphiné (1688–9), and in the sieges of Mons (1691) and Namur (1692). In 1710 he was commissioned by Leopold, Duke of Lorraine (*reg* 1698–1729), to create a series of cartoons depicting the life of his father, Charles V, nominal Duke of Lorraine; the *Victories of Charles V* (1711–18; Vienna, Ksthist. Mus.; *see* FRANCE, fig. 93) were woven in Nancy. Later Jean-Baptiste Martin and Pierre-Denis Martin were among the 12 artists employed in the decoration of the hôtel belonging to the Duc de Bourbon, Grand Maître de la Maison du Roi, at Versailles, which was overseen by the architect Robert de Cotte. Each provided two large and two small views of royal palaces (now Versailles, Château and Mairie; *see* VERSAILLES, fig. 3). Jean-Baptiste's son, also called Jean-Baptiste Martin (*d* after 1741), completed the *Siege of Mons* and the *Siege of Namur* (both Versailles, Château) after his father's death.

Jal; Mariette

BIBLIOGRAPHY
J.-L. Bordeaux: 'L'Hôtel du Grand Maître à Versailles', *Gaz. B.-A.*, n. s. 5, civ (1984), pp. 113–26
P. Guerra: 'Mons et Namur, tableaux des Conquestes du Roy', *Rev. Hist. Versailles*, lxix (1985), pp. 35–46
L. C. Starcky: *Paris, Mobilier national: Dessins de van der Meulen et de son atelier*, Inventaire des collections publiques françaises, 33 (Paris, 1988)

□

Martin, John (*b* Haydon Bridge, Northumb., 19 July 1789; *d* Douglas, Isle of Man, 17 Feb 1854). English painter and printmaker. Known as 'Mad Martin', he was one of England's most significant 19th-century painters of sublimely Romantic themes. Many of his canvases are extremely large in scale, which enhances their tremendous visual impact. He often made prints, notably mezzotints, from his paintings.

1. BEFORE 1815. His career as a painter began in 1803 when he was apprenticed to a coachmaker in Newcastle upon Tyne shortly after his parents moved there. In 1804 he became a pupil of Boniface Moss or Musso, an Italian painter originally from Piemonte, who gave him lessons in drawing and painting. In 1805 he went to London to work with Musso's son, Charles Muss [Musso] (1779–1824), a ceramics painter. Finding that Muss was unemployed, Martin began to support himself by selling drawings of views of his native Northumberland until, in 1807, he was finally taken on by Muss in a new glass- and ceramics-painting business. Muss went bankrupt in 1809, but both he and Martin were employed by William Collins, who owned a well-established glass-painting studio in the Strand, London. Here he spent the hours after work 'sitting up at night till 2 or 3 o'clock ... acquiring that knowledge of perspective which has since been so valuable to me' (Martin, p. 176). He realized that his best chance of a successful artistic career was as a painter of serious subjects. His first oils, small in scale, were classical landscapes inspired by Claude and date from about 1807 (e.g. *Classical Landscape with Ruined City*, priv. col., see Feaver, p. 14). They constitute a conventional looking-back at the paintings of the Old Masters, an accepted norm at that period, but they also echo the 'elegant pastorals' of the *Liber Studiorum* (London, 1807–19), a series of prints after Turner's paintings, which started appearing at about this time and which could have influenced Martin in his choice and handling of subject. It was not until 1810 that he sent *Clytie* (priv. col., see Feaver, p. 23), a substantial work in a similar vein, to the exhibition of the Royal Academy. The painting was, however, rejected, but when Martin left Collins's workshop in late 1811 after a dispute with his colleagues, he was able to devote his energies exclusively to painting pictures that he hoped would be successful at the Academy.

With *Sadak in Search of the Waters of Oblivion* (St Louis, MO, A. Mus.), in which the tiny figure of the hero struggles in a craggy, volcanic landscape that threatens to overwhelm him, Martin arrived at a formula that he was to exploit throughout the rest of his career. The painting was well-received when it was shown at the Academy in 1812. It was sold after the exhibition and launched his career as a major artist. For the next four years he exhibited paintings with classical and biblical themes and populated with minute figures (e.g. *Adam's First Sight of Eve*, 1812; Glasgow, A.G. & Mus.). Also from this period are a number of small *plein-air* oils of landscapes of London and its environs (e.g. *Distant View of London*, 1815; Glasgow, A.G. & Mus.). Technically, he lacked the painterly skills that were a highly regarded feature of British painting at the time. His colours in these works tend to be rather cold and the handling hard, qualities that characterize all of his oil paintings.

2. 1815 AND AFTER. His early training in commercial art led to an interest in printmaking and publishing. He learnt to etch and his earliest-known print in this medium—*Classical City* (e.g. New Haven, CT, Yale Cent. Brit. A.)—is dated 1816. As with his paintings, the theme was inspired by the example of Claude and shows a view of a city framed by a repoussoir of trees. In it, he employed his virtuoso technique of perspective for the first time and coupled it with the repetition of accurately delineated architectural motifs in order to draw the viewer into the picture, a treatment that was to become the hallmark of his art. His method of underpinning pictorial narrative added novelty and authenticity to the genre of history painting and provided spectators with an immediately comprehensible sense of the sublime. His first real success with this technique was the large canvas *Joshua Commanding the Sun to Stand Still upon Gideon* (1.49×2.31 m, London, The United Grand Lodge of England), exhibited first at the Royal Academy in 1816 and then at the British Institution in 1817. His first commercial venture—seven etchings issued under the title of *Characters of Trees*—was

published in London in that year. He was also commissioned to make a number of views, later etched and privately published (n.p., *c.* 1818), of the newly completed Sezincote (*c.* 1805) in Gloucestershire. The house and its grounds, designed by Samuel Pepys Cockerell with Humphry Repton and Thomas Daniell, were among the first examples in Britain of the taste for Indian design. Martin's contact with it provided him with a source of exotic images that frequently recur in later works.

He achieved his greatest critical and financial success with *Belshazzar's Feast* (1821; priv. col.; see fig.). Using descriptions from the Bible and information from available archaeological research as his sources, he depicted a view of the palace of Belshazzar, a Babylonian king, and by showing the disposition of the moon and planets he created a sense of the precise moment of his destruction, which had an element of historical truth about it. Constable called it a 'pantomime', yet over a period of about six months, more than 50,000 people paid to see it at the British Institution. A solo show of his paintings at the Egyptian Hall in Piccadilly in 1822 was only a partial success.

Thereafter he devoted much of his time to the making and publishing of prints, mostly mezzotints, after his works (*see also* MEZZOTINT, §2). In all, he designed and engraved more than 130 prints, of which just over 100 were mezzotints. He first used this medium in *c.* 1824, and with its particular ability to convey rich contrasts of light and shade it was ideally suited to his dramatic subject-matter. His skill in manipulating mezzotint places him among the greatest of all 19th-century printmakers. He

John Martin: *Belshazzar's Feast*, oil on canvas, 1.60×2.49 m, 1821 (private collection)

engraved subjects taken mostly from the Bible or from Milton, as with his series of illustrations for *Paradise Lost* (2 vols, London, 1827), and these were issued either as large separate plates or as smaller prints that were issued in parts. His most ambitious project was *Illustrations to the Bible* (London, 1831–5), though only half of the proposed 40 works were published. The relatively high cost of his work, and the regular infringement of his copyright by imitators, affected both the publication of this series and his printmaking career in general, and by the late 1830s had brought about financial ruin.

Martin also devoted a great deal of his time to projects, the visionary nature of which rivalled the subject-matter of his grand historical and biblical canvases. The most notable of these involved a proposed embankment for the Thames and a plan to improve London's water supply and its sewers; none of these ideas was realized. During the 1830s and 1840s he continued to paint large canvases, including the *Coronation of Queen Victoria* (2.38×1.85 m, 1839; London, Tate). As his strength waned he increasingly turned to small-scale works, producing a remarkable series of highly poetical watercolours of the valley of the River Wye (e.g. the *Wye near Chepstow*, 1844; UK, priv. col.). In his last years (1851–3) he did three paintings representing the *Last Judgement* (e.g. the *Great Day of His Wrath*, c. 1853; London, Tate).

WRITINGS

'Mr. John Martin', *Illus. London News* (17 March 1849), p. 176

BIBLIOGRAPHY

M. L. Pendred: *John Martin, Painter: His Life and Times* (London, 1923)
T. Balston: *John Martin, 1789–1854* (London, 1947)
W. Feaver: *The Art of John Martin* (Oxford, 1975)
'*Darkness Visible': The Prints of John Martin* (exh. cat. by J. Wees with M. Campbell, Williamstown, MA, Clark A. Inst.; Lawrence, U. KS, Spencer Mus. A.; Oberlin Coll., OH, Allen Mem. A. Mus.; 1986–7)
John Martin, 1789–1854: 'Belshazzar's Feast', 1820 (exh. cat. by R. Hamlyn, London, Tate, 1989)
John Martin: Visionary Printmaker (exh. cat. by M. Campbell, York, C.A.G., 1992)

ROBIN HAMLYN

Martin, Sir (John) Leslie (*b* Manchester, 17 Aug 1908). English architect, theorist and teacher. After graduating from the School of Architecture, University of Manchester, in 1930, he joined the teaching staff there until becoming Head of the School of Architecture, Hull, from 1934 to 1939.

In 1933 he set up in private practice, subsequently designing the nursery school (1937–8), Northwich, and the Morton House (1937–9), Brampton, which were tentative examples of Modern Movement architecture in England. In 1935 he married the architect Sadie Speight, who became a lifelong collaborator. In 1937 he was co-editor, with Ben Nicholson and Naum Gabo, of *Circle: International Survey of Constructive Art*, which attempted to define common preoccupations of Constructivist painters, sculptors and architects on a European scale. In 1939 his work entered a new phase when he was engaged by the London, Midland and Scottish Railway Company, and from 1949 to 1956 he worked for the London County Council (LCC). With the LCC he led the design team working under Robert Matthew on the Royal Festival Hall (1948–51; *see* LONDON, fig. 10). The final design of the building reflected the process of overcoming problems connected with the limited site and high levels of soundproofing required for a concert hall. Succeeding to the post of Architect to the LCC in 1953, Martin organized his department into a highly productive professional team of great integrity, whose work was influential internationally.

In 1956 the third phase of Martin's career began, when he was appointed the first Professor of Architecture at the University of Cambridge and also established a private practice at nearby Great Shelford. He began to design a series of university buildings during the 1950s and 1960s, in which his prime concern was to reflect the general cultural and technical context of the time. The results were integrated, well-finished ensembles using traditional materials in low-rise configurations. Examples include College Hall (from 1956; with Trevor Dannatt), Knighton, University of Leicester, and, with Colin St John Wilson and others, Harvey Court (from 1958), Gonville and Caius College, Cambridge; the William Stone Building (from 1960), Peterhouse, Cambridge; the University Library Buildings (from 1959), Manor Road, Oxford; and the first British Museum Library project (1962; unexecuted), London. In the 1970s Martin also established the Centre for Land Use and Built Form Studies (now Martin Centre), Cambridge. Here, with Lionel March, he explored architectural design as a rational process, in which the final artistic expression was logically entailed by determining factors such as function and context. He also helped to promote a reassessment of the prevailing concepts of high-rise, high-density occupancy, and to argue for a more efficient and more humane standard in housing policies. He was among the first to demonstrate conclusively that tall buildings can make uneconomical use of land in certain circumstances.

By the time Martin left the University of Cambridge in 1972, the department of architecture had been transformed from a small academic teaching unit into an outstanding institution. Notable buildings of Martin's later career include the Music School (from 1974; with Ivor Richards), at the University of Cambridge, where the plan reflected the need for a stage-by-stage building process. Smaller scale works, such as Kettles Yard Gallery (from 1969; with David Owers), Cambridge, demonstrate the application of Martin's design principles at a domestic scale. He was Slade Professor of Fine Arts at the University of Oxford from 1965 to 1966 and subsequently a visiting professor of architecture at Yale University from 1973 to 1974. He was knighted in 1957 and received the RIBA Gold Medal in 1973.

WRITINGS

ed., with B. Nicholson and N. Gabo: *Circle: International Survey of Constructive Art* (London, 1937/*R* 1971)
ed., with S. Speight: *The Flat Book* (London, 1939)
'An Architect's Approach to Architecture', *RIBA J.*, lxxiv/5 (1967), pp. 191–200
ed., with L. March: *Urban Space and Structures* (Cambridge, 1972)
'Notes on a Developing Architecture', *Archit. Rev.* [London], clxiv/977 (1978), pp. 10–17
Buildings and Ideas, 1933–83: From the Studio of Leslie Martin and his Associates (Cambridge, 1983)

BIBLIOGRAPHY

T. Stephens: 'The Third Force in English Architecture', *Archit. Des.*, xxxv (1965), pp. 429–48

MICHAEL SPENS

Martin, Mungo [Nakapenkem: 'Eight Times a Chief'] (*b* Fort Rupert, BC, *c*.1879; *d* 16 Aug 1962). Native Canadian Kwakiutl chief and sculptor. As a child he exercised his dexterity with a knife and adze, was apprenticed to CHARLIE JAMES and learnt the traditional values and totemic skills of Kwakiutl culture (see fig.). He married Abayah (Tlakawakilayokwai), and the two united effectively in their efforts to preserve the fast disappearing traditional way of life of the Kwakiutl people. In 1921 the Canadian government launched a drive against the potlatch (a rank confirmation ceremony in which goods are distributed as gifts and sometimes also deliberately destroyed) and seized the bulk of the tribe's inherited possessions, jailing many of the people who had participated. A reversal of the policy in the late 1940s made a dramatic change in native life, and Martin was invited in 1950 to oversee the restoration programme at the University of British Columbia, a responsibility he eagerly accepted. He and his wife guided this renaissance in native arts and culture for many years, working at Thunderbird Park, Victoria, until his death. Not only a master sculptor, Martin was also an outstanding teacher and tribal historian. One of his major creations was the 39 m-high Beacon Hill pole, one of the tallest extant. He was also commissioned to carve a ceremonial pole honouring the centennial visit of Queen Elizabeth II in 1958; this is 30.48 m tall and stands in Thunderbird Park. Martin drowned tragically in 1962.

For general discussion of 20th-century developments in Native North American art *see* NATIVE NORTH AMERICAN ART, §XV.

BIBLIOGRAPHY
F. J. Dockstader: *Great North American Indians* (New York, 1977), pp. 167–8

FREDERICK J. DOCKSTADER

Mungo Martin: *Cannibal Bird*, articulated mask, painted wood with cedar-bark fringe, 345×1230×921 mm (including fringe), 1953 (Victoria, BC, Royal British Columbia Museum)

Martin, Paul (Augustus) (*b* Herbeuville, Alsace-Lorraine, 16 April 1864; *d* London, 7 July 1944). English photographer of French birth. At the age of sixteen he was apprenticed to a wood-engraver. He took up photography as a hobby in 1884, though working as an engraver, using a Fallowfield Facile hand camera to take unusual snapshots of the Victorians bathing, paddling, or playing on the sand at Yarmouth in 1892 (London, V&A). The camera, camouflaged as a brown paper parcel, was held under the arm; Martin encased his in leather and improved its mechanism. He recorded street life in London by taking photographs of the sherbet- and water-sellers, Billingsgate fish porters and the police making an arrest. In 1896 he gained the Royal Photographic Society's Gold Medal for his pioneering night photography. This preceded Alfred Stieglitz's better-known scenes of New York. Martin's *Eros in Piccadilly Circus* (1896; Austin, U. TX, Human. Res. Cent., Gernsheim Col.) required a 15-minute exposure with the lens shielded from the lights of passing traffic. He presented these as lantern slides, tinted yellow and blue to heighten the effect of the gas street lamps. His work provides a link between 19th-century pictorialism and 20th-century realism.

WRITINGS
Victorian Snapshots (London, 1939/*R* New York, 1972) [autobiography]
BIBLIOGRAPHY
B. Jay: *Victorian Candid Camera: Paul Martin 1864–1944* (Newton Abbot, 1973)
R. Flukinger, L. Schaaf and S. Meacham: *Paul Martin: Victorian Photographer* (London, 1978)

WILLIAM BUCHANAN

Martin and George of Kolozsvár. Hungarian family of sculptors and bronze-casters. The only sources for the activity (before 1372 to 1390) of Martin [Martón] and George [György] Kolozsvár are the unreliable inscriptions on copies of their mostly lost works. Their names are always given in the same order, which may either be a mark of seniority or reflect their perceived artistic ranking. One may have specialized in modelling, the other in casting. The 17th-century copies of the full-size statues (originals destr. 1660) of the canonized Hungarian kings Stephen, Emeric and László from the cathedral of Nagyvárad (now Oradea, Romania) were inscribed *per Martinum et Georgium filios magistri Nicolai pictoris de Colosvar*. This inscription, now lost, gives the most detailed information; the accompanying date, although this may well have been false, has been variously read as 1364, 1366 or 1371, indicating that the figures were cast during the reign of King Louis I (*reg* 1342–82) and the bishopric of Demeter Futaki (1345–72). The lost shield on their only surviving work, the bronze equestrian statue of *St George* (Prague, N.G., Convent of St George) gave the date 1373 with the inscription *per Martinum et Georgium de Clussenberch conflatum est*. The last reference to them was in the inscription of the bronze equestrian statue of *St László* (destr. 1660) erected in 1390 in front of Nagyvárad Cathedral.

The figure of *St George* is first recorded in Prague Castle in 1541; the theory that it was recast during the 16th century has been disproved by metallurgical studies (Kotrba). Attempts have been made to derive the brothers' style from German or Czech sculpture: Pinder related it on technical grounds to the work of the ducal workshop at the Stephansdom, Vienna (*see* VIENNA, §V, 1(i)), and Kutal claimed that the model for the statue was made by Heinrich Parler von Gmund, attributing only the actual bronze-casting to Martin and George. This theory, however, takes no account of their work in Nagyvárad. Balogh's relation of the style and technique of the Prague statue to the bronze Evangelist symbols on the façade of Orvieto Cathedral (*see* ORVIETO, §2(ii)(b)) provides a more plausible source, and the brothers may have been trained in Italy around the middle of the 14th century.

BIBLIOGRAPHY

W. Pinder: *Die deutsche Plastik vom ausgehenden Mittelalter bis zum Ende der Renaissance*, i (Wildpark-Potsdam, 1924), pp. 88–92
J. Balogh: *Márton és György Kolozsvári szobrászok* [Martin and George, sculptors of Kolozsvár] (Cluj, 1934)
A. Kutal: *České gotické sochařství, 1350–1450* [Bohemian Gothic sculpture, 1350–1450] (Prague, 1962)
V. Kotrba: 'Die Bronzeskulptur des heiligen Georg auf der Burg zu Prag', *Anz. German. Nmus.* (1969), pp. 9–28
Die Parler und der Schöne Stil, 1350–1400: Europäische Kunst unter den Luxemburgern (exh. cat., ed. A. Legner; Cologne, Schnütgen-Mus., 1978)

ERNŐ MAROSÍ

Martín de Solórzano (*fl* 1482; *d* Palencia, 1506). Spanish architect. He came from a family of builders, and he worked in Castile from 1482 until his death. His activity is documented at the cathedrals of Coria (*c.* 1496–8), Plasencia and Palencia (*c.* 1504–6), and on a library (now the Capilla del Cardenal) in the cloister of Ávila Cathedral. S Tomás of Ávila is generally attributed to him because of its similarities with the Capilla del Cardenal and its mention in his commission at Coria.

The foundation of S Tomás was established in the will of the Royal Treasurer, Hernan Nuñez Arnalte, and the terms were executed by his wife, Maria Dávila, and the Dominican inquisitor Tomás de Torquemada. The convent soon won royal favour, housing a summer residence and the tomb of Prince Juan (1478–97), the only son of Ferdinand and Isabella of Spain. Work began in 1482 and advanced rapidly with the installation of the community in 1493.

The church has a Latin cross plan with a star-vaulted nave of five bays and lateral chapels. An unusual raised presbytery complements the western choir loft. Sober decoration emphasizes the clarity of the plan: only the multiple mouldings of responds interrupt the plain, granite walls. On the exterior, simple ball ornament prevails, and the arms of Ferdinand and Isabella dominate the façade. An open porch shelters the portal, which is framed by an ogee arch and decorated with multiple mouldings and branches of pomegranates. Figures of saints stand under canopies on the walls of the porch. The convent includes three cloisters, in which the restrained decoration centres on emblems of the Dominican Order, ball ornament, pomegranates and, in the Patio de los Reyes, the arms of Ferdinand and Isabella. The limited extent of Martín de Solórzano's work and the uncertainty surrounding his role elsewhere complicate efforts to credit him with the austere aspect of S Tomás. Local traditions, the predominant granite and Torquemada's tastes may, however, have influenced the character of the building.

In 1495 Martín de Solórzano designed a library, now the Capilla del Cardenal, in the cloister of Ávila Cathedral. The project was carried out under his son Juán de Solórzano and Pedro de Rasínes, and completed in 1499. Martín had left Ávila to work on the choir of Coria Cathedral. He may have designed the north portal there, in the florid style that reappears on the lavishly decorated walls enclosing the choir of Palencia Cathedral, with which he is also associated.

BIBLIOGRAPHY

M. Gómez Moreno: *Catálogo monumental de la provincia de Ávila*, 3 vols (Madrid, 1901–2; rev. by A. de la Morena and T. Pérez de Higuera, 1983)
L. Torres Balbás: *Arquitectura gótica*, A. Hisp. (Madrid, 1952)
F. Chueca Goítia: *Arquitectura del siglo XVI*, A. Hisp. (Madrid, 1953)

JAMES D'EMILIO

Martineau, Robert Braithwaite (*b* London, 19 Jan 1826; *d* London, 13 Feb 1869). English painter. The son of a successful solicitor, he embarked on a legal career before turning to art. He studied at F. S. Cary's drawing school (1846–8) and in 1848 entered the Royal Academy Schools, where he was awarded a silver medal for drawing. In 1851 he became a pupil of William Holman Hunt, with whom he maintained a close friendship. Martineau was closely associated with the Pre-Raphaelite circle. He modelled for the gentleman in Madox Brown's *Work* (1852, 1856–63; Manchester, C.A.G.). He exhibited at the Pre-Raphaelite exhibition in Russell Place, London, in 1857, and he was treasurer of the short-lived Hogarth Club (1858–61).

Martineau's most celebrated work, *The Last Day in the Old Home* (1862; London, Tate), a critical success when exhibited at the International Exhibition in London in 1862, reflects the Pre-Raphaelite interest in moralizing modern-life subjects, with its depiction of a family forced to leave its home because of the gambling debts of the father. Martineau exhibited 11 small-scale works at the Royal Academy between 1852 and 1867. These included portraits and genre scenes with one or two figures, such as the *Last Chapter* (1863; Birmingham, Mus. & A.G.), and literary subjects, for example *Kit's Writing Lesson* (1852; London, Tate) from Dickens's *The Old Curiosity Shop* and *Katherine and Petruchio* (1855; Oxford, Ashmolean) from Shakespeare's *The Taming of the Shrew*. At the time of his death, Martineau was working on a large canvas with a historical theme, *Christians and Christians* (unfinished; Liverpool, Walker A.G.). Martineau's patrons included Edward Mudie of Mudie's circulating library; James Leathart; Kirkman Hodgson, the Governor of the Bank of England; and Holman Hunt's patron Sir Thomas Fairbairn.

BIBLIOGRAPHY

DNB
P. Gurland: *Robert Braithwaite Martineau's 'The Last Day in the Old Home'* (MA thesis, Courtauld Inst., U. London, 1986) [contains full bibliog.]

PENELOPE GURLAND

Martinelli, Anton Erhard (*b* Vienna, 1684; *d* Vienna, 1747). Austrian master builder and architect. He is mentioned in connection with many of the most notable building schemes of the period as a master builder. However, it is difficult to discover if Martinelli was also involved in their actual design. For instance, he was the master builder at the spectacular Karlskirche in Vienna (1715–37; *see* AUSTRIA, fig. 6 and VIENNA, §V, 2), the joint work of Johann Bernhard Fischer von Erlach and Joseph Emanuel Fischer von Erlach, and later also of the Schwarzenberg Palace in Vienna (by Johann Bernhard Fischer von Erlach and Johann Lukas von Hildebrandt; begun 1697). The list of Martinelli's works compiled in 1726 (Vienna, Archv Baumeistergenossenschaft) also includes the renovation of the Esterházy Palace on the Walnerstrasse, Vienna; the church of the Teutonic Order, St Elisabeth, built at the expense of Graf von Stahrenberg; the Moravian palaces of Duke Schwarzenberg; and Gräfin Althan's two Styrian and two Hungarian palaces in Csáktornya (now Čakovec, Croatia) and Magyarbél (the former Csáky Palace). The original central range of the ducal palace at Fertöd (1721; rebuilt 1764–6 by Melchior Hefele) for the Esterházy family was also Martinelli's work, and he was constantly employed by the Esterházy family as well as by Wenceslas, Prince of Liechtenstein, mainly on his Moravian estates. One of Martinelli's most distinguished works is the Italianate hospital for disabled soldiers (1727–35; now Town Hall) in Pest, on foundations laid by Fortunato da Prati. Although of monumental size, its façade projections, pilastered over a horizontally articulated plinth storey, barely protrude beyond the general plane of the elevation.

UNPUBLISHED SOURCES

Vienna, Archv Baumeistergenossenschaft [list of Martinelli's works, 1726]

BIBLIOGRAPHY

A. Schoen: *A budapesti Központi Városháza* [The Central Town Hall of Budapest] (Budapest, 1930)

P. Voit: *Der Barock in Ungarn* (Budapest, 1971)

——: 'Les Inspirations françaises de l'art baroque en Hongrie', *Baroque revue internationale* (Montauban, 1976)

PÁL VOIT

Martinelli, Domenico (*b* Lucca, 30 Nov 1650; *d* Lucca, 11 Sept 1718). Italian architect, active in central Europe. He was ordained a priest in Lucca in 1673, then trained as a land surveyor and subsequently studied architecture. In 1678 he moved to Rome, where he attended the Accademia di S Luca; in 1679 and 1680 he won the first prize for architecture there and was elected Professor of Architecture and Perspective in 1683. Apart from some small designs for Lucca (altars in S Andrea and S Nicolao, *c*. 1685), some gigantic fantasy projects for King John Sobieski of Poland (1624–96) have survived on paper from this period (memorial church and great country house of Francavilla, *c*. 1684).

Although he had hardly any practical experience as an architect, Martinelli was summoned to Vienna by counts Ferdinand Bonaventura Harrach (1637–1706) and Dominik Andreas Kaunitz (1655–1705) in 1690, and he spent the next 15 years north of the Alps, producing the major part of his architectural oeuvre there. At first he was mainly engaged in building or altering palaces in Vienna and its environs. In 1690 he designed the façade of the Harrach Palace in Vienna, a front articulated strictly by colossal pilasters with slightly projecting end wings surmounted by pediments; this scheme served as a model for palace façades in Vienna for decades to come.

In 1691 Martinelli came into contact with the imperial diplomat Count Dominik Andreas Kaunitz, his most important patron in the following years, for whom he carried out alterations to his palace in Vienna (now the Liechtenstein Palace) in a classicizing Roman Baroque style, which dominated secular architecture in Vienna in the last decade of the 17th century. The design, with its powerfully projecting centre, derives indirectly from Gianlorenzo Bernini's Palazzo Chigi in Rome. Martinelli applied the same style to suburban architecture in the large Liechtenstein Garden Palace in Vienna (from 1692; a modified version of an earlier project by Domenico Egidio Rossi).

When Kaunitz was sent on a diplomatic mission to Holland (1696–8), he took Martinelli with him to study the breweries, mills and brick kilns that he wanted to introduce on his own Moravian estates. Martinelli was also introduced to a number of German princes as an architect in the service of the imperial diplomatic service, and he produced designs for the residences of two of the Electors, Johann Wilhelm von der Pfalz of the Palatinate (1658–1716) and Lothar Franz Schönborn. Although these projects were not executed, they are important and influential documents of the 'Italianizing' architecture of central Europe around 1700.

On his return to Vienna in 1698 Martinelli received only a few commissions, notably the great country house of Landskron (Lanškroun) in Bohemia for Prince Johann Adam Andreas of Liechtenstein (from 1698), a strongly articulated structure with columniated loggias clearly reminiscent of Martinelli's native Lucca (and surviving only as fragments today). He also designed a large palace for Norbert Leopold Count Kolowrat (*d* 1716) in Prague (1701, not executed) and was involved in the construction of the Martinitz Palace in Prague (from 1700, to a plan by Carlo Fontana). However, Martinelli's activity became confined more and more to that of 'house architect' to Count Kaunitz, for whom he planned a revised layout for Austerlitz (Slavkov u Brna in Moravia) on the model of Bernini's Chigi Forum in Ariccia and fundamental alterations to the castle (both from 1698, only partially completed). In addition he worked intensively on modest building projects on Kaunitz's extensive estates in Moravia: the parish churches of Letonitz (Letonice) and Rausnitz (Rousínov) and the stud farm at Neu-Kaunitz (Palárikovo).

After Count Kaunitz's death in 1705 Martinelli was obliged to return to Italy. For some years he worked as a teacher at the Accademia di S Luca but returned around 1710 to his native town of Lucca, where he died in impoverished circumstances. His extensive legacy of drawings is to be found today largely in Lucca (Bib. Stat.) and Milan (Civiche Raccolte d'Arte Antica, Castello Sforzesco, Collezione Martinelli).

As a teacher at the Roman academy, where he worked with Carlo Rainaldi, Mattia de Rossi and Carlo Fontana, Martinelli was closely familiar with the Roman architecture of Bernini's successors. His importance lies in having mediated this 'strict' tendency of Roman late Baroque classicism (the period immediately prior to Neo-classicism, which featured an architecture of classical trends but of great versatility and occasional unorthodoxy) directly to central Europe after 1690. Even though many of his projects were not realized, his creations had a direct influence on the development of Baroque architecture in the Habsburg countries, as well as an indirect influence through other architects who followed.

BIBLIOGRAPHY

[G. B. Franceschini]: *Memorie della vita di Domenico Martinelli, sacerdote lucchese e insigne architetto* (Lucca, 1772)

H. Tietze: 'Domenico Martinelli und seine Tätigkeit in Österreich', *Jb. Ksthist. Inst. Wien*, xiii (1919), pp. 1–46

Z. Rewski: 'Architekci G. B. Colombo i D. Martinelli a Jan III Sobieski', *Biul. Hist. Sztuki*, ix (1947), pp. 322–40

V. Richter: 'Náčrt činnosti Domenica Martinelliho na Moravě', *Sborn. Prac. Filoz. Fak. Brn. U.*, 7 (1963), pp. 49–88

H. Lorenz: 'Domenico Martinelli und Prag', *Umění*, xxx (1982), pp. 21–34

——: 'Zur Internationalität der Wiener Barockarchitektur', *Wien und der europäische Barock*, vii of *Akten des XXV. internationalen Kongresses für Kunstgeschichte: Wien 1983*, pp. 21–30

——: *Domenico Martinelli und die österreichische Barockarchitektur* (Vienna, 1991)

HELLMUT LORENZ

Martinelli, Fioravante (*b* Rome, *c.* 1599; *d* Rome, 24 July 1677). Italian writer and antiquarian. He was born into a poor family and entered the priesthood. At about the age of 30 he met Orazio Giustiniani (*d* 1649), then priest of the congregation of the Oratory, who was made a cardinal in 1645. It was probably Giustiniani who procured for Martinelli an appointment as Hebrew (1636) and later Latin (1637) secretary at the Vatican Library, where he appears to have worked until 1661 (the date of the last payment in his name). The library holds many of his unpublished writings. Martinelli's first published works are short, extremely erudite monographs on single monuments. In 1644 he published *Roma ricercata nel suo sito*, which was popular because of its conciseness. The guide explicitly uses information taken from Vasari's *Vite*, Pompilio Totti's *Ritratto di Roma antica* (Rome, 1627), Gaspare Celio's *Memoria delli nomi dell'artifice i delle pitture che sono in alcune chiese, facciate e palazzi di Roma* (Naples, 1638) and Giovanni Baglione's *Le nove chiese di Roma* (Rome, 1639). It was followed by *Roma ex ethnica sacra*, a scholarly guide in Latin in which the author clearly relied on sources and manuscripts from the Vatican Library; it gives a detailed account of all the churches of Rome, with their building history, and is particularly valuable for its record of the inscriptions in them, now in part lost.

Martinelli was a friend, admirer and supporter of Francesco Borromini, whom he had probably met in the 1630s, when they were both in contact with the Filippino oratory. In the third edition of *Roma ricercata* (1653) Martinelli gave more attention to Borromini than in the 1650 edition, and Connors suggests that Dominique Barrière's engravings illustrating the text are based on drawings by Borromini. Borromini reconstructed the villa of Monte Mario, given to Martinelli by Giustiniani, and Martinelli here wrote *Roma ornata dell'architettura, pittura e scoltura*, which was later revised by Borromini. Again, Martinelli quoted from Vasari, Celio and especially Baglione (often transcribing his errors), but he also added further information about works produced in Rome between 1642 and 1660. The book also discusses topics on which no-one had written before, including a full history of the Sapienza (the university of Rome) and the Vatican Library and descriptions of the villas Ludovisi and Montalto. However, perhaps the most important contents are Borromini's notes, of which there are about a hundred. These, with Martinelli's observations, make *Roma ornata* an important text for understanding Borromini's ideas. In order to counter the accusations made against Borromini by his contemporaries, Martinelli mentions repeatedly that Borromini followed in the footsteps of Michelangelo while still working in an original way, that he was familiar with the work of the ancients and that he understood the principles established by Vitruvius. It is unclear why Martinelli's book was not printed: it may have been either because Gasparo Alveri published an encyclopedic guide in 1664 or because of its defence of Borromini.

UNPUBLISHED SOURCES

Rome, Vatican, Bib. Apostolica Lat. 8231, Assemani papers, fols 344r–51r [*Breve relazione della vita del Cardinale Giustiniani*]

WRITINGS

Ecclesia S Laurentii in fonte di Vico Patricio (Rome, 1629)

Imago B Mariae Virginis, quae apud Venerandas SS Sixti e Dominici Moniales ... cultu osservaretur (Rome, 1635)

Diaconia S Agathae in Subura (Rome, 1638)

Roma ricercata nel suo sito (Rome, 1644)

Roma ex ethnica sacra (Rome, 1653)

V. D'Onofrio, ed.: *Roma ornata dell'architettura, pittura e scoltura* (Rome, 1969) [contains complete list of Martinelli's writings, pp. xxiv–v]

BIBLIOGRAPHY

P. Mandosio: *Bibliotheca Romana*, ii (Rome, 1672–92), pp. 52–3

L. Schudt: *Le guide di Roma* (Vienna and Augsburg, 1930/*R* Farnborough, 1971), pp. 62–9

C. D'Onofrio: *Roma nel seicento* (Rome, 1969)

J. Bignami-Odier: *La Bibliothèque Vaticane de Sixte IV à Pie XI* (Vatican City, 1973), pp. 131–2

A. Blunt: *Borromini* (Cambridge, 1979), pp. 26–7, 84, 194, 226–8

J. Connors: *Borromini and the Roman Oratory* (Cambridge, 1980), pp. 75, 222, 263–4

ALESSANDRA ANSELMI

Martinelli, Giovanni (*b* Montevarchi, Arezzo, 1600 or 1604; *d* Florence, 1 Jan 1659). Italian painter. He had moved to Florence by 1621, and in 1623 is documented as living in the house of Jacopo Ligozzi. No works from this early period survive, and his first documented works were a fresco and other paintings (untraced) executed in 1622 for the church of S Leonardo at Grosseto. These were commissioned by Francesco dell'Antella (1567–1624), commander of the Order of Malta, who was a patron of Caravaggio during the latter's stay in Malta. Martinelli is not documented in Florence over the next ten years, and it is now widely accepted that he visited Rome in the latter part of the 1620s. By the mid-1630s he was established in Florence, where he worked mainly for private collectors, and in 1636 he enrolled in the Accademia del Disegno, and became a member in 1637. The earliest dated work to survive is the *Miracle of the Mule* (1632; Pescia, S Francesco), based on Lodovico Cigoli's painting of the same subject (1597; Cortona, S Francesco), and composed with a characteristically Florentine clarity and lucidity. Yet the painting's naturalism and effects of light are perhaps indebted to Roman art. Other works of this period, such as *Death Appearing to the Banqueters* (New Orleans, LA, Delgado Mus.), and the companion pieces the *Violin Player* (Atlanta, GA, High Mus. A.) and the *Spinet Player* (Clermont-Ferrand, Mus. Bargoin), bear a strong resemblance to the art of such Florentine painters as Filippo Tarchiani (1576–1645) and Anastagio Fontebuoni (1580–1626), both of whom had lived for a long

Giovanni Martelli: *Belshazzar's Feast*, oil on canvas, 2.28×3.42 m, *c.* 1653 (Florence, Galleria degli Uffizi)

while in Rome. Martinelli was also indebted to such French and Neapolitan followers of Caravaggio as Valentin de Boulogne, Simon Vouet and Massimo Stanzione. Vouet's influence is apparent in the *Judgement of Solomon* (USA, priv. col., see Gregori and Schleier, fig. 453) and the *Woman of Samaria* (Terranuova Bracciolini, Arezzo, Prepositura), both of which may be dated to *c.* 1638. In these paintings the luminous quality of the whites and brightness hark back to a Roman Caravaggesque tradition, and particularly to the art of Orazio Gentileschi. In the 1630s Martinelli also developed a fresco style that is close to that of Giovanni da San Giovanni and similarly influenced by the naturalism and narrative simplicity of Bernardino Poccetti. His frescoes of the 1630s include four *Allegories*, completed by 1638, at the Certosa del Galluzzo, near Florence.

In the 1640s and 1650s Martinelli painted some altarpieces, but most of his works are allegorical pictures of moral and philosophical themes; these show little stylistic development and are difficult to date. Altarpieces of the 1640s include *St Nicholas in Glory* (1640; Poppiano, Florence, Castello Guicciardini) and the *Virgin of the Rosary* (1646–7; Pozzolatico, Florence, S Stefano). Such works as *Young Student Tempted by the Senses* (Berlin, von Klopmann priv. col., see Del Bravo, p. 1588), *Music and the Vanity of Power* (Florence, Gal. Corsini), and the two allegorical pictures of *Vanity* (Rome, Zeri priv. col., see Gregori and Schleier, fig. 454) suggest the influence of the moralizing allegories popularized in Rome in the 1620s by such artists as Angelo Caroselli and Pietro Paolini. These

subjects were also fashionable at literary academies in Florence, and have parallels in the works of Lorenzo Lippi and Cesare Dandini. Martinelli also painted still-lifes, but the only undoubted example is the *Still-life with Roses, Asparagus, Peonies and Carnations* (Florence, Depositi Gal.), an attribution based on similarities with the roses in the *Virgin of the Rosary*. His works of the 1650s include his most famous work, *Belshazzar's Feast* (see fig.), an elaborate composition with a sumptuous architectural setting, and frescoes of scenes from the *Life of the Blessed Bonaventure Buonaccorsi* (1654; Pistoia, SS Annunziata) and from the *Life of Mary Magdalene* (1655; Pistoia, S Domenico). The repetitive and less competent paintings of the *Miracle of St Zenobius* (Pistoia, Basilica dell'Umiltà) and *Noah's Sacrifice* (West Wycombe Park, Bucks, NT) also date from the 1650s.

BIBLIOGRAPHY

F. Sricchia: 'Giovanni Martinelli', *Paragone*, iv/39 (1953), pp. 29–34

C. Del Bravo: 'Lettera sulla natura morta', *An. Scu. Norm. Sup. U. Pisa*, ser. 3, iv/4 (1974), pp. 1565–91

G. Cantelli: 'Proposte per Giovanni Martinelli', *Paradigma*, ii (1978), pp. 135–43

Painting in Florence, 1600–1700 (exh. cat. by C. McCorquodale, London and Cambridge, 1979), pp. 88–9

G. Cantelli: *Repertorio della pittura fiorentina del seicento* (Florence, 1983), pp. 107–8

Il seicento fiorentino: Arte a Firenze da Ferdinando I a Cosimo III, 3 vols (exh. cat., Florence, Pal. Strozzi, 1986), *Pittura*, pp. 325–7; *Disegno*, pp. 302–4; *Biografie*, pp. 114–17

A. Nesi: 'Un'aggiunta al catalogo di Giovanni Martinelli', *Paragone*, xxxix/457 (1988), pp. 62–5

M. Gregori and E. Schleier, eds: *La pittura in Italia: Il seicento*, 2 vols (Milan, 1989) [with bibliog.]

G. Leoncini: 'Giovanni Martinelli', *La natura morta in Italia*, ed. F. Porzio, ii (Milan, 1989), pp. 556–7

F. Falletti, ed.: *Chiostri seicenteschi a Pistoia* (Pistoia, 1992), pp. 56, 72

CHIARA D'AFFLITTO

Martinelli, Niccolo. *See* TROMETTA.

Martinelli, Vincenzo (*b* Bologna, 20 June 1737; *d* Bologna, 20 April 1807). Italian painter. He was a nephew and pupil of Carlo Lodi (1701–65), and a member of the Accademia Clementina from 1759 to 1762. He worked for a long period with his uncle, and on the latter's death inherited the workshop and continued the tradition of decorative landscape painting. His works are more naturalistic, particularly in their treatment of light and shade, than Lodi's arcadian scenes, as is evident in the *Landscape with the Villa Boschi* (1766; Bologna, Villa La Sampiera, see Roli, pl. 374a). Similar characteristics inform the three tempera paintings, with figures by Nicola Bertuzzi, in the Casino Marsigli, Bologna. In 1769 Martinelli was in Parma, on the occasion of Ferdinando di Borbone's marriage to Amalia d'Austria, and subsequently visited several European capital cities, producing a vast number of decorative landscapes, often in collaboration with figure painters such as Domenico Pedrini (1728–1800), Filippo Pedrini, Emilio Manfredi (*d* 1801) and Gaspare Bigari. He also worked as a scene painter for theatres in Bologna.

Towards the end of the 1770s Martinelli's style changed, and, through his contact with contemporary Venetian artists, he lightened his palette and created more spacious landscapes, as in the *Coastal View with Gypsy Encampment* (Bologna, Pin. N.) and in the tempera paintings of scenes from the *Life of Moses* in the Palazzo del Monte Matrimonio, Bologna, with figures by Filippo Pedrini. His decoration of the Palazzo Dondi and his scenes of *Dido and Aeneas* in the Palazzo Salina, with quadratura by Petronio Fancelli (1734–1800) and figures by Pietro Fabbri, are characterized by more vivid colour and stronger tonal contrasts. Later he enjoyed a long collaboration with Pietro Fancelli (1764–1850) and moved towards Neoclassicism, a development in harmony with the naturalism of his landscape painting. His output was prolific and his pupils numerous. Among them were Antonio Basoli and Luigi Busatti who, in 1805, worked with him on the decorations for the festivities organized to welcome Napoleon Bonaparte to Bologna.

BIBLIOGRAPHY

P. Giordani: *Elogio di Vincenzo Martinelli nell'Accademia di Belle Arti in Bologna* (Bologna, 1809)

G. Zucchini: *Paesaggi e rovine nella pittura bolognese del settecento* (Bologna, 1947), pp. 48–62

R. Roli: *Pittura bolognese, 1650–1800: Dal Cignani ai Gandolfi* (Bologna, 1977)

L'arte del settecento emiliano: Architettura, scenografia, pittura di paesaggio (exh. cat., Bologna, Pal. Re Enzo, 1980)

G. Bergomi: 'Pietro Fancelli e Filippo Pedrini, figuristi nei "paesi" di Vincenzo Martinelli', *Il Carrobbio*, xiv (1988), pp. 19–28

UGO RUGGERI

Martinet, François-Nicolas (*b c.* 1725; *d c.* 1804). French engraver and draughtsman. He was related to the engravers Charles Dupuis (1685–1742) and Nicolas-Gabriel Dupuis. In 1756 he was working as Graveur du Cabinet du Roi, under the auspices of the Menus Plaisirs du Roi. For this he engraved after the drawings of members of the Slodtz family (e.g. *May Ball at Versailles during the Carnival of 1763*). After Charles-Michel-Ange Challe he engraved the catafalque of the *Dauphin* (1766), that of *Elisabeth Farnese* (1766) and that of the *Dauphine Marie-Josèphe* (1767). At the same time Martinet produced illustrations for plays or comic operas by such contemporaries as Marmontel, Voltaire and Philidor; some of these he engraved himself, while others were drawn by him but engraved by his sister Thérèse Martinet (*b c.* 1731). He also engraved some portraits, such as that of the *Maréchal de Villars* after Antoine Coypel, and landscapes and genre scenes (e.g. the *Gallant Gardener* and the *Rash Lover*), which he sometimes arranged in suites (e.g. the *Five Senses*).

Martinet also produced books of ornamental drawings and engravings, such as *Livre des ornements inventés par Martinet*, as well as book illustrations (e.g. Jean-Jacques Rousseau's *Le Contrat social*, 1762 and Voltaire's *La Henriade*, 1775). He failed to complete his *Descriptions historiques de Paris*, intended as an introduction to the *Histoire de Paris et de la France* by M. Béguillet (Paris, 1779–81), but produced many illustrations for scientific works, in particular some 1000 plates for Buffon's *L'Histoire naturelle*, which were used by the Sèvres Porcelain Factory to execute (1782–99) the so-called Buffon service. It was as a natural-history illustrator and designer of ornaments that Martinet did his best work, displaying sureness and skill, whereas in his figural scenes his draughtsmanship and composition could sometimes appear clumsy.

BIBLIOGRAPHY

Portalis–Beraldi

C. Le Blanc: *Manuel de l'amateur d'estampes*, ii (Paris, 1856)

D. Guilmard: *Les Maîtres ornemanistes* (Paris, 1881)

L. Hautecoeur: 'Quelques documents relatifs à François-Nicolas Martinet, dessinateur et graveur du Cabinet du Roy', *Archvs A. Fr.*, n. s. 1, i (1907), pp. 280–309

G. Lechevallier-Chevignard: *La Manufacture de porcelaine de Sèvres* (Paris, 1908)

F. Souchal: *Les Slodtz: Sculpteurs et décorateurs du roi* (Paris, 1967)

L. Hautecoeur: 'Une Famille de graveurs et d'éditeurs parisiens: Les Martinet et les Hautecoeur', *Paris & Ile-de-France: Mémoires* (1970), pp. 205–340

HÉLÈNE GUICHARNAUD

Martinet, Louis (*b* 1810; *d* 1894). French painter, administrator and dealer. He was the son of a Corsican architect called Martinetti and became a pupil of Antoine-Jean Gros. He painted chiefly on commission, mainly copies of religious subjects destined for provincial churches. An eye infection caused him to give up painting, and he moved to the Direction des Beaux-Arts, in charge of exhibitions and public fêtes. He is best remembered, however, for his role as organizer of independent exhibitions held in his Paris gallery at 26 Boulevard des Italiens, premises adjoining Richard Seymour-Conway, 4th Marquess of Hertford's house and owned by him. The first of these, held in 1859, was a posthumous showing of the work of Ary Scheffer. The following year, when there was no Salon, he held a small exhibition at which some pictures refused by the jury in 1859 were shown, as well as several paintings by Ingres, who no longer sent his work to the official Salon. Also in 1860 Martinet collaborated with Jean-Marie Durand-Ruel and Francis Petit in a photographic publication in ten volumes called *L'Album*. In this were reproductions of 100 contemporary works of art accompanied by critical commentaries. Later in the year Petit organized an exhibition at Martinet's gallery of 300 works, mainly 18th-century, from private collections. Dr Louis La Caze, the Duc de Morny and Hertford were among the lenders. The exhibition was on a scale not previously seen in France and was the first of a small series.

In June 1861 Martinet launched a publication called *Le Courrier artistique* to promote the interests represented by his gallery. In 1862 he proposed the creation of a Société Nationale des Beaux-Arts to sponsor exhibitions of contemporary painting. The Comte Alexandre Walewski (1810–68) was honorary president, Théophile Gautier was acting president, and the vice-presidents were the sculptor Auguste Préault and Martinet himself, who saw his role as essentially that of an artist among equals, rather than as a dealer. The Exposition Permanente, as it was called, opened in September 1861. Edouard Manet, a founder-member, sent an important series of works, including the *Spanish Singer* (1860; New York, Met.). He continued to exhibit there, sending 14 pictures in 1863. Charles Baudelaire, who reviewed the exhibition in 1862, praised Martinet for achieving the apparently impossible task of setting up a permanent exhibition, commented favourably on two works by Alphonse Legros, but characteristically reserved his greatest enthusiasm for Eugène Delacroix, who showed a small version of his *Death of Sardanapalus* (1827; Paris, Louvre).

Martinet's aim was not to set up an alternative Salon. Indeed, in a letter to Manet in 1863, he declared that he could not provide a repository for pictures refused at the Palais de l'Industrie. His scheme was intended as a presentation of the achievement of French art, both past and present. Thus, following the death in 1863 of Delacroix, a founder-member of the Société Nationale, Martinet formed a committee, again headed by Walewski, to organize a great posthumous exhibition of his work, to be held on the Boulevard des Italiens, when Alexandre Dumas *père* made the opening speech.

Martinet also arranged concerts at the gallery, though these were not popular with artists, but in 1864 abandoned his gallery scheme to turn the premises into a small theatre, the Fantaisies Parisiennes. It is probable that the competition from the Salon, to which most artists continued to send their best work, undermined the success of his venture. In 1870 he took on the direction of the Théâtre Lyrique, but was ruined when it was burnt down during the Commune. Late in life he returned to painting, particularly landscapes, and was occasionally rewarded by an official purchase.

BIBLIOGRAPHY

Notice-préface au catalogue de la vente au profit de Mme Martinet (sale cat., Paris, 17–18 May 1887)

G. Ribeaucourt: *Une Figure d'artiste, Louis Martinet* (Paris, 1894)

E. G. Holt: *The Art of All the Nations 1850–73* (Princeton, 1982)

L. Huston: 'Le Salon et les expositions d'art: Réflexions à partir de l'expérience de Louis Martinet', *Gaz. B.-A.*, n. s. 5, cxvi (1990), pp. 45–50

LINDA WHITELEY

Martinez. Native American artists. Julian Martinez (*b* San Ildefonso Pueblo, NM, 1885; *d* San Ildefonso Pueblo,

1943) and his wife, Maria Martinez [née Montoya] (*b* San Ildefonso Pueblo, 1887; *d* San Ildefonso Pueblo, 1980), made and decorated pottery in San Ildefonso Pueblo, NM; in all their work together Maria was the potter and Julian the painter. Maria first learnt pottery-making from her aunt Nicolasa Peña Montoya (1863–1904) in the early 20th century. There were few other potters at the Tewa pueblo of San Ildefonso. In 1907 the newly founded School of American Archaeology (now School of American Research, Santa Fe, NM) began excavations in nearby Rio de los Frijoles canyon, whose sites are ancestral to the people of San Ildefonso. Maria was among the people of San Ildefonso hired to assist with the examination of excavated sherds, and she was encouraged by Edgar Lee Hewett (1865–1946), the director, to replicate the ancient pottery forms. Maria shaped, slipped and polished pots, and Julian painted them.

Hewett also encouraged San Ildefonso men to paint watercolours on paper. Julian may have made crayon drawings as early as 1908, and by 1920 he had developed his own style. He was influenced by close association with the San Ildefonso painter Crescencio Martinez (1879–1918), who married Maria's sister Maximiliana (1885–1955). While Julian's paintings of San Ildefonso dancers are awkward and naive compared to those of his best contemporaries, his abstracted *avanyus* (water serpents) and other animals are often finely detailed. Nevertheless, his work on paper and on pottery was complementary. While Maria became the undisputed best potter of San Ildefonso, Julian became the undisputed best painter of pottery (see fig.).

Maria and Julian became masters of traditional San Ildefonso Polychrome, Polished Black and Polished Red pottery. In 1915 they demonstrated in San Diego at the Panama–California exposition, where the anthropological exhibits were organized by Hewett. The School of American Research and the Museum of New Mexico continued to support Maria's work, and by 1918 they were buying

Maria Martinez and Julian Martinez: *Snake Pot*, polychrome pottery water-jar, h. 288 mm, 1927 (Taos, NM, Millicent Rogers Museum)

her pottery for promotional resale to other museums. In the winter of 1919–20 Maria and Julian invented a new type: Black-on-black, a highly polished black ware with decoration in matt-black paint. Examples were exhibited at the Art Museum in Santa Fe. Early pieces had surfaces covered almost entirely with matt-black paint, leaving negative designs, but Julian soon changed the style so that the surface was predominantly polished black whether the designs were positive or negative. Maria and Julian shared the process readily: by 1925 Black-on-black was the most commonly made type at San Ildefonso and was rapidly adopted by potters in other Tewa pueblos, particularly Santa Clara, and in the Keres pueblo of Santo Domingo.

Maria and Julian also continued to work in polychrome, and many of their most beautiful polychrome vessels were made between 1925 and 1930. During this period Julian favoured exceedingly fine detail, which would not show to advantage on their black pottery. After Julian's death, Maria collaborated first with her daughter-in-law Santana (*b* 1909), wife of Maria's and Julian's son Adam (*b* 1903); and then with her son Popovi Da (1921–71). These later efforts are often as fine as earlier ones, but the most notable difference from earlier pieces by Maria and Julian is that Maria stopped making large jars. She ceased pottery-making entirely in 1970.

Maria was the first Pueblo potter to sign her work regularly. A few pieces, signed about 1918, bear her Tewa name, *Po've'ka*: 'Pond Lily'. Such pieces are rare. She ceased signing again until *c.* 1923, when she began to use 'Marie'. About 1925, she began to sign 'Marie + Julian', and from that date always identified collaborative efforts. Nevertheless, several pieces made with Julian, identifiable by his style or in photographs, as late as 1926 are unsigned. Pieces made with Popovi Da are both signed and numbered with a code expressing the date of firing. The signatures were made on the base while the pieces were leather-hard. However, Maria also signed, with a felt pen, numerous turn-of-the-century pots not made by her, when brought to her by people who hoped they had one of her pots, presumably out of generosity and a desire not to disappoint.

BIBLIOGRAPHY
C. Guthe: 'Pueblo Pottery Making: A Study at the Village of San Ildefonso', *Papers of the Southwestern Expedition*, ii (New Haven, 1925)
A. Marriott: *Maria: The Potter of San Ildefonso* (Norman, 1948)
K. M. Chapman: *The Pottery of San Ildefonso Pueblo* (Albuquerque, 1970)
D. Lyon: 'The Polychrome Plates of Maria and Popovi', *Amer. Ind. A.*, i/2 (1976), pp. 76–9
S. Peterson: *The Living Tradition of Maria Martinez* (Tokyo, 1977)
R. Spivey: *Maria* (Flagstaff, 1979, rev. 1989)

JONATHAN BATKIN

Martínez, Alfredo Ramos. *See* RAMOS MARTÍNEZ, ALFREDO.

Martínez, Domingo (*b* Seville, 1688; *d* Seville, 1749). Spanish painter. He was the leading painter in Seville during the first half of the 18th century. He trained under Lucas Valdés Leal and is known to have been affable, energetic and intelligent, which enhanced his reputation as an artist. When Philip V moved the court to Seville in 1727, Martínez became a friend of the French painter Jean Ranc, who recommended him to the King for appointment as a court painter when the court returned to Madrid in 1734. Martínez refused the appointment, preferring to remain in Seville, where he had a large workshop, in which he taught such artists as Juan de Espina, Andrés Rubira (*d* 1760) and Pedro Tortolero.

Martínez's style combines echoes of Murillo with French influences that derive in particular from his association with Ranc and Louis-Michel van Loo. He had a great facility for composition and a discerning command of colour, producing attractive paintings with balanced compositions, in which form and atmosphere are rendered in bright colours. His principal works are in Seville, where he produced large series of decorative paintings. The first of these was executed *c.* 1724 for the chapel of the Palacio de S Telmo, a naval cadet training college (*in situ*); the paintings depict episodes from the life of Christ connected with childhood, suitable for an institution concerned with the education of boys and youths. About 1730 he decorated the presbytery of the convent church of S Paula with two scenes from the life of the saint (*in situ*). The retable of the church of Buen Suceso in Seville contains paintings depicting the biblical characters of the Tree of Jesse (1733; *in situ*). In 1738 he executed the series of large paintings that adorn the chapel of the Virgen de la Antigua in Seville Cathedral for the Archbishop of Seville, Louis de Salcedo y Azcona, of whom he painted a portrait (*c.* 1738–40; Seville, Pal. Arzobisp.). His last large series is a cycle of eight paintings for the Royal Tobacco Factory in Seville (*c.* 1748; Seville, Mus. B.A.). The scenes depict the procession of eight allegorical carts that took place in Seville in 1747 to celebrate the accession of Ferdinand VI in the previous year.

BIBLIOGRAPHY
S. Soro: *Domingo Martínez* (Seville, 1982)
A. Pérez Sánchez: *Pintura barroca en España, 1600–1750* (Madrid, 1992), pp. 420–24

ENRIQUE VALDIVIESO

Martínez (y Lurbe), Jusepe (*b* Saragossa, 6 Dec 1600; *d* Saragossa, 6 Jan 1682). Spanish painter, engraver and writer. He was a son of the Flemish painter Daniel Martínez (*d* 1636), with whom he first trained, following late Mannerist trends. In 1623 he went to Italy, and in 1625 he was in Rome, where he met Guido Reni, Domenichino and, shortly afterwards in Naples, Jusepe de Ribera. This contact with Italian classicism and naturalism influenced his work, and he always maintained a preference for classical balance and structure. He combined this with chromatic tones and a chiaroscuro that became progressively softer. The extensive documentation on Martínez deals only intermittently with his paintings, and it is not always possible to trace his stylistic development. His earliest recorded work is the series of five engravings on the *Life of St Pedro Nolasco* (*c.* 1625), which were engraved in Rome by Johann Friedrich Greuter (*d* 1662) after Martínez's drawings (untraced). In 1627 he returned to Saragossa and in 1632, together with Juan Galván (*d* 1658), he was nominated by the Diputación de Aragón to examine the copies of portraits of the kings of Aragon made for Philip IV. Also about 1632 he entered the circle of the collector Vincencio Juan de Lastanosa, to whom he sent some engravings, perhaps the series on the *Life of St Pedro Nolasco*. In 1634 Martínez travelled to Madrid, where he came into contact with Eugenio Cajés, Francisco Pacheco and Alonso Cano. Treating the same subject as in his earlier engraving series, in 1635–40 he painted *St Pedro Nolasco* (Saragossa, Mus. Prov. B.A.; see fig.), though the dating is uncertain. His relationship with the Court was renewed when Philip IV visited Catalonia and stayed in Saragossa in 1642, accompanied by Diego Velázquez. Martínez was nominated Pintor del Rey *ad honorem* in 1643 and entrusted with the artistic education of Don Juan José de Austria. Velázquez became friendly with Martínez and occasionally used his workshop.

The largest number of documented works by Martínez belong to the 1640s and 1650s. These include, all in Saragossa, the altarpiece of the Agustinos Descalzos (1646–8; untraced), that of Nuestra Señora la Blanca en la Seo (1646–7) and the allegory of the *Sadness of Saragossa* made for the funeral of the Príncipe-Baltasar Carlos (1646). From the Lastanosa family he received the commission for paintings (1646; all untraced) for the family chapel in Huesca Cathedral, including various portraits. The large canvas of the *Virgin of Monserrat with the Patron Saints of Huesca* (*c.* 1646; Huesca Cathedral) was a commission from Juan Martin Ramirez. The paintings for the altarpieces of the parishes of La Almunia de Doña Godina and of Santa María de Uncastillo date from 1647.

Such works as *Christ Appearing to St Cayetano* (*c.* 1643–49; Saragossa, S Isabel), the portrait of the honorary

Jusepe Martínez: *St Pedro Nolasco*, oil on canvas, 2.26×1.45 m, 1635–40 (Saragossa, Museo Provincial de Bellas Artes)

archbishop *Fray Juan Cebrián* (*c.* 1658–62; Saragossa, Pal. Arzobisp.) or the *Apparition of the Virgin to St Filippo Neri*—after the painting by Reni in S Maria in Vallicella, Rome—and the *Penitent St Jerónimo with the Angel of Justice* (*c.* 1669; both San Miguel de los Navarros), intended for the artist's funerary chapel, show how Martínez's style remained dependent on monumentality, firm draughtsmanship and a varied colouring of somewhat dull tones, applied with compressed brushstrokes. From about 1670 Martínez ceased painting and turned to writing his *Discursos practicables del nobilísimo arte de la pintura* (*c.* 1673), which was not published until 1866 in Madrid. This contains the artist's theory of painting, together with accounts of his journeys to Italy and Madrid, and of his relationship with other painters and Aragonese contemporaries. Martínez's son, Jerónimo Jusepe Bautista Martínez, became a painter and Carthusian friar, and his works include the *Self-portrait Painting Jusepe Martínez* (Saragossa, Mus. Zaragoza).

WRITINGS

Discursos practicables del nobilísimo arte de la pintura (*c.* 1673); ed. J. Gállego (Madrid, 1989)

BIBLIOGRAPHY

V. González Hernández: *Jusepe Martínez (1600–1682)* (Saragossa, 1981)
Jusepe Martínez y su tiempo (exh. cat. by J. L. Morales y Marin, A. E. Pérez Sánchez and J. Rogelio Buendía, Saragossa, Inst. Mus. Camon Aznar, 1982)
A. Ansón Navarro: 'Un cuadro inédito de Jusepe Martínez en la Basílica de San Lorenzo de Huesca: La Virgen de Monserrat con San Orencio, Santa Paciencia y sus hijos los Santos Lorenzo y Orencio, obispo de Auch', *Aragonia Sacra*, iv (1989), pp. 7–11

ISMAEL GUTIÉRREZ PASTOR

Martínez, Oliverio (*b* Piedras Negras, Mexico, 1901; *d* Mexico City, 21 Jan 1938). Mexican sculptor. He studied at the Academia de San Carlos, Mexico City (1928–30), under the sculptor José María Fernández Urbina (1898–1975). He was one of the pioneers of innovative trends in 20th-century Mexican sculpture and maintained links with the Mexican muralists, with whom he shared an exalted nationalism and a taste for monumental forms, celebrating the heroes of the Mexican Revolution in, for example, his monument to *Zapata* (1932) in the main square of Cuahutla, Mexico. In 1933 Martínez won a competition to execute four sculptural groups for the monument to the *Revolution* (1933) for the Palacio Legislativo, Mexico City. Carlos Obregón Santacilia designed the structure of the central cupola and arches of the building, and Martínez intended to place three energetic and geometrically solemn figures on the upper part of each of the four corners. Although the Palacio Legislativo was never built, the monument was completed in 1933 and built on the foundations intended for it. These stone sculptures, each 11.5 m high, depicted *Independence*, *Reform*, the *Publication of the Agrarian Laws of the Revolution* and the *Publication of the Labour Laws of the Revolution*.

BIBLIOGRAPHY

M. Monteforte Toledo: *Las piedras vivas* (Mexico City, 1965), pp. 202–3, 205
E. O'Gorman and others: *Cuarenta siglos de plástica mexicana*, 3 vols (Mexico City, 1971)

ESPERANZA GARRIDO

Martínez Barrio, Antonio (*b* Huesca, 1750; *d* Madrid, 1798). Spanish goldsmith. The son of a goldsmith of the same name, he went to Saragossa in 1764 to attend the classes in painting and drawing given by the painter José Luzán y Martínez (1710–85). In 1769 he went to study at the Real Academia de Bellas Artes de S Fernando in Madrid. In 1775 Martínez deposited with Charles III a number of gold and silver pieces, made by himself, as a guarantee for a loan to subsidize a visit to Paris and London. On his return to Spain in April 1776 he brought models of gold and silver objects and a good knowledge of the most modern styles. In October 1777 he presented to the King a proposal for a school—later also a factory—of goldsmithing. The Real Escuela de Platería received royal sanction in April 1778 and functioned until 1869, its directors all being distinguished goldsmiths. Many craftsmen trained in the school, some as Martínez's own pupils, including Josep Martí and Josep Rovira of Barcelona, and the Basques Domingo Conde (*fl* 1798–1808) and José Ignacio de Macazaga (*fl* 1790; *d* 1820), the last two marrying sisters of Martínez. His chief assistant was the Frenchman Nicolàs Chameroi (*d* 1832).

The Real Fábrica de Platería produced gold pieces both for private commissions and to satisfy the demand for such mass-produced small gold objects as handles for walking-sticks, buttons, boxes and needle-cases. The same was true of the production of such silver objects as trays, *trembleuses*, vinaigrettes, buckles and plates, decorated with hammering, cut-card work and pierced work. Among larger commissions fulfilled by the factory in Martínez's lifetime was the set of about 30 pieces made for Caballero Góngora, Bishop of Córdoba (1794; Córdoba, Iglesia de la Asunción de Priego). Secular objects produced by the factory are characterized by fluted cylindrical bodies, ram's head or pineapple finials, ferrules and other classical motifs inspired by 18th-century Parisian and Adam decoration. Some original types of object were produced, for example *especieros de corazón* (heart-shaped spice-boxes) and inkstands surmounted by a cup-bearing cupid.

BIBLIOGRAPHY
J. M. Cruz Valdovinos: *La Real Escuela de Platería de don Antonio Martínez* (Madrid, 1988)
——: 'Datos para una historia económica de la Real Fábrica de Platería de don Antonio Martínez', *An. Inst. Estud. Madril.*, xxxiii (1993), pp. 73–122

For further bibliography *see* SPAIN, §IX, 1.
JOSÉ MANUEL CRUZ VALDOVINOS

Martínez de Arrona, Juan (*b* Vergara, 1562; *d* Lima, 1635). Spanish architect and sculptor active in Peru. He was trained as a sculptor by Cristóbal Velázquez (*d* 1616), a Mannerist of the school of Alonso Berruguete. He arrived in Lima *c.* 1599 and carved the life-sized reliefs of *Christ and the Apostolate* (1608) in cedar above the chests in the sacristy of the cathedral. They are imposing but do not strive for realism, betraying the influence of the Antique, particularly in the disposition and layout of the channelled folds and drapery and through references to Renaissance classicism. In 1614 he was appointed *maestro mayor* of Lima Cathedral, a post which he retained until his death. He is also known to have worked on the stone façade of S Lázaro. Following the earthquakes of 1606 and 1609, various architects were consulted on how to re-roof the cathedral. Wooden vaults were rejected and Martínez de Arrona proposed Gothic ribbed vaults, executed in brick. This proposal was followed and the church was completed by 1622 and the towers installed in 1624, when work was also carried out on the portals and choir-stalls. Francisco Becerra's plan was retained, although the Gothic vaults and Ionic columns were altered slightly. They were eventually replaced by an identical structure in wood and plaster following the 1746 earthquake. Seven of the cathedrals' portals were designed by Martínez de Arrona in 1626, combining Baroque with Classical elements through the use of Corinthian columns. The niches and ornamentation were more strongly related to Baroque fashions, and this is particularly the case with the main entrance, with its abrupt changes in the niches between contours, planes and broken pediments.

BIBLIOGRAPHY
H. E. Wethey: *Colonial Architecture and Sculpture in Peru* (Cambridge, MA, 1949)
G. Kubler and M. Soria: *Art and Architecture in Spain and Portugal and their American Dominions 1500 to 1800* (Harmondsworth, 1959), pp. 130–31
E. Harth-Terré: *Perú: Monumentos hispánicos y arqueológicos* (Mexico City, 1975), p. 40
J. B. Ballesteros: *Arte hispanoamericano de los siglos XVI a XVIII* (Madrid, 1987), p. 306
V. Fraser: *The Architecture of Conquest: Building in the Viceroyalty of Peru, 1535–1635* (London, 1990), p. 106
W. IAIN MACKAY

Martínez de Hebert, Pedro. *See* HEBERT, PEDRO.

Martínez de Hoyos, Ricardo (*b* Mexico City, 28 Oct 1918; *d* 1983). Mexican painter. He came from a family of artists and was self-taught. He initially concentrated on landscapes and metaphysical themes, as in *The Astronomer* (1944; priv. col., see Bonifaz Nuño, fig. 5). However, the figure of the Indian was a constant element in his production of large-format paintings. Indigenous male and female figures are set dramatically against dark backgrounds; their semi-illuminated bodies are emphasized by the use of a single pure colour, such as blue, red or orange (e.g. *The Sorcerer*, 1971; Mexico City, Mus. A. Mod.). These colossal images draw their inspiration from Pre-Columbian hieratic sculpture, and their highly individual use of colour and fine draughtsmanship distinguish Martínez from his contemporaries.

BIBLIOGRAPHY
R. Bonifaz Nuño: *Ricardo Martínez* (Mexico City, 1965)
L. Cardoza y Aragón: *Ricardo Martínez: Una selección de su obra* (Mexico City, 1981)
XAVIER MOYSSÉN

Martínez del Mazo, Juan Bautista. *See* MAZO, JUAN BAUTISTA MARTÍNEZ DEL.

Martínez de Oviedo, Diego (*b* Cuzco; *fl* 1664–80). Peruvian architect and sculptor. He was the son of the architect Sebastián Martínez (*d c.* 1660), from whom he received his training. After his native city was destroyed in the earthquake of 1650, he rebuilt the façade and towers (which he may also have designed) of the Jesuit church of La Compañía, one of the finest in Peru, in 1664–8. His carving of the façade in the form of a retable in stone shows similarities to his work in wood for the retables inside this church. Martínez de Oviedo's remarkable achievement as an architect and sculptor is seen in his designs for the cedarwood retable, pulpit and façades of S Teresa, Cuzco, completed in 1676. Other works in Cuzco are in the churches of S Domingo (choir screen, 1665), S Sebastián near Cuzco (principal retable, 1679) and the Cathedral (side altar, 1667). His work in the cloister of the monastery of La Merced, Cuzco, on which he collaborated with his father in 1663, resembles a wood-carving carried out in stone. Together with Francisco Chávez y Arellano, Juan Tomás Tuyru Tupac Inca and Martín de Torres, Martínez de Oviedo was responsible for the artistic renewal in Cuzco, prompted by Archbishop Mallinedo (*d* 1699), in the last third of the 17th century.

BIBLIOGRAPHY

H. Wethey: *Art and Architecture in Peru* (Cambridge, 1949)
J. Cornejo Bouroncle: *Derroteros del arte cusqueño* (Cuzco, 1956)
E. Marco Dorta: *La arquitectura barroca en el Perú* (Madrid, 1957)

RAMÓN GUTIÉRREZ

Martínez Gutierrez, Juan (*b* Bilbao, 1901; *d* Chile, 1976). Chilean architect of Spanish birth. He moved to Chile as a child and studied architecture at the Universidad de Chile in Santiago from 1917 to 1922. In 1927 he won the first architectural competition to be organized in Chile, for the Chilean Pavilion at the Exposicion Ibero-Americana 1929. He visited Europe in 1928–31 and absorbed the influence of Rationalism, the Bauhaus and other modern developments. In 1931 he became Profesor de Taller (workshop teacher) at the Escuela de Arquitectura of the Universidad de Chile. He became its Director in 1932 and reformed the teaching programme. In 1936 he won a competition for the Escuela de Derecho building (completed 1938) in the Universidad de Chile. Equal to the best architecture of its time worldwide, the building is Rationalist with expressionistic elements in the main curved façade and well-articulated south elevation. After such projects as the Escuela Militar in Santiago (1943), which is an early example of exposed concrete on exterior and interior walls, he designed the Unión Española de Seguros building (1948), which anticipated some of the Gropius/TAC schemes in Boston and also incorporates local material, such as copper, in the façades. Martínez—who was an excellent watercolourist—paved the way for the transformation of architectural teaching in Chile. In 1969 he was awarded the Premio Nacional de Arquitectura and in 1975 became Emeritus Professor of the Universidad de Chile. He stressed the principal that good architecture is the result of conscientious study of its 'function', although his best works in fact transcend this view.

BIBLIOGRAPHY

H. Eliash and M. Moreno: *Arquitectura y modernidad en Chile, 1925–1965* (Santiago, 1989)

RAMÓN ALFONSO MÉNDEZ

Martínez Pedro, Luis (*b* Havana, 1910). Cuban painter. He studied architecture at the University of Havana (1930), before moving to the USA in 1931, where he studied at the Arts and Crafts Club, New York (1932). He returned to Cuba in 1933. The most individual of Cuba's Constructivist painters, he is best known for *Territorial Waters*, a series that reached its climax in the early 1960s and that

used geometric forms to describe the wave patterns of water (e.g. *Territorial Waters 5*, 1962; Havana, Mus. N. B.A.). Although such a referential use of hard-edge forms was common among Latin American artists, Martínez Pedro's interest in water as subject-matter is surprisingly rare. By the early 1970s he began to concentrate on enlarged images of tropical flora in a style derivative of Pop art, for example *Coral-tree Flower* (1975; Havana, Mus. N. B.A.).

BIBLIOGRAPHY

A. H. Barr, jr: 'Modern Cuban Painters', *MOMA Bull.*, xi/5 (1944), pp. 2–14
J. Gómez-Sicre: *Pintura cubana de hoy* (Havana, 1944)

RICARDO PAU-LLOSA

Martínez Pérez, Sebastián (*b* Treguajantes, Soria, 25 Dec 1747; *d* 24 Nov 1800). Spanish merchant and collector. He came from a *hidalgo* background in Rioja and moved to Cádiz in adolescence to make his fortune in the Indies trade. Cádiz, culturally rich and cosmopolitan, was at the height of its prosperity at that period, a city in which it was not unusual for merchants to appreciate and collect works of art. Martínez Pérez bought houses, books, silver and English furniture as well as many prints and paintings. When an inventory was made of his collection after his death it contained 746 paintings, of which 26% were landscapes and seascapes, 21% religious subjects, 11% still-lifes and 8% portraits. There was a strong Neoclassical element in Martínez's taste. He had bronze busts of *Anton Raphael Mengs* and his Spanish friend *José Nicolás de Azara*, many mythological pictures and sculptures, one or two antiquities and paintings of ruins and other 'classical' subjects. He also had prints after Raphael's series of Old Testament scenes in the Logge of the Vatican and of Giovanni Battista Piranesi's *Vedute* and *Antichità*. He evidently liked nudes and Dutch genre paintings too, and he had a signed interior by Pieter de Hooch. Francisco de Goya stayed with him for several months in the first half of 1793 to recuperate from illness and had painted his portrait (1792; New York, Met.) when Martínez was in Madrid the previous year. Earlier Goya had painted three overdoors for Martínez, generally identified as the *Sleeping Woman* (Dublin, N.G.), a smaller picture of the same subject (Hartford, CT, Wadsworth Atheneum) and another of *Two Women Talking* (Madrid, MacCrohon priv. col.).

BIBLIOGRAPHY

M. Pemán: 'La colección artística de Sebastián Martínez, el amigo de Goya, en Cádiz', *Archv Esp. A.*, li (1978), pp. 53–62
N. Glendinning: 'Goya's Patrons', *Apollo*, cxiv (1981), pp. 236–47
A. García Baquero: *Libro y cultura burguesa en Cádiz: La biblioteca de Sebastián Martínez* (Cádiz)
M. Pemán: 'Estampas y libros que vio Goya en casa de Sebastián Martínez', *Archv Esp. A.*, cclix–cclx (1992), pp. 303–20

NIGEL GLENDINNING

Martínez Sánchez, José (*fl* Valencia and Madrid, 1858–68). Spanish photographer. Although he maintained a studio in Valencia, he was more commonly known as one of the photographers based in Madrid's central Puerta del Sol. In partnership with Antonio Cosmes, he made a set of photographs that constitutes Spain's first serial photographic reportage of a single news event, depicting the arrival by sea of their majesties to Valencia's Port of Grau

(1858; Madrid, Bib. N.); included in this series was the first photograph in Spain of dawn. His best work was produced in association with Juan Laurent. Photographs in their album *Obras públicas* (*c.* 1867) indicate that many of Laurent's unsigned masterworks may actually have been by Martínez Sánchez. Both were technically innovative and presented their invention, *leptografía*, a new paper process for photographic prints, before the Société Française de Photographie in November 1866, aiming to displace common albumen paper. Their invention was adopted by Julio Beauchy, Franck (Alexander Gobinet de Villecholso) and André-Adolphe-Eugène Disdéri.

BIBLIOGRAPHY
L. Fontanella: *La historia de la fotografía en España desde sus orígenes hasta 1900* (Madrid, 1981)
LEE FONTANELLA

Martini, Alberto (*b* Oderzo, nr Treviso, 24 Nov 1876; *d* Milan, 8 Nov 1954). Italian painter and engraver. His early paintings, such as the *Sacred River Isonzo* (1892; Milan, priv. col., see Bellini, p. 43), were not given serious consideration by critics at the time. He is more highly regarded for the vast number of drawings that he produced and that gained him his first recognition at the Venice Biennale in 1897, where he had on display 14 drawings from the anthology *La corte dei miracoli*. He concentrated mainly on illustrating famous literary works such as Pulci's *Morgante maggiore*, Tassoni's *La secchia rapita* (1895), the *Divina commedia* (1901–2) and the *Tales of E. A. Poe*, which occupied him until 1909. His drawings for these publications show the influence of Bosch, Pieter Bruegel I, Dürer, Lucas Cranach I and Albrecht Altdorfer, whose work he had studied in Munich. This is particularly noticeable in the recurrent depiction of a real world controlled by spirits and monstrous and deformed demonic beings. For these reasons critics have treated Martini, together with de Chirico and Alberto Savinio, as one of the precursors of Surrealism, though he never officially subscribed to it despite his lengthy stay in Paris from 1928 onwards and his direct acquaintance with André Breton. The series *Women–Butterflies* (1915–20) bears witness to his proto-Surrealism, expressed as a synthesis of Symbolist references combined with Liberty stylization and elegance and dreamlike distortions, as in the black-and-white lithograph, subsequently hand-coloured, entitled *Felina* (1915; Oderzo, Pin. Com. Alberto Martini).

BIBLIOGRAPHY
M. Lorandi: *Alberto Martini* (Milan, 1985)
P. Bellini, ed.: *Alberto Martini: Mostra antologica* (Oderzo, 1988)

Martini, Arturo (*b* Treviso, 11 Aug 1889; *d* Milan, 22 March 1947). Italian sculptor. He was self-taught as a sculptor, though he started work in Treviso as an apprentice ceramist, an occupation to which he returned later in life. From 1906 to 1907 he attended the studio in Treviso of a local sculptor, A. Carlini (1859–1945), and subsequently studied at the Accademia di Belle Arti in Venice where he was taught by the Italian sculptor Urbano Nono (1849–1925). In 1909 he met Gino Rossi and with him took part in exhibitions at the Ca' Pesaro in Venice, organized by the art critic Nino Barbantini.

In order to keep himself up to date with new tendencies Martini travelled and, in particular, stayed in Paris where in 1912 seven of his carvings were displayed with work by Rossi and Modigliani at the Salon d'Automne. Typical of this period is the coloured terracotta *The Prostitute* (1909–13; Venice, Ca' Pesaro), which shows the influence of Gauguin with its thick dark line enclosing the areas of colour. He was also influenced by the Jugendstil on a study trip in 1909 to Munich, where he met Adolf von Hildebrand. Between 1920 and 1930 he produced works such as the *Prodigal Son* (1926) and *La Pisana* (1928–9; both Acqui Terme, Ottolenghi priv. col., see Perocco), which attracted critical approval at the Venice Biennale in 1932. In 1938–9 he devoted himself primarily to painting, but returned to sculpture soon afterwards. In 1945 he published his book *La scultura lingua morta*, which was an influence on young artists like M. De Luigi (1901–78), Alberto Viani and Mirko. His later sculptures include *Woman Swimming Underwater* (1941–2; Milan, Lucchetti priv. col., see Perocco) and *Il Palinuro* (1946; U. Padua).

WRITINGS
La scultura lingua morta (Venice, 1945)

BIBLIOGRAPHY
G. Perocco: *A. Martini* (Rome, 1962)
G. Mazzotti: *Arturo Martini, catalogo della mostra* (Treviso, 1967)
SAVERIO SIMI DE BURGIS

Martini, Cristofano di Michele. *See* ROBETTA.

Martini, Ferdinando (*b* Florence, 30 July 1841; *d* Monsummano Terme, nr Pistoia, 24 April 1928). Italian writer and politician. He began his career as a playwright in the early 1860s and subsequently took up journalism. He became a liberal member of the Italian parliament in 1876 and, after holding various posts, was appointed Minister of Education in 1892 and finally a senator in 1923. From 1871 he had contributed to the Florentine daily newspaper *Il fanfulla*. In 1879 he founded its Sunday edition, *Il fanfulla della domenica*, and was its Director until 1882. In that year it became a weekly publication, *La domenica letteraria*. He wrote a small number of articles on art, the majority of which appeared in *Il fanfulla*. In them he dealt primarily with logistical problems associated with the organization of exhibitions and with the relationship between artists and governing bodies. He was opposed to the idea of valuable works of art being moved about in travelling exhibitions and he campaigned for a prudent administration of the Italian artistic patrimony in order to save it from uncontrolled export abroad. He also advocated government aid to help with the development of public collections. His most important articles were collected and published as *Fra un sigaro e l'altro* (1876) and *Di palo in frasca* (1891). Throughout his life he wrote numerous short stories and between 1922 and 1928 wrote his memoirs, *Confessioni e ricordi*.

WRITINGS
Fra un sigaro e l'altro (Milan, 1876)
Di palo in frasca (Modena, 1891; rev. Milan, 1931)
Confessioni e ricordi (Florence, 1922–5; rev. Milan, 1929)
Regular contributions to *Il fanfulla* (1871–82)

BIBLIOGRAPHY
A. Donati: *Ferdinando Martini* (Rome, 1925)
C. Cappuccio, ed.: 'Ferdinando Martini', *Memorialisti dell'ottocento*, La letteratura italiana: Storia e testi, LIX/ii (Milan and Naples, 1958), pp. 955–63
C. A. Madrignani: '*La domenica letteraria*' *di F. Martini e di A. Sommaruga* (Rome, 1978)

GIULIANA TOMASELLA

Martini, Francesco di Giorgio. *See* FRANCESCO DI GIORGIO MARTINI.

Martini, Ndoc (Andon) (*b* Shkodër, 14 June 1871; *d* Paris, 6 Dec 1916). Albanian painter. After studying at the School of Arts and Crafts in Shkodër he worked in his family's atelier as a designer of bridal outfits and accessories. He later graduated from the Arbëreshi College at S Demetrio Corone in Calàbria, where he painted frescoes in one of the halls. He finished his studies at the Académie des Beaux-Arts in Paris (1904–9), where he painted the portrait of *President Loubet* and frescoes for the Chambre des Députés in the Palais Bourbon. In Paris Martini also continued to depict Albanian subjects, for example *Skanderbeg* (1912; Istanbul, International Trade Exhibition; destr. 1913). He was noted for the psychological depth of his portraiture. On the whole Martini adhered to traditional realist style and composition, but his work was gradually influenced by French Impressionism, as in *Dr Prela* (1916; Tiranë, A.G.).

BIBLIOGRAPHY
Artet Figurative Shqiptare [Albanian figurative art] (Tiranë, 1978)
K. Buza: 'Edhe një vepër e Ndoc Martini' [Another painting by Ndoc Martini], *Drita* (10 April 1983), p. 11

SULEJMAN DASHI

Martini, Simone (*b c.* 1284; *bur* Avignon, ?4 Aug 1344). Italian painter. Active in central Italy (mostly Siena), Naples and Avignon, he ranks, in terms of professional skill and manual dexterity, as one of the outstanding painters of the 14th century anywhere in Europe. His grand formal altarpieces encompass at the most exalted professional level a range of decorative techniques that were simply beyond the reach of most of his contemporaries. While always beguiling as a pictorial raconteur, he varied both the pitch and the pace of his story-telling in a manner similarly without parallel in the century, moving from the discursive and ambivalent drama of his frescoes in S Francesco, Assisi (*see* §I, 2(iii) below), to the claustrophobic and excited composition of his Antwerp Polyptych (*see* §I, 4 below). In short, Simone's documented work is far richer in contrasts than the comparable output of any other 14th-century artist, revealing a restless and innovative temperament. His work was certainly based on precedent (though the closest antecedents are a matter for debate), and there is a recognizable 'Simone style' in the various polyptychs associated with him and his workshop. Beyond that, however, the most striking aspects of his painting lie in its novelty and invention.

Although compared with other 14th-century artists, the life of Simone Martini is well-documented (rather more, for instance, is known about him than about Giotto), there are still unsolved problems concerning the attribution and chronology of his works, which, in turn, have important repercussions on the interpretation of his career.

I. Life and work. II. Working methods and studio organization. III. Posthumous reputation.

I. Life and work.

1. Artistic formation, before *c.* 1315. 2. Siena, Naples and Assisi, *c.* 1315–20. 3. Siena, Orvieto, San Gimignano and Pisa, *c.* 1320–35. 4. Avignon, *c.* 1335–44.

1. ARTISTIC FORMATION, BEFORE *c.* 1315. It is now normal to accept, in the absence of other documentation, the evidence of a memorial inscription seen by Vasari in S Francesco, Siena, from which it would appear that Simone was born in 1284. Since the earliest archival record of Simone's existence dates from 1315, the first 30 years of his life, including his training, are a matter of debate and speculation. The basis of this speculation lies in the view taken of his earliest surviving work, from *c.* 1315 (*see* §2 below), about which there is no complete agreement. The traditional view is that Simone was a true Sienese painter trained in the workshop of Duccio; furthermore, it has been argued that he painted a substantial section of Duccio's *Maestà* (Siena, Mus. Opera Duomo). According to this view, Simone's initial style, determined by Duccio, was modified during the second decade by the influence of Giotto, and the familiar style as seen in Simone's *Maestà* (Siena, Pal. Pub.; *see* §2(i) below) or the *St Louis* altarpiece (Naples, Capodimonte; *see* §2(ii) below) is an amalgam of these two sources. There are obvious problems raised by this approach. Is it likely that Simone at the age of about 25 would still be painting in a style virtually indistinguishable from Duccio's? Against that, it may be argued that Vasari's inscription may have been mistaken and that Simone may have been born in the 1290s. The absence, however, of any evidence before 1315 in the Sienese archives for the existence of Simone or his father, Martino, also needs an explanation, the simplest being that the family was not living in Siena during the early years of the century. This leads on to the alternative view of Simone's youth and training: that in the early works the resemblances to Duccio are superficial and that the structure of the figures, the layout of narrative scenes and the command of three-dimensional perspective are those of a painter fundamentally influenced by the practices of Roman mural painters—especially those known through the earlier decorations at S Francesco, Assisi. From this point of view, Vasari's statement that Simone was a pupil of Giotto seems to be unexpectedly near the mark, though it is open to question whether Giotto himself painted at Assisi (*see* ASSISI, §II, 2(iv)). Vasari, in fact, suggested that Simone trained under Giotto in Rome. Simone's penchant for imitating precious materials, his experiments with raised gesso modelling, his knowledge of some unusual details of northern Gothic architecture, the indubitable and pronounced northern Gothic figure and drapery style, as well as other details, all suggest access to northern 'court' art from the Anglo-French milieu of Paris and London. There is, in fact, considerable agreement over the presence of these elements in his style. It is not, however, certain that he went north of the Alps in the late 13th century, since it has been argued that these pictorial interests might

have been stimulated in Rome at the same period or indeed in Naples, for at this time both were centres of French cultural influence. These debates matter to the extent that the reader has to choose the basis on which to introduce Simone into the story of Trecento painting. There is a predominantly Sienese view that he should be seen primarily as the great continuator of the grand tradition of Duccio. The other view, in its various shades, sees the most interesting things in his painting as generated by a world lying beyond the borders of Tuscany and even beyond the borders of Italy.

2. SIENA, NAPLES AND ASSISI, *c.* 1315–20.

(i) The 'Maestà'. The surviving evidence shows that Simone finished painting his *Maestà* (*see* WALL PAINTING, colour pl. II, fig. 2, and SIENA, fig. 10), which covers virtually the entire end wall of the Great Hall (nicknamed the Sala del Mappamondo) of the Palazzo Pubblico, Siena, in 1315–16. It is likely, however, to have been begun earlier than that, for the first and major building phase of the palazzo came to a close in 1311. Simone and his workshop repaired the fresco in 1321. The subject is clearly derived from Duccio's *Maestà*, an enormous panel painting installed on the high altar of Siena Cathedral in June 1311. Many of the saintly figures are manifestly similar, and the tiered arrangement whereby the heads of the figures in front do not obscure those of the figures behind has also been followed. The impression is, however, fundamentally altered: it is, put simply, more secular. Iconographically this is apparent in the magnificent canopy that carries on it the arms of Siena (the so-called *balzana*), the arms of the Sienese *popolo* (a lion) and of the Neapolitan royal house of Anjou. The Virgin engages in an exchange of greetings with the four kneeling saints who, as patrons of Siena, have been chosen as the accredited representatives of the Commune. (The speeches are—or were—inscribed within the composition.) The secularity of the scene is emphasized by the pictorial illusion of the wall. The painting embraces the entire surface from wall to wall and ceiling to floor. The wall surface has apparently been pierced to reveal the court of the Virgin drawn up under the great canopy—itself a space-defining device that instantly gives the figure group a material presence totally beyond the purposes of Duccio's masterpiece. This materiality is enhanced by the modelling of decorative patterns in gesso relief and by the insertion of pieces of coloured glass, a few fragments of which survive in the throne, to make the surface still more sparkling.

(ii) The 'St Louis' altarpiece. It is generally agreed that the *St Louis of Toulouse* altarpiece (Naples, Capodimonte; *see* GOTHIC, fig. 78), signed by Simone, is connected with the celebrations of 1317 to mark the completion of the canonization of St Louis of Toulouse (*d* 1299), a member of the royal house of Anjou. Simone probably went to Naples to execute it, but it is very unlikely that he is identical with a knight called Simone Martin, fortuitously present in Naples at the same time. The altarpiece contains much family heraldry and a portrait of King Robert (*reg* 1309–43), Louis' younger brother. In its emphasis on minute and splendid surface detail, the altarpiece confirms the impression of the *Maestà*. It also demonstrates a close

observation of texture and a taste for the exotic in the carpet, a crozier of a design that would have been unusual in 1317 and a wooden podium decorated with intarsia work (features that prefigure the painting of Jan van Eyck). At the base of the altar is a narrative *predella*—the first to survive intact, though probably with antecedents in the work of Duccio and Cimabue. It gives the earliest information about Simone's narrative style, which is very simple and direct. The scenes, illustrating the life, death and miracles of the saint, are played out on a shallow stage. These scenes were 'new', there being no pre-existing iconography for St Louis. The basis would seem to be the official *Life* of the saint, but the identification of the third and fifth scenes is not entirely clear. The detail is minutely observed, but the figures are sturdy and solid. This is not like the style of Duccio, as seen in the cathedral *Maestà*. The altarpiece as a whole, therefore, tends to lessen the impression of a close relationship between the styles of the two artists.

(iii) The chapel of S Martino, S Francesco, Assisi. As with most of the mural decoration of S Francesco, there is virtually no contemporary evidence for the painting of the chapel of S Martino (*see* ASSISI, §II, 2(vi)), and the attribution to Simone (now universally accepted) dates only from the early 19th century. The patron was a Franciscan cardinal, Gentile Partino da Montefiore del'Aso. He died in 1312, having previously given a large sum of money for the chapel. That money, 600 florins, while far in excess of the amount needed to execute the mural decoration, does not seem quite enough to have paid for the construction of the building. The absence of other evidence, therefore, leaves unclear the state of the site in 1312, and hence the date of the frescoes. There is, however, some consensus that they were painted before 1319–22, a period in which political strife rendered unlikely further decoration of the basilica. The presence of a haloed image of St Louis of Toulouse in the soffit of the entrance arch has normally been accepted as an indication of a date of *c.* 1317, though it does not, in fact, preclude an earlier date.

The subject, the *Life of St Martin*, is of great rarity in Italy and, effectively working without precedents, Simone was again creating a new iconography. The scenes chosen, perhaps by the patron's executors, stressed St Martin's relationship with the secular world and gave Simone a series of splendid opportunities for painting moments of secular and ecclesiastical pageantry and ritual (see fig. 1). Many of the techniques used occur also in the Siena *Maestà* (for instance the raised patterning), and the narrative layout, normally confined to a narrow stage, is similar to that found in the *St Louis* altarpiece. The larger scale of the frescoes, however, gave more scope for the description of costume, and there are some hats that have been convincingly identified as Hungarian in style (e.g. that worn by the central figure in fig. 1; *see also* ASSISI, fig. 6). Perhaps most remarkable of all is the astonishing array of characterizations of the human face and expression.

The formal layout of the chapel of S Martino owes much to pre-existing decoration in S Francesco, both in the Upper Church and in the chapel of S Nicola (finished

1. Simone Martini: *Renunciation of Arms* (*c.* 1317), fresco, Chapel of St Martin,
S Francesco, Assisi

before 1307). The closest antecedents to Simone's narrative style probably lie in the work of the *St Francis* cycle
in the Upper Church, where the emphasis on material,
secular splendour and courtly ritual is also to be found. A
few of Simone's details are manifestly imitated from this
source. The chapel of S Martino also contains snatches of
illusionism derived from the earlier painting—the galleries
of half-length saints in the windows and the angel figures
that gesticulate from their tiny porthole-like medallions.
Above the entrance arch, Cardinal Gentile is painted
kneeling before his patron St Martin under a ciborium.
The saint gravely receives the bare-headed Cardinal, who
has tactfully laid his hat aside on the parapet. All of this
supports the view that by *c.* 1310 the mural painting of
Assisi was at least as important a factor in the artistic
formation of Simone as the tradition of Duccio and that
the most distinctive elements in his training were received
outside Siena.

Perhaps the most striking piece of illusion, however,
occurs in the decoration of the chapel of S Elisabetta in
the right transept of the Lower Church. Above the altar
(now removed), against a splendid stamped, gilt ground,
the Virgin and Child appear from behind a parapet,
between two crowned saints, perhaps Louis of France and
Ladislas of Hungary. On the side wall, five further saints
stand behind a parapet, apparently in an open loggia set
against a blue sky. They assist—somewhat casually—at the
altar, turning gravely towards each other. St Louis of
Toulouse, at the instance of his neighbour St Francis, has

laid down his royal crown on the parapet so that the
fleurons appear to protrude into the transept.

3. SIENA, ORVIETO, SAN GIMIGNANO AND PISA,
c. 1320–35. During this period, the Sienese civic archives
give a fairly full picture of Simone's life in Siena and his
work for the Commune. He married the sister of Lippo
Memmi in 1324 and bought a house. He worked consistently for the Commune, mainly on small jobs. His major
works for the city during this period were probably a
Crucifix (1321) and an altarpiece of uncertain date, both
for the Cappella de' Nove in the Palazzo Pubblico (both
untraced); the fresco of *Guidoriccio da Fogliano before
Montemassi* (normally dated 1330 but perhaps of 1333),
which faces the *Maestà* in the Sala del Mappamondo (*see*
SIENA, figs 10–11); the *Annunciation* for the S Ansano
altar of Siena Cathedral (1333; Florence, Uffizi); and a
second altarpiece (untraced), which remained in the cathedral until the early 17th century. There is less agreement
about the attribution of the fresco of the so-called *New
Town* (perhaps Arcidosso, painted 1331), recently rediscovered immediately below the image of Guidoriccio.

Although attempts have been made since 1977 (by
Moran, Mallory and others) to disassociate the image of
Guidoriccio from the work of Simone (for further details
of this unusually heated debate, see bibliography), the
evidence is not cumulatively compelling. The painting,
however, suggests workshop intervention and had also
been much repaired and restored. The figure, a spirited
equestrian study, was probably intended to embody the
military pretensions and aspirations of the Sienese Commune; it is strange that there is no inscription to Guidoriccio, who was Capitano della Guerra (1328–33), here
identifiable only by his heraldry and perhaps to his
contemporaries by his face. The panoramic landscape is
remarkable when compared with anything previously
painted in Siena—the most apposite comparisons are to
be found in the earlier paintings at Assisi. Simone included
in the scene a 'portrait' of the town of Montemassi, a view
of some temporary siegeworks (the so-called *battifolle* in
the centre) and a view of the Sienese camp on the right.
The emblematic nature of the image is emphasized by the
absence of any other human in the fresco, which makes
the scene curiously unreal. Like much of Simone's work,
this was a highly unusual commission, apparently without
precedent and demanding the creation of a new type of
iconography.

The S Ansano altarpiece of the *Annunciation* (1333;
Florence, Uffizi) is more routine in its subject but equally
original in its treatment. The requirements were novel—a
major altarpiece in the new Gothic style containing a
narrative event in its main panel. The effects are now
marred by a grossly over elaborate late 19th-century frame.
The altarpiece is, however, still dominated by its two
central figures. Technically, the painting is a *tour de force*
equalled only by the earlier *St Louis* altarpiece. All Simone's
formidable technical skill was deployed; the differentiation
of costly materials and textures and the painting of the lily
seem to anticipate the skill of Jan van Eyck. Yet the
altarpiece also contains a dramatic confrontation of rare
sensitivity: Gabriel, mouth open, enunciates the fateful
words, which are embossed in the gold-leaf background,

2. Simone Martini: St Catarina Altarpiece, tempera on panel, 1.95×3.40 m, c. 1320 (Pisa, Museo Nazionale di S Matteo)

and the Virgin on her splendid throne draws back in alarm. This is drama in the grand manner of Pietro Cavallini but executed with the perceptive touch of the Isaac Master.

Alongside Simone's civic work, there was a large number of private commissions, some executed by his workshop, which probably provided a higher proportion of his income. Only one appears to have been painted in Siena: the altarpiece (Siena, Pin. N.) that decorated the coffin of the Blessed Agostino Novello in S Agostino, Siena. Its format, which derives from the 13th century, is unexpected and presumably reflects the wishes of a mildly old-fashioned patron. Several other altarpieces of a more normal 14th-century format were executed principally for churches in Orvieto, San Gimignano and Pisa. Following Duccio's precedents, they were made up of one or more rows of half-length figures of saints, normally with images of the Virgin and Child in the centre. The earliest seems likely to be the altarpiece done for the church of S Agostino, San Gimignano (now divided between Cambridge, Fitzwilliam; Cologne, Wallraf-Richartz Mus.; and an Italian priv. col.). The totally 'un-gothicized' architectural design is very close to the surviving altarpieces from Duccio's workshop, and much of the decorative repertory is familiar from other works. In the 16th century the painting was reported as being signed, though the inscription is now lost.

Simone's most brilliant surviving polyptych, signed on the central panel, was painted c. 1320 for the Dominican church of S Caterina, Pisa (Pisa, Mus. N. & Civ. S Matteo;

see fig. 2; the date is recorded in the annals and chronicle of the convent). Although it too bears a resemblance to a Duccesque prototype, it goes far beyond any previous achievement in scale, brilliance of colour and inventiveness. Despite being shorn of almost all its detachable architectural components (pilasters, pinnacles, crockets) and split up into smaller units (even the predella has been sawn into seven parts), it is still remarkable for the uniformly high quality of its painting and the variety of its 44 figures. The Dominican emphasis on learning and preaching is illustrated by the fact that most of the figures carry books or scrolls.

Three further altarpieces survive that are directly connected with both Simone and the town of Orvieto. One, signed and with an incomplete date, perhaps 1324, was painted for the church of S Domenico (parts Orvieto, Mus. Opera Duomo). Its fragmentary remains of good, though somewhat routine, quality show a significant change in the organization of the architecture. The S Caterina Altarpiece is organized in clearly divided horizontal tiers—a common feature of Sienese altarpieces at that time. In the S Domenico Altarpiece, the pointed arches pierce the upper gable after the manner of a Gothic ciborium. The same feature is visible in a second altarpiece for Orvieto, this one painted for S Maria dei Servi (Boston, MA, Isabella Stewart Gardner Mus.). Of the third altarpiece for Orvieto, said to come from S Francesco, only the central panel survives (also Orvieto, Mus. Opera Duomo). In format it is different from the others, though

3. Simone Martini: *St John the Evangelist*, tempera on panel, 420×302 mm, 1320 (University of Birmingham, Barber Institute of Fine Arts)

with its curious tri-gabled upper silhouette it too seems to refer back to the designs of Duccio. This group of altarpieces by Simone is sufficient to give a vivid impression of the variety of invention that he could impart into creations that were all too often routine (if expensive) both in conception and execution.

The *St John the Evangelist* (U. Birmingham, Barber Inst.; see fig. 3), dated 1320, also belongs to this period. It is thought originally to have formed part of a triptych with figures of the Virgin and the dead Christ (untraced). The scale and intimacy of this panel, with its delicately observed emotion, set it apart from the grandiose paintings discussed above. This type of small private commission became more common in Simone's later work.

During this period Simone may be judged prosperous. Apart from the sums of money he put up for his marriage, he became the owner of one house and the part owner, with his brother Donato, of a second. Between 1321 and 1333 his is the only important painter's name to appear in the communal accounts. After 1333, however, there is no firm evidence for his presence in Siena, and by 1336 at the latest he had moved to Avignon. The circumstances in which he was persuaded to move are now hard to imagine. Inducements from Avignon may have been assisted by serious competition after *c.* 1328 from the Lorenzetti workshop in Siena itself.

4. AVIGNON, *c.* 1335–44. Paradoxically, all the archival evidence for Simone's life at Avignon comes from the Sienese archives. Nothing survives at Avignon itself, and it is not clear whether anything remains to be found in the papal archives at Rome. The latter records, however, do seem to show that he was never employed by the popes. Therefore the likelihood is that he either joined the household of a member of the papal curia or was privately supported, for example by a sinecure. The inducements to leave Siena must have included position and security; they were also materially sufficient to enable Simone—apparently—to abandon almost entirely his 'public' commissions (and his workshop) and to work on a restricted number of small private paintings. Apparently only his wife and his brother Donato moved with him to the papal city.

Simone's only known public work at Avignon was the decoration of the inside of the porch of the cathedral, Notre-Dame-des-Doms, for Cardinal Giacomo Gaetani Stefaneschi. The programme originally included a famous painting of *St George and the Dragon* (destr. ?1828) on the south wall and apparently a *Miracle of Andrea Corsini*, an event that occurred in 1333, on the north wall; no more is known about the latter, which had vanished by the mid-17th century. The paintings over the portal, however, though much decayed, were recently discovered to have beneath them some superb *sinopie*, perhaps the most distinguished examples of draughtsmanship to have survived from the 14th century. Where possible, frescoes and *sinopie* have been transferred to the papal palace. The *sinopie* are unusually detailed and exhibit many changes of composition and iconography. This might suggest that the patron, Stefaneschi, took a close interest in them. The tympanum has the earliest surviving example of the subject of the *Madonna of Humility* (in which the Virgin is seated on the ground); Jacopo Stefaneschi kneels before her.

The remaining paintings by Simone from this period are all small in scale, private in destination and unexpected or unusual in content. Typical is the only signed and dated panel from the period, the *Christ Discovered in the Temple* of 1342 (Liverpool, Walker A. G.; see FRAME, fig. 5). The painting records Mary's complaint to Christ after he had tarried arguing with the Doctors in the Temple: 'Son, why hast thou dealt with us thus', and it appears to be unique in its subject. The circumstances of the commission have not been satisfactorily explained (and there are no indications of its original owner), but the way in which the painter has caught the nuance of a family row is masterly. It is reminiscent of the skill and sensitivity of the *Annunciation* (Florence, Uffizi) and the *St John the Evangelist* (U. Birmingham, Barber Inst.). The panel is painted on the reverse to look like marble and was not attached to any other painting.

In 1338, Simone painted a frontispiece for a manuscript of the works of Virgil (Milan, Bib. Ambrosiana) owned by his friend FRANCESCO PETRARCH; the authenticity is attested by an inscription in the margin. This, a painting on vellum of subdued colouring and exceptional delicacy, is so unusual in the context of Trecento manuscript painting that only exceptional circumstances may account for it. Many of the special features are most easily understood if the frontispiece was intended as a 'classical' picture suited to the Classical texts that succeed it. The subject-matter must have been devised by Petrarch. At the top, the poet Virgil sits in the act of inspiration. As the inscription explains, his secrets are uncovered by his commentator, Servius, who symbolically draws back a brilliantly painted diaphanous curtain. Round about stand those persons to whom the main poems are addressed: a warrior (the *Aeneid*), a farmer (the *Eclogues*) and a rustic (the *Georgics*).

Simone's work at Avignon contains other surprises. It probably included the tiny panel of *St Ladislas* (Altomonte, S Maria della Consolazione) and the portraits of Petrarch's love, *Laura*, and of *Cardinal Napoleone Orsini* (both untraced). These are the first recorded individual portraits in Italian art. The most controversial work probably from this period is the so-called Antwerp or Orsini Polyptych (divided between Antwerp, Kon. Mus. S. Kst., Berlin, Gemäldegal., and Paris, Louvre). This is a tiny two-sided devotional piece, less than 300 mm high and comprising four panels. When open, one side showed the *Annunciation*, the other a scene from Christ's *Passion* (see fig. 4). Unlike Simone's other paintings, brilliantly coloured, disturbingly dramatic and packed with tumultuous action. Although it has been dated by different scholars to almost every part of Simone's life, it does not look at all similar to his other earlier narrative paintings, and the extreme sophistication of the dramatic groupings makes it likely to be a fully mature work.

If this is a correct picture of Simone's output at Avignon, it is of a highly individual painter working at leisure for a set of discriminating and intelligent private patrons. There is little sign of more public commitments. There is no evidence that he painted, for instance, in the papal palace and little indication that he influenced those who did paint there.

II. Working methods and studio organization.

Simone painted in books, on panel and on walls. The basic techniques used in the paintings associated with his workshop are, for the most part, normal for the period and similar to the processes described at the end of the 14th century by Cennino Cennini. It seems clear, however, that one of the important or special areas of expertise in the workshop was the apposite use of, or imitation of, materials of contrasted substance and texture. This led to the insertion (especially on thrones or items of regalia) of translucent coloured glass to look like handstones, the use of *verre eglomisé* to counterfeit enamel and the employment of gold, silver and tin-foil on raised gesso to imitate, for instance, the metallic appurtenances of dress such as belts and buckles. Simone's manipulation of paint is also remarkable in this respect. In the *St Louis* altarpiece (Naples, Capodimonte), for example, the smooth intarsia work of the wooden platform on which St Louis sits is vividly distinguished in texture from the rough Middle Eastern carpet lying on the floor. A similarly vivid transition is to be found in the *Annunciation* (Florence, Uffizi) between the delicacy of the Virgin's lily and the gilded vase in which it stands. The reverse sides of many of his panels are painted to look like marble. This expertise was never equalled by any other 14th-century Italian painter.

A further area of experiment was the application in his wall paintings of stamped patterns on the gesso or *intonaco*. Some of these patterns, for example those in the *Guidoriccio* (Siena, Pal. Pub.) and in the frescoes in the chapel of S Elisabetta, S Francesco, Assisi, seem to have been applied as a means of differentiating textures, imitating, for instance, stamped leather. One example, the reverse of an *Annunciation* diptych (Washington, DC, N.G.A.; St Petersburg, Hermitage), appears calculated to look like a bookcover. However, Simone's most innovative decorations are undoubtedly the stamped patterns used extensively in the gold grounds of his panel paintings, especially on haloes and round the borders. It is not known what led to this development, and, confusingly, the earliest examples of these highly elaborate patterns seem to have been used in fresco paintings: the *Maestà* (Siena, Pal. Pub.) and the paintings in the Lower Church, S Francesco, Assisi. The possibilities for panel painting were already explored in the *St Louis* altarpiece (Naples, Capodimonte), and by the time of the S Domenico Altarpiece (perhaps 1324; Orvieto, Mus. Opera Duomo) patterns were being created involving the deployment of 21 separate metal punches, each with its own motif. The effects were almost at once imitated by other painters, both in Florence and Siena, and the migration of the punch tools between workshops and between cities promises to throw fresh light on the movements of painters. Unfortunately, the study of punch-marks produces formidable problems. It is, however, clear that after *c.* 1320 the older method (used,

4. Simone Martini: *Road to Calvary*, tempera on panel, 295×205 mm, *c.* 1340 (Paris, Musée du Louvre)

for instance, by Duccio) of decorating gold leaf with inscribed patterns almost entirely ceased.

Simone has also been credited with designing things in other media. It has sometimes been argued that he was responsible for the design of the stained glass in the chapel of S Martino, S Francesco, Assisi. This hypothesis, though superficially plausible, is not supported by the style of the glass. More intriguing is the design of the crozier held by St Louis of Toulouse in the *St Louis* altarpiece: its crook contains a figure group and is supported by the twisting figure of an angel attached to the staff. A small group of surviving croziers spread across Europe have a similar pattern (e.g. Città di Castello, Mus. Capitolare; Cologne Cathedral, Treasury), but Simone's representation in the *St Louis* altarpiece (Naples, Capodimonte) seems to pre-date them.

The evidence concerning the personnel of Simone's workshop is very imprecise. Among his contemporaries, his brother Donato and his brothers-in-law Lippo and Tederigho were all painters, as was also his father-in-law Memmo di Filippuccio. Lippo Memmi is documented in collaboration with Simone on the *Annunciation* (Florence, Uffizi). Payments to Simone in the communal archives of Siena several times note the existence of unnamed collaborators, but their numbers cannot be calculated. The finished output of the workshop veers from the surprising diversity of style and quality of the *Maestà* (Siena, Pal. Pub.) to the remarkable uniformity of the S Caterina altarpiece (Pisa, Mus. N. & Civ. S Matteo). Some paintings have been grouped together as the work of hypothetical painters such as the Master of the Palazzo Venezia Madonna, the Master of the Straus Madonna and Barna da Siena, who are seen as collaborators or followers of Simone. However, almost none of the work is dated and the position over attributions remains fluid.

These problems refer exclusively to the Sienese workshop of Simone. There is no evidence that any of its members apart from his brother Donato travelled with him to Avignon, and the 'public' side of Simone's career—that part normally involving collaborators—dwindled at Avignon almost to nothing. The ability of Donato is unclear, since his only documented commission is for signs and notices on the walls of the bath-houses of mineral spas near Siena. Though trained as a painter, he may have worked for his brother principally in an administrative capacity.

III. Posthumous reputation.

There is no doubt that Simone's reputation lived on into the 15th century in Siena. It also seems clear that the polyptychs painted *c.* 1320 became models for later 14th-century artists both in their formal composition and decorative repertory. Arguably he set new technical standards, though much of his painting for private patrons would have been inaccessible to other artists. The relevance of his work to the second half of the century is hard to demonstrate. On his departure for Avignon, Simone's Sienese practice fell almost at once into the hands of the Lorenzetti workshop, and it seems that it was the style especially of Ambrogio Lorenzetti that exercised a dominant influence on Sienese painters for the remainder of the century. There is evidence, nevertheless, that an altarpiece by Simone in the Palazzo Pubblico was carefully repaired and enlarged *c.* 1448, while Ghiberti's Sienese informants in the early 15th century stated that Simone was, among their painters, not merely 'molto famoso' but 'il migliore'. Simone's departure for Avignon and his sojourn there are full of ambiguities, not least in their implications for the ultimate impact of his art on Siena. Moreover, the influence of his style cannot be traced with certainty to any surviving panels from Avignon or Provence; the suggestion, for instance, that the so-called Master of the Rebel Angels was an Avignonese follower of Simone Martini remains speculative. His wider influence is even more enigmatic. There is a general tendency to stress the importance of his presence in Avignon for the development of European art. This appears, however, to be wishful thinking.

The traditions that persisted about Simone's life and painting between the 14th and 18th centuries were confused and, in certain important respects, wrong. The recovery from the archives of details concerning his life began in the pages of the *Lettere sanesi* of Lorenzo della Valle, though the findings were to some extent distorted by della Valle's determination to assert the primacy of the 'Sienese school of painting' over that of Florence. This was a reaction against the Vasarian view that the recovery of art began with Cimabue and Giotto. A more balanced view was achieved during the 19th century, partly through the intervention of non-Italians such as Rumohr and Schnaase; and partly through the far more systematic and professional research in the archives by Milanesi. This research served to expel from the canon of Simone's work certain major errors introduced by Vasari (such as the attribution to him of the frescoes in the Spanish Chapel, S Maria Novella, Florence). As is often the case, a kind of watershed was reached in the writing of Crowe and Cavalcaselle. Since *c.* 1900 the oeuvre of Simone himself has not been significantly increased, and scholars have occupied themselves particularly in establishing the chronology of the undated works and in the stylistic appraisal and grouping of the works from the studio.

However, the influence of Vasari's views on the history of Italian painting lived on with the consequential problem of assimilating the style of Simone to a mainstream that runs from Giotto through Masaccio to Michelangelo. Simone keeps company more easily with the great court artists of the Renaissance, such as Gentile da Fabriano, Pisanello and Raphael, and in near-contemporary terms, his vivid characterizations and discursive narrative find readier parallels in the varied fresco painting in S Francesco, Assisi. His oeuvre contains diverse commissions and a range of technique unequalled in the 14th century; it is perhaps the continuing re-appraisal of that diversity that is the most interesting historiographical development of recent years. This has involved investigations in a number of areas, notably those concerned with patronage, with hagiographical needs and the creation of new images, with contemporary devotional trends and, in a rather different direction, with secular iconography and decoration. Simone's painting in its diversity reflects many aspects of 14th-century life, politics and culture; and these new developments allow his formidable ability to be seen in a broader and better-informed historical perspective.

BIBLIOGRAPHY

EARLY SOURCES AND DOCUMENTS

G. Vasari: *Vite* (1550, rev.2/1568); ed. G. Milanesi (1878–85)

G. Milanesi: *Documenti per la storia dell'arte senese* (Siena, 1854–5)

K. Burdach: *Aus Petrarcas ältestem deutschen Schülerkreise* (Berlin, 1929) [for the evidence for the lost portrait of Napoleone Orsini]

P. Bacci: 'L'elenco delle pitture, sculture e architetture di Siena compilato nel 1625–6 da Mons. Fabio Chigi poi Alessandro VII', *Bull. Sen. Stor. Patria*, n.s. x (1939), pp. 197–213

A. Peter: 'Quand Simone est-il venu en Avignon?', *Gaz. B.-A.*, xxi (1939), pp. 153–74

P. Bacci: *Fonti e commenti per la storia dell'arte senese* (Siena, 1944) [a number of errors are corrected in the articles listed below]

J. Rowlands: 'The Date of Simone Martini's Arrival in Avignon', *Burl. Mag.*, cvii (1965), pp. 25–6

E. C. Southard: 'Simone Martini's Lost *Marcus Regulus*: A Document Rediscovered and a Subject Clarified', *Z. Kstgesch.*, xlii (1979), pp. 217–19

A. S. Hoch: 'A New Document for Simone Martini's Chapel of St Martin at Assisi', *Gesta*, xxiv (1985), pp. 141–6

GENERAL

G. B. Cavalcaselle and J. A. Crowe: *Storia della pittura in Italia* (Florence, 1885, Eng. trans., 1908) [offered the first 'modern' account of Simone's life and work]

E. Borsook: *The Mural Painters of Tuscany* (London, 1960, rev. 2, Oxford, 1980), pp. 19–27 [good illus. of the artist's work in Siena and Assisi]

E. Carli: *La pittura senesi del trecento* (Venice, 1981)

Il gotico a Siena (exh. cat., Siena, Pal. Pub., 1982)

L'Art gothique siennois (exh. cat., Avignon, Mus. Petit Pal., 1983)

MONOGRAPHIC WORKS

A. Gosche: *Simone Martini* (Leipzig, 1899)

R. van Marle: *Simone Martini et les peintres de son école* (Strasbourg, 1920)

A. De Rinaldis: *Simone Martini* (Rome, 1936)

G. Paccagnini: *Simone Martini* (Milan, 1955) [the first important monograph summarizing much 20th-century writing]

G. Contini and M. C. Gozzoli: *L'opera completa di Simone Martini* (Milan, 1970) [an invaluable and for the most part reliable catalogue of the biographical data and paintings; includes Petrarch's sonnets referring to the lost portrait of *Laura*]

Simone Martini e 'champagne' (exh. cat., Siena, Pin. N., 1985)

A. Martindale: *Simone Martini* (Oxford, 1987) [incl. summary of recent discussions, cat. rais., summary of sources and good illus.]

SPECIALIST STUDIES
To 1320

L. Coletti: 'The Early Works of Simone Martini', *A. Q.*, xii (1949), p. 291

F. Bologna: *Gli affreschi di Simone Martini a Assisi* (Milan, 1966)

I. Hueck: 'Frühe Arbeiten des Simone Martini', *Münchn. Jb. Bild. Kst*, xix (1968), p. 29 [looks to the Roman painters at Assisi]

F. Bologna: *I pittori alla corte angioina di Napoli, 1266–1414* (Rome, 1969)

J. Gardner: 'Saint Louis of Toulouse, Robert of Anjou and Simone Martini', *Z. Kstgesch.*, 39 (1976), p. 12

J. H. Stubblebine: *Duccio di Buoninsegna and his School* (Princeton, 1979) [argues that Simone worked on Duccio's *Maestà*]

A. Perrig: 'Formen der politischen Propaganda der Kommune von Siena in der ersten Trecento-Hälfte', *Bauwerk und Bildwerk im Hochmittelalter*, ed. K. Clausberg and others (1981), pp. 213–33 [for an important reappraisal of the imagery]

I. Hueck: 'Die Kapellen der Basilika San Francesco in Assisi: Die Auftraggeber und die Franziskaner', *Patronage and Public in the Trecento: Proceedings of the St Lambrecht Symposium, 1984*

——: 'Ein Dokument zur Magdalenekapelle der Franziskuskirche von Assisi', *Scritti di storia dell'arte in onore di Roberto Salvini* (Florence, 1984), pp. 191–6

J. Brink: 'A Sienese Conceit in a Painting by Simone Martini at Assisi', *Simone Martini: Atti del convegno: Siena, 1985* (Siena, 1988), pp. 67–73

A. Garzelli: 'Peculiarità di Simone Martini ad Assisi: Gli affreschi della capella di San Martino', *Simone Martini: Atti del convegno: Siena, 1985* (Siena, 1988), pp. 55–65

'Guidoriccio da Fogliano' and 'New Town' frescoes

U. Feldges-Henning: 'Zu Thema und Datierung von Simone Martini's Fresko *Guido Riccio da Fogliano*', *Mitt. Ksthist. Inst. Florenz*, xvii (1973), p. 273

G. Moran: 'An Investigation Regarding the Equestrian Portrait of *Guidoriccio da Fogliano* in the Siena Palazzo Pubblico', *Paragone*, xxviii/333 (1977), p. 81

L. Bellosi: 'Castrum pingatur in palatio, 2: Duccio e Simone Martini pittori di Castelli senesi a l'esempio come erano', *Prospettiva*, 28 (1982), pp. 41–65

M. Seidel: 'Castrum pingatur in palatio, 1: Ricerche storiche e iconografiche sui castelli dipinti nel Palazzo Pubblico', *Prospettiva*, 28 (1982), pp. 17–40

J. Polzer: 'Simone Martini's *Guidoriccio da Fogliano*: A New Appraisal in the Light of a Recent Technical Examination', *Jb. Berlin. Mus.*, xxv (1983), pp. 103–41

F. Zeri: *L'inchiostra variopinto: Cronache e commenti dai flasi Modigliano al falso Guidoriccio* (Milan, 1985)

M. Mallory and G. Moran: 'New Evidence Concerning *Guidoriccio*', *Burl. Mag.*, cxxviii (1986), pp. 250–56

A. Martindale: 'The Problem of Guidoriccio', *Burl. Mag.*, cxxviii (1986), pp. 259–73

M. Mallory and G. Moran: 'The Border of *Guido Riccio*', *Burl. Mag.*, cxxix (1987), p. 187 [letter]

P. Torriti: Letter to the Editor, *Burl. Mag.*, cxxxi (1989), p. 485; reply by M. Mallory and G. Moran, *Burl. Mag.*, cxxxiii (1991), p. 37

M. Mallory and G. Moran: 'Did Siena Get its *Carta* before its Horse?', *J. A.* [USA] (May, 1991), p. 76

——: 'Resistance to Critical Thinking', *Syracuse Schol.* (Spring 1991), pp. 39–63

Other works, 1320–35

K. Steinweg: 'Beiträge zu Simone Martini und seiner Werkstatt', *Mitt. Ksthist. Inst. Florenz*, vii (1953–6), p. 162

C. de Benedictis: 'Sull'attività orvietana di Simone Martini e del suo seguito', *Ant. Viva*, vii (1968), p. 3

H. W. van Os: *Marias Demut und Verherrlichung in der Sienesiche Malerei, 1300–1450* (The Hague, 1969) [comments on the place of the S Ansano altarpiece in the pietistic imagery of the period]

J. Cannon: 'Simone Martini, the Dominicans and the Early Sienese Polyptych', *J. Warb. & Court. Insts*, xlv (1982), pp. 69–93

H. W. van Os: *Sienese Altarpieces, 1215–1460, I* (Groningen, 1984) [discusses S Ansano altarpiece in relation to the decorative programme of Siena Cathedral]

I. Hueck: 'Simone intorno al 1320', *Simone Martini: Atti del convegno: Siena, 1985* (Siena, 1988)

1335–44

F. Enaud: 'Les Fresques de Simone Martini en Avignon', *Les Monuments Historiques de la France* (1963), pp. 114–80 [the fundamental publication of the rediscovered *sinopie*]

D. Denny: 'Simone Martini's *Holy Family*', *J. Warb. & Court. Insts*, xxx (1967), p. 138

H. W. van Os and M. Rinkleff-Reinders: 'De reconstructie van Simone Martini's zgn polyptiek van de *Passie*', *Ned. Ksthist. Jb.*, xxiii (1972), pp. 1–14

B. Degenhart: 'Das Marienwunder von Avignon: Simone Martini's Miniaturen für Kardinal Stefaneschi und Petrarch', *Pantheon*, xxxiii (1975), p. 191

J. Brink: 'Simone Martini's "Orsini Polyptych"', *Jb. Kon. Mus. S. Kst.* (1976), p. 7

——: 'Francesco Petrarch and the Problem of Chronology in the Late Paintings of Simone Martini', *Paragone*, xxviii/331 (1977), p. 3

——: 'Simone Martini, Francesco Petrarch and the Humanistic Program of the Virgil Frontispiece', *Mediaevalia*, iii (1977), pp. 83–117

M. Laclotte and D. Thiébaut: *L'Ecole d'Avignon* (1983)

TECHNIQUE AND WORKSHOP PRACTICE

Catalogo della IV mostra di restauri (exh. cat., Naples, Pal. Reale, 1960) [contains the conservation report on the *St Louis* altarpiece]

M. Frinta: 'Unsettling Evidence in some Panel Paintings of Simone Martini', *La pittura nel XIV e XV secolo: il contribuito dell'analisi tecnica alla storia dell'arte*, ed. H. van Os and J. R. J. van Asperen de Boer (Bologna, 1983), pp. 211–25

E. Skaug: 'Punchmarks—What Are They Worth? Problems of Tuscan Workshop Inter-relationships in the Mid-14th Century: The Ovile Master and Giovanni da Milano', *La pittura nel XIV e XV secolo: Il contributo dell'analisi tecnica alla storia dell'arte*, ed. H. W. van Os and J. R. J. van Asperen de Boer (Bologna, 1983), pp. 253–82

L. Tintori and S. A. Fehm jr: 'Observations on Simone Martini's Frescoes in the Montefiori Chapel at Assisi', *La pittura nel XIV e XV secolo: Il contributo dell'analisi tecnica alla storia dell'arte*, ed. H. W. van Os and J. R. J. van Asperin de Boer (Bologna, 1983), pp. 175–9

SIMONE'S FOLLOWERS

K. Steinweg: 'Beiträge zu Simone Martini und seiner Werkstatt', *Mitt. Ksthist. Inst. Florenz*, vii (1953–6), p. 162
C. De Benedictis: *La pittura senese, 1330–1370* (Florence, 1979) [for the most recent attempt to bring to order the large group of paintings linked stylistically with the work of Simone]

ANDREW MARTINDALE

Martinique. *See under* ANTILLES, LESSER.

Martino da Udine. *See* PELLEGRINO DA SAN DANIELE.

Martinoski, Nikola (*b* Kruševo, 18 Aug 1903; *d* Skopje, 7 Feb 1973). Macedonian painter. In 1919 he attended lectures on art at the icon-painting workshop of Dimitar Andonov-Papradiški (1859–1954) in Skopje. In 1920 he moved to Bucharest, where he graduated from the Academy of Fine Arts in 1927. He lived in Paris (1927–8), frequenting the Académie de la Grand Chaumière as well as studying under Roger Bissière and Moïse Kisling at the Académie Ranson. He then settled in Skopje, acting as a corresponding member of the Belgrade group Oblik. In the 1930s Martinoski developed a version of Expressionism that, despite its derivation from the ÉCOLE DE PARIS, was strongly related to the painterly procedures and the social and political commitment of NEUE SACHLICHKEIT. During the 1930s his work evolved from portraits and religious subjects to social issues and evocative monumental compositions executed in several public locations and private residences in Skopje. In 1935 he decorated his family's coffee-house, Okean (destr.) in Skopje, with 12 explicitly erotic wall paintings. After 1945 he helped establish the Art Gallery in Skopje, and he became its director. He is considered one of the most gifted pioneers of modern Macedonian art.

BIBLIOGRAPHY

B. Petkovski: *Nikola Martinoski* (Skopje, 1982) [with Fr. summary]

BOJAN IVANOV

Martinus 'opifex' (*fl* 1440; *d* Regensburg, ?1456). Illuminator, active in Germany. Most scholars, except Ziegler (1988), place at the beginning of his career his contribution, dated 1440, to a manuscript (before 1440–66; 295×210 mm; Munich, Bayer. Staatsbib., Cgm. 3974) executed at various workshops. A manuscript with the text of Thomas von Cantimpré's *De natura rerum* and extracts from Ibn Butlan's *Tacuinum sanitatis* (*c.* 1445; 455×325 mm; Granada, Bib. U., MS. C.67) also belongs to this early phase. From 1446 to 1449 Martinus is known to have been active at the court of Frederick III in Vienna. To this period belong a *Golden Legend* (1446–7; 540×360 mm; Vienna, Österreich. Nbib., Cod. 326) and a Breviary (1447–8; 530×365 mm; Vienna, Österreich. Nbib., Cod. 1767), which were both executed for Frederick III in collaboration with three other court illuminators and their workshops. In early 1451 Martinus 'opifex' is attested in Regensburg.

Other extant works by Martinus 'opifex' are the Peutinger Prayerbook (*c.* 1450; 142×100 mm; Stuttgart, Württemberg. Landesbib., MS. brev. 91; completed in 1499 by Berthold Furtmeyer) and a manuscript of Guido da Columna's *Trojan War* (before 1456; 375×275 mm; Vienna, Österreich. Nbib., Cod. 2773); the latter bears the signature *Martinus opifex* written in gold at the bottom edge of the first folio. These manuscripts reveal him as the head of a large workshop but who personally executed only a small part of its output. Martinus 'opifex' was a leading representative of early south German and Austrian realism. His importance lies in his original handling of landscape and space and the novelty of his disposition of objects and figures. The origins of his style are controversial; Schmidt and Suckale maintained a Bavarian origin, while Ziegler (1977, 1988) placed his stylistic roots in the Vienna region *c.* 1400 and identified him as the artist of the *Christ Carrying the Cross* (*c.* 1430; 232×181 mm; Chicago, IL, A. Inst.) traditionally assigned to the Master of the Worcester panel.

BIBLIOGRAPHY

G. Schmidt: 'Die Buchmalerei', *Gotik in Österreich* (exh. cat., Krems an der Donau, Minoritenkirche, 1967), pp. 134–8, nos 97–100
C. Ziegler: *Studien zur Stilherkunft und Stilentwicklung des Buchmalers Martinus Opifex* (diss., U. Vienna, 1974)
——: 'Zur österreichischen Stilkomponente des Buchmalers Martinus Opifex', *Cod. MSS*, iii/3 (1977), pp. 82–94
R. Suckale: 'Die Regensburger Buchmalerei von 1350 bis 1450', *Regensburger Buchmalerei: Von frühkarolingischer Zeit bis zum Ausgang des Mittelalters* (exh. cat., eds F. Mütherich and K. Dachs; Regensburg, Städt. Gal., 1987), pp. 94–9, nos 97–100
C. Ziegler: *Martinus Opifex: Ein Hofminiator Friedrichs III.* (Vienna, 1988)

ULRIKE LIEBL

Martirosyan, Harut'yun Artashes [Arutyun Artashesovich] (*b* Leninakan [now Kumayri], 1 May 1921; *d* Yerevan, 28 July 1977). Armenian archaeologist and art historian. He graduated from the history department at Yerevan University, then went to Leningrad (now St Petersburg) as a postgraduate student and worked under Boris Piotrovsky at the State Hermitage Museum. In 1959 he was appointed head of the early archaeology section at the Institute of Archaeology and Ethnography. His particular interest was the prehistoric archaeology and culture of Armenia and the archaeology of Urartu. He took part in the excavations of Karmir Blur and led a general expedition to study the caves and petroglyphs of Armenia. His archaeological research is outlined in his doctoral thesis on Armenia in the Bronze and Early Iron Ages and in his monograph on the excavation of an Urartian city, Argishtikhinili. His specialist works are devoted to Armenian petroglyphs.

WRITINGS

Armeniya v epokhu bronzy i rannego zheleza [Armenia in the Bronze and Early Iron Ages] (Yerevan, 1965)
Ush bronzedaryan bnakavayrer ev dabaranadashter [Settlements and sepulchres of the Late Bronze Age] (Yerevan, 1969) [Eng. summary]
Geghama lerneri zhayrapatkernere [The petroglyphs of the Geghamian mountain range] (Yerevan, 1971) [Eng. summary]
Hayastani nakhnadaryan nshanagrere ev nrants urartahaykakan krknaknere [The prehistoric petroglyphs of Armenia and their Urartian–Armenian types] (Yerevan, 1973) [Eng. summary]
Argishtikhinili (Yerevan, 1974) [Eng. summary]

BIBLIOGRAPHY

'Arutyun Artashesovich Martirosyan', *Sov. Arkheol.*, ii (1978), pp. 331

V. YA. PETRUKHIN

Martorana. Italian family of artists and decorators. Pietro Martorana (*b* Palermo, 1705; *d* Palermo, 1759) worked in Palermo. He was a follower of Gaspare Serenari (1694–1759), and painted fresco cycles in the churches of S Rosalia (untraced), S Carlo and S Chiara. In 1736 he worked on the palace of Michele Gravina Branciforte, Prince of Butera, in collaboration with Olivio Sozzi (1696–1765), who is notable for having introduced the style of Sebastiano Conca to Palermo. Gioacchino Martorana (*b* Palermo, 1735; *d* Palermo, 1779), Pietro's son, worked in Rome and Sicily. At the age of 17 he moved to Rome to study with Giuseppe Vasi, a former pupil of his father. Vasi arranged for him to stay with Marco Benefial. Gioacchino admired the painting of Conca and the classicism of Batoni. He worked in Rome until the 1770s, and among the works executed there (many for Palermo) are the *Virgin, St Gaetano and Giuseppe Calasanzio* (Rome, S Dorotea), eight scenes from the *Life of St Benedict* (Palermo, Gal. Reg. Sicilia) painted for S Rosalia, Palermo, four scenes from the *Life of St Francis Xavier* (1765; Palermo, S Francesco Saverio) and frescoes and an altarpiece (1768–9; Palermo, S Ninfa) for the church of the Padri Crociferi. The altarpiece is clearly influenced by Conca and by Batoni. Gioacchino Martorana's work in Palermo began with the execution of a series of portraits, for example those of the architect *Venanzio Marvuglia* (Palermo, Bib. Com.) and the *Viceroy Fogliani and his Consort* (Palermo, Pal. Normanni), both dated to the 1770s. He also accepted commissions for fresco decorations, a few of which survive, for example those in the Palazzo Costantino and the Palazzo Comitini. These were influenced by the French Rococo, a style that had been brought to Palermo by Elia Interguglielmi. Martorana's frescoes (*c.* 1780) in Palazzo Butera, Palermo, are firmly in the cosmopolitan Rococo style.

BIBLIOGRAPHY

S. Lo Monaco: *Pittori e scultori siciliani dal '600 al primo '800* (Palermo, 1940), p. 84
S. Rudolph, ed.: *La pittura del '700 a Roma* (Milan, 1983), p. 786
C. Siracusano: *La pittura del '700 in Sicilia* (Rome, 1986), pp. 325–9, 334 [with bibliog.]
——: 'La pittura del '700 in Sicilia', *La pittura in Italia: Il settecento*, ed. G. Briganti, ii (Milan, 1989, rev. 1990), pp. 516–30, 787

DONATELLA GERMANÒ SIRACUSA

Martorel, María (*b* Salta, 18 Jan 1909). Argentine painter. She studied in her home province under Ernesto Scotti (1900–57), painting at that time in a figurative style. Her first journey to Europe in 1952 led her to subject landscape to a geometric treatment and also to elaborate more purely abstract forms. While living in Paris in 1955, for example, she made works out of coloured paper suggestive of her experience of the Metro system. Soon after her return to Argentina in 1957 her work became completely geometrical, showing the influence of the work and theories of such artists as László Moholy-Nagy, Josef Albers, Max Bill, Georges Vantongerloo and Friedrich Vordemberge-Gildewart. Polygonal shapes predominated in the dynamic spiralling compositions that she produced in 1959–60, while colour became the most important element of the pictures she made in 1961 in New York.

As in the paintings of Robert Delaunay, colour determines outline, space and volume in Martorel's work. These create precise and clearly defined dynamic rhythms that transform the composition as a whole into a kind of sign. Curves echo or approach each other, sometimes multiplied in parallel patterns; they ascend in graceful verticals or take on a more horizontal emphasis, stopping just before the edge of the canvas or taking unexpected turns above or below, with bands of different widths contrasting dynamically with each other. *Ekho A* (1968), an oil painting in diptych form, and *Ekho C* (1968; both Buenos Aires, Mus. A. Mod.), a triptych painted in acrylic, exemplify this period of her development. The objective relationships within a limited space that she conveyed in her first geometric works gave way to a sense of infinite space undulating in unison with the serene forms represented. Like Paul Klee and Bill, she based her systematical explorations of form on the analogy of musical variations, and in the 1960s she created environments using panels in which coloured bands imposed a dynamic rhythm. The logic of form and colour in Martorel's work testifies to the determining presence of a harmonious balance of rationality and sensitivity.

BIBLIOGRAPHY

María Martorel y la pintura (exh. cat. by N. Perazzo, Buenos Aires, Gal. A. Centoira, 1985)

NELLY PERAZZO

Martorell, Antonio (*b* Santurce, nr Bilbao, 1939). Puerto Rican printmaker, painter, draughtsman, illustrator and performance artist of Spanish birth. He studied in Spain in 1961–2 under Julio Martín Caro and with Lorenzo Homar at the graphic arts workshop of the Instituto de Cultura Puertorriqueña (1962–5). He inherited a social and political commitment from Puerto Rican artists working in the 1950s, but introduced wit and irony to his satirical treatment of political themes in prints, posters and illustrations. From the late 1960s, for instance, he produced portfolios of woodcuts in which he combined texts and images as a way of commenting on social and political events.

Martorell founded the Taller Alacrán in 1968 with the aim of mass-producing at affordable prices. In the 1970s he began to experiment with innovative printmaking techniques, for example in a series of cut-out works influenced by Pop art, in which he played on stereotypes of authoritarianism in Latin America. In subsequent prints he explored the painterly qualities of woodcuts on a monumental scale. From the late 1970s, however, he was increasingly concerned with innovative live performances that combined printmaking and painting with the movement of actors. From 1978 to 1984 he lived in Mexico City, where he taught printmaking and drawing at the Escuela Nacional de Bellas Artes. He was appointed artist-in-residence at the Universidad de Puerto Rico in Cayey in 1986.

BIBLIOGRAPHY

M. Traba: 'Los Salmos de Martorell', *Rev. Inst. Cult. Puertorriqueña* (July–Sept 1972), pp. 5–9
Antonio Martorell: Obra gráfica, 1963–1986 (exh. cat. by A. Díaz-Royo, N. Rivera and J. A. Torres Martinó, San Juan, Inst. Cult. Puertorriqueña, 1986)

MARI CARMEN RAMÍREZ

Martorell, Bernat [Master of St George; Master of S Jordi; Master of S Jorge] (*b* Sant Celoni; *fl* 1427; *d*

Barcelona, between 13 and 23 Dec 1452). Catalan painter. The name Master of S Jorge was coined by Bertaux to refer to the painter of the altarpiece of *St George* (Chicago, IL, A. Inst.; Paris, Louvre). This was the most spectacular of a group of works attributed to an anonymous artist who was recognized as one of the finest Catalan painters of the 14th and 15th centuries. His works made a transition between those of Lluís Borrassà and Jaume Huguet, and it was thought that he could be identified with Bernat Martorell, the painter recorded as most in demand in Catalonia between 1427 and 1452. The identification was finally proved by the publication in 1938 (Duràn i Sanpere) of the contract for the Púbol altarpiece of *St Peter Enthroned* (Girona, Mus. Dioc.; see fig. 2 below).

1. Life and work. 2. Working methods, style and technique.

1. LIFE AND WORK. By 1427 Martorell must have been a mature and independent artist, for in that year he painted two important altarpieces: one for the convent of S María de Pedralbes, Barcelona, and the other, signed jointly with the sculptor Antoní Claperos the elder, for the high altar of the convent church of S María de Jesús, Barcelona. The latter was commissioned by the bridlemakers' guild of St Stephen, the guild to which painters were attached, indicating the prestige that Martorell enjoyed among his peers. Both works are untraced.

From this time documentary evidence shows that Bernat Martorell headed the most important workshop in Barcelona and had contacts throughout Catalonia. It is significant that his appearance on the artistic scene coincided with the death of Lluís Borrassà (1424–5). Commissions came to Martorell from a wide area: the regions around Barcelona, around Girona (Sp. Gerona), Vic and central Catalonia, and a broad area between Lleida and the monastery of Poblet, within the present-day province of Tarragona. Altarpieces painted by him are recorded for such Barcelona guilds as the bridlemakers (1427), shoemakers (1437), fishermen (1437), silversmiths (1439), ships' captains (1442) and master builders (1449), as well as for the silversmiths of Vic (1436). Occasionally he worked for the royal house (1434), for the Generalitat de Catalunya (e.g. the altarpiece for S María in Montsó, 1437) and the Casa de la Ciutat (the town hall) in Barcelona, for which he carried out various tasks, including colouring sculptures, for example the figure of *St Raphael* over the central portal (1433). He also received important ecclesiastical commissions, such as those for works in the cathedrals of Barcelona (e.g. 1437) and Lleida (1441).

The works commissioned from Martorell were very varied. As well as altarpieces, which were the main category, his workshop illuminated manuscripts, designed embroidery, stained glass and flags, painted coats of arms, polychromed sculpture and, on at least one occasion, decorated a clockface (1434). Of this, only a group of altarpieces, two illuminated manuscripts and an embroidered altar hanging, supposedly designed by the master, have survived.

Only one work by Martorell, the altarpiece of *St Peter Enthroned* for the church of Púbol Castle (1437–42; Girona, Mus. Dioc.), can be securely dated. Nonetheless, it has been possible to establish an approximate chronology

for the works attributed to him on the basis of stylistic development. The altarpiece of *St John the Baptist*, from the parish church in Cabrera de Mataró, near Barcelona (Barcelona, Mus. Dioc.), is thought to be his earliest surviving work, although it already shows his refined style. The altarpiece of *St George Killing the Dragon* (Chicago, IL, A. Inst.; see fig. 1; and Paris, Louvre) shows a surprising change: it seems to be a youthful work (*c.* 1425–30), yet it is a confident and enthusiastic painting, in which Martorell displays his artistic abilities, seen especially in the draughtsmanship, the detailed description of the surroundings and the expression on the horse's face, all of which reveal an acute study of nature. Other paintings thought to be from the same period share this impetuous quality, although less intensely. These include parts of the altarpiece of *SS John the Baptist and Eulalia* for Vic Cathedral (Vic, Mus. Episc.), a triptych of the *Descent of the Cross with Saints* (Lisbon, Mus. N. A. Ant.), an altarpiece of *St Lucy* (Paris, priv. cols; Barcelona, priv. cols; for illustrations see Gudiol and Alcolea Blanch, figs 645–7) and the altarpiece of *St Eulalia*, apparently from the monastery of Poblet (Barcelona, Mus. A. Catalunya).

The Púbol Altarpiece was painted at the mid-point of Martorell's career; the contract was signed with the nobleman Bernat de Corbera on 6 July 1437. In the centre St

1. Bernat Martorell: *St George Killing the Dragon*, tempera on panel, 1423×965 mm, *c.* 1425–30 (Chicago, IL, Art Institute of Chicago)

Peter is shown enthroned surrounded by cardinals, with the donors kneeling at his feet (see fig. 2); above the central panel is a *Calvary*; and on the predella and lateral panels are depicted scenes from the *Life of St Peter* and other saints. Some of the upper sections seem to be the work of assistants, but the vitality of treatment elsewhere (particularly in the expressive donor portraits and the predella scene from the *Life of St Paul*) indicates Martorell's authorship. The miniatures in a Book of Hours believed to be from the convent of S Clara in Barcelona (Barcelona, Inst. Mun. Hist.; fols 15*v*, 149*r*, 163*v*) are of a similar date.

Martorell's later works can be characterized by the increased participation of assistants. This does not mean, however, that the master had started to decline. Such compositions as the predella scenes of *Christ and the Woman of Samaria* and *Christ with a Man Possessed* of the altarpiece of the *Transfiguration* in Barcelona Cathedral are among the most exceptional works of Catalan Gothic painting and show how Martorell's observation of reality and everyday life had intensified. Parts of another late work, the altarpiece of the *Archangel Michael* from S Miguel de Pobla, Cèrvoles (Tarragona, Mus. Dioc.; Barcelona, Mus. A. Catalunya), are also of superb quality. At the end of his life Martorell still undertook very large projects, such as the altarpiece for the high altar of S Maria del Mar, Barcelona (1435–47; destr.). Two panels probably forming part of this work, representing the *Resurrection* and *Pentecost*, survived until 1936; they each measured 3.60×1.75 m, which gives an idea of the size of the whole.

On 17 October 1452 Martorell contracted to paint an altarpiece for the island of Sardinia. His will was made on 13 December 1452 and he was dead by 23 December. Martorell's widow and eldest son maintained the activity of his workshop by subletting it to other painters.

2. WORKING METHODS, STYLE AND TECHNIQUE. The scale of Martorell's undertakings must have necessitated the collaboration both of assistants and of other painters, but only one painter who was attached to his workshop, Ramon Isern (*fl* 1437–54), is known by name. When Martorell went to Lleida in 1441 to paint the main altarpiece for the Cathedral, he took on two painters who had their own workshops in that city, Jaume Ferrer the younger (*fl* 1430; *d* after 1457) and Pere Teixidor (*fl* 1437; *d* after 1441). Similarly, when Martorell was commissioned by the magistrates (*Concellers*) of Barcelona to illuminate a manuscript of Jaume Marquilles's *Comentaris sobre els usatges de Barcelona* (1448; Barcelona, Inst. Mun. Hist.) he handed it over to the illuminator Bernat Rauric (*fl c.* 1448-59).

Martorell's style is so distinctive that it is relatively easy to differentiate his work from that of his collaborators. Even in his early days, compared with the lively arabesques of rich colour in the works of his predecessors Borrassà and Joan Mates (*fl* 1391; *d* 1431), Martorell's paintings appear serene, with softer, more subtle colours. He also achieved a high degree of narrative interest in the variety of emotional response of his characters and the minute description of their surroundings.

Martorell must be considered the first Catalan painter to explore the effects of light. His works frequently include backlighting, angled light and reflections, which could only be the result of a direct observation of nature. This enabled him to suggest differences in surface texture in spite of working in tempera. The realism evident in his compositions was a joint consequence of his study of nature and his gifts as a draughtsman.

BIBLIOGRAPHY
J. Puiggari: 'Noticia de algunos artistas catalanes inéditos de la edad media y del renacimiento: Apuntes leidos en la sesión del 17 de junio de 1871', *Mem. Real Acad. B. Let. Barcelona*, iii (1880), pp. 73–103, 267–306
E. Bertaux: 'Les Primitifs espagnols', *Rev. A.*, xx (1905), pp. 417–36; xxii (1907), pp. 107–26, 241–62 and 339–60; xxiii (1908), pp. 269–79
S. Sanpere i Miquel: *Los cuatrocentistas catalanes* (Barcelona, 1906)
J. Mas i Domènech: 'Notes sobre antichs pintors a Catalunya', *Bol. Real Acad. B. Let. Barcelona*, vi (1911–12), pp. 216–21, 250–60, 307–21 and 430–40
A. Duràn i Sanpere: 'En Bernat Martorell illuminador de llibres', *Bull. Bib. Catalunya*, iv (1917)
C. R. Post: *A History of Spanish Painting* (Cambridge, MA, 1930–66), ii; vii/2, pp. 753–5; xii, pp. 570–73
A. Duràn i Sanpere: 'El maestro del retablo de San Jorge', *La Vanguardia* (16 Feb 1938)
J. Gudiol Ricart: *Pintura gótica*, A. Hisp., ix (Madrid, 1955)

2. Bernat Martorell: *St Peter Enthroned*, central panel of the Púbol Altarpiece, tempera on panel, 1437–42 (Girona, Museu Diocesà de Girona)

F. P. Verrié: 'La pintura (gótica)', *L'Art català*, ed. J. Folch i Torres (Barcelona, 1955)

J. Gudiol: *Bernardo Martorell* (Madrid, 1959)

J. Domínguez Bordona and J. Ainaud de Lasarte: *Miniatura. Grabado. Encuadernación*, A. Hisp., xviii (Madrid, 1962)

Trésors de la peinture espagnole: Eglises et musées de France (exh. cat. by M. Laclotte, Paris, Louvre and Mus. A. Déc., 1963)

P. Bohigas: *La ilustración y la decoración del libro manuscrito en Cataluña* (Barcelona, 1965)

J. Sutrà i Viñas: 'El retablo de San Pedro de Púbol', *Rev. Gerona*, 54 (1971), pp. 44–50

A. Duràn i Sanpere: *Barcelona i la seva història*, iii: *L'art i la cultura* (Barcelona, 1975), pp. 116–34

M. Grizzard: 'An Identification of Martorell's Commission for the Aragonese Courts', *A. Bull.*, lxiv (1982), pp. 311–14

J. Gudiol and S. Alcolea Blanch: *Pintura gótica catalana* (Barcelona, 1986), pp. 121–32, cat. 377–97

SANTIAGO ALCOLEA BLANCH

Martorell, Bohigas, Mackay [MBM]. Spanish Catalan architectural partnership founded in 1951 by Josep (Maria) Martorell (Codina) (*b* Barcelona, 21 May 1925) and Oriol Bohigas (Guardiola) (*b* Barcelona, 20 Dec 1925) and extended in 1962 to include David Mackay (*b* Eastbourne, 25 Dec 1933). Martorell and Bohigas went into partnership together after graduating from the Escuela Tecnica Superior de Arquitectura, Barcelona, where they both later received doctorates (1963), and where Bohigas became a professor (1971) and Director (1977–80); both also studied urban planning at the Instituto de Estudios de la Administracion Local (1961). Mackay graduated from the Northern Polytechnic School of Architecture, London (1958), and the Escuela Tecnica Superior de Arquitectura, Barcelona (1968).

As founding members of GRUPO R (1951), with Antoni de Moragas, José Ma Sostres Maluquer and others, Martorell and Bohigas reacted against the status quo of Spanish architecture in favour of a return to the rationalist Modernism terminated in Spain by the Civil War. The Escorial housing block (1952–62; with F. Mitjans, M. Ribas, J. M. Ribas and J. Alemany) in Barcelona and the Casa Guardiola (1954–5) in Argentona both represent this attempt to retrieve a Modernist language through the adoption of a consciously modest rationalism, though with popular roots, using building practices drawn from local craft traditions. By the early 1960s, however, dissatisfaction with an uncritical acceptance of the rationalist heritage led MBM to a new ideology, which was set out by Bohigas in a manifesto, 'Cap a una arquitectura realista'. The manifesto was in sympathy with the emerging views of Team Ten and the Neo-Realist and New Brutalist philosophies they produced; these required architecture to be consistent with a country's economic and technical capabilities, resulting in an honesty that valued the exercise of individual responsibility by each architect for his work. This new, pragmatic and carefully detailed approach to architecture was expressed in the group of dwellings (1959) in Calle Pallars; the Max Cahner House (1959–62); the competition-winning Oficina de Visado (1961), Colegio de Arquitectos; and a 12-storey block of flats (1959–65), Avenida Meridiana, all in Barcelona. The flats all have protruding

Martorell, Bohigas, Mackay: Villa Olimpica, housing in the Olympic Village, Barcelona, 1992

pointed bays, with angled windows positioned in a complex pattern to provide a variety of lighting environments in rooms of similar size and orientation, as well as an apparent randomness in the elevation. A pavement arcade of bold, segmented arches adds to the unique urban character of the tiled street façades.

At this time MBM became the undisputed force behind Catalan architecture, following a path marked out by Bohigas as a respected theorist and critic. The practice began to acquire an international reputation within the group of architects known as the Barcelona school and among students and young professionals who were attracted to train in their office. A growing range of commissions throughout the decade enabled MBM to develop its pluralistic Modernism, always related to context and materials, in such buildings as the Casa del Pati housing development (1964), the Xaudiera housing (1964–70) and other blocks of flats such as that in Calle Caspe (1967–9), all in Barcelona. The versatility of the practice can be seen by contrasting the neo-vernacular complexity of the Santa Agueda holiday flats (1966–7), Benicasín, Castellón, or the summer camps for schoolchildren (1961–5), Canyamars, Maresme, with the compact simplicity and obvious quality of the nearby housing for teachers (1967–9), Pineda, the informal functionality of the Escuela Garbí (1968), Esplugues, or the boldly industrial buildings for the Fábrica Piher, Badalona, designed and built by MBM over more than a decade (1958–70). All these last buildings are near Barcelona.

Nevertheless, as MBM moved into the 1970s it became sensitive to the changes that brought about the disintegration of the Barcelona school, and it adapted to new trends. Even though the practice continued to produce individual expressions related to building programmes, it played a part in the subversion of rationalist principles and the development of a new sensitivity to urban context that characterized late Modernism in the 1970s. Its work continued to be elegant, stimulating and receptive to outside innovations, still pluralist in attitude yet more eclectic. A great deal of housing was produced during this period, including flats (1971–3) in Pals, Gerona, with their references to context that are reminiscent of Robert Venturi; and the Casa de la Torre (1971–5), Santa Perpetua de la Moguda; the Casa Almirall (1975–7), La Garriga; and the Neo-Expressionist housing development (1974–80) in Calle Marti l'Humà, Sabadell, where parallel, curving blocks reproduce the local, urban context. By contrast, the Escola Thau (1972–4) in Barcelona retains a Brutalist image, though somewhat softened by neo-vernacular references.

Although Bohigas remained a firm believer in a continuing Modernism, some works betray formal and ideological tensions and ambiguities. The housing (1975–9) in the Sarria district of Barcelona broke new ground, its glass-covered alley a relevant urbanistic innovation; the Casa Serras (1977), Canovellas, is a linear house with references to Mies van der Rohe in its glass living-room and emphasized first-floor structure. From 1981 to 1984 Bohigas was Director of Planning for Barcelona and prepared a new urban plan for the city for the occasion of the Olympic Games in 1992 with the aim of restoring and exhibiting the city's buildings and open spaces. Meanwhile, MBM's practical brand of eclecticism continued in Barcelona in such works as the housing (1983) at Mollet, the park and swimming-pool (1984) at Creueta del Coll, and in the Olympic Village (see fig.), part of a comprehensive residential and leisure redevelopment of El Poble Nou, an obsolete industrial area overlooking the sea.

WRITINGS
O. Bohigas: 'Cap a una arquitectura realista', *Serra Or* (1962), May, pp. 50–52
——: *Arquitectura modernista* (Barcelona, 1968)
——: *Reseña y catalogo de la arquitectura modernista* (Barcelona, 1972)
J. M. Martorell: *Guia d'arquitectura de Menorca* (Barcelona, 1978)
O. Bohigas: *Reconstrucción de Barcelona* (Barcelona, 1985)
D. Mackay: *Modern Architecture in Barcelona, 1854–1939* (Oxford, 1989)

BIBLIOGRAPHY
Martorell-Bohigas-Mackay: Arquitectura, 1953–1978, intro. H. Pinón and C. Jencks (Madrid, 1979)
Martorell, Bohigas, Mackay: 30 años de arquitectura, 1954–1984, intro. K. Frampton (Madrid, 1985)
J. M. Martorell, O. Bohigas, D. Mackay and A. Puigdomenech: *Transformation of a Seafront: The Olympic Village, 1992* (Barcelona, 1992)
JORDI OLIVERAS

Martos, Ivan (Petrovich) (*b* Ichnya, Chernihiv province, 1754; *d* St Petersburg, 7 April 1835). Ukrainian sculptor, active in Russia. He was the son of an impoverished landowner and studied at the Academy of Arts in St Petersburg from 1764 to 1773 under Louis Rolland (1711–91) and Nicolas-François Gillet. Between 1773 and 1779 Martos completed his education in Rome under Carlo Albacini (*fl* 1770s–1800) and adopted the Neo-classical style. He returned to Russia in 1779 and began to teach in the sculpture class at the Academy of Arts, where, in 1794, he became Senior Professor and in 1814 Rector of Sculpture.

Martos's most important work was for funerary and memorial sculpture. His first tombstones make much use of bas-relief figures, for example the tomb for *Marfa Petrovna Sobakina* (marble, 1782; Moscow, Donskoy Monastery). In the tomb for *Yelena Stepanovna Kurakina* (marble, 1792; St Petersburg, Mus. Sculp.) a relief portrait of the deceased is accompanied by a weeping figure sculpted in the round. In the tomb for the Emperor, *Paul I* (bronze, 1807; Pavlovsk, Mausoleum), sculptural and architectural elements are combined. While all these works lie within the traditions of Neo-classicism, they are distinguished by their various solutions to the problem of expressing profound emotion within the confines of a necessarily restrained style. Martos's masterpiece is his monument to *Kuz'ma Minin and Dmitri Pozharsky* in Moscow (bronze, 1804–18; Red Square), in which two Russian figures from the 17th-century wars are presented as heroes from Antiquity. This monument is especially notable for the power of its massive, austere forms, and in this it is one of the most distinctive works of Russian Neo-classicism.

Among other works by Martos, the most notable are a figure of *Actaeon* (gilded bronze, 1800–01) for the Grand Cascade at Peterhof, and the statue of *John the Baptist* (bronze, 1804–7) and the relief *Moses Striking Water from the Rocks* (Pudozh stone, 1804–7), both for Kazan' Cathedral. Martos was an extremely prolific artist, and his work was of a consistently high quality throughout most of his life. In the late works, however, such as the monuments to *Armand Emmanuel Richelieu* in Odessa (bronze, 1823–8; Primorsky Boulevard) and *Mikhail Vasil'yevich Lomonosov* in Arkhangel'sk (bronze, 1826–8; Lomonosov Place), there is a certain rigidity, which seems to reflect a crisis in the tradition of Neo-classicism. Nonetheless, Martos remains one of the most important Neo-classical sculptors of the Russian empire, and certainly one of the most influential.

BIBLIOGRAPHY

N. Kovalenskaya: *Zhizn' i tvorchestvo russkogo skul'ptora I. P. Martosa* [The life and work of the Russian sculptor I. P. Martos] (Moscow and Leningrad, 1938)
Istoriya russkogo iskusstva [The history of Russian art], viii/1 (Moscow, 1963), p. 287
I. M. Gofman: *Ivan Petrovich Martos* (Leningrad, 1970)

SERGEY ANDROSSOV

Martu. *See* AMORITE.

Martyn, Ferenc (*b* Kaposvár, 10 June 1899; *d* Pécs, 11 April 1986). Hungarian painter, sculptor, designer and illustrator. He spent his childhood in Kaposvár in the house of the Secessionist painter József Rippl-Rónai. His early works are figurative. During the 1920s he painted arcadian scenes, but he was soon influenced by Surrealism, often combining experienced events with subconscious visions. Martyn lived in Paris from 1926 to 1940 and moved towards abstraction, joining the CERCLE ET CARRÉ group, and then in 1931 ABSTRACTION-CRÉATION, taking part in their exhibitions. He painted cityscapes and portraits, and was influenced by Constructivism. His nonfigurative works were painterly and expressive of his Hungarian temperament and used the rhythm of expansive arched forms. He can be seen as an intermediary between the Ecole de Paris and Hungarian art; he often returned to Budapest to organize exhibitions of Hungarian abstract painters living in Paris.

Martyn's abstract work largely derived from his experience of Paris, southern French towns, Mediterranean landscapes, the sea, bird life, and his frequent visits to Spain and Hungary. His horror at World War II was seen in *War* (1943; Pécs, Martyn Ferenc Col.); when he was conscripted in 1944 he went into hiding. During this period he produced an expressive series of nine drawings about horror and fear, the *Fascist Hydra* (Pécs, Martyn Ferenc Col.), in which Fascism was symbolized by monsters rendered in broken lines. In 1946–9 he was involved with the Abstract Group, which had broken away from the European school. After the war, he settled in Pécs where he produced numerous drawings. His sculptural works range from wooden constructions to monumental works in plaster (e.g. *Four Figures*, 1941; Pécs, Pannonius Mus.). In 1950 he produced a series of historical paintings on the 18th-century nationalist leader Ferenc Rákóczi. Martyn continued painting still-lifes that incorporated Hungarian folk elements (e.g. *Wine-cask Hooper Tools*, 1960; Pécs, Martyn Ferenc Col.). He also produced illustrations, for example for the poems of Stéphane Mallarmé (1964; Pécs, Martyn Ferenc Col.). He dedicated a series of works to perspectival problems (e.g. *Standing Forms*, 1965; Pécs, Martyn Ferenc Col.), and designed vases and plates for the Zsolnay porcelain factory in Pécs. In the last decade of his life he returned to gestural and geometric abstraction.

BIBLIOGRAPHY

E. Hárs: 'Ferenc Martyn', *Acta Hist. A. Acad. Sci. Hung.*, xiv/3–4 (1968), pp. 275–306
——: *Martyn* (Budapest, 1970)
——: *Martyn Ferenc* (Budapest, 1975)
——: *Martyn Ferenc: Oeuvre catalogue* (Pécs, 1983)

ÉVA BAJKAY

Martyrium [Gr. martyrion]. Term referring to a site that bears witness to the Christian faith, such as a significant event in the life and Passion of Christ, the tomb of a saint or martyr, and his or her place of suffering or testimony. It is also used to mean the structure erected over such a site. Monumental martyria form an important category of Early Christian architecture, and were built according to a variety of plans.

Martyrion is derived from the Greek *martys*, meaning witness in the legal sense, and first appears in the Septuagint as the evidence for something. By the mid-2nd century AD *martys* or martyr came to mean someone whose testimony was sealed with suffering and death for the Christian faith, and by *c.* 350 *martyrion* or martyrium was commonly used to refer to the location of a martyr's tomb and the commemorative shrine or church constructed over it. That it had also come to mean a place revered in the scriptures is implied by Eusebius' description (*c.* 337) of the Tomb of Christ as 'the venerable and most holy martyrium of the Saviour's resurrection'.

The earliest known martyrium is probably the shrine of St Peter (*see* ROME, §V, 14(i)(a)), which was built in a courtyard of the Vatican Hill necropolis in the late 2nd century AD (see fig. 1). The aedicula in front of the niche apparently lay above the saint's tomb and was referred to as his *tropaeum*, the monument of his victory over death and paganism. Simple, open-air martyrial precincts were also set up on the Via Appia (honouring the festival of SS Peter and Paul) and in the Christian cemeteries in Bonn, Germany, and Salona (now Marusinac), Croatia. One martyrium below ground is the so-called Chapel of the

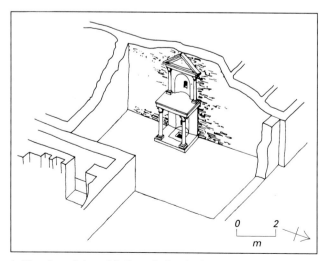

1. Martyrium, shrine of St Peter, St Peter's, Rome, late 2nd century AD; reconstruction drawing

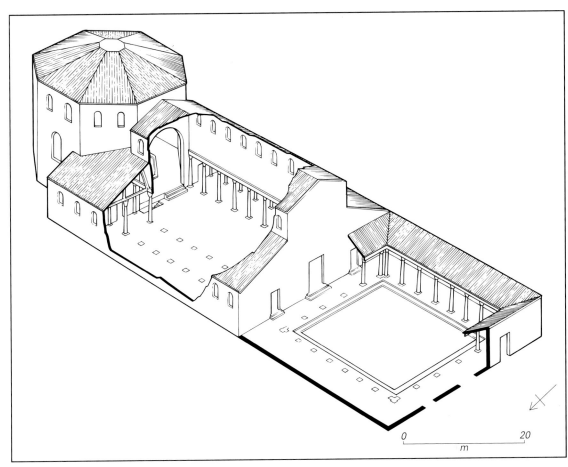

2. Martyrium, church of the Nativity, Bethlehem, AD 333; isometric reconstruction

Popes in the Catacombs of St Calixtus, Rome, which was modestly decorated by 250 and provided with an altar in the 4th century. Following pagan antecedents in *heroa* (heroes' shrines) and mausolea, these martyria were equipped with a *mensa* (table) for funeral banquets or *refrigeria* in honour of the deceased. After the Edict of Milan (AD 313), these celebrations assumed increased importance.

During the 4th century open-air precincts gave way to monumental martyria, as for example the Anastasius Mausoleum in Salona (*c.* 305–10; *see* SALONA, §2). This two-storey, apsed building sheltered the martyr's body below the apse, and the remainder of the crypt contained the tombs of the founders. The upper level served for memorial services and banquets, apparently with an altar above the martyr's tomb, thus establishing that a martyrium's purpose could be both 'evidential' and liturgical. The combination of these two aspects can be seen in several buildings in Rome, among the most impressive of which are the so-called cemetery basilicas outside the city walls. Those of St Lawrence on the Via Tiburtina (*c.* 330), SS Peter and Marcellinus on the Via Labicana (*c.* 324–36), and St Agnes on the Via Nomentana (337–50), were built near martyrs' tombs, while the Basilica Apostolorum (*c.* 313–37), later dedicated to St Sebastian, on the Via

Appia, replaced the precinct martyrium of SS Peter and Paul. The most outstanding example, however, was the huge basilica of Old St Peter's (119×64 m; *c.* 319–29; *see* ROME, §V, 14(i)) built by Constantine to house the Apostle's shrine, which was marked by a baldacchino in the middle of the transept, opposite the eastern apse. Because of its size, the building was also accessible to large crowds of pilgrims and offered space for funeral services near the Apostle's tomb.

Old St Peter's was the only one of Constantine's martyria (*see* CONSTANTINE THE GREAT) that actually enclosed a martyr's shrine. The others built by him commemorated holy places in Palestine (see fig. 2) and may be considered as the prototypes of martyria in the East. In each case the building's layout had to be adapted to the exigencies of the site. At Bethlehem the octagon enshrining the cave of the Nativity lay at the east end of a five-aisled basilica, while at Jerusalem a courtyard separated the basilica of the Holy Sepulchre (dedicated 336) from the rock of Calvary and the Anastasis (Resurrection) Rotunda, where the Sepulchre was housed. At Constantine's Eleona on the Mount of Olives, a different approach was adopted with the construction of a simple basilica above the cave where Christ taught the Apostles before the Ascension.

By the second half of the 4th century a custom had developed in the East of transporting or 'translating' relics from one place to another. The earliest recorded example is the removal of St Babylas' remains to Kaoussié, near Antioch (now Antakya), Syria, in 351–4. The bodies of SS Timothy, Andrew and Luke were brought to Constantinople in 356–7 by Emperor Constantius (*reg* 337–61) and placed in the cruciform church of the Holy Apostles (*see* ISTANBUL, §III, 9(i)), adjoining the circular mausoleum of Constantine. Thus any church, whether commemorative or parochial, could become a martyrium, and the possession of some relics became increasingly important for new foundations.

The influence of the Constantinian centralized martyria and the cruciform church of the Holy Apostles may be seen in numerous later buildings. Examples of centralized martyria include a rotunda (diam. 18 m) built by a Roman lady, Pomoenia (*c.* 370), to mark the site of the Ascension on the Mount of Olives, and the 5th-century octagonal martyria constructed over what were believed to be the house of St Peter at Capernaum (now Tall Hum), Palestine, and the tomb of St Philip at Hierapolis (now Pamukkale), Turkey. The latter two buildings were also equipped for the celebration of the liturgy. In the church of St Simeon at QAL'AT SIM'ĀN, Syria (*c.* 480–90), the octagonal martyrium formed the central feature, enshrining the column on which the saint spent the last years of his life. Examples of martyria that followed the cruciform plan of the Holy Apostles include that of St Babylas (begun *c.* 379) at Kaoussié (*see* ANTIOCH (i), §3), where the saint's relics were finally brought to rest; the redesigned structure (after 400) over the tomb of St John at Ephesos (*see* EPHESOS, §I, 3), and possibly that of St Menas (completed *c.* 490) at ABU MINA, Egypt. Adomna, writing *c.* 685 (Wilkinson), described another cruciform building above the Well of Jacob near Shechem (now Tall Balatah), Palestine.

In his pioneering study of the martyrium, Grabar proposed that the development of the domed cube as the standard Byzantine church form reflected the introduction of relics into the building. There is, however, little evidence to support this, for although the octagonal church of the Theotokos (484) at Mount Garizim (now Gerizim), Palestine, and numerous churches in Syria reflect the influence of earlier centralized martyria, the veneration of relics played a minor role in Byzantine liturgical planning. In Constantinople, for example, neither Hagia Sophia nor Hagia Eirene held relics of any significance during the early centuries, although, as the city's cathedral, Hagia Sophia later became a great repository of relics. Moreover, given their various functions and the limitations of the sites on which they were built, it is difficult to consider martyria as a specific architectural type. In addition to the octagons, rotundas and cruciform basilicas already cited, several centralized martyria in the shape of trefoils are known from North Africa, such as those at Tebessa, Algeria (*c.* 400), and Damous al-Karita, near Carthage, Tunisia (?4th century). One of the best-documented martyrial shrines is the five-aisled basilica of Hagios Demetrios, Thessaloniki (*c.* 450 or early 6th century: *see* THESSALONIKI, §III, 3), in which the main object of veneration was not the crypt, said to be left over from the

baths where Demetrius was murdered, but the freestanding ciborium in the nave.

Martyria built in Rome after Constantine began to develop along separate lines. Following the introduction of a permanent altar above the grave of St Peter, functional problems developed in the basilica, with both the liturgical celebration and pilgrim traffic focusing on the same point. This was remedied by Pope Gregory I (*reg* 590–604), who introduced a two-level arrangement with an elevated sanctuary above an annular crypt. It exerted considerable influence in the development of Western European architecture, where the relationship of the altar and major relic was largely maintained as more elaborate varieties of crypts and chevets were created.

BIBLIOGRAPHY

EARLY SOURCES

Eusebius of Caesarea: *The Tricennalia of Constantine* (*c.* 337); in *Eusebius Werke*, i, ed. I. Heikel (Leipzig, 1902)

GENERAL

H. Leclercq: 'Martyrium', *Dictionnaire d'archéologie chrétienne et de liturgie*, ed. F. Cabrol and H. Leclercq, x/2 (Paris, 1932), pp. 2512–23
A. Grabar: *Martyrium: Recherches sur le culte des reliques et l'art chrétien antique*, 2 vols (Paris, 1943–6); review by R. Krautheimer in *A. Bull.*, xxxv (1953), pp. 57–61
R. Krautheimer: 'Mensa-Coemeterium-Martyrium', *Cah. Archéol.*, xi (1960), pp. 15–40
——: *Early Christian and Byzantine Architecture*, Pelican Hist. A. (Harmondsworth, 1965, rev. 4/1986)
H. Strathmann: 'Martus', *Theologisches Wörterbuch zum Neuen Testament*, ed. G. Kittel, iv (Grand Rapids, 1967; Eng. trans, 1968), pp. 474–508
F. W. Deichmann: 'Martyrerbasilika, Martyrion, Memoria, und Altargrab', *Röm. Mitt.*, lxxvii (1970), pp. 144–69
T. F. Mathews: *The Early Churches of Constantinople: Architecture and Liturgy* (University Park, PA, and London, 1971)
W. E. Kleinbauer: 'The Origin and Functions of the Aisled Tetraconch Churches in Syria and Northern Mesopotamia', *Dumbarton Oaks Pap.*, xxvii (1973), pp. 89–114
J. Wilkinson: *Jerusalem Pilgrims before the Crusades* (Warminster, 1977), p. 193
P. Brown: *The Cult of the Saints: Its Rise and Function in Latin Christianity* (Chicago, 1981)
Y. Duval: *Loca sanctorum Africae*, 2 vols (Paris, 1982)
R. Ousterhout: 'The Temple, the Sepulchre, and the Martyrion of the Savior', *Gesta*, xxix (1990), pp. 44–53

ROBERT OUSTERHOUT

Maruscelli [Marucelli], **Paolo** (*b* Rome, 1596; *d* ?Rome, 17 Oct 1649). Italian architect and engineer. He was one of the few Romans to practise architecture in his native city at a time when the high Baroque style was being formed there by immigrant Lombards such as Carlo Maderno and Francesco Borromini and Tuscans such as Pietro da Cortona. He may have been trained in the circle of Giovanni Battista Soria, but his repertory of ornament shows some affinities with the Milanese work of Francesco Maria Ricchini. His contact with the Oratorians, the followers of S Filippo Neri, began in 1622 and led to his first important commission, the Chiesa Nuova (1626–65), Perugia, a provincial church combining the plan of Jacopo Vignola's Gesù with the façade type introduced by Maderno at S Susanna, both in Rome. The Oratorians also commissioned Maruscelli to produce an ambitious project (1627) for the rebuilding of their house next to S Maria in Vallicella, Rome. On this scheme he worked in close collaboration with Virgilio Spada, and the final plan (Rome, Vatican, Bib. Apostolica and Archv S Maria in Vallicella) synthesizes stylistic elements from three earlier institutional buildings: Andrea Palladio's Convent of the Carità, Venice; Pellegrino Tibaldi's Palazzo Arcivescovile, Milan; and Soria's Palazzo della Famiglia Borghese, Rome. The new building, if fully completed, would have been grander than a monastery but not as imposing as a prince's or cardinal's palace. The sacristy was built according to Maruscelli's project, but Borromini took over for the oratory itself, producing a masterpiece of the Roman Baroque (*see* BORROMINI, FRANCESCO, §I, 4 and fig. 4).

Maruscelli was also the architect of at least four other buildings for religious orders in Rome. In 1629 he began work on the Theatine convent at S Andrea della Valle, where such details as door frames and the general layout of the sacristy show his style. Between 1631 and 1636 Maruscelli was active, with Benedetto Molli, in the planning of the new wing of the Jesuit Collegio Germanico opposite the façade of S Agostino. In 1636 he replaced Oratio Torriani (*fl* 1602–57) as the architect of the sacristy (completed 1642) of S Maria dell'Anima, Rome, where his style can be seen in the rich stucco ornament, including cornucopias and the imperial eagle. From 1638 to 1643 he built the east and north wings of the Dominican convent at S Maria sopra Minerva, a design of unremitting functionalism that, in the history of Roman institutional building, stands somewhere between the convent of S Marcello al Corso by Antonio Casone (1559–1634) and Borromini's Propaganda Fide.

From 1633 until his death Maruscelli was active in the rebuilding of the Palazzo Capodiferro (Palazzo Spada) for Cardinal Bernardino Spada, Virgilio's older brother. The present atrium of the palace is his, as well as the picture gallery and the rooms on the south-west side of the courtyard. His most interesting contribution was an illusionistic display of architectural perspective painted on the garden wall in 1641–2; this may be linked to illusionistic paintings in French gardens, such as the fictive arch of Constantine painted on a wall of Cardinal Richelieu's garden at Rueil in the 1630s. It was replaced by Borromini's perspective colonnade in 1653. Other work by Borromini elsewhere in the palace obliterated some work by Maruscelli.

Cardinal Carlo de' Medici provided Maruscelli with his most significant commission, the rebuilding of the Palazzo Madama, Rome, between 1637 and 1642 (see fig.). Originally built in the late 15th century for Sinulfo di Castel Ottieri and acquired in 1505 by the Medici, the palace had been the family seat in Rome during the pontificate of Leo X. Various proposals, including schemes by Giuliano da Sangallo and Lodovico Cigoli, had been made for reconstructing the palace before Maruscelli began work in 1637. The majestic façade (1638–9) is a heavily decorated version of the standard Roman palace type, replete with images of Hercules (symbolizing the virtuous ruler) and lions (referring to the pontificates of Leo X and Leo XI). On the interior Maruscelli restructured the old apartments and added new ones, created a grand staircase and built a two-storey *salone* as the ceremonial centrepiece of the palace. Efforts to acquire all the houses on the property and to establish an *isola medicea* were blocked by the French, who refused to sell houses near their churches of S Luigi dei Francesi and S Salvatore in Thermis. A new street, the

Paolo Maruscelli: façade of the Palazzo Madama, 1637–42; engraving from G. Vasi: *Delle magnificenze di Roma antica e moderna*, iv (Rome, 1754), pl. 70

Corsia Agonale, opened a vista to the palace door, however, and gave the Medici their long-sought link with the Piazza Navona, where they enjoyed a brief hegemony until the rise of the Pamphili family in 1644. Although Maruscelli's façade was not as innovative as such later work as Bernini's Palazzo Chigi (1664), it did leave its stamp wherever luxury and magnificent display were a prime consideration. Among its immediate progeny are the façades of Camillo Arcucci's Palazzo Pio in the Campo dei Fiori, Felice della Greca's projects for the Palazzo Chigi in Piazza Colonna, and Carlo Rainaldi's Palazzo Mancini al Corso, all in Rome.

Maruscelli left behind a library of 123 volumes, including most of the classics of architecture, books on hydraulics, engineering and military architecture, on optics and mathematics, and dictionaries in various languages. His main achievement was to create an architectural repertory adapted to the whole spectrum of Roman 17th-century patronage, from Theatine austerity through the middle style of the Oratorians to Medici splendour.

BIBLIOGRAPHY
Thieme–Becker
L. Neppi: *Palazzo Spada* (Rome, 1975), pp. 133–74
J. Connors: *Borromini and the Roman Oratory* (Cambridge, MA, 1980), pp. 107–12
E. Fumagalli: *La 'fabbrica' di Palazzo Medici in Piazza Madonna a Roma* (diss., U. Florence, 1986)
——: 'La Villa Médicis au XVIIe siècle, *La Villa Médicis*, ed. A. Chassel and P. Morel, ii (Rome, 1991), p. 578, no. 55

JOSEPH CONNORS

Marussig, Piero (*b* Trieste, 10 May 1879; *d* Pavia, 13 Oct 1937). Italian painter. He was the son of a wealthy businessman and collector. He went to Vienna and Munich, where he joined the Secession. He then lived in Rome for two years (1903–5) and spent a year in Paris (1905), where he studied Post-Impressionism and Fauvism. On his return to Italy in 1906 he lived in Trieste and until about 1919 painted in a loosely expressionistic style. Marussig adopted a technique of outlining his figures with bold contours. Works of this period, such as *The Sisters* (Milan, Gal. A. Mod.), are imbued with melancholic overtones, produced by the combination of heavily impastoed brushwork, strong colours and subdued light.

In 1919 Marussig had a one-man show at the Galleria Vinciana in Milan where he met Carlo Carrà and the critic Margherita Sarfatti. He was a founder-member of the Novecento group (1922), with which he exhibited at the Venice Biennale of 1924. Later he joined the steering committee of the reformulated NOVECENTO ITALIANO and participated in its exhibitions of 1926 and 1929 in Milan. He also had numerous shows abroad. Despite this involvement, Marussig's art never truly embraced the monumentality or archaism of other members of the group such as Mario Sironi or Achille Funi (1890–1972). His work of the 1920s, such as *The Bather* (1925; Gallarate, priv. col., see 1986 exh. cat., no. 40), shows an increased emphasis on space and volume, the use of earthy tones and a renewed interest in pictorial values. His repertory of intimate domestic scenes was extended in the 1930s to include a series of landscapes similar in atmosphere to the peaceful images of the Lombard countryside painted by Arturo Tosi (1871–1956), a close friend.

In 1930, with Funi and the sculptor Timo Bortolotti (1884–1954), Marussig opened a studio in Milan based on Renaissance principles for training young artists.

BIBLIOGRAPHY

R. Bossaglia: *Il novecento italiano: Storia, documenti, iconografia* (Milan, 1979)

Piero Marussig dalla provincia mitteleuropea al novecento italiano (exh. cat., ed. G. Mascherpa; Iseo, Pal. Arsenale, 1986)

SIMONETTA FRAQUELLI

Maruyama Ōkyo [Isshō; Ōkyo; Ōsui Gyofu; Rakuyō Sanjin] (*b* Kameoka [now Kyoto Prefecture] or Kyoto, 1733; *d* Kyoto, 1795). Japanese painter. Although born into a farming family, he showed an early talent for drawing. His parents, after trying unsuccessfully to have him become a monk, apprenticed him first to a clothing shop in Kyoto and then to a toymaker there, for whom he painted dolls. Ōkyo frequented a cosmetics shop for which he designed accessories, and it was at the instigation of the shop's customers that he undertook formal training as a painter.

1. TRAINING AND EARLY WORKS, *c.* 1745–65. Ōkyo's teacher, Ishida Yūtei (1721–86), had been a pupil of Tsuruzawa Tangei (1688–1769), a painter in the style of the KANŌ SCHOOL, whose father had been trained by Kanō Tan'yū (*see* KANŌ, (11)). Yūtei's style was typical of Kanō artists of his time, being a synthesis of the Kanō and Tosa (*see* TOSA SCHOOL) traditions with additional elements derived from the Rinpa school and touches of naturalism. Under Yūtei's direction Ōkyo copied the works of earlier painters and learnt to paint large-scale works based on carefully conceived small sketches. He inherited his teacher's interest in diverse painting styles, and four sketchbooks (Tokyo, N. Mus.) containing copies of sketches from life by Watanabe Shikō are evidence of his admiration for Shikō's combination of Rinpa, Kanō and naturalistic elements. From his late teens Ōkyo also studied Dutch prints, learning the principles of linear perspective and modelling the human form.

From a similar age until he was about 30, Ōkyo produced *ukie* (perspective pictures), in which space was observed from a single viewpoint. His earliest extant paintings of this kind are *meganee* ('eyeglass pictures'), the distorted views used in a perspective box (Jap. *nozoki karakuri*), which were presumably produced for the toy shop in Kyoto where he worked in the 1750s. His *meganee* were based on Chinese woodblock prints made in the Suzhou area, themselves derived from Dutch copperplate engravings, and depicted both Chinese and Japanese scenery using chiaroscuro effects and vanishing-point perspective, as in *Archery Contest at Sanjūsangendō* (Hyōgo, Yabumoto priv. col.). In this picture the target is placed at the rear of the composition so as to draw the viewer's attention to the vanishing perspective point. Over the same period Ōkyo also produced paintings in more usual formats, culminating in works such as the hanging scroll *Old Pine Tree in the Snow* (*Setsushō zu*; 1765; Tokyo, N. Mus.). In these he experimented with the naturalistic treatment of detail and the use of ink in a way that foreshadows his mature style, but they lack the consistency of vision which marks the latter.

2. EMMAN'IN PERIOD, 1765–74. In about 1765 Ōkyo became friends with Yūjō (1722–73), the abbot of the Emman'in, a temple in Ōtsu (now Shiga Prefecture). Soon after, the abbot invited Ōkyo to Emman'in and encouraged him to continue his technical experiments. Ōkyo produced a vast number of sketches, copied Chinese bird-and-flower paintings and analysed the work of other artists, including ink paintings of the Muromachi period (1333–1568) as well as of those in the Kanō and Rinpa styles.

Ōkyo's observations about painting, recorded by Yūjō in his diary (*Manshi*, 'Myriad records'; 1761–73), show his concern with definition of space both in the picture as a whole and in the description of individual forms. His view that an artist must determine the 'bone structure' of a figure before attaching the clothing, for example, reflected his familiarity with the Western basis of figure drawing. He is known to have studied and copied foreign books on surgery. In pursuit of accuracy he advocated sketching directly from nature and copying models rather than drawing from the imagination, but he used mirrors and other optical devices to help him visualize three-dimensional forms on two-dimensional surfaces. His scientific interests included the Chinese-derived pseudo-science of *ninsōgaku* ('physiognomy'), which clearly influenced the appearance of the figures in the scroll *Supplement of the Encyclopedia of Correct Descriptions of Human Figures* (1770; Tenri, Nara Prefect., Lib.), for example.

Ōkyo also studied methods for using inks, pigments and brushes, refining a number of techniques used in *mokkotsu* ('boneless') ink painting, such as the application of shading with a slanted brush (*tsuketate*) to define the various planes of individual forms. To express volumetric forms he used the techniques of *kataguma* ('one-sided shading') in which the ink was applied on a single side of the form, and *sotoguma* ('external shading'), in which non-linear washes in gradated tones delineated the form in reserve.

3. MATURE WORK, 1774–85. By the time Ōkyo returned to Kyoto in 1774, he had successfully fused these diverse elements into a distinctive personal style. Its main feature was the combination of naturalism and stylization, as in the hanging scroll *Peacock, Hen and Peonies* (1776;

Maruyama Ōkyo: *Waterfall and Pine Trees*, wall painting, ink and colours on paper, 1794 (Kagawa Prefecture, Kotohira Shrine, Omote Shoin)

Kyoto, Imp. Pal.). He did not copy directly from nature but modified natural forms and their arrangement through the use of special brush techniques and a consistent angle of vision to create an illusion of naturalism. His style represented a break with earlier painting traditions and was sometimes referred to as *shaseiga* ('life-drawing painting'). His scientific curiosity gave his work an intellectual rather than an intuitive air; this proved popular with his clientele, but Ōkyo was criticized by his rivals for lack of inner spirit.

In the later 1770s he began to produce paintings in greater numbers and in larger formats, eventually establishing a workshop that continued to produce paintings in his style after his death. Ōkyo painted some of his most important large-scale works for temples such as Daijōji (Hyōgo Prefecture) and Kongōji in Kameoka, and in 1790 he took part in the restoration of the imperial palace in Kyoto. He contracted an eye disease in 1793 but continued working, and the wall painting *Waterfall and Pine Trees* (1794; see fig.), executed for the Omote Shoin at Kotohira Shrine in Kagawa Prefecture, is considered one of his best compositions. By following the course of the waterfall as it flows into a pond, the viewer is drawn into the picture and has the impression of standing on the verandah in the foreground.

Ōkyo's workshop attracted many pupils, among them his son Maruyama Ōzui (1766–1829), who succeeded him as head of the Maruyama school, Nagasawa Rosetsu, Komai Genki (1747–97), Watanabe Nangaku (1767–1813) and Mori Tetsuzan (1775–1841). Many underdrawings by Ōkyo were retained and used by his pupils. The work of Ōkyo and his followers was later combined with that of the Shijō workshop founded by Matsumura Goshun in the so-called Maruyama–Shijō school (*see* JAPAN, §VI, 4(viii)).

UNPUBLISHED SOURCES

Yūjō: *Manshi* ['Myriad records'] (1761–73)

BIBLIOGRAPHY

J. Hillier: *The Uninhibited Brush: Japanese Art in the Shijō Style* (London, 1974)

T. Yamagawa: *Ōkyo, Goshun*, Nihon bijutsu kaiga zenshū [Complete collection of Japanese painting], xxii (Tokyo, 1980)

Ōkyo and the Maruyama–Shijō School of Japanese Painting (exh. cat. by J. Sasaki, St Louis, MO, A. Mus., 1980)

J. Sasaki: 'Ōkyo kankei shiryō *Manshi* bassui' [Materials on Ōkyo: selections from the *Myriad Records*], *Bijutsushi*, xxxi/111 (1981), pp. 46–60

——: 'Maruyama Ōkyo no kaigaron: *Manshi* o chūshin ni shite' [Maruyama Ōkyo's writings on painting, centering on the *Myriad Records*], *Kyōtō Daigaku Bungakubu Bigaku Bijutsushi Kenkyūshitsu Kenkyū Kiyō*, iii (1982)

——: 'Maruyama Ōkyo no jinbutsu zu ni kansuru ichi kōsatsu' [An initial examination of Maruyama Ōkyo's figure paintings], *Kyōtō Daigaku Bungakubu Bigaku Bijutsushi Kenkyūshitsu Kenkyū Kiyō*, vi (1985), pp. 1–34

——: 'Maruyama Ōkyo no sansuiga ni tsuite' [Concerning Maruyama Ōkyo's landscape paintings], *Bijutsushi*, cxx (1986), pp. 113–32

PATRICIA J. GRAHAM

Marv [Marw, Mary]. *See* MERV.

Marville, Charles (*b* Paris, 18 July 1816; *d* between Jan 1878 and 20 Sept 1879). French photographer and illustrator. He first worked as an illustrator in the medium of wood-engraving and was associated with Tony Johannot. With the writer Charles Nodier (1780–1844) and publishers such as Curmer and Bourdin he took part in the creation of great Romantic illustrated editions of such works as *Paul et Virginie* by Bernardin de Saint-Pierre. He was, however, primarily a landscape artist known as an illustrator of travel books. By 1851 he had become a photographer, concentrating on religious sites and religious architecture, particularly for Louis-Désiré Blanquart-Evrard, who published *c.* 100 of his calotypes. He worked for the Louvre and reproduced drawings by major French and Italian artists. Collaborating with architects such as Paul Abadie, he photographed the different stages of construction or of restoration of civil and religious monuments. He also photographed the new Bois de Boulogne.

Marville's most accomplished work was the album of *c.* 400 images of roads condemned by Baron Georges-Eugène Haussmann's restructuring of Paris, for example *Rue des Prêtres-St-Séverin (5e Arrondissement)* (albumen print, *c.* 1865; Paris, Carnavalet). At the request of the municipality, he took a systematic census of them before their demolition (*see* PHOTOGRAPHY, fig. 10). Ten years later, he returned to the same sites where he was again commissioned to photograph the new main roads in order to present Haussmann's Paris at the Exposition Universelle of 1878.

BIBLIOGRAPHY
M. de Thézy: 'Charles Marville et Haussmann', *Photographie et architecture: Monuments historiques*, 110 (1980), pp. 13–17
Charles Marville, photographe de Paris de 1851 à 1879 (exh. cat. by M. de Thézy, Paris, Bib. Hist., 1980)
C. C. Hungerford: 'Charles Marville, Popular Illustrator: The Origins of the Photographic Sensibility', *Hist. Phot.*, ix/3 (1985), pp. 227–46
M. de Thézy and R. Debuisson: *Marville, Paris* (Paris, 1994)

MARIE DE THÉZY

Marville, Jean de [Marvile]. *See* JEAN DE MARVILLE.

Marx, Erich (*b* Berlin, 25 April 1921). German collector. A law graduate, he worked in publishing before setting up his own business in Berlin. In his collecting, which he began in 1975, he favoured artists of his own generation and took advice from the exhibition organizer Heiner Bastian (*b* 1943). The Marx collection includes works by Joseph Beuys, Robert Rauschenberg, Cy Twombly and Andy Warhol.

BIBLIOGRAPHY
Joseph Beuys, Robert Rauschenberg, Cy Twombley, Andy Warhol (exh. cat. by H. Bastian, W. Berlin, Tiergarten. N.G.; Mönchengladbach, Städt. Mus. Abteiberg; 1982)

Marx, Roger (*b* Nancy, 1859; *d* Paris, 1913). French civil servant, writer and collector. He began his career as a journalist in Nancy, writing on the arts for the *Progrès de l'Est* from 1878, and in 1882 he published a series of studies of local painters, *Etudes d'art lorrain*. In the same year he was appointed Secrétaire des Beaux-Arts in Paris and five years later succeeded Jules Castagnary as Directeur de l'Administration des Beaux-Arts; in 1889 he became Inspecteur des Musées de Province. He organized the great Exposition Universelle in 1889; among other reforms, he instituted a new section for the decorative arts at the Salon from 1891. He was in charge of the paintings at the Exposition Universelle in 1900 and persuaded the reluctant Impressionists Claude Monet, Auguste Renoir and Camille Pissarro to exhibit there. In addition, Marx was a prolific writer, often coming to the defence of the avant-garde. He was a friend of many artists, among them Paul Cézanne, Henri de Toulouse-Lautrec, Auguste Rodin and particularly Eugène Carrière, whom he met in 1884 and who painted portraits of *Roger Marx* (1885) and of his son *Pierre Roger-Marx* (1886; both Paris, Mus. d'Orsay). Marx was a contributor to the *Gazette des beaux-arts* from 1895, becoming its editor in 1905. He also edited *L'Image* and *Les Maîtres de l'affiche*, and was one of the founders of *L'Estampe originale*. During his career he amassed considerable collections of drawings and prints by his contemporaries; many of these were sold after his death. His son Claude Roger-Marx (1888–1977) collected

in a similar manner and donated important groups of drawings to the Louvre in 1974 and 1978.

WRITINGS
Etudes d'art lorrain (Paris, 1882)
Henri Regnault (Paris, 1886)
Etudes sur l'école française (Paris, 1903)
L'Art social (Paris, 1913)
Maîtres d'hier et d'aujourd'hui (Paris, [1914])

BIBLIOGRAPHY
P. Jamot: 'Roger Marx (1859–1913)', *Gaz. B.-A.*, n. s. 3, xi (1914), pp. 1–10
F. Lugt: *Marques* (1921), p. 417
G. Wildenstein: 'Pour le centenaire de Roger Marx', *Gaz. B.-A.*, n. s. 5, liv (1959), pp. 1–3
Donations Claude Roger-Marx (exh. cat., Paris, Louvre, 1980–81)
S. Monneret: *L'Impressionnisme et son époque: Dictionnaire international*, i (Paris, 1987), pp. 505–6

Marx, Samuel A(braham) (*b* Natchez, MS, 27 Aug 1885; *d* New York, 17 Jan 1964). American collector and architect. He trained in Boston and Paris and had a distinguished career as an architect and interior designer. Although he was previously interested in the arts, he began, with his wife Florene, to collect 20th-century paintings by the Ecole de Paris only after marrying in 1937. The Marx collection always remained relatively small, *c.* 48 paintings and 12 sculptures, ranging from Roger de La Fresnaye's *Artillery* (1911) to Miró's *Painting* (1936). The Marxes' first purchases, in 1939, were Picasso's *Woman Combing her Hair* (1908) and Braque's *Yellow Tablecloth* (1935). Works by Picasso and Braque were to remain the cornerstones of the collection over the next 20 years, together with those by Matisse, who was represented by larger, more Cubist-influenced work such as *Woman on a High Stool* (1913) and *The Moroccans* (1916). The majority of these Matisses were eventually presented to MOMA, New York, of which Samuel Marx was a trustee, and whose Director of Collections, Alfred H. Barr, jr, thought highly of their choice from this artist's work. In later life Florene Marx, as Mrs Wolfgang Schoenborn, was also a trustee of MOMA, but a number of her acquisitions, notably Picasso's *Bust of a Woman* (1906), were given to the Art Institute of Chicago.

BIBLIOGRAPHY
The Collection of Sam and Florene Marx (exh. cat., New York, MOMA, 1965)

A. DEIRDRE ROBSON

Marxism. Term for the body of social theory based on the work of the German socialist and political economist Karl Marx (1818–83) and his collaborator Friedrich Engels (1820–95). In addition to giving rise to an important political movement, it has also had profound implications for the understanding of art.

1. Introduction. 2. Social theory. 3. Marx's writings on art. 4. Influence on art history.

1. INTRODUCTION. As a student in Berlin, Marx associated with a group of radicals inspired by the idealist philosophy of Hegel. After university he worked for the liberal Cologne paper *Rheinische Zeitung*; the paper was suppressed in 1843, and Marx moved to Paris, where he became involved in communist politics. In 1844 he met Engels, and the two subsequently summarized their basic

ideas in the *Communist Manifesto* (1848), a pamphlet for the short-lived Communist League. Both returned to Germany to work on the *Neue Rheinische Zeitung*, but after the defeat of the European revolutions of 1848–9 they suspended their political and revolutionary activities. Marx moved to London and pursued his economic studies at the British Library, while Engels worked for 20 years for his family's manufacturing firm in Manchester. In 1864, Marx helped found the International Working Men's Association, the purpose of which was to provide a basis for cooperation among trade unions and working-class parties in Britain and on the Continent. Although conflicts between the supporters of Marx and Engels and those of anarchist Mikhail Bakúnin (1814–76) led to the demise of the International in the 1870s, the following years saw a growth of national workers' parties of a more or less Marxist character, of which the German Social Democratic Party was the largest, and in 1889 the Second International was founded. Like the First International, this was a loose federation of European trade unions and socialist parties but it was much larger than its predecessor and represents the golden age of Marxism. World War I tore it apart, however, and after the Russian Revolution of 1917 Marxism split into two distinct political movements as Soviet-inspired Communist parties divorced themselves from the less revolutionary Social Democratic parties of the day. Marxist theory has had important implications for the understanding of art and its relation to society, primarily through the concept of IDEOLOGY, which became particularly influential following the posthumous publication in 1927 (Eng. trans. 1936) of Marx's *Die deutsche Ideologie*. Marx himself also took a direct interest in art at various stages of his life and, although he did not expound a coherent, unified critical doctrine, left an abundance of writings from which specifically Marxist views on aesthetics have been derived.

2. SOCIAL THEORY. Marx's critique of capitalism and his general theory of history and society—the latter often known as 'the materialist conception of history' or 'historical materialism'—are central to Marxism. The critique of capitalism was the subject of Marx's magnum opus, *Das Kapital*, the first volume of which was published in 1867 (subsequent volumes were published posthumously). Here Marx analysed the basic nature of capitalism as the exploitation of the labour of the worker by the capitalist and argued that capitalism's internal contradictions would eventually lead to its demise. Marx's 'historical materialism', on the other hand, was an attempt to explain the general contours of social evolution, which, in the words of Engels (1892 introduction to *Socialism: Utopian and Scientific*): 'located the ultimate cause and great moving power of all important historic events in the economic development of society, in the changes in the modes of production and exchange, and in the consequent division of society into distinct classes, and in the struggles of these classes against one another'.

Marx and Engels first elaborated this theory of history, which became the guiding thread of their subsequent studies, in *Die deutsche Ideologie*, written in Brussels in 1845–6. A compact statement of it appears in the preface to *Zur Kritik der politischen Ökonomie* (1859), in which Marx contends that the economic structure of society, constituted by its relations of production, is the real foundation of society. It is the basis 'on which rises a legal and political superstructure and to which correspond definite forms of social consciousness'. On the other hand, society's relations of production themselves 'correspond to a definite state of development of [society's] material productive forces'. In this manner 'the mode of production of material life conditions the social, political and intellectual life process in general'. As society's productive forces develop, they clash with existing production relations, which fetter their growth. 'Then begins an epoch of social revolution' as this contradiction rifts society and as people become, in a more or less ideological form, 'conscious of this conflict and fight it out'. This conflict is resolved in favour of the productive forces, and new, higher relations of production, whose material preconditions have 'matured in the womb of the old society itself', emerge that accommodate more successfully the continued growth of society's productive capacity. The 'bourgeois mode of production' (i.e. capitalism) represents the most recent of several progressive epochs in the economic formation of society, but it is the last antagonistic form of production. With its demise the prehistory of humanity will come to a close.

According to Marx, then, the expansion of the productive forces (that is, of the means of production and of the skill and expertise of human labour power) determines society's relations of production. These relations, however, also influence the momentum and qualitative direction of the development of productive forces; capitalism in particular is distinguished by its tendency to raise society to a productive level undreamt of before. Still, Marx's materialist conception assigns explanatory primacy to the development of the productive forces, envisioning, for instance, the emergence of capitalism as a response to the level of the productive forces existing at the time of its origin. While the development of society's productive capacity thus determines the main contours of its socio-economic evolution, the various resulting economic structures in turn shape society's legal and political institutions, or superstructure. Which other social institutions are properly part of the superstructure is a matter of debate, but Marx certainly thought that all the various spheres and realms of society reflect the dominant mode of production and that the general consciousness of an epoch is shaped by the nature of its production. The Marxist theory of ideology contends, in part, that certain ideas originate or are widespread because they support existing social relations or promote particular class interests. The economy's determination of legal and political forms, however, will tend to be relatively direct, while its influence over other social realms, culture, art and consciousness generally is more attenuated and nuanced.

In the social organization of production, people stand in different relations to the forces and products of production, and in any given mode of production these relations will be of certain characteristic sorts. People's economic positions—as understood in terms of the existing social production relations—give them certain material interests in common with others and determine their class. Under capitalism, the two major classes are the bourgeoisie (or capitalist class) and the proletariat (or working class). The bourgeoisie own the means of production, while the proletariat own only their labour power and are consequently obliged to work for the capitalist class. A central thesis of Marxism is that class position, so defined, determines the characteristic consciousness or world view of its members. For example, Marx's discussion of the Legitimists and Orléanists in *Der achtzehnte Brumaire des Louis Bonaparte* (1852) emphasizes that on the basis of its socio-economic position each class creates 'an entire superstructure of distinct and peculiarly formed sentiments, illusions, modes of thought and views of life'. The differing material interests of classes divide them and lead to their struggle. Classes differ in the extent to which their members perceive themselves as a class, so that antagonisms between classes may not be discerned by the participants, or may be understood only in a mystified or ideological manner.

Marx and Engels wrote that 'the history of all hitherto existing society is the history of class struggles'. The ultimate success or failure of a class is, however, determined by its relation to the advance of the productive forces. In the words of *Die deutsche Ideologie*, 'the conditions under which definite productive forces can be applied are the conditions of the rule of a definite class of society'. The class that has the capacity and the incentive to introduce or preserve the relations of production required to accommodate the advance of the productive forces has its hegemony ensured. Marx viewed class rule as having been both inevitable and necessary to force the productivity of the direct producers beyond the subsistence level. The productive progress brought by capitalism, however, eliminates both the feasibility of and the historical rationale for class rule. Since the state is primarily the vehicle by which a class secures its rule, it will wither away in a post-class society.

In *Das Kapital*, Marx maintained that under capitalism workers, despite their legal freedom to work for whomever they choose, are exploited by the dominant economic class just as serfs and slaves had been exploited in earlier modes of production. Marx thought that his theory of surplus value was the key to understanding this exploitation, in which the worker's labour, unlike other factors of production, contributes more value to the final product than the free market obliges the capitalist to pay the worker for his labour. This surplus value is the source of capitalist profit in all its different forms, and the pursuit of profit drives the capitalist system. *Das Kapital* also sees capitalism as subject to various internal contradictions leading to cyclical but increasingly severe economic crises. Capitalism is unable to resolve its internal difficulties, and no reform of the system can change its basic exploitative character. On the other hand, capitalism does prepare the material conditions that make socialism possible and spawns an increasingly large and well-organized working class, which eventually seeks through either peaceful or violent political revolution to replace capitalism by a system of cooperative production (socialism) that is more hospitable to its needs—a system 'in which the free development of each is the condition for the free development of all'. Marx wrote little about this future society. He did believe that after the proletarian revolution, society as a whole would

control the means of production, and each individual worker would receive from the common stock of society's produce in proportion to the work he had done. Furthermore, Marx foresaw this socialist society evolving to a higher, purely communistic level in which neither money, market nor state as conceived at present would exist. Characterized by material plenty, this future communist society would be governed by the slogan 'from each according to his ability, to each according to his needs'.

Marx and Engels always viewed their theories as scientific and derided the teachings of other socialistic and communistic parties as 'utopian', because they were based on abstract ethical appeals and unrealistic schemes for the future rather than on an accurate understanding on the nature of capitalism and the course of historical development. It should be borne in mind, however, that Marx and Engels did not see historical development as a mechanical process, nor did they pretend to be able to explain its every detail. For instance, while Marx's preface to *Zur Kritik der politischen Ökonomie* designates the Asiatic, ancient, feudal and modern bourgeois modes of production as the major epochs in humanity's advance, these mark the general stages of socio-economic evolution as a whole—not steps that every nation should climb. It even seems likely that Marx would have been willing to revise his particular tabulation of historical periods (or at least the pre-feudal ones), since he did not analyse in detail humanity's early modes of production. Moreover, certain social and cultural phenomena are beyond Marxism's explanatory range, and from its broad purview, many historical events, and certainly the specific forms they take, are accidental. Nor did Marx and Engels seek to explain fully and scientifically individual behaviour, although they always attempted to situate that behaviour within its sociological confines.

3. MARX'S WRITINGS ON ART. In 1835–6, while still a student of criminal law at the University of Bonn, Marx attended the lectures of the Romantic critic and writer August Wilhelm Schlegel and the Professor of Art History Eduard d'Alton. It is likely that through these lectures Marx became acquainted with the ideas and works of the Nazarenes and then became interested in the role of the artist in society. In 1837 he is known to have read Winckelmann's *Geschichte der Kunst des Alterthums* and Lessing's *Laokoon*. After joining the Doktorenklub at Berlin in 1837, he was invited by the philosopher Bruno Bauer to contribute to a publication on Hegel's teachings on art. The title for this contribution was originally proposed as 'Hegel's Hatred of Religious and Christian Art and his Dissolution of all Positive State Laws', which suggests his belief at the time that Hegel was a Hellenist who would have been antipathetic to the Romantic Christianity that was current at that time and even a part of the political policy of Frederick William IV (*reg* 1840–61). Only part of Marx's contribution was published, however, as an article in the *Rheinische Zeitung*. At the time he was writing on art, he studied the writings of Benjamin Constant (1767–1830) and Ludwig Feuerbach (1804–72), and he may well have been influenced by the ideas of the Utopian socialist the Comte de Saint-Simon (1760–1825), who saw the artist as playing an important

role in the productive capacities of a nation and as an avant-garde leader of men.

In 1844, Marx published his *Ökonomische und philosophische Manuskripte*, in which he set out his concept of alienated labour, but at this point in his career he had not developed an idea of art as simply a form of economic production. It was only in their *Die deutsche Ideologie* that Marx and Engels together developed a more explicitly 'Saint-Simonian' concept of art as a form of productive labour. Here they attacked the élitist view of art as something to be created only by great individuals and wrote that 'whether an individual such as Raphael succeeds in developing his talent depends wholly on demand, which in turn depends on the division of labour and the conditions of human culture resulting from it'. They diverted attention away from the art object and concentrated instead on the circumstances of its production, thereby abolishing the distinction between art and labour that had been central to the aesthetics of Kant, Schiller and Hegel.

Marx and Engels believed that ideas of professional specialization in art were a consequence of the division of labour and that it was essential that the practice of art should be democratized, in order that it cease to be an exclusive practice:

> The exclusive concentration of artistic talent in certain individuals, and its consequent suppression in the broad masses of the people, is an effect of the division of labour … With a communist organization of society, the artist is not confined by the local and national seclusion which ensues solely from the division of labour, nor is the individual confined to one specific art, so that he becomes exclusively a painter, a sculptor etc; these very names express sufficiently the narrowness of his professional development, and his dependence on the division of labour. In a communist society, there are no painters, but at most men who, among other things, also paint.

It is clear from this passage from *Die deutsche Ideologie* that Marx and Engels believed that everyone had the capacity for some form of artistic work. On the other hand, Marx remained a believer in the superior status of Greek art, and in the introduction to the *Grundrisse* (1857) he returned to the subject of aesthetics. In a much-quoted passage, he faced the uneasy relationship between the development of a given society and the type and style of art it produced: 'In the case of the arts, it is well known that certain periods of their flowering are out of all proportion to the general development of society, hence also to the material foundation, the skeletal structure as it were of its organization'. From this, it is evident that at least by 1857 he had rejected a simplistic equation between the forms of art and systems of social organization.

While Marx was working on *Zur Kritik der politischen Ökonomie* he was invited to contribute an article on aesthetics to the *New American Encyclopedia*. In his notebooks for this entry (which he never completed), he was obviously considering the problematic relationship between objects and the ways in which they are perceived aesthetically, and he wrote a detailed synopsis of *Ästhetik* by Friedrich Theodor Vischer (1807–87). The metaphor of base and superstructure was first mentioned in the introduction to *Zur Kritik der politischen Ökonomie*; art was explicitly stated to be part of the superstructure and one of the 'ideological forms' in which class conflict is carried out.

4. INFLUENCE ON ART HISTORY. Because Marx did not leave a coherent body of writings on the subject of art and aesthetics, it was left to his followers to elaborate on the implications of the concept of ideology for our understanding of art. The use of Marxist ideas within the discipline of art history is perhaps most clear in the studies of the production of art from a sociological point of view (*see* SOCIOLOGY OF ART) and studies of the social background to artists and periods (*see* SOCIAL HISTORY OF ART). However, the overall impact of Marxism on art history is difficult to define, mainly because subsequent writers have emphasized different aspects of Marxist theory and linked them to other concerns. The most significant writer to develop Marxist ideas of art in the early part of the 20th century was GEORGYI PLEKHANOV, who had translated the *Communist Manifesto* into Russian in 1882. In his *Iskusstvo i obshchestvennaya zhizn'* of 1912 (Eng. trans. *Art and Social Life*, London, 1936) he proposed a strictly deterministic view of the practice of art: 'the art of any people has always, in my opinion, an intimate causal connection with their economy'. This was a severely reductionist view, suggesting that art was nothing more than a reflection of social relations and class structure. A more sophisticated version of Marxist aesthetics was developed in Hungary by György Lukács (1885–1971), who devoted his life to the study of literature and aesthetics. Lukács developed Marx's views of commodity fetishism, whereby it was believed that capitalism reduced all forms of cultural production to economic servitude; on the other hand, he believed that it was possible for works of art to penetrate beyond the level of social appearances in order to expose what was described as the social totality. In the USSR the idea of developing an appropriate form of proletarian art led to the creation of a sterile aesthetic doctrine and a rigid adherence, enforced by Stalin and Zhdanov, to the stylistic principles of SOCIALIST REALISM. In Germany, by contrast, in the period between the two world wars, Marxist ideas were associated with the avant-garde. The Institute for Social Research, founded at the University of Frankfurt in 1923, became an important centre for the development of Marxist critical theory; among the significant writers associated with the Frankfurt School were Theodor Adorno, Max Horkheimer, Herbert Marcuse and WALTER BENJAMIN, who in his essay on 'The Work of Art in the Age of Mechanical Reproduction' (1936) developed a view of art as inseparable from its environment of technology and social class. Max Raphael, on the other hand, in his book *Proudhon, Marx, Picasso* returned to the analysis of the problem raised by Marx in the *Grundrisse* as to the relationship between mythology and art and the 'disproportionate development' of material production and art.

In Britain and the USA during the early and mid-20th century, the dominant ideology was that art is the product of the mind, and that the individual mind has a degree of intellectual freedom to express a statement of private consciousness. Art was assumed to derive from artistic belief and intention and not just be determined by the economic conditions of its production. As a result, Marxist ideas were only occasionally, and to a limited degree, applied to the study of art history; it was assumed that works of art originated in the changing vocabulary of style and aesthetic consciousness, not in their conditions of production. However, even in Britain and the USA there were significant practitioners of a Marxist view of art history. For example, in 1948 FREDERICK ANTAL published his *Florentine Painting and its Social Background*, which developed a detailed view of the relationship of Italian painters to their social and economic circumstances; and Francis Klingender, who read economics at the London School of Economics and whose PhD thesis was on 'The Black-coated Worker in London', undertook what he described as 'theoretical and historical studies designed to elucidate the role of art as one of the great value-forming agencies in the social structure and social change'. This resulted in the publication of his book on *Art and the Industrial Revolution*. In 1951 ARNOLD HAUSER published his *Social History of Art*, and in the 1950s Meyer Schapiro (*b* 1904) gained prominence for his socio-cultural studies of artists and styles.

The standard critical view of the social history of art during the 1950s is evident in the hostile review of Hauser's work by Ernst Gombrich (repr. in the latter's *Meditations on a Hobby Horse*), but since that time, although Marxism has declined as a political force, it has gained momentum within the understanding and practices of art history. In 1972 the British Marxist critic John Berger (*b* 1926), in his book *Ways of Seeing*, addressed issues ranging from artists' finances to the portrayal of women in both Old Masters and modern advertising. Another eminent British figure in the development of a Marxist art history was T. J. Clark, who set up a school of art history strongly influenced by Marxist ideas at the University of Leeds in the mid-1970s. In the USA, similar ideas and developments were associated with the Department of Art History at the University of California, Los Angeles (*see also* UNITED STATES OF AMERICA, §XVII).

As a result of these and other writings influenced by Marxist ideas during the 1970s, Marxism ceased to be a minor, and possibly eccentric, sideline within the practice of art history and became a dominant mode of interpretation both explicitly in the work of declared Marxists on both sides of the Atlantic (especially in California) and implicitly in the works utilizing semiotics, deconstruction, feminist and other perspectives, which are collectively labelled the New Art History (*see* ART HISTORY, §III). In particular, there was a developing interest in popular art and the 'culture industry' under the influence of the writers associated with the Frankfurt School, and, despite its demise as a political force in Eastern Europe, Marxism continued to flourish in the academies of the West.

BIBLIOGRAPHY
M. Lifshitz: *The Philosophy of Art of Karl Marx* (New York, 1938)
L. Baxandall: *Marxism and Aesthetics: A Selected Annotated Bibliography* (Sussex, 1968)
T. Adorno: *Aesthetische Theorie* (Frankfurt, 1972)
H. Arvon: *Marxist Aesthetics* (London, 1973)
N. Hadjinocolaou: *Histoire de l'art et lutte des classes* (Paris, 1973)
D. McLellan: *Karl Marx: His Life and Thought* (New York, 1973)
F. Klingender: *Marxism and Modern Art* (London, 1975)
D. Laing: *The Marxist Theory of Art* (Brighton, 1978)
H. Marcuse: *The Aesthetic Dimension: Towards a Critique of Marxist Aesthetics* (Boston, 1978)
P. Bourdieu: *La Distinction: Critique sociale du jugement* (Paris, 1979)
M. Raphael: *Proudhon, Marx, Picasso: Trois études sur la sociologie de l'art* (London, 1980)
L. Kolakowski: *Main Currents of Marxism*, 3 vols (Oxford, 1981)
J. Todd: 'Insight and Ideology in the Visual Arts', *Brit. J. Aesth.*, xxi/4 (1981), pp. 305–17
J. Wolff: *The Social Production of Art* (London, 1981)
P. H. Feist: 'Künstler und Gesellschaft: Ein theoretisches und methodisches Problem der Kunstwissenschaft', *Kunst und Reformation* (Leipzig, 1982)
G. Pollock: 'Women, Art and Ideology', *Women's A.J.*, iv/1 (1983), pp. 39–47
M. A. Rose: *Marx's Lost Aesthetic: Karl Marx and the Visual Arts* (Cambridge, 1984)
T. J. Clark: *The Painting of Modern Life* (New York and London, 1985)
H. Kramer: 'T. J. Clark and the Marxist Critique of Modern Painting', *New Criterion*, iii/7 (1985), pp. 1–8
A. Rifkin: 'Marx's Clarkism', *A. Hist.*, viii/4 (1985), pp. 488–95
A. Callinicos: *Against Postmodernism: A Marxist Critique* (Oxford, 1989)
T. Eagleton: *The Ideology of the Aesthetic* (Oxford, 1990)

WILLIAM H. SHAW, CHARLES SAUMAREZ SMITH

Marx von Esslingen. *See* BÖBLINGER, (4).

Mary, Duchess of Burgundy. *See* BURGUNDY, (6).

Mary, Queen of Hungary. *See* HABSBURG, §I(7).

Mary II, Princess of Orange and Queen of England and Scotland. *See* ORANGE NASSAU, (6).

Mary Anne of Austria, Queen of Spain. *See* HABSBURG, §II(8).

Mary Christina, Duchess and Regent of Savoy. *See* SAVOY, §II(7).

Mary Joanna, Duchess of Savoy. *See* SAVOY, §II, (9).

Marzabotto. Modern name of an Etruscan city, the ancient name of which is unknown. Situated *c.* 50 km south of Bologna, in the central valley of the River Reno on a terrace called Pian di Misano, at the exit of the Apennine mountain passes, it was part of the Etruscan colonization of the plain around the River Po in the second half of the 6th century BC and was connected via the River Reno with Felsina (Bologna) and Spina. Marzabotto is the only Etruscan city to have been extensively excavated and studied. Its layout is based on a formal grid plan (see fig.), divided along orthogonal axes according to ancient rules. These axes comprise a main north–south street and three east–west streets, all of which were 15 m wide. There were also subsidiary north–south streets only 5 m wide. The precise extent of the inhabited area cannot be calculated because of fluvial erosion and the absence of any walls. Two monumental structures to the east and north, however, appear to have been city gates. The blocks formed by the intersection of the streets were occupied by both private dwellings and manufacturing establishments, in particular pottery and metal workshops, but nothing is known of the area given over to public buildings. The single-storey dwellings faced on to the streets, and the rooms were arranged internally around a central courtyard, open to the sky and usually containing a well. The roofs must have been ridged, since rain-water was intended to run off into collection pipes. These houses were built on foundations of river pebbles, and the walls were of compressed clay on a wooden framework (*opus craticium*). (*See also* ETRUSCAN, §II, 2 and fig. 8f.) The temple area, set apart on raised ground to the north-east and dominating the city, consisted of a three-cella structure and cult altars arranged in parallel according to the astronomical orientation of the city. The necropoleis are outside the urban area, to the north and east. They include tombs both for inhumation and for cremation, though always for individuals rather than families. The earliest tombs lack identifying inscriptions, but later examples have incised river boulders, bulb-shaped stone markers and, finally, commemorative stone slabs.

Archaeological evidence from Marzabotto reveals a process of colonial transplantation, with settlers arriving from central Etruria. The letter forms in inscriptions, for example, are similar to those found at Chiusi. Its geographical position and its workshops suggest that Marzabotto was a trading and industrial, rather than agricultural, centre. It was destroyed during the Gallic invasion of Italy in the mid-4th century BC, possibly before the construction of the city had been completed. It remained deserted until Imperial times, when a farm was established in what had been the north-eastern area of the Etruscan city.

BIBLIOGRAPHY
G. A. Mansuelli: *Guida alla città etrusca e al Museo di Marzabotto* (Bologna, 1966, 2/1978)
——: 'Marzabotto: Dix années de fouilles et de recherches', *Mél. Archéol. & Hist.: Ecole Fr. Rome*, lxxxiv (1972), p. 111

MARCO RENDELI

Marziale, Marco (*fl* 1492–1507). Italian painter. He was first recorded in 1492 as one of several assistants to Giovanni Bellini in the Doge's Palace in Venice; in an inscription on his earliest known work, a damaged *Virgin and Child with Saints and a Donor* (1495; Zadar, St Mary, Treasury), he called himself a pupil of Gentile Bellini. Visual confirmation of his close association with both Bellini brothers is provided by the rather large number of his signed and dated works, many of which are closely based on compositional motifs by Giovanni, but which in their linearity and angularity more closely resemble the style of Gentile. The influence of German art, and of Dürer in particular, has often been noted in the sharply focused and densely packed details, the harsh modelling and the expressive ugliness found in much of Marziale's work.

In 1500 he seems to have moved to Cremona, perhaps at the behest of the poet and jurist Tommaso Raimondi, who is portrayed with his wife as a donor in Marziale's *Circumcision* altarpiece (1500; London, N.G.), painted for the local church of S Silvestro. The artist's last recorded work, a *Virgin and Child with Saints* (1507; London, N.G.), was also painted for a church in Cremona; it shows the influence of both Lombard painting and Perugino's *Virgin Enthroned with Saints*, painted in 1494 for S Agostino, Cremona. Marziale in turn seems to have stimulated a taste in Cremona for an anti-classical angularity and eccentricity that was later reflected in the work of Altobello Melone.

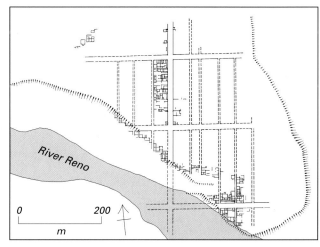

Marzabotto, plan of the acropolis hill and part of the town, showing a grid pattern of streets, second half of the 6th century BC

BIBLIOGRAPHY
Thieme–Becker
G. Ludwig: 'Archivalische Beiträge zur Geschichte der venezianischen Malerei', *Jb. Kön.-Preuss. Kstsamml.*, suppl. xxvi (1905), pp. 34–6 [doc.]
B. Geiger: 'Marco Marziale und der sogenannte nordische Einfluss in seinen Bildern', *Jb. Kön.-Preuss. Kstsamml.*, xxxiii (1912), pp. 1–22, 122–48
B. Berenson: *Venetian School* (1957), i, p. 112
H. W. van Os and others, eds: *The Early Venetian Paintings in Holland* (Maarssen, 1978)

PETER HUMFREY

Masaccio [Tommaso di Ser Giovanni di Mone Cassai] (*b* San Giovanni Val d'Arno, 21 Dec 1401; *d* Rome, before late June 1428). Italian painter. He is regarded as the founder of Italian Renaissance painting, a view established within a decade of his death. Vasari correctly perceived that Masaccio 'always followed as best he could in the footsteps of Brunelleschi and Donatello, even though he worked in a different medium'. Among the painters of his time, he was the first to organize his compositions according to the system of linear perspective developed by Brunelleschi. He thus transposed into painting the mathematically proportioned spaces and Classical architectural vocabulary of Brunelleschi's buildings, as well as the realistic anatomical structure, heavy draperies and human grandeur of Donatello's statues. He was also inspired by the paintings of Giotto and the art of antiquity. Masaccio's revival of Giotto's monumentality and concentration on volume was, like the writings by humanists on Florentine history, an affirmation of the greatness and enduring values of the Florentine past.

The features that distinguish Masaccio's work most sharply from that of Giotto are his rendering of objects and figures as fully three-dimensional solids with gravitational weight; the measurability of his pictorial space; his depiction of light and shadow as if light were entering this space from a single source; and his portrayal of figures as conscious individuals who confront issues of profound moral moment and exist and act in real time as well as real space.

I. Life and work. II. Working methods and technique. III. Critical reception and posthumous reputation.

I. Life and work.

1. Training and early years, to *c.* 1426. 2. *c.* 1427 and after. 3. Lost undated works. 4. Disputed attributions.

1. TRAINING AND EARLY YEARS, TO *c.* 1426. Masaccio's father was the notary Ser Giovanni di Mone (Simone) Cassai (*d* 1406), after whose death his mother, Jacopa di Martinozzo di Dino (*b* 1381), married Tedesco di Feo, an apothecary in Masaccio's native San Giovanni, which is situated between Florence and Arezzo in the upper Arno Valley. By the age of 16 Masaccio was referred to as a painter in Florence in a document of 14 October 1418. On 7 January 1422 he was inscribed in the Florentine painters' guild, the Arte de' Medici e Speziali, giving as his residence the parish of S Niccolò sopr'Arno. In 1424 his name appears in a register of the Compagnia di S Luca, the professional association of Florentine painters. He is documented in Florence twice in 1425: on 5 June he and another painter were paid for gilding processional candlesticks for the canons of Fiesole Cathedral, and on 18 July he was cited for a debt to a sausagemaker.

Writers from Vasari (1568) to van Marle (1928) believed that Masaccio's master was MASOLINO, with whom he later often collaborated. This is hardly possible, however, since Masolino was not registered in the painters' guild—and could therefore not have accepted apprentices—until 1423. Moreover, there are no links between the Late Gothic style of Masolino's early works, such as his *Madonna of Humility* (1423; Bremen, Ksthalle), and the works now regarded as autograph paintings by Masaccio. On the contrary, during the years in which the two artists are believed to have worked together (*c.* 1424–8), Masolino's style clearly shows the influence of the younger Masaccio.

(i) Lost early works. (ii) The S Giovenale Triptych. (iii) The S Ambrogio Altarpiece. (iv) The Carnesecchi Triptych. (v) The Pisa Altarpiece.

(i) Lost early works. According to 15th- and 16th-century sources, Masaccio painted a fresco of the *Consecration of St Maria del Carmine* (destr. 1598–1600)—Vasari referred to it as the *Sagra*—over the interior portal of the cloister abutting the church of St Maria del Carmine in Florence. The consecration of the church was celebrated on 9 April 1422, and it is probable that the artist executed or began the fresco in that year. Vasari described it as painted in greenish monochrome (*di verde terra*) and as showing the Piazza del Carmine with rows of five or six figures proportionally decreasing in perspective. Groups of these figures were copied in drawings by Michelangelo (Vienna, Albertina), by Michelangelo's assistant Antonio Mini (Florence, Casa Buonarroti) and by four anonymous 16th-century Florentine draughtsmen (priv. col., see Berti, 1962/rev. 1967, fig. 43; Florence, Uffizi and Ugo Procacci priv. col., see Berti, 1988, p. 211; and Folkestone, Mus. & A.G.). Behind the religious procession, according to Vasari, came numerous Florentine citizens, among them Brunelleschi, Donatello, Masolino, Niccolò da Uzzano, Giovanni di Bicci de' Medici, Bartolomeo Valori and Antonio Brancacci, whom Vasari wrongly believed to have commissioned the Brancacci Chapel frescoes (*see* §2(ii) below).

Vasari also reported that there were portraits by Masaccio of the same Florentines in the house of Simone Corsi; they may have been the prototypes for a group of five profile portraits of men wearing *mazzocchi* (turban-like hats) of the second quarter of the 15th century (Boston, MA, Isabella Stewart Gardner Mus.; Chambéry, Mus. Benoit-Molin; Norfolk, VA, Chrysler Mus.; two in Washington, DC, N.G.A.). Three of these (the panels in Boston and Chambéry, and one in Washington) have been stylistically associated with or attributed to Masaccio himself. Of these, the portrait in Boston, which was cleaned in 1980–81, is by far the most consistent with Masaccio's style in breadth of design, solidity of form and distribution of light and shade. Nevertheless, none can confidently be given to him. Another lost work by Masaccio, the *Virgin in a Tabernacle*, is mentioned in a Florentine document dated 23 August 1426; it is not known for whom or where it was painted.

(ii) The S Giovenale Triptych. It is widely believed that Masaccio's earliest extant work is a gold-backed triptych (Regello, nr Florence, S Giovenale di Cascia) with the *Virgin and Child and Two Angels* flanked on the left by *SS Bartholomew and Blaise* and on the right by *SS Giovenale and Anthony Abbot*. Cleaning of the triptych, discovered in the late 1950s, revealed the date 23 April 1422 on the strip below its three panels. The attribution to Masaccio has in its favour the stark three-dimensionality and realism of the Virgin and the nude Child; the broad handling of the pink garments of the angels; the bold perspective construction of the Virgin's throne; and the resemblances in physiognomic type and expression between the Virgin and Child in the triptych and those in the S Ambrogio Altarpiece (Florence, Uffizi; *see* §(iii) below) and the central panel of the Pisa Altarpiece (London, N.G.; see §(v) below). The attribution of the S Giovenale Triptych is nevertheless problematic. The pairs of saints are far less three-dimensional than the central *Virgin and Child*, suggesting that they may be by a different author or authors. But even the *Virgin and Child* presents difficulties. Whereas in the S Ambrogio Altarpiece and in the *Virgin and Child* from the Pisa Altarpiece light enters the pictorial space as if from a single source, the vanishing-point for the perspective construction is at the level of the Virgin's knees, and the spatial projection of the robes covering her legs is emphasized by the highlight on her left knee, in the S Giovenale *Virgin and Child* light strikes the figures from the left, front and right, the vanishing-point is at the Virgin's chin, and the block of the Virgin's legs placed against the steeply rising throne platform lacks convincing volumetric definition. It has been argued that at the age of 19 Masaccio had not yet attained the mastery of three-dimensional form that he displayed about two years later in the S Ambrogio Altarpiece, but this does not entirely resolve the problem.

(iii) The S Ambrogio Altarpiece. The altarpiece of the *Virgin and Child with St Anne* (Florence, Uffizi) was attributed to Masaccio by Vasari (1568) when it was in the Florentine church of S Ambrogio. An early attempt to clean the painting, probably in the 18th century, caused serious

losses that were subsequently repainted. Cleaning and restoration between 1935 and 1954 revealed areas that had survived in nearly their original condition, most notably the Child and the heads of the Virgin and St Anne. These show that the painting was probably executed by at least two hands. It is now widely believed that the throne and its platform, the Virgin and Child and perhaps the angel at the upper right are by Masaccio and that St Anne, the cloth of honour behind her and the other four angels were painted by Masolino. It could also be argued that all five angels, which exhibit stylistic inconsistencies between each other as well as in relation to the main figures, were executed by assistants.

In the picture's present state the Virgin and Child are far more robust and sculpturally rounded than the figure of St Anne (the pose of the Child closely resembles that of an Etruscan bronze votive statue, 3rd century BC; Rome, Vatican, Mus. Gregoriano Etrus.). They seem to be the first known reflections of Masaccio's mature style. Even though this is consistent with the presumed division of labour, the view that Masaccio was the picture's sole author has not been abandoned. The issue is complicated by disagreement concerning the precise role of each artist in the other projects—the Carnesecchi Triptych (see §(iv) below), the Brancacci Chapel frescoes and the S Maria Maggiore Altarpiece (see §2(iii) below)—in which they are believed to have collaborated. Although it is not known from whom the S Ambrogio Altarpiece was commissioned, it is generally agreed that it was painted between 1423 and 1425, either before 2 November 1424, when Masolino received a payment for frescoes in the chapel of the Compagnia della Croce in S Stefano at Empoli, or between that date and 1 September 1425, when he went to Hungary. Because the *Pietà* (Empoli, Mus. Collegiata) painted by Masolino in Empoli seems to show the strong influence of Masaccio, the earlier date is the more likely (for the opposite view see MASOLINO, §1–2).

(iv) The Carnesecchi Triptych. Vasari (1568) also attributed to Masaccio a triptych in the Carnesecchi Chapel of S Maria Maggiore, Florence, with the *Virgin and Child, St Catherine* and *St Julian* above a predella with the *Nativity*, a scene from the *Life of St Catherine* and a panel in which 'St Julian kills his mother and father'. (In 1550 he had stated that Masaccio was responsible only for the predella.) However, the *Virgin and Child* (ex-S Maria di Novoli, nr Florence, stolen c. 1924) and the *St Julian* (Florence, Pal. Arcivescovile) are now thought to be by Masolino.

The scene from the *Life of St Julian* described by Vasari may well be identical with a severely damaged predella panel of the *Legend of St Julian* (Florence, Mus. Horne). Although the attribution to Masaccio is contested, it is supported by the restriction of the palette to reds, earth colours, grey and black; by the illumination of the figures from a single light source and by the three-dimensional conception and sculptural roundness of the figures. A predella panel of the *Attempted Martyrdom of St Catherine* in an altarpiece of 1437 by Andrea di Giusto (Florence, Accad.) may be a copy based on Masaccio's scene from the *Life of St Catherine*. Masolino's participation in the Carnesecchi Triptych probably ended with his departure for Hungary. If Masaccio painted the predella afterwards,

it is likely that he did so before 19 February 1426, when he signed the contract for the Pisa Altarpiece.

(v) The Pisa Altarpiece. The work was commissioned by the Pisan notary Giuliano di Colino degli Scarsi da San Giusto for a chapel in S Maria del Carmine, Pisa. Construction of the chapel by the mason Pippo di Gante began on 29 November 1425. The wooden, gilded framework of the altarpiece was begun on 25 November 1425 by the Sienese wood-carver Antonio di Biagio, whose last payment was recorded on the same day, 19 February 1426, as the first payment to Masaccio. This sequence of payments indicates that the form of the altarpiece, including the number, placement, size and shape of its compartments, was determined not by Masaccio but by Antonio di Biagio. Masaccio received his final payment on 26 December 1426, but he was recorded in Pisa again on 23 January 1427, when he was a witness to a notarial act.

The altarpiece was dispersed after S Maria del Carmine was remodelled in the late 16th century. Vasari (1568) described the polyptych as containing a *Virgin and Child*, with angels playing music at the Virgin's feet, between figures of SS Peter, John the Baptist, Julian and Nicholas;

1. Masaccio: *Virgin and Child Enthroned*, central panel from the Pisa Altarpiece, tempera on panel, 1355×730 mm, 1426 (London, National Gallery)

2. Masaccio: *Adoration of the Magi*, predella panel from the Pisa Altarpiece, tempera on panel, 210×610 mm, 1426 (Berlin, Gemäldegalerie)

a predella with scenes from the lives of these saints and an *Adoration of the Magi* in the middle; and above the main storey 'many saints in additional panels' surrounding a *Crucifixion*. The surviving panels of the altarpiece are the *Virgin and Child Enthroned* (London, N.G.; see fig. 1); the predella panels of the *Adoration of the Magi* (see fig. 2), the *Crucifixion of St Peter*, the *Beheading of St John the Baptist*, the *Legend of St Julian* and *St Nicholas and the Poor Man's Daughters* (all Berlin, Gemäldegal.); four small figures (*St Augustine*, *St Jerome* and two Carmelite saints) from the pilasters at either side of the main storey (all

3. Masaccio: *Crucifixion*, panel from the Pisa Altarpiece, tempera on panel, 770×640 mm, 1426 (Naples, Museo e Gallerie Nazionali di Capodimonte)

Berlin, Gemäldegal.); the *Crucifixion* (Naples, Capodimonte; see fig. 3); and half-length figures of *St Paul* (Pisa, Mus. N. S Matteo; see fig. 4) and *St Andrew* (Malibu, CA, Getty Mus.) from among the panels on either side of the *Crucifixion*. The predella panels of the *Legend of St Julian* and *St Nicholas and the Poor Man's Daughters* are thought to be by Andrea di Giusto, who on 24 December 1426 was paid for work on the Pisa Altarpiece as Masaccio's apprentice (*garzone*).

In the centre of the *Adoration of the Magi* Masaccio included the standing profile portraits of the donor and his son. The son, swathed in a cloak, with one hand on his hip and the other folded across his chest, assumes the pose of a Classical statue of *Sophocles* (Roman marble copy of a 4th-century BC Greek original, Rome, Vatican, Mus. Gregoriano Profano). Although there is no evidence that Masaccio could have seen this statue or others of the same type, its arm postures could have been transmitted to him through Hellenistic terracotta figurines such as a *Winged Genius* (Munich, Staatl. Antikensamml., 6800).

Shearman (1966) proposed that the enthroned Virgin and Child surrounded by angels and the four standing saints in the main storey, instead of being separated by colonettes as was the custom in polyptychs of this date, were placed on three platforms receding into a continuous space, which was unified by a perspective construction consistent with that of the Virgin's throne, the vanishing-point being just below Christ's left foot. However, documentary, technical and stylistic evidence (see Gardner von Teuffel, 1977) conclusively shows that the main storey had the traditional form of compartments divided by colonettes. The question remains whether these colonettes were placed only between the Virgin and Child and the saints, as in polyptychs by Starnina or Piero della Francesca, or whether, as in altarpieces by Giovanni del Biondo or Giovanni di Paolo, they also formed separate compartments for each saint.

2. *c.* 1427 AND AFTER. On 29 July 1427, six months after he was last recorded in Pisa, Masaccio filed a tax declaration with the Florentine *catasto* office in which he stated that he, his mother and his younger brother, the painter Giovanni di Ser Giovanni, called SCHEGGIA, were

diminish and are foreshortened so well that the wall seems to be hollowed out'. The vanishing-point of the foreshortened barrel vault is at the top of the raised step behind the kneeling donors, roughly at the spectator's eye-level, and the Virgin and St John (though not God the Father and Christ) are also rendered as if seen from below. Because the Classical forms and ornaments framing the space of the chapel or mausoleum (left ambiguous by Masaccio) recall the bays at either side of the Florentine Ospedale degli Innocenti (begun 1420) by Brunelleschi, who is credited with the invention of Renaissance linear perspective, it has been thought that Brunelleschi may have designed or collaborated with Masaccio on a cartoon for the painted architecture. There is, however, no documentary evidence that the two artists ever collaborated.

The *Trinity* is thought to have been commissioned by a member of the Lenzi family. The tombstone of Domenico Lenzi and his family, dated 1426, was formerly in front of the fresco; Domenico's son Benedetto was Prior of S Maria Novella from June 1426 until September 1428; and the kneeling donor at the left wears the red robes of the Florentine *gonfaloniere di giustizia*, an office held in August and September 1425 by Domenico's cousin Lorenzo di Piero Lenzi (*d* 1442), who was buried in the church of Ognissanti, Florence.

At an unknown date after the completion of the fresco, an altar was placed in front of the image of 'death'—a skeleton on a catafalque surmounted by the inscription: IO FU G[I]A QUEL CHE VOI S[I]ETE EQUEL CHISON[O] VOI

4. Masaccio: *St Paul*, panel from the Pisa Altarpiece, tempera on panel, 610×340 mm, 1426 (Pisa, Museo Nazionale di S Matteo)

living in a house in Florence on the Via dei Servi; that he was renting 'part of a workshop' on the Piazza S Apollinare; that his cash assets were 'approximately six soldi'; and that he owed various creditors about forty-five fiorini, including a debt of six fiorini to his apprentice Andrea di Giusto 'for the balance of his salary'. A few weeks before Masaccio filed this tax declaration, Masolino had returned from Hungary. Documents (see Procacci, 1980) suggest that in August 1427 the two artists probably began the paintings on the walls of the Brancacci Chapel in S Maria del Carmine, Florence. But before that, more likely in the early part of 1427 than during the two preceding years, as the majority of writers have maintained, Masaccio painted the fresco of the *Trinity* (see fig. 5) in the third bay of the left aisle of S Maria Novella, Florence.

(i) The *Trinity*. (ii) The Brancacci Chapel frescoes. (iii) The S Maria Maggiore Altarpiece.

(i) The 'Trinity'. The work was first recorded in *Memoriale di molte statue e picture di Florentia* (1510) by Francesco Albertini, who called it 'a Crucifixion, that is a Trinity with death at the foot'. Vasari (1568) described it as a Trinity with the Virgin and St John the Evangelist 'contemplating the crucified Christ' and 'a barrel vault represented in perspective, and divided into squares full of bosses, which

5. Masaccio: *Trinity* (*c.* 1425–7), fresco, S Maria Novella, Florence

A[N]CO[RA] SARETE ('I was once that which you are and that which I am you will also be').

In 1570, when redesigning the church's interior, Vasari covered the upper part of the fresco with one of his altarpieces; it was rediscovered during renovations *c.* 1860 and transferred to the entrance wall. The altar in front of the lower part was removed in 1951, and in 1952 the two parts of the fresco were reunited, cleaned and restored.

Masaccio's fresco is unique in Italian painting in its representation of the Trinity within an illusionistic, Classically inspired interior framed by the motif of a triumphal arch instead of against a gilded or landscape background. It may thus have been the prototype for the design by Brunelleschi's adopted son Buggiano for the Cardini Chapel in S Francesco at Pescia (1446), where a triumphal arch similar to Masaccio's frames a barrel-vaulted interior containing a wooden crucifix.

(ii) The Brancacci Chapel frescoes. Neither the commission nor the execution of the frescoes is documented. The Brancacci Chapel in S Maria del Carmine was founded by Pietro Brancacci (*d* 1366–7), and a bequest was left to it in his son Antonio's will dated 16 August 1383. Since between 1422 and 1434 it was owned by Pietro's nephew FELICE BRANCACCI, it has been thought that he commissioned the fresco decorations. Felice's first will (26 June 1422) transferred ownership of the chapel to his sons on his death, designated the chapel as his burial site and extended burial rights to other family members on condition of paying a tribute of 25 fiorini. His second will (5 September 1432) stipulated that if the decoration of the chapel were still unfinished at the time of his death, his heirs should be responsible for its completion. But in 1434 Felice went into exile in Siena, and the frescoes remained incomplete until the intervention 50 years later of Filippino Lippi (*see* LIPPI, (2)).

According to Vasari, the earliest frescoes in the chapel were Masolino's *Four Evangelists* in the vault and the *Calling of SS Peter and Andrew*, the *Denial and Remorse of St Peter* and *Christ Walking on the Water* in the lunettes (all destr. 1746–8). He also attributed to Masolino *St Peter Preaching* on the altar wall and *St Peter Curing a Cripple and the Raising of Tabitha* (*see* MASOLINO, fig. 2) in the upper tier of the wall to the right of the altar. Masaccio, according to Vasari, then painted *St Peter Baptizing Neophytes* and *St Peter Healing with his Shadow* (*see* FLORENCE, fig. 6) on the altar wall, the *Tribute Money* (see fig. 6) in the upper tier of the wall to the left of the altar, and below it the *Raising of the Son of the Prefect of Antioch and St Peter Enthroned as Bishop of Antioch* (for illustration *see* CARMELITE ORDER), which was left unfinished and completed by Lippi between *c.* 1481 and 1485.

In addition to the scenes described by Vasari, the decoration of the chapel includes the *Distribution of the Goods of the Church and the Death of Ananias* on the altar wall and the *Expulsion from Paradise* in the upper tier of the left entrance pier, both by Masaccio, and opposite it the *Temptation of Adam and Eve* by Masolino. The figure of Eve in the *Expulsion* assumes the arm and hand gestures of the *Venus de' Medici* (Florence, Uffizi), a Roman copy of a Praxitilean original, first recorded in the Villa Medici in Rome in 1638. Masaccio may have known the statue of a similar type that the humanist Benvenuto da Imola saw in a Florentine house in the second half of the 14th century, or he may have derived the gestures from the earlier antique adaptation in the standing, nude figure of *Prudence* at the base of Giovanni Pisano's pulpit (1302–10) in Pisa Cathedral.

The chronology of the Brancacci Chapel is problematic. Those writers who follow Vasari believe that Masolino painted all his sections of the chapel in a single campaign between November 1424 and September 1425, working alone on the vault and lunettes and in tandem with Masaccio on the walls (for this view *see* MASOLINO, §2). However, the documentary evidence for the two artists' movements and activities can also be interpreted to suggest that there were two campaigns: one during which Masolino

6. Masaccio: *Tribute Money* (*c.* 1427), fresco, Brancacci Chapel, S Maria del Carmine, Florence

decorated the vault and the lunettes (before Sept 1425), and another in which he and Masaccio jointly executed their frescoes on the walls when he had returned from Hungary (some time after 7 July 1427); the wall frescoes would then have been left unfinished when Masolino and Masaccio went to Rome. (Masolino is thought to have gone in spring 1428, Masaccio after 11 May of that year.) It has been objected that the period from perhaps August 1427 to May 1428 would not have been enough time for the two artists to execute nine frescoes. But even allowing for the suspension of work during winter, when it was too cold to paint on wet plaster, there would have been ample time. The total number of *giornate* (work sessions corresponding to sections of plaster discernible by their rims) is 131, and given the area of Masaccio's contribution (roughly twice that of Masolino's), the frescoes could have been painted in less than a hundred sessions.

The frescoes were restored first *c.* 1565, again in 1782 after they were severely damaged by a fire in the church in 1771 and a third time by Filippo Fiscali in 1902–4. A fourth conservation campaign (1982–8) brought to light two heads in circular frames between bands of acanthus ornament on the embrasures of the window over the altar, and a small fragment of a landscape and the back of a male figure on the wall above the altar. The left embrasure with the head of a woman has been given to Masolino, and the fragment above the altar and the right embrasure with the head of a man to Masaccio; but there is no consensus over these attributions. Two fragmentary *sinopie* were discovered on the left and right sides of the lunette over the altar wall, although their subjects do not correspond to the *Denial of St Peter* painted there, according to Vasari, by Masolino. All earlier restorations as well as a viscous coat that darkened the colours of the wall paintings were removed (1986–8), revealing previously obscured passages and the original clear, bright colours.

The subjects of the wall paintings appear to have been taken mainly from the Acts of the Apostles and the chapters on the three feasts of St Peter in the *Golden Legend* by Jacopo da Voragine. The account in the *Golden Legend* of the feast of the Chairing of Peter, for example, was probably the source for the frescoes on the lower tier of the left wall, from *St Peter Imprisoned* to his *Enthronement as Bishop of Antioch*. Debold von Kritter (1975) suggested that the combination of the *Temptation* and the *Expulsion* on the entrance piers with the cycle of scenes from the *Life of St Peter* in the interior of the chapel corresponds to comparisons of Peter with Adam and Eve in theological texts by Nicholas of Lyra and Maximus of Turin, according to which the original sinners Adam and Eve have their counterpart in St Peter, the redeemed sinner who through his own example and the institutions of the Church becomes the gatekeeper of paradise and leads mankind to redemption. Interpretations of the wall paintings as reflections of contemporary events are all based on contradictory and inconclusive evidence.

The placement of the Apostles in the *Tribute Money* in a semicircular arc with Christ in the middle, which imparts to the figures of the central group unprecedented spatial unity and psychological concentration, has been convincingly related (Meiss, 1963) to Brunelleschi's use of the circular plan in the domes of the Old Sacristy of S Lorenzo (begun 1421) and the Pazzi Chapel (begun 1443), both Florence, to symbolize in mathematical form the Christian conception of God's grace as radiating from the centre of the perfect form of the circle.

Longhi (1940) recognized that the head of Christ, which covers the fresco's vanishing-point and was the last area to be plastered and painted, is in the style of Masolino, a view supported by the most recent cleaning of the fresco; he also suggested that the perspective and lighting of the architectural background in the *Raising of Tabitha*, which was painted in a single session, are characteristic of Masaccio, but this proposal has been questioned since the cleaning. Watkins (1973) presented technical evidence that the two artists could have worked on the frescoes of the second tier at the same time.

(iii) The S Maria Maggiore Altarpiece. The work, now dispersed, was a double-sided triptych, with the *Foundation of S Maria Maggiore* (Naples, Capodimonte), flanked by *SS Jerome and John the Baptist* (London, N.G.) and *An Evangelist and St Martin of Tours* (Philadelphia, PA, Mus. A.); and on the other side the *Assumption of the Virgin* (Naples, Capodimonte) flanked by *A Pope and St Matthias* (London, N.G.) and *SS Peter and Paul* (Philadelphia, PA, Mus. A.). Vasari saw the altarpiece in a small chapel near the sacristy of the Roman church of S Maria Maggiore and attributed the central panel of the *Virgin of the Snow* (destr.) to Masaccio. The altarpiece was apparently commissioned by Pope Martin V (*reg* 1417–31), probably for the main altar of the church rather than for the small chapel where it was seen by Vasari. The features of St Martin of Tours are believed to be those of the Pope, and a column, the emblem of the Colonna family to which the Pope belonged (*see* COLONNA, (1)), appears six times in the border of St Martin's vestment and in the form of the staff held by St John the Baptist.

Since its rediscovery in 1951, the panel with *SS Jerome and John the Baptist* has been regarded, with some dissent (see Davies, 1961), as the only one of the triptych's six known compartments that was painted, though not completely finished, by Masaccio. The other five are attributed to Masolino. However, technical examination of the two panels in Philadelphia has revealed that they were probably designed by Masaccio, who seems to have painted the hands and feet of SS Peter and Paul. Masolino apparently painted at least the faces of the Evangelist and of St Martin of Tours, after which the programme of the altarpiece and the design of the two panels were altered. The *SS Jerome and John the Baptist*—with its unbroken, regular contours, meticulous rendering of detail and luminous, evenly textured surfaces—is the most refined of Masaccio's paintings. It has been thought an early work, on the grounds that it lacks the formal breadth and robustness of Masaccio's other paintings; this assumption is difficult to sustain, however, considering both the limited knowledge of Masaccio's stylistic evolution and the clear colours and precise execution revealed by the cleaning of the Brancacci Chapel frescoes. Moreover, documentary evidence (Procacci, 1953 and 1980) strongly suggests that the S Maria Maggiore Altarpiece was begun only after Masaccio and Masolino arrived in Rome, probably in spring 1428. The decorative elegance of Masaccio's panel, rather than indicating an early date, was more likely a response to the aesthetic preferences of the papal court and of Martin V, who in 1427 had commissioned Gentile da Fabriano, the most refined painter of his generation, to fresco the nave (destr.) of S Giovanni in Laterano. Masaccio's work on the altarpiece was cut short by his death, news of which reached Florence before the end of June 1428, and it was finished by Masolino.

3. LOST UNDATED WORKS. Two paintings are listed in the inventory of the Medici collection compiled in 1492 after the death of Lorenzo the Magnificent: a *desco da parto* with a 'skirmish' (*una schermaglia*) and a panel with *SS Peter and Paul*. Albertini (1510) listed a fresco by Masaccio of the *Last Judgement* in the second cloister of S Maria degli Angeli, Florence, which may be reflected in the nude figures of a *Last Judgement* by Giovanni di Paolo (Siena, Pin. N.). Vasari, following earlier sources, attributed to Masaccio a fresco of *St Paul* (destr. 1675–83) on a pier next to the Serragli Chapel in S Maria del Carmine, and he praised the figure's forceful expression and foreshortening from below and identified it as a portrait of Bartolo di Angiolino Angiolini.

Other lost works of Masaccio recorded by Vasari are a fresco in the Badia, Florence, of *St Ivo of Brittany* (destr. 1627) 'in a niche with his feet foreshortened, seen from below', beneath whom there were 'widows, children and poor assisted by him in their want'; a panel with a male and female nude in the Palazzo Rucellai; and a painting of *Christ Exorcizing a Possessed Man* in the house of Ridolfo Ghirlandaio with 'buildings so drawn in perspective that the interior and exterior are represented at the same time'. Vasari's description of the latter fits the architectural setting of Francesco d'Antonio's *Christ and the Apostles in a Temple* (Philadelphia, PA, Mus. A.), which may be a copy or reflection of Masaccio's lost picture. Vasari also noted an *Annunciation* 'painted in tempera' on the rood screen of S Niccolò sopr'Arno, Florence, with 'a building filled with columns drawn in perspective', which he believed to be by Masaccio. The painting is thought to have been the prototype for compositions of the *Annunciation* with symmetrically arranged perspective colonnades by Fra Angelico (Florence, Mus. S Marco), Domenico Veneziano (Cambridge, Fitzwilliam) and Piero della Francesca (Perugia, G.N. Umbria). (It has been identified by some as a late work by Masolino, Washington, DC, N.G.A., although this is not generally accepted.)

4. DISPUTED ATTRIBUTIONS. Among the works formerly attributed to Masaccio since Crowe and Cavalcaselle (1864) is a panel with the *Agony in the Garden* and the *Communion of St Jerome* (Altenburg, Staatl. Lindenau-Mus.), which seems to be by an artist who attempted to imitate but did not fully understand Masaccio's style. A *desco da parto* (Berlin, Gemäldegal.) showing the interior of a convent (not, as is generally claimed, a palace, for the columns of the courtyard rest on a low wall or stylobate, as is usual in convents but not in palaces) is a not wholly successful imitation of Masaccio's style, probably of the late 1430s; it has a birth scene on one side and a courtyard in perspective with figures of a herald, men bearing gifts,

nuns and fashionable ladies on the other. On the back a naked boy who resembles the Child in the S Giovenale Triptych kneels on a meadow of flowers and instructs a sharp-toothed dog. The same anonymous artist may have been responsible for a small panel of the *Virgin and Child* (Florence, Pal. Vecchio), although in the picture's present restored state an attribution seems hazardous. On its back is the coat of arms of Antonio Casini (*d* Florence, 1439), a native of Siena who was made a cardinal on 24 May 1426. The panel was probably painted towards the end of the Cardinal's life. An impressive damaged and restored fresco of *Christ on the Cross* (Florence, S Maria del Carmine) that came to light after the Florentine flood of 1966 would seem to be the work of another Florentine follower of Masaccio active in the 1430s. A crudely painted roundel of *God the Father* (London, N.G.) is by a follower or imitator of Masaccio of uncertain date, while a fresco of the *Virgin and Child with SS Michael and John the Baptist* (Montemarciano, Oratory) has been recognized since the 1950s as a work of *c.* 1425–30 by Francesco d'Antonio. The fresco decoration of the chapel of St Catherine in S Clemente, Rome, given to Masaccio by Vasari, has been attributed to Masolino since the late 19th century, and, although Longhi (1940) proposed that Masaccio may have been responsible for the riders in the middle zone of the *Crucifixion*, there is no compelling stylistic or technical evidence of this, either in the fresco itself or in the *sinopia* discovered when the work was detached in the 1950s. A *Madonna of Humility* (Washington, DC, N.G.A.) is difficult to attribute because of its current repainted state, although photographs taken in 1929–30 before it was restored suggest that it may well have been painted by Masaccio.

II. Working methods and technique.

In fresco as well as in tempera Masaccio followed the methods described in Cennino Cennini's *Libro dell'arte*, although for the underpainting of flesh he employed a greyish tone rather than the greenish *verdaccio* recommended by Cennini. In contrast to the rich colouring of Late Gothic painting, Masaccio's palette is restricted and repetitive. In his figures it is dominated by tonalities of blue and red, generally within close range of a middle value, with a preference for vermilion, and in his architectural and landscape backgrounds by warmer or cooler greys. The chromatic range of the *Virgin and Child* from the Pisa Altarpiece and the *Trinity* at S Maria Novella is composed entirely of gradations of these three colours. In the three predella panels from the Pisa Altarpiece this scheme of colours is augmented sparingly by a golden orange-yellow and an occasional black, and in the Brancacci Chapel frescoes by orange-yellows and muted greens.

The *Trinity* and the frescoes by Masaccio in the Brancacci Chapel were very largely executed in *buon fresco* on sections of wet plaster, with additions in *fresco a secco* (after the plaster had dried) for the gilded haloes and, in the Brancacci Chapel, for the foliage of the trees. Whether Masaccio used *sinopie* is not known. The *intonaco* of the wall frescoes in the Brancacci Chapel has never been detached, and the *arriccio* beneath the *Trinity* was destroyed when it was detached *c.* 1860. Vestiges on the surface of the *Tribute Money* of vertical plumb lines snapped into the plaster by cords in order to establish the axis of the standing figures—the earliest known example of what later became common studio practice—and of incised lines to mark the straight edges of the architecture have been taken as indications that Masaccio there worked directly on the wall without a cartoon.

Attempts to reconstruct Masaccio's method of painting the foreshortened architecture in the *Trinity* have reached two different conclusions. One is that he first drew a modular ground-plan of the coffered vault, as if he were designing a Brunelleschian building, and then projected this ground-plan in perspective on a squared cartoon from which, when enlarged to full scale, the foreshortened design was transferred to the painting. The other, more likely solution is that by means of a ruler and compass and relatively simple operations of Euclidean geometry he drew the foreshortened forms of the architecture directly on a cartoon, enlarging sections of it for transfer to the wall for each work session and controlling the design of the whole by means of a plumb line and other snapped cords, traces of which remain on the surface of the *intonaco*. Evidence of Masaccio's use of cartoons in the *Trinity* is restricted to *spolveri* (dusted pounce marks) in the entablature of the architecture. An incised grid of squares and rectangles across the face of the Virgin and incised guidelines for foreshortened architectural ornaments, the rear arch and the curved bands of the vault suggest that Masaccio executed at least parts of the fresco directly on the wall, as he also may have done in the Brancacci Chapel.

III. Critical reception and posthumous reputation.

In the dedicatory letter to Brunelleschi at the beginning of *Della pittura* (1436), Leon Battista Alberti declared that when he returned to Florence from exile (*c.* 1429) he perceived in Brunelleschi, Donatello, Lorenzo Ghiberti, Luca della Robbia and Masaccio 'a genius for every laudable enterprise in no way inferior to any of the ancients who gained fame in these arts'. It is widely thought that Alberti had Masaccio's compositions in mind when in the first two books of *Della pittura* he recommended to painters how pictures should be designed and executed in order to command the same admiration as Greek and Roman authors bestowed on paintings of antiquity.

The first Renaissance writer to attempt to characterize Masaccios's style was the Florentine humanist Cristoforo Landino. In his commentary (1481) on Dante's *Divine Comedy*, Landino praised Masaccio for his imitation of the true appearance of objects in nature (*imitazione del vero*), the roundness (*rilievo*) he gave to his figures, the harmony and coherence of his compositions, his dedication to the clarity of three-dimensional form at the cost of ornamental grace (*puro senz'ornato*), his mastery of perspective and his assurance in dealing with technical problems (*facilità*). In its concise definition of the essential components of Masaccio's style, Landino's text has not been surpassed.

Masaccio's work had an immediate and profound impact on his contemporaries. Not only his collaborator Masolino and his apprentice Andrea di Giusto, but also Gentile da Fabriano and minor Florentine masters, such

as Bicci di Lorenzo, Francesco d'Antonio, Giovanni del Ponte, Giovanni Toscani and Paolo Schiavo, accommodated the decorative Giottesque or Late Gothic traditions in which they were trained to the sober, sculptural realism of Masaccio. The principal artists to assimilate Masaccio's innovations were Fra Angelico, Fra Filippo Lippi and Andrea Castagno—who are reported by Vasari to have studied the frescoes in the Brancacci Chapel—as well as Paolo Uccello, Domenico Veneziano, Piero della Francesca and Andrea Mantegna. But it was Leonardo da Vinci who first fully understood and incorporated into his own style Masaccio's depiction of objects under conditions of light and shade as they are observed in nature. In one of his notebooks, Leonardo wrote that Masaccio 'showed by his perfect works how those who take for their standard anyone but nature, mistress of masters, were labouring in vain'.

In his *Vite* Vasari divided the history of Italian painting into three periods and designated Giotto, Masaccio and Leonardo their founders. By then nature was no longer considered painting's sole mistress. The works of Classical antiquity and of Raphael and Michelangelo were thought to rival and surpass nature as the most worthy models, for they were perceived as rectifying nature's imperfections. In Vasari's judgement, the only earlier Italian painter who could still be imitated with profit was Masaccio, because it was he who 'paved the way for the good style of our own day', having understood, among other things, 'that all figures which do not stand with their feet flat and foreshortened, but are on the tips of toes, are destitute of all excellence in style (*maniera*) in essentials, and show an utter ignorance of foreshortening'. Vasari reported that the Brancacci Chapel became the school of Florentine painters, and he named 25, including Leonardo, Michelangelo and Raphael, who studied and copied its wall paintings. The only such copies to have survived are drawings by Michelangelo of *St Peter Paying the Tax Collector* (Munich, Staatl. Graph. Samml.) from the *Tribute Money* and of *Adam and Eve* (Paris, Louvre) from the *Expulsion*, although the attribution is not unanimously accepted.

Vasari placed Raphael at the summit of the 'good style' towards which Masaccio had paved the way. This view, that Masaccio laid the groundwork for what Raphael perfected and that he might have achieved what Raphael did had he been born later or lived longer, prevailed until the end of the 19th century. Joshua Reynolds wrote in his 12th Discourse (1784) that Raphael

> had carefully studied the work of Masaccio; ... [whose] manner was dry and hard, his compositions formal, and not enough diversified according to the custom of painters in that early period, yet his works possess that grandeur and simplicity which accompany, and even sometimes proceed from, regularity and hardness of manner.

In 1830 Eugène Delacroix wrote in the *Revue de Paris* that, although Masaccio 'wrought by himself the greatest revolution painting ever experienced', posterity has hidden him 'behind the rays with which it had surrounded Raphael'. Yet 'who can say', Delacroix continued, 'what new perfections he might have discovered in later years;

and who can affirm that he might not have put even Raphael in the shade'.

Bernard Berenson (1896) finally removed Masaccio from the shadow of Raphael, perceiving in him an artist unrivalled among Italian painters in power of three-dimensional form and in gravity, dignity and resoluteness of expression. Masaccio, according to Berenson, 'gave Florentine painting the direction it pursued to the end' and surpassed all other painters of his age. Although later painters were capable of 'greater science, greater craft, and greater perfection of detail', there was never a 'greater reality' or 'greater significance' than in the works of Masaccio.

Brockhaus (1929–32) was the first scholar who sought to place these works in the context of 15th-century political and social currents. During Masaccio's lifetime Florence was engaged in a series of wars with Milan and other Italian states; the city-state succeeded against great odds in maintaining its independence and republican form of government. Humanist writers, comparing Florence to the Roman republic of antiquity, celebrated the city for its defence of civic freedom and human dignity. Hartt (1964) suggested that the figures in Masaccio's paintings were classically inspired embodiments of these ideals. Masaccio's sober, realistic, unornamented style—in contrast to the ornate, courtly style of Gentile da Fabriano—was interpreted by Antal (1947) as an affirmation of the ascendancy in early 15th-century Florence of a newly influential upper middle-class bourgeoisie. Because these interpretations deal with style, they have the merit of addressing decisions and choices controlled by the artist. The situation is different in the case of attempts to discover in Masaccio's works iconographic allusions to contemporary social or political issues and events, since the determination of subjects and iconographic programmes was in the hands not of the artist but of the patron.

BIBLIOGRAPHY

EARLY SOURCES AND DOCUMENTS

L. B. Alberti: *De pictura* (MS. 1435); It. trans. as *Della pittura* (MS. 1436); ed. L. Mallè (Florence, 1950), p. 54; Eng. trans. by J. Spencer as *On Painting* (London, 1956), p. 39
C. Landino: *Commento di Cristoforo Landino fiorentino sopra la Commedia di Dante* (Florence, 1481); ed. R. Cardini: *Scritti critici e teorici*, i (Rome, 1974), p. 124
G. Santi: *La vita e le geste di Federico da Montefeltro duca d'Urbino* (MS. c. 1492); ed. L. Michelini Tocci (Rome, 1985), ii, p. 674
F. Albertini: *Memoriale di molte statue e picture di Florentia* (Florence, 1510)
G. Santi: *Il Codice Magliabechiano* (MS. c. 1540); ed. C. Frey (Berlin, 1892), pp. 81–2, 315–19; ed. C. Fabriszy as *Il Codice dell'anonimo Gaddiano* (Florence, 1893)
A. Billi: *Il libro di Antonio Billi* (MS. c. 1550); ed. C. Frey (Berlin, 1892), pp. 16–17
G. Vasari: *Vite* (1550, rev. 2/1568); ed. G. Milanesi (1878–85), ii, pp. 305–25
J. Reynolds: *Discourses on Art* (London, 1778); ed. R. R. Wark (San Marino, CA, 1959/*R* New Haven and London, 1975), pp. 216–21
E. Delacroix: *Oeuvres littéraires*; ed. E. Faure (Paris, 1923), ii, pp. 12–13
U. Procacci: 'Documenti e ricerche sopra Masaccio e la sua famiglia', *Riv. A.*, xiv (1932), pp. 489–503; xvii (1935), pp. 91–111
——: 'Sulla cronologia delle opere di Masaccio e di Masolino tra il 1425 e il 1428', *Riv. A.*, xxviii (1953), pp. 3–55
P. Murray: *An Index of Attributions before Vasari* (Florence, 1959), pp. 110–12
U. Procacci: 'Nuove testimonianze su Masaccio', *Commentari*, xxvii (1976), pp. 223–37
J. Beck: *Masaccio, the Documents* (Locust Valley, NY, 1978)

U. Procacci: 'Masaccio e la sua famiglia negli antichi documenti', *Stor. Valdarno*, ii (1981), pp. 553–9

GENERAL
EWA; Thieme–Becker
J. A. Crowe and G. B. Cavalcaselle: *A New History of Painting in Italy*, i (London, 1864), pp. 519–50
B. Berenson: *The Florentine Painters of the Renaissance* (London, 1896), pp. 27–31
M. Dvořák: *Geschichte der italienischen Kunst im Zeitalter der Renaissance* (Munich, 1927), pp. 47–62
R. van Marle: *Italian Schools*, x (1928), pp. 251–307
F. Antal: *Florentine Painting and its Social Background* (London, 1947/*R* 1986), pp. 305–28
U. Baldini: 'Masaccio', *Mostra di quattro maestri del primo rinascimento* (exh. cat., ed. M. Salmi; Florence, Pal. Strozzi, 1954), pp. 3–17
J. White: *The Birth and Rebirth of Pictorial Space* (London, 1957, rev. Cambridge, 3/1987), pp. 135–41
E. Borsook: *The Mural Painters of Tuscany* (Oxford, 1960, rev. 2/1980), pp. 58–67
F. Hartt: 'Art and Freedom in Quattrocento Florence', *Essays in Memory of Karl Lehmann* (New York, 1964), pp. 114–31
B. Cole: *Masaccio and the Art of the Early Renaissance* (Bloomington, 1980)
P. Hills: *The Light of Early Italian Painting* (New Haven, 1987), pp. 129–45

MONOGRAPHS
A. Schmarsow: *Masaccio-Studien*, 2 vols (Kassel, 1895–99)
E. Somaré: *Masaccio* (Milan, 1924)
O. H. Giglioli: *Masaccio* (Bergamo, 1929)
M. Salmi: *Masaccio* (Rome, 1932, rev. Milan, 2/1948)
M. Pittaluga: *Masaccio* (Florence, 1935)
K. Steinbart: *Masaccio* (Vienna, 1948)
U. Procacci: *Tutta la pittura di Masaccio* (Milan, 1951, rev. 2/1952)
L. Berti: *Masaccio* (Milan, 1962, rev. University Park, PA, 2/1967)
A. Parronchi: *Masaccio*, Diamanti A. (Florence, 1966)
P. Volponi and L. Berti: *L'opera completa di Masaccio*, Class. A. (Milan, 1966)
C. Del Bravo: *Masaccio* (Florence, 1969)
U. Procacci: *Masaccio* (Florence, 1980)
L. Berti: *Masaccio* (Florence, 1988) [with photos of the restored frescoes of the Brancacci Chapel]

THE S GIOVENALE TRIPTYCH
L. Berti: 'Masaccio 1422', *Commentari*, xii (1961), pp. 84–107
——: 'Masaccio a S Giovenale di Cascia', *Acropoli*, ii (1962), pp. 149–65
J. Stubblebine and others: 'Early Masaccio: A Hypothetical Lost Madonna and a Disattribution', *A. Bull.*, lxii (1980), pp. 217–25
Masaccio e l'Angelico: Due capolavori della diocesi di Fiesole (exh. cat., ed. E. Micheletti and A. Maetzke; Fiesole, Pal. Mangani, 1984), pp. 14–29

THE PISA ALTARPIECE
W. Suida: 'L'altare di Masaccio, già nel Carmine a Pisa', *L'Arte*, ix (1906), pp. 125–7
M. Davies: *The Earlier Italian Schools*, London, N.G. cat. (London, 1951, rev. 2/1961/*R* 1986), pp. 269–72
E. Borsook: 'A Note on Masaccio in Pisa', *Burl. Mag.*, cxxxiii (1961), pp. 212–15
J. Shearman: 'Masaccio's Pisa Altarpiece: An Alternative Reconstruction', *Burl. Mag.*, cviii (1966), pp. 449–55
C. Gardner von Teuffel: 'Masaccio and the Pisa Altarpiece: A New Approach', *Jb. Berlin. Mus.*, xix (1977), pp. 23–68

THE 'TRINITY'
G. J. Kern: 'Das Dreifaltigkeitsfresko von S Maria Novella: Eine perspektivisch architekturgeschichtliche Studie', *Jb. Preuss. Kstsamml.*, xxiv (1913), pp. 36–58
C. de Tolnay: 'Renaissance d'une fresque', *L'Oeil*, xxxvii (1958), pp. 37–41
U. Schlegel: 'Observations on Masaccio's *Trinity* Fresco in Santa Maria Novella', *A. Bull.*, xiv (1963), pp. 19–33
J. Coolidge: 'Further Observations on Masaccio's *Trinity*', *A. Bull.*, xlviii (1966), pp. 382–4
O. von Simson: 'Über die Bedeutung von Masaccios Trinitätsfresko in S Maria Novella', *Jb. Berlin. Mus.*, viii (1966), pp. 119–59
H. W. Janson: 'Ground Plan and Elevation in Masaccio's *Trinity* Fresco', *Essays in the History of Art Presented to Rudolf Wittkower* (London, 1967), pp. 83–8

J. Polzer: 'The Anatomy of Masaccio's *Holy Trinity*', *Jb. Berlin. Mus.*, xiii (1971), pp. 18–59

C. Dempsey: 'Masaccio's *Trinity*: Altarpiece or Tomb', *A. Bull.*, liv (1972), pp. 279–81

E. Hertlein: *Masaccios 'Trinität'* (Florence, 1979)

R. Goffen: 'Masaccio's *Trinity* and the Letter to the Hebrews', *Mem. Domenicane*, xi (1980), pp. 489–504

R. Liebermann: 'Brunelleschi and Masaccio in Santa Maria Novella', *Mem. Domenicane*, xii (1981), pp. 127–39

W. Kemp: 'Masaccios *Trinità* im Kontext', *Marburg, Jb. Kstwiss.*, xxi (1986), pp. 45–72

A. Perrig: 'Masaccios *Trinità* und der Sinn der Zentralperspektive', *Marburg. Jb. Kstwiss.*, xxi (1986), pp. 11–43

THE BRANCACCI CHAPEL FRESCOES

J. Mesnil: 'Per la storia della cappella Brancacci', *Riv. A.*, x (1912), pp. 34–40

H. Brockhaus: 'Die Brancacci-Kapelle in Florenz', *Mitt. Ksthist. Inst. Florenz*, iii (1929–32), pp. 160–82

P. Meller: 'La cappella Brancacci: Problemi rittrattistici e iconografici', *Acropoli*, i (1960–61), pp. 186–227, 273–312

C. de Tolnay: 'Note sur l'iconographie des fresques de la Chapelle Brancacci', *A. Lombarda*, x (1965), pp. 69–74

H. von Einem: *Masaccios Zinsgroschen* (Cologne, 1967)

L. B. Watkins: 'Technical Observations on the Frescoes of the Brancacci Chapel', *Mitt. Ksthist. Inst. Florenz*, xvii (1973), pp. 65–74

A. Debold von Kritter: *Studien zum Petruszyklus in der Brancacci Kapelle* (Berlin, 1975)

A. Molho: 'The Brancacci Chapel: Studies in its Iconography and History', *J. Warb. & Court. Inst.*, xl (1977), pp. 50–98

W. Welliver: 'Narrative Method and Narrative Form in Masaccio's *Tribute Money*', *A.Q.* [Detroit], n. s. 1 (1977–8), pp. 40–58

D. Amory: 'Masaccio's *Expulsion from Paradise*: A Recollection of Antiquity', *Marsyas*, xx (1979–80), pp. 7–10

U. Procacci and U. Baldini: *La cappella Brancacci nella chiesa del Carmine a Firenze* (Milan, 1984)

O. Casazza: 'Il ciclo delle storie di San Pietro e la *Historia salutatis*', *Crit. A.*, ix (1985), pp. 77–82

W. Jacobsen: 'Die Konstruktion der Perspektive bei Masaccio und Masolino in der Brancaccikapelle', *Marburg. Jb. Kstwiss.*, xxi (1986), pp. 73–92

U. Baldini: 'Le figure di Adamo e Eva formate affatto ignude in una cappella di una principal chiesa di Fiorenza', *Crit. A.*, liii/1 (1988), pp. 72–7

O. Casazza: 'La grande gabbia architettonica di Masaccio', *Crit. A.*, liii/1 (1988), pp. 78–97

U. Baldini and O. Casazza: *La cappella Brancacci* (Milan, 1990)

K. Christiansen: 'Some Observations on the Brancacci Chapel Frescoes after their Cleaning', *Burl. Mag.*, cxxxiii (1991), pp. 5–20

THE S MARIA MAGGIORE ALTARPIECE

K. Clark: 'An Early Quattrocento Triptych from Santa Maria Maggiore, Rome', *Burl. Mag.*, cxiii (1951), pp. 339–47

M. Davies: *The Earlier Italian Schools*, London, N.G. cat. (London, 1951, 2/1961/R 1986), pp. 272–80

M. Meiss: 'London's New Masaccio', *ARTnews*, li/2 (1952), pp. 24–5

J. Pope-Hennessy: 'The Sta Maria Maggiore Altarpiece', *Burl. Mag.*, xciv (1952), pp. 31–2

D. Gioseffi: 'Domenico Veneziano: L'esordio masaccesco e la tavola con i SS Girolamo e Giovanni Battista della National Gallery di Londra', *Emporium*, lxviii (1962), pp. 51–72

M. Meiss: 'The Altered Program of the S Maria Maggiore Altarpiece', *Studien zur toskanischen Kunst* (Munich, 1964), pp. 169–89

C. B. Strehlke and M. Tucker: 'The Santa Maria Maggiore Altarpiece: New Observations', *A. Crist.*, lxxv (1987), pp. 105–24

OTHER SPECIALIST STUDIES

J. Mesnil: 'Masaccio and the Antique', *Burl. Mag.*, xlviii (1926), pp. 91–8

——: *Masaccio et les débuts de la Renaissance* (The Hague, 1927)

——: 'Die Kunstlehre der Frührenaissance im Werke Masaccios', *Vorträge der Bibliothek Warburg, 1925–26* (Leipzig, 1928), pp. 122–46

O. H. Giglioli: 'Masaccio: Saggio di bibliografia ragionata', *Boll. Reale. Ist. Archeol. & Stor. A.*, iii/4–6 (1929), pp. 55–101

M. Pittaluga: 'Masaccio e L. B. Alberti', *Rass. It. A.*, xxiv (1929), pp. 779–90

——: 'La critica e i valori romantici di Masaccio', *L'Arte*, xxxiii (1930), pp. 139–64

H. Lindberg: *To the Problem of Masolino and Masaccio*, 2 vols (Stockholm, 1931)

R. Oertel: 'Die Frühwerke des Masaccio', *Marburg. Jb. Kstwiss.*, vii (1933), pp. 191–28

——: 'Masaccio und die Geschichte der Freskotechnik', *Jb. Preuss. Kstsamml.*, lv (1934), pp. 229–40

R. Longhi: 'Fatti di Masolino e di Masaccio', *Crit. A.*, v (1940), pp. 151–66

U. Procacci: 'Il Vasari e la conservazione degli affreschi della cappella Brancacci al Carmine e della Trinità in S Maria Novella', *Scritti di storia dell'arte in onore di Lionello Venturi* (Rome, 1956), pp. 211–22

R. Offner: 'Light on Masaccio's Classicism', *Studies in the History of Art Dedicated to William Suida* (London, 1959), pp. 66–73

M. Meiss: 'Masaccio and the Early Renaissance: The Circular Plan', *Studies in Western Art*, ii (Princeton, 1963), pp. 123–45

M. Boskovits: 'Giotto Born Again', *Z. Kstgesch.*, xxix (1966), pp. 51–66

R. Freemantle: 'Masaccio e l'antico', *Crit. A.*, xxxiii (1969), pp. 39–56

C. Gilbert: 'The Drawings Now Associated with Masaccio's *Sagra*', *Stor. A.*, iii (1969), pp. 260–78

J. Polzer: 'Masaccio and the Late Antique', *A. Bull.*, liii (1971), pp. 36–40

J. Beck: 'Fatti di Masaccio', *Essays in Archaeology and the Humanities in Memoriam Otto Brendel* (Mainz, 1976), pp. 211–14

B. Cinelli and F. Mazzocca: *Fortuna visiva di Masaccio* (Florence, 1979)

E. Maurer: 'Masaccio–Cavallini–Spätantike', *Ars Auro Prior* (Warsaw, 1981), pp. 155–60

——: 'Masaccio: Vom Himmel gefallen?', *15 Aufsätze zur Geschichte der Malerei* (Basle, 1982), pp. 75–89

T. Verdon: 'La Sant'Anna Metterza: Riflessioni, domande, ipotesi', *Uffizi, Stud. & Ric.*, v (1988), pp. 33–58

P. Joannides: *Masaccio and Masolino: A Complete Catalogue* (London, 1993)

HELLMUT WOHL

Masada [Heb. Mezadah]. Fortress on a flat-topped rock on the eastern side of the Judean Desert in Israel; to the east, the rock terminates in a sheer cliff 400 m above the Dead Sea. According to the Jewish Roman historian Josephus Flavius (AD 37–after 93), whose account of Masada is the only extant one, it was built (probably *c.* 37–31 BC) by Herod the Great. During the period of the Jewish War (AD 66–73), it was garrisoned by the Jewish Zealots, who made their last stand there against the Romans. Three years after the capture of Jerusalem, the defenders of Masada, having held the fortress during a three-year siege, destroyed themselves when it was about to fall.

Masada was encircled by a dolomite stone wall with casemates: the space between the two walls was partitioned into 70 compartments. Each of the four gates consisted of a room with an inner and an outer entrance and benches along the walls. Rising from small casemates, the 30 towers were built at unequal distances, according to the rock's topography. An elaborate water-supply system consisted of numerous cisterns linked by channels; there were also several pools, some probably associated with ritual bathing.

Eight palaces have been found in the northern and western parts of the rock. Herod's Northern palace or villa, on the northern edge of the cliff, had three storeys, the lower two with terraces; it had its own small bathhouse. Next to it was a smaller palace, the public storehouses and a large bathhouse. The Western palace, largest of the buildings, was a ceremonial and administrative centre; the main hall had a decorative mosaic floor. One group of three small palaces probably served the royal family, while a further group served as residences for high officials and as administrative buildings. The Masada palaces exhibited the basic elements of Hellenistic architecture, being characterized by a simple central court and a columned hall leading to a *triclinium*, usually in the southern part of the court.

A building believed to have served as a synagogue was added during the Zealot period. It was part of the casemate wall, with one main entrance, and measured 12.5×10.5 m, being divided by two rows of columns. It was built in two phases, in the second of which mud-plastered benches were added along the walls.

BIBLIOGRAPHY

Y. Yadin: 'The Excavation of Masada, 1963/64: Preliminary Report', *Israel Explor. J.*, xv (1965), pp. 1–20

——: *Masada* (London and New York, 1966)

——: 'The Synagogue at Masada', *Ancient Synagogues Revealed*, ed. L. I. Levine (Jerusalem, 1981)

E. Nezer: *Masada III: The Yigael Yadin Excavations, 1963–1965, Final Reports* (Jerusalem)

RACHEL HACHLILI

Masahiro Rokkaku. *See* ROKKAKU, KIJŌ.

Masahisa Fukase. *See* FUKASE, MASAHISA.

Masai. *See* MAASAI.

Masana, Josep (*b* Granollers, nr Barcelona, 17 March 1894; *d* Barcelona, 4 Jan 1979). Spanish Catalan photographer. His first studio was in Granollers, but he established his name when he settled in Barcelona. He had close links with a number of film companies and founded the Savoy cinema in Barcelona. His photography was in part influenced by the sophisticated compositions and subject-matter characteristic of Pictorial photography, seen in *Untitled* (bromoil, *c.* 1927). His commercial work, however, in particular his photomontages, such as another *Untitled* (also from *c.* 1927), was more avant-garde.

BIBLIOGRAPHY

Idas y caos: Aspectos de las vanguardias fotográficas en España (exh. cat., ed. J. Fontcuberta; Madrid, Min. Cult., 1984); Eng. trans. as *Ideas and Chaos: Trends in Spanish Photography, 1920–1945*, pp. 102–9, 122, 133–7

Masana, fotògraf (exh. cat. by M. Galmes, Granollers, Cent. Cult. Caixa Pensions, 1985)

M. Gili: 'Our Photographic Forefathers', *Barcelona: Metròpolis Medit.*, 3 (1987), pp. 72–7

JOAN FONTCUBERTA

Masanobu (i). *See* KANŌ, (1).

Masanobu (ii). *See* HEINOUCHI MASANOBU.

Masanobu (iii). *See* OKUMURA MASANOBU.

Masanobu (iv). *See* KITAO MASANOBU.

Maşathöyük [Maşat Höyük]. Site in Turkey of an ancient city that flourished during the Hittite period in the 2nd millennium BC, where one of the earliest Hittite archives was discovered (*see* ANATOLIA, ANCIENT, §I, 2(ii)(a)). The city was situated in the northern part of the land of the Hittites, 312 km north-east of modern Ankara. It was established on a natural outcrop of rock and consisted of a citadel and a lower town. The mound measures 450×225 m and rises 29 m above the level of the plain. Excavations began in 1973 and continued until 1984. Most of the finds are in the Museum of Anatolian Civilizations in Ankara.

The first settlement at Maşathöyük was established on the summit of the rocky massif during the Early Bronze Age in the 3rd millennium BC. The next settlement (level V, *c.* 18th century BC) was contemporary with levels Ia–b of the trading district (*karum*) of KÜLTEPE (Kanesh). Its pottery, rhyta, stamp seals and metalwork are equal to those of Kültepe, Alişar and Boğazköy. The settlement was destroyed by fire in circumstances that appear to have affected many of the settlements of central Anatolia. However, during the Hittite Old Kingdom, from the 17th to the 15th centuries BC (levels IVa–b), Maşathöyük became a great city.

The earliest known example of Hittite monumental architecture was discovered at Maşathöyük in the citadel in level III. It measured 72×65 m, and 45 rooms have been excavated at basement level. Its plan and the discovery of an archive in two of its rooms prove that it was a palace with both administrative and living quarters (see fig.). The building had two storeys built of mud-brick and wood on foundations of stone. Large storage jars were found in some of the long, narrow storerooms; some of the tablets in the archive have provided information on what was stored. Around the central courtyard of the palace there was a colonnade, the roof of which was supported by wooden columns that rested on beautifully worked stone bases (found *in situ*). The palace was on the frontier with the land of the Kashka, the Hittites' greatest enemies, and represented the military, political and administrative might of a frontier commander who communicated directly with the king. A temple of the same date as the palace was discovered in the lower city; most of the storerooms surrounding its open courtyard have been excavated. The script on the tablets found in the palace archive is Middle Hittite, and, according to the seal impressions on them, the tablets are contemporary with Tudhaliya II (*reg c.* 1410–1380 BC). Palace, temple and city were burnt down and destroyed by the Kashka during the reign of this king; indeed, letters between the king and the commander mention the Kashka threat. Level II in the Hittite period has been dated by a seal impression of

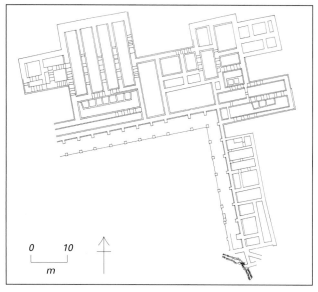

Maşathöyük, plan of the surviving remains of the Hittite palace, level III, destroyed *c.* 1410–*c.* 1380 BC

Suppiluliuma I (*reg c.* 1380–1335 BC), and the last Hittite level (level I) has been attributed to the 13th century BC with the help of a further cuneiform tablet. The city burnt down during the last decade of that century. Finds include 'Mycenaean IIIB' imported pottery as well as seal impressions bearing hieroglyphic Hittite inscriptions.

There are three Phrygian and Iron Age levels (numbered III–I), which lasted from the 8th century BC to the 4th, when only a section of the citadel was occupied. Besides the painted ceramics that characterized central Anatolia at this date, there was an increase in the number of finds showing the influence of East Greek pottery.

BIBLIOGRAPHY

T. Özgüç: *Maşat Höyük kazıları ve çevresindeki araştırmalar/Excavations at Maşat Höyük and Investigations in its Vicinity* (Ankara, 1978) [bilingual text]

S. Alp: 'Remarques sur la géographie de la région du haut Yeşil-Irmak d'après les tablettes hittites de Maşat-Höyük', *Florilegium Anatolicum: Mélanges offerts à Emmanuel Laroche* (Paris, 1979), pp. 29–35

K. Emre: 'Maşathöyük'de Eski Tunç Çağı/The Early Bronze Age at Maşathöyük', *Belleten*, xliii/169 (1979), pp. 21–48

S. Alp: 'Die hethitischen Tontafelentdeckungen auf dem Maşathöyük', *Belleten*, xliv/173 (1980), pp. 25–59

T. Özgüç: 'Excavations at the Hittite Site Maşat Höyük: Palace, Archives, Mycenaean Pottery', *Amer. J. Archaeol.*, lxxxiv (1980), pp. 305–9

——: *Maşat Höyük II, Boğazköy'un kuzey-doğusundaki bir Hitit merkezi/A Hittite Center Northeast of Boğazköy* (Ankara, 1982) [bilingual text]

TAHSIN ÖZGÜÇ

Masato Otaka. *See* OTAKA, MASATO.

Mascaron. Decorative grotesque mask, usually over a door or fountain (*see* GROTESQUE).

☐

Mascherino [Mascarino], **Ottaviano** [Ottavio dei Nonni] (*b* Bologna, *bapt* 3 Sept 1536; *d* Rome, 6 Aug 1606). Italian architect, sculptor and painter. He was the son of Giulio Mascherino, a mason who worked with Jacopo Vignola in 1547. Vignola's influence is clear in Ottaviano Mascherino's earliest attributed work, the Porta Pia (Porta di S Isaia) in Bologna (1567–71; destr. 20th century), and it has been suggested that he merely executed Vignola's design (Wasserman, 1966). He is documented in 1568 as the architect supervising the construction of the Fountain of Neptune in Bologna. A year later he joined the Consiglio dei Bombasari e Pittori in Bologna, and his first documented works are paintings. Also in 1569, with Lorenzo Fiorini, in the Cubiculum Artistarum of the Archiginnasio (the university) he painted frescoes representing the *Liberal Arts* (partially destr. 1944) and executed the niche and statue of *Apollo* for the entrance. There are echoes of Parmigianino, Lorenzo Sabatini and Giambologna in these works. In the Villa Guastavillani at Barbiano (nr Bologna), there are frescoes and a statue of *Bacchus* attributed to him (Negro, 1990). He probably also planned this villa, which was begun in 1575 by Cardinal Filippo Guastavillani (1540–87), a nephew of Pope Gregory XIII (*reg* 1572–85).

Mascherino is documented in Rome in 1574, where he was instrumental in introducing the style of the Bolognese

Ottaviano Mascherino: casino in the courtyard of the Palazzo del Quirinale, Rome, from 1582

school. He was first employed as a painter at the Vatican, working on the loggias of Gregory XIII; he also painted *quadrature* in the Sala del Bologna (Negro, 1990). As a painter, he was elected to the Accademia di S Luca in 1576 and to the Virtuosi al Pantheon in 1580. From 1574 he is also mentioned as an architect; he probably assisted the papal architect Martino Longhi the elder, whom he succeeded in 1577. At the Vatican he modified the east side of the Cortile di S Damaso and began what became the palace of Pope Sixtus V. Other projects there included the construction of the Galleria delle Carte Geografiche above the west corridor of the Cortile del Belvedere (from 1578), the Torre dei Venti (1578–80), the west loggia in the upper court of the Belvedere (1582–5) and the restructuring of S Marta (1582; destr. 1930). From 1582 to 1585 he planned the restructuring of a summer palace, the Vigna d'Este, on the Quirinal Hill in Rome, for Gregory XIII, including a casino with a two-storey loggia and side wings, surmounted by a central tower (now part of the Palazzo del Quirinale; see fig.). His oval staircase in the casino was one of the first to be constructed. A predilection for the oval form, and for centrally planned structures in general, is evident in many of his unrealized designs.

Mascherino held the post of papal architect until the death of Gregory XIII (in 1585) and again under Innocent IX (*reg* 1591). This gave him access to a large clientele. Ecclesiastical works in Rome for other important patrons included the Bandini Chapel in S Silvestro al Quirinale (1580–85), the restructuring of S Caterina della Ruota (1585–before 1591), the church and cloister of SS Giovanni Evangelista e Petronio (from 1582), the supervision of the construction of S Maria in Traspontina, designed (1581–7) by Giovanni Sallustio Peruzzi, and the oval steps leading to the cloister of the Ospedale di S Spirito in Sassia. In the nave of S Salvatore in Lauro (after 1591) the use of free-standing, paired columns has contributed much to Mascherino's fame, although the attribution is not unanimous (Heydenreich and Lotz, p. 284). He also worked on the reconstruction of Roman palaces, including the Albero (destr.), Alessandrino, Ginnasi, Aldobrandini, Verospi and the Monte di Pietà (Wasserman, 1966). The dates and the extent of his participation in these projects are uncertain, however. Although many aspects of Mascherino's work remain to be clarified, according to Wasserman, he is particularly interesting for his way of organizing interior spaces, for example the use of different designs for the sides of a courtyard, and for the juxtaposition of urban and suburban architectural elements. He was certainly appreciated by his contemporaries, as is clear from his nomination in 1604 as Principe of the Accademia di S Luca.

BIBLIOGRAPHY

J. S. Ackerman: *The Cortile del Belvedere* (Rome, 1954)
J. Wasserman: 'The Palazzo Sisto V in the Vatican', *J. Soc. Archit. Hist.*, xxi (1962), pp. 26–35
——: 'The Quirinal Palace in Rome', *A. Bull.*, xlv (1963), pp. 205–44
——: *Ottaviano Mascarino and his Drawings in the Accademia Nazionale di San Luca* (Rome, 1966); review by K. Schwager in *Z. Kstgesch.*, xxxi (1968), pp. 246–68
L. H. Heydenreich and W. Lotz: *Architecture in Italy, 1400–1600*, Pelican Hist. A. (Harmondsworth, 1974)
I. Sjöström: *Quadratura: Studies in Italian Ceiling Painting* (Stockholm, 1978)
E. Negro: 'Cubiculum Artistarum et Cubiculum Juristarum: La decorazione pittorica cinquecentesca delle aule', *L'archiginnasio, il palazzo, l'università, la biblioteca*, ed. G. Roversi, i (Bologna, 1988), pp. 145–58
N. Margot: *Gregory XIII's Tower of the Winds in the Vatican* (diss., New York U.; microfilm, Ann Arbor, 1990)
E. Negro: 'Ottaviano Mascherino pittore e scultore', *Lelio Orsi e la cultura del suo tempo*, ed. J. Bentini (Bologna, 1990), pp. 161–72

ALESSANDRA ANSELMI

Mascherone. *See* GARGOYLE.

Masci, Girolamo. *See* NICHOLAS IV.

Mas d'Azil. Cave site in France, near Ariège. It has yielded important remains dating from the Late Upper Palaeolithic period (*c.* 20,000–*c.* 10,000 BP) and later, and it is the type site for the Azilian tradition (*c.* 9000–*c.* 7500 BC). The huge cave, 450 m long and 50 m wide, was created in a limestone cliff by the River Arize; it was discovered in 1859 and excavated by Edouard Piette (1887–96), HENRI BREUIL (1901–2), and Marthe Péquart and Saint-Juste Péquart (1935–42). Parts of the collection are at the site (Mas d'Azil, Mus. Ladevèze) and in Saint-Germain-en-Laye (Mus. Ant. N.).

The left river terrace yielded several Magdalenian, Azilian, Mesolithic and Neolithic levels; on the right bank, Aurignacian and Solutrean levels were overlain by four Magdalenian and Azilian levels (*see* PREHISTORIC EUROPE, §§I and II, 1). One of the cave galleries, known as the Breuil Gallery, is decorated with Magdalenian paintings and engravings, but these are not well preserved. The excavated evidence indicates that at least some of the portable art found was produced at Mas d'Azil itself, and that it was one of the frequently reoccupied sites of the Upper Palaeolithic period. The richness of the art objects indicates a special function within a more general settlement pattern.

The Magdalenian levels have yielded most of the portable art. To the Middle Magdalenian phase are attributed many famous art objects: decorated pierced discs, batons, spear-throwers with animal heads (mainly horses, some even with skinned features, and ibexes) and many engravings, for example on animal shoulder-blades. Of the many spear-throwers, a complete example is decorated with a young ibex, its head turned back towards an emerging turd on which two birds are sitting (l. 334 mm; Saint Brieuc, Péquart priv. col.; *see* PREHISTORIC EUROPE, §II, 3(ii) and fig. 12). A similar piece to this startling scene has been found in the cave of Bédeilhac. Another probable spear-thrower is decorated by three horse heads, one of them possibly skinned, at the hook end. Pierced batons are decorated with signs and animal motifs, mainly horses. There was also a wealth of jewellery, mostly decorated, including bone discs cut from animal shoulder-blades. The Upper Magdalenian phase included more engravings, such as horses and a bison superimposed on a shoulder-blade.

The Azilian levels contained 1444 pebbles, some of which were flaked, painted with red ochre. Motifs include dots, rows of transverse lines and more complex patterns. Complex motifs and pebbles both painted and engraved are rare. A certain selection for size, form and decoration seems to have been exercised (Couraud, 1985).

BIBLIOGRAPHY
E. Piette: *L'Art pendant l'âge du renne* (Paris, 1907)
A. Alteirac and D. Vialou: 'La Galerie Breuil de la grotte du Mas d'Azil', *Préhist. Arièg.*, xxxv (1980), pp. 3–63
J. Clottes, A. Alteirac and C. Servelle: 'Oeuvres d'art mobilier magdalé-niennes des anciennes collections du Mas d'Azil', *Préhist. Arièg.*, xxxvi (1981), pp. 1–40
A. Alteirac and D. Vialou: 'Grotte du Mas d'Azil', *L'Art des cavernes: Atlas des grottes ornées paléolithiques françaises* (Paris, 1984), pp. 389–94
C. Couraud: 'L'Art azilien: Origine-survivance', *Gallia-Préhist.* (1985) [suppl.]

JOACHIM HAHN

Masegne, dalle [Masignis, de]. Italian family of sculptors and architects. Jacobello [Giacomello; Jacobellus; Jaco-melo] dalle Masegne (*fl* from 1383; *d* after 1409) and his brother Pierpaolo dalle Masegne (*fl* from 1383; *d c.* 1403) were the sons of Antonio dalle Masegne, a stonemason in Venice. They usually undertook and signed their major commissions together, as was the common practice in Venice for family partnerships. However, although there is no documentary evidence to prove it, it is possible to recognize their individual styles in separate sections of their collaborative works.

The Masegne brothers were in Mantua in 1383 when Francesco I Gonzaga recommended that the brothers should be imprisoned for molesting a woman (Rambaldi, 1920). On 3 August 1386 Pierpaolo was accused of adultery in Bologna. He was then living in the house of the scholar Giovanni da Legnano, who had died in 1383 and whose tomb (Bologna, Mus. Civ. Med.), originally in S Domenico, Bologna, was signed by both brothers. However, a comparison of the drapery style of the local remains of the tomb monument with that of the Apostles in the central section of the iconostasis in S Marco, Venice, attributed to Jacobello alone, suggests that the tomb was also Jacobello's work. It follows the traditional Bolognese design for scholars' tombs, such as that of *Giovanni d'Andrea Calderini* dating from the mid-14th century (Bologna, Mus. Civ. Med.). In October 1386 the brothers were living in Venice and were commissioned to carve the portal of the Dominican church in Modena. Judging from the Tuscan traits in his sculpture, Pierpaolo possibly visited Tuscany at this time.

In November 1388 Jacobello and Pierpaolo jointly signed a contract to construct the high altar at S Francesco, Bologna (finished 1392; *in situ*). Jacobello's role in its execution is difficult to define, partly because it has been heavily restored, but it may have been marginal; the predominant style is that of Pierpaolo. The richly ornate marble altar is arranged like a painted polyptych on two tiers crowned by high, slender finials. A relief of the *Coronation of the Virgin* in the centre is flanked by full-length saints in niches, the upper tier has *God the Father*

1. Jacobello dalle Masegne and Pierpaolo dalle Masegne: central section (dated 1394) of the iconostasis, S Marco, Venice

enthroned, flanked by half-length busts of saints, each divided from the next by rows of smaller saints also in tabernacles. Above, the *Crucifixion with the Virgin and St John* is set on a tall pinnacle. Along the base, like a predella, are nine narrative scenes from the life of St Francis.

In 1390 the Masegne brothers were in Bologna, and in 1391 Pierpaolo (referred to as a stonemason) undertook to carve pilaster bases for S Petronio. They were both in Bologna again in 1392; but they may both have been in Venice before the work on S Francesco was completed. Both brothers signed the central section of the iconostasis (choir screen; see fig. 1) in S Marco, Venice, in 1394, which would suggest that they must have begun this large project *c.* 1392–3. The iconostasis sculptures reveal two radically different styles. One group is formed by the twelve marble Apostles of the central section. These show marked similarities with mid-14th-century Lombard sculpture, particularly with works of Bonino da Campione, who was active in Verona. The strongly expressive physiognomy of the Apostles' faces is close to the angels' faces on the tomb (Padua, Eremitani) of *Ubertino da Carrara* (*d* 1345) by Andriolo de' Santi of Venice, to such mid-14th-century mosaics in S Marco as those in the baptistery and also to Paolo Veneziano's paintings. This would suggest that this sculptor's roots lay in northern Italy. The marble female figures on the lateral sections facing the chapel of S Clemente and the chapel of S Pietro are in a different style (see fig. 2). Their similarity to Tuscan sculpture, particularly to the work of artists in the circle of Nino Pisano, is so strong that it would suggest that the sculptor stayed for a considerable time in Tuscany and continued working in the Tuscan style on his return to Venice. Given that Pierpaolo was absent from Venice *c.* 1394 and that Jacobello was absent *c.* 1397, the figures in the central section, which is dated 1394, can be attributed to Jacobello and the lateral sections, dated 1397, to Pierpaolo. Both sculptors used assistants, and the stylistic differences within their sections are due mainly to different qualities of execution, not to independent designs.

In October 1395 Jacobello was commissioned by Francesco I Gonzaga to erect the façade (destr.) of Mantua Cathedral. Work progressed so slowly that in 1397 Francesco Gonzaga reminded the sculptor of his contractual obligations, and the commission passed to Pierpaolo; a clause in Pierpaolo's contract left him free to change his brother's design. It was finished by 1403, but payments continued until 1409. The original appearance of the façade is known from Domenico Morone's painting of the *Expulsion of the Bonacolsi* (Mantua, Pal. Ducale; *see* MANTUA, fig. 2). It was built of red brick in the Venetian Gothic style, the central section was faced in marble, and its gable was surmounted by five aediculae, each holding a statue. Two lions from the portico have survived.

In 1396 Jacobello executed another commission for Mantua (finished 1398), of which nothing survives. Before May 1399 Jacobello signed an initial agreement with Francesco Gonzaga to carve the tomb for his second wife, Margherita Malatesta (*d* Feb 1399), for S Francesco, Mantua, but on 5 April 1400 the contract for the tomb was signed by Pierpaolo. Only the effigy of Margherita survives (Mantua, Pal. Ducale). There is documentary evidence that in 1396 Jacobello intended to go to Milan.

2. Pierpaolo dalle Masegne: *Saint*, marble, from one of the lateral sections (1397) of the iconostasis, S Marco, Venice

The same year the authorities of Milan Cathedral granted 'Giacomelo da Venezia e suo fratello' a three-month trial period at the cathedral. Another document describes Jacobello as an engineer ('*inzenario*'). The documents may refer to the Masegne brothers, although it is not certain. A number of unconvincing attributions of sculpture at Milan Cathedral have been made to the Masegne brothers, and it has also been postulated that they had a decisive influence on Lombard art in the early 15th century.

In the later 1390s the Masegne brothers seem to have signed several contracts independently, although they may have executed the work jointly. According to one hypothesis, the brothers were working independently by the end of the 14th century. In October 1400 Pierpaolo signed a contract to decorate the large window in the Sala del Maggior Consiglio in the Doge's Palace, Venice. In 1403 he made a will when he was ill and probably died soon after. Jacobello was mentioned in Bologna in 1409 when he was claiming outstanding payments for the high altar of S Francesco. Other attributions to Jacobello include two marble statues of *St John the Baptist* and *St Anthony of Padua* (both Venice, S Stefano, sacristy) that may be early works, *c.* 1380. The carving of the gaunt face and tightly clasped hand of the marble statue of the kneeling Doge Antonio Venier (*c.* 1394; Venice, Correr) is also characteristic of Jacobello.

BIBLIOGRAPHY

Thieme–Becker

M. Caffi: 'Chatalapiera scultori veneziani del secolo XVI di nome imaginario ed altri artefici poco noti', *Nuovo Arch Ven.*, i/2 (1891), pp. 181–90

P. Paoletti: *L'architettura e la scultura del rinascimento a Venezia*, 2 vols (Venice, 1893)

A. Venturi: *Storia*, iv (1901–40), pp. 797–842

P. Torelli: 'Jacobello e Pietropaolo dalle Masegne a Mantova', *Rass. A.*, xiii (1913), pp. 67–71 [docs]

I. Supino: 'La pala d'altare di Jacobello e Pier Paolo dalle Masegne nella chiesa di S Francesco in Bologna', *Mem. Reale Accad. Sci. Ist. Bologna, Classe Sci. Morali*, ix (1914–15), pp. 111–55 [docs]

L. Planiscig: 'Geschichte der venezianischen Skulptur im XIV. Jahrhundert', *Jb. Ksthist. Samml. Allhöch. Ksrhaus.*, ccciii/2 (1916), pp. 31–212; ccciii/3 (1916), pp. 176–92

P. L. Rambaldi: 'Nuovi appunti sui maestri Jacobello e Pietro Paolo da Venezia', *Venezia, Stud. A. & Stor. Dir. Mus. Civ. Correr*, i (1920), pp. 63–88 [docs]

R. Krautheimer: 'Zur venezianischen Trecentoplastik', *Marburg. Jb. Kstwiss.*, v (1929), pp. 193–212

S. Bettini: 'L'ultima e la più bella opera di Pier Paolo dalle Masegne', *Dedalo*, xii (1932), pp. 347–59

C. Gnudi: 'Jacobello e Pietro Paolo da Venezia', *Crit. A.*, ii (1937), pp. 26–38

G. Mariacher: 'Orme veneziane nella scultura lombarda: I fratelli Dalle Masegne a Milano', *Ateneo Ven.*, cxxxvi (1945), pp. 25–7

C. Gnudi: 'Nuovi appunti sui fratelli dalle Masegne: Un capolavoro di Pierpaolo, grandezza di Jacobello', *Proporzione*, iii (1950), pp. 48–55

J. Pope-Hennessy: *Italian Gothic Sculpture* (London, 1955, rev. 3/1985), pp. 37–8, 204–5

C. Bocciarelli: 'Di una probabile opera di Jacobello dalle Masegne a Milano', *A. Lombardo*, iii (1958), pp. 72–6

E. Mariani: 'Nuovi documenti mantovani su Jacomello e Pietropaolo dalle Masegne', *Atti & Mem. Accad. Virgil. Mantova*, 2nd ser., xxxii (1960), pp. 71–102 [docs]

R. Roli: *La pala marmorea di S Francesco in Bologna* (Bologna, 1964)

W. Wolters: 'Über zwei Figuren des Jacobello dalle Masegne in S Stefano zu Venedig', *Z. Kstgesch.*, xxviii (1965), pp. 113–20

C. Seymour jr: *Italian Sculpture, 1400–1500*, Pelican Hist. A. (Harmondsworth, 1966)

L. Heusinger: *Jacobello und Pierpaolo dalle Masegne* (diss., U. Munich, 1967)

W. Wolters: *La scultura veneziana gotica, 1300–1460* (Milan, 1976), pp. 62–74, 212–14

WOLFGANG WOLTERS

Maser, Villa Barbaro. Italian villa at Maser, a village in the Veneto between Cornuda on the River Piave and the fortified town of Asolo, in the foothills of the Dolomites *c.* 60 km north-west of Venice. The villa, designed by Andrea Palladio and built in 1554–8 for the Barbaro family, lies to the east of the village and faces south. It incorporates the remains of a medieval *castello* tower as a forward-projecting two-storey central block; this tower may have been built *c.* 1339, when Venice conquered the province of Treviso and the Barbaro family acquired the property. Its rebuilding and enlargement by Palladio (*see* PALLADIO, ANDREA, §I, 1(ii)) were commissioned in 1549 by two of

Maser, Villa Barbaro by Andrea Palladio, 1554–8; aerial view looking north-east, showing the nymphaeum to the right

the most important humanist statesmen and artistic patrons of the Venetian republic: Daniele Barbaro, Ambassador to England and Patriarch Elect of Aquileia, and his married brother Marc'Antonio Barbaro, a Venetian senator and Ambassador to Constantinople (*see* BARBARO). Palladio's first plan sketches (London, RIBA) date from May 1549; the villa was definitively designed between 1551 and 1554.

Palladio substituted new vaults for the former beamed ceilings in an intermediate storey of the tower, extending its spaces into the original top storey (which survives only as an unfloored, windowless attic), and covered it with a monumental pitched roof, presenting a pedimented gable towards the long approach avenue of lime trees. This pediment is supported by four giant Ionic half-columns rising through both levels of fenestration to treat the projecting façade as an antique temple-front attached to the entrance wall of the main block, the full form of which thus assumes, in angled or distant views, the three-dimensional aspect of an ancient temple. The villa backs on to a wooded hillside (see fig.), which Palladio concealed with tall lateral arcades ending in high dovecots. These narrow east–west wings function as retaining walls to mask a private garden lying behind residential suites on the upper level of the wings, with service rooms on the lower level, which connect on both floors across the reception rooms of the central block. The south façade thus becomes a five-part composition, its central block connected by lower arcades to terminal pavilions crowned with pedimented frontispieces: that adjoining the entrance forecourt to the east (projected, unfeasibly, for stables) still contains a carriage-house, while wine-cellars and kitchens formerly occupied its twin, opening on to gardens and orchards to the west.

As noted by Vasari, the garden and grotto structures (1552) by Bartolomeo Ammanati at the Villa Giulia in Rome are paralleled at the Villa Barbaro by the nymphaeum, a fountain hemicycle and grotto chamber in the enclosed upper garden. These combine architecture, sculpture and fresco painting in a programmatic reconstruction of a Greek oracular sanctuary described by Pausanias, dedicated to the genius of the place and to beneficent Fortune (Lewis, 1980). The engineering of this element, the structural reworkings of the site and the medieval tower, and Palladio's new wings, must have been executed in 1554–8, as literary references of 1558 and 1559 (see Puppi, 1973) state that the villa was in use, with the decoration of the nymphaeum complete. The most striking feature of the nymphaeum, as well as of the façade pediment, pavilion niches and the chimney-pieces of four of the largest rooms, is a lavish cycle of nearly three-dimensional stucco sculptures; these display the style of a sophisticated amateur in the circle of Alessandro Vittoria, and in fact were contemporaneously attributed to Marc'Antonio Barbaro (Ludovico Roncone, in Scamozzi).

The axial suites of private rooms on the upper storey of Palladio's wings open northwards directly on to the nymphaeum garden and also look south through windows situated under the arcades of the main elevation. These rooms were later frescoed with unexceptional cycles of imagery depicting Venus and Hercules, attributed to followers of Battista Zelotti; the westernmost room, with its *Labours of Hercules*, was repainted by Girolamo Pellegrini (*d* 1700) around 1670 (Pallucchini). The upper floor of the central block was arranged by Palladio to provide reception rooms and staircases in its corners, divided by a cruciform hall lit from balconied windows set in the east, south and west façades; on the north side the hall opens through a triumphal arch into the main *salone*, the Sala dell'Olimpo, which, with two flanking vestibules, provides access to the lateral wings. These vestibules (a 'Room of Faith' leading to Daniele Barbaro's eastern suite, a 'Room of Fortune' leading to that of Marc'Antonio Barbaro and his family on the west), the Sala dell'Olimpo, the Crociera and two corner chambers along the main façade (a south-eastern 'Room of the Family' and a south-western room inscribed 'To the Genius of the Place and to the Household Gods') were all painted with a magnificent cycle of frescoes (*c.* 1561) by Veronese, his masterpiece in this medium and the most distinguished fresco cycle in any Italian Renaissance private palace (*see* VERONESE, PAOLO, §I, 3(i) and ILLUSIONISM, colour pl. IV). The painted decoration is organized within an elaborate *trompe l'oeil* architecture of columnar screens, recessed niches, pedimented portals, sculptured attics and projecting cornices, all designed by Palladio (Lewis, 1982). Among these frameworks are illusionistic landscapes with Classical ruins, based on engravings (1561) by Battista Pittoni (*c.* 1520–83) (Oberhuber, 1968), as well as simulated sculptures and reliefs in fictive marble, bronze, gilt and coloured stones. Finally, interspersed within *trompe l'oeil* doorways, balconies and cornices revealing distant vistas of open sky, is a large population of life-like human figures in full colour, occasionally representing real people (among them

Marc'Antonio Barbaro's wife, children, servants and friends, including a huntsman traditionally identified as Veronese), but mostly comprising idealized figures of allegories, virtues, and personifications of the Christian and Olympian gods. The overall iconographic theme presented by these emblematic figures, which are mainly derived from *Le imagini de i dei degli antichi* (Venice, 1556) by Vincenzo Cartari, is the immanence of Christian humanism in the moral philosophy of the Classical world (Lewis, 1990).

At the end of his life Palladio designed a free-standing private chapel for the villa, the chapel of the Redeemer (built 1580–84), as a scaled-down realization of his unexecuted 'rotunda project' (1576) for the votive church of the Redentore in Venice—an alternative design strongly promoted by Marc'Antonio Barbaro. The chapel at Maser has extensive stucco sculptures (1584–8) by Giannantonio da Salo and Pietro di Benvegnudo (both *fl c.* 1584–1603; Lewis, 1981). The plan and elevation of this Tempietto Barbaro, ultimately inspired by the Pantheon in Rome, may even have contributed a long-standing feature to its great model: Palladio's twin bell-towers above the pedimented portico at Maser seem likely to have inspired the similar 'donkey's ears' added to the Pantheon by Bernini.

Because Palladio acted at Maser in large part as an inspired executant of concepts originated by his two most extraordinary patrons (Huse), the residential complex is hardly an independent demonstration of his own ideas: Marc'Antonio Barbaro, in addition to modelling all the sculptures, undoubtedly supervised the villa's complex engineering (his speciality in the Senate); and Daniele Barbaro certainly invented its immensely sophisticated iconographic programme. Nevertheless, Palladio published the plan and elevation of the villa as his own in his treatise *I quattro libri dell'architettura* of 1570, from which its persuasive five-part configuration had a profound influence on the Palladian revivals of the 18th and 19th centuries, especially in northern Europe and Great Britain. Its miraculous cycle of architectural and figural frescoes by Palladio and Veronese contributed to a revolution in the concept of mural painting and indirectly inspired such milestones of *di sotto in sù* illusionism as Roman Baroque ceiling paintings by Cortona and Andrea Pozzo, as well as the late Baroque masterworks of Giambattista Tiepolo and his many followers.

BIBLIOGRAPHY

G. Vasari: *Vite* (1550, rev. 2/1568); ed. G. Milanesi (1878–85), vii, p. 530

A. Palladio: *I quattro libri dell'architettura* (Venice, 1570, 3/1601/*R* Newcastle upon Tyne, 1971; Eng. trans. by I. Ware, London, 1738/*R* New York, 1965), ii, p. 51

G. D. Scamozzi, ed.: *Tutte l'opere d'architettura di Sebastiano Serlio* (Venice, 1584/*R* Bologna, 1978) [introductory letter by Lodovico Roncone]

B. Berenson and others: *Palladio, Veronese e Vittoria a Maser* (Milan, 1960) [unique monograph; fine illus.]

R. Wittkower: *Architectural Principles in the Age of Humanism* (London, 1962), pp. 135–6 [analysis of harmonic proportions of plan]

U. Basso: *Cronaca di Maser: Delle sue chiese e della villa palladiana dei Barbaro* (Montebelluna, 1968)

K. Oberhuber: 'Hieronymous Cock, Battista Pittoni und Paolo Veronese in Villa Maser', *Munuscula discipulorum: Kunsthistorisches Studien Hans Kauffmann* (Berlin, 1968), pp. 207–24 [discovery of engraved sources for landscape frescoes]

D. Lewis: 'Disegni autografi del Palladio', *Boll. Cent. Int. Stud. Archit. Andrea Palladio*, xv (1973), pp. 369–79

L. Puppi: *Andrea Palladio*, 2 vols (Milan, 1973); Eng. trans. as 1 vol. (New York, 1975, London, 2/1986)

N. Huse: 'Palladio und die Villa Barbaro in Maser', *A. Ven.*, xxviii (1974), pp. 106–22

U. Basso: *La villa e il tempietto dei Barbaro a Maser di Andrea Palladio* (Montebelluna, 1976)

R. Pallucchini and others: *Gli affreschi nelle ville venete dal seicento all'ottocento*, 2 vols (Venice, 1978), i, pl. 183, no. 94; ii, figs 147–51

D. Lewis: 'Il significato della decorazione plastica e pittorica a Maser', *Boll. Cent. Int. Stud. Archit. Andrea Palladio*, xxii (1980), pp. 203–13; repr. and rev. as 'Classical Texts and Mystic Meanings: Daniele Barbaro's Program for the Villa Maser', *Klassizismus, Epoche und Probleme: Festschrift für Erik Forssman*, ed. J. Meyer zur Capellen and G. Oberreuter-Kronabel (Hildesheim, 1987), pp. 289–307

——: *The Drawings of Andrea Palladio* (Washington, DC, 1981), pp. 45–6, 154–8, 192–4

L. Larcher Crosato: 'Considerazioni sul programma iconografico di Maser', *Mitt. Ksthist. Inst. Florenz*, xxvi (1982), pp. 211–56 [excellent general survey]

D. Lewis: 'Palladio's Painted Architecture', *Vierhundert Jahre Andrea Palladio (1580–1980): Colloquium* (Heidelberg, 1982), pp. 59–74 [Palladio's documented drawings for architectural frescoes]

I. J. Reist: 'Divine Love and Veronese's Frescoes at the Villa Barbaro', *A. Bull.*, lxvii (1985), pp. 614–35

D. Lewis: 'The Iconography of Veronese's Frescoes in the Villa Barbaro at Maser', *Nuovi studi su Paolo Veronese*, ed. M. Gemin (Venice, 1990), pp. 317–22

DOUGLAS LEWIS

Masereel, Frans (*b* Blankenberge, 30 July 1889; *d* Avignon, 3 Jan 1972). Belgian printmaker, illustrator, draughtsman and painter. He came from a well-to-do Ghent family and studied briefly at the Académie des Beaux-Arts in Ghent before settling in Paris, where in 1914 he published his first album of woodcuts, a work that gave no indication of his future style. He left for Switzerland in 1914 and was based until the end of World War I in Geneva, where he was associated with the circle of writers around the French novelist Romain Rolland (1866–1944). Throughout World War I he contributed to the Geneva daily newspaper *La Feuille*, supplying it with drawings that provided a critical commentary on the vicissitudes of war, denouncing those responsible and especially high finance. Using a brush and black ink, Masereel emulated the idiosyncratic style of his woodcuts, rejecting traditional hatching and confining himself to contrasts of black and white, with a novel emphasis on the expressive potential of the black areas. While living in Geneva he and his friend the poet René Arcos founded les Editions du Sablier, which published the work of writers with pacifist tendencies, such as Rolland, Charles Vildrac, Georges Duhamel, Pierre-Jean Jouve, Andreas Latzko and Stefan Zweig, in beautiful editions illustrated with woodcuts by Masereel. Masereel also published, with great success internationally, several books that consist solely of woodcuts, such as *Mon Livre d'heures* (167 woodcuts, Geneva, 1919), *Le Soleil* (63 woodcuts, Geneva, 1919), *Histoire sans paroles* (60 woodcuts, Geneva, 1920) and *Idée: Sa Naissance, sa vie, sa mort* (83 woodcuts, Paris, 1920).

Masereel remained particularly devoted to this form of illustrated book and continued producing such works with little stylistic variation, often composing the images around a central figure as pivot and demonstrating a rebellious spirit sometimes verging on satire. His initial concern with the horrors and misery of war later gave way to an exposure of the defects of capitalist society. A Communist sympathizer, he visited the USSR and China but never formally joined the Party. In addition to these politically inspired works, he produced others that reveal a real zest for life, sometimes tinged with irony, and occasionally even tenderness, as in *Souvenirs de mon pays* (Geneva, 1921). He also worked in a similar style in large woodcuts that were perhaps even more striking by virtue of their size. Masereel's woodcuts were highly influential on Belgian printmakers, especially on Henri Van Straten (1892–1944), Joris Minne (1897–1988), Jozef Cantré and Jan Cantré (1886–1931), in spite of the fact that he was unable to return there for many years since he had to do his military service. Together they were sometimes referred to as De Vijf in recognition of their role as a group in reviving the Flemish tradition of the woodcut, in spite of the apparent differences in their work.

Although Masereel is known mainly for his prints, he also worked in other media. As a painter he first depicted sailors and solidly built young women (e.g. *Seated Woman*, 1930; Paris, Pompidou) without achieving the powerful expressiveness of the Belgian painters of the same period who came to be referred to as the Flemish Expressionists. Later on he became interested mainly in landscape, without giving it any distinctive imprint of his own. He remained committed, however, to ink drawing and to watercolour, giving his usual subject-matter a more optimistic note by his occasional inclusion of Rubensian nudes. He also worked sporadically as a stage designer and potter. After World War II he settled in Nice.

BIBLIOGRAPHY

Frans Masereel: Malerei und Graphik, 1917–1957 (exh. cat., ed. G. Pommeranz-Liedtke; W. Berlin, Akad. Kst., 1957)

Frans Masereel und das Buch, intro. T. Pinkus (Berlin and Leipzig, 1961)

Frans Masereel (exh. cat., Pau, Mus. B.-A., 1966)

R. Avermaete: *Frans Masereel* (Antwerp and Paris, 1975; Eng. trans., London, 1977)

ROGER AVERMAETE

Masey, Francis (Edward) (*b* London, 18 Nov 1861; *d* Salisbury, Rhodesia [now Harare, Zimbabwe], 3 Sept 1912). English architect active in South Africa and Rhodesia. He was apprenticed to his father, the architect Philip Masey, in London for two years before entering the office of Alfred Waterhouse (1878). In 1887 he became a student in the Royal Academy Schools, London, and he won several prizes that enabled him to visit France (1889) and Italy (1891). In 1896 he went to Cape Town on a three-year contract with the Public Works Department, but soon after his arrival he met HERBERT BAKER, broke his contract and entered practice with him; the partnership of Baker & Masey was formed in 1899. Their first success was winning the competition for the City Club (1896–7), Cape Town, built to a classical design with Baroque gables and domes. Masey's studies in Italy were a major influence on the use of the Italianate style frequently adopted by the practice, particularly before Baker's visit to see Classical sites in Europe in 1900 at the expense of Cecil Rhodes. Masey also worked on the Italian Romanesque designs for St Philip's (1898), Cape Town, and the Memorial Church of St John the Evangelist (1901–2), Mafeking. In 1902 Baker went to Johannesburg and Masey took sole responsibility for the partnership's buildings in Cape Town, including the Renaissance-inspired Rhodes Building (1900–8) for De Beer's, with an internal courtyard and

Flemish gables on the façade, and Marks Building (1903–5) with rusticated stonework at ground-floor level, as well as the simple, gabled St George's Grammar School (1904), part of the scheme for Baker's St George's Cathedral (1897–1957). Masey was also involved in the design of Baker's classical monuments: the Shangani Memorial (1898), the Kimberley Siege Memorial (1904) and the Rhodes Memorial (1905–8), Table Mountain, Cape Town. In 1910 Masey left his partnership with Baker and settled in Salisbury; he is credited with the introduction of the Italianate courtyard building into Rhodesia with designs such as the Salisbury Club (1912). His work, obscured by Baker's reputation, made a significant contribution to the colonial architecture of southern Africa. He was a founder-member of the Cape Institute of Architects (1901) and its first president; he was also a respected teacher.

WRITINGS
Regular contributions to *The State* (1909–10)
'Rhodesian Buildings and the Central Court', *Archit. Rev.* [London], xxxi/186 (1912), pp. 266–9

BIBLIOGRAPHY
Obituary, *RIBA J.*, xix/20 (1912), pp. 750–51
D. E. Grieg: *Herbert Baker in South Africa* (Cape Town, 1970)

C. J. M. WALKER

Mashhad [Meshed]. City in north-east Iran. The city grew around the tombs of the Abbasid caliph Harun al-Rashid (*reg* AD 786–809) and, more importantly, the eighth Shi'ite imam, 'Ali ibn Musa al-Riza, believed to have been poisoned in 818 and buried near the caliph's head. Imam Riza's tomb was not only responsible for the name of the town (Arab. *mashhad*: 'place of martyrdom') but also its transformation into one of the most venerated Shi'ite centres. The mausoleum was expanded as early as the 11th century, when Ghaznavid rulers rebuilt the tomb and constructed a wall around the settlement. Three impressive mihrabs of glazed ceramic with lustre decoration were added to the tomb chamber, two in 1215 and a third in 1242. Along with dados of star-and-cross tiles, these constitute one of the finest ensembles of ceramic decoration from medieval Iran (*see* ISLAMIC ART, §II, 9(ii)(b)). The city grew in importance following the Mongol invasions of Khurasan in the early 13th century and the decline of the nearby cities of Tus and Nishapur.

Under the Timurid dynasty major new buildings were added to the holy precinct (Arab. *haram al-sharīf*; *see* ISLAMIC ART, §II, 6(i) and SHRINE, colour pl. IV, fig. 1). One of the most significant was the Friday Mosque (1416–18) commissioned by Gawharshad, wife of Shahrukh, from the architect Qavam al-Din Shirazi. The structure, with four iwans arranged around an open court (26×31 m), is notable for its superb decoration in tile mosaic. The deep sanctuary iwan on the south-west side of the court is flanked by cylindrical minarets. From a shallow iwan on the north-east side opens the *dar al-siyāda*, a building for descendants of the Prophet linking the mosque to the inner sanctuary, and the *dar al-huffāz*, a square chamber for recitation of the Koran, also commissioned by Gawharshad. Other notable Timurid constructions include two madrasas, the Bala-yi sar ('Above the head'; 1426) and Du-dar (1439), and the iwan (1467) added by 'Alishir

Nava'i to the Old Court, itself to the north-east of the mosque.

Members of the Safavid dynasty lavished much attention on Mashhad. The main addition to the shrine in the 16th century was the gilded minaret added by Tahmasp on the north-east side of the Old Court. The Safavid policy of transforming the city, like Qum, into a major pilgrimage centre for Shi'ites became more urgent during the reign of 'Abbas I (*see* SAFAVID, (2)), when the Ottomans gained control of Karbala and Najaf, the major Shi'ite shrines in Iraq. In 1601 Shah 'Abbas undertook the restoration and expansion of the shrine complex. He built an esplanade (1603) through the Old Court and had the dome of the mausoleum redecorated (1606). Near the southern corner of the Old Court, the commander-in-chief of his army, Allahverdi Khan, commissioned a dome chamber (1612), which is notable for its fine tile revetment. The blind iwan (1659) erected by 'Abbas II on the north-east side of the same court is equally impressive for its decoration.

Embellishment of the shrine precinct has continued. The Afsharid ruler Nadir Shah (*reg* 1736–47) had the minaret in the Old Court regilded and the iwan of 'Alishir tiled with gold. The Qajar ruler Fath 'Ali Shah (*reg* 1797–1834) began construction of a New Court on the south-east side of the sanctuary; it included a gold iwan. The shrine complex also includes numerous other dependencies such as caravanserais, public kitchens, madrasas and a five-storey library–museum (1977), which displays some of the impressive collection of Islamic manuscripts, printed books and works of Islamic art belonging to the shrine. Mashhad was also a centre of book production under the Timurids and Safavids (*see* ISLAMIC ART, §III, 4(vi)(a)).

BIBLIOGRAPHY
Enc. Iran: 'Āstān-e Qods-e Rażawī [Complex of buildings around the shrine of Imam 'Ali al-Riza]; *Enc. Islam*
Muhammad Hasan Khān Sani' al-Dawla: *Matla' al-shams*, 3 vols (Tehran, 1883–5/*R* Iran. Solar 2535/1976) [vol. 2 devoted to history and top. of Mashhad]
D. M. Donaldson: 'Significant Mihrābs in the Haram at Mashhad', *A. Islam.*, ii (1935), pp. 118–27
A. U. Pope and P. Ackerman, eds: *Survey of Persian Art* (2/1964–7), pp. 1201–11
B. Saadat: *The Holy Shrine of Imam Reza, Mashhad*, 4 vols (Shiraz, 1976) [Pers. and Eng. text]

MASSUMEH FARHAD

Mashkov, Il'ya (Ivanovich) (*b* Mikhaylovskaya-on-Don, 29 July 1881; *d* Moscow, 20 March 1944). Russian painter. He studied at the Moscow School of Painting, Sculpture and Architecture (1900–10) under Valentin Serov and Konstantin Korovin. In 1909–10 he exhibited with the Third Golden Fleece and in 1910 was a founder-member of the avant-garde exhibiting society the Jack of Diamonds, of which he remained a leader until 1915. In these early years his still-lifes, landscapes and portraits were particularly influenced by Fauvism. Characteristic is the magnificent portrait of *Mme Kirkal'da* (1910; Moscow, Tret'yakov Gal.), which demonstrates a witty sense of humour and a love of bold colouring and crude figure drawing. A series of still-lifes, including *Loaves of Bread* (1912; St Petersburg, Rus. Mus.), was inspired by Russian folk art. In 1914 Mashkov moved away from these influences; paintings such as *Still-life with Horse's Skull* (St Petersburg, Rus.

Mus.) reveal lighter brushwork, a restrained palette and new sensitivity to the different material qualities of objects.

Following the Revolution of 1917, Mashkov became a professor at Svomas (Free Art Studios). He exhibited at the third series of World of Art (Mir iskusstva) exhibitions in 1922 in Petrograd (now St Petersburg) and those of the Society of Moscow Artists (1927–8). In 1924 he joined the Association of Artists of Revolutionary Russia (AKhRR) and during the mid- to late 1920s his creative output and teaching echoed the realist tendencies espoused by this group. *Moscow Meal: Meat, Game* (1924; Moscow, Tret'yakov Gal.) is a masterpiece of realism.

BIBLIOGRAPHY
V. Perel'man: *Il'ya Mashkov* (Moscow, 1957)
G. Arbuzov and V. Pushkarov: *Il'ya Mashkov* (Moscow, 1973)
I. S. Bolotina: *I. I. Mashkov: Khudozhestvennoye naslediye* [I. I. Mashkov: artistic heritage] (Moscow, 1977)

ANTHONY PARTON

Mašić, Nikola (*b* Otočac, 28 Nov 1852; *d* Zagreb, 4 June 1902). Croatian painter. He began studying art in 1872 at the Vienna Akademie der Bildenden Künste, continuing in Munich in the same year, first in the drawing class of Alexander Wagner (1826–94) and then in the painting classes of Anton Seitz (1829–1900) and Wilhelm von Lindenschmidt (1829–95). In 1878 he studied in Paris, at the Académie Julian and with William Bouguereau. For the next two years he travelled through Croatia, executing his most successful paintings: small studies of riverbanks, pasture-lands and clouds, with human and animal figures on the distant horizon (examples Zagreb, Gal. Mod. A.). He also painted the peasants of Lika and Posavina, their houses, barns and yards with geese and turkeys, their gardens with pumpkins and sunflowers (examples Zagreb, Gal. Mod. A.). These paintings represent the beginning of *pleinairisme* in Croatia. While in Capri (1880) he painted landscapes full of light and vigour and in Munich (1880–83) he executed some of his most representative work, for example *Gooseherd on the Sava River* (1880–81) and *Summer's Idyll* (1883; both Zagreb, Gal. Mod. A.). In these paintings Mašić realized the potential of both studio and *plein-air* approaches but failed to surpass the limitations of the anecdotal realism characteristic of the European painting of his time. In 1884 he returned to Zagreb, where he taught drawing at the newly opened School for Arts and Crafts. From 1894 until his death he was the director of the Strossmayer Gallery of Old Masters.

BIBLIOGRAPHY
M. Peić: *Nikola Mašić* (exh. cat., Belgrade, Serb. Acad. Sci. & A., 1975)

ZDENKO RUS

Masip. *See* MAÇIP.

Masjid-i Solaiman. *See* ELYMAIS, §2.

Maskana [Mesken; Meskene; Miskina]. Small town in north Syria on the south bank of the River Euphrates near an ancient site known in antiquity as Emar, in Byzantine times as Barbalissos and in Islamic times as Balis. It lay on an ancient trade route between the Mediterranean, Anatolia and Mesopotamia. The site was excavated in 1929 and again between 1971 and 1976 during salvage operations accompanying the building of the Tabqa Dam. The minaret was dismantled and rebuilt on higher ground, but the ancient site and Maskana itself have been flooded by Lake Assad. Finds are in the National Museum, Aleppo, and the Musée du Louvre, Paris; objects looted from the site are in numerous private collections.

1. EMAR. This Bronze Age city flourished during the 3rd and 2nd millennia BC as a staging-post on a major trade route, where not only goods but also ideas and influences were exchanged. The city is mentioned in the Ebla texts of the second half of the 3rd millennium BC, and the Mari correspondence and late Nuzi texts confirm its importance in the 2nd millennium BC; the excavators found neither the Early nor the Middle Bronze Age levels, however.

Under the Hittite king Suppiluliuma I, who dominated north Syria in the middle of the 14th century BC, Emar was transferred to the edge of the plateau, and a new city was built on a specially prepared and terraced site. At the same time a huge defensive ditch, 500 m long, 50 m wide and 20 m deep, was cut into the rock to the west of the site. At the highest point, to the south-west, a religious complex was built, consisting of two temples *in antis* on either side of a street leading to a sacred enclosure behind the temples. The king's palace was built at the second highest point, dominating the River Euphrates from the north-west. The city was surrounded by a wall, and a citadel was built on a rock outcrop some 12 km downstream at Tell Faq'ous. The city was destroyed *c.* 1200 BC, probably by the Sea Peoples (*see* SYRIA-PALESTINE, §I, 2(iv)(c)).

Numerous tablets were found during the excavations, inscribed in the cuneiform script of Mesopotamia and bearing the impressions of some 240 stamp and cylinder seals (*see* ANCIENT NEAR EAST, §II, 1(i)(b) and (ii)). The seal designs illustrate the many composite influences within the city—Hittite, Mesopotamian and local Syrian—which are also to be seen in other artistic fields. The four temples excavated at Emar resemble the Syrian version of the megaron, later found in Greek temple architecture. The palace was an early example of the *bit hilani*, with a broad reception-room, columned portico and staircase, which was later favoured in the Neo-Hittite and Aramaic kingdoms of the early 1st millennium BC. Private houses probably resembled the numerous house models that have been found (see fig.), with an upper storey opening on to a flat roof. Similar houses had been characteristic of the area for several centuries and have also been found in Cappadocia (central Anatolia) and along the Levantine coast; other house models resemble towers. Numerous clay figurines were found, mostly female, some male and some animal. There are also fragments of clay masks and a fine caprid horn (Aleppo, N. Mus.) carved in several registers with processions of animals, and ritual and hunting scenes. Glass and faience objects and jewellery found in the temples bear witness to the city's wealth.

BIBLIOGRAPHY
D. Beyer, ed.: *A l'occasion d'une exposition, Meskéné-Emar: Dix Ans de travaux, 1972–1982*, Editions Recherche sur les Civilisations (Paris, 1982)

J.-C. MARGUERON

Emar (Maskana), architectural model of a house, terracotta, 440×600 mm, 13th century BC (Paris, Musée du Louvre)

2. BALIS [Bālis]. Until it was conquered by the Muslim Arabs in the 7th century AD, the site was a frontier town between Sasanian Iran and the Byzantine empire. Pillaged several times by the Persians, it was rebuilt by Justinian (*reg* AD 527–65). Under the Muslims it regained its strategic importance as a major stage on the route from Antioch to Iraq, and it remained prosperous until Balis was destroyed by the Mongols in the 13th century. Near the impressive brick fortifications and praetorium attributed to the re-building by Justinian and the brick minaret of the congregational mosque (1210) were found pottery, coins and stucco decoration dating from the 1070s. This stucco decoration, a simple architectonic arcade with foliated kufic inscriptions and crisp vegetal scrolls, belonged to a Shi'ite shrine (Arab. *mashhad*). The minaret, erected in 1210–11 in the name of the Ayyubid ruler al-Malik al-'Adil Abu Bakr, has a rectangular base supporting an octagonal shaft (h. 27 m). It is decorated with four ornamental inscriptions in simple relief brickwork and elaborately carved ceramic plaques, using both cursive and elaborately foliated angular scripts. The minaret is a western example of the brick architecture typical of Mesopotamia under the Abbasids (*see* ISLAMIC ART, §II, 5(ii)(e)).

BIBLIOGRAPHY

Enc. Islam/2: 'Bālis'
F. Sarre and E. Herzfeld: *Archäologische Reise im Euphrat- und Tigrisgebiet*, 4 vols (Berlin, 1911–20), i, pp. 2–3, 114, 123–9
G. Salles: 'Les Décors en stuc de Balis', *Mémoires du IIIe Congrès international d'art et d'archéologie iraniens: Leningrad, 1935*, pp. 221–6
D. Sourdel and J. Sourdel-Thomine: 'Notes d'épigraphie et de topographie', *An. Archéol. Syrie*, iii (1953), pp. 103–5
——: 'Un Sanctuaire chiite de l'ancienne Balis', *Mélanges d'islamologie dédié à la mémoire de Armand Abel*, ed. P. Salmon (Leiden, 1974), pp. 247–53
G. Hennequin and M. A. al-'Ush: *Les Monnaies de Bālis* (Damascus, 1978)

□

Maskhuta, Tell el- [Gr. Heroöpolis]. Egyptian site in the Wadi Tumilat, 110 km north-east of Cairo. In 1883 Edouard Naville excavated a devastated temple with a square enclosure (210×210 m) and extensive storerooms, which he assigned to the 19th Dynasty (*c.* 1292–*c.* 1190 BC). Naville and Alan Gardiner identified the site with biblical cities on the route of the Exodus, particularly Succoth and Pithom (Exodus 1:11 and 12:37). This was accepted by scholars until the University of Toronto excavation of the 1970s, which yielded finds proving the city to date to the 3rd–2nd century BC, a millennium later than Naville had believed. Settlement at Tell el-Maskhuta in the 7th century BC was connected with the first canal constructed through the Delta to export Indian products to Mediterranean markets via the Red Sea. High-quality artefacts, such as an Attic Black-figure kylix with incised palmette decoration, Syrian glass unguentaria and a faience inkwell shaped like a double cartouche, demonstrate its mercantile importance. Wealthy grave goods included jewellery and frit amulets (all Isma'ilia Mus.). Under the Ptolemaic dynasty (304–30 BC), Tell el-Maskhuta continued as a trading centre, and in the Roman period Emperor Trajan rebuilt the canal. A text on an ostracon from an Antonine period (AD 138–92) burial in the necropolis has the earliest known occurrence of the chi-rho monogram for Christ's name. The site seems to have been abandoned in the mid-2nd century AD.

BIBLIOGRAPHY

LÄ: 'Tell el-Maschuta'

E. Naville: *The Store-city of Pithom and the Route of the Exodus* (London, 1885, 4/1903)

J. S. Holladay jr: *Tell el-Maskhuta: Preliminary Report on the Wadi Tumilat Project, 1978–9* (1982), iii of *Cities of the Delta* (Malibu, CA, 1980–)

DOMINIC MONTSERRAT

Masó, Luis Bonifás y. *See* BONIFÁS Y MASÓ, LUIS.

Maso di Banco (*fl* 1335–50). Italian painter. He was first identified (as Maso) by Ghiberti, who claimed he was a pupil of Giotto and a great master of painting, but the issue was complicated for many centuries by Vasari, who confused Maso with an artist he called Tommaso di Stefano, nicknamed GIOTTINO. Maso di Banco is mentioned in several Florentine documents: in 1341 some of his paintings and equipment were seized against an uncompleted commission; in 1346 he joined the Arte de' Medici e Speziali. Although none of the output attributed to him is signed or dated, a major fresco cycle, other more fragmentary frescoes and some panels of the 1330s and 1340s can be firmly attributed to him on stylistic grounds.

Maso's most important surviving frescoes are in the Bardi di Vernio Chapel in Santa Croce, Florence, built in 1310 by a branch of the powerful banking family. Work by Maso and his shop was under way by 1335, for the frescoes incorporate the Bardi arms as they were before being modified in that year. The niche housing the great Gothic marble tomb shows Maso's interest in the relationship between architecture and painting; the fresco shows the figure of an unidentified member of the Bardi family, as if rising directly from the actual tomb in which he is buried, and kneeling in a rocky landscape. Above is *Christ in Majesty* surrounded by angels in the manner of a Last Judgement. The programme stresses the growing importance of the laity, whose tombs were normally placed outside a church, and who had not previously been depicted as participants in a Christological scheme. Maso painted the rest of the chapel with scenes from the *Life of St Sylvester*, the 4th-century pope who converted Emperor Constantine to Christianity. The cycle includes *Constantine and the Magicians*, the *Dream of Constantine*, the *Baptism of Constantine by St Sylvester*, *St Sylvester Resurrecting an Ox* and *St Sylvester with the Dragon* (see fig.). The paintings are characterized by Maso's use of simultaneous narrative, and by his distinctive articulation of space through the oblique setting of buildings in relation to the picture plane and the use of vertical foreshortening. The architecture is also used to assist the narrative, by focusing attention on the main characters. Maso's powers of observation are shown by the meticulous depiction of the Roman Forum in the ruined state in which he must have seen it. Grave and dignified figures gesticulate in the foreground. They have unusually long fingers and characteristic facial features, with full-lipped mouths, rather large ears and narrow eyes with a horizontal upper lid.

Maso used contrasts between light and dark tones to emphasize the design, and, despite recent restoration, the original colour scheme, which includes pink, grey, red and

Maso di Banco: *St Sylvester with the Dragon* (?1330s), fresco, Bardi di Vernio Chapel, Santa Croce, Florence

white, is clear and echoes the palette of Giotto's later period. The stained-glass windows in the chapel have sometimes been attributed to Maso, but they were probably painted by Taddeo Gaddi, another of the Giottesque artists working in the church.

The remains of another fresco by Maso (Florence, Mus. Opera Santa Croce) show the *Coronation of the Virgin with Saints, Angels and Donors*. It was painted above a portal in the right aisle, and its shape reflects the form of the lunette; the spandrels are filled with floral patterns. Maso may have worked as an assistant to Giotto at the Castelnuovo, Naples; details in some of the fragmentary frescoes there recall the *St Sylvester* paintings. Certain frescoes in Assisi, at S Chiara and at S Francesco (both in the church and in the Sala del Capitolo), have also been attributed to Maso, but the identification of the various Giottesque hands there is not clear. It is possible that the scheme of the St Stanislas Chapel in the Lower Church was originally planned by Giotto, and that Maso painted one of the frescoes there, the *Crucifixion with the Virgin and St John*. His panel paintings include a pentaptych (ex-Altes Mus., Berlin) of which only a lateral panel with *St Anthony of Padua* (New York, Met.) survives. In a closely related style is a polyptych in Santo Spirito, Florence, showing the *Virgin and Child with SS Mary Magdalene, Catherine, Andrew and Julian*. Despite the conventional elaborate Gothic frames and gold background, the figures have a sense of weight and even three-dimensionality. The Virgin is shown half-length, in a frontal pose well suited to the tall and narrow central panel. She tenderly grasps the Child, who in turn is holding a goldfinch, symbolizing the Crucifixion. Despite the difference of medium, these panels relate closely to the Bardi frescoes.

Maso was the most successful continuator of Giotto's style, able to convey both the volume of the figures and their individual expression. His work is less dramatic than Giotto's, and has a more austere and restrained quality. It also displays a much greater preoccupation with the depiction of architecture. Maso was able to create the illusion of deep space that engaged the spectator, while his use of subtle colour tones to create pattern also contributed to the overall clarity of design. He was aware of the work of contemporary Sienese painters, and his output reflects the elegant line of Simone Martini's paintings and the ambitious scale of works by Pietro and Ambrogio Lorenzetti. Of his contemporaries, Taddeo Gaddi was the most influenced by his style. Maso had no immediate followers, since there was a general reaction against the sort of expressiveness for which he and Giotto had been striving, perhaps a result of the political and social changes of the 1340s. There was a deliberate revival of some of his motifs and forms at the end of the 14th century, but his real heirs were Masaccio and, particularly, Piero della Francesca, whose clear designs and emphasis on the structuring role of architecture seem to suggest a direct knowledge of Maso's work.

BIBLIOGRAPHY

R. Offner: 'Four Panels, a Fresco and a Problem', *Burl. Mag.*, liv (1929), pp. 224–45
P. Toesca: *Gli affreschi della Cappella di San Silvestro in Santa Croce a Firenze* (Florence, 1944)
M. Meiss: *Painting in Florence and Siena after the Black Death* (Princeton, 1951)
E. Borsook: *The Mural Painters of Tuscany* (London, 1960)
B. Berenson: *Florentine School* (1963)
M. A. Bianchini: *Maso di Banco*, Maestri del Colore (Milan, 1968)
D. Wilkins: 'Maso di Banco and Cenni di Francesco: A Case of Late Trecento Revival', *Burl. Mag.*, cxi (1969), pp. 83–4
A. Smart: *The Assisi Problem and the Art of Giotto* (Oxford, 1971)
B. Cole: *Giotto and Florentine Painting, 1280–1375* (New York, 1975)
R. Fremantle: *Florentine Gothic Painters from Giotto to Masaccio* (London, 1975)

CAROLA HICKS

Maso [Tommaso; Masaccio] **di Bartolommeo** (*b* Capannole, nr Valdambra, Arezzo, 1406; *d c.* 1456). Italian sculptor. He is first recorded working with Donatello and Michelozzo between 1434 and 1438 on the installation and decorative relief-carving of the external pulpit of Prato Cathedral. From 1438 to 1442 he executed part of the bronze grille of the Cappella del Sacro Cingolo in the cathedral, until a dispute halted his work. It is gothicizing in style, with a pattern of delicate rosettes and elegantly twisted stems of naturalistic plant forms interspersed with animals and putti. In 1447 Maso made a gilded bronze reliquary inlaid with bone and tortoiseshell for the same chapel. It is decorated with a frieze of leaden putti dancing clumsily behind a colonnade and is ultimately derived from Donatello's *Cantoria* made for Florence Cathedral (Florence, Mus. Opera Duomo).

Two account-books, which Maso kept between 1447 and 1452, record many of his smaller decorative commissions from important Florentine patrons. For Piero de' Medici he made a pair of candlesticks and two gilded bronze eagles for the Cappella del Crocefisso in S Miniato al Monte and the bronze railings (1447) around the miraculous *Annunciation* in SS Annunziata. For Cosimo de' Medici he designed the frieze (1452) for the courtyard of the Palazzo Medici in Florence; and for the Arte del Cambio a stone tabernacle. Maso worked on a wide variety of projects and employed many assistants. The portal of S Domenico in Urbino, which he designed in 1449 and whose light architectural forms encrusted with elaborate surface decoration show the influence of Michelozzo, appears to have been entirely executed by assistants, while the reliefs in the lunette and pediment were commissioned from Luca della Robbia. Other commissions included the provision and repair of armaments for Federigo da Montefeltro II and the Republic of Florence.

In 1446 Maso received a joint commission with Luca della Robbia and Michelozzo for the bronze doors of the New Sacristy in Florence Cathedral. Work was suspended after Maso's death until his brother Giovanni took over his part in 1461.

BIBLIOGRAPHY

G. Vasari: *Vite* (1550, rev. 2/1568), ed. G. Milanesi (1878–85), ii, p. 172, n. 1, p. 291, n. 2
C. E. Yriarte: *Le Livre de souvenirs de Maso di Bartolommeo* (Paris, 1894)
G. Marchini: 'Di Maso di Bartolommeo ed altri', *Commentari*, iii (1952), pp. 108–27
——: 'Maso di Bartolommeo', *Donatello e il suo tempo: Atti dell' VIII convegno internazionale di studi sul rinascimento: Firenze, 1966*

ROSIE-ANNE PINNEY

Masó i Valentí, Rafael (*b* Girona, 16 Aug 1880; *d* Girona, 13 July 1935). Spanish Catalan architect. As a poet with connections with literary circles, he was soon in touch with promoters of NOUCENTISME. Early in his career, when he was searching for his own architectural language, he introduced references to European styles in such buildings as the Farmacia Masó (1908) and the Farinera Teixidor (1911), both in Girona. In his second, more original period (1912–22), he became a complete *noucentista*, creating buildings characterized by a greater sense of architectural use of innovative elements, with an expressiveness achieved by using ceramic material. Outstanding examples include the Athenea building, Girona (1913), the Casa Masramón (1914), Olot, the Casa Cendra (1915), Anglés; the Casa Casas (1916), Playa de Sant Pol; and the Casa Teixidor (1918), Girona. His last period reflected a greater classical influence, with the introduction of traditional elements and a loss of his earlier originality, as can be seen in the housing estates of Teixidor (1928), Girona, and S'Agaró (1929), S Feliu de Guixols.

BIBLIOGRAPHY

Almanac dels Noucentistes (Barcelona, 1911)

J. Tarrús: *Rafael Masó* (Barcelona, 1971)

JORDI OLIVERAS

Masolino (da Panicale) [Tommaso di Cristofano Fini] (*b* Panicale, Umbria, 1383; *d* after 1435). Italian painter. He is one of the pivotal figures of Florentine painting. Not only does his career span the two decades during which the basis of Renaissance painting was forged, but for a time he collaborated with its protagonist, MASACCIO, most notably in a cycle of frescoes in the Brancacci Chapel in S Maria del Carmine, Florence, a landmark in the history of European art. Paradoxically, his collaboration with Masaccio has obscured his own achievement. Vasari originated the idea that Masolino was the teacher of Masaccio, and he also attributed a number of Masolino's works to an early phase of Masaccio's. Not until the 20th century was the work of the two artists convincingly distinguished. Masolino's most extensive independent fresco cycle in the Lombard town of Castiglione Olona (a work unknown to Vasari) was recovered in 1843, and a century later the fresco fragments and the *sinopie* of another, documented cycle were discovered in the church of S Stefano, Empoli. These have thrown further light on a career that remains enigmatic and subject to a variety of interpretations.

1. Training and early career, to *c*. 1424. 2. The Brancacci Chapel frescoes and collaboration with Masaccio, *c*. 1424–5. 3. Last years, *c*. 1426 and after.

1. TRAINING AND EARLY CAREER, TO *c*. 1424. His birth date is based on the date given in the 1427 *catasto* (land registry declaration) of his father. (Whether he was born in Panicale di Val d'Elsa, as stated by Vasari, or a suburb of San Giovanni Val d'Arno, the birthplace of Masaccio, has not, however, been established.) He must therefore have been about 39 when he was first recorded as a painter on 7 September 1422; *c*. four months later he matriculated in the Florentine painters' guild, the Arte de' Medici e Speziali, on 18 January 1423, the year of his earliest certain work, the *Madonna of Humility* (Bremen, Ksthalle). Masolino's training and earlier career are largely conjectural: according to Vasari, he was a pupil of Lorenzo Ghiberti, 'and in his youth a very good goldsmith, and the best assistant Lorenzo had in the work on the [Baptistery] doors ... He devoted himself to painting at the age of 19

... learning colouring from Gherardo Starnina'. Both points remain hypothetical. Payments were made to a 'Maso di Cristofano' for work on Ghiberti's first set of bronze doors for the Baptistery in Florence from 1404 until some time after 1407; whether this was Masolino has been disputed. Starnina returned to Florence from Spain between 1401 and 1404 and was one of the most prominent artists in the city until his death *c*. 1413. Masolino could thus well have been employed by Ghiberti before an apprenticeship with Starnina, which might explain the absence of independent works before 1423. (It has also been suggested that the information in the *catasto* is erroneous and that Masolino was born *c*. 1400; there is, however, no cogent reason for this.) In any case, Ghiberti's sculpture was a source of inspiration for Masolino throughout his career, and there are undeniable affinities between Masolino's earliest paintings and those of Starnina. In the *Madonna of Humility*, for example, the pose of the child and the relationship of his face to that of the Virgin seem to derive from a Ghibertian prototype, possibly a half-length terracotta *Virgin and Child* in which the child stood on a plinth rather than straddled his mother's knee and left hand. The splayed drapery folds of the Virgin's cloak, on the other hand, are not unlike those favoured by Starnina.

An equally important place in Masolino's artistic formation must be accorded to Gentile da Fabriano. Gentile is now known to have been living in Florence by October 1420 and may have been active there as early as late September 1419, two to three years before Masolino joined the painters' guild. The refinement of Gentile's figure types, with their delicately modelled features and naturalistically rendered details are the pre-condition to Masolino's *Madonna of Humility*, which can be compared with Gentile's *Virgin and Child* (*c*. 1420; Washington, DC, N.G.A.). Indeed, Gentile's influence was the determining factor in Masolino's art, far outlasting that of Masaccio. (Earlier comparisons of Masolino's work with Lombard painting are irrelevant in the light of what is now known of Gentile's early activity in Florence.)

Masolino's most significant commission before the Brancacci Chapel fresco cycle was for the decoration of a side chapel in S Stefano, Empoli, belonging to the Compagnia della Croce, for which he was paid 74 florins on 2 November 1424. This is a small chapel, the tall, narrow lateral walls of which are divided into four horizontal fields with the *Story of the True Cross* depicted on the upper three zones and, apparently, portraits of the donors viewed through an arcade on the bottom zones. Of the narrative scenes, only the *sinopie* survive. Considering the available space and the fact that two episodes are shown in some of the individual picture fields, the narrative clarity is remarkable. This is due, above all, to the fact that the compositions were conceived in terms of figural action. Buildings and the suggestion of a spatial setting were peripheral to the creation of simple figure groups invariably placed close to the picture plane. There is no hint in these scenes of the use of a coherent perspective system such as Masolino consistently employed in his subsequent work. Rather, the compositions recall the work of Starnina: the *Beheading of Chosroes* should be compared with Starnina's fresco of the *Resurrection of Lazarus* (Florence, Mus.

Opera Santa Croce), and the scene of *Chosroes Enthroned* with Starnina's *Death of St Jerome*, recorded in an engraving in Séroux d'Agincourt's *L'Histoire de l'art*.

One of the few frescoed portions in the chapel still intact is a recess with, on its back wall, a still-life of liturgical books and two flasks of wine and water on shelves. Again, there is no hint of perspectival logic, although Masolino's depiction of cast shadows—such as appear in Gentile da Fabriano's *Adoration of the Magi* (1423; Florence, Uffizi)—reveals a precocious interest in naturalistic effects. The remains of two other frescoes in the same church, one of the *Virgin and Child with Two Angels* in a lunette over the sacristy door and the other of a saint flanked by young girls, are both contained in highly effective Gothic architectural surrounds for which Starnina's surviving frescoes in the Carmine, Florence, again offer a precedent.

Perhaps the most impressive early work by Masolino is the detached fresco of the *Pietà* painted for the baptistery of the Collegiata in Empoli (Empoli, Mus. S Andrea; see fig. 1), in which the assertive form of the sarcophagus introduces a jarringly realistic note into an otherwise hieratic and planar composition. Masolino's source was, again, a Late Gothic work: Lorenzo Monaco's *Pietà* (1404; Florence, Accad.).

2. THE BRANCACCI CHAPEL FRESCOES AND COL-LABORATION WITH MASACCIO, *c.* 1424–5. Whether Masolino had established contact with Masaccio by 1424 is not known. The Empoli frescoes suggest he had not. (Longhi, 1940, argued the contrary case with regard to the *Pietà* at Empoli; *see also* MASACCIO, §I, 1(iii).) Collaboration with Masaccio seems to have begun with the fresco cycle in the Brancacci Chapel. The frescoes, carried out by Masolino and Masaccio in the 1420s and completed by Filippino Lippi *c.* 1481–5, mark a watershed in the history of European art. Originally there were figures of the *Four Evangelists* (destr.) in the vault (attributed by Vasari to Masolino), scenes of the *Temptation of Adam and Eve* and the *Expulsion from Paradise* (by Masolino and Masaccio respectively) on the lateral walls of the entrance and 17 episodes from the *Life of St Peter* (by Masolino and Masaccio, later added to by Filippino Lippi) in 12 separate picture fields on the lateral and back walls (the back wall is divided by a biforate Gothic window). Individual fields are separated by Corinthian pilasters and a dentilled moulding, a complete novelty at this date. Construction of a new vault and window in 1746–8 destroyed the four uppermost scenes in the lunettes and the figures of the *Evangelists* in the vault. The frescoes were further altered by repeated restorations and the effects of a fire that swept the church in 1771. A full restoration was undertaken in 1982–8. In addition to revealing an unsuspected brilliance of colour in the surviving portions, the restoration campaign recovered *sinopie* for two of the destroyed scenes on the altar wall, the decorations of the window embrasure, and, below the window, fragments of a scene that is not mentioned in any of the early descriptions of the chapel (its identification remains speculative). These discoveries and the clarification of styles resulting from the cleaning bear directly on the conjectures regarding the commission

1. Masolino: *Pietà*, detached fresco, 2.8×1.2 m, from the baptistery of the Collegiata, Empoli, *c.* 1424 (Empoli, Museo della Collegiata di Sant'Andrea)

of the cycle, the attribution of the individual scenes and on the iconographic programme.

That the prominent Florentine citizen FELICE BRAN-CACCI was probably the patron of the chapel is suggested by his two wills, the first dated 26 June 1422 and the second 5 September 1432. There is, however, no known document related to the commission, which is not likely to have been arranged before Brancacci's return from an embassy to Egypt in February 1423. Masaccio would have been available at any time after that, but Masolino can hardly have begun work before completion of the frescoes in Empoli. On 8 July 1425 Masolino was paid by the Compagnia di S Agnese for work on props for the Ascension Day miracle play (Ascension Day actually fell on 17 May 1425). This has reasonably been adduced as evidence that Masolino was already working in the Brancacci Chapel at the time. On 1 September 1425 Masolino gave power of attorney to a banker and entered the service of the condottiere Filippo Scolari (Pippo Spano) in Hungary. He did not return until some time between 7 July 1427 and 11 May 1428 (Molho, 1977). His activity in the Brancacci Chapel is, therefore, confined to the period between November 1424 and September 1425 or, less likely, some time after July 1427 (in Christiansen's opinion the latter date can be excluded for reasons of style; for a different interpretation *see* MASACCIO, §I, 2(ii)). That it was he and not Masaccio who received the commission, as recorded by Vasari and sustained by most recent critics, was confirmed by the recovery of the decoration of the window embrasure. The window extends into the uppermost zone of the original fresco cycle, and its decoration would have been conceived along with those first scenes. It is virtually identical with the border surmounting Masolino's *Pietà* at Empoli and antithetical to the Corinthian pilasters framing the surviving scenes. Moreover, the two *sinopie* that have been recovered from the altar wall, one showing the *Repentance of St Peter* and the other the *Feed my Sheep* (a scene not mentioned by Vasari who, however, attributed all of the uppermost scenes to Masolino), again accord with Masolino's work at Empoli. (The attempt to attribute one of the *sinopie* to Masaccio is without basis.) It is, therefore, probable that Masolino began work on the Brancacci Chapel independently in 1425 and that Masaccio's collaboration was sought on completion of the four scenes in the lunettes. The reason

behind the collaboration can only be surmised. Perhaps it was simply an effort to expedite work in view of the far more prestigious commission Masolino had from Pippo Spano. At the time Masaccio was probably relatively unknown, although if he had completed his fresco of the *Consecration of St Maria del Carmine* (the *Sagra*; destr.) in the church's cloister, this may have recommended his services. Whatever the explanation, the results were momentous.

From the outset the two artists took their different styles into account and made an effort to minimize the disparities by alternating the authorship of the frescoes. Thus, Masaccio undertook the large scene of the *Tribute Money* on a lateral wall, while Masolino painted the adjacent *St Peter Preaching*; Masolino painted *St Peter Curing a Cripple and the Raising of Tabitha* on the opposite lateral wall, while Masaccio painted the adjacent *St Peter Baptizing Neophytes*. Interestingly, the recent cleaning suggests that a further effort was made to unify the scenes, Masolino painting the conical hills in *St Peter Baptizing*, while Masaccio continued the naturalistic hills and sky of the *Tribute Money* into Masolino's fresco of *St Peter Preaching*. Longhi's suggestion that Masolino also painted Christ's head in the *Tribute Money* also seems correct, although the hypothesis that Masaccio painted the background buildings in the *Raising of Tabitha* is no longer tenable. The most important result of this collaboration was in Masolino's adoption of Renaissance pilasters to divide the scenes and a one-point perspective system to organize the narratives. There can be no doubt that these were Masaccio's innovations, and the degree to which Masolino understood their implications is debatable.

In *St Peter Curing a Cripple and the Raising of Tabitha* (see fig. 2), the main lines of the various buildings recede to a point somewhat to the right of the two richly clothed youths in the centre of the composition. Superficially, the scheme seems identical with that employed by Masaccio in the *Tribute Money*, but whereas in Masaccio's scene the vanishing-point coincides with the narrative focus—

2. Masolino: *St Peter Curing a Cripple and the Raising of Tabitha* (c. 1425), fresco, Brancacci Chapel, S Maria del Carmine, Florence

Christ's head—in Masolino's fresco space and narrative operate independently of each other, with the result that the two miracles of St Peter are reduced to peripheral events. Architecture is used exclusively to generate an expansive (and superfluous) space rather than to clarify the action and the sequence of the narrative, as in Masaccio's scene. Masolino apparently adopted what he perceived as a technical innovation—the use of strings snapped from a single point on the wall at the height of the foreground figures (an improvement on the system recorded in Cennino Cennini's *Libro dell'arte*)—without perceiving that this perspectival system was only the scaffolding for a new kind of realistic painting, which was based on the study of modelled figures viewed under controlled lighting conditions and the use of elaborate architectural drawings to ensure structural logic and verisimilitude. Masolino's work in the chapel was less advanced than Sassetta's contemporary predella for his altarpiece for the Arte della Lana in Siena (Siena, Pin. N.), in which figure and setting are perfectly integrated; and it was aesthetically inferior to Gentile's predella panel of the *Presentation in the Temple* (Paris, Louvre) from the *Adoration of the Magi* (Florence, Uffizi). Given Masolino's love of naturalistic detail, it is not surprising that he should lavish such extraordinary attention on genre details in the background. The stones on the ground, which cast shadows, are depicted like elements in a still-life, and the figure behind Tabitha's bed with one hand upraised wears a blue robe that originally had a gilt decoration. Masolino's debt to Gentile was a continuing factor in his art.

The church's Carmelites were staunch supporters of the papacy, and a cycle devoted to St Peter would have met with their approval; members of the Order are shown in the scenes of *St Peter Preaching* (by Masolino) and *St Peter Enthroned as Bishop of Antioch* (by Masaccio; for illustration *see* CARMELITE ORDER). The choice of scenes is not unusual: nine of the episodes represented are listed in Jacopo da Voragine's *Golden Legend*, including the *Tribute Money* (which Meiss, 1963, attempted to relate to the establishment of the *catasto* in 1427). The remaining scenes all underscore Peter's privileged position among the Apostles (except for the scene of his repentance). The inclusion of scenes of the *Temptation* and *Expulsion* indicate that the underlying theme is that of salvation through the Church, whose head is Peter. The scenes are not strictly chronological, but have been arranged to form complementary pairs: the *Calling of St Peter* opposite *Christ Walking on the Water* (both destr.); *St Peter Preaching* next to *St Peter Baptizing*, the *Tribute Money* opposite *St Peter Curing a Cripple and the Raising of Tabitha*; *Peter Imprisoned* opposite *Peter Released by an Angel*. This is the same expedient adopted later by Filippo Lippi in his frescoes in Prato Cathedral and by Piero della Francesca in the cycle in S Francesco, Arezzo, and it points to an exegetical approach to the theme. That Masolino's collaboration with Masaccio went beyond sharing the commission of the Brancacci Chapel is shown by the contemporary altarpiece for S Ambrogio, Florence, with the *Virgin and Child with St Anne* (Florence, Uffizi), in which Masolino was probably responsible for the figure of St Anne and four angels, while Masaccio painted the Virgin and Child and one angel (Vasari again

attributed the work to Masaccio). However, there is no evidence that a formal partnership was established, and, in Christiansen's opinion, it would be incorrect to postulate an association that extended beyond Masolino's departure for Hungary in September 1425, when he left the Brancacci Chapel frescoes incomplete.

3. LAST YEARS, *c.* 1426 AND AFTER. Masolino's work in the decade following his collaboration in the Brancacci Chapel, though frequently relegated to a position of secondary importance, is of considerable historical interest and is aesthetically superior to what he produced earlier. Nothing remains of the work in Hungary for Pippo Spano, who died on 28 December 1426. Masolino returned to Florence between 7 July 1427, when his father stated that he was still in Hungary, and 11 May 1428, the day before he was finally emancipated from his father's guardianship at the age of about 45. The only work that can be dated with reasonable certainty to this period is the *Annunciation* (Washington, DC, N.G.A.), now identified (Damiani, 1982) with the altarpiece that Vasari saw in the church of S Niccolò sopr'Arno, Florence, and formerly attributed to Masaccio. The chapel in the rood screen (*tramezzo*) for which it was painted was provided for in the will of Michele Guardini dated 8 March 1427. The scene, framed by a feigned carved stone arch, is depicted in an elaborate, brightly coloured architectural setting with a low viewpoint that has the effect of enhancing the decorative character of the work rather than of generating a sense of realism. The picture marks a retreat from Masaccio's innovations and a renewed interest in the courtly aspects of Gentile da Fabriano's work—the brocade dress of the angel depends on the central panel of the *Virgin and Child* in Gentile's altarpiece for S Niccolò sopr'Arno (British Royal Col., on loan to London, N.G.). This is attributable partly to Masolino's natural predilection and partly to the impact of Late Gothic Bohemian painting that he would have seen in Hungary.

Some time after May 1428, and possibly not until 1429, Masolino was summoned to Rome. The date is a matter of surmise, not fact (no documents can be connected with Masolino's extensive activity in Rome). His three principal patrons in Rome were Martin V (*see* COLONNA, (1)), who was promoting a restoration and redecoration of the Roman basilicas, Cardinal Castiglione Branda and Cardinal Giordano Orsini. For the first Masolino completed a double-sided triptych for S Maria Maggiore that was begun by Masaccio and probably left incomplete at his death in Rome before late June 1428 (central panels, Naples, Capodimonte; side panels, London, N.G., and Philadelphia, PA, Mus. A.; for a different reconstruction *see* MASACCIO, §I, 2(iii)). This altarpiece is sometimes dated as early as 1423 and is also viewed—incorrectly in Christiansen's opinion—as evidence of a continued collaboration between Masolino and Masaccio (for a good analysis, see Meiss, 1964). For Cardinal Branda's titular church of S Clemente, Masolino frescoed a chapel with scenes from the *Life of St Catherine* and the *Life of St Ambrose* as well as a *Crucifixion*. For Orsini's palace on Monte Giordano, Rome he painted a cycle of famous men (destr.), for which related drawings survive (see Mode, 1972). There is evidence that the Orsini commission was finished in 1432, which accords with what little is known of Masolino's movements in these years. In Rome the standard of taste had been set not by Masaccio, but by Gentile da Fabriano, who at his death in 1427 left several unfinished works. It was in this environment that Masolino took decisive steps in adapting the heroic style of the Brancacci Chapel to the exigencies of courtly art. One-point perspective is used to create tunnelling, box-like interiors or elaborate, stepped exterior views that generate abstract surface patterns and a heightened sense of unreality (most notable in the *Annunciation* over the entrance arch of Branda's chapel in S Clemente). Judged in terms of the naturalism of the Brancacci Chapel, these works are regressive. In the *Foundation of S Maria Maggiore* (see fig. 3), the central panel of the S Maria Maggiore altarpiece, figures have a doll-like delicacy, despite several recognizable portraits (including that of Martin V), and the landscape background, which includes topographical details of great

3. Masolino: *Foundation of S Maria Maggiore*, central panel from the S Maria Maggiore Altarpiece, tempera and gold on panel, 1.44×0.76 m, after 1428 (Naples, Museo e Gallerie Nazionali di Capodimonte)

beauty, lacks substance. In the frescoes of the *Life of St Catherine* in S Clemente, the lighting and space are surprisingly inconsistent. However, judged as narratives, these works mark a significant advance. They reveal a greater command of expression, and the compositions are more focused.

To carry out this extensive work, Masolino must have hired a number of assistants. Domenico Veneziano has been mentioned in connection with the frescoes at S Clemente, and Paolo Uccello has been proposed as an assistant or collaborator at the Palazzo Orsini. A number of figure types at S Clemente recall the later work of Vecchietta, who certainly later worked with Masolino at Castiglione Olona. Longhi believed Masaccio carried out part of the *Crucifixion* in S Clemente, but this seems highly unlikely (the fresco is in a ruinous state but the detached *sinopia* is consistent with Masolino's work).

In 1432–3 Masolino painted a fresco of the *Virgin and Child and Two Angels* in S Fortunato, Todi, for which he received payments on 17 October 1432 and 30 June 1433. The work is inspired by a fresco of 1426 by Gentile da Fabriano in Orvieto Cathedral, in which the figures are similarly viewed *di sotto in su*, but Masolino rejected the naturalistic premise of Gentile's work, opting instead for a composition of geometric purity. Masolino's last major undertaking was a series of frescoes for Cardinal Branda in his home town of Castiglione Olona, Lombardy. He decorated the ribbed vault of the choir of the Collegiata (the church was consecrated in 1425 and still undecorated in 1431; the frescoes are signed) and the interior of an adjacent small baptistery (the building became a baptistery only in 1431; the frescoes are dated 1435). The Collegiata frescoes appear to have been painted earlier than those in the baptistery. In the triangular, concave surface of the vaults, Masolino returned to the principle of architecture as a foil for figural compositions; the result is a series of unprecedentedly evocative scenes in which carefully described details (an open cupboard with stacked books in the *Annunciation*; the flock of sheep in the background of the *Nativity*) animate scenes conspicuous for their refined figure types and blond tonality. In the *Marriage of the Virgin*, in which the steps of the temple fill the awkward spandrels at the base of the vault while an ingeniously conceived second storey accommodates the scene in the pointed apex, Masolino was able for the first time to integrate fully figural action and architecture. The other scenes show a new awareness of the possibility of using illusionistic space and surface pattern to achieve a unified composition.

Masolino's real stature emerges in the cycle of the *Life of St John the Baptist* in the small baptistery (main area, approximately 5×5.5 m; see fig. 4), in which spatial effects are handled with consummate facility. Even the irregularities of the floor-plan are utilized to achieve surprising, illusionistic effects. In *St John's Imprisonment*, for example, the front wall of the prison is shown on the lateral wall, while on the window jamb is depicted a view of the saint through a barred window. A comparison of the scene of the *Banquet of Herod* with *St Catherine on the Wheel* in S Clemente, in which both settings are defined by a receding

4. Masolino: *Life of St John the Baptist* (1435), fresco, baptistery, Castiglione Olona, Lombardy

arcade to the right and back and by a two-storey loggia to the left, reveals Masolino's increased sophistication. Although Masolino determined the rate of diminution only approximately, the isocephaly of the *Banquet of Herod* suggests familiarity with the basic tenets of Alberti's perspective system (which assured a greater unification of figure with setting). Coupled with this increased mastery of space, there is a firmer grasp of anatomy, especially evident in the *Baptism*, in which the figure of Christ is based on Ghiberti's bronze relief for the Siena baptismal font, and in the portraits in the scene of *St John Preaching*. The tooled areas of gold and silver leaf (now badly damaged) are brilliantly exploited to imitate rich brocades and cut velvet. It is not surprising that Masolino found favour with a native of Lombardy, where realism and courtly refinement were the basis of Late Gothic art. And yet, if the scene of *St John Preaching* in the baptistery is compared with that of *St Peter Preaching* in the Brancacci Chapel, it is extraordinary the degree to which Masolino abandoned Masaccio's attempt to make painting an extension of the visible world and to imagine biblical events in terms of human experience. The change would seem inexplicable were the same phenomenon not observable in the work of other contemporary Tuscan artists, such as Sassetta and Uccello. Masolino's collaboration with Masaccio was a necessary but aberrant prelude to the creation of a new post-Gothic style later in the century.

Vecchietta, Masolino's principal assistant at Castiglione Olona, and Paolo Schiavo completed the decoration of the choir of the Collegiata, presumably after Masolino's death, and it is to Vecchietta, not Masolino, that a landscape decoration in Cardinal Branda's palace is probably due; he also decorated a chapel in the palace. Whereas in Florence Masolino had no significant influence—apart from Paolo Schiavo and, possibly, the young Domenico Veneziano—in Siena, through Vecchietta, his work struck a responsive chord.

BIBLIOGRAPHY

G. Vasari: *Vite* (1550, rev. 2/1568); ed. G. Milanesi (1878–85), ii, pp. 305–25

P. Toesca: *Masolino da Panicale* (Bergamo, 1908)

R. Longhi: 'Fatti di Masolino e di Masaccio', *Crit. A.*, xxv–xxvi (1940), pp. 145–80

K. Clark: 'An Early Quattrocento Triptych from Santa Maria Maggiore, Rome', *Burl. Mag.*, xciii (1951), pp. 339–43

U. Procacci: 'Sulla cronologia delle opere di Masaccio e di Masolino tra il 1425 e il 1428', *Riv. A.*, xxviii (1953), pp. 3–55

G. Urbani: 'Restauro di affreschi nella cappella di S Caterina a S Clemente in Roma', *Boll. Ist. Cent. Rest.*, xxi–xxii (1955), pp. 13–20

R. Krautheimer: *Lorenzo Ghiberti* (Princeton, 1956) [incl. analysis of S Clemente frescoes]

E. Micheletti: *Masolino da Panicale* (Milan, 1959)

E. Borsook: *The Mural Painters of Tuscany from Cimabue to Andrea del Sarto* (London, 1960, rev. Oxford, 1980)

M. Meiss: 'Masaccio and the Early Renaissance: The Circular Plan', *Acts of the Twentieth International Congress of the History of Art: Princeton, 1963*, ii, pp. 123–45

R. Oertel: 'Perspective and Imagination', *Acts of the Twentieth International Congress of the History of Art, Princeton, 1963*, ii, pp. 146–59

M. Meiss: 'The Altered Program of the Santa Maria Maggiore Altarpiece', *Festschrift L. Heydenreich* (Munich, 1964), pp. 169–90

B. Cole: 'A Reconstruction of Masolino's True Cross Cycle in Santo Stefano, Empoli', *Mitt. Ksthist. Inst. Florenz*, xiii (1967), pp. 289–300

E. Wakayama: 'Novità di Masolino a Castiglione Olona', *A. Lombarda*, xvi (1971), pp. 1–16

R. Mode: 'Masolino, Uccello, and the Orsini *Uomini Famosi*', *Burl. Mag.*, cxiv (1972), pp. 369–78

L. B. Watkins: 'Technical Observations on the Frescoes of the Brancacci Chapel', *Mitt. Ksthist. Inst. Florenz*, xvii (1973), pp. 65–74

A. Debold-von Kritter: *Studien zum Petruszyklus in der Brancaccikapelle* (Berlin, 1975)

R. Freemantle: 'Some New Masolino Documents', *Burl. Mag.*, cxvii (1975), pp. 658–9

A. Molho: 'The Brancacci Chapel: Studies in its Iconography and History', *J. Warb. & Court. Inst.*, xl (1977), pp. 50–98

E. Wakayama: 'Il programma iconografico degli affreschi di Masolino nel battistero di Castiglione Olona', *A. Lombarda*, l (1978), pp. 20–32

A. Braham: 'The Emperor Sigismund and the Santa Maria Maggiore Altarpiece', *Burl. Mag.*, cxxii (1980), pp. 106–11

G. Damiani: *San Niccolò Oltrarno: La chiesa, una famiglia di antiquari* (Florence, 1982), pp. 29–30, 57–9

F. Santi: 'Momenti della scultura e della pittura', *Il tempio di San Fortunato a Todi* (Milan, 1982), 149–50

U. Baldini: *La Cappella Brancacci nella chiesa del Carmine a Firenze* (Milan, 1984)

A. Natali: 'La chiesa di Villa a Castiglione Olona e gli inizi del Vecchietta', *Paragone*, xxxv/407 (1984), pp. 3–14

P. Joannides: 'A Masolino Partially Reconstructed', *Source: Notes Hist. A.*, iv/4 (1985), pp. 1–5

O. Casazza: 'Il ciclo delle storie di San Pietro e la "Historia Salutis": Nuova lettura della Cappella Brancacci', *Crit. A.*, li (1986), pp. 69–82

M. Boskovits: 'Il percorso di Masolino: Precisazioni sulla cronologia e sul catalogo', *A. Crist.*, 718 (1987), pp. 47–66

J. Manca: 'A Remark by Pliny the Elder as a Source for Masolino's Landscape Mural in Castiglione Olona', *A. Crist.*, 719 (1987), pp. 81–4

F. Mazzini: 'Stacco e ricollocamento di affreschi di Masolino nel battistero di Castiglione Olona: Le sinopie', *A. Crist.*, 719 (1987), pp. 85–98

C. Strehlke and M. Tucker: 'The Santa Maria Maggiore Altarpiece: New Observations', *A. Crist.*, 719 (1987), pp. 105–24

E. Wakayama: 'Masolino o non Masolino: Problemi di attribuzione', *A. Crist.*, 719 (1987), pp. 125–236

U. Baldini and O. Casazza: *La Cappella Brancacci* (Milan, 1990)

K. Christiansen: 'Some Observations on the Brancacci Chapel Frescoes after their Cleaning', *Burl. Mag.*, cxxxiii (1991), pp. 5–20

P. Joannides: *Masaccio and Masolino: A Complete Catalogue* (London, 1993)

KEITH CHRISTIANSEN

Mason (i). Craftsman who builds in stone or brick. From the Middle Ages until the 18th century a mason also designed masonry buildings and performed the functions that, in modern times, would be divided between architect, engineer, contractor and builder.

I. Introduction. II. The masons. III. Lodge organization. IV. Techniques.

I. Introduction.

Modern efforts to establish the history of the organization and methods of medieval building have had to overcome several myths about masons, in particular the notion that the social fraternity of Freemasonry is a direct outgrowth of medieval freemasonry, which in turn had its historical roots in ancient times, traceable back through the Romans to the Egyptians and the building of the pyramids. This myth was dismissed by Knoop and Jones, historians of both the medieval masons' craft and the modern fraternity of Freemasons, in their publications of 1937 and 1947. 'Freemason' is a medieval English word that originally distinguished masons who carved in freestone (i.e. sandstone or limestone that could be sawn or carved freely both with and against the grain). By the 15th century the word was used interchangeably with 'mason' as a generic term for a craftsman who built in stone, while more specialized terms denoted masons assigned to specific tasks in the building process. Furthermore, the term 'freemason' continued to be applied to these craftsmen until at least the beginning of the 18th century, by which time the Freemasons' fraternity was coming into being. It is not within the purview of this article to discuss the origins of Freemasonry, which was a post-medieval social development that had little to do with the socio-economic conditions or technical practices of the medieval masons' craft.

Attempts to trace the origins of the medieval masons' craft from Roman building practices and traditions have been closely connected with erroneous accounts of the genesis of modern Freemasonry. The determination to establish a pedigree of 'Freemasonry' going back to the builders of the Egyptian pyramids required that a direct link be found between medieval and Classical builders in stone; but very few documents concerning masons survive from the five centuries or so between the disintegration of the Roman Empire in western Europe and the revival of towns, trade and widespread building in stone after AD 1000. Whereas a history of the stone buildings of this period can be written on the basis of extant monuments, the same cannot be done for the builders, for there is a lack of evidence about who they were, where they came from and how they were trained and organized. There are sporadic references after AD 643 to the so-called *magistri Comacini*, but little is actually known about them. There are also tantalizing references in Carolingian documents to masons brought 'from across the Alps' to participate in the spate of monastic and royal building inspired by Charlemagne. A continuous history of the masons' craft begins only after 1000, when contemporary financial records from building construction begin to supplement, and then largely to replace, monastic chronicles as the primary sources of information on the constructional history of buildings, and on technical, economic and social questions regarding the building craftsmen.

Modern scholarship has also corrected the misapprehension that monasteries and churches were often built by monks themselves, aided by pious folk who contributed manual labour in the CULT OF CARTS. While it is possible that some monks served as building craftsmen before 1000, the question is debatable; and in the surge of building after *c.* 1000 it is clear that stone construction required technical building skills that neither monks nor untrained laymen would have possessed. However, it is equally uncertain how masons, who functioned in the vernacular languages, would have gained access to the literary content of the Latin-dominated ecclesiastical culture of the monasteries and churches. Evidence of their education indicates that the great majority would not have been sufficiently literate in Latin to have read, as is often presumed, either the Classical books by Vitruvius (*see* VITRUVIUS, §3(i)) and Euclid (*c.* 300 BC) or the voluminous theological and scientific literature of ancient and medieval Christian scholars.

BIBLIOGRAPHY
F. B. Andrews: *The Mediaeval Builder and his Methods* (Oxford, 1925)
M. S. Briggs: *The Architect in History* (Oxford, 1927)
D. Knoop and G. P. Jones: *The Mediaeval Mason* (Manchester, 1933, 3/1967)
——: *An Introduction to Freemasonry* (Manchester, 1937)
N. Pevsner: 'The Term "Architect" in the Middle Ages', *Speculum*, xvii (1942), pp. 549–62
D. Knoop and G. P. Jones: *The Genesis of Freemasonry*, Publications of the University of Manchester, ccxxix (Manchester, 1947)
P. du Colombier: *Les Chantiers des cathédrales: Ouvriers, architectes, sculpteurs* (Paris, 1953, rev. 1990)
P. Booz: *Der Baumeister der Gotik* (Munich, 1956)
J. Gimpel: *Les Bâtisseurs des cathédrales* (Paris, 1958; Eng. trans., New York, 1961)
J. H. Harvey: *The Mediaeval Architect* (London, 1972)
S. K. Kostoff, ed.: *The Architect: Chapters in the History of the Profession* (New York, 1977)
A. Saint: *The Image of the Architect* (New Haven, 1983)

II. The masons.

1. Roles and responsibilities. 2. Wages and social standing. 3. Education and training.

1. ROLES AND RESPONSIBILITIES. The terminology of the three languages used in the financial building records of medieval England demonstrates the great variety in the technical roles of the masons. *Cementarius* and *lathomus* in Latin, *masoun* in Norman French and 'mason' in English were general terms, while several words or phrases were used to indicate specialized functions: hewers (Lat. *cissores*, *taylatores*; Norman Fr. *tailleurs*) and setters (Lat. *positores*, *cubitores*; Norman Fr. *couchours*), wallers (Lat. *muratorii*; Eng. 'roughmasons'), paviors (Norman Fr. *pavours*), marblers (Lat. *marmorarii*), freestone masons (Lat. *lathomi liberarum petrarum*; Norman Fr. *masouns de franche peer*; Eng. 'freemasons', 'hardhewers'). The role of the master mason himself differed from that of the modern architect. It is difficult and perhaps misleading to draw a composite picture of the medieval master mason, for the roles and responsibilities, social standing and economic rewards of

these men varied considerably across the centuries of Romanesque and Gothic building, and among contemporary master masons within any particular period. In general the master mason was responsible for only those parts of the building in stone or brick. Carpenters, glaziers and plumbers each had master craftsmen responsible for construction in wood, glass and lead. The master mason might well be first among equals, but he did not supervise the work of these other masters. It is thus misleading to speak of the master mason as the 'architect' of a cathedral or castle. Within his sphere, the master mason was responsible for both design and construction, which again differs from modern practice, in which the architect designs the building and then supervises the work of contractors who execute the designs. Finally, the great majority of master masons stayed on site while construction was underway, contrary to most modern architects who hire supervisors to ensure that the contractors construct the building according to the drawings and specifications of the architect. Their presence significantly affected the design process. Fully detailed building plans did not have to be completed before construction began. Indeed, medieval building could be effected without architectural drawings, as was normally the case before 1200, although drawings played an increasingly prominent role in Gothic building from the 13th century onwards (*see* ARCHITECTURAL DRAWING, §1).

The physical presence of the patrons during construction, or at least of their clerical officials, allowed ongoing consultations with the master mason, a factor that also played a vital part in design and construction decisions. This symbiotic working relationship between patron and builder was often represented in medieval miniatures, which showed the patron and the master mason consulting on site (see fig. 1). The design process was also influenced by the traditional spatial requirements of the monks, parish and cathedral clergy, and castle-building kings and nobles.

1. Mason and patron consulting during the foundation and construction of the city of Berne in 1191; miniature from Diebold Schilling: *Spiezer/Chronik*, 220×240 mm, *c.* 1485 (Berne, Burgerbibliothek Bern, MS. Hist. Helv. I.16, fol. 55)

It was the accommodation of these traditions that provided much of the continuity in medieval architectural designs. Because so much was already mutually understood and agreed within these traditions, patrons and builders could concentrate on developing the seemingly endless variations on themes that are found in surviving medieval monuments.

The master mason also worked closely with journeymen masons within the traditional building practices of the craft. Sharing a common education and technical vocabulary, the master mason was able to convey his intentions to the working masons, who executed them with a minimum of instruction. This was particularly true in the use of templates as the primary means of transmitting essential technical information between the designer and the working masons (*see* TEMPLATE). The splendid large-scale architectural drawings by 14th- and 15th-century master masons were probably intended more for the benefit of patrons than for constructional usage.

As technical supervisor of construction, the master mason was concerned with three major centres for the masons' activities: the quarry, the masons' lodge and the building fabric itself. On large projects these centres might involve scores of craftsmen and labourers. Their efforts had to be carefully coordinated to produce the right stones from the right quarries and to get these transported to the building lodge; there the rough-hewn stones were precisely cut to the guidelines provided by the templates and then moved again and set into their exact location in the building. The master mason often appointed an under-master or warden (Ger. *Parlier*; Fr. *appareilleur*; Sp. *aparejedor*) both to assist him and to be in charge of the masons if he was away from the site. By the 14th century the absences of the more famous masters could be frequent or extended, for they were sometimes engaged on other projects as consultants, or they might be responsible for two or more major projects simultaneously.

Some master masons developed businesses as materials and building contractors. This was especially true in England, where surviving contracts provide a vivid and detailed picture of what has been described as one of the earliest of medieval capitalistic enterprises (Knoop and Jones, 1936). The traditional economic structure of medieval building was the direct labour system, in which patrons provided funds for payrolls and purchase of materials, with these funds administered by an official of the patron who was often called the CLERK OF WORKS. In 13th-century England some masters began to receive payments for 'taskwork', to be accomplished by masons who worked directly for the master rather than the patron. This practice eventually developed into full-scale contracting for the supply of raw or finished materials and for building construction, all for a price previously agreed.

2. WAGES AND SOCIAL STANDING. The variety of technical roles among masons was also reflected in their wages. In 14th-century England the daily wages of masons varied from 2d. to 5d., the rate depending on both the type of work and their skills. In London a mason arriving on a job for the first time was evaluated by the master and other masons to determine his level of skill before he was assigned to work and his wages were set. Journeymen

normally received wages only for days worked, with the exception of a few holidays each year. Master masons were paid weekly salaries and received their pay regardless of workdays missed owing to weather or holidays. The master mason's salary was usually set as a function of the journeymen's wages, ranging from 2d. to 8d. more per day than the highest paid journeymen received. This constraint on the master's salary was offset by periodic bonuses, which were awarded in cash payments, gifts of clothing, wine and food, or meals with the building patrons. The biggest income differentials between masters and journeymen, however, went to those who became materials or building contractors or who, because of their reputations, were able to accept multiple commissions and appointments as master masons or to serve as consultants on projects directed by other masters.

The wages of both master masons and journeymen were very low compared with the incomes not only of the feudal, ecclesiastical and merchant classes that commissioned their works, but also of the stewards and clerks who administered building projects. As an example, in England in 1378 the King's Master Mason, Henry Yevele, received a salary of 1s. per day, while the King's Clerk of Works, John Blake, received 2s. per day. Furthermore, an able clerk might expect further advancement in royal or ecclesiastical service with even higher remuneration, while the King's Master Mason was at the peak of his craft and career.

It is difficult to assess the socio-economic status of the masons' craft in medieval society. Owing to the itinerant nature of their work—many of the largest masonry projects, such as castles and monasteries, were built in the countryside, resulting in a very small number of resident masons continuously living and working in the same town—masons did not readily fit into the craft and merchant guild structure of urban life. Moreover, their travels from one project to another made it difficult for them to accumulate the urban properties that constituted an important basis for social standing in town life. Those who did, such as Henry Yevele and Burkhard Engelberg, were exceptional. Those masons who were appointed masters of the great cathedral workshops often bought a house in which to settle during their years of service, but these men rarely became prominent leaders in the political life of the towns; whatever urban offices they held were usually related to their technical abilities as masons and involved the oversight and maintenance of town defences, bridges and drainage systems (see GERTHENER, MADERN).

3. EDUCATION AND TRAINING. The socio-economic status of medieval masons reflected their educational background and training, and vice versa. While masons, and especially master masons, were highly trained and skilful craftsmen, their skills centred on physical rather than literary activities. They acquired those skills through apprenticeship, with the oral transmission of technical information, rather than through written documents, though by the later Middle Ages many master masons were literate in their vernacular language, and perhaps a few in Latin as well.

The young apprentice mason might begin in the quarry and then work his way through all the stages of building in stone. He would learn to be a rough layer and then a setter of finely carved stones. He could then be transferred to the masons' lodge, where he learnt to carve stones to the shape of the templates provided by the master mason. The more gifted young masons or sons of master masons could be apprenticed to a master, from whom they learnt the advanced techniques of design and construction that they needed to become masters of the craft.

By the mid-15th century German masons had formalized the *Wanderjahr* as a routine part of their education. After several years working at a particular building lodge, a young mason would spend a year or more travelling to other sites where he worked as a journeyman (*Gesell*), learning the building techniques of the different lodges. In the regulations developed in Germany (*see* §III, 2(ii) below) it was virtually mandatory for a mason to have completed his *Wanderjahr* before learning advanced design and construction techniques. Masons in other parts of Europe do not seem to have undertaken the *Wanderjahr* in so formal a sense, but the place of itinerant masons in a local lodge was still a matter of concern: English 14th-century records show that authorities both within and outside the craft wrestled with the problem of how to certify the technical skills of a mason who arrived unknown at a site and presented himself as a trained and competent journeyman mason.

BIBLIOGRAPHY

V. Mortet and P. Deschamps: *Receuil de textes relatifs à l'histoire de l'architecture et à la condition des architectes en France, au moyen âge*, 2 vols (Paris, 1911–28)

D. Knoop and G. P. Jones: 'Masons' Wages in Mediaeval England', *Econ. Hist.*, ii (1930–33), pp. 473–99

O. Kletzl: *Titel und Namen von Baumeistern deutscher Gotik*, Schriften der deutschen Akademie in München, xxvi (Munich, 1935)

D. Knoop and G. P. Jones: 'The Rise of the Mason Contractor', *RIBA J.*, 3rd ser., xliii (1936), pp. 1061–71

L. F. Salzman: *Building in England down to 1540* (Oxford, 1952/R 1967)

M. Aubert: 'La Construction au moyen âge', *Bull. Mnmt.*, cxviii (1960), pp. 241–59; cxix (1961), pp. 7–42, 81–120, 181–209, 297–323

H. M. Colvin, ed.: *The Middle Ages*, 2 vols (1963), i and ii of *The History of the King's Works* (London, 1963–82)

L. R. Shelby: 'The Role of the Master Mason in Mediaeval English Building', *Speculum*, xxxix (1964), pp. 387–403

——: 'The Education of Medieval English Master Masons', *Med. Stud.*, xxxii (1970), pp. 1–26

J. James: *The Contractors of Chartres*, 2 vols (Dooralong, 1979; Wyong and London, 1981)

L. R. Shelby: 'The Contractors of Chartres', *Gesta*, xx (1981), pp. 173–8

For further bibliography *see* §I above.

III. Lodge organization.

1. The lodge. 2. The 'Constitutions of Masonry'.

1. THE LODGE. On a large building project the masons' organization was focused on their workshop, the masons' lodge. Only in the largest cities were there sufficient resident masons to maintain a guild. Even in London the masons' guild apparently did not exist before 1356, when the city officials approved certain 'Regulations for the Trade of Masons'. By 1376 the masons' mistery, or guild, was represented by four masons on the London Common Council, but little is known about its development before 1481, when a set of ordinances for the masons was approved by the mayor and aldermen. Meanwhile, scattered evidence reveals that London masons of the 14th century were creating a 'fraternity of masons', referred to

2. Masons transporting stones from the masons' lodge to the construction site of a church at Vézelay; miniature from *Histoire de Charles-Martel et de ses successeurs*, 1448–65 (Brussels, Bibliothèque Royale Albert 1er, MS. 6, fol. 554*v*)

also as the 'fellowship of freemasons of London'. This development paralleled the practice of many London crafts in generating a social and religious fraternity as an ecclesiastical institution alongside their craft mistery or guild, which was a civic institution.

The masons' lodge, around which their work was organized, was normally built of wood. There the free-masons cut and shaped the stones that they, or mason setters, would later place into the building (see fig. 2; for further illustration *see* MASTERS, ANONYMOUS, AND MONOGRAMMISTS, §I: MASTER OF THE CITÉ DES DAMES). The lodge could accommodate 15 to 20 masons working at their bankers, and on the walls were hung the scores of templates required for the piers, shafts, vaults, moulded doorways and window tracery. Insights into the specific organization and activities of the masons in their building lodges are provided by several sources. The series of ordinances issued by the chapter of York Minster in 1352, 1370 and 1408 regulated the activities of the masons working in the building lodge. The ordinance of 1352 begins with an invocation to the ancient customs (*consuetudines antiquae*) that pertained to the masons in the construction of the Minster. It then gives detailed regulations on the hours of the day for beginning and ending work, rules for lunch and nap times, and stipulations on how far from the lodge the masons might go during rest periods. All these activities were regulated by the ringing of bells.

2. THE 'CONSTITUTIONS OF MASONRY'. Other documents more directly reveal the perspectives of the masons themselves. These are the 'Constitutions of Masonry', which continued to be composed until the 18th century and which are the documentary links between the modern social fraternity of Freemasonry and the medieval masons' craft. They survive in medieval English and German forms.

(i) England. The earliest surviving examples of 'Constitutions of Masonry' are the so-called Regius MS. (London, BL, Bibl., Reg., 17A.I) and the Cooke MS. (London, BL, Add. MS. 23198), which were composed around 1400. Each begins with a history of the craft, followed by the

'Articles and Points of Masonry'. The latter are codifications of customs that had long regulated the masons' activities and that, as stated by the authors, were previously contained in 'old books of masonry' and 'the book of charges' that had been 'written in Latin and in French both'.

Four types of mason are named in these documents (masters, wardens, fellows and apprentices), and the 'Articles and Points' were intended to regulate their relationships both with each other and with their patrons. Particular attention was given to the responsibilities of master masons towards apprentices, who were to be selected from able-bodied and free men, carefully trained in the skills of the craft for their full seven-year term, and paid appropriately for their developing skills, so that patrons would not be overcharged for the apprentices' work. The master mason was also enjoined to pay the fellows, or journeymen, wages appropriate to the type of work they did; to replace a less capable mason with a more capable one if the latter should arrive at the site; and to settle disputes between fellow masons on the job. The warden was encouraged to serve the master and building patron well during the absence of the master and to be a mediator between the master and fellows and between disputing fellows when the master was away. Fellow masons were urged to love their masters and fellows as their own brothers; to give a full day's work for their pay; to accept the tasks assigned them by the master; to hold the art of masonry in honour; not to covet the wife or daughter of the master or of their fellows; and to keep the counsel of their fellows 'in lodge and in chamber and in every place thereas masons be'.

This reference to the masons' lodge was to a place, the actual workshop, rather than to a social or organizational group of masons, and this use seems to have been employed elsewhere in the 'Articles and Points'. The formal organization of the masons, however, is not clear. The role of regional 'Congregations' of masters and fellow masons was emphasized: these were to be held every year or every three years, at which the 'masters should be examined of the articles after written, and be ransacked whether they be able and conning to the profit of the lords them to serve, and to the honour of the foresaid art'. Yet, despite extensive searches, Knoop and Jones found no positive evidence that such congregations of masons were actually held in England.

(ii) Germany. Until the middle of the 15th century German masons seem to have been organized much like their English peers. There were a few towns with guilds (*Zünfte*) of masons registered with town officials, but, as with English masons, the local building lodges (*Bauhütten*) constituted the organizational centres of the craft. By 1450 these German lodges had acquired a more formalized character than the 'lodge' of the English 'Articles and Points of Masonry', for they had become the local institutions that regulated and governed the professional lives of the masons who belonged to them. Each lodge operated according to its own rules, but there were many common practices and customs resulting from the shared experiences of masons who wandered from one lodge to another.

During the 1450s masons in southern Germany made several attempts to coordinate and codify these common rules and customs. Discussion meetings were held at Speyer and Strasbourg before 1459; a third meeting at Regensburg in that year produced the Ordinance (*Ordnung*), which was revised at another meeting in Speyer in 1464. This was based on the law and customs (*Recht und Herkommen*) of the local lodges (*Hütten*); the particulars of the Ordinance were called points and articles (*Punkte und Artikel*), and they were written down at Regensburg in the Book (*Buch*), which constituted the official record of the Regensburg meeting. A copy of the Book was made available only to certain lodges where it was placed under the authority of the master mason, who was to protect it from unauthorized persons or copying and to see that it was read to the masons of the lodge at least once a year.

Three types of lodge were recognized in the Ordinance: the simplest lodges, which did not possess a copy of the Book; regular lodges, which did hold a copy; and chief lodges, which not only had a copy but held rather vaguely defined jurisdictional authority over other lodges. All of these were referred to in the Ordinance simply as *Hütten*. Masons who promised to uphold the Ordinance of Regensburg were said to belong to the Brotherhood (*Bruderschaft*) of the masons' handicraft (*Handwerk der Steinmetzen*). This Brotherhood was not quite a fraternity in the usual medieval sense, for it lacked a localized centre as well as the fiscal and administrative machinery of even the simpler forms of socio-religious fraternities; nor was it a craft guild, for it was not regulated by municipal authorities. It was not even like the Congregations proposed in the English 'Articles and Points of Masonry', for there were no provisions for regular regional meetings of the Brotherhood, and, after the first round of sessions in which the Ordinance was composed, no more general meetings of the Brotherhood were held during the 15th century.

The Regensburg Ordinance is longer and more detailed than the English 'Articles and Points of Masonry', and it is more systematically organized, with separate sections devoted to the master (*Meister* or *Werkman*), warden and journeymen (*Parlier und Gesellen*) and apprentice (*Diener*). One of the key features was the practice of *Fürdrung* (mod. Ger. *Förderung*), which, although not defined in the Ordinance, meant the process by which the journeymen could advance from one level to another among the masons of the lodge, although the specific levels of promotion were not spelt out. *Fürdrung* sometimes meant appointment to a specific position, such as master mason of the lodge. The Ordinance indicated that not all lodges had a *Hüttenfürdrung*; this would probably have been the case on smaller projects where there were only a few masons at work. If a lodge did maintain this advancement or promotion procedure, it was carefully guarded by the lodge traditions: one of the articles states that a new master of a lodge 'should uphold and maintain the *Fürdrung* according to the law and customs of the lodge and of masonry, as is usual and customary in that region'.

The *Fürdrung* was also used as a means of certification for journeymen, for a mason who had been through the *Fürdrung* could be expected to possess certain skills in masonry. In particular, anyone considered for appointment as a master mason was expected to know one of the critical techniques for late medieval German masons, namely, how to take 'measures' from the ground-plan:

> If someone wants to devise a stone structure by means of measures (*Masse*) or by the extrapolation device (*Auszug*), and he does not know how to take them out of the basic figure (*Grund*), and he has not apprenticed to a workman nor been through advancement (*Fürdrung*), then he should not take up the task in any way. However, if such a one does undertake it, then no journeyman should stand by him or support his appointment (*Fürdrung*).

BIBLIOGRAPHY

RDK: 'Bauhütte'

C. Heideloff: *Die Bauhütte des Mittelalters in Deutschland* (Nuremberg, 1844)

J. Raine, ed.: *The Fabric Rolls of York Minster*, Surtees Soc., xxxv (Durham, 1859)

F. Janner: *Die Bauhütten des deutschen Mittelalters* (Leipzig, 1876)

J. Neuwirth: *Die Satzungen des Regensburger Steinmetzentages im Jahre 1459 auf Grund der Klagenfurter Steinmetzen und Maurerordnung von 1628* (Vienna, 1888)

A. L. von Ebengreuth: 'Das Admonter Hüttenbuch und die Regensburger Steinmetzordnung vom Jahre 1459', *Mitt. Ksr.-Kön. Zent.-Comm. Erforsch. & Erhaltung Kst- & Hist. Dkml.*, n.s., xx (1894), pp. 168–71, 227–41

J. Neuwirth: 'Die Satzungen des Regensburger Steinmetzentages nach dem Tiroler Hüttenbuche von 1460', *Z. Bauwsn*, xlvi (1896), pp. 175–218

W. Jüttner: *Ein Beitrag zur Geschichte der Bauhütte und des Bauwesens im Mittelalter* (Cologne, 1935)

D. Knoop, G. P. Jones and D. Hamer, eds: *The Two Earliest Masonic MSS: The Regius MS and the Cooke MS*, Publications of the University of Manchester, cclix (Manchester, 1938)

D. Knoop and G. P. Jones: 'The London Masons' Company', *Econ. Hist.*, iv (1938–40), pp. 157–66

R. Wissell: 'Die älteste Ordnung des Grossen Hüttenbundes der Steinmetzen von 1459 (nach der Thanner Handschrift)', *Gesch. Oberrheins*, n.s., lv (1942), pp. 51–133

E. Egg: 'Die Bruderschaft der Steinmetzen und Maurer in Tirol', *Neue Beitr. Gesch. Landesknd. Tirols*, i/2 (1969), pp. 69–83

IV. Techniques.

1. Introduction. 2. The geometry of the masons. 3. The Expertise. 4. The end of the medieval tradition.

1. INTRODUCTION. Evidence, either verbal or graphic, from masons themselves on the technical aspects of their work is not abundant. It scarcely exists from before the 13th century, and it starts to become voluminous only in the 15th. Surviving templates and drawings give some idea of how they designed the individual ashlars and mouldings for each building, but their understanding of the structural behaviour of masonry can be inferred only from the surviving buildings and from the limited documentary evidence, which includes writings by a few masons and records of Expertises (*see* §3 below). It is also difficult to establish to what extent documents from the late medieval period reflect earlier medieval methods of design and construction.

Although much regarding the technical expertise of medieval masons is still not understood, three characteristics of their craft are evident: it was essentially traditional, empirical and experimental. The combination of these traits provided much of the dynamics of Romanesque and Gothic building. Masons literally built on what had come down to them from previous generations; but their continuous stylistic and technical innovations show that they were not craft-bound to build in exactly the same way as their forefathers. They accepted, on the basis of empirical evidence, what had worked in the past, but they were willing to experiment with variations on received tradition. If the experiment worked, that is, if the building stood up and the change was well received, the empirical evidence of success permitted the addition of this particular experimental change into the received traditions of the craft. Stylistic and technical innovation might occur through the experiments of a particularly gifted master mason, through the quality of work of a prominent lodge of journeymen, or sometimes through the impetus given by an energetic and sensitive building patron. At any one time many separate centres were conducting experiments within existing traditions.

Lorenz Lechler's *Instructions* to his son, though written in 1516, near the end of the medieval period, clearly represent the type of skill that characterized the mason's craft (*see* LECHLER, LORENZ, §2). The *Instructions* were generally prescriptive, but Lechler also urged his son to make his own judgements on certain design questions. However, while leaving room for experiments, he frequently warned that, whatever the design, it should sustain the building's structural integrity: 'An honourable work glorifies its master if it stands up.'

2. THE GEOMETRY OF THE MASONS.

(i) The myth of 'sacred geometry'. Many scholars have been convinced that medieval masons maintained a craft 'secret' on which their building designs and construction techniques were based, and numerous efforts have been devoted to reconstructing the 'sacred geometry' that is thought to have been the content of this secret. The evidence for a masons' craft secret, however, rests largely on two passages in the Regensburg Ordinance, both concerned with the technique of deriving the elevation from the ground-plan (*see* §III, 2(ii) above). Yet neither of these texts justifies such an interpretation. The first article simply states that the technique was used as a means of certifying who was qualified to design stone structures. The second article presumed that the technique was known to every major grade of the masons' craft above apprentice; what was forbidden was to teach the technique to anyone who was not a mason. 'Item, no workman, master, warden, or journeyman should instruct anyone on how to take the elevation out of the ground-plan, anyone, that is to say, who is not of our handicraft'. The implication is that any mason could legitimately be taught the technique by another mason who knew it, and any mason who pretended to be knowledgeable about masonry should know how to use it. There was nothing exclusive or esoteric about this matter within the craft.

Perhaps the masons themselves did not expect the exhortation denying the technique to anyone outside their craft to have much impact. They suggested no sanctions against transgressors and could not have enforced the rule, for they had no effective institutional mechanisms for maintaining a 'trade secret'. An urban guild might have been able to do so, but the nature of the building industry made it virtually impossible to keep a 'trade secret' truly secret even in southern Germany, let alone across Europe. If anyone who was not a mason wanted to learn the

technique, he could have done so from any mason willing to teach it to him. The technique was set forth in at least two late 15th-century pamphlets on the design of pinnacles and gables: Mathes Roriczer's *Büchlein von der Fialen Gerechtigkeit*, published in Regensburg in 1486 (*see* RORICZER, (3), §2), and the *Fialenbüchlein*, written by the goldsmith HANNS SCHMUTTERMAYER and printed in Nuremberg shortly after 1486. In the latter Schmuttermayer stated that he learnt the technique from famous master masons, such as the Junker of Prague, Master Ruger and Nicholas of Strasbourg. It was of interest to gold- and silversmiths, who used it to design tiny pinnacles, gablets and buttresses for the micro-architecture of reliquaries and monstrances. Indeed many of the famous goldsmith drawings of Basle (Basle, Kstmus.; *see* SCHMUTTERMAYER, HANNS), which contain numerous examples of this design technique, were drawn during the very period that the German masons were drafting the exhortation to restrict knowledge of the technique to masons.

See also ARCHITECTURAL PROPORTION, §II, 1(ii).

(ii) Constructive geometry. Geometry was a fundamental element in the expertise of medieval masons: all their surviving writings on building are concerned with geometrical applications. To them, the stability of a building was governed by its shape: if the proportions were right, the building would stand up (*see also* MASONRY, §III). The importance of geometry was underscored in the introduction to the English 'Articles and Points of Masonry' (*see* §III, 2(i) above), which states 'that among all the crafts of the world of man's craft, masonry has the most notability and most part of this science of geometry'. This account describes Euclid as the founder of the masons' craft. The geometry of the masons was hardly Euclidian, however, as is clear from Roriczer's *Geometria deutsch* (1498), in which he solved some simple problems in geometry by manipulating geometrical forms with masons' drawing tools: straightedge, triangle, dividers etc. This was non-mathematical geometry, in which Roriczer felt no obligation to demonstrate the correctness of his solutions. The procedure was essentially arbitrary and could not be mathematically reasoned: each step had to be memorized. The arbitrariness allowed variation and creativity in a design technique that otherwise seems mechanical: while their procedures were very similar, Roriczer and Schmuttermayer generated pinnacles and gablets that were noticeably different from each other (see figs 3 and 4).

This non-mathematical geometry of the masons could be described as constructive geometry. It was applied to all aspects of the design, from determining overall dimensions of ground-plans, façades and cross-sections of buildings down to the dimensions and shapes of individual stones that fitted into vault ribs and window mullions. All the measurements could be generated from a single measure. This 'great measure' was part of an ancient building tradition referred to in the Old Testament. Ezekiel 40:42 records at considerable length the dimensions of all details of a great temple, as if part of a building manual of *c.* 600 BC has been bound in with the books of the Bible. Ezekiel 40:3 and 5 describes a man holding what was evidently a great measure, six cubits long and probably marked with a subdivision of palms. With this he could

3. Geometric grid for a gablet and pinnacles by Mathes Roriczer; from his *Wimpergbüchlein* (Regensburg, 1486–90)

establish the major dimensions of rooms as well as small individual measurements, using merely the numbers listed so diligently in the chapters of Ezekiel. Once such numbers had been recorded, either in a manual or on a drawing, they could be transferred to the site when the great measure had been physically constructed.

The essential feature of the great measure was that it was part of the building. It was not an absolute yardstick; if it were cut slightly smaller initially, a slightly smaller building would result from the same building plan. Vitruvius, writing in the late 1st century AD, made this clear in his discussion of *ordinatio*, one of six main concepts in his theory of architecture (*On Architecture*, I.i; *see* VITRUVIUS, §2). *Ordinatio* is the great measure, and it is made up of *quantitas*, that is, modules taken from the building. Once the dimension of a particular component has been fixed, all other components can be expressed in terms of the first, and this unit of measure becomes the module. All this may seem unnecessarily complicated, when every modern building worker has a knowledge of decimals and has his standard folding metre rule; but Greek, Roman and medieval buildings were constructed not with standard yardsticks but with a local great measure established at the start of the campaign. The ground-plan was laid out with

the great measure, and all components of the building, the height and width of the columns and the intercolumniations, were expressed in terms of the modules that made up the *ordinatio*.

The portfolio of Villard de Honnecourt (Paris, Bib. N., MS. Fr. 19093) contains ground-plans for churches that can be read instantly by any present-day architect. Elevations, however, seem out of scale, giving exaggerated prominence to particular architectural features, as a convention designed to emphasize one section of the work. This was precisely Villard's aim, and the medieval architect would have had no difficulty in interpreting these elevations. Once the ground-plan has been fixed, and a set of numbers established by which, in proportion, the dimensions of every member of the building can be constructed, there is no ambiguity about any of the vertical dimensions.

Proportions based on irrational numbers cannot be derived from the great measure. Arithmetically based proportions were used extensively in the medieval period as a continuation of the Roman tradition, and the methods used to obtain them were the same as those given by Vitruvius, who was aware that the square root of two, as an irrational number, could not be expressed on a great measure but could be geometrically constructed. He gave the construction for doubling the square, which was followed immediately by a discussion of the Pythagorean 3:4:5 triangle.

Lorenz Lechler presented many of these design and construction techniques in his *Instructions*. In his prescriptions for designing a hall church with a single-aisled choir,

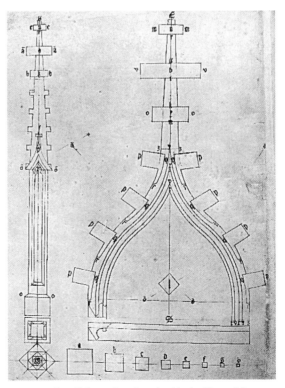

4. Geometric grid for a pinnacle and gablet by Hanns Schmutter-mayer; from his *Fialenbüchlein* (Nuremberg, late 1480s)

Lechler used the width of the choir to determine, by means of arithmetical ratios, both the major dimensions of the church and smaller components. He also used the width of the choir to set the dimensions of a square that was then rotated on itself to provide the dimensions and shapes of the vault ribs and window mullions. He combined geometrical configurations and arithmetical ratios for producing basic measurements of all parts of the building and for settling structural questions pertaining to the choir vault and its buttressing system.

BIBLIOGRAPHY

C. von Drach: *Das Hütten-Geheimniss vom gerechten Steinmetzen-Grund* (Marburg, 1897)
L. Keller: *Zur Geschichte der Bauhütten und der Hüttengeheimnisse* (Berlin, 1898)
C. F. Discher: *Die deutschen Bauhütten im Mittelalter und ihre Geheimnisse* (Vienna, 1932)
P. Frankl: 'The Secret of the Mediaeval Masons', *A. Bull.*, xxvii (1945), pp. 46–60
D. H. S. Cranage: *Cathedrals and How they Were Built* (Cambridge, 1951)
L. R. Shelby: 'The 'Secret' of the Medieval Masons', *On Pre-modern Technology and Science: Studies in Honor of Lynn White, Jr.*, ed. B. Hall and D. West, Humana Civilitas: Sources and Studies Relating to the Middle Ages and Renaissance, i (Malibu, 1976), pp. 201–19
Les Bâtisseurs des cathédrales gothiques (exh. cat., ed. R. Recht; Strasbourg, Anc. Douane, 1989)

LON R. SHELBY

3. THE EXPERTISE. If structural problems developed in a medieval building, the patrons might bring together an Expertise or delegation of several master masons, to seek advice either from the group as a whole or from each separate member. Official reports from several of these Expertises have survived, and the three at Chartres, Girona and Milan provide particular insights into late medieval ideas about structure and design.

(i) Chartres Cathedral. In 1316 the authorities of Chartres Cathedral in France assembled three outside masters (two masons and a carpenter), all high-ranking Parisian craftsmen, to consult with their counterparts at Chartres concerning the maintenance and repair of the cathedral (most of which had been completed the previous century). The visitors rendered their opinions as a committee, and the technical questions that were posed to them can be inferred from their answers. They apparently surveyed most of the structure, noting repairs needed in various parts of the building. The primary concern, however, seems to have been with the high vaults and flying buttresses. The experts assured the cathedral authorities that, while the piers, ribs and keystones of the vaults were sound, parts of the webs might need to be replaced, and the crossing vault needed urgent repair. Furthermore, the flying buttresses needed repair before they endangered the stability of the vaults.

(ii) Girona Cathedral. A quite different set of problems faced the gathering of experts at Girona Cathedral, Spain, in 1416 (*see* GIRONA, §1(i)). In the 14th century the Cathedral Chapter had begun the process of replacing the Romanesque cathedral by building a new Gothic choir, but plans for the nave were not made until 1416, when the architect, Guillermo Boffiy, designed a single-cell nave that was to be as wide as the choir and aisles together. It was intended that the nave vault would have an unprecedented span of 22.25 m, and the Chapter convoked an Expertise of eleven masters to advise them on the feasibility of Boffiy's plan. The Chapter posed three questions: would a wide, single-cell nave fall down; if a three-aisled nave were built, how could it be made congruent with the three-aisled choir, and how high should it be; and which of the two designs would be more compatible with the choir and better proportioned to it?

Each of the masters responded separately and under oath. They unanimously agreed that, structurally speaking, Boffiy's design for the single-cell nave could be built if he continued with the care with which he had begun. To the second set of questions the masters gave varied answers, as might be expected, for there were several solutions available. To the third question, seven of the masters favoured a three-aisled nave, while four supported Boffiy's plan. When Boffiy was called before the Chapter several months later to answer the same set of questions, he defended his plan for a single-cell nave. A week later the Chapter allowed him to proceed, the nave was built, and its survival is the empirical validation of Boffiy's experiment.

(iii) Milan Cathedral. The most celebrated series of medieval Expertises took place in Milan in Italy at the end of the 14th century. The new cathedral begun by the Milanese in 1386 was to be one of the largest in Europe (*see* MILAN, §IV, 1(i)(a)), and a building council was appointed to oversee the project. When the local masons ran into difficulties with the foundations, the council brought in the first of a series of master masons from Germany and France to advise the council and the local masons on how to proceed. The conflicts between the Milanese and foreign consultants, the hesitancies of the council and the periodic changes of design for the cathedral provide a classic study of the potential problems inherent in the medieval building tradition, emphasized as they were in Milan by the deliberate choice of a design that was intended to reflect northern, rather than local, characteristics. The Milanese could operate only within the conservative traditions of Lombardy, and they had little preparation for taking on a project of this size and little understanding of, or sympathy with, the ideas and criticisms of the northern masters. Consequently, the first consultant, a French architect named Nicolas de Bonaventure, was dismissed within a year of his appointment in 1389.

The next consultant, a German master named Hans von Freiburg (Freiburg im Breisgau), entered into a protracted debate over the geometrical scheme to be applied to the cross-section of the building. The original design had been *ad quadratum*: the cross-section was to be inscribed within a square, and the height of the work to the top of the high vault should be the same as the total width of the nave and four aisles. To establish the height of the main vaults and those of the aisles, Hans proposed a design *ad triangulum*, based on an equilateral triangle, to replace the previously agreed dimensions. This proposal created dimensional problems arising from the irrational numbers inherent in equilateral triangles, and in 1391 a mathematician, Gabriele Stornaloco from Piacenza, was called in to resolve them (*see* MILAN, fig. 13). The clear internal width of Milan Cathedral is 96 braccia (the braccio, the Milanese cubit, is *c.* 600 mm). A true equilateral triangle on a base of 96 braccia has an irrational height, not measurable on a great measure of *c.* 83.1 braccia. Stornaloco proposed that this figure should be rounded up to 84 braccia. The original design *ad quadratum* had intended to use a great measure of eight braccia. Stornaloco's proposal eliminated the irrational root 3 but fixed the great measure at seven braccia. This proposal was disputed, and Heinrich Parler von Gmünd was called in to advise. He proposed a return to the *ad quadratum* scheme.

The council responded by calling an Expertise of 14 Italian masters in 1392, who unanimously rejected Parler's proposal and reduced the height of the nave to 76 braccia, which effectively replaced the equilateral triangle as well. They accepted Stornaloco's figure of 28 braccia for the height of the piers of the outer aisles, but above this level they worked to a great measure of 6 braccia. Since the horizontal great measure was unalterable at 8 braccia, the mensuration above the level of the piers was 'Pythagorean'. The 1392 Expertise was concerned, then, with establishing the great measure for the work so that the overall dimensions of the various components of the building could be decided. In the event, three great measures were used, one for the horizontal dimensions and two for the different stages of the vertical dimensions.

Parler was dismissed, and the Milanese proceeded unhindered by foreign consultants (except for a visit in 1394 by Ulrich von Ensingen, who achieved little) until 1399, when major decisions needed to be made about various structural questions. Three consultants were summoned from Paris, including Jean Mignot (*d* 1410) and Jacques Coene, although Mignot was soon left on his own. Detailed arguments took place in a series of meetings between 1399 and 1401. Mignot found fault with the construction of the foundations and urged that they be enlarged. He also criticized the proportions of the bases and capitals of the main piers, and he argued that the external buttresses should be made three times the thickness of the piers, on the grounds that the buttresses as designed would not be adequate to resist the thrust of the vaults. Finally, he proposed that the equilateral triangle be restored as the geometric basis of the cross-section, which would raise the height of the nave back to 84 braccia.

The Italians hotly defended everything that they had built so far, and in the discussions they supported the technical capability of their craft against what they saw as Mignot's geometrical theorizing. In the most famous exchange of all, the Italians declared, 'Scientia est unum et ars est aliud' ('Theory is one thing, practice another'), to which Mignot replied, 'Ars sine scientia nihil est' ('Practice is nothing without theory'). Here *'scientia'* meant the theory embodied in the rules known by the master architect. *'Ars'* meant the craft of the stone mason, the practice of construction. The Italians were telling Mignot that his theoretical rules were all very well, but they knew in practice how a cathedral should be built.

Both sides were working within the traditions of medieval masonry from different perspectives. Mignot's *'scientia'* was constructive geometry, which he found wanting in the work at Milan. His specific criticisms of the Milan structure reflected the building traditions of northern masons, based on centuries of empirical validation. His worries about the dimensions of the buttresses were not based on calculations of stress but on design traditions, and he mixed together aesthetic and structural criticisms in a way that demonstrated no very clear grasp of either. The local builders could not apply the geometrical rules of northern experts, but they were confident that their craft tradition would enable them to solve the design problems arising from the regionally unprecedented size and shape of Milan Cathedral. They doggedly rejected all external advice on major problems of construction and built the cathedral according to their own rules. The cathedral has remained standing for six centuries.

4. THE END OF THE MEDIEVAL TRADITION. Medieval masons, ignorant of the sophisticated mathematical techniques of modern engineers and architects, relied on myriad rules of thumb and geometrical manipulations that experience had shown to be effective. These traditions continued long after the Middle Ages, both in practice and in theory. Until Britain adopted the metric system *c.* 1970, British carpenters measured their work in eights or sixteenths of an inch, subdividing the basic module in a way that had been current for two millennia; and in France François Blondel's rule of 1683 for the widths of piers of arches consists only of geometry. It was not until a century later that Jean-Rodolphe Perronet reduced drastically the size of the river piers of his bridges from those given by the medieval rules of proportion.

The design traditions of the lodges were not suddenly eclipsed, but their importance was reduced by different developments. When Roriczer's *Büchlein von der Fialen Gerechtigkeit* was published in 1486, Arabic numerals were passing into common use, and the irrational value of root 2 could be measured to a degree of practical accuracy on a decimally subdivided rule. Vitruvian ideas of proportion were rediscovered by the princes, scholars and gentlemen of 15th-century Italy; the publication of an illustrated edition of Vitruvius (1511), following the reinforcement of his ideas in Leon Battista Alberti's *De re aedificatoria* (*c.* 1450), enabled men other than architects to design buildings. Guided by these rules and illustrations, an educated man could successfully try his hand at architecture without the trouble of learning how to build. A sign that by the 16th century Gothic theory was diverging from Gothic practice is the treatise of Rodrigo Gil de Hontañón (*see* GIL DE HONTAÑÓN, (3)): in this work the sketches of vaults and buttresses are not consistent within themselves, and it gives the impression that Rodrigo, who was a practising architect, was here copying mechanically something that he had learnt by rote.

By 1675 Robert Hooke knew of the hanging chain theory (*see* MASONRY, §III, 3(iv)), and Sir Christopher Wren applied the idea spectacularly, and in a way inconceivable to the Gothic architect, in his design of the inclined drum of St Paul's Cathedral, London. The medieval tradition had, however, already been broken: in 1638 Galileo Galilei gave the first recognizably modern account of structural analysis. His first 'new science', treating of the resistance that solid bodies offer to fracture, started a science based on rational mechanics rather than the empirical, geometrical rules of ancient and medieval times.

BIBLIOGRAPHY

S. Garcia: *Compendio de arquitectura y simetría de los templos* (1681, with insertion by R. Gil de Hontañón), ed. J. Camón (Salamanca, 1941)

J.-B.-A. Lassus: *Album de Villard de Honnecourt, architecte du XIIIe siècle: Manuscrit publié en facsimile* (Paris, 1858/R 1976)

R. Willis: *Facsimile of the Sketchbook of Wilars de Honecourt* (London, 1859) [trans. of Lassus, with add. commentary]

G. E. Street: *Some Account of Gothic Architecture in Spain* (London, 1865)

V. Mortet: 'L'Expertise de la cathédrale de Chartres en 1316', *Congr. Archéol. France*, lxvii (1900), pp. 308–29

H. Stein: 'Une Expertise du XVIe siècle', *Bib. Ecole Chartes*, lxx (1909), pp. 447–55

A. H. Thompson: 'Medieval Building Documents, and What We Learn from Them', *Proc. Somerset. Archaeol. & Nat. Hist. Soc.*, lxvi, 3rd ser., vi (1920), pp. 1–25

J. Ackerman: '*Ars sine scientia nihil est*: Gothic Theory of Architecture at the Cathedral of Milan', *A. Bull.*, xxxi (1949), pp. 84–111

P. Frankl: *The Gothic: Literary Sources and Interpretations through Eight Centuries* (Princeton, 1960)

L. R. Shelby: 'The Geometrical Knowledge of Medieval Master Masons', *Speculum*, xlvii (1972), pp. 395–421

L. R. Shelby, ed. and trans.: *Gothic Design Techniques: The Fifteenth-century Design Booklets of Mathes Roriczer and Hanns Schmuttermayer* (Carbondale, IL, 1977)

L. R. Shelby and R. Mark: 'Late Gothic Structural Design in the "Instructions" of Lorenz Lechler', *Architectura* [Munich], ix (1979), pp. 113–31

R. Mark: *Experiments in Gothic Structure* (Cambridge, MA, 1982)

S. L. Sanabria: 'The Mechanization of Design in the 16th Century: The Structural Formulae of Rodrigo Gil de Hontañón', *J. Soc. Archit. Hist.*, xli (1982), pp. 281–93

F. B. Toker: 'Gothic Architecture by Remote Control: An Illustrated Contract of 1340', *A. Bull.*, lxvii (1985), pp. 67–95

For further bibliography *see* LECHLER, LORENZ, §2 and RORICZER, (3).

LON R. SHELBY, with JACQUES HEYMAN

Mason (ii). American family of architects. George C(hamplin) Mason sr (*b* Newport, RI, 17 July 1820; *d* Philadelphia, PA, 31 Jan 1894) set up practice in Newport in 1858 and was the city's leading architect in the 1860s and 1870s. His son, George C(hamplin) Mason jr (*b* Newport, 8 Aug 1850; *d* Ardmore, PA, 22 April 1924), became his partner in 1871 after a varied career as a merchant, artist, journalist and estate agent; he was a prolific writer, publishing primarily on Newport topics. The Masons were part of a well-established Newport family, a situation that assisted them in setting up their architectural practice. George C. Mason sr's work was largely residential. The August Belmont summer house (begun 1860; destr.), Bythesea, RI, was a typical example: a large and unprepossessing, hip-roofed clapboard structure with a cross-gabled pavilion accenting the symmetrical, three-bay entrance front.

With the emergence of the younger Mason as chief designer, the firm's designs became more ambitious. The earliest commission ascribed to him, the Thomas Cushing house (1869–70), Newport, is an elaborate essay in the STICK STYLE. Mason jr studied American colonial architecture and published many books on the subject. He designed the earliest Colonial Revival house in the USA, the Frederick Sheldon residence (1871–2; destr.), Newport, and he was the first American architect to achieve prominence for his restoration projects. His best-known work was his restoration from 1895 to 1913 of Independence Hall (1731–53), Philadelphia.

WRITINGS

G. C. MASON SR

Newport and its Environs (Newport, 1848)

The Application of Art to Manufactures (New York, 1858)

Newport and its Cottages (Boston, 1875) [contains fine heliotype photographs of many Mason buildings]

The Old House Altered (New York, 1878)

G. C. MASON JR

'An American Country House', *Bldg & Engin. J.*, xxxix/1070 (1875), p. 36

'The Old Stone Mill at Newport', *Mag. Amer. Hist.*, iii/9 (1879), pp. 541–9

Thoughts on Architecture, its Literature and Practice (Newport, 1879)

'Colonial Architecture', *Amer. Archit. & Bldg News*, x/294 (1881), pp. 71–4; x/295 (1881), pp. 83–5

Architects and their Environment (Philadelphia, 1907)

BIBLIOGRAPHY

A. F. Downing and V. J. Scully jr: *Architectural Heritage of Newport, Rhode Island* (Cambridge, MA, 1952, rev. 2/New York, 1967)

D. Chase: 'Mason, George Champlin, Sr.' and 'Mason, George Champlin, Jr.', *Buildings on Paper: Rhode Island Architectural Drawings*, ed. W. Jordy and C. Monkhouse (Providence, 1982), pp. 222–4

DAVID CHASE

Mason [née Trumbull], **Alice (Bradford) Trumbull** (*b* Litchfield, CT, 1904; *d* New York, 1971). American painter. In her youth she travelled extensively in Europe, studying at the British Academy in Rome in 1923. She then trained with the painter Charles W. Hawthorne (1872–1930) at the National Academy of Design, New York, where she formed a friendship with artists Ilya Bolotowsky and Ephyr Slobodkina (*b* 1914), who were later co-founders of the Abstract American Artists group (AAA) in 1937. Mason continued her studies until 1931, attending courses at the Grand Central Art Galleries, New York, given by the Abstract Expressionist painter Arshile Gorky. In December 1930 she married and subsequently had two children. Before resuming painting (1934) she took up poetry and a literary correspondence with such leading artistic figures as Gertrude Stein. Stein's belief in the self-generative power of non-representational language accorded with Mason's own experiments in visual abstraction. Mason became a key figure in the AAA, acting as Treasurer and President between 1939 and 1963. During the 1940s and 1950s she exhibited occasionally at the Rose Fried Gallery, Twentieth Century Gallery and Hanse Gallery, New York. Her work created an important bridge for succeeding abstract and conceptual artists, laying its emphasis on structural elements of pure geometric form in closely organized and contemplative designs that typified Mason's natural reserve and lyrical sensibility.

BIBLIOGRAPHY

Alice Trumbull Mason (exh. cat. by R. Pincus-Witten, New York, Whitney, 1973)

Alice Trumbull Mason (exh. cat. by M. Brown, Tulane, U. LA, 1982)

Alice Trumbull Mason (exh. cat., New York, Washburn Gal., 1985)

Mason, George Heming (*b* Fenton Park, Staffs, 11 March 1818; *d* London, 22 Oct 1872). English painter. He lived in Rome from 1845. When his father's Staffordshire pottery firm failed in 1848, his allowance terminated and he turned seriously to painting. In the early 1850s he met Giovanni Costa and Frederic Leighton; Costa moulded Mason's style, and Leighton provided life-long financial support. He was also influenced by the work of the French artists that he saw at the Paris Exposition Universelle (1855), particularly Ernest Hébert, Jules Breton and Alexandre-Gabriel Decamps. The best of Mason's early works, such as *Ploughing in the Campagna* (1857; Liverpool, Walker A.G.), record picturesque scenes with an unpretentious sunlit naturalism.

In 1858 Mason married and settled in the family home at Wetley Abbey, Staffs. After a depressed and unproductive period, he was encouraged by Leighton and Costa to begin painting local scenes. *Wind on the Wold* (*c.* 1863; London, Tate), for example, depicting a girl driving calves, embodies a poetic and evocative mood. Mason moved to London in 1864. The large *Evening Hymn* (exh. 1868; ex-Wyndham priv. col.; etching, see 1982 exh. cat., no. 45) gained him his ARA in 1869. His last painting, *Harvest Moon* (1873; London, Tate), exemplifies his mature style. A procession of harvesters returns through twilit fields, carrying sheaves, scythes and musical instruments. Their dynamic poses and simplified costumes suggest that, like Fred Walker at this date, Mason wished to use the British peasant to depict the beauty of classical form. He was a great influence on the development of the Etruscan school.

DNB

BIBLIOGRAPHY

S. Reynolds: 'George Heming Mason and the Idealised Landscape', *Apollo*, cxiii (1981), pp. 106–9
George Heming Mason (exh. cat., ed. R. Billingham; Stoke-on-Trent, City Mus. & A.G., 1982)

HILARY MORGAN

Mason, Raymond (*b* Birmingham, 2 March 1922). English sculptor, active in France. He trained as a painter from 1937 at Birmingham College of Art and the Royal College of Art, but he turned to sculpture while at the Slade (1943–6). In 1946 he moved to Paris; having nowhere else to work, he made the street his subject. His drawings were strongly influenced by his mentor, Giacometti.

In the reliefs Mason exhibited at the Beaux-Arts Gallery, London, in the mid-1950s, the image was gouged into the plaster as a kind of drawing; but in *Barcelona Tram* (1953; Paris, Pompidou) he developed the figures into three dimensions, while in *Crossroads at the Odéon* (1958–9; Paris, Pompidou) the more complex and animated forms threatened to break the box enclosure altogether. He devoted much of the 1960s to *The Crowd* (1963–8; Paris, Fonds N. A. Contemp.), a bronze mass of figures; yet he found that the forms were rendered inert when translated into metal and that they ceased to be a scene and became an object.

Mason first used bright colour in the *Expulsion of Fruit and Vegetables from the Heart of Paris 28 February, 1969* (1969–71; Paris, St Eustache), both to 'animate the space' and, he said, to 'humanize the figures' (see Brenson interview in 1977 exh. cat.); the whole thrust of his art has been to eliminate the distance between the work and the spectator. Both here and in *Tragedy in the North: Winter Rain Tears* (1975–7; Paris, Gal. Claude Bernard) Mason attempted to create a whole world, a microcosm, in tableaux of life-size figures. The architectural setting is built up rather as the terraces of a stadium, and figures separately cast in epoxy resin are slotted in. These bulging-eyed characters, strident in colour and gesture, populist in flavour, are reminiscent of Daumier's polychrome busts of the Deputies, and of James Gillray and the English humorists. In 'translating a painter's vision into three dimensions' (see 1982 exh. cat., p. 13), Mason successfully

challenged the prevailing orthodoxies of contemporary sculpture.

BIBLIOGRAPHY

Raymond Mason (exh. cat., Paris, Gal. Claude Bernard, 1977) [incl. interview with M. Brenson]
Raymond Mason (exh. cat., intro. M. Peppiatt; ACGB, 1982)
Raymond Mason (exh. cat. by G. Régnier, Paris, Pompidou, 1985)
H. Lessore: *A Partial Testament* (London, 1986)

□

Mason, William (i) (*b* Hull, 12 Feb 1725; *d* Aston, S. Yorks, 5 April 1797). English clergyman, writer and garden designer. Educated at St John's College, Cambridge, he was ordained in 1754 and was a royal chaplain from 1757 to 1772. His friends and acquaintances included such literary and artistic figures as the poet Thomas Gray, Horace Walpole (later 4th Earl of Orford), William Gilpin, the garden designer 'Capability' Brown and the painters Paul Sandby and Joshua Reynolds, the last of whom provided material for his 'Anecdotes' (posthumously published in W. Cotton's anthology in 1859) and for Mason's translation of *De arte graphica* (1668) by Charles-Alphonse Du Fresnoy.

Mason's best-known written works are his verse history *The English Garden* and his satirical attacks upon the royal architect William Chambers. *The English Garden*, organized in four books after Virgil's *Georgics* (completed 29 BC), a didactic poem on agriculture, brought together advice on the mundane activities of practical gardening and historical and critical commentary on the past and present art of landscape design, all of which was strongly coloured by Mason's affinity with the aesthetics of the PICTURESQUE. His widely applauded verse satire *An Heroic Epistle to Sir William Chambers* poured scorn upon the Tory architect's enthusiasm for Chinoiserie as expressed in his *Dissertation on Oriental Gardening* (1772). Chambers claimed first-hand experience of gardens in China and sought to promote the development of an imitative European type. Through his parodic versions of the garden contrivances described in the *Dissertation* and ridicule of their value as objects of Associationism, Mason deeply humiliated Chambers; the *Dissertation* had its supporters nevertheless, and became an influential text abroad, particularly in France.

Mason's most admired contribution to garden design was probably his flower-garden at Nuneham, Oxon, laid out from 1772 with assistance from George Simon Harcourt, Viscount Nuneham (1736–1809), an amateur landscape painter who inherited the estate on becoming 2nd Earl Harcourt in 1777. It consisted of a series of irregular flower-beds, lawns and serpentine walks in a small and sheltered area between the Palladian house and the Neoclassical All Saints Church (1764), built in the grounds for the first Earl by James 'Athenian' Stuart; there was also a classical Temple of Flora and several herms around its periphery. In keeping with the late 18th-century preoccupation with subjective expression the garden had a sentimental character, with a plethora of melancholy verse epitaphs and remembrances incised on seats and masonry tablets. Aquatint views of the garden were made by Paul Sandby and published in *The Virtuosi's Museum* (1778).

WRITINGS

The English Garden, 4 vols (London, 1772–81), rev. W. Burgh (York, 1783)

An Heroic Epistle to Sir William Chambers (London, 1773)

trans: C.-A. Du Fresnoy: *De arte graphica* (Paris, 1668) as *The Art of Painting* (London, 1783)

The Works of William Mason, M.A., 4 vols (London, 1811)

'Anecdotes of Sir Joshua Reynolds, Chiefly Relative to his Manner of Coloring', *Sir Joshua Reynolds's Notes and Observations on Pictures . . . Extracts from his Italian Sketchbooks*, ed. W. Cotton (London, 1859)

BIBLIOGRAPHY

J. W. Draper: *William Mason: A Study in Eighteenth-century Culture* (New York, 1924)

M. L. Batey: *Nuneham Courtenay*, guidebook (Oxford, 1970, rev. 1979)

——: 'William Mason: English Gardener', *Gdn Hist.*, i/2 (1973), pp. 11–25

A Candidate for Praise: William Mason (exh. cat. by B. Barr and J. Ingamells, York, C.A.G., 1973)

MICHAEL SYMES

Mason, William (ii) (*b* Ipswich, 24 Feb 1810; *d* Dunedin, New Zealand, 22 June 1897). New Zealand architect of English birth. He was articled in Ipswich to his father, George Mason (1782–1865), but soon moved to London where he was a pupil of Edward Blore. After a period of practice in Ipswich during which he designed several churches (most notably St Botolph's, Colchester, 1837–8), parsonages and poorhouses, he emigrated in 1838 to New South Wales. There he worked in the office of Mortimer Lewis, Colonial Architect.

In March 1840, as Superintendent of Works, he joined Lieutenant-Governor Hobson in New Zealand, where he was a key participant in the founding of Auckland. He began a private practice in Auckland in 1841 and remained there until 1862. He then moved to Dunedin where he practised until 1876, latterly with Nathaniel Young Armstrong Wales (1832–1903).

Mason exemplified the early Victorian approach to architecture; his churches were neo-Gothic, his public buildings Neo-classical, while his houses were in a late Georgian style readily adapted to colonial conditions and the preferences of the client. Old Government House (1855–7), Auckland, and St Matthew's Church (1873), All Saints' Church (1865–73), Bishopscourt (1871–2; now Columba College) and the Bank of New South Wales (1866), all in Dunedin, are among his most notable surviving buildings. Mason was the first architect to live and work in New Zealand, and he established professional standards of benefit to later architects. He was active in public life, as President of the Board of Works in Auckland, as Mayor and Chief Magistrate in Dunedin and as an MP.

Colvin

BIBLIOGRAPHY

J. Stacpoole: *William Mason: The First New Zealand Architect* (Auckland and Oxford, 1971)

JOHN STACPOOLE

Masone [Massone], **Giovanni.** *See* MAZONE, GIOVANNI.

Masonry. Assemblage of stones, bricks or sun-dried mud (adobe), fitted together for construction, with or without mortar.

I. Introduction. II. Types. III. Structure.

I. Introduction.

Masonry can be either quarried and artificially shaped (dressed and ashlar; *see* §II below), or natural (dry-stone and flint walling). Dry-stone walling is an ancient masonry technique, using well-chosen frost-shattered or splintered rocks carefully interlocked. The resulting structures are most frequently used for field walls and crude huts. South Italian trulli, with their beehive domes, are remarkable survivors of this continuous tradition. The dry-stone walling of GREAT ZIMBABWE, however, shows that it could also be used in ceremonial buildings.

The ancient Egyptians first exploited cut stone, using primitive tools to extract and shape rectangular blocks and harder granites to grind and polish smooth surfaces and perfect joints. Their extraordinary skill permitted substantial masonry structures to be erected without any form of bonding or mortar. Aswan granite was quarried using wedges, heat and rapid cooling, whereby the Egyptians created substantial monolithic blocks, such as the obelisk (h. 30 m) now in the Piazza di S Giovanni in Laterano, Rome.

Ancient Greek and Roman masonry shows variants upon Egyptian, including use of rustication (*see* §II below), concrete and brickwork, the commonest Roman form. The Romans often combined masonry, concrete and brick in complex ways (*see* ROME, ANCIENT, §II, 1(ii)(c)), as in the Pantheon (*c.* AD 120), Rome. Ancient Greek and Roman masonry depended on the quality of the stone and the methods of extraction. Medieval European architecture often lacked one or the other, and commonly both, hence the predominance of rubble (*see* §II below), which consisted of virtually anything to hand. The Byzantine and Islamic civilizations were the true inheritors of the Classical tradition, and Islam reintroduced such Roman refinements as the hardened chisel and the drill into 11th-century Europe. Gothic architecture was heavily dependent upon good masonry technology (*see* §III below), although some areas, notably England, persevered with older rubble-based techniques. By the early Renaissance most ancient Roman masonry techniques, with the important exception of concrete, had been re-learnt, and masonry became the mainstay of European architecture until the advent of cast-iron and steel beams in the 18th and 19th centuries. Modern steel construction has reduced masonry to mere cladding, with brick or stone infilling.

Islamic civilizations used many masonry techniques including ashlar, brick and rubble. The buildings of the Ottoman Turks exhibit outstanding cutting and finish. The 16th-century Selimiye Cami at EDIRNE is one of the greatest structural achievements of world architecture. In Islamic Iran brick was favoured, but in India the climate made sandstone a suitable, desirable and durable building material. Marble cutting achieved a remarkable level of sophistication, with the intricate undercutting in the 11th- and 12th-century temples at Mt Abu (*see* MT ABU, §2) approaching the level of filigree. The Taj Mahal at Agra (*see* AGRA, §II, 1) is perhaps the finest example of marble cutting in the world.

Masonry became important to the ceremonial architecture of Mesoamerica from about the 6th century BC, but, although cutting techniques were refined, the post-and-lintel construction precluded much development. The Pueblo Indians of CHACO CANYON, NM, had constructed elaborate masonry buildings by the mid-11th century AD.

Traditional Chinese, Japanese and Korean architecture was almost entirely timber-based, stone being reserved for foundations and platforms. The most significant role for masonry was in fortification and subterranean tombs (*see* CHINA, §II, 6(ii); JAPAN, §III, 1; KOREA, §II, 3(ii)). The GREAT WALL OF CHINA is the largest masonry structure in the world.

See also STONE (i), §II.

II. Types.

There follows an alphabetical listing with descriptions of masonry types. Cross-references within this article are indicated in the form 'See *Opus testaceum*'; cross-references to other articles in the Dictionary are in the usual form '*see* STRIPWORK'.

Ashlar. Fine-jointed, regularly shaped stone blocks, with a smooth, dressed exposed face. The term generally applies to tight-fitting oblong blocks laid in horizontal courses. Ashlar was introduced (*c.* 2620 BC) by the ancient Egyptians in the step pyramid of Djoser at Saqqara and employed universally thereafter for public or high-quality architecture. English Portland stone is considered one of the finest materials for ashlar. Ashlar is often used as a veneer concealing another material, such as rubble or brick.

Cloisonné. Rectangular stone blocks set within 'frames' of another material, usually brick, for colour contrast. Cloisonné was especially popular in Byzantine architecture (e.g. the church of the Theotokos, Hosios Loukas, Phocis, 946–55, and Hagioi Theodoroi, Athens, mid-11th century).

Cyclopean [polygonal]. Method of using large irregular blocks, seen in several structures of the Greek Late Bronze Age, *c.* 1300–1200 BC. The rocks were smoothed and finished, then interlocked skilfully to accommodate their polygonal shapes. The walls of Mycenae, Greece (*c.* 1250 BC), preserve the best examples. The Etruscans built cyclopean walls from the 6th century BC, and the Romans continued the tradition down to the last centuries BC (e.g. Aletrium [now Alatri], 3rd century BC; Praeneste [now Palestrina], Temple of Fortuna Primigenia, *c.* 80 BC).

Dressed. Term for any stone block with a finished or smoothly worked surface. Normally made for use in ashlar walling, dressed stone may also be used for quoins or long and short work (see below).

Dry-stone. Use of stone blocks or slabs without mortar or cement bonding. Dry masonry may be either ashlar, cyclopean or rubble. The ancient Egyptians were able to lay their ashlar dry, each block resting directly upon the next with exceptionally fine joints. The Greeks also employed dry-stone techniques, although the Romans, with their liking for brick and concrete, favoured mortar and cement. Few later architectural periods had sufficiently good stone-cutting technology to permit dry ashlar walling, although the rusticated façades of the Westgate (1380) of Canterbury, England, were constructed entirely without mortar.

Dry-stone rubble walling, either for boundary walls or for structures, is an ancient tradition still found in much of Europe. The Aran islands off Co. Galway, Ireland, have many miles of dry-stone walling, while in areas of England such as Derbyshire and the Cotswolds dry-stone walls and buildings abound. Other notable areas for dry-rubble masonry are southern Africa, for example Great Zimbabwe (11th–15th centuries), and, in modern times, south Italy and the Canary Islands (Spain). Dry-stone walling is not dressed but cut into slabs that are laid in irregular courses. In buildings, dry-stone walls are thickly plastered inside.

Flushwork. Technique in which knapped flint is contrasted with ashlar to make patterns in the masonry, as at, for example, the gatehouse (*c.* 1320–25) of Butley Priory, Suffolk (*see* HERALDRY, fig.17). The split side of the flint is set flush with the surface.

Galleting. Technique whereby sherds or fragments of a material are inserted into the mortar to fill gaps left by rubble or irregular masonry blocks. It is most common in flint buildings of eastern and southern England, where walls abound with sharp black splinters, and is also found in areas where volcanic debris is employed, such as the Canary Islands.

Herringbone. Pattern of brick or stone courses laid obliquely in alternating rows, creating interlocking zigzags, each pair of rows resembling the backbone of a fish. Occasionally, a horizontal course is inserted between layers, creating a 'spine'. It is very common in Anglo-Saxon buildings, using either re-used Roman brick or slabs of ragstone. Roman rubble cores sometimes approximate herringbone patterns (e.g. Richborough Castle, Kent; 280s). Anglo-Saxon examples were often plastered over, suggesting that the intent was structural rather than decorative. Perhaps the most extensive use is the west tower of St Margaret, Marton (Lincs), probably built in the 11th century. English herringbone continued after the Norman Conquest of 1066: in brick in the south transept of St Albans Abbey (now Cathedral), and in the rubble repairs to Pevensey Castle (E. Sussex), both 1070–80.

Decorative herringbone reappeared in late medieval English domestic building, employed in the brick nogging infill of timber-framing, as at Ockwells Manor (1450s), Bray (Berks): it is most commonly found in thin brick fire-backs of early chimney-stacks. Decorative brick herringbone was briefly popular in late Byzantine architecture: Hagia Theodora, Arta (Greece), and the south church of Fenarı Isa Cami (church of Constantine Lips), Istanbul (Turkey), both late 13th century.

Long and short. Arrangement of stone blocks that is both structural and decorative, in which individual dressed stones alternate vertically, one lengthwise, the next on end etc. The origin may be Roman, as Ostia exhibits many examples of vertical strips of tufa jigsawed into regular brick masonry. The method is particularly associated with Anglo-Saxon architecture in England, where it is employed for angle quoins, or as STRIPWORK within a wall. The advantage of long and short angles within a rubble structure comes from the greater strength and longevity of cut-stone masonry corners, plus the deep bedding of the rectangular short blocks into the wall, which gives extra support to the rubble structure at every second block. Long and short work often appears as stripwork decoration within a façade, where it is both decorative and stiffens the fabric. Long and short work seems to have been well established by *c.* 1000: the tower of All Saints, Earls Barton (Northants), is the most famous example (for illustration *see* STRIPWORK).

Although it occurs seldom in continental Europe, one example exists on the west façade of S Simpliciano, Milan (Italy), where a stone narthex (probably 12th century) employing long and short technology has been embedded into the Late Antique brickwork.

Opus Africanum. Type of masonry used in Roman North Africa, in which a framework of dressed stone is infilled with panels of mud brick or rubble.

Opus incertum. Small, irregular blocks inserted into thick mortar to create a crude masonry surface to a rubble or concrete wall. It appears in Roman Republican architecture, certainly by the 3rd or 2nd century BC at Ostia, and perhaps earlier (*see also* ROME, ANCIENT, §II, 1(ii)(c)).

Opus mixtum. See *Opus testaceum.*

Opus reticulatum. Roman decorative device using small, square slabs of stone embedded into a regular, tightly knit diamond pattern, used by 55 BC in the Theatre of Pompey, Rome. The Torhalle of Lorsch Abbey (*c.* 800; *see* LORSCH ABBEY, §2) has multi-coloured *opus reticulatum* on its upper façade.

Opus testaceum. Concrete faced with regular courses of brick, used in the Roman period, as in the Theatre of Marcellus, Rome (13 BC; *see* ROME, ANCIENT, §II, 1(ii)(c)). When panels of *opus reticulatum* are combined with vertical strips of *opus testaceum* the technique is known as *opus mixtum.*

Polygonal. See *Cyclopean.*

Rubble. The most common masonry technique, incorporating any material found or recovered, such as dressed blocks, broken fragments, brick or flint. The success of rubble depends on the thickness of the wall and the strength of the binding mortar. If either is too thin, the structure will fail. As it is almost impossible to construct a thin rubble wall, owing to the irregularity of the material and the size of the gaps to be filled by the mortar, in areas or building traditions lacking dressed stone and ashlar technology, rubble walls are likely to be very thick, with all the consequent architectural disadvantages.

Rubble was, however, the key to the Roman use of concrete, which was a contained rubble core drenched in a lime mortar mix (*see* ROME, ANCIENT, §II, 1(ii)(c)). Builders in later architectural periods, such as the Romanesque, having no practical knowledge of Roman concrete, enclosed massive rubble walling within two skins of dressed ashlar (*see* THICK-WALL STRUCTURE). English Romanesque and Gothic buildings are notorious for their employment of heavy rubble walling. Rubble has been generally avoided in sophisticated architecture since the

13th century, and modern concrete is made from a different mix. Rubble has, however, survived as the mainstay of simple vernacular masonry building worldwide.

Rustication. Ancient decorative treatment of ashlar, where the exposed surface is deliberately roughened to suggest the original strength of the natural rock. The rugged texture contrasts strongly with the fine-jointing of the coursing. The Greeks first exploited rustication, commonly on fortified walls or platforms, for example the temple complex at Pergamon (Turkey), since when it has been associated with expressions of power. Although a rusticated wall may be more difficult to scale, the defensive effectiveness is not great. Appearance is all. Almost every Classically based style in architectural history has employed rustication for effect, usually for the basement or lower storeys of important public buildings, for example the Porta Rosa (4th century BC) at Velia and the Palazzo Medici-Riccardi (begun 1444) in Florence, both in Italy, and the 17th-century palace of Versailles, France. Completely rusticated façades are less common but usually express some aggressive intent: the 13th-century walls of Aigues-Mortes, France, the Palazzo Vecchio (begun 1298) in Florence, Newgate Prison (1770–78; destr. 1902) in London and the Marshall Field Wholesale Store (1885–7; destr.; *see* RICHARDSON, H. H., fig. 4) in Chicago, USA. Rustication became almost obligatory in all 18th- and 19th-century public buildings in Europe and the USA. Other forms include smooth blocks raised above wide 'cement' bonding lines, as with the Radcliffe Camera (finished 1749), Oxford, England; individual blocks with sharply bevelled angles; and another form that enjoyed a brief popularity, Diamond Point, which has smooth-sided pyramids projecting from each show-face, as at the 17th-century Czernin Palace (Prague, Czech Republic).

Spolia [Lat.: 'spoils']. Masonry derived from a previous building; a term commonly applied to the re-use of Greek or Roman fragments. The respond bases within the aisles of S Lorenzo Maggiore, Milan (Italy), are up-turned Corinthian capitals. The chancel arch of ESCOMB CHURCH (7th–9th century), in England, is apparently a 4th-century arch dismantled and removed from a Roman fort. Classical and earlier spolia occasionally appear in the foundations of later buildings: the New Kingdom statues (*c.* 1539–*c.* 1075 BC) excavated from beneath the forecourt of the Greco-Roman Temple of Horus at EDFU, and the apse foundation of Notre-Dame-de-Nazareth, the 12th-century former cathedral of Vaison-la-Romaine (Provence), packed with fluted column sections and other Roman fragments.

Vermiculated [Lat. *vermiculus*: 'little worm']. Variety of rustication, where the exposed surface is carved into intricate, worm-like patterns, sometimes in high relief, which may occupy the entire block or be framed within a plain border. Popular in some Renaissance architecture, for example Giulio Romano's house (1538–44) in Mantua, Italy, it was especially liked in England: the 18th-century doorcases of Bedford Square (built 1775–80) and the New Government Offices (1898–*c.* 1912), both in London.

BIBLIOGRAPHY

W. C. Huntington and R. E. Mickadeit: *Building Construction* (New York, 1929, 4/1975)

A. Behringer and F. Rek: *Das Mauerbuch* (Ravensburg, 1953)

F. Rainsford-Hannay: *Dry Stone Walling* (London, 1957/R 1976)

A. Clifton Taylor: *The Pattern of English Building* (Frome, 1962, rev. 4/1987)

J. Bowyer: *A History of Building* (London, 1973)

J. S. Ackerman: 'The Tuscan/Rustic Order: A Study in the Metaphorical Language of Architecture', *J. Soc. Archit. Hist.*, xlii (1983), pp. 15–34

L. G. Redstone: *Masonry in Architecture* (New York, 1984)

M. London: *Masonry* (Washington, DC, 1988)

A. Shadmon: *Stone: An Introduction* (London, 1989)

For further bibliography *see* ANCIENT NEAR EAST, §I, 1; ARABIA, §II, 2(i); EARLY CHRISTIAN AND BYZANTINE ART, §II, 1; GREECE, ANCIENT, §II, 1(ii); INDIAN SUBCONTINENT, §III, 1; ISLAMIC ART, §II, 1; MESOAMERICA, PRE-COLUMBIAN, §II, 1(i); PREHISTORIC ART, §§IV, 2, V, 3 and VI, 2; and ROME, ANCIENT, §II, 1(ii)

FRANCIS WOODMAN

III. Structure.

The general principles of the structural behaviour of masonry, developed below with respect to the simple arch, apply to any form of masonry construction, and they may be illustrated by that clear feat of structural engineering, the Gothic great church. The problems are encountered in their most critical form in the attenuated structure of Gothic; from the pre-Gothic period only the dome presents any structural challenge that is not present in Gothic itself, and no masonry structure built after the Middle Ages presented new problems.

1. Introduction. 2. Structural theory. 3. Structural elements. 4. The Gothic structure.

1. INTRODUCTION. The outstanding feature of masonry buildings, even those erected many years ago, is their ability to survive. Minor failures have occurred, and there have been major catastrophes, but the masonry structure is essentially extremely stable. Two severe earthquakes only slightly damaged Hagia Sophia, Istanbul (*see* ISTANBUL, §III, 1(ii)(a)); the bombardments of World War II often resulted in a slightly damaged medieval cathedral surrounded by a modern city that was totally destroyed, as at Cologne. At a much less severe level of disturbance, the continual shifts and settlements of foundations experienced over the centuries seem to cause the masonry structure little distress, although, as will be seen, there may be an initial high-risk period of about a generation.

Gothic churches were designed by men who were both architects and engineers. The master mason's educational path contrasts sharply with that of modern practice, which is based on the post-medieval concept of the 'gentleman' architect, who needs a technical adviser for his structure, if this is at all complex (*see* MASON (i), §II, 1). The evolutionary tree of the modern structural engineer has its roots in the medieval period (and earlier), that of the modern architect in developments of the 15th century to the 17th. Until the end of the Middle Ages the architect knew, in the fullest technical sense, how to build, as well as how to give his building an 'architectural' design. The question seems to be obscured by the visual evidence; for example, by the differences in form between each of the great ring of High Gothic cathedrals round Paris; or again, the records of the late 14th-century Expertise at Milan

Cathedral (*see* MILAN, §IV, 1(i)(a) and MASON, §IV, 3(iii)), which led Ackerman (1949) to the tempting conclusion that structure played 'a secondary role in the process of creation'. This conclusion may be true for part of the work at Milan, but once it is believed to be true for any great church, attitudes are no longer those of Gothic builders but of Renaissance architects. According to Harvey (1958) the 'Gothic rules were so complicated that no one who had not served a long apprenticeship and spent years of practice could master them; whereas the rules of Vitruvius were so easy to grasp that even bishops could understand them, and princes could try their hand at design on their own'.

Within the outward appearance of a great cathedral building there lies a stone skeleton whose anatomy, while showing evolutionary differences brought about by place and time, may be analysed and discussed in common terms. The medieval rules ensured that the skeleton was effective, and decorative elements could then be applied with safety. The quadripartite rib vault, for example, and the lierne vault, the tierceron vault, the star vault and even the fan vault have a common basic structural action (*see* VAULT: RIB). Since medieval cathedrals survive, this confirms that such rules as may be deduced from an examination of the medieval sources were both effective and correct.

2. STRUCTURAL THEORY.

(i) The material. (ii) The voussoir arch. (iii) The master theorem (the 'safe theorem'). (iv) Settlement and cracking. (v) Timescale for settlement. (vi) Models.

(i) The material. Masonry is a collection of dry stones (or bricks etc), sometimes squared and well-fitted, sometimes left unworked, that are placed one on another to form a stable structure. Mortar may be used to fill interstices, but this mortar will have been weak initially, may have decayed with time and cannot be assumed to add strength to the construction. Thus an arch built by assembling wedge-shaped stones (voussoirs) upon centering will stand when the centering is removed. Gravity ensures that each stone presses on the next, and a state of compression exists throughout the masonry. If the arch were inverted it would fly apart, unless there were strong adhesive (mortar) between the stones that would help them to resist the disintegrating tensile forces. Stability of a whole masonry structure is assured by the compaction under gravity of the various elements; a general state of compressive stress exists, but only feeble tensions can be resisted.

All this would have been well understood by medieval builders, although they would not have had numerical concepts of stress or of the strength of their material. A modern engineer would perhaps begin by making calculations to relate these quantities. In this connection a parameter established by Yvon Villarceau in 1854 and used by engineers in the design of great masonry arches is illuminating. An indirect quantity was used to express the strength of stone: the height to which a prismatic column might (theoretically) be built before crushing at the base under its own weight. This height may be predicted easily; a medium sandstone might have a unit mass of 2000 kg/m³ and a crushing stress of 400 kg/cm². Dividing one figure

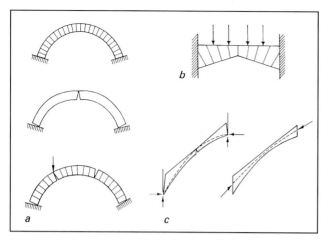

1. Masonry arches: (a) (from top to bottom): fitting perfectly between abutments; cracking to accommodate an increased span; at collapse by the formation of four 'hinges'; (b) flat arch; (c) flying buttress: (left) passive state; (right) working state

by the other gives the height of the self-crushing column as 2000 m.

The pier in an attenuated Gothic cathedral carries more than its own weight: it must support the high vault and the timber roof above and will be subjected to additional loads from wind (and perhaps earthquake). Even a crossing pier, however, which carries the central tower and is among the most highly stressed elements of a masonry structure, will not be subjected to a high level of stress compared with the potential crushing strength of the material. The piers will have average compressive stresses not more than one-tenth of the crushing strength of the material, and the main portions of the load-bearing structure (flying buttresses or the webs of masonry vaults, for example) will be working at one-hundredth of the crushing strength. Infill panels or walls, which carry little more than their own weight but which must always be in compression if they are to be stable, may be subject to a stress as low as one-thousandth of the potential of the material. This low background of compressive stress ensures that the small pieces of stone are compacted by gravity into a certain overall shape designed by the architect, but that shape can be maintained only if the stones do not slip one on another. The elements may interpenetrate to some extent, but the main instrument of stability is the low compressive stress that will allow friction forces to develop, locking the stones against slip.

Thus the behaviour of the masonry structure can be examined in the light of three simplifying assumptions, each one of which is not strictly true, and each of which must in any case be tested in the light of contrary experience with a particular building. The three assumptions are that masonry has no tensile strength, that stresses are so low that masonry has effectively an unlimited compressive strength and that sliding failure does not occur. The first assumption will clearly lead to an underestimate of the strength of a structure, but it is not unduly conservative. Individual blocks of stone may be strong in tension (and corbelled construction relies on this), but

mortar between stones is indeed weak. An attempt to impose tensile forces would pull the work apart. The assumption that the material has unlimited compressive strength will be approximately correct for average stresses. Stress concentrations can arise, however, which will lead to local distress evidenced by surface spalling (splintering), but the overall structure will not fail (see §3(ii) below). Finally, individual stones can slip, but generally the masonry structure retains its shape remarkably well; only a very small compressive prestress is necessary to avoid the dangers of slip and loss of cohesion. Particular precautions are occasionally taken to avoid slip (see PINNACLE, §1), but a masonry structure is rarely distressed in this way. It is possible to build a comprehensive structural theory on the basis of these assumptions and to illuminate the behaviour of a large masonry structure. The masonry arch is a particularly simple example, and its action repays detailed examination.

(ii) The voussoir arch. The voussoir arch (see fig. 1a top) is supposed to be made from identical wedge-shaped stone voussoirs, assembled without mortar on temporary supporting formwork (centering), and fitting exactly between its abutments. When the centering supporting the masonry is removed, the arch starts to thrust horizontally, and the abutments give way slightly. The arch must accommodate itself to the increased span within the framework of the three basic material assumptions: while the voussoirs retain their initial coherence they do not slip against each other (or against the abutments); the stone does not crush; and tensile forces cannot be resisted. The geometrical accommodation is made by cracking of the arch (1a middle; greatly exaggerated). The voussoirs cannot slip, but they can hinge about a point of contact either on the intrados or the extrados. The resulting cracks, which will always occur in a real stone structure, are not signs of incipient collapse but merely indicate that the structure has responded to some unpredictable but inevitable shift in the external environment.

Indeed, the cracked three-pinned arch (1a middle) is a well-known and perfectly satisfactory structural form. When such a stable arch is subjected to a single point load (1a bottom), which is slowly increased so that its magnitude becomes steadily more important compared with the dead weight of the arch, some pre-existing cracks might close and new cracks might open, but none of this need lead to loss of structural integrity. The arch can fail only when sufficient hinges have formed to create a mechanism of collapse, as shown in the four hinges of fig. 1a bottom. There are some forms of arch for which such a mechanism of collapse cannot be constructed: the flat arch (*plate-bande*; 1b) and the arch form employed in a flying buttress (1c). Within the limitations of the present assumptions, these types of arch are infinitely strong. They will fail only when loads increase to such an extent that overall crushing occurs, or alternatively by one of the stones sliding out of the construction.

These arguments are kinematic in nature, being based upon ideas of mechanisms of collapse; but masonry structures can also be understood through statics. The equilibrium state of an arch may best be studied by the funicular polygon, which describes geometrically the way forces are transmitted (in compression) from section to section of the arch, giving the shape of the line of thrust. The shape of the compressive funicular polygon is exactly the same as that of a weightless cord in tension. If such a cord is imagined to be hung from two points, and subjected to the same loads that act on the arch, then 'as hangs the flexible line, so, but inverted, will stand the rigid arch' (Hooke, 1675). Since, in the real arch, compressive forces can be transmitted between stones but tension cannot, the funicular polygon must lie within the actual boundaries of the masonry.

(iii) The master theorem (the 'safe theorem'). Ideas of a hanging cord, corresponding to the line of thrust in an arch, give a vivid picture of the way in which such a simple structure behaves. There is, however, a master theorem of masonry, which, although it applies to any assemblage, no matter how complex, will be presented for the simple arch. The first inescapable fact is that the system of compressive forces in the structure, equilibrating the self-weight of the building and carrying wind and other live loads to the ground, must lie completely within the boundaries of the masonry. The three simplifying assumptions (no tensile strength, great compressive strength, no slip) enable an account of the behaviour of masonry to be embraced within the modern so-called plastic theory of structures. The plastic theorems are then available, of which, for masonry, the 'safe theorem' is the master. The simple statement of the theorem is that if a line of thrust can be found to lie within the masonry (for example the funicular arch within the real arch), then the structure can never collapse under the given loads. The statement may seem self-evident, but it has important consequences.

The power of the safe theorem lies in the fact that the satisfactory thrust line found by the analyst need not be the actual thrust line, which will necessarily shift as small, unpredictable changes occur in the environment, causing the structure to respond by a shift in its pattern of cracks. The actual state of a structure will constantly alter. All the analyst need calculate is just one possible satisfactory state, and the real structure will also be able to find such a state for itself. There are no conceivable settlements or other disturbances that can cause the thrusts to shift outside the masonry, as can be seen by considering in detail some of the consequences of settlement, together with some practical applications of the safe theorem.

(iv) Settlement and cracking. The abutment spread of a masonry arch (*see* §(ii) above) was imagined to lead to a tidy set of hinges. Settlements in a highly complex structure will lead to a correspondingly complex pattern of cracks: a nave pier might settle by perhaps 100 mm relative to its neighbours, giving rise to a visually alarming set of cracks just above the pier. This is not, however, a sign of danger.

An outline drawing of a cathedral building, to a scale of 1:100, could be accommodated on a relatively modest size of paper. If two such drawings, the first of the building in its original perfect state and the second showing the settlement of the nave pier by 100 mm were superimposed, the defect of 100 mm in the real structure would be represented by 1 mm on the drawing board, barely more than the thickness of a pencil line. The geometry of the original building, before any settlement occurred, is known

to have been satisfactory. The cathedral stood, which is experimental evidence that a set of forces could be found within the boundaries of the masonry. The geometry of the distorted building is almost unchanged: the force paths sketched on the original drawing will lie within the masonry of the second drawing. The conclusion from the safe theorem is that, despite perhaps visually alarming cracking, the deformed building has virtually the same margin of safety as it had in its perfect state. Masonry will, inevitably, crack, and any actual cracks visible in a structure merely indicate that the building has at some time been subjected to imposed movements from the external environment.

(v) Timescale for settlement. The five-minute theorem for masonry may be stated for, say, a flying buttress: if the work stands for five minutes after the timber centering of the flying buttress is removed on completion of the stonework, then it will stand for 500 years (an upper limit depending on the decay of the material). This is all that is needed to satisfy the safe theorem by confirming experimentally, on the real structure, that the shape of the flying buttress is correct. This flamboyant statement assumes that the loads on the flying buttress are static, arising from self-weight and dead thrusts from the nave vaulting. It does not necessarily apply to the upper flying buttresses in some large Gothic churches, the function of which (*see* §4 below) is to resist wind forces acting on the great timber roof; and it concentrates only on the masonry, ignoring any possible interaction with the foundations, whose settlement is measured in years, even a decade or so, rather than minutes.

Foundation settlements can lead to geometry changes rather larger than those envisaged so far. Under the crossing tower of a great church there are almost always indications of gross distortions: the once horizontal courses of masonry in the nave, choir and transepts abutting a crossing may indicate settlements of as much as *c.* 300 mm (now rather more than the thickness of a pencil line on the drawing board). This is both common-place and straightforward; the crossing piers, themselves highly stressed (at one-tenth of the strength of the material), require high bearing stresses from the soil for their support. The whole of the plan area at the crossing typically requires such a high mean supporting stress that the modern engineer, concerned to prevent cracks developing in his design, would use piles to limit foundation movement. The high stresses under the medieval structure ensure that consolidation of the soil and resultant settlement will inevitably occur. If the settlement can be tolerated, however, the stresses are not so high as finally to distress a stiffish clay.

The 'soil-mechanics' timescale for consolidation of a tower in relation to the surrounding portions of a structure is one generation. There are numerous records of towers collapsing within 20 years of their completion, for example the first central tower of Winchester Cathedral. These collapses resulted from uneven settlements, not necessarily grossly upsetting the geometry of the tower itself, but throwing extremely high loads on abutting masonry. In some cases this masonry has been reinforced to restore stability, sometimes with concealed internal raking buttresses, occasionally spectacularly, as with the strainer arches of *c*. 1338 at Wells Cathedral (*see* WELLS, §1(i)). Once the risk period of a generation is past, and the tower has survived either untouched or with reinforcement—and provided there are no changes in the general soil condition, such as would be caused by alterations in the level of the water table (which may have led to the collapses at the cathedrals of Ely in 1322 and Chichester in 1861)—the tower may well be deemed to be structurally safe.

(vi) Models. This view of the masonry structure is based firmly on geometry, that is, the stability of the structure will be assured primarily by its shape and not at all (or only very marginally) by the strength of the component material. Modern stress rules play no part in a structural view of masonry. Medieval architects knew nothing of stress; they were concerned with the proper proportions of a structure (*see* MASON (i), §IV, 3). The diameter of a nave pier should bear a certain relation to its height, the breadth of a main buttress should be a certain fraction of its depth and so on. Rules like these are essentially numerical and lead to a geometry of structure that is independent of scale. Thus a design could be built to any size. Once the unit of measure had been established, all individual dimensions for all parts of the building followed according to simple rules of proportion. In particular, a model could be used not only to solve problems of construction, such as problems of stereotomy, but also to simulate the overall structure. The use of models is well-attested: the late 14th-century brick and plaster model (destr. 1406) of S Petronio, Bologna (*see* BOLOGNA, §IV, 2), was over 18 m long. Such a model can be used with complete confidence to check the stability of the whole or any part of the structure, since questions of stability, depending as they do on relative proportions (i.e. on geometrical shape), can be checked at any scale. By contrast, questions of strength cannot be scaled in this way, as Galileo Galilei was aware, and his exposure in 1638 of the square-cube law was the first scientific demonstration that a scale model will always be misleadingly strong. A cathedral built to a height of 2000 m would crush under its own weight; it is the fact that stresses are low in a cathedral of human scale that makes geometrical rules effective.

3. STRUCTURAL ELEMENTS.

(i) Walls. (ii) Piers. (iii) Vaults. (iv) Domes. (v) Spires. (vi) The flying buttress.

(i) Walls. It is obvious intuitively that a wall must not be too thin compared to its height and length; some sort of geometrical requirement seems to be imposed on its design. A thin wall may be built vertically and remain upright in precarious equilibrium under its own weight, but it must have some reasonable margin of safety against settlement and accidental tilt of its foundations. The centre of gravity of the wall must not move outside the verticals drawn through the limits of its base, and a certain minimum ratio of thickness to height will give the required margin. Equally, a free-standing wall must not be blown flat by high winds, and this again leads to a (calculable) minimum thickness of construction that requires no other support. A thinner wall of great length may, however, be stabilized

by buttressing, which effectively thickens the wall at intervals along its length. If the wall forms part of a building, such as the aisle wall of a church, the buttresses will also absorb lateral forces arising from the timber roof or masonry vaults. Mean stresses in such walls are, as has been noted, very small.

The calculation of a mean stress can be misleading. The medieval construction of a wall, perhaps 1 m thick, or even 2 m for some great towers, consists of two outer skins of good coursed ashlar (the skins being *c*. 200–300 mm thick), with random rubble and mortar fill contained between them. There is little tensile strength inherent in such a construction, and two devices were commonly used to try to provide reinforcement. The first, which gives little connection between the skins, consists of baulks of timber laid horizontally at the centre of the wall and embedded in the rubble and mortar. The second involves the use of 'through stones', larger blocks of masonry passing right through the wall at mostly regular intervals in the construction. For thicker walls, as in towers, sufficiently large pieces are not available to act as through stones, and the two skins tend to drift apart, a tendency exacerbated by the action of wind and by the forces engendered by bell ringing. The internal faces of the tower form a square that cannot be reduced in size, and interact with each other to prevent movement. Externally the outward drift of the four skins of the tower walls may have to be prevented by tie-bars anchored in iron plates (*see* TIE-BAR).

(ii) Piers. Attached wall shafts should be regarded as local thickening, required mainly to stabilize the construction. The case is very different for arcade piers, and above all for crossing piers that carry the weight of a tower. The typical large medieval pier is constructed from a well-cut stone skin and a rubble and mortar core. Any outward movement of the skin will, as with the wall, lead to voids in the core and a possible slump of the internal material. Since a crossing pier carries a high mean stress, any such decay of the core will lead to very large stresses being engendered in the skin. Two consequent local mechanisms of distress can be observed. In the first, pressure points force off wedges of stone, and roughly triangular spalled areas may be seen in the skin. Alternatively, high pressures between the stones can lead to vertical cracking of the stones forming the skin. Neither mechanism is necessarily a sign of imminent collapse. An extreme example of spalling and cracking was observed during the construction of the Panthéon, Paris (*see* PARIS, §V, 9), in the last years of the 18th century (Heyman, 1985). Here very tight joints were achieved by careful working of the outer 100 mm of the stones, with the interior cut back and stuffed loosely with mortar. As a result, the weight of the central work was carried on an effective 100 mm skin of masonry, with corresponding excessive stresses.

(iii) Vaults. The behaviour of a masonry vault does not depend on the method of construction (*see* VAULT).

(a) Barrel vault. (b) Groin vault. (c) Rib vault. (d) Fan vault.

(a) Barrel vault. A semicircular barrel vault may be built in a straightforward way from horizontal courses of stone

(see fig. 2a left), a type of construction that needs temporary formwork to support the masonry; or, as with the Byzantine barrel vault, it can be built from tiles without the use of centering (2a right). The tiles are laid back at an angle, each course acting as (permanent) formwork for the next course to be laid. Each of the vaults is, however, a semicircular arch, and the structural action is the same; each will behave in the way discussed above (see fig. 1a above). For example, if the supports spread, the vault will develop a hinging crack more or less along its crown (for a description of some of the pathology of the masonry vault *see* §4 below). Similarly, the webs of vaults may be coursed in the 'French' or the 'English' way (2b), but the completed 'shell' structure has the same basic action independent of its construction.

The 'monolithic' concrete barrel vault built by the Romans from brick tiles and mortar might be thought to be free of thrust, and to deliver only vertical loads to its supports; but movement apart of the supports will crack the vault, just as the concrete of the Roman Pantheon (*c.* AD 120; *see* ROME, §V, 8) was cracked (*see* §(iv) below); the concrete barrel vault will once again have been transformed into an arch (see fig. 1a middle above). The barrel vault may be thought of, then, as a series of parallel arch rings, delivering a continuous line of thrust to the supporting walls, which must be sufficiently massive to provide the required support. Early medieval builders were very reluctant to pierce these walls with windows sufficiently large to give adequate illumination to the church. The transverse arches that were sometimes provided in articulation with the nave arcades below did not concentrate the forces of the barrel; the arches are really constructional in nature, being built first, and acting as permanent formwork for the barrels, which could then be erected bay by bay on movable temporary supports. The barrel itself continued to act as before. Moreover, a semicircular arch requires a massive thickness for stability, at just over one-tenth of the radius as a minimum (Amiens Cathedral, begun 1220, has a nave width of 14 m, so that a semicircular barrel to cover this span would require a minimum thickness of more than 700 mm). Because in practice the vaults need not be fully semicircular, thicknesses can be reduced markedly; and the construction can be stabilized by filling the haunches with rubble, similar to the fill in the conoids of a Gothic vault (2c).

(b) Groin vault. The significant step in lightening construction came from the use of two barrels intersecting at right angles, to create the three-dimensional vault proper rather than a mere repetition of two-dimensional arches. This, the groin vault, was employed by the Romans in concrete, for example in the basilica of Maxentius (begun 307; *see* ROME, §V, 11), with a span of over 25 m. Such a vault needs support only at the corners, and windows can be introduced into the walls below the vault. Further, much smaller thicknesses of vaulting material could eventually be used for such intersecting vaults, thus reducing weights on piers and lateral thrusts on external buttresses.

The simplest form of groin vault results from the intersection of two equal semicylindrical barrels; the resulting bay of vaulting is square in plan, and the diagonals of the square define the groins. There are geometrical

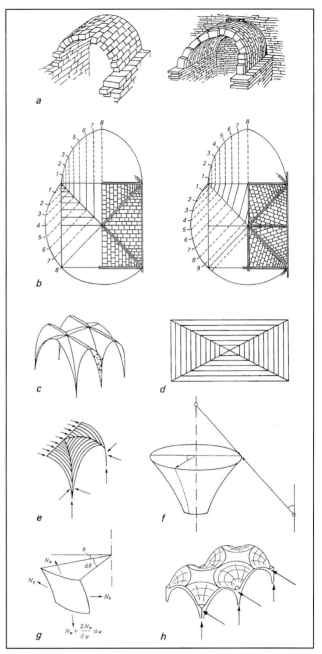

2. Masonry vaults: (a) semicircular barrel vault: (left) built with supporting formwork; (right) built without support; (b) stonework coursing for vaults: (left) French way; (right) English way; (c) quadripartite vault; (d) rectangular vault thought of as a series of arches; (e) forces necessary to maintain the equilibrium of a quadripartite vault; (f) basic shell of revolution defining the surface of a fan vault; (g) stress resultants acting on an element of a fan vault; (h) basic assembly of a complete fan fault

difficulties inherent in the cutting of the stones meeting at the groins (2b), and there are further severe geometrical difficulties if the two barrels intersecting to form the vault have different spans, so that the bay is rectangular rather than square. A first simplification was introduced by allowing the webs of the vault, between the groins, to be domed; the groins were not then fixed uniquely by the intersection of two given semicircular barrels but could be designed to some extent by the architect. The vaulting webs could then in turn be designed to fit the boundary arcs, that is, those at the four edges of the bay and those of the groins.

The groins themselves, however, were still difficult to cut, and Romanesque builders finally started their construction of groin vaults by cutting the groins independently and building the rubble masonry webs to match. Masonry arches were erected on the diagonals of the bay and then embedded, either wholly or partially, within the masonry of the vault webs. It was only a short step to build the groin arches as independent ribs and to construct the vault webs on the back of these so that the ribs were visible from below. The meeting edges of the vault could then be cut without much care, since irregular joins could be filled with mortar and hidden from view by the rib.

(c) Rib vault. The simplest form of masonry rib vault is the quadripartite vault (2c), divided into four severies (webs) by the diagonals on the rectangular plan. In order to determine primary vault forces, modern shell theory may be used on the skeletal structure. In its simple form the theory is indifferent as to whether forces are tensile or compressive, and, as tensile forces cannot develop in the real masonry vault, the theory must not be pushed too far. The main conclusions from shell theory are certainly valid: for example, that stresses in a smoothly curving vault are of the order Rw, where R is the local radius of curvature of the shell and w is the unit mass of the material.

A pointed vault over a nave of 15 m span might have a radius R of 10 m. Taking the unit mass of a medium sandstone as $w = 2000 \text{ kg/m}^3$, the product Rw becomes 2 kg/cm^2, to be compared with the crushing strength of 400 kg/cm^2. (It may be noted that the value of stress is independent of the thickness of the vault; doubling the thickness will double the gravity forces, but the resisting area is also doubled.) The ambient stress in the shell is so low that the strength of the stone is of little relevance; the level is little more than that of the small compressive stress necessary to lock the stones together by friction. Thus vault webs could be constructed of light stone (for example of weak tufa in the choir of Canterbury Cathedral, 1174–89), and thick mortar joints of poor strength could be used.

These remarks apply to smoothly curving shells. At shell intersections (e.g. at the groins of a vault) there will be large stress concentrations. A crease in a shell introduces a discontinuity into the force field and is a line of weakness; a reinforced crease (e.g. ribs applied to a groin vault), however, confers rigidity on the whole shell structure. There is, of course, conflicting evidence as to the role of the ribs, some of which seem very small (e.g. Reims Cathedral, from 1210), and there is the example of Longpont Abbey (begun *c.* 1210), Aisne, where fallen ribs still allowed the webs to stand. Numerical calculation helps to resolve the conflict. To take a hypothetical example, a quadripartite vault, 200 mm thick and slightly pointed, may be used to span a rectangular bay 15×7.5 m. Such a vault, with its ribs, will have a mass of about 80,000 kg,

and the main shells will be stressed to about 2 kg/cm^2. If the vaulting webs are supported on diagonal ribs, the maximum force in a diagonal rib will be about one-quarter of the total mass of the vault (i.e. *c.* 20,000 kg). A rib of, say, 25×20 cm has an area of 500 cm² and would be stressed to 40 kg/cm^2, or to one-tenth of the crushing strength of 400 kg/cm^2. This would seem to be a safe level. If this vault were built without ribs, or were built on ribs that subsequently fell, the analysis indicates that the primary shell stress of about 2 kg/cm^2 will increase sharply in the neighbourhood of the groins to perhaps 40 kg/cm^2. There will be a high stress concentration, but if the diagonal intersections of the webs are sufficiently regular, and the mortar sufficiently strong, the vault will not collapse; in a sense it will have succeeded in constructing its own ribs.

The rib, then, serves a structural purpose as a necessary, but perhaps not finally essential, reinforcement for the groins; it enables vaulting compartments to be laid out more easily; it enables much of the constructional formwork to be dispensed with; and it covers ill-matching joints at the groins. As a bonus, the rib has been thought to be aesthetically satisfying, and all of these functions may be thought of as the 'function' of the rib. The structural purpose is, however, clear: a sharp crease in a shell demands reinforcement. Thus in a quadripartite vault formed by intersecting barrels (pointed or not) with a level soffit, the deep diagonal creases (2c), increasing in sharpness towards the springing of the vault, require reinforcement, and the diagonal ribs, whether exposed or hidden, emerge as the effective members carrying the whole vault. By contrast, there will be no creases in the shell at the nave walls or at the positions of the transverse arches; neither the wall arches (formerets) nor the main transverse arches are required to carry anything but their own weights. If the soffit of the vault is not level, as, for example, when each bay is gently domed, a crease will appear at the transverse arches, which then emerge as true structural elements.

The simple view of the quadripartite vault, four vaulting compartments supported on diagonal ribs, suggests an equally simple way of envisaging the primary forces in the vault (2d). The cylindrical barrels of the vault have been sliced into independent arches, not interacting with each other and supported therefore solely from the diagonal cross-ribs reinforcing the groins. Although this simplified sliced structure will have a pattern of behaviour that will not necessarily be experienced by the real unsliced vault, it gives a realistic picture of actual behaviour (*see* §4 below). Part of the sliced vault may be shown in perspective (2e), together with the forces necessary to maintain equilibrium. At the crown, the horizontal propping forces in the vault webs are engendered by the other half of the vault: the two halves lean against each other to preserve stability. These horizontal forces must be resisted, as will be seen, by the buttresses. It emerges clearly from this simplified analysis, and is confirmed by much fuller studies, that the resisting horizontal forces act some way above the base of the vault (2e). The thrusts do not follow the lines of the diagonal ribs but act progressively above these as the springing is approached, thus compelling the placing of fill in the vaulting pockets (cf. fig. 2c) in order to provide a compressive path for the forces.

This basic behaviour of the quadripartite vault is reflected in the similar action of apparently much more complex patterns of vault. In the Middle Ages the developments in rib vaulting (the lierne and tierceron vaults in England and the net and star vaults of southern Germany, Austria and Bohemia) were largely decorative, rather than structural. The extra ribs, applied to a smoothly turning surface, were not required to reinforce creases, and they can be stripped away from the smooth vault surface to reveal the basic quadripartite form.

(d) Fan vault. One English development, however, departs radically from the standard form: the fan vault. Here, although the ribs are applied to a smoothly turning surface and are therefore decorative, the shell beneath is fundamentally different. A shell surface has two principal curvatures. Thus the vaulting webs in fig. 2e are curved in the direction of the sliced arches, but they are flat in the direction at right angles. In mathematical terms one of the curvatures is zero, so that the product at each point of the two principal curvatures (known as the Gaussian curvature) is also zero. Where the curvatures of both lines meeting at right angles are concave (as in a domed vaulting severy), the Gaussian curvature is positive. By contrast the fan vault (shown as a complete shell of revolution in fig. 2f) has a negative Gaussian curvature; of two lines on the surface, one will be concave and one convex. Such a fan vault, of given shape, can be analysed readily by modern shell theory: statics may be used to give the values of the hoop (or circumferential) stress resultant ($N\Theta$ in fig. 2g) and the meridional (or longitudinal) stress resultant ($N\phi$) for each element of the shell. (The theory may require tensile forces to be developed for certain shapes of fan, and such solutions would once again be inadmissible for a masonry vault.)

Of great interest are 'inverse' solutions that can be obtained for which the hoop stress resultant is zero. That is, if this condition is imposed, the equations may be solved to give the corresponding appropriate profile of the fan vault. Such a vault carries its loads by compressive forces along the meridional lines, with no forces in the horizontal plane; it can therefore be cut into two halves by a vertical plane without forces being introduced at the cut. The vault in fact requires compressive forces round the top edge, but equilibrium can be maintained by vertical and horizontal thrusts at the springing. Separate fans can then be assembled into a complete vault (2h). The spandrels at the crown of the vault, effectively shallow arches bridging the fans, will provide the necessary compressive forces round the top edges, and heavy bosses along the centre line of the vault will further improve the stability. Inverse solutions derived in this way, 'perfect' profiles that carry only meridional forces, are containable within the profiles of actual vaults, for example those of Bath Abbey (begun 1499), Henry VII's Chapel at Westminster Abbey (1503–9), King's College Chapel (1512–15), Cambridge, and Peterborough Cathedral (finished c. 1518), to name the four vaults that span 8 m or more. The basic action of these vaults is the same in each case; the vault in fig. 2h must be supported in the same way as the intersecting barrel vault in fig. 2e—both vaults thrust down and out.

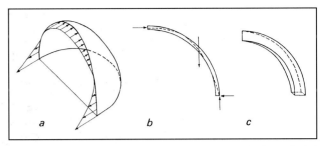

3. Masonry domes: (a) membrane hoop stresses acting in a thin hemispherical dome; (b) minimum thickness for a sliced masonry dome; (c) an 'arch' isolated from a dome by meridional cuts

(iv) Domes. Masonry domes also thrust down and out, and the resulting horizontal forces must be absorbed either internally, by encircling ties or chains, or externally by buttresses. The basic pattern of behaviour can be appreciated by starting once again from modern shell theory. A thin hemispherical dome subjected to the action of its own weight will be stressed in two directions at right angles. The meridional stresses (acting along the lines of longitude) are always compressive and increase towards the base of the dome. The circumferential or hoop stresses, acting along parallel circles (lines of latitude), are compressive in the upper part of the dome but start to become tensile at an angular distance 51.8° from the crown, and large tensile stresses are developed near the base. A sectioned half-dome would therefore be subjected to the hoop-stress distribution on the cut edge shown (see fig. 3a). These stresses are determined unequivocally for a thin dome, and, since masonry cannot withstand tension, the necessary (and correct) conclusion is that an unreinforced, thin hemispherical dome cannot be built from masonry.

The necessary tensile forces implied by fig. 3a can be supplied, as noted above, by circumferential chains. If these are absent, a dome of finite thickness can indeed stand, but the internal thrusts must depart from the hemispherical surface. Viewed in cross-section (3b), the dome is maintained in equilibrium by a horizontal thrust at the base. The dotted line, within the thickness of the hemispherical masonry, gives the trace of a vanishingly thin, non-circular dome, which would, in theory, just stand without anywhere developing tensile stresses. The horizontal thrust in this example must be resisted by external buttressing, either rising directly from the ground, as in the Pantheon, Rome, or, in the case of the Byzantine church, by abutting arches and semidomes (as at Hagia Sophia, Istanbul, begun 532). In either case, as with the two-dimensional voussoir arch, the abutments will tend to give way. To accommodate itself to the increased span, the dome, like the arch, must crack, and it is the natural state of masonry domes to exist with cracks along the meridians (e.g. the Pantheon, Rome; Florence Cathedral, 1420–34; and St Peter's, Rome, begun 1506).

It was the cracking at St Peter's that led to Giovanni Poleni's report of 1748 on the state of that dome; his comprehensive work, in which he surveyed the existing knowledge of masonry construction, can hardly be bettered as a description of the basic mechanics of the subject.

He was aware of Hooke's observation (*see* §2(ii) above) that the shape of a hanging chain will give, inverted, the shape of the corresponding arch. In an astonishing anticipation of the master 'safe theorem', Poleni stated explicitly that the stability of a structure can be established unequivocally if it can be shown that the thrust line lies completely within the masonry. He noted that the cracks at St Peter's had already divided the dome into portions approximating half-spherical lunes (orange slices). He sliced the dome hypothetically into 50 such lunes and then considered the stability of, effectively, a two-dimensional arch composed of two lunes (for a schematic illustration of one such lune see fig. 3c). He determined the thrust line for the arch experimentally (see fig. 4) by loading a flexible string with unequal weights, each weight calculated to be proportional to a segment of the lune, with due allowance made for the lantern. The thrust line determined in this way does in fact lie within the thickness of the dome of St Peter's; by comparison, the thrust line corresponding to a uniformly loaded chain is shown passing outside the masonry. Poleni established in this way a solution for which the hoop-stress is zero; the notionally separate lunes act independently and transmit neither tension nor compression in the circumferential direction. Moreover, he took account of the real, and in fact common, state of a dome. The same orange-slice technique can be used to obtain minimum thicknesses for spherical domes, as, for example, when the thrust line is only just containable within the masonry (see fig. 3b above).

Sir Christopher Wren, co-surveyor with Robert Hooke for London after the Great Fire of 1666, understood all this, although he disliked its aesthetic implications. His

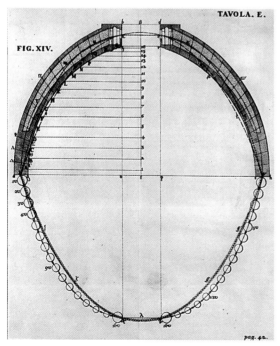

4. Experimental demonstration of the stability of the dome of St Peter's, Rome; from G. Poleni: *Memorie istoriche della gran cupola del Tempio Vaticano* (Padua, 1748)

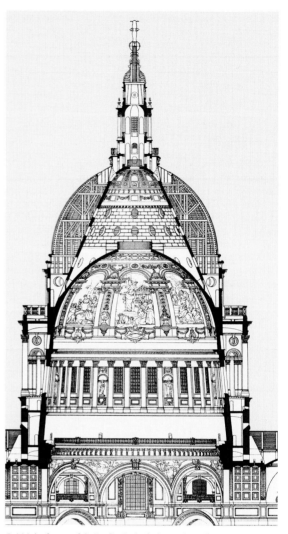

5. Triple dome of St Paul's Cathedral, London; from Arthur F. E. Poley: *St Paul's Cathedral* (London, 1927), pl. IX

triple dome at St Paul's Cathedral (see fig. 5) consists of a timber outer structure (capable of resisting tensile forces), the true conical dome supporting the massive lantern and the inner dome with a central eye, as at the Roman Pantheon, which is all that is seen from inside the building. Iron chains help to contain the thrust, but the main buttressing is provided by the inclined surfaces of the whole internal supporting structure, disguised externally by the vertical colonnades of the drum.

Byzantine domes were constructed not as full hemispheres but shallower; the remodelled central dome of Hagia Sophia embraces about 140° rather than 180°. Moreover, it is thickened towards the springing, and the whole forms a very stable structure. The earthquake of 989 brought down one-quarter of the dome, and this behaviour was repeated (with failure of a different quarter of the repaired dome) in 1346. This sort of stability can be examined satisfactorily by an application of Poleni's slicing technique.

See also DOME, §1.

(v) Spires. A right circular cone, standing under its own weight, will be subjected only to compressive stresses, one set acting in the directions of the straight generators and one set at right angles in the circumferential (hoop) direction. Thus masonry, a structural material incapable of carrying tension, may be employed satisfactorily to construct a conical SPIRE. Moreover, if the stone were of the thicknesses commonly used in the construction of spires, and the geometry were also not unusual (that is, not too narrow a cone angle leading to an excessively slender spire), then the spire would behave satisfactorily in wind. The self-weight of the masonry would be sufficient to prevent the spire overturning under lateral wind forces, and large tensile stresses would not develop. (Consideration of the effect of wind leads to the provision of extra mass at the tip of the spire; the masonry must be solid for *c.* 1 m, or extra weight introduced into the construction in other ways.)

A masonry spire is almost invariably octagonal in cross-section rather than circular. The supporting square tower is converted to an octagon near its top by the use of squinches, the octagon serving as a base for the construction of the flat-sided spire. A circle can be contained within an octagonal shell provided that the shell has a thickness greater than about 1/26 of the diameter. An octagonal spire of this minimum thickness could thus contain within its constituent masonry the conical thrust surface of the right circular spire. The master 'safe theorem' then confirms the stability of the octagonal spire. Practical rules for the design of plain octagonal spires envisage a thickness of 1/24–1/30 of the diameter, and many spires have thicknesses at least as great as this. Thinner spires need reinforcement. Decorative treatment of the angles (quoins) usually involves some enlargement of the masonry shell in these regions and effectively reduces the span of each face of the spire. In an extreme case, the faces can be reduced to zero thickness, leaving a skeletal spire of eight quoins, but these must now be braced by horizontal ribs. Each face of the spire is divided into rectangular (strictly, trapezoidal) compartments, and this, with decorative infill, is the construction at, for example, Freiburg im Breisgau Cathedral (*c.* 1300). Similar spires exist at the cathedrals of Ulm (1390s) and Cologne (designed *c.* 1320, built 1842–80).

(vi) The flying buttress. Masonry vaults thrust down and out and must be restrained laterally. If there are no side aisles the main buttresses can directly abut the nave walls, but where there are aisles the flying buttress (*see* BUTTRESS, §2) is effectively a compressive prop passing over the aisles between the vault and the main buttress, containing within its masonry the line of thrust that passes through space above the aisle. If the flying buttress were weightless, its best form, by analogy with the weightless cord in tension (*see* §2(ii) above), would be a straight line. Antoni Gaudí adopted this logical solution in some of his constructions, such as the Bishop's Palace (1887–93) at Astorga, now the Museo de los Caminos. The typical Gothic flying buttress has indeed a flat extrados and, as has been noted, this flat-arch form has no mechanism of collapse. The typical line of thrust of fig. 1c right, in which a thrust is collected from the high vault and transmitted to the external buttress, cannot be placed to correspond to a pattern of hinges leading to collapse.

On the contrary, for a typical buttress the thrust can be increased to a very high value (of the order of 1000 tonnes) before crushing of the stone occurs; but a minimum value of thrust is necessary to maintain the flying buttress in place (see figs 1c left and 1a middle above). Slight spread has been supposed between nave and main buttress, and the flyer has cracked to accommodate the increased span. In this 'passive' state (using rough figures) a 10-tonne flyer will lean against the nave wall with a minimum thrust of about 3 tonnes. It can, however, easily absorb a typical vault thrust of 10 or 20 tonnes. Indeed, since this value is substantially higher than that needed to ensure stability, the hinge pattern of fig. 1c left is not likely to occur in practice. Under exceptional circumstances, however, the pattern may be observed when the flyer is heavier than necessary and the external buttresses are subject to settlement, as was found to be the case in 1985 at the chapter house at Lincoln Cathedral.

There are many variations of the standard form of flying buttress, from the almost horizontal flyers of Palma de Mallorca Cathedral (begun 1306) to the nearly vertical props at Bath Abbey or the tower of St John the Baptist (begun *c.* 1400), Cirencester. All, however, have the essential property that a straight line of thrust may be drawn entirely within the masonry, so that the strength of any flyer is limited only by the crushing strength of the material. Occasionally this requirement was lost sight of, as at Amiens Cathedral. Buttresses similar to those at the chevet of Amiens Cathedral (see fig. 6) were originally provided in the nave, but these failed by upward buckling, and they

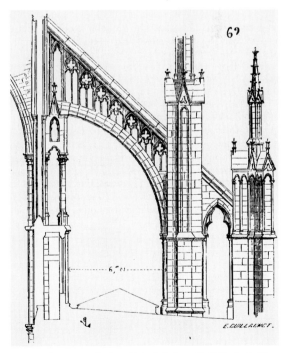

6. Flying buttresses, Amiens Cathedral; from E.-E. Viollet-le-Duc: *Dictionnaire raisonné de l'architecture française du XIe au XVIe siècle* (Paris, 1854–68)

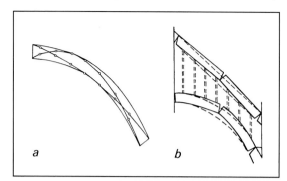

7. Flying buttresses at Amiens Cathedral: (a) limiting positions for the thrust lines in the lower rib; (b) possible buckling mode of failure

were replaced in the 15th century by a different two-tier design (see fig. 8 below). There are really two buttresses: the curved lower rib, positioned at the TAS-DE-CHARGE to pick up the steady vault thrust, and the straight upper rib, normally unloaded, but with an essential function as a brace against wind loads (*see* §4 below). The two ribs are connected by tracery. The curved lower rib is an arch requiring a minimum horizontal thrust of about 5 tonnes for stability; the corresponding line of thrust passes through the intrados at the two ends of the rib and touches the extrados between, as indicated in fig. 7a. The vault thrust at Amiens approaches 20 tonnes, and this higher value implies a straightening of the thrust line. At about 20 tonnes the thrust line has straightened to the extent that it can only just be accommodated within the masonry (7a). Thus the rib is forced to operate between the thrust limits of 5 and 20 tonnes. The lower value is the minimum necessary for stability, while at the upper limit the rib buckles upwards. This was the probable mode of failure at Amiens (7b); as the curved rib buckles upwards, the tracery connection ensures that the straight rib is also pushed aside, allowing the nave wall eventually to lean out.

4. THE GOTHIC STRUCTURE. The exposed external skeleton of a Gothic great church was classified by Julien Azais Guadet as the propped-up style of architecture, and this structure, so readily apparent, can be thought of in almost a two-dimensional way. The main structural elements of pier, buttress and flyer, all dedicated to the task of supporting the high vault, are assembled in planes at regular intervals down the nave and choir. If the cathedral has transepts, then the same construction is repeated, but at right angles, the planes now running east–west rather than north–south.

There are, of course, forces acting out of the main structural planes: although at Amiens Cathedral the rectangular bays of the high vault of the nave have their main thrusts in the north–south direction, which are transmitted to the main buttress by the lower flying buttress (see fig. 8), the vault also thrusts east–west. Bay by bay down the axis of the building the thrusts and counterthrusts are equal; the masonry at the crossing can support the thrusts on each side, but finally there are unbalanced forces at the east and at the west end of the church. At the east end the French solution was to provide an apsidal termination;

the smoothly turning chevet is supported by the same flying buttress system carried round in a semicircle. The usual square termination of English Gothic necessitates buttresses placed directly against the fabric (if no aisle or eastern projection, such as a Lady chapel, intervenes). At the west end some other massive construction, perhaps incorporating corner towers, could provide stability. Similar buttressing is needed at the square terminations of transepts.

This discussion of the Gothic structure has been made in terms of static forces, of the thrusts and counterthrusts engendered by the steady action of gravity. The lower flying buttress at Amiens is positioned not at the apparent springing of the vault but perfectly in the region of the *tas-de-charge*, where the vault thrust escapes from the masonry (cf. fig. 8 and fig. 2e above). Other forces, however, can act on the structure, notably those due to wind and earthquake (of significance even in northern Europe). A northern gale acting on the tall timber roof above the high vault will engender large forces acting on

8. The Gothic structure, Amiens Cathedral, nave; from E.-E. Viollet-le-Duc: *Dictionnaire raisonné de l'architecture française du XIe au XVIe siècle* (Paris, 1854–68)

the masonry at parapet level, which must be brought down to the ground. The upper flying buttress in fig. 8 is placed there mainly for this purpose. When the wind is not blowing the buttress is idle, leaning against the fabric with a minimum passive thrust, and perhaps helping to support any thrust engendered by the timber roof itself; in a gale, it will react instantly to any lateral force. The original design at Amiens attempted to combine the vault thrust buttress and the wind buttress in a single element (see fig. 6 above), which, as has been seen, proved unsatisfactory.

The passive pattern of forces under gravity loading is revealed by an examination of the pathology of the Gothic structure. For example, it was seen that the circular voussoir arch, supported from abutments that move slightly under load, would crack in the pattern of fig. 1a (middle). Had the arch been pointed, the single crack at the crown would, theoretically, be replaced by two hinges displaced from the crown (see fig. 9a). In practice any slight asymmetry of the arch will lead to the suppression of one or other of these displaced hinges.

A simple extension of these basic ideas leads to an understanding of the mechanics of the vault. As a first step towards this understanding, fig. 9b (top) shows the cross-section of a uniform cylindrical barrel vault, drawn roughly to scale (say a vault thickness of 300 mm with a span of 15 m). The vault is supposed to be maintained by the buttresses. As drawn, the vault is in fact too thin to carry its own weight; fill, backing the haunches of the barrel, is therefore shown, allowing a pathway for the vault forces in their 'escape' from the vault proper. The external buttressing system will, almost inevitably, give way slightly under the imposed thrusts from the vault, and movements will occur during the first few years of the structure's life. In general, movement of the buttresses will virtually cease when the soil under the foundations has consolidated under the bearing pressures. During this process, however, the vault will have had to accommodate itself to the increased span, and the resulting crack pattern is shown in fig. 9b (bottom). Had the barrel vault had a pointed cross-section, then the crack near the crown of the vault would have been slightly off-centre (9a). Typical cracks of this sort near the crown of a slightly pointed quadripartite vault (see fig. 10) are the first kind of chronic defect exhibited in practice by masonry vaults, but other cracks also occur.

The vault in fig. 9b is essentially two-dimensional, in the sense that the cross-section was supposed to be the same down the length of the church. Fig. 9c shows, schematically, a single square bay of a quadripartite vault formed by the intersection of cylindrical barrels. In fig. 9c (top), an elevation of the vault is shown, looking west down the length of the church; the fill, which serves the same function as before, is placed in the vaulting conoids (cf. the plan of fig. 9c (bottom left); the vault is supposed to extend for several bays, as indicated in the plan). If now the buttressing system of the vault gives way, the portion that runs east/west will crack as before (9c (middle)), and the single hinge line at or near the crown will be visible from within the church. The change in geometry is accommodated by rotation of the three hinges, with a consequent drop of the crown of the vault.

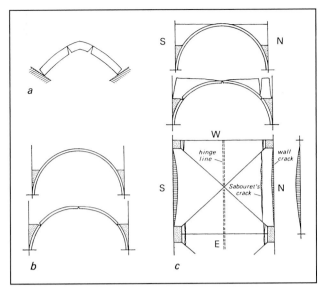

9. Crack development: (a) pointed arch; (b) barrel vault; (c) quadripartite vault

A severe geometrical constraint is, however, imposed on the intersecting vault that runs north–south. The horizontal soffit of this vault was built to the original dimension of the span, but the span has now increased.

10. Typical cracking of a Gothic vault

At the plane of the buttressing system, the mismatch in dimensions is zero, but it increases to a maximum at the crown (9c (bottom right)). The general effect of this mismatch is evident in the elevation (9c (middle)); from the left (south) side of the plan it will be seen that the whole of the geometrical incompatibility could be taken up by a gap opening between the vault and the wall. This would, however, place the masonry of the north–south vault adjacent to the wall in a severe state of strain. A crack pattern that allows the vault to deform in more or less strain-free monolithic pieces is sketched in the right (north) side of the plan (9c (bottom right)). A secondary crack, classified by Pol Abraham as Sabouret's crack, after the French architect who drew attention to its significance in 1928, has opened parallel to the wall crack (see fig. 10). A Sabouret's crack and a wall crack will effectively isolate a portion of the north–south vault, and this portion will then be free to act as a simple arch running east–west and spanning roughly between adjacent vaulting conoids. Thus, cracks near the crown are traces of hinge lines in a portion of the vault through which compressive forces are being carried, the forces in fact acting approximately perpendicular to the hinge lines. By contrast, the wall cracks and Sabouret's cracks represent complete separation of the masonry, through which a hand may often be passed. No forces can be transmitted across such fissures, and the compressive forces run parallel to the cracks.

The behaviour modelled in fig. 9c is based on an idealized quadripartite cylindrical vault having square bays. The general pathology of all vaults is of the same nature and may be observed in groin and rib vaults with rectangular bays, and indeed in fan vaults. The isolation of several compartments of the vault by crack patterns leads to the possibility of very precise calculation of the vault forces, both in magnitude and location. It is these considerations that led to the sketches of figs 2d and 2e above as suitable models for estimation of the action of high vaults; in turn, once the action of the vault is known, the analysis of the rest of the structure, including the piers, flying buttresses, external buttresses and foundation pressures, can be determined with some accuracy.

BIBLIOGRAPHY

Galileo Galilei: *Discorsi e dimostrazioni matematiche, intorno a due nuove scienze attenenti alla mecanica e i movimenti locali* (Leiden, 1638)
R. Hooke: *A Description of Helioscopes, and Some Other Instruments* (London, 1675)
F. Blondel: *Cours d'architecture enseigné dans l'Académie royale d'architecture*, 2 vols (Paris, 1675–83)
G. Poleni: *Memorie istoriche della gran cupola del Tempio Vaticano* (Padua, 1748)
Y. Villarceau: *Sur l'établissement des arches de pont* (Paris, 1853)
E. E. Viollet-le-Duc: *Dictionnaire raisonné de l'architecture française du XIe au XVIe siècle*, 10 vols (Paris, 1854–68)
J. A. Guadet: *Éléments et théorie de l'architecture*, 4 vols (Paris, n.d.)
T. G. Jackson: *Gothic Architecture in France, England, and Italy* (Cambridge, 1915)
——: *Byzantine and Romanesque Architecture* (Cambridge, 1920)
V. Sabouret: 'Les Voûtes d'arêtes nervurées', *Génie Civ.* (3 March 1928)
P. Abraham: *Viollet-le-Duc et le rationalisme médiéval* (Paris, 1934)
J. S. Ackerman: '*Ars sine scientia nihil est*: Gothic Theory of Architecture at the Cathedral of Milan', *A. Bull.*, xxxi (1949), pp. 84–111
J. Harvey: 'Mediaeval Design', *Trans. Anc. Mnmt Soc.*, n. s., vi (1958), pp. 55–72
P. Frankl: *The Gothic: Literary Sources and Interpretations through Eight Centuries* (Princeton, 1960)
J. Fitchen: *The Construction of Gothic Cathedrals* (Oxford, 1961)
J. Heyman: 'The Stone Skeleton', *Int. J. Solids & Structures*, ii (1966), p. 249
——: 'On Shell Solutions for Masonry Domes', *Int. J. Solids & Structures*, iii (1967), pp. 227–41
——: 'Spires and Fan Vaults', *Int. J. Solids & Structures*, iii (1967), pp. 243–57
——: 'On the Rubber Vaults of the Middle Ages, and Other Matters', *Gaz. B.-A.*, lxxi (1968), p. 177
——: *Equilibrium of Shell Structures* (Oxford, 1977)
R. Mark, K. D. Alexander and J. F. Abel: 'The Structural Behaviour of Medieval Ribbed Vaulting', *J. Soc. Archit. Hist.*, xxxv (1977), pp. 241–51
J. Heyman: *The Masonry Arch* (Chichester, 1982)
R. Mark: *Experiments in Gothic Structure* (Cambridge, MA, 1982)
J. Heyman: 'Chronic Defects in Masonry Vaults: Sabouret's Cracks', *Monumentum*, xxvi (1983), p. 131
——: 'The Crossing Piers of the French Panthéon', *Structural Engin.*, lxiii/1 (1985), pp. 230–34
R. Mark: *High Gothic Structure: A Technological Reinterpretation* (Princeton, 1985)
——: *Light, Wind and Structure: The Mystery of the Master Builders* (Boston, MA, 1990)

JACQUES HEYMAN

Masrur. Site of rock-cut temples in Himachal Pradesh, India. The only notable example of rock-cut architecture in the Himalayan region, the group of temples dominates a hill crest and faces a ritual bathing tank. The central shrine is the tallest and the only one with an excavated interior; originally dedicated to Shiva but now housing modern images of Rama, Lakshmana and Sita, it has a large forehall with four massive columns and side staircases leading to a terrace. The exteriors of the shrines are in various states of completion; while much fine detail appears on door frames, niches and sections of the superstructures, the overall impression is of temple forms emerging from solid rock. The monuments are generally dated to the early 9th century on the basis of their similarity to temples of the Pratihara period (*see* INDIAN SUBCONTINENT, §III, 5(i)(a)). The style of the figurative sculpture shows Kashmiri influence (*see* INDIAN SUBCONTINENT, §V, 7(ii)), while the decorative motifs relate to the local wood-carving tradition. Although no inscriptions have been found at Masrur, the Karkota dynasty of Kashmir may have been patrons. Few of the Masrur sculptures survive *in situ*, but several pieces are held by the Himachal State Museum, Simla.

BIBLIOGRAPHY

C. Sivaramamurti: *The Art of India* (New York, 1977)
M. G. Singh: *Art and Architecture of Himachal Pradesh* (Delhi, 1983)
G. Michell: *Buddhist, Hindu, Jain*, i of *Penguin Guide to the Monuments of India*, 2 vols (London, 1989)
M. W. Meister, M. A. Dhaky and K. Deva, eds: *North India: Period of Early Maturity, A.D. 700–900* (1991), ii/2 of *Enc. Ind. Temple Archit.* (Delhi and Philadelphia, 1983–)
S. Aryan: *Himadri Temples* (Shimla, 1994)

WALTER SMITH

Massalia. *See* MARSEILLE.

Massard, Jean (*b* Bellême, Orne, 22 Aug 1740; *d* Paris, 16 March 1822). French printmaker. He studied engraving under François-Nicolas Martinet and Jean-Georges Wille, establishing his reputation as an engraver of book illustrations by contributing 16 plates to the edition by Pierre-François Basan and Noël Le Mire of Ovid's *Metamorphoses* (1767–71). However, it is in his engravings after Jean-Baptiste Greuze that the velvet-like texture of his work can be seen to best advantage, notably in *La Mère bien aimée* (1775; London, BM, Portalis 6) and *La Dame bienfaisante* (1778; London, BM, Portalis 4). Massard's plates have always been criticized for being overworked, but an anonymous writer of 1779, thought to be the engraver Charles-Etienne Gaucher, blamed this partly on Greuze, who overemphasized the importance of tone in line-engraving and took such an interest in the engraving of his own works that he would often add the finishing touches himself. It seems that Greuze did in fact retouch Massard's plates. Massard also engraved genre scenes after Pierre-Antoine Baudouin, including *Le Lever* (1771; London, BM, Portalis 1), one of his best plates. As well as continuing to engrave for some of the most luxurious editions of the period, Massard collaborated on several of the publications on museum collections, such as Jean-Baptiste Wicar's *Galerie de Florence* (1789–1807) and S.-C. Croze-Magnan's *Musée français* (1803–9). In 1785 he became an associate of the Académie Royale de Peinture et de Sculpture, but he did not become an academician. He was a devout Roman Catholic and a staunch royalist, resuming his former title of Graveur du Roi with the restoration of the monarchy in 1814.

Massard was the founder of a dynasty of engravers that included his sons Jean-Baptiste(-Louis) (1772–*c.* 1815), (Jean-Baptiste-)Félix (*b* 1773), (Jean-Baptiste-Raphaël-)Urbain (1775–1843); Alexandre(-Pierre-Jean-Baptiste) (*b* 1777); his grandson, Alexandre's son (Jean-Marie-Raphaël-)Léopold (1812–89); and Léopold's two sons Jules-Louis (*b* 1848) and Horace (*b* 1854).

BIBLIOGRAPHY

Lettre d'un voyageur, à Paris, à son ami Sir Charles Lovers, demeurant à Londres. Sur les nouvelles estampes de M. Greuze, ... Publiées par M. N*** (Paris, 1779)

R. Portalis and H. Béraldi: *Les Graveurs du dix-huitième siècle*, iii (Paris, 1882), pp. 45–56

H. Béraldi: *Les Graveurs du XIXe siècle*, ix (1889), pp. 239–45

E. Dacier: *La Gravure en France au XVIIIe siècle: La Gravure de genre et de moeurs* (Paris, 1925), p. 114

F. Arquié-Bruley: 'Documents notariés inédits sur Greuze', *Bull. Soc. Hist. A. Fr.* (1981), pp. 125–54

M.-E. HELLYER

Massari, Giorgio (*b* Venice, 13 Oct 1687; *d* Venice, 20 Dec 1766). Italian architect. His father, Stefano Massari, was a joiner or carpenter, and Massari's first patron was a friend of the family, Paolo Tamagnini, a rich Venetian merchant who commissioned him to build a villa (1712) at Istrana in the region of Treviso. The influence of Palladio, which characterized Massari's work, was already apparent in this early building, particularly in the triple Palladian window in the central section. Massari went on to produce a large number of works for a variety of patrons, especially ecclesiastical ones, and he became one of the most important Venetian architects of the first half of the 18th century. Most of his buildings were executed in the Veneto region, but an early exception was the church of S Maria della Pace (1719), Brescia, for the Philippine Fathers. Built in two storeys, it has a five-bay façade with four large columns, and it served throughout the 18th century as a model for church architecture in the Veneto.

Massari's best-known church is S Maria del Rosario (1725–36), the church of the Gesuati, built on the Giudecca canal, Venice, to a rectangular plan with cut-off corners. Its pedimented façade, with four giant engaged Corinthian columns and a minor order for the portal, has many Palladian echoes, although the clustered pilasters at the angles exhibit an undulating Rococo quality. The aisleless nave has three interconnected chapels on each side, articulated with a triumphal arch motif, while the choir features free-standing columns as in Palladio's Il Redentore. Rococo effects are particularly notable in the ceiling treatment at the Gesuati, particularly in the frames surrounding Giambattista Tiepolo's fresco decorations (1739; *see* TIEPOLO, (1)). Lighting is exclusively from clerestory windows, leaving the chapels in shadow.

From 1727 Massari was also involved at the church and hospital of the Catecumeni and the Scuola di S Giovanni Evangelista, Venice, where he raised the ceiling of the Gran Salone and introduced Rococo decoration. The church of S Antonio (1731–2), Udine, however, is one of his most purely Neo-classical works; like that of the Gesuati, the façade has four Corinthian columns on high pedestals supporting an entablature and pediment. In 1735 Massari won a competition for the design of the new church and hospital of S Maria della Pietà, Venice. The hospital was never built, although the drawings survive (Venice, Correr), but work on the church continued from 1745 to 1760 (façade completed 20th century). The church is a simplified version of the Gesuati, planned as an aisleless rectangle with curved corners, against which the four chapels are set. The nave was used as a concert auditorium, and a vestibule was provided at the front to insulate against noise from the street.

Massari produced numerous villas, including the Villa Cordellina (1735), Montecchio Maggiore, Vicenza, the elevation of which echoed the central block of Palladio's Villa Badoer, Fratta Polesine; the service blocks, however, were grouped as free-standing units around their own courts instead of being linked to the house in the manner of Palladio's *barchesse*. Massari's most important secular work is the Palazzo Grassi (1748), on the Grand Canal, Venice, which has a traditional Venetian façade made more restrained by the use of pilasters instead of columns. The internal courtyard, however, is surrounded by Tuscan columns supporting a straight entablature, with a first-floor arcade on narrow coupled pilasters. Massari also completed the Ca' Rezzonico (formerly the Palazzo Bon; *see* VENICE, fig. 5), opposite the Palazzo Grassi, begun in 1649 by Baldassare Longhena, who completed only the ground floor. Massari continued the work from 1748, adding a second atrium at the far end of the courtyard, with a grand staircase beyond; the second storey added by Massari is probably based on Longhena's design, but the attic storey, with oval windows, reveals Massari's own hand.

Among many smaller works, Massari can also be credited with the design of S Eufemia, Brescia, built in the last years of Venetian rule. This building was formerly attributed to Abbot Pietro Faita, the patron and administrator of the project, but, according to a document by the Abbot, recently discovered, a scheme by Massari was accepted after Massari had rejected three designs submitted to him for judgement. Massari's work has been variously described as 'Baroque', 'Rococo' and 'Neo-classicist', but a comprehensive study of his oeuvre shows that it reflects all three characteristics. He can best be characterized as an heir to the Venetian classicist tradition that began with Palladio, continued with Longhena and ended by interpreting in a particularly Venetian manner the first stimuli of the Enlightenment.

BIBLIOGRAPHY

V. Moschini: 'Giorgio Massari, architetto veneto', *Dédalo* (1932)
C. Renato: 'La nuova paternità di Villa Cordellina a Montecchio Maggiore', *Vita Vicentina* (Sept 1954)
E. Bassi: *Architettura del sei e settecento a Venezia* (Naples, 1962)
——: 'Il volto architettonico di Venezia nel seicento: Giorgio Massari: L'architettura della prima meta del '700 a Venezia', *Boll. Cent. Int. Stud. Archit. Andrea Palladio*, iv (1962)
A. Massari: 'Giorgio Massari e la facciata della chiesa della Pietà', *Ateneo Ven.*, iv/3 (1966)
——: *Giorgio Massari: Architetto veneziano del settecento* (Vicenza, 1971)
V. Volta: 'Quel piccolo disegno per l'Abate Faita: Un giornale di cantiere permette di attribuire a Giorgio Massari la settecentesca chiesa di S Eufemia', *G. di Brescia* (17 Aug 1989)

VALENTINO VOLTA

Massari, Lucio (*b* Bologna, 1569; *d* Bologna, 1633). Italian painter. He was taught by Bartolomeo Passerotti, from whom he developed a naturalistic Late Mannerist style. The most important influence on his early development, however, was Bartolomeo Cesi, whose revival of the classicism of the High Renaissance remained of fundamental importance to Massari's art. In 1592, on the death of Passerotti, Massari moved into the orbit of the Carracci family, attracted by Annibale and Agostino's lucid treatment of space and form rather than by Lodovico's emotional and romantic style. This can be seen in his frescoes (1600) of the oratory of S Colombano, Bologna, where the *Crucifixion* is characterized by an archaizing symmetry and clarity. The altarpiece of the *Virgin with Saints* (1603) in S Maria dei Poveri, Bologna, while drawing closer to Annibale Carracci, looks back directly to the classicism of Raphael; Massari's contributions (1604–5) to the decoration of the cloister of S Michele in Bosco, Bologna, are more indebted to Ludovico Carracci, although the classical architectural framing of each scene seems to foreshadow his later contacts with Domenichino. In his *Visitation* (1607; Bologna, S Caterina) Massari was directly inspired by Annibale Carracci and developed a classical and purist style that was reinforced by a visit to Rome, probably around 1610. His experience of Domenichino's frescoes of the *Meeting of St Nilus and Emperor Otto III* and the *Building of the Abbey Church* (1609–10; Grottaferrata Abbey) encouraged the development of carefully composed scenes, as in the *Triumph of David* (Rome, Gal. Pallavicini), with its lucid treatment of space; another, even more striking, example is the fresco decoration of the chapel of the Relics in the Certosa del Galluzzo, near Florence, left unfinished by Bernardino Poccetti in 1597 and completed by Massari around 1612. There, in the *Martyrdom of St Lawrence* and the *Martyrdom of St Stephen*, the artist established a clear spatial setting reminiscent of Domenichino's *Legends of St Nilus*, and the work is permeated by an extreme classicism. The *Massacre of the Innocents* on the other hand is influenced by Guido Reni's painting of that subject (1612; Bologna,

Pin. N.), which was already famous enough to act as a model for others.

On his return to Bologna Massari painted his *Mystic Marriage of St Catherine* (after 1614; Bologna, S Benedetto), in which he developed the pure classicism of Domenichino; the space is articulated by austerely modelled figures, the colours are clear and precise and the result reminiscent of Bartolommeo Cesi. In 1616 Massari worked with Francesco Albani and Lorenzo Garbieri at Mantua, yet these artists did not significantly affect his work, and his two scenes from the *Life of St Margaret* (1616; Mantua, S Maurizio) were again deeply influenced by Domenichino. The *Communion of St Jerome* (Bologna, S Paolo Maggiore), which is also indebted to Agostino Carracci, and the scenes from the *Life of the Blessed Corradino Ariosti* (1625) in the same church draw on the same source, and from this date Massari's style remained so stable that it is difficult to establish a chronology for his late works.

These late paintings include the *St Gaetano* (1630; Bologna, S Bartolomeo) and the large *Disputation of St Cyril*, in a *quadratura* setting by Girolamo Curti, in the Libreria of S Marco, Bologna; the latter work is distinguished by the archaizing revival of Raphael's classicism that is fundamental to Massari's art. This is also characteristic of his easel pictures, from both this and earlier periods, such as *Aeolus and Juno* (Rome, Gal. Doria-Pamphili) and the *Holy Family with St John* (Florence, Pitti), and of his altarpieces, such as the *Virgin with Saints* (Bologna, SS Giorgio and Siro), where the influence of Guido Reni and Annibale Carracci can also be seen. Massari's last works, such as the *Road to Calvary* (Bologna, Certosa) or the *St Carlo Borromeo* of the Madonna del Barracano, Bologna, attain an austere simplicity that may be compared with contemporary works by Sevilian artists such as Eugenio Caxés and Francisco de Zurbaran, although the sources and intent are undoubtedly different.

BIBLIOGRAPHY

C. C. Malvasia: *Felsina pittrice* (1678); ed. G. Zanotti (1841), i, pp. 389–96
C. Volpe: 'Lucio Massari', *Paragone*, lxxi/6 (1955), pp. 3–18
F. Arcangeli: 'Una "gloriosa gara"', *A. Ant. & Mod.*, iii (1958), pp. 236–54, 354–72
C. Volpe: 'Lucio Massari', *Maestri della pittura del seicento emiliano* (exh. cat., ed. F. Arcangeli, M. Calvesi, G. C. Cavalli, A. Emiliani and C. Volpe; Bologna, Pal. Archiginnasio, 1959)
N. Clerici Bagozzi: 'Due opere di Lucio Massari in San Maurizio a Mantova', *Paragone*, xxxvii/317–19 (1976), pp. 136–44
C. Chiarelli and G. Leoncini: *La Certosa del Galluzzo a Firenze* (Milan, 1982)
Brera dispersa: Quadri nascosti di una grande raccolta nazionale (Milan, 1984)
D. Benati: *L'arte degli Estensi: La pittura del seicento a del settecento a Modena e Reggio* (exh. cat., ed. A. Emiliani; Modena, Pal. Musei, 1986), pp. 153–5

UGO RUGGERI

Massé, Jean-Baptiste (*b* Paris, 29 Dec 1687; *d* Paris, 26 Sept 1767). French engraver, miniature painter and draughtsman. He first trained in Jean Jouvenet's Paris workshop but then joined the miniature painter Louis de Châtillon (1639–1734), under whose influence his main fields of endeavour became engraving, drawing and miniature painting. Massé's official career began in 1717 with his admission to the Académie Royale de Peinture et de Sculpture; as his *morceau de réception* he submitted an engraving of *Antoine Coypel*, the Académie's director, after a self-portrait. Massé's masterwork was the series of engravings begun in 1723 of the 'Grande Galerie de Versailles et les deux Salons qui l'accompagnent, peints par Charles Le Brun premier peintre de Louis XIV dessinés par Jean-Baptiste Massé Peintre et Conseiller de l'Académie Royale de Peinture et de Sculpture et gravés sous ses yeux par les meilleurs maîtres du tems'; it demanded from him not only artistic ability but also organizational talent: a whole string of engravers, most of them first-rate artists and members of the Académie, worked from his drawings, which had been created over a period of eight years. The great folio volume, containing over 50 plates, which finally appeared in 1753, did not achieve the expected financial success, but Massé received some official recognition when Louis XV acquired the 53 preparatory drawings (Paris, Louvre). As 'peintre en miniature du roi', Massé often represented the young King in miniature portraits that bear witness to the artist's exceptional skill in the technique. Two snuff-boxes (1726; Paris, Louvre) show portraits of *Louis XV* on the inside of the lid: despite the diminutive format, these portraits, executed after engraved models, display great subtlety of execution and strong plasticity and expressive power. They belie Mariette's characterization of Massé's art as technically perfect but devoid of content.

BIBLIOGRAPHY

Mariette; Portalis–Beraldi; Thieme–Becker

A. P. F. Robert-Dumesnil: *Le Peintre-graveur français* (1835–71)

E. Campardon: *Un Artiste oublié: J. B. Massé peintre de Louis XV* (Paris, 1880)

L. Schildlof: *Die Bildnisminiatur in Frankreich im XVII., XVIII., XIX. Jahrhundert* (Leipzig, 1911)

S. Grandjean: *Catalogue des tabatières, boîtes et étuis des XVIIIe et XIXe siècles du Musée du Louvre* (Paris, 1981)

CATHRIN KLINGSÖHR-LE ROY

Massey, (Charles) Vincent (*b* Toronto, 20 Feb 1887; *d* London, 30 Dec 1967). Canadian statesman and patron. He was president of the family business, the Massey–Harris Co., from 1921 to 1925. As Minister to the United States (1926–30), High Commissioner to London (1935–46) and Governor-General of Canada (1952–9), he gave high priority to the strengthening of the artistic life of the nation. In 1925 he was appointed a trustee of the National Gallery of Canada and for the rest of his life was a principal adviser to a succession of directors. He and his wife were friends and patrons of the Group of Seven and during the 1930s were instrumental in promoting the work of David Milne. He formed a comprehensive collection of contemporary British painting, which he later presented to the National Gallery of Canada. In 1941 he was made a trustee of the National Gallery, London, and in 1943 became its chairman. He also chaired a committee to examine the functions of the National Gallery, the Tate Gallery and the Victoria and Albert Museum. He maintained his involvement with Canadian painting, initiating the show of Canadian art at the Tate Gallery in 1938 and acting as chief organizer of the Canadian war artists' programme in 1943. Shortly after his return to Canada, he was appointed chairman of the Royal Commission on National Development in the Arts, Letters, and Sciences. The main recommendation of the report (1951) was the establishment of a central body that would provide financial support for scholarship and the arts; this was implemented in 1957 with the formation of the Canada Council. Canadian painters, who hitherto received meagre financial support, have been the principal beneficiaries of the Council's programmes.

BIBLIOGRAPHY

Report of the Royal Commission on National Development in the Arts, Letters, and Sciences, 1949–1951 (Ottawa, 1951)

C. Bissell: *The Young Vincent Massey* (Toronto, 1981)

——: *The Imperial Canadian: Vincent Massey in Office* (Toronto, 1986)

CLAUDE BISSELL

Massignon, Pierre-Henry-Ferdinand. *See* ROCHE, PIERRE.

Massimo [Massimi; Massimo alle Colonne]. Italian family of nobles, bankers and patrons. It is one of the oldest Roman families, and its members have held important offices in the secular and ecclesiastical administration of Rome and the Church. In 1826 Pope Leo XII conferred on them the rank of Principe. According to tradition, as recorded by Onofrio Panvinio *c.* 1550, the family owes its origins to the Roman general Fabius Maximus (3rd century BC). By the 12th century they owned a house in the Parione district of Rome, on the site of the present Palazzo Massimo alle Colonne, Corso Vittorio Emanuele. Pietro Massimo (*d* 1489) housed the printing firm of Konrad Sweynheim and Arnold Pannartz in his palazzo in Rome (destr. 1527), and founded the chapel of St Peter Martyr in S Maria della Strada (destr. 16th century), Rome. His son Domenico Massimo (*d* 1531/2) amassed enormous riches and expanded the palazzo. After his death, Domenico's sons Pietro Massimo (*d* 1544), Luca Massimo (*d* 1550) and Angelo Massimo (*d* 1550) divided his properties, and each decided to build new residences on or close to the site of the old palazzo. Pietro had Baldassare Peruzzi erect the Palazzo Massimo alle Colonne, which was begun in 1532 (*see* PERUZZI, BALDASSARE, §3 and fig. 4). Its walls and ceilings were painted under the direction of Perino del Vaga with scenes from Classical history and mythology, while Daniele da Volterra decorated the *sala grande* with a painted frieze showing the Roman ancestors of the family, including Fabius Maximus. Pietro's wife, Faustina Rusticelli (*d* 1571), founded the Massimo Chapel in the Basilica di S Giovanni Laterano. Antonio da Sangallo designed another palazzo (destr. *c.* 1880) in Rome (Florence, Uffizi, UA 944) for Luca Massimo, and this became famous for its collection of Classical sculpture and inscriptions.

Luca's grandson (1) Camillo Massimo was a distinguished patron in the 17th century, especially of Nicolas Poussin and Claude Lorrain. Successive members of the family were all descended from Angelo and his son Fabrizio Massimo (*d* 1633). Angelo built the Palazzo di Pirro (completed *c.* 1537), Rome, designed by Giovanni Mangone, next to Pietro's palazzo, and had it frescoed by followers of Perino del Vaga, who continued their work for Angelo's son Massimo Massimo (*d* 1579), Archbishop of Amalfi. Angelo also founded the Massimo Chapel in Trinità dei Monti, with decorations by Perino del Vaga (destr.; one fresco London, V&A). In 1574 Fabrizio became Lord of Arsoli (nr Tivoli), where he had various buildings erected, including SS Salvatore, designed by Giacomo della Porta.

Various members of the Massimo family continued to occupy prominent positions in both the ecclesiastical and civil life of Rome. In 1789 Francesco Camillo VII Massimo (1730–1801) bought the 16th-century Villa Montalto (destr.) near the Baths of Diocletian. Meanwhile, his son Carlo Massimo (1766–1827) bought the Villa Giustiniani (now Villa Massimo Lancelotti), Rome, and had it decorated (1819–27) by Friedrich Overbeck, Peter Cornelius and other members of the Nazarenes with scenes from the works of Dante, Torquato Tasso and Ludovico Ariosto (*see* OVERBECK, FRIEDRICH). Cardinal Francesco Massimo (1806–46) was the promoter of the Museo Gregoriano Egizio (1839) in the Museo del Vaticano. After 1659, when it was acquired by Fabrizio Camillo IV Massimo (*d* 1693), the Palazzo Massimo alle Colonne was connected with the Palazzo di Pirro and expanded, especially in the 19th century. Although no longer connected in the late 20th century, each palazzo is still owned by members of the Massimo family.

BIBLIOGRAPHY
O. Panvinio: *De Fabiorum familia, de Maximorum familia* (MS. *c.* 1550; Rome, Vatican, Bib. Apostolica, Archv Capitolare S Pietro, Cod. Lat. 6168); ed. A. Mai in *Spigilegium romanum*, ix (1843), pp. 543–91
P. Litta: *Famiglie celebri italiane*, IV/xlv (Milan, 1837)
K. Gerstenberg: *Die Wandgemälde der deutschen Romantiker im Cassino Massimo zu Rom* (Berlin, 1934)
Ceccarius: *I Massimo*, Le Grandi Famiglie Romane, viii (Rome, 1954)
H. Wurm: *Der Palazzo Massimo alle Colonne* (Berlin, 1965)
C. L. Frommel: *Der römische Palastbau der Hochrenaissance*, Römische Forschungen der Bibliotheca Hertziana, xxi, 3 vols (Tübingen, 1973)
                                                                J. L. DE JONG

(1) Cardinal **Camillo (Carlo) Massimo** (*b* Rome, 1620; *d* Rome, 1677). He assumed the name Camillo from his cousin, Vincenzo Giustiniani's nephew, whose estate he inherited in 1640. He had a deep love of Classical antiquity, and the most celebrated classical artists in 17th-century Rome were inspired by his learning. As a patron and collector, he emulated Giustiniani and Cassiano dal Pozzo, whom he knew. Probably in the late 1630s he took drawing lessons from Nicolas Poussin, and a contemporary inscription on Poussin's *Self-portrait* drawing (*c.* 1630; London, BM) states that Poussin gave the drawing to Massimo.

In the reign of Pope Innocent X Massimo rose quickly in the Curia, acquiring the position and wealth that allowed patronage on a grand scale. In the mid-1640s he commissioned two erudite and austere pictures from Poussin—*Moses Trampling on Pharaoh's Crown*, an extremely rare subject, and *Moses Changing Aaron's Rod into a Serpent* (both Paris, Louvre)—and acquired a number of Poussin drawings, mainly of Ovidian themes (*c.* 1622–3; Windsor Castle, Royal Lib.), which had been commissioned by Giambattista Marino. He also commissioned mythological pictures from Claude Lorrain: *Argus Guarding Io* (*c.* 1644; Holkham Hall, Norfolk) and *Coast View with Apollo and the Cumean Sibyl* (*c.* 1646; St Petersburg, Hermitage).

Massimo was among the ten representatives of the papal court who sat to Diego Velázquez during the painter's stay in Rome in 1649. The resulting portrait (Kingston Lacy, Dorset, NT) shows him in the peacock-blue robes of the Cameriere Segreto to which he had been appointed in 1646. In 1654 he was appointed papal nuncio to Spain, but Philip IV, suspecting him of sympathy with the French, would not receive him. Velázquez, however, wrote to welcome him. He was finally received in 1655, and it was probably in this period that he acquired portraits by Velázquez of the Spanish King and Queen and two princesses (untraced).

Massimo had evidently expressed anti-French sentiments at the Spanish court, but Alexander VII, who became Pope in April 1665, wished to maintain relations with France and so recalled Massimo to Rome, where he remained without office for 12 years. This doubtless allowed him more time to concentrate on his collection of antiques and his library. He remained close to Poussin, visited him in his studio and probably made his library available to the painter, who in 1664 gave him one of his most recondite works, the unfinished *Apollo and Daphne* (Paris, Louvre).

With the election of Pope Clement X (1670), who made him a cardinal, Massimo again became a powerful patron. In the 1670s he advised the papal family, the Altieri, to commission Carlo Maratti, whose classical style he admired, to fresco a ceiling in their Roman palace with the *Triumph of Clemency*. He commissioned two large pictures from Claude, the *View of Delphi with a Procession* (1673; Chicago, IL, A. Inst.), an erudite treatment of a subject from Classical antiquity, and the *Coast View with Perseus and the Origin of Coral* (1674; Holkham Hall, Norfolk), a rare subject from Ovid, whose unusual composition may have been inspired by ancient painting. Both these works re-created the Classical world for which he held such fervent regard, a regard that led him also to commission PIETRO SANTE BARTOLI to make drawings of ancient Roman mosaics and paintings (one of three volumes remains, Glasgow, U. Lib.), intended for eventual publication. In 1677 Bartoli was commissioned to copy the illustrations in the Late Antique manuscript, the Vatican Virgil (Rome, Vatican, Bib. Apostolica, Cod. Vat. 3867).

BIBLIOGRAPHY
A. Blunt: 'The Massimi Collection of Poussin Drawings in the Royal Library at Windsor Castle', *Master Drgs*, xiv/1 (1976), pp. 3–31
C. Pace: 'Pietro Santi Bartoli: Drawings in Glasgow University Library after Roman Paintings and Mosaics', *Pap. Brit. Sch. Rome*, xlvii (1979), pp. 117–55
F. Haskell: *Patrons and Painters: A Study in the Relations between Italian Art and Society in the Age of the Baroque* (New Haven and London, 1980), pp. 114–19   ☐

Massina, Pino da. *See* JACOBELLO D'ANTONIO.

Massingham. English family of sculptors. Although the Massinghams are the only substantially documented late medieval English sculptors, little of their recorded work survives.

(1) John Massingham (i) (*fl* 1409–50). In 1438 John (i) was paid for an inn sign for the Sun Tavern in Canterbury, and from 1438 to 1442 he was master carver at All Souls College, Oxford, founded by Henry Chichele (Archbishop of Canterbury, 1414–43). Similarities between the six statues of kings on the Canterbury Cathedral choir-screen and the carvings of Henry VI and the Archbishop and of the Resurrection (all replaced) on the College gateway suggest that Massingham may have made all these works, together with the lost imagery of the College chapel's great reredos. The very weathered figures from the gateway show many similarities with the Canterbury kings. In 1448–9 Massingham, now working in London, carved an image of the *Virgin* for Eton parish church (Berks). In 1449 he worked on the effigy of *Richard Beauchamp, Earl of Warwick*, for his burial chapel in St Mary's, Warwick, probably carving the wooden model from which the gilt-latten figure was cast. It has been conjectured that he made some of the extant freestone imagery for the east window of the chapel, and that he also produced imagery for the chantry chapel of Henry V in Westminster Abbey (*see* LONDON, §V, 2(ii)(a)), the two works that introduced Netherlandish–Burgundian realism into English sculpture.

(2) John Massingham (ii) (*fl* 1438–78). Son of (1) John Massingham (i). He worked with his father at All Souls College, Oxford, and his first independent work was an inn sign, for The Angel at Andover (1452–3). In 1465–6 he painted the late 14th-century *Virgin and Child* from the outer gate of Winchester College, and in 1469–70 he sculpted the images for the chapel reredos. Between 1475 and 1478 he carved and painted the crucifix and companion figures of *Mary* and *John* for the new roodloft, designed by William Hunt.

BIBLIOGRAPHY

Harvey

L. Stone: *Sculpture in Britain: The Middle Ages*, Pelican Hist. A. (Harmondsworth, 1955, rev. 1972)

PHILLIP LINDLEY

Mass Observation. British investigative organization founded in 1937 to examine aspects of popular culture. Although Mass Observation was neither an art movement nor a particular school or style, it did attract artists, photographers and film makers who were involved in realist, Surrealist and social documentary practices. Anthropologist Tom Harrisson (1911–76), poet and journalist Charles Madge (*b* 1912) and painter, poet and documentary film maker Humphrey Jennings (1907–50) announced its formation by calling for volunteers to observe and gather data on subjects ranging from anti-Semitism to the aspidistra cult.

The methodology of Mass Observation was threefold: inviting the 'masses' to send in diary-form reports of their everyday lives; gathering scientifically observed data from full- and part-time volunteers; and involving poets, writers and artists by demanding their creative responses to 'ordinary life'. By 1938 Mass Observation boasted over 1500 observers. Madge and Jennings in particular were involved in British Surrealism in the 1930s. Applying the methods of anthropology to their culture by studying its customs, superstitions, habits and phobias appealed to their desire to explore the national mood and the shared subconscious desires and beliefs. The intellectual left

Mass Observation photograph by Humphrey Spender: *Open Market, Bolton*, 1937 (Brighton, University of Sussex, Mass Observation Archive)

supported Mass Observation enthusiastically. Similar concerns were being explored in art by the ARTISTS INTERNATIONAL ASSOCIATION; in literature (e.g. George Orwell's *Road to Wigan Pier*, 1937); and in Jennings's films for the General Post Office Film Unit, which captured the 1930s documentary movement at its height.

While Madge and Jennings conducted surveys on national events in London, Mass Observation's most exhaustive survey was conducted by Harrisson in Bolton (referred to as 'Worktown') and Blackpool during the summer in 1937 and 1938. In 1937 Harrisson invited Humphrey Spender to photograph Bolton, for example *Open Market* (see fig.). The camera was regarded as a democratic tool with which to document and record fact. It was also recognized that ordinary 'fact' could take on a strange countenance through its fantastic transformation into an *objet trouvé*: the Surrealist sense of the uncanny in the commonplace often appears in Spender's documentation of *Street Life* in Bolton or his *Blackpool* series. Spender's photographs have become the most extensive and valuable source of visual documentation of Mass Observation.

The painter Julian Trevelyan (*b* 1910) went to Bolton in 1937. He was fully aware of the Surrealist potential for urban metaphor and fantasy and produced witty cityscape collages from newspapers, magazines and waste paper (all untraced). William Coldstream and Graham Bell went to Bolton in 1938. Both Bell's *Bolton* series, which duplicated many subjects in Spender's photographs, and Coldstream's *Bolton* (1938; Ottawa, N.G.) were typical of the realism practised by the EUSTON ROAD SCHOOL, which was sparing in its use of colour and paint and subtle in its linear drawing. Few works survive from their two-week stay.

Influenced by Trevelyan's collage techniques, Harrisson became interested in art practices that did not require the cultural sophistication of art school training. Harrisson's interest in groups of 'worker' artists, such as the Ashington Group of miners in Northumberland, was also linked to notions of art for and by the masses. After visiting the group in 1938, Harrisson and Trevelyan organized the successful exhibition *Unprofessional Painting* in the Bensham Grove Settlement in Gateshead, including work by London draper George Downs, pavement artist David Burton, bus driver Henry Stockley and St Ives painter Alfred Wallis.

The poetic nature of Mass Observation disappeared at the outbreak of World War II, and thereafter there was no attempt to organize any visual documentation. By 1940 Mass Observation was working for the Ministry of Information assessing levels of morale at home. In 1949 Mass Observation was registered as a limited company, later becoming a subsidiary of the British Market Research Bureau, with no formal connection with the Mass Observation Archive now housed at Sussex University.

WRITINGS
T. Harrisson, H. Jennings and C. Madge: 'Anthropology at Home', *New Statesman & Nation* (30 Jan 1937) [letter]

BIBLIOGRAPHY
Humphrey Spender: Worktown, Photographs of Bolton and Blackpool taken for Mass Observation, 1937–38 (exh. cat. by I. Jeffrey, D. Mellor and D. Smith, Brighton, U. Sussex, Gardner Cent. Gal., 1977)
D. Mellor: 'Mass Observation: The Intellectual Climate', *Cam. Work*, 11 (1978)
M.-L. Jennings: *Humphrey Jennings: Film Maker, Painter, Poet* (London, 1982)
J. Mulford, ed.: *H. Spender: Worktown People, Photographs of Northern England, 1937–1938* (London, 1982) [excellent pls]
A. Calder and D. Sheridan: *Speak for Yourself: A Mass Observation Anthology, 1937–49* (London, 1984)
Mass Observation (exh. cat. by R. Varley, London, Watermans A. Cent., 1987)
W. Feaver: *The Ashington Group* (London, 1988)

INGRID SWENSON

Masson, André (*b* Balagne, 4 Jan 1896; *d* Paris, 28 Oct 1987). French painter, draughtsman, printmaker and stage designer. His work played an important role in the development of both SURREALISM and ABSTRACT EXPRESSIONISM, although his independence, iconoclasm and abrupt stylistic transitions make him difficult to classify. Masson was admitted to the Académie Royale des Beaux-Arts et l'Ecole des Arts Décoratifs in Brussels at the age of 11. Through his teacher Constant Montald, he met the Belgian poet Emile Verhaeren (1855–1916), who persuaded Masson's parents to send him to Paris for further training. Masson joined the French infantry in 1915 and fought in the battles of the Somme; he was gravely wounded, and his wartime experiences engendered in him a profound philosophy about human destiny and stimulated his search for a personal imagery of generation, eclosion and metamorphosis.

Masson's early works, particularly the paintings of 1922 and 1923 on a forest theme (e.g. *Forest*, 1923; see Leiris and Limbour, p. 93), reflected the influence of André Derain, but by late 1923 he had moved away from Derain towards Analytical Cubism. His first solo exhibition, organized by Daniel-Henri Kahnweiler at the Galerie Simon in Paris (1923), attracted the attention of André Breton, who purchased *The Four Elements* (1923–4; Paris, priv. col., see 1976 exh. cat., p. 102) and invited Masson to join the Surrealist group. Influenced by Surrealist ideas, both Masson and Joan Miró began experimenting with automatic drawing (for illustration *see* AUTOMATISM), and the Cubist imagery of Masson's painting soon resonated with symbolic content. Two drawings were reproduced in the first issue of *Révolution surréaliste* in December 1924. By late 1929 the Cubist syntax of Masson's paintings had become more schematic, the compositions more open, and the imagery developed from random 'automatic' gestures (*see* AUTOMATISM). By sprinkling coloured sands on canvas, prepared by drawing 'automatically' with glue, he was able to retain the spontaneity of the drawings, yet build a complex poetic imagery. One of the first, and most successful, sand paintings is *Battle of the Fishes* (1927; New York, MOMA; see fig.), in which a primordial eroticism is revealed through an imagery of conflict and metamorphosis, poetically equating the submarine imagery with its physical substance.

Between 1924 and 1929 (when Breton expelled Masson from the Surrealist group) the biomorphic abstractions of Miró and Masson dominated Surrealist painting. Masson spent much of the period between 1930 and 1937 in the south of France and in Spain. During this period he explored themes and subjects drawn from Greek mythology, Spanish literature and the Spanish Civil War. From 1931 to 1933 the theme of massacres prevailed and led to a series of violent, orgiastic drawings filled with sharp, jagged pen strokes (e.g. *Massacre*, 1933; ex-artist's col., see

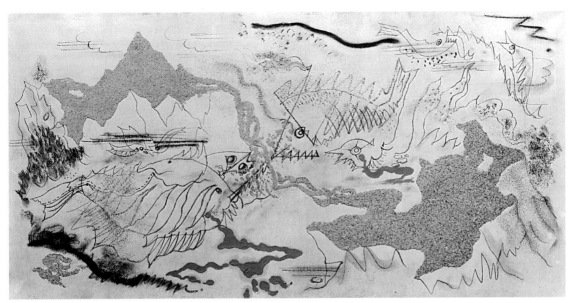

André Masson: *Battle of the Fishes*, sand, gesso, oil, pencil and charcoal on canvas, 362×730 mm, 1927 (New York, Museum of Modern Art)

Hahn, p. 15). A group of expressionistic scenes of ritual-istic erotic killings based on Greek mythology followed. In 1933 Masson executed the drawings *Sacrifices* including *The Crucified One*, *Mithra*, *Osiris* and *Minotaur* (published as etchings, as *Sacrifices*, Paris, 1936) to accompany a text by Georges Bataille. That same year he completed the first of a group of stage designs and costumes for the ballet *Les Présages*, choreographed by Léonide Massine for the Ballets Russes de Monte Carlo, followed by designs for Knut Hamsun's *La Faim* (1939), the production by Jean-Louis Barrault (*b* 1910) of Cervantes's *Numance* (1937) and Darius Milhaud's *Medea* (1940), among others.

Masson's return to Paris in 1937 and his reconciliation with Breton were marked by a move towards greater representation and deep illusionistic spaces in his art, perhaps influenced by the prominence of Salvador Dalí, René Magritte and Yves Tanguy in the Surrealist move-ment at that time. Images of erotic violence and death mingle with mythological and literary themes drawn from ancient Greece and from Sigmund Freud's writings on the dream and the unconscious, in *Gradiva* (1939; Knokke-le-Zoute, Casino Com.), *Metamorphoses* (1939; Paris, Gal. Ile de France) and other major paintings of these years. The myth of Theseus and the Minotaur provided the theme for numerous paintings and drawings and finally led Masson away from illusionism and back to a form of automatism in which the unity of the human and natural worlds is achieved through the process of drawing itself.

Automatism continued as the basis of Masson's work during his years in New York during World War II. The series of telluric paintings, rich in the colours of the autumn landscape in Connecticut, where Masson was living at the time, including *Meditation on an Oak Leaf* (1942; New York, MOMA), *Iroquois Landscape* (1942; Paris, Simone Collinet priv. col., see 1976 exh. cat., p. 164) and *Indian Spring* (1942; New York, Mr and Mrs William Mazer priv. col., see 1976 exh. cat., p. 165), reveal a

spontaneous and integrated relationship between colour, line and form. *Leonardo da Vinci and Isabella d'Este* (1942; New York, MOMA) can be cited as an important influence on Arshile Gorky's move toward biomorphic abstraction in the early 1940s. Although direct influences are more difficult to determine, there are strong affinities with Jackson Pollock's work of those years, which he may have seen at S. W. Hayter's Atelier 17 where both artists worked in the 1940s.

Masson returned to France in 1946, settling in Aix-en-Provence until 1955. In 1950 a series of his essays was published as *Le Plaisir de plaindre* (Nice). A series of trips to Italy from 1951 resulted in the album of colour lithographs *Voyage à Venise* (1952) and other works on the theme of the Italian landscape. Although Masson did not participate in the last major international exhibition of Surrealism (Paris, 1947), he was cited in the catalogue as one of the 'Surrealists in spite of themselves' (also included in this group were Picasso, Dalí and Oscar Domínguez). The paintings of the post-war period, however, reflect Masson's growing interest in Impressionism, J. M. W. Turner and Zen Buddhism. Combining Impressionist style with Oriental technique and imagery, and drawing on his whole repertory of themes and techniques, as well as branching out into new areas opened up by his study of Zen, Masson abandoned chiaroscuro for all-over luminos-ity, soft transparent pastels and a personal and gestural calligraphy. A large retrospective exhibition with Alberto Giacometti in Basle in 1950 was followed, five years later, by the Grand Prix National.

Masson's most important commission was his invitation from André Malraux to paint the ceiling of the Théâtre de l'Odéon in Paris (1965). Masson continued to divide his time between Paris and the south of France. The course of his work was marked less by stylistic unity than by his commitment to art as a poetic, philosophical and psycho-logical exploration. His last work expanded the themes of transformation and metamorphosis that he began in 1922.

WRITINGS

with J.-L. Barrault, Georges Bataille and others: *André Masson* (Rouen, 1940)

Mythologies (Paris, 1946) [contains 'Mythologie de la nature', 'Mythologie de l'être' and 'L'Homme emblématique', with 41 full-page drgs]

BIBLIOGRAPHY

M. Leiris and G. Limbour: *André Masson and his Universe* (Geneva, 1947)

G. Charbonnier: *André Masson: Entretiens avec Georges Charbonnier* (Paris, [*c.* 1959])

W. Rubin: 'Notes on Masson and Pollock', *Arts* [New York], xxxiv/2 (1959), pp. 36–43

O. Hahn: *André Masson* (London, 1965)

W. Chadwick: 'Masson's *Gradiva*: The Metamorphosis of a Surrealist Myth', *A. Bull.*, lii/4 (1970), pp. 415–22

J. P. Clébert: *Mythologies d'André Masson* (Geneva, 1971) [thematic study]

F. Will-Levaillant: 'André Masson et le livre: Dessin, gravure, illustration', *Bull. Biblioph.*, 2 (1972), pp. 129–55

——: 'Catalogues des ouvrages illustrés par André Masson, de 1924 à février 1972', *Bull. Biblioph.*, 2 (1972), pp. 156–80; 3, pp. 272–304

André Masson (exh. cat. by W. Rubin and C. Lanchner, New York, MOMA, 1976) [contains full bibliog. and chronology]

Masson: Opere dal 1920 al 1970 (exh. cat., Florence, Orsanmichele, 1981)

André Masson (exh. cat. by S. A. de Turenne, M. Leiris and F. Will-Levaillant, Nîmes, Mus. B.-A., 1985)

D. Ades: *André Masson* (New York, 1994)

WHITNEY CHADWICK

Masson, Antoine (*b* Loury, 1636; *d* Paris, 30 May 1700). French engraver, draughtsman and pastellist. Beginning with chasing and damascene work for armour, he came to devote himself wholly to engraving. In 1679 he was received (*reçu*) by the Académie Royale de Peinture et de Sculpture in Paris and exhibited at the Salon of 1699. He made seven reproductive engravings of religious subjects, after Titian (the *Disciples at Emmaus*), Carlo Maratti and Peter Paul Rubens. Of his 63 portrait engravings, some are after his own compositions, others after Nicolas Mignard (*Henri de Lorraine, Comte d'Harcourt*, also known as the *Young Man with a Pearl*, RD 34), Charles Le Brun (*Louis XIV*, RD 43–4), Gilbert de Sève and Thomas Blanchet. He excelled in the rendering of materials and the vivacity of expressions, but sometimes gave way to a gratuitous virtuosity, as in his portrait of *Guy Patin* (RD 59), in which the nose is formed from a single spiral cut. The few drawings that are now attributed to him include pastels of *Charles II, King of England* (Dijon, Mus. Magnin) and *Pierre Dupuis* (Paris, Louvre).

BIBLIOGRAPHY

A. P. F. Robert-Dumesnil: *Le Peintre-graveur français*, ii (Paris, 1836), pp. 98–139 [RD]

J. Danton: *Notice sur A. Masson suivie du catalogue de l'oeuvre de Masson et d'un document inédit* (Orléans, 1866)

Artistes orléanais du XVIIe siècle (exh. cat., ed. J. Pruvost Auzas; Orléans, Mus. B.-A., 1958), pp. 40–51

VÉRONIQUE MEYER

Masson, Luis León (*fl* Seville, 1858; *d* ?Seville, ?1874). Spanish photographer. He was one of Seville's earliest established photographers and worked with his wife. Unlike contemporary photographers in Seville, such as Francisco de Leygonier y Haubert, Masson travelled throughout Andalusia to Málaga, Granada, Córdoba and Algeciras as well as to Madrid to make photographs. His series on Gibraltar is notable for its completeness and because the many photographs he made there are not the customary views of the rock and bay, but the colony itself: military docks and fortifications, specific military and civil buildings, and the topography of the territory. He and his wife considered photographs of cadavers to be their speciality and Masson's bullfight images are regarded as among the earliest on the subject.

BIBLIOGRAPHY

Photography in Spain in the Nineteenth Century (exh. cat. by L. Fontanella, Dallas, Delahunty & Fraenkel Gals, 1984)

LEE FONTANELLA

Massot, Firmin (*b* Geneva, 5 May 1766; *d* Geneva, 16 May 1849). Swiss painter, draughtsman and teacher. His first teacher was his sister, the portrait painter and engraver Pernette Massot (1761–1828). In 1788 Massot visited Rome with the painter Jean-Pierre Saint-Ours as a guide. On his return Massot was commissioned to produce several charcoal drawings, including two miniature portraits in profile (*c.* 1790; priv. col.), probably depicting two young women of the Chavanne family. From 1794, in order to escape the turbulence of the French Revolution he sought refuge at Coppet with Jacques Necker, former French Minister of Finance under Louis XIV, and his wife Suzanne, who introduced him to Lausanne society, where he established a new clientèle.

Having returned to Geneva he worked with Wolfgang Adam Töpffer, Jacques-Laurent Agasse and his own brother-in-law Nicolas Schenker (?1760–1848). Massot executed several works in collaboration with Töpffer and Agasse, Massot painting the figures. Töpffer painted the backgrounds for Massot's miniature bust portraits of Genevan society figures or of such aristocratic foreign visitors as the Polish Zamoyski and Czartoryski families. In these there is a marked contrast between the naturalism of Töpffer's landscapes and the artificial lighting of Massot's faces. One of his major commissions was the portrait of *Empress Josephine Bonaparte* (1812), of which he painted *c.* 25 versions. From 1805 Massot taught Amélie Romilly (1788–1875). From 1814 his output was on a par with that of a factory; he printed a list of 'set prices' that were determined solely by the sex of the sitter and the format of the painting. Massot rarely signed and dated his works; approximate dates can be deduced only by an examination of the dress of the sitters. Other artists working in Geneva painted in a similar style, among them Marianne Fol-Straub (1802–46); their work is often ascribed to him.

BIBLIOGRAPHY

D. Baud-Bovy and F. Boissonas: *Peintres genevois du XVIIIe et du XIXe siècle* (Geneva, 1903–4)

Jacques-Laurent Agasse, 1767–1849, ou La Séduction de l'Angleterre, (exh. cat., ed. R. Loche; Geneva, Mus. A. & Hist.; London, Tate; 1988–9)

VINCENT LIEBER

Massoudy, Hassan (*b* Najaf, 1944). Iraqi calligrapher, painter, printmaker and writer, active in Paris. He studied painting and calligraphy in Baghdad from 1960 to 1969, and in 1969 exhibited his work at the Iraqi Artists' Society exhibition and at the French Cultural Centre in Baghdad. The same year he went to Paris and studied at the Ecole des Beaux-Arts until 1975. Thereafter he lived in Paris. Although influenced by traditional calligraphy, he developed his own calligraphic style, which incorporated painterly elements. In many of his works, for example *Je suis le feu tapi dans la pierre. Si tu es de ceux qui font jaillir l'étincelle alors frappe* (1984; Paris, Inst. Monde Arab.), he employed proverbs and quotations from a range of sources. He also researched and wrote about Arabic calligraphy.

WRITINGS

Calligraphie arabe vivante (Paris, 1981)

BIBLIOGRAPHY

The Influence of Calligraphy on Contemporary Arab Art (exh. cat., London, Iraqi Cult. Cent., 1980)

M. Tournier: *Hassan Massoudy: Calligraphe* (Paris, 1986)

Mass production. Production of a large number or mass of a single given object, either by hand or machine. The term mass production usually also implies machine production and the division of human or automated labour to reduce the cost of production when a sufficient quantity is produced.

1. Before *c.* 1900. 2. *c.* 1900 and after.

1. BEFORE *c.* 1900. Mass production developed in pockets of the Western capitalist economy before the factory system, before machine production and even before a detailed division of labour. There is some evidence of large-scale hand-production of basic pottery in both ancient Egypt and ancient Rome, and a division of labour was beginning to emerge in the furniture workshops of mid-18th-century London in such firms as those of John Linnell (i) and Thomas Chippendale (i), where chair and table legs and feet were made by hand in batch, if not mass, production. The large-scale development of mass production came with the introduction of machinery, the factory system and the division of labour on the one hand and the growth of the domestic and overseas middle-class market on the other. The main developments took place from the mid-18th century. From 1769, for example, Josiah Wedgwood (*see* WEDGWOOD) introduced a detailed division of labour to speed up production, employ fewer skilled workers and produce more uniform products at his Etruria works. Mass production led to the success of his 'Queen's Ware' range, which filled the gap in the market between very expensive foreign porcelain and the poor-quality everyday tableware then available from British potteries.

By the mid-19th century it was still only the British textile industry that had been extensively mechanized. In other industries higher levels of production were often at the expense of an increased division of labour, and low prices were the result of poor-quality materials and unskilled labour. For example, there was little division of labour in the largely bespoke furniture trade until the second half of the 19th century when it began to cater for the growing middle-class market, which demanded high-quality goods but at greatly reduced cost. This was achieved through the 'sweated labour' system that developed in the East End of London where the increased production of cheap furniture was based on low wages, poor working conditions, cheap materials and an intense subdivision of labour. Production was by hand rather than machine because, despite the enormous demand, wages were so low that it was not worthwhile for employers to introduce expensive machinery, the initial cost of which took years to recoup. In the USA, however, high labour costs and a shortage of craft skills encouraged manufacturers to replace people with machines. These factors, coupled with developments in precision tool-making, encouraged the growth of the American System of Manufactures, in which goods using standardized and interchangeable parts were mass-produced by machine. Fire-arms, locks, clocks, watches, sewing-machines and cars were all produced by this system, and the results in a country with an enormous domestic market were remarkable: for example, by the end of the 19th century Robert H. Ingersoll (1859–1928) produced a wrist-watch that cost only one dollar. The growth in population had led to a greater demand for all kinds of domestic goods, and from the early 19th century glassmakers, for example, experimented with new technology to mass produce cheap pressed-glass tableware; such companies as the LIBBEY GLASS CO. developed mass-produced industrial glass products.

In 1857 MICHAEL THONET opened his purpose-built factory in Koritschan-bei-Gaya, Moravia, where he employed unskilled local workers, whom he trained in his new methods of mass-producing bentwood furniture, designed for commercial use in hotels, restaurants etc and produced on a huge scale for an international market. It was shipped unassembled for easier transportation. In 1857 the factory produced 10,000 articles, mainly chairs; in 1859 the first Thonet catalogue was issued showing 26 items, and by 1860 the factory produced over 50,000 pieces of furniture including armchairs, settees and tables (*see* INDUSTRIAL DESIGN, fig. 3).

2. *c.* 1900 AND AFTER. One of the best-known examples of standardized mass production was the 'Model T' car produced in 1908 by Henry Ford (1863–1947). An unchanging design, standardized parts and (from 1914) a moving assembly line all helped reduce costs dramatically, from £850 in 1910 to £360 in 1916 (see fig. 1). By 1927 nearly 15 million 'Model T' cars had been sold, but declining sales forced Ford to respond to market demands for new models—an early example of the problem of standardization in mass production bringing lower costs, which then have to be offset by demands for novelty and rapid changes in fashion. In the USA in the late 1920s and 1930s these conflicting demands of economy and novelty were resolved by emphasizing superficial changes in the appearance of goods—a system that came to be known as 'styling'.

Yet the problem of the uniformity associated with standardization remained. It was not only the American System of Manufacture that emphasized standardization and the interchangeability of parts. From 1905 RICHARD RIEMERSCHMID, a German designer, experimented with his *Typenmöbel*, which he saw as a prototype furniture for standardized machine mass production that would bring good design to the general public. Riemerschmid was a member of the DEUTSCHER WERKBUND, an organization of manufacturers, designers and retailers formed in Germany in 1907 to stimulate the German economy by increasing its share of world markets in well-designed large-scale or mass-produced quality goods, be they hand- or machine-made. The issue of standardization was debated in 1914, with Henry Van de Velde (a Belgian designer then working in Germany) arguing for the place

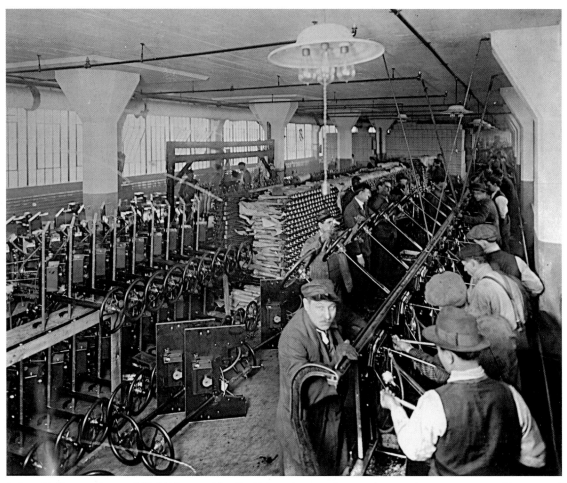

1. Assembly-line manufacture of 'Model T' automobiles, Ford Motor Company, Detroit, 1914 (Dearborn, MI, Henry Ford Museum and Greenfield Village)

of individuality and creative freedom against Hermann Muthesius, who stressed that the way to transform everyday objects lay with standardization. For the consumer the problem was wanting a fashionable, uniform, mass-produced object that was in some way different. Wedgwood's solution had been to offer his customers a choice of a variety of patterns that could be added to a standard pottery shape (*see* INDUSTRIAL DESIGN, fig. 1). In the USA in the 1930s, the answer was a selfconscious revamping of the appearance of an object without redesigning the product itself, for example the Coldspot refrigerator by RAYMOND LOEWY, which re-cased an existing Sears Roebuck Co. product in 1935, and Cadillac cars, which were restyled annually in the 1950s by Harley T. Earl (1893–1969) and his design team.

The restyling of well-known mass-produced products to stimulate sales continues: new styles of famous brand-name sports training-shoes are launched every few months; hairdryers are being 'gendered' for the male market, which will accept a metallic grey gun-shaped model but not a pastel-coloured one designed for the female market. Another response to the uniformity of standardization demanded by mass production has been

to 'customize' uniform products, especially cars. The famous Volkswagen 'Beetle' car, 20 million of which were produced in the 40 years after World War II, has been customized in many different and inventive ways by owners over the years, as have Levi jeans. The replacement of the unique object by the mass-produced one has simply offered new challenges to the consumer's individualism and inventiveness.

Despite the dominance of the machine aesthetic and modernism in art and design, non-mass-produced items are seen as superior: uniqueness has a high market value. Certain machine mass-produced mugs even have glazes that mimic the imperfections resulting from hand production. Although the quality of the materials used and the care taken during production may be equal in a machine-made and a handmade object, the latter is seen as somehow superior. The idea that hand production is somehow morally better than machine production because it does not involve the alienation resulting from the division of labour derives from the ARTS AND CRAFTS MOVEMENT, which developed in Britain from the 1860s in response to the worst excesses of capitalist development, including the division of labour, machine production and the use of shoddy materials, and spread through Europe and North America. It sought to retain the satisfaction obtained when a craftworker makes a single item from beginning to end and sometimes also designs it. One result of the increased production of the relatively cheap objects that graced the houses of the new middle class in the 19th century was the alienation of the workers who made them, either because their skills had been replaced by machines or because subdivision of labour made them little more than parts of a machine. The Arts and Crafts Movement also equated hand production with quality production because it developed at the time when machine production was in its infancy and was frequently concerned with manufacturing cheap imitations of expensive handmade products. By the early 20th century it was clear that the Arts and Crafts Movement was unable to move beyond the production of highly priced, well-made, one-off objects.

The Deutscher Werkbund and the Design and Industries Association (DIA; founded in Britain in 1915) set out to make well-designed quality goods available to the general public. Both organizations grew out of the Arts and Crafts Movement, retained an emphasis on quality but insisted that it should apply to both hand and machine mass-produced goods. They focused on commercially viable everyday goods, from electric light bulbs and fans to teapots with spouts that poured without dripping, all of which were mass-produced. The work of these and other institutions, together with the Modern Movement in art and design, which argued that machine forms as well as

machine production were appropriate for the new machine age, helped the acceptance after World War I of the idea that mass production could mean quality production. The teamwork of designers and manufacturers committed to quality mass production by machine, such as the chairs designed by Charles Eames and Ray Eames (*see* EAMES) for Herman Miller Inc. in the USA (*see* INDUSTRIAL DESIGN, fig. 6) and by ROBIN DAY for Hille International of Great Britain from the 1950s to the 1970s (see fig. 2), transformed public attitudes towards mass-produced items that proclaimed their machine origins instead of trying to look like handmade items. These mass-produced objects have become collectors' items.

The increase in prosperity and home ownership from the 1960s created a market for good quality, well-designed, mass-produced furniture for discerning first-time buyers. In 1964 Terence Conran opened the first Habitat shop in Fulham Road, London, which, together with numerous later branches, catered for this market with great success. From the late 1980s Habitat was challenged by the Swedish firm of IKEA (founded by Ingmar Kamprad in 1943), which offers a huge variety of Swedish-designed mass-produced home furnishings, most of which are supplied flat-packed for self-assembly, from its enormous superstores in the UK, as well as in other European countries, the Far East and North America. In 1992 Habitat was bought by Stichting Ingka, the Dutch company that also owned IKEA.

2. Mass-produced chairs, polypropylene with metal legs, designed by Robin Day for Hille International, 1963; (background and right foreground) stacking chairs, (left foreground) armchair and armless chair, each with single-stem base

BIBLIOGRAPHY

S. Giedion: *Mechanization Takes Command* (New York, 1948)
R. Banham: *Theory and Design in the First Machine Age* (London, 1972)
J. Heskett: *Industrial Design* (London, 1980, 2/1984)
E. Lucie-Smith: *A History of Industrial Design* (Oxford, 1983)
A. Forty: *Objects of Desire: Design and Society, 1750–1980* (London, 1986)
J. Heskett: *German Design, 1870–1918* (New York, 1986)
P. Sparke: *An Introduction to Design and Culture in the Twentieth Century* (London, 1986)
D. Miller: *Material Culture and Mass Consumption* (New York and Oxford, 1987)

PAT KIRKHAM

Massys. *See* METSYS.

Mastaba. Type of ancient Egyptian tomb in which the burial chamber is surmounted by a rectangular superstructure built of mud-brick or stone. It is named after its resemblance to a low mud-brick bench (Arab. *mastaba*). Mastabas were used throughout the Early Dynastic Period (*c.* 2925–*c.* 2575 BC) and the Old Kingdom (*c.* 2575–*c.* 2150 BC) and were the commonest tomb type for Old Kingdom private burials. They are therefore found predominantly in the royal cemeteries of Memphis, capital at that time, which stretched across the desert plateau between Cairo and the Faiyum. Mastabas consist of three main elements: the burial chamber, the superstructure and the offering chapel.

Very simple mastabas are known from the 1st Dynasty (*c.* 2925–*c.* 2775 BC), such as Tomb 1845 at Tarkhan, which comprise a pit burial covered by a brick-faced mastaba filled with rubble. A much more elaborate example from early in the 1st Dynasty is that of Queen Neithhotpe at Naqada. This contains a burial chamber and storerooms built at ground level within the brick superstructure. The best-known 1st Dynasty mastabas are those at SAQQARA. These may be genuine royal tombs or cenotaphs (the 1st-Dynasty kings also had elaborate pit graves at Abydos), or the tombs of high officials. In each case a deep pit was excavated out of the rock and subdivided with brick walls to form a burial chamber flanked by storerooms. Tombs from the reign of King Den (*reg c.* 2850 BC) onwards have a stairway leading down to the burial chamber. The superstructures were built of mud-brick and contained more storerooms. The exterior faces were constructed as a series of stepped niches known as 'palace façade' design.

The superstructures of 2nd Dynasty (*c.* 2775–*c.* 2650 BC) mastabas are solid with smooth sides. The burial chamber and storerooms were all tunnelled underground, running off a central corridor, as in the mastaba of Ruaben (Tomb 2302) at Saqqara. Early 3rd Dynasty (*c.* 2650–*c.* 2575 BC) examples are similar. Gradually, the number of subterranean rooms was reduced until, by the 4th Dynasty (*c.* 2575–*c.* 2465 BC), tombs have a single large burial chamber. The stairway approach was retained at first but gave way to a vertical shaft. In early examples the burial chamber was tunnelled into the south face of the shaft, but from the 4th Dynasty it was always on the west. There was some revival of the palace façade design in the 3rd Dynasty, usually only on the east side, as in the mastaba of Hesyre at Saqqara (*see* HESYRE, TOMB OF), but this trend was short-lived, and later mastabas are plain. After the development of royal pyramid tombs in the 3rd Dynasty, mastabas were used exclusively for burials of courtiers,

officials and lesser members of the royal family. Most were of solid brick or brick with a rubble filling, but the 4th Dynasty mastabas at GIZA were made entirely of stone.

The most important aspect of mastaba development was the evolution of the offering chapel. Some 1st Dynasty mastabas had simple built-on brick chapels, such as Tomb 852 at Tarkhan. In the 2nd Dynasty the east face contained two offering niches, the southern one usually larger. Some 3rd Dynasty tombs, for example Tomb 3070 at Saqqara, emphasized this by having a wall built along the entire east side, thus forming a corridor to the southern niche (known as a corridor chapel). The offering niche also gradually took on the form of a room within the superstructure, often cruciform in shape. In the 5th and 6th Dynasties (*c.* 2465–*c.* 2150 BC) the number of rooms increased in wealthier tombs until the superstructure became one large mortuary chapel, such as in the mastaba of Mereruka at Saqqara (*see* MERERUKA, TOMB OF). These chapels were decorated with carved reliefs (*see* EGYPT, ANCIENT, §IX, 3(iii)(b)). The important elements of the chapel were the 'false door', through which the deceased could pass to partake of offerings (*see* STELE, §2); the altar, on which offerings were made; and the *serdab*, a room completely sealed off except for two eye-slits, and containing a statue of the deceased, which could act as a substitute body if the mummy was destroyed.

BIBLIOGRAPHY

J. de Morgan: *Ethnographie préhistorique* (Paris, 1897), ii of *Recherches sur les origines de l'Egypte* (Paris, 1896–7), pp. 147–268
N. de G. Davies: *The Mastaba of Ptahetep and Akhethetep*, 2 vols (London, 1900–01)
W. M. F. Petrie: *Gizeh and Rifeh* (London, 1907)
G. Steindorff: *Das Grab des Ti* (Leipzig, 1913)
W. M. F. Petrie: *Tarkhan II* (London, 1914)
J. E. Quibell: *Archaic Mastabas* (Cairo, 1923)
H. Junker: *Giza: Grabungen auf dem Friedhof des Alten Reiches bei den Pyramiden von Giza*, 12 vols (Vienna, 1929–55)
G. A. Reisner: *The Development of the Egyptian Tomb* (Oxford, 1936)
P. Duell: *The Mastaba of Mereruka*, 2 vols (Chicago, 1938)
W. B. Emery: *The Tomb of Hemaka* (Cairo, 1938)
——: *Hor-aha* (Cairo, 1939)
G. A. Reisner: *A History of the Giza Necropolis*, 2 vols (Cambridge, MA, 1942–55)
W. B. Emery: *Great Tombs of the First Dynasty*, 3 vols (Cairo, 1949; London, 1954–8)
——: *Archaic Egypt* (Harmondsworth, 1961)

PHILIP J. WATSON

Mastara. Village in the T'alin region of Armenia, on the western slope of Mt Aragats, noted for its well-preserved Armenian church of St Hovhannes (John). That it was built in the mid-7th century is suggested by certain architectural details and the names on five undated inscriptions on the south and west façades. These state that the church was built for the salvation of the monk Grigoras during the time of Bishop T'eodoros of the Gnuni family. The Bishop is known to have been a signatory of the acts of the Council of Dvin (*c.* AD 645). According to Manuch'aryan, however, the Greek inscription on the south wall and the church's large foundation walls indicate that the present structure replaced a larger 5th-century building. The only dated inscription (891) is on the south portal lintel and refers to the rebuilding of the portal; Gregoras and the son of a Brother Gregor are identified as patrons.

The church, raised on a three-stepped platform, is a domed, centrally planned building in the form of a square with four projecting horseshoe-shaped apses, which are pentagonal on the exterior. The eastern apse is flanked by two rectangular chambers enclosed within the rectilinear east end. The church can be considered a variant of the free-standing cruciform churches constructed in Armenia during the 7th century, such as the small church of the Mother of God (Astvatsatsin) at T'ALIN, the churches at Alaman and S Step'anos at Lmbat. The form of the transition from the spacious central space to the drum above is unusual in Armenian architecture. Eight squinches alternate with semi-domes to create an octagonal base for the drum, which becomes circular through the construction of sixteen squinches. Another unusual feature is the division of the interior of the dome into 12 panels with ribs terminating in circles. The two portals on the south and west façades are like those in other 7th-century Armenian churches, with projecting arches resting on double columns with cubic capitals. The arch above the west portal frames the sculptural relief of an equal-armed cross and one of the foundation inscriptions. A dove is carved at the top of each of the arch's colonettes. The same composition of two birds flanking a cross appears on the eastern apse and in the royal mausoleum (364) at Aghts', the 5th-century wall at the cathedral at ĒDJMIAD-ZIN, and other churches from the 7th to the 14th centuries. All Mastara's windows are decorated with sculptured cornices made up of various motifs such as vine scrolls, sinuous spirals and braided and diamond-shaped ornaments. Mastara may have been the model for such 7th-century Armenian churches as the cathedral at Art'ik, St Grigor at Harichavank and Voskepar. The church of the Holy Apostles (Arak'elots'; 928–53) at Kars resembles Mastara even more closely.

BIBLIOGRAPHY

A. A. Manuch'aryan; *K'nnut'yan Hayastani IV–XI dareri shinararakan vkayagreri* [A study of building documentation in the IV to XI centuries in Armenia] (Erevan, 1977), pp. 57–8

S. Der Nersessian: *L'Art arménien* (Paris, 1977/*R* 1989; Eng. trans., London, 1978), p. 38

A. Eremyan: *O vzaimootnosheniyakh armyanskoi i byzantiiskoi arkhitekturi IV–VII vv* [On the interrelationship of Armenian and Byzantine architecture of the 4th to 7th centuries AD] (Erevan, 1978)

L. Der Manuelian: *Armenian Architecture*, intro. by K. Maksoudian, Armenian Architectural Archives, ed. V. L. Parsegian, i (Zug, 1981)

P. Cuneo: *Architettura armena dal quarto al diciannovesimo secolo*, i (Rome, 1988), pp. 224–5

J.-M. Thierry and P. Donabedian: *Armenian Art* (New York, 1989), p. 555

LUCY DER MANUELIAN, ARMEN ZARIAN

Mastelletta [Donducci, Giovanni Andrea] (*b* Bologna, 1575; *d* Bologna, 1655). Italian painter. He trained under the Carracci, most notably Ludovico (Malvasia), but he also responded to the more expressive art of Pietro Faccini and Annibale Castelli. The spontaneity and freedom of his *Mystic Marriage of St Catherine* (Rome, Gal. Spada) emphasizes his closeness to these painters, while his *Assumption of the Virgin* (Bologna, Pin. N.) is closer to Ludovico Carracci's style, though with overtones of a Mannerist elegance that is characteristic of Mastelletta. Annibale Carracci died in 1609, and after 1610 Mastelletta went to Rome, where he probably turned to the group of artists around Adam Elsheimer, Carlo Saraceni and Agostino Tassi, all of whom painted landscapes enlivened by small, vivid figures. Mastelletta's *Crossing of the Red Sea* (see fig.), *Moses Parting the Waters*, *Fête Champêtre* and *Soldiers on the March* (all Rome, Gal. Spada) are the stylistically mature product of this relationship, yet they also reveal his responsiveness to Emilian Mannerist painters, among them Parmigianino, Jacopo Zanguidi, Giovanni Bertoia and, in particular, Nicolò dell'Abate. In the same period Mastelletta painted 12 scenes from the *Lives of Saints* (Bologna, Pin. N.), probably to adorn a Franciscan church. These feature larger figures but still retain the Mannerist insubstantiality apparent in the works in the Galleria Spada.

Mastelletta also travelled to Venice, probably in 1612, which brought him into contact with late Venetian Mannerism as exemplified in the work of such artists as Domenico Tintoretto and Palma Giovane. His two vast paintings of the *Miracle of the Forty Drowned Men* (1613) and the *Resurrection of Napoleone Orsini* (1614) in the Arca Chapel of S Domenico, Bologna, certainly date from after this trip. Their distinguishing characteristic is a dramatic use of light that could only be derived from a close knowledge and study of the work of Tintoretto, probably of his decoration for the Scuola di S Rocco, Venice, while the flickering paint surface is comparable to Titian's late works. Mastelletta's frescoes on the pendentives and half-lunettes and the undersides of the arches (1615) successfully completed the chapel's decoration, which is distinguished by its deeply felt religious pathos. A similar feeling pervades the *Stigmatization of St Francis* and *Death of the Saint* (both ex-S Petronio, Bologna; Casalmaggiore Cathedral), in which the agitated handling of the paint matches the pathos of the subject. On the other hand, in *St Bonaventura* (Bologna, S Petronio), a companion to these paintings, there is a more controlled quality, partly due to Mastelletta's awareness of contemporary developments, such as Guido Reni's *Pietà dei Mendicanti* (1613–16; Bologna, Pin. N.), from which he derived the symmetrical balance of his composition and its division into two levels. The extraordinary *Meeting of Aspasia and Artaxerxes* (Venice, priv. col., see Coliva, p. 117), in which the underlying mood is inspired by Reni, is refined and ethereal in handling. Other small paintings, however, such as his *Rest on the Flight into Egypt* (Bologna, Pin. N.), the *Triumph of David* and the *Discovery of Moses* (both Rome, Pal. Doria-Pamphili), mark a return by Mastelletta to his early style, with an emphasis on firmness and clarity, which also characterizes his sacred paintings of the period, such as the *Birth of the Baptist* (Bologna, S Maria dei Servi). The key works demonstrating this renewed classical tendency are paintings in S Maria della Pietà, Bologna, which reveal close links with Reni yet retain elements inspired by Faccini and something of the extraordinary spontaneity of the earliest of Mastelletta's works, most marked in the lively and airy *Flight into Egypt* and its brilliant preparatory sketch (Darmstadt, Hess. Landesmus.).

The works of Mastelletta's later years are less evocative. In the 1620s and 1630s he appears to have sought inspiration in the works of the great interpreters of Bolognese classicism rather than relying on his own resources. The *Resurrection* (Bologna, S Salvatore) is clearly based on the painting of this subject by Annibale Carracci (Paris, Louvre), while his *Delivery of the Keys to St Peter*

Mastelletta: *Crossing of the Red Sea*, oil on canvas, 1.04×1.27 m, *c.* 1610–12 (Rome, Galleria Spada)

(Budrio, S Lorenzo) adopts the compositional layout of a painting by Reni (1633–4; Perpignan, Mus. Rigaud), and the late *Virgin with Saints* (Verucchio, Collegiate Church) contains elements derived from Ludovico Carracci's *Ascension* (Bologna, S Cristina). These paintings continue to be highly competent but there is a decline in quality, as can most clearly be seen in the paintings that treat subjects Mastelletta had painted in his youth, such as the *Baptist Preaching* and the *Baptism* (both *c.* 1630; Bologna, S Maria dei Servi), in which the artist's 'flickering, smoky, brilliant and enchanting spirit' (Marangoni) has acquired tired, expressionless cadences through over-repetition.

BIBLIOGRAPHY
C. C. Malvasia: *Felsina pittrice* (1678); ed. G. Zanotti (1841), ii, pp. 67–72
M. Marangoni: 'Il Mastelletta', *L'Arte*, xv (1912), pp. 174–82
V. Alce: 'Cronologia delle opere d'arte della Cappella di S Domenico in Bologna', *A. Ant. & Mod.*, iii (1958), pp. 394–406
Maestri della pittura del seicento emiliano (exh. cat., Bologna, Pal. Archiginnasio, 1959), pp. 65–73
R. Longhi: 'Momenti della pittura bolognese', *Paragone*, xiii/155 (1962), pp. 44–52
F. Monai: 'Un pittore secessionista del seicento bolognese: G. A. Donducci detto il Mastelletta', *Studi di storia dell'arte in onore di A. Morassi* (Venice, 1971), pp. 219–26
U. Ruggeri: 'Una *Maddalena* del Mastelletta', *Crit. A.*, xxxvii/130 (1973), pp. 74–6
A. Coliva: *Il Mastelletta: Giovanni Andrea Donducci, 1575–1655* (Rome, 1980)

UGO RUGGERI

Master. For named artists with this prefixed title and no surname (eg. Master Bertram) *see under* the artist's given name. For anonymous artists who have been assigned nicknames by art historians (e.g. the Master of the Beaufort Saints or the Bedford Master) *see under* MASTERS, ANONYMOUS, AND MONOGRAMMISTS, §I.

Masterpiece. Term with three main meanings, successively of diminishing precision: (a) a test-piece of work submitted to a craft organization as qualification for entry as a master (e.g. 'Hans submitted his masterpiece to the guild in 1473'); (b) a work considered an artist's best and/or most representatively central (e.g. 'Hans's masterpiece is surely the *Passion* cycle in Berlin'); (c) simply a work considered very good and/or canonical, either absolutely ('Hans's *Passion* cycle is a masterpiece') or in some particular respect ('a masterpiece of colour'). The first meaning is discussed in §1 below, the other two in §2 below. A further complication of definition is that the various western European synonyms—particularly the

French *chef d'oeuvre*, Italian *capolavoro*, German *Meister-stück* and *Hauptwerk*—have had different histories and still have different nuances. The English word 'master-piece' is a 16th-century derivation from the German *Meisterstück*, probably by way of the Dutch derivative, but its later development has run more in parallel with uses of the French *chef d'oeuvre*. The terminological complexities are excellently documented and disentangled by Cahn (1979), whose book is the standard study of the masterpiece.

1. The test-piece. 2. The outstanding work.

1. THE TEST-PIECE. From the late 13th century in France and the 14th century in Germany references are found to craft guilds demanding test-pieces of journeymen and immigrant workers for entry to the rank of 'master', itself a recent usage for the senior controlling members of city craft unions. In southern Europe the practice existed too, often with less regularity and rigour, but did not bear as heavily on such craftsmen as painters and sculptors: thus, in Italy tests or *prove* were sometimes imposed, but the Italian word *capolavoro* is a post-Renaissance imitation of the French *chef d'oeuvre* in its more general senses, (b) and (c). In northern Europe, however, the masterpiece often became a favoured means of control by established craftsmen, and as early as the 14th century was being extended to painters and sculptors. By the 15th century there was a wide range of practice, from guilds demanding no masterpiece to guilds demanding several: an example of the latter extreme is the guild of painters and sculptors in Kraków, which from 1490 demanded a *Virgin and Child*, a crucifix, and a figure of *St George*. It will be noted that, as well as representing common subjects of the artist, these three cover a range of principal representational skills—drapery and nude figure, matt and lustre, and so on.

Formally the craft masterpiece was a defensible test of skill, a means of guarding the public from incompetent manufactures, but in practice it lent itself to various kinds of protectionist abuse: exemptions for sitting masters' kin, stipulations of prohibitively expensive conditions (pre-cious materials, specially rented workshops, feasts for the masters) and arbitrary assessment. From the 15th century on there were frequent protests from city councils and princes about craft guild protectionism depressing trade and, sometimes, quality and innovation; from the same time it also became increasingly common for princes to insist on painters and sculptors whom they wished to employ at their courts being exempted from regulation by city or guild. By the 17th century painters and sculptors in some great guild-ridden centres were attaining a degree of freedom from guild control through the institution, often with government support, of the ACADEMY. A paradigm of this new kind of academy was the Académie Royale de Peinture et de Sculpture founded in Paris in 1648, which from the start was envisaged by the State as a counter to the guild, or *maîtrise*, from whose regulations academicians were explicitly exempt.

In very many cities, however, the painters and sculptors had never been submitted to the masterpiece demand, even when other crafts were, sometimes simply because their number was too few to form their own guild or a substantial section within a conglomerate guild. The more conspicuous guild masterpieces surviving and identifiable in museums are pieces from such crafts as those of locksmiths and clockmakers, not painters and sculptors. Issues arise of how far painting and sculpture were at the time considered special cases, how far the guild aesthetic and ideology associable with the general institution of the masterpiece was compatible with their and our concep-tions of 'art', and what this aesthetic and ideology was.

It might be expected that the masterpiece be associated with uniform or conservative local styles and craftsman-like standards of facture, and there does look to have been some such tendency. Strong guilds, however, had more effective means of limiting idiosyncrasy or distinction—inspection and marking of wares, control of raw materials, regulation of workshop size and marketing—and the existence of a masterpiece demand may well be more a symptom of a strong guild than a primary cause of well-made mediocrity. More subtly, the institution of the masterpiece could focus and formalize issues of a quite modern kind about artistic achievement and its basis. In particular, there was a question in such crafts of design as painting and sculpture about whether a masterpiece should be of the craftsman's own, original conception, or whether it was enough to produce a technically secure replica of an already existing pattern.

In 1516 there was an exemplary dispute about this within the painters' and sculptors' guild at Strasbourg. One faction proposed that 'the candidate shall make his piece an independently [*frei*] designed one, without using any model pattern, but rather out of his own intelligence and ability'; this design would then be his, for making replicas. Another faction, composed of what seem smaller or less successful masters, objected to this demand, arguing from a proper respect for past masters: 'We are troubled about the masterpiece, that it is to be made independently, without any model pattern, as they propose, which is unheard of; knowers and lovers of art, whether religious or secular, have never despised or been ashamed of taking their forebears' art and learning from it.' They name four distinguished Strasbourg painters and sculptors of the previous half-century who had been more generous in their attitude to people copying masterpieces from their or others' designs (see Rott, 1938). The first group's position entails a sense of artistic originality, of intellectual property and of a distinction between mere executive competence and inventive creativity. The second group assumes a collective city repertory of designs that both exploits and honours the inventions of outstanding past masters. The structure of the issue, however, was a clear signal that the way to distinction was individual design and creation of patterns.

The demand for a qualifying test-piece survived some way into the age of academies. At first the Académie Royale still demanded a '*chef d'oeuvre*', and subsequently a piece called the '*morceau de réception*' on much the same basis. There was a range of practices in other academies; in England the Royal Academy of Arts, from 1768, accepted a 'Diploma Work' after election, and in a more relaxed spirit. In art pedagogy the test-piece principle still persists in various guises such as students' final-year diploma exhibits, although, as is often noted, the true medieval masterpiece ideal is more clearly represented by the art historian's doctoral thesis. But the active life of the term 'masterpiece' has long been in the wider senses (b) and (c) as defined above.

2. THE OUTSTANDING WORK. Almost from the first the English word was used also in extended and transferred senses—thus Shakespeare in 1606 (*Macbeth*, 2, iii, 67): 'Confusion now hath made his masterpiece!'—and there may have been several reasons for this. One certainly lay in the fact that, as Cahn demonstrated, the French *chef d'oeuvre* had come to be used in the 16th century also of great buildings, prodigies of art, and French use affected English use here as in much else. Another is that there is a suggestive instability in the dual-substantive structure 'master-piece': it may be still (i) the piece that renders someone a master of a guild, but it may also, and in English rather more naturally, be (ii) a master- or controlling piece, a little as in 'master key' or 'master plan', or (iii) it may be simply the piece of a real master, whatever is meant by that. There may even be a latent sense (iv) that the piece is a master in that it instructs us, in an art or a culture. The lexical history of the word is laid out and exemplified in the *Oxford English Dictionary*, though naturally in references crisply differentiated. Contemporary use is in practice slovenly—as in such titles as 'Masterpieces of Modern Art'—and often ambiguous; but since there is no point in deploring usage, the question is whether it entails assumptions that, on reflection, might seem problematic for the users' conceptions of art. There seem at least two zones of such assumption.

In the sense (b), of an artist's best or most central or climactic piece of work, sometimes also the *magnum opus* or the physically grandest, 'masterpiece' involves some suggestion of the artist's oeuvre being integral in character and almost parabolic in trajectory. The masterpiece is, presumably, where that character is most expansively, completely and tautly realized, and where that trajectory is at a peak; the life-project is of-a-piece but also linearly goal-directed, and so at some moment most nearly achieved. Such an idea is in some tension both with many actual current notions of personal creative identity and with the shape of many artists' oeuvres, or lives' work. Fisher (1991) analysed the contradictions between the sense of masterpiece and a modern conception, partly determined by our museum culture, of works of art existing in series, not to mention in phases, each work therefore inherently incomplete. There are also tensions with the esteem widely given to the sketch (as in drawings and *bozzetti*), for visibility of the process of facture, and for turning-point works that exhibit problem-solving in progress (as in Picasso's *Demoiselles d'Avignon*, 1907; New York, MOMA) and are therefore imperfect.

In the sense (c), of an indisputably very good or great piece of work, 'masterpiece' presupposes a scale of value, but not in such a way as to offer a frame for reflection on the problems and criteria of evaluation; it just forecloses discussion. Although it has less focus than such terms as 'classic', 'touchstone' or 'paragon', it does imply and invite thought about 'the canon', in the sense of a repertory of exemplary works embodying the best of the culture. Cahn,

again, demonstrates how far the development of the concept of 'masterpiece' in the 17th and 18th centuries was associated with the formation of canons both of Classical sculpture and of High Renaissance and Early Baroque painting, and, although these canons lost much of their cogency in the 19th century, the term still gave a form to the appetite for the indisputably fine cultural achievement.

The concept of the canon has been studied more fully in relation to literary history and the claims of socio-cultural engineering than in relation to visual art. The formation of canons of artistic masterpieces has been rather different from that of sacred books through a selection of authentic, canonical texts, although it may be coloured by some connotations from this. The prototype artistic canon was the Late Antique selection of those Classical texts considered suitable models for imitation and, in schools, an educational convenience: the criterion for inclusion was representative linguistic or stylistic correctness—not uniqueness, brilliance or articulated richness of human content. At least something of this survived into the 17th- or 18th-century canons of Classical sculpture and early modern painting. With the gradual disintegration of the Neo-classical episteme during the 19th century, an evolving and locally variable canon of European artistic masterpieces came to represent much more than correctness: genius, originality, human wisdom and plenitude, even prowess of the racial or national culture, and thus inevitably sectional and class values. If exclusive, unchanging and unreflective, masterpiece canons may have a socializing effect that is anything from aesthetically impoverishing to politically sinister, it is argued; the remedy would be historical and critical scrutiny, and a resistance to closure. In any event, the shifty term 'masterpiece' is likely to prove more symptomatic than illuminating.

BIBLIOGRAPHY

H. Huth: *Künstler und Werkstatt der Spätgotik* (Augsburg, 1925/*R* Darmstadt, 1967)
H. Bechtel: *Wirtschaftsstil des deutschen Spätmittelalters* (Munich and Leipzig, 1930)
H. Rott: *Quellen und Forschungen zur südwestdeutschen und schweizerischen Kunstgeschichte im 15. und 16. Jahrhundert*, iii; *Oberrhein, Quellen*, i (Stuttgart, 1938), pp. 221–2 [docs for Strasbourg dispute of 1516]
W. Cahn: *Masterpieces: Chapters on the History of an Idea* (Princeton, 1979) [the standard work]
R. von Hallberg, ed.: *Canons* (Chicago, 1984)
P. Fisher: *Making and Effacing Art* (New York and Oxford, 1991), ch. 6

MICHAEL BAXANDALL

Master printers. Term used to describe a variety of professional people collaborating with artists in the creation of prints and paperworks. Although study and training programmes that led to the designation of 'master printer' existed in the late 20th century, the title was more generally used with reference to printers who achieved a level of critical success and respect based on their collaborations, regardless of their backgrounds. At this time many of the best-known collaborators resisted the label owing to its outdated historical reference to the separation of roles of artist and printer. Other printers felt that their roles as directors of presses, which incorporated a range of responsibilities far beyond the actual collaborative process, did not adequately describe their function. While the term 'master printer' has continued to be used as a title of respect, it is unlikely that universal consensus on its definition will ever be reached. The phenomenon of the master printer is almost exclusively Western, and this account therefore concentrates on developments in the West and in particular the USA. For information on the collaborative role of the artist–printmaker and the professional printmaker in other cultures, *see under* the appropriate sections of regional survey or civilization articles.

I. Creation and replication. II. The influence of lithography. III. Specialization and collaboration. IV. Printmaking in the USA before *c.* 1960. V. Developments since *c.* 1960. VI. Master printers since *c.* 1960.

I. *Creation and replication.*

As printing workshops sprang up throughout Europe in the 16th century, the craft of printing was fostered through a traditional apprenticeship system. Master printers, with shops containing printing presses and other equipment, would hire young apprentices who, after years of training and experience, might eventually aspire to the position of master printer. In both Eastern and Western printmaking traditions, divisions of labour developed that segregated the various stages in producing a print and assigned them to a number of individuals (*see* PRINTS, §IV). Japanese woodblock prints, for example, employed the skills of artisans, who would transfer an artist's drawing to several woodblocks, carve the blocks and print them. Engravings produced in 16th-century European workshops often included the names of the various participants. The name of the person who designed the image was followed by the Latin *invenit* ('he designed'; abbreviated to *inv.*, *invt* or *in.*), or by *pinxit* ('he painted'; abbreviated to *pinx.* or *pinxt*), if the original image for the print was taken from a painting. The person who drew or transferred the image on to the printing matrix was indicated by the word *delineavit* ('he drew'; abbreviated to *delin.*, *delt* or *del.*). The person who cut the woodblock or engraved the lines on a plate was designated by the term *sculpsit* ('he engraved'; abbreviated to *sculp.*, *sculpt* or *sc.*), *fecit* ('he made'; abbreviated to *fec.*) or *incidit* ('he engraved'; abbreviated to *incid.* or *inc.*). Finally, the name of the printer was indicated by *impressit* ('he printed'; abbreviated to *imp.*). Often the name of the publisher would also be included, followed by *excudit*.

Before the 19th century there were certainly numerous examples of artists who were intimately involved in the conception, execution and printing of their images, including Albrecht Dürer (*see* DÜRER, (1)) and Rembrandt (*see* REMBRANDT VAN RIJN). The history of printmaking in the 16th, 17th and 18th centuries has also preserved the names of countless printers noted for their exceptional skills in relief and intaglio printmaking processes (*see* PRINTS, §III, 1 and 2). Clearly, many outstanding early prints were the result of the combined vision of an artist and the skill of a printer, with the printer's contribution often overlooked.

The vast majority of prints produced, however, tended to be reproductive or didactic, with the primary purpose of conveying and disseminating information. This practical function also promoted the association of printmaking with the mechanical arts and the crafts tradition, rather than the elevated 'fine art' stature enjoyed by painting and sculpture. This attitude was reinforced by a Renaissance-based emphasis on individualism and the promotion of the artist as a solitary, creative genius. The relationship between artist and printer remained, for the most part, one of creator and replicator rather than of intimate collaboration.

II. *The influence of lithography.*

Fundamental changes taking place in 19th-century Europe began to alter the role of the master printer. The Industrial Revolution, with its emphasis on mechanization of production and accompanying division of labour, reinforced the distinction between artists and artisans, between mind and hand. The Romantic movement, which celebrated the sole creator, the cult of genius and a heroic model of the artist, continued to relegate the printer to a lesser status. Simultaneously, the invention of lithography by Alois Senefelder in 1798 (*see* LITHOGRAPHY, §II) created additional separation in the roles of artist and printer, for it demanded far greater technical skill and knowledge in preparing and printing the lithographic stones than had earlier relief and intaglio processes. Unlike in these earlier processes, an artist could easily create a drawing directly on to a lithographic stone, just as he or she would draw on a piece of paper. Only the task of fixing the image on the stone and printing the edition fell to the master printer. This development brought new definition to the concept of the 'original print' as an original image that had been created directly by an artist on lithographic stones or woodblocks or intaglio plates. The role of the master printer in instructing the artist as to the best ways in which to put his or her marks on the stone, and the experimentation that led to new tonal, linear and textural effects, were again ignored as the artist was allotted total responsibility and credit for the creation of the image.

Throughout the 19th century artist–printmaker movements and revivals of interest in various printmaking media occurred, as artists experimented with the preparation of printing matrices. Generally the printing of the plates, stones or blocks would still be handed over to trained and experienced printers for the production of the edition. The notion of an image as an 'original' print remained intact as long as the division of mind and hand, of mental and manual labour, of idea and execution, was kept clear and separate. The idea of artistic collaboration has always been problematic and often denied by both printer and artist, as well as by critics uneasy with the concept of joint creativity. André Mellerio, one of the earliest historians to write about printmaking collaboration and a major figure in the promotion of late 19th-century artistic printmaking, was nonetheless harsh in his treatment of printers who overstepped their roles or imposed artistic judgements on projects ('La Lithographie en couleurs', 1898).

The invention of lithography, however, owing to its complex and technical nature, at the same time laid the groundwork for a closer artist-and-printer collaboration. By the beginning of the 19th century artists of all types began to seek the services of master printers and to experiment with the expressive possibilities of the new medium. Christoph Wilhelm Reuter in Germany and

D. J. Redman in Britain were among the first to establish presses and to work with artists on original prints in the first two decades of the century. In France the printshops of Godefroy Engelmann and Charles de Lasteyrie (1759–1849) were established in Paris by 1816 and were soon followed by such printing establishments as those of François-Séraphin Delpech (1778–1825), Villain, Charles Motte, Langlumé and Auguste Bry. At the same time Charles Joseph Hullmandel began a career as printer and author of *The Art of Drawing on Stone* (London, 1824), which secured him a place as the most important British printer of the first half of the 19th century, working with such artists as J. M. W. Turner, Samuel Prout, John Frederick Lewis and Théodore Gericault.

Artists throughout Europe turned to lithography with enthusiasm, and outstanding examples of early original lithographs were produced by Jean-Baptiste Isabey and Eugène Isabey, Carle Vernet and Horace Vernet, Antoine-Jean Gros, Eugène Delacroix, Francisco de Goya, Thomas Shotter Boys and scores of other artists. Technical experimentation and innovation also continued with relief and intaglio processes, and artists as diverse as William Blake, Turner and Goya created masterpieces using etching, engraving, aquatint and mezzotint techniques. Also during the 1830s and 1840s an impressive body of lithographs of strong social and political content was created. Led in France by Honoré Daumier and Paul Gavarni, artists found outlets for their biting satire and commentary in illustrated newspapers and magazines such as *Le Charivari* and *La Caricature* (*see also* CARICATURE, §3). This tradition of artist–illustrator re-emerged in the 1880s as a host of young artists, including Théophile-Alexandre Steinlen, Henry Somm and Adolphe Willette, collaborated with printers to produce editions of prints as well as illustrations for wide-ranging political, artistic and literary publications, including *Le Courrier français*, *Gil Blas*, *Le Chat noir*, *Le Chambard* and *La Feuille*. Because of the strong point of view and distinctive styles of these artists, the originality and artistic merit of these images were never questioned. However, there were obvious variations in these prints, due to the contributions of their many printers.

III. Specialization and collaboration.

A second wave of artistic interest in lithography began in the 1860s and 1870s with such artists as Edouard Manet, Henri Fantin-Latour, James McNeill Whistler and Odilon Redon all defining new expressive possibilities for the medium in styles and movements progressing from Realism and Impressionism to Symbolism. Despite outstanding prints produced by these and other artists, an explosion

1. Henri de Toulouse-Lautrec: *L'Estampe originale*, colour lithograph of the printer Père Cotelle at the firm of Edward Ancourt, Paris, 589×791 mm, 1893 (Milwaukee, WI, Milwaukee Art Museum)

of demand for images and the advent of colour lithography created a huge print industry that also produced a flood of mediocre commercial images. Technological advances and the application of photographic processes to print production led to increasing mechanization (*see* PHOTOGRAPHY, §I).

One result of these changes was that the large lithographic firms with the most advanced technology and sophisticated equipment were increasingly unwilling to take on labour-intensive, low-profit projects for artists. By the end of the century there was a clear division between the large commercial printing establishments and the smaller lithography workshops, in which printers were sensitive to the needs of artists. There were a few exceptions, of course. At the firm of Edward Ancourt in Paris, the printer Père Cotelle worked with Henri de Toulouse-Lautrec to create both prints and posters, and the shop became a favourite meeting-place for artists fascinated by lithography (see fig. 1). Eugène Carrière and others also collaborated with the printer Edouard Duchâtel at the huge Lemercier establishment, also in Paris.

As a market for prints grew, print workshops were opened by printers who specialized in working with artists, and opportunities for closer and more sustained artist–painter collaboration increased. One of the earliest 19th-century printers to open a print studio was Auguste Delâtre, whose experiments with etching, colour etching and monotype processes were shared with artists including Félix Bracquemond, Félicien Rops, Charles Meryon, Whistler and the Impressionists. His son Eugène Delâtre (1854–1938) established a reputation as a printer–collaborator *par excellence* and played a fundamental role in the revival of interest in colour etching. An artist himself, as well as a technician and instructor, Eugène Delâtre not only collaborated and printed for such artists as Charles Maurin, Auguste Lepère, Emmanuel Robbe, Steinlen, Henri Evenepoel and Picasso but also sold small etching presses to Camille Pissarro, Edgar Chahine (1874–1947), Robbe and others. The firm of Delâtre was without equal, although there were other intaglio printers of note beginning to collaborate with artists and producing, for example, the extraordinary suite of colour etchings (1890–97; see fig. 2) by Mary Cassatt, who worked with the printer Léon Leroy for the publisher Alfred Cadart (1828–75).

Crucial to the success of the smaller print workshops in Paris was support from publishers and dealers, such as Cadart, Durand-Ruel, Edmond Sagot, Auguste Lepère, André Marty (*b* 1857), Charles Hessèle, Kleinmann, Georges Petit, Gustave Pellet (1859–1919) and Ambroise Vollard, all of whom commissioned, published and promoted both individual prints and portfolios. The two *L'Estampe originale* portfolios (1888, 1893–5) and *L'Estampe moderne* (1895–6) exemplify the numerous portfolios and albums of prints that helped introduce a wide range of established and emerging artists to the public.

Auguste Clot (1858–1936), a printer who had apprenticed with the huge firm of Lemercier before establishing a lithography studio in Paris in the early 1890s, enjoyed regular support from many of the same publishers, particularly Ambroise Vollard. Clot's collaborations of the 1890s resulted in stunning colour lithographs by artists of the Nabis group, including Pierre Bonnard, Edouard Vuillard,

2. Mary Cassatt: *The Bath*, colour etching, 318×248 mm, 1890–91 (New York, Metropolitan Museum of Art)

Maurice Denis and Ker-Xavier Roussel, and by artists as stylistically diverse as Toulouse-Lautrec, Edvard Munch, Odilon Redon, Paul Signac, Theophile-Alexandre Steinlen, Edmond Aman-Jean and Paul Cézanne. Extensive surviving correspondence attests to close collaboration and extensive experimentation on many projects, with Clot not only supplying technical brilliance and innovative solutions but also providing artists with options including exotic papers and offering experimentation with relief-printing processes. Clot's experiments with relief printing and transferring wood-relief images to lithography with Henri Heran (Paul Herrmann) and Munch in 1896 pointed to some of Munch's later innovative mixed-process prints.

In Paris the firm of Mourlot conducted business from the 1850s. Mourlot's printers, including Tuttin, Sorleir, Deschamps and Fernand Mourlot, became legendary for their lithographic collaborations with artists including Picasso, Georges Braque, Maurice Utrillo, Fernand Léger, Henri Matisse, Marc Chagall, Joan Miró, Alexander Calder and Ben Shahn during the 1940s and 1950s. Edmond Desjobert, who had started his career printing lithographs for Steinlen and Jean-Louis Forain at the turn of the century, opened the Atelier Desjobert in 1920 and collaborated with artists including Picasso, Raoul Dufy, Kees van Dongen, Léger, Matisse, Georges Rouault, Hans Arp, Adolf Dehn (1895–1968), Yasuo Kuniyoshi and Reginald Marsh. The Imprimerie Lacourière, founded by the master printer Roger Lacourière (1892–1966) in 1929, specialized in printing intaglio images by Picasso, André Derain, Georges Braque, Joan Miró, Alberto Giacometti, Alexander Calder, Henry Moore and André Masson. Picasso's

3. Pablo Picasso: *Ostrich*, lift-ground aquatint, 369×280 mm, 1936 (Toledo, OH, Museum of Art); one of 31 illustrations by Picasso from Georges Louis Leclerc, Comte de Buffon: *Histoire naturelle (Textes de Buffon)* (Paris, 1942), leaf inserted after p. 105

incomparable *Vollard Suite* (1936) was produced in the Lacourière workshop, as were his illustrated books *La Tauromaquia* (Paris, 1959) and the *Histoire naturelle* (Paris, 1942; see fig. 3) of Georges Louis Leclerc, Comte de Buffon (1707–88). Other workshops in Paris, including those of Marcel Durassier, Georges Leblanc, Aldo Crommelynck and Gerard Patris, continued to offer collaborative printing services to artists after World War II.

The Englishman S. W. HAYTER left a career as a chemist and geologist to establish a workshop in Paris in 1927, which in 1933 he named Atelier 17. As an artist and printmaker dedicated to re-establishing intaglio printmaking as an original art form, Hayter promoted an exchange of ideas between artists and stressed the artist's direct and spontaneous interaction with the intaglio plate. This manner of working particularly suited many of the Surrealist artists, who would visit the studio to experiment with multiple etching and engraving techniques and with complicated multi-layered inking methods. Legions of artists worked with Hayter in Paris until 1940, when the studio relocated to the USA during the war years, and again from 1950 until Hayter's death in 1988.

IV. Printmaking in the USA before c. 1960.

Throughout the 18th and 19th centuries American printmaking remained primarily a commercial venture, and examples of collaborative printmaking were relatively rare. There was no shortage of highly skilled and experienced printers working in printing establishments across the country, such as those of Louis Prang in Boston, Kurz & Allison in Chicago and Currier & Ives in New York, but

their skills were applied primarily to reproductive work. One of the earliest examples of artist–printer collaboration was in John James Audubon's *The Birds of America*, an ambitious portfolio of 435 hand-coloured aquatints based on Audubon's watercolours, which was printed by the English master printmaker Robert Havell (*d* 1832) and his son Robert Havell jr. Audubon closely monitored every stage of the project as the printmakers experimented with combinations of etching, aquatint, line-engraving and hand-colouring, and the resulting prints reflected the close communication and contribution of each collaborator. There were revivals of interest in various forms of printmaking throughout the 19th century. Most of the activity took place as artists, many of whom had travelled to Europe and perhaps worked with European printers, returned home and began to experiment with printmaking processes. While such artists as Thomas Moran, Mary Nimmo Moran (1842–99), Robert Swain Gifford (1840–1905) and Stephen Parrish (1846–1938) created an extraordinary body of etchings throughout the 1880s, most projects were printed by the artists themselves. It was not until the early 20th century that demand led to the establishment of printmaking workshops based on the French tradition.

In the USA the first printer to establish a true collaborative lithography workshop was George C. Miller (1892–1964), who had been apprenticed to the commercial American Lithographic Company at the age of 14. After assisting such artists as Albert Sterner (1863–1946), George Bellows, Joseph Pennell and Arthur B. Davies with their lithographic experimentation, Miller opened his own workshop shortly after World War I and during the 1930s printed hundreds of editions with Thomas Hart Benton, John Steuart Curry, Grant Wood, Bellows, Louis Lozowick (1892–1973), Stuart Davis, Childe Hassam, Rockwell Kent and Reginald Marsh.

The artist Bolton Brown (1864–1936) also played a vital role in defining new possibilities for the artist–printer relationship. Brown's experiments with lithography, learnt during a year spent studying in London, led him from 1918 to begin assisting artists, including Bellows, John Sloan and Albert Sterner in printing their lithographs. Brown often claimed that artists' lithographs were best printed by other artists, and that the printer was a full collaborator in both technical and aesthetic matters. Miller was far more circumspect in offering technical information and perfection in printing and in making a careful distinction between the roles of artist and printer. As master printers the skills of these two men are unquestioned. Their differing attitudes towards collaboration, however, provided examples for a wide range of print workshops between 1925 and 1960. Grant Arnold in Woodstock, NY, Lawrence Barrett (1897–1973) in Colorado Springs, Lynton Kistler in Los Angeles and Theodore Cuno in Philadelphia all established collaborative workshops. Demand for their services came from a variety of artists. Some were young Americans who had travelled to Europe and who had made prints in workshops such as the Atelier Edmond Desjobert; they included Adolf Dehn (1895–1968), Marsden Hartley, Kuniyoshi, Stuart Davis and John Storrs (1885–1956). Others were European émigrés, such as Max Weber, Abraham Walkowitz, Lozowick and Jean Charlot, who were already accomplished printmakers.

The 1930s, the years of the Great Depression in the USA, were also the period of the creation of the Federal Art Project (FAP) to help support artists and to keep the fine arts alive during a time of severe economic hardship. The printmaking workshops established in 1935 were instrumental in promoting the development of colour printing as an artistic medium. Collaborative experiments with colour relief printing, lithography and screenprinting provided many artists with their first opportunities to work with skilled printers and to explore printmaking processes. Some FAP printers also printed privately for artists; Theodore Wahl, for example, printed Jackson Pollock's first lithographs in the mid-1930s. By 1936 sixteen print workshops had been formed in nine states.

One of the most influential intaglio print workshops was Hayter's Atelier 17 during its period in New York (1940–50). As in his Paris intaglio studio, Hayter believed in a collaborative environment in which artists and artist–printers would work together, sharing ideas and expertise. The studio attracted not only a host of expatriate European artists, including Max Ernst, Jacques Lipchitz, Salvador Dalí, Marc Chagall, Le Corbusier, Joan Miró and André Masson, but also many of the young American artists who went on to revolutionize the art world, including Robert Motherwell, Jackson Pollock, Willem De Kooning, Alexander Calder and Louise Nevelson. Advances in intaglio technology and process came rapidly, and soon many of those who had collaborated at Atelier 17 went on to establish strong printmaking programmes at colleges and universities; these artist–printers included Mauricio Lasansky at the University of Iowa, Iowa, and Gabor Peterdi (*b* 1915) at the Brooklyn Museum, New York, Hunter College, New York, and finally Yale University, New Haven, CT. The model of artist–printer and the promotion of artistic collaboration among equals was thus reinforced and continued as scores of art students began intensive training in printmaking.

Robert Blackburn (*b* 1920), an African-American artist–printmaker whose exposure to printmaking including study at the Harlem Community Arts Center and the Arts Students League in New York and two years working for the Desjobert firm in Paris, established a print workshop in New York in 1949. The Printmaking Workshop, as it came to be called in 1959, was also a cooperative venture. In addition to collaborating and printing editions with artists, Blackburn offered classes, and artists could pay to use the facilities. The non-profit workshop, still in operation, has become a multicultural centre of printmaking activity and a training ground for the scores of young printers who opened studios in the 1970s and 1980s.

V. Developments since c. 1960.

By 1960 the definition of a master printer had diversified to include printers who had apprenticed in the traditional manner, artist–printers who came to specialize in collaborative printmaking because of their extraordinary skills and sensitivity to the needs of other artists, young printers who were graduating from university printmaking programmes, and printers who were primarily self-taught.

Artists also had diverse backgrounds, some having worked as printers or having extensive knowledge and experience using print processes, and others with virtually no exposure. Given the range of skills and backgrounds, continuing attempts to segregate strictly the roles of printer and artist were often a futile exercise. Fundamental post-war social, political and economic factors were creating a radically new cultural and artistic climate and laying the groundwork for an explosion of interest in printmaking. While the focus of the 'print renaissance' had shifted to the USA by the late 1960s, impetus for a new interest in printmaking was clearly an international phenomenon. Post-war prosperity in the USA had led to the growth industries of advertising and marketing, resulting in a barrage of visual images from the commercial print media, television, film and numerous other sources that were quickly exported to major European capitals. In this Technological Revolution artists responded to evolving intellectual and aesthetic concerns by creating new styles and formats geared to the world around them. The print, a repeatable visual image that could embody, reflect and interpret new and borrowed images, was seen by many artists as an appropriate vehicle by which to embrace change, to explore new ideas and technologies and to provide access to art for expanding audiences. Dealers, curators, publishers and educators promoted the study and purchase of prints.

The key to the intense interest in collaborative printmaking was the fact that many artists, such as Robert Rauschenberg, Claes Oldenburg, Andy Warhol and Jim Dine, had already become regular collaborators as they participated in new art forms such as happenings and performance art, and as they worked with others on theatre, dance, film and literary collaborations. New theories of pluralist aesthetics, feminist art criticism and Marxist interpretation, and an emphasis on interdisciplinary approaches, began to redefine originality based on the content and format of the finished work and not on a restrictive formula for those collaborating. Many young artists viewed printers at collaborative presses as colleagues and welcomed opportunities to explore new technologies to expand both their own repertories and conventional definitions of works of art on paper.

The changing operation and organization of many new printshops also had an impact on the collaborative artist–printer relationship. While some workshops continued to operate as 'contract' shops, collaborating with artists and producing editions for third-party publishers and other financial backers, many presses began publishing their own projects (*see* PRINTS, §IV, 2). Printer–publishers expanded their commitment to artists by assuming new research, marketing and promotional roles in addition to producing editions. With a new interest in the distribution and sales of the finished prints, printer–publishers began to play a greater creative role in the selection and definition of projects. Printer–publishers could choose the artist with whom they wished to work, furthering the careers of artists whose work they admired while at the same time providing a showcase for the talents and facilities of their printmaking workshops. Research and experimentation often took place independently of specific collaborations, so that studios could remain competitive and attract the most innovative, exciting and marketable artists. The printer–publishers also led the way towards increased professionalism by creating more formal written documentation and description of projects.

VI. Master printers since c. 1960.

The two print workshops that set the standards for three decades of growth were already in operation by 1960. In West Islip, NY, the Russian émigrée Tatyana Grossman (1904–82) had founded Universal Limited Art Editions (ULAE) in 1957, with the goal of publishing artists' books and of introducing a select group of artist to printmaking. The firm was unique in its goal of seeking out artists and underwriting all the costs of production and marketing. Not a printer herself, Grossman asked Robert Blackburn to commute to Long Island from his Manhattan printshop to work on the press's first collaborative project, an artists' book combining the talents of the artist Larry Rivers and writer Frank O'Hara. No expenses were spared on *Stones* (New York, 1957–9) as sheets of paper were hand-made and hours of time spent as Blackburn proofed and printed the 12 black-and-white, word-and-image lithographs.

While Grossman's total dedication to the artist was more in the 19th-century tradition of the French studio, the collaborations of the printers Blackburn, Zigmunds Priede, Donn Steward (1921–86) and others were decidedly 20th-century in their daring and in their willingness to break the rules and push the boundaries of traditional printmaking. One by one, established and emerging artists, including Rauschenberg, Jasper Johns, Barnett Newman, Grace Hartigan, Motherwell, Lee Bontecou and Helen Frankenthaler came to ULAE to make prints. Photographic processes were explored as artists borrowed images from newspapers and magazines, and the studio expanded to incorporate offset lithography and intaglio facilities to accommodate projects. Blackburn's last project at ULAE before he returned to his Printmaking Workshop full-time was on Rauschenberg's *Accident* (1963; see fig. 4). True to its name, the lithographic stone had cracked and broken during proofing. When Blackburn's successor, Priede, created a second plate, which incorporated evidence of the broken stone and printed the edition, the image quickly came to represent the concept of the 'happy accident' that allowed for and capitalized on unforeseen developments during the collaboration.

In Los Angeles the artist June Wayne had a slightly different set of priorities in establishing the Tamarind Lithography Workshop in 1959. An artist and accomplished printmaker herself, she had experienced difficulties in finding lithographers to work with in the USA. Believing lithography to be a dying art form, she set out to create a lithography workshop that could train lithographers, promote artistic collaboration, stimulate a market for prints, raise the status of the master printer, and help train printers to establish independent workshops and to advance lithography as an artistic medium. Wayne joined with the extraordinary talents of Clinton Adams (*b* 1918) and Garo Antreasian (*b* 1922), both master printers as well as accomplished artists and teachers, and they began an ambitious programme of inviting printers and artists to collaborate at the press. Well-established artists, including Josef Albers, Rico Lebrun (1900–64), Louise Nevelson

4. Robert Rauschenberg: *Accident*, lithograph, 1048×750 mm, 1963 (West Islip, NY, Universal Limited Art Editions)

and Adja Yunkers, were among the early collaborators at Tamarind; younger artists, including Ed Ruscha, Vija Celmins, Nicholas Krushenick (*b* 1929) and Nathan Oliveira, also came to experiment with lithographic techniques. In 1970 the Tamarind Institute was created at the University of New Mexico in Albuquerque, and the press continued to train printers, collaborate with artists, conduct extensive research into the processes and materials of the lithographic medium and publish journals and technical papers.

As ULAE and Tamarind Lithography Workshop were beginning their operations in the USA, new collaborative workshops had also opened in Europe. Britain's avant-garde artistic community responded rapidly to the pop phenomenon and led the way with the establishment of several collaborative printshops that offered new options for artists to make prints. A wave of interest in SCREEN-PRINTING, the print process that became most closely identified with the prints of the major Pop artists, was finding a host of practitioners on both sides of the Atlantic. Kelpra Studio, founded in London by Christopher Prater in 1957, was one of the earliest collaborative workshops to utilize and adapt commercial screenprint techniques to the creation of fine art. Just as ULAE had begun to find ways to transfer photographically the found images of Rauschenberg to lithographic stones and to incorporate photographic processes for both technical and creative purposes, Prater's technical experiments with screenprint and photographic technology gave artists, including Eduardo Paolozzi, Richard Hamilton and David Hockney, new freedom to borrow images and interpret signs and symbols from the everyday world. Many American artists also collaborated with Prater at Kelpra, including R. B. Kitaj, Alan d'Arcangelo (*b* 1930), Robert Motherwell, Larry Rivers and Jim Dine.

Lithography also benefited from renewed interest in Britain. Inspired by pioneering experiments in lithography by Ceri Richards, Stanley Jones opened Curwen Studio in London as an outgrowth of the successful Curwen Press publishing firm. Printing for British artists, including John Piper, Ceri Richards and Henry Moore, Stanley Jones was one of the first printers to introduce the special qualities of offset lithography to artists. Other presses established in Great Britain also had a tremendous impact on artists on both sides of the Atlantic. Editions Alecto Limited was established by the printers Joe Studholme and Paul Cornwall Jones in 1962. In 1963 the partners were joined by the print dealer and promoter Robert Erskine, and Editions Alecto added a gallery space and became an educational centre revolving around the contemporary print. As printer–publishers, Alecto developed and pioneered many new advertising and marketing approaches quickly adopted by other print workshops, as they developed new corporate, private and institutional markets. Numerous printers were hired to collaborate with artists, and facilities for intaglio, lithography and screenprinting processes were created. Artists' quarters were added to the complex, as were office spaces for the curating and marketing of the more than 800 editions Alecto published during its first 10 years, with artists including David Hockney, Eduardo Paolozzi, Jim Dine, Ed Ruscha and Claes Oldenburg. In 1970 Paul Cornwall Jones left Editions Alecto to found Petersburg Press, an international collaborative workshop that employed both European and American printers and worked with an impressive roster of artists in print studios in both London and New York.

Elsewhere in Europe, printmaking workshops were established by printers with wide-ranging backgrounds to accommodate the expressive needs of avant-garde artists. In Stuttgart Luitpold Domberger established Editions Domberger in the late 1950s to provide collaborative screenprinting opportunities for artists as diverse as Robert Indiana, Josef Albers, Victor Vasarely, Richard Anuszkiewicz, Marisol and Richard Estes. Domberger, followed by his son Michael Domberger, specialized in the intricate hand-cutting of stencils and made extensive experimental use of fluorescent inks and other new materials in their collaborations. The screenprinter Hans-Peter Haas also collaborated with artists in Stuttgart, while in Munich the lithographer Kurt Lohwasser also collaborated with numerous young artists. In Italy, Floriano Vecchio's screenprinting collaborators included the Americans Grace Hartigan and Andy Warhol in the late 1950s, and screenprinting collaboration was also offered by Sergio Tosi and Fausta Tosi in Milan. In Rome, Valter Rossi and Eleonora Romeo Rossi opened 2RC Editrice in 1965, specializing in multiple printmaking processes. In Zurich, Emil Matthieu had developed a strong reputation for his collaborations on lithographic projects. These were only a few of the studios, large and small, that began to collaborate with artists during the late 1950s and early 1960s.

In the USA during the 1960s there was a remarkable burst of collaborative printmaking activity. The first graduates of the master-printer programme at Tamarind were beginning to establish their own presses, and other printers with diverse backgrounds and printmaking specialities were also setting up collaborative workshops across the country. Those who published their own projects tended to set the pace in an increasingly competitive art market. Ken Tyler's technical genius had produced improved presses, new types of equipment and better systems for print registration and other improved techniques and practices during his years at Tamarind; he set up his own workshop in Los Angeles in 1965 and was joined by two partners in 1967 to become Gemini GEL. With solid financial backing, Tyler's goal to improve existing printmaking technology and his absolute passion for collaboration led to collaborations with artists that immediately redefined the contemporary print. Such projects as Albers's meticulously printed *White Line Squares* series (1966), Rauschenberg's *Booster and 7 Studies* series (1967), Johns's *Color Numeral* series (1968–9) and Claes Oldenburg's *Profile Airflow* (1969) not only brought new standards to the field of contemporary printmaking but also played important roles in the developing oeuvres of artists who went on to become seminal figures in the history of late 20th-century art. The workshop expanded also to facilitate intaglio, screenprinting, sculpture and other projects, and the studio also made contracts with independent printers, plastic fabricators and other specialists for complicated, multi-process works on paper. After Tyler left Gemini in 1974, the studio continued with the printer Ron

5. Master printer Ken Tyler (left) and artist Frank Stella (right) pulling a print impression of *The Affidavit* from the assembled intaglio plate; photographed at Tyler Graphics Ltd, New York, 1992

6. Robert Longo: *Men in the Cities (Joanna and Larry)*, set of two lithographs in three black colours, each 1.82×0.98 m, 1983 (New York, Edition Schellmann & Kluser); printed in collaboration with Maurice Sánchez, Derrière L'Etoile Studios, New York

McPherson coordinating projects, followed by Serge Lozingot (*b* 1936), who became head printer at Gemini in 1971.

With Lozingot, the master-printer tradition had in many ways come full circle. He had been a printer's apprentice at Les Orphelins d'Auteuil in Paris (1949–53) before leaving to print editions for Jean Dubuffet in the artist's studio for five years. He went to work at the Atelier Mourlot in 1963, and in 1966 he moved to Los Angeles to work first at the Tamarind Lithography Workshop and then for June Wayne at her Tamstone Press, before accepting the head position at Gemini GEL.

Tyler moved on to new challenges and more successes after his departure from Gemini. He settled in New York

to set up a studio closer to many of the artists with whom he was collaborating, and Tyler Graphics Ltd was established in Bedford Village, New York. Beginning in 1974 with sophisticated new equipment and facilities for papermaking as well as printmaking, Tyler initiated collaborative projects with artists that reflected his own intense interest in paper as both a support and an artist's medium. Cast paper and pulp painting were added to the options available for artists to work with, and soon innovative paperworks were being created by Frank Stella (see fig. 5), Kenneth Noland, Hockney and James Rosenquist, whose *Welcome to the Water Planet* series (1987) of mixed-process prints rivalled his major paintings in their scale and complexity.

Numerous other Tamarind printers also established collaborative presses from 1960, including Irwin Hollander (*b* 1927; with Hollander's Workshop in New York), Jean Milant (with Cirrus Editions in Los Angeles) and Jack Lemon (*b* 1936; in Nova Scotia and then Chicago as Landfall Press). Many went to work at existing collaborative workshops, and still other new Tamarind master printers went on to become associated with university professional workshops, including GraphicStudio at the University of South Florida-Tampa and the Nova Scotia College of Art in Halifax.

Screenprinting, which does not require complicated technical processes or equipment, attracted printers with diverse backgrounds. Some came directly from commercial printing firms; some were primarily self-taught; a few had experimented with screenprinting techniques in the FAP graphics workshops, and some had even learnt basic screenprinting in the armed services. Sheila Marbain of Maurel Studios and Steven Poleskie of Chiron Press in New York, Sirocco Screenprints in New Haven, CT, and Styria Studios in California and then New York were among the earliest studios to specialize in working with artists on screenprint projects in the 1960s. Offset lithography, another printmaking process with commercial overtones, was offered to artists as a creative medium by

7. Richard Bosman: *Man Overboard*, wood-relief print, 698×482 mm, 1981 (New York, Brooke Alexander Editions); printed by Chip Elwell

printers including Eugene Berman of Falcon Press in Philadelphia and Hiroshi Murata (*b* 1941) of the non-profit Art–Research–Technology workshop at the University of Massachusetts, in Amherst. Following in their footsteps and given examples of offset lithographs coming from Curwen Press and Petersburg Press in London, many American workshops added offset equipment to their facilities throughout the 1970s. Johns, for example, was the first to use the new offset press at ULAE in 1971, and the resulting *Decoy* showcased new expressive possibilities made realizable by offset equipment and processes.

Although screenprinting and lithography dominated the printmaking scene throughout the 1960s, intaglio printmaking remained the printmaking medium of choice for many artists (*see* PRINTS, §III, 2). Kathan Brown, who had studied printmaking in London and worked there in the print studio of Birgit Skiold, returned to establish Crown Point Press in Oakland, CA, in 1962. In doing so, she brought new standards of technical precision and professionalism to the field of intaglio printmaking and reawakened many American artists to the special tonal, linear and textural qualities of intaglio processes. By the early 1970s, as styles and aesthetics shifted away from the flat, mechanical look favoured by many of the Pop and Op artists of the previous decade, intaglio printshops once again flourished. In New York, Condeso-Brokopp, Prawat Laucheron, Mohammad O. Khalil, Kathleen Caraccio (*b* 1947) and Catherine Mosley were among the many printers who opened collaborative printshops specializing in etching, aquatint, engraving, drypoint and other intaglio techniques.

While intaglio, lithography and screenprint processes continued to evolve along with changing aesthetics (see fig. 6), in the early 1980s a renewed interest in relief printing developed as artists shifted away from the Realist, Conceptualist and Minimalist concerns of the decade earlier and began to focus on painterly and emotionally involved styles that quickly came to be labelled Neo-Expressionism, New Narrative or New Figure painting (*see* PRINTS, §III, 1). Interest in wood-relief printing manifested itself in both traditional and innovative applications. Chip Elwell (1940–86), who began collaborating in New York in 1975 with such artists as Richard Bosman (*b* 1944; see fig. 7) Louisa Chase (*b* 1951), Joan Snyder (*b* 1940) and Gregory Amenoff (*b* 1948), and Michael Berdan, who in 1980 opened Mulberry Press in Boston to collaborate with artists utilizing traditional Japanese relief-printing techniques, represent vastly different approaches and attracted very different types of artists.

Throughout the 1970s and 1980s, collaborative studios of every description opened across the USA, until by 1993 there were more than 300. Fundamental to this growth was the extraordinary growth of the print market place. Press publishers, independent publishers, dealers, individual artists and even institutions were publishing prints and marketing them to individuals, corporations and museums in ever-increasing numbers. The secondary market place of gallery and auction houses realized enormous prices for well-known prints, and the idea of art as an investment caused many who knew little about prints to purchase them as one might purchase stocks and bonds. Entire editions of prints from well-known presses or by internationally known artists were often sold out before the editions were actually printed. Although many collectors had turned to print-buying as the price of the paintings and sculpture of their favourite contemporary artists became prohibitive, many prints were also selling for prices that made them inaccessible to all but the wealthy.

Necessary readjustment in the contemporary print world came in the form of a major worldwide economic recession and an accompanying crash of the international art market in the late 1980s. Printers and printer–publishers were forced to scale back their operations drastically; however, very few collaborative workshops actually went out of business, which was a testimony to the tenacity and dedication of many large and small presses.

BIBLIOGRAPHY

GENERAL

J. Pennell and E. R. Pennell: *Lithography and Lithographers: Some Chapters in the History of the Art* (London, 1898, 2/1915)

R. M. Burch: *Colour Printing and Colour Printers*, intro. R. McLean (London, 1910/*R* Edinburgh, 1983) [incl. chap. by W. Gamble on modern processes]

L. Delteil: *Manuel de l'amateur d'estampes des XIXe et XXe siècles pour servir de complément au Manuel de l'amateur d'estampes*, 2 vols (Paris, 1926)

P. Gilmour: *Modern Prints* (New York, 1970)

D. Stein and D. Karshan: *'L'Estampe originale': A Catalogue Raisonné* (New York, 1970)

M. Knigin and M. Zimiles: *The Contemporary Lithography Workshop around the World* (New York, 1974)

F. Eichenberg: *The Art of the Print: Masterpieces, History, and Techniques* (New York, 1976)

P. Gilmour: *The Mechanized Image: An Historical Perspective of 20th Century Prints* (London, 1978)

M. Melot: *Grand graveurs* (Paris, 1978); Eng. trans. as *Graphic Art of the Pre-Impressionists* (New York, 1981)

G. Antreasian: 'Some Thoughts about Printmaking and Print Collaborations', *A. J.* [New York], xxxix (1980), pp. 180–88

K. Beall: 'The Interdependence of Printer and Printmaker in Early 19th Century Lithography', *A. J.* [New York], xxxix (Spring 1980), pp. 195–201

U. E. Johnson: *American Prints and Printmakers* (New York, 1980)

D. Phillips: 'Artist and Printer: "A Coincidence of Sympathies"', *ARTnews Annu.*, lxxx (March 1981), pp. 100–06

C. Saft: 'The Growth of Print Workshops and Collaborative Printmaking since 1956', *Prt Rev.*, xiii (1981), pp. 55–68

J. Ludman and L. Mason: *Fine Print References: A Selected Bibliography of Print-related Literature* (Millwood, NY, and London, 1982)

F. Mourlot: 'The Artist and the Printer', *La Lithografia* (Milan, 1982); Eng. trans. as *Lithography: 200 Years of Art, History and Technique*, ed. D. Porzio (New York, 1983), pp. 183–9

American Impressions: Prints since Pollock (exh. cat. by R. Castleman, New York, MOMA, 1985)

C. T. Butler and M. Laufer: *Recent Graphics from American Printshops* (Mt Vernon, IL, 1986)

'Collaboration East and West: A Discussion', *Prt Colr Newslett.*, xvi (1986), pp. 196–205

P. Gilmour: 'Picasso and his Printers', *Prt Colr Newslett.*, xviii (July–Aug 1987), pp. 81–90

Lasting Impressions: Lithography as Art (exh. cat., ed. P. Gilmour; Canberra, N. G., 1988)

P. D. Cate and M. Grivel: *From Pissarro to Picasso: Color Etching in France* (New Brunswick and Paris, 1992)

C. Pulin: *Guide to Printmaking Workshops in Canada and the United States* (Washington, DC, 1993)

HISTORIES

H. Beraldi: *Les Graveurs au XIXe siècle*, 13 vols (Paris, 1885–92)

C. Roger-Marx: *La Gravure originale en France de Manet à nos jours* (Paris, 1939; Eng. trans., 1939)

J. Adhémar: *L'Estampe française: La Lithographie française au XIXe siècle* (Paris, 1944)

F. H. Man: *150 Years of Artist's Lithography, 1803–1953* (London, 1954)

C. Roger-Marx: *La Gravure originale au XIXe siècle* (Paris, 1962)

J. Adhémar: *La Gravure originale au 18e siècle* (Paris, 1963; Eng. trans., New York, 1964)

——: *La Gravure originale au XXe siècle* (Paris, 1967)

F. Man: *Artists' Lithographs: A World History from Senefelder to the Present Day* (London and New York, 1970)

M. Twyman: *Lithography, 1800–1850: The Technique of Drawing on Stone in England and France and their Application in Works of Topography* (London, New York and Toronto, 1970) [the most thorough and reliable account in Eng.]

C. Spencer: *A Decade of Printmaking* (London and New York, 1973)

J. Adhémar: 'Les Imprimeurs lithographes au XIXe siècle', *Nouv. Est.* (Nov–Dec 1975), pp. 8–9

Prints of the Twentieth Century: A History (exh. cat. by R. Castleman, New York, MOMA, 1976)

P. D. Cate and S. H. Hitchings: *The Color Revolution: Color Lithography in France, 1890–1900* (Santa Barbara, 1978) [incl. Eng. trans. by M. Needham of Mellerio's 'La Lithographie originale en couleurs']

R. T. Godfrey: *Printmaking in Britain: A General History from its Beginnings to the Present Day* (New York, 1978)

J. A. Flint: *Art for All: American Print Publishing between the Wars* (Washington, DC, 1980)

Printed Art: A View of Two Decades (exh. cat. by R. Castleman, New York, MOMA, 1980)

P. D. Cate: *Circa 1800: The Beginnings of Modern Printmaking, 1775–1835* (New Brunswick, NJ, 1981)

C. Adams: *American Lithographers, 1900–1960: The Artists and their Printers* (Albuquerque, 1983)

J. Watrous: *A Century of American Printmaking: 1880–1990* (Madison, WI, 1984)

The Artistic Revival of the Woodcut in France, 1875–1900 (exh. cat. by J. Baas and R. S. Field, Ann Arbor, U. MI, Mus. A., 1984)

J. Bailly-Herzberg: *Dictionnaire de l'estampe en France, 1830–1950* (Paris, 1985)

C. Adams: *Printmakers in New Mexico, 1980–1990* (Albuquerque, 1991)

INDIVIDUAL MASTER PRINTERS

A. Lejard: 'Mourlot: A Centre of Lithographic Art in Paris', *Graphis*, xi (1955), pp. 500–05

A. Freund: 'Mourlot, Master Printer of Lithographs', *ARTnews Annu.*, lxxii (March 1973), pp. 30–32

J. Flint: *George Miller and American Lithography* (Washington, DC, 1976)

A. Maurice: 'George C. Miller and Son: Lithographic Printers to Artists since 1917', *Amer. A. Rev.* (March–April 1976), pp. 133–144

Eugene Feldman, 1921–75 (exh. cat. by R. Fine, Philadelphia, PA, Temple U., Tyler Sch. A., 1976)

J. Baas: *Auguste Lepère and the Artistic Revival of the Woodcut in France, 1875–1895* (Ann Arbor, 1982)

Charles Hullmandel and James Duffield Harding: A Study of the English Art of Drawing on Stone, 1818–1850 (exh. cat. by C. Swanson, Northampton, MA, Smith Coll. Mus. A., 1982)

G. von Groschwitz and C. Adams: 'Mourlot: Life and Work: Thoughts of an Artist–Printer, A Conversation with Irwin Hollander', *Tamarind Pap.*, viii (1985), pp. 34–43

N. Parris: *Through a Master Printer: Robert Blackburn and the Printmaking Workshop* (Columbia, SC, 1985)

P. Gilmour: *Ken Tyler, Master Printer and the American Print Renaissance* (New York and Canberra, 1986)

——: 'Curiosity, Trepidation, Exasperation, Salvation! Ceri Richards, his Australian Printer and Stanley Jones', *Tamarind Pap.* (Spring 1987), pp. 28–37

N. Smale: 'Thomas R. Way: His Life and Work', *Tamarind Pap.* (Spring 1987), pp. 17–27

Seven Master Printmakers: Innovations in the Eighties (exh. cat. by R. Castleman, New York, MOMA, 1991)

WORKSHOPS AND STUDIOS

G. Blanchard: *Les Lithographies originales des peintres de l'atelier Clot* (Paris, 1965)

American Graphic Workshops: 1968 (exh. cat. by M. W. Baskett, Cincinnati, OH, A. Mus., 1968)

Tamarind: Homage to Lithography (exh. cat. by V. Allen and W. S. Lieberman, New York, MOMA, 1969)

G. Antreasian and C. Adams: *The Tamarind Book of Lithography: Art & Techniques* (New York, 1971)

M. Bloch: *Tamarind: A Renaissance of Lithography* (Washington, DC, 1971)

Made in California: An Exhibition of Five Workshops (exh. cat. by M. Bloch, Los Angeles, UCLA, Dickson A. Cent., 1971)

Technics and Creativity: Gemini G.E.L. (exh. cat. by R. Castleman, New York, MOMA, 1971)

Atelier Lacourière (exh. cat. by J. Adhémar, Montbéliard, Maison A. & Loisirs, 1972)

Artists at Curwen (exh. cat. by P. Gilmour, London, Tate, 1977)

Art of the Picture Press: Tyler Graphics Ltd. (exh. cat. by J. Goldman, Hempstead, NY, Hofstra U., Lowe Gal., 1977)

M. Lovejoy: 'The National Experimental Graphics Workshop of Cuba: Printmaking in Cuba Today', *Prt Rev.*, ix (1979), pp. 80–90

Kelpra Studio: Artists' Prints, 1961–1980 (exh. cat. by P. Gilmour, London, Tate, 1980)

R. Fine: *Gemini G.E.L.: Art and Collaboration* (New York, 1984)

M. Devon: 'The Scottish Printmaking Workshops', *Tamarind Pap.*, viii (1985), pp. 31–43

L. Goodman: 'Print Workshops in Italy', *Prt News* (Winter 1986), pp. 14–18

Tyler Graphics: The Extended Image (exh. cat. by E. Armstrong, Minneapolis, MN, Walker A. Cent., 1987)

E. Sparks: *Universal Limited Art Editions: A History and Catalogue, the First Twenty-five Years* (Chicago and New York, 1989)

R. Fine and M. L. Corlett: *GraphicStudio: Contemporary Art from the Collaborative Workshop at the University of South Florida* (Washington, DC, 1991)

TRUDY V. HANSEN

Masters, anonymous, and monogrammists. Collective terms for artists who have not been identified with a documented, named individual, but whose oeuvre has been recognized by art historians (for discussion of anonymous Greek vase painters *see* VASE PAINTERS, §II). The various sources from which their identifying names have been derived is reflected in the subdivision of the following article.

Anonymous masters (§I) covers those artists whose association with, for example, a particular work, place or patron, or stylistic and iconographic characteristic has led art historians to refer to them by a descriptive name. These are listed alphabetically by the identifying part of the name, ignoring the preliminary 'Master' and intervening prepositions and articles. (Anonymous masters should not be confused with *named* artists with the prefixed title 'Master' and no surname, as in Master Bertram; for entries of the latter type *see under* the artist's given name elsewhere in the dictionary.) Dated anonymous masters (§II), who are most usually named from the date of the sample work, are entered chronologically. Anonymous monogrammists (§III) are listed alphabetically by the initials of the monograms that appear on their work.

I. Anonymous masters. II. Dated masters. III. Monogrammists.

I. Anonymous masters.

Master of the Aachen Altar (*fl c.* 1485–1515). German painter. He is named after the great winged altarpiece with scenes from the *Passion* (*c.* 1510; Aachen, Domschatzkam.), painted for the Carmelite church in Cologne. The central panel depicts an agitated *Crucifixion* scene in front of a broad landscape background and under a dramatic sky (see fig.). On the inner sides of the wings is an *Ecce homo* to the left and a *Lamentation* to the right. Other events from the Passion appear as subsidiary scenes in the middle-ground. The strongly individualized faces, animals, plants, architecture and landscape elements create a narrative feel. The colours are richly contrasted and of sonorous tone, underscored by the bold painting style.

The Master's paintings show a decided strength of form and expressive ability. Stange compared the intentions of his work to those of a popular preacher, while Friedländer saw parallels with the early 16th-century Antwerp Mannerists. Many influences are blended in his work: from the

Master of the Aachen Altar: *Crucifixion*, central panel from the *Passion* altarpiece painted for the Carmelite church in Cologne, oil on panel, 1.43×2.42 m, *c.* 1510 (Aachen, Domschatzkammer)

Master of the Holy Kinship in Cologne, in whose work-shop it is likely the painter was trained, as well as from the Wesel painter Derick Baegert and Jan Joest of Kalkar. Influences from Netherlandish art (e.g. Hugo van der Goes) are also present. Rensing's attempt to decipher the various rows of letters found in the Master's paintings as the signature of a Cologne goldsmith is not convincing, but Anzelewsky's suggestion that the Master of the Aachen Altar can be identified with the monogrammist MASTER P.W. OF COLOGNE (*see* §III below) is more likely, owing to the strong similarities between their respective paintings and engravings. These indicate an early influence from the Augsburg painter Jörg Breu the elder and the workshop of the Frueauf family, particularly in the way in which the Master of the Aachen Altar creates faces and landscape forms. Dürer's influence is also evident in the works of both artists.

Other works attributed to the Master include an altar-piece with *Passion* scenes, comparable to that in Aachen, painted for St Columba, Cologne (centre panel, London, N.G.; wings, Liverpool, Walker A.G.), dating from *c.* 1495. Two depictions of the *Adoration of the Magi* (Bonn, priv. col., see Rensing, p. 213, and south Germany, priv. col.), which are indebted to Hugo van der Goes, are also from this early period. On the right-hand edge of the Bonn panel is the half-length figure of a young man looking out of the picture, which is probably a self-portrait. What is probably the same figure, albeit rather older, appears in a third version of the *Adoration of the Magi* (*c.* 1505; Berlin, Gemäldegal.) and on the left wing of the Aachen altarpiece. The Master also worked as a portrait painter, as can be seen by his portrait of the merchant *Johann von Melem* (*c.* 1495; Munich, Alte Pin.). His works are orientated toward the profane, despite their religious themes, and show new, all-encompassing figure arrangements that make full use of the picture space.

BIBLIOGRAPHY

M. J. Friedländer: *Die altniederländische Malerei* (Berlin, 1924–37); Eng. trans. as *Early Netherlandish Painting* (Leiden, 1967–76)

H. Kisky: 'Der Meister des Aachener Altares', *Der Meister des Bartholo-mäusaltares—Der Meister des Aachener Altares: Kölner Maler der Spätgotik* (exh. cat., Cologne, Wallraf-Richartz-Mus., 1961), pp. 44–50

T. Rensing: 'Der Meister des Aachener Altares', *Wallraf-Richartz-Jb.*, xxvi (1964), pp. 229–50

A. Stange: *Die deutschen Tafelbilder vor Dürer: Kritisches Verzeichnis*, i (Munich, 1967), pp. 106–11

F. Anzelewsky: 'Zum Problem des Meisters des Aachener Altars', *Wallraf-Richartz-Jb.*, xxx (1968), pp. 185–200

HANS M. SCHMIDT

Master of the Abbey of Dilighem (*fl* Antwerp, *c.* 1500–30). Name given to the artist of a triptych of *Christ in the House of Simon* (Brussels, Mus. A. Anc.), formerly in the abbey of Dilighem. It now seems likely that he can be identified with Jan van Dornicke, otherwise known as JAN MERTENS.

CARL VAN DE VELDE

Master of Adelaide of Savoy [Master of MS. Poitiers 30] (*fl c.* 1450–*c.* 1470). French illuminator. He is named after his principal work, a Book of Hours (Chantilly, Mus. Condé, MS. 76) that was at one time in the possession of Marie-Adélaïde of Savoy, Duchesse de Bourgogne (1685–1712), who was the wife of Le Petit Dauphin Louis and

Master of Adelaide of Savoy: *December*, colours on parchment, 219×150 mm; calendar illustration from a Book of Hours, 1460–70 (Chantilly, Musée Condé, Château de Chantilly, MS. 76, fol. 12*v*)

grand-daughter-in-law of Louis XIV. The artist was a contemporary of Jean Fouquet, and the works attributed to him show that he was one of the most original illuminators active in western France during the second half of the 15th century. He was possibly trained in the Loire region and began his career in Angers. His style evolved from the complex group of manuscripts by the Master of Jouvenel des Ursins and his associates. This relationship can be seen in his earliest attributed work, Giovanni da Colonna's *Mare historiarum* (Paris, Bib. N., MS. lat. 4915, fols 80–160), executed *c.* 1447–8 for Chancellor Guillaume Jouvenel des Ursins; in particular, his sensitive and atmospheric treatment of light is derived from the Jouvenel group. During this early period the Adelaide Master executed several miniatures in the so-called Hours of Mary Stuart (Paris, Bib. N., MS. lat. 1405), in which he collaborated with, among others, the Master of the Geneva Boccaccio.

The Master of Adelaide of Savoy is thought to have been subsequently active chiefly in Poitiers. To emphasize the artist's connection with this town, König (1982) has renamed him the Master of MS. Poitiers 30, after a Missal for the use of Poitiers (1450–60; Poitiers, Bib. Mun., MS. 30). The two miniatures executed by the Master in this volume (fols 167*v* and 168*r*) are close in style to his other work and appear to confirm his presence in Poitiers. During this period he seems to have either collaborated on, or more likely, completed, a Book of Hours (Paris,

Bib. N., MS. Rothschild 2534), in which three miniatures in the Office of the Passion (fols 124*r*, 126*r*, 132*v*) are by the Master of Margaret of Orleans.

The Master of Adelaide of Savoy illustrated mainly religious texts, the finest example being the Chantilly Book of Hours. His illustrations on the *verso* and *recto* of the calendar pages are especially celebrated; these depict various seasonal activities and games (see fig.). An influential compositional device appears in this manuscript in the miniatures of the Offices of the Dead, whereby one scene is superimposed over a full-page illustration. This motif, possibly derived from the work of the Master of the Geneva Boccaccio, appears in the work of subsequent Poitiers illuminators in the period from 1470 to 1480. It occurs in the early works of Robinet Testard, a follower of the Master, who also adopted his decorative floral borders and flat, unmodulated use of colour. One of the few secular manuscripts illustrated by this Master is the *Roman du Graal* (*c.* 1450–?1455; Paris, Bib. N., MS. fr. 96). This ambitious and extensive cycle of illustrations displays the salient characteristics of his style: his attention to the atmospheric effects of light, his essentially flat and bright palette and the geometric construction of forms. Also attributed to the Master, but later in date, are nine leaves from a Book of Hours (*c.* 1460–?1470; Chicago, IL., Everett and Ann McNear priv. col.).

BIBLIOGRAPHY

V. Leroquais: *Les Livres d'heures manuscrits de la Bibliothèque Nationale* (Paris, 1924), iii, pp. 80–81

Y. Bouissounouse: *Jeux et travaux d'après un livre d'heures du XVe siècle* (Paris, 1925)

E. König: *Französiche Buchmalerei um 1450: Der Jouvenal-Maler, der Maler des Genfer Boccaccio und die Anfänge Jean Fouquets* (Berlin, 1982), pp. 33, 93, 108, 225–31, 235–7, 256, figs 6–7, 22–7

——: *Les Heures de Marguerite d'Orléans* (Paris, 1991), p. 101, fig. 11

Les Manuscrits à peintures en France, 1440–1520 (exh. cat. by F. Avril and N. Reynaud, Paris, Bib. N., 1993–4), pp. 123–6

Master of Afflighen Abbey. *See* MASTER OF THE JOSEPH SEQUENCE below.

Master of the Aix Annunciation (*fl* 1442–5). Painter active in France. He is named after a panel of the

Master of the Aix Annunciation: *Annunciation*, panel, 1.55×1.76 m, *c.* 1442–5 (Aix-en-Provence, Ste Marie-Madeleine)

Annunciation (Aix-en-Provence, Ste Marie-Madeleine; see fig.). The painting has been connected with a series of wills executed on behalf of the draper Pierre Corpici (*b* ?1388; *d* before ?1465), an inhabitant of Aix. In the earliest surviving will, dated 9 December 1442, known only from a copy made by Henri Requin (Labande), Corpici expressed a wish to be buried in Aix Cathedral and bequeathed 100 florins to pay for an altarpiece depicting the Annunciation or the Virgin Annunciate. The painting was to have a *supercelo* (crowning panel) and a *scabelo* (predella) and bear both the Corpici arms and the sign of his shop. Although not a contract, the will is quite specific regarding the subject-matter of the altarpiece. There is no mention, however, of it being a triptych with wings nor of the name of the artist who was to execute the work. On 5 January 1443, Corpici was granted permission by the cathedral chapter to construct an altar (destr. 1618), which was located to the right of the entrance of the west choir (built *c.* 1285–*c.* 1425). A further will of 14 July 1445 reiterates Corpici's desire to be buried in the cathedral; no reference is made to the altarpiece in this document, suggesting it was completed by this date. Further wills of 13 February 1449, 19 April 1458 and a final one of 8 November 1465 refer to the 'altar of the *Annunciation*', indicating that the altarpiece was installed by then. It has been suggested that the Aix *Annunciation* was originally a triptych, with *Isaiah* (Rotterdam, Mus. Boymans–van Beuningen) as the left wing, with *St Mary Magdalene Kneeling* on the reverse, and *Jeremiah* (Brussels, Mus. A. Anc.) as the right wing, with *Christ* on the reverse; a *Still-Life with Books* (Amsterdam, Rijksmus.) was originally at the top of the *Isaiah* panel. The association of these lateral panels has been disputed (Hochstetler-Meyer). By 1551 the *Annunciation* seems to have lost its crowning panel and predella, and in 1618 it was moved from the Corpici altar to the Espagnet family altar in the cathedral baptistery; it was transferred to the sacristy of Ste Marie-Madeleine between 1791 and 1818. Numerous attempts have been made to identify the artist of the *Annunciation* or determine his nationality. An early attribution was to the Neapolitan Niccolò Colantonio on the basis of the resemblance to his *St Jerome in his Study Removing a Thorn from the Lion's Paw* (Naples, Capodimonte), but this has long since been discounted. The painter of the *Annunciation* was a near contemporary of the Master of Flémalle, Jan van Eyck, Stephan Lochner, Konrad Witz and Lukas Moser, and the painting bears a stylistic relationship with the work of these artists, for example with Witz's *SS Catherine and Mary Magdalene in a Church* (Strasbourg, Mus. Oeuvre Notre Dame) and with the *Annunciation* (Madrid, Prado) attributed to the Master of Flémalle, although whether the relationship is due to direct influence or common prototypes is unclear. Comparisons have also been drawn with the work of the sculptor Claus Sluter, for example his *Weepers* from the tomb of *Philip the Bold* (Dijon, Mus. B.-A.) have been compared with the *Prophet* panels. The *Annunciation* is stylistically conservative, and the diversity of theories as to its origins is the result of its eclectic character. Whether the painter was Netherlandish, Burgundian, Provençal or from further afield is a matter of conjecture. He has been tentatively identified with several artists including the

Provençal Jean Chapus and three Flemish artists active in Provence: Guillaume Dombet, Arnoul de Cats [Arnolet de Catz] (*fl* 1430–35) and BARTHÉLEMY D'EYCK.

BIBLIOGRAPHY
L. H. Labande: 'Notes sur quelques primitifs de Provence, L'Annonciation d'Aix', *Gaz. B.-A.*, n. s. 5, vii (1932), pp. 392–7
J. Boyer: 'Le Maître de l'Annonciation d'Aix est-il identifié? Documents inédits sur le Maître de l'Annonciation', *Gaz. B.-A.*, n. s. 5, liv (1959), pp. 301–14
B. Hochstetler-Meyer: 'A Reexamination of the *Triptyque de l'Annonciation d'Aix*', *Gaz. B.-A.*, n. s. 5, xcv (1980), pp. 97–106
M. Laclotte and D. Thiébaut: *L'Ecole d'Avignon* (Paris, 1983), pp. 218–22
J. Boyer: 'Nouveaux documents sur le triptyque de l'Annonciation d'Aix', *Gaz. B.-A.*, n. s. 5, cvi (1985), pp. 189–94

☐

Master of the Albrecht Altar (*fl c.* 1430–50). Austrian painter. He is named from an altar dedicated to the Virgin executed for the Carmelite church on the square 'am Hof' in Vienna (28 of the 32 panels survive, now at Klosterneuburg, Mus. Chorherrenstifts). The work was once thought to have been commissioned by the Holy Roman Emperor Albert II as Duke Albert V of Austria (*reg* 1404–39), but the removal of later paint from the outer wings revealed scenes from the history of the Carmelite Order, together with the coat of arms of Oswald Oberndorffer, a high-ranking finance official and a friend of Albert, who was clearly the real patron. The altarpiece is stylistically dated between 1438 and the early 1440s. The iconographic range of the work is especially remarkable, including scenes of the Carmelite Order on the outside and of the *Life of the Virgin* on either side of the (lost) shrine. On the Sunday side of the wings two rows of eight panels each have devotional pictures of the Virgin as *Queen of Heaven* (corresponding to the Litany of Our Lady). The stereotype arrangement of the Mother of God (always presented frontally) among the heavenly host gives a uniform effect.

A work that precedes the altarpiece stylistically is the 'little Albrecht Altar', of which five panels remain (Budapest, Mus. F.A.; Vienna, Belvedere; *Annunciation*, Berlin, Kaiser-Friedrich Mus., destr. 1945). The coats of arms in the *Presentation of Christ* also justify the dating of the small altarpiece before the large one, between 1435 and 1438.

There are strong allusions to local painters, such as the Master of the Presentation of Christ and the Master of the Schloss Lichtenstein, but both altarpieces show such clear references to Netherlandish painting that the painter must have travelled to the west. The *Nativity* on the large Albrecht Altar alludes to the *Nativity* (Dijon, Mus. B.-A.) by the MASTER OF FLÉMALLE (*see* below), as can be seen from a comparison of the Virgin's white garment or the shepherds in both pictures. The use of light on one of the external panels presupposes a knowledge of the most recent achievements in the Netherlands, such as the *Portrait of a Woman* attributed to the Master of Flémalle (London, N.G.).

See also KASCHAUER, JAKOB.

BIBLIOGRAPHY
W. Suida: 'Die Wiener Malschule von 1420 bis 1440', *Belvedere*, viii (1925), pp. 53–8
O. Pächt: *Österreichische Tafelmalerei der Gotik* (Augsburg, 1929), pp. 13–16
L. Baldass: 'Das Ende des Weichen Stils in der österreichischen Tafelmalerei', *Pantheon*, xiv (1934), pp. 378–81

W. Buchowiecki: 'Der einstige Hochaltar der ehemaligen Karmeliterkirche auf dem Platz "Am Hof" in Wien', *Carmelus*, iii/2 (1956), pp. 243–74

Gotik in Österreich (exh. cat., Stein an der Donau, Minoritenkirche, 1967), pp. 73–4, 105–6

E. Baum: *Katalog des Museums mittelalterlicher österreichischer Kunst, Unteres Belvedere, Wien* (Vienna, 1971), pp. 39–40

B. Bonard: *Der Albrechtsaltar in Klosterneuburg bei Wien: Irdisches Leben und himmlische Hierarchie—Ikonographische Studie* (Munich, 1980)

A. Rosenauer: 'Zum Stil des Albrechtsmeisters', *Der Albrechtsaltar und sein Meister*, ed. F. Röhring (Vienna, 1981), pp. 97–122

MONIKA DACHS

Alexander Master [Master of the Alexander Romance] (*fl c.* 1420–50). Illuminator, active in France. He is named after the Romance of Alexander (London, BL, Royal MS 20.B.XX), which was connected by Pächt and Alexander with the miniatures in two Books of Hours of Paris Use (*c.* 1420–30; Oxford, Bodleian Lib., MS. Liturg. 100; and Stonyhurst, Lancs, MS. 33). All three of these manuscripts as well as others were thought by Meiss to be the later work of the MASTER OF THE HARVARD HANNIBAL (*see* below).

BIBLIOGRAPHY

O. Pächt and J. J. G. Alexander: *Illuminated Manuscripts in the Bodleian Library, Oxford*, i (Oxford, 1966), p. 52, no. 663

M. Meiss: *French Painting in the Time of Jean de Berry: The Limbourgs and their Contemporaries*, 2 vols (London, 1974), esp. pp. 207–8, 390–92

CATHERINE REYNOLDS

Master of Alkmaar (*fl c.* 1475–*c.* 1515). North Netherlandish painter. He was named after a polyptych of seven panels representing the *Seven Acts of Mercy* (Amsterdam, Rijksmus.; *see* URBAN LIFE, fig. 1), commissioned by the Confraternity of the Holy Ghost in Alkmaar for the Laurenskerk. These panels are dated 1504 and signed with a monogram. The figure types and spacious settings are similar to works by the Haarlem painter Jan Mostaert, suggesting that the Master may have been trained in Mostaert's milieu *c.* 1475.

It is generally believed that the Master was Cornelis Buys the elder (*fl* 1490–1524), active in Alkmaar between 1490 and 1524. According to van Buchell, Buys was the first teacher of Jan van Scorel; van Mander stated that Buys was the brother of JACOB CORNELISZ. VAN OOSTSANEN. The similarity between Jacob Cornelisz.'s monogram and the monogram appearing on the *Acts of Mercy* supports the identification of the Master with Buys. Another proposal, that the Master was the Haarlem painter Pieter Gerritsz., is unlikely, since Gerritsz. was probably active until 1540, and the works ascribed to the Master do not seem later than *c.* 1515.

The Master's style is somewhat provincial. Figures are doll-like with simplified facial features and stiff movements. Works such as the *Adoration of the Magi* (Amsterdam, Rijksmus.) reveal the interest in the depiction of clearly defined space and the strong feeling for atmospheric effects of light and shadow characteristic of later Dutch painting. His portraits include those of *Jan van Egmond* (*d* 1516) and Egmond's wife *Magdalena van Waerdenburg* (both New York, Met.), which should be dated after 1504 because of Jan's aged appearance.

BIBLIOGRAPHY

K. van Mander: *Schilder-boeck* ([1603]–1604), fol. 207

A. van Buchell: *Res pictoriae, 1583–1639*; ed. G. J. Hoogewerff and I. Q. van Regteren Altena (The Hague, 1928)

M. J. Friedländer: *Die altniederländische Malerei* (Berlin, 1924–37), x (1932), pp. 33–44; Eng. trans. as *Early Netherlandish Painting* (Leiden, 1967–76), v, p. 96; x, pp. 24–9, *passim*; xii, p. 83

G. J. Hoogewerff: *De Noord-Nederlandsche schilderkunst*, ii (The Hague, 1937), pp. 352–8

Middeleeuwse kunst der Noordelijke Nederlanden (exh. cat., Amsterdam, Rijksmus., 1958), pp. 89–90; review by K. G. Boon in *Burl. Mag.*, c (1958), p. 376

J. Bruyn: 'De Abdij van Egmond als opdrachtgeefster van kunstwerken in het begin van de zestiende eeuw', *Oud-Holland*, lxxxi (1966), p. 199

J. Snyder: *Northern Renaissance Art* (New York, 1985), pp. 446–8

ELLEN KONOWITZ

Master of the Almshouse of the Seven Electors. *See* MASTER OF THE AMSTERDAM DEATH OF THE VIRGIN below.

Master of Amiens (*fl c.* 1515–25). South Netherlandish or northern French painter. Friedländer in 1937 first proposed the Master as the author of three panels with Marian subjects (all Amiens, Mus. Picardie) commissioned by the Puy de Notre-Dame of Amiens in 1518, 1519 and 1520 (NS 1519–21). Around the Amiens panels he grouped three other paintings that he attributed to the artist: a *Death of the Virgin* (Antwerp, Mus. Mayer van den Bergh), a *Virgin in the Temple* (ex-P. Cassirer priv. col., Berlin, see Friedländer (1967–76), pl. 68) and a *Nativity* (San Francisco, CA, de Young Mem. Mus.). Foucart (see 1965 exh. cat.) noted that a fourth panel for the Amiens Puy, executed in 1521 (NS 1522) and surviving only in poor condition (Amiens, Mus. Picardie), was by the same hand.

Friedländer recognized the Master's strong stylistic links with ANTWERP MANNERISM but left open the question of the artist's origin: Antwerp, the southern Netherlands, or northern France. The Antwerp connection, and in particular the close affinity of the Amiens panels to the work of Jan de Beer, has been emphasized in the recent literature. Ewing has suggested that, prior to travelling to Amiens, the Master worked as an assistant in de Beer's Antwerp studio. The Master's style is characterized by brilliant chromatic juxtapositions, an exuberant playfulness and fantasy, and a flickering, nervous technique. Although only a few works are known, they reveal an artist of genuine force and originality. Of all the Late Gothic mannerist painters outside Germany, the Master of Amiens is the most mannered and his virtuosic technique one of the most daring.

BIBLIOGRAPHY

M. J. Friedländer: *Die altniederländische Malerei* (Berlin 1924–37), xiv (1937), pp. 123–4; Eng. trans as *Early Netherlandish Painting* (Leiden, 1967–76), x, pp. 35–6, 66 [complete reproductions]

Le XVIe Siècle européen: Peintures et dessins dans les collections publiques françaises (exh. cat., ed. M. Laclotte; Paris, Petit Pal., 1965), pp. 144–9 [entries by J. Foucart; good bibliog.]

M. A. Lecoq: 'Le Puy d'Amiens de 1518: La Loi du genre et l'art du peintre', *Rev. A.* [Paris], xxxviii (1977), pp.63–74 [hist. and iconographic study of the 1518 panel]

D. Ewing: *The Paintings and Drawings of Jan de Beer*, 2 vols (diss., Ann Arbor, U. MI, 1978), pp. 56–8, 158, 178–87

Y. Pinson: 'Les "Puys d'Amiens", 1518–1525: Problèmes d'attribution et d'évolution de la loi du genre', *Gaz. B.-A.*, n.s. 5, cix (1987), pp. 47–61 [history and purpose of Amiens Puy and the paintings; argues that only the 1518 and 1519 panels are by the Master of Amiens]

DAN EWING

Master of Ampurias [Master of Castelló d'Empúries] (*fl* second quarter of the 15th century). Catalan painter. He is named after the altarpiece of the *Archangel Michael* from S Maria, Castelló d'Empúries, near Girona, of which six scenes survive (Girona, Mus. A.). His other principal surviving work is a large panel representing *SS John the Baptist and Stephen* (Barcelona, Mus. A. Catalunya), which formed the main section of an altarpiece, probably from the Dominican church in Puigcerdà. These works show that the Master was a representative of the final stages of the so-called International Gothic style and was particularly attracted by the problems of naturalistic interpretation. The compositions show his interest in human physiognomy, costumes and landscape. His minute attention to detail resulted, however, in a lack of integration of the different elements of the composition. He had a fine sense of colour and sound technical skill, enabling him to exploit the qualities of the tempera medium.

A chronology for the Master must be deduced from his style, which suggests that he was essentially a contemporary of Bernat Martorell and Joan Antigó. The provenances of his surviving works indicate that he belonged to the school of Girona.

BIBLIOGRAPHY

J. Subias i Galter: *Les taules gòtiques de Castelló d'Empúries* (Girona, 1930)
C. R. Post: *A History of Spanish Painting* (Cambridge, MA, 1930–66), ii, pp. 430–32; vii, pp. 773–5
J. Gudiol and S. Alcolea Blanch: *Pintura gótica catalana* (Barcelona, 1986), p. 142, nos 430, 430 bis

SANTIAGO ALCOLEA BLANCH

Master of the Amsterdam Cabinet. *See* HOUSEBOOK MASTER below.

Master of the Amsterdam Death of the Virgin [Master of the Almshouse of the Seven Electors] (*fl c.* 1500). Netherlandish painter. He was named (by Friedländer) after a panel of the *Death of the Virgin* (*c.* 1500; Amsterdam, Rijksmus.), which portrays the Virgin and the Apostles in a complex interior space, warm and intimate in mood, and populated by small, gesturing figures with tiny hands and heads but bulky, drapery-clad torsos. Hoogewerff, however, preferred the name the Master of the Almshouse of the Seven Electors, after the institution that gave the painting to the Rijksmuseum. Hoogewerff also attributed some of the panels that Friedländer had grouped around this painter to another, shadowy artist: the Master of the Lantern. There is also disagreement over his domicile: Friedländer related him stylistically to Amsterdam, Hoogewerff to the Utrecht school of book illustrators (*see* UTRECHT, §2). The painter's delicate execution, minute details and enclosed settings certainly recall a miniaturist tradition. A *Last Supper* (Amsterdam, Rijksmus.) attributed to him closely resembles an illumination of the same subject in the Hours of Catherine of Cleves (New York, Pierpont Morgan Lib., MS. M. 917, fol. 142*v*), which was executed in Utrecht *c.* 1440. The double portrait of a Utrecht burgomaster and his wife, *Dirk Borre van Amerongen and Maria van Snellenberg* (Rotterdam, Mus. Boymans–van Beuningen), also suggests that the artist had ties to that city. Furthermore, his small *Adoration* triptych (ex-Glitza priv. col.,

Hamburg) includes the distinctive tower of Utrecht Cathedral in the background of the right exterior shutter.

BIBLIOGRAPHY

M. J. Friedländer: *Die altniederländische Malerei* (Berlin, 1924–37); Eng. trans. as *Early Netherlandish Painting* (Leiden, 1967–76), x (1973)
G. J. Hoogewerff: *De Noord-Nederlandsche schilderkunst*, i (The Hague, 1936)
Middeleeuwse kunst der Noordelijke Nederlanden (exh. cat., Amsterdam, Rijksmus., 1958)

JANE L. CARROLL

Master of the André Virgin (*fl* Bruges, *c.* 1500). South Netherlandish painter. His name is derived from the *Virgin and Child* (Paris, Mus. Jacquemart-André), and this, another *Virgin and Child* (Scranton, PA, Everhart Mus.) and a *Virgin and Child with Four Angels Standing in an Arch* (Madrid, Mus. Thyssen-Bornemisza) are the only three paintings attributed to the Master. The background to the Thyssen *Virgin* shows Bruges, which suggests that the Master was active in that city. The obvious source for this painting is Jan van Eyck's *Virgin at the Fountain* (Antwerp, Kon. Mus. S. Kst.), which is echoed in Petrus Christus's *Standing Virgin and Child* (Budapest, Mus. F.A.). There are very close stylistic similarities between the work of Gerard David and the Master, and, intriguingly, the view in the Thyssen *Virgin* corresponds to that from David's studio in Bruges. A similar, somewhat larger composition of the same subject as the Thyssen panel is in the Metropolitan Museum of Art, New York, an even larger copy of which was previously on the New York art market (sold Sotheby Parke Bernet, 14 December 1977, lot 155A). Ebbinge Wubben attributed the Metropolitan painting to the Master of the André Vigin, but Fahy and Van Miegroet accepted it as a late autograph work by Gerard David, dating from *c.* 1515–20. David's authorship is suggested, among other things, by the delicately applied *sfumato*, refined modelling and the distinct porcelain-like quality of the flesh, which is not typical of the Master of the André Virgin. Furthermore, the consistency and subtlety in the use of mass and void are comparable to David's equally late *Rest on the Flight into Egypt* (Washington, DC, N.G.A.).

BIBLIOGRAPHY
Thieme–Becker

M. J. Friedländer: *Die altniederländische Malerei* (Berlin, 1924–37); Eng. trans. as *Early Netherlandish Painting* (Leiden, 1967–76), ix/2 (1971), p. 117
D. De Vos: 'Meester van de André-Madonna', *Anonieme Vlaamse primitieven* (exh. cat., ed. D. De Vos and others; Bruges, Groeningemus., 1969), p. 68
The Thyssen-Bornemisza Collection, Lugano, Col. Thyssen-Bornemisza cat. (Castagnola, 1969), pp. 206–7 [opinions of Ebbinge Wubben and Fahy on attribution]
G. Borghero: *Thyssen-Bornemisza Collection: Catalogue Raisonné of the Exhibited Works of Art* (Lugano and London, 1986)
H. J. Van Miegroet: *Gerard David* (Antwerp, 1989), pp. 246–54, 304

HANS J. VAN MIEGROET

Master of Anne of Brittany. *See* MASTER OF THE UNICORN HUNT below.

Master of the Annunciation to the Shepherds (*fl* ?*c.* 1620–40). ?Spanish painter. He was named by Bologna in 1958 after the painting of the *Annunciation to the Shepherds* in the City of Birmingham Museum and Art Gallery (see fig.). In succeeding years a large, homogeneous group of pictures, of very high quality, have been associated with this work and with a stylistically similar *Annunciation to the Shepherds* in the Museo e Gallerie Nazionali di Capodimonte, Naples. He was a strong and original artist who, in the 1620s and 1630s, created works whose expressive power and warm humanity find parallels in Jusepe de Ribera's works of the same period. The Naples *Annunciation to the Shepherds* was probably painted in the mid-1620s; it is distinguished by the harsh realism of the figures, their clothes ragged and their skin weatherbeaten; the work conveys a sympathy with the world of the poor and the suffering. Similarities with the figures in Velázquez's *Feast of Bacchus* (*The Drunkards*, 1628–9; Madrid, Prado) suggest that the artist may be Spanish. The impasto is rich, and the colouring sombre. Two versions of the *Prodigal Son* (Naples, Capodimonte) are in a similar style, while the *Artist's Studio* (Paris, priv. col., see Gregori and Schleier, fig. 722), an extraordinary and complex allegory of the relationship of art to nature, may date from the early 1630s. In this period the Master of the Annunciation to the Shepherds dominated a vigorous naturalistic movement in Neapolitan art, to which Francesco Fracanzano and Francesco Guarino also adhered. In the mid-1630s the artist, in common with Ribera and other Neapolitan painters, began to develop a more delicate and painterly

style, evident in the *Adoration of the Magi* (ex-Matthiessen F.A., London; see 1982 exh. cat., fig. 83) and the *Birth of the Virgin* (Castellammare di Stabia, S Maria della Pace); in both these works the elegant, graceful figures and silvery light suggest a close relationship with the art of Bernardo Cavallino. The Master also painted single figures and studies of heads, among them *Girl with a Rose* (Naples, De Vito priv. col., see 1982 exh. cat., fig. 84) and *Man Reading* (Lecce, Mus. Prov. Sigismondo Castromediano). Despite his undoubted and powerful influence on Neapolitan painters, the Master has hitherto resisted attempts at identification. Three names have been suggested: Bartolomeo Bassante, the painter of a signed *Adoration of the Shepherds* (?1640s; Madrid, Prado); Giovanni Do and Nunzio Rossi. None has been generally accepted. In the 17th century Celano described a picture of the *Adoration of the Shepherds* then in the church of S Giacomo degli Spagnoli, Naples, which he attributed to a Bartolomeo Bassante or Passante. A picture (untraced) of this subject, and of the same dimensions, appeared on the French art market in the mid-1980s, which may perhaps be the picture described by Celano, and which is attributed to the Master of the Annunciation to the Shepherds. It is possible to see, moreover, that the damaged signature on the *Artist's Studio* begins with a B. It has been suggested (N. Spinosa, in Gregori and Schleier, p. 474) that the Master of the Annunciation may be the Bartolomeo Bassante, mentioned by Celano; he is not, however, to be confused with the artist of the same name whose signed *Adoration of the Shepherds* (Madrid, Prado) is in a lyrical, charming style that contrasts sharply with that of the Master of the Annunciation.

BIBLIOGRAPHY

C. Celano: *Notizie del bello, dell'antico e del curioso della città di Napoli* (Naples, 1692); ed. G. Chiarini (Naples, 1856–60/*R* 1970), iii, p. 1617

A. Mayer: *Jusepe de Ribera* (Leipzig, 1923)

R. Longhi: 'I pittori dell' realtà in Francia, overro i Caravaggeschi francesi del seicento', *Italia Lett.*, xi (1935), p. 1

F. Bologna: *Francesco Solimena* (Naples, 1958)

R. Longhi: 'G. B. Spinelli e i naturalisti napoletani del seicento', *Paragone*, xx/227 (1969), pp. 42–52

M. Marini: *Pittori a Napoli, 1610–1656* (Rome, 1974)

Painting in Naples, 1606–1705: From Caravaggio to Giordano (exh. cat., ed. C. Whitfield and J. Martineau; London, RA, 1982), pp. 190–95

J. Neumann: 'Unbekannte neapolitanische Gemälde im Schloss in Opoçno', *Akten des XXV. internationalen Kongresses für Kunstgeschichte: Wien, 1983*, vii, pp. 139–45

Civiltà del seicento a Napoli (exh. cat., ed. S. Cassani; Naples, Capodimonte, 1984–5), i, p. 158, 341–8

G. De Vito: 'Alla ricerca del vello d'Oro (appunti di un viaggio)', *Ricerche sul '600 napoletano*, ed. R. Causa (Milan, 1986), pp. 119–58

M. Gregori and E. Schleier, eds: *La pittura in Italia: Il seicento* (Milan, 1988, rev. 1989), ii

N. Spinosa: 'Qualche aggiunte e alcune precisazione per il Maestro dell'Annuncio ai Pastori', *Scritti di storia dell'arte in onore de Raffaello Causa* (Naples, 1988), pp. 181–8

Master of Antoine of Burgundy [Master of the Schwarzes Gebetbuch] (*fl* Bruges, *c.* 1460–80). South Netherlandish illuminator. The name was given to the painter of three manuscripts made for Antoine of Burgundy: a two-volume French translation of Valerius Maximus, *Faits et dits mémorables* (Berlin, Staatsbib., MS. Dep. Breslau 2), a *Chronicle* by Aegidius de Roya (The Hague, Rijksmus. Meermanno–Westreenianum, MS. 10.A.21) and

Master of the Annunciation to the Shepherds: *Annunciation to the Shepherds*, oil on canvas, 1.81×1.26 m, mid-1620s (Birmingham, City of Birmingham Museum and Art Gallery)

a *Livre de bonnes moeurs* by Jacques le Grand (Paris, priv. col.). The artist also worked for other patrons, contributing, for example, to the illumination of a four-volume copy of Froissart's *Chronicles* (Paris, Bib. N., MS fr. 2643–6) for Louis de Gruuthuse. His most beautiful work is the Schwarzes Gebetbuch ('Black prayerbook'; Vienna, Österreich. Nbib., Cod. 1856), a Book of Hours with both the lettering and the illumination in inks and paints of gold and silver on parchment dyed black.

The style of the Master of Antoine of Burgundy is distinctive: while the interiors are depicted in a relatively conventional way, with a pronounced high viewpoint and exaggerated foreshortening, the landscape backgrounds often have convincing depth. The artist shows a complete mastery of such effects as the depiction of still water or of nocturnal scenes, but his painting is most effective in the graphic portrayal of his large figures with their mobile facial expressions. The actions and reactions of the participants are often caught with astonishing vivacity. Nonetheless the figures themselves are often somewhat wooden, with extremely long, puppet-like legs and spherical knee-joints. Tall, rounded fur hats, caps and extremely long, pointed shoes are typical features of the costume. In many respects the style of the Master of Antoine of Burgundy is close to that of the Master of the Dresden Prayerbook. Jenni and Thoss have stressed the need for a critical review of the artist's oeuvre; the Schwarzes Gebetbuch could provide a point of departure for this. Whether the Master of Antoine of Burgundy can be identified with PHILIPPE DE MAZEROLLES on the basis of this manuscript remains questionable.

BIBLIOGRAPHY

F. Winkler: *Die flämische Buchmalerei* (Leipzig, 1925/*R* Amsterdam, 1978), pp. 79–85

Q. Smital: *Das Schwarze Gebetbuch des Herzogs Galeazzo Maria Sforza*, 2 vols (Vienna, 1930) [facs.]

A. De Schryver and F. Unterkircher: *Gebetbuch Karls des Kühnen vel potius Stundenbuch der Maria von Burgund*, Codices selecti, xiv (Graz, 1969) [facs.]

J. Harthan: *Books of Hours and their Owners* (London, 1977), pp. 106–13

U. Jenni and D. Thoss: *Das Schwarze Gebetbuch* (Frankfurt am Main, 1982) [facs.]

G. Dogaer: *Flemish Miniature Painting in the 15th and 16th Centuries* (Amsterdam, 1987), pp. 120–24

Flämische Buchmalerei: Handschriftenschätze aus dem Burgunderreich (exh. cat. by D. Thoss, Vienna, Österreich. Nbib., 1987), pp. 48–50

BODO BRINKMANN

Master of the Antwerp Adoration (*fl c.* 1520). South Netherlandish painter. The conventional name was given by Friedländer (1915) and derives from a triptych depicting the *Adoration of the Magi* (Antwerp, Kon. Mus. S. Kst.). The artist belongs to the group of the so-called Antwerp Mannerists (*see* ANTWERP MANNERISM). His oeuvre consists of small triptychs and panels, apparently for private devotion. The discovery, on the Master's triptych of the *Adoration of the Magi* (Brussels, Mus. A. Anc.), of a monogram G and a presumed self-portrait, probably at the age of *c.* 25, has led to speculation about his identity.

BIBLIOGRAPHY

M. J. Friedländer: 'Die Antwerpener Manieristen von 1520', *Jb. Kön.-Preuss. Kstsamml.*, xxxvi (1915), pp. 65–91

——: *Die altniederländische Malerei* (Berlin, 1924–37); Eng. trans. as *Early Netherlandish Painting* (Leiden, 1967–76), xi (1974), pp. 26, 72

P. Philippot: 'Le Monogrammiste G, Maître de l'Epiphanie d'Anvers', *Bull. Mus. Royaux B.-A. [Belgique]*, vi (1956), pp. 157–66

P. Vanaise: 'Nadere identiteitsbepaling van de Meester der Antwerpse Aanbidding' [Further information on the identification of the Master of the Antwerp Adoration], *Bull. Inst. Royal Patrm. A.*, i (1958), pp. 132–45

——: 'De hersamenstelling van een zoekgeraakte compositie van de Meester der Antwerpse Aanbidding' [The reconstruction of a lost composition by the Master of the Antwerp Adoration], *Bull. Inst. Royal Patrm. A.*, ii (1959), pp. 34–40

Anonieme Vlaamse primitieven [Anonymous Flemish primitives] (exh. cat., ed. D. De Vos and others; Bruges, Groeningemus., 1969), pp. 156–61

E. De Corte: 'Triptyque de la Passion monogrammé et daté 1527, de l'entourage du Maître de l'Adoration d'Anvers et du Maître de 1518, inspiré des cycles gravés de Dürer: Une Approche de la technique picturale', *Rev. Archéologues & Historiens A. Louvain*, xxi (1988), p. 230

CARL VAN DE VELDE

Apocalypse Master. *See* MASTER OF THE BERRY APOCALYPSE below.

Master of the Arcimboldi Missal (*fl* Milan, *c.* 1492). Italian illuminator. He is named after the spendidly illuminated Missal (Milan, Bib. Capitolare, MS. X.D.I.13) that bears the coat of arms and the portrait of Guidantonio Arcimboldi, Archbishop of Milan (1489–97). The manuscript was probably donated to Arcimboldi by Ludovico Sforza ('il Moro'), Duke of Milan; the frontispiece bears a miniature of the Duke and his court during the coronation ceremony, which took place in S Ambrogio, Milan, on 26 March 1495. The Missal must therefore have been decorated after that date, and it is attributed to a Milanese artist strongly influenced by the work of Ambrogio Bergognone and Cristoforo de Predis.

The Master of the Arcimboldi Missal is also credited with the Hours of Ascanio Sforza (Oxford, Bodleian Lib., MS. Douce 14), produced at a later date than the Milanese manuscript. Here his pictorial language has become less dry and sharp, the modelling is softer and the rendering of landscape more refined; the style partly reflects the new experience of Leonardo da Vinci's painting. Other miniatures have been attributed to the Master, including three initials (Paris, Wildenstein Inst., 25–7), a *St Stephen* (London, Wallace, M. 330) and *St John the Baptist* (Venice, Fond. Cini, inv. 2111). Alexander identified the Master with MATTEO DA MILANO. The Arcimboldi Missal could therefore document Matteo's early career in Milan in the 1490s, before he is first documented in Ferrara in 1502.

BIBLIOGRAPHY

F. Malaguzzi Valeri: *Gli artisti lombardi* (1917), iii of *La corte di Ludovico il Moro*, 3 vols (Milan, 1913–17), pp. 175–82

R. Cipriani: 'Maestro del Messale Arcimboldi', *Arte lombarda dai Visconti agli Sforza* (Milan, 1958), pp. 157–9

O. Pächt and J. J. G. Alexander: *Italian School* (1970), ii of *Illuminated Manuscripts in the Bodleian Library Oxford* (Oxford, 1966–73), p. 97

G. Mariani Canova: *Miniature dell'Italia settentrionale nella Fondazione Giorgio Cini* (Vicenza, 1978), pp. 58–9

J. J. G. Alexander: 'Italian Illuminated Manuscripts in British Collections', *La miniatura italiana tra gotico e rinascimento: Atti del II congresso di storia della miniatura italiana: Cortona, 1983*, i, p. 113

M. P. Lodigiani: 'Per Matteo da Milano', *A. Crist.*, lxxix (1991), pp. 287–300

J. J. G. Alexander: 'Matteo da Milano illuminator', *Pantheon*, l (1992), pp. 32–45

MILVIA BOLLATI

Master of the Augsburg Visitation. *See* MASTER OF THE FREISING VISITATION below.

Master of the Augsburg Legend of St Benedict. *See* BURGKMAIR, (1).

Master of the Augsburg Legend of Ulrich (*fl c.* 1450). German painter. He is named after two cool-coloured paintings of the *Legend of Ulrich* (*c.* 1450; Augsburg, SS Ulrich and Afra). Their backs being unpainted, it is thought they were part of a wall cladding. Each shows three scenes concerning the patron saint of Augsburg: those on the first panel take place in the choir and the ambulatory sides of a large Romanesque church, which presumably is the old SS Ulrich und Afra (destr. 1474). First two angels appear to the sick Bishop Ulrich, bringing him chalice and paten; then, while he celebrates Mass before two deacons (who seem portraits), the hand of God appears to him alone. Finally he blesses throngs of the poor. The second panel is organized around two interiors with windows giving on to an intermediate landscape. On the left, the sleeping Ulrich is commanded by St Afra, the town's other patron saint, to apply to the Emperor for consecration of the monastery. On the right, Ulrich rewards a messenger with goose-meat, which the hostile Duke Arnulf, in the centre, hopes to use as evidence of Friday fast-breaking, but as it is handed to him it turns into a fish. The Duke's followers' Burgundian costumes and the buildings' pointed turrets suggest knowledge of the art of the Master of Flémalle and book illuminations influenced by him such as those by the Master of Girart de Roussillon. An Antwerp copy (New York, Met.) of a lost painting from Robert Campin's circle indicates how the Master improved on the church's architecture. Yet more comparable is the foreground of a Dutch painting, in the tradition of Rogier van der Weyden, of the *Dream of Pope Sergius* (New York, Friedsam priv. col.).

The influence of van der Weyden also appears in two later altar wings, again undated, with scenes from the *Life of the Virgin* (Nuremberg, Ger. Nmus.) and two *Passion* scenes with painted backs (Brussels, Mus. A. Anc.). The sharply etched portrait of *Pius Joachim* (Basle, Kstmus.) again shows Dutch influence. (An untraced frame inscription, perhaps fictitious, claimed the artist was a Basle Anabaptist.) The more restrained portrait of *Hans von Rechberg zu Schramberg* (*d* 1464; Vienna, Kstmus.) is likewise superb. In all his paintings the Master contributed a comfortable Swabian narrative tone to his Netherlandish models.

BIBLIOGRAPHY
E. Buchner: 'Der Meister der Ulrichslegende', *Beitr. Gesch. Dt. Kst*, ii (1928), pp. 7–30
——: *Das deutsche Bildnis der Gotik und der frühen Dürerzeit* (Berlin, 1953), pp. 69ff, nos 56, 57

HANS GEORG GMELIN

Master of the Augsburg Portraits of Painters. *See* §III: MONOGRAMMIST BB below.

Master of the Augustinian Altar (*fl c.* 1470–87). German painter. He is named after a picture-screen (Nuremberg, Ger. Nmus.), parts of which originate from the monastery church of the Augustinian Hermits in Nuremberg. One side shows, on four wings, eight scenes from the *Legend of St Vitus*; these are broken by two wings showing scenes from four other saints' lives. Four pairs of male and female saints are painted on the reverse, and two predella covers also survive. The interpolation of subject-matter suggests a combination of two different

but stylistically related altarpieces: first an altar of the *Ten Thousand Martyrs* or *Auxiliary Saints* from the Cistercian chapel of the Ebracher Hof in Nuremberg, from 1482 (hence the Cistercian coat of arms under the *Vision of St Bernard*); secondly an altar of *St Vitus* produced in 1487 for the Augustinian Hermits. These works were assembled in their present form in 1932.

Given the lack of documentary evidence, all information about the paintings is stylistic. They are not all executed by the same hand (although there is a unity of design) but are of a quality unique in Nuremberg painting of the time. Various features are adopted from the leading Nuremberg masters Hans Pleydenwurff and Michel Wolgemut. But the Master originated from the Upper Rhine area: a fragmentary panel, considered an early work (*c.* 1470; Berne, Kstmus.), shows the influence of Martin Schongauer in the firm figure construction, and the Nuremberg *Martyrdom of St Sebastian* adopts an intricately contorted nude figure from Schongauer's engraving (B. 59). The Master must have had sufficient reputation to persuade Rueland Frueauf and his son of that name to come from Salzburg to Nuremberg to collaborate on the *St Vitus* altar. The signature 'RF' can be seen on the first scene of the legend, where St Vitus repudiates idolatry. A large *Madonna of Mercy* (Nuremberg, Ger. Nmus.) was also produced, with a significant contribution by Frueauf.

The Master is distinguished in the closely interwoven world of Nuremberg altar-painting because of his generous, less trivial style of depiction, with its sure grasp of material structure and the human figure. It would appear that after working as an itinerant artist, doing church commissions throughout Middle Franconia in the 1480s, the Master settled permanently in Nuremberg, founding an important workshop.

BIBLIOGRAPHY
J. Rosenthal-Metzger: *Das Augustinerkloster in Nürnberg* (diss., U. Erlangen, 1930)
F. Lahusen: *Der Hochaltar der ehemaligen Augustinerkirche S. Veit in Nürnberg* (diss., U. Freiburg im Breisgau, 1957)
E. Pfeffer: 'Der "Augustiner-Hochaltar" und vier weitere Nürnberger Altare des ausgehenden 15. Jahrhunderts', *Mitt. Ver. Gesch. Stadt Nürnberg*, lii (1963/4), pp. 305–98
A. Stange: 'Die deutschen Tafelbilder vor Dürer', *Kritisches Verzeichnis*, iii, ed. P. Stricher and H. Härtle (Munich, 1980), pp. 83–8, nos 168–79, esp. no. 172

HANS GEORG GMELIN

Master of Ávila (*fl* second half of the 15th century). Spanish painter. He painted a small triptych (*c.* 1470–75; Madrid, Mus. Lázaro Galdiano), which shows on the interior the *Nativity*, the *Annunciation to the Shepherds* and the *Magi's Vision of the Star*; on the exterior is the *Annunciation.* The Master of Ávila may possibly have visited the Netherlands, because the painting is an adaptation of the Middleburg triptych of the *Nativity* (Berlin, Gemäldegal.) attributed to Rogier van der Weyden; Netherlandish influence is also apparent in the Virgin's draperies and the orange-yellows and reds in St Joseph's coat, which are typical of the Master of Flémalle. The Master of Ávila also evidently painted several works for Ávila (hence his name), including a panel of the *Meeting of Joachim and Anna at the Golden Gate* in the north transept of S Vicente, and three panels of the *Meeting at the Golden Gate, Christ among the Doctors* and the *Death of the Virgin* in the parish church of Barco de Ávila. The Master was a technically accomplished artist, who fused virile types with a gentle and fresh way of looking at things (Post). Attempts have been made to identify him with Pedro Díaz de Oviedo (Mayer) and García de Barco (*fl c.* 1476; Tormo), who came from the region where the paintings were found, but neither identification has been generally accepted.

Ceán Bermúdez
BIBLIOGRAPHY
A. Mayer: *Geschichte der spanischen Malerei* (Leipzig, 2/1922)
E. Tormo: 'Excursión colectiva a Arenas de San Pedro, Candelodia, Trujillo, Plasencia, Barco de Ávila y Piedrahita', *Bol. Soc. Esp. Excurs.*, 36 (1928)
C. R. Post: *A History of Spanish Paintings*, iv/2 (Cambridge, MA, 1933)
                                                    J. R. L. HIGHFIELD

Master of Badia a Isola (*fl c.* 1290–1320). Italian painter. This anonymous artist, named after the *Virgin and Child Enthroned with Two Angels* in SS Salvatore e Cirino, Badia a Isola (nr Monteriggioni, Siena), is a problematic figure. At the one extreme, the Badia a Isola panel and related works have been viewed as early works by Duccio di Buoninsegna; at the other, a much expanded corpus of works for the artist has been proposed (Stubblebine). A number of critics agree in grouping a *Virgin and Child* (Siena, Pin. N., 593), a polyptych that once contained a *St Paul*, a *St John the Evangelist* and a *St Peter* (South Hadley, MA, Mount Holyoke Coll. A. Mus.), a *St John the Baptist* (Cologne, Wallraf-Richartz-Mus., 608), a *Virgin and Child* (Utrecht, Catharijneconvent), a *Redeemer* and four *Angels* (untraced) and a *Virgin and Child Enthroned with Four Angels* (Venice, Fond. Cini), but other attributions are widely debated. The painter of the Badia a Isola panel, a distinct and independent artistic personality, was conservative, blending elements from the tradition of Guido da Siena with the newer style of Duccio. His early work is markedly sculptural and spatially assertive; his later production is less so. The Badia a Isola panel is the most important of the Master's surviving works insofar as it seems to document stylistic features of Sienese art in the 1290s that are less visible elsewhere.

Thieme–Becker
BIBLIOGRAPHY
R. van Marle: *Italian Schools* (1923–38), ii, pp. 77–9
C. Brandi: *Duccio* (Florence, 1951), pp. 141–3
J. Stubblebine: *Duccio di Buoninsegna and his School*, ii (Princeton, 1979), pp. 75–85
J. White: *Duccio: Tuscan Art and the Medieval Workshop* (London, 1979), pp. 150–51
                                                    H. B. J. MAGINNIS

Master of the Balaam (*fl c.* 1440–50). German or Burgundian French engraver. He is named after the engraving *Balaam on his Ass and the Angel* (Dresden, Kupferstichkab.; Lewis, no. 1). Also attributed to him are some ten prints, each of which survives in a single example. The attribution is not certain in all cases: for example the main engraving, *St Elegius in his Workshop* (Amsterdam, Rijksmus.; L 16), has also been attributed to the MASTER OF THE WEIBERMACHT and the MASTER OF THE GARDENS OF LOVE (*see* below). Most of the small, often circular engravings recall niello work and may have been preparatory sketches for goldsmiths. The Master probably worked in either the Upper Rhine region or Burgundy.

BIBLIOGRAPHY
Hollstein: *Dut. & Flem.*
M. Lehrs: *Geschichte und kritischer Katalog des deutschen, niederländischen und französischen Kupferstichs im XV. Jahrhundert*, (Vienna, 1908), pp. 327–36 [L]
M. Geisberg: *Die Anfänge des deutschen Kupferstiches und der Meister E.S., Meister der Graphik*, ii (Leipzig, 1909), p. 55
——: *Die Anfänge des Kupferstiches, Meister der Graphik*, ii (Leipzig, 1923), pp. 60–63
                                                    HOLM BEVERS

Master of the Bamberg Altar (*fl* Nuremberg, *c.* 1420–40). German painter. He is named after an altarpiece of *Passion* scenes (1429; ex-Franciscan church, Bamberg; Munich, Bayer. Nmus.) in which the style is derived from that of the Nuremberg Master of the Altarpiece of the Virgin (*fl* 1400–10; *c.* 1410; Nuremberg, Ger. Nmus.). The Master of the Bamberg Altar collaborated with the Master of the Deichsler Altarpiece in the Imhoff Altar (*c.* 1418–22; Nuremberg, Lorenzkirche; *see* MASTER OF THE IMHOFF ALTAR below). The *Man of Sorrows with the Virgin and St John* (Nuremberg, Ger. Nmus.) by the Master of the Bamberg Altar forms the reverse panel of the Imhoff Altar. It is a good example of his solemn style, with figure mass and simplicity of composition. Another of his paintings, the *Man of Sorrows Standing with the Virgin* (*c.* 1420; Nuremberg, Ger. Nmus.), shows his mastery of restrained presentation of a devotional subject. Like the Master of the Deichsler Altarpiece (possibly Berthold Landauer), he was strongly dependent for his facial types and figure style on Bohemian painting, particularly that of the Master of Třeboň, though his more block-like figure forms and solidity of figure grouping contrast with the elegant, elongated figures of the Master of Třeboň, moving further away from the International Gothic style of Prague. In his work may be traced some influence from late-14th-century north Italian painting, such as that of Altichiero.

Thieme–Becker
BIBLIOGRAPHY
A. Stange: *Deutsche Malerei der Gotik*, ix (Munich, 1958/R Nendeln, 1969), pp. 12–15, figs 10–17
——: *Kritisches Verzeichnis der deutschen Tafelbilder vor Dürer*, iii (Munich, 1978), pp. 30–32, nos 31–5
Gothic and Renaissance Art in Nuremberg 1300–1550 (exh. cat., New York, Met., 1986), nos 28, 29
                                                    NIGEL J. MORGAN

Bamberg Master (*fl c.* 1225–37). German sculptor and architect. Name conferred by Wilhelm Boeck on the artist in charge of work on Bamberg Cathedral in the period after 1230 (*see* BAMBERG, §2(ii)). It arises from the desire to attribute important works of the so-called younger sculpture workshop to a specific artist. Apart from smaller works, Boeck attributed the sculptures of the *Rider* (*see* BAMBERG, fig. 3), an *Old Woman*, the *Synagogue* and *Eve* (Bamberg, Diözmus.) to the Master. The *Virgin* and the general conception of the Princes' Portal, however, should be seen as being executed to his designs in collaboration with three independent, younger sculptors and their assistants. By this theory, he would have been schooled artistically on older works in the cathedral, such as the choir-screen reliefs, and then spent time at the Reims Cathedral workshops, where he became acquainted with the assimilation of antique art, before returning to Franconia.

Boeck's fine distinctions between the work of different sculptors, based on subtle stylistic analyses and speculative psychological intuition, have not been widely accepted. The younger workshop is seen as a centre where older and more artistically progressive craftsmen, coming especially from Reims, worked together. Apart from the stylistic distinctions, there are evident differences of quality. Models drawn from French sculpture are modified according to individual needs; the Bamberg style was especially derived from the sculptures in the north transept at Reims. It is possible that only one sculptor mediated these forms, but there seems to be little point in isolating the contributions of particular artists as it is impossible to form a definite judgement on the degree of specialization and cooperation within the Bamberg workshop. The chronology of the building of Bamberg Cathedral and the dating of the works at Reims can hardly be reconciled by current research; this suggests that the Bamberg sculptures should be dated from c. 1225 to the consecration of the cathedral in 1237.

BIBLIOGRAPHY

W. Boeck: *Der Bamberger Meister* (Tübingen, 1960)

W. Sauerländer: 'Reims und Bamberg: Zu Art und Umfang der Übernahmen', *Z. Kstgesch.*, xxxix (1976), pp. 167–92

R. Suckale: 'Die Bamberger Domskulpturen: Technik, Blockbehandlung, Ansichtigkeit und die Einbeziehung des Betrachters', *Münchn. Jb. Bild. Kst*, n. s. 3, xxxviii (1987), pp. 27–82

H.-C. Feldmann: *Bamberg und Reims: Die Skulpturen, 1220–1250* (Ammersbeck bei Hamburg, 1992)

M. Schuller: *Das Fürstenportal des Bamberger Domes* (Bamberg, 1993)

KLAUS NIEHR

Master of the Bambino Vispo [Master of the Lively Child] (*fl* Florence, early 15th century). Italian painter, possibly identified as STARNINA. Sirén (1904) assembled a group of paintings under the name the Master of the Bambino Vispo. These included the *Virgin and Child with Saints and Angels* (Florence, Accad.), the *Virgin of Humility* (Philadelphia, PA, Mus. A.), a triptych of the *Virgin and Child with Music-making Angels and Four Saints* (Rome, Pal. Doria-Pamphili) and an altarpiece wing with *SS Mary Magdalene and Lawrence and a Cardinal Donor* (Berlin, Bodemus.). He chose the name on account of the particularly lively expression and movement of the Christ Child in the paintings. He associated the altar wing with a documented altarpiece of *St Lawrence*, which, it was then believed, had been donated to Florence Cathedral by Cardinal Pietro Corsini in 1422. This date provided the starting-point from which to relate the Master to other 15th-century Florentine painters. Sirén believed the painter to be a distant follower of Lorenzo Monaco and noted his apparent interest in the psychology of the figures as well as a marked sense for the decorative that set him apart from his contemporaries. The Master was accepted by art historians, but Sirén's attempts to identify the painter with Pietro di Domenico da Montepulciano or Parri Spinelli were not seriously pursued. The question was raised as to whether the Master's obvious indebtedness to the Late Gothic style could be explained solely by the influence of Lorenzo Monaco, or whether it might result from direct contact with the centres of Late Gothic painting, particularly Valencia.

Pudelko (1938) attempted to chart the Master's stylistic development. He pointed to the close thematic and stylistic similarities between the *Last Judgement* (Munich, Alte Pin.), attributed to the Master, and early 15th-century Valencian painting, such as the retable of the *Crucifixion* and *Stories of the True Cross* attributed to the Gil Master and Bonifacio Ferrer's retable of the *Crucifixion, Conversion of St Paul* and *Baptism* (both Valencia, Mus. B.A.). Pudelko concluded that the *Last Judgement* was painted c. 1415 in Valencia. This would suggest that the Master was in Valencia before 1422, the date previously proposed for the *St Lawrence* altarpiece. While there, he was deeply influenced by the Late Gothic style before becoming the most important representative of this style in Florence, together with Lorenzo Monaco. Pudelko believed that the *St Lawrence* altarpiece reveals how the Master subsequently evolved a more grandiose style, under the influence of Gentile da Fabriano, that later declined into meaningless mannerisms, as in another triptych of the *Virgin and Child with Music-making Angels and Four Saints* (U. Würzburg, Wagner-Mus.). This development was generally accepted, although scholars could not agree on the Master's identity nor his exact connection with Spanish painting. Longhi ascribed to the Master several Valencian paintings that previously had constituted the oeuvre of the Gil Master (named after an altarpiece donated by Vicente Gil; fragments in New York, Met.; New York, Hisp. Soc. America) and suggested that they had been painted in Spain. Nevertheless, Longhi insisted on the Tuscan, or specifically Florentine, origins of the artist.

De Saralegui suggested that the Gil Master could be identified with the Valencian MIGUEL ALCANYIS, and at this stage the problem of the identity of the Master of the Bambino Vispo appeared to be resolved. However, Alcanyis is documented in Barcelona, Valencia and Mallorca between 1415 and 1447, and Oertel saw no specific connection between the Master's work and Spanish painting and, like Sirén, regarded him as a pupil of Lorenzo Monaco.

Berti and Bellosi noticed the striking similarities between the work of the Master of the Bambino Vispo and that of Starnina, and this prompted van Waadenoijen and Syre to claim the Master and Starnina as the same person. The premise for this identification was new evidence that the *St Lawrence* altarpiece could be dated much earlier than had previously been supposed. It was proved that it was donated by Cardinal Angelo Acciauoli (1349–1408) to a chapel in the Certosa del Galluzzo, near Florence (not by Cardinal Corsini to the Cathedral in 1422). Consequently, the altarpiece was painted in 1404–7 and the oeuvre of the Master has to be dated considerably earlier than had previously been assumed. Van Waadenoijen and Syre attempted to integrate the works of the Master into the documented oeuvre of Starnina and to establish a chronology. This led to a complete reassessment of the Master's style. His indebtedness to Late Gothic style was no longer regarded as retardataire; instead it corresponded to the most advanced artistic currents of the early 15th century. Both scholars believe that not all the works attributed to the Master of the Bambino Vispo are by Starnina: some should be ascribed to his followers and members of his workshop, or even to other masters. The connection with

Valencian painting could be explained by the fact that Starnina is documented in Valencia. In general, scholars have accepted van Waadenoijen's and Syre's theory. Boskovits, however, believed the Master to be Miguel Alcanyis, who, he suggested, worked with Starnina in Spain and subsequently followed his master to Florence.

BIBLIOGRAPHY

O. Sirén: 'Di alcuni pittori fiorentini che subirono l'influenza di Lorenzo Monaco: Il Maestro del Vispo Bambino', *L'Arte*, vii (1904), pp. 349–52

——: 'Florentiner Trecentozeichnungen', *Jb. Preuss. Kstsamml.*, xxvii (1906), pp. 208–23

——: 'A Late Gothic Poet of Line', *Burl. Mag.*, xxiv (1913–14), pp. 323–30; xxv (1914), pp. 15–24

G. Pudelko: 'The Maestro del Bambino Vispo', *A. America*, xxvi (1938), pp. 47–63

R. Longhi: 'Fatti di Masolino e di Masaccio', *Crit. A.*, v (1940), pp. 145–91 (183–5)

L. de Saralegui: 'Comentarios sobre algunos pintores y pinturas de Valencia', *Archv Esp. A.*, xxvi (1953), pp. 237–52

L. Berti: *Masaccio* (Milan, 1964), pp. 137–8, n. 152

R. Oertel: 'Der Laurentius-Altar aus dem Florentiner Dom: Zu einem Werk des Maestro del Bambino Vispo', *Studien zur toskanischen Kunst, Festschrift für L. H. Heydenreich* (Munich, 1964), pp. 205–20

L. Bellosi: 'La mostra di affreschi staccati al Forte Belvedere', *Paragone*, xvii/201 (1966), pp. 73–9

J. van Waadenoijen: 'Proposal for Starnina: Exit the Maestro del Bambino Vispo?', *Burl. Mag.*, cxvi (1974), pp. 82–91

M. Boskovits: 'Il Maestro del Bambino Vispo: Gherardo Starnina o Miguel Alcañiz?', *Paragone*, xxvi/307 (1975), pp. 3–15

C. Syre: *Studien zum 'Maestro del Bambino Vispo' und Starnina* (diss., U. Bonn, 1979)

J. van Waadenoijen: *Starnina e il gotico internazionale a Firenze* (Florence, 1983)

CORNELIA SYRE

Master with the Banderoles (*fl c.* 1450–75). North Netherlandish engraver. He is named after a group of engravings that incorporate long banderoles (speech banners) with Latin captions. Because three scenes from the story of the *Creation* (Lehrs, 1921, nos 1–3) have inscriptions in Dutch, he is thought to have worked in the northern Netherlands, perhaps Geldern or Overijssel. About 130 engravings are attributed to him. They are engraved in a crude, mechanical way; the draughtsmanship is weak and clumsy. Most of them are large-format, broadsheet-style engravings of religious and secular subjects. Unparalleled in north European engravings are the

large allegorical pictures with explanatory inscriptions, such as the *Redemption of the World through Christ's Death on the Cross* (L 85). Some of these engravings are based on Italian models, so it is possible that the Master visited Italy. His oeuvre consists largely of copies and compilations from the work of other engravers (e.g. the Master of the Playing Cards, the Master E.S.) and of reproductions of early panel paintings from the Netherlands (the Master of Flémalle, Rogier van der Weyden) and Germany (Stefan Lochner).

BIBLIOGRAPHY

Hollstein: *Dut. & Flem.*; Thieme–Becker

M. Lehrs: *Der Meister mit den Bandrollen: Ein Beitrag zur Geschichte des ältesten Kupferstiches in Deutschland* (Dresden, 1886)

——: *Geschichte und kritischer Katalog des deutschen, niederländischen und französischen Kupferstichs im XV. Jahrhundert*, iv (Vienna, 1921), pp. 1–164 [L]

M. Geisberg: *Die Anfänge des Kupferstiches, Meister der Graphik*, ii (Leipzig, 1923), pp. 74–7

Fifteenth-century Engravings of Northern Europe from the National Gallery of Art (exh. cat., ed. by A. Shestack; Washington, DC, N.G.A., 1967–8), nos 29, 30

A. I. Lockhart: 'Four Engravings by the Master with the Banderoles', *Bull. Cleveland Mus. A.*, lx (1973), pp. 247–55

M. Hébert: *Bibliothèque Nationale, Département des Gravures: Inventaire des gravures des écoles du Nord 1440–1550*, i (Paris, 1982), pp. 175–6

HOLM BEVERS

Master of Banyoles [Sp. Bañolas]. *See* ANTIGÓ, JOAN.

Master of the Barbarigo Reliefs (*fl c.* 1486–*c.* 1515). Italian sculptor. He is named after the three bronze reliefs of the *Coronation of the Virgin* (see fig.), the *Assumption of the Virgin* and the *Twelve Apostles* (Venice, Ca' d'Oro) that formerly decorated the altar donated by the BARBARIGO family for a double tomb in the church of S Maria della Carità in Venice (now the Galleria dell'Accademia). Other fragments surviving from the tombs (dismantled 1808) include a marble kneeling effigy of *Doge Agostino Barbarigo* (Venice, ante-sacristy of S Maria della Salute) and a limestone relief of the *Resurrection* (Venice, Scu. Grande S Giovanni Evangelista). The Barbarigo tomb is recorded in an engraving of 1692 (Venice, Correr, Raccolta Ghesso, iii, no. 435), which shows that the reliefs decorated the altar of the central barrel-vaulted bay, flanked on either

Master of the Barbarigo Reliefs: *Coronation of the Virgin*, bronze relief, *c.* 1515 (Venice, Ca' d'Oro)

side by the kneeling figures of *Marco Barbarigo* and *Agostino Barbarigo*. In each adjacent bay was a reclining effigy on a bier supported by a console. Documentary evidence suggests that work on the tombs began *c.* 1486, the date of Doge Marco Barbarigo's death, and that the reliefs were completed by 1515.

The attribution of these bronze reliefs has caused much scholarly discussion. Leo Planiscig (1921) coined the anonymous sculptor's present title, suggesting that he may be identified with Tullio Lombardo. Other suggestions have included Alessandro Leopardi (Paoletti, 1893), Antonio Lombardo (Bode, 1907) and Paolo di Matteo Savin (Pope-Hennessy, 1963). The present consensus is that the reliefs are probably the work of a sculptor working within the circle of Antonio Lombardo and Tullio Lombardo. The classicizing modelling of the figures and draperies and the distinctive punching of the grounds of these reliefs have been recognized in a number of other anonymous works, including a bronze half-length relief of *Christ Blessing*, a relief of *Cupid* (both Berlin, Skulpgal.), a bronze statuette of *Charity* (Vienna, Ksthist. Mus.) and a *St Jerome* (Brescia, Mus. Civ. Crist.), all of which bear similarities of facture and modelling.

BIBLIOGRAPHY

P. Paoletti: *L'archittetura e la scultura del rinascimento in Venezia* (Venice, 1893), pp. 184–5

W. Bode: *The Italian Bronze Statuettes of the Renaissance* (English edn 1907, rev. New York, 1980)

L. Planiscig: *Venezianische Bildhauer der Renaissance* (Vienna, 1921), pp. 209–15

E. F. Bange: *Staatliche Museen zu Berlin: Die italienischen Bronzen der Renaissance und des Barock*, ii (Berlin and Leipzig, 1922), pp. 4–5; cat. nos 23–5

G. Fogolari, U. Nebbia and V. Moschini: *La R. Galleria Giorgio Franchetti alla Ca' d'Oro* (Venice, 1929), p. 148

Italian Bronze Statuettes (exh. cat., ed. J. Pope-Hennessy; London, V&A, and elsewhere, 1961), cat. nos 91–2

J. Pope-Hennessy: 'An Exhibition of Italian Bronze Statuettes—I', *Burl. Mag.*, cv (1963), pp. 14–23

A. Markham Schulz: 'Pietro Lombardo's Barbarigo Tomb in the Venetian Church of S Maria della Carità', *Art the Ape of Nature: Studies in Honour of H. W. Janson*, ed. M. Barasch and L. Freeman Sandler (New York, 1981), pp. 171–92

ANTONIA BOSTRÖM

Master of the Barberini Panels (*fl c.* 1445–75). Italian painter. The two eponymous works (New York, Met.; Boston, MA, Mus. F.A.) were painted in Urbino, whence they were removed to Rome by Cardinal Antonio Barberini (*see* BARBERINI, (4)) in 1631. The pictures, which have been the subject of much debate and speculation, are exceptional both for their ambitious architectural settings and their genre-like treatment of narrative. It is now generally conceded that they represent, in a highly unorthodox fashion, the *Birth of the Virgin* and the *Presentation of the Virgin*; that the elaborate architecture, with its wealth of Classical allusion, reflects the influence of Alberti; and that their author was either trained or deeply influenced by Fra Filippo Lippi in Florence *c.* 1445–50 and then fell under the spell of Piero della Francesca, aspects of whose palette and figure types he imitated in a superficial fashion. Other works attributed to the artist include, in their presumed order of execution, an *Annunciation* (Washington, DC, N.G.A.), a second *Annunciation* (Munich, Alte Pin.), a *Crucifixion* (Venice, Fond. Cini), three related

panels with saints (Milan, Brera and Bib. Ambrosiana; Loreto, Santuario Santa Casa) and a painted alcove (Urbino, Pal. Ducale). The *Annunciation* in Munich bears the arms of the French banker Jacques Coeur and was probably painted in Florence during the financier's trip to Italy in 1448. The alcove has, on the basis of its armorial devices, been dated after 1474, but this is by no means certain. It does, however, establish that the artist was employed by Federigo II, Duke of Urbino. The Barberini panels have been presumed to have decorated the Palazzo Ducale; this is unlikely since the panels are not mentioned in any inventory or description of the palace. They have also been supposed, almost certainly incorrectly, to have formed part of a larger series dealing with the Life of the Virgin, but the *Presentation of the Virgin* panel includes subsidiary representations of the Annunciation and the Visitation, thereby eliminating these two crucial scenes from any hypothetical series. Alternatively, it has been suggested that one or both of the Barberini panels formed part of an altarpiece of the *Birth of the Virgin* commissioned in 1467 from FRA CARNEVALE for the church of S Maria della Bella in Urbino. Vasari mentioned the altarpiece in his life of Bramante, and it was later confiscated by Cardinal Antonio Barberini. Surprisingly, the identification has been dismissed, despite the fact that both panels are attributed to Fra Carnevale in a 1644 inventory of Barberini's possessions. Even more surprisingly, Zeri's identification of the Master of the Barberini Panels with Giovanni Angelo di Antonio da Camerino (*fl* 1451–61) has been widely accepted, despite the fact that Giovanni's activity as a painter is completely undocumented. Identifications of the anonymous master with Bramante and with Alberti have been rightly dismissed.

BIBLIOGRAPHY

R. Offner: 'The Barberini Panels and their Painter', *Mediaeval Studies in Memory of A. Kingsley Porter* (Cambridge, MA, 1939), pp. 205–53

F. Zeri: *Due dipinti, la filologia e un nome: Il Maestro delle Tavole Barberini* (Turin, 1961)

K. Christiansen: 'For Fra Carnevale', *Apollo*, cix (1979), pp. 198–201

Urbino e le Marche prima e dopo Raffaello (exh. cat., ed. M. G. Ciardi Duprè dal Poggetto and P. dal Poggetto; Urbino, Pal. Ducale, 1983), pp. 43–55

KEITH CHRISTIANSEN

Master of the Bardi St Francis (*fl* Florence, *c.* 1225–50). Italian painter. Garrison was the first to attribute a group of works to the author of the large panel on the altar of the Capella Bardi, Santa Croce, Florence, representing *St Francis and 20 Scenes from his Legend*. He included a *Crucifix* (Florence, Uffizi, 434) in this group and identified these paintings (previously thought to belong to the Lucca school) as Florentine in origin and showing signs of contact with the Bigallo Master. Prehn (1976) noted that two distinct painters worked on the *St Francis* panel, a fact that was more obvious after restoration, and that neither of them could be identified with the painter of the *Crucifix*. Boskovits, however, defined the principal Master of the Bardi St Francis as a precursor of Coppo di Marcovaldo, who, during the first half of the 13th century, moved away from the figurative tradition of painting in Lucca and developed a style characterized by the description of form through strongly marked patterns of light and dark. According to Boskovits, Coppo could have been one of the assistants who painted the scenes beneath the figure of the saint in the Santa Croce panel. The impressive painting of a *Virgin and Child Enthroned, with Scenes from the Virgin's Life* (Moscow, Pushkin Mus. F.A.) also has obvious stylistic and compositional affinities with the Santa Croce panel.

BIBLIOGRAPHY

E. B. Garrison: *Italian Romanesque Panel Painting: An Illustrated Index* (Florence, 1949), p. 12
C. L. Ragghianti: *Pittura del Dugento a Firenze* (Florence, 1955), pp. 36–40
E. T. Prehn: *A 13th Century Crucifix in the Uffizi and the Maestro del San Francesco Bardi* (Edinburgh, 1958)
M. Boskovits: *Cimabue e i precursori di Giotto: Affreschi, mosaici e tavole* (Florence, 1976)
E. T. Prehn: *Aspetti della pittura medioevale toscana* (Florence, 1976), pp. 39–55
A. Tartuferi: 'Pittura fiorentina del duecento', *La pittura in Italia: Le origini*, ed. E. Castelnuovo (Milan, 1985, rev. in 2 vols, 1986), pp. 267, 270–71

ANGELO TARTUFERI

Master of the Baroncelli Portraits (*fl* Bruges, *c.* 1489). South Netherlandish painter. He is named from double portraits (Florence, Uffizi), identified by Warburg in 1902 as *Pierantonio Bandini Baroncelli*, successor of Tommaso Portinari of the Medici bank in Bruges, and his wife *Maria Bonciani*. The Master was a contemporary of both the Master of the Legend of St Lucy and the Master of the Legend of St Ursula (i) and worked in a style close to that of Hans Memling and rather reminiscent of that of Petrus Christus. His manner is dry and rather austere, with static figures painted under harsh lighting. The rest of the Master's small oeuvre is grouped around this portrait pair and a *Female Saint (?Joan of Valois) with a Donor and Two Women* (U. London, Courtauld Inst. Gals). The donor in the latter may be Giacomo di Giovanni d'Antonio Loiani of Bologna, who married a Flemish woman. A panel with the *Annunciation* (Antwerp, Kon. Mus. S. Kst.), attributed by Hulin de Loo to the Master of the Baroncelli Portraits and comparable to a similar *Annunciation* (Brussels, Mus. Royaux A. & Hist.), has now been given to an anonymous master of *c.* 1500.

BIBLIOGRAPHY

Thieme–Becker
A. Warburg: 'Flandrische Kunst und florentinische Frührenaissance', *Jb. Kön.-Preuss. Kstsamml.*, xxiii (1902), pp. 247–66
G. Hulin de Loo and E. Michel: *Les Peintures primitives du XIVe, XVe et XVIe siècles de la collection Renders à Bruges* (Bruges, 1927)
P. Murray: *Catalogue of the Lee Collection: Courtauld Institute of Art, University of London* (London, 1958, rev. 1962), pp. 14–15
D. De Vos and J. Vervaet: 'Meester van de Baroncelli Portretten', *Anonieme Vlaamse primitieven* (exh. cat., Bruges, Groeningemus., 1969), pp. 56–7, 210–11
M. J. Friedländer: *Early Netherlandish* (1967–76), vi/1 (1971), p. 62; vi/2 (1971), p. 123
P. Vandenbroeck: *Catalogus schilderijen 14e en 15e eeuw*, Antwerp, Kon. Mus. S. Kst. cat. (Antwerp, 1985), pp. 12–14

HANS J. VAN MIEGROET

Bartholomew Master. *See* MASTER OF THE ST BARTHOLOMEW ALTAR below.

Master of the Beaufort Saints (*fl c.* 1400–10). Illuminator, active in the southern Netherlands. He is named after a series of remarkable miniatures with hagiographic scenes in the Beaufort Hours (London, BL, Royal MS. 2. A. XVIII), in which HERMAN SCHEERRE painted an *Annunciation*, accompanied by his motto. The Master of the Beaufort Saints also illuminated another Book of Hours with Scheerre (Oxford, Bodleian Lib., MS. lat. liturg. f.2), which suggests that they worked in the same workshop. His style is quite different from that of Scheerre, however, but it fits in directly with south Netherlandish miniature painting and also shows an affinity with the work of Melchior Broederlam. It seems likely, therefore, that the Master was of south Netherlandish origin. Apart from blue, red and pink, his lively palette includes contrasting colours, for example deep red and yellow or yellow and green. The compositions are dynamic, with powerful, divergent lines, and the faces are well modelled, usually with special accents on the nose and at the corners of the mouth. This style recurs in a number of manuscripts, including a Missal in Antwerp (Mus. Plantin–Moretus, MS. 15.8/192), a Book of Hours in London (BL, Add. MS. 18213; with Flemish rubrics), a Psalter in Le Mans (Bib. Mun., MS. B. 249) and a Book of Hours at Stonyhurst, Lancs (MS. 70). It was once thought that he visited England and illuminated Books of Hours for English patrons; however, more recent research has shown that he probably did not leave the Netherlands but that his miniatures were sent to England to be incorporated in manuscripts. Later, he worked with the GOLD SCROLLS GROUP (*see* below).

BIBLIOGRAPHY

B. Cardon: 'The Illustrations and the Gold Scrolls Group', *Typologische taferelen uit het leven van Jezus* [Typological scenes from the life of Jesus]: *A Manuscript from the Gold Scrolls Group (Bruges, c. 1440) in the Pierpont Morgan Library, New York, MS. Morgan 649*, Corpus van Verluchte Handschriften uit de Nederlanden [Corpus of illuminated manuscripts from the Low Countries], i (Leuven, 1985), pp. 157–61
——: *Vlaamse miniaturen voor van Eyck: Catalogus*, Corpus van Verluchte Handschriften uit de Nederlanden, vi (Leuven, 1993), pp. 40–48, nos 14, 15

BERT CARDON

Bedford Master [Master of the Bedford Hours; Master of the Breviary of the Duke of Bedford] (*fl c.* 1405–65). Illuminator or workshop of illuminators and painters active in France.

1. History of the attributions. 2. Workshop style and practice. 3. Localizing the workshop.

1. HISTORY OF THE ATTRIBUTIONS. The name was first proposed in 1914 by Winkler for the artist responsible for illuminating a Breviary and a Book of Hours for John of Lancaster, Duke of Bedford, English Regent in France from 1422 to 1435. The Book of Hours (London, BL, Add. MS. 18850) with portraits of the Duke and his wife, Anne of Burgundy, who were married in 1423, was presented to King Henry VI of England in 1430. The unfinished Bedford or, from its liturgical use, Salisbury Breviary (Paris, Bib. N., MS. lat. 17294) was begun *c.* 1424 (the start of the tables for computing Easter) and was still in progress in 1433, the year of the Duke's marriage to Jacquetta of Luxembourg, whose arms appear in the manuscript. These and a third manuscript, wrongly identified as a Pontifical (destr. 1871 but published in the mid-19th century, e.g. Vallet de Viriville, 1866), are all richly illuminated in a similar style and all bear or bore the Duke's arms, badges and mottoes.

Around these three manuscripts Durrieu (1904; 1905–29) assembled an earlier and a later group of illuminations in this style. The earlier group included miniatures in Jean, Duc de Berry's Grandes Heures, completed in 1409 (Paris, Bib. N., MS. lat. 919); the Térence des Ducs (Paris, Bib. Arsenal, MS. 664) owned by the Dauphin Louis, Duc de Guyenne, at his death in 1415; a Bible bought by John the Fearless, Duke of Burgundy, in 1415 (Brussels, Bib. Royale Albert 1er, MSS 9024–5); and the undated but related *Livre de chasse* by Gaston de Foix (Paris, Bib. N., MS. fr. 616). He associated these works with the painter Haincelin de Hagenau, recorded in Paris from 1403 to 1415 working for the Queen, Isabella of Bavaria, Philip the Bold, Duke of Burgundy, and Louis, Duc de Guyenne. The group of later works he associated with one Jean Haincelin, documented as an illuminator in Paris between 1448 and 1450. Winkler proposed a Master of the Duke of Bedford as an artist distinct from Durrieu's Haincelin de Hagenau and responsible only for the middle-period manuscripts, but as the name gained currency, receiving formal recognition in Ring's corpus of 15th-century French painting (1944), the limits of Winkler's definition became blurred.

The early group of manuscripts was attributed to a separate artist by Spencer, who, while stressing the collaborative nature of book illumination, used the identification of individual hands to divide the later oeuvre into different phases of a continuous workshop history. In her reconstruction, the Bedford Master himself was active *c.* 1415–30; his work is first discernible in the Breviary made for a Dauphin of France, probably Louis de Guyenne and thus pre-1415 (Châteauroux, Bib. Mun., MS. 2); he painted the best miniatures in the Bedford Hours, the related earlier Lamoignon Hours (Lisbon, Mus. Gulbenkian, MS. L.A. 237) and Vienna Hours (Vienna, Österreich. Nbib., Cod. 1855), the later Sobieski Hours (Windsor Castle, Royal Lib.) and the first phase of the Salisbury Breviary. He gradually gave way to his 'Chief Associate' who ran the workshop until its final productions, such as the *L'Arbre des batailles* (1460; Paris, Bib. N., MS. fr. 1276), the *Guerres puniques* (1457–61; Paris, Bib. Arsenal, MS. 5086) and the *Cas des nobles hommes et femmes* (1465; Chantilly, Mus. Condé, MS. 401).

Other scholars (e.g. Byrne) have accepted the idea of the 'Chief Associate' to cover the later work. The earliest group of manuscripts was examined by Meiss, who discerned an embodiment of the style from which the Bedford Master developed and so ascribed them to a 'Bedford Trend'. Their overall decoration has yet to be analysed to see if a more precise relationship can be established with the Bedford workshop of *c.* 1415–65. Attempts are thus being made to reconstruct the long history of the workshop responsible for the Bedford manuscripts, even though it is impossible to disentangle the work of a single Bedford Master from its finished products.

2. WORKSHOP STYLE AND PRACTICE. The distinctive style of the Bedford Hours (see fig. 1) and the major part of the Salisbury Breviary is that of a painter rather than a draughtsman. Forms are established through colour, line being used to reinforce or clarify where necessary, as in

1. Bedford Master: *Duke of Bedford before St George*; miniature from the Bedford Hours, 260×180 mm, *c.* 1423 (London, British Library, Add. MS. 18850, fol. 256*v*)

the small border medallions. Women, angels and youths are more elegant than the squatter male figures, which have wide faces and bulbous noses. Compositions are often highly complex, as with the multi-scene narratives of the Breviary, where careful design and colour patterning ensure that meaning is not submerged in anecdote (see fig. 2). Over the years, compositions were simplified and detail was eliminated, the loss in surface pattern not usually being counterbalanced by a gain in three-dimensional illusion. Execution became increasingly summary, so that what had been a careful layering and juxtaposition of paint degenerated into a blurry indistinctness. Colour moved from light, bright greens, blues and oranges to duller pink-reds and heavy combinations of brown and gold.

An examination of the subsidiary decoration of the Bedford Hours, the Salisbury Breviary and many other manuscripts with miniatures in the Bedford style shows that they are the products of a continuous workshop rather than a series of independent painters. The calligraphy of the borders allows for attributions to separate hands in a way not possible with the miniatures: the same border illuminator can be found in the Salisbury Breviary, the Missal of the Bishops of Paris (Paris, Bib. Arsenal, MS. 621) and the Sobieski Hours; another can be traced in later sections of the Salisbury Breviary, the Dunois Hours (London, BL, Yates Thompson MS. 3), the Coëtivy Hours (1443–4; Dublin, Chester Beatty Lib., MS. W. 82), an unfinished Bible (Paris, Bib. N., MSS fr. 20065–6) and

2. Bedford Master: *St Anne and the Three Marys*; miniature from the Salisbury Breviary, 255×175 mm, *c.* 1424 (Paris, Bibliothèque Nationale, MS. lat. 17294, fol. 518*r*)

other Books of Hours (e.g. Oxford, Keble Coll. Lib., MS. 39). The persistence of workshop patterns, particularly illustrations for the Hours of the Virgin, further supports the idea of a central workshop, where personnel might change but the stock of designs was carefully preserved. As an example, the mis-spelling *peur* for *puer natus est* on the angel's scroll in the *Annunciation to the Shepherds* is faithfully repeated from the Lamoignon to the Coëtivy Hours and in at least four other instances. Although the workshop produced at least one panel painting, the *Last Judgement* (Paris, Mus. A. Déc.), it seems to have excelled at illumination, exploiting to the full the illustrative potential of texts and the challenge of integrating word and image—both formally, as in the elimination of the borders to the miniatures in the Sobieski Hours, and in significance, as in the Salisbury Breviary border medallions, where each is based on a quotation from the text of the Office. Its artists also borrowed extensively from the Boucicaut Master and the de Limbourg brothers and from Netherlandish types originated by the Master of Flémalle, Rogier van der Weyden and Jan van Eyck.

Several distinct stylistic groups have been separated from the label of the Bedford Master: those of the Master of the Munich Golden Legend, the Master of Jean Rolin II and the Master of the Salisbury Breviary St Stephen. The Bedford workshop not only influenced such painters, with whom it shared commissions, but also provided the patterns of layout and compositions adopted by the Master of Jouvenal des Ursins and his circle. Through the Master of Jean Rolin II, if such an individual can be identified, the Bedford workshop is directly linked to Maître François, whose style dominated Parisian illumination into the last decade of the 15th century.

3. LOCALIZING THE WORKSHOP. The early manuscripts of the 'Bedford Trend' group seem to have been made in Paris, the trading centre for illuminated manuscripts and other luxuries. Throughout the history of the style, the Use of Paris overwhelmingly predominates in liturgical manuscripts, and, apart from the Duke of Bedford's commissions and a Book of Hours of Sarum Use (sold London, Sotheby's, 21 June 1988, lot 99), the workshop does not appear to have exploited the English market or to have had firm ties with any French provincial centre. While anyone might have turned to Paris for a book, the political divisions within France make the allegiance of its clients important evidence for the workshop's history. Unfortunately, the patrons of many manuscripts are unknown or uncertain, as is the case with the series of large Hours including the Vienna Hours and the Lamoignon Hours, both of which predate the Treaty of Troyes (1420), which made Paris the capital of English France. The Bedford Hours may have been begun for another, unidentified, patron, but its completion for the Duke and Duchess of Bedford and the Duke's commissioning of the Breviary and so-called Pontifical show the workshop's acceptance of English rule.

The workshop's decoration of the Missal of the Bishops of Paris, begun for Jacques du Châtelier, bishop from 1427 to 1438, when Paris was under English rule, and completed for the French-appointed Denis du Moulin (*reg* 1439–47), suggests that its artists remained in the capital and returned to French allegiance at the surrender of Paris in 1436. The workshop subsequently made Books of Hours for Bedford's military opponent Jean, Comte de Dunois (London, BL, Yates Thompson MS. 3), as well as Dunois's companion in arms, the Admiral Prigent DE COËTIVY (*c.* 1443–4; Dublin, Chester Beatty Lib., MS. W. 82).

The influence of Bedford workshop layouts and compositions has been noted to the south and west of Paris, particularly in Poitiers; if this influence is the result of direct contact, it was most likely during the extremely hard years of the later 1430s that the workshop was driven from the capital. If this was the case, the evidence of liturgical books *c.* 1440–60 and the Paris colophon of the *L'Arbre des batailles* of 1460 suggests that the illuminators returned to contribute to Paris's revival.

Several manuscripts were illuminated by the workshop over considerable periods: perhaps 15 years for the so-called Pontifical, 10 to 15 years for the Missal of the Bishops of Paris, some 20 years for the unfinished Bible (Paris, Bib. N., MSS fr. 20065–6) and approaching 40 years for the Salisbury Breviary. The considerable capital tied up in these undertakings suggests that the financer of the workshop was acting as a book producer rather than simply as an illuminator. It is perhaps in such a figure that a single Bedford Master could best be sought.

BIBLIOGRAPHY

G. de Bure: *Catalogue des livres de la bibliothèque de feu M. le duc de la Vallière*, 9 vols (Paris, 1783)

R. Gough: *An Account of a Rich Illuminated Missal Executed for John, Duke of Bedford* (London, 1794)

Vallet de Viriville: 'Notice de quelques manuscrits précieux', *Gaz. B.-A.*, xx (1866), pp. 255–85, 453–65; xxi (1866), pp. 471–87

P. Durrieu: *La Peinture à l'exposition des primitifs français* (Paris, 1904), pp. 72–3

A. Michel, ed.: *Histoire de l'art* (Paris, 1905–29), iii, pp. 165–6; iv, pp. 706–8 [articles by P. Durrieu]

F. Winkler: 'Zur Pariser Miniaturamalerei im dritten und vierten Jahrzehnt des 15. Jahrhundert', *Beitr. Forsch.: Stud. & Mitt. Antiqua. Jacques Rosenthal*, iv–v (1914), pp. 114–20

G. Ring: *A Century of French Painting* (London, 1944), nos 76–9

E. Trenkler: *Livre d'heures, Vienne, Österreichische Nationalbibliothek cod. 1855* (Vienna, 1948)

J. Porcher: *French Miniatures from Illuminated Manuscripts* (London, 1960), pp. 67–8

E. Spencer: 'L'Horloge de sapience', *Scriptorium*, xvii/2 (1963), pp. 607–12

K. Perls: 'Le Tableau de la famille des Juvenal des Ursins au Louvre: Le Maître du duc de Bedford et Haincelin de Hagenau', *Rev. A. Anc. & Mod.*, lxviii (1965), pp. 173–80

E. Spencer: 'Gerson, Ciboule and the Bedford Master's Shop', *Scriptorium*, xix/1 (1965), pp. 104–8

——: 'The Master of the Duke of Bedford: The Bedford Hours', *Burl. Mag.*, cvii (1965), pp. 495–502

——: 'The Master of the Duke of Bedford: The Salisbury Breviary', *Burl. Mag.*, cxix (1966), pp. 607–12

M. Meiss: *French Painting in the Time of Jean de Berry: The Late 14th Century and the Patronage of the Duke* (New York, 1967)

——: *French Painting in the Time of Jean de Berry: The Boucicaut Master* (New York, 1968)

A. von Eeuw and J. Plotzek: *Die Handschriften der Sammlung Ludwig* (Cologne, 1971–85), ii, pp. 103–14; iv, pp. 235–6

M. Meiss: *The de Lévis Hours* (New Haven, 1972)

D. Byrne: 'The Hours of Admiral Prigent de Coëtivy', *Scriptorium*, xxvii/2 (1974), pp. 248–61

M. Meiss: *French Painting in the Time of Jean de Berry: The Limbourgs and their Contemporaries* (New York, 1974), pp. 363–8

E. Spencer: *The Sobieski Hours: A Manuscript at Windsor Castle*, Roxburghe Club, 239 (London, 1977)

J. Backhouse: 'A Re-appraisal of the Bedford Hours', *BL J.*, vii (1981), pp. 47–61

E. König: *Die französische Buchmalerei um 1450: Der Jouvenal Maler, der Maler des Genfer Boccaccio und die Anfänge Jean Fouquets* (Berlin, 1982)

The Last Flowering: French Painting in Manuscripts 1420–1530 from American Collections (exh. cat. by J. Plummer, New York, Pierpont Morgan Lib., 1982)

J. Marrow: 'Miniatures inédites de Jean Fouquet: Les Heures de Simon de Varie', *Rev. A.*, lxvii (1985), pp. 7–35

C. de Hamel: *A History of Illuminated Manuscripts* (Oxford, 1986), pp. 173, 176, 178–9, 182

C. Reynolds: *The Salisbury Breviary, Paris, BN, MS. lat. 17294, and Some Related Manuscripts* (diss., U. London, 1986)

C. Sterling: *La Peinture médiévale à Paris, 1300–1500* (Paris, 1987), pp. 419–60

C. Reynolds and J. Stratford: 'Le Manuscrit dit "Le pontifical de Poitiers"', *Rev. A.*, lxxxiv (1989), pp. 61–80

J. Backhouse: *The Bedford Hours* (London, 1990)

CATHERINE REYNOLDS

Master of the Béguins [Maître aux Béguins] (*fl c.* 1650–70). Painter, active in Paris. The pictures now given to this artist were formerly attributed to the Le Nain brothers. In 1922 Jamot pointed out the differences of inspiration and style, compared with the work of the Le Nain, of a number of works now classed under this heading. It was left to Thuillier (see exh. cat.) to isolate a distinct artistic personality and body of work, which he collected under the name of the 'Maître aux Béguins', a reference to the type of peasant bonnet (*béguin*) worn by many of the female figures in these paintings. The 20 or so pictures attributed to this Master, which to judge by their often prestigious provenance were highly prized in the 17th century and the 18th, are almost all outdoor rustic genre scenes. They include *Peasants by a Drinking Trough* (versions Paris, Louvre; U. Glasgow, Hunterian A.G.), *Mother Nursing her Child during the Grape Harvest* (Cleveland, OH, Mus. A.), *Peasant Family with a Ram* (Princeton U., NJ, A. Mus.) and *Village Scene* (Moscow, Pushkin Mus. F.A.). The compositions of these works are somewhat repetitive: the figures are usually grouped before a fragment of rustic architecture, with a glimpse of landscape beyond. These backgrounds give little sense of depth or reality. The figures are scrupulously delineated, but their expressions are stereotyped. The greater emphasis is placed on the picturesque description of costume and accessories. The latter, composed of dishes, pots, baskets or fruit and vegetables, often form still-life compositions in the foregrounds. A painting of *Charity* (New York, Met.), with stylistic and formal affinities to the foregoing paintings inspired by the Le Nain, presents a different type of subject-matter, perhaps derived from a theatrical performance, since the male figure in this obscure scene has the air of a portrait. It would seem to indicate that this Master may have tackled a wider variety of subjects. The realism of the figural and still-life elements and the heaviness of the features of many of the figures suggest that the Master of the Béguins was a Flemish painter who took up the type of painting made fashionable by the Le Nain. Martin has identified him with Abraham Willemsens (*fl* 1627–72) by means of comparison with a signed genre scene (sold London, Christie's, 19 April 1991, lot 90).

BIBLIOGRAPHY

P. Jamot: 'Sur les frères Le Nain, II: Essai de classement de l'oeuvre des Le Nain', *Gaz. B.-A.*, n. s. 4, v (1922), pp. 293–308

Les Frères Le Nain (exh. cat. by J. Thuillier, Paris, Grand Pal., 1978), pp. 318–29, nos 69–77

L. G. Martin: 'The Maître aux Béguins: A Proposed Identification', *Apollo*, cxxxiii (1991), pp. 113–14

THIERRY BAJOU

Master of the Beheading of St John the Baptist (*fl* ?Milan, *c.* 1500–*c.* 1525). Italian engraver. Galichon first assembled the small oeuvre of this Master by attributing five engravings, previously ascribed to several different printmakers, to the author of the *Beheading of St John the Baptist*. Four of these engravings form a clearly unified group and are certainly the work of one hand.

Little of substance is known about the Master, although his connections with Milanese art are evident, making it reasonable to assume that he was active in Milan. The most ambitious of his engravings, *Allegorical Theme: Combat of Animals*, is related to a pen drawing of *Animals Fighting and a Man with a Burning Glass* (Paris, Louvre) by Leonardo da Vinci, which is assignable to the first of Leonardo's two Milanese periods (*c.* 1483–99), probably to the early 1490s. The portions of the engraving that are not based directly on the Louvre drawing are related to other works by Leonardo. Scholars have also noted that the figure and drapery style of the *Beheading of St John the Baptist* are comparable to works by Marco d'Oggiono, one of Leonardo's Milanese followers, although the other engravings by the Master are not as close to d'Oggiono's style.

The Master's manner of engraving reflects the stippling technique developed by Giulio Campagnola to achieve a soft, tonal quality in his prints, evident in his *Doe Resting* and *Stag Browsing*. It has been proposed that the Master was also influenced by Andrea Mantegna and that he was responsible for two engravings of the *Man of Sorrows* and *Hercules and the Hydra* now assigned to Mantegna's school, although these attributions have been disputed.

BIBLIOGRAPHY

E. Galichon: 'De quelques estampes milanaises', *Gaz. B.-A.*, xviii (1865), pp. 546–52
A. M. Hind: *Early Italian Engraving: A Critical Catalogue* (London, 1938–48), v, pp. 97–9
J. A. Levenson, K. Oberhuber and J. L. Sheehan: *Early Italian Engravings from the National Gallery of Art* (Washington, DC, 1973), pp. 437–8
M. J. Zucker: *The Early Italian Masters, Commentary (1984)*, 25 [XIII/ii] of *The Illustrated Bartsch*, ed. W. Strauss (New York, 1978–), pp. 108–10, 123–4

JAY A. LEVENSON

Bellaert Master. *See* MASTER OF JACOB BELLAERT below.

Master of the Berlin Passion (*fl* late 15th century). German or Netherlandish engraver. He was named (Lehrs, 1889) after a *Passion* cycle of nine engravings, of which seven were glued in a manuscript (1482; Berlin, Kupferstichkab.) from the Lower Rhine, written in the convent of the Sisters of the Common Life at Arnheim. His long-standing identification (Geisberg, 1903) as Israhel van Meckenem (i) (*see* MECKENEM, (1)) has been questioned by the claims that his centre of activity was the Limbourg area (Marrow, 1978) and that he was Dutch, not German (Hollstein: *Dut. & Flem.*; Robels in 1970 exh. cat.).

To the 117 engravings attributed to the Master (see Lehrs, 1915; Hollstein: *Dut. & Flem.*) should be added the *Mass of St Gregory* (*c.* 1465; Lehrs, 1934, no. 346) and *St Barbara* (Lehrs, 1934, no. 388), both previously attributed to Israhel van Meckenem (ii). The Master's early cycle of the *Life of Christ* (L 14–25) was copied many times, proving the popularity that the engraver enjoyed. The *Hortus conclusus* (L 37), the Master's largest surviving engraving, together with the animal figures and decorative engravings (L 82–117) created to serve as models in the workshops of painters, miniaturists and goldsmiths, forms part of the artist's late work; he had by this stage reached the climax of a technique that also links him in part to the Master of the Playing Cards.

The Master of the Berlin Passion's role in the region of the Lower Rhine was comparable to that of the Master E.S., and his works were copied by engravers who were perhaps members of the same shop—the Master with the Flower Borders, the Master of St Erasmus, the Master of the Dutuit Mount of Olives and the Master of the Martyrdom of the Ten Thousand (all of whom *fl* mid-15th century)—as well as by the Master with the Banderoles and Israhel van Meckenem (ii). His draughtsmanship is of a quality lower than that of the Master E.S., but the modelling is extremely delicate, and his skill as a goldsmith is evident in the decoration in his ornamental works, among the earliest of their kind. His engravings, often of modest dimensions and hand-coloured, were certainly intended for the most part to be affixed in manuscripts.

BIBLIOGRAPHY

Hollstein: *Dut. & Flem.*; Hollstein; *Ger.*; Thieme–Becker
M. Lehrs: 'Der deutsche und niederländische Kupferstich des fünfzehnten Jahrhunderts in den kleineren Sammlungen', *Repert. Kstwiss.*, xi (1889), pt I, pp. 47–56; pt II, pp. 213–39
M. Geisberg: *Der Meister der Berliner Passion und Israhel van Meckenem: Studien zur Geschichte der westfälischen Kupferstecher im 15. Jahrhundert*, xlii of Studien zur deutschen Kunstgeschichte (Strasbourg, 1903/R Nendeln, Liechtenstein, 1979)
M. Lehrs: *Geschichte und kritischer Katalog des deutschen, niederländischen und französischen Kupferstichs im 15. Jahrhundert*, iii (Vienna, 1915) [L]; ix (Vienna, 1934)
Herbst des Mittelalters: Spätgotik in Köln und am Niederrhein (exh. cat., Cologne, Kstver., 1970), pp. 144–50, nos 336–67 [entries by H. Robels]
J. Marrow: 'A Book of Hours from the Circle of the Master of the Berlin Passion: Notes on the Relationship between Fifteenth-century Manuscript Illumination and Printmaking in the Rhenish Lowlands', *A. Bull.*, lx/4 (1978), pp. 590–616

BÉATRICE HERNAD

Master of the Berlin St Jerome. *See under* GASPARO PADOVANO.

Master of the Berlin Sketchbook (*fl* second quarter of the 16th century). Painter and draughtsman, active in the northern Netherlands and Germany. He takes his name from an unpublished sketchbook of 48 folios (Berlin, Kupferstichkab., 75C 2a/119), which can be dated *c.* 1523–6 on the basis of inscriptions and sketches recording two dated paintings by Jacob Cornelisz. van Oostsanen. Jacob's panels, the *Virgin and Child* (1526; Stuttgart, Staatsgal.) and the *All Saints* (1523; Kassel, Schloss Wilhelmshöhe), are copied with a degree of care that suggests that the artist of the sketchbook, presumably an assistant in Jacob's Amsterdam studio, produced it as a means of preserving motifs and compositions by his master.

The Master's idiosyncratic style is characterized by nervous lines and dainty forms. The figures have egg-shaped faces, as befits the inheritor of the tradition of Geertgen tot Sint Jans and Jacob Cornelisz. Their features are tiny, and the fluttering hands are impossibly small, even for these ethereal bodies. Heads tilt at a slight angle, creating a wistful expression and making the start of the S-curve that dominates their pose. These and other stylistic features enable other works to be attributed to the Master, among them an *Annunciation* (Indianapolis, IN, Mus. A.) and the *Portrait of a Scholar* (Antwerp, Kon. Mus. S. Kst.). Three other panels once formed a tiny Marian triptych: the *Coronation of the Virgin* (ex-Sotheby Mak van Waay, Amsterdam), which would have been flanked by the *Virgin on the Crescent Moon* (Strasbourg, Mus. B.-A.) and the *Virgin and Child with St Anne* (ex-David Carritt, London).

All the paintings assigned to the Master are executed on pine, a type of wood not used in the Netherlands in the early 16th century but popular in Germany. This support suggests that the Master returned or moved to a German city on leaving Jacob's studio. The delicacy and precision of his style points to either Cologne or the Lower Rhine as his Teutonic home. His art, which spans the transition from a Late Gothic aesthetic to early Mannerism, also helps to establish artistic links between Germany and the Netherlands in the 16th century.

BIBLIOGRAPHY

K. Steinbart: 'Nachlese im Werk des Jacob Cornelisz. von Amsterdam', *Marburg. Jb. Kstwiss.*, v (1929), pp. 213–60 [repr. of those fols that copy Jacob's works]

J. L. Carroll: *The Paintings of Jacob Cornelisz. van Oostsanen, 1472?–1533* (diss., Chapel Hill, U. NC, 1986)

JANE L. CARROLL

Berner Nelkenmeister. *See* CARNATION MASTERS below.

Master of the Berne St John Altarpiece. *See under* CARNATION MASTERS below.

Master of the Berry Apocalypse [Apocalypse Master] (*fl c.* 1408–20). French illuminator. He is named after an Apocalypse in French (New York, Pierpont Morgan Lib., MS. M. 133), his finest work. The manuscript belonged to Jean, Duc de Berry, as shown by his *ex libris* on fol. 87*v*, but it does not appear in any of the inventories of the ducal library. Jean de Berry may have been the first owner of the manuscript, which was probably begun shortly before his death, in 1414 or 1415. It comprises a cycle of 83 illustrations, each framed by a scene from the Life of St John against a red background. The size of the miniatures varies from half a page, with the text in two columns beneath, to full-page pictures with no text. As in the second Apocalypse of the so-called Master of the Medallion of similar date (Chantilly, Mus. Condé, MS. 28; see Meiss), the sequence of illustrations largely departs from older models.

The Master's technique differs from that of contemporary Parisian illuminators. The drawing has a more spontaneous effect and is usually animated only by a wash tint, with a restrained palette of magenta, brown and green. In his later works the highlights in the landscape backgrounds are often executed in gold. In addition to this manuscript, Jean de Berry acquired in 1413 a copy of *Le Brut d'Angleterre* (Paris, Bib. N., MS. fr. 1454), also illuminated by the Apocalypse Master. The only dated manuscript (1416) with miniatures by the Master is a fragment, comprising 33 folios, of a *Trésor des histoires* (Paris, Bib. N., MS. nouv. acq. fr. 14285).

BIBLIOGRAPHY
C. A. J. Nordenfalk: *Kung praktiks och drottning teoris jaktbok: Le Livre des déduis du roi Modus et de la reine Ratio* (Stockholm, 1955), pp. 61, 94
M. Meiss: *French Painting in the Time of Jean de Berry: The Limbourgs and their Contemporaries* (New York, 1974), pp. 252, 256, 298, 342, 368ff [with worklist]

GABRIELE BARTZ

Master of Berry's Cleres Femmes (*fl* 1403–15). Name associated with a south Netherlandish or German workshop of illuminators, active in Paris. The name was coined by Meiss (1967) after the 109 miniatures in a manuscript of Boccaccio's *De mulieribus claris* in French translation, *Des Cleres et Nobles Femmes*, or, more accurately, *Des Femmes nobles et renommées* (1404; Paris, Bib. N., MS. fr. 598; see fig.); this is a refinement of Martens's classification, the 'Master of 1402', which included other illuminators (*see* MASTER OF THE CORONATION OF THE VIRGIN below), all seemingly affiliated with the Paris-based publisher Jacques Rapondi. The Paris manuscript is a copy of another (1403; Paris, Bib. N., MS. fr. 12420), produced for Philip the Bold, Duke of Burgundy, and the former was presented to Jean, Duc de Berry, by Jean de la Barre, a tax official. Three principal individuals may be

Master of Berry's Cleres Femmes: *Thamyris, the Daughter of Mikon, Painting the Virgin and Child*, 75×65 mm; miniature from Boccaccio: *Des Cleres et Nobles Femmes*, 360×250 mm, 1404 (Paris, Bibliothèque Nationale, MS. fr. 598, fol. 86)

identified within the Master of Berry's Cleres Femmes workshop. Manuscripts attributed to the workshop include: a copy of Livy's *Histoire romaine* (*c.* 1405; Geneva, Bib. Pub. & U., MS. 77), a *Lancelot du lac* (*c.* 1404; Paris, Bib. N., MSS fr. 117–20; for illustration *see* ROMANCE, MANUSCRIPT), a second *Lancelot* and a *Bible historiale* (1405–6; Paris, Bib. Arsenal, MSS 3479–80 and 5057–8, respectively) and another *Des Femmes nobles et renommées* (*c.* 1410; Brussels, Bib. Royale Albert 1er, MS. 9509). The style of the workshop can be traced until *c.* 1415 in such manuscripts as a *Bible historiale* (Brussels, Bib. Royale Albert 1er, MSS 9024–5) and a Book of Hours (Baltimore, MD, Walters A.G., MS. W. 265). Although adapted to Parisian patronage, these works reflect the Northern taste for stubby, gesturing figures; backgrounds are shallow with little interest in foreshortening.

BIBLIOGRAPHY
B. Martens: *Meister Francke* (Hamburg, 1929)
M. Meiss: *French Painting in the Time of Jean de Berry: The Late XIV Century and the Patronage of the Duke*, 2 vols (London, 1967, rev. 1969)
——: *French Painting in the Time of Jean de Berry: The Boucicaut Master* (London, 1968)
——: *French Painting in the Time of Jean de Berry: The Limbourgs and their Contemporaries*, 2 vols (New York, 1974)

P. M. de Winter: *La Bibliothèque de Philippe le Hardi, duc de Bourgogne (1364–1404): Etude sur les manuscrits à peintures d'une collection princière à l'époque du 'Style Gothique International'* (Paris, 1985)

PATRICK M. DE WINTER

Berswordt Master (*fl c.* 1400–*c.* 1435). German painter. He is named after a *Crucifixion* triptych (1431; Dortmund, Marienkirche) that bears the coat of arms of the local patrician family of Berswordt and appears to have been part of an endowment made in 1431 by the family for their newly acquired chapel. An investiture document of 1437 mentions the 'newly erected altar of the Holy Cross'. The wings show *Christ Carrying the Cross* and the *Deposition*, with the *Annunciation* on the reverse sides. All altarpieces by the eclectic Berswordt Master reflect designs from other workshops, mainly those of Master Bertram and Conrad von Soest. These are assimilated, however, into a personal style with the usually generalized forms of his sharp-nosed protagonists showing broad, rapid brushstrokes.

The Bielefeld Altarpiece (?1400; central panel, Bielefeld, Neustädter Marienkirche) has also been attributed to the Master from surface characteristics and underdrawing style, although the uneven artistic quality suggests inexperience or workshop participation. The frame (untraced) was inscribed with the date 1400. The altarpiece features a central *sacra conversazione*, flanked by 12 scenes from the *Childhood and Passion of Christ*. The wings each showed nine scenes from the cycle (Berlin, Gemäldegal.; Oxford, Ashmolean; New York, Met.; priv. cols). Recent examination by infra-red photography revealed that the *St Nicholas* panel (*c.* 1410–20; Soest, Nikolaikapelle), formerly attributed to Conrad von Soest, derives from the same workshop.

BIBLIOGRAPHY

F. Jacobs: 'Der Meister des Berswordt-Altares', cxvii of *Göppinger akademische Beiträge* (diss., U. Münster; Göppingen, 1983)
B. Corley: *Conrad von Soest: His Altarpieces, his Workshop and his Place in European Art* (diss., U. London, Courtauld Inst. and Birkbeck Coll., 1991) [incl. infra-red reflectograms and cat. entry for the altarpieces]
——: *Conrad von Soest, Painter among Merchant Princes* (London, 1996)

BRIGITTE CORLEY

Biadaiolo Master (*fl* Florence, *c.* 1325–35). Italian illuminator and painter. He is named from the manuscript known as Il Biadaiolo (Florence, Bib. Medicea-Laurenziana, MS. Tempi 3), which contains nine miniatures, all attributed to him. The text, written by Domenico Lenzi and entitled *Specchio umano*, documents grain prices and the resulting human consequences for the years 1320 to 1335 in Florence. The *biadaiolo*, or grain merchant, was an effective witness to this period, which was one of both prosperity and hardship; it was also chronicled by Giovanni Villani (*c.* 1275–1348). The moralistic overtones of Lenzi's text are complemented in the miniatures by the depiction of angels and demons, signs that man has little control over events but must react appropriately to them. The Master records the events with much topical detail, and particular care is taken to portray accurately such scenes as the open-air grain market in Piazza Orsanmichele (fol. 79*r*) and the skylines of Siena and Florence (fols 57*v*–58*r*). This pictorial precision, with the Master's narrative abilities, makes the scenes instructive yet charming. Two paintings are also attributed to the Master: a gabled panel with five scenes (the *Virgin and Child with Saints*, the *Glorification of St Thomas Aquinas*, the *Nativity*, *Crucifixion* and *Last Judgement*; 590×428 mm; New York, Met.) and a damaged tabernacle with, on the central panel, the *Virgin and Child with Four Saints and Angels* (ex-Joseph Lindon Smith priv. col., New York, see Offner and Steinweg, section III/ii/1, pl. XX). Offner considered the Biadaiolo Master to be a product of the 'miniaturist' tendency that was fostered by the workshop of PACINO DI BONAGUIDA, and he noted the closeness of the Master's style to that of the MASTER OF THE DOMINICAN EFFIGIES (*see* below). Boskovits (Offner and Steinweg, III/ix), however, concluded that the works attributed to the Biadaiolo Master, datable to *c.* 1325–35, should be considered instead as the early production of the Master of the Dominican Effigies, whose documented career spans the period *c.* 1328–50.

BIBLIOGRAPHY

R. Offner and K. Steinweg: *Corpus* (1930–79) [section III/ix by M. Boskovits]
G. Muzziolo: *Mostra storica nazionale della miniatura* (Florence, 1954)
D. Robb: *The Art of the Illuminated Manuscript* (Philadelphia, 1973)
L. Miglio: 'Per una datazione del Biadaiolo fiorentino', *La Bibliofilia*, lxxvii (1975), pp. 1–36
G. Pinto: *Il libro del Biadaiolo* (Florence, 1978)
S. Partsch: *Profane Buchmalerei der bürgerlichen Gesellschaft im spätmittelalterlichen Florenz* (Worms, 1981)

DOMENICO G. FIRMANI

Master of Bielke (*fl c.* 1611–32). Swedish painter. His name is derived from his portraits of *Niels Bielke of Åkerö* (1614; Stockholm, Skokloster Slott) and his children *Thure Bielke* and *Sigrid Bielke* (both *c.* 1622 or earlier). An earlier, full-figure portrait of *Karl IX, King of Sweden* (*c.* 1605–11; Romrod, Schloss) shows traces of the Master's style. With his retardataire manner, in the style of *c.* 1500, the Master of Bielke is closely related to the Master of Bysta (*fl c.* 1610–20), but in comparison with the latter's sober, simple work, the Master of Bielke's pictures are mannered and stylized. Together they are considered the most interesting Swedish portrait painters of the early 17th century, and there is strong reason to believe that one of them, probably the Master of Bielke, can be identified as the Swedish court painter Holger (Holgerdt) Hansson (*b* before 1570; *d* 1624), who is known to have worked for Niels Bielke (1569–1639). In 1622 Hansson received orders for interiors and portraits for the royal apartments in the Kungliga Slott in Stockholm; the portraits, which included *Duke John and his Consort* and *Gunilla Bielke* (both ?1624), have not survived, and no other portraits were signed by Hansson. Although the Master of Bielke was prolific, no further work can be identified today except a portrait etching of *Gustav II Adolf, King of Sweden* (1618; Strömbom, fig. 160) in a church Bible.

BIBLIOGRAPHY
SVKL
S. Strömbom: *Svenska kungliga porträtt i svenska porträttarkivets samlingar* [Swedish court portraits in Swedish portrait collections], i (Stockholm, 1943)

MARTA GALICKI

Bigallo Master (*fl* Florence, *c.* 1225–55). Italian painter. Offner reconstructed the career of the painter of the Bigallo *Crucifix* (*c.* 1225–30; Florence, Mus. Bigallo), whose work shows the moderate plasticity and warm tones typical of much Florentine 13th-century painting. Certain stylistic features of the Bigallo *Crucifix* are similar to those found in the work of Berlinghiero Berlinghieri from Lucca, although perhaps too much attention has been paid to this. The painter's ability to keep up with developments in contemporary painting is shown by the reflection of Giunta Pisano's expressionism in another *Crucifix* (*c.* 1230–40; Chicago, IL, A. Inst.). The measured composition and breadth of plan in the dossal of *St Zenobius*, with four scenes from his life (Florence, Mus. Opera Duomo), demonstrates the Master's competence as a narrative painter. Another painting attributed as a late work, a beautiful painted *Crucifix* (*c.* 1240s; Rome, Pal. Barberini), documents the links between the Bigallo Master and contemporary painting in Umbria and Lazio (see, for example, Marcucci).

BIBLIOGRAPHY

R. Offner: 'The mostra del tesoro di Firenze sacra: I', *Burl. Mag.*, lxiii (1933), p. 76

E. B. Garrison: *Italian Romanesque Panel Painting: An Illustrated Index* (Florence, 1949), pp. 12–13

C. L. Ragghianti: *Pittura del duecento a Firenze* (Florence, 1955), pp. 11–12

L. Marcucci: *Gallerie nazionali di Firenze: I dipinti toscani del secolo XIII* (Rome, 1958), pp. 25–7

A. Tartuferi: *La pittura a Firenze nel duecento* (Florence, 1990), pp. 13–15, 71–2

ANGELO TARTUFERI

Master of the Birago Hours (*fl c.* 1465). Italian illuminator. He was recognized by Alexander and De La Mare as the illuminator of a Book of Hours formerly in the Abbey Collection (MS. J.A. 6960) that bears the coat of arms of the Birago family. He illuminated all the pages of the manuscript except for folio 125*r*, which is attributed to Belbello da Pavia. The Master's hand is also clearly recognizable in some pages of another Book of Hours (Paris, Bib. N., MS. fond. Smith-Lesouëf 22) and in a manuscript containing a treatise by the jurist Girolamo Mangiaria, *Opusculum de impedimentis matrimonii ratione consanguinitatis et affinitatis* (Paris, Bib. N., MS. Lat. 4586), which was read at Pavia University in 1465. The frontispiece (fol. 1*r*) depicts Galeazzo Maria Sforza, Duke of Milan, to whom the manuscript is dedicated, receiving the book from the author. In both the Birago and the Smith-Lesouëf Hours the Master collaborated with BELBELLO DA PAVIA, and he may have been trained in Belbello's workshop. This would explain the accentuated expressiveness of some of his figures, the strong and brilliant colouring and, above all, the use of certain decorative motifs, such as branches of leaves and flowers against a gold background, which is typical of Belbello and his workshop.

BIBLIOGRAPHY

G. Swarzenski and R. Schilling: *Die illuminierten Handschriften und Einzelminiaturen des Mittelalters und der Renaissance in Frankfurter Besitz* (Frankfurt am Main, 1929), pp. 247–8

J. J. G. Alexander and A. C. De La Mare: *The Italian Manuscripts in the Library of Major J. R. Abbey* (London, 1969), pp. 147–50

F. Avril: *Dix siècles d'enluminure italienne* (Paris, 1984), p. 156

E. Kirsch: *Five Illuminated Manuscripts of Gian Galeazzo Visconti* (Philadelphia, PA, 1991), p. 100

MILVIA BOLLATI

Master of the Boccaccio Illustrations (*fl c.* 1470–90). South Netherlandish engraver. The name was given by Passavant to the anonymous engraver of nine illustrations in a French translation of Boccaccio, *De La Ruine des nobles hommes et femmes*, published by Colard Mansion (Bruges, 1476). This is the earliest surviving printed book to be illustrated with pasted-in engravings; of the few extant copies, the most complete, which contains eight hand-coloured prints, is in Boston, MA (Mus. F.A.). It is now clear that the nine illustrations are by different hands: Passavant, no. 5/Lehrs, no. 4, P 6/L 5, P 8/L 7–8 and possibly P 10/L 10 can be attributed to the illuminator known as the MASTER OF THE DRESDEN PRAYERBOOK (*see* below); P 3/L 2, P 7/L 6 and P 9/L 9 can be attributed to the Master of the White Inscriptions. The latter probably also executed P 4/L 3, which is a copy after the fragmentary print in the Bibliothèque Nationale in Paris, formerly attributed to the Housebook Master.

BIBLIOGRAPHY

Hollstein: *Dut. & Flem.*

J. D. Passavant: *Le Peintre-graveur* (Leipzig, 1860–64), ii, pp. 3–10, 250 [P]

M. Lehrs: *Geschichte und kritischer Katalog des deutschen, niederländischen und französischen Kupferstichs im XV. Jahrhundert* (Vienna, 1908–34), iv, pp. 165–87; vii, pp. 390–400 [L]

F. Anzelewsky: 'Die drei Boccaccio-Stiche von 1476 und ihre Meister', *Festschrift Friedrich Winkler* (Berlin, 1959), pp. 114–25

Livelier than Life: The Master of the Amsterdam Cabinet or the Housebook Master (exh. cat., ed. J. P. Filedt Kok; Amsterdam, Rijksmus., 1985), pp. 191–2 [incl. bibliog.]

J. P. FILEDT KOK

Master of Boethius BN fr. 809. *See under* MASTER OF JOUVENEL DES URSINS below.

Master of the Boqueteaux [Master of the Jean de Sy Bible; Master of the Umbrella-trees] (*fl c.* 1350–80). French illuminator or group of illuminators. The name was first used by Martin, who identified the work of a single workshop in a number of Parisian manuscripts of the second half of the 14th century. The leading master was so-named after the little groups of trees, or copses (*boqueteaux*), with umbrella tops, that characterize the work of this school. Although the precise division of labour within the group is controversial, the manuscripts forming the main core of work attributable to a leading master, perhaps to more than one, have been established. Some more recent critics, however, have preferred the designation Master of the Jean de Sy Bible, considering that the characteristic tree motif was first introduced by the Remède de Fortune Master *c.* 1350 and quickly adopted by other Parisian illuminators.

The 'Boqueteaux' style is identifiable early on in a large two-volume *Bible historiale* (London, BL, Royal MS. 17. E. VII), the text of which is dated 1357, and in the early unfinished sketches of the Bible translated by Jean de Sy (Paris, Bib. N., MS. fr. 15397), which was commissioned by King John II but probably not illustrated until the early 1360s. The other works of this group include a dated Bible (1368; Berlin, Staatsbib. Preuss. Kultbes., MS. Phillipps 1906), the two tinted drawings at the beginning of the works of Guillaume de Machaut (Paris, Bib. N., MS. fr. 1584), a *Bible historiale*, presented to Charles V in 1372 (The Hague, Rijksmus. Meermanno-Westreenianum, MS. 10. B. 23), the first volume of another *Bible historiale* (Paris, Bib. Arsenal, MS. 5212), part of the Grandes Heures of Philip the Bold, Duke of Burgundy (1376–7;

vol. 1: Cambridge, Fitzwilliam, MS. 3–1954; Brussels, Bib. Royale Albert 1er, MSS 11035–7; vol. 2: Brussels, Bib. Royale Albert 1er, MS. 13092), the *Songe du verger* (1378; London, BL, Royal MS. 19 C. IV) and a copy of St Augustine's *City of God* (London, BL, Add. MS. 15244). The style of these manuscripts shows a move away from the still prevalent courtly influence of Jean Pucelle towards a greater realism, particularly in the representation of nature and landscape. Animals, birds and flowers abound, as well as the characteristic clumps of umbrella-trees. Figures are small and squat, lively and natural in their attitudes; they do not dominate the landscape but are set into it. A striking feature of these works is the peculiarly vigorous and dramatic narrative style. The miniatures are often executed in semi-grisaille, which became popular at this time.

The 'Boqueteaux' style gave a new impetus to Parisian manuscript illumination, spreading over much of northern France. The Master's workshop became the most productive in Paris during the reign of Charles V (*see* VALOIS, (2)) and often provided work for the King, sometimes in collaboration with the Master of the Coronation Book of Charles V (*see also* GUILLAUME DE MACHAUT). Many more manuscripts can be associated with the 'Boqueteaux' style, but most are of lower artistic quality; later manuscripts in the group show a decline in vigour and an increasingly repetitive style. In all, perhaps as many as 12 illuminators contributed to this workshop. The identification of the principal illuminator as JAN BOUDOLF, who signed the frontispiece of the Hague Bible, has been disputed.

BIBLIOGRAPHY

H. M. R. Martin: *La Miniature française du XIIIe au XVe siècle* (Paris, 1923), pp. 44–54
E. Panofsky: *Early Netherlandish Painting: Its Origins and Character*, i (Cambridge, MA, 1953), pp. 36–41; rev. L. M. J. Delaissé in *Scriptorium*, xi (1957), pp. 109–18
M. Meiss: *French Painting in the Time of Jean de Berry: The Late Fourteenth Century and the Patronage of the Duke* (London, 1967), pp. 20–23, 96, 162, 181, 198, 287–8, 388
P. M. de Winter: 'The Grandes Heures of Philip the Bold, Duke of Burgundy: The Copyist Jean L'Avenant and his Patrons at the French Court', *Speculum*, lvii/4 (1982), pp. 786–842
C. Sterling: *La Peinture médiévale à Paris, 1300–1500* (Paris, 1987)

Border Limner. *See* PHILLIPS, AMMI.

Master of Borsjö (*fl c.* 1625–7). Sculptor, active in Sweden. The name derives from a group of works associated with Borsjö Manor House in Skåne, southern Sweden (under Danish rule in the 17th century). The latest work in this group is a sandstone and limestone pulpit dated 1626. Stylistically this pulpit is close to two earlier pulpits produced in Skåne, one for Lund Cathedral by Johannes Ganssog (1592) and the other, dated 1599, by Daniel Thommisen (*d* 1603), in the church of St Peter, Malmö. All three make use of north German Renaissance ornament, and their similar relief compositions are reminiscent of the work of Hans van Steenwinckel the younger. The assured solution of technical and spatial problems in the Borsjö pulpit, however, suggests an original hand. Various works originally at Borsjö or associated with its owners, the Marsvin family, follow the style of the pulpit. These include a relief of the *Crucifixion* (1627; Sofvestad

Church), an oak relief of the *Last Supper* (Borsjö Chapel), a series of 12 oak pew ends depicting *Christ and the Apostles* (Lund U., Kstmus.; formerly Balkåkra Church), the pulpit at Sjörup parish church (formerly at Borsjö) and the monument to *Frederik Ulfeld and his Family*, originally in Borsjö old parish church (now Balkåkra Church). This carved and painted oak monument, displaying the deceased (*d* 1622) and his children kneeling before a triumphal arch, is enhanced by an elaborate, scrolling, Baroque frame decorated with the evangelists, putti and reliefs of the *Crucifixion* and the *Resurrection*. It is signed A.S., the only clue to the sculptor's identity.

BIBLIOGRAPHY

O. Rydbeck: *Två märkliga konstnärer: Adam van Düren och Mästaren med signaturen A.S.* [Two remarkable artists: Adam van Düren and the Master with the signature A.S.] (Stockholm, 1918), pp. 77–141

ANTONIA BOSTRÖM

Boucicaut Master (*fl c.* 1390–1430). Illuminator, active in Paris. The anonymous artist known as the Boucicaut Master is named after his work in the Book of Hours of Paris Use (274×190 mm; Paris, Mus. Jacquemart-André, MS. 2; see MANUSCRIPT, colour pl. IV), which was commissioned by Jean II le Meingre de Boucicaut, Marshal (*maréchal*) of France (1365–1421).

1. Book of Hours of Maréchal de Boucicaut. 2. Related works. 3. Influence.

1. BOOK OF HOURS OF MARÉCHAL DE BOUCICAUT. After the death of Maréchal de Boucicaut the manuscript passed to his brother Geoffroy, who left it in 1430 to his son Jean III le Meingre. The last-named had folios 240–42 added, which include two miniatures attributed to PIERRE VILLATE. After Jean III le Meingre's death (1490), the manuscript was owned by Aymar de Poitiers, who had most of the arms and mottoes of the Marshal replaced with his own. The Book of Hours can be dated after 1401, when Boucicaut went to Genoa as French governor. It includes a suffrage to St Bridget of Sweden, whose cult was popular in Italy but not in the kingdom of France because of her enmity towards the French crown. Furthermore, the youngest king in the *Adoration of the Magi* (fol. 83*v*) is, unusually, dressed in black and wears a chain closely resembling the *bâton noueux* chosen in 1403 by Louis d'Orléans as the device for the anti-Burgundian party. This implies that at least parts of the manuscript were completed after the murder of Louis d'Orléans on 23 November 1407.

Some of the requirements of the patron set the Boucicaut Hours apart from most other Books of Hours produced for princely or royal patrons. The suffrages are placed at the beginning instead of the end of the manuscript; the saints are not ordered according to the litany but have a strong biographical emphasis; and the full-page miniatures of standing saints are unique for their time. The artistic innovations, however, in both the decoration and illustration, are the most notable features of the manuscript. The miniatures of the Boucicaut Hours, all full-page, are remarkable for the interest shown in perspective and light, and Panofsky noted their importance for the origins of early Netherlandish painting. The handling of the figures is more conventional; the faces are stereotyped, with eyes, mouths and noses often registered only with grey brushstrokes; similarly, the modelling of flesh is generally rather minimal, as for example in the *Martyrdom of St Lawrence* (fol. 20*v*). The strength of the Boucicaut Master lies in the depiction of architecture with an empirical perspective that achieves astonishing spatial effects. Often the scene is framed by an arch that is not logically connected to the rest of the architecture, thus distancing the onlooker from the sacred event or subject. The landscape elements inserted in the foreground of the outdoor scenes have a similar function. There are also significant achievements in the depiction of landscape. The middle ground (often depicting a lake with swans on it) becomes paler in colour and more blurred as it leads into the background, in which diminutive figures are sometimes set. The far landscape extends to the horizon, above which is a band of blue with delicate accents of vermilion and grey. When the landscape is shown under strong light, as in the *Flight into Egypt* (fol. 90*v*; see fig. 1), which also has one of the earliest examples of a sunrise, the background is highlighted with gold, as if the light were reflected back from the landscape and the figures in it.

The Boucicaut Master uses very bright colours with a new luminosity and more subtle tones than earlier manuscript illuminators. The use of colour is developed from the fundamental contrast between blue and red. There are almost no pastel shades apart from pink, and yellow is hardly ever used. The borders are fairly uniform. Besides

1. Boucicaut Master: *Flight into Egypt*; illumination from the Book of Hours of Maréchal de Boucicaut, 274×190 mm, begun after 1401 (Paris, Musée Jacquemart-André, MS. 2, fol. 90*v*)

the golden ivy leaves on penwork tendrils, there are especially fine early examples of acanthus foliage sprouting from the ends or middles of the three-sided baguettes. The formation of the *bas-de-pages* suggests that the manuscript occupies an early position in the Master's oeuvre.

2. RELATED WORKS. On the basis of the Boucicaut Book of Hours, a large but not wholly homogeneous corpus of works has been assembled for the Master and his workshop. The Book of Hours of Paris Use (215×160 mm; Oxford, Bodleian Lib., MS. Douce 144) dated 1407 (1408 new style) on fol. 27*r* has some miniatures similar to the style of the Boucicaut Master. Nevertheless there are differences, above all in the flesh tones, which are underlaid with green, and the broader, more roundly modelled heads and bodies. The palette is wider, and green is used not only for landscape but also for clothing and architecture. Black is used as a colour, and white clothing is heightened with chromatic colours. Closely related to this style are a few miniatures (fol. 84*r*; fol. 100*r*) and initials attributed to the Boucicaut Master or his workshop in the Grandes Heures of Jean, Duc de Berry (400×300 mm; Paris, Bib. N., MS. lat. 919), which was completed in 1409. The three miniatures in the *Réponses de Pierre Salmon* (280×205 mm; Paris, Bib. N., MS. fr. 23279) are, however, much closer in style to the Boucicaut Hours. The text was written in 1409 for Charles VI, King of France, and the Paris manuscript was a presentation copy completed that year. Another copy (265×195 mm; Geneva, Bib. Pub. & U., MS. fr. 165) was illuminated by the same painter but after 1411, because it includes a letter of that date (fol. 100*v*); however, the sources for the illuminations have no connection with those of the Paris copy. The miniature on fol. 4*r* (*Charles VI with the Author and Three Nobles*; see fig. 2) is one of the most important works of the Boucicaut Master himself and has a unique border composed of emblems of the King. The later part of the manuscript, from fol. 109*v*, was completed in the mid-15th century. It is known from the inventory of 1413 of Jean, Duc de Berry, that the richly illustrated *Livre des merveilles* (420×298 mm; Paris, Bib. N., MS. fr. 2810) was given to him by John the Fearless, Duke of Burgundy, whose arms, devices and portrait appear on fol. 226*r*. The manuscript has 265 miniatures painted in a style that resembles that of the Book of Hours in Oxford (Douce 144) and the Grandes Heures (MS. lat. 919) but is rather distant from the Boucicaut Hours itself. All this suggests that a workshop was involved, which employed illuminators working in two distinct but related styles.

Besides the commissions from the French princes, the high reputation enjoyed by the Boucicaut Master in his lifetime is demonstrated by other surviving manuscripts. These include the Breviary made for a Dauphin, assumed to be Louis, Duc de Guyenne (*d* 1415), of which only the summer section survives (280×195 mm; Châteauroux, Bib. Mun., MS. 2). The chief illuminator here was the BEDFORD MASTER (*see* above), who is sometimes identified as Haincelin of Hagenau, *enlumineur et varlet de chambre* of this Dauphin from 1409 to 1415. The Breviary is remarkable for its numerous high-quality historiated initials, as well as for miniatures that, in spite of being extremely small, are unprecedented in their rich detail. Fol. 265*r*

2. Boucicaut Master: *Charles VI with the Author and Three Nobles*; illumination from Pierre Salmon: *Réponses de Pierre Salmon*, 265×195 mm, after 1411 (Geneva, Bibliothèque Publique et Universitaire de Genève, MS. fr. 165, fol. 4*r*)

shows, for example, a procession leading into the portal of a church, which must be intended to represent the west portal of Notre-Dame, Paris; and fol. 364*r*, depicting the *Martyrdom of St Denis at Montmartre*, has a detailed view of Paris in the background. Both these miniatures were painted by the Boucicaut Master. A third collaborator on this manuscript was named by Meiss as the Orosius Master, after the *Histoire ancienne* (Paris, Bib. N., MS. fr. 301), executed before 1400.

The Lectionary from the Sainte Chapelle in Bourges (505×305 mm; Bourges, Bib. Mun., MSS 33–6) contains the arms, devices and portrait of Jean de Berry (MS. 35, fol. 17*v*; the Duke kneeling before St Andrew). In these manuscripts the same illuminator as in the Grandes Heures appears, again working in collaboration with the PSEUDO-JACQUEMART (*see* below), an illuminator working in an archaic style from the circle of Jacquemart de Hesdin. The similarities with the Grande Heures in decoration and the choice of saints in the calendar are particularly striking.

A Missal executed for a member of the merchant family of Trenta from Lucca (336×256 mm; Lucca, Bib. Stat., MS. 3122) bears their arms in the border of fol. 7*r*, and members of the family are probably depicted at Mass in the miniature on this folio. Lorenzo Trenta is the most likely of the four Trenta brothers who can be considered

as possible patrons of the book (all of whom were residing in northern Europe as merchants), because only his patron saint seems to be honoured in a miniature in the Missal (Meiss). The smaller miniatures (including the *Mass* on fol. 7*r*, the finest in the book) are notable for their brilliant colour and sense of atmosphere. The large pages of the canon, especially the *Crucified Christ*, are more solid in effect, and their compositions are very conservative.

The extensive influence of the workshop of the Boucicaut Master is reflected still more strongly in a Book of Hours of the Use of Rome made for the Visconti of Milan (195×140 mm; Turin, Bib. Reale, MS. Var. 77; historiated initials belonging to it, MS. Var. 74). The illustrations are confined to historiated initials, but the beginnings of the Offices of the Passion and the Dead are distinguished by the addition of *bas-de-page* scenes. Although both the script and layout of the manuscript are Italian, it may not have been made in Italy; singularly, the corpse in the miniature for the Office of the Dead (fol. 49*r*) wears a royal crown. The Visconti Book of Hours, which may have been produced a little earlier than the Boucicaut Hours, is also notable because it contains contributions from both stylistic groups discernible in the Boucicaut workshop. The choice of colour in a detached initial from this manuscript corresponds to that in the Book of Hours in Oxford and the Grandes Heures of Jean, Duc de Berry, for example the use of violet against beige and the clothing of St Joseph in the *Nativity* scene (fol. 16*r*), who is entirely wrapped in red draperies with a black head-covering. This illuminator, who is not encountered in the Boucicaut Hours itself, also executed the miniature illustrating the Penitential Psalms (fol. 37*r*).

Other books by the Boucicaut Master's workshop include the *Livre de la propriété des choses* of Bartholomaeus Anglicus (385×295 mm; Paris, Bib. N., MS. fr. 9141), which still contains the arms of Beraud III, Comte de Clermont (*d* 1426). Admiral Prigent DE COËTIVY possessed two manuscripts from the workshop of the Boucicaut Master, although he may not have been their first owner as he was born *c.* 1400: Boccaccio, *Des Cleres et Nobles Femmes* (409×292 mm; Lisbon, Mus. Gulbenkian, MS. L. A. 143) and *Le Livre du trésor des histoires* (386×280 mm; Paris, Bib. Arsenal, MS. 50777). The Boucicaut Master's collaboration with Jacquemart de Hesdin on the Très Belles Heures of Jean, Duc de Berry (Brussels, Bib. Royale Albert 1er, MS. 11060/61), is now generally disputed, but the proposal was one factor in the tentative identification of the Boucicaut Master with JACQUES COENE, a theory that has received somewhat wider support.

It seems certain that the Boucicaut workshop was active in Paris, but its period of activity is less clear. The only dates that can be verified are for the short period between 1407 and the beginning of 1413, and Meiss accordingly limited the Boucicaut Master's activity to the first and second decades of the 15th century, beginning with the Boucicaut Book of Hours. Some Books of Hours are clearly earlier than either the Boucicaut Hours or the Book of Hours in Oxford of 1407, however, which suggests that the beginnings of the style should be dated before 1400. On the other hand, a small but artistically outstanding Book of Hours of Paris Use (159×114 mm; London, BL,

Add. MS. 16997), later owned by Etienne Chevalier, probably dates from the mid-1420s.

The collaborator of the Boucicaut Master in the Book of Hours in Oxford went on from his tentative attempts to penetrate and fill the entire picture page to develop an imaginative and animated type of border incorporating medallions. This finds its most mature expression in his principal work, the Book of Hours of Paris Use (250×175mm; Paris, Bib. Mazarine, MS. 469), which probably dates from *c.* 1415 (the illuminator of a Breviary of John the Fearless collaborated as a subordinate in the manuscript). The Mazarine Hours have miniatures and texts that are clearly English additions. Another Book of Hours (London, BL, Egerton MS. 1070), which was once owned by Rene I, King of Naples, and a *Bible historiale* (London, BL, Royal MS. 15 D III), both including illuminations from the Boucicaut Master's workshop, were also in England by the late 15th century. Other works in the style of the Boucicaut Master include a Book of Hours (Florence, Gal. Corsini) in which many northern French saints are prominently named in the calendar, suggesting a northern French patron, and a Book of Hours of Paris Use (ex-D. and J. Zwemmer priv. col.) that contains calendar miniatures executed by the Master of the Rohan Hours, at a time when he was active in Troyes or Angers. An *Histoire romaine* by Livy (ex-Aachen, Suermondt-Ludwig-Mus.; not that now in Malibu, CA, Getty Mus.) was written by a scribe of Breton origin, Raoul Tainguy.

3. INFLUENCE. Through the wide dissemination of his works and the training of successive generations of illuminators, the Boucicaut Master decidedly influenced the whole of French 15th-century manuscript illumination. The realistic representation of space, the lighting effects and the straightforward interaction between the figures by means of clear, concise gestures offered considerable advantages over the works of equally famous contemporaries such as the Fastolf Master and the Master of Margaret of Orleans. Succeeding generations gave the physiognomies more character than either the Boucicaut Master or the illuminator responsible for the Mazarine Hours, however. Even Jean Fouquet employed the Boucicaut Master's illuminations as a basis for his own; and his predilection for colour schemes built on the contrasts between blue and red were derived from the same source, even if he did not know the Boucicaut Master himself.

BIBLIOGRAPHY

P. Durrieu: 'Le Maitre des Heures du Maréchal de Boucicaut', *Rev. A. Anc. & Mod.*, xix (1906), pp. 401–15; xx (1906), pp. 21–35

E. Panofsky: *Early Netherlandish Painting: Its Origin and Character*, 2 vols (Cambridge, MA, 1953), pp. 53–61

M. Meiss: *French Painting in the Time of Jean de Berry: The Boucicaut Master* (London, 1968)

D. Byrne: 'The Boucicaut Master and the Iconographical Tradition of the *Livre des propriétés des choses*', *Gaz. B.-A.*, n. s. 6, xci (1978), pp. 149–60

B. König: *Französische Malerei um 1450: Der Jouvenel-Maler, der Maler des Genfer Boccaccio und die Anfänge Jean Fouquets* (Berlin, 1982), pp. 113–35

C. Sterling: *Enguerrand Quarton: Le Peintre de la 'Pietà d'Avignon'* (Paris, 1983), pp. 167–71

GABRIELE BARTZ

Master of the Bourbons. *See* MASTER OF MOULINS below.

Master of the Brandon Portrait (*fl c.* 1530). South Netherlandish painter. He worked in Bruges and owes his name to his portrait of *Charles Brandon, Earl of Suffolk* (*c.* 1530), courtier to Henry VIII, King of England. It is clear from this one painting that his work is south Netherlandish in character. Apart from this piece, Friedländer attributed five other portraits with similar characteristics to the Master. The calm dignity expressed by these portraits and the careful, neat manner in which they were executed suggests that they were painted by a follower of Gerard David. The style of this Master is also reminiscent of that of Adriaen Isenbrandt, although the former's sitters are more sharply individualized, and there is a more distinctive and even glassy range of colours in his work. One further distinguishing feature of these portraits is the striking use of light in the modelling of the sitters' heads. Generally, the portraits show a tendency towards geometrical stylization, which makes them look rather empty and bare. This effect is partly due also to certain details, such as the tightly closed mouth, with vertical lines on either side, and the glazed expression of the sitters. Friedländer mentioned a number of south Netherlandish painters who were working in England at the court of Henry VIII between 1520 and 1530 and who might therefore be identified with the Master of the Brandon Portrait. The first artist he suggested was JAN RAF, who became a member of the painters' guild in Bruges in 1512 and who was living in England *c.* 1530. Two other artists mentioned by Friedländer are Gerard Horenbout (*see* HORENBOUT, (1)) and his son Lucas Horenbout (*see* HORENBOUT, (2)), who moved to London some time between 1521 and 1526.

BIBLIOGRAPHY

Bénézit

M. J. Friedländer: 'Ein vlamischer Portraitmaler in England', *Gent. Bijdr. Kstgesch.*, iv (1937), pp. 5–18

JETTY E. VAN DER STERRE

Master of the Breisach Altar. *See* §III: MASTER H.L. below.

Master of the Breviary of Jean sans Peur (*fl c.* 1406–20). Illuminator, active in France. This name was given by Meiss (1956) to the main illuminator of a large and richly decorated two-volume Breviary (London, BL, Add. MS. 35311 and Harley MS. 2897) made for John the Fearless (Jean sans Peur), Duke of Burgundy, between 1413 and 1419. The illumination in this manuscript shows a thorough knowledge of the art of the de Limbourg brothers, with whom the Master appears to have collaborated on the TRÈS RICHES HEURES (*c.* 1411/13–16; Chantilly, Mus. Condé, MS. 65), painting many initials and the finest of the borders. Apart from these manuscripts, his style is rarely found. One miniature in a manuscript dated 1406 (Paris, Bib. N., MS. fr. 926) and several illuminations in Books of Hours produced *c.* 1410–20 (Baltimore, MD, Walters A.G., MS. W. 219; Vienna, Österreich. Nbib., Cod. s.n. 2613; Palermo, Bib. Cent. Regione Siciliana, MS. 1.A.15) have been attributed to him. These manuscripts show his collaboration with such Parisian painters as the Boucicaut Master and the Egerton Master (*fl* 1400–20) and with artists associated with north-east France, such as the Master of Walters 219, which suggests that he

Master of the Brunswick Diptych: diptych with the *Virgin and Child with St Anne* and a *Carthusian Monk Presented by St Barbara*, each panel 350×230 mm, *c.* 1490 (Brunswick, Herzog Anton Ulrich-Museum)

may have worked in both areas. Although employing many figure types and compositions from the Limbourgs, the Breviary Master did not copy their models slavishly and was capable of adapting and on occasion improving on them. His borders in the Très Riches Heures reveal an accurate and detailed observation of plants and animals not found to the same extent in their work.

The Master employed a distinctive technique of modelling forms with a feathery stippling of colour, which extends to areas of delicately punched burnished gold. In the Book of Hours in Baltimore this technique verges on a form of pointillism, with line abandoned and form defined purely with colour. The shimmering effect of his illuminations is aided by his luminous palette, which combines yellows, reds and blues with burnished metals.

BIBLIOGRAPHY

M. Meiss: 'The Exhibition of French Manuscripts of the XIII–XVI Centuries at the Bibliothèque Nationale', *A. Bull.*, xxxviii (1956), pp. 187–96

——: 'The Master of the Breviary of Jean sans Peur and the Limbourgs', *Proc. Brit. Acad.*, lvi (1970), pp. 111–29

——: *French Painting in the Time of Jean de Berry: The Limbourgs and their Contemporaries*, 2 vols (London and New York, 1974)

O. Pächt and D. Thoss: *Die illuminierten Handschriften der Österreichischen Nationalbibliothek: Französische Schule I*, 2 vols (Vienna, 1974), p. 138

L. M. C. Randall and others: *France, 875–1420* (1990), i of *Medieval and Renaissance Manuscripts in the Walters Art Gallery* (Baltimore, 1990–), pp. 280–85

SUSIE NASH

Bruges Master of 1473. *See* §II: MASTER OF 1473 below.

Master of the Brunswick Diptych (*fl c.* 1480–1510). North Netherlandish painter. He was named by Friedländer after a diptych in Brunswick of the *Virgin and Child with St Anne* in a spacious garden setting on the left panel and a kneeling *Carthusian Monk Presented by St Barbara* on the right (see fig.). The reverse of the right wing has a standing figure of *St Bavo*. The donor has been identified (van Luttervelt) as Hendrik van Haarlem, prior of the Charterhouse of Amsterdam until 1490, but this cannot be confirmed. The diptych was formerly attributed to Geertgen tot Sint Jans, although reminiscences of the style of the Master of the Tiburtine Sibyl appear in the barren architectural background and in certain drapery conventions. The composition closely resembles one of the same subject by a follower of Hugo van der Goes (Brussels, Mus. A. Anc.).

A number of other paintings attributed to the Master of the Brunswick Diptych have been described as early works of Geertgen, but the Master of the Brunswick Diptych employed a lighter palette than Geertgen, with blond tones and soft pinks predominating. His treatment of the draped figure is less plastic and three-dimensional, and spatial settings are frequently abstracted into flat, colourful patterns that lack the clarity of Geertgen's constructions. There is a miniature-like quality to his compositions. Three panels that were part of an altarpiece dedicated to the infancy of Christ, the *Annunciation* (Glasgow, A.G. & Mus.), the *Nativity* (Amsterdam, Rijksmus.) and the *Presentation* (Minneapolis, MN, Inst. A.), are typical of his more decorative style and are considered to be among his earliest works. In each panel Mary wears a colourful blue and white floral brocade, and Joseph is portrayed as a young man. An *Adoration of the Magi* (Amsterdam, Rijksmus.), usually attributed to Geertgen tot Sint Jans, has been identified as the central panel of the triptych, but this seems unlikely. Among the other works attributed to the Master of the Brunswick Diptych are two tall wings from a *Passion* (?Crucifixion) triptych, the *Arrest of Christ* and the *Entombment* (Brussels, Mus. A. Anc.). The compositions, with the summary treatment of the figures and the steeply rising landscape backgrounds spotted with tiny figures, are related to manuscript illumination. The standing figures in niches on two panels, *St Valerian* and *St Cecilia* (Amsterdam, Rijksmus.), typify the doll-like character of his saints, a quality that is especially evident in the charming *Holy Family at Supper* (Cologne, Wallraf-Richartz-Mus.). A new type of subject-matter for panel painting, domestic genre, appears in this intimate household scene with a young mother feeding soup to her child. The Cologne painting has also been attributed to Jan Mostaert, and this association has led some art historians to identify the Master of the Brunswick Diptych as the teacher of Mostaert (Châtelet). According to van Mander (*Het schilder-boeck*, 1604), Mostaert was trained by Jacob van Haarlem, perhaps the painter Jacob Jansz. van Haarlem, whose activity in Haarlem is documented from 1483 until his death in 1509. Whether or not this identification is acceptable or the Master and Jacob van Haarlem are the same artist, the works of the Master of the Brunswick Diptych do link the art of Geertgen to that of Mostaert in Haarlem.

BIBLIOGRAPHY

L. Balet: *Der Frühholländer Geertgen tot Sint Jans* (The Hague, 1909)
M. J. Friedländer: *Die altniederländische Malerei* (Berlin, 1924–37); Eng. trans. as *Early Netherlandish Painting* (Leiden, 1967–76), v, pp. 31–2
J. J. H. Kessler: *Geertgen tot Sint Jans: Zijne herkomst en invloed in Holland* [Geertgen tot Sint Jans: his origins and influence in Holland] (Utrecht, 1930)
G. J. Hoogewerff: *De Noord-Nederlandsche schilderkunst* [North-Netherlandish painting], ii (The Hague, 1937), pp. 194–202
W. Vogelsang: *Geertgen tot Sint Jans* (Amsterdam, 1945)
R. van Luttervelt: 'Schilderijen met Karthuizers uit de late 15de en de vroege 16de eeuw' [Paintings with Carthusians from the late 15th to the early 16th century], *Oud-Holland*, lxvi (1951), pp. 75–92
Middeleeuwse kunst der noordelijke Nederlanden (exh. cat., Amsterdam, Rijksmus., 1958), pp. 55–8
A. Châtelet: *Les Primitifs hollandais* (Paris, 1980); Eng. trans. as *Early Dutch Painting* (Oxford, 1981), pp. 124–33

JAMES SNYDER

Master of the Brussels Initials (*fl* Paris and Bologna, *c.* 1390–1410). Illuminator. His name and a corpus of works attributed to him are derived from the 15 historiated initials in the Très Belles Heures of Jean, Duc de Berry (Brussels, Bib. Royale Albert 1er, MSS 11060–61), possibly executed before 1402. Pächt's identification of the Master as Zebo or Zanobi da Firenze on the basis of an inscription in the Hours of Charles the Noble (Cleveland, OH, Mus. A., MS. 64.40) is no longer accepted.

With the exception of the entirely Italian Statute Book illuminated by the Master for the Compagnia dello Spedale di S Maria della Vita (Bologna, Bib. Com. Archiginnasio, Fondo Ospedali MS. 6), which can be dated to 1408, his work appears alongside that of French illuminators in

Master of the Brussels Initials: *Pentecost*, miniature; from a Book of Hours, 220×155 mm, early 15th century (London, British Library, Add. MS. 29433, fol. 111*v*)

manuscripts produced in or around Paris in the first decade of the 15th century. At times the Master simply worked on manuscripts that appear to have been left unfinished, as in the case of the Brussels Hours, in which his historiated initials are decorated with brilliantly coloured acanthus leaves and peopled by energetic figures with green flesh tones, standing out in marked contrast to the more subdued French miniatures and borders. In a Book of Hours of *c.* 1390 (Parma, Bib. Palatina, MS. lat. 159), perhaps his first work in France, the Master executed calendar illustrations and five other miniatures, all inserted in borders typically French in style and format and appearing with the work of French illuminators. Occasionally, as in a Book of Hours in Oxford (Bodleian Lib., MS. Douce 62), the French borders around his miniatures were erased and replaced by lavishly coloured acanthus and gold medallions peopled by nude putti in the Italian manner. In the Hours of Charles the Noble and in another Book of Hours (London, BL, Add. MS. 29433; see fig.) the Master is the dominant artistic personality, having control of the decoration as well as the illuminations on most of his miniature pages, but adding historiated initials to text pages with the distinctive French ivy borders.

The Master of the Brussels Initials is important for having introduced to Paris a repertory of Italian iconographic motifs, luxurious and brightly coloured acanthus borders, fanciful and luminously coloured architectural settings, some derived from frescoes by Altichiero in Padua, and a lively narrative style that transformed the aesthetic effect of the French manuscripts on which he worked. The influence of his Italianate style supplanted that of earlier 14th-century Italian art that had previously pervaded French illumination, and it decisively contributed to the rich and exotic qualities of the internationalism that was developing in French manuscript illumination at this time.

BIBLIOGRAPHY
O. Pächt: *The Master of Mary of Burgundy* (London, [1948]), p. 52
W. Wixom: 'The Hours of Charles the Noble', *Bull. Cleveland Mus. A.*, lii/3 (March 1965), pp. 50–83
M. Meiss: *French Painting in the Time of Jean de Berry: The Late Fourteenth Century and the Patronage of the Duke* (New York, 1967), pp. 229–46
R. Calkins: 'An Italian in Paris: The Master of the Brussels Initials and his Participation in the French Book Industry', *Gesta*, xx/1 (1981), pp. 223–32
P. de Winter: 'Art, Devotion and Satire: The Book of Hours of Charles III, the Noble, King of Navarre, at the Cleveland Museum of Art', *Gamut*, ii (1981), pp. 42–59
R. Calkins: *Illuminated Books of the Middle Ages* (Ithaca, 1983), pp. 250–81

ROBERT G. CALKINS

Master of Burgo de Osma (*fl* first half of the 15th century). Spanish painter. The anonymous painter named after the altarpiece of the *Virgin* (*c.* 1430–40; now dismembered, panels in Burgo de Osma, Mus. Catedralicio, and Paris, Louvre) made for the high altar of the cathedral of El Burgo de Osma, Castile, was a follower of Pere Nicolau and an important representative of Valencian painting of the early 15th century. The *Virgin* altarpiece in the parish church of Rubielos de Mora (Teruel) of *c.* 1410–20 is the painter's most characteristic work, in which the elegance of the elongated forms combines with a vigorous expressionism. The *Entombment* (Seville, Mus. B.A.) and *Deposition* (Barcelona, Pal. Puig), all panels from a dismembered retable, are in a similar style. The Master's later manner was more subdued, and the late *Quo Vadis* (*c.* 1440–50; Madrid, Mus. Arqueol. N.) shows his interest in naturalistic features.

BIBLIOGRAPHY
L. de Saralegui: 'Miscelanea de remembranzas vicentinas', *Archv A. Valenc.*, xxvi (1955), pp. 19–26
M. Hériard Dubreuil: 'Gótico internacional', *Historia del arte valenciano*, ii (Valencia, 1988), pp. 182–235

MATHIEU HÉRIARD DUBREUIL

Master of the Burgundian Prelates (*fl c.* 1470–90). Illuminator, active in France. Reynaud assembled a large group of manuscripts under this name, including two Missals (Paris, Bib. N., MS. lat. 879; Siena, Bib. Com. Intronati, MS. X.V.I.), a Pontifical (Autun, Bib. Mun., MS. 129) and a Breviary (Chaumont, Bib. Mun., MSS 32–3). They were made between 1475 and 1490 for several high-ranking Burgundian church officials, after whose patronage the Master is named. He may also have been employed by one of them, Ferry de Clugny (*d* 1483), to paint the frescoes in the Chapelle Dorée of Autun Cathedral between 1473 and 1480, although their ruined state makes attribution difficult. This, and the liturgical use of the other manuscripts associated with his hand, such as the Book of Hours of Autun Use (London, BL, Sloane MS. 2419), suggests that the Master was based in the Burgundian region, working for a prestigious but predominantly local clientele. His style is characterized by its calm sobriety, created partly by a distinctive palette of dull rose, dark blue, grey and matt gold. His figures are still, with softly modelled faces that are meditative rather than expressive and with eyes averted or turned towards Heaven in restrained gestures of piety and awe. Drapery is hatched with a mesh of gold lines; architecture and landscapes are often outlined with touches of white. The Master's compositions are static and show little interest in drama or narration, but his style is ideally suited to devotional images, such as the full page *Crucifixion* in the Missal of Richard Chambellan (Paris, Bib. N., MS. lat. 879). This illumination, like several others attributed to this Master, is large in size and independent from any text or subsidiary decoration, which lends it the character of a small panel rather than a decorated page. It is his most accomplished work and reaches a standard not found in all the manuscripts of this group.

BIBLIOGRAPHY
L. Cloquet and A. de Lagrange: 'Manuscrits de Ferry de Clugny', *Rev. A. Chrét.* (1889), pp. 77–80
Y. Bonnefoy: *Peintures murales de la France gothique* (Paris, 1954), p. 27
N. Reynaud: 'Un Peintre français de la fin du XVe siècle: Le Maître des prélats bourguignons', *Etudes d'art français offertes à Charles Sterling* (Paris, 1975), pp. 151–63
The Last Flowering: French Painting in Manuscripts 1420–1530 from American Collections (exh. cat. by J. Plummer and G. Clark, New York, Pierpont Morgan Lib., 1982), pp. 75–6, nos 97–8
R. S. Wieck: *Late Medieval and Renaissance Manuscripts, 1350–1525, in the Houghton Library* (Cambridge, MA, 1983), pp. 36–7, no. 17
Le Livre au siècle de Rolin (exh. cat., Autun, Bib. Mun., 1985), pp. 45–9, nos 32–6

SUSIE NASH

Bysta Master. *See under* ARENDTZ, CORNELIUS.

Master of Cabestany (*fl c.* 1130–80). Sculptor, active in Italy, France and Spain. He is named after the tympanum representing the *Assumption of the Virgin* at Ste Marie, Cabestany (Roussillon). He worked in an idiosyncratic and expressive style, characterized by animated figures with stocky bodies, large hands and heads with distinctive features. His violent use of the drill is also characteristic of his work (see fig.). He was a prolific sculptor and evidently had a long career, working over a large area; sculptures have been attributed to him in Catalonia (S Pere de Galligants, Girona; Sant Pere de Rodes (Sp. San Pedro de Roda) and Sant Esteve d'En Bas), Roussillon (Ste Marie, Cabestany, and Ste Marie, Le Boulou), Pays d'Aude (Saint-Papoul, Saint-Hilaire d'Aude, Lagrasse Abbey and the Assomption de Notre-Dame, at Rieux-Minervois), Tuscany (Sant'Antimo and S Giovanni, Sugana) and Navarre (Errondo and Villaveta). The variations in quality seen in these works (e.g. Lagrasse Abbey and Villaveta) have suggested that the Master had an associate, but this would be surprising in an artist whose work is remarkable for its consistency and discipline. It also seems unlikely that a workshop was involved, because the style of the sculpture is very individual.

A starting-point for the Master of Cabestany's work may be the reliefs at St Pierre, La Réole (Gironde), and

Master of Cabestany: *Christ Walking on the Waves*, from the west portal of Sant Pere de Rodes, mid-12th century (Barcelona, Museu Frederic Marés)

some capitals in S Caprais, Agen (Lot-et-Garonne), and Notre-Dame, Lescar (Basses-Pyrénées). He was also influenced by sculpture at Toulouse, but it was the Early Christian sarcophagi in St Feliú, Girona, which the Master would have known through his work in Sant Pere de Galligants (*c.* 1131), that radically transformed his work. With unusual antiquarian discernment he followed Late Antique models, from which derives his characteristic use of the drill. The influence of the Roda Bible (Paris, Bib. N., MS. lat. 6) may perhaps be detected in the capital at Saint-Papoul relating the punishment of Daniel's accusers; the art of Catalonia was clearly also an important formative influence. The Master of Cabestany's travels exemplify the general spread of influence from Toulouse. The importance of his work in Tuscany can be compared with that of the 'proto-Renaissance' sculpture of Biduino at S Cassiano, Settimo, near Pisa, but the iconography of the Master is more original. The *Assumption of the Virgin* on the tympanum at Cabestany is an early example of a Marian theme and includes the apocryphal motif of the Virgin's girdle, venerated as a relic at Prato Cathedral (Tuscany). In the tympanum from Errondo (New York, Cloisters) the motif of Christus Victor derived from a sarcophagus in Girona is combined with the influence of exegetical texts that link the *Temptations of Christ* to his allegorical triumph, as sung in Psalm 90.

BIBLIOGRAPHY
J. Gudiol: 'Los relieves de la portada de Errondo y el maestro de Cabestany', *Príncipe Viana*, xiv (1944), pp. 9–16
M. Durliat: 'L'Oeuvre du maître de Cabestany', *Actes du congrès régional des fédérations historiques du Languedoc: Carcassone, 1952*, pp. 185–93
——: *La Sculpture romane en Roussillon*, iv (Perpignan, 1954)
J. Ainaud de Lasarte: 'Noticias de San Pedro de Roda', *Rev. Gerona*, v (1959), pp. 33–5
E. Junyent: 'L'Oeuvre du maître de Cabestany', *Actes du 96e congrès national des sociétés savantes, section d'archéologie: Montpellier, 1961*, pp. 169–78
J. Raspi-Serra: 'Contributo allo studio di alcune sculture dell'abbazia di Sant'Antimo', *Commentari*, xv (1964), pp. 135–65
G. Zarnecki: 'A Sculptured Head Attributed to the Maître de Cabestany', *Burl. Mag.*, cvi (1964), pp. 536–7
L. Pressouyre: 'Une Nouvelle Oeuvre du 'maître de Cabestany' en Toscane: Le Pilier sculpté de San Giovanni in Sugana', *Bull. Soc. Nat. Antiqua. France* (1969), pp. 30–55
C. Bargellini: 'More Cabestany Master', *Burl. Mag.*, cxii (1970), pp. 140–44
M. Durliat: 'Du Nouveau sur le maître de Cabestany', *Bull. Mnmtl.*, cxxix (1971), pp. 193–8
——: 'Le Maître de Cabestany', *Cah. Saint-Michel de Cuxa*, iv (1973), pp. 116–27
J. Nougaret: 'L'Oeuvre languedocien du maître du tympan de Cabestany', *Languedoc roman*, Nuit Temps (La Pierre-qui-Vire, 1975), pp. 355–60
J. Gardelles: 'L'Oeuvre du Maître de Cabestany et les reliefs du château de la Réole', *Bull. Mnmtl.*, cxxxiv (1976), pp. 231–7
V. Kupfer: 'The Iconography of the Tympanum of the Temptation of Christ at the Cloisters', *Met. Mus. J.*, xii (1978), pp. 21–31
D. L. Simon: 'Still More by the Cabestany Master', *Burl. Mag.*, cxxi (1979), pp. 108–11
J. Barrachina: 'Dos relleus fragmentaris de la portalada de Sant Pere de Rodes del mestre de Cabestany', *Quad. Estud. Med.*, i (1980), pp. 60–61
S. Moralejo: 'La reutilización e influencia de los sarcófagos antiguos en la España medieval', *Colloquio sul reimpiego dei sarcofagi romani nel Medioevo: Pisa, 1982*, pp. 187–203
——: 'Artistas, patronos y público en el arte del Camino de Santiago', *Compostellanum*, xxx (1985), pp. 395–430 (402–5)

S. MORALEJO

Master of the Cambrai Altarpiece. *See under* STOCKT, VRANCKE VAN DER.

Master of Canapost [Master of Seu d'Urgell] (*fl* late 15th century). Catalan painter. Although he has been known by two different names, his artistic personality is apparent in a small group of works: the altarpiece of the *Virgin* from S Esteve, Canapost, near Girona (Girona, Mus. A.); the paintings of the reliquary donated in 1496 by Bishop Berenguer de Pau (*reg* 1486–1506) to Girona Cathedral (Girona, Mus. Catedralici); the canvases decorating the organ shutters of Seu d'Urgell Cathedral (Barcelona, Mus. A. Catalunya; priv. cols); two sections (an *Annunciation* and a *Penitent St Jerome*) from an altarpiece from the chapel of Nostra Senyora de Gràcia, Puigcerdà (Barcelona, Mus. A. Catalunya); and the great altarpiece of the *Trinity* from the Loge de Mer in Perpignan, dated 1489 (Perpignan, Mus. Rigaud).

The provenances of these paintings suggest that the Master of Canapost worked mainly in the region between Girona and Perpignan. It is possible, however, that he may have been trained under Jean Fouquet at Tours, because Fouquet's influence is apparent in his early works: compare, for example, the *Virgin and Child* in the altarpiece from S Esteve, Canapost, with Fouquet's diptych of *Etienne Chevalier* of *c.* 1452 (Antwerp, Kon. Mus. S. Kst.; Berlin, Gemäldegal.). The development of the Master's style, showing sound mastery of drawing and of the technique of oil painting, can be seen in such later works as the *Presentation of Christ in the Temple*, one of the canvases for the organ at Seu d'Urgell and the *Penitent St*

Jerome from the altarpiece in Puigcerdà, in which the Master painted picturesque landscape scenery.

BIBLIOGRAPHY

C. R. Post: *A History of Spanish Painting* (Cambridge, MA, 1930–66), vi, pp. 7–10; vii, pp. 35–9, 604–8; xii, pp. 672–4, 681

M. Durliat: *Arts anciens du Roussillon* (Perpignan, 1954)

——: 'La Peinture à Perpignan autour de 1500', *Actes du 86ème congrès national des Sociétés savantes: Section d'archéologie: Montpellier, 1961*, pp. 339–41

J. Gudiol and S. Alcolea Blanch: *Pintura gótica catalana* (Barcelona, 1986), pp. 200–01, nos 654–5

SANTIAGO ALCOLEA BLANCH

Candlelight Master [Maître à la Chandelle] (*fl c.* 1620–40). French or Dutch painter, active in Rome. The identity and even the existence of this early Baroque painter have prompted much debate. In 1960 Benedict Nicolson attributed a stylistically coherent group of 39 unsigned and undated Caravaggesque night scenes to an anonymous painter he called the 'Candlelight Master'; these works had been variously attributed to Gerrit van Honthorst, Matthias Stom, Georges de La Tour and other followers of Caravaggio. Nicolson proposed that the Candlelight Master had been born *c.* 1600 in or around Aix-en-Provence and had been an apprentice in Utrecht before settling in Rome. In 1964 Nicolson and Jean Boyer independently identified the Candlelight Master as TROPHIME BIGOT, a native of Aix, who lived in Rome in the 1620s and early 1630s, and further identified Bigot with the mysterious painter of nocturnes whom Joachim von Sandrart called 'Trufemondi'.

This identification proved questionable, however. The paintings executed by Bigot in Rome between 1620 and 1634 are typically small, single-figure night scenes in the manner of Caravaggio, while those signed by Bigot in Provence after 1634 are larger, multiple-figure compositions in a late Mannerist style. Nicolson (1972) and Thuillier (1973) resolved this discrepancy by positing two Bigots: Bigot the elder (*b* 1579; *d* after 1649), who was responsible for the Provençal paintings, and Bigot the younger, resident in Rome 1620–34, who was responsible for the pictures that Nicolson had ascribed to the Candlelight Master. In 1979 Jean-Pierre Cuzin maintained that there was only one Trophime Bigot, who had worked both in Provence and Rome and had executed only those few Roman nocturnes that seemed closest in style to the Provençal works, while the remainder of the nocturnes belonged to the more prolific and competent Candlelight Master, whose identity might be linked to a certain 'Mr Jacomo pittore', named in the archives of S Maria in Aquiro as the painter of a work already believed to be by the Candlelight Master and an assistant.

In 1988 Jean Boyer published new documentary evidence that confirmed the existence of only one Bigot, who had been the author of the Provençal paintings and at least some of the Roman nocturnes. However, it is still not known whether Bigot and the Candlelight Master are the same artist or whether, as Cuzin proposed, they are two separate painters, most of the disputed works being attributable to the Candlelight Master. Even if the existence of the Candlelight Master is accepted, it is not known whether he was connected with 'Maestro Jacomo' or even whether he was French, as Nicolson believed, or Dutch,

as suggested by the strong influence on his works of Honthorst, Stom and Adam de Coster (*c.* 1586–1643).

The Candlelight Master's depictions of single or paired half-length figures illuminated by an artificial light constitute an independent persona among Caravaggio's followers in Rome. The subjects are flea pickers, smokers, singers, doctors and penitent saints, all dramatically illuminated by the flame of a candle or oil lamp as they perform simple tasks, such as pouring oil or singing. A superb example is the *Young Boy Singing* (see fig.), in which a turbaned youth sings by the light of a suspended lamp, which illuminates his face and renders his sheet music translucent, so that several notes from the reverse side are visible in silhouette. Typical of the Candlelight Master's works are exquisite light effects that simultaneously sculpt and dematerialize forms, as in the sharply articulated lamp bracket and the singer's doughy hands. Such curious light effects are not, however, an end in themselves but a means of enhancing the figure's contemplative state and the dreamlike atmosphere. *Young Boy Singing* is probably related to a series of four paintings in Rome that have similar subjects and bold lighting: *Boy Singing*, *Young Girl Singing*, *Boy Holding a Bat* and *Boy Pouring Oil into a Lamp* (all *c.* 1620–35; Rome, Gal. Doria-Pamphili). These are among the Candlelight Master's best works. His painting of a *Doctor Examining a Sample of Urine* (*c.* 1620–35; Oxford, Ashmolean) also stands out for its straightforward depiction of contemporary medical practice. The larger, more ambitious nocturnes of religious subjects credited to the same

Candlelight Master: *Young Boy Singing*, oil on canvas, 675×495 mm, *c.* 1620–35 (San Francisco, California Palace of the Legion of Honor)

artist (e.g. *St Sebastian Tended by St Irene*, *c.* 1630–40; Bordeaux, Mus. B.-A.) are generally weaker and less inventive than his genre scenes. The Candlelight Master worked in a style that hovered between Honthorst and Georges de la Tour, and although he never attained their mastery he produced some of the finest luminist paintings of his day.

BIBLIOGRAPHY

B. Nicolson: 'The "Candlelight Master": A Follower of Honthorst in Rome', *Ned. Ksthist. Jb.*, xi (1960), pp. 121–64

J. Boyer: 'Un Caravagesque français oublié: Trophime Bigot', *Bull. Soc. Hist. A. Fr.* (1964), pp. 35–51

——: 'Nouveaux Documents inédits sur le peintre Trophime Bigot', *Bull. Soc. Hist. A. Fr.* (1964), pp. 153–8

B. Nicolson: 'Un Caravagiste aixois: Le maître à la chandelle', *A. France*, iv (1964), pp. 117–39

——: 'The Rehabilitation of Trophime Bigot', *A. & Lit.*, iv (1965), pp. 66–105

——: 'Caravaggesques at Cleveland', *Burl. Mag.*, cxiv (1972), pp. 113–7

J. Thuillier: *Tout l'oeuvre peint de Georges de La Tour* (Paris, 1973), p. 47

B. Nicolson: *The International Caravaggesque Movement: Lists of Pictures by Caravaggio and his Followers throughout Europe from 1590 to 1650* (Oxford, 1978); rev. in 3 vols as *Caravaggism in Europe*, ed. L. Vertova (Turin, 1989), i, pp. 59–64 [rev. edn has excellent pls]

Le Peinture en Provence au XVIIe siècle (exh. cat., ed. H. Wytenhove; Marseille, Mus. B.-A., 1978), pp. 3–10 [Bigot text by Jacques Thuillier]

A. Blunt: 'Trophime Bigot', *Burl. Mag.*, cxxi (1979), p. 444

J.-P. Cuzin: 'Trophime Bigot in Rome: A Suggestion', *Burl. Mag.*, cxxi (1979), pp. 301–5

France in the Golden Age: Seventeenth-century French Painting in American Collections (exh. cat. by P. Rosenberg, Paris, Grand Pal.; New York, Met.; Chicago, IL, A. Inst.; 1982)

C. Del Bravo: *Le riposte dell'arte* (Florence, 1985)

P. Rosenberg and M. Stewart: *French Painting, 1500-1825*, San Francisco, CA, F.A. Museums Cat. (San Fransisco, 1987), pp. 41–3

J. Boyer: 'The One and only Trophime Bigot', *Burl. Mag.*, cxxx (1988), pp. 355–7

LAURIE G. WINTERS

Master of the Cappella Medici Polyptych [Master of Terenzano] (*fl c.* 1315–35). Italian painter. Identified in the 20th century and at first named the Master of Terenzano (Berenson), this painter is now named after a polyptych (*c.* 1320s) that originally stood in the Medici Chapel of Santa Croce in Florence. Its panels of half-length saints are now separated and occupy a secondary position as pinnacles for the altarpiece on the high altar of the same church. In his own day the artist must have held a respectable, if modest, position, forming part of a line of painters descended from the St Cecilia Master and Pacino di Bonaguida, whose work, although influenced by Giotto's, stands in contrast to it. Although the painters of the so-called 'miniaturist tendency' (Offner) excelled at manuscript illustration, the Master of the Cappella Medici Polyptych is known only through a dozen panels, which include larger objects of some importance, for instance a Crucifix (Stuttgart, Staatsgal., 2635), as well as such small devotional works as the *Virgin and Child Enthroned with Four Saints* (Detroit, MI, Inst. A.), once the centre of a portable triptych. The limited evidence of these works perhaps fails to show his full range and talent but indicates that he was probably trained in Pacino's workshop during the second decade of the century. The Master's sweet, timid and doll-like figures reveal a kinship with the younger, more prolific and more important Master of the Dominican Effigies, with whom he was initially confused and may have collaborated. His debt to Giotto is evident in, for example, a *Crucifixion* (New York, Wildenstein's)

and *Virgin Enthroned* (Raleigh, NC Mus. A.), and from the 1320s the influence of Jacopo del Casentino and Bernardo Daddi can be seen also in such work as his *Virgin and Child* from the central panel of the Medici Chapel polyptych (*in situ*) and the *Virgin and Child* tabernacle (U. Würzburg, Wagner-Mus., 88). Unlike Bernardo, however, he was less successful in bridging the gap between a training that emphasized small-scale painting and the more monumental style of Giotto.

BIBLIOGRAPHY

R. Offner and K. Steinweg: *Corpus* (1930–79), III/ii (1930), pt i, pp. 73–86, and III/vii (1957), pp. v, 83–92; rev. M. Boskovits, III/ii (1987), pp. 21–2, 356–80

B. Berenson: 'Quadri senza casa: Il trecento fiorentino, I', *Dédalo*, xi (1930–31), pp. 957–88 (978–82)

A. Ladis: 'An Early Trecento Madonna Uncovered', *Ant. Viva*, xxii/1 (1983), pp. 5–10

M. Boskovits: *Corpus* (1984), pp. 54–5, 280–82

ANDREW LADIS

Master of Cappenberg. *See* BAEGERT, (2).

Carnation Masters [Berner Nelkemeister] (*fl c.* 1475–*c.* 1500). Swiss painters. A series of altar paintings, produced mainly in Berne but also in Zurich, Fribourg and Baden im Aargau, shows prominently placed carnations of several types: a pair of red and white carnations, a carnation with panicle and a carnation with a stem of lavender. Although the carnations are generally seen as disguised signatures, they do not identify a single artist but seem to serve as an emblem for one or more painters' brotherhoods. While in some cases the sign might also refer to the patron (Nägeli = Nelke = carnation), this is not the case for all.

The earliest and best of these works, a high-altarpiece depicting the *Crucifixion* (after 1480; Fribourg, Franziskanerkirche), clearly reveals a south Netherlandish training in the tradition of Rogier van der Weyden and has been distinguished (Moullet, Stange) from the work of other Carnation Masters as deriving from 'the workshop of Bartholomäus Ruthenzweig' (*fl* before 1480). The altarpiece was completed by Paul Löwensprung (*fl c.* 1475; *d* 1499), who was in Berne after 1493 and who also used a carnation signature on his works, such as his altar of the *Virgin* (*c.* 1490; ex-Barfüsserkirche, Basle; Basle, Kstmus.). Another artist with a carnation signature, and with a clear, simple style of picture composition, was the Master of the Berne Altarpiece of St John (*fl c.* 1490–1510; altarpiece *c.* 1490; ex-Dominikanerkirche, Berne; middle section untraced; wings, Berne, Kstmus.; Zurich, Ksthaus; Budapest, Mus. F.A.). A further Carnation Master, the Berne Master of St Beatus, is named after an altar wing depicting that saint (*c.* 1494; ex-Beatuskirche, Beatenberg; Sarnen, Heimatmus.). The *Adoration of the Shepherds* in the Kunsthaus, Zurich, signed with a carnation, may be by Hans Leu the elder.

BIBLIOGRAPHY

Thieme–Becker

P. Moullet: *Les Maîtres à l'oeillet* (Basle, 1943)

A. Stange: *Die deutschen Tafelbilder vor Dürer*, ii (Munich, 1970), pp. 77–80

C. Klemm: 'Züricher Nelkenmeister: Enthauptung eines jugendlichen Heiligen', *Ksthaus Zürich. Ges., Jber.* (1986), pp. 89–94

BRIGITTE HERRBACH

Master of the Carrand Triptych. *See* GIOVANNI DI FRANCESCO (i).

Master of Castelló d'Empúries. *See* MASTER OF AMPURIAS above.

Master of the Castello Nativity (*fl* Florence, *c.* 1445–*c.* 1470/75). Italian painter. He was named by Berenson (1913) after the *Nativity* (Florence, Accademia) that came from the Medici villa at Castello. There are no datable works by the Master, but the earliest attributable works indicate stylistically that he was probably a pupil of Filippo Lippi and trained in his studio in Florence in the 1440s, before Lippi's move to Prato.

The altarpiece of the *Virgin and Child Enthroned with SS Justus and Clement* (Prato, Mus. Opera Duomo) would appear to be an early work datable to the mid-15th century (Procacci). In its composition, drapery style and architectural setting it is heavily dependent on Lippi's work of the 1440s; the figure of St Clement is derived from Lippi's *Annunciation* (*c.* 1445; Munich, Alte Pin.). Two scenes from the *Lives of SS Justus and Clement* (Philadelphia, PA, Mus. A.) and a *Nativity* (London, N.G.) originally formed the predella of the altarpiece. The iconography of the *Nativity* is based on the *Revelations* of St Bridget, popular in Florence at this date, and shows the Virgin's hands covered by a veil, a detail present in many of the Master's devotional works.

The Master apparently collaborated with Lippi on the predella panel of the *Nativity* (Washington, DC, N.G.A.), which is usually considered to belong to the Munich *Annunciation*: the figure of St Joseph and the typology of the Christ Child, both characteristic of the Master, are almost identical with their counterparts in the London *Nativity*. Also stylistically close to the Prato Altarpiece is the *Virgin of Humility with Two Musician Angels* (Pisa, Mus. N. & Civ. S Matteo).

The Castello *Nativity* cannot, in fact, have been executed for the Medici villa at Castello since it appears in inventories only after 1610 (Shearman). In 1638, however, the coats of arms on the base of the altarpiece (now illegible) were recorded as being those of the Medici and the Tornabuoni families. It is presumed that it was made for Piero de' Medici and his wife Lucrezia Tornabuoni. Certainly, the sumptuous decoration of the Virgin's robe accords with Piero's taste for ornate works of art, while the intense devotional aspect of the work—emphasized by the presence of the young Baptist and God the Father in a glory of seraphim—is consistent with Lucrezia's fervent piety. The painting probably dates from *c.* 1460, contemporary with the work of Domenico Veneziano and with Lippi's and Gozzoli's decoration in the chapel of the Palazzo Medici, Florence. All these artists were favoured by Piero.

The corpus of paintings attributed to the Master is frequently repetitive in subject-matter and composition, yet the works are carefully executed and probably catered for the demands of patrons who were, for the most part, educated as well as rich. This would seem to be confirmed by the existence of several portraits by the Master of apparently noble Florentine women, such as the *Portrait of a Woman* (New York, Met., 49.7.6), strongly influenced by Lippi, and another elegant and decorative female portrait (Boston, MA, Isabella Stewart Gardner Mus.). These portraits seem to date from the end of the Master's career.

BIBLIOGRAPHY

C. Gamba: 'Due opere d'arte nella R. villa di Castello', *Ant. Viva.*, iii (1903), pp. 81–2
B. Berenson: *Catalogue of Italian Paintings in the John G. Johnson Collection, Philadelphia*, i (Philadelphia, 1913), p. 17
——: *Italian Pictures of the Renaissance* (Oxford, 1932), p. 343
U. Procacci: 'Opere sconsciute d'arte toscana', *Riv. A.*, xvii (1935), pp. 405–11
M. Salmi: 'Aggiunte al tre e al quattrocento fiorentino', *Riv. A.*, xvii (1935), pp. 411–21
——: 'Il Maestro della Natività di Castello', *Liburni Civitas*, ii (1938), pp. 217–56
B. Berenson: *Florentine School* (1963), i, pp. 141–2
M. Meiss: 'A Lunette by Master of Castello Nativity', *Gaz. B.-A.*, lxx (1967), pp. 213–18
F. Zeri and E. Gardner: *The Metropolitan Museum of Art: Italian Paintings, Florentine School* (New York, 1971), p. 114
Arte nell'aretino (exh. cat. by L. Boccia and others, Arezzo, S Francesco, 1974), pp. 91–2
E. Carli: *Il Museo di Pisa* (Pisa, 1974), pp. 97–8
G. Marchini: *Filippo Lippi* (Milan, 1975), pp. 119, 234–5
J. Shearman: 'The Collection of the Younger Branch of the Medici', *Burl. Mag.*, cxvii (1975), pp. 12–27 (16, 20)
F. Zeri: *Italian Paintings in the Walters Art Gallery*, i (Baltimore, 1976), pp. 74–6
Early Italian Painting (exh. cat., London, Matthiesen F.A., 1983), pp. 57–8

ANNA PADOA RIZZO

Master of Catherine of Cleves (*fl* ?Utrecht, *c.* 1435–60). North Netherlandish illuminator. He was named for a manuscript that was for many years in the possession of the Duc d'Arenberg and was known as the Book of Hours of Catherine of Cleves because it includes a donor portrait of Catherine of Cleves, Duchess of Gelders.

1. THE BOOK OF HOURS OF CATHERINE OF CLEVES. After World War I the manuscript was inaccessible, and for over 50 years research was dependent on a handful of photographs made in 1904. Nonetheless, the iconographic rarity and extraordinary artistic quality of the book's decoration were recognized. In 1958 the manuscript entered the Guennol Collection in New York. Five years later the Pierpont Morgan Library in New York acquired a fragment of a Book of Hours that had been in the collection of Baron Maurice de Rothschild in the 1930s. The comparison of this new acquisition and the fragment in the Guennol Collection revealed that these were not only by the same illuminator but were in fact matching parts of a single and extraordinarily richly decorated Book of Hours, which had been taken apart in the 19th century, when the sequence of the miniatures was disturbed. Plummer first reconstructed the original form of the volume. In 1970 the Pierpont Morgan Library acquired the other portion from the Guennol Collection, but the manuscript remains in two volumes (the Rothschild portion, MS. M. 917; the Arenberg/Guennol portion, MS. M. 945).

The Hours of Catherine of Cleves originally contained 168 miniatures, of which 11 are now lost. The large number results from a decorative scheme that allows a complete opening with a full-page miniature on the *verso* and a half-page miniature above the text on the facing *recto* to mark the beginning of each major office or prayer.

In addition, each minor textual division is marked by a head-piece miniature. The unusually rich textual content of the book caused many of the peculiar iconographic aspects of the illustrations.

Each hour of the two most important offices, the Office of the Virgin and the Office of the Holy Cross, is decorated with two illustrations so that each office required a cycle of sixteen pictures. The opening miniature of the Office of the Virgin (see Plummer, no. 1) shows the owner of the book, Catherine, Duchess of Gelders, kneeling before the Virgin and Child in glory. Following this is a cycle from the *Annunciation to Joachim* (P 2) to the *Assumption of the Virgin* (P 15). The Office of the Holy Cross contains an elaborate cycle of the Passion with several rarely encountered scenes (P 16–31). The offices and masses connected with the days of the week follow. The texts for Friday constitute an exception: the Hours of the Holy Cross, which would be common at this place, had already been included at the beginning of the manuscript and were replaced by the Office of the Compassion of the Lord. This rare text is illustrated by scenes from the legend of the *Tree of Mercy*, the branch from the Tree of Life that was planted in the mouth of Adam and grew to provide the wood for the Cross of Christ (P 79–86). The mass appended is the usual Mass of the Holy Cross (P 87). The beginning of each office and mass is decorated with a full two-page opening, while the beginning of each hour within the offices has a head-piece miniature. These are followed by the Penitential Psalms and the Office of the Dead, which are introduced with a fully illustrated opening (P 98–100). The suffrages to the saints are illustrated by 57 (originally 61) head-piece miniatures (P 101–57), usually showing the standing saints with their attributes, or more rarely in a scene from their legend.

All the miniatures in the Hours of Catherine of Cleves are by the same painter. The *Deposition* (P 28) is related to the composition by the Master of Flémalle, known from a copy (Liverpool, Walker A.G.), and the detailed observation characteristic of early Netherlandish painting is also evident in these miniatures. The Master of Catherine of Cleves succeeded not only in introducing the achievements of panel painters into manuscript illumination but also in adding a new depth of human understanding to the realism found in panel paintings. He showed the Holy Family at their household chores (P 92 and P 149; see fig. 1) or at a meal (P 93) with great sympathy; these scenes offer excellent information on the furnishing of domestic rooms in the 15th century. These paintings represent family life more directly than any others before the genre painting of the 17th century. This directness is characteristic of the scenes in the *bas-de-page* miniatures, as for example the baker at his work (P 111) or an innkeeper sampling his wine (P 110). Often these scenes relate to the miniature on the page and supplement or comment on the action represented there, sometimes humorously. For example, in the death scene a young dandy at the death bed appears again in the *bas-de-page* already helping himself from the chest containing the inheritance (P 41). The Master of Catherine of Cleves was also capable of gravity. In the fourth miniature of the *Tree of Mercy* cycle (P 82), the branch of the Tree of Life is shown growing through Adam's shattered gravestone into a great tree that stands

1. Master of Catherine of Cleves: *Holy Family at Work*, 192×130 mm, miniature from the Hours of Catherine of Cleves, *c.* 1440 (New York, Pierpont Morgan Library, MS. 917, fol. 149)

alone in a desolate, severe landscape with an evening sky tinted orange and yellow. The miniature is one of the earliest pure landscapes and is also striking for its strict geometrical composition and the intensity of its mood. The artist clearly wished to refer to the turning-point between the mercy denied to Adam and the plan of salvation in which the tree, as the wood of Christ's cross, played a direct part.

The representations of the saints in the suffrages afforded no opportunity for such intensity, and the illuminator gave greater attention to the borders in this part of the book. Instead of ivy leaf and acanthus borders, a variety of objects are depicted with the care of a still-life, linked up or arranged in geometric forms around the text and miniature. On certain pages, objects such as a Paternoster (P 116), a collection of coins and medals (P 117), a piece of jewellery (P 147) or feathers (P 151) give the impression of resting on the parchment, an effect that corresponds to later *trompe l'oeil* painting. Often, however, the arrangements are fantastic or grotesque, such as a chain of fish swallowing each other's tails (P 128) or an arrangement of mussels and a crab (see fig. 2). There are a few early versions of such border decoration, as in the Très Riches Heures by the Limbourg brothers (Chantilly, Mus. Condé, MS. 65, fol. 168*v*), but the Book of Hours of Catherine of Cleves is unique in the variety of the objects represented. Its extravagant border decoration had an

2. Master of Catherine of Cleves: *St Ambrose*, border decorated with mussels and a crab, 192×130 mm, miniature from the Hours of Catherine of Cleves, *c*. 1440 (New York, Pierpont Morgan Library, MS. 917, fol. 244)

influence on later book painters in Ghent and Bruges, such as the Master of Mary of Burgundy and his followers. For an illustration *see* CALVARY.

2. DATING AND LOCATION. Since the portrait of Catherine of Cleves at the beginning of the book shows her coat of arms as Duchess of Gelders, the manuscript must date from after her marriage in 1430. The style of the miniatures, however, points to a slightly later date, *c*. 1440–45. Although some of the landscapes (e.g. P 4) partially reiterate formulae originating in Parisian illumination of *c*. 1400, others (e.g. P 16) are surprisingly progressive, with a low horizon and a convincing structure of hills, plains and paths winding into a far distance. His figures act with great freedom and have a surprising physical presence. Their plasticity is emphasized by strong highlighting, particularly in the flesh tones; the figures bend and move, sometimes quite dramatically. Draperies are rather sharply folded, underlining the figures' movement, but often these develop a dynamic and spacious quality of their own.

The painting of 14 manuscripts has been attributed either wholly or in part to the Master of Catherine of Cleves. The earliest phase of his career is represented by a number of datable works including a Book of Hours dated

1438 (The Hague, Rijksmus. Meermanno–Westreenianum, MS. 10.E.1). The sketchlike execution, with very loose application of paint and visible brushstrokes, the pale colouring, awkward faces and dramatic movements give the 12 full-page miniatures of this manuscript a remarkably expressive quality. This is very unlike the later miniatures in the Hours of Catherine of Cleves, with their bright and varied palette and their firmly modelled surfaces. Other early works include 8 miniatures in the Hours of Kaetzaert van Zaer, dated 1439 (Leiden, Bib. Rijksuniv., MS. B.P.L.224), and the 7 finest pen drawings of the 117 that illustrate a historiated Bible, also of 1439 (Munich, Bayer. Staatsbib., MS. germ. 1102). Another Bible illustrated in the same technique (London, BL, Add. MS. 38122) contains a few drawings by the Master of Catherine of Cleves, but, whereas his drawing style in the Munich Bible is enlivened by a nervous, agitated, even shaky line, the pen drawings in the London manuscript suggest an effort to achieve a painterly effect through the use of finely nuanced hatching and consequently have been dated much later. Both Bibles were made for members of the Lokhorst family of Utrecht. Calkins identified the hand of the Master of Catherine of Cleves in six historiated initials, a miniature and a border in the Greiffenclau Missal (Baltimore, MD, Walters A.G., MS. W. 174). Since the principal painter of the Missal is the Master of Zweder van Culemborg, it is assumed that the Master of Catherine of Cleves was connected with and perhaps even trained in this workshop.

The Master of Catherine of Cleves probably painted the nine full-page miniatures in the Hours of Katharina von Lokhorst (Münster, Westfäl. Landesmus., MS. 530), perhaps *c*. 1448, the year of the marriage of the owner and shortly after the artist's masterpiece, the Hours of Catherine of Cleves. The Hours of the Burggraf Willem van Montfort, Provost and Archdeacon of Utrecht Cathedral (Vienna, Österreich. Nbib., Cod. s.n. 12878), must have been completed *c*. 1450, as its astronomical tables begin in this year. The borders are without parallel in other manuscripts decorated by the Master of Catherine of Cleves, and only 3 of the 23 miniatures were painted by him. The others are in the style associated with Willem Vrelant. In this case it is possible that the Master delivered only three individual folios to the workshop responsible for the rest of the book. The Pontifical from Onze-Lieve-Vrouw, Utrecht (Utrecht, Bib. Rijksuniv., Hs. 400), is of similar date and is notable for the genre-like representations of craftsmen at work in the borders. The historiated initial 'I' in the first volume of a Bible (Brussels, Bib. Royale Albert 1er, MS. 9158–9167), commissioned by Abbot Henri de Cherauz for his monastery of St Lawrence near Liège in 1456, has been identified as an important late work (Scillia). The three surviving miniatures as well as the borders in the front section of a Book of Hours (The Hague, Rijksmus. Meermanno–Westreenianum, MS. 10.F.50), probably painted for another member of the Lokhorst family, are by the Master of Catherine of Cleves. The border decoration of the later part of this Book of Hours is by another illuminator identified by Boon as Philippe de Mazerolles. Such close collaboration with the Master of Catherine of Cleves suggests that Mazerolles was then a member of his workshop. The works from this latest phase often look somewhat mannered, with a monotonous repetition of sharp rectangular drapery folds.

Although the Master may have been itinerant for a period, both his patrons and the artists with whom he collaborated suggest that his workshop was in Utrecht. This would most easily explain his relationship to later Flemish manuscript illumination, for the influence of Utrecht illumination in Flanders is clearly documented.

BIBLIOGRAPHY

K. G. Boon: 'Nieuwe gegevens over de Meester van Katharina van Kleef en zijn atelier' [New information on the Master of Catherine of Cleves and his workshop], *Bull. Kon. Ned. Oudhdknd. Bond*, n. s. 6, xvii (1964), cols 241–54

P. Pieper and others: 'Das Stundenbuch der Katharina von Lochorst und der Meister der Katharina von Kleve', *Westfalen: Hft. Gesch., Kst & Vlksknd.*, xliv/2 (1966), pp. 97–164 [issue ded. to exh. cat., Münster, Westfäl. Landesmus., 1966]

J. Plummer, ed.: *The Hours of Catherine of Cleves* (New York, 1966) [partial facs. with reproductions of all miniatures and a selection of text pp.] [P]

L. M. J. Delaissé: *A Century of Dutch Manuscript Illumination* (Berkeley and Los Angeles, 1968), pp. 28–30, 32, 37–41, 81–6

F. Gorissen: *Das Stundenbuch der Katharina von Kleve: Analyse und Kommentar* (Berlin, 1973) [commentary vol. suppl. Plummer, 1966]

R. G. Calkins: 'Parallels between Incunabula and Manuscripts from the Circle of the Master of Catherine of Cleves', *Oud-Holland*, xcii (1978), pp. 137–60

D. G. Scillia: 'A Late Work from the Circle of the Master of Catherine of Cleves', *Oud-Holland*, xcii (1978), pp. 1–6

R. G. Calkins: 'Distribution of Labor: The Illuminators of the Hours of Catherine of Cleves and their Workshop', *Trans. Amer. Philos. Soc.*, lxix/5 (1979), pp. 3–83

J. H. Marrow: *A Descriptive and Analytical Catalogue of Dutch Illustrated Manuscripts of the 14th, 15th and 16th Centuries*, 2 vols (Doornspijk, 1990)

BODO BRINKMANN

Master of the Cellini Madonna. *See under* BASSANTE, BARTOLOMEO.

Cesi Master (*fl* 1308). Italian painter. He was named by Garrison after a dossal now in S Maria, Cesi, in Umbria, dated by inscription to 1308. It shows the *Virgin and Child Enthroned* with a kneeling female donor named in the inscription as Domina Elena; on either side are two registers of small-scale standing saints and two angels swinging censers. The panels of a large rectangular triptych, now arranged as a pair of doors (Saint-Jean-Cap-Ferrat, Villa–Mus. Ile de France, Fond. de Rothschild), showing scenes from the *Life of the Virgin*, have also been attributed to the Master. The centre panel, the *Assumption of the Virgin*, has the distinctive Umbrian iconography of the Virgin leaning her head and arm on Christ's shoulder. Small narrative scenes from the *Life and Death of the Virgin* are on the wings. The triptych is probably identifiable with one seen in the Convento della Passione, Spoleto, in the 19th century and probably painted for Spoleto Cathedral. The Cesi Master was active in the region around Spoleto, and a painted Crucifix (Spoleto, Pin. Com.) is also attributed to him. This is unusual in that it shows the living Christ crucified with only three nails. A fragmentary rectangular dossal from S Maria, Ponte, near Spoleto, is sometimes attributed to him. It shows *Christ in Majesty* within a mandorla supported by five roundels containing the four Evangelist Symbols and an *Agnus Dei*; on either side are two registers with small-scale standing saints and

censer-swinging angels, and the remains of an *Annunciation* and *Nativity*. Works by the Cesi Master show the influence of the Roman Master (*fl c.* 1260–80) at Assisi, and a Roman origin under the influence of Pietro Cavallini has been suggested (Longhi). His works contain many iconographical echoes of the frescoes of S Francesco, Assisi, for example the St Nicholas Chapel in the Lower Church and the stylistic influence of the St Cecilia Master in the Upper Church. He was also much influenced by earlier local painters such as Simeone and Machilone da Spoleto (*fl* 1230–57).

BIBLIOGRAPHY

E. B. Garrison: *Italian Romanesque Panel Painting: An Illustrated Index* (Florence, 1949), p. 14

R. Longhi: 'Un dossale italiano a Saint-Jean-Cap-Ferrat', *Paragone*, xii/141 (1961), pp. 11–19

M. Meiss: 'Reflections of Assisi: A Tabernacle and the Cesi Master', *Scritti di storia dell'arte in onore di Mario Salmi*, ii (Rome, 1962), pp. 75–111

F. Todini: *La pittura umbra dal duecento al primo cinquecento* (Milan, 1989), i, p. 114; ii, pp. 127–9

DILLIAN GORDON

Master of Chaource (*fl c.* 1510–30). French sculptor. He worked in the Champagne region, near Troyes. Koechlin and Marquet de Vasselot named him the Master of St Martha, after a celebrated stone statue of *St Martha* in the church of La Madeleine, Troyes. The serenity of this figure, its seriousness of expression and the fluidity of its draperies made an original departure from the stiffness of Late Gothic sculpture. Devaux (1956) identified similar characteristics in the *Entombment* (Chaource, St Jean-Baptiste), a stone group produced in 1515 for Nicolas de Moustier, Captain of Chaource; he consequently named the artist the Master of Chaource. the *Entombment* is among the most poignant examples of the genre. It still conforms to the Gothic tradition, but, in the grouping of the figures and their naturalness of movement and gesture, the sculptor has introduced a new expressiveness and a dramatic tension. The sober and statuesque style and the distinctive facial type, with flat planes of the forehead, cheeks and chin, are found in a number of other examples of sculpture from this period, such as the *Pietà* in St Jean, Troyes, and two groups of *Donors with Saints* (Troyes, St Nicolas). The composition of the *Entombment and Deposition* in the church of Villeneuve-L'Archevêque, which came from the Cistercian abbey of Vauluisant, clearly shows the influence of Italian examples, while the two *Holy Women* (New York, Cloisters) may be the work of a follower. The work of the Master of Chaource shows the persistence of the Gothic spirit, while more decorative, emphatic and mannered tendencies were gradually developing. Devaux (1959 and 1970) has proposed that the Master of Chaource may have been Nicolas Halins (*fl* 1502/3–41).

BIBLIOGRAPHY

R. Koechlin and J.-J. Marquet de Vasselot: *La Sculpture à Troyes et dans La Champagne méridionale au seizième siècle: Etude sur la transition de l'art gothique à l'italianisme* (Paris, 1900), pp. 96–110

L. Morillot: *Une Belle Statue de l'eglise de la Madeleine à Troyes, son identification* (Dijon, 1904)

E. Devaux: *Le Maître de Chaource* (St Léger-Vauban, 1956) [photographs]

R. Devaux: 'Suite à Chaource', *Zodiaque*, 40 (1959)

——: '2e suite à Chaource', *Zodiaque*, 84 (1970)

W. H. Forsyth: *The Entombment of Christ: French Sculptures of the Fifteenth and Sixteenth Centuries* (Cambridge, MA, 1970)

Vie Champagne, 309 (1981) [issue dedicated to Troyes sculpture]

C. Avery: *Studies in European Sculpture*, ii (London, 1988), pp. 103–35 (130–31)
PHILIPPE ROUILLARD

Master of Charles VIII. *See* PERRÉAL, JEAN.

Master of Charles of Angoulême. *See* TESTARD, ROBINET.

Master of Charles of France (*fl c.* 1455–75). French illuminator. His chief work is in a Book of Hours (Paris, Bib. Mazarine, MS. 473) produced for Charles, Duc de Berry, younger brother of King Louis XI. The artist was a follower of Jean Fouquet, whose stage settings he adapted with inventive *trompe l'oeil* effects. In all probability the master is to be identified with JEAN DE LAVAL, recorded in Charles's accounts. Overpainted heraldry suggests that the Mazarine Hours were begun in 1465 for Louis, Bâtard de Bourbon, and Joanna of Valois, a natural daughter of Louis XI. The manuscript was then continued for Charles of France, with special impetus in the campaign to mark his induction as Duke of Normandy that year. The book was planned with an ambitious programme, but many of its illustrations were not carried out beyond the drawing stage. The most elaborate composition is on an excised double folio (1465; New York, Cloisters, 58.71 a–b). Here, the facing sides form a diptych of the *Annunciation* (see fig.) set before the portal of a church with profuse sculptural decoration outlined in white and gleaming in various shades of gold, as if a huge shrine. Behind is a

landscape in which figure prominently the castle of Mehun-sur-Yèvre and an unusual procession of angels descending from Heaven. On the *verso* of the second folio, the text and its historiated initial are framed to give the illusion of a panel suspended from a chain in the interior of a portal before the *Visitation* set in a landscape. The artist's *tableaux* are generally banal, but he is distinguished by some surprising effects, which were largely carried out on the frames: in one miniature of the Mazarine manuscript, the *Journey to Bethlehem* (fol. 72 bis), the wide panoramic landscape is framed by borders depicting sentries in full armour; in another, the *Nativity* (fol. 85*v*), the framing device comprises an aviary on which perch magnificent peacocks. Also characteristic of this artist are the round faces of his figures, rather puffed out, with high foreheads and eyes that seem half open.

A modest corpus of miniatures has been attributed to the Master of Charles of France. His early work is represented by an *Annunciation* of *c.* 1455 in a Book of Hours (Stonyhurst Coll., Lancs, MS. 38, fol. 40), and a Psalter–Hours (New York, Pierpont Morgan Lib., MS. M. 67) of *c.* 1455–60. His mature style is exemplified by the miniatures in a *Roméléon* made in 1461 for Charles of France (Coligny, Fond. Martin Bodmer, MS. 143), with one of the compositions incorporating a close rendering of Fouquet's portrait of *King Charles VII* (Paris, Louvre); a copy of works by Seneca and Cicero (St Petersburg, Rus. N. Lib., MS. fr. F.v.III, 1); and Charles's Hours. The artist's late style is represented by the *Vierge aux fleurs*,

Master of Charles of France (?Jean de Laval): *Annunciation*, tempera and gold on parchment, left leaf 172×123 mm, right leaf 170×125 mm; from the Hours of Charles of France, 1465 (New York, The Cloisters, 58.71 a–b)

added to a Book of Hours (The Hague, Kon. Bib., MS. 74), and probably by the Hours of Marguerite of Rohan, widow of Jean d'Orléans, Comte d'Angoulême (*c.* 1475; Princeton U., NJ, Lib., Garrett MS. 55), in which compositions have become more tightly controlled.

BIBLIOGRAPHY

L. Delisle: 'Un Feuillet des Heures de Charles, frère de Louis XI', *Manuscrit*, i/2 (1894), pp. 147–8

H. Stein: *Charles de France, frère de Louis XI* (Paris, 1919)

M. B. Freeman: 'The Annunciation from a Book of Hours for Charles of France', *Bull. Met.*, n. s., xix (1960–61), pp. 105–18

The Last Flowering: French Painting in Manuscripts, 1420–1530 (exh. cat. by J. Plummer, New York, Pierpont Morgan Lib., 1982)

PATRICK M. DE WINTER

Chief Associate of Maître François. *See* MASTER OF JACQUES DE BESANÇON.

Master of the Chiostro degli Aranci. *See* GIOVANNI DI CONSALVO.

Master of the Church Sermon. *See* AERTGEN VAN LEYDEN.

Master of the Cité des Dames (*fl c.* 1400–15). Illuminator, active in Paris. One of the most prolific illuminators in Paris during the first two decades of the 15th century, he was named by Meiss after the five or more copies of Christine de Pisan's *Cité des dames* illustrated by him and his workshop. His early work is closely related to that of Jacquemart de Hesdin, with whom he executed the Barcelona Hours (*c.* 1401; Barcelona, Bib. Central, MS. 1850). Both artists used the same Italianate method of modelling flesh tones with green underpaint, and many of Jacquemart's figures and compositions were adopted by the Master of the Cité des Dames. Although the Italian elements in his work are pronounced, Sterling argued that he came from the Netherlands, drawing particular attention to the artist's evocation of realistic detail in scenes of domestic and city life, his innovative treatment of landscape and his distinctive rendering of interior space and architectural settings.

The first illustrations for the *Cité des dames*, which appeared in 1405, seem to have been composed by the Master under the direction of Christine herself, and all the copies from his workshop follow the same model. The opening miniature (Paris, Bib. N., MS. fr. 607, fol. 2*r*; see fig.) demonstrates how key concepts of the author's text are given effective visual expression. The composition is divided into two sections: in the interior on the left, Christine stands behind a table on which are displayed both open and closed books. Reading has fuelled her frustration at not having been born a man, a frustration that she communicates to Droiture, Raison and Justice who present themselves before her. The static nature of this scene, in which figures and objects are crowded into a relatively small internal space, emphasizes the author's mood. By contrast, on the right, in an expansive exterior, Christine, assisted by Raison, has already begun to build the walls of the City of Women. The energetic activity of 'bricklaying', in which the two female figures are engaged, tellingly emphasizes the allegorical theme of the book— the construction of an enduring edifice, indeed a whole city, out of eminent deeds accomplished by women.

Master of the Cité des Dames: frontispiece miniature from Christine de Pisan: *Cité des dames, c.* 1405 (Paris, Bibliothèque Nationale, MS. fr. 607, fol. 2*r*)

The Cité des Dames Master collaborated with other Parisian illuminators and workshops, and the influence of the Boucicaut Master, which became increasingly marked in his work, was probably the result of such collaboration. For example his striking frontispiece for the *Works* of Christine de Pisan (London, BL, Harley MS. 4431, fol. 2*r*; for illustration *see* CHRISTINE DE PISAN), presented to Isabeau of Bavaria *c.* 1412–15, is clearly influenced by the Boucicaut Master's dedication miniature in the second version of Pierre Salmon's *Réponses de Pierre Salmon* (after 1411; Geneva, Bib. Pub. & U., MS. fr. 165, fol. 4*r*; *see* BOUCICAUT MASTER above, fig. 2); the artists had collaborated on an earlier edition of the *Réponses*. The remarkable representation of space in the frontispiece to the *Works* has been analysed (White) and, in certain elements, the influence of 14th-century Italian artists such as Maso di Banco and Pietro and Ambrogio Lorenzetti discerned; but the northern illuminator's distinctive handling of colour has also been noted (Sterling). On either side of the room, beds draped in red create a powerful impression of movement into depth, while the semicircle of seated women behind the kneeling Christine helps to preserve the surface cohesion of the composition. The setting of the presentation scene in a royal bedchamber, together with such details as the open shutters on the rear wall and the framing diaphragm arch, are derived from the Boucicaut Master.

The spacious settings for many of the compositions of the Cité des Dames Master have prompted comparisons with monumental wall painting. While his landscapes are sometimes based on rather archaic patterns, they convincingly convey the sense of an extensive terrain and are enlivened by the rendering of closely observed detail or the presentation of events from unusual angles. Windswept clouds fill the sky in an illlustration of the countryside in Salmon's *Réponses* (*c.* 1409; Paris, Bib. N., MS. fr. 23279, fol. 69*r*); and the *Death of Queen Brunehilde* in Boccaccio's *Des Cas des nobles femmes* (*c.* 1415; Paris, Bib. N., MS. fr. 16994, fol. 307*r*) is presented with striking immediacy through a close-up bird's-eye view of a city street, which includes not only the queen's demise but also a glimpse of the disturbed citizens, who witness the event from the doorways of their houses.

The Cité des Dames Master was responsible for the supervision and organization of a large workshop, which specialized in the illumination of historical, romantic and allegorical texts, many of which were secular in nature. These included the *Grandes Chroniques de France*, French translations of Livy and Boccaccio, and several other writings of Christine de Pisan. Hindman and Hedeman have argued that the notable ability of this team to render accurately such details as contemporary dress, settings and ceremonial was an important factor in their popularity. The learned advisers responsible for drawing up extensive visual programmes often exploited these talents to provide a contemporary political or moral gloss on a particular historical or allegorical text.

BIBLIOGRAPHY
M. Meiss: 'The Exhibition of French Manuscripts of the XIII–XVI Centuries at the Bibliothèque Nationale', *A. Bull.*, xxxviii (1956), pp. 187–96
——: *French Painting in the Time of Jean de Berry: The Late XIV Century and the Patronage of the Duke*, 2 vols (London and New York, 1967, rev. 1969)
J. White: *The Birth and Rebirth of Pictorial Space* (London, 1967)
M. Meiss with K. Morand and E. W. Kirsch: *French Painting in the Time of Jean de Berry: The Boucicaut Master* (London and New York, 1968)
M. Meiss with S. O. Smith and E. Beatson: *French Painting in the Time of Jean de Berry: The Limbourgs and their Contemporaries*, 2 vols (New York and London, 1974)
P. de Winter: 'Christine de Pizan, ses enlumineurs et ses rapports avec le milieu bourguignon', *Actes du 104e congrès national des sociétés savantes: Paris, 1979*, pp. 335–75
S. L. Hindman: *Christine de Pizan's 'Epistre Othea': Painting and Politics at the Court of Charles VI* (Toronto, 1986), pp. 16, 63, 69, 73, 97
C. Sterling: *La Peinture médiévale à Paris, 1300–1500*, i (Paris, 1987), pp. 286–95
A. D. Hedeman: *The Royal Image: Illustration of the Grandes Chroniques de France, 1274–1422* (Berkeley and Los Angeles, 1991), pp. 153–77

MARGARET M. MANION

Master of Città di Castello (*fl c.* 1305–20). Italian painter. He is named after the *Virgin and Child Enthroned with Saints* (Città di Castello, Pin. Com.), which may derive from a lost composition by Duccio di Buoninsegna. The painting is the earliest work of a corpus that also includes a dismembered polyptych of the *Virgin and Child* (Siena, Mus. Opera Duomo, 24) and *SS Augustine, Paul, Peter and Anthony Abbot* (Siena, Pin. N., 29–32); a polyptych of the *Virgin and Child with SS Francis, John the Evangelist, Stephen and Chiara* (Siena, Pin. N., 33); and a third altarpiece composed of a *Virgin and Child* (Copenhagen, Stat. Mus. Kst), *St Peter* and *St John the Baptist* (New Haven, CT, Yale U. A.G., 1943. 242 and 1943. 243), as well as a *St Francis* (ex-Lanckoronski priv. col., Vienna). A *Virgin and Child* in Detroit (Detroit, MI, Inst. A., 24.96) is a closely related shop work. Although inclined to borrow heavily from Duccio and perhaps also from Segna di Bonaventura and Ugolino di Nerio, the Master had a distinctive style rooted in late 13th-century Sienese painting, and his works continued to reflect these origins well into the second decade of the 14th century. He was an interesting colourist, with a preference for subtle variations and pale hues, but his work had little impact on a younger generation in Siena.

BIBLIOGRAPHY
Thieme–Becker
C. Brandi: *Duccio* (Florence, 1951), pp. 148–50
P. Torriti: *La Pinacoteca Nazionale di Siena: Dipinti dal XII al XV secolo* (Genoa, 1977), pp. 66–8
J. Stubblebine: *Duccio di Buoninsegna and his School*, i (Princeton, 1979), pp. 85–9

H. B. J. MAGINNIS

Master of the Cloisters Unicorn. *See* MASTER OF THE UNICORN HUNT below.

Master of the Coburg Roundels [Master of the Drapery Studies] (*fl* Strasbourg, *c.* 1470–1500). German draughtsman and painter. His name derives from two sketches for roundels (*c.* 1485; Coburg, Veste Coburg), considered to be cornerstones of his stylistic development. He is also known as the Master of the Drapery Studies because many of his works are detailed studies of the folds of clothing (sleeves, loincloths) or of whole garments. He is attributed with about 180 sheets (notably Coburg, Veste Coburg; Berlin, Kupferstichkab.; Madrid, Bib. N.; Paris, Louvre), most of them covered on both sides, one of the largest groups of drawings attributed to an artist of the pre-Dürer era. As there are several drawings after Strasbourg stained glass paintings of *c.* 1460, it has been suggested (Wentzel, Rott, Andersson) that the draughtsman was a designer in a glass-painting workshop; since some show similarities to products of workshops within the sphere of Peter Hemmel von Andlau, one window design might be attributable (Anzelewsky) to this leading master of the Strasbourg glass-painting industry, by whom the Master may have been employed (Fischel).

The Master's drawings also include studies of works from the Netherlands or Cologne, of paintings, sculptures and plans for altars. Opinions vary considerably as to the chronological order of the sheets. Buchner (1927) considered that he was stylistically indebted to the Housebook Master and that he was active in the Middle Rhine area; Fischel (1933–4) added further panels and some mural fragments to his oeuvre, contending that he was trained under the Strasbourg Master of the Karlsruhe Passion. The principal paintings comprise ten panels of a *Passion* cycle (1488; Strasbourg, St Pierre-le-Vieux) and a similar *Passion* (1490s: Mainz, Landesmus.), a *Trinity* (Lyon), sections of an altar of *St Mary Magdalene* (before 1490; Karlsruhe, Staatl. Ksthalle; San Francisco, CA, de Young Mem. Mus.) and altar wings showing the *Legend of St Margaret* (1490s; Dijon, Mus. B.-A.; priv. cols). There are also a few individual panels depicting saints (1490s; Strasbourg, Mus. Oeuvre Notre-Dame).

BIBLIOGRAPHY

E. Buchner: 'Studien zur mittelrheinischen Malerei und Graphik der Spätgotik und Renaissance, III. Der Meister der Coburger Rundblätter', *Münchn. Jb. Bild. Kst.*, n. s. 1, iv (1927), pp. 284–300

F. Winkler: 'Skizzenbücher eines unbekannten rheinischen Meisters um 1500', *Wallraf-Richartz-Jb.*, n. s. i ([vi] 1930), pp. 123–52

L. Fischel: 'Die Heimat des "Meisters der Coburger Rundblätter" (Studien in der altdeutschen Abteilung der Badischen Kunsthalle, ii)', *Oberrhein. Kst.*, vi (*c.* 1933/34), pp. 27–40

——: 'Der Meister der Karlsruher Passion; sein verschollenes Oeuvre (Studien in der altdeutschen Abteilung der Badischen Kunsthalle, iii)', *Oberrhein. Kst.*, vi (*c.* 1933–4), pp. 41–60

H. Rott: *Quellen und Forschungen zur südwestdeutschen und schweizerischen Kunstgeschichte im XV. und XVI. Jahrhundert. III. Der Oberrhein* (Stuttgart, 1937), pp. 73–9, nos 34–8

H. Wentzel: 'Glasmaler und Maler im Mittelalter', *Z. Kstwiss.*, iii (1949), pp. 53–62 (61)

L. Fischel: *Die Karlsruher Passion und ihr Meister* (Karlsruhe, 1952), pp. 31f, 62f

F. Anzelewsky: 'Peter Hemmel und der Meister der Gewandstudien', *Z. Dt. Ver. Kstwiss.*, xxviii (1964), pp. 43–53

From a Mighty Fortress (exh. cat., ed. C. Andersson and C. Talbot; Detroit, MI, Inst. A.; Ottawa, N.G.; Coburg, Veste Coburg; 1981–2), pp. 108–44; pp. 388–93 (C. Andersson: 'Excursus: The Master of the Coburg Roundels'); nos 28–44

MICHAEL ROTH

Master of the Codex Coburgensis (*fl* 1550–55). Italian draughtsman. He executed a collection of 282 drawings of antiquities, with a preponderance of reliefs, which was acquired on the Roman art market in 1870 and 1872 by the Frankfurt dealer Jacob Gerson (1821–1903), Consul General for Saxony, and presented by him to Duke Ernst II of Saxe-Coburg and Gotha (*reg* 1844–93) as a gift. It has since been known as the Codex Coburgensis, although it is a portfolio, and is today housed in the Kupferstichkabinett der Kunstsammlungen der Veste Coburg, Coburg (inv. no. Hz 2). Little is known of its history before its acquisition by Gerson; however, watermarks on the paper of the drawings and the locations where the antiquities depicted were earlier preserved both indicate a mid-16th-century origin in Rome and its neighbourhood. It is likely that the collection of drawings was commissioned by Cardinal Marcello Cervini (1501–55), who reigned as Pope Marcellus II for a few days in 1555. He was a great scholar, with an interest in the study of antiquity, who is known to have commissioned editions of antique inscriptions and illustrated works on antique sculpture in connection with the foundation of a Vitruvian academy. The dates of discovery of some of the antiquities depicted in the Codex Coburgensis suggest that the work was undertaken towards the end of his life.

Although the sequence of the drawings was wholly disarranged before Gerson's acquisition of the collection, traces of earlier display and ensuing neglect (before 1806) allow certain conclusions about the original arrangement of the contents. These are confirmed by the Codex Pighianus in the Staatsbibliothek Preussischer Kulturbesitz in Berlin (MS. Lat. 2° 61), which contains a partial, later expanded copy of the Codex Coburgensis, with 172 of its drawings and also 50 sheets bearing copies of originals lost from the Codex Coburgensis. Further evidence suggests that the Coburg collection formerly consisted of considerably more than 300 sheets. It was originally arranged in chapters on genealogies of gods, astronomy and calendrical lore, heroic mythology, death and sacrificial ritual, insignia of office and circus shows. Thus the Codex

Coburgensis may be called the first, systematically presented work of archaeological illustration, long predating Johann Joachim Winckelmann.

There has hitherto been no actual certainty concerning the identity of the artist, or several artists, who executed the drawings of the Codex Coburgensis. Examination of the state of preservation of the drawings, very variable in parts, has led to the conclusion that with five exceptions they are all by the same hand. No further drawings by the artist of the Codex Coburgensis have been found elsewhere, other than four contained in the Codex Pighianus, probably placed there in error during the process of copying; hence the name of Master of the Codex Coburgensis must suffice as the artist's designation.

This master is distinguished from all other Renaissance artists who drew antiquities by his understanding of archaeology and stylistic closeness to his models; he is pre-eminent above all in the faithfulness with which he records the state of preservation of his originals and in his rendering of exact detail. His regular procedure was first to depict an object precisely in black chalk and then to execute the drawing with a pen in brown ink, adding grey wash with a brush. The light always falls from above left to below right, proof that the drawings were executed in a workshop, with a theoretical and didactic purpose in mind. Free relief background to the objects depicted is provided by vertical wash strokes. He evolved a special method of presenting extended depictions involving unfolding or unrolling paper. Among his stylistic characteristics are blank eyes, certain details of toe- and fingernails, and the avoidance of crosshatching in pen and arbitrary stippling. Clearly ordered compositions of a classical appearance, with a minimum of receding planes, were most to the liking of this artist; he mastered restless, more complex subjects with somewhat greater difficulty. He had an especial preference for Hellenic reliefs, whose religious content must have held interest for his client. Whether the inscriptions on the monuments depicted are by this artist or whether he engaged a lettering specialist for the task remains to be established.

BIBLIOGRAPHY

F. Matz: 'Über eine dem Herzog von Coburg-Gotha gehörige Sammlung alter Handzeichnungen nach Antiken', *Mber. Kön. Preuss. Akad. Wiss. Berlin* (Sept–Oct 1871)

Der Codex Coburgensis: Das erste systematische Archäologiebuch (exh. cat., ed. H. Wrede and R. Haprath; Coburg, Veste Coburg, 1986)

RICHARD HARPRATH

Master of the Codex of St George (*fl* first half of the 14th century). Italian illuminator and painter. His cognomen is derived from an illuminated Missal, known as the St George Codex (Rome, Vatican, Bib. Apostolica, Archv Capitolare S Pietro, MS. C. 129). From the time of DeNicola, who first connected this Master with the Vatican manuscript, until the early 1950s, he was thought to have been trained by a Sienese master, specifically, a follower of Simone Martini. The arguments centred around his association with Simone in Avignon and the importance of both artists for the development of the International Gothic style. Simone Martini's lost fresco of *St George* in Notre-Dame-des-Doms, Avignon, was considered to be the model for the St George Master's illustration on folio *85r* of the Vatican manuscript: on that page, St George frees the Cappadocian princess in the margins of Cardinal Giacomo Stefaneschi's text on 'The Miracles and Martyrdom of St George' (see fig.). Most scholars, however, now consider that the Master received his early training in Florentine art and that he was active in the first half of the 14th century, possibly as early as the first decade. A chronology of his career was established by Howett, but different dates were suggested by Boskovits (1984), because he associated the artist with the career of the elusive Lippo di Benivieni.

Early works attributed to the St George Master, such as the initial with *St Peter Venerated by a Pope* (Boulogne, Bib. Mun., MS. 86, fol. *2r*), demonstrate that his style combined the traditions of Sienese art, which entered Florence through the works of Duccio, with the native Florentine style of the period before Giotto, designated the 'miniaturist' tendency by Offner (*see* PACINO DI BONAGUIDA). Howett (1976) noted spatial and compositional problems that evolved out of these monumental and lyrical traditions and dated this early period *c.* 1325–30. Boskovits, however, believed that the Master's career began some 10–15 years earlier, listing as an example a Gradual (Rome, Santa Croce in Gerusalemme, MS. Cor. D) made in 1315 for the Badia di San Salvatore a

Settimo; he reproduced folio *272v*, an initial D with *St Clement Enthroned*. The spatial deformities were described by Boskovits as typical of the Master's approach, which was never as rational as that of Giotto's followers. Howett considered that the illumination in this manuscript was later in date, belonging to what he designated the Master's transitional period of *c.* 1335–40.

Within this transitional period, the Master attempted to put more substantive figures in a more convincing space. The figures in 17 cuttings (Berlin, Kupferstichkab., nos 1987, 1989, 1993–4, 1997, 2000, and Berlin, Bodemus., nos 1984–6, 1988, 1990–92, 1995–6, 1998–9) are more outwardly vivid, and the spatial settings are further developed, as in the initial F with the *Birth of the Virgin* (no. 2000). Boskovits proposed that the Berlin miniatures were executed soon after the earliest works of *c.* 1310–15, barely predating the Codex of St George itself. Both Boskovits and Howett recognized that the eponymous Codex represented the Master's mature style, but the former considered that certain stylistic features suggested an early date, while the latter dated the manuscript to the late period of *c.* 1340–45. The works of this stage in the Master's career reflect the increasing influence of Bernardo Daddi in Florence, and Howett proposed that the influence of Jacopo del Casentino and Pacino di Bonaguida was eclipsed by the increasingly pervasive sway of Daddi. The diptych of the *Crucifixion* and *Lamentation* (New York, Cloisters) and other late works show Daddi's lyric sweetness without a loss of spatial clarity or a reversion to surface pattern.

BIBLIOGRAPHY

G. DeNicola: 'L'affresco di Simone Martini ad Avignone', *L'Arte*, ix (1906), pp. 336–44
J. Howett: *The Master of the St George Codex* (diss., U. Chicago, 1968)
——: 'Two Panels by the Master of the St George Codex in the Cloisters', *Met. Mus. J.*, xi (1976), pp. 85–102
G. Pinto: *Il libro del Biadaiolo* (Florence, 1978)
M. G. Ciadri Dupre dal Poggetto: *Il Maestro del Codice di San Giorgio e il Cardinal Jacopo Stefaneschi* (Florence, 1981)
M. Boskovits: *Corpus* (1984)

DOMENICO G. FIRMANI

Master of Coëtivy (*fl c.* 1455–75). Illuminator, painter and tapestry designer, active in France. He is named after the Book of Hours with the portraits and armorial bearings of Olivier de Coëtivy and his wife, Marie Marguerite de Valois (Vienna, Österreich. Nbib., MS. 1929), made between their marriage in 1458 and Marie's death in 1473. This smart prayerbook is, in terms of page layout and border decoration, typical of French books of this period, but the style of the miniatures, all the work of the Coëtivy Master, does not appear to derive from the French tradition, suggesting instead a Netherlandish, and more specifically a north Netherlands, origin.

Although the Coëtivy Master illuminated other devotional books, such as a Book of Hours made for the Rivoire family (Paris, Bib. N., MS. nouv. acq. lat. 3114) and a Psalter (Baltimore, MD, Walters A.G., MS. W.297), these books do not show the artist at his best. The small scale of most of these pictures seems to have restricted his sense of composition, and his preference to work on a somewhat larger scale may be seen in several non-liturgical books convincingly attributed to him. These are all elaborately decorated and allow a clearer appreciation of his

Master of the Codex of St George: *St George Slaying the Dragon* in margins, *St George Venerated by Cardinal Giacomo Stefaneschi* in initial D, 370×249 mm; illuminated folio from the Codex of St George, *c.* 1315–45 (Rome, Vatican, Biblioteca Apostolica, Archivio Capitolare di S Pietro, MS. C. 129, fol. *85r*)

Master of Coëtivy: *Raising of Lazarus with Donors*, oil on panel, 785×1440 mm, *c.* 1455–60 (Paris, Musée du Louvre)

style. The only one that can be closely dated from internal evidence, and which may be the earliest of these manuscripts, is a copy of Dante's *Divine Comedy* (Paris, Bib. N., MS. ital. 72) made for Charles of France, younger son of King Charles VII, when he held the title Duc de Berry (1461–5). Other secular texts illuminated by the Master include an *Histoire universelle* by Orosius (Paris, Bib. N., MS. fr. 64), a *Compendium romanorum* (Paris, Bib. N., MS. fr. 730), a *Miroir historial* (Rome, Vatican, Bib. Apostolica, MS. Vat. reg. lat. 767) and two copies of Boethius's *Traité de la consolation*, one made for Jean Budé (*d* 1501), a royal secretary (Paris, Bib. N., MS. fr. 1098), and the other with no indications of original patronage (New York, Pierpont Morgan Lib., MS. M.222).

All these manuscripts display the Coëtivy Master's skill in adapting a wide variety of compositional techniques, often combining elements of landscape and interior setting within a single miniature to connect spatially several narrative scenes (e.g. MS. Vat. reg. lat. 767, fol. 6*r*). The artist was particularly successful in handling dramatic situations involving numerous figures, and exciting battle scenes, full of movement and vigour, may be considered his speciality. The subject-matter of the Orosius, for example, offered him the opportunity to develop this skill (e.g. fols 55*v*, 345*r*, 411*r*): soldiers with grimacing faces, wearing mock antique armour, some wielding swords, lances or banners, others riding rearing horses, convey a feeling for lively action. Although the Master tended to avoid difficulties of foreshortening, he was not uninterested in issues concerning perspective; landscape settings reveal a wonderful sense of distance and atmosphere, while interiors are quite spacious and coherent, although they use no definable rules of perspective.

The Master of Coëtivy's use of rather vibrant colour schemes is one of his most distinct characteristics and one that distinguishes him from contemporary French illuminators. He favoured colours such as orange modelled in dark red, and a deep blue, particularly evident in the skies of his landscapes. His figure style is also distinctive: male figures tend to be short and thick-set, uncouth and often menacing in appearance, with exaggerated facial features; women are less grotesque and are usually elegant, with handsome, though bland features and narrow waists. The atmospheric qualities of the Coëtivy Master's work suggest the influence of contemporary French artists such as Jean Fouquet, but the basic earthiness of his approach has more in common with art from the northern Netherlands. Comparison of his work with such artists as the Master of Catherine of Cleves and Geertgen tot Sint Jans indicates that he probably trained in the north Netherlandish tradition.

The illustrations in the *Miroir historial* are basically pen drawings, showing the Master's work at its most sensitive and detailed. In the *Compendium romanorum* the drawing is tinted with watercolour, an unusual technique for the period but one also used in eight large drawings of uniform character (Paris, Louvre, 2140–47) that are obviously by the same artist. These drawings are of great interest because they are clearly designs for part of a set of tapestries depicting the *Story of the Trojan Wars*. Evidently the Master also worked on a large scale. Several tapestries related to these drawings survive (e.g. four panels in Zamora Cathedral, Spain), and others are mentioned in inventories, indicating that this Trojan war series was one of the most popular sets of tapestries of the 15th century: one set was presented to Charles the Bold, Duke of Burgundy, in 1472 and another delivered to King Henry VII of England in

1488. The drawings are probably of earlier date since the paper has watermarks attributable to the 1460s. Like his miniatures, the Master's tapestry designs have a very cluttered effect but succeed in conveying a great sense of action. On the basis of these drawings, the design of other tapestries has been attributed to him, including an *Embarkation of Titus and Vespasian* (Lyon, Mus. A. Déc.), although the original drawings do not survive. One panel painting, a *Raising of Lazarus with Donors* (Paris, Louvre; see fig.), is also by the Master. This painting is less fussy and more emotional than his other work and firmly establishes his Netherlandish origins.

Since many of the Coëtivy Master's patrons were connected with the French court, it seems likely that the artist worked chiefly in the region of the Loire valley where the court resided. Further evidence suggests that the Coëtivy Master may be identified with the artist Henri de Vulcop (*see* VULCOP, (2)). At the time that Charles of France's *Divine Comedy* was illuminated (1461–5) Vulcop was one of two painters in his service. The other, Jean de Laval, may be associated with miniatures dated 1465 made for Charles's Book of Hours (New York, Cloisters, 58.71 a, b), and it is not unreasonable to assume that the *Divine Comedy*, which is stylistically quite unlike the Hours, was executed by Vulcop. Furthermore, Vulcop is a Netherlandish name, which agrees with the character of the Coëtivy Master's work. Nevertheless, the identification cannot yet be considered certain. The Coëtivy Master had several followers, most notably the Master of the Unicorn Hunt.

BIBLIOGRAPHY

P. Durrieu: 'Les Heures de Coëtivy à la bibliothèque de Vienne', *Bull. Soc. N. Antiqua. France* (1921), pp. 301–17
N. Reynaud: 'La *Résurrection de Lazare* et le Maître de Coëtivy', *Rev. Louvre*, xv (1965), pp. 171–82
——: 'Un Peintre français cartonnier de tapisseries au XVe siècle: Henri de Vulcop', *Rev. A.* [Paris], xxii (1973), pp. 7–22
O. Pächt and D. Thoss: *Die illuminierten Handschriften der Österreichischen Nationalbibliothek: Französische Schule*, 2 vols (Vienna, 1974), pp. 29–32, pls 32–41
N. Reynaud: 'Complément à la *Résurrection de Lazare* du Maître de Coëtivy', *Rev. Louvre*, xxvii (1977), pp. 222–4
G. Wingfield Digby: *The Tapestry Collection, Medieval and Renaissance*, London, V&A cat. (London, 1980), pp. 14–18
S. Hindman and G. M. Spiegel: 'The Fleur-de-lis Frontispieces to Guillaume de Nangis's *Chronique abrégée*: Political Iconography in Late Fifteenth-century France', *Viator*, xii (1981), pp. 381–407
The Last Flowering: French Painting in Manuscripts, 1420–1530, from American Collections (exh. cat. by J. Plummer and G. Clark, New York, Pierpont Morgan Lib., 1982)

THOMAS TOLLEY

Master of the Coronation Book of Charles V (*fl* Paris, *c.* 1350–78). French illuminator. He worked primarily for the court and was the most prolific illuminator in Paris after the Master of the Boqueteaux, with whose workshop he often collaborated. His lively compositions, graphically delineated, are appealing for their juxtaposition of hues. The figures have a portrait-like quality, but no concern is shown for foreshortening or perspective. The Master's earliest known illuminations are in a manuscript of the works of GUILLAUME DE MACHAUT (Paris, Bib. N., MS. fr. 1586). Shortly before 1356 he illustrated for King John II a *Bible historiale* (London, BL, Royal MS. 19 D. II). For the Dauphin, Charles, he produced the frontispiece of the *Livre des neuf juges* (1361; Brussels, Bib. Royale

Albert 1er, MS. 10319) and the illustrations of another *Bible historiale* (1363; Paris, Bib. N., MS. fr. 5707). In 1365 for the same patron, now King Charles V, he executed 38 miniatures in a book recording the coronation ceremony (London, BL, Cotton MS. Tib. B. VIII). Among other volumes for Charles V, in 1375–6 the Master contributed to two copies of the *Grandes Chroniques de France* (Paris, Bib. N., MS. fr. 2813; Britain, priv. col.), to a copy of St Augustine's *City of God* (Paris, Bib. N., MSS fr. 22912–3) and to manuscripts combining Aristotle's *Politics* and the pseudo-Aristotelian *Oeconomics* (Paris, Waziers priv. col.; Brussels, Bib. Royale Albert 1er, MSS 11201–2). For Jean, Duc de Berry, he partially illustrated another copy of the *Grandes Chroniques* (sold London, Sotheby's, 8 Dec 1981, lot 94). In 1376–8 he collaborated on the Grandes Heures of Philip the Bold, Duke of Burgundy (vol. 1: Cambridge, Fitzwilliam, MS. 3-1954; Brussels, Bib. Royale Albert 1er, MSS 11035–7; vol. 2: Brussels, Bib. Royale Albert 1er, MS. 13092); his work here shows signs of senescence and was completed by others.

BIBLIOGRAPHY

E. S. Dewick: *The Coronation Book of Charles V of France (Cotton MS. Tiberius B. VIII)*, Henry Bradshaw Society, xvi (London, 1899)
La Librairie de Charles V (exh. cat., ed. F. Avril and J. Lafaurie; Paris, Bib. N., 1968)
Les Fastes du gothique: Le Siècle de Charles V (exh. cat., entries by F. Avril and others, Paris, Grand Pal., 1981)
P. de Winter: 'The Grandes Heures of Philip the Bold, Duke of Burgundy: The Copyist Jean L'Avenant and his Patrons at the French Court', *Speculum*, lvii (1982), pp. 786–842
——: *La Bibliothèque de Philippe le Hardi, Duc de Bourgogne (1364–1404)* (Paris, 1985)

PATRICK M. DE WINTER

Master of the Coronation of the Virgin [Coronation Master; Master of the Livre des femmes nobles et renommées] (*fl* 1402–4). French illuminator. He is named after the frontispiece miniature, depicting the *Coronation of the Virgin* surrounded by numerous saints, of a manuscript of the revision of 1402 of the *Golden Legend* (392×287 mm; Paris, Bib. N., MS. fr. 242). Meiss assembled a corpus of works for this artist, whom he believed to have been trained in the Netherlands, from a group of manuscripts that Martens had attributed to an anonymous artist named the Master of 1402 (the rest of the group was ascribed to the MASTER OF BERRY'S CLERES FEMMES; *see* above). This comprises especially the Book of Hours that, according to its colophon (fol. 216v), originated at Nantes in 1402 (140×100 mm; New York, Pierpont Morgan Lib., MS. M. 515); some miniatures in a *Bible historiale* mentioned in the inventory of Jean, Duc de Berry, in 1402 (Paris, Bib. N., MS. fr. 159); Hayton de Courcy's *Fleur des histoires de la terre d'Orient* (Paris, Bib. N., MS. fr. 12201), one of three copies acquired by Philip the Bold, Duke of Burgundy, in 1403; and Boccaccio's *Des cleres et nobles femmes* (Paris, Bib. N., MS. fr. 598), which Jean de Berry received in February 1404. De Winter rejected the designation 'Coronation Master' and chose the name Master of the Livre des femmes nobles et renommées, in whose oeuvre he included the above-mentioned works.

BIBLIOGRAPHY

B. Martens: *Meister Francke* (Hamburg, 1929), pp. 192–3, 241
M. Meiss: *French Painting in the Time of Jean de Berry: The Limbourgs and their Contemporaries*, 2 vols (New York, 1974), pp. 98, 104, 287–8, 336, 383–4

P. de Winter: *La Bibliothèque de Philippe le Hardi, Duc de Bourgogne (1364–1404)* (Paris, 1985), pp. 98–106

GABRIELE BARTZ

Master of the Counts Palatinate and Margraves. *See* BESSER, HANS.

Masters of the Craterographia. *See under* ZÜNT, MATTHIAS.

Master of the Crayfish. *See* CRABBE, FRANS.

Master of the Crocifisso dei Bianchi (*fl* 1500–20). Italian painter. The name is given to the painter of the *Mystic Marriage of St Catherine with SS Anthony Abbot and James* (Lucca, Curia Arcivescovile), originally in the church of the Crocifisso dei Bianchi, Lucca, and formerly attributed to the Master of the Lathrop Tondo. However, this painting and others stylistically close to it, such as the *Virgin and Child with SS Stephen and Jerome* (Berlin, Gemäldegal.) and the fresco of *Famous Men and Women* (Lucca, Cathedral Library), are not of the quality of the Master of the Lathrop Tondo (Ferretti) and would seem to be the work of a painter active *c.* 1510 and influenced by the Master and by Amico Aspertini, who was working in Lucca at that date. Baracchini and others have proposed that the Master of the Crocifisso dei Bianchi can be identified as the painter Ranieri di Leonardo da Pisa, documented in Lucca from 1502 to 1521, who painted with Vincenzo Frediani a *Virgin and Child* in S Gennaro di Capannori, near Lucca (see Tazartes). He was a minor painter, active in Frediani's workshop. The *Virgin and Child with SS Roch and Frediano* (Torre, S Frediano) and the *Virgin and Child with SS John the Baptist, Colombano, Catherine and Sebastian* (S Colombano, parish church) can be attributed to him on stylistic grounds.

BIBLIOGRAPHY
M. Ferretti: 'Percorso lucchese', *An. Scu. Norm. Sup. Pisa*, n.s. 2, v/3 (1975), pp. 1059–60
M. Tazartes: 'Anagrafe lucchese', i, *Ric. Stor. A.*, xxvi (1985), pp. 10–11
C. Baracchini and others: 'Pittori a Lucca tra '400 e '500', *An. Scu. Norm. Sup., Pisa*, n.s. 2, xvi (1986), pp. 769–72, 813–14
G. Concioni, C. Ferri and G. Ghilarducci: *I pittori rinascimentali a Lucca* (Lucca, 1988), pp. 185–95

MAURIZIA TAZARTES

Master of the Crucifixion Altar. *See* MASTER OF THE ST BARTHOLOMEW ALTAR below.

Master of the Cueur d'amour espris. *See* MASTER OF KING RENÉ OF ANJOU below.

Master of the Cypresses (*fl c.* 1420–40). Spanish illuminator. He was named by Angulo Iñiguez after the characteristic cypress trees that frequently appear in a series of miniatures in vols 29 and 66 of the Choirbooks of Seville Cathedral (Seville, Archv Catedral). Angulo Iñiguez dated these illuminations to the early years of the 15th century and noted the influence of Giotto apparent in the artist's work; however, the influence of Netherlandish painting can also be observed in addition to Italianate elements. The wall paintings in the monastery of S Isidoro del Campo, Santiponce, near Seville, have also been attributed to the Master, as has a Bible in Madrid (Madrid, Escorial, MS. 1.13) that is richly decorated with miniatures.

It has been suggested that the Master of the Cypresses may perhaps be identified with Pedro de Toledo (*fl* 1434); if so, the work of the Master would establish strong artistic links between Seville and Toledo. The style of the illuminations attributed to the Master in any case bears striking similarities to that of the DE CARRIÓN workshop and could provide a clue to the artistic origins of Juan and Pedro de Carrión.

BIBLIOGRAPHY
D. Angulo Iñiguez: 'La miniatura en Sevilla: El Maestro de los Cipreses', *Archv Esp. A. & Arqueol.*, iv (1928), pp. 65–96
——: 'Miniaturas del segundo cuarto del siglo XV: Biblia Romanceada, 1.1.3 de la Biblioteca de El Escorial', *Archv Esp. A. & Arqueol.*, v (1929), pp. 225–31

LYNETTE BOSCH

Master of the Dangolsheim Madonna (*fl* 1460s). German sculptor. The name is given to the carver of a wooden statue of the *Virgin and Child* (h. 1.02 m; Berlin, Bodemus., inv. no. 7055). The statue is made of walnut with the original polychrome partly preserved and a reliquary container within the figure. It came from a private collection in Dangolsheim, Lower Alsace, supposedly originating from a monastery in Strasbourg. It is dated to the 1460s.

The subject, of the naked child lying in the hands of his mother and playfully half-hiding behind her veil, is similar to the Hammerthaler *Virgin and Child* of *c.* 1450 (Munich, Heiliggeistkirche), and the motif of the cloak's folds turned up at the front is found in simplified form in an engraving (Lehrs 79) by MASTER E.S. (*see* §III below), which was most probably done during the 1450s and may well refer to an older statue of a Virgin and Child of this type. Although in many respects the Dangolsheim *Virgin and Child* is close to the works of Nicolaus Gerhaert, it is distinguished from them principally by the treatment of the draperies, which are developed as abstract and metallic rather than as a rendering of the texture of the cloth. Fischel emphasized the pre-Gerhaert character of the *Virgin and Child* and tentatively identified the Master with the Strasbourg sculptor Hans Jöuch (*d* between 1462 and 1466); but more recent scholars have linked the figure stylistically to the standing figures of the high altar of 1462 in the Georgskirche, Nördlingen (*see* MASTER OF NÖRDLINGEN below), the attribution of which is contested.

BIBLIOGRAPHY
Thieme–Becker
L. Fischel: 'Zur kunsthistorischen Stellung des Meisters der Dangolsheimer Maria', *Jb. Staatl. Kstsamml. Baden-Württemberg*, iii (1966), pp. 51–68 [with bibliog.]
M. Baxandall: *The Limewood Sculptors of Renaissance Germany* (New Haven, 1980), pp. 250–51
R. Recht: *Nicolas de Leyde et la sculpture à Strasbourg, 1460–1525* (Strasbourg, 1987), pp. 152–85, 346–50
Die Dangolsheimer Muttergottes nach ihrer Restaurierung (exh. cat., Berlin, Staatl. Museen Preuss. Kultbes., 1989)
B. Buczynski and H. Krohm: 'Die Dangolsheimer Muttergottes: Technologische Untersuchung und Restaurierung', *Z. Ksttech. & Konserv.*, iii (1989), pp. 165–89
M. Nass: 'Der Kupferstich der Muttergottes mit Maiglöckchen L. 79 des Monogrammisten E. S. und die Beziehungen zur Dangolsheimer Muttergottes', *Jb. Berlin. Mus.*, xxxiii (1991), pp. 239–51

E. Zimmermann and others: 'Zuschreibungsprobleme: Beiträge des Berliner Colloquiums zur Dangolsheimer Muttergottes', *Jb. Preuss. Kultbes.*, xxviii (1992), pp. 223–67

EVA ZIMMERMANN

Master of the Darmstadt Passion (*fl c.* 1435/40–1455/60). German painter. Around 1450 he was the outstanding painter in the Middle Rhine region; Panofsky called him 'perhaps the most accomplished colourist and luminarist outside the Netherlands'. His oeuvre has been assembled from relatively few works. Thode (1900) named the Master on the basis of two altar panels (both Darmstadt, Hess. Landesmus.) showing on the insides *Christ Carrying the Cross* (see fig.) and a crowded *Calvary*, with a patterned gold ground, with fragments of an *Annunciation* and *Adoration of the Infant Jesus* on the outsides. These two panels are probably from a church in Hessen.

1. OEUVRE. To the two Darmstadt panels Thode linked two altar-wing paintings in Berlin (Gemäldegal.), which when he wrote were already divided into four panels. They show on the former insides the *Adoration of the Kings* and the *Veneration of the Holy Cross*, with the *Virgin Enthroned with the Child* and the *Trinity* on the outsides. The Berlin paintings were later linked by Stange and others to a large *Calvary* in the St Martin-Kirche in Bad Orb, near Aschaffenburg, the Berlin works being its former wings.

A number of further panels have been attributed to the painter; these originate—as Stange surmised and as has

now been ascertained—from a large retable in the former Cistercian church at Baindt, north of Lake Constance. The panels depict saints and scenes from the Life of the Virgin on a partly patterned gold ground: on the altar's insides, *SS Fabian and Sebastian*, the *Communion of St Onophrius* and the *Meeting at the Golden Gate* (Zurich, Ksthaus) and *SS Dorothy and Catherine* (Dijon, Mus. B.-A.); on the outsides, scenes mostly of the miracles of Jesus, such as the *Marriage at Cana*, the *Healing of a Blind Man* (Stuttgart, Staatsgal.) or the *Awakening of the Young Man at Nain* (Munich, Alte Pin.). Finally, two interrelated panels with three-quarter-length depictions of *King David* and *St John the Baptist* (priv. col.), close to the retable panels, have been attributed to the oeuvre.

2. CHRONOLOGY AND STYLE. The former Baindt retable has usually been dated in the 1420s or 1430s, that is, before the other works of the artist. This suggests that his origin lay in the Lake Constance region. The *SS Fabian and Sebastian* at Zurich reflects paintings by Konrad Witz such as *Abishai, Sibbechai and Benaiah* (*c.* 1435; Basle, Kstmus.; for illustration *see* WITZ, KONRAD).

Some uncertainties in the treatment of the figures—the postures and their spatial relations—suggest they are the work of a young artist. The attempt to attribute the insides and outsides of the Baindt retable to different hands (Wolfson) is unconvincing: in many 15th-century altarpieces a different conception of the image was used on the insides and outsides of the retable. The fragmentary work that survives from Baindt indicates the mind and hand of a single artist.

The *Calvary* panel of Bad Orb (destr. 1983) may be dated, like its former wings now in the Gemäldegalerie in Berlin, to the years 1445–50, about a decade after the Baindt retable—taking into account, for example, the roughly contemporaneous works of Stefan Lochner, who also came from Lake Constance, in Cologne. As compared to the early work, the figures have taken on a statuesque definition, while colour (particularly in carefully balanced shades of red and green), space and surface, as well as the interrelations of the figures, are brought together in a clear, coherent and rhythmical order. Mature humanity is also expressed by the figures, as in the splendid figure of the Good Captain in the *Calvary* or the bishop in the *Veneration of the Holy Cross*. The characters now have the quality of portraits. These individualized figures make it conceivable that the artist also produced separate portraits. A highly developed interest in objective reality, seen in the figure types, costumes, implements, features of Gothic or Romanesque architecture and in the legible Hebrew inscriptions, points forward to a new epoch.

As compared to the Bad Orb/Berlin triptych (which cannot be regarded as two separate works, as Wolfson suggests), the Darmstadt panels herald a new monumental conception and a deeper seriousness. The additive quality to be found in the earlier work has given way to a unified composition throughout the work. The resultant stiffness of the figures is not the result of artistic incapacity. The carefully calculated treatment of light and colour displays an artist working at the height of his powers. They are the latest products of this painter, and can be dated hardly earlier than the mid-1450s.

Master of the Darmstadt Passion: *Christ Carrying the Cross*, altar panel, 1.56×1.19 m, *c.* 1455 (Darmstadt, Hessisches Landesmuseum)

The Master can thus be seen as originating from the Lake Constance area and coming to work in the mid-Rhine region, perhaps at Mainz or Aschaffenburg. Early influences, not least that of Konrad Witz, were soon overlaid by impressions from the great Netherlandish artists such as Robert Campin or Jan van Eyck. Some Italian experiences seem also to have left traces in his work. Probably slightly younger than Konrad Witz and Stefan Lochner, he had a stature of his own transcending regional boundaries; his work had a special resonance in Middle Rhenish art, even if it had no directly tangible consequences.

BIBLIOGRAPHY
H. Thode: 'Die Malerei am Mittelrhein im XV. Jahrhundert und der Meister der Darmstädter Passionsszenen', *Jb. Kön.-Preuss. Kstsamml.*, xxi (1900), pp. 59–74, 113–35
A. Stange: *Deutsche Malerei der Gotik*, iii (Berlin, 1938), pp. 148–54
——: *Kritisches Verzeichnis der deutschen Tafelbilder vor Dürer*, ii (Munich, 1970), pp. 100–2, nos 441–4
H. M. Schmidt: 'Zum Meister der Darmstädter Passion', *Kst Hessen & Mittelrhein*, xiv (1974), pp. 7–48
M. Wolfson: 'Der Meister der Darmstädter Passion', *Kst Hessen & Mittelrhein*, xxix (1989), pp. 7–104

HANS M. SCHMIDT

Master of the David and St John Statuettes (*fl* Florence, late 15th century or early 16th). Italian sculptor. Conventional name for the sculptor of two stylistically coherent groups of statuettes produced in terracotta and in some numbers, under the influence of Verrocchio. The group of statuettes of *David* are characterized by elaborately decorated, pseudo-Roman armour reminiscent of that shown on Ghiberti's *Gates of Paradise* and are derived from Verrocchio's bronze statue of *David* (*c.* 1475; Florence, Bargello). They have the left elbow bent, the right arm hanging down with a sword in its hand, and Goliath's head between the feet. The other group, which is stylistically related and appears with minor variations and in some numbers, comprises statuettes of the *Young St John the Baptist*, who is shown seated on some rocks in the desert. Classic examples of both compositions are in the Victoria and Albert Museum, London; a nude *St Sebastian* in the same collection also appears to originate from the same workshop, together with a superior version located in the Kunstgewerbemuseum, Leipzig. All the statuettes are highly detailed and partially hollowed out for firing, while some bear traces of polychromy; these features indicate that they were not *bozzetti* but finished statuettes, produced commercially for domestic altars or as interior decoration, for example to be displayed on mantelpieces.

'The authorship of the statuettes presents a problem of great difficulty', wrote John Pope-Hennessy (1964, p. 193). He ruled out earlier attributions based on comparisons between the terracottas of St Sebastian and major statues of the same saint by Baccio da Montelupo and Leonardo del Tasso (1466–?1500), arguing that the supposed similarities were 'generic, and not substantiated by other authenticated works' by either sculptor. A connection with the style of the young Jacopo Sansovino has also been suggested. However, there is no record of his having been involved in such productions, although he was a gifted and prolific modeller. Connections with Andrea della Robbia and Giovanni della Robbia, whose workshop was

then producing glazed terracotta sculpture in a not dissimilar style, should also be considered. There may also be links with other series of Florentine terracotta statuettes that are currently grouped by subject, for example those ascribed to the Master of the Unruly Children, including groups of warriors struggling with horsemen in the style of Leonardo da Vinci and a series of recumbent river gods inspired by Michelangelo. The latter sculptures suggest a late date for the work of the Master of the David and St John Statuettes, in the 1520s at the earliest. It has also been argued that works attributed to the Master of the David and St John Statuettes or to the Master of the Unruly Children may be by Pietro Torrigiani.

BIBLIOGRAPHY
J. Pope-Hennessy: *Catalogue of Italian Sculpture in the Victoria and Albert Museum* (London 1964), nos 169–72
La civiltà del cotto (exh. cat., ed. A. Paolucci; Impruneta, 1980), pp. 85–6, 96–8, cat. nos 2.7, 2.8
B. Boucher: *The Sculpture of Jacopo Sansovino* (New Haven and London, 1991), p. 313, cat. nos 1, 2
A. P. Darr: 'Verrocchio's Legacy: Observations Regarding his Influence on Pietro Torrigiani and other Florentine Sculptors', *Verrocchio and Late Quattrocento Italian Sculpture*, ed. S. Bule, A. P. Darr and F. S. Gioffredi (Florence, 1992), pp. 125–39

CHARLES AVERY

Master of the Death of the Virgin (*fl c.* 1440–50). Engraver, probably active in south Germany. Some ten prints have been attributed to him, including the *Death of the Virgin*, after which he was named by Lehrs. He was formerly believed to have come from the southern Netherlands but is now thought to have lived in south Germany. The artist, probably a goldsmith, was one of the first generation of engravers. His style is rather awkward and lacks the refinement of his contemporary, the Master of the Playing Cards. His prints are characterized by stiff drapery and a limited suggestion of space, giving the impression that the figures are floating in mid-air. Besides a few prints of religious subjects, there is a large *Battle Scene* (unique impression, Paris, Louvre), set in a broad landscape with 80 or more soldiers, mounted or on foot, engaged in a tumultuous battle.

BIBLIOGRAPHY
Hollstein: *Dut. & Flem.*
M. Lehrs: *Geschichte und kritischer Katalog des deutschen, niederländischen und französischen Kupferstichs im XV. Jahrhundert* (Vienna, 1908–34/R Nedeln, 1969), i, pp. 279–87
M. Geisberg: *Die Anfänge des Kupferstichs*, Meister der Graphik (Leipzig, 1923), pp. 6, 68–71
T. Musper: 'Der früheste Stecher: Ein Oberdeutscher', *Pantheon*, xxviii (1941), pp. 203–7

J. P. FILEDT KOK

Master of the Decapitation of St John. *See under* MERKLIN, KONRAD.

Master of the Deichsler Altarpiece. *See under* MASTER OF THE IMHOFF ALTAR below.

Master of Delft (*b c.* 1470; *fl c.* 1490–1520). North Netherlandish painter. He is stylistically related to the Master of the Virgo inter Virgines, who is believed to have been active in Delft. His association with Delft is also suggested by the inclusion of the tower of the Nieuwe Kerk (completed 1496) in the background of his early

Crucifixion triptych with other scenes from the *Passion* (London, N.G.), a full-dress Calvary of the sort popular in the Rhineland and the northern Netherlands during the 15th century. With its large crowds of highly animated and brilliantly dressed spectators and participants and with its particular emphasis on the presence of children, this altarpiece strongly reflects the practical piety of Geert Grote and the teachings of Thomas à Kempis, which stressed the importance of the imitation of Christ in daily life and the vital necessity to educate the young. A kneeling donor in Carthusian dress at the lower left of the central panel—the only immobile figure in this painting apart from the crucified Christ—led Châtelet to propose that the altarpiece may have been painted for the abbey of Bartholomausdael, near Delft. A further connection with Delft is suggested by a pair of altarpiece wings (Cologne, Franzen priv. col., see Friedländer, pls 48–9) painted in the Master's workshop about 1510, bearing the arms and portraits of Dirk van Beest (*d* 1545), Mayor of Delft, and his wife, Gertruyt van Diemen, as well as portraits of their five children, including their son, Theodore, a Carthusian monk. (Only the portraits of the patron saints, John the Baptist and Mary Magdalene, appear to be by the Master's own hand; the wings form a triptych with a central panel depicting the *Virgin and Child with St Anne* by the Master of Frankfurt.)

One of the key works by the Master of Delft, datable to *c.* 1500 on the basis of costumes, is his triptych with the *Virgin and Child with Saints* (Amsterdam, Rijksmus.; see fig.). An unusually elaborate *Hortus conclusus* of the Song of Songs—a metaphor for Mary's virginity—is presented in the form of a raised flowerbed situated within the paved courtyard of a palace. The spectacular vision of a tabernacle

at upper right seems to refer to the 'more perfect tabernacle, not made with hands' that is described in St Paul's letter to the Hebrews (9:11)—an explanation of the replacement of the Old Covenant and its rituals by a new institution made possible by Christ's crucifixion. The Delft Master's figures are charming and animated, and his manner is slightly playful. The ladies' costumes feature the inventive and improbable headgear often found in Lower Rhenish painting at the turn of the century. His colours are light and silvery, featuring a characteristic pointillé method of applying tiny dots of red pigment on a light ground. The wings of the Amsterdam triptych contain portraits of an anonymous donor and his wife. The anonymous donor's patron, St Martin, bears the likeness of David of Burgundy, Bishop of Utrecht (*d* 1496). The donatrix is sponsored by St Cunera, identifiable by the scarf with which she was strangled. The outer wings depict an *Annunciation* in grisaille, which was not painted by the Master himself but may be by the workshop hand that painted the van Beest family portraits.

According to Friedländer, the Master possibly designed 16 woodcut illustrations for Olivier de la Marche's *Le Chevalier délibéré* (Gouda, [n.d.], 2/Schiedam [*c.* 1498]), although more recently the illustrations have been attributed to the Master of Spes Nostra, a painter from the circle of the Master of Delft. Friedländer also speculated that the Master of Delft, or perhaps his teacher, might have designed the illustrations for the 'legend of St Lidwina' (Schiedam, 1498) and for the devotional books printed at the convent of Den Hem, near Schoonhoven, in the last years of the 15th century. These works had previously been attributed to the young Jacob Cornelisz. van Oostsanen. A further connection with the graphic arts

Master of Delft: triptych with the *Virgin and Child with Saints*, oil on panel, central panel 845×680 mm, wings 845×300 mm, *c.* 1500 (Amsterdam, Rijksmuseum)

is apparent in the compositions of the Master's paintings of the *Deposition* (Oxford, Christ Church Lib.) and the *Virgin and Child with St Bernard* (Utrecht, Catharijneconvent), both of which reflect the influence of the Dutch engraver known as Master I.A.M. of Zwolle.

BIBLIOGRAPHY

M. J. Friedländer: *Die altniederländische Malerei* (Berlin, 1924–37); Eng. trans. as *Early Netherlandish Painting* (Leiden, 1967–76), x, pp. 30–33, 75–6, 86, pls 42–53

M. J. Schretlen: *Dutch and Flemish Woodcuts of the Fifteenth Century* (London, 1925), pls 77–80

P. J. J. van Thiel and others: *All the Paintings of the Rijksmuseum in Amsterdam* (Amsterdam, 1976)

A. Châtelet: *Les Primitifs hollandais* (Paris and Fribourg, 1980); Eng. trans. as *Early Dutch Painting: Painting in the Northern Netherlands in the Fifteenth Century* (Oxford and New York, 1981), pp. 155–7

JANE CAMPBELL HUTCHISON

Master of the della Rovere Missals (*fl c.* 1475–1505). Illuminator, active in Italy and France. This name was given by Levi d'Ancona (1959) to an artist whose principal work is a richly decorated four-volume Missal produced for Cardinal Domenico della Rovere (*d* 1501), which includes his portrait, arms and devices (New York, Pierpont Morgan Lib., MS. 306; Turin, Archv Stato, MSS J. b. II.2–4). Originally one liturgical whole, it was destined for use in the Sistine Chapel, Rome (Dykmans). In the first volume (New York), the Master collaborated with, or possibly took over the project from, an artist who signed himself *Franciscus Betyni* and is presumably the Veronese Francesco di Bettini (*fl c.* 1481–1539). The della Rovere Master was working in Rome by 1478, as his style is recognizable in a Theophylactus (Rome, Vatican, Bib. Apostolica, MS. Vat. lat. 263) of that year dedicated to Pope Sixtus IV (*reg* 1471–84). The della Rovere Missals were probably produced in Rome between 1484 and 1490 as they appear to include a portrait of Pope Innocent VIII (*reg* 1484–92).

These works show a mature artist with a thorough knowledge of contemporary Italian painting, especially that of Melozzo da Forlì, active in the Vatican until 1481. He is capable of producing convincing settings, as for example in the miniature depicting the *Priest Reciting Mass* (New York, Pierpont Morgan Lib., MS. 306, fol. 119*r*; see fig.). His miniatures are full of rich architectural effects and imposing classical elements. Arcades and columns are adorned with precious stones and pearls and festooned with garlands of pomegranates, and at their bases nude putti with chubby faces and blond, curly hair, again reminiscent of Melozzo, frequently appear. The figures are tall and slender with small, mildly expressive faces that tend to gaze skyward in attitudes of wonder. They are clothed in heavy robes that fall in strong vertical lines, like the flutes of a column, although this characteristic becomes progressively less marked.

All four volumes must have been completed by 1490, because by that date the Master was in Provence, where he collaborated on a Book of Hours (New York, Pierpont Morgan Lib., MS. 348) with the Master of René II of Lorraine, identified as Georges Trubert, who sold his house in Provence and moved to Lorraine that year. Soon after, the della Rovere Master left the south of France for Tours, where he worked on two Books of Hours for use

Master of the della Rovere Missals: *Priest Reciting Mass*, 348×263 mm, miniature from the first volume of the della Rovere Missal, *c.* 1485 (New York, Pierpont Morgan Library, MS. 306, fol. 119*r*)

there (Paris, Bib. Arsenal, MS. 432; Modena, Bib. Estense, MS. A.K.7.2). The latter includes the device *AEIOU* (Austriae Est Imperare Orbi Universo), belonging to the Holy Roman Emperor Frederick III and his successor, the Holy Roman Emperor Maximilian I, with the initials *PK*, which may stand for the Latin form (Phillipus Karolus) of the forenames of Philip the Fair, King of Castile, Maximilian's son. If this book was made for Philip the Fair (Levi d'Ancona, 1953), it must have been produced in Tours by 1506, the year in which he died and the latest date ascribable to any of this Master's surviving works. The works produced in Tours are clearly influenced by the style of Jean Bourdichon. The miniature depicting the *Visitation* in the Hours in Modena (fol. 46*v*) adopts a device favoured by Bourdichon of concentrating the attention on half-length figures, which fill the frame and emphasize the drama of the event. Facial types in both this book and the Paris Hours are also influenced by Bourdichon's models, with female figures exhibiting the distinctive high, thin eyebrows and heavily lidded eyes and heads turned slightly to one side. The blond putti, garlands and architectural settings, familiar from the works produced in Italy, are still in evidence and appear to be the hallmark of this artist.

The della Rovere Master may have been of French or Italian origin. While most, if not all, of his early works were produced in Italy and show a thorough understanding of contemporary Italian art, certain elements suggest a knowledge of southern French painting, and his later departure for France and easy assimilation of the style of Bourdichon suggest he may have been French by birth.

BIBLIOGRAPHY

M. Levi d'Ancona: 'Il Codice A.K.7.2. della Biblioteca Estense di Modena', *Commentari*, iv (1953), pp. 16–21
——: 'Le Maître des missels della Rovere: Rapports entre la France et l'Italie vers la fin du XVe et le début du XVIe siècle', *Actes du XIXe congrès international d'histoire de l'art: Paris, 1959*, pp. 256–63
R. Brenzoni: 'Il messale di Domenico della Rovere nella Pierpont Morgan Library di New York e il suo miniatore Francesco de Castello', *L'Arte*, lxi (1963), pp. 139–47
Fifth Centenary of the Vatican Library (Vatican City, 1975), p. 26, no. 58, pl. 8
The Last Flowering: French Painting in Manuscripts, 1420–1530, from American Collections (exh. cat. by J. Plummer and G. Clark, New York, Pierpont Morgan Lib., 1982), pp. 79–81, nos 102–3
M. Dykmans: 'Le Missel du Cardinal Dominique de la Rovere pour la Chapelle Sixtine', *Scriptorium*, xxxvii (1983), pp. 205–38
The Painted Page: Italian Renaissance Book Illumination, 1450–1550 (exh. cat., ed. J. J. G. Alexander; London, RA, 1994)

SUSIE NASH

Dido Master. *See* APOLLONIO DI GIOVANNI.

Master of the Die (*fl c.* 1530–*c.* 1560). Engraver and print designer, active in Italy. Name given to an artist in the workshop of Marcantonio Raimondi in Rome who signed his prints with a small die, or the letters BV. Suggested identifications include Benedetto Verino, Daddi or Dado, Marcantonio's natural son, or, more recently, TOMMASO VINCIDOR, one of Raphael's assistants. The Master collaborated with many of the artists in Marcantonio's studio working on Raphaelesque designs and made scores of prints, mainly reproducing Raphael's decorations for the Vatican (e.g. *Coronation of the Virgin*, B. 29). The Master also produced sheets of grotesque decorative panels in imitation of the antique prototypes reinvented by Raphael (e.g. B. 80–85); these served as patterns for north European decoration. He is best known for a suite of four designs, *Playing Putti* (1532; B. 32–5). These prints were made after tapestry designs by Giovanni da Udine and cartoons by Vincidor (Munich, Staatl. Graph. Samml.), finished in 1521, which expressed the dream of a Golden Age under the pontificate of Leo X. Each shows three winged putti engaged in symbolic play on heavy swags of verdure. The cartoons were sent with Vincidor to Brussels to be woven, and the finished tapestries hung in the Sala di Constantino in the Vatican. The new genre was popular: 20 similar compositions by other artists are known in drawings or engravings. In the 1530s the Master's engravings were themselves used as cartoons for tapestry sets after Raphael's *Life of the Virgin*, ordered by such patrons as the Prince–Bishop of Liège, Cardinal Evrard de la Marck. The Master's works therefore reveal the extraordinary productivity of the Marcantonio workshop at this date and the high standard of craftsmanship used to disseminate Raphael's oeuvre.

BIBLIOGRAPHY

S. Boorsch: *Italian Masters of the Sixteenth Century*, 29 [XV/ii] of *The Illustrated Bartsch*, ed. W. Strauss (New York, 1982), pp. 159–241 [B.]
L. Zentai: 'On Baldassare Peruzzi's Compositions Engraved by the Master of the Die', *Acta Hist. A. Acad. Sci. Hung.*, xxix/1–4 (1983), pp. 51–104
Raphael invenit (exh. cat. by G. B. Pezzini, S. Massari and S. P. V. Rodino, Rome, Ist. N. Graf., 1985), pp. 137–8, 584–6, 805, 820–25

LOUISE S. MILNE

Doheny Master. *See under* §II: THE 1520S HOURS WORKSHOP below.

Master of the Dominican Effigies [Master of the Lord Lee Polyptych] (*fl c.* 1328–50). Italian painter and illuminator. At one time named after a polyptych in the Lee Collection (?1345; U. London, Courtauld Inst. Gals), he is now named after his most unusual panel, *Christ and the Virgin Enthroned with Seventeen Dominican Saints* (*c.* 1336; Florence, S Maria Novella). He has been identified with Ristoro di Andrea (*fl c.* 1334–64) or some other illuminator associated with S Maria Novella, but this is unproven. It has also been suggested (Boskovits) that the work of another illuminator, the BIADAIOLO MASTER (*see* above), may constitute an early phase of his career; if correct, this would reinforce his position as the chief heir to PACINO DI BONAGUIDA, with whom he may have trained and certainly collaborated. Like Pacino, his work derives ultimately from the St Cecilia Master and forms part of what has been called the 'miniaturist tendency' (Offner), a group of painters often associated with small-scale anecdotal narratives. Like his slightly older contemporaries Jacopo del Casentino and the MASTER OF THE CAPPELLA MEDICI POLYPTYCH (*see* above), he responded to the ideas of Giotto without entirely understanding them. The work of Giotto's pupil Bernardo Daddi, however, provided a more accessible source of inspiration for his panels. His most successful work is in manuscripts, where, despite a delightful simplicity, his miniatures reveal strongly controlled designs animated by vivacious figures and lively patterns of colour, for example the *Nativity and Annunciation to the Shepherds* on a single leaf from a *laudario* or vernacular choir-book (Washington, DC, N.G.A., B-15, 393). This artist executed a wide variety of commissions for various Florentine patrons, both lay and religious. These include such service books as an Antiphonary commissioned for S Maria Novella between 1328 and 1334 (Florence, S Maria Novella, Cor. H Inv. No. 1357) and secular works, for example a fine series of miniatures for Dante's *Divine Comedy* (*c.* 1337; Milan, Castello Sforzesco, MS. 1080).

BIBLIOGRAPHY

R. Offner and K. Steinweg: *Corpus* (1930–79), III/ii, pt i, pp. 49–68, and pt ii, pp. 239–61; III/vii, pp. iii–v, 27–82; rev. M. Boskovits (1987), III/ii, pp. 271–354, 582–7
B. Berenson: 'Quadri senza casa: Il trecento fiorentino, I', *Dédalo*, xi (1931), pp. 978–82
M. Boskovits: *Corpus* (1984), pp. 54–7, 283–95

ANDREW LADIS

Master of the Drapery Studies. *See* MASTER OF THE COBURG ROUNDELS above.

Master of the Dresden Prayerbook (*fl c.* 1460–1520). Netherlandish illuminator and engraver. He was named by Winkler after the Book of Hours in Dresden (Dresden, Sächs. Landesbib., MS. A311; two detached miniatures, Paris, Louvre, inv. no. 20694, 20694bis). The book was slightly damaged by water in 1945. Its format and composition are typical of Books of Hours produced in Bruges, but it differs in the illustration of the calendar, with 12 full-page miniatures of the occupations of the months.

These miniatures show the Master of the Dresden Prayerbook to have been one of the first illuminators to capture differing moods and atmosphere in landscapes, for example a fresh May morning or a gathering storm on a hot day in July. His finest achievements in landscape painting are the calendar miniatures of the Voustre Demeure Hours (Madrid, Bib. N., MS. Vit. 25–5), where the *Signs of the Zodiac* are represented as heavenly apparitions in landscapes that reflect the changing seasons. In view of this expertise, it is not surprising that, on several occasions, the Master of the Dresden Prayerbook undertook, as a specialist, the calendar sections of Books of Hours illustrated by other illuminators (e.g. London, BL, Add. MS. 38126 and Egerton MS. 1147). At the same time his own workshop, with *c.* 40 known manuscripts, was one of the most productive in the Netherlands.

The Master of the Dresden Prayerbook's thick-set, somewhat rotund figures with clumsy hands and feet and massive heads, are distinctive. His narrative style is lively and rich in detail. He gave his figures dramatic postures and gestures, often so boldly foreshortened that the effect is exaggerated. He used bright and glowing colours, in particular a vivid orange, light red, yellow and purple as well as occasional large unbroken areas of black. His miniatures lack the refined finish of the contemporary Ghent-Bruges school of illumination; individual brush-strokes and stippling remain visible, and broad areas of colour are left untouched.

The Master's original style suggests that he trained in the northern Netherlands, possibly in Utrecht *c.* 1460. He subsequently went to Bruges, where, apparently under the influence of the Master of Antoine of Burgundy, he developed his new concept of landscape painting. Here, *c.* 1470, he produced the Dresden Book of Hours (see fig.), also that in The Hague (Rijksmus. Meermanno–Westreenianum, MS. 10.F.1) and two *Valerius Maximus* manuscripts, one for Jean de Gros, treasurer of the Order of the Golden Fleece (Leipzig, Bib. U., MS. Rep. I.11b), and one for Jan Crabbe, Abbot of Ter Duinen Abbey in Bruges (Bruges, Mus. Groot Semin., MSS 157/188, 158/189, 159/190). The Master probably then went to Valenciennes in order to work with Simon Marmion on the Louthe Hours (Leuven, U. Catholique, Archvs, MS. A.2), the Huth Hours (London, BL, Add. MS. 38126) and further Books of Hours (London, V&A, MS. Salting 1221; Cambridge, MA, Harvard U., Houghton Lib., MSS Typ. 443/443.1). In the 1480s he was back in Bruges, where he painted most of the miniatures in the Breviary of Isabella the Catholic, Queen of Spain (unfinished; London, BL, Add. MS. 18851). It seems likely that the Master undertook one further journey, as he illuminated the Cartulary of the hospital of St Jacques, Tournai, written in 1489 (Tournai, Bib. Ville, Cod. 4A), and still later a Book of Hours (Paris, Bib. N., MS. lat. 1416) and an Evangeliary (Paris, Bib. Arsenal, MSS 661/662) for the use of Amiens. Apparently he finally settled in Bruges between 1490 and 1500. During this period he produced his finest works, a Book of Hours (London, BL, Add. MS. 17280) for Philip I and his wife, Joanna, Queen of Castile-León, and the Crohin-de la Fontaine Hours (Malibu, CA, Getty Mus., MS. 23). After 1500 his painting became increasingly two-dimensional; the drapery looks sacklike, the figures seem incorporeal

Master of the Dresden Prayerbook: *June*, watercolour on parchment, 135×95 mm; page from Book of Hours, *c.* 1470 (Dresden, Sächsische Landesbibliothek, MS. A.311, fol. 6*v*)

and the faces stereotyped and usually distorted (Berlin, Gemäldegal., MS. 78.B.14; Cambridge, Fitzwilliam, MS. 1058–1975, fol. 15*r*). Two openings in the Spinola Hours of 1515 (Malibu, CA, Getty Mus., MS. Ludwig IX.18, fols 109*v*/110*r*, 119*v*/120*r*) can be counted among his last works. None of the attributed manuscripts can be dated stylistically later than 1520.

Anzelewsky has established, by a comparison of styles, that the Master of the Dresden Prayerbook was also active as an engraver. Some of the illustrations in a French translation of Boccaccio, *De la ruine des nobles hommes et femmes*, published by Colard Mansion (Bruges, 1476), are attributed to him (*see* MASTER OF THE BOCCACCIO ILLUSTRATIONS above).

BIBLIOGRAPHY

R. Bruck: *Die Malereien in den Handschriften des Königreichs Sachsen* (Dresden, 1906), pp. 337–45 [reproduces calendar of Dresden Prayerbook]

F. Winkler: 'Der Brügger Meister des Dresdener Gebetbuches und seine Werke', *Jb. Kön.-Preuss. Kstsamml.*, xxxv (1914), pp. 225–44

——: *Der Leipziger Valerius Maximus: Mit einer Einleitung über die Anfänge des Sittenbildes in den Niederlanden* (Leipzig, 1923)

——: *Die flämische Buchmalerei* (Leipzig, 1925/R Amsterdam, 1978), pp. 94–101

E. Kästner: *Bekränzter Jahreslauf: Ein festlicher Kalender für alle Zeit* (Leipzig, 1935/R 1979) [colour pls of the calendar illustrations of the Dresden Prayerbook]

F. Anzelewsky: 'Die drei Boccaccio-Stiche von 1476 und ihre Meister', *Festschrift Friedrich Winkler* (Berlin, 1959), pp. 114–25

B. Brinkmann: *Der Meister des Dresdner Gebetbuchs und sein Kreis: Leben und Werk eines burgundischen Buchmalers zwischen Utrecht, Brügge und Amiens* (Berlin, 1990)

BODO BRINKMANN

Master of the Ehningen Altar (*fl c.* 1470–80). German painter. He is named after a winged altarpiece (Stuttgart, Staatsgal.) from St Maria, Ehningen, near Stuttgart, the chancel of which dates from 1476. It bears the coat of arms of Countess Palatine Matilda (1419–82), widow of Count Ludwig V of Württemberg and then residing in nearby Rottenburg. The altarpiece, which is in all essentials a faithful copy of a lost triptych by Dieric Bouts (*see* BOUTS, (1)), belongs equally to the histories of Netherlandish and German painting. It is painted in tempera with oil glazes on spruce and depicts on the centre panel the *Resurrection* with in the background the *Noli me tangere* and the *Procession of the Holy Women to the Sepulchre*, on the left-hand wing *Christ Appearing to his Mother* with the *Ascension* in the background and on the right-hand wing the *Incredulity of Thomas* with the *Pentecost* in the background. The outer surfaces of the wings show the *Annunciation* with, in the tympanum of the painted gateway, a relief of the *Fall* and, next to this, Matilda's coat of arms. The untraced predella showed *Christ and the Apostles* (ex-Stuttgart, Württemberg. Landesmus.). The artist undoubtedly learnt the rudiments of his art from Bouts himself; only in the slightly compressed proportions and the solidly anchored bodies (especially the nude half-figure of the Resurrected Christ) are his possible south German origins, perhaps around Lake Constance or Ulm, suggested.

No other works by the Master of the Ehningen Altar are known, although some products of his workshop may have been identified, and it appears from these that the painter became increasingly acclimatized to the traditional Württemberg milieu. Whether he also produced the frescoes in the winter refectory of the Cistercian monastery at Bebenhausen remains an open question.

BIBLIOGRAPHY
J. Baum: *Altschwäbische Kunst* (Augsburg, 1923)
M. J. Friedländer: *Die altniederländische Malerei* (Berlin, 1924–37); Eng. trans. as *Early Netherlandish Painting* (Leiden, 1967–76)
W. Schöne: *Dieric Bouts und seine Schule* (Berlin and Leipzig, 1938)
A. Stange: *Schwaben in der Zeit von 1450 bis 1500* (1957), viii of *Deutsche Malerei der Gotik* (Munich and Berlin, 1934–61)
Dieric Bouts (exh. cat., Brussels, Pal. B.-A.; Delft, Stedel. Mus. Prinsenhof; 1957–8)
B. Bushart: 'Studien zur Altschwäbischen Malerei', *Z. Kstgesch.*, xxii (1959), pp. 133–57
A. Stange: *Oberrhein, Bodensee, Schweiz, Mittelrhein, Ulm, Augsburg, Allgau, Nordlingen, von der Donau zum Neckar* (1970), ii of *Kritisches Verzeichnis der deutschen Tafelbilder vor Dürer* (Munich and Berlin, 1967–78)

DETLEF ZINKE

Master of the Embroidered Foliage (*fl* Brussels, *c.* 1495–1500). Painter, active in the southern Netherlands. This name was given by Friedländer to the artist of a number of works that include foliage depicted in an almost mechanical technique, with small luminous raised marks, reminiscent of embroidery stitches (although this motif should not be the sole criterion for attribution). The influence of Rogier van der Weyden is evident in the Master's paintings of the Virgin, which are conflations or copies of van der Weyden's own work. The main, generally accepted, attributions are the *Virgin and Child in a Garden* (see fig.), the triptych of the *Virgin and Child with Angels* (Lille, Mus. B.-A.) and the *Virgin and Child* (1510–20) from the Johnson Collection (Philadelphia, PA, Mus. F.A.)—this last being an embellished copy, and the earliest

Master of the Embroidered Foliage: *Virgin and Child in a Garden*, oil on panel, 1.04×0.86 m, *c.* 1495–1500 (Amsterdam, E. Proehl private collection)

one known, of van der Weyden's *Virgin and Child in a Niche* (Madrid, Prado). All three of these very similar works show the Virgin holding the Child in her lap, while he plays with the pages of a Bible. The *St Peter* on the back of the right wing of the Melbourne Altarpiece (Melbourne, N.G. Victoria) is also generally attributed to this Master. Two other works that can be assigned to the same artist, the triptych with the *Virgin and Child with Angels and SS Catherine and Barbara* (before 1496; Polizzi Generosa, S Maria degli Angeli) and the *Virgin and Child with Angels* (ex-Groz priv. col.; Paris, Louvre), reveal the influence of Hugo van de Goes.

In the Master's work spiritual content is subordinated to the anecdotal, characterized by a concentration on the depiction of landscape in which trees with stylized foliage and straight, smooth trunks are arranged in regular lines. Other features, typical of his work, are the concern with decorative detail (peacocks, flowers, a cottage), the inclined head of the Virgin, her eyes hidden by heavy lids, and the arrangement of drapery with repeating designs. The tranquillity of the compositions is achieved by the use of horizontal, parallel planes derived from the Bruges school. De Callataÿ attempted to identify the Master and revise the attributions to him, but this work has not been followed up. Callataÿ also suggested that the Master was a specialist in landscape painting and may have executed work in collaboration with other artists (*see also* MASTER OF THE LEGEND OF ST CATHERINE and MASTER OF THE LEGEND OF ST BARBARA below).

BIBLIOGRAPHY
M. J. Friedländer: *Die altniederländische Malerei* (Berlin, 1924–37); Eng. trans. as *Early Netherlandish Painting* (Leiden, 1967–76), iv (1969), pp. 65, 81–82, 86–7, 91–2, 100–101; xiv (1976), pp. 12–13

E. Larsen: 'The Monogrammist ADR, alias the Master with the Embroidered Foliage', *Oud-Holland*, lxxvi (1961), pp. 201–2

J. Białostocki: *Les Musées de Pologne: Gdańsk, Kraków, Warszawa* (1966), ix of *Les Primitifs flamands, I: Corpus de la peinture des anciens Pays-Bas méridionaux au quinzième siècle* (Brussels, 1951–), pp. 12–13

R. A. Koch: 'Copies of Roger van der Weyden's Madonna in Red', *Rec. A. Mus., Princeton U.*, xxvi/2 (1967), p. 49

Primitifs flamands anonymes: Maîtres aux noms d'emprunt des Pays-Bas méridionaux du XVe au début du XVIe siècle (exh. cat., ed. A. Janssens de Bisthoven and others, Bruges, Groeningemus., 1969), pp. 150–54, 281–6

D. De Vos: 'De Madonna-en-Kindtypologie bij Rogier van der Weyden en enkele minder gekende Flemalleske Voorlopers', *Jb. Berlin. Mus.*, xiii (1971), pp. 60–161

V. Hoff and M. Davies: *The National Gallery of Victoria, Melbourne* (1971), xii of *Les Primitifs flamands, I: Corpus de la peinture des anciens Pays-Bas méridionaux au quinzième siècle* (Brussels, 1951–), pp. 20–24

E. de Callataÿ: 'Etude sur le maître au feuillage en broderie', *Mus. Royaux B.-A. Belgique: Bull.*, xxi (1972), pp. 17–39

C. Périer-D'Ieteren: *Colyn de Coter et la technique picturale des peintres flamands du XVe siècle* (Brussels, 1985), p. 45, ill. 79

C. PÉRIER-D'IETEREN

Master of Empúries. *See* MASTER OF AMPURIAS above.

Master of the Erfurt Regler Altar (*fl* ?Erfurt, *c.* 1450–75). He is named after the high altar in the Reglerkirche in Erfurt, which has paintings depicting the *Passion*. Its outer sides and predella were probably executed by another artist, following this Master's design. Characteristic of the Master of the Erfurt Regler Altar are figures, set in narrow, confined spaces, who seem frozen in the middle of violent movements, their faces often grotesquely distorted (as with the tormentors of Christ, for example). On the one hand he seems to have been influenced by painters of the Middle Rhine area, such as the Master of the Oberstein Altar (Oberstein an der Nahe, Felsenkirche), also known as the Master of the Mainz Derision; on the other, the Master of the Tucher Altar (Nuremberg, Franenkirche) seems to have made a direct impression on him. He himself was a formative influence, for example on the painter who produced the wings for the *Passion* altarpiece of the Klosterkirche at Bad Hersfeld (Kassel, Schloss Wilhelmshöhe). Also attributed to the Master are wings from an altar of the *Virgin* (Munich, Alte Pin.) and two depicting the *Crucifixion* and *Ascension* (Karlsruhe, Staatl. Ksthalle) that were possibly sections of two corresponding altarpieces, of unknown origin.

Kindler

BIBLIOGRAPHY

A. Stange: *Kritisches Verzeichnis der deutschen Tafelbilder vor Dürer*, ii (Munich, 1970), pp. 101–2, nos 445–7

GISELA GOLDBERG

Erminold Master [Master of Erminold] (*fl c.* 1270–84). German sculptor. He was active in Regensburg from *c.* 1275 until after 1280 and is named after his principal work, completed on documentary evidence in 1283: the funerary figure of the *Blessed Erminold of Hirsau* (*d* 1121), the founding abbot of the Benedictine monastery at Prüfening, near Regensburg. The figure lies in front of the former rood altar in the abbey church (now the parish church of St Georg). It is 1.98 m high and made of sandstone (the crook of the crosier is lead, and there are remains of the original tempera painting). French cathedral sculpture (of e.g. Reims or Paris) was probably the most significant stylistic influence on the Erminold Master, and it may be presumed that he served his apprenticeship in the 1250s or 1260s, perhaps in Mainz and Strasbourg. His personal style becomes fully apparent only in the small red sandstone figures of prophets and angels in the archivolts of the west portal of Basle Minster (*c.* 1270).

The monumental sandstone statues of the *Virgin* and the *Angel Annunciate* of *c.* 1280 on the inner sides of the two west crossing piers in Regensburg Cathedral can definitely be attributed to the Erminold Master. Large areas of the original painting survive, and stylistically the group belongs to the Strasbourg and Upper Rhine tradition dating from around the mid-13th century. It ranks among the greatest achievements of German sculpture of the period.

The seated figure of *St Peter*, *c.* 1284, formerly in the main choir of Regensburg Cathedral (sandstone, remnants of the original painting; Regensburg, Stadtmus.), is generally regarded as a late work by the Erminold Master. He was the last significant figure in German monumental sculpture of the late 13th century, achieving a strongly individual style while drawing on older artistic forms of expression.

BIBLIOGRAPHY

G. Schmidt: 'Beiträge zum Erminoldmeister', *Z. Kstwiss.*, xi/3–4 (1957), pp. 141–74

A. Hubel: 'Der Erminoldmeister und die deutsche Skulptur des 13. Jahrhunderts', *Beitr. Gesch. Bistums Regensburg*, viii (1974), pp. 53–241

MICHAEL STUHR

Master of the E-Series Tarocchi (*fl* Ferrara, *c.* 1465). Italian engraver. Levenson gave the name to the author of a series of 50 engravings that constitutes one of the finest achievements of Italian printmaking in the 15th century. The series is subdivided into five sets of ten engravings; each image is titled and numbered within its set, and a letter indicates to which set it belongs. The sets consist of the *Conditions of Man* (E), *Apollo and the Muses* (D), the *Liberal Arts* (C), the *Cosmic Principles* (B) and the *Firmaments of the Universe* (A). A second version of the series exists in which the 'E' of the first group is replaced with the letter 'S'. It has been generally accepted that the E-series is the original set and that the S-series is derived from it. Two figures from the E-series were copied in a manuscript of 1467 (Bologna, Archv Stato, *Costituzione dello studio bolognese*), which provides a *terminus ante quem* for the dating of the series.

Both the E-series and the S-series were traditionally referred to as 'Mantegna's Tarocchi', but the engravings cannot have been intended to serve as *tarocchi* (tarot cards), since they do not correspond to the game either in number or in iconography; it is debatable if they formed a game at all, since some examples are bound together in a kind of pictorial encyclopedia (e.g. Paris, Bib. N.). The original designs for the cards can be attributed neither to Mantegna nor to one of his pupils but to an artist active in Ferrara, almost certainly identifiable as the Master of the E-Series Tarocchi who engraved the series. The Master is also responsible for two other engravings, the *Death of Orpheus* and *Cupids at the Vintage*, the latter of which is copied in a manuscript of 1466 (Vienna, Österreich. Nbib., Ser. nov. 4643, frontispiece).

The Master was extremely skilled technically, and his refined style is well suited to the erudite humanist subjects he illustrated. His work has more in common with manuscript illumination than with monumental painting. The plasticity of the figures is emphasized by the use of clear outlines and delicate shading, as can be seen in the *Emperor* of the E-Series Tarocchi. The iconographic programme of this series is particularly complete, and the series has been used as a source of iconographic borrowings. Copies of some of the figures appear in two versions of the poem *De imaginibus gentilium deorum* by the humanist Ludovico Lazzarelli (Rome, Bib. Vaticana, Cod. Urb. Lat. 716, 717), one of which can be dated 1471, and also in Dürer's early drawings.

BIBLIOGRAPHY
P. Kristeller: *Die Tarocchi* (Berlin, 1910)
H. Brockhaus: 'Ein edles Geduldspiel: "Die Leitung der Welt oder die Himmelsleiter", die sogennanten Taroks Mantegnas vom Jahre 1459–60', *Miscellanea di storia dell'arte in onore di Igino Benvenuto Supino* (Florence, 1933), pp. 397–410
K. Clark: Letter, *Burl. Mag.*, lxii (1933), p. 143
A. M. Hind: *Early Italian Engraving: A Critical Catalogue* (London, 1938–48), i, pp. 221–40
K. Rathe: 'Sulla classificazione cronologica di alcuni incunabuli calcografici italiani', *Maso Finiguerra*, v (1940), pp. 3–13 (7–10)
E. Panofsky: *The Life and Art of Albrecht Dürer* (Princeton, 1943, rev. 2/1948), i, p. 31; ii, pp. 102–3
L. Donati: 'Le fonti iconografiche di alcuni manoscritti urbinati della Biblioteca Vaticana: Osservazioni intorno ai cosiddetti "Tarocchi del Mantegna"', *La Bibliofila*, lx (1958), pp. 48–129
E. Ruhmer: *Francesco del Cossa* (Munich, 1959), pp. 66–8
J. Levenson, K. Oberhuber and J. Sheehan: *Early Italian Engravings from the National Gallery of Art* (Washington, DC, 1973), pp. 81–157

MARCO COLLARETA

Master of Evert van Soudenbalch (*fl* Utrecht, *c.* 1460–70). Illuminator, active in the northern Netherlands. This name was given to the major illuminator of a two-volume Bible (Vienna, Österreich. Nbib., Cod. 2771–2), made for Evert van Soudenbalch, a canon of Utrecht Cathedral from 1445 to 1503, who is shown being presented to the Virgin on fol. 10*r* of the first volume (see fig.). The text, in Middle Dutch, is a compilation of texts from the Bible and historical works including the Alexander romance and extracts from Flavius Josephus, with commentaries from Petrus Comestor's *Historia scolastica*. As a consequence of those contents, the 244 miniatures and 33 historiated initials are iconographically most unusual. The Master of Evert van Soudenbalch devised the scenes with a psychological insight comparable with Rembrandt's treatment of biblical history two centuries later and was perhaps the first artist to give convincing expression to such feelings as jealousy, consternation, self-doubt and resignation (Delaissé, 1968). His achievements in technique are equally notable: the use of small brushstrokes of colour achieves a variety of surface effects, so that objects appear strongly modified by light and shade. This enabled him to differentiate facial expressions, to achieve an astonishing three-dimensionality of modelling and to give a lively appearance to drapery surfaces. The contrasting of complementary shades that characterizes his use of colour is nonetheless combined with a sensitivity to middle tones. Thus steel blue is set against ochre and dark blue-green against violet. Flesh tones are highlighted orange and shaded olive green. Figures are mobile and show his command of unusual viewpoints: they are often seen from behind or from below to heighten the dramatic quality of his compositions. The most astonishing demonstration of the individuality of characterization and the vivid quality of the Master's work is in a manuscript on paper, a Middle Dutch work of natural history (Wolfenbüttel, Herzog August Bib., Cod. Guelf. 18.2. Aug. 4°).

Although the Master of Evert van Soudenbalch was the best among them, he often worked in collaboration with other illuminators. In the Vienna Bible the work of six different painters can be distinguished. The Master of Evert van Soudenbalch painted most of the miniatures in the first volume but none in the second. A few miniatures of the first volume and some of the later ones of the second were produced by a painter who has been called the Master of the Fleecy Clouds. As the distinctive cloud formation is not included in other manuscripts, however, this painter should more properly be called the Master of the London Passional after another of his works (London, BL, Add. MS. 18162). The painter of the beginning of the second volume of the Bible also painted all but one of the miniatures in a Book of Hours (U. Liège, Bib. Gén., MS.

Master of Evert van Soudenbalch: *Creation* scenes, *Evert van Soudenbalch Being Presented to the Virgin and Child*, and the *Fall*; miniatures from the Bible of Evert van Soudenbalch, 395×288 mm, *c.* 1460 (Vienna, Österreichische Nationalbibliothek, Cod. 2771, fol. 10*r*)

Wittert 13) made no later than *c.* 1460 for Gijsbrecht van Brederode, Bishop of Utrecht. The exceptional miniature of the *Last Judgement* (fol. 39*v*) was produced by the Master of Evert van Soudenbalch himself.

The most important Book of Hours in this group is the manuscript known from its second owner as the Hours of Mary van Vronenstein (Brussels, Bib. Royale Albert 1er, MS. II. 7619). The book had belonged first to Jan van Amerongen, and the 12 full-page pictures by the Master of Evert van Soudenbalch were perhaps added when it changed hands. Several historiated initials and borders were painted by the Master of the London Passional. The date 1460 is marked on an astronomical chart in the manuscript, providing a point of reference for the chronological classification of this group of manuscripts. Two other Books of Hours contain illumination attributable to these artists: one in Liège (U. Liège, Bib. Gén., MS. Wittert 34), with historiated initials by the Master of Gijsbrecht van Brederode and border decoration by the Master of the London Passional, and another (Malibu, CA, Getty Mus., MS. Ludwig IX. 10) with a miniature of the *Coronation of the Virgin* by the Master of Evert van Soudenbalch surrounded by a border with music-making angels (fol. 15*v*).

Both owners and liturgical aspects of these manuscripts link them to Utrecht, and, in addition, Scillia established links between them and woodcuts in Utrecht, incunabula. These illuminators therefore undoubtedly worked in Utrecht, where they comprised the most important workshop of the period around 1460.

They also had connections with the southern Netherlands. Marrow attributed a whole series of manuscripts certainly produced in Ghent to the Master of the London Passional. These can be dated after his Utrecht works: it appears he had moved to Ghent. A most curious connection with Flanders on the one hand and with England on the other is provided by a Book of Hours in Oxford (Bodleian Lib., MS. Auct. D.inf.2.13), which has exquisite pictures painted in grisaille by the Master of Evert van Soudenbalch. The Office of the Virgin is for the Use of Sarum, and the manuscript was therefore undoubtedly intended for the English market. The borders framing the miniatures are either English or at least imitate English decoration. The facing text pages have the same borders along with historiated initials, painted in grisaille in the style of the south Netherlandish illuminator WILLEM VRELANT.

In addition to the manuscript illuminations, a panel painting has been attributed to the Master of Evert van Soudenbalch. This triptych (Utrecht, Cent. Mus.) has a central *Crucifixion* with the *Mass of St Gregory* and a *St Christopher* depicted on the wing panels. When closed the wings show an *Annunciation* in grisaille. There is a view of Utrecht in the background of the *Crucifixion* showing the cathedral under construction, as it was *c.* 1457–67. Boon connected a *Mount of Calvary* (Providence, RI, Sch. Des., Mus. A.) with the Utrecht *Crucifixion*. Both works follow the same models, which were also the basis for miniatures on similar themes in the Hours of Mary van Vronenstein (fols 123*v* and 54*v*).

Boon also attributed two further works to the painter of these panels: a *Nailing to the Cross* (Liverpool, Walker

A.G.) and a *Tree of Jesse* (Utrecht, Buurkerk), which is thought to have borne the date 1451. He suggested the possibility of identifying this 'Master of the Tree of Jesse in the Buurkerk' with the Master of Evert van Soudenbalch. The relationship of these paintings to the miniatures is indisputable.

BIBLIOGRAPHY

L. M. J. Delaissé: 'Le Livre d'heures de Mary van Vronenstein, chef-d'oeuvre inconnu d'un atelier d'Utrecht, achevé en 1460', *Scriptorium*, iii (1949), pp. 230–45

K. G. Boon: 'Een Utrechtse schilder uit de 15de eeuw, de Meester van de Boom van Jesse in de Buurkerk', *Oud-Holland*, lxxvi (1961), pp. 51–60

L. M. J. Delaissé: *A Century of Dutch Manuscript Illumination* (Berkeley and Los Angeles, 1968), pp. 41–9

La Miniature hollandaise (exh. cat., Brussels, Bib. Royale Albert 1er, 1971), pp. 36–8, 55–6

O. Pächt and U. Jenni: *Die illuminierten Handschriften und Inkunabeln der Österreichischen Nationalbibliothek: Holländische Schule*, 2 vols (Vienna, 1975), i, pp. 43–85; ii, pls 80–261

D. G. Scillia: 'The Master of the London Passional: Johann Veldener's "Utrecht Cutter"', *The Early Illustrated Book: Essays in Honor of Lessing J. Rosenwald* (Washington, DC, 1982), pp. 23–40

J. H. Marrow: 'Prolegomena to a New Descriptive Catalogue of Dutch Illuminated Manuscripts', *Miscellanea Neerlandica: Opstellen voor Dr Jan Deschamps ter gelegenheid van zijn zeventigste verjaardag*, i (Leuven, 1987), pp. 295–309

BODO BRINKMANN

Master of the Évora Altarpiece (*fl c.* 1490–1500). South Netherlandish painter, active in Portugal. He is named after his only known work, a polyptych of the *Life of the Virgin*, in nineteen panels, all but four of which are in the Museu Regional in Évora. The large central panel shows the *Virgin in Glory*. Twelve side panels narrate the *Life and Death of the Virgin*; four of these are in Lisbon: the *Presentation of the Virgin*, the *Marriage of the Virgin*, the *Presentation in the Temple* and the *Death of the Virgin* (Lisbon, Mus. N. A. Ant.). Six relatively small panels with scenes from the *Passion of Christ* supposedly comprise part of the predella.

The altarpiece was commissioned for the choir of Évora Cathedral, and the plan for this monumental work may have been conceived during the marriage celebrations for the Infante Don Alfonso of Portugal (1475–91) in 1490. Reis-Santos thus dated the central panel to *c.* 1490, while the other parts were probably painted some ten years later, a theory based on stylistic differences between the central and side panels.

There has been some discussion as to whether the predella scenes ever belonged to the same altarpiece, though apparently made by the same artist who painted the side panels; there are, according to Reis-Santos, similarities between the two groups in the style of faces, gestures and postures.

According to Friedländer, the polyptych was painted by an outstanding south Netherlandish artist, familiar with the work of Hugo van der Goes, and with the help of assistants. He suggested that the painting of the *Virgin in Glory* is derived from a lost original by van der Goes. Others have proposed Gerard David and his workshop. De Figueiredo attributed the altarpiece to the workshop of David, working in cooperation with an artist who painted in the style of Albert Bouts. In support of this thesis, he cited a ten-month stay in Portugal during 1501 by Roelof van Velpen (*fl* 1491–1501), who was a native of Leuven.

BIBLIOGRAPHY

M. J. Friedländer: *Die altniederländische Malerei* (Berlin, 1924–37); Eng. trans. as *Early Netherlandish Painting* (Leiden, 1967–76), iv, p. 89

J. de Figueiredo: 'Metsys e Portugal', *Melangen Hulin de Loo* (Brussels and Paris, 1931), pp. 163–4

M. J. Friedländer: 'Eine Zeichnung von Hugo van der Goes', *Pantheon*, viii (1935), pp. 99–104

L. Reis-Santos: *Obras-primas da pintura flamenga dos seculos XV e XVI em Portugal* (Lisbon, 1953; Eng. trans, 1962), pp. 67–72 [preface by M. J. Friedländer]

FEMY HORSCH

Master of the Fabriano Altarpiece. See PUCCIO DI SIMONE.

Fastolf Master [Master of Sir John Fastolf] (*fl c.* 1420–60). Illuminator, active in France and England. The Master's name comes from a manuscript containing the *Livre des quatre vertus* and the *Epître d'Othéa* (Oxford, Bodleian Lib., MS. Laud. misc. 570) made for Sir John Fastolf (*d* 1459), who had added substantial profits from the French wars to his English inheritance. The book was produced in England and was dated 1450 by the English scribe Ricardus Franciscus, but the miniatures were thoroughly French in style. They combine an emphasis on surface, from reinforced outlines and flat patterning, with some effect of volume from the drapery modelling of his often angular, elongated figures and a degree of three-dimensional illusion in the architectural settings. Landscapes are flatter compilations of stylized natural details, where any recession through overlapping forms is negated by the gold of the starry skies.

Early in his career the Fastolf Master seems to have worked in Paris, since miniatures by him and the Boucicaut Master are found together in a Book of Hours of Paris Use datable *c.* 1420 (New York, Pierpont Morgan Lib., MS. M. 100). He continued to use his extensive knowledge of Boucicaut Master compositions after he had left the capital for the greater prosperity of Rouen, a centre of English administration and settlement. Miniatures in several liturgical manuscripts for Rouen and other Norman uses, such as Coutances (Paris, Bib. Arsenal, MS. 560), have been attributed to the Fastolf Master. The earliest, datable from the calendar before 1424, is a Book of Hours of Rouen Use (New York, Pierpont Morgan Lib., MS. M. 27), ordered for a member of the Guerin or Garin family, probably Jean, a canon of Rouen Cathedral. The patron who commissioned a handsome French Missal (Oxford, Keble Coll. Lib., MS. 38) is unknown.

The Fastolf Master was also employed by English patrons such as Sir William Porter, last cited in France in 1431, for his Book of Hours (New York, Pierpont Morgan Lib., MS. M. 105) and the anonymous owner of another Hours of Sarum Use (Oxford, Bodleian Lib., MS. Auct. D inf. 2 II). Perhaps some years before the surrender of Rouen in 1449 he definitively allied himself to his English clients and crossed to England. The liturgical manuscripts to which he contributed, such as the Psalter with a London calendar (Oxford, Bodleian Lib., MS. Hatton 45), suggest that he settled in London, the likely home of Ricardus Franciscus, with whom he collaborated on at least one other book (London, BL, Harley MS. 2915).

Despite his apparent popularity in England, the Fastolf Master does not seem greatly to have influenced native artists, who continued to work in the style largely formed by Netherlandish and Rhenish immigrants and sustained by the growing trade in Netherlandish manuscripts. The Fastolf Master himself contributed to a Book of Hours of Sarum Use (New York, Pierpont Morgan Lib., MS. G. 9) where the chief miniaturist was a Netherlander, English illuminators supplying the subsidiary decoration. Despite the predominance of the Low Countries, some trade in books continued, or was re-established, with Rouen, and it was there that the Fastolf Master had most impact, both directly and through the TALBOT MASTER (*see* below). His linear clarity made his compositions easy to reproduce, and his style was an important element in the expanding Rouen book trade, which was already developing the techniques for the repetitive mass production characteristic of its later output.

BIBLIOGRAPHY

J. J. G. Alexander: 'A Lost Leaf from a Bodleian Book of Hours', *Bodleian Lib. Rec.*, viii (1971), pp. 248–51

J. D. Farquhar: *Creation and Imitation: The Work of a Fifteenth Century Manuscript Illuminator*, Nova University Studies in the Humanities, i (Fort Lauderdale, 1976), pp. 59–60

M. Parkes: *The Medieval Manuscripts of Keble College, Oxford* (London, 1977), MS.38

E. P. Spencer: *The Sobieski Hours: A Manuscript in the Royal Library at Windsor Castle* [Roxburghe Club, no. 239] (London, 1977)

The Last Flowering: French Painting in Manuscripts, 1420–1530, from American Collections (exh. cat. by J. Plummer and G. Clarke, New York, Pierpnt Morgan Lib., 1982), pp. 1–2, no. 1, pp. 15–16, nos 21–3

CATHERINE REYNOLDS

Master of the Female Half-lengths (*fl* ?Antwerp, first half of the 16th century). South Netherlandish painter or group of painters. The name is given to what was apparently a large workshop that specialized in small-scale panels of aristocratic young ladies in half-length and devotional scenes: they are shown reading, writing or playing musical instruments, usually in a wood-panelled interior or against a neutral background. Some of the women are represented with an ointment jar, the attribute of Mary Magdalene.

1. IDENTIFICATION. The Master was first distinguished as an individual artist in the 19th century. Friedländer included 67 paintings in his catalogue of the artist, and about 40 more have since been published, mainly panels in Spanish collections that were probably produced for export. None of these paintings is signed or dated, but two panels from the workshop (both Antwerp, Kon. Mus. S. Kst.) are copied after a lost *Man of Sorrows* designed by Jan Gossart in 1527.

The Master's identity and the place and period of his activity have been widely disputed. Writers have attempted to place him in Antwerp, Bruges, Ghent, Mechelen and the French court, dating his activity from the early to the late 16th century. It has been suggested that he was the French court painter Jean Clouet, because of the poetry of Clement Marot that can be read in songbooks held by the ladies in some of the paintings, but French music was also popular in Flanders at that time. The Master was also thought to be the poet and painter Lucas de Heere, who was active in Ghent. Benesch believed that the Half-length Master was one Hans Vereycke, who was described by van Mander as a landscape and portrait painter in Bruges.

Benesch's theory is based on a landscape drawing (Paris, Louvre) that he ascribed to the Master, which is inscribed with Vereycke's name in a later hand. However, according to Hulin de Loo (see 1902 exh. cat.), Vereycke is identical with a painter named Jan van Eeckele, who first registered in the Guild of St Luke in Bruges in 1534 and died there in 1561, thus too late for the style of the landscapes in the paintings assigned to the Master. Bergmans (see 1963 exh. cat.) located the Master in the cultural centre of Mechelen because of the emphasis on music and art that he saw in the paintings of the young women.

More persuasively, Friedländer and Koch placed the artist in Antwerp and Mechelen in the 1520s and 1530s, owing to the closeness of the landscapes to those of Joachim Patinir and the similarity of the female types to those of Bernart van Orley. Koch believed that the artist may have been trained in Patinir's shop in Antwerp *c.* 1520. This proposal has since been accepted by a number of writers, who have tried to identify the Master's hand in the background landscapes of paintings by Antwerp artists such as Quentin Metsys (e.g. the *Virgin and Child in a Landscape*, Poznań, N. Mus.). Furthermore, the compositions and use of Italianate architectural ornament in panels of the *Adoration of the Magi* by the Master (e.g. Munich, Alte Pin.; Berlin, Bodemus.) suggest contact with Antwerp artists such as Jan de Beer, Pseudo-Bles and other members of the so-called Antwerp Mannerists. It is now generally accepted that the paintings ascribed to the Master are by not one but several artists. No attempt has been made to sort out the hands, although it has been suggested that Marcellus Coffermans may have been one of the painters in the workshop.

2. WORKS. Little is known about the original function of these panels of half-length ladies. Several women may be shown together, as in two panels depicting a *Concert* (Rohrau, Schloss; St Petersburg, Hermitage), or single figures may be depicted alone, as in the *Magdalene Reading* (Paris, Louvre; see fig.). The inventory of King Henry VIII of England lists paintings of similar subjects, for instance a picture of a woman playing a lute, with a book and a pot of lilies. A passage in Pierre de Bourdeille Brantôme's *Vie des dames galantes* describes paintings of women with flutes that were brought from Flanders to France and hung above fireplaces in inns and taverns.

The Master's female type is very distinctive, with a heart-shaped face, often turned in three-quarter view, with lowered eyes, a straight, thin nose and high, narrow eyebrows. Typically, the women wear a close-fitting velvet dress with a low neckline, and their hair is parted in the centre and partly covered by a cap. The same figure type appears in the devotional panels of the Virgin, which the workshop produced in great numbers. The Virgin usually wears a transparent veil over her hair and, almost as a trademark, a small metallic button on her bodice or headband. The Christ Child is nude, slightly elongated and muscular; Joseph is bald with a long, forked beard. Characteristic are the two panels of the *Rest on the Flight into Egypt* (London, N.G.; Philadelphia, PA, Mus. A., Johnson Col.) and the *Virgin and Child with a Book* (St Petersburg, Hermitage).

Master of the Female Half-lengths: *Magdalene Reading*, oil on panel, 540×420 mm, early 16th century (Paris, Musée du Louvre)

The Master and his workshop also produced replicas of standardized compositions such as the *Crucifixion*, the *Deposition*, the *Virgin of Sorrows*, *St Jerome* and *Lucretia*. There are also a few paintings of mythological subjects, for example the *Judgement of Paris* (Amsterdam, Rijksmus., on loan to The Hague, Mauritshuis), and several portraits of anonymous sitters are attributed to him (Budapest, Mus. F.A.; Vienna, Ksthist. Mus.). Compositions are frequently borrowed from other Netherlandish artists, for instance the *Man of Sorrows* after the lost work by Gossart mentioned earlier; several panels of the *Virgin and Child with a Book* (e.g. ex-Gal. Pallavicini, Rome) are after a design by van Orley of *c.* 1520. As was the vogue in Netherlandish art in the early 16th century, the Master often derived the poses of the Virgin and Child from panels of the 15th-century artist Rogier van der Weyden, undoubtedly as a reference to the great heritage of the past. Italian prints were also occasionally a source. Panels of *Venus and Cupid* and *Neptune and Thetis* (both Berlin, Gemäldegal.) are after engravings by Gian Giacomo Caraglio.

The landscape backgrounds in paintings of the Half-length group follow the general formula developed by Patinir and also borrow specific details. For instance, in the Master's versions of the *Rest on the Flight into Egypt* (e.g. Vienna, Ksthist. Mus.), he quoted from Patinir the scenes of the Miracle of the Wheatfield and the Fall of the Pagan Idol. Koch ascribed six panels to the Master that were formerly considered to be by Patinir. Among the other paintings for which the Master is thought to have provided the landscape background are another *Rest on* the *Flight into Egypt* (Toronto, A.G.), with figures in the style of van Orley, and Gossart's signed and dated *Virgin and Child* (1521; Cleveland, OH, Mus. A.).

BIBLIOGRAPHY

K. van Mander: *Schilder-boeck* ([1603]–1604)
Exposition des tableaux flamands des XIVe, XVe et XVIe siècles (exh. cat. by G. Hulin de Loo, Bruges, Groeningemus., 1902)
M. J. Friedländer: *Die altniederländische Malerei* (Berlin, 1924–37); Eng. trans. as *Early Netherlandish Painting* (Leiden, 1967–76), xii, pp. 18–21
O. Benesch: 'The Name of the Master of the Half-lengths', *Gaz. B.-A.*, xxiii (1943), pp. 269–82
J. H. Perrera: 'Museo Español del Maestro de las Medias Figuras', *Goya*, 49 (1962), pp. 2–11
Le Siècle de Bruegel: La Peinture en Belgique au XVIe siècle (exh. cat., Brussels, Mus. A. Anc., 1963), pp. 170–72 [entries by S. Bergmans]
R. A. Koch: *Joachim Patinir* (Princeton, 1968) [with further bibliog.]
M. Diaz Padrón: 'Nuevas pinturas del Maestro de las Medias Figuras', *Archv Esp. A.*, ccx (1980), pp. 169–84
——: 'Pinturas flamencas del XVI: Tablas del Maestro de las Medias Figuras identificadas en España', *Archv Esp. A.*, ccxix (1982), pp. 273–86

ELLEN KONOWITZ

Master of the Figdor Deposition [Master of the Martyrdom of St Lucy; Master of the Page beneath the Cross; Pseudo-Geertgen] (*fl* late 15th century). North Netherlandish painter. His name is derived from a painting of the *Deposition*, formerly in the collection of Dr Albert Figdor, Vienna, and sold in 1930 to the Staatlichen Museen, Berlin, where it was destroyed in 1945. The Master was a follower of Geertgen tot Sint Jans and played an important role in the development of painting in Haarlem. The Master mirrors Geertgen's style, as is evident in a comparison of Geertgen's *Burning of the Bones of St John the Baptist* (Vienna, Ksthist. Mus.) with the Master's *Martyrdom of St Lucy* (Amsterdam, Rijksmus.): composition, figures, colour and landscape are very alike, yet the Master's drawing is not as good, and in the *Deposition* he shows a new tendency towards sometimes extreme mobility of the figures.

The *Deposition* and the *Martyrdom of St Lucy* constitute the core of the Master's oeuvre. Both panels were originally the same size and were probably the two sides of the left wing of an altarpiece. Hoogewerff coined the name 'Master of the Page beneath the Cross' after a figure in a *Crucifixion* (Amsterdam, Rijksmus.) that he ascribed to the same artist. This painting, however, is clearly of lesser quality than the others, and its authenticity has been disputed by authorities including Friedländer. Friedländer saw in the Master's work a connection between the Haarlem and Amsterdam schools and suggested that the painter may have been a teacher of Jacob Cornelisz. Several identifications have been made: Valentiner thought that he might have been one of the brothers Mouwerijn (*fl* before 1473; *d* 1509) or Claes Simonsz. van Waterlandt (*fl* 1485–90), a hypothesis further expanded by Châtelet; another possibility is the young JACOB CORNELISZ, but this has not been widely accepted as Kunze argued against it; Hoogewerff tried to identify the Master with Jan Gerritsz. Swegher (*d* 1514).

BIBLIOGRAPHY

Thieme–Becker
W. R. Valentiner: *Aus der niederländischen Kunst* (Berlin, 1914), pp. 68–71
M. J. Friedländer: *Die altniederländische Malerei* (Berlin, 1924–37); Eng. trans. as *Early Netherlandish Painting* (Leiden, 1967–76), v, pp. 77, 96

G. J. Hoogewerff: *De Noord-Nederlandsche schilderkunst*, 5 vols (The Hague, 1937–47), ii, pp. 192, 211–20, 291, 389, 427; iii, pp. 11, 22, 76, 78, 81, 92, 95, 144; iv, p. 1; v, pp. 54–5
I. Kunze: 'Neuerwerbungen niederländischer Gemälde', *Berlin. Mus.: Ber. Staatl. Mus. Preuss. Kulthes.*, lx (1939), pp. 8–13
A. Châtelet: *Early Dutch Painting: Painting in the Northern Netherlands in the Fifteenth Century* (Amsterdam, 1980), pp. 138–40, 144, 227–8

FEMY HORSCH

Master of Figline. *See* MASTER OF THE FOGG PIETÀ below.

Master of the First Prayerbook of Maximilian. *See* MASTER OF THE OLDER PRAYERBOOK OF MAXIMILIAN below.

Master of the Fleecy Clouds. *See under* MASTER OF EVERT VAN SOUDENBALCH above.

Master of Flémalle (*fl c.* 1420–*c.* 1440). South Netherlandish painter. With Jan van Eyck and Rogier van der Weyden, he determined the course of Netherlandish and thence much of European painting in the 15th century. There is good reason for identifying him with ROBERT CAMPIN of Tournai, the master of van der Weyden.

1. Works. 2. Identity. 3. Working methods and technique. 4. Posthumous reputation.

1. WORKS.

(i) The Flémalle panels and related works. (ii) Other attributions.

(i) The Flémalle panels and related works. The Master of Flémalle was named by von Tschudi in 1898 from three surviving panels (Frankfurt am Main, Städel. Kstinst. & Städt. Gal.) of a lost ensemble. The panels, depicting the *Virgin and Child* (1600×680 mm; see fig. 1), *St Veronica Holding the Vernicle* (1515×610 mm) and a grisaille *Trinity*, were bought in 1849 from Ignaz van Houten of Aachen; he had obtained them from a priest in Liège who apparently said that they had come from an 'abbey of Flémalle, near Liège' and that the central panel had been destroyed at the Battle of Neerminden (1793). On the reverse of the *Virgin and Child* is a 17th- or 18th-century grisaille *Mater dolorosa*, which may repeat a lost original design. A large and expensive commission, the ensemble must have been intended for a location of some prestige and significance. Unfortunately, no abbey of Flémalle ever existed, nor did an 'abbey of Falin, near Sedan', an alternative version of van Houten's information recorded by Sulpiz Boiserée. Reinach suggested that 'Falin' might be a corruption of Elant, the only abbey near Sedan and a suitable place for so splendid a work since it was the funerary church of the Counts of Nevers.

Von Tschudi also associated with the so-called Flémalle panels a fragment of a *Crucified Thief with Two Onlookers* (Frankfurt am Main, Städel. Kstinst. & Städt. Gal.; see fig. 2), a connection already recognized by Passavant in 1858. The bloodless corpse of the *Crucified Thief* invites comparison with the dead Christ in the grisaille *Trinity*, while the exotic bystanders match the Virgin and St Veronica in the rich colouring and detailing of costume. A grisaille saint on the reverse of the *Crucified Thief* shows that the fragment came from a folding wing of a triptych. A greatly reduced copy of the later 15th century (Liverpool,

1. Master of Flémalle: *Virgin and Child*, oil on panel, 1.60×0.68 m, *c.* 1430–40 (Frankfurt am Main, Städelsches Kunstinstitut und Städtische Galerie)

Walker A.G.) preserves the entire composition in triptych form. The central panel shows the *Deposition*, and the other thief and a female bystander are on the left wing, where there is an unidentified kneeling donor who may

either reflect the position of a donor on the original or be an insertion by the copyist. In the copy the sky is painted naturalistically, unlike the elaborately patterned but severely damaged gold background of the original fragment. The proportions have also been altered: the figures are spaced more widely, lessening the impact of the original tightly welded central group. Drawn copies of the *Crucified Thief* on the left wing (Cambridge, MA, Fogg) and of the central *Deposition* (Cambridge, Fitzwilliam) probably preserve the quality of the original more successfully than does the harshly executed painted copy. Calculating from the dimensions of the original surviving *Thief* (1330×925 mm), the central panel of the triptych must have measured 2.5×2.5 m; like the Flémalle panels, it must have formed part of a very large altarpiece.

The original painted *Crucified Thief* cannot be traced before 1811, when, already a fragment, it was in Aschaffenburg. It has been argued that the copy of the complete triptych came from the hospital of St Julian in Bruges, because of the grisaille figure of *St Julian* on the outer wing and the coat of arms, previously thought to be that of Bruges (now seen as possibly that of the Troche family). Certainly Bruges painters knew the composition: elements were used in the central *Crucifixion* of the scenes from the *Passion of Christ* in St Salvator, Bruges, and by Ambrosius Benson in his *Deposition* altarpiece (Segovia Cathedral). Miniatures in the Hours of Catherine of Cleves (New York, Pierpont Morgan Lib., MSS M. 917 and M. 945) and the TURIN–MILAN HOURS, which also derive from the altarpiece, show that the design was familiar in the northern Netherlands and suggest that the original may date before *c.* 1430. The less assured drawing of the figures in the *Crucified Thief* fragment has led to general agreement to date it earlier than the Flémalle panels.

The Flémalle wings show that the Master was a great artist whose masterpieces of design fuse three-dimensional illusionism and decorative surface pattern to forceful emotional and intellectual effect. The youthful Virgin suckling the Child is movingly contrasted with the aged Veronica holding the vernicle. The figures convey credible feelings and are surely based on life drawings: the accuracy of their delineation is matched by the careful manipulation of tone so that light–dark contrasts maximize the bulk of the figures and the plausibility of the space they inhabit, a space both marked out and denied by the careful detailing of the flowery ground and forcefully curtailed by ornately patterned textile backdrops.

The equally realistic rendering of both plants and hangings makes their 'unreal' combination one of the factors that ensures that naturalistic effects do not detract from the paintings' spiritual impact. Believable as people, the figures are yet removed from the mundane by their grandeur and serenity and by the rich splendour of colour and gilding in clothes and settings. The divine is only obviously symbolized in the miraculous image of the face of Christ on the vernicle and the haloes around the Virgin and Child.

Despite their technical brilliance and dramatic impact, the Flémalle compositions seem to have had few repercussions, perhaps because they were comparatively inaccessible. A bust-length tondo composition of a similarly veiled *Virgin Suckling the Child* (e.g. Philadelphia, PA,

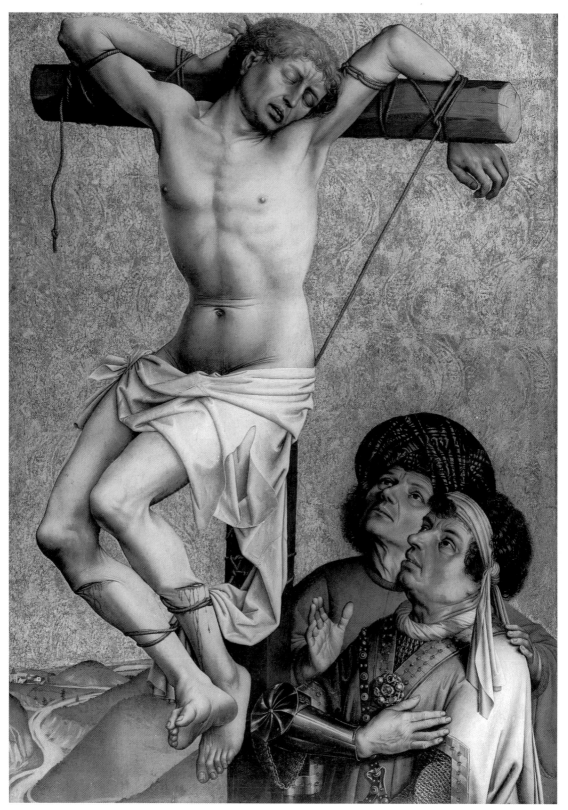

2. Master of Flémalle: *Crucified Thief with Two Onlookers*, oil on panel, 1330×925 mm, *c.* 1420–30 (Frankfurt am Main, Städelsches Kunstinstitut und Städtische Galerie)

Mus. A.) may have originated from the Master as a cheap variant of the Flémalle *Virgin and Child*. No surviving picture approaches the quality of the Flémalle panels, and the differences between versions make it hard to be certain of the composition's original form. A very successful image of the *Virgin Suckling the Child*, shown standing in the apse with attendant angels, which seems to have been favoured into the 16th century, relates to the Flémalle Virgin in basic concept only. The awkwardness of the apse in what seems the most faithful version (London, N.G.) as well as the more obtrusively contrived elegance of the Virgin's support of the veil suggest that, if the design did originate with the Master of Flémalle, it would considerably antedate the Flémalle altarpiece.

A broader-format version of the grisaille *Trinity*, with the Father enthroned, seems to have been better known than the composition of the Flémalle wing itself. The figures are grouped under a baldachino on the left wing of a small diptych (each panel, 285×185 mm; St Petersburg, Hermitage), surrounded by angels with instruments of the Passion, in a widely imitated design best recorded in another panel (Leuven, Mus. Vander Kelen-Mertens). In all three, the dead Christ still raises one hand to display the wound in his side, but in the Flémalle grisaille alone one foot is tilted so that the nail hole is seen, more horrifyingly, in the sole. The other wounds are almost lost in the deadness of the pose, in contrast to the careful arrangement of hands and feet in the variants. The jarring angularity of Christ's legs is reinforced by the shadow of his left knee on his right leg, just as the power of the upright Father is stressed by the shadow of his head. Umbra and penumbra are meticulously distinguished, and the cast shadows combine with the more subtle depictions of light and shade to create a limited but plausible space. The compression of the two figures preserves a notion of carving from the block, a sculptural effect increased by the incised inscription on the pedestal and the anchoring of the dove to Christ's shoulder.

(ii) Other attributions. While the exceptional quality of the Flémalle panels and the *Crucified Thief* and their exhibition in the same public collection ensured that von Tschudi's naming of the Master of Flémalle gained widespread acceptance, there has been equally widespread disagreement about the precise limits of the artist's oeuvre. Von Tschudi subsumed into his Master of Flémalle the works attributed by Bode to his MASTER OF MERODE (*see* below). Yet once the separate authorship of the Merode Triptych (New York, Cloisters) is accepted, it is possible to establish which works belong with the principal works by the Master of Flémalle and which, while stylistically related, should be assigned to other artists working under his influence or direction. Such attributions are bound to remain controversial, given the inadequate knowledge of 15th-century workshop practice. Any picture, particularly on the scale of the Flémalle panels, is likely to have been worked on by assistants, so that the hand of the Master has to be sought in the overall design and in the execution of at least the principal parts. Scale has also to be taken into consideration when comparing smaller paintings associated with the Master's name.

In what is hypothetically considered the Master's earliest work, the Seilern Triptych (London, Courtauld Inst. Gals), his genius for visual expression is combined with as yet incomplete technical skill. This small folding triptych (600×499 mm when closed) has the *Entombment* on the central panel, with the *Two Thieves* and the empty Cross on the left wing above an unidentified donor and the *Resurrection* on the right. Despite the difference in scale and the proposed early date—in the 1420s, judging by the donor's costume—the Seilern Triptych resembles the lost *Deposition* triptych, not only in the presence and appearance of the thieves and the body of Christ but also in fundamental principles of design. In both, the figures of the crowded central panel are thrown into even greater relief by the imagined depth of the landscapes in the wings, although the *Deposition* wings are articulated with considerably greater skill and have a gold ground instead of a sky. The orientalizing costume takes on a more literally descriptive role in the *Entombment* since Christ is being buried in a striped prayer shawl in accordance with Jewish custom. The desire for spatial coherence is evident yet still not satisfactorily met: the fence curving round the tomb of the *Resurrection* extends into the central panel to mark off the depiction of the same tomb. Comparable in scale and probably in date is a fragment representing *St John the Baptist* from a small wing panel (Cleveland, OH, Mus. A.), which, as in the Flémalle wings, shows the saint against a rich textile hanging.

A small panel of the *Nativity* (870×700 mm; Dijon, Mus. B.-A.) shows many features of the Flémalle panels in conception and many compositional devices from the *Deposition* triptych. In both, the figures are basically arranged in two rows with a foreground figure seen unusually in back view; fluttering angels with sharply pointed wings animate the upper areas; and a landscape of conical hills is linked to the middle ground by a wide road. The elaboration and exploitation of narrative detail are seen again in the presence of the two midwives; their less familiar role is explained in the curling banderoles, which act as focusing devices and as a unifying force in the coherence of surface decoration with spatial illusionism. The orientalizing costumes of the midwives again show the Master's awareness of the New Testament as a record of events in the East, and the meticulous depiction of the more fantastic detail ensures that the figures lose none of their credibility.

A painting of the *Adoration of the Magi* (Berlin, Gemäldegal.) seems to be an accurate copy of an earlier composition by the Master of Flémalle, best recorded in a drawing (Berlin, Kupferstichkab.). Painted versions (Verona, Castelvecchio, and Cambridge, Fitzwilliam), in which the stable is more simply set parallel to the picture plane, are less faithful to the presumed original. Unlike the Dijon *Nativity*, which ambitiously links the background, middle ground and foreground, in this composition the tightly grouped figures obscure the middle ground, leaving a distant landscape view to appear in isolation in the upper left corner.

The two-event narrative of the *Miracle of the Rods and the Marriage of the Virgin* (765×880 mm; Madrid, Prado; *see* SYMBOL, fig. 1) led the Master to separate yet link the scenes by elaborate architectural settings. The result lacks the certainty of the *Nativity*, but the figure types, expressive gestures, back-view figures and exotic costumes all reveal his hand, evident also in the delicate execution. On the right, the Virgin is married in an incomplete Gothic portal, not yet properly joined to the adjacent, vaguely Romanesque temple, a careful visualization of the separateness yet interdependence of the Old and New dispensations. From the rightwards emphasis, the panel must have formed the left wing of some folding ensemble to which an *Annunciation* (Madrid, Prado), also given to the Escorial by Philip II, would seem to have belonged. Cut down (765×702 mm) and with a planed reverse, it is hard to re-create its relationship with the *Marriage* and whatever other panels may have existed. The Virgin Annunciate and Gabriel show the Master of Flémalle's characteristically broad and bulky figure types, and the churchlike structure is entirely congruent with the architectural fantasies of the *Marriage of the Virgin*. Nevertheless, the execution is inferior, and the *Annunciation* is usually considered a workshop product. The *Annunciation* (Brussels, Mus. A. Anc.) in which the Virgin sits in a contemporary domestic interior, has claims to be considered an original by the Master. There are significant changes between the underdrawn design and the paint surface, particularly in the fireplace. The many derivatives, in sculpture as well as painting, including the Merode Triptych, follow the painted composition, suggesting that the Brussels *Annunciation* marks the origin of the design on which the other versions depend.

It is likely that domestic scenes of the Virgin and Child in an interior also originated from the Master of Flémalle, although no specific composition can be credited to him with any certainty. The right wing of the diptych in St Petersburg shows the Child lying across his mother's knee while she warms her hand at the fire. There is a variant of this composition (London, N.G.), seemingly of much higher quality. In the Salting *Virgin and Child* (London, N.G.), attributed to JACQUES DARET, the Virgin suckles the Child before a firescreen that acts as a halo. Her exaggeratedly wide face, with its ugly, stylized features, is a coarsened version of the broad shapes of the Flémalle Virgin, with her curving downcast eyelids, and the empty artificiality of the Child's gesture contrasts markedly with the tender expressiveness of the Flémalle panel.

When compared with the immaculately detailed heads of the Flémalle panels, the pendant *Portrait of a Man* and *Portrait of a Woman* (see fig. 3; both London, N.G.) can also safely be attributed to the Master, their extraordinary quality being even more apparent after cleaning in 1987. Using the three-quarters view, as did van Eyck, the Master of Flémalle angled the bodies more acutely to emphasize volume and shaded the far side of the face for maximum relief. The *Portrait of a Fat Man* (Berlin, Gemäldegal.), inconclusively identified as Robert de Masmines (*d* 1430), shows a similar treatment of the form of the head. Copies made in the 16th century of portraits of *Bartholomy Alatruye* and his wife (dep. Tournai, Mus. B.-A.) retain characteristics of the Master of Flémalle; judging from the costume, the originals must have been later than the closely comparable National Gallery pendants, whose dress seems appropriate for the 1430s.

3. Master of Flémalle: *Portrait of a Woman*, oil and tempera on panel, 407×279 mm, *c.* 1430 (London, National Gallery)

Other than portraits, secular works attributable to the Master of Flémalle have not survived. A scene of the *Vengeance of Tomyris*, imitated into the 17th century, was preserved in a picture that came from Spain (ex-Kaiser-Friedrich Mus., Berlin; destr. World War II); it clearly showed its origins with the Master of Flémalle in figure types, compositional devices and decorative detail. The bloody story from Herodotus of Tomyris' vengeance on the King of Persia for the death of her son is forcefully conveyed with all the Master's narrative skill, the horror mitigated by the gentleness of the curves orchestrating the composition. It was possibly part of a series to which also belonged a composition with *Jael and Sisera*, a subject close in content to that of Tomyris, which is preserved in a Flémallesque-style drawing (Brunswick, Herzog Anton Ulrich-Mus.).

Other pictures with Flémallesque characteristics do not display the Master's genius for purposeful composition and must be the work of followers or assistants of varying skills: the *Virgin and Child in a Glory* (Aix-en-Provence, Mus. Granet), for instance, is extremely well painted, the *Virgin and Child in a Garden* (Berlin, Gemäldegal.) less so. The *Crucifixion* (Berlin, Gemäldegal.) combines thoroughly Flémallesque figure types and costumes into an incoherent whole, as does the *Virgin and Child with Saints* (Washington, DC, N.G.A.).

2. IDENTITY. None of the pictures by the Master of Flémalle or the copies that appear to be faithful records of his inventions has a certain date or provenance. Barthelmy Alatruye, married in 1411, came from a Lille family but travelled widely as a leading member of the Burgundian administration and was at The Hague when he died in 1446. One Flémallesque work does have a named patron and date: the wing panels of *St John the Baptist* with Heinrich Werl, and *St Barbara* (Madrid, Prado), Werl's name and the date 1438 being recorded in an inscription. The empty gestures, the weakly conceived donor figure and the incoherent fussiness of setting remove these from the Master of Flémalle to a closer association with the Master of Merode, but they do provide a certain date with some relation to the Flémalle oeuvre. Given this lack of firm historical evidence, any attempt to localize and date the work of the Master of Flémalle must be based on stylistic comparisons.

The works of Rogier van der Weyden (*see* WEYDEN, VAN DER, (1)) reveal a pervasive awareness of the Master of Flémalle's feeling for the emotional content of a picture and its expression through facial features and gestures as well as more subtle configurations of line, shape and colour. There are also instances of direct quotations. For example, van der Weyden's great *Deposition* (before 1443; Madrid, Prado) is almost a reworking of the Master of Flémalle's central *Deposition* panel. More curiously, the face of the *Fat Man* was used by Rogier for the figure usually identified as Nicodemus, suggesting access to the Master's studio drawings. Moreover, the central panel of the *Nativity* in van der Weyden's Bladelin Triptych (Berlin, Gemäldegal.) reflects the Master's Dijon *Nativity*, a relationship even clearer in the underdrawing of the van der Weyden composition, which includes a banderole like that in the Dijon *Nativity*. More literal still are the correspondences between the work of the Master of Flémalle and the documented wings from the St Vaast altarpiece by Jacques Daret. The physical types are very similar, with features and costumes drawn from a range of prototypes, while the compositions reuse specific originals: Daret's *Nativity*, the Master's Dijon *Nativity*; his *Adoration of the Magi*, the work recorded in a copy in Berlin; his *Presentation in the Temple*, the temple structure and some of the figures of the Prado *Marriage of the Virgin*.

Both Jacques Daret and Rogier van der Weyden were apprenticed to the Tournai painter Robert Campin. The simplest explanation of the profound yet independent influence of the Master of Flémalle on the art of both is to identify the Master of Flémalle with Campin.

Campin's dates, *c.* 1375–1444, are compatible with what is known of the Flémalle oeuvre. He was prosperous and known outside Tournai to such an extent that the Countess of Hainault intervened on his behalf. Campin's and van der Weyden's wives may have been related. The fragments of a mural *Annunciation* (Tournai, St Brice) are the only surviving paintings with a claim to being authenticated works by Campin. Despite differences in scale, the simplified mural technique and its linear emphasis make it possible to compare the surviving angel's face, with the exaggerated semicircular hooding of the eyelid and lower eye socket, with the similar formulation of faces such as that of the thief in the Seilern Triptych. While the uncertain

documentation and date of the *Annunciation* make it untenable as proof or disproof of Campin's identity with the Master of Flémalle, it is at least compatible with the Flémalle oeuvre.

Little is known of Tournai painting outside the Daret–van der Weyden circle, but Tournai sculpture shows considerable stylistic affinities to the Flémalle works. Campin is documented as having undertaken the polychromy of statues; the Angel and Virgin of the *Annunciation* group by Jean Delemer, which he coloured in 1428, survive in a very damaged and restored form (dep. Tournai, Mus. B.-A.). Whether or not the Master of Flémalle was himself active in Tournai's flourishing sculpture trade, his work—especially his grisailles and his painted architecture—shows considerable sensitivity to sculptural form. Moreover, the Flémalle paintings seem to have been particularly accessible to Tournai sculptors, who certainly repeated not only the *Annunciation* but also elements of the *Marriage of the Virgin*. Thus while inadequate survival and the movement of artists and designs make local style an inadequate criterion for assigning the Master to any one town, Tournai appears to provide a plausible setting for his work.

Given the problems of re-creating the career of Rogier van der Weyden, it is not surprising that an artist of equal genius, the Master of Flémalle, should have his identity recreated from suggestive but not totally conclusive evidence. Nevertheless, his anonymity has perhaps been over-scrupulously preserved, when there are so many points of contact with the career of Robert Campin. By the early 1990s there was an increasing tendency to identify the painter outright as Campin (e.g. a symposium held at London, N.G., 1993).

3. WORKING METHODS AND TECHNIQUE. The desire to clarify the attributional problem within the Flémalle group of paintings has motivated much of their technical investigation. Until more scientific analyses are available, only tentative observations can be made. Paintings attributable to the Master of Flémalle and Rogier van der Weyden, however, have been sufficiently investigated to disprove any belief in the Master of Flémalle as the young van der Weyden, a theory in any case untenable on grounds of chronology and individual stylistic development.

The Master of Flémalle could not have undertaken his major projects without the assistance of a competent and well-organized workshop, the existence of which can be deduced from the divergence in quality between the Prado *Marriage of the Virgin* and *Annunciation* panels. The precise role of assistants within pictures that seem overwhelmingly attributable to the Master is bound to remain controversial. The workshop was probably extensively employed in the preparation of panels for painting. Wherever the Master of Flémalle trained, he received a thorough grounding in the skills of his craft, which he passed on to, or expected from, his workshop. Not only was paint skilfully prepared and applied, but panels were prepared and gilded with great delicacy and technical mastery. The intricate gilded patternings of the Seilern Triptych and the damaged *Thief* testify to the Master's knowledge of traditional techniques that went out of fashion during the 15th century, as gold was increasingly used as a pigment or burnished on the flat, if employed at all. Thus van der Weyden's willingness to exploit the qualities of gold, despite its denial of spatial illusion, can presumably be linked to the Master of Flémalle.

The careful planning of the design of a panel would, by contrast, have been predominantly the work of the Master himself. Such detailed paintings would have required extensive preparatory drawing from life for individual figures and details. Yet the making and collecting of drawings as patterns for reuse make it hard to know whether surviving examples are carefully finished preparatory studies or records of a figure or composition to be preserved for future reworking. The beautiful drawing of the Flémalle *St Veronica* (Cambridge, Fitzwilliam) carefully repeats the painting, whereas other drawings, such as those from the lost *Deposition* triptych or the *Jael and Sisera*, seem to be less accomplished records by other artists either from drawn or painted originals or some intermediary source.

The underdrawing of the Flémalle *Virgin and Child* is bold: contours are defined with broad strokes, and modelling is indicated by closely placed hatching in areas of shadow. The Master tended to expand his underdrawn forms in the paint layer, consistently emphasizing volume and bulk. Significant changes do occur between underdrawing and painting. For example, in the Seilern Triptych the donor's face was repositioned, as was the foot of the resurrected Christ to link him more clearly to the ground. The concern for clarity of spatial construction is shown in the completeness of the drawing of the receding tomb in the right wing, a detail largely obscured by figures in the finished painting. In the case of the *Portrait of a Fat Man*, a correction from more detailed observation probably underlies the change in the line of the ear between underdrawing and painting. This change suggests that this panel is the original and that another version (Madrid, Mus. Thyssen-Bornemisza), which follows the final painted composition, is a contemporary replica.

The Master of Flémalle appears to have painted in a refined oil medium. Paint samples from the pendant portraits in the National Gallery, London, show the use of egg as well as linseed oil, probably in separate layers. His brushwork is not as minute as van Eyck's, but he too exploited the medium to establish tiny nuances of change in colour and tone. He took less advantage of its translucence: X-rays reveal that rather than leaving white ground to read through glazes in light areas, he employed white lead heavily. In this, his technique relates to that of the earlier work of van der Weyden.

4. POSTHUMOUS REPUTATION. The works of the Master of Flémalle were collected throughout Europe and imitated into the 17th century, his influence extending beyond Campin's pupils and the Netherlands, to Germany, Spain, and in France to the monumental panel painters of the south as well as the miniaturists of the north. He provided a model fusion of the new illusionistic techniques with a more traditional awareness of surface pattern, but this aspect of his art tended to be neglected for the more easily imitated figures with their telling expressions and gestures. Because none of the major works survives intact, it takes an effort of imagination to recapture their grandeur

of conception and dramatic impressiveness. Yet the breathtaking emotional and aesthetic appeal of his mature work establishes him as one of the greatest artists of the 15th century. The survival of his works in any form, unhelped by a personality cult, is proof of their enduring power, which, to the viewer, renders the identity of their creator an art-historical irrelevance.

BIBLIOGRAPHY

J. D. Passavant: 'Der Maler Roger van der Weyden', *Z. Christ. Archäol. Kst*, ii (1858), pp. 1–20, 120–30, 178–80

H. von Tschudi: 'Der Meister von Flémalle', *Jb. Kön.-Preuss. Kstsamml.*, xix (1898), pp. 8–34, 89–116

E. Firmenich-Richartz: 'Neues von "Meister von Flemalle"', *Mhft. Kstwiss.*, vi (1913), pp. 377–8

F. Winkler: *Der Meister von Flémalle und Rogier van der Weyden* (Strasbourg, 1913)

M. J. Friedländer: *Die altniederländische Malerei* (Berlin, 1924–37); Eng. trans. as *Early Netherlandish Painting* (Leiden, 1967–76), ii

S. Reinach: 'Ni Flémalle ni Falin', *Rev. Archéol.*, n. s. 2, xxxii (1930), pp. 223–4

C. de Tolnay: *Le Maître de Flémalle et les frères van Eyck* (Brussels, 1939)

E. Panofsky: *Early Netherlandish Painting*, 2 vols (Cambridge, MA, 1953)

J. Taubert: 'La *Trinité* du Musée de Louvain: Une Nouvelle Méthode de critique des copies', *Bull. Inst. Royal Patrm. A.*, ii (1959), pp. 20–33

M. J. Frinta: *The Genius of Robert Campin* (The Hague, 1966)

J. G. van Gelder: 'An Early Work by Robert Campin', *Oud-Holland*, lxxxii (1967), pp. 1–17

M. Sonkes: *Dessins du XVe siècle: Groupe van der Weyden* (1969), v of *Les Primitifs flamands, III: Contributions à l'étude des primitifs flamands* (Antwerp, 1952–)

——: 'Le Dessin sous-jacent chez Roger van der Weyden et le problème de la personnalité du Maître de Flémalle', *Bull. Inst. Royal Patrm. A.*, xiii (1971–2), pp. 161–206

M. Davies: *Rogier van der Weyden* (London, 1972)

L. Campbell: 'Robert Campin, the Master of Flémalle and the Master of Merode', *Burl. Mag.*, ccxvi (1974), pp. 634–46

Le Dessin sous-jacent dans la peinture, Colloque III: Septembre 1979: Le problème Maître de Flémalle–van der Weyden, Louvain, 1979

J. R. J. van Asperen de Boer and others: 'A Progress Report on the Investigation of the Underdrawings in the Paintings of the Group van der Weyden–Flémalle', *Le Dessin sous-jacent dans la peinture, Colloque IV: Octobre 1981: Le Problème de l'auteur de l'oeuvre de peintre, Louvain, 1981*

C. Périer-d'Ieterer: *Colyn de Coter et la technique picturale des peintres flamands du XVe siècle* (Brussels, 1985)

M. Comblen-Sonkes: *Le Musée des Beaux-Arts de Dijon*, xiv of *Les Primitifs flamands, I: Corpus de la peinture des anciens Pays-Bas méridionaux au XVe siècle* (Brussels, 1986), pp. 159–208

J. O. Hand and M. Wolff: *The Collection of the National Gallery of Art: Early Netherlandish Painting* (Washington, DC, 1986)

J. Mills and R. White: 'Analyses of Paint Media', *N.G. Tech. Bull.*, xi (1987), pp. 92–5

J. R. J. van Asperen de Boer and others: 'Underdrawing in Paintings of the Rogier van der Weyden and Master of Flémalle Groups', *Ned. Ksthist. Jb.*, xli (1990)

J. Dijkstra: *Origineel en kopie: Een onderzoek naar de navolging de Meester van Flémalle en Rogier van der Weyden* (diss., U. Amsterdam, 1990)

M.-L. Lievens-de Waegh: *Le Musée National d'Art Ancien et le Musée National des carreaux de faïence*, xvi of *Les Primitifs flamands, I: Corpus de la peinture des anciens Pays-Bas méridionaux au XVe siècle* (Brussels, 1991), pp. 106–27

J. Sander: *Niederländische Gemälde im Städel, 1400–1550* (Mainz, 1993), pp. 88–153 [with bibliog.]

D. Bamford and others: 'The Virgin of the Firescreen', *N.G. Tech. Bull.*, xv (in preparation)

CATHERINE REYNOLDS

Master of Flora [Maître de Flore] (*fl c.* 1555–70). Painter, active in France. Grouped under this name are a small number of paintings and drawings executed by an artist probably of Italian origin who is known to have worked in France between 1555 and 1570. A painting representing *Flora* (ex-d'Albenas priv. col., Montpellier;

San Francisco, CA Pal. Legion of Honor) has given its name to this remarkable heir to the first Fontainebleau school. Together with this painting, three other works permit a firm appreciation of the personality and style of the Master: the *Triumph of Flora* (Vicenza, Canera de Salasco priv. col.; see exh. cat., no. 130), which is considered to be a workshop production; the *Birth of Cupid* (New York, Met.; see fig.); and the *Allegory of Abundance* (Ravenna, Accad. B.A.). All these works show strong affinities with the style of Rosso Fiorentino and Francesco Primaticcio and also with that of Nicolò dell'Abate, who arrived in Fontainebleau in 1552. In these paintings the principal figure, passive and occupying a large part of the picture space, is contrasted with other more dynamic figures: putti in the *Triumph*, servants in the *Birth* and children in the *Abundance*. As in the work of Nicolò dell'Abate, but in a more anecdotal way, nature is very much present, particularly in the flowers strewn around in such profusion that they could almost be seen as the signature of the artist.

The extreme elegance of the figures, whose feet and hands are treated in a distinctive fashion, and the sensuality and voluptuousness that emanate, demonstrate the precious and refined Mannerist style practised in the court painting of the period. This style is executed with a broad, lush touch. Certain parallels have been drawn in the compositions with the work of Bronzino or with the motifs that were created by Giulio Romano and adapted at the château of Fontainebleau by Primaticcio in the Galerie d'Ulysse. A further work attributed to the Master of Flora is *The Concert* (Paris, Louvre), a copy of part of a fresco painted by Nicolò dell'Abate after Primaticcio in the Salle de Bal at Fontainebleau.

The same emphasis on linear rhythm in composition, the same graphic elegance, elongation and grace in the nude figures, the characteristic profile in the faces—all signs that this artist was a very close follower of Primaticcio—are to be found among his drawings given to the Master of Flora. These include *Procris and Cephalus* (New York, Pierpont Morgan Lib.) and *Apollo and the Muses* (Paris, Louvre), which is a project for one of the medallions in the Chambre des Arts at the château of Ancy-Le-Franc (Yonne).

Two names have been proposed to identify the artist: Ruggiero de Ruggieri, from Bologna, the most prominent

Master of Flora: *Birth of Cupid*, oil on canvas, 1.08×1.30 m, *c.* 1560–65 (New York, Metropolitan Museum of Art)

artist at Fontainebleau after the death of Nicolò dell'Abate (he is documented there from 1557 to 1597), or Giulio Camillo dell'Abate (1552–82), the son and partner of Nicolò. It has also been proposed that these works may be by one of the Cousin family.

BIBLIOGRAPHY

S. Béguin: L'Ecole de Fontainebleau: Le Manièrisme à la cour de France (Paris, 1960)

L'Ecole de Fontainebleau (exh. cat. by S. Béguin and others, Paris, Grand Pal., 1972); rev. as Fontainebleau: Art in France, 1528–1610, 2 vols (exh. cat. by S. Béguin and others, Ottawa, N.G. 1973)

PHILIPPE ROUILLARD

Master of Fogdö [Union Master] (*fl* first quarter of the 15th century). Scandinavian painter. He executed wall paintings in Fogdö Church and in the Lady chapel in Strängnäs Cathedral, both in Södermanland, Sweden. He has sometimes been thought to be the master responsible for paintings in the church at Undløse in Sjaelland, Denmark, and the name Union Master derives from the supposition that he worked in both Sweden and Denmark, which were then politically united. Although there are some similarities in the figure style and ornamentation between these works, there are also differences, and the identification cannot be proved.

The Master of Fogdö's style is closely related to the *Schöne Stil* and is of pronounced elegance, seen especially in the Apostles at Fogdö. Their elongated bodies, enveloped in softly draped mantles, form graceful S-curves, and their faces sometimes have slightly superior expressions. The figures are surrounded by vines, and their costumes are often patterned to simulate precious fabrics. The impression of sophistication is enhanced by the subtle colouring. The Fogdö Master probably worked only occasionally in Sweden and may have been summoned from abroad.

BIBLIOGRAPHY

B. G. Söderberg: De gotländska passionsmålningarna och deras stilfränder [The Gotland Passion paintings and their stylistic family] (Lund, 1942), pp. 244–68

——: Svenska kyrkomålningar från medeltiden [Swedish church paintings from the Middle Ages] (Stockholm, 1951), pp. 146–54

Å. Nisbeth: 'Strängnäs domkyrka' [Strängnäs Cathedral], Sveriges Kyrkor, clxxxix (Stockholm, 1982), pp. 63–89

A. Nilsén: Program och funktion i senmedeltider kalkmåleri: Kyrkmålningar i Mälarlandskapen och Finland, 1400–1534 [Programme and function in late medieval wall painting: paintings in churches in the Mälar provinces and Finland, 1400–1534] (Stockholm, 1986), pp. 14, 77–8, 263

ANNA NILSÉN

Master of the Fogg Pietà [Master of Figline] (*fl* first half of the 14th century). Italian painter. He derives his name from a predella panel of the *Lamentation* (Cambridge, MA, Fogg; see fig.), around which Offner grouped a series of works. He is also known as the Master of Figline after the large-scale *Virgin and Child with Saints and Angels* in the Collegiata at Figline Valdarno, just south of Florence. Opinion regarding his origins has ranged widely. He has been considered Roman, Emilian or Umbrian, or even Lombard, Burgundian or from Avignon. More specifically he has been identified with Giovanni di Bonino, a glass painter who worked at Assisi and Orvieto in the first half of the 14th century. There is a similar lack of agreement on the dates of his activity. Offner suggested

that he was Florentine and active from *c.* 1320 onwards. Others saw 15th-century elements in his work and drew comparisons with Andrea del Castagno and Piero della Francesca.

Recent scholars, however, charted a career for the painter from the late years of the 13th century through the first half of the 14th. Although influenced by Giotto's formal innovations he evolved a strongly individual style. The existence of Sienese elements in his work has been corroborated by Muller's technical examination of two panels with *SS Francis and Philip* (Worcester, MA, A. Mus.), which concluded that the carpentry, tooling and painting techniques were more Sienese than Florentine and could be closely associated with the work of Pietro Lorenzetti and his associates *c.* 1340. Works generally attributed to the Master include fourteen panels and frescoes, with another ten or so less firmly accepted paintings, and designs for stained-glass windows in the lower church of S Francesco, Assisi, and in Santa Croce, Florence.

The Master's earliest surviving work is probably a fresco, dated to the first decade of the 14th century, in the sacristy of the lower church at Assisi. This *Virgin and Child with SS Francis and Clare and Two Angels* clearly records his debt to Giotto in the substantial bulk of the figures and their simple and compact forms. The composition and the eccentric scale of the angels, however, indicate that the Master at this stage had yet to assimilate or was uninterested in the sophisticated spatial realism of Giotto and the painters of the upper church. The Master's style is already marked by certain distinctive features: he tends to favour pastel shades of pink and green, surface pattern and a calligraphic treatment of hair, emphatic gestures and characteristic facial features, with large, prominent eyes in the troubled, often wistful, faces. The result is solemn and expressive in a way that recalls Florentine painting before Giotto.

The altarpiece in Figline Valdarno marks a development of this combination of the decorative and expressive while showing more confidence in the handling of scale and space, especially in the ambitious design of the throne. The emphatic contours that define individual forms open the way for the more linear late style of the Master as represented in the painted Crucifix in Santa Croce, Florence, the *St John the Baptist* (Ferrara, Pin. N.) and the saints, including *SS Philip and Francis* (Worcester, MA, A. Mus.), from a dismembered polyptych reconstructed by Volpe. Accompanying this more graphic treatment, most effectively employed to silhouette the large and expressive hands and feet, is a coarsening of facial features and the representation of the body in a more monumental form. The dramatic intensity and the consummate technical skill justify the assessment of the Master as 'the most authoritative alternative to Giotto in Florence in the early decades of the Trecento' (Bellosi, 1980–81 exh. cat.).

BIBLIOGRAPHY

R. Offner: 'The Master of the Fogg Pietà', A. America, xiv (1926), pp. 160–76

R. Offner and K. Steinweg: Corpus (1930–), III/vi, pp. 65–100

C. Volpe: 'Ristudiando il Maestro di Figline', Paragone, xxiv/277 (1973), pp. 3–23

Master of the Fogg Pietà: *Lamentation*, tempera on panel, 423×500 mm, *c.* 1330 (Cambridge, MA, Fogg Art Museum)

N. E. Muller: 'Lorenzettian Technical Influences in a Painting of *St Philip* by the Master of Figline', *Atti del XXIV congresso internazionale di storia dell'arte, Bologna: 1979*, iii, pp. 283–95

Il Maestro di Figline (exh. cat., ed. L. Bellosi and others; Figline Valdarno, Vecchio Pal. Com., 1980–81) [with bibliog.]

M. Boskovits: *Corpus* (1984), pp. 60–66, 317–34, pls cxliii–clx

Capolavori a Figline: Cinque anni di restauri (exh. cat., ed. C. Caneva and others; Figline Valdarno, Vecchio Pal. Com., 1985–6), pp. 45–63

BRENDAN CASSIDY

Master of the Franciscan Breviary (*fl c.* 1440–60). Italian illuminator. He is named after a two-volume Breviary of Franciscan Use (Bologna, Bib. U., MS. 337), which was probably written *c.* 1446. His work is also found in several other manuscripts, including a splendid Gradual entirely illuminated in his style (Ithaca, NY, Cornell U., Lib., MS. B 50++), a Breviary (Parma, Bib. Palatina, MS. 6) and a Psalter (Rome, Vatican, Bib. Apostolica, MS. Barb. lat. 585), and in many cuttings from choir-books (e.g. Berlin, Kupferstichkab., nos 1234 and 6694; Venice, Fond. Cini, nos 2172 and 2207; Paris, Mus. Marmottan, no. 27). The Vatican Psalter was commissioned by Cardinal Ioannes Bessarion, papal legate for Bologna 1450–55, and

is probably part of the great series of choir-books that he commissioned during his residence in Emilia. This series of at least 20 large-format volumes was the work of several artists and was presented to the convent of S Maria Annunziata in Cesena after its foundation in 1458. The Master of the Franciscan Breviary's contribution to this series has been identified in two surviving Antiphonals (Cesena, Bib. Malatestiana, Corale 3; and sold Amsterdam, Mensing–Muller, 5 April 1935, lot 19) and in folios cut from dismembered books (Venice, Fond. Cini, nos 2096–7). Features of the Master's highly decorative style, such as the smoothly modelled round faces and the flowing contours of figures and drapery, place him among the followers of the Lombard painter Michelino da Besozzo. His identification as Ambrogio da Cermenate or as Jacopino Cietario cannot be sustained. He apparently had access to the designs of Giovannino de Grassi and Belbello da Pavia as he repeated many of their motifs, especially extravagantly structured architectural initials. Notable is his unusual and subtle manipulation of monochrome: black with gold, light brown with white or light blue, pinks and greens. When he used a full palette the results were spectacular, particularly the brilliant, glowing colours of his fluid draperies highlighted with touches of gold. His style is characteristic of the colourful and charming illumination produced in and around Milan throughout the first 60 years of the 15th century.

BIBLIOGRAPHY

Arte lombarda dai Visconti agli Sforza (exh. cat., Milan, Pal. Reale, 1958), pp. 79–80

R. Calkins: 'The Master of the Franciscan Breviary', *A. Lombarda*, 16 (1971), pp. 17–36

G. Mariani Canova: *Miniature dell'Italia settentrionale nella Fondazione Giorgio Cini* (Venice, 1978), pp. 39–44

ROBERT G. CALKINS

Master of Frankfurt (*b* 1460; *d* ?1533). South Netherlandish painter. He takes his name from two paintings commissioned by patrons from Frankfurt am Main. His chief importance lies in his continuing the great tradition of 15th-century Netherlandish painting (particularly the compositions of Rogier van der Weyden and Hugo van der Goes) well into the 16th century, his development of a markedly earthy figure type, his apparently innovative management of a large workshop that 'mass-produced' paintings for the open market and his status (with his greater contemporary, Quentin Metsys) as a founder of the distinguished tradition of painting in Antwerp.

The Master of Frankfurt has been tentatively identified with Hendrik van Wueluwe, active in Antwerp from 1483 until his death there in 1533. Van Wueluwe may have come from Woluwe, near the region outside Brussels where van der Goes spent his last days. The Master's style suggests close contact with the art of van der Goes and, to a lesser extent, the Lower Rhine. Van Wueluwe emerges from the documents as a prominent Antwerp artist. He was Dean of the artists' guild six times and had seven apprentices. Earlier identifications of the artist with Conrad Fyol (*d* 1499–1500) and Jan de Vos (*fl* 1489–1521) are no longer tenable.

Two of the Master's paintings are among the earliest that can be documented in Antwerp. The *Festival of the Archers* (Antwerp, Kon. Mus. S. Kst.; *see* DRESS, fig. 33) carried an inscription on its original frame (destr.) indicating that the painting was given to the city in 1493. The panel, rich in the folklore of the military guilds, was long housed in the guildhall of the Antwerp crossbowmen. The *Portrait of the Artist and his Wife* (Antwerp, Kon. Mus. S. Kst.; see fig.) is in its original frame, which carries the date 1496 and both their ages; it follows from this that he was born in 1460, she in 1469. This painting also bears the arms of the Antwerp Guild of St Luke.

Around 1503 the Master painted his great altarpiece of the *Holy Kinship* for the Dominican church in Frankfurt (Frankfurt am Main, Hist. Mus.). Here the artist's gruff, down-to-earth figures found full expression. Other important commissions followed, such as the *Crucifixion* triptych (Frankfurt am Main, Städel. Kstinst. & Städt. Gal.) for the Frankfurt patrician family of Claus Humbracht (1440–1504), whose son was resident in Antwerp by 1503. There is some evidence that the artist visited Frankfurt, but the fact that he painted on oak panels virtually rules out his working in the Frankfurt area. These

Master of Frankfurt: *Portrait of the Artist and his Wife*, panel, 380×260 mm, 1496 (Antwerp, Koninklijk Museum voor Schone Kunsten)

successful commissions early in the century coincided with Antwerp's own remarkable rise in economic power.

Many of the paintings from the Master's workshop after this 'Frankfurt period' were multiples of time-honoured compositions produced for the open market, in which the Master's own hand becomes increasingly difficult to identify among those of his assistants. Certain motifs, such as standardized brocade patterns, have helped identify works made in this large workshop. The works of the highest quality *c.* 1510–20 are the small panels entirely from the Master's own hand, primarily portraits (the latest dated 1518) and panels showing the Virgin and Child. Late altarpieces, such as the *Lamentation* triptych (Munich, Alte Pin.) and *Holy Family* triptych (Liverpool, Walker A.G.; The Hague, Mauritshuis), sometimes betray a knowledge of the new taste in landscape (influenced by Joachim Patinir) and of the fanciful costumes of the Antwerp Mannerists. The Master's figures, however, remain the same rough-hewn types. There is little evidence of the Master of Frankfurt after *c.* 1520, and he had no significant following.

BIBLIOGRAPHY

H. Weizsäcker: *Die Kunstschätze des ehemaligen Dominikaner-Klosters in Frankfurt a. M.* (Munich, 1923), pp. 126–40

M. J. Friedländer: *Die altniederländische Malerei* (Berlin, 1924–37); Eng. trans. as *Early Netherlandish Painting* (Leiden, 1967–76), vii, pp. 54–7

A. J. J. Delen: 'Wie was de Meester van Frankfurt?', *Miscellanea Leo van Puyvelde* (Brussels, 1949), pp. 74–83

S. Goddard: 'The Master of Frankfurt and his Shop', *Acad. Anlct.: Kl. S. Kst.*, xlvi/38 (Brussels, 1984)

——: 'Brocade Patterns in the Shop of the Master of Frankfurt: An Accessory to Stylistic Analysis', *A. Bull.*, lxvii (1985), pp. 401–17

D. Ewing: 'Archival Notes: Jan de Beer and Hendric van Wueluwe (The Master of Frankfurt)', *Jb.: Kon. Mus. S. Kst.* (1994), pp. 32, 34 [work done for the Antwerp church of St James]

STEPHEN H. GODDARD

Master of the Frankfurt Crucifixion. *See* MASTER OF RIMINI below.

Master of the Frankfurt Garden of Paradise (*fl c.* 1410–30). German painter. He is named after a small panel painting of the *Garden of Paradise* (*c.* 1410; Frankfurt am Main, Städel. Kstinst. & Städt. Gal.), barely as big as two hands, which captivated people in the Romantic period through its tender, intimate lyricism. It has been linked with a small *Annunciation* (Winterthur, Samml. Oskar Reinhart), the larger *Virgin among the Strawberries* (Solothurn, Kstmus.) and several woodcuts. This group of works is also connected to the fragment of a *Head of the Virgin* (ex-Adelhausen, Dominican convent) and to panels of the *Virgin* (*c.* 1430; ex-Tennenbach, monastery; Freiburg im Breisgau, Augustinmus.) and their original reverses of *Passion* scenes (Karlsruhe, Kunsthalle). It can be inferred that the Master and his workshop worked in Colmar or—more probably—Basle.

The small *Garden of Paradise* is like a large miniature, with deep, bright blues in the sky and the cloaks of the Virgin and St Barbara, who fetches water, a light, gentle red in those of St Dorothy, picking apples, and St Catherine, teaching the infant Jesus to play the zither, and a lush, fresh green in the grassy bank with its wealth of spring plants—snowbells, daisies, strawberries. The garden is bounded by a crenellated wall along which grow summer plants—irises, pinks and roses. The women and the group of SS Michael, George and Oswald look less like saints, more like courtiers from a contemporaneous garden of love. The arcadian mood is reminiscent of the miniatures in a 15th-century French *Boccaccio* (Paris, Bib. Arsenal), which have the same deep blue, while the figure of the Virgin relates to a single woodcut print in Colmar (Bib.). In the Winterthur *Annunciation*, the angel and the Virgin are portrayed equally tenderly, as large figures within the more energetically containing framework of an interior with receding ceiling beams. Caskets, small maiolica jugs and a pot plant enliven the barren floor in front of a bench covered with a green blanket. The sense of confinement is further emphasized in the *Virgin among the Strawberries*, with a small donor in the foreground, while in the later scenes from the Tennenbach altar the plumper, less youthful figures completely dominate their surroundings.

BIBLIOGRAPHY

G. F. Hartlaub: *Das Paradiesgärtlein von einem oberrheinischen Meister um 1410* (Berlin, 1944)

A. Stange: *Deutsche Malerei der Gotik*, iv (Munich, 1951), pp. 61–8

E. M. Vetter: 'Das Frankfurter Paradiesgärtlein', *Heidelberg Jb.*, ix (1965), pp. 102–46

HANS GEORG GMELIN

Freake Painter (*fl* Boston, 1670–*c.* 1680). American painter. He is sometimes incorrectly known as 'The Freake Limner', a term restricted in the 17th century to painters of miniatures, which he is not known to have produced.

Freake Painter: *Mrs John (Elizabeth) Freake and her Baby, Mary*, oil on canvas, 1080×934 mm, dated 1670, altered 1674 (Worcester, MA, Worcester Art Museum)

A group of eight portraits painted in oil on canvas in or near Boston between 1670 and 1678 appear to have been made by the same hand. They represent *John Freake* (n.d.; Worcester, MA, A. Mus.), *Mrs John (Elizabeth) Freake and her Baby, Mary* (1670; Worcester, MA, A. Mus.), *Henry Gibbs* (1670; priv. col., see 1982 exh. cat., pl. xxi), *Margaret Gibbs* (1670; priv. col., see 1982 exh. cat., pl. xxii), *Robert Gibbs* (1670; Boston, MA, Mus. F.A.), the *Mason Children* (1670; San Francisco, CA, de Young Mem. Mus.), *Edward Rawson* (Boston, MA, New England Hist. Geneal. Soc.) and the *Rev. John Davenport* (New Haven, CT, Yale U. A.G.). Six of these paintings bear the date 1670 lettered in a similar manner. All are stylistically and structurally related; they form the largest (and among the most sophisticated) group of portraits made by the same artist or studio/shop in 17th-century New England. All of these paintings, which represent sitters slightly smaller than life, are characterized by precise delineation of features similar to that found in 16th-century English portraiture. The most famous portrait of this group, *Elizabeth Freake and her Baby* (see fig.), is enhanced by a brilliant range of colours. Vermilion and lead–tin yellow are found in the dress, coral beads and ribbons; lead white in the caps, lace and aprons. Mrs Freake is seated on a chair bearing Turkey work upholstery and is holding a six-month-old child. The portrait of the child was added in 1674, three years after the painting was first made. Previously Mrs Freake had been represented with hands in her lap holding a fan; her collar and ribbons were also substantially different. The portrait of the Boston merchant *John Freake* (Elizabeth's husband) is the pendant to this. Carefully wrought details such as the almond-shaped eyes and linear, pursed lips are characteristic of the artist's work. His imagery is spatially flat but not lacking in subtle shading.

Although the identity of the Freake painter is a mystery, Samuel Clement (1635–c. 1678), who was known as a painter in Boston, may well have been responsible for the Freake portraits and the other related works. He was the son of Augustine Clement (1600–74) of Reading, Berks, who trained in England (as a painter–stainer) and arrived in New England in 1635. He settled in Dorchester, MA, near the residence of the surgeon Dr John Clark, whose portrait now hangs in the Boston Medical Library in the Francis A. Countway Library of Medicine. Since Clark and the elder Clement were neighbours, it seems possible that the portrait of the surgeon was painted by Augustine. This painting bears the date 1664 and is one of the two earliest dated examples of New England painting. Comparisons between the Clark portrait and the Freake paintings suggest an altogether different artist practising in Boston for a few years following the death of Augustine Clement.

BIBLIOGRAPHY

XVIIth Century Painting in New England (exh. cat. by L. Dresser, Worcester, MA, A. Mus., 1935), pp. 81–3
L. Dresser: 'The Freake Portraits', *Worcester A. Mus. Bull.*, xxix/5 (1964)
——: 'Portraits in Boston, 1630–1720', *Archv Amer. A. J.*, vi (1966), pp. 1–34
S. Gold: 'A Study in Early Boston Portrait Attributions: Augustine Clement, Painter-stainer of Reading, Berkshire, and Massachusetts Bay', *Old-Time New England*, lviii/3 (1968), pp. 61–78
A. L. Cummings: 'Decorative Painting in Early New England', *American Painting to 1776: A Re-appraisal*, ed. I. M. G. Quimby (Charlottesville, 1971), pp. 91–101
S. E. Strickler: 'Recent Findings on the Freake Portraits', *Worcester A. Mus. J.*, v (1981–2), pp. 48–55
J. L. Fairbanks: 'Portrait Painting in Seventeenth Century Boston', *New England Begins: The Seventeenth Century*, iii (exh. cat. by J. L. Fairbanks and R. F. Trent, Boston, MA, Mus. F.A., 1982), pp. 413–53
W. Craven: *Colonial American Portraiture* (Cambridge, 1986), pp. 38–48, 85–8

JONATHAN L. FAIRBANKS

Master of the Freising Visitation [Master of the Augsburg Visitation] (*fl* second half of the 15th century). German painter. He is named after the painting of the *Visitation* from the abbey church of St Johann (Domberg), Freising, and now in Augsburg Cathedral. Two other paintings from the church, depicting the *Massacre of the Innocents* (Nuremberg, Ger. Nmus.) and the *Death of the Virgin* (priv. col.), belonged to the same altarpiece. In 1461 a Master Sigismund (from Freising) received payments for the side wings of the high altar of St Johann, and Ramisch considered that the three fragments belonged to this work. Stylistically, however, they seem to date from the 1480s. Perhaps Master Sigismund can be presumed to be identical with the Sigmund Huetter from Freising who is documented as having executed many works for the cathedral and monastic churches in Freising between 1451 and 1490; it cannot therefore be ruled out that this master was responsible for the paintings. The Master's work appears to be closer to the painting of Salzburg and Munich than to Swabia, and Stange included him among the painters of Lower Bavaria. A more thorough investigation of his origins is, however, needed. Two depictions of the *Crucifixion* (Detroit, MI, Inst. A., and Freising,

Diözmus.), probably dating from the 1470s, are also attributed to the Master.

BIBLIOGRAPHY

E. Buchner: 'Der Augsburger Tafelmalerei der Spätgotik: Der Meister der Augsburger Heimsuchung', *Beitr. Gesch. Dt. Kst*, ii (1928), pp. 56ff
A. Stange: *Salzburg, Bayern und Tirol in der Zeit vom 1400 bis 1500* (1960), x of *Deutsche Malerei der Gotik* (Munich and Berlin, 1933–61), pp. 122ff
Hans Holbein der Ältere und die Kunst der Spätgotik (exh. cat., Augsburg, Rathaus, 1965), pp. 131–2
H. Ramisch: 'Meister der Freisinger Heimsuchung (Sigmund Huetter)' (exh. cat., Freising, Diözmus., 1984), pp. 72–3

GISELA GOLDBERG

Master of the Games [Maître des Jeux] (*fl c.* 1645–55). Painter, active in Paris. In 1978 Cuzin grouped together under this name 13 paintings previously attributed to the Le Nain brothers. With the exception of a *Portrait of a Man* (Le Puy, Mus. Crozatier), the pictures are genre scenes, some of them representing games of chance (hence the Master's appellation). The stylistic traits shared by these paintings include a reduction of space to simple geometric volumes in which forms are delineated in bright light and shadows that are heavily accentuated, though not always corresponding very closely to the forms that cast them. The emphasis on scrupulously observed reality in the depiction of faces and draperies led Cuzin to propose that the artist responsible for these pictures was a northern, most likely Flemish, follower of the Le Nain working in Paris. The dating proposed was based on affinities with works by the latter and on the costumes represented. Among the pictures attributed to the Master of the Games are *Soldiers Playing Cards* (U. Birmingham, Barber Inst.), *Dice Players* (Amsterdam, Rijksmus.), *Backgammon Players* (Paris, Louvre) and *The Cheats* (Reims, Mus. St Denis). Further works are *The Gardener* (Cologne, Wallraf-Richartz-Mus.), the *Family Meal* (Toledo, OH, Mus. A.), the *Rustic Meal* (Detroit, MI, Inst. A.) and three outdoor scenes of *Children's Dances* (e.g. Cleveland, OH, Mus. A.). Some of these scenes may be actual portraits.

BIBLIOGRAPHY

J.-P. Cuzin: 'A Hypothesis Concerning the Le Nain Brothers', *Burl. Mag.*, cxx (1978), pp. 875–6
Les Frères Le Nain (exh. cat. by J. Thuillier, Paris, Grand Pal., 1978)
La Peinture française du XVIIe siècle dans les collections américaines (exh. cat. by P. Rosenberg, Paris, Grand Pal.; New York, Met.; Chicago, IL, A. Inst.; 1982), pp. 363–4

THIERRY BAJOU

Gansevoort Limner (*fl c.* 1730–45). American painter. He was one of several portrait painters, known as the Patroon Painters, active during the first half of the 18th century in the Dutch-settled lands along the Hudson River from New York to Troy. He may have derived his compositions freely from British and Dutch mezzotints, but his style is strongly individualistic. The faces of his sitters are simplified and delicately rendered, while their figures are flat and geometrical, thinly painted in warm colours. His best-known portraits are *Pau de Wandelaer* (c. 1730; Albany, NY, Inst. Hist. & A.) and *Deborah Glen* (c. 1737; Williamsburg, VA, Rockefeller Flk A. Col.).

Black proposed that the Gansevoort Limner was Pieter Vanderlyn, grandfather of the American painter John Vanderlyn, and has since attributed to him around 20 portraits painted between *c.* 1730 and *c.* 1745 in or near Albany and Kingston, NY. Pieter Vanderlyn, born in the Netherlands *c.* 1687, arrived in New York in 1718, probably by way of Curaçao. He resided in or near Albany and Kingston in the years of the Gansevoort Limner's work in those places and died in Shawangunk, NY, in 1778. Black's identification of Vanderlyn as the Gansevoort Limner contradicts Flexner's earlier proposal that Vanderlyn was the De Peyster Limner; Black suggests that the De Peyster Limner was Gerardus Duyckinck (1695–1746).

BIBLIOGRAPHY

J. T. Flexner: 'Pieter Vanderlyn, Come Home', *Antiques*, lxxv (1959), pp. 546–9, 580
M. Black: 'Pieter Vanderlyn and Other Limners of the Upper Hudson', *American Painting to 1776*, ed. I. Quimby (Charlottesville, VA, 1971), pp. 217–49
R. H. Saunders and E. Miles: *American Colonial Portraits* (Washington, DC, 1987), pp. 144–5, 161–2

DAVID TATHAM

Master of the Gardens of Love (*fl* Netherlands, *c.* 1430–40/45). Netherlandish engraver. One of the very earliest copper-engravers, he is named after two engravings of *Gardens of Love* (Lehrs, 1908, nos 20 and 21). He may have worked in the northern Netherlands, perhaps The Hague. His surviving oeuvre is extremely small, some of his *c.* 26 attributed engravings remaining unauthenticated. With one exception, the engravings are all unique. Their small format may suggest that they were used as illustrations for manuscripts or as models for miniatures. The Master's engraving technique is very crude: heavy outlines and strong hatching (often schematic cross hatching) predominate. The figures are characterized by angular, stiff movements.

The Master covered both religious and secular subjects. The *Passion* series (L 6–13) is very close in style and composition to a group of Dutch illuminations of *c.* 1440, which suggests a common Netherlandish source. The Master's most famous work, the *Large Garden of Love* (Berlin, Kupferstichkab.; L 21), also provides an indication as to his origins, as its theme and style show the influence of Burgundian-Netherlandish courtly art. The composition possibly derives from a wall hanging in the style of the Bardac Tapestries (*c.* 1420; New York, Met.) or from a fresco of courtly society. It has been maintained that the composition reflects some documented but untraced works by Jan van Eyck in the palace at The Hague (*c.* 1422–4); this remains unproven, however. The *Small Garden of Love* (L 20; Boston, MA, Mus. F.A.) depicts an allegory of courtly love.

BIBLIOGRAPHY

Hollstein: *Dut. & Flem.*
M. Lehrs: *Der Meister der Liebesgärten. Ein Beitrag zur Geschichte des ältesten Kupferstichs in den Niederlanden* (Leipzig, 1893)
——: *Geschichte und kritischer Katalog des deutschen, niederländischen und französischen Kupferstichs im XV. Jahrhundert*, i (Vienna, 1908), pp. 304–26 [L]
D. P. Bliss: 'Love-gardens in the Early German Engravings and Woodcuts', *Prt Colr Q.*, xv (1928), pp. 91–109
I. Schüler: *Der Meister der Liebesgärten. Ein Beitrag zur frühholländischen Malerei* (Amsterdam, 1933)
——: 'Ein unbekannter Stich des Meisters der Liebesgärten', *Wallraf-Richartz-Jb.*, xxx (1968), pp. 345–8
R. S. Favis: *The Garden of Love in Fifteenth-century Netherlandish and German Engraving: Some Studies in Secular Iconography in the Late Middle Ages and Early Renaissance* (diss., Philadelphia, U. PA, 1974)

M. Hébert: *Bibliothèque nationale, Département des gravures: Inventaire des gravures des écoles du Nord, 1440–1550*, i (Paris, 1982), p. 159

HOLM BEVERS

Master of the Gardner Annunciation (*fl c.* 1450–1500). Italian painter. In 1927 Longhi assigned this name to an unknown 15th-century central Italian artist who executed a small group of panel paintings and frescoes, Umbrian in character. The most noteworthy among the group is the *Annunciation* (Boston, MA, Isabella Stewart Gardner Mus.), from which the artist's provisional name is derived. Early paintings attributed to the Master, which include the *Virgin and Child with Two Seraphim* (Baltimore, MD, Walters A.G.) and the *Virgin and Child with a Pomegranate* (1481; Berlin, Gemäldegal), show the influence of Pietro Perugino and Fiorenzo di Lorenzo, while the later works are infused with Roman influences.

Although scholars agree on the oeuvre proposed by Longhi, the identity of the artist has remained controversial. The Boston *Annunciation*, for example, bought by Isabella Stewart Gardner in 1900 through Bernard Berenson as a work by Fiorenzo di Lorenzo, was later catalogued at the Gardner Museum as a work by Antoniazzo Romano. In 1953 Zeri rejected this attribution and instead proposed Piermatteo (Lauro de' Manfredi) d' Amelia (*c.* 1450–1503/8). Subsequent documentary and circumstantial evidence supports Zeri's argument. Archival records found in 1978 show that the Gardner *Annunciation* was originally made for the main altar of the Franciscan church in Amelia, Piermatteo's native city, not for S Maria degli Angeli in the Porziuncola, a district near Assisi, where Berenson acquired it in the late 19th century. Another document, discovered in 1986, identifies the *Virgin and Child Enthroned with Saints* (1485; Terni, Mus. & Pin. Civ.), a major altarpiece traditionally attributed to the Master of the Gardner Annunciation, as a work by Piermatteo d'Amelia.

Piermatteo d'Amelia was a pupil and collaborator of Filippo Lippi at Spoleto between 1467 and 1469. Other influences on his style are reflected by the attributions of the Gardner *Annunciation*: Fiorenzo di Lorenzo during Piermatteo's early period and Antoniazzo Romano during the mid-1480s. He is documented in Rome in 1480, working on the decoration of the Sistine Chapel, and in Civita Castellana in 1502–3. Zeri also observed his style in the fresco depicting the *Mass of St Gregory* at Orvieto Cathedral, where Piermatteo is recorded working in 1480–81. Although Piermatteo's activities are well documented, it was not until the last decades of the 20th century that any of his paintings were successfully identified.

BIBLIOGRAPHY

R. Longhi: 'In favore di Antoniazzo Romano', *Vita artistica*, ii (1927), pp. 226–33 (228)
F. Zeri: 'Il Maestro dell'Annunciazione Gardner', *Boll. A.*, 2nd ser., xxxviii (1953), pp. 125–39, 233–49
B. Berenson: *Central and North Italian Schools* (1968), i, pp. 251–2; iii, pls 1070–72
L. Canonici: 'L'Annunciazione Gardner alla Porziuncola', *Archv Franciscanum Hist.*, lxxi (1978), pp. 459–62
F. Zeri: 'Postilla al Maestro dell'Annunciazione Gardner', *Paragone*, xxxvi/429 (1985), pp. 3–6

A. Ricci: 'Pier Matteo d'Amelia e la pala dei Francescani: Un documento notarile per identicare l'autore dell'opera', *Arte sacra in Umbria e dipinti restaurati nei secoli XIII–XX* (Perugia, 1986), pp. 47–9

GENETTA GARDNER

Master of the Gathering of Manna (*fl c.* 1460–75). North Netherlandish painter. Named by Haverkamp Begemann after the painting of the *Gathering of Manna* (Douai, Mus. Mun.), the artist appears to have been a Haarlem painter and close follower of Albert van Ouwater. A second panel, the *Fire Offering of the Jews* with a grisaille figure of *St Peter* on the reverse (Rotterdam, Mus. Boymans–van Beuningen), is closely related in style and size. The two probably formed the wings of an altarpiece celebrating the Eucharist, since both are familiar Old Testament antetypes (Exodus 16:14–15 and 13:10–12) for the Last Supper. This typology and the style of the squat figures, cramped into exaggerated spatial settings, suggest that the artist was familiar with woodcut illustrations in blockbooks often believed to have been produced in Haarlem, *c.* 1465–75, the *Biblia pauperum* and the *Speculum humanae salvationis*. The same style characterizes the miniatures in Utrecht manuscripts of the period (e.g. the Bible of Evert van Soudenbalch; *c.* 1465; Vienna, Österreich. Nbib., Cod. 2771–2). A *Crucifixion* (Saint-Germain-en-Laye, priv. col., see Friedländer, iii, pl. 55) has also been associated with the panels in Douai and Rotterdam as part of the same altarpiece. A fourth painting by the Master, the *Healing of the Blind Man of Jericho* (Blaricum, Kleiweg de Zwaan-Vellema priv. col.), is typical of narrative paintings in the northern Netherlands and has four episodes of the story (Mark 10:46–52) set in a deep landscape along a winding road. Borrowings from Ouwater's *Raising of Lazarus* (Berlin, Gemäldegal.; for illustration *see* OUWATER, ALBERT VAN) are evident, but the treatment of the figures is less accomplished. The Master's paintings, together with the woodcuts and the Utrecht miniatures, form an important body of works linking Ouwater's generation to that of Geertgen tot Sint Jans in Haarlem painting.

For possible identifications *see* NETHERLANDS, THE, §III, 2.

BIBLIOGRAPHY

M. J. Friedländer: *Die altniederländische Malerei* (Berlin, 1924–37); Eng. trans. as *Early Netherlandish Painting* (Leiden, 1967–76)
K. G. Boon: 'Een Hollands altaar van omstreeks 1470' [A Dutch altar of around 1470], *Oud-Holland*, lxv (1950), pp. 207–15
E. Haverkamp Begemann: 'Een Noord-Nederlandsche primitief', *Bull. Mus. Boymans*, ii (1951), pp. 51–7
Middeleeuwse kunst der noordelijke Nederlander: 150 jaar Rijksmuseum jubileumtentoonstelling (Amsterdam, 1958), pp. 55–8
J. Snyder: 'The Early Haarlem School of Painting', *A. Bull.*, xlii (1960), pp. 48–9
A. Châtelet: *Les Primitifs hollandais* (Paris and Fribourg, 1980); Eng. trans. as *Early Dutch Painting* (Oxford and New York, 1981), pp. 88–90

JAMES SNYDER

Master of the Geneva Boccaccio. *See under* MASTER OF JOUVENEL DES URSINS below.

Master of the Geneva Latini. *See* MASTER OF THE ROUEN ECHEVINAGE below.

Master of Gerlamoos. *See* ARTULA VON VILLACH, THOMAS.

Master of the Getty Epistles. *See under* §II: THE 1520S HOURS WORKSHOP below.

Gil Master. *See* ALCANYIS, MIGUEL.

Master of the Girart de Roussillon [Girart Master; Meister der Chronik von Jerusalem] (*fl c.* 1450–70). South Netherlandish illuminator. His name is derived from the *Roman de Girart de Roussillon* (Vienna, Österreich. Nbib., Cod. 2549), which was copied in 1448 in the workshop of Jean Wauquelin in Mons and illuminated shortly afterwards. The Girart Master is generally identified as the Bruges illuminator DREUX JEAN, who worked for Philip the Good, Duke of Burgundy. The Master also painted miniatures in grisaille and in colour in such manuscripts as the *Chroniques de Jérusalem abrégiées* (Vienna, Österreich. Nbib., Cod. 2533); the *Entry into Jerusalem* (fol. 5r) in grisaille at the beginning of Jean Gerson's *Passion de Nostre Seigneur* (Brussels, Bib. Royale Albert 1er, MSS 9081–2) was painted for the Duke of Burgundy. A single leaf (Berlin, Kstbib. & Mus., no. 4005, 6) has been attributed to the Girart Master; miniatures by his hand also occur in, among others, a prayerbook (Paris, Bib. N., MS. nouv. acq. fr. 16428) and the *Passion de St Adrien* (Paris, Col. Count de Waziers).

BIBLIOGRAPHY

Thieme–Becker
A. de Schryver: 'Pour une meilleure orientation des recherches à propos du Maître de Girart de Roussillon', *Rogier van der Weyden en zijn tijd. Internationaal colloquium: Brussel, 1964*, pp. 43–75
G. Dogaer: *Flemish Miniature Painting in the 15th and 16th Centuries* (Amsterdam, 1987), pp. 15, 65, 69, 77–82, 109, 133

HANS J. VAN MIEGROET

Girona Master (*fl* Bologna, *c.* 1260–*c.* 1290). Illuminator, active in Italy. He may be identifiable as the scribe Bernardino da Modena (*fl* Bologna, 1268–9). Conti named this illuminator after his work in the Girona Bible or Bible of Charles V (Girona, Bib. Capitolare), which is signed by the scribe MAGISTER BERNARDINUS DE MUTINA/ FECIT: since the inscription and its decoration are entirely in ink, this may refer only to the writing and layout. The Master's earliest surviving work, executed with the help of one or two assistants, is probably a Psalter (Bologna, Bib. U., MS. 346), containing a calendar of Paduan Use and a *Passion* cycle with perhaps the first extensive landscape settings in Italian or western European art. The painterly execution, use of the finest blue and violet pigments and the decoration of the richly decorated text provide the closest reflection of Palaiologan art in Italy; the artist seems to have had first-hand knowledge of Byzantine or Armenian court art, and he may have been of Greek origin.

In addition to the Girona Bible, the artist illuminated another sumptuous Bible (Madrid, Escorial, Bib. Monasterio S Lorenzo, Cod. a. I. 5) and at least two series of choir-books. The illumination of those for S Francesco, Bologna (Bologna, Mus. Civ. Med., MSS 525–7), has conventionally been described as Cimabuesque; it is, however, far closer to its Byzantine sources than Cimabue's own work, and most of the Master's work is earlier than Cimabue's and probably an influence on it. The *Calling of SS Peter and Andrew* (Bologna, Mus. Civ. Med., MS 526, fol. 7*r*) is remarkable for including an ancient vessel with projecting prow and an evocative rocky shore. Even finer painting is found in the choir-books of S Jacopo a Ripoli (Florence, S Marco, MSS 561–2). The iconography used by this artist in a copy of Gratian's *Decretals* (Princeton U., NJ, Lib., Garret MS. 97) allows it to be dated earlier than the copy (Rome, Vatican, Bib. Apostolica, MS. Vat. lat. 1375) signed by JACOPINO DA REGGIO, who is documented between 1269 and 1286. The Girona Master is the finest Bolognese illuminator and the principal creator of the so-called 'Second Style' of Bolognese illumination (*see* BOLOGNA, §II, 1). He is probably responsible for the extensive influence of contemporary Palaiologan art on such Roman and Tuscan painters as Cimabue and Duccio.

BIBLIOGRAPHY

M. Jacoff: 'The Bible of Charles V and Related Works: Bologna, Byzantium and the West in the Late Thirteenth Century', *Il medio oriente e l'occidente nell'arte del XIII secolo. Atti del XXIV congresso: Bologna, 1979*, ii, pp. 163–72

A. Conti: *La miniatura bolognese: Scuole e botteghe* (Bologna, 1981), pp. 39–54, pls 8–9, 11, figs 61–111

R. Gibbs: 'Landscape as Property: Bolognese Law Manuscripts and the Development of Landscape Painting', *Il codice miniato laico. Atti del IV congresso di storia della miniatura italiana: Cortona, 1992*

ROBERT GIBBS

Master of the Glorification of the Virgin (*fl* Cologne, *c.* 1470–94). German painter. He is named after a large panel, densely filled with numerous figures, showing the *Glorification of the Virgin* (*c.* 1475; ex-St Brigida, Cologne; Cologne, Wallraf-Richartz-Mus.). His inflexible concept of form, archaic compositional patterns and numerous references to the work of Stefan Lochner point to his starting work in mid-century. A small panel showing the *Virgin and Infant Jesus on a Bench* (Berlin, priv. col.) was very likely produced before the *Glorification*. A *Portrait of a Young Man* (*c.* 1480; Penrhyn, nr Bangor, priv. col.) shows a matter-of-fact and thorough style following the example of the portraits of Dieric Bouts and Hans Memling. The south Netherlandish Master of Flémalle's Werl Altarpiece, then in Cologne, influenced the Master's *Annunciation* (*c.* 1490; Cologne, Wallraf-Richartz-Mus.), and other Netherlandish influences—perhaps the Columba Triptych by Rogier van der Weyden (*c.* 1450; ex-Columba, Cologne; Munich, Alte Pin.; *see* WEYDEN, VAN DER, (1), fig. 3) and works by Hugo van der Goes—left traces in his works. The various components come most clearly to light in the magnificent *Adoration of the Magi* (?1493; ?ex-Franziskanerkirche, Brühl, Aachen, Suermondt-Ludwig-Mus.). Large panels showing *St Christopher*, the city patrons *SS Gereon and Peter* and *St Anne, the Virgin and the Infant Jesus* (after 1493; Cologne, Wallraf-Richartz-Mus.) offer a fine representation of sculpturally conceived saints before a true-to-life view of Cologne and its environs, seen from the Rhine. Not until Anton Woensam's woodcut *vedute* (1531; Cologne, Wallraf-Richartz-Mus.) was this prospect of the city surpassed.

BIBLIOGRAPHY

L. A. Scheibler: *Die hervorragendsten anonymen Meister und Werke der Kölner Malerschule von 1460 bis 1500* (diss., U. Bonn, 1880), pp. 44–7

A. Stange: *Deutsche Malerei der Gotik*, v (Munich, 1952), pp. 16–21

H. M. Schmidt: 'Zum Werk des Meisters der Verherrlichung Mariae', *Schülerfestgabe für Herbert von Einem zum 16. Februar 1965* (Bonn, 1965), pp. 249–60

A. Stange: *Die deutschen Tafelbilder von Dürer: Kritisches Verzeichnis*, i (Munich, 1967), pp. 55–7, nos 140–48

Herbst des Mittelalters: Spätgotik in Köln und am Niederrhein (exh. cat., Cologne, Ksthalle, 1970), p. 43

HANS M. SCHMIDT

Master of the Golden Panel of Lüneburg (*fl c.* 1431–5). German painter. He is named after the high altarpiece of the Benedictine monastery of St Michael in Lüneburg. The Golden Panel was a Romanesque gold antependium (destr. after 1698) that housed relics and treasures from the monastery. Its painted double wings (Hannover, Niedersächs. Landesmus.) are likely to have been added in 1431 to mark the completed reconstruction of the partially destroyed church. The closed wings (oak, 2.31×1.84 m each) showed the *Crucifixion* juxtaposed with its typological parallel, the *Brazen Serpent*. The inside of the outer wings and the outside of the inner wings depict 36 scenes from the *Life of the Virgin* and the *Passion of Christ*, starting with an *Annunciation* and culminating in the *Coronation of the Virgin*. On the inside, the inner wings are decorated with carved and gilded figures of saints and prophets.

Blaschke argued that the painted panels were the work of two successive painters. However, examination by infra-red photography has revealed a consistent vigorous underdrawing style indicating a single designer (Corley). Surface characteristics, on the other hand, reflect at least three hands, presumably in workshop collaboration. The design and style, the variety of hues and the painterly application of colours all suggest intimate knowledge of the work of Conrad von Soest. The sometimes haphazard use of models from Conrad's workshop may suggest that the painter trained with Conrad. It is interesting to note that a 'Cord von Soest' is recorded in the Lüneburg records between 1426 and 1451.

BIBLIOGRAPHY

M. Kempfer: 'Die Farbigkeit als Kriterium für Werkstattbeziehungen, dargestellt an zehn Altären aus der Zeit zwischen 1370 und 1430', *Giessen. Beitr. Kstgesch.*, ii (1973), pp. 7–49

R. Blaschke: *Studien zur Malerei der Lüneburger 'Goldenen Tafel'* (diss., Bochum, Ruhr-Univ., 1976)

B. Corley: *Conrad von Soest: His Altarpieces, his Workshop and his Place in European Art* (diss., U. London, Courtauld Inst. A. and Birkbeck Coll., 1991)

——: *Conrad von Soest, Painter among Merchant Princes* (London, 1996)

BRIGITTE CORLEY

Gold Scrolls Group (*fl c.* 1415–55). Group of south Netherlandish illuminators. First identified by Winkler as the Master of the Gold Scrolls, it has subsequently been recognized that the catalogue of works attributed to this figure has assumed such proportions that it must be the product of a group of artists instead. The name derives from the manner in which the backgrounds of the miniatures are often painted: in flat colour, decorated with golden foliated ornament. Further stylistic characteristics are the representation of the figures, which look rather like little dolls with oval faces in which nose, mouth and eyes are only summarily treated. They are drawn with supple, unbroken lines and make stereotyped gestures. The folds of their garments are straight and sometimes fall softly in waves to the ground. Shallow pocket pleats formed above the belts are also typical, and the forms are modelled with hatched pen-strokes or by gradations in the

Gold Scrolls Group: *St Ursula and a Bishop with Donors*; miniatures from a collection of religious exercices, *c.* 145×109 mm, ?1530s (London, British Library, MS. Add. 39638, fol. 31*v*)

paint. The dominant colours are green, blue, red and orange. The scenes take place in coulisse-type landscapes or fairly elaborate interiors. The depiction of cloth printed with small circles is also characteristic of the group.

The Gold Scrolls Group was particularly active in Bruges but in its early years appears to have had strong connections with Paris. This is apparent in the Hours of Edward I of Portugal (1433–8; Lisbon, Arquiv. N., MS. 140), where the influence of the Boucicaut Master is clear. The Hours of Joseph Bonaparte (Paris, Bib. N., MS. lat. 10538), left incomplete in the workshop of the Boucicaut Master *c.* 1415, was later completed by the Gold Scrolls Group. The influence of the workshop of Jacquemart de Hesdin has also been established, and there are connections with the work of the MASTER OF THE BEAUFORT SAINTS (*see* above). The Gold Scrolls miniatures are also indebted to early 15th-century south Netherlandish illumination. In a few manuscripts, such as the Missal probably created for a church in Genoa (before 1431; New York, Pierpont Morgan Lib., MS. M. 374), both Parisian and south Netherlandish influences are apparent. This also applies to a Book of Hours in The Hague (The Hague, Kon. Bib., MS. 133. D. 14) and another in Brussels (Brussels, Bib. Royale Albert 1er, MS. 18270).

Typical Gold Scrolls manuscripts from the years after 1425 include richly illuminated Books of Hours that form a distinctive group (e.g. Baltimore, MD, Walters A.G., MS. W. 211; New York, Pub. Lib., MS. 28; and Paris, Bib. Ste Geneviève, MS. 1274). It can be deduced from these that the artists in the group were collaborating freely and in constantly varying combinations. Manuscripts with identification marks stamped in the borders near the miniatures—a protectionist practice that arose out of the Bruges municipal statutes of 1426—also date from this period (e.g. Rouen, Bib. Mun., MS. Leber 135). This suggests that the artists worked under the guidance of a book dealer.

The Gold Scrolls Group also illuminated tracts such as *Le Livre du gouvernement des rois et des princes* (Brussels, Bib. Royale Albert 1er, MS. 9474), Bibles (e.g. 1432; London, BL, Yates Thompson MS. 16) and manuscripts of religious exercises (London, BL, Add. MS. 39638; see fig.). There is also a distinct group of manuscripts, the so-called Pen and Ink Group, which have been illustrated with pen drawings. They consist of a manuscript with scenes from the *Life of Christ* (New York, Pierpont Morgan Lib., MS. M. 649) and three copies of the *Speculum humanae salvationis* (New York, Pierpont Morgan Lib., MS. M. 385; Paris, Bib. N., MS. fr. 188; and Copenhagen, Kon. Bib., MS. GK.S. 79).

Around 1450 the Gold Scrolls Group illuminated more luxurious manuscripts, such as the Montfort Book of Hours (Vienna, Österreich. Nbib., Cod. s.n. 12878), the Llangatock Book of Hours (Malibu, CA, Getty Mus., MS. Ludwig IX 7) and the Hours of Isabella the Catholic (Madrid, Bib. Pal.). During this period the group's style was assimilated by a new generation of illuminators, including the Master of the Magdalen Missal (*fl* mid-15th century), providing a transition to the types of book production dominated by Willem Vrelant in the third quarter of the 15th century.

BIBLIOGRAPHY
Thieme–Becker
F. Winkler: *Die flämische Buchmalerei des XV. und XVI. Jahrhunderts* (Leipzig, 1925/*R* Amsterdam, 1978), pp. 25–7
A. W. Byvanck: 'Aanteekeningen over handschriften met miniaturen ix: De Noordnederlandsche kunst en de miniaturen uit Zuid-Nederland en uit Noord-Frankrijk' [Notes on manuscripts with miniatures ix: northern Netherlandish art and the miniatures from the southern Netherlands and northern France], *Oudhdknd. Jb.*, x (1930), pp. 104–15
——: 'Kroniek der Noord-Nederlandsche miniaturen ii' [Chronicle of the northern Netherlandish miniatures ii], *Oudhdknd. Jb.*, n. s. 3, iv (1935), pp. 15–16
E. Panofsky: *Early Netherlandish Painting*, 2 vols (Cambridge, MA, 1953), pp. 121–3
De Vlaamse miniatuur: Het mecenaat van Filips de Goede [The Flemish miniature: the patronage of Philip the Good] (exh. cat. by L. M. J. Delaissé, Brussels, Bib. Royale Albert 1er, 1959), pp. 18–19, 28–33
J. D. Farquhar: 'Identity in an Anonymous Age: Bruges Manuscript Illuminators and their Signs', *Viator*, xi (1980), pp. 371–83
M. Smeyers and B. Cardon: 'Vier eeuwen Vlaamse miniatuurkunst in handschriften uit het Grootseminarie te Brugge' [Four centuries of Flemish miniature art in manuscripts from the Seminary in Bruges], *De Duinenabdij en het Grootseminarie te Brugge* [The Abbey of the Dunes and the Seminary in Bruges] (Tielt-Weesp, 1984), pp. 161–6
B. Cardon: 'The Illustrations and the Gold Scrolls Group, Typologische Tafereleren uit het Leven van Jesus [Typological scenes from the Life of Christ]: A Manuscript from the Gold Scrolls Group (Bruges, *c.* 1440) in the Pierpont Morgan Library, New York, MS. Morgan 649', *Corpus*

of Illuminated Manuscripts from the Low Countries, i, ed. M. Smeyers (Leuven, 1985), pp. 119–204

G. Dogaer: *Flemish Miniature Painting in the 15th and 16th Centuries* (Amsterdam, 1987), pp. 27–31

BERT CARDON

Master of the Goslar Sibyls (*fl c.* 1508–10). German painter. He is named after the paintings on the panelling of the conference room (the 'Huldigungssaal') in the Rathaus at Goslar. Twelve kings and emperors are portrayed alternately with sibyls in contemporary dress, each pair of rulers turning towards the sibyl between them but divided from her by a thin wooden pillar and surrounded by rich tracery. The sibyls stand on grass, the rulers on paved floors, against a background of drapes and landscapes. Painted curtains affixed to poles border the lower edge of the pictures. Each picture on the ceiling has a richly ornamented frame. The scenes are dominated by red, blue and a brownish, modulating yellow. The damask patterns of the garments were printed on, using templates.

The unique imagery of the paintings (which were discovered in 1854, behind filing cabinets) illustrates the sibyls' prophecy of the coming of Christ and (simultaneously) of the emperors and kings (see Vöge). The conference chamber has been likened (Goldberg) to a medieval shrine, here turned in on itself. Its theme of prophets and sibyls first appeared in the late Middle Ages on choir-stalls (1469–71; Ulm Cathedral), then penetrated into the secular sphere, initially in the conference hall at Überlingen (1492), where it combines with picture cycles of historical rulers, and then in stained-glass windows, cathedral façades, exterior walls of town halls and the Fürstensaal (1530) of the Lüneburg Rathaus. In Goslar, the *Ara coeli* legend of the Emperor Augustus, to whom the Tiburtine sibyl prophesied the advent of a new world order, is transferred to the representative of the free imperial town of Goslar, and the hope of salvation is fulfilled in Christ.

On the north and west walls of the conference chamber local saints are painted on the surfaces of the window-openings. On the west wall one panel shows a patron, possibly Johann Papen, Burgomaster (1498–1509) of Goslar, kneeling before (on another panel) the Apocalyptic Virgin on a crescent moon. Opposite this, on the east side, are doors painted on both sides, with a *Man of Sorrows* and *Mater dolorosa* on the reverse sides giving on to the Trinity Chapel, the walls of which have seven pictures (including scenes of the *Passion*) painted in secco technique. On the chapel's ceiling are four panels depicting the *Childhood of Christ*, surrounded by the *Evangelists* and twelve *Prophets*. None of the documents relating to the construction of the conference chamber names a painter who could be connected with its decoration. Ascriptions have included Michael Wolgemut, Hans Pleydenwurff, Hans Raphon and the elusive figure Hans Witten of Cologne. The date of the work is suggested by the fact that a new altar was built over the underlying charnel-house on 31 March 1505, and also by the recent identification of motifs in the Trinity Chapel borrowed from Hans Schäufelein's *Speculum passionis* woodcut series (1507). Some evidence supports the theory (Goldberg) that the principal painter, responsible for all the pictures, moved to Goslar from Thuringia or Saxony, the painter

of the Trinity Chapel being a stylistically dependent journeyman.

The Calenberg Altar (*c.* 1515; ex-Burg Calenburg; priv. col.) is without doubt another work by the Master of the Goslar Sibyls. The middle panel is thought to show the family of Duke Erich I of Brunswick-Calenberg (1470–1540), praying before a seated Virgin flanked by two male and two female saints. On the insides of the wings, presenting St Maurice with retinue and three auxiliary saints, the rich draughtsmanship, with elongated, templated garments, is again more imposing than the actual painting of the work. Possible influences can be ascertained in contemporary painting at HILDESHEIM, in the cathedral altar (*c.* 1515; Brunswick, Herzog Anton Ulrich-Mus.) and in the high altar (1519) of the former Cistercian convent church at Wienhausen.

BIBLIOGRAPHY

J. M. Kratz: *Hildesheim. Allg. Anz.*, 269 (3 Sept 1858)

W. Vöge: *Jörg Syrlin der Ältere und seine Bildwerke*, ii (Berlin, 1950), p. 96

T. Tappen and H. G. Uhl: 'Hans Witten von Cöln?', *Fröhlich-Festschrift* (Goslar, 1952), p. 104

H.-G. Griep: 'Der Goslarer "Huldigungssaal-meister"', *Harz-Z.*, xi (1959), p. 113

G. Goldberg: *Der Huldigungssaal im Rathaus zu Goslar* (diss., U. Munich, 1960)

Master of the Göttinger Barfüsseraltar (*fl* 1424). German painter. He is named after an enormous altarpiece (1424; Hannover, Niedersächs. Landesmus.) from the Franciscan Barfüsserkirche (destr. 1820–24) in Göttingen. All surfaces of the work are painted, and it comprises a central panel, two pairs of wings and remnants of supports, presenting scenes of the *Passion*, *SS Francis and George and the Virgin* (third view), the *Apostles with the Texts of the Creed* (second view), four allegories of *Christ's Deeds for Mankind* (first view) and, on the supports, *Female Saints*. The altarpiece was apparently a late work, in which the Master's draughtsmanship and painting skills had become rigid and fossilized. It shows a strong influence from the Master of the Golden Panel of Lüneburg and, in the large Mount Calvary breaking through the rows of images, a knowledge of Conrad von Soest's Wildungen Altarpiece (1403; Bad Wildungen, St Maria, Elizabeth und Nikolaus). For this work the Master's patron was probably Brother Luthelmus, who is portrayed in miniature kneeling under the cross, with Henricus Duderstat. Whether the latter was the painter remains uncertain, but it is assumed that the Master was a Franciscan patronized by the nobility (coats of arms on the *Creed* panels). The altarpiece brings the 'soft style' of painting (see GERMANY, §III, 2) in Lower Saxony to a close.

Two wings of an altar of *St Mary Magdalene* (1416; ex-Magdalenenkirche, Hildesheim; Hamburg, Ksthalle; Stuttgart and Münster, priv. cols; central panel untraced) are considered earlier works of the same artist. The wings show that the painter was influenced initially by the work of Master Bertram, as is evident for example in a comparison of the dense arrangement of the figures in the *Supper with Simon* with Master Bertram's *Last Supper* (before 1383; Paris, Mus. A. Déc.). In a small altarpiece (*c.* 1420) in the chapel at Offensen near Holzminden, with panels of the *Annunciation* and *Nativity* (central panel, Bielefeld, Neustädter Marienkirche), the influence of Westphalian painting is evident in the *Annunciation* and in the baldacchino motif.

BIBLIOGRAPHY

R. Behrens: *Der Göttinger Barfüsser-Altar: Ein Beitrag zur Geschichte der niedersächsischen Malerei des frühen 15. Jahrhunderts* (Bonn, 1939)

——: 'Der Altar in Offensen', *Niederdt. Beitr. Kstgesch.*, iv (1965), pp. 89–100

HANS GEORG GMELIN

Gregory Master. *See* MASTER OF THE REGISTRUM GREGORII below.

Master of the Griggs Crucifixion. *See* TOSCANI, GIOVANNI.

Griselda Master (*fl c.* 1490). Italian painter. He was named after a set of three *spalliera* panels (London, N.G.) devoted to Boccaccio's story of Patient Griselda (*Decameron*, X.10). They had been assigned to Pinturicchio, and the Master's style is rightly linked to Umbria, although he was active chiefly in Siena. The tall, spindly figures on the panels show vibrant movement and are dressed in elegant costumes, despite their crude, sticklike, sketchy execution. The artist's personality was established by the discovery of the same hand at work in small background scenes in a set of panels of single figures standing on pedestals with landscape backgrounds. Eight panels of the set by various artists have been identified. Four of the panels are by Sienese painters: Matteo di Giovanni's *Judith* (Bloomington, IN U. A. Mus.); Neroccio de' Landi's *Claudia Quinta* (Washington, DC, N.G.A.; *see* ITALY, fig. 29); Francesco di Giorgio's *Scipio Africanus* (Florence, Bargello); and Pietro Orioli's *Sulpicia* (Baltimore, MD, Walters A.G.). The other four were first attributed to Signorelli but now are given by consensus to an artist dependent on him, plausibly considered to be the Griselda Master himself: *Artemisia* (Milan, Mus. Poldi Pezzoli); *Eunostos* (Washington, DC, N.G.A.); *Alexander* (U. Birmingham, Barber Inst.); and *Tiberius Gracchus the Elder* (Budapest, Mus. F.A.). Though more suave and sculptural, the main figures share the smaller ones' finicky, dancer-like refinement. The shared theme of persons behaving virtuously to the opposite sex is that of the Griselda panels too, and the figures were probably made for a grand house, perhaps for a marriage; the Piccolomini and Spanocchi families of Siena have been suggested. The frequent comparison with Castagno's series of *Nine Famous Men and Women* (Florence, Uffizi) can be enhanced, in that both sets include one half-length figure, the only Biblical one, in each case an Old Testament heroine (in this case *Judith*, for Castagno *Esther*). Hence *Judith* may, like *Esther*, have been over a door in the middle of the wall, the central and highest-ranking figure. There would then have had to have been a ninth panel. It is consistent that the seven surviving secular panels comprise two male Romans and two male Greeks (in both cases one military, one civil), two female Romans (one virgin, one wife) and one female Greek (a wife). A candidate for a ninth figure, as a Greek virgin, is Hippo. The usual reconstruction regards the set of eight as complete, because there are four men and four women, and assumes that the *Judith* has been cut. That the ethnic clusters are significant is also suggested in that the Greek figures are all by the Griselda Master, whereas the other

five are each by a different artist, including one by him; the work is often said to have begun with the better-known artists assisted by the Griselda Master for backgrounds, after which the Master took over and completed the set.

The logical place to seek other work by the Griselda Master is in the backgrounds of paintings by LUCA SIGNORELLI (as Longhi suggested); there are little scenes by him in the background of Signorelli's *Last Days of Moses* in the Sistine Chapel, Rome (1481–2), and some large figures in the foreground of the same scene. The Sistine cycle is notorious for complex collaborations between masters and assistants. Signorelli and his followers are often credited with parts of Perugino's *Giving of the Keys*, and the Griselda Master seems to have painted the Tribute Money group in the background of that scene and an elegant portrait figure in front of it. Of all the distinctive styles in the chapel, the Griselda Master's is the only one not fitted with an artist's name, and so he may well be the only artist named by Vasari as working in the chapel by whom no works are known, Rocco Zoppo. As confirmation, this man worked with Perugino (so explaining the Umbrian style) but was born in Belforte, close to Siena, thus matching the Master's career. The portrait figure in the *Giving of the Keys* is a clue to the specific origins of his style in the Peruginesque San Bernardino panels (Perugia, G.N. Umbria).

BIBLIOGRAPHY

A. Venturi: 'I quadri di scuola italiana nella Galleria Nazionale di Budapest', *Arte*, iii (1900), pp. 185–240 (237–8)

G. De Nicola: 'Notes on the Museo Nazionale of Florence, v: Fragments of Two Series of Renaissance Representations of Greek and Roman Heroes', *Burl. Mag.*, xxxi (1917), pp. 224–8

F. Canuti: *Il Perugino* (Siena, 1931) [on Rocco Zoppo]

R. Longhi: 'Un intervento raffaelesco nella serie "eroica" di Casa Piccolomini', *Paragone*, xv/175 (1964), pp. 5–8

B. Berenson: *Central and North Italian Schools* (1968), i, p. 252

E. Zafran: *Fifty Old Master Paintings from the Walters Art Gallery* (Baltimore, 1988), no. 13 [for late 20th-century opinions on the Master and important bibliog.]

A. Barriault: '*Spalliera*' *Paintings of Renaissance Tuscany* (University Park, PA, 1994)

CREIGHTON E. GILBERT

Master of Grossgmain. Austrian painter. He is named from four wing panels (1499; Grossgmain, nr Salzburg, Maria Himmelfahrt) of a dismantled altar of the Virgin and two very tall panels depicting the *Virgin and Child* and *Salvator mundi* perhaps produced in conjunction with them. The wing panels depict the *Presentation in the Temple*, *Christ among the Doctors*, the *Descent of the Holy Ghost* and the *Death of the Virgin*; the normally exposed faces have been destroyed apart from a few fragments that have been removed. The close stylistic relation with the work of Rueland Frueauf (i) was noted early on and superseded the incorrect attribution to Bartholomäus Zeitblom. The independent Master of Grossgmain is now widely regarded as the 'dominant personality in a workshop that must probably be seen as an extension or a branch of the Frueauf workshop' (Demus). His origin in the artistic milieu of Salzburg is not usually contested. The common use of the same punch for the decoration of the backgrounds of paintings confirms a direct link with Frueauf (Zimmermann), of whom he is thought to have been a pupil.

With the Master of Grossgmain, loosely dispersed figures or chains of figures entered Salzburg painting for the first time; these figures occupy a space with an accentuated but uneven perspective that, like the scattered, still-life-like objects, intensifies the still and subdued quality of the whole conception. The lack of interest in convincing spatial relationships is deliberately demonstrated by the close spacing of distant points, resulting in highly compressed perspective views.

Other works attributed to the Master of Grossgmain are the *Virgin Enthroned with St Thomas and Donors* (1483; Prague, N. Mus.), the *Coronation of the Virgin* (Prague, N. Mus.), *St Augustine* and *St Ambrose* (perhaps the predella of the Grossgmain Altar; both Vienna, Belvedere) and the *Education of Christ* (Boston, MA, Mus. F.A.). Disputed works are the Pretschlaipfer Triptych (ex-Berchtesgadenerhof, Salzburg; Vienna, Belvedere) and *St Jerome* (Madrid, Mus. Thyssen-Bornemisza).

BIBLIOGRAPHY

L. Baldass: *Conrad Laib und die beiden Rueland Frueauf* (Vienna, 1946), pp. 71–3, nos 73, 110–27

A. Stange: *Deutsche Malerei der Gotik*, x (Berlin, 1960), pp. 43–6, nos 70–75

O. Demus: 'Zu den Tafeln des Grossgmainer Altars', *Österreich. Z. Kst & Dkmlpf.*, xix (1965), pp. 43–5, pls 34–9

E. Baum: *Katalog des Museums Mittelalterlicher Österreichischer Kunst*, i of *Kunst der Österreichische Galerie Wien* (Vienna and Munich, 1971), pp. 102–3

Spätgotik in Salzburg: Die Malerei, 1400–1530 (exh. cat., ed. A. Rohrmoser; Salzburg, Mus. Carolino Augusteum, 1972)

E.-M. Zimmermann: *Studien zur Frueauf-Problem (Rueland Frueauf der Ältere und der Meister der Grossgmain)* (diss., U. Vienna, 1975)

ALBIN ROHRMOSER

Master of Grosslobming (*fl c.* 1380–1420). Sculptor, active principally in Austria. He derives his name from five of the figures from the choir of the parish church of Grosslobming (Styria), which may be from a cycle commissioned by Ernst von Lobming *c.* 1400–03 in connection with his tomb (except for the *Virgin Annunciate* (Frankfurt am Main, Liebieghaus), all Vienna, Belvedere). Since Kris, these have been considered among the main representatives of the *Schöne Stil* ('Beautiful style'). The Grosslobming figures appear, however, to be the works of two artists, whose parts cannot be divided exactly: one carved figures of *St George*, *St Lambertus* (the titular saint of the church) and the *Virgin Annunciate*; the other made the figures of *St John* and the *Angel Annunciate*. Both sculptors are indebted to Western prototypes, but only the sculptor of the *St George* appears actually to have been trained in the Netherlands. His work is technically of very high quality, and he vests his figures with a certain 'psychological' insight.

These characteristics are also found in a *Man of Sorrows* (Vienna, Belvedere) from Pfenningberg near Linz and in three portal figures at Steyr parish church. Two figures in Linz, a *Virgin* (Bischöf. Diözmus.) and a bishop (priv. col., on loan to Oberösterreich. Landesmus.), probably belonged to the same ensemble, which may originally have been in a chapel of the church. These works are related to a *Virgin and Child* in Falkenstein church (Lower Austria) and a saint formerly in the Hinrichsen Collection. The latter shows closer similarities than any other to the paintings of the Třeboň Abbey altar (frags, Prague, N.G.),

made *c.* 1378–85, but also to contemporary Viennese glass painting. The earliest work of this circle has also been preserved in Vienna: a bust of the *Virgin* that was added *c.* 1380 to an older figure of *St Anne* on the south tower of the Stephansdom (Vienna, Hist. Mus.).

Although the Master of Grosslobming's style shows Franco-Flemish influence, he probably also knew the work of the Prussian-Silesian Master of the Schöne Madonnen, such as the Hedwig boss in Holy Cross Church, Wrocław. That the Master of Grosslobming had actually travelled to eastern Germany is demonstrated by the head of *St John* from the south portal of Meissen Cathedral (Berlin, Staatl. Museen Preuss. Kultbes.), which is closely related to his style. The *Man of Sorrows* called 'Zahnwehherrgott' (Christ as healer of toothache) in the Stephansdom, Vienna, can be attributed to his workshop. A *St Peter* in the monastery of St Lambert and a *Pietà* in the crypt of Lienz parish church (eastern Tyrol) are not entirely by his hand, and other shop work includes two saints (Klosterneuburg Abbey, Lapidarium) and a *Virgin* from the Schulhof in Vienna (Vienna, Hist. Mus.), these showing distinct similarities to the style of the Parler family.

The Master and some other sculptors were probably called to Buda *c.* 1410 to decorate the palace of King Sigismund with a lavish cycle of figures (perhaps on the occasion of his coronation). A number of these statues, which were excavated in 1974, are related to the group at Steyr (*Virgin*, head of maid), while others are dependent on the figures in Grosslobming (herald, bishop), although they have far greater plasticity. This new style is also represented by the effigy of *Ulrich II von Schaunberg* (*d* 1398) in Wilhering Church near Linz and the figures of the *Annunciation* in New York (Met.; Cloisters), all probably dating to the period just before the Buda sculptures were made.

A group of three figures preserved in the presbytery of S Marco, Venice, represents the last phase of the Master's activity. This shows distinct early Renaissance tendencies. That a northern artist could show such sympathies is demonstrated by a model book in the Galleria degli Uffizi, Florence, which has been attributed to a Netherlandish artist and not only shows stylistic links to the Master's work but also appears to have travelled a route that corresponds remarkably well to the regions in which he is presumed to have worked. HANS VON JUDENBURG was a follower of the Master.

BIBLIOGRAPHY

E. Kris: 'Über eine gotische Georgs-Statue und ihre nächsten Verwandten', *Jb. Ksthist. Samml. Wien*, n. s., 4 (1930), pp. 121–54

E. Baum: *Katalog des Museums Mittelalterlicher Österreichischer Kunst* (Vienna and Munich, 1971), pp. 22–7, nos 4–8

K. Ginhart: *Die Fürstenstatuen von St Stephan in Wien und die Bildwerke aus Grosslobming* (Klagenfurt, 1972)

E. Marosi: 'Vorläufige kunsthistorische Bemerkungen zum Skulpturenfund von 1974 in der Burg von Buda', *Acta Hist. A. Acad. Sci. Hung.*, xxii (1976), pp. 333–73

H. Beck and H. Bredekamp: 'Kompilation der Form in der Skulptur um 1400: Beobachtungen an Werken des Meisters von Grosslobming', *Städel-Jb.*, n. s., 6 (1977), pp. 139–57

Gotik in der Steiermark (exh. cat., Graz, Kultreferat Steiermärk. Landesregierung, 1978), pp. 203–4, 225–7, 230–33, 240–41

M. Horvath, ed.: *Der Königspalast und die gotischen Statuen des mittelalterlichen Buda* (Budapest, 1980)

L. Schultes: 'Der Meister von Grosslobming und die Wiener Plastik des Schönen Stils', *Wien. Jb. Kstgesch.*, xxxix (1986), pp. 1–40, 223–44

L. Zolnay and E. Marosi: *A budavári szoborlelet* [Sculpture from the castle of Buda] (Budapest, 1989)

L. Schultes: 'Der Meister von Grosslobming und Hans von Judenburg: Zeit- und Individualstil um 1400', *Internationale Gotik in Mitteleuropa*, ed. G. Pochat and B. Wagner (Graz, 1990), pp. 253-68

Der Meister von Grosslobming (exh. cat. by A. Saliger, Vienna, Belvedere, 1994) [colour illus.]

LOTHAR SCHULTES

Master of the Guild of St George (*fl c.* 1485–1504). Painter, active in Mechelen. He was named by Friedländer after the *Portrait of the Members of the Guild of St George* (*c.* 1495; Antwerp, Kon. Mus. S. Kst.), one of the earliest surviving group portraits in Netherlandish painting. He has sometimes been identified with Boudewijn van Battel (*fl* 1465–1508), also known as van der Wyct, but this remains conjectural. Other paintings (both portraits and narratives) have been attributed to him on stylistic grounds: *Jean de Mol* (*c.* 1485; U. London, Courtauld Inst. Gals); a diptych showing *Philip the Fair and Margaret of Austria* (*c.* 1494; Vienna, Ksthist. Mus.); panels illustrating the *Legend of St Rombaut* (*c.* 1500–03; Mechelen Cathedral); the triptych of *Charles V and his Sisters as Children* (*c.* 1502; Vienna, Ksthist. Mus.); and the *Seigneur of Bricquegny* (*c.* 1504; Ghent, Despiegelaere priv. col.). His style and technique are highly personal. Narrative compositions are a montage of individual images; the demands of the narrative sequence are given precedence over perspectival unity, and consequently there is only a limited sense of spatial illusion. In the portraits the emblematic element determines the composition. Realism and convention are combined by individualizing the faces within a standard formula and by varying the handling of the modelling. The stiff figures are ill-proportioned, with tiny bodies, large heads and stubby hands; the drapery is composed of tight, angular folds. Compositions are sketched with areas of colour used as the base tone of the pictorial design; rough outlines in the underdrawing are reinforced on the surface by heavy lines. Together with the systematic alterations to the composition during execution, these features indicate the prime importance for the artist of the painting process in the elaboration of the forms.

BIBLIOGRAPHY

G. Van Doorslaer: 'Un Portraitiste malinois du XVème siècle', *Bull. Cerc. Archéol., Litt. & A. Malines* (1921), pp. 14–20

M. J. Friedländer: *Die altniederländische Malerei* (Berlin, 1924–37); Eng. trans. as *Early Netherlandish Painting* (Leiden, 1967–76), iv (1969); xiv, p. 67, suppl., pp. 13–14

G. Delmarcel and C. Périer-D'Ieteren: 'De laatgotische schilderkunst te Mechelen', *Aspekten van de laatgotiek in Brabant* (exh. cat., Leuven, Brouwerijmus., 1971), pp. 244–59

C. Périer-D'Ieteren: 'Le Portrait d'un seigneur de Bricquegny dû au Maître de la Gilde de Saint-Georges', *Rev. Belge Archéol. & Hist. A.* (1972), pp. 39–53

——: 'Le Triptyque de Charles-Quint et de ses deux soeurs enfants: Une Oeuvre du Maître de la Gilde de Saint-Georges', *Bull. Inst. Royal Patrm. A.*, xiv (1973–4), pp. 105–17

——: 'Le Maître de la Gilde de Saint-Georges: Catalogue critique de cinq des panneaux de la Légende de Saint-Rombaut', *Jb.: Kon. Mus. S. Kst.* (1975), pp. 153–201

P. Vandenbroeck: 'Meester van de Mechelse St. Jorisgilde', *Catalogus schilderijen 14e en 15e eeuw*, Antwerp, Kon. Mus. S. Kst. cat. (Antwerp, 1985), pp. 84–9

C. PÉRIER-D'IETEREN

Master of Guillebert de Metz (*fl c.* 1415–60). South Netherlandish illuminator. He is named after his work in two manuscripts signed by the scribe Guillebert de Metz. He painted the frontispiece in one, a collection containing Guillebert's description of the city of Paris, dated 1434, and works by Christine de Pisan and others (Brussels, Bib. Royale Albert 1er, MS. 9559–64). The other codex is a copy of Laurent de Premierfait's French translation of Boccaccio's *Decameron* (Paris, Bib. Arsenal, MS. 5070), in which Guillebert names his place of residence as Grammont (Flem. Geeraardsbergen) in East Flanders. The majority of the 100 miniatures in this book were produced by the Master of Mansel, but the Master of Guillebert de Metz illuminated the beginning of the codex, including such miniatures as *Richard and Catelle* (see fig.). Guillebert de Metz is also mentioned as living in Grammont in an account of 1432 relating to two books for Philip the Good, Duke of Burgundy. In a third manuscript (The Hague, Kon. Bib., MS. 133. A. 2) Guillebert describes himself as 'libraire de M. le duc Jean de Bourgogne'. According to this, he was already in the service of the Burgundian dukes before the death of John the Fearless in 1419.

The exact nature of the connection between Guillebert and the illuminator who worked principally for him is unclear. Illuminators' instructions in Flemish that still survive under a few of the *Decameron* miniatures reveal that the Master of Guillebert de Metz was also south Netherlandish. His style is unmistakable: prominent black outlines surround the bright, thick, enamel-like areas of colour in his miniatures. Black is also used in the drawing of drapery, particularly in the dark shaded areas, emphasizing the volume of the figures despite the basic flatness of the compositional style. The fall of the folds is simple and clear, however, and conforms to the Soft style. The faces often have the colour and solidity of alabaster and are shaded with olive green in a manner that strikingly recalls 14th-century Italian painting. The Master of Guillebert de Metz favoured intense shades of green and blue and liked to include large areas of silver, in armour or the sky, for example. His marginal decoration is distinguished by its colourful, broad-leaved acanthus, springing from the four corners of the border area in heavy coils, forming clusters rather than continuous tendrils. In some works, most obviously in a Book of Hours (Malibu, CA, Getty Mus., MS. 2), the foliage becomes disproportionate in size and extremely three-dimensional in appearance. The use of naturalistic elements gives it an illusionistic effect, while the colouring remains entirely abstract. There is also an extraordinary wealth of imaginative, humorous motifs.

In historical terms the Master of Guillebert de Metz occupies an important transitional place between Paris illumination after 1400 and the independent Flemish tradition: to the former he owes his compositional schemes, to the latter his original use of motifs. The interchange was probably mediated by the Burgundian library. The miniatures of the Paris *Decameron* reproduce (exactly, in most cases) a Boccaccio illuminated in Paris around 1415 (Rome, Vatican, Bib. Apostolica, MS. Pal. lat. 1989). The Rome *Decameron* was once part of the library of John the Fearless and, according to a note by the bookbinder Lievin Stuart, must have been in Bruges about a century later. The Master of Guillebert de Metz also added miniatures to a Breviary illuminated for John the Fearless by a painter from the circle of the Limbourgs

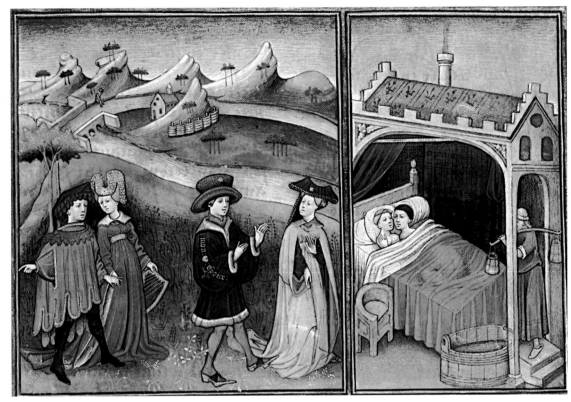

Master of Guillebert de Metz: *Richard and Catelle*; miniature from Boccaccio: *Decameron*, 130×190 mm, *c.* 1440 (Paris, Bibliothèque de l'Arsenal, MS. 5070, fol. 116)

and by the Egerton Master (London, BL, Add. MS. 35311 and Harley MS. 2897). Other illuminations (Germany, priv. col.) also reveal the Master's familiarity with models used by the workshop of the Boucicaut Master. The Paris Book of Hours of John the Fearless (Paris, Bib. N., MS. nouv. acq. lat. 3005) could also be an early work by the Master of Guillebert de Metz. Yet commissions from the Burgundian court form only one part of the extensive production of the Master's workshop, which also included manuscripts for patrons in Ghent and Bruges, such as the Book of Hours for the Ghent patrician Daniel Rym (Baltimore, MD, Walters A.G., MS. W. 166). Some of the numerous Books of Hours from this workshop were certainly produced for the open market. Among the most beautiful and richly decorated are the Book of Hours in Malibu already mentioned and two others, in Bologna (Bib. U., MS. 1138) and in the Vatican (Rome, Vatican Bib. Apostolica, MS. Ottobon. lat. 2919).

BIBLIOGRAPHY
F. Winkler: 'Studien zur Geschichte der niederländischen Miniaturmalerei des XV. und XVI. Jahrhunderts, ii: Eine flandrische Lokalschule um 1420–1460', *Jb. Ksthist. Samml. Allhöch. Ksrhaus.*, xxxii (1915), pp. 306–24
——: *Die flämische Buchmalerei* (Leipzig, 1925/*R* Amsterdam, 1978), pp. 28–30
Le Siècle d'or de la miniature flamande (exh. cat. by L. M. J. Delaissé, Brussels, Pal. B.-A.; Amsterdam, Rijksmus.; Paris, Bib. N.; 1959), pp. 21–7
M. Meiss: 'The First Fully Illustrated *Decameron*', *Essays in the History of Art Presented to Rudolf Wittkower* (London, 1967), pp. 56–61
G. Dogaer: *Flemish Miniature Painting in the 15th and 16th Centuries* (Amsterdam, 1987), pp. 33–7
Andachtsbücher des Mittelalters aus Privatbesitz (exh. cat. by J. M. Plotzek, Cologne, Schnütgen-Mus., 1987), pp. 172–5

BODO BRINKMANN

Guinigi Painter. *See* MASTER OF THE LATHROP TONDO below.

Master of the Guiron le courtois (*fl c.* 1370). Italian illuminator. The illustration of a fragmentary copy of the Arthurian romance *Guiron le courtois* (Paris, Bib. N., MS. nouv. acq. fr. 5243), after which this Master is named, is one of the most accomplished and sophisticated examples of 14th-century manuscript illumination. All but one of the scenes are restricted to the margins of the lower half of the folio, below and sometimes to either side and between the two columns of text. There are no frames, and the text areas appear as screens hanging in front of the illustrated narrative. Occasionally there is a playfulness in the depiction of represented space relative to the surface of the page that became common only in late 15th-century manuscripts: for example on folio 26*v* Arthur's hand curls around and holds the edge of the text area as he peers out from behind it. The delicacy and precision of drawing are equalled by the close attention to narrative accuracy and the interaction of the protagonists. The exceptional quality of these illustrations was recognized by the Master of Latin 757, who absorbed characters and decorative details from the *Guiron* manuscript and reused them throughout his career. The flourished initials contain the arms and monogram of Bernabò Visconti, Lord of Milan, for whom the manuscript was presumably made. Both the flourished and the painted initials can be paralleled in a manuscript (Paris, Bib. N., MS. lat. 7880I) that Petrarch had illuminated in Milan in 1369. It was presumably in this city and around this date that this exceptional illuminator worked. Another illuminated copy of *Guiron le courtois* (priv. col.) is his only other known work.

BIBLIOGRAPHY

P. Toesca: *La pittura e la miniatura nella Lombardia dai più antichi monumenti alla metà del quattrocento* (Milan, 1912/R Turin, 1966), pp. 162–3

A. Quazza: 'Miniature lombarde intorno al 1380', *Boll. A.*, n. s. 4, 1/1 (1965), pp. 67–72

Dix Siècles d'enluminure italienne (exh. cat., ed. Y. Załuska and others; Paris, Bib. N., 1984), pp. 94–5

K. Sutton: 'Milanese Luxury Books: The Patronage of Bernabò Visconti', *Apollo*, cxxxiv (1991), pp. 322–6

KAY SUTTON

Master of the Habsburgs (*fl c.* 1490–1520). Austrian painter. He is named from a panel painting of the *Adoration of the Magi* (1493–1508; Vienna, Belvedere), in which the middle king and one of the retinue behind him have been given the features of the Habsburg emperors Maximilian I and Frederick III. (The right-hand edge of the picture with the young king has been cut off.) Elements derived from the Netherlands—facial types, especially those of the Virgin and infant Jesus, the faithful rendering of facts, distant landscapes in the background and superb colouring—suggest his training there and distinguish this artist from run-of-the-mill Tyrolean painters, though he was later to some extent influenced by Marx Reichlich.

Among the works ascribed to the Master are three half-length paintings of the *Virgin and Child* (Vienna, Belvedere; Innsbruck, Tirol. Landesmus.; Venice, Correr) and several panels donated by noble families from North and South Tyrol with the *Virgin and Saints* (ex-Weiherburg, nr Innsbruck, and ex-Landeck: both Innsbruck, Tirol. Landesmus.; ex-Prösels, nr Völs: Nuremberg, Ger. Nmus.) and *St Anne with SS Joachim and Joseph* (Bolzano, Mus. Civ.); the half-length Virgins are in Paduan or Venetian settings, which suggests that the painter may have travelled to North Italy. He has been identified with Niklas Reiser (*fl* 1498–1512 in Schwaz).

BIBLIOGRAPHY

E. Egg: 'Zur maximilianischen Kunst in Innbruck, I. Der Habsburger Meister (Nikolaus Reiser?)', *Veröff. Tirol. Landesmus. Ferdinandeum*, xlvi (1966), pp. 11–35

E. Baum: *Katalog des Museums Mittelalterlicher Österreichischer Kunst: Unteres Belvedere Wien* (Vienna, 1971), pp. 146–7, 168

E. Egg: *Gotik in Tirol, die Flügelaltäre* (Innsbruck, 1985), pp. 336–9

JANEZ HÖFLER

Master of Hakendover (*fl* Brussels, *c.* 1400–20). South Netherlandish sculptor. He was one of the outstanding 15th-century Netherlandish sculptors and directed a large, influential workshop. Four major ensembles have been attributed to him: an altarpiece in St Salvator, Hakendover (Brabant; *c.* 1400–04); a series of archivolt prophets and historiated consoles from the Belfry portal of the Brussels Town Hall (1404–5; Brussels, Mus. Com.); a series of life-size *Apostles* (*c.* 1408–9) and a wall tabernacle (1409) in

the choir of NOTRE-DAME-DE-HAL; and a *Calvary* altarpiece (*c.* 1410–15) in the Reinoldikirche, Dortmund (Westphalia).

A large number of wooden altarpiece fragments may also be attributed to the artist or his workshop, including a *Virgin* and a *St Joseph* from an *Adoration of the Magi* group (Brussels, Musées Royaux A. & Hist.); a female saint (Huppaye church, Brabant); a series of seated prophets (Ath, Mus. Athois; Frankfurt am Main, Liebieghaus; Utrecht, priv. col.); two Apostle statuettes (priv. col.); a *Pentecost* group (New York, Met.); and a *Gethsemane* group (Amsterdam, Rijksmus.).

The Hakendover Altarpiece combines the late 14th-century tradition of ANDRÉ BEAUNEVEU with a greater spatial depth characteristic of the years around 1400. Over the following decade, the master's sculpture developed increasing amplitude and realism, as can be seen in his work for the church in Hal, where his versatility and expressive range extend from the heightened intensity of the monumental and strikingly life like Apostle statues to the sharply observed genre details of the intricately carved wall tabernacle reliefs. The Master was at his best in small-scale works. This is also evident in his finest work, the Dortmund Altarpiece, which consists of a central chapel-like space with sculpture, framed by hinged shutters with painted scenes, and which introduced a type that became standard in Brabantine sculpture for over a century. The Dortmund group, which includes several Apostle statuettes of a type identical to his earlier works but interpreted in a more evolved style, ranks with the finest examples of the fully developed 'Soft style' in the Netherlands. His late style, represented by the *Pentecost* group in New York, reveals a highly personal manner of great purity and introspection, dominated by abstract drapery rhythms.

BIBLIOGRAPHY

R. Maere: 'Le Retable d'Haekendover', *An. Acad. Royale Archéol. Belgique*, n. s. 6, viii (1920), pp. 70–97

R. Hamann: 'Spätgotische Skulpturen der Wallfahrtskirche in Hal', *Belgische Kunstdenkmäler*, ed. P. Clemen, i (Munich, 1923), pp. 214–33

D. Roggen: 'Het Retabel van Hakendover', *Gent. Bijdr. Kstgesch. & Oudhdknd.*, i (1934), pp. 108–21

I. Geisler: 'Studien zur niederländischen Bildhauern des ausgehenden 14. und frühen 15. Jahrhunderts', *Wallraf-Richartz-Jb.*, xviii (1956), pp. 146–8

I. Achter: 'Schrein und Flügelgemälde eines gotischen Altares, jetzt in der Kath. Pfarrkirche zu Rheinberg', *Jb. Rhein. Dkmlpf.*, xxiii (1960), pp. 214–15

Flanders in the Fifteenth Century. Art and Civilization: Masterpieces of Flemish Art: Van Eyck to Bosch (exh. cat., Detroit, MI, Inst. A., 1960), pp. 231–4, cat. nos 69–70

A. von Euw: 'Der Kalvarienberg im Schnütgen-Museum', *Wallraf-Richartz-Jb.*, xxviii (1965), pp. 111–16

R. Marijnissen and H. Van Liefferinge: 'Les Retables de Rheinberg et de Hakendover', *Jb. Rhein. Dkmlpf.*, xxvii (1967), pp. 75–89

J. Steyaert: *The Sculpture of St Martin's in Halle and Related Netherlandish Works* (diss., U. Michigan, 1974), pp. 111–48

Die Parler und der Schöne Stil, 1350–1400: Europäische Kunst unter den Luxemburgern (exh. cat., ed. A. Legner; Cologne, Schnütgen-Mus., 1978), i, pp. 88–90, 94–5

K. Morand: 'Claus Sluter: The Early Years', *Liber Amicorum Herman Liebaers* (Brussels, 1984), pp. 561–84

J. STEYAERT

Master of the Halepagen Altar. *See* DEDEKE, WILM.

Master of the Hamilton Xenophon (*fl* Florence, 1470s and 1480s). Italian illuminator and ?painter. He is named after a manuscript illuminated (after 1475) for Ferdinand I of Aragon (Berlin, Kupferstichkab., MS. Hamilton 78.C.24), a Latin translation of Xenophon's *Kyroupaideia*. The Master was an artist of some note, whose prestigious patrons included the Medici and Federigo II da Montefeltro, and whose work ranged from the illustration of Books of Hours to humanistic texts. His early style is best represented by some folios of two Antiphonaries (begun in 1463; Florence, Bib. Medicea-Laurenziana, MSS Edili 148 and 150), to which Zanobi Strozzi and Francesco di Antonio del Chierico, in whose bottega he worked until 1478, also contributed. Other early collaborative projects include the frontispiece of Jerome's *Commentary on Ezechiel* (Rome, Vatican, Bib. Apostolica, MS. Urb. lat. 57, fol. 2r) with Domenico Ghirlandaio and Poggio Bracciolini's *Storia di Firenze* (Rome, Vatican, Bib. Apostolica, MS. Urb. lat. 491) with Francesco Rosselli. Reflections of Ghirlandaio's work emerge again in the Bible for Federigo da Montefeltro (completed 1478; Rome, Vatican, Bib. Apostolica, MSS Urb. lat. 1–2), in which he collaborated with del Chierico; the Master's own unmistakable style has also been recognized in some of its miniatures previously attributed to Attavante Attavanti.

The two main frontispieces of the codex of the vernacular version of Leonardo Bruni's *Historia fiorentini populi* (Florence, Bib. N. Cent., Banco Rari 53) were painted in 1480. These show a combination of monumental composition and minute rendering of surface and volume, approaching Netherlandish work, while the refined technique is suggestive of goldsmiths' work. This was followed by a series of Books of Hours, probably datable before the end of 1480. The possibility that the Master also worked as a panel painter should not be excluded: some of his illustrations show evidence of a large repertory of portraits and groups of figures, painted in particular colour harmonies that suggest experience in painting on a larger scale.

BIBLIOGRAPHY

A. Garzelli: *La Bibbia di Federico da Montefeltro* (Rome, 1977), pp. 144–56
——: *Miniatura fiorentina del rinascimento, 1440–1525: Un primo censimento*, 2 vols (Florence, 1985), pp. 157–62

PATRIZIA FERRETTI

Harris Master. *See* SÁNCHEZ.

Master of the Harvard Hannibal (*fl c.* 1415–40). Illuminator, active in France. He was named by Meiss after the miniature of the *Coronation of Hannibal* in a French translation of Livy (Cambridge, MA, Harvard U., Houghton Lib., Richardson MS. 32, fol. 263r). Based on a design by the Boucicaut Master (Paris, Bib. N., MS. fr. 259, fol. 253r), it is the only miniature in this style; the others are associated with the Boucicaut and Bedford masters. The Harvard Hannibal Master worked with the Boucicaut Master in such other manuscripts as the copy of Boccaccio's *Des Cleres et Nobles Femmes* (Lisbon, Fund. Gulbenkian, MS. L.A. 143) and alone, as in a Book of Hours of Paris Use (New York, Pierpont Morgan Lib., MS. M. 455). Meiss considered these to be the earlier works, datable *c.* 1415, of the illuminator who subsequently painted miniatures in, among other books, a Romance of Alexander (London, BL, Royal MS. 20.B.XX) and two Books of

Hours of Paris Use (Oxford, Bodleian Lib., MS. Liturg. 100; and Stonyhurst, Lancs, MS. 33). Pächt and Alexander had signalled the connection between these three manuscripts, and later Plummer noted the difficulties in identifying their artist with that of the 'earlier' Harvard Hannibal group. It seems more plausible to consider the styles of these 'earlier' and 'later' groups as originating from two separate artists, the first influenced by the Boucicaut Master, the second more strongly influenced by the Limbourg brothers. The confusion between the two has inevitably led to confusions in attribution so that miniatures by many other artists have been ascribed to the Master of the Harvard Hannibal.

Both painters illuminated books of Paris Use and would seem to have trained and worked in Paris. With the decline of Paris as a centre for luxury goods, the later artist, that of the Alexander manuscript, seems to have moved to the south Netherlands, where he worked on the Hours of Guillebert de Lannoy (Waddesdon Manor, Bucks, NT, MS. 4), and then to have returned to France under English rule. He contributed some of the miniatures added to a Psalter (London, BL, Cotton MS. Domitian A. XVII), presumably when it was altered for presentation to Henry VI *c.* 1430, and illuminated a Book of Hours of Sarum Use (London, BL, Sloane MS 2468) owned by the English Umfray family by 1453. The centre for this activity may have shifted from Paris to Rouen, since his hand is also found in an Hours of Rouen Use (Baltimore, MD, Walters A.G., MS. W. 259), and his style is still evident in a manuscript (Paris, Bib. N., MS. fr. 126), mostly in the style of the Talbot Master, made for the *echevins* of Rouen in 1449 or later.

Both artists used clear, bright colours and shared an interest in highly decorated architectural and landscape settings. The artist of the Alexander manuscript, however, employed more complex details, and his characteristically sharp-nosed figure types and his painterly technique, apparently derived from the Bedford Master, also distinguish him from the Harvard Hannibal Master, whose tendency to an immaculate finish resembles the work of the Boucicaut Master. The careful modelling and precise elaboration of detail in the work of the former ensured the continuation of earlier Parisian illumination into the mid-15th century.

BIBLIOGRAPHY

G. F. Warner and J. P. Gilson: *Catalogue of the Western Manuscripts in the Old Royal and King's Collections*, ii (London, 1922), pp. 369–70
J. Porcher: *Les Belles Heures de Jean de France, duc de Berry* (Paris, 1953), pp. 27, 48
——: *Manuscrits à peintures offerts à la Bibliothèque Nationale par le comte Guy du Boisrouvray* (Paris, 1961), no. 14
O. Pächt and J. J. G. Alexander: *Illuminated Manuscripts in the Bodleian Library, Oxford*, i (Oxford, 1966), p. 52, no. 663
M. Meiss: *French Painting in the Time of Jean de Berry: The Limbourgs and their Contemporaries*, 2 vols (London, 1974), esp. pp. 207–8, 390–92
Medieval and Early Renaissance Treasures in the North West (exh. cat., ed. J. J. G. Alexander and P. Crossley; U. Manchester, Whitworth A.G., 1976), p. 24, no. 31
L. M. J. Delaissé, J. Marrow and J. de Wit: *The James A. de Rothschild Collection at Waddesdon Manor: The Illuminated Manuscripts* (Fribourg, 1977), pp. 65–94
The Last Flowering: French Painting in Manuscripts, 1420–1530, from American Collections (exh. cat. by J. Plummer and G. Clark, New York, Pierpont Morgan Lib., 1982), pp. 5–6, nos 6–7

R. S. Wieck: *Late Medieval and Renaissance Illuminated Manuscripts, 1350–1525, in the Houghton Library* (Cambridge, MA, 1983), pp. 10–15, nos 5–6

J. Backhouse: *Books of Hours* (London, 1985), p. 52

R. S. Wieck: *The Book of Hours in Medieval Art and Life* (London, 1988), pp. 184–5, nos 29–30

Sale cat., London, Sotheby's: 29 Nov 1990, lot 136

CATHERINE REYNOLDS

Master of the Heisterbach Altar (*fl* Cologne, *c.* 1440– *c.* 1450). German painter. His name is derived from the original location of a large altarpiece (?before 1448) with double pairs of wings, the Cistercian abbey of Heisterbach near Bonn (dissolved 1806; partly destr. 1809). The untraced central section, which may have been carved, purportedly showed *Christ and Six Apostles.* The pairs of wings can be clearly reconstructed. In its closed state it showed *St Ursula* (Cologne, Wallraf-Richartz-Mus.) and *St Gereon* (?*Cassius*; Munich, Alte Pin.), with their companions. The first set of wings showed 16 scenes from the *Life of Christ* (12, Munich, Alte Pin.; 4, Cologne, Wallraf-Richartz-Mus.) and the second set of wings *Apostles* and *SS Benedict and Bernard,* were shown in painted tabernacles (Munich, Alte Pin.). This inner view, with relic skulls behind tracery openings in the lowest level, evidently followed the layout of relic-bearing altarpieces. Although the elongated, soft and somewhat spiritless figure types were still clearly orientated towards prototypes from *c.* 1400 to *c.* 1435, there are also unmistakable references to Stefan Lochner's paintings. Also attributed to the Master are two intimate panels of the *Virgin and Child* (priv. col.) and an altarpiece triptych with a central *Crucifixion* and at the sides the *Virgin with the Twelve Apostles* (*c.* 1445; Munich, Alte Pin.; ?ex-Cologne). The Master of the Heisterbach Altar was a conservative painter, not particularly creative and probably without contact with the progressive forces of Netherlandish art. Still bound by the Cologne tradition exemplified by the Master of St Lawrence (*c.* 1415–*c.* 1430), he could not distance himself from the style of Lochner, though he can hardly have been the latter's pupil as was formerly conjectured.

BIBLIOGRAPHY
C. Aldenhoven: *Geschichte der Kölner Malerschule* (Lübeck, 1902), pp. 162–4

A. Stange: *Deutsche Malerei der Gotik*, v (Munich, 1952), pp. 4–7

——: *Die deutschen Tafelbilder vor Dürer, Kritisches Verzeichnis*, i (Munich, 1967), pp. 46–8, nos 108–12

G. Goldberg and G. Scheffler: *Altdeutsche Gemälde, Köln und Westdeutschland, Gemäldekataloge, Alte Pinakothek München*, xxiv (Munich, 1972), pp. 145–57, 244–74

R. Budde: *Köln und seine Maler, 1300–1500* (Cologne, 1986), pp. 88–90

M. Wolfson: 'Vor "Stefan Lochner"—über den Maler des Kölner Dombildes und den Meister des Heisterbacher Altares', *Stefan Lochner, Meister zu Köln—Herkunft, Werke, Wirkung* (exh. cat., ed. F. G. Zehnder; Cologne, Wallraf-Richartz-Mus., 1993), pp. 97–107

HANS M. SCHMIDT

Master of the Herpin. *See under* §III: MASTER w‡s.

Master of the Hersbruck High Altar (*fl c.* 1475–1500). German painter. He is named from an altarpiece (*c.* 1480–90) in the parish church of Hersbruck, near Nuremberg. Although the altarpiece is now dismembered, with the sculptural shrine removed (Nuremberg, Ger. Nmus.), the panels from the two pairs of movable wings are still preserved in the church at Hersbruck. These

comprise a *Nativity* and *Death of the Virgin* on the panels flanking the shrine, eight scenes from the *Passion* displayed on the first opening of the wings, and four by another hand on the exterior, showing scenes from the *Life of the Virgin.* The *Passion* scenes, by which the Master is best known, are crowded with figures, activated by gesture and twisted postures, complicated movements of line in the drapery and contours, and abrupt shifts from foreground to distance. On the basis of the figures, compositions and colouring, the Master is associated with Hans Pleydenwurff and Michael Wolgemut of Nuremberg. Certain characterizations and proportions of figures also suggest that he was acquainted with Bavarian painting. Repeated but inconclusive efforts have been made to identify him with Wolfgang Katzheimer, whose activity in Bamberg is documented from 1465 to 1508. Even among writers who acknowledge the separate existence of this anonymous master, there is little unanimity about all the works that should be assigned specifically to him, except the Hersbruck high altar itself.

BIBLIOGRAPHY
Thieme–Becker

H. Thode: *Die Malerschule von Nürnberg im 14. und 15. Jahrhundert in ihrer Entwicklung bis auf Dürer* (Frankfurt am Main, 1891), pp. 144–6

F. Dörnhöffer: 'Beiträge zur Geschichte der älteren Nürnberger Malerei', *Repert. Kstwiss.*, xxix (1906), pp. 441–67

N. Bonsels: 'Wolfgang Katzheimer von Bamberg', *Stud. Dt. Kstgesch.*, cccvi (1936), pp. 57–68

A. Stange: *Deutsche Malerei der Gotik*, ix (Munich, 1958), pp. 94–9

W. Schwemmer: *Die Kunstdenkmäler von Bayern: Mittelfranken, x. Landkreis Hersbruck* (Munich, 1959), pp. 129–32

F. Anzelewsky: 'Eine spätmittelalterliche Malerwerkstatt: Studien über die Malerfamilie Katzheimer in Bamberg', *Z. Dt. Ver. Kstwiss.*, xix (1965), pp. 142–6

A. Stange with P. Strieder and H. Härtle: *Kritisches Verzeichnis der deutschen Tafelbilder vor Dürer*, iii, ed. N. Lieb (Munich, 1978), pp. 115–17

Master of the Historia Friderici et Maximiliani [Master of Pulkau; Master of the Historia] (*fl c.* 1508–25). German or Austrian draughtsman and painter. He executed 46 drawings in a manuscript of the above title and has been attributed with a varying body of other drawings and paintings. All these works possess stylistic traits associated with the Danube school, although stylistic variations among them allow for much conjecture about the unity of their authorship.

The *Historia Friderici et Maximiliani* (*c.* 1515; Vienna, Haus-, Hof- & Staatsarchiv, MS. Böhm no. 24) is a life history of Emperor Maximilian I, who commissioned the work, and of his father, Emperor Frederick III. Composed by the humanist Joseph Grünpeck and illustrated with unsigned drawings, the manuscript was intended for presentation to Maximilian's grandson, the future Charles V. The latest date it refers to is 1508, but most commentators have concluded for other reasons that it should be dated *c.* 1515. While the drawings closely resemble Albrecht Altdorfer's draughtsmanship of *c.* 1508, they diverge from the developments of his manner over the following decade.

The body of work now assembled under the Master's name includes other paintings and drawings that are neither Altdorfer's nor any other identified artist's. Voss (1907) attributed three other drawings to him; two (Berlin, Kupferstichkab.; Vienna, Albertina) are now generally assigned to Altdorfer and one, the *Beheading of St Catherine*

(Vienna, Akad. Bild. Kst.; Winzinger no. 134), remains considered as the Master's. Voss named him Master MZ (separately from the engraver known by that monogram) after initials on this last drawing, which he did not recognize as a later addition. Dodgson (1924) and Halm (1930) attributed the *Historia* drawings to Altdorfer, but when a number of clearly non-Altdorfian panels came to be attributed to the artist (Buchner, 1938; Benesch and Auer, 1957; and Stange, 1964), a separate identity was required.

Now seen as a painter, the artist also became known as the Master of Pulkau (Oettinger, 1939), from an altarpiece (*c.* 1520) in the Heilig-Blut-Kirche, Pulkau, Lower Austria. This Austrian attribution divided opinions as to whether the artist was primarily located in Regensburg, with Altdorfer, or in Vienna. Taking both locales into account, Dworschak (1965) proposed that the Master was Niclas Preu (*fl* 1502–33), a contemporary Augsburg artist of otherwise uncertain production who is documented as at both Regensburg and Vienna. Most recently Mielke (see 1988 exh. cat.) has argued more forcefully than anyone previously that the *Historia* drawings and those most closely related to them are indeed by Altdorfer. He thus rejects the attribution of the Pulkau panels to the same hand and gives reasons why a date of 1508 is valid for the *Historia* manuscript.

BIBLIOGRAPHY

Thieme–Becker: 'Master of Pulkau'

H. Voss: *Der Ursprung des Donaustils: Ein Stück Entwicklungsgeschichte deutscher Malerei* (Leipzig, 1907), pp. 195–7

C. Dodgson: [review of H. Tietze: *Deutscher Meister: Albrecht Altdorfer* (Leipzig, 1924)], *Burl. Mag.*, xlv (1924), pp. 93–4

P. Halm: 'Die Landschaftszeichnungen des Wolfgang Huber', *Münchn. Jb. Bild. Kst*, n. s. 1, vii (1930), pp. 65–6

Albrecht Altdorfer und sein Kreis (exh. cat. by E. Buchner, Munich, 1938), pp. 147–9

K. Oettinger: 'Die Malereien des Pulkauer Altars', *Pantheon*, xxiii (1939), pp. 161–70

F. Winzinger: *Albrecht Altdorfer: Zeichnungen* (Munich, 1952), pp. 54–6, 101–4

O. Benesch and E. M. Auer: *Die Historia Friderici et Maximiliani* (Berlin, 1957) [complete illus. of *Historia* drgs and other attributed works]

A. Stange: *Malerei der Donauschule* (Munich, 1964), pp. 111–15, figs 42, 204–18

F. Dworschak: *Die Kunst der Donauschule, 1490–1540* (exh. cat., ed. O. Wurzel; St Florian, Stiftssamml.; Linz, Schlossmus.; 1965), pp. 96–104 [identified as Niclas Preu]

Albrecht Altdorfer: Zeichnungen, Deckfarbenmalerei, Druckgraphik (exh. cat. by H. Mielke, Berlin, Kupferstichkab., 1988), pp. 325–7 [identified as Albrecht Altdorfer; ten colour illus. from *Historia*]

CHARLES TALBOT

Master of the Holy Blood [Maître du Saint-Sang] (*fl* ?Bruges, *c.* 1530). South Netherlandish painter. Name given by Hulin de Loo (1902 exh. cat.) to the anonymous painter of the triptych of the *Lamentation* (Bruges, Mus. Heilige Bloed) that belonged to the Bruges Brotherhood of the Holy Blood. Friedländer attributed 30 works to the Master, whom he characterized as a competent but unassuming practitioner, active in Bruges *c.* 1530. The paintings also show strong Antwerp influence, but the *Lamentation* triptych and that of the *Glorification of the Virgin* (Bruges, St Jacobskerk), both of which belong to the group of attributed works, have always been in Bruges, thus supporting the idea that the studio of the Master was there. The paintings also show affinities with the works of

Gerard David, Albert Cornelis (*c.* 1500–32), Ambrosius Benson and Jan Provoost, who were also active in Bruges. According to Friedländer, the absence of donor portraits in the triptychs indicates that they were not made on commission but were produced for the open market, presumably for export.

The oeuvre attributed to the Master was also strongly influenced by the work of Quinten Metsys and shares characteristics with that of other Antwerp painters such as the Master of Frankfurt. This could be explained by an apprenticeship in Antwerp before the Master's period of activity in Bruges. The paintings often combine compositions influenced by Hans Memling with figure types that stiffly rework the style of Metsys. Their design and execution are frequently rough, with angular rhythms and inaccurate anatomy. The derivative nature of this artist's oeuvre makes his artistic personality difficult to assess. Moreover, the lack of stylistic homogeneity in the works attributed to him by Friedländer suggests that they are the work of more than one hand. There is a small core of ten paintings, including the two triptychs in Bruges, that are distinguished by a relatively more refined treatment. Other examples include the *Annunciation* (Madrid, Prado), the *Virgin with Three Angels* (Antwerp, Kon. Mus. S. Kst.), the *Virgin and Child* (New York, Met.), the *Crucifixion* (Greenville, SC, Bob Jones U. Gal. Sacred A.), two wing panels with *St Catherine* and *St Barbara* (Cleveland, OH, Mus. A.) and three versions of *Lucretia* (Munich, Alte Pin.; Brussels, Mus. A. Anc.; and Vienna, Gemäldegal. Akad. Bild. Kst.).

BIBLIOGRAPHY

Thieme–Becker

W. H. J. Weale: 'Gérard David', *Le Beffroi*, i (1863), pp. 223–33

Exposition des tableaux flamands des XIVe, XVe et XVIe siècles (exh. cat. by G. Hulin de Loo, Bruges, Groeningem., 1902), pp. 33, 39, nos 126, 155; review by M. J. Friedländer in *Repert. Kstwiss.*, xxvi (1903), p. 149

M. J. Friedländer: *Die altniederländische Malerei* (Berlin, 1924–37); Eng. trans. as *Early Netherlandish Painting* (Leiden, 1967–76), ix, pp. 95–8, 118–20

E. Panofsky: *Early Netherlandish Painting: Its Origins and Character*, i (Cambridge, 1953), p. 266

G. Marlier: 'Une *Montée au Calvaire* du Maître du Saint-Sang', *Les Beaux-Arts* (Oct 1956), p. 13

V. Bruncel: 'Une *Lucrèce* du Maître du Saint-Sang', *Les Beaux-Arts* (Oct 1957), p. 8

Anonieme vlaamse primitieven: Zuidnederlandse meesters met noodnamen van de 15de en het begin van de 16de eeuw (exh. cat., Bruges, Groeningemus., 1969), pp. 74–87, 223–4

C. Van Den Bergen-Pantens: 'Une Oeuvre inédite du Maître du Saint-Sang', *Hand. Genoot. Gesch. 'Soc. Emul.' Brugge*, cxiii (1976), pp. 229–49

D. De Vos: *Catalogus schilderijen 15de en 16de eeuw*, Bruges, Groeningemus. cat. (Bruges, 1979), pp. 144–6

CHRISTINE VAN MULDERS

Master of the Holy Kinship (*fl* Cologne, *c.* 1475–*c.* 1510). German painter. He is named after an altarpiece depicting the *Holy Kinship* (*c.* 1500–03; Cologne, Wallraf-Richartz-Mus., ex-Dominican Kloster St Achatius). In this assembly of the relatives of the Virgin, a central group with St Anne and the Infant Jesus is flanked by SS Barbara and Catherine, the latter depicted as the Mystic Bride of Christ. On the inner sides of the wings, in front of a broad landscape, are (left) SS Roch and Nikasius with the donor, Nikasius Hackeney, and (right) SS Gudula and Elizabeth with his wife Christina. Here the Master's art is at its zenith. Solid bourgeois comfort and steadiness character-ize the figures. The composition of the triptych is, as with most of his work, unassuming. However, it is pervaded by a sensitivity to colour values, shades of red being dominant.

One of the last Late Gothic artists in Cologne, the Master produced panel and glass-painting, the most exten-sive oeuvre surviving from his epoch in Cologne. This was with the participation of a large workshop, so that attribution and evaluation are fraught with problems. Rode's proposed identification of the Master with the Cologne painter Lambert von Luytge (Liège; *d* 1508)—through stylistic comparison with his stained glass in the northern nave aisle of Cologne Cathedral (1507–8)—suggests that the origin of his artistic language might lie in the area of the River Meuse.

Through comparison with the *Holy Kinship*, the Mas-ter's earliest works are deemed to include a winged altarpiece of the *Seven Joys of Mary* (*c*. 1475; Cologne, Benedictine monastery of the Maccabees). It closely fol-lows Stefan Lochner's altarpiece (1447; Darmstadt, Hess. Landesmus.; ex-Cologne, Katharinenkirche), which illus-trates the Cologne base of his style, as does the *Lamentation* (*c*. 1480; Munich, Alte Pin.), leading back to the Master of the Life of the Virgin. His later work, open to various influences, bears traces of contact with the art of his contemporary, the Master of the St Bartholomew Altar. In the strongly symmetrical votive panel of *Graf Gumprecht von Neuenahr and his Family* (before 1484; Cologne, Wallraf-Richartz-Mus.), the conception and style point to an accommodation with Netherlanders such as Rogier van der Weyden and Hans Memling. The work of the Lower Rhenish-Westphalian painter Derick Baegert was appar-ently the model for his crowded, agitated *Calvary* (*c*. 1490; Brussels, Mus. Royaux A. & Hist.; ex-parish church, Richterich, nr Aachen), with the *Adoration of the Magi* and *Resurrection* (Valkenburg, nr Maastricht, Jesuitenkolleg) as wing pictures, the former recalling the work of Hugo van der Goes. Indeed, in these wing panels it is difficult to reconcile the sense of landscape and pictorial space with what is known of the Master's art. Perhaps the subse-quently independent Master of the Aachen Altar was involved.

Also attributed to the Master of the Holy Kinship are a *Mass of St Gregory* (1486; Utrecht, Catharijneconvent), a two-piece epitaph (Nuremberg, Ger. Nmus.) for Jakob Udemann of Erkelenz (*d* 1492), the *St Sebastian* altarpiece (1493–4; Cologne, Wallraf-Richartz-Mus.), a sort of group portrait showing the master's ability as a portrait painter, and an altarpiece with the *Circumcision* (1503–7; Munich, Alte Pin.; ex-St Kolumba, Cologne). A small winged altarpiece with *SS Barbara and Dorothy* in the central picture (before 1510; Cologne, Wallraf-Richartz-Mus.) is thought to have been one of his last works. His workshop was a reservoir of various talents, perhaps including the Master of St Severin and the Master of the Aachen Altar.

BIBLIOGRAPHY

A. Stange: *Deutsche Malerei der Gotik*, v (Munich, 1952), pp. 73–90
——: *Die deutschen Tafelbilder vor Dürer, Kritisches Verzeichnis*, i (Munich, 1967), pp. 90–96, nos. 262–89
H. Rode: 'Die Namen der Meister der hl. Sippe und von St. Severin, eine Hypothese, zugleich ein Beitrag zu dem Glasmalereizyklus im nör-dlichen Seitenschiff des Kölner Doms', *Wallraf-Richartz-Jb.*, xxxi (1969), pp. 249–54
G. Goldberg and G. Scheffler: *Altdeutsche Gemälde, Köln und Westdeutsch-land, Gemäldekataloge, Alte Pinakothek München*, xiv (Munich, 1972), pp. 411–61
U. Westfehling: *Die Messe Gregors des Grossen* (exh. cat., Cologne, Schnütgen-Mus., 1982), pp. 46–59
R. Budde: *Köln und seine Maler, 1300–1500* (Cologne, 1986), pp. 19, 119–27, 249–51, nos 83–5
F. G. Zehnder: *Katalog der Altkölner Malerei*, xi of *Katalog des Wallraf-Richartz-Museums* (Cologne, 1990), pp. 271–315

HANS M. SCHMIDT

Master of Hoogstraten (*fl* Antwerp, *c*. 1505). Neth-erlandish painter. He is named after a series of seven panels of the *Sorrows of the Virgin* (Antwerp, Kon. Mus. S. Kst.), which were in the church of St Catherine, Hoogstraten, until 1825, and which were possibly painted for it *c*. 1505. Volskaja identified the artist as one of Memling's pupils at Bruges, Passcier van der Mersch (*d c*. 1500), although Gerard David seems a closer source of inspiration for the Master, and this in turn might support the suggestions by Hoogewerff and Châtelet that he was of Dutch origin. Other works by the Master include the *Adoration of the Magi* formerly in the Johnson Collec-tion (Philadelphia, PA, Mus. A.), which has similar figures with pale faces, long fingers and noses shown in incorrect profile.

BIBLIOGRAPHY

M. J. Friedländer: *Die altniederländische Malerei* (Berlin, 1924–37); Eng. trans. as *Early Netherlandish Painting* (Leiden, 1967–76), vii, pp. 51–3, 72–4, 90
L. Philippen and J. Ernalsteen: *Rond het Hoogstraatsche altaarstuck van het Antwerpsch Museum* [Round the Hoogstraten altarpieces of the Antwerp Museum] (Brecht, 1928)
G. J. Hoogewerff: *De Noord-Nederlandsche schilderkunst*, i (The Hague, 1936), pp. 517–18; ii (1937), p. 582
S. Leurs: 'Meester van Hoogstraten: *Christus in de tempel*, en Sint-Germanuskerk te Tienen', *Eigen Schoon Braband*, 37 (1954), pp. 54–7
H. Comstock: 'Panels from a Flemish Altar Painting', *Connoisseur*, cxxxix (1957), pp. 203–4
V. L. Volskaja: 'A Picture of a Netherlandish Artist of the 15th Century in the A. S. Pushkin Museum', *Festschrift Lazarev* (Moscow, 1960), pp. 232–42
A. Châtelet: *Les Primitifs hollandais* (Paris and Fribourg, 1980); Eng. trans as *Early Dutch Painting* (Oxford and New York, 1981)
C. Scaillièrez: 'Un *Christ en Croix* du Maître de Hoogstraeten du Musée des beaux-arts d'Angers', *Rev. Louvre*, xxxvi (1986), pp. 192–6

CARL VAN DE VELDE

Master of the Horloge de Sapience. *See under* MAS-TER OF JEAN ROLIN below.

Master of the Hortulus Animae (*fl* after 1510). Name devised by Winkler to cover the supposed artist of a group of south Netherlandish illuminations that has subsequently been attributed among various artists. The central manu-script of the group was a German translation by Sebastian Brandt of the *Hortulus animae* (Vienna, Österreich. Nbib., Cod. 2706) copied from the editions printed in Strasbourg in 1510. The codex is richly decorated with 36 full-page pictures, 29 smaller miniatures, 29 historiated borders and 2 historiated initials. Winkler tentatively identified the Master of the Hortulus Animae as Gerard Horenbout. This hypothesis was demolished when Georges Hulin de Loo discovered documented works by Horenbout. After this the miniatures of the Vienna *Hortulus animae* were attributed (even by Winkler himself) to Simon Bening. The Older Prayerbook of Maximilian (Vienna, Österreich.

Nbib., Cod. 1907), which was included in Winkler's original group, became the central manuscript of a group defined by Hulin de Loo as the work of the Master of the Older Prayerbook of Maximilian. Both the attribution of the *Hortulus animae* to Simon Bening (*see* BENING, (2), fig. 2) and the partial replacement of the Master of the Hortulus Animae by the Master of the Older Prayerbook of Maximilian are generally accepted.

BIBLIOGRAPHY
F. Dörnhöffer: *Seelengärtlein: Hortulus Animae: Cod. Bibl. Pal. Vindobon, 2706*, 4 vols (Frankfurt am Main, 1907–11) [facs. edn]
F. Winkler: *Die flämische Buchmalerei* (Leipzig, 1925/*R* Amsterdam, 1978), pp. 118–25
——: 'Neuentdeckte Altniederländer, i: Sanders Bening', *Pantheon*, xv (1942), pp. 261–71
W. Hilger: *Das ältere Gebetbuch Maximilians I* (Graz, 1973), pp. 45–54 [facs. edn]
Flämische Buchmalerei: Handschriftenschätze aus dem Burgunderreich (exh. cat. by D. Thoss, Vienna, Österreich. Nbib., 1987), pp. 104–6, 119–21

BODO BRINKMANN

Master of the Hours of Isabella of Castile. *See under* TOMASINO DA VIMERCATE.

Housebook Master [Master of the Amsterdam Cabinet] (*fl* Middle Rhineland, *c.* 1470–1500). German printmaker, draughtsman and painter. The most important works attributed to him are two groups, from which he derives his two alternative names: the so-called Medieval Housebook (Swabia, Waldburg-Wolfegg priv. col., see 1985 exh. cat., no. 117), an illustrated manuscript with 40 pen-and-ink drawings of profane themes, and a group of 89 drypoints, the majority preserved in the print room of the Rijksmuseum in Amsterdam. To this corpus many varied works of art have been added, including woodcuts, paintings, miniatures, sculptures and stained-glass windows. Over the past century debate concerning the Master's oeuvre as well as his identification has earned him the accolade of being the most argued-about German artist of the 15th century.

1. IDENTITY. The Master has been identified both with obscure artists, such as Martin Hess, Nicolaus Schit (*fl c.* 1500), Hans Hirtz, Heinrich Mang, Wolfgang Peurer and Nikolaus Nievergalt von Worms (*c.* 1450–1511), and with more famous names, such as Bartholomaus Zeitblom, Hans Holbein the elder, Matthias Grünewald and Wilhelm Pleydenwurff. None of these tentative identifications, however, is still accepted. The most likely candidate seems to be ERHARD REUWICH, a painter from Utrecht, but the differences between Reuwich's documented oeuvre and that of the Master are too numerous to make the proposed identification entirely convincing. All that can be deduced from the Master's work is that he worked in the Middle Rhine area, including Mainz and Heidelberg, and that he must have received commissions from noblemen and church authorities. Rather than attempting to identify him with a known artist, late 20th-century scholars have concentrated on describing his artistic personality as evidenced in the surviving work.

2. WORK.

(i) The drypoints. Apart from traditional religious themes, the 89 drypoints, the attribution of which has never been

seriously doubted, represent worldly subjects such as amorous couples, hunting scenes, noblemen, peasants, wild men etc—images that reflect with surprising directness a late medieval courtly culture of which little has been preserved. These prints form the best starting-point for a reconstruction of the Master's work and development. Altogether only 122 impressions of the drypoints are known. The Amsterdam group of 80 prints, 61 of which are unique impressions, comes from the 18th-century collection of Pieter Cornelis, Baron van Leyden (1717–88); their earlier provenance is unknown. The free manner of drawing and the spontaneous character of the prints—as well as the limited number of impressions—can be partly explained by the technique of DRYPOINT, in which the lines are drawn directly on to the metal plate with a sharp needle (leaving a ridge of metal, or burr, that initially retains the ink but quickly wears away). After a hesitant beginning, the artist succeeded in applying this technique, which was not otherwise used in the 15th century, with such precision and subtlety that the result differs little from the few silverpoint drawings also attributed to him (*see* §(iii) below).

None of the drypoints is dated, but they reveal a clear artistic development, from *c.* 1470 to 1490. The earliest

1. Housebook Master: *Young Man and Death*, drypoint, 141×87 mm, *c.* 1485–90 (Amsterdam, Rijksmuseum)

prints, such as *Samson and the Lion* (Lehrs, 1893–4, no. 5), datable *c.* 1470–75, are small in format, the drawing is hesitant and the composition simple. Yet these early works already display the Master's highly individual details in pose, dress and so on, features especially evident in the small prints of *Infants Playing* (L 59–61; *see* PRINTS, fig. 3) and the *Dog Scratching Himself* (L 78).

In the work of his mature middle phase he developed a greater sense of space, refinement and delicacy, which was combined with a more assured technique; this is nowhere more apparent than in prints such as *Solomon's Idolatry* (L 7), *Aristotle and Phyllis* (L 54) and the *Amorous Couple* (L 75), sheets that can be dated between 1480 and 1488. During this period the Master also produced several prints showing a wealthy and carefree courtly dreamworld, inhabited by slim, elegantly dressed youths. These seem to reflect an outmoded chivalric culture still fashionable at certain German courts. That the Master had contacts specifically with the royal court at Heidelberg is suggested by a drawing plausibly attributed to him in a manuscript translation of *Die Kinder von Limburg* (Heidelberg, Ubib., Cod. pal. germ. 87); the drawing, dated 1480, shows the moment at which the manuscript itself was presented to the Count Palatine Philip the Sincere (*reg* 1476–1508) by Johan van Soest, his court poet. Whether the drypoints were produced at this same court remains uncertain.

The transience of such a courtly life is depicted in a highly probing manner in the *Young Man and Death* (L 58; *see* fig. 1), one of the finest pieces from this period, which, like others, was drawn with a very fine drypoint needle. In sharp contrast to the idealized picture of courtly life is the negative, satirical manner in which peasants, tramps and other lowlife subjects are represented, especially in the prints with coats of arms (L 79–89). Themes such as 'Unequal Love' and the 'World turned upside down' are depicted for the first time in the Master's prints.

An unusual aspect of the religious prints is the emphasis on intimate details from the life of the Virgin and Christ. This approach played an important role in late medieval devotional practice and mysticism, linking the worshipper to the sacred event. In the touching and original *Holy Family by the Rosebush* (L 28), a crouching, half-hidden Joseph amuses the Child by rolling apples towards him. This print, generally thought to have inspired Dürer's engraving of the *Holy Family with the Dragonfly* (*c.* 1495; B. 44), is one of the Master's late works, *c.* 1490. Executed with less virtuosity and refinement than the earlier works, these show a sketchy and more painterly use of the drypoint.

(ii) The Housebook. This is a leather-bound volume, with 64 folios of fine parchment in 9 gatherings; it has been kept in Schloss Wolfegg in southern Germany since the 17th century. Besides pen drawings, some coloured, there are several miniatures. The title given to the manuscript in the 19th century is somewhat misleading, since the book contains little information about household matters—only one gathering deals with domestic remedies—but much more about military matters and mining, both accompanied by instructive technical drawings. These sections seem to have been intended for (and were probably written by) a munitions master. Preceding these technical

2. Housebook Master: *Luna*, pen and brown and black ink, 290×186 mm; from the Medieval Housebook, *c.* 1480 (Wolfegg, Schloss Wolfegg, Kupferstichkabinett, fol. 17a)

sections is a group of drawings of the planets and their children (fols 11*r*–41*r*) and another of courtly scenes (fols 18*v*–24*r*), each contained within one gathering. These sections were not originally from the same manuscript, and each of the three groups of illustrations has a characteristic style. Thus it is debated whether they are by a single artist.

The scenes of courtly life are partly coloured pen drawings that cover both sides of the page opening; in subject-matter and dress they correspond to the Master's secular prints, but the draughtsmanship is rather stereotyped and different from that of the drypoints and the drawings of the planets. Although the latter are largely based on earlier blockbook illustrations, the pen drawings represent the figures in an original and often humorous way. *Mercury* (fol. 16*r*), for instance, includes a schoolmaster flogging a pupil's bare bottom and a painter being embraced by his mistress while he paints the Virgin and St Catherine. Even within this group of drawings there are stylistic differences: the best ones, *Mars*, *Sol* and *Luna* (see fig. 2), seem closely related to the Master's mature drypoints both in figure type and manner of drawing; the others are more akin to his early prints.

(iii) Other attributions. Only a limited number of other works of art can be attributed to the Master with any certainty. These include two silverpoint drawings of an

Amorous Couple (both *c.* 1485; Berlin, Kupferstichkab.; Leipzig, Mus. Bild. Kst.), which are similar in style to the prints with courtly subjects as well as the drawings of *Sol, Luna* and *Mars*. A looser style is evident in two pen drawings (both Berlin, Kupferstichkab.): the *Striding Man* (*c.* 1490) and the historically important, but not entirely undisputed sheet with *Maximilian I at a Peace Banquet in Bruges, 16 May 1488*. Besides the dedication page of 1480 in *Die Kinder von Limburg*, the miniatures with the *Four Evangelists* in a Gospel Book (*c.* 1475–80; Cleveland, OH, Mus. A.) are also attributed to the Master.

Since the end of the 19th century most experts have assumed that the artist who made the drypoints and worked on the Housebook was primarily a painter; however, there has been little agreement concerning which paintings should be ascribed to him. The least doubtful seems to be the so-called Speyer *Passion* altarpiece, of which three panels, the central *Crucifixion*, the *Ecce homo* and *Christ before Caiaphas*, are preserved together in Freiburg im Breisgau (Augustinerm.); three others are dispersed: the *Resurrection* (Frankfurt am Main, Städel. Kstinst. & Städt. Gal.), *Christ Washing the Feet of the Disciples* (Berlin, Gemäldegal.) and the *Last Supper* (Berlin, Bodemus.). Not only are the figure types and the lively manner of painting reminiscent of the Master's mature work of *c.* 1480–85, but the detailed underdrawing revealed by infra-red reflectography shows close parallels with the crosshatching seen in the prints.

The *Resurrection*, in particular, shows the painter at his best, with a lively manner of drawing and a rich and powerful colour scheme. Less original are the nine panels of the so-called Mainz *Life of the Virgin* (one dated 1505; Mainz, Landesmus.), which includes images related to late prints by the Master. Probably only the best of the panels, such as the *Nativity* and the *Adoration of the Magi*, are autograph, the rest being workshop products, possibly executed after the Master's death. Less doubtful is the authenticity of the famous *Amorous Couple* (*c.* 1484; Gotha, Schloss Friedenstein); both its style and subject-matter—an ideal picture of 'courtly' love—fit in well with the Master's work.

The Master was a major influence in the region of the Middle Rhine. Besides paintings there are many works in stained glass that reflect his subjects and style, although it remains uncertain whether he actually produced stained glass or merely provided the designs. The stained-glass panel of the *Virgin and Child on the Crescent Moon* (*c.* 1485–90; New York, Cloisters) is very closely related to the style of his prints, while *A Patrician's Tournament* (*c.* 1480; Germany, priv. col., see 1985 exh. cat., no. 135), a window possibly from the house of the Alten-Limpurg Society in Frankfurt, is strongly reminiscent of the courtly scenes in the Housebook.

BIBLIOGRAPHY

M. Lehrs: *Der Meister des Amsterdamer Kabinetts* (Berlin, 1893–4) [L]

H. T. Bossert and W. F. Storck: *Das mittelalterliche Hausbuch nach dem Originale im Besitze des Fürsten von Waldburg-Wolfegg-Waldsee* (Leipzig, 1912)

M. Lehrs: *Geschichte und kritischer Katalog des deutschen, niederländischen und französischen Kupferstichs im XV. Jahrhundert*, 9 vols (Vienna, 1908–34/R Nedeln, 1969), viii, pp. 1–164

E. Graf zu Solms-Laubach: 'Der Hausbuch-Meister', *Städel-Jb.*, ix (1935–6), pp. 13–93

J. Graf Waldburg-Wolfegg: *Das mittelalterliche Hausbuch* (Munich, 1957)

A. Stange: *Der Hausbuchmeister* (Baden-Baden and Strasbourg, 1958)

J. Campbell Hutchison: *The Hausbuchmeister: Sources of his Style and Iconography* (diss., U. WI, 1964)

——: *The Master of the Housebook* (New York, 1972) [complete bibliog.]

J. P. Filedt Kok: 'The Prints of the Master of the Amsterdam Cabinet', *Apollo*, cxvii (1983), pp. 427–36

Livelier than Life: The Master of the Amsterdam Cabinet or the Housebook Master, ca. 1470–1500 (exh. cat. by J. P. Filedt Kok and others, Amsterdam, Rijksmus., 1985)

D. Hess: *Meister um das mittelalterliche Hausbuch: Studien zur Hausbuchmeisterfrage* (Mainz, 1994)

J. P. FILEDT KOK

Master of the Hutz Portrait. *See under* MERKLIN, KONRAD.

Illustratore (*fl c.* 1330–47). Italian illuminator. Erbach von Fürstenau first distinguished this artist from Niccolò di Giacomo da Bologna, calling him the Pseudo-Niccolò. The name 'Illustratore' was proposed by Longhi, but hypotheses as to his identity (which have included Andrea da Bologna) have proved difficult to substantiate.

Around 1330 the Illustratore collaborated with an artist working in an archaic style on a copy of Dante's *Divine Comedy* (Florence, Bib. Riccardiana, MS. 1005; Milan, Bib. N. Braidense, MS. AG.XII). The initials and small miniatures in the Florence volume, the one executed by the Illustratore, have stocky, expressive figures of great narrative force, which distinguish the illustrations as some of the most lively examples made for Dante's works. The *Infortiatum* of Justinian (Cesena, Bib. Malatestiana, MS. S.IV.2) and the *Accursius, Glossa in codicem* (Rome, Vatican, Bib. Apostolica, MS. Vat. lat. 1430) are also from this early period, while the *Decretals* of Gregory IX (Rome, Vatican, Bib. Apostolica, MS. Vat. lat. 1389) and the *Liber sextus decretatium* (Markt St Florian, Stiftsbib., MS. III.7), decorated for Bishop Albert von Passau (*d* 1342), date from *c.* 1335.

The Illustratore's narrative style is closely linked to that of Giotto, but it shows the impact of the strongly expressive manner of contemporary Bolognese painting. The page decoration is sombre (in the tradition of Bolognese illumination of the 1320s), ornamented by small gold bosses, sometimes with 'tails' attached. The illuminations at the head of the texts either have frames with some architectural detail or figures that gesture to others in the margins, enlivening the whole page. In the earliest works, the background is decorated with gold foliage on blue. Later, wide bands of decoration on a blue background are inserted in the margins between the text and the gloss, an arrangement also used by the Master of 1328, with whom the Illustratore collaborated. At the same time the foliage and tailed gold bosses become less common. The traditional decoration of the initials with small male and female heads, in both text and gloss, is usually the work of assistants.

The Illustratore's narrative skill is seen in the *Decretals* of Gratian (Rome, Vatican, Bib. Apostolica, MS. Vat. lat. 1366; see fig.), executed *c.* 1335–40 in collaboration with the Master of 1328 (*see* §II below) and the so-called Master of the Paris Gratian, named after another copy of this work (Paris, Bib. N., MS. Nouv. acq. lat. 2508). Other manuscripts dating from the same period, the *Institutions* (Paris, Bib. N., MS. lat. 14343) and the *Accursius, Glossa*

Illustratore in collaboration with the Master of 1328: *Girl Refusing to Enter the Convent*; miniature from Gratian: *Decretals, c.* 1335–40 (Rome, Vatican, Biblioteca Apostolica, MS. Vat. lat. 1366, fol. 198*r*)

in Codicem (Rome, Vatican, Bib. Apostolica, MS. Vat. lat. 1409), also show the participation of the latter. Other texts revealing the collaboration of artists working in the style of the Illustratore are often of poorer quality (e.g. a copy of Gratian's *Decretals*, Munich, Bayer. Staatsbib., Clm. 23552). The Illustratore's collaboration with artists with individual styles gradually decreased, however, and manuscript decoration became organized within a single workshop, with the assistants copying the style of the Master.

The *Constitutions of Clement V* (1343; Padua, Bib. Capitolare, MS. A25) contain a large miniature decorated by the Illustratore with *Scenes from the Life of St Catherine of Alexandria*; its companion volume, the *Decretals of Boniface VIII* (Padua, Bib. Capitolare, MS. A24), has a page illuminated with *Scenes from the Life of St Stephen, King of Hungary*. Both manuscripts were probably decorated in Padua, and their style suggests renewed contact with the work of Giotto.

The exact date at which the Illustratore ceased to be active as an illuminator, once he had handed his workshop over to the Master of 1346, named after the Statutes of the Drapers' Guild of that year (Bologna, Archv Stato., MS. min. 12), is difficult to establish. Some illuminations, such as those in two copies of Gratian's *Decretals* (Rome, Vatican, Bib. Apostolica, MS. Urb. lat. 161, fol. 125*v* and Geneva, Bib. Pub. & U., MS. lat. 60, fol. 127*r*), demonstrate

his continued presence, and he may have become involved in the administration of the workshop. During this phase, his workshop returned to motifs he had earlier abandoned, such as the tailed gold bosses.

The choice of texts illustrated reflects the changes in patronage after the repeal of the University's privileges in 1337. Examples are the Missal of Cardinal Bertrand de Deux (*d* 1355; Rome, Vatican, Bib. Apostolica, MS. Cap. 63B); a medical treatise by Galvano da Levanto (Rome, Vatican, Bib. Apostolica, MS. Vat. lat. 2463); the *Compendium moralis philosophiae* of Luca Manelli (*c.* 1346–8; Paris, Bib. N., MS. lat. 6467), dedicated to Bruzio Visconti; and the *Metamorphoses* of Apuleius (Rome, Vatican, Bib. Apostolica, MS. Vat. lat. 2194). These last two works show stylistic affinities between the Illustratore's workshop under the Master of 1346 and the early career of Niccolò di Giacomo da Bologna. A late work of sustained quality from the workshop is a copy of St Jerome, which belonged to Bishop Giovanni di Andrea (1346–7; Bologna, Coll. Spagna, MS. 273). There are no further traces of the workshop's activity after the Black Death of 1348.

BIBLIOGRAPHY

A. Erbach von Fürstenau: 'La miniatura bolognese: Studi su Niccolò di Giacomo', *L'Arte*, xiv (1911), pp. 1–12
Guida alla mostra della pittura bolognese del trecento (exh. cat. by R. Longhi, Bologna, Pin. N., 1950), pp. 11–24 (15); repr. in *Opere complete di Roberto Longhi*, vi (Florence, 1973), pp. 155–87 (159–60)
F. Flores d'Arcais: 'Le miniature del Riccardiano 1005 e del Braidense AG.XII.2', *Stor. A.*, 33 (1978), pp. 105–14
A. Conti: *La miniatura bolognese: Scuole e botteghe* (Bologna, 1981), pp. 87–96
Dix siècles d'enluminure italienne (exh. cat. by F. Avril, Paris, Bib. N., 1984), pp. 79–84

ALESSANDRO CONTI

Master of the Imhoff Altar (*fl c.* 1410–20). German painter. He is named after an altarpiece (*c.* 1418–22) commissioned by Konrad Imhoff (*d* 1449) for the Lorenzkirche in Nuremberg, where the central panel with the *Coronation of the Virgin* and wings with *Apostles* are still preserved, though partially disassembled. The donor appears with the first three of his four wives on the inner wings, flanking the *Coronation*. Originally on the back of the altarpiece was the *Man of Sorrows, with the Virgin and St John* (Nuremberg, Ger. Nmus.), now generally regarded as the work of the Master of the Bamberg Altar. The work of the Imhoff painter has been subsumed (Stange, 1958, 1978) under the name of the Master of the Deichsler Altarpiece, known from the panels of two surviving wings (Berlin, Gemäldegal.). Earlier attributions of both the Imhoff Altar and Deichsler Altarpiece to BERTHOLD LANDAUER are based only on his well-documented activity in Nuremberg at that period. The Deichsler panels, which must predate the Imhoff Altar by five or ten years, show the hand of an artist schooled on Bohemian painting of *c.* 1400. The Imhoff Altar, while still representative of the 'soft style', reveals a shift towards a more firm and spare manner of painting and the use of stronger colours, qualities that in part distinguish the painting of Nuremberg in this period.

BIBLIOGRAPHY

Thieme–Becker

H. Thode: *Die Malerschule von Nürnberg im 14. und 15. Jahrhundert in ihrer Entwicklung bis auf Dürer* (Frankfurt am Main, 1891), pp. 19–22

C. Gebhardt: *Die Anfänge der Tafelmalerei in Nürnberg*, Stud. Kstgesch., ciii (1908), pp. 31–5

E. Lutze and E. Wiegand: *Die Gemälde des 13. bis 16. Jahrhunderts*, Nuremberg, Ger. Nmus. cat. (Leipzig, 1937), pp. 92–3, no. 116

A. Stange: *Deutsche Malerei der Gotik*, ix (Munich, 1958), pp. 9–12 [under Meister des Deichsler-Altars]

H. T. Musper: *Gotische Malerei nördlich der Alpen* (Cologne, 1961), pp. 140–41

A. Stange, with P. Strieder and H. Härtle: *Kritisches Verzeichnis der deutschen Tafelbilder vor Dürer*, iii, ed. N. Lieb (Munich, 1978), pp. 25–9

E. Ullmann: *Geschichte der deutschen Kunst, 1350–1470* (Leipzig, 1981), p. 249

Gothic and Renaissance Art in Nuremberg, 1300–1550 (exh. cat., New York, Met., 1986), pp. 82, 152–4

C. Schleif: *Donatio et Memoria: Stifter, Stiftungen und Motivationen an Beispielen aus der Lorenzkirche in Nürnberg* (Munich, 1990), pp. 52–4

P. Strieder: *Tafelmalerei in Nürnberg, 1350–1550* (Königstein im Taunus, 1993), pp. 26–9

CHARLES TALBOT

Master of the Immaculate Conception. *See* FREDIANI, VINCENZO.

Ippolita Master (*fl c.* 1459–65). Italian illuminator. Numerous manuscripts survive by this Master, who was mainly active at the Sforza court in Milan. In 1459 he was employed on the decoration of the *Trattato di caccia e falconeria* (Chantilly, Mus. Condé, MS. 368/1375) for Francesco Sforza, Duke of Milan. In the same and subsequent years he was commissioned to decorate other manuscripts, mostly Classical texts (Paris, Bib. N., MSS lat. 7703 and 7779) for the education of the young Galeazzo Maria Sforza. The *De practica seu arte tripudi* ('Of the practice or art of dancing') by Guglielmo da Pesaro (Paris, Bib. N., MS. it. 973), illuminated in 1463, is also dedicated to Galeazzo.

The Ippolita Master is linked with a group of manuscripts (Paris, Bib. N., MS. it. 1712; U. Valencia, Bib., MS. 780) commissioned in 1465 by Francesco Sforza and Bianca Maria Visconti as a wedding gift for their daughter Ippolita. In these and in the other manuscripts mentioned he shows himself to be much indebted to Late Gothic Lombard illumination, in particular that of the MASTER OF THE VITAE IMPERATORUM (*see* below). His manuscripts also show a decidedly humanistic taste in their more orderly coordination of text and decoration. The Master's predilection for strong, brilliant colours and orderly, symmetrical compositions, in which the landscape is always subsidiary to the narrative, and above all his striking decorative taste mark him as a pleasing and gracious illuminator justly favoured by the ducal family.

BIBLIOGRAPHY
R. Cipriani: 'Maestro di Ippolita', *Arte lombarda dai Visconti agli Sforza* (Milan, 1958), pp. 89–92

E. Pellegrin: *La Bibliothèque des Visconti et des Sforza ducs de Milan* (Florence and Paris, 1969), pp. 56–7

A. C. de la Mare: 'Further Italian Illuminated Manuscripts in the Bodleian Library', *La miniatura italiana tra gotico e rinascimento: Atti del II congreso di storia della miniatura italiana: Cortona, 1983*, pp. 145, 148

F. Avril: *Dix Siècles d'enluminure italienne* (Paris, 1984), pp. 152–5

20 Illuminated Manuscripts from the Celebrated Collection of William Waldorf Astor, First Viscount Astor (sale cat., London, Sotheby, 21 June 1988), pp. 48–54

G. Toscano: 'La librairie des rois d'Aragon à Naples', *Bull. Biblioph.*, ii (1993), pp. 265–83

The Painted Page: Italian Renaissance Book Illumination, 1450–1550 (exh. cat., ed. J. J. G. Alexander; London, RA, 1994)

MILVIA BOLLATI

Master of Irrsdorf. *See* §III: MASTER I.P. below.

Isaac Master (*fl* Assisi, *c.* 1290s). Italian painter. His name is derived from the frescoes depicting *Isaac Blessing Jacob* and *Isaac and Esau* (each 3×3 m; see fig.) in the Upper Church of S Francesco, Assisi; the frescoes occupy the middle register of the third bay from the crossing on the north wall of the nave (*see* ASSISI, §II, 2(iii)). By assigning these scenes to the young Florentine Giotto, Thode (1885), while refuting Vasari's attribution to Cimabue, sparked the controversy over the identity and origin of the Isaac Master. Subsequent attempts to identify him with either the Roman artist Pietro Cavallini or with another Florentine, Gaddo di Zanobi Gaddi (see Mather), have been unpersuasive. Present consensus is divided between scholars accepting the attribution to GIOTTO and those advocating that the Isaac Master came from Rome, where he had absorbed the art of Cavallini. Notwithstanding the effort to assert Giotto's primacy in Assisi, iconographic and stylistic details in the Isaac Master's frescoes attest to his Roman background.

The design of the Isaac scenes and their horizontal left-to-right arrangement within an Old Testament cycle reflect the organization of such cycles in Early Christian basilicas in Rome. The figure of the aged, blind and partially recumbent Isaac that commands the foregrounds of both episodes was ultimately derived from a mid-5th-century fresco, *Isaac Blessing Jacob*, once embellishing S Paolo fuori le Mura, Rome. This fresco (destr. but reproduced in a 17th-century watercolour: Rome, Vatican, Bib. Apostolica, MS. Barb. lat. 4406, fol. 39*r*) had been renewed by Cavallini probably during the 1280s. Between *c.* 1291 and 1293 he painted a similar fresco in the Roman church of S Cecilia in Trastevere. Further reliance on Cavallini for

Isaac Master: *Isaac and Esau* (mid-1290s), fresco, 3×3 m, Upper Church, S Francesco, Assisi

compositional models appears in the Isaac Master's transformation of St Anne from Cavallini's *Birth of the Virgin* mosaic (early 1290s; Rome, S Maria in Trastevere) into the resting Isaac. The postures of St Anne's two female attendants were reversed and the figures recast as Esau and Rebecca in *Isaac and Esau*. Even the overall interior from the mosaic was appropriated. Against these elements derived from Cavallini, the Isaac Master's sensitive use of light accentuated the dramatic emotions of the figures. Though composed of broad, smooth, continuous brushstrokes, the even drapery folds have a three-dimensional character resembling late 13th-century sculpture by Arnolfo di Cambio in Rome and Orvieto. An inherent classicism also points to a Roman background for the Isaac Master. A reclining River God as an additional source for the patriarchal Isaac represents his most conspicuous borrowing from the Antique.

The absence of documents prevents the specific dating of the Isaac Master's Assisi frescoes. Despite Stubblebine's radically late allocation to the 1320s, these scenes are usually associated with the demand made by the first Franciscan Pope, Nicholas IV, in his Bull of 14 May 1288, that the decoration of S Francesco be completed. The Isaac Master's depiction on the nave vault beside the entrance of the *Four Latin Doctors of the Church*, whose cult Pope Boniface VIII (*reg* 1294–1303) promulgated in the *Liber Sextus* of 1298, does not necessarily provide a *terminus post quem*. White's examination of the frescoes in the Upper Church established that work on the Old and New Testament cycles along the nave followed the painting of the choir, crossing and transepts begun *c*. 1280 by Cimabue. The Isaac Master joined the project on the third bay and proceeded towards the inside wall of the façade, completing the cycles. This sequence generally went from west to east but not without interruption. The Isaac Master overpainted sections of the *Presentation in the Temple* in the third bay of the south nave wall, which implies some delay before he began work on the decoration during the mid-1290s.

There is a rudimentary perspective in the *Isaac* scenes, where a foreshortened, boxlike structure, open at the front, encloses figures seen from a constant high viewpoint, and furniture is shown foreshortened. These features present a pictorial space heralding the advances of the Master of the Legend of St Francis in the fresco cycle below. The Isaac Master's technique contributed equally to the development of fresco painting. Wall surfaces were divided into areas frequently following the figures' contours drawn on rough plaster (*arriccio*). These work-stages (*giornate*), paintable in one day, would be covered with a thin layer of wet plaster (*intenazo*) upon which fresh colours were applied directly. This procedure made the Isaac Master one of the earliest practitioners of the true fresco technique (*see* FRESCO, §1) formulated during the last quarter of the 13th century in Rome.

In 1980 areas of the walls that had suffered considerable paint loss because of humidity were stabilized to check further deterioration. In addition to the two renowned *Isaac* scenes and the *Four Latin Doctors of the Church*, *Joseph Lowered into the Well* and *Joseph before his Brothers*, on the north wall of the nave, and *Pentecost*, on the inside wall of the façade, are among the better-preserved frescoes

designed and executed by the Isaac Master with workshop assistance. These images exemplify the soundest attributions to him.

The Isaac Master was one of the Roman painters active in Assisi who brought a classically inspired art to the mother church of the Franciscans. His work transcended the schematic 13th-century Italo-Byzantine style and introduced figures imbued with human qualities set inside receding space. Such features had a distinct influence on Giotto. The Isaac Master thus personified a major stylistic transition that altered the course of Late Gothic Italian painting.

BIBLIOGRAPHY

Thieme–Becker

G. Vasari: *Vite* (1550, rev. 2/1568); ed. G. Milanesi (1878–85), i, pp. 252–3

L. da Pietralunga: *Descrizione della basilica di San Francesco e di altri santuari di Assisi* [MS.; *c*. 1570–80]; ed. P. Scarpellini (Treviso, 1982), pp. 399–427, 453–8 [bibliog.]

H. Thode: *Franz von Assisi und die Anfänge der Kunst der Renaissance in Italien* (Berlin, 1885, rev. 2/1904), pp. 240–54

A. Venturi: *La basilica di Assisi* (Rome, 1908), pp. 105–14

A. Nicholson: 'The Roman School at Assisi', *A. Bull.*, xii (1930), pp. 270–300

F. J. Mather jr: *The Isaac Master: A Reconstruction of the Work of Gaddo Gaddi* (Princeton, 1932)

R. Oertel: 'Wandmalerei und Zeichnung in Italien: Die Anfänge der Entwurfszeichnung und ihre monumentalen Vorstufen', *Mitt. Ksthist. Inst. Florenz*, v (1940), pp. 217–314

P. Toesca: *Gli affreschi del Vecchio e del Nuovo Testamento nella Chiesa Superiore del santuario di Assisi* (Florence, 1948)

R. Oertel: *Die Frühzeit der italienischen Malerei* (Stuttgart, 1953, rev. 2/1966); Eng. trans. as *Early Italian Painting* (London, 1968)

J. White: *The Birth and Rebirth of Pictorial Space* (London, 1957, rev. 3/1987)

M. Meiss: *Giotto and Assisi* (New York, 1960)

——: *The Great Age of Fresco: Discoveries, Recoveries and Survivals* (New York, 1970), pp. 38–9

A. Smart: *The Assisi Problem and the Art of Giotto: A Study of the Legend of St Francis in the Upper Church of San Francesco, Assisi* (London, 1971, rev. New York, 2/1983)

——: 'Some Unpublished Copies of Frescoes at Assisi', *Apollo*, xcix (1974), pp. 228–31

H. Belting: *Die Oberkirche von San Francesco in Assisi: Ihre Dekoration als Aufgabe und die Genese einer neuen Wandmalerei* (Berlin, 1977)

P. Hetherington: *Pietro Cavallini: A Study in the Art of Late Medieval Rome* (London, 1979), p. 157

J. White: 'Cimabue and Assisi: Working Methods and Art Historical Consequences', *A. Hist.*, iv (1981), pp. 355–83; also in: *Studies in Late Medieval Italian Art* (London, 1984), pp. 135–65

S. Nessi: *La basilica di San Francesco in Assisi e la sua documentazione storica* (Assisi, 1982)

C. Brandi: *Giotto* (Milan, 1983)

L. Bellosi: *La pecora di Giotto* (Turin, 1985)

J. Poeschke: *Die Kirche San Francesco in Assisi und ihre Wandmalereien* (Munich, 1985) [excellent pls]

J. H. Stubblebine: *Assisi and the Rise of Vernacular Art* (New York, 1985)

E. Castelnuovo, ed.: *La pittura in Italia: Il duecento e il trecento* (Milan, 1986) [vol. ii contains articles by E. Lunghi and F. Todini]

A. M. Romanini: 'Gli occhi di Isacco: Classicismo e curiosità scientifica tra Arnolfo di Cambio e Giotto', *A. Med.*, i (1987), pp. 1–56

ADRIAN S. HOCH

Master of Jacob Bellaert (*fl c*. 1484). North Netherlandish woodcutter. He was one of the best woodcut designers in the late 15th-century Netherlands and worked on books printed by Jacob Bellaert at Haarlem between 1484 and 1486. His designs are notable for their painterly style, preoccupation with natural phenomena and lively narrative. The borrowing of figures, motifs and compositional schemes from paintings attributed to the Master of the Tiburtine Sibyl supports the conclusion that his designs originated in that Master's workshop. After Bellaert's press ceased operation in 1486, the Bellaert Master's style became the dominant influence in Antwerp book illustration and remained so into the 1490s.

BIBLIOGRAPHY

Hollstein: *Dut. & Flem.*
J. Snyder: 'The Early Haarlem School of Painting, I', *A. Bull.*, xlii (1960), pp. 39–55 (53–5)

THOMAS J. GOMBAR

Master of Jacques de Besançon [Chief Associate of Maître François; Jacques de Besançon] (*fl c.* 1480–98). French illuminator. He was the last in a succession of three artists who headed the most prolific workshop for book illumination in Paris in the second half of the 15th century. His name has been subjected to considerable change since Durrieu first studied this school (1892) and called the master responsible for its comprehensive development Jacques de Besançon. Durrieu attributed nearly 50 manuscripts, produced over a period of more than 40 years, and illustrations in 28 printed books to the illuminator of a miniature depicting *St John and the Poisoned Cup* in an *Office of St John* (Paris, Bib. Mazarine, MS. 461, fol. 9*r*). A colophon (fol. 33*v*) in this book records the donation of the work to the confraternity of St John the Evangelist by Jacques de Besançon 'enlumineur' and 'batonnier' of the said confraternity, which was dedicated to the craft of the book. In 1898 Thuasne cited a letter written by Robert Gaguin in August 1473, which referred to the completion of an illuminated *City of God* for Charles de Gaucourt by the 'egregius pictor Franciscus'. Identified through its coats of arms as Paris, Bib. N., MSS fr. 18–19, this had been among the manuscripts attributed to Jacques de Besançon; Durrieu therefore re-named his artist Maître François. Spencer (1963, 1974), however, distinguished three chronologically successive artistic personalities as responsible for the workshop, a theory that has received general acceptance: the MASTER OF JEAN ROLIN (*see* above), *c.* 1440–65; MAÎTRE FRANÇOIS ('pictor franciscus'), *c.* 1460–80; and the Chief Associate of Maître François, *c.* 1480–98. Sterling (1990) and Reynaud (1993 exh. cat.) restored the name Jacques de Besançon to the last of the trio, although Reynaud modified it to the Master of Jacques de Besançon, arguing that it is not clear whether the donor of the Mazarine *Office of St John* actually executed its two miniatures or whether his title 'enlumineur' referred specifically to the craft of embellishing initials, as Durrieu, Spencer and others have interpreted it; this would mean that Jacques had commissioned the miniatures for his confraternity.

The Master of Jacques de Besançon used the iconographical and compositional schemes established by his predecessors. Certain characteristics, however, distinguish his style from that of Maître François: for example, more elongated and willowy figures with softer and smoother features; a lighter palette in which blond and rose tones are more predominant and are offset by broad expanses of blue and gold; and a more static, even monumental quality of composition in contrast to the dramatic liveliness of Maître François's work. The Master's patrons included monarchs and their immediate households, as well as wealthy aristocrats and bureaucrats. Among his most

splendid works are: a French translation of the *Golden Legend* (*c.* 1480–90; Paris, Bib. N., MSS 244–5) in which he collaborated with Maître François, further elaborating themes borrowed from contemporary theatre, such as the *Procès de paradis*, which had become a hallmark of the workshop; a Greek Lectionary (*c.* 1480–82; Paris, Bib. N., MS. gr. 55) for Cardinal Charles of Bourbon; the *Statutes of the Order of St Michael* (*c.* 1492–4; Vienna, Österreich. Nbib., Cod. 2637), possibly for Charles VIII; and a resplendent Missal (*c.* 1492; Paris, Bib. Mazarine, MS. 412), the illustration of which incorporates an unusual number of typological and allegorical themes and is largely based on a repertory inherited from Maître François. The Master was also employed by the publisher Antoine Verard and painted numerous frontispieces in presentation copies of printed books for royal and other wealthy patrons.

BIBLIOGRAPHY

Thieme–Becker: 'Jacques de Besançon'
P. Durrieu: *Un Grand Enlumineur parisien au XVe siècle: Jacques de Besançon et son oeuvre* (Paris, 1892)
L. Thuasne: 'François Fouquet et les miniatures de la *Cité de Dieu* de Saint Augustin', *Rev. Bib.*, viii (1898), pp. 33–57
L. Thuasne, ed.: *Roberti Gaguini epistolae et orationes*, i (Paris, 1903), p. 225
E. P. Spencer: 'L'horloge de sapience', *Scriptorium*, xvii, (1963), pp. 277–99; xix (1965), pp. 104–8
O. Pächt and D. Thoss: *Französischen Schule* (1974), I/i of *Die illuminierten Handschriften und Inkunabeln der Österreichischen Nationalbibliothek* (Vienna, 1974), pp. 80–93, 152–61
E. P. Spencer: 'Dom Luis de Busco's Psalter', *Gatherings in Honor of Dorothy E. Miner* (Baltimore, 1974), pp. 227–40
——: 'Le Lectionnaire du Cardinal Charles II de Bourbon', *Doss. Archéol.*, xvi (1976), pp. 124–9
The Last Flowering: French Painting in Manuscripts, 1420–1530, from American Collections (exh. cat. by J. Plummer, New York, Pierpont Morgan Lib., 1982)
C. Sterling: *La Peinture médiévale à Paris, 1300–1500*, ii, (Paris, 1990), pp. 177–80, 215–29
Les Manuscrits à Peintures en France, 1440–1520 (exh. cat. by F. Avril and N. Reynaud, Paris, Bib. N., 1993–4)

MARGARET M. MANION

Master of James IV of Scotland (*fl c.* 1500–30). South Netherlandish illuminator. He was named by Winkler after a Book of Hours (Vienna, Österreich. Nbib., Cod. 1897) with a full-page miniature of James IV of Scotland, kneeling at a prie-dieu under a green canopy, commended by his patron saint (fol. 24*v*; see fig.). He is turned towards an altar that has an antependium showing the Scottish royal coat of arms and the motto *In my defens* and is crowned by a painted retable with a half-figure of the Saviour on the central panel. The counterpart to this miniature, towards the end of the book (fol. 243*v*), shows the Queen, Margaret Tudor, in prayer before a vision of the Mother of God. There is also a page with a coat of arms (fol. 14*v*). The work must have been produced between the marriage of the royal couple in 1503 and the death of James IV in 1513. However, the book presents many problems: the folios with the patrons' portraits are not integrated in the gatherings as was usual in Flanders, and they may have been later additions. Yet, because the initials and mottoes of the pair appear in other borders of the book, it must have been made for James and Margaret, even if the decision to include full-page portraits was made only after the original commission. It is also curious that the portrait miniatures were produced by different artists.

Master of James IV of Scotland: *James IV of Scotland in Prayer with St James*, 200×140 mm; miniature from the Hours of James IV and Margaret Tudor, *c.* 1503–15 (Vienna, Österreichische Nationalbibliothek, Cod. 1897, fol. 24*v*)

The drawing on fol. 243*v* is significantly softer than that on fol. 24*v*, with lighter contours; the heads are less exaggerated and the eyes are smaller than those in fol. 24*v* and are not defined with strong outlines. The difference is also evident in the depiction of buildings. Winkler recognized this at first, although he later agreed with Durrieu in attributing both pictures to the same painter. In fact only the portrait of the King was produced by the Master of James IV of Scotland, who therefore owes his name to this miniature and not to the manuscript as a whole. At least two more miniatures of Codex 1897, however, can be attributed with certainty to the same artist: the *Rest on the Flight into Egypt* (fol. 104*v*) and *Christ among the Doctors* (fol. 109*v*). The latter miniature follows a model by Simon Marmion (Naples, Bib. N., MS. I.B.51, fol. 289*v*).

While the Master of James IV of Scotland made only a minor contribution to the Book of Hours that gave him his name, other works were produced almost entirely by him (London, BL, Add. MS. 35313), and he contributed largely to extensive group efforts such as the Spinola Book of Hours (Malibu, CA, Getty Mus., MS. 83) and the Grimani Breviary (Venice, Bib. N. Marciana, MS. lat. I.

99). His most important contribution to illumination in Ghent and Bruges seems to have been in developing an almost symmetrical layout for important text openings: as well as the usual full-page picture on the *verso*, a large miniature was added to the top of the facing *recto*. The text was reduced to a few—often only two—lines. Borders with matching motifs complete the unified character of the page opening. In the Spinola Book of Hours the Master of James IV of Scotland went further and placed the few opening lines of text in equal areas on *recto* and *verso*, thus achieving the greatest possible symmetry in format. When historiated borders are also incorporated, as in the Spinola Book of Hours, he was able to use almost the whole surface of the double-page spread for skilfully interwoven arrangements and figure compositions, in which the aesthetic boundaries between miniature, text and border are cleverly reinterpreted.

The question of whether the Master of James IV of Scotland can be identified with Gerard Horenbout (*see* HORENBOUT, (1)) has long been discussed. Although the only documented work by Horenbout, the Sforza Book of Hours in London (BL, Add. MS. 34294), is stylistically quite different from the works of the Master of James IV of Scotland, it is a special case because of the circumstances of the commission. Dogaer agreed with the identification, while Plotzek and Kren weighed up the evidence without reaching a decision.

BIBLIOGRAPHY
P. Durrieu: 'Les Heures de Jacques IV, Roi d'Ecosse', *Gaz. B.-A.*, n. s. 5, iii (1921), pp. 197–212
——: *La Miniature flamande* (Brussels, 1921), p. 70
F. Winkler: 'Neuentdeckte Altniederländer, ii: Gerard Horenbout', *Pantheon*, xvi/31 (1943), pp. 54–64
L. MacFarlane: 'The Book of Hours of James IV and Margaret Tudor', *Innes Rev.*, xi (1960), pp. 3–20
A. von Euw and J. M. Plotzek: *Die Handschriften der Sammlung Ludwig*, ii (Cologne, 1982), pp. 256–85, figs 387–468
Renaissance Painting in Manuscripts: Treasures from the British Library (exh. cat., ed. T. Kren; Malibu, CA, Getty Mus.; New York, Pierpont Morgan Lib.; London, BL; 1984), pp. 40–48, 63–8
G. Dogaer: *Flemish Miniature Painting in the 15th and 16th Centuries* (Amsterdam, 1987), pp. 161–7
F. Unterkircher: *Das Gebetbuch Jakobs IV. von Schottland und seiner Gemahlin Margaret Tudor* (Graz, 1987) [facs. edn]
                                                    BODO BRINKMANN

Master of the Jarves Cassoni. *See* APOLLONIO DI GIOVANNI.

Master of Jean de Mauléon. *See under* §II: THE 1520s HOURS WORKSHOP.

Master of the Jean de Sy Bible. *See* MASTER OF THE BOQUETEAUX above.

Master of Jean Rolin [wrongly known as the Master of the Horloge de Sapience] (*fl c.* 1440–65). Illuminator, active in France. This anonymous master was named by Spencer (1963) after his work in manuscripts that belonged to or were associated with Cardinal Jean II Rolin (1408–83), third son of Nicolas Rolin, Chancellor of Burgundy: the Missals in Autun (Autun, Bib. Mun., MSS 108A and 114A) and Lyon (Lyon, Bib. Mun., MS. 517). Certain elements in the Rolin Master's style may derive from the work of Jan van Eyck and even from that of Rogier van der Weyden, but he appears to have been trained in a

Parisian atelier. His work is found with that of an illuminator working in the style of the Bedford Master in a Book of Hours in London (BL, Add. MS. 25695) and with the Bedford Master himself in another Book of Hours in Vienna (Österreich. Nbib., Cod. 1840; see fig.). The Rolin Master's compositional structures are often archaic, and formats in Missals and Books of Hours (e.g. the Book of Hours in Baltimore, MD, Walters A.G., MS. Walters 251) recall those of the Boucicaut and the Bedford Masters. The layouts in an *Horloge de sapience* (Brussels, Bib. Royale Albert 1er, MS. IV 111) are more imaginative. The 34 miniatures in this French version of the *Horologium sapientiae* by the Dominican mystic Heinrich Seuse, alias Suso (*c.* 1300–66), are the epitome of the Rolin Master's style.

The Master's use and control of space is measured. Inanimate objects are clearly separated from human forms, horizon lines are consistently set high and landscapes are panoramic and realistic. They characteristically include formal hedgerows and quinquepartite clumps of ground-hugging ferns, while the densely foliated, stumpy trees are placed in regimented lines. Rocky outcrops leaning to the right and lit from the left are placed in the middle ground, and paths meander over undulating terrain to the crests of hills. Buildings are firmly and precisely drawn. Sparsely lit rear chambers, narrow passageways and curious spiral staircases often add a touch of mystery to the Master's interior views, especially when they are glimpsed through doorways. The painter's interest and attention to detail are also apparent in clothing, cloths and wall hangings. Characters of high social rank have elegant physiques and are generally well proportioned. Their heads have broad cheek-bones and generous temples, small mouths and chins and boldly drawn ears, accented with two dots. In contrast, people of lower social rank are shown as short, with low foreheads and thick and prominent noses. Attempts to show faces in profile or from an oblique angle are often unsuccessful. Throughout his works the artist used brilliant colours and might juxtapose a figure wearing a vermilion gown and blue cloak with a boldly patterned red and gold cloth of honour or with an intricately designed green tiled floor. Mixed hues fascinated him, particularly shades of grey tinted with such colours as violet, citrus-green and soft orange. The Master's concerns were more aesthetic than naturalistic or expressive, and he appears to have influenced contemporary artists such as the Master of Vienna (Vienna, Österreich. Nbib., Cod. s.n. 13237), the Master of Wolfenbüttel (Wolfenbüttel, Herzog August Bib., Cod. Guelf. 32.6 Aug. 2°) and the prolific Maître François.

Master of Jean Rolin: *St Luke*, 127×67 mm; miniature from a Book of Hours, tempera and gold leaf on vellum, 250×178mm, *c.* 1445–60 (Vienna, Österreichische Nationalbibliothek, Cod. 1840, fol. 14*v*)

——: 'Pictorial Programmes in Manuscripts of the French Version of Suso's *Horologium sapientiae*', *Archv Fratrum Praedicatorum*, lvii (1987), pp. 31–43

C. R. Sterling: *La Peinture médiévale à Paris, 1300–1500* (Paris, 1990), ii, pp. 176–89

P. R. Monks: *The Brussels Horloge de sapience: Iconography and Text of Brussels, Bibl. Roy., MS. IV 111* (Leiden, 1990)

——: 'The Rolin Master's Hand in London, British Library, MS. Add. 25695', *Medieval Texts and Images*, ed. M. M. Manion and B. Muir (Melbourne, 1991), pp. 57–70

P. R. Monks: 'The Master of Jean Rolin II as the Illuminator of the *Gages de bataille* in Paris, Bibl. Nat., MS. fr. 2258', *Scriptorium*, xlvi/1 (1992), pp. 50–60 [4 pls]

L. M. C. Randall and others: *France, 1420–1540*, ii of *Medieval and Renaissance Manuscripts in the Walters Art Gallery* (Baltimore and London, 1992), 1, pp. 128–32, 174–80; 2, figs 227, 228, 245, pls XIIB, XIVB

J. H. Marrow with contr. by F. Avril: *The Hours of Simon de Varie* (London, 1994) [facs. edn]

P. R. Monks: 'Some Doubtful Attributions to the Master of Jean Rolin II', *Medieval Codicology, Iconography, Literature and Translation: Studies for Keith Val Sinclair* (Leiden, 1994), pp. 143–50, figs 48–58

——: *Piety and Chivalry: The Medieval World of a Parisian Artist* (in preparation)

PETER ROLFE MONKS

BIBLIOGRAPHY

'L'*Horloge de sapience* d'Henri Suso: France, vers 1455', *Bull. Bib. Royale Belgique*, v (1961), pp. 48–58

E. P. Spencer: 'L'*Horloge de sapience*, Bruxelles, Bibliothèque Royale, MS. IV 111', *Scriptorium*, xvii (1963), pp. 277–99

'Henri Suso, *Buchlein der ewigen Weisheit*, version française', *Bruxelles, Bibliothèque Royale Albert 1er: Quinze Années d'acquisitions* (Brussels, 1969), pp. 84–6

The Last Flowering: French Painting in Manuscripts, 1420–1530, from American Collections (exh. cat. by J. Plummer and G. Clark, New York, Pierpont Morgan Lib., 1982), pp. 62–4

P. R. Monks: 'Reading Fifteenth-century Miniatures: The Experience of the *Horloge de sapience* in Brussels, Bibl. Roy., MS. IV 111', *Scriptorium*, xl (1986), pp. 242–8, pls 13–16

Joseph Master (*fl* Reims, *c.* 1245–55). French sculptor. The name was coined by Vöge to single out the sculptor of the figure of Joseph from the *Presentation in the Temple* group on the left jamb of the central portal of the west façade of Reims Cathedral. The Joseph Master's hand may be detected also in the Maidservant on the same jamb, the 'smiling angel' from the *Annunciation* group on the right jamb and the angel who escorts a martyred saint, probably St Denis, on the left jamb of the north portal. The sculptures were probably carved *c.* 1245–55.

The style of the Joseph Master embodies the self-assurance and mannered elegance found in such Parisian work as the *Last Judgement* tympanum of Notre-Dame (*c.* 1225–30), the figure of 'Childebert' from St Germain-des-Prés (*c.* 1240; Paris, Louvre) and the *Apostles* from the Sainte-Chapelle (1240s). The influence of this style was tempered, however, by that of the atelier that produced the bold figures of the Queen of Sheba, Solomon and David on the west façade of Reims. The figure of Joseph exemplifies the Master's work. Pivoting on his column as he proffers the sacrificial doves, the heavy folds of his drapery accentuate the rhetoric of his pose; his face is enlivened both by the smile that plays on his lips and by the jaunty corkscrew curls of his beard and hair (*see* REIMS, fig. 5). The pointed physiognomies and courtly coiffures of the Parisian styles are here combined with the swirling mantles and slight swagger of existing sculpture at Reims to create an animated and expressive style.

The style of the Joseph Master was the most influential of all those at Reims, inspiring the many smiling angels and elegant Virgins, rendered in precious metals, ivory and illuminated manuscripts, produced in Paris in the 13th and 14th centuries.

BIBLIOGRAPHY

W. Vöge: *Die Anfänge des monumentalen Stils im Mittelalter* (Strasbourg, 1894)
W. Medding: 'Der Josephmeister von Reims', *Jb. Preuss. Kstsamml.*, l (1929), pp. 299–318
R. Hamann-MacLean: 'Stilwandel und Persönlichkeit: Der Priester-Meister', *Recl Mus. N.* [Belgrade], iv (1964), pp. 243–53
A. E. Brandenburg: 'La Sculpture à Paris au milieu du XIIIe siècle', *Bull. Soc. Hist. Paris & Ile-de-France* (1970), pp. 31–41
W. Sauerländer: *Gotische Skulptur in Frankreich, 1140–1270* (Munich, 1970; Eng. trans., London, 1972)

DONNA L. SADLER

Master of the Joseph Sequence [Master of Afflighem Abbey] (*fl* Brussels, *c.* 1495–1500). South Netherlandish painter. He was named by Friedländer (1923) after a series of tondi illustrating the *Legend of St Joseph* (Berlin, Bodemus.; Munich, Alte Pin.; New York, Met.). Friedländer (1924–37) subsequently attributed eight panels with scenes from the *Life of Christ* and the *Life of the Virgin* (*c.* 1493–1508; Brussels, Mus. A. Anc.) to the same painter. These came from the abbey of Afflighem and gave the artist his alternative name. The inscription TE BRUESELE on the *Circumcision*, the buildings and the style of painting suggest that the artist worked in Brussels *c.* 1500. The portraits of *Philip the Fair* and *Joanna the Mad* on the wings of the *Last Judgement* triptych from Zierickzee (*c.* 1496–1506; Brussels, Mus. A. Anc.) and the wings of the *Legend of St Barbara* (Baltimore, MD, Walters A.G.) are also attributed to this artist. The wings of the Strängnäs I *Passion* altarpiece, sometimes credited to him, are attributed to Colijn de Coter by C. Périer-D'Ieteren.

The narrative compositions, where events are placed side by side, are governed by alternating vertical and horizontal accents. Figures are elongated, postures stiff and movements angular; the smooth faces, often seen in profile, have long, straight noses and close-set slit eyes. His handling of paint is essentially graphic and gives a decorative aspect to the closely woven brocades, where small impastoed strokes of yellow imitate embroidery. The stylistic peculiarities of the artist are found in several Brussels tapestries, which suggests that he may have designed cartoons for weavers. Friedländer identified the Master as Jacob van Lathem, but the question remains open.

BIBLIOGRAPHY

M. J. Friedländer: 'Die Brüsseler Tafelmalerei gegen den Ausgang des 15. Jahrhunderts', *Belg. Kstdkml.*, ed. P. Clement; i (Munich, 1923), pp. 313–17
——: *Die altniederländische Malerei* (Berlin, 1924–37); Eng. trans. as *Early Netherlandish Painting* (Leiden, 1967–76), iv, pp. 63–5, 80–81
Primitifs flamands anonymes: Maîtres au noms d'emprunt des Pays-Bas méridionaux du XVe et du début du XVIe siècle (exh. cat., Bruges, Groeningemus., 1969), pp. 124–5
C. Sterling: 'La Peinture de tableaux en Bourgogne au XVe siècle', *An. Bourgogne*, l/1 (1978), pp. 5–17, (p. 12, n. 14)
C. Coppens: 'Het Afflighem retabel', *Eigen Schoor Brabander*, lxvi/4–5–6 (1983), pp. 191–9
C. Périer-D'Ieteren: *Les Volets peints des retables bruxellois conservés en Suède et le rayonnement de Colyn de Coter* (Stockholm, 1984), pp. 25–7
F. Joubert: 'La Tenture de choeur de Saint-Etienne d'Auxerre et la peinture bruxelloise vers 1500', *Rev. A.*, 75 (1987), pp. 37–42

C. PÉRIER-D'IETEREN

Master of Jouvenel des Ursins (*fl c.* 1447–60). French illuminator. He is named after Guillaume Jouvenel des Ursins, Chancellor of France from 1447 to 1472 and patron of a copy of Giovanni Colonna's compilation, the *Mare historiarum* (1447–55; Paris, Bib. N., MS. lat. 4915). This impressive manuscript contains significant work by the Jouvenel Master, but the differing styles of its illustrations indicate that a number of other artists were also involved. The manuscript has 730 miniatures, including 7 large-format paintings marking the beginning of each book, and represents one of the most ambitious programmes for the illustration of a history text ever undertaken at that time. The variety of artists at work was not recognized until relatively late, first by Schaefer and then more systematically by König (1982), who distinguished as many as 11 different hands. The illuminators' methods of working manifestly developed as the project progressed: the first half of the manuscript reveals a close collaboration, with several painters working with the greatest care within a single gathering, but the last part was illustrated fairly hastily by a single illuminator from folio 290 onwards. No illustrated manuscript of the same text seems to have served as a model for Jouvenel's copy, which raises the question of where the inspiration for this impressive cycle came from.

The whole work is fairly consistent in style, and it gives the impression of having been executed under the influence of the Jouvenel Master's dominant artistic personality. All the other artists who collaborated on the manuscript, with three notable exceptions, appear to have developed their work more or less directly from his, although his personal contribution was limited. He painted only two of the large miniatures: one at the beginning of book II in which Guillaume Jouvenel is depicted both as Chancellor and as a knight, at the feet of the Trinity (fol. 21*r*), and one in book III depicting the story of *David and Solomon* (fol. 46*v*); his contribution to the small miniatures does not extend beyond folio 62. The Jouvenel Master produced densely worked paintings in luminous and intense colours, and his landscapes (and even some of his figures) show that he still adhered quite strongly to the aesthetic of the great Parisian illuminators of the first quarter of the century: his palette in particular owes a great deal to the Bedford Master. His monumental figures, however, clothed in their ample drapery, are indicative of a more developed artistic vision, associated with the new Netherlandish style. He attracted several illuminators of a younger generation, whose styles were similar although distinct from his own, to work with him. The two principal figures among them, the Master of the Geneva Boccaccio and the Master of Boethius BN fr. 809, each painted two of the large paintings: the former was responsible for those of books III and IV (fols 86*r* and 149*r*), while the latter executed those of books VI and VII (fols 250*r* and 319*r*). The Boethius Master was also responsible for the scene on folio 1 showing Chancellor Jouvenel in his copyist's studio. König believes that the two worked together to produce the large painting in book V (fol. 196*r*). These two artists can be distinguished from the Jouvenel Master by their vigorous execution and the marked dynamism of their figures. Together with the Jouvenel Master, they formed a close team, their bonds perhaps strengthened by family ties.

This fascinating manuscript has given rise to a long and continuing debate concerning its origins and the identity of its illustrators. Durrieu believed that some of its miniatures belonged to Jean Fouquet's early work from before his journey to Italy (i.e. before 1447), but Porcher demonstrated that this was impossible by referring to the 1449 date recorded by the scribe at the end of book V. The *Mare historiarum* then became the point of reference for a group of manuscripts that Porcher attributed to the Jouvenel Master, a contemporary of Fouquet's rather than Fouquet himself. Schaefer suggested that the principal artist should be identified with Coppin Delf, a painter in the service of the house of Anjou. König made the vital distinction between the Jouvenel Master properly speaking and his two closest emulators, the Boccaccio and Boethius Masters, and became the first to precisely map out the different hands involved in the illustration of the manuscript. After a tightly constructed argument, which nevertheless is not universally accepted, he concluded that the work was executed in Nantes. Sterling has attempted to identify the Jouvenel Master and the Geneva Boccaccio Master with André d'Ypres (*fl* 1435–44) and his son Nicolas Dipre (Colin d'Amiens) respectively, two eminent Picard painters known to have been in Paris during the third quarter of the 15th century. All the evidence suggests, however, that the Jouvenel Master and his associates worked exclusively in western France, between Angers and Tours. This is supported by several arguments, including the fact that the Geneva Boccaccio Master's hand is present in a number of manuscripts executed for the Anjou family. It is also strengthened by the discovery of an important new work by the Jouvenel Master, which

was certainly contemporary with the *Mare historiarum*: a Book of Hours of the Use of Angers (*c.* 1450–55; Paris, Bib. N., MS. nouv. acq. lat. 3211). The Jouvenel Master produced 15 of the surviving 18 miniatures, and these show him at the peak of his stylistic development.

The Jouvenel Master's hand has also been recognized in a *Bible moralisée* (*c.* 1402–4, 1450–65 and 1485–93; Paris, Bib. N., MS. fr. 166), a work left unfinished by the Limbourg brothers in 1404 (*see* LIMBOURG, DE, fig. 1). The contribution of a team of Angers artists, including the Boccaccio Master, can be seen from the fourth gathering onwards (fols 25–32); the Jouvenel Master systematically repainted the heads of existing figures executed by a collaborator in the next gathering, on folios 33*v* and 40*r*. Two elements allow his hand to be identified: first, the powerful figure of the naked Christ in the second, right-hand scene on folio 40*r* is an inverted copy of the Christ supported by God the Father in the miniature of the *Merciful God* that he painted in a Book of Hours of the Use of Nantes (London, BL, Add. MS. 28785, fol. 58*r*); and second, the canon at the foot of the same folio recalls a figure in the *Stigmatization of St Francis* that Fouquet painted in the London Hours of the Use of Angers (see above). The canon's right-hand sleeve, with its elaborate folds, repeats line for line that of the canon shown praying in the miniature of *St Francis*, a miniature with which the Jouvenel Master was certainly familiar, since he himself had been the principal illustrator of this manuscript.

The Jouvenel Master worked again with the Boethius and Geneva Boccaccio Masters on a Book of Hours of Roman Use (*c.* 1455–60; Paris, Bib. N., MS. Rothschild 2530), but this time his two younger associates took charge of the project. They divided most of the illustrations equally between them, executing 15 each. The Jouvenel Master still exerted a strong influence, especially on the Geneva Boccaccio Master, whose *Adoration of the Magi* (fol. 60*r*), for example, was borrowed directly from the miniature of the same subject in the Angers Book of Hours. The Jouvenel Master himself executed only the last four miniatures in the Rothschild Hours: the *Visitation* (fol. 46*r*), the *Coronation of the Virgin* (fol. 115*r*), *Pentecost* (fol. 128*v*) and the *Adoration of the Cross* (fol. 173*v*). These miniatures, together with a Book of Hours of the Use of Rennes (Amsterdam, Bib. Philos. Hermetica), were possibly his last works but show that, despite aging, the artist retained all the brilliant colouring that was such an unmistakable distinguishing feature of his work.

BIBLIOGRAPHY

P. Durrieu: 'La Question des oeuvres de jeunesse de Jean Fouquet', *Recueil de mémoires publié par la Société Nationale des Antiquaires de France à l'occasion de son centenaire* (Paris, 1904), pp. 111–19

Les Manuscrits à peintures en France du XIIe au XVIe siècle (exh. cat. by J. Porcher, Paris, Bib. N., 1955)

J. Porcher: 'L'Homme au verre de vin et le Maître de Jouvenel des Ursins', *Rev. Fr. de l'élite européenne* (July 1955), pp. 117–24

C. Schaefer: 'Deux Enluminures du Maître de Jouvenel des Ursins à la Biblioteca Nacional à Lisbonne', *Arquivs Cent. Cult. Port.*, vii (1974), pp. 117–47

——: 'Le Maître de Jouvenel des Ursins (Coppin Delf?), illustrateur du *Speculum Historiale* de Vincent de Beauvais (ms. 126 de la Biblioteca Nacional à Lisbonne)', *Arquivs Cent. Cult. Port.*, viii (1974), pp. 81–114

E. König: *Französische Buchmalerei um 1450: Der Jouvenel-Maler, der Maler des Genfer Boccaccio und die Anfänge Jean Fouquets* (Berlin, 1982)

S. Maddalo: 'Castellum quod dicitur Capitolium: Roma immaginata, Parigi, Lat. 4915', *A. Med.*, 2nd ser., iv/1 (1990), pp. 71–97

——: *In figura Romæ: Immagini di Roma del libro medioevale* (Rome, 1990)

C. Sterling: *La Peinture médiévale à Paris, 1300–1500*, ii (Paris, 1990)

P. S. Lewis: 'The Chancellor's Two Bodies: Note on a Miniature in BNP Lat. 4915', *J. Warb. & Court. Inst.*, lv (1992), pp. 263–5

N. Reynaud: 'Sur la Double Représentation de Guillaume Jouvenel et sur ses emblèmes', *Rev. Bib. N.*, 44 (Summer 1992), pp. 50–57

FRANÇOIS AVRIL

Master of the Judgement of Solomon (*fl* Rome, 1620–30). Painter. In 1943 Roberto Longhi grouped ten pictures around an anonymous work, the *Judgement of Solomon* (*c.* 1620; Rome, Gal. Borghese) and titled the artist the Master of the Judgement of Solomon. This small oeuvre included five *Apostles* from the Casa Gavotti in Rome (Florence, Fond. Longhi) and a *Denial of St Peter* (Rome, Pal. Barberini). In 1957 it was enlarged by the discovery of a spectacular *Christ among the Doctors* (Langres, St Martin), which may have come from the collection of Vincenzo Giustiniani. The *Judgement of Solomon* and the *Christ among the Doctors*, distinguished by classical compositions, gravity of expression and a limited range of greys and browns, suggest a powerful and original artist who was active in Rome between 1620 and 1630. The artist's nationality remains controversial, although it is accepted that he was not an Italian. Longhi attempted to identify him as a French painter; it has also been suggested that he may be Gérard Douffet, a painter from Liège who was in Rome between 1614 and 1622, but this remains a complex problem since there are no documented works from Douffet's Roman period. The anonymous Master's works, however, have close affinities with those of Dirck van Baburen, who was in Rome between 1613 and 1620, and with those of Jusepe de Ribera and his followers Giovanni Do and Bartolomeo Passante (1614–78), and scholars now tend to see him as a northern painter who was responsive to Flemish, Roman and Neapolitan influences. He remains one of the most mysterious artists of the international Caravaggesque movement, whose oeuvre bears witness to the difficulties of determining the direction of exchanges and of influences between Naples and Rome, Italy and Flanders.

BIBLIOGRAPHY

R. Longhi: 'Ultimi studi sul Caravaggio e la sua cerchia', *Proporzioni*, i (1943), pp. 5–63

Caravaggio and his Followers (exh. cat., Cleveland, OH, Mus. A., 1971), pp. 134–5 [with bibliog.]

B. Nicolson: *The International Caravaggesque Movement* (Oxford, 1979), pp. 73–4

ARNAULD BREJON DE LAVERGNÉE

Karlsruhe Master (*fl c.* 1440–60). Italian painter. The *Adoration of the Child* (Karlsruhe, Staatl. Ksthalle) was taken by Pudelko (1935) as the stylistic basis on which to build the oeuvre of an unidentified artist active in Florence and Prato in the 1440s and 1450s. In Pudelko's opinion, his career probably began in the workshop of Paolo Uccello. The works attributed to him are strongly influenced by Domenico Veneziano, but later examples make clear reference to Alesso Baldovinetti. The catalogue of frescoes, panels and drawings created by Pudelko for the Karlsruhe Master corresponds very closely to the oeuvre that Salmi (1934) provisionally assigned to the Master of the Quarata Predella, and many of the works attributed to Pudelko's Karlsruhe Master continue to be ascribed to Paolo Uccello or have been claimed for Giovanni di Francesco or the Master of the Castello Nativity. Some have also been described as school of Andrea del Castagno or Florentine school. The frescoes of the *Dispute of St Stephen*, the *Birth of the Virgin* and the *Presentation of the Virgin* in the chapel of the Assunta, Prato Cathedral, were initially acceptable to Pope-Hennessy as part of the Karlsruhe Master's oeuvre, and he therefore renamed the latter the PRATO MASTER (*see* below), dating the Karlsruhe *Adoration* to an earlier phase of the unknown artist's career, long before the Prato frescoes. Later (1969) Pope-Hennessy amalgamated the work of his Prato Master with parts of the oeuvre of Salmi's Master of the Quarata Predella but rejected the Karlsruhe *Adoration* and created around this yet another catalogue of works, whose author, identified as active 1440–60, he now called the Karlsruhe Master, as Pudelko had done in 1935. Owing to the close stylistic links with the work of Paolo Uccello, Parronchi (1974) sought to identify the Karlsruhe Master with Uccello's daughter Antonia (1456–91), whom Vasari and Gaetano Milanesi referred to as a Carmelite nun and painter. Parronchi's argument rests on the inscription SOROR ANTONIA P. on a panel showing a clerical scene, from S Donato, Polverosa (Florence, Uffizi). Parronchi interpreted the inscription as either 'Sister Antonia, daughter of Paolo' or 'painted by Sister Antonia'. To this female artist he attributed the Karlsruhe *Adoration*; the *Thebaid* (Florence, Accad. B.A. & Liceo A.), also in Pudelko's list; the *Virgin and Child* (Greenwich, CT, T. S. Hyland priv. col., see Parronchi, pl. 25a), also in Pope-Hennessy's list; and a triptych of the *Crucifixion* (ex-Knoedler's, New York, see Parronchi, pl. 24a). Parronchi's proposition, particularly with regard to his dating of the works to the second half of the 15th century, remains unconvincing.

BIBLIOGRAPHY

G. Vasari: *Vite* (1550, rev. 2/1568); ed. G. Milanesi (1878–85)

C. Gamba: 'Di alcuni quadri di Paolo Uccello o della sua scuola', *Riv. A.*, vi (1909), pp. 19–30

R. Longhi: 'Ricerche su Giovanni di Francesco', *Pinacotheca*, i (1928), pp. 34–48

M. Marangoni: 'Gli affreschi di Paolo Uccello a San Miniato al Monte a Firenze', *Riv. A.*, xii (1930), pp. 403–17

L. Venturi: 'Paolo Uccello', *L'Arte*, xxxiii (1930), pp. 52–87

R. van Marle: 'Eine unbekannte Madonna von Paolo Uccello', *Pantheon*, ix (1932), pp. 76–80

R. Offner: 'The Mostra del Tesoro di Firenze Sacra', *Burl. Mag.*, lxiii (1933), pp. 72–84, 166–78

M. Salmi: 'Paolo Uccello, Domenico Veneziano, Piero della Francesca e gli affreschi del duomo di Prato', *Boll. A.*, xxviii (1934), pp. 1–27

G. Pudelko: 'Der Meister der Anbetung in Karlsruhe, ein Schüler Paolo Uccellos', *Das siebte Jahrzehnt: Festschrift für Adolph Goldschmidt* (Berlin, 1935), pp. 123–30

J. Pope-Hennessy: *Paolo Uccello* (London, 1950, rev. 1969)

J. Lauts: *Meisterwerke der Staatlichen Kunsthalle Karlsruhe* (Honnef, 1957)

——: *Katalog Alter Meister*, Karlsruhe, Staatl. Ksthalle cat. (Karlsruhe, 1966)

A. Parronchi: *Paolo Uccello* (Bologna, 1974)

D. Lüdke, G. Reising and K. Simons-Kockel: *Ausgewählte Werke der Staatlichen Kunsthalle Karlsruhe: 150 Gemälde vom Mittelalter bis zur Gegenwart* (Stuttgart, 1988)

JOHANNES TRIPPS

Master of the Karlsruhe Passion (*fl c.* 1435–65). German painter. He was active in the region around Strasbourg and is named after a *Passion* altarpiece dated *c.* 1440–50. Seven panels have survived: the *Agony in the*

Garden, *Crowning of Christ with Thorns*, *Christ Carrying the Cross*, *Disrobing* and *Christ being Nailed to the Cross* (all Karlsruhe, Staatl. Ksthalle); the *Betrayal* (Cologne, Wallraf-Richartz-Mus.); and the *Flagellation* (priv. col., see Muller, no. 70). Along with Konrad Witz, Caspar Isenmann and the Master E.S., the Master was one of the most significant artists of the Upper Rhine area of this period. The identification with HANS HIRTZ, however, who was in Strasbourg between 1421 and 1462, is hypothetical. The stained glass in St Wilhelm and Alt St Peter, Strasbourg, has also been attributed to him, as has a fresco of scenes of the *Passion* for the Dominican church in the same city that survives only in an engraving of 1621 by Bartholomäus Dietterlin (Munich, Staatl. Graph. Samml.).

The Master's style is astonishingly expressive, distinguished by a pronounced realism and an unprecedented graphic quality, although his sense of perspective and proportion and his figure style appear old-fashioned. The dramatic narrative style is innovative, however. Figures are clearly characterized as good or evil, with a wide variety of emotion depicted: next to the uncomplaining, suffering Christ and his quietly mourning companions in the scenes from the altarpiece the artist places aggressive thugs and noisy onlookers. Undisguised prejudice, directed at the Jews in particular, is expressed in their exaggerated gestures and grimaces. The restless, noisy atmosphere of the scenes is emphasized by the strong colour, the massed, intersecting figures and heads that fill the picture space and by the bewildering profusion of precisely depicted, detailed costumes and weapons. These features contribute to the fascination of the pictures, which reflect the spiritual and social unrest of the late Middle Ages.

BIBLIOGRAPHY

Kindler: 'Hirtz, Hans'; Thieme–Becker

F. Muller: *Versteigerungskatalog der Sammlung Raedt von Oldenbarnevelt* (Amsterdam, 1902)

E. Buchner: 'Über eine mittelrheinische Zeichnung der Spätgotik', *Pantheon*, i (1928), pp. 314–15

O. Fischer: 'Der Meister von Waldersbach im Elsass', *Z. Kstgesch.*, ii (1933), pp. 333–47; iii (1934), pp. 281–3

H. Rott: *Der Oberrhein* (1936–8), iii of *Quellen und Forschungen zur südwestdeutschen und schweizerischen Kunstgeschichte des 15. und 16. Jahrhunderts* (Stuttgart, 1933–8), pp. 55–60

A. Stange: *Südwestdeutschland von 1400 bis 1450* (1951), iv of *Deutsche Malerei der Gotik* (Munich and Berlin, 1934–61), pp. 77–81

L. Fischel: *Die 'Karlsruher Passion' und ihr Meister* (Karlsruhe, 1952)

J. Lauts: *Alte Meister*, Karlsruhe, Staatl. Ksthalle cat. (Karlsruhe, 1966)

G. Schiller: *Ikonographie der christlichen Kunst*, ii (Gütersloh, 1968)

F. Blasius: *Bildprogramm und Realität: Untersuchungen zur oberrheinischen Malerei um die Mitte des 15. Jahrhunderts am Beispiel der 'Karlsruher Passion'* (Frankfurt am Main, Berne and New York, 1986)

DIETMAR LÜDKE

Master of the Kefermarkt Altar (*fl* c. 1470–1510). Painter and sculptor, active in Austria. He takes his name from the high altarpiece of the pilgrimage church of Kefermarkt (Upper Austria), for which Christoph von Zelking, one of Emperor Frederick III's retainers, provided an annual payment in his will of 1490. From the text of the will and a confirmation of the payment of the balance, which has not survived, it can be presumed that the altarpiece was begun before 1490 and completed in 1497. Its paintwork was almost entirely removed in 1852–5 during the restoration organized by Adalbert Stifter.

The altar has been attributed to every important woodcarver from Michael Pacher to Veit Stoss I and Tilman Riemenschneider. That it should be attributed to the busy Passau workshop of Martin Kriechbaum is further confirmed by a *Virgin* at Windigsteig (Waldviertel, Lower Austria) that has occasionally been related to the Kefermarkt Master. This comes originally from the high altar (consecrated in 1500) of the pilgrimage church of Maria Rafings, which belonged to the Windigsteig parish. In the same year Kriechbaum was a witness to the resignation of the parish priest of Windigsteig. Therefore the *Virgin* is the only surviving work that can be attributed to Kriechbaum with some probability. *See also* KRIECHBAUM, (2).

For bibliography *see* KRIECHBAUM.

LOTHAR SCHULTES

Kent Limner. *See* PHILLIPS, AMMI.

Master of the Khanenko Adoration (*fl* Ghent and/or Bruges, *c.* 1490–1500). South Netherlandish painter. Friedländer assembled the Master's small oeuvre in 1926: the artist is named after a diptych with the *Adoration of the Magi* (Kiev, Mus. W. & Orient. A.), previously in the Khanenko (Chanjenko) collection. Other works published by Friedländer consist of a half-length *Virgin and Child* (Dessau, Staatl. Gal.), a drastically cut down triptych of the *Adoration of the Magi*, also depicted half-length (Saint-Omer, Mus. Hôtel Sandelin), and, finally, a *Virgin Suckling the Child in a Landscape* (Stuttgart, Staatsgal.), with a background similar to the landscapes of Gerard David and Joachim Patinir. However, there is no general agreement concerning these attributions. Neither Winkler nor Fenyö accepted the Stuttgart and Dessau panels as by the Khanenko Master, while Fenyö added to the Master's corpus another *Adoration of the Magi* (Budapest, priv. col., see Fenyö, pp. 24–6), previously given to Hugo van der Goes. He noted that the Master's style was shaped by that of Hugo van der Goes and Hans Memling, but that its main source was the oeuvre of the Master of Flémalle. The moon-shaped head of the Virgin, which is indeed reminiscent of the Master of Flémalle, recurs in the Dessau, Kiev, Saint-Omer and Stuttgart compositions. Boon's suggestion that the Khanenko Master and the Master of the Turin Crucifixion are identical has not found general acceptance. However, an *Adoration* (Hulshorst, W. H. de Monchy priv. col.), questioned by Friedländer, was exhibited in 1970 as by the Master of the Turin Crucifixion (Amsterdam, P. de Boer, no cat. no.).

BIBLIOGRAPHY

Thieme–Becker

M. J. Friedländer: *Die altniederländische Malerei* (Berlin, 1924–37); Eng. trans. as *Early Netherlandish Paiting* (Leiden, 1967–76)

K. G. Boon: 'Meester van de Khanenko-Aanbidding of Meester van de Kruisiging te Turijn', *Oud-Holland*, lxviii (1953), pp. 209–16

F. Winkler: *Das Werk des Hugo van der Goes* (Berlin, 1964), p. 291

D. De Vos, M. Baes-Dondeyne and P.-G. Chabert: 'Meester van de Khanenko-Aanbidding', *Anonieme Vlaamse primitieven* (exh. cat., Bruges, Groeningemus., 1969), pp. 65–8, 216–20

I. Fenyö: 'Über ein Gemälde des Meisters der Khanenko-Anbetung', *Miscellanea I.Q. van Regteren Altena* (Amsterdam, 1969), pp. 24–6

Gent: Duizend jaar kunst en cultuur (exh. cat., Ghent, Mus. S. Kst., 1975), pp. 128–9, 186–7

HANS J. VAN MIEGROET

Master of King René of Anjou [Master of the Cueur d'amour espris] (*fl* Anjou and Provence, *c.* 1440/45– *c.* 1470). Illuminator. He is named after his patron René I, King of Naples (*reg* 1438–42) and Duke of Anjou (*reg* 1434–80), for whom he produced his principal work, the *Livre du cueur d'amour espris* (Vienna, Österreich. Nbib., Cod. 2597).

1. Works. 2. Identification.

1. WORKS. The text of the *Livre du cueur d'amour espris* was composed by René I in 1457, with additions (fols 57– 87) dated to 1477, and is dedicated to the King's nephew John II, Duke of Bourbon. The *Livre du Cueur* is an allegorical narrative in the tradition of the 13th-century *Roman de la rose*. Of the 29 miniatures planned as illustrations, an exceptionally large number for a secular manuscript, only 16 were completed by the René Master. The story begins with René's dream, which is depicted in the frontispiece, *Amour Comes to the Bed of the Lovesick King and Takes his Heart away, Giving it to Desire* (fol. 2*r*; for illustration *see* ANJOU, §II(4)). One of the most remarkable aspects of the miniatures is the extraordinary skill in the depiction of the various times of the day and night: for example the elongated shadows cast by the

1. Master of King René of Anjou: *Emilia in her Garden*; miniature from René I: *Théséide*, 266×200 mm, *c.* 1460–65 (Vienna, Österreichische Nationalbibliothek, Cod. 2617, fol. 53*r*)

rising sun in *The Reading of the Inscription of the Fountain* (fol. 15*r*) and the two virtuoso nocturnes, *Cueur and Desire Resting under an Aspen Tree* (fol. 12*v*) and the *Embarkation of Cueur and Desire with Two Female Companions for the Isle of Love* (fol. 55*r*). The naturalistic compositions show the artist's characteristic close observation of natural phenomena, dress, animals and vegetation. The scenes are simply composed, generally with only two or three figures, their proportions in relation to the settings and the bold lighting all contributing to an effect of monumentality and possibly indicating an artist accustomed to working on a large scale.

Five later copies of the text exist, none of which is illuminated by the René Master. One of these (Paris, Bib. N., MS. fr. 24399) has a complete cycle of miniatures, which, although indebted to the miniatures by the René Master, are not identical. This has given rise to the suggestion that a complete first version of the miniatures was produced by the René Master shortly after the text's composition in 1457 and was used as the source for both the Vienna and Paris manuscripts. The former is generally dated *c.* 1465–70, but it is not known whether it was executed in Provence or Anjou. The Paris version has been dated 1480 (Mérindol, 1980).

Attributed to the René Master is the *Théséide* (Vienna, Österreich. Nbib., Cod. 2617), a French translation of Boccaccio's epic poem of the legend of Theseus written in 1334–41 and possibly translated by Louis de Beauvau, adviser to King René. The volume is dedicated to a young unidentified woman, possibly associated with René's court, who appears on the dedication page (fol. 14*v*). It is illustrated with 16 miniatures, 7 of which are accepted to be by the René Master (fols 14*v*, 17*r*, 18*v*–19*r*, 39*r*, 53*r*, 64*r* and 102*r*). The remaining illustrations were executed by another artist at a later date, *c.* 1470, undoubtedly working from the René Master's designs, who has been traditionally identified as the Master of Jouvenel des Ursins or more specifically the Master of the Geneva Boccaccio. One miniature, *Emilia Setting off for the Hunt* (fol. 76*v*), appears to have been begun by the René Master and completed by the later illuminator. Like those in the *Cueur* manuscript, the illustrations of the *Théséide* are closely integrated with the narrative. They include an ambitious double-page miniature, the *Battle between the Greeks and the Amazons* (fols 18*v*–19*r*) and *Emilia in her Garden* (fol. 53*r*; see fig. 1), in which the artist depicts botanically accurate plants and flowers specific to a single place of origin. The manuscript has been variously placed: *c.* 1460 from Anjou or 1460–65 from Provence. Like the *Cueur*, the *Théséide* was left incomplete by the René Master, perhaps as a result of his death (Robin, 1985).

The third, and only complete, series of illustrations by the René Master is in the *Traité de la forme et devis d'un tournois* (Paris, Bib. N., MS. fr. 2695), a description of an ideal tournament written by René and dedicated to his younger brother Charles of Anjou, Comte du Maine (*d* 1472). Known as the *Livre des tournois*, the text has been variously dated to *c.* 1450 (Delaissé) and *c.* 1460 (Avril, 1986). The manuscript, with its 36 tinted illustrations, is unusually executed on paper and is possibly a model on which the final parchment version was to be based. There are five 15th-century copies of the *Livre des tournois*, two of which (Paris, Bib. N., MSS fr. 2692 and

2. Master of King René of Anjou: *The Prize-giving*; 385×300 mm, miniature from René I: *Traité de la forme et devis d'un tournois*, *c.* 1450–65 (Paris, Bibliothèque Nationale, MS. fr. 2695, fol. 103*v*)

2693) closely follow the original and were made for the bibliophile Louis de Gruuthuse of Bruges. In the *Tournois* the artist's interest in the effects of light (e.g. *The Prize-giving*, fol. 103*v*; see fig. 2) and his love of pageantry, heraldry and ritual are apparent. The rapid, bold and free use of brushstrokes perhaps suggests an artist who also undertook large-scale panel paintings. The colour washes describe form and create atmosphere, rather than purely decorative effects, and the images themselves are treated as an integral part of the text, not as mere ornamentation. The *Tournois* has been given various dates in the 1450s, or has been placed later, 1460–65, and thus contemporary with the *Théséide*. A relative chronology and exact place of execution have yet to be clearly established for all the Master's works: they form a stylistically homogeneous group and may indeed have been executed close in date.

Avril (1977) proposed the addition to the René Master's oeuvre of a number of miniatures from a Book of Hours (New York, Pierpont Morgan Lib., MS. M. 358), the rest of which are attributed to Enguerrand Quarton. The two artists may have worked on the book successively rather than simultaneously, while the border decoration seems to date from a later period (after 1455–60). The miniatures show familiarity with the work of Jan van Eyck and the Master of Flémalle. The manuscript has been dated *c.* 1440–45, was possibly executed in Provence and might, therefore, be the earliest work by the René Master.

Several other works have been attributed to the René Master with varying degrees of acceptance. The Hours of René of Anjou (1409–10; London, BL, MS. Egerton 1070) contains five added miniatures (fols 4*v*, 5*r*, 53*r*, 110*r* and 139*r*) that have been attributed by some scholars (Pächt, 1956; Reynaud, 1989) to the René Master and placed early in his career, between 1435 and 1442. Their stylistic relationship to the Master's later works, however, is not easily reconciled, nor is it certain that they are all by the same hand. It is perhaps more likely that they are the work of a skilled artist working at René's court in the 1430s, who may have come from the same artistic milieu as the René Master and appears to have been familiar with the work of Jan van Eyck; it has even been proposed that the René Master was this artist's pupil (Robin, 1985).

The illustrations of the *Pas de Saumur* (St Petersburg, Rus. N. Lib., MS. fr. F. P.XI,4) have been compared to the work of the René Master, in particular to the *Tournois* manuscript, and may reflect a lost work by him. The *Pas d'arme de la bergère de Tarascon* (Paris, Bib. N., MS. fr. 1974), made for either Louis de Luxembourg or the author of the poem, Louis de Beauvau, is illustrated with one miniature of a *Seated Shepherdess Guarding her Flock* (fol. 1*r*), which is strongly reminiscent of the work of the René Master. The illustration has been dated *c.* 1449–50 and attributed to the atelier of the René Master (Avril) or even to the master himself (Gousset, 1981). *Le Mortifiement de vaine plaisance*, an allegorical poem written by René in 1455, is illustrated in a number of copies, the finest of which is in Metz (Metz, Bib. Mun.). Five of the miniatures (detached) have been compared to the work of the René Master and thus regarded as preserving lost compositions by this artist, which could have been executed 1455–7. Given that the René Master illustrated the King's other works, it is likely that he illustrated this text as well. The influence of the artist has been seen in a miniature of *St John on the Island of Patmos* (Waddesdon Manor, Bucks, NT, MS. 21, fol. 13*r*) in a Book of Hours executed by the illuminator Georges Trubert. The design may derive from a now lost version of this subject by the René Master.

2. IDENTIFICATION. The identity of this artist has been the subject of considerable speculation. His proposed origins have ranged from the southern Netherlands to the Loire Valley and Tours; he has also been considered a pupil or collaborator of Jean Fouquet. It has been suggested (Châtelet, 1980) that Guillaume Porchier is the author of the miniatures in the Vienna *Livre du cueur*, since there are records of payments made to him during 1479 for the illumination of a *Livre du cueur*, for which he received in total the considerable sum of 210 florins and 11 gros. This thesis is unconvincing as 1479 is too late for the Vienna *Cueur*, and it is more likely that the payments refer to the decorative borders of the Vienna manuscript or possibly the miniatures of the Paris version. Traditionally, the miniatures are ascribed to René himself, as it has been argued that the close relationship between the text and images is the result of a single author (Pächt, 1956, 1973, 1977; and Thoss, 1974, 1978); yet the attribution of the *Cueur* text itself to René is not absolutely certain, and

there is little concrete evidence of René's direct involvement in the production of works of art to substantiate this theory.

Durrieu (1911) first proposed BARTHÉLEMY D'EYCK as the author of the miniatures of the Vienna *Cueur* and, by extension, the other work associated stylistically with this Master. There are no works known to be by Barthélemy. Ducal accounts for 1454–69, the period when the manuscripts are generally thought to have been made, make no reference to Barthélemy. The limited documentary evidence indicates that he held a position of responsibility, arranging for the payment of other artists and purchasing materials. His identification with the René Master has been accepted by a number of scholars and is the most plausible given his long and close association with the King: he was at René's court for at least 23 years, from *c.* 1447, and on 7 May 1449 was described as 'peintre et varlet de chambre'; he often travelled with the King and even worked adjacent to his apartments. In addition, Barthélemy was of Netherlandish origin and active in France; he is documented in Aix-en-Provence on 19 February 1444, acting as witness to the painter Enguerrand Quarton, with whom the René Master collaborated on the Pierpont Morgan Hours. Barthélemy's documented presence in Aix-en-Provence has led some scholars to identify him as the MASTER OF THE AIX ANNUNCIATION (*see* above), the painter of a panel (Aix-en-Provence, Ste Marie-Madeleine), executed 1443–5. The patron of the panel was the draper Pierre Corpici (?1388–before 1465), who in October 1447 and July 1449 is documented as a supplier of cloth to René. The *Annunciation* would thus be an early work by the René Master, while he was still under the influence of such Netherlandish artists as Jan van Eyck and the Master of Flémalle. The panel is contemporary with the suggested date for the Morgan Book of Hours, and it seems closer in style with that manuscript than with the later secular works; the relationship of this panel to the rest of the René Master's works is, however, problematic, and the scale of the work and the subject-matter complicates comparisons. Both works are of high quality and equally idiosyncratic. Whether Barthélemy d'Eyck was indeed the Master of the Aix Annunciation and the Master of King René of Anjou remains to be resolved.

BIBLIOGRAPHY

G. F. Waagen: *Die vornehmsten Kunstdenkmäler in Wien*, 2 vols (Vienna, 1867), pp. 83ff

O. Smital and E. Winkler: *Livre du Cuer d'amours espris*, 3 vols (Vienna, 1926), [vol. 3, colour facs.]

O. Pächt: 'René d'Anjou et les Van Eyck', *Cah. Assoc. Int. Etud. Fr.*, 8 (1956), pp. 40–67

L. J.-J. Delaissé: 'Les Copies flamandes du Livre des tournois de René d'Anjou', *Scriptorium*, xxiii (1969), pp. 187–98

O. Pächt: 'René d'Anjou: Studien, I and II', *Jb. Ksthist. Samml. Wien*, n. s., xxxiii (1973), pp. 85–126; xxxvii (1977), pp. 7–106

O. Pächt and D. Thoss: *Französische Schule*, 2 vols (1974), i of *Die illuminierten Handschriften und Inkunabeln der österreichischen Nationalbibliothek*, ed. O. Pächt (Vienna, 1974–), pp. 32–48, pls 43–73

F. Avril: 'Manuscrits à peintures d'origine française à la Bibliothèque nationale de Vienne', *Mél. Bull. Mnmtl*, cxxxiv (1976), pp. 329–38

——: 'Pour l'enluminure provençale: Enguerrand Quarton, peintre de manuscrits?', *Rev. A.*, 35 (1977), pp. 9–38

D. Thoss: *Französische Gotik und Renaissance in Meisterwerken Buchmalerei* (Vienna, 1978), n. 35

A. Châtelet: 'Le Problème du Maître du Coeur d'Amour épris: Le Roi René ou Guillaume Porchier?', *Bull. Soc. Hist. A. Fr.* (1980), pp. 7–14

C. de Mérindol: 'Deux Cycles iconographiques du Coeur d'Amour épris: Essai de datation', *Bull. Soc. Hist. A. Fr.* (1980), pp. 15–19

M.-Th. Gousset, D. Poirion and F. Unterkircher: *Le Coeur d'Amour épris* (Paris, 1981)

Le Roi René en son temps, 1382–1481 (exh. cat., Aix-en-Provence, Mus. Granet, 1981), nos D1–6, D20

N. Coulet, A. Planche and F. Robin: *Le Roi René* (Aix-en-Provence, 1982), pp. 145–215

F. Robin: *La Cour d'Anjou-Provence: La Vie artistique sous le règne de René* (Paris, 1985), pp. 187–208

F. Avril and others: *Le Livre des tournois du roi René de la Bibliothèque Nationale (MS. fr. 2695)* (Paris, 1986)

M.-Th. Gousset: 'Le Jardin d'Emilie', *Rev. Bib. N.*, vi/2 (1986), pp. 7–24

A. Demarquary Rook: 'Georges Trubert, the René Master and Waddesdon MS. 21', *Burl. Mag.*, cxxx (1988), pp. 352–5

N. Reynaud: 'Barthélemy d'Eyck avant 1450', *Rev. A.*, 84 (1989), pp. 22–43

□

Master of the Krainburg Altar (*fl c.* 1510). Austrian painter. He is named after two altarpiece wings (*c.* 1510; Vienna, Belvedere) from Krainburg, near the Karawanken Alps. The wings, painted on both faces, show the flight and martyrdom of the local *SS Cantius, Cantianus and Cantianilla* on the inner faces and the *Agony in the Garden* and the *Resurrection* on the outer faces. The scenes with the saints, under lunettes decorated with sculptures of the prophets painted in gold, are the most striking example of Late Gothic influence from the Netherlands in Austria. The main characters are painted in bright, almost garish colours, now darkened with age; the surrounding landscape is of a clayey hue. As well as having similarities with the style of the Master of the Virgo inter Virgines, the rich damasks and pointed faces are strongly reminiscent of that of the Master of the St Bartholomew Altar. Emotions, from a paralysing certainty of death (in the arrest scene) to sadistic brutality (the executioners), are sympathetically portrayed. The head of a judge (which recalls Hans Baldung's self-portraits) shows the painter on the threshold of the Renaissance, but his still basically Late Gothic perception is poignantly illustrated in the primitive figures in Gethsemane.

Attributed to the same Master by stylistic analysis, single altar pictures (all *c.* 1500) of the *Legend of St Florian* (Graz, Steirmärk. Landesmus.) and the *Nativity*, the *Adoration of the Magi* and the *Massacre of the Innocents* (all Chicago, IL, A. Inst.) pre-date the wings from the Krainburg altarpiece. The ethereal bodies in light colours in the *Body of St Florian Guarded by the Eagle*, for example, are flatly embedded in extensive elements of landscape. The influence of the Master of the Virgo inter Virgines can already be detected (e.g. *Adoration of the Magi*) in the types of head, their eyes protruding from taut skin. The huge frescoes (*c.* 1515–20) in the church of St Primus on the southern slope of Mala Planina, Slovenia, demonstrate the artist's mastery of monumental surfaces with the inclusion of a wealth of detail and invite comparison with Jerg Ratgeb. A powerful depiction of the *Adoration of the Magi* forms the main painting and contains a splendid cavalcade surmounted by Netherlandish curtain arches. A second, dilapidated fresco depicts the atrocities perpetrated by the Turks in 1471, with a well preserved central group of the patron saints and Virgin.

BIBLIOGRAPHY

O. Benesch: 'Der Meister des Krainburger Altars I', *Wien. Jb. Kstgesch.*, vii (1930), pp. 120–41
——: 'Fortsetzung und Schluss', *Wien. Jb. Kstgesch.*, viii (1932), pp. 50–67
F. Stelè: *Monumenta artis Slovenicae I: La Peinture murale au moyen âge* (Ljubljana, 1935), p. 47
E. Baum, ed.: *Katalog des Museums mittelalterlicher österreichischer Kunst* (Munich, 1971), p. 136

HANS GEORG GMELIN

Master of Lanaja. *See* GRAÑEN, BLASCO DE.

Lancelot Master. *See* MASTER OF LATIN 757 below.

Master of the Last Judgement. *See under* TAÜLL, S CLIMENTE AND S MARIA.

Master of the Lathrop Tondo [Guinigi Painter] (*fl c.* 1490–1520). Italian painter. He was named by Berenson (1906) after the tondo of the *Virgin and Child, with SS Jerome and Catherine and a Donor* (*c.* 1496–1502; Malibu, CA, Getty Mus.), which from 1906 to 1929 had belonged to Francis Lathrop, a New York collector. The painting was commissioned by the Guinigi and Buonvisi families of Lucca (whose coats of arms are included), probably to commemorate the marriage of Michele Guinigi and Caterina Buonvisi in 1496. Berenson collected a corpus of paintings around this work, suggesting that the Master was active in Lucca and influenced by Domenico Ghirlandaio, Filippino Lippi and Flemish painting. Ragghianti (1955) added five more works to the Master's oeuvre and renamed him the Guinigi Painter. He believed that the artist was particularly influenced by the Bolognese painter Amico Aspertini, who was active in Lucca *c.* 1506–8/9. Fahy (1965) added 23 paintings to the Master's supposed output, but Ferretti (1975) gave a number of them to the MASTER OF THE CROCIFISSO DEI BIANCHI (*see* above). A preliminary chronology for the Master of the Lathrop Tondo was proposed by Natale (1980). A panel of *St Anthony Enthroned with SS Andrew, Dominic, Francis and Bartholomew* (Lucca, S Pietro Somaldi), attributed to him by Ferretti and Kiel (both 1972), was dated to *c.* 1497 and identified as the work of MICHELANGELO DI PIETRO by Tazartes (1985); the Master's chronology, however, remains uncertain.

The earliest works attributed to the Master, such as a pair of panels with *St Blaise and a Male Donor* and *St Lucy and a Female Donor* (*c.* 1490; Lucca, Marchese Pietro Mazzarosa priv. col., see Fahy, pl. 7) show the influence of Florentine painters in the morphology of the saints and in the niche settings, which are tempered by some Lucchese traits, while the unidealized portraits of the kneeling donors have an affinity with Flemish portraiture. The style is decorative and characterized by an enamelled, metallic finish, which is also found in the Lathrop Tondo. The *Virgin of the Girdle* (*c.* 1500; Sarasota, FL, Ringling Mus. A.) has iconographical and stylistic links with other Lucchese works such as Vincenzo Frediani's altarpiece of the *Immaculate Conception* (1503; Lucca, Villa Guinigi) and the wooden altarpiece of the *Assumption of the Virgin* (Lucca, S Frediano) by Masseo di Bartolomeo Civitali (*d* after 1511). It also shows the influence of paintings that were then in Lucca but painted by artists from further afield, such as Sebastiano Mainardi's *Virgin and Child with*

SS Apollonia and Sebastian (Philadelphia, PA, Mus. A.) and Perugino's *Virgin and Child with SS Jerome and Peter* (*c.* 1500–05; Chantilly, Mus. Condé). The influence of Perugino is also evident in the *Virgin and Child with SS Lawrence and Jerome* (Lucca, Villa Guinigi), in the *Annunciation* (Lucca, SS Annunziata), which shows more Flemish influence, and in the *Virgin and Child with SS Cassiano and Blaise* (Lucca, S Cassiano a Vico).

During his last period (1510–20) the Master of the Lathrop Tondo seems to have been influenced by Amico Aspertini, whose eccentric, bizarre manner was grafted on to the Master's earlier classicizing style, transforming it into something harsh, grotesque and exaggerated. These traits are exemplified in the *Virgin and Child with SS James and Christopher* (*c.* 1510; Lammari, nr Lucca, S Cristoforo) and in the *Virgin and Child with SS Augustine, Monica, Anthony of Padua and Jerome* (*c.* 1510; Lucca, Villa Guinigi), from S Agostino in Lucca.

BIBLIOGRAPHY

B. Berenson: 'La pittura in Italia nella raccolta Yerkes', *Ant. Viva.*, vi (1906), pp. 37–8
C. L. Ragghianti: 'Il pittore nei Guinigi', *Crit. A.*, ii/8 (1955), pp. 137–44
R. Longhi: 'Uno sguardo alle fotografie della mostra "Italian Art and Britain" alla Royal Academy di Londra', *Paragone*, xi/125 (1960), p. 61
E. Fahy: 'A Lucchese Follower of Filippino Lippi', *Paragone*, xvi/185 (1965), pp. 9–20
G. Ardinghi: 'Altri dipinti per il Maestro del Tondo Lathrop', *Prov. Lucca*, viii/1 (1968), pp. 85–95
G. Monaco, L. Bertolini Campetti and S. Meloni Trkulja: *Museo Nazionale di Villa Guinigi* (Lucca, 1968), pp. 162–3
G. Ardinghi: 'Una pala d'altare nella parrocchiale di Marlia', *Prov. Lucca*, ix/3 (1969), pp. 99–100
——: 'Madonna col Bambino nella chiesa di Ombreglio', *Prov. Lucca*, xii/1 (1972), pp. 114–15
M. Ferretti: 'Mostra del restauro, Pisa 1972', *An. Scu. Norm. Sup. Pisa*, n.s. 2, ii/2 (1972), p. 1057
H. Kiel: 'Pisa, mostra del restauro 1972', *Pantheon*, xxx (1972), p. 508
M. Ferretti: 'Percorso lucchese', *An. Scu. Norm. Sup. Pisa*, n.s. 2, v/3 (1975), pp. 1055–60
——: 'Di nuovo sul percorso lucchese', *An. Scu. Norm. Sup. Pisa*, n.s. 2, viii/3 (1978), pp. 1248–50
M. Natale: 'Note sulla pittura lucchese alla fine del '400', *Getty Mus. J.*, viii (1980), pp. 37–43
M. Tazartes: 'Committenza popolare in S Frediano di Lucca', *Ric. Stor. A.*, 13–14 (1981), pp. 111–18
——: 'Anagrafe lucchese, I. Vincenzo di Antonio Frediani "pictor de Luca": Il Maestro dell'Immacolata Concezione?', pp. 4–17, 28–39
——: 'Anagrafe lucchese, III. Michele Angelo (del fu Pietro "Mencherini"): Il Maestro del Tondo Lathrop?', *Ric. Stor. A.*, 26 (1985)

MAURIZIA TAZARTES

Master of Latin 757 [Lancelot Master] (*fl c.* 1380–95). Italian illuminator. Toesca first grouped together as the work of a single Lombard artist the illumination in three manuscripts (all Paris, Bib. N.): a combined Book of Hours and Missal (MS. lat. 757), the so-called *Lancelot du lac* (MS. fr. 343) and several folios of a health handbook, *Tacuinum sanitatis* (MS. nouv. acq. lat. 1673). Several other manuscripts have since been added to this group, but only the Hours/Missal was completed in a single campaign in a homogeneous style.

One of the most lavish and extensively decorated of medieval manuscripts, this book was almost certainly made for Bertrando de' Rossi, Conte di San Secondo (*d* 1396), whose arms and monogram are part of the original decoration. On folio 109*v* he is shown kneeling before the Virgin and Child wearing the livery collar of Gian Galeazzo

Master of Latin 757: *Burial of a Bishop Saint*, 265×205 mm; miniature from a Book of Hours and Missal, after 1385 (Paris, Bibliothèque Nationale, MS. lat. 757, fol. 114*v*)

Visconti, Count of Pavia and Lord, later Duke, of Milan. As Bertrando allied himself with Gian Galeazzo after May 1385, becoming his 'first counsellor', the illumination of the Hours/Missal must have been completed after this date. Its illustration and decoration are painted in clear, rich colours, with a plentiful use of burnished gold. The painting style has great charm; highly finished miniatures are peopled with lively, rather doll-like figures, often placed in detailed and complicated settings. Both the fashionable dress and the architecture reflect the environment of artist and patron: the *Burial of a Bishop Saint* (fol. 114*v*; see fig.), for example, is set within a depiction of the basilica of S Ambrogio, Milan. Similarly, in the earliest of the Books of Hours illuminated in this style (written 1383; Modena, Bib. Estense, MS. alpha S. 2. 31, lat. 862), the *Nativity* (fol. 37*v*) is set outside the walls of a city bearing Milan's coat of arms and containing its most prominent monuments.

As well as drawing upon the world around him, the Master of Latin 757 relied on a wide range of artistic sources. Many figures and groups in the *Lancelot* were derived from an earlier romance, the *Guiron le courtois* (Paris, Bib. N., MS. nouv. acq. fr. 5243), made for Bernabò Visconti (*see* VISCONTI (i), (2)), for whom the *Lancelot* may have been intended. Many compositions and one of the border styles in the Hours in Modena, and also in Latin 757, reveal the Master's close knowledge of the work of GIOVANNI DI BENEDETTO DA COMO, with whom he may have trained. Other figures or groups can be identified

from sculpture or murals in churches in Milan or its environs. Although motifs and types are often recognizable from one manuscript to another, they are inventively reused and recombined; variety and rich detail were primary concerns.

It is clear that the Master collaborated with others. In such instances as the *Tacuinum sanitatis* he was responsible for discrete sections of the book; in others, for example the stunning sequence of *Creation* scenes that opens the Hours/Missal, all the miniatures were drawn in a uniform style, but details of finish indicate that they were painted by two artists. In a copy of Lucan's *De bello civile* (Paris, Bib. N., MS. lat. 8045), folio 2*r* has a border and historiated initial in the style of the Hours/Missal and an inscription in gold in the margin, *iohannes de castagno pinxit*. It is not clear whether this identifies the Master or a collaborator.

The Master of Latin 757 appears to have been the favoured illuminator producing luxury manuscripts for members of the Visconti court, and his influence is obvious in the work of several Milanese illuminators of the next generation. Among his latest works are initials in a copy of Dante's *Divine Comedy* (Florence, Bib. N. Cent., MS. Banco Rari 39), which also contains illumination by Tomasino da Vimercate. He was perhaps the closest and most prolific follower of the Master of Latin 757; through him the amiable and decorative qualities of the Master's style were transmitted to become characteristic of Milanese illumination throughout the first half of the 15th century.

BIBLIOGRAPHY

P. Toesca: *La pittura e la miniatura nella Lombardia dai più antichi monumenti alla metà del quattrocento* (Milan, 1912/R Turin, 1966), pp. 131–5, 155, 160–3

A. Quazza: 'Miniature lombarde intorno al 1380', *Boll. A.*, n. s. 4, 1/1 (1965), pp. 67–72

L. Cogliati Arano: 'Due libri d'ore Lombardi eseguiti verso il 1380', *A. Lombarda*, xv (1970), pp. 37–44

K. Sutton: 'The Original Patron of the Lombard Manuscript Latin 757 in the Bibliothèque Nationale, Paris', *Burl. Mag.*, cxxiv/1 (1982), pp. 88–94

Dix Siècles d'enluminure italienne (exh. cat., ed. Y. Załuska and others; Paris, Bib. N., 1984), pp. 96–101

K. Sutton: 'Codici di lusso a Milano: Gli esordi', *Il millennio Ambrosiano: La nuova città dal Comune alla Signoria*, ed. C. Bertelli (Milan, 1989), pp. 110–39

KAY SUTTON

Master of the Legend of St Barbara (*fl c.* 1470–1500). South Netherlandish painter and draughtsman. The name was given by Friedländer to the artist of a panel, now divided in two, illustrating the *Legend of St Barbara* (*c.* 1475; Bruges, Mus. Saint-Sang; Brussels, Mus. A. Anc.). Two drawings by the Master for this work survive (Paris, Louvre; New York, Met.). The rather perfunctory treatment of the modelling in the panel indicates that it was probably executed with an assistant.

That the Master probably worked in Brussels is suggested by his collaboration on altarpieces with other masters active in the city. He collaborated with the MASTER OF THE VIEW OF ST GUDULE (*see* below) on panels illustrating the *Legend of St Géry* (Dublin, N.G.; The Hague, Mauritshuis) and with the MASTER OF THE LEGEND OF ST CATHERINE (*see* below) on an altarpiece (Cologne, Wallraf-Richartz Mus.), for which he painted the scenes from the *Life of Job*. It is also likely that he collaborated on the right wing of an altarpiece (Melbourne, N.G.

Victoria), depicting the *Resurrection of Lazarus*, which also shows stylistic analogies with the work (two panels, Brussels, Mus. A. Anc.; Warsaw, N. Mus.) of the Master of the Martyrdom of SS Crispin and Crispinian. Reynaud has suggested that these are the same painter, perhaps the Master himself at two points in his career or one of his close collaborators. Several other altarpiece panels have traditionally been attributed to him: the *Coronation of Henry II* (Nuremberg, Ger. Nmus.), the *Battle of Henry II against the Pagans* (Münster, Stadtmus.) and two wings from a triptych of the *Adoration of the Magi* (New York, Met.), which probably also shows the intervention of assistants.

An imitator of Rogier van der Weyden, the Master's own style is characterized by elegant female figures, with fixed gazes, high, arched eyebrows and large foreheads, and the crude appearance of the male faces, with their shaggy hair and dark beards. Several of his works show the influence of Dieric Bouts, particularly in the postures of the figures. The Master's work was the first to suggest two stylistic innovations that were later to be developed by the Master of the View of St Gudule: the composition of narrative scenes, in which spatial continuity replaces the simple juxtapositions typical of the Master of the Legend of St Catherine, and the agitated, expressive placing of figures in architectural settings.

BIBLIOGRAPHY

Thieme–Becker
M. J. Friedländer: 'Der Meister der Barbaralegende', *Jb. Kstwissen.*, ii–iii (1924–5), pp. 20–25
——: *Die altniederländische Malerei* (Berlin, 1924–37); Eng. trans. as *Early Netherlandish Painting* (Leiden, 1967–76), iv (1969), pp. 60–62, 78–9, 85, 89, 98–9; xiv (1975), p. 11
D. Gaiffier: 'Le Triptyque du Maître de la légende de Sainte Barbe: Sources littéraires de l'iconographie', *Rev. Belge Archéol. & Hist. A.*, xxviii (1959), pp. 3–23
J. Białostocki: *Les Musées de Pologne: Gdańsk, Kraków, Warszawa* (1966), ix of *Les Primitifs flamands, I. Corpus de la peinture des anciens Pays-Bas mériodionaux au quinzième siècle*, (Brussels, 1951–), pp. 12–13
Primitifs flamonds anonymes: Maîtres aux noms d'emprunt des Pays-Bas mériodionaux du XVe et du début du XVIe siècle (exh. cat., ed. A. Janssens de Bisthoven and others; Bruges, Groeningemus., 1969), pp. 105–6, nos 46, 48–9, 50–52; review by N. Reynaud and J. Foucart in *Rev. A.*, viii (1970), pp. 68–9
M. Sonkes: 'Quelques dessins attribué au Maître de la Légende de Sainte Barbe', *Mélanges d'archéologie et d'histoire de l'art offerts au professeur J. Lavalleye* (Leuven, 1970), pp. 281–9
R. Guislain-Witterman: 'L'Oeuvre du Maître de la Légende de Sainte Barbe', *Bull. Inst. Royal Patrm. A.*, xvii (1978–9), pp. 89–105

C. PÉRIER-D'IETEREN

Master of the Legend of St Benedict (*fl* 1510–30). German sculptor. He may have been apprenticed to Tilman Riemenschneider or Hans Witten; his *Pietà* (Hildesheim, Pelizaeus-Mus.) draws on that of Witten at Goslar. He worked for the older Master of St Epiphanius before becoming the leading wood-carver in Hildesheim, Lower Saxony. In 1518 he made the *St Benedict* altarpiece for the Benedictines of St Godehard monastery, Hildesheim, from which he is named. Its open-mouthed figures have a vitality related to the revival in religious feeling at the onset of the Reformation. All the pieces attributed to him are in limewood and were polychromed; none is *in situ*. Most have rough or flat backs and were intended for niches in altarpieces.

Of ten original altarpieces postulated from extant fragments (see von der Osten), the earliest and best preserved is the *Education of the Virgin* (*c.* 1510; Philadelphia, PA, Mus. A.), in which the Virgin and St Anne sit on a steep double chair, holding the rhomboid books that characterize Hildesheim carving. The Master's interest in depicting age, his unique carving of hair (bundles of intricate spirals) and his predilection for acute foreshortening (particularly of furniture) are fully developed here. Two unidentified saints (Waddesdon Manor, Bucks, NT) may once have flanked this work. His capacity to reinvent religious themes is seen in the centre of the altarpiece of the *Holy Kinship* (Everloh, nr Hannover, Lutheran Chapel), an unusual treatment showing the family at table. Later works show him turning, as did Tilman Riemenschneider, to the ravaged faces of age and experience, for example in a free-standing *St Mary Magdalene* (Hildesheim, Pelizaeus-Mus.). Three other wood-carvers emerged from the Benedict Master's shop: the Master of St Johannes, the Master of the Holtruger Madonna and the Master of St Urban.

BIBLIOGRAPHY

F. Stuttmann and G. von der Osten: *Niedersächsische Bildschnitzerkunst des späten Mittelalters* (Berlin, 1940), pp. 34–52
T. Hodgkinson: *The James A. de Rothschild Collection at Waddesdon Manor, Sculpture* (London, 1970), pp. 146–9, pl. 52
G. von der Osten: '*The Education of the Virgin*: A Masterpiece of German Sculpture', *Bull. Philadelphia Mus. A.*, lxxvii (1981), pp. 1–10

Master of the Legend of St Catherine (*fl* Brussels, 1470–1500). South Netherlandish painter. The name was given by Friedländer to the painter of a panel illustrating scenes from the *Legend of St Catherine* (Brussels, van der Elst priv. col.; see Friedländer, 1949). The Master's narrative compositions combine the anecdotal with the expressive, and his style is a stereotyped version of that of Rogier van der Weyden. Faces are narrow with large, high-set ears, elongated eyes with vacant expressions and long noses. The Master shows a pronounced taste for architectural representations, and greyhounds and griffins appear frequently in his works. The evident links with the work of Rogier van der Weyden have led Friedländer and subsequent art historians to identify the Master as Rogier's son Pieter, who continued to run his father's studio. Some of the compositions and landscapes, however, are reminiscent of those used by the Bruges school of painting. Works attributed to the Master on the basis of style include, among others: the triptych of the *Last Supper* (Bruges, Mus. Groot Semin.), a dramatic composition lacking the sacred quality of its prototype by Dieric Bouts; the *Miracle of the Loaves and Fishes*, which is the central panel of the Melbourne Triptych (*c.* 1492–5; Melbourne, N.G. Victoria); the scenes from the *Life of St Peter* and the *Visitation with the Donor Claudio Villa* from the *Job* altarpiece (*c.* 1485–90; Cologne, Wallraf-Richartz-Mus.); the altarpiece of the *Virgin* (*c.* 1490; Granada, Capilla Real); and the triptych of the *Virgin Enthroned with Angels and SS Catherine and Agnes* (Bourges, Hôtel Jacques Coeur). On two of these, the Melbourne and *Job* altarpieces, he collaborated with the Master of the Legend of St Barbara. In 1978 two wings were added to the Master's oeuvre: the *Annunciation* and the *Presentation in the Temple* (both Florence, Bargello). In his reconstruction of a single triptych, Deroubaix included these with a newly discovered *Adoration of the Magi* (Switzerland, priv. col.) as the central panel and a *Nativity* (Brussels, Mus. A. Anc.) as the upper right wing.

BIBLIOGRAPHY

Thieme–Becker: 'Weyden, Pieter van der'

M. J. Friedländer: 'Der Meister der Katharinen-Legende und Rogier van der Weyden', *Oud-Holland*, lxiv (1949), pp. 156–61

P. Philippot: 'La Fin du XVe siècle et les origines d'une nouvelle conception de l'image dans la peinture des Pays-Bas', *Bull. Mus. Royaux B.-A.*, xxi (1962), pp. 3–38

M. J. Friedländer: *Die altniederländische Malerei* (Berlin, 1924–37); Eng. trans. as *Early Netherlandish Painting* (Leiden, 1967–76), iv (1969), pp. 57–60, 76–8, 85, 89, 90, 98; xiv (1976), p. 11

I. Hiller and H. Vey: *Katalog der deutschen und niederländischen Gemälde bis 1550* (Cologne, 1969), pp. 82–6

Primitifs flamands anonymes, maîtres aux noms d'emprunt des Pays-Bas méridionaux du XVe et du XVIe siècle (exh. cat., ed. A. Janssens de Bisthoven and others; Bruges, Groeningemus., 1969), pp. 87–9, 100–02, 233–4, 237–42; review by N. Reynaud and J. Foucart in *Rev. A.*, viii (1970), p. 68

V. Hoff and M. Davies: *Les Primitifs flamands: Corpus de la peinture des anciens Pays-Bas méridionaux au quinzième siècle. The National Gallery of Victoria, Melbourne* (Brussels, 1971), pp. 20–24

C. Deroubaix: 'Un Triptyque du Maître de la Légende de Sainte Catherine (Pieter van der Weyden) reconstitué', *Bull. Inst. Royal Patrim. A.*, xvii (1978–9), pp. 153–72

C. Perier-D'Ieteren: 'Contributions to the study of the Triptych with the *Miracles of Christ*: The *Marriage at Cana*', *A. Bull. Victoria*, xxxi (1990), pp. 2–19

——: 'Genèse de l'oeuvre et dessin sous-jacent dans les peintures du Maître de la Légende de Sainte Catherine', *Le Dessin sous-jacent dans la peinture*, X: *Louvain, 1993*

——: 'Contributions to the Study of the Melbourne Triptych II', *A. Bull. Victoria*, xxxiv (1994), pp. 5–24

C. PÉRIER-D'IETEREN

Master of the Legend of St Francis (*fl* Assisi, *c.* 1290s). Italian painter. The cycle of paintings of the *Legend of St Francis* (*see* GOTHIC, fig. 77) in the nave of the Upper Church of S Francesco, Assisi, consists of 28 narrative scenes illustrating events from St Bonaventura's *Legenda maior* (1260–63), proclaimed the official biography of St Francis in 1266. Italian literary tradition ascribed these frescoes to GIOTTO and dated them *c.* 1300. Rintelen (1912) and Offner (1939) rejected this attribution, and since then Italian scholars have tended in general to support the conventional assignment to Giotto and his workshop, while others have recognized the work of at least three different painters (*see* ASSISI, §II, 2(iv)). The Master of the Legend of St Francis is the comprehensive title for the principal painter, who probably designed and supervised the execution of the fresco cycle in the Upper Church. His work includes most of the episodes, from *St Francis Donating his Cloak to a Beggar* (scene II; see fig.) to the *Stigmatization of St Francis* (scene XIX). The scenes are grouped in separate units conforming to the church's architecture. Each of the four bays along the north and south walls of the nave contains three episodes (each 2.7×2.3 m) arranged from left to right above the dado. Two additional scenes are below the east galleries beside the entrance, and two (each 2.7×2 m) cover the inside wall of the façade. The cycle begins on the north wall of the nave in the bay closest to the crossing and ends on the south wall opposite. Like the biblical cycles above them, the organization of the St Francis cycle recalls Roman models. The prototype may have been Pietro Cavallini's lost *St Francis* cycle in S Francesco a Ripa, Rome (Paeseler).

Three episodes deviate from St Bonaventura's chronology in order to emphasize parallels with Christ. The landscapes depicting the *Miracle of the Spring* (scene XIV) and *St Francis Preaching to the Birds* (scene XV) are on the inside wall of the façade, while the *Apparition at Arles* (scene XVIII) on the south wall of the nave precedes the *Stigmatization*. This rearrangement of Francis's legend enabled his ministry to proceed uninterrupted, culminating in the celebrated affirmation of his miracles, arranged to correspond typologically with episodes in the New Testament cycle above. Such a meticulous balance also produced a sophisticated interaction between bays where rigid and loose symmetrical design alternates throughout the cycle.

Pictorial and stylistic details reveal the Master of the Legend of St Francis's Roman origins. The profusion of fictive COSMATI decoration and the resemblance of the ciborium in the *Institution of the Crib at Greccio* (scene XIII) to the altar canopies by Arnolfo di Cambio in S Paolo fuori le Mura (1285) and S Cecilia in Trastevere (1293) indicate a knowledge of contemporary Roman monuments. Moreover, comparisons with Giotto's Arena Chapel frescoes (begun after 1303) reveal the Master of the Legend of St Francis's preference for drier brush-strokes, allying him to the Roman artist Pietro Cavallini. Additional characteristics of his style are the illumination of the scenes by a strong light falling consistently to one side and the juxtaposition of buildings presented frontally and shown foreshortened with those shown obliquely. The scenes of the *Legend of St Francis*, with their sharply outlined figures inhabiting unprecedented landscapes or architectural interiors, were the forerunners of Giotto's increasingly naturalistic compositions.

Proposed datings of the so far undocumented *Legend of St Francis* cycle span the period from 1288 to 1350. Although these were the latest frescoes painted in the Upper Church, Stubblebine's suggestion that they date from the late 1320s and 1330s is implausible. Vasari's assertion that Giotto had been commissioned to paint these frescoes by Giovanni da Murrovalle while he was Franciscan Minister General from 1296 until 1304 is questionable, but various circumstances endorse this period as the date of execution. Murray noted the similarity of the Lateran portico mosaics in the *Dream of Innocent III* (scene VI) to real church refurbishment ordered by the first Franciscan Pope Nicholas IV in 1291. This *terminus post quem* for the fresco would accord with the papal Bull of 14 May 1288 calling for the completion of S Francesco's embellishment. Moreover, the Sala dei Notari frescoes of 1296–7 in the Palazzo dei Priori, Perugia, seem to be dependent on this cycle. White observed the reproduction of Assisi images in Giuliano da Rimini's signed and dated *Virgin and Child with Saints* altarpiece (1307; Boston, MA, Isabella Stewart Gardner Mus.), and Meiss discerned comparable borrowings in the altarpiece of the *Virgin and Child with Saints* (1308; Cesi, S Maria) by the Cesi Master. Given these confines, the Master of the Legend of St Francis probably began painting during the later 1290s, soon after the Isaac Master finished the frescoes of the upper level. The cycle is composed of approximately 300 *giornate* (daily work stages) and, on the basis of this, it seems likely that the work would have taken at least two years. Tintori and Meiss (1962) found

Master of the Legend of St Francis: *St Francis Donating his Cloak to a Beggar* (late 1290s), fresco, 2.7×2.3 m, Upper Church, S Francesco, Assisi

that work had begun with *St Francis Donating his Cloak to a Beggar* (scene II) and progressed eastwards following the narrative sequence. The installation of the rood-beam undoubtedly caused the delay in painting the first scene, *St Francis and the Madman of Assisi*, which was among the last frescoes painted by the St Cecilia Master. An extensive use of lead white characterizes the episodes assigned to the Master of the Legend of St Francis. The oxidization of this pigment has resulted in dark opaque areas in several scenes on the north nave wall. Also, although most surfaces had been prepared or painted on wet plaster (*buon fresco*), considerable areas, such as the blue backgrounds and the twisted columns separating the

episodes, were finished on dry plaster (*a secco*). The Master of the Legend of St Francis, like the Isaac Master, had a distinctive style, which marked the threshold of realistic observation. He created a fresco cycle that, dominating the decoration of the mother church of the Franciscan Order, became the model for representations of St Francis well into the 14th century.

BIBLIOGRAPHY
Thieme–Becker
G. Vasari: *Vite* (1550, rev. 2/1568); ed. G. Milanesi (1878–85), i, pp. 376–8
L. da Pietralunga: *Descrizione della basilica di San Francesco e di altri santuari di Assisi* (MS.; *c.* 1570–80); ed. P. Scarpellini (Treviso, 1982), pp. 427–58 [bibliog.]

F. Rintelen: *Giotto und die Giotto-Apokryphen* (Munich, 1912, rev. Basle, 2/1923), pp. 177–210

A. Schmarsow: *Kompositionsgesetze der Franzlegende in der Oberkirche zu Assisi* (Leipzig, 1918)

E. Moltesen: *Giotto und die Meister der Franzlegende* (Copenhagen, 1930)

L. Maurtius: *Die Franzlegende in der Oberkirche von S. Francesco in Assisi und ihre Stellung in der Kunstgeschichtlichen Forschung* (Berlin, 1932)

R. Offner: 'Giotto, Non-Giotto', *Burl. Mag.*, lxxiv (1939), pp. 259–68; lxxv (1939), pp. 96–113

F. J. Mather jr: 'Giotto's St Francis Series at Assisi Historically Considered', *A. Bull.*, xxv (1943), pp. 97–111

A. Nicholson: 'Again the St Francis Series', *A. Bull.*, xxvi (1944), pp. 193–5

P. Toesca: *Gli affreschi della vita di San Francesco nella chiesa cuperiore del santuario di Assisi* (Florence, 1946)

P. Murray: 'Notes on Some Early Giotto Sources', *J. Warb. & Court. Inst.*, xvi (1953), pp. 58–80

J. White: 'The Date of the Legend of St Francis at Assisi', *Burl. Mag.*, xcviii (1956), pp. 344–50; also in J. White: *Studies in Late Medieval Italian Art* (London, 1984), pp. 96–109

——: *The Birth and Rebirth of Pictorial Space* (London, 1957, rev. 3/1987), pp. 33–47

M. Meiss: *Giotto and Assisi* (New York, 1960)

——: 'Reflections of Assisi: A Tabernacle and the Cesi Master', *Scritti di storia dell'arte in onore di Mario Salmi*, ii (Rome, 1962), pp. 75–111

L. Tintori and M. Meiss: *The Painting of the Life of St Francis of Assisi with Notes on the Arena Chapel* (New York, 1962)

J. White: *Art and Architecture in Italy 1250–1400*, Pelican Hist. A. (Harmondsworth, 1966, rev. 2/1987)

Giotto e il suo tempo. Atti del congresso internazionale per il VII centenario della nascita di Giotto: Roma, 1967 [articles by C. Brandi and W. Paeseler]

A. Smart: *The Assisi Problem and the Art of Giotto: A Study of the Legend of St Francis in the Upper Church of San Francesco, Assisi* (London, 1971, New York, 2/1983)

G. Ruf: *San Francesco e S Bonaventura: Un'interpretazione storico-salvifica degli affreschi della navata nella chiesa superiore di San Francesco in Assisi alla luce teologica di San Bonaventura* (Assisi, 1974)

H. Belting: *Die Oberkirche von San Francesco in Assisi: Ihre Dekoration als Aufgabe und die Genese einer neuen Wandmalerei* (Berlin, 1977), pp. 80–86, 142–5

L. Tintori: 'Il bianco di piombo nelle pitture murali della basilica di San Francesco ad Assisi', *Studies in Late Medieval and Renaissance Painting in Honor of Millard Meiss*, 2 vols (New York, 1977), pp. 437–44

S. Nessi: *La basilica di San Francesco in Assisi e la sua documentazione storica* (Assisi, 1982)

D. Blume: *Wandmalerei als Ordenspropaganda: Bildprogramme im Chorbereich franziskanischer Konvente Italiens bis zur Mitte des 14. Jahrhunderts* (Worms, 1983), pp. 37–41, 167–8

L. Bellosi: *La pecora di Giotto* (Turin, 1985)

J. Poeschke: *Die Kirche San Francesco in Assisi und ihre Wandmalereien* (Munich, 1985), pp. 34–40, 84–95 [excellent pls]

G. Rocchi: 'La più antica pittura nella basilica di S Francesco ad Assisi', *Racar*, xii (1985), pp. 169–73

J. H. Stubblebine: *Assisi and the Rise of Vernacular Art* (New York, 1985)

ADRIAN S. HOCH

Master of the Legend of St George

Master of the Legend of St George (*fl c.* 1460–90). Painter, active in Germany. Apparently an immigrant in Cologne, possibly of Netherlandish origin, he is named after the *St George* altarpiece (Cologne, Wallraf-Richartz-Mus.). Its central panel is divided into four sections with multiple narrative scenes from the *Life of St George*. This cycle continues on the inside of the wings, while the reverse sides contain single subjects, the *Holy Family* and the *Ecce homo*, which incorporate portraits of the donor, Peter Kannegiesser (*d* 1473), and his family. The increased monumentality and artistic competence shown in the reverse side of the wings may indicate that they were painted later, after the patron's demise. References there to the Portinari Altarpiece (*c.* 1471–6; Florence, Uffizi) by Hugo van der Goes support this hypothesis.

This imitative artist was influenced mainly by Rogier van der Weyden and his followers but also by contemporary art in Cologne. Lively storytelling is matched by technical competence but often suffers from indifferent artistic quality. A detailed description of nature, including landscapes with aerial perspective, is contrasted by an awkward presentation of figures. His works are further characterized by a somewhat dry style and by cool colours. The Master of the Legend of St George has been credited, not always convincingly, with a considerable oeuvre.

BIBLIOGRAPHY

H. M. Schmidt: *Der Meister des Marienlebens und sein Kreis: Studien zur spätgotischen Malerei in Köln* (Düsseldorf, 1978)

K. J. Dorsch: 'Georgszyklen des Mittelalters', *Kunstgeschichte* (Frankfurt am Main, Berne and New York, 1983), xxviii of *Europäische Hochschulschriften*

R. Budde: *Köln und seine Maler, 1300–1500* (Cologne, 1986)

BRIGITTE CORLEY

Master of the Legend of St Godelieve

Master of the Legend of St Godelieve (*fl* 1470–80). South Netherlandish painter. He is named after a polyptych (New York, Met.), of which the main panel shows the *Feast of the Count of Boulogne*, the *Marriage of St Godelieve and Bertolf* and the *Treachery of Bertolf and his Mother*. The left wing has two panels showing further scenes from the life of the saint, and the right wing has scenes of the saint's death and miracles. The exterior has a *Saint (?Roch) and Donor*, *St Nicholas of Bari*, *John the Baptist and a Donor* and *St Quirinus* (or possibly St Arnout, with whom Godelieve is often paired). Godelieve, an exclusively Netherlandish saint who came from Gistel near Bruges, is rarely portrayed. In this work the scenes of the saint's life and miracles are presented in a detailed and clear manner. Although the style resembles the work of two Bruges artists, the Master of the Legend of St Ursula and the Master of the Legend of St Lucy, it is less refined and flatter. The altarpiece was commissioned for a chapel in Bruges and hung in the church of Notre-Dame until the end of the 18th century. A copy, dated 1622, is in the Musée des Antiquités at Bruges.

BIBLIOGRAPHY

M. English: *Godelieve van Gistel* (Bruges and Brussels, 1944)

H. B. Wehle and M. Salinger: *A Catalogue of Early Flemish, Dutch and German Paintings*, New York, Met. (New York, 1947), pp. 84–8

JEREMY GRIFFITHS

Master of the Legend of St Lucy

Master of the Legend of St Lucy (*fl c.* 1475–1505). South Netherlandish painter and draughtsman. This name was coined by Friedländer to identify the artist responsible for a group of paintings linked stylistically to the panel of the *Legend of St Lucy* (1480; Bruges, St Jacob). Some 45 to 50 paintings are associated with this master, although variations among them suggest workshop participation in certain cases. Some silverpoint drawings have also been attributed to him (Roberts). Depictions of the city of Bruges in the background of some of his paintings record changes in the belfry, which was being remodelled from 1483 to *c.* 1502. Verhaegen noted four distinct forms of the belfry recorded in them, and on this and the stylistic evidence of the paintings themselves she proposed a chronology for the artist's works. The *Virgin among Holy Women* (Brussels, Mus. A. Anc.; see fig.), dated to *c.* 1490, typifies his mature style: ponderous figures occupy a

Master of the Legend of St Lucy: *Virgin among Holy Women*, oil on panel, 1.08×1.71 m, *c.* 1490 (Brussels, Musée d'Art Ancien)

shallow space near the picture plane in a static, symmetrical composition with lush foliage and brocaded garments that display a detailed rendering of surface textures characteristic of 15th-century Netherlandish art. The Master's paintings are technically proficient reworkings of established themes. As a narrative, the *Legend of St Lucy* is unusual among the artist's surviving works, as most of them are devotional images, including, in particular, many images of the Virgin, such as the Brussels *Virgin among Holy Women*, a *Virgin and Child Enthroned* (Los Angeles, CA, Co. Mus. A.) and a half-length *Virgin and Child* (Williamstown, MA, Clark A. Inst.). The static compositions, cool colours and subdued emotion of his works (e.g. the triptych of the *Lamentation*; Minneapolis, MN, Inst. A.) give his paintings a solemn, rather than expressive, effect.

The patrons of the Master came not only from Bruges but also from centres with commercial ties to the city, such as Estonia (altarpiece of the *Black Heads*; Tallinn, A. Mus. Estonia), Italy (altarpiece of *St Catherine of Alexandria*; Pisa, Mus. N. & Civ. S Matteo) and Spain (*Assumption of the Virgin*; Washington, DC, N.G.A.). This foreign patronage influenced his style; for example, an Italian patron probably required the Italian format, with predella and gable, of the Pisan altarpiece. The number of his paintings with a Spanish provenance suggests that he may have visited Spain, as several of his works reflect Spanish compositions or include Spanish decorative motifs (e.g. *St Nicholas Enthroned*, 16th-century copy of original; Bruges, Groeningemus.). Like many of his contemporaries, he was an eclectic artist who borrowed compositions and motifs from many sources, including works by such

artists as Jan van Eyck, Rogier van der Weyden and Hugo van der Goes, and many of his works were once assigned to the school of Dieric Bouts. He worked in Bruges at the same time as Hans Memling; the two painters operated in the same milieu and worked for similar patrons, and their works also display similarities of style, composition and theme. Several of his works influenced his younger contemporaries in Bruges, including Gerard David and Jan Provoost.

BIBLIOGRAPHY

N. Verhaegen: 'Le Maître de la Légende de Sainte Lucie: Précisions sur son oeuvre', *Bull. Inst. Royal Patrm. A.*, ii (1959), pp. 73–82

M. J. Friedländer: *Die altniederländische Malerei* (Berlin, 1924–37); Eng. trans. as *Early Netherlandish Painting* (Leiden, 1967–76)

D. De Vos: 'Nieuwe toeschrijvingen aan de Meester van de Lucialegende, alias de Meester van de Rotterdamse Johannes op Patmos', *Oud-Holland*, xc (1976), pp. 137–61

A. M. Roberts: *The Master of the Legend of Saint Lucy: A Catalogue and Critical Essay* (diss., Philadelphia, U. PA, 1982)

J. Hand and M. Wolff: *Early Netherlandish Painting*, Washington, DC, N.G.A. cat. (Washington, DC, 1986), pp. 177–83

A. M. Roberts: 'North Meets South in the Convent: The Altarpiece of Saint Catherine of Alexandria in Pisa', *Z. Kstgesch.*, xlx (1987), pp. 187–206

A. M. ROBERTS

Master of the Legend of St Mary Magdalene (*fl* Brussels, *c.* 1490–*c.* 1526). South Netherlandish painter. This name was given by Friedländer on the basis of two panels from a dismembered polyptych of the *Legend of St Mary Magdalene* (*c.* 1515–20): *St Mary Magdalene Hunting* (ex-Kaiser-Friedrich Mus., Berlin, destr. 1940–45; see Friedländer, 1975, pl. 7) and the *Sermon of St Mary Magdalene* in the Johnson Collection (Philadelphia, PA, Mus. F.A.). Maquet-Tombu 'reconstructed' the polyptych

Master of the Legend of St Mary Magdalene: *Raising of Lazarus*, detail from the *Legend of St Mary Magdalene*, oil on panel, 1.26×1.15 m, *c.* 1515–20 (Copenhagen, Statens Museum for Kunst)

by adding four more panels: a *Noli me tangere* and *Louis IX of France with Donors and St Margaret of Antioch* (both Schwerin, Staatl. Mus.), the *Feast in the House of Simon the Pharisee* (Budapest, N. Mus.) and the *Raising of Lazarus* (Copenhagen, Stat. Mus. Kst; see fig.). There have been several attempts to identify this Master with the Master of the Portraits of Princes, Pieter van Coninxloo and Bernard van der Stockt (*fl* before 1469–after 1538), none of which has been generally accepted. The examination of the Master's prolific output, in fact, reveals obvious stylistic differences, perhaps the result of the involvement of other artists—although by the 1990s these had yet to be identified.

The Master's work occupies a middle position between the archaicizing tradition of Rogier van der Weyden (found especially in paintings of the *Virgin and Child*, which are often set against a background dotted with gold) and the italianizing formulae introduced by Bernard van Orley. The Master's style is characterized by a schematic rendition of both the compositional elements and the figures and follows the general simplification of pictorial technique found in more minor Masters towards the late 15th century. The morphology of faces, shown in three-quarters view, follows a pattern: the men's are sturdy, triangular and very wide across the cheekbones, while the women's are round, with thick, rounded chins and almost closed, swollen eyelids. Both have dark, inexpressive and almond-shaped eyes, and noses forming an emphatic oblique line leading to mouths with full lower lips. The backs of the hands have a slightly swollen appearance, and the fingers

lack joints. The artist's interest in the depiction of decorative details compensates for a lack of variation in the modelling of the flesh tints and also appears in the treatment of the landscape, in particular in the foliage and the ground.

Among those works still attributed to the Master are: the altarpiece of the *Annunciation* (Brussels, Mus. A. Anc.); the *Rest on the Flight into Egypt*, the left wing of the Melbourne Altarpiece (Melbourne, N.G. Victoria); the *Holy Family* (Antwerp, Kon. Mus. S. Kst.); the *Virgin Annunciate* (Münster, Westfäl. Landesmus.); two wings of the triptych known as the *Golden Fleece*—a *Donor with St Thomas* and a *Female Donor with St Margaret*; and a panel from the *Legend of St Rumoldus—Offerings to and Worship of the Relics of St Rumoldus* (Mechelen Cathedral). So many portraits of different types are attributed to the Master that it is impossible to form a clear picture of his style in this genre. However, the portrait of *Margaret of Austria* (Paris, Louvre), the *Portrait of a Man* (Dijon, Mus. B.-A.), the *Portrait of a Man in Armour* (Berlin, Gemäldegal.) and the portrait of *Katharina van der Stockt* (Münster, Stadtmus.) are all conventionally presented half-figures and seem acceptable attributions. None of these portraits has anything in common with the more tightly executed works of the Master of the Portraits of Princes.

BIBLIOGRAPHY
M. J. Friedländer: *Repert. Kstwiss.*, xxiii (1900), p. 256
——: *Die altniederländische Malerei* (Berlin, 1924–37); Eng. trans. as *Early Netherlandish Painting*, xii (1975), pp. 13–17, 90–95, 130, 133; xiv, (1976), p. 25
J. Maquet-Tombu: 'Un Triptyque du Maître de la légende de Marie Madeleine', *Gaz. B.-A.*, n. s. 4, xv (1927), pp. 299–310
——: 'Le Maître de la légende de Marie Madeleine', *Gaz. B.-A.*, n. s. 5, ii (1929), pp. 258–91; iii (1930), pp. 190–93
Primitifs flamands anonymes: Maîtres aux noms d'emprunt des Pays-Bas méridionaux du XVe et du début du XVIe siècle (exh. cat., ed. A. Janssens de Bisthoven and others; Bruges, Groeningemus., 1969), pp. 66–9, 130–50; review by N. Reynaud and J. Foucart in *Rev. A.*, viii (1970), p. 69
R. Grosshans: 'Zwei Bildnisse Adolfs von Cleve und der Mark, Herrn zu Ravenstein und Wynnendael, 1425–1492', *Berlin. Mus.: Ber. Staatl. Mus. Preuss. Kulthes.*, xxii/1 (1972), pp. 6–7
C. Périer-D'Ieteren: 'Contribution à l'étude des volets du triptyque dit de *Toison d'Or*, attribué au Maître de la légende de Marie Madeleine', *Oud-Holland*, lxxxix/3 (1975), pp. 129–41
N. Reynaud: 'Les Maîtres à "noms de convention"', *Rev. A.*, xlii (1978), pp. 41–52 (46, 52; n. 53)

C. PÉRIER-D'IETEREN

Master of the Legend of St Ursula (i) (*fl* ?Bruges, *c.* 1470–1500). South Netherlandish painter. The artist was named by Friedländer after the altarpiece of eight panels illustrating the *Legend of St Ursula*, with two additional panels showing *The Church* and *The Synagogue* (before 1482; all Bruges, Groeningemus.), formerly in the convent of the Augustinian Black Sisters in Bruges. Among several surviving portraits, the *Portrait of a Donor* (*c.* 1479; Philadelphia, PA, Mus. A.) apparently portrays Lodovico Portinari; it was originally part of a diptych, accompanied by a *Virgin and Child* (Cambridge, MA, Fogg). Among important surviving works, the *Virgin and Child with Three Donors* (Antwerp, Kon. Mus. S. Kst.) is dated 1486. A number of the paintings include depictions of the city of Bruges and may be dated to before 1483 or between 1493 and 1499, depending on the state of the belfry, which underwent additions and alterations at these times. The artist's style is apparently derived from Rogier van der

Weyden but also shows the influence of Hans Memling. Many of the Master's works were formerly attributed to Hugo van der Goes. The central panel of the triptych of the *Nativity* (*c.* 1495–1500; Detroit, MI, Inst. A.) shows the influence of Memling's compositions, while the left wing indicates a knowledge of the *Visitation* panels (Leipzig, Mus. Bild. Kst., and Turin, Gal. Sabauda) that have been attributed to van der Weyden.

BIBLIOGRAPHY

M. J. Friedländer: *Die altniederländische Malerei* (Berlin, 1924–37); Eng. trans as *Early Netherlandish Painting* (Leiden, 1967–76), vi (1971), pp. 44, 122–3, pls 113–47

P. Bautier: 'Le Maître brugeois de la Légende de Sainte Ursule', *Mus. Royaux B.-A. Belgique: Bull.* [Belgique], v (1956), pp. 3–12

G. Marlier: 'Le Maître de la Légende de Sainte Ursule', *Jb.: Kon. Mus. S. Kst.* (1964), pp. 5–40

H. Pauwels: 'Maître de la Légende de Sainte Ursule', *Primitifs flamands anonymes: Maîtres aux noms d'emprunt des Pays-Bas méridionaux du XVe et du début du XVIe siècle* (exh. cat., Bruges, Groeningemus., 1969), pp. 29–46, 195–204

JEREMY GRIFFITHS

Master of the Legend of St Ursula (ii) (*fl c.* 1480–1510). German painter. He stands out among the Late Gothic painters of Cologne through his uncommon colouristic talent. His work is now distinctly separated (Aldenhoven) from that of the MASTER OF ST SEVERIN (*see* below), to whom it was formerly attributed. He is named after a cycle of 19 known oil paintings depicting the *Legend of St Ursula* (1492–6; Bonn, Rhein. Landesmus.; Cologne, Wallraf-Richartz-Mus.; Cologne, Erzbischöf. Diöz.-Mus.; London, V&A; Paris, Louvre, and others). Although eight paintings were in St Severin, Cologne, until 1880, it is thought that the former parish church of St Brigid was the cycle's original location. Painted with a relatively dry technique, weak in oil, on a barely primed canvas, the cycle combines a bold pictorial conception with a detailed reproduction of costumes, buildings and diverse forms of landscape. Characteristic are the pale flesh tones of some figures, emphasizing an extreme ideal of beauty, and the generally dignified, serious atmosphere, in which there is a melancholy hitherto unusual in Cologne. The iconography of the cycle reveals the painter's knowledge of earlier representations of the *Legend of St Ursula* (1456; Cologne, St Ursula; *c.* 1440; Cologne, Wallraf-Richartz-Mus.) and of other Cologne works, overlaid with dominant influences from Netherlandish art.

The earliest preserved evidence of the Master is a winged altarpiece (*c.* 1480–85; Frauenberg, Kreis Euskirchen, St Georg) of which the central panel depicts the *Holy Kinship*, at the edges the donor couple, and the wing panels the *Annunciation* and *Adoration of the Magi*. The reverse sides of the wings (*Crucifixion* and *Lamentation*) are thought (Wallrath) to have been painted by an assistant in the manner of the early works of the Master of St Severin, who himself later used the Frauenberg scene as a model for his *Adoration of the Magi* (*c.* 1505–10; Cologne, Wallraf-Richartz-Mus.) and who may have been a pupil of the Master of the Legend of St Ursula. The latter Master's poise and sophisticated use of colour are impressively asserted in another early work, a panel of the *Virgin and Child with Female Saints in the Hortus Conclusus* (1480s; Cologne, Wallraf-Richartz-Mus.). His ability to bring figures and landscapes into a lively relationship emerges

convincingly in the central panel of an altarpiece showing the *Stigmatization of St Francis* (*c.* 1500; Cologne, Wallraf-Richartz-Mus.). The coolly restrained *Portrait of a Young Woman* (*c.* 1500; Cologne, Wallraf-Richartz-Mus.), ascribed to the Master, also belongs to this period. His later style is seen in the dense, agitated pattern of the *Lamentation* (*c.* 1510; Cologne, Erzbischöf. Diöz.-Mus.), formerly the right-hand wing panel from a large altarpiece of the *Passion* (its reverse being a fragment of the *Last Judgement*; the central panel, *Calvary*, was destroyed in Berlin, 1945).

The Master's characteristic use of colour, distinct figure types and specific relationship to pictorial space suggest that his idiom derived not only from Cologne but also from the northern Netherlands—possibly from the circle of Geertgen tot Sint Jans and the Master of the Virgo inter Virgines—though it also took from influences by the art of the southern Netherlands, perhaps from the circle of Hugo van der Goes. Proposed connections with Venetian painting (e.g. Carpaccio) are as yet unclear. Of the Master's Cologne contemporaries, only the Master of the St Bartholomew Altar could really compare with him in range.

BIBLIOGRAPHY

Kindler (Wallrath)

C. Aldenhoven: *Geschichte der Kölner Malerschule* (Lübeck, 1902), pp. 292–314

H. Brockmann: *Die Spätzeit der Kölner Malerschule* (Bonn, Leipzig, 1924), pp. 123–225

A. Stange: *Deutsche Malerei der Gotik*, v (Munich, 1952), pp. 91–103

C. M. Kauffmann: *The Legend of Saint Ursula*, Victoria and Albert Museum Monographs (London, 1964)

A. Stange: *Die deutschen Tafelbilder vor Dürer: Kritisches Verzeichnis*, i (Munich, 1967), pp. 96–100, nos 292–301

HANS M. SCHMIDT

Master of the Legend Scenes (*fl* early 16th century). Austrian painter and woodcutter. He is named after two altarpiece wings with three scenes from the *Legend of SS Cosmas and Damian*: the *Miraculous Healing of the Leg*, *A Husband Commending his Wife to the Saints* and the *Delivery of the False Message by the Devil* (Vienna, Ksthist. Mus.). He is thought to have been the earliest disciple of Lucas Cranach the elder in Austria and to have been later influenced by both Albrecht Altdorfer and Jörg Breu the elder. His rather stately figures are in splayed-out, often affected poses, with the feet and knees twisted outwards, appearing almost dislocated. The heads have high foreheads and flat, slightly upturned noses; long shadows run down in parallel lines from the eyes.

Research suggests that the Master of the Legend Scenes is identical with the Master of the Miracles of Mariazell, named after a series of 25 woodcuts (Berlin, Kupferstichkab.) influenced by Lucas Cranach, one of which bears the date 1503. Six panels depicting the *Miracles of the Virgin of Mariazell* (1512; Graz, Steiermärk. Landesmus.) may be by the same artist. The woodcuts have little connection with the pictures: only three of the painted scenes are repeated in the woodcuts. Other works attributed to the Master are a *Kneeling Saint* (Munich, Bayer. Nmus.) and three panels with the standing figures of *St Stephen*, *St Mary Magdalene* and *St Sebastian* (all Klosterneuburg, Mus. Chorherrenstiftes).

BIBLIOGRAPHY

O. Benesch: 'Zur altösterreichischen Tafelmalerei', *Jb. Ksthist. Samml. Wien*, n. s. i (1928), pp. 63–118, table 154

J. Meder: 'Der Meister der Legendenszenen der Mariazeller Wunder', *Z. Dt. Ver. Kstwiss.*, iii (1936), pp. 7–10

SONJA WEIH-KRUGER

Master of Liesborn (*fl* Liesborn, nr Lippstadt, *c*. 1460–90). German painter. He is named after an altarpiece in the Benedictine monastery of Liesborn. In 1465 Abbot Heinrich von Cleve (*d* 1490) dedicated five altars there, including the high altar, for which he subsequently commissioned a painted altarpiece. In the 18th century it was removed and dismantled, and in 1804, following secularization of the monastery, 14 parts were dispersed (ex-priv. cols; London, N.G.; Münster, Westfäl. Landesmus.; Münster, Westfäl. Kstver.). Reconstruction from fragments and from two scenes that are still intact reveals that it was a fixed altarpiece, with no wings, showing the *Crucifixion* (centre), with saints on either beneath the cross; above the saints' heads were four angels catching the blood of Christ. The remaining side sections show the *Annunciation*, the *Adoration of the Infant Jesus*, the *Adoration of the Magi* and the *Presentation in the Temple*. As the standing saints are positioned supposedly in the Cologne tradition, the work has been thought to come from Cologne; however, the choice of picture did not originate with the artist but with Abbot Heinrich von Cleve, and its emphasis on the sacrifice made by Christ as giving meaning to the Mass accords with texts belonging to the Bursfeld Benedictine congregation.

BIBLIOGRAPHY

W. König: 'Studien zum Meister von Liesborn', *Quellen & Forsch. Gesch. Kreises Beckum*, vi (Beckum, 1974)

P. Pieper: *Die deutschen, niederländischen und italienischen Tafelbilder bis um 1530: Bestandskatalog Westfälisches Landesmuseum für Kunst und Kulturgeschichte* (Münster, 1986)

Der Kalvarienberg des Meisters von Liesborn (exh. cat., Münster, Stadtmus., 1988)

J. Luckhardt: 'Der Heiligen unter dem Kreuz: Eine inhaltliche Interpretation des Liesborner Altares', *Niederdt. Beitr. Kstgesch.*, xxxi (1992), pp. 50–67

R. Brandl: 'The Liesborn Altar-piece, a New Reconstruction', *Burl. Mag.*, cxxxv (1993), pp. 180–89

JOCHEN LUCKHARDT

Master of the Life of Lydwina (*fl c*. 1496–8). South Netherlandish woodcutter. He designed the illustrations for Johannes Brugman's *Vita Lidwinae*, an account of the life of a local holy woman, printed at Schiedam in 1498. He may also be responsible for the title-page woodcuts in two books published at Gouda: *Leven van Liedwy* (1496) and the *Historie vanden heiligen patriarch Joseph* (1496 or later). Elements in his style derive from the somewhat earlier Master of the Chevalier Délibéré, and some of his figure types resemble those in paintings attributed to the Master of Delft, with whose workshop he may have been associated. His clear relationship to the early work of Jacob Cornelisz. is one of influence rather than identity.

BIBLIOGRAPHY

Hollstein: *Dut. & Flem.*

A. Châtelet: *Les Primitifs hollandais* (Paris and Friburg, 1980); Eng. trans. as *Early Dutch Painting* (Oxford and New York, 1981), pp. 163, 240–41

THOMAS J. GOMBAR

Master of the Life of the Virgin (*fl c*. 1460–80). German painter. He is named from a winged altarpiece (*c*. 1465; Cologne, St Ursula) with panels depicting scenes from the *Life of the Virgin* (one, *Presentation in the Temple*, London, N.G.; seven, Munich, Alte Pin.), the reverse side of its wings being damaged and dismembered. The altarpiece was donated by the Cologne patrician Johann von Hirtz (councillor 1440–74; *d* 1481), whose portrait is prominent in the *Visitation*. Although the Master of the Life of the Virgin's collaboration (Stange, 1967) and even identity (Förster) with the Master of the Lyversberg Passion has been suggested, there is more reason to believe that the Master of the Legend of St George was involved.

The formative influence on the Master of the Life of the Virgin was Netherlandish: the work of Rogier van der Weyden and Dieric Bouts I was known in Cologne soon after *c*. 1450, notably through imported works such as the former's Columba Triptych (*c*. 1455; ex-Cologne, St Kolumba; Munich, Alte Pin.; *see* WEYDEN, VAN DER, (1), fig. 3) and the panels of the Master of the Munich Arrest of Christ. He was for his generation the pace-setting artist in the Rhineland metropolis, his style clearly separated from that of Stefan Lochner.

The oeuvre attributed to the Master is characterized by its idealistic, dignified and cool poise, in which classical stylization resonates. His earliest known work is a *Passion* triptych (*c*. 1460; Bernkastel-Kues, St Nikolaus Hospital, chapel), commissioned by Cardinal Nikolaus Cusanus (1400–64), who is depicted as donor. It blends Cologne, Netherlandish and, apparently, Italian motifs (such as are also seen in the *Birth of the Virgin* in his eponymous altarpiece). In expansive scenes, constructed more contemplatively than dramatically, the central panel depicts the *Crucifixion*, the left-hand wing the *Mocking of Christ* and the right-hand the *Entombment*.

Other attributed works by the Master, dated through comparison with the *Life of the Virgin* altarpiece, include the *Vision of St Bernard* (*c*. 1480; Cologne, Wallraf-Richartz-Mus.), which is permeated with great intimacy, and a panel of the *Virgin* (*c*. 1470–75; Berlin, Gemäldegal.). His *Portrait of an Architect* (1470; Munich, Alte Pin.) and the *Portrait of a Man*, perhaps a scholar (1480; Karlsruhe, Staatl. Ksthalle), as well as various donor portraits in the altar panels, are evidence of his ability not only to depict human physiognomy but to heighten its expression, a talent that made him a popular portrait painter in Cologne. His work rose to a classical clarity in the *Lamentation*, the central panel of the Cologne De Monte Triptych (after 1480; Cologne, Wallraf-Richartz-Mus.), for which his former workshop assistant, the Master of the Legend of St George, subsequently executed wing panels.

The Master's attributed oeuvre has now been reduced by attributions to the Master of the Lyversberg Passion, the Master of the Legend of St George and the Master of the Bonn Diptych (*fl c*. 1485): none of these artists could evade his influence. He is thought also to have influenced stained-glass painting and woodcut book illustration in Cologne; this is only beginning to be researched. In the pictorial world of the Master of the Life of the Virgin, late medieval vision and feeling achieved a relatively harmonious and valid expression, despite diverse new influences heralding a more restless and more strongly subjective epoch.

BIBLIOGRAPHY

O. H. Förster: 'Der Linzer Altar und die Frühwerke des Meisters des Marienlebens', *Wallraf-Richartz-Jb.*, iii/iv (1926–7), pp. 152–73
A. Stange: *Deutsche Malerei der Gotik*, v (Munich, 1952), pp. 25–57
——: *Kritisches Verzeichnis der deutschen Tafelbilder vor Dürer*, i (Munich, 1967), pp. 61–6, nos 167–85
H. M. Schmidt: *Der Meister des Marienlebens und sein Kreis: Studien zur spätgotischen Malerei in Köln* (Düsseldorf, 1978), pp. 19–54, 174–93
R. Budde: *Köln und seine Maler, 1300–1500* (Cologne, 1986), pp. 95–106
F. G. Zehnder: *Katalog der Altkölner Malerei*, xi of *Katalog des Wallraf-Richartz-Museums* (Cologne, 1990), pp. 466–84

HANS M. SCHMIDT

Lippi-Pesellino Imitators. *See under* PSEUDO-PIER FRANCESCO FIORENTINO below.

Master of the Livre des femmes nobles et renommées. *See* MASTER OF THE CORONATION OF THE VIRGIN above.

Master of the London Passional. *See under* MASTER OF EVERT VAN SOUDENBALCH above.

Master of the London Pliny. *See under* GASPARO PADOVANO.

Master of the Lord Lee Polyptych. *See* MASTER OF THE DOMINICAN EFFIGIES above.

Master of Lourinhã (*fl* 1510–25). North Netherlandish painter, active in Portugal. Two of the most representative works by this anonymous Master are now at Lourinhã (Estremadura), from where he takes his name. He worked between 1510 and 1512 in collaboration with Frei Carlos on the triptych of the *Infantes* (Lisbon, Mus. N. A. Ant.), which includes portraits of the sons of Manuel I, Dom John (the future John III) and Dom Luís. The altarpiece of Funchal Cathedral, Madeira, has 12 panels relating to the *Eucharist*, the *Life of the Virgin* and the *Passion* (1510–15). It shows the influence of engravings by Martin Schongauer, Albrecht Dürer and Jacob Cornelisz. of Amsterdam, as well as the aesthetic of Dutch painting.

Around 1513 the Master of Lourinhã worked at the convent of Madre de Deus, Xabregas (Lisbon), from which are known two panels of Franciscan saints, *SS Francis and Anthony* and *SS Clare and Colette* (Lisbon, Mus. N. A. Ant.). The two panels now at the Misericórdia, Lourinhã, from a monastery on the island of Berlenga off the west coast of Portugal, are of great interest. One shows *St John the Baptist* and the other *St John on Patmos*, which has for background a blue–green landscape of sea and mountains, with a walled city, and is characteristic of the Haarlem school of the early 16th century. It appears that here the Master was inspired by the treatment of the same subject by the Master of the Taking of Christ (*fl* 1455–75; Rotterdam, Mus. Boymans–van Beuningen), who was a pupil of Dieric Bouts, which would confirm the northern origins of the Master of Lourinhã. Between 1520 and 1525, in collaboration with other Portuguese artists, he painted the *Altarpiece of the Order of Santiago* (Lisbon, Mus. N. A. Ant.) for the church of the castle at Palmela, which belonged to the Military Order of Santiago.

BIBLIOGRAPHY

L. Reis-Santos: *Estudos de pintura antiga* (Lisbon, 1943), pp. 189–96, 278
G. Kubler and M. Soria: *Art and Architecture in Spain and Portugal and their American Dominions, 1500 to 1800*, Pelican Hist. A. (Harmondsworth, 1959)
L. Reis-Santos: *O mestre de Lourinhã* (Lisbon, 1963)
A. Châtelet: *Les Primitifs hollandais* (Paris and Fribourg, 1980); Eng. trans. as *Early Dutch Painting* (Oxford and New York, 1981)

DAGOBERTO L. MARKL

Louthe Master. *See* MARMION, SIMON.

Master of the Louvre Annunciation. *See under* BRACCESCO, CARLO.

Master of the Lübeck Bible (*fl c.* Lübeck, 1489–94). Woodcutter. He was the principal designer of woodcut illustrations for one of the most extraordinary examples of German incunabula, the Low German Bible printed by Stephan Arndes at Lübeck in 1494, and was responsible for most of the woodcuts in the Pentateuch. The remaining woodcuts are by a related but inferior hand. Only one other work can be confidently attributed to him, a *Dance of Death* published anonymously at Lübeck in 1489. His style, with its painterly approach and sophisticated rendering of landscape, has no precedents in Lübeck art and bespeaks Netherlandish origins, so he may have been an itinerant artist. He is the harbinger of a new style that shares features with the early work of Jacob Cornelisz. and Lucas van Leyden.

BIBLIOGRAPHY

Hollstein: *Dut. & Flem.*

THOMAS J. GOMBAR

Luçon Master (*fl* Paris, 1401–17). French illuminator. A leading artist working in Paris in the Late Gothic style, he was named by Meiss after the cycle of miniatures in the Missal–Pontifical (*c.* 1405–7; Paris, Bib. N., MS. lat. 8886) of Etienne Loypeau, Bishop of Luçon. His works are distinguished by meticulous finish, elegance and subtle tonalities. Characteristic are his sinuous figures echoed by curling arabesques in the backgrounds. He specialized in the production of Books of Hours as suggested by the 21 extant examples known, mostly in public collections. A volume written in 1401 (Barcelona, Bib. Catalunya, MS. 1850), is the earliest dated Hours in which his work appears. His activity, however, also extended to other liturgical and devotional volumes, the latter exemplified by the compendium of moral treatises (Paris, Bib. N., MS. fr. 926) that Marie de Berry received in 1406 from her confessor Simon de Courcy. By 1406 the Master and his workshop also began illustrating secular texts destined for Jean, Duc de Berry, and John the Fearless, Duke of Burgundy, and their retainers. Among this more diversified production are volumes of the works of Aristotle (Brussels, Bib. Royale Albert Ier, MSS 9089–90; Paris, Bib. N., MS. fr. 208), Virgil's *Eclogues and Georgics* (Holkham Hall, Norfolk, MS. 307), the *Décades* of Valerius Maximus (Paris, Bib. N., MS. lat. 6147), Boccaccio's *Cas des nobles hommes* (Geneva, Bib. Pub. & U., MS. 190) and Gerbert de Montreuil's *Roman de la violette* (St Petersburg, Rus. N. Lib., MS. fr. Q.v.XIV, 3). Typical of the Luçon Master's later works are the drapery borders of burnished and delicately tooled gold.

BIBLIOGRAPHY

M. Meiss: *French Painting in the Time of Jean de Berry: The Late XIV Century and the Patronage of the Duke*, 2 vols (London, 1967, rev. 1969)

——: *French Painting in the Time of Jean de Berry: The Limbourgs and their Contemporaries*, 2 vols (New York, 1974)

PATRICK M. DE WINTER

Master of Luxembourg-Martigues. *See under* DUVAL, MARC.

Master of the Lyversberg Passion (*fl* Cologne, *c.* 1460–*c.* 1480). German painter. He is named from two panels showing eight scenes of the *Passion* (?1464; Cologne, Wallraf-Richartz-Mus.) that entered the collection of the Cologne merchant Jakob Johann Lyversberg (*d* 1834) around 1800. It is thought that they were originally the inner sides of the wings of a large carved altarpiece donated in 1464 to the Carthusian church in Cologne by the merchant and city councillor Johann Rinck (*d* 1466) and his son Peter (*d* 1501). The paintings on the outer sides of the wings show the *Annunciation* and *Adoration of the Magi* (Nuremberg, Ger. Nmus.). The motifs, sprightly narrative style, richly contrasting colours and crowded profusion of figures in conventional compositional arrangements suggest that the Master was linked to earlier Cologne painting in the tradition of Stefan Lochner. Not only the depiction of the details of fabrics but also individual picture formulae indicate contact with contemporary Flemish works then to be seen in Cologne churches, such as Rogier van der Weyden's St Columba altarpiece (1450s; ex-Cologne, St Kolumba; Munich, Alte Pin.) and above all works from the circle of Dieric Bouts I. These influences are clearly seen in early works attributed to the Master, for example the altarpiece of the *Virgin* (1463; Linz am Rhein, Pfarrkirche). A miniature on parchment depicting the *Crucifixion with the Virgin and St John* (before *c.* 1461; Cologne, Wallraf-Richartz-Mus.) verifies that early in his career, at least, he had worked as a manuscript illuminator. His gift for exact observation fitted him for some of the earliest portrait work in Cologne. His last preserved work is the asymmetrical panel of the *Crucifixion with the Virgin and SS John and Mary Magdalene* (*c.* 1475; Cologne, Wallraf-Richartz-Mus.), formerly regarded as a work of the Master of the Life of the Virgin; now it is thought to show the definite influence of that more important artist on the Master of the Lyversberg Passion.

BIBLIOGRAPHY

L. A. Scheibler: *Die hervorragendsten anonymen Meister und Werke der Kölner Malerschule von 1460 bis 1500* (diss., U. Bonn, 1880)

O. H. Förster: 'Der Linzer Altar und die Frühwerke des Meisters des Marienlebens', *Wallraf-Richartz-Jb.*, iii/iv (1926–7), pp. 152–73

A. Stange: *Kritisches Verzeichnis der deutschen Tafelbilder vor Dürer*, i (Munich, 1967), pp. 68–71, nos 196–206

H. M. Schmidt: *Der Meister des Marienlebens und sein Kreis: Studien zur spätgotischen Malerei in Köln* (Düsseldorf, 1978), pp. 58–74

R. Budde: *Köln und seine Maler, 1300–1500* (Cologne, 1986), pp. 106–12

F. G. Zehnder: *Katalog der Altkölner Malerei*, xi of *Katalog des Wallraf-Richartz-Museums* (Cologne, 1990), pp. 345–55

HANS M. SCHMIDT

Master of the Madonna of the Seven Sorrows. *See under* ISENBRANDT, ADRIAEN.

Master of the Madre de Deus. *See under* AFONSO, JORGE.

Magdalen Master (*fl* Florence, *c.* 1265–90). Italian painter. One of the most influential artists in 13th-century Florence, he was named by Sirén (1922) after a panel showing a standing figure of St Mary Magdalen flanked by eight small scenes from her life (Florence, Accademia). Sirén first attributed three pictures of the *Virgin and Child* (Berlin, Gemäldegal.; S Michele in Rovezzano, nr Florence; ex-S Fedele, Poppi, now Arezzo, Gal. & Mus. Med. & Mod.) to this Master and emphasized the apparent influence of Coppo di Marcovaldo. In 1926 he added another group of paintings to the Magdalen Master's oeuvre, including the altarpiece of the *Virgin Enthroned between SS Andrew and James* (Paris, Mus. A. Déc.). This, one of the painter's most beautiful and important works, had already been linked by Toesca to the panel in the Accademia. Offner (1927) identified other early works, such as the dossal of the *Virgin and Child Enthroned between SS Leonard and Peter* (New Haven, CT, Yale U. A.G.) and the tabernacle showing the *Virgin and Child Enthroned with SS Peter and Paul* (New York, Met.).

The assessment of the Magdalen Master's importance and the chronology of his paintings have given rise to widely divergent hypotheses: some scholars have suggested that the large group of works attributed to him should be allocated to more than one painter and have emphasized the popular, almost artisan character of the works. If, however, the quality of the work is debatable, the originality of the style cannot be so easily questioned; it must be the product of an individual master, who was the head of one of the most important and well-organized workshops in Florence in the second half of the 13th century. It satisfied the demands of a lay, bourgeois clientele, as the frequent presence of donors in the paintings shows. Their inclusion was still fairly unusual in the 13th century. The chronology proposed by Offner (1927) and by Coor–Achenbach (1947) is still generally valid. The latter divided the Magdalen Master's work into three successive stages: first showing the influence of the Bigallo Master and the painter of the *Virgin and Child* in S Andrea at Rovezzano, as in the dossal in Yale University; then closer to the more courtly style of such Florentine painters as Coppo di Marcovaldo, as in the Berlin *Virgin and Child*; and finally showing the renewed influence of Cimabue, as in the *Virgin and Child* from Poppi.

It has been suggested that the Magdalen Master participated in the mosaic decoration of the dome of the Florentine Baptistery, but his exact contribution is difficult to identify owing to the mosaic's poor state of preservation and heavy restoration. The Magdalen Master's lively narrative scenes may have been a source of inspiration for Florentine illuminators at the end of the 13th century, when the influence of Cimabue was still strong. There seems to have been a reciprocal influence between the Magdalen Master and such artists as Meliore and Corso di Buono (*fl c.* 1275), which did much to revitalize Florentine painting between 1270 and 1280.

BIBLIOGRAPHY

Thieme–Becker: 'Meister der hl. Magdalena'

O. Sirén: *Toskanische Malerei im XIII Jahrhundert* (Berlin, 1922), pp. 264–75

P. Toesca: 'Gli affreschi del duomo di Aquileia', *Dédalo*, vi (1925–6), pp. 43–4

——: 'Peintures toscanes inconnues du XIIIe siècle', *Gaz. B.-A.*, n. s. 5, xiii (1926), pp. 347–60

R. Offner: *Italian Primitives at Yale University*, Yale U. A.G. cat. (New Haven, 1927), pp. 11–14

G. Coor-Achenbach: 'A Neglected Work by the Magdalen Master', *Burl. Mag.*, lxxxix (1947), pp. 119–29

E. B. Garrison: *Italian Romanesque Panel Painting: An Illustrated Index* (Florence, 1949)

C. L. Ragghianti: *Pittura del dugento a Firenze* (Florence, 1955), pp. 100–06

L. Marcucci: *Gallerie nazionali di Firenze: I dipinti toscani del secolo XIII* (Rome, 1958), pp. 49–56

A. Tartuferi: 'Pittura fiorentina del duecento', *La pittura in Italia: Il duecento e il trecento*, ed. E. Castelnuovo, i (Milan, 1986), pp. 267–82

——: *La pittura a Firenze nel duecento* (Florence, 1990), pp. 42–5

ANGELO TARTUFERI

Master of Mansel (*fl c.* 1420–60). South Netherlandish illuminator. The name is given to the illuminator of the majority of the 65 miniatures in a two-volume *Fleur des histoires* by Jean Mansel (Brussels, Bib. Royale Albert 1er, MSS 9231–2). Some of the miniatures, however, particularly in the second volume, were painted by SIMON MARMION. Two volumes of a three-volume copy of the same text were also illuminated by the Master of Mansel (Vienna, Schottenkirche, Stiftsgal., MSS 167/139–168/140). As Mansel wrote the text around 1440, and the manuscripts—particularly those in Vienna—date from soon after this, a direct connection between the author and the illuminator's workshop is possible.

In a copy of Laurent de Premierfait's French translation of Boccaccio's *Decameron* (Paris, Bib. Arsenal, MS. 5070) the Master of Mansel worked with the Master of Guillebert de Metz; both artists closely followed the illustration of a Boccaccio produced around 1415 in Paris. The Master of Mansel's style also shows the clear influence of the Bedford Master, another illustrator who worked in Paris. In common with this artist, he had a predilection for depicting small houses, open at the front, allowing the inclusion of several scenes in one picture field; steeply raked landscapes, with a high horizon line to give an impression of depth; and certain figure types, such as the old man with a long shaggy beard.

The presence of wave-shaped clouds, brushed with silver, moving from left to right across the even, rich blue of his skies, is almost a trademark of the Master of Mansel. The light, airy colouring and the atmospheric effect of the landscapes are also characteristic of this artist. These qualities connect him with contemporary illumination in Amiens. It has also been suggested that he worked in Valenciennes, because of Simon Marmion's participation in the Brussels *Fleur des histoires* and because Marmion's style follows on directly from that of his predecessor.

BIBLIOGRAPHY

F. Winkler: *Die flämische Buchmalerei* (Leipzig, 1925/*R* Amsterdam, 1978), pp. 34–6

Le Siècle d'or de la miniature flamande (exh. cat. by L. M. J. Delaissé, Brussels, Pal. B.-A.; Amsterdam, Rijksmus.; Paris, Bib. N.; 1959), pp. 60–66

G. Dogaer: *Flemish Miniature Painting in the 15th and 16th Centuries* (Amsterdam, 1987), pp. 43–7

Flämische Buchmalerei: Handschriftenschätze aus dem Burgunderreich (exh. cat. by D. Thoss, Vienna, Österreich. Nbib., 1987), pp. 43–5

BODO BRINKMANN

Master of the Mansi Magdalene (*fl* ?Antwerp, *c.* 1515–25). South Netherlandish painter. He was named after a painting of the *Magdalene* (Berlin, Gemäldegal.), formerly in the collection of the Marchese Battista Mansi at Lucca, where it was wrongly attributed to Quinten Metsys. In this painting the Master imitated the broad heads and long fingers of Metsys's figures, but the rigid frontality, monochromatic colouring and panoramic landscape framing the figure are characteristics of his own style, found also in the Master's *Saviour* (Philadelphia, PA, Mus. A.). There the figure is placed in the centre foreground of a landscape that is partly derived from Albrecht Dürer's engraving of the *Vision of St Eustace*. The Master's frequent use of Dürer's prints helps date his period of activity: the *Entombment* (Ghent, Mus. S. Kst.) is derived from Dürer's woodcut of the scene from the *Small Passion* of 1511. The Master also copied Italian prints, as in his *Virgin and Child* (Madrid, Mus. Thyssen-Bornemisza), based on an engraving by Marcantonio Raimondi. The artist's identity remains uncertain, but Friedländer suggested that he may have been Willem Muelenbroec, who registered in the Antwerp painters' guild as a pupil of Metsys in 1501.

BIBLIOGRAPHY

M. J. Friedländer: *Die altniederländische Malerei* (Berlin, 1924–37); Eng. trans. as *Early Netherlandish Painting* (Leiden, 1967–76), vii, pp. 45–7

ELLEN KONOWITZ

Master of the Marble Madonnas (*fl c.* 1470–1500). Italian sculptor or group of sculptors. The name was coined by Bode (1892–1905) for an anonymous sculptor, apparently Tuscan, possibly trained in the workshop of Mino da Fiesole and influenced by Antonio Rossellino. Numerous sculptures have been attributed to him on the basis of related compositions, drapery forms, ornamental motifs and pronounced mannerisms. Chief among the latter is a peculiar feline smile from heavy-lidded eyes and a taut jaw, at its best radiating inward joy but often acerbic or bordering on the manic. The Master's eclectic shop and followers produced marble reliefs of the *Virgin and Child*, busts and reliefs of the suffering Christ and busts of children. Bode had noted (1886) that many of these were of Florentine or Tuscan provenance.

The chief documented monument that is stylistically associated with the Master's work is the Numai tomb (1502) at S Pellegrino, Forlì. This has led to the Master's identification as either Tommaso Fiamberti (de Nicola, 1922) or Giovanni Ricci (*d* after 1523; Balogh, 1933), but whichever of these Lombards made the Forlì reliefs seems, rather, to have been a late, somewhat clumsy follower of the Master. Numerous attributions in Emilia–Romagna, Urbino, Hungary and Dalmatia might indicate that either the Master or a close follower was active in those regions. Balogh (1975) gives the most complete list of attributed works.

The sculptures attributed to the Master are the product of various hands, and several may be collaborative works. Even the best works and most frequent types are not necessarily all by a single hand. Two marble reliefs of the *Virgin and Child* (Florence, Bargello and S Stefano al Ponte) are representative of the most characteristic composition. They reflect a prototype by Mino da Fiesole exemplified by the *Virgin and Child* relief on the monument to Conte Ugo of Tuscany (1469–81; Florence, Badia), but Rossellino's influence shows in softer flesh and drapery passages, freer movement, curling hair and background motifs. The Bargello relief is stiff, almost frontal and close to Mino, whereas the S Stefano relief has soft, fluid handling and a warm expression, with signs of Verocchio influence in the smiles. This may be due to a distinct personality in the workshop. In related reliefs the Virgin has an ovoid head with a high plucked forehead and long, pointed chin, with a spreading hood and a mantle with a sinuous, hatched border; the Christ Child is shown seated, holding a bird or orb, and paired background angels proffer a crown or fruit. Good examples include one close to the S Stefano relief (Paris, Louvre) and one with its old polychromy (Ottawa, N.G.), a link to Urbino; a third is in Canberra (N.G.). A bust of the youthful *St John the Baptist* (Washington, DC, N.G.A.) and a half-length youthful *St John the Baptist* (Kansas City, MO, Nelson–Atkins Mus. A.) are close to the Madonna reliefs in expression and the handling of details. Most accomplished of the related works is a bust *Ecce homo* (Switzerland, priv. col., see Middeldorf, 1973), with rich, open and fluid carving, sharply ornamental locks of hair and remarkable expressive intensity.

The three reliefs of the *Virgin and Child* (Urbino, Pal. Ducale) are arguably by at least three sculptors, one of whom (see Rotondi, 1950–51, fig. 445) probably also carved the fine relief of the *Virgin and Child* (Pistoia, Mus. Civ.). A collaborator on the Urbino *Virgin and Child beneath an Arch* (Rotondi, fig. 447) may have carved a related composition of the same subject (U. London, Courtauld Inst. Gals) as well as the strange busts of boys (Budapest, N.G.; Urbino, Pal. Ducale) with harsh smiles and knobbly curls. An important group of works in Hungary, Dalmatia (dated *c.* 1480–92 by Balogh, 1980) and Forlì has stockier figure-types, compositions frequently reflecting the lunette above Desiderio da Settignano's Marsuppini tomb (Florence, Santa Croce) and a Child often wearing a short tunic. Striking patterns of ornament and drillwork occur in these. The *Virgin and Child with Cherubim* (Berlin, Skulpgal., 94) appears close to the works in Dalmatia and Hungary, as does a group of reliefs by yet another hand (e.g. New York, Mortimer Schiff priv. col.), in which the Virgin is shown tenderly caressing the Child; the faces are coarser, and the drapery is brittle and angular.

BIBLIOGRAPHY

Thieme–Becker
W. von Bode: 'Die italienischen Skulpturen der Renaissance in den königlichen Museen zu Berlin, VI: Die Florentiner Marmorbildner in der zweiten Hälfte des Quattrocento', *Jb. Kön.-Preuss. Kstsamml.*, vii (1886), pp. 29–32
——: *Denkmäler der Renaissance: Sculptur toscanas* (Munich, 1892–1905), i, pp. 130–31
G. de Nicola: 'Tommaso Fiamberti: Il Maestro delle Madonne di Marmo', *Rass. A.*, ix (1922), pp. 73–81
J. Balogh: 'Uno sconosciuto scultore italiano presso il Re Mattia Corvino', *Riv. A.*, xv (1933), pp. 272–97
P. Rotondi: *Il Palazzo Ducale di Urbino* (Urbino, 1950–51), i, pp. 392, 467, 473–6; ii, figs 443–51
J. Pope-Hennessy: *Catalogue of Italian Sculpture in the Victoria and Albert Museum*, i (London, 1964), pp. 151–2, 197–8
——: 'Three Marble Reliefs in the Gambier-Parry Collection', *Burl. Mag.*, cix (1967), pp. 117–18
U. Middeldorf: 'An *Ecce homo* by the Master of the Marble Madonnas', *Album Amicorum J. G. van Gelder* (The Hague, 1973), pp. 234–6; also in U. Middeldorf: *Raccolta di scritti*, ii (Florence, 1980), pp. 345–9
J. Balogh: *Die Anfänge der Renaissance in Ungarn: Matthias Corvinus und die Kunst* (Graz, 1975), pp. 179–83 [lists most works attributed to the Master, with references]
U. Middeldorf: *Sculptures from the Samuel H. Kress Collection: European Schools, XIV–XIX Century* (London, 1976), pp. 29–30
J. Balogh: 'A márvanymadonnák mestere: Mátyás király szobrásza' [The Master of the Marble Madonnas: King Mátyás's sculptor], *Épités-Épitészettudomány*, xii (1980), pp. 77–86 [discussion of Hung. and Dalmat. career, reaffirms identity with Ricci]
G. Gentilini: 'Maestro delle Madonne di Marmo: Madonna col Bambino e angeli', *Misericordia di Firenze: Archivio e raccolta d'arte*, ed. C. Toricelli and others (Florence, 1981), pp. 248–9
J. Balogh: 'Der Meister der Marmormadonnen: Giovanni Ricci', *Matthias Corvinus und die Renaissance in Ungarn, 1458–1541* (exh. cat., Schallaburg, Schloss, 1982), pp. 385–91

ALISON LUCHS

Master of Margaret of Orleans (*fl c.* 1428–65). French illuminator. He was one of the more individual artists to emerge from the milieu of the Limbourg brothers and the Boucicaut and Bedford masters. Although few works can be ascribed to him with certainty, his ingenious and imaginative borders and repertory of decorative motifs were highly influential on manuscript illumination in north-western France, and in particular on the work of the Master of Jouvenel des Ursins. Attempts have been made to reconstruct the Master's itinerant career (König, 1991), which included an initial period in Paris, where he responded to the works of the Boucicaut Master, and subsequent periods in Bourges, Rennes and Poitiers. His two earliest commissions are placed during the Bourges stay: a *Grandes Chroniques de France* (Paris, Bib. N., MS. fr. 2605), possibly made for Charles VII, and a copy of Boccaccio's *Le Livre des cas des nobles hommes et femmes* (Chantilly, Mus. Condé, MS. 858), formerly owned by the Breton admiral, Prigent de Coëtivy. Also from this period is a *Livre des secrets de l'histoire naturelle* (Paris, Bib. N., MSS fr. 1377–9), which is dated in an ex-libris to 1428.

The illuminator is named after his principal work, a Book of Hours (Paris, Bib. N., MS. lat. 1156 B) made for Margaret of Orleans (1404–68). The text was copied in 1421, probably by the scribe Yvonnet de La Mote, and the illumination begun after Margaret's marriage in 1426 to Richard de Bretagne, Comte d'Etampes (*b* 1395). The calendar illustrations were probably executed in Rennes by another local artist *c.* 1426, while the following 41 miniatures by the Master are dated *c.* 1430. It has been proposed that the manuscript was illuminated in either Anjou or Brittany, perhaps in the ancient Breton capital of Rennes (König, 1982). The assurance and exuberance of this work, seen especially in the decorated borders, distinguishes it from contemporary manuscript illumination. The inhabited borders possess an extraordinary vitality and a rich and varied palette. Some are purely decorative, comprising schematic or naturalistic flowers, others depict profane subject-matter unrelated to the main image. The narrative borders are unparalleled in their inventiveness, and include hunting scenes (fol. 163r), cavalcades of lively figures travelling through forests of giant flowers (fol. 168r), and a vivid battle scene (fol. 171r). The border of *Christ before Pilate* (fol. 135r; see fig.) depicts figures sweeping up letters of the alphabet that are scattered across a plain gold background. These lively marginal decorations and certain details of style recall the work of the Bedford Master. Illuminators active in Rennes were profoundly influenced by this manuscript, and several of its compositions were borrowed.

A subsequent stay in Poitiers (c. 1440–50) is plausible given that the Master's work appears also to have been familiar to illuminators there. This can be seen in two manuscripts (Rome, Vatican, Bib. Apostolica, MS. Ross. 119, and Paris, Bib. N., MS. Rothschild 2534), the latter completed by the Master of Adelaide of Savoy, who was active in Poitiers 1450–60. A further work attributed to the Master of Margaret of Orleans is a Book of Hours (dispersed; New York, Pierpont Morgan Lib., MS. M. 190; Paris, Bib. N., MS. lat. 1170; Tours, Bib. Mun., MS. 217; Edinburgh, N. Lib.), executed for Marie de Rieux after her marriage to Louis d'Amboise, Vicomte de Thouars. The manuscript is variously dated between 1440 and 1450 and localized to Brittany or Anjou. Dated to this final period of activity is another *Grandes Chroniques de France* (Châteauroux, Bib. Mun., MS. 5, and fragments Paris, Bib. N., Cab. Est. Ad. 133). There is evidence here of collaboration with another illuminator, who in c. 1450 worked on an *Arbre des batailles* (Paris, Bib. Arsenal, MS. 2685) for the Constable of France, Arthur de Richemont.

BIBLIOGRAPHY

V. Leroquais: *Les Livre d'heures manuscrits de la Bibliothèque nationale*, 2 vols (Paris, 1927), i, pp. 67–70

Les Manuscrits à peintures en France du XIIIe au XVIe siècle (exh. cat. by J. Porcher, Paris, Bib. N., 1955), pp. 113–15, nos 241–7

E. König: *Französische Buchmalerei um 1450, Der Jouvenal-Maler, der Maler des Genfer Boccaccio und die Anfänge Jean Fouquets* (Berlin, 1982), pp. 53–6, 64–6, 72, 116–17, 122–4, 134, 217, 255, figs 116, 118–19, 251, 273, 297–8

——: *Les Heures de Marguerite d'Orléans* (Paris, 1991)

Les Manuscrits à peintures en France, 1440–1520 (exh. cat. by F. Avril and N. Reynaud, Paris, Bib. N., 1993–4), pp. 28–9

□

Master of the Martyrdom of St Lucy. *See* MASTER OF THE FIGDOR DEPOSITION above.

Master of Mary of Burgundy (*fl* Ghent, *c*. 1469–*c*. 1483)). South Netherlandish illuminator, painter and draughtsman. He is named after his most celebrated work, the Hours of Mary of Burgundy (Winkler, 1915; *see* §1(ii) below). He was one of the most original of the early Netherlandish artists, and his work, for such patrons as Margaret of York (1446–1503), wife of Charles the Bold, Duke of Burgundy, and his daughter, Mary of Burgundy, movingly reflects the introverted spirituality of the Burgundian dynasty's last decade. The numerous iconographic and formal innovations of his manuscripts determined the highly accomplished style of the GHENT-BRUGES SCHOOL of illuminators well into the 16th century.

1. Life and work. 2. Working methods and technique. 3. Critical reception and posthumous reputation.

1. LIFE AND WORK.

(i) Training and early work, before c. *1477.* The Master's patrons and his familiarity with the panel painting of Ghent place his activity in that city, but he may have trained first in Brussels with DREUX JEAN, who is probably

Master of Margaret of Orleans: *Christ before Pilate*; miniature from the Hours of Margaret of Orleans, 209×148 mm, *c*. 1430 (Paris, Bibliothèque Nationale, MS. lat. 1156 B, fol. 135*r*)

to be identified with the Master of the Girart de Roussillon. Jean may have inspired the Master's dark palette, visible strokes of black and red to model flesh areas and borders of *trompe l'oeil* vegetation on a gold ground. The painter of a *Calvary* triptych (*c*. 1468; Ghent, St Bavo), usually identified as Justus of Ghent, exerted a more important influence on the Master. His mixed colours and use of exotic dress are similar to those of the triptych, and he used the same devices for creating space in a deep landscape: averted figures and foreground ledges used as repoussoirs and overlapping hills of greens and blues progressively desaturated towards a white horizon.

The Master's earliest extant work is a miniature of the *Presentation in the Temple* (early 1470s; Berlin, Kupferstich-kab., no. 1754), on a leaf detached from a lost Book of Hours produced in the workshop of Lieven van Lathem. This was followed by a Book of Hours (early 1470s; Vienna, Österreich. Nbib., Cod. 1988) for a lady named Ysabeau, in which the Master painted 34 historiated initials, while other artists, perhaps including Geertgen tot Sint Jans, executed the 4 full-page miniatures. The borders have the flowering blue and brownish gold acanthus painted on bare parchment that is characteristic of this

1. Master of Mary of Burgundy: *Mary of Burgundy with a Vision of a Mass of the Virgin and Child*, 225×150 mm; frontispiece miniature from the Hours of Mary of Burgundy, *c.* 1477 (Vienna, Österreichische Nationalbibliothek, Cod. 1857, fol. 14*v*)

period. Sometime before 1477 the Master decorated a Breviary (Cambridge, St John's Col., MS. H. 13; London, BL, Cotton MS. Tib. A.II, fol. 1) belonging to Margaret of York. He painted the seven surviving miniatures and most of the borders. These are in both the earlier style of foliage against a bare parchment ground and the new style of flowering acanthus *en trompe l'oeil* on a gold ground, evident before only in the Girart Master's *Chroniques de Jerusalem abregiées* (Vienna, Österreich. Nbib., Cod. 2533) and in a few works for Charles the Bold from the circle of van Lathem.

(ii) Mature work, c. 1477 and after. In January 1477, according to an introductory rubric, a close follower or assistant of the Master of Mary of Burgundy painted the gold-ground borders and frontispiece (fol. 1*v*) of a Register (Windsor Castle, Royal Lib.) for the Ghent Confraternity of St Anne, whose patrons were Margaret of York and Mary of Burgundy. Although the drawing is uncertain and the execution weak, the design may be attributed to the Master. The intercessory relationship between the images of the deans painted in the border and the miniature, which shows Margaret and Mary in a church praying before an image of the Virgin and Child and St Anne, recurs in the Master's eponymous work, the Hours

of Mary of Burgundy (Vienna, Österreich. Nbib., Cod. 1857); his involvement in the completion of this important book was almost certainly the reason for delegating the execution of the Register.

The Hours of Mary of Burgundy is uniformly written in the elegant hand of Claes (Nicholas) Spierinc; the decoration, however, is remarkably heterogeneous, probably the result of several campaigns. Four artists began the work on a luxurious, but conventional programme: LIEVEN VAN LATHEM, Willem Vrelant, another north Netherlandish artist and a follower of the Girart Master. Each began one of the principal offices but finished no more than the first opening. In a second, or perhaps continuing, campaign, van Lathem carried on with borders, drolleries and miniatures, including those of the calendar, while the artist usually identified as Simon Marmion contributed miniatures of the *Virgin and Child* (fol. 35*v*) and *St John on Patmos* (fol. 27*r*). Among the drolleries, a lion holding an English standard implies that the book was commissioned by Margaret of York; the costumes suggest a date in the early 1470s. A pair of blank gold shields on the second opening of each office indicates that the book was to be a gift to Margaret's stepdaughter, Mary, on the settlement of her marriage negotiations, when the appropriate armorial charges could be painted over the thin gold washes.

In the final campaign the first 32 leaves and the book held by St John in the *Patmos* scene were repainted in black; in addition, some margins were expanded, a few of the inserted miniatures were replaced by more original scenes, and the remainder were finished. The black pages suggest that the book was now planned to serve the owner in the period of mourning for her father during the early months of 1477. Five of the inserted miniatures and the suffrage pages were assigned to the Master and an assistant. The four by his hand include an innovative *Nailing of Christ to the Cross* (fol. 43*v*), instead of the traditional *Crucifixion*, and, facing a prayer to the Virgin, the famous frontispiece (fol. 14*v*) showing a lady reading in front of a window opening on to a church, representing a vision, in which the Virgin and Child are adored by a group of noblewomen (see fig. 1). A partial anagram, RIM, on the lady's steeple headdress, the irises symbolizing the Virgin Mary and a pair of engagement carnations on the window-sill identify the reader as Mary herself. The event depicted in the church is the censing of the altar during Mass, a time of intercession for the absent faithful. The censing deacon, seen from the back, is probably Mary's unofficial fiancé, Maximilian of Austria, whose portraits show similar features, and the lady kneeling with her attendants opposite is probably Margaret of York.

The Master next contributed a small miniature of *King David Praying* (fol. 36*r*) and two borders to a Breviary (Brussels, Bib. Royale Albert 1er, MS. IV. 860), written in 1477 for the Rodeklooster, the Augustinian monastery in Brussels. A second Rodeklooster Breviary (London, BL, Add. MS. 11863) was decorated by an assistant. His most complete work, the Hours of Engelbert of Nassau (Oxford, Bodleian Lib., Douce MSS 219–20) is datable to the late 1470s by the costumes seen in the unusual drollery sequence, representing a falcon hunt and subsequent joust (see fig. 2), that runs through two of the offices. The text

2. Master of Mary of Burgundy: *Lion and Wild Man Jousting*; drollery scene from the Hours of Engelbert of Nassau, late 1470s (Oxford, Bodleian Library, MS. Douce 219, fol. 132*v*)

format without a border; van Lathem painted two more and Marmion five. The 12 others are by assistants and one of the so-called 'Ghent Associates': they include copies (nos 17, 7) of the Master's *Naming of St John the Baptist* (fol. 122) and *Presentation in the Temple* (fol. 151) in Margaret's Breviary; a copy (no. 5) of Hugo van der Goes's *Annunciation to the Shepherds* from his *Nativity* panel (Berlin, Gemäldegal.; *see* GOES, HUGO VAN DER, fig. 5); and an *Elevation of the Host* (no. 15), in which the letters 'C[harles]' and 'M[argaret]' on the altar steps suggest that it was painted before the death of Charles the Bold. It may have been the Master of Mary of Burgundy's departure from the project that necessitated this collection of miniatures by other artists, copies of the Master's work and older leaves.

Some years later the Master painted on a single leaf an unusual composition of the *Mass of St Gregory*, shown from the side in a large church choir (Brussels, Bib. Royale Albert 1er, MSS II.3654–6). The tall, borderless format had previously appeared, in the *St Barbara* from the Voustre Demeure Hours, but the space represented is now much deeper. A small panel, the *Building of the Tower of Babel* (The Hague, Mauritshuis), may probably be attributed to the Mary Master. It is dated to the late 1470s or 1480s on the basis of style.

2. WORKING METHODS AND TECHNIQUE. An accomplished narrator, the Master of Mary of Burgundy

was once again transcribed by Spierinc. Although the armorials of Engelbert II are visible beneath those of a subsequent owner, Philip the Fair, later King of Spain (*reg* 1504–6), Engelbert was not the first owner since his shield occurs in one of the *trompe l'oeil* borders (fol. 133) that were painted over the original borders of flowering acanthus on bare parchment. This overpainting was probably done in order to obliterate the emblems of the first owner. Miniature versions of the armorials of the original owner or donor are evident on the collars of three dogs in the drollery hunt: the only known bearers of these arms, the Bollioud de Saint Julien family of the Forez, were in Picardy around 1400.

The Master's most innovative work, *c*. 1481, was in a Book of Hours for a patron who used the initial 'n', or a double 'i', and the motto *Voustre demeure* (Madrid, Bib. N., MS. Vit. 25–5); Spierinc was again the scribe. The Master painted most of the coloured or gold-ground borders, nearly all the small miniatures and the five borders containing a pictorial scene or narrative, a border type that had been developed only recently in France (see fig. 3). He also added innovative empty landscapes opposite the *Labours of the Months* in the calendar by the Master of the Dresden Prayerbook. The Master of Mary of Burgundy painted only two of the full-page miniatures originally inserted in the manuscript (Berlin, Kupferstichkab., MS. 78. B. 13): a *Crucifixion* (no. 10) and the slightly later *Disputation of St Barbara* (no. 18), both in a new, tall

3. Master of Mary of Burgundy: scenes from the *Passion*, miniature from the Voustre Demeure Hours, *c.* 1481 (Madrid, Biblioteca Nacional, MS. Vit. 25–5, fol. 14)

frequently designed new compositions for traditional devotional subjects. He also expanded traditional cycles with new, subsidiary scenes, such as Mary on her way to see Elizabeth after the *Annunciation*, 'pondering all these things in her heart' (Nassau Hours, fols 97*v*–98*r*). His short, humble figures express an innocence and fundamental sadness through stooping postures, thrusting gestures and a wide-eyed gaze. Pensiveness, melancholy and suffering are the Master's true subjects. He also perfected important innovations in the layout of the decorated page, which served both to unify the text, border and miniature, and to engage the reader's attention.

His first development was to treat the miniature as a visualization of the content of the owner's prayer, by depicting him or her in one of the borders. This is based on precedents in French Books of Hours, in the Hours of Daniel Rhym from Ghent (Baltimore, MD, Walters A.G., MS. 166) and in the works of Hermann Scheere. In Margaret's Breviary, the Master of Mary of Burgundy took this idea further. He painted the vegetation of the border casting shadows on the gold ground as if the foliage existed within the reader's world. The illusion was enhanced by a shadow on the upper left diagonal to suggest light falling from the reader's right. He also lightened the ground colour at the inner edge to make the text area resemble a sheet of parchment laid on top of the border. The flatness is pierced by a little miniature showing the deep and hazy world of the devotional scene. The reader's presence is made explicit in the depiction of the owners in the Confraternity Register and in the Hours of Mary of Burgundy. In the latter the miniature is specifically shown as a window. Building on precedents from France and perhaps on the Church's interpretation of the Song of Songs II.9, 'Behold he standeth behind our wall, he looketh forth at the windows, showing himself through the lattice', as referring to Christ's incarnation, the artist surrounded three of his miniatures with the architectural frame of a chapel or the enamelwork of a monstrance. The reader's presence is also implied in the later works. The skull-filled niches around the cemetery scene (fol. 92*r*) in the Nassau Hours invite the reader to be identified with the deceased in the tomb looking back on this world. On the *Crucifixion* leaf (see fig. 4) from the Voustre Demeure Hours the luminosity of the oval miniature, which appears both as a bubble hovering over and as an opening in the surrounding dark Gethsemane, brings the reader imaginatively into the event itself.

The Master's second major innovation, the illusion of the text hanging in front of a narrative border, is also evident in the Gethsemane border. Again, he built on and simplified French precedents, which had shown the text as a placard before a complicated building or landscape. On the less significant pages he lightened the value of the inner edge of the *trompe l'oeil* borders, to make the text seem to come forward. On the *Funeral* page (fol. 238*r*), the church scene is an island of light within the dark terrors of Hell that fill the border. Four other borders are filled by a rocky landscape containing the episodes of the Passion or a saint's life, while the written space is treated as a placard hanging in front of the landscape by ropes or rods from a narrow frame at the edge of the border (see fig. 3 above). The device shows the text as a mediator

4. Master of Mary of Burgundy: *Crucifixion* and scenes of Gethsemane; miniature from the Voustre Demeure Hours, *c.* 1481 (Berlin, Kupferstichkabinett, MS. 78. B. 13)

between the events and the reader. These inventions support the idea of the book as an art object rather than as a vehicle for the text. That this was intentional is seen in Mary's Hours, in which a decorated margin on an unwritten blank page (fol. 83*v*) reveals that, contrary to the usual practice, the illuminators of the first campaign worked before the scribe; clearly, the handsome script was meant to contribute to the artistic effect. The most unified work in the Master's oeuvre, however, is the Nassau Hours, in which Spierinc's script was originally accompanied by borders of acanthus and other leafwork on every *recto* and *verso*, except on the cemetery page. Although the principal borders are repainted, the drollery sequences that link the pages of two consecutive offices and the miniatures display the nearly uniform execution of the hand of the Master and one close assistant. The Voustre Demeure Hours were apparently intended to have a similar unity.

Despite his innovations, the Master was also at times influenced by other artists. The melancholy tone of his work, for example, approaches that of Hugo van der Goes, who also provided the artist with a few motifs. The figures of St John supporting the Virgin in the *Nailing of Christ to the Cross* (fol. 43*v*) in Mary's Hours copy the figures in Hugo's *Lamentation* (Vienna, Ksthist. Mus.; *see* GOES, HUGO VAN DER, fig. 3), and certain of the apostles in the *Death of the Virgin* (fol. 170*v*) in the Nassau Hours are derived from Hugo's panel of this subject (Bruges, Groeningemus.). In addition, the setting of the *Death of the Virgin* is based on the *Annunciation* (Paris, Louvre) attributed to Rogier van der Weyden and is one of several indications of the Master's knowledge of Rogier's work. These borrowings are rare, however, and well integrated in the Master's characteristic style of freely painted, assymmetrical compositions.

The Master's technique differs from the usual illuminator's practice of a smooth application of the gouache within sharp outlines: the paint is layered in fine but visible strokes that become less distinct as they model and define. The palette is mainly dark: purples, browns and greys, with black to model faces and hands, and bright accents of salmon pink or saturated red, green or blue in the figures' clothing. The likelihood that the Master also worked on panel is supported by the aerial perspective that illuminates the darkness for the Gethsemane scenes and makes a hazy sunlight for the scenes of Calvary. Many of the tiny miniatures, for example the *Last Judgement* (fol. 181*v*) in the Nassau Hours, with a fused mass of naked bodies tumbling into a cleft beneath a great circle of the Blessed around the Saviour–Judge in the sky, have the scope and quality of much larger paintings.

Something of the Master's working procedure can be observed in the reuse of his compositions, especially in the work of the Ghent Associates. The use made of his one surviving drawing, a *Pentecost* (Paris, Ecole N. Sup. B.-A., 2670), is most interesting. The tiny dimensions of the composition (60×50 mm), quickly drawn with brush and ink with added strokes of white to suggest a strong light from the left, are precisely those of the miniatures in the small Books of Hours produced by his workshop. The conclusion that the drawing was made to be copied *in toto* is borne out by its appearance with the whole setting included in the Hours of Mary and Maximilian (Berlin, Kupferstichkab., MS. 78. B. 12, fol. 31*v*) painted by the Ghent Associates in 1482. This procedure is new in Netherlandish illumination and accounts for the high degree of standardization in the manuscripts of the Ghent Associates: breaking with the practice of his predecessors, who composed directly on the parchment or whose assistants did so by combining partial patterns, in preparing whole miniatures on separate sheets the Master left his assistants no room for invention.

3. CRITICAL RECEPTION AND POSTHUMOUS REPUTATION. The Ghent Associates began to imitate the Mary of Burgundy Master before 1477 in the first Hastings Hours (Madrid, Mus. Lázaro Galdiano, inv. 15503) and in 1477/8 in Louis XI's *Life of St Adrian* (Vienna, Österreich. Nbib., Cod. s.n. 2619), repeating his compositions and layouts while ignoring the iconographic relationships among the elements. The Master's influence was greatest in the 1480s and 1490s, extending not only to the Ghent Associates but to the younger panel painters of the time. The church scene in the frontispiece of Mary's Hours was imitated in Geertgen's early *Holy Kinship* (Amsterdam, Rijksmus.). The *Ecce homo* (fol. 69*r*) in the Nassau Hours was reproduced on an anonymous panel (Prague, N.G., Sternbek Pal.) and, more freely, in Hieronymus Bosch's first version of the subject (Frankfurt am Main, Städel. Kstinst. & Städt. Gal.). Bosch also imitated the Master's continuous narrative Passion scenes on the frame around St Gregory's vision of the Man of Sorrows, on the exterior

of the *Adoration of the Magi* triptych (Madrid, Prado). Gerard David borrowed figures from the Mary Hours for his early *Nailing of Christ to the Cross* (London, N.G.). The Master's designs continued to be used in the 16th century, in larger and often half-length form, by Gerard Horenbout and Simon Bening. The models were received through copies as well as through original drawings. Two such copies exist after his narrative borders: one (London, BM) reproduces that of *Mary and Joseph at the Inn* in the Voustre Demeure Hours and the other (Paris, Ecole N. Sup. B.-A.) a lost *Life of David*.

This illuminator's work has been highly valued since the 19th century, when Waagen drew attention to the remarkable quality of the miniatures of the Nassau Hours. A large oeuvre was assembled by Winkler and Hulin de Loo in the early decades of the 20th century and discussed in Pächt's monograph. Lieftinck, however, reanalysed most of the manuscripts, distinguishing the Master's hand from the bland execution of the earlier Master of Margaret of York and from the polished but imitative work of the Ghent Associates. The Master's identity has been the subject of controversy. Hulin de Loo proposed that the Master was Alexander, or Sanders, Bening (*see* BENING, (1)). The latter entered the Ghent painters' guild in 1469 (under the sponsorship of Joos van Wassenhove and Hugo van der Goes), married Katherijn, probably a relative of Hugo, joined the Bruges guild in 1486 and died in 1519; his sister married Gosswijn van der Weyden, Rogier's grandson. This would account for the Master's affinity with the two sponsors, his knowledge of Rogier's designs and the reuse of so many of his compositions by Alexander's son Simon (*see* BENING, (2)). The chief objection to this thesis is that no works after the 1480s have been attributed to the Master of Mary of Burgundy, whereas Sanders Bening was active after 1500.

BIBLIOGRAPHY

F. Waagen: *Treasures of Art in Great Britain*, iii (London, 1854), pp. 82–4

F. Winkler: 'Studien zur Geschichte der niederländischen Miniaturmalerei des XV und XVI Jahrhunderts', *Jb. Ksthist. Samml. Allhöch. Ksrhaus.*, xxxii (1915), pp. 279–342

——: *Die flämische Buchmalerei* (Leipzig, 1925, rev. Amsterdam, 1978), pp. 103–13, 203–4

G. Hulin de Loo: 'La Vignette chez les enlumineurs gantois entre 1470 et 1500', *Bull. Cl. B.-A., Acad. Royale Sci., Lett. & B.-A. Belgique*, xxi (1939), pp. 158–80

F. Winkler: 'Neuentdeckte Altniederländer I: Sanders Bening', *Pantheon*, xxx (1942), pp. 261–71

P. Wescher: 'Sanders and Simon Bening and Gerard Horenbout', *A. Q.*, ix (1946), pp. 191–211

O. Pächt: *The Master of Mary of Burgundy* (Oxford, 1948)

S. Sulzberger: 'Jérome Bosch et les maîtres de l'enluminure', *Scriptorium*, xvi (1962), pp. 46–9

G. I. Lieftinck: *Boekverluchters uit de omgeving van Maria van Bourgondië*, c. *1475*–c. *1485*, Verhandlingen van de Koninklijke Vlaamse Academie voor Wetenschappen, Letteren en Schone Kunsten van België, Klasse der Letteren, xxxi/66 (Brussels, 1969) [incl. almost all the Master's miniatures]

F. Unterkircher and A. de Schryver, eds: *Gebetbuch Karls des Kühnen vel potius Stundenbuch der Maria von Burgund: Codex Vindobonensis 1857 der Österreichischen Nationalbibliothek* (Graz, 1969) [facs. and commentary]

J. J. G. Alexander: *The Master of Mary of Burgundy: A Book of Hours for Engelbert of Nassau* (New York, 1970)

A. H. van Buren: 'The Master of Mary of Burgundy and his Colleagues: The State of Research and Questions of Method', *Z. Kstgesch.*, xxxviii (1975), pp. 286–309

Gent: Duizend jaar kunst en cultuur: Boekdrukkunst, boekbanden, bor-duurkunst, edelsmeedkunst, miniatuurkunst, ii (exh. cat., Ghent, Oudhknd. Mus. Bijloke, 1975), nos 607–10 [entries by A. de Schryver]

P. M. de Winter: 'A Book of Hours of Queen Isabel la Católica', *Bull. Cleveland Mus. A.*, lxvii (1981), pp. 342–427

J. A. Testa: *The Beatty Rosarium: A Manuscript with Miniatures by Simon Bening* (Doornspijk, 1986), pp. 53–64

Flämische Buchmalerei: Handschriftenschätze aus dem Burgunderreich (exh. cat. by T. Thoss, Vienna, Österreich. Nbib., 1987)

ANNE HAGOPIAN VAN BUREN

Master of the Mascoli Altar (*fl* Venice, *c*. 1430). Italian sculptor. His name is derived from the marble altarpiece of the *Virgin and Child with SS Mark and James* in the Mascoli Chapel, S Marco, Venice (see fig.). An inscription above the altar dates the foundation of the chapel to 1430, and both the figures and the architectural frame of the altar were probably commissioned at that time. Most authors also attribute the relief of the *Virgin and Child with Two Angels* over the exterior portal of the Corner Chapel (after October 1422) in S Maria dei Frari, Venice, to the Master of the Mascoli Altar. In both works the tightly pulled drapery reveals the lines of the body, accenting the pose and movement of the figures; the rather conventional Gothic frames were probably designed and executed by Venetian masons. It appears that the three sections of the Corner Chapel relief and also the figures for the Mascoli Chapel were adapted to fit into their respective frames, suggesting that the carvings did not originate in Venice but were imported and inserted into existing frames.

The style of the works attributed to the Mascoli Master has been the subject of controversy. Most authors have identified him as a Venetian, suggesting a number of well-known sculptors including Pierpaolo dalle Masegne, Giovanni Buon and Bartolomeo Buon, but the strong stylistic similarity to works by Lorenzo Ghiberti indicates instead that the Master was active in Florence. For example, the style of SS Mark and James in the Mascoli altar is derived from figures in Ghiberti's reliefs for the first bronze door for the Florentine Baptistery, and the Virgin for the Corner Chapel appears to have been modelled on Ghiberti's figures of St John the Evangelist and St Ambrose, also on the Baptistery doors. The Virgin for the Mascoli Altar, however, is based on models from Nino Pisano's circle. The Florentine origin of these figures is particularly clear when works by the Mascoli Master are compared with Venetian copies, such as the Virgin in the south transept of S Marco, and with Venetian works showing his influence, such as the pair of angels on the front of the Mascoli Altar or a figure of Gabriel (New York, Met.).

The Mascoli Master's works in Venice, and through them some of the formal characteristics of Ghiberti's work, influenced a number of artists in Venice during the 1440s, including Bartolomeo Buon. Others translated his style into a calmer mood expressing psychological states through glance and gesture.

BIBLIOGRAPHY

L. Planiscig: 'Die Bildhauer Venedigs in der ersten Hälfte des Quattrocento', *Jb. Ksthist. Samml. Wien*, iv (1930), pp. 47–120 (113)

J. Pope-Hennessy: *Italian Gothic Sculpture* (London, 1955, 3/1985), pp. 49, 221, 286

W. Wolters: *La scultura veneziana gotica, 1300–1600* (Milan, 1976), pp. 110, 276 [gives summary of research, bibliog. and illus.]

WOLFGANG WOLTERS

Master of the Mass of St Gregory (*fl* ?Berne, *c*. 1500). Swiss painter. The anonymous painter is named after a winged altar (Berne, Schweizer. Landhaus), the outer faces of which represent the Mass of St Gregory. He was one of a number of Late Gothic Swiss painters who 'signed' their works by including carnations in their pictures in a variety of ways. Besides the altar after which he is named and other more or less related works, a *Nativity* (Zurich, Ksthaus) consisting of two sections can also be ascribed to him; the same carnation 'mark' can be seen on the reverse side. As this mark does not contain a concealed signature, there is no workshop link with the other CARNATION MASTERS (*see* above), whose style is more akin to that of Zurich. The origin and style of his works suggest that he lived in Berne and had been influenced by the painter Hans Fries, who worked in Freiburg. Supposedly Alsatian elements in his work have led to identification (Stange) of this Master with Paul Löwensprung of Strasbourg (*d* 1499), who is known to have been in Berne from 1493 but to whom no work can authoritatively be ascribed.

BIBLIOGRAPHY

W. Hugelshofer: 'Zu einigen neuen altschweizerischen Gemälden', *Jb. Kst & Kstpf. Schweiz*, iv (1925–7), pp. 226–38

M. Moullet: *Les Maîtres à l'oeillet* (Basle, 1943), pp. 57–63

A. Stange: *Deutsche Malerei der Gotik*, vii (Berlin and Munich, 1955), p. 69

L. H. Wüthrich: *Spätgotische Tafelmalerei, 1475 bis 1520* (Berne, 1969), p. 18

JANEZ HÖFLER

Master of the Mascoli Altar: *Virgin and Child with SS Mark and James*, marble, h. 1.3 m, *c*. 1430 (Venice, S Marco)

Master of the Mauer Altar (*fl c.* 1500–30). German wood-carver, possibly a member of the KRIECHBAUM family. He is named from the carved limewood altar of the Virgin in the pilgrimage church of Mauer (consecrated 1509) near Melk (Lower Austria). The altar, which was produced *c.* 1510 either for Mauer or for Göttweig Abbey (erected 1510), is not uniform stylistically and was later altered. The predella is untraced. The subject, which combines themes of the *Crucifixion* and the *Life of the Virgin*, is not necessarily as originally planned. The shrine (central panel) has a multifigured composition depicting the *Coronation of the Virgin* with the *Intercession of the Saints*. The almost classical, strictly symmetrical design possibly indicates knowledge of Albrecht Dürer's Heller Altarpiece (1509; destr. 1729) and his woodcut of the *Assumption* (B. 94) from the cycle of the *Life of the Virgin* (Nuremberg, 1510), the earlier scenes of which provided a direct model for the reliefs on the wings (*Annunciation* and *Visitation*). The scene of the *Nativity*, however, follows an engraving by Martin Schongauer. (The reliefs and figures of prophets in the upper part are evidently by a different hand from the group on the shrine.) In addition, the animated figures of the souls and their intercessors are reminiscent of the turbulent dramatic quality of Dürer's *Large Passion* print cycle (Nuremberg, *c.* 1497–1500), which may also be the source of a certain predilection for caricatured, grotesquely exaggerated faces.

This style was anticipated *c.* 1505 in a figure of *St Michael* from the area around Freistadt and in a *Johannesschüssel* (Head of St John the Baptist: Linz, Oberösterreich. Landesmus.). This clearly reveals the Master's training in the Kefermarkt workshop. The probable identification with Stefan Kriechbaum is based on the use of a distinctive Augsburg style of ornamentation. A figure of *St Anne with the Virgin and Child* (Vienna, Dom- & Diözmus.) from the Annenkirche, Vienna, shows that the Master also knew at first hand the work of Veit Stoss, to whom this figure has also been attributed. Other works by the Mauer Master include a *St Vitus in the Cauldron* and a *St Leopold* (both Krems, Hist. Mus.), a Crucifix in the parish church of Spitz (Lower Austria) and a figure of the *Virgin Enthroned* (Frankfurt am Main, Liebieghaus).

Finally, the predilection for the grotesque, particularly evident in the singing angels at Mauer, dominates the former high altar at Zwettl Abbey (Lower Austria), previously dated 1525. The central panel of this work has survived in the parish church at Adamov (Czech Republic). Schindler also attributed the St Bernard Altar at Zwettl Abbey, produced in 1500, to the Master (who evidently carved some of the saints' heads in Mauer). The characteristic metallic drapery style can also be seen in the Valentine altar in the crypt of St Peter, Vienna. The following works might provide a link between the style of the altars of Mauer and Zwettl: the altar of *All Saints* at Altmünster near Gmunden (Upper Austria), dated 1518; a *Coronation of the Virgin* on the Baroque high altar of the church of Grossreinprechts (Lower Austria); and a relief of the *Mount of Olives* in the parish church at Melk. An unusually expressive Crucifix at Maria Laach might be connected with the 'carved panel' that Stefan Kriechbaum was due to deliver there in 1518; it shows such an affinity

to the Zwettl shrine that a contribution by a member of the Kriechbaum family appears probable.

BIBLIOGRAPHY
A. von Bartsch: *Le Peintre-graveur* (1803-21) [B.]
E. Völter: 'Der Schnitzaltar von Mauer bei Melk', *Z. Bild. Kst*, n. s., lxi (1927–8), pp. 309–13
H. Seiberl: 'Der Zwettler Altar und die Auswirkungen des Kefermarkter Stiles im 16. Jahrhundert', *Jb. Ksthist. Samml. Wien*, n. s., x (1936), pp. 105–30
K. Oettinger: *Anton Pilgram und die Bildhauer von St Stephan* (Vienna, 1951), pp. 60–72
R. Feuchtmüller: *Der Schnitzaltar in Mauer bei Melk* (Vienna, 1955/R St Pölten, 1975)
W. Paatz: *Süddeutsche Schnitzaltäre der Spätgotik* (Heidelberg, 1963)
M. Baxandall: *The Limewood Sculptors of Renaissance Germany* (New Haven and London, 1980), p. 308
W. L. Strauss: *Sixteenth-century German Artists*, 10 [7-1] of *The Illustrated Bartsch*, ed. W. L. Strauss (New York, 1980) [B.]
H. Schindler: *Donaubairisches: Vorträge zur Kunstgeschichte* (Passan, 1982), pp. 69–86
900 Jahre Stift Göttweig, 1083–1983: Ein Donaustift als Repräsentant benediktinischer Kultur (exh. cat., Gottweig, 1983), pp. 507–11
H. Schindler: *Meisterwerke des Spätgotik* (Regensburg, 1989), pp. 186-93
L. Schultes: 'Zu Identität und Werk des Meisters des Kefermarkter Altars', *Der Meister des Kefermarkter Altars*, ed. L. Schultes (Linz, 1993), pp. 59-72

LOTHAR SCHULTES

Maximilian-Master. *See* MASTER OF THE OLDER PRAYERBOOK OF MAXIMILIAN below.

Master of the Maximilian Schoolbooks (*fl c.* 1445–75). Austrian illuminator. He is named from three manuscripts intended for the instruction of the future Maximilian I (*c.* 1465–8; Vienna, Österreich. Nbib., MSS 2368, s.n. 2617, 2289). They comprise a reading-book in German and Latin, a Latin grammar and the *Doctrinale puerorum* (*c.* 1200) by Alexander de Villa Dei. Apart from one other imperial commission, a prayerbook (*c.* 1465–7; Vienna, Österreich. Nbib., MS. 1942) for Maximilian's mother, Eleonor of Portugal (1434–67), he worked for influential citizens of Vienna and high ecclesiastics, the canons of Klosterneuburg and even for Matthias Corvinus, King of Hungary, for whom he illuminated a missal (1469; Rome, Vatican, Bib. Apostolica, Ross. 1164).

By 1450 the Master had replaced the rather conservative Illuminator of Duke Albrecht (*fl c.* 1430–50) as the foremost representative of his craft in Vienna. While he strictly adhered to his predecessor's patterns of vegetal ornament, the style of his miniatures was definitely innovative. In his early work there is evidence of familiarity with contemporary south Netherlandish panel painting and with recent French book illumination. Thus his single miniature of the *Lamentation of Christ* (Berlin, Kupferstichkab.) paraphrases a composition by Rogier van der Weyden, and some of the background landscapes in his early manuscripts are reminiscent of the Boucicaut Master. From *c.* 1460 his art became increasingly provincial, his stocky figures rather stereotyped and with less of their former liveliness; nonetheless his works continued to be much in demand until the early 1470s.

BIBLIOGRAPHY
H. Fichtenau: *Die Lehrbücher Maximilians und die Anfänge der Fraktur-schrift* (Hamburg, 1961)
Gotik in Österreich (exh. cat. by G. Schmidt, Krems-Stein, Minoritenkirche, 1967), pp. 173–6

A. Rosenauer: 'Zu einer niederländischen Beweinungskomposition . . .', *Wien. Jb. Kstgesch.*, xxii (1969), pp. 157–66

GERHARD SCHMIDT

Master of Mérode (*fl c.* 1400–50). South Netherlandish painter. Bode named the Master in 1887 from a triptych only twice exhibited before it passed from the Mérode family to the Metropolitan Museum of Art, New York. (It is now on display in The Cloisters, New York.) An *Annunciation* in a contemporary domestic interior is flanked, on the left wing, by a donor couple imagined to be in the garden of the Virgin's house and, on the right wing, by St Joseph in his carpenter's workshop. One of the coats of arms in the stained glass of the central panel has been identified as that of the Ingelbrechts family of Mechelen, and the man behind the donors bears the badge of the town of Mechelen. He and the donatrix were added over a completely painted background indicating a complex initial history. The lady's costume suggests a date in the 1430s.

The works attributed by Bode to his Master of Mérode were given by von Tschudi (denied access to the Mérode Triptych) to the MASTER OF FLÉMALLE (*see* above). Despite its infelicities of design and draughtsmanship, the triptych was accepted as a key work in the Flémalle oeuvre until Campbell pointed out that it was inferior to the Flémalle panels and that the composition was a pastiche of other Annunciations originated by the Master of Flémalle, the *Annunciation* in the Musée d'Art Ancien, Brussels, in particular being regarded as the principal source for the composition. Another of these, attributed to his workshop (Madrid, Prado), probably belongs, together with the autograph *Marriage of the Virgin* (also Prado), to a larger ensemble that could have included the original of the striking composition of St Joseph as a carpenter. The Master of Mérode's hand has been detected in the Prado *Annunciation* and the reverse of the *Marriage of the Virgin*, and he presumably acquired his knowledge of the Master of Flémalle's style and compositions while a member of his workshop.

The Salting *Virgin and Child* (London, N.G.) and the Werl wing panels, dated 1438 (Madrid, Prado), share characteristics of the Mérode Triptych, such as clumsily assembled but minutely observed and executed detail. The triptych inspired independent copies, and the Master's meticulously crafted but awkward derivations served to disseminate the art of the Master of Flémalle.

BIBLIOGRAPHY

W. Bode: 'La Renaissance au musée de Berlin, iii: L'Ancienne Ecole flamande', *Gaz. B.-A.*, n. s. 1, xxxv (1887), pp. 209–20, 423–34
H. von Tschudi: 'Der Meister von Flémalle', *Jb. Kön.-Preuss. Kstsamml.*, xix (1898), pp. 8–34, 89–116
A. Hocquet: 'Le Maître de Flémalle, quelques documents', *An. Acad. Royale Archéol. Belgique*, lxxiii (1925), pp. 5–17
Bull. Met., xvi/4 (1957) [issue devoted to the Mérode Triptych]
L. Campbell: 'Robert Campin, the Master of Flémalle and the Master of Mérode', *Burl. Mag.*, ccxvi (1974), pp. 634–46
M. Laszlo, R. Nachtigall and A. F. Gutman: *Literature on the Mérode Altarpiece* (New York, 1974)

CATHERINE REYNOLDS

Master of Messkirch. *See* STRÜB, (2).

Master of the Milan Adoration. *See* BEER, JAN DE.

Master of the Miracle of the Apostles. *See* AERTGEN VAN LEYDEN.

Master of the Miracles of Mariazell. *See* MASTER OF THE LEGEND SCENES above.

Master of the Missal of Borso d'Este. *See under* GIORGIO D'ALEMAGNA.

Master of the Modena Hours. *See under* TOMASINO DA VIMERCATE.

Master of Mondsee (*b* ?Salzburg; *fl c.* 1497). Austrian painter. He is named after a number of panels from a winged altar top in the former Benedictine abbey church of Mondsee, near Salzburg. These can be dated from an altar consecration in 1497. The winged altar had a programme of large painted scenes from the *Childhood of Christ*. Traces on the backs of the wings show that this was completed by the *Coronation of the Virgin* and scenes from the *Life of the Virgin* in low relief. The large panels of the *Circumcision* (Vienna, Belvedere), placed above the *Presentation of Christ* (German priv. col.), on the left, faced those of the *Adoration of the Magi* (German priv. col.), placed above *Christ among the Doctors* (Vaduz, Samml. Liechtenstein). Two graded wings, painted on both sides (Vienna, Belvedere), showed on the outside *St Ambrose* and *St Augustine* and on the inside the *Flight to Egypt* and the donor in front of the Virgin in a dress of corn-ears. The last two panels have a gold background. The coat of arms identifies the donor as Benedikt Eck von Vilsbiburg (abbot, 1463–99). The entire altar is a simplified version of the winged altar in Teichstätt, near Strasswalchen (consecrated 1479; destr. but known through drawings), and the high altar of St Wolfgang (1481) by Michael Pacher, also commissioned by the abbot of Mondsee.

The four large panels in shiny, cold, clear, luminescent colours display a marked contrast with Pacher's work at St Wolfgang and with the fragments (Vienna, Belvedere) of the former high altar of the Franciscan church in Salzburg from almost the same period. The three scenes placed inside Late Gothic churches have an awkward perspective, while the *Adoration* and *Flight to Egypt* introduce simple yet atmospheric elements of landscape. Thematic references such as the presence in the *Adoration* of Jacob's ladder underneath a sheaf on the stable floor were later taken up in Mondsee by Albrecht Altdorfer, who imaginatively altered them in his *Nativity* (1507; Bremen, Ksthalle). The free use of perspective and the imaginative fluttering of the robes already show the influences of the Danube school. This hitherto unknown Master belongs among the most significant Austrian painters of 1500, on a par with Rueland Frueauf and the Master of Grossgmain.

BIBLIOGRAPHY

O. Benesch: 'Der Meister des Krainburger Altares', *Wien. Jb. Kstgesch.*, vii (1930), p. 120
S. Florian: *Der Meister von Mondsee* (diss., U. Vienna, 1950)
S. Krasa-Florian: 'Der Meister von Mondsee', *Das Mondseeland: Geschichte und Kultur* (exh. cat., Mondsee, Stift; Linz, Oberösterreich. Landesmus.; 1981), pp. 139–48

HANS GEORG GMELIN

Master of the Morrison Triptych (*fl* first quarter of the 16th century). Netherlandish painter. He is named after a triptych of the *Virgin and Child* (Toledo, OH, Mus. A.), formerly in the Morrison Collection, Fonthill, Wilts, which is partly derived from a triptych of the same subject by Hans Memling (Vienna, Ksthist. Mus.). Friedländer ascribed other paintings to the Master on the basis of this panel, including the *Virgin and Child with Saints in a Garden* (London, N.G.), a scene bathed in sunlight, and an *Adoration of the Magi* (Philadelphia, PA, Mus. A.). The latter represents a view of Antwerp in the background with the unfinished cathedral tower, suggesting a date of *c.* 1510. Friedländer noted the influence of Quentin Metsys's figure types, and there are also similarities in the oval heads and smooth modelling to works by artists of the early Haarlem school, especially Geertgen tot Sint Jans.

Friedländer suggested that the artist was the pupil of Metsys who registered as 'Adriaen' in the Antwerp painters' guild in 1495; he further believed that this Adriaen was the same artist who entered as a master in 1503. Nieto Gallo also identified the Master as Metsys's pupil Adriaen but proposed that he was one Adriaen Skilleman, who became a master in 1499. Valentiner argued that the Master was a north Netherlandish painter named Simon van Harlem, who was active in Antwerp from 1502–24, which would explain the similarities to Dutch art. However, Davies doubted that the London painting was by the same hand as the Morrison Triptych and questioned, in fact, whether most of the panels ascribed to the Master were by one artist.

BIBLIOGRAPHY

M. J. Friedländer: *Die altniederländische Malerei* (Berlin, 1924–37); Eng. trans. as *Early Netherlandish Painting* (Leiden, 1967–76), vii, pp. 41–5

G. Nieto Gallo: 'El retablo de *San Juan Bautista* en la iglesia del Salvador de Valladolid: Quentin Metsys o Adriaen Skilleman?', *Bol. Semin. Estud. A. & Arqueol.*, xiii–xxi (1941), pp. 47–70

W. R. Valentiner: 'Simon van Herlem, the Master of the Morrison Triptych', *Gaz. B.-A.*, xlv (1955), pp. 5–10

M. Davies: *The Early Netherlandish School*, London, N.G. cat. (London, 1968), p. 122

ELLEN KONOWITZ

Master of Moulins [Master of the Bourbons] (*fl* *c.* 1480–*c.* 1500). Painter, probably of south Netherlandish origin, active in France. He is named after the triptych of the *Virgin and Child Adored by Angels with Saints and Donors* in Moulins Cathedral (see fig. 1). Many of the works attributed to the Master can be associated with members of the Bourbon court at Moulins, and he may have been their court painter. Given the poor survival rate of French 15th-century panels, a surprisingly large number of works can be attributed to him, allowing for workshop intervention. They show a master whose revealing images of powerful intensity combine the daring colour and compositional ideas of van der Goes with the looser technique and Italianate motifs fashionable in France. He has been plausibly identified as Jean Hey.

1. The Moulins Triptych. 2. Other attributed works. 3. Identification.

1. THE MOULINS TRIPTYCH. The painting was presumably presented by Peter II, Duke of Bourbon, and his wife Anne of Beaujeu, daughter of Louis XI, who are depicted on the interior of the wings with their daughter Suzanne (*see* BOURBON, §I(3) and (4)). Born in 1491, Suzanne appears to be about seven years old, allowing the work to be dated *c.* 1498. The object of their devotion on the centre panel is the Virgin and Child adored by angels, two of whom hold a crown surmounted by twelve stars over the Virgin's head. The imagery is associated with the Immaculate Conception, for which the Bourbons had a particular reverence: the crescent moon is beneath the Virgin's feet, and behind her is a golden radiance that,

1. Master of Moulins: *Virgin and Child Adored by Angels with Saints and Donors*, oil on panel, h. 1.59 m, *c.* 1498 (Moulins Cathedral)

even in its damaged state, suggests the glory of the sun. Her identity with the woman clothed by the sun of St John's apocalyptic vision is made explicit by the two lowest angels, who hold a scroll with the text from Revelation. The left-hand angel points to the inscription, the right-hand angel to the Virgin. The rich reds and blues of the Virgin's draperies are repeated by the ceremonial robes of the donors, who, despite Christ's gesture of blessing towards the Duke, are otherwise clearly separated from the celestial court by the luxurious red and green striped hangings. St Peter, the Duke's patron, is shown as pope rather than apostle, with the Bourbon motto *Esperance* on his cope, his keys clutched in his right hand and his left indicating his protégé to the Virgin and Child. St Anne, with no traditional attribute, points out the Duchess and her daughter. When the wings are shut, their exterior faces reveal an *Annunciation*, the Virgin placed unusually on the left with two angels hovering above her, and Gabriel, attended by a further four angels, on the right. Though painted in grisaille, the floating angels, the elegantly attenuated hands of the Virgin and the lily in the vase behind her are all unconvincing as stone sculptures, despite their traceried niches. The format of the folding triptych with grisaille exterior is thoroughly Netherlandish, and the closest parallels are found in the work of Hugo van der Goes, both for the concept of 'living sculptures' on the exterior and for the design of the interior, which is based on a combination of the exteriors and interiors of van der Goes's Edinburgh wing panels (*c.* 1473–8; Edinburgh, N.G.).

The Moulins Triptych is not, however, in its original state. Discrepancies in the fictive architecture of the *Annunciation* demonstrate that the wings have been cut down, the left more at the bottom and the right more at the top. Originally Mary and Gabriel would have been on roughly the same level, mitigating the now rather menacing downward swoop of the archangel. The reason for the unequal cutting is seen on the interior faces, where both panels end just below the donors' robes; since the Duchess's mantle falls further forward than the Duke's, more was taken from the top of her panel. The wings retain their original width of 669 mm, but their present height of 1.59 m is exactly that of the centre panel (1.33 m wide); initially they seem to have been at least 100 mm higher. When first reproduced and recorded in the 1830s, the wings were already cut and exhibited on piers in the choir, their interior faces alone visible. Their frames were said to be of the 17th century, but the uncut centre panel still has its original, classicizing frame with, on the lower edge, the initials P and A buckled together. Similar straps, though unfastened, appear in the fictive spandrels of the *Annunciation*. While it is highly likely that a folding triptych would be dismantled in the 17th century, here the wings seem to have been cut while still associated with the central panel, an event for which no plausible explanation has yet been proffered.

2. OTHER ATTRIBUTED WORKS. The Master of Moulins painted an earlier, much smaller, triptych for Peter II and Anne of Beaujeu, not long after the birth of Suzanne, of which only the wings survive. The left wing depicts the *Duke and St Peter*, the right the *Duchess and St John the Evangelist* and, originally part of the same panel, their infant daughter in her baby clothes (755×658 mm, 730×530 mm and 268×162 mm respectively; Paris, Louvre). The right wing still has traces of its marbled reverse under later overpainting, and on the original frame of the left wing are listed the Duke's titles and the date of his succession to the Duchy, 1488. Appropriately for what would seem a more private devotional work, the donors are not in state robes, but the similarity of the treatment of their faces with the Moulins Triptych leaves little doubt of the identity of the artist, allowing for workshop assistance.

Peter II again appears, in reverse, in a miniature attributed to the Master: the frontispiece to a manuscript copy of the statutes of the royal order of St Michael made for presentation to Charles VIII (Paris, Bib. N., MS. fr. 14363, fol. 3*r*). Since the Duke is the only recognizable attendant on the King as he greets St Michael, he may have been the donor. The other illuminations are stylistically unrelated, and the Master may have been called on to execute only the miniature with portrait figures.

Suzanne de Bourbon may be the sitter in the panel, probably always an independent portrait, in New York (320×230 mm; Met.). She is shown to waist length holding a pearl rosary in a setting opening on to landscape not unlike that of the Bourbon wings in the Louvre, a standard device in the Netherlands. Her lavish ermine-lined gown, decorated with gold beads and embroidery, and the fleur-de-lis-shaped ruby and pearl jewel hanging from her neck indicate a member of the French royal family, and Suzanne is the only suitable candidate. Her more sickly features in the Moulins Triptych are not incompatible with this portrait, and the identification receives some support from its Bourbon provenance.

The Master of Moulins also portrayed *Cardinal Charles de Bourbon, Archbishop of Lyon* (Munich, Alte Pin.; see fig. 2), shown at prayer in his stall and identified by the coat of arms included in the carved decoration and in the borders of the brocade backcloth. The portrait has a marbled reverse and was presumably the right wing of a devotional diptych with the *Virgin and Child* on the left wing. Charles was made Cardinal in 1476 and died in 1488. As he here seems younger than in a medal dating from the end of his life, the portrait may have been commissioned *c.* 1480, probably before the Master had become attached to the Bourbon court.

The surviving left wing of a diptych or triptych, datable by the costume to the 1490s, depicts *Madeleine de Bourgogne*, the illegitimate daughter of Philip III, Duke of Burgundy (550×400 mm; Paris, Louvre). Kneeling facing to the right, she is identified by her patron saint, St Mary Magdalen, and by the Burgundian badge incorporated in the jewel at her neck. Madeleine was a member of the Bourbon court at Moulins and married Bompar de Laage; the picture was owned by the de Laage family in the 19th century. The rich colouring and the treatment of donatrix and patron saint are comparable to those in the right wing of the Moulins Triptych.

An inscription dated December 1494 identifies the portrait of the *Dauphin Charles-Orland* (397×368 mm; Paris, Louvre), son of Charles VIII and nephew of Anne of Beaujeu. The child was then 26 months old, and this

2. Master of Moulins: *Cardinal Charles de Bourbon, Archbishop of Lyon*, panel, 340×250 mm, *c.* 1480 (Munich, Alte Pinakothek)

private picture was sent to his father on his Italian campaign but lost to the Venetians at the Battle of Fornovo. Although this is not a formal portrait, the figure of the Dauphin can be compared to the infant Suzanne in the Louvre wing: in his baby clothes, he is given some sort of precocious dignity by his rosary beads and brocade backcloth.

The Master of Moulins's other known patron was Cardinal Jean II Rolin, Bishop of Autun. He is shown kneeling in his red robes in the *Nativity* (530×730 mm; Autun, Mus. Rolin) and is identified by his coat of arms, by his cardinal's hat, which hangs from a nail in the stable doorway, and by his motto, which forms part of the gold decoration filling the spandrels. The sitter's apparent age would suggest a date around 1480, roughly contemporary with the portrait of *Charles de Bourbon*. In all the Master's works the white flesh tones and physical types recall those of Hugo van der Goes; here the composition, with its cut-off figures, illogical scale and shepherds in the background, contains direct quotations from the Ghent painter. Yet the painting is looser than van der Goes's, particularly in the summary detailing of the landscape, which is very like that in the Louvre wings and the New York portrait.

A richly dressed ecclesiastic accompanied by a military saint (?St Victor or St Maurice) appears against a landscape without intervening architecture in the right wing of a diptych (820×480 mm; Glasgow, A.G. & Mus.). They are at half length but are otherwise more closely related to the assured handling of the Moulins Triptych than to the Louvre Bourbon wings, where saint and donor are carefully separated. In the Glasgow panel, as at Moulins, the donor is practically enclosed within the saint's contour. The artist's sensitivity to shape is clearly demonstrated in the changes to the fluttering pennon that counterpoints the pattern of the figures' heads. The patron has not been conclusively identified.

Two panels cut from the sides of a larger picture also have an unknown provenance: the *Meeting of SS Joachim and Anne at the Golden Gate with Charlemagne* (720× 590 mm; London, N.G.) and the *Annunciation* (730× 500 mm; Chicago, IL, A. Inst.). At the right edge, part of a cloth of honour draped over the wall next to Charlemagne suggests a central image of an enthroned saint or, more probably, the Virgin and Child. The picture would then have presented a coherent image of Salvation through the birth of the Virgin and the birth of Christ, and the emphasis on the Immaculate Conception, St Anne and Charlemagne possibly indicates another Bourbon commission. This idea is strengthened by the presence of Charlemagne on an enamelled diptych (480×350 mm; London, Wallace) that repeats very closely the donor wings of the Moulins triptych: Charlemagne is paired with St Louis of France, who could, therefore, have been the figure originally beside the *Annunciation*. Despite these possible Bourbon connections, the picture would have been too wide to have had the Louvre panels as its wings.

Some idea of the type of Virgin and Child that probably accompanied the Louvre wings, the *Charles de Bourbon* and the Glasgow ecclesiastic can be gained from a panel showing the Virgin at half length behind a carpet-draped surface on which the Child is supported by one of four attendant angels (385×295 mm; Brussels, Mus. A. Anc.). It is the panel most easily compared with the centre of the Moulins Triptych, where the same physical types, colour range and projection of volume against a flat background (here of gold) are all found.

3. IDENTIFICATION. A damaged panel of the *Ecce homo* (390×300 mm; Brussels, Mus. A. Anc.), showing Christ with bound hands, crown of thorns and reed sceptre, displayed at half length between parted curtains, is so close in style to paintings attributed to the Master of Moulins that it seems to be by the same artist. The inscription on the reverse identifies the painter as Jean Hey, *teutonicus* and *pictor egregius*, and records that it was painted in 1494 for Jean Cueillette, *notaire* and *secretaire* to Charles VIII. This Jean Hey was included by the poet Jean Lemaire de Belges in his *Plainte du Désiré* of 1504 in a list of the greatest living painters, in a way that suggests he was then inactive through ill health.

In addition to the stylistic similarities between this one authenticated work by Hey and those attributed to the Master of Moulins, the few ascertainable details of Hey's life do fit the biography that can be deduced for the Master. Both Hey's name and the epithet *teutonicus* show that he was of Netherlandish origin, and the Master's works are permeated by Netherlandish traditions and conventions; in particular they reveal a wide-ranging knowledge of works by Hugo van der Goes painted in the 1470s. From employment in Burgundy with Jean Rolin and in Lyon with Cardinal Charles de Bourbon *c.* 1480, the Master seems to have moved to the court of Peter II, Duke of Bourbon. Jean Cueillette, Hey's one known patron, had made his career with the Bourbons, and, although in 1494 his royal titles took precedence over his office as Treasurer of Bourbon, the royal chancery was then located in Moulins, during Charles VIII's absence in Italy. Jean Lemaire de Belges was from 1498 to 1503 largely based at the Bourbon court in Moulins and was unlikely to exclude their chief painter from his list of artists. It seems reasonable to identify the Master of Moulins with the Bourbons' court painter, when so many of his surviving works can be associated with them and the members of their court. If this assumption is correct, the Master's name was certainly Jean, because a surviving account for 1502–3 includes in the Bourbon household *Maistre Jehan le peintre*, ranking with such officials as the doctor; other painters, distinguished by surnames, appear lower down among barbers and cobblers. Other Jeans have been proposed, apart from Jean Hey, but none of these alternative identifications is satisfactory. Jean Perréal's works have finally been identified and are incompatible. Jean Prévost, apparently chiefly active as a glass painter, was appointed master glazier of Lyon Cathedral in 1471 and so cannot have been profoundly influenced by the works of Hugo van der Goes produced in the 1470s. On the current evidence there seems little doubt that *Maistre Jehan le peintre* was Jean Hey and that the artist of the Moulins Triptych painted the *Ecce homo*. The position and contacts of Jean Hey, who was apparently in failing health in 1504, coincide with those of the Master of Moulins, for whom no works are known beyond the earliest years of the 16th century.

BIBLIOGRAPHY

M. Huillet d'Istria: *Le Maître de Moulins* (Paris, 1961), i of *La Peinture française à la fin du moyen âge* [full bibliography]
A. Châtelet: 'A Plea for the Master of Moulins', *Burl. Mag.*, civ (1962), pp. 517–24
M. Hours: 'Le Maître de Moulins: Etude radiographique', *A. France*, iii (1963), pp. 63–74
N. Reynaud: 'Les Portraits des Bourbons au Louvre: Reconstitution d'un panneau du Maître de Moulins', *Rev. Louvre*, xiii (1963), pp. 159–66
C. Sterling: 'Du nouveau sur le Maître de Moulins', *L'Oeil*, cvii (1963), pp. 2–15, 65–8
H. Zerner and S. Katić: *Il Maestro di Moulins*, Maestri Colori (Milan, 1966)
N. Reynaud: 'Jean Hey, peintre de Moulins, et son client, Jean Cueillette', *Rev. A.*, 1–2 (1968), pp. 34–7
C. Sterling: 'Jean Hey, le Maître de Moulins', *Rev. A.*, 1–2 (1968), pp. 27–33
W. Wells: 'Abbot Nicaise de l'Orme and Jean Perréal: Glasgow's Master of Moulins Reconsidered', *Apollo*, cxiv (1981), pp. 148–55
L. Campbell: *Renaissance Portraits* (New Haven and London, 1990), pp. 214, 271
J. Dunkerton and others: *Giotto to Dürer: Early Renaissance Painting in the National Gallery* (London, 1991), pp. 358–9

CATHERINE REYNOLDS

Master of MS. Poitiers 30. *See* MASTER OF ADELAIDE OF SAVOY above.

Master of the Munich Arrest of Christ (*fl c.* 1455–*c.* 1480). Netherlandish painter. Schöne attributed two works, the *Arrest of Christ* and the *Resurrection* (both Munich, Alte Pin.), traditionally ascribed to Dieric Bouts I (*see* BOUTS, (1)), to an anonymous artist whom he called the Master of the Munich Arrest of Christ. (In 1906 Voll

had attributed them to Albert van Ouwater.) Schöne included ten other paintings usually attributed to Bouts in the oeuvre of this painter, whom he considered to be a close follower of Bouts and Ouwater. Among these were the altarpiece of *St Hippolytus* (Bruges, St Sauveur) and the *Coronation of the Virgin* (Vienna, Gemäldegal. Akad. Bild. Kst.). The main works in Munich were originally part of a larger altarpiece from the St Lorenzkirche in Cologne. On the reverse of the panels are grisaille figures of *St John the Evangelist* (Munich, Alte Pin.) and *St John the Baptist* (Cleveland, OH, Mus. A.).

The Master's *Arrest of Christ* is a compact composition, perhaps derived from prints or miniatures, with unusual nocturnal effects where the huddled figures are arbitrarily illuminated by moonlight and the torch held by one of the henchmen. The *Resurrection* is very closely related to the right panel of Bouts's altarpiece of the *Deposition* (Granada, Capilla Real). Schöne's attributions have been rejected by many scholars. The paintings grouped about the Munich panels are uneven in quality and are, for the most part, lesser works by followers of Bouts. Châtelet accepted Schöne's attribution, emphasizing the Master's connections with the Haarlem school of painting, but he greatly modified the list of paintings ascribed to him.

BIBLIOGRAPHY

K. Voll: *Die altniederländische Malerei von Jan van Eyck bis Memling* (Leipzig, 1906), pp. 156–8
M. J. Friedländer: *Die altniederländische Malerei* (Berlin, 1924–37); Eng. trans. as *Early Netherlandish Painting* (Leiden, 1967–76), iii [as Dieric Bouts]
W. Schöne: *Dieric Bouts und seine Schule* (Berlin and Leipzig, 1938), pp. 37–42, 163–5
E. Panofsky: *Early Netherlandish Painting*, i (Cambridge, MA, 1953), p. 315 [as Bouts]
A. Châtelet: *Les Primitifs hollandais* (Paris and Fribourg, 1980); Eng. trans. as *Early Dutch Painting* (Oxford and New York, 1981), pp. 80–84, 212–14

JAMES SNYDER

Master of the Munich Golden Legend (*fl c.* 1420–60). Illuminator, active in France. This master was named by Spencer from a copy of the French translation of the *Golden Legend* in Munich (Munich, Bayer. Staatsbib., Cod. gall. 3). It has an extensive cycle of illustrations, all in the same style, notable for the use of line to hatch flat areas of colour and to define facial features and other details. The style appears in numerous manuscripts, first collected by Spencer, in miniatures of varying degrees of competence; it seems that at least at certain stages of his career the Master was working with associates who ably copied his easily repeated linearity. Perhaps attributable to a distinct assistant are the miniatures that show more modelling in colour and less reliance on black line for detail, as in a Book of Hours of Paris Use (Baltimore, MD, Walters A.G., MS. W. 288).

The style can be traced in a long sequence of manuscripts, of which the Munich *Golden Legend*, datable *c.* 1420, would seem to be one of the earliest, while among the latest are a Franciscan Breviary (Paris, Bib. Arsenal, MSS 596–7), which includes St Bernadino, canonized in 1450, and a Book of Hours datable to around 1460 (Paris, Bib. N., MS. Rothschild 2534). The origins of the style are not known, but the clarity of outline suggested to Spencer a link with German traditions. It seems initially, however, to have been centred on Paris, as indicated by the liturgical use of such books as the Hours in Vienna (Österreich. Nbib., Cod. s. n. 2614) and the Eales Hours (U. Reading Lib., MS. 2067) and by the several manuscripts with miniatures also in the style of the BEDFORD MASTER (*see* above). These include Books of Hours (London, BL, Add. MS. 18192, Egerton MS. 2019, and Paris, Bib. N., MS. nouv. acq. lat. 3111) and the Sobieski Hours (Windsor Castle, Royal Lib.). The miniatures added after 1427 to Hours for the Neville family (Paris, Bib. N., MS. lat. 1158) show the style flourishing in English France, possibly in Rouen, as suggested by the Rouen Use of two Books of Hours (Minneapolis, MN, priv. col., and Naples, Bib. N., MS. I B 27), while its influence continued in Paris after English rule, as seen in the votive panel of the Jouvenel des Ursins family (Paris, Louvre, on dep. Paris, Mus. Cluny), painted between 1445 and 1449.

The centre of the style seems to have moved into French France by the 1440s, although the Master(s) may have been fairly itinerant since it is difficult to pinpoint any one place of origin for the manuscripts so far discussed. A Book of Hours for the Use of Reims and written by the wife of a scribe in Reims (Paris, Bib. Arsenal, MS. 1189) has miniatures in the style of the Munich *Golden Legend*. Angevin connections are suggested by the reuse of the Master of the Munich Golden Legend's designs for the *Passion* cycle of the Sobieski Hours in the Psalter of Jeanne de Laval (Poitiers, Bib. Mun., MS. 241), while a small Book of Hours (New York, Pierpont Morgan Lib., MS. M. 241) has some offices for the Use of Angers. Its calendar has a few Breton saints, and the ermine badge in the border decoration has been cited as proof of Breton ownership. An ermine also appears, however, beside the unknown female owner of one of the London Hours (Add. MS. 18192), which otherwise shows no Breton connections and is textually closely related to another Hours, apparently of Parisian production (Baltimore, MD, Walters A.G., MS. W. 247), which has two miniatures in the Munich *Golden Legend* style (see fig.). A connection with Brittany is more certainly indicated by the influence of the Master of Marguerite of Orléans on some of the borders in a Book of Hours (Milan, Castello Sforzesco, MS. 2164).

At least a decade later this Master contributed to the Rothschild Hours, as did the Master of Adelaïde of Savoy, localized by König at this date in Poitiers, which could perhaps have been a base for the Master of the Munich Golden Legend. Although his work is often found in the same manuscripts as the Bedford Master workshop, often reworking Bedford workshop designs, the Master of the Munich Golden Legend is stylistically closer to the Fastolf and Talbot Masters, yet he would seem to have been only briefly active in Rouen. Further research is needed to disentangle the history of the Munich *Golden Legend* style outside Paris and its relationship to illumination in Normandy, Brittany and the royal centres around the Loire.

BIBLIOGRAPHY

C. Santoro: *I codici miniati della Biblioteca Trivulziana* (Milan, 1958), pp. 111–13, no. 116
J. Porcher: *Manuscrits à peintures offerts à la Bibliothèque Nationale par le comte Guy du Boisrouvray* (Paris, 1961), no. 16
M. Rotili: *Miniatura francese a Napoli, miniatura e arte minori in Campania*, Collana di saggi e studi, ii (Rome, 1968), pp. 42–3, nos 7–8

Master of the Munich Golden Legend: *Visitation*; miniature from a Book of Hours, 180×134 mm, *c.* 1435–40 (Baltimore, MD, Walters Art Gallery, MS. W. 247, fol. 39*r*)

O. Pächt and D. Thoss: *Die illuminierte Handschriften und Inkunabeln der österreichische Nationalbibliothek, französische Schule*, i (Vienna, 1974), pp. 139–41 [list of attributed MSS]
E. P. Spencer: *The Sobieski Hours: A Manuscript in the Royal Library at Windsor Castle*, Roxburghe Club, ccxxxix (London, 1977), esp. pp. 20, 51
Medieval Illumination, Glass and Sculpture in Minnesota Collections (exh. cat., ed. A. Stones and J. Steyaert; Minneapolis, U. MN, A. Mus., 1978), pp. 58–66, no. 14
E. König: *Die französische Buchmalerei um 1450: Der Jouvenel Maler, der Maler des Genfer Boccaccios und die Anfänge Jean Fouquets* (Berlin, 1982), esp. pp. 16, 64, 213, 225–31
The Last Flowering: French Painting in Manuscripts, 1420–1530, from American Collections (exh. cat. by J. Plummer and G. Clark, New York, Pierpont Morgan Lib., 1982), pp. 6–8, nos 9–10
G. Morello: *Die schönsten Stundenbücher aus der Biblioteca Apostolica Vaticana* (Zürich, 1988), p. 108, no. 130
R. S. Wieck: *The Book of Hours in Medieval Art and Life* (London, 1988), no. 34

CATHERINE REYNOLDS

Naumburg Master (*fl* 13th century). Sculptor, active in Germany. Works attributed to his apprenticeship are in France (cathedrals of Reims, Noyon, Metz, Amiens and Strasbourg), but his personal contribution to sculptures at Mainz Cathedral (perhaps completed by 1239), Naumburg Cathedral (*c.* 1250–60) and Meissen Cathedral (*c.* 1268–80) is clear. His only surviving works from Mainz are the reliefs of the *Last Judgement* and the *Bandaged Head* (both Mainz, Bischöf. Dom- & Diözmus.; *see* MAINZ, fig. 2) and *St Martin and the Beggar* (Bassenheim, St Martin), known as the 'Bassenheim Rider'. Seven over life-size statues in the choir and vestibule of the cathedral are attributed to him at Meissen.

In Naumburg the Master and the workshop produced the 12 life-size founders' statues in the west choir, the reliefs on the so-called west rood screen and the *Crucifixion* group in its portal, as well as much of the architectural ornament of the building (*see* NAUMBURG, §1(ii)); he was probably also closely involved in the architectural design. In addition, the Naumburg Master completed individual commissions: the tomb of *Bishop Dietrich II* (*d* 1272), the statue of a deacon (both Naumburg Cathedral) and a tomb (possibly of a founder) in Merseburg Cathedral.

While earlier scholarship was mainly concerned with identifying the Naumburg Master's personal contribution to each piece, the contribution of workshops is now given more emphasis. The oeuvre as a whole shows a stylistic development from Early to High German Gothic, which might as easily have been the development of an individual artist as of a workshop. The naturalistic treatment of the Naumburg Master's figures in Mainz and Naumburg is unique in the mid-13th century. They combine skill in carving with a sense of objective reality and an understanding of an individual's psychology and actions that is very unusual in this period. In the late works in Meissen the realism of the statues is already overlaid by Gothic stylization.

See also CRUCIFIX, fig. 4.

BIBLIOGRAPHY

H. Giesau: *Die Meissner Bildwerke: Ein Beitrag zur Kunst des Naumburger Meisters* (Burg bei Magdeburg, 1936)
H. Küas: *Die Naumburger Werkstatt* (Berlin, 1937)
E. Lehmann and E. Schubert: *Der Meissener Dom: Beiträge zur Baugeschichte und Baugestalt bis zum Ende des 13. Jahrhunderts* (Berlin, 1968)
E. Schubert: *Der Naumburger Dom* (Berlin, 1968)
D. Schubert: *Von Halberstadt nach Meissen: Bildwerke des 13. Jahrhunderts in Thüringen, Sachsen und Anhalt* (Cologne, 1974)
W. Sauerländer: 'Die Naumburger Stifterfiguren: Rückblick und Fragen', *Die Zeit der Staufer: Geschichte, Kunst, Kultur* (exh. cat. by R. Haussherr and others, Stuttgart, Württemberg. Landesmus., 1977), v, pp. 169–245
E. Schubert: 'Zur Naumburg-Forschung der letzten Jahrzehnte', *Wien. Jb. Kstgesch.*, xxxv (1982), pp. 121–38

ERNST SCHUBERT

Master of Nördlingen (*fl* 1460s). German sculptor. The name is given to the carver of the wooden figures of the high altar of the Georgskirche, Nördlingen, Germany. The group consists of a Crucifix (h. 1.72 m), the *Virgin* (h. 1.47 m) and *St John* (h. 1.51 m), two (originally probably four) grieving angels (one, uncertainly attributed, in Kaiserslautern, Pfalzgal.), *St George* (h. 1.55 m) and *St Mary Magdalene* (h. 1.49 m). All the figures are of walnut with original polychrome. The paintings on the altar wings (Nördlingen, Stadtmus.) and the fragments of painting preserved on the shrine are by Friedrich Herlin. The wings were removed in 1683 and the shrine was enveloped in a Baroque casing, with the figures of *St George* and *St Mary Magdalene* standing near by.

The most important earlier attributions, based on documentary references, were to sculptors working in the 1470s: Simon Lainberger, the Nuremberg wood-carver, because he received a reminder from the town of Nördlingen in 1478 to deliver sculptures promised to Friedrich Herlin; and the sculptor Hans Kamensetzer from Ulm: a

Hans Kamensetzer (without details of his profession) is also found in Nördlingen in 1476.

When the Baroque casing was dismantled in 1971, the Late Gothic shrine was revealed, with Herlin's signature and the date 1462. This discovery reopened discussions about a connection with the Strasbourg sculptor NICOLAUS GERHAERT, whose sandstone Crucifix of 1467 (Baden-Baden, Stiftskirche) is closely related to that of Nördlingen. Some researchers attribute all the Nördlingen figures to Gerhaert; others see in the standing figures at least, with their powerful expressiveness and the ornamental style of their drapery folds, characteristics perhaps deriving from an earlier stylistic current from Strasbourg, possibly under Gerhaert's influence.

Most scholars now believe that the Nördlingen standing figures and the Dangolsheim *Virgin and Child* (*see* MASTER OF THE DANGOLSHEIM MADONNA above) are the work of the same sculptor, and Recht follows Fischel in associating the name of Hans Jöuch (documented in Strasbourg 1427, *d* between 1462 and 1466) with the Master of the Dangolsheim Madonna.

BIBLIOGRAPHY
Thieme–Becker

L. Fischel: 'Zur kunsthistorischen Stellung des Meisters der Dangolsheimer Maria', *Jb. Staatl. Kstsamml. Baden-Württemberg*, iii (1966), pp. 51–68 [with bibliog.]
E. Zimmermann: 'Spätgotik am Oberrhein, Meisterwerke der Plastik und des Kunsthandwerks, 1450–1530; Forschungsergebnisse und Nachträge zur Ausstellung im Badischen Landesmuseum, 1970', *Jb. Staatl. Kstsamml. Baden-Württemberg*, ix (1972), pp. 109–14
A. Schädler: 'Studien zu Nicolaus Gerhaert von Leiden: Die Nördlinger Hochaltarfiguren und die Dangolsheimer Muttergottes in Berlin', *Jb. Berlin. Mus.*, n. s., xvi (1974), pp. 46–82
E. D. Schmid: *Nördlingen: Die Georgskirche und St Salvator* (Stuttgart and Aalen, 1977), pp. 97–123
J. Taubert, F. Buchenrieder and K. W. Bachmann: 'Friedrich Herlins Nördlinger Hochaltar von 1462', *Farbige Skulpturen, Bedeutung, Fassung, Restaurierung*, ed. J. Taubert (Munich, 1978), pp. 150–66
M. Baxandall: *The Limewood Sculptors of Renaissance Germany* (New Haven, 1980), pp. 249–50
R. Recht: *Nicolas de Leyde et la sculpture à Strasbourg, 1460–1525* (Strasbourg, 1987), pp. 116–17, 125–8, 152–85, 341, 346–50
H. Krohm: 'Bemerkungen zur kunstgeschichtlichen Problematik des Herlin-Retabels in Rothenburg o.T.', *Jb. Berlin. Mus.*, n. s., xxxiii (1991), pp. 185–208
J. Nicolaisen and S. Schellenberger: 'Vorschlag für eine Neuaufstellung im Nördlinger Hochaltarretabel des Friedrich Herlin', *Jb. Berlin. Mus.*, n.s., xxxiii (1991), pp. 209–12
E. Oellermann: 'Die Schnitzaltäre Friedrich Herlins im Vergleich der Erkenntnisse neuerer kunsttechnologischer Untersuchungen', *Jb. Berlin. Mus.*, n. s., xxxiii (1991), pp. 213-38

EVA ZIMMERMANN

Master of the Novella. *See under* CORTESE, CRISTOFORO.

Master of the Older [First] **Prayerbook of Maximilian** [Maximilian Master] (*fl c.* 1480–1515). South Netherlandish illuminator. This name was given to the illuminator, of the Ghent–Bruges school, who painted the personal prayerbook of Maximilian I, Holy Roman Emperor from 1508 (Vienna, Österreich. Nbib., Cod. 1907). The book is identifiable as Maximilian's through the coat of arms in the miniature depicting him in prayer before St Sebastian (fol. 61*v*; see fig.). In addition there are prayers relating to a ruler and a calendar entry (in his hand) of the name day of his father Frederick III. The manuscript can be dated precisely since this form of his arms was applicable only

Master of the Older Prayerbook of Maximilian: *Maximilian in Prayer before St Sebastian*, miniature from the *Older Prayerbook of Maximilian*, 190×133 mm, 1486–7 (Vienna, Österreichische Nationalbibliothek, Cod. 1907, fol 61.*v*)

from 1486, and in 1487 unrest broke out in Flanders, which led to Maximilian's imprisonment. The manuscript is known as the Older Prayerbook of Maximilian to distinguish it from the prayerbook printed by Johann Schönsperger (Augsburg, 1513) on the Emperor's instructions. A strikingly large number of texts are common to both books. The printed text, however, represents a complete Book of Hours, whereas Maximilian's manuscript lacks the essential components of the Office of the Virgin and the Office of the Dead and contains instead a long series of Latin and Flemish prayers for the most diverse occasions. It is uncertain therefore whether the manuscript as it survives (88 fols) is a fragment or represents Maximilian's specific choice of texts.

The texts of the Older Prayerbook determine the number of illustrations: only five miniatures and three historiated initials. Although this makes the basis for comparison small, numerous miniatures in other manuscripts have been attributed to this illuminator. Most of these were previously considered the work of the Master of Mary of Burgundy. The Master of the Older Prayerbook of Maximilian is now regarded as this Master's most

productive pupil. De Winter attributed twenty-two manuscripts to him, of which two (Madrid, Mus. Lázaro Galdiano, Inv. No. 15503; London, BL, Add. MS. 54782) are Books of Hours made for William, Lord Hastings, who was executed in 1483. While there are art-historical problems concerning the life and work of the Master of the Older Prayerbook of Maximilian, it seems clear that he was among the first illuminators to use the new *trompe l'oeil* border of the Ghent–Bruges school, filling the margins of his manuscripts with flowers, insects and many other objects apparently lying on a coloured ground. His colouring is remarkably delicate, with a tendency towards a pastel-like tonality. The settings in his miniatures project deeply into the picture space, often with a somewhat exaggerated perspective. Faces are alike and frequently have a slightly dull expression and rounded eyes. The flesh tones have strong white highlighting that provides an intense three-dimensional quality but often makes the skin look a little pale.

Other works of significance attributed to the Master are two Books of Hours for Philipp of Cleves (Brussels, Bib. Royale Albert 1er, MS. IV.40; Vienna, Österreich. Nbib., Cod. S.n.13239), a Book of Hours for Isabella, Queen of Castile and León (Cleveland, OH, Mus. A., CMA 63.256), and a breviary dated 1494 (Glasgow, U. Lib., MS. Hunter 25). The Rothschild Hours (Vienna, Österreich. Nbib., Cod. S.n.2844), produced around 1515, is one of the latest manuscripts with miniatures attributed to the Master of the Older Prayerbook of Maximilian. Since van Buren and Brinkmann pointed to fundamental differences within the works grouped under the Master's name, it is possible that they may be distributed among several artists. Instead of the name 'Master of the Older Prayerbook of Maximilian', van Buren used the term 'Ghent Associates' of the MASTER OF MARY OF BURGUNDY (*see* above). The opinion that the Master of the Older Prayerbook of Maximilian is to be identified with the documented illuminator Sanders Bening is purely hypothetical.

BIBLIOGRAPHY
W. Hilger: *Das ältere Gebetbuch Maximilians I* (Graz, 1973) [facs. edn]
A. H. van Buren: 'The Master of Mary of Burgundy and his Colleagues: The State of Research and Questions of Method', *Z. Kstgesch.*, xxxviii (1975), pp. 286–309
E. Trenkler: *Rothschild Gebetbuch* (Graz, 1979) [facs. edn]
P. de Winter: 'A Book of Hours of Queen Isabel la Católica', *Bull. Cleveland Mus. A.*, lxvii (1981), pp. 342–427
Renaissance Painting in Manuscripts: Treasures from the British Library (exh. cat., ed. T. Kren; Malibu, CA, Getty Mus.; New York, Pierpont Morgan Lib.; London, BL; 1984), pp. 21–30
B. Brinkmann: 'The Hastings Hours and the Master of 1499', *BL J.*, xiv (Spring 1988), pp. 90–106

BODO BRINKMANN

Master of the Open-mouthed Boys [Maître des Enfants à la Bouche Ouverte; Maître des Petits Garçons à la Bouche Entr'ouverte] (*fl* Rome, *c.* 1615–25). Painter, active in Italy. Nicolson (1979) gave this name to the artist presumed responsible for a small number of Caravaggesque paintings of heads and half-length figures first grouped together by Bréjon de Lavergnée and Cuzin. They considered him to have been possibly a French pupil of Carlo Saraceni. The appellation derives from the distinctive open-mouthed expression of the young, male subjects of the pictures. These include a pair of tondi representing

Jacob and Esau and *David with the Head of Goliath* (ex-Hazlitt, Gooden & Fox, London, 1967), two paintings of the *Head of a Young Man* (Stanford, CA, U. A.G. & Mus.; Hartford, CT, Wadsworth Atheneum) and a *Small Boy Frightening a Little Girl with a Crab* (untraced). Rosenberg added to these *Concert with a Singer, Theorbo Player and Woman with a Crown* (Richmond, VA Mus. F.A.), while Fohr, less convincingly, attributed a *Triumph of David* (Tours, Mus. B.-A.) to this painter.

Old attributions of these paintings to Francesco Cairo, Rutilio Manetti, Daniele Crespi and Pietro Paolini give some indication of their refinement of style. In them precision of drawing is tempered by delicate modulation of chiaroscuro, which does not, however, hide a certain clumsiness. These attributions also affirm the complexity of the influences working on the artist. Because of the resemblances of the work to that of Saraceni (who is known to have had a number of French pupils, including Guy François and Jean Leclerc) as well as its French Caravaggesque character, the painter is generally believed to have been a Frenchman belonging to the second generation of the followers of Caravaggio working in Rome around 1615–25.

BIBLIOGRAPHY

B. Nicolson: 'Caravaggio and the Caravaggesques: Some Recent Research', *Burl. Mag.*, cxvi (1974), pp. 603–16
Valentin et les caravaggesques français (exh. cat. by A. Bréjon de Lavergnée and J.-P. Cuzin, Paris, Grand Pal., 1974)
B. Nicolson: *The International Caravaggesque Movement: A List of Pictures by Caravaggio and his Followers throughout Europe from 1590–1650* (London, 1979)
R. Fohr: *Catalogue des tableaux français et italiens du XVIIe siècle du Musée des Beaux-Arts de Tours* (Paris, 1982), no. 197, p. 133
La Peinture française du XVIIe siècle dans les collections américaines (exh. cat. by P. Rosenberg, Paris, Grand Pal.; New York, Met.; Chicago, IL, A. Inst.; 1982), p. 664

THIERRY BAJOU

Master of the Ordini. *See under* GIACOMO DI MINO DEL PELLICCIAIO.

Master of the Ortenberg Altar (*fl* after 1417). German painter. He is named after a small altarpiece from Ortenberg am Vogelsberg (after 1417; Darmstadt, Hess. Landesmus.) depicting the *Virgin among Virgins* on the middle panel and the *Nativity* and *Adoration of the Magi* on the inner faces of the wings. (There is an *Annunciation* by a later painter on the outer faces of the wings.) The subject-matter chosen for the main panel—the Virgin and her relatives, with female saints—suggests that it was destined for a convent, perhaps that of the Premonstratensian canonesses at St Maria Konradsdorf, near Ortenberg, and was perhaps commissioned to become the main altar after a fire at the convent church in 1417. Evidence for this is the inclusion of St Servatius, a cousin of the Virgin and patron saint of viticulture, which was also practised in Ortenberg. All the historical data suggest that the altar was made in Mainz. Among surviving examples of Middle Rhine panel painting in the 'Soft style' (*see* GERMANY, §III, 2), the Ortenberg Altar is alone of its type. It is distinctive in the courtliness of its basic attitude, inspired from western book illumination and stained glass, and in its association of the Virgin's nearest female relatives with three major woman saints, Agnes, Barbara and Dorothy.

In conjunction with the gold background of the painted surface, the use of silver leaf as a foil for the robes produces a metallic appearance. Two badly damaged panels from a Marian altar, a *Nativity* (Lézignan, Aude, parish church) and *Adoration of the Magi* (Aschaffenburg, Schloss Johannisburg Staatsgal.), may be early works by the same Master.

BIBLIOGRAPHY

G. Bott: *Der Ortenberger Altar in Darmstadt* (Stuttgart, 1966)

HANS GEORG GMELIN

Master of the Osservanza (*fl ?c.* 1440–80). Italian painter. Longhi recognized that two triptychs, formerly attributed to Sassetta, were the work of another hand. The *Virgin and Child with SS Jerome and Ambrose* (Siena, Osservanza; see fig.) and the *Birth of the Virgin* (Asciano, Mus. A. Sacra), formerly in the Collegiata, Asciano, both have a stylistic affinity with Sassetta's works but, in terms of narrative expression, still belong to the Late Gothic tradition. Longhi observed that a further group of paintings was closely related to these works. This included the predella of the Osservanza Altarpiece (Siena, Pin. N., 216), a predella of *St Bartholomew* (Siena, Pin. N.), scenes of the *Passion* (Rome, Pin. Vaticana; Philadelphia, PA, Mus. A.; Cambridge, MA, Fogg) and the scenes from the *Life of St Anthony Abbot* (dispersed; e.g. panels in Washington, DC, N.G.A.; New York, Met.; Wiesbaden, Mus. Wiesbaden) previously also attributed to Sassetta. These last panels are difficult to integrate into the group. The full-length painting of *St Anthony Abbot* (Paris, Louvre), which scholars have attempted to integrate with the small scenes from the saint's life into a multipartite altarpiece, seems to come from another altarpiece.

Graziani named the painter the Master of the Osservanza after the altarpiece in that church and reconstructed his oeuvre around this work, ranging between the *Pietà with St Sebaldus and a Devotee* (Siena, Monte Dei Paschi priv. col.), datable 1432–3, and the painted cover of the Gabella (tax records) showing the *Archangel Michael* (Siena, Pal. Piccolomini, Archv Stato), dated 1444. Graziani proposed that the Master took as his models Giovanni da Milano, Gregorio di Cecco and Masolino, thereby combining Sienese and Florentine stylistic elements. Graziani's theory was accepted by Zeri, Carli, Volpe, Laclotte, Benati, Angelini and Christiansen.

A different theory was proposed by Berenson, who suggested that the Master's oeuvre was the early work of SANO DI PIETRO, known to have been active from 1428 but whose earliest dated work is the Gesuati Polyptych of 1444 (Siena, Pin. N.; for illustration *see* SANO DI PIETRO). This was accepted by Brandi (1949), Pope-Hennessy (1956), Torriti and Boskovits.

A third hypothesis was put forward by Alessi and Scapecchi (1985). They established that the Osservanza panel was painted for S Maurizio, Siena, and that the date on the painting, 1436, refers to the foundation of the chapel by its patron, the grocer Manno d'Orlando (*d* 1442), and not necessarily to the year in which the altarpiece was painted. They suggested that the Osservanza Altarpiece and the *Birth of the Virgin* date from the late 1440s and that the Master was active from the 1440s to the 1470s and was influenced by developments in Florentine painting

Master of the Osservanza: *Virgin and Child with SS Jerome and Ambrose*, tempera on panel, 2.16×1.62 m, late 1440s [dated 1436] (Siena, Convent of St Bernardino dell'Osservanza)

of that date, particularly by Fra Angelico and Uccello. They further proposed that the Master could be identified with FRANCESCO DI BARTOLOMEO ALFEI, a well-documented artist who was associated with Sano di Pietro but whose work has not been identified. While Pope-Hennessy (1987) did not accept the identification of the Master with Alfei, he accepted Alessi's and Scapecchi's attribution of additional works to the Master. These include the *Virgin and Child* (New York, Met.) and two paintings of the *Virgin of Humility* (Altenburg, Staatl. Lindenau-Mus.; New York, Brooklyn Mus.).

BIBLIOGRAPHY

R. Longhi: 'Fatti di Masolino e di Masaccio', *Crit. A.*, v (1940), pp. 145–91 (188, n. 26)

B. Berenson: *Sassetta: Un pittore senese della leggenda francescana* (Florence, 1946), pp. 51–2

C. Brandi: 'Introduzione alla pittura senese del primo quattrocento', *Rass. Italia* (1946), p. 31

A. Graziani: 'Il Maestro dell'Osservanza', *Proporzioni*, 2 (1948), pp. 75–88

C. Brandi: *Quattrocentisti senesi* (Milan, 1949), pp. 69–87; review by J. Pope-Hennessy in *A. Bull.*, xxxiii (1951), pp. 141–3

F. Zeri: 'Il Maestro dell'Osservanza: Una crocefissione', *Paragone*, v/49 (1954), pp. 43–4

J. Pope-Hennessy: 'Rethinking Sassetta', *Burl. Mag.*, xcviii (1956), pp. 364–70

E. Carli: *Il Sassetta e il Maestro dell'Osservanza* (Milan, 1957), pp. 89–121; review by C. Volpe in *A. Ant. & Mod.*, 4 (1958), pp. 344–5

M. Laclotte: 'Sassetta, le Maître de l'Observance et Sano di Pietro: Un Problème critique', *Inf. Hist. A.*, ii (1960), pp. 47–53

H. M. von Erffa: 'Der Nürnberger Stadtpatron auf italienischen Gemälden', *Mitt. Ksthist. Inst. Florenz*, xx (1976), pp. 1–12

P. Torriti: *La Pinacoteca Nazionale di Siena: I dipinti dal XII al XV secolo* (Genoa, 1977), pp. 248–52

D. Benati: 'Il Maestro dell'Osservanza', *Il gotico a Siena* (exh. cat., Siena, Pal. Pub., 1982), pp. 393–8; review by M. Boskovits in *A. Crist.*, lxxi (1983), pp. 259–76 (267)

P. Scapecchi: 'Quattrocentisti senesi nelle Marche: Il polittico di Sant'Antonio Abate del Maestro dell'Osservanza', *A. Crist.*, lxxi (1983), pp. 287–90 [with Eng. summary]

C. Alessi and P. Scapecchi: 'Il Maestro dell'Osservanza: Sano di Pietro o Francesco di Bartolomeo', *Prospettiva*, 42 (1985), pp. 13–37

Sassetti e i pittori toscani tra XIII e XV secolo (exh. cat. by A. Angelini, Siena, Col. Chigi-Saracini, 1986), pp. 43–7

J. Pope-Hennessy: *Italian Paintings in the Robert Lehman Collection*, New York, Met. cat. (Princeton, 1987), pp. 105–11

Painting in Renaissance Siena (exh. cat., New York, Met., 1988), pp. 99–136 [entry by K. Christiansen]

Restauri, 1983–1988 (exh. cat., Siena, 1988), pp. 20–27 [entry by C. Alessi]

Catherine de Sienne, (exh. cat., Avignon, 1992), pp. 253–4 [entry by C. Alessi]

CECILIA ALESSI

Master of Otto van Moerdrecht [Master of the Seraph] (*fl c.* 1420–30). North Netherlandish illuminator. He provided two miniatures in a copy of the *Postilla in Prophetas* (1423–5; Utrecht, Bib. Rijksuniv., MS. 252) by Nicolas de Lyre, commissioned by Otto van Moerdrecht while he was a novice at the Nieuwlicht Charterhouse near Utrecht and donated to the monastery after his profession. One miniature, about a third of the height of the text, shows the author seated in a landscape against an ornamented background (fol. 44*r*); on the facing *verso* (fol. 43*v*), a full-page representation of a six-winged angel, with inscriptions on its wings identifying them with aspects of a godly life, is described in a caption as 'Moralisacio seraph'. The painter of this very unusual picture, derived from a text by Alanus de Insulis, has been named the 'Master of the Seraph' but is more often called the Master of Otto van Moerdrecht. It was once thought that the

scribe and illuminator of this manuscript were monks at Nieuwlicht and that the painter might have been Otto van Moerdrecht himself. Everything known of the charterhouse, however, argues against the presence there of an established scriptorium. It is now generally assumed that the Master of Otto van Moerdrecht worked in an urban workshop in Utrecht.

The two miniatures of the Utrecht manuscript show a clear allegiance to the late phase of the Soft style. The landscape is the most archaic component of both pictures. Hills seem to be composed of clods of earth heaped on one another. Tiny crowns and long, flexible, stemlike trunks give the trees the appearance of bizarre flowers. There is no relation of setting to figure-scale. The modelling, however, is extraordinarily soft throughout. The subdued colouring is striking, with only grey and beige, apart from two muted shades of green and a little ochre of the angel's hair. Even the flesh colour is pale and soft. Both pictures, particularly that of the seraph, were painted as washed ink drawings, and the atypical technique and unusual iconography make a stylistic comparison with other manuscript illumination difficult.

Numerous miniatures have been connected with the Master of Otto van Moerdrecht, but they were certainly not all produced by the painter of the two miniatures in the Utrecht codex. On the contrary, the work of about half-a-dozen painters, varying in quality and appearing to belong to slightly different generations, can be distinguished. This 'Moerdrecht style' reflected an important facet of Utrecht book illumination in the 1420s and 1430s. Only rarely do illuminations in this style show a sensitivity equal to that of the page-opening from the Utrecht manuscript. In fact, they are characterized by bright, often harsh, colouring, based on contrasting red, orange and blue tones. The figures are bold in design but always appear completely flat. Garments are divided into many parallel sweeping folds. Heads are characteristically egg-shaped with narrow, slit eyes. The figures often have either no neck at all, or a neck that is inelegantly wide. A Bible in Brussels written in 1431 (Bib. Royale Albert 1er, MS. 9018–23) and another (undated) in The Hague (Kon. Bib., MS. 78.D.38) both contain many excellent examples of this style, although other artists contributed to both works. The five-volume Bible (Darmstadt, Hess. Landes- & Hochschbib., Hs 324), written by Thomas à Kempis between 1427 and 1439 in the Augustinian monastery of Agnietenberg near Zwolle, is also illuminated in the Moerdrecht style, as are miniatures in the book known as the Egmond Breviary (New York, Pierpont Morgan Lib., MS. M. 87) and the Breviary of Mary of Guelders (Berlin, Staatsbib. Preuss. Kultbes., MS. germ.qu.42). The four miniatures in the latter, in a section added to the manuscript around 1425, are among the most exquisite of this group. Missals (Heidelberg, Ubib.) and Books of Hours (Rome, Vatican, Bib. Apostolica, MS. Ross.61) also contain illumination in this style.

BIBLIOGRAPHY

J. P. Gumbert: *Die Utrechter Kartäuser und ihre Bücher im frühen fünfzehnten Jahrhundert* (Leiden, 1974), pp. 129–31, 181–5

W. H. Beuken and J. H. Marrow: *Spiegel van den Leven ons Heren* (Doornspijk, 1979), pp. 65–99

Handschriften en oude drukken van de Utrechtse Universiteitsbibliotheek (exh. cat., Utrecht, Bib. Rijksuniv., 1984), pp. 38–44

J. H. Marrow: 'Prolegomena to a New Descriptive Catalogue of Dutch Illuminated Manuscripts', *Miscellanea Neerlandica: Opstellen voor Dr. Jan Deschamps ter gelegenheid van zijn zeventigste verjaardag* [Dutch miscellanea: drawn up for Dr. Jan Deschamps on the occasion of his 70th birthday], i (Leuven, 1987), pp. 295–309

——: *A Descriptive and Analytical Catalogue of Dutch Illustrated Manuscripts of the 14th, 15th and 16th Centuries*, 2 vols (Doornspijk, 1990)

BODO BRINKMANN

Ovile Master. *See* BULGARINI, BARTOLOMMEO.

Master of the Page beneath the Cross. *See* MASTER OF THE FIGDOR DEPOSITION above.

Master of the Pala Sforzesca (*fl* Milan, *c.* 1490–*c.* 1500). Italian painter. The Master's oeuvre centres around the Pala Sforzesca (Milan, Brera), which was painted for the church of S Ambrogio ad Nemus, Milan, on the orders of Ludovico Sforza, il Moro, guardian of the Duke of Milan and, in 1494, Duke of Milan himself. It depicts the Virgin and Child, the four Doctors of the Church, Ludovico il Moro, his wife, Beatrice d'Este, and Ludovico's two sons. The painting is identifiable with an artist's plan that the Duke's secretary Stanga submitted to Ludovico on 22 January 1494 (Malaguzzi Valeri, p. 45). The painter's name is not mentioned, and attempts to identify him with Vincenzo Foppa, Bernardino de Conti, Ambrogio de Predis and others are untenable on stylistic grounds (Malaguzzi Valeri; Romano, Binaghi and Collura, 1978).

In the deliberately archaizing altarpiece the Master depicted Ludovico and his family in stark profile, kneeling at the feet of the Virgin. He liberally employed gold and lapis lazuli in painting the figures' jewel-encrusted garments. This lavish ostentation was typical of the Milanese court at that date. The Master's paintings take elements from the works of Foppa, Bergognone and Leonardo, from Ferrarese painters *c.* 1475 and from artists working at the Certosa di Pavia in 1490–1500. Stylistically, he was an individual and idiosyncratic painter with considerable skill in depicting space and volume but inept at representing movement and Leonardo's *sfumato*.

About 15 paintings can be grouped around the Pala Sforzesca. Zeri and Romano (1982) have convincingly dated the Master's works, placing them between the *Virgin and Child* (Baltimore, MA, Walters A.G.) and the frescoed chapel with the *Crucifixion with Saints* in S Giorgio in Annone, Brianza, Como, spanning a period from before 1490 to after 1500.

BIBLIOGRAPHY
C. Bianconi: *Nuova guida di Milano per gli amanti delle belle arti* (Milan, 1787), p. 366
F. Malaguzzi Valeri: 'Il Maestro della Pala Sforzesca', *Ant. Viva*, ix (1905), pp. 44–8
L. Giordano: 'Il duomo di Monza e l'arte dall'età viscontea al cinquecento', *Storia di Monza e della Brianza: L'arte dall'età romana al rinascimento*, ii (Milan, 1973), pp. 441–2
F. Zeri: *Italian Paintings in the Walters Art Gallery*, i (Baltimore, 1976), pp. 290–91
G. Romano: 'Il Maestro della Pala Sforzesca', *Processo per il museo* (exh. cat., ed. F. Russoli; Milan, Brera, 1977)
G. Romano, M. T. Binaghi and D. Collura: *Il Maestro della Pala Sforzesca* (Florence, 1978)
G. Mulzzani: 'Un'aggiunta al Maestro della Pala Sforzesca', *A. Lombarda*, 51 (1979), pp. 22–3
G. Romano: 'Maestro della Pala Sforzesca: S Giacomo, S Bartolomeo, e tre Apostoli', *Zenale e Leonardo* (exh. cat., Milan, Mus. Poldi Pezzoli, 1982), pp. 54–7

M. T. BINAGHI OLIVARI

Master of the Palazzo S Gervasio (*fl ?c.* 1620–1640s). Italian painter. His name derives from the location of the most important work attributed to him, the *Still-life with Fruit, Flowers and a Dove in Flight* (Venosa, Pal. S Gervasio), an opulent and decorative still-life featuring a rich display of fruits and flowers on a table draped with a brilliant red cloth. The naturalism of the objects and the quality of light on flowers, grapes and glass carafes indicate a familiarity with the still-lifes of Caravaggio and his Roman followers, while the ornamental and elaborate arrangement suggests a date in the 1620s. The frontal composition and the intensity of the observation hint at a connection with Spanish still-life. Various attempts have been made to identify the artist. Bottari's attribution of the picture to Aniello Falcone, based on its similarity to the still-life details in that artist's *Concert* and *Christ Driving the Money-changers from the Temple* (both Madrid, Prado), is not generally accepted. Causa attributed to the Master a group of still-lifes, including the *Still-life with Pigeons and Game* (Cremona, Mus. Civ. Ponzone), *Still-life with Fruit* (San Francisco, CA, de Young Mem. Mus.), *Still-life with Grapes, Pomegranates, Figs and Butterfly* and *Still-life with Pigeons, Artichokes and Vase of Flowers* (both Florence, Fraschetti priv. col., see 1984–5 exh. cat., p. 350), and also suggested that he may have collaborated with Falcone on the frescoes (1641–2) in the Firrao Chapel in S Paolo Maggiore, Naples. Marini proposed a possible identification with the Roman nobleman, Giovanni Battista Crescenzi (*see* CRESCENZI, (2)). The question of the Master's identity remains unresolved.

BIBLIOGRAPHY
S. Bottari: *Caravaggio* (Florence, 1966), pp. 143–6
R. Causa: 'La natura morta a Napoli nel sei e settecento', *Storia di Napoli*, V/iii (Cava dei Tirreni, 1972), pp. 1004–5
M. Marini: 'Caravaggio e il naturalismo internazionale', *Storia dell'arte italiana*, ed. F. Zeri and G. Previtali, ii (Turin, 1981), pp. 347–445
Painting in Naples, 1606–1705: From Caravaggio to Giordano (exh. cat., ed. C. Whitfield and J. Martineau; London, RA, 1982), pp. 195–6 [with bibliog.]
Civiltà del seicento a Napoli (exh. cat., ed. S. Cassani; Naples, Capodimonte, 1984–5) [with bibliog.]

□

Master of Panzano (*fl c.* 1360–90). Italian painter. The oeuvre of this Sienese painter was grouped by Berenson round a small triptych of the *Mystic Marriage of St Catherine, SS Peter, Paul and Other Saints* (Panzano, S Leolino). A conjectural development under the influence of Pietro Lorenzetti is based on accepting as his a small *Maestà* of *c.* 1355 (Siena, Pin. N., no. 585); but this attribution and the accompanying arguments are not wholly convincing. The stylistic traits of the *Mystic Marriage* point instead to some contact with Bartolo di Fredi and Andrea Vanni but most clearly to Paolo di Giovanni Fei, of whom the Master of Panzano may be regarded as an imitator. The general features of the Panzano Virgin and St Catherine, the former with a markedly retroussé nose, recall Fei, although the sacklike, inexpressive faces have none of his elegance. Similarly, the long-faced Panzano St Peter, large head set at a precarious tilt, is a mannerist response to such figures as the St James of Fei's *Birth of the Virgin* (Siena, Pin. N., no. 116), but without the structural logic or the expressive power. The pinnacle figures of SS Anthony Abbot and Blaise above the flanking panels, all set within a crisp intersecting arcade, exactly echo the postures of the saints below. The intricate and spirited convolutions of St Catherine's draperies in the central panel of the Panzano triptych show the Master at his most accomplished.

BIBLIOGRAPHY

B. Berenson: 'Quadri senza casa: Il trecento senese, II', *Dédalo*, xi (1930), pp. 329–62
——: *Central and North Italian Schools*, i (1968), pp. 254–5
G. Moran: 'Il Maestro di Panzano', *Not. Chianti Class.* (Oct 1975), p. 4
P. Torriti: *La Pinacoteca Nazionale di Siena: I dipinti dal XII al XV secolo* (Genoa, 1977/*R* 1980), p. 210

JOHN RICHARDS

Master of the Parement de Narbonne (*fl* last third of the 14th century). Painter and illuminator, active in France. He is named after the *Parement de Narbonne* (Paris, Louvre; see fig.), a large drawing in black ink on white silk (samite) found in Narbonne at the beginning of the 19th century. It shows, primarily, scenes of the *Passion* and was, most probably, the *table d'en haut*, to be suspended above and behind the altar, from a *chapelle* of hangings and vestments used to decorate a chapel during Lent. The early provenance of the work is uncertain: the portraits of the King of France, *Charles V* (*d* 1380), and his wife *Joanna of Bourbon* (*d* 1378) and the monogram K in the border prove that it was a royal commission. Its presence in Narbonne was the only reason for believing it to be a gift from the sovereign to the Cathedral of St Just, Narbonne, which housed the tomb of the entrails of Philip III (*d* 1285). No documentary evidence records such a donation or the presence of the *Parement* in the Cathedral.

The drawing, almost 3 m long, is of surprising monumentality and is the work of an exceptional artist, who must also have produced panel painting, even if no such work has survived. His style is based in the art of JEAN PUCELLE and his followers: the treatment in black and white—dictated by the purpose of the *Parement*—evokes the grisaille decoration of the Hours of Jeanne d'Evreux (*c.* 1325–8; New York, Cloisters, MS. 54.1.2.; *see* GOTHIC, fig. 80). There is the same concern for formal clarity in arranging figures, a remarkable sense of linear rhythms and a use of light and shade that confers a strong physical presence on the figures (*see* GOTHIC, fig. 70). The marked interest in the representation of space and volume in the articulation and positioning of the figures can only be explained by assuming contact with Italian painting more recent than that which had provided models for Pucelle. Probably painted between 1375 and 1380, the work reflects

that naturalistic tendency that ran through French manuscript illumination from the middle of the century: the variety of facial types and the emphasis placed on their characterization confer a remarkable expressive force on the *Parement*.

Some of the miniatures of the Très Belles Heures de Notre-Dame of Jean, Duc de Berry (Paris, Bib. N., MS. nouv. acq. lat. 3093), from the first campaign of illustration, probably begun *c.* 1380 for the Duc, are generally accepted as the work of the same Master: eight large miniatures for the Hours of the Virgin, those of the Office of the Dead and the Prayers of the Passion, and the first four for the Hours of the Cross. Done in collaboration with another illuminator (close to the Master of the Coronation Book of Charles V), who painted the *bas-de-pages* and the historiated initials, these scenes are exceptionally innovative, painted in intense and contrasting colours, and according to Avril represent 'that which is most advanced in French painting' of their time. A drawing representing an archer (Oxford, Christ Church Pict. Gal.) has also been attributed to this artist. Several known painters have been suggested as possible identifications for the Master, in particular André Beauneveu and Jean d'Orléans.

BIBLIOGRAPHY

F. de Guilhermy: 'Iconographie historique: Le roi Charles V et la reine Jeanne de Bourbon', *An. Archéol.*, xxii (1862), pp. 61–76
G. Hulin de Loo: *Heures de Milan: Troisième Partie des très belles Heures de Notre-Dame enluminées par les peintres de Jean de France, duc de Berry et par ceux du duc Guillaume de Bavière, comte de Hainaut et de Hollande* (Brussels, 1911), pp. 11–16
E. Panofsky: *Early Netherlandish Painting*, i (Cambridge, MA, 1953), pp. 42–6
T. Teasdale Smith: 'The Use of Grisaille as Lenten Observance', *Marsyas*, ix (1959), pp. 43–5
M. Meiss: *French Painting in the Time of Jean de Berry: The Late Fourteenth Century and the Patronage of the Duke*, i (London, 1967), pp. 99–134, 337–40
Les Fastes du gothique: Le siècle de Charles V (exh. cat., Paris, Grand Pal., 1981–2), pp. 339–41, 371–3 [entries by F. Avril and D. Thiébaut]
C. Sterling: *La Peinture médiévale à Paris, 1300–1500*, i (Paris, 1987), pp. 218–44

DOMINIQUE THIÉBAUT

Paris Master (*fl* Florence, *c.* 1440–60). Italian painter. He was named by Schubring after the anonymous painting of the *Judgement of Paris* (Glasgow, A. G. & Mus.) and attributed with 22 other cassone paintings of mythological or historical subjects. This is not, however, a stylistically coherent group; only three of the works can be securely given to the same workshop as the *Judgement of Paris*: the

Master of the Parement de Narbonne: *Parement de Narbonne*, monochrome ink on samite, h. 937 mm, *c.* 1375–*c.* 1380 (Paris, Musée du Louvre)

Sleep of Paris and the *Rape of Helen* (ex-Lanckoronski priv. col., Vienna; see Wohl, pls 185, 186) and a *Diana and Actaeon* (see Wohl, pl. 188). To these four may be added two cassone panels of the story of *Patient Griselda* (Bergamo, Gal. Accad. Carrara). The six panels have at various times been associated with or attributed to Domenico Veneziano, Pesellino and Domenico di Michelino; but, although they share a common pictorial language with these artists, they have an artistic identity of their own. The *Judgement of Paris* and *Diana and Actaeon* were among the first Italian paintings of Classical mythology in which the nude figure predominates, but the new Classical subject-matter was painted in the Gothic style, and the artist probably also drew on Netherlandish illuminations containing nude figures.

BIBLIOGRAPHY

P. Schubring: *Cassoni* (Leipzig, 1915), pp. 109, 260–65
H. Wohl: *The Paintings of Domenico Veneziano, ca. 1410–1461: A Study in Florentine Art of the Early Renaissance* (New York, 1980), pp. 154–8, 192–3

HELLMUT WOHL

Passion Master. *See* JEAN LE NOIR.

Master of the Passion of Christ (*fl* first half of the 15th century). Swedish painter or group of painters. The differences in skill between the 40 or so wall paintings in the island of Gotland attributed to this Master suggest that a workshop rather than a single artist was responsible for them. The same pattern with small variations has, however, been used everywhere for the *Nativity* and the *Passion of Christ* and was probably inspired by a German woodcut series. The arrangement of the paintings in a row along the wall, very much like wall hangings, has parallels in northern Germany but is rare on the Swedish mainland. The length of the series varies, and sometimes the legend of a saint is added, for example St Margaret of Antioch and St Catherine of Alexandria or, more often, a number of separate saints, placed in painted niches along the walls. St George and St Martin seem to have been the most popular.

The style of the Master of the Passion of Christ has its roots in 14th-century painting. The figure drawing is somewhat naive but very expressive, for example the suffering face of Christ, who is shown bleeding profusely from his wounds, in the *Passion* scenes. Few colours are used, brownish-red and greyish-black being predominant. The paintings are noted above all for their strong religious expressiveness. It has been conjectured that the Master could have had connections with a supposed workshop in the Brigittine convent of Vadstena, but the arguments for this are very hypothetical.

BIBLIOGRAPHY

B. G. Söderberg: *De gotländska passionsmålningarna och deras stilfränder* [The Gotland Passion paintings and their stylistic family] (Lund, 1942) [contains a cat. and illustrations; claims Brigittine influence]

ANNA NILSÉN

Master of the Pearl of Brabant (*fl c.* 1470–90). Netherlandish painter. The *Pearl of Brabant* is a triptych of the *Adoration of the Magi* with wings showing *St John the Baptist in the Wilderness* (left) and *St Christopher Crossing a River* (right) (Munich, Alte Pin.), traditionally ascribed to Dieric Bouts the elder (*see* BOUTS, (1)). This attribution was questioned by Heiland and Voll, who judged it to be the work of a close follower of Bouts, perhaps his elder son, Dieric Bouts the younger, who inherited his father's workshop *c.* 1475. Friedländer regarded the Munich triptych as definitely by the hand of Dieric Bouts the elder and considered the reattribution an 'irresponsible folly'. Schöne revived the attribution of Heiland and Voll and assembled a number of works under the authorship of the Master of the Pearl of Brabant, whom he also tentatively identified as Dieric Bouts the younger. According to Schöne, the works of the Master are stylistically close to Dieric Bouts the elder's paintings, but he found a lack of compositional unity between figures and space, an over precious quality in the treatment of the small figures and an intensity in the local colours that he felt were habits of an intimate workshop assistant and not the Master himself. Among the paintings that Schöne grouped about the Munich triptych are *Moses and the Burning Bush* (Philadelphia, PA, Mus. A.), *Christ in the House of Simon* (Munich, Alte Pin.) and the *Virgin and Child Enthroned with SS Peter and Paul* (London, N.G.). Davies considered the London painting an authentic work by Dieric Bouts the elder, and, for the most part, scholars have been reluctant to sever the Munich triptych from his oeuvre. A number of the paintings attributed to the Master by Schöne are considered works of lesser followers of Bouts the elder.

BIBLIOGRAPHY

P. Heiland: *Dierick Bouts und die Hauptwerke seiner Schule* (Potsdam, 1902)
K. Voll: *Die altniederländische Malerei von Jan van Eyck bis Memling* (Leipzig, 1906), pp. 124–31
M. J. Friedländer: *Die altniederländische Malerei* (Berlin, 1924-37); Eng. trans. as *Early Netherlandish Painting* (Leiden, 1967–76), iii, p. 21 [as Dieric Bouts the elder]
W. Schöne: *Dieric Bouts und seine Schule* (Berlin and Leipzig, 1938), pp. 43–9, 179–89
M. Davies: *Early Netherlandish School*, London, N.G. cat. (London, 1945, rev. 2/1955, rev. 3/1968), pp. 19–20

JAMES SNYDER

Master of the Pellegrini Chapel. *See* MICHELE DA FIRENZE.

Master of Petrarch (*fl* Augsburg, *c.* 1515–*c.* 1522). German woodcut designer. He is named from his most famous work, the woodcuts illustrating the German edition of Petrarch's *De remediis utriusque fortunae*. Those for the first part were completed in 1519, those for the second in 1520. They were produced for the Augsburg publishers Sigmund Grimm (*fl* 1496; *d* before 1532) and Marx Wirsung (*fl* 1518–23). The woodcuts did not appear until 1532, when they were published in two volumes under the title *Von der Artzney bayder Glück, des guten vnd widerwertigen*, by Heinrich Steyner (*fl* 1522; *d* 1548) of Augsburg. Also known as the *Glücksbuch* or *Trostspiegel*, this was an extremely popular work that came out in many editions; the last was published by Vincentius Steinmeyer (*fl* 1608) in 1620 (Frankfurt am Main). Its popularity was due mainly to the lively and witty illustrations (for example *see* AUGSBURG, fig. 5), which constitute one of the most important visual sources for the cultural history of 16th-century Germany. Their topicality, at the time of the

Reformation and Peasant Wars, is especially pungent and has led to interpretation in sociological or political (often Marxist) terms. For later artists they provided a rich pictorial source, as attested by Rubens's numerous copies. It has been argued that the visual conception of the book was due to Sebastian Brant (1458–1521) who, in the introduction to vol. I, is credited with the role of pictorial adviser: since the translation of Petrarch's original into German was not completed until 1621, so that the artist did not have the full German text before him, and since it is unlikely that the artist knew Latin, Brant would have had an important role as an adviser.

Several of the woodcuts were reused in the German edition of Cicero's *Officia*, commissioned by Johann, Freiherr zu Schwarzenberg (1463–1528), and executed for Grimm and Wirsung but published by Steyner in 1531, with further illustrations, which the same Master had apparently designed shortly after the Petrarch woodcuts. Smaller projects for Grimm and Wirsung included the illustrations to translations by Albrecht von Eyb (1420–75) of Plautus' comedies *Bacchides* and *Menaechmi* and of the *Philogenia* (1518) by Ugolino Pisani, to the German translation of *Calisto and Melibea* (1520) by Fernando de Rojas, to Cicero's *De senectute* (1522) and to various religious works, foremost the *Devotissimae meditationes de vita et passione J. Christi* (1520). Among the Master's works for other Augsburg publishers, the devotional book known as *Gilgengart* (Schönsperger, 1520) and the *Nemo* and *Epigrammatum liber* by Ulrich von Hutten (Miller, 1518 and 1519 respectively) are best known. Attributions also include many single-leaf woodcuts, such as a popular children's alphabet (1521), which shows the same inventiveness and diversity as the Petrarch illustrations. Attempts to attribute drawings and paintings to the Master have not been entirely successful: the much-discussed *Tree of Fools* (*c.* 1525; Coburg, Veste Coburg) and *Wheel of Fortune* (*c.* 1520; British priv. col.) show a kinship to the *Glücksbuch* in subject-matter rather than in style.

Despite his prolific career and great popularity, the Master's name was already forgotten in the next century. Discovery of the monogram H.W. on two of the Cicero woodcuts led to identification (Röttinger, 1904) of the Master with Hans Weiditz (*see* WEIDITZ, (2)), but for lack of further evidence the two artists are here treated separately.

LK

BIBLIOGRAPHY
W. von Seidlitz: 'Der Illustrator des Petrarca', *Jb. Kön.-Preuss. Kstsamml.*, xii (1891), pp. 158–66
H. Röttinger: *Hans Weiditz, der Petrarkameister*, 50 of Studien zur Kunst (Strasbourg, 1904)
T. Musper: *Die Holzschnitte des Petrarkameisters: Ein kritisches Verzeichnis* (diss., 1922; Munich, 1927)
E. Buchner: 'Der Petrarkameister als Maler, Miniator und Zeichner', *Festschrift Heinrich Wölfflin* (Munich, 1924), pp. 209–31
W. Fraenger: *Altdeutsches Bilderbuch: Hans Weiditz und Sebastian Brant*, 2 of *Denkmale der Volkskunst* (Leipzig, 1930)
W. Scheidig: *Die Holzschnitte des Petrarca-Meisters: Zu Petrarcas Werk 'Von der Artzney bayder Glück'* (Berlin, 1955)
U. Steinmann: 'Die politische Tendenz des Petrarca-Meisters: Seine Stellungnahme gegen die Wahl Karls V. und sein Verhalten zu den Ereignissen in Württemberg', *Forsch. & Ber.: Staatl. Mus. Berlin*, vi (1964), pp. 40–90
F. Petrarcha, ed. and commentary by M. Lemmer: *Von der Artzney bayder Glück, des guten vnd widerwertigen* (Hamburg, 1984)
H.-J. Raupp: 'Die Illustrationen zu Francesco Petrarca, *Von der Artzney bayder Glueck des guten vnd widerwertigen*' (Augsburg, 1532), *Wallraf-Richartz-Jb.*, xlv (1984), pp. 59–112

KRISTIN LOHSE BELKIN

Master of the Petrarch Triumphs (*fl c.* 1503). Illuminator, active in France. He is named after a newly translated copy of Petrarch's *Trionfi* (Paris, Bib. N., MS. fr. 594), which he illuminated. This manuscript must be close in date to a French version of Petrarch's *De remediis utriusque fortunae* (Paris, Bib. N., MS. fr. 225), which was translated in 1503; both manuscripts were commissioned in Rouen, possibly by Georges I d'Amboise (1460–1510), Cardinal and Archbishop of Rouen, for presentation to Louis XII. On this evidence Ritter and Lafond proposed the Master as the chief personality of a 'Rouen school' sustained by the patronage of the Cardinal, who assembled a large number of artists for building, decorating and furnishing his palace at Gaillon (nr Rouen). The Master is more likely, however, to have worked in Paris, since his hand is found in manuscripts also illuminated by the Parisian Jean Pichore (e.g. a Book of Hours; Ecouen, Mus. Ren., MS. E. Cl. 1251) and other Paris-based illuminators. Stylistic features in the *Trionfi* manuscript suggest knowledge of work from the circle of Jean Bourdichon and Jean Poyet in the Tours area. The so-called Petites Heures of Anne of Brittany (Paris, Bib. N., MS. nouv. acq. lat. 3027) is among the Master's finest works (although the link with Anne is not firm). His other manuscripts include a Book of Hours (New York, Pierpont Morgan Lib., MS. M. 356) illuminated for Claude Molé from Troyes.

BIBLIOGRAPHY
G. Ritter and J. Lafond: *Manuscrits à peintures de l'école de Rouen* (Paris, 1913)
The Last Flowering: French Painting in Manuscripts, 1420–1530, from American Collections (exh. cat. by J. Plummer and G. Clark, New York, Pierpont Morgan Lib., 1982)
I. Delaunay: 'Les *Heures* d'Ecouen du Musée national de la renaissance: Echanges entre manuscrits et imprimés autour de 1500', *Rev. Louvre*, 4 (1993)
Les Manuscrits à peintures en France, 1440–1520 (exh. cat. by F. Avril and N. Reynaud, Paris, Bib. N., 1993–4)

ROWAN WATSON

Master of the Pfullendorf Altar (*fl c.* 1500). German painter. He is named after a double-winged altarpiece (*c.* 1500), supposedly from the parish church at Pfullendorf, of which eight panels of the *Life of the Virgin* and *Prophets* have survived. In reconstruction the cycle presents two rows, one above the other, each with four panels depicting the *Life of the Virgin* (Sigmaringen, Fürst. Hohenzoll. Samml. & Hofbib.; Stuttgart, Staatsgal.; Frankfurt am Main, Städel. Kstinst. & Städt. Gal.), which together formed the second view of the altarpiece. When closed, it showed four scenes of the *Passion* (now almost completely destr.), on the reverse sides of the outer wings. The shrine that belonged to the third view is lost, but there is evidence that it contained carved relief figures of *St Ottilie* and a second female saint. The eight surviving half-length pictures of *Prophets* (Stuttgart, Staatsgal.) may have been next to the scenes from the *Life of the Virgin*, as the figures are positioned outside the picture axis of the painted scenes (Bushart), or may have formed the front and reverse of upper side extensions that covered the higher central shrine (Rettich).

The Master was active at first in Bartholomäus Zeitblom's workshop, probably in Ulm, but a former identification with the young Bernhard Strigel has been refuted (Bushart). In the *Presentation in the Temple* and the *Death of the Virgin*, one above the other on the reverse side of the surviving right wing (before *c.* 1500; Bingen, nr Sigmaringen, parish church) of an altarpiece (destr. 1790), the artist's style is already fully developed, but the execution is still somewhat clumsy. In both pictures a prophet, looking outwards, is connected with the scene (which supports Bushart's suggested reconstruction of the Pfullendorf Altar). The figures of SS Peter and John the Evangelist (in profile, attending to the dying Virgin) provide a good point of comparison with the corresponding figures in the Pfullendorf *Death of the Virgin*. The Pfullendorf Altarpiece presupposes a knowledge of Zeitblom's altarpiece at Heerberg (1497–8; Stuttgart, Staatsgal.), as the heads of the Virgin in each are very closely related, although the head of Joseph, with its pointed nose and watchful eyes, is an entirely original invention by the Pfullendorf artist, whose draughtsmanship was more vivacious and fiery, superior to that of both Zeitblom and Strigel. Above all, in his sense of space, spatial gradation of objects and clearly organized vegetation, the Master of the Pfullendorf Altar influenced Strigel in his works after 1506. The Master of Sigmaringen, now identified as Hans Strüb, also learnt from him.

BIBLIOGRAPHY
B. Bushart: '"Meister des Pfullendorfer Altars" oder Bernhard Strigel', *Z. Kstgesch.*, xxi (1958), pp. 230–42
E. Rettich: 'Bernhard Strigel: Rezension zu Stange 8', *Z. Kstgesch.*, xxii (1959), p. 158

HANS GEORG GMELIN

Master of the Piccolomini Madonna [Piccolomini Master] (*fl* Siena, ?1450–1500). Italian sculptor or group of sculptors. A number of reliefs of the Virgin and Child have been collected together under this name. All show the Virgin turned three-quarter face, standing behind a parapet upon which the Infant Christ reclines, raising his hand in benediction. Variations occur in the decoration of the parapet and the presence or absence of candelabra and putti's heads in the sky. In some examples the Virgin holds a cartouche. By the 1990s nine marble examples were known: Siena, Col. Chigi-Saracini; Paris, Louvre, 609; Pesaro, Mus. Civ.; Florence, Mus. Bardini; Paris, Louvre, ex-Arconati Visconti priv. col.; Benneboek, Pannwitz priv. col.; London, V&A; Pianiga (Padua), parish church; and New York, Met. There is also one in stucco (Florence, priv. col.).

The reliefs in the Louvre (609) and Collezione Chigi-Saracini in Siena both have the Piccolomini coat of arms on the parapet, and both originally came from properties belonging to the Chigi family. They would seem to be of higher quality than the others and may be by the same hand. The existence of so many variants of a single composition is rare, and it has been suggested that they may all derive from a common prototype that was originally in Siena, either a lost relief by Donatello of *c.* 1457–8 (Bode, Pope-Hennessy) or the Chigi-Saracini relief itself. This, in turn, has led to the attribution of the latter relief

to il Vecchietta (Valentiner), to a sculptor in the circle of Giovanni di Stefano (Bode, Schubring), and even to the claim that it is a work of the early 16th century by Lorenzo Marrina (1476–1534; Curajod).

It is extremely unlikely that all the reliefs are the work of a single sculptor. The Chigi-Saracini and the Louvre (609) reliefs do, however, have the appearance of being Sienese, datable *c.* 1475–1500. Stylistically they are close to paintings by Neroccio de' Landi and Francesco di Giorgio, particularly in the rhythmic outlines of the delicate, semi-transparent drapery and the facial characteristics with fine arched eyebrows and almond-shaped eyes.

BIBLIOGRAPHY
L. Curajod: 'Récentes Acquisitions du Musée de la sculpture moderne au Louvre', *Gaz. B.-A.*, n.s. 1, xxiii (1881), pp. 203–6
W. von Bode: *Denkmäler der Renaissance: Sculptur toscanas*, (Munich, 1892–1905), i, p. 159
P. Schubring: *Die Plastik Sienas in Quattrocento* (Berlin, 1907)
W. Valentiner: 'Marble Reliefs by Lorenzo Vecchietta' *A. America & Elsewhere*, xiii (1924), pp. 55–62
F. Negri Arnoldi: 'Sul Maestro della Madonna Piccolomini', *Commentari*, xiv (1963), pp. 8–16
J. Pope-Hennessy: *Catalogue of Italian Sculpture in the Victoria and Albert Museum*, i (London, 1964), pp. 261–3; review by F. Negri Arnoldi in *Commentari*, xxi (1970), pp. 201–18
M. Salmi: *Il palazzo e la collezione Chigi-Saracini* (Siena, 1967), pp. 230–32
A. Parronchi: 'Une Madonne donatellienne de Jacopo Sansovino', *Rev. A.* [Paris], xxi (1973), pp. 41–3
E. Neri Lusanna and L. Faedo: *Le sculture*, ii of *Il museo Bardini a Firenze* (Milan, 1986), pp. 269–70
G. Gentilini: 'Il Maestro della Madonna Piccolomini', *Collezione Chigi-Saracini. La scultura: Bozzetti in terracotta, piccoli marmi e altre scultura dal XIV al XX secolo*, ed. G. Gentilini and C. Sisi (Siena, 1989), i, pp. 80–98

FRANCESCA PETRUCCI

Pierpont Limner (*fl* ?Boston, *c.* 1710–16). English painter, active in the USA. Two of the finest portraits painted in New England during the early 18th century, *The Rev. James Pierpont* and *Mrs James Pierpont* (New Haven, CT, Yale U. A.G.), remain unattributed to a named artist. The Rev. Pierpont, a Congregationalist minister, helped to found the Collegiate School of Connecticut in 1701, which became Yale College in 1718. The pendant portraits of him and his third wife, Mary Hooker, are both dated 1711 and are rendered in the elegant, high style then practised in England by Sir Godfrey Kneller and his followers. A portrait of *Caleb Heathcote* (New York, NY Hist. Soc.), a wealthy colonial leader, executed in a similarly painterly manner, has been attributed to the Pierpont Limner and probably dates from about 1711–13, when Heathcote was mayor of New York. Portraits of *Edward Collins* (*c.* 1716; Albany, NY, Inst. Hist. & A.) and of *Edward Savage* (*c.* 1711–15; priv. col.) are also included in recent discussions of the Pierpont Limner's oeuvre. Pierpont family tradition maintains that the artist was English and painted in Boston between about 1710 and 1716.

BIBLIOGRAPHY
'Caleb Heathcote (1666–1721)', *American Portraits in the New York Historical Society* (New Haven, 1974), i, pp. 344–5
W. Craven: *Colonial American Portraiture* (Cambridge, 1986), pp. 121–3

CARRIE REBORA

Master of the Playing Cards (*fl c.* 1425–50). German engraver. The most accomplished and influential member of the first generation of engravers, he is named after a series of engravings with number cards and figure cards arranged in suits of flowers, birds, deer (see fig.), wild men and beasts of prey, preserved largely in the Bibliothèque Nationale, Paris, and the Kupferstichkabinett, Dresden. From the numerous copies of the suit symbols in datable manuscripts, his cards can be dated shortly before 1440.

Lehrs attributed additional engravings to the Master, and his attributions were further refined by Geisberg (1924). Fischel pointed out some stylistic inconsistencies within this group, considering them the result of diverse models. The fact that the engravings survive in unique or very rare impressions, sometimes from recut plates, complicates the problem. Van Buren and Edmunds showed that many of the surviving impressions of the cards are from later editions printed with combinations of plate segments juxtaposed to make up the number cards. Number cards with the suit symbols engraved on a single plate represent the original design of the cards and date from the earliest editions. Wolff re-examined the body of attributed works in relation to the playing cards themselves, concluding that only three other engravings should be given to the engraver of the cards: the *St George* (Lehrs, no. 35), the *Betrayal of Christ* (L 2) and the *Virgin Standing on the Snake* (L 29, unique impression from reworked plate, Padua, Bib. Semin.). Like the playing cards, these prints are characterized by clear, elegant contours and short, parallel hatching flecks rather than crosshatching. These delicate strokes give a shimmering effect of light

and surface texture in the best-preserved impressions but were rapidly worn down in the printing process.

The Master of the Playing Cards' facility with the burin suggests that he, in common with most early engravers, was trained as a goldsmith. He was traditionally thought to have worked in the Upper Rhine, in part because of similarities in graphic technique and figure type with other engravers from this region, such as the Master of the Nuremberg Passion and Master E.S. This localization is confirmed by analogies between Upper Rhenish painting and the cards and the other three engravings attributable to the Master. The engravings are particularly close to the paintings of the Master of the Frankfurt Paradise Garden, who seems to have worked in Alsace, probably in Strasbourg.

For the animals and birds of the playing cards at least, the engraver drew on established models. Motifs from these suits occur in earlier illuminated manuscripts, particularly in the Parisian production of the Bedford Master, by the second decade of the century. The repetition of these designs in earlier manuscripts points to the existence of a repertory of patterns suitable for decorative use. The Master of the Playing Cards, in elegantly reproducing an engraved version of these presumed patterns and passing them on to other artists, played a role that was prophetic of the later development of the engraving medium. The influence of the playing cards is attested to by engraved copies of the cards and widespread copies after the suit symbols in later manuscript borders and other areas requiring decorative or naturalistic motifs.

BIBLIOGRAPHY

M. Geisberg: *Das älteste gestochene deutsche Kartenspiel vom Meister der Spielkarten (vor 1446)* (Strasbourg, 1905)
M. Lehrs: *Geschichte und kritischer Katalog des deutschen, niederländischen, und französischen Kupferstichs im XV. Jahrhundert*, i (Vienna, 1908) [L]
M. Geisberg: *Die Anfänge des Kupferstiches* (Leipzig, 1923, rev. 1924)
L. Fischel: 'Oberrheinische Malerei im Spiegel des frühen Kupferstichs', *Z. Kstwiss.*, i (1947), pp. 23–38
H. Lehmann-Haupt: *Gutenberg and the Master of the Playing Cards* (New Haven, 1966) [his assoc. of the Master with Mainz and the prod. of Gutenberg Bibles is no longer accepted]
A. H. van Buren and S. Edmunds: 'Playing Cards and Manuscripts: Some Widely Disseminated Fifteenth-century Model Sheets', *A. Bull.*, lvi (1974), pp. 12–30
M. Wolff: 'Some Manuscript Sources for the Playing-card Master's Number Cards', *A. Bull.*, lxiv (1982), pp. 587–601
——: 'Observations on the Master of the Playing Cards and Upper Rhenish Painting', *Essays in Northern European Art Presented to Egbert Haverkamp-Begemann*, ed. A.-M. Logan (Doornspijk, 1983), pp. 299–302

MARTHA WOLFF

Master of the Playing Cards: *Queen Wearing a Bourrelet* (or *Queen of Deer*), engraving, 135×90 mm, *c.* 1435–40 (Boston, MA, Museum of Fine Arts)

Master of the Polling Panels (*fl c.* 1439–52). German painter. He was one of the most distinctive artists in early Bavarian painting and worked in the area around Munich and Kremsmünster. His oeuvre, which can be assembled with certainty on stylistic grounds, includes the panels of two winged altarpieces from the Augustinian monastery at Polling in Upper Bavaria, after which he is named. Four of these come from an altarpiece of scenes from the *Life of the Virgin* and are dated 1444. The altarpiece was donated by Duke Albert II of Bavaria (*reg* 1438–60) and his wife, Anna (1420–74). The surviving panels are an *Annunciation* and *Adoration of the Magi* (Munich, Alte Pin.) and a *Nativity* and *Presentation in the Temple* (Munich, Bayer. Nmus.). Two further panels come from an altarpiece of the Holy Cross; they are a *Crucifixion* and three scenes of the *Discovery of the True Cross* (Munich, Bayer. Nmus.). Four further panels from an altarpiece of the *Life of the Virgin*, dated 1439, are in the Stiftsgalerie, Kremsmünster. Two well-preserved panels with *St Peter* and *St Paul* are also extant (Cassani priv. col.).

The paintings are distinguished by their use of advances made in early Netherlandish painting in the depiction of landscapes and of architectural interiors. They are also characterized by the heightened expressiveness of the figure types and landscape forms: in this the influence of the Wurzach Altar (1437; Berlin, Reichenhofen in the Allgäu) by HANS MULTSCHER can be seen. The Master of the Polling Panels has sometimes been identified with the documented Munich painter Gabriel Angler, who in turn should be identified with the Master of the Tegernsee Altar (for a different view *see* MASTER OF THE TEGERNSEE ALTAR below). The identification with Conrad Sachs suggested by Liedke on stylistic and chronological grounds is more doubtful.

BIBLIOGRAPHY
A. Stange: *Deutsche Malerei der Gotik*, x (Munich and Berlin, 1959), pp. 61–3
J. M. Ehresmann: 'The Master of the Polling Altars: An Austrian Contribution to the Bavarian School', *Marsyas*, xiv (1968–9), pp. 17–28
V. Liedke: 'Die Münchner Tafelmalerei und Schnitzkunst der Spätgotik: II', *A. Bavar.*, xxix–xxx (1982), pp. 45–84
——: 'Zwei bis lang unbekannte Gemälde des Meisters der Pollinger Tafel in einer Münchner Privatsammlung', *A. Bavar.*, lxvii–lxviii (1992), pp. 7–14

JANEZ HÖFLER

Master of the Portraits of Princes (*fl c.* 1470–*c.* 1492). South Netherlandish painter. He was named by Friedländer after three portraits of noblemen dated between 1480 and 1487: *Englebert of Nassau* (Amsterdam, Rijksmus.), the *Young Man of the Fonseca Family* (Rotterdam, Mus. Boymans–van Beuningen) and the *Portrait of a Young Man*, recently identified as Jan Bossaert (ex-N. Mus., Poznań; priv. col.). These hieratic portraits are identically presented, the half-length figures being shown in three-quarter view to the left and against plain backgrounds. The relatively two-dimensional treatment of the torsos has a decorative quality and contrasts with the individuality of the faces. Their expressions conform to a standard type: heavy and constructed from planes, with long, prominent noses and a distant look in the wide-open eyes. The schematic handling of paint nonetheless appears meticulous: this is typical of late 15th-century Netherlandish painting and of Brussels in particular. The painted frame is an integral part of the composition. The reverse of each panel is painted with the sitter's coat of arms. The originality of these portraits lies in the obvious desire for realism, inspired perhaps by the strongly modelled portraits of Hugo van der Goes but transformed into a formula. Other works attributed to the Master are the portraits of *Louis of Gruuthuse* (*c.* 1472–80; Bruges, Groeningemus.; *see* BRUGES, fig. 4), *Adolphe of Cleves* (*c.* 1490; Berlin, Gemäldegal.) and the portrait of the same sitter included in the triptych of the *Marriage at Cana* (*c.* 1492; Melbourne, N.G. Victoria).

The identity of this Master remains doubtful: Pieter van Coninxloo (*fl* 1479–1513), Bernard van der Stockt (before 1469–after 1538), Lieven van Lathem, the Master of the Legend of St Mary Magdalene and Jan van Coninxloo I

(*fl* Brussels, *c.* 1491) have all been proposed. Whatever his identity, there is a clear connection with the Ghent–Bruges school of illumination.

BIBLIOGRAPHY
BNB: 'Vrancke Van der Stockt'
A. J. Wauters: 'Marguerite d'Autriche gouvernante des Pays-Bas et le peintre Pierre van Coninxloo', *Bull. Mus. Royaux Cinquantenaire*, n.s., xiii (1914), p. 7
M. J. Friedländer: *Die altniederländische Malerei*: (Berlin, 1924–37); Eng. trans. as *Early Netherlandish Painting* (Leiden, 1967–76), iv, p. 59
J. Maquet-Tombu: 'Le Maître de la légende de Marie-Madeleine', *Gaz. B.-A.*, ii (1929), p. 281; iii (1930), p. 190
P. Wescher: 'Das höfische Bildnis von Philip dem Guten bis zu Karl V', II, *Pantheon*, xxviii (1941), p. 274
J. Białostocki and M. Walicki: *Europäische Malerei in polnischen Sammlungen, 1300–1800* (Warsaw, 1957), p. 475
J. Duverger: 'Hofschilder Lieven van Lathem (ca 1430–1493)', *Jb.: Kon. Mus. S. Kst.* [Antwerp] (1969), pp. 97–104
Primitifs flamands anonymes: Maîtres aux noms d'emprunt des Pays-Bas méridionaux du XVe et du début du XVIe siècle (exh. cat., Bruges, Groeningemus., 1969), pp. 127–30, 257–62
V. Hoff and M. Davies: *The National Gallery of Victoria, Melbourne*, Les Primitifs flamands: I. Corpus, 12 (Brussels, 1971), p. 19
R. Grosshans: 'Zwei Bildnisse Adolfs van Cleve und der Mark, Herrn zu Ravenstein und Wynnendael (1425–1492)', *Berlin. Mus.*, n. s., xxii (1972), pp. 3–10
N. Reynaud: 'Les Maîtres à "noms de convention"', *Rev. A.* [Paris], 42 (1978), pp. 41–52
J. Rivière: 'Réévaluation du mécénat de Philippe le Beau et de Marguerite d'Autriche en matière de peinture', *Activités artistiques et pouvoirs dans les états des ducs de Bourgogne et des Habsbourgs et les régions voisines* (Basle, 1985), no. 25, p. 114
C. Périer-D'Ieteren: 'Une Oeuvre retrouvée du Maître des Portraits Princiers', *An. Hist. A. & Archéol.*, viii (1986), pp. 43–56
C. van den Bergen-Pantens: 'Description et identification des armoiries du revers', *An. Hist. A. & Archéol.*, viii (1986), pp. 57–8
C. Périer-D'Ieteren: 'Apports à l'étude du retable de la multiplication des pains de Melbourne', *An. Hist. A. & Archéol.*, xiv (1992), pp. 7–25

C. PÉRIER-D'IETEREN

Master of the Prado Redemption (*fl* Brussels, *c.* 1470). South Netherlandish painter. He is named after a triptych of the *Redemption* (Madrid, Prado; for illustration *see* STOCKT, VRANCKE VAN DER), which was at one time incorrectly believed to be the altarpiece (untraced) for St Aubert, Cambrai, commissioned from Rogier van der Weyden. Hulin de Loo (*BNB*) proposed that the Master of the Prado Redemption was the same person as VRANCKE VAN DER STOCKT. This identification was initially resisted but is now widely accepted.

BIBLIOGRAPHY
BNB: 'Stockt (Vrancke van der)'

FEMY HORSCH

Prato Master (*fl c.* 1440–50). Italian painter. Pope-Hennessy (1950) assigned this name to an anonymous artist closely allied with Paolo Uccello. In collaboration with another artist, he painted frescoes of the *Lives of the Virgin and St Stephen* in the chapel of the Assunta, Prato Cathedral. Specifically attributed to the Prato Master are the scenes depicting the *Birth of the Virgin*, the *Presentation of the Virgin*, the *Dispute of St Stephen*, most of the figures in the borders surrounding the scenes, images of the *Virtues* on the ceiling and some of the saints on the entrance arch. The fresco of the full-length figure of *Jacopone da Todi*, discovered in 1871 behind a Baroque altar in the same chapel, can also be attributed to him. The mediocre collaborator responsible for the lower scenes on both walls is almost unanimously recognized as Andrea di Giusto.

Suggested dates for the cycle vary considerably. Parronchi, for example, believed they were begun in 1435 or 1436 in order to place the frescoes within the transitional phase of Uccello's career following his return to Florence from Venice in 1430. Pope-Hennessy, on the other hand, attributed the frescoes to an artist trained in Uccello's workshop. They would have been painted after Uccello's clockface of 1443 (Florence Cathedral), since the Prato Master borrowed the heads in it as prototypes for his own work. Because the upper frescoes would have almost certainly been painted first, the death of Andrea di Giusto (1450) provides a *terminus ante quem* for the entire fresco cycle.

Former attributions of the Prato frescoes to Domenico Veneziano or Giovanni di Francesco have been largely discarded, but their inclusion in Uccello's oeuvre is maintained by many. The frescoes, however, display several peculiar qualities. The exaggerated facial expressions in the *Dispute* almost, though perhaps unintentionally, caricature Uccello's interest in physiognomy as a scientific subject. They are contrasted by the more stylized features of other figures. Unusual colours are likewise juxtaposed in original combinations, and the tendency to treat them as flat, large fields intensifies their decorative role. Interest in embellishment is further evident in the smaller details. The artist's shifting attention between decorative line and plastic effect is notable. Unsystematic perspective, inexactly constructed figures and an inconsistent handling of space and volumes all point to an artist who enthusiastically followed the advances being made by his contemporaries but developed none himself.

The Prato Master has at times been identified with the KARLSRUHE MASTER (*see above*) and the Master of the Quarata Predella. Scholarly opinion on the subject is varied and sometimes conflicting. The connections, if any, among these three masters remain unclear and so, too, does the association of the Prato Master with such works as the *Virgin and Child* (Dublin, N.G.), a *Female Saint with Two Children* (Florence, Pitti) and *St George and the Dragon* (London, N.G.). While most scholars assign these works to Uccello, perhaps they should be attributed to the still enigmatic Prato Master.

BIBLIOGRAPHY

R. van Marle: *Italian Schools*, ix (1927)
J. Pope-Hennessy: *Paolo Uccello* (London, 1950, rev. 2/1969)
G. Marchini: *Il duomo di Prato* (Milan, 1957)
E. Borsook: *The Mural Painters of Tuscany: From Cimabue to Andrea del Sarto* (London, 1960, rev. Oxford, 1980), pp. 79–84
C. Shell: 'The Early Style of Fra Filippo Lippi and the Prato Master', *A. Bull.*, xliii (1961), pp. 197–209
M. Meiss: *The Great Age of Fresco: Discoveries, Recoveries and Survivals* (New York, 1970)
A. Parronchi: *Paolo Uccello* (Bologna, 1974)

DONNA T. BAKER

Master of Pratovecchio (*fl* Florence, *c.* 1450). Italian painter. Longhi gave the name to an anonymous Florentine painter active in the mid-15th century who was influenced by Domenico Veneziano and, to a lesser extent, by Andrea del Castagno. His most important surviving work is a dismembered triptych consisting of an *Assumption of the Virgin* (Pratovecchio, S Giovanni Evangelista, on dep. Arezzo, Soprintendenza alle Gallerie), side panels of *SS Michael and John the Baptist* and a *Bishop and Female Martyr* as well as side pilasters, tondi and pinnacles (all London, N.G.). Longhi suggested that the *Death of the Virgin* (Boston, MA, Isabella Stewart Gardner Mus.) originally formed the predella, but this is debatable.

Longhi also attributed to the Master the *Virgin and Child with SS Bridget and Michael*, known as the Poggibonsi Altarpiece (Malibu, CA, Getty Mus.), and this has been accepted by later scholars. Using a document of 1439, Fredericksen tried to identify the Poggibonsi Altarpiece with one painted by GIOVANNI DI FRANCESCO (i) for the Convent of Paradiso, Pian di Ripoli, near Florence, and suggested that the Master's works were early works by Giovanni di Francesco. However, this identification is difficult to sustain, since the two groups of paintings assigned to the Master and to Giovanni di Francesco are clearly distinct in style. The identification of the Poggibonsi Altarpiece with that mentioned in 1439 also remains unproven: the subject named in the document does not tally with the Poggibonsi painting, which, in any case, would seem to date to *c.* 1450. Certainly it is very close in style to the *Assumption of the Virgin*. Longhi also attributed other works to the Master. These include *Three Archangels* (Berlin, Gemäldegal.), two panels of the *Virgin and Child* (Cambridge, MA, Fogg; Florence, Vittorio Frascione priv. col.) and a *Virgin and Child with Angels* (New York, Pierpont Morgan Lib.). Also attributable to the Master is a fresco fragment with a frieze of putti heads, part of the decoration of the Lenzi Chapel, Ognissanti, Florence (*in situ*), which was decorated by Bicci di Lorenzo and Neri di Bicci between 1446 and 1451. Presumably the Master completed the work with Neri di Bicci after Bicci di Lorenzo became ill.

Given the quality of the Master's work and the narrow time band into which it apparently falls, Longhi suggested that he may have died young. Padoa Rizzo's hypothesis is that he may be identified with JACOPO DI ANTONIO, who died aged 27 in 1454.

BIBLIOGRAPHY

M. Davies: *The Earlier Italian Schools*, London, N.G. cat. (London, 1951, 2/1961/*R* 1986), pp. 541–4
R. Longhi: 'Il "Maestro di Pratovecchio"', *Paragone*, iii/35 (1952), pp. 10–37
F. Hartt: 'The Earliest Works of Andrea del Castegno, Part Two', *A. Bull.*, xli (1959), p. 234
F. Zeri: *Due dipinti, la filologia e un nome* (Turin, 1961), p. 45
F. Zeri and B. Fredericksen: *Census of Pre-Nineteenth Century Italian Paintings in North American Public Collections* (Cambridge, MA, 1972), p. 135
B. Fredericksen: *Giovanni di Francesco and the Master of Pratovecchio* (Malibu, 1974)
P. Hendy: *European and American Paintings in the Isabella Stewart Gardner Museum* (Boston, 1974), pp. 107–10
Disegni italiani del tempo di Donatello (exh. cat., ed. A. Angelini; Florence, Uffizi, 1986), pp. 32–3
A. de Marchi: 'Maestro di Pratovecchio', *Pitture di luce* (exh. cat., ed. L. Bellosi; Milan, 1990), pp. 149–52
A. Padoa Rizzo: 'Ristudiando i documenti: Proposte per il Maestro di Pratovecchio e la sua tavola eponima', *Atti de convegno internazionale di studi di storia dell'arte nel centenario della nascita di Mario Salmi* (in preparation)
——: *Aggiunte al Maestro di Pratovecchio* (in preparation)

ANNA PADOA RIZZO

Master of the Prayerbooks of *c*. 1500 (*fl c*. 1500). South Netherlandish illuminator. The name was devised by Winkler to reflect the fact that miniatures by this artist are found in many south Netherlandish Books of Hours of the period around 1500. A typical example of his consistent and distinctive style is Codex 1862 of the Österreichische Nationalbibliothek, Vienna. The relatively crude figures have stereotyped faces: those of the women often distinctly egg-shaped, those of the men with straight noses, low foreheads and hair that sits on the head like a cap. In the landscape backgrounds, the thickly painted clouds and the trees stand out. The trees have either round, vivid green leaves or (even in summer landscapes) no leaves at all. Bare trees and pale hills, which look like chalk cliffs, recur throughout the works of the Master. Garments are often painted in pastel shades such as pale violet or light wine-red; the Master particularly liked to include a garment in shell-gold, shaded with orange. Also, his figures are often grey- or white-haired. Thick wine-red ink lines often surround the picture area.

His debt to the Master of the Dresden Prayerbook is especially evident in his calendar illustrations. Yet Winkler's opinion that he was a pupil of this Master is contradicted by an entirely independent early work (The Hague, Rijksmus. Meermanno-Westreenianum, MS. 10.F. 12). He added miniatures painted in grisaille to a prayerbook of Philip the Good, Duke of Burgundy. His most beautiful illuminations, executed with exceptional delicacy, are, however, to be found in secular manuscripts. Notable among these are an opulently illustrated manuscript of the *Roman de la rose* made for Engelbert II of Nassau (London, BL, Harley MS. 4425), a Monstrelet, *Chronique de France*, at Leiden (Bib. Rijksuniv., MS. Voss. Gall. 2), two full-page miniatures added to a Virgil written for Jan Crabbe, abbot of the abbey of Duinen, near Bruges (Holkham Hall, Norfolk, Lib., MS. 311), and a Xenophon, *Cyropaedia*, in Geneva (Bib. Pub. & U., MS. fr. 75). Judging by the costumes depicted, these works can be dated between 1490 and 1505–10.

BIBLIOGRAPHY

F. Winkler: 'Studien zur Geschichte der niederländischen Miniaturmalerei des XV. und XVI. Jahrhunderts, iv: Der Gebetbuchmeister und seine Stellung in der Miniaturmalerei um 1500', *Jb. Ksthist. Samml. Allhöch. Ksrhaus.*, xxxii (1915), pp. 334–42
——: *Die flämische Buchmalerei* (Leipzig, 1925/*R* Amsterdam, 1978), pp. 128–9
P. Schatborn: '39 Grisailles in the Book of Hours of Philip the Good in The Hague: An Attribution to the "Gebetbuchmeister um 1500"', *Oud-Holland*, lxxxv (1970), pp. 45–8
Renaissance Painting in Manuscripts: Treasures from the British Library (exh. cat., ed. T. Kren; Malibu, CA, Getty Mus.; New York, Pierpont Morgan Lib.; London, BL; 1984), pp. 49–58
G. Dogaer: *Flemish Miniature Painting in the 15th and 16th Centuries* (Amsterdam, 1987), pp. 159–60
Flämische Buchmalerei: Handschriftenschätze aus dem Burgunderreich (exh. cat. by D. Thoss, Vienna, Österreich. Nbib., 1987), pp. 107–12

BODO BRINKMANN

Master of the Privileges (*fl* Palma de Mallorca, *c*. 1334–49). Catalan illuminator and painter. He is named after the work with which he is most closely identified, a *Libro de Privilegios* (Palma de Mallorca, Archv Hist.) illuminated *c*. 1334. He was apparently the head of a thriving and important Mallorcan workshop responsible for the production of illuminated manuscripts and panel paintings. Other works attributed to him include a *Leyes Palatinas* of King James II of Mallorca (Brussels, Bib. Royale Albert 1er, MS. 9169), datable to *c*. 1337, the retable of *St Eulalia* in Palma de Mallorca Cathedral and the retable of *St Quiteria* (Palma de Mallorca, Soc. Arqueol. Lul-Liana). The retable of *St Eulalia* was commissioned by Bishop Berenguer Batlle (*d* 1349). All these works are linked by a style revealing Italian influence, notably that of the Sienese school. Although the Master evidently closely studied the works of Duccio, Simone Martini and Pietro Lorenzetti, he also retained a strong attachment to Spanish traditions. This is seen in his hieratically arranged, frontal and highly formal compositions and in the use of strong, vibrant primary colours.

BIBLIOGRAPHY

M. Meiss: 'Italian Style in Catalonia and a Fourteenth Century Catalan Workshop', *J. Walters A.G.*, iv (1941), pp. 45–87
J. Domínguez Bordona: *Miniatura*, A. Hisp., xviii (Madrid, 1962), p. 147

LYNETTE BOSCH

Master of the Privileges of Ghent and Flanders (*fl c*. 1440–60). South Netherlandish illuminator. He was named by Winkler after a codex in Vienna (Österreich. Nbib., Cod. 2583), which is a unique historical document containing transcriptions of the privileges and statutes for the town of Ghent and the country of Flanders from 1241 to 1454. The manuscript is illuminated with 15 miniatures and marginal decoration of exceptionally high quality. The coats of arms and mottoes of Philip the Good, Duke of Burgundy, are included in many of the borders. The Duke's victory over the rebellious citizens of Ghent in 1453, depicted in the only two full-page miniatures of the codex, was probably the reason for the production of this magnificent manuscript, which may even have been intended as a work of atonement.

All the miniatures of Cod. 2583 were produced by the Master of the Privileges of Ghent and Flanders. At first sight his style appears almost archaic and influenced by the designs and motifs of French illumination *c*. 1400, for example in the depiction of landscapes. The scenes are entirely two-dimensional: figures and horses are always shown either in profile or viewed from the front or rear. Even the grouping of figures hardly conveys an impression of space. Nonetheless the miniatures are extremely subtle in effect, because of the use of colour: bright, resonant shades are balanced against each other; rich blue, grass green and a striking salmon-red are just as prominent as the large areas of silver. The crude bodies and faces are modelled with exceptional delicacy; the pale flesh tone is shaded with red and olive green. The figure- and head-types are reminiscent of those of the Master of Guillebert de Metz, from whose workshop the Master of the Privileges of Ghent and Flanders probably originated.

Judging by the style of the borders of Cod. 2583, the Master of the Privileges of Ghent and Flanders may have worked in Ghent. He painted a Gradual (1469; Ghent, Bib. Rijksuniv., MS. 14) for Jacob van Brussel, Abbot of St Bavo in Ghent. On the other hand he painted miniatures in a copy of St Augustine's *City of God* (1445; Brussels, Bib. Royale Albert 1er, MSS 9015–16) written for Jean Chevrot, Bishop of Tournai.

BIBLIOGRAPHY

F. Winkler: 'Studien zur Geschichte der niederländischen Miniaturmalerei des XV. und XVI. Jahrhunderts, ii: Eine flandrische Lokalschule um 1420–1460', *Jb. Ksthist. Samml. Allhöch. Ksrhaus.*, xxxii (1915), pp. 306–24

——: *Die flämische Buchmalerei* (Leipzig, 1925/R Amsterdam, 1978), p. 31

O. Pächt, U. Jenni and D. Thoss: *Die illuminierten Handschriften und Inkunabeln der Österreichischen Nationalbibliothek: Flämische Schule*, 2 vols (Vienna, 1983), i, pp. 23–34; ii, pls II, 28–44

G. Dogaer: *Flemish Miniature Painting in the 15th and 16th Centuries* (Amsterdam, 1987), pp. 56–9

Flämische Buchmalerei: Handschriftenschätze aus dem Burgunderreich (exh. cat. by D. Thoss, Vienna, Österreich. Nbib., 1987), pp. 29–31

BODO BRINKMANN

Master of the Prodigal Son (*fl* Antwerp, *c.* 1530–60). Flemish painter. His name is derived from the *Parable of the Prodigal Son* (Vienna, Ksthist. Mus.), which was originally ascribed to JAN MANDIJN by Gustav Glück but reattributed to this anonymous master by Georges Hulin de Loo in his catalogue of 1909 of the museum of Ghent. Ring, who first published a list of possible attributions to the artist, observed that one of the paintings had the monogram LK (see Marlier, p. 80), which she thought could be that of Leonaert Kroes, an artist mentioned by Karel van Mander as one of the teachers of Gillis van Conincxloo III. The authenticity of the monogram and the status of the picture as an autograph work have been doubted, however, and the identification with Kroes has therefore been dismissed. Subsequent additions to the artist's oeuvre, notably by Marlier, and the regular appearance of several versions of the same compositions have made it clear that the Master must have been the head of an extremely busy studio. Many of his works have biblical subjects, often taken from the Old Testament. Some of these, presumably the earliest, are close in style to the work of Pieter Coecke van Aelst and Pieter Aertsen, but in other paintings the influence of such artists as Pieter Pourbus and Frans Floris becomes apparent, while the antique ruins in some of the landscape backgrounds indicate the Master's knowledge of Hieronymus Cock's engravings of 1550–51. This suggests a career extending from the 1530s until at least the 1550s. Only one painting actually has a date, of 1535. Volckaert has also shown that the Master executed cartoons (Paris, Louvre) for a series of ten tapestries of the *Story of Tobias*, woven in Brussels (Gaasbeek, Kasteel, and Tarragona, Mus. Dioc.).

NBW

BIBLIOGRAPHY

G. Glück: article in *Jb. Kön.-Preuss. Kstsamml.*, xxv (1904), p. 175

G. Hulin de Loo: *Catalogue du Musée des Beaux-Arts de Gand* (Ghent, 1909)

G. Ring: 'Der Meister des verlorenen Sohnes, Jan Mandyn und Lenaert Kroes', *Repert. Kstwiss.*, xliv (1923), pp. 196–201

J. G. Hoogewerff: '*Italiaansche rhapsodie*, een merkwaardig werk van den "Meester van den Verloren Zoon"' [*Italian Rhapsody*, a remarkable work by the 'Master of the Prodigal Son'], *Meded. Ned. Hist. Inst. Rome* (1931), pp. 109–16

G. Marlier: 'L'Atelier du Maître du Fils Prodigue', *Jb.: Kon. Mus. S. Kst.* (1961), pp. 75–111

L. Reis-Santos: 'Suzanna no banho da oficina do "Mestre do filho pródigo"', *Museu* (1961), pp. 54–9

M. Diaz Padron: 'Nuevas pinturas identificadas del Maestro del hijo pródigo', *Goya* (1980–81), pp. 130–39

——: 'Dos nuevas pinturas identificadas del Maestro del hijo pródigo', *Archv Esp. A.*, liv (1981), pp. 369–73

——: 'Un tríptico inédito del Maestro del *Hijo pródigo* en el Museo de Pontevedra', *Bol. Mus. Prado*, ii (1981), pp. 5–10

M.-L. de Contenson-Hollopeau: 'La Parabole du Festin par "Le Maître du fils prodigue"', *Rev. Louvre*, xxxi (1982), pp. 273–7

A. Volckaert: '"De Meester van de Verloren Zoon en de Brusselse wandtapijtkunst" [The Master of the Prodigal Son and the tapestry of Brussels], *Jb.: Kon. Mus. S. Kst.* (1987), pp. 93–106

CARL VAN DE VELDE

Pseudo-Antonio da Monza. *See* BIRAGO, GIOVANNI PIETRO.

Pseudo-Bles [Pseudo-Blesius] (*fl c.* 1520). South Netherlandish painter. His paintings form the principal foundation of the style now called ANTWERP MANNERISM. His name is taken from the apocryphal signature HENRICVS BLESIVS F, which has since been erased, on the *Adoration of the Magi* (Munich, Alte Pin.). It was on the basis of this work that many paintings were formerly attributed to Herri met de Bles. Michiels and Glück pointed out that this signature was probably false and showed that the group of paintings associated with it were not the work of one hand and could certainly not be attributed to met de Bles.

Friedländer grouped a number of works, which he called the Pseudo-Bles group, around the *Adoration of the Magi*. In these paintings (e.g. the *Beheading of St John the Baptist*, Berlin, Gemäldegal.; for illustration *see* ANTWERP MANNERISM) the subject is placed in an architectural setting, characterized by an exaggerated Gothic perpendicularity but at the same time containing many Renaissance elements. The very slim figures are rather small in relation to the architecture. The violence of movement, which makes them appear almost panic-stricken, and the imperfect knowledge of anatomy revealed in the small ears, deep-set eyes and long noses, illustrate, according to Friedländer, that these paintings are the work of a young master whom he attempts to identify as the young Jan de Beer. This hypothesis, which implies that these works were produced *c.* 1505–10, receives almost no support in art-historical literature. While there is undeniably a degree of stylistic affinity between the work of the Pseudo-Bles and that of Jan de Beer, the verticality in the architecture and the angularity of gesture are absent from de Beer's work. Moreover, stylistically these works would seem to have been produced *c.* 1520, which would coincide chronologically with the mature work of Jan de Beer rather than his early work.

BIBLIOGRAPHY

A. Michiels: *Histoire de la peinture flamande*, iv (Paris, 1866), p. 421

G. Glück: 'Beiträge zur Geschichte der Antwerpener Malerei im XVI. Jahrhundert', *Jb. Ksthist. Samml. Allhöch. Ksrhaus.*, xxii (1901), p. 8

M. J. Friedländer: *Die altniederländische Malerei* (Berlin, 1924–37); Eng. trans. as *Early Netherlandish Painting* (Leiden, 1967–76), xi

D. C. Ewing: *The Paintings and Drawings of Jan de Beer*, i (Ann Arbor, 1978), pp. 137–9, 167–9

HANS DEVISSCHER

Pseudo-Boccaccino. *See* GIOVANNI AGOSTINO DA LODI.

Pseudo-Geertgen. *See* MASTER OF THE FIGDOR DEPOSITION above.

Pseudo-Jacopino (di Francesco Bavosi dei Papazoni) (*fl c.* 1320–60). Italian painter or group of painters. Jacopino di Francesco Bavosi was a well-documented artist active 1360–83 whose work has not been satisfactorily identified. In 1365 Jacopino and his son Pietro, who was also a painter (*fl* 1365–83), were employed as junior partners of Andrea de' Bartoli on frescoes for the Visconti Palace at Pavia. Attempts have been made to identify this Jacopino with the 'Jacobus' who, in a similar collaboration with Simone dei Crocefissi, painted and signed frescoes of the *Circumcision, Adoration of the Magi* and *Presentation in the Temple* from S Apollonia, Mezzaratta (*c.* 1360; Bologna, Pin. N.).

The Mezzaratta frescoes have been linked with a substantial group of fresco and panel paintings formerly dated to the later 14th century but now dated *c.* 1320–50. The revised dating excludes the authorship of Jacopino Bavosi for most of these works. Rather than the product of an individual, they appear to be the work of an autonomous Bolognese school of painting, influenced by Bolognese manuscript illumination and Riminese painting.

The first work of the principal artist of the earlier works of this group is a small *Crucifixion* (Avignon, Mus. Petit Pal.), in which strong Riminese influence is evident in the incised diapered gold background, close-set, vertical drapery folds and the olive greens and pinks. The lively gestures and distinctive dress of the protagonists are typical of the works produced *c.* 1320–40, including the *Coronation of the Virgin* (Bologna, Pin. N.) and five predella panels (Raleigh, NC Mus. A.). The most refined examples are the *Death of St Francis* (Rome, Pin. Vaticana) and a fresco fragment probably of St Thomas Aquinas (Bologna, S Domenico). Two Virgins, painted in imitation of Italo-Byzantine prototypes (Florence, S Maria Maggiore and Fond. Longi), show the extraordinary versatility of this artist.

The heart of the Pseudo-Jacopino corpus is made up of three polyptychs (Bologna, Pin. N.), which are later in date, *c.* 1340–50. These show few Riminese traits and may be by a different hand from the previous group. In the polyptych of the *Coronation of the Virgin* and *Crucifixion*, the doll-like figures of the Virgin and Christ contrast with the refinement and elegance of the two knightly saints. Such a contrast is used for expressive effect in the *Pietà* that crowns the polyptych of the *Presentation of Christ in the Temple*, where Christ's foreshortened body emphasizes the Virgin's impassioned embrace, and her slit eyes stress her tears. The scene of *Christ among the Doctors* in the polyptych of the *Death of the Virgin* includes large numbers of texts and shows violent discussion in which some of the elders fling down their books in disgust. The composition is reminiscent both of local university debates and of Bolognese manuscript illumination. It is the painter of these polyptychs who possibly painted the Magi and donor in the Mezzaratta *Adoration of the Magi*, signed *Jacobus et Symon.*

BIBLIOGRAPHY
F. Filippini: 'Iacopo Avanzi, pittore bolognese del "300"', *Atti & Mem. Reale Deput. Stor. Patria Emilia & Romagna*, n. s. 4, ii (1912), pp. 397–432 (422–4)
E. Sandberg Vavalà: 'Some Bolognese Paintings outside Bologna and a Trecento Humorist', *A. America*, xx (1931), pp. 12–37
L. Coletti: *I Padani* (1947), iii of *I primitivi*, Stor. Pitt. (Novara 1941–7)
F. Filippini and G. Zucchini: *Miniatori e pittori a Bologna: Documenti dei secoli XIII e XIV* (Florence, 1947), pp. 8, 120–25, 130, 195–6
R. Longhi: *Lavori in Valpadana*, Opera Completa, vi (Florence, 1973)
L. Bellosi: *Buffalmacco e il Trionfo della Morte* (Turin, 1974), pp. 84–7, 104
F. Arcangeli: *Pittura bolognese del '300* (Bologna, 1978), pp. 106–35, 136–49 [notes by P. G. Castagnoli and A. Conti]
C. Volpe: 'La pittura emiliana del trecento', *Tomaso da Modena e il suo tempo: Atti del convegno, Treviso, 1979*, pp. 237–48
A. Conti: *La miniatura bolognese* (Bologna, 1981), pp. 77–80
L. Lodi: 'Note sulla decorazione punzonata di dipinti su tavola di area emiliana', *Mus. Ferrar.: Boll. Annu.*, 11 (1981), pp. 14–39
ROBERT GIBBS

Pseudo-Jacquemart (*fl c.* 1380–1410). French or Franco-Flemish illuminator. Meiss singled out this artist as an independent personality from the work attributed to JACQUEMART DE HESDIN and his circle. The strong similarities in style between the Pseudo-Jacquemart and Jacquemart de Hesdin are explained by a collaboration lasting more than 20 years. Meiss described the Master as 'a sort of workhorse' who displayed little creativity and imagination of his own but borrowed not only from Jacquemart but from diverse artists including Jean Pucelle and other illuminators in the service of his employer, Jean, Duc de Berry.

As early as *c.* 1380 Pseudo-Jacquemart may have collaborated on the Très Belles Heures de Notre-Dame of the Duc (Paris, Bib. N., MS. nouv. acq. lat. 3093), which certainly became an important source for his art. His earliest certain work is in a *Golden Legend* (London, BL, Royal MS. 19. B. XVII) from 1382. Nine other manuscripts contain work attributable to him, including the Psalter of Berry (*c.* 1386; Paris, Bib. N., MS. fr. 13091), the Petites Heures (before 1390; Paris, Bib. N., MS. lat. 18014) and the Grandes Heures (before 1409; Paris, Bib. N., MS. lat. 919), all owned by the Duc. Although the Pseudo-Jacquemart was not responsible for the most important decoration in any of these manuscripts, he did paint most of the surviving work in the Grandes Heures, where both decorative elements and miniatures were copied from various manuscripts in Jean de Berry's collection, giving the work a retrospective quality. In one of the illuminator's last works, the Lectionary of the Sainte-Chapelle in Bourges (*c.* 1410; Bourges, Bib. Mun., MSS 33–6), there are miniatures by the Boucicaut Master, and the Pseudo-Jacquemart even used his drawings as models.

The Pseudo-Jacquemart's style was routine and changed little over the years, but his work is important for the insight it gives into the composition of a workshop, the phenomenon of collaboration and the use of models in the art of *c.* 1400.

BIBLIOGRAPHY
M. Meiss: *French Painting in the Time of Jean de Berry: The Late Fourteenth Century and the Patronage of the Duke*, i (London, 1967), pp. 151–4
Les Fastes du gothique: Le Siècle de Charles V (exh. cat., ed. G. Pélegrin; Paris, Grand Pal., 1981), pp. 341–7, 430–31
M. SMEYERS

Pseudo-Niccoló. *See* ILLUSTRATORE above.

Pseudo-Ortkens (*fl* Brussels, *c.* 1500). Name associated with a south Netherlandish workshop of painters and draughtsmen. The work of this group was formerly attributed to a single artist, Aert Ortkens of Nijmegen (*see* ARNOULT DE NIMÈGUE). In 1917 Friedländer attributed to Ortkens a tapestry design (London, BM), annotated by a later hand *Adam van Ort, 1424*, which he believed misread a lost inscription with the name *Aert* and the date *1524*. On the basis of this sheet, he also ascribed to Ortkens a group of drawings at Leipzig, previously thought to be by the Master of the Leipzig Cabinet. Subsequent writers assigned to Ortkens and his school about 50 drawings (largely designs for glass roundels), 20 painted glass roundels, windows such as the *Tree of Jesse* now at St George's, Hanover Square, London, and the designs of a tapestry series of the *Aeneid* (London, Hampton Court, Royal Col.). All these works have doll-like figures with rounded faces and circular, heavily lidded eyes; drapery that falls in deep folds, sometimes bunched on the ground in zigzag shapes; and spatial relationships that are often awkward. The subjects are varied and include religious scenes (e.g. *Samuel Anointing David*; Paris, Fond. Custodia, Inst. Néer.), illustrations of Classical texts (e.g. the second of Virgil's *Eclogues*; Oxford, Ashmolean) and secular subjects (e.g. *Man Struggling with Death*; New York, Pierpont Morgan Lib.). The drawings, usually in pen and ink, employ parallel lines and extensive cross-hatching rather than wash to indicate shading. The similarities in figure type to the works of Bernard van Orley and Jan van Coninxloo II suggest that the drawings were made in Brussels.

It is now generally believed that the artist to whom Friedländer ascribed the drawings cannot be the glass painter Aert Ortkens of Nijmegen, who signed windows now in Rouen and Tournai. Stylistically the works are different from these documented windows, in which the compositions are flatter and the figures more static. Moreover, Ortkens borrowed frequently from engravings, while the drawings do not; Ortkens was a renowned imitator of Italian design, but the Italianate decoration found in his windows is never present in the group of drawings and painted glass roundels, which remains Gothic in style; and Ortkens was active in Antwerp, while the works, as noted, have stylistic links with Brussels. Wayment proposed to re-identify the 'Pseudo Ortkens' artist as Adriaen van den Houte (*c.* 1459–1521), the glass painter to Margaret of Austria in Mechelen. Boon, however, suggested that Pseudo-Ortkens may have been active primarily as a designer of tapestries rather than of monumental stained glass.

The drawings and painted roundels are, in fact, not by one artist but by several, and the Master must have engaged a relatively large workshop. Frequently, a single composition exists in several versions by different hands of varying competence. *Susanna and the Elders* is known in drawings in the Lugt Collection, Paris, and, weaker in execution, at the Pierpont Morgan Library, New York, as well as in three painted glass roundels, the most accomplished being in the Victoria and Albert Museum, London; a cruder version is in the Musée des Antiquités, Rouen, and another, probably later in date, in the Lugt Collection.

BIBLIOGRAPHY

M. J. Friedländer: 'Der niederländische Glasmaler Aerdt Ortkens', *Amtl. Ber. Kön. Kstsamml.*, xxxviii (1917), cols 161–7
——: *Die altniederländische Malerei* (Berlin, 1924–37); Eng. trans. as *Early Netherlandish Painting* (Leiden, 1967–76), xii, p. 31
A. E. Popham: 'Notes on Domestic Glass Painting, II', *Apollo*, x (1929), pp. 152–4
H. Wayment: 'A Rediscovered Master: Adriaen van den Houte (*c.* 1459–1521) and the Malines/Brussels School, I: A Solution to the "Ortkens" Problem', *Oud-Holland*, lxxxii (1967), pp. 172–202
——: 'A Rediscovered Master: Adriaen van den Houte (*c.* 1459–1521) and the Malines/Brussels School, II: Adriaen van den Houte as a Tapestry Designer', *Oud-Holland*, lxxxiii (1968), pp. 71–94
——: 'A Rediscovered Master: Adriaen van den Houte (*c.* 1459–1521) and the Malines/Brussels School, III: Adriaen's Development and his Relation with Bernard van Orley', *Oud-Holland*, lxxiv (1969), pp. 257–69
K. G. Boon: *Netherlandish Drawings of the Fifteenth and Sixteenth Centuries* (The Hague, 1978), ii, pp. 137–8

ELLEN KONOWITZ

Pseudo-Pier Francesco Fiorentino (*fl* second half of the 15th century). Italian painter or group of painters. The name was given by Berenson (1932) to an unknown artist whose work was previously confused with that of PIER FRANCESCO FIORENTINO, a follower of Benozzo Gozzoli and Neri di Bicci. The numerous pictures attributed to the anonymous master do not in fact resemble Pier Francesco's oeuvre. They are instead well-crafted, albeit mechanical, adaptations of paintings by Pesellino and Filippo Lippi. A few are copies of whole compositions, such as the *Virgin Adoring the Christ Child* in the chapel of the Palazzo Medici-Riccardi, Florence, which replaced Lippi's original (Berlin, Gemäldegal.). The Pseudo-Pier Francesco works derived from Lippi's designs only (all from paintings dating from the 1450s) often combine motifs from more than one composition. Pesellino's Madonnas (e.g. Toledo, OH, Mus. A.; ex-Edouard Aynard priv. col., Lyon) were another frequent resource. Works by Pseudo-Pier Francesco are all marked by a lavish, archaic use of gold leaf, and many include elaborate rose-hedge backgrounds, probably derived from Domenico Veneziano.

Zeri (1958) was the first to suggest that this body of works was not produced by one painter but rather by a workshop. He published a *Virgin and Child* (Italy, art market), in which the figure of the Virgin is taken from Antonello da Messina's *Virgin Annunciate* (Munich, Alte Pin.). He also called attention (1976) to a tondo (Arezzo, Gal. & Mus. Med. & Mod.) derived from Leonardo's Benois *Madonna and Child* (St Petersburg, Hermitage), which is probably one of the last products of the workshop. Zeri's title for the painters of these mass-produced works (who also polychromed stucco reliefs of the Madonna that had been mass-produced; see Middeldorf) is more accurate than Berenson's, namely 'The Lippi-Pesellino Imitators'.

BIBLIOGRAPHY

B. Berenson: 'Quadri senza casa. Il quattrocento fiorentino, II', *Dedalo*, xii/3 (1932), pp. 665–702 (692–7)
F. Zeri: 'Un riflesso di Antonello da Messina a Firenze', *Paragone*, ix/99 (1958), pp. 16–21
B. Berenson: *Florentine School*, i (1963), pp. 171–4
F. Zeri: *Italian Paintings in the Walters Art Gallery* (Baltimore, 1976), pp. 80–85
U. Middeldorf: 'Some Florentine Painted Madonna Reliefs', *Collaboration in Italian Renaissance Art*, ed. W. S. Stead and J. T. Paoletti (New Haven, 1978), pp. 77–90 (80–81)

ELIOT W. ROWLANDS

Master of Pulkau. *See* MASTER OF THE HISTORIA FRIDERICI ET MAXIMILIANI above.

Master of the Putti (*fl* Venice, *c.* 1469–75). Italian illuminator. Stylistic evidence and visual clues, such as family crests on attributed works, indicate that he decorated printed books for Venetian typographers from 1469 and that he was active in Venice during the first half of the 1470s. The Master of the Putti's manuscripts, for example a copy of Pliny (1472; Padua, Bib. Semin., MS. K.I.), are decorated with imagination and refinement *all'antica*, with touches of tempera, a technique that remained typical of his production. The antiquarian motifs of satyrs, epigraphs, sarcophagi, vases and putti, from which his name is derived, are taken from Classical reliefs of the Imperial period. There are close similarities to the drawings of Jacopo Bellini and to the work of Mantegna and precedents also in the antiquarian interests of the Venetian and Paduan illuminators of the preceding decade. Adopting the faceted initials favoured by the latter group, the Master created splendid mythological scenes. Another Paduan characteristic appears in his illusionistic frontispieces, where the text appears to be inscribed on a parchment scroll supported by architectural elements (*see* VENICE, §III, 1).

The artist's crisp, nervous style is close to the drawing style of Antonio Pollaiuolo, but even more so to that of Marco Zoppo. The influence of Giovanni Bellini is evident in the energy of the modelling and in the expression and emotional intensity of the figures. The debt to Bellini is still more apparent in the Master's use of colour in the two-volume *Bibbia italica* (1471; New York, Pierpont Morgan Lib., MS. Inc. 26983). The Master of the Putti's late work has not yet been clearly defined.

BIBLIOGRAPHY

G. Mariani Canova: *La miniatura veneta del rinascimento, 1450–1500* (Venice, 1969)

L. Armstrong: *Renaissance Miniature Painters and Classical Imagery: The Master of the Putti and his Venetian Workshop* (London, 1981)

The Painted Page: Italian Renaissance Book Illumination, 1450–1550 (exh. cat., ed. J. J. G. Alexander; London, RA, 1994)

FEDERICA TONIOLO

Master of Raigern (*fl c.* 1415–20). Bohemian painter. He was one of the most influential painters in southern Bohemia during the early 15th century and is named after an altarpiece from the Benedictine monastery at Raigern (now Rajhrad). Dated before 1420, the six surviving panels (five in Brno, Mus. City; one in Prague, N.G., Šternberk Pal.) are his only authenticated work and appear to combine scenes from the *Passion* with scenes from the *Legend of the Holy Cross*. He attained a vivid narrative realism through the accumulation of dramatically active figure-groups and heightened expression, for example in *Christ Carrying the Cross* (Brno) and the *Crucifixion* (Prague). The Master of Raigern seems to have had a large workshop and influenced painting not only in southern Bohemia but also in neighbouring countries, for example, in Vienna, the work of the MASTER OF THE ST LAMBERT VOTIVE ALTARPIECE (*see* below).

BIBLIOGRAPHY

A. Matějček and J. Pešina: *Bohemian Gothic Painting* (Prague, 1950)

K. M. Swoboda, ed.: *Gotik in Böhmen* (Munich, 1969), pp. 259–60

JANEZ HÖFLER

Master of the Regent [Master of the Stadholder Maria] (*fl c.* 1540). South Netherlandish painter. He was court painter, either in Brussels or in Mechelen, to Queen Mary of Hungary, who was Regent and Stadholder of the Netherlands from 1531 to 1555. He was one of the weaker portrait painters who worked in the tradition of Hans Holbein (ii). The Master's paintings are small or average in size, and the sitters are portrayed from the waist upwards, against a flat, neutral background. The sitters' hands—often with stretched fingers and gloved—are depicted motionless at the bottom edge of the image (e.g. *William, 1st Baron Paget*, ?1549; London, N.P.G.). A characteristic feature of this Master is the way in which the eyes of the sitters are rendered: a shadow in the outer corner of the lower eyelid pushes the eye forward; towards the temple the upper and lower eyelids overlap, and the lines around the eye are very pronounced. The sitter's lips are usually pressed together so that his expression tends to be one of gruff pride. The Master's style of painting is characterized by short brushstrokes and a rough application of paint. Another typical feature that distinguishes this south Netherlandish Master from many Holbein followers from elsewhere is the shadow in the background cast by the sitter's head. Friedländer discovered dates on two portraits, one of 1537 and the other of 1538. The Master of the Regent can possibly be identified with GUILLIM SCROTS, a painter mentioned in the inventories of Mary of Hungary.

Thieme-Becker

BIBLIOGRAPHY

M. J. Friedländer: *Die altniederländische Malerei* (Berlin, 1924–37); Eng. trans. as *Early Netherlandish Painting* (Leiden, 1967–76)

G. Ring: 'Three Works by the "Regent Master" at the Royal Academy', *Burl. Mag.*, xciii (1951), pp. 88–92

JETTY E. VAN DER STERRE

Master of the Registrum Gregorii [Gregory Master] (*fl c.* AD 980–96). Ottonian illuminator. He is named after two detached leaves of a manuscript of the *Registrum Gregorii* (984; Trier, Stadtbib., MS. 117/1626, and Chantilly, Mus. Condé, MS. 14 *bis*) given by Egbert, Archbishop of Trier, to Trier Cathedral. Work in a group of late 10th-century codices, most of them produced for churches in Trier between 980 and 996, is also attributed to this artist. A Sacramentary made for Lorsch Abbey, perhaps *c.* 980 (Chantilly, Mus. Condé, MS. 1447), may be among his earliest works, while his last known work is a Gospel Book in Manchester (John Rylands U. Lib., MS. 98). Its miniatures are now missing but are attributed to the Gregory Master on the grounds of the full-page incipits to the Gospels, characteristically laid out with medallions of emperors in square frames in the borders. Since Otto III is portrayed as an emperor, the manuscript cannot have been produced before 996, the date of his imperial coronation. The Master has also been linked with Ottonian ivory-carving (*see* OTTONIAN ART, §VI).

Verses in the surviving fragment of the *Registrum Gregorii* suggest that it possibly commemorates the death of Otto II, in 983. The Chantilly leaf shows an emperor enthroned under a ciborium flanked by personifications of the four provinces of the empire offering homage. It has been argued that this must represent Otto II, since at his death his son was only three years old, but it need not be a specific portrait. On the Trier leaf (see fig.), St Gregory the Great is shown seated at a lectern and inspired by the dove of the Holy Spirit as he dictates to a monk

Master of the Registrum Gregorii: *St Gregory the Great Dictating*; single leaf from St Gregory the Great: *Letters*, AD 984 (Trier, Stadtbibliothek, MS. 117/1626)

standing behind him. The figures have small, carefully modelled heads and attenuated bodies and like the architecture and hanging draperies are organized in a series of superimposed planes that suggest shallow space.

One of the most magnificent Ottonian manuscripts, the Codex Egberti (Trier, Stadtbib., MS. 24), contains full-page miniatures of the *Presentation of the Book of Egbert* and the *Four Evangelists*, as well as fifty-one framed New Testament illustrations dispersed throughout the text, of which the Gregory Master contributed seven. His miniatures stand out from the other narrative scenes in the Codex Egberti in their close relationship to such Early Christian manuscripts as the Quedlinburg Itala fragment (Berlin, Dt. Staatsbib., MS. theol. lat. 485), seen in both the figure style and the graded wash backgrounds (*see* EARLY CHRISTIAN AND BYZANTINE ART, §V, 2(i)).

This artist also made additions to older manuscripts. For example, an early 9th-century Gospel Book from St Martin's Abbey, Trier (Prague, Strahov Abbey & N. Lit. Mem., MS. D.F. III, 3), contains four Evangelist portraits added in his hand, and the detached leaf of *St Mark* (Harburg, Schloss, Cod. I, 2, lat. qu. 2) is the only survival of the Evangelist portraits that he inserted into a pre-Carolingian manuscript from Echternach. These miniatures rely heavily on Carolingian models: the Schwarzwald leaf, for example, may be compared for its design with the Matthew portrait in the Cleves Gospels (Berlin, Dt. Staatsbib., MS. theol. lat. 2. 260), although the Gregory

Master's Evangelist has none of the sketchy illusionism of the Carolingian work. In the Sainte-Chapelle Gospels (Paris, Bib. N., MS. lat. 8851), datable by a series of emperor medallions to 967–83, the *Christ in Majesty* by the Gregory Master is of similar format to that in the Carolingian Tours Bibles (*see* CAROLINGIAN ART, §IV, 3), notably the Vivian Bible (Paris, Bib. N., MS. lat. 1). A rectangular frame encloses a field of graded wash background, symmetrically articulated by medallions containing Evangelist symbols and corner fields with Evangelist portraits, surrounding Christ in a mandorla in the centre. Unlike its Carolingian predecessors, the figures and borders are more sharply delineated, and the identifying rubrication is used liberally.

BIBLIOGRAPHY

H. V. Sauerland and A. Haseloff: *Der Psalter Erzbischof Egberts von Trier, Codex Gertrudianus in Cividale* (Trier, 1901)
C. Nordenfalk: 'Der Meister des Registrum Gregorii', *Münchn. Jb. Bild. Kst*, iii/1 (1950), pp. 61–77
H. Schiel: *Codex Egberti der Stadtbibliothek Trier* (Basle, 1960)
C. R. Dodwell: *Painting in Europe, 800–1200*, Pelican Hist. A. (Harmondsworth, 1971), pp. 56–60
F. Mütherich: 'L'Art ottonien', *Le Siècle de l'an mil*, ed. L. Grodecki and others (Paris, 1973), pp. 87–188
H. Mayr-Harting: *Ottonian Book Illumination*, 2 vols (London, 1991)

RONALD BAXTER

Master of the Reichenhall Altar (*fl* Salzburg, *c.* 1520). Austrian painter. He is named after a winged altarpiece (Munich, Bayer. Nmus.) that supposedly came from the Salinenkapelle at Reichenhall; according to the inscription on the lower frame of the inside faces of the wings, it was donated by Leinhart Kuefpeck and his wife, Margret, in 1521. When closed, it shows *SS Dorothy, Sebastian, Florian and Margaret*, when open *SS Leonard, Sebastian, Florian and Bartholomew*; a predella shows *SS Peter and Paul Holding St Veronica's Handkerchief*, with an *Angel with the Instruments of the Passion* beside each; the donor and his wife kneel beside St Leonard and St Bartholomew respectively. The clothes and distinguished bearing of the saints suggest the influence of the Italian-inspired Renaissance painting of Augsburg, as does the whole altar construction with its ornamented framework.

Also attributed to the Master are a panel (1521; Salzburg, Mus. Carolino Augusteum) from Bergheim depicting *St Felicity Enthroned with her Sons Januarius, Felix and Philippus* and on the reverse *St Elizabeth Feeding the Sick*, and a picture of a *Church Dignitary* (?1522–4; Salzburg, St Peter) in a fully illustrated setting kneeling in front of a prie-dieu. This probably represents Johann Staupitz (*c.* 1470–1524), abbot (1522–4) of St Peter in Salzburg. Attribution to the same master of the paintings on the carved main altar of the church of Mariä Himmelfahrt at Gröbming, Styria, should probably be rejected.

BIBLIOGRAPHY

Thieme–Becker
O. Fischer: *Die altdeutsche Malerei in Salzburg* (Leipzig, 1908), pp. 154–62
Katalog der Gemälde des Bayerischen Nationalmuseums (Munich, 1908), pp. 69–71
Spätgotik in Salzburg: Die Malerei, 1400–1530 (exh. cat., Salzburg, Mus. Carolino Augusteum, 1972), pp. 187–9

JANEZ HÖFLER

Master of Rhenen (*fl c.* 1500). North Netherlandish painter. He is named from a panel depicting the *Conquest* *of Rhenen by Jan II of Cleves in 1499* (Amsterdam, Rijksmus.). Schmidt-Degener identified him in 1933 with the Master of the St Elisabeth Panels, but Buijsen has shown on stylistic grounds that they were two artists. One other work, *Christ Presented to the People* (Amsterdam, Rijksmus.), has been attributed to the Master of Rhenen. The two scenes reveal an interest in anecdotal detail and are painted in a similar style (Buijsen, figs 1 and 2) that is especially noticeable in the figures and architectural features. The figures are characterized by their wooden movements and emphatic gestures and in some cases show the same physical features and poses.

BIBLIOGRAPHY
F. S-D [F. Schmidt-Degener]: article in *Jversl. Ver. Rembrandt* (Amsterdam, 1933), p. 19
G. J. Hoogewerff: *De Noord-Nederlandsche schilderkunst*, 5 vols (The Hague, 1936–47), i, pp. 498–509; v, p. 116
E. Buijsen: 'De Meester van Rhenen en de Meester van de St.-Elisabeth-panelen: Niet een maar twee personen', *Bull. Rijksmus.*, xxxvi/3 (1988), pp. 133–8 [contains further bibliog.]

JETTY E. VAN DER STERRE

Master of Rimini [Master of the Frankfurt Crucifixion] (*fl* second quarter of the 15th century). Sculptor, probably of south Netherlandish origin. His name is derived from the alabaster *Crucifixion* altar from S Maria delle Grazie, Rimini (*c.* 1430; Frankfurt am Main, Liebieghaus). The altar was probably made for the church's consecration in 1432; it was later incorporated into a Baroque altar but may originally have been part of a shrine or a choir-screen. It comprises a centre section with the *Crucifixion*, the crosses of the Good and Bad Thieves and groups beneath. The Twelve Apostles are ranged in pairs on either side. The altar is generally agreed to have been made in the southern Netherlands or northern France, almost certainly in a workshop that specialized in producing alabaster sculpture for export. Stylistic comparison with early 15th-century Netherlandish painting such as the work of Rogier van der Weyden and the Master of Flémalle confirms this hypothesis. The altar also reflects the evolution of Netherlandish sculpture during the early 15th century: from soft, graceful compositions to the more rigid forms that became popular in the mid–1430s. Also attributed to the Master of Rimini is the small alabaster *Pietà* in S Francesco, Rimini (the Tempio Malatestiano), known as the Madonna dell'Acqua. This was said to have miraculous powers over rainfall and became a focus of pilgrimage. Dated *c.* 1440, it is stylistically close to the later style of the Frankfurt altar. The same master may also have been responsible for a *Pietà* from Lorch am Rhein (Frankfurt am Main, Städel. Kstinst. & Städt. Gal.) and a statuette of *St Christopher* (ex-Mus. Civ., Padua; untraced after World War I). Defoer has further attributed an alabaster head of *St John the Baptist* now in St Willibrordus, Utrecht, to the Master of Rimini.

BIBLIOGRAPHY
Thieme–Becker
H. L. M. Defoer: 'Een alabasten Johannes-in-disco in de St. Willibrordus te Utrecht', *Miscellanea I.Q. van Regteren Altena* (Amsterdam, 1969), pp. 17–19 [with Eng. summary]
A. Legner: 'Der Alabasteraltar aus Rimini', *Städel-Jb.*, n. s., ii (1969), pp. 101–68
M. Maek-Gerard, ed.: *Liebieghaus-Museum alter Plastik: Nachantike grossplastische Bildwerke*, ii (Melsungen, 1981), pp. 148–75

Master of the Rohan Hours (*fl c.* 1410–40). ?French illuminator. He is named after his contribution to the illumination of the Rohan Hours (Grandes Heures de Rohan, *c.* 1430–33; Paris, Bib. N., MS. lat. 9471), which contains the arms of the Rohan Family (gules with seven gold macles) on several pages (notably fol. 26*v*), although it is not certain that these arms are original. Several scholars, including Avril, associate the production of the Rohan Hours with the Angevin court and with Yolande of Aragon, wife of Louis II, Duke of Anjou. Some of the miniatures indicate familiarity with the work of the Limbourg brothers in the Belles Heures of Jean, Duc de Berry (*c.* 1405–8; New York, Cloisters; *see* LIMBOURG, DE, fig. 3), which Yolande purchased after the Duc's death in 1416. The Rohan Hours also incorporates an extensive biblical cycle based on a *Bible moralisée* (Paris, Bib. N., MS. fr. 9561), brought from Naples to the court of Anjou by Louis II. It is thought that Yolande may have commissioned the Rohan Hours in 1431 to celebrate the marriage of Charles of Anjou, Comte du Maine, to a daughter of Alain IX de Rohan; the marriage, however, never took place.

The 11 extant full-page miniatures of the Rohan Hours and the image of the *Virgin and Child* accompanying the prayer 'O intemerata' (fol. 33*v*) provide the touchstone for identifying the oeuvre of the Rohan Master, although there is disagreement among scholars about the extent to which assistants were also involved in several of these paintings. While the Master's work reveals knowledge both of Italian developments in spatial representation, probably mediated through the Boucicaut Master and his workshop, and of the mannered elegance of the Limbourgs, his own very personal style is distinguished by its expressive quality. To this end he did not hesitate to distort perspective or to communicate emotion through forceful line and dramatic contrasts in scale, as in the famous opening illustration to the Office of the Dead (fol. 159*r*; see fig.), where the communication between the Lord in the heavens and the prone figure, laid out on a fine cloth on the ground, is one of extraordinary pathos and tenderness. The theme of a naked corpse in the graveyard had been used in the workshops of the Troyes and Boucicaut Masters; but in the hands of the Rohan Master it is transformed: the emaciated figure, surrounded by bones and skulls, radiates an inner beauty, and the finely modelled head is raised trustingly towards a merciful judge. The Latin inscription on the accompanying scroll echoes this trust: 'Into thy hands O Lord I commend my spirit; thou hast redeemed me, O Lord God of truth'; and the stereotyped bust of God becomes a large compassionate presence, whose bent head and concentrated gaze reinforce both the judgement and the assurance contained in his response (in French): 'For your sins you shall do penance. On the day of judgement you shall be with me'. In the face of this elemental exchange, the battle between the archangel Michael and the devil for the soul of the deceased, against a backdrop of angels in blue and gold, some of whom assist in the attack on their fallen counterpart, is presented as a restrained and more limited expression of the struggle between the forces of good and evil, both the reduced scale and lateral placement of this episode ensuring its subsidiary role.

Master of the Rohan Hours: miniature illustrating the Office of the Dead, 290×208 mm; from the Rohan Hours, *c.* 1430–33 (Paris, Bibliothèque Nationale, MS. lat. 9471, fol. 159*r*)

Similarly, the theme of Mary lamenting over her dead son, which illustrates the Hours of the Cross (fol. 135*r*), is not new; but the Rohan Master's combination of this with the figure of St John holding the swooning Virgin, a motif that is usually part of the Crucifixion scene, results in a moving expression of grief and anguished love. As the Virgin sinks towards the ground, sustained only by the apostle's arms around her waist, her drooping arms are transformed into a gesture of endearment towards the dead Christ at her feet; and John, too, plays a dual role: grasping the sorrowing mother, he looks back intently to God in the heavens, thus involving the Deity in the human pathos of the event. Although different illuminators executed the smaller paintings in the Rohan Hours, including the extensive series of scenes modelled on the Angevin Bible, most scholars believe that the Rohan Master played a major role in designing the illumination of this book. The positioning of the lines of introductory text in the full-page miniatures at the base of the page, and often in a very confined space, would seem to indicate that as chief illuminator he was also able to plan aspects of the page layout with the scribe.

The Rohan Master seems to have worked regularly with a large number of assistants and to have collaborated with various groups of illuminators. This compounds the difficulty of trying to trace his career, about which there is considerable disagreement, although Meiss (1974) attributed *c.* 40 manuscripts to him and his workshop. The current state of research has been summarized (Avril), indicating that, while the Rohan Master's origins are unknown, his earliest work was in the Champagne area, where he illuminated a number of Books of Hours, several of them being for the Use of Troyes. The earliest manuscript associated with this Champagne period is the Giac Hours (*c.* 1410; Toronto, Royal Ont. Mus., Lee of Fareham col.). Although for the Use of Rome, it shows the Rohan Master adopting motifs and compositions from the local workshop of the Troyes Master (*fl* 1390–1415), as well as revealing a familiarity with developments in late 14th-century Paris. Around 1415–20, the Rohan Master moved to Paris, where his work included the illumination of a number of secular manuscripts by such authors as Valerius Maximus, Giovanni Boccaccio and Jean Froissart. These reflect his contacts with the Bedford Master and his circle and the Master of the Berry Apocalypse; but he was most strongly influenced by the Boucicaut Master. More Books of Hours for the Use of Troyes indicate that the Master returned to Champagne for some time before the climax of his career during which period, in addition to the Rohan Hours, he was involved in the Hours of René of Anjou (Paris, Bib. N., MS. lat. 1156A) and the so-called Hours of Isabella Stuart (Cambridge, Fitzwilliam, MS. 62).

Scholarly opinion favours Angers and the Angevin court as the centre for these activities, although Meiss (1974) suggested Bourges. Meiss also indicated an earlier date, in the 1420s, for the Master's mature period; but Avril argued for 1430–40, on the grounds that the Hours of René of Anjou are dated by internal heraldic and historical evidence to 1435–6. Durrieu's suggestion that the Rohan Master was the illuminator Adenet Lescuyer, resident in Angers from 1457–71, has not been substantiated; and while the Rohan Master could have been a panel painter as well as an illuminator, the attempt by Ring to attribute to him a fragment of a retable (Laon, Mus. Archéol. Mun.), although endorsed by Meiss, has not received general acceptance.

BIBLIOGRAPHY

P. Durrieu: 'Le Maître des *Grandes Heures de Rohan* et les Lescuier d'Angers', *Rev. A. Anc. & Mod.*, ii (1912), pp. 81–98, 161–83

V. Leroquais: *Les Livres d'heures manuscrits de la Bibliothèque nationale* (Paris, 1927), pp. 281–90, pls xxxviii–xliii

A. Heimann: 'Der Meister der *Grandes Heures de Rohan* und seine Werkstatt', *Städel-Jb.*, vii–viii (1932), pp. 1–61

——: 'The Giac Book of Hours', *Burl. Mag.*, lxxi (1937), pp. 83–4

E. Panofsky: 'Re-integration of a Book of Hours Executed in the Workshop of the "Maître des Grandes Heures de Rohan"', *Medieval Studies in Memory of A. Kingsley Porter*, ii (Cambridge, 1939), pp. 479–99

J. Porcher: 'Two Models for the *Heures de Rohan*', *J. Warb. & Court. Inst.*, viii (1945), pp. 1–6

E. Panofsky: 'The de Buz Book of Hours', *Harvard Lib. Bull.*, iii (1949), pp. 163–82

G. Ring: *A Century of French Painting* (London, 1949), pp. 202–4

J. Porcher: *The Rohan Book of Hours* (London, 1959)

M. Meiss and M. Thomas: *The Rohan Book of Hours* (London, 1973)

M. Meiss with S. O. Smith and E. Beatson: *French Painting in the Time of Jean de Berry: The Limbourgs and their Contemporaries*, 2 vols (London and New York, 1974), pp. 256–77, 352–3

Les Manuscrits à peintures en France, 1440–1520 (exh. cat. by F. Avril and N. Reynaud, Paris, Bib. N., 1992–3) [essays by F. Avril, pp. 25–6]

MARGARET M. MANION

Rolin Master. *See* MASTER OF JEAN ROLIN above.

Rosenwald Master. *See under* §II: THE 1520S HOURS WORKSHOP below.

Master of the Rotterdam St John on Patmos. *See* MASTER OF THE LEGEND OF ST LUCY above.

Master of the Rouen Echevinage [Master of the Geneva Latini] (*fl c.* 1460–80). French illuminator. The Master of the Geneva Latini, named after Brunetto Latini's *Li Livres dou trésor* (Geneva, Bib. Pub. & U., MS. Fr. 160), is more appropriately known as the Master of the Rouen Echevinage: the name derives from the sumptuous manuscripts that he illustrated for the Bibliothèque des Echevins in Rouen (Paris, Bib. N., MSS Fr. 2685, 2623, 129, 2629, 2596). The Master was the dominant illuminator in Rouen after the departure of the English in 1449, when the city became a flourishing centre of manuscript production. Among the numerous Books of Hours painted by him, the finest is that sold in 1983 (London, Sotheby's, 6 Dec 1983, lot 82).

The Master's iconographic and stylistic sources lie in Parisian illumination of the first half of the 15th century, transmitted especially through the work of the Master of the Golden Legend (Munich, Bayer. Staatsbib., Clm. gall. 3). Both the miniatures and their rich borders are distinguished by the use of bright colours, a lavish use of gold and the emphasis given to patterns of angular lines. In the Master's conventional and repetitive compositions, mannered figures with stereotyped gestures are set in front of luminous townscapes. These backgrounds, as well as his fondness for certain material objects, indicate his familiarity with Flemish painting. In his later works this affected and mannered approach softens and yields to a more monumental style, seen for example in the Hours of Jacques d'Estouteville (Turin, Bib. Reale, MS. Var. 88), the large miniatures in the Breviary of Charles de Neufchâtel, Bishop of Besançon (Besançon, Bib. Mun., MS. 69), and in the illustration of the *Livre des trois âges* by Pierre Choisnet of Rouen, which was probably intended for Louis XI or one of his children (Paris, Bib. N., MS. Smith-Lesouëf 70).

The style of the Master of the Rouen Echevinage made a profound impression on the illumination of contemporary Books of Hours in Rouen. It was perpetuated in an impoverished and mechanical form in numerous copies at the end of the 15th century (see Watson) and occasionally in the engraved illustrations of Rouen incunabula. The influence of his compositions is still discernible in the early 16th-century Books of Hours of the 'Rouen school', in which Italian Renaissance motifs were introduced into Normandy.

BIBLIOGRAPHY

O. Pächt and D. Thoss: *Die illuminierten Handschriften der Österreichischen Nationalbibliothek, französische Schule*, i (Vienna, 1974), pp. 57–8

L. M. J. Delaissé, J. Marrow and J. de Wit: *The James A. de Rothschild Collection at Waddesdon Manor: Illuminated Manuscripts*, viii (London, 1977), cat. no. 11, pp. 229–46; cat. no. 12, pp. 247–64

The Last Flowering: French Painting in Manuscripts, 1420–1530, from American Collections (exh. cat., ed. J. Plummer and G. Clark; New York, Pierpont Morgan Lib., 1982), nos 87–8

Catalogue of Western Manuscripts and Miniatures to Be Sold with the Gospels of Henry the Lion, London, Sotheby's, 6 Dec 1983, lot 82

R. Watson: *The Playfair Hours: A Late Fifteenth Century Illuminated Manuscript from Rouen (Victoria & Albert Museum, L.475–1918)* (London, 1984)

C. Rabel: 'Artiste et clientèle à la fin du Moyen Age: Les Manuscrits profanes du Maître de l'échevinage de Rouen', *Rev. A.*, lxxxiv (1989), pp. 48–60

F. Avril and N. Reynaud: *Les Manuscrits à peintures en France, 1440–1520* (Paris, 1993), pp. 168–73

CLAUDIA RABEL

Master of Roussillon [Rosselló] (*fl* first half of the 15th century). Catalan painter. The earliest work attributed to him is the damaged retable of *SS John the Baptist and John the Evangelist* from the chapel at Bastida, the residence of the lords of Evol, and now in the church at Evol, near Olette, west of Perpignan. The donor in the central panel can be identified from the coat of arms as Guillem de So, Vescomte d'Evol, who died in 1428. Other works attributed to the Master include the retable of *St Andrew* from Perpignan (New York, Cloisters), the retable of *SS Justus and Pastor* now in the American church in Paris and a pinnacle from an altarpiece depicting the *Crucifixion* (h. 1.13 m; Basle, Kstmus.). These works all show the traditions of the Serra brothers mediated through Lluís Borrassa and at the same time reflect the influence of the Master of St George and Franco-Flemish manuscript illumination. There are close links, for example, between the narrative scenes in the *St Andrew* retable and Borrassa's altarpiece of *St Peter* (1411–13; Terrassa, S Pedro). The Master's colours are intense and vivid, often set against gold diapered backgrounds with delicate floral motifs, and his compositions are clear and coherent, with great delicacy of detail. He also employed distinctive figure types, especially an old man with a sharp nose and a beard. In his work, 'romantic and dramatic episodes are translated into the lively and picturesque brightness of contemporary life' (Post). Various identifications have been proposed for the Master, including Arnau Pintor (*fl* 1401–40), Bartomeu Capdevila (*fl* 1411–60) and, more plausibly, Jaubert Gaucelm (*fl* 1393–1434), who was apprenticed to Pedro Serra in 1393.

BIBLIOGRAPHY

C. R. Post: *A History of Spanish Painting*, 14 vols (Cambridge, MA, 1930–66), ii and vii/2

N. de Dalmases and A. José i Pitarch: *L'art gòtic s. xiv–xv*, Historia de l'Art Català, iii (Barcelona, 1984)

J. R. L. HIGHFIELD

Master of St Anastasio. *See under* BERNARDINO DEL CASTELLETTO.

Master of St Augustine (*fl c.* 1490). Painter, active in the southern Netherlands. He is named after the fragmentary *St Augustine* altarpiece, the central panel of which (1.30×1.53 m; New York, Cloisters) shows scenes from the *Life of St Augustine*, culminating in his coronation as Bishop of Hippo. The right wing (1.36×0.65 m; Dublin, N.G.) shows *St Augustine's Vision of St Jerome* and the *Death-bed of St Augustine*. Another cut-down fragment depicting *SS Augustine and Paul* (990×665 mm; Aachen, Mus. B.-A.) matches the Dublin wing. To this corpus, Friedländer added three male portraits and a *St Nicholas Enthroned* (999×804 mm; Bruges, Groeningemus.). In the background of the latter are scenes of Bruges, including the towers of the belfry, which were remodelled four times between 1480 and 1502, thus enabling Friedländer to date the painting to *c.* 1490 and assign the Master to Bruges. Other scholars, however, have shown that the *St Nicholas* is a 16th-century copy of an earlier work (Janssens de Bisthoven and Parmentier), and there has been a tendency (Huyghebaert) to revert to the earlier attribution to the MASTER OF THE LEGEND OF ST LUCY (*see* above), who often depicted the belfry in his backgrounds. If this is correct, there is no basis for placing the Master of St Augustine in Bruges. Unidentified coats of arms on the Dublin wing of the *St Augustine* altarpiece may provide a new provenance for this Master, whose expert rendition of surfaces is typical of 15th-century Netherlandish art. His depictions of ecclesiastical robes are minutely observed, and his portrait heads are precise and detailed in a style reminiscent of Jan van Eyck and others, but they remain somewhat wooden, as do his figure-groups.

BIBLIOGRAPHY

M. J. Friedländer: 'The Bruges Master of St Augustine', *A. America*, xxv (1937), pp. 47–54

A. Janssens de Bisthoven with R. Parmentier: *Le Musée Communal de Bruges: Les Primitifs flamands: Corpus de la peinture des anciens Pays-Bas méridionaux au quinzième siècle*, i (Antwerp, 1951), pp. 71–3

N. Huyghebaert: 'Le Retable "brugeois" du Maître de Saint Augustin', *Hand. Genoot. Gesch. 'Soc. Emul.' Brugge*, cviii (1971), pp. 74–6

□

Master of St Auta (*fl* 1522–5). South Netherlandish painter, active in Portugal. He was identified by van Puyvelde among the Netherlandish painters active in Portugal in the first half of the 16th century. There are influences of Antwerp Mannerism and of illuminated manuscripts and also characteristics of the Lisbon workshops in the altarpiece of *St Auta* (Lisbon, Mus. N. A. Ant.). It is probable that the Master represents a group of painters who were followers of or collaborators with JORGE AFONSO.

The altarpiece of *St Auta* was commissioned by Queen Eleanor, the widow of John II and sister of Manuel I, for the convent of Madre de Deus, Xabregas, Lisbon, which she founded in 1509. It dates from between 1522, when a brief of Pope Leo X, confirmed by Adrian VI, authorized the iconographic portrayal of St Auta, a companion of the Virgin and the martyr St Ursula, and 1525, the year of Queen Eleanor's death. One of the panels shows the departure from Cologne of the relics of the Saint, which had been presented to the Portuguese Queen by Emperor Maximilian I, and another, painted in brilliant colours and details, their arrival in 1517 in procession, watched by Queen Eleanor, at the Madre de Deus Convent, the Manueline façade of whose church is represented realistically. The other panels show episodes from the *Life and Martyrdom of St Ursula and her Companions.* In the *Marriage of St Ursula to Prince Conan* a group of black minstrels playing brass instruments is an interesting reflection of festive occasions at the Portuguese court.

BIBLIOGRAPHY

L. van Puyvelde: *La Peinture flamande au siècle de Bosch et Breughel* (Paris, 1962)

N. C. Guedes, A. P. Ravara and M. A. Beaumont: *Retábulo de Santa Auta: Estudo de investigação* (Lisbon, 1972)

DAGOBERTO L. MARKL

Master of the St Bartholomew Altar [Bartholomew Master; Christoph Master; Master of the Crucifixion Altar; Master of the Thomas Altar] (*fl* Cologne, *c.* 1470–1510). Painter and illuminator, active in Germany. Although he established himself as one of the leading painters in Cologne, he also had links with Gelderland, Arnhem and Utrecht, and his style shows considerable Netherlandish influences. This has led many scholars to speculate that he originally came from the eastern Netherlands. His small oeuvre consists predominantly of religious panel paintings, although some portraits have also been attributed to him.

The Master is named after a large triptych known as the *St Bartholomew* altar (ex-St Kolumba, Cologne; Munich, Alte Pin.; see fig.). The central panel shows *SS Agnes, Bartholomew and Cecilia with a Donor*, the left inner wing *SS John the Evangelist and Margaret* and the right wing *SS James the Younger and Christine*. The donor, who became visible only after the panel was cleaned (1949–51), wears a Carthusian habit, and it is now generally accepted that the altarpiece was painted for the Cologne Kartäuserkirche. Two escutcheons added later can be identified as those of the Cologne merchant Arnt von Westerburg (*fl* 1471–1531) and his wife, Druitgen von Andernach. It has been suggested that the panel of *SS Peter and Dorothy* with the *Virgin and Child with St John the Evangelist* on the reverse (London, N.G.) also formed part of this ensemble, but this thesis is no longer accepted. The London panel is probably the left wing of another altarpiece of which the right wing is *SS Andrew and Colomba* (Mainz, Röm.–Ger. Zentmus.).

Probably to be considered among his early works are the 13 magnificent full-page miniatures inserted into the Hours of Sophia van Bylant (also known as the Homoet Hours; 1475; Cologne, Wallraf-Richartz-Mus., 1961/32). Sophia van Bylant and her deceased husband, Reynalt van Homoet (*d* 1458/9), are depicted facing the Hours of Eternal Wisdom (p. 188) and the Matins of the Holy Spirit (p. 150), respectively. It is possible that the Master of St

Master of the St Bartholomew Altar: *SS Agnes, Bartholomew and Cecilia with a Donor*, central panel of the *St Bartholomew* altar, 1.29×1.61 m, 1500–?1510 (Munich, Alte Pinakothek)

Bartholomew was still living in Arnhem when he painted the miniatures for Sophia van Bylant, who herself lived near Arnhem at Doorwerth Castle. Manuscripts produced in Arnhem (Gelderland) rarely contain illustrations, and this Book of Hours is the most noteworthy exception.

The *Virgin and Child with St Anne* (Munich, Alte Pin.), painted before 1480, is typical of the Master's early style, as are two panels with the *Holy Family* (Budapest, Mus. F.A.; Frankfurt am Main, Städel. Kstinst. & Städt. Gal.) in which St Joseph holds the child. Another early work, the *Marriage at Cana* (Brussels, Mus. A. Anc.; *see* GERMANY, fig. 35), is loosely inspired by Dieric Bouts the elder, while Justus of Ghent's *Adoration of the Magi* (New York, Met.) probably inspired the Master's own version of the subject (*c.* 1480; Munich, Alte Pin.). Perhaps the *Adoration of the Magi* (Paris, Petit Pal.) and a fragment with *St James the Elder* (ex-von Pannwitz col., Heemstede; untraced) also belong to his early production. However, the attribution to the Bartholomew Master of the *Mass of Pope Gregory* (Trier, Bischöf. Dom- & Diözmus.) remains debatable.

Of his mature works, the *Virgin and Child with a Nut* (Cologne, Wallraf-Richartz-Mus.) was probably painted around the same time as the *Virgin with SS Augustine and Adrian* (Darmstadt, Hess. Landesmus.), which was made for the Augustinian hermits in Cologne. Two paintings of the *Deposition* (London, N.G., 6470; Paris, Louvre, 2787) are somewhat archaic reflections of Rogier van der Weyden's well-known *Descent from the Cross* (Madrid, Prado; *see* WEYDEN, VAN DER, (1), fig. 2). They may have been the central panels of a triptych or some other ensemble. Like Rogier's widely copied composition, the use of gold framing devices and the tiered composition emulate the form of a carved altarpiece in polychrome wood. The London *Deposition* is sometimes dated as late as 1501–5.

In addition to the *St Bartholomew* altar, two other triptychs (both Cologne, Wallraf-Richartz-Mus.) constitute the Master's major works. The first, of *c.* 1499, has a *Crucifixion* in the centre, *SS John the Baptist and Cecilia* on the left wing, *SS Agnes and Alexius* on the right wing, and on the outer wings in grisaille an *Annunciation* and *SS Peter and Paul*. The second, the *St Thomas* altar of *c.* 1501, has the *Miracle of St Thomas* in the middle, *SS Mary Magdalene and John the Evangelist* on the left wing and *SS Hippolytus and Afra* on the right; the outer wings have grisaille representations of *St Felicitas* and *St Symphorosa*. Both altarpieces were commissioned by the Rector of Cologne University, Peter Rinck, for the Cologne Charterhouse. The *Baptism* (Washington, DC, N.G.A.), originally in Arnhem Cathedral, may have been painted either in the 1490s or *c.* 1500, between the *Crucifixion* and *St Thomas* altars. Clearly its stylistic and thematic interpretation is derived from the Netherlandish pictorial tradition as is the case with the panel of the *Virgin and Christ with St Agnes* (Nuremberg, Ger. Nmus.), which has close affinities to the *Mystic Marriage of St Agnes* (*c.* 1470–80; Esztergom, Dioc. Mus.), painted by a Utrecht artist. Another Netherlandish reference occurs in a *Portrait of a Man* (Cologne, Wallraf-Richartz-Mus.), in which the view from the window is of Utrecht Cathedral from the north-west. The depiction of the nave roof and windows, installed only *c.* 1515, suggests an approximate date for the portrait.

Another *Portrait of a Man* (*c.* 1492; Munich, Alte Pin.) is no longer accepted as by the Bartholomew Master.

BIBLIOGRAPHY

Thieme–Becker

A. Stange: *Deutsche Malerei der Gotik: Köln in der Zeit von 1450 bis 1515*, v (Berlin and Munich, 1952/*R* Nendeln, 1969), pp. 61–73

P. Pieper: 'Das Stundenbuch des Bartholomäus-Meisters', *Wallraf-Richartz-Jb.*, xxi (1959), pp. 97–158

——: 'Der Meister des Bartholomäusaltares', *Der Meister des Bartholomäusaltares. Der Meister des Aachener Altares. Kölner Maler der Spätgothik* (exh. cat., Cologne, Wallraf-Richartz-Mus., 1961), pp. 22–100

R. Walrath: 'Bildnis eines Unbekannten vom Meister des Bartholomäusaltares', *Wallraf-Richartz-Jb.*, xxvii (1965), pp. 389–94

——: 'Der Meister des Bartholomäusaltares in den Niederlanden und in Köln', *Kunstchronik*, xix (1966), pp. 281–2

G. Goldberg and G. Scheffler: *Altdeutsche Gemälde Köln und Nordwestdeutschland*, Munich, Bayer. Staatsgemäldesammlungen cat. (Munich, 1972), pp. 223–43

Alte Pinakothek München: Erlauterungen zu den ausgestellten Gemälden (Munich, 1983), pp. 315–17

The Golden Age of Dutch Manuscript Painting (exh. cat. by H. L. M. Defoer, A. S. Korteweg and W. C. M. Wüstefeld, New York, Pierpont Morgan Lib., 1990), pp. 15, 89, 245, 265, 267

N. MacGregor: *A Victim of Anonymity: The Master of the Saint Bartholomew Altarpiece* (London, 1994)

HANS J. VAN MIEGROET

Master of St Beatus. *See* MASTERS, ANONYMOUS, AND MONOGRAMMISTS, §I: CARNATION MASTERS above.

Master of the St Bertin Altar. *See* MARMION, SIMON.

St Cecilia Master (i) (*fl c.* 1290–1320). Italian painter. One of the major painters of the early 14th century, he is named after the panel of *St Cecilia Enthroned* (Florence, Uffizi), originally from the altarpiece of *St Cecilia*, Florence, and almost certainly painted before 1304; the saint is flanked by scenes from her life (see fig.). In addition to a group of stylistically homogeneous panels located in and around Florence, four frescoes from the cycle of the *Legend of St Francis* in the Upper Church of S Francesco, Assisi, are widely accepted as his. The work of this painter belongs to and possibly initiated a strand of Florentine painting running parallel to, but distinct from, that influenced by Giotto. Descriptions of his style that emphasize its miniaturist tendencies ignore other and more monumental aspects. These are seen in the central figure of the *St Cecilia* altarpiece and to a lesser extent in a panel of the *Virgin and Child with Saints* (Florence, S Margherita a Montici). The design and modelling of the face of St Cecilia are not far removed from that of the Virgin in the Altarpiece Badia attributed to Giotto (Florence, Uffizi), and the St Cecilia Master may have had more contact with Giotto than has often been allowed. The narrative scenes of the *St Cecilia* panel and a panel of *St Margaret with Six Scenes from her Life* (Florence, S Margherita a Montici) reveal a contrasting and quite un-Giottesque character. Figures are dainty, tapering up to small heads, and they move with a nervous but graceful urgency. The scenes from St Cecilia's life are set within remarkably refined and attenuated architectural settings, realized with great precision. A panel of *St Peter Enthroned* (Florence, S Simone), which has the same sharply receding throne and is in other ways very close to this group, is dated 1307.

The St Cecilia Master's frescoes in the Upper Church at Assisi were painted after the rest of the *Legend of St Francis* and exemplify the great speed and fluency of his

St Cecilia Master: *St Cecilia Enthroned*, tempera on panel, 0.85×1.81 m, before 1304 (Florence, Galleria degli Uffizi)

technique. They consist of the first scene of the cycle, on the fourth bay of the north wall of the nave, and the whole of the fourth bay of the south wall, which closes the cycle. The broadly symmetrical designs, the figure style and the general architectural character closely resemble those of the *St Cecilia* panel, though the architecture of the frescoes is less abstract. The opening *St Francis and the Madman of Assisi* features unmistakable depictions of the Torre del Comune and the Temple of Minerva in Assisi, though the former is reinvented in a Gothic style and the latter according to the spindly proportions of the St Cecilia narratives. The figured spiral column of the *Liberation of Peter the Heretic* suggests first-hand knowledge of Trajan's Column, Rome, and the delicate and spacious settings of the *Healing of the Wounded Man* and the *Confession of the Woman of Benevento* even suggest some contact with ancient Roman painting styles. The clarity of design and warmth of colour are unsurpassed in the *St Francis* cycle.

The St Cecilia Master's origins are unclear, as is his exact relationship with the rest of the painters of the *Legend of St Francis*, but he may have emerged from a Roman rather than a Florentine background. His influence on Bernardo Daddi and other Florentine painters was considerable. The architectural settings of his frescoes influenced the painter of the *Presentation in the Temple* (Rimini, S Agostino), and Paolo Veneziano's panels from the cover for the 'Pala d'Oro' (Venice, S Marco) seem to reflect a clear, if unaccountable, acquaintance with the *St Cecilia* altarpiece narratives.

BIBLIOGRAPHY
R. Offner: 'A Great *Madonna* by the St Cecilia Master', *Burl. Mag.*, l (1927), pp. 91–104
R. Offner and K. Steinweg: *Corpus* (1931), I/iii [whole vol.]
A. Smart: 'The St Cecilia Master and his School at Assisi', *Burl. Mag.*, cii (1960), pp. 405–13, 431–7
L. Tintori and M. Meiss: *The Painting of the 'Life of St Francis' in Assisi* (New York, 1962)
J. White: *Art and Architecture in Italy, 1250–1400*, Pelican Hist. A. (Harmondsworth, 1966, rev. 2/1987), pp. 215–18
A. Smart: *The Assisi Problem and the Art of Giotto* (Oxford, 1971)
R. Fremantle: *Florentine Gothic Painters* (London, 1975), pp. 35–44 [full bibliog.]

JOHN RICHARDS

St Cecilia Master (ii). *See under* CONCHA, ANDRÉS DE LA.

Master of the St Elisabeth Panels. *See under* MASTER OF RHENEN above.

Master of St Francis [Maestro di S Francesco] (*fl c.* 1260–80). Italian painter. This painter of frescoes and panels and, perhaps, designer of stained glass in the district around Perugia was named by Thode after a panel of *St Francis with Angels* in S Maria degli Angeli, Assisi. Much of the work attributed to him was part of the early phase in the decoration of S Francesco, Assisi (*see* ASSISI, §II, 2 and fig. 2), and includes the fresco cycle in the nave of the Lower Church with five scenes from the *Passion* on the right wall and five scenes from the *Life of St Francis* on the left. (These were damaged by the later opening of the side chapels.) In spite of the obvious participation of assistants, the entire cycle seems to have been planned by a single artist and can be considered as homogeneous and characteristic of his style. This was largely based on the later works of Giunta Pisano but also shows the influence of such Umbrian artists as Rainaldetto di Ranuccio, Simeone and Machilone and of contemporary manuscript illumination, for example the Gospel Book of Giovanni da Gaibena (Padua, Bib. Capitolare). The Master of St Francis embodies an important aspect of the contact between Italian and Byzantine art of this period: Byzantine elements, particularly of iconography, are found with western forms of ornamentation and a use of colour that is far from Byzantine.

The scenes from the *Life of St Francis* are based on the *Vita secunda* (1247) by Tommaso da Celano. In 1266 this was replaced by the *Legenda maior* (1260–63) of St Bonaventura as the only authorized source for the Saint's iconography. The cycle must therefore be earlier than

1266, because the frescoes include some iconographic details derived from Celano and discarded in the *Legenda* (e.g. the seraph in the *Stigmatization of St Francis*, which in the *Legenda* was replaced by a Crucifix); but the paralleling of the scenes from the lives of St Francis and Christ depends on Bonaventura's idea of St Francis as *alter Christus*. The frescoes seem therefore to date from the first half of the 1260s, before the authorization of the *Legenda maior* and corresponding perhaps with the frequent presence of St Bonaventura in Umbria from 1260 to 1263.

The Master's workshop was also employed in the Upper Church of S Francesco: on the execution of the stained glass for the window in the right transept, the *Appearances of Christ*, in collaboration with northern masters (*see* ASSISI, §II, 3 and fig. 7). This phase of the work has been dated to about the same time as the frescoes in the same transept by the Northern Master (*fl c.* 1260–80). The stained-glass workshop may have also executed some of the windows of the upper nave (the scenes from the *Lives of SS Bartholomew and Matthew* and the scenes from the *Lives of SS Francis and Anthony*) within a period that covers at least the 1270s.

A number of panel paintings have been attributed to the Master of St Francis and his workshop. The panel of *St Francis with Angels* (Assisi, S Maria degli Angeli) is traditionally attributed to the Master's own hand, as is the double-sided polyptych possibly executed for S Francesco al Prato, Perugia, and now dispersed. It includes a *St Francis*, *St Matthew* and *St Anthony*, a *Deposition* and a *Lamentation* (Perugia, G.N. Umbria), an *Isaiah* (Assisi,

Tesoro Mus. Basilica S Francesco), *St Peter* (Brussels, Stoclet priv. col.), *SS Simon and Bartholomew* (New York, Met.) and *SS James and John the Evangelist* (Washington, DC, N.G.A.). The style of the polyptych obviously echoes the Assisi frescoes and dates from the end of the 1260s. A *Crucifix* (London, N.G.; see fig.) and another in Paris (Louvre) are probably also mostly by the Master of St Francis and recall the dramatic tendencies of the *Deposition* and *Lamentation* at Assisi. The London version is the more dramatic, with a more complex composition, and might be the earlier of the two, but they both date from about the end of the 1260s. The latest of the works attributed to the Master of St Francis is a *Crucifix* (Perugia, G.N. Umbria; *see* GILDING Colour pl. 057) dated 1272, an example of his mature style. It is also the earliest to include the figure of St Francis at the foot of the cross.

BIBLIOGRAPHY
H. Thode: *Franz von Assisi und die Anfänge der Kunst der Renaissance in Italien* (Berlin, 1885, 2/1904)
J. Cannon: 'Dating the Frescoes by the Maestro di San Francesco at Assisi', *Burl. Mag.*, cxxiv (1982), pp. 65–9
D. Gordon: 'A Perugian Provenance for the Franciscan Double-sided Altarpiece by the Maestro di San Francesco', *Burl. Mag.*, cxxiv (1982), pp. 70–77
S. Romano: 'Le storie parallele di Assisi: Il Maestro di San Francesco', *Stor. A.*, xliv (1982), pp. 63–82
Francesco d'Assisi: Codici e miniature (exh. cat., Foligno, Mus. Archeol., 1982)
D. Blume: *Wandmalerei als Ordenspropaganda* (Worms, 1983)
S. Esser: *Die Ausmalung der Unterkirche von S Francesco in Assisi durch den Franziskusmeister* (diss., U. Bonn, 1983)
J. Poeschke: 'Der "Franziskusmeister" und die Anfänge der Ausmalung von S Francesco in Assisi', *Mitt. Ksthist. Inst. Florenz*, xxvii (1983), pp. 125–70
D. Gordon: 'Un *Crucifix* du Maître de San Francesco', *Rev. Louvre* (1984), pp. 253–61
S. Romano: 'Pittura ad Assisi, 1260–1280: Lo stato degli studi', *A. Med.*, ii (1984), pp. 109–41
SERENA ROMANO

Master of the Francis Legend. *See* MASTER OF THE LEGEND OF ST FRANCIS above

Master of St George. *See* MARTORELL, BERNAT.

Master of St Giles (*fl* Paris, *c.* 1490–1510). French painter. He is named after two small panel paintings depicting episodes from the *Life of St Giles*, the reverses of which are painted in grisaille and show figures in niches: *St Peter* on the reverse of the *Mass of St Giles* and a *Bishop Saint* (perhaps St Loup) on the back of *St Giles Protecting a Hind* (both London, N.G.). Two further panels of similar character and format, also originally with grisaille figures on the reverses (apparently separated in recent times and now untraced), are evidently by the same artist. On the reverse of the *Baptism of King Clovis by St Rémi* (also identified as the *Baptism of the Nobleman Lisbius by St Denis*) was formerly *St Denis*, and on the reverse of an *Episode from the Life of a Bishop Saint* (identified either as *St Loup Curing the Children*, or, more probably, as *St Rémi Converting the Arian Bishop Genebaut*) was *St Giles* (both Washington, DC, N.G.A.). The costumes depicted in all four panels provide some basis for dating them. Certain Italianate details in the dress imply a date after 1495, when Charles VIII returned from his Italian campaign, while the bulky garments worn by the men and their long hair suggest a date close to 1500.

Master of St Francis (attrib.): *Crucifix*, tempera on panel, 921×750 mm, late 1260s (London, National Gallery)

Master of St Giles: *Mass of St Giles*, oil on panel, 615×455 mm, *c.* 1500 (London, National Gallery)

Although no documentary evidence survives concerning the original provenance of these paintings, it seems likely that they were executed in Paris, since they feature topographical portraits of Paris and neighbouring towns. The *Mass of St Giles* (see fig.), in which an angel appears with a note miraculously pardoning a sin of King Charles Martel at the moment of the elevation of the Host by St Giles, takes place in the royal abbey of Saint-Denis to the north of the city. Details of the painting depict with exceptional archaeological accuracy some of the original furnishings of the abbey, most of which no longer exist. Serving as a retable on the altar is the gold altar-frontal, sumptuously decorated with reliefs and gems, given by Charles the Bald and destroyed during the French Revolution. Above this is the Cross (untraced) considered to have been made by St Eligius (*d* 658–9) and donated to Saint-Denis Abbey by King Dagobert (*d* 639), whose elaborately carved tomb, executed in the 13th century and still *in situ*, is included on the right of the picture. The background of *St Giles Protecting a Hind*, in which the Saint is shown accidentally hit by an arrow shot by a royal huntsman, is identifiable as a view of Pontoise, to the west of Paris. In the *Episode from the Life of a Saint*, the Bishop stands on the steps of St-Jean-le-Rond, which in the 15th century adjoined the north-west tower of Notre-Dame,

Paris, which is shown behind, sharply foreshortened, next to the chapel of the Hôtel-Dieu. In the distance is a view of the south bank of the Seine, including the tower of Ste Geneviève. The *Baptism of King Clovis* is set in the lower chapel of the Sainte-Chapelle with a view through the portal to the Palais de la Cité. Many of the details of the setting, however, such as the statue of Christ on the trumeau, are taken from the upper chapel. This is curious, since infra-red reflectography has revealed that the artist's original intention was to show just the lower chapel, which indicates that changes were made in order to suggest a grander setting.

Since the four panels were originally painted on both sides, they probably formed part of the shutters of a folding altarpiece or similar structure. Attempts to reconstruct its form have proved problematic because so much of the original ensemble has been lost, and the shape of the niche containing the *St Giles* is not consistent with the remaining panels. It has been suggested that this panel was independent of the others, though its size and iconography suggest otherwise. One explanation is that it belonged to a different tier of the ensemble. The character of the niches suggests, however, that the panels were arranged in a single tier, like the altarpiece of St Bertin attributed to SIMON MARMION, which had a central section made of precious metals. Similar works were not uncommon in northern France, whence the artist may have come. Whatever the arrangement of the panels, their subjects indicate that they were possibly commissioned for the Parisian church of St Leu-St-Gilles. Although the panels contain numerous references to the theme of kingship and were partly inspired by a *Life of St Denis* (1317) written by a monk from the royal abbey, this is insufficient to support the theory that they originally formed part of the decoration protecting the high altar at Saint-Denis. Such references are equally relevant to St Leu-St-Gilles, which was situated on the Rue St-Denis.

Among other works attributable to the Master of St Giles are portraits of a man and a woman (Chantilly, Mus. Condé), probably fragments of a much larger work, and a portrait of *Philip the Fair, Duke of Burgundy* (ex-Winterthur, Samml. Oskar Reinhart), who visited Paris in 1501. A *Presentation in the Temple* (Rotterdam, Boymans–van Beuningen) is partly derived from the Prevedari engraving by Bramante (1481), while a *Betrayal of Christ* (Brussels, Pal. B.-A.) is interesting as a rare example for this date of a night scene, a lantern being the only source of light. The meticulously detailed style of the Master of St Giles indicates a period of training in the Netherlands, perhaps in a workshop influenced by Gerard David, whose work he seems to have known. He was also familiar with works by Rogier van der Weyden. His *Virgin and Child* (Paris, Louvre), probably an early work, is copied from a composition originating in Rogier's workshop. Technical examinations have confirmed that his technique is essentially Netherlandish. Aspects of his style, however, suggest that he was actually a Frenchman. For example, portraiture of buildings and night scenes are more frequently found in French than in Netherlandish art and may be traced back to the work of the DE LIMBOURG brothers in the early 15th century. The Master's facial types and choice of colours are also suggestive of a French origin and may be compared with works by Jean Fouquet.

BIBLIOGRAPHY

M. J. Friedländer: 'Der Meister des Hl. Ägidius', *Amtl. Ber. Kön. Kstsamml.*, xxiv (1912–13), pp. 187–9
J. Held: 'Zwei Ansichten von Paris beim Meister des Heiligen Ägidius', *Jb. Preuss. Kstsamml.*, iii (1932), pp. 3–15
J. Dupont: 'Une Vierge du Maître de Saint-Gilles', *Bull. Mus. France* (July 1936), pp. 108–9
M. J. Friedländer: 'Le Maître de Saint-Gilles', *Gaz. B.-A.*, lxxix (1937), pp. 221–31
M. Davies: *The Early Netherlandish School*, London, N.G. cat. (London, 1945, rev. 3/1968), pp. 107–13
C. Sterling: *Les Peintres du moyen âge* (Paris, 1945)
M. Hébert: 'Les Monuments parisiens dans l'oeuvre du Maître de Saint-Gilles', *Mém. Féd. Soc. Hist. & Archéol. Paris & Ile-de-France*, i (1949), pp. 213–36
G. Ring: *A Century of French Painting, 1400–1500* (London, 1949)
W. M. Hinkle: 'The Iconography of the Four Panels by the Master of Saint Giles', *J. Warb. & Court. Inst.*, xxviii (1965), pp. 110–44
——: 'The King and the Pope on the Virgin Portal of Notre-Dame', *A. Bull.*, xlviii (1966), pp. 5–8
D. Bomford and J. Kirby: 'Two Panels by the Master of Saint Giles', *N.G. Tech. Bull.*, i (Sept. 1977), pp. 49–56
C. Eisler: *Paintings from the Samuel H. Kress Collection: European Schools Excluding Italian* (London, 1977), pp. 239–43
J. O. Hand and M. Wolff: *Early Netherlandish Painting*, Collections of the National Gallery, Washington (Cambridge, MA, 1986), pp. 163–76

THOMAS TOLLEY

Master of St Ildefonso (*fl* Valladolid, second half of the 15th century). Spanish painter. He is named from *St Ildefonso's Reception of a Chasuble from the Virgin Mary* (Paris, Louvre), which is traditionally held to come from Valladolid; it may even have come from the chapel of S Ildefonso in the Colegiata there. The style, characterized by harmony of colour and intense expressions, resembles that of four panels of *St Athanasius*, *St Louis of Toulouse*, both enthroned, *SS Peter and Paul* and *SS Andrew and James the Great*, which probably came from the convent of La Merced, Valladolid (see Post, p. 402). They have been attributed to the Master of Ávila, but Post considered them to be the work of the Master of St Ildefonso, a more sophisticated painter, although both artists modified the harshness of their Netherlandish models. There are also similarities with Jacomart's triptych of *St Anne* in the Colegiata, Játiva, but these may be coincidental. Other works attributed to the Master include *St Anne* and *St Anthony of Padua* (Valladolid, Mus. N. Escul., see Post, p. 408), eight lateral panels of the retable of Don Alvaro de Luna in Toledo Cathedral and an effigy of the *Virgin of the Immaculate Conception* from S Pablo at Peñafiel, a little to the east of Valladolid.

BIBLIOGRAPHY

P. Vidal: *Histoire de la ville de Perpignan* (Paris, 1897)
S. Sanpere y Miquel: *Los cuatrocentistas catalanes* (Barcelona, 1906)
C. R. Post: *A History of Spanish Painting*, iv/2 (Cambridge, MA, 1933)
J. G. Ricart: *Pintura gótica*, A. Hisp., ix (Madrid, 1955)

J. R. L. HIGHFIELD

Master of the St John Altarpiece (*fl* Gouda, 1480–1500). North Netherlandish painter and designer of stained-glass windows and ?woodcuts. He was named by Hannema after three panels: the *Birth of St John the Baptist*, the *Flight of St Elizabeth* (both Rotterdam, Boymans–van Beuningen) and the *Meeting of St John the Baptist and Christ* (Philadelphia, PA, Mus. A.). These must have been part of an altarpiece, possibly the high altar of the St Janskerk, Gouda, which was devoted to St John the Baptist. The most striking features of the works attributed to the Master and his workshop are the solid, angular figures, the occasionally grotesque, craggy faces and the rather deep landscape views in the background. These also occur in the early prints of Lucas van Leyden, and for this reason the Master has been identified with HUGO JACOBSZ., Lucas van Leyden's father, who is known to have worked in Gouda in 1488. As the St John panels are generally dated before 1500, this hypothesis seemed acceptable. However, things became more complicated when dendrochronological research suggested a date for the panels of *c*. 1512, which would make their style very traditional and old-fashioned. While neither the rather flat technique of these panels, with areas of strong local colour, nor the under-drawing (revealed by infra-red reflectography) show any direct similarities to the early paintings by Lucas, there is a close resemblance between the underdrawing and the draughtsmanship of the earliest surviving glass cartoons from the St Janskerk (on loan to Amsterdam, Rijksmus.), dated *c*. 1510, which in the past have been attributed to Lucas van Leyden.

Other works attributed to the Master and his workshop include two versions of the *Nativity* (Brussels, Mus. A. Anc.; Esztergom, Mus. Christ.) and an *Entombment* (Budapest, Mus. F.A.). The Master was presumably also responsible for the designs of the woodcut illustrations to Olivier de la Marche's *Chevalier délibéré* (Gouda, 1486–90).

BIBLIOGRAPHY

D. Hannema: 'De Meester van het Johannes altaar', *Bull.: Mus. Boymans*, i (1937), pp. 3–4
I. Q. van Regteren Altena: 'Hugo Jacobsz.', *Ned. Ksthist. Jb.*, vi (1955), pp. 101–7
Middeleeuwse kunst der Noordelijke Nederlanden (exh. cat., ed. R. Luttervelt; Amsterdam, Rijksmus., 1958), pp. 72–4, cat. nos 62–6
K. G. Boon: 'De vroegste glascartons uit de St Janskerk te Gouda', *Bull. Rijksmus.*, xxi (1973), pp. 151–75
A. Châtelet: *Les Primitifs hollandais* (Paris and Fribourg, 1980); Eng. trans. as *Early Dutch Painting* (Oxford and New York, 1981), pp. 157–62, 237–40
K. G. Boon: 'The Life and Work of Hugo Jacobsz. before 1500', *Essays in Northern European Art Presented to Egbert Haverkamp-Begemann on his Sixtieth Birthday* (Doornspijk, 1983), pp. 43–8
Van Eyck to Bruegel, 1400–1550: Dutch and Flemish Painting in the Collection of the Museum Boymans–van Beuningen (Rotterdam, 1994), nos 25–26, pp. 128–36

J. P. FILEDT KOK

Master of St John the Baptist (*fl* Upper Rhine, *c*. 1450–60). German engraver. He has been named after the large-format engraving *St John the Baptist with the Agnus Dei* (L 11). A further ten engravings are attributed to him, *St Sebastian* (L 10) and nine sheets of a series of standing *Apostles* (L 1–9). His work is closely related to that of the Master of the Passion of Christ, and he was one of the best successors of the Master of the Playing Cards on the Upper Rhine. His relation to the Master E.S., and therefore the question of the dating of his work, has not been clarified.

BIBLIOGRAPHY

M. Lehrs: *Geschichte und kritischer Katalog des deutschen, niederländischen und französischen Kupferstichs im XV. Jahrhundert*, i (Vienna, 1908), pp. 263–72

M. Geisberg: *Die Anfänge des deutschen Kupferstiches und der Meister E.S., Meister der Graphik*, ii (Leipzig, 1909), pp. 47–8

L. Fischel: 'Werk und Name des Meisters von 1445', *Z. Kstgesch.*, xiii (1950), pp. 105–24

HOLM BEVERS

Master of the St Lambrecht Votive Altarpiece (*fl c.* 1410–40). Austrian painter. He is named after an International Gothic style panel formerly in the abbey of St Lambrecht, Styria (*c.* 1425–30; Graz, Alte Gal.), in which Abbot Heinrich Moyker (1419–55), the donor, kneels before the Virgin of Mercy, with St Hemma of Gurk (or St Hedwig), in a landscape setting showing the Hungarians' victory over the Turks. Other works have been ascribed to this artist, some in contention with attributions to the Master of the Linz Crucifixion (Linz, Oberösterreich. Landesmus.), to Hans von Judenburg and to Hans von Tübingen (*fl* Wiener Neustadt, *c.* 1433–62). Tübingen's activity seems too late to be identified with the Master of St Lambrecht's group of paintings, normally dated *c.* 1410–40. Among the panels that have been attributed to the Master and his workshop are the *Trinity wih Christ Crucified* ('*Throne of Mercy*') or *Gnadenstuhl Trinity, c.* 1410–20; London, N.G.) and the *Trinity Pietà* (*c.* 1430; Vienna, Belvedere). A stained-glass window (*c.* 1430–40; St Lambrecht, St Peter), with Old Testament parallels to the life of Christ, has also been attributed to him. This group of works, some perhaps by closely related members of a workshop, show some features of the soft style of the Bohemian International Gothic, but other aspects are reminiscent of the Cologne and Westphalian schools. They are closely connected to Viennese paintings of the International Gothic. In addition, the elegance and courtly costume of the figures, their refined poses and gestures and the turreted, castellated architectural forms have parallels with contemporary French and Burgundian painting and the work of Simone Martini.

BIBLIOGRAPHY

Thieme–Becker
O. Benesch: 'Zur altösterreichischen Tafelmalerei, I: Der Meister der Linzer Kreuzigung', *Jb. Ksthist. Samml. Wien*, n. s. ii (1928), pp. 63–76; *R* in O. Benesch: *Collected Writings*, iii (London, 1972), pp. 16–30
——: 'Neue Materialien zur altösterreichischen Tafelmalerei, I: Die Flügel der Linzer Kreuzigung', *Jb. Ksthist. Samml. Wien*, n. s. iv (1929), pp. 155–68; *R* in O. Benesch: *Collected Writings*, iii (London, 1972), pp. 77–88
K. Oettinger: *Hans von Tübingen und seine Schule* (Berlin, 1938)
A. Stange: *Deutsche Malerei der Gotik*, xi (Munich, 1961/*R* Nendeln, 1969), pp. 11–19, figs 9–18
G. Schmidt: 'Die österreichische Kreuztragungstafel in der Huntington Library', *Österreich. Z. Kst & Dkmlpf.*, xx (1966), pp. 1–15
E. Baum: *Katalog des Museums Mittelalterlicher Österreichischer Kunst* (Vienna, 1971), pp. 30–35; suppl. (Vienna, 1981), pp. 12–13
J. Oberhaidacher: 'Der Meister der St. Lambrechter Votivtafel und Simone Martini', *Wien. Jb. Kstgesch.*, xlv (1972), pp. 173–81, 303–8
J. Wegh: 'Die heilige Hemma? Zur Ikonographie der Votiftafel von St. Lambrecht', *Acta Hist. A. Acad. Sci. Hung.*, xxiv (1978), pp. 123–31
E. Bacher: *Die mittelalterliche Glasgemälde in der Steiermark, I, Graz und Strassengel, CVMA Österreich*, iii (Vienna, 1979), pp. xliv–xlvi, 91–3

NIGEL J. MORGAN

Master of St Martha. *See* MASTER OF CHAOURCE above

Master of SS Paul and Barnabas. *See under* MANDIJN, JAN.

Master of St Philip. *See* CIAMPANTI, (2).

Master of St Sebastian (i) (*fl* ?Lower Rhine, *c.* 1470–90). German engraver. He is named after a large-format engraving of *St Sebastian* (Lehrs, 4). Nine other engravings, including patterns for ornamentation, are attributed to him; few copies of each exist. The question whether the *Family of St Anne* (Lehrs, 1) is a 19th-century work has not been resolved. Stylistically the somewhat coarsely engraved sheets show a similarity with the work of the Master b ⋉ 8 (*see* §III below) and the Master of the Boccaccio Illustrations, with whom he was once identified, probably erroneously.

BIBLIOGRAPHY

M. Lehrs: *Geschichte und kritischer Katalog des deutschen, niederländischen und französischen Kupferstichs im XV. Jahrhundert*, iv (Vienna, 1921), pp. 188–99
Fifteenth-century Engravings of Northern Europe from the National Gallery of Art (exh. cat., ed. A. Shestack; Washington, DC, N.G.A., 1967–8), nos 32–3
M. Hébert: *Bibliothèque Nationale, Département des Gravures: Inventaire des gravures des écoles du Nord, 1440–1550*, i (Paris, 1982), p. 67

HOLM BEVERS

Master of St Sebastian (ii). *See* LIEFERINXE, JOSSE.

Master of St Severin (*fl* Cologne, *c.* 1485–*c.* 1515). German painter. He is named after the location of two panels depicting *SS Agatha and Cornelius, Stephen and Helena* (*c.* 1500; Cologne, St Severin), notable for their sculptural figure conception and warm colour. His work was distinguished by Aldenhoven in 1902 from the qualitatively superior paintings of the Master of the Legend of St Ursula (ii). Rode (1969) identified the Master of St Severin with the Cologne civic painter Master Clais (*fl* 1507), who probably designed some stained glass that clearly bears connections with his work in the northern nave of Cologne Cathedral (1508, 1509). The Master of St Severin evidently led a large workshop, a factor that would support this identification: Clais was in office as city painter from 1508.

The Master's ostentatious but rather dry art followed in a workmanlike fashion, a retardataire Cologne tradition learnt from the Master of the Holy Kinship but stemming from Stefan Lochner. A winged altarpiece (?1490s; ex-Johanniterkirche SS Johannes und Cordula, Cologne; Boston, MA, Mus. F.A.) has a central panel depicting *Calvary* and wing panels showing events from the *Life and Death of St John the Baptist*. Its resemblance to a *Calvary* (?*c.* 1480; Brussels, Mus. A. Anc.) by the Master of the Holy Kinship suggests that the latter may have been the Master of St Severin's teacher. From *c.* 1500 are the *Rosary* altarpiece (ex-Dominican church, Cologne; Cologne, St Andreas) and panels depicting the *Passion* (ex-St Severin, Cologne), comprising *Christ before Pilate* (Cologne, Wallraf-Richartz-Mus.), the *Agony in the Garden*, *Lamentation* and *Assumption of the Virgin* (all Munich, Alte Pin.) and the *Ascension* (Bonn, Rhein. Landesmus.). Also attributed to the Master are the *Portrait of a Young Man* (*c.* 1500; Swiss priv. col.) and the *Portrait of an Old Woman* (*c.* 1490; London, N.G., on loan from Polesden Lacey, Surrey, NT), which testify that he was a portrait painter of some significance, despite his often very dull, pious figures.

The influence of the Master of the Legend of St Ursula (ii) can be seen especially in the rich, soft-toned colour spectrum of the Master of St Severin's later works and in certain of his figure types. He followed the example of the Master of the Legend of St Ursula's *Adoration of the Magi* (*c.* 1480–85; Frauenberg, St Georg) in two depictions of that theme (both Cologne, Wallraf-Richartz-Mus.). The earlier picture (*c.* 1505–10) marked a highpoint in his creation: he achieved an extremely fine colour composition and intimate mood. The larger and later (1512) of the panels, donated by Christian Conreshem (*d* after 1530), later rector of Cologne University, which was probably originally destined for St Ursula, Cologne, characterizes the Master's late style, in his conventional striving towards representation. A large number of pictures can only count as workshop productions where in individual cases there are boundaries of style between the different artists, from time to time also touching on the circle of the Master of the Legend of St Ursula. Examples of this are a *Last Judgement* (after 1500; Cologne, Wallraf-Richartz-Mus.) and the 20-part cycle of the *Legend of St Severin* (1500; Cologne, St Severin, Wallraf-Richartz-Mus.). The young Bartholomaeus Bruyn I may have worked for the Master of St Severin from 1512.

BIBLIOGRAPHY

C. Aldenhoven: *Geschichte der Kölner Malerschule* (Lübeck, 1902), pp. 279–85

H. Brockmann: *Die Spätzeit der Kölner Malerschule* (Bonn, Leipzig, 1924), pp. 17, 27, 76, 150–90

A. Stange: *Deutsche Malerei der Gotik*, v (Munich, 1952), pp. 103–14

——: *Die deutschen Tafelbilder vor Dürer: Kritisches Verzeichnis*, i (Munich, 1967), pp. 102–6, nos 308–25

H. Rode: 'Die Namen der Meister der hl. Sippe und von St Severin: Eine Hypothese, zugleich ein Beitrag zu dem Glasmalereizyklus im nördlichen Seitenschiff des Kölner Doms', *Wallraf-Richartz-Jb.*, xxxi (1969), pp. 249–54

HANS M. SCHMIDT

Master of St Veronica (*fl c.* 1395–?after 1425). German painter. He is named from the panel depicting *St Veronica with the Sudarium* (*c.* 1415; Munich, Alte Pin.; see fig.). The most influential painter in Cologne in the early 15th century, he appears to have been an immigrant who introduced the International Court style and thus initiated the 'school of Cologne'. On stylistic grounds it is generally assumed that he settled in Cologne *c.* 1400. The quality of his work has been acclaimed by such perceptive authors as Goethe, Dehio and Stange.

1. IDENTITY AND FORMATION. No document can plausibly be connected with the Master, and attempts to identify him with recorded painters, including Master Wilhelm of Cologne, Herman Wynrich von Wesel (*d c.* 1413) and Herman de Coulogne (*fl* 1389–1417), had to be abandoned. Suggestions that he served his apprenticeship in Cologne depend largely on dating two stylistically related altarpieces to *c.* 1370–80. However, both the *Elizabeth* altarpiece (Cologne, Wallraf-Richartz-Mus.; Ludwigshafen, Hack-Mus. & Städt. Kstsamml.) and the *St Clare* altarpiece (Cologne Cathedral) can be shown to have been 'modernized', and the latter completed, by the Master of St Veronica and his workshop after 1400. It can, however, be inferred that the Master worked for a

Master of St Veronica: *St Veronica with the Sudarium*, tempera (with traces of oil and resin) on prepared panel, 781×482 mm, *c.* 1415 (Munich, Alte Pinakothek)

time as a journeyman in the workshop of Conrad von Soest in Dortmund in Westphalia.

Striking similarities in the styles of these two artists, including analogous facial features, have encouraged the attribution of certain panels (now generally regarded as early works by the Master of St Veronica) to Conrad von Soest. Recent research has confirmed the Cologne Master's specific knowledge of Conrad's workshop practices, for example in his adoption of a cloud punchmark, which is otherwise an idiosyncratic feature only of autograph works by Conrad von Soest (Corley). Furthermore the Master of St Veronica introduced into Cologne certain technical characteristics at variance with German practice but observable in Conrad's work, such as the use of red bole and the colours ultramarine and lead-tin yellow. The sojourn as journeyman in Conrad's workshop seems plausible; however, his softly modelled forms, more generalized description of figures and muted tempera palette diverge from Conrad's vigorous and precise technique and suggest an apprenticeship with a different master.

2. WORK. The Veronica Master's acquaintance with Westphalian painting can be demonstrated in the *Calvary*

(*c.* 1408; Cologne, Wallraf-Richartz-Mus.), a small oak panel for private devotions featuring the peculiar Westphalian cross-type with two horizontal bars for the thieves. The poignant juxtaposition and characterization of the various groups under the cross denote a gifted storyteller. Another panel, the *Trinity* (1400–05; Cologne, Wallraf-Richartz-Mus.), has frequently been ascribed to Conrad von Soest, but the soft modelling of the forms, the juxtaposition of fine long and short brushstrokes, and the punched frame of large circles in the gold ground indicate the Master of St Veronica. A small *Crucifixion* (*c.* 1405; Washington, DC, N.G.A.) appears to have been commissioned by a Dortmund patrician, Segebodo Berswordt, to commemorate his brother Conrad Berswordt, a monk in the Carthusian monastery of St Barbara in Cologne.

Other patrons favoured small images of the Virgin, such as the *Virgin with the Pea Blossom* (*c.* 1410–15; Nuremberg, Ger. Nmus.). Closely related in style and features is the eponymous *St Veronica with the Sudarium* (*c.* 1415; Munich, Alte Pin.; see fig.), in which the saint, presumably kneeling, holds the sudarium displaying Christ's image in heraldic size. Although surface decoration has precedence over realistic description in these Court style paintings, spatial recession is plausibly indicated here through receding tiles and colour perspective. The increased monumentality of the forms points to the middle period of the artist's career. In a further development of this image of *St Veronica*, the Master painted the saint in three-quarter view (*c.* 1420; London, N.G.), pushed right up against the picture plane.

In the large *Crucifixion* (*c.* 1425; Cologne, Wallraf-Richartz-Mus.) showing Christ flanked by the Virgin, St John and seven apostles, painted with workshop assistance, the Master grafted the indigenous elongated figure style on to his own courtly images. The torso of Christ still follows the pattern of the *Crucifixion* of *c.* 1405, and the cloud punchmark continues to be used to decorate the gold ground. The Master of St Veronica attracted a considerable number of followers. His style prevailed in Cologne until the arrival there *c.* 1440 of Stefan Lochner.

BIBLIOGRAPHY

Vor Stefan Lochner: Die Kölner Malerei von 1300–1430, 2 vols (exh. cat., Cologne, Wallraf-Richartz-Mus., 1974–7)

F. G. Zehnder: *Der Meister der heiligen Veronika* (Sankt Augustin, 1981)

R. Budde: *Köln und seine Maler, 1300–1500* (Cologne, 1986)

B. Corley: *Conrad von Soest: His Altarpieces, his Workshop and his Place in European Art* (diss., U. London, Courtauld Inst. and Birkbeck Coll., 1991)

——: *Conrad von Soest: Painter among Merchant Princes* (London, 1996)

BRIGITTE CORLEY

Samson Master (*fl c.* 1190–*c.* 1220/30). German sculptor or workshop. Active in the Cologne and Middle Rhine area, he or it is named after the fragment of a figure of *Samson Fighting a Lion* (shell-limestone, h. 560 mm, *c.* 1220; Maria Laach Abbey). The designation is now thought to apply to a workshop, rather than an individual, which produced a group of figural sculptures and capitals in a somewhat varied Late Romanesque style (the Paradise capitals in Maria Laach; the double capital, probably from St Maria ad Gradus in Cologne, now Cologne, Erzbischöf. Diöz.-Mus.).

The main influences on the 'Samson Master style' seem to have been northern French cathedral sculpture (e.g. Saint-Denis Abbey; Notre-Dame, Paris; Chartres Cathedral), the goldwork and small bronze sculpture of the Rhine–Meuse area (e.g. RAINER OF HUY, NICHOLAS OF VERDUN) and Byzantine figure compositions transmitted through pattern books. Characteristic of the style are the alignment of the figure with the stone block, the stereometric arrangement of figure, surface and setting, draperies chiselled with great virtuosity and a pronounced feeling for 'ideal' proportion and beauty of the human figure.

The following sculptures are also attributed to the Samson Master: two relief fragments with depictions of a lap-fiddler (limestone, traces of colour, 840×460 mm, *c.* 1200) and of a dancer (limestone, traces of colour, 650×500 mm, *c.* ?1190; both Cologne, Schnütgen-Mus.); the figures on two choir-stall ends, a *Writing Angel* and a *Writing Devil* (limestone, 750×155 mm and 150×530 mm, *c.* 1210–20; Bonn, Minster); and the fragments of an *?Angel Annunciate* found in 1947 in the bombed church of St John the Baptist in Cologne (limestone, 680×290 mm, *c.* 1210–20; Cologne, Schnütgen-Mus.).

BIBLIOGRAPHY

K. A. Wirth: 'Beiträge zum Problem des "Samsonmeisters"', *Z. Kstgesch.*, xx (1957), pp. 25–51

Rhein und Maas: Kunst und Kultur, 800–1400 (exh. cat., Cologne, Ksthalle; Brussels, Mus. Royaux A. & Hist.; 1972), i, pp. 336–7

Die Zeit der Staufer, Geschichte-Kunst-Kultur (exh. cat., Stuttgart, Württemberg. Landesmus., 1977), i

R. Budde: *Deutsche romanische Skulptur, 1050–1250* (Munich, 1979), pp. 174–6

B. Kaelble: *Untersuchungen zur grossfigurigen Plastik des Samsonmeisters* (Düsseldorf, 1981)

A. Legner: *Deutsche Kunst der Romanik* (Munich, 1982)

Ornamenta Ecclesiae: Kunst und Künstler der Romanik in Köln (exh. cat., ed. A. Legner; Cologne, Josef-Haubrich-Ksthalle, 1985), ii, pp. 384–9

MICHAEL STUHR

Master of S Climente. *See under* TAÜLL, S CLIMENTE AND S MARIA.

Master of San Davino. *See under* GUALTIERI DI GIOVANNI.

Master of S Jorge. *See* MARTORELL, BERNAT.

San Juan de la Peña Master. *See under* SAN JUAN DE LA PEÑA.

Master of San Lorenzo della Costa (*fl* Bruges, *c.* 1490–1500). South Netherlandish painter. The Master is known only from three ogive-shaped panels of equal dimensions (1.50×0.92 m) with the *Martyrdom of St Andrew* in the centre, the *Marriage at Cana* on the left and the *Raising of Lazarus* on the right (1499; all San Lorenzo della Costa, church). The central panel contains donor portraits. The altarpiece was commissioned by the Genoese merchant Andreas de la Coste (Andrea della Costa; *d* 1542), who became a citizen of Bruges in 1483 and to whom the Master was probably related. The merchant's wife, Agnes Adornes, whom he married in 1492, came from an influential Flemish-Genoese family. Although the three panels were executed in Bruges, on their completion they were shipped to Genoa and placed on the altar of St

Andrew in the church built by Lorenzo della Costa, located in the small town of San Lorenzo della Costa near Santa Margherita Ligure, on the coast near Genoa.

The panels are characterized by a funnelling perspective, which tends to draw the eye into the middle distance and background, and by faces rendered in *sfumato* and an overall chiaroscuro effect, which is sometimes considered uncharacteristic of the period. However, both the iconography and the design of the *Marriage at Cana* apparently inspired Gerard David, who had probably seen the paintings in Bruges. The Master of San Lorenzo della Costa is sometimes considered to be a Flemish painter active in Portugal, possibly a certain Frans Hendrickx or Francisco Henriques, who appeared there about 1502, but this proposition remains hypothetical.

BIBLIOGRAPHY

M. J. Friedländer: *Die altniederländische Malerei* (Berlin, 1924–37); Eng trans. as *Early Netherlandish Painting* (Leiden, 1967–76), vi/2 (1971), p. 125, Supp. 246

Mostra della pittura antica in Liguria (exh. cat. by A. Morassi, Genoa, Pal. Reale, 1946), pp. 51–2

A. Morassi: *Trittico fiammingo a San Lorenzo della Costa* (Florence, 1947)

N. Geirnaert and A. Vandewalle: *Adornes en Jeruzalem: Internationaal leven in het 15de- en 16de-eeuwse Brugge* (Bruges, 1983), pp. 32–4

H. J. Van Miegroet: *Gerard David* (Antwerp, 1989), pp. 307–8

HANS J. VAN MIEGROET

Master of S Marco (*fl* Barcelona, mid-14th century). Catalan illuminator and painter. He is named after the triptych of *St Mark* (Manresa, Mus. Hist. Catedral), which has been used as the basis of further attributions. There is no consensus, however, on either his identity or his oeuvre. He was first identified by Soler y March, who considered him to be a follower of Jaime Serra; others have identified him as Arnau de la Peña (a follower of Serra), Bernat Martorell or Arnau Bassa (*see* BASSA, (2)). Works attributed to the Master include a polyptych of the *Passion of Christ* (New York, Pierpont Morgan Lib.), part of the illumination of the *Llibre vert* (*c.* 1380–85; Barcelona, Arxiu Mun.), a *De regimine principi* by Egidio Colonna (U. Valencia, Bib., MS. 435) and the *Usatges de Barcelona* (Lleida, Ayuntamiento). Works belonging to the workshop include a Psalter (Paris, Bib. N., MS. lat. 8846), a copy of Gratian's *Decretals* (London, BL, Add. MSS 15274–5) and a Missal from Ripoll Abbey (Barcelona, Arxiu Corona Aragó, MS. 18). The style of the Master of S Marco is a synthesis of the native Catalan tradition with the style of Simone Martini.

BIBLIOGRAPHY

A. Soler y March: *La Peinture catalane à la fin du moyen âge* (Paris, 1933), pp. 39–40

M. Meiss: 'Italian Style in Catalonia and a Fourteenth Century Catalan Workshop', *J. Walters A.G.*, iv (1941), pp. 45–87

Spanish Painting (exh. cat., Toledo, OH, Mus. A., 1941), pp. 15–18

LYNETTE BOSCH

Master of S Maria. *See under* TAÜLL, S CLIMENTE AND S MARIA.

Master of S Trovaso (*fl* Venice, *c.* 1470). Italian sculptor. The artist is named after three superlative reliefs of unknown origin now set into an altar frontal in S Trovaso, Venice. Two of the reliefs depict *Angels Playing Musical Instruments* and the third shows *Angels Carrying the Instruments of the Passion* (there are anonymous copies

of the reliefs in Berlin, Dahlem, Skulpsamml.). Attempts to attribute the works of the Master of S Trovaso to Agostino di Duccio (Venturi) have not found favour. Pope-Hennessy thought it possible that a relief depicting the *Head of St John the Baptist* in the sacristy of S Maria del Giglio, Venice, was by the same Master. Paoletti (1893) stressed the similarities with works by Antonio Rizzo. Comparison of the S Trovaso panels with Rizzo's reliefs (executed after 1486) for the Scala dei Giganti in the courtyard of the Doge's Palace, Venice, adds weight to the hypothesis that the Master can be identified with Rizzo, but this suggestion—more convincing than any other—has gained little support.

BIBLIOGRAPHY

P. Paoletti: *L'architettura e la scultura del rinascimento a Venezia* (Venice, 1893), p. 159

L. Planiscig: 'Pietro Lombardi ed alcuni bassirilievi veneziani del '400', *Dedalo*, x (1929–30), pp. 461–81

A. Venturi: 'Pietro Lombardi e alcuni bassirilievi veneziani del '400', *L'Arte*, i (1930), pp. 191–205

J. Pope-Hennessy: *Italian Renaissance Sculpture* (London, 1958, 3/1985), pp. 92, 337

N. Huse and W. Wolters: *Venedig, die Kunst der Renaissance: Architektur, Skulptur, Malerei, 1460–1590* (Munich, 1986), p. 161

WOLFGANG WOLTERS

S Zeno Masters (*fl c.* 1310–60). Italian painters. Simeoni and Sandberg-Vavalà grouped a number of Veronese painters comprising the first and second phases of 14th-century painting in Verona under the labels First and Second S Zeno Master. Cuppini later divided the First S Zeno Master's work between three distinct hands: the Redentore Master, who painted frescoes in S Fermo Maggiore, Verona, in 1319–20, as well as other works in S Zeno Maggiore and Santa Trinità in Verona; the Master of Corte Lepia, named after a series of frescoes in S Giuliano di Corte Lepia, Vago di Lavagno, but who also worked in S Zeno Maggiore; and the Master of the Presentation, painter of the eponymous fresco and others in S Zeno. Of these the Redentore Master, who painted imposing portraits of the Franciscan *Prior Daniele Gusmerio* and the donor *Guglielmo Castelbarco* in S Fermo, is the most striking. His bulky figures, solidly modelled and with large staring eyes, correspond to the style of Paduan painting after Giotto. The Second S Zeno Master (probably representing a number of workshops) was responsible for frescoes throughout Verona, including more than 20 in S Zeno itself. With the exception of a dainty but strikingly undramatic *St George and the Princess* and three *Scenes from the Life of St Nicholas* in S Zeno, these are almost invariably votive renderings of the *Virgin and Child*, with or without saints, of a standard type repeated with little variation. This master's, or group's, style is more refined, with more consciously rhythmic drapery folds. The simple wooden thrones of the earlier frescoes are occasionally embellished with more intricate Gothic detail, and the pallid and staring frontal *Virgins* of the Corte Lepia Master are replaced by a more gracious and humane model. A dated fresco of the *Virgin and Child with Saints* (1354) in S Anastasia, Verona, is a little more ambitious in scale and scope and probably represents the latest phase of the second S Zeno style, which towards 1360 blends almost imperceptibly into a style influenced by Turone.

BIBLIOGRAPHY
L. Simeoni: *La basilica di S Zeno a Verona* (Verona, 1909)
E. Sandberg-Vavalà: *La pittura veronese del trecento e del primo quattrocento* (Verona, 1926), pp. 44–100
M. T. Cuppini: 'Pitture del trecento in Verona', *Commentari*, xii (1961), pp. 75–83
——: La pittura e la scultura in Verona al tempo di Dante', *Dante e Verona* (exh. cat., ed. R. Gozzi; Verona, Castelvecchio, 1965), pp. 175–98

JOHN RICHARDS

Master of Schloss Lichtenstein (*fl c.* 1430–50). Austrian painter. He is named after Schloss Lichtenstein in Baden-Württemberg, Germany, the location of two panels of a winged altarpiece of the *Death* and *Coronation of the Virgin*. Two further cycles of pictures can be grouped around this pair of panels: fourteen panels with scenes from the *Lives of Christ and the Virgin* (Vienna, Belvedere; Vienna, Ksthist. Mus.; Philadelphia, PA, Mus. A.; ex-Kaiser-Friedrich Mus., Berlin; Moscow, Pushkin Mus. F.A.; Tallinn, A. Mus. Estonia; Munich, Alte Pin.; Warsaw, N. Mus.) and seven scenes from the *Passion* (Basle, Kstmus.; Esztergom, Mus. Christ.; Augsburg, Schaezlerpal.; Munich, Alte Pin., on dep. Augsburg, Schaezlerpal.). These panels were probably produced before the larger, more minutely executed panels at Schloss Lichtenstein; it is not known whether they belong to a single altarpiece or to several. The vertical format of the panels (some with surviving wooden framework) is pronounced, and the tall, thin figures are always placed in the very foreground of the picture. The backgrounds show selective indications of interiors or steep, simplified landscapes. The fact that the panels are in Russian, Swabian, Hungarian and Estonian collections increases the difficulty of locating this master. Pächt and Baldass were the first to assign him to the Viennese school of painting on the grounds of stylistic and iconographic similarities with the works of the Master of the Albrecht Altar and the Viennese Master of the Presentation of Christ (*fl c.* 1420–40). Like these two painters, the Master of Schloss Lichtenstein worked within the Transitional style that characterized the 1430s and 1440s. He was also influenced by contemporary Netherlandish painting and by 14th-century Italian art.

BIBLIOGRAPHY
H. Feuerstein: *Verzeichnis der Gemälde der fürstlich Fürstenbergischen Sammlungen zu Donaueschingen* (Donaueschingen, 1921), pp. 62–3
L. Baldass: 'Wiener Tafelmalerei II', *Der Cicerone*, xxi (1929), pp. 129–31
O. Pächt: *Österreichische Tafelmalerei der Gotik* (Augsburg, 1929), pp. 15–18
L. Baldass: 'Der Marienaltar des Meisters von Schloss Lichtenstein', *Jb. Preuss. Kstsamml.*, lvi (1935), pp. 6–21
S. Karling: *Einige Werke des Meisters von Schloss Lichtenstein in Tartu und Moskau* (Tartu, 1940)
A. Rosenauer: 'Meister v. Schloss Lichtenstein', *Gotik in Österreich* (exh. cat., Krems an der Donau, Minoritenkloster, 1967), pp. 104–5
E. Baum: *Katalog des Museums Mittelalterlicher Österreichischer Kunst*, Vienna, Belvedere cat. (Vienna, 1971), pp. 42–7

MONIKA DACHS

Master of Schöppingen (*fl* Westphalia, 1440–70). German painter. He is named after a *Passion* altarpiece in the parish church at Schöppingen. The only work associated with him that can be provisionally dated is a *St Nicholas* panel with four Church Fathers (1443; Münster, Westfäl. Landesmus.; ex-Gutes Althaus, Nordwalde). It is an excellent example of his style: richly robed figures with

small doll-like heads stand on grassy ground, brightly coloured but painted with restraint.

Of the Master's three known *Passion* altarpieces, the Haldern Altar (Münster, Westfäl. Landesmus.; ex-parish church, Haldern) is thought to be earliest, pre-dating the *St Nicholas*. The *Passion* is shown on the inner faces of both wings, with the outer faces scenes from the *Life of St John the Baptist* and from the *Legend of St Ludger*. It already shows all the distinguishing features of his style: in the *Crucifixion*, although gold ground is still used for the sky, an elevated viewpoint reveals numerous echelonned figures and landscape levels, while the subsidiary scenes are depicted with spare realism. The work is recognizably based on the Westphalian tradition of the Münster master who painted the altars at Warendorf, Darup and Isselhorst, but features such as the Salome show an acquaintance with the Master of Flémalle (cf. the latter's drawing in Brunswick, Herzog Anton Ulrich-Mus.), suggesting journeyman years spent in the Netherlands. In the Schöppingen Altar (*c.* 1454–7) the three *Passion* scenes are linked by interlocking spaces. The Haldern Altar's unity of time and space survives only in the two external faces of the wings, the *Annunciation* and the *Nativity*. The interior in the former is one of the first examples in Germany of the consistent realism characteristic of the Netherlands, and the scene glows with colour. Thirdly, an altar from a Soest church (destr. Berlin, 1945), weaker in all its details, must date from the late 1450s. The influence of Master Francke is apparent. The letters 'zur Way' written on the Soest *Crucifixion* have led to a suggested identification of the Master of Schöppingen as the Coesfeld painter Dietrich zur Wayge (*fl* 1429).

The effects of the realism that the Master introduced into German painting were widely felt: in the Schlägler Altar (Cleveland, OH, Mus. A.), attributed to the Hamburg painter Konrad von Vechte (*fl c.* 1425–44); the Unna Altar (before 1473; Frankfurt am Main, Cathedral), attributed to Hans Bornemann; the altar at Steinhagen (*c.* 1450–60; Protestant church); and in Johann Koerbecke's Langenhorst Altar (*c.* 1450; Münster, Westfäl. Landesmus.).

BIBLIOGRAPHY
T. Rensing: *Der Meister von Schöppingen* (Munich and Berlin, 1959)

HANS GEORG GMELIN

Master of the Schwarzes Gebetbuch. *See* MASTER OF ANTOINE OF BURGUNDY above.

Master of Seeon (*fl c.* 1420–40). German sculptor. His name is derived from the Benedictine abbey at Seeon, which formerly housed the *Virgin and Child Enthroned* (h. 1.08 m, *c.* 1428–35; Munich, Bayer. Nmus.). He was probably trained in Salzburg as a stone-carver, perhaps in the workshop that produced a column statue of the *Virgin* (*c.* 1425; Salzburg, Peterskirche). He must also, however, have studied with a wood-carver, as limewood became his chosen medium. The geographical distribution of the works attributed to him suggests that he settled in Mühldorf, south-east Bavaria.

The Master did not renounce the Salzburg *Schöne Stil* (*see* GOTHIC, §III, 1(iii)(c) and 2(iii)), but the drapery of his figures has sharp folds, rather than gentle waves, often piled up in parallel. The Virgin's cape on the Seeon example and others (e.g. *c.* 1425; Wasserburg am Inn, Frauenkirche) characteristically has plentiful, broad, inter-connecting groups of tubular folds. Facial features are prominent and often linearly delimited, with hair carefully rendered. Except for the Kolumban Christ Child (*c.* 1425 or earlier; Altenhohenau, SS Peter and Paul), children's bodies are usually hardly differentiated. Ears are strikingly simplified, and heads have a prominent crescent-moon shape. The heads of male saints (e.g. *St Erasmus*, after 1435; Pittenhart, St Nikolaus; *St Pancratius*, *c.* 1430–35; Niederbergkirchen, St Blasius) are characterful, with hair composed of strong, bulging curls. The latter example closely resembles the *St Nicholas* tympanum (1432–43) in the west portal of St Nikolaus, Mühldorf, which is the only stone sculpture attributed to this Master. It is also associated with a silver bust of *St Zeno* (remade 1467; Munich, Bayer. Nmus.) from the collegiate church at Isen, near Wasserburg, for which the Master may have made the wooden model. The numerous works that show his influence, including some of high quality, indicate a sizeable workshop, although only his extension of the *Schöne Stil* to free-standing wooden figures in association with altars is of more than local significance.

BIBLIOGRAPHY

H. K. Ramisch: 'Zur Salzburger Holzplastik im zweiten Drittel des 15. Jahrhunderts', *Mitt. Ges. Salzburg. Landesknd.*, civ (1964), pp. 1–87

Schöne Madonnen, 1350–1450 (exh. cat., ed. D. Grossmann; Salzburg, Dommus., 1965), pp. 41–4

D. Grossmann: 'Der Meister von Seeon', *Marburg. Jb. Kstwiss.*, xix (1974), pp. 85–138

Spätgotik in Salzburg: Skulptur und Kunstgewerbe, 1400–1530 (exh. cat., ed. J. Gassner; Salzburg, Mus. Carolino Augusteum, 1976), pp. 56, 104–10, nos 77, 128 [entries by W. Steinitz and A. Rohrmoser]

DIETER GROSSMANN

Master of the Seraph. *See* MASTER OF OTTO VAN MOERDRECHT above.

Master of Seu d'Urgell. *See* MASTER OF CANAPOST above.

Master of Sigmaringen. *See* STRÜB, (1).

Silver Birch Master. Name coined by Anthony Blunt (1950) for the artist he thought responsible for a group of small landscape paintings that show rocky, Italianate scenes in which trees with silvery bark and feathery foliage create decorative patterns against the sky. The group was then attributed to Gaspard Dughet by Shearman (1963), who argued that it represented the earliest phase of Dughet's development. Subsequently, Whitfield (1979) attributed all these paintings to Nicolas Poussin, arguing that Poussin began to paint landscapes earlier than had hitherto been believed and that these works might represent his first works in this genre. The problem was discussed by French (1980), when a work from this group, the *Landscape with Birch Trees and a Goatherd* (London, Colnaghi's; see 1980 exh. cat., fig. 1), was exhibited with early works by Dughet, the *Hagar and Ishmael* (Wilton House, Wilts) and the *Landscape with Hunters* (Keele U.). Other works from Blunt's Silver Birch group are the *Italian Landscape with a Cowherd* (London, N.G.) and the *Landscape with a Goatherd* (priv. col. see Whitfield, fig. 9), both of which are close to Poussin's *Landscape with St*

Jerome (Madrid, Prado), which Blunt accepted as by Poussin in 1959. The question of the attribution of the group of pictures thus remains open. Despite this artist's name, the silver birch is hardly found in Italy (where both Dughet and Poussin were active).

For further discussion *see* DUGHET, GASPARD and POUSSIN, NICOLAS.

BIBLIOGRAPHY

A. Blunt: 'Poussin Studies, V: The Silver Birch Master', *Burl. Mag.*, cxii (1950), pp. 69–73

A. Blunt and J. Shearman: *The Landscape Drawings*, iv/4 of *The Drawings of Nicolas Poussin* (London, 1963)

L. Salerno: *Pittori di paesaggio del seicento a Roma* (Rome, 1977–8), ii, nos 86.1–86.3

C. Whitfield: 'Poussin's Early Landscapes', *Burl. Mag.*, cxxi (1979), pp. 10–19

Gaspard Dughet Called Gaspar Poussin (1615–75) (exh. cat. by A. French, London, Kenwood House, 1980)

A. Blunt: 'Letter to the Editor: The Silver Birch Master, Nicolas Poussin, Gaspard Dughet and Others', *Burl. Mag.*, cxxii (1980), pp. 577–82

M. N. Boisclair: *Gaspard Dughet* (Paris, 1986)

Master of the Small Landscapes (*fl* mid-16th century). Flemish draughtsman. Name given to the anonymous artist who produced a series of drawings (e.g. Cambridge, Fitzwilliam; Chatsworth, Derbys; Darmstadt, Hess. Landesmus.) from which 44 landscape etchings were made, probably by Jan and Lucas van Doetechum. The etchings were published in Antwerp by Hieronymus Cock in two series, the first (1559) consisting of 14 sheets with the title *Multifarium casularum*, the second (1561), containing 30 sheets, entitled *Praediorum villarum*; an enlarged edition with both series was also issued in 1561. Cock did not name the artist, but the designs are attributed to Cornelis Cort in a third edition (Antwerp, 1601) published by Theodor Galle (although *see also* CORT, CORNELIS).

In 1612 CLAES JANSZ. VISSCHER published copies of the etchings, which he claimed were after designs by Pieter Bruegel the elder. The Master of the Small Landscapes has also been identified with Cock himself, as well as with Joos van Liere (*d* 1583; see E. Haverkamp-Begemann in 1975 exh. cat.), Hans Bol and Cornelis van Dalem, while others have regarded the artist as an independent anonymous master. The drawings, which are in reverse to the etchings, were retouched and extra figures added, perhaps by an artist in Cock's studio *c.* 1560. Liess separated them into two groups and concluded that most are by a follower of Bruegel, possibly Cort, with the remaining 18 by Bruegel himself, forming part of the *naer het leven* ('after the life') figure studies, which have themselves been attributed by other scholars to Roelandt Savery. He further suggested that the studies were taken from nature and may have been preparatory drawings for Bruegel's winter scenes, including the *Hunters in the Snow* (1565; Vienna, Ksthist. Mus.), but this view has not been widely accepted.

BIBLIOGRAPHY

Pieter Bruegel d. Ä. als Zeichner: Herkunft und Nachfolge (exh. cat. by F. Anzelewsky and others, W. Berlin, Kupferstichkab., 1975)

R. Liess: 'Die kleinen Landschaften Pieter Bruegels d. Ä. im Lichte seines Gesamtwerks', *Ksthist. Jb. Graz*, xv–xvi (1979–80), pp. 1–116; xvii (1981), pp. 35–150

Master of the Stadholder Maria. *See* MASTER OF THE REGENT above.

Master of the Stauffenberg Altar (*fl* mid-15th century). German painter. He is named after the Stauffenberg Triptych (Colmar, Mus. Unterlinden). When open, this shows a *Pietà* (1.27x0.97 m), flanked by scenes of the *Annunciation* and the *Nativity* (both 1.27x0.42 m), and when closed the *Crucifixion*, with donors who can be identified from their coats of arms as Hans Erhard Bock of Stauffenberg, Bailiff of Rouffach (nr Colmar), and his wife, Aennelin of Oberkirch. The year of their marriage, 1454, and that of 1460, when Aennelin is mentioned as a widow, help to date the work. Sterling (1980), however, dated the main *Pietà* panel slightly earlier than the wings. The *Pietà* panel shows the influence of Rogier van der Weyden and is distinguished by its imposing grandeur. The triptych also shows traces of the so-called International Gothic style and a tendency towards lyricism that is peculiar to Colmar. These features suggest that the Master was active in Alsace in the mid-15th century, after Konrad Witz but just before Martin Schongauer, at the time when Netherlandish influence was penetrating the Upper Rhine. Bauch thought that the Master should be identified with the young Schongauer (*see* SCHONGAUER, (1)), but Stange considered that he was an independent painter and attributed to him the Bergheim Predella, which depicts *St John the Baptist Preaching* and *St George and the Dragon* (tempera on pine; Colmar, Mus. Unterlinden). He also regarded him as a formative influence on the Housebook Master. Sterling (1979–82) has since, however, defined his role more clearly and has placed his activity in the artistic milieu of Hans Hirtz, Jost Haller (to whom he attributed the Bergheim predella), Caspar Isenmann and the Master of the *Man of Sorrows* (Boston, MA, Mus. F.A.), which was important for Schongauer's early development.

BIBLIOGRAPHY
I. Futterer: 'Eine Gruppe oberrheinischen Tafelbilder des 15. Jahrhunderts', *Oberrhein. Kst*, ii (1926–7), p. 24
K. Bauch: 'Schongauer Frühwerke', *Oberrhein. Kst*, v (1932), pp. 171–83
A. Stange: *Die deutschen Tafelbilder vor Dürer*, ii (Munich, 1970), no. 66
C. Sterling: 'Jost Haller, Maler zu Strassburg und zu Saarbrücken in der Mitte des 15. Jahrhunderts', *Wien. Jb. Kstgesch.*, xxxiii (1980), pp. 99–126
——: 'Jost Haller, peintre à Strasbourg et à Sarrebrück au milieu du XVe siècle', *Bull. Soc. Schongauer* (1979–82), pp. 53–111 [rev. of article of 1980]

CHRISTIAN HECK

Master of the Sterzing Altarpiece (*fl c.* 1450–70). Austrian painter. He painted the wings (Vipiteno, Mus. Multscher) of the 1456–8 altarpiece in Sterzing (now Vipiteno, Italian Tyrol), whose centrepiece is formed of wood sculptures of the standing *Virgin and Child* flanked by saints, by HANS MULTSCHER (all Vipiteno, Unserer Lieben Frau im Moos). Some writers have identified him as Multscher, but most reject this. The altarpiece survives only in fragments but can be in part reconstructed. The paintings were on the wings of the triptych altarpiece. The inner panels showed the *Annunciation*, the *Nativity*, the *Adoration of the Magi* and the *Death of the Virgin*, and when closed the outer panels showed the Passion scenes of *Gethsemane*, the *Flagellation*, the *Crowning with Thorns* and the *Way of the Cross*. Multscher's sculpture was surmounted by a standing *Man of Sorrows* flanked by the *Virgin* and *St John the Evangelist*. The painter of the wings, like Multscher, worked in Ulm, but the strong influence of Rogier van der Weyden shows a trend away from earlier Ulm painting such as the expressive and harsh realism of the Wurzach Altarpiece (1437; Berlin, Gemäldegal.), controversially thought to be by Multscher. In the Sterzing panels' representation of interior space and landscape, and in the elongated figure poses and facial types, the influence of Rogier van der Weyden is evident, but the figure compositions have a compression and hard clarity of outline different from that of the Flemish master. Other works by the Master of the Sterzing Altarpiece are the Heiligkreuztal Altarpiece depicting the *Death of the Virgin* (1450–60; Karlsruhe, Staatl. Ksthalle; Stuttgart, Staatsgal.), the *Bridal Pair* (*c.* 1470; Cleveland, OH, Mus. A.) and a *St Mary Magdalene* (*c.* 1470; Oberlin Coll., OH, Allen Mem. A. Mus.).

BIBLIOGRAPHY
Thieme–Becker
A. Stange: *Deutsche Malerei der Gotik*, viii (Munich, 1956/R Nendeln, 1969), pp. 5–9, figs 3–15
N. Rasmo: *Der Multscheraltar in Sterzing* (Bolzano, 1963)
M. Tripps: *Hans Multscher* (Weissenhorn, 1969), pp. 125–31, 263–8, figs 241–8
A. Stange: *Kritisches Verzeichnis der deutschen Tafelmalerei vor Dürer*, ii (Munich, 1970), pp. 124–7, nos 568–79
U. Söding: 'Hans Multschers Sterzinger Altar', *Münchn. Jb. Bild. Kst*, xl (1989), pp. 39–44, 68–71

NIGEL J. MORGAN

Stratonice Master (*fl c.* 1470–1510). Italian painter. He was named by Berenson (1931) after two cassone panels with scenes from the *Story of Antiochus and Stratonice* (San Marino, CA, Huntington A.G.). Berenson also attributed to the Master two large panels of the *Rape of Proserpina* and the *Story of Orpheus and Eurydice* (ex-priv. col., Vienna, see Berenson, 1931, pp. 736–7) and a group of paintings that combine Sienese and Florentine stylistic elements. Berenson's suggestion that he was a Sienese master active from 1475 to 1490, influenced by Francesco di Giorgio Martini, Filippino Lippi and Botticelli, was accepted by van Marle and Waterhouse. However, Fahy (1965) suggested that the Master might have had connections with Lucca and (1966) distinguished three phases in his career. From 1470 to 1480 there was the first, Sienese, phase when he was influenced by Liberale da Verona and Francesco di Giorgio Martini (see fig.). During a second, Florentine, phase the Master absorbed (*c.* 1480) the styles of Filippino Lippi and Botticelli, while in a third, Lucchese, phase (*c.* 1480 onwards) he had close links with contemporary painters in Lucca.

Meloni Trkulja attributed a triptych of the *Virgin and Child with SS John the Baptist, Vitus, Modestus and Peter* (Montignoso, nr Massa, SS Vito and Modesto) to the Master's Lucchese phase, but Tazartes (1985) found the contract for the triptych, made in 1482 between the Operai of the church and the painter Michele Ciampanti of Lucca (*see* CIAMPANTI, (1)), thus leading to the attribution of some of the Stratonice Master's work to that artist. The Stratonice Master's Florentine and Lucchese phases coincide perfectly, in terms of chronology and style, with Ciampanti's career. The *Virgin and Child with SS Ursula, Agatha and Angels* (Birmingham, AL, Mus. A.), attributed

Stratonice Master: *Virgin and Child with an Angel*, tempera on canvas, 1470–80 (Vienna, Lederer Collection)

E. K. Waterhouse: 'Two Panels from a Cassone by Montagna in the Ashmolean Museum', *Burl. Mag.*, lxxxix (1947), pp. 46–7
F. Zeri: 'The Beginnings of Liberale da Verona', *Burl. Mag.*, xciii (1951), pp. 114–15
E. Fahy: 'A Lucchese Follower of Filippino Lippi', *Paragone*, xvi/185 (1965), pp. 14–16
——: 'Some Notes on the Stratonice Master', *Paragone*, xvii/197 (1966), pp. 17–28
B. Fredericksen: 'The Earliest Painting by the Stratonice Master', *Paragone*, xvii/197 (1966), pp. 53–5
L. Bellosi: 'Un "S Sebastiano" del Maestro di Stratonice', *Paragone*, xviii/207 (1967), pp. 62–3
S. Meloni Trkulja: article in *Boll. A.*, n.s. 5, liii/1 (1968), p. 53
B. Berenson: *Central and North Italian Schools* (1968), vol. ii, pp. 256–7
M. Ferretti: 'Percorso lucchese', *An. Scu. Norm. Sup. Pisa*, n.s. 2, v/3 (1975), pp. 1046–52
——: 'Di nuovo sul percorso lucchese', *An. Scu. Norm. Sup. Pisa*, n.s. 2, viii/3 (1978), pp. 1247–8
M. Natale: 'Note sulla pittura lucchese alla fine del quattrocento', *Getty Mus. J.*, 8 (1980), pp. 5–58
C. Ferri: 'Nuove notizie documentarie su autori e dipinti del'400 lucchese', *Actum Luce*, xi/1–2 (1982), pp. 53–72
M.Tazartes: 'Anagrafe lucchese, II. Michele Ciampanti: Il Maestro di Stratonice?', *Ric. Stor. A.*, 26 (1985), pp. 18–27
——: 'Nouvelles Perspectives sur la peinture lucquoise du quattrocento', *Rev. A.*, 75 (1987), pp. 29–36

MAURIZIA TAZARTES

Master of the Straus Madonna (*fl c.* 1385–1415). Italian painter. His oeuvre has been reconstructed (Longhi; Offner) around a *Virgin and Child* (ex-Percy S. Straus priv. col., New York; Houston, TX, Mus. F.A., 44.565) formerly confused with a 14th-century Sienese panel (44.566) with the same provenance and in the same museum. Of over 30 surviving panels painted in Florence and its environs, the Master's only dated work is the small, incisive *Man of Sorrows* (1405; Warsaw, N. Mus.). One of the most individual and lyrical Late Gothic Tuscan painters, he bridges the gap between Agnolo Gaddi and Lorenzo Monaco. His slender, pale figures blend spiritual evanescence with Giottesque solidity of form and are at their most expressive in the *Man of Sorrows with Instruments of the Passion* of *c.* 1395 and the *Annunciation* of *c.* 1405 (both Florence, Accad.), in which a highly refined sense of design balances perfectly with a poetic and vivid sense of colour. Striking touches of realism, as seen in the cockerel of the Passion or Gabriel's lilies, enliven these scenes. The subtly modelled *Virgin and Child with Two Angels* in the church at Sagginale (nr Borgo San Lorenzo), originally flanked by *SS John the Baptist* and *Dominic* (both Oxford, Christ Church Pict. Gal.), is one of the Master's finest mature works. Like Starnina and influenced in part by Spinello Aretino and the Giottesque revival, his graceful yet quietly compelling figures were important for the generation of Masolino in the last years of the Late Gothic style.

BIBLIOGRAPHY
R. Longhi: 'Ricerche su Giovanni di Francesco', *Pinacotheca*, i (July–Aug 1928), pp. 34–8; rev. as '*Me Pinxit*' e quesiti caravaggeschi, *1928–1934* (Florence, 1968)
R. Offner: 'La mostra del tesoro di firenze sacra', *Burl. Mag.*, lxiii (1933), pp. 166–78
L. Bellosi: 'Da Spinello Aretino a Lorenzo Monaco', *Paragone*, 187 (Sept 1965), pp. 18–43
F. Zeri: 'Italian Primitives at Messrs. Wildenstein', *Burl. Mag.*, cvii (1965), pp. 252–6
Arte nell'Aretino (exh. cat. by A. M. Maetzke, Arezzo, S Francesco, 1974–5), pp. 72–4, cat no. 24
M. Boskovits: *Pittura fiorentina alla vigilia del Rinascimento, 1370–1400* (Florence, 1975), pp. 136–8, 362–6

to the Master by Berenson (1931), has echoes of Botticelli and contemporary Lucchese masters such as Vincenzo Frediani (the former Master of the Immaculate Conception), the Master of the Lathrop Tondo and the sculptor Matteo Civitali. The works attributed to the Stratonice Master's early Sienese period (1470–80), however, are hard to reconcile with the works grouped around Ciampanti's Montignoso Triptych, and their chronology is difficult to establish. The Master's last years are also difficult to categorize. Ferretti (1975 and 1978) suggested that a group of paintings dependent on Sienese and Umbro-Tuscan sources, including the *Virgin and Child with Saints* (Avignon, Mus. Petit Pal.) and the *Virgin and Child with SS John the Baptist and Mary Magdalene* (Paris, Heim & Cie), date from the last phase of the Master's career at the end of the 15th century. This phase might coincide with Michele Ciampanti's last period. Natale (1980), however, attributed this group of works to the Master of St Philip (later identified as Ciampanti's son, Ansano di Michele Ciampanti; *see* CIAMPANTI, (2)).

BIBLIOGRAPHY
R. van Marle: *Italian Schools* (1923–38), xvi, pp. 509–13
B. Berenson: 'Quadri senza casa: Il quattrocento senese', *Dedalo*, xi (1931), pp. 735–46

A. Tartuferi: 'Qualche considerazione sul Maestro della Madonna Straus e due tavole inedite', *A. Crist.*, lxxv/720 (1987), pp. 161–8
——: 'Master of the Strauss Madonna', *The Martello Collection: Further Paintings, Drawings and Miniatures, 13th–18th Centuries* (Florence, 1992), pp. 132–5, no. 31

FRANK DABELL

Talbot Master [Master of John Talbot] (*fl* Normandy, *c.* 1430–60). Illuminator. The Master takes his name from two manuscripts commissioned by John Talbot, 1st Earl of Shrewsbury, one of the English army leaders in France during the final stages of the Hundred Years War (1337–1453). The Shrewsbury Book (London, BL, Royal MS. 15. E. VI), a collection of romances and didactic texts, was presented by Talbot to Margaret of Anjou, almost certainly as she passed through Rouen in 1445 on her way to marry the English king Henry VI. The finest miniatures, including two with representations of Talbot himself, are best taken as the basis for the style of the Talbot Master, since they are of higher quality than any in the other manuscript, a Book of Hours (Cambridge, Fitzwilliam, MS. 40–1950), which probably dates to within ten years of the Earl's marriage to Margaret Beauchamp in 1425.

The obvious place for Talbot to order French books was Rouen, the capital of English Normandy until 1449. Liturgical books associable with the Talbot Master, for example the Book of Hours of Rouen Use (Paris, Bib. N., MS. lat. 13283), support this localization. A compilation dating perhaps from the first half of the 1450s, bearing the arms of the *échevins* of Rouen and including anti-English propaganda by the loyalist French writer Alain Chartier (Paris, Bib. N., MS. fr. 126), contains miniatures by the Talbot Master. This shows that he did not follow the English retreat across the Channel—unlike the Fastolf Master, from whom his style seems to derive and with whom he has been confused. Both shared a love of emphatic outline and surface pattern, but the Talbot Master seldom attempted the more complex modelling of the Fastolf Master, preferring flat areas of colour. His figures are characterized by pursed red lips and stiff gestures. Linearity made his style easy to imitate. With lesser artists, the style degenerated into a repetitive and awkward simplicity, evident in the Shrewsbury Book itself, yet its accessibility ensured the continuing influence of the Talbot Master's technique and compositions as Rouen's flourishing book trade expanded to make it a major centre for French illumination.

BIBLIOGRAPHY
F. Wormald and P. Giles: *A Descriptive Catalogue of the Additional Illuminated Manuscripts in the Fitzwilliam Museum Acquired between 1895 and 1979 (Excepting the McClean Collection)*, 2 vols (Cambridge, 1982), ii, pp. 444–8 [contains full bibliog.]
The Last Flowering: French Painting in Manuscripts, 1420–1530, from the American Collections (exh. cat. by J. Plummer and G. Clark, New York, Pierpont Morgan Lib., 1982), p. 17, no. 24 [contains full bibliog.]

CATHERINE REYNOLDS

Master of the Tegernsee Altar (*fl c.* 1440–60). German painter. He is named after the main altarpiece (1444–5) at the former Benedictine monastery of St Quirinus at Tegernsee. Since the altarpiece was documented as the *tabula magna*, he is also called the Master of the Tegernsee Tabula Magna. He was thought to be the Munich painter Gabriel Mälesskircher until it was demonstrated (Buchner, 1938–9) that he belonged to a generation preceding that of Mälesskircher, whose 13 altarpieces for the Tegernsee Monastery were painted from 1474. Recently discovered archival evidence (Liedke, 1982) points to the Munich painter Gabriel Angler the elder (*c.* 1405–?1462) as the artist in question. The centre of the now dismembered *tabula magna* consisted of two oblong panels set one above the other, the *Crucifixion* (Nuremberg, Ger. Nmus.) above *Christ Carrying the Cross* (Munich, Bayer. Nmus.). Four other *Passion* scenes appeared on the interior of the flanking wings, and four scenes from the *Life of St Quirinus* were seen when the wings were closed. The unidealized, rude and bulky figures reveal the Master to have been an unrestrained and highly expressive exponent of a particular kind of realism, also associated with the Master of the Tucher Altar and with Hans Multscher. In the late 17th century the backgrounds of the principal panels were repainted with dark and stormy skies, which produces an effect not altogether out of keeping with the original emotional tenor. In another large *Crucifixion* from Tegernsee (1439–40; Munich, Alte Pin.) he painted the scene in grisaille with an elaborate architectural frame, as if the painting were a stone retable.

BIBLIOGRAPHY
Thieme–Becker; *AKL*
Die Anfänge der Münchner Tafelmalerei (exh. cat. by K. Feuchtmayr, Munich, Neue Staatsgal., 1935), pp. 24–34
E. Buchner: 'Der wirkliche Gabriel Mälesskircher', *Münchn. Jb. Bild. Kst*, n. s. 1, xiii (1938–9), pp. 36ff
W. Pinder: *Die deutsche Kunst der Dürerzeit* (Leipzig, 1940), pp. 44–50
K. Oettinger: 'Die Blütezeit der Münchner gotischen Malerei', *Z. Dt. Ver. Kstwiss.*, viii (1941), pp. 17–20
E. Buchner: *Malerei der deutschen Spätgotik* (Munich, 1960), pp. 16–17
A. Stange: *Deutsche Malerei der Gotik*, x (Munich, 1960), pp. 63–8
C. A. zu Salm and G. Goldberg: *Altdeutsche Malerei*, Munich, Alte Pin. cat., ii (1963), pp. 152–3
V. Liedke: 'Die Münchner Tafelmalerei und Schnitzkunst der Spätgotik, II: Vom Pestjahr 1430 bis zum Tod Ulrich Neunhausers 1472', *A. Bavar.*, xxix/xxx (1982), pp. 1–34

CHARLES TALBOT

Master of Terenzano. *See* MASTER OF THE CAPPELLA MEDICI POLYPTYCH above.

Master of the Thomas Altar. *See* MASTER OF THE ST BARTHOLOMEW ALTAR above.

Master of the Tiburtine Sibyl (*fl c.* 1470–90). North Netherlandish painter. He was one of the major artists active in Haarlem during the last quarter of the 15th century. He was named by Friedländer after the *Vision of Augustus and the Tiburtine Sibyl* (*c.* 1476; Frankfurt am Main, Städel. Kstinst. & Städt. Gal.; see fig.); the unusual subject-matter relates to the doctrine of the Immaculate Conception, an issue then current among the theologians at the University of Leuven. It is likely to have been painted soon after the Master left the Leuven workshop of Dieric Bouts I, where he is thought to have trained. Notable departures from Bouts's style are evident in the isolation of groups within a broad courtyard and the slightly mannered treatment of the doll-like figures. Soon after the Master arrived in Haarlem (*c.* 1480–82), where he established a large workshop, he painted the *Raising of Lazarus* (Mexico City, Mus. S Carlos). The influence of paintings of the same subject by Haarlem artists such as Albert van Ouwater and Geertgen tot Sint Jans is evident

Master of the Tiburtine Sibyl: *Vision of Augustus and the Tiburtine Sibyl*, oil on panel, 689×857 mm, *c.* 1476 (Frankfurt am Main, Städelsches Kunstinstitut und Städtische Galerie)

in some of the figures. A number of smaller panels produced by the Master and his workshop depict the Virgin and Child seated in an enclosed garden before an expansive view of a palace complex that resembles the background in the *Raising of Lazarus* (e.g. *Virgin and Child in a Garden*; Hayward's Heath, Sussex, R. Clarke priv. col., see Friedländer, iii, pl. 95).

Two large panels, the *Crucifixion* (Detroit, MI, Inst. A.) and the *Marriage of the Virgin* (Philadelphia, PA, Mus. A.), are representative of the artist's mature style, *c.* 1485–90. The *Crucifixion* is based on a widely copied type that originated in Bouts's workshop but incorporates an allegorizing landscape: beyond the tormentors on the right are a stagnant pond, a sandy gully with serpents and lizards and a rocky precipice with the proverbial dry tree of death and sterility, while behind the faithful mourners on the left is a verdant meadow in bright sunlight, symbolizing the promise of rebirth and salvation. Distinctive drapery patterns are repeated throughout his works, including the elaborate chevron pleats in the mantle of the male figure seen from behind. The Master also enriched his landscapes with a variety of flora and fauna that seem more picturesque than symbolic.

These features characterize many of the woodcuts in the printed books of Jacob Bellaert, published in Haarlem between 1484 and 1486, and it is thought that the Master provided the designs for them. Several figures from the paintings are repeated in them in exact detail, for example the male tormentor, seen from behind in the *Crucifixion*, is repeated in the *Raising of Lazarus* in the *Life of Christ*. Many of the illustrations of the *Book on the Properties of Things*, taken from the 13th-century treatise on natural history by Bartholomaeus Anglicus, reflect the Master's interest in nature. The frontispieces before the chapters on the properties of the sky, sea and earth are devoted entirely to the creatures that populate them: birds, fish and animals rendered with an astonishing realism. The frontispiece for the chapters on the divisions of the earth is a vast global landscape that anticipates the cosmic landscapes of the Antwerp Mannerists of the 1520s.

BIBLIOGRAPHY
M. J. Friedländer: *Die altniederländische Malerei* (Berlin, 1924–37); Eng. trans. as *Early Netherlandish* (1967–76), iii, pp. 41–2
W. R. Valentiner: 'Aelbert van Ouwater', *A. Q.* [Detroit], vi (1943), pp. 74–91
Middeleeuwse kunst der noordelijke Nederlanden (exh. cat., Amsterdam, Rijksmus., 1958), pp. 46–7

J. Snyder: 'The Early Haarlem School of Painting', *A. Bull.*, xlii (1960), pp. 49–55

D. Scillia: 'Three New Panels by the Master of the Tiburtine Sibyl', *Oud-Holland*, xciv (1980), pp. 1–10

A. Châtelet: *Les Primitifs hollandais* (Paris and Fribourg, 1980); Eng. trans. as *Early Dutch Painting* (Oxford and New York, 1981), pp. 140–43

JAMES SNYDER

Master of Tortuna (*fl c.* 1490–1503). Painter, active in Sweden. His known work comprises only the wall paintings of Tortuna Church in Västmanland, two painted wooden crosses (Falun, Dalarnas Mus.; Dalarna, Evertsberg Chapel) and the painted wings of an altarpiece in Venjan Church, Dalarna. He was apparently active in Sweden only for a short time. The paintings of Tortuna Church are among the most interesting medieval Swedish paintings to survive. Parts of them have been destroyed, but enough remains to give an idea of the style and of the programme, which is extremely well conceived. The paintings are expressive and highly original, covering the entire space like a tapestry. The figural scenes, separated by slender arcades, play against a background of leaves and large, elaborate flowers on the vaults and piers. The colours were red, turquoise, yellow, green, black and white, but most are now changed or faded. The figure style is mannered, stylized or very realistic, depending on the subject-matter. The programme strongly promotes the doctrine of Transubstantiation and the Eucharist and stresses the importance of the Rosary and the necessity of praying for souls in Purgatory. An expressive representation of the *Last Judgement* with the Nine Orders of Angels and the Seven Mouths of Hell (the Capital Sins) was placed opposite the original entrance. The programme is unique both in the choice of motifs and in its effect; the artist may perhaps have been a cleric.

BIBLIOGRAPHY

H. Cornell and S. Wallin: *Schwedische Kirchenmalereien des 16. Jahrhunderts* (Stockholm, 1954), pls 1–23

A. Nilsén: 'Kalkmålningarna i Tortuna kyrka' [The wall paintings in Tortuna Church], *Imagines medievales*, Acta Universitatis Upsaliensis, Ars Suetica, vii (1983), pp. 293–336

——: *Program och funktion i senmedeltida kalkmåleri: Kyrkmålningar i Mälarlandskapen och Finland, 1400–1534* [Programme and function in late medieval wall painting: painting in churches in the Mälar provinces and Finland, 1400–1534] (Stockholm, 1986)

ANNA NILSÉN

Master of Třeboň (*fl* last quarter of the 14th century). Bohemian painter. His name is taken from the small town (Ger. Wittingau) in south Bohemia from which his best-known work originated. This is the altarpiece painted for the church of St Giles in the Augustinian monastery in Třeboň, which must have been executed after 1380, when work on the church vaults was begun. The three surviving panels (Prague, N.G., Convent of St George) are from the wings and show scenes from the *Passion*: the *Agony in the Garden*, with *SS Catherine, Mary Magdalene* and *Margaret* on the outer side, the *Entombment* (*see* PRAGUE, fig. 7) with *SS Giles, Gregory* and *Jerome*, and the *Resurrection* (see fig.) with *SS James the Less, Bartholomew* and *Philip*. The modelling of the figures is achieved through a skilful use of colour and light, so that they appear to float in front of the stylized rocky backgrounds, giving the paintings a shimmering, visionary quality. The sense of depth is also

Master of Třeboň: *Resurrection*, tempera on canvas and panel, detail from the Třeboň Altarpiece, after 1380 (Prague, National Gallery, Convent of St George)

conveyed by light, with a strong diagonal emphasis that reinforces the feeling of insubstantiality.

On stylistic grounds a small group of works can be attributed to the Master of Třeboň or to his workshop. They are a damaged, double-sided panel of the *Virgin Mourning* and *St Christopher* (Církvice Parish Church, nr Kutná Hora, *in situ*); the *Adoration of the Magi* (Hluboká nad Vltavou, Castle); the *Crucifixion* (Prague, N.G., Convent of St George) from the chapel of St Barbara, near Třeboň; the *Virgin and Child* (Prague, N.G., Convent of St George) from Roudnice nad Labem; and the Aracoeli *Madonna* (Prague, N.G., Convent of St George), whose painted frame, the earliest of its kind in Bohemia, shows female saints and prophets that are close in style to the figures on the backs of the Třeboň panels. Most of the works come from provincial locations in Bohemia, but it seems probable that the Master of Třeboň worked in Prague, and several facts point to his close connections with the court: the provost of the chapel of All Saints in Prague Castle, Peter of Rožmberk, was a patron of the Augustinian monastery in Třeboň and may have been instrumental in commissioning the altarpiece for the church; the summer residence of the archbishops of Prague was at Roudnice. The consciously archaic figure of the Virgin of the Aracoeli *Madonna* is based on a painting (*in situ*) in the treasury of Prague Cathedral, said to be a gift from Pope Urban V (*reg* 1362–70) to Emperor Charles

IV and itself a copy of the venerated painting of the Virgin in S Maria in Aracoeli, Rome.

While some affinity with Franco-Netherlandish painting can be traced in the work of the Master of Třebon, his style is firmly grounded in the works of earlier Bohemian court painters, notably the *Apocalypse* cycle (partly destroyed) in the chapel of the Virgin at Karlštejn Castle and the chapel paintings in Prague Cathedral. His impact on Bohemian art was considerable and far-reaching. The main elements of his style, the elegant figures, soft colouring and elaborate, looping draperies, were adopted by his contemporaries almost immediately, in both panel painting and manuscript illumination, and were continued well into the 15th century, although with an increasing degree of stylization. His ideals were as rapidly assimilated by sculptors, and the *Schöne Stil*, which evolved in Central Europe at the end of the 14th century, owed much to his original vision.

BIBLIOGRAPHY

A. Kutal: *Gothic Art in Bohemia and Moravia* (London, 1971)
R. Chadraba, ed.: *Dějiny českého výtvarného umění* [History of Czech fine art], I/i (Prague, 1984)

AMANDA SIMPSON

Master of the Tree of Jesse in the Buurkerk. *See under* MASTER OF EVERT VAN SOUDENBALCH above.

Master of the Trinity of Turin (*fl* 1470–90). French painter. He is named after a *Trinity* in Turin (Mus. Civ. A. Ant.), a monumental panel (1.72×0.82 m) that shows Christ lying across the knees of God, who supports him with both hands. Several panels have been grouped around this work: a *Presentation in the Temple* (Greenville, SC, Bob Jones U. Gal. Sacred A.), a *Death of the Virgin* (Turin, Balbo Bertone priv. col.), a *Female Donor Presented by St Anthony* (Switzerland, priv. col.) and a *Female Donor Presented by St John the Baptist* (Switzerland, priv. col.), while a *Nativity* (Antwerp, Mus. Mayer van den Bergh) is attributed variously to the Master, to a disciple or to the workshop. The Master's origins are unclear: he may have been a Provençal painter (Castelnuovo) or a French artist with a Burgundian background (Sterling). The source for the unusual iconography of the *Trinity* has been traced to a miniature in the Hours of Saluces (1460–70; London, BL, Add. MS. 27697, fol. 175), one of the finest and most innovative manuscripts of the period, made for a female member of the House of Saluces. It has been suggested that both works are by the same artist (Avril; Romano). On this basis, a possible identification has been proposed of Antoine de Lonhy (*fl* 1460–62), an artist documented in Barcelona, Toulouse and Avigliana, near Turin, who undertook both miniature and large-scale work.

BIBLIOGRAPHY

E. Castelnuovo: 'Ragguaglio provenzale: Una "Ecole d'Avignon" di Michel Laclotte', *Paragone*, xl/131 (1960), pp. 35–49
C. Sterling: 'Etudes savoyardes, II: Le Maître de la Trinité de Turin', *L'Oeil* (Nov 1972), pp. 14–27
J. Gudiol and S. Alcolea i Blanch: *Pintura gótica catalana* (Barcelona, 1986), pp. 199–200
F. Avril: 'Le Maître des Heures de Saluces: Antoine de Lonhy', *Rev. A.* [Paris], 85 (1989), pp. 9–34
G. Romano: 'Sur Antoine de Lonhy en Piémont', *Rev. A.* [Paris], 85 (1989), pp. 35–44

□

Master of the Triumph of Death (*fl* first half of the 14th century). Italian painter. He was named by Thode after the *Triumph of Death*, part of the largest cycle of 14th-century frescoes in the Camposanto of Pisa. Other frescoes in the cycle attributable to him are the *Last Judgement*, *Hell*, the *Thebaid*, the *Resurrection*, *Christ Appearing to the Apostles* and the *Ascension*. They were severely damaged during World War II. The cycle is distinctive for its large scale, unique iconography and imaginative interpretation. The frescoes are executed in a violent and highly animated style, showing an inclination to irony and a use of the grotesque, distant both from the equilibrium and control of the figural language of Giotto and from the refinement of Sienese painting.

The *Triumph of Death* constitutes the most complex representation of this iconographic theme, combining the traditional motif of the Three Living and Three Dead (here enriched by the presence of hermits following the monk Macarius and by the lively and elegant procession behind the Three Living) with an image of Death flying over a pile of corpses towards a group of revelling youths and maidens (see fig.); depicted in the sky is a battle between angels and devils over the possession of souls. The eschatological significance of this vast work, painted on the walls of a cemetery, is confirmed by its juxtaposition to the *Last Judgement* and *Hell*, while the *Thebaid* is associated with the image of eremitical life, seen also in the *Triumph*. The unusual iconographic programme was probably inspired by the Dominicans of Pisa, among

Master of the Triumph of Death: *Triumph of Death* (detail; 1330s), fresco, Camposanto, Pisa

whom was the notable personality of Domenico Cavalca (*d* 1342).

The stylistic unity of the frescoes is now recognized, although Vasari attributed them to various artists, including Orcagna, Pietro Lorenzetti and Buffalmacco. They were once commonly attributed to Francesco Traini, the most important Pisan painter of the 14th century, an attribution that was affirmed by Meiss (1933) but contested by Longhi (1935), who proposed that the Master of the Triumph of Death was a Bolognese painter. His argument was based on certain similarities discerned between the frescoes and Bolognese painting, notably the work of Vitale da Bologna. Two frescoed figures of saints on a pier in S Paolo a Ripa d'Arno in Pisa have also been attributed to him. While the frescoes show characteristics typical of paintings of both Bologna and Pisa and also of Arezzo and Florence, their style is too heterogeneous to be assigned specifically to any one of these. More recently the Master of the Triumph of Death has been identified as BUFFALMACCO (Bellosi), who is recorded in the early literature as one of the greatest of 14th-century painters, although no authenticated work by him survives. He was of Florentine origin and worked in Pisa, Arezzo and Bologna, which would account for the plurality of styles evident in the frescoes.

Once dated after the middle of the 14th century and associated with the changed moral climate after the Black Death of 1348 (Meiss, 1951), the fresco cycle has more recently been dated earlier (Polzer; Meiss, 1971). Furthermore, the costumes and the appearance of the figures suggest that it was executed in the mid-1330s.

BIBLIOGRAPHY

G. Vasari: *Vite* (1550, rev. 2/1568); ed. G. Milanesi (1878–85), i, pp. 145, 161, 182–4

H. Thode: 'Der Meister vom *Triumphe des Todes* in Pisa', *Repert. Kstwiss* (1888), pp. 13–20

M. Meiss: 'The Problem of Francesco Traini', *A. Bull.*, xv (1933), pp. 97–173

R. Longhi: *La pittura padana del trecento* (Bologna, 1935); repr. in *Opere complete di R. Longhi*, vi (Florence, 1973), pp. 3–90 (35–51)

D. Guerry: *Le Thème du triomphe de la mort dans la peinture italienne* (Paris, 1950)

R. Longhi: 'La mostra del trecento bolognese', *Paragone*, v (1950), pp. 5–23 (12)

M. Meiss: *Painting in Florence and Siena after the Black Death* (Princeton, 1951)

L. Réau: *Iconographie de l'art chrétien*, ii (Paris, 1957), pp. 642–5

E. Carli: *Pittura pisana del trecento*, i (Milan, 1958)

M. Bucci: *Camposanto monumentale di Pisa: Affreschi e sinopie* (Pisa, 1960), pp. 35–65

J. Polzer: 'Aristotle, Mohammed and Nicholas V in Hell', *A. Bull.*, xlvi (1964), pp. 457–69

M. Meiss: 'Notable Disturbances in the Classification of Tuscan Trecento Paintings', *A. Bull.*, liii (1971), pp. 178–87

L. Bellosi: *Buffalmacco e il 'Trionfo della morte'* (Turin, 1974)

LUCIANO BELLOSI

Master of the Tucher Altarpiece (*fl c.* 1430–50). German painter. He is named after an altarpiece (*c.* 1445–50) that has been in the Frauenkirche, Nuremberg, since the early 19th century and known as the Tucher Altarpiece since at least 1615, when the Tucher family paid for its restoration on transfer from its original location in the Augustinerkirche to the Kartäuserkirche, both in Nuremberg. The Master belonged to a generation of painters, including Konrad Witz and Hans Multscher, recognized for their tough, sculptural-seeming realism. Unlike Witz, however, he eschewed the representation of space and concentrated on solid form, especially that of the human figure, as exemplified by the three scenes that make up the altarpiece's central panel, a *Crucifixion* flanked by an *Annunciation* (left) and *Resurrection* (right). The figures are placed with a minimum of *mise-en-scène* against a tooled gold ground. Elaborate, Late Gothic tracery in the form of a running baldacchino projects out over the figures as if they actually existed in relief and were not just painted. Frequently noted is the still-life that appears as part of the setting for the *Vision of St Augustine*, painted on the exterior of the right wing. Distributed on two shelves in the saint's study, this still-life resembles those placed in niches above the figures of prophets by the Master of the Aix Annunciation (1445; Brussels, Mus. A. Anc.; Amsterdam, Rijksmus., on loan to Paris, Louvre). However, neither the similarity of these motifs nor other stylistic evidence has been sufficient to reconstruct a clear history of this master outside Nuremberg. Eight works have been attributed to him (Stange, 1978), including multi-panelled altarpieces.

BIBLIOGRAPHY

P. Strieder: 'Der Tucheraltar in der Nürnberger Frauenkirche', *Kst & S. Heim*, xlviii (1950), pp. 173–7

A. Stange: *Deutsche Malerei der Gotik*, ix (Munich, 1958), pp. 23–31

P. Strieder: 'Miszellen zur Nürnberger Malerei des 15. Jahrhunderts', *Anz. Ger. Nmus.* (1975), pp. 44–6

A. Stange with P. Strieder and H. Härtle: *Kritisches Verzeichnis der deutschen Tafelbilder vor Dürer*, iii, ed. N. Lieb (Munich, 1978), pp. 40–46

Gothic and Renaissance Art in Nuremberg, 1300–1550 (exh. cat., New York, Met., 1986), no. 30, p. 474

P. Strieder: *Tafelmalerei in Nürnberg, 1350–1550* (Königstein im Taunus, 1993), pp. 37–44 [with colour illus.]

CHARLES TALBOT

Master of the Umbrella-trees. *See* MASTER OF THE BOQUETEAUX above.

Master of the Unicorn. *See* DUVET, JEAN.

Master of the Unicorn Hunt [Maître de la Chasse à la Licorne; Master of the Cloisters Unicorn; Master of Anne of Brittany] (*fl c.* 1480–1510). French designer of tapestries, illuminator, designer of woodcuts and stained glass. He was the principal designer of seven magnificent tapestries representing the pursuit and capture of a unicorn (New York, Cloisters), which costume details suggest were designed *c.* 1500. The tapestries were probably woven in Brussels, the pre-eminent centre for tapestry production *c.* 1500, but their style and provenance indicate the Master was of French origin. Although the initials AE found on all seven panels have been used to connect them with Queen Anne of Brittany, whose collection of tapestries was considerable, there is no clear indication for whom they were commissioned. They are first recorded in 1680 in Paris among the possessions of Duc François VI de La Rochefoucauld. The letters FR (restored, but original) on one of the tapestries suggests the possibility that the set was originally connected with François I de La Rochefoucauld (*d* 1516), a prominent member of the French court. Records of lost tapestries made *c.* 1500 for this family (Oxford, Bodleian Lib., MS. Gough DRW. Gaignières 16, fols 58–9), however, have not confirmed this theory.

Two of the *Unicorn Hunt* tapestries have *millefleurs* backgrounds, and the action takes place against a field composed largely of flowers. In the other five the figures are set in a proper landscape with sky (modern replacement) above. The Master's workshop may have been responsible for the design of all seven tapestries, but, if so, his own part was restricted to those with landscapes, the design of which is more accomplished.

He was particularly skilful in conveying a sense of excitement and occasion. In the *Unicorn Defends himself* (see fig.), for example, he brought out the vigour of the scene by showing the unicorn both kicking an assailant who attempts to spear it and at the same time disembowelling a hound with its horn. The action is complemented by great attention to colourful detail, especially the carefully observed costumes and wildlife. The artist's figure style is also distinctive: the women are dignified and elegant, whereas the men tend to be shown in movement or gesticulating, often with menacing or grimacing expressions.

Many of these characteristics are apparent in other tapestries of the period, some of which may be attributed to the Master of the Unicorn Hunt, including the remains of a set of *Famous Women* (Boston, MA, Mus. F.A.), made for Cardinal Ferry de Clugny between 1480 and 1483, and the *Story of Perseus* (France, priv. col., see Freeman, p. 204) bearing the arms of Charles Guillard (1456–1537). Similarities of style between these works and the five *millefleurs* tapestries known as the *Lady and the Unicorn* series (Paris, Mus. Cluny; *see* TAPESTRY, colour pl. I, fig. 1), probably commissioned by Jean IV Le Viste between 1484 and 1500, have led to the suggestion that the Master of the Unicorn Hunt also designed this set. There is at present insufficient evidence for such a theory.

Master of the Unicorn Hunt: the *Unicorn Defends himself*, tapestry, no. 4 of the *Unicorn Hunt* series, 3.68×4.01 m, *c.* 1500 (New York, The Cloisters)

The style of the Master of the Unicorn Hunt is evident in numerous woodcuts decorating printed books. Although it is unclear whether the Master was personally responsible for their design, all the major Parisian publishers produced books with illustrations in his style, suggesting his work enjoyed wide public acclaim. The date and place of publication of most of these books are known, establishing the Master's activity in Paris between *c.* 1480 and *c.* 1510. Apart from works of moral edification such as *L'Art de bien vivre* (Verard, 1492), most of the woodcut designs in the Master's style are in Books of Hours. In one example printed by Philippe Pigouchet for Simon Vostre (1498) the margins feature a stag hunt close to scenes in the *Unicorn* tapestries. Compositions similar to several of the woodcuts reappear in a small group of illuminated Books of Hours, all clearly painted by the same artist, who is probably identical with the Master. Because one of these, known as the Très Petites Heures (Paris, Bib. N., MS. nouv. acq. lat. 3120), was made for Anne of Brittany, some time after her marriage to Charles VIII of France in 1491, the Master of the Unicorn Hunt is sometimes known as the Master of Anne of Brittany. He executed at least one other royal commission, the stained glass of the rose window of the Sainte-Chapelle in Paris datable to 1485–98. Between 1485 and 1510 the Master was involved in at least one other glazing project in Paris, the chapel in the hôtel of the abbots of Cluny (now the Musée Cluny).

Anne of Brittany's accounts include a payment to Jean de Cormont, a Parisian painter, who in 1493 undertook work in connection with the Queen's Chapel. But this is no reason to attribute the illuminations in the Très Petites Heures to the same artist, and the Master of the Unicorn Hunt remains unidentified. The origin of the Master's style, however, can be traced with some confidence. His figure style, types and preference for crowded scenes have much in common with works by the Master of Coëtivy, a painter, illuminator and tapestry designer, active in the Loire Valley region *c.* 1455–75. The Coëtivy Master seems likely therefore to have trained the Master of the Unicorn Hunt, who probably inherited his model books. At an early stage in his career, *c.* 1480, the Master of the Unicorn Hunt would have moved to Paris, which was slowly regaining status as the seat of government. Although his style dominated Parisian art of the late 15th century, it attracted few imitators after *c.* 1510. By this date his clientele had become preoccupied with the fashion for Italian styles, which were not easily reconciled with his own manner. He did, however, occasionally make use of Italianate motifs. Winged putti holding swags, for example, appear in the Très Petites Heures, but this seems to have been more a concession to royal taste than a serious attempt to change the character of his output.

BIBLIOGRAPHY

F. Perrot: 'Un Panneau de la vitrerie de la chapelle de l'hôtel de Cluny', *Rev. A.*, x (1970), pp. 66–72

N. Reynaud: 'Un Peintre français, cartonnier de tapisseries au XVe siècle: Henri de Vulcop', *Rev. A.*, xxii (1973), pp. 6–21

G. Souchal: 'Un Grand Peintre français de la fin du XVe siècle: Le Maître de la Chasse à la Licorne', *Rev. A.*, xxii (1973), pp. 22–49

Chefs-d'oeuvre de la tapisserie du XIVe au XVIe siècle (exh. cat. by G. Souchal, intro. F. Salet; Paris, Grand Pal., 1973)

M. Freeman: *The Unicorn Tapestries* (New York, 1976)

A. Erlande-Brandenburg: *La Dame à la licorne* (Paris, 1979)

G. Souchal: ' "Messeigneurs les Vistes" et la "Dame à la licorne" ', Bib. Ecole Chartes, cxli (1983), pp. 209–67

THOMAS TOLLEY

Union Master. *See* MASTER OF FOGDÖ above.

Master of the Unruly Children (*fl* Florence, early 16th century). Italian sculptor. Conventional name for an anonymous sculptor much influenced by Verrocchio and Benedetto da Maiano, who produced a stylistically coherent group of statuettes in terracotta, the common feature being one or more mischievous children. These were first integrated by Wilhelm von Bode in connection with examples in the Altes Museum in Berlin, while later discussions concentrated on a *Charity* (see fig.) in the Victoria and Albert Museum, London (Pope-Hennessy, 1964), and a *Virgin and Child* in the Fogg Art Museum, Cambridge, MA (Avery, 1981). The terracottas ascribed to the Master of the Unruly Children are composed with complete assurance and convey a sense of movement and physical presence that indicates an accomplished sculptor. He executed a series of variations on the basic theme of a seated woman with children about her. Some examples with three children conform to the standard iconography of the Christian virtue of Charity. Others, with only one boy, apparently represent the *Virgin and Child*, in some

Master of the Unruly Children: *Charity*, terracotta, early 16th century (London, Victoria and Albert Museum)

of which he playfully reveals one of his mother's breasts as she reads. The similar facial features of the women, the disposition of their feet with knees swung to their left, their loose robes and ample cloaks, and the treatment of their drapery folds, especially across their knees and their feet along the bases, relate all of them to the same master. The modelling of the children, with the fleshiness of their cheeks, necks, arms, legs and abdomens, as well as their facial expressions and swirling curls of hair, also relate them to the same hand. In some compositions children appear on their own, quarrelling. All have rocky bases and, where necessary, are hollowed out behind to prevent cracking when being fired in the kiln. They are also often painted naturalistically. Close in style and subject to the statuettes by the Master of the Unruly Children are the glazed terracotta figures of the Christian Virtues, especially the *Charity*, made for the frieze depicting the *Seven Works of Mercy* on the external loggia of the Ospedale dell Ceppo in Pistoia. The curious ribbed and pointed halo, like an umbrella blown inside out, with which the *Charity* in Pistoia is endowed, frequently features in the work of the Master of the Unruly Children. Santi Buglioni is credited with glazing the figures at Pistoia between 1526 and 1528, but it is not known whether he actually modelled them.

It is unlikely that a sculptor as competent as the Master of the Unruly Children restricted himself to producing such a limited range of subjects, and the particular groups from which he derives his nickname form probably only one facet of a more extensive activity. Two other distinct series of statuettes in terracotta, on much the same scale and in a similar style, should perhaps be attributed to him: both manifest a tendency to produce a series of variations on a particular theme, and are clearly not *bozzetti* but finished sculptures made for collectors. One series takes the theme of a mêlée of soldiers fighting around a horseman. These have sometimes been attributed to Giovanni Francesco Rustici, a close associate of Leonardo da Vinci. The terracotta groups are indeed reminiscent of Leonardo's sketches for his fresco, the *Battle of Anghiari* (*c.* 1503–5; Florence, Pal. Vecchio; destr.). According to Vasari, Rustici executed terracotta groups of horses with men on or under them. There is thus ample evidence for an attribution of at least some of these works to Rustici, but others are very close in style, facial types and technique to works by the Master of the Unruly Children.

The other series that is related in style to the *Unruly Children* consists of reclining male figures with various attributes, often upturned urns, signifying that they are river gods. Again, there are the characteristics of form and movement, facial expression, and rendering of flesh, hair and drapery folds that appear in the *Unruly Children*. Examples of the *River Gods* are located in the Museum of Art, Rhode Island School of Design, and the Detroit Institute of Arts: some are reworkings of Michelangelo's models and drawings of the 1520s for the unexecuted *River Gods* intended for the tombs in his New Sacristy in S Lorenzo, Florence. They have sometimes been connected with Jacopo Sansovino, on the strength of their similarities with his Venetian works, especially the statuettes of the *Four Evangelists* on the altar-rail in S Marco's, Venice, and the terracotta *bozzetto* of *St John* in the Staatliche Museen Preussischer Kulturbesitz, Berlin. The work of the Master of the Unruly Children has also been compared with that of the Master of the David and St John Statuettes, and furthermore it has been suggested that sculptures attributed to these masters may be by Pietro Torrigiani. It has remained difficult to decide between the several candidates, one of whom may ultimately prove to be concealed behind the anonymity of the Master of the Unruly Children.

BIBLIOGRAPHY

J. Pope-Hennessy: *Catalogue of Italian Sculpture in the Victoria and Albert Museum* (London, 1964), nos 425–6

La civiltà del cotto (exh. cat., ed A. Paolucci; Impruneta, 1980), nos 2.16–2.18

C. Avery: *Fingerprints of the Artist: European Terra-cotta Sculpture from the Arthur M. Sackler Collections* (Washington, DC, and Cambridge, MA, 1981), no. 9

B. Boucher: *The Sculpture of Jacopo Sansovino* (New Haven and London, 1991), cat. nos 101, 118, 125–6

A. P. Darr: 'Verrocchio's Legacy: Observations Regarding his Influence on Pietro Torrigiani and other Florentine Sculptors', *Verrocchio and Late Quattrocento Italian Sculpture*, ed. S. Bule, A. P. Darr and F. S. Gioffredi (Florence, 1992), pp. 125–39

M. Ferretti: *Master of the Fretful Children* (Turin, 1992)

CHARLES AVERY

Master of Uttenheim (*fl* Tyrol, *c.* 1450/70–80). Austrian painter. He is named after a painting of the *Virgin and Child with SS Margaret and Barbara* (*c.* 1470; ex-parish church, Uttenheim in Pustertal; Vienna, Ksthist. Mus.). Other works by him are eight panels of the *Life of St Augustine* and one of *Joachim's Offering Rejected in the Temple* (both *c.* 1470) in the Augustinian convent of Neustift (now Novacella, Italy) near Brixen (now Bressanone, Italy); the *Coronation of the Virgin* (*c.* 1475–80; ex-Neustift; Munich, Alte Pin.); and scenes of the *Life of St Stephen* (*c.* 1470; Moulins, Mus. Dépt. A. & Archéol.). His connection with Michael Pacher is controversial: who influenced whom? Both produced dramatic perspective, strong contrasts of lighting and low viewpoints derived from north Italian painters such as Mantegna. It seems most probable that Pacher introduced these features to the region and that the Master of Uttenheim was his follower. Although some believe that his earliest works may be of *c.* 1450–60, all are likely to be later than *c.* 1470, first following Pacher's *St Lawrence* Altar (Vienna, Belvedere) in the *St Stephen* panels and then his *Fathers of the Church* Altar (*c.* 1475; Munich, Alte Pin.) in the *Coronation of the Virgin*.

The Master of Uttenheim has tentatively been identified with Marx Scherhauff (*fl* 1474–84), son of the painter Leonhard Scherhauff (*fl* 1460–74) of Brixen. In 1474–84 both gave money to Neustift, where Marx's brother Jerome Scherhauff was a canon. The several works by the Master of Uttenheim for Neustift may have resulted from close family connections with the convent.

BIBLIOGRAPHY

Thieme–Becker

O. Pächt: *Österreichische Tafelmalerei der Gotik* (Augsburg, 1929)

A. Stange: *Deutsche Malerei der Gotik*, x (Munich, 1960/*R* Nendeln, 1969), pp. 161–7, pls 253–60

I. Kmentt: *Der Meister der Uttenheimer Tafel* (Vienna, 1967)

Gotik in Österreich (exh. cat., Krems, Minoritenkirche, 1967)

N. Rasmo: *Michele Pacher* (Milan, 1969); Eng. trans. by P. Waley (London, 1971), pp. 198–210, 243

Spätgotik in Tirol (exh. cat., Vienna, Belvedere, 1973), no. 4

NIGEL J. MORGAN

Master of the Vatican Homer. *See under* GASPARO PADOVANO.

Master of the Vienna Schottenstift (*fl* Vienna, 1470s). Austrian painter. He is named after the altarpiece painted for the high altar of the Schottenkirche in Vienna (Vienna, Belvedere, and Schottenkirche, Stiftsgal.). All but 3 of the 24 panels have survived, most of them in their original state with paintings on both sides. Of these panels the sides for working days show 8 scenes of the *Passion*, and the Sunday sides show 16 scenes from the *Life of the Virgin*. The insides of the wings, which originally showed reliefs of standing saints, and the central shrine (probably a *Coronation of the Virgin*) have been lost.

The date 1469 over the depiction of the town gateway in the *Entry into Jerusalem* almost certainly refers to the start of the work. The scenes of the *Life of the Virgin* may well have been produced during the course of the 1470s. Fundamental to the narrative technique are the unified scene and concentration on the focus of the action. A predilection for landscape is also characteristic, with town and street views of Vienna and Krems incorporated in the *Visitation*, *Flight into Egypt* (*see* VIENNA, fig. 2) and *Christ Carrying the Cross*.

The altarpiece is an important example of Late Gothic Viennese painting, the character of which during the 1460s and 1470s can also be seen in such works as the panels in Maria am Gestade, Vienna. The extremely close connection with Netherlandish art is also perceptible in the Schottenkirche Altar. Elements are incorporated from the *Last Supper* (1467; Leuven, St Pieter) by Dieric Bouts I, and the composition of the *Lamentation* is derived from Rogier van der Weyden (Miraflores Triptych, Berlin, Gemäldegal.; *see* WEYDEN, VAN DER, (1), fig.1). Some of the panels also show links with the circle around Michael Wolgemut and Hans Pleydenwurff. The two stylistic trends suggest that at least two masters contributed to the altarpiece, but their contributions have not been certainly identified; one master was possibly responsible for the *Passion* scenes and the other for the *Life of the Virgin*. Nonetheless a single artist probably devised the overall plan. Of other works attributed to this master, two panels depicting the *Legend of St Barbara* (York, C.A.G.; Upton House, Warwicks, NT) seem the most plausible.

BIBLIOGRAPHY
B. Kurth: 'Über den Einfluss der Wolgemuth-Werkstatt in Österreich und im angrenzenden Süddeutschland', *Jb. Ksthist. Inst. Ksr.-Kön. Zent.-Komm. Dkmlpf.*, x (1916), pp. 89–90
O. Pächt: *Österreichische Tafelmalerei der Gotik* (Augsburg, 1929), pp. 19–21
F. Grossmann: 'Der gotische Hochaltar der Wiener Schottenkirche', *Kirchenkunst*, iv (1932), pp. 13–16
E. Strohmer: 'Die Malerei der Gotik in Wien', *Geschichte der bildenden Kunst in Wien*, ed. R. K. Donin (Vienna, 1955), pp. 26–33
A. Rosenauer: 'Zu einer niederländischen Beweinungskomposition und ihren Reflexen in der österreichischen Malerei des 15. Jhdts.', *Wien. Jb. Kstgesch.*, xxii (1969), pp. 157–66
E. Baum: *Katalog des Museums Mittelalterlicher Österreichischer Kunst, Unteres Belvedere, Wien* (Vienna, 1971), pp. 96–7

M. DACHS

Master of the View of Ste Gudule (*fl* Brussels, *c.* 1470–90). South Netherlandish painter. Friedländer gave this name to the painter of the '*Pastoral Sermon*' (*St Géry Preaching*; Paris, Louvre; see fig.), which includes a view of the cathedral of Ste Gudule in Brussels. The north tower is shown as unfinished, suggesting that the work was painted before 1480, a date confirmed by the style of dress. Other works attributed to the Master include: the *Virgin and Child with St Mary Magdalene and a Female Donor* (*c.* 1475–80; Liège, Mus. A. Relig. A. Mosan), which shows the influence of both Jan van Eyck and Rogier van der Weyden in its composition; the *Clothing of the Beggars* (Madrid, Mus. Thyssen-Bornemisza) and the *Liberation of the Prisoners* (Paris, Mus. Cluny), two panels from a series on the theme of mercy; the *Portrait of a Young Man* (London, N.G.), with the portal of Notre-Dame-du-Sablon in Brussels in the background; and the *Marriage of the Virgin* (Utrecht, Catherijneconvent). Several of these show the painter's interest in architecture and the buildings of Brussels, particularly those in Brabantine Gothic style.

The expressive style of the Master of the View of Ste Gudule tends towards caricature in the treatment of faces, which are often grimacing. Particular attention is paid to the mannered movements of the figures, with their agitated, outstretched hands and long, spreading fingers. Sometimes subjected to violent contortions, these figures are shown in arrested poses with no sense of communication between them. These peculiarities confer on the compositions a dynamism new to Netherlandish painting, further enhanced by the search for continuity between interior and exterior space. His pictorial idiom, although

Master of the View of Ste Gudule: '*Pastoral Sermon*' (*St Géry Preaching*), oil on panel, 950×680 mm, before 1480 (Paris, Musée du Louvre)

simplified in its structure, conforms to the general tendency among minor Brabantine masters of the end of the 15th century, and is relatively concise. It is characterized by an incisive vocabulary, subject to a formal play of lines, by the precision of detail, nervous and graphic touches to animate the surface of fabrics, modelling effects to enhance expressivity and, finally, by fine shadows in delicate relief, which accentuate the edges of clothing and the contours of faces and architecture. The Master's extravagant style can be distiguished from the more hardened style of his contemporaries, whose works were dominated by their Netherlandish predecessors, while the Master's expressionist tendency has stronger links with German work.

The Master's considerable oeuvre, which includes a number of altarpiece wings made for export, indicates a large workshop with many collaborators. For example the panel of *St Catherine and the Philosophers* (Dijon, Mus. B.-A.) and its pendant, the *Dispute of St Catherine* (Oberlin Coll., OH, Allen Mem. A. Mus.), the *Genealogy of St Anne* (U. Paris V, Fac. Médec.), the wings of the *Passion* altarpiece (Geel, St Dimpnakerk) and the *Presentation of the Virgin* (Brussels, Mus. A. Anc.) are workshop productions related in different degrees to the style of the Master but marked by a looser execution and a drier handling of paint. The Master may have collaborated with the Master of the Legend of St Barbara on an altarpiece illustrating the *Legend of St Géry*, as there are analogies in format and composition between the panels of this Legend (The Hague, Mauritshuis; Dublin, N.G.) attributed to the Legend of St Barbara Master and *St Géry Preaching*.

BIBLIOGRAPHY

Thieme–Becker: 'Meister von Sainte Gudule'
M. J. Friedländer: *Die Brüsseler Tafelmalerei gegen den Ausgang des 15. Jahrhunderts*, Belg. Kstdkml., i (Munich, 1923), pp. 317–20
——: *Die altniederländische Malerei* (Berlin, 1924–37); Eng. trans. as *Early Netherlandish Painting* (Leiden, 1967–76), iv (1969), pp. 62–3, 79–80, 85–6, 90, 99–100; xiv (1976), p. 12
P. Lefevre and O. Praem: 'Le Narthex et les tours de la collégiale Sainte-Gudule à Bruxelles', *Bull. Soc. Royale Archéol. Bruxelles* (1936), pp. 22–6
M. J. Friedländer: 'Der Meister von Sainte Gudule: Nachträgliches', *Annu. Mus. Royaux B.-A. Belgique*, ii (1939), pp. 23–31
J. Lavalleye: 'L'École bruxelloise de peinture au XVe siècle', *Bruxelles au XVe siècle* (exh. cat., Brussels, Mus. Com., 1953), pp. 165–87
M. Davies: *Early Netherlandish School*, London, N.G. cat. (London, 1968), pp. 113–15
Primitifs flamands anonymes: Maîtres aux noms d'emprunt des Pays-Bas méridionaux du XVe et du début du XVIe siècle (exh. cat., ed. A. Janssens de Bisthoven and others; Bruges, Groeningemus., 1969), pp. 114–15, 250–55; review by N. Reynaud and J. Foucart in *Rev. A.*, viii (1970), pp. 67–8
C. Sterling: 'Le Maître de la Vue de Sainte Gudule: Une Enquête', *Mus. Royaux B.-A. Belgique: Bull.* (1974–80), pp. 9–28
C. Périer-D'Ieteren: *Les Volets peints des retables bruxellois conservés en Suède et le rayonnement de Colyn de Coter* (Stockholm, 1984), pp. 95–6
——: *Colyn de Coter et la technique picturale des peintres flamands du XVe siècle* (Brussels, 1985), pp. 45, 47; figs 47, 80
M. Comblen-Sonkes: *Le Musée des Beaux-Arts de Dijon* (1987), xiv of *Les Primitifs flamands, I: Corpus de la peinture des anciens Pays-Bas méridionaux au quinzième siècle* (Brussels, 1951–), pp. 255–65

C. PÉRIER-D'IETEREN

Virgil Master. *See* APOLLONIO DI GIOVANNI.

Master of the Virgo inter Virgines (*fl* Delft, *c.* 1483–98). North Netherlandish painter and woodcut designer. He is named after the altarpiece of the *Virgin with SS Catherine, Cecilia, Ursula and Barbara* (Amsterdam, Rijksmus.), formerly in the convent at Konigsveld, near Delft. First distinguished as an individual artist in 1903 by Friedländer, who subsequently assembled a considerable oeuvre around the altarpiece in Amsterdam, the Master is the least concerned with elegance and the most uncompromisingly 'realist' of the early Netherlandish masters and has been characterized as a forerunner of the Dutch school.

Stylistic affinities between the Master's paintings and prints in books published in Delft between 1483 and 1498 by Jacob van der Meer, Christiaan Snellaert and Eckert van Homburch locate the artist in that city and indicate that he was also a woodcut designer. He may possibly be identified with Dirc Jansz. (*fl* 1474–95), one of the only two painters mentioned in the Delft archives during the later 15th century. The provenance of three of the Master's major works suggests that he, like his contemporaries Joos van Wassenhove and Hugo van der Goes, undertook commissions for foreign clients: the *Adoration of the Magi* triptych (Salzburg, Mus. Carolino Augusteum), formerly in Salzburg Cathedral, the *Crucifixion* triptych (Barnard Castle, Bowes Mus.), before *c.* 1840 in Lucca, and the *Crucifixion* (Florence, Uffizi), at Poggio a Caiano by 1792.

It is unclear to what extent analogies between the Master's work and that by some of the leading painters in the southern Netherlands reflect his own travels or a common, lost north Netherlandish source. Dieric Bouts painted spindly, poignant figures with curiously restrained but eloquent gestures, and these provide in many respects a point of departure for the more expressive and emotional characters of the Master of the Virgo inter Virgines. There are also compositional analogies between his Salzburg *Adoration of the Magi* and Hugo van der Goes's Monforte Altarpiece of the same subject (before 1473; Berlin, Gemäldegal.; *see* GOES, HUGO VAN DER, fig. 2). The Master's solemn, long-faced figures, often incongruously clad in gorgeous, fantastic dress, recall those in Joos van Wassenhove's *Calvary* triptych (Ghent Cathedral), and it has been pointed out that the figure of the Virgin and the eldest king in the Master's *Adoration of the Magi* (Berlin, Gemäldegal.) derive from Joos's painting of the same subject (New York, Met.), which was probably painted at Antwerp in 1460–64.

The narrow but highly distinctive range of facial types—with long necks, high cheekbones, prominent foreheads and slit-like mouths—makes the hand of the Master of the Virgo inter Virgines immediately apparent in such works as the Berlin *Adoration of the Magi*, the *Annunciation* (Rotterdam, Mus. Boymans–van Beuningen) and the *Entombment* (St Louis, MO, A. Mus.). In one of his finest works, the Liverpool *Entombment* (Liverpool, Walker A.G.; *see* fig.), the faces of the Virgin and her companions seem puffy and washed out with grief. Their ravaged expressions contrast dramatically with the exquisite gestures and delicate, measured steps of the two interlocked groups of protagonists. Similarly, the rich fur, brocade and gauze of Joseph of Arimathea's elaborate costume emphasize the pasty monochrome of the dead Christ's body and the barren grey–brown landscape background. This precise narrative has few equals in 15th-century painting. By contrast, the Master's Uffizi *Crucifixion* and the *Massacre*

Master of the Virgo inter Virgines: *Entombment*, 550×563 mm, oil on oak panel, *c.* 1483–98 (Liverpool, Walker Art Gallery)

of the Innocents from the inner shutters of his Salzburg Altarpiece have an uninhibited emotionalism that verges on the grotesque, inviting comparison with Hieronymus Bosch.

By comparison with the greatest north Netherlandish painter of his day, Geertgen tot Sint Jans, the Master of the Virgo inter Virgines lacked breadth of vision and was less refined and cosmopolitan. Nevertheless, the distribution of his works as far afield as Austria and Tuscany goes against the notion that he was in any sense a provincial artist. The predominantly emotional tenor of the Master's style would have recommended his work to Italian commentators, who praised Netherlandish painters above all for 'devoutness' and the skilful portrayal of feelings. His compositions have a sincerity in tune with the 'psychological realism' of the *Devotio moderna*. This popular movement among lay groups and ecclesiastical communities in the northern Netherlands stressed personal religious experience and encouraged meditation on the Life and Passion of Christ, strongly influencing contemporary manuscript illumination; as an illustrator of devotional books published at Delft, the Master would have known its programme.

BIBLIOGRAPHY

M. J. Friedländer: 'Die Brügger Leihausstellung von 1902', *Repert. Kstwiss.*, xxvi (1903), pp. 147–75

——: 'Die verzameling von Kaufmann te Berlijn', *Onze Kst*, x (1906), p. 39

——: 'Die Meister der Virgo inter Virgines', *Jb. Kön.-Preuss. Kstsamml.*, xxi (1910), pp. 64–72

C. M. J. H. I. Smits: *De iconografie van de Nederlandse primitieven* (Amsterdam, 1933), pp. 153–4

A. M. Hind: *An Introduction to the History of Woodcut* (London, 1935/R New York, 1963), ii, pp. 571–4

G. J. Hoogewerff: *De Noord-Nederlandsche schilderkunst*, ii (The Hague, 1937), pp. 241–3

R. van Luttervelt: 'De Herkomst van de Meester van de Virgo inter Virgines', *Bull.: Mus. Boymans*, iii (1952), pp. 57–71

E. Panofsky: *Early Netherlandish Painting*, i (Cambridge, MA, 1953), pp. 323–4

Middeleeuwe kunst der Noordlijke Nederlanden (exh. cat., ed. R. van Luttervelt; Amsterdam, Rijksms., 1958), pp. 65–71

K. G. Boon: 'De Meester van de Virgo inter Virgines', *Oud-Delft*, ii (1963), pp. 5–35

F. Winkler: *Das Werk des Hugo van der Goes* (Berlin, 1964), pp. 176–8

C. D. Cuttler: *Northern Painting from Pucelle to Bruegel* (New York, 1968), pp. 165–7

L. M. J. Delaissé: *A Century of Dutch Manuscript Illumination* (Berkeley and Los Angeles, 1968), pp. 8–12, 73, 87–96

A. Châtelet: *Les Primitifs hollandais* (Paris and Fribourg, 1980); Eng. trans as *Early Dutch Painting* (Oxford and New York, 1981), pp. 146–57, 231–6

D. Wolfthal: *The Beginnings of Netherlandish Canvas Painting, 1400–1530* (Cambridge, 1989), p. 42

MARK L. EVANS

Master of the Vitae Imperatorum (*fl* 1430–50). Italian illuminator. He is named after the manuscript of the Italian translation of Suetonius' *Vitae imperatorum* (Paris, Bib. N., MS. it. 131), copied in 1431 for Filippo Maria Visconti, 3rd Duke of Milan. The artist's style continues the Lombard tradition of the late 14th century and the early 15th, and he may have trained with Tomasino da Vimercate. Both illuminators painted in clear, bright colours, and they shared a repertory of decorative features combined in elaborate initials and borders, incorporating both naturalistic and fantastic foliage. The stylized figures that people the initials and miniatures painted by the Master of the Vitae Imperatorum appear to be direct descendants of those in the work of the earlier illuminator, although they are shown with a more controlled animation and a greater interest in modelling. The influence of Michelino da Besozzo may account for the Master's fluid drapery style, in which deep and curling folds are combined within a simplified contour. In general, his highly finished and precisely painted miniatures are not naturalistic in style, their emphasized lines contributing to an overall sense of pattern and decorativeness.

Although a Missal (New York, H. N. Strauss Col. dated 1413) has been attributed to the Master, the bulk of his extant work dates from the period 1430–50. He was one of the favourite illuminators of Filippo Maria Visconti and painted many manuscripts produced for the Duke and members of his family and court. One of the earliest of these, *c.* 1430–34, is the Breviary (Chambéry, Bib. Mun., MS. 4) made for Filippo Maria's second wife, Maria of Savoy (*d* 1447), which also contains initials (fols 436*v*–438*v*) painted by Belbello da Pavia. The *Vitae imperatorum* is the earliest of the dated manuscripts illustrated by the Master for the Duke. It is the most lavish survival of several Roman histories that Filippo Maria had copied in translation and then illustrated or decorated by this illuminator. Although this style seems to have been favoured by many Lombard humanists for the decoration of their Classical texts, the most remarkable miniatures that the Master produced for the Duke illustrate Dante's *Inferno*. The manuscript of this poem (*c.* 1438; Paris, Bib. N., MS. it. 2017 and Imola, Bib. Com., MS. 32) with the commentary of the Milanese humanist Guiniforte Barzizza (1406–63) and containing Filippo Maria's coat of arms is now dismembered and partly defaced. Originally it had 115 miniatures showing the progress of the Poet and Virgil through Hell. The dramatic compositions, all shown taking place under the earth's crust, demonstrate an invention, control and expressive range unsurpassed in the Master's work.

Besides working for members of the Visconti court, the Master worked also for prominent Milanese citizens. Between 1433 and 1438 he illuminated a Pontifical (Cambridge, Fitzwilliam, MS. 28) for Francesco Pizolpasso, Archbishop of Milan, and in the 1440s he painted two manuscripts for Cristoforo da Cassano, keeper of the Albergo del Pozzo, an inn that survived until 1918. One of these, Fazio degli Uberti's *Il dittamondo* (1447: Paris, Bib. N., MS. it. 81), contains a series of images of constellations that reveal the Vitae Imperatorum Master as a subtle and accomplished draughtsman with special skill in the representation of animals. A large number of manuscripts has been attributed to the Master, and it has been proposed (Melograni) that he had assistants who worked under his close supervision. He was once thought to be the author of an initial 'C' of the *Communion of the Apostles* (Venice, Fond. Cini, no. 2099) that is inscribed as having been made in 1439 by an Olivetan of Milan. This initial and other works in the same style, however, have been identified as the work of a second illuminator, known as the Olivetan Master. The influence and features of the style of the Master of the Vitae Imperatorum were widespread in Lombardy and persisted into the next generation of Milanese illumination, for example in the work of the Ippolita Master, the anonymous illuminator whose role at the court of Francesco Sforza, Duke of Milan, was analogous to that played by the Vitae Imperatorum Master at the court of the third Duke.

BIBLIOGRAPHY

P. Toesca: *La pittura e la miniatura nella Lombardia dai più antichi monumenti alla metà del quattrocento* (Milan, 1912/R Turin, 1966), pp. 528–32

A. Stones: 'An Italian Miniature in the Gambier-Parry Collection', *Burl. Mag.*, cxi (Jan 1969), pp. 7–12

E. Cappugi: 'Contributo alla conoscenza dell'Inferno Parigi-Imola e del suo miniatore detto il Maestro delle Vitae Imperatorum', *La miniatura italiana tra gotico e rinascimento. Atti del II congresso di storia della miniatura italiana: Cortona 1983*, pp. 285–96

S. Bandera Bistoletti: 'La datazione del ms. *italien* 2017 della Bibliothèque Nationale di Parigi miniato dal "Magister Vitae Imperatorum"', *Scritti di storia dell'arte in onore di Roberto Salvini* (Florence, 1984), pp. 289–92

Dix Siècles d'enluminure italienne (exh. cat., Paris, Bib. N., 1984), pp. 148–51

Arte in Lombardia tra gotico e rinascimento (exh. cat., Milan Pal. Reale, 1988), pp. 122–9

A. Melograni: 'Appunti di miniatura lombarda: Ricerche sul "Maestro delle Vitae Imperatorum"', *Stor. A.*, lxx (1990), pp. 273–314

F. Todini: *Una collezione di miniature italiane dal duecento al cinquecento* (Milan, 1993), pp. 56–99

The Painted Page: Italian Renaissance Book Illumination, 1450–1550 (exh. cat., ed. J. J. G. Alexander; London, RA, 1994)

□

Master of the von Groote Adoration (*fl* Antwerp, 1510–20). South Netherlandish painter. The name was given by Friedländer in 1915 and derived from a triptych of the *Adoration of the Magi* (ex-Freiherr von Groote priv. col., Kitzburg; see Friedländer, 1915, pls 36–7). The same subject is treated in several other altarpieces attributed to the Master, as is the *Lamentation* (e.g. Vienna, Akad. Bild. Kst.), although the homogeneity of the works attributed to this Master presents serious problems.

BIBLIOGRAPHY

M. J. Friedländer: 'Die Antwerpener Manieristen von 1520', *Jb. Kön.-Preuss. Kstsamml.*, xxxvi (1915), pp. 65–91

——: *Die altniederländische Malerei* (Berlin, 1924–37); Eng. trans. as *Early Netherlandish Painting* (Leiden, 1967–76), xi (1974), pp. 24–6, 70–71

J. Roosval: 'Les Peintures des retables néerlandais en Suède', *Rev. Belge Archéol. & Hist. A./Belge Tijdschr. Oudhdknde & Kstgesch.*, iv (1934), pp. 311–20

R. Ehmke: 'Die Predella des Paffendorfer Passionsaltares', *Jb. Rhein. Dkmlpf.*, xxiii (1960), pp. 302–7

M. E. Ricker: 'Une *Lamentation* maniériste anversoise de l'entourage du Maître de l'Adoration van Groote: Etude de l'oeuvre et situation dans la production de son époque', *Rev. Archéologues & Historiens A. Louvain*, xvii (1984), p. 302

CARL VAN DE VELDE

Master of the Vyšší Brod Altar (*fl* mid-14th century). Bohemian painter. The altarpiece from which this anonymous artist takes his name originally came from the Cistercian monastery in Vyšší Brod (Ger. Hohenfurth), southern Bohemia. It consists of nine panels (now in Prague, N.G., Convent of St George), which were once probably arranged thematically in three tiers. The lower row showed scenes from the *Infancy of Christ*—the *Annunciation*, *Nativity* and *Adoration of the Magi*; the centre row, *Passion* scenes—the *Agony in the Garden*, *Crucifixion* and *Lamentation*; and the top row was composed of the *Resurrection*, *Ascension* and *Pentecost*. Although nothing is known of the artist, a small figure in the lower right-hand corner of the *Nativity* panel provides a possible identity for the donor. The kneeling nobleman holds the model of a church, and prominently displayed beside him are the Rožmberk arms. Peter I of Rožmberk died in 1347, and his patronage of the monastery at Vyšší Brod—itself on Rožmberk lands—earned him the title 'secundus fundator'.

The panels exemplify one of the most vital elements in the development of 14th-century Bohemian painting: a thorough understanding of contemporary Italian painting, particularly that of Florence and Siena. Bohemian painting from the first half of the century, with its emphasis on linear rhythms, was largely indebted to the art of western Europe. The activities of Charles IV, Holy Roman Emperor, and his courtiers opened the way for new influences on Bohemian artists. Charles himself was a frequent visitor to Italy during the 1330s and 1340s; the last bishop of Prague, Jan of Dražice, had spent years of exile at the papal court in Avignon; and the first archbishop of Prague, Arnošt of Pardubice, had studied at the law schools of Padua and Bologna. Italian models are clearly the source for most of the Vyšší Brod panels. Although the elaborate drapery folds are still derived from western Europe, the fully modelled faces are entirely Italianate. The gold backgrounds and minimal rocky landscapes refer back to the Italo-Byzantine tradition, but the spatial representation of such elements as the Virgin's throne in the *Annunciation*, or the shed in the *Nativity*, show a first-hand knowledge

of contemporary Italian developments, as does the emotional tension between the figures and the clear, bright colours.

The slight variations in style found in the panels point to a division of work between three or even four hands, reflecting the usual workshop practice for a work of this scale and importance. The overall design, however, must be credited to the main master, who painted the *Annunciation*, *Nativity*, *Adoration* and *Resurrection*. Only one other panel, the *Virgin and Child* (Prague, N.G., Convent of St George) from the castle of Veveří in Moravia, can be attributed with any certainty to his workshop, and this on purely stylistic grounds. Nevertheless, this master's balanced synthesis of western and Italian elements provided a major contribution to the formation of the court style of the 1350s and 1360s.

BIBLIOGRAPHY

A. Matějček and J. Pešina: *Gothic Painting in Bohemia* (Prague, 1956)

A. Kutal: *Gothic Art in Bohemia and Moravia* (London, 1971)

R. Chadraba, ed.: *Dějiny českého výtvarného umění* [History of Czech fine art], I/i (Prague, 1984)

AMANDA SIMPSON

Master of the Washington Coronation (*fl* Venice, 1324). Italian painter. He is named after a panel with the *Coronation of the Virgin* (1324; Washington, DC, N.G.A.). This work and an associated group of paintings were attributed to PAOLO VENEZIANO by Sandberg-Vavalà and most other authorities up to Pallucchini. Muraro and Lazareff, however, have distinguished this group from Paolo's, Muraro tentatively proposing that they might be by Paolo's brother Marco di Martino da Venezia (*fl* 1335–45), by whom no documented work is known to survive. Marco is recorded with Paolo in 1335 by a notary of Treviso, Oliviero Forzetta, and as a resident of the same parish in Venice in 1345. Lucco has argued, however, that these paintings are the work of an earlier artist, perhaps the brothers' father, Martino, rather than Marco.

A *Virgin and Child* panel (Padua, Mus. Civ.) is certainly by the Master of the Washington Coronation, as is a damaged fresco of the *Virgin and Saints* on the façade of S Francesco, Treviso. The figures in the panel paintings have distinctively long faces and classicizing drapery that distinguish them from Paolo's known work. The frames have very finely moulded profiles and steeply cusped arches, probably derived from French architecture and very different from the rich mouldings of Paolo's frames, for which the façade of S Marco in Venice is generally considered to have been the dominant influence. The *Virgin* (Moscow, Pushkin Mus. F.A.) attributed to Marco appears to be an earlier work of the author of the altarpiece of *St Leo* (Vodnjan, St Blaise), while another in Belgrade (N. Mus.) has affinities with the work of Paolo and that attributed to Marco.

Muraro attributed a group of Crucifixes to this master: that in the Istituto Ellenico di Studi Bizantini e Postbizantini, Venice, is readily distinguished from Paolo's work by its linear treatment of the ribcage and the tightly crossed legs, features that associate it with the more specifically Romanesque mosaic of the *Crucifixion* in the baptistery of S Marco. Those in St Nicholas, Trogir, and the Borla

Collection, Trino (nr Vercelli), are probably more advanced works by him. The embroidered antependium in St Mary's, Zadar, and the stained glass in the chapel of St John the Baptist, S Francesco, Assisi, are less secure attributions, although they may be identifiable with Marco's 'pannos theutonicos' and 'fenestre vitree' recorded by Forzetta in the Franciscan churches of Venice and Treviso.

BIBLIOGRAPHY

E. Sandberg-Vavalà: 'Master Paolo Veneziano', *Burl. Mag.*, lvi (1930), pp. 160–83

R. Pallucchini: *La pittura veneziana del trecento* (Venice and Rome, 1965), pp. 17–60 pls. I–VII, XII, figs. 16–211; review by V. Lazareff in *A. Bull.*, xlviii (1966), pp. 119–21

M. Muraro: *Paolo da Venezia* (Philadelphia and London, 1970)

L. Gargan: *Cultura e arte nel Veneto al tempo del Petrarca* (Padua, 1978), pp. 56–61, 265–8

G. Gamulin: *The Painted Crucifixes in Croatia* (Zagreb, 1983)

R. Gibbs: 'A Fresco by Marco or Paolo Veneziano in Treviso', *Stud. Trevi.*, 1–2 (1984), pp. 27–31

F. D' Arcais: 'Venezia', *La pittura nel Veneto: Il trecento*, ed. M. Lucco, i (Milan, 1992), pp. 21–4, 47–52

M. Lucco: 'Marco di Martino da Venezia', *La pittura nel Veneto: Il trecento*, ed. M. Lucco, ii (Milan, 1992), p. 541

ROBERT GIBBS

Master of Wavrin (*fl* ?Lille, *c*. 1450–75). Illuminator, active in the southern Netherlands. He is named after Jean de Wavrin, Lord of Forestel (*d c*. 1475), a military officer and compiler of chronicles, for whom he illuminated a number of manuscripts; many of these bear the Wavrin coat of arms and signature. The works to which the Master of Wavrin contributed are almost all chivalric romances, generally elaborately illustrated with numerous miniatures. The *Roman de Florimont* (Paris, Bib. N., MS. fr. 12566), for example, includes 105 miniatures. Others with extensive cycles are the *Histoire des seigneurs de Gavre*, the *Roman de Girart de Nevers* (Brussels, Bib. Royale Albert 1er, MSS 10238 and 9631), the *Histoire d'Oliviers de Castille* (Ghent, Bib. Rijksuniv., MS. 470) and the *Chatelain de Couchy* (Lille, Bib. Mun., Fond. Godefroy, MS. 134).

Unlike his contemporary illuminators, the Master of Wavrin worked on paper and consciously chose an illustrative technique that suited this medium: pen drawing heightened with washes of colour. With just a few nervous strokes of the pen he drew simple but charming scenes, almost cartoon-like in character, with just a minimum of detail. His emphasis was always on the central action, omitting secondary scenes that might divert attention from the main subject.

The interiors tend to be simple, resembling stage sets in composition, with only a few figures. The Master's restrained use of colour, employing carefully placed touches of pigment in a narrow range (usually blue, brown, yellow and red), produced a studied austerity in his work. Characteristic of his female figures are their fashionable dress, with long robes falling in angular pleats and tall, conical hats with veils. His knights tend to be portrayed with pointed noses and chins and unusually short necks, dressed in doublets and tight-fitting trousers, with pointed shoes; soldiers, with helmets covering their eyes, are usually represented frontally.

The Master was also meticulous in his depiction of animals, mostly horses in battles or tournaments. His landscapes are sober, reduced to a few elementary lines,

the green foliage of the trees invariably dotted with red or black. Only rarely did he include rocks in his landscape backgrounds, and architecture is limited to the odd schematic tower or gatehouse.

Several manuscripts painted in the master's style are probably workshop products executed under his supervision. A more colourful version of his style is evident in the work of the Master of the Champion des Dames, who is named after the illustrated edition of Martin Le Francs' text (Grenoble, Bib. Municipale, MS. 875).

BIBLIOGRAPHY

J. Porcher: 'Les Peintres de Jean de Wavrin', *Rev. Fr. Elite Eur.* (April 1956), pp. 17–22

G. Dogaer: *Flemish Miniature Painting in the 15th and 16th Centuries* (Amsterdam, 1987), pp. 91–2

Les Manuscrits à peintre en France, 1440-1520 (exh. cat. by F. Avril and N. Reynaud, Paris, Bib. N., 1993–4)

G. DOGAER

Master of the Weibermacht (*fl* ?Lower Rhine, *c*. 1450–60). German engraver. He is named after his main work, the large-format engraving of the *Weibermacht* ('*Power of Women*'; see Lehrs, 1908, no. 16). From another engraving, bearing the handwritten date 1462, he was also given the name Master of 1462, and he is attributed with a further group of engravings, depicting religious and secular subjects, closely related to each other in their somewhat coarse draughtsmanship and their engraving technique. They are usually assigned to various hands—the MASTER WITH THE BANDEROLES, the MASTER OF THE PLAYING CARDS and his followers, the MASTER OF THE GARDENS OF LOVE and the MASTER OF BALAAM (*see* above). Many of these engravings are copies from earlier patterns and may have originated from the Lower Rhine.

BIBLIOGRAPHY

M. Lehrs: *Geschichte und kritischer Katalog des deutschen, niederländischen und französischen Kupferstichs im XV. Jahrhundert*, i (Vienna, 1908), pp. 163–5, 226–48

M. Geisberg: *Die Anfänge des deutschen Kupferstiches und der Meister E.S., Meister der Graphik*, ii (Leipzig, 1909), pp. 36–41

M. Lehrs: 'Beiträge zum Werk der primitiven Kupferstecher', *Jb. Preuss. Kstsamml.*, xli (1920), pp. 192–9

M. Geisberg: *Die Anfänge des Kupferstiches, Meister der Graphik*, ix (Leipzig, 1923), pp. 38–47

M. Hébert: *Bibliothèque Nationale, Département des Estampes: Inventaire des gravures des écoles du nord, 1440-1550*, i (Paris, 1982), p. 37

HOLM BEVERS

Master of the White Inscriptions. *See* MASTER OF THE BOCCACCIO ILLUSTRATIONS above.

Master of the Wolfgang Altarpiece (*fl c*. 1450–70). German painter. He is named after an altarpiece (*c*. 1460; Nuremberg, St Lorenz) depicting *St Wolfgang* with other saints and scenes of the *Resurrection*. Other works are an altarpiece of the *Virgin* (ex-St Elizabeth, Wrocław; Warsaw, N. Mus.), a *Passion* altar (*c*. 1460; Nuremberg, St Lorenz, on loan to the Dreieinigkeitskirche) and a *St Catherine* altar (1465; Schwabach, SS John and Martin). He has tentatively been identified with Valentin Wolgemut (father of Michael Wolgemut), who was mentioned in Nuremberg records from 1461 and died *c*. 1469–70.

The Wolfgang Altarpiece shows some slight influence from Netherlandish painting, in the treatment of light, space, head types and figure poses of the sort that transformed Nuremberg painting from *c.* 1450, leading to a break with work such as that of the Master of the Tucher Altar (*c.* 1450; Nuremberg, Frauenkirche). The same development is seen more fully in contemporary work by Hans Pleydenwurff, working in Nuremberg 1457–72 and also influenced by Dieric Bouts.

The Master of the Wolfgang Altarpiece seems to have strongly influenced several artists working in Nuremberg *c.* 1450–75, whose works are distinct from those of Pleydenwurff and his followers. Examples of the work of these artists are the *Epitaph of Friedrich Schön* (*d* 1464; Nuremberg, St Lorenz) and the altarpiece of *St Vitus* (*c.* 1450–55; Schwabach, SS John and Martin).

Thieme–Becker   BIBLIOGRAPHY

A. Stange: *Deutsche Malerei der Gotik*, ix (Munich, 1960/*R* Nendeln, 1969), pp. 38–41, figs 55–63
——: *Kritisches Verzeichnis der deutschen Tafelmalerei vor Dürer*, iii (Munich, 1978), pp. 47–53, nos 72–91

NIGEL J. MORGAN

Master of the Worcester Panel. *See under* MARTINUS 'OPIFEX'.

Master of Zweder van Culemborg (*fl c.* 1420–40). North Netherlandish illuminator. He is named after a Missal with a canon page showing a bishop, commended by St Martin, the patron of Utrecht, worshipping Christ on the Cross (Bressanone, Bib. Semin. Maggiore, MS. C.20(N.62)). The bishop is identified by a coat of arms in the border as Zweder van Culemborg, who was nominated Bishop of Utrecht in 1423 but was unable to enter the town until 1425. He left for the Council of Basle in 1431 and died there in 1433. It is most probable that the Missal was produced *c.* 1425, soon after the Bishop's appointment. It contains 16 historiated initials, and 13 of these were painted by the illuminator known as the Master of Zweder van Culemborg, who was probably active in Utrecht. The canon page itself, however, is not by the Zweder Master.

This master is the most significant representative of the declining Soft style in north Netherlandish manuscript illumination. The slim, curvilinear figures are modelled with fine, short brushstrokes of local colour and subtly placed white highlights. The light, clear colouring is striking and includes a strong mid-blue, a bright orange and a soft, slightly green, light yellow. There is a surprising variety and expressiveness of facial type, and portraits have clearly individualized features. This is true of the female owner of a Book of Hours in Stockholm (Nmus., inv. no. B1646, fol. 110*v*), who is portrayed kneeling before St Catherine, and above all of the portrait of Cardinal Hugues de Lusignan in the dedicatory added to Peter von Herenthal's *Commentary on the Psalms*, written in 1416 (Paris, Bib. N., MS. lat. 432, fol. 2*v*). The miniature was presumably added in 1434, before the codex was presented to the Cardinal at the Council of Basle.

The Master of Zweder van Culemborg's workshop used two characteristic types of border decoration: one, where gold trefoils on ink lines, mostly round and bunched in threes, are accompanied by green drops; and a *de luxe* border, where a narrow bar of burnished gold is entwined

with illusionistically depicted blossoms and leaves, interspersed with cherubs on clouds. The best examples are in a Bible in Vienna (Nbib., Cod. 1199–1202, Cod. 1200, fol. 1*r*), a Missal written for Everardus von Greiffenclau (Baltimore, MD, Walters A.G., MS. W.174, fol. 152*v*) and a Book of Hours, also in Baltimore (MS. W.168, fols 52*v*, 76*v*); the latter, however, is thought to be the work of a follower.

Among about two dozen manuscripts attributed to the Master of Zweder van Culemborg's workshop is a strikingly large number of Missals. Apart from those already mentioned, they include one written in 1415 for the Teutonic Order (Zwolle, Prov. Overijssels Mus.), the Missal of the Cleve court chapel (Düsseldorf, Nordrhein-Westfäl. Hauptstaatsarchv, MS. G.III.3) and the Hoya Missal (Münster, Ubib., MS. 41), which epitomizes the master's late work, after 1430. The folio facing the canon of the mass (fol. 94*v*) shows not only the most developed Crucifixion composition but also the most pronounced naturalism in the plants of the border. As well as the Books of Hours in Baltimore and Stockholm, others in Cambridge (Fitzwilliam, MS. 141), Utrecht (Bib. Rijksuniv., Hs. 1037) and The Hague (Kon. Bib., MS. 74.G.34) belong to this group.

With other artists, the Master of Zweder van Culemborg painted in a Bible made for a member of the Lokhorst family (Cambridge, Fitzwilliam, MS. 289) and in the Egmond Breviary (New York, Pierpont Morgan Lib., MS. M. 87; single detached miniatures from the manuscript are in Utrecht, Bib. Rijksuniv., Hs.12.C.17, and Cambridge, Fitzwilliam, MS. 1-1960). The illuminator who painted the canon miniature with the portrait of Zweder van Culemborg in the Bressanone Missal also worked in the Lokhorst Bible and may have been active in the Master of Zweder van Culemborg's workshop. It has been suggested that the Master of Catherine of Cleves contributed to the Greiffenclau Missal, the Egmond Breviary and MS. W. 168. Although the only attribution generally accepted is a few miniatures in the Greiffenclau Missal, it is indisputable that the Master of Catherine of Cleves, with his realistic approach and his naturalistic border decoration, draws on the work of the Master of Zweder van Culemborg.

BIBLIOGRAPHY

G. J. Hoogewerff: 'Geldersche miniaturschilders in de eerste helft van de XVde eeuw', *Oud-Holland*, lxxvi (1961), pp. 3–49
U. Finke: 'Utrecht: Zentrum nordniederländischer Buchmalerei', *Oud-Holland*, lxxviii (1963), pp. 27–66
L. M. J. Delaissé: *A Century of Dutch Manuscript Illumination*, CA Stud. Hist. A., vi (Berkeley, 1968), pp. 20–26
C. Limentani Virdis, ed.: *Codici miniati fiamminghi e olandesi nelle biblioteche dell'Italia nord-orientale* (Vicenza, 1981), pp. 35–9
J. H. Marrow: *A Descriptive and Analytical Catalogue of Dutch Illustrated Manuscripts of the 14th, 15th and 16th Centuries* (Doornspijk, 1990)

BODO BRINKMANN

II. Dated masters.

Master of 1328 (*fl* Bologna, *c.* 1320–40). Italian illuminator. His name derives from the date on his *Matricola dei merciai* (Tradesmen's register; Bologna, Mus. Civ., MS. 633). His work in the choir-books (Antiphonal 11) for the convent of S Domenico, Bologna, is earlier and can be dated to the first half of the 1320s, as can a copy of Gratian's *Decretals* (Madrid, Bib. N., MS. Vit. 21–2) and his participation in the *Rhetorica ad Erennium* (Holkam Hall, Norfolk, Lib. MS. 373), which is of particular interest for its history of the Classical world. The style of the Master of 1328 is close to that of Nerio in its compact areas of colour, divided into what are almost uniform zones; yet in his treatment of narrative and space he was clearly influenced by the later works (after 1317) of Giotto, and he was the first to apply these influences coherently to Bolognese manuscript illumination. The Master of 1328, like the so-called Illustratore Master, reached the height of his career in the 1330s, when he concentrated on legal texts (e.g. Vienna, Österreich. Nbib., Cod. 2040 and 2047 and New York, Pierpont Morgan Lib., MSS M. 821 and M. 716). He worked with Illustratore on a copy of Gratian's *Decretals* (Rome, Vatican, Bib. Apostolica, MS. lat. 1366; for illustration *see* §I: ILLUSTRATORE above). His last known work is probably the Turin Digest (Turin, Bib. N. U., MS. E. I. 1), which possesses the greatest narrative content of any of his works and dates from *c.* 1340. The illustration of the *Martyrdom of St Catherine* (fol. 4) suggests a knowledge of the early works of Vitale da Bologna.

BIBLIOGRAPHY

M. Harrsen and G. K. Boyce: *Italian Manuscripts in the Pierpont Morgan Library* (New York, 1953), nos 33–5, 37

G. Mariani Canova: *Miniatura dell'Italia settentrionale nella fondazione Giorgio Cini* (Vincenza, 1978), nos 15, 16

A. Conti: *La miniatura bolognese: Scuole e botteghe* (Bologna, 1981), pp. 82–5

P. M. de Winter: 'Bolognese Miniatures at the Cleveland Museum', *Bull. Cleveland Mus. A.*, lxx (1983), pp. 314–52 (318–25, note 23, p. 48)

Dix Siècles d'enluminure italienne (exh. cat. by F. Avril, Paris, Bib. N., 1984), p. 79

ALESSANDRO CONTI

Master of 1419 (*fl* Florence, *c.* 1419–30). Italian painter. The artist was first identified by Pudelko (1938), who constructed a corpus around the *Virgin and Child with Angels* (Cleveland, OH, Mus. A.; see fig.), the central panel of a dismembered triptych. The work is dated 1419, hence the name by which the Master is known. This corpus was not entirely coherent, however, and the artist was more clearly defined by Longhi (1940), who recognized that he was probably trained in the circle of Lorenzo Monaco, later absorbing the more conservative innovations of the Renaissance represented by Masolino. The triptych of *St Julian Enthroned with Two Saints* (San Gimignano, Mus. Civ.), originally in the Collegiata, can be dated to this phase in his development and shows an extremely precocious response in the 1420s to Masaccio's early work, such as the S Giovenale Triptych (Reggello, S Giovenale in Cascia) and the *Virgin and Child with St Anne and Angels* (Florence, Uffizi), in its attempt to show the figures in perspective and to render their bodies volumetrically. Critics have emphasized the importance of the Master's role in the development of the Late Gothic style in Florence and have suggested links with Rosello di Jacopo Franchi, Giovanni Toscani and also with some controversial works attributed to Paolo Uccello, such as the frescoed tabernacle of *Lippi and Macia* (Macia, Mater Dei).

Master of 1419: *Virgin and Child with Angels*, 1.96×0.68 m, 1419 (Cleveland, OH, Cleveland Museum of Art)

Carli suggested that the Master could be identified with Ventura di Moro (*fl* 1419–56), a Florentine painter known chiefly through documents. Ventura is documented working as a painter in San Gimignano around 1427; it has been suggested that the triptych of *St Julian* also dates from this year and might have been part of that campaign of work. Those who have accepted this identification have enlarged the artist's corpus to include documented works attributed to Ventura such as the frescoes on the façade of the oratory of the Bigallo in Florence, now barely legible. However, a comparison between the original nucleus of works attributed to the anonymous Master and those subsequently added makes it apparent that the identification should be rejected. The underlying artistic formation of the two groups of works is so dissimilar that they cannot be the work of the same painter, even in two phases of his career.

BIBLIOGRAPHY

G. Pudelko: 'The Maestro del Bambino Vispo', *A. America*, xxvi (1938), pp. 47–63
R. Longhi: 'Fatti di Masolino e Masaccio', *Crit. A.*, v (1940), pp. 145–91 (177, 183, 185)
B. Nicolson: 'The Master of 1419', *Burl. Mag.*, xcvi (1954), p. 181
P. Pouncey: 'Letters: A New Panel of the Master of 1419', *Burl. Mag.*, xcvi (1954), pp. 291–2
W. Cohn: 'Notizie storiche intorno ad alcune tavole fiorentine del '300 e '400', *Riv. A.*, xxxi (1956), pp. 41–72
H. S. Francis: 'Master of 1419', *Bull. Cleveland Mus. A.*, xliii (1956), pp. 211–13
A. Parronchi: *Studi sulla dolce prospettiva* (Milan, 1964), pp. 132–3
S. Skerl Del Conte: 'Una tesi di laurea su "Il Maestro del 1419 e Paolo Uccello"', *A. Friuli, A. Trieste*, iii (1979), pp. 175–84
E. Carli: *San Gimignano* (Milan, 1982), p. 94
H. W. van Os: 'Discoveries and Rediscoveries in Early Italian Painting', *A. Crist.*, lxxi (1983), pp. 69–80

CECILIA FROSININI

Master of 1456 (*fl* 1456). Painter, possibly of south Netherlandish origin. He is named after the *Portrait of a Man* dated 1456 (510×420 mm; Vaduz, Samml. Liechtenstein), acquired in 1677 by Prince Karl Eusebius von Liechtenstein. Nothing is known of the sitter, the painter or the commission. The nature of the support (parchment glued probably after the fact on to a pine panel) sheds no light on the stylistic origin of the portrait, which is one of the most exceptional of the 15th century, the only one known in which the sitter is shown bust-length, almost frontally, with life-like proportions; in this it differs from previous south Netherlandish portraits, and in particular those by Jan van Eyck, which have cramped shoulders. The south Netherlandish training of the artist is attested, however, by the adoption of a neutral background, the use of a parapet in the foreground on which the hand rests and the direct gaze of the sitter, the concern for naturalistic detail in the features and the sensuous rendering of textures. Although the panel is larger and less rectangular in shape than south Netherlandish panels, it is still far from the square format employed by JEAN FOUQUET in his portrait of *Charles VII* (Paris, Louvre) and from its life-size, waist-length figure.

The attribution of the work has long been controversial. It has been attributed to Fouquet himself, sometimes being considered a self-portrait, close to that painted on enamel (Paris, Louvre). The sense of monumentality and the astonishing stability of the image found in the work both of Fouquet and the Master of 1456 have also been noted, although the former's concern for formal construction and geometricization of forms is lacking. The *Portrait of a Man* may also be linked to Portuguese painting, on

which Jan van Eyck's visit made a deep impression; the portrait has been associated with the *Man with a Wine Glass* (Paris, Louvre), the faces of which are close to those in the polyptych of *St Vincent*, attributed to Nuño Gonçalvès (Lisbon, Mus. N. A. Ant.). In the *Portrait of a Man* and the *Man with a Wine Glass*, the figures are both dressed in sombre clothes and stand out against a brownish background, and a calligraphic Gothic inscription runs similarly on either side of the faces. Now enlarged at the sides, however, the panel in the Musée du Louvre originally had longer proportions and was consequently more faithful to the northern tradition; its modelling is also less vigorous and the execution coarser than the portrait of 1456. Hulin de Loo suggested that the Master of 1456 was of south Netherlandish origin, but that he may have worked in Burgundy or Provence. He compared the panel with miniatures in the *Livre du cueur d'amour éspris* (Vienna, Österreich. Nbib., Cod. 2597) and the *Annunciation* triptych (Aix-en-Provence, Ste Marie-Magdalene; Brussels, Pal. B.-A.; Rotterdam, Mus. Boymans–van Beuningen; Amsterdam, Rijksmus.), which he increasingly tended to attribute to the same artist (*see* §I: MASTER OF THE AIX ANNUNCIATION and MASTER OF KING RENÉ OF ANJOU above; *see also* BARTHÉLEMY D'EYCK). The style of this master can be recognized by his taste for powerful forms, his attentive description of surfaces and, above all, his energetic use of light, particularly when it falls on the faces, showing up their inner structure. This hypothesis seems the most likely of the three, but it is no longer generally accepted.

BIBLIOGRAPHY

M. J. Friedländer: 'Die Votivtafel des Estienne Chevalier von Fouquet', *Jb. Kön.-Preuss. Kstsamml.*, xvii (1896), pp. 206–14
G. Hulin de Loo: *L'Exposition des 'Primitifs français' au point de vue de l'influence des frères van Eyck sur la peinture française et provençale* (Brussels, 1904), pp. 30–32
C. Sterling: *La Peinture française: Les Primitifs* (Paris, 1938), pp. 86–7
E. von Strohmer: 'Der Meister von 1456 in der Galerie Liechtenstein in Wien', *Pantheon*, xxxi/2 (1943), pp. 25–34
G. Künstler: 'Jean Fouquet als Bildnismaler', *Wien. Jb. Kstgesch.*, xxviii (1975), pp. 26–35
D. Thiébaut: 'French Artist (Provençal?), 1456: *Portrait of a Man*', *Liechtenstein: The Princely Collections* (exh. cat., New York, Met., 1985–6), p. 185 [excellent pl.]
C. Sterling: 'Un Portrait provençal méconnu', *Hommage à Hubert Landais: Art, objets d'art, collections* (Paris, 1987), p. 96

DOMINIQUE THIÉBAUT

Master of 1462. *See* §I: MASTER OF THE WEIBERMACHT above.

Master of 1473 [Bruges Master of 1473] (*fl* Bruges, 1473). South Netherlandish painter. His name is derived from the date on his only known work, the Jan de Witte Triptych (Brussels, Mus. A. Anc.). This work consists of three hinged panels of equal size. The central panel, with a delicate *Virgin and Child*, is flanked by panels showing the kneeling donors. These have been identified as Jan de Witte, later the Lord of Rudervoorde, and his second wife, Marie Hoose. De Witte was Burgomaster of the Aldermen of Bruges (1472–3) and Burgomaster of Bruges (1482) and was also a counsellor of Charles the Bold, Duke of Burgundy. On the reverse of the right panel there was originally a painting in grisaille of the *Crucifixion*. There are inscriptions on the frames: under de Witte *Etatis*

XXX anom ('thirty years of age'); under the Virgin *Hoc Opus pfectu a MIIII LXXIII—XXVII die julii* ('this work was finished on the 27th day of July 1473'); under Marie de Hoose *Etatis XVI anom* ('sixteen years of age'). The exact specification of the day of completion probably indicates that the triptych was created for a special occasion, presumably the marriage of the donors. The triptych shows stylistic kinship with the work of Rogier van der Weyden and Hans Memling. Unity of setting within the panels is preserved by placing the figures within a walled garden. Friedländer considered that the artist was an outstanding contemporary of Memling, perhaps also a pupil of van der Weyden. The influence of Dieric Bouts the elder has also been suggested.

BIBLIOGRAPHY

M. J. Friedländer: *Die altniederländische Malerei* (Berlin, 1924–37); Eng. trans. as *Early Netherlandish Painting* (Leiden, 1967–76), vi, pp. 38, 59
Primitifs flamands et maîtres du 16e au 19e siècle (exh. cat., Brussels, Gal. Robert Finck, 1962), no. 1, pp. I–VII

FEMY HORSCH

Master of 1499 (*fl c.* 1499). South Netherlandish painter. The date of 1499 is inscribed on a small diptych (311×146 mm; Antwerp, Kon. Mus. S. Kst.) made for Christiaan de Hondt, Abbot of Ter Duinen, in West-Flanders from 1495 to 1509. The left wing is a copy of Jan van Eyck's *Virgin in a Church* (Berlin, Gemäldegal.; *see* EYCK, VAN, (2), fig. 5) and the right wing, showing the abbot in prayer in a detailed interior, probably reflects the lost right wing of van Eyck's diptych. Between 1515 and 1557 Abbot Robrecht de Clercq was painted on the reverse of the right wing, and the *Salvator mundi* on the reverse of the left was retouched. The changes from van Eyck are chiefly additions to increase decorative detail and emphasize the foreground. The painting technique retains something of the finesse necessary to copy van Eyck, but the sharper modelling is more akin to Hugo van der Goes, with whom the Master of 1499 could have worked, since three other pictures from his hand are based on Hugo's designs: the *Virgin Enthroned with Female Saints* (Richmond, VA Mus. F.A.), the triptych of the *Coronation of the Virgin* (Brit. Royal Col.) and the diptych of the *Annunciation* (Berlin, Bodemus.). The derivative nature of his work allows the Master of 1499 to be localized in Ghent, the home of van der Goes, but makes it difficult to date. A donor couple with the *Virgin and Child* (Paris, Louvre) wear the fashions of the 1490s. A *pasticheur* who lacked the originality to revivify his borrowings, the Master of 1499 has been less studied in his own right than for the light he sheds on van der Goes.

BIBLIOGRAPHY

F. Winkler: 'Ein Nachfolger des Hugo van der Goes', *Amtl. Ber. Kön. Kstsamml.*, xxxvii (1916), pp. 69–76
M. J. Friedländer: *Die altniederländische Malerei* (Berlin, 1924–37); Eng. trans. as *Early Netherlandish Painting* (Leiden, 1967–76), iv
Primitifs flamands anonymes (exh. cat., Bruges, Groeningemus., 1969), nos 18–21 [contains full bibliog.]
F. Winkler: *Das Werk des Hugo van der Goes* (Berlin, 1964)
L. Campbell: *The Early Flemish Pictures in the Collection of Her Majesty the Queen* (Cambridge, 1985), nos 32 and 43 [contains full bibliog.]

CATHERINE REYNOLDS

Master of 1515 (i) (*fl c.* 1515). ?Italian engraver and draughtsman. The Master's name is taken from the date on an engraving of *Cleopatra with a Herm*. A further 40 engravings are generally accepted as the work of the same artist; all are characterized by a preference for the depiction of architecture, decorative details and figures inspired by the Antique. Of these engravings, six (presumably the earliest) are executed with the burin alone, while the rest show traces of drypoint burrs. Among the remaining 34 is the *Allegory with Roman Monuments* (possibly an *Allegory of Fortitude*), an unfinished engraving that has traces of drypoint and is a kind of Antique architectural caprice: it includes the statue of Marcus Aurelius and Trajan's Column. It is the best illustration of the Master's style, a highly personal interpretation of the technique using close parallel lines for shading popularized by Mantegna.

The Master's distinctive originality in terms of style, technique and iconography makes it difficult to place him in the history of engraving. At first he was assumed to be Italian; later he was thought to be a northern European artist, possibly the sculptor Hermann Vischer the younger, or a dilettante from the Rechenmeister family of Nuremberg. The discovery that architectural elements in a number of his engravings were taken directly from a sketchbook (Berlin, Kupferstichkab.) plausibly attributed to the Milanese sculptor Agostino Busti seems to have settled the problem of his identity (Dreyer and Winner). Yet, although the engravings certainly reproduce the drawings attributed to Busti, it does not necessarily follow that Busti was the engraver. Moreover, a comparison of the drawings attributed to Busti with the only drawing generally accepted as being by the Master of 1515 (1520; Berlin, Kupferstichkab., with an inscription in old German on the back) highlights their considerable stylistic discrepancies. It would therefore be prudent to consider the Master an anonymous artist, with evident contacts with contemporary north Italian art.

BIBLIOGRAPHY

P. Kristeller: 'Eine Zeichnung des Meisters von 1515', *Amtl. Ber. Kön. Kstsamml.*, xxxii (1910–11), cols 60–62
——: *Der Meister von 1515* (Berlin, 1916)
K. Simon: 'Der Meister von 1515 = Hermann Vischer?', *Italienische Studien, Paul Schubring zum 60. Geburtstag gewidmet* (Leipzig, 1929), pp. 123–37
A. M. Hind: *Early Italian Engraving: A Critical Catalogue* (London, 1938–48), v, pp. 279–90
P. Dreyer and M. Winner: 'Der Meister von 1515 und das Bambaja-Skizzenbuch in Berlin', *Jb. Berlin. Mus.*, vi (1964), pp. 53–94
J. Levenson, K. Oberhuber and J. Sheehan: *Early Italian Engravings from the National Gallery of Art* (Washington, DC, 1973), pp. 456–64
M. J. Zucker: *Early Italian Masters, Commentary (1984)*, 25 [XIII/ii] of *The Illustrated Bartsch*, ed. W. Strauss (New York, 1978–), pp. 571–95

MARCO COLLARETA

Master of 1515 (ii). *See under* AFONSO, JORGE.

Master of 1518. *See* MERTENS, JAN.

The 1520s Hours Workshop (*fl c.* 1520–50). Workshop of French manuscript illuminators. Four individual hands can be distinguished within this group, which began its activity in the French Renaissance, probably in the area of Tours: the Rosenwald Master; the Master of Jean de Mauléon; the Master of the Getty Epistles; and the Doheny Master. Their distinctive style emerged from the Loire Valley tradition of fine manuscripts to which they added complex borrowings from the Antwerp Mannerists,

Albrecht Dürer and Marcantonio Raimondi. Some 25 religious and secular manuscripts are known, dating from the early 1520s to the mid-1530s, with others from the middle of the century. These are mainly Books of Hours, the calendar illumination, main miniatures, saints' vignettes and decorative motifs (both traditional and classicizing) of which show a continuing stylistic tradition. The Masters were also commissioned to provide frontispieces for the vernacular archival compilations and translated humanist texts produced c. 1522–35 for the court of Francis I by court secretaries from Tours. The 1520s Hours Workshop has long been associated with Geofroy Tory, the Bourges-born Parisian humanist, publisher and printer. A fresh look at the manuscripts and Tory's publications reveals that he used the talents of the workshop rather than working among them as artist and scribe.

The Masters are named after their most typical manuscripts. The two earliest Masters worked before 1525. The Rosenwald Master's Book of Hours (1524; Washington, DC, Lib. Congr., Rosenwald Col., MS. 52) is the most obviously Flemish of all the workshop manuscripts. The Master used a repertory of Antwerp Mannerist drawings that was eagerly adopted and added to by subsequent miniaturists. The Book of Hours by the Master of Jean de Mauléon (c. 1524; Baltimore, MD, Walters A.G., MS. W.449) is no less northern in source, and his style merges smoothly with the work of the Doheny Master, named after a Book of Hours of c. 1528, formerly in the Estelle Doheny Collection (sold London, Christie's, 2 Dec 1987, lot 174). The namepiece of the Master of the Getty Epistles (Malibu, CA, Getty Mus., MS. Ludwig I.15) features a more restrained Italianate grace that effortlessly anticipates the style of the mid-century, which was dominated by the school of Fontainebleau.

In contrast to other contemporary French manuscript illumination, the work of the 1520s Hours Workshop is distinguished by finely detailed characterization of graceful and lively figures, subtly modelled drapery, delicately painted backgrounds and decorative systems of restrained luxuriousness. Only the roughly contemporary Master of Claude de France (fl c. 1515–26), with whom the workshop collaborated at least once (on the Epistles of St Paul with the Canonical Epistles; London, V&A, MS. L. 1721–1921), was as talented.

BIBLIOGRAPHY

M. Orth: 'Geofroy Tory et l'enluminure: Deux Livres d'heures de la collection Doheny', Rev. A., 1 (1981), pp. 40–47
The Last Flowering: French Painting in Manuscripts, 1420–1530, from American Collections (exh. cat. by J. Plummer and G. Clark, New York, Pierpont Morgan Lib., 1982), pp. 101–4
Renaissance Painting in Manuscripts: Treasures from the British Library (exh. cat., ed. T. Kren; Malibu, CA, Getty Mus.; New York, Pierpont Morgan Lib.; London, BL; 1983–4), pp. 187–92 [entry on BL, Add. MS. 35318 by M. Orth]
M. Orth: 'French Renaissance Manuscripts: The 1520s Hours Workshop and the Master of the Getty Epistles', Getty Mus. J., xvi (1988), pp. 33–60
——: 'Antwerp Mannerist Model Drawings in French Renaissance Books of Hours: A Case Study of the 1520s Hours Workshop', J. Walters A.G., xlvii (1989), pp. 61–90

MYRA D. ORTH

Master of 1527. See AERTGEN VAN LEYDEN.

Master of the 1540s (fl ?Antwerp, c. 1541–51). South Netherlandish painter. Name given by Friedländer to the painter of c. 30 portraits bearing dates falling between 1541 and 1551. The identity of one of the sitters, Gillis van Schoonbeke Aged 25 (1544; priv. col., on loan to Antwerp, Kon. Mus. S. Kst.), guardian of the Antwerp hospital, suggests that the artist was active in Antwerp. Compared with such painters as Anthonis Mor and Willem Key, the Master of the 1540s was probably a rather modest artist patronized by the upper middle classes. However, his works demonstrate great ability and considerable cultivation.

Probably because his patrons were not of the nobility or aristocracy, the Master's paintings lack coats of arms, signs and inscriptions that might betray the identities of the sitters, most of whose ages are given. Examples on public view include the Portrait of a 49-year-old Man, and its pendant, the Portrait of a 54-year-old Woman (both 1542; Turin, Gal. Sabauda), the pendant portrait of Schoonbeke's 17-year-old wife (also 1544; priv. col., on loan to Antwerp, Kon. Mus. S. Kst.), the Portrait of a 62-year-old Man (1544; Cambridge, MA, Busch-Reisinger Mus.) and the Portrait of a 25-year-old Woman (1544; Cologne, Wallraf-Richartz Mus.). Each sitter's pose is governed by social convention, and little or nothing of the inner character is revealed. Yet the features are shown with great objectivity and skill. The juxtaposition of strong linear features with hazy areas of shadow is typical. The sitters are placed in front of a background of medium brightness so that the flesh areas, as well as the very dark, silky clothing, are well defined, thus enhancing the sense of three-dimensionality.

Friedländer claimed the works of the Master were once regarded as early paintings by Nicolas Neufchatel, but Neufchatel is recorded as the pupil of Pieter Coecke van Aelst in 1539, and Friedländer thought it virtually impossible that he could have been an independent master by 1541. However, Friedländer suggested that Neufchatel may have been influenced by the Master and possibly even worked in his studio c. 1543.

BIBLIOGRAPHY

F. Winkler: Altniederländische Malerei (Berlin, 1924), p. 290
M. J. Friedländer: Die altniederländische Malerei (Berlin, 1924–37), iii, pp. 84–93; Eng. trans. as Early Netherlandish Painting (Leiden, 1967–76), xiii, pp. 46–50, 93–5
R. A. Peltzer: 'Nicolas Neufchatel und seine Nürnberger Bildnisse', Münchn. Jb. Bild. Kst, n. s. 1, iii (1926), pp. 187–231
R. H. Wilenski: Flemish Painters, 1430–1830 (New York, 1960), pp. 120–21

CHRISTINE VAN MULDERS

III. Monogrammists.

Monogrammist AC. See CLAESZ., ALLAERT.

Master A.S. See under §I: MASTER OF BORSJÖ above.

Master A.W. (fl 1525–46). German draughtsman and woodcutter. His monogram formerly led to confusion between him and Anton Woensam. In the plates from his main work, Luthers Kirchenpostille, originally published

(Wittenberg, 1528) by Hans Lufft (1495–1584), subsequently in a new edition (Wittenberg, 1530) by Georg Rhau (1488–1548), he showed great versatility in his way of looking at and depicting things. In the calligraphic manner of some of the woodcuts he followed the stylistic characteristics of Georg Lemberger; in others he displayed a broad, painterly, large-scale approach. Again in the 3 pictures of *St Paul with Emissaries* and 21 illustrations of the *Apocalypse* in the edition of Luther's New Testament (Wittenberg, 1529) printed by Hans Lufft, Master A.W. showed his debt to Lemberger, copying works by him, some the same way round, some reversed, with only minor changes in the detail. Other important series include illustrations of the *Ten Commandments, Three Articles of Faith* and *Lord's Prayer* for Luther's catechism (Wittenberg, 1532); 13 illustrations of the *Articles of Faith* and *Sacraments*; and a series of 37 illustrations for Luther's New Testament (Erfurt, 1535) printed by Melchior Sachse. Fourteen illustrations for the Old Testament (Leipzig, 1541), which complete a sequence by Lucas Cranach (ii), were probably the last series. Many title borders have been attributed to Master A.W.

BIBLIOGRAPHY

H. Zimmermann: 'Beiträge zur Bibelillustration des 16. Jahrhunderts', *Stud. Dt. Kstgesch.*, ccxxvi (1924), pp. 37–57, nos 15–22
H. Schreiber: 'Betrachtungen zur sächsischen Buchkunst im 16. Jahrhundert', *B. & Schr.*, n. s., ii (1939), pp. 1–15

SONJA WEIH-KRÜGER

Monogrammist BB [Master of the Augsburg Portraits of Painters] (*fl* 1502–15). German draughtsman and painter. Twenty portrait drawings (1502–15) and an oil portrait (1505) are connected by the monogram BB, perhaps denoting Barthel Beham, added at a considerably later date. The majority of the subjects (twelve, Berlin, Kupferstichkab.; two, Hamburg, Ksthalle; one, Weimar, Schlossmus.; four, Gdańsk, N. Mus.; one, Copenhagen, Stat. Mus. Kst) are artists and their apprentices, fourteen named and their place of origin noted. Since some of the subjects have been identified as Augsburg figures, it has been supposed that the series was commissioned or preserved by the Augsburg guild of painters. In comparison with portrait studies by Hans Holbein (i), these portraits, all reflecting the impact of the Renaissance, display a stylistic approach and diversity indicating one or more artists of the younger generation. Definite ascription has not proved possible; the greater number are stylistically congruous and resemble the work of Leonhard Beck, to whom the whole series has been ascribed (Winkler). The oil painting, however, is clearly by a lesser hand.

BIBLIOGRAPHY

Thieme-Becker
F. Winkler: *Augsburger Malerbildnisse der Dürerzeit* (Berlin, 1948)
E. Buchner: 'Meister mit Notnamen und Monogrammisten', *Z. Kst*, iv (1950), pp. 320–21
H. Zimmermann: 'Ein Gemälde vom Meister der Augsburger Malerbildnisse', *Z. Dt. Ver. Kstwiss.*, xviii (1964), pp. 73–80

TILMAN FALK

Master B.F. (*fl* Milan, *c.* 1486–1545). Italian illuminator and painter. The initials B.F. appear on a group of miniatures painted by a Lombard artist, clearly a follower of Leonardo da Vinci. They include an *Adoration of the Magi* (New York, Pierpont Morgan Lib., MS. M. 725) and

an *Entombment* (London, BM, Add. MS. 18196), as well as a number of other miniatures dispersed in various museums and private collections. A number of different hypotheses have been proposed, and some scholars now tend to accept Wescher's identification of the Master as Francesco Binasco, an illuminator documented at the court of Francesco Maria Sforza, Duke of Milan (*reg* 1521–35). Binasco was also a goldsmith and an engraver, and in 1513 he was working at the Milan mint in the service of Massimiliano Sforza (Levi D'Ancona).

Although many manuscripts have been attributed to the Master, a chronology has not been definitely established. His earliest works certainly include the *Liber hiemalis ordinis SS Ambrosii* (1486; Milan, Archv Capitolare) for Pietro de Casolis, Canon of St Ambrogio, Milan, the *Romanzo di Paolo e Daria* by Gasparo Visconti (Berlin, Kupferstichkab., MS. 78. C. 27) and a three-volume Bible (Milan, Archv Capitolare), in which the *explicit* bears the date 19 April 1507.

Of somewhat later date is the decoration of the *Lives of the Archbishops of Milan* (Milan, Bib. Ambrosiana, MS. H. 87. Sup.), which shows the arms of Agostino Ferrero, Bishop of Vercelli (1511–36). A number of miniatures cut from choir-books commissioned by the Olivetans of SS Angelo e Nicolò at Villanova Sillaro near Milan and probably illuminated in the years 1500–10 have been traced (London, BL, Add. MSS 18196, 18197b, 39636; Berlin, Kupferstichkab., 626 and 1246; London, Wallace, M. 325-6, 333-5 (miniatures of the *Life of Christ*); Philadelphia, PA, Free Lib., M 72,11, M 28,19, M 72,116, M 72,49–54). Binasco worked for the Olivetan monastery of S Vittore in Corpo, Milan, the provenance of three choir-books decorated after 1542 (Milan, Castello Sforzesco, Biblioteca Trivulziana, corali nos 1–3).

The close link discerned between manuscripts illuminated by this Master and contemporary Lombard painting, especially the work of Leonardo and Bernardino Luini, has been confirmed by the analysis of the panel paintings now attributed to him: a *Circumcision* (Philadelphia, PA, Mus. A.) and two predella panels of the *Nativity* and the *Presentation in the Temple* (Scotland, priv. col., see Frangi, figs 7–8). These works show clear references to the painting of Luini, as well as to that of Martino Piazza of Lodi (*d* 1527).

BIBLIOGRAPHY

DBI
G. Nicodemi: 'I codici miniati dell'Archivio Santambrogiano', *Rass. A.*, i (1914), pp. 91–6
R. Benson: *The Holford Collection: Dorchester House*, i (London, 1927), pp. 35–8
P. Toesca: *Monumenti e studi per la storia della miniatura italiana, I: La collezione di Ulrico Hoepli* (Milan, 1930), pp. 117–19
P. Wescher: *Beschreibendes Verzeichnis der Miniaturen, Handschriften und Einzelblätter des Kupferstichkabinetts der Staatlichen Museen Berlin* (Leipzig, 1931), pp. 133–4
M. Harrsen and G. K. Boyce: *Italian Manuscripts in the Pierpont Morgan Library* (New York, 1953), pp. 55–6
P. Wescher: 'Francesco Binasco Miniaturmaler der Sforza', *Jb. Berlin. Mus.*, ii (1960), pp. 75–91
M. Levi D'Ancona: *The Wildenstein Collection of Illuminations: The Lombard School* (Florence, 1970), pp. 97–105
G. Mariani Canova: *Miniature dell'Italia settentrionale nella Fondazione Giorgio Cini* (Vicenza, 1978), pp. 59–63

Zenale e Leonardo: Tradizione e rinnovamento della pittura lombarda (exh. cat., Milan, Mus. Poldi Pezzoli, 1982), pp. 60–62 [entry by M. Natale and A. Zanni]

F. Frangi: 'Vincenzo Civerchio: Un libro e qualche novità in margine', *A. Crist.*, lxxv (1987), pp. 325–30

J. J. G. Alexander: 'The Livy (MS. 1) Illuminated for Gian Giacomo Trivulzio by the Milanese Artist B. F.', *Yale U. Lib. Gaz.*, lxvi (1991), pp. 219–34

P. G. Mulas: *B. F. et il Maestro di Paolo e Daria* (Pavia, 1991)

MILVIA BOLLATI

Master B. G. At least two German engravers used this monogram. Nagler identified one monogrammist active in the 15th century (N 2079) and a second in the 16th (N 1850, *fl c.* 1589). The earlier artist was formerly mistakenly identified as Barthel Schongauer but was probably Berthold Gobel (*b* 1467), a goldsmith of Frankfurt am Main, who became a citizen in 1495 and was documented there in 1499. This identification, first proposed by Geisberg, was based on an engraving (1490s) with the coat of arms of the Rohrbach-Holzhausen family. Close to fifty engravings by the master are known (see Bartsch, Evans, Passavant, and Lehrs) including seven separate copies after compositions of Martin Schongauer's engraved *Passion* cycle in a technique very close to his. The later master, now thought to have been active earlier (*fl c.* 1561), has been tentatively identified as Georg Balk; the identification as Georg Brentel (*fl* Lauingen, *c.* 1603) is not generally accepted. Only two engravings by him are recorded: the *Martyrdom of St Catherine*, a copy after Albrecht Dürer's composition (B. 120), and *Coat of Arms with the Symbols of the Passion* (1561; Nuremberg, Ger. Nmus.), with the monogram B. G. in the lower left corner.

BIBLIOGRAPHY

Thieme–Becker

A. von Bartsch: *Le Peintre-graveur*, vi (1808), pp. 68–76; viii (1808), pp. 152–63 [22 entries] [B.]

A. E. Evans: *The Fine Art Circular and Print Collector's Manual* (London, 1857), p. 38 [add. 4 entries]

G. K. Nagler: *Monogrammisten*, i (1858), nos 1850, 2079 [N]

J. D. Passavant: *Le Peintre-graveur*, ii (Leipzig, 1860), pp. 118–23 [18 entries add. to Bartsch]

W. Strauss: *Die deutsche Einblatt Holtzschnitz* (Munich, 1923–30); Eng. trans. rev. as *The German Single-leaf Woodcut, 1550–1600*, iii (New York, 1975), pp. 1217–18

M. Lehrs: *Geschichte und kritischer Katalog des deutschen, niederländischen und französischen Kupferstichs im XV. Jahrhundert*, viii (Vienna, 1932), pp. 165–219 [44 attribs; locations of all known impressions, copies, watermarks; bibliog.]

T. A. Riggs: *The Print Council Index to Oeuvre-Catalogues of Prints by European and American Artists* (New York and London, 1983), p. 522

W. Prein: *Handbuch der Monogramme in der europäischen Graphik vom 15. bis zum 18. Jahrhundert* (Munich, 1989), p. 40

HANS J. VAN MIEGROET

Master b ⚭ 8 (*fl* ?Frankfurt am Main, *c.* 1470–90). German engraver. The 45 prints attributed to this engraver, the majority signed with the monogram b ⚭ 8, include five copies after prints by Martin Schongauer and seven after prints by the Housebook Master. It is assumed that practically all the others are based on lost works by the latter. The subject-matter of these prints is almost exclusively secular and includes courtly lovers and satirical scenes with peasants. In style and content they are very close to the drypoints of the Housebook Master, although the images are more stereotyped and the manner of engraving is rather dry. Prints such as one with the coats

of arms of the Rohrbach and Holzhausen families from Frankfurt (*c.* 1480) were probably designed by the monogrammist himself, and it can be assumed from this that he worked in Frankfurt am Main. The suggested identification with the Frankfurt goldsmith Bartholomeus Gobel, about whom nothing is known, requires further examination.

BIBLIOGRAPHY

M. Lehrs: *Geschichte und kritischer Katalog des deutschen, niederländischen und französischen Kupferstichs im XV. Jahrhundert* (Vienna, 1908–34/*R* Nendeln, 1969), viii, pp. 165–219

J. C. Hutchinson: *The Master of the Housebook* (New York, 1972), pp. 74–80, 159–85

J. P. Filedt Kok: *Livelier than Life: The Master of the Amsterdam Cabinet or the Housebook Master* (exh. cat., Amsterdam, Rijksmus., 1985), pp. 193–212

J. P. FILEDT KOK

Master B±R (*fl* ?Lower Rhine, *c.* 1480–90). German engraver. The initials B and R, with a trademark in the form of an anchor between them, are found on 17 rare engravings. They comprise both religious subjects (influenced by Martin Schongauer) and secular, for example satires on rustic life (Lehrs, 1927, nos 11–12). The Master's best-known engraving is the *Chess-game between Death and the King* (L 16), an allegory on the transience of the human condition. His portrait of *Emperor Frederick III* (L 17), of which only one example survives, is thought to be the earliest engraved portrait of a ruler.

BIBLIOGRAPHY

M. Lehrs: 'Der älteste Bildnisstich', *Belvedere*, viii (1925), pp. 133–5

——: *Geschichte und kritischer Katalog des deutschen, niederländischen und französischen Kupferstichs im XV. Jahrhundert*, vi (Vienna, 1927), pp. 291–313 [L]

M. Hébert: *Bibliothèque nationale, Département des gravures: Inventaire des gravures des écoles du nord, 1440–1550*, i (Paris, 1982), pp. 104–5

HOLM BEVERS

Brunswick Monogrammist (*fl* second quarter of the 16th century). Flemish painter. He was active in Antwerp and is named after the *Feeding of the Poor* (Brunswick, Herzog Anton Ulrich-Mus.), which is signed with a monogram found only on this panel and apparently composed of the interlocked letters J, V, A, M, S and L. His identity has been greatly disputed. Some consider his works as youthful paintings by Jan van Hemessen (Eisenmann, Graefe, Puyvelde and Friedländer), but most recent scholars have linked him with JAN VAN AMSTEL (Hoogewerff, Genaille, Faggin, Schubert and Wallen). Bergmans has suggested the name of Meyken Verhulst (*d* 1600), wife of Pieter Coecke van Aelst, and restricts the oeuvre to four paintings.

The Brunswick Monogrammist is best known for his paintings of biblical subjects, composed of many small figures arranged in loose groups with great freedom of movement. The backgrounds usually consist of architectural settings with carefully designed perspective, as in the Brunswick painting and *Ecce homo* (Amsterdam, Rijksmus.), or delicately painted landscapes in such works as the *Entry into Jerusalem* (Stuttgart, Staatsgal.) and *Christ Carrying the Cross* (Basle, Kstmus.; Paris, Louvre). He is an important precursor of Pieter Bruegel the elder in his use of landscape and also in his interest in genre details of contemporary life. Paintings of a *Merry Company* (Berlin,

Gemäldegal.; Frankfurt, Städel. Kstinst.) show brothel interiors, while even in his biblical works Flemish costumes and peasant activities are often included. His oeuvre has been recently enlarged by the addition of a number of paintings with large-scale figures (Faggin, Schubert and Wallen).

BIBLIOGRAPHY

Thieme–Becker
O. Eisenmann: [review of W. Bode: *Studien zur Geschichte des holländischen Malerei* (Brunswick, 1883)], *Repert. Kstwiss.*, vii (1884), pp. 207–26
F. Graefe: *Jan Sanders van Hemessen* (Leipzig, 1909)
G. J. Hoogewerff: *De Noord-Nederlandsche schilderkunst*, iv (The Hague, 1941–2)
R. Genaille: 'Jan van Amstel, le monogrammiste de Brunswick', *Rev. Belge Archéol. & Hist. A.*, xix (1950), pp. 147–53
S. Bergmans: 'Le Problème Jan van Hemessen-Monogrammiste de Brunswick', *Rev. Belge Archéol. & Hist. A.*, xxiv (1955), pp. 133–57
L. van Puyvelde: *La Peinture flamande au siècle de Bosch et Breughel* (Brussels, 1962)
G. T. Faggin: 'Jan van Amstel', *Paragone*, xv (1964), pp. 43–51
S. Bergmans: 'Le Problème du Monogrammiste de Brunswick', *Mus. Royaux B.-A. Belgique: Bull.*, xiv (1965), pp. 143–62
D. Schubert: *Die Gemälde des Braunschweiger Monogrammisten* (Cologne, 1970)
M. J. Friedländer: *Die altniederländische Malerei* (Berlin, 1924–37); Eng. trans. as *Early Netherlandish Painting* (Leiden, 1967–76), xii (1975)
B. Wallen: *Jan van Hemessen* (Ann Arbor, 1983)

ELISE L. SMITH

Master C.A. (*fl* early 16th century). German woodcutter, painter and draughtsman. He cut most of the 54 illustrations (Stumm, nos 145, 147, 149, 151, 153) for the satirical poem *Geuchmatt* (Basle, 1519) by Thomas Murner (1475–1537), which was printed by Adam Petri (*fl* 1509–27); some are monogrammed. The woodcuts are indebted to the style of Urs Graf, and for his female figures Master C.A. used as a model the series of woodcuts of the *Wise and Foolish Virgins* (1518; Stumm, nos 144, 146, 148, 150, 152) by Niklaus Manuel Deutsch I; some of the portraits of fashionably dressed women, exaggerated in a slightly Mannerist way, are direct copies with details omitted. Master C.A. contributed three woodcuts to the *Familienchronik des Grafen Truchsessen von Waldburg* by Matthäus von Pappenheim (n.p., *c.* 1519/*R* Memmingen, 1777–85, 2 vols). In the monogrammed painting *St Jerome in the Wilderness* (1519; Basle, Kstmus.) the saint is a staffage figure in a sketchy, brown-coloured rocky wilderness built up in the style of Hans Leu II.

BIBLIOGRAPHY
L. Stumm: 'Ein Nachahmer Niklaus Manuels', *Anz. Schweiz. Altertknd.*, n. s., x (1908), pp. 326–31
P. Ganz: *Malerei der Frührenaissance in der Schweiz* (Zurich, 1924), p. 120, table 81

SONJA WEIH-KRÜGER

Master C.C. (*fl* Lyon, 1546–55). Engraver, generally identified with the Dutch painter CORNEILLE DE LYON, who was active in France in the mid-16th century. Robert-Dumesnil attributed to him 86 prints on religious, mythological and allegorical subjects, signed with the monogram C.C. Most bear the inscription 'Lugd. Ar' (i.e. printed in Lyon, at the house of the bookseller and print publisher B. Arnoullet, who died in 1555). Among the engravings is the *Massacre of the Innocents*, which forms part of a suite to which Jean de Gourmont (i) and Georges Reverdy also contributed. Master C.C. also illustrated two books, the *Epitome gestarum LVIII regum Franciae*, which was published in Lyon by Arnoullet in 1546, with 59 portraits, and the *Livre extraordinaire des architectures de Sebastien Serlio*, published by Jean de Tournes in 1551 with 50 plates. Like Reverdy, the Master C.C. contributed to the introduction to Lyon of the Mannerist style of the Fontainebleau school.

BIBLIOGRAPHY
A.-P.-F. Robert-Dumesnil: *Le Peintre-graveur français*, vi (1842), pp. 7–32
J. Adhémar: *Bibliothèque nationale, Département des estampes: Inventaire du fonds français, graveurs du seizième siècle*, ii (Paris, 1938), pp. 270–74

MARIANNE GRIVEL

Master DS (*fl* 1501–13). Swiss woodcutter and painter. A few signed and dated woodcuts provide a basis for compiling his works. He has been identified (Fischel) with a 'Daniel Schwegeler von baselln, appelles' who in 1503 paid to become a freeman of Leipzig. Documents on this Schwegler's family have been taken (Fischel, see 1984 exh. cat.) with stylistic facets of the woodcuts to present a coherent plausible identity for DS. Gregor Schwegler, his father, was a notary in the episcopates of Konstanz and Basle. Daniel Schwegler (*c.* 1482–1543) matriculated as a citizen of Konstanz at Basle University in 1496–7. His elder brother Hartmann Schwegler preceded him to Leipzig, held a vicariate near Mainz from 1502 and in 1504 received a living at the Petersstift in Basle. A connection with Mainz appears in the works of DS, insofar as they are the only ones from Basle to show stylistic affinities to the Middle-Rhenish art of the time, especially to Grünewald; while some murals painted *c.* 1509 in the Kaplänersakristei of the Basle Petersstift were attributed either to DS (Riggenbach) or to an artist related to him (Schmid) before these connections were known. By 1506 Daniel Schwegler is documented as a member of the episcopal court of Basle. From 1513, when no further work by DS is known, he served as episcopal procurator.

Only a few woodcuts by DS are signed: a large printer's mark of the Basle association of Amerbach/Petri/Froben (1511; Bock, no. 35); Archbishop Leonhard von Keutschach's escutcheon (1510; B 26); a double scene of one man dying piously and another dying dissolutely (before 1508; B 13); the large paired *Man of Sorrows* and *Virgin and Child* (B 39 and 38); a large *St Anne, the Virgin and the Christ Child* with a prayer, signed by the printer SRF, by Pamphilus Gengenbach (1513; B 40); a *St Gregory at Mass*, signed SD (B 34); and the mighty *Crucifixion* (B 41). In the last a warrior looking backwards out of the picture indicates the artist's self-portrait. A second printer's mark (1511; B 36) is securely attributable to DS. *Christ Crucified between the Virgin and St John*, found in missals (pubd Jacob and Thomas Wolff, 1510–21; Missale Speciale, no. 27), is secured on stylistic grounds.

Other attributions, datable from the print, comprise ten comic woodcuts from Paulus Olearius's *De fide concubinarum in sacerdotes* and Jacobus Hartlieb's *De fide meretricum* (pubd Jacob Wolff or Michael Furter, from 1501–2; B 1–10); the frontispiece for a St Ambrose (pubd Adam Petri, 1506; B 12); six woodcuts, including battle scenes and William Tell shooting the apple, for the *Kronika Peterman Etterlyns* (pubd Furter, 1507; B 14–17 and 47–

8); three woodcuts for Gregor Reisch's *Margarita philosophica* (pubd Furter and Schott, 1508; B 19–21, Ptolemy in ed. Heinrich Petri, 1535); coats of arms woodcuts in the Würzburg and the Brixen missals of 1509 (B 24) and 1511 (B 30, 31); a large *St James as a Pilgrim* (pubd Heinrich Petri, *c.* 1530; B 23); and a broadsheet by Niclaus Moler (Furter, 1507; fragmentary copies in London, BM, and Basle, U. Basle). Disputed attributions include a large single-leaf woodcut of the *Battle of Dornach* of 1499 (*c.* 1500; B 44) and woodcuts for various chronicles, devotional collections, editions of Albertus Magnus, Guillermus von Paris, prophetic poems etc (B 45, 46, 49, 50, 51, 54, 55, 57, 59, 60 etc). Further convincing attributions are a miniature in the matricule of Basle University for the rector of winter 1510–11, Heinrich Lutenwang, a drawing of the *Crucifixion* (Koegler), a *Crucifixion* in the Schweizerisches Landesmuseum, Zurich (Koegler), and a *Resurrection*, certainly from the same lost altarpiece, in the Kunstmuseum, Basle.

An expressive and never beautifying depiction of ugliness, poverty, ageing and suffering, as well as of joy, especially in angels and children closely related to those of Grünewald, has always been seen as characteristic of DS's style. The powerful depiction in the Petersstift murals reinforces the connection with Daniel Schwegler made by documentation. A *Passion* cycle from St Ulrich, Basle (destr.), and murals (1509; discovered 1982) in a nearby private house show close affinities to his style.

BIBLIOGRAPHY

H. Koegler: 'Vorläufiger Bericht über neue Blätter des Meisters DS', *Kunstchronik*, n. s., xviii (1906–7), no. 19, pp. 289–91
——: 'Die *Kreuzigung* im Landesmuseum, wahrscheinlich ein Gemälde des Meisters DS', *Anz. Schweiz. Altertknd.*, n. s., ix (1907), pp. 314–25
C. Dodgson: 'Die Holzschnitte des Baseler Meisters DS', *Jb. Kön.-Preuss. Kstsamml.*, xxviii (1907), pp. 21–33
H. Koegler: 'Eine Zeichnung des Basler Meisters D.S.', *Repert. Kstwiss.*, xxxix (1916), pp. 1–10
E. Bock: *Holzschnitte des Meisters DS* (Berlin, 1924) [B]
H. A. Schmid: *Die Werke Hans Holbeins in Basel* (Basle, 1930), pp. 7–8
L. Fischel: 'Neue Mitteilungen über den Basler Monogrammisten DS', *Münch. Jb. Bild. Kst*, n. s. 2, v (1954), pp. 111–19
P. L. Ganz: *Die Miniaturen der Basler Universitätsmatrikel* (Basle, 1960), pp. 122–3, table 3
R. Riggenbach: 'Ausstattung...', *Kunstdenkmäler Basel-Stadt*, v (Basle, 1966), pp. 110–13, nos 157–60
J. Rowlands: 'Some Notable Early Prints', *BM Yb.*, 1 (1976), pp. 260–70
Oberrheinische Buchillustration 2: Basler Buchillustration, 1500–1545 (exh. cat., Basle, 1984), pp. viii–xv and *passim*

FRANK HIERONYMUS

Master D✗V. *See* VELLERT, DIRK.

Master E.S. (*fl c.* 1450–1467). German engraver and draughtsman. He is named after the initials on what are now recognized as the first known engravings with a monogram. About 318 engravings, the earliest from *c.* 1450, the latest dated 1466 and 1467, are attributed to him, although his work is estimated to have originally comprised about 500 engravings. Of the surviving engravings, 95 are unica; for many only two or three impressions exist. After Israhel van Meckenem (ii), he was the most productive engraver of the 15th century.

The Master E.S. has occasionally been identified with Erhard Schön, E. Stern, Gillis (Egidius) Stechlin, Erwin von Stege (*fl* 1456–75), Erhard Schongauer and with a member of the Ribeisen family from Strasbourg. The only certain fact is that he was active in the Upper Rhineland, presumably in Konstanz, Basle, Freiburg or—most probably—Strasbourg. Three engravings of the *Virgin of Einsiedeln* (1466; Lehrs, nos 68, 72 and 81) suggest that he also had some connection with the Swiss Benedictine monastery at Einsiedeln; he may have stayed there and in Konstanz between 1465 and 1466. Like many 15th-century engravers, he may have been trained as a goldsmith; it remains uncertain whether he was also active as a painter on panel or glass. He was evidently famous as a printmaker in his lifetime. His engravings were exported to distant parts of Europe: contemporary copies or adaptations of his works can be found, for example, in Italy. The large number and range of engravings produced suggest that he ran a workshop and that he was possibly also active as a commercial distributor.

The thematic repertory of the engravings themselves is unusually large. There are conventional religious scenes from the *Life of the Virgin* and the *Passion of Christ* (e.g. the *Crucifixion*, *c.* 1465; see fig.), as well as images of saints and devotional sheets; a few of these may have been ecclesiastical commissions, as were the three versions of the *Virgin of Einsiedeln*. There are also secular subjects: the *Garden of Love* (L 207, 214–15), playing cards, women with heraldic emblems, ornamental sheets and a series of alphabet letters with figures, which covers 23 sheets (L 283–305). These were principally intended for prosperous nobles and patricians.

Master E.S.: *Crucifixion*, engraving, 228×155 mm, *c.* 1465 (Berlin, Dahlem, Kupferstichkabinett)

The engravings attributed to the Master E.S. also display great diversity in technique and form—so much so that they have not always been accepted as the work of one artist: in the 19th century a small group was attributed to the MASTER OF THE TIBURTINE SIBYL (*see* §I above), named after the large-format depiction of the *Tiburtine Sibyl and Emperor Augustus* (*c.* 1450; L 192). Although the chronology is not always clear, the engravings with fine strokes and delicate modelling (e.g. the *Nativity, c.* 1450; L 22) are usually dated as early works by the Master E.S.; those with long strokes and bold hatching, or with crosshatching (e.g. the series of *Seated Apostles, c.* 1460; L 112–23), are usually considered late. Variations in style are sometimes due to the influence of different models. A few subjects adapt forms from earlier illuminated manuscripts and pattern-books: for instance the *Ars moriendi* (*c.* 1450; 175–85) are based on illuminated manuscripts from *c.* 1430 and the alphabet letters on late 14th- and early 15th-century sources. However, most of the models come from contemporary painting and sculpture of the Upper Rhineland and Flanders. Some engravings correspond closely in composition and style with the work of Konrad Witz and his circle: the *Tiburtine Sibyl and Emperor Augustus*, for example, with the panel *St Augustine* (*c.* 1435; Dijon, Mus. B.-A.) from Witz's Heilsspiegel Altarpiece. There are also similarities with the work of other Upper Rhenish painters, such as the Master of 1445, the Master of the Karlsruhe Passion and Jost Haller. In many cases, however, Netherlandish influences predominate. The composition of the *Holy Trinity* (L 186) draws closely on a panel with the *Trinity* by the Master of Flémalle (*c.* 1430–32; Frankfurt am Main, Städel. Kstinst.), and a second version of the *Tiburtine Sibyl* (L 191) follows Rogier van der Weyden's left wing of the Bladelin Altar (*c.* 1452; Berlin, Gemäldegal.). Moreover, there are close, possibly reciprocal, connections with Nicolaus Gerhaert of Leyden and Strasbourg sculpture of *c.* 1460; the model for the magnificent engraving of the standing *St Sebastian* (L 159) can be traced to a wooden figure from Gerhaert's circle (*c.* 1460; Berlin, Skulpgal.). However, the Master E.S. did not follow his models slavishly but with astonishing freedom and flexibility.

Although various drawings have been attributed to the Master E.S., only two are now accepted: the *Girl with a Ring* (Berlin, Kupferstichkab.) and the *Baptism* (early 1450s; Paris, Louvre); the former remains particularly enigmatic with regard to its size and purpose.

The graphic work of the Master E.S. forms the transition between the earliest known engravings of the 1430s and 1440s (e.g. by the Master of the Playing Cards) and the fully developed line-engravings of the late 15th century (as produced by Martin Schongauer). He influenced the technical development of engraving and produced the earliest known white-line engraving, the *Virgin on a Grassy Bank* (*c.* 1465–7; L 70), the only example from the 15th century. His artistic originality resides in his free and accomplished adaptation of new artistic forms of expression—particularly from the Netherlands. Through the wide distribution of his engravings, he had a considerable impact on the artistic production, especially in sculpture, of his own generation and the next.

BIBLIOGRAPHY

M. Geisberg: *Die Anfänge des deutschen Kupferstiches und der Meister E.S.*, Meister der Graphik, ii (Leipzig, 1909)
M. Lehrs: *Geschichte und kritischer Katalog des deutschen, niederländischen und französischen Kupferstichs im XV. Jahrhundert*, ii (Vienna, 1910) [L]
W. Pinder: 'Zur Vermittler-Rolle des Meisters E.S. in der deutschen Plastik', *Bild. Kst*, n.s., xxxii (1921), pp. 129–32
M. Geisberg: 'The Master E.S.', *Pr. Colr. Q.*, ix (1922), pp. 203–35
——: *Die Kupferstiche des Meisters E.S.* (Berlin, 1923)
——: *Der Meister E.S.*, Meister der Graphik, x (Leipzig, 1924)
L. Fischel: 'Le Maître E.S. et ses sources strasbourgeoises', *Archv Alsac. Hist. A.*, xiv (1935), pp. 185–229
E. Hessig: *Die Kunst des Meisters E.S. und die Plastik der Spätgotik*, Forsch. Dt. Kstgesch., i (Berlin, 1935)
L. Fischel: *Nicolaus Gerhaert und die Bildhauer der deutschen Spätgotik* (Munich, 1944), pp. 163–7
——: *Die Karlsruher 'Passion' und ihr Meister* (Karlsruhe, 1952), pp. 35–48
E. W. Hoffman: 'Some Engravings Executed by the Master E.S. for the Benedictine Monastery at Einsiedeln', *A. Bull.*, xliii (1961), pp. 231–7
Master E.S.—Five Hundredth Anniversary Exhibition (exh. cat., ed. A. Shestack; Philadelphia, PA, Mus. A., 1967)
J. C. Hutchison: *Early German Artists*, 8 [VI/i] of *The Illustrated Bartsch*, ed. W. Strauss (New York, 1980), pp. 9–123
K. P. F. Moxey: 'Master E.S. and the Folly of Love', *Simiolus*, xi (1980), pp. 125–48
Meister E.S.: Ein oberrheinischer Kupferstecher der Spätgotik (exh. cat., ed. H. Bevers; Munich, Staatl. Graph. Samml.; Berlin, Kupferstichkab.; 1986–7)

Master F.C. *See* CRABBE, FRANS.

Master FVB (*fl c.* 1475–1500). South Netherlandish engraver. He has been named after a group of engravings, which bear the initials FVB on the lower edge. Although he has been identified as Franz von Bocholt or as F. of Bruges, there is no clear evidence to support this. His known work consists of 59 engravings (*see* BELGIUM, fig. 14), their subjects including scenes from the Old Testament, the Virgin and saints, with genre scenes and a few ornamental sheets. The engravings are distinguished by their technical brilliance, for example in the consistent use of crosshatching, which was modelled on the work of Martin Schongauer. The figures were conceived monumentally and drawn with conviction. Most of the compositions and individual figures were drawn from works by Schongauer or, in particular, from early Netherlandish painting. Connections can be seen with Rogier van der Weyden (for example the *Annunciation*; Lehrs, 1930, no. 3), Hans Memling and Dieric Bouts I. The master's principal work, the *Judgement of Solomon* (L 2), like the treatment of the same subject by the Master E.S. (L 7), may have derived from a lost panel of *Justice* by the Dieric Bouts I.

BIBLIOGRAPHY

Hollstein: *Dut. & Flem.*; Thieme–Becker
M. Lehrs: 'The Master FVB', *Prt Colr Q.*, x (1923), pp. 3–30, 149–61
——: *Geschichte und kritischer Katalog des deutschen, niederländischen und französischen Kupferstichs im XV. Jahrhundert*, vii (Vienna, 1930), pp. 102–64 [L]
Fifteenth-century Engravings of Northern Europe from the National Gallery of Art (exh. cat., ed. A. Shestack; Washington, DC, N.G.A., 1967–8), nos 126–33
G. Smith: 'The Exterior of the Bladelin Altarpiece and the Master FVB', *Oud-Holland*, lxxxv (1970), pp. 115–16
M. Hébert: *Bibliothèque nationale, Département des Gravures: Inventaire des gravures des écoles du Nord, 1440–1550*, i (Paris, 1982), pp. 165–8

HOLM BEVERS

Master GJ. *See* VELLERT, DIRK.

Monogrammist HA. *See* AESSLINGER, HANS.

Master H.E. *See* MASTER H.F.E. below.

Master H. F. (*fl* Basle, 1490s–*c.* 1520). Swiss draughtsman and wood-engraver. His initials have suggested Hans Furtenbach (*fl* 1514–19), Hans Franck (*fl* 1514–26), HANS FUNK I or HANS FRIES. His known works, generally monogrammed, include drawings (1516–18; six: Basle, Kstmus.; one: Berlin, Kupferstichkab.) in which his style resembles that of Ambrosius Holbein, suggesting that he may have been a pupil of Hans Baldung. He also executed ten wood engravings (1516), generally initialled, which were used to illustrate a book entitled *Die Brösamlin doct. Keisersperg. uffgelesen von Frater Johann Paulin* (Strasbourg, 1517), and a further ten (1518) for the *Buch der Sunden des Munds* (Strasbourg, 1518) by Geyler von Kaysersberg (1478–1510). Later, *c.* 1520, he worked for Johann Froben (1460–1527) and other publishers in Basle.

BIBLIOGRAPHY

G. K. Nagler: *Monogrammisten*, iii (1863) [identifies as Hans Furtenbach]
H. A. Schmid: 'Der Monogrammist H. F. und der Maler Hans Franck', *Jb. Kön.-Preuss. Kstsamml.*, xix (1898), pp. 64–76 [identifies as Hans Franck or Hans Funk]
M. J. Friedländer: *Der Holzschnitt* (Berlin, 1917), p. 130 [cautious of all attribs]
M. Hébert: *Bibliothèque nationale, Département des gravures: Inventaire des gravures des écoles du nord, 1440–1550* (Paris, 1982), pp. 308–9

VINCENT LIEBER

Master H.F.E. [H.E.] (*fl* mid-16th century). Italian engraver. He has often been confused with Domenico Beccafumi. Tietze-Conrat suggested identification of the initials with Hieronymus Fagiuoli Emilianus, the Bolognese engraver Girolamo Faccioli (*fl c.* 1530; *d* 1573), mentioned several times by Vasari in connection with Parmigianino and Francesco Salviati. Bartsch listed five engravings signed with these initials: *Adoration of the Shepherds* (B. 1); *Christ among the Doctors* (B. 2) after Lodovico Mazzolino; *Marine Gods* (B. 3), perhaps after a drawing by Raphael; *Parnassus Profaned* (B. 4); and the *Effect of Wine* (B. 5), possibly after a drawing by Salviati. Passavant attributed a sixth engraving to him, *Two Cupids Riding Sea-monsters*, in the style of Mantegna.

BIBLIOGRAPHY

J. D. Passavant: *Le Peintre-graveur*, vi (Leipzig, 1864), p. 153
E. Tietze-Conrat: '*Les Vendangeurs*: An Engraving by the Monogrammist H.F.E.', *Gaz. B.-A.*, n. s. 6, xxv (1944), pp. 187–9
Renaissance in Italien 16. Jahrhundert (exh. cat., intro. K. Oberhuber; Vienna, Albertina, 1966), pp. 170–71
S. Boorsch and J. T. Spike: *Italian Artists of the Sixteenth Century* (1986), 31 [XV/iv] of *The Illustrated Bartsch*, ed. W. Strauss (New York, 1978–) [B.]

FRANÇOISE JESTAZ

Master H.L. (*fl* 1511–26). German sculptor, engraver and wood-carver. He is known by the initials with which he signed a carved altarpiece (1523–6; Breisach, Cathedral), twenty-four engravings and seven woodcuts.

1. IDENTITY. His activity span, at least 1511–26, is documented by dated engravings (1511, 1519, 1522) and the Breisach Altarpiece. Several of the engravings were dated or redated 1533 by someone else, who may have acquired the plates following the artist's death. The altarpieces at Breisach and Niederrotweil am Kaiserstuhl and other closely related sculpture locate him as working around the Upper Rhine, especially in or near Freiburg im Breisgau. He apparently first trained and worked in Austria and perhaps Lower Bavaria and Franconia. The Austrian connection is seen in resemblances between the Breisach Altarpiece and the altar of the *Virgin of the Green Meadow* (1505) in the pilgrimage church of Mauer bei Melk, but differences in drapery and compositional rhythm resist the theory that he carved both works.

Efforts to identify the artist by name remain highly speculative. The name is tantalizingly omitted from a letter that he carried in 1523 from the town councillors of Breisach to those in Freiburg, concerning materials for the Breisach Altarpiece (Baxandall, pp. 30–31): 'We have engaged the master who bears this letter to carve an altarpiece in the choir of our church, for which we are in need of some wood we cannot get in our city.' The monogram on the prints was formerly mistakenly taken for the signature of Hans Leinberger. A drawing for an altarpiece (Ulm, Stadtarchv), closely related to the work of Master H.L., includes a figure of St Joachim with a banderole inscribed with the letters HLOI, believed by Schindler (1981) to signify Hans Loi, but there is no certifiable work by Hans Loy (*fl* 1519–21) for comparison, and the Breisach letter of 1523 does not refer to the artist as might be expected had he been, as Loy was, a guild member in Freiburg as recently as 1520.

2. WOOD-CARVINGS. The Breisach Altarpiece (1523–6) is an unpolychromed lime-wood triptych. Trefoil-shaped at the top, the corpus or shrine contains the *Coronation of the Virgin* (see GERMANY, fig. 30) carved in deep relief. In each of the flanking wings stand two saints: *St Stephen* and *St Lawrence* (left), *St Protasius* and *St Gervasius* (right). Four busts of the *Church Fathers*, busily writing, appear in the predella. Six more sculptures (*Christ as the Man of Sorrows*, the *Virgin and Child with St Anne*, *SS Vitalis and Valeria* and two angels) occupy the canopy that rises above the shrine. The exterior of the wings was left bare. The composition with the *Coronation of the Virgin*, surrounded by countless squirming little angels, resembles the central panel of the main altarpiece (1512–16), painted by Hans Baldung, in Freiburg Cathedral. However, the drapery that swirls over and around the figures at Breisach distinguishes this work and its carver. The patterns of drapery correspond to the stylistic trend (*c.* 1510–30) of parallel folds, but Master H.L. used the motion of drapery as if it were a cosmic force concentrated into visible and tactile form. Such unrelenting motion finds its organic counterpart in the floral ornament, a wide band of which rises and falls over the figures across the entire upper part of the altarpiece. The carved figures in the canopy are easily recognized as the work of a different hand, which has suggested that Master H.L. was a painter/engraver who designed the altarpiece and then subcontracted a wood-carver, possibly the Austrian Master of the Mauer Altar.

An unsigned, carved triptych (*c.* 1525–30; Niederrotweil am Kaiserstuhl, Friedhofskirche St Michael) is the only other extant altarpiece generally accepted to be at least in part by the hand of Master H.L., and that part pertains to the reliefs on the wings rather than to the central shrine. As in Breisach, the central shrine contains a *Coronation of the Virgin*, but this time executed by another carver working in the manner of Master H.L., perhaps identical with the Master of the St Anne Altarpiece (*fl* 1515–16) in Freiburg Cathedral. There are two scenes in relief on each wing: on the left *St Michael Weighing Souls* above and the *Baptism* below; on the right, the *Beheading of St John the Baptist* above and the *Fall of the Rebel Angels* below. The first impression conveyed by the reliefs is one of utter confusion, increased by the fact that parts of the scenes run together vertically with no separation between them; but close examination reveals masterful control of all the figures and drapery and of the complex relationships between them. No consensus exists about whether this altarpiece was made before or after the one at Breisach, but in the boxwood group of *Adam and Eve in Paradise* (*c.* 1520; Freiburg im Breisgau, Augustinmus.), attributed to Master H.L., similarities to figures by Conrat Meit, Jan Gossart and Bernard van Orley have been noted, prompting speculation that, following the Peasant War and onset of Protestant iconoclasm, Master H.L. moved to the Netherlands before the Niederrotweil Altarpiece was completed.

3. PRINTS AND RELATED STATUES. It is not difficult to associate the linear complexity of the reliefs at Niederrotweil or the movements of drapery at Breisach with the sensibility of a graphic artist. Master H.L. was a master engraver, whose sources in turn were also engravings. His earliest dated print, *Angels Bearing Instruments of the Passion* (1511; Lossnitzer, no. 7), shows a composition based on Mantegna's *Soldiers Carrying Trophies* (1480–95; London, Hampton Court, Royal Col.) and burin work in the manner of Dürer. The arresting images, density of the design and strong chiaroscuro are characteristic of his own vision. The engraving of *St Peter* (1522; L 16) calls to mind certain figures of Grünewald, such as the grisaille panel of *St Lucy* (*c.* 1511–12; Frankfurt am Main, Städel. Kstinst. & Städt. Gal.), with a similar torque in the body, moving light and rippling pleats. Such expressive qualities reveal the same hand in two statues, *St John the Baptist* and *St John the Evangelist* (Nuremberg, Ger. Nmus.), presumably of about the same date. An engraving of *St George as Victor* (1533; L 13) likewise serves as evidence for attributing to this artist a carved figure of the same subject (*c.* 1510–15; Munich, Bayer. Nmus.).

BIBLIOGRAPHY
M. Lossnitzer: *Hans Leinberger: Nachbildungen seiner Kupferstiche und Holzschnitte* (Berlin, 1913) [L]

T. Demmler: 'Der Meister des Breisacher Hochaltars', *Jb. Kön.-Preuss. Kstsamml.*, xxxv (1914), pp. 103–35

O. Schmitt: *Oberrheinische Plastik im ausgehenden Mittelalter* (Freiburg im Breisgau, 1924), pp. 44–53 [commentary to plates, pp. 14–16]

C. Sommer: 'Der Meister des Breisacher Hochaltars', *Z. Dt. Ver. Kstwiss.*, iii (1936), pp. 245–74

I. Schroth: 'Die Herkunft des Meisters H.L.', *Kunstchronik*, xiii (1960), pp. 283–4

G. von der Osten: 'Über den Monogrammisten H.L.', *Jb. Staatl. Kstsamml. Baden-Württemberg*, iii (1966), pp. 69–82

E. Zimmermann: 'Meister H.L.' and 'Umkreis des Meisters H.L.', *Spätgotik am Oberrhein* (exh. cat., Karlsruhe, Bad. Landesmus., 1970), pp. 201–8

I. Krummer-Schroth: 'Der Schnitzaltar in Niederrotweil a. K.', *Jb. Staatl. Kstsamml. Baden-Württemberg*, viii (1971), pp. 65–96

J. Rasmussen: 'Zum Meister H.L.', *Jb. Hamburg. Kstsamml.*, xviii (1973), pp. 55–68

H. Schindler: *Der Schnitzaltar* (Regensburg, 1978, rev. 2/1982)

M. Baxandall: *The Limewood Sculptors of Renaissance Germany* (New Haven and London, 1980), pp. 30–31, 299–301

H. Brommer: 'War Hans Loy der Meister HL?', *Freiburg. Diöz.-Archv*, c (1980), pp. 161–202

H. Schindler: *Der Meister HL = Hans Loy?* (Königstein im Taunus, 1981)

H. Gombert: 'Untersuchungen zum Werk des Meister H.L.', *Das Münster*, xxxiv (1981), pp. 17–31

M. J. Liebmann: *Die deutsche Plastik 1350–1550* (Leipzig, 1982), pp. 387–9

Sculptures allemandes de la fin du moyen âge dans les collections publiques françaises 1400–1530 (exh. cat., Paris, Louvre, 1991–2), pp. 266–9

CHARLES TALBOT

Master H. S. (*fl* 1534–65). Swiss or German designer, cabinetmaker and wood-engraver. His mark consisted of the initials H. S. on either side of two arrows surmounted by a set square. Although these heraldic charges appeared in the armorial bearings of the Meichssner family of Nuremberg, it is unlikely that he belonged to it. It is contended that he could have been Hans Stegel (*fl c.* 1500) of Nuremberg or, more plausibly, Heini Seewagen (*fl* 1522; *d* after 1544) of Berne, who was in Italy in 1522. All five known wood-engravings marked with the H. S. monogram depict furnishings, apparently in the style of Augsburg. Each appears on a leaf of which the obverse side is printed with an engraving by another anonymous artist, Master H. G. (*fl* 1563–5). As H. G. appears to have been a Nuremberg artist, it is thought that H. S. worked in the same city. Several Swiss public collections have furnishings bearing the monogram of Master H. S., including a wardrobe (1565), two chests (Zurich, Schweizer. Landesmus.) and wooden wall panels (Zum goldenen Hirschen, St Gall; now in St Gall, Hist. Mus.). These pieces were generally decorated with views of architecture, executed in marquetry in an apparently Venetian style, which supports the contention that Master H. S. was Heini Seewagen.

BIBLIOGRAPHY
Thieme-Becker

G. K. Nagler: *Die Monogrammisten* (1858–1920)

O. von Falke: *Deutsche Möbel des Mittelalters und der Renaissance*, iii (Stuttgart, 1924), pp. 153–5

C. Dodgson: *Catalogue of Early German and Flemish Woodcuts. . .in the British Museum*, i (London, 1980)

VINCENT LIEBER

Master H W (*fl* 1501–20). German sculptor and wood-carver. The evidence of his identity rests on three works dated between 1501 and 1512, monogrammed H W, around which a group of stylistically similar sculptures has been collected. Hentschel identified H W with Hans Witten on the basis of an entry in the Annaberg council records concerning the settlement of a tavern brawl in April 1511 between 'Master Balczer the painter and Hans Widenn his adversary, also a painter.' Hertzsch has, however, disproved Henschel's suggestion that he was the same person as the 'meister Hanss (moler) von Cöln', active between 1501 and 1528 in Chemnitz and Annaberg. Tappen and Uhl found the name Hans Witten several times in the tax register of the priest of St Jakobi, Goslar, between 1490 and 1525, but with no indication of his profession. Thus Master H W's artistic development must be reconstructed solely on the basis of his known and attributed works.

Master H W's career as a wood-carver apparently began in the artistic milieu of Brunswick and Goslar. In the early 1490s he seems to have travelled to south Germany and the Upper Rhine as far as Strasbourg, and he may have learnt to carve stone in the workshop of Adam Kraft in Nuremberg. Detectable influences are, however, not stylistic but organic. Although his 'Lower Saxon early period' has been subject to much stylistic analysis, it is still disputed. Assigned to the end of it is the figure of *St Helena Discovering the True Cross* (sandstone, remains of the original polychromy; h. *c.* 1.55 m; Halle, Staatl. Gal. Moritzburg), produced in 1501 for the old Rathaus (destr. 1945) in Halle an der Saale. It is signed on the pedestal. The early phase includes the reliefs on the pulpit of the Ägidienkirche in Brunswick, datable after 1501, a work of high quality from which emerges a mature personal style. The portrait monument to *Dietrich von Harras* (d 1499) in the Stiftskirche at Chemnitz/Ebersdorf (probably 1502–5; porphyry, traces of the original paint; *c.* 2×1 m) is carved almost entirely out of the base-plate, emphasizing its three-dimensionality.

In 1501, or 1504 at the latest, the Master moved to Chemnitz and in 1508–10 to Annaberg. His main period of activity coincided exactly with the years of prosperity of the Saxon and Bohemian silver-mining towns and of their burgeoning municipal culture. About 1504–5 he took over the commission for the sculptural decoration of the north portal of the Benedictine abbey church of St Maria in Chemnitz (now the castle church; portal re-erected inside in 1973–4), but it is uncertain whether he was responsible for the overall design of the *Astwerk* decoration of the door frame, over 11 m high and interspersed with figures. Only four of the five statues of saints in the middle storey, the *Virgin* and *SS John the Baptist, Benedict* and *Scholastica* (porphyry, traces of paint; h. *c.* 1.4 m), are by his hand. They show his knowledge both of the 'early classical' figurative style of Michel and Gregor Erhart (*see* ERHART), as on the Blaubeuren altar (Blaubeuren, Benediktinerkloster), and of the sculpture of the successors of NICOLAUS GERHAERT in the Upper Rhine area.

Master H W made the plan for the portable altar (1507–12; wood, original polychromy and gilding; h. overall *c.* 6.8 m) of St Nikolai, Ehrenfriedersdorf, and the figures of both the central panel and the relief work. The other carving and decorative work was carried out by studio assistants; the panel paintings were by Hans von Cöln. It is one of the outstanding Upper Saxon retables of the period. The sculptor's preference for freely figurative 'micro-architecture' is embodied in the so-called *Tulpenkanzel* ('Tulip pulpit') in Freiberg Cathedral (1508–10; porphyry with a limewood cover; h. 3.9 m). As an imaginative composition in stone, yet free from architectural constraints and soaring in the broad, light space of the hall church, the pulpit is unique. The meaning and symbolism of the decorative figure work possibly allude to the local mining fable of Daniel, who tried to find ore on trees but was put on the right path by the angel. It could also represent the 'tree of the New Paradise'. The high altar retable (wood, gilded polychromy; h. *c.* 10 m) of the Marienkirche, Borna, near Leipzig, is signed H W and dated 1511. The shrine composition, the *Visitation*, is nowhere else represented in this central position.

In 1512 Master H W signed and dated the lintel of the 'Beautiful Portal' (porphyry, originally painted; h. *c.* 4 m; now Annaberg, Annenkirche) that he made for the Franciscan church in ANNABERG. The iconography of the ogee-shaped tympanum (see fig.) refers to the 'Portiuncula Indulgence', which was believed to have been revealed to St Francis in a dream. The choirs of angels flanking the Throne of Grace seem almost to anticipate the expressive pathos of Baroque ecclesiastical sculpture in their enthusiastically devotional rapture. Their head type resembles two lectern caryatids, an angel and a deacon (limewood, original polychromy; deacon, h. 1.75 m; angel, h. 2.03 m), in the Stiftskirche of Chemnitz/Ebersdorf. With the Crucifix (limewood, traces of original polychromy; figure, h. *c.* 2 m) in the same church, they can be dated 1513. Hardly much later must be the monumental *Scourging* column (limewood, polychromy; h. *c.* 3.6 m), now in the choir of the castle church at Chemnitz. With pictures around its whole surface, it has no comparable prototype in German sculpture.

The artist's late work includes a font of *c.* 1515 (porphyry, originally painted; h. 1.2 m; Annaberg, Annenkirche), which is a large-scale version of a silver gilt lidded bowl of a type illustrated, for example, in Albrecht Dürer's 'Dresden Sketchbook' (Dresden, Sächs. Landesbib., fol. 193); the grandiose *Vesperbild* (*c.* 1515–20; limewood, original polychromy; 1760×1630 mm) in St Jakobi, Goslar; a keystone depicting the *Story of Daniel* (*c.* 1520; porphyry; diam. *c.* 1 m and a *Crucifixion* relief (*c.* 1520; porphyry; 900×770 mm; both Annaberg, Annenkirche). His bold, effervescent, inventive talent, coupled with his technical assurance, made him the leading representative of Late Gothic stone sculpture and wood-carving in Upper Saxony and enabled him constantly to revivify traditional themes.

BIBLIOGRAPHY

W. Hentschel: *Hans Witten: Der Meister H.W.* (Leipzig, 1938)
G. von der Osten: 'Das Frühwerk des Hans Witten', *Jb. Preuss. Kstsamml.*, lxiii/3 (1942), pp. 90–104

Master H W: 'Beautiful Portal', detail of the tympanum, porphyry, *c.* 4.00×2.85 m, 1512 (Annaberg, Annenkirche)

T. Tappen and H.-G. Uhl: 'Hans Witten von Cöln?', *Frölich-Festschrift: Karl Frölich zur Vollendung des 75. Lebensjahres am 14. April 1952*, Beitr. Gesch. Stadt Goslar, xiii (Goslar, 1952), pp. 104–16

E.-H. Lemper: 'Spätgotische Plastik in Sachsen', *Sächs. Heimatbl.*, viii/4 (1962), pp. 301–31

H.-D. Beeger and W. Quellmalz: 'Geologisch-Mineralogische Untersuchungen an den Porphyrtuffen des Nordportales der Schlosskirche zu Karl-Marx-Stadt: Mit einer kunstgeschichtlichen Einführung von Heinrich Magirius', *Jb. Staatl. Mus. Mineral. & Geol. Dresden* (1964), pp. 249–90

H. Magirius: *Die Stiftskirche zu Karl-Marx-Stadt/Ebersdorf,* Christ. Dkml, lxxxii (Berlin, 1971)

E. Fründt: *Der Bornaer Altar von Hans Witten: Das Leben Mariens und die Passion Christi in Bildern vom Hochaltar der Marienkirche* (W. Berlin, 1975)

G. Lammel: 'Das Portal der Schlosskirche in Chemnitz (Karl-Marx-Stadt)', *Sächs. Heimatbl.*, xxi/6 (1975), pp. 249–57

H. Magirius: *Die Annenkirche zu Annaberg*, Christ. Dkml, xcvii/xcviia (Berlin, 1975, 2/1985)

W. Grundmann: *Der Meister H.W.: Das Schaffen Hans Wittens* (W. Berlin, 1976)

W. Hertzsch: *Die Gemälde des Ehrenfriedersdorfer Altars und Hans von Cöln* (diss., Leipzig, Karl-Marx-U., 1976)

H. Magirius: *Die Kunigundenkirche und die Marienkirche in Borna*, Christ. Dkml, xcviii (Berlin, 1976)

——: *Der Dom zu Freiberg* (W. Berlin, 1977)

D. Beeger and H. Prescher: 'Die Tulpenkanzel im Dom zu Freiberg: Geschichte der Restaurierung, Gesteinsmaterial und auftretende Schäden: Mit einer kunstgeschichtlichen Einführung von Heinrich Magirius', *Abh. Staatl. Mus. Mineral. & Geol. Dresden*, xxvii (1977), pp. 41–62

H. Burkhardt: 'Kruzifixe und Kreuzigungsgruppen in der St Annenkirche zu Annaberg: Eine notwendige Bestandsaufnahme', *Sächs. Heimatbl.*, xxvii/6 (1981), pp. 275–83

M. Stuhr: *Die Bildwerke des Meisters H.W.* (Leipzig, 1985)

MICHAEL STUHR

Master IAM of Zwolle (*fl* Zwolle, *c.* 1470–95). North Netherlandish engraver. The master, whose prints are signed with the monogram IA or IAM and usually the place name Zwoll(e), was the most original 15th-century engraver in the northern Netherlands. The maker's mark, which is worked into the monogram on a number of prints, makes the identification with the painter Jan van den Mijnnesten (*d* 1504) very likely; the latter was frequently recorded in Zwolle between 1462 and 1504, but none of his works is known. Many of the Master's prints include the sign of a drill that was used for working on silver: this may indicate that they were engraved by a goldsmith after the painter's designs.

The 26 extant prints by the monogrammist include only one copy (after Martin Schongauer) and reveal an original and independent artist. He worked to a relatively large format, and the prints are engraved in a broad and rather coarse manner, in which shadows tend to be heavy and are indicated by close cross-hatching. The early prints, including a *Lamentation* and a *Crucifixion*, were strongly influenced by Rogier van der Weyden's work. Later prints are more expressive and have strong chiaroscuro effects. The three prints of the *Last Supper*, *Christ on the Mount of Olives* and the *Arrest of Christ*, probably from an unfinished *Passion* series, show a sense of drama combined with a rather crude realism. The scenes are placed within richly decorated Late Gothic architectural frames. The prints may have been intended as models for sculpted reliefs.

Hollstein: *Dut. & Flem.*

M. Lehrs: *Geschichte und kritischer Katalog des deutschen niederländischen und französischen Kupferstichs im XV. Jahrhundert* (1908–34/R 1969), vii, pp. 165–218

Middeleeuwse kunst der noorderlijke Nederlanden (exh. cat., ed. R. Luttervelt; Amsterdam, Rijksmus., 1958), pp. 158–62

E. Finkenstaedt: *The Master IAM of Zwoll* (diss., Cambridge, MA, Harvard U., 1963)

——: 'Some Notes on the Early Chronology of the Master IAM of Zwoll', *Simiolus*, i (1966–7), pp. 121–7

Fifteenth-century Engravings of Northern Europe from the National Gallery of Art, Washington (exh. cat. by A. Shestack, Washington, DC, N.G.A., 1967–8), pp. 134–7

B. Dubbe: 'Is Johann van den Mynnesten de "Meester van Zwolle"', *Bull. Rijksmus.*, xviii (1970), pp. 55–65

A. Châtelet: *Les Primitifs hollandais* (Paris, 1980; Eng. trans. as *Early Dutch Painting*, Oxford, 1981), pp. 168–71

J. P. Filedt Kok: 'Master IAM of Zwoll: The Personality of a Designer and Engraver', *Festschrift to Erik Fischer: European Drawings from Six Centuries* (Copenhagen, 1990), pp. 341–56

J. P. FILEDT KOK

Master I.B. (*fl* 1523–30). German engraver. One of the most important of the Nuremberg Little Masters, he produced engravings, monogrammed I.B., that show close familiarity with the graphic works of Dürer and the Behams. He is distinct from the Lombard painter and engraver Giovanni Battista Palumba, known as Master I.B. with the Bird from his signature on eleven woodcuts of the 1500s (*see* WOODCUT, §II, 3). There are dated works between 1523 and 1530 around which the German artist's surviving oeuvre fits reasonably. Friedländer identified him as the youthful GEORG PENCZ, from the undoubted fact that his activity ceased at the time Pencz's first engravings appeared, *c.* 1530, from their evident common training in the 'school' of Dürer and from stylistic and thematic links between Master I.B.'s last works and Pencz's earliest. However, Landau, demonstrating the stylistic and expressive distance between Master I.B.'s highly assured and precise handling of the burin *c.* 1530 and Pencz's relatively clumsy and tentative productions of the same period, refuted this theory. Other attempts to identify the artist—with Jakob Binck, with the sculptor Hans Peisser, who modelled several of his works after engravings by Master I.B., notably the latter's print of the *Forge of the Heart* (1529; B. 30), and with Giovanni Britto—have been equally inconclusive. The best working hypothesis remains that Master I.B. was a discrete and as yet anonymous artist.

The subject-matter of the prints varies widely, from (early) copies after Dürer and religious and genre scenes in a style characteristic of the Nuremberg Little Masters to allegorical and mythological subjects: a series of the *Planets* (B. 11–17), the *Virtues* (B. 23–9), a *Triumph of Bacchus* (B. 19), a *Battle of Gladiators* (B. 21) and *Putti Gathering Grapes* (B. 18). These works reveal a close acquaintance with Italian printmakers, particularly those of northern Italy, though certain prints are literal copies after Raphael. Three wholly decorative ornamental sheath designs, one dated 1529 (B. 50–52), show him adopting an entirely Italianate mannerism of a kind that is directly comparable to, and suggests some relationship with, the designs of Heinrich Aldegrever. In the majority of his figurative works, however, the Italianate quality is tempered by a manner and technique formed in the circle of

Dürer. The proximity to Dürer is most closely revealed in Master I.B.'s best-known print, the *Forge of the Heart*, which is based on a drawing (London, BM) executed by Dürer shortly before his death in 1528 for his friend Willibald Pirckheimer. Master I.B. extended the design, surrounding it with an elaborate border, suspending it from a column, adding a couple of putti and a dog and altering the identity of the female figures who take part in this elaborate allegory.

BIBLIOGRAPHY

J. von Sandrart: *Teutsche Academie* (1675–9); ed. A. R. Peltzer (1925)
A. von Bartsch: *Le Peintre-graveur* (1803–21) [B.; 52 attribs]
G. K. Nagler: *Monogrammisten* (1858–1920) [71 attribs]
J. D. Passavant: *Le Peintre-graveur* (Leipzig, 1860) [59 attribs]
M. J. Friedländer: 'Georg Pencz, Jörg Pencz, der Meister I.B.', *Repert. Kstwiss.*, xx (1897), pp. 130–32
G. Pauli: 'Der Meister I.B. und Georg Pencz', *Repert. Kstwiss.*, xx (1897), pp. 298–300
E. W. Braun-Troppau: 'Hans Peissers Plaketten und der Nürnberger Kleinmeister I.B.', *Archv Medaillen- & Plakettenkd.*, iii (1923), pp. 104–14
D. Landau: *Catalogo completo dell'opera grafica di Georg Pencz* (Milan, 1978)

ANDREW MORRALL

Master IO.FF (*fl c.* 1480–1515). Italian sculptor. Various candidates have been proposed for the bronze plaquette sculptor who signed his works IO.FF, including Giovanni delle Corniole (*c.* 1470–*c.* 1516), Gian Francesco di Boggio (*fl* 1538) and Giovanni Francesco Ruberti (1486–1526); current opinion favours Giovanni Paolo Fonduli.

The subjects most frequently depicted on this master's plaquettes are allegorical and mythological scenes in circular frames, such as the *Judgement of Paris*, *Ariadne on Naxos* and an *Allegory with a Woman on a Dragon*, and in cartouche frames subjects including the *Trial of Mucius Scaevola*, the *Death of Marcus Curtius* and an *Unidentified Scene with the Breaking of Sticks* (all Washington, DC, N.G.A.). Originally they probably functioned as decorations for sword pommels, and some of these compositions have been recognized in the decoration of daggers and scabbards, including one (*c.* 1493–8; London, V&A) made for Cesare Borgia. They were also used in fine bookbindings produced 1510–15 for Jean Grolier.

BIBLIOGRAPHY

W. Terni de Gregory: 'Giovanni da Crema and his "Seated Goddess"', *Burl. Mag.*, xcii (1950), pp. 159–61
C. B. Fulton: *The Master of IO.FF and the Function of Plaquettes*, Stud. Hist. A., xxii (1982), pp. 143–62 [bibliog. and pls]

□

Master I.P. [Master J.P.] (*fl c.* 1520). Bavarian or Austrian wood-carver. He was one of a group of carvers active in Salzburg, Passau and Prague who made small, elegant, highly refined reliefs in boxwood, limewood and pearwood. These items were in many ways a northern counterpart to the small bronze statuettes produced in Italy for wealthy private collectors. The Master of Irrsdorf, the earliest of the group, has sometimes been identified with Master I.P.; Gert von der Osten has suggested that he be identified as J. Pocksberg. The only dated work by Master I.P. is a pearwood relief of the *Fall of Man* (160×125 mm; Vienna, Belvedere, Österreich. Gal.), a version of Albrecht Dürer's engraving of 1504 in which Eve's back is turned to the viewer. Both nudes are more

animated and sensuous than Dürer's, and the Garden of Eden is fully developed in a convincing perspective based on depth of undercutting. A related work, inscribed *Adam D.* (which may or may not be a signature), is in the Palazzo Pitti in Florence, while still others are in Gotha (Schloss Friedenstein), Prague (N.G., Convent of St George) and Frankfurt am Main (Liebieghaus); a statuette of *Adam* alone is in Moscow (Pushkin Mus. F.A.).

BIBLIOGRAPHY
Thieme–Becker

E. F. Bange: *Die Kleinplastik der deutschen Renaissance in Holz und Stein* (Munich, 1928), pp. 59–60
Die Kunst der Donauschule, 1490–1540 (exh. cat., ed. Otto Wutzel; Linz, Schlossmus., 1965), pp. 278, 281
G. von der Osten and H. Vey: *Painting and Sculpture in Germany and the Netherlands, 1500–1600*, Pelican Hist. A. (Harmondsworth, 1969), pp. 251–2

JANE CAMPBELL HUTCHISON

Master I♀V (*fl* Fontainebleau, *c.* 1543–4). French engraver. He has been identified as Jean Vignay, a painter employed at the château of Fontainebleau between 1537 and 1540 at the rate of 20 sols a day, or as Jean Vaquet, another painter who worked at Fontainebleau between 1540 and 1550 and received 13 livres a month (Adhémar). Herbet, who emphasized the problems involved in such attributions based on payment records, attributed 28 reproductive engravings to this master. The Master I♀V seems to have specialized in reproducing the decorations in Fontainebleau and the works of Giulio Romano, Rosso Fiorentino, Andrea del Sarto and Polidoro da Caravaggio. According to Zerner, he introduced the Flemish-style panoramic landscape to Fontainebleau. His manner of engraving developed over the years, becoming close to that of Antonio Fantuzzi, but there is originality in his rather strange, minutely detailed sense of line.

BIBLIOGRAPHY

A. von Bartsch: *Le Peintre-graveur* (1803–21), xvi/2 (1901)
F. Herbet: *Les Eaux-fortes nommées ou marquées*, iv of *Les Graveurs de l'école de Fontainebleau* (Fontainebleau, 1896–1902)
J. Adhémar: *Graveurs du seizième siècle* (1938), ii of *Inventaire du fonds français*, Paris, Bib. N., Cab. Est. cat. (Paris, 1930–), pp. 148–52
H. Zerner: *Ecole de Fontainebleau: Gravures* (Paris, 1969)
L'Ecole de Fontainebleau (exh. cat., ed. S. Béguin; Paris, Grand Pal.; Ottawa, N.G.; 1972–3), nos 358–62 [entries by H. Zerner]
H. Zerner: *Italian Artists of the Sixteenth Century* (1979) 33 [XVI/ii] of *The Illustrated Bartsch*, ed. W. Strauss (New York, 1978–)

MARIANNE GRIVEL

Master J.P. *See* MASTER I.P. above.

Master J.S. *See* SILBER, JONAS.

Master L.Cz. [?L.Cm.] (*fl c.* 1485–1500). German printmaker and painter. Ten of the twelve surviving engravings by this artist are signed with the monogram. Two are also dated: a design for a decorative piece, the *Maiden and the Unicorn* (1492; see Lehrs, no. 12), and *SS Peter and Paul* (1497; L 9). The early engravings, for example *St George* (*c.* 1485–90; L 7), are somewhat derivative of Martin Schongauer and the Housebook Master; later works, such as the *Temptation of Christ* (late 1490s; L 2), show the Master's own style. As he used aquatint to achieve tone, so that his engravings resemble painting, it is thought that he was not a goldsmith but a painter. Consequently he has been attributed with the works of the Master of the Strache Altar, named from four *Passion* scenes (*c.* 1485–90), of which three—*Christ before Pilate* (Berlin, Gemäldegal.), the *Flagellation* (Paris, Louvre) and *Christ Carrying the Cross* (Nuremberg, Ger. Nmus.)— were in the collection of Hugo Strache. The suggestion that they were on two wings forming part of an *Agony in the Garden* (after 1497–before 1504; Darmstadt, Hess. Landesmus.) cannot be correct, as the latter was not painted until the end of the 15th century and the measurements do not correspond.

The thoroughly lurid depiction of the *Passion* has some connection with the *Passion* cycles painted in Bamberg in the mid-1480s and 1490s, and a *Crucifixion* (*c.* 1485; Nuremberg, Ger. Nmus.) is also associated with Bamberg, through the donor, Canon Stibar, which suggests that Master L.Cz. worked in Bamberg. The L.Cz. signature (recently interpreted as L.Cm.) suggests that he might have been the painter Lorenz Katzheimer, though he was documented in Bamberg only in 1505 and 1510, or that the oeuvre might be the early work of Lucas Cranach the elder, who came from nearby Kronach.

BIBLIOGRAPHY
Thieme–Becker
M. Lehrs: 'Der Meister L Cz und der Meister WB', *Veröff. Graph. Ges.*, xxv (Berlin, 1922) [L]
M. Weinberger: 'Über die Herkunft des Meisters L Cz', *Festschrift Heinrich Wölfflin* (Munich, 1924), pp. 169–82
B. Saran: *Der Meister L.Cz.: Ein Wegbereiter Albrecht Dürers in Bamberg* (Bamberg, 1939)
E. Schenk-Gotha: 'Der Meister L Cz', *Z. Kst*, i/4 (1947), pp. 26–30
E. Buchner: 'Zum Malwerk des Meisters L Cz', *Festgabe für Seine Königliche Hoheit Kronprinz Rupprecht von Bayern* (Munich, 1953), pp. 85–9
A. Stange: *Deutsche Malerei der Gotik*, ix (Munich, Berlin, 1958), pp. 105–8
F. Anzelewsky: 'Eine spätmittelalterliche Malerwerkstatt: Studien über die Malerfamilie Katzheimer in Bamberg', *Z. Dt. Ver. Kstwiss.*, xix (1965), pp. 146–50
A. Shestack: *Master L Cz and Master WB* (New York, 1971)
D. Koepplin and T. Falk: *Lucas Cranach: Gemälde, Zeichnungen, Druckgraphik*, ii (Basle and Stuttgart, 1976), pp. 760–61
A. Stange: *Kritisches Verzeichnis der deutschen Tafelbilder vor Dürer*, iii (Munich, 1978), pp. 123–5

RENATE BAUMGÄRTEL-FLEISCHMANN

Master L.D. *See* DAVENT, LÉON.

Master MZ (*fl c.* 1500). German engraver. Twenty-two engravings are signed with the initials MZ, six of them dated (1500, 1501, 1503). In the absence of appreciable stylistic or technical development and because the artist's sources—Albrecht Dürer's prints from the 1490s in particular—are no later than the dated prints, it is thought that all the production was concentrated *c.* 1500. The prints are equally divided between religious and secular subjects. Often a state of disquiet inhabits the figures, accompanied by eccentric use of perspective and abrupt changes in scale, as seen for example in *The Embrace* (Lehrs, 1932, no. 16) and *Solomon's Idolatry* (L 1). Most of his works have landscape backgrounds executed with a delicate, atmospheric touch that suggests a precursor of Albrecht Altdorfer and other painters of the Danube school. *The Ball* and *The Tournament* (1500; L 17–18), companion pieces that represent a court festival in Munich, are the principal evidence that the artist was active in that city. The same hand may have engraved a reliquary plaque

(1501; Andechs, pilgrimage church of Mariae Verkündigung) commissioned by the Munich Brotherhood of Butchers. This similarity has supported the contention that the Monogrammist MZ was the Munich goldsmith Matthäus Zasinger (*fl* 1498–1555), though the burin work more readily suggests the hand of a painter than that of an engraver. Accordingly the Master has been attributed with eight panels with scenes from the *Life of St Lawrence* (*c.* 1505–7; Berching, Lorenzkirche). Noting the similarities of form and expression between the engravings of Master MZ and the paintings of Master MS (*fl* 1521), who was active in Hungary and is also associated with the Danube school, it has been argued that the paintings and engravings are by the same hand. None of these or other proposed identities is yet persuasive.

BIBLIOGRAPHY
Thieme–Becker
H. Voss: *Der Ursprung des Donaustiles* (Leipzig, 1907), pp. 107–27
M. Lehrs: 'The Master MZ', *Prt Colr. Q.*, xvi (1929), pp. 205–50
——: *Geschichte und kritischer Katalog des deutschen, niederländischen und französischen Kupferstichs im XV. Jahrhundert*, viii (Vienna, 1932), pp. 330–78 [L]
Fifteenth-century Engravings of Northern Europe from the National Gallery of Art (exh. cat., ed. A. Shestack; Washington, DC, N.G.A., 1967–8), nos 143–53
A. Lenz: *Der Meister MZ* (diss., U. Munich, 1972)
M. Mojzer: 'Um Meister MZ', *Acta Hist. A.*, xxi (1975), pp. 371–428
——: 'Um Meister MZ: II. Teil', *Acta Hist. A. Acad. Sci. Hung.*, xxvii (1981), pp. 247–79
C. Andersson and C. Talbot: *From a Mighty Fortress: Prints, Drawings and Books in the Age of Luther, 1483–1546* (exh. cat., Detroit, MI, Inst. A., 1983), pp. 312–17

CHARLES TALBOT

Monogrammist NH. *See* HOGENBERG, (1).

Monogrammist PC (*fl* 1524–41). North Netherlandish draughtsman. The monogram, usually read as 'PC' but possibly to be interpreted as 'DC', appears on a homogeneous group of Leiden school drawings, mostly stained-glass designs in pen and ink. Among these are three series of drawings representing the Seven Acts of Mercy, one group dated 1524, of which six designs survive: *Giving Drink to the Thirsty* (Paris, Fond. Custodia, Inst. Néer.); the *Feeding of the Hungry* and the *Sheltering of the Pilgrims* (both Berlin, Kupferstichkab.); *Caring for the Dying* and the *Burying of the Dead* (both Amsterdam, Rijksmus.); and the *Freeing of the Prisoners* (London, BM). Only one window, after the latter drawing, has survived (Paris, Louvre). Two drawings from the second series, which is dated 1531, are preserved: the *Burying of the Dead* (Munich, Staatl. Graph. Samml.) and the *Feeding of the Hungry* (Rotterdam, Mus. Boymans–van Beuningen). Of the third group, dated 1532, three sheets are extant: the *Burying of the Dead* and *Caring for the Dying* (both Berlin, Kupferstichkab.) and *Freeing of the Prisoners* (ex-Holkham Hall, Norfolk). The artist's draughtsmanship is characterized by vigorous hatching and crosshatching, comparable to the work of Lucas van Leyden and Cornelis Engebrechtsz.

The artist was traditionally identified as Engebrechtsz.'s eldest son, PIETER CORNELISZ. KUNST, who, according to van Mander, made designs for stained glass. According to Bangs, however, the monogram does not correspond to that which appears after the name of Pieter Cornelisz. Kunst on a list from 1515 of housemarks intended for the buckets used by Leiden firemen. Bangs further suggested that the monogram might belong instead to the Leiden glass painter 'Meester' Pieter Hugenz. van Cloetinge (*fl* 1518–38), whose mark is unknown. This argument has not been universally accepted: Boon has pointed out that other artists who did not sign their work with a monogram also appear on the list with their housemarks, and, furthermore, housemarks on practical objects cannot necessarily be equated with signatures or monograms on works of art.

BIBLIOGRAPHY

K. van Mander: *Schilder-boeck* ([1603]–1604)

F. Dülberg: 'Die Persönlichkeit des Lucas van Leyden', *Oud-Holland*, xvii (1899), pp. 65–83 (66)

J. D. Bangs: 'The Leiden Monogrammist PC and Other Artists' Enigmatic Fire Buckets', *Source: Notes Hist. A.*, i/1 (1981), pp. 12–15

Kunst voor de Beeldenstorm: Noordnederlandse kunst, 1525–1580 [Art for the iconoclasm: north Netherlandish art, 1525–1580] (exh. cat., ed. J. P. Filedt Kok, W. Halsema-Kubes and W. Th. Kloek; Amsterdam, Rijksmus., 1986), pp. 167–8, nos 49–50

The Age of Bruegel: Netherlandish Drawings in the Sixteenth Century (exh. cat. by J. O. Hand and others; Washington, DC, N.G.A.; New York, Pierpont Morgan Lib.; 1986–7), pp. 122–6, nos 40–41

K. G. Boon: *The Netherlandish and German Drawings of the XVth and XVIth Centuries of the Frits Lugt Collection* (Paris, 1992), i, pp. 235–7, no. 132, iii, pl. 25

JANE SHOAF TURNER

Master PM (*fl* ?Lower Rhine, 1480–90). German engraver. His initials are found on the engraving of the *Man of Sorrows on the Grave with Two Angels* (see Lehrs, 1927 no. 4). Four unsigned engravings, few copies of which have survived, are attributed to him. They include a study sheet, unusual among early engravings, with figures of *Adam and Eve* (L 1). The good figure drawing and delicate engraving style suggest they may have been occasional works by a painter, rather than by a professional engraver. His style is very closely related to that of Master B.R.

BIBLIOGRAPHY

M. Lehrs: 'Der Meister PM', *Jb. Kön-Preuss. Kstsamml.*, xix (1898), pp. 135–8

——: *Geschichte und kritischer Katalog des deutschen, niederländischen und französischen Kupferstichs im XV. Jahrhundert*, vi (Vienna, 1927), pp. 281–90 [L]

M. Hébert: *Bibliothèque nationale, Département des gravures: Inventaire des gravures des écoles du nord, 1440–1550*, i (Paris, 1982), p. 105

HOLM BEVERS

Master P.S. (i) (*fl* first half of 16th century). German draughtsman and etcher. His work was dependent on the Danube school in both style and choice of theme, as in the etching of a *Pair of Lovers under a Tree* (1538; sold Berne, Gutekunst & Klipstein, 1903). His distinctive stylistic peculiarities bring together a number of previously unassigned compositions, such as the etching in the manner of Jakob Binck of a *Seated Naked Woman and Child in Landscape with Town and River* (1539; Amsterdam, Rijksmus.), or the etching of *Samson Supporting the Gates of Gaza* (1539; Berlin, Kupferstichkab.). These vary in technique. The hatching on *Samson* is much softer and less dense, giving greater depth, than the broad, summary treatment of the landscape. The etching technique remains reminiscent of rigid woodcut. The unsigned etching of a *Fortified Town on the Water* (1536; Kaliningrad, Reg. Local Hist. Mus.) has close stylistic links with the Amsterdam etching. Two unsigned drawings dated 1535 are connected with it—*Jonas beneath the Fig Tree on the Hills outside Nineveh* (Dresden, Kupferstichkab.) and *Daniel in the Lions' Den* (Leiden, Rijksuniv., Pretenkab.): these must have belonged to a series of the *Prophets*. Two landscape drawings (1527; Haarlem, ex-Koenigs priv. col.; Weimar, Schlossmus.) are also attributed to the Master. His oeuvre suggests an artist mainly attracted by the beauty of the way water and land cut into each other. In this he adopted from the Danube school the elements in which their romantic feeling for nature was expressed: typically, S-shaped curving bridges, winding roads and paths, and the placement of settlements on a riverbank.

BIBLIOGRAPHY

J.O. de Gelder: 'Tekeningen toegeschreven aan Jakob Binck' [Drawings attributed to Jakob Binck], *Oudhdknd. Jb.*, n. s. 3, ii (1933), pp. 44–5, fig. 1

H. van den Wall: 'Graphische Arbeiten des Monogrammisten P.S.', *Graph. Kst.*, n. s. 1, iv (1939), pp. 47–61

Zeichnung in Deutschland: Deutsche Zeichner, 1540–1640, i (exh. cat. by H. Geissler, Stuttgart, Staatsgal., 1979), pp. 176–7

SONJA WEIH-KRUGER

Master P.S. (ii). *See under* PRÉVOST, JACQUES.

Master PW of Cologne (*fl* Cologne, *c.* 1500). German engraver. Some 97 prints are attributed to him, of which the most the important are large-format *Swiss War* (see Lehrs, no. 18), a depiction of a theatre of war in the Lake Constance area in 1499 printed with six large copperplates, and the *Round Card Game* (L 20–91). Though he was once thought to be a south German engraver, it appears that he worked in Cologne. The *Raising of Lazarus* (*c.* 1500; Berlin, Kupferstichkab.) is probably by his hand. It is possible that he is identical with the MASTER OF THE AACHEN ALTAR (*see* §I above), who worked in Cologne and served his apprenticeship in the circle of the Frueaufs and Jörg Breu I.

BIBLIOGRAPHY

M. Lehrs: *Die ältesten deutschen Spielkarten des Königlichen Kupferstichkabinetts zu Dresden* (Dresden, 1885), pp. 27–38

——: 'Der Meister PW von Köln', *Repert. Kstwiss.*, x (1887), pp. 254–70

——: *Geschichte und kritischer Katalog des deutschen, niederländischen und französischen Kupferstichs im XV. Jahrhundert*, vii (Vienna, 1930), pp. 250–330

E. Schleuter: *Der Meister PW*, 305 of *Stud. Dt. Kstgesch.* (Strasbourg and Leipzig, 1935)

F. Anzelewsky: 'Der Meister des Aachener Altars und der Monogrammist PW', *Studien aus dem Berliner Kupferstichkabinett*, ed. H. Möhle (Berlin, 1966), pp. 16–20

——: 'Zum Problem des Meisters des Aachener Altars', *Wallraf Richartz-Jb.*, xxx (1968), pp. 185–200

M. Hébert: *Bibliothèque nationale, Département des gravures: Inventaire des gravures des écoles du nord, 1440–1550*, i (Paris, 1982), pp. 108–9

HOLM BEVERS

Master S (*fl c.* 1520). South Netherlandish engraver. So-called because he usually signed his engravings with the monogram S, the Master was the author of an extensive group of prints representing mainly religious themes. Stylistically his work is closely linked to ANTWERP MANNERISM. Some of his prints were inspired by the engravings of Albrecht Dürer, Lucas van Leyden, Dirk Vellert and others. The compositions are often rather stiff, and in general the work appears archaic. Master S was certainly not a first-class engraver; his historical significance lies in the fact that he headed an active workshop in which prints were mass-produced for the first time in the southern

Netherlands. The small engravings were sometimes glued into manuscripts and served as cheap 'ersatz' miniatures. Over 450 prints have been attributed to him, but many are the work of collaborators or pupils.

Glück (1926) identified him hypothetically with the Antwerp goldsmith Alexander van Brugsal (*d* before 1545), who was admitted to the Antwerp Guild of St Luke in 1515/16. He was a prominent citizen and met Dürer on several occasions during the latter's stay in Antwerp in 1520/21. There is, however, no evidence to support the identification.

BIBLIOGRAPHY

Hollstein: *Dut. & Flem.*

A. J. J. Delen: *Histoire de la gravure dans les anciens Pays-Bas et dans les provinces belges des origines jusqu'à la fin du 18ème siècle* (Paris, 1924–35), iii/2, pp. 36–8

G. Glück: 'Eine Vermutung über den Meister S', *Festschrift der National-bibliothek in Wien* (Vienna, 1926), pp. 401–5; repr. in *Aus drei Jahrhunderten Europäischer Malerei* (Vienna, 1933), pp. 130–35

R. A. K[och]: 'Two Engravings by Monogrammist "S" (Alexander van Bruessele?)', *Rec. A. Mus., Princeton U.*, x (1951), pp. 12–19

H. Schwarz: 'Two Unrecorded Engravings by Master S', *Bull. Inst. Royal Patrm. A.*, vi (1957), pp. 39–42

M. Hébert: *1450–1550* (1983), ii of *Inventaire des gravures des écoles du nord*, Paris, Bib. N., Cab. Est. cat., pp. 297–312

JAN VAN DER STOCK

Master SC (*fl* earlier 16th century). German engraver. He probably came from the Danube region of Bavaria. His work seems influenced by the engravings of Albrecht Dürer but also, in overall pictorial effect and a painterly richness of light and dark, by Albrecht Altdorfer. Three fine engravings are known: *St John on Patmos* (first state 1517; second state 1521; Nagler, iv, 3979, no. 3), *Archer with a Woman*, known as *The Savages* (1520; Koch, p. 177), and *The Flag-thrower* (Koch, p. 178). The pen-and-ink drawing *Decorative Jug with Winged Mermaids and a Shield-bearer on the Lid and a Dolphin as the Spout* (*c.* 1530; Erlangen, Ubib.), marked with the monogram SC, was clearly influenced by Altdorfer's etched designs for vessels. Although the painterly and stylistically very confident effect of the engravings suggests that Master SC was also a painter, the attribution to him of the painting *Battle between Mercenary Infantrymen* (1514; Würzburg, Wagner-Mus.) remains controversial. There are nonetheless many obvious stylistic connections between it and the engravings, not only in the strained positions of the wild, unkempt-looking infantrymen as they lunge and move, and in their strikingly chiselled jaw- and cheekbones, but in the whole artistic attitude to form.

BIBLIOGRAPHY

G. K. Nagler: *Monogrammisten* (1858–1920)

E. Buchner: 'Bemerkungen zum "Historien- und Schlachtenbild" der deutschen Renaissance', *Beitr. Gesch. Dt. Kst*, i (1924), pp. 240–59

——: 'Zwei oberdeutsche Meister der Reformationszeit, I. Der Monogrammist SC', *Z. Bild. Kst*, n. s. 1, lix (1925/6), pp. 49–54

E. Bock: *Die Zeichnungen in der Universitätsbibliothek Erlangen* (Frankfurt am Main, 1929), no. 1020

K. Oettinger: 'Der Meister der Würzburger Schlacht', *Pantheon*, xii (1939), pp. 89–94

R. A. Koch.: *Early German Masters (1980)*, 14 [VIII/i] of *The Illustrated Bartsch*, ed. W. Strauss (New York, 1978–)

V. Hoffmann and K. Koppe, eds: *Martin von Wagner Museum der Universität Würzburg: Gemäldekatalog* (Würzburg, 1986), no. 315

SONJA WEIH-KRÜGER

Master W〰 (*fl* ?eastern Netherlands, *c.* 1465–90). South Netherlandish engraver and ?gold- and silversmith. He signed his prints with the letter W and a house mark in the form of a stylized key. Over 80 engravings survive: besides a number of conventional religious subjects and two exceptional series, one of ships and one of the Burgundian army, they are mainly decorative prints. His designs for chalices, reliquaries, monstrances and architectural features in a Late Gothic style are sometimes large format and extremely detailed. The more unusual prints of Gothic church interiors were probably designs for tabernacles and similar items and would have been intended for the use of shrinemakers or masons. Since one of his engravings represents the coat of arms of Charles the Bold, Duke of Burgundy (which may be dated before 1472), it is generally thought that the Master had contacts with the Duke's court in Bruges; but there are reasons to believe that he worked near the border of Germany, not far from Zwolle.

BIBLIOGRAPHY

Hollstein: *Dut. & Flem.*

M. Lehrs: *Meister* W〰 (Leipzig, 1895)

——: *Geschichte und kritischer Katalog des deutschen, niederländischen und französischen Kupferstichs im XV. Jahrhundert*, 9 vols (Vienna, 1908–34/R Nedeln, 1969), vii, pp. 1–101

W. Boerner: *Meister* W〰 (Leipzig, 1923)

J. P. FILEDT KOK

Master WB (*fl* 1586–1612). Swiss stained-glass artist. He signed several stained-glass works with the interlacing monogram WB. There is some debate about his identity. He was probably Wolfgang Breny (Bräni) from a glass-painting family in Rapperswil. For a long time research followed Lehmann's assumption that Master WB was Wolfgang Bühler (Büler), a glass-painter who settled in Wil in 1585 as a *nüwer Schiltbrenner* ('new sign smith'), then moved to Rapperswil and is reported to have died there. Wyss, however, has proved that the Wolfgang Bühler, an associate of Hans Fallenter (*fl c.* 1570; *d* 1612) in Lucerne, who is mentioned in these sources, has no link with the monogrammist WB. His theory, based on an entry in the tax book of Wil (1591, p. 63; see Boesch, 1949, p. 22), is that WB is rather Wolfgang Breny (Bräni) of Rapperswil (*d* 1613), who signed many panes of glass between 1586 and 1612. In 1586 Master WB made a monogrammed stained-glass panel (Nostell Priory, W. Yorks; Boesch, 1937, no. 38) for Pastor Stössel in Mosnang, and he is attributed with a glass panel (1599; Wragby, St Michael; Boesch, 1937, no. 436) for Pastor Diethelm Uli from Wil in Mosnang. There are records of a commission for a stained-glass panel of the *Adoration* (1586; priv. col.; Boesch, 1935, no. 25, fig.) from Caspar Spitzly. A heraldic panel of *Abbot Joachim Opser with SS Gallus and Othmar* (1588; St Gall, Hist. Mus.) and a votive panel (1594; ex-Kstgewmus., Berlin; Schmitz, i, p. 206; ii, pl. 58) belonging to the town clerk Hans Falck, the mayor of Wil and a town councillor, are monogrammed, as is a superb heraldic panel (1605; sold Munich, Gal. Hugo Helbing, 1913) depicting the bishop of Chur with two angels in long robes. Other heraldic panels (Basle, Hist. Mus.; St Gall, Hist. Mus.) are attributed to Master WB.

BIBLIOGRAPHY

Thieme–Becker

H. Lehmann: *Die ehemalige Sammlung schweizerischer Glasmalereien in Toddington Castle, England, Sammlung Studeley* (Munich, 1911), p. 111

H. Schmitz: *Die Glasgemälde des Kunstgewerbe-Museums Berlin*, 2 vols (Berlin, 1913)

P. Boesch: 'Die Toggenburger Scheiben' *Neujbl. Hist. Ver. Kant. St Gallen*, lxxvii (1935)

——: 'Schweizer Glasgemälde im Ausland: Die Sammlung in Nostell Church', *Anz. Schweiz. Altertknd.*, n. s., xxxix (1937), pp. 14, 298

F. Wyss: 'Einige Streiflichter auf die Glasmalerei in Rapperswil und Weesen', *Z. Schweiz. Archäol. & Kstgesch.*, 24 (1946), pp. 80–91

P. Boesch: 'Die Wiler Glasmaler und ihr Werk', *Neujbl. Hist. Ver. Kant. St Gallen*, lxxxix (1949)

F. FORTER

Master W‡B (*fl* ?Mainz, *c.* 1450–1500). German painter, engraver and designer of stained-glass windows and wood-cuts. The monogram, with a *Schlangenstab*, or snake twisted round a staff between the letters, appears on two portrait engravings. These and two others have sometimes been taken for impressions from reworked plates of the House-book Master, for the engraving is similar to the direct and lively style of the latter's drypoints. This gives the heads, which were probably intended as character studies rather than portraits, a forceful appearance. The same style recurs in a number of painted portraits (Frankfurt am Main, Städel. Kstinst. & Stadt. Gal.; 1484 Madrid, Mus. Thyssen-Bornemisza). Other attributions include panels with scenes from the *Life of St Sebastian* in Mainz Cathedral, stained-glass windows in the choir of the Marienkirche in Hanau and a number of drawings and designs for the woodcuts in the *Chronicles of Saxony* (Mainz, 1492). His work is characterized by a lively realism and vivid expressions. The attributed works seem to come from a typical late medieval painter's workshop in Mainz, in which various crafts were practised side by side. This makes it difficult to distinguish the Master's own contributions from those of other artists.

Some scholars have identified the Master with Wolfgang Beurer, a name that occurs with the date 1484 in Albrecht Dürer's handwriting on a drawing of a *Man on Horseback* (Gdańsk, N. Mus.), but of whom no further biographical details are known. This identification has led to a regrouping of the oeuvre attributed to the Master: some works have now been ascribed to Arnold Beurer and some to the Master of the Herpin.

BIBLIOGRAPHY

M. Lehrs: *Geschichte und kritischer Katalog des deutschen, niederländischen und französischen Kupferstichs im XV. Jahrhundert*, 9 vols (Vienna, 1908–34/*R* Nedeln, 1969), vi, pp. 343–9

E. Buchner: 'Studien zur Mittelrheinischen Malerei und Graphik der Spätgotik und Renaissance', *Münchn. Jb. Bild. Kst*, n.s. 1, iv (1927), pp. 229–325

A. Shestack: *Master LCz and Master* W‡B (New York, 1971)

F. Anzelewsky: 'Eine Gruppe von Malern und Zeichnern aus Dürers Jugendjahren', *Jb. Berlin. Mus.*, xxvii (1985), pp. 35–59

J. P. Filedt Kok: *Livelier than Life: The Master of the Amsterdam Cabinet or the Housebook Master* (exh. cat., Amsterdam, Rijksmus., 1985), pp. 53–4, 213–16, nos 113–16

J. P. FILEDT KOK

Master WG (*fl* 1572). Name given to the author, compiler or copyist of an extensive architectural pattern book (Frankfurt am Main, Städel. Kstinst. & Städt. Gal., Cod. 2026). The volume (220×155×55 mm) has a leather case with stamped decoration (dated 1560) and two metal fastenings; the monogram W*G and the year 1572 were later embossed in the type area of the front cover. The volume contains 314 pages (*c.* 200×150 mm), partly inter-leaved. The watermarks are of the paper-mill at Landshut in the mid-16th century and probably of the paper-mill of Munich-Au. This indicates that the volume could have been produced in Bavaria. The date 1572, which may be the date of completion, appears on fols 9 and 279, and the initials WG on fols 7, 9 and 44. The endpapers bear entries by 19th-century owners. The book is generally well preserved, but there are minor water traces; one sheet, between fols 188 and 189, has been lost. There is no explanatory text.

The codex contains pen-and-ink drawings and cut-out designs of vaults (including designs suitable for centralized and secular buildings), arches, window tracery, elevations, house gables, geometric constructions, spiral staircases and sundials; the last follow Albrecht Dürer's instructions regarding measurement. The drawings are incised and coloured in greenish-brown above or near the incisions, with occasional red washes; fols 3, 4, 9 and 10 are red chalk drawings. Even the cut-out pages have incisions; narrow paper strips are sometimes torn out and stuck back. The vault designs are largely conventional, and insofar as they can be identified, they are related to south German buildings of the last quarter of the 15th century or at least resemble such buildings; fols 10, 14 and 202, for example, show the designs of the aisle vaulting in the Frauenkirche, Munich. Stylistically they often reveal post-Gothic features, and there are also many very dense or rather asymmetrically arranged designs that are equally post-Gothic in character. Much, however, looks back to earlier material: for instance, the design on fol. 225 resembles that of the Cistercian abbey church at Zwettl, Lower Austria. Vault ribs are sometimes curvilinear.

Master WG is as yet unidentified. The amateurish sketchiness of the drawings and cut-out designs and the errors in the construction diagrams suggest that the volume could scarcely have been drawn up or copied by a mason from a traditional background: there is no understanding of or feeling for structural principles. The mark ⸗, which appears five times, need not necessarily be a mason's mark but could also be a mark of ownership. Whether it belongs to the monogrammist WG or was taken from the patterns is an open question.

BIBLIOGRAPHY

P. Booz: *Der Baumeister der Gotik* (Munich and Berlin, 1956), p. 42

W. Müller: 'Verkommen und Variationen einer Rippenkonfiguration Nürnberger Meisterstücke in der österreichischen Spätgotik', *Österreich. Z. Kst & Dkmlpf.*, xxvii (1973), pp. 132–9

F. Bucher: *Architector: The Lodge Books and Sketchbooks of Medieval Architects*, i (New York, 1979), pp. 195–373 [complete facs.]

E. Pauken: *Das Steinmetzbuch WG 1572 im Städelschen Kunstinstitut zu Frankfurt am Main* (Cologne, 1979); review by W. Müller in *Z. Kstgesch.*, lxiv (1981), pp. 97–9

R. Recht: 'Les "Traités pratiques" d'architecture gothique', *Les Bâtisseurs des cathédrales gothiques* (exh. cat., ed. R. Recht; Strasbourg, Musées Ville, 1989), p. 282

FRIEDRICH KOBLER

Master W.S. with the Maltese Cross. *See* STETTER, WILHELM.

Mastic. Natural resin widely used as a varnish for paintings, as well as an additive to oil paint or a medium in its own right (*see* RESIN, §1). It has been obtained from the bark of a Mediterranean tree of the genus *Pistacia* since at least the 9th century. For use as varnish, it is dissolved in turpentine or linseed oil but suffers from both the defects of increased yellowness with age and a tendency to BLOOM. It has now been superseded by dammar or synthetic resin varnishes.

RUPERT FEATHERSTONE

Mastini. *See* AMASTINI.

Mastroianni, Umberto (*b* Fontana Liri, 21 Sept 1910). Italian sculptor and painter. In 1924 he moved to Rome, where he studied drawing at the Accademia di San Marcello and sculpture in the studio of his uncle Domenico Mastroianni. In 1926 he moved to Turin, where he produced his first works of figurative sculpture, mainly nudes and portraits, inspired by the art of the Italian Renaissance. In 1940 he totally abandoned figurative art in favour of abstraction influenced by Futurism. His use of stone and marble favoured large-scale works and in 1946, in Turin, he created the monument to the *Fallen for Liberty*, also known as the monument to *The Partisan* (stone, 8.9×3.5 m) in the Campo della Gloria in Turin. His friendship with Luigi Spazzapan brought him closer to the European avant-garde. In 1951 he had his first one-man show at the Galerie de France in Paris, where he achieved some success. In 1955 Mastroianni produced his first bronzes, which were characterized by a dynamic structure around a central core. At the Venice Biennale of 1958 his exhibits included his first wall-panels based on his experiments with such new materials as wood and sacking (e.g. *Sediments*, mixed media and sacking, 1961; Rome, G.N.A. Mod.). These works, which brought him closer to the innovations of Alberto Burri, were followed by *Plastic Reliefs* (1959–62). After experimenting with engraving (1962–3), he returned to large metal works: in 1964 the municipality of Cuneo commissioned the monument to the *Italian Resistance* (bronze, 18×20×12 m), with which he was involved until 1969. During the 1970s he concentrated on painting, using a range of materials and colours and sometimes achieving an almost decorative rhythm. His bronze sculptures and monumental steel works of the 1970s also developed a flat frontal quality. He continued his experiments with mixed media and paints into the 1980s.

BIBLIOGRAPHY

Umberto Mastroianni (exh. cat., ed. P. Bucarelli; Rome, G.N.A. Mod., 1974)
Umberto Mastroianni, 2 vols (exh. cat. by F. Moschini, Florence, Forte Belvedere, 1981)

DANIELA DE DOMINICIS

Masucci, Agostino (*b* Rome, 1690; *d* Rome, 19 Oct 1768). Italian painter and draughtsman. He was apprenticed in Rome, first to Andrea Procaccini and later to Maratti. His work is characterized by a classicism derived from Guido Reni and ultimately from Raphael. According to Pio, he was 'nourished first by the perfect milk of Maratti, and then saturated with the divine nectar of Raphael'. One of the last artists of Maratti's school, he was also a precursor of the movement known as Proto-Neo-classicism, which flourished in the Roman art world during the 1720s and 1730s, and the inventor of the new code of portraiture that evolved from the Maratti school.

Masucci entered the competitions held by the Accademia di S Luca, Rome, and won prizes in 1706, 1707 and 1708 with the *Killing of Tarpeia*, the *Battle between the Horatii and the Curiatii*, *Ancus Marcius* and *Accius Nevius*; on becoming an academician in 1724, he painted the *Martyrdom of St Barbara* as his *morceau de réception* (all Rome, Gal. Accad. N. S Luca). Among Masucci's prestigious clients was Monsignor Niccolò del Giudice (1660–1743), the papal Major-domo and Prefect of the Sacred Palaces. Masucci also had a long relationship with the Rospigliosi family. An *Adoration of the Magi*, donated by Prince Giuseppe Rospigliosi in 1807 to S Lorenzo at Zagarolo, near Rome, dates from *c*. 1710 or shortly afterwards (Negro, 1989). Masucci's first public works were the altarpieces depicting *St Venantius Freed by the Angel* and *St Venantius Bringing forth the Water* for the main chapel of the church of SS Venanzio ed Ansuino del Camerinesi (destr.) in Rome, where the high altarpiece was by Luigi Garzi. These paintings, commissioned by the Marchesa Girolama Bichi Ruspoli and documented by a payment dated 31 December 1717, are now in the modern church of SS Fabiano e Venanzio in the Tuscolano quarter of Rome. In them Masucci's style is clearly based on that of Maratti, but it also shows a perfect assimilation of the teaching of Garzi. For the church of S Maria in Via Lata, Rome, Masucci produced a series of ovals, notable among which are the *Annunciation* and the *Adoration of the Magi*. These works, mentioned by Pio and hence painted before 1724, show impeccable draughtsmanship and an interest in Rococo subtleties.

In 1728–9 Masucci is documented as working on the decoration of Domenico Clemente Rospigliosi's audience chamber on the third floor of the Palazzo Rospigliosi–Pallavicini, Rome. There he painted the large canvas of *Hercules Received on Olympus*, in which the solemn and monumental rendering of the figures is accompanied by perfect draughtsmanship and a crystalline clarity of tones. A drawing of *Jupiter Enthroned with a Female Figure* (Berlin, Kupferstichkab.) may be connected with this ceiling. A small canvas of the *Christ Child and St John the Baptist* (Rome, Gal. Pallavicini) can be dated to the same period, as can the famous portrait of *Cardinal Banchieri* (1728; ex-Rospigliosi priv. col.), which belongs to the courtly tradition of portraiture derived from Maratti. Other documented portraits were commissioned by the family: one of the young *Camillo Rospigliosi* (1737; untraced) and another of *Giuseppe Rospigliosi* (sold Rome, Tavazzi, 12–24 Dec 1932, lot 472).

In the 1730s Masucci was the most important painter of the classicist tradition: he became the official heir of the Maratti school after the death of Giuseppe Bartolomeo Chiari (1727) and held the important official posts of regent of the Congregazione dei Virtuosi al Pantheon (1735) and principe of the Accademia di S Luca (1737–8). An excellent example of Masucci's mature work from this period is the *Judgement of Solomon* (signed and dated 1738; Turin, Mus. Civ. A. Ant.), which is characterized by lucid clarity of composition and terse use of colour. He enjoyed prestigious commissions from the courts of Turin, Spain and Portugal, becoming a favourite painter of King John

V of Portugal. For the basilica at Mafra he produced a *Coronation of the Virgin* (untraced) and a *Holy Family* (1730; Mafra, Pal. N.), as well as three paintings for the famous chapel of St John the Baptist in S Roch, Lisbon (commissioned in 1742; installed in 1747). One of these was an *Annunciation*, the probable modello for which survives (Minneapolis, MN, Inst. A.; see fig.).

In Rome, together with Panini and Batoni, Masucci was commissioned by Pope Benedict XIV to decorate the ceiling of the Coffee House in the grounds of the Palazzo del Quirinale with canvases of the *Four Prophets* and *Christ Entrusting his Flock to Peter* (both 1742–3).

Besides the Rospigliosi portraits already mentioned, Masucci painted the *Portrait of a Boy in Oriental Costume* and the *Portrait of a Woman* (both Baltimore, MD, Walters A.G.), the portrait of *Duca Camillo Rospigliosi on Horseback* (Rome, Pal. Braschi) and that of *James Ogilvie, Lord Deskford* (1740; priv. col.; see Clark, 1967, fig. 118), which shows great mastery. He also produced a large group of portrait drawings intended to illustrate Pio's *Vite* (Stockholm, Nmus.; see Clark, 1967) and remained an accomplished draughtsman throughout his career. Unfortunately, the fame Masucci gained in the field of portraiture declined after the cold reception of his portrait of *Pope Benedict XIV* (1743; Rome, Gal. Accad. N. S Luca), painted for a competition won by Pierre Subleyras.

During the 1740s Masucci was overtaken by such painters as Batoni, or to a lesser extent by Placido Costanzi, and gradually excluded from the most important commissions. He continued to have success with his devotional pictures, for example the oval of *St Anthony Adoring the Virgin and Child* (1751; Forano, nr Rieti, S Sebastiano). This picture repeats, at least a quarter of a century later, the compositional plan of the *Adoration of the Magi* in S Maria in Via Lata, Rome. Masucci was buried in S Salvatore ai Monti, Rome. His two most important pupils were Batoni and Gavin Hamilton. His son, Lorenzo Masucci (*d* Rome, 3 July 1785), became a minor painter.

BIBLIOGRAPHY

Thieme–Becker

N. Pio: *Vite* (1724); ed. C. Enggass and R. Enggass (1977), pp. 145–6, 254–5, 313–5
A. M. Clark: 'Agostino Masucci: A Conclusion and a Reformation of the Roman Baroque', *Essays in the History of Art Presented to Rudolf Wittkower*, i (London, 1967), pp. 259–64; also in *Studies in Roman Eighteenth-century Painting*, ed. E. P. Bowron (Washington, DC, 1981), pp. 90–102
——: 'The Portraits of Artists Drawn for Nicola Pio', *Master Drgs*, v (1967), pp. 3–23
O. Susinno: 'I ritratti degli accademici', *Accademia Nazionale di San Luca* (Rome, 1974), p. 232
V. Casale: 'Diaspore e ricomposizioni: Gherardi, Cerruti, Grecolini, Garzi, Masucci ai Santi Venanzio e Ansuino in Roma', *Scritti di storia dell'arte in onore di Federico Zeri*, ii (Milan, 1984), pp. 736–54
A. Negro: 'Agostino Masucci: Un soffitto in palazzo Rospigliosi Pallavicini ed alcune aggiunte', *Per Carla Guglielmi: Scritti di allievi* (Rome, 1989), pp. 125–35
F. Rangoni: 'Masucci Agostino', *La pittura in Italia: Il settecento*, ed. G. Briganti, ii (Milan, 1989), 788–9
S. Vasco Rocca, T. Borghini and P. Ferreris, eds.: *Roma lusitana, Lisbona romana* (Rome, 1990) [a guide]

ANA MARIA RYBKO

Masuda. Japanese family of seal-carvers, known as the Jōhekikyo school. They were masters of the Archaic style of seal-carving. The first member was Masuda Kinsai [Un'en, Jōhekikyo] (*b* Edo [now Tokyo], 1764; *d* Edo, 1833). Kinsai was succeeded by his adopted son, Masuda (Yamaguchi) Gūsho [Tōrei, Jōhekikyo II] (*b* Edo, 1797; *d* Edo, 1860). Gūsho's son Kōen (1836–1921) continued the line, which was thereafter taken up by Kōen's nephew Kōetsu (some of whose work is in the National Museum in Tokyo). Masuda Kinsai was also a skilled calligrapher and student of orthography. He was familiar with the tradition of the Early Edo-school seal-carvers such as Hosoi Kōtaku and Ikenaga Dōun (*see also* Japan, §XVI, 20), and combined the style with Chinese styles of the Ming (1368–1644) and Qing (1644–1911) periods, to be found in such albums as *Feihong tang yin pu*, thus creating seals marked by a new subtlety and grace. Together with Hamamura Zoroku II (*see* Zoroku), he is ranked as one of the Two Great Seal-carvers of the Edo period. His seals were highly treasured, and he was commissioned by the aristocracy as well as by literati and painters. Kinsai was also a connoisseur of calligraphy, painting and ancient pottery; he studied Chinese verse with Ichikawa Kansai and was considered one of the 'ten talents' of his poetry society, the Kōkosha. In his later years he did not travel much but dedicated himself to work, even carving three seals on his deathbed. He was buried at Jōshinji, a temple in Komagome. His seal albums include *Jōhekikyo inpu* ('Book of seals by Jōhekikyo') and *Kinsai inzon* ('Extant

Agostino Masucci: *Annunciation*, oil on canvas, 985×683 mm, *c.* 1742–7 (Minneapolis, MN, Minneapolis Institute of Arts)

seals of Kinsai'). Before his death he had prepared an unpublished work on the study of seal-carving, which he passed on to his adopted son and successor, Masuda Gūsho.

Gūsho studied calligraphy from a young age with Nagahashi Tōgen. He became apprenticed to Kinsai to learn seal-carving, and, after succeeding him, he took the name Jōhekikyo II. He studied Archaic seal script (Jap. *tensho*; Chin. *zhuanshu*) from such albums as *Xianmin yinlüe* and *Qin Han yincun*, combining this with the brush techniques of the great modern masters. He is known for his finely detailed and elegant style and considered artistically equal to the Chinese carvers Chen Zaizhuan and Zhou Zifen. In 1819 he was ordered to carve two official seals for the shogunate. He was buried near his adoptive father in Jōshinji. He was succeeded by his eldest son Masuda Kōen, who enjoyed a high reputation among Meiji period (1868–1912) seal-carvers in Japan. Seals carved by all three generations are to be found in the collection *Jōhekikyo shūin* ('Collection of seals of the Jōhekikyo'; 1922).

BIBLIOGRAPHY

K. Nakai: *Nihon in hitozute* [Accounts of Japanese seal-carvers] (1915)
Y. Nakata, ed.: *Nihon no tenkoku* [Japanese seal-carving] (Tokyo, 1966)

NORIHISA MIZUTA

Masuko Shinoda. *See* SHINODA, TŌKŌ.

Masuo Ikeda. *See* IKEDA, MASUO.

Masyaf [Maṣyāf; Masyad]. Castle and town 45 km east of Hama, Syria. Mentioned as early as the late 11th century, the fortress was built on a rocky promontory on the eastern slopes of the Jabal al-Nusayriyya and displays an impressive vertical mass buttressed with rectangular towers. It is an excellent example of military architecture of the medieval Islamic period, with a curtain wall and numerous rectangular salients and a central keep. Masyaf successfully resisted crusader attacks and was briefly the property of the Banu Munqidh of Shayzar before becoming an Isma'ili stronghold. In 1260 the fortress was plundered by the Mongols and in 1270 it was taken by the Mamluk sultan Baybars (*reg* 1260–76), who incorporated it into his domain.

BIBLIOGRAPHY

Enc. Islam/2: 'Maṣyād'
M. van Berchem: 'Épigraphie des assassins de Syrie', *J. Asiat.*, 9th ser., ix (1897), pp. 453–501
T. S. R. Boase: *Castles and Churches of the Crusading Kingdom* (London, 1967)

HAFEZ K. CHEHAB

Masyutyn, Vasyl' (Mykolayovych) [Masyutin, Masyuta-Soroka; Vasyl' Nikolayevich] (*b* Chernihiv, 1884; *d* Berlin, 15 Dec 1955). Ukrainian printmaker, sculptor, medallist and art historian, active in Germany. He studied at the Moscow School of Painting, Sculpture and Architecture under Vasyl' Maté (1856–1917). After the 1917 Revolution he taught briefly at Vkhutemas (Higher Art and Technical Studios), moving to Berlin in 1921. He frequently sent works back to Ukraine to participate in the exhibitions of the Association of Independent Ukrainian Artists (ANUM), of which he became a member when it was formed in Lwów (L'viv) in 1931. His early graphic work includes etchings treated as symbolic fantasies bordering on the grotesque. He also produced a cycle of engravings, the *Seven Deadly Sins*, and illustrations to Aesop's fables and to the works of Gogol and Balzac. He sculpted busts of Balzac and several hetmans and produced an entire series of commemorative medallions of the Cossack leadership, medieval princes and contemporary cultural figures, a total of 63 portraits rendered with historical accuracy. Examples of his work are in the Pushkin Museum of Fine Arts in Moscow. He also contributed to art pedagogy with his manual on engraving and lithography (1922), and contributed articles to the ANUM journal, *Mystetstvo* (Art), published in Lwów.

WRITINGS

Gravyura i litografiya [Printmaking and lithography] (Moscow and Berlin, 1922)

BIBLIOGRAPHY

N. Romanov: *Oforty V. N. Masyutina* [Etchings of V. N. Masyutin] (Moscow, 1920)

MYROSLAVA M. MUDRAK

Mat. *See* MOUNTING, §1.

Matabei. *See* IWASA MATABEI.

Mataré, Ewald (*b* Aachen, 25 Feb 1887; *d* Büderich, nr Düsseldorf, 29 March 1965). German sculptor, printmaker and art dealer. He studied modelling, painting and drawing privately in Aachen. In 1907 he studied painting at the Akademie der Bildenden Künste in Berlin and entered the studio of Lovis Corinth in 1914, leaving six months later because of lack of inspiration. In 1915 he became a pupil of the German history painter Arthur Kampf (1864–1950). After a short period in the army he was awarded a grant that guaranteed an income. In 1918 he joined the Novembergruppe. In 1920 he began making woodcuts, and his early works, usually portraits or animals, used simplified and strongly reduced forms, which recall Expressionist examples, in particular those of Die Brücke (e.g. *Cows in the Dunes*, 1920; Düsseldorf, Kstmus.). Occasionally the strong black-and-white contrast was softened with watercolour accentuations. In the early 1920s he made an intense study of Adolf von Hildebrand's programmatic essay *Das Problem der Form in der bildenden Kunst* (Strasbourg, 1905) but felt that its theses went counter to his own intentions. For Mataré it was the tactile rather than the optical aspect of sculpture that was important. He started his sculptural work in 1922. When he had no boards for his woodcuts, he began to carve; at first he used driftwood but later he selected fine woods. He placed great importance on the natural grain of his material. Mataré made a series of heads and portrayals of animals and figures, whose meditative mood recalls prehistoric idols, for example *Female Head: Portrait of Hanna Hasenbäumer* (1922; Düsseldorf, Kstmus.) and *Chicken* (bronze cast from wooden model, 1924; Cologne, Mus. Ludwig). The pre-war works are characterized by the closure of the form, the clear contours and the smoothness of the surface, for example *Female Torso* (1932; Cologne, Mus. Ludwig; see fig.); the animal sculptures, in particular cattle, are characterized by their volume and attitude.

Mataré travelled a great deal and was heavily influenced in the mid-1920s by the frescoes of Giotto in Assisi. He

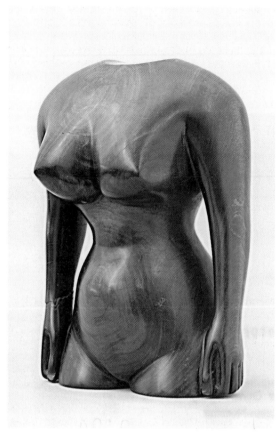

Ewald Mataré: *Female Torso*, teak, h. 200 mm, 1932 (Cologne, Museum Ludwig)

analysed the composition and colouring of the Italian painter's work, whose clarity became an important factor in his later religious work. In the 1930s he began to make colour prints, the basic black plate enhanced by warm, clay-like earth colours or green tones. At the suggestion of Paul Klee, who taught at the Kunstakademie in Düsseldorf from 1931, Mataré became professor of sculpture there in 1932. He held the post for only seven months, however, since he was dismissed by the Nazis in 1933.

Mataré had little success with his first works for the church; the sculpture *St Thomas Aquinas* (1932–3; see 1987 exh. cat., p. 32), made in Berlin and decorated with mosaic, was rejected by the Bishop's Palace and removed from its setting. It was then given as a present to Pastor Vaahsen in the St Remigius-Kirche in Wittlaer, Düsseldorf. Even here it was not met with a great deal of official approval and had to be walled in; it was destroyed during World War II. Mataré's friendship with Pastor Vaahsen marks an important point in his life, because it led to numerous church commissions, which were to determine his work until the end of his life. The clergyman, whose church had been decorated by Jan Thorn-Prikker and Heinrich Nauen, commissioned a tabernacle from Mataré.

Although in 1934 Mataré was able to deliver his monumental basalt figure for the war memorial in Cleve (removed 1938; returned in an altered state, 1981) and

exhibited it in Krefeld a year later, his existence—especially after he was represented in the 'degenerate art' exhibition (1936; *see* ENTARTETE KUNST)—was jeopardized. Private commissions became as important as church commissions. In the works of the late 1930s and the 1940s, the rounded forms gave way to more angular facets (e.g. *Triangle Cow I* (1942; bronze version, priv. col., see 1987 exh. cat., pl. 4) or derive from Roman and Gothic models, for example *Christ Triumphant* (1938), in St Elizabeth's Hohenlind, Cologne, and *Crucifixion Group* (1938) in St Remigius, Wittlaer, Düsseldorf.

After the collapse of the Third Reich, Mataré was reinstated as a professor at the Academy in Düsseldorf, but he refused the directorship of the institution. He also rejected an offer from the Technische Hochschule in Stuttgart (1948). The period of Germany's reconstruction brought Mataré a large number of public commissions. He produced doors for, among others, the Alte Kirche in Krefeld (1952), for Cologne Cathedral (1947–54), for the Church of World Peace in Hiroshima (1953–4) and for the Rathaus in Aachen (1962–4). He worked with Giacomo Manzù and Toni Schneider-Manzell on Salzburg Cathedral and *Gate of Hope* (bronze with enamel inlay, 1956–8). Mataré designed the entire interior decoration of the St Rochuskirche in Düsseldorf. The artist had already produced liturgical objects such as chalices and crucifixes in the 1940s, and renewed orders followed. He also produced medals, plaques and mosaics, for example the *Doves' Fountain* in Cologne (1953) and the bronze-cast *Owl* with mosaic inlay (1963–4; Neuss, Clemens-Sels-Mus.), rounded off Mataré's work. The post-war works could be seen as Mataré's attempt to synthesize all his earlier efforts. He placed a major emphasis on decoration and ornament, which he had emphatically avoided in his early work.

BIBLIOGRAPHY

H. Peters: *Ewald Mataré: Das graphische Werk* (Cologne, 1957)
Mataré und seine Schüler: Beuys, Haese, Heerich, Meistermann (exh. cat. by F. J. van der Grinten and H. van der Grinten, W. Berlin, Akad. Kst.; Hannover, Kestner-Ges.; 1979)
A. Klapheck: *Ewald Mataré: Aquarelle, 1920–1958* (Munich, 1983)
S. M. Schilling: *Ewald Mataré* (Cologne, 1987)
Ewald Mataré Retrospektive—das plastische Werk (exh. cat., Cologne, Kstver., 1987)

SEPP KERN

Matas, Niccola (*b* Ancona, 6 Dec 1799; *d* Florence, 11 March 1872). Italian architect and writer. He studied at the Accademia di Belle Arti in Rome before spending some time in Vicenza and in Venice, where he knew the art critic and theorist Conte Leopoldo Cicognara; he then moved to Florence in 1825. During his studies in the Veneto he completed his Neo-classical training begun in Rome and at the same time made a careful study of medieval architecture. These two stylistic influences prevailed from his earliest architectural projects (a parade ground for Vicenza and a theatre for Hamburg) and from his first executed works: the restoration of the Palazzo Ginori (1826) in the Piazza Santa Croce, Florence, the façade of S Francesco (1829) at Bibbiena, near Arezzo, and, at Ancona, the decoration of the Teatro delle Muse and the restoration of the dome and campanile of the cathedral (both 1835). Matas's Neo-classicism was infused by an eclecticism that is particularly evident in his works for the Demidov family, which included the completion of the Villa di S Donato, Florence, and a project for a mausoleum (unexecuted; both from 1837) and the Napoleon Museum (1852) at San Martino, Elba, paid for by Prince Anatole Demidov. Matas's interest in medieval architecture was expressed in his unexecuted designs (1842) for the façade of S Maria del Fiore, Florence, and in his work on the protracted restoration and completion of Santa Croce, Florence (begun 1837; Gothic Revival façade 1857–63). At the same time he was working on the restoration (1851) of S Stefano dei Cavalieri at Pisa and the plan of the monumental cemetery (1848–59) at S Miniato al Monte, Florence (completed by Mariano Falcini).

WRITINGS
Dimostrazione del progetto per compiere colla facciata l'insigne basilica di S Maria del Fiore (Florence, 1843)
Pubblico cimitero monumentale per la città di Firenze a S Miniato al Monte (Florence, 1848)
Elogio di Baldassare Peruzzi (Pisa, 1850)

BIBLIOGRAPHY
T. Buccolini: *Niccola Matas, architetto anconitano, discorso* (Ancona, 1880)
E. Brües: 'Die Fassade von S Croce in Florenz: Ein Werk des Architekten Matas', *Mitt. Ksthist. Inst. Florenz*, xii (1965), pp. 151–69
M. Maffioli: 'Niccola Matas: Architetto del Principe', *Ant. Viva*, xxiv/4 (1985), pp. 34–9
——: 'La facciata di Santa Croce: Storia di un cantiere', *Santa Croce nell'800* (exh. cat., ed. M. Maffioli; Florence, Santa Croce, 1986), pp. 41–79
C. Cresti, M. Cozzi and G. Carapelli: *Il duomo di Firenze, 1822–1887: L'avventura della facciata* (Florence, 1987), pp. 31–52
Due granduchi, tre re e une facciata (Florence, 1987), pp. 91–5 [S Maria del Fiore di Firenze]

MARIO BENCIVENNI

Matazō Kayama. *See* KAYAMA, MATAZŌ.

Matcham, Frank [Francis] (*b* Newton Abbot, Devon, 22 Nov 1854; *d* Southend, Essex, 17 May 1920). English architect. He first trained in the office of George S. Bridgeman (1839–*c*. 1900) at Paignton, Devon. Later Matcham moved to London and joined the practice of Jethro T. Robinson, architect to Hengler's Circus and Theatre Consultant to the Lord Chamberlain. From the latter connection Matcham derived a thorough grounding in theatre building regulations. He was always to be concerned for safety, ventilation and sight-lines, and his eventually large practice was to employ engineering staff.

Matcham married Robinson's daughter in 1877 and on Robinson's death in 1878 completed the Elephant and Castle Theatre in south London (1879; rebuilt). Developing friendships with theatre owners and managers, including Sir Oswald Stoll (1866–1942) and Edward Moss (1852–1912), brought in commissions not only in London but in the industrial North. He designed theatres in Bolton (Theatre Royal, 1888; destr. 1963; Grand, 1894; destr. 1963), Nottingham (Theatre Royal, 1897; rebuilt 1978), Leeds (Grand Opera, 1898) and in expanding ports and resorts such as Southport (Opera House, 1891; destr. 1931), Portsmouth (1900) and Everton (Olympus, 1905; rebuilt 1949), as well as in Belfast (1895), Cardiff (Empire Palace, 1896–1900; destr. 1961) and Glasgow (King's Theatre, 1904; Coliseum, 1905). By the 1890s, as theatres attracted investors and the work rolled in, he was perfecting the music-hall and light-opera interior as fantasy world, for example at the Edinburgh Empire Palace (1892; destr.

1911) and the Buxton Opera House (1903). Structurally he created an organic flow of boxes and balconies, overlaid with central European blends of decoration in fibrous plaster and lush Second Empire upholstery. In his legitimate theatres such as the Grand Theatre, Blackpool (1894), the Lyric Opera House, Hammersmith, London (1895–9; rebuilt 1979) and the Richmond Theatre, Surrey (1899), the interiors were also masterpieces of dynamic three-dimensional design. His Blackpool Ballroom (1896; rest. 1958) is spectacularly opulent. However, the bravura of his façades was less convincing in the hard light of day (London Hippodrome, 1899).

As architectural taste veered towards classicism, Matcham dignified his Edwardian fronts (London Coliseum, 1904), perhaps influenced by Sachs's book on opera houses and theatres (1896–8). Although he did not belong to the RIBA and his scenic genius was misunderstood by young critics such as Sachs, Matcham had arrived at exactly the moment to house the late Victorian and Edwardian stage with more brio (and more theatres) than any of his rivals, and his interiors were part of every performance.

BIBLIOGRAPHY
E. O. Sachs: *Modern Opera Houses and Theatres*, 3 vols (London, 1896–8)
B. M. Walker, ed.: *Frank Matcham: Theatre Architect* (Belfast, 1980) [incl. list of works]

PRISCILLA METCALF

Matchitt, Paratene Moko Puorongo (*b* Tokomaru Bay, 10 Aug 1933). New Zealand painter and sculptor. He studied art at Dunedin Teachers' College in 1957. He was one of a group of young Maori arts and crafts advisers who were encouraged to develop art forms drawing on their Maori cultural heritage and growing knowledge of Western art. Contact with the master carver Pine Taiapa from 1960 to 1972 helped deepen Matchitt's awareness of Maori art. His major works are either community-orientated projects or series centred on a common theme. Among his community projects are painted murals in the dining-halls at Whangaparaoa, Cape Runaway, and at Turangawaewae Marae, Ngaruawahia. A subject central to his output from 1967 was the 19th-century Maori religious leader Te Kooti Rikirangi, exemplified by the mixed-media wall sculpture *Te Kooti* (1986; U. Auckland). Matchitt was a leader in the renaissance of Maori art, which draws on the resources of Maori traditional culture and history in the shaping of contemporary work.

BIBLIOGRAPHY
K. Mataira: *Maori Artists of the South Pacific* (Raglan, 1984)

MICHAEL DUNN

Matejko, Jan (*b* Kraków, 24 June 1838; *d* Kraków, 1 Nov 1893). Polish painter. He studied from 1852 to 1858 at the School of Fine Arts in Kraków and, during this time, started exhibiting historical paintings with the Society of Friends of the Fine Arts there (e.g. *Sigismund I Bestowing Nobility on the Professors of the University of Kraków in 1535* (1858; Kraków, Jagiellonian U., Mus. F.A.). After studying in Munich (1859) under the history painter Hermann Anschütz (1802–80) and then briefly and less successfully in Vienna, Matejko returned to Kraków, where he was based for the rest of his life. In 1860 Matejko issued an illustrated album, *Ubiory w Polsce* ['Costumes in

Jan Matejko: *Homage of Prussia*, oil on canvas, 388×785 mm, 1880–82 (Kraków, National Museum)

Poland from 1200 to 1795'] (later editions 1875 and 1901), a project reflecting his intense interest in historical records of all kinds and his desire to promote such interest among the Polish people in an effort to intensify their patriotic feelings. This role first became widely associated with Matejko with his painting of *Stańczyk* (1862; Warsaw, N. Mus.), the court jester to King Sigismund I (1437–1548), to whom Matejko gave his own features. The jester is presented as a symbol of the nation's conscience: he sits glumly in a chair apart from the other figures, alone in seeing that events during the wars against Moscow would ultimately end in tragedy.

In 1863 Matejko was deeply saddened by the outcome of the January Uprising, during which one of his brothers was killed, and he painted the *Year 1863—Polonia* (1864; Kraków, N. Mus.). From this point on historical scenes, invariably of some contemporary relevance, were Matejko's main concern, and he was celebrated abroad as well as at home for his colourful, detailed and imaginative evocation of the great moments of Polish history. The *Sermon of Skarga* (1864; Warsaw, Royal Castle), despite its subject-matter, which was not easily accessible, was highly praised when shown in Paris in 1865. But there was not always unanimous support for Matejko's often critical attitude towards the behaviour of his compatriots: the Polish aristocracy were indignant at *Rejtan—The Fall of Poland* (1866; Warsaw, Royal Castle), concerned with events between 1773 and 1793, which implied that their attitude had delivered the nation into the hands of its enemies. With the *Union of Lublin* (Warsaw, N. Mus.), painted in 1869 to mark the third centenary of the union of Poland and Lithuania, Matejko embarked on a series of pictures of Poland's greatest political and military successes. These were to include *Batory at Psków* (1871; Warsaw, N. Mus.), in which he introduced a more harmonious colour scheme with a predominance of gold tones, the *Raising of the 'Sigismund' Bell in the Cathedral*

Tower in Kraków in 1521 (1874; Warsaw, N. Mus.) and the most powerful and visionary of Matejko's historical compositions: *Battle of Grunwald* (1875–8; Warsaw, N. Mus.), showing the victory over the Teutonic Knights secured in the 15th century by the Poles and Lithuanians and their allies under the Polish king Władysław Jagiellon. While meeting with an enthusiastic public response, Matejko's approach to history paintings as seen in such works also had a profound influence on a generation of students in Kraków where, from 1873, Matejko was Director of the School of Fine Arts. Familiarity with works by both Tintoretto and Veronese, seen by Matejko on his first journey to Venice in 1878–9, prompted a more sedate treatment of composition and a softer, richer colouring in works of the early 1880s, such as the *Homage of Prussia* (1880–82; Kraków, N. Mus.; see fig.). The incisiveness and critical approach to characterization seen earlier in Matejko's many portraits, for example those of his *Three Children* (1870; Warsaw, N. Mus.) and of *Princess Marcelina Czartoryska z Radziwitt* (1874; Kraków, N. Mus.), a pianist and pupil of Chopin, also added a good deal to the overall effect of such large-scale scenes.

Matejko's work during his last 15 years was often related to official anniversaries: the *Constitution of 3 May* (1891; Warsaw, N. Mus.) was painted for the centenary of the ratification of the Fourth Parliament in 1788–92. It shows a ceremonial procession to St John's Cathedral in Warsaw and lacks the positive dramatic urgency of earlier works. Matejko died while at work on the *Vows of Jan Kazimierz in Lwów Cathedral in 1656* (Wrocław, N. Mus.). Other activities during his last years included a cycle of 12 paintings, the *History of Civilization in Poland* (1888–9; Warsaw, N. Mus.), for which he wrote an accompanying commentary, and the polychromatic decoration of St Mary's Church in Kraków, which he carried out in 1889–91 with two of his pupils, Stanisław Wyspiański and Józef Mehoffer. He also produced throughout his career a number of drawings, mainly sketches and studies for oil paintings, and watercolours. By the time of his death Matejko had become a cult figure to the nation at large (three years later, his house at Florianska 41 in Kraków was made into the Matejko Museum, now part of Kraków, N. Mus.) and an overpowering symbol of achievement for a younger generation of artists.

WRITINGS
M. Szukiewicz, ed.: *Listy Jana Matejki do żony Teodory* [Letters from Jan Matejko to his wife Teodora] (Kraków, 1927)

BIBLIOGRAPHY
PSB; Thieme–Becker
M. Gorzkowski: *O artystycznych czynnościach Jana Matejki* [On the artistic activities of Jan Matejko] (Kraków, 1882)
——: *Jan Matejko: Epoka lat jego najmłodszych* [Jan Matejko: the earliest period of his life] (Kraków, 1896)
S. Tarnowski: *Matejko* (Kraków, 1897)
M. Gorzkowski: *Epoka lat dalszych do końca życia artysty, z dziennika prowadzonego w ciągu 17 lat* [The later period to the end of the artist's life, from the diary written over a period of 17 years] (Kraków, 1898)
I. Pawłowicz Jabłonski: *Wspomnienie o Janie Matejce* [A memoir of Jan Matejko] (Lwów, 1912)
S. Witkiewicz: *Matejko* (Lwów, 1912)
M. Treter: *Matejko* (Lwów, 1939)
M. Porębski: *Jana Matejki 'Bitwa pod Grunwaldem'* [Jan Matejko's *Battle of Grunwald*] (Warsaw, 1953)
——: *Jana Matejki 'Kazanie Skargi'* [Jan Matejko's *Sermon of Skarga*] (Warsaw, 1953)
S. Serafińska: *Jan Matejko: Wspomnienia rodzinne* [Jan Matejko: a family memoir] (Kraków, 1955)
Polnische Malerei von 1830 bis 1914 (exh. cat., Kiel, Christian Albrechts-U., Ksthalle; Stuttgart, Württemberg. Kstver.; Wuppertal, von der Heydt-Mus.; 1978–9), pp. 231–6
J. Starzyński: *Jan Matejko* (Warsaw, 1979)
La Peinture polonaise du XVIe au début du XXe siècle, Warsaw, N. Mus. cat. (Warsaw, 1979), pp. 285–303

WANDA MAŁASZEWSKA

Mateo (*fl* 1168–?1217). Spanish architect and possible sculptor. He was Master of the Works of the cathedral of Santiago de Compostela, and he was granted a life pension in connection with this work by Ferdinand II of León in 1168. His name also appears in the inscription on the lintels of the Pórtico de la Gloria, installed on 1 April 1188, attributing to him the direction of building work. Other possible references to him occur in documents from 1189 to 1217.

Although Mateo is known in the art-historical literature primarily as a sculptor, the inscription refers to him in the capacity of an architect. This activity was not restricted to the portal and the façade of which it is a part, however, but may also have included the completion of the cathedral itself. As a whole, except for those details where the design conforms to what had already been built, the architecture of this campaign reveals the influence of Burgundian buildings. The sculptural decoration, however, is less unified: initially it shows links with Burgundian work (La Charité-sur-Loire, Avallon) but then a second, more varied style appears, which has been attributed to Mateo himself. It would be more accurate, however, to attribute the architecture to him, because it is more homogeneous than the sculpture, and Mateo was the master responsible for the work from its inception. Mateo's intervention in the sculptural programme should not be excluded, however, and he may even have contributed designs.   The distinction of being included in the dedicatory inscription of a royal endowment, without mentioning the names of the patrons, would be unusual at this period for a supposedly manual worker. To his work as an architect, Mateo probably also added that of *magister operis*, with responsibility for the finances of the project. According to his contract (1175), Mateo's contemporary Raymond the Lombard carried out both these roles at Seu d'Urgell; and the term *magisterium* that was applied to Mateo's work had also been used to designate the functions of Bernardo, the Treasurer of the work at Santiago (1134).

BIBLIOGRAPHY
Ceán Bermúdez
E. Llaguno y Amírola: *Noticias de los arquitectos y arquitectura de España desde su restauración . . . ilustradas y acrecentadas con notas por D. Juan Agustín Ceán Bermúdez*, i (Madrid, 1829), pp. 31–2, 252
A. Neira de Mosquera: 'Historia de una cabeza: 1188', *Monografías de Santiago* (Santiago, 1850, 2/1950), pp. 27–42 [a legendary recreation of Mateo's activity and a source for some mistakes in subsequent stud.]
A. López Ferreiro: *El Pórtico de la Gloria* (Santiago, 1886, 3/1975)
J. Filgueira Valverde: 'Datos y conjeturas para la biografía del maestro Mateo', *Cuad. Estud. Gallegos*, iii (1948), pp. 49–69
F. Bouza-Brey: 'El maestro Mateo en la tradición popular de Galicia', *Compostellanum*, iv (1959), pp. 5–18
M. Ward: *Studies on the Pórtico de la Gloria at the Cathedral of Santiago de Compostela* (diss., New York U., 1978)
S. Moralejo: 'El 1 de abril de 1188: Marco histórico y contexto litúrgico en la obra del Pórtico de la Gloria', *El Pórtico de la Gloria: Música, arte y pensamiento* (Santiago de Compostela, 1988), pp. 19–36

S. MORALEJO

Mateo, Julio (*b* Havana, 16 April 1951). Cuban painter and printmaker, active in the USA. He arrived in the USA in 1960 and grew up in Philadelphia, PA. He obtained his BFA from the University of Florida, Gainesville, in 1973 and his MFA from the University of South Florida, Tampa, in 1978. He came from an artistic family, and in his work he drew successfully on his dual Latin- and North-American legacies. From North America he derived his cultivation of constructed and flat, painted surfaces, a legacy of Abstract Expressionism and Minimalism. From Latin America he derived a love of signs and a preoccupation with the functions of language, pioneered by Joaquín Torres García. Mateo's abstractions, for example *Untitled* (1986; see 1987–8 exh. cat., p. 11), are in his words about the '"grammar" of rhythm and process' in the plastic sense, and how 'the limitations of a physical space can determine structure and form'.

BIBLIOGRAPHY
J. Milani: 'Julio Mateo/Printmaker, Sculptor', *Floridian Mag.* (1 Aug 1982), pp. 8–10
R. Hagenberg and others, eds.: *Eastvillage 85* (New York, 1985)
Abstract Visions (exh. cat., New York, Mus. Contemp. Hisp. A., 1987–8), p. 11

RICARDO PAU-LLOSA

Mates, Joan (*fl* 1391–?1431). Catalan painter. He completed a retable of *SS Thomas and Anthony*, which had been left unfinished at Pedro Serra's death, for Barcelona Cathedral in 1409. Mates undertook a number of distinguished commissions for altarpieces in Barcelona and as far afield as Huesca in Aragon (e.g. the retable of *St Engracia*, ordered on 18 Jan 1416; untraced). His documented surviving works are the retable of *SS Martin and Ambrose* in Barcelona Cathedral (1411), the retable of *St Sebastian* (1417; Barcelona, Mus. A. Catalunya) for the chapel of Pia Almoina, Barcelona, and the high altar retable of S Maria, Vila-rodana (1422). Other works attributed to him include the retables of *SS Lucy and Michael* (Barcelona, priv. col.), *St Jaume de Vallespinosa* (Tarragona Cathedral) and the *Entombment* (Barcelona, Mus. A. Catalunya). Mates was an expressive painter, who used contrasts of line for intensity of effect. His interests were focused on the human figure rather than the architectural setting, and he produced refined and elegant works that show the influence of Franco-Flemish manuscript illumination.

Joan Mates made a will in 1431, but Sanpere proposed that he should be identified with the artist of the same name who was paid for a retable in 1440 in Collioure, Roussillon (untraced). This artist was still active in Roussillon in 1451, dying at Perpignan in 1463; his son Jorge Mates became an apprentice of Jaume Huguet in 1469.

BIBLIOGRAPHY

S. Sanpere i Miguel: *Los quatrocentistas catalanes*, 2 vols (Barcelona, 1906)
C. R. Post: *A History of Spanish Painting*, vii (Cambridge, MA, 1938)
N. de Dalmases and A. José i Pitarch: *L'art gòtic s. xiv–xv*, Història de l'Art Català, iii (Barcelona, 1984)

J. R. L. HIGHFIELD

Matham, Jacob (*b* Haarlem, 15 Oct 1571; *d* Haarlem, 20 Jan 1631). Dutch engraver, draughtsman and painter. When the pre-eminent engraver Hendrick Goltzius married Matham's mother in 1579, he took Jacob on as an apprentice. Matham worked more closely with Goltzius than others of his circle, engraving many of the master's drawings and paintings and closely imitating his teacher's manner. Despite Matham's prolific output, his artistic personality does not emerge clearly, and the oeuvres of both engravers contain unsigned works, which deserve reattribution.

Matham's early engravings from *c*. 1588 reflect the impact on the Haarlem Mannerists of drawings by Bartholomeus Spranger and Jan Speeckaert. His series of the *Standing Virtues and Vices* (B. 264–77) and the *Four Elements* (B. 278–85) capture the strong chiaroscuro, as well as the abrupt, hooked contours of limbs and musculature and frozen swags of drapery in these artists' figure drawings. Matham's most ambitious work is his *Tablet of Cebes*, after a Goltzius design (1592; B. 139) re-creating an ancient painting described by Plato. In the richly detailed image, pilgrims move along a twisting path leading from past temptations to the domain of virtue. In this print, made from three folio-sized plates, Matham shows a more fluent and subtle burin technique. Even here, however, he does not fully master the device of building up secondary patterns and textures, such as the reflective surface of satin, with crosshatching.

After his stepfather's return from Italy, Matham himself went there between 1593 and 1597, working mainly in Venice and Rome in the company of the painter Frans Badens (1571–1618). Several prints after Tintoretto, Palma Giovane, Taddeo Zuccaro and other Italian painters occupied him for decades afterwards, as did engravings after Abraham Bloemaert and the revered earlier masters Pieter Aertsen and Albrecht Dürer. He became dean of the Guild of St Luke, Haarlem, in 1605, and the signature on his engraving of *Moses and Aaron* (Hollstein, XI, no. 5) indicates that he was court engraver in The Hague one year before his death.

A systematic catalogue of Matham's drawings has not been attempted. However, a small group of signed and dated drawings reveals the influence of Goltzius and Spranger on both his pen and chalk techniques. Some pen drawings of mythological or fantastic figures (e.g. *Head of a Man with a Peaked Cap*, Edinburgh, N.G.; *Fantastic Portrait*, U. London, Courtauld Inst. Gals) show his interest in the bold, burin-like use of the pen as developed by Goltzius and Jacques de Gheyn II. Matham displayed his virtuosity as a draughtsman in the remarkable 'pen painting' of the *Brewery and Country House of Jan Claesz. Loo* (1627; Haarlem, Frans Halsmus.). This imaginary scene, juxtaposing Loo's country and city properties, is the precursor of a group of works that created the same effects of a linear painting on a gessoed panel by counterproofing a print. While there is no evidence that Matham also painted extensively, one still-life by this master is now in a Dutch private collection.

Jacob Matham trained his sons to engrave according to techniques learnt from Goltzius's shop. Adriaen Matham (*b* Haarlem, *c*. 1599; *d* The Hague, 23 Nov 1660) recorded a diplomatic trip to Morocco in drawings and engravings and engraved political events at the Hague court. Jan Matham (*b* Haarlem, Jan 1600; *d* Haarlem, July 1648) made prints of genre scenes after Adriaen Brouwer and other artists and was a still-life painter. Theodor Matham (*b* Haarlem, 1605/6; *d* Amsterdam, 1676) engraved numerous figural scenes and portraits and participated in large projects for reproducing in prints the Giustiniani sculpture gallery in Rome and the art collection of Gerrit and Jan Reynst in Amsterdam.

BIBLIOGRAPHY

Hollstein: *Dut. & Flem.*; Thieme–Becker
E. K. J. Reznicek: *Die Zeichnungen von Hendrick Goltzius* (Utrecht, 1961)
Graphik der Niederlande, 1508–1617 (exh. cat. by K. Renger, Munich, Staatl. Graph. Samml., 1979), pp. 61–2
W. Strauss: *Netherlandish Artists*, 4 [XII/ii] of *The Illustrated Bartsch*, ed. W. Strauss (New York, 1980) [B.]
D. Freedberg, A. Burnstock and A. Phenix: 'Paintings or Prints? Experiens Sillemans and the Origins of the *Grisaille* Sea Piece', *Prt Q.*, i/3 (1984), pp. 148–68
L. Widerkehr: 'Jacob Matham Goltzij Privignus. Jacob Matham graveur et ses rapports avec Hendrick Goltzius,' *Ned. Ksthist. Jb.*, xlii–xliii (1991–2), pp. 219–60

DOROTHY LIMOUZE

Matheson, Robert M(ichael). *See under* TOWNLEY AND MATHESON.

Matheus de Layens (*b* ?Henegouwen *c*. 1400; *d* Leuven, 5 Dec 1483). South Netherlandish architect. Almost all his career was spent in Leuven and elsewhere in Brabant. He played an important part in realizing the new city plan for Leuven that had been inaugurated at the beginning of the 15th century: it was centred on the new main marketplace, demarcated by the rebuilt collegiate St Pieterskerk, the new town hall, which rivalled that of Brussels (begun 1401), and the Tafelrond guild house. He may have been trained by Sulpitius van Vorst on St Pieterskerk (*c*. 1425–39). In 1445 he succeeded Jan Keldermans II both as supervisor of the works at St Pieterskerk and as city architect to Leuven. He probably worked on the vaulting of the transept and nave of St Pieterskerk and also designed a west tower complex to replace the one damaged by fire in 1458: however, only the foundations were executed.

The building's striking homogeneity indicates that he was faithful to his predecessors' plans, although the frequently imitated tabernacle (1450) is his own. In 1448 he continued work on the new town hall, also begun by Sulpitius, but he had to alter his predecessor's design as the foundations would not support a belfry. The result (completed 1468–9) is an original, richly sculptured shrine-like building with four slim corner towers, which long stood as an exemplar in the Netherlands (*see* TOWN HALL, fig. 2). Finally, he oversaw the construction of the Tafelrond (1480–87; altered 19th century; rest. 1916–27) by Maxime Winders until his death. It comprised three houses, which served partly as rented housing and partly as an assembly hall for the citizens. As city architect, moreover, he directed numerous works, from the construction of the Groote Toren (1463–9; destr.; for illustration see *Sketchbook of Leuven*, MS., *c.* 1600; Brussels, Bib. Royale Albert 1er) and new locks (from 1465; destr.) to the restoration in 1459 of the Lakenhalle (Cloth Hall, begun 1317; partly destr. 1914; rest. 1922), subsequently taken over by the university, and renovation work on the town walls (1478–80; mostly destr.). His earliest known independent work was the outer Mechelen gate (1445; destr.). In Leuven the choir of St Quintenskerk (completed 1453) is attributed to him, as are the choir (destr.) and transept of St Jacobskerk (1467–84).

Matheus de Layens was frequently consulted as an expert: for example, he inspected the large new staircase towers of the Coudenberg Palace (1468–9; destr.) in Brussels and the design for the collegiate church of St Waudru (begun 1450) in Mons. Eventually he provided the definitive design for this (*see* BELGIUM, fig. 3), which is very close to that of the choir of St Pieterskerk, and he directed the works (1457–*c.* 1462). His name is also found at St Sulpitius (1452–3), Diest, Vilvoorde Castle (?1459; destr.), Mons Town Hall (1479), and St Lambert's Cathedral (1480; destr. 1794), Liège. Furthermore he continued the work on the church of Onze Lieve Vrouw ten Poel (*c.* 1448–*c.* 1470) at Tienen and designed, among other elements, the baptistery (1455) and tabernacle (1469–70; destr.) at St Leonarduskerk in Zoutleeuw. Matheus de Layens was one of the most important of the architects who gave shape to Brabantine Gothic.

BIBLIOGRAPHY
BNB
E. van Even: *Louvain dans le passé et le présent* (Leuven, 1895)
D. Roggen and J. Withof: 'Grondleggers en grootmeesters der Brabantse gotiek' [Founders and architects of the Brabantine Gothic style], *Gent. Bijdr. Kstgesch.*, x (1944), pp. 83–206
A. Maesschalck and J. Viaene: 'Het stadhuis van Leuven: Mensen en bouwkunst in Boergondisch Brabant', *Arca Lovan.*, vi (1977), pp. 1–255
R. M. Lemaire and H. Godts: 'De gotische bouwkunst', *Arca Lovan.*, vii (1978), pp. 293–315
M. Cheyns: *De Stadsmeester-metsers te Leuven, 1425–1526* (diss., Leuven, Katholieke U., 1979)
K. J. Philipp: 'Sainte-Waudru in Mons (Bergen, Hennegau): Die Planungsgeschichte einer Stiftskirche, 1449–1450', *Z. Kstgesch.*, li (1988), pp. 372–413

KRISTA DE JONGE

Mathew [Matthew], **Sir Tobie** [Tobias] (*b* Salisbury, 3 Oct 1577; *d* Ghent, 13 Oct 1655). English connoisseur. The most Italianate gentleman of the early Stuart age and the first of the English virtuosi, he was educated at Christ Church, Oxford, afterwards becoming an MP in 1601. He spent three years travelling (1604–7) and got to know the courts of Europe better than any of his compatriots. On his return to England, he announced his conversion to Roman Catholicism and was banished abroad for 10 years. He lived in Madrid, Brussels and Rome, and became an important contact for English tourists abroad, including Thomas Howard, 2nd Earl of Arundel, the foremost English collector of the age. Mathew also came to know Peter Paul Rubens intimately as a consequence of his acting as picture agent for Sir Dudley Carleton, later 1st Viscount Dorchester, the English ambassador at The Hague. Despite having been ordained as a priest while in Rome, Mathew was allowed home in 1617. Subsequently he was involved in marriage negotiations undertaken by George Villiers, 1st Duke of Buckingham, and others between Charles, Prince of Wales (later Charles I), and the Spanish Infanta. In 1623 Mathew travelled to Madrid with those working to bring about this (unrealized) project; there he acted as the English party's guide to the Habsburg collections. In 1640 Mathew's unwavering allegiance to the Catholic faith at a time of continued unease in England over religious questions led to his second banishment, and he retired to the English College at Ghent. Although his published writings and translations are entirely devoted to religious subjects, Mathew was in his lifetime an example to those English courtiers who sought to obtain a sophisticated knowledge of the European arts.

WRITINGS
J. Donne, ed.: *A Collection of Letters Made by Sir Tobie Mathew* (London, 1660)

BIBLIOGRAPHY
W. N. Sainsbury: *Original Unpublished Papers Illustrative of the Life of Peter Paul Rubens, as an Artist and Diplomatist* (London, 1859)
D. Mathew: *Sir Tobie Mathew* (London, 1950)
D. Howarth: *Lord Arundel and his Circle* (London, 1985)

DAVID HOWARTH

Mathey [Matheus, Mathieu, Matthei], **Jean Baptiste** [Giovanni Battista] (*b* ?Dijon, *c.* 1630; *d* Paris, *c.* 1696). French architect and painter, active in Bohemia. He went to Rome *c.* 1655, where he became a member of Claude Lorrain's circle of northern painters. In 1668 he became painter-in-ordinary to Johann Friedrich von Wallenstein, Bishop of Hradec Králové, during the Bishop's stay in Rome. When Wallenstein was appointed Archbishop of Prague in 1675, Mathey followed him to Bohemia, where he concentrated on architecture. Because Mathey had trained as a painter, he experienced many problems with the builders' guild and could only supervise the execution of his designs by builders' companies instead of working with his own team. He worked mostly for the Archbishop and other members of the Wallenstein family but also accepted commissions from other Czech noblemen such as Count Thun and Count Šlik. He also worked for the Church and religious orders.

Mathey was the most important architect of foreign origin among those active in Bohemia in the last quarter of the 17th century. Unlike most of his Prague-based north Italian colleagues, he worked in a Roman classical Baroque style in the manner of late Carlo Rainaldi and Carlo Fontana, blending this with early French classicism, notable for its shallow detailing. His first project after his

Jean Baptiste Mathey: Troja country house, near Prague, 1679–91

arrival in Prague was an extensive rebuilding (1675–9) of the Archbishop's Palace. Its three-storey façade is characterized by simple, strict forms, creating a slow dignified rhythm distinct from Borromini's style of dynamic Baroque, which was then very popular throughout Europe. The church of St Francis of the Crusader Knights was built in 1679–88 by Carlo Lurago's company to Mathey's design and is the latter's most important work of church architecture. Together with the Klementinum, the former Jesuit college, it forms an intimate square at the Old Town end of the Charles Bridge (*see* PRAGUE, fig. 4). The church is oval in plan, with a drummed dome, cruciform arms and a saucer-domed choir, and it dominates its surroundings with a large dome that forms a fine contrast to a rather flat façade articulated by clustered pilasters and niches with statues.

The Troja country house (1679–91; see fig.) on the outskirts of Prague was commissioned by Count Václav Vojtěch Šternberk. Here Mathey based his scheme on a countryside villa he knew from Rome. The Troja country house shows Mathey's ability to design a building in full harmony with its surroundings. The central three-storey hall is flanked by two-storey pavilions surmounted by towers and is set off externally by an oval staircase embracing a grotto. This open layout in the French tradition contrasts with the usual Italo-Bohemian solid block with evenly spaced bays, or courtyard type buildings. Mathey's town-house style is represented by the Toscana Palace (1689–90), built on the Hradčany for Michael Osvald Thun-Hohenstein. It has a flat elevation articulated by pilaster strips. Mathey began to work for the Cistercian Order in Plasy in 1685 and designed the abbot's house (begun 1698) in Plasy as a variant of the Troja three-wing building with a central hall. Mathey then went on to design

churches in Manětín, Litvínov and Jitřín, as well as the riding school in Prague Castle. After Mathey left Prague for France in 1694, his legacy was taken up by a number of architects active in Bohemia, the most important of whom was Giovanni Battista Alliprandi, but his most significant influence was that evinced in the work of Johann Bernhard Fischer von Erlach.

BIBLIOGRAPHY
J. Morper: *Der Prager Architekt Jean Baptiste Mathey* (Munich, 1927)
J. Neumann: *Český barok* [Czech Baroque] (Prague, 1969)
P. Preiss: *Italští umělci v Praze: Renesance manýrismus baroko* [Italian artists in Prague: Renaissance, Mannerism, Baroque] (Prague, 1986)
J. Dvorsky, ed.: *Od počátků renesance do závěru baroka* [From the beginning of the Renaissance to the end of Baroque], ii/1 and ii/2 of *Dějiny českého výtvarného umění* [History of Czech fine arts] (Prague, 1989)
D. KÖSSLEROVÁ

Mathias of [Mathieu d'] **Arras** (*b* Arras; *fl* 1342; *d* Prague, 1352). French architect. Two inscriptions in Prague Cathedral identify him as the first architect of the present building. One, engraved on his tomb, gives his death date and name and identifies him as *magister oper*[*is*]. The other, originally accompanying a portrait bust in the triforium, identifies him as a native of Arras, stating that Charles of Luxembourg (later Emperor Charles IV) brought him from Avignon to direct the construction of the cathedral, and that Mathias began building from the foundations in 1342, directing the work until his death.

Mathias must have trained in northern France and then made his way south, probably encountering Charles during the latter's visit to Avignon in 1340. At Prague Cathedral Mathias built and vaulted the ambulatory and radiating chapels, two south choir chapels and one north chapel. The hemicycle piers are also his design. He drew from northern and southern French buildings of the late 13th century and early 14th, such as S Germain, Auxerre, and the Cathedrals of Narbonne, Rodez and Toulouse. Prague Cathedral's plan and moulded, beaked capitals with fillets reflect Rodez; its thin, shafted chapel piers and the panel connecting the ambulatory side of the main arcade piers resemble Narbonne; the main arcade piers recall those of S Germain; and the triforium passage turns outward over the ambulatory vaults as at Narbonne, Rodez and Toulouse.

Mathias brought to Prague an appreciation of sharpness and angularity, of continuity and interpretation of line, plane and curve, formed in the workshops of southern France and anticipating the visual effects of Late Gothic.

BIBLIOGRAPHY

L. Cavrois: 'Mathias d'Arras, architecte du XIVe siècle', *Mém. Acad. Sci., Lett. & A. Arras*, n.s. 2, xx (1889), pp. 326–45
O. Kletzl: 'Die Grabsteine der Dombaumeister von Prag', *Z. Bild. Kst.*, lxiv (1930–31), pp. 175–80
P. Héliot and V. Mencl: 'Mathieu d'Arras et les sources méridionales et nordiques de son oeuvre à la cathédrale de Prague', *La Naissance et l'essor du gothique méridional au XIIIe siècle*, Cahiers de Fanjeaux, ix (Toulouse, 1974), pp. 103–25

VIVIAN PAUL

Mathieu, Georges (*b* Boulogne-sur-Mer, 27 Jan 1921). French painter, sculptor, designer and illustrator. He left Boulogne-sur-Mer in 1933 to attend the Lycée Hoche in Versailles, where he learnt Greek, Russian and Spanish. Over the next few years he was educated at various secondary and university institutions in Rouen, Cambrai and Douai, studying law at Douai in 1941. He started to paint landscapes and portraits in oils in 1942 and the following year taught English at the Lycée in Douai. He worked as an interpreter for the US Army at Cambrai in 1944 and in that year read Edward Crankshaw's *Joseph Conrad: Some Aspects of the Art of the Novel* (London, 1936), which impressed upon him the importance of style; he cited it as an influence on his first experiments with abstraction, such as *Inception* (1944; artist's col., see Quignon-Fleuret, p. 9), with dark amorphous forms suggestive of primordial creation. The following year he began to use drip techniques, as in *Evanescence* (1945; artist's col., see Quignon-Fleuret, p. 10). After spending several months in Paris in 1945, later that year he became professor of French at the Université Americaine in Biarritz, a post he held until 1946.

In 1947 Mathieu moved to Paris, where he became head of the public relations department of the American company United States Lines. The same year, realizing the significance of the work he and other artists such as Wols and Camille Bryen were then doing, which he called 'lyrical abstraction', he began vigorously to promote the new style in opposition to the previously dominant style of geometric abstraction, whose exponents had recently regrouped at the first Salon des Réalités Nouvelles in 1946. In 1947 Mathieu organized an exhibition of 14 painters entitled *L'Imaginaire* (Paris, Gal. Luxembourg); the catalogue preface by Jean-José Marchand, 'Vers l'abstraction lyrique', made use of his term. Continuing his campaign on behalf of lyrical abstraction, in 1948 Mathieu organized two further exhibitions, *H.W.P.S.M.T.B.* (Paris, Gal. Allendy) followed by *White and Black* (Paris, Gal. Deux Iles). By the early 1950s this work was seen as part of a more general tendency towards geometric abstraction referred to as ART INFORMEL.

Noting the similarity of direction between the work of European artists such as Wols, Bryen, Hans Hartung, himself and Americans such as Jackson Pollock, Mark Tobey, Mark Rothko and Willem de Kooning, Mathieu planned an exhibition of works by these and other artists at the Galerie Montparnasse in Paris, a project that was partly realized in an exhibition there in October 1948. In 1949 he took part in an exhibition, *Huit Oeuvres nouvelles* (Paris, Gal. René Drouin) together with Jean Fautrier, Jean Dubuffet, Wols, Roberto Matta, Henri Michaux and others. By 1949, in paintings such as *White Reign* (1949; New York, MOMA), Mathieu had developed a technique of spontaneous, broad brushstrokes, arriving at a style that became known as TACHISM. Soon afterwards his work was also presented in the context of ART AUTRE. Within a year or so he had begun to use thick paint, often straight from the tube, applied in a calligraphic, gestural style sometimes compared to Chinese or Japanese calligraphy, as in *Tache noire* (1952; New York, Guggenheim). With minor variations this approach remained characteristic of his mature style, with the compositions generally centred well within the framing edge, often on a vast scale, as in *Capetians Everywhere* (1954; Paris, Pompidou; see fig.).

In 1950 Mathieu held his first one-man show (Paris, Gal. René Drouin), and in the following year he travelled to Italy. During this time he claimed there was a relationship between lyrical abstraction and Gestalt theory in psychology; contrary to general semantic theory, he also asserted rather perversely that in his painting the sign preceded its signification, a relationship that he regarded as philosophically revolutionary. In 1953 he founded a journal for avant-garde theories in the arts and other fields, the *United States Lines Paris Review*, which he ran for the next ten years. In 1955 he designed sets for Emmanuel Looten's play *Saga de Lug Halhvynn*, staged in Paris at the Théâtre du Creuset d'Artel.

At the Festival International d'Art Dramatique held in Paris in May 1956, Mathieu was invited to paint a large canvas before an audience. This took place at the Théâtre Sarah Bernhardt during the Nuit de la Poésie on 28 May and, while poetry was read front-stage, Mathieu executed the vast painting *Homage to the Poets of the Whole World* (4×12 m, 1956; destr., see Mathey, p. 76) in a mere 30 minutes. He later performed similar feats, though even at this time speed was an essential of his technique, emphasizing his instinctive, intuitive approach to painting. This public event prefigured Yves Klein's painting demonstrations using live models and Happenings by American artists in the late 1950s and 1960s.

In 1962 Mathieu extended his style into three dimensions for an exhibition, *L'Objet* (Paris, Mus. A. Déc.), for example in a group of five sculptures designed to ornament the gateway (see Mathey, pl. 171). These works marked the beginning of his involvement with a variety of other media, although he remained particularly devoted to painting, charting the development of Tachism and describing its wider significance in his book *Au-delà du tachisme* (1963). In 1966 he received two important commissions: one for a tapestry cartoon from the Manufacture Nationale des Gobelins for the *Expo '67* exhibition

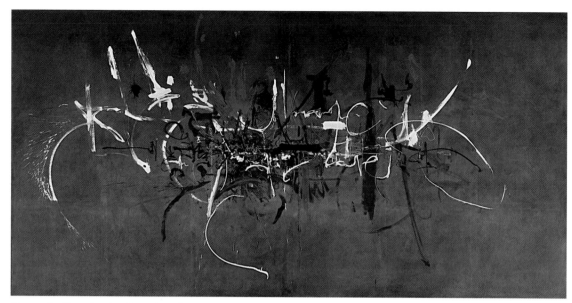

Georges Mathieu: *Capetians Everywhere*, oil on canvas, 2.95×6.00 m, 1954 (Paris, Pompidou, Musee National d'Art Moderne)

in Montreal, and another to design a factory and grounds at Fontenay-le-Comte. The factory, Tranformateurs B.C., was realized from his models. In his paintings of the 1960s he continued generally to work in the style of the previous decade, although works such as *Battle of Gilboa* (1962; artist's col., see Quignon-Fleuret, p. 49) had a more minimal, controlled design. The historical title given to this and other paintings, coupled with their large size, makes them curiously reminiscent of the academic history paintings of the 19th century. Involving himself in a wide range of activities—designing stage sets, tapestries, posters and coins, including the new 10-franc coin in 1974—he persistently advocated Tachism, not only in paintings such as *Matta Salums* (1978; see 1978 exh. cat., pl. 39) but also by relating it as a concept to areas beyond the narrow aesthetic realm. He also applied himself directly to wider social issues, such as the indifference of politicians towards spiritual matters and the poor design of towns. Pursuing his earlier view of the semantic importance of Tachism, he also engaged in disputes over the validity of structuralism, the claims for which he tried to refute.

WRITINGS
Analogie de la non-figuration (Paris, 1949)
Au-delà du tachisme (Paris, 1963)
Le Privilège d'être (Paris, 1967)
De la Révolte à la Renaissance (Paris, 1973)

BIBLIOGRAPHY
Mathieu (exh. cat. by T. del Renzio, London, ICA, 1956)
Lyrical Abstraction in New Paintings (exh. cat. by J. Fitzsimmons, New York, Kootz Gal., 1957)
Mathieu (exh. cat. by M.-C. Dane, Paris, Mus. A. Mod. Ville Paris, 1963)
Mathieu (exh. cat. by G. Schehade and F. Mathey, Paris, Gal. Charpentier, 1965)
Mathieu: Gemälde, Gouachen, Aquarelle, Collagen (exh. cat. by W. Haftmann, Cologne, Kstver., 1967)
F. Mathey: *Mathieu* (Paris and Milan, 1969)
D. Quignon-Fleuret: *Mathieu* (Paris, 1973)
Mathieu: Oeuvres anciennes 1948–1960 (exh. cat. by D. Quignon-Fleuret, Paris, Gal. Beaubourg, 1974)
Mathieu: Quelques oeuvres peintes de 1963 à 1978 (exh. cat. by R. Arnoud, Paris, Grand Pal., 1978)
For further bibliography *see* ART AUTRE; ART INFORMEL; TACHISM.

PHILIP COOPER

Mathura [Mathurā; Madhupura, Madhupurī, Madhurā, Mahurā, Mathulā Muttra, Uttar Mathurā]. City on the Yamuna River, 150 km south of Delhi in Uttar Pradesh, India, established *c.* 6th century BC. During the 1st–3rd centuries AD Mathura achieved renown as the first centre of a school of art serving the three major Indian religions—Hinduism, Buddhism and Jainism—as well as several folk cults. The influence of Mathura dominated Indian art for several centuries, thereby establishing the first artistic conventions that can be described as 'pan-Indian'. The Mathura model consisted of a codified visual language expressing divine power as well as a distinctive sculptural style using the characteristic local plain or spotted red sandstone. Although it was once a major centre with many important monuments, only fragments of the buildings of Mathura survive. However, a large number of sculptures have been retrieved. Many were found in wells and the Yamuna, where they appear to have been thrown for safekeeping during upheavals and invasions. Others were recovered in the course of urban construction, notably the extraordinary finds of Buddhist art unearthed at Govindnagar on the western outskirts of the city in 1976. Important archaeological excavations include the work of the West German Archaeological Mission under the direction of Herbert Härtel, who conducted a campaign at Sonkh, *c.* 20 km south of Govardhan, Mathura District, in 1966–74; between 1973 and 1977, the Archaeological Survey of India under the direction of M. C. Joshi excavated a number of sites in Mathura city. The chief collections of Mathura art are at the Government Museum in Mathura and the State Museum in Lucknow, although examples are also found in museums and private collections in the USA, Europe and Japan.

1. Early period (to 1st century AD). 2. Kushana period (1st–3rd centuries AD). 3. Gupta period (4th–6th centuries AD). 4. Medieval period (7th–12th centuries). 5. Late period (12th century and after).

1. EARLY PERIOD (TO 1ST CENTURY AD). Mathura began as a village close to the Yamuna near the northern end of the modern city and grew into an extensive settlement (c. 3.9 km sq.) from the end of the 4th century to the 2nd BC. During this period terracotta figurines, notably mother goddess and elephant types, were made on a large, perhaps commercial, scale. More unusual finds include a terracotta head of a man, dating to the end of the 4th century BC, from Sonkh. Such terracotta figurines, as well as the anthropomorphic pots found at both Mathura and Sonkh, may have helped to lay the foundation of the Mathura sculptural style.

From the 2nd century BC, Mathura experienced economic growth and cultural diversity, probably owing to population shifts from the east and north-west; these in turn stimulated artistic expansion. Architectural activity at Mathura is documented from c. the 2nd century BC: the Mathura lion capital inscription (London, BM) mentions the erection of a Buddhist stupa and monastery. Surviving fragments include gateway crossbars bearing carved scenes including an enshrined *bodhi* tree, the worship of the Wheel of the Law (*dharmacakra*), the adoration of a stupa and a scene of the god Indra paying homage to Buddha seated in a cave (Mathura, Govt Mus., M3). Railing pillars and coping stones from the outer enclosure of a stupa are carved with episodes from *jātaka* (Mathura, Govt Mus., 15.586) stories and symbolic representations of the Buddha such as the *bodhi* tree within a railing and three umbrellas (e.g. Mathura, Govt Mus., 14–15–438, 14.431). These examples testify to the gradual introduction of Buddha figures in place of symbols referring to his presence. Towards the end of this period, construction began on a large Jaina stupa at Kankali Tila (*see also* STUPA, §1); Hindu building activities can also be documented. According to the Mora well inscription of the early 1st century AD, a stone shrine dedicated to the five *vṛṣṇi* heroes, whose cult preceded the Hindu Vaishnava sect, stood at Mora, a village on the outskirts of the town. Two inscribed statues (Mathura, Govt Mus., 87.145 and 87.146) datable by inscription to the third quarter of the 1st century AD, probably of doorkeepers, intimate that they guarded a Hindu shrine, since one of the doorkeepers represents the god Agni. A Shiva shrine represented in reliefs (Mathura, Govt Mus., 52.3525; Lucknow, State Mus., B 141) shows the god's highest sign (*liṅga*), the phallic emblem, attesting to his cosmic creative supremacy, placed on an altar in the shade of a tree.

Isolated sculptures of between the 2nd century BC and the latter part of the 1st century AD represent divinities in whose honour religious structures were built; it cannot, however, be assumed that the following divinities were housed in the structures mentioned above. Sculptural fragments from Mora include two male figures of from around the second part of the 1st century AD and a female figure, dated to the Kushana period (Mathura, Govt Mus., E20–22); the two males may represent *vṛṣṇi* heroes,

Vasudeva–Krishna and the female Samkarshana/Balarama, and the future their sister Ekanamsha. Shiva icons include monumental *liṅga*s (e.g. Lucknow, State Mus., 1970×260 mm) and large, realistic *liṅga*s with a head of the god emerging from them (*ekamukhaliṅga*s; e.g. Philadelphia, PA, Mus. A., 70.221.1, h. 781 mm; Bharatpur, State Mus., 52, h. 1.38 m). A colossal, free-standing, ithyphallic image of Shiva (h. 1.48 m) holding a water-pot in his left hand and making the gesture of reassurance (*abhaya mudrā*) with his right that was found in Bharata Mandir, Rishikesh, Uttar Pradesh, was probably also made in Mathura. Pre-Kushana Buddha images from Mathura comprise two main types: the standing type seen on a relief from Kankali Tila (Lucknow, State Mus., J531) and the seated type that occurs on the architrave mentioned above (Mathura, Govt. Mus., M3), on which the Buddha appears seated with crossed legs in a cave. The former shows a rather corpulent Buddha with a deep navel, wearing a long, sarong-type lower garment (*dhotī*) and with a thin folded shawl over his bare torso; his right hand is raised in the gesture of reassurance, and he has a cranial bump (*uṣṇīṣa*) and a plain nimbus surrounding the head and shoulders. But for the pose, the seated type resembles the standing type. One indicator of an early date is the loose and rather clumsy position of the crossed legs; in sculpture of the Kushana period (*see* §2 below) the legs are tightly locked into the more formal yogic meditative pose (*padmāsana*). The same loosely poised crossed legs characterize seated representations of Jaina *tīrthaṅkara*s, which were first produced at Mathura (Lucknow, State Mus., J 354, J 609; c. 2nd century BC). The nude *tīrthaṅkara* figures do not have the haloes or the *śrīvatsa* (an emblem composed of two opposed S-shapes on the chest; *see* INDIAN SUBCONTINENT, §II, 3) found on later sculptures (*see* §2 below); the same is true of representations on the 1st-century BC Jaina tablets of homage (*āyāgapaṭa*s) found at the Kankali Tila stupa. A male deity filled with life's energy (*yakṣa*) is portrayed in a similar fashion to Buddha figures, since both represent 'Great Beings' (*mahāpuruṣa*s). For example, the *yakṣa* found at Parkham near Mathura (Mathura, Govt Mus., C1; c. 1st century BC) has, like the standing Buddha type, a massive body built up by a series of rounded, interlocking forms; a sash around the upper abdomen further emphasizes his powerful, inflated figure (*see* INDIAN SUBCONTINENT, fig. 141). Female counterparts (*yakṣī*s) of the same period include one representing the *yakṣī* Layava seated on a wicker stool in the earliest example of the 'European' fashion with both legs hanging down (*pralambapādāsana*; Mathura, Govt Mus., 72.5).

2. KUSHANA PERIOD (1ST–3RD CENTURIES AD). During this period Mathura became a cosmopolitan city characterized by cultural, religious and ethnic diversity: in addition, as an important centre of the far-flung KUSHANA empire, the city achieved considerable political stature and had a dynamic economy. The arts proliferated, demonstrating unmistakable evidence of ideas originating both in the north-west and locally.

The sites of Mat and Sonkh clearly reflect Mathura's urban complexity during this period. At Mat, c. 14 km north of Mathura, there was a brick-built shrine where royalty worshipped the deity or deities that protected them; razed in antiquity, all that remains of it is a rectangle (*c.* 30×18 m) with a circular sanctuary in the north-west. This site yielded fragmentary sculptures of Kushana kings or dignitaries wearing their native Scythian dress; these include figures of Kanishka (h. 1.7 m; *see* INDIAN SUBCONTINENT, fig. 152) and Vima Khadphises (h. 2.1 m; Mathura, Govt Mus., 213, 215). Royal statuary, foreign to early Indian art, reflects the Central Asian influences brought in by the Kushanas. A contemporary brick-built apsidal temple at Sonkh was dedicated to an important local serpent (*nāga*) cult and decorated with numerous high-quality reliefs of serpent themes. The temple was surrounded by a peristyle and enclosed by a stone railing; the entrance gateway was decorated with a figure of a nubile woman holding a branch (*śālabhañjikā*; see fig. 1).

During this period the Mathura school led the development of Hindu imagery. It perfected the four-armed icon of Vasudeva–Krishna holding the mace (*gadā*) and wheel (*cakra*) in his raised extra hands, rendered in both standing and seated forms (Mathura, Govt Mus., 2487 and 39.2858). Other themes included the incarnations of Vishnu, notably as a boar, as the horse Hayagriva and as Trivikrama (Mathura, Govt Mus., 65.15;4846 and 50.3550). The sculptors of Mathura also developed the Vaishnava *caturvyūha* image, conceived to express the concept that the 'transcendental supreme Lord' emits four emanations (*vyūha*) who perpetuate cosmic creation. Though fragmented, this image originally showed the first *vyūha* Vasudeva giving rise to the other emanations from his shoulders and head (Mathura, Govt Mus., 392–5). In Shaiva art Mathura continued to produce large, realistic *liṅga*s, while evolving new two-headed and four-headed (*mukhaliṅga*) forms (e.g Mathura, Govt Mus., 462; New Delhi, N. Mus., 65.172; Varanasi, Banaras Hindu U, Bharat Kala Bhavan, 22.755). Mahesha, the first fully manifest god responsible for further creations, is rendered as a four-headed figure sometimes with addorsed bodies (e.g. Zurich, René Russek priv. col., 177 IMG; Mathura, Govt Mus., E12), while representations of the androgynous Lord Ardhanarishvara achieved considerable sculptural refinement (e.g. Los Angeles, CA, Co. Mus. A., L83.46); sculptures of the Divine Couple convey the lithe, yet robust, forms of Shiva and his consort (e.g. Mathura, Govt Mus., G52). Mathura appears to have had a monopoly on making icons of the Warrior Goddess, but why this is so remains a puzzle. Numerous sculptures of this deity, both small and large, were made in stone and terracotta; indeed, the Kushana-period representations of the goddess found at Mathura outnumber those of any other deity. She is portrayed in two modes, the first of which shows her restoring cosmic order by killing the buffalo–demon. In this form she has four, six or eight arms; with her two natural arms she grips the struggling buffalo, while the raised extra hands hold such weapons as the trident, shield, spear or sword and, rarely, the sun and moon (e.g. Berlin, Mus. Ind. Kst, MIK5817). Sometimes, as in the last-mentioned piece, the innermost extra arms hold a wreath above the head as if performing a self-coronation gesture. Despite her martial air, the goddess is dressed and adorned as a typical Indian woman. In the second mode, she stands straight and alone; only her lion-vehicle may be seen at

1. Carved bracket representing a young woman holding a branch (*śālabhañjikā*), sandstone, h. 780 mm, from Sonkh, near Mathura, 1st–2nd centuries AD (Mathura, Government Museum)

her feet (Berlin, Mus. Ind. Kst, MIK 5894). This iconography is a blend of local and foreign elements typifying the amalgamation of cultures and ideas that characterized Mathura under Kushana rule.

The development of the Buddha image likewise reflects Mathura's inter-regional ascendancy during this period. Early images were fashioned according to an indigenous (*kapardin*) type. The best example of this is a stele from the Katra mound representing the Buddha seated on a lion-throne beneath the *bodhi* tree and showing the upper soles of both feet decorated with the Wheel of the Law and the Three Jewels (*triratna*; Mathura, Govt Mus., A1; *see* INDIAN SUBCONTINENT, fig. 152). The Buddha, surrounded by a scalloped-edged nimbus and flanked by attendants with fly-whisks, faces directly outward, with wide-open eyes, narrow eyebrows broken by a round protrusion in the centre of the forehead (*ūrṇā*), a slight smile, elongated ears and no hair save a top knot (*kaparda*) shaped like a snail. His corpulence can be seen through the thin *dhotī* and the scarf gathered on the left shoulder. He makes the gesture of addressing an audience (*vyāvṛtta mudrā*) with his right hand, while the left, in a commanding gesture, rests on the thigh. Another good example of this hierarchically frontal type is the Mathura Buddha (Sarnath, Archaeol. Mus., B1), which was installed at Sarnath, Uttar Pradesh, in year three of Kanishka's reign, assumed by many scholars to commence in AD 78.

This early, indigenous Buddha type was subsequently influenced by the Buddha images developed in GANDHARA. The result can be seen in the seated Buddha from Anyor (Mathura, Govt Mus., A65), Mathura District, dated by inscription to year 51 (perhaps AD 129), in which the hair has rows of short curls and the garment has become a heavy monk's robe covering the whole body. Several symbols of the 'Great Being' have been replaced. The right hand now assumes the gesture of reassurance, while the left holds the hem of the robe in front of the chest. A new gesture, the *dhyāna* (meditation) *mudrā* in which the hands rest in the lap, is seen on a seated (now headless) Buddha from Govindnagar (Mathura, Govt Mus., 76.19). Gandharan influences also led to an increase in narrative themes portraying the life of the Buddha. Kushana-period sculptures from Mathura were widely disseminated throughout the north, east and central areas of the subcontinent: for example, in 1985 excavations at SANGHOL in the Punjab yielded 117 Mathura sculptures that originally formed part of a stupa railing.

The Jaina art of Mathura comprises seated and standing figures of *tīrthaṅkara*s. All the early figures are nude (*digambara*) and have the *śrīvatsa* mark in the centre of the chest and an *ūrṇā* between the brows. A number of fourfold images (*sarvatobhadrikā*; 'auspicious from all sides') are known; these are composed of four standing figures of different *tīrthaṅkara*s arranged on the four sides of a pillar to face the cardinal points and were worshipped by circumambulation.

3. GUPTA PERIOD (4TH–6TH CENTURIES AD). Although Mathura continued to produce images for all the major religions during the GUPTA period, it was but one among several great centres. Previously unknown religious art forms appeared, and a new, more refined, style was developed. Hindu art of the period displays a wider iconographic spectrum; in a large, broken image of Vishnu (1.02×0.66 m; New Delhi, N. Mus., SR 242), the god is identified by a long garland of forest flowers (*vanamālā*). On a stone post Krishna is shown lifting Mount Govardhana (Mathura, Govt Mus., D47). The Mathura sculptors also formulated the complex icon of Vishnu's omniform, Vishvarupa (Mathura, Govt Mus., 42–43.298). In Shaiva art sculptures include images of the androgynous Ardhanarishvara (Mathura, Govt Mus., 772) and the Divine Couple (Mathura, Govt Mus., 2084; Zurich, René Russek

priv. col., IMG 545); new forms include Vinadhara (e.g. Zurich, René Russek priv. col., IMG 569), Lakulisha (e.g. Mathura, Govt Mus., 3211), Harihara (e.g. Mathura, Govt Mus., 1336) and a five-faced *pañcamukha-liṅga* (Mathura, Govt Mus., 516).

Mathura is known for the graceful and ethereal Buddha images produced in the Gupta period (e.g. Mathura, Govt Mus., A5). The slim, elegant form of the standing Buddha conveys spiritual harmony. The Buddha's eyes are lowered, implying introspection; the drapery of his monastic robe cascades in rippling folds all over his body. His 'conchlike' neck marked with three lines, his perfectly ovoid head and the form of his shoulders and arms all portray superhuman perfection. One of the few intact Gupta-period images of a *tīrthaṅkara* (Lucknow, State Mus., J118; see fig. 2) indicates that the same stylistic developments observed in Hindu and Buddhist images also occurred in Jaina sculpture. The nude saint, poised in yogic concentration, sits on an elaborate lion–throne. His large, ornate nimbus offsets the quietude of his meditative pose.

Architectural fragments of the Gupta period have been found in considerable numbers and include carved pillars, portions of temple doors, mouldings, dormers and excavated fragments of walls. No intact temples have survived.

4. MEDIEVAL PERIOD (7TH–12TH CENTURIES). After the 7th century Mathura declined in importance as

2. Seated *tīrthaṅkara*, spotted red sandstone, h. 950 mm, from Mathura, 3rd–4th centuries AD (Lucknow, State Museum, J118)

sculptural production became increasingly decentralized. Although Hindu, Jaina and, to a lesser extent, Buddhist images were still carved at Mathura, the images were no longer exceptional and conformed to general conventions of iconography and style. Stelae carved in high relief replaced free-standing images, and the mottled red sandstone so characteristic of early Mathura sculpture was often replaced by a buff-coloured stone, as in a figure of the Jaina goddess Chakreshvari from Kankali Tila (Mathura, Govt Mus.). While the Huna incursions of the late 5th century may have contributed to the abandonment of Mathura's ancient shrines and disrupted the production of sculpture, far more devastating was the sack of the city and its temples by the armies of Mahmud of Ghazna in 1018. That some reconstruction took place after the raid is evidenced by several images and a pair of 10th-century pillars from Mahaban (Lucknow, State Mus.).

5. LATE PERIOD (12TH CENTURY AND AFTER). With the establishment of the Delhi Sultanate, Mathura became a city of secondary importance. The 15th century, however, was marked by the resurgence of devotional Vaishnavism, particularly the worship of Krishna. Some illustrated manuscripts, such as the dispersed *Bhagavata Purāṇa* of *c.* 1520–30, may have been produced in the city. The renowned Hindu saint Chaitanya visited Mathura and 'rediscovered' sites traditionally connected with the early life of Krishna, including Gokul, Govardhan, Vishram Ghat and VRINDAVAN. While temples were built from the 15th century, the city suffered damage under Sikandar Lodi (*reg c.* 1489–*c.* 1517) and again under the Mughal ruler Aurangzeb (*reg* 1658–1707); in consequence, most of the existing temples are 19th-century reconstructions. The principal building of the Mughal period is the Jami' Mosque (1660–61), which is similar to contemporary buildings at Lucknow and Varanasi. Another 17th-century mosque stands on the ruins of the Keshava Deva Temple, which was destroyed on the orders of Aurangzeb; portions of the temple's foundations are still visible. Among the monuments of the colonial period, the most interesting is the Roman Catholic church of the Sacred Heart (1870) designed by F. S. Growse, who also founded the Government Museum in 1874.

See also INDIAN SUBCONTINENT, §IV, 4(i), 5(i), 6(i) and 7(i).

BIBLIOGRAPHY

V. S. Agrawala: 'Pre-Kushāna Art of Mathurā', *J. U. P. Hist. Soc.*, vi (1933), pp. 81–120
——: 'Mathurā Terracottas', *J. U. P. Hist. Soc.*, viii–ix (1935–6), pp. 6–39
——: 'Buddha and Bodhisattva Images in the Mathura Museum', *J. U. P. Hist. Soc.*, xxi (1948), pp. 43–98
J. E. van Lohuizen-de Leeuw: *The 'Scythian' Period* (Leiden, 1949)
V. S. Agrawala: *A Catalogue of the Brahmanical Images in the Mathura Museum* (Lucknow, 1951)
——: *Mathura Museum Catalogue: Jaina Tirthankaras and Other Miscellaneous Figures* (Lucknow, 1952)
H. Lüders: *Mathurā Inscriptions*, ed. K. L. Janert (Göttingen, 1961)
V. S. Agrawala: *Mathura Museum Catalogue: Architectural Pieces* (Varanasi, 1963)
N. P. Joshi: *Mathura Sculptures* (Mathura, 1966)
J. M. Rosenfield: *The Dynastic Arts of the Kushans* (Berkeley, 1967)
J. C. Harle: *Gupta Sculpture* (Oxford, 1974)
H. Härtel: 'Some Results of the Excavation at Sonkh: A Preliminary Report', *German Scholars on India*, ii (Bombay, 1976), pp. 69–99
M. C. Joshi and C. Margabandhu: 'Some Terracottas from Excavations at Mathurā: A Study', *J. Ind. Soc. Orient. A.*, n. s., viii (1976–7), pp. 16–32
J. E. van Lohuizen-de Leeuw: 'New Evidence with Regard to the Origin of the Buddha Image', *South Asian Archaeology 1979* (Berlin, 1981), pp. 376–400
D. M. Srinivasan: 'Early Krṣṇa Icons: The Case at Mathurā', *Kalādarśana: American Studies in the Art of India*, ed. J. G. Williams (New Delhi, 1981), pp. 127–36
J. G. Williams: *The Art of Gupta India: Empire and Province* (Princeton, 1982)
R. Göbl: *System und Chronologie der Münzprägung des Kušānreiches* (Vienna, 1984)
R. C. Sharma: *Buddhist Art of Mathurā* (Delhi, 1984)
S. P. Gupta, ed.: *Kushāna Sculptures from Sanghol (1st–2nd Century A.D.): A Recent Discovery*, i (New Delhi, 1985)
H. Härtel: 'The Concept of the Kapardin Buddha Type of Mathurā', *South Asian Archaeology 1983* (Naples, 1986), pp. 653–78
G. Kreisel: *Die Śiva-Bildwerke der Mathurā-Kunst* (Stuttgart, 1986)
H. Härtel: 'Archaeological Evidence on the Early Vāsudeva Worship', *Orientalia Iosephi Tucci memoriae dedicata*, ed. G. Gnoli and L. Lanciotti (Rome, 1987), pp. 573–87
D. M. Srinivasan: 'A Unique Mathurā Eight-armed Viṣṇu Image of the 4th Century A.D.', *Orient. A.*, xxxiv/4 (1988–9), pp. 276–81
——: *Mathurā: The Cultural Heritage* (New Delhi, 1989)
——: 'Newly Discovered Inscribed Mathurā Sculptures of Probable Doorkeepers, Dating to the Kṣatrapa Period', *Archvs Asian A.*, xliii (1990), pp. 63–9 [epigraphic analysis by L. Sander]
——: *Origins of Divine Multiplicity in Indian Art: Meaning and Form* (Leiden, in preparation)

DORIS METH SRINIVASAN

Mathurins. *See* TRINITARIANS.

Matilda of Canossa, Countess of Tuscany (*b c.* 1045; *d* 1115). Italian patron. She is now recognized as an extremely influential patron. Her prominence is well documented in the *Vita Mathildis* (Rome, Vatican, Bib. Apostolica, MS. Lat. 4922), the illuminated biography completed in 1111–12 by her chaplain Donizo. He labelled her 'the worthy daughter of Peter', and she is best known for her politics as the staunchest papal supporter in the Investiture Dispute. She was also interested in Cluniac reform. By donating her extensive possessions to the Church, she not only strengthened the Papacy but also helped north Italian cities (especially those under her influence in Emilia-Romagna) in their struggle for independence from the Empire. Matilda's status as the first promoter of the Italian city-state (*comune*) is later reflected in Dante's *Divine Comedy*, where he elevates Matilda to a place of honour as Beatrice's guide to Paradise.

Matilda's involvement in the rebuilding of Modena Cathedral (1099–1106) is well documented and illustrated in the *Relatio translationis corporis Sancti Geminiani* (Modena, Archv Capitolare). The two-storey porch-portal (*protiro*) was first introduced here, with an iconography that may contain allusions to the papal allegiance of the bishops and citizens. This allegiance was shared by the cathedrals of Reggio Emilia, Piacenza, Ferrara and Verona, the church of S Zeno Maggiore, Verona, and the Cluniac monasteries of S Benedetto Polirone, Rome, and Nonantola, all of which were built by related workshops under the patronage of Matilda or her family. Large-scale sculptural programmes were commissioned for the façades of these churches by their bishops and abbots from such sculptors as Wiligelmo and Nicholaus. They bear similarities both in figure style and iconography to the illuminations of the two manuscripts commissioned by Matilda surviving from the once huge personal library at Canossa: the *Vita Mathildis* cited above and the *Gospels of Matilda*

(New York, Pierpont Morgan Lib., MS. M.492), dated 1115; also to the floor mosaics of Reggio Emilia Cathedral and those showing the Four Cardinal Virtues at S Benedetto Polirone, laid to surround the tomb of Matilda which has now been removed to the Vatican.

BIBLIOGRAPHY

Donizo: *Vita Mathildis* (*c*. 1111–12); ed. in *PL*, cxlviii (1853), cols 949–1036; facs. *Vita Mathilde von Canossa*, 2 vols (New York, 1982)

A. Overman: *Graefin Mathilde von Tuscien: Ihre Besitzungen, Geschichte ihres Gutes von 1115–1230 und ihre Regesten* (Innsbruck, 1895)

G. Warner: *The Gospels of Mathilda, Countess of Tuscany* (New York, 1917)

Studi Matildici, 3 vols (1964–78) [congress reports, held in Modena and Reggio Emilia]

R. Rough: *The Reformist Illuminations in the Gospels of Matilda, Countess of Tuscany: A Study in the Art of the Age of Gregory VII* (The Hague, 1973)

P. Piva: *Da Cluny a Polirone: Un recupero essenziale del romanico europeo*, Biblioteca Polironiana di Fonti e Studi, iv (San Benedetto Po, 1980)

Lanfranco e Wiligelmo: Il Duomo di Modena (Modena, 1984) [incl. articles by A. Peroni, R. Salvini, W. Sauerländer and A. C. Quintavalle]

C. Verzar Bornstein: *Portals and Politics in the Early Italian City-state: the Sculpture of Nicholaus in Context* (Parma, 1988)

CHRISTINE VERZAR

Matisse, Henri (Emile Benoît) (*b* Le Cateau-Cambrésis [now Le Cateau], nr Cambrai, Picardy, 31 Dec 1869; *d* Nice, 3 Nov 1954). French painter, draughtsman, sculptor, printmaker, designer and writer. He came to art comparatively late in life and made his reputation as the principal protagonist of FAUVISM, the first avant-garde movement at the turn of the century. He went on to develop a monumental decorative art, which was innovative both in its treatment of the human figure and in the constructive and expressive role accorded to colour. His long career culminated in a highly original series of works made of paper cut-outs, which confirmed his reputation, with Picasso, as one of the major artists of the 20th century.

1. Training and work, to 1896. 2. 1897–1904. 3. The Fauvist period, 1904–6. 4. 1906–10. 5. 1910–17. 6. Nice, 1918–30. 7. The 1930s. 8. 1940–54.

1. TRAINING AND WORK, TO 1896. Matisse was born in his grandparents' home and grew up in the neighbouring village of Bohain-en-Vermandois, where his father's general store had developed into a grain business. He worked first as a solicitor's clerk in the local town of Saint-Quentin before taking a degree in law in Paris from October 1887 to August 1889, without apparently showing the slightest interest in art; on returning home he resumed work as a solicitor's clerk. Bored by the routine of office life, he attended drawing classes at the Ecole Quentin Latour before going to work.

In winter 1889 Matisse took up painting during a prolonged period of convalescence from appendicitis. He abandoned law and obtained his father's grudging permission to study painting in Paris. He registered at the Académie Julian on 5 October 1891 and entered the class of the highly successful Salon painter William-Adolphe Bouguereau to prepare for the entrance examination to the Ecole des Beaux-Arts. From October 1892, after failing this examination, he took courses in drawing and perspective at the Ecole des Arts Décoratifs. Like other students, he also hoped to be invited to work informally in the studio of one of the professors by drawing in the glass-enclosed court of the Ecole des Beaux-Arts from casts of Greek and Roman sculpture. Among the few surviving drawings of this type is *Hermes Adjusting his Sandal* (*c*. 1892; Nice, Mus. Matisse), after a statue by Lysippos.

In 1892 Matisse was invited to join the studio of Gustave Moreau, who had been appointed professor in January of that year. He passed the official entrance examination of the Ecole des Beaux-Arts in 1895 and remained in Moreau's studio until his marriage to Amélie Parayre in January 1898. As a student he despised Bouguereau's rather mindless insistence on the mechanical imitation of surface appearances, but he developed great respect and affection for Moreau, who gave him sympathetic encouragement and who stressed the power of the imagination and of feeling. Moreau was unusual as a teacher in wishing his students to begin by painting in order to develop their gifts as colourists.

Following Moreau's emphasis on the study of Old Masters, Matisse copied at least 19 paintings in the Louvre from 1893 to 1900; he produced, among other works, *The Ray* (1894–1900; Le Cateau, Mus. Matisse), after Jean-Siméon Chardin. Although he later reacted against his academic training, he continued later in life to make direct reference to earlier paintings and to emphasize the primacy in his art of drawing from the human figure.

The style and subject-matter of Matisse's first original paintings, culminating in such works as *The Reader* (1895; Paris, Pompidou) and *Interior with a Top Hat* (1896; Paris, priv. col., see Watkins, 1984, p. 21), owe little or nothing to his teachers. They are for the most part modest still-lifes and interiors, firmly based on reality, in a restricted tonal palette influenced above all by his copies after Dutch masters and Chardin and by exhibitions he had seen of the work of Jean-Baptiste-Camille Corot and Edouard Manet. *The Reader*, purchased by Mme Félix Faure, wife of the President of the Republic, for the official summer residence at Rambouillet, was one of the four paintings selected from his submission of seven for exhibition at the Salon de la Société Nationale des Beaux-Arts in 1896. Matisse became an associate member of the Salon in that year and, at the age of 26, appeared to be destined to a future as a conservative and moderately successful painter.

2. 1897–1904. Following his success at the Salon, Matisse set himself on an experimental course during which he investigated new developments in painting in a bid to establish himself as a modern artist. Under the influence of Impressionism he had gradually adopted a lighter palette and bolder brushwork while working outdoors in 1896, during the second of three successive summer painting trips to Belle-Ile, off the coast of Brittany. These discoveries were synthesized on his return to Paris that winter, possibly at Moreau's instigation, in his first major exhibition painting, the *Dinner Table* (1897; Paris, S.IIS. Niarchos priv. col., see Watkins, 1984, p. 29), for the Salon de la Société Nationale des Beaux-Arts in spring 1897; with it he hoped to consolidate his reputation and to demonstrate his maturity as a painter capable of sustaining work on a large scale. It represents his mistress Caroline Joblaud (who also posed for *The Reader*) hovering over the centre of a table in order to put the final touches to a bouquet of flowers. The surface of the painting, pitted

and scored with scrapings-out and reworkings, testifies to the difficulties experienced by Matisse in reconciling his new interest in Impressionism with his previous technique.

Matisse was undaunted by the hostile reception accorded to this picture, and, like Cézanne, van Gogh and Gauguin before him, he turned for advice to Camille Pissarro. At Belle-Ile that summer he renewed contact with the Australian painter John Peter Russell, a friend of Claude Monet, and acquired from him a drawing by van Gogh; in paintings such as *Rocks and Sea (Belle-Ile)* (1897; Paris, priv. col., see Watkins, 1984, p. 32) he adopted the principal features of an Impressionist *plein-air* technique: pale grounds, broken brushwork, bright colour and informality of composition. These methods were also applied to domestic interiors such as *First Orange Still-life* (1899; Paris, Pompidou), which bear comparison with the *Intimisme* of Pierre Bonnard and Edouard Vuillard, whose work he had recently come to know.

On his return to Paris at the end of 1897, Matisse went through an equally momentous change in his personal life. He left Caroline Joblaud, who had given birth to his daughter Marguerite on 3 September 1894, and on 8 January 1898 married Amélie Noémie Alexandrine Parayre. Following Pissarro's advice, the Matisses spent their brief honeymoon in London, where they looked at the work of J. M. W. Turner; on returning to France, Matisse decided to spend a year painting in the south, initially in Corsica. He broke his visit there in mid-June to see exhibitions by Monet and Pissarro in Paris, and in August he and his pregnant wife moved on to Fenouillet, near Toulouse, to stay with her parents. Their son, Jean, was born there on 10 January 1899.

In Corsica Matisse explored different approaches to landscape painting, from conservative, well-constructed compositions to exuberant small-scale experiments in the expressive manipulation of colour. The first signs of his new maturity as a painter in Toulouse stemmed from a systematic pursuit of pictorial problems from painting to painting, and from his reading of Paul Signac's treatise, 'D'Eugène Delacroix au Néo-impressionisme', serialized in *La Revue blanche* from May to July 1898. In the astonishingly bold *Still-life with Oranges* (1899; St Louis, MO, Washington U., Gal. A.), flat shapes of colour supply both sensations of light and the painting's structure. He had finally moved beyond Impressionism.

Despite his straitened circumstances, on his return to Paris in February 1899 Matisse purchased from the dealer Ambroise Vollard several works by other artists: *Three Bathers* (c. 1881–4; now Paris, Petit Pal.) by Cézanne, a van Gogh drawing, Gauguin's *Young Man with Flower* (1891; Shaker Heights, OH, Mr & Mrs H. Greenberg priv. col., see G. Wildenstein, *Gauguin*, Paris, 1964, i, p. 164) and a plaster cast of Auguste Rodin's bust of *Henri de Rochefort* (1884; untraced). Rodin and Cézanne, in particular, set the artistic agenda that Matisse was to pursue in his treatment of the human figure in different media over the next few years. In order to have regular access to models, Matisse worked in a succession of public and private art schools: the Ecole des Beaux-Arts, which eased him out on the grounds that he was too old to be a student at 30; the Académie Julian, where the students defaced one of his drawings; the Académie Camillo, which closed

for lack of funds; and the Académie Colarossi. In order to clarify his ideas as a painter, he took up sculpture, taking lessons from 1899 to 1901 at the Ecole Communale de la Ville de Paris, showing Rodin some of his drawings and going to Emile-Antoine Bourdelle's studio for technical advice.

Matisse's return as a more experienced adult to a student environment led to his becoming the leader of a group of younger artists, notably André Derain, whom he had met at the Académie Camillo and who in turn introduced him to Maurice de Vlaminck at the van Gogh exhibition held at the Galeries Bernheim-Jeune in 1901. Together Matisse, Derain and Vlaminck soon became the principal figures of a new movement, Fauvism, the origins of which lay in Impressionism. In reviving the study of the nude human figure, however, Matisse was in part reacting against what he perceived as Impressionism's neglect of this traditional subject. From 1900 to 1903 he occasionally treated the figure as a vehicle for striking colour contrasts, but in general during this period he favoured two contrasting courses in both his paintings and his sculptures. In some works he emphasized the arabesque or overall rhythm of the figure, as in *Nude Study in Blue* (c. 1899–1900; London, Tate) and the cast bronze sculpture, *Madeleine I* (1901; Baltimore, MD, Mus. A.). In other cases the dominant impression is of the figure's craggy mass, as in two studies of a muscular model who also posed for Rodin: the painting *Male Model* (c. 1900; New York, MOMA) and his first major sculpture, *The Serf* (1900–03; Nice, Mus. Matisse).

From 1900 to 1903 Matisse worked under difficult conditions. Unable to sell his art, he took a brief job with Derain painting decorative garlands for the 1900 Exposition Universelle at the Grand Palais in Paris. Suffering from bronchitis in the winter of 1900–01, he was taken by his father to Villards-sur-Ollon, Switzerland, for his convalescence. The poor reception accorded to the first works shown by him at the Salon des Indépendants in April 1901 led to the withdrawal of his allowance from his father. His wife, who had given birth to their second son, Pierre (*see* MATISSE, PIERRE), on 13 June 1900, was herself exhausted and in poor health, and she was thus unable to continue with the small milliner's shop that she had opened in October 1899. Matisse was obliged to billet his family with relations and to work at his parents' home at Bohain-en-Vermandois in the winter of 1902–3.

During this period Matisse painted fewer works, but they were more finished in technique and tended to restrict bright colour to telling descriptive accents. For his figure compositions he chose more obviously pleasing subjects than had earlier been the case, perhaps to make his paintings more saleable but also in emulation of Manet. Such is the case with two portraits of his wife: *La Coiffure* (1901; Washington, DC, N.G.A.), in which she is seen from behind, arranging her hair in front of the mirror, and *The Guitarist* (1903; New York, Mrs R. F. Colin priv. col., see Watkins, 1984, p. 48), in which she assumes the identity of a musician in Spanish costume. The model in *Carmelina* (1903; Boston, MA, Mus. F.A.), placed in a full-frontal pose, challenges the viewer to inspect her body in as brazen a manner as Manet's *Olympia* (1863; Paris, Mus. d'Orsay).

Of the numerous landscapes painted by Matisse during this period, *Path in the Bois de Boulogne* (1902; Moscow, Pushkin Mus. F.A.) is the most deliberately structured. He also produced a number of views of Notre-Dame and the River Seine from the window of his room at 19, Quai St Michel, combining in such works as *Notre-Dame* (*c.* 1901; London, Tate) the Impressionist practice of painting in front of the motif with the traditional process of slowly building up the paint surface in the studio. Views of rooms, for example *Interior with Harmonium* (*c.* 1900; Nice, Mus. Matisse), are notable for their treatment of depth by means of a high vantage point, with forms aligned at dynamic angles as in Japanese 19th-century woodcuts. Some of the still-lifes are carefully constructed in a palette of silvery blues and greys, while others are more experimental in their boldly applied colour.

3. THE FAUVIST PERIOD, 1904–6. From his first one-man exhibition, which opened at Vollard's gallery on 1 June 1904, Matisse obtained neither critical nor commercial success. Yet, rather than return to a traditional realist mode, he continued to explore the expressive potential of colour. He spent two summers painting in small Mediterranean ports, at St Tropez in 1904 and in 1905 at Collioure, close to the Spanish border; each succeeding winter in Paris he synthesized his discoveries about colour in large paintings from his imagination: *Luxe, calme et volupté* (1904–5; Paris, Pompidou), the title of which was taken from the repeated refrain of Baudelaire's poem *L'Invitation au voyage*, and the *Joy of Life* (1905–6; Merion Station, PA, Barnes Found.).

Matisse and his wife stayed at St Tropez with the leading Neo-Impressionist painter, Paul Signac. The renewed experience of Mediterranean light resulted in an immediate brightening of Matisse's palette and in his subsequent decision to abandon brown underpainting. It was to the work of Cézanne, however, rather than to Neo-Impressionism, that Matisse looked most for inspiration at St Tropez, and his use of broad brushstrokes in the *Terrace, St Tropez* (1904; Boston, MA, Isabella Stewart Gardner Mus.) led to a quarrel with Signac. The imagery of idealized nudes posed by the sea in *Luxe, calme et volupté*, Matisse's only major painting in a Neo-Impressionist style, may have been suggested by the work of another Neo-Impressionist painter, Henri Edmond Cross, resident in the neighbouring town of Saint-Clair. Matisse's setting is based on a landscape painted at St Tropez, *By the Sea* (1904; Düsseldorf, Kstsamml. Nordrhein-Westfalen), which shows his wife and son Pierre on the beach below Signac's house. On his return to Paris that winter Matisse followed Signac's academic process for large landscapes by proceeding from a painted study and cartoon to the final work. *Luxe, calme et volupté* was exhibited in March 1905 at the Neo-Impressionist-dominated Salon des Indépendants and was purchased by Signac.

1. Henri Matisse: the *Joy of Life*, oil on canvas, 1.74×2.38 m, 1905–6 (Merion Station, PA, Barnes Foundation)

Despite Matisse's later strictures about the expressive limitations of working to a system, the Neo-Impressionist concept of the colours on the painter's palette as approximations of the pure hues of the visible spectrum suggested to him a way of organizing bright colours in terms of autonomous relationships that were independent of any descriptive function. At Collioure in the summer of 1905, stimulated by Derain and by the example of van Gogh and Gauguin, Matisse developed this new language of colour in a more spontaneous way. the *Open Window, Collioure* (1905; New York, Mr and Mrs J. H. Whitney priv. col., see Watkins, 1984, p. 61) and the portrait of *Derain* (1905; London, Tate; *see* OIL PAINTING, fig. 3), when exhibited at the Salon d'Automne in October 1905 along with works by Derain, Vlaminck and others, appeared to the public as brash and primitive. Matisse and his colleagues were branded the *fauves* ('wild beasts'), from which the movement known as Fauvism took its name. Some of the most daring works associated with the style, such as Matisse's picture of his wife known as the *Portrait with the Green Stripe* (1905; Copenhagen, Stat. Mus. Kst), date from this period.

Before the reactions had died down, Matisse was hard at work on his second great imaginary composition, the *Joy of Life* (see fig. 1), in a large space which he had rented in a former convent, the Couvent des Oiseaux, at 56, Rue de Sèvres, and which he kept as his studio until 1908. In this key work, which depicts a harem of Oriental women transposed to the West, broad areas of unmodulated colour are conjoined with sinuous linear arabesques. The sources for the painting are a complex compendium of his own work—including his student copies after Watteau and Poussin, Japanese woodcuts, Persian miniatures, the poetry of Stéphane Mallarmé—and earlier representations of an earthly paradise such as Titian's *The Andrians* (1523–5; Madrid, Prado), Agostino Carracci's engraving *Love in the Golden Age* (*c.* 1589–95), Ingres's the *Age of Gold* (1843–9; Dampierre, Château) and, above all, Gauguin's sensuous treatment of the subject in such paintings as *Te arii vahine (Queen of Beauty)* (1896; Moscow, Pushkin Mus. F.A.). As with *Luxe, calme et volupté*, Matisse established the setting in a landscape painted directly from the motif (*Landscape at Collioure*, 1905; Copenhagen, Stat. Mus. Kst) and in Paris proceeded from studies and sketches to a full-scale rehearsal in a cartoon. The final painting was his only exhibit at the Salon des Indépendants in March 1906. Even Matisse's own supporters were shocked. Pure, flat colours had been seen before, but not on such a large scale.

4. 1906–10. Matisse's rising critical reputation as leader of the Fauves was accompanied by increased sales. The success of his second one-man exhibition, held at the Galerie Druet in March 1906, enabled him to visit Algeria (Algiers, Constantine, Batna and Biskra) and to spend longer that year at Collioure. After visiting Italy in 1907, he went to Germany twice, in 1908 and again in 1910 to see the great Islamic exhibition in Munich. His art began to be exhibited and published abroad. Gertrude, Sarah and Leo STEIN, who were the first Americans and among the first collectors anywhere to buy his work, introduced him to other collectors, notably Claribel and Etta CONE,

and to artists, notably Picasso in 1906; Matisse's intermittent rivalry with Picasso was to prove a lasting feature of his career. In 1908 Sarah Stein, with Hans Purrmann, helped to found Matisse's school, which operated until 1911. Leo Stein, who later lost interest in Matisse, bought three of his most difficult paintings: the *Joy of Life*, *Woman with Hat* (1905; San Francisco, priv. col., see Watkins, 1984, p. 69) and *Blue Nude—Souvenir of Biskra* (1907; Baltimore, MD, Mus. A.). The Russian merchant Sergey Shchukin (*see* SHCHUKIN, (1)) became the most important collector of Matisse up to 1914, commissioning two of his major canvases of the period, *Dance II* (1909–10) and *Music* (1910; both St Petersburg, Hermitage).

Partly in response to Picasso's challenge for the leadership of the avant-garde and as a defence against criticism directed at his work, on 25 December 1908 Matisse published 'Notes d'un peintre', an artistic credo of which the basic tenets remained valid throughout his later development. Fundamental to his theory of art was an insistence that 'expression', as the ultimate goal of the artist, 'must not be considered as separate from his pictorial means' but that, on the contrary, it was the composition—'the entire arrangement' of the picture—that was expressive. 'The simplest means', he insisted, 'are those which best enable an artist to express himself' and his temperament. Banishing both anecdote and excessive literalness from his representations, he explained in a statement that has since been much quoted: 'What I dream of is an art of balance, of purity and serenity devoid of troubling or depressing subject-matter . . . a soothing, calming influence on the mind, something like a good armchair which provides relaxation from physical fatigue'.

Earlier in 1908 Matisse had moved his home, school and studio to the Hôtel Biron, the former Couvent du Sacré Coeur, Boulevard des Invalides, Paris, where Rodin was also among those who rented studio space. With the commission from Shchukin for *Dance* and *Music* in 1909, Matisse and his family first rented and then bought a house at Issy-les-Moulineaux, a suburb of Paris, and built a studio in its large garden. In September 1909 Matisse signed a contract with the Galeries Bernheim-Jeune, and his financial security appeared assured.

Matisse's work during this period falls into three categories: figure compositions, still-lifes and interiors, and portraits. On his return to Collioure from North Africa in 1906, he moved away from the Fauve style of the previous year and experimented with a new language of the human figure stimulated primarily by Gauguin's primitivism, but also by Cézanne's compositions of bathers, by classical decorations, by African tribal sculpture and by the challenge of Picasso. In general terms, he sought to integrate the types of figure seen in the *Joy of Life* into the surface design so that the idyllic quality of the subject-matter could be experienced in the very form of the work.

Sculpture and painting were closely bound in this programme. Matisse's continued treatment of the human figure in two modes, one brutal and immediate, concerned with structure and modelling, the other curvilinear and more graceful, is illustrated by a comparison of *Blue Nude—Souvenir of Biskra*, his only exhibit at the 1907 Salon des Indépendants, with *Luxury I* (1907; Paris, Pompidou), shown at the Salon d'Automne later that year. The expanded volumes of *Blue Nude*, contained by a heavy blue contour, are forcefully displayed across the canvas surface, whereas the figure in *Luxury I*, attended by her handmaidens, is executed in a linear style of classical simplicity. The differences extend also to the working methods used for the two pictures. The genesis of *Blue Nude* was closely related to that of a cast bronze sculpture, *Reclining Nude I* (1907; Paris, Pompidou; see fig. 2), in which he explored the visual balance of contrasting forms in space. *Luxury I*, on the other hand, followed a process of linear refinement from preliminary drawings to a full-scale cartoon. Matisse went on to paint a second, even more simplified, version (Copenhagen, Stat. Mus. Kst), probably later in the same year.

Bathers with a Turtle (1908; St Louis, MO, A. Mus.) is the first major painting of Matisse's maturity and the first in a series of large decorative paintings in which nudes are silhouetted against an elemental background of blue and green bands. *Music* (1907; New York, MOMA), a sketchy painting that represents a dancing couple as well as a crouching figure and a standing violinist, apparently featured in his discussions with Shchukin for two large-scale canvases. To clinch the commission, Matisse painted *Dance I* (1909; New York, MOMA), basing his circle of dancers on the figures seen in the background of the *Joy of Life*. He then went to great lengths to rethink the

composition and to treat the contours of the figures in a more fluid way in order to express more completely the idea of movement. In the bronze *La Serpentine* (1909; Baltimore, MD, Mus. A.), he took his formal ideas to an extreme, distorting and elongating female anatomy so as to treat it as a visual balance of opposing rhythms and volumes.

Matisse's original conception for the Shchukin commission appears to have been for a cycle of three paintings; one of these, a composition of bathers by a waterfall, was later transformed into the great *Bathers by a River* (1916; Chicago, IL, A. Inst.). Eventually Matisse produced the pair of canvases, *Dance II* (1909–10) and *Music* (1910; both St Petersburg, Hermitage), which perfectly complement each other in both subject-matter and composition: one a pounding Bacchic dance, the other a tranquil vision of harmony. When exhibited at the Salon d'Automne of 1910, before being sent to Moscow, they were judged by critics and the public to be a confusing combination of archaic and remote subject-matter with a distorted and immediate means of expression.

Broadly speaking, Matisse's figure compositions were conceived in his imagination and confirmed in studies of the nude; his development of a monumental decorative genre based on the still-life in an interior, on the other

2. Henri Matisse: *Reclining Nude I*, bronze, 342×502×286 mm, 1907 (Paris, Pompidou, Musée National d'Art Moderne)

hand, arose out of his inventive transformation of objects into relationships of form and colour achieved through the process of painting itself. The outcome of this development was the *Dinner Table (Harmony in Red)* (1908; St Petersburg, Hermitage), which was also bought by Shchukin. In a dining-room permeated by red, a maid places a fruit dish on an equally red table. This suffusion of the interior with a single colour is balanced by the predominant green of the garden, seen through the window on the left. Matisse again drew on his previous works, notably on the *Dinner Table* (1897), but also on his changing response to the painting itself as it evolved; its unrelieved flatness of presentation had been anticipated in his Cézanne-like *Blue Still-life* (1907; Merion Station, PA, Barnes Found.).

Given that Matisse was more interested in developing his art and in expressing his, rather than the sitter's, personality, he tended to avoid portraits, especially commissions. Instead he preferred to paint his family and friends, who were unlikely to try to dictate the final result. He was, nevertheless, sensitive to the mood and personality of the sitter or model, and he came to depend on them for inspiration. In his efforts to progress beyond a literal likeness, however, he would either bring out an aspect of the sitter's character through exaggeration, and sometimes through association with objects or flowers, or he would resort to a more structured mode, striving through form to express some eternal human essence. Matisse's portraits of adults are usually in the tradition of Renaissance three-quarter-length portraits. He turned for guidance to Paolo Veronese's *Portrait of a Woman with Child and Dog* (late 1540s; Paris, Louvre) when painting his friend and pupil *Greta Moll* (1908; London, N.G.). During ten three-hour sittings this portrait changed considerably, particularly in its colour scheme.

5. 1910–17. Driven on by the challenge of Cubism as the leading avant-garde movement, during this period Matisse achieved what many critics now regard as the greatest works of his career. While he did not relinquish the ambition to paint imaginary compositions with nudes, he concentrated on subjects that grew out of his direct experience of his sitters and surroundings, spurred also by his travels. Stimulated by his visit to the great Islamic exhibition in Munich in October 1910, from mid-November through to mid-January 1911 he travelled in Spain, concentrating on the Moorish cities of the south: Seville, Córdoba and Granada. In October 1911 he visited St Petersburg and Moscow before spending the winter months of early 1912 and 1912–13 in Morocco.

Inspired by these travels and by Persian miniatures, Matisse reacted against Cubism by making his paintings larger, more exotic and richer in colour. He spent most of 1911 on four separately conceived large paintings of roughly similar format, each treating the transformation of an interior (studio, home and holiday environment) into a monumental decorative display. The first of these, the *Pink Studio* (Moscow, Pushkin Mus. F.A.), represents Matisse's own art and other props ranged along the back wall of his outdoor studio at Issy. The *Painter's Family* (St Petersburg, Hermitage), completed by the end of May, groups family members around the fireplace in the living-room at Issy. *Interior with Aubergines* (Grenoble, Mus.

Peint. & Sculp.), the largest and most decorative of the four despite the removal of a floral border, was executed that summer at the holiday home at Collioure. Finally the *Red Studio* (New York, MOMA), completely novel in its all-over redness, was painted in his outdoor studio at Issy in October. Together, these four magnificent canvases are sometimes referred to as the 'symphonic interiors'.

Following the extreme effort of his year's work, Matisse hoped that Morocco would prove sufficiently exotic to encourage him to make direct contact again with nature. It also allowed him to examine Cubism with greater detachment. His primary concern was to convey the dreamlike atmosphere of brilliant light and colour enveloping both figures and objects. Two paintings from this first visit, *Window at Tangier* (1912) and the *Kasbah Gate* (1912), were incorporated with *Zorah on the Terrace* (1912) from his second stay into a triptych (Moscow, Pushkin Mus. F.A.) for Shchukin's rival Muscovite collector, Ivan Morosov. Although not sold as a triptych, *Park at Tangier* (1912; Stockholm, Mod. Mus.) similarly relates to the later *Moroccan Garden* (1912; New York, MOMA) and *Palmleaf, Tangier* (1912; Washington, DC, N.G.A.) to form a trio of garden paintings. Partly as a further reaction against Analytical Cubism, the paintings of his second stay, such as *Arab Café* (1913; St Petersburg, Hermitage), a large canvas showing six Arabs contemplating a bowl of goldfish and a vase of flowers, are if anything flatter and more abstract (for discussion of Matisse's use of contradictory depth, *see* PERCEPTION).

Matisse's paintings from the summers of 1912 and 1913 at Issy-les-Moulineaux, while more literal in their descriptions of the motif, maintained the air of reverie and the emphatic use of blue of the Moroccan pictures. In the summer of 1912 he painted four related interiors with a goldfish bowl, including *Goldfish and Sculpture* (New York, MOMA), previously dated to 1911, with the objects melodically arranged in a field of blue. In the *Blue Window* (1913; New York, MOMA) the interior of his bedroom at Issy merges with a view of the garden into a bold geometric structure again filled with variations of a single hue. A similar blue colour scheme was used to great effect in the portrait of *Mme Matisse* (1913; St Petersburg, Hermitage), which, after over 100 sittings, was exhibited at the 1913 Salon d'Automne.

Matisse's exhibition of 13 of his Moroccan paintings at Bernheim-Jeune in March 1913 was generally well received, but it was with the structural treatment of the portrait of *Mme Matisse* that he began to be accepted again by the avant-garde and to explore, in his own way, the formal language of Cubism. This engagement with Cubism, combined with a return to favourite motifs on again renting a studio at 19, Quai St Michel in the autumn of 1913, resulted in a succession of masterpieces painted during his winters there from 1914 to 1917: *Interior with Goldfish* (1914; Paris, Pompidou), *Studio, Quai St Michel* (1916; Washington, DC, Phillips Col.) and the *Painter and his Model* (1917; Paris, Pompidou). In 1914 he installed a hand-press at 19, Quai St Michel, using it to produce in that year about 60 etchings, drypoints and monotypes, mostly portraits of friends, and 9 transfer lithographs of nudes, for example *Standing Nude, Face Half-hidden* (1914; New York, MOMA).

3. Henri Matisse: *The Moroccans*, oil on canvas, 1.83×2.79 m, 1916 (New York, Museum of Modern Art)

Several portraits are among Matisse's most austere and formally structured paintings of 1914: *Woman on a High Stool* (New York, MOMA), a portrait of Germaine Raynal, whose husband Maurice Raynal was known for his critical promotion of Cubism; *Mlle Yvonne Landsberg* (Philadelphia, PA, Mus. A.), with sweeping incised lines emanating from the figure, perhaps in response to his printmaking rather than to Futurist lines of force; and *Head, White and Pink* (Paris, Pompidou), based on his daughter Marguerite. The rigorous structure of such paintings may owe something to a series of five portrait sculptures of a neighbour at Issy, Jeanne Vaderin, known as *Jeannette I–V* (Nice, Mus. Matisse). The first two were modelled from life in 1910; the intermediate pieces were finished by October 1911; and the last of the bronzes was developed, perhaps as late as 1916, from a cast of the third state.

On the outbreak of World War I in August 1914 Matisse volunteered for military service but was rejected because, at 45, he was near the upper age limit. The example of Juan Gris, whom he met at Collioure in September, probably acted as a catalyst in the production of one of his most abstract paintings, *Open Window, Collioure* (1914; Paris, Pompidou), a highly simplified reprise of a subject he had treated nearly a decade earlier. On his return to Paris at the end of the year, Matisse further developed his personal response to Cubism, taking as a starting-point his own paintings and familiar motifs: *Goldfish* (1914–15; New York, MOMA) relates to *Interior with Goldfish* (1914; Paris, Pompidou), while *Variation on a Still-life by de Heem* (1915; New York, MOMA) is based on the *Dinner Table*

(*c.* 1893; Nice, Mus. Matisse), his student copy of Jan de Heem I's *Still-life* (1640; Paris, Louvre).

Matisse applied these modern methods of construction to the completion in 1916 of *Bathers by a River* (Chicago, IL, A. Inst.), originally conceived in 1909 as a 'scene of repose', and *The Moroccans* (New York, MOMA; see fig. 3). To help in solving his recurring problem of relating the human figure to a flat background, he executed three life-size bronze reliefs known as *The Back I–III* (1909, 1913 and 1916; all London, Tate) contemporaneously with the three stages of *Bathers by a River*. (A fourth relief (London, Tate) followed in 1930–31 while he was working on a mural commission for Albert C. Barnes.) *The Moroccans* similarly evolved in distinct stages in September 1913 and November 1915; when it was finally completed in the summer of 1916, the anecdotal quality of a late-afternoon scene of Arabs reclining on a terrace was transformed into another highly structured and virtually abstract design.

Matisse returned to a more literal treatment of the subject in *The Window* (1916; Detroit, MI, Inst. A.) and *Piano Lesson* (1916; New York, MOMA), both painted in the living-room at Issy in the summer of 1916. The realism of such works was accompanied by his reassessment of Gustave Courbet and Manet. In a ravishing series of paintings of the Italian model Laurette, such as the *Painter and his Model* (1917; Paris, Pompidou), Matisse first gave form to a sustained meditation on the theme of the artist and his model, with particular emphasis on relaying her personality through both style and mood. The sequence culminated in the *Three Sisters* triptych (1917; Merion

Station, PA, Barnes Found.), in which Laurette is accompanied by her two sisters. Another painting of the same year, *Music Lesson* (Merion Station, PA, Barnes Found.), provided a final record of all his family together.

6. NICE, 1918–30. Matisse first stayed in Nice in the last days of 1917, and his annual winter sojourns in hotels and rented accommodation were extended until he more or less became a resident of the town, only returning to Paris for the four midsummer months to avoid the intense heat. In the autumn of 1921 he rented an apartment at 1, Place Charles-Félix, which became his home in Nice until his move in 1938 to palatial rooms in the former Hôtel Régina on the hill at Cimiez behind the town.

In the decade following his arrival in Nice, Matisse temporarily abandoned the monumental scale and modern methods of construction that he had used in his great decorative compositions in favour of a more naturalistic style first hinted at in the Laurette series. Apparently wishing to leave behind the war, bad weather, the avant-garde and even his family, he concentrated on the female form and on other subjects that gave him pleasure: not only secluded interiors, landscapes and still-lifes of flowers, but light itself. Matisse's obsession with the effects of light on objects led him to re-evaluate aspects of Impressionism and of the work of contemporaries such as Albert Marquet and Bonnard. He and Marquet corresponded with Monet and probably met him in May 1917. Matisse made his first visit to Renoir, whose treatment of the female nude he particularly admired, on 31 December 1917. He went to Cherbourg in the summer of 1918 and, like Monet before him, painted at Etretat on the Normandy coast in the summers of 1920 and 1921. The only major interruptions to this routine came in September 1919 and January 1920, when he travelled to London at the invitation of Serge Diaghilev to work on sets and costumes for a production of Igor Stravinsky's ballet *Le Chant du rossignol*, which was staged in Paris in 1920 and revived in 1925.

4. Henri Matisse: *Large Seated Nude*, bronze, h. 781 mm, *c.* 1924–5 (Baltimore, MD, Baltimore Museum of Art)

With a few possible exceptions, Matisse's habit during this period of working outdoors, rejuvenating his art through contact with nature, did not result in major works. Similarly, his still-lifes were extraordinarily beautiful but minor paintings, climaxing in 1924 in a series that included *Interiors, Flowers and Parrots* (Baltimore, MD, Mus. A.) and *Interior with a Phonograph* (priv. col., see Watkins, 1984, p. 163). Matisse's principal subject throughout his first years in Nice remained the female model, not only in painting but in other media. In the ravishing studies of Antoinette Arnoux, who began modelling for him at the end of 1918, the process of refinement went from drawing into painting and back into drawing. Matisse's favourite model from 1920 to 1927, Henriette Darricarrère, a musician who had also trained as a ballet dancer, excelled in the different roles she was asked to play, from Oriental odalisque to domestic companion, musician and dancer.

After a trip to southern Italy and Sicily in the summer of 1925, Matisse painted fewer canvases and with greater difficulty. He appears to have set himself the task of resolving in drawings, sculptures, prints and paintings the articulation and balance of mass of the seated and reclining female nude. His bronze sculpture, *Large Seated Nude* (*c.* 1924–5; Baltimore, MD, Mus. A.; see fig. 4), where the figure is caught between sitting and reclining, evolved in at least three states from his exploration of the pose in painting and printmaking and was in turn taken up in a highly structured painting, *Decorative Figure on an Ornamental Background* (1925–6; Paris, Pompidou). The theme of the reclining nude was similarly elaborated in drawings, paintings and prints, and in the sculptures *Reclining Nude II* (1927) and *Reclining Nude III* (1929; both Nice, Mus. Matisse).

In 1929 Matisse virtually gave up painting to concentrate on a series of over 200 etchings, drypoints and lithographs, for example *Reclining Nude from the Back* (transfer lithograph, 1929; London, V&A). In a sense these prints represent the most complete expression of two of the principal qualities sought by Matisse in this period: flooding light, as represented by the overall whiteness of the page, and a visual equivalence for the emotion aroused in him by his models, through the treatment of their figures in linear arabesques.

Matisse's paintings of 1920 to 1925 were instrumental in the growth of his popular reputation in the following decade; a particularly voluptuous example of his work from this period, *Odalisque with Red Culottes* (1921; Paris, Pompidou), was bought for the Musée du Luxembourg in Paris in 1922, the first purchase by the state of one of his paintings since *The Reader* (1895). The prices specified in 1923 in Matisse's fifth and final three-year contract with Bernheim-Jeune were substantially higher than in his previous contract, and most of the paintings in his 1924 exhibition were sold in advance of the official opening. Important retrospective exhibitions of his work were held in Copenhagen in 1924, Berlin in 1930, and Paris, Basle and at the recently founded Museum of Modern Art in New York in 1931. In 1920 the first of many monographs was published, confirming Matisse's place in the history of art. His heroic, innovative days appeared to be over.

7. THE 1930S. Rather than continuing with the commercially successful style of the 1920s, Matisse made a complete break in the 1930s, not only in terms of his work but also in the circumstances of his life. In 1930 he went to Tahiti, via New York and San Francisco, and later that year made a second journey to the USA to serve on the jury of the Carnegie International Exhibition. As so often happened to Matisse on his travels, his initial reaction to Tahiti was one of disappointment. He was far more impressed by New York, rapturously describing the effects of light on the skyscrapers. Despite this, his experiences of Tahiti filtered through into his consciousness as one of the main sources of his subject-matter in the last decade of his life.

In 1930 he also received two commissions which were to occupy him for the next three years and which determined the twin directions of his art in the 1930s. The first commission, from the publisher Albert Skira, was for an edition of the poems of Stéphane Mallarmé, *Poésies* (Lausanne, 1932; see fig. 5), illustrated with original etchings. The second, from Albert C. Barnes, was for a mural decorating the main hall of the Barnes Foundation in Merion Station, PA.

For the Mallarmé etchings Matisse evolved a classical drawing style in which forms were synthesized into precise outlines through a process of long deliberation. He considered book design in the same terms as painting, judging his main formal problem to be balancing the predominance of white in the illustration with the relative blackness of the text. Moreover, he used the poems as an excuse to rephrase favourite poses and themes, particularly in his

5. Henri Matisse: *Baudelaire*, pen and ink; *c.* 1930 (Paris, Bibliothèque Littéraire Jacques Doucet); for an etching to illustrate *Poésies* by Stéphane Mallarmé (Lausanne 1932)

treatment of the nude. The illustration preceding the poem *La Chevelure*, for example, evolved from the sculptures *Jeanette II–V* (1910–15), the kittenish pose of *Laurette with a Cup of Coffee* (1916–17; priv. col., see 1986 exh. cat., p. 67) and the rounded volumes of *Tiari* (1930; Baltimore, MD, Mus. A.), a sculpture that fused the image of a Tahitian girl with flowing hair with that of the gardenia from which it takes its title.

For the Barnes murals Matisse returned to the subject of the dance first treated in the background of the *Joy of Life* (1905–6), a painting by then displayed in the very hall for which the murals were destined. The proposed site, calling for three lunettes above glazed doors leading on to a garden, was extremely awkward; on his return to Nice he made little progress until he developed a new flexible method of working based on the system that he had evolved while designing Diaghilev's production of *Le Chant du rossignol* in 1920. He began by drawing the enormous figures directly on the canvas with charcoal clamped to the end of a long bamboo pole, pinning cut-out pieces of paper around them and making final adjustments when he replaced the paper with paint. As he was nearing completion of *Dance I* (1931–3; Paris, Mus. A. Mod. Ville Paris) in 1932, he discovered that he had been given incorrect measurements, so he produced a completely new variation, *Dance II* (3.57×14.32 m overall, 1932–3; Merion Station, PA, Barnes Found.), with eight instead of six dancers.

Drawing is essential to Matisse's paintings of the later 1930s, as is an expressive distortion of the female form in order to capture the mood or personality of the model, for example by exaggerating the length of her body in languid repose. The 22 photographs documenting the successive states of *Pink Nude* (1935; Baltimore, MD, Mus. A.) provide vivid evidence of the process by which Matisse expanded the figure, beginning with the sixth state, by pinning cut-out paper shapes to the canvas until the forms filled the surface with the full weight of relaxation. In other works, such as *The Dream* (1935; Paris, Pompidou), a mood of reverie is conveyed by the profundity of the model's sleep.

Through his work on the Barnes murals, Matisse came increasingly to use colour in easel paintings such as *Lady in Blue* (1937; Philadelphia, PA, Mus. A.) to advertise and emphasize shape in a simplified palette with an ever greater heraldic intensity, allowing line to etch out a more autonomous existence. In the *Rockefeller Overmantel Decoration* (1938; New York, priv. col., see Watkins, 1984, p. 186) and *Music* (1939; Buffalo, NY, Albright–Knox A.G.), he complicated his series of women in interiors by adding a second model. His paintings of the 1930s were usually preceded by studies and accompanied by exquisite independent drawings, which he continued to regard as equal in status with his painting.

8. 1940–54. In January 1941 Matisse underwent an operation for a tumour, which left him an invalid. Unable to travel abroad, he constructed his own tropical environment in his palatial apartment in the Hôtel Régina, on the hill above Nice in the suburb of Cimiez, where he had lived since 1938. Just as his first period of prolonged convalescence in 1890 had brought him into painting, so

the second led to his late style: to grand interior paintings from 1946 to 1948, to the decoration of the Chapelle du Rosaire at Vence in 1948–51 and to a series of paper cut-outs which were his final works.

Matisse began with drawing, an ideal medium for a convalescent because of the less strenuous physical demands imposed by it. In 1941 and 1942 he concentrated almost exclusively on a series of 158 drawings, divided into 17 groups, collectively called *Themes and Variations*; one such series, called *H1* (1941; Grenoble, Mus. Peint. & Sculp.), represented ivy trailing out of a Chinese vase. Matisse's absorption with drawing also found an outlet in a succession of books that he designed and illustrated throughout, as he had with Mallarmé's *Poésies*. These were: *Pasiphaé* by Henri de Montherlant (Paris, 1944); *Visages* by Pierre Reverdy, *Lettres portugaises* by Marianna Alcaforado and Baudelaire's *Les Fleurs du mal* (all Paris, 1946); *Repli* by André Rouveyre and his own book *Jazz*, published by Tériade, which consisted of vividly coloured stencil prints after cut-out paper maquettes (both Paris, 1947); *Florilège des amours de Ronsard* by Pierre de Ronsard (Paris, 1948); *Poèmes* by Charles d'Orléans (Paris, 1950); and *Echos*, with texts by Jacques Prévert, André Verdet and Nazim Hikmet, and *Apollinaire* by André Rouveyre (both Paris, 1952). Three further illustrated books were published posthumously: *Une Fête en Cimmérie* (Paris, 1963), *Poésies antillaises* (Paris, 1972) by John-Antoine Nau and a revised edition of *Pasiphaé* (Paris, 1981) containing all 90 linocuts originally executed for it in 1944. In addition, Matisse contributed at least one original print to about 12 other publications. Like his earlier edition of Mallarmé's *Poésies*, these books cost him enormous effort and should not be regarded as minor works.

In 1942 Matisse began to paint seriously again, concentrating on the female model, either dressed as a dancer or posed in an armchair before the huge shuttered windows of the Régina. The technique that enabled him to develop a radically new form of decorative art came, however, with the commission in 1942 for an illustrated album in colour; this resulted five years later in Matisse's first major project using the cut-out paper technique, *Jazz*. Instead of using cut-out paper simply as an aid in the gestation of a work, as he had earlier done, Matisse decided to base stencils for prints directly on such designs. The 20 plates, supplemented by pages of handwritten text, incorporate memories, dream imagery, references to earlier pictures and current concerns, coupled with an intense excitement about the freedom and intensity of colour of the new medium. Matisse recognized the concrete reality of the medium, and cutting directly into the coloured surface resolved the conflict that he had earlier experienced between line and colour, making each dependent on the other.

Fearing an Allied bombardment, Matisse had left Nice for the neighbouring hill-town, Vence; he did not return to the Régina until 1949, when he needed its space to work on designs for the Chapelle du Rosaire at Vence. In summer 1945 he returned to Paris to find himself honoured, with Picasso, as part of the promotion of a new independent France; the Musée National d'Art Moderne in Paris began belatedly at this time to form a representative collection of his work. Matisse's art was, however, at that time going through a transitional phase. Commissions for two overtly decorative works—the first from Zika Ascher for two screenprinted hangings, *Oceania, the Sea* and *Oceania, the Sky*, the other from the tapestry factory at Beauvais for two tapestries, *Polynesia, the Sea* and *Polynesia, the Sky* (all 1946; Paris, Pompidou)—led him to develop the lagoon imagery found in three plates of *Jazz* into mural-scale paper cut-outs. During the summer of 1946 the many cut-out images intended for the *Oceania* pair were pinned directly to adjoining walls in his Paris apartment. The system devised by Ascher for the printing of the silkscreens in London, involving the repositioning of the cut-out shapes in accord with tracings made by Matisse, was later adapted to the large-scale paper cut-outs made in Nice, which were reassembled and glued to their supports by specialists in Paris.

Matisse's understanding of the expressive potential of formal elements and of the fact that light could be conveyed by means of colour, renewed by his experiments with paper cut-outs, had a salutary influence both on his oil paintings and on brush drawings, such as *Interior with Window and Palm* (1948; priv. col., see Watkins, 1984, p. 213). Oil paint remained his favoured medium for registering his responses to the light and atmosphere of his studio-home at Vence. His final series of oil paintings, announced by *Yellow and Blue Interior* (1946; Paris, Pompidou), was concluded with *Large Red Interior* (1948; Paris, Pompidou).

The Chapelle du Rosaire at Vence, on which Matisse worked almost exclusively from 1948 to 1951, provided him with an opportunity to crown his career with a synthesis of light, colour, drawing and sculpture within an architectural setting. The chapel acts as a celestial prism, with the filtered light from his great stained-glass windows on the south side drenching with colour the simple white interior decorated with line drawings in ceramic (*see* STAINED GLASS, fig. 7). By moving the altar from the east to the west end, he freed the east wall, which was attached to the main building, for a series of ceramic drawings of the *Stations of the Cross*, and completed his design of the west wall with an apse window.

Once he had discovered the techniques of working to mural scale, Matisse could no longer be satisfied by easel painting. His brush drawing technique, employed in the ceramic murals, culminated with a series of trees and acrobats; these in turn affected his paper cut-outs of the human figure, such as *Blue Nude IV* (1952; Nice, Mus. Matisse), in which he set out to reconcile the sculptural integrity of the human figure with the formal freedom of the new medium. His final paper cut-out compositions, such as *Memory of Oceania* (1953; New York, MOMA; see fig. 6), many of which were maquettes for decorative projects, literally evolved on the walls around him in the Régina. In *The Snail* (1952–3; London, Tate), the coloured panels of the earlier paper cut-out grids were released from their background role in order to become the elements of the image itself. One of Matisse's final paper cut-out decorations, *Ivy in Flower* (1953; Dallas, TX, Mus. F.A.), was a maquette for a stained-glass window commissioned for the mausoleum of Albert Lasker and fabricated by Paul Bony.

Matisse was buried in the cemetery at Cimiez, not far from the Roman arena where the Villa des Arènes now

6. Henri Matisse: *Memory of Oceania*, gouache and crayon on cut-and-pasted paper over canvas, 2.84×2.86 m, 1953 (New York, Museum of Modern Art)

houses the Musée Matisse. Since his death his reputation has steadily increased as one of a select group of artists who radically redefined the language of painting in the 20th century.

WRITINGS

'Notes d'un peintre', *Grande Rev.*, lii/24 (1908), pp. 731–45
J. Clair, ed.: 'Correspondance Matisse-Bonnard', *Nouv. Rev. Fr.*, xviii (1970), no. 211, pp. 82–100; no. 212, pp. 53–70
D. Giraudy, ed.: 'Correspondance Henri Matisse–Charles Camoin, 1925–1946', *Rev. A.* [Paris], xii (1971), pp. 7–34
D. Fourcade, ed.: *Henri Matisse, écrits et propos sur l'art* (Paris, 1972)
J. D. Flam, ed.: *Matisse on Art* (London, 1973) [extensive bibliog.]
D. Fourcade, ed.: 'Autres propos de Henri Matisse', *Macula*, i (1976), pp. 92–115

BIBLIOGRAPHY

MONOGRAPHS

M. Sembat: *Henri Matisse* (Paris, 1920)
A. Basler: *Henri Matisse* (Leipzig, 1924)
A. C. Barnes and V. de Mazia: *The Art of Henri Matisse* (New York, 1933)
P. Courthion: *Henri Matisse* (Paris, 1934)
R. Fry: *Henri Matisse* (London, 1935)
A. H. Barr jr: *Matisse: His Art and his Public* (New York, 1951)
G. Diehl: *Henri Matisse* (Paris, 1954)
C. Greenberg: *Matisse* (New York, 1955)
R. Escholier: *Matisse ce vivant* (Paris, 1956)
J. Lassaigne: *Matisse* (Geneva, 1959)
R. Escholier: *Matisse from the Life* (London, 1960)
J. Selz: *Matisse* (Paris, 1964)
F. Brill: *Matisse* (London, 1967)
J. Guichard-Meili: *Matisse* (London, 1967)
J. Russell: *The World of Matisse, 1869–1954* (New York, 1969)
J. Leymarie: *Matisse* (Paris, 1970)
J. Jacobus: *Matisse* (New York, 1972)
N. Watkins: *Matisse* (Oxford, 1977)
L. Gowing: *Matisse* (London, 1979)
P. Schneider: *Matisse* (Paris, 1984) [extensive bibliog.]
N. Watkins: *Matisse* (Oxford, 1984)
L. Delectorskaya: *Henri Matisse: L'Apparente Facilité* (Paris, 1986)
J. Flam: *Matisse: The Man and his Art, 1869–1918* (London, 1986) [extensive bibliog.]
J. Elderfield: *Henri Matisse: A Retrospective* (London and New York, 1992)

EXHIBITION CATALOGUES

Matisse, 1869–1954 (exh. cat., ed. L. Gowing; London, Hayward Gal., 1968)

Henri Matisse: Exposition du centenaire (exh. cat., ed. P. Schneider; Paris, Grand Pal., 1970)

Matisse as a Draughtsman (exh. cat., ed. V. I. Carlson; Baltimore, MD, Mus. A., 1971)

Henri Matisse: Dessins et sculptures (exh. cat., ed. D. Fourcade; Paris, Pompidou, 1975)

The 'Wild Beasts': Fauvism and its Affinities (exh. cat., ed. J. Elderfield; New York, MOMA, 1976)

Henri Matisse: Paper Cut-outs (exh. cat., ed. J. Cowart and others; St Louis, MO, A. Mus.; Detroit, MI, Inst. A.; 1977)

Henri Matisse: Das goldene Zeitalter (exh. cat., Bielefeld, Städt. Ksthalle, 1981)

Henri Matisse, 1869–1954: Gravures et lithographies (exh. cat., ed M. Hahnloser-Ingold and R. M. Mayou; Fribourg, Mus. A. & Hist., 1982)

Henri Matisse (exh. cat., ed. P. Schneider; Zurich, Ksthaus, 1982)

Henri Matisse: The Early Years in Nice, 1916–1930 (exh. cat., ed J. Cowart and D. Fourcade; Washington, DC, N.G.A., 1986)

Henri Matisse: Matisse et l'Italie (exh. cat., ed. P. Schneider; Venice, Correr, 1987)

Les Chefs-d'oeuvre du Musée Matisse et les Matisses de Matisse (exh. cat., ed N. Watkins and X. Girard; Tokyo, Isetan Mus. A., 1987)

Matisse in Morocco: The Paintings and Drawings, 1912–13 (exh. cat., ed. J. Cowart; Washington, DC, N.G.A.; New York, MOMA; Moscow, Pushkin Mus. F.A.; Leningrad, Hermitage; 1990–91)

Henri Matisse 1904–1917 (exh. cat. by Y.-A. Bois, Paris, Pompidou, 1993)

MUSEUM CATALOGUES

J. Elderfield: *Matisse in the Collection of the Museum of Modern Art* (New York, 1978)

A. Izerghina: *Henri Matisse: Paintings and Sculptures in Soviet Museums* (Leningrad, 1978)

I. Monod-Fontaine: *Oeuvres de Henri Matisse (1869–1954)*, Paris, Pompidou (Paris, 1979) [extensive bibliog.]

Cahiers Henri Matisse, 4 vols, Musée Matisse (Nice, 1986)

SPECIALIST STUDIES

M. Schapiro: 'Matisse and Impressionism', *Androcles*, i/1 (1932), pp. 21–36

W. S. Lieberman: *Matisse: Fifty Years of his Graphic Art* (New York, 1956)

M. Wheeler: *The Last Works of Henri Matisse: Large Cut Gouaches* (New York, 1961)

R. J. Moulin: *Henri Matisse: Dessins* (Paris, 1968)

A. Bowness: *Matisse et le nu* (Paris, 1969)

M. Pleynet: *L'Enseignement de la peinture* (Paris, 1971)

L. Aragon: *Henri Matisse: A Novel*, 2 vols (London, 1972)

A. E. Elsen: *The Sculpture of Henri Matisse* (New York, 1972)

S. Lambert: *Matisse Lithographs* (London, 1972)

N. Calmel: *Matisse: 'La Chapelle du Rosaire des Dominicaines de Vence et de l'Espoir'* (Digne, 1975)

J. H. Neff: 'Matisse and Decoration: The Shchukin Panels', *A. America*, lxiii/4 (1975), pp. 39–48

W. Tucker: 'Matisse's Sculpture: The Grasped and the Seen', *A. America*, lxiii/4 (1975), pp. 62–6

G. C. Bock: *Henri Matisse and Neo-Impressionism* (Los Angeles, 1977)

J. Elderfield: *The Cut-outs of Henri Matisse* (London, 1978)

M. Duthuit-Matisse, C. Duthuit and F. Garnaud: *Catalogue raisonné de l'oeuvre gravé*, 2 vols (Paris, 1983)

J. Elderfield: *The Drawings of Henri Matisse* (London, 1984)

J. Guichard-Meili: *Matisse: Paper Cut-outs* (London, 1984)

I. Monod-Fontaine: *The Sculpture of Henri Matisse* (London, 1984)

C. Duthuit and F. Garnaud: *Catalogue raisonné des ouvrages illustrés* (Paris, 1988)

GENERAL WORKS

G. Duthuit: *The Fauvist Painters* (New York, 1930)

NICHOLAS WATKINS

Matisse, Pierre (*b* Bohain, Aisne, France, 13 June 1900; *d* St-Jean-Cap-Ferrat, 10 Aug 1989). American dealer. He was the second son of HENRI MATISSE. He worked initially in a Paris gallery but decided in the mid-1920s to go to New York. Here he organized a number of shows of recent European painting at the Valentine Gallery of Valentine Dudensing. In 1932 Matisse opened his own gallery, the Pierre Matisse Gallery, in New York at 41 East 57th Street. Here he was a major outlet for the work of his father, though he never held an exhibition of his work. Introduced to Surrealist art in the 1920s by Pierre Loeb, Matisse was significant as one of the most important early supporters of Surrealist artists in America, in particular Miró, whose work he showed almost annually from 1932 to 1983. Other painters whose work he handled for many years were Balthus (from 1938 to 1977), Alexander Calder (1932–43), Chagall (1941–82), Alberto Giacometti (1948–64) and Wifredo Lam. He helped Yves Tanguy to the United States in 1939, and subsequently showed his work until 1963. Other Surrealists he showed in the 1940s were Roberto Matta, Leonora Carrington and the American painter Kay Sage (*b* 1898), Tanguy's wife. Matisse took on few artists after World War II; among these were Dubuffet, whom he began to show in 1947, Jean-Paul Riopelle, whom he introduced in 1954, Loren MacIver, Manolo Millares and Theodore Roszak.

BIBLIOGRAPHY

A. D. Robson: *The Market for Modern Art in New York in the 1940s and 1950s* (PhD thesis, U. London, 1988), pp. 110–30

R. Mason: Obituary, *The Independent* (17 Aug 1989)

A. DEIRDRE ROBSON

Matos. Portuguese family of ceramic artists and tile painters. A document of 1575 records that Marçal de Matos (*fl c.* 1550–1600) was then painting an arch for a chapel in the Lisbon workshop of the Flemish painter Felip de Goes. Although Marçal's work has not been clarified with any certainty, he has been attributed with some of the Mannerist figured *azulejo* (glazed tile) paintings (1565 and later) in the Quinta da Bacalhoa in Azeitão (*in situ*), near Setubal. In the water pavilion there are scenes of *Susanna and the Elders* (1565), the *Rape of Hipodémia* and the *Allegory of the River Tagus*. On the west verandah are *Allegories of the Rivers Euphrates, Nile, Danube, Douro and Mondego*, all framed with Flemish Mannerist strapwork, and in the garden is a tiled scene of the *Rape of Europa*. Marçal has also been credited (Santos Simões) with the important panel from the chapel of Nossa Senhora da Vida, Lisbon (*c.* 1580; Lisbon, Mus. Azulejo), which takes the form of an altarpiece with the *Adoration of the Shepherds* in the centre, while on either side in simulated niches are *St John* and *St Luke* and above a scene of the *Annunciation*.

The tiles in Nossa Senhora da Vida have also been attributed to Francisco de Matos (*fl c.* 1575–1600), who was possibly the nephew of Marçal and whose only known work is the signed tile covering (1584) of the interior of an aisle chapel in S Roque, Lisbon. The ensemble consists of decorative elements painted in blue and white on a strong yellow ground, with a central medallion in polychrome depicting the *Miracle of St Roch*. The panels are the most important *azulejo* works of their period, both in their exceptional technical quality and in the complexity of their design.

BIBLIOGRAPHY

V. Correia: 'As primeiras faianças e azulejos lisos em Lisboa', *Azulejos* (Lisbon, 1956), pp. 114–21

J. M. dos Santos Simões: *Azulejaria em Portugal nos séculos XV e XVI* (Lisbon, 1969)
Azulejos de Lisboa (exh. cat., ed. J. Meco; Lisbon, Câmara Mun., 1984)

JOSÉ MECO

Matos, Francisco Vieira de. *See* VIEIRA LUSITANO, FRANCISCO.

Matrakçi Nasuh. *See* NASUH, MATRAKÇI.

Matsa [Mácza], Ivan [Iogann; János] (Lyudvigovich) (*b* Alsó Hrabócz, nr Varanno [Nižny Hrabovec, nr Vranov, Slovakia], 4 Aug 1893; *d* Moscow, 1974). Hungarian critic, active in the USSR. In Budapest in 1917, as János Mácza, he became one of the main contributors to the journal *MA* (Today). In 1919 he emigrated to Czechoslovakia, in 1922 rejoined *MA* colleagues in Vienna and in 1923 followed *MA*'s avant-garde contacts to Moscow. In 1928 he was a founder-member of the October Group that sought a synthesis of Modernism, especially Constructivism, with proletarian art. In 1929, moving further towards the Party line, he became a founder and chairman of the board of the All-Union Alliance of Associations of Proletarian Architects, VOPRA, which explicitly rejected Constructivism. From 1930 Matsa was engaged in university teaching as well as architectural criticism. In 1931 he represented VOPRA on the editorial board of *Soviet Architecture*, entering actively into theoretical debates. Throughout the later 1930s and World War II, Matsa wrote extensively on Socialist Realism, though always managing to avoid totally vilifying former Modernists. Even in 1937 he dared point out to the 1st Congress of Soviet Architects the relative lack of theory underlying the new aesthetic. Ten years later the art press started to attack him, and a resolution of the Academy of Arts on 1 February 1949 named Matsa, Nikolay Punin, David Arkin (1899–1957) and other critics as 'rootless cosmopolitans' and 'aestheticizing anti-patriots', not just for supporting the avant-garde but for admitting any merit even in Impressionism. Matsa alone continued to teach and write thereafter.

WRITINGS

[J. Mácza:] *A teljes színpad* [The complete stage] (Vienna, 1922); Fr. trans. as 'Le Théâtre total', *L'Activisme hongrois*, ed. C. Dautrey and J.-C. Guerlain (Paris, 1979), pp. 204–19
[I. L. Matsa:] *Iskusstvo sovremennoy Evropy* [The art of contemporary Europe] (Moscow, 1926)
[——:] *Sovetskoy iskusstvo za 15 let: Materialy i dokumentatsiya* [Soviet art of the last 15 years: materials and documentation] (Moscow, 1933)
[J. Mácza:] *Legendák és tények* [Legends and facts] (Budapest, 1972)

BIBLIOGRAPHY

The Hungarian Avant-garde: The Eight and the Activists (exh. cat. by J. Willet and others, London, Hayward Gal., 1980)

CATHERINE COOKE

Matschinsky-Denninghoff. German sculptors. Brigitte Matschinsky-Denninghoff (née Meier-Denninghoff) (*b* Berlin, 2 June 1923) studied at the Hochschule der Künste, Berlin, and the Akademie der Bildenden Künste, Munich, between 1943 and 1946. In 1948 she became an assistant to Henry Moore in England, and at his instigation she studied the archaic sculpture at the British Museum. Under Moore's influence she explored organic forms employing stone, wood and terracotta. Between 1949 and 1950 she stayed in Paris on a grant to work for Antoine Pevsner, at

which time she turned to sculpture in metal and became a founder-member of the group ZEN 49. Martin Matschinsky (*b* Grötzingen, nr Karlsruhe, 4 July 1921) trained both as a photographer (1938–40) and as an actor (1948–50). Self-taught as a sculptor (although he had studied soldering technique), he began to sculpt in 1955 and in that year married Meier-Denninghoff. In 1955 he and his wife began to work together as a team, and from 1970 they signed their sculptures jointly. They lived in Munich from 1954 to 1961 and in Paris from 1961 to 1970, before settling in West Berlin. They employed sheaves of thin brass rods soldered together with tin, in poetic explorations of abstract form in small-scale, life-size and large, outdoor works (up to 9 m h.). The sheaves consist of rods and tubular elements and, until the mid-1970s, they were arranged to interact with space and evoke flight, assembled as monolithic, enclosed units, or grouped as curvilinear 'screens' appearing to rotate around each other (e.g. *Twopart*, 1.2×0.9×0.8 m, 1964; Düsseldorf, Kstmus.). The use of rod-like surfaces shows the pronounced legacy of Pevsner. After 1967 the tubes were integrated with random geometric steel shapes creating assemblages conceptually aligned with international Minimalism, as in the outdoor sculpture *Harlequin* (steel, h. 4 m, 1972; Sindelfingen, Germany). Since the mid-1970s the sculptors also worked with extremely pliable sheaves in a pure flow of undulating form, as in *Berlin* (chromium-plated nickel and steel, 8×9×5 m, 1985–7; Berlin, Tautzienstrasse). Each artist's abstract works on paper (which are signed individually) complement the sculptures. Brigitte's drawings, collages and etchings emphasize microscopic versus macroscopic structures, while Martin's drawings, gouaches and watercolours deal largely with the dynamics of line and gesture. Among important exhibitions in which they participated were the Venice Biennale of 1962, *Documenta II* in 1959 and *Documenta III*, Kassel, in 1964.

BIBLIOGRAPHY

M. de la Manfred, ed: *Matschinsky-Denninghoff* (Bonn, 1980)
——: *Matschinsky-Denninghoff* (exh. cat., Heidelberg, Kstver., 1984)
Matschinsky-Denninghoff: Skulpturen und Zeichnungen, 1955–1985 (exh. cat., ed. E. Busche and R.-F. Raddatz; W. Berlin, Akad. Kst., 1985) [retro. with contribs by E. Roters, W. Hofmann, J. Langner and others]
G.-W. Költzsch, ed.: *Matschinsky-Denninghoff* (Cologne, 1992) [incl. cat. rais. of sculptures comp. A. Schwarz with contribs by E. Roters and J. Langner]

ERICH G. RANFFT

Matsue. Japanese city on the Ohashi River, which flows from Lake Shinji to the Japan Sea coast. Now capital of Shimane Prefecture, it was an Edo-period (1600–1868) castle town (*jōkamachi*) of the Matsudaira clan. The earliest known settlement in the region, 5 km south of Matsue, is the village Fudoki no oka, the capital of Izumo Province. Yaegaki Shrine there is reputed to be the home of the Shinto gods Susano'o and Kushinadahime. In the area are also several ancient burial mounds (*kofun*), reconstructions of Kofun-period (*c.* AD 300–710) houses, the ruins of the Nara-period (710–94) Izumo Kokubunji and Kamosu Shrine, whose main hall (*honden*), built in 1346, is Japan's oldest surviving Taisha ('grand shrine') style structure (*see* JAPAN, §III, 3(i)). Matsue's more recent history revolves around the Matsudaira clan. After the Battle of Sekigahara (1600), the victorious Tokugawa

Ieyasu (1543–1616) gave the area around Matsue to Horio Yoshiharu (1543–1611), who built the first Matsue Castle from 1607 to 1611. Matsudaira Naomasa (1601–66), grandson of Tokugawa Ieyasu, then received Matsue in 1638 and finished rebuilding the three-storey castle tower in 1642. Despite plans to destroy it in 1875, the castle retains its original appearance. The tombs of nine generations of the Matsudaira are at the temple Gesshōji on the west side of Matsue. North of the castle, one street preserves some 18th-century samurai residences. In 1966 authorities moved the Meimeian tea house (chashitsu) and garden to the same area. It was originally built in 1799 by Matsudaira Fumai (1751–1818), daimyo of Izumo Province and the best-known tea master of his time. Fumai's Kanden'an tea house is north-east of Matsue. The life of Japanophile writer Lafcadio Hearn (Koizumi Yakumo; 1850–1904), who taught English at Matsue Middle School in 1890–92, is commemorated at Matsue's Koizumi Yakumo Kin'enkan (Koizumi Yakumo Memorial Hall).

BIBLIOGRAPHY
L. Hearn: Kokoro (New York, 1896)
——: Glimpses of Unfamiliar Japan (New York, 1904)

KEN BROWN

Matsukata, Kōjirō (b Kagoshima, 1 Dec 1865; d Kamakura, Kanagawa Prefect., 24 June 1950). Japanese businessman and collector. From 1884 to 1890 he studied in the USA and in France. After his return to Japan he became involved in politics for a short period, but later turned to business, becoming the first head of the Kawasaki Ship Building Co. in 1896. By his retirement in 1928 he had greatly contributed to the company's growth. He was also successful as director of other businesses. From 1936 he was elected for four terms as a member of the Lower House (Shūgiin), remaining active in the business world.

Between 1916 and 1926 Matsukata acquired, primarily in London and Paris, the works that made up the Matsukata Collection. It included c. 8000 ukiyoe ('pictures of the floating world') prints (now Tokyo, N. Mus.) bought from Henri Vever and c. 2000 European works, mainly 19th-century French sculpture and painting. In amassing his collection he obtained the cooperation of the English painter Frank Brangwyn, the director of the Musée du Luxembourg, Paris, Léonce Bénédite, and the Japanese art historian Yukio Yashiro (1890–1975).

Matsukata's aim in collecting was to be able to show works to Japanese art students and lovers of art who did not generally have the opportunity to see Western art. To this end he asked Brangwyn to plan the building of an art museum in Tokyo (unexecuted). More than 1000 examples of European art that Matsukata had collected were shipped to Japan. However, when the Kawasaki Ship Building Co. was reorganized, because of financial difficulties that reached a peak in 1927, the collection was dispersed. The c. 300 works that remained in London were destroyed by fire in 1939 at the warehouse where they were stored; those in Paris were confiscated by the French government as goods of the enemy. In 1959, 308 paintings and 63 sculptures were returned by the French government and the National Museum of Western Art in Tokyo, designed by Le Corbusier, was inaugurated.

BIBLIOGRAPHY
Y. Yashiro: Geijutsu no patoron [Art patrons] (Tokyo, 1958)
S. Takashina: Kindai no bijutsu 2: Matsukata korekushon [Modern art 2: Matsukata collection] (Tokyo, 1971)
N. Minato: 'Matsukata Kōjirō to sono bijutsukan kōsō ni tsuite (jō) (ge)' [Kōjirō Matsukata and his museum project (1) (2)], Museum [Tokyo], 395–6 (Feb–March 1984)

TORU ASANO

Matsumoto, Shunsuke (b Tokyo, 19 April 1912; d Tokyo, 8 June 1948). Japanese painter. He lost his hearing when he was 15. In 1929 he entered the Pacific Painting Institute, Tokyo. In 1935 he was selected to submit works to the 22nd exhibition of the Nikakai (Second Division Society) and he continued to submit works annually until 1942. He also showed works in other exhibitions, for example with the NOVA Bijutsu Kyōkai (NOVA Art Society) and Form. In 1936 with his wife Sachiko he published the monthly journal Zakkichō, which contained miscellaneous writings and designs. Numerous cultural figures and painters contributed to it and 12 issues were published in 1937. In 1940 he joined the Kyūshitsukai (Nine-Room Society) which was a gathering of avant-garde painters from the Nikakai. When the arts magazine Mizue published the article 'Kokubo kokka to bijutsu' ('The military state and art') in January 1941, a discussion concerning the cooperation of painters in the war, Matsumoto contributed the rebuttal 'Ikite-iru gakka' ('The living painter') in April 1941 in the same journal. Amid the inevitable interruption of exhibitions by artists' groups caused by World War II, Matsumoto, with seven other painters, including Ai Mitsu and Tsuruoka Masao (b 1907), formed the Shinjin Gakai (New People's Painting Society) in 1943. After the war, in 1947, he joined the Jiyū Bijitsukai (Free Art Society); however, the following year he contracted tuberculosis.

Matsumoto's early paintings were influenced by the paintings of Georges Rouault, Modigliani and later George Grosz, Noda Hideo (1910–39) and Fujita Tsugoharu; they incorporated a modernist style that freely applied the technique of montage and that illustrated a poetic image of the urban landscape. They depicted the architecture and profile of a desolate urban landscape affected by the spread of war damage in a realist style. After the war, he turned away from realism and created paintings that anticipated a change towards abstraction. Nevertheless, the common elements in all his works are the sharp line and the strong textures. The approach to his work is humanistic, of a will which held fast to the individual's viewpoint of life, not of that of the conditions that underlay the war.

BIBLIOGRAPHY
Ningen fūkei [A view of people] (1982)
Matsumoto Shunsuke (exh. cat., Tokyo, N. Mus. Mod. A., 1986)

ATSUSHI TANAKA

Matsumoto Castle [Matsumotojō; Fukashijō; Gakojō (Goose Lake Castle); Karasujō (Raven Castle)]. Japanese site in the city of Matsumoto, central Nagano Prefecture. The castle, which was of the hirajiro ('castle on a plain') type, was important as an example of Azuchi–Momoyama-period (1568–1600) and Edo-period (1600–1868) architecture. The only surviving original buildings are in the donjon complex, consisting of a main donjon and a lesser donjon (both *c.* 1590s), a connecting gallery and two turrets (1633–8) adjoined to the main donjon. The complex has been designated a National Treasure. Most of the buildings in the castle were auctioned and demolished in 1872 after the abolition of domainal rule. The donjons were sold for some 235 *ryō*, but a petition of stay succeeded in preserving them. Repairs were carried out in 1903 by a local preservation society and in 1950–55 by the government. The restoration of 1950–55 used early photographs and other sources to restore 25 sections, primarily windows, staircases, pillars and loopholes.

The city of Matsumoto was a commercial and political centre in Nagano Prefecture from the time of the Muromachi period (1333–1568), and its original castle was built by the Shimadate family in 1504. The growth of a significant castle town, however, dates from the occupation of the area by the daimyo Ogasawara Sadayoshi (1546–95). Construction of the present castle was begun by Ishikawa Kazumasa (*d* 1592), the daimyo of Matsumoto from 1591. His heir Yasunaga ([Mitsunaga], *d* 1642) continued construction, reputedly adding stone walls to the original earthworks, widening the moats, adding the main and lesser donjons as well as new turrets and covered galleries on the stone walls and rebuilding the gates, some time before 1600. Two turrets, a two-storey, south-eastern turret (*tatsumi yagura*) and a one-storey, moon-viewing turret (*tsukimi yagura*), were adjoined to Yasunaga's main donjon by the daimyo Matsudaira Naomasa (1601–66) between 1633 and 1638 (see fig.).

For its defence, the castle depended on the rivers of the Matsumoto Basin, which is flanked by the Hida and Chikuma mountains, and on man-made structures. It was compactly built with three rectangular enceintes, the Main Enceinte (Honmaru) being enclosed on three sides by the Second Enceinte (Ninomaru). This was again separated by an inner moat from the Third Enceinte (Sannomaru), which encompassed both inner enceintes. The outer moat around the Third Enceinte had a circumference of only 2 km. *Umadashi* (protective walls for mounted warriors sallying out) originally lay in front of the outer gates. The low stone walls of the surviving buildings are characterized by a random masonry technique and rise at a low angle with no concave curve from the base. The marshland on which the buildings stand dictated the unusual shape of their walls and made it necessary in places to add artificial wooden foundations under the stones to reinforce them, particularly on the south-western side of the base of the donjons.

The donjon complex lies in the south-western corner of the Main Enceinte overlooking the moat on its western and southern sides. The main donjon has six internal storeys and five exterior levels or roof layers, this discrepancy being typical of the structural limitations of the *Bōrō* ('Watch-tower') style (*see also* HIMEJI, §2). It rises 25 m from its stone base, which is 6 m above the water-level of the moat. The lesser donjon has three storeys rising to a height of 14 m. The donjon walls rise directly up from the edge of the stone base, which, because of the weakness of its foundation, forms two parallelograms with slightly concave sides linked by the connecting gallery. The donjons' exteriors therefore follow the same irregular shape.

Matsumoto Castle, main donjon, south-eastern and moon-viewing turrets seen from the south, 1633–8

The main donjon (*tenshukaku*) is architecturally important, representing a mature stage of the *Bōrō* style of castle building, while also including elements of the later *Sōtō* ('Layered-tower') style. The Japanese donjon developed from a simple watch-tower added to, and structurally independent of, the daimyo's living quarters in the main enceinte. The watch-tower at Matsumoto Castle was added to a larger base structure, as at many other places, but the donjon originally had no provision for living quarters and served mainly as a storehouse, one characteristic of the *Sōtō* style (*see* JAPAN, §III, 4(ii)(c)). The residential and administrative centre of the castle was in the palace of the Main Enceinte, built in *shoin zukuri* ('book hall or study construction'). When this burnt down in 1727, it was not rebuilt, and the centre shifted to the Second Enceinte.

The base of the main donjon is 15.2 m along each side. Sixteen supporting wooden pillars go through the stone base so that the weight of the donjons rests directly on the underlying foundation. Inside, the main supporting pillars of the first and second, third and fourth, and fifth and sixth floors also go through both floors, so that structurally the main donjon consists of a set of three two-storey structures. The roofs of the main donjon have only five gables; most of the roof surfaces conform to the undecorated *yosemune zukuri* ('hipped-gable roof construction'). Another five gables originally existed but, compared to Himeji Castle's 15 and Nagoya's 20, Matsumoto's roof line is closer in appearance to that of the ungabled *Sōtō* style. Moreover, only one of the main donjon's original gables, on the northern side of the second-storey roof, was structurally necessary. Their decorative value aside, gables served the important structural function of fitting the roof to its building before the time when architectural advances made it possible to build the more common *Sōtō*-style donjon. The structural need for gables was obviated by using staggered corners (*furesumi*), with different degrees of inclination for spacing beams and crossbeams, and different angles of inclination on each roof. Marks found during 20th-century restorations indicated that the original structure had a lower position for the fourth-level roof.

The entrance to the donjons lies in the gallery that connects them, and, while the door itself is unfortified, it could be protected by missile fire from both donjons. The donjons' windows are few and undecorated, with heavy protective grilles, although the surface is riddled with loopholes. Machicolations (*ishi otoshi*) jut out from near the first storey, adding movement to the base-line of the structure, while being eminently functional. The top floor of the main donjon lacks the decorative balcony and windows typical of *Bōrō*-style donjons such as Himeji; the windows are purely functional. The basic surface is covered with white plaster up to and under the eaves, while the lower half of the outer walls is covered with black-lacquered weatherboards, a form common in earlier donjons. This stark contrast in coloration and overall Spartan construction earned the castle its popular name of Raven Castle. The two turrets were constructed as one building. A decorative balcony opens on to the moat on three sides of the moon-viewing turret. The refined character of this turret contrasts sharply with the severe functionality of the complex's overall design.

BIBLIOGRAPHY

M. Fujioka: *Shiro to shoin* [Castles and palaces], xii of *Genshoku Nihon no bijutsu* [Arts of Japan, illustrated] (Tokyo, 1968)

K. Hirai: *Jōkaku I* [Castles I], xiv of *Nihon kenchikushi kiso shiryō shūsei* [Collection of the basic materials in Japanese architectural history], ed. H. Ōta (Tokyo, 1978)

J. F. MORRIS

Matsumura Goshun [Gekkei; Toyoaki; Yūho] (*b* Kyoto, 1752; *d* Kyoto, 1811). Japanese painter. He founded the Shijō school of painting, which combined elements of *shaseiga* ('life-drawing painting'), developed by MARUYAMA ŌKYO, and *Bunjinga* ('literati painting'), practised by his early mentor YOSA BUSON (*see* JAPAN, §VI, 4(vi)(e) and (viii)). The name Shijō school reflects the location of Goshun's painting studio on Shijō (fourth) street in Kyoto.

In 1769 Goshun went to work in the Kyoto mint, as had four generations of his family before him. He began painting *c.* 1770 under the tutelage of Ōnishi Suigetsu, a popular artist in Kyoto, whose works are no longer known. Around 1772 Goshun left his post at the mint to become a full-time painter. Suigetsu had died, and Yosa Buson accepted Goshun as his student of *Bunjinga* painting and *haiku* (17-syllable form) poetry. They also practised *haiga* (illustrated *haiku*). From the early 1770s until 1781 Goshun used another set of names, principally Gekkei, for both *haiku* and painting. In 1777 he painted his earliest recognized work, *Rakan* ('Arhat'; pair of scrolls, Ikeda, Itsuō A. Mus.). This period was the peak of Buson's career, and Goshun derived his style directly from the master's best works. In 1781 Goshun's wife and father died, and to help Goshun recover Buson sent him to the country town of Ikeda in Settsu (now Osaka Prefecture). There he began to use the artist's name Goshun, and from that time until his return to Kyoto in 1787 he produced his best known literati-style works. These are calligraphically effective, show mature confidence in construction methods and display a full sense of environment and atmosphere. A prime example is the *Hibiscus and Blue*

Heron on a Tree-stump (1782; Hyōgo, Kurokawa Inst. Anc. Cult. Res.; see fig.).

On Buson's death in 1783, Takai Kitō (1741–1789), his main *haiku* disciple, inherited his 'Yahantei' *haiku* studio seal and Goshun his painting seal, 'Sankadō'. Clearly Goshun was meant to carry on Buson's manner. Buson's other painting disciple, Ki Baitei (1734–1810), and Goshun took responsibility for settling Buson's affairs. Goshun continued to paint in Buson's style with the encouragement of Kitō, though he experimented with a wide range of brush techniques and types of composition. Throughout the mid-1780s he had frequent contact with Maruyama Ōkyo. In 1787 Goshun participated in a project by the Maruyama school to decorate Daijōji temple (Hyōgo Prefecture), though his work was still in Buson's manner. That year he moved back from Ikeda to Kyoto, but the great fire of January 1788 displaced Goshun and Ōkyo from their homes. They sought refuge in the Kiun'in temple, and there Ōkyo tried to convince Goshun to join

Matsumora Goshun,: *Hibiscus and Blue Heron on a Tree-stump*, hanging scroll, ink and light colours on silk, 1.26×0.60 m, 1782 (Hyōgo, Kurokawa Institute of Ancient Cultural Research)

his school. In 1789 Goshun's colleague Kitō died, and Goshun switched to the *shaseiga* style. *Shiroume* ('White plum trees'; a pair of folding screens, ink on rough indigo dyed silk; Ikeda, Itsuō A. Mus.) is a transitional work.

Goshun joined Ōkyo's studio to learn *shaseiga*, then in 1793 opened his own studio in the Shijō area. When Ōkyo died in 1795, Goshun formally separated from the main Maruyama school and promoted his own style, which was more elegant and atmospheric than Ōkyo's structurally and spatially analytical manner. His handscroll *Peach Blossom Spring* (Saitama, Tōyama Kinenkan Fūzoku Mus.) is exemplary of Shijō style.

BIBLIOGRAPHY

C. H. Mitchell: *The Illustrated Books of the* Nanga, *Maruyama, Shijō and Other Related Schools of Japan* (Los Angeles, 1972)
R. Okada: *Haiga no bi* [The art of *haiga*] (Osaka, 1973)
C. L. French: *The Poet-painters: Buson and his Followers* (Ann Arbor, 1974)
J. R. Hillier: *The Uninhibited Brush: Japanese Art in the Shijō Style* (London, 1974)
T. Yamagawa: *Ōkyo, Goshun*, Nihon bijutsu kaiga zenshū [Complete collection of Japanese painting], xxii (Tokyo, 1980)
Ōkyo and the Maruyama-Shijō School of Japanese Painting (exh. cat. by J. Saski, St Louis, MO, A. Mus., 1980)
R. Okada: *Goshun: Catalogue of Paintings by Matsumura Goshun*, Ikeda, Itsuō A. Mus. cat. (Ikeda, 1983)
A Myriad of Autumn Leaves: Japanese Art from the Kurt and Millie Gitter Collection (exh. cat., ed. S. Addiss and others; New Orleans, LA, Mus. A.; Baltimore, MD, Walters A.G.; 1983–4)

HOLLIS GOODALL-CRISTANTE

Matsumura Keibun [Kakei] (*b* Kyoto, 1779; *d* Kyoto, 26 May 1843). Japanese painter. He was a leading figure in the Shijō school established by his half-brother, MATSUMURA GOSHUN (*see* JAPAN, §VI, 4(viii)). Their father, a fourth-generation official of the Kyoto gold mint, died when Keibun was two years old, making it likely that he would follow Goshun, 27 years his senior, into an artistic career. Keibun mastered the techniques of painting taught at Goshun's studio at Shijō-Sakaimachi in Kyoto. He studied the work of MARUYAMA ŌKYO, whose blend of realism and decorative beauty exerted a major influence on him. Keibun's numerous sketchbooks reveal his lifelong adherence to Ōkyo's dictum to draw from nature. Additionally, he was familiar with Chinese literati painting (*Bunjinga*) and art theories of the Ming (1368–1644) and Qing (1644–1911) periods. In his later years he associated with Koishi Genzui (1793–1865), a leading figure of Confucian literati circles in Kyoto (*see* JAPAN, §VI, 4(vi)(d)). In 1797 Keibun's work was chosen for exhibition by the leading literati scholar and painter, Minagawa Kien (1734–1807) who from 1792 sponsored twice-yearly exhibitions of new works of painting. By 1801 his designs were being included with those of Goshun and other Kyoto artists in woodblock-printed picture-books (*ehon*). After Goshun's death in 1811 Keibun shared the leadership of the Shijō school with fellow-pupil OKAMOTO TOYOHIKO, and the two became the most popular painters in Kyoto. Keibun was particularly noted for his bird-and-flower (*kachō*) compositions. Typical of these is *Spring Blossoms and Autumn Foliage*, a pair of six-panel folding screens (Kyoto, Akiko Kato priv. col.; see Harada, illus. no. 8). These brilliantly coloured screens depict seasonal birds and flowers with detailed realism. In place of

expressive brushwork, Keibun stressed the elegant disposition of closely observed forms against a gold background.

Having emerged as a master in his own right, Keibun worked to consolidate Goshun's legacy. He organized a memorial exhibition of his brother's paintings in 1817. Keibun emphasized his local ties in 1829 by painting a flock of birds on the inner ceiling of the *Naginataboko*, the Shijō neighbourhood's float for the annual Gion festival. His block-printed picture album of 1830, *Go Keibun gafu* ('Picture album by Keibun'; Paris, Bib. N.) brought the Shijō style to a wide audience. After his death in 1843 his students, including Nishiyama Hoen (1804–67), Maekawa Gorei (1806–76) and Yokoyama Seiki (1792–1864), and their pupils extended Keibun's influence into the Meiji period (1868–1912).

BIBLIOGRAPHY

H. Harada, ed.: *Kyōto gadan: Edomatsu Meiji no gajintachi* [The Kyoto art world: painters of the late Edo and Meiji periods] (Kyoto, 1975)
Ōkyo and the Maruyama–Shijō School of Japanese Painting (exh. cat. by J. Sasaki, St Louis, MO, A. Mus., 1980)

MARK H. SANDLER

Matsys. *See* METSYS.

Matta (Echaurren), Roberto (Antonio Sebastián) (*b* Santiago, 11 Nov 1911). Chilean painter, printmaker and draughtsman. He was educated at the Sacré Coeur Jesuit College and at the Catholic University of Santiago, where he studied architecture (1929–31). In 1933 he went to Europe and worked in Le Corbusier's atelier in Paris. At the end of 1934 Matta visited Spain where he met the poet and playwright, Federico García Lorca (1898–1936), and Salvador Dalí. The following year he went to Scandinavia (where he met the architect Alvar Aalto) and to Russia, where he worked on housing design projects. He was in London for a short period in 1936 and worked with Walter Gropius and László Moholy-Nagy. Employment with the architects of the Spanish Republican pavilion at the Paris International Exhibition (1937) brought him into close contact with Picasso's *Guernica* (1937; Madrid, Prado), which greatly impressed him. Another important influence at this time was Marcel Duchamp whose work he first saw in 1936 and whom he met shortly afterwards.

At this time Matta made only drawings, for example *Inside Drive* (1939; see 1984 exh. cat., p. 10). Their vitality and freshness brought his work to the attention of the Surrealists and André Breton invited him to take part in the Exposition Internationale du Surréalisme (1938). At the suggestion of his friend the painter Gordon Onslow Ford (*b* 1912) he began to paint. On the outbreak of World War II Matta went to New York. He spoke fluent English and made contact with American contemporaries such as Jackson Pollock, Arshile Gorky and Mark Rothko. In summer 1941 Matta travelled with Robert Motherwell to Mexico where he was deeply impressed by the dramatic landscape and the work of the Mexican mural painters David Siqueiros, Diego Rivera and José Clemente Orozco.

Matta's first exhibition, at the Pierre Matisse Gallery in New York (1942), was praised by Breton as one of the high points of the Surrealist vision; the originality of works such as *Listen to Living* (1941) made a powerful impact on the American Abstract Expressionists. In 1944 he painted *Vertigo of Eros*, one of the first of his works to

Robert Matta: *Le Vertige d'Eros/Le Vert Tige des roses*, oil on canvas, 1.96×2.52 m, 1944 (New York, Museum of Modern Art)

have a pun in the title (*Le Vertige d'Eros/Le Vert Tige des roses*); it was immediately acquired by the Museum of Modern Art, New York (see fig.). Influenced by *Guernica* and the works of the Mexican mural painters he began to paint on a far larger scale than his American contemporaries, who later followed his example and began to produce the monumental works for which they are known.

After his initial success in New York, Matta began to attract the disapproval of powerful American critics such as Clement Greenberg, who objected to the figurative elements in Matta's painting, and of the Surrealists, who considered that his work no longer adhered to their tenets. In 1947 Matta had his first exhibition in Paris at the Galerie René Drouin. He returned to Europe in 1948 when the beginning of cold war politics made life increasingly difficult in the USA for an artist with Matta's strongly held political views. In the same year he was expelled by Breton from the Surrealist group. He lived in Rome, London and Paris but travelled widely outside Europe. He returned briefly to Chile during the period of the Allende government and later divided his time between Paris and Tarquinia in Italy.

Matta's influences include the work of Picasso, Duchamp and Kandinsky, but also such diverse sources as architectural and engineering drawings, science fiction illustrations and films, comic books and graffiti. As a result his painting became epic in scale and subject-matter, as in *Coigitum* (4.12×10.36 m, 1972–3; see 1977 exh. cat.). Retaining his strong political commitment (he was particularly active in denouncing the Pinochet regime in Chile and the US involvement in Latin American politics) Matta has often exhibited in factories and in the public buildings of left-wing municipalities rather than in art galleries. He also produced numerous prints, including his series of etchings *Hom'mère* (1970), an autobiographical exercise, and many drawings. The subject-matter was often political, or based on literary sources including Arthur Rimbaud, Antonin Artaud, Rabelais and Shakespeare. *The Banquet* (1982, pastel on paper; see 1984 exh. cat., cover) is part of the *Storming the Tempest* series of large pastels, whose theme is the conquest of the New World by the Old, or the exploitation of the Third World by the First.

BIBLIOGRAPHY
A. Breton: *Le Surréalisme et la peinture* (Paris, 1928, rev. 1965; Eng. trans., London and New York, 1972), pp. 82, 146, 149, 182–94
A. Jouffroy: *Une Révolution du regard* (Paris, 1965)
Matta: Coigitum (exh. cat., London, Hayward Gal., 1977)
G. Ferrari: *Matta: Index dell'opera grafica dal 1969 al 1980* (Viterbo, 1980)
Roberto Matta: Paintings and Drawings, 1971–1979 (exh. cat. by P. Selz and J.-M. Tasende, La Jolla, CA, Tasende Gal., 1980)

Matta, the Logic of Hallucination (exh. cat. by R. Malbert and P. Overy, ACGB, 1984)
Matta (exh. cat. by A. Sayas and C. Schweisguth, Paris, Pompidou, 1985)

PAUL OVERY

Mattarnovy [Mattannowy], **Georg Johann** [Maternovy, Ivan Stepanovich] (*fl* 1714; *d* St Petersburg, 2 Nov 1719). German architect, active in Russia. He arrived in St Petersburg on 8 February 1714 at the recommendation of the Prussian architect Andreas Schlüter, who was one of many foreigners engaged by Peter I, Tsar and Emperor of Russia (*reg* 1682–1725), to build his new capital there. His first project was the design of a grotto, in which he said he specialized, and a gallery for the gardens of the Summer Palace, where Schlüter was also working. Mattarnovy's major works were the Second Winter Palace (1716–19; destr. 1780s) on the Neva embankment and the first stone cathedral of St Isaac of Dalmatia (1717–27; destr.). His only extant building is Peter I's Imperial Library and Museum (the Kunstkamera; 1718–34) on Vasil'yevsky Island, completed by Nicolaus Friedrich Härbel (*d* 1724), Gaetano Chiaveri and Mikhail Zemtsov. The original conception may have been Schlüter's. A tiered octagonal tower supporting an observatory is flanked by two identical annexes, the façades articulated with plain panels and platbands. The Kunstkamera later became the Academy of Sciences and today is the Peter the Great Museum of Anthropology and Ethnography. Mattarnovy is also known to have worked on a customs house and dockyard. His sons Johann Christian Mattarnovy and Philip Georg Mattarnovy were educated in Russia and continued to work there as painters and engravers.

BIBLIOGRAPHY

I. Ye. Graba': *Arkhitektory-inostrantsy pri Petre Velikom* [Foreign architects at the time of Peter the Great] (Moscow, 1911); also in I. Ye. Graba': *O russkoy arkhitekture* (Moscow, 1969), pp. 263–83
I. Ye. Graba' and others: *Russkaya arkhitektura pervoy poloviny XVIII veka: Issledovanyya i materialy* [Early 18th-century Russian architecture: studies and materials] (Moscow, 1954)
J. Cracraft: *The Petrine Revolution in Russian Architecture* (Chicago, 1988) [background and illus.]

LINDSEY HUGHES

Matte, Rebeca (*b* 1875; *d* 1929). Chilean sculptor. After studying at the Academia de Bellas Artes in Santiago she lived for many years in Europe, going to Paris in 1900 where she studied under Denys Puech and Paul Dubois (i) at the Académie Julian. She also studied with Giulio Monteverde in Rome, finally settling in Florence, in a Renaissance mansion. Working in marble and bronze, she concentrated on the human figure, seeking to represent volume in a rigidly formal manner yet consistently conveying an emotional charge.

Matte formed part of a generation that assimilated academic canons of monumentality in the Greek tradition. Her subject-matter consisted of biographical, historical, allegorical or mythological events. She also produced public monuments, including some government commissions in Chile (e.g. the monument *Héroes de la concepción* at the Parque Cementerio General in Santiago; marble, h. 2.5×l. 3.0 m, 1920) and one for the Vredespaleis in The Hague (*Grupo la guerra*; marble, 2.0×1.5 m). She was given a teaching post at the Accademia di Belle Arti in 1918, and

on her death the Italian government requested one of her works (in marble) for the Palazzo Pitti in Florence.

BIBLIOGRAPHY

M. Ivelič: *La escultura chilena* (Santiago, 1979), pp. 12–15
V. Carvacho Herrera: *Historia de la escultura chilena* (Santiago, 1983), pp. 207–11

CARLOS LASTARRIA HERMOSILLA

Mattei. Italian family of patrons and collectors. Claiming descent from Innocent II (*reg* 1130–43), the Mattei were an ancient Roman family of merchants and civic officials who prospered economically in the 16th century. Towards the middle of the 16th century two branches of the family, the Mattei, Dukes of Paganica, and the Mattei, later Duchi di Rocca Sinibaldi and Duchi di Giove, began to erect a formidable group of four contiguous urban palaces that became known as the *isola dei Mattei* in the S Angelo district of Rome. The architectural complex was believed to have been built on the site of the ancient Circus Flaminius: in fact it was located on the site of the Teatro di Balbo and the Crypta Balbi (both 19 BC). Palazzi of the Mattei–Paganica occupied the southern and western portions of the *isola*. The Palazzo Mattei di Paganica, erected by Ludovico Mattei, Duca di Paganica, was constructed in 1540 to designs ascribed to Jacopo Vignola. The interior contains frescoed friezes possibly executed by Taddeo Zuccaro and Federico Zuccaro. The smallest of the new Mattei palaces was erected to designs ascribed to Nanni di Baccio Bigio on a contiguous site, facing the Piazza dei Mattei, in or perhaps a little before 1540 by Giacomo Mattei, younger brother of Ludovico. The austere façade was decorated with chiaroscuro frescoes (destr.) depicting scenes from the *Life of Furio Camillo* executed (1548) by Taddeo Zuccaro (Vasari). Giacomo subsequently commissioned Taddeo Zuccaro to execute frescoes representing the *Passion* (*c.* 1556; see ZUCCARO, (1), fig. 1) in the Mattei Chapel, S Maria della Consolazione (*in situ*). Muzio Mattei (*d* Crete, *c.* 31 May 1668), the son of Giacomo Mattei, is known to have strongly influenced the Comune of Rome in their decision to commission from Taddeo Landini the so-called Fontana delle Tartarughe (marble and bronze; 1581–8) in the Piazza dei Mattei, adjacent to the *isola*: he appears to have chosen the site and perhaps determined the fountain's materials. He also undertook to maintain the new fountain, as well as the piazza. A catafalque (untraced; drawing, London, BM) for Muzio was designed in Bernini's studio in 1668.

The second branch of the Mattei consisted of Alessandro Mattei (*d* 1580); his brother Paolo Mattei (*d* 2 or 4 March 1592), the Duca di Giove; and Alessandro's three sons: (1) Ciriaco Mattei, Duca di Rocca Sinibaldi; Cardinal Girolamo Mattei (*b* Rome, 1546; *d* Rome, 1603); and (2) Asdrubale Mattei, Duca di Giove and, after Ciriaco's death, also Duca di Rocca Sinibaldi. Their palazzi occupied the northern and eastern areas of the *isola dei Mattei*. The palazzo of Alessandro Mattei, now the Palazzo Mattei–Caetani, bears the date 1564 on an inscription above the main entry portal. The architect was formerly identified as Bartolomeo Ammannati, although Claudio Lippi di Caravaggio, the son of Nanni di Baccio Bigio, has also been suggested. Alessandro commissioned ceiling frescoes (1559–60; some *in situ*), from Taddeo Zuccaro, which were executed with Federico Zuccaro and which depict scenes from the *Life of Alexander the Great*. In the *grand salone* there are frescoes by Giovanni Alberti with landscapes by Paul Bril. During 1564–5 Alessandro Mattei also had a family burial chapel, subsequently decorated through the patronage of Ciriaco Mattei, constructed in a Tuscan style by Giacomo del Duca in S Maria in Aracoeli.

Paolo Mattei acquired a site on the Palatine in 1552, on which he erected a small villa called the 'Palatina' (destr.), in part frescoed with grotesques and mythological scenes, possibly by Baldassare Peruzzi and subsequently engraved by Marcantonio Raimondi. At the Palatina, Paolo also collected antiquities, some of which were later recorded at his nephew Asdrubale's Palazzo Mattei di Giove. In 1585 Paolo acquired burial rights in and agreed to have decorated the chapel of the Pietà in S Maria in Aracoeli. The fresco scheme (*in situ*) executed (1588–90) for him by Cristoforo Roncalli consists of a complex Christological programme with a doctrinal interpretation of the Passion as its central theme. Girolamo Mattei, of the order of Observant Franciscans, became the first Mattei Cardinal, elevated by Sixtus V. It is thought that Girolamo commissioned the fresco of the *Flagellation* (1573; *see* ZUCCARO, (2), fig. 1) bearing the Mattei coat of arms in conjunction with a cardinal's hat, from Federico Zuccaro in the oratory of the Gonfalone. He was a reserved and austere man, whose patronage was limited; nonetheless, for about two years (1601–*c*. 1603) Caravaggio was a guest in his palace.

BIBLIOGRAPHY

G. Vasari: *Vite* (1550, rev. 2/1568); ed. G. Milanesi (1878–85), vii, pp. 78, 83–4
G. Baglione: *Vite* (1642); ed. V. Mariani (1935), pp. 50, 56, 87, 289, 309, 343, 346, 379
G. P. Bellori: *Vite* (1672); ed. E. Borea (1976)
F. Titi: *Descrizione delle pitture. . .in Roma* (Rome, 3/1763), pp. 86–91, 187, 189–96, 469–70, 473
L. Heutter: 'I Mattei custodi dei Ponti', *Capitolium*, vii (1929), pp. 347–55
G. Antici–Mattei: 'Cenni storici sulle nobili e antiche famiglie Antici, Mattei, e Antici–Mattei', *Riv. Coll. Araldica*, xxxix–xlii (1941–4)
M. Worsdale: 'Bernini's Studio Drawings for a Catafalque and Fireworks, 1668', *Burl. Mag.*, cxx (1978), p. 462
C. Benocci: *Il Rione S Angelo* (Rome, 1980), pp. 57–78
——: 'Taddeo Landini e la fontana delle Tartarughe in Piazza Mattei a Roma', *Stor. A.*, lii (1984), pp. 187–203
S. Finocchi Vitale and R. Samperi: 'Nuovi contributi sull'insediamento dei Mattei nel Rione S Angelo e sulla costruzione del Palazzo Mattei Paganica', *Stor. Archit.*, viii (1985), pp. 19–36

(1) Ciriaco Mattei (*b* Rome, 12 Aug 1545; *d* Rome, 10 Oct 1614). He was a distinguished patrician and city official. He had the renowned Villa Celimontana, with its complex garden scheme, constructed (1581–6) on vineyards inherited from Giacomo Mattei on the Monte Celio. The architect of the principal casino was Giacomo del Duca. The gardens, much visited by foreign travellers, were arranged in a formal scheme *all'antica*, which included terraces and ramps, avenues and hedges, as well as a labyrinth for amusement. A highly celebrated collection of antique and contemporary statuary and fountains, (destr. and dispersed) in addition to a rich collection of antique inscriptions, were originally part of the design. Only the Capitoline Obelisk given to Ciriaco by the City of Rome in 1582 remains *in situ*. MacDougall's reconstruction of the gardens reveals an allegorical and emblematic scheme organized around the theme of the antique Roman circus, a conspicuous reference to the myth of the Circus

Flaminius. The gardens were meant to evoke the glories of ancient Rome, and demonstrate the Mattei's links with that era. During the 17th century they were enlarged and embellished with a series of emblematic fountains (destr.; see Falda; Belli Barsali), probably designed by Bernini.

Ciriaco also assembled a collection of antiquities (see Venuti; Lanciani) at the Palazzo Mattei (now Mattei-Caetani). This was dispersed in the 18th century, and many pieces, including the Mattei *Ceres* (marble; *c*. 3rd century BC; Rome, Vatican, Gal. Candelabri) and the acclaimed *Pudicity* (marble; late 1st century AD; Rome, Vatican, Braccio Nuo.), entered the Museo Pio-Clementino. In 1584 Ciriaco obtained the municipal appointment of Conservatore in Rome. In the Mattei Chapel, S Maria in Aracoeli, he had a decorative scheme executed (1586–9; incomplete) by Girolamo Muziano, with the assistance of Giacomo del Duca. The principal paintings are five large oils (*in situ*) depicting scenes from the *Life of St Matthew*, the family's patron saint.

In 1592 Clement VIII granted jointly to Ciriaco and Asdrubale Mattei the fief of Rocca Sinibaldi. Ciriaco thus obtained the title of marchese along with the estate castle, which was probably designed by Baldassare Peruzzi. Three works by Caravaggio are documented as having been painted for Ciriaco: the *Supper at Emmaus* (London, N.G.), payment January 1602; *St John the Baptist* (Rome, Pin. Capitolina), payments July and December 1602; and the *Taking of Christ* (Dublin, N.G.), payment 2 January 1603. Baglione stated that the *Incredulity of St Thomas* (Potsdam, Schloss Sanssouci) was painted for him, but it is more likely that this work was painted in the Palazzo Mattei for Vincenzo Giustiniani.

BIBLIOGRAPHY

G. B. Falda: *Le fontane di Roma* (Rome, 1675, rev. 1690–91), iii, pls 18–19
R. Venuti: *Vetera monumenta quae in hortis Caelimontanis et in aedibus Matthaeiorum adservantur*, 3 vols (Rome, 1776–9)
R. Lanciani: *Storia degli scavi di Roma e notizie intorno le collezioni romane di antichità*, iii (Rome, 1907), pp. 83–6, 88–97 [Ciriaco's testament, 1610; the inventory of his possessions, 1614]
L. Hautecoeur: 'La Vente de la collection Mattei et les origines du Musée Pio-Clémentin', *Mél. Archéol. & Hist.*, xxx (1919), pp. 57–75
M. Borda: 'Sculture antiche a villa Celimontana', *Capitolium*, xxxi (1956), pp. 43–54
I. Belli Barsali: *Ville di Roma: Lazio I* (Milan, 1970), pp. 54, 384–5
E. B. MacDougall: *The Villa Mattei and the Development of the Roman Garden Style* (diss., Cambridge, MA, Harvard U., 1970)
F. Haskell and N. Penny: *Taste and the Antique: The Lure of Classical Sculpture, 1500–1900* (New Haven and London, 1981/*R* 1982), pp. 66, 141–3, 181–2, cats 4, 22, 74
J. Heideman: *The Cinquecento Chapel Decorations in S Maria in Aracoeli in Rome* (Amsterdam, 1982)
H. Hibbard: *Caravaggio* (London, 1983)
E. B. MacDougall: 'A Circus, a Wildman and a Dragon: Family History and the Villa Mattei', *J. Soc. Archit. Historians*, xlii (1983), pp. 121–30
F. Cappelletti and L. Testa: *Identificazione di un Caravaggio: Nuove tecnologie per una rilettura del 'S Giovanni Battista' di Roma* (Rome, 1990)
F. Cappelletti: 'The Documentary Evidence of the Early History of Caravaggio's *Taking of Christ*', *Burl. Mag.*, cxxxv (1993), pp. 742–6

(2) Asdrubale Mattei (*b* Rome, 1556; *d* Rome, 1638). Brother of (1) Ciriaco Mattei. In 1592 he inherited from his uncle Paolo the small villa on the Palatine, as well as property in the *isola* on which he eventually built his own palace. In 1598 he became the Duca di Giove and *c*. 1598 commissioned CARLO MADERNO to design and erect the Palazzo Mattei di Giove, the last of the family palaces to enrich the *isola dei Mattei* (see Panofsky-Soergel). It is celebrated for the courtyards, embellished with free-standing antique statuary and inset antique low reliefs, and it was almost certainly designed to accommodate Asdrubale's vast collection of antique marbles (*in situ*; Guerrini; Venuti). This rich collection derived from the villa on the Palatine, from the site of the *isola* where they appear to have been discovered during excavations for the Mattei palaces, and from Ciriaco Mattei's Villa Celimontana.

In 1600 the initial stage of interior decoration in the palace was executed on the *piano nobile*. This consists of a series of frescoes by different artists depicting scenes from the *Life of Joseph* (all *in situ*): Antonio Circignani, the *Triumph of Joseph*; scenes and grotesques by Paul Bril and Prospero Orsi (?1558–*c*. 1633); *Joseph's Family in Egypt* by Cristoforo Greppi; feigned architecture with emblematic devices of the Mattei by Tarquinio Ligustri. The chapel was also adorned at this time with an altarpiece (untraced) by Cristoforo Roncalli, depicting *St Francis*. Between 1606 and *c*. 1608 a second decorative phase was accomplished. The ceiling of the Sala of Rachel and Jacob was painted (1607) under the supervision of Francesco Albani: Giovanni Lanfranco and Domenichino also contributed to these decorations. The third major decorative phase comprised four ceiling frescoes (1614–15) by Lanfranco, two of which survive (*in situ*). The final decorations of the Palazzo Mattei di Giove began in 1622 with the commission given initially to Pietro Paolo Bonzi and subsequently to Pietro da Cortona to fresco the vault of the *galleria* with scenes of the *Story of Solomon*.

Asdrubale was also a keen collector of paintings, with an adventurous and undogmatic interest in contemporary art, in landscape and in north European artists such as Paul Bril. He owned works by many Caravaggesque painters, among them GIOVANNI SERODINE and Antiveduto Gramatica, and a *St Sebastian* (untraced) by Caravaggio himself. There is a portrait of *Asdrubale Mattei* (Chantilly, Mus. Condé), attributed to Alessandro Turchi.

BIBLIOGRAPHY

G. Panofsky-Soergel: 'Zur Geschichte des Palazzo Mattei di Giove', *Röm. Jb. Kstgesch.*, xi (1967–8), pp. 109–88

L. Guerrini: 'Sculture di Palazzo Mattei: Le statue del cortile', *Stud. Misc.*, xx (1972), pp. 19–43

——: *Palazzo Mattei di Giove: Le antichità* (Rome, 1982)

M. Bertoldi, M. Marinozzi, L. Scolari and C. Varagnoli: 'Palazzo Mattei di Giove: Le fasi della costruzione e l'individuazione delle lavorazioni caratteristiche', *Ric. Stor. A.*, xx (1983), pp. 65–76

J. M. Merz: 'A Possible Identification: The Mattei Brothers', *Apollo*, cxxii (1985), p. 406

F. Cappelletti and L. Testa: 'I quadri di Caravaggio nella collezione Mattei: I nuovi documenti e i riscontri con le fonti', *Stor. A.*, lxix (1990), pp. 75–84

F. Cappelletti: 'La committenza di Asdrubale Mattei e la creazione della Galleria nel Palazzo Mattei di Giove a Roma', *Stor. A.*, lxxvi (1992), pp. 256–95

Caravaggio: The Master Revealed (exh. cat. by S. Benedetti, Dublin, N.G., 1993)

□

Matteis, Paolo de (*b* Piano del Cilento, Salerno, 9 Feb 1662; *d* Naples, 26 Jan 1728). Italian painter and silversmith. He was important to the history of painting in Naples in the transitional period between the 17th and 18th centuries. His elegant art encouraged the movement away from Baroque drama towards a more tender, rocaille style in harmony with the earliest manifestations in Naples of the Arcadian school of poetry and of the Enlightenment. He painted frescoes, altarpieces and allegorical and mythological pictures.

1. Early years: Rome and Naples, to 1701. 2. International success: Paris, Rome and Naples, 1702–28.

1. EARLY YEARS: ROME AND NAPLES, TO 1701. He arrived in Naples while still young and received his first artistic training in the workshop of Luca Giordano. He was in Rome before 1683, where he was the pupil of Giovanni Maria Morandi (1622–1717), a still-life painter, and here he became a protégé of the 7th Marqués del Carpio, Gaspar de Haro y Guzmán, the Spanish Ambassador, who had already begun to form an impressive art collection. In Rome the influence of Giordano was modified by the formal elegance of the painting of Carlo Maratti. De Matteis's earliest known work, the *Allegory of Divine Wisdom Crowning Painting as the Sovereign of the Arts* (1680s; ex-library ceiling, Convent of SS Gerolamo and Francesco, Genoa; Malibu, CA, Getty Mus.; see fig. 1), represents a balanced synthesis of Baroque and classical styles. When the Marqués del Carpio was nominated Viceroy of Naples in 1683, de Matteis followed him there, and the first important works that follow his return to Naples continue in this vein. They include a *Virgin and Child* (1690; Naples, S Giovanni dei Fiorentini), a series of six canvases of scenes from the *Lives of SS Francis and*

1. Paolo de Matteis: *Allegory of Divine Wisdom Crowning Painting as the Sovereign of the Arts*, oil on canvas, 3.56×2.55 m, 1680s (Malibu, CA, J. Paul Getty Museum)

Clare (1690–95; Cocentaina, Spain, Convent of the Clarisas), the overdoors with the *Baptism of Christ* and the *Resurrection* for the Casa de Campo in Madrid (1696; Madrid, Real Acad. S Fernando, Mus.) and lastly the fresco of *St Bruno Interceding with the Virgin Mary for Suffering Humanity* (1699), which decorates the vault of the pharmacy of the Certosa di S Martino, Naples. He sent other works to Pistoia at the request of the bishop G. M. Marchetti: the altarpiece depicting the *Vision of St Gaetano Thiene* (signed and dated 1693) in S Paolo in Pistoia and two canvases, *Pan and Syrinx* and *Apollo and Marsyas* (both 1695), for the Marchetti family's palace (*in situ*). The painter's fame, when he was only a little over 30, had clearly spread beyond Naples.

In these years de Matteis created a delicate, graceful style that broke with the vigour of the Baroque. Even when his compositions were directly indebted to Giordano, as in *Olinda and Sofronia Rescued by Clorinda* (dated 169?; Norfolk, VA, Chrysler Mus.), which is derived from Giordano's painting of the same subject from Torquato Tasso's *Gerusalemme liberata* (Genoa, Pal. Reale), de Matteis's treatment, without high drama, has an 18th-century elegance and lightness. His art encouraged the classical tendencies of established artists such as Francesco Solimena, although Solimena's classicism became more rigidly academic.

2. INTERNATIONAL SUCCESS: PARIS, ROME AND NAPLES, 1702–28. De Matteis, a successful artist with an international reputation, was appreciated by the most refined connoisseurs. He was invited by Victor-Marie, Comte d'Estrées (1660–1737), to go to Paris, where he stayed from 1702 to 1705 and worked for the Dauphin, among others, and in the gallery of the palace of the Compagnie des Indes Orientales (destr.). No works from this Parisian visit have survived. The contact with the elegant art of 18th-century Paris confirmed de Matteis in the style he had already developed. In 1707, during the War of the Spanish Succession (1701–14), Naples became part of the Austrian Empire, and de Matteis was one of the favourite artists of the new governors. The first of the Austrian viceroys, W. Philipp Lorenz, Graf von Daun (1669–1741), commissioned him to paint a ceiling for one of the rooms of his palace in Vienna; the grandiose subject for this work was *Justice, Fortune and Valour Helping Hercules, Crowned by Glory, while Time and Truth Defeat Slander and Envy* (Vienna, Pal. Daun–Kinsky, 1714–19). Through the viceroys of Naples, Paolo de Matteis had important commissions from leading members of the Austrian aristocracy, among them Emperor Joseph I (*reg* 1705–11), for whom he executed, before 1711, the altarpiece for the chapel of the Hofburg, Vienna, showing *St John of Nepomuk and King Wenceslas* (*in situ*).

This was the most fruitful period of de Matteis's life. He was in touch with the most advanced intellectual circles in Europe and in 1712 received a particularly important commission from ANTHONY ASHLEY COOPER, 3RD EARL OF SHAFTESBURY, who considered him the best painter in Italy. To demonstrate his own aesthetic theories on the nature of history painting, Lord Shaftesbury gave de Matteis precise instructions for a painting of *Hercules at the Crossroads between Virtue and Vice*. He later published

this programme, under the title *A Notion of the Historical Draught or Tablature of the Judgement of Hercules* (London, 1713). Paolo de Matteis followed Shaftesbury's instructions closely, fulfilling at the same time his own interest in complex philosophical concepts. A drawing (Paris, Louvre) suggests that Annibale Carracci's celebrated *Hercules at the Crossroads* (*c.* 1596; Naples, Capodimonte), painted for the Camerino in the Palazzo Farnese in Rome, was one of several sources. There are three versions of de Matteis's final composition (St Giles House, Dorset; one signed and dated 1712, Leeds, Temple Newsam House, see fig. 2; and Munich, Alte. Pin.). Other works from these years have similarly literary and mythological themes, among them *Night* (Quimper, Mus. B.-A.), *Diana and the Hunt* (Paris, Louvre), the *Venus Giving Arms to Aeneas* (1714; ex-Pal. Buonaccorsi, Macerata) and the *Self-portrait in the Act of Painting, an Allegory of the Peace of Utrecht (1713) and the Peace of Rastadt (1714)* (*c.* 1714; fragment, Naples, Capodimonte; sketch for whole scene, U. Houston, TX, Sarah Campbell Blaffer Gal.). His contemporaries and later de Dominici criticized the bizarre nature of the latter invention, which is rich in emblematic allusions: the painter shows himself, wearing a dressing-gown, accompanied by a monkey—an allusion to *Mimesis*—and by other allegorical figures. However, de Matteis particularly liked this subject and elaborated it in another large picture from which the self-portrait is missing (Mainz, Landesmus.). An *Annunciation* (1712; St Louis, MO, A. Mus.) and an *Adoration of the Shepherds* (Richmond, VA. Mus. F.A.), both of which are less complex formally and iconographically, were inspired by Arcadian literary principles; they were painted for Aurora Sanseverino, Duchess of Laurenzano (1669–1730), a poetess, and under the bucolic pseudonym Lucinda Coritesia, the moving spirit behind the Naples literary Arcadian society.

Throughout this period de Matteis also executed many works for churches: frescoes with the *Immaculate Conception* and the *Assumption of the Virgin with the Queen of Sheba and Solomon* in the cupola of the church of Il Gesù Nuovo in Naples (1713; frescoes destr. 1776; small oil sketches, Naples, Capodimonte, and W. Berlin, Gemäldegal., respectively); the fresco in the cupola of the large chapel of Taranto Cathedral depicting the *Glorification of St Catald* (1713); and the canvases in the abbey of S Martino delle Scale, Palermo, with the *History of St Benedict and other Benedictine Saints* (1725). These works are large and complex decorative schemes in which the well-established devices of Baroque decorative painting are brought up to date by a delicate and airy touch; their style suggests how important the last frescoes by Luca Giordano in the Cappella del Tesoro (1704) at the Certosa di S Martino, Naples, were, even to de Matteis. There is no disparity of style between these religious works and his freer allegories, mythological scenes and paintings of subjects from Tasso's *Gerusalemme liberata*, or from other literary sources, which continued to be in demand from the most enlightened aristocratic and bourgeois collectors. De Matteis was resident in Rome between 1723 and 1725, when he painted the *Blessed Andrea Conti d'Anagni Performing a Miracle* (Paris, priv. col.) for Pope Innocent XIII and was commissioned by Benedict XIII to paint an altarpiece with the *Virgin and Child Appearing to St*

2. Paolo de Matteis: *Hercules at the Crossroads between Virtue and Vice*, oil on canvas, 641×768 mm, 1712 (Leeds, Temple Newsam House)

Dominic in the Orsini Chapel of S Maria sopra Minerva, Rome (*in situ*).

In the final years of his life de Matteis made models for sculpture in silver. There is the well-known bust of *St Sebastian*, cast by Gaetano Starace (1727), in S Sebastiano a Guardia Sanframondi, Benevento, and the design for the completion of the altar frontal of the Trinità delle Monache in Naples, which was originally projected (1725) by another painter, Giacomo del Po. A group of marble figures with the *Virgin and Child and St Joseph* (untraced) was, according to de Dominici, directly sculpted by de Matteis.

BIBLIOGRAPHY

L. Pascoli: *Vite de' pittori, scultori ed architetti moderni*, ii (Rome, 1736), p. 135

B. de Dominici: *Vite* (1742–3), iii, pp. 518–50

B. Croce: 'Shaftesbury in Italia', *Uomini e cose della vecchia Italia* (Bari, 1927), pp. 272–309

F. Bologna: *Francesco Solimena* (Napoli, 1958), pp. 143–5

F. Haskell: *Patrons and Painters* (London, 1963), pp. 198–200

A. E. Pérez Sánchez: *Pintura italiana del siglo XVII en España* (Madrid, 1965), pp. 405–13

O. Ferrari: 'Le arti figurative', *Storia di Napoli* (Cava dei Tirreni, 1970), VI/ii, pp. 1221–363

M. Chiarini: 'Un episodio giordanesco a Pistoia', *Festschrift Klaus Lankheit* (Cologne, 1973), pp. 173–4

V. de Martini: 'Introduzione allo studio di Paolo de Matteis', *Napoli Nob.*, xiv (1975), pp. 209–28

G. Borrelli: 'Il modello del pittore de Matteis per il S Sebastiano in argento di Guardia Sanframondi', *Napoli Nob.*, xv (1976), pp. 121–3

O. Ferrari: 'Considerazioni sulle vicende artistiche a Napoli durante il viceregno austriaco', *Stor. A.*, xxxv (1979), pp. 11–38

E. Schleier: 'Paolo de Matteis, e non Marchesini, Trevisani o Amigoni', *Paragone*, ccclv (1979), pp. 66–70

A. Brejon de Lavergnée: 'La Peinture napolitaine du dix-huitième siècle', *Rev. A.* [Paris], 52 (1981), pp. 63–76

C. Siracusano: 'L'opera di Paolo de Matteis a San Martino delle Scale e la sua fortuna in Sicilia', *Quad. Ist. Stor. A. Med. & Mod.*, v–vi (1981–2), pp. 61–6

N. Spinosa: *Pittura napoletana del settecento: Dal barocco al rococò* (Naples, 1986), pp. 31–6, 129–38

E. Schleier: 'Opere di Paolo de Matteis in Germania', *Scritti di storia dell'arte in onore di Raffaello Causa* (Naples, 1988), pp. 305–310

A. Brejon de Lavergnée: 'Plaidoyer pour un peintre "de pratique": Le Séjour de Paolo de Matteis en France (1702–1705)', *Rev. A.* [Paris], 88 (1990), pp. 70–79

L. Pistilli: 'Lord Shaftesbury e Paolo de Matteis: *Ercole al bivio tra teoria e practica*', *Stor. A.*, 68 (1990), pp. 95–121

ORESTE FERRARI

Matteo, Giorgio di. *See* GIORGIO DA SEBENICO.

Matteo, Pasquino di. *See* PASQUINO DA MONTEPULCIANO.

Matteo, Sano di. *See* SANO DI MATTEO.

Matteo da Campione. *See under* CAMPIONESI.

Matteo (di Pietro di Giovanni di Ser Bernardo) da Gualdo (*b* Gualdo Tadino, *c.* 1435; *d* Gualdo Tadino, after 20 Jan 1507). Italian painter and notary. He was a minor master who worked on the fringes of the artistic activity in Umbria and the Marches. He was rediscovered in the 19th century, but his original, easily recognizable style, with its tendency to distortion and its lively popular sentiment, has ensured him a popularity that perhaps exceeds his merits.

Matteo is documented in his place of birth between 29 May 1463, when he entered into a marriage contract with Pellegrina di Pietro d'Angelello, and 21 January 1507, when he added a codicil to his will. His first securely attributed work, the *Virgin and Child with St Anne* (*c.* 1460; Gualdo Tadino, S Francesco), derives its compositional structure and linear rhythms from the work of Girolamo di Giovanni da Camerino and Bartolomeo di Tommaso da Foligno respectively. The signed and dated altarpiece depicting the *Virgin and Child Enthroned with SS Francis, Bernard, Margaret and Catherine of Alexandria* (1462; ex-S Margherita, Gualdo Tadino; Gualdo Tadino, Pin. Com.) points to contact with Padua and the work of Mantegna. The same stylistic elements appear in his most significant work, the fresco (1468) on the end wall of the oratory of the Pellegrini, Assisi, depicting the *Virgin and Child Enthroned with SS Anthony Abbot and James and the Annunciation*. Matteo's later activity in and around Gualdo Tadino was very intense. His works include triptychs for S Nicolò (1471) and S Maria di Pastina (1477) (both Gualdo Tadino, Pin. Com.) and another for S Lorenzo in Coldellanoce, as well as numerous frescoes. Although these paintings clearly show his assimilation of the ideas and motifs of such contemporaries as Carlo Crivelli and Niccolò di Liberatori, they also utilize Late Gothic forms and rhythms. The same motifs, more crudely and expressionistically rendered, recur in the *Annunciation* and the *Tree of Jesse* (both Gualdo Tadino, Pin. Com.) and the *Meeting of Joachim and Anna* (Nocera Umbra, Pin. Com.), all executed in the last decades of the 15th century. While currently attributed to Matteo, they may have been painted by his son Girolamo da Gualdo (*fl* 1st quarter of 16th century), who, like his father, also practised as a notary, as did his own son, Bernardo da Gualdo (*fl* 1500–30).

BIBLIOGRAPHY

G. B. Cavalcaselle and J. A. Crowe: *Storia della pittura in Italia*, ix (1902), pp. 96–102
P. Scarpellini: 'Un paliotto di Matteo da Gualdo', *Paragone*, xxvii/313 (1976), pp. 54–61
G. Donnini: 'La vicenda pittorica di Matteo da Gualdo', *Gualdo Tadino* (Gualdo Tadino, 1979), pp. 81–107
F. Todini: *La pittura umbra dal duecento al primo cinquecento* (Milan, 1989), i, pp. 211–14; ii, pp. 383–6

P. SCARPELLINI

Matteo da Milano (*b* ?Milan; *fl c.* 1492–1523). Italian illuminator. He is first documented in November 1504 among the artists working on the Breviary of Ercole I d'Este (1502–5; Modena, Bib. Estense, MS. VG. 11, lat. 424). He appears in the Este accounts until 1512. Hermann identified Matteo as the illuminator of numerous historiated initials in the Breviary, as well as four full-page miniatures that were cut out of the manuscript (Zagreb, Yug. Acad. Sci. & A.). Matteo's style is characterized by a late 15th-century Lombard sense of three-dimensional form and modelling, suggesting that his earliest training took place in Milan. His use of classical motifs is often superficial and decorative. Matteo's familiarity with the prints of Albrecht Dürer is apparent in quotations in the background of the full-page miniature of the *Calling of SS Peter and Andrew* from the Breviary, in cuttings from the Hours of Alfonso I d'Este (Zagreb, Yug. Acad. Sci & A.) and in the architectural background of the miniature from the Hours of Bonaparte Ghislieri (London, BL, Yates Thompson MS. 29, fol. 74*v*). The last-mentioned manuscript also reveals Matteo's knowledge of northern manuscript traditions and has borders with *trompe l'oeil* flowers and fantastic beasts arrayed against a continuous gold background in the Flemish manner. Alexander attributed a number of manuscripts and cuttings to Matteo, including the Missal of Cardinal Arcimboldi of Milan (Milan, Bib. Capitolare, MS. II.D.I.13; *see* MASTERS, ANONYMOUS, AND MONOGRAMMISTS, §I: MASTER OF THE ARCIMBOLDI MISSAL), which he dated to *c.* 1492, and a Missal written in Rome in 1520 for Cardinal Giulio de' Medici (Berlin, Kupferstichkab., MS. 78. D. 17).

BIBLIOGRAPHY

H. J. Hermann: 'Zur Geschichte der Miniaturmalerei am Hofe der Este in Ferrara', *Jb. Ksthist. Samml. Allhöch. Ksrhaus.*, xxi (1900), pp. 117–271
J. J. G. Alexander: 'Italian Illuminated Manuscripts in British Collections', *La miniatura italiana tra gotico e rinascimento: Atti del II congresso di storia della miniatura italiana: Cortona, 1983*, i, pp. 110–13
C. M. Rosenberg: 'The Influence of Northern Graphics on Painting in Renaissance Ferrara: Matteo da Milano', *Mus. Ferrar.: Boll. Annu.*, xv (1985–7), pp. 61–74
J. J. G. Alexander: 'Matteo da Milano, Illuminator', *Pantheon*, l (1992), pp. 32–45

CHARLES M. ROSENBERG

Matteo da Viterbo. *See* GIOVANETTI, MATTEO.

Matteo de' Pasti. *See* PASTI, MATTEO DE'.

Matteo di Cione. *See* CIONE, (3).

Matteo di Giovanni (*b* Borgo Sansepolcro, *c.* 1430; *d* Siena, 1495). Italian painter. His large surviving oeuvre exemplifies the development of Sienese painting in the 15th century from an emphasis on line and pattern to an early interest in the innovations of contemporary Florentine art. It has been suggested that he was first influenced by Umbrian painting of the mid-15th century, but he was already active in Siena by the early 1450s. This was a decade of transition in the artistic life of the city after the death of Sassetta, Domenico di Bartolo and Pietro di Giovanni d'Ambrogio and before the influx of new ideas during the pontificate of Pius II. Matteo is first documented in Siena in 1452, when he was commissioned to gild an angel carved in wood by Jacopo della Quercia for Siena Cathedral. In 1457 he decorated the chapel of S Bernardino there. The modest nature of these projects suggests that he was still an apprentice. In this period he collaborated with Giovanni di Pietro (ii), the brother of il

Vecchietta, which supports the hypothesis that his early training was in the circle of il Vecchietta.

Giovanni di Pietro is known mainly through documents, and attempts to establish his artistic identity have involved works traditionally attributed to Matteo in his early period, notably the altarpiece of the *Annunciation with SS John the Baptist and Bernardino* (Siena, S Pietro Ovile; still largely *in situ*), painted in a style close to il Vecchietta. The centre panel, a copy of Simone Martini's *Annunciation* (Florence, Uffizi) from Siena Cathedral, has been attributed to Matteo by some scholars and to Giovanni by others, while the side panels of *St John the Baptist* and *St Bernardino*, which show the strong influence of Domenico di Bartolo and Pietro di Giovanni d'Ambrogio, are generally accepted as by Matteo. The archaic style of the Ovile altarpiece has certain elements in common with Matteo's first dated work, an altarpiece painted in 1460 (Siena, Mus. Opera Duomo).

Stylistic affinities are also apparent between the Ovile altarpiece panels and Matteo's predella with scenes from the *Life of St John the Baptist* and side panels with *St Peter* and *St Paul* (all Sansepolcro, Mus. Civ.), all of which once surrounded Piero della Francesca's *Baptism* (London, N.G.), works datable on stylistic grounds to the mid-1450s. A slightly later work is the altarpiece of the *Virgin and Child with SS James, Augustine, Bernardino and Margaret* (Asciano, Mus. A. Sacra). The *Annunciation* in the pinnacle, and the predella, include elements derived from Domenico di Bartolo and il Vecchietta, as well as details typical of Matteo's later works: geometric paving, fine fabrics and certain facial expressions, often melancholy.

Matteo's first dated work, the signed altarpiece of 1460, the *Virgin and Child Enthroned with SS Anthony of Padua and Bernardino and Angels* (Siena, Mus. Opera Duomo; see fig.), was recorded in 1478 in the chapel of S Antonio in the Baptistery, Siena. The pairs of angels behind the Virgin recall those in Piero della Francesca's *Baptism*, which suggests that the *Baptism* altarpiece was completed earlier. The Siena painting, with its careful depiction of space and sculptural figures, marks perhaps the most intense period in Matteo's artistic career.

Matteo, with masters of the previous generation, Giovanni di Paolo, Sano di Pietro and il Vecchietta, was commissioned by Pius II to paint two altarpieces for Pienza Cathedral (*in situ*). The first, the *Virgin and Child with SS Jerome, Ambrose, Augustine and Nicholas* (1462–4), shows a new element of fantasy, with archaeological overtones, in the throne of the Virgin. The second panel, painted somewhat later and signed, the *Virgin and Child with SS Catherine, John, Bartholomew and Lucy*, suggests a broader range of influences, particularly the manuscript illumination of Liberale da Verona, who was in Siena from 1466. The Virgin's throne is surrounded by saints clothed in dazzling colours; the drawing is softer and more flexible, elegantly defining the faces, and the graceful and delicate figures are typical of Matteo's mature works. In the *Flagellation* in the pinnacle, the floggers are an early reference to the Florentine painting of Antonio del Pollaiuolo; the figure of Christ, seen from below and slightly foreshortened, evokes the work of Piero della Francesca.

Matteo di Giovanni: *Virgin and Child Enthroned with SS Anthony of Padua and Bernardino and Angels*, oil on panel, 1460 (Siena, Museo dell'Opera del Duomo)

The delightful *Virgin and Child with Angels* (1470; Siena, Pin. N.) is still full of youthful freshness and charm, both in the delicate definition of the faces and hands and in the vivacity of the colours. The angels are reminiscent of those painted by Domenico di Bartolo in the *Madonna of Humility* (1433; Siena, Pin. N.; for illustration see DOMENICO DI BARTOLO) but with softer modelling, more fluid forms, enamel-like colours and careful attention to detail. These qualities characterize Matteo's work of the 1470s and 1480s, which is full of charm and elegance but has an increasingly narrow vision. In the 1470s he produced some of his most ambitious works, including the Placidi Altarpiece (1476) and the *St Barbara* altarpiece painted in 1479 for the bakers' guild (both Siena, S Domenico), the *Assumption* (London, N.G.) for S Agostino, Asciano, and the Cinughi Altarpiece (Siena, S Maria della Neve). All these are ornate compositions of great splendour, with a prevalence of decorative, flat forms, rather than the sense of space and volume found in his early works. He seems to have become increasingly conservative in this period, creating works of undoubted charm but somewhat insular and aristocratic in tone. This tendency may reflect the many commissions he received from noble families for pictures for private devotion, for example, two paintings of the *Virgin and Child with Saints* (both Washington, DC, N.G.A.).

In his last phase Matteo made greater use of workshop assistance to execute the increasing number of his commissions. Important works of these years include three versions of the *Massacre of the Innocents* (Naples, Capodimonte; Siena, S Maria dei Servi; Siena, S Agostino), in which his late style is clearly defined. These paintings show the high level of Matteo's final phase, the tendency to abstraction, a recurring interest in fictive bas-reliefs inspired by the beautiful stoups in Siena Cathedral attributed to Antonio Federighi, and accents of lively imagination. Among his last works are the *Virgin and Child with Saints* (Siena, Mus. Opera Duomo) for the altar of the Celsi family in Siena Cathedral, the large *St Michael* altarpiece (Montepescali, S Lorenzo), the lunette over Francesco di Giorgio Martini's *Nativity* (Siena, S Domenico) and the *Virgin and Child with Saints* (Anghiari, S Agostino). The number and importance of Matteo's commissions indicate that he was highly esteemed in his lifetime, although his reputation later was overshadowed by such contemporaries as Francesco di Giorgio Martini.

BIBLIOGRAPHY

G. Milanesi: *Documenti per la storia dell'arte senese*, 3 vols (Siena, 1854–6), ii, p. 279

S. Borghesi and L. Banchi: *Nuovi documenti per la storia dell'arte senese* (Pisa, 1898), pp. 254–5

G. F. Hartlaub: *Matteo da Siena und seine Zeit* (Strasbourg, 1910)

P. Bacci: 'I primi ricordi del pittore Matteo di Giovanni in Siena', *Riv. A.*, xi (1929), pp. 128–31

M. Gengaro: 'Matteo di Giovanni', *La Diana*, ix (1934), pp. 149–85

C. Brandi: *Quattrocentisti senesi* (Milan, 1949), pp. 142–8

J. Pope Hennessy: 'Matteo di Giovanni's *Assumption* Altarpiece', *Proporzioni*, iii (1950), pp. 81–5

——: 'A *Crucifixion* by Matteo di Giovanni', *Burl. Mag.*, cii (1960), pp. 63–7

E. Trimpi: '"Johannem Baptistam Hieronymo aequalem et non maiorem": A Predella for Matteo di Giovanni's Placidi Altarpiece', *Burl. Mag.*, cxxv (1983), pp. 457–66

C. B. Strehlke: 'Sienese Paintings in the Johnson Collection', *Paragone*, xxxvi/427 (1985), pp. 8–15

La pittura in Italia: Il quattrocento (Milan, 1987), i, pp. 329–32, 335, 337; ii, pp. 706–7 [entry by A. Angelini]

Painting in Renaissance Siena, 1420–1500 (exh. cat. by K. Christiansen, L. Kanter and C. B. Strehlke, New York, Met., 1988–9), pp. 270–81

La pittura senese del rinascimento (Milan, 1989), pp. 284–95 [entry by C. Strehlke]

P. Torriti: *La Pinacoteca Nazionale di Siena* (Genoa, 1990), pp. 258–65

GIOVANNA DAMIANI

Matteo di Nuccio Vagnoli. *See* NUTI, MATTEO.

Matteo Giovanetti. *See* GIOVANETTI, MATTEO.

Matter painting. Term applied to a style of painting that originated in Europe in the 1950s, often abstract in form, emphasizing the physical quality of thick impasto into which tactile materials such as metal, sand, shells and cement might be added. More specifically it refers to the work of Dutch painters such as Bram Bogart and Jaap Wagemaker and Belgian painters such as Bert de Leeuw (*b* 1926), René Guiette (*b* 1893) and Marc Mendelson (*b* 1915). This expressive style was not bound to any specific aesthetic and was used by each artist to different ends. In Wagemaker's *Cruel Desert* (1965; Bochum, Mus. Bochum, Kstsamml.), for example, the effect is violent and brutal through the incorporation of teeth into the composition. The works of Guiette, however, were more contemplative and abstract, intended as meditations on the nature of painting and its materials, as in *Work in White* (1958; see exh. cat.). Among the other European painters in relation to whose work the term is often used are Jean Dubuffet, Jean Fautrier, René Burri and Antoni Tàpies (for illustration *see* TÀPIES, ANTONI).

BIBLIOGRAPHY

Guiette (exh. cat. by A. Bosquet, Paris, Gal. Int. A. Contemp., 1958)

K. J. Geirlandt: *L'Art en Belgique depuis 45* (Antwerp, 1983)

□

Matteson, Tompkins Harrison (*b* Peterborough, NY, 9 May 1813; *d* Sherburne, NY, 2 Feb 1884). American painter. He lived most of his life in Sherburne, with the exception of the years 1841 to 1850, which he spent in New York, and is known primarily for his genre and historical paintings. A good draughtsman, he painted popular motifs from colonial and revolutionary history, and many of his domestic scenes were engraved for women's magazines, especially those with sentimental themes, such as *Taking the Advantage* (a courtship scene) and *The Doctor*. Two of his later works are typical of popular rural genre themes: *Justice's Court in the Backwoods* (1850; Cooperstown, NY, Mus. State Hist. Assoc.), in which the local postmaster–shoemaker is hearing a trial; and the *Turkey Shoot* (1857; Cooperstown, NY, Mus. State Hist. Assoc.), taken from James Fenimore Cooper's best-selling novel, *The Pioneers*. Matteson preferred to live in the country at Sherburne, where he brought up a large family and was active in local affairs and politics.

BIBLIOGRAPHY

A. Jones: *Rediscovered Painters of Upstate New York, 1700–1875* (Utica, 1958), pp. 65–7

ELIZABETH JOHNS

Matte' Trucco, Giacomo (*b* 1869; *d* 1934). Italian naval architect and engineer. His fame rests on a single major work, the Fiat car factory (1915–21) at Lingotto, Turin. This huge reinforced concrete structure of 400,000 sq. m was a forerunner of the concrete aesthetic of Pier Luigi Nervi and Riccardo Morandi. The enormously long, five-storey building has two daring helicoidal ramps leading to a banked test track for cars on the roof. The factory's audacious design made a tremendous impression on foreign as well as Italian observers. Le Corbusier used an illustration of the factory to demonstrate the principles set out in *Vers une architecture* (Paris, 1923), while Gruppo 7 considered it one of the few industrial buildings in Italy possessing architectural value. Although Matte' Trucco was never personally involved in the Rationalist movement, the Fiat building figured prominently in the first Esposizione dell'Architettura Razionale in Rome (1928).

BIBLIOGRAPHY

A. Pica: *Architettura moderna in Italia* (Milan, 1967)

M. Pozzetto: *La Fiat-Lingotto: Un'architettura torinese d'avanguardia* (Turin, 1975)

K. Frampton and Y. Futagawa: *Modern Architecture, 1851–1919* (New York, 1981), p. 195

LIBERO ANDREOTTI

Matthäus [Mattheus] **von Esslingen** [Esselingen]. *See* BÖBLINGER, (3).

Mattheuer, Wolfgang (*b* Reichenbach, Vogtland, 7 April 1927). German painter, printmaker and sculptor. Although self-taught as a painter, he served an apprenticeship in lithography and continued his training as a printmaker at the Hochschule in Leipzig. He taught at the Hochschule für Graphik und Buchkunst in Leipzig from 1956 to 1974, and from the 1960s he played a prominent role in the development of East German art. In order to express the dilemmas facing society and the individual in a difficult period, he made references to familiar myths, as in the *Flight of Sisyphus* (1972; Dresden, Gemäldegal. Neue Meister), and invented his own allegories; he achieved a distancing effect in these works by employing a restrained method of painting derived from poster art and characterized by smooth surfaces, sharp contours and garish, artificial colours. While referring to nature as a source of balance, he specialized in suburban landscapes that suggest opposition, tension and difficulty, as in *Bratsker Landscape* (1967; Berlin, Staatl. Museen, N.G.).

Mattheuer explored such themes in a variety of media, often using prints, including woodcuts, linocuts, lithographs and screenprints, to propose images and compositions that he later adapted to his paintings. From the 1970s he also produced sculptures, often using masks of sheep's heads to represent laziness and stupidity.

BIBLIOGRAPHY
D. Gleisberg, H. Penndorf and I. Krüger: *Wolfgang Mattheuer: Das druckgraphische Werk, 1954–1977* (Altenburg, 1977)
Wolfgang Mattheuer: Ein Künstler in der DDR (exh. cat. by U. W. Schneede and H. Schönemann, Hamburg, Kstver., 1977)
H. Schönemann: *Wolfgang Mattheuer* (Leipzig, 1988)
Wolfgang Mattheuer: Malerei, Grafik, Zeichnung, Plastik (exh. cat., E. Berlin, N.G., 1988)

GUDRUN SCHMIDT

Mattheus [Matheis; Matheus; Mathieu], **Georg** (*fl* ?1551–72). German woodcutter. Active in Augsburg and seemingly in Lyon, he worked principally after Italian masters, without developing an independent style of draughtsmanship. He carved religious and mythological subjects: his line is hard, and his figures are stiff and lifeless. Some woodcuts he signed fully, for example the chiaroscuro woodcut of the *Flight into Egypt* (Vienna, Albertina): 'JORG MATHEIS FVRMSCHNEIDER VA. AUGSPURG'; others he signed only with M, such as *Martha Leading Mary Magdalene into the Temple* (London, BM). It has been suggested that he was the artist who signed a woodcut portrait of *Martin Luther* with '*Jörg Formschneider 1551*' and who stayed in Wittenberg after 1551.

BIBLIOGRAPHY
Hollstein: *Ger.*
G. K. Nagler: *Neues allgemeines Künstler-Lexikon*, viii (Munich, 1839), pp. 433–4

VERONIKA BRAUNFELS

Matthew, Robert (Hogg). *See under* ROBERT MATTHEW, JOHNSON-MARSHALL & PARTNERS.

Matthias, Holy Roman Emperor. *See* HABSBURG, §I(12).

Matthias Corvinus, King of Hungary (*b* Klausenburg [now Cluj-Napoca], 1443; *reg* 1458–90; *d* Vienna, 1490). Hungarian patron and collector. He was the son of Governor John Hunyadi (*d* 1456) and took over both the political and cultural affairs of Hungary with great energy and determination. The buildings, collections and workshops set up by him testify to his powers of organization and co-ordination. His patronage was concerned with art as an enhancement of his nation's glory and he also exploited the decorative arts to represent the power of the state through pageants and festivals, delegations and sumptuous gifts. Owing to his patronage, Hungarian art (*see* HUNGARY, §V, 1) became pre-eminent in the cultural development of central Europe, with the early introduction of Renaissance ideas and styles drawn directly from the great Italian centres, Florence in particular.

Matthias Corvinus was driven by his own thirst for knowledge, his love of books and his passion for building and collecting. Mantegna painted his portrait (destr.), and Lorenzo de' Medici commissioned Verrocchio to make bronze reliefs of *Alexander the Great* and *Darius* (destr.) for Matthias Corvinus. He bought works abroad and set up local workshops employing both Hungarians and Italians. Local artists who trained there disseminated the new styles throughout the country, ensuring their rapid and easy assimilation. He personally directed the development of his library, employing as librarian in the 1480s a Florentine humanist, Taddeo Ugoleto, to build up the Greek and Latin holdings. The collection of Greek works allegedly made the Biblioteca Corviniana the model for Lorenzo de' Medici's library in Florence. Three manuscripts dated 1467 were copied for the King in Florence; in the 1480s many books were illuminated for him in the workshops of the most famous Florentine illuminators: Attavante degli Attavanti, Boccardino Vecchio, Gherardo and Monte di Giovanni del Foro (*see* FORO, DEL, (1) and (2)). The Buda workshop was, however, more significant for Hungarian art, as the Lombard illuminators, including Franciscus de Castello Italico de Mediolano (*fl* 1465), together with Hungarian artists in the 1480s, also worked for humanist senior clerics and lay members of the court. In the Buda workshop, the King's coat of arms was painted in every book and a special binding, often enhanced with gilding, was employed. The book collection, which was not allowed to decay after Matthias's death, was broken up and dispersed only after the Turkish victory of 1526.

The focus of Matthias Corvinus's patronage was, however, architecture. His most important work was the reconstruction of the royal palace in the castle of Buda between 1470 and 1479. Most of the Renaissance remains are Florentine in style, some echoing the forms of Brunelleschi, Alberti, Michelozzo and Bernardo Rossellino, while others show the influence of the new generation of sculptors, Desiderio da Settignano, Benedetto da Maiano and Verrocchio. Vasari records that the King's Florentine architect, Chimenti di Leonardo Camicia (1431–before 1505) remained a long time in Hungary at the head of a royal workshop including Italian, Dalmatian and Hungarian masons.

All the other buildings initiated by Matthias Corvinus mark major developments in the Hungarian Renaissance. His alterations to the summer palace at VISEGRÁD created a masterpiece of architecture terraced harmoniously into the natural surroundings; his commissions for villas, at, for example, Nyék (destr.), introduced a new genre. Sculpture was always given prominence. Most of the statues in Buda were of bronze, including six life-size or over-life-size statues (destr.) erected in the castle: *Hercules* in the monumental forecourt of the palace (a pioneering idea), two nude warriors flanking the entrance to the gatehouse, and the standing figures of the three Hunyadis (John, Ladislaus and Matthias) on the façade of the wing built by Matthias. The palace also had a bronze gate with a relief showing the *Labours of Hercules*, a frieze with battle of the Lapiths tapestry hangings designed by Antonio del Pollaiuolo for the throne and an elaborate support for a *Calvary* (Treasury, Esztergom Cathedral), attributed to the goldsmith Caradossa who worked in Buda in 1489.

Matthias Corvinus's patronage included in its scope Gothic ecclesiastical art; the impressive enlargements of the coronation church at Székesfehérvár and the foundation of the (former) Franciscan church in Klausenburg in 1486 mark the culmination of Gothic architecture in Hungary.

BIBLIOGRAPHY

J. Teleki: *A Hunyadiak kora* [The age of the Hunyadi family], 12 vols (Pest, 1853–7)
V. Fraknói: *Magyar diplomáciai emlékek Mátyás király korából* [Hungarian diplomatic documents from the age of King Matthias Corvinus], 4 vols (Budapest, 1875–8)
——: *Mathias Corvinus, König von Ungarn, 1458–1490* (Freiburg im Breisgau, 1891)
——: *Mátyás király levelei* [The letters of King Matthias Corvinus], 2 vols (Budapest, 1893–5)
E. Hoffmann: *Régli magyar bibliofilek* [Old Hungarian bibliophiles] (Budapest, 1929)
I. Lukinich, ed.: *Mátyás király emlékkönyv* [Memorial volume of King Matthias Corvinus], 2 vols (Budapest, 1940)
J. Balogh: *A művészet Mátyás király udvarában* [Art at the court of King Matthias Corvinus], 2 vols (Budapest, 1966)
C. Csapodi and K. Gárdonyi-Csapodi: *Bibliotheca Corviniana* (Budapest, 1967, rev. 4/1990; Eng. trans., 1969)
J. Balogh: 'Mattia Corvino ed il primo rinascimento ungherese', *Actes du XXIIe congrès international d'histoire de l'art: Budapest, 1969*, i, pp. 611–21; iii, pls 188–9, figs 1–6
C. Csapodi: *The Corvinian Library: History and Stock* (Budapest, 1973)
J. Balogh: *Die Anfänge der Renaissance in Ungarn: Matthias Corvinus und die Kunst* (Graz, 1975)
Matthias Corvinus und die Renaissance in Ungarn, 1458–1541 (exh. cat., Schallaburg, Schloss, 1982)
J. Balogh: *Mátyás király és a művészet* [King Matthias Corvinus and the arts] (Budapest, 1985)

GYÖNGYI TÖRÖK

Matthieu [Mathieu], **Georg David** (*b* Berlin, 20 Nov 1737; *d* Ludwigslust, 3 Nov 1778). German painter and engraver. He received his training as a painter from his father, the Prussian court painter David Matthieu (1697–1755), and his stepmother and aunt, the painter Anna Rosina Lisiewska (?1713/16–83). He apparently travelled outside Germany and is known to have gone to Stralsund with the painter Philipp Hackert in 1762. His portraits from this period, including one of *Princess Charlotte of Mecklenburg-Strelitz*, who married King George III of England, recall the style of Antoine Pesne.

Matthieu was appointed court painter to Duke Frederick of Mecklenburg-Schwerin in 1764, and he remained at the ducal residences of Ludwigslust and Schwerin until shortly before his death. The duchy of Mecklenburg-Schwerin was totally impoverished following the Seven Years' War between Prussia and Austria and cultural life at the strictly Pietist court was restricted. As court painter Matthieu was inundated with commissions for group or individual portraits of members of court society, which he executed diligently in simple, conventional compositions. The sitters always seem serenely cheerful, and Matthieu does not dwell on the rather muted splendour of court life. The paintings evoke the unworldly spirit of court Rococo, with little suggestion of any Enlightenment influence. There are only a few more probing portraits, painted in a naturalistic manner, for example *Professor A. J. D. Äpinus* and *Duchess Louise Friederica*. Although the narrow horizons of the court diminished Matthieu's creativity, he was the most important painter of 18th-century Mecklenburg. Many of his works are kept by the Staatliches Museum in Schwerin.

BIBLIOGRAPHY
Thieme–Becker

E. Steinmann and H. Witte: *Georg David Matthieu* (Leipzig, 1911)
Porträtausstellung Georg David Matthieu (exh. cat., Schwerin, Staatl. Mus., 1911)
Katalog der Malerei des 18. Jahrhunderts (exh. cat., Schwerin, Staatl. Mus., 1954)

VOLKER HELAS

Mattioli, Gianni (*b* 1903). Italian collector. He lived and worked as an economist, mainly in Milan. Mattioli began by acquiring works from an important private Italian collection that was about to be dispersed. Later he enriched his patrimony with other works, by Old Masters and modern art, until it eventually comprised *c*. 100 pieces. Apart from collecting paintings by such European artists as Henri Rousseau, Braque, Picasso, Kandinsky, Klee and Léger, he assembled the first collection of modern Italian art. For each artist Mattioli chose a few works of high quality that were representative of a particular phase of the artist's development and of the art-historical period in general. He acquired more than 30 Futurist works, including *Matter* (1912) by Umberto Boccioni, the *Interventionist Demonstration* (1914) by Carlo Carrà and the *Ballerina in Blue* (1912) by Gino Severini (all Milan, Mattioli priv. col, see 1967–72 exh. cat., pp. 19, 27 and 36). He also obtained works by other Italian artists such as de Chirico, Giorgio Morandi, Modigliani, Scipione, Ottone Rosai and Mario Sironi. After his death his collection was inherited by his daughter Laura Mattioli Rossi and remains in Milan.

WRITINGS
'Come ho formato la mia raccolta', *Biennale Venezia*, 3 (1951), pp. 25–6

BIBLIOGRAPHY

C. L. Ragghianti: *Arte moderna in una raccolta italiana* (Milan and Florence, 1953)
G. Ponti: *Milano oggi* (Milan, 1957), pp. 30–31
M. Valsecchi: *Capolavori d'arte moderna nelle raccolte private* (Turin, 1959)
Masters of Modern Italian Art from the Collection of Gianni Mattioli (exh. cat. by F. Russoli, Washington, DC, Int. Exh. Found., 1967–72)

DANIELA COIA

Mattioli, Lodovico (*b* Crevalcore, 2 Jan 1662; *d* Bologna, 20 Nov 1747). Italian painter and engraver. He was a pupil of Giuseppe Maria Crespi and was active in Bologna (where he painted a landscape fresco for the former orphanage of S Bartolomeo) and in Parma, Modena and Ferrara. Buscaroli attributed to him the *Landscape with Ploughmen* and the *Landscape with Travellers* (both Bologna, Leoni priv. col.; for illustrations, see Buscaroli). Mattioli's engravings, based on his own designs or those by other artists, among them Guido Reni, include landscapes, allegorical scenes, portraits, book illustrations and festival decorations. Most famous are his illustrations for the republication of Giulio Cesare Croce's *Bertoldo e Bertoldino* (Bologna, 1736) after an original set of etchings by Crespi. Other reproductive prints by Mattioli include the *Woman of Samaria* after Annibale Carracci, *St Jerome* and the *Agave* after Crespi (for illustrations, see Merriman), the *Immaculate Conception* after Donato Creti and numerous landscapes after Guercino.

BIBLIOGRAPHY

Bolaffi
R. Buscaroli: *Pittura di paesaggio in Italia* (Bologna, 1935), pp. 366, 377–8
M. P. Merriman: *Giuseppe Maria Crespi* (Milan, 1980), pp. 149–58, 180, 253, 268; figs 89–108, 123, 145, 148

ANNAMARIA NEGRO SPINA

Máttis Teutsch, János (*b* Braşov, 13 Aug 1884; *d* Braşov, 17 March 1960). Hungarian painter, printmaker, woodcarver, sculptor and writer. He studied at the School of Craft and Design in Budapest (1901–2), and at the Akademie der Bildenden Künste in Munich (1902–5). In 1906–8 he lived in Paris, carving picture frames. As a painter and printmaker he was influenced by the work of Matisse, Cézanne, van Gogh, Munch and Gauguin, as well as by German Expressionism. He was preoccupied with the force of colour and the effect of one colour on another. In his oil paintings, watercolours and linocuts he strove to express the emotions he experienced through landscape (e.g. *Bright Landscape*, oil on canvas, 1916; Pécs, Pannonius Mus.), but he did not go as far as Kandinsky towards total abstraction. He was associated with various avantgarde groups, including the Activists, the MA GROUP, and Der Sturm in Berlin, and he had numerous one-man shows in Europe. His *Soul Flowers* paintings of 1916–24 (e.g. *Stylized Flower, c.* 1921; Budapest, Mus. F.A.) contrasts the calm of the horizontal and the energy of the vertical with cold and warm colours and convex and concave forms, in order to explore compositional and dynamic rhythmic possibilities. He also made painted clay and wood sculptures (e.g. *Composition with Two Figures*, painted wood, h. 340 mm, 1921; Budapest, Mus. F.A.). In 1923 he became an active member of the Romanian avant-garde, and in 1925 he started working for the periodical *Integral*. His work began to show a stronger structural order and a more objective symbolic world. The human figure dominates the maquettes he made in middle age. From 1928 to 1931 he spent his summers at the NAGYBÁNYA COLONY. In his theoretical writings he revealed a similar artistic vision to that of Klee and Kandinsky; these were published under the title *Kunstideologie* (1931). He advocated an expressionist musicality and a lyrical abstraction. Between 1930 and 1940 he designed murals (unexecuted) on the themes of work and motherhood. During World War II he gave up working, but between 1945 and 1948 he began a realistic period with Surrealist elements; his work in the early 1950s became more realist in accordance with the official cultural policy of the period.

WRITINGS
Kunstideologie. Stabilität und Aktivität im Kunstwerk (Potsdam, 1931)

BIBLIOGRAPHY
L. Kassák: *Máttis Teutsch János* (diss., Loránd Eötvös U., Budapest, 1917)
Z. Banner: *Máttis Teutsch* (Bucharest, 1974)
K. Passuth: 'Les Oeuvres de Mattis Teutsch au Musée de Beaux-Arts', *Bull. Mus. F.-A.*, xlv–xlvi (1977), pp. 105–34
J. Szabó: *Máttis Teutsch* (Budapest, 1983) [incl. Ger. summary]

ÉVA BAJKAY

Mattoir [macehead]. Printmaking tool with a rounded spiked head, used particularly for STIPPLE engraving.

☐

Matvejs, Voldemārs Hans. *See* MARKOV, VLADIMIR.

Matveyev, Aleksandr (Terent'yevich) (*b* Saratov, 25 Aug 1878; *d* Moscow, 22 Oct 1960). Russian sculptor. He studied at the Moscow School of Painting, Sculpture and Architecture (1899–1902) under Sergey Volnukhin (1859–1921) and Paolo Troubetskoy. He took part in the World of Art and Blue Rose exhibitions. The influence of the impressionistic sculpture of Troubetskoy is particularly noticeable in Matveyev's early works (e.g. the sculpture of the painter *Viktor Borisov-Musatov*, plaster, 1900; Moscow, Tret'yakov Gal.). Matveyev borrowed from this impressionism a sensitivity to texture and to the 'breathing' surface of forms, and from Symbolism and Art Nouveau an inclination towards images of sleep and of outward contentment along with inward anxiety, a shaky equilibrium on the boundaries of dream and reality, life and a deathly torpor. Although as a result Matveyev was called the 'Russian Maillol', his work is nearer to the painting of Gauguin and the sculpture of George Minne. The figures of naked adolescent boys (marble and Inkerman stone, 1908–11; destr.; fragments in St Petersburg, Rus. Mus.) that decorated the villa of Ya. Ye. Zhukovsky in Kuchukskoye, Crimea, evoke a mood of harmony ineluctably merged with an an anxious longing, as does the sleeping figure of a boy (granite, 1910) that decorates the gravestone of Borisov-Musatov in Tarusa near Moscow. The latter not only conveys magnificently the melancholic spirit of Borisov-Musatov's work but also shows a virtuoso use of texture and the exploitation of *nonfinito* effects.

After the October Revolution of 1917 Matveyev took part in Lenin's plan of monumental propaganda, sculpting a monument to *Karl Marx* (plaster, 1918; destr.) in Petrograd (now St Petersburg) that is impressive in its energy and its terse generalization of forms. Neo-classical tendencies are seen in the harmoniously balanced group *October* (plaster, 1927; St Petersburg, Rus. Mus.; bronze cast, 1958), in which a soldier, a peasant and a worker depicted according to the principle of 'heroic nudity' symbolize the three leading social strengths of the Revolution. The classicism of Matveyev's work is never purely stylized and external but underpins the architectonics and inner grandeur of real-life subjects, as in the remarkable bronze figure of the *Standing Woman* (1937; St Petersburg, Rus. Mus.), in which the Classical compositional canon is combined naturally with modest, everyday sentiments and a heroic, vital energy.

Against the background of the pompous decorative tendencies that permeated Russian sculpture between the 1930s and the 1950s, Matveyev's work represents an example of great artistic integrity. In the *Self-portrait* (bronze, 1939; St Petersburg, Rus. Mus.) the features of a death-mask are dramatically combined with a penetratingly lively gaze. Matveyev's plans for monumental works at that time remained unrealized, but his sketches of monuments acquired an independent significance, subdued and inwardly expressive, and in particular in the 1940s and 1950s he turned more than once to the image of the poet

Aleksandr Pushkin, bringing out the psychological characteristics with particular clarity. In the 1920s Matveyev worked for the Petrograd State porcelain factory (after 1925 the Lomonosov porcelain factory), making refined small-scale sculptures and producing variations on the nude female figure. Matveyev's oeuvre is comparatively small in volume, but he had an enormous influence on Russian art, and he taught numerous sculptors at the Academy of Arts, Leningrad (now St Petersburg), from 1918 to 1948 and at the Surikov Art Institute, Moscow.

BIBLIOGRAPHY

A. I. Bassekhes: *A. T. Matveyev* (Moscow, 1960)

A. T. Matveyev: Výstavka proizvedeniy k 100-letiyu so dnya rozhdeniya [A. T. Matveyev: exhibition to mark the 100th anniversary of his birth] (exh. cat., Leningrad, Rus. Mus., 1978)

Ye. B. Murina, ed.: *Aleksandr Matveyev* (Moscow, 1979) [with illus.]

M. N. SOKOLOV

Matveyev, Andrey (*b* 1701/2; *d* St Petersburg, 4 May 1739). Russian painter. In 1716 he received a grant to visit Holland, and from 1717 he studied art in Amsterdam under Arnold Boonen and at the Koninklijke Academie voor Schone Kunsten in Antwerp. While still a student he painted an *Allegory of Painting* (1725) and *Venus and Cupid* (?1726; both St Petersburg, Rus. Mus.), which show that he had already absorbed much of the technique and style of European painting, an achievement of great importance to the development of a new style in Russian art.

Matveyev returned to Russia in 1727 and became a member of the Office of Buildings in St Petersburg, receiving the title of Master in 1731. For nine years he was head of the department of painting there. He was an outstanding director, proposing and advising on the numerous monumental and decorative projects for the churches and palaces in St Petersburg and its suburbs, as well as Moscow; he also concerned himself with the decoration of triumphal arches. His surviving monumental and decorative works, including those in the Cathedral of SS Peter and Paul in St Petersburg, reveal the influence of European Baroque. Matveyev's portraits, together with those of Ivan Nikitin, mark a new stage in the development of Russian art. These include a portrait of *Peter I* (St Petersburg, Hermitage), based on an original by Karel de Moor. An assured self-confidence is detectable in the *Self-portrait with the Artist's Wife* (?1729; St Petersburg, Rus. Mus.), executed in a spirited painterly manner, while a relatively complex characterization is attempted in the companion portraits of *Ivan Golitsyn* and his wife *Anastasiya* (both 1728; Moscow, priv. col., see Il'ina and Rimskaya-Korsakova, pls 42 and 43).

BIBLIOGRAPHY

N. Moleva and E. Belyutin: *Zhivopisnykh del mastera: Kantselyariya ot stroyeniy i russkaya zhivopis' pervoy poloviny XVIII veka* [Masters of painting: the Office of Buildings and Russian painting in the first half of the 18th century] (Moscow, 1965)

T. V. Il'ina and S. V. Rimskaya-Korsakova: *Andrey Matveyev* (Moscow, 1984)

O. S. Yevangulova: *Izobrazitel'noye iskusstvo v Rossii pervoy chertverti XVIII veka: Problemy stanovleniya khudozhestvennykh printsipov Novogo vremeni* [The fine arts in Russia in the first quarter of the 18th century: problems of establishing the artistic principles of the modern age] (Moscow, 1987)

ANDREY A. KAREV

Matveyev, Fyodor (Mikhaylovich) (*b* St Petersburg, 1758; *d* Rome, 1826). Russian painter. In 1764 he was enrolled at the newly opened Educational College attached to the St Petersburg Academy of Arts, and he later studied in the academy's landscape class, in 1776 under Semyon Fyodorovich Shchedrin (1745–1804). On completing his academy studies in 1778 he was acclaimed the best student of his year, and he received the major gold medal for landscape painting. In 1779 he received a grant to study in Rome, where he remained based for the rest of his life. During the first years of his stay in Italy, Matveyev copied works by the German landscape painter Philipp Hackert, who also advised him. In 1807 Matveyev was awarded the title of Academician in St Petersburg for his painting *View of the Environs of Naples* (1806; St Petersburg, Rus. Mus.).

In 1809 Matveyev received a pension from the Russian state and began to travel around Italy and Switzerland, accompanied by Russian aristocrats, many of whom provided him with commissions. The general European enthusiasm for Italy ensured the popularity of Matveyev's landscape views, but he remained dependent on the dominant conception of the Italian countryside as a type of grandiose open-air museum, full of scenes informed by both historical memory and the artistic associations connected with Nicolas Poussin and Claude Lorrain. Matveyev's work tends to repeat the same formula and thus is characterized by symmetry of construction, the use of decorative silhouettes of trees as a framing device in the foreground, a moderately bright middle plane and a background in the form of a hilly ridge painted in much cooler tones. Such pictures as *View of Lake Maggiore* (1808), *View of Lake Nemi near Rome* (1821; both St Petersburg, Rus. Mus.) and *View of Rome, Colosseum* (1816; Moscow, Tret'yakov Gal.) typify this approach. Of the Russian landscape artists of his period, Matveyev was the most consistently classicist. Although his landscape views lack an element of mythology, they retain a sense of the magic of the perfection of architectonic and decorative order.

BIBLIOGRAPHY

A. A. Fyodorov-Davydov: 'Fyodor Matveyev', *Russkiy peyzazh XVIII—nachala XX veka* [Russian landscape painting from the 18th century to the beginning of the 20th century] (Moscow, 1986), pp. 51–78

M. M. ALLENOV

Matyushin, Mikhail (Vasil'yevich) (*b* Nizhny Novgorod, 1861; *d* Leningrad [now St Petersburg], 14 Oct 1934). Russian painter, patron, musician, writer and publisher. He pursued a highly original line of artistic thought and practice and developed an organic perception of the world, deriving his inspiration from nature rather than machines, unlike many of his Russian Constructivist contemporaries.

Matyushin trained initially as a musician at the Moscow Conservatory (1878–81) and played the violin in the Court orchestra in St Petersburg from 1881 to 1913. In 1889 he began to attend the School of the Society for the Encouragement of the Arts in St Petersburg, where he studied painting with Yan Tsionglinsky (*d* 1914). In Tsionglinsky's studio he met the artist and writer Yelena Guro, whom he married. Later (1906–8) he studied with the World of Art (Mir Iskusstva) painters Léon Bakst and Mstislav Dobuzhinsky at the Zvantseva School of Art in St Petersburg.

In 1909 Matyushin briefly joined the circle around Nikolay Kul'bin and the following year he founded the UNION OF YOUTH (Soyuz Molodyozhi) group with Guro. He contributed only occasionally to Union of Youth exhibitions (1911, 1913–14). After meeting Malevich and the Futurist poets Aleksey Kruchonykh and Vladimir Mayakovsky in 1912, Matyushin's and Guro's flat became an important meeting place and intellectual centre for the avant-garde. In the summer of 1913 the first congress of Russian Futurists, attended by Malevich and Kruchonykh, was held at Matyushin's *dacha* in Uuskirkko, Finland. Matyushin had contributed to Futurist publications such as the first volume of *Sadok sudey* ('Trap for judges'; St Petersburg, 1912) and in 1913 he set up his own imprint, Crane (Zhuravl'), under which he published several works including *The Three* in memory of Guro, who died that year. He also published the second volume of *Sadok sudey* (1913) and Malevich's *From Cubism and Futurism to Suprematism* (1915). In 1913 Matyushin composed the music for the Futurist opera *Victory over the Sun*, for which Velimir Khlebnikov had written the prologue, Kruchonykh the libretto, and for which Malevich had designed the sets and costumes. The following year he composed the music for Kruchonykh's *Conquered War*.

In 1913 Matyushin edited and published a translation of Albert Gleizes's and Jean Metzinger's *Du Cubisme*. He also wrote and published an extended commentary on the book's central ideas, in which he linked Cubism firmly to the concept of the FOURTH DIMENSION as formulated by the Russian philosopher Pyotr Uspensky. This commentary provides an important indication of how Cubism was interpreted by some painters of the Russian avant-garde, including Malevich, and highlights Matyushin's concern over the next ten years with the spatial and spiritual realities of the fourth dimension and its place in art.

Matyushin's early interest in the growth of organic form led him to study the roots and branches of trees. He showed some of these studies in 1911 at the Union of Youth exhibition, arguing that these forms were the most perfect manifestation of growth and the movement of matter. The perception of such growth entailed the development of what Matyushin called 'spatial realism'. This was intimately bound up with his system of extended vision called *zorved* ('see–know'). *Zorved* combined the development of man's physical vision with that of his spiritual intuition, ultimately releasing him from the spiritual and physical cage of three dimensions. Matyushin argued that the current perception of three-dimensional space was inadequate because it was unidirectional, limited by the position of the eyes in the front of the head. To appreciate space fully, man had to acquire total vision encompassing 360°, which would be directionless and therefore limitless. The artist was to develop this awareness through physical exercise of the eyes and spiritual discipline, and then to depict this totality of vision in his work. Through this intensified awareness of three-dimensional space, a further fourth dimension would become perceptible.

Matyushin attempted to express his ideas in paintings such as *Movement in Space* (1917–18; St Petersburg, Rus. Mus.), where a swathe of coloured bands moves diagonally across a white ground, the combinations and variations within the banding producing dynamic energy across the plane of the canvas. *Painterly Musical Construction* (1918; Athens, George Costakis priv. col.) has a far more rhythmical and swirling sense of space, built up from myriad touches of bright colour; it expresses Matyushin's interest in the analogy between the abstract expressive language of painting and that of music. In 1923 Matyushin exhibited an intricately constructed wooden cube, extended on all sides as if a hypercube, to demonstrate how an object grows into another dimension. This experiment in spatial realism was clearly related to such paintings as *Crystal* (1919–20; Moscow, Tret'yakov Gal.; see fig.), in which the facets of rectilinear form are evidently intended to evoke the growth of a crystal developing simultaneously in all directions; here Matyushin suggests the fourth dimension through the intense expression of three-dimensional space.

Matyushin taught in the State Free Art Studios (Svomas) in Petrograd (now St Petersburg) and later in the painting department of the Academy of Arts, where he organized his studio of spatial realism (1918–26). He also directed the Department of Organic Culture at the Petrograd State Institute of Artistic Culture (Ginkhuk), where he continued to develop his theories of *zorved*. His concern for underlying organic unity led him to investigate the interrelationship of form and colour, and its physical and psychological effect on the viewer. In 1932 his research into colour was published as *Zakonomernost' izmenyayemosti tsvetovykh sochetaniy: Spravochnik po tsvetu* [The laws governing the variability of colour combinations: a reference book on colour] (Moscow and Leningrad, 1932).

Mikhail Matyushin: *Crystal*, oil and paper on canvas, 680×500 mm, 1919–20 (Moscow, Tret'yakov Gallery)

Matyushin was preparing a second volume for publication when he died.

WRITINGS

'O knige Gleza i Metsanzhe *o Kubisme*' [Concerning Gleizes's and Metzinger's book *Du Cubisme*], *Soyuz Molodyozhi*, 3 (1913), pp. 25–34; Eng. trans. in L. Henderson: *The Fourth Dimension and Non-Euclidean Geometry in Modern Art* (Princeton, 1983), pp. 368–75

'An Artist's Experience of the New Space', *The Structurist*, xv–xvi (1975–6), pp. 74–7

BIBLIOGRAPHY

L. Zhadova: 'Tsvetovaya sistema Matyushina' [Matyushin's colour system], *Iskusstvo* (1974), no. 8, pp. 38–42

A. Povelikhina: 'Matyushin's Spatial System', *The Structurist*, xv–xvi (1975–6), pp. 64–71

C. Lodder: *Russian Constructivism* (New Haven, 1983), chap. 7

A. Z. Rudenstine, ed.: *Russian Avant-garde Arts: The George Costakis Collection* (London, 1983), pp. 268–322

CHRISTINA LODDER

Mauch, Daniel (*b* ?Ulm, 1477; *d* Liège, 16 Nov 1540). German wood-carver and sculptor. He was a master in Ulm by 1503. His earliest authenticated work, an altar depicting the *Holy Family* (1510; Bieselbach, Chapel), has distinctly contemporary features such as the use of an advanced altar form, Renaissance decoration and unpainted figures. However, in his next altar, dedicated to *St Sebastian* (*c.* 1520; Geislingen, St Maria), he reverted to a conventional Late Gothic chapel shrine. In 1529 Mauch left Ulm, where the Reformation had spawned a hostility to images, and settled in Liège. Here he made and signed

Christoph Maucher: *Triumph of Emperor Leopold I and his Son Joseph I*, ivory with ebony base, 1700 (Vienna, Kunsthistorisches Museum)

a small *Virgin and Child* for the monk Berselius (1529–35; Liège, Mus. A. Rélig. A. Mosan), the finest example of his use of the 'parallel fold' style of drapery. Most of his work in the southern Netherlands was in stone, as impressively demonstrated by the tombstone of *Abbot Jean de Coronmeuse* (ex-St Jacques, Liège; Paris, Louvre) attributed to him. Several small sculptures closely influenced by Conrat Meit must also date from this period. Moreover, the stylistic peculiarities of some goldsmith pieces suggest that Mauch prepared models for them.

BIBLIOGRAPHY

G. Otto: *Die Ulmer Plastik der Spätgotik*, vii of *Tübinger Forschungen zur Archäologie und Kunstgeschichte* (Reutlingen, 1927), pp. 310–27

L. Göbel: *Beiträge zur Ulmer Plastik der Spätgotik*, xiii of *Tübinger Forschungen zur Kunstgeschichte* (Tübingen, 1956), pp. 9–24

S. Wagini: *Der Ulmer Bildschnitzer Daniel Mauch (1477–1540)*; Forsch. Gesch. Stadt Ulm (Stuttgart, 1995)

SUSANNE WAGINI

Maucher. German family of ivory-, amber- and wood-carvers. Johann Georg Maucher (*b* Osterhofen, 1604; *d* Schwäbisch Gmünd, 1680) was a wood-carver who specialized in decorating the stocks of muskets. Of his sons, (1) (Johann) Christoph Maucher and (2) Johann Michael Maucher both followed in their father's profession and also extended their work into other media.

(1) (Johann) Christoph Maucher (*b* Schwäbisch Gmünd, 24 Oct 1642; *d* after 1721). He moved to Danzig (now Gdansk, Poland) *c.* 1670 and practised there until 1705, when continuing protests from the city's guilds forced him to leave. His earliest known work is an ivory group of *Hercules Overpowering the Hydra of Lerna and the Nemean Lion* (1682; Berlin, Skulpgal.), in which the combatants are locked together in bitter struggle. Maucher's only signed work is an elaborate allegorical group in ivory on an ebony base set with ivory reliefs, which depicts the *Triumph of Emperor Leopold I and his Son Joseph I* (1700; Vienna, Ksthist. Mus.; see fig.). It was made in celebration of Leopold's victory over the Turks and Hungarians, which culminated in the Treaty of Karlowitz (1699). Above the turmoil of Turks and various allegorical figures, which include *Falsehood* and *Malevolence*, the enthroned Leopold and his designated successor hold sway under the imperial eagle, seen clutching a turban and crescent (symbols of the defeated Turks) in its talons. All the figures in this ivory group are remarkably stocky in their proportions.

During his time in Danzig Maucher learnt the art of amber-carving, perhaps from Nikolaus Turow. He may have participated in making the amber chair (1677) given to Leopold by Elector Frederick III of Brandenburg, of which only fragments survive (Vienna, Ksthist. Mus.). Other works in amber attributed to Maucher include statuettes of *Dido* and *Cleopatra* (Vienna, Ksthist. Mus.) and two Old Testament heroines, *Judith* and *Jael* (Modena, Gal. & Mus. Estense).

(2) Johann Michael Maucher (*b* Schwäbisch Gmünd, 16 Aug 1645; *d* Würzburg, 1701). Brother of (1) Christoph Maucher. In 1688 he left Schwäbisch Gmünd, ostensibly because of his immoral conduct, to work in Augsburg, where he presented Emperor Leopold with a musket he had decorated. In 1693 he settled in Würzburg, where he remained. Over 30 hunting guns decorated and signed by Maucher survive (examples Munich, Bayer. Nmus.; Vienna, Ksthist. Mus.; Karlsruhe, Bad. Landesmus.; New York, Met.; and elsewhere). Such guns were made as collectors' items rather than for hunting itself: the high relief of the ivory plaquettes mounted on their stocks would have been damaged had they been used. Maucher's subject-matter for his ivory reliefs mostly derives from 16th- and 17th-century prints by such artists as Jost Amman, Adriaen Collaert (*c.* 1560–1618) and Phillip Galle. The characteristic features of his works can be seen on the fruitwood stock of one musket in Vienna (Ksthist. Mus.): the stock is carved and also decorated with ivory plaquettes of hunting scenes and two larger reliefs of the Roman hero Marcus Curtius (after a print by Amman) and *Pluto and Proserpina* (see fig.). The powerfully modelled nudes with their voluptuously swelling forms are in keeping with the contemporary German Baroque style.

Maucher also decorated dishes, pots and bowls with hunting scenes. He sometimes described himself as a sculptor, and although no large-scale works by him had been identified by the 1990s, contemporary documents suggest that in 1696–7 he produced sculptures for the monastery at Oberzell. The decoration on the organ loft

Johann Michael Maucher: *Pluto and Proserpina*, ivory plaquette on a carved fruitwood musket stock, l. 1.05 m, 1670–80 (Vienna, Kunsthistorisches Museum)

of the cathedral of the Holy Cross in Schwäbisch Gmünd may also be his work.

BIBLIOGRAPHY

W. Klein: *Johann Michael und Christoph Maucher, zwei Gmünder Elfenbein Schnitzer des Barock* (Schwäbisch Gmünd, 1920)

——: 'Die Elfenbeinschnitzerfamilie Maucher', *Gmünd. Heimatbl.* (1933)

R. Verres: 'Der Elfenbein- und Bernsteinschnitzer Christoph Maucher', *Pantheon*, xii (1933), pp. 244–6

S. V. Grancsay: 'Carved Gunstocks by Johann Michael Maucher', *J. Walters A.G.*, ii (1939), pp. 43–53

E. Petrasch: 'Über einige Jagdwaffen mit Elfenbeinschnitzerei im Badischen Landesmuseum: Marginalien zum Werk des Büchsenschäfters Johann Michael Maucher', *Waf.- & Kostknd* (1960), pp. 11–26

C. Theuerkauff: 'Kaiser Leopold im Triumph wider die Türken: Ein Denkmal in Elfenbein von Christoph Maucher, Danzig', *Hamburg. Mittel- & Ostdt. Forsch.*, iv (1963), pp. 61–93

H. Schedelmann: *Die grossen Büchsenmacher* (Brunswick, 1972)

Barockplastik in Norddeutschland (exh. cat., ed. J. Rasmussen; Hamburg, Mus. Kst & Gew., 1977)

M. Trusted: 'Four Amber Statuettes by Christoph Maucher', *Pantheon*, xlii/3 (1984), pp. 245–50

JOHANNES RAMHARTER

Mauclair, Camille [Faust, Séverin] (*b* Paris, 29 Dec 1872; *d* Paris, 23 April 1945). French writer, theorist and critic. Writing under the pseudonym of Camille Mauclair, his first book was *Eleusis* (1894). Though a comparative latecomer to Symbolism, he here expounded his version of its aesthetic. He broadly defined the symbol as 'tout ce qui paraît' and emphasized the importance of the dream. Mostly the work is influenced by Stéphane Mallarmé, whom he greatly admired, and is, in its philosophical aspects, derived from Arthur Schopenhauer. He was sympathetic to the Pre-Raphaelites, Edward Burne-Jones and others in England, and saw the Symbolists as achieving similar results in France.

Throughout his life Mauclair remained dogmatically entrenched within a Symbolist perspective. He admired the Impressionists whilst hoping that their stylistic innovations could be turned to Symbolist effect. In 1892 he took over the *Mercure de France* from Albert Aurier and rapidly used his column to attack Post-Impressionists such as Gauguin, Cézanne and others. Later he saw himself as engaged in a crusade against modern art and as a defender of the French tradition, *La Farce de l'art vivant* (1929–30) being the clearest example of this. He hysterically attacked everything from Fauvism onwards, though the criticism is notably uninformed. He used the terms 'fauve' and even 'cubisto-fauve' as generic forms of abuse, whilst suspecting art dealers of a subversive conspiracy to undermine public taste. His literary output remained prodigious until his death.

WRITINGS

Eleusis (Paris, 1894)

Servitude et grandeur littéraires (Paris, 1922)

La Farce de l'art vivant (Paris, 1929–30)

BIBLIOGRAPHY

G. J. Aubry: *Camille Mauclair* (Paris, 1905)

A. G. Lehmann: *The Symbolist Aesthetic in France, 1885–1895* (Oxford, 1968)

Maufe, Sir **Edward (Brantwood)** (*b* Ilkley, Yorks, 12 Dec 1883; *d* Shepherd's Hill, Buxted, E. Sussex, 12 Dec 1974). English architect. He was articled to William A. Pite in 1899 before going up to St John's College, Oxford, in 1904. His first major commission, Kelling Hall (1912) at

Kelling, Norfolk, for Sir Henry Deterding shows his early links with the Arts and Crafts Movement. After service in World War I, he came to prominence in 1924 with his design for the Palace of Industry at the British Empire Exhibition, Wembley (1924–5). Two churches, St Bede's (1922–3), Clapham, London, and St Saviour's (1924–6), Acton, London, are of the simplified Gothic Revival kind and show affinities with contemporary Swedish architecture, of which Maufe was a constant champion.

Maufe's domestic work of the inter-war period had a stylish 'alternative' modernity in direct contrast with the new functionalism. His interiors show built-in fitments and pastel colour schemes, with silver-lacquered furniture and mirrors: characteristic works are Yaffle Hill (1929), Broadstone, Dorset, and the Studio for Religious Services (1931; destr.) at Broadcasting House, London. In 1932 Maufe won the competition for the new Guildford Cathedral (1936–61), Surrey, with a design that carried the simplification of Gothic forms still further than Giles Gilbert Scott's Liverpool Cathedral (initially designed 1903). Its effect of monumentality and austerity, of building anew on tradition, with references to the English Gothic are characteristics of Maufe's work. He was chief architect to the Imperial War Graves Commission (1941–69), and after World War II rebuilt Gray's Inn and Middle Temple in London in a scholarly Neo-Georgian style. In 1944 he received the Royal Gold Medal for Architecture, and he was knighted in 1954.

WRITINGS
Modern Church Architecture (London, 1946)

BIBLIOGRAPHY
DNB
Obituary, *Building*, ccxxvii (1974), p. 27
Obituary, *Architects' J.*, clxi (1975), pp. 67–8
J. Cornforth: 'Shepherd's Hill', *Country Life* (9 Oct 1975), pp. 906–9

MARGARET RICHARDSON

Maufra, Maxime(-Camille-Louis) (*b* Nantes, 17 May 1861; *d* Poncé, Sarthe, 23 May 1918). French painter and printmaker. He began painting under the guidance of local painters in Nantes such as the brothers Charles Leduc (*b* 1831) and Alfred Leduc (*c.* 1850–1913) and the landscape painter Charles Le Roux (1841–95). Having originally intended to go into business, he turned to painting after a visit in 1883 to Britain, where he first saw the work of Turner. He exhibited for the first time in 1886 at Nantes and in the Paris Salon with critical approval. He travelled throughout Brittany and met Gauguin at Pont-Aven in 1890. Maufra settled in Paris in 1892 at the Bateau-Lavoir but returned to Brittany each year, in particular to the Quiberon region. In 1894 Le Barc de Boutteville mounted an exhibition of his work which revealed his individual talents to a wider public. He subsequently exhibited with Durand-Ruel, to whom he remained under contract for the rest of his life. His art was enriched by his travels in the Dauphiné (1904), the Midi (1912), Algeria (1913) and Savoy (1914), and also by his exploration of etching and lithography.

Maufra painted primarily landscapes and marine views. He was influenced initially by Impressionism, although he completely rejected the Impressionists' investigation of instantaneous sensations. For some time he was affected by meeting the artists of the Pont-Aven school, and he retained a pronounced liking for synthesis, strong colour and powerful drawing. These qualities are most strikingly evident in his prints and drawings. Maufra remained an independent and intuitive painter wedded to recording the truths of nature.

BIBLIOGRAPHY
V. E. Michelet: *Maufra: Peintre et graveur* (Paris, 1908)
A. Alexandre: *Maxime Maufra: Peintre marin et rustique* (Paris, 1926)
D. Morane: *Maufra: Catalogue de l'oeuvre gravé* (Pont-Aven, 1986)
P. Ramade: *Maufra Maufra* (Douarnenez, 1988)

PATRICK RAMADE

Mauger, Jean (*b* Dieppe, *c.* 1648; *d* Paris, 9 Sept 1722). French medallist. He worked at the Paris mint from 1685 until his death. The most prolific and technically accomplished medallist of his generation, he was responsible for 250 of the 286 medals reproduced in the medallic history of Louis XIV, published in 1702. He provided his own portraits for these medals (and for his earlier large-scale ones); their reverses, however, are skilful renditions of detailed drawings by Sébastien Le Clerc the elder (London, BL, Add. MSS 31.908) and Antoine Coypel (Paris, Acad. Inscr. & B.-Lett.), on behalf of the Petite Académie. Mauger's brilliantly successful image of *Louis XIV*, shown in profile to the left, laureate and wearing Roman armour, was used with a number of the reverse dies produced for the large-scale series of medals executed in the late 1680s and early 1690s and was imitated by medallists throughout Europe. Examples of Mauger's medals are in the British Museum, London, and in the Bibliothèque Nationale, Cabinet des Médailles, Paris.

BIBLIOGRAPHY
Thieme–Becker
Médailles sur les principaux événements du règne de Louis Le Grand, Académie des Inscriptions (Paris, 1702)
A. Jal: *Dictionnaire critique de biographie et d'histoire* (Paris, 1867, 2/1872)
J. J. Guiffrey: 'Jean Mauger', *Rev. Numi.* (1889), pp. 273–309
La Médaille au temps de Louis XIV (exh. cat., ed. J. Jacquiot; Paris, Hôtel de la Monnaie, 1979), pp. 175–201

MARK JONES

Maugis, Claude, Abbé (*b c.* 1600; *d* 12 July 1658). French administrator, collector and amateur artist. He was Trésorier and Surintendant des Bâtiments to the Regent, Marie de' Medici, and Conseiller from 1630 to her son Louis XIII. Maugis was considered a great collector and is known to have had a large and beautifully arranged cabinet of *objets d'art*, paintings, prints and cameos as well as a library. He may have influenced the taste of Armand-Jean du Plessis de Richelieu who, as Surintendant of Marie's household, worked with Maugis at the Palais du Luxembourg, Paris, in the 1620s. In 1650 Roger de Piles saw Peter Paul Rubens's oil sketches for the *Life of Marie de' Medici* cycle in Maugis's collection. Although none of the extant sketches has a provenance that can be traced back to him, it is entirely possible that some were once in his possession. As Surintendant des Bâtiments to Marie, Maugis was responsible for her artistic commissions, and advised her to choose Rubens to paint the *Life of Marie de' Medici* cycle (1622–5; Paris, Louvre) for the Luxembourg, declaring that he was the only painter in Europe capable of carrying through such an ambitious project. Rubens's correspondence reveals Maugis's role as a go-between—transmitting Richelieu's decisions concerning the cycle's iconography, urging Rubens on, sending measurements to Antwerp, vetting sketches and even suggesting details (although his proposal of the zodiacal sign of Taurus for the *Birth of Marie* was rejected). As Richelieu cooled in 1625 over the proposal that Rubens also paint the *Life of Henry IV* cycle, Maugis delayed writing to the artist and angered him by altering the specifications. The project was dropped, but Rubens nevertheless described Maugis as courteous, good and sincere, though dilatory, and reported that when Louis XIII first viewed the *Life of Marie de' Medici* Maugis interpreted the controversial subjects 'with a most skillful alteration and concealment of its true meaning'. Maugis was in fact probably involved in the substitution of the anodyne *Felicity of the Regency* (*see* HISTORY PAINTING, fig. 2), for a politically risky proposal, the *Flight of Marie*.

Félibien records that Maugis was pleased by Philippe de Champaigne's decorative paintings (*c.* 1622–6) at the Palais du Luxembourg under the direction of Nicolas Duchesne, and that he recalled Champaigne from Brussels in 1628 to succeed Duchesne as Premier Peintre to Marie. Champaigne's subsequent portrait of *Claude Maugis* (1630) was engraved by Lucas Vorsterman (i). After Maugis's death, his collection of prints and drawings by Dürer went to his friend Michel de Marolles; a small group of drawings by Dürer (Paris, Bib. N.), which includes the *Water-mill near Nuremberg*, are believed to have once formed part of Maugis's collection.

BIBLIOGRAPHY

A. Félibien: *Entretiens sur les vies et les ouvrages des plus excellens peintres anciens et modernes* (Paris, 1666–8, rev. 1725/R London, 1967)
C. de Ris: *Les Amateurs d'autrefois* (Paris, 1877)
E. Bonnaffé: *Dictionnaire des amateurs français au XVIIe siècle* (Paris, 1884), pp. 207–8
M. Rooses and C. Ruelens, eds: *Correspondance de Rubens*, iii (Antwerp, 1898)
R. S. Magurn, ed.: *The Letters of Peter Paul Rubens* (Cambridge, MA, 1955)
J. Thuiller and J. Foucart: *Rubens's 'Life of Marie de' Medici'* (New York, 1969)

ANNE THACKRAY

Maulbertsch [Maulpertsch], **Franz Anton** (*b* Langenargen am Bodensee, 7 June 1724; *d* Vienna, 7 Aug 1796). Austrian painter. His work as a painter of both oil paintings and frescoes on religious, mythological and occasionally worldly themes spanned the second half of the 18th century, adapting a Late Baroque training to the onset of Neo-classicism but remaining strikingly individual throughout. His fresco work, mostly still *in situ* in widespread central European locations, came at the end of an artistic tradition and was for long neglected, being far from major cultural centres; but it is now seen to establish him as one of the leading painters of his century and a colourist comparable to Giambattista Tiepolo.

1. LIFE AND WORK.

(*i*) *To 1765*. After training with his father, Anton Maulbertsch (1684–1748), he studied in Vienna at the Akademie Kaiserliche (1739–45 and 1749–50) and also, apparently, with the painter Peter van Roy (*c.* 1706–45) with whom he lodged in the city. The *Adoration of the Magi* (1745–50; Cluj, Romania, St Michael), with its wild flares of lighting, diagonal composition and interest in eccentric detail,

shows Maulbertsch's early style, influenced by the Akademie and in particular by the work of his teacher Paul Troger. Maulbertsch's painting the *Academy with its Attributes at the Feet of Minerva* (untraced; grisaille sketch, Munich, priv. col.; see Garas, 1960, pl. 15) was awarded first prize in the Akademie competition of 1750.

Maulbertsch's first independent frescoes, for the Piaristenkirche of Maria Treu in Vienna (1752–3), have a visionary, passionate expression and make dynamic use of illusionistic architecture, especially in the *Glory of the Virgin* in the central dome. A more relaxed, Rococo style appears in the ceiling paintings for Schloss Suttner at Ebenfurth, Lower Austria (1754), with their lighter colours and playful execution. Those in the church of Heiligenkreuz–Gutenbrunn, Lower Austria (1757; *see* AUSTRIA, fig. 15) present an extraordinary aerial choreography in the *Finding of the True Cross*. Altar paintings of this period, such as the *Assumptions of the Virgin* at the Cistercian church at Zirc, Hungary (1754) and at St Quintin, Mainz (1758), also show a Rococo approach, with gracefully elongated figures reminiscent of Giovanni Battista Piazzetta.

These developments reach their height in the masterly ceiling and altar frescoes of the parish church at Sümeg, Hungary (1757–8). In the high altar fresco of the *Ascension* Maulbertsch's figures transcend both solid and illusory framing devices, and with them the physical world. Equally impressive, however, are the many subordinate scenes where figure groups are used as decorative elements. The side altar frescoes too are compelling in their drama and pathos, especially the *Crucifixion* with its frightened bucking horse, spearman and arched torso of the dying Christ. The work at Sümeg is notable, above all, for its richness of invention and detail, for example the many figures surrounding *St Peter Preaching*.

An equally spectacular unity of purpose and execution marks the ceiling painting of the *Glorification of Bishop Leopold Eck and the Bishopric* (1759) in the Feudal Hall of the bishop's summer residence at Kroměříž, Moravia, where ethereal figures soar into illusory space, detaching themselves from groups of worldly personages in elaborate 17th-century dress who in turn mingle with mythological and imaginary creatures looking on from *trompe l'oeil* architectural elements at the join of wall and ceiling. The brilliance of Maulbertsch's work here, with its poetic individuality and atmospheric subtlety of light and colour, was readily acknowledged and he was henceforth assured of further commissions. The same year he became a member of the Akademie in Vienna as 'history painter and fresco painter', his reception piece being an *Allegory of the Arts* (Vienna, Alte Universität, Ratsaal).

Maulbertsch's painting of the earlier 1760s encompasses the very attractively painted naturalistic details of plants, trees and waterfalls in the *Progress and Fruits of the Sciences* (1760; *in situ*) on the ceiling of the library of the Barnabitenkloster at Mistelbach, Lower Austria, and the dramatic figure composition of the *Glorification of the Premonstratensian Order* (destr.; oil study Vienna, Belvedere, Österreich Gal.; see fig. 1) in the refectory of the monastery at Klosterbruck (now Louka, Czech Republic). In these works, as in the ceiling paintings in the chapel at Trenčianske Bohuslarice castle (1763), the parish church

1. Franz Anton Maulbertsch: *Glorification of the Premonstratensian Order*, oil on canvas, 560×750 mm, *c.* 1765; sketch for frescoes (destr.) in the refectory of the Premonstratensian monastery at Klosterbruck (now Louka, Czech Republic) (Vienna, Belvedere, Österreichische Galerie)

at Schwechat, Lower Austria (1764; destr.) and the Jagdschloss at Féltorony Halbturn, Austria (1765), his first large-scale imperial commission, Maulbertsch assigned a dominant role to light, as the main means of expression. The enhanced expressiveness also characterizes the oil paintings produced for altarpieces during this period, for instance *Christ Appearing to St Thomas* (1762–4; Brno, St Thomas). Oil sketches, such as that for the *Assumption of Mary* at Schwechat (1762–4; Vienna, Belvedere, Österreich. Gal.) have a virtuosic sense of liberation and brightly luminous colour. Maulbertsch also essayed some etchings at this time (e.g. *Christ and the Centurion of Capernaum*, *c.* 1762–4; Vienna, Albertina).

(ii) After 1765. In the later 1760s a change of style in Maulbertsch's work becomes evident: largely in response to the advance of Neo-classicism, and at his patrons' implicit or explicit request, he introduced greater balance, more static composition and a more uniform light. In the frescoes of 1766 for the church of Hradiště, Czech Republic, the imagery aligns itself with the real architectural structure, rather than defying it. The *Baptism* (*c.* 1766) in the frescoed barrel vault of the ceiling of the Theologien-saal of Vienna University is another relatively self-contained image, as is the ceiling painting, the *Institution of the Order of St Stephen* (1768; Vienna, Hungarian Embassy), commissioned by Empress Maria Theresa. The ceiling

frescoes (1767) for the Carmelite church at Székesfehér-vár, Hungary, use an elaborate picturesque illusionism, with a central figure giddily climbing upwards beyond its highest parapets in the *Allegory of Salvation*. In 1769 Maulbertsch was commissioned to select works for copying by students at the recently founded Kupferstecher-akademie, led by Jakob Schmutzer whose daughter he was to marry in 1780. In 1770 Maulbertsch himself became a member of this body with his grisaille painting *Allegory on the Destiny of Art* (Vienna, Gemäldegal. Akad. Bild. Kst).

During the 1770s the new style is increasingly evident in Maulbertsch's work: he was attempting to combine the Baroque traditions of monumental painting with the new demands for clarity, comprehensibility and truth to historical fact. The results can be seen in altar paintings, often completed with the help of assistants, such as the *Last Supper* (1773) at the Augustinerkirche, Korneuburg, Lower Austria. Ceiling paintings become more like panel paintings—well demarcated, firmly structured and uniformly lit—as in his works at the Hofburg, Innsbruck (1775–6). From the early 1780s most of Maulbertsch's commissions came from the Hungarian part of the Empire, where the art of fresco continued to flourish later than elsewhere. They followed relatively explicit instructions from patrons such as Károly Esterházy, Bishop of Eger, or Ferenc Zichy, Bishop of Győr, who were influenced by the prevailing Neo-classical taste and demanded historical truthfulness as well as clarity. The ceiling painting for the main nave of Győr Cathedral (1781) clearly responds to these requirements but the epitome of Maulbertsch's uninterrupted mastery in the new context is to be found in the frescoes of *St Stephen* (1782–3) for the ceiling of the choir in the parish church at Pápa, with their bold use of architectural illusionism and impressive richness of colour.

During the last decade of his life, Maulbertsch received far fewer large-scale commissions, and some of his more interesting work from this time is intimate in character as well as scale, revealing new capacities. He produced genre scenes, for example the *Peep-show Man* (painting, 1785; Nuremberg, Ger. Nmus.; etching, 1785; Vienna, Albertina), strongly reminiscent of 17th-century Dutch work. He painted small biblical senes in the manner of Rembrandt (e.g. *Esther and Hatchah*, 1785–6; Vienna, Belvedere, Österreich. Gal.) and historical and mythological compositions such as *Coriolanus before Rome* (1790–93; Stuttgart, Staatsgal.; see fig. 2). The etching *Zodiac* (1780–84; Vienna, Albertina) reveals a strong fantastical imagination and employs a wide range of stroke; another etching, the *Picture of Tolerance* (1785; Vienna, Albertina), paraphrases Joseph II's Edict of Tolerance. In his only securely attributed *Self-portrait* (c. 1794–5; Vienna, Belvedere, Österreich. Gal.) Maulbertsch achieved an image both confident and touching.

The late sketches for fresco commissions, such as the *Martyrdom of St Quirinus* (1791; Vienna, Belvedere, Österreich. Gal.) for Szombathely Cathedral, retain something of Maulbertsch's earlier liveliness, but the fresco work he carried out in his last years is marked on the whole by unmistakable weariness and obvious reliance on assistants. These failings show through in the *Allegory of the Sciences* (1794) on the library ceiling in the Strahov monastery, Prague, while Maulbertsch's schemes for the newly erected Cathedral at Szombathely were completed after his death by his most important pupil, Josef Winterhalder the younger.

2. WORKING METHODS AND TECHNIQUE. With fresco and altar projects, Maulbertsch always worked from a concrete commission; in accordance with Late Baroque artistic custom, the patron predetermined the subject-matter, the dimensions, etc, often setting out the concepts and layouts in writing—as in the works at Kroměříž and Strahov. Following these specifications, the artist would complete various sketches, drawings, colour-studies, and oil sketches, which the patron might correct and accept. The final sketch or model served as the contractual basis, which determined the working process and the conditions. Maulbertsch worked on frescoes during spring and summer, and in winter on altar pictures in his studio in Vienna,

2. Franz Anton Maulbertsch: *Coriolanus before Rome*, oil on panel, 350×455 mm, 1790–93 (Stuttgart, Staatsgalerie)

mostly with help from pupils or assistants. Contemporaries praised his extraordinarily swift, virtuoso working method. He generally received large fees, but since he also had high overheads he made little profit. He lived with his family in the Josefstadt, Vienna, in his own house, in secure, though modest middle-class circumstances; he died in high esteem.

BIBLIOGRAPHY

Thieme–Becker

G. J. Dlabacz: *Allgemeines Künstler-Lexikon für Böhmen* (Prague, 1815)

J. Kapossy: *A szombathelyi székesegyház és mennyezetképei* [The Szombathely cathedral and its ceiling] (Budapest, 1922)

A. Pigler: *A pápai plébániatemplon és mennyezetképei* [The Pápa parish church and its ceiling] (Budapest, 1922)

O. Benesch: 'Maulbertsch: Zu den Quellen seines malerischen Stils', *Städel-Jb.*, iii–iv (1924), pp. 107–76

F. Gerke: *Die Fresken des F. A. Maulbertsch zu Sümeg* (Mainz, 1950)

H. Tintelnot: *Die barocke Freskomalerei in Deutschland* (Munich, 1951)

K. Garas: *Magyarországi festészet a XVIII. században* [Hungarian painting of the 18th century] (Budapest, 1955)

——: *Franz Anton Maulbertsch* (Budapest, 1960) [with cat. rais. and extensive bibliog.]

——: 'Nachträge und Ergänzungen zum Werk F. A. Maulbertschs', *Pantheon*, xxi (1963), pp. 29–37

F. Gerke: *Die Mainzer Marienauffahrt des Franz Anton Maulbertsch* (Mainz, 1966)

B. Bushart: 'Offenbarung der göttlichen Weisheit: Zur Augsburger Ölskizze des F. A. Maulbertsch', *Alte & Mod. Kst*, cxv (1971), pp. 7–31

K. Garas: 'Franz Anton Maulbertsch: Neue Funde', *Mitt. Österreich. Gal.*, xv (1971), pp. 7–35

E. A. Maser: 'Franz Anton Maulbertsch as Portraitist', *Pantheon*, xxix (1971), pp. 292–307

J. A. Friesen: 'Franz Anton Maulbertsch und sein Bild der Duldung', *Mitt. Österreich. Gal.*, xvii (1973), pp. 15–55

Franz Anton Maulbertsch (exh. cat., Vienna, Piaristenkloster, 1974)

Franz Anton Maulbertsch és kora [Franz Anton Maulbertsch and his age] (exh. cat., Budapest, Mus. F. A., 1974)

K. Garas: *Franz Anton Maulbertsch: Leben und Werk* (Salzburg, 1974)

I. Krsek: *František Antonín Maulbertsch* (Prague, 1975)

P. Cannon Brookes: 'The Oil Paintings of Franz Anton Maulbertsch in the Light of the 1974 Exhibitions', *Burl. Mag.*, cxix (1977), p. 18

F. M. Haberditzel: 'Franz Anton Maulbertsch', *Mitt. Österreich. Gal.*, xxi (1977), pp. 1–582

P. Preiss: *Katalog: Österreichische Barockmaler aus der National Galerie in Prag* (Vienna, 1977–8)

E. Braum: *Katalog des Österreichischen Barockmuseums im Unteren Belvedere in Wien* (Vienna, 1980)

Deutsche Barockgalerie: Katalog der Gemälde (Augsburg, 1984)

Franz Anton Maulbertsch und sein Kreis in Ungarn (exh. cat., Budapest, Mus. F.A.; Budapest, N.G.; Esztergom, Mus. Christ.; Sigmaringen, Mus. Langenargen am Bodensee; 1984)

KLÁRA GARAS

Maulbronn Abbey. Former Cistercian monastery in Baden-Württemberg, Germany. The abbey, founded by Ritter Walter von Lomersheim in 1138, was relocated at Maulbronn, in the narrow Salzach Valley on the southern slope of the Stromberg, and approved by Pope Eugenius III (*reg* 1145–53) on 29 March 1148. The abbey achieved great renown, with up to 100 monks in the late Middle Ages. In 1556 it was dissolved and became a Protestant theological school; it is now a Protestant boarding school. The precinct (3.8 ha) is still surrounded by a wall (l. 850 m) with five towers and moats dating from the first half of the 13th century and renovated in 1361–7 by Abbot Johann von Rottweil.

1. ABBEY CHURCH. Dedicated to St Mary and consecrated in 1178, the abbey church is a basilica with strong characteristics of mid-12th-century Cistercian churches: it has a straight-ended choir and a series of narrow transept chapels 3.6 m wide, but no towers, crypt or galleries. The vaulted eastern part was started *c.* 1147 under the influence of Worms Cathedral. In the south transept there is a *Totenpforte* (Door for the Dead), and the night stairs occupy the north transept. The nave, which is in the Swabian tradition emanating from Hirsau, originally had a flat ceiling, which has been partly preserved above the decorated vaulting built in 1424; it consisted of thick planks nailed up below the roof timbers with small boards inserted into grooves in the planks. The original rood screen separating the monks' choir from that of the lay brothers is still in place at the fifth bay of the nave. It has two round-arched passageways and picks up the profiles of the nave pier bases, carrying them around the doorways in a way typical of Swabia and the Upper Rhine.

The upper west façade is articulated with corner pilasters and hanging arches. The entrance porch, or 'paradise', is datable on stylistic grounds to 1210–15, and it was designed by a master trained in northern France. The porch is one of the most elegant creations of the transitional period from Romanesque to Gothic. The three square bays are vaulted with semicircular ribs, those of the diagonal ribs being set lower than the wall ribs so that their crowns are of equal height. The supports therefore consist of a bundle of taller and shorter columns, visually tied together with shaft rings, which results in a lively play between the members. The water-holding bases and the profiles of the ribs and the shaft rings were influenced by the Noyon and Soissons area of northern France, which also inspired the crocket capitals. The paradise opens to the west through a double doorway flanked by two unglazed windows set between buttresses; the windows have trefoiled twin openings under containing arches. The open, moulded effect is a Gothic idea expressed in Romanesque forms, and it differentiates the porch from the rich frame of the church door, which uses Alsatian forms from *c.* 1150. The mature style developed by the Master of the Paradise in adapting French forms to the local tradition was widely influential: it is found at the Cistercian abbey of Walkenried near Brunswick and the Bischofsgang in the choir of Magdeburg Cathedral.

2. MONASTIC BUILDINGS. The monastery is laid out on the usual Cistercian plan, but with the claustral buildings north of the church; the domestic offices, mostly half-timbered buildings put up between the 16th century and the 18th, are to the west. The hunting-lodge of Duke Ludwig VI of Württemberg (*reg* 1568–93), built in 1588, is north-east of the enclosure opposite the guest-house. The cloisters north of the church were built in sections. The south walk was built *c.* 1210–20 under the influence of the Master of the Paradise. While the outer walls have the bundles of linked shafts, on the church side the ribs are supported on columns and bundles of columns, some of which are tapered off while others end at the shaft rings with half-moon-shaped consoles. There were originally benches for evening readings; and the two stone water-spouts indicate that this was where the monks customarily washed their feet on Saturdays.

The west walk, which dates from *c.* 1300, has early examples of window tracery. The east and north walks

1. Maulbronn Abbey, monks' refectory, c. 1220

were built by c. 1320. With its large windows and nine-ribbed star vault, the octagonal fountain house, which was built c. 1340–50 on a circular base dating from 1210, is one of the most elegant spaces created in the Gothic period.

The monastic buildings were built from the early 13th century. The vaulted storeroom in the west range next to the church is dated by an inscription to 1201. North of it a barrel-vaulted passageway with a Romanesque door gives access to the cloister garth. The lay brothers' refectory, started in 1201, lies north of the passage; its double columns and rib vaulting date from c. 1215 (renovated in the 19th century). Above the refectory is the lay brothers' dormitory, which was converted to a winter refectory for the monks c. 1512–18. The kitchen, built c. 1220, is set in the north-west corner serving both the lay brothers' refectory and that of the monks.

The monks' refectory (27.3×11.8 m; see fig. 1), which is set at right angles to the cloisters opposite the fountain house, was built c. 1220. Apart from the paradise it is architecturally the most important feature of the abbey, a masterpiece of the Transitional style and the most lavish surviving 13th-century dining-hall. The eight bays are divided by circular piers of alternately thick and thin cross-section with shaft rings and capitals, supporting sexpartite vaults. The ribs, which are decorated with dogtooth ornament, are corbelled into the walls. The reading desk, accessible by a spiral stair, is on the east wall. The room is given its character by the graduated varied forms, by its height, which is almost the same as the width, and by the

strong through-light afforded by tall, slender, round-arched windows.

The remainder of the north range is taken up by the warming room of c. 1250, the parlour and the dormitory (renovated c. 1320–30) above. The passage to the garden leads into the parlour built in 1493 by the lay brother Konrad von Schmie, with an oratory above added in 1495. These Late Gothic additions have net vaults with lively painting and curvilinear window tracery. The Herrenhaus, the monastery guest-house, built in 1512–18, contains remains of the early 13th-century Romanesque infirmary, but the hall, with its wooden supports, dainty oriel and spiral staircases, was designed by Brother Konrad in 1493 and continued by Brother Augustin in 1517.

The chapter house (14.3×8.4 m; see fig. 2) with the chapel of St John the Baptist in the east range is the other architecturally distinguished building in the monastic complex. It is divided by three columns and opens to the cloister through slender arcading. It has a star vault with triradial ribs; the rib profile, the vaulting itself and the very style of the angel blowing an animal horn and the Evangelists carved on the keystones suggest a date in the 1320s. The tracery forms of both chapter house and cloister show influences from the Upper and Middle Rhine Valley, and the early 14th-century buildings at Maulbronn show German High Gothic in its maturity.

BIBLIOGRAPHY

E. Paulus: *Die Cisterzienser-Abtei Maulbronn* (Stuttgart, 1873, 3/1889)

P. Schmitt: *Maulbronn: Eine Studie zur deutschromanischen Bauentwicklung des XII. Jahrhunderts* (diss., U. Strasbourg, 1903)

A. Mettler: 'Zur Klosteranlage der Zisterzienser und zur Baugeschichte Maulbronns', *Württemberg. Vjheft. Landesgesch.*, n. s., xviii (1909)

I. Dörrenberg: *Das Zisterzienser-Kloster Maulbronn* (Würzburg, 1937/R 1938) [with bibliog.]

C.-W. Clasen: *Die Zisterzienserabtei Maulbronn im 12. Jahrhundert und der bernhardische Klosterplan* (diss., Kiel, Christian-Albrechts U., 1956)

B. Seitz: *Maulbronner Impressionen* (Maulbronn, 1977)

W. Irtenkauf, ed.: *Kloster Maulbronn, 1178–1978* (Maulbronn, 1978)

R. Henk: *Abtei Maulbronn* (Heidelberg, 1979/R 1980)

G. Binding and M. Untermann: *Kleine Kunstgeschichte der mittelalterlichen Ordensbaukunst in Deutschland* (Darmstadt, 1985)

G. Frank: *Das Zisterzienserkloster Maulbronn* (Hildesheim, 1993)

GÜNTHER BINDING

2. Maulbronn Abbey, chapter house, c. 1320–30

Maulouel, Jean. *See* MALOUEL, JEAN.

Mauperché, Henri (*b* ?Paris, *c.* 1602; *d* Paris, 26 Dec 1686). French painter and printmaker. He may have studied under Daniel Rabel at some period before 1634, in which year he travelled to Rome with Louis Boullogne (i). There, almost certainly, they became acquainted with Jean Blanchard, Sébastien Bourdon and Herman van Swanevelt. Mauperché was back in Paris in 1639, working with Blanchard for Armand-Jean du Plessis, Cardinal de Richelieu, at the Palais-Royal; the contract (12 March 1639) for the works to be undertaken mentions topographical views and landscapes with ruins, a contract in which Mauperché is described as Peintre Ordinaire du Roy. About 1646–7 he painted a *Landscape with Traveller* (Paris, Louvre) as part of the commission to decorate the interiors of the Cabinet de l'Amour at the Hôtel Lambert, Paris, where he worked alongside Swanevelt, Jan Asselijn and Pierre Patel (i). He was married for the first time in 1647, with Blanchard as one of the witnesses. In 1648 he was among the group of artists accepted (*agréé*) by the Académie Royale de Peinture et de Sculpture. In 1654 he engraved his only dated work, the *Plan of Liancourt* (see Robert-Dumesnil, no. 51), a bird's-eye view of the château and gardens (destr.) in Oise owned by the du Plessy family. The following year he became a professor at the Académie Royale.

During the 1660s Mauperché's commissions included eight landscapes (1660; untraced) for the apartments in the Louvre, Paris, of Louis XIV's wife, Maria-Theresa, and fourteen large landscapes for Anne of Austria's Grand Cabinet at the château of Fontainebleau, on which he worked with Jean Cotelle; only two survive, the *Pilgrims at Emmaus* and *Christ and the Woman of Samaria* (both 1663; Sofia, N. Archaeol. Mus.). Among his other works are a number depicting religious subjects, including the *Landscape with Tobias and the Angel* (Lisieux, Mus. Vieux-Lisieux) and the *Rest on the Flight into Egypt* (1671; Paris, Louvre). Mauperché's careful attention to the effects of atmospheric perspective in these and other pictures is the result of his strong links with other French landscape painters in Paris during the late 1640s, in particular Pierre Patel (i), with whose works some by Mauperché have occasionally been confused.

Mauperché is best known for his complex and spirited engravings (some 50 survive), for which he was dubbed 'the French Swanevelt'. Apart from the bird's-eye view of Liancourt, none is dated, but most were made during the period in which he lived in the Ile Saint-Louis (1639–56); they include the series of six prints each of the *Life of the Virgin* (RD 16–21), the *Story of Tobias* (RD 2–7) and the *Prodigal Son* (RD 10–15). This period was one of intense stylistic experiment for Mauperché, in the course of which he absorbed the classicizing style of the years of Anne of Austria's Regency, leading to an emphasis on perspective and balanced compositions; he thus came close to the compositional formulae of both Patel and Laurent de La Hyre. This general quest for the mood of the time was enriched by Mauperché's own individual touches.

BIBLIOGRAPHY

A.-P.-F. Robert-Dumesnil: *Le Peintre-graveur français* (1835–71) [RD]
F. Engerand: *Inventaires des collections de la couronne: Inventaire des tableaux du Roy rédigé en 1709–1710 par Nicolas Bailly* (Paris, 1899)
J.-M. Barielle: *Henri Mauperché (1602–1685)* (diss., U. Paris IV, 1979)

NATALIE COURAL

Maura y Montaner, Bartolomé (*b* Palma de Mallorca, 1844; *d* Madrid, Dec 1926). Spanish printmaker. He studied at the Academia de Bellas Artes in Palma de Mallorca, and from 1868 at the Real Academia de Bellas Artes de S Fernando in Madrid. His teachers included Federico de Madrazo y Küntz, Domingo Martínez and Carlos de Haes. He won the Concurso Nacional in 1872 with his print of *The Spinners* (engraving, 1872) after the painting (Madrid, Prado) by Velázquez. He was the administrator of the Calcografía Nacional, Madrid, from 1878 to 1893, when he became artistic director of the Fábrica Nacional de Moneda y Timbre in Madrid. He was appointed chief engraver at the Banco de España in 1898, and became a member of the Real Academia de S Fernando the following year. He was an excellent interpretative printmaker with an extensive output that included copies of Old Master paintings and portrait etchings of leading contemporary and historical figures such as *Philip IV* (1871), after Velázquez.

BIBLIOGRAPHY

J. J. Tous: *Grabadores mallorquines* (Palma de Mallorca, 1977), pp. 68–76
E. Paez Rios: *Repertorio* (1981–3)
J. Vega: *El aguafuerte en el siglo XIX* (Madrid, 1985)

BLANCA GARCÍA VEGA

Maurel. *See* MOREL.

Maurer, Alfred H(enry) (*b* New York, 21 April 1868; *d* New York, 4 Aug 1932). American painter. He studied at the National Academy of Design, New York, in 1884 and briefly at the Académie Julian, Paris, during 1897. He received critical success with academic paintings of single female figures in interiors and genre scenes of café society, which reflected the influence of the work of James Abbott McNeill Whistler and William Merritt Chase, for example *At the Café* (*c.* 1905; St Petersburg, Hermitage). His long residence in Paris from 1897, his participation in various independent salons and his association with Leo and Gertrude Stein led to his interest in avant-garde art. He may have been one of a group of Americans who studied briefly with Henri Matisse. By 1907 he was producing vigorously painted Fauvist landscapes, such as *Landscape with Red Tree* (*c.* 1907–8; New York, Mr and Mrs John C. Marin jr priv. col., see exh. cat., p. 42), which he exhibited in New York at Alfred Stieglitz's gallery, 291, in 1909 and at the Folsom Gallery in 1913.

Maurer returned permanently to New York in 1914 and continued to paint Fauvist landscapes into the 1920s. During his last decade he also painted still-lifes that were synthetic Cubist table-top arrangements and enigmatic studies of heads that indicated his distraught emotional state, for example *Two Heads (Abstraction)* (1931/2; Williamstown, MA, Williams Coll. Mus. A.). The single and paired heads had large eyes and elongated faces; under the influence of analytic Cubism, Maurer sometimes fragmented them. These stylized heads became his most personal contribution to modernism. Maurer's modernist art was largely ignored until 1924, when the Weyhe Gallery in New York accorded him the first of several one-man exhibitions, which met with critical success.

BIBLIOGRAPHY
'Maurer and Expressionism', *Int. Studio*, xlix/193 (March 1913), p. viii
E. McCausland: *A. H. Maurer* (New York, 1951)
Alfred H. Maurer, 1868–1932 (exh. cat. by S. Reich, Washington, DC, N. Col. F.A., 1973)
N. Madorno: 'The Early Career of Alfred Maurer: Paintings of Popular Entertainment', *Amer. A. J.*, xv/1 (Winter 1983), pp. 4–34

ILENE SUSAN FORT

Maurice, Stadholder and Prince of Orange. *See* ORANGE NASSAU, (2).

Maurice of Savoy, Cardinal. *See* SAVOY, §II(6).

Maurin, Charles (*b* Le Puy, 1 April 1856; *d* Grasse, 22 July 1913). French painter and printmaker. In 1875 he won the Prix Crozatier, which enabled him to study in Paris, at the Ecole des Beaux-Arts under Jules Lefebvre in 1876–9 and also at the Académie Julian, where he later taught. He exhibited at the Salon des Artistes Français, becoming a member in 1883. Among his paintings are the *Prelude to Lohengrin* and *Maternity* (both Le Puy, Mus. Crozatier). Inspired by the work of Japanese artists and the growing popularity of the 18th-century print, he was one of a small group of artists who experimented with colour plates and in 1891 he patented a new technique of colour printing. His best works are his lightly washed grey and pink etchings of nudes, such as *After the Bath*, *The Model* and *Child with a Pink Ribbon*, which show a high standard of drawing and modelling. He also produced wood-engravings, for instance *Head of a Young Girl in a Landscape* (1890; see 1980 exh. cat., p. 17), and others set in low-life cafés and music-halls.

BIBLIOGRAPHY
F. L. Leipnik: *History of French Etching* (London, 1924)
Charles Maurin, 1856–1914 (exh. cat., Le Puy, Mus. Crozatier, 1978)
Post-impressionist Graphics: Original Prints by French Artists, 1880–1903 (exh. cat., ACGB, 1980)

ETIENNE LYMBERY

Mauritania, Islamic Republic of [République Islamique de Mauritanie]. Country on the north-west coast of Africa. It is bordered to the north by Western Sahara, to the north-east by Algeria, to the east and south by Mali, and to the south-west by Senegal. The capital is Nouakchott. Most of Mauritania's 1,030,700 sq. km is low-lying desert that supports a livestock-based nomadic existence, although there is some arable farming along the fertile banks of the Senegal River. There was much urban migration in the 1980s and 1990s, but still only a small amount of industrial development, the economy continuing to be based on agriculture with some mineral exports.

Mauritania's early history is marked by the incursion of Berber tribes from the north, which forced the indigenous population of Fulani, Soninke and Berber peoples southwards. In the 15th century nomadic Arab tribes moving south began to eclipse Berber power while the Portuguese, and later the Dutch and the French, also showed interest in the area. The Senegal Treaty of 1817 recognized the coastal territory as a French sphere of influence, and in 1903 a French protectorate was extended over Mauritania. In 1904 the region became part of French West Africa, remaining a French colony until independence in 1960.

Most of Mauritania's population of *c.* 1,970,000 (UN estimate, 1989) are Arab-Berber or of Sudanic origin and speak Hassaniyya, an Arabic-based dialect. The black African minorities, still concentrated in the south, have retained their respective languages. The official languages are Arabic and French, and nearly all Mauritanians are Muslims of the Malekite sect. This entry covers art in Mauritania since colonial times. For the arts of the area in earlier times, including prehistoric rock art, *see* AFRICA, §VII, 3(i).

Artistic activity in Mauritania following colonization has centred on its strong craft traditions, since there have been few developments in painting or sculpture. Metalworking is of largely Arab derivation, an exception being the goldworking techniques acquired from the ancient empire of Ghana. Among the objects produced are locks (some inlaid with silver), anklets, bracelets, caskets, chests and teapots. Carved-wood and silver chests are made in Mederdra. Although in decline, leatherwork was still an important craft in the early 1990s, and such painted and tooled leather items as saddles and large decorated travelling bags, usually made of five sheepskins, were still part of nomadic tribal life. Weaving techniques similar to those of southern Morocco are used to make carpets, cushions and brightly coloured rugs of camel- and goat-hair, the latter from Boutilimit. Mats are also woven from palm-cane. In the south there are wood-carving traditions. Arabic calligraphy is used as decoration for several media, and a footprint motif is characteristic. These crafts are, in general, the responsibility of a caste of craftsmen (*mu'alimin*) who traditionally have formed families or groups working exclusively for particular clients. In an attempt to promote and commercialize their labours, the government created the Bureau de l'Artisanat (early 1960s).

Traditional architecture in Mauritania can be seen in such medieval stone cities as Chinguetti in the Adrar region, an important Muslim centre from the 13th century onwards, and Tichitt, in the Tagant region, a fortress, now largely in ruins, on a high cliff. In both, the house-building techniques are Berber, featuring chevron patterns of the stone within the structure and the use of dark stones placed individually or in layers. At Oualata the mud-plastered walls of the stone buildings have distinctive decorations of two types: white, painted low-relief moulding and flat painted motifs in red on a white ground, the latter possibly a later innovation. The designs consist of motifs, for which there is a comprehensive terminology, composed of curved lines possibly deriving from leather-work. Traditionally, the doors of houses, which are made of vertical planks of wood supported by transverse pieces, are decorated with metal bosses.

Modern, Western-inspired architecture has been introduced to Mauritania to a limited extent. Although the capital, Nouakchott, was built on empty coastal dunes at the time of independence, the modern buildings are mainly in a traditional Berber style, and, at Tidjikdja, in a fort built before 1905 by a French official, Xavier Coppolani, a typically Saharan style was used. One modern building of interest is Nouakchott's central hospital, designed shortly after independence by the recently formed architectural studio Atelier de Montrouge (*see* RENAUDIE, JEAN), in which wards are linked by inner courtyards.

Apart from the Bureau de l'Artisanat, patronage in Mauritania is scarce. A craft centre in Nouakchott produces silver jewellery and daggers and wood and silver chests, while other handicrafts can be purchased in the markets. Although there are no art galleries or museums, there are collections of manuscripts in the National Library, Nouakchott (founded 1965), and the libraries in Oualata, an ancient centre of learning, Boutilimit, Kaédi, Mederdra, Tidjikdja and Chinguetti.

See also BAMANA, BERBER and FULANI.

BIBLIOGRAPHY
G. J. Duchemin: 'A propos des décorations murales des habitations de Oualata (Mauritanie)', *Bull. Inst. Fr. Afrique Noire*, xii/4 (1950), pp. 1095–110
O. du Puigaudeau: 'Contribution à l'étude du symbolisme dans le décor mural et l'artisanat de Walâta', *Bull. Inst. Fr. Afrique Noire*, xix/1–2 (1957), pp. 137–83
——: 'Architecture maure', *Bull. Inst. Fr. Afrique Noire*, xxii/1–2 (1960), pp. 92–133
M.-F. Delarozière: *Formes et couleurs en Mauritanie* (Nouakchott, 1976)
J. Corral: *Ciudades de las caravanas: Alarifes del Islam en el desierto*, El diseño del entorno (Madrid, 1985)
M.-F. Delarozière: *Les Perles de Mauritanie* (Aix-en-Provence, 1985)

☐

Mauro di Codussis. *See* CODUSSI, MAURO.

Maurya [Mauryan]. First imperial dynasty of India. It flourished *c.* 321 BC–*c.* 232 BC, continuing to rule some areas until *c.* 185 BC. Chandragupta Maurya, founder of the house, formed his empire by gaining control of much of the prosperous kingdom of the Nanda dynasty in eastern India and filling the vacuum in the north-west left by Alexander's retreat in 325 BC. He campaigned successfully as far south as the Vindhyas, returning to Gandhara in the north-west between 305 and 303 BC to defeat Seleukos Nikator, Alexander's general who had gained control of much of the region. Pataliputra (modern PATNA) became Chandragupta's capital after the final overthrow of the Nandas. Chandragupta's mentor was Kautilya, the famous author of the *Arthaśāstra*, a treatise on statecraft.

Chandragupta was succeeded by Bindusara *c.* 297 BC, who probably extended the empire in the Deccan. He was followed by his son Ashoka *c.* 269 BC. Ashoka attacked Kalinga, one of the few parts of the subcontinent not under Mauryan rule, winning a bloody victory. Ashoka's remorse at the suffering and loss of life, mentioned in his edicts, is taken as an indication of his conversion to Buddhism.

The edicts, carved on rocks and pillars throughout the empire, are the earliest historical epigraphs from the subcontinent and are found from Shabazgarhi in the north-west to Brahmagiri in Karnataka (*see also* INDIAN SUBCONTINENT, §I, 4). They consist primarily of Ashoka's official proclamations and instructions to his subjects. The pillars on which many of the edicts are found are monolithic shafts of sandstone once surmounted by animal capitals. They are true examples of imperial dynastic art, being uniform in material, style and technique. Through

Ashoka's agency the third Buddhist council took place, and Buddhism began its expansion within the subcontinent. Ashoka died *c.* 232 BC, after which his empire began to disintegrate. The Gangetic heartland remained under Mauryan rule until the SHUNGA dynasty replaced it *c.* 185 BC.

BIBLIOGRAPHY
V. Smith: *Aśoka* (Oxford, 1903)
E. Hultzsch: *Inscriptions of Aśoka*, Corp. Inscr. Indic., i (London, 1925)
K. A. Nilakantha Sastri: *The Age of the Nandas and Mauryas* (Varanasi, 1952)
R. P. Kangle: *The Kauṭilīya Arthaśāstra*, 3 vols (Bombay, 1960–63)
R. Thapar: *Aśoka and the Decline of the Mauryas* (Oxford, 1961)
S. P. Gupta: *The Roots of Indian Art* (Delhi, 1980)
J. Strong: *The Legend of King Aśoka: A Study and Translation of the Aśokāvadāna* (Princeton, 1983)

J. MARR

Maus, Octave (*b* Brussels, 12 June 1856; *d* Brussels, 26 Nov 1919). Belgian lawyer and critic. His first employment was with the lawyer and writer Edmond Picard (1836–1924), dealing with the legal problems of artists and writers. In 1881 he co-founded the weekly periodical *Art moderne* with Picard, the writer and lawyer Victor Arnould (1838–93) and Eugène Robert, and eventually became its sole director. Published until 9 August 1914, *Art moderne* was the most avant-garde Belgian periodical of its time, covering both native and foreign trends in art, literature and music. The first issue proclaimed the social importance of art and its evolutionary development, coupling these notions with a belief in the independence and originality of the artist. Music was given generous coverage, with a bias towards the music and ideas of Richard Wagner (Maus himself was keenly interested in music and had been an early visitor to Bayreuth). In 1884 Maus was invited to become secretary of the newly founded group Les XX (*see* <VINGT>, LES). Effectively the group's unifying force, he was in charge of the publicity and organization of the exhibitions, the first of which opened on 2 February 1884 at the Palais des Beaux-Arts in Brussels. He also arranged for lectures and musical concerts to be included during the exhibitions and invited suitable non-members to exhibit with the group; Théo Van Rysselberge painted a portrait of him at this time (*Octave Maus*, 1885; Brussels, Musées Royaux B.-A.; see BELGIUM, fig. 51). In 1893 Maus proposed a vote that Les XX be dissolved and promptly founded its successor, LIBRE ESTHÉTIQUE, in 1894. The outbreak of World War I brought both *Art moderne* and Libre Esthétique to an end. Maus spent most of the war in Lausanne where he set up L'Office Belge to aid Belgian refugees in Switzerland; he also organized profit-making exhibitions for the benefit of Belgian artists. His plans to revive both *Art moderne* and Libre Esthétique after the war were cut short by his illness and then death.

WRITINGS
L'Espagne des artistes (Brussels, 1887)
Souvenirs d'un Wagnériste: Le Théâtre de Bayreuth (Brussels, 1888)
Les Préludes: Impressions d'adolescence (Brussels, 1921)
Regular contributions to *A. Mod.* (1881–1914)

BIBLIOGRAPHY
M. O. Maus: *Trente années de lutte pour l'art, 1884–1914* (Brussels, 1926) [an account by Maus's wife]
A. V. Linden: *Octave Maus et la vie musicale belge, 1875–1914* (Brussels, 1950)

☐

Mausoleum. Monumental form of tomb. Its name is derived from one of the most famous buildings of antiquity, the funerary monument completed *c.* 350 BC at Halikarnassos in Asia Minor (*see* HALIKARNASSOS, §2) in honour of Mausolos, Satrap of Caria (*reg* 377–353 BC), and his wife Artemisia (*d* 351 BC). A mausoleum is a house of the dead, although it is often as much a symbol as a sepulchre. Following the example at Halikarnassos, this term has been employed for large, monumental and stately tombs, usually erected for distinguished or prominent individuals. It first appeared in English in 1546, applied by Thomas Langley (*d* 1581) specifically to the tomb of Mausolos. In his translation of Livy (London, 1600), Philemon Holland (1552–1637) extended the meaning of the term to cover a stately burial-place for a person of distinction, and by 1688 it simply meant a stately tomb. The concept of an imposing burial-place, as established in ancient times, is to be distinguished from a CENOTAPH or monument.

The idea of the mausoleum, and some of its visual trappings, has persisted for some 4500 years, from 3rd-Dynasty Egypt to 20th-century Moscow. During some periods, especially Middle and New Kingdom Egypt and medieval Christian Europe, impressive architectural monuments for the tombs of distinguished persons were not the norm, but the mausoleum has been one of the recurring themes in the architectural history of the Western world.

For further discussion and for information on mausolea in other areas *see* TOMB; see also the architectural sections of individual country, regional and cultural surveys.

I. Ancient world, *c.* 3000 BC –*c.* AD 330. II. Early Christian, *c.* AD 330–*c.* 600. III. Medieval, *c.* AD 600–*c.* 1500. IV. Renaissance, 16th century. V. 17th century. VI. 18th century. VII. 19th century. VIII. 20th century.

I. *Ancient world,* **c.** *3000* BC–c. AD *330.*

1. EGYPT. Disposal of the dead by cremation or inhumation was usual in antiquity. By the 1st Dynasty (*c.* 2925–*c.* 2775 BC) of Early Dynastic Period Egypt, however, tombs for rulers and nobles began to appear above ground, especially at ABYDOS and SAQQARA. These took the form of a MASTABA (named after an Arabic term for a low, mud-brick bench); this was generally rectangular or trapezoidal and housed not only the bodies of important individuals but possessions that might be needed in the next world, although the burial itself was still underground. In the 3rd Dynasty (*c.* 2650–*c.* 2575 BC) IMHOTEP, working for King Djoser (*reg c.* 2630–*c.* 2611 BC), developed the idea of placing a series of mastabas on top of each other to create a more monumental tomb and to enable the dead ruler to achieve more readily his destined union with the stars (*see* PYRAMID, §1). The result was a six-stepped pyramid, erected at Saqqara (*see* SAQQARA, fig. 1), the first truly monumental tomb—or what would later be called a mausoleum. The first true pyramid, at MAIDUM, has been ascribed to Huni (*reg c.* 2599–*c.* 2575 BC). It was followed, during the 4th Dynasty of the Old Kingdom, by the 'Red Pyramid' and 'Bent Pyramid' of Sneferu (*reg c.* 2575–*c.* 2551 BC) at Dahshur, and then by the three great pyramids at GIZA, built by Cheops (*reg c.* 2551–*c.* 2528 BC), Chephren (*reg c.* 2520–*c.* 2494 BC) and Mycerinus (*reg*

c. 2490–*c.*2472 BC). Built of limestone, these three mausolea took the form of four equilateral triangles rising to an apex from a square base. No more tombs were built in Egypt on such a monumental scale because, after the end of the Middle Kingdom (*c.* 1630 BC), monarchs became increasingly worried about the security of the tombs and their possessions and opted for hidden burial-places rather than dramatic pyramids.

2. ASIA MINOR. Although it has its ancestry and heritage in ancient Egypt, the mausoleum essentially evolved from the tradition of the tomb house or HEROÖN, a shrine over the tomb of a hero, which occurred in Asia Minor and in Greece itself from the Archaic to the Hellenistic periods. Early examples appeared in Lycia in the 5th century BC in the form of funeral monuments on high podia. This conception may have derived from the idea that the dead would be taken to heaven by winged creatures, as depicted on the so-called Harpy Tomb at Xanthos (*c.* 480 BC), where a flat-roofed tomb house was hollowed out at the top of a monolithic tower. An example from Trysa, also in Lycia (first half of the 5th century BC; architectural sculpture in Vienna, Ksthist. Mus.), featured, within a walled court, a sarcophagus with a gabled top. By the end of the 5th century BC, as in the Nereid Monument at Xanthos (*c.* 425–400 BC; London, BM), which took the shape of a temple raised on a podium (for illustration *see* XANTHOS), the tomb house seems to have reached a characteristic form. Later, in the Lion Tomb at Knidos (3rd or 2nd century BC, sometimes dated as early as 390–370 BC; *see* TOMB, fig. 1; lion statue now in London, BM), an Egyptian-style pyramid was added to the top of these structures.

This tradition, though vastly expanded in scale, produced the Mausoleum at Halikarnassos in Caria, bordering on Lycia. This gigantic monument, which became the standard model, combined a high base, a temple-like structure and a pyramid, topped by a quadriga. This basic formula was used on a smaller scale in Asia Minor at BELEVI (3rd century BC; *see* GREECE, ANCIENT, fig. 30), near Ephesos, in the Tomb of Hamrath (*c.* 75 BC) at Soada (now Es Suweidiya), Syria, and at Gümüşkesen (first half of the 2nd century AD), Mylasa. Further afield, such monuments could be found in Greece itself—that to Pythianice, erected by Harpalus (*c.* 355–323 BC) on the sacred way from Eleusis to Athens—and in Sicily—the so-called Tomb of Theron (*c.* first half of the 1st century BC) at Akragas (now Agrigento).

3. ROME. The mausoleum as an architectural type flourished especially in Rome, where examples in an enormous range of sizes abound from the heyday of the Republic to the collapse of the Empire. Round forms were probably the most popular type and seem to have evolved from Etruscan tumulus-type tombs (7th century BC onwards), which were earth mounds up to 48 m in diameter, sometimes resting on rock-cut or stone foundations. The Roman versions were either simple cylinders, like the Etruscan prototypes, or cylinders set on a square podium. Perhaps the most famous surviving example in the latter category, at least on a smaller scale, is the Tomb of Caecilia Metella (*c.* 20 BC) on the Via Appia; its present battlements

MAVSOLEVM·HADRIANI·ET·PONS·AELIVS·ROMA·

1. Mausoleum of Hadrian (now the Castel Sant'Angelo), Rome, AD 130–39; reconstruction drawing

2. Tomb of the Julii, Saint-Rémy-de-Provence, third quarter of the 1st century BC

were added in the 13th century. Others on this scale include the Mausoleum of C. Ennius Marsus (second half of the 1st century BC) at Sepino, the tombs at Gaeta of L. Sempronius Atratinus (marble facing now in Gaeta Cathedral) and L. Munatius Plancus (both *c.* 20 BC), and the so-called Tor de' Schiavi (early 4th century AD), Via Praenestina, Rome. Larger examples in Rome can be seen in the tombs of two emperors, the mausolea of Augustus (begun 28 BC; partially extant) and Hadrian (AD 130–39; now the Castel Sant'Angelo; see fig. 1; *see* ROME, §V, 9). A variant is provided by the Tomb of Romulus, also known as the Mausoleum of Maxentius (*c.* AD 307), beside the Circus of Maxentius on the Via Appia. Little survives, but reconstructions by Sebastiano Serlio and Andrea Palladio in the 16th century and modern archaeological investigations (see Rasch) suggest that it was a round, domed mausoleum but preceded by a portico, the whole set in an arcaded precinct of rectangular shape.

There were also rectangular mausolea, rather like tomb temples. In the case of that formerly assigned to Annia Regilla (*c.* AD 160; *see* ROME, ANCIENT, fig. 14), near the Via Appia, the gable-roofed temple on a low podium was articulated with four pilasters on all sides, although with the inner pair on the south side recessed into the walls as octagonal columns. Other examples include the so-called Oratory of Phalaris (*c.* 85 BC), Akragas; the Tomb of Absalom (early 1st century AD), Jerusalem; and the tomb house illustrated on a relief (Rome, Vatican, Mus. Gregoriano Profano) from the tomb of the Haterii, Centocelle. Octagonal structures were less common, but a very imposing one was the Mausoleum of Diocletian (*c.* AD 300; now Split Cathedral; *see* SPLIT, §1) at Spalato. Recalling the familiar Egyptian format, there were also at least two pyramidal tombs in Rome itself, including the extant burial monument of Caius Cestius (*c.* 12 BC), the proportions of which are more attenuated than those of

Giza, but there is no doubt about its ancestry. Another type of Roman mausoleum took the form of a tower of multiple stages. This tendency may be seen in the Tomb of the Julii (third quarter of the 1st century BC; see fig. 2) at Glanum (now Saint-Rémy-de-Provence) and the so-called Conocchia (third quarter of the 1st century AD) on the Via Appia at Santa Maria Capua Vetere.

II. Early Christian, c. AD 330–c. 600.

Various Roman types of mausoleum continued to be built after the triumph of Christianity, but increasingly the mausoleum came to be allied to a church. Between the 4th and 6th centuries, the traditional concept of the mausoleum became linked with the idea of the MARTYR-IUM. Two of the early examples of round mausolea-cum-martyria for Christian burial are provided by the tombs in Rome of Constantine the Great's mother and daughter. The former, the Mausoleum of Helena (*d c.* 330) on the Via Casilina (now the Tor Pignattara), was a domed, circular structure, with alternating rectangular and circular niches, actually attached to the east end of the basilica built over the catacomb of SS Marcellino e Pietro. The latter, the Mausoleum of Constantia (*d* 354), was set against the south side of the church of S Agnese and featured a taller, domed, central circular section surrounded by a vaulted ambulatory; it is now the church of S Costanza (*see* ROME, §V, 18).

Their format was apparently related to the mausoleum of Constantine himself, a round tomb (356–7; destr. 536) that was part of the church of the Holy Apostles in Constantinople, and the Holy Sepulchre in Jerusalem, which consisted of the tomb of Christ in the garden of Joseph of Arimathea, over which Constantine had erected the Anastasis Rotunda (326–35; altered 1048), separated from a basilica by a courtyard (*see* JERUSALEM, §II, 2(i)). This conception of the Holy Sepulchre merged with the fairly common cylindrical Roman mausoleum as a model especially appropriate for a martyrium, and for a time it encouraged the erection of round mausolea–martyria. Variations might include the Mausoleum of Theodoric (*c.* AD 526) at Ravenna (*see* RAVENNA, fig. 3), which features a domed drum set above a ten-sided lower storey with a cruciform, vaulted interior, and the contemporary Tomb of Clovis I (*reg* 481–511) behind the present Pan-théon in Paris, dedicated to the Holy Apostles and intended as the Frankish king's mausoleum. Not all Early Christian and Byzantine tombs used this format, however. Equally symbolic but quite different is the Greek cross employed for the Mausoleum of Galla Placidia (*c.* AD 425–6; *see* RAVENNA, fig. 2), Ravenna, although it was probably originally a martyrium and not used as her tomb.

III. Medieval, c. AD 600–c. 1500.

Despite its flowering as a combined mausoleum–martyr-ium in the first centuries of the Christian Church, however, the mausoleum as a separate architectural entity largely disappeared after the Early Christian period. Increasingly, burial of the famous and distinguished took place in a church, and sculptural monuments replaced architectural ones. Towards the end of the Middle Ages a few monu-ments and chapels with some resemblance to mausolea

began to appear, such as the Tombs of the Glossators (late 13th century) outside S Francesco, Bologna, and the large, free-standing della Scala monuments (14th century) outside S Maria Antica, Verona (*see* VERONA, §3(iii); for illustration *see* SCALA, DELLA). Similarly, in France in the late Middle Ages, funerary chapels—often with space for burial underneath—were sometimes attached to churches, though surviving examples from the 16th century fre-quently have a Renaissance character. Funerary chapels derived from what was known of the Anastasis Rotunda in Jerusalem seem also to have existed in central Europe at this time (*see* JERUSALEM, §II, 2(ii) and EASTER SEPUL-CHRE), but free-standing mausolea in the Roman sense did not appear.

IV. Renaissance, 16th century.

The pseudo-mausolea found in the late Middle Ages continued into the Renaissance; examples in France in-clude the Ferrand family chapel (1530) outside St Jean, Joigny, and the chapel of Jean Forget (1549) at St Etienne, Toul. Sometimes they came even closer to free-standing sepulchres. In Poland a circular mausoleum with four apses at right angles was erected *c.* 1520 next to Gniezno Cathedral for Archbishop Jan Łaski. However, as befits a culture imbued with the revival of antiquity, consciousness of ancient mausolea also appeared in the Renaissance; thus an engraving of the Mausoleum at Halikarnassos, based on Pliny the elder's description (*Natural History* XXXVI.xxx–xxxi), was included in the edition of *Hypne-rotomachia Poliphili* (attributed to Francesco Colonna) published in Venice in 1499. Inspired by Pliny, and possibly also inspired by this engraving, Antonio da Sangallo (ii) drew a mausoleum that featured a square base flanked by four porticos, surmounted by a stepped pyramid and topped with a finial (Florence, Uffizi). It is also possible that the Chigi Chapel (designed *c.* 1512–13) at S Maria del Popolo in Rome may have been intended by Raphael and his patron Agostino Chigi as a reconciliation of the ancient tradition of the mausoleum with the Christian idea of a chapel.

Michelangelo, too, seems to have turned to this antique theme, not only in the New Sacristy (1519–34) attached to the north transept at S Lorenzo, Florence, but also in his original idea for the tomb of Pope Julius II, conceived as a tomb house (*c.* 11×7 m) to be placed inside St Peter's, Rome. Although this work was radically altered before its erection in S Pietro in Vincoli, Rome, the original scheme certainly harked back to ancient prototypes.

Another large, 16th-century royal funerary chapel sim-ilarly approached the grandeur and conception of ancient mausolea, although, as it was attached to an existing church, it did not actually repeat the antique formula. Undoubtedly inspired by her family's chapel in Florence, Catherine de' Medici commissioned from Francesco Pri-maticcio the Valois Chapel for her husband Henry II and herself, to be annexed to the end of the north transept at Saint-Denis Abbey, the French royal necropolis. This large, circular chapel, with a central domed rotunda and six trefoil-shaped alcoves, was begun in 1559 but never completed (destr. 1719).

V. 17th century.

Dynastic funerary chapels similarly characterized much of the following century, including the octagonal Chapelle Ronde (1607–35) for the dukes of Lorraine at the church of the Cordeliers, Nancy, and the Panteón de los Reyes (1617–18) for the Habsburgs at the Escorial, near Madrid. A semi-octagonal chapel-cum-mausoleum (1632–4) was designed for Gustav II Adolf (*reg* 1611–32) in the Riddarholmskyrka, Stockholm. Others in Sweden include a Greek-cross space (1666) for Lars Kagg, added to the 12th-century church at Floda by Erik Dalbergh, and the Caroline Mausoleum (1671–1743) in the Riddarholmskyrka, designed by Nicodemus Tessin (i), which is also a Greek cross in plan and features free-standing Doric columns; its dome was redesigned in the 1740s by Carl Hårleman.

In France, the Bourbon Louis XIV attempted to outdo his Valois predecessors with plans to build a funeral chapel attached to the east end of Saint-Denis. François Mansart's design of *c.* 1663 combined a taller central domed space surrounded by four oval chapels alternating with four smaller circular ones, but it was never carried out. Like so many other such buildings, both projected and executed, it belonged to the tradition of the chapel–martyrium rather than the ancient free-standing mausoleum.

A martyrium–mausoleum for Charles I, planned for the grounds of Windsor Castle to the designs of Christopher Wren (1678; Oxford, All Souls Coll., Codrington Lib.), would have marked a return to the antique formula, for it was to have been a completely independent, domed, cylindrical mausoleum. It was authorized by Parliament, but money for its construction was never forthcoming. Although it drew on Renaissance and post-Renaissance sources, including Michelangelo's dome for St Peter's and Donato Bramante's Tempietto at Rome, the basic conception of a circular building as a memorial house of the dead was certainly antique. This attempt to return to the ancient world for an appropriate monument to the martyred monarch should be viewed alongside Wren's fascination with the Mausoleum of Halikarnassos, his endeavour to work out its details from Pliny's description, and his discourses on the presumed Etruscan tomb of Porsenna (Pliny: *Natural History* XXXVI.xiii), the pyramids and the Tomb of Absalom in Jerusalem.

Other British schemes for mausolea in the last half of the 17th century can also be identified. In 1657 John Webb (i) designed a cylindrical 'depository' for Sir Justinian Isham (1610–74) to be built next to the chancel of All Saints, Lamport, near Lamport Hall, Northants, the seat of the Isham family. Although not executed, this structure was viewed by Webb as 'rarely new', with its exterior rusticated, 'for so the Ancients used' (Bold). An octagonal mausoleum with a low ogee dome in Greyfriars churchyard, Edinburgh, was designed by James Smith for Sir George Mackenzie of Rosehaugh (1636–91) and completed in time for his funeral.

VI. 18th century.

1. EARLY 18TH CENTURY. The mausoleum received dramatically renewed attention in England from Wren and his successors Sir John Vanbrugh and Nicholas Hawksmoor. Like Wren, Vanbrugh was unable to erect a mausoleum, although he may have designed one, and he argued eloquently in 1722 in support of such a monument for Blenheim: 'Sure if ever any such thing as erecting Monuments in open spaces was right, it wou'd be so in this case' (Webb).

Hawksmoor's mausoleum at Castle Howard, N. Yorks, is perhaps the first grand, imposing and free-standing example since antiquity. Like his former master, Wren, he was thoroughly familiar with the tombs of the ancient world, and his design (Oxford, All Souls Coll., Codrington Lib.) for the steeple of St George's (1716–27), Bloomsbury, London, for example, is his own reconstruction of the Mausoleum of Halikarnassos. He had previously (*c.* 1702) planned a mausoleum for William III (*reg* 1688–1703). For Castle Howard he built two, the first of which, a pyramid (1728–9), was in effect a mausoleum for Charles Howard, 1st Earl of Carlisle (*d* 1686). The second, for Charles Howard, 3rd Earl of Carlisle, is Hawksmoor's masterpiece—a great, dour, domed cylindrical structure (h. 23 m) with a ring of Doric columns (*see* HAWKSMOOR, NICHOLAS, fig. 4). It is closer to Bramante's Tempietto than to such ancient examples, cited by Hawksmoor in correspondence with his client, as the Tomb of Caecilia Metella (see above), but its powerful sombre quality and idea are indeed Roman. Begun in 1729 and completed in 1742, it is a major, although a fairly isolated, example of an English mausoleum.

Other English examples were produced before the mid-18th century. In the churchyard at Chiddingstone, Kent, is a mausoleum of 1736 surmounted by a pyramidal roof, designed by Henry Streatfield for his family; and in 1740 an octagonal one dedicated to Marwood William Turner, designed by James Gibbs, was added to the north end of the chancel of St Cuthbert's, Kirkleatham, Cleveland. Alessandro Galilei designed a cylindrical mausoleum *c.* 1718, possibly for William Stanus of Carlingford, Co. Louth, although it was not executed.

There is also evidence of Italian interest in the subject. In 1725 the Accademia di S Luca in Rome held a competition for a sepulchre for a prince of the Church that would equal those of the Egyptians. And Filippo Juvarra designed a complex five-part structure as a mausoleum for the kings of France, perhaps in 1720–21 when he was in Paris. Although engraved in 1739, it was never executed.

2. ROME, MID-CENTURY. After almost 14 centuries of neglect, in the mid-18th century architects and patrons again became intensely interested in mausolea as part of the revival of antiquity that marks Neo-classicism. This renewed efflorescence occurred first in Rome, arising from the archaeological enthusiasm and new approach to design that developed there in the 1740s and 1750s. The revitalization of antiquity through archaeology was epitomized in the engravings of Giovanni Battista Piranesi, who was one of the central figures in the revival of the mausoleum. In his first volume of engravings, *Prima parte di architetture e prospettive* (Rome, 1743), Piranesi published a plate that he called an antique sepulchre with obelisks and sepulchral urns. Its multiplicity of Roman forms and megalomaniacal

scale, characteristic of almost all his work, did not necessarily serve as a model for later mausolea, but his thematic suggestion and the wealth of such details as urns, obelisks, colonnades and rusticated surfaces were highly influential. His largest and most comprehensive undertaking, *Le antichità romane* (Rome, 1756), published in four volumes, was originally planned *c.* 1753 as a publication devoted primarily to tombs, urns and funeral inscriptions, essentially an expanded version of his *Camere sepolcrali degli antichi romani* (1750).

Others in Rome, especially the young scholarship holders at the French Academy there, shared Piranesi's interest—or were inspired by it. These included Jean-Laurent Legeay (who may even have anticipated Piranesi), Louis-Joseph Le Lorrain, Charles Michel-Ange Challe, Nicholas-Henri Jardin and Marie-Joseph Peyre, all of whom reflected a new style in which the influence of Piranesi seems decisive. Not all of them designed mausolea, but their conceptions of these years are closely related to Piranesi's *sepolcro antico*. Only the scale of a design by Jardin for a mausoleum (1748) resembles the work of Piranesi, but its pyramidal shape is a highly appropriate antique sepulchral form, possibly drawn from the monument of Caius Cestius at Rome (see §I, 3 above). In the 1750s Peyre conceived a sepulchral chapel based on another extant Roman mausoleum, the Tomb of Caecilia Metella. His description of this design in *Oeuvres d'architecture* (Paris, 1765) not only mentions that monument but, in his words, 'shows how, in imitating this ancient form, one could lay out, according to our usage, monuments consecrated to the glory of great men'. By 1755 the theme of the sepulchral chapel was sufficiently esteemed by the French Academy in Paris for it to be chosen for that year's Prix de Rome competition (see Pérouse de Montclos, 1984).

Young architects of other nationalities in Rome were also aroused by this theme. In 1751–2 William Chambers, inspired by the death of Frederick, Prince of Wales (1707–51), and the examples of Piranesi and the French students in Rome, created a design for a mausoleum (London, V&A) employing a large, cylindrical, domed structure flanked by obelisks. This design, too, remained unexecuted but clearly resembled those of his Roman contemporaries. Robert Adam did not actually design any mausolea while in Italy in the 1750s, but his drawings of such antique or Early Christian mausolea as the pyramid of Cestius, various tombs of the Via Appia and the Via Latina, and the mausolea of Helena and Theodoric provided valuable material after his return to England.

3. LATE 18TH CENTURY. Despite the extensive French fascination with the mausoleum in the 1740s and 1750s in Rome, its full flowering in France occurred only in the 1780s in the fantastic conceptions of Etienne-Louis Boullée—for example his enormous drawings for a funerary chapel in the form of a low pyramid (Paris, Bib. N.; Florence, Uffizi)—and those who followed. There were a number of indications of continuing French interest in this theme throughout the second half of the 18th century: in 1785 a sepulchral chapel was again the subject for the Prix de Rome, which was won by Jean-Charles-Alexandre Moreau (1762–1810) and Pierre-François-Léonard Fontaine; and it was also the subject for the monthly *prix*

d'émulation in August 1767 and June 1780. The publication of designs for mausolea in Peyre's *Oeuvres d'architecture* and various supplements of François de Neufforge's *Recueil élémentaire d'architecture* (Paris, 1757–80), particularly in 1777, created further interest.

In Prussia in the 1780s and, especially, the 1790s there were a number of unexecuted designs for mausolea, of which at least six were in response to the Akademie's competition in 1796–7 for a monument to *Frederick the Great* in Berlin. The most impressive was that of Friedrich Gilly, which combined a great Greek Doric temple on top of a high podium, flanked by obelisks and set within a precinct formed by powerful colonnades and arcaded entrances (for illustration *see* GILLY, (2)). Carl Gotthard Langhans, Heinrich Gentz, Friedrich Wilhelm Erdmannsdorff, and Aloys Hirt also submitted designs. Other surviving mausoleum designs were made by Hans Christian Genelli, Heinrich Christoph Jussow and Karl Friedrich Schinkel. Executed examples in both France and the various German states are much rarer.

In England, on the other hand, not only was there an enormous outpouring of mausoleum designs in the last four decades of the 18th century but substantial numbers were erected. Between 1768 and 1793 at least 46 designs were shown at exhibitions in London. Although most date from after 1780, several drawings and buildings were also executed in the previous two decades, with most of the famous architects of the period, including Chambers, Adam, James Paine, George Dance (ii), James Wyatt, Joseph Bonomi and John Soane, indulging in the subject. Examples range from Adam's first scheme for the mausoleum to John Fitzmaurice, 1st Earl of Shelburne (*d* 1761), at Bowood House, Wilts—based on a variety of ancient and Renaissance models but especially the mausoleum of Diocletian at Split, which Adam and his assistants had measured and drawn—to Bonomi's executed pyramidal mausoleum (1794) for John Hobart, 2nd Earl of Buckinghamshire (1723–93), at Blickling, Norfolk (see fig. 3). In between are a host of cylinders, squares, Greek

3. Mausoleum, by Joseph Bonomi, Blickling, Norfolk, 1794

crosses, towers and complex combinations, both projected and erected. In the first category, for example, is James Wyatt's mausoleum (1787–94) at Brocklesby Park, Lincs, with its ring of Doric columns surrounding an internal cylinder crowned by a low dome (*see* WYATT, (2), fig. 1). In the second is Wyatt's mausoleum (1782) at Cobham, Kent, which features canted corners sporting sarcophagi on paired Doric columns, an elegantly refined coffered interior and a dramatic pyramidal top. Adam's executed building at Bowood and James Paine's at Gibside, Durham (both early 1760s) are Greek-cross mausolea. The Rockingham Mausoleum (1783–8) at Wentworth Woodhouse, S. Yorks, by John Carr of York, employs a towered format, derived from such buildings as the Tomb of the Julii at Saint-Rémy.

Unlike the preceding types, the complex mausoleum designs of late 18th-century England have, in their combination of parts, no antique model, although the individual components recall specific ancient features. Soane was even more enthralled by the subject than his fellow Neoclassicists. His unexecuted designs of *c.* 1776–7 in memory of James King, of 1779 for William Pitt, 1st Earl of Chatham (1708–78), and of *c.* 1800 for a sepulchral chapel at Tyringham, Bucks, are typical. They employ cylinders, squares, pyramids, porticos and sarcophagi; but only at Tyringham are the parts fully integrated and the whole synthesized into a powerful, mature design.

VII. 19th century.

1. EARLY 19TH CENTURY. The continued, even heightened devotion to antiquity that characterized the first quarter of the 19th century was, not unnaturally, accompanied by a continued absorption with the mausoleum. Soane, for example, executed two schemes of this

4. Mausoleum for Sir Peter Francis Bourgeois by John Soane, Charlotte Street (now Hallam Street), London, 1807–8 (destr.); interior perspective by the Soane Office, watercolour, 555×630 mm, 1807 (London, Sir John Soane's Museum)

kind, the more complete being the mausoleum for Sir Peter Francis Bourgeois and Mr and Mrs Noel Desenfans at Dulwich College Picture Gallery (1811–14). Like the Tyringham design, it alluded to antiquity, but greatly modified in a highly original manner. On the interior, Soane combined a dark, circular *tholos* ringed with Greek Doric columns and a three-armed tomb chamber flooded with hidden light. On the exterior, primitivist tendencies turned columns into simple brick piers, intercolumniations into slits and striations, and the Greek Revival into a wholly original creation. Soane produced another five mausoleum designs in the first three decades of the 19th century, including one for Sir Peter Francis Bourgeois at his house in Charlotte Street (see fig. 4), of which the Dulwich Mausoleum is a close copy. Other British designs include Charles Heathcote Tatham's mausoleum (1807–8) for Granville Leveson-Gower, 1st Marquess of Stafford (1721–1803), at Trentham Hall, Staffs; Archibald Elliot's Forbes Mausoleum (1816) at Callander House, Central; and a towered mausoleum to Richard Budd, erected from *c.* 1824 in St Matthew's churchyard, Brixton, London, to the designs of R. Day (*fl* 1827–41). Tatham's powerful, square mausoleum, with tapered sides and a smaller but still strong second stage, was described in the caption to his 1808 engraving of it as situated 'After the manner of Roman tombs...on the roadside', thus illustrating the continuing potency of ancient influence.

German examples include various designs by Schinkel, Friedrich Weinbrenner, Giovanni Salucci and Jussow. Designs by the last two were executed at Rotenberg, near Stuttgart (1820–24), for Queen Catherine of Württemburg (1788–1819), and at Kassel in 1826 for Wilhelmine Caroline (*d* 1820), respectively. The most interesting case involves that for Queen Luise (1776–1810) in the park at Schloss Charlottenburg (*see* BERLIN, §IV, 1). It was built between 1810 and 1812, Heinrich Gentz erecting a classical Greek Doric temple front by Schinkel, despite Schinkel's design of and exhortation for a Gothic conception. This style, which was already a significant leitmotif and later grew in importance, indicates the romanticism that seemed especially appropriate for the theme of death.

The St Louis Chapel at Dreux (1816–22), which was erected as a royal funeral chapel for Louise-Marie-Adélaïde de Bourbon, the Dowager Duchesse d'Orléans (1753–1821), also involves the contrasting classical and Gothic styles, but with a quite different outcome. Originally it was a cylinder with four arms, like a Greek cross, in essence a classical rotunda; in 1839–46, however, it was Gothicized by Pierre Bernard LeFranc (1795–1856) by order of King Louis-Philippe, indicating the changing taste approaching the mid-19th century.

In addition to the original form of the Orléans chapel and such tombs as the dome set on a cube in C.-M.-A. Froelicher's monument (1820–22) to Ferdinand, Duc de Berry (1778–1820), at Rosny-sur-Seine, probably the most significant French contribution to early 19th-century mausolea was the foundation of Père Lachaise in Paris, the first cemetery created as if in a landscape garden. Begun by Alexandre-Théodore Brongniart in 1804, this new conception for a burial ground was to include various kinds of graves and eventually a multitude of mausolea. Among Brongniart's designs was a pyramidal chapel (built *c.* 1812), which united this approach with the traditional types of individual structures. Other early mausolea at Père Lachaise include the two-stage tomb (1818) of Pierre Monge, designed by Pierre Clochar (1774–before 1855). Mausolea here tended to be relatively smaller in size, as was appropriate to their setting.

2. MID-19TH CENTURY. By the mid-19th century, similar picturesquely landscaped cemeteries had been established elsewhere. These also began to sprout mausolea—somewhat smaller structures, as can be seen at Kensal Green and Highgate, London; Mt Auburn in Cambridge, MA, and its progeny in Philadelphia, New York and other American cities; Mt Royal in Montreal; and others in Germany and elsewhere. Examples of mausolea in these new cemeteries range from the towered monument (1837) to Andrew Ducrow in Kensal Green to Eugène-Emmanuel Viollet-le-Duc's tomb (1865–6) for Charles-Auguste-Louis-Joseph, Duc de Morny (1811–65), at Père-Lachaise—a small, square mausoleum with four elaborate altar finials. There even occur cast-iron tombs, such as the rectangular example with rusticated piers (*c.* 1871) for John M. Helm in the City Cemetery of Natchez, MI.

Larger, more independent mausolea continued to appear in these years, reflecting the parade of styles that became common in the mid-19th century. Georg Ludwig Friedrich Laves, for example, designed both a pyramidal mausoleum (a traditional and time-honoured treatment) at Derneburg *c.* 1839 for Graf Ernst Friedrich Herbert von Münster and an even more overtly Egyptoid mausoleum (1841) with cavetto mouldings and other easily recognizable motifs for Queen Frederica (1778–1841) in the Berggarten, Herrenhausen, Hannover. The latter design was not executed, Laves substituting a square mausoleum with a low dome, small apse and Doric portico (1841–7), inspired by that for Frederica's sister, the Prussian Queen Louise, at Charlottenburg (see §7(i) above). Similarly, Albert Jenkins Humbert (1822–77) and Ludwig Grüner (1801–82) designed a domed columnar rotunda in 1861 for Victoria, Duchess of Kent (1786–1861), at Frogmore House, Berks, but the following year they began a Romanesque mausoleum at the same place for the Prince Consort, Albert of Saxe-Coburg (completed 1868; *see* TOMB, fig. 19). Another Romanesque design was the St Fernand Chapel at Neuilly, created by Fontaine in 1843 for Ferdinand, Duc d'Orléans (1810–42). Other examples range from a tempietto for the mausoleum (1826) to John Peter Van Ness in Oak Hill Cemetery, Washington, DC, by George Hadfield, to a stepped, rusticated entrance and narrowing column for the Molson Mausoleum in Mt Royal Cemetery, Montreal, completed in 1863 to the designs of George Browne (1811–85).

3. LATE 19TH CENTURY. In the 1880s and 1890s, smaller and not-so-small mausolea continued to proliferate in the picturesque landscaped cemeteries that were an important facet of middle-class and upper-middle-class life. These new cemeteries, with gentle hills and tree-framed lakes, were peppered with pyramids, miniature temples and other tomb houses in contemporary architectural styles. New tendencies also appeared here, as in the

work of Louis Sullivan at Graceland Cemetery, Chicago, and Bellefontaine Cemetery, St Louis, MO. The former contains his two-stage pyramid (1887–9) for Martin Ryerson and his Getty Tomb (1890), which is a squarish monument with a slightly broader top, bearing an exquisite series of stylized and naturalized bands carved in stone and cast in bronze on its gates. The profusion of delicate decoration on the Wainwright Tomb (1891–2) in Bellefontaine Cemetery is related to that on his Wainwright Building (also 1891), St Louis, but here is combined with two geometric shapes—a rectangular block and a dome. A grander family, the Vanderbilts, representing an older generation of captains of industry, commissioned a Romanesque mausoleum for the Moravian Cemetery at New Dorp on Staten Island, NY, from their favourite architect, Richard Morris Hunt, in 1885–6.

Traditional forms, such as the pyramid, continued to be employed, though often with more elaborate ornamentation. Such was certainly the case with the unexecuted mausoleum designed by the Englishman Thomas Willson (*b* 1814) in 1882 as a tribute to the assassinated American president James A. Garfield (1831–81). To the basic pyramidal form Willson added not only battered entrances but also crosses, an obelisk finial and an elaborate Renaissance Revival domed interior. Grant's Tomb, New York (1891–7), designed by John H. Duncan (1855–1929) as the monument to President Ulysses S. Grant (1822–85), is a large mausoleum of impressive grandeur, rivalling those of antiquity. Various prepossessing configurations were suggested in the second competition of 1890, but Duncan's winning design was based on the Mausoleum at

5. Grant's Tomb by John H. Duncan, New York, 1891–7

Halikarnassos, albeit somewhat modified. This enormous structure combines a square base with four Greek Doric porticos, topped by a recessed Ionic colonnaded cylinder with a conical top (see fig. 5).

VIII. 20th century.

The late 19th-century pattern of building both smaller family mausolea in landscaped cemeteries, echoing the prevailing architectural styles, and grand national monumental tombs continued into the 20th. The latter type, emphasizing size, grandeur and national symbolism, were reserved for special individuals. Thus the tomb of another assassinated American president, William McKinley (1843–1901), erected by H. van Buren Magonigle (1867–1935) in Canton, OH, in 1905–06, is a modern version of the Tomb of Caecilia Metella. It is a great cylinder, separated from a dome by a drum and faced with a flat plane in which is inserted the arched entrance and a commemorative panel. Similarly, the Bismarck Monument in Szczecin (1913–15) by Wilhelm Kreis is another mausoleum of the ancient type but combining German and classical details.

A modernized version of antiquity might also characterize the most famous 20th-century mausoleum, that in Red Square, Moscow, for Vladimir Ilyich Lenin (1870–1924). This was originally designed by Aleksey Shchusev as a temporary building for the funeral early in 1924, then as a wooden building that May; it was finally rebuilt in 1929–30 in reinforced concrete and brick, with a granite exterior (see fig. 6). Although it lacks the decorative detail of antique prototypes, its shapes are familiar: a rectangular block topped by a four-stepped pyramid upon which rests a simplified version of a classical temple.

BIBLIOGRAPHY

EWA

C. Wren: *Tracts and Discourse on Architecture* [late 17th–early 18th century]; *Wren Soc.*, xix (1942), pp. 138–45

W. Wood: *An Essay on National and Sepulchral Monuments* (London, 1808)

W. B. Dinsmoor: *The Architecture of Ancient Greece and Rome* (New York, 1902); rev. as *The Architecture of Ancient Greece* (New York, 1927, rev. 3/1950)

G. Webb, ed.: 'The Letters and Drawings of Nicholas Hawksmoor Relating to the Building of the Mausoleum at Castle Howard, 1726–1742', *Walpole Soc.*, xix (1931), pp. 111–64

A. Grabar: *Martyrium: Recherches sur le culte des reliques et l'art chrétien antique*, 2 vols (Paris, 1943–6)

A. Blunt: *Art and Architecture in France, 1500 to 1700*, Pelican Hist. A. (Harmondsworth, 1953)

L. Hautecoeur: *Mystique et architecture: Symbolisme du cercle et de la coupole* (Paris, 1954)

H. s'Jacob: *Idealism and Realism: A Study of Sepulchral Symbolism* (Leiden, 1954)

K. Downes: *Hawksmoor* (London, 1959, rev. 2/1979)

E. Panofsky: *Tomb Sculpture* (New York, 1964)

J. Harris: 'Le Geay, Piranesi and International Neo-classicism in Rome, 1740–1750', *Essays in the History of Architecture Presented to Rudolf Wittkower*, ed. D. Fraser, H. Hibbard and M. J. Lewine (London, 1967), pp. 189–96

T. Kraus: *Das römische Weltreich*, Propyläen-Kstgesch., ii (Berlin, 1967)

J.-M. Pérouse de Montclos: *Etienne-Louis Boullée, 1728–1799: De l'architecture classique à l'architecture révolutionnaire* (Paris, 1969; abridged Eng. trans., New York, 1973)

A. M. Vogt: *Boullées Newton-Denkmal: Sakralbau und Kugelidee* (Basle, 1969)

J. Curl: *The Victorian Celebration of Death* (Newton Abbot, 1972)

A. J. Braham and W. P. J. Smith: *François Mansart, 1598–1666*, 2 vols (London, 1973)

P. Ariès: *Essais sur l'histoire de la mort en Occident, du moyen âge à nos jours* (Paris, 1975)

D. Stillman: 'Death Defied and Honor Upheld: The Mausoleum in Neo-classical England', *A. Q.* [Detroit], n. s., i (1978), pp. 175–214

J. Curl: *A Celebration of Death* (London, 1980)

6. Lenin Mausoleum by Aleksey Shchusev, Moscow, 1924–30

M. Ragon: *Espace de la mort* (Paris, 1981); Eng. trans. as *The Space of Death: A Study of Funerary Architecture, Decoration and Urbanism* (Charlottesville, VA, 1983)

K. Jeppesen and others: *The Maussolleion at Halikarnassos*, 2 vols (Århus, 1981–6)

P. Ariès: *The Hour of our Death* (New York, 1982)

G. Erouard: *Jean-Laurent Legeay: Un Architecte français dans l'Europe des lumières* (Paris, 1982)

D. Kahn: 'The Grant Monument', *J. Soc. Archit. Historians*, xli (1982), pp. 212–31

A. Erlande-Brandenburg: 'Mausolées', *Mnmts Hist. France*, cxxiv (1982–3), pp. 27–32

R. A. Beddard: 'Wren's Mausoleum for Charles I and the Cult of the Royal Martyr', *Archit. Hist.*, xxvii (1984), pp. 36–49

R. A. Etlin: *The Architecture of Death: The Transformation of the Cemetery in 18th-century Paris* (Cambridge, MA, 1984)

J.-M. Pérouse de Montclos: *'Les Prix de Rome': Concours de l'Académie royale d'architecture au XVIIIe siècle* (Paris, 1984)

J. Rasch: *Das Maxentius-Mausoleum an der Via Appia in Rom* (Mainz, 1984)

J. Bold: *John Webb: Architectural Theory and Practice in the Seventeenth Century* (Oxford, 1989)

H. Colvin: *Architecture and the After-life* (New Haven, 1991)

DAMIE STILLMAN

Mausolos (*reg* 377–352 BC). Ancient Greek ruler. He was the Satrap (i.e. vassal of the King of Persia) of Caria in Asia Minor, now western Turkey, and a member of the Hekatomnid dynasty. Although Carian by birth, Mausolos greatly admired Greek culture and art. He was famous for having moved his capital from Mylassa to the coastal site of HALIKARNASSOS, where there was a good harbour. He laid out the new capital in the natural hollow by the harbour, as described by Vitruvius (*On Architecture* II. 811ff), with his tomb, the Mausoleum, at the centre. He employed the most famous Greek architects and sculptors of his time to build and decorate this, but he died before it was completed. The Mausoleum was finished by his wife and half-sister, Artemisia, who reigned after him. A fine portrait statue from the Mausoleum (London, BM, 1001) has been thought to represent Mausolos, though there is no proof of this.

BIBLIOGRAPHY

C. M. Robertson: *A History of Greek Art*, 2 vols (Cambridge, 1975), p. 447

S. Hornblower: *Mausolus* (Oxford, 1982)

MARGARET LYTTELTON

Mauve, Anton [Anthonij] (*b* Zaandam, 18 Sept 1838; *d* Arnhem, 5 Feb 1888). Dutch painter. He came from a large family of clergymen in the province of North Holland. At the age of 16 he was apprenticed to the animal painter Pieter Frederik van Os (1808–92): animals (especially sheep, but also cows and horses) became Mauve's preferred theme. He then trained for a few months with Wouterus Verschuur, who gave him his love of horses, in the style, at least, of Paulus Potter and Philips Wouwerman. Initially Mauve painted horses above all else—not the shining animals Verschuur painted, but worn-out plodding beasts. In 1858 Mauve joined his much older friend Paul Gabriël on a trip to Oosterbeek, the Dutch Barbizon, where he met Gerard Bilders and Willem Maris, two artists who were to have an enormous influence on him. The premature death of Bilders, a painter with whom he shared emotionalism and fickleness of mood, came as a great shock to Mauve. Apart from Bilders, Willem Maris, who was six years his junior, was a lifelong friend. There are a number of similarities between their work as well as essential differences: Mauve tended to add human figures to his animal pieces, whereas the youngest of the Maris brothers did not; Mauve's cows, horses and sheep seem more peaceful than Maris's—at times almost listless. For a long time Mauve was impressed by Maris's virtuosity as a painter, although he eventually adopted a different style. There is a clear relationship between man and animal or between the animals themselves in Mauve's paintings, a noticeable difference from Maris's pictures.

Mauve is considered one of the finest HAGUE SCHOOL painters. His oeuvre can be divided into three periods: the early years, which coincide with his stay in Oosterbeek; the mature years in The Hague (from 1871 onwards); and the late period in Laren from 1885 until his death. The transitions between these periods occurred very gradually. The first period is characterized by dependence on his former teachers, Verschuur and van Os, and by a fondness for summery landscapes; for example, *Cows by a Pool near Oosterbeek* (Arnhem, Gemeentemus.). In The Hague his style began to crystallize. Although his forms started to flow one into the other, they still retained their structure. Instead of using picturesque elements to create a mood, Mauve came to rely on the general characteristics of the landscape and thereby achieved a greater degree of simplicity. The human figure assumed an increasingly prominent role, while such motifs as beach life and the dunes, taken from the coastal landscapes, occur frequently: *Morning Ride on the Beach* (1876; Amsterdam, Rijksmus.; see fig.) and *Fishing Boat on the Beach at Scheveningen* (1876; Dordrecht, Dordrechts Mus.) are typical examples. During his Hague period Mauve began to apply the paint in thinner layers and indicated colour gradations by placing distinct touches of paint next to one another, so anticipating the techniques of the Neo-Impressionists. During his years in The Hague, Mauve used the shellfish-gatherer theme favoured by such Hague school artists as Jacob Maris and J. H. Weissenbruch; his *Shellfish-Gatherer* (Paris, Louvre), with its full range of grey tones, is a classic example. Apart from the various aspects of beach life, Mauve continued to paint animal subjects during this period. *Cows by a Ditch* (Munich, Neue Pin.) shows how he had managed to free himself from the style of his teachers: the brushstrokes are much freer and the composition no longer offers a distant view of the horizon because a row of trees screens off the background.

In 1881 and 1882 Vincent van Gogh worked in Mauve's studio. Mauve's wife, Ariëtte Carbentus, was his cousin so when van Gogh decided to become a painter and moved to The Hague, he went to Mauve for instruction. Van Gogh was the only workshop assistant Mauve ever had. In March 1882 there was a complete break between the two painters. Nevertheless van Gogh's work clearly shows that he learnt a good deal during this brief period: such themes as diggers, potato harvesters and wood merchants all originate from Mauve. During his period in The Hague, Mauve was active in artistic society. In 1876, together with Willem Maris and Hendrik Mesdag, he founded the Hollandsche Teeken-Maatschappij ('Dutch Drawing Society'); in 1878 he became first art inspector of the Pulchri Studio and later, until 1883, its treasurer.

Anton Mauve: *Morning Ride on the Beach*, oil on canvas, 450×700 mm, 1876 (Amsterdam, Rijksmuseum)

In about 1880 Mauve started to look for another place to live; he deplored the urbanization of The Hague, which interfered with his artistic activities. After wandering through Drenthe and Gelderland for a while he eventually settled in Laren. He was particularly fascinated by the intimacy of the village, its interiors, the peasant families and the workers in the fields. In 1885 his wife and children came to join him, and the Mauve family moved into the house next door to the artist Albert Neuhuys, who, together with Jozef Israëls, had originally discovered Laren as a painters' village. Mauve also contributed to the fame of the Laren school, which, although it never attained the same success as the Hague school, for a short time enjoyed an international reputation through such artists as Israëls, Neuhuys, Mauve and Max Liebermann; but on the whole the village was home to painters of lesser importance.

In Laren, Mauve could still feel that he was in direct contact with nature. He added a glass extension to his house (to enlarge his studio) and began to paint directly from nature without making preliminary sketches. This third period was dominated by the influence of François Millet and the rise of Realism. Although the influence of the great French painter should not be exaggerated, it is striking that human figures assumed an even greater importance in Mauve's paintings. His landscapes with sheep included more figures during this period, and he painted more and more themes from peasant life: for example *Women Binding Sheaves* (Wassenaar, priv. col., see 1983 exh. cat., p. 250), *Women Digging Potatoes* (Montreal, Mus. F.A.) and the *Vegetable Garden* (1887; Rotterdam, Mus. Boymans–van Beuningen). An important difference from Millet, who tended to depict the struggle of man

against nature, is that Mauve emphasized the bond between them. One group of Mauve's paintings that has received little attention is his winter landscapes; especially in his watercolours (e.g. *Old Coach in Snow*, 1885; Philadelphia, PA, Mus. A.) he excelled in capturing the silence of winter. The work painted during this final period had a strong influence on Liebermann and Giovanni Segantini. In 1888, having been ordered to rest for a while, Mauve died suddenly after a stroke. His son, Anton Rudolf Mauve (1876–1962), was also a painter.

FRANSJE KUYVENHOVEN

BIBLIOGRAPHY
Scheen
H. L. Berckenhoff: *Anton Mauve* (Amsterdam, 1890)
E. Fles: 'Anton Mauve and the Modern Dutch School, 1838–1888', *Mag. A.* (1896), pp. 71–5
R. Bouyer: *Anton Mauve: Sa Vie, son oeuvre* (Paris, 1898)
M. Rooses, ed.: *Het schildersboek: Nederlandsche schilders der negentiende eeuw, in monographieën door tijdgenoten* [The book about painters: Dutch painters of the 19th century, in monographs by contemporaries], iii (Amsterdam, 1900), pp. 3–36
F. Rutter: 'A Consideration of the Work of Anton Mauve', *The Studio*, xlii (1907), pp. 2–18
Selected Works by James Maris, Anton Mauve, H. Fantin Latour (exh. cat., London, French Gal., 1910)
K. Scheffler: 'Zeichnungen von Anton Mauve', *Kst & Kstler*, xi (1913), pp. 383–4
E. Hancke: 'Anton Mauve', *Kst & Kstler*, xiii (1915), pp. 356–68
Herdenkingstentoonstelling Anton Mauve, 1838–1888 [Anton Mauve memorial exhibition, 1838–1888] (exh. cat., The Hague, Gemeentemus., 1938)
H. P. Baard: *Anton Mauve* (Amsterdam, 1946)
Anton Mauve (exh. cat., Laren, Singer Mus., 1959)
J. W. Keefe: 'Drawings and Watercolors by Anton Mauve', *Mus. News: Toledo Mus. A.*, n.s., ix (1966), pp. 75–94
E. P. Engel: *Anton Mauve (1838–1888): Bronnenverkenning en analyse van zijn oeuvre* [Anton Mauve (1838–1888): a study of sources and analysis of his oeuvre] (Utrecht, 1967)

C. J. de Bruyn Kops: 'Anton Mauve als beginneling en het geschilderde portretje van zijn leermeester', *Bull. Rijksmus.*, xvii (1969), pp. 37–43

J. de Gruyter: *Haagse school*, ii (Rotterdam, 1969), pp. 61–72 [with Eng. summary]

The Hague School: Dutch Masters of the 19th Century (exh. cat., ed. R. de Leeuw, J. Sillevis and C. Dumas; London, RA; Paris, Grand Pal.; The Hague, Gemeentemus.; 1983)

De Haagse School: De collectie van het Haagse Gemeentemuseum (exh. cat., The Hague, Gemeentemus., 1988)

GEERT JAN KOOT

Mauzaisse, Jean-Baptiste (*b* Corbeil, Seine-et-Oise, 1 Nov 1784; *d* Paris, 15 Nov 1844). French painter and lithographer. The son of a poor organist, he entered the Ecole des Beaux-Arts in Paris on 16 November 1803 as a pupil of François-André Vincent. He first exhibited at the Salon in 1812, with the painting *Arab Weeping over his Horse* (Angers, Mus. B.-A.), which was a great success and won him a first class medal. He specialized in history subjects, particularly battle scenes, as well as genre scenes and portraits (e.g. portrait of the miniature painter *Muneret*, 1812; Paris, Louvre). He also worked with Antoine-Jean Gros on several of the latter's paintings.

Mauzaisse was commissioned to produce various decorative paintings for public buildings. He worked in the Louvre, where he executed ceiling decorations in the gallery of antique jewellery and elsewhere, and also a number of grisailles in the vestibule of the Galerie d'Apollon. These decorations tended to be allegorical, as in *Time and the Seasons* (1822) for the jewellery gallery (*in situ*), or mythological, as in *Prometheus Animating Man* in the gallery of antiquities (*in situ*). For the Salle Louis XVIII in the Louvre he produced the ceiling painting *Divine Wisdom Giving Laws to the Kings and Legislators of the Earth* (1827; *in situ*). He received a few commissions for religious paintings, such as the *Martyrdom of St Etienne* (1824; Bourges, Hôtel Jacques Coeur) for the cathedral of Bourges, and *St Clarus Healing the Blind* (1831) for the cathedral of Nantes (*in situ*).

When Louis-Philippe declared the Château de Versailles a national museum of French history, Mauzaisse received numerous commissions to paint portraits and battle scenes. These include the full-length portrait of *Comte Philippe d'Artois*, the *Battle of Fleurus* (1837) and *Napoleon at Eylau* (all Versailles, Château). He was also one of the earliest practitioners of lithography, in which medium he produced such portraits as that of the Director General of the French museums under Napoleon, *Baron Vivant Denon*. In addition, he made lithographs of historical subjects and genre scenes, as well as illustrations for the publication *La Henriade, ornée de dessins lithographiques avec les portraits* (Paris, 1823) by F.M.A. de Voltaire.

BIBLIOGRAPHY

Bellier de La Chavignerie–Auvray; Bénézit; Hoefer; Thieme–Becker

C. Gabet: *Dictionnaire des artistes de l'école française au XIXe siècle* (Paris, 1831)

P. Larousse, ed.: *Grand Dictionnaire universel du XIXe siècle*, x (Paris, 1873), p. 1369

H. Beraldi: *Les Graveurs du XIXe siècle*, ix (Paris, 1889), pp. 252–3

ATHENA S. E. LEOUSSI

Maverick, Peter Rushton (*b* Cheshire, CT, 1 April 1755; *d* Newark, NJ, 12 Dec 1811). American silversmith and engraver. After training as a silversmith, he responded to the growing demand for copperplate-engraving by launching his own business in Newark in the 1770s, advertising in the New York and New Jersey newspapers as an engraver of tea sets and as a copperplate printer. Engraving bookplates, broadsides and occasional portraits provided his staple income; in later years, after American Independence, he was also able to meet the demand of nascent banks for individualized, intricately designed banknotes to counter forgery. Although the ephemeral nature of his work makes it difficult to evaluate his talent within the broader context of contemporary engraving, he achieved sufficient status to be elected as the representative of the Engravers' Association to the Federal Procession of 1788. Three of his sons, Samuel Maverick, Andrew Maverick and the best-known, Peter Maverick (1780–1871), also became printmakers. The last established a partnership with Asher B. Durand between 1817 and 1820, producing bookplates, maps, banknotes and book and magazine illustrations. He used lithography as early as 1824, when he designed the plates for the *Annals of the Lyceum of Natural History of New York*.

BIBLIOGRAPHY

S. DeWitt Stephens: *The Mavericks: American Engravers* (New Brunswick, NJ, 1950)

DAVID M. SOKOL

Mavo. Japanese group of artists, active in Tokyo from 1923 to 1925. The most important figure in the formation of the group was TOMOYOSHI MURAYAMA, who met Hewarth Walden in Berlin in 1922 and became associated with Constructivism and other European avant-garde movements. He exhibited at the Erste Internationale Kunstausstellung at the Haus Leonard Tietz, Düsseldorf, and participated in the first Kongress des Internationalen Fortschrittlichen Künstler, before returning to Japan in January 1923 in an attempt to establish a new arts movement there. The leading avant-garde groups active in Tokyo at that time were the Futurist Art Society (Miraiha Bijutsu Kyōkai), which was greatly influenced by David Burlyuk, and the Action group, in which Tai Kanbara was involved. Murayama became acquainted with several members of the Futurist Art Society, including Masamu Yanase (1900–45), Kamenosuke Ogata (1900–42), Shūzo Ōura and Kunio Kadowaki, and together they formed the Mavo group. The group's activities had a strong Dadaist character and were intended to provoke and disturb. In July 1923 at their first group exhibition they issued a manifesto declaring: 'We will be the avant-garde forever. We are not restrained. We are radical. We are revolutionizing.' Other artists later joined, but few of the group's works remain, other than Yanase's *A Morning in May and myself before Breakfast* (1923: Tokyo, priv. col.), which uses flat surfaces, and a number of works in which printed matter, hair and other *objets trouvés* are pasted to the surface, and some three-dimensional compositions. In 1924 several members of the group left to form the Three Division Society (Sanka), which disbanded, however, in 1925 after two exhibitions, partly as a result of the anarchic tendencies that characterized both groups.

The group also produced seven issues of the *Mavo* magazine between July 1924 and late 1925, with Murayama as the principal editor. It was large format (305×230 mm), with translations, poems, essays and numerous illustrations by Murayama, Tatsuo Okada and Kyōjirō Hagiwara. It also included contributions by other artists such as anarchist poets. The magazine's design and layout were highly original, but its unusual typography made it difficult to read, and the use of a provocative collage entitled *Image of a Mistress* on the cover of the third issue resulted in its sale being banned.

WRITINGS
T. Murayama: *Engekiteki jijoden* [Dramatical autobiography], ii (Tokyo, 1971)

BIBLIOGRAPHY
DADA in Japan: Japanische Avantgarde, 1920–1970 (exh. cat. by Y. Shirakawa and others, Düsseldorf, Kstmus., 1983)
T. Omuka: 'The Sanka in Theater: An Avant-Garde Performance in the Taisho Era', *Bull. Stud. Philos. & Hist. A. U. Tsukuba* (Tsukuba, 1987), no. 5

TORU ASANO

Mawangdui [Ma-wang-tui]. Site in Hunan Province, China, about 4 km east of the city of Changsha. Three tombs of the Western Han period (206 BC–AD 9) were excavated here in 1972–4. Grave goods from the tombs display the influence of the southern state of Chu, which controlled the area before the unification of China into an empire in 221 BC. The Mawangdui site constitutes one of the most important tomb complexes found in China.

Tomb 1, which was undisturbed, contained the remains of a woman of about 50 years of age. Her many grave goods were inscribed 'Majordomo of household of Marquis of Dai', and coins and funeral money found in the grave date the tomb to before 140 BC. The *Shiji* ('Records of the historian'), by the Han historian Sima Qian (*c.* 145–*c.* 90 BC), states that Li Cang, Prime Minister of Changsha, was granted the marquisate of Dai in 193 BC and died in 186 BC, and the occupant of Tomb 1 has been identified as his widow, the Marchioness of Dai. Tomb 2, adjacent to Tomb 1, is identified as that of Li Cang himself. Tomb 3, south of Tomb 1 and dated to 168 BC, is that of a male of about 30 years of age, possibly a younger son of Li Cang. These latter tombs predate Tomb 1. The vertical pit construction is typical of the Chu area and follows the older tradition of Zhou-period (*c.* 1050–256 BC) graves (*see* CHINA, §II, 6).

Tomb 1 consists of an earth mound, with tomb passage, pit and chamber; the top of the pit measures 19.5×17.8 m. The pit and chamber were filled with white clay, charcoal and soil rammed hard and were thus completely insulated, such that the contents, including the body, were extraordinarily well preserved. The chamber is divided into a coffin room and side compartments for grave goods. Four wooden coffins, fitting one inside the other, were precisely jointed and have wooden nails. The coffins are of painted lacquer and feature mythological scenes in black or polychrome on a red or black background, the innermost one decorated with embroidery and glued feathers. The occupant was covered in bedding and garments and dressed in an embroidered and painted robe of red and yellow silk. Grave goods included a silk painting, pottery, wooden figures, musical instruments, bamboo cases, toilet boxes, lacquerware, silk clothing, food, medicines and burial money. Tombs 2 and 3 were less well sealed and had been robbed, and burial objects were not so numerous nor in such good condition as those in Tomb 1. Li Cang's tomb

contained lacquerware, burial money, gold ingots, pearls, ceramics and some gold-inlaid bronzes. Tomb 3 was furnished with lacquerware, crossbows, clothing, wooden effigies, musical instruments, silk paintings and books made of bamboo and silk.

Silk paintings from Mawangdui constitute the earliest complete Chinese paintings known. A T-shaped banner placed over the innermost coffin in Tomb 1 is important for its conveying of spatial recession and its depiction of contemporary beliefs. The subject-matter relates to the belief that the individual possesses two souls, one that stays with the body and burial goods after death and another that goes on to an afterlife. The theme of the painting is the guiding of the ascending soul (*hun*) on its journey. Of four silk paintings from Tomb 3, one is also T-shaped. Fragments of other paintings from Tomb 3 show scenes possibly relating to the dead man's life and are important for the history of portrait painting. Other paintings may show Daoist deep-breathing exercises.

The textiles in the tombs, the earliest known from the Western Han period, are of great variety and exceptional quality. They are in the form of lined and unlined clothes, socks, shoes, gloves, curtains, silk wrappers and damask and fancy gauze pieces, altogether over 20 different coloured silks of printed and painted designs, displaying superior weaving, printing and dyeing techniques (*see also* CHINA, §§XII, 2(i), XIII, 8(ii) and fig. 294). The 162 wooden human effigies from Tomb 1, of varying sizes, are particularly important for their depiction of contemporary life of the region. Some are painted, and one is fully dressed in silk (*see also* CHINA, §XIII, 26). Some depict musicians with miniature instruments, and altogether they represent the retinue of a person of rank. Of 184 lacquerware pieces from Tomb 1 and 316 from Tomb 3 (*see* CHINA, fig. 244), many, decorated in yellow and red patterns, painted or incised on a black background, are in matching sets and fit into each other. There are 16 different kinds of object, including both domestic and ritual vessels, and several items are also depicted in the ceremonial scenes on the painted banner from Tomb 1. Inscriptions indicate the function and capacity of objects, and seal impressions show whether the workshop of origin was private or government controlled.

Records written on bamboo strips include inventories of grave goods and, in Tomb 3, a medical treatise. The books written on silk found at Mawangdui are some of the earliest found in China. More than 20 are works previously considered lost, even by the time of the Eastern Han period (AD 25–220; *see also* CHINA, §XIII, 3). The 51 ceramic items include boxes and vases made from plain or painted grey pottery or a type of hard pottery decorated with a stamped design. Some pieces contained the remains of food and medicines. Miscellaneous items found at the site include clay coins, full-sized musical instruments, bamboo cases tied with hemp cords, wooden staffs, bronze mirrors and tin bells.

BIBLIOGRAPHY
B. Watson: *Records of the Grand Historian of China*, 2 vols (Columbia, 1961)
Changsha Mawangdui yi hao Han mu [Han Tomb 1 at Mawangdui, Changsha], 2 vols (Beijing, 1973)
Yu Weichao and Li Jiahao: 'Mawangdui yi hao Han mu chutu qiqi zhi di zhu men' [Some problems concerning the place of manufacture of the

lacquerware unearthed from Han Tomb 1 at Mawangdui], *Kaogu* (1975), no. 6, pp. 344–8

M. Loewe: 'Manuscripts Found Recently in China: A Preliminary Survey', *T'oung Pao*, lxiii/2–3 (1977), pp. 99–136

A. Bulling: 'Ancient Chinese Maps: Two Maps Discovered in a Han Dynasty Tomb from the Second Century B.C.', *Expedition*, xx/2 (Winter 1978), pp. 16–125

M. Loewe: *Ways to Paradise: The Chinese Quest for Immortality* (London, 1978)

CAROL MICHAELSON

Ma-wang-tui. *See* MAWANGDUI.

Mawsil. *See* MOSUL.

Mawson, Samuel Moses (*b c.* 1793; *d* London, 23 Aug 1862). English dealer. His particular interest lies in the influence he exerted over the great collection formed by Richard Seymour-Conway, 4th Marquess of Hertford (*see* SEYMOUR-CONWAY, (2)). He was acting as Lord Hertford's agent by 1848 and continued until 1861, their partnership being recorded in a series of letters preserved in the Wallace Collection library. (All pictures mentioned hereafter are also in the Wallace Collection, London.) Mawson, based in London, brought desirable acquisitions to the attention of Lord Hertford, based in Paris, who increasingly relied on his judgment. By 1854 Hertford was writing to him: 'I have quite a little collection of pictures to see that I am totally unacquainted with & that you will introduce me to on my return to London' (they include Velázquez's *Baltasar Carlos in Infancy* and Murillo's *St Thomas of Villanueva*). Perhaps Mawson's most remarkable purchases were the 17 pictures from the Phipps and Northwick sales of 1859, which Hertford never saw, and which include Jan Steen's *Harpsichord Lesson*, Joshua Reynolds's *Mrs Robinson* and Cima da Conegliano's *St Catherine*. Mawson became virtually the Curator of Hertford House (Hertford's London residence and now the Wallace Collection); he arranged the pictures and delighted in showing them off to distinguished visitors. 'Pardon all the trouble I give you', Hertford wrote to him in 1856, 'but I know the friendly interest you take in my little Collections that owe so much to your kindness as well as to your taste & judgment.'

UNPUBLISHED SOURCES

London, Wallace [archives]

BIBLIOGRAPHY

J. Ingamells, ed.: *The Hertford Mawson Letters* (London, 1981)

JOHN INGAMELLS

Max. Bohemian family of artists. Anton Max (1734–1808) and his son Josef Franz Max (1765–1838) were both sculptors. Of the latter's three sons, Josef Calasanza Max (1804–55) and (1) Emanuel Max were sculptors, working for a time in partnership. Josef Calasanza Max's sons, (2) Gabriel Max and Heinrich Max (1847–1900), were both painters, and his daughter Caroline Max married the painter Gyula Benczur. Gabriel Max's elder son, Corneille Max (1875–1924), was a painter and etcher, and his younger son, Columbus Josef Max (*b* 1877) was a painter.

BIBLIOGRAPHY

Thieme–Becker

(1) Emanuel Max, Ritter von Wachstein (*b* Bürgstein, Bohemia [now Sloup, Czech Republic], 19 Oct 1810; *d* Prague, 21 Feb 1901). Sculptor. He studied at the Academy of Fine Arts, Prague (1827–31), under Josef Bergler and František Waldherr (1784–1835). He lived in Vienna (1833–7) and Rome (1839–49), working on commissions, mainly for members of the Austrian and Bohemian gentry. These included portraits (e.g. *Wolfgang Amadeus Mozart*, 1837; Prague, Libs Facs & Insts Charles U.), allegorical and religious statuary (*St Ludmila*, 1849; Prague Cathedral) and monuments. After his return to Prague in 1849, he was able to adapt to the conventions of the time, helped partly by his brother, Josef Calasanza Max (1804–55), who ran a sculptor's workshop. The Max brothers' activity constituted an essential stylistic shift away from Neoclassicism and the Empire style and towards a Romantic form of realism. Among the largest projects in Prague on which the brothers collaborated were the monument to *Francis I* and the monument to *Marshal Josef Radecký* (1858; both Prague, Lapidarium Hist. Mus.). From 1853 to 1861 they also replaced seven of the Baroque sculptures (destr. 1848) on the Charles Bridge in Prague. Many sculptors of the following generation trained in the brothers' studio.

BIBLIOGRAPHY

E. Max: *Zweiundachtzig Lebensjahre* (Prague, 1893)

V. Volavka: *Sochařství devatenáctého století* [Sculpture of the 19th century] (Prague, 1942); repr. in *České malířství a sochařství 19. století* [Czech painting and sculpture of the 19th century] (Prague, 1968), pp. 212–16

(2) Gabriel (Cornelius), Ritter von **Max** (*b* Prague, 23 Aug 1840; *d* Munich, 24 Nov 1915). Painter, illustrator and teacher, nephew of (1) Emanuel Max. He studied at the Academy of Fine Arts, Prague (1855–8), and the Akademie der Bildenden Künste, Vienna (1858–61), and under Karl Theodor von Piloty at the Akademie der Bildenden Künste, Munich (1863/4–7). He settled in Munich, where he opened a private school of painting in 1869. His paintings and book illustrations of the second half of the 1860s show an affinity with the late Romanticist movement. He illustrated works of German literature by Wieland, Lenau and Schiller, as well as producing illustrations for Goethe's *Faust* (1867–8; Prague, N.G., Kinský Palace). As well as literary and even musical sources, religious themes frequently occur in his work, including his first great success, the *Crucifixion of St Julie* (1867; ex-Sotheby's, London, 1976). In numerous female figures and portraits Max explored the tension between the inner state and the charm of the physical appearance or surroundings of his subjects. His interest in the artistic perception of relationships between physical reality and the spiritual world led him to a study of anthropology and contemporary occultism and mysticism, as in his portraits of the *Seer of Prevorst* (Prague, N.G., Convent of St Agnes) and the *Ecstasy of Kateřina Emmerichová* (1885; Munich, Neue Pin.).

Through his studio, especially during the 1870s, Max influenced a number of artists in Austria and Germany. He also had an important influence in Bohemia and on Hungarian artists, and from 1879 to 1883 he was professor of historical painting at the Akademie in Munich. However, whereas in his paintings of the 1870s and 1880s Max made sensitive use of a naturalistic style, he later rejected artistic sensuality in favour of the symbolic and allegorical aspects of painting. His interest in the metaphysical significance of painted reality was expressed in *Apes as an Artistic Jury* (1889; Munich, Neue Pin.).

BIBLIOGRAPHY

A. Klemt: 'Gabriel Max und seine Werke', *Graph. Kst.*, ix (1886–7)
N. Mann: *Gabriel Max' Kunst und seine Werke* (Leipzig, 1888, 2/1890)
H. Ludwig, ed.: *Münchner Maler im 19. Jahrhundert*, iii (Munich, 1982), pp. 122–6

ROMAN PRAHL

Maxence, Edgard (*b* Nantes, 17 Sept 1871; *d* La Bernerie-en-Retz, Loire-Atlantique, 1954). French painter. He was a pupil of Jules-Elie Delaunay and Gustave Moreau at the Ecole des Beaux-Arts, Paris, and helped to popularize Symbolism in the 1890s by applying a highly finished academic technique to Symbolist subjects. His best-known paintings, which include *Girl with a Peacock* (before 1896; Paris, G. Levy priv. col., see Jullian, p. 2) and the *Soul of the Forest* (*c.* 1897; Nantes, Mus. B.-A.), are decorative, vaguely religious or allegorical images of beautiful women in medieval dress, influenced by early Italian Renaissance and late English Pre-Raphaelite art. Maxence often enriched the surface of his works with gold or silver foil and gilt plaster relief and mounted them in elaborate frames of his own design. He also painted fashionable portraits such as *Woman with an Orchid* (1900; Paris, A. Lesieutre priv. col., see 1986 exh. cat., p. 29) and Impressionist landscapes. Though he participated in the avant-garde Salon de la Rose + Croix between 1895 and 1897, Maxence exhibited successfully at the conservative Salon des Artistes Français from 1894 to 1939 and frequently served on its committees and juries. Maxence's work changed little in style and content after the turn of the century and, despite the condemnation of progressive critics, continued to enjoy strong middle-class patronage until the late 1930s.

BIBLIOGRAPHY

H. Focillon: 'Le Salon de la Société des Artistes Français', *Rev. A. Anc. & Mod.*, xxxiii (1913), pp. 425–52
E. Ripert: 'Antibes: Ville de soldats, de marins et de poètes', *L'Illustration*, clxxiv (1929), pp. 331–4 [good colour reprs of Impressionist landscapes]
P. Jullian: *The Symbolists* (London, 1973)
Le Symbolisme et la femme (exh. cat., ed. I. Millman and D. Montalant; Paris, Dél. Action A., 1986)

For further bibliography *see* SYMBOLISM.

KENNETH NEAL

Maximian [Maximianus; Maximinian; Maximinianus] (*d c.* AD 557). Dalmatian ecclesiastic and patron. According to the 9th-century chronicle of Agnellus, he was a native of Dalmatia and was consecrated a deacon in Pola (now Pula, Croatia), where he built the basilica of St Marija Formosa (also known as S Maria in Canneto; *see* PULA, §II). He travelled to Alexandria and later to Constantinople, where he remained until AD 546, when Justinian I created him Archbishop of Ravenna. As the imperial nominee to the see, he was only reluctantly accepted by the inhabitants of the recently reconquered city (540) and at first he was forced to reside outside its walls.

In the mosaic panel on the north side of the apse in S Vitale, Ravenna (consecrated in 547; *see* RAVENNA, §2(viii)), where the Emperor is portrayed at the centre of his military, civil and ecclesiastical entourage, Maximian occupies a prominent position at Justinian's left hand. He wears the *pallium* (bishop's stole), only recently granted to the bishops of Ravenna, and is the only figure to be identified by inscription. He was a key figure in the growth of Byzantine influence in Ravenna during the 6th century, and the nature of his authority may be deduced from the iconography of the exquisite ivory throne that carries his monogram (Ravenna, Mus. Arcivescovile; *see* EARLY CHRISTIAN AND BYZANTINE ART, §VII, 5; and THRONE, fig. 1). This was produced by an Eastern, probably imperial, workshop and includes a number of narrative panels telling the biblical story of Joseph in Egypt, perhaps implying that Maximian's role was as much administrative and political as ecclesiastical. Although Agnellus describes his many gifts to the churches and implies active participation in construction campaigns, such as that of the basilica of S Stefano (destr.), Ravenna, Maximian is no longer seen as the all-important patron of his times. The church of S Vitale, for example, was founded under one of his predecessors, Ecclesius (521/2–531/2), and was financed by the wealthy banker Julianus Argentarius; its construction and decoration seem to have proceeded without interruption, indicating that most of the work had been completed before the arrival of Maximian. On the other hand, while the church of S Apollinare in Classe (*see* RAVENNA, §2(v)) was founded by Julianus, the project probably soon came to a halt and remained unfinished until completed by Maximian in 549. It seems that he did not introduce any spectacular innovations, but simply continued the trends reflecting Byzantine influences that had been present in Ravenna since *c.* 500, when Theodoric (*reg* 493–526), whose tastes had similarly been formed in the East, exercised his patronage in the city.

BIBLIOGRAPHY

Pauly-Wissowa

Agnellus: *Liber Pontificalis ecclesiae Ravennatis* (first half of the 9th century); ed. O. Holder-Egger, *Scriptores rerum Langobardicarum et Italicarum saec.vi–ix*, Mnmt. Ger. Hist. (Hannover, 1878)
F. W. Deichmann: *Ravenna: Hauptstadt des spätantiken Abendlandes*, ii/2 (Wiesbaden, 1976)

P. J. NORDHAGEN

Maximilian, Archduke of Austria. *See* HABSBURG, §I(13).

Maximilian I, Duke and Elector of Bavaria. *See* WITTELSBACH, §I(5).

Maximilian I, Holy Roman Emperor. *See* HABSBURG, §I(3).

Maximilian II, Holy Roman Emperor. *See* HABSBURG, §I(8).

Maximilian II Emanuel, Elector of Bavaria. *See* WITTELSBACH, §I(7).

Maximilian III Joseph, Elector of Bavaria. *See* WITTELSBACH, §I(10).

Maxman, Susan (Abel) (*b* Columbus, OH, 30 Dec 1938). American architect. She received her Master of Architecture degree from the University of Pennsylvania, Philadelphia, in 1977, and established her own firm there in 1984. Much of her work involved restoration and interior design, such as the Vernon House (*c.* 1750–1805), Germantown, PA, and the interior architecture for the Criminal Justice Center, Philadelphia. Her Philadelphia office (123 S. 22nd Street) is her own renovation (1984) of a townhouse (1886) by Frank Furness. In 1992 Maxman became the first woman president of the American Institute of Architects, an appointment she saw as symbolic of the potential impact women can make on the architectural profession. In this role she advocated two issues that she regarded as complementary: a greater environmental awareness and accountability on the part of architects; and urban revitalization. She encouraged the 'recycling' of buildings through renovation and restoration in place of new construction, and through increasing the efficiency of buildings, while enlivening the urban fabric. She encouraged architects to work with such groups as the Audubon Society, the Department of Energy and the Environmental Protection Agency in order to lend an architectural voice to environmental policy. Regarding urban revitalization, Maxman supported an interactive, holistic approach and called on architects to transcend the 'single-building mentality' developing instead 'an interdisciplinary approach to the design, planning, and infrastructure of entire cities'.

WRITINGS
'Toward a New Urban Vision', *Architecture* [USA], lxxxii/1 (1993), pp. 37–9

BIBLIOGRAPHY
D. K. Dietsch: 'Presidential Precedent', *Architecture* [USA], lxxx/7 (1991), p. 13
K. Salmon: 'AIA Inaugurates First Woman President', *Architecture* [USA], lxxxi/11 (1992), p. 19
D. Prowler: 'Interview with AIA President Susan Maxman', *Prog. Archit.*, lxxiv/2 (1993), p. 107

WALTER SMITH

Maxwell. Canadian family of architects, of Scottish descent. Edward R. Maxwell was a carpenter who emigrated to Canada from Jedburgh, Scotland, before 1836. His son Edward John Maxwell (*b* Montreal, 1836) set up his own lumber company in Montreal and had four children, two of whom became architects. Edward Maxwell (*b* Montreal, 31 Dec 1867; *d* Montreal, 14 Nov 1923) served an apprenticeship in Montreal with Alexander F. Dunlop (1842–1923) but received his main training in Boston, MA, where he worked from 1888 to 1891 for the firm of Shepley, Rutan & Coolidge, the successors to the firm of H. H. Richardson. He set up his own practice in Montreal in 1892, immediately attracting commissions from influential clients in the financial and commercial circles of Montreal for palatial city residences and country homes as well as banks, offices, schools and churches. The influence of Richardson and his own training in Boston are evident in Edward's early work, but such early buildings as the London and Lancashire Life Assurance Building (1899) also reflected the trend among North American architects towards French Beaux-Arts design. William Sutherland Maxwell (*b* Montreal, 14 Nov 1874; *d* Montreal, 25 March 1952) began his career as a draughtsman in Edward's office before moving to Boston, where he worked for the firm of Winslow and Wetherell from 1895 to 1898. He then spent 16 months in Paris, in the studio of Jean-Louis Pascal. On his return he began working with his brother, and in 1902 the two became partners. William's training in Paris emphasized the influence of Beaux-Arts planning and design in their architecture, most notably in their design for the Art Association of Montreal Gallery (1912;

now the Montreal Museum of Fine Arts) and the Parliament Buildings (1912), Regina, Saskatchewan. An excellent draughtsman, William was often responsible for designing the architectural ornament and interior furnishings of their buildings, but their draughting room also provided training for many young local architects. After Edward's premature death, William carried on the firm's activities in partnership with Gordon MacLeod Pitts (1886–1954). In 1940 he moved to Haifa, Palestine (now Israel), where his daughter had married the head of the Bahai faith, but he returned to Montreal in 1951.

BIBLIOGRAPHY
I. Murray, ed.: *Edward & W. S. Maxwell: Guide to the Archive* (Montreal, 1986) [with extensive bibliog.]
R. Pepall: *Construction d'un musée beaux-arts: Montréal, 1912/Building a Beaux-arts Museum* (Montreal, 1986)
Country Houses for Montrealers, 1892–1924: The Architecture of E. and W. S. Maxwell (Montreal, 1987)
The Architecture of Edward and W. S. Maxwell (exh. cat., Montreal, Mus. F.A., 1991)

ROSALIND M. PEPALL

Maxwell, William Stirling-. *See* STIRLING-MAXWELL, WILLIAM.

Maxy, Max Herman (*b* Braila, 26 Oct 1895; *d* Bucharest, 19 July 1971). Romanian painter. He studied first in Bucharest (1913–15) under Camil Ressu and Iosif Iser, then in Berlin (1922) under Arthur Segal. In Berlin he exhibited with the Novembergruppe. Such works as *Diagonal Construction* (1922; priv. col., see exh. cat., no. 12) show Maxy's complete assimilation of late Cubism and his awareness of wider currents of abstraction. On his return to Romania he became one of the leading members of the avant-garde, introducing Cubism and organizing with Marcel Janco, Victor Brauner and Corneliu Michăilescu the exhibitions of the Contimporanul group in 1924, 1930 and 1935, in which the work of Romanian artists was shown with that of major figures in the European avant-garde, such as Klee. At the same time Maxy was editor of *Integral* and the organizer of the Group of New Art (Grupul de Artă Nouă). In 1924 he co-founded the Academy of Modern Decorative Arts in Bucharest, which was intended as a Romanian version of the Bauhaus and which continued until 1928; despite its short existence, it gave Maxy an opportunity to establish himself as a designer and to exhibit his work at the Official Salon of Architecture and Decorative Arts (1931). His best-known paintings date from the 1930s and are in a Cubist style. After World War II he was director of the Museum of Art in Bucharest. In his late works he made thematic and stylistic concessions to artistic demands of the Communist regime (e.g. *Refinery at Brazi*, 1963; Simu, Mus. A.).

BIBLIOGRAPHY
M. H. Maxy: Expoziția retrospectivă (exh. cat. by G. Dinu, Bucharest, Gal. A. Dalles, 1965)
P. Oprea: *M. H. Maxy* (Bucharest, 1974)

ALINA-IOANA ȘERBU

May, Cliff (*b* San Diego, CA, 29 Aug 1908; *d* Los Angeles, 18 Oct 1989). American architect–builder. His education in business administration at San Diego State College (1929–30) was interrupted by the Depression. He subsequently applied his woodworking skills to the design and construction of late Craftsman furniture. While in San Diego he turned to architecture and by the mid-1930s had established a new practice in Los Angeles as an architect-builder. From his first house in San Diego (1931–2) to the hundreds that followed throughout the USA and in other countries, his work reflects the American and Hispanic styles current in California, while incorporating current technological amenities. The house for John A. Smith, La Habra, CA (1934–6), used landscaped courtyards surrounded by informal interiors flanked by galleries. His own residence in West Los Angeles (1952–6; later additions) epitomizes his work after World War II by its open plan and large areas of glass set beneath a broad, low-pitched roof.

Two architectural pattern books published by *Sunset* magazine, *'Sunset' Western Ranch Houses* (San Francisco, 1946) and *Western Ranch Houses by Cliff May* (Menlo Park, 1958), contributed to the wide appeal of May's work, as have modest sample houses sponsored by other magazines and a nationally available low-cost house (1952–3), designed in collaboration with the Los Angeles architect Chris Choate (1905–81). May was a major exponent of the suburban ranch house whose designs are more familiar than his name. In common with his academic counterparts, however, in his later work, such as the Robert Wian house in Pear Blossom, CA (1969–71), he tended to make a more direct use of historical motifs.

BIBLIOGRAPHY

D. Bricker: *Built for Sale: Cliff May and the Low Cost California Ranch House* (MA thesis, Santa Barbara, U. CA, 1983)
M. L. Laskey: *The California Ranch House* (Los Angeles, 1984)
J. Greenwald: 'Cliff May (1908–1989)', *LA Architect* (Dec 1989), p. 8
D. Bricker: Ranch Houses by Cliff May: 'Restore the Romance and Charm of Early California Design to Modern Living', *The Art and Craft of California Architecture*, ed. R. Winter (Washington, DC, 1995)

DAVID BRICKER

May, Ernest (*b* Strasbourg, 16 July 1845; *d* Paris, 28 Oct 1925). French banker and collector. In 1879 he married and set up residence in the Avenue de Villiers, near the Parc Monceau, Paris. Degas painted him as part of a group portrait in *Portraits at the Stock Exchange* (1878–9; Paris, Mus. d'Orsay), which was shown at the Impressionist exhibition in 1879. Degas wrote somewhat satirically about him to Félix Bracquemond, relating that May had thrown himself into artistic activity, was organizing a charity auction in aid of an artist (Louis Hippolyte Mouchot, 1846–93) and had arranged a gallery in his house to display his collection. Presumably a friend of the wealthy painter Gustave Caillebotte, May had plans for a joint sponsorship with him of an art review to be called *Jour et nuit* and to be devoted to prints, but their backing never materialized due to Caillebotte's differences with Degas. May apparently admired Degas, commissioning from him a painting of his wife and newborn son (1881; inc.; ex-Gal. Petit, Paris, 1919) and buying several of his ballet subjects, including *Rehearsal of the Ballet on the Stage* (?1874; New York, Met.). He was a customer of the dealer Paul Durand-Ruel but also dealt directly with Manet, Monet and Degas. In the early years of his collecting, and after 1890, he bought several paintings by Old Masters and 18th-century

artists at auction, but his collection was dominated primarily by Impressionist works, including Manet's *Guitar-player* (1867; Farmington, CT, Hill-Stead Mus.), bought from the artist in 1879. The sale of his collection in 1890 (Paris, Gal. Petit, 4 June) included 14 early landscapes by Corot. At this time he bought back several pictures, including Camille Pissarro's *Entrance to the Village of Voisins* (1872; Paris, Mus. d'Orsay), which was one of several Impressionist paintings in his collection that entered the Musée du Louvre after May's death.

BIBLIOGRAPHY

M. Pantazzi: *Degas* (exh. cat., ed. H. Loyrette; Paris, Grand Pal.; Ottawa, N.G.; New York, Met.; 1988–9), pp. 316–18
A. Distel: *Les Collectionneurs des impressionnistes: Amateurs et marchands* (Dudingen, 1989)
M. Laclotte: *Les Donateurs du Louvre* (Paris, 1989)

LINDA WHITELEY

May, Ernst (*b* Frankfurt am Main, 27 July 1886; *d* Hamburg, 12 Sept 1970). German urban planner, architect and writer. He was educated in London at University College (1907–8) and at the Technische Hochschule in Darmstadt (1908–10). After military service in Darmstadt he returned to London where he worked (1910–12) for Raymond Unwin. His work with Unwin was important for shaping his views on housing and planning, and in encouraging a sympathy for the social reforming attitudes that underlay Unwin's views. In 1912 May returned to study under Theodor Fischer in Munich at the Technische Hochschule (1912–13), but his attempts to establish a private practice in Frankfurt were cut short by World War I. In 1918 May became architect to a non-profit housing organization in Silesia, Schlesische Heimstätten. Working on small rural developments there he was able to develop further the garden city ideas that he had explored with Unwin. In the plan for Breslau submitted for a competition in 1919, he abandoned the established system of stepped density zoning and proposed instead to accommodate the city's new growth in a number of self-contained satellite communities, linked to the existing centre by tram or rail.

In 1924 May was invited by the mayor of Frankfurt am Main, Ludwig Landmann, to take up the post of city architect. His work there was thoroughly documented, particularly in May's magazine *Das neue Frankfurt*, which gave the impression of the unique quality of May's programme, although much of what he achieved in Frankfurt could be matched elsewhere: the widespread standardization of plans and components, the use of limited prefabrication and non-traditional forms of construction, and the volume of housing built. What was special to Frankfurt was Landmann's organizational framework and political support, for, as May readily admitted, his achievements were dependent on the system that concentrated decisions on planning and architectural and building policy in his hands. May's general development plan for the city extended the ideas first tried in Breslau: Praunheim (1927–30), Niederrade (late 1920s; see fig.), Römerstadt (1926–30), Westhausen (1930) and the other estates of the 1920s were treated as satellite communities, planned in a conscious relationship with the natural landscape, with views along the banks of the Nidda River or across open fields to the Taunus mountains in the distance, and linked to the city centre by direct tram routes. These overall planning principles may be traced back to the Garden City movement, but in terms of detailed planning these schemes exemplify the Modernist concept of *Zeilenbau*, in which long blocks of flats are laid out in parallel on a strict grid formation. The individual dwellings were equipped with fittings of a quality to match the best products of the Bauhaus or the Deutscher Werkbund. And this was not simply a superficial aesthetic. The prefabricated Frankfurt Kitchen, designed by Grete Schütte-Lihotzky, was highly influential on contemporary modernist designers. It was designed on the mass-production principles of Scientific Management, as were the Römerstadt houses, whose form was presented as a product of a precast panel system intended to save skilled labour and erection time.

May's achievements were widely recognized in international planning and housing circles and it was appropriate that CIAM II's 'The Minimum Dwelling', the first full meeting of CIAM, should take place in Frankfurt. In 1930, when his reputation was at its height, he was invited to the USSR to work on city planning and the preparation of standard designs for housing and communal living blocks. May was assisted by a 'brigade', drawn largely from his team from Frankfurt. Working and living in two railway coaches for much of their years in the USSR, May and his brigade prepared plans for a number of new and expanding cities, including Magnitogorsk (1930), Altostroy (1930) and Stalingrad. In 1932 they entered a plan for a limited competition for the expansion of Moscow along satellite city lines. The frustrations of working in the USSR seemed, however, endless: not only was the context in which they were asked to plan or prepare their designs subject to frequent and apparently arbitrary change, but much of their work was ignored or even actively sabotaged by the Russians with whom they were meant to collaborate; by early 1933 May and most of the brigade had decided to leave.

Unable to return to Nazi Germany, May travelled to Kenya where he farmed and worked as an architect until interned in 1940. Released after two years with the help of Unwin's widow, he gradually resumed practice, preparing a master-plan for Kampala and building a variety of buildings in Kampala, Mombasa and around Lake Victoria. After World War II he was urged to assist with the task of reconstruction in Germany. It was not until 1953, however, after many refusals, that he agreed to return to work for the Neue Heimat housing association in Hamburg. Appointed as a professor at Darmstadt in 1956, he continued to write and lecture until his death. His most important post-war work was the range of large-scale housing developments and planning projects that he carried out during the 1950s and early 1960s for cities such as Rheinhausen and Mainz (both 1953).

WRITINGS
F. Block, ed.: *Probleme des Bauens: Wohnbau* (Potsdam, 1928)
'Die Wohnung für das Existenzminimum', *Neue Frankfurt*, 1 (1929), p. 209
'Fünf Jahre Wohnungsbautätigkeit in Frankfurt am Main, Siedlung Mämmolshainerstrasse', *Neue Frankfurt*, 4–5 (1930), p. 130
'Der Bau neuer Städte in der USSR', *Neue Frankfurt*, 7 (1931), p. 133
'Die sozialistische Stadt—Wie sehen die neuen russischen Städte aus?', *Bauwelt*, 24 (1931), p. 817

Ernst May: Niederrade estate, Frankfurt am Main, late 1920s

BIBLIOGRAPHY
J. Buekschmitt: *Ernst May: Bauten und Planungen* (Stuttgart, 1963)
C. Castex, J.-C. Depaule and P. Panerai: 'Le Nouveau Frankfurt et Ernst May', *Cah. Rech. Archit.*, 1 (1977), pp. 18–31
C. Borngräber: 'Foreign Architects in the USSR: Bruno Taut and the Brigades of Ernst May, Hannes Meyer, Hans Schmidt', *Archit. Assoc. Q.*, xi/1 (1979), pp. 50–62
——: 'The Social Impact of the New Architecture in Germany and the Building of the New Frankfurt', *Archit. Assoc. Q.*, xi/1 (1979), pp. 39–43
F. Kramer: 'Das neue Frankfurt', *Archit. Assoc. Q.*, xi/1 (1979), pp. 44–9

NICHOLAS BULLOCK

May, Hugh (*b* Mid Lavant, W. Sussex, *bapt* 2 Oct 1621; *d* Mid Lavant, 21 Feb 1684). English architect. He was from a family of Sussex gentry, several of whom gained court appointments after the restoration of Charles II. He seems to have started his career in the household of George Villiers, 2nd Duke of Buckingham (in 1650–51 he was involved in removing the Duke's works of art from York House to the Low Countries). He also met the painter Peter Lely around this time and for 25 years was to be his close friend. May's artistic interests, combined with services presumably rendered to the exiled king during the Commonwealth, were appropriately rewarded in 1660, when he was appointed Paymaster in the Office of Works. In 1665–6 May was a member of the committee that made proposals for the repair of St Paul's Cathedral, proposals rendered obsolete a few months later by the Great Fire. Following this, he was active as one of six surveyors appointed to supervise the rebuilding of the City. In 1668 he was promoted to Comptroller in the Office of Works, but the following year he was passed over for the Surveyorship when it was conferred on Christopher Wren. In November 1673 he was appointed Comptroller of the Works at Windsor; with this he gained the great architectural opportunity of his lifetime, the remodelling of Windsor Castle.

May's importance for British architecture in the late 17th century was threefold. Of most widespread value was the encouragement he gave John Evelyn to publish his *Parallel of the Antient Architecture with the Modern* (1664), translated from Roland Fréart's *Parallèle de l'architecture antique et de la moderne* (Paris, 1650). It proved to be the most useful handbook of classical architecture in English for the next 50 years. Second, in his designs from the mid-1660s for a group of private houses, May established, with Roger Pratt, a new norm for domestic architecture. These are all of two storeys, with windows of regular (classical) proportions and bold hipped roofs. May introduced a pedimented centrepiece to each principal façade, with or without pilasters to carry the pediment. This Palladian idea he took perhaps from Jacob van Campen, whose Mauritshuis (1633–44) in The Hague must have been familiar to him; but the curving quadrants and wings that flanked his most prominent house, Berkeley House (1665; destr. 1733), Piccadilly, London, were recognized at the time as deriving directly from Palladio.

May's interior planning, however, did not follow Palladian principles. At Eltham Lodge (1664), Kent, a compact villa three rooms deep and his only house to survive without drastic remodelling, rooms are slotted informally into the rectangular envelope; and the range added to Cornbury (c. 1666–7), Oxon, belonging to Edward Hyde, 1st Earl of Clarendon, and bearing the Latin inscription *Deus haec otia fecit* ('God made this repose') clearly had a comparable function as a place of retirement. By contrast, Cassiobury (c. 1677–80; destr. 1922), Herts, for Arthur Capel, 1st Earl of Essex, and Holme Lacy (1674–5), Hereford & Worcs, the house of John, 1st Viscount Scudamore, almost certainly built to May's design, are of a greatly extended H-plan. The single-pile ranges of the latter were distinctly old-fashioned, and such plans were presumably adopted to make the greatest possible external show and to give internal enfilades of state rooms.

May's third area of influence resulted from his remodelled state apartments at Windsor Castle (1675–84) for Charles II, work that also brought together the decorative painter Antonio Verrio and the virtuoso wood-carver Grinling Gibbons. Together they created spectacular suites of rooms, culminating in the King's Chapel and St George's Hall. These were widely imitated in great houses until the early 18th century. Windsor's state rooms were largely destroyed by Jeffry Wyatville after 1824, but their effect can still be appreciated today at Chatsworth, Derbys, and Burghley, Cambs, as well as at Wren's Hampton Court. For the exteriors at Windsor, May took a classical approach towards the internal court, but he cast into a type of neo-Norman those parts that would be seen in conjunction with pre-existing medieval work. These he built with simple blocks and towers. The round-headed windows, classically detailed but with deep-set concave surrounds, were clearly intended to harmonize with the earliest parts of the castle. In due course John Vanbrugh was to recognize the potential of this 'castle air', as he called it, and May's work at Windsor proved to be the progenitor of the castle style so favoured in the Picturesque period a century later.

BIBLIOGRAPHY
Colvin
H. A. Tipping: 'Country Homes, Gardens Old & New: Eltham Lodge', *Country Life*, xlvi (9 Aug 1919), pp. 168–74
G. F. Webb: 'Baroque Art', *Proc. Brit. Acad.*, xxxiii (1947), pp. 131–48
C. Hussey: 'Cornbury Park, Oxfordshire, the Seat of Mr. O. V. Watney', *Country Life*, cviii (22 Sept 1950), pp. 922–6
K. Downes: *English Baroque Architecture* (London, 1966)
H. Colvin, ed.: *A History of the King's Works*, v (1976)

JOHN NEWMAN

May, Morton D(avid) (*b* St Louis, MO, 1914; *d* St Louis, 13 April 1983). American businessman and collector. His family wealth came from the May Department Stores. His collecting encompassed two separate strands. He was an enthusiastic collector of art from Africa, the Pacific Islands and Central America, and he donated many such works to the St Louis Art Museum over the years. He also became well known as one of the earliest American collectors of German Expressionism, a style in which he developed an interest in the mid-1940s, when there were few dealers handling such work in the USA.

May's collection eventually included more than 90 works. It comprised a selection by the artists of Die Brücke, such as Ernst Ludwig Kirchner, Emil Nolde and Max Pechstein, and works by artists associated with Der Blaue Reiter, for example Alexei Jawlensky and Vasily Kandinsky. Approximately one half of the collection, however, consisted of works by Max Beckmann, whom May came to know when Beckmann was teaching in St Louis in the late 1940s, ranging from *Stormy Day at Sea* (1908) to the triptych *Acrobats* (1939) and a portrait of him (1949). Many works from his collection were donated to the St Louis Art Museum upon his death.

BIBLIOGRAPHY
German Expressionist Paintings from the Collection of Morton D. May (exh. cat., Denver, CO, A. Mus., 1960)
The Morton D. May Collection of German Expressionist Paintings (exh. cat., Austin, U. TX, A. Mus., 1974)

A. DEIRDRE ROBSON

May, Phil(ip William) (*b* New Wortley, Leeds, 22 April 1864; *d* London, 5 Aug 1903). English illustrator. He was one of the most widely appreciated of the generation of pen-and-ink illustrators that arose with the commercially successful introduction of the photomechanical means of reproducing illustrations (line block and half-tone block) in the 1880s and 1890s. So widespread was May's appeal, both to the public and to other artists, that Whistler said that 'modern black & white art could be summed up in two words—Phil May'.

May was not formally trained as an artist, but after some hardship in early life he found success with his caricature of the actors *Irving, Bancroft and Toole* (1883), which led to commissions from *Society* magazine. Illustrations for the *St Stephen's Review* sustained him in his early years. In 1885 he left for Australia because of bad health and worked there very productively for the *Sydney Bulletin* until 1888. He returned to Britain in 1892, having spent some time studying in Paris, and secured commissions from magazines such as the *Graphic*, the *Illustrated London News*, *Sketch*, *Punch* and *English Illustrated Magazine*. He also contributed drawings for commercial advertising campaigns.

In 1892 May began publishing collections of his drawings in annuals (there were 15 in all by 1903). In 1895 *Phil May's Sketch Book* was published and in 1896 his definitive *Guttersnipes* appeared. On the strength of these works May was elected a member of The Royal Institute of Painters in Watercolours. So popular was May's work that collections of his drawings continued to be published in both Britain and Australia for some time after his death.

May was in a direct line of descent from earlier Victorian illustrators who took characters and situations observed in the city streets and countryside as their subjects, notably John Leech and Charles Keene. He was essentially an illustrator of types rather than individuals. David Low considered him not so much a cartoonist or caricaturist as a master of the illustrated joke, where the drawing is subordinate to the caption.

May's style of pen-and-ink drawing can be described as an economy of means expressed in smoothly flowing lines. The characteristic simplicity of his early drawings and their apparent spontaneity belie much painstaking compositional work in pencil before the process of selectively picking out essential lines in pen and ink was done. In excluding everything that was inessential to the humour May paid little or no attention to background details: frequently his characters look as if they were suspended in space. To a greater degree perhaps than any other popular illustrator May introduced his own likeness into his work.

The best description of May's attitudes to both work and life is his own: 'draw firm and live jolly'. He was a bon viveur who enjoyed the Bohemian London life of artists' clubs in the 1890s.

DNB

BIBLIOGRAPHY

H. Jackson: *The 1890s* (London, 1913)
J. Thorpe: *Phil May: Master-draughtsman & Humorist 1864–1903* (London, 1932)
Drawings by Phil May (exh. cat. by A. Robertson, Leeds, C.A.G., 1975)

LEO JOHN DE FREITAS

Maya. Pre-Columbian Mesoamerican peoples, whose civilization flourished in parts of what are now Mexico, Guatemala, Belize, Honduras and El Salvador from *c.* 300 BC to the 16th century AD. The ancient Maya region is usually divided by archaeologists into two areas, the Lowlands and the Highlands, according to geographical and cultural differences (see fig. 1). Culturally, the Lowland and Highland areas shared much, although the Highland Maya differed in four principal factors (*see* §2 below). The Spaniards destroyed much of Maya élite culture at the time of the Conquest, such as the practice of hieroglyphic writing and a variety of religious rituals; however, other aspects of Maya culture, including their language and various folk customs, survived. Maya-speaking peoples living today in Mesoamerica number more than four million.

See also PRE-COLUMBIAN MESOAMERICA.

1. Lowlands. 2. Highlands.

1. LOWLANDS. The Lowland Maya area comprised the tropical lowlands of southern Mexico, Guatemala, Belize and Honduras (see fig. 1). It is subdivided into a Northern Lowland area (the Mexican states of Yucatán, Quintana Roo and northern Campeche) and a Southern Lowland area (southern Campeche, eastern Tabasco and northern Chiapas in Mexico, northern and central Guatemala, Belize and Western Honduras). These two Lowland areas are sometimes termed Northern and Central Maya, with a third, Southern (i.e. Highland) area.

(i) c. 1000 BC–*c.* AD *300.* The sedentary agricultural village base upon which Maya civilization was built has been traced back to as early as *c.* 1000 BC at the site of Cuello in northern Belize. During the succeeding 700 years, settlements were established in most parts of the lowlands and the Lowland Maya began trading with adjacent areas for materials that were lacking in the lowland zone. Between *c.* 600 BC and *c.* 300 BC the populations at individual sites began to increase and the first public architecture was built.

During this population expansion, there is some evidence of a rise in competition and conflict among those sites witnessing the most rapid growth. In the midst, or perhaps as a result, of these developments, social organization became more complex, and truly urban civilization began to emerge by *c.* 300 BC, at the beginning of the Late Pre-Classic period (*c.* 300 BC–*c.* AD 250). Large-scale, labour-intensive public architecture was constructed, and a high-art style began to develop at a number of lowland sites. Some of these settlements, for example EL MIRADOR in Guatemala and Cerros in Belize, appear to have had a brief but impressive florescence at the beginning of this phase, while others, such as TIKAL in Guatemala and LAMANAI in Belize, built on their early prosperity to become major political, religious and commercial centres for many more centuries. Whether these cultural developments were due to indigenous growth or to external influences (and, if the latter, from where) is a matter of debate among scholars, but most experts agree that there was a combination of internal trends and external influences from the southern Highland area of Guatemala and El Salvador.

Among the early architectural achievements are large pyramidal structures with stucco masks flanking the stairways that lead to the tops. Spectacular examples were built at both Lamanai and Cerros, where the pyramids exceeded 30 m and 20 m, respectively, in height. The largest Late Pre-Classic site, however, was El Mirador, where most of the principal construction was completed by the end of the Late Pre-Classic period. The core of the site comprised a series of platforms topped by pyramids, including one that is 55 m high and another that is 40 m. To the west of the core lies a huge complex rising 70 m above the jungle floor. The stucco masks found on the pyramids and platforms of many of these Pre-Classic buildings represent important Maya deities and indicate that a distinct iconography and style had developed by this time. Early wall paintings found at Tikal also date to this period. There appears to have been much communication among sites at the beginning of the Late Pre-Classic period, reflected in similarities in architecture, ceramics and site plans, as well as by the presence of a wide variety of imported goods, including obsidian (black volcanic glass, chipped to make sharp cutting and scraping tools), a resist-painted pottery known as Usulután Ware from the southern Highland Maya area and sting-ray spines, used in bloodletting ceremonies, from the Pacific Coast. Goods traded between Cerros in northern Belize and Komchén in the

1. Map of the Maya region before AD 1521; those areas with separate entries in this dictionary are distinguished by CROSS-REFERENCE TYPE

Northern Lowland area have also been identified, and salt was one of the perishable commodities thought to have been moved from north to south.

(ii) c. AD *300–c. 900.* By *c.* AD 300 significant changes began to occur. Sites such as El Mirador and Cerros declined. Tikal became the largest site in the Southern

Lowland area, while another site, DZIBILCHALTÚN, emerged as a major centre in the Northern Lowland area. At the same time, the expanding influence of TEOTIHUACÁN, the most prominent city in the Basin of Mexico, in the Mesoamerican Central Highlands (*see* MESOAMERICA, PRE-COLUMBIAN, §II, 3(ii)), began to be felt in the Maya

2. Maya Lowland region, Copán, view of the ballcourt, constructed during the Classic period, *c.* AD 400–*c.* 800

region. Stelae with hieroglyphic inscriptions were erected for the first time, using the Maya Long Count calendrical system. The earliest such monument known at Tikal corresponds to the year AD 292. Hieroglyphic writing was clearly derived in the lowlands from earlier developments in the highlands. Polychrome pottery with elaborate geometric designs and distinctive plate and bowl forms was also developed and wall painting continued. In architecture, stone temples on platforms or pyramids predominated in the ceremonial centres of the principal sites, some of which, such as Tikal, had reached urban proportions. Even without metal tools, the Maya displayed considerable skill in quarrying and shaping the limestone blocks that went into their temples and other structures.

One of the major breakthroughs in the decipherment of Maya hieroglyphs has been the discovery, first made by Tatiana Proskouriakoff, that the monumental inscriptions were not purely esoteric but had significant historical and political content. Since the 1970s and 1980s, scholars have been able to isolate the presence of ruling lineages at a series of sites and have studied their histories. Before the end of the 4th century AD, the first ruling dynasty in the Southern Lowland area was established at Tikal. The influence of Teotihuacán is particularly clear at Tikal, where an élite individual, who was closely aligned with the Mesoamerican Central Highlands, married into the dynasty soon after its establishment. Teotihuacán-related motifs appear on stelae at Tikal, especially Stele 31 (AD 435), and Teotihuacán-influenced architecture and ceramics are also found.

Maya population continued to increase in the Lowlands through the Early Classic period (*c.* AD 300–*c.* 600), and, with the demise of the influence of Teotihuacán by the

beginning of the 7th century AD, many more large urban centres began to develop alongside Tikal. Near the southern frontier of the Southern Maya Lowland area, COPÁN (see fig. 2) grew in size and power. The inscriptions on its distinctive 'in-the-round' monumental style indicate the establishment of a powerful ruling élite there by the 5th century. PALENQUE, on the western frontier of the Maya region, became prominent soon after, under a ruler named Pacal (*reg* AD 615–84; *see* JADE, colour pl. II, fig. 1), who extended Palenque's influence in the western lowlands and was buried in a spectacular tomb beneath the Temple of the Inscriptions (*see* MESOAMERICA, PRE-COLUMBIAN, fig. 17). His successors strengthened Palenque's power and built some of its most spectacular monuments, including the palace complex with its unique tower, the Temple of the Sun and the Temple of the Foliated Cross. ALTUN HA in Northern Belize also grew significantly in size; its rulers and élite citizens were buried in a series of rich tombs. Maya aesthetic and craft achievements reached new heights during these centuries, notably in exquisitely painted polychrome cylinder vases that often depict the Maya élite.

Throughout the 7th and 8th centuries, the number of large, multi-roomed range structures or palaces built at Maya sites increased. The ratio of palaces to temples shifted significantly in favour of the former and a number of factors indicate that the gulf between commoner and élite was growing. In sculpture (in both captor–captive scenes and in inscriptions) and in wall paintings, such as those at BONAMPAK (*see* COLOUR, colour pl. I, fig. 1), the rising importance of warfare, raiding and competition among sites is evident. Continued population growth throughout the lowlands caused increasing reliance on intensive forms of agriculture. In the 9th century, from their homeland in the Gulf Coast lowlands of Tabasco and Campeche, a mercantile-oriented group of Chontal Maya, also known as the Putún, began to extend their influence economically and militarily into both the Southern and Northern Lowland areas. The Putún were also in contact with the Mesoamerican Central Highlands, as evidenced in the art and architecture of sites taken over or influenced by them, such as Southern Lowland SEIBAL, Northern Lowland UXMAL and other Puuc region sites, and CHICHÉN ITZÁ. They also produced a distinctive temperless pottery known as Fine Orange Ware, which they traded widely throughout the lowlands.

(iii) c. *900–1521.* The combination of pressure on resources, environmental degradation and external disruption of trade routes appears to have been mainly responsible for the demise of a number of the closely linked centres in the Southern Lowland area. Classic Maya civilization did not 'collapse', however, as is sometimes suggested, but shifted its demographic and cultural focus from the south to the north over a period of time from the Late Classic period (*c.* AD 600–*c.* 900) to the Early Post-Classic period (*c.* 900–*c.* 1200). While Tikal, Copán and Palenque were being abandoned in the south, Uxmal, KABÁH, SAYIL, LABNÁ and Chichén Itzá, among others, were increasing their political and economic powers in the north.

The buildings constructed during this period at Puuc region sites are some of the finest architectural achievements anywhere in Pre-Columbian America. Structures such as the Palace of the Governors and the Nunnery Quadrangle at Uxmal, the Codz Poop at Kabáh, the Great Palace at Sayil and the Arch at Labná show the characteristic traits of the Puuc style: carefully cut veneer masonry, mosaic façades with both geometric and naturalistic designs, elaborate roof-combs and an overall sense of proportion and relation to neighbouring buildings and terrain. A few hieroglyphic inscriptions are found at sites in the Puuc region but only in the early part of their occupation.

The contemporaneous site of Chichén Itzá in the centre of the Yucatán Peninsula also has some fine architecture, including the Church, the Caracol (or Observatory), the Castillo (the main pyramid), the Great Ballcourt and the Temple of the Warriors. Re-examination of the dating of Chichén Itzá in the 1980s indicated that its florescence almost totally coincided with that of the Puuc region sites, although it continued somewhat longer (until the beginning of the 13th century AD). This research has also indicated that the 'Toltec' occupation of Chichén Itzá was contemporaneous and spatially integrated with the Maya occupation of the site. Many scholars doubt that Chichén Itzá was actually conquered by Toltecs from their capital of Tula in the Mesoamerican Central Highlands, as traditional interpretations have claimed. An alternative interpretation is that such Central Highland influences as *chacmools* (stone statues of figures reclining on their backs), warrior columns and the prowling jaguar motif may have been brought to Chichén Itzá through intermediaries such as the Putún Maya. Hieroglyphic inscriptions were used

early in the sequence at Chichén Itzá; at least one inscription from the 10th century AD has been found.

The Late Post-Classic period (*c.* AD 1200–1521) was marked by the decline of Chichén Itzá and the rise of MAYAPÁN, a densely settled, walled city to the west of it, in the early 13th century. This phase is sometimes called the Decadent period, after an apparent decline in architectural and artistic standards. At Mayapán, the capital of a confederacy encompassing much of the Northern Lowland area, TULUM, on the east coast of the Yucatán Peninsula, and San Gervasio, the principal centre on the island of Cozumel, buildings were constructed of crudely cut stones and covered with heavy coats of plaster. Temples were considerably smaller than before, there was a new emphasis on worship at the family level and dedicatory caches were often reused. Elaborate ceramic incense-burners depicting various deities were manufactured at Mayapán and other sites and used in family worship. Parts of these burners were apparently mass-produced. The economic and political systems of the period were nevertheless as complex as in earlier periods. Thus, although the high arts were de-emphasized, Late Post-Classic period Maya culture was far from decadent.

The Mayapán-led confederacy collapsed *c.* AD 1450 as a result of political infighting. The following short period before the Spanish Conquest in the early 16th century was one of conflict among various groups in the Northern Lowland area. The Spanish Conquest of Yucatán took more than two decades, the Spanish finally wresting control from the Maya by the end of 1546. The Maya suffered considerable population loss during this period, due mainly to diseases introduced by the Spanish, and this loss, along with the policies of their conquerors, effectively brought their great civilization to a close.

BIBLIOGRAPHY

S. G. Morley, G. W. Brainard and R. J. Sharer: *The Ancient Maya* (Stanford, 1946, rev. Palo Alto, 4/1983)

T. Proskouriakoff: *An Album of Maya Architecture*, Carnegie Institution Publication, dlviii (Washington, DC, 1946, rev. Norman, 2/1963)

M. D. Coe: *The Maya* (London and New York, 1966, rev. 5/1993)

T. P. Culbert, ed.: *The Classic Maya Collapse* (Albuquerque, 1973)

G. F. Andrews: *Maya Cities: Placemaking and Urbanization* (Norman, 1975)

R. E. W. Adams, ed.: *The Origins of Maya Civilization* (Albuquerque, 1977)

P. D. Harrison and B. L. Turner II, eds: *Pre-Hispanic Maya Agriculture* (Albuquerque, 1978)

W. Ashmore, ed.: *Lowland Maya Settlement Patterns* (Albuquerque, 1981)

J. S. Henderson: *The World of the Ancient Maya* (Ithaca, 1981)

N. Hammond: *Ancient Maya Civilization* (New Brunswick, 1982)

A. F. Chase and P. M. Rice, eds: *The Lowland Maya Postclassic* (Austin, 1985)

Maya: Treasures of an Ancient Civilization (exh. cat., ed. E. Gallenkamp and R. E. Johnson; New York, Amer. Mus. Nat. Hist.; Los Angeles, CA, Nat. Hist. Mus.; Dallas, TX, Mus. A.; and elsewhere; 1985–7)

The Blood of Kings: Dynasty and Ritual in Maya Art (exh. cat. by L. Schele and M. E. Miller, Fort Worth, Kimbell A. Mus., 1986)

J. A. Sabloff and E. W. Andrews V, eds: *Late Lowland Maya Civilization: Classic to Postclassic* (Albuquerque, 1986)

P. A. Urban and E. M. Schortman, eds: *The Southeast Maya Periphery* (Austin, 1986)

N. Hellmuth: *Monster und Menschen in der Maya-Kunst* (Graz, 1987)

G. R. Willey: *Essays in Maya Archaeology* (Albuquerque, 1987)

M. D. Coe: 'Ideology of the Maya Tomb', *Maya Iconography*, ed. E. P. Benson and G. G. Griffin (Princeton, 1988), pp. 222–35

——: 'The Hero Twins: Myth and Image', *The Maya Vase Book*, i, ed. J. Kerr (New York, 1989), pp. 161–84

L. Schele and D. Friedel: *A Forest of Kings: The Untold Story of the Ancient Maya* (New York, 1990)

M. D. Coe: *Breaking the Maya Code* (New York, 1992)

C. C. Coggins: *Artefacts from the Cenote of Sacrifice: Chichen Itza, Yucatan* (Cambridge, MA, 1992)

The Art of Ancient Mexico (exh. cat., ed. M. Ryan; London, Hayward Gal., 1992)

D. Friedel, L. Schele and J. Parker: *Maya Cosmos: Three Thousand Years on the Shaman's Path* (New York, 1993)

D. A. Hodell, J. H. Curtis and M. Brenner: 'Possible Role of Climate in the Collapse of Classic Maya Civilization', *Nature*, ccclxxv (1995), pp. 391–4

J. A. Sabloff: 'Drought and Decline', *Nature*, ccclxxv (1995), p. 357

JEREMY A. SABLOFF

2. HIGHLANDS. The Highland Maya area (sometimes termed Southern Maya) comprised the highlands of southern Chiapas, Mexico, of southern Guatemala and Honduras and western El Salvador (see fig. 1 above). The cool upland basins and valleys of this area have been densely populated for millennia, and many of its inhabitants still adhere to traditional beliefs that relate to Pre-Columbian Maya civilization. In the Pre-Columbian period, occasional influxes of new rulers altered the style and content of art as an official medium; yet there has been remarkable continuity of language and ethnicity within often sharply demarcated territories. Each territory, from the Late Pre-Classic period (*c.* 300 BC–*c.* AD 250) to the Spanish conquest of the Highland Maya area in 1524, had a principal urban site with a core of public buildings; today, each Maya municipality has a town centre with a church, municipal buildings, a market place and residential population.

Though similar in many respects to the culture of the Lowland Maya area (*see* §1 above), Highland Maya culture differed generally in the following: the stele–altar architectural complex was absent, and the corbel arch was little used, except in the Post-Classic period (*c.* AD 900–1521) for substructural tombs; the influence of central Mesoamerican culture, especially from the Central Highlands, was most marked during the Classic period (*c.* AD 250–*c.* 900) and Post-Classic period (*c.* 900–1521); and the system of Maya Long Count dates was used only in the Late Pre-Classic period. This calendar, with its 256-year cycle (*see* MESOAMERICA, PRE-COLUMBIAN, §II), was a basis for uniting Maya political organization throughout the region.

The political disintegration of Southern Lowland Maya civilization during the Late Classic period (*c.* AD 600–*c.* 900) and Early Post-Classic period (*c.* 900–*c.* 1200; *see also* §1 above) brought refugee lineages into the Maya Highland area and the Mesoamerican Central Highlands, for example to CACAXTLA, as well as the Maya Northern Lowland area. However, while approximately 120 of the Maya Highland Post-Classic period civic centres with monumental architecture in the Guatemalan highlands (see below) have been identified with communities described in 30 Maya ethnohistoric chronicles of the 16th century, few of their counterparts for the earlier Pre-Columbian periods have been recorded or explored. Independent traditions of monumental sculpture had developed in the Alta Verapaz basins and in the Valley of Guatemala, and to the west along the Pacific coastal slope at IZAPA (Mexico) and ABAJ TAKALIK (Guatemala) by the

Late Pre-Classic period, accompanied by incipient hieroglyphic writing. At sites such as Los Cerritos in Chiché, El Quiché, Guatemala, and at SEIBAL and Dos Pilas in the Rio Negro Valley, where Highland and Southern Lowland areas meet, monumental architecture was spread over several square kilometres. At KAMINALJUYÚ, in what is now Guatemala City, wall paintings adorn the architectural façades, especially those built during the 6th-century mid-Classic period. Construction at Kaminaljuyú was in a syncretic Maya–Mesoamerican Central Highland style, but executed by local masons and artists, whose efforts were apparently directed by emigrants from the metropolis of TEOTIHUACÁN in the north-east Basin of Mexico. While speculation abounds as to the nature of the Mexican entourage—long-distance traders, a military garrison or a marriage alliance between a Maya princess from a patrilineage bereft of male heirs—the presence of Teotihuacán ceramics and central Mesoamerican green obsidian (volcanic glass) indicates that formal trade linkages cemented the socio-political bond. Nevertheless, through the Classic period most of the Maya Highland area remained peripheral, and did not participate in the development of hieroglyphic writing carved on stelae, nor in the production of elaborate polychrome ceramics, wall painting, sculpture or construction of lofty corbel-vaulted temples that characterized the Maya Lowland area.

With the end of the Late Classic period, a major influx of peoples, the ancestors of the Quichean groups, moved into the Highland area from the western periphery of the Southern Lowland area. At one time under the political tutelage of Palenque, these peoples may have settled for one or two generations at Seibal until the early 10th century. New dynasties in the Guatemalan and Chiapas Highlands, established by the 10th century, signalled the beginning of the Post-Classic period by the establishment of confederacies of Quiché, Cakchiquel, Tzutujil and Chiapanec Maya, and by revised political messages in new styles of material culture and arrangements of buildings. Most of the archaeological sites once within this Quiché state have been surveyed and identified with specific lineages. Archaeological investigations at the first sites mentioned in the ethnohistories, such as Chixab—where the 13 migratory lineages first gathered at the headwater of the Usumacinta River, upriver from Palenque and Seibal—and Jakawitz, have revealed that the migratory groups were quite small, perhaps with only a few dozen people in each patrilineage.

The Highland Maya confederacy endured for some six centuries. The Quichean peoples built temples, ballcourts, lineage houses (long structures) and palaces mixing elements of style from both Classic Maya and central Mesoamerican traditions, including twin temples, I-shaped ballcourts and colonnaded lineage houses, all lavishly covered in lime plaster as at the Aztec capital of Tenochtitlán in the Basin of Mexico. At the same time Maya-style corbel-vaulting was used for tombs within the substructures, radial stairways were occasionally built on all four sides of temples and structures were aligned to the horizon's rising and setting points of the solar equinoxes, solstices and Venusian conjunctions, as at Pre-Classic and Classic Maya sites. During the Early Post-Classic period the highest ranked lineages built sites with radial temples and ballcourts occasionally orientated 15.25° east of north, virtually as miniature versions of Northern Lowland Chichén Itzá. The best-known community, Tujalja, one day's walk north of Jakawitz, and the sites of Chutinamit and Chutixtiox, were headed by the Toltecat (Toltec) and Xiu lineages, apparently branches of the same families at Chichén Itzá, and by a priestly office (K'ucumatz) that translated as the Feathered Serpent (Northern Lowland Maya Kukulkán; central Mesoamerican Quetzalcóatl). Ceramics at the higher ranked sites included carved wares with step-frets and outer surfaces red-slipped and carved with designs painted white. Notable frequencies of Tohil Plumbate trade ware with effigies of Tláloc (central Mesoamerican god of rain) also characterize sites with radial temples. In contrast, the predominant ceramics at sites of less highly ranked lineages, such as Jakawitz of the Ajaw and Cawek lineages, or Amak Tam of the Tamub lineage, were coarse grained wavy-lined incised ware, apparently a provincial rendition of the Toltec Mazapan ware of the Mesoamerican Central Highlands.

The confederacy had evolved into a segmentary state by the beginning of the Late Post-Classic period. From the Quiché capital Utatlán comes the New World's longest aboriginal text, the *Popol Vuh*, transcribed from a Maya screenfold codex into Latin characters in 1554. Like the Quiché culture, the subject-matter is syncretic. The first three creation myths described reflect a more Cholan Maya syntax of the Classic period Lowland area. The deities who created the realms of the Upperworld, Underworld (*Xibalba*) and Middleworld (earth) are identified with specific constellations in newly recorded petroglyphic friezes, continuing the Lowland Maya stelae tradition and style. The fourth section is historiographic, framed within repetitious celestial cycles, and describing events specific to places and peoples, which have been borne out archaeologically.

Quichean wall paintings were also essentially a central Mesoamerican overlay on Maya forms, part of the MIX-TECA-PUEBLA style. At the Cakchiquel capital IXIMCHÉ (*c.* AD 1400–1527) the two-dimensional codex-like figures appear painted on altars. The palace of the Ahaw lineage at Utatlán, built with a multi-storey tower resembling the tower at Palenque, has exterior wall paintings in the curvilinear Classic Lowland Maya style—especially of mythical figures from the early sections of the *Popol Vuh*—as well as interior wall paintings in the Mixteca–Puebla style—especially of warriors. Paralleling the creation tablets of the Cross Group at Palenque, the creation scenes of the *Popol Vuh* were carved near by in a panel that depicted for the first time the creator gods Tepeu and K'ucumatz, and the culture heroes Hun-Hunahpu and his twin progeny, Hunahpu and Ixbalanque, playing the ball-game against One-Death, supreme lord of the Underworld. Paired with this frieze is a sky chart of the positions of the constellations at winter solstice, when the forces of the true light begin to win the cosmic battle as daylight hours lengthen. Orion, leader of the favourable constellations, traditionally reigned overhead at the beginning of the cosmic war. Appropriately, Late Post-Classic ceramics within the Quiché state are characterized by the white-painted spiral style called Fortress White-on-Red, which has been identified with the constellation Orion. To the east, beyond the Quiché state boundaries, brightly painted ceramic bichromes and polychromes depict various modes of an open-mouthed Feathered Serpent.

BIBLIOGRAPHY

A. V. Kidder, J. Jennings and E. M. Shook: *Excavations at Kaminaljuyú, Guatemala*, Carnegie Institution Publication, dlxi (Washington, DC, 1946)

G. F. Guillemín: 'The Ancient Cakchiquel Capital of Iximché', *Expedition*, ix/2 (1967), pp. 22–35

M. S. Edmonson: *The Book of Counsel: The Popol Vuh of the Quiché Maya of Guatemala*, Tulane University Middle American Publication Series, xxxv (New Orleans, 1971)

D. W. Sedat and R. J. Sharer: 'Archaeological Investigations in the Northern Maya Highlands: New Data on the Maya Preclassic', *Studies in the Archaeology of Mexico and Guatemala*, ed. J. A. Graham (Berkeley, 1972), pp. 23–35

R. Carmack, J. Fox and R. Stewart: *La formación del reino Quiché* (Guatemala City, 1975)

J. W. Fox: *Quiché Conquest: Centralism and Regionalism in Highland Guatemalan State Development* (Albuquerque, 1978)

R. M. Carmack: *The Quiché Mayas of Utatlán* (Norman, 1981)

J. W. Fox: 'The Postclassic Eastern Frontier of Mesoamerica: Cultural Innovation along the Periphery', *Current Anthropol.*, xxii (1981), pp. 321–46

A. Ichon and others: *Rabinal et la vallée moyenne du Río Chixoy* (Paris, 1982)

J. W. Fox: *Maya Postclassic State Formation* (Cambridge, 1987)

——: 'On the Rise and Fall of the Tulans and Maya Segmentary States', *Amer. Anthropologist*, xci (1989), pp. 656–81

W. L. *Scribes, Warriors and Kings: The City of Copón and the Ancient Maya* (London and New York, 1991)

J. W. Fox, D. Wallace and K. Brown: 'The Emergence of the Quiché Elite: The Putún-Palenque Connection', *Mesoamerican Elites, an Archaeological Assessment*, ed. D. Z. Chase and A. F. Chase (Norman, 1992), pp. 169–90

J. W. Fox: 'Political Cosmology among the Quiché Maya', *Factional Competition and Political Development in the New World*, ed. E. M. Brumfiel and J. W. Fox (Cambridge, 1994), pp. 158–70

JOHN W. FOX

Mayaklik-Tarishlak. *See under* KHOTAN.

Mayakovsky, Vladimir (Vladimirovich) (*b* Bagdadi, Georgia, 19 July 1893; *d* Moscow, 14 April 1930). Russian poet, critic, graphic designer and painter of Georgian birth. Although best known as a poet and playwright he studied painting at the Moscow School of Painting, Sculpture and Architecture (1911–14) and, as a member of the Futurist group Hylea, was a pioneer of what later became known as PERFORMANCE ART. Mayakovsky's family moved to Moscow on the death of his father in 1906, and he soon became involved in left-wing activities, for which he was repeatedly arrested. On passing the entrance examination of the Moscow School of Painting, Sculpture and Architecture in August 1911, his political activities shifted their focus to bohemian épatage. In the class for figure painting Mayakovsky met David Burlyuk, who with his brothers Nikolay Burlyuk (1890–1920) and Vladimir Burlyuk (1886–1917) and the 'aviator poet' Vasily Kamensky (1864–1961), formed the core of the Russian Futurist movement. Adopting a stance similar to that of Marinetti, whose Futurist manifesto (*see* FUTURISM) had been published in Russian in 1909, these artists, although they denied an Italian Futurist connection, rejected what they felt was the bourgeois compromise of the old world in order to embrace the pitiless technology of the new. Wearing the uniform of a dandy, or a parody of the traditional clothes of the Russian peasant and populist intellectual, they painted their faces with arcane symbols and travelled the length and breadth of Russia giving poetry readings and impromptu performances merely by appearing in public in incongruous attire. They intended, as the title of David Burlyuk's manifesto *Poshchechina obshchestvennomu vkusu* (Moscow, 1912) makes clear, to render 'a slap in the face of public taste'. There are surviving academic studies produced by Mayakovsky at art school (now Moscow, V. V. Mayakovsky Mus.) and a series of fanciful sketches of giraffes, bears and other animals, as well as portraits of the artist and his friends. Many of these were made with improvised materials on scraps of paper. Most of his energy at this time, however, went into the writing and performance of his poetry, which incorporated neologisms and non-verbal sound effects; but his most important achievement as a visual artist were his drawings for the books produced by Burlyuk and his circle. *Trebnik troikh* ('The missal of the three', Moscow, 1913), for example, contains a particularly interesting example of a primitivist *Still-life* (facing p. 42).

In February 1914 Mayakovsky and Burlyuk were expelled from art school. A number of small Cubo-Futurist oil paintings (Moscow, V. V. Mayakovsky Mus.; Moscow, priv. col.) by Mayakovsky date from 1915 and 1916. At the same time he began to work on a series of crude, cartoon-like anti-German and anti-Turkish war propaganda posters, to which he added humorous, rhyming verses. The enthusiasm of the avant-garde for the War soon evaporated, and when the Revolution took place in October 1917, Mayakovsky, then living in Petrograd (now St Petersburg), was one of the first to welcome it. The Futurists supported the Bolsheviks and put all their energies into propaganda for the new state (*see* AGITPROP). During 1918 Mayakovsky wrote scripts for films in which he played a leading role; he also completed and performed in the 'medieval' agit-play *Misteriya-Buffa*, with sets designed by Kazimir Malevich. He wrote and performed many new revolutionary poems and submitted three works to the first exhibition of the Union of Russian Artists in Moscow. From this time until the mid-1920s the Futurists, now Com-Fut (Communist-Futurists), enjoyed a privileged relationship with ANATOLY LUNACHARSKY, Head of NARKOMPROS, who provided state patronage for their newspapers and journals and who insulated them from criticism from Lenin and other party leaders who felt that their avant-gardism was élitist. Aware of their vulnerability, the avant-garde sought to serve the Revolution by moving away from fine art to designing objects or images that were useful or changed the way people thought. From October 1919 Mayakovsky worked in Moscow for the Russian Telegraph Agency (ROSTA) on a series of large-scale, stencilled posters with simple serial images, which provided up-to-date news on the progress of the Red Army in the Civil War, or information on the government's public health and literacy campaigns, for example (see fig.). The posters, which were displayed in empty store windows and at telegraph offices, were very eye-catching, looked like vast newspaper cartoons and could be understood by the barely literate; Mayakovsky worked on these until February 1922.

When the Civil War ended in 1921 Mayakovsky became the leader of the Moscow LEF (Left Front of the Arts) group and the editor of its journal; this became the main

Vladimir Mayakovsky: *Remember Red Army Barracks Day*, ROSTA window poster, no. 729, 1.00×0.79 m, December 1920 (Moscow, V. V. Mayakovsky State Museum); the captions read: 'Remember the Day of the Red Barracks'; '1) We hammered the Russian White Guards this time. It is not enough:'; '2) The monster of World Capitalism is still alive'; '3) Thus a new Red Army is necessary'; '4) Thus we must act decisively to help it.'

mouthpiece for Productivism (*see* CONSTRUCTIVISM, §2), a tendency that involved avant-garde artists as propagandists and designers for industry. The group held together until spring 1925, when Mayakovsky embarked on an extended journey to Cuba, Mexico and the USA via Germany and France. Under Lenin's New Economic Policy (NEP; instigated 1922) Mayakovsky had joined with ALEKSANDR RODCHENKO in writing and designing advertisements for the press, and billboards to promote the large state-run department stores and the goods and services of nationalized industries. As with the ROSTA posters, Mayakovsky matched images to a humorous rhyming text. They also worked together on illustrated volumes of Mayakovsky's verse (e.g. *Pro eto*, 'About this', Moscow, 1923, and *Siflis*, 'Syphilis', Tiflis, 1926). In 1927 the LEF group reformed as Novy LEF (New LEF) but, in keeping with the changing cultural and economic climate, it manifested a new interest in documenting the profound changes in agriculture and heavy industry that were beginning. LEF saw itself as the guardian of revolutionary values and roundly condemned bourgeois NEP mentality as well as the proliferating bureaucracy of the state. Mayakovsky's satirical plays *Klop* ('The bedbug', 1929) and *Banya* ('The bathhouse', 1930) levelled their sights on such targets; however, Lunacharsky, Mayakovsky's protector, had been dismissed, and Mayakovsky was no longer immune from counter-attack, particularly from the state-backed associations of self-designated proletarian writers and critics who pronounced that his work, as well as that of his LEF colleagues, was élitist, formalist and 'unintelligible to the masses'. Such accusations were deeply wounding to an artist who had consciously modelled himself as the poet of the revolution. In February 1930 he organized a one-man retrospective, *Dvadtsat let rabot* ('Twenty years of work'; Moscow and Leningrad), which showed the wide range of his creative output and was intended to prove that his work was still popular and relevant to the present; the new literary establishment ignored the exhibition. Devastated by this as well as a series of unhappy love affairs, Mayakovsky shot himself in his apartment. Crowds of over one hundred and fifty thousand people thronged the Moscow streets at his funeral. Vladimir Tatlin and the students of Vkhutein (*see* VKHUTEMAS) designed his catafalque. Mayakovsky's work quickly fell into disregard until it was rehabilitated at the express wish of Stalin in 1936, with an official version of Mayakovsky's life that was a tendentious rewriting of what actually happened. On the letter with which he gave his authorization, Stalin wrote: 'Indifference to his memory is a crime.'

WRITINGS
Polnoye sobraniye sochineniy [Complete works], 13 vols (Moscow, 1955–61)

BIBLIOGRAPHY
Literaturnaya Gazeta (30 April 1930); Eng. trans., ed. D. Elliott, as *Mayakovsky Memorial Edition of Literaturnaya Gazeta* (Oxford, 1982)
R. Jakobson: *Smerta poeta* (Berlin, 1931); Eng. trans. as 'On a Generation that Squandered its Poets', *Major Soviet Writers: Essays in Criticism*, ed. E. J. Brown (Oxford, 1973), pp. 7–32
O. Brik: 'Mayakovsky: Redaktor i organizator (Materialy k literaturnoy biografii)' [Mayakovsky: editor and organizer (materials for a literary biography)], *Lit. Krit.*, 4 (1936), pp. 113–46
V. Shklovsky: *O Mayakovskom* (Moscow, 1940); Eng. trans. as *Mayakovsky and his Circle* (London, 1974)
V. A. Katanian: *V. Mayakovsky* (Moscow, [c. 1941])
H. Marshall, ed. and trans.: *Mayakovsky* (London, 1965)
W. Woroszylski: *The Life of Mayakovsky* (New York, 1970)
E. J. Brown: *Mayakovsky: A Poet in the Revolution* (Princeton, 1973)
W. Duwakin: *Majakowski als Dichter und bildender Künstler: ROSTA Fenster* (Dresden, 1975)
B. Jagenfeldt: *Majakovskij and Futurism, 1917–1921* (Stockholm, 1977)
D. Elliott, ed.: *Mayakovsky: Three Views* (Oxford, 1982)
——: *Mayakovsky: Twenty Years of Work* (Oxford, 1982)

DAVID ELLIOTT

Mayall, John Jabez Edwin [Meal, Jabez] (*b* Manchester, 17 Sept 1813; *d* Southwick, nr Brighton, 6 March 1901). English photographer. He became established as a daguerreotypist in Philadelphia, PA, but returned to England in 1846, rapidly emerging as one of the top daguerreotypists in London. His association with the USA was tenacious; even Queen Victoria, a regular patron, said of him: 'the oddest man I ever saw. . .but an excellent photographer. . .he is an American'. She was not alone in her observation of Mayall's eccentric but charismatic behaviour.

Mayall's forceful monochromatic portrait images were the equal of Antoine Claudet's and successful competitors of William Kilburn's hand-coloured daguerreotypes. Mayall exhibited portraits of the famous at his Daguerreotype Institution, and many of his sitters, including *Sir John Herschel, Professor Alfred Swain Taylor* (1806–80) and *Sir David Brewster* (1781–1868), were intimately connected

with the early history of photography. Mayall also resolutely expanded the scope of the daguerreotype beyond portraiture. His panorama of *Niagara Falls* (1845) excited tremendous interest, including praise from J. M. W. Turner, and he was renowned for his efforts to develop a new branch of photographic fine art by using the daguerreotype in historical allegory. An early series of ten daguerreotypes illustrating the Lord's Prayer was completed while he was in Philadelphia, and in England he compiled a 'Shakespearian Series' (see 1848 exh. cat.).

Mayall remained active as a photographer throughout his life, becoming, among other things, an early specialist in full-length life-size portraits. He moved his main studio to Brighton (where he became the mayor), while maintaining his London operations. His later work is often confused with that of his son, the photographer John Mayall (1842–91).

WRITINGS
Catalogue of Daguerreotype Panoramas, Falls of Niagara, Shakespeare's Birth-place Tomb, Relics, Photographic Pictures, Portraits of Eminent Persons, &c. in the Gallery of the Daguerreotype Institution (London, 1848)

BIBLIOGRAPHY
L. J. Schaaf: 'Mayall's Life-size Portrait of George Peabody', *Hist. Phot.*, ix (1985), pp. 279–88
L. L. Reynolds and A. T. Gill: 'The Mayall Story', *Hist. Phot.*, ix (1985), pp. 89–107
——: 'The Mayall Story—A Postscript', *Hist. Phot.*, xi (1987), pp. 77–80

L. J. SCHAAF

Mayapán. Site of Pre-Columbian MAYA city of the Late Post-Classic period (*c.* AD 1200–1521), 40 km south-east of Mérida in Yucatán, Mexico. The name means 'Standard of the Maya'. According to Bishop Landa, a Spanish observer writing in the 16th century, Mayapán was established by a ruler from CHICHÉN ITZÁ named Kukulcán, who decreed that henceforward all the native lords of Yucatán would reside there. Ethno-historical sources agree that the city was founded between 1263 and 1283 by the Itzá, a Maya group from Chichén Itzá. Between 1362 and 1382 Mayapán was ruled by the Cocom, an Itzá lineage under whom it became the capital of the northern plains region of Yucatán. However, the Cocom became so oppressive that the other resident lords, led by the Tutul Xiu lineage, murdered and deposed them sometime between 1441 and 1461. Mayapán was traditionally referred to as *Ichpa* ('within the enclosure'), and archaeological investigations confirmed that it was indeed a fortified walled city. It contained some 3500 structures within 4 sq. km, about 100 of which were large masonry temples or ceremonial structures. An estimated population of 11,000–12,000 was accommodated in housing ranging from substantial residences to perishable huts.

At the heart of the city is a radially symmetrical pyramid temple with four stairways, known as the 'Castillo' or 'Temple of Kukulcán'; it is a smaller and shoddier imitation of the Castillo at Chichén Itzá. The central civic-religious precinct also included a circular, tower-like structure reminiscent of but smaller than the Caracol at Chichén Itzá. Several of the plazas grouped around these central temples were fronted by colonnaded halls. Resting on low platforms, these were constructed on a roughly rectangular plan with a double colonnade at the front and benches along the rear wall. They have been interpreted as temporary quarters for priests and acolytes. Elaborate élite residences were built of masonry and located near the city centre. Their plans typically comprise an open front room, sometimes entered through a colonnade, and one or more enclosed rear chambers, which sometimes contain small altars that may have served as family shrines. These 'palaces' are less well constructed than earlier Maya architecture, employing crude block walls and beam-and-mortar roofs; thick plaster concealed faults in the masonry. Architectural sculpture was generally of modelled stucco, although a few structures displayed reused elements of Puuc Maya carved-stone sculpture. At the opposite end of the social scale were over 2000 irregularly spaced houses surrounding the city centre. Most were of partial masonry construction with perishable upper walls and thatched roofs. Surrounded by low, dry-stone boundary walls, such dwellings probably accommodated extended families.

The Maya stele cult was revived at Mayapán, and some 13 carved monuments were erected there. Stele 1 depicts the aged Sun god seated on a throne accepting an offering. The presence of a calendrical glyph and stylistic and iconographic correspondences with the Paris Codex of *c.* 1300–*c.* 1500 (Paris, Bib. N.) indicate a probable date in the Maya Long Count system (*see* MESOAMERICA, PRE-COLUMBIAN, §II) corresponding to 1441. Mayapán ceramics are distinguished by large polychrome, hollow figurine censers (Mérida, Mexico, Mus. Reg. Antropol. Yucatan), known as the Chen Mul Modelled type, which resemble other Late Post-Classic types produced from southern Veracruz to Belize and inland as far as Lake Petén Itzá. The figures represent traditional Yucatec Maya deities such as Itzamna, Chac and Ek Chuah, as well as central Mexican gods such as Quetzalcóatl and Xipe Totec.

BIBLIOGRAPHY

D. de Landa: *Relación de las cosas de Yucatán* (*c.* 1565); Eng. trans. as *The Maya: Diego de Landa's Account of the Affairs of Yucatán*, ed. A. R. Pagden (Chicago, 1975)

H. E. D. Pollock and others: *Mayapán, Yucatán, Mexico*, Carnegie Inst. Washington, pubn 619 (Washington, DC, 1962)

R. E. Smith: *The Pottery of Mayapán: Including Studies of Ceramic Material from Uxmal, Kabah and Chichén Itzá*, Pap. Peabody Mus. Archaeol. Ethnol., 66, 2 vols (Cambridge, MA, 1971)

JEFF KARL KOWALSKI

Maybeck, Bernard (Ralph) (*b* New York, 7 Feb 1862; *d* Berkeley, CA, 3 Oct 1957). American architect. He attended the Ecole des Beaux-Arts, Paris (1882–6), and from then on employed academic design principles with spirit and conviction. Concurrently he was influenced by theories as divergent as those of Eugène-Emmanuel Viollet-le-Duc and Gottfried Semper, while also pursuing many of the aims of the Arts and Crafts Movement. On his return from Paris, he worked for the firm of Carrère & Hastings, New York (1886–9). He moved to California in 1890, holding a number of minor jobs in the San Francisco region until he opened his own office in 1902. Maybeck continued in active practice until World War II, mostly in partnership with his brother-in-law, Mark White. Their office remained small, with suburban and rural houses comprising the majority of realized commissions.

Maybeck's oeuvre resists categorization. As he drew from many sources for ideas, so he relished diversity in expression. No project was too small or unimportant, too grand or ambitious. Informal, rustic dwellings, such as the Flagg house, Berkeley (1900–01), may be composed with a clear sense of order and unity, or may appear to be a fanciful collage, as did Wyntoon, Phoebe Hearst's great mountain lodge on the McLoud River in northern California (1902–3, destr. 1933). Space may unfold in neat, axial sequences, as in the Roos house, San Francisco (1908–9), or in loose, circuitous paths, as in the Senger house, Berkeley (1906–7). Maybeck sought to emphasize the expressive qualities of structure, sometimes defying rational solutions. But structure could also give lucid coherence to the entire scheme, as with the reinforced concrete Lawson house, Berkeley (1907). Post-medieval vernacular architecture in central Europe provided the major source for Maybeck's imagery, yet he also drew on the buildings of Imperial Rome.

Many of these dissimilar characteristics are synthesized in the First Church of Christ Scientist, Berkeley (1909–11). Here a simple rectangular plan gains three-dimensional complexity through a tiered cruciform interior space, the lower portion of which is plain, the upper portions richly detailed. Outside, the structure is more or less symmetrical, but divided into small sections—some rendered as fragments—and covered with vines. Its appearance suggests a folk building added to and embellished over time, yet the underlying organization is rigorous and highly sophisticated.

Maybeck long sought commissions for large civic and other institutions. Only a few such projects came his way, however, partly because his approach was so unconventional. The Palace of Fine Arts, San Francisco, built in 1913–15 for the Panama–Pacific International Exposition and reconstructed in the 1960s, is without precedent. The gallery proper, a curving, steel-trussed shed, lies behind a giant Corinthian peristyle and an open rotunda—part Pantheon, part triumphal arch—set amid lush plants and fronted by a lagoon. No scheme better embodies Maybeck's belief that architecture should be principally a purveyor of mood and sentiment; whether tailored to an individual client or to the public, architecture should aim to transcend the value of aesthetic, technical and social ideologies.

Maybeck's romantic view is demonstrated in two remarkable commissions for the car dealer Earle C. Anthony, the Packard Automobile Showrooms at San Francisco (1926) and at Oakland, CA (1928, destr. 1974). The former suggests a Roman ruin into which a concrete, steel and glass cage has been inserted. The latter was mostly a concrete fantasy, its showroom like an enormous crypt, its ramps like ziggurats. Parts of both buildings could be compared with an elaborate stage set; elsewhere, a dramatized past collides with the machine age in playful tension: a frank, if unusual, response to the changing modern world. Maybeck executed part of his plan for the pastoral campus of Principia College, Elsah, IL, between 1931 and 1937, but during the Depression he was offered little other work. Towards the end of his life he began to receive the national recognition long due.

WRITINGS

Palace of Fine Arts and Lagoon, Panama–Pacific International Exposition, 1915 (San Francisco, 1915)

'Architecture of the Palace of Fine Arts and the Panama–Pacific International Exposition', *CA Mag.*, i (1916), pp. 161–4

BIBLIOGRAPHY
Contemp. Architects
C. Keeler: *The Simple Home* (San Francisco, 1904, rev. with intro. D. Shipounoff, Santa Barbara, 2/1979)
I. F. M[orrow]: 'The Earle C. Anthony, Inc., Packard Building, San Francisco', *Archit. & Engin. CA*, xc/1 (1927), pp. 60–67
D. Gillum: 'The Earle C. Anthony Building, Oakland, California', *Archit. & Engin. CA*, xcvi/2 (1929), pp. 35–42, 67–73
J. M. Bangs: 'Bernard Ralph Maybeck, Architect, Comes into his Own', *Archit. Rec.*, cii/1 (1948), pp. 72–9
E. McCoy: *Five California Architects* (New York, 1960/R 1975), pp. 1–57
W. H. Jordy: *American Buildings and their Architects: Progressive and Academic Ideals at the Turn of the Twentieth Century* (Garden City, NY, 1972/R New York, 1986), pp. 275–313
R. M. Craig: *Maybeck at Principia: A Study of an Architect–Client Relationship* (diss., Ithaca, NY, Cornell U., 1973)
J. Beach: 'The Bay Area Tradition 1890–1918', *Bay Area Houses*, ed. S. Woodbridge (New York, 1976), pp. 23–98
K. H. Cardwell: *Bernard Maybeck: Artisan, Architect, Artist* (Santa Barbara, 1977)
J. Maybeck: *Maybeck: The Family View* (Berkeley, CA, 1980)
R. Longstreth: *On the Edge of the World: Four Architects in San Francisco at the Turn of the Century* (New York, 1983)
S. Woodbridge: *Bernard Maybeck: Visionary Architect* (New York, 1992)
RICHARD LONGSTRETH

Mayekawa, Kunio. *See* MAEKAWA, KUNIO.

Mayer, A(ugust) L(iebmann) (*b* Darmstadt, 1885; *d* Nice, France, 1943). German art historian. Educated at the University of Leipzig, where he obtained his doctorate with a thesis on Jusepe de Ribera (pub. Leipzig, 1920), Mayer concentrated his historical research on Spanish art, as one of a group of German specialists dedicated to the archaeology and art of the Iberian peninsula, that included Carl Justi and Julius Meier-Graefe. Mayer also published works on Diego Velázquez (1924) and Francisco de Goya (1923) and made important contributions to our knowledge of El Greco (pub. 1926) and Tintoretto. Concerned more with documentary and philological work than with critical and aesthetic questions, Mayer, who knew Spain extremely well and made at least five long trips there, also published important surveys of the history of Spanish art, including *Die Sevillaner Malerschule* (1911) and *Geschichte der Spanischen Malerei* (1913).

WRITINGS
Die Sevillaner Malerschule (Leipzig, 1911)
Geschichte der Spanischen Malerei (Leipzig, 1913)
Francisco de Goya (Munich, 1923); Eng. trans. (London, 1924) [with cat. of works]
with E. von der Bercken: *Jacopo Tintoretto*, 2 vols (Munich, 1923)
Diego Velazquez (Berlin, 1924); Eng. trans. as *Velazquez, a Catalogue Raisonné of the Pictures and Drawings* (London, 1936)
Dominico Theotocopuli, El Greco (Munich, 1926)

BIBLIOGRAPHY
H. Kehrer: *Deutschland in Spanien: Beziehung, Einfluss und Abhängigkeit* (Munich, 1953)
FRANCISCO CALVO SERRALLER

Mayer, Albert (*b* New York, 29 Dec 1897; *d* New York, 14 Oct 1981). American architect, engineer and urban planner. He received his architectural training at the Massachusetts Institute of Technology, Cambridge, MA, graduating in 1919. His particular interest was housing reform, and in the 1930s he joined with Catherine K. Bauer (1905–64), Lewis Mumford, Clarence Stein and Henry Wright in devising conceptual models of improved housing that would create a sense of community and provide abundant light, fresh air and space. As a result of their activities, in 1937 the United States Housing Authority was formed. Mayer formed a partnership with Julian Whittlesey in 1935, which William Glass joined later. They designed such innovative apartment houses as 240 Central Park South (1941), New York.

While serving as an army engineer during World War II Mayer met Indian Prime Minister Jawaharlal Nehru and as a result was engaged in 1946 to advise on planning *c.* 300 rural Indian villages, beginning in Uttar Pradesh. He also worked with Matthew Nowicki on the original scheme for Chandigarh (1949–50), designing four residential superblocks inspired by the work of Stein and Wright in their community of Radburn (1929), NJ. His views on planning were expounded in *The Urgent Future* (1967) in which he argued against uncontrolled urban expansion forming what he termed 'megalopolis'. Instead he favoured moderate-sized cities and a decentralization of metropolitan areas. One of his last planning projects was the new town of Kitimat, British Columbia, begun *c.* 1954. After his retirement from practice (1961) he remained active as a planning consultant.

WRITINGS
with H. Wright and L. Mumford: *New Homes for a New Deal: A Concrete Program for Slum Clearance and Housing Relief* (New York, 1934)
The Urgent Future (New York, 1967)
'It's Not Just the Cities', *Archit. Rec.*, cxlv (1969), no. 7, pp. 151–62; cxlvi (1969), no. 3, pp. 171–82; no. 5, pp. 139–46; no. 6, pp. 105–10; cxlvii (1970), no. 7, pp. 137–42; cxlviii (1970), no. 1, pp. 101–6

BIBLIOGRAPHY
'Industry Builds Kitimat', *Archit. Forum*, ci (1954), no. 1, pp. 128–48; no. 4, pp. 158–61
N. Evanson: *Chandigarh* (Berkeley, 1966)
M. Marriott and R. L. Park: *The Story of Rural Development at Etawah, Uttar Pradesh* (Westport, CT, 1973)
R. C. Emmett: *Guide to the Albert Mayer Papers on India in the University of Chicago Library* (Chicago, 1977)
LELAND M. ROTH

Mayer, (Marie-Françoise-)Constance [la Martinière] (*b* Paris, 1775; *d* Paris, 26 May 1821). French painter. Constance Mayer's name is closely associated with that of PIERRE-PAUL PRUD'HON, with whom she collaborated on many works often catalogued under his name. She was one of an increasing number of women artists who worked mainly as painters of miniatures, portraits and genre scenes. In the middle years of her career, under the impact of Prud'hon's influence, she turned to allegorical subjects. She studied first under Joseph-Benoît Suvée and then Jean-Baptiste Greuze, whose sentimental subjects and soft handling left a deep and lasting impression on her work, but especially on the early Salon exhibition pictures of children and young girls. It was as a pupil of Suvée and Greuze that she signed her Salon submission of 1801, *Portrait of the Artist with her Father; He Points to a Bust of Raphael* (Hartford, CT, Wadsworth Atheneum), although that year she took lessons from Jacques-Louis David. His teaching accounts for the greater clarity, incisiveness and serious tone of the work. Despite the bust of Raphael and antique fragments on the studio wall in this painting, Mayer never really incorporated these models into her own work and remained closer in subject and sentiment to Greuze than to David.

In 1802 Mayer entered Prud'hon's studio as a pupil but soon became his friend, housekeeper, childminder and mistress. His wife, who was seriously unbalanced, was placed in a nursing home in 1803 and Prud'hon was given custody of the children. The usual distinction between teacher and pupil, master and assistant was not clearcut with Prud'hon and Mayer. Nor is it easy to assess their respective contributions to Salon paintings. Prud'hon normally produced the early drawings and sketches and Mayer then worked them up into paintings with varying degrees of assistance from Prud'hon. For the Salon exhibit of 1804, *Innocence Preferring Love to Wealth* (St Petersburg, Hermitage), he produced at least 12 sketches but she executed most of the painting and exhibited it under her name. A later allegory of a subject painted by Greuze in the late 1770s, *Innocence Drawn by Love and Followed by Regret* (priv. col., see J. Guiffrey: *L'Oeuvre de P. P. Prud'hon*, 1924, pp. 4–5), was begun by Mayer but finished by Prud'hon and catalogued under his name. Empress Josephine commissioned the *Sleep of Venus and Cupid, Disturbed by Zephyrs* (London, Wallace), which Mayer exhibited in 1806 and to which she added a pendant in 1808. These were both sold at later dates as Psyche subjects by Prud'hon.

The *Happy Mother* (exh. Salon 1810; Paris, Louvre; see fig.) and the *Unfortunate Mother* (exh. Salon 1812; Paris, Louvre) are instances of the early 19th-century concern with motherhood, a much-debated subject since the novels of Jean-Jacques Rousseau and the pronouncements of Enlightenment thinkers of the mid-18th century. The *Happy Mother* is a powerful depiction of the pleasure of breast-feeding, while the *Unfortunate Mother* evokes a sense of loss, the mother shown mourning at the tomb of her dead child. Both paintings are set in wooded landscapes and emphasize the private nature of maternal experience. Adverse criticism of these attempts at serious subject-matter led Mayer to turn again to portraiture, mostly paintings of her women friends (e.g. *Mme Voiart*, exh. Salon 1814; Nancy, Mus. B.-A.). For the Salon of 1819 she returned to an allegorical subject, the *Dream of Happiness* (Paris, Louvre), showing a couple and child in a boat being taken down the River of Life by Love and Fortune. It was a happiness that Mayer never experienced. Although she had made a reputation for herself as an artist and had been given lodgings in the Sorbonne, she never had children of her own and became depressed and ill with her personal circumstances. When Prud'hon refused to contemplate the idea of remarriage should his wife's illness become fatal, Mayer cut her own throat with his razor. Prud'hon completed her painting The *Poverty-stricken Family* (M. G. Jakobi priv. col., see Weston, p. 16), a work much admired by Stendhal for its convincing depiction of despair. It was exhibited with her other works in 1822, in a posthumous exhibition which Prud'hon organized as a tribute to her.

BIBLIOGRAPHY

C. Clément: *Prud'hon, sa vie, ses oeuvres, sa correspondance* (Paris, 1872)
C. Gueullette: 'Constance Mayer', *Gaz. B.-A.*, n.s. 1, xix (1879), pp. 476–90; xx (1879), pp. 525–38

Constance Mayer: *Happy Mother*, oil on canvas, 1.94×1.47 m, exh. Salon 1810 (Paris, Musée du Louvre)

J. Doin: 'Constance Mayer', *Rev. A. Anc. & Mod.*, xxix (1911), pp. 49–60
E. Pilon: *Constance Mayer (1775–1821)* (Paris, 1927)
H. Weston: 'The Case for Constance Mayer', *Oxford A. J.*, iii/1 (1980), pp. 14–19

HELEN WESTON

Mayer, Louis. *See* VAUXCELLES, LOUIS.

Mayer, Rudolf (*b* Teschen [now Cieszyn, Poland], 12 June 1846; *d* Karlsruhe, 24 June 1916). Austrian medallist and engraver, active in Germany. He trained under Otto König (1838–1920) at the Kunstgewerbeschule in Vienna and worked there after 1871 as a freelance artist. In 1873 he became a professor at the Kunstgewerbeschule in Stuttgart, and from 1886 until 1913 he was Professor of Engraving at the Kunstgewerbeschule in Karlsruhe. Mayer first became known for the bowls, goblets and boxes that he made of precious metals, winning prizes at several exhibitions; very few are known to be extant. After 1896 he worked mainly as a medallist, producing numerous medals and plaques portraying artists, both living and dead; from 1897 onwards these medals were produced in Pforzheim at the technically advanced minting works of B. H. Mayer. Some of Mayer's medals were produced in great numbers and exerted a powerful influence on contemporary medal art. Mayer studied the French medal art of his day but also imitated the style of the German

Renaissance medal. His efforts to produce works of high artistic quality as a counterpoise to the mass production of medals were rewarded with numerous prizes. From 1902 onwards he also cut dies for the coins, to be minted at Karlsruhe, of the Grand Dukes of Baden.

BIBLIOGRAPHY

Forrer; Thieme–Becker

Rudolf Mayer: Medaillen und Metallarbeiten der Jahrhundertwende (exh. cat. by M. Bachmayer and P. H. Martin, Karlsruhe, Bad. Landesmus., 1977)

S. Salaschek: *Katalog der Medaillen und Plaketten des 19. und 20. Jahrhunderts im französischen und deutschen Sprachraum in der Hamburger Kunsthalle* (Hamburg, 1980), pp. 262–4

HERMANN MAUÉ

Mayerhoffer. Hungarian family of masons and architects. Andreas [András] Mayerhoffer (*b* Salzburg, 1690; *d* Pest, 1771) was for a long time Master of the Guild of Masons, Stone-dressers and Carpenters in Pest. He was an active master mason whose name is recorded as early as 1702. Only one surviving work, however, can be authenticated with certainty, the small Péterffy Palace (1755; now a restaurant, Százéves vendéglő) in Pest. It is a two-storey, seven-bay block with atlantids flanking the central doorway and supporting a balcony. The window heads are picked out with Rococo decoration. Mayerhoffer was formerly believed to be the architect of the church of the Pauline Order (1722–42; now the university church) in Pest and the palace (1744–7; altered after 1867) for Graf Antal Grassalkovich (1694–1771) at Gödöllő and was therefore considered the greatest Hungarian architect of the first half of the 18th century. It now appears, however, that he was involved only in minor technical aspects of the construction process. Establishing the extent of his oeuvre is difficult because of his close and documented association with his talented sons János Mayerhoffer (*b* Pest, 1721; *d* Pest, 1780), himself a master mason, and András Mayerhoffer (*b* Pest, 1725; *d* Pest, 1785). The brothers worked on several palaces for the Hungarian nobility, such as Nagytétény (1765–71), Pécel (*c.* 1770–75), Gács (*c.* 1770–75), Hatvan (1754–63 for Antal Grassalkovich; now a hospital) and Gernyeszeg, all in a style based on the Grassalkovich Palace at Gödöllő, itself derived from the royal palace in Buda attributed to Jean-Nicolas Jadot de Ville-Issey.

BIBLIOGRAPHY

E. Réh: *A régi Buda és Pest építőmesterei Mária Terézia korában* [Master builders of old Buda and Pest in the time of Maria Theresa] (Budapest, 1932)

M. Mojzer: 'Adatok Mayerhoffer András művészetéhez' [Some contributing facts to the art of András Mayerhoffer], *Művészettörténeti Értesítő* (1956)

P. Voit: *Der Barock in Ungarn* [The Baroque in Hungary] (Budapest, 1971)

PÁL VOIT

Mayerne, Théodore Turquet de. *See* TURQUET DE MAYERNE, THEODORE.

Mayhew, John. *See under* INCE & MAYHEW.

Mayito [García Joya, Mario] (*b* Santa María del Rosario, 28 July 1938). Cuban photographer. He studied fine arts at the Escuela Superior de Arte San Alejandro, Havana (1955–7), and subsequently studied at the Cuban Institute of Film Art and Industry (1963–4), where he was Director of Photography in 1961–8. He worked for several advertising agencies in Havana (1957–8), and in 1959 he was one of the founder-members of the photographic team on the newspaper *Revolución*. As an important photographic reporter, he not only worked in Cuba but also made a moving report on Nicaragua. His name was further enhanced by his work on films such as Tomás Gutiérrez Alea's *La ultima cena* (1975) and Miguel Latín's *El recurso del método* (1977) and by one-man exhibitions such as *Cuba Va!* at the Museo Nacional de Bellas Artes in Havana (1970). He has also carried out research into the history of Cuban photography.

BIBLIOGRAPHY

E. Billeter: *Fotografia Lateinamerika* (Zurich and Berne, 1981)

——: *Canto a la realidad fotografie Lateinamerika, 1860–1993* (Barcelona and Berne, 1993–4)

ERIKA BILLETER

Maykop [Maikop]. Town in the northern Caucasus in Russia and site of a burial mound dating to the Early Bronze Age (mid-3rd millennium BC). It was excavated by Nikolai I. Veselovsky (1848–1918) in 1897. Beneath a hemispherical embankment (h. 10.6 m) was a rectangular burial chamber covered by a layer of beams and partitioned into three sections. The skeleton of a man covered in red ochre was found in the larger, southern section. Several magnificent necklaces were found in the region of his neck and chest; the beads are of gold and silver, bored lazurite, cornelian, meerschaum and turquoise. On the man's head was a conical tiara of gold hoops decorated with gold rosettes, similar to finds at Ur. There was originally a canopy over the body with silver tubes as supports; large figurines of bulls, two cast in gold and two in silver, in a style reminiscent of Sumerian sculpture, were affixed to the lower part of four of the supports. The curtains of the canopy were hung with 38 rings or hoops and 87 chased gold medallions, of which 68 represent lions and 19 represent bulls.

Other finds include local spherical clay pots, a spherical stone vessel with a gold lid and gold upper section, two gold vessels and fourteen spherical and pear-shaped silver vases, as well as two large silver goblets with spherical bodies and high necks, decorated with chased images of animals. The pictorial motif on one of the goblets is traditional in Ancient Near Eastern art: on the body of the vessel is a string of animals, with two goats, two sheep, a bull and a bird. The other goblet is highly unusual. In addition to a string of four animals (two bulls in a heraldic composition, a lion and a horse) on its body, there is a circular design with goats, sheep, lions and boars around the foot. This entire composition is set in a landscape: the neck of the vessel is incised with a range of mountains, including two main peaks, and two trees. Between the trees is a bear, while from the mountains flow two streams that separate the bulls from the horse and lion and flow into a lake around the foot of the vessel. The traditional interpretation of the scene is that it is a landscape of the Caucasus Mountains, but it is more likely to be a cosmological composition: mountains, land animals and water (the streams flowing into the lake) are three cosmic regions on a vertical plane, while on the horizontal plane the four animals represent the earthly region. All artefacts are now in the Hermitage, St Petersburg. The Maykop barrow is a monument to the early influence of Near Eastern civilizations on the art and culture of the Caucasus. There are similar, less rich burial mounds in the northern Caucasus that, together with contemporaneous fortified settlements, form part of the Early Bronze Age Maykop culture.

BIBLIOGRAPHY
Otchot arkheologicheskoy komissii za 1897 god [Archaeological Commission report for 1897] (St Petersburg, 1900)
Otchot arkheologicheskoy komissii za 1898 god [Archaeological Commission report for 1898] (St Petersburg, 1901)
B. Farmakovsky: 'Arkhaicheskiy period v Rossii' [The archaic period in Russia], *Mat. Arkheol. Ros.*, xxxiv (1914)
F. Hančar: *Urgeschichte Kaukasiens* (Vienna, 1937)
M. V. Andreyeva: 'Ob izobrazheniyakh na serebryanykh maykopskikh sosudakh' [On the images of Maykop silver vessels], *Sov. Arkheol.*, i (1979), pp. 22–34

V. YA. PETRUKHIN

Maymont, Paul (*b* Paris, 1926). French architect. He graduated in architecture from the Ecole des Beaux-Arts, Paris, and in 1959 went on a scholarship to Kyoto University where he was in direct contact with the ideas and proponents of Metabolism. During this time he began to study the possibility of erecting megastructures floating on caissons. In 1962, concerned with the unprecedented demographic growth of the Paris region, he proposed establishing an elaborate underground city beneath the River Seine, and in 1963 he proposed a floating city, Thalassa, to be built off the coast of Monaco; this project incorporated some of the formal sophistication of the Metabolists. Although hailed in the 1960s by some critics, these utopian ideas remained marginal to mainstream French architectural debate.

WRITINGS
'L'Urbanisme flottant à la conquête des espaces', *Les Visionnaires de l'architecture* (Paris, 1965), pp. 86–109
BIBLIOGRAPHY
R. Banham: *Megastructure: Urban Futures of the Recent Past* (London, 1976, rev. New York, 1977)

ISABELLE GOURNAY

Maymurru, Narritjin (*b* ?1922; *d* Yirrkala, 1982). Australian Aboriginal painter and sculptor. He was a member of the Manggalili clan of the Yolngu-speaking peoples. He grew up in the Caledon Bay region of north-east Arnhem Land, Northern Territory, before European colonization. In the 1930s he moved to the newly established mission of Yirrkala and in 1938 helped to establish the Aboriginal settlement of Umbakumba on Groote Eylandt. After World War II he began to produce paintings for sale through the Yirrkala Mission store. He lived in Darwin for some time and won prizes in the Aboriginal art category at the Darwin Eisteddfod. In 1962 he was one of the main painters of the Yirritja moiety panel for Yirrkala Church. In 1963 he travelled with an Aboriginal dance group to perform in the southern states of Australia; on this trip he became determined that Aboriginal art should gain the same recognition in Australia as European art. By the 1970s his paintings (e.g. *Gunyan Crab in Djarrakpi Landscape*, 1975; Melbourne, N.G. Victoria) were highly sought after by collectors (*see* ABORIGINAL AUSTRALIA, fig. 10 for an example of his work), and in 1978, with his son Banapana Maymurru (1944–86), he was jointly awarded a visiting artistic fellowship at the Australian

National University, Canberra. They were the first Aboriginal artists to be awarded such a position. Like Mawalan Marika, Narritjin played a major role in encouraging women to produce sacred paintings: several of his daughters, including Naminapu Maymurru (*b* 1952), Bumiti Maymurru (*b* 1948) and Nyapililngu Maymurru (*b* 1937) became well-known painters. With his brother Nanyin Maymurru (?1918–69) and under the tutelage of Birkidji (1898–1983), he developed a characteristic style of painting using a distinctive technique of dashed infill. With Mawalan Marika and Munggurrawuy Yunapingu he developed a method of representing myths in episodic form in large complex paintings, which, although based on traditional art, involved a considerable elaboration of the figurative component (e.g. *Bamapama*, see Morphy, fig. 9.5).

BIBLIOGRAPHY
Manggalili Art (exh. cat. by H. Morphy, Canberra, Austral. N. U., 1978) [references throughout]
H. Morphy: *Ancestral Connections: Art and an Aboriginal System of Knowledge* (Chicago, 1991), pp. 214–91
VIDEO RECORDINGS
I. Dunlop: *The Narritjin at Djarrakpi* (Sydney, 1981)

HOWARD MORPHY

Mayn, John de la. *See* MAIANO, DA, (3).

Maynard [Maeneard], Alan [Allen] (*fl* 1563–*c*. 1584). French architect and sculptor, active in England. He was engaged by Sir John Thynne to work on his country house, Longleat, Wilts, in 1563, and he was active there intermittently until the building attained its final form *c*. 1580. He carved chimney-pieces in 1563, 1565 and 1566, and by 1570 he was again at Longleat for the rebuilding of the house after a fire in 1567. With Robert Smythson he was mason in charge of further reconstruction begun in 1572, when new façades were erected that the two men claimed to have designed. Maynard's contribution may have been the elaborate cresting on the parapet and most of the carved details of the walls and windows, all of which are in a flimsy Renaissance idiom and suggest the author was familiar with French architecture. The three original chimney-pieces in the present house, those in the hall, upper gallery and old kitchen, are probably his work and have some highly distinctive features, notably the term with two tails intertwined on the hall overmantel. This figure recurs in a slightly different form on a design, attributed to Maynard, for the elevation of a two-storey building in the French style of the early 16th century (Longleat, Wilts, Archv).

Among the work that Girouard suggested Maynard might have done when away from Longleat are a façade of Chalcot House, Wilts; a tomb-chest bearing the arms of the Delamere family in All Saints, Nunney, Somerset; and the stately canopied tomb of *John Leweston and his wife* (*c*. 1584; Sherborne Abbey, Dorset). Maynard became an English citizen in 1566.

BIBLIOGRAPHY
M. Girouard: 'New Light on Longleat: Allen Maynard, a French Sculptor in England in the 16th Century', *Country Life*, cxx (20 Sept 1956), pp. 594–7
——: *Robert Smythson and the Elizabethan Country House* (London, 1966, rev. New Haven, 1983), pp. 44–5, 49, 51–2, 54, 62–5, 70–76, 295–6

ADAM WHITE

Mayne, Roger (*b* Cambridge, 5 May 1929). English photographer. He is known principally for his images of British street life, which date from 1956 to the early 1960s. His inspired photographs of Teddy boys (a youth subculture of the late 1950s) and their girlfriends, of adults and of children playing have been widely exhibited and published. His extended study of Southam Street, North Kensington, was the result of five years of photography (1956–61) in one London street; in total, he produced around 1400 negatives. Other subjects included theatre portraiture and especially landscape, in Spain, Greece and Britain, in monochrome and in colour. His photographs for the *Shell Guide to Devon* were published in London in 1975, with a text by his wife Ann Jellicoe. From the mid-1960s Mayne was interested in documenting the growth of his children. He later developed an interest in drawing and etching.

PHOTOGRAPHIC PUBLICATIONS

Shell Guide to Devon, text by A. Jellicoe (London, 1975)

BIBLIOGRAPHY

Roger Mayne: Photographs 1964–73 (exh. cat., intro. D. Piper; London, Phot. Gal., 1974)

M. Haworth-Booth: *The Street Photographs of Roger Mayne* (London, 1986, rev. 1993)

MARK HAWORTH-BOOTH

Mayo, Juan de. *See* VERMEYEN, JAN CORNELISZ.

May of Notre-Dame de Paris. Name given to the 76 specially commissioned devotional paintings given, one each May, from 1630 to 1708 by the goldsmiths' corporation of Paris to the cathedral of Notre-Dame (none was commissioned in 1683 or 1684). The paintings were approximately 3.50×2.75 m in size and usually drew their subjects from the Acts of the Apostles. The commissions were awarded to established artists or, occasionally, to younger painters, indicating their rising reputation. Until the 'Mays' were dispersed during the French Revolution they were hung on the arcades of the choir and nave of the cathedral. A number are untraced, but eight have been returned to the side chapels of Notre-Dame, including works by Jacques Blanchard (*Descent of the Holy Ghost*, 1634); Sébastien Bourdon (*Crucifixion of St Peter*, 1634) and Charles Le Brun (*Stoning of St Stephen*, 1651). Another eleven, including Bon Boullogne's *Jesus Healing the Sick* (1678) and Joseph Parrocel's *St John the Baptist in the Desert* (1694), are in the Musée des Beaux-Arts, Arras. Others can be found in the museums of Rouen, Toulouse, Marseille and Clermont-Ferrand, as well as in the churches of St Thomas-d'Aquin, Paris; St Louis, Versailles; and St Pierre-St-Etienne, Toulouse.

BIBLIOGRAPHY

J.-J. Guiffrey: 'Les "Mays" de Notre-Dame de Paris d'après un manuscrit conservé aux Archives Nationales', *Mém. Soc. Hist. Paris & Ile-de-France*, xiii (1886), pp. 289–316

P.-M. Auzas: 'Les Grands "Mays" de Notre-Dame de Paris', *Gaz. B.-A.*, n. s. 5, xci (1949), pp. 177–200

——: 'Précisions nouvelles sur les "Mays" de Notre-Dame de Paris', *Bull. Soc. Hist. A. Fr.* (1956), pp. 40–44

MARC JORDAN

Mayr [Mair; Meyr], **Johann Ulrich** (*b* Augsburg, 1630; *d* Augsburg, 11 June 1704). German painter. He was the son of Christoph Georg Mayr, a rich merchant in Augsburg, and Susanne Fischer (1600–74), a painter and engraver. In the 1640s he studied with Rembrandt in Amsterdam and with Jacob Jordaens in Antwerp and also travelled to England and Italy. He specialized in portraiture, sometimes depicting his models in historical costumes. His earliest works date from the 1650s, for example *Self-portrait* (Nuremberg, German. Nmus.). Rembrandt's guidance is evident in the profile *Portrait of a Poet* (1653; Vaduz, Samml. Liechtenstein). The influence of Jordaens can be seen in his conception of the half-length *David with the Head of Goliath* (Augsburg, Schaezlerpal.), in which Mayr combined portraiture with an Old Testament theme. In the late 1650s he worked for the electoral court in Munich and made a series of portraits of *Elector Ferdinand Maria*, his wife *Henriette Adelaide* and his brother *Maximilian Philipp and his Family* (Munich, Residenzmus.; reproduced in engravings by Melchior Küsel I in 1659). His portraits, modelled on the English examples of Anthony van Dyck, met the demands of aristocratic taste, and from 1660 Mayr worked for the Viennese aristocracy, among his commissions the full-length portrait of *Count Ferdinand Bonaventura von Harrach* (1660; Nechanice, Nech Castle). His works of this period are characterized by steady composition, refined colour, freedom of execution and an emphasis on brushwork.

In 1662 Mayr married in Augsburg and in 1665 became a master in the painters' guild there. Two years later Cosimo III de' Medici visited Mayr to express his admiration for his work. In 1674 he painted Emperor *Leopold I* and his wife *Claudia Felicitas* (both Bolzano, Pal. Mercantile). With the painter Siegismund Müller (*fl* 1643, 1673–90) and Joseph Werner II, he founded the Kunstakademie in Augsburg, becoming Director in 1684.

BIBLIOGRAPHY

E. Buchner: 'Über einige Bilder des Augsburger Malers Johann Ulrich Mair', *Schwäb. Mus.*, ii (1926), pp. 176–84

G. Heinz: 'Studien zur Portrait-Malerei an den Höfen der österreichischen Erblande', *Jb. Ksthist. Samml. Wien*, lix (1963), pp. 174, 181, 206, 209

Deutsche Maler und Zeichner des 17. Jahrhunderts (exh. cat., ed. W. J. Müller; W. Berlin, Schloss Charlottenburg, 1966), p. 61

G. Adriani: *Deutsche Malerei im 17. Jahrhundert* (Cologne, 1977), pp. 123–4, 187

W. Sumowski, ed.: *Gemälde der Rembrandt-Schüler*, 4 vols (Landau-Pfalz, 1983), iii, pp. 2175–8

G. Krämer: *Deutsche Barockgalerie* (Augsburg, 1984), pp. 180–83

HANA SEIFERTOVÁ

Mayreder. Austrian family of architects, urban planners and engineers. Karl Meyreder (*b* Vienna, 13 June 1856; *d* Graz, 9 Sept 1935) and his brother Julius Mayreder (*b* ?1860; *d* ?1911) both studied at the Technische Hochschule in Vienna under Heinrich von Ferstel and Karl König (1841–1915). Karl in particular worked in the prevalent late 19th-century Historicist manner of his teachers. The brothers worked together on a number of projects, including the Kreuzherrenhof (1898), the Palais Isbary (1900) and the Borgfeldt Mausoleum (1904) in the Kaltenleutgeben, all in Vienna. Karl was also a prominent urban planner, being chief architect of the Vienna planning department between 1894 and 1902. He was successful in a number of urban-planning competitions, and between 1894 and 1911 he prepared plans for Krnov (Ger. Jägerndorf) and Karlovy Vary (Ger. Karlsbad; both now in Czech Republic) and for Rovereto, Italy. Together with his youngest brother Rudolf (1864–1937), municipal councillor in Vienna between 1895 and 1904, he was involved in the new general development plan for Vienna, from 1893. Unlike the redevelopment of Paris by Georges-Eugène Haussmann, the plans for Vienna were more cautious. They aimed at improving existing layouts rather than wholesale demolition and rebuilding. Little is known about Julius Mayreder, but he worked in a more progressive style than his brother Karl and was one of the founding members of the Vienna Secession in 1897, with such artists as Josef Hoffmann, Joseph Maria Olbrich and Gustav Klimt. In the 1990s the construction and engineering firm founded by the brothers was still in business as Mayreder, Keil, List Gmbh.

BIBLIOGRAPHY

R. Schwietzer: 'Der Generalregulierungsplan für Wien (1893–1920)', *Ber. Raumforsch. & Raumplan.*, xiv (1970), pp. 23–41

W. Mayer: *Gebietsänderungen in Raume Wien, 1850–1910, und die Debatten um das Entstehen eines Generalregulierungsplanes von Wien* (diss., U. Vienna, 1972)

R. Schwietzer: 'Bibliographie für Städtebau und Raumplanung, 1850–1918', xvii, *Schrreihe Inst. Städtebau, Raumplan. & Raumordnung, Tech. Hochsch. Wien* (1972)

Maystorov, Nikolay (*b* Sofia, 7 Aug 1943). Bulgarian painter and etcher. He studied painting under Nenko Balkanski (1907–77) and graduated from the National Academy of Arts (Natsionalna Hudozhestvena Academia) in Sofia in 1969. His paintings and prints are noted for their dynamic style, their technical perfection and their clearly stated messages containing philosophical undertones. In the early 1970s he was one of a number of artists who overcame the limitations of Socialist Realism and arrived at his own solutions by an unconventional path. He avoided narrative subjects, didactic themes and pseudointellectually complicated images, preferring instead to use paradox, irony and the grotesque, the sources of which lie in parables and phantasmagoria. He used biblical stories to illustrate the eternal theme of the conflict between good and evil that is the subject of his metaphorical compositions. Many of his best-known works were executed in the 1970s: *Crucifixion* (1970; Sofia, N.A.G.), the series *Intervention, Resistance, Twentieth Century* (all 1975) and the triptych *Conception; Birth; Circus* (1976; Sofia, C.A.G.). His paintings are highly expressive and combine deformity with elevated poetics (e.g. *Temptation*, 1987; Sofia, N.A.G.). In 1979 he executed a cycle of etchings as illustrations for Baudelaire's *Les Fleurs du mal* (1857). *The Conversion*, a series of etchings from 1980, is inspired by ancient Bulgarian history.

BIBLIOGRAPHY

Z. Genov, ed.: *Entsiclopedia na isobrasitelnite iskustva v Bulgaria* [Encyclopedia of Bulgarian art], ii (Sofia, 1987)

Bulgarsk nutidskunst [Modern Bulgarian fine art] (exh. cat. by E. Heide and J. Jensen, Copenhagen, Charlottenborg, 1988)

JULIANA NEDEVA-WEGENER

Ma Yuan [Ma Yüan]. *See* MA, (1).

Mayumi Miyawaki. *See* MIYAWAKI, MAYUMI.

Mazarin. French family of patrons and collectors of Italian origin. Cardinal (1) Jules Mazarin used his influence at court to secure his family's position in France. His brother Michel Mazarin (1607–48) was appointed Archbishop of Aix-en-Provence and initiated work on the Quartier Mazarin (begun 1646). Their niece Laura Mancini (1635–57) was married to Louis, Duc de Vendôme (1612–69), a grandson of Henry IV, King of France, and marriages were also made into the royal house of Savoy. (2) Louise-Jeanne de Durfort was of Mazarin descent by birth and through marriage. In 1771 her daughter Louise (1759–1826) married the future Honore IV, Prince of Monaco (*reg* 1814–19), and the Mazarin family papers became part of the Grimaldi collection.

(1) Cardinal **Jules Mazarin** [Giulio Mazarini] (*b* Pescina, 14 July 1602; *d* Vincennes, 9 March 1661). Educated at the Collegio Romano and in Spain at the university in Alcalá, he joined the papal army in 1625. A brilliant negotiator, he soon became a papal diplomat. In 1630 he met Cardinal Armand-Jean du Plessis de Richelieu; in 1632 and again in 1634–6 he was papal nuncio extraordinary in France; and in 1642 he was made a cardinal by Louis XIII. He rose rapidly at Court, becoming first minister to Anne of Austria, who acted as Regent from 1643 to 1651, when Louis XIV gained his majority. At that time Mazarin became the King's first minister. His administrative career was complicated by war with the Austrian and Spanish Habsburgs (1635–59) and by the Frondes, a series of civil wars between 1648 and 1653. The Frondes forced Mazarin into bouts of exile and caused the dispersal of his possessions, although most were recovered after he re-established his and the King's authority in 1653.

Life in Pope Urban VIII's Rome had convinced Mazarin early in his career that art patronage carried enormous prestige and influence. In Paris he encouraged support for Italian art, music, opera, ballet, furnishings and even perfumes; one such promotion, *The Marriage of Orpheus and Eurydice* by the Italian composer Luigi Rossi, performed in Paris in 1647, was the capital's first staged opera. Several years earlier Mazarin had helped arrange for Gianlorenzo Bernini to sculpt a marble bust of *Cardinal Richelieu* (1640–41; Paris, Louvre), but he was unable to lure Bernini from Italy to Paris for other projects he devised over the next few years. Nor would Pietro da Cortona travel to Paris to decorate Mazarin's library; instead, Cortona's pupil Giovanni Francesco Romanelli decorated the ceiling of the upper of two superimposed galleries added by François Mansart to the Hôtel de Chevry-Tubeuf. Although he initially rented it (from 1643), Mazarin subsequently purchased the Hôtel, which became known as the Palais Mazarin, to contain his collections, guests and relatives, although he himself dwelt in royal residences to avoid assassination. While the Hôtel's lower gallery contained some of Mazarin's 350 pieces of antique sculpture—which included a *Narcissus*, a *Demeter* and a *Dancing Satyr* (all now Paris, Louvre)—Romanelli's upper gallery (subsequently transformed to become the Galerie Mazarine at the Bibliothèque Nationale) displayed further examples of Mazarin's sculpture collection in a setting that combined the ceiling's painted mythologies (e.g. *Zeus and the Titans*) with gilded decoration and stucco figures by Michel Anguier (see fig.). Romanelli's work is reminiscent of Pietro da Cortona's ceilings for the Pitti

Mazarin in the Upper Gallery of his Palace by Robert Nanteuil and François Chauveau, engraving, 476×569 mm, 1659 (Paris, Bibliothèque Nationale)

Palace, Florence, but with a French bias towards greater naturalism.

Mazarin employed French artists both for interior decorations and for portraiture; he sat to Philippe de Champaigne, Mathieu Le Nain, Pierre Mignard (example Chantilly, Mus. Condé) and, repeatedly, to Robert Nanteuil. He did not, however, bring the fledgling Académie Royale de Peinture et de Sculpture under his protection until 1655 and chose to refuse Charles Le Brun the opportunity to compete for Simon Vouet's former rooms at the Louvre. His particular preference was for French artists whose training was Italian, for example Nicolas Poussin, whose *Inspiration of the Poet* (*c.* 1628–9; Paris, Louvre) was one of the 77 French paintings Mazarin owned. Another 283 paintings (out of a total of 546) were by Italian artists, and included Raphael's *Baldassare Castiglione*, Titian's *Venus of Pardo* (Paris, Louvre; previously in Charles I's collection in London) and Correggio's *Mystic Marriage of St Catherine*, the last of which was a present, given in 1650, from Cardinal Antonio Barberini, whom Mazarin sheltered during his exile. All these paintings are now in the Louvre along with various *objets d'art* listed in inventories of 1653 and 1661, although most of Mazarin's luxurious furnishings are untraced. He also owned a massive collection of books and manuscripts and these 40,000 items were made available to scholars from the 1640s. The library in which they were housed survives as the Bibliothèque Mazarine, Quai de Conti, Paris, to where both it (with the original décor of Corinthian columns) and the contents were transferred from Pierre Le Muet's original building (designed 1646) in the Rue de Richelieu.

Mazarin died at Vincennes, where his agent Jean-Baptiste Colbert had overseen the extension by Louis Le Vau of the old château between 1654 and 1661 (Le Vau also worked on the Hôtel de la Saltpêtrière, Paris, founded by Mazarin in 1656). His enormous estate (in excess of 37 million livres) was offered to the King, but Louis accepted only some paintings and diamonds. The remainder, along with the Palais Mazarin, was divided between Mazarin's heirs, his nephew the Duc de Nevers, and his niece and her husband, the Duchesse and Duc de La Meilleraye (the latter becoming the Duc de Mazarin). The 300,000 livres

Mazarin bequeathed to the Theatine order (his confessors) to fund the construction of Guarino Guarini's church of Ste Anne-la-Royale, Paris (destr.), proved insufficient to complete it, while his hope that the proposed Collège des Quatre-Nations (begun 1662 by Le Vau, *see* LE VAU, LOUIS, fig. 3; now the Institut de France)—which he had endowed—would educate an elite drawn from regions newly absorbed within France was thwarted by the Sorbonne. The King bought 40,000 livres' worth of art treasures and furnishings from Mazarin's heirs and took both Colbert and Louis Le Vau into his own service. What they had collectively learnt from Mazarin concerning patronage of the arts began to bear fruit at the château of Versailles by the end of the 1660s.

BIBLIOGRAPHY

A. L. A. Franklin: *Histoire de la Bibliothèque Mazarine et du Palais de l'Institut* (Paris, 1860, 2/1901)

Duc d'Aumale: *Inventaire de tous les meubles du Cardinal Mazarin dressé en 1653 et publié d'après l'original par le duc d'Aumale* (London, 1861)

A. Chéruel and Vicomte B. D'Avenel: *Lettres du Cardinal Mazarin pendant son ministère . . . documents inédits*, 9 vols (Paris, 1872–1906)

A. Chéruel: *Histoire de France pendant la minorité de Louis XIV*, 4 vols (Paris, 1879–80)

——: *Histoire de France sous le ministère de Mazarin* (Paris, 1882)

L.-G. Cosnac: *Les Richesses du Palais Mazarin, inventaire dressé après la mort 1661* (Paris, 1884)

Mazarin: Homme d'état et collectionneur, 1602–1661 (exh. cat., intro. J. Cain; Paris, Bib. N., 1961)

R. A. Weigert: 'Le Palais Mazarin: Architectes et décorateurs', *A. France*, ii (1962), pp. 147–69

G. Dethan: *Mazarin et ses amis: Choix de lettres inédits* (Paris, 1968)

D. Alcouffe: 'The Collection of Cardinal Mazarin's Gems', *Burl. Mag.*, cxvi (1974), pp. 514–26

M. Laurain-Portemer: *Etudes Mazarines* (Paris, 1981)

A. Brejon de Lavergnée: *L'Inventaire Le Brun de 1683: La Collection des tableaux de Louis XIV* (Paris, 1987)

ANNE THACKRAY

(2) Louise-Jeanne de Durfort, Duchesse de **Mazarin** (*b* 1 Sept 1735; *d* Paris, 16 March 1781). She was the daughter of Emmanuel Felix de Durfort, Duc de Duras. In 1747 she married Louis-Marie-Guy, Duc d'Aumont (*d* 1799); they separated in 1763. Her tastes were probably formed by her father-in-law, Louis-Marie-Augustin, Duc d'Aumont (1700–1782). Her main interests were Kakiemon porcelain from Japan and Sèvres porcelain, mounted hardstones and rare marbles, as well as furniture decorated with lacquer or with porcelain plaques and richly ornamented with gilt bronzes. In 1767 she bought the Hôtel de La Roche-sur-Yon (destr. 1855), Paris; its redecoration (*c.* 1777–80), under the direction of François-Joseph Bélanger and Jean-François Thérèse Chalgrin was accompanied by an updating of her collections, so that all the pieces would fit perfectly into the new surroundings that she had created. Many of these pieces, or replicas of them, are extant, including fire-dogs decorated with eagles (Philadelphia, Pennsylvania Mus. of F.A.), fire-dogs with perfume-burners (1775; Malibu, CA, Getty Mus.), a laurel-branch candelabra (1781; Malibu, CA, Getty Mus.), a large *bleu turquin* marble console table (1751; New York, Frick) designed by Chalgrin, and a chimney-piece (1781; New York, Met.) modelled by Jean-Joseph Foucou. All the bronzes on these objects are by or attributed to Pierre Gouthière. Six pieces of furniture with porcelain plaques, some by Martin Carlin, match Joseph Baumhauer's Japanese lacquer commode (1770) and cabinets (after 1768)

and a sécretaire with doors (1755–65; all Windsor Castle, Berks, Royal Col.), also in lacquer, by Bernard van Risamburgh (ii) (*b* before 1730; *d* 1766).

BIBLIOGRAPHY

J. Stern: *À l'Ombre de Sophie Arnauld: François-Joseph Bélanger, architecte des menus plaisirs, premier architecte du Comte d'Artois*, i (Paris, 1930), pp. 150–56

C. Baulez: 'Pierre Gouthière (1732–1813)', *Vergoldete Bronzen: Die Bronzarbeiten des Spätbarock und Klassizismus*, ed. H. Ottomeyer and P. Proschel, ii (Munich, 1986), pp. 561–642 (582–6)

A. Pradère: *French Furniture Makers* (London, 1989)

T. Dell: *Furniture and Gilt Bronzes, French* (1992), v/1 of *The Frick Collection: An Illustrated Catalogue* (New York 1968–), pp. 104–33

JEAN-DOMINIQUE AUGARDE,
JEAN-NÉRÉE RONFORT

Maze. *See* LABYRINTH AND MAZE.

Mazeline, Pierre (*b* Rouen, 1632; *d* Paris, 7 Feb 1708). French sculptor. He was received (*reçu*) into the Académie Royale in 1668, with an oval, marble bas-relief of *St John the Evangelist* (Paris, Louvre). Immediately after, he was inundated with commissions for interior and exterior decorations for the French royal residences and he worked for the Bâtiments du Roi for the rest of his career. This work included models and ornaments for fountains (especially for the châteaux of Versailles and later of Marly), statues and vases, and sculptures for the church of Notre-Dame and for the Grand Commun (now Hôpital Militaire) at Versailles, as well as for the Invalides, Paris. At his death, Mazeline was still working on trophies for the chapel at the château of Versailles.

Many of Mazeline's works for the gardens at Versailles were collaborative undertakings, initially with the sculptor Noël Jouvenet (*d* 1716) and later with Simon Hurtrelle. The finest examples still *in situ* include an allegorical marble statue of *Europe* (1675–9)—a majestic work overencumbered by draperies—which formed part of Charles Le Brun's 'Grande Commande' of 1674 for the Parterre d'Eau; the animated *Putti Fishing* (1678–80), executed as part of a lead fountain; and a fine marble copy of the antique *Apollo Pythius* (1683). Three important commissions undertaken in 1688–92 with Hurtrelle's assistance are notable indicators of the esteem in which Mazeline was held by the Surintendant des Bâtiments du Roi, Jules Hardouin Mansart: the marble and bronze tombs of *Chancellor Michel Le Tellier* (1686–8; Paris, St Gervais) and *Charles, Duc de Créqui* (1688–9; main group Paris, St Roch; statues of the *Virtues*, Paris, Dôme des Invalides) and the bronze equestrian statue of *Louis XIV* for Montpellier (destr. 1792; plaster model Stockholm, Kun. Slottet). All three monuments were based on designs by Hardouin Mansart. Mazeline's solemn *Virtues* enveloped in draperies—*Justice* and *Prudence* on the Le Tellier monument, and *Religion*, *Liberality* and *Magnificence* on the Créqui monument—exemplify a type of classicism that has more correctness than originality.

BIBLIOGRAPHY

Guiffrey; Lami; Souchal

F. Souchal: 'Le Monument funéraire du Duc de Créqui à l'Eglise des Capucines', *Archvs A. Fr.*, n. s., xxv (1978), pp. 173–80

FRANÇOISE DE LA MOUREYRE

Mazenta [Magenta]**, Giovanni Ambrogio** (*b* Milan, 1565; *d* Rome, 1635). Italian architect. He came from a distinguished Milanese family, and he was educated as a humanist scholar; Mazenta entered the Barnabite Order in 1591, becoming General in 1612, a post he held for five years. The Order's extensive building programme took Mazenta to various parts of Italy, but his most important works were in Bologna in the first quarter of the 17th century; his role in later projects, however, seems to have been only advisory. Mazenta designed three churches in Bologna: S Salvatore, S Pietro and S Paolo. S Salvatore was completed to Mazenta's design of 1605 by Tommaso Martelli (*fl* 1575–1617) in 1623. The plan appears to be based on that of Il Gesù (1568), Rome, by Jacopo Vignola, although Mazenta cited the Baths of Diocletian, restored by Michelangelo in 1561 as S Maria degli Angeli, as the source of the free-standing interior columns. The nave bays, with their side chapels, are of unequal length; the longer, central bay is groin-vaulted. This, together with the tall arches to the side chapels, creates a transeptal effect in the nave, so that the impression conveyed is of a compact Greek-cross unit, with the crossing and sanctuary, both without columns, as an addition; early drawings show this clearly. The interior remains monochromatic as originally designed, spared the addition of decoration common to early Baroque churches. The façade was also based on Il Gesù, but the unadorned brick wall surface, with the entrance portal unconstrained within the architectonic frame, shows north Italian tendencies. S Salvatore was influential for later Baroque churches. Mazenta's other two Bolognese churches were less robustly articulated. In his design of 1605 for the rebuilding of the cathedral of S Pietro, Mazenta retained the choir (1575) by Domenico Tibaldi, and he added a separate nave with alternating high and low nave-arcade arches. He later added bays to each end to integrate it with the choir. Work was started in 1608 by Floriano Ambrosini (*fl* 1596–1615) and was continued by Nicolò Donati (*d* 1618), who altered Mazenta's design, from 1612. The church of S Paolo (1606; altered 1634) conformed more faithfully to the Gesù type but with distinctive lateral illumination in the vault.

From 1612 to 1620 Mazenta lived in Milan; he made designs for the churches of S Carlo ai Catinari, Rome, with a Greek-cross nave supported by free-standing columns, later executed (*c.* 1612) by Rosato Rosati with piers; and for S Giovanni delle Vigne (1618; altered 1736), in Lodi, Lombardy, also with a row of free-standing columns. While serving the Order in Rome between 1620 and 1626, he designed S Paolo in Macerata, Marches (executed 1623–1655 by Antonio Ursuzio), which was a modest version of S Salvatore. From 1626 Mazenta travelled extensively as a Visitor; he made designs for the churches of S Giovanni (*c.* 1627) in Acqui, Piedmont; S Carlo (*c.* 1635), Arpino, Latium, with an octagonal plan similar to Borromini's S Carlo alle Quattro Fontane (1638–41), Rome; and, his last work, S Carlo alle Mortelle (1635) in Naples.

UNPUBLISHED SOURCES

Milan, Archv S Barnabas [drawings for S Salvatore, 1605; designs for S Carlo, Arpino, *c.* 1635]

Rome, Archv S Carlo ai Catinari [designs for S Carlo ai Catinari, *c.* 1612; designs for S Carlo, Arpino, *c.* 1635]

BIBLIOGRAPHY

R. Wittkower: *Art and Architecture in Italy, 1600–1750*, Pelican Hist. A. (Harmondsworth, 1958, rev. 1991)

G. Mezzanotte: 'Gli architetti Lorenzo Birago e Giovanni Ambrogio Mazenta', *L'Arte*, lx (1961), pp. 231–94

R. Ricci and G. Zucchini: *Guida di Bologna* (Bologna, 1968)

J. Varriano: *Italian Baroque and Rococo* (New York, 1986)

□

Mazer, Carl [Karl] **Peter** (*b* Stockholm, 9 March 1807; *d* Naples, 18 Jan 1884). Swedish painter, draughtsman and photographer. The son of a French emigrant, he studied at the Kungliga Akademi för de Fria Konsterna in Stockholm and then for several years, from 1825, with Antoine-Jean Gros in Paris. Mazer was not, however, notably influenced by the style of Gros, although he was entrusted with the underpainting in some of Gros's historical compositions. Mazer is believed to have fought at the barricades in Paris during the revolution of 1830; several of his drawings show fighting in the streets. After a stay in Italy he spent the years 1835–8 in Sweden and Finland painting portraits. The tonality of these works is generally dark and their psychological expression sometimes intense. Several of them portray well-known Nordic writers and artists such as the poet *C. J. L. Almquist* (1835; Stockholm, Nordiska Mus.). From 1838 to 1854 Mazer lived in various parts of the Russian Empire: in St Petersburg, Yaroslavl', Nizhny Novgorod, Kazan', Siberia and the Ukraine. He also spent three years in China. In his autobiographical notes and letters his activities during this period are well documented, but the many portraits he painted are largely untraced. Some, such as *Chinese Merchants* (Stockholm, Nmus.), are notable for adhering to Far Eastern compositional and colouristic devices.

Numerous drawings, however, have been preserved (mainly in Stockholm, Nordiska Mus.; also three sketchbooks and *c.* 150 loose sheets, Stockholm, Nmus.). Mazer's drawings were made partly from nature and partly in Paris at a later date when he planned to publish a *Voyage pittoresque* based on his travels; unfortunately these plans came to nothing. In the drawings he records, with marked precision, cities, churches, monasteries, camps and trading places, as well as people of various types, from Muscovites to the people of Kirghizstan. Eventually, when the daguerreotype was introduced in Russia (*c.* 1840), Mazer obtained the necessary equipment and made portrait photographs in his Moscow studio. He continued to earn a living mainly as a photographer after his return to Stockholm in 1856 and also during the last years of his life, which were spent in Paris and then in Italy. He wrote a textbook on photography that was published in Sweden in 1864.

BIBLIOGRAPHY

Bénézit; Thieme–Becker

B. Magnusson: 'Carl Peter Mazer', *Kontakt med Nmus.*, 15 (1974), pp. 9–18

PONTUS GRATE

Mazerolles, Philippe de. *See* PHILIPPE DE MAZEROLLES.

Mazev, Petar (*b* Kavadarci, 10 Feb 1927; *d* Skopje, 13 March 1993). Macedonian painter. In 1953 he graduated from the Academy of Arts in Belgrade, where he studied under the painter Zoran Petrović (1894–1962). He then moved to Skopje and participated in several group exhibitions. In 1958–9 he lived in Paris, and in 1960 he was co-founder in Skopje of the short-lived group Mugri. In the mid-1960s, Mazev started to include in his non-figurative paintings, executed in muted colours and rendered in dense and grainy impasto, materials such as burnt wooden plates, glass, scrap-metal sheets, sand and even some of his earlier smaller-format paintings, which he usually reworked on the spot. During the second half of the 1960s, he completed a series of monochrome paintings, concluding his 'white period'. During the 1970s he turned to a figurative interpretation of ABSTRACT EXPRESSIONISM, yet with more violent brushwork and thick black contours. After accomplishing several monumental projects in the late 1960s and 1970s, Mazev executed the large (200 sq. m), four-part mosaic decoration in the memorial charnel-house (1979–80) in Titov Veles. He spent the last decade of his career as a professor at the Academy of Fine Arts in Skopje.

BIBLIOGRAPHY
B. Petkovski: 'Petar Mazev', *Otkrivanja* [Discoveries] (Skopje, 1977), pp. 95–106
Denešnoto tvoreštvo na Petar Mazev [Recent work of Petar Mazev] (exh. cat. by B. Petkovski, Skopje, A.G., 1982) [with Eng. text]
BOJAN IVANOV

Mazi Dağ. *See* TUR 'ABDIN.

Mazo, Juan Bautista Martínez del (*b* Cuenca Province, *c.* 1613; *d* Madrid, 9 Feb 1667). Spanish painter. He is generally believed to have been born in the province of Cuenca, as his father was from Alarcón and his mother from Beteta. The first record of him concerns his marriage on 21 August 1633 to Francisca Velázquez, the daughter of DIEGO VELÁZQUEZ. From this it can be assumed that Mazo was then already a disciple of Velázquez, and from that date he was closely associated with his father-in-law. Velázquez, who then held the position, arranged for Philip IV to appoint Mazo as Ujier de Cámara in 1634, and Mazo and his bride are known to have lived in the same house as Velázquez.

The protection of Velázquez enabled Mazo to enter palace circles, where he was entrusted with important duties, most significantly as professor of painting and painter to the Infante Balthasar Carlos from 1643 until the latter's death in 1646. During this time Mazo often accompanied the Prince on journeys throughout the Peninsula. He painted the *View of Saragossa* (1647; Madrid, Prado; for illustration *see* SARAGOSSA) for the Infante, finishing the work after the latter's death. Velázquez's daughter died before 1657, the year in which Mazo is documented as obtaining the important palace position of Ayuda de la Furriera and travelling to Naples on a journey that must have lasted until at least the middle of 1658. After the death of Velázquez (1660), in April 1661 Mazo succeeded him as Pintor de Cámara, in which post he was obliged to make portraits of Philip IV and his queen, MariaAnna of Austria. Mazo married again, became a widower once more in 1665 and immediately remarried, almost certainly so that his children could be looked after.

Although Mazo's life is relatively well documented, his oeuvre is problematic. There are very few works preserved that can be firmly attributed to him, something compounded by the fact that for many years he collaborated closely with Velázquez. Those works in the style of Velázquez that lack the master's excellence are frequently attributed to Mazo. In his portraits he followed Velázquez's models and techniques, and he probably painted many of the existing copies of Velázquez's official portraits of the sovereigns, in particular those of Philip IV and Queen MariaAnna. The various known portraits by Mazo of *Maria Anna of Austria* after she was widowed in 1665 (London, N.G.; Toledo, Casa & Mus. El Greco; and Ponce, Mus. A.) are clearly signed. The finest, the version dated 1666 in London, is the prototype for the others as well as for the later portraits of the Queen by other court painters, particularly Juan Carreño de Miranda and Claudio Coello. In the *Portrait of the Painter's Family* (Vienna, Ksthist. Mus.; see fig.), an important work signed with the coat of arms of the Mazo family, there is a clear echo of Velázquez's *Las Meninas* (1656; Madrid, Prado). In the background of this interesting and singular group portrait is a living-room or artist's studio, where a painter is depicted in front of an easel on which is shown an unfinished portrait of the *Infanta Margarita* similar to that attributed to Velázquez (Madrid, Prado). The painter has been thought to be Velázquez, but is more probably Mazo himself. The *Child Wearing Ecclesiastical Robes* (Toledo, OH, Mus. A.) was formerly attributed to Velázquez but is now unanimously accepted as the work of Mazo.

Two other portraits by Mazo are those of the *Infante Balthasar Carlos* (Madrid, Prado) showing the Infante at 16 years of age and probably painted in 1645 when he was still dressed in mourning for his mother, Isabel de Valois, who had died in 1644, and that of the *Infanta Margarita* (Madrid, Prado), also shown in mourning. The latter was almost certainly painted after the death of Margarita's father in 1665, probably on the occasion of her betrothal to Emperor Leopold I of Austria in 1666. All these portraits show the deliberate imitation of Velázquez's loose technique, although they miss the master's secure handling and precision. Sometimes Mazo's highly sketchy treatment becomes so extreme that the painted textures are flimsy and lacking in volume. In the Vienna group portrait the composition is clumsy and fails to achieve the harmonious spatial function of its model, Velázquez's *Las Meninas*; despite this, in the context of contemporary Spanish painting the picture is a rare and unusual example of group portraiture set in an interior.

Mazo's landscape paintings with small figures are more personal in style, and his extraordinary ability in this genre was recognized by his contemporaries, particularly Palomino. Both the signed *View of Saragossa* and the documented *Hunt of the Tabladillo at Aranjuez* (Madrid, Prado) show Mazo's skill in the representation of landscape and his graceful depiction of the gestures and expressions of the numerous groups of figures. However, the figure groups are not integrated into the compositions and almost seem to have been added on or arranged in the manner of a frieze. They appear somewhat disconnected from the fine spatial settings, which are executed with extraordinary depth and—in the case of the *View of Saragossa*—with great topographical accuracy. The *View of Pamplona* (1647), painted on the occasion of Mazo's journey to

Juan Bautista Martínez del Mazo: *Portrait of the Painter's Family*, oil on canvas, 1.48×1.75 m, *c*. 1660 (Vienna, Kunsthistorisches Museum)

Aragón and known through copies of sections (Madrid, Mus. Lázaro Galdiano, and London, Apsley House), must have been of similar interest. Mazo's journey to Italy in 1657 no doubt allowed him to study the evolution of Italian landscape painting, which was moving towards the more dynamic Baroque style, and also enabled him to incorporate the luminosity inherent in the classicist tradition of Claude Lorrain into his own work. The beautiful *Arch of Titus* (Madrid, Prado) dates from this time; it was once attributed to Velázquez but is now unanimously accepted as being by Mazo. The composition, which is oblique and a little unbalanced, together with the lack of definition of the foreground figures, distinguish it from the work of Velázquez.

Though of uncertain dates, there are other landscapes that can certainly be attributed to Mazo as they appear under his name in the inventories of the Palacio de Madrid from the beginning of the 18th century. They are the *Retiro Lake*, the *Palace Garden*, the *Calle de la Reina at Aranjuez* and *Mercury and Hermes* (all Madrid, Prado). Even more clearly, these show echoes of Claude's style, which was definitely a determining influence in the work of the landscape painter Benito Manuel de Agüero

(*c*. 1620–68), a follower of Mazo. Mazo is also known to have copied the works of other artists, particularly Rubens and Titian, with such a degree of perfection that, according to Palomino, it was 'almost impossible to distinguish the copies from the originals'. The Museo del Prado preserves a series of excellent smaller copies, attributed to Mazo, of Rubens's mythological paintings (1636) for the hunting-lodge of the Torre de la Parada. In the same museum are two faithful copies, again attributed to Mazo, of Titian's paintings of *Diana and Actaeon* and *Diana and Callisto* (1550s–60s; Edinburgh, N.G.).

See also MADRID, fig. 7.

BIBLIOGRAPHY

A. A. Palomino de Castro y Velasco: *Museo pictórico* (1715–24), p. 961

M. L. Caturla: 'Sobre un viaje de Mazo a Italia hasta ahora ignorado', *Archv Esp. A.*, xxviii (1955), p. 73

E. du Gué Trapier: 'Martínez del Mazo as a Landscapist', *Gaz. B.-A.* (1955), p. 73

J. A. Gaya Nuño: 'Juan Bautista del Mazo, el gran discípulo de Velázquez', *Varia Velazqueña*, i (Madrid, 1960), pp. 471–81

J. Lopez Nanio: 'Matrimonio de Juan B. del Mazo con la hija de Velázquez', *Archv Esp. A.*, xxxiii (1960), pp. 387–420

N. Ayola Mallory: 'Juan Bautista Martinez del Mazo: Retratos y paisajes', *Goya*, 221 (1991), pp. 265–76

ALFONSO E. PÉREZ SÁNCHEZ

Mazois, Charles-François (*b* Lorient, 12 Oct 1783; *d* Paris, 20 Dec 1826). French architect and writer. He studied at the Ecole Centrale in Bordeaux (from 1803) and in Paris under Charles Percier, before being appointed Directeur des Bâtiments de la Couronne (1809–15) to Joachim Murat, King of Naples (*reg* 1808–15). Mazois's major work in Naples was the restoration of the royal palace at Portici. In 1809 he began the research for his most influential publication, *Les Ruines de Pompeii*. Publication began in 1812 and the plates were exhibited in Paris at the Salon of 1824. After Mazois's death, the remaining parts were edited by Franz Christian Gau, who brought the work to completion in 1838. In 1816 Pierre-Jean-Louis-Casimir, Duc de Blacas d'Aulps, the French Ambassador in Rome, named Mazois architect to the Embassy and supported his Pompeian research. Mazois's most important Roman projects were the direction of the restoration in 1817 of Domenichino's frescoes in S Luigi de' Francesi, a royal French church, by Vincenzo Camuccini (1771–1844), and the restoration of Trinità dei Monti, another royal French foundation, and the Spanish Steps (1816). In 1819, having returned to France, he was appointed Inspecteur to the Conseil des Bâtiments Civils, in which capacity he restored (1824–5) the archbishop's palace at Reims and the screens in the cathedral choir as part of the preparations for the coronation (1825) of Charles X (*reg* 1824–30). For this work he was made a Chevalier of the Légion d'Honneur. His buildings in Paris between 1819 and his death include the Passage Saucède (*c.* 1825; destr. 1857), four houses in the Ville de François I of the Champs Elysées; and his only surviving work, the Passage Choiseul (1825–7).

WRITINGS

Les Ruines de Pompeii: Dessinées et mesurées par F. M. pendant les années 1809–11 (Paris, 1812–38)
Le Palais de Scaurus (Paris, 1819)

BIBLIOGRAPHY

Bauchal; Thieme–Becker
F.-X. Feller, ed.: *Biographie Universelle* (1844), viii
L. Neis: *Ultra-Royalism and Romanticism: The Duc de Blacas's Patronage of Ingres, Delacroix and Horace Vernet* (diss., Madison, U., WI, 1987)

LAURA HICKMAN JONES

Mazone [Masone; Massone; Mazzoni], **Giovanni** (*fl* Liguria, 1453–1510/12). Italian painter and wood-carver. Though originally from Alessandria, he was released from the bonds of *patria potestà* in Genoa in 1453 by his father, Giacomo Mazone (*fl* 1434–53), who was also a painter. Giovanni's first recorded commission dates from 1463, when he was engaged to make a relief-carving on an altar (untraced) for the chapel of S Giovanni Battista in Genoa Cathedral. Wood-carving, mentioned again in 1476 in a contract for the renovation of the main altar of Genoa Cathedral, constantly occupied his workshop, which specialized in polyptych frames. Mazone's earliest activity was centred on the now dispersed polyptych depicting the *Apotheosis of St Nicholas of Tolentino* (1466; ex-S Maria in Cellis, Sampierdarena; Milan, Bib. Ambrosiana; Zurich, Ksthaus; Italy, priv. cols). The panels are Mediterranean in character with their profusion of tooled gold and decorative relief work. The Late Gothic style is attenuated in the rendering of the flesh, where there is a greater sense of volume. This reflects the influence of the first visit to

Liguria (1461) of Vincenzo Foppa, who was specified as a model in Mazone's contract of 1463.

The polyptych of the *Annunciation* (Genoa, Nostra Signora del Monte), formerly attributed to Giacomo Serfolio or to the Master of the Annunciation of the Monte, illustrates a moment in Mazone's complex stylistic development before he had absorbed the new ideas of Foppa. Apart from its Late Gothic Lombard elements, the painting displays a Netherlandish influence in the central scene, which is especially reminiscent of the *Annunciation* (1451; Genoa, S Maria di Castello) by Justus of Ravensburg, and aspects of Provençal art in the treatment of landscape. The polyptych of the *Virgin and Child Enthroned with the Four Evangelists* (Pontremoli, SS Annunziata) presents a similar range of cultural references, with, additionally, some signs of Paduan influence (possibly indirect) and parallel signs of intervention by workshop assistants. In those years assistants such as Galeotto Nebbia da Castellazzo Bormida (*c.* 1446–after 1495) are documented. Mazone's only signed and dated work is the triptych of the *Noli me tangere* (1477; Alençon, Mus. B.-A. & Dentelle), painted around the same time as the signed triptych of the *Nativity* (Savona, Pin. Civ.); these are more unambiguously derived from the Lombard tradition, which was strongly represented in Liguria by such painters as Francesco da Verzate (*fl* 1465–1500) and Cristoforo de' Mottis (*fl* 1460–86). Any Cremonese influence is merged with the Provençal style of Jacques Durandi.

In a series of works that Mazone probably produced in the 1480s there is a new interest in perspective and the rendering of volume in figure painting. This was fostered by the presence of works by Foppa and his followers, such as de' Mottis, but is also a reflection of Tuscan art, especially that of Andrea del Castagno and Domenico Ghirlandaio. These paintings include the *Virgin and Child Enthroned* (Genoa, S Maria delle Vigne), *St Mark with Four Saints* (Liverpool, Walker A.G.), a polyptych with the *Annunciation* (Genoa, S Maria di Castello), a polyptych with the *Virgin and Child Enthroned with Six Saints* (Miami Beach, FL, Bass Mus. A.) and *St John the Baptist* (Milan, Bib. Ambrosiana). Between 1483 and 1489 Mazone also executed frescoes in the Sistine Chapel, near Savona Cathedral. Some of these have become detached, while others are covered by 18th-century stuccowork. They contained sacred scenes decorated with friezes in the Lombard style. The *Calvary* (ex-S Giuliano d'Albaro, Genoa; Genoa, Gal. Pal. Bianco) is probably contemporaneous. Its figures seem closely related to those of the Liverpool *St Mark*, but they are imbued with a deeper dramatic sense, suggestive of Netherlandish influence, and its landscapes show a heightened sense of spatial depth. This last characteristic has led some scholars to suggest that part of the painting was done by Nicolò Corso, who is documented in Mazone's workshop around 1484.

A more radical break from Netherlandish and Mediterranean traditions, in favour of a Paduan style of naturalism with elements from the work of Mantegna and Foppa, appears in the triptych of the *Nativity* (main sections, Avignon, Mus. Petit Pal.), which Mazone painted in 1489 at the request of Cardinal Giuliano della Rovere (later Pope Julius II) for the Sistine Chapel, near Savona

Cathedral. In the minute rendering of some of the drapery folds and faces, however, the intervention can be discerned of an unknown collaborator, to whom other works painted in the following years and formerly attributed to Mazone can be assigned. These include the polyptych of *St Lawrence* (1492; Cogorno, S Lorenzo), the side panels of the triptych of the *Annunciation* (1493; Savona, Pin. Civ.) and parts of a polyptych for S Giorgio, Moneglia. Among Mazone's last works is the panel depicting the *Four Doctors of the Church* (Paris, Mus. Jacquemart-André), which is probably a section of the altarpiece painted in 1491 for Baldassarre Lomellini in S Teodoro, Genoa.

BIBLIOGRAPHY
G. V. Castelnovi: 'Il quattro e il primo cinquecento', *La pittura a Genova e in Liguria dagli inizi al cinquecento*, ed. C. Bozzo Dufour, i (Genoa, 1970, rev. 1987), pp. 84–95, 143–4
A. M. Folli: 'Giovanni Mazone pittore genovese del quattrocento', *Studi Genuensi*, viii (1970–71), pp. 163–90
M. Migliorini: 'Appunti sugli affreschi del convento di Santa Maria di Castello a Genova', *Argomenti Stor. A.* (1980), pp. 49–63
Zenale e Leonardo (exh. cat., Milan, Mus. Poldi Pezzoli, 1982), pp. 85–90 [entry by M. Natale]
C. Varaldo: 'Giovanni Mazone nella cappella Sistina a Savona', *Sabazia*, iv (1983), pp. 8–12
L. Martini: 'Ricerche sul quattrocento ligure: Nicolò Corso tra lombardi e fiamminghi', *Prospettiva*, xxxviii (1984), pp. 42–58
G. V. Castelnovi: 'Su Giovanni Mazone e il "cosidetto Serfolio" ', *Riv. Ingauna & Intemelia*, xxxix (1984), pp. 1–13
G. Algeri: 'Galleria Nazionale di Palazzo Spinola', *Interv. Rest.: G.N. Pal. Spinola*, 9 (1986), pp. 19–24
O. Bergomi: 'Contributo a Giovanni Mazone', *Paragone*, xxxvii/431–3 (1986), pp. 41–4
M. Boskovits: 'Nicolò Corso e gli altri: Spigolature di pittura lombardo-ligure di secondo quattrocento', *A. Crist.*, lxxv (1987), pp. 351–86
M. Natale: 'Pittura in Liguria nel quattrocento', *La pittura in Italia: Il quattrocento*, ed. F. Zeri, 2 vols (Milan, 1987), i, pp. 15–30 (19–20)
A. De Floriani: 'Verso il rinascimento', *La pittura in Liguria: Il quattrocento*, ed. G. Algeri and A. De Floriani (Genoa, 1991), pp. 238–46, 287–300, 417–24

VITTORIO NATALE

Mazza, Giuseppe (*b* Bologna, 13 May 1653; *d* Bologna, 6 June 1741). Italian sculptor. He was the son of the sculptor Camillo Mazza (1602–72) with whom he trained for a time. However, he preferred to learn the art of painting, studying with the Bolognese fresco painter Domenico Maria Canuti and attending Carlo Cignani's life classes. None of his paintings seems to have survived. Mazza probably made the transition to sculpture after leaving Canuti's studio in the company of the painter Giovanni Gioseffo dal Sole. Both resumed their training at Count Alessandro Fava's private school in the Palazzo Fava in Bologna.

While Bologna remained very much Mazza's home, around 1670 or 1671 he financed a first trip to Venice with the funds from his initial commission, a stucco framework of putti for a painting of the *Madonna and Child* (Bologna, SS Cosimo e Damiano; destr.). Although much impressed with Venice, Mazza returned to Bologna in 1672 to study with another painter, Lorenzo Pasinelli, who proved to be a significant influence. Pasinelli strengthened the young sculptor's already painterly tendencies, which are particularly evident in such relief carvings as the stucco *Communion of St Juliana* and *Decapitation of St Niccolini Manzoli* (both *c.* 1681; Bologna, S Giacomo Maggiore). Mazza inherited a rich stock of motifs from Bolognese painters, and in these two carvings he quoted from both Alessandro Tiarini and Reni.

In 1692 John Adam Andreas, Prince of Liechtenstein, invited Mazza to come to Vienna for an extended stay. Mazza declined the honour but over the next decade completed several works for the Prince, including over life-size marble busts of *Venus* (see fig.) and *Ariadne* (1692; Vaduz, Samml. Liechtenstein). Throughout his life Mazza enjoyed fruitful collaborations with painters. Around 1693 he joined Marcantonio Franceschini to decorate Bologna's church of the Corpus Domini. There Mazza's stucco *Madonna of the Mystery of the Rosary* (destr.) for the altar of the Fontana Chapel, distinguished by its framework of 15 terracotta medallions illustrating the *Mystery of the Rosary*, established him as the pre-eminent Bolognese sculptor of the time. He enjoyed that position for the rest of his life, fulfilling many important commissions for churches as well as for royalty.

A large number of Mazza's works exist in Venice, where he travelled annually from Bologna. While there in 1704 he created not only religious pieces, such as the bronze low relief of the *Adoration of the Shepherds* (Venice, S Clemente), but also secular decorations, such as the embellishment of the Palazzo Widmann's ceilings and overdoor spaces with stucco putti. In his maturity he indulged in an even livelier Baroque decorative scheme as with the animated life-size stucco figures and billowing adornments for a room in the Palazzo Bianconcini, Bologna. It was during a later Venetian sojourn that Mazza created what many consider to be his masterpiece: six monumental bronze reliefs showing scenes from St Dominic's life (*c.* 1717–20; Venice, SS Giovanni e Paolo). He

Giuseppe Mazza: *Venus*, marble, h. 760 mm, 1692 (Vaduz, Sammlungen des Fürsten von Liechtenstein)

represented the saint's story as a series of restrained, elegant and compositionally balanced events. This rejection of Baroque drama in favour of a Bolognese classicizing style extends even to the positioning of the reliefs in arched wall spaces where they complement rather than compete with the church architecture.

Among Mazza's last works are four life-size stucco *Cardinal Virtues* (*c.* 1728; Bologna, S Domenico) and monumental stucco statues of the *Four Evangelists* (*c.* 1733; Modena, S Domenico). At the age of 69 he travelled to Rome, but neither the sights there nor a meeting with the sculptor Camillo Rusconi appeared to change his style. Mazza helped establish Bologna's Accademia Clementina and served as its director in 1710, 1722 and 1724. He reinvigorated the 18th-century Bolognese school of sculpture and influenced his pupils Andrea Ferreri (1673–1744) and Angelo Gabriello Piò, as well as Filippo Scandellari (1717–1802).

BIBLIOGRAPHY

G. Zanotti: *Storia dell'accademia Clementina di Bologna*, ii (Bologna, 1739)
R. Wittkower: *Art and Architecture in Italy, 1600–1750*, Pelican Hist. A. (Harmondsworth, 1958, rev. 3/1973), pp. 450, 569, n. 48
J. Fleming: 'Giuseppe Mazza', *Connoisseur*, cxlviii (1961), pp. 206–15 [includes oeuvre catalogue]
Mostra della scultura bolognese del settecento (exh. cat., ed. E. Riccòmini: Bologna, Mus. Civ., 1966), pp. 45–69
C. Semenzato: *La scultura veneta del seicento e del settecento* (Venice, 1966)
C. Puglisi: 'The Capella di San Domenico in Santi Giovanni e Paolo, Venice, pt. I', *A. Ven.*, xl (1986), pp. 230–38

ROBIN A. BRANSTATOR

Mazzafirri, Michele (*b* Florence, *c.* 1530; *d* Florence, 1597). Italian medallist, goldsmith, silversmith and sculptor. He worked primarily as a goldsmith for the second and third Medici Grand Dukes of Tuscany, Francesco I and Ferdinand I, as well as for Vincenzo I Gonzaga of Mantua. His works of plate and jewellery, gold reliefs and seals are documented, but have not survived. He was involved in the casting in silver in 1580 of some of the figures from a series of the *Labours of Hercules* (e.g. Florence, Bargello; Dublin, N.G.; Vienna, Ksthist. Mus.), using models by Giambologna. He is also suggested as the author of a stone bust of *Vincenzo I Gonzaga* (Milan, Castello Sforzesca), and he produced a series of wax reliefs showing events from the life of Francesco I (London, BM). Also in wax is a group of models for medals and coins (London, BM), in particular a relief in white wax on black slate showing *Hercules Slaying a Centaur*, based on one of the series by Giambologna for the Tribuna in the Galleria degli Uffizi, and not on the marble version of 1595–1600 (now Florence, Loggia Lanzi), as stated by Pollard. This scene was subsequently used for the reverse of a medal of Ferdinand I de' Medici (see Armand, i, p. 284), signed by Mazzafirri and dated 1588. It was later re-used, with minor changes, by Gasparo Mola (i) in 1598 for another medal of Ferdinand. Mazzafirri's medals demonstrate an attention to the small details of armour and dress in a style that is dry and precise. His portraits are accurate, but without life, and his reverses are unimaginative and brittle versions of official emblems. Only on some of the well-struck medals (Florence, Bargello) with portraits on the obverse and reverse respectively of Ferdinand I and his consort, Christina of Lorraine, can one appreciate the value of the artist's precision and make some connection with the subject.

BIBLIOGRAPHY

Forrer
A. Armand: *Les Médailleurs italiens* (2/1883–7), i, pp. 283–5
G. Guidetti: 'La breve vita di una medaglia Gonzaghesca del '500', *Medaglia*, ii/3 (1972), pp. 19–21
G. Pollard: *Italian Renaissance Medals in the Museo Nazionale del Bargello*, ii (Florence, 1985), pp. 806–30

STEPHEN K. SCHER

Mazzanti, Ludovico (*b* Rome, 5 Dec 1686; *d* Orvieto, nr Terni, 29 Aug 1775). Italian painter. He served his apprenticeship under Giovanni Battista Gaulli from 1700 onwards and was influenced by the classicism of Maratti as well as by the Baroque tendencies of Lanfranco in the refined form found in the work of Giovanni Battista Beinaschi (1638–88). His painting was produced in the cultural climate of the Society of Arcadia and the Accademia di S Luca, which included Odazzi and other Roman decorative artists. He took part in the Concorsi Clementini in 1703–5 and 1708, becoming a member of the Accademia di S Luca in 1744 and of the Accademia Clementina in 1748.

Mazzanti's first works were executed in Rome and Orvieto, the Umbrian town from which his parents had originated. There he designed the composition for the upper mosaic (1713–14) on the façade of the cathedral, of which a print survives (Orvieto, Cassa Risparmio). In Rome between 1720 and 1722, together with Sebastiano Conca, Francesco Trevisani and others, he worked on the important cycle of paintings for the Palazzo de Carolis. Mazzanti himself was responsible for the *Zephyrs Chasing the Winter Away* and *Spring*, formerly attributed to Odazzi. In 1720 for S Ignazio in Rome he carried out his first major commission from the Jesuit Order, the frescoes representing the *Assumption of the Virgin*, the *Adoration of the Shepherds*, the *Presentation in the Temple* and *David and Jeremiah* (all *in situ*). These reveal the influence of Gaulli as well as stylistic elements derived from Odazzi. Following this, from 1721 to 1726 Mazzanti executed paintings for S Andrea al Quirinale, Rome (see fig.), which demonstrate a marked leaning towards the style of Maratti and an adherence to the methods of Ignaz Stern.

Mazzanti's works executed in Naples, where he settled in 1733, reveal his assimilation of Solimena's work as well as a preference for the clear chromatic range of Paolo de Matteis and, at the same time, for the works of Lanfranco and Beinaschi. Between 1733 and 1736 he painted the *Evangelists* in the pendentives beneath the dome as well as other frescoes (signed and dated) in the church of the Gerolamini, and also the seven paintings featuring scenes from the *Life of the Virgin* for the Abbey of Montevergine (these have been overpainted to a large degree during restoration work carried out at the end of the 19th century). The climax of his Neapolitan period was further paintings dealing with the *Life of the Virgin* (1736–9) in the church of the Jesuit Novitiate at Pizzofalcone (better known as the church of the Nunziatella). At the same time he painted canvases for the Collegiata of Santa Maria delle Grazie at Marigliano and the *Martyrdom of St Stanislaus Kostka* (signed; Naples, Paternò priv. col.).

Ludovico Mazzanti: altarpiece in the chapel of S Ignazio di Loyola, S Andrea al Quirinale, Rome, 1721–6

In the 1740s Mazzanti was active in Rome, Orvieto, Viterbo and the Marches. At Città di Castello he executed paintings for the monastery of Santa Chiara, and in the cathedral he signed and dated the *Evangelists* (1751) in the pendentives beneath the dome, works that are related to those in the church of the Gerolamini at Naples. After settling definitively in Rome during 1752–3, as well as painting canvases and decorative panels above doorways, Mazzanti executed frescoes of mythological and marine scenes (of which no traces survive) for the palace of Monsignor Bonacorsi (1708–76). A contract dated 1757 made between the artist and Paolo Borghese documents the execution of paintings and decorative panels for overdoors. Mazzanti's fame must have been considerable since he also gained commissions abroad. His *St Francis Xavier in Agony* (initialled; Düsseldorf, Stadtmus.) was exported to Poland. In France, the painting of the *Virgin and St Teresa* in the Carmelite church of Gray has also been attributed to him.

BIBLIOGRAPHY

P. Santucci: *Ludovico Mazzanti, 1686–1775* (L'Aquila, 1981) [with bibliog.]

A. Brejon de Lavergnée: 'Un Ensemble de tableaux romains peints pour les églises de Franche-Comté. Costanzi, Pietri, Mazzanti, Conca, Trevisani', *Il se rendit en Italie: Etudes offertes à André Chastel* (Rome, 1987), pp. 537–50

N. Spinosa: *Pittura napoletana del settecento dal rococò al classicismo* (Naples, 1987), i, pp. 31, 118–19; ii, p. 145 nos 233–4

IRIARTE: Antico e moderno delle collezioni del gruppo IRI (exh. cat. by A. Bacchi, Rome, Pal. Venezia, 1989), pp. 108–10

V. Casale: 'La pittura del settecento in Umbria', *La pittura in Italia: Il settecento*, i (Milan, 1990), pp. 351–70

A. M. Rybko: 'Mazzanti, Ludovico', *La pittura in Italia: Il settecento*, ii (Milan, 1990), p. 790

ANA MARIA RYBKO

Mazzola [Mazolla; Mazzuoli]. Italian family of painters. They came from Pontremoli, but moved to Parma in 1305. Bartolomeo II Mazzola (*fl* 1461–*c.* 1505), who may have been a painter, had three sons who were painters: Filippo Mazzola (*b* Parma, *c.* 1460; *d* Parma, before 30 June 1505), Pier'Ilario II Mazzola (*b c.* 1476; *d* after 30 May 1545) and Michele Mazzola (*b c.* 1469; *d* after 1529). Filippo may have trained with Francesco Tacconi (*fl* 1458–1500) of Cremona. His signed paintings, which include the *Virgin Enthroned with Saints* (1491; Parma, G.N.), the *Baptism* (1493; Parma Cathedral) and the *Conversion of Saul* (1504; Parma, G.N.), are closely related to the works of contemporary Venetian painters, latterly Alvise Vivarini in particular. He was also an accomplished portrait painter, producing such works as the *Portrait of a Man* (Milan, Brera) and *Alessandro da Richao* (Madrid, Mus. Thyssen-Bornemisza). Pier'Ilario and Michele collaborated on commissions, including frescoes in the chapel of S Niccolò (1515) in S Giovanni Evangelista, Parma. Filippo's son, Girolamo Francesco Maria Mazzola, known as PARMIGIANINO, became a leading Mannerist painter. Parmigianino's pupil, who added the Mazzola surname to his own, was GIROLAMO MAZZOLA BEDOLI. Bedoli's son Alessandro Mazzola Bedoli (*b* 2 Sept 1547; *d* 1612), also a painter, worked mainly in Parma.

BIBLIOGRAPHY

G. Vasari: *Vite* (1550, rev. 2/1568); ed. G. Milanesi (1878–85), v, pp. 217–38

C. Ricci: *Filippo Mazzola* (Trani, 1898)

L. Testi: 'Pier Ilario e Michele Mazzola', *Boll. A.*, iv (1910), pp. 49–67, 81–104

B. Berenson: *Venetian School*, i (1957), pp. 112–14

F. Zeri: 'Filippo Mazzola e non Alvise Vivarini', *Diari di lavoro*, i, (Bergamo, 1971), pp. 54–5

□

Mazzola, Girolamo Francesco Maria. *See* PARMIGIANINO.

Mazzola Bedoli, Girolamo. *See* BEDOLI, GIROLAMO MAZZOLA.

Mazzolino, Ludovico (*b* Ferrara, *c.* 1480; *d* Ferrara, after 27 Sept 1528). Italian painter. He may have served an apprenticeship with Ercole de' Roberti (Morelli) before he left Ferrara to study in Bologna with Lorenzo Costa (i). The earliest surviving documentation is from 20 May 1504, when he received a first payment for frescoes (destr. 1604) in eight chapels in S Maria degli Angeli, Ferrara, commissioned by Ercole I d'Este, Duke of Ferrara and Modena. Between 1505 and 1507 he was paid for works, presumably decorative, in the Este *guardaroba* and the *camerini* of the Duchessa Lucrezia Borgia in Ferrara Castle (untraced). His first surviving dated painting is the triptych of the *Virgin and Child with SS Anthony and Mary Magdalene* (1509; Berlin, Gemäldegal.), which shows the influence of his training with Costa and of the German-orientated circle of Jacopo de' Barbari and Lorenzo Lotto.

The archaizing tendency of Mazzolino's work has led to the suggestion (Zamboni) that in his youth, perhaps before 1509, he was in Venice in direct contact with Giorgione. After that year he resided permanently in Ferrara, where he produced mainly small paintings in oil on panel. In 1511 he signed and dated the *Holy Family with SS Sebastian and Roch* (sold London, Christie's, 9 March 1923), which again employs the style of Costa but introduces a new, restless asymmetry. The anti-classical tendency apparent in the work may derive from Albrecht Dürer, who was in Ferrara in 1506 on his way to Bologna. The landscape in the signed and dated *Pietà* (1512; Rome, Gal. Doria Pamphili), painted for Lucrezia Borgia, shows a strong influence of Giorgione. The diverse components of Mazzolino's artistic background were united in his most important work of this period, the *Adoration of the Magi* (1512; sold London, Sotheby's, 11 March 1964, no. 129).

In the *Holy Family* (1516; Munich, Alte Pin.) the influence of Lotto can still be felt, as well as that close stylistically. The *Crossing of the Red Sea* (1521; Dublin, N.G.) also shows evidence of his familiarity with north European prints, particularly of Lucas Cranach the elder. The altarpiece *Christ among the Doctors* (Berlin, Gemälde-gal.) for S Francesco in Bologna is signed and dated 1524. Also from that year is the small altarpiece the *Tribute* (Poznań, N. Mus.) painted for the Bolognese writer Gerolamo Casio (1465–1533). Many of Mazzolino's paintings after 1520, such as the *Virgin and Child with St Anthony Abbot* (1525; Chantilly, Mus. Condé), reflect the manner of Dosso Dossi, who dominated Ferrarese painting in this period. Mazzolino's efforts to adopt modern models were not sustained, however, and the *Circumcision* (Vienna, Ksthist. Mus.) and the *Pietà* (St Petersburg, Hermitage), both dated 1526, show that in his last years he returned to the style of Costa. He died of the plague, aged 49 (Baruffaldi).

BIBLIOGRAPHY

G. Vasari: *Vite* (1550, rev. 2/1568); ed. G. Milanesi (1878–85), iii, pp. 138–9

G. Baruffaldi: *Vite de' pittori e scultori ferraresi* (Ferrara, c. 1697–1722); ed. G. Boschini (Ferrara, 1844–6), i, pp. 126–30

G. Morelli: *Le opere dei maestri italiani nelle gallerie di Monaco, Dresda e Berlino* (Bologna, 1886), p. 254

A. Venturi: 'Nuovi documenti: Ludovico Mazzolino pittore nella chiesa di Santa Maria degli Angeli', *Archv Stor. A.*, ii (1889), p. 86

——: 'Ludovico Mazzolino', *Archv Stor. A.*, iii (1890), pp. 449–64

R. Longhi: *Officina ferrarese* (1934, rev. Florence, 1956), pp. 68–70

S. Zamboni: *Ludovico Mazzolino* (Milan, 1970)

LUCA LEONCINI

Mazzoni, Angiolo (*b* Bologna, 21 May 1894; *d* Rome, 28 Sept 1979). Italian architect and engineer. The son of a government official in the state railways, he attended the Scuola di Applicazione per Ingegneri in Rome and completed his training in architecture at the Accademia di Belle Arti in Bologna, graduating in 1923. Following a brief apprenticeship in the office of Marcello Piacentini, he began working for the state's railway and postal services, where he rose quickly to the position of general inspector. From the mid-1920s he designed a great number of railway stations and post offices, including those for Nuoro, Palermo, Agrigento, La Spezia, Bergamo, Pola, Littoria, Siena, Ferrara, Abetone, Trento and Reggio Emilia. It is estimated that he built between 30 and 40 works between 1928 and 1943, spanning a wide range of styles. Some, including the central post offices in Palermo (*c.* 1929–34) and Trento (*c.* 1934–6), are notable for their elegant, richly furnished interiors and for the sculptures, murals and stained-glass windows by such artists as Mario Sironi, Enrico Prampolini and Fortunato Depero. Mazzoni's style varied widely depending on the circumstances of the commission. His metaphysical Villa Rosa Maltoni Mussolini (1928–35) in Calabrone, near Livorno, contrasts sharply with the Constructivist power house for the Florence Railway Station (*c.* 1934) and the neo-Roman Termini Station (1938–43) in Rome. This eclecticism notwithstanding, many of Mazzoni's buildings display a consistent restraint and a generally robust sense of form. In 1944 he accepted the offer of a teaching position at the Columbian State University in Bogotà, where he lived from 1947 to 1962, and was apparently involved in the development of the country's highway and railway systems. In 1962 he retired with his wife to Rome, where he spent his remaining years in isolation.

BIBLIOGRAPHY

C. Severati: 'Un progetto inedito del 1936 per la stazione principale di Roma', *L'Architettura*, v/18 (March, 1973), pp. 754–64

A. Forti: *Angiolo Mazzoni architetto tra fascismo e libertà* (Florence, 1978)

F. Solmi and others: *Angiolo Mazzoni (1894–1979) architetto nell'Italia tra le due guerre* (Bologna, 1984)

R. Etlin: *Modernism in Italian Architecture, 1890–1940* (Cambridge, MA, 1991)

LIBERO ANDREOTTI

Mazzoni, Guido [Modanino, Paganino] (*b* Modena, ?1450; *d* Modena, 12 Sept 1518). Italian sculptor, painter, mask-maker and festival director. He was brought up by a paternal uncle, Paganino Mazzoni, a Modenese notary and official of the Este bureaucracy. This connection with the ducal court of Ferrara throws some light on the artist's early training, which is otherwise obscure. A document of 1472 refers to him as a painter, and his first sculpture strongly echoes the figural style in Francesco del Cossa's frescoes (1466–the mid-1470s) at the Palazzo Schifanoia outside Ferrara. Mazzoni may have worked at the Palazzo Schifanoia in association with the stucco master Domenico di Paris, where he may have learnt to model papier-mâché props for the court masques that contemporary sources say he directed and designed. A related activity of these years was making the realistic and caricatural festival masks (*volti modenesi*) for which Modena was famous.

It was in the synthesis of these diverse talents that Guido Mazzoni made his name as a master of dramatic ultra-realism in sculpture. He specialized in composing groups of life-size, naturalistically pigmented terracotta figures whose gestures and facial expressions convey intense emotional involvement. His works on the theme of the *Lamentation* include portrait figures of donors as biblical personages and incorporate life casts of the subject's face and hands, often reworked to fit the action of the scene. Mazzoni's standard format for this theme is distinct from the Deposition and Entombment tableaux of Franco-German tradition, and shows seven mourners around the corpse of Christ, expressing varying degrees of grief. The figures of the Virgin Mary, Mary Magdalene, Mary Cleofa, Mary Salome, St John the Evangelist, Joseph of Arimathaea and Nicodemus are usually arranged in a shallow semicircle facing the viewer set within a large and slightly elevated niche, which may originally have been painted to depict Calvary. The groups were designed to be seen from several viewpoints including from below.

In the earliest group attributable to Mazzoni (the *Lamentation*, c. 1475; Busseto, nr Parma, S Maria degli Angeli), the broad handling of form and strident characterization betray his beginnings as a mask-maker. By the early 1480s, however, he began using life casts to imbue his figures with a sense of immediacy and to enhance their functional value as *ex votos*. The *Head of a Man* (Modena, Gal. & Mus. Estense) is the earliest example of this shift from allusive naturalism to the use of reality itself, in which every scar and wrinkle, even the roughened skin of the subject's shaved cheeks, is faithfully reproduced. The decisive development that followed is shown in two works of about 1485; the *Adoration of the Virgin and Child* (Modena Cathedral) and *Lamentation* (Modena, S Giovanni Battista). In both works Mazzoni subordinated mechanical mimesis to drama, reformulating the inert data furnished by casts into facial expressions and gestures of poetic eloquence. Also apparent in these works, and in the fragments of the *Lamentation* (Padua, Mus. Civ.) made for Venetian patrons, is a fluidity of movement and lyrical introspection reminiscent of Giovanni Bellini. Finally, in the best-known of his groups, the *Lamentation* (1492; Naples, S Anna dei Lombardi) made for the Duke of Calabria (later Alfonso II), Mazzoni achieved a formal monumentality and grandeur of mood that reflects the humanist climate of the Neapolitan court and the artist's exposure to Classical sculpture and contemporary Tuscan art (see fig.).

Like many other Italian artists, Mazzoni emigrated to France when Charles VIII returned there in 1496 after his coronation as King of Naples. Mazzoni was court sculptor first to Charles VIII and then to his successor Louis XII of France. His major work of this period, the tomb of *Charles VIII* (see Verdon, 1978, figs 87–90) in Saint-Denis, Paris, was destroyed in 1789, but pre-revolutionary illustrations and descriptions confirm that Mazzoni's gift for realism in dramatically activated portrait sculpture was also brought to bear on the royal effigy, made of polychrome enamel and gilded bronze and set on a black marble base. This monument and Mazzoni's project for a two-tier tomb for Henry VII of England (a different design was subsequently commissioned from Pietro Torrigiani in 1512) influenced later French funerary sculpture. Other works attributable to him in these years, all associated with the French court, seem to be collaborative projects. The effigies on the sepulchral monument of *Philippe de Commynes* (ex-Grands Augustins, Paris; fragments Paris, Louvre) and individual figures in the life-size *Death of the Virgin* (Fécamp, Abbaye de la Trinité), which are carved in stone rather than modelled, are close to Mazzoni's style but have many non-Italian features; the same is true of an equestrian statue of *Louis XII* (destr.; see Verdon, 1978, fig. 94), which stood over the entrance of the Château de Blois, Loir-et-Cher, and is known now

only from drawings. Mazzoni also acted as consultant and entrepreneur for the decoration of the façade of Château de Gaillon, near Rouen, procuring *all'antica* medallions (Paris, Louvre and Ecole N. Sup. B.-A.) from Italy, and may have directed the decoration with painting and sculpture of the abbot's chapel at the Hôtel de Cluny, Paris (now Paris, Mus. Cluny). In France his role seems to have been that of director of an international workshop, entrusted with fusing the new Italian style with local Late Gothic realism. He had the highest salary of the dozens of Italian artists working at the court and was knighted by Charles VIII. On the death of Louis XII in 1515, Mazzoni returned to Modena, where he had a house and business investments.

Mazzoni had probably already worked outside Modena before his journeys to Naples and France, since he would have accompanied his figures (which were fired in horizontal sections) to be reconstructed and painted on site. He employed assistants, including his wife and daughter, and was well paid and highly regarded. Documents record personal gifts to Mazzoni and his wife from the Dukes of Ferrara, and Vasari said that the Duke of Calabria held Mazzoni in the greatest veneration. His social standing may have been partly due to the special character of his art, which called for intimacy with the patron whose private religious feelings it interpreted. Mazzoni was part-artist, part-confessor and part-stage-director, 'casting' the patron in a key role in this sculptural *sacra rappresentazione*. The increasing psychological subtlety of Mazzoni's interpretation of his themes probably reflects first-hand involvement in religious drama productions.

Mazzoni should be distinguished from Niccolò dell'Arca, whose *Lamentation* group in Bologna (S Maria della Vita) has sometimes been seen as the source of his style. Although it is difficult to establish chronological precedence, Mazzoni's groups bear little resemblance to Niccolò dell'Arca's stylized tableau beyond general similarities of theme and format. Mazzoni strove for an integral illusion of reality in the service of religious sentiment, whereas Niccolò dell'Arca's figures are typically Ferrarese in their expressionism. Mazzoni's appeal lay in his ability to situate patron and viewer in an utterly believable context of shared feeling. He was the most celebrated practitioner of this artistic genre, influencing both the ultra-realistic ensembles of 16th-century northern Italy—the sacromonti ('holy mountains') at Varallo and elsewhere—and the development of the multiple-figure Neapolitan crèche.

BIBLIOGRAPHY

A. Pettorelli: *Guido Mazzoni da Modena, plasticatore* (Turin, 1925)

C. Gnudi: 'L'arte di Guido Mazzoni', *Boll. Stor. A.*, ii (1952), pp. 98–113 [crit. interpretation of earlier lit.]

H. Dow: 'Two Italian Portrait Busts of Henry VIII', *A. Bull.*, xlii (1960), pp. 291–6

M. Beaulieu: 'Note sur la chapelle funéraire de Philippe de Commines au Couvent des Grands Augustins de Paris', *Rev. Louvre Mus. Fr.*, xvi (1966), pp. 65–75

O. Morisani: 'Mazzoni e no', *Scritti in onore di Edoardo Arslan* (Milan, 1966), pp. 475–9

E. Riccòmini: *Guido Mazzoni*, I maestri della scultura (Milan, 1966) [colour pls]

G. Hersey: *Alfonso II and the Artistic Renewal of Naples, 1485–1495* (New Haven, 1969), pp. 112–21

C. Mingardi: 'Problemi mazzoniani', *Contributi dell'Istituto di storia dell'arte medievale e moderna dell'Università Cattolica del Sacro Cuore* (Milan, 1972), pp. 163–87

Guido Mazzoni: *Duke of Calabria* [later Alfonso II] *as Joseph of Arimathaea Mourning the Dead Christ*, detail from the *Lamentation* group, terracotta, life-size, 1492 (Naples, S Anna dei Lombardi)

T. Verdon: *The Art of Guido Mazzoni*, Outstanding Diss. F.A. (New York, 1978) [exhaustive bibliog.]

N. Gramaccini: 'Guido Mazzonis Beweinungsgruppen', *Städel-Jb.*, n. s., ix (1983), pp. 7–40

T. Verdon: 'Guido Mazzoni in Francia: Nuovi contributi', *Mitt. Ksthist. Inst. Florenz*, xxxiv (1990), pp. 139–64

A. Lugli: *Guido Mazzoni e la rinascita della terracotta del quattrocento* (Modena, 1991)

TIMOTHY VERDON

Mazzoni, Sebastiano (*b* Florence, ?1611; *d* Venice, 22 April 1678). Italian painter. His probable date of birth casts doubt on the assertion by Tommaso Temanza that he studied with Cristofano Allori. In 1632 and 1633 he is recorded in the studio in Florence of the eclectic and idiosyncratic Baccio del Bianco, who had a profound influence on his art. In 1638 he entered the Accademia del Disegno, Florence, and in the same year signed and dated *Venus and Mars Surprised by Vulcan* (priv. col., see 1986 exh. cat., pl. 1.203), his first secure work. The allegories of *Summer* and *Winter* (Florence, Pal. Arcivescovile) are possibly earlier. In these works he responded, in a manner that strikingly recalls Stefano della Bella and Cecco Bravo, to the wit, grace and humorous neo-Mannerist fantasy of Giovanni da San Giovanni. He shared with Cecco Bravo, an artist of similar temperament, a precocious interest in Venetian painting; Mazzoni's art in particular was directly indebted to that of Bernardo Strozzi, and he was also influenced by Domenico Fetti and Francesco Maffei. In the 1640s he painted small and medium-sized pictures for private collectors, such as the *Venus and Cupid* (New York, Navarro priv. col., see Pallucchini, ii, pl. 729) and the *Leda and the Swan with Nymphs and Cupids* (Florence, priv. col., see 1986 exh. cat., pl. 1.204); the works are in a playfully affected style, and perhaps suggest, as does the *Charity* (ex-Briganti priv. col., Rome; see Pallucchini, ii, pl. 727), a response to the sensual art of Francesco Furini and Cesare Dandini.

Between 1646, when he is documented in Florence, and 1648, Mazzoni moved to Venice. There he signed and dated two altarpieces for the church of S Benedetto: *St Benedict Presenting a Priest to the Virgin* (1648) and *St Benedict in Glory among the Theological Virtues* (1649; both *in situ*). *Susanna and the Elders* (priv. col., see 1979 exh. cat., p. 93) is also dated 1649. In Venice he became a close friend of Pietro Liberi, and, influenced by Fetti, Johann Liss and, above all, Strozzi, led the painterly, Baroque movement that became established in Venice at that time. His works of the 1650s, which include the *Annunciation* (Venice, Accad.) and the *Disputation on the Arts* (two versions; Venice, priv. col.; Chaalis, Mus. Abbaye), are already Baroque in feeling, and the works painted around 1660, which include *Cleopatra's Banquet* (1660; Washington, DC, Smithsonian Inst., on loan to Washington, DC, N.G.A.), the *Sacrifice of Jephtha* (Kansas City, MO, Nelson–Atkins Mus. A.) and the *Death of Cleopatra* (Rovigo, Accad. Concordi), are distinguished by dramatic movement and violent contrasts of light and dark. In their grandiose, theatrical effects and vibrant, broken brushwork, these pictures brilliantly anticipate aspects of 18th-century Venetian painting. In Mazzoni's last works, such as the *Dream of Pope Honorius III* (1669; Venice, S Maria del Carmine), space is unclear and irrational and the increasingly visionary mood is inspired by Tintoretto.

BIBLIOGRAPHY

N. Ivanoff: 'Sebastiano Mazzoni', *Saggi & Mem. Stor. A.*, ii (1958–9), pp. 209–80 [with bibliog.]

G. Ewald: 'Hitherto Unknown Works by Cecco Bravo', *Burl. Mag.*, dclxxxix (1960), pp. 344–7

——: 'Inediti di Sebastiano Mazzoni', *Acropoli*, i (1960–61), pp. 139–44

E. A. Safarik: 'Per la pittura veneziana del seicento: Sebastiano Mazzoni', *A. Ven.*, xxviii (1974), pp. 157–68

Painting in Florence (exh. cat. by C. McCorquodale, London, RA; Cambridge, Fitzwilliam; 1979)

R. Pallucchini: *La pittura veneziana del seicento*, 2 vols (Milan, 1981), i, pp. 226–31; ii, pp. 752–65

Il seicento fiorentino: Arte a Firenze da Ferdinando I a Cosimo III, 3 vols (exh. cat., Florence, Pal. Strozzi, 1986), i, pp. 374–7; iii, pp. 120–21

A. Barsanti: 'Mazzoni, Sebastiano', *La pittura italiana: Il seicento*, ed. R. Contini and C. Ginetti, 2 vols (Milan, 1989), ii, p. 810 [with bibliography]

ELISA ACANFORA

Mazzucchelli, Pier Francesco. *See* MORAZZONE.

Mazzucotelli, Alessandro (*b* Milan, 30 Dec 1865; *d* Milan, 29 Jan 1938). Italian metalworker. His family were dealers in iron, and a change of financial circumstances forced him to give up his studies to work with the blacksmith Defendente Oriani in Milan, whose business he later took over (1891). He had great success in the first Esposizione Internazionale d'Arte Decorativa in Turin in 1902. In 1903 he travelled throughout Europe with the cabinetmaker Eugenio Quarti and on his return began teaching in the crafts school of the Società Umanitaria in Milan. Mazzucotelli's wrought-iron provides the distinguishing character in many buildings in the *Stile Liberty* style in Italy, Germany and Thailand, where he provided ironwork for Annibale Rigotti's buildings (1907–26) in Bangkok. From 1902 to 1908 he worked in the firm Mazzucotelli-Engelmann and thereafter independently. From 1922 he ran the Scuola d'Arte Decorativa di Monza in Milan. He designed jewellery for Calderoni and fabrics for the weaving factory at Brembate (exh. 1906, Esposizione Internazionale del Sempione, Milan), and he exhibited at both the Exposition Universelle et Internationale in Brussels (1910) and the Exposition Internationale des Arts Décoratifs et Industriels Modernes in Paris (1925). He is best-known for his wrought ironwork, mainly designed as decorative features for buildings. It is in a vigorous *Stile Liberty*, with flowing semi-figurative botanical forms reminiscent of those in the Victor Horta houses of the early 1890s. It appears in balustrades and handrails of such buildings as the Palazzo della Borsa (1907; now Post Office) in Milan by Luigi Broggi, Palazzo Castiglioni (1900–03), Corso Venezia 47 and Villa Romeo (1908; now Clinica Columbus), both in Milan and by Guiseppe Sommaruga, and in the lamps in the Piazza del Duomo in Milan, as part of Gaetano Moretti's renovations of 1927–8.

BIBLIOGRAPHY

U. Oietti: *Ferri battuti di Alessandro Mazzucotelli* (Milan, 1911)

Alessandro Mazzucotelli (exh. cat. by V. Pica, Milan, 1925)

A. Hammacher and R. Bossaglia: *Mazzucotelli: L'artista italiano del ferro battuto liberty* (Milan, 1971)

VINCENZO FONTANA

Mazzuoli. Italian family of sculptors. (1) Giuseppe Mazzuoli was active in Siena and Rome, continuing the style of Gianlorenzo Bernini well into the 18th century. His brother (2) Giovanni Antonio Mazzuoli, though younger, taught him to sculpt. Giovanni Antonio remained in Siena, where he was also active as a stuccoist.

(1) Giuseppe Mazzuoli (*b* ?Volterra, 1 Jan 1644; *d* Rome, 7 March 1725). Soon after his birth he moved with his family to Siena, where his father, Dionysio Mazzuoli, an architect and engineer, undertook to rebuild Prince Mattia's palazzo. Giuseppe's earliest training was provided by his younger brother (2) Giovanni Antonio, who remained behind in Siena when he himself went to Rome. There Giuseppe entered the workshop of Ercole Ferrata but worked directly under Melchiorre Caffa. So, probably sometime in the mid-1660s (Caffa died in an accident in 1667), this Sienese sculptor became part of a rich artistic culture in Rome. His first project involved the funerary monument to *Alexander VII* in St Peter's, supervised by Bernini, to which he contributed the marble figure of *Charity* (*bozzetto* prepared by Bernini *c.* 1673). In 1675 Mazzuoli became a member of the Congregazione dei Virtuosi al Pantheon and in 1679 a member of the Accademia di S Luca.

Mazzuoli emerged from a matrix of late 17th-century Italian styles, all generally within what traditionally has been called the High Baroque, and produced many statues throughout his long career. At least 80 were identified by Suboff, although a number of those outside Rome can no longer be traced. His commissions were characteristic for the age: tombs (or funerary monuments), portrait busts, putti and angels, devotional images (e.g. the *Virgin*, marble, 1677, Siena, S Martino; the *Dead Christ*, marble, *c.* 1673, Siena, S Maria della Scala), apostles and allegorical figures, more or less evenly distributed between Siena and Rome. Pascoli claimed that the sculptor worked in Siena during the summer and in Rome in the winter. Although Mazzuoli continued the general tradition of Bernini and Ferrata through the end of the 17th century and into the 18th, he did practise within the perimeters of classicism, broadly defined. His portrait of *Flavio Chigi* (marble; Rome, Musei Vaticani) is firmly in the tradition of Renaissance and post-Renaissance portraiture, especially as practised by his master Ferrata and contemporaries Lorenzo Ottoni and Domenico Guidi: the bust-length figure turns his head slightly from the central axis, as if responding to some exterior presence. The carving of the face and hair shows restraint and a sense that physiognomy is less important than grace and delicacy of treatment. Although his monumental statue of *St Philip* (marble, *c.* 1703–12; Rome, S Giovanni in Laterano; see fig.), for the famous series of *Apostles*, shows the deep pockets of shadow and dramatic, diagonal patterns for drapery typical of the Baroque, nonetheless it is part of the classical tradition of over life-size statues, framed loosely by a niche and either gesturing to the faithful or performing a characteristic act.

Giuseppe Mazzuoli carried this uniquely Roman style of sculpture to Siena. Among the churches there that have sculpture by him are the cathedral, S Maria della Scala, S Martino, S Agostino and S Donato. There are also busts of the Sansedoni family in the Palazzo Sansedoni and

Giuseppe Mazzuoli: *St Philip*, marble, *c.* 1703–12 (Rome, S Giovanni in Laterano)

religious sculpture in its chapel. Further major works in Rome are the marble figures of *St John the Baptist* and *St John the Evangelist* in the church of Gesù e Maria; collaboration with Ferrata and others on the tomb of *Clement X* in St Peter's; marble busts on the Poli Monument in S Crisogono (*c.* 1680); figures on the marble monuments to the *Rospigliosi Family* and the *Pallavicini Family* in S Francesco a Ripa; a marble statue of *St Teresa* in S Silvestro in Capite (*c.* 1700); and the marble funeral monument to *Angelo Altieri and his Wife Laura Carpegna* in S Maria in Campitelli (after 1709).

Mazzuoli was also responsible for sculptural projects elsewhere: one of his early works is a marble group of the *Baptism* in S Giovanni at Valletta, Malta; in 1677 he decorated the villa of Cetinale, near Siena, for Cardinal Flavio Chigi, and he sent a group representing the *Death of Cleopatra* to Lisbon for the gardens of the Colonial Hospital. The latter work shows some of the quieter stylistic tendencies of the Settecento. His nephew Bartolomeo Mazzuoli (*d* 1749) carried on his style into the mid-18th century.

BIBLIOGRAPHY

Thieme–Becker

L. Pascoli: *Vite*, ii (Rome, 1736), pp. 477–87

G. della Valle: *Lettere sanesi*, iii (Rome, 1786), pp. 444–6

V. Suboff: 'Giuseppe Mazzuoli', *Jb. Preuss. Kstsamml.*, iii (1928), pp. 33–47

F. Pansecchi: 'Giuseppe Mazzuoli', *Commentari*, x (1959), pp. 33–43

U. Schlegel: 'Some Statuettes of Giuseppe Mazzuoli', *Burl. Mag.*, cix (1967), pp. 388–95

——: *Die italienischen Bildwerke*, i (Berlin, 1978), pp. 70–77

A. Nava Cellini: *La scultura del seicento* (Turin, 1982), pp. 106–8, 249

A. Negro: 'Nuovi documenti per Giuseppe Mazzuoli e bottega nella Cappella Pallavicini Rospigliosi a San Francesco a Ripa', *Boll. A.*, lxxii (1987), pp. 157–78

(2) Giovanni Antonio Mazzuoli (*b* Volterra, 1644; *d* ?Siena, after 1706). Brother of (1) Giuseppe Mazzuoli. Apart from stucco decorations in the church of Gesù e S Lucia in Montepulciano, his work is in Siena, where he seems to have been a prosperous and highly valued sculptor. Della Valle provided a biography and a comprehensive list of Mazzuoli's work and wrote about the high quality of his marbles and stuccos. Giovanni Antonio's sculpture is for the most part public and religious. One of his most important works is the stucco relief of the *Assumption with Angels* (*c.* 1700) on the Triumphal Arch of Siena Cathedral. Other work of note includes the marble tombs of *Conte Orso d'Elci* (*c.* 1668; Siena, S Agostino), two wall monuments, of *Virgilio de' Vecchi* and *Camillo de' Vecchi* (marble, both *c.* 1706; Siena, S Martino), and one of *Antonio Rospigliosi* (Siena, S Virgilio). In addition there are reliefs of the *Miracle of Ambrogio Sansedoni* in the chapel of the Palazzo Sansedoni. Much of Mazzuoli's sculpture is small-scale and decorative: putti, angels, candelabra, altar embellishments and work in gilt stucco. Had he gone to Rome with his brother Giuseppe, to whom he gave his earliest training, he probably would have become a prominent sculptor working in the style of the late work of Bernini and Ercole Ferrata. By remaining in Siena, he kept his reputation local and his art provincial.

Thieme–Becker
BIBLIOGRAPHY
L. Pascoli: *Vite de' pittori, scultori, ed architetti moderni*, ii (Rome, 1736), pp. 478, 486
G. Pecci: *Relazione storica dell'origine e progresso della festosa Congrega. de' Rozzi di Siena* (Siena, 1757), pp. 23, 26, 35, 44, 48, 50, 57, 86, 90, 124
G. della Valle: *Lettere sanesi*, iii (Rome, 1786), pp. 447–8
A. E. Brinckmann: *Barock-Bozzetti*, ii (Frankfurt am Main, 1924), pp. 75–6

VERNON HYDE MINOR

Mbangwé [Mba Nwē]. *See* BANGWA.

Mbatha, Azaria (*b* Zululand, 1941). South African printmaker and textile designer. His interest in art and design was fostered when he was in Ceza Mission Hospital with tuberculosis in the early 1960s. The Swedish textile designer Peder Gowenius was teaching art and craft at the hospital as a therapy for the patients; he taught Mbatha the technique of linocut. In 1962 Mbatha began to study art at the Evangelical Lutheran Church Art and Craft Centre at Umpumulo in Natal, later moving with the centre to Rorke's Drift, Natal. There he expressed an interest in drawing, which was discouraged because, unlike printmaking, it was not considered an economically 'useful' technique; instead great emphasis was placed on the translation of the narratives and oral history of rural Zululand into the design of prints for textiles and illustrations. Mbatha established a personal style of dividing the format of his prints into a series of tableaux making up a complete narrative dealing with biblical subjects, as in the *Revelation of St John* (*c.* 1965; Johannesburg, U. Witwatersrand). In his prints he employed a range of personally developed symbols that expressed the alienation and oppression experienced in contemporary black society. He graduated from Rorke's Drift in 1964, later winning a

scholarship to study at the Konst Fack Art School in Stockholm (1965–7). He returned to South Africa in 1968, teaching for a brief period at Rorke's Drift, but in 1970 he moved back to Sweden, where he studied fine arts and social sciences at the University of Lund.

For illustration of a linocut *see* SOUTH AFRICA, fig. 4.

BIBLIOGRAPHY
W. Eichel: *Azaria Mbatha: Im Herzen des Tigers: Südafrikanische Bilder* (Wuppertal, 1986)
Rorke's Drift and After: An Exhibition of Prints, Tapestries and Paintings (exh. cat., U. Cape Town, Cent. Afr. Stud., 1990)

BEVERLY MARKS-PATON

MBM. *See* MARTORELL, BOHIGAS, MACKAY.

Mbundu. *See* CHOKWE AND RELATED PEOPLES, §4.

Mead, Dr **Richard** (*b* Stepney, London, 1 Aug 1673; *d* London, 16 Feb 1754). English physician, patron and collector. One of the most enlightened patrons and collectors in early 18th-century England, Mead was a distinguished physician, practising medicine in London from 1696. He became an FRS in 1703 and was appointed physician to George II in 1727. A trip to Italy in the 1690s inspired a love for antiquities and for contemporary art and he bought Greek and Roman coins, gems and statuary, including the so-called *Homer*, a Greek bronze head of the 3rd century BC formerly in the collection of Thomas Howard, 2nd Earl of Arundel, and now identified as *Sophocles* (London, BM). He also owned six mural paintings (untraced) from the Baths of Titus, Rome.

Mead's first purchase of a painting was the *Flaying of St Bartholomew* by Jusepe de Ribera (untraced), and his collection grew to embrace works by Isaac Oliver (*Portrait of an Unknown Young Man*), Hans Holbein (portrait of *Erasmus*, priv. col.; see *Apollo*, cxiv, 1981, p. 331), Quinten Metsys (portrait of *Aegidius*), Carlo Maratti (*Holy Family*), Peter Paul Rubens (portrait of *Dr Mayerne*, Raleigh, NC Mus. A.), and eight oil sketches for the *Life of Achilles* (Rotterdam, Mus. Boymans—van Beuningen) as well as two small landscapes (untraced) by Claude Lorrain. He also owned works by contemporary artists, including Panini, from whom he commissioned the *Landing of Aesculapius at Rome in the Time of the Plague* (possibly that picture now in an Italian priv. col., illus. in F. Avisi, *Gian Paolo Panini*, 1961, fig. 186), as well as Canaletto and Mead's friend Sir Godfrey Kneller, whose oil sketch for *Queen Anne Presenting the Plans of Blenheim to Military Merit* (1708; Blenheim Pal., Oxon) was in his collection. In 1719 Antoine Watteau went to England to consult Mead about his tubercular illness, and left behind two paintings, *L'amour paisable* (*c.* 1720; untraced) and *Italian Comedians* (*c.* 1720; possibly the picture in Washington, DC, N.G.A.). Both of these pictures were engraved by Bernard Baron and helped to further the growing interest in England in French Rococo painting.

Mead commissioned portraits of himself from Allan Ramsay (1747; London, Foundling Hosp.) and Jonathan Richardson the elder (untraced), and there are portrait busts of him by Louis François Roubiliac (plaster, London, BM) and Peter Scheemakers II (marble, 1754; London, Westminster Abbey). He was also a governor of the

Foundling Hospital, which besides its charitable work became one of the first institutions where artists could exhibit their work to the public; pictures presented to it by William Hogarth, Francis Hayman, Joseph Highmore, George Lambert, Richard Wilson and Thomas Gainsborough were on display. Mead's own collection was in a gallery attached to his house in Great Ormond Street, and was the only public art collection in London to be open in the mornings to artists and copyists. Despite financial difficulties, Mead kept his art collection and his library of 10,000 books intact until his death. It was dispersed in a series of sales in March 1754, many works passing into notable collections, including those of Jacob de Bouverie, Thomas Hollis, Lyde Brown, Horace Walpole, Thomas Coke, 1st Earl of Leicester, and Charles Wyndham, 2nd Earl of Egremont.

BIBLIOGRAPHY

DNB
[M. Maty]: *Authentic Memoirs of the Life of Richard Mead, MD* (London, 1755)
W. T. Whitley: *Artists and their Friends in England,* 2 vols (London, 1928)
M. Eidelberg: 'Watteau's Paintings in England in the Early Eighteenth Century', *Burl. Mag.*, cxvii (1975), pp. 576–82
R. Raines: 'Watteau and "Watteaus" in England before 1760', *Gaz. B.-A.*, 6th ser., lxxxix (1977), pp. 51–64
D. Sutton: 'Aspects of British Collecting, I/iv: The Age of Sir Robert Walpole', *Apollo*, cxiv (1981), pp. 328–39

SHEARER WEST

Mead, William Rutherford. *See under* McKIM, MEAD & WHITE.

Meadmore, Clement (*b* Melbourne, 9 Feb 1929). Australian sculptor and designer, active in the USA. He studied aeronautical engineering and later industrial design at the Royal Melbourne Institute of Technology, but left without finishing the course. From 1949 to 1953 he worked as an industrial designer, specializing in furniture. Marketed widely in Australia during these years, his furniture was distinguished by its simplicity. It was constructed with plain, undisguised materials such as steel rods, timber laminates and cord; his tables, chairs and shelving systems exercised a delight in linear and open structure that conveyed an impression of virtual weightlessness. In his free time Meadmore began to produce sculptures, carving wooden shapes whose forms were similar to those of tensioned strings, and from 1950 to 1953 experimenting with mobiles. After extensive travel in 1953 in Europe, where he was particularly impressed by modern sculptures that he saw in Belgium, he produced his first large abstract sculptures in welded steel. Some of these, for example *Duolith III* (steel, h. 1.26 m, 1962; Melbourne, N.G. Victoria) were influenced by photographs of the prehistoric sites of Carnac, Stonehenge and Avebury, most obviously in their textured surfaces and in the monolithic quality of their massive, perpendicular steel slabs. From 1959 to 1961 Meadmore was Director of Gallery A in Melbourne, before moving to Sydney. In 1959 he visited Japan, where he saw an exhibition of modern American painting that included works by Mark Tobey, Robert Motherwell, Barnett Newman and Mark Rothko; he was especially struck by Newman's work. He continued to work in welded metal until he moved in 1963 to the USA, where he met Newman and came under the spell of the

monumental, geometrical sculpture then being produced there. Working in Cor-Ten steel he simplified his forms and began to use curves in his sculptures, as in *Bent* (steel, h. 0.87 m, 1966; Melbourne, Joseph Brown Gal.). He developed this style in such dynamic works as *Fling* (1971; see 1971 exh. cat.), using long, extensively twisted, square-faced elements. He also made many huge public sculptures, such as *Dervish* (1975; Melbourne, N.G. Victoria), in which it appears that huge rectangular blocks have been convoluted under pressure from colossal, unseen forces.

BIBLIOGRAPHY
Clement Meadmore (exh. cat., Chicago, Richard L. Feigen, 1971)
G. Sturgeon: *The Development of Australian Sculpture, 1788–1975* (London, 1978), pp. 147–50
A. McCulloch: *Encyclopedia of Australian Art*, ii (Melbourne and London, 1984), pp. 784–5

GEOFFREY R. EDWARDS

Meadows, Algur Hurtle (*b* Vidalia, GA, 24 April 1899; *d* Dallas, TX, 10 June 1978). American businessman, collector and patron. In 1928 he co-founded a financial services corporation, that helped to develop the east Texas oil field and that later grew into the General American Oil Co., one of the largest independent oil companies in the USA. In the late 1950s he was invited to prospect for oil in Spain. Although the search proved futile, his stay in Madrid near the Prado Museum introduced him to Spanish art, of which he became an avid collector.

In 1962 Meadows donated his collection of Spanish pictures, and funds for a building to house them, to Southern Methodist University, Dallas, TX, in memory of his first wife, Virginia Garrison Stuart Meadows (1901–61). The museum opened in 1965. Responding to doubts about the attribution of many of the paintings (as well as of others in his private collection of Impressionist paintings), Meadows, with characteristic openness, sought the advice of three experts, Diego Angulo Iñiguez, José López-Rey and William B. Jordan. In 1967 Meadows hired Jordan as Director of the museum, and over 11 years they built what has been called 'the finest encyclopedic collection of Spanish art outside of Spain' (Burke, p. 3), including Diego Velázquez's *Sibyl with Tabula Rasa* (1644–8), five works by Bartolomé Esteban Murillo (e.g. *Jacob Laying the Peeled Rods before the Flocks of Laban*; *c.* 1660), Goya's *Madhouse at Saragossa* (1794), Picasso's *Cubist Still-life in a Landscape* (1915) and Joan Miró's *Queen Louise of Prussia* (1929).

In addition to the museum, Meadows founded the Elizabeth Meadows Sculpture Garden (with works by Auguste Rodin, Aristide Maillol, Henry Moore, Isamu Noguchi and David Smith) in honour of his second wife and endowed the Meadows School of the Arts, both at the university.

BIBLIOGRAPHY
W. B. Jordan: *The Meadows Museum: A Visitor's Guide* (Dallas, 1974)
M. B. Burke: *A Selection of Spanish Masterworks from the Meadows Museum* (Dallas, 1986)

MARCUS BURKE

Meadows, Bernard (William) (*b* Norwich, 19 Feb 1915). English sculptor. After studying at Norwich School of Art from 1934 to 1936, Meadows became Assistant to Henry Moore (1936–40). He studied at the Royal College of Art from 1938 to 1940 and from 1946 to 1948 (serving with the RAF 1941–6). From 1948 to 1960 Meadows taught at the Chelsea School of Art and from 1960 to 1980 he was Professor of Sculpture at the Royal College of Art. Meadows's main work is in bronze and, like Moore, he made drawings before sculpture. Unusual in his oeuvre are the two figures representing the *Spirit of Trade Unionism* (1958), Trades Union Congress building, London. In his early work predominant subjects were the cock (e.g. 1953) and cockerel (e.g. 1955; both AC Eng) and the crab (e.g. 1953; Cambridge, Clare Coll. and Jesus Coll.); these sharply angled bronzes, usually under 1.2 m in height, came near abstraction but retained the nature of their subject. In the 1960s titles as *Standing Armed Figure* (1962; London, Brit. Council) stress both aggression and vulnerability. Towards the late 1960s a change emerged in round smooth shapes inspired by fruit, such as apples, and suggestive of human forms. Polished round forms added light and contrast when next to angular opaque surrounds, as in the sculpture for the Eastern Counties Newspaper Building, Norwich (*c.* 1968–9). He exhibited regularly, from the time of the Festival of Britain exhibition in London in 1951, at major exhibitions at home and abroad, and a series of one-man exhibitions have been held in London and New York.

PRINTS
S. Beckett: *Molloy* (Geneva, 1966) [34 etchings and a box]

BIBLIOGRAPHY
W. J. Strachan: 'The Sculptor and his Drawings: (2) Bernard Meadows', *Connoisseur*, clxxxv (April 1974), pp. 288–93

SARAH WIMBUSH

Meadows, (Joseph) Kenny (*b* Cardigan, 1 Nov 1790; *d* London, Aug 1874). Welsh illustrator and watercolourist. The son of a naval officer, he was active as an illustrator in London by 1823. Working in collaboration with Isaac and Robert Cruikshank on *The Devil in London* (1832), he belonged to the older generation of comic illustrators who expressed caricature rather than humour in their work. Meadows was an early and proficient advocate of drawing on the wood for wood-engraving and recommended the process to publishers. His most notable single work is *Portraits of the English* (London, 1840), a series of character sketches of the working, middle and upper classes treated in a broad caricature style. His *Shakespeare* (London, 1843), a three-volume collection of over 1000 illustrations of the plays, is considered his masterpiece. His work appeared in such magazines as *Punch* (1841) and the *Illustrated London News*. From 1843 to 1845 he was the principal artist of the *Illuminated Magazine*, contributing fine decorative work as well as humorous pictures. Meadows was a talented watercolourist (see *Light of the Harem*, London, V&A) and exhibited in London from 1830 to 1853.

DNB   BIBLIOGRAPHY
M. H. Spielmann: *The History of Punch* (London, 1895), pp. 446–9

SIMON HOUFE

Meal, Jabez. *See* MAYALL, JOHN JABEZ EDWIN.

Meander [maeander; fret; Greek key design]. Decorative motif consisting of a line turned back on itself in a series of rectangular bends. There are several variations, for example involving two continuous intersecting lines (see

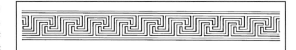

Carved meander from the entablature of the Temple of Jupiter, Baalbek, 1st century AD; reconstruction drawing

fig.). The meander occurs on ancient Greek painted pottery from the Geometric period onwards (for example on a belly-handled amphora of the 8th century BC; *see* GREECE, ANCIENT, fig. 85), and it was widely used, in painted or carved form, on flat-profile architectural mouldings in ancient Greek buildings of all periods and as a border design in floor mosaics. In Roman times it continued to occur on buildings and occasionally in mosaics, and it has remained in the decorative repertory of many art forms into modern times.

MARGARET LYTTELTON

Meatyard, Ralph Eugene (*b* Normal, IL, 15 May 1925; *d* Lexington, KY, 7 May 1972). American photographer. An optician by profession, he made photographs that portray mysterious circumstances through blurred motion or masked faces. He studied with Van Deren Coke (*b* 1921) at the University of Kentucky, Lexington, from 1944 to 1955 and with Henry Holmes Smith (1909–86) and Minor White at Indiana University, Bloomington, IN, in 1956. His early work consisted of experiments with focal length and long exposure, using bits of landscape as subject. Later, he developed a personal imagery, in which costumed figures emerge from murky backgrounds in a combination of black humour and pathos. His best-known work is the book *The Family Album of Lucybelle Crater*, published posthumously in Highlands, NC, in 1974, in which all of the snapshots are of masked family and friends.

BIBLIOGRAPHY
Ralph Eugene Meatyard: Caught Moments—New Viewpoints (exh. cat., London, Olympus Gal., 1983)
Ralph Eugene Meatyard: An American Visionary (exh. cat., ed. B. Tannenbaum; Akrom, OH, A. Mus.; New York, NY, Rizzoli; 1991)

SHERYL CONKELTON

Mebes, Paul (*b* Magdeburg, 1872; *d* Berlin, 1938). German architect. He studied at the Technische Hochschule in Magdeburg before setting up practice in Berlin. Among his early works were the Oberrealschule (1909–10), Beuckestrasse 27, Zehlendorf, and offices for the Nordstern insurance company (1913–15), Badensche Strasse/Meraner Strasse, Schöneberg, Berlin. In 1907 he was appointed director of the Beamten-Wohnungs-Verein zu Berlin, a large housing cooperative. Among his early works for this client were housing blocks at Fritschweg/Rückertstrasse/Grillparzerstrasse, Steglitz; at Grabbeallee/Paul-Franke-Strasse, Niederschönhausen; and at Horstweg/Knobelsdorffstrasse, Charlottenburg (all 1908). After 1911 Mebes worked with his brother-in-law, the architect Paul Emmerich (1876–1958), and the two were responsible in the 1920s and early 1930s for a large number of housing estates in Berlin, notable for their rational planning, undemonstrative elevations and generous provision of windows. Among the best-known schemes were the Heidehof (1923–4), Niklasstrasse, Zehlendorf, and blocks at Bergstrasse (1927–31), Steglitz; in the Friedrich-Ebert-Siedlung (1929–31) at Müllerstrasse and Afrikanische Strasse, Wedding; in the Forschungssiedlung Spandau-Haselhorst (1930–32), Gartenfelder Strasse; and the Spreesiedlung (1932) at Hainstrasse, Niederschöneweide.

Mebes and Emmerich also built estates in other cities, such as the Grosssiedlung Leipzig-Gohlis-Nord (1929–30). Among their public buildings were the Deutsche Länderbank (1922–3), Pariser Platz, Berlin; the administration building (1923–4) of the Mannesmann company in the Tiergartenviertel, Berlin; and schools at Apolda in Thuringia (1928–30) and at Zoppot (1929–31; now Sopot, Poland). Mebes's more lasting fame rests, however, on his book *Um 1800* (1908), an elegant survey of the simple Neo-classicism that had flourished in Germany, Denmark and the Netherlands in the late 18th century and the early years of the 19th. The several hundred illustrations range from the Nymphenburg Palace in Munich to fishermen's cottages on the Baltic and also include interiors and furniture from the period. On the basis of this rich pictorial evidence, Mebes argued that the only way to escape from the impasse of late 19th-century historicism and *Jugendstil* would be to return to the models of 1800, which, he said, were essentially modern in their simplicity. This was a controversial notion in 1908, but one that had gained wide acceptance by the time a second, modified edition of the book appeared in 1918. The simple cottage style of 1800 was adopted in one of the last schemes by Mebes and Emmerich, housing in Potsdam for disabled servicemen, built in the mid-1930s.

WRITINGS

Um 1800: Architektur und Handwerk im letzten Jahrhundert ihrer traditionellen Entwicklung, 2 vols (Munich, 1908); rev. with W. C. Behrendt (Munich, 1918, 3/1920)

BIBLIOGRAPHY

'Dreissig Jahre neuer Wohnbau dargelegt an Bauten von Mebes und Emmerich', *Mhft. Baukst & Städtebau*, 22 (1938), pp. 233–40

E. Meyer: *Paul Mebes: Miethausbau in Berlin, 1906–1938* (Berlin, 1972)

IAIN BOYD WHYTE

Mecarino [Mecherino], **Domenico.** *See* BECCAFUMI, DOMENICO.

Mec art. Term coined in 1965 as an abbreviation of 'mechanical art' by Alain Jacquet and Mimmo Rotella and promoted by the French critic Pierre Restany (*b* 1930) to describe paintings using photographically transferred images that could be produced in theoretically unlimited numbers. The term was first publicly used of works by Serge Béguier (*b* 1934), Pol Bury, Gianni Bertini (*b* 1922), Nikos (*b* 1930), Jacquet and Rotella at an exhibition at the Galerie J in Paris entitled *Hommage à Nicéphore Niépce*. In contrast to the use of screenprinting by Americans such as Robert Rauschenberg and Andy Warhol to incorporate photographic images, the Mec artists projected images directly on to canvases coated with photosensitive emulsion, and they generally used the method to alter rather than merely reproduce the original photographic image. In his *Cinétizations*, for example, Bury cut and turned concentric rings in the original photograph before rephotographing the image and transferring it on to canvas, as

in *La Joconde* (1964; see 1989 exh. cat., p. 61). Having earlier used the method of *décollage*, Rotella continued to rely on torn surfaces when he began in 1964 to produce works that he termed *reportages*, rephotographing his altered material before projecting it on to the sensitized canvas. Jacquet, for his part, broke down the photographic image in paintings such as his *Déjeuner sur l'herbe* series (1964; e.g. Paris, Fonds N. A. Contemp.) into a pattern of coloured spots to imitate the process of printing by four-colour separations used in the mass media.

BIBLIOGRAPHY

Alain Jacquet (exh. cat. by O. Hahn, Zurich, City-Gal., 1965)

A. Bonito Oliva and others: *Mimmo Rotella: 'Lamière'* (Milan, 1989)

Pol Bury (exh. cat. by P. Cabanne, Paris, Gal. 1900-2000, 1989)

Mecca [Makka]. City in Saudi Arabia and the holiest city in Islam. Only Muslims may enter it. Located in a mountain valley at the foot of the Hijaz Highlands, Mecca has a well, Zamzam, which made life possible in this desert area. A town and trading community, known to Ptolemy as Macoraba, arose in ancient times at the juncture of trade routes to Syria, Iraq, the Yemen and the Red Sea. It contained a pagan sanctuary (Arab. *ḥaram*) and was a major centre of pilgrimage, particularly at the time of its annual fair. In its earliest form the sanctuary consisted only of the Ka'ba (Arab. 'cube'), a simple unroofed rectangular structure, but it was reconstructed *c.* 608 by the Quraysh tribe, the guardians of Mecca, as a rectangular structure of alternating courses of masonry and wood 18 cubits high. The single door was raised above ground-level to protect the shrine from hostile intruders and flood waters.

Muhammad, the Prophet of Islam, was born in Mecca *c.* 570 AD, but he was forced to emigrate with his fellow Muslims in 622 to Yathrib (*see* MEDINA). With the victory of the Muslims over Quraysh resistance in 629–30, Mecca's holy shrine became the centre of Islamic pilgrimage. The Koran states that the Ka'ba had been raised initially by the prophets Ibrahim (Abraham) and Isma'il, and Muslims believe that the institution of Islam restored the Ka'ba to its original monotheistic role. Muslims revere the Black Stone, set in its east corner, which they believe had been given to Ibrahim by the Archangel Gabriel. When Muhammad entered Mecca, he left the sanctuary untouched but had the idols in it destroyed. In early 624 the direction of Muslim prayer (Arab. *qibla*) was changed from Jerusalem to Mecca, and all Muslims are enjoined in the Koran to pray five times daily towards the Ka'ba. All who are able must make the pilgrimage to Mecca (Arab. *ḥajj*) at least once, during which they circumambulate the Ka'ba (Arab. *ṭawāf*) and perform other rites. With the Prophet's final pilgrimage in 632, the pilgrim rites were definitively established.

To accommodate the increasing number of pilgrims, the open area around the Ka'ba was enlarged in 638 by the second caliph, 'Umar (*reg* 634–44), and again by his successor 'Uthman (*reg* 644–56), who built colonnades around the esplanade within which the Ka'ba stands. This mosque, the Masjid al-Haram, encompassed the well of Zamzam and two sites associated with the founders of the first Ka'ba, the Maqam Ibrahim and Hijr of Isma'il.

Adjacent to the mosque is the Mas'a (Arab. 'place of running'), the course between the hills of al-Safa' and al-Marwa, along which Ibrahim's wife Hajar had run to find water in the desert before Zamzam sprang up. In 683 the Ka'ba was burnt and the surrounding mosque damaged when the army of the Umayyad caliphs (*reg* 661–750) besieged the city, held by the counter-caliph 'Abdallah ibn al-Zubayr. Ibn al-Zubayr rebuilt the Ka'ba, using Meccan stone and Yemeni mortar and extending it to include the Hijr. The Black Stone, which had been split into three by the fire, was reinstalled in a silver band. Ibn al-Zubayr's alterations lasted only until 693, when the Umayyads took the city and rebuilt the Ka'ba in its form at the time of Muhammad. The Umayyad caliph al-Walid (*reg* 705–15) had the mosque decorated with marble, gold leaf and mosaics, which were probably like those decorating the Dome of the Rock (*see* JERUSALEM, §II, 1(iii)) and the Great Mosque of Damascus (*see* DAMASCUS, §3). By the 7th century the Ka'ba was covered with the *kiswa*, a great cloth that was replaced annually.

Under the early Abbasid caliphs (*reg* 749–1258) the mosque was greatly enlarged. Work was begun by al-Mansur (*reg* 754–75) and completed under his son al-Mahdi (*reg* 775–85); several of the columns in the mosque bear inscriptions in the latter's name. The mosque retained this form for centuries. It was recorded in some detail by the traveller Ibn Jubayr in 1183. Under the patronage of the Mamluk Sultan of Egypt, Qa'itbay (*reg* 1468–96), a madrasa was built against one side of the mosque, and under the Ottoman sultans Süleyman (*reg* 1520–66) and Selim II (*reg* 1566–74) the entire structure was extensively remodelled. The Ka'ba itself was entirely rebuilt in 1631 after it had been demolished in floods the previous year. The mosque comprised a vast esplanade with arcades on four sides; it had seven minarets, the largest number of any mosque in Islam. At the centre was the Ka'ba, with the Maqam Ibrahim and the semicircular Hijr close by. The well of Zamzam was roofed. The Mas'a, which had become the main commercial street of Mecca, was relatively wide. This Ottoman form was recorded in drawings and plans by the travellers 'Ali Bey and J. L. Burckhardt in the early 19th century; it was first photographed in the latter part of the century. In 1955 the Saudi government began to extend the mosque to provide an estimated 300,000 worshippers with a clear view of the Ka'ba. In its current form the mosque covers an area of 16 ha, including the Mas'a, which has been roofed. The door of the Ka'ba (1982) is made of solid gold. The *kiswa*, which had formerly been made in Egypt and sent with the hajj caravan, is made annually in Saudi Arabia.

Several other ancient mosques and sites exist in Mecca, although most of them have been rebuilt in the 20th century. Among them is the Rayya Mosque, where the Prophet raised his standard on the day of the victory of the Muslims at Mecca, the Jinn Mosque, the Ajaba Mosque, the Abu Bakr Mosque and the mosque of Hamza; these are all basically modern buildings and little is known of their earlier appearance. The mosque of Bilal, the Prophet's muezzin, may be somewhat older. Several other religious sites and graves were venerated in earlier times. Other sites and mosques are found on the road to and around Mt 'Arafat where the pilgrimage rites are completed. Few

of the traditional houses of Mecca, with their turned wooden screens (Arab. *rawashin*, *mashrabiyya*), have survived in this modern city.

See also under SAUDI ARABIA.

BIBLIOGRAPHY
Enc. Islam/2: 'Ka'ba', 'Makka' [Mecca]
Ibn Jubayr: *Rihla* [Travels] (1183–5); Eng. trans. by R. J. C. Broadhurst as *The Travels of Ibn Jubayr* (London, 1952)
'Ali Bey (Domenico Badia y Leblich): *Travels of Ali Bey in Morocco, Tripoli, Cyprus, Egypt, Arabia, Syria and Turkey, between the Year 1803 and 1807* (London, 1816)
J. L. Burckhardt: *Travels in Arabia* (London, 1829/*R* 1968)
C. Snouck Hurgronje: *Mekka*, 2 vols (The Hague, 1888–9); Eng. trans. of ii by J. H. Monahan as *Mecca in the Latter Part of the 19th Century* (Leiden and London, 1931)
I. Rifa'at Pasha: *Mir'at al-haramayn* [Mirror of the two sanctuaries] (Cairo, AH 1344/1925)
K. A. C. Creswell: *Early Muslim Architecture*, I/i (Oxford, 1932/*R* and enlarged 1969)
H. A. Basalama: *Ta'rikh 'imarat al-masjid al-haram* [History of the building of the Masjid al-Haram] (n.p., AH 1354/1935–6/*R* Jiddah, AH 1400/1980)
E. Esin: *Mecca the Blessed, Madinah the Radiant* (London, 1963)
A. A. 'Attar: *al-Ka'ba wa'l-kiswa mundhu arba'at alaf sinna hata al-yawm* [The Ka'ba and the kiswa for 4000 years until today] (Mecca, AH 1397/1977)
S. A.Bakr: 'al-Buqa' al-muqaddisa' [The holy places], *Ashhar al-Masajid fi'l-Islam* [The most famous mosques in Islam], i (Jiddah, AH 1400/1980)
H. A. Basalama: *Ta'rikh al-ka'ba al-ma'azzama* [History of the splendid Ka'ba] (*R* Jiddah, AH 1400/1980)
F. H. Matar: *Ta'rikh 'imarat al-haram al-sharif* [History of the building of the noble sanctuary] (Jiddah, AH 1402/1982)
G. R. D. King: *The Historical Mosques of Saudi Arabia* (London, 1986)
G. R. D. KING

Mechel, Christian von (*b* Basle, 4 April 1737; *d* Berlin, 4 Nov 1817). Swiss engraver, publisher and dealer, active in France and Germany. Although he was apprenticed in 1753 to the engraver Georg Daniel Heumann (1691–1759) in Nuremberg, his friendship with the brothers Johann Justin Preissler (1698–1771) and Georg Martin Preissler (1700–1754) was of greater importance. He continued his education (1755–7) with Johann Georg Pintz (1697–1767) in Augsburg, then went to Paris in 1757, to the academy of Jean-Georges Wille, who not only nurtured his taste for realistic representation of a landscape but also transformed him into a courtier and shrewd businessman. From 1760 to 1764 Mechel ran his own engraving studio in Paris, printing and distributing his own work and that of such engravers as L. de Montigny, Elie Mesnil (*b* 1728), Joseph Jean Halle (1740–1805), Jean-Baptiste de Lorraine (*b* 1731) and Antoine Louis Romanet (1742/3–1810), who reproduced the paintings of Charles Eisen, Philipp Hieronymus Brinckmann, Franz Edmund Weirotter, Philippe Jacques de Loutherbourg, Jean-Honoré Fragonard and others. Through such friends as Fragonard, Eisen, Carle Vanloo, François Boucher and Jean-Baptiste Greuze, he gained patrons and is thought to have won admittance to the court.

Mechel left Paris in 1764, taking with him portfolios of his own and others' engravings and many original paintings. He settled in Basle, where he printed and distributed finished plates by Johann Ludwig Aberli, Adrian Zingg (1734–1816) and Salomon Gessner. In 1766 he travelled to Florence, Rome and Naples, in search of business contacts. Although his guide in Rome, Johann Joachim

Winckelmann, instilled in him a great interest in antiquity, he was more impressed with Renaissance paintings and those of such contemporary artists as Anton Raphael Mengs, Pompeo Girolamo Batoni, Gavin Hamilton and Anton von Maron, which he studied in depth.

Mechel returned to Basle in 1766, having forged important business links, acquired a Roman agent and purchased many works of art, and immediately had the façade of his recently acquired Gothic house (1767) remodelled in Classical style, the first such example in Basle; in 1776 he inserted a portal, the work of his friend Nicolas de Pigage. Mechel's first major work was the series *Oeuvre du Chevalier Hedlinger ou recueil des medailles de ce célèbre artiste* (Basle, 1776–8), based on reproductions of the medallions of Johann Karl Hedlinger. It was followed by *La Galerie électorale de Düsseldorf* (Basle, 1778) and *Oeuvre de Jean Holbein* (Basle, 1780–95). For the former, Nicolas de Pigage had inadequate outline drawings (Basle, Kstmus.) of the paintings in the Elector's gallery at Düsseldorf made for Mechel's engravers Balthasar Anton Duncker (1746–1807), Johann Joseph Störklin (*d* 1778), Johann Heinrich Troll (1756–1824), Isaac Jacob Lacroix (1751–1800), Gottfried Eichler I, Philipp Gottfried Pintz (*fl* 1766–76), Bartholomäus Hübner (1727–95), Karl Matthias Ernst (1758–1830), Ludwig Sommerau (1756–86) and Carl Guttenberg. These are of more artistic value than the distorted engravings by Christian von Mechel.

With the work on Hans Holbein (ii), Mechel contributed to the revival of interest in the work of that artist and won the favour of the Holy Roman Emperor Joseph II (1741–90), who invited him to Vienna. After 1778 he made three lengthy visits to Vienna, finding a patron in Prince Wenzel Anton Kaunitz-Rietburg, to whom he owed the contract to reorganize the Belvedere Gallery and to produce a catalogue (1778) of the paintings. He divided the pictures according to the history of style and in so doing envisaged art education for the public (*see* GERMANY, §XIV). His engraving *La Galerie Impériale . . . de Vienne* (London, BL; *see* MUSEUM, fig. 2) was published in Basle in 1784. As a member of the Akademie der Bildenden Künste in Vienna, he served as an intermediary between the Academy and Viennese artists working in Rome, for example Franz Anton Zauner, Heinrich Füger and Christoph Unterberger.

Between 1783 and 1793 Mechel's studio in Basle prospered. Among the many engravers working for him, some came from the Mannheim School of Egid Verhelst (i). Mechel was constantly travelling in Germany and the Spanish southern Netherlands, and he also visited Paris and London at this time. The war in Switzerland, however, led to the decline and eventually the closure of his business (1802–8). In 1800 he settled in Berlin, becoming a member of the Akademie der Künste and a Prussian royal counsellor and planning the reorganization of the collection of pictures and antiques in the palace of Sanssouci at Potsdam. Among his series of engravings from this period are the *Bildnisse sämtlicher zu dem Throne von Frankreich zurückberufenen Bourbons* (Berlin, 1814), *Lucas Cranachs Stammbuch* (Berlin, 1814) and *Die eiserne Hand des Ritters Götz von Berlichingen* (Berlin, 1815).

BIBLIOGRAPHY

L. H. Wüthrich: *Christian von Mechel* (Basle and Stuttgart, 1956)
——: *Das Oeuvre des Kupferstechers Christian von Mechel* (Basle and Stuttgart, 1959)
Von Gessner bis Turner: Zeichnungen und Aquarelle von 1750–1850 im Kunsthaus Zürich Graphische Sammlung (exh. cat., by B. von Waldkirch, Zurich, Ksthaus, 1988), pp. 63–7

INGRID SATTEL BERNARDINI

Mechelen [Fr. Malines]. City in northern Belgium, known for its production of gold, silver and lace. By 1254 the gold- and silversmiths of Mechelen constituted an independent group within the collective guild of St Eloi. The earliest documents relating to a separate union and statutes date from the 14th century. Gold- and silversmiths as well as other artists experienced a period of great prosperity in the following centuries, encouraged partly by the temporary residency of Margaret of York, Duchess of Burgundy. Margaret of Austria, Duchess of Savoy and Regent of the Netherlands (*see* HABSBURG, §I(4)), had her permanent residence there in the 16th century. After a period of decline at the end of the 16th century and in the 17th, the number of silversmiths increased significantly in the 18th century, as did the influence exerted by this centre. The most prominent gold- and silversmiths were members of the van Steynenmo(e)len family, active from the 15th to the 18th centuries, and the van den Bosche and van Beveren families. The city mark consists of the city coat of arms: three pillars with the imperial eagle in a heart-shaped shield. One engraved plate with makers' names and marks, beginning in 1749, survives (Mechelen, Stedelijk Mus.); the names of two silversmiths of Lier, who, since the early medieval period, had been obliged to have their work assayed in Mechelen, are also included. Lace was produced in Mechelen in the 17th and 18th centuries.

See BELGIUM, §§IX, 1(ii) and XI, 3.

BIBLIOGRAPHY

G. Van Doorslaer: *La Corporation et les ouvrages des orfèvres malinois* (Antwerp, 1935)

LEO DE REN

Meckenem. German or Netherlandish family of engravers and goldsmiths. They are thought to have originated in Meckenheim near Bonn, but (1) Israhel van Meckenem (i) is associated mainly with Bocholt in Westphalia, where (2) Israhel van Meckenem (ii), presumed to be his son, was active as an engraver. The two artists used an identical housemark or hallmark (a caltrop with a small horizontal cross-stroke) on their engravings, which are similar in style and technique. Israhel van Meckenem (ii) made several copies of works by Israhel van Meckenem (i) and by the so-called Master of the Berlin Passion, with whom Israhel the elder has been identified.

(1) Israhel van Meckenem (i) (*fl* Bocholt, *c.* 1457; *d c.* 1465–70). He probably arrived in Bocholt *c.* 1457, possibly after having worked in the Netherlands. In 1458–9 he received a salary from the town, and in 1464 he was in Bonn in connection with the sale of a house. He may subsequently have made brief stays in Bocholt and Cleve. For his work as an engraver, he has been identified as the MASTER OF THE BERLIN PASSION (*see* MASTERS, ANONYMOUS, AND MONOGRAMMISTS, §I).

(2) Israhel van Meckenem (ii) (*b* Meckenheim, *c*. 1440–45; *d* Bocholt, 10 Nov 1503). Son of (1) Israhel van Meckenem (i). He is thought to have trained from 1457 with his father at Bocholt. An engraving (Lehrs, ix, no. 605) suggests that he was in Cleve in 1465, though this date has been questioned (Koreny, in Hollstein: *Ger.*). The many copies he executed of works by the Master E.S. make it likely that he visited southern Germany *c.* 1466 and became apprenticed to this master, plausibly until the Master E.S.'s death *c.* 1467–8. Israhel van Meckenem may then have purchased and subsequently retouched the Master's plates.

An *Agnus Dei* casket (Munich, Bayer. Nmus.), a piece of goldsmith's work attributed to Israhel and executed for Konrad Leen, vicar of the Marienkirche at Theuerstadt, suggests his presence in the Bamberg region in 1470. He may have worked under the Master W with the Key (*fl* 1465–85) in the southern Netherlands during the 1470s (Geisberg, 1903) or, alternatively, while staying in Neuss during its siege in 1475 (Warburg). But during the 1470s Israhel returned to Bocholt, where he appears to have settled permanently, apart from possible short trips to the southern Netherlands. His name is recorded in Bocholt archives from 1480, for example in 1482, 1487, 1488, 1492, 1497, 1498 and 1499, for the execution of town commissions for goldsmith's work.

Geisberg (1905) attributed 570 engravings to Israhel; Lehrs gave a list of 624 attributions, revised by Koreny (Hollstein: *Ger.*). A very prolific artist, Meckenhem copied avidly from the Master of the Berlin Passion, the Master E.S., Martin Schongauer, the Housebook Master, the Master P.W. of Cologne, the Master bg (*fl* late 15th century), the Master W with the Key, the Master F.V.B. and the young Albrecht Dürer; he also worked from drawings by Hans Holbein the elder. Yet as an engraver he was also capable of originality and showed himself to be highly skilled, for example in the *Daily Life* cycle (L 499–510) or in the *Dance of Herodias* (L 367), where the religious subject becomes the background and pretext for a profane representation, showing contemporary secular life in the Lower Rhine region. His *Self-portrait with his*

Wife, Ida (?Ida Ernstes; L 1; see fig.), an engraving perhaps influenced by a Swabian painter (Shestack) or by a drawing by Hans Holbein (Koreny, 1968), is the first signed self-portrait and also the first double portrait executed as an engraving. His decorative works (e.g. L 690, where his forename is included in the composition) express his taste for ornamentation.

During his early career Israhel was drawn by the expressive qualities of the Master of the Berlin Passion, the Master E.S. and Westphalian painters such as Johann Koerbecke and the Master of Schöppingen. In the late 1470s and early 1480s he was inspired by the work of Martin Schongauer and especially by Netherlandish art, developing perspective spaces under the influence of Rogier van der Weyden, Dieric Bouts and their followers Aelbrecht Bouts, the Master of the Legend of St Catherine and the Master of the Legend of St Barbara. His engravings, often narrative in character, bring together several scenes surrounded by a landscape and structuring architectural elements. During the 1480s Israhel's technique, previously quite stiff, became freer, bolder and more original, achieving pictorial effects of contrast and great richness. His delicately modelled figures, with their regular silhouettes, stand out clearly. The collaboration with Hans Holbein the elder brought a certain monumentality to his work and is the earliest example in Germany of an engraver reproducing a painter's drawings. His productivity, his brilliant technique, his skill at retouching, his originality and his activity as a copyist all attest to Israhel van Meckenem's importance as an engraver (*see also* ENGRAVING, §II, 2).

BIBLIOGRAPHY
Hollstein: *Dut. & Flem.*; Hollstein: *Ger.*; Thieme–Becker
M. Lehrs: 'Der deutsche und niederländische Kupferstich des fünfzehnten Jahrhunderts in den kleineren Sammlungen', *Repert. Kstwiss.*, xi (1889), pt I, pp. 47–56; pt II, pp. 213–39
M. Geisberg: *Der Meister der Berliner Passion und Israhel van Meckenem. Studien zur Geschichte der westfälischen Kupferstecher im 15. Jahrhundert*, xlii of Stud. Dt. Kstgesch. (Strasbourg, 1903/*R* Liechtenstein, 1979)
——: *Verzeichnis der Kupferstiche Israhel van Meckenem + 1503*, lvii of Stud. Dt. Kstgesch. (Strasbourg, 1905)
M. Lehrs: *Geschichte und kritischer Katalog des deutschen, niederländischen und französischen Kupferstichs im 15. Jahrhundert*, iii (Vienna, 1915), ix (Vienna, 1934) [L]
M. Geisberg: 'Israhel van Meckenem', *Prt. Colr Q.*, xvii (1930), pp. 212–37
A. Warburg: *Israhel van Meckenem: Sein Leben, sein Werk und seine Bedeutung für die Kunst des ausgehenden 15. Jahrhunderts*, vii of Forsch. Kstgesch. Westeuropas (Bonn, 1930)
M. Geisberg and others: 'Israhel van Meckenem, Goldschmied und Kupferstecher: Zur 450. Wiederkehr seines Todestages', *Unser Bocholt* (1953) [double issue]
Israhel van Meckenem (exh. cat., Cologne, Wallraf-Richartz-Mus., 1953–4)
Prentenkunst van Martin Schongauer, Albrecht Dürer, Israhel van Meckenem (exh. cat., Rotterdam, Mus. Boymans, 1955)
A. Wagner: 'Meister der Grafik, Israhel van Meckenem, ein spätmittelalterlicher Kupferstecher und Goldschmied', *Kst & S. Heim*, lxv (1966–7), pp. 607–10
A. Shestack: *Fifteenth-century Engravings of Northern Europe from the National Gallery of Art* (Washington, DC, 1967–8)
F. Koreny: *Über die Anfänge der Reproduktionsgraphik nördlich der Alpen* (diss., U. Vienna, 1968)
L. Behling and others: *Israhel van Meckenem und der deutsche Kupferstich des 15. Jahrhunderts*, *Unser Bocholt* (1972) [double issue]
Spielkarten: Ihre Kunst und Geschichte in Mitteleuropa (exh. cat. by F. Koreny, P. Kopp and D. Hoffmann, Vienna, Albertina, 1974), pp. 66–7, 69–70, 233–4; nos 22, 24, 176

Israhel van Meckenem (ii): *Self-portrait with his Wife, Ida*, engraving, 124×173 mm, *c.* 1490–95 (Vienna, Graphische Sammlung Albertina)

J. Marrow: 'A Book of Hours from the Circle of the Master of the Berlin Passion: Notes on the Relationship between Fifteenth-century Manuscript Illumination and Printmaking in the Rhenish Lowlands', *A. Bull.*, lx/4 (1978), pp. 590–616

J. Schnack: 'Der *Passionszyklus* in der Graphik Israhel von Mechenems und Martin Schongauers', *Bocholt. Quellen & Beitr.*, ii (1979)

F. Koreny and J. C. Hutchinson: *Early German Artists*, 9 [VI/ii] of *The Illustrated Bartsch*, ed. W. Strauss (New York, 1981)

BÉATRICE HERNAD

Medal. Piece of metal (or sometimes other material) that is usually coin-like, with an image and/or inscription, usually on both sides. It is generally a commemorative object. Large ancient Roman presentation pieces of bronze, silver and gold, produced between the 2nd and the 5th century AD, are generally called medallions; the term is also somewhat loosely applied to particularly large Renaissance and later medals (*see* MEDALLION).

I. Introduction. II. History.

I. Introduction.

Medals are usually discs of gold, silver, copper alloy (bronze or brass) or lead, bearing images. In the 20th century artists greatly expanded this range of materials and the shapes and forms of medals. Traditionally, the images included on the obverse a portrait with identifying inscription, and on the reverse a text or some sort of figure or scene associated with the subject of the portrait. The production of medals is not subject to the same official controls that govern COINS: they are not used as currency and can be made at the request of private individuals. The medal's primary function is to honour, commemorate, glorify, criticize or even satirize its subject through an extended pictorial and verbal message that usually covers both of its surfaces. It is reproduced in varying numbers and distributed, in the manner of a book or print, to what may be a large public. The message begins with the portrait, which is fully identified by an inscription providing name, titles, profession, social status, honours and other relevant facts. The reverse may contain text alone, in the form of mottoes, epigrams and historical data; this may be placed around the edge and also fill the field. More common are narrative scenes, coats of arms, symbolic devices, allegories, representations of the subject engaged in some significant action or emblems expressing in cryptic language a particular idea, attribute or intention of the subject.

Medals may be cast or struck. With few exceptions, until the second half of the 16th century medals were produced by the casting method. The artist generally made a preparatory drawing, using this as the basis for carving a model in wax, plaster, stone or wood. Lettering was added by direct modelling, by cutting the letters into a ring that was then pressed into the modelling material, or with incuse punches that would produce raised letters in the same way. Punches that had the letters in relief could be used to add the letters directly on to the mould. The artist then pressed the model into a soft material, often composed of sand and glue, or gesso, pumice, water and sizing material, creating a negative image; this was the mould. The obverse and reverse moulds were dried and fitted together, with appropriate openings for the introduction of the molten metal and for the escape of air and gases.

The metal was poured into the mould and allowed to cool. The two halves of the mould were then broken away or separated, and the rough medal extracted for finishing and patination.

After the mid-16th century, medals were increasingly produced by striking as well as casting. Striking is impressing on to a metal blank, called a planchet or flan, images and letters that have been cut or stamped in negative on to the faces of obverse and reverse dies. This was accomplished by means of the screw press, in which the upper die, or trussel, was placed in the base of a long screw that descended through the top of a frame; on this was set a long arm with heavy counterweights at each end. The pile, or lower die, was held in the base of the press, and the planchet was placed on it. The descending screw impressed the images simultaneously on both sides of the planchet.

See also METAL, §V, and PLAQUETTE.

II. History.

1. 15th century. 2. 16th century. 3. 17th and 18th centuries. 4. 19th century. 5. 20th century.

1. 15TH CENTURY. The philosophical and spiritual foundation for the appearance of the medal in Italy is composed of two indissolubly linked factors: the Renaissance philosophy of man, and the re-evaluation of Classical antiquity, or humanism. The uniqueness of human physiognomy, character and achievements needed to be celebrated in a way that would survive the erosion of time and the fragility of men's memories. Based, in part, on surviving ancient Roman coinage, the medal, with its portrait, supporting images and inscriptions, was the ideal means of achieving earthly immortality and became extremely popular from the moment of its appearance.

The first true Renaissance medal was created *c.* 1438 by Pisanello, perhaps with the collaboration of Leon Battista Alberti; it shows the portrait of the penultimate Byzantine emperor, *John VIII Palaeologus*, who was visiting Ferrara (*see* PISANELLO, fig. 4). During the following 22 years Pisanello produced some 26 medals for a variety of patrons, most of his work being done in the courts of Mantua, Ferrara, Rimini and Naples. Working in delicate low relief, he modelled sensitive portraits, combined with evocative reverses that distilled, in beautifully conceived images, a particular attribute of the sitter. Most memorable among his medals are those of *Leonello d'Este, Marquess of Ferrara* (see fig. 1), *Novello Malatesta* and *Cecilia Gonzaga*; and in Naples, *Alfonso I of Aragon*, and *Don Inigo d'Avalos*.

By the second half of the 15th century cast medals were being produced in all of the major Italian centres of artistic activity, by goldsmiths, die-engravers, sculptors and painters, for sitters representing all the higher levels of society. Pisanello's invention was enthusiastically picked up in those cities where he had worked. In Rimini, Sigismondo Pandolfo Malatesta ordered a large number of several types of medal from the painter, miniaturist and architect Matteo de' Pasti, one of the best of the early imitators of Pisanello. The courts of Mantua and Ferrara, which

1. Medal by Pisanello: *Leonello d'Este, Marquess of Ferrara* (left, obverse; right, reverse), cast bronze, diam. 100.5 mm, 15th century (Washington, DC, National Gallery of Art)

continued to be important centres of patronage, nurtured artists who dispersed to other cities, as well as attracting artists from elsewhere. A passion for antiquity is evident in Mantua in the active production of small plaquettes and medals in the Classical mode, and even in the names of two of the noted artists in this manner, Antico and Moderno. The medals of this school display precision and elegance of lettering, crisp details, finely drawn portraits and an almost academic reference to Classical subjects.

Among the native Mantuan artists who spent most of their careers elsewhere was Cristoforo di Geremia, active in Rome. His work, which shows the influence of Mantegna, in turn inspired the medals of another important Mantuan, Bartolommeo Melioli (1448–1514). Both artists combined fine portraits with beautiful Latin epigraphy and graceful, yet forceful, interpretations of Classical forms. One of the most popular, prolific and characteristic medallists of the Renaissance, the goldsmith and sculptor Sperandio Savelli (*c.* 1425–1504), was also a Mantuan. His style derived from that of Pisanello, but was much heavier and more robust; it showed little relationship to the work of other Mantuan medallists. He worked chiefly in Ferrara, Bologna and Venice. His portraits are powerful and expressive, though not subtle; he worked in large scale and high relief, so that his medals display a distinctly sculptural style, as opposed to the more painterly approach of Pisanello, from whom he often, quite shamelessly and awkwardly, borrowed reverse compositions. Among the medallists from other parts of Italy who worked for some time in Mantua was Gian Cristoforo Romano, also a sculptor and architect, who was one of the favourites of the Mantuan court (for an illustration of his medal of *Isabella d'Este*, see GIAN CRISTOFORO ROMANO).

In Venice, among a diversity of styles that cannot necessarily be characterized as Venetian, could be found the distinct personality of such artists as Giovanni Boldu (*fl* 1454–*c.* 1477), with his taut portraiture and vigorous

reverse compositions, and Vittore Gambello, a sculptor, jeweller, die-engraver and armourer, the precision and delicacy of whose medals reflect these various professions. Included in the Venetian school is Fra Antonio da Brescia (*fl* 1487–1513), who recorded with simple fidelity and charming realism some of the prominent citizens of Venice. The medals attributed to Maffeo Olivieri show an elegance and refinement appropriate to his portraits of Venetian patricians; but his range also included the powerful modelling and high relief seen in his medal of *Altobello Averoldi*, one of the masterpieces of Renaissance medallic art. The work of Giulio delle Torre (*c.* 1480–*c.* 1530) of Padua, a jurist and amateur medallist, is notable for its quality; his style had obvious associations with those of the Venetian medallists, particularly Olivieri.

Rome was another centre of activity to which many artists gravitated. The relative stability of the papal court, the existence of a mint and the need for effective means of propaganda were all important elements in the development of technical innovations, such as machinery for striking, and in the unbroken production of coins and medals. In the Quattrocento, most of the medals were cast, and they retained often admirable stylistic identities; such were the sometimes awkward, but honest and effective portraits by Andrea Guazzalotti (1435–94/5), who produced medals for four successive popes in the second half of the century.

Like Cristoforo di Geremia, Lysippus the younger was a Mantuan artist who did much of his work in Rome, producing a series of sharply modelled portraits of members of the papal curia, combined with beautiful examples of Latin epigraphy. The career of Giovanni Candida, who was clearly influenced by Lysippus, shows that medallic art was avidly and successfully pursued by amateurs. Candida, a member of an aristocratic Neapolitan family, spent his life in the diplomatic service but nevertheless managed to dabble in medal-making. Although he cannot be attached to any particular school, he was very talented and exerted considerable influence on the development of the medal in France at the end of the 15th century.

Surprisingly, in Florence, the city most closely associated with all phases of the Renaissance, interest in medals began only in the last quarter of the 15th century. The first significant Florentine medallist, Bertoldo di Giovanni, was a bronze sculptor, said by Vasari to have been a pupil of Donatello and Michelangelo's master. On the basis of one signed medal, a group of medals has been attributed to him; it shows a very distinctive, if not altogether attractive style, with very low relief and a field crowded with many agitated figures, as in the medal commemorating the *Pazzi Conspiracy* (1478). Bertoldo's efforts hardly foreshadow the greatest of all Florentine medallists, Niccolò de Forzore Spinelli, whose style characterizes the entire Florentine school of medals throughout the remainder of the 15th century. His manner is established in five signed pieces, such as the bronze medal of *Alfonso I d'Este* (1492; for illustration *see* SPINELLI, (3)). A number of other medals have been attributed either to him or to his school. For the most part, the scale of his medals is large, and the portraits, including remarkably handsome portraits of women, are bold and strongly characterized; yet the reverses are surprisingly indifferent in quality, with one or two notable exceptions, such as the *Three Graces* on the reverse of the beautiful medal of *Giovanna Albizzi Tornabuoni*.

In the 15th century there was virtually no medallic activity in any country but Italy, although, at the very end of the century, Lyon, a wealthy, commercial city with strong ties to Italy, on several occasions commemorated royal visits with impressive medals that show a significant combination of Late Gothic and Renaissance elements. Italians working outside Italy produced a few scattered medals, often of questionable quality. It was not until other elements of the Italian Renaissance had been imported enthusiastically into other countries that medals likewise began to be produced in great numbers.

2. 16TH CENTURY.

(i) Italy. The introduction of the screw press for striking coins and medals, drastic changes in the political landscape and shifts in taste all affected the development of the medal. With increasing frequency, medals became the product of an official mint, and they were produced in large quantities and used extensively for propaganda, and they became the exclusive responsibility of die-engravers. The result was some decline in quality and a desiccation of style that was inherent in the technique, regardless of the source of the design. This is not to say that all struck medals lacked quality, but it is still in the cast medal that the finest and most exciting work is found. The medals produced by the papal mint in Rome are prime examples of the sort of work done by official die-engravers and merit little attention (*see* CELLINI, BENVENUTO, fig. 1). A few artists, such as Alessandro Cesati, Giovanni Bernardi and Giovanni Antonio de' Rossi at times rose above the common level, but they could not match the accomplishments of contemporary medallists elsewhere in Europe.

2. Medal by Pastorino Pastorini: *Lucrezia de' Medici* (uniface), cast lead, diam. 69 mm, 16th century (private collection)

Even in cities of major artistic importance, such as Florence and Venice, few medals of any distinction were made. In Padua, which continued as a major centre of bronze-casting, there were several medallists who concentrated on imitating sestertia (Roman coins) or producing fantasy pieces in a classicizing style. The best known of these artists, Giovanni Cavino (1500–70), not only produced an entire series of imitation sestertia, but also designed a number of struck medals with portraits of contemporaries that are excellent in their refined technique and precise characterizations. The grand-ducal court in Florence provided another source of patronage, and several of the more praiseworthy medallists of the period, such as Giampaolo Poggini, Jacopo da Trezzo, Pietro Paolo Galeotti and Gasparo Mola spent varying amounts of time there, but, except for Mola, chiefly worked elsewhere.

Pastorino Pastorini, born in Siena, lived most of his life in Florence and was widely available as a medallist, becoming one of the most productive and representative medallists of the 16th century. In over 200 cast medals, most of them uniface, he recorded, in a coldly precise, detached manner, the features of members of practically every prominent family in Italy (e.g. *Lucrezia de' Medici*, see fig. 2), and of many personalities from beyond the Alps. The virtuosity with which Pastorino described the minutest details of dress and adornment is a characteristic that dominates the best 16th-century Italian medals and particularly influenced the development of the medal in other countries.

The most important of all Italian centres of medallic production in the 16th century was Milan, largely because of Leone Leoni, a rare example of a major sculptor who was also active as a medallist. In both sculpture and medals, Leoni swung from a stiff and mannered awkwardness, related to his fulfilment of court commissions, to more sympathetic products, such as his medals of *Michelangelo*, *Andrea Doria the Elder* and *Ippolita Gonzaga*, which were unimpeded by the constraints of the courtier. Important followers of Leoni include Jacopo da Trezzo and Antonio Abondio. The activities of all three artists were not confined to Milan, but included extended periods spent in various parts of the Habsburg Empire, including the Netherlands, Spain, Germany, Bohemia (Prague) and Austria, countries where their highly sophisticated work exerted great influence on the development of the medal.

A fascinating group of Mannerist wax-modellers was centred on Reggio Emilia. The leading artists of this school were Alfonso Ruspagiari, Gian Antonio Signoretti (*fl* 1540–1602) and Bombarda (probably Andrea Cambi; *fl c.* 1560–75). With an oblique reference to Leoni's earlier medal of *Ippolita Gonzaga*, the Emilian medallists, whose work was usually uniface and cast in a lead alloy, produced a series of bizarre and delightful portraits that are unforgettable in their originality. Their subjects are dressed in agitated, filmy garments and are richly coiffured, as if they were participating in some elaborate court masque. They are often represented as ancient busts, set on elaborate pedestals. By the end of the century, the Italian cast medal had become so rarified that it could go no further in its own country and only provide a source for artists in other countries.

(ii) Germany. Medals began to appear in Germany only in the 16th century and were distinctly different from Italian ones. Although cast, they were generally made from stone and wood models carved by goldsmiths, die-engravers and wood- and stone-carvers, whose techniques were highly refined and tended towards exact detail. Despite their

foundation in humanism, they rarely displayed the complex imagery and intellectual sophistication found in Italian medals. Only in rare cases did the reverse show anything other than a heraldic achievement; attention was focused instead on the portrait, which was usually uncompromisingly, even brutally, realistic.

The enormous number of medals produced is evidence that this form enjoyed great success in Germany, beginning in the second decade of the 16th century. Nuremberg and Augsburg were the main centres of medallic production throughout the century, with some important work also being done in Saxony. Nuremberg's flourishing production of medals in the 1520s and 1530s was dominated by the work of Mathes Gebel, followed in the next two decades by such artists as Joachim Deschler and Hans Bolsterer (*d* 1573). Augsburg produced in Hans Schwarz one of the most significant and powerful of the early German medallists (for an illustration of his bronze medal of *Melchior Pfinzing*, *see* SCHWARZ, HANS). Like most contemporary artists, he travelled extensively and worked in other cities. The Augsburg school was dominated by the work of Christof Weiditz (i) and Friedrich Hagenauer, both master wood-carvers; their models and medals show astonishing precision and refinement. The sculptor Hans Daucher of Augsburg designed in the 1520s a number of outstanding medals (which he did not cast himself), such as that of *Philip, Count Palatine of the Rhine* (see fig. 3).

Superior carving techniques are evident among other leading artists in various regions. In Saxony, Hans Reinhart produced several adequate portraits but displayed the full range of his craft in beautiful heraldic reverses and in a number of religious medals, dominated by the spectacular *Trinity* medal (1544; Trier, Domschatz) a *tour de force* betraying his activity as a goldsmith. In the latter part of the 16th century medals continued to be produced in great numbers but with a certain monotony of style and presentation.

(iii) France. The development of the medal in France was almost wholly dependent on the patronage of the crown and its need to use the royal mint as an effective means of propaganda. There was little of the widespread and popular commissioning of medals that took place in Italy and Germany. The full influx of Italian culture into France had begun in 1494, with the Italian wars; from then on, particularly during the reign of Francis I, Italian humanism and art were quite deliberately imported. The presence of Italian artists affected medallic production, although with less than memorable results. However, in the early 16th century the city of Lyon continued to foster the production of medals by native artists, and some of these are worthy of consideration.

Under Henry II royal involvement in the production of coins and medals became firmly established. In 1573 Charles IX (*reg* 1560–74) appointed the great sculptor Germain Pilon to the new post of Contrôleur Général des Effigies at the mint, where he could execute portraits for coins and medals and oversee their production. During this period Pilon also cast a series of large medallions with portraits of the Valois kings and members of the court. Little else that was noteworthy was done before the beginning of the 17th century.

3. Medal by Hans Daucher: *Philip, Count Palatine of the Rhine* (obverse), cast silver, diam. 51.7–51.9 mm, 16th century (Berlin, Bodemuseum, Münzkabinett)

(iv) England and the Low Countries. English Renaissance art, including medals, was relatively sparse and often the product of non-English artists. A number of medals of *Henry VIII* were from German sources; others of the same subject have been thought to be later restitutions. Jacopo da Trezzo's admirable medal of *Queen Mary Tudor* was probably based on a portrait by Antonis Mor. In the reign of Elizabeth I this pattern continued with small, undistinguished struck and cast medalets and counters, often produced by the mint from designs by foreign artists. Only rarely did works of quality emerge, such as those produced by Steven van Herwijck during his visit to England in 1562. The dominance of painting in English art is seen in the best of Elizabeth's medals, based on or actually designed by the greatest miniaturist of the period, Nicholas Hilliard.

A similar situation can be found in the Low Countries; Italian Renaissance innovations such as the portrait medal were not fully developed until a later period. In the 15th century the dukes of Burgundy had employed Italian artists to produce medals of their family and members of their court; the Emperor Charles V and his son Philip II, King of Spain, also favoured Italian artists, who strongly influenced the few native medallists active during the second half of the 16th century. As an isolated instance, and without much influence on subsequent medallists, the renowned Flemish painter Quinten Metsys produced at least one medal, a portrait of *Desiderius Erasmus* dated 1519, which deserves to be numbered among the greatest examples of the art.

The most prominent medallists in the Netherlands in the 16th century include the sculptor Jacques Jonghelinck, whose work was always extremely proficient technically but whose inspiration varied, resulting in portraits that are often lifeless, and reverse compositions that only occasionally reach a superior level of design. Van Herwijck's medals were of a more sympathetic character; he was widely travelled and seems to have thus been exposed to a greater range of outside influences. He combined excellent technique with sensitive portraiture and accomplished design. It was not until the middle of the next century that the medallic form enjoyed a revival.

BIBLIOGRAPHY

G. F. Hill: *Medals of the Renaissance* (London, 1920, rev. 1978)
G. Habich: *Die Medaillen der italienischen Renaissance* (Stuttgart and Berlin, 1924)
J. Babelon: *La Médaille et les médailleurs* (Paris, 1927)
G. F. Hill: *A Corpus of Italian Medals of the Renaissance before Cellini*, 2 vols (London, 1930/R Florence, 1984)
M. Jones: *The Art of the Medal* (London, 1979)
The Currency of Fame: Portrait Medals of the Renaissance (exh. cat., ed. S. K. Scher; New York, Frick, 1994) [includes extensive bibliography]

STEPHEN K. SCHER

3. 17TH AND 18TH CENTURIES. Although the expediency of striking resulted in fewer cast medals being made, the mechanization of the process enabled the medal-making industry to develop; it established professions for engravers and engineers and, as a business, attracted promoters and publishers. Cast medals continued to be made and enjoyed periods of popularity. In both technique and composition they most effectively captured the spirit of the Renaissance and appealed to those with a taste for Classical art, which the Grand Tour did much to stimulate.

Details of how the engravers' workshops and their apprentices operated are not clear, but, since for much of the 17th century there were relatively few centres of activity, a medallist in search of training was often obliged to travel to a foreign mint in order to acquire the necessary skills. In some cases technique and expertise were handed down in families from one generation to the next; in this way several dynasties of medallists became established. Experienced medallists travelled to different courts to carry out commissions and to exploit new markets; by these means medal-making skills spread further afield, although the activity remained largely Europe-based for much of the 18th century.

The portrait continued to serve as a central feature in medals, although it played little or no part in some of the purposes to which medals were being put, such as propaganda. During the 18th century the usefulness of the medal as an instrument of encouragement and reward was recognized by academies, institutions and societies throughout western Europe. In its commemorative role, the medal frequently documented scientific and other advances. The medallist's art became an accepted part of the Paris Salons and the Royal Academy's annual exhibitions in London.

Series of medals were a practical means of recording a nation's history and achievements, while representing a fitting diplomatic gift; they formed the backbone of many engravers' work. A number of princely medal collections have as their core the series that royalty had themselves commissioned, as well as those of other countries presented by visiting ambassadors. In the 18th century a number of important medal cabinets were formed, including those of Frederick the Great of Prussia, Louis XV of France and George III of Britain. At their foundation in the middle of the century, the Hunterian Museum in Glasgow and the British Museum in London were endowed with significant medal collections.

(i) Italy. Among the most prominent medallists working in Italy in the first half of the 17th century were Gasparo Mola (*see* §2(i) above) and Francesco Travani. Mola worked at the mints in Florence and Rome, and his struck medals include a finely executed portrait of *Charles Emanuel I, Duke of Savoy*, with the Duke's badge on the reverse, and one of *Cosimo II de' Medici*. Travani made cast medals of *Pope Urban VIII* and *Pope Alexander VII*; his name also occurs on struck medals of *Ferdinando II de' Medici* and *Cosimo III de' Medici*. Some of the reverses of Mola's and Travani's medals were designed by Gianlorenzo Bernini.

Giovanni Battista Guglielmada (*fl* 1665–88) was active in Rome, where his medals include those for various popes; some of the medals he made for Queen Christina of Sweden, who settled in Rome following her abdication and conversion to Catholicism, may represent the beginnings of a proposed series recording events in her life. The most prolific dynasty of Italian medallists was that of the HAMERANI family. Giovanni Hamerani worked at the papal court for Clement X and Clement XI, where he cut a large number of medal dies. Other medallists of his family included his sons Ermenegildo Hamerani, who engraved a medal of *Nicolas Duodo*, Venetian Ambassador

4. Medal by Ottone Hamerani: *Princess Maria Clementina* (obverse), struck silver, diam. 48 mm, 1719 (private collection)

at Rome, and Ottone Hamerani, whose medals included portraits of *James Stuart*, the Old Pretender (1688–1766), and one of his wife-to-be *Princess Maria Clementina* (1702–35), to commemorate her escape from Innsbruck in 1719 (priv. col.; see fig. 4). Ferdinand de Saint-Urbain, whose work displays a distinctive clarity in its engraving, produced a large number of medal dies for the mints in Bologna and Rome in the 1680s and 1690s, and subsequently worked at the mint in Nancy, producing an extensive series of medals recording the dukes and duchesses of Lorraine. His portrait medals of contemporaries include those of *Philip V of Spain* and the English physician *John Freind*.

The large cast medal made a resurgence in Italy under the Florentine sculptor and medallist Massimiliano Soldani, who studied in Rome under the painter Ciro Ferri and the sculptor Ercole Ferrata and became a medallist at the mint in Florence, working for Cosimo III de' Medici and Queen Christina. He made a number of medals carrying retrospective portraits of the Medici family, as well as personal portraits of contemporary artists and scientists, including the poet, philosopher and naturalist *Francesco Redi*. Most prolific among Soldani's followers was Antonio Francesco Selvi, whose output included another series, of 111 medals, of the Medicis, as well as medals of *Galileo* and the connoisseur *Andrew Fountaine*. These Florentine medals embody in their size and technique an essentially Renaissance tradition, while their compositions represent a revival of interest in the Antique and Classical taste.

(ii) France. The work of the French medallist Guillaume Dupré is among the finest of all post-Renaissance cast medals. He worked both in France and in Italy, where he was influenced by the work of Leone Leoni, Jacopo da Trezzo and Mola (*see* §III, 1 above). His medals, many uniface and of large diameter, display a brilliant technique in chasing and excel in their attention to detail. They include those of *Francesco de' Medici* (1614–34), *Louis XIII of France, Marcantonio Memmo, Doge of Venice* and *Jean de Saint-Bonnet, Marquis de Toiras* (see fig. 5). The other notable French medallist of the 17th century was

Jean Warin. His cast medals include a bronze portrait (1630) of *Armand-Jean du Plessis, Cardinal de Richelieu*; on the reverse, Fame drives a chariot in which France is seated. Warin also executed a large number of struck medals, including those of *Louis XIV*, his mother, *Anne of Austria* (1601–66), and *Cardinal Jules Mazarin*. A painting attributed to François Lemaire (*c.* 1620–88) depicts Warin showing a medal to a young Louis XIV.

The Petite Académie, established in the 1660s, directed the striking of medallic series commemorating the events of the reign of Louis XIV. The first series was published in 1702; among those to work on it were Jean Mauger, who engraved many of the standard portraits of Louis XIV, as well as some of the reverses, Thomas Bernard (1650–1713), Michel Molart (*fl* 1650–1710) and Hiérome Roussel (1663–1713). The Petite Académie was responsible for the choice of medals, approving the inscriptions and designs, many of which were executed by Sébastien Le Clerc (i). This formalized system resulted in medals that were widely regarded as the most advanced of their time; contemporary foreign medallists used the designs as prototypes for their own work. The Petite Académie's last series was published in 1723, although the format continued to influence the work of such engravers as the prolific Jean Duvivier, who contributed to the series several medals of Louis XV, Joseph Roettier and François Marteau (*c.* 1720–59).

In the last quarter of the 18th century French medallists were free of formal academic constraints. Among the medals of Benjamin Duvivier, the son of Jean Duvivier, were portraits of *Louis XVI*, *Napoleon* and *George Washington*. The American War of Independence was a familiar theme among the medals of Augustin Dupré, whose work includes the celebrated *Libertas Americana* and a portrait of the naval commander *John Paul Jones*. Nicolas-Marie Gatteaux (1751–1832) also produced a number of medals

5. Medal by Guillaume Dupré: *Jean de Saint-Bonnet, Marquis de Toiras* (obverse), cast copper, diam. 59 mm, 1634 (sold Sotheby's, London, 5–6 October 1989, lot 257)

commemorating events in the USA, such as the surrender of General John Burgoyne at Saratoga in 1777, and the storming of Stony Point in 1779; in addition, several of his medals commemorate the foundation of the French Republic.

(iii) The Netherlands. Dutch medallists of the late 16th century and the early 17th owed little to their antecedents (*see* §2(iv) above). The medals they produced, struck, unsigned and without portraits, are distinguished by their low relief and the narrative content of their elaborate compositions. G. van Bijlaer (*fl* 1587–1605) was the most prolific medallist of the genre that recorded religious and military conflicts and alliances in northern Europe (e.g. *Victory of Prince Maurice of Nassau over the Spaniards at Nieuport*, 1600). In marked contrast, both stylistically and compositionally, are a number of high-relief medals comprising silver repoussé plates joined by a broad rim at their edge. Exponents of this school included Pieter van Abeele, whose work includes a portrait of the infant *Prince William III of Orange Nassau*, the border swathed in a wreath of oranges; another was Wouter Müller (*fl* 1653–88), whose medals record the Anglo-Dutch naval battles of the 1660s and include a full-facing bust of *Admiral Martin Tromp.*

The prolific school of Dutch medallists that emerged in the 1680s included Jan Smeltzing, Jan Luder (*fl* 1685–1710) and Jan Boskam (*fl* 1689–1708). Their work, much of which is closely based on contemporary French medal design, commemorates many of the long-running conflicts between France and the Netherlands, and frequently ridicules Louis XIV. In the Low Countries medallic art evolved little in the 18th century. Typical was the work of Martin Holtzhey (1697–1764) and his son Johann George, which includes medals for the centenary in 1748 of the Peace of Westphalia and a prize awarded by the Amsterdam life-saving society in 1767.

(iv) Germany. In the first half of the 17th century the principal centres of medal-making in Germany remained Augsburg and Nuremberg; however, by the mid-17th century, and largely as a result of the Thirty Years War, their influence declined. Christian Maler (*fl* 1603–45) took over his father's medal and goldsmithing business in Nuremberg and produced a number of struck medals of prominent city figures, as well as some for German nobility and Holy Roman Emperors. From the Emperor Ferdinand II he received permission, *cum privilegio*, to strike medals in his own house, as noted on an oval medal of *Queen Elizabeth of Bohemia.* Sebastian Dadler served various court mints in Germany; his medals, many of them large and well detailed, include those of the *Death of Gustav II Adolf of Sweden* (1632), and *Jean Calvin.*

Prominent in the mid-17th century was Johann Blum (*fl* 1630–60), who executed medals for the courts of Brunswick, Saxony and Orange-Nassau, including a medal celebrating the marriage in 1641 of William II of Orange-Nassau and Princess Mary of England. Another noted medallist was Johann Höhn (*fl* 1637–85), whose medals, executed for electoral courts, include a portrait of *Frederick William, Margrave of Brandenburg.*

Philipp Heinrich Müller, who worked at the Augsburg, Nuremberg and Salzburg mints, typifies German medallists of the late 17th century and the early 18th. He produced a large number of medals on various subjects, including the *Battle of La Hogue* (1692), which borrows heavily from a French prototype, and *John William, Elector Palatine of the Rhine* (1711). Many of these medals, and those of contemporary medallists, such as Martin Brunner (1659–1725), Georg Hautsch (1664–1736) and Georg Wilhelm Vestner were published by Freiderich Kleinert (1633–1714), a Nuremberg silversmith and coin dealer; the illustrations may have been produced in collaboration with Caspar Lauffer (*fl* 1700–45), master of the mint at Nuremberg, who issued a catalogue of medals. One of the most successful promoters of the medal in Germany and elsewhere in the early 18th century was Christian Wermuth, who worked for various ducal houses. His output can be numbered in the hundreds and includes a series of Roman emperors, as well as satirical medals, including some of the financier John Law, to mark the collapse of his organization in 1720.

(v) Britain. The anonymous, small-scale and low-relief medals for the coronation of James I in 1603, and for the death of Henry, Prince of Wales, in 1612 were produced at the Royal Mint in London by engravers trained to engrave coinage dies. Nicolas Briot, an experienced coin and medal engraver from the mint in Paris, came to London in the 1620s and worked at the mint. His medals of Charles I include a struck medal for his coronation in 1626 and a large cast medal, dated 1630 and celebrating the King's *Dominion of the Seas.* Thomas Rawlins, who was trained by Briot, made in the 1640s a number of cast badges of Charles I and the Parliamentary generals in the Civil War; these are usually of crude manufacture, in sharp contrast to the work of Abraham Simon and Thomas Simon, which was among the finest produced by medallists in Britain. Their cast medals of politicians, diplomats and the nobility, including *John, Baron de Reede* and *John Thurloe* (for illustration *see* SIMON), display sensitivity and sureness of touch. It would appear that Thomas Simon executed the chasing of the medals, which were based on Abraham Simon's wax models; Thomas also engraved medal dies for Oliver Cromwell, as well as those for the coronation of Charles II (1661) and to celebrate his dominion of the seas (1665).

John Roettier, whose family probably represents the largest dynasty of European medallists, came from the Low Countries to work at the mint for Charles II, producing medals marking events in his reign, including the Restoration. He was subsequently assisted by his sons Norbert Roettier and James Roettier (i), who engraved medals relating to King William III of Orange and Queen Mary II and to the followers of the exiled James II in France. George Bower (*fl* 1660–89), who also worked at the mint, engraved a number of medals commemorating the Protestant–Catholic conflicts of the 1680s, including a medal marking the destruction in 1689 of Catholic chapels in London. John Croker was the chief engraver at the mint; many of his medals, which were principally of British campaigns against France, were based on French medallic designs, for example that for the *Capture of Lille* in 1708.

In the second half of the 18th century medals were largely produced by private medallists. Those by John Kirk (*fl* 1745–75) include *Joshua Reynolds*, while many by

Thomas Pingo the younger (1714–76) were prize medals for various institutions. By the 1790s Birmingham was becoming prominent in medal-making; it was there that medals by Conrad Heinrich Küchler (*c.* 1740–1810) were struck, at Matthew Boulton's factory.

(vi) Other countries. Arvid Karlsteen (1654–1718) of Sweden and Anton Meybusch of Denmark both studied engraving in Paris; they subsequently executed a number of medals at their respective mints in Stockholm and Copenhagen. The Swiss-born Johann Karl Hedlinger was in demand at several European courts and was chief engraver in Stockholm; he produced a large number of medals, including a portrait of *George II of England*, with a terrestrial globe on its reverse.

At St Petersburg the mint attracted German medallists, such as Johann Lorenz Natter, who had also worked in Florence and London. In the 1740s a school of engraving was established, where Samuel Judin (*fl* 1740–80) and Timothey Ivanov (1729–1802), both of whom became prolific medallists of the Russian school, studied die-engraving skills. Elsewhere in Europe during the 18th century medal-making was taking place on a limited scale. In Lisbon Antonio Mengin (*fl* 1720–60) was medallist to John V, of whom he made a medal. In Madrid Tomás Prieto (1716–82) directed production at the court of Charles III; his work includes a medal celebrating the marriage in 1765 of the future Charles IV. To some extent mints in Mexico and Peru benefited from the export of technical expertise from Spain in striking proclamation medals of Charles III. There is evidence of earlier medal-making activity, in the form of an anonymous and crudely cast silver medal for the proclamation of Philip V in 1701, which would seem to be the work of a silversmith. Similarly, cast Indian chiefs' medals made in New York in the 1760s were the work of a silversmith, Daniel Christian Fueter (*fl* 1753–69). Only in the 1790s did a fully fledged medal-making industry become established in the USA, at the mint in Philadelphia.

BIBLIOGRAPHY
Forrer
G. F. Hill: *Medals of the Renaissance* (London, 1920, rev. 1978)
A. S. Norris and I. Weber: *Medals and Plaquettes from the Molinari Collection at Bowdoin College* (Brunswick, ME, 1976)

CHRISTOPHER EIMER

4. 19TH CENTURY. The most successful and influential example of 19th-century medallic Neo-classicism was the *Histoire métallique* of some 90 medals commemorating events from the Napoleonic Wars, struck (1804–14) at the Monnaie des Médailles in Paris, under the direction of Vivant Denon. The medals, designed by such artists as Alexandre Evariste Fragonard and Antoine-Denis Chaudet and engraved by the likes of Bertrand Andrieu, Nicolas-Guy Brenet and Romain-Vincent Jeuffroy, became, after the end of hostilities, highly popular souvenirs of a dramatic period of European history and spawned at least two imitations. In Russia Count Fyodor Tolstoy produced a series of 19 medals, while in Britain the series of National Medals issued in 1820 by James Mudie commemorated British successes between 1794 and 1817; it is ironic that Mudie, unable to secure sufficient numbers of British die-engravers, had to turn to French artists for many of his

designs. British medallists who did contribute included the young William Wyon, who was responsible for the reverse of the medal (1818) commemorating the earliest event to be depicted, the victory over the French fleet off Ushant in 1794 (Brown, 1980, no. 387). Wyon later produced the first of the series of 30 medals for the Art-Union of London; issued over 60 years, they constitute the most significant example of medallic patronage in Victorian Britain.

Wyon's great rival, Benedetto Pistrucci, who was working in London from 1815, also produced medals in the Neo-classical taste, but fewer of them; and, although both artists had influential supporters, Pistrucci's medals were generally regarded as less successful than Wyon's. A comparison between Wyon's portrait of *Queen Victoria* on the medal commemorating her visit to the City of London in 1837 (Brown, 1987, no. 1775) and Pistrucci's design for the official coronation medal in 1838 (Brown, 1987, no. 1801) reveals a certain degree of lifelessness in the latter. Besides producing allegorical scenes in the Neo-classical style, Wyon could satisfy a taste for the Gothick, as in his rendition of *Bodiam Castle* (1830; Brown, 1980, no. 1456), and was capable of a detailed realism, as in the view of Newcastle upon Tyne on his *Newcastle to Carlisle Railway* medal (1840; see fig. 6; Brown, 1987, no. 1983). Compatriots of Pistrucci who worked in the Neo-classical style included Luigi Manfredini (1771–1840)—who made a number of medallic portraits of Napoleon—and Francesco Putinati (*c.* 1775–1848), both of whom were active in Milan; Gerolamo Vassallo (1771–1819), who worked in Genoa; Tommaso Mercandetti (1758–1821) in Rome; and Giovanni Antonio Santarelli in Florence. In Switzerland the principal exponent of the style was Henri François Brandt (1789–after 1845), who had studied under Jacques-Louis David in Paris and with Antonio Canova and Bertel Thorvaldsen in Rome.

6. Medal by William Wyon: *Newcastle to Carlisle Railway* (obverse), struck silver, diam. 50 mm, 1840 (London, British Museum)

In France the Neo-classical tradition remained dominant throughout the greater part of the 19th century in the medals of such artists as Emile Rogat (1770–1852), Jean-Pierre Montagny (1789–1862), Jean-Jacques Barré (1793–1855) and Valentin Maurice Borrel. The tendency to greater elaboration and more realistic detail that is discernible in their work is also pronounced in the medals of other countries. Aleksandr Lyalin (1802–62) in St Petersburg, Joseph Daniel Boehm (1794–1865) and Konrad Lange (1806–56) in Vienna, Wilhelm Kullrich (1821–87) in Berlin, Laurent Joseph Hart (1810–60) in Brussels and Leonard Charles Wyon (son of William Wyon) in London were all skilled engravers and highly accomplished portraitists, while the Belgian Léopold Wiener (1823–91) and his brothers produced a series of architectural medals, with highly detailed views of interiors and exteriors of historic buildings. In the 19th century there was more serious medal production in the USA, with such artists as the Hungarian-born Moritz Fürst (1782–after 1838) and later Charles Barber (1840–1917), a native of London, serving as engravers to the United States Mint in Philadelphia.

Alongside the work of such artists, increased mechanization led to a proliferation of mass-produced medals and medalets, generally of inferior quality. The application of steam power to the striking process, developed in the late 18th century by Matthew Boulton and James Watt, and improved upon in the early 19th century by Diedrich Uhlhorn, made possible the production of large numbers of medals in cheap, usually white-metal alloys. Edward Thomason (1769–1849), who had learnt his trade under Boulton, was able to produce over 50,000 medals for the Yorkshire parliamentary election of 1807 (Brown, 1980, nos 623–4). Later in the century, no coronation, jubilee or other major public celebration passed unaccompanied by a large number of souvenir medals, and other events were recorded in medals issued by companies, institutions and individuals. Prize medals, issued by societies and educational establishments, grew in popularity, and in many countries the use of medals as military awards was now systematized.

The increasing use of the reducing machine had a profound impact on medal production. Previously, medal dies had been produced by engravers, who, whether following their own designs or those of another artist, either cut direct into the steel die or engraved punches from which the dies were made up. With the advent of the pantographic reducing machine, a punch could be produced from a sculptor's larger model. William Wyon owned a reducing machine, and by the end of the century mechanical reduction was the standard practice. This made it possible for sculptors and modellers to produce medals without the intervention of a die-engraver. In Britain in the 1880s and 1890s exponents of the New Sculpture, such as Alfred Gilbert, George Frampton and William Goscombe John, produced medals in this way, the softly modelled forms, lyrical compositions and matt finish of which echo contemporary developments on the Continent, where the French medallists Jules-Clément Chaplain and Oscar Roty were the first to introduce these characteristics. Medals were extremely popular in late 19th-century France; such artists as Georges Prud'homme,

Daniel Dupuis (1849–99), Georges Dupré and Ovide Yencesse (1869–1947) produced numerous medals, many of which have no commemorative function but are simply objects of beauty. The major centre of medal production that rivalled Paris was Vienna, where Anton Scharff (1845–1903) was Court Medallist and Stefan Schwartz taught at the Kunstgewerbeschule; the latter's many distinguished pupils included Rudolph Marschall (b 1873). The Austrian Emil Fuchs brought the Viennese style to Britain and later worked in the USA, where Augustus Saint-Gaudens, who had studied in Paris, was the most important artist working in the field.

Parallel with the 19th-century proliferation of the struck medal, and partly as a reaction against its commercialization, was the revival of the cast medal. The leading figure in this development was the French sculptor David d'Angers, who began a series of medallic portraits in the 1820s, continuing to add to it until the 1850s. Other French artists who took up the idea included Auguste Préault, Henri Chapu, Alexandre Charpentier and Gustave Deloye (1838–99). Alphonse Legros, resident in London from 1863, introduced the cast medal to Britain in the 1880s, and a number of British artists, including Edward John Poynter and Hamo Thornycroft, followed his example; moreover, as Professor of Fine Art at London's Slade School, Legros was able to introduce the subject to a generation of students. A number of the students of his compatriot Edouard Lanteri, who taught at the South Kensington schools, also went on to produce medals.

BIBLIOGRAPHY

De la 1ère à la 3e République, ii of *Catalogue général illustré des éditions de la Monnaie de Paris* (Paris, n.d.)

R. Marx: *Les Médailleurs français contemporains* (Paris, n.d.)

——: *Les Médailleurs français depuis 1789* (Paris, 1897)

H.-J. de Dompierre de Chaufepié: *Les Médailles et plaquettes modernes*, 3 vols (Haarlem, 1899–1907)

La Médaille en France de Ponscarme à la fin de la Belle Epoque (exh. cat. by Y. Goldenberg, Paris, Hôtel de la Monnaie, 1967)

J. Taylor: *The Architectural Medal: England in the Nineteenth Century* (London, 1978)

L. Brown: *British Historical Medals, 1760–1837* (London, 1980)

La medaglia neoclassica in Italia e in Europa: Atti del quarto convegno internazionale di studio: Udine, 1981

E. B. Sullivan: *American Political Badges and Medalets, 1789–1892* (Laurence, MA, 1981)

D. Fearon: *Victorian Souvenir Medals* (Princes Risborough, 1986)

L. Brown: *British Historical Medals, 1837–1901* (London, 1987)

A. Griffiths: 'The Design and Production of Napoleon's *Histoire métallique*', *The Medal*, 16 (1990), pp. 16–30

——: 'The Origins of Napoleon's *Histoire métallique*', *The Medal*, 17 (1990), pp. 28–38

——: 'The End of Napoleon's *Histoire métallique*', *The Medal*, 18 (1991), pp. 39–49

J. de Caso: *David d'Angers: Sculptural Communication in the Age of Romanticism* (Princeton, 1992)

Artistic Circles: The Medal in Britain, 1880–1918 (exh. cat. by P. Attwood, BM, 1992)

5. 20TH CENTURY. Early in the 20th century there was little change in the prevailing classicizing, naturalistic style of the struck medal that was established by Chaplain and Roty. In France such artists as Marie-Alexandre-Lucien Coudray, Jules Legastelois, Georges Prud'homme and Séraphin Vernier (1852–1927) continued to produce such medals up to, and even after World War I. Likewise, such European artists as the Belgian Pierre Theunis (1883–1950), the Czech Heinrich Kautsch (1859–1943) and

Stanislav Sucharda, and the Swedish Erik Lindberg (1873–1966) produced beautiful medals that were increasingly out of step with the times. The unprecedented carnage of World War I led German medallists to develop a radically new style that paralleled the Expressionism of other arts of the period. Some artists, such as Joseph Gangl and Karl Xaver Goetz, the most prolific of the contemporary German medallists, incorporated propaganda messages into their medals, but the horror of war underlies all their work (e.g. medal struck to commemorate the sinking of the *Lusitania*). Its principal features were an uncompromising and at times brutal style, the predominance of the image of the skeleton and the revival of the medieval Dance of Death theme and the use of cast iron rather than the more usual bronze. The medals of Ludwig Gies (see fig. 7) and Erzsébeth Esseö (1883–1954) are particularly haunting. This type of medal was not made outside Germany and did not long survive the war, although Goetz continued to make satirical and propaganda medals up to and throughout World War II. The inter-war period was dominated by the emergence of the hard-edged, stylized Art Deco medal. France was the major producer of such medals and Pierre Turin (1891–1968) the most accomplished practitioner, although other artists adapted their style to accord with the new fashion. Belgium was also an important centre, with such artists as Josuë Dupon (1864–1935) producing fine work. In Britain a group of young medallists worked in a similar style, encouraged by the Deputy Master of the Royal Mint, Sir Robert Johnson, who was indefatigable in promoting the art of the medal; Percy Metcalfe and J. Langford Jones were the foremost of his protégés. In the USA the industrial designer Norman Bel Geddes produced a memorable image for General Motors; less adventurous were the medal designs of Paul Manship and Carl Paul Jennewein (1890–1978).

The production of cheap, mass-produced, inartistic medals has remained a feature of the 20th century, as it was of the 19th. However, since World War II there has been a dramatic broadening in both the form and the function of the medal, with artists increasingly using the medium as a means of personal expression. The rise of the art medal has been accompanied by growing public interest and an increasing number of collectors. This process has been aided by the Fédération Internationale de la Médaille (FIDEM), founded in 1937, which brings together artists, manufacturers, art historians and collectors; since the 1960s it has organized biennial international exhibitions of contemporary medals in different locations around the world. Societies devoted to the art of the medal have arisen in many countries, including the Netherlands, France, Finland, Great Britain, Japan and the USA. They promote the subject by commissioning new medals and encouraging greater public interest. Particularly prominent in the post-war period have been the countries of eastern Europe. State support of the arts, combined with a tendency by communist governments not to oversee medal design with the rigour applied to other media, left artists relatively free in their medal work. A vast amount of creative endeavour placed Poland, Hungary and Czechoslovakia in the forefront of the international contemporary medal scene, and from the 1980s the medal was established as a significant art form in Bulgaria, a country with no long-standing medallic tradition. The overthrow of communism in Europe in the late 1980s increased the range of themes available to medallists and itself became a subject commemorated by many medallists. Artists from both West and East Germany produced a large number of medals celebrating the removal of the Berlin Wall and the subsequent reunification of their country.

In the late 20th century many of the defining characteristics of the medal were stripped away, as artists dispensed with traditional notions of the medal. Abstraction and minimalism have altered many artists' approach, and the boundaries between the medal and other art forms have become blurred. Medals may now be made of glass, as, for example, those of the Hungarian Maria Lugossy (*b* 1950), who was active from the 1970s and went on to add bronze elements to her work. The Dutch artist Lijsbeth Teding van Berkhout (*b* 1946) used glass, charcoal and steel in her medals. Ready-made objects are also found, as in the work of the French artist Roger Bezombes, who produced arresting images by incorporating, for example, ball-bearings. The American James Malone Beach (*b* 1947) went further, using coins, beads, toys, enamelwork and photographic images to create evocative and poignant images. The use of enamelled colour, especially by such jewellers as Britain's Fred Rich (*b* 1954), has added to the possibilities provided by the variations of patina. Construction has been added to the traditional techniques of casting and striking, while in the Netherlands in the late 20th century the application of industrial techniques to medal manufacture has resulted in an extraordinary body of work that defies the contemporary move away from abstraction towards the figurative.

The medal is now also firmly established in many countries outside Europe and the USA. In some cases this development can be traced to the influence of one particular artist. Andor Meszaros (1900–1972) fled his native Hungary in 1939 to live in Australia, where he and subsequently his son Michael Meszaros (*b* 1945) worked

7. Medal by Ludwig Gies: *Dance of Death* (obverse), cast iron, diam. 120 mm, 1917 (London, British Museum)

as medallists. Likewise, Dora de Pedery-Hunt (*b* 1913) from Budapest was single-handedly responsible for introducing the concept of the art medal to Canada. Certain Far Eastern countries, notably Japan and Korea, have active medallists. The increasing number of countries participating in the FIDEM exhibitions demonstrates the vibrancy of the medium and its relevance to the modern world.

BIBLIOGRAPHY

De 1945 à nos jours, iv of *Catalogue général illustré des éditions de la Monnaie de Paris* (Paris, n.d.)

Catalogue of the International Exhibition of Contemporary Medals (exh. cat., intro. A. Baldwin; New York, Amer. Numi. Soc., 1910)

Médailles, Fédération Internationale de la Médaille (1938–)

M. Jones: *The Dance of Death* (London, 1979)

The Medal, British Art Medal Society (1982–)

Contemporary British Medals (exh. cat. by M. Jones, London, BM, 1986)

E. Smite: *Medalu maksla* (Riga, 1987)

The Beaux-Arts Medal in America (exh. cat. by B. A. Baxter, New York, Amer. Numi. Soc., 1987)

Aufbruch-Durchbruch: Zeitzeichen in der deutschen Medaillenkunst (exh. cat. by W. Steguweit and I. S. Weber; Munich Staatl. Münzsamml.; Berlin, Bodemus.; 1990)

Die Kunstmedaille der Gegenwart in Deutschland (exh. cat. by W. Steguweit and I. S. Weber, Berlin, Bodemus., 1992)

PHILIP ATTWOOD

Illustration Acknowledgements

We are grateful to those listed below for permission to reproduce copyright illustrative material and to those contributors who supplied photographs or helped us to obtain them. The word 'Photo:' precedes the names of large commercial or archival sources who have provided us with photographs, as well as the names of individual photographers (where known). It has generally not been used before the names of owners of works of art, such as museums and civic bodies. Every effort has been made to contact copyright holders and to credit them appropriately; we apologize to anyone who may have been omitted from the acknowledgements or cited incorrectly. Any error brought to our attention will be corrected in subsequent editions. Where illustrations have been taken from books, publication details are provided in the acknowledgements below.

Line drawings, maps, plans, chronological tables and family trees commissioned by the *Dictionary of Art* are not included in the list below. All of the maps in the dictionary were produced by Oxford Illustrators Ltd, who were also responsible for some of the line drawings. Most of the line drawings and plans, however, were drawn by one of the following artists: Diane Fortenberry, Lorraine Hodghton, Chris Miners, Amanda Patton, Mike Pringle, Jo Richards, Miranda Schofield, John Tiernan, John Wilson and Philip Winton. The chronological tables and family trees were prepared initially by Kate Boatfield and finalized by John Johnson.

Machuca, Pedro Photo: Anthony Kersting, London

Machu Picchu *1* Ancient Art and Architecture Collection, London/ Photo: J. Stevens

Machzor Bodleian Library, Oxford (MS. Laud Or. 321, fol. 127*v*)

Maçip: (2) Juan de Juanes Museo del Prado, Madrid

Macke, August Städtische Galerie im Lenbachhaus, Munich

McKim, Mead & White *1–2* Library of Congress, Washington, DC; *3* New-York Historical Society, New York

Mackintosh, Charles Rennie *1, 3* Royal Commission on Ancient Monuments, Scotland/© Crown Copyright; *2, 4* Hunterian Art Gallery, University of Glasgow

Maclise, Daniel National Gallery of Ireland, Dublin

Madagascar *1* Photo: Hilary Bradt; *2* Photo: John Mack; *3* Trustees of the British Museum, London; *4* Field Museum of Natural History, Chicago, IL (neg. no. 109022)

Madarász, Viktor Hungarian National Museum, Budapest

Maderno, Carlo *1* Photo: Archivi Alinari, Florence

Maderno, Stefano Photo: Archivi Alinari, Florence

Madonnero Photo: Archivi Alinari, Florence

Madras Photo: Philip Davies

Madrasa *1–2* Photo: W. Denny

Madrazo: (1) José de Madrazo y Agudo Museo del Prado, Madrid

Madrazo: (2) Federico de Madrazo y Küntz Museo del Prado, Madrid

Madrid *1, 3–4* Photo: Ampliaciones y Reproducciones MAS, Barcelona; *2, 8* Photo: Robert Harding Picture Library, London; *5–6* Biblioteca Nacional, Madrid; *7* Photo: Patrimonio Nacional Archivo Fotográfico, Madrid

Madurai Photo: © American Institute of Indian Studies, Varanasi

Maekawa, Kunio Photo: Yoshio Watanabe

Maes, Nicolaes *1* Board of Trustees of the Victoria and Albert Museum, London; *2* Bayerische Staatsgemäldesammlungen, Munich

Maes Howe Photo: © Historic Scotland

Maffei, Francesco Photo: Gabinetto Fotografico, Soprintendenza ai Artistici e Storici, Venice

Mafra Photo: Conway Library, Courtauld Institute of Art, London

Magdeburg *1–2* Photo: Bildarchiv Foto Marburg

Magnasco: (2) Alessandro Magnasco Musée des Beaux-Arts, Bordeaux/Photo: Alain Danvers

Magritte, René *1* Museum of Modern Art, New York (Kay Savage Tanguy Fund)/© ADAGP, Paris, and DACS, London, 1996; *2–3* Musée National d'Art Moderne, Paris

Ma Hezhi Metropolitan Museum of Art, New York (Gift of J. Pierpont Morgan, by exchange; no. 1973.121.3)

Mahlstick Board of Trustees of the Victoria and Albert Museum, London

Maiano, da: (1) Giuliano da Maiano Photo: James Austin, Cambridge

Maiano, da: (2) Benedetto da Maiano Photo: Archivi Alinari, Florence

Maidum Egyptian Museum, Cairo

Maillart, Robert Architectural Association, London

Maillol, Aristide Photo: © RMN, Paris

Maimonides manuscripts Library of the Hungarian Academy of Sciences, Budapest (MS. Kaufmann A77/II, fol. 48a)

Mainardi, Bastiano Indianapolis Museum of Art, Indianapolis, IN (Gift of Mrs Booth Tarkington in memory of her husband)

Maino, Juan Bautista Museo del Prado, Madrid

Mainz *1* Photo: Bildarchiv Foto Marburg; *2* Bischöfliches Dom- und Diözesanmuseum, Mainz

Majiayao Photo: Cultural Relics Publishing House, Beijing

Makart, Hans Kunstmuseum, St Gall

Makonde Photo: Mohammed Peera

Maksimov, Vasily Photo: NOVOSTI Photo Library, London

Málaga Photo: Ampliaciones y Reproducciones MAS, Barcelona

Malawi Ministry of External Affairs, Blantyre/Photo: Willie Nampeya, Blantyre

Malaysia *2–3* Photo: Helen I. Jessup; *4* British Library, London (Or. MS. 13295); *5* Photo: Susan Conway; *6* © Tettoni, Cassio and Associates Pte Ltd, Singapore; *7* Photo: Victor T. King

Malbork Castle Photo: Bildarchiv Foto Marburg

Malczewski, Jacek Photo: Henryk Pieczul

Maler, Hans (i) Society of Antiquaries of London

Mälesskircher, Gabriel Bayerische Staatsbibliothek, Munich

Malevich, Kazimir *1* Stedelijk Museum, Amsterdam; *2* Museum of Modern Art, New York

Malhoa, José Museu da Cidade, Lisbon/Photo: Antonio Rafael

Mali *1–2* Museum für Völkerkunde, Basle

Mallia Ekdotiki Athenon SA, Athens

Malouel, Jean Photo: © RMN, Paris

Malta *1* © Malta Government Tourist Board, Valletta; *2* Photo: Quentin Hughes; *3–4* Museum of Fine Arts, Valletta; *5* Photo: Malta National Tourist Office, London; *6* Department of Information, Valletta

Mamallapuram *1–2* Photo: Michael D. Rabe

Mamluk, §II: (3) Al-Nasir Muhammad Trustees of the British Museum, London

Mamluk, §II: (10) Qa'itbay Photo: Ancient Art and Architecture Collection, London

Mancadan, Jacobus Sibrandi Groninger Museum, Groningen

Mancheng Photo: Robert Harding Picture Library, London

Manchester *1* Lawrence and Wrightson, London; *2* Photo: Manchester Public Libraries, Central Library, Manchester

Mander, van: (1) Karel van Mander I *1* British Library, London (no. 1401.g.53); *2* Bibliothèque Royale Albert 1er, Brussels; *3* Kunsthalle, Bremen; *4* Städelsches Kunstinstitut, Frankfurt am Main

Mandu Photo: Robert Harding Picture Library, London

Manet, Edouard *1* Photo: © RMN, Paris; *2* Staatliche Museen zu Berlin, Preussischer Kulturbesitz; *3* Courtauld Institute Galleries, London; *4* Harvard University Art Museums, Cambridge, MA

Manetti, Rutilio Pinacoteca Nazionale, Siena/Photo: Jean du Champ Gioco della Morra

Manfredi, Bartolomeo *1* Art Institute of Chicago, IL/© 1996. All rights reserved; *2* Photo: Arch. Phot. Paris /© DACS, 1996

Mangbetu London Library

Manguin, Henri Musée National d'Art Moderne, Paris

Manila Cultural Center of the Philippines, Manila

Mannerism *1–2* Photo: Archivi Alinari, Florence

Mannheim Reiss-Museum der Stadt Mannheim

Manohar Cincinnati Art Museum, Cincinnati, OH (Gift of John J. Emery)

Manpukuji Obakusan Manpukuji Bunkaden, Kyoto

Man Ray Museum of Modern Art, New York (Purchase)/© Man Ray Trust/ADAGP, Paris, and DACS, London, 1996

Mansart: (1) François Mansart *1* Bibliothèque Nationale de France, Paris; *2* Country Life Picture Library, London/Photo: Frederick Evans; *3* Photo: Bildarchiv Foto Marburg; *4* Photo: Conway Library, Courtauld Institute of Art, London

Mansart: (2) Jules Hardouin Mansart *1*, *3* Photo: James Austin, Cambridge; *2* Photo: British Architectural Library, RIBA, London; *4* Photo: Arch. Phot. Paris/© DACS, 1996

Mansur Board of Trustees of the Victoria and Albert Museum, London

Mantegazza Board of Trustees of the Victoria and Albert Museum, London

Mantegna, Andrea *1* Photo: Overseas Agenzia Fotografica, Milan; *2* Photo: Archivi Alinari, Florence; *3*, *5* Photo: © RMN, Paris; *4* Staatliche Museen zu Berlin, Preussischer Kulturbesitz; *6* Trustees of the National Gallery, London

Manteño Photo: © ACL Brussels

Mantua *1–3* Photo: Foto Giovetti, Mantua

Manual, manuscript Niedersächsische Staats- und Universitätsbibliothek, Göttingen

Manuscript *1* Trustees of the British Museum, London; *2* British Library, London (Or. MS. 5309); *3* British Library, London (Or. MS. 6660.71); *4* British Library, London (Ind. Ch. MS. 4); *5* Bodleian Library, Oxford; *6*, *14* Photo: Conway Library, Courtauld Institute of Art, London; *7*, *9* Bibliothèque Nationale de France, Paris; *8* Board of Trustees of the Victoria and Albert Museum, London; *10* Syndics of Cambridge University Library/Photo: Conway Library, Courtauld Institute of Art, London; *11* British Library, London (MS. 2897, fol. 188); *12* Stonyhurst College, Clitheroe, Lancs; *13* Photo: Bildarchiv, Österreichische Nationalbibliothek, Vienna; *15* Bodleian Library, Oxford (MS. Douce 180, fol. 92)/Photo: Conway Library, Courtauld Institute of Art, London

Manzoni, Piero Museum of Modern Art, New York (Gift of Fratelli Fabbri Editori and Purchase)

Manzù, Giacomo Tate Gallery, London

Maori *1–2* Institute and Museum, Auckland; *3* Etnografiska Museum, Stockholm/Photo: Bo Gabrielsson; *4* Museum of New Zealand Te Papa Tongarewa, Wellington (neg. no. B18760); *5* Photo: City Art Gallery, Auckland

Map *1* British Library (MS. 28681, fol. 9*r*); *2* Hereford Cathedral; *3* Photo: Ms Susan Kish; *4* Photo: Archivi Alinari, Florence

Maqsūra Creswell Archive, Ashmolean Museum, Oxford (EMA II, pl. 89a; neg. no. C. 530)

Marajó South American Pictures, Woodbridge, Suffolk/Photo: Tony Morrison

Maratti, Carlo *1* Photo: © ACL Brussels; *2* Photo: Archivi Alinari, Florence; *3* Vatican Museums, Vatican City, Rome; *4* Photo: National Trust Photo Library, London

Marburg, Elisabethkirche Photo: Bildarchiv Foto Marburg

Marc, Franz Städtische Galerie im Lenbachhaus, Munich

Marçal de Sas, Andrés Photo: Ampliaciones y Reproducciones MAS, Barcelona

Marchant, Nathaniel Trustees of the British Museum, London

Marchesi, Pompeo Photo: Bildarchiv, Österreichische Nationalbibliothek, Vienna

Marchionni, Carlo Photo: Archivi Alinari, Florence

Marcks, Gerhard Christie's, London/Photo: A.C. Cooper Ltd, London

Mardel, Carlos Art Archive of the Calouste Gulbenkian Foundation, Lisbon/Photo: Carlos de Azevedo

Marées, Hans von Bayerische Staatsgemäldesammlungen, Munich

Margarito d'Arezzo National Gallery of Art, Washington, DC (Samuel H. Kress Collection)

Mari *1* Musée du Louvre, Paris/Photo: Vuillet; *2* Mission Archéologique Française, Tell-Hariri

Mariana Islands Bernice P. Bishop Museum Archives, Honolulu, HI/Photo: Hans Hornbostle

Marieschi, Michele Giovanni Trustees of the National Gallery, London

Mariette: (4) Pierre-Jean Mariette Ashmolean Museum, Oxford

Marilhat, Prosper Photo: Giraudon, Paris

Marine painting Trustees of the National Gallery, London

Marinetti, Filippo Tommaso © DACS, 1996

Marini, Marino Fondazione Marino Marini, Pistoia

Maris: (1) Jacob Maris Rijksdienst Beeldende Kunsten, Amsterdam, on loan to the Centraal Museum, Utrecht

Maris: (3) Willem Maris Haags Gemeentemuseum, The Hague

Marks *1* Photo: © ACL Brussels; *3* Pierpont Morgan Library, New York (no. I,97); *4* Pierpont Morgan Library, New York (no. IV,79c)

Marlik Iran Bastan Museum, Tehran

Marly Photo: © RMN, Paris

Marmion, Simon *2* Bibliothèque Royale Albert 1er, Brussels

Marmitta, Francesco National Gallery of Scotland, Edinburgh

Marot: (1) Jean Marot I British Library, London (no. 61.d.5)

Marot: (2) Daniel Marot I Rijksmuseum Paleis Het Loo, Apeldoorn

Marquesas Islands Photothèque du Musée de l'Homme, Paris

Marquet, Albert Musée National d'Art Moderne, Paris/© ADAGP, Paris, and DACS, London, 1996

Marquetry *1* Rijksmuseum, Amsterdam; *2* Royal Collection, Windsor Castle/© Her Majesty Queen Elizabeth II; *3* National Trust, Waddesdon Manor, Bucks

Marseille *1* Photo: © Yves Gallois Photographie Acclam, Marseille; *2–3* Musée d'Histoire de Marseille

Martin, John Private collection, United Kingdom

Martin, Mungo Royal British Columbia Museum, Victoria, BC (no. CPN 7857)

Martinelli, Giovanni Photo: Scala, Florence

Martinez Millicent Rogers Museum, Taos, NM

Martínez, Jusepe Photo: Ampliaciones y Reproducciones MAS, Barcelona

Martini, Simone *1* Sacro Convento di San Francesco, Siena/Photo: P. Gerhard Ruf; *2* Photo: Scala, Florence; *3* Barber Institute of Fine Arts, University of Birmingham; *4* Photo: Andrew Martindale

Martorell, Bernat *1* Art Institute of Chicago, IL/© 1996. All rights reserved; *2* Photo: Ampliaciones y Reproducciones MAS, Barcelona

Martorell, Bohigas, Mackay Photo: Ampliaciones y Reproducciones MAS, Barcelona

Maruscelli, Paolo British Library, London (no. 177.f.18)

Maruyama Ōkyo National Research Institute, Tokyo

Masaccio *1* Trustees of the National Gallery, London; *2* Staatliche Museen zu Berlin, Preussischer Kulturbesitz; *3* Museo e Gallerie Nazionali di Capodimonte, Naples/Photo: Overseas Agenzia Fotografica, Milan; *4–6* Photo: Archivi Alinari, Florence

Mascherino, Ottaviano Photo: Archivi Alinari, Florence

Masegne, dalle *1–2* Photo: Osvaldo Böhm, Venice

Maser, Villa Barbaro Centro Palladiano, Vicenza

Maskana Photo: © RMN, Paris

Maso di Banco Photo: Archivi Alinari, Florence

Masolino *1*, *3–4* Photo: Archivi Alinari, Florence; *2* Photo: Gabinetto Fotografico, Soprintendenza ai Beni Artistici e Storici, Florence

Mason (i) *1* Burgerbibliothek Bern, Berne; *2* Bibliothèque Royale Albert 1er, Brussels; *3* Universitätsbibliothek Würzburg (no. 4 an I.t.q.XXXX); *4* Germanisches Nationalmuseum, Nuremberg

Masonry *4* British Library, London (no. 61.i.3); *5* British Library, London (no. 1899.g.2); *6*, *8*, *10* Photo: British Architectural Library, RIBA, London

Mass Observation Photo: Humphrey Spender, 1937

Masson, André Museum of Modern Art, New York (Purchase)/© ADAGP, Paris, and DACS, London, 1996

Mass production *1* Henry Ford Museum and Greenfield Village, Dearborn, MI; *2* Hille International

Mastelletta Photo: Gabinetto Fotografico Nazionale, Istituto Centrale per il Catalogo e la Documentazione, Rome

Master printers *1* Milwaukee Art Museum, Milwaukee, WI (Gift of Mrs Harry Lynde Bradley); *2* Metropolitan Museum of Art, New York (Gift of Arthur Sachs, 1916; no. 16.3.1); *3* Toledo Museum of Art, Toledo, OH (Gift of Molly and Walter Bareiss in honour of Barbara K. Sutherland); *4* Universal Limited Art Editions, West Islip, NY; *5* Photo: © ARS, New York, and DACS, London, 1996 *6* Edition Schellmann, Cologne and New York/© DACS, 1996; *7* Brooke Alexander Editions, Inc., New York/Photo: Eric Pollitzer, Hempstead, NY

Masters, anonymous, and monogrammists, §I:

Master of the Aachen Altar Domkapitel Aachen/Photo: Ann Munchow

Master of Adelaide of Savoy Photo: Giraudon, Paris

Master of the Aix Annunciation Photo: Giraudon, Paris

Master of the Annunciation to the Shepherds City of Birmingham Museum and Art Gallery

Master of the Barbarigo Reliefs Photo: Osvaldo Böhm, Venice

Bedford Master *1* British Library, London (Add. MS. 18850); *2* Bibliothèque Nationale de France, Paris

Master of Berry's Cleres Femmes Bibliothèque Nationale de France, Paris

Boucicaut Master *1* Musée Jacquemart-André, Paris; *2* Bibliothèque Publique et Universitaire, Geneva

Master of the Brunswick Diptych Herzog Anton Ulrich-Museum, Brunswick

Master of the Brussels Initials British Library, London (Add. MS. 29433)

Master of Cabestany Museu Frederic Marés, Barcelona

Candlelight Master Fine Arts Museums of San Francisco, CA (Gift of Archer M. Huntington in memory of Collis P. Huntington)

Master of Catherine of Cleves *1–2* Pierpont Morgan Library, New York

Master of Charles of France Metropolitan Museum of Art, New York (Cloisters Collection, 1958)

Master of the Cité des Dames Bibliothèque Nationale de France, Paris

Master of the Codex of St George Biblioteca Apostolica Vaticana, Rome

Master of Coëtivy Photo: © RMN, Paris

Master of the Darmstadt Passion Hessisches Landesmuseum, Darmstadt

Master of Delft Rijksmuseum, Amsterdam

Master of the della Rovere Missals Pierpont Morgan Library, New York

Master of the Dresden Prayerbook Sächsische Landesbibliothek, Dresden

Master of the Embroidered Foliage Photo: © ACL Brussels

Master of Evert van Soudenbalch Photo: Bildarchiv, Österreichische Nationalbibliothek, Vienna

Master of the Female Half-lengths Photo: © RMN, Paris

Master of Flémalle *1–2* Städelsches Kunstinstitut, Frankfurt am Main; *3* Trustees of the National Gallery, London

Master of Flora Metropolitan Museum of Art, New York (Rogers Fund, 1941; no. 41.48)

Master of the Fogg Pietà Harvard University Art Museums, Cambridge, MA (Gift of Meta and Paul J. Sachs)

Master of Frankfurt Photo: © ACL Brussels

Freake Painter Worcester Art Museum, Worcester, MA (Gift of Mr and Mrs Albert W. Rice)

Gold Scrolls Group British Library, London (Add. MS. 39638)

Master of Guillebert de Metz Bibliothèque Nationale de France, Paris

Housebook Master *1–2* Rijksmuseum, Amsterdam

Illustratore Biblioteca Apostolica Vaticana, Rome

Isaac Master Photo: Archivi Alinari, Florence

Master of James IV of Scotland Photo: Bildarchiv, Österreichische Nationalbibliothek, Vienna

Master of Jean Rolin Photo: Peter Rolfe Monks

Master of King René of Anjou *1* Photo: Bildarchiv, Österreichische Nationalbibliothek, Vienna; *2* Bibliothèque Nationale de France, Paris

Master of Latin 757 Bibliothèque Nationale de France, Paris

Master of the Legend of St Lucy Photo: © ACL Brussels

Master of the Legend of St Mary Magdalene Statens Museum for Kunst, Copenhagen

Master of Margaret of Orleans Bibliothèque Nationale de France, Paris

Master of Mary of Burgundy *1* Photo: Bildarchiv, Österreichische Nationalbibliothek, Vienna; *2* Bodleian Library, Oxford (MSS Douce 219-20, fol. 132*v*); *3* Biblioteca Nacional, Madrid; *4* Staatliche Museen zu Berlin, Preussischer Kulturbesitz/Kupferstichkabinett

Master of the Mascoli Altar Photo: Archivi Alinari, Florence

Master of Moulins *1* Photo: Giraudon, Paris; *2* Bayerische Staatsgemäldesammlungen, Munich

Master of the Munich Golden Legend Walters Art Gallery, Baltimore, MD

Master of the Older Prayerbook of Maximilian Photo: Bildarchiv, Österreichische Nationalbibliothek, Vienna

Master of the Osservanza Photo: Archivi Alinari, Florence

Master of the Parement de Narbonne Photo: Scala, Florence

Master of the Playing Cards Museum of Fine Arts, Boston, MA

Master of the Prado Redemption Museo del Prado, Madrid

Master of the Registrum Gregorii Stadtbibliothek, Trier

Master of the Rohan Hours Bibliothèque Nationale de France, Paris

Master of the St Bartholomew Altar Bayerische Staatsgemäldesammlungen, Munich

St Cecilia Master (i) Photo: Archivi Alinari, Florence

Master of St Francis Trustees of the National Gallery, London

Master of the St Francis Legend Photo: Archivi Alinari, Florence

Master of St Giles Trustees of the National Gallery, London

Master of St Veronica Bayerische Staatsgemäldesammlungen, Munich

Silver Birch Master Trustees of the National Gallery, London

Stratonice Master Photo: Maurizia Tazartes

Master of the Tiburtine Sibyl Städelsches Kunstinstitut, Frankfurt am Main

Master of Třeboň National Gallery, Prague/Photo: Vladimir Fyman

Master of the Triumph of Death Photo: Archivi Alinari, Florence

Master of the Unicorn Hunt Metropolitan Museum of Art, New York (Cloisters Collection; Gift of John D. Rockefeller Jr, 1937; no. 37.80.4)

Master of the Unruly Children Board of Trustees of the Victoria and Albert Museum, London

Master of the View of Ste Gudule Photo: © RMN, Paris

Master of the Virgo inter Virgines Board of Trustees of the National Museums and Galleries on Merseyside, Liverpool

Masters, anonymous, and monogrammists, §II: Master of 1419 Cleveland Museum of Art, Cleveland, OH

Masters, anonymous, and monogrammists, §III: Master E.S. Staatliche Museen zu Berlin, Preussischer Kulturbesitz

Masters, anonymous, and monogrammists, §III: Master H W Photo: Michael Stuhr

Masucci, Agostino Minneapolis Institute of Arts, Minneapolis, MN

Mataré, Ewald Photo: Rheinische Bildarchiv, Cologne

Matejko, Jan National Museum, Kraków

Mathey, Jean Baptiste Institute of Art PAN, Prague

Mathieu, Georges Musée National d'Art Moderne, Paris

Mathura *1–2* Photo: © American Institute of Indian Studies, Varanasi

Matisse, Henri *1* © Succession H. Matisse/DACS, 1996; *2* Musée National d'Art Moderne, Paris/© Succession H. Matisse/DACS, 1996; *3* Museum of Modern Art, New York/© Succession H. Matisse/DACS, 1996; *4* Baltimore Museum of Art, Baltimore, MD (Cone Collection, formed by Dr Claribel Cone and Miss Etta Cone of Baltimore, MD); *5* Photo: J.-L. Charmet/© Succession H. Matisse/DACS, 1996/Bibliothèque Littéraire Jacques Doucet, Paris; *6* Museum of Modern Art, New York (Gift of Mr and Mrs Samuel A. Marx)/© Succession H. Matisse/DACS, 1996

Matsumoto Castle Photo: Yoshiyuki Kawahigashi, Tokyo

Matsumura Goshun Kurokawa Kenkyusho, Hyōgo

Matta, Roberto Museum of Modern Art, New York/© ADAGP, Paris, and DACS, London, 1996

Matteis, Paolo de *1* J. Paul Getty Museum, Malibu, CA; *2* Leeds City Art Galleries

Matteo di Giovanni Photo: Fotografia Lensini Fabio, Siena

Matyushin, Mikhail Tret'yakov Gallery, Moscow

Maucher: (1)Christoph Maucher Kunsthistorisches Museum, Vienna

Maucher: (2) Johann Michael Maucher Kunsthistorisches Museum, Vienna

Maulbertsch, Franz Anton *1* Photo: Bildarchiv, Österreichische Nationalbibliothek, Vienna; *2* Staatsgalerie, Stuttgart

Maulbronn Abbey *1–2* Photo: Bildarchiv Foto Marburg

Mausoleum *1* Photo: British Architectural Library, RIBA, London; *2* Photo: Bildarchiv Foto Marburg; *3* Photo: RCHME/© Crown Copyright; *4* Trustees of Sir John Soane's Museum, London; *5* US Department of the Interior, National Park Service; *6* SCR Photo Library, London

Mauve, Anton Rijksmuseum, Amsterdam

May, Ernst Photo: British Architectural Library, RIBA, London

Maya *2* Photo: Arnold Nelson/OmniQuests

Mayakovsky, Vladimir Photo: Stephen White

Mayer, Constance Photo: © RMN, Paris

Mazarin: (1) Jules Mazarin Bibliothèque Nationale de France, Paris

Mazo, Juan Bautista Martínez del Kunsthistorisches Museum, Vienna

Mazza, Giuseppe Sammlungen des Fürsten von Liechtenstein, Schloss Vaduz

Mazzanti, Ludovico Bibliotheca Hertziana, Rome (Rigamonti)

Mazzoni, Guido Photo: Archivi Alinari, Florence

Mazzuoli: (1) Giuseppe Mazzuoli Photo: Archivi Alinari, Florence

Meckenem: (1) Israhel van Meckenem (i) Graphische Sammlung Albertina, Vienna

Medal *1–2* National Gallery of Art, Washington, DC; *3* Staatliche Museen zu Berlin, Preussischer Kulturbesitz; *4–5* Photo: Sotheby's, London; *6–7* Trustees of the British Museum, London